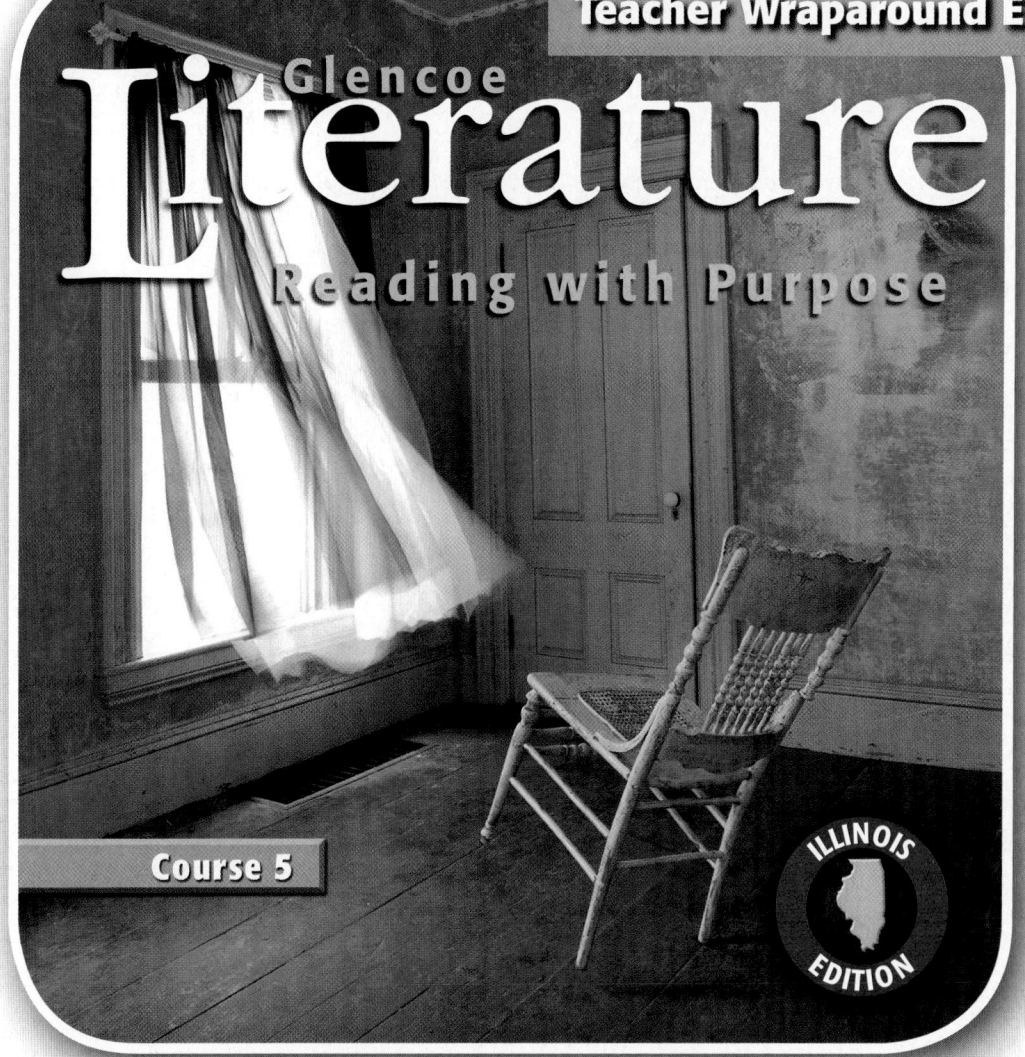

Glencoe
Literature
Reading with Purpose

Course 5

ILLINOIS EDITION

Program Consultants

Jeffrey D. Wilhelm, PhD

Douglas Fisher, PhD

Beverly Ann Chin, PhD

Jacqueline Jones Royster, DA

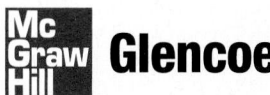

McGraw Hill **Glencoe**

New York, New York   Columbus, Ohio   Chicago, Illinois   Peoria, Illinois   Woodland Hills, California

Acknowledgments

Grateful acknowledgment is given authors, publishers, photographers, museums, and agents for permission to reprint the following copyrighted material. Every effort has been made to determine copyright owners. In case of any omissions, the publisher will be pleased to make suitable acknowledgments in future editions.

Acknowledgments continued on page R76.

Image Credit: IL3 Getty Images, **IL16** © David R. Frazier Photolibrary/Alamy

Glencoe

The *McGraw·Hill* Companies

Send all inquiries to:
Glencoe/McGraw-Hill
8787 Orion Place
Columbus, OH 43240-4027

ISBN-13: 978-0-07-878009-7
ISBN-10: 0-07-878009-8

Printed in the United States of America.

1 2 3 4 5 6 7 8 9 071 12 11 10 09 08 07 06

Illinois Teacher Reviewers

Illinois Learning Standards	Pages
STATE GOAL 1: Read with understanding and fluency.	
A. Apply word analysis and vocabulary skills to comprehend selections.	
1.A.4a Expand knowledge of word origins and derivations and use idioms, analogies, metaphors and similes to extend vocabulary development.	Author's Language and Style 410 Literary Element 971, 985 Revising Check 410 Vocabulary Practice 30, 65, 71, 74, 81, 83, 91, 97, 109, 111, 118, 163, 178, 185, 249, 252, 263, 276, 289, 351, 359, 361, 371, 374, 382, 397, 419, 427, 436, 442, 451, 484, 489, 558, 561, 568, 598, 601, 625, 674, 850, 865, 885, 1008, 1044, 1050, 1133, 1136, 1149, 1153, 1157 Vocabulary Workshop 372, 1052, 1068 Writing About Literature 1239
1.A.4b Compare the meaning of words and phrases and use analogies to explain the relationships among them.	Vocabulary Practice 83, 91, 97, 109, 163, 178, 249, 276, 351, 359, 361, 371, 436, 442, 484, 489, 558, 561, 598, 601, 625, 850, 865, 1044, 1050, 1153, 1157
B. Apply reading strategies to improve understanding and fluency.	
1.B.4a Preview reading materials, clarify meaning, analyze overall themes and coherence, and relate reading with information from other sources.	Comparing the Big Idea 226, 482, 685, 939, 1087, 1160 Daily Life and Culture 248, 350, 590, 884, 984, 1061 Preview the Article 186, 491, 664, 763, 1020, 1172 Reading Check 7, 315, 525, 711, 965, 1115 Reading Strategy 121, 129, 252, 263, 338, 351, 453, 463, 484, 489, 535, 539, 551, 555, 568, 618, 621, 653, 658, 670, 674 1020, 1025, 1030, 1039, 1042, 1121, 1133, 1165, 1171, 1241, 1255 Responding and Thinking Critically 17, 29, 47, 61, 70, 80, 90, 108, 117, 128, 146, 160, 177, 185, 190, 205, 220, 236, 248, 262, 275, 288, 334, 350, 358, 370, 381, 387, 396, 408, 416, 426, 434, 441, 450, 463, 481, 488, 493, 498, 533, 539, 549, 554, 561, 567, 572, 576, 581, 590, 596, 600, 609, 614, 620, 625, 629, 633, 637, 641, 644, 651, 657, 663, 667, 674, 717, 739, 760, 766, 769, 791, 811, 833, 849, 864, 884, 892, 895, 911, 931, 984, 1007, 1018, 1023, 1030, 1034, 1042, 1050, 1061, 1067, 1075, 1083, 1132, 1148, 1157, 1163, 1170, 1175, 1180, 1202, 1226, 1239, 1255

Illinois Learning Standards	Pages
1.B.4b Analyze, interpret and compare a variety of texts for purpose, structure, content, detail and effect.	Comparing Author's Cultures 207, 1151 Persuasive Text 465 Reading Check 963 Reading Strategy 13, 18, 21, 30, 31, 51, 62, 74, 81, 121, 129, 132, 147, 149, 161, 181, 185, 186, 228, 237, 240, 249, 252, 263, 265, 276, 279, 289, 321, 335, 338, 351, 354, 359, 361, 371, 374, 382, 384, 389, 397, 403, 409, 412, 417, 419, 427, 430, 434, 436, 442, 447, 451, 453, 463, 466, 481, 484, 489, 491, 495, 499, 531, 533, 536, 539, 541, 544, 547, 549, 558, 561, 570, 572, 574, 576, 578, 582, 587, 591, 594, 596, 598, 601, 602, 611, 615, 623, 625, 627, 629, 631, 633, 635, 637, 642, 649, 651, 653, 658, 661, 663, 664, 670, 674, 719, 739, 740, 761, 763, 771, 791, 792, 811, 812, 833, 850, 865, 871, 885, 889, 892, 893, 897, 912, 915, 931, 971, 985, 989, 1008, 1010, 1019, 1020, 1025, 1030, 1031, 1039, 1042, 1044, 1051, 1054, 1062, 1064, 1070, 1075, 1078, 1083, 1121, 1133, 1136, 1149, 1153, 1157, 1161, 1177, 1180, 1185, 1203, 1207, 1227, 1241, 1255 Responding and Thinking Critically 17, 29, 47, 61, 70, 80, 90, 108, 117, 128, 146, 160, 177, 185, 190, 205, 220, 236, 248, 262, 275, 288, 334, 350, 358, 370, 381, 387, 396, 408, 416, 426, 434, 441, 450, 463, 481, 488, 493, 498, 533, 539, 549, 554, 561, 567, 572, 576, 581, 590, 596, 600, 609, 614, 620, 625, 629, 633, 637, 641, 644, 651, 657, 663, 667, 674, 717, 739, 760, 766, 769, 791, 811, 833, 849, 864, 884, 892, 895, 911, 931, 984, 1007, 1018, 1023, 1030, 1034, 1042, 1050, 1061, 1067, 1075, 1083, 1132, 1148, 1157, 1163, 1170, 1175, 1180, 1202, 1226, 1239, 1255 Speaking, Listening, and Viewing Workshop 298-299, 1265 Test Preparation and Practice 302-304, 512-514, 698-700, 952-954, 1102-1104, 1268-1270 Writers on Reading 6-7, 314-315, 524-525, 710-711, 964-965, 1114-1115 Writing About Literature 19, 30, 48, 63, 71, 81, 92, 109, 161, 206, 250, 263, 289, 335, 352, 359, 371, 383, 398, 417, 428, 451, 490, 499, 539, 545, 556, 568, 582, 592, 616, 625, 629, 637, 641, 674, 811, 833, 866, 886, 892, 912, 986, 1008, 1051, 1063, 1134, 1149, 1157, 1171, 1204, 1228, 1239, 1255 Writing Workshop 290-297, 1257

Illinois Learning Standards	Pages
1.B.4c Read age-appropriate material with fluency and accuracy.	Comparing the Big Idea 685, 939 Comparing Author's Viewpoints 464 Daily Life and Culture 248, 590 Independent Reading 300-301, 510-511, 696-697, 950-951, 1100-1101, 1266-1267 Literary Analysis Model 4, 5, 312, 313, 522, 708, 962, 1112 Reading Further 335, 442, 499, 128 Reading Strategy 13, 18, 21, 30, 97, 109, 206, 209, 220, 240, 249, 252, 263, 321, 335, 338, 351, 361, 371, 389, 397, 412, 417, 430, 434, 436, 442, 453, 463, 484, 489, 495, 499, 536, 539, 551, 555, 558, 561, 618, 621, 623, 625, 627, 629, 635, 637, 653, 658, 763, 792, 811, 834, 849, 1020, 1054, 1062, 1136, 1149, 1165, 1171, 1172, 1231, 1239, 1241, 1255 Selection 14, 22, 37, 52, 66, 75, 84, 98, 112, 122, 133, 150, 164, 182, 196, 210, 229, 241, 253, 266, 280, 32, 339, 355, 362, 375, 384, 390, 403, 413, 420, 431, 437, 447, 454, 467, 470, 474, 478, 485, 495, 532, 537, 542, 548, 552, 559, 565, 566, 571, 575, 579, 588, 589, 595, 599, 612, 613, 619, 624, 628, 632, 636, 640, 642, 650, 654, 656, 662, 664, 671, 672, 673, 676, 677, 681, 716, 720, 741, 763, 768, 772, 793, 813, 835, 851, 873, 890, 893, 898, 916, 932, 933, 972, 990, 1011, 1020, 1025, 1032, 1040, 1045, 1055, 1064, 1071, 1079, 1084, 1086, 1122, 1137, 1154, 1158, 1159, 1161, 1166, 1172, 1178, 1186, 1208, 1232, 1242 Test Preparation and Practice 302, 512, 698, 952, 1102, 1269
C. Comprehend a broad range of reading materials.	
1.C.4a Use questions and predictions to guide reading.	Connecting 13, 21, 36, 51, 65, 74, 83, 97, 111, 121, 132, 149, 163, 181, 195, 209, 228, 240, 252, 265, 279, 321, 338, 354, 361, 374, 389, 403, 412, 419, 430, 436, 447, 453, 466, 484, 495, 531, 536, 541, 547, 551, 558, 564, 570, 574, 578, 587, 594, 598, 611, 618, 623, 627, 631, 635, 639, 649, 653, 661, 670, 719, 771, 792, 812, 834, 850, 871, 889, 897, 915, 971, 989, 1010, 1025, 1039, 1044, 1054, 1070, 1078, 1121, 1136, 1153, 1165, 1185, 1207, 1231, 1241 Literature Groups 63 Preview the Article 186, 491, 664, 763, 1020, 1172 Reading Strategy 195, 206, 374, 419, 430, 551, 555, 670, 834, 849, 889, 1231, 1239

Illinois Learning Standards	Pages
1.C.4b Explain and justify an interpretation of a text.	Comparing Author's Purpose 685 Comparing Author's Viewpoints 482 Comparing Cultures 939 Comparing Cultural Beliefs 1087 Comparing Description 1160 Comparing Narrator 226 Discussion Starter 223, 477, 684, 932, 1086 Literary Criticism 19, 71, 544, 582, 651 Listening and Speaking 866 Primary Visual Artifact 90, 117 Reading Check 313, 523, 1113 Reading Strategy 83, 91, 228, 237, 570, 572, 602, 719, 739, 1153, 1157 Responding and Thinking Critically 17, 29, 34, 47, 61, 70, 80, 90, 108, 117, 128, 146, 160, 177, 185, 190, 205, 220, 236, 248, 262, 275, 288, 334, 350, 358, 370, 381, 387, 396, 408, 416, 426, 434, 441, 450, 463, 481, 488, 493, 498, 533, 539, 543, 549, 554, 561, 567, 572, 576, 581, 590, 596, 600, 609, 614, 620, 625, 629, 633, 637, 641, 644, 651, 657, 663, 667, 674, 717, 739, 760, 766, 769, 791, 811, 833, 849, 864, 884, 892, 895, 911, 931, 984, 1007, 1018, 1023, 1030, 1034, 1042, 1050, 1061, 1067, 1075, 1083, 1132, 1148, 1157, 1163, 1170, 1175, 1180, 1202, 1226, 1239, 1255 Quickwrite 225, 480 Test Preparation and Practice 307, 517, 703, 957, 1107, 1273 Writing About Literature 19, 30, 48, 63, 71, 81, 92, 109, 161, 206, 250, 263, 289, 335, 352, 359, 371, 383, 398, 417, 428, 451, 490, 499, 539, 545, 556, 568, 582, 592, 616, 625, 629, 637, 641, 674, 811, 833, 866, 886, 892, 912, 986, 1008, 1051, 1063, 1134, 1149, 1157, 1171, 1204, 1228, 1239, 1255 Writing Workshop 290-297, 940-947, 1088-1095 You're the Critic 61, 177, 396, 426, 554, 614
1.C.4c Interpret, evaluate and apply information from a variety of sources to other situations (e.g., academic, vocational, technical, personal).	Daily Life and Culture 350, 884, 984, 1061 Interdisciplinary Activity 576 Reading Strategy 97, 109, 240, 249, 252, 263, 279, 289, 389, 397, 412, 417, 564, 568, 639, 641, 642, 893, 897, 912, 1010, 1019, 1078, 1083, 1165, 1171, 1172 Responding and Thinking Critically 769

Illinois Learning Standards	Pages
1.C.4d Summarize and make generalizations from content and relate them to the purpose of the material.	Literary Analysis 108, 128, 146, 370 Reading Handbook R23 Reading Strategy 321, 335, 361, 371, 627, 629, 631, 633, 670, 674, 740, 761, 871, 885 Responding and Thinking Critically 29, 111, 118, 160, 177, 220, 248, 262, 275, 463, 596, 760, 833, 1050, 1180 Writing About Literature 129
1.C.4e Analyze how authors and illustrators use text and art to express and emphasize their ideas (e.g. imagery, multiple points of view).	Author's Language and Style 92, 383, 410, 490, 545, 592, 659, 886, 986, 1228 Comparing Description 1161 Comparing Persuasive Appeals 482 Comparing Sound Devices 685 Revising Check 92, 383, 410, 490, 545, 592, 659, 886, 986, 1228 Literary Element 21, 29, 51, 62, 65, 70, 91, 163, 178, 181, 185, 240, 249, 389, 397, 409, 416, 447, 450, 453, 463, 466, 481, 484, 489, 498, 536, 539, 541, 544, 547, 549, 551, 555, 558, 581, 587, 591, 596, 598, 618, 620, 623, 625, 627, 629, 631, 633, 635, 637, 649, 651, 653, 658, 661, 663, 670, 674, 871, 885, 971, 985, 1010, 1018, 1054, 1062, 1133, 1153, 1157, 1165, 1170, 1177, 1180, 1231, 1239 Literary Analysis Model 4-5, 522-523, 708-709, 962-963, 1112-1113 Primary Source Quotation 381, 657 Primary Visual Artifact 117 Reading Strategy 228, 237, 265, 276, 354, 359, 384, 430, 434, 447, 451, 491, 547, 549, 561, 570, 572, 574, 576, 594, 602, 611, 615, 627, 629, 631, 633, 635, 637, 649, 651, 719, 739, 812, 833, 870, 885, 893, 1031, 1064, 1136, 1149, 1153, 1157, 1177, 1180, 1207, 1227 Responding and Thinking Critically 17, 29, 47, 90, 108, 117, 128, 146, 160, 185, 205, 220, 248, 275, 334, 350, 381, 387, 396, 408, 426, 441, 450, 481, 488, 493, 498, 533, 539, 549, 554, 567, 572, 576, 581, 590, 596, 609, 614, 620, 625, 629, 637, 641, 644, 651, 657, 663, 674, 760, 1132, 1170, 1180, 1239 Selection 467, 602, 1031 Speaking, Listening, and Viewing Workshop 508-509 TIME 491-493 Writing About Literature 30, 147, 119, 206, 250, 352, 359, 398, 451, 463, 490, 499, 568, 625, 637, 659, 674, 833, 912, 1134, 1149, 1239 Writing Workshop 291-292, 294-295, 501-502, 504-505, 687-688, 690-691, 941-942, 944-945, 1091-1095, 1257-1259, 1261 You're the Critic 61

Illinois Learning Standards	Pages
1.C.4f Interpret tables, graphs and maps in conjunction with related text.	Author's Language and Style 250, 277, 352, 410, 428, 490, 592, 616, 659, 762, 866, 986, 1063, 1135, 1204, 1228
	Comparing Author's Culture 226
	Comparing Author's Viewpoints 482
	Literary Element 18, 29, 47, 62, 80, 91, 108, 128, 146, 160, 178, 205, 236, 249, 262, 288, 334, 351, 370, 382, 397, 409, 416, 427, 441, 450, 489, 498, 555, 567, 581, 591, 594, 598, 600, 602, 615, 618, 620, 658, 761, 866, 885, 911, 985, 1007, 1050, 1062, 1133, 1170, 1203, 127
	Meet the Author 1024
	Persuasive Text 465
	Quickwrite 95, 715, 869
	Reading Strategy/Tip 13, 21, 51, 74, 83, 97, 111, 121, 132, 149, 181, 186, 195, 209, 228, 240, 252, 265, 279, 321, 338, 354, 361, 374, 384, 389, 403, 412, 427, 430, 436, 447, 453, 466, 484, 491, 495, 531, 536, 541, 544, 547, 551, 558, 564, 570, 574, 578, 587, 602, 611, 623, 627, 631, 635, 639, 642, 649, 653, 661, 664, 670, 719, 740, 763, 771, 792, 812, 834, 850, 871, 889, 897, 915, 971, 989, 1020, 1025, 1031, 1039, 1044, 1054, 1070, 1078, 1121, 1136, 1153, 1161, 1165, 1172, 1177, 1185, 1207, 1231, 1241
	Speaking, Listening, and Viewing Workshop 695
	Test Preparation and Practice 1103
	Visual Literacy 408, 760
	Vocabulary Workshop 49, 130, 372, 1052, 1068
	Writing About Literature 19, 30, 48, 63, 71, 81, 92, 109, 119, 129, 147, 161, 179, 206, 237, 250, 263, 289, 335, 352, 371, 383, 410, 417, 442, 490, 499, 545, 556, 568, 582, 592, 601, 616, 621, 659, 762, 866, 886, 912, 986, 1008, 1019, 1051, 1063, 1134, 1149, 1171, 1204
	Writing Workshop 290, 500, 503, 686, 689, 940, 942, 943, 1088, 1089, 1090, 1256, 1260
	You're the Critic 275, 426, 614

Illinois Learning Standards	Pages

STATE GOAL 2: Read and understand literature representative of various societies, eras and ideas.

A. Understand how literary elements and techniques are used to convey meaning.

2.A.4a Analyze and evaluate the effective use of literary techniques (e.g., figurative language, allusion, dialogue, description, symbolism, word choice, dialect) in classic and contemporary literature representing a variety of forms and media.	Author's Language and Style 63, 410, 428, 490, 659, 866, 1229 Comparing Description 1160 Comparing Persuasive Appeals 464 Comparing Sound Devices 685 Literary Analysis Model 52, 523, 1112, 1113 Literary Element 13, 18, 21, 29, 47, 51, 62, 65, 70, 74, 80, 83, 91, 97, 108, 111, 118, 163, 178, 181, 185, 205, 240, 249, 389, 397, 416, 427, 447, 450, 453, 463, 466, 481, 484, 489, 498, 531, 533, 536, 539, 541, 544, 547, 549, 551, 555, 581, 587, 591, 600, 618, 620, 623, 625, 627, 629, 631, 633, 635, 637, 649, 651, 653, 658, 661, 663, 740, 761, 771, 791, 792, 811, 834, 849, 885, 897, 911, 915, 931, 971, 985, 989, 1007, 1018, 1025, 1030, 1054, 1062, 1078, 1083, 1121, 1133, 1153, 1157, 1165, 1170, 1231, 1239 Literary Focus 192, 193, 444, 445, 528, 529, 584, 585, 646, 647, 868, 869, 1118, 1119, 1182, 1183 Reading Strategy 83, 91, 228, 237, 265, 276, 547, 549, 570, 572, 574, 576, 578, 582, 594, 596, 598, 601, 611, 615, 631, 633, 649, 651, 661, 663, 719, 739, 812, 833, 1064, 1153, 1157, 1207, 1227 Responding and Thinking Critically 17, 29, 47, 70, 80, 90, 108, 117, 220, 248, 275, 334, 350, 370, 381, 396, 408, 426, 450, 481, 488, 498, 539, 549, 554, 567, 572, 576, 591, 600, 625, 629, 637, 641, 651, 667, 674, 760, 791, 884, 911, 984, 1007, 1132, 1157, 1170, 1202, 1226, 1239, 1255 Test Prep and Practice 304, 513, 699, 700, 953, 954, 1104 Writing About Literature 119, 129, 352, 398, 463, 490, 499, 568, 624, 637, 659, 663, 833, 886, 912, 1134, 1149, 1239

Illinois Learning Standards	Pages
2.A.4b Explain relationships between and among literary elements, including character, plot, setting, theme, conflict and resolution and their influence on the effectiveness of the literary piece.	Author's Language and Style 428 Comparing Narrator 226 Comparing Theme 939 Literary Analysis Model 4, 5, 708, 709, 962, 963 Literary Element 18, 29, 36, 47, 62, 80, 121, 128, 132, 146, 149, 160, 195, 205, 236, 252, 262, 265, 276, 288, 338, 351, 358, 498, 564, 567, 598, 600, 615, 670, 674, 719, 739, 761, 812, 833, 850, 864, 889, 892, 911, 1007, 1039, 1042, 1044, 1050, 1070, 1075, 1136, 1148, 1170, 1207, 1227, 1241, 1255 Literary Focus 10, 11, 94, 95, 714, 715, 868, 869, 968, 969, 1036, 1037 Reading Strategy 13, 18, 21, 30, 36, 48, 51, 62, 65, 71, 74, 81, 111, 118, 121, 129, 132, 147, 149, 161, 163, 178, 181, 185, 186, 279, 289, 338, 351, 361, 371, 436, 442, 453, 463, 495, 499, 536, 539, 541, 544, 664, 670, 674, 771, 791, 792, 811, 850, 865, 889, 892, 897, 912, 915, 931, 989, 1008, 1010, 1018, 1039, 1042, 1044, 1051, 1954, 1062, 1161, 1185, 1203, 1241, 1255 Responding and Thinking Critically 17, 29, 70, 117, 128, 146, 177, 185, 205, 220, 350, 371, 381, 387, 441, 488, 539, 549, 554, 567, 572, 591, 609, 614, 620, 625, 633, 637, 641, 667, 739, 760, 791, 884, 911, 1007, 1023, 1061, 1132, 1180, 1202, 1226, 1255 Test Preparation and Practice 304, 513, 514, 700, 954, 1104 Writing About Literature 19, 30, 48, 63, 71, 81, 92, 109, 147, 161, 179, 185, 206, 237, 263, 289, 335, 359, 371, 383, 428, 451, 556, 582, 592, 616, 641, 811, 866, 931, 986, 1008, 1051, 1083, 1157, 1171, 1204, 128
2.A.4c Describe relationships between the author's style, literary form (e.g., short stories, novels, drama, fables, biographies, documentaries, poetry, essays) and intended effect on the reader.	Grammar and Style 19, 63, 92, 119, 179, 250, 277, 352, 383, 398, 410, 428, 490, 545, 592, 659, 762, 866, 886, 986, 1063, 1134, 1204, 128 Literary Element 83, 91, 240, 249, 279, 288, 321, 334, 354, 358, 361, 370, 374, 382, 412, 416, 419, 427, 436, 441, 495, 498, 558, 561, 570, 572, 574, 576, 578, 581, 594, 596, 611, 615, 639, 641, 771, 791, 871, 885, 985, 1010, 1018, 1203 Reading Strategy 374, 382, 409, 1070, 1075 Writing About Literature 147, 352, 371, 463, 539, 545, 568, 621, 674, 892, 1063, 1075, 1134, 1255
2.A.4d Describe the influence of the author's language structure and word choice to convey the author's viewpoint.	Literary Element 83, 91, 240, 249, 374, 382, 397, 447, 450, 627, 629, 635, 637 Reading Strategy 447, 451, 466, 484, 489, 594, 596, 1070, 1075 Reading Tip 564 Writing About Literature 463, 539, 762

Illinois Learning Standards	Pages
B. Read and interpret a variety of literary works.	
2.B.4a Critique ideas and impressions generated by oral, visual, written and electronic materials.	Literary Criticism 71, 549, 582, 651 Primary Source Quotation 381, 652, 1132 Primary Visual Artifact 17, 90, 864, 1226 Reading Strategy 491, 602 Responding and Thinking Critically 17, 29, 34, 47, 61, 70, 80, 90, 108, 117, 128, 146, 160, 177, 185, 190, 205, 220, 236, 248, 262, 275, 288, 334, 350, 358, 370, 381, 387, 396, 408, 416, 426, 434, 441, 450, 463, 481, 488, 493, 498, 533, 539, 543, 549, 554, 561, 567, 572, 576, 581, 590, 596, 600, 609, 614, 620, 625, 629, 633, 637, 641, 644, 651, 657, 663, 667, 674, 717, 739, 760, 766, 769, 791, 811, 833, 849, 864, 884, 892, 895, 911, 931, 984, 1007, 1018, 1023, 1030, 1034, 1042, 1050, 1061, 1067, 1075, 1083, 1132, 1148, 1157, 1163, 1170, 1175, 1180, 1202, 1226, 1239, 1255 Visual Literacy 1202 Writing About Literature 359, 490, 499, 886, 1149 Writing Workshop 290–297 You're the Critic 61, 177, 396, 426, 554, 614
2.B.4b Analyze form, content, purpose and major themes of American literature and literature of other countries in their historical perspectives.	Comparing Author's Purpose 668, 685 Comparing Cultural Beliefs 1076, 1087 Comparing Cultures 913, 939 Comparing Theme 913, 939 Daily Life and Culture 248, 350, 590, 884 Literary Focus 94–95, 121, 128, 132, 146, 321, 334, 338, 351, 361, 370, 495, 498, 528–529, 1070, 1075 Reading Strategy 31, 65, 71, 384, 419, 427, 639, 641, 740, 761, 871, 885, 1177, 1180 Responding and Thinking Critically 17, 29, 34, 47, 61, 70, 80, 90, 108, 117, 128, 146, 160, 177, 185, 190, 205, 20, 236, 248, 262, 275, 288, 334, 350, 358, 370, 381, 387, 396, 408, 416, 426, 434, 441, 450, 463, 481, 488, 493, 498, 533, 539, 543, 549, 554, 561, 567, 572, 576, 581, 590, 596, 600, 609, 614, 620, 625, 629, 633, 637, 641, 644, 651, 657, 663, 667, 674, 717, 739, 760, 766, 769, 791, 811, 833, 849, 864, 884, 892, 895, 911, 931, 984, 1007, 1018, 1023, 1030, 1034, 1042, 1050, 1061, 1067, 1075, 1083, 1132, 1148, 1157, 1163, 1170, 1175, 1180, 1202, 1226, 1239, 1255 Review 262, 358, 1170 Writing About Literature 185, 417, 545

Illinois Learning Standards	Pages
2.B.4c Discuss and evaluate motive, resulting behavior and consequences demonstrated in literature.	Literary Element 97, 108, 109, 178, 1185, 1203 Reading Strategy 132, 178, 279, 289, 338, 771, 791, 850, 1010, 1019 Responding and Thinking Critically 17, 29, 61, 70, 80, 91, 128, 146, 160, 177, 185, 205, 220, 236, 262, 288, 350, 351, 358, 371, 381, 397, 533, 539, 590, 614, 620, 625, 641, 663, 739, 760, 811, 833, 864, 884, 911, 984, 1007, 1018, 1061, 1075, 1132, 1148, 1239, 1255

STATE GOAL 3: Write to communicate for a variety of purposes.

A. Use correct grammar, spelling, punctuation, capitalization and structure.

3.A.4 Use standard English to edit documents for clarity, subject/verb agreement, adverb and adjective agreement and verb tense; proofread for spelling, capitalization and punctuation; and ensure that documents are formatted in final form for submission and/or publication.	Grammar and Style 19, 63, 92, 119, 179, 250, 277, 352, 383, 398, 428, 545, 556, 592, 616, 762, 866, 886, 986, 1063, 1134, 1204, 1228 Grammar Workshop 72, 238, 336, 562, 887, 987, 1150, 1205 Test Preparation and Practice 306–307, 516–517, 702–703, 956–957, 1106–1107, 1272–1273 Writing About Literature 19, 30, 48, 63, 71, 80, 92, 109, 119, 129, 147, 161, 179, 185, 206, 237, 250, 263, 277, 289, 335, 352, 371, 383, 398, 410, 417, 428, 442, 451, 490, 539, 545, 556, 568, 582, 592, 601, 616, 621, 637, 659, 674, 866, 886, 912, 986, 1008, 1019, 1051, 1063, 1134, 1149, 1171, 1204, 1228 Writing Workshop 296–297, 506–507, 692–693, 946–947, 1096–1097, 1262–1263 Writing Handbook R32

B. Compose well-organized and coherent writing for specific purposes and audiences.

3.B.4a Produce documents that exhibit a range of writing techniques appropriate to purpose and audience, with clarity of focus, logic of organization, appropriate elaboration and support and overall coherence.	Comparing the Big Idea 482, 685, 939, 1087, 1160 Test Preparation and Practice 307, 517, 703, 957, 1107, 1273 Writing About Literature 19, 30, 48, 63, 71, 80, 92, 109, 119, 129, 147, 161, 179, 185, 206, 237, 250, 263, 277, 289, 335, 352, 359, 371, 383, 398, 410, 417, 428, 442, 451, 463, 499, 533, 539, 545, 556, 568, 572, 582, 592, 596, 601, 616, 621, 625, 637, 641, 659, 663, 674, 762, 811, 833, 866, 886, 892, 912, 931, 986, 1008, 1019, 1051, 1063, 1075, 1083, 1134, 1149, 1157, 1171, 1204, 1228, 1239, 1255 Writing Workshop 290–297, 500–507, 686–693, 940–947, 1088–1097, 1256–1263 Writing Handbook R35

Illinois Learning Standards	Pages
3.B.4b Produce, edit, revise and format work for submission and/or publication (e.g., manuscript form, appropriate citation of sources) using contemporary technology.	Writing Workshop 297, 507, 693, 947, 1097, 1263 Writing Handbook R34, R39–R41
3.B.4c Evaluate written work for its effectiveness and make recommendations for its improvement.	Grammar and Style 19, 63, 250, 277 Grammar Workshop 72, 238, 562, 887, 987, 1150, 1205 Quickwrite 585 Test Preparation and Practice 306–307, 516–517, 702–703, 956–957, 1106–1107, 1272–1273 Writing About Literature 19, 30, 48, 63, 71, 81, 92, 109, 119, 129, 147, 161, 179, 185, 206, 237, 250, 263, 277, 335, 352, 359, 371, 383, 398, 410, 417, 428, 442, 451, 490, 539, 545, 556, 568, 582, 592, 601, 616, 621, 637, 659, 674, 866, 886, 912, 986, 1008, 1019, 1051, 1063, 1134, 1149, 1171, 1204, 128 Writing Workshop 290–297, 500–507, 686–693, 940–947, 1088–1097, 1256–1263

C. Communicate ideas in writing to accomplish a variety of purposes.

3.C.4a Write for real or potentially real situations in academic, professional and civic contexts (e.g., college applications, job applications, business letters, petitions).	Writing About Literature 410 Learning for Life 289, 451, 1171 Writing Workshop 940–947 Writing Handbook R42–R45
3.C.4b Using available technology, produce compositions and multimedia works for specified audiences.	Interdisciplinary Activity 371 Performing 556 Speaking, Listening, and Viewing Workshop 298–299, 508–509, 694–695, 1098–1099

STATE GOAL 4: Listen and speak effectively in a variety of situations.

A. Listen effectively in formal and informal situations.

4.A.4a Apply listening skills as individuals and members of a group in a variety of settings (e.g., lectures, discussions, conversations, team projects, presentations, interviews).	Activities 966 Comparing Sound Devices 685 Listening and Speaking 48, 250, 398, 592 Speaking, Listening, and Viewing Workshop 299
4.A.4b Apply listening skills in practical settings (e.g., classroom note taking, interpersonal conflict situations, giving and receiving directions, evaluating persuasive messages).	Learning for Life 81, 206 Listening and Speaking 633 Literature Groups 63 Performing 481 Speaking, Listening, and Viewing Workshop 1265
4.A.4c Follow complex oral instructions.	Listening and Speaking 912, 1149 Speaking, Listening, and Viewing Workshop 949, 1265

Illinois Learning Standards	Pages
4.A.4d Demonstrate understanding of the relationship of verbal and nonverbal messages within a context (e.g., contradictory, supportive, repetitive, substitutive).	Speaking, Listening, and Viewing Workshop 299, 509, 695, 949, 1099, 1265
B. Speak effectively using language appropriate to the situation and audience.	
4.B.4a Deliver planned informative and persuasive oral presentations using visual aids and contemporary technology as individuals and members of a group; demonstrate organization, clarity, vocabulary, credible and accurate supporting evidence.	Interdisciplinary Activity 659 Listening and Speaking 1149 Speaking, Listening, and Viewing Workshop 298–299, 508–509, 694–695, 948–949, 1098–1099
4.B.4b Use group discussion skills to assume leadership and participant roles within an assigned project or to reach a group goal.	Activities 8, 316, 1116 Comparing Narrator 226 Comparing Persuasive Appeals 482 Comparing Sound Devices 685 Comparing Theme 939 Discussion Starter 223, 477, 684, 932, 1086, 1158 Learning for Life 1171 Literary Criticism 651 Literature Groups 63, 92, 109, 129, 277, 359, 410, 417, 568, 621, 791, 1008, 1051, 1134 Primary Source Quotation 381 Primary Visual Artifact 17, 90 Speaking, Listening, and Viewing Workshop 1264–1265 Visual Literacy 760, 1202 You're The Critic 61, 177, 275, 396, 426, 614
4.B.4c Use strategies to manage or overcome communication anxiety and apprehension (e.g., developed outlines, notecards, practice).	Listening and Speaking 119, 912 Performing 481, 1042, 1204 Speaking, Listening, and Viewing Workshop 298–299, 508–509, 694–695, 948–949, 1098–1099
4.B.4d Use verbal and nonverbal strategies to maintain communication and to resolve individual and group conflict.	Speaking, Listening, and Viewing Workshop 1264–1265

STATE GOAL 5: Use the language arts to acquire, assess and communicate information.

A. Locate, organize, and use information from various sources to answer questions, solve problems and communicate ideas.

5.A.4a Demonstrate a knowledge of strategies needed to prepare a credible research report (e.g., notes, planning sheets).	Interdisciplinary Activity 383, 428, 1063 Internet Connection 161, 263, 352, 739, 986 Writing Handbook R36–R41 Writing Workshop 503, 1088–1097

Illinois Learning Standards	Pages
5.A.4b Design and present a project (e.g., research report, scientific study, career/higher education opportunities) using various formats from multiple sources.	Interdisciplinary Activity 30, 371, 428, 849 Learning for Life 206 Speaking, Listening, and Viewing Workshop 1098–1099
B. Analyze and evaluate information acquired from various sources.	
5.B.4a Choose and evaluate primary and secondary sources (print and nonprint) for a variety of purposes.	Interdisciplinary Activity 659 Primary Source Quotation 381, 1132 Speaking, Listening, and Viewing Workshop 508–509 Writing Handbook R36–R37 Writing Workshop 1089
5.B.4b Use multiple sources and multiple formats; cite according to standard style manuals.	Internet Connection 263, 352 Writing Handbook R38, R39–R41 Writing Workshop 1089, 1095
C. Apply acquired information, concepts and ideas to communicate in a variety of formats.	
5.C.4a Plan, compose, edit and revise information (e.g., brochures, formal reports, proposals, research summaries, analyses, editorials, articles, overheads, multimedia displays) for presentation to an audience.	Interdisciplinary Activity 371, 428, 1063 Internet Connection 161, 263 Speaking, Listening, and Viewing Workshop 1098–1099
5.C.4b Produce oral presentations and written documents using supportive research and incorporating contemporary technology.	Learning for Life 451 Speaking, Listening, and Viewing Workshop 508–509, 948–949, 1098–1099
5.C.4c Prepare for and participate in formal debates.	Literary Criticism 19 Literature Groups 92, 237 Debating 434

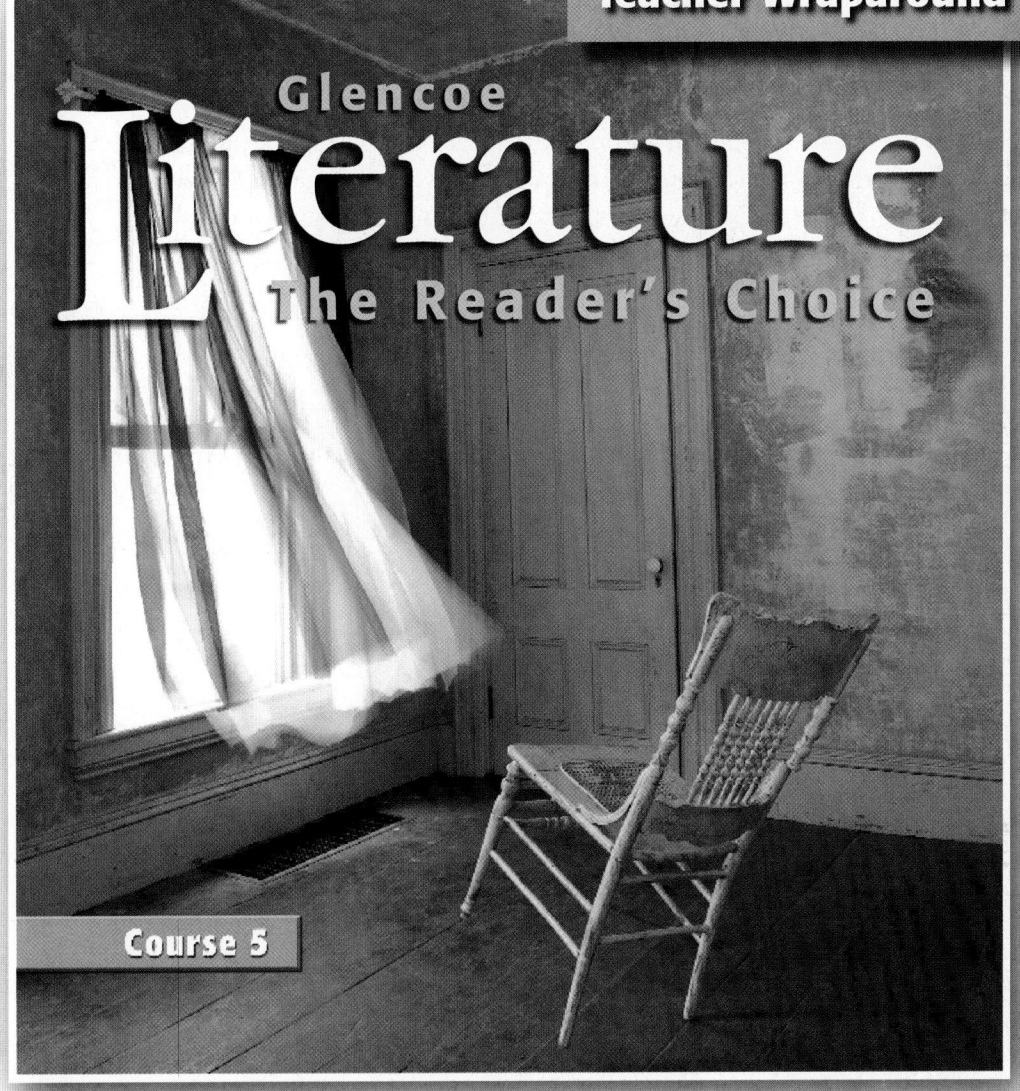

Glencoe
Literature
The Reader's Choice

Course 5

Program Consultants

Jeffrey D. Wilhelm, PhD

Douglas Fisher, PhD

Beverly Ann Chin, PhD

Jacqueline Jones Royster, DA

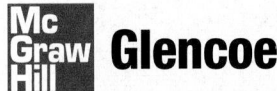

McGraw Hill **Glencoe**

New York, New York   Columbus, Ohio   Chicago, Illinois   Peoria, Illinois   Woodland Hills, California

ACKNOWLEDGMENTS

Grateful acknowledgment is given authors, publishers, photographers, museums, and agents for permission to reprint the following copyrighted material. Every effort has been made to determine copyright owners. In case of any omissions, the publisher will be pleased to make suitable acknowledgments in future editions.

Acknowledgments continued on page R101.

 Glencoe

The *McGraw·Hill* Companies

Send all inquiries to:
Glencoe/McGraw-Hill
8787 Orion Place
Columbus, OH 43240-4027

ISBN-13: (student edition) 978-0-07-845480-6
ISBN-10: (student edition) 0-07-845480-8
ISBN-13: (teacher edition) 978-0-07-845491-2
ISBN-10: (teacher edition) 0-07-845491-3

Printed in the United States of America.

2 3 4 5 6 7 8 9 071/043 12 11 10 09 08 07 06

Senior Program Consultants

Jeffrey D. Wilhelm, PhD, a former middle and secondary school English and reading teacher, is currently Professor of Education at Boise State University. He is the author or coauthor of numerous articles and several books on the teaching of reading and literacy, including award-winning titles such as *You Gotta BE the Book* and *Reading Don't Fix No Chevys*. He also works with local schools as part of the Adolescent Literacy Project and recently helped establish the National Writing Project site at Boise State University.

Douglas Fisher, PhD, is Professor of Language and Literacy Education and Director of Professional Development at San Diego State University, where he teaches English language development and literacy. He also serves as Director of City Heights Educational Pilot, which won the Christa McAuliffe Award from the American Association of State Colleges and Universities. He has published numerous articles on reading and literacy, differentiated instruction, and curriculum design. He is coauthor of the book *Improving Adolescent Literacies: Strategies That Work* and coeditor of the book *Inclusive Urban Schools*.

Program Consultants

Beverly Ann Chin, PhD, is Professor of English, Director of the English Teaching Program, former Director of the Montana Writing Project, and former Director of Composition at the University of Montana in Missoula. She currently serves as a Member at Large of the Conference of English Leadership. Dr. Chin is a nationally recognized leader in English language arts standards, curriculum, and assessment. Formerly a high school teacher and adult education reading teacher, Dr. Chin has taught in English language arts education at several universities and has received awards for her teaching and service.

Jacqueline Jones Royster, DA, is Professor of English and Senior Vice Provost and Executive Dean of the Colleges of Arts and Sciences at The Ohio State University. She is currently on the Writing Advisory Committee of the National Commission on Writing and serves as chair for both the Columbus Literacy Council and the Ohioana Library Association. In addition to the teaching of writing, Dr. Royster's professional interests include the rhetorical history of African American women and the social and cultural implications of literate practices. She has contributed to and helped to edit numerous books, anthologies, and journals.

TEACHER REVIEWERS

The following teachers contributed to the review of *Glencoe Literature*.

Bridget M. Agnew
St. Michael School
Chicago, Illinois

Monica Anzaldua Araiza
Dr. Juliet V. Garcia
    Middle School
Brownsville, Texas

Katherine R. Baer
Howard County Public Schools
Ellicott City, Maryland

Tanya Baxter
Roald Amundsen High School
Chicago, Illinois

Danielle R. Brain
Thomas R. Proctor
    Senior High School
Utica, New York

Yolanda Conder
Owasso Mid-High School
Owasso, Oklahoma

Gwenn de Mauriac
The Wiscasset Schools
Wiscasset, Maine

Courtney Doan
Bloomington High School
Bloomington, Illinois

Susan M. Griffin
Edison Preparatory School
Tulsa, Oklahoma

Cindi Davis Harris
Helix Charter High School
La Mesa, California

Joseph F. Hutchinson
Toledo Public Schools
Toledo, Ohio

Ginger Jordan
Florien High School
Florien, Louisiana

Dianne Konkel
Cypress Lake Middle School
Fort Myers, Florida

Melanie A. LaFleur
Many High School
Many, Louisiana

Patricia Lee
Radnor Middle School
Wayne, Pennsylvania

Linda Copley Lemons
Cleveland High School
Cleveland, Tennessee

Heather S. Lewis
Waverly Middle School
Lansing, Michigan

Sandra C. Lott
Aiken Optional School
Alexandria, Louisiana

Connie M. Malacarne
O'Fallon Township
    High School
O'Fallon, Illinois

Lori Howton Means
Edward A. Fulton
    Junior High School
O'Fallon, Illinois

Claire C. Meitl
Howard County Public Schools
Ellicott City, Maryland

Patricia P. Mitcham
Mohawk High School (Retired)
New Castle, Pennsylvania

Lisa Morefield
South-Western
    Career Academy
Grove City, Ohio

Kevin M. Morrison
Hazelwood East High School
St. Louis, Missouri

Jenine M. Pokorak
School Without Walls
    Senior High School
Washington, D.C.

Susan Winslow Putnam
Butler High School
Matthews, North Carolina

Paul C. Putnoki
Torrington Middle School
Torrington, Connecticut

Jane Thompson Rae
Cab Calloway High School
    of the Arts
Wilmington, Delaware

Stephanie L. Robin
N. P. Moss Middle School
Lafayette, Louisiana

Ann C. Ryan
Lindenwold High School
Lindenwold, New Jersey

Pamela Schoen
Hopkins High School
Minnetonka, Minnesota

Megan Schumacher
Friends' Central School
Wynnewood, Pennsylvania

Fareeda J. Shabazz
Paul Revere Elementary School
Chicago, Illinois

Molly Steinlage
Brookpark Middle School
Grove City, Ohio

Barry Stevenson
Garnet Valley Middle School
Glen Mills, Pennsylvania

Paul Stevenson
Edison Preparatory School
Tulsa, Oklahoma

Kathy Thompson
Owasso Mid-High School
Owasso, Oklahoma

Instructional Planning and Support

BOOK OVERVIEW

Reference Section

CONTENTS

> "Round about California in that day were scattered a host of these living dead men . . ."
>
> —Mark Twain

"*Seize him and unmask him—that we may know whom we have to hang at sunrise . . .*"

—Edgar Allan Poe

"*For an instant he hung suspended between balance and falling . . .*"

—Jack Finney

"She washed us in a river
of make-believe . . ."

—Alice Walker

"The mud was like quicksand around
her, and anyone attempting to reach
her was in danger of sinking."

—Isabel Allende

UNIT TWO # NONFICTION

— PART 1 — *THE POWER OF MEMORY* 317

"Living life as art requires a readiness to forgive."

—Maya Angelou

"I was thrilled by the wildness of the ocean . . ."

—Jewelle L. Gomez

— **PART 3** — KEEPING FREEDOM ALIVE 443

"It is no longer a choice between violence and nonviolence in this world; it's nonviolence or nonexistence."

—Martin Luther King Jr.

UNIT THREE Poetry

— **PART 1** — The Energy of the Everyday

> "Violent socks, my feet were
> two fish made of wool"
>
> —Pablo Neruda

> "Mortality is your shadow
> and your shade."
>
> —N. Scott Momaday

"I am offering this poem to you,
since I have nothing else to give."

—Jimmy Santiago Baca

UNIT FOUR DRAMA

*"The dearest profit is sometimes
all too dear."*

—Sophocles

"We all stand up against the spirit
of Caesar, and in the spirit
of men there is no blood."

—William Shakespeare

— PART 2 — PORTRAITS OF REAL LIFE

UNIT FIVE *Legends and Myths*

— **PART 1** — *Acts of Courage* 967

"Sir Launcelot, I know that Queen Gwynevere loves you, and you her."

—Sir Thomas Malory

"If you have something to give, give it forever."

—Jenny Leading Cloud

> "His jaws chattered and his limbs shook as the poison
> flooded through him like a rising Nile."
>
> —Geraldine Harris

UNIT SIX Genre Fiction

— PART 1 — The Extraordinary and Fantastic ...1117

> *"Destroy this one man,
> and you destroy a race, a people,
> an entire history of life."*
> —Ray Bradbury

— PART 2 — The Uncanny and Mysterious 1181

"*I must impress upon you that you are in very grave danger.*"

—Agatha Christie

Reference Section

SELECTIONS BY GENRE

Fiction

Short Story

Myth and Folktale

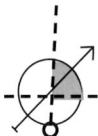

PERSPECTIVES

*Award-winning nonfiction book excerpts
and primary source documents*

TIME

High-interest, informative magazine articles

Comparing Literature
Across Genres

FEATURES

Comparing Literature: *Different Viewpoints*

INDEPENDENT READING

TEST PREPARATION AND PRACTICE

LITERARY FOCUS

Literary History

SKILLS WORKSHOPS

Writing Workshops

Speaking, Listening, and Viewing Workshops

Grammar Workshops

Vocabulary Workshops

Why do I need this book?

Glencoe Literature: The Reader's Choice is more than just a collection of stories, poems, nonfiction articles, and other literary works. Every unit is built around **Big Ideas,** concepts that you will want to think about, talk about, and maybe even argue about. Big Ideas help you become part of an important conversation. You can join in lively discussions about who we are, where we have been, and where we are going.

Organization

The literature selections you will read are organized by literary element and genre into six units: The Short Story, Nonfiction, Poetry, Drama, Legends and Myths, and Genre Fiction.

Each unit contains the following:

A **UNIT INTRODUCTION** provides you with the background information to help make your reading experience more meaningful.

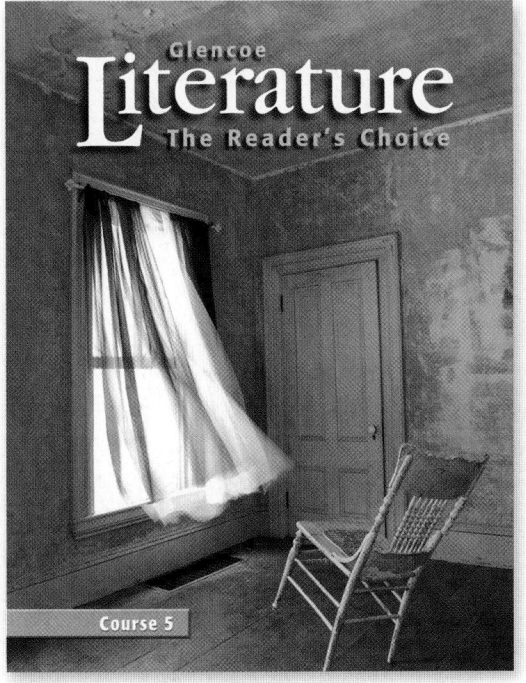

- **GENRE FOCUS** defines the literary elements that make up a unit.
- **THE LITERARY ANALYSIS MODEL** uses an example to help you identify different literary elements and analyze their use within the text.
- **WRITERS ON READING** gives you genre-specific reading tips from famous authors.
- **BIG IDEAS** target three concepts that you can trace as you read the literary selections.

LITERATURE SELECTIONS follow each Unit Introduction. The selections are organized as follows.

Reading and Thinking

The main selections in your textbook are arranged in three parts.

- Start with **BEFORE YOU READ.** Learn valuable background information about the selection and preview the skills and strategies that will guide your reading.

MEET THE AUTHOR presents a detailed biography of the writer whose work you will read and analyze.

LITERATURE PREVIEW and **READING PREVIEW** list the basic tools you will use to read and analyze the selection.

- Next, read the **LITERATURE SELECTION.** As you flip through the selections, you will notice that parts of the text are highlighted in different colors. At the bottom of the page are color-coded questions that relate to the highlighted text. Yellow represents a *Big Idea*, magenta represents a *Literary Element*, and blue represents a *Reading Strategy*. These questions will help you gain a better understanding of the text.

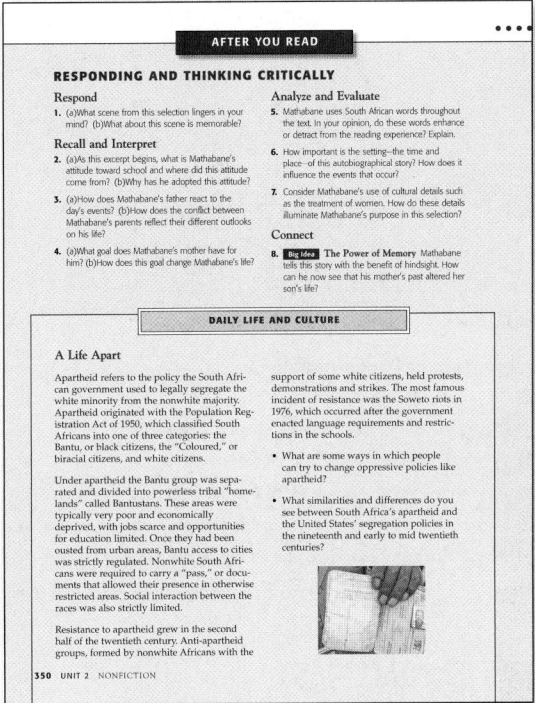

- Wrap up the selection with **AFTER YOU READ.** Explore what you have learned through a wide range of reading, thinking, vocabulary, and writing activities.

Vocabulary

VOCABULARY WORDS that may be new or difficult for you are chosen from most selections. They are introduced on the **BEFORE YOU READ** page. Each word is accompanied by its pronunciation, its part of speech, its definition, and the page number on which it appears. The vocabulary word is also used in a sample sentence. Vocabulary words are highlighted in the Literature Selection.

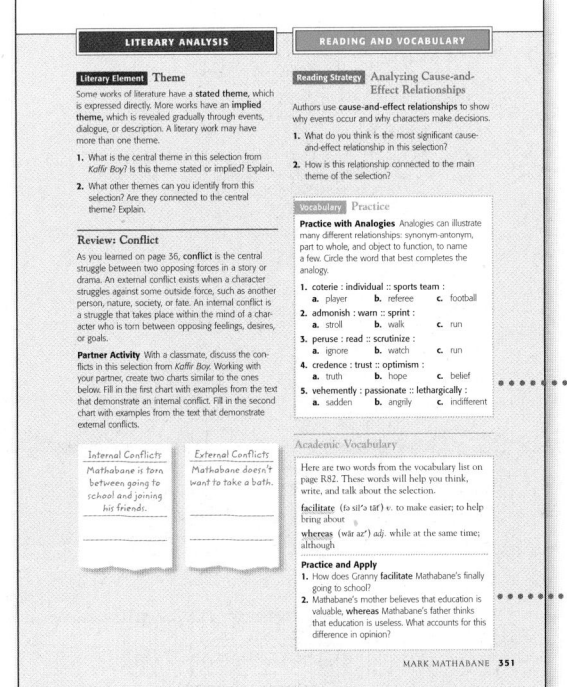

VOCABULARY PRACTICE On the **AFTER YOU READ** pages, you will be able to practice using the vocabulary words in an exercise. This exercise will show you how to apply a vocabulary strategy to understand new or difficult words.

ACADEMIC VOCABULARY Many of the **AFTER YOU READ** pages will also introduce you to two words that are frequently used in academic work. You will be prompted to apply the definitions of these words to answer questions about the selection that you have just read.

Writing Workshops

Each unit in *Glencoe Literature: The Reader's Choice* includes a Writing Workshop. The workshop walks you through the writing process as you work on an extended piece of writing related to the unit.

- You will create writing goals and apply strategies to meet them.

- You will pick up tips and polish your critical skills as you analyze professional and workshop models.

- You will focus on mastering specific aspects of writing, including organization, grammar, and vocabulary.

- You will use a rubric to evaluate your own writing.

Revising

Use the rubric below to help you evaluate your writing.

Rubric: Writing an Effective Persuasive Speech

☑ Do you state your opinion clearly?

☑ Do you include both logical and emotional appeals?

☑ Do you use reasons and facts to support your opinion?

☑ Do you present your ideas in a logical order?

☑ Do you include and respond to counterarguments?

☑ Do you clarify your opinion as needed and restate it in your conclusion?

Test Preparation and Practice

At the end of each unit, you will be tested on the literature, reading, and vocabulary skills you have just learned. Designed to simulate standardized tests, this test will give you the practice you need to succeed while providing an assessment of how you have met the unit objectives.

Test Preparation and Practice

English–Language Arts

Reading: Drama

Carefully read the following passage. Use context clues to help you define any words with which you are unfamiliar. Pay close attention to the mood, theme, and characters. Then, on a separate sheet of paper, answer the questions on pages 953–954.

from *Oedipus the King* by Sophocles

TIME AND SCENE: *The royal house of Thebes. Many years have passed since Oedipus ascended the throne of Thebes, and now a plague has struck the city. A Chorus, the citizens of Thebes, along with Oedipus and Jocasta, are on stage.*

Chorus. My king

I've said it once, I'll say it time and again—
I'd be insane, you know it,
senseless, ever to turn my back on you.

5 You who set our beloved land—storm-tossed, shattered—
straight on course. Now again, good helmsman,
steer us through the storm!

[*The Chorus draws away, leaving Oedipus and Jocasta side by side.*]

Jocasta. For the love of god,
Oedipus, tell me too, what is it?
Why this rage? You're so unbending.

10 **Oedipus.** I will tell you. I respect you, Jocasta,
much more than these men here . . . [*Glancing at the Chorus.*]
Creon's to blame. Creon schemes against me.

Jocasta. Tell me clearly, how did the quarrel start?

Oedipus. He says I murdered Laius—I am guilty.

15 **Jocasta.** How does he know? Some secret knowledge
or simply hearsay?

Oedipus. Oh, he sent his prophet
to do his dirty work. You know Creon,
Creon keeps his own lips clean.

Jocasta. A prophet?
Well then, free yourself of every charge!
Listen to me and learn some peace of mind.

Organizing Information

Graphic organizers—such as Foldables™, diagrams, and charts—help you keep your information and ideas organized.

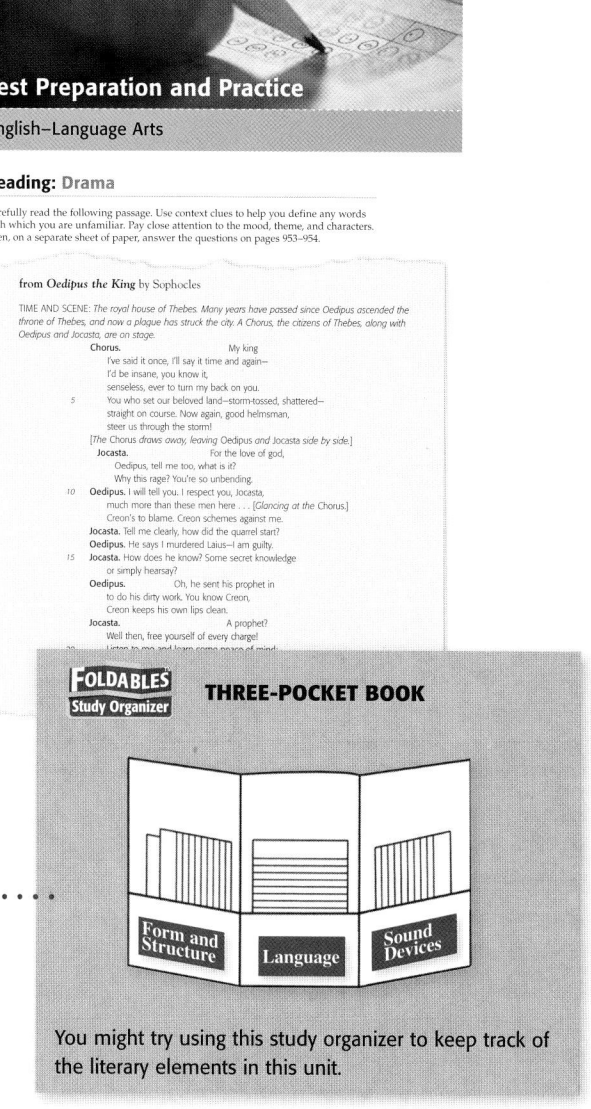

FOLDABLES Study Organizer

THREE-POCKET BOOK

Form and Structure Language Sound Devices

You might try using this study organizer to keep track of the literary elements in this unit.

SCAVENGER HUNT

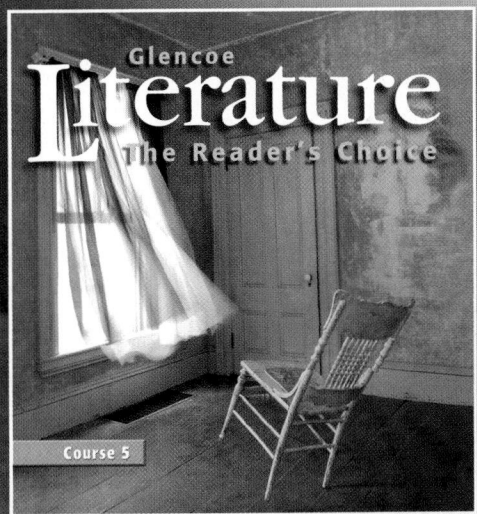

Glencoe Literature: The Reader's Choice contains a wealth of information. The trick is to know where to look to access all of that information. If you go through this scavenger hunt, either alone or with teachers or parents, you will quickly learn how the textbook is organized and how to get the most out of your reading and study time.

Let's get started!

1 How many units and parts are there in this book?
Six units and fifteen parts

2 What is the difference between the Glossary and the Index?
The Glossary lists vocabulary words and definitions. The Index lists skills, authors, titles, art, and artists.

3 There is a section on Test-Taking Strategies in the Reference Section in the back of the textbook. Where else in the book can you find help for test preparation?
In the Test Preparation and Practice section at the end of each unit

4 In what special feature can you find biographical information about a specific author?
In Meet the Author in the Before You Read pages

5 If you want to find all of the selections in the book that are short stories, where would you look?
In the Selections by Genre section at the front of the book

6 If you wanted to find a definition of the term *allegory*, where would you look?
In the Literary Terms Handbook at the back of the book

7 Where can you find the Big Ideas for each unit?
At the beginning of each unit and part

8 The Web site for this book is referred to throughout the book. What sort of information does the Web site contain that might help you?
Additional information about the literature and the authors and additional skills practice

9 Which of the book's main features will provide you with the strategies for developing your writing skills?
The Writing Workshops

After you answer all the questions, meet with a partner or a small group to compare answers.

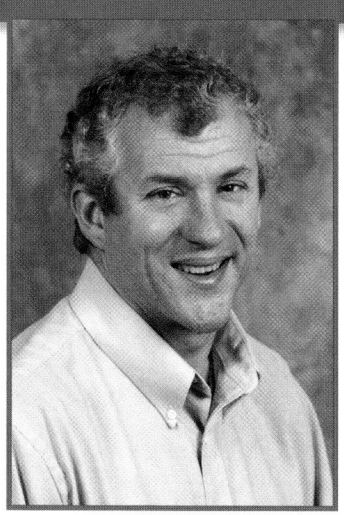

Philosophy Statement

Glencoe Literature: The Reader's Choice

by Jeffrey D. Wilhelm, PhD
Professor of English Education, Boise State University

G *lencoe Literature: The Reader's Choice* is a uniquely powerful program for helping to engage and teach your students. Why? It is an inquiry-based program, featuring differentiated instruction and using an integrated "Big Ideas" approach.

An Inquiry-Based Approach

Inquiry is a research-based approach that gives students significant reasons or purposes for reading. It is the most powerful instructional treatment for both engaging students and assisting them to learn essential concepts and strategies. Based on his review of research, George Hillocks has famously argued that all reading and writing are forms of inquiry and that they are best taught and learned through inquiry. *The Reader's Choice* provides a historical, cultural, and social context for every literary selection, thereby producing a framework for inquiry and discovery. This kind of inquiry not only informs students' thinking about the literature but also informs their thinking about issues in our contemporary world.

Differentiated Instruction

All classroom teachers understand that their students bring different interests and abilities to class. They have different motivations and needs. However, in most classrooms, every student is asked to do the same thing at the same time. With an inquiry-based approach, individual students can read texts that are appropriate to their interests and abilities, engage in more or less practice with particular strategies, work in different small groups, and yet still be part of the common classroom project of pursuing an inquiry. In fact, with this type of learning environment, difference becomes an asset and a resource,

because those who read different things and learn different concepts and strategies have a unique contribution to offer the group (Wilhelm 2006). In *The Reader's Choice,* we introduce various resources, such as graphic novels and informational texts, which appeal to a variety of learners' needs and can be used with individual students or small groups. We also suggest ways to pursue various selections and activities with students so that the power of differentiation can be tapped.

The Big Ideas

The Reader's Choice also employs the exclusive **Big Ideas** approach that organizes, motivates, and guides student learning. The **Big Ideas,** which guide each unit, are personally relevant to students and socially significant in the world. Teachers can achieve curricular coherence because all instructional materials, whether conceptual or procedural, are organized around understanding the central ideas. For example, stories and poems that were once taught in isolation from each other now inform each other as they address the central guiding ideas. Using this approach, students are much more likely to understand important concepts that they can apply both to their lives and to their future reading and writing.

Motivation

Motivating students is the greatest challenge facing teachers today, particularly when it comes to reading and writing. The seminal research of John Guthrie (2002), my own award-winning research on boys and literacy development (Smith and Wilhelm 2002, 2006), and various national reports and reviews have demonstrated this.

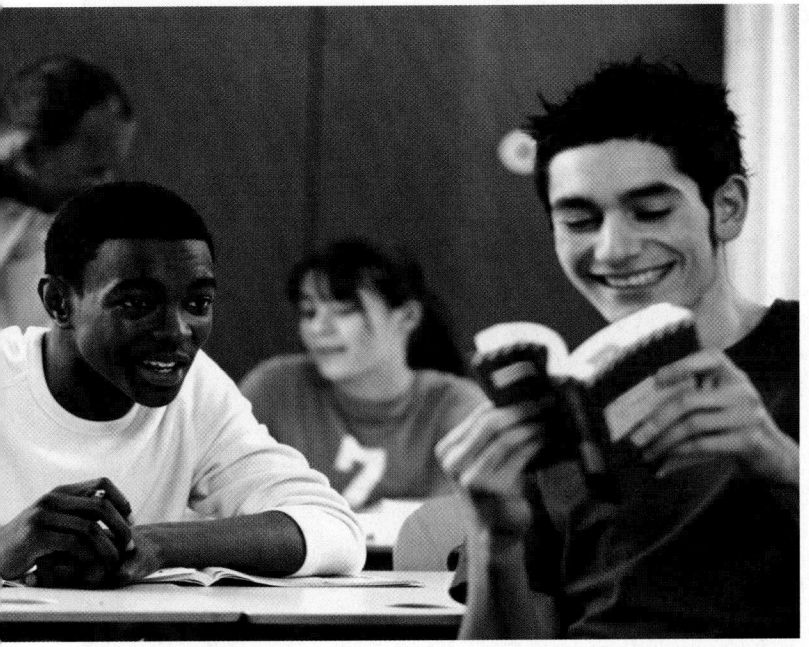

When Michael Smith and I undertook our studies of boys' literacy, we found that before students would engage with a literacy task, they needed to understand the purpose and to know that they would receive the necessary assistance for success. They also needed to know that they would become more competent in obvious ways, that they would be able to exert more control over their own lives as a result, and that they would engage in social activity. The research of Czikszentmihalyi (1990), Gee (2003), and others indicates that these conditions are also crucial for the learning of young women. *The Reader's Choice* is designed first and foremost to meet these motivational prerequisites to engagement and learning.

Works Cited

Applebee, A. N., Burroughs, R., and Stevens, A. S. 2000. Shaping Conversations: A study of continuity and coherence in high school literature curricula. *Research in the Teaching of English* 34:396–429.

Brown, J., Collins, A., and DuGuid, P. 1989. Situated cognition and the culture of learning. *Educational Researcher* 18, 32–42.

Caskey, M. 2006. The evidence for core curriculum—past and present. *Middle School Journal* (37)3, 48–54.

Csikszentmihalyi, M. 1990. Flow: *The Psychology of Optimal Experience.* New York: Harper & Row.

Gee, J. 2003. *What Video Games Have to Teach Us About Learning and Literacy.* New York: Palgrave Macmillan.

Guthrie, J. 2002. Classroom contexts for engaged reading: An overview. http://www.cori.umd.edu/Research/Papers/Classroom.htm.

Hidi, S., and Harackiewicz, J. M. 2000. Motivating the academically unmotivated: A critical issue for the twenty-first century. *Review of Educational Research* 70, 151–180.

Hillocks, G. 1995. *Teaching Writing as Reflective Practice.* New York: Teachers College Press.

Hillocks, G., Jr. 1999. *Ways of Teaching/Ways of Learning.* New York: Teachers College Press.

Jacobs, Heidi Hayes. 1989. *Interdisciplinary Curriculum: Design and implementation.* Washington, DC: ASCD.

Smith, M. W., and Wilhelm, J. D. 2006 *Going with the Flow: How to engage boys (and girls) in their literacy learning.* Portsmouth, NH: Heinemann.

Smith, M. W., and Wilhelm, J. D. 2002 *Reading Don't Fix No Chevys: Literacy in the lives of young men.* Portsmouth, NH: Heinemann.

Tyler, R. 1949. *Basic Principles of Curriculum and Instruction.* Chicago: University of Chicago Press.

Wertsch, J. 1998. *Mind as Action.* New York: Oxford University Press.

Wiggins, G., and McTighe, J. 2003. *Understanding by Design.* Washington, DC: ASCD.

Wilhelm, J. D., Baker, T., and Dube-Hackett, J. 2001. *Strategic Reading.* Portsmouth, NH: Heinemann.

Wilhelm, J. D. 2006. *Inquiring Minds Learn to Read and Write: Inquiry, questioning and discussion strategies to improve reading and writing.* New York: Scholastic.

The *Reading Next* Report

What Is the Focus of the Report?

In 2004 the Carnegie Corporation released *Reading Next— A Vision for Action and Research in Middle and High School Literacy: A Report to Carnegie Corporation of New York.* Authored by Harvard researchers Gina Biancarosa and Dr. Catherine Snow and published by the Alliance for Excellent Education in Washington, D.C., the report responds to the growing literacy crisis among middle and high school students.

The contours of this problem are troubling. For example, in the United States today, more than eight million students in grades 4–12 lack the ability to read proficiently (U.S. DOE 2003). Every day, more than three thousand students drop out of high school (Alliance for Excellent Education 2003)—largely because they lack the literacy skills to keep up (Kamil 2003; Snow and Biancarosa 2003). Only seventy percent of high school students graduate on time, and fewer than sixty percent of all African American and Latino students get their diplomas (Greene 2002). Clearly, these numbers paint a picture of a system in crisis.

The driving force behind the *Reading Next* report is simple. Students who lack literacy skills face serious disadvantages in almost every aspect of their lives—at school, at work, and in the community. Research indicates that most middle and high school readers decode well; that is, they are able to sound out the words on a given page of text. However, many of these readers are unable to conceptualize what they read or to connect new words and ideas to those they already know. Unable to comprehend the various texts they encounter, these students quickly fall behind in the three areas—school, work, and community—that matter most.

The *Reading Next* report draws attention to this problem and seeks to dispel the outdated notion that struggling and reluctant middle and high school readers are unable to benefit from literacy instruction. Instead, the report asserts, these students can and *do* benefit— significantly—from literacy instruction. According to the report, educators and other interested parties should, then, work hard to develop effective literacy programs for struggling middle and high school students.

Why Is the *Reading Next* Report Important?

The report identifies fifteen characteristics of an effective literacy program. The first nine characteristics, or recommendations, are instructional—ideas and activities that teachers can implement. The remaining six are infrastructural—ideas and activities that can be realized at the schoolwide level or in the student's home or community.

According to the report, effective literacy programs for struggling readers share the following **instructional** components:

1. **Direct, explicit comprehension instruction,** or teaching core reading strategies
2. **Effective instructional principles embedded in content,** or teaching students to use reading skills in all content areas
3. **Motivation and self-directed learning,** or motivating students to read (now and after graduation), and to become independent, lifelong learners
4. **Text-based collaborative learning,** or teaching students to interact with one another vis-à-vis a variety of texts
5. **Strategic tutoring,** or giving students intense, individualized instruction when necessary
6. **Diverse texts,** or using texts whose genre, topic, and level of difficulty vary
7. **Intensive writing,** or offering instruction that relates to the writing tasks students will perform at the high school level and beyond
8. **A technology component,** or using technology as a tool for and topic of literacy instruction
9. **Ongoing formative assessment of students,** or conducting frequent, informal assessments of student progress under current instructional practices

The report also notes that effective literacy programs share the following **infrastructural** components:

10. **Extended time for literacy,** or offering two to four hours of interdisciplinary (cross-classroom and cross-content area) literacy instruction per day

11. **Professional development,** or offering long-term and ongoing support for teachers

12. **Ongoing summative assessment of students and programs,** or evaluating students and educators in order to build accountability and improve systems

13. **Teacher teams,** or forming interdisciplinary groups that discuss and are accountable for students' progress

14. **Leadership,** or the execution of program goals by teachers and principals who understand their students and their reading and writing curriculum

15. **A comprehensive and coordinated literacy program,** or the formation of a literacy program that draws strength from various disciplines, departments, and community organizations

Glencoe Literature: The Reader's Choice and the Reading Next Report

The *Reading Next* report recommends nine instructional improvements, and *The Reader's Choice* program equips teachers to implement all of them—when, where, and how they choose. Developed with these improvements in mind, *The Reader's Choice* gives teachers the instructional tools they need to help students in the ways that matter most.

The Reading Next Report recommends...	The Reader's Choice features...
direct, explicit comprehension instruction.	**Before You Read** pages, which clearly teach reading skills, literary elements and analysis, and vocabulary development.
effective instructional principles embedded in content.	**Vocabulary Workshops, Grammar Workshops, Writing Workshops**, which focus on the teach-model-practice-assess mode of instruction.
motivation and self-directed learning.	**Independent Reading** pages, which motivate students to explore literary works on their own.
text-based collaborative learning.	several types of partner and group activities, which encourage students to work together and share opinions about the text.
strategic tutoring.	peer review activities in the **Writing Workshops**, which give students the opportunity to work in small mentoring groups.
diverse texts.	a wide range of literary selections from various genres.
intensive writing.	**Writing Workshops** and **Writing About Literature** activities, which help students develop the connection between reading and writing.
a technology component.	a variety of technology-based components, such **Glencoe.online** products, the *Student Works* **CD-ROM,** and the *Skill Arcade* **CD-ROM,** which help students build proficiency.
ongoing formative assessment of students.	end-of-unit **Test Preparation and Practice** pages, which are designed to gauge students' mastery of reading, writing, and vocabulary skills.

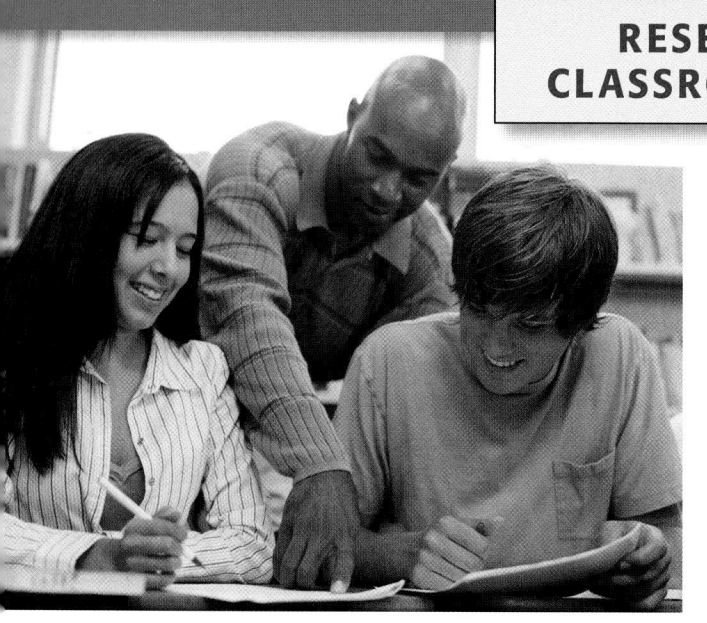

Inquiry-Based Learning

The Power of Inquiry for Teaching Reading and Writing

by Jeffrey D. Wilhelm, PhD
Professor of English Education,
Boise State University

The late MIT physicist Jerrold Zaccharias once defined education as "the raising of questions worth arguing about." As my research has shown, many students would agree (Smith and Wilhelm 2003). They do not want to "play guess what the teacher already knows"—they want to pursue questions that really matter to them personally and in the world.

Our foremost educators since John Dewey's time have argued against information-transmission modes of instruction and for "hands-on" and "minds-on" learning. Surveys of students and research in the field support the use of inquiry approaches instead of information transmission. Inquiry approaches have been shown to improve student engagement, attitude, achievement, and learning in a wide spectrum of areas.

What Is Inquiry?

Inquiry is the problem-oriented exploration of questions that drive and organize the disciplines. Through inquiry students learn essential concepts and strategies for doing work and applying understanding in the real world. They engage in the same kinds of conversations, problem solving, and applications that real practitioners do and make use of the same tools.

Finding out about existing information is part of true inquiry, but it is only the initial step. Inquirers then proceed to many other steps that help them interpret, generate, and shape information into knowledge. Human beings want to make meanings, not just receive them. Students want to be agents and actors in the world and do not want their actions dictated by teachers' directions and past ways of understanding. They want to mark their own identities, not merely take on other people's identities, ideas, and ways of doing things.

Inquiry-oriented, active, discussion-based learning, particularly when abetted by a purposeful curriculum of connected activities, works to build deep understandings over time and an emphasis on high academic achievement.

Inquiry-Based Learning and *Glencoe Literature: The Reader's Choice*

There are numerous advantages to using the inquiry approach (see Hillocks 1999; Wiggins and McTighe 1998). Here we'll touch briefly on what seem to me to be the most important: motivation, context, and curricular coherence.

Motivation

In my own research (Smith and Wilhelm 2002; 2006; Wilhelm and Friedemann 1998), I've found that inquiry approaches organized around essential questions that embed reading and composing as meaningful inquiry-oriented activities have many benefits. These include increased student engagement, comprehension, better behavior and assignment completion, and deeper learning. In *Glencoe Literature: The Reader's Choice*, each unit is organized around the **Big Ideas,** designed to make learning matter to students in immediate ways.

Context

Many of the reading, composing, and language activities in *The Reader's Choice* are organized around real problems and issues, providing a meaningful context for students. Grammar, vocabulary, and reading and writing strategies are taught in the context of immediate use and are in service to reading or composing something that is personally relevant and that addresses the inquiry question.

Curricular Coherence

Inquiry teaching characterizes what Applebee, Burroughs, and Stevens (2000) call an *integrated* curriculum, that is, a curriculum in which students develop a set of skills, strategies, or tools that they apply with increasing sophistication across a range of activities. Everything that is learned is learned sequentially and in an integrated way by addressing the **Big Ideas.** Through inquiry a congruence of means and ends is achieved (Wiggins and McTighe 1998). Reading and writing help students personally address historically and socially significant issues. Likewise, grammar is taught in the context of the literary selections and students' own writing so that it is situated and meaningful. Care has been taken to teach grammatical constructs when it will help students with the kinds of writing they are engaged in at that time. In this way, reading and writing become integrated as forms of inquiry taught in a context of inquiry. By using this exciting approach, your students will see all of the benefits that accompany inquiry approaches.

Works Cited

Please Note: Some elements of this white paper appear in *Going with the Flow,* Smith and Wilhelm, and *Inquiring Minds Learn to Read and Write,* Wilhelm. Used with permission. Interested readers can find fuller treatments of the ideas presented here, along with relevant supporting research, by referring to these books.

Applebee, A. N., Burroughs, R., and Stevens, A. S. 2000. Shaping Conversations: A study of continuity and coherence in high school literature curricula. *Research in the Teaching of English* 34:396–429.

Dewey, J. 1916. *Democracy in Education.* New York: The Free Press.

Hillocks, G., Jr. 1999. *Ways of Thinking, Ways of Teaching.* New York: Teachers College Press.

Smith, M. W., and Wilhelm, J. D. 2002 *Reading Don't Fix No Chevys: Literacy in the lives of young men.* Portsmouth, NH: Heinemann.

Smith, M. W. and Wilhelm, J. D. 2006. *Going with the Flow: How to engage boys (and girls) in their literacy learning.* Portsmouth, NH: Heinemann.

Wiggins, G., and McTighe, J. 1998. *Understanding by Design.* Alexandria, VA: ASCD.

Wilhelm, J. D. 2003. *Reading IS Seeing.* New York: Scholastic.

Wilhelm, J. D., and Friedemann, P. 1998. *Hyperlearning: Where projects, inquiry, and technology meet.* York, ME: Stenhouse.

Differentiated Instruction

Meeting the Diverse Needs of Our Students

by Douglas Fisher, PhD
Professor of Education and Director of Professional Development,
San Diego State University

Today's classroom contains students from a variety of backgrounds and with a variety of learning styles, strengths, and challenges. With careful planning, you can address the needs of all students in the literature classroom, using *Glencoe Literature: The Reader's Choice.* The basis for this planning is differentiated learning.

Differentiated Instruction Is a Key to Access

To differentiate instruction, teachers must acknowledge and react accordingly to students' differences in background knowledge, interests, needs, learning styles and preferences, and current reading, writing, and English language skills. The general guidelines for differentiating instruction include:

- **Linking assessment with instruction** Assessments should occur before, during, and after instruction to ensure that the curriculum is aligned with what students do and do not know. Using assessments in this way allows you to plan instruction for whole groups, small groups, and individual students.

- **Clarifying key concepts and generalizations** Students need to know what is essential and how this information can be used in their future learning. In addition, students need to develop a sense of the **Big Ideas**—historical, cultural, or social concepts that structure each unit in *The Reader's Choice.*

- **Emphasizing critical and creative thinking** The content, process, and products used or assigned in the classroom should require that students think about what they are learning. While some students may require support, additional motivation, varied tasks, materials, or equipment, the overall focus on critical and creative thinking allows for all students to participate in the lesson.

- **Including teacher- and student-selected tasks** A differentiated classroom includes both teacher- and student-selected activities and tasks. At some points in the lesson, the teacher must provide instruction and assign learning activities. At other points, students should be provided choices in how they engage with the content. This balance increases motivation, engagement, and learning.

Supporting Individual Students

The vast majority of students will thrive in a classroom based on differentiated instruction. However, wise teachers recognize that no single option will work for all students and that there may be students who require unique systems of support to be successful.

Tips for Instruction

The following tips for instruction can support your efforts to help all students reach their maximum potential.

- Survey students to discover their individual differences. Use interest inventories of their unique talents so you can encourage contributions in the classroom.

- Be a model for respecting others. Adolescents crave social acceptance. The student with learning differences is especially sensitive to correction and criticism, particularly when it comes from a teacher. Your behavior will set the tone for how students treat one another.

- Expand opportunities for success. Provide a variety of instructional activities that reinforce skills and concepts.

- Establish measurable objectives and decide how you can best help students meet them.

- Celebrate successes and make note of and praise "work in progress."

- Keep it simple. Point out problem areas if doing so can help a student effect change. Avoid overwhelming students with too many goals at one time.

- Assign cooperative group projects that challenge all students to contribute to solving a problem or creating a product.

How Do I Reach Students with Learning Disabilities?

- Provide support and structure. Clearly specify rules, assignments, and responsibilities.
- Practice skills frequently. Use games and drills to help maintain student interest.
- Incorporate many modalities into the learning process. Provide opportunities to say, hear, write, read, and act out important concepts and information.
- Link new skills and concepts to those already mastered.
- If possible, allow students to record answers on audiotape.
- Allow extra time to complete assessments and assignments.
- Let students demonstrate proficiency with alternative presentations, including oral reports, role plays, art projects, and musical presentations.
- Provide outlines, notes, or tape recordings of lecture material.
- Pair students with peer helpers and provide class time for pair interaction.

How Do I Reach English Language Learners?

- Remember that students' ability to speak English does not reflect their academic abilities.
- Try to incorporate the students' cultural experiences into your instruction. The help of a bilingual aide may be effective.
- Avoid any references in your instruction that could be construed as cultural stereotypes.

- Preteach important vocabulary and concepts.
- Encourage students to preview text, such as noting headings, before they begin reading.
- Remind students not to ignore graphic organizers, photographs, and maps since there is much information in these visuals.
- Use artifacts and photographs whenever possible to build background knowledge and understanding. An example of this would be coins in a foreign currency or a raw cotton ball to reinforce cotton's importance in history.

How Do I Reach Gifted Students?

- Make arrangements for students to take selected subjects early and to work on independent projects.
- Ask "what if" questions to develop high-level thinking skills. Establish an environment safe for risk taking in your classroom.
- Emphasize concepts, theories, ideas, relationships, and generalizations about the content.
- Promote interest in the past by inviting students to make connections to the present.
- Let students express themselves in alternate ways such as creative writing, acting, debates, simulations, drawing, or music.
- Provide students with a catalog of helpful resources, listing things such as agencies that provide free or inexpensive materials, appropriate community services and programs, and community experts who might be called upon to speak to your students.
- Assign extension projects that allow students to solve real-life problems related to their communities.

References

Fisher, D. 2005. The missing link: standards, assessment, and instruction. *Voices From the Middle.* 13(2), 8–11.

McTighe, J., Seif, E., and Wiggins, G. 2004. You can teach for meaning. *Educational Leadership* 62(1), 26-30.

Pflaum, S. W., and Bishop, P. A. 2004. Student perceptions of reading engagement: learning from the learners. *Journal of Adolescent and Adult Literacy* 48(3), 202–213.

Tomlinson, C. A., and McTighe, J. 2006. *Integrating Differentiated Instruction & Understanding by Design: Connecting content and kids.* Alexandria, VA: ASCD.

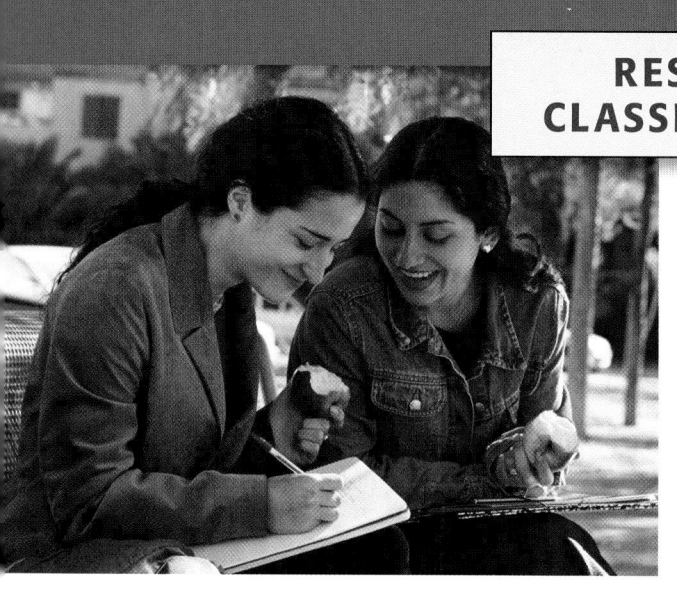

Content Literacy

Ensuring that Students Access the Text to Build Reading, Writing, and Thinking Skills

by Douglas Fisher, PhD,
Professor of Education
and Director of Professional Development,
San Diego State University

Considerable research evidence exists regarding "what works" in helping students understand difficult concepts and content. The evidence to date clearly indicates that teachers must activate students' background and prior knowledge, teach students how to take notes and use graphic organizers, focus on vocabulary, and help students develop their thinking through writing. As such, our instructional goals are multifaceted. Students must read, write, speak, listen, and view in order to understand the content. This requires that we provide content literacy instruction that is evidence based and results in increased achievement.

Activating Background and Prior Knowledge

Decades of research strongly suggest that learning is dependent on attention and interest. When we have and hold students' attention and interest, they think about the content of our classes, and they learn. To gain their attention, we have to activate both background knowledge and prior knowledge (Dochy, Segers, & Buehl 1999).

Although they are sometimes used interchangeably, *background knowledge* and *prior knowledge* are different yet complementary ideas. Background knowledge is the information that students have because of who they are and what they have experienced. Prior knowledge is the information that students should know based on their participation in previous schooling experiences. Activating and building both background and prior knowledge focus students' attention on the topic at hand, a powerful way to begin a standards-aligned unit of study.

Note Taking

The ability to take and organize notes is a significant predictor of student success. Notes serve an external storage function, which builds comprehension and understanding of the content. Over time, and with instruction, students not only use their notes for external storage of information, but also for encoding their ideas. Pauk (1974) has observed that note taking is a critical skill for college success. Peverly, Brobst, Graham, and Shaw (2003) showed that background knowledge and note taking were significant predictors of success on tests.

In other words, note taking is a critical skill. But the question remains: what kind of note-taking system works? According to a number of studies, a two-column format, such as Cornell note taking, is effective (Fisher, 2001). With this format, students take notes and complete the tasks on the right side of the page while the left side provides a guide to key points. These key points help students quickly find information, locate references, and study for exams. As Faber, Morris, and Lieberman (2000) found, the Cornell note-taking system increases comprehension (and test scores!).

Graphic Organizers

Graphic organizers, such as concept maps, semantic webs, and cause-and-effect charts, also help students visually organize information presented in text format (Fisher, Frey, & Williams 2002). In addition, graphic organizers are a good way to summarize information and will aid students in remembering and recalling content (Irwin-DeVitis & Pease 1995; Wilson 2002).

Graphic organizers have been used successfully by many different kinds of learners, including English language learners, struggling readers, students with disabilities, and students who are gifted and talented. The usefulness of graphic organizers is well documented, and they are a powerful way to ensure that students learn and understand content.

Vocabulary

The vocabulary demands in secondary schools are intense. Students are expected to learn thousands of words per year in multiple content areas. In a study of secondary students, Espin and Foegen (1996) found vocabulary to be a significant predictor of content-area performance. Farket and Elmore (1992) found vocabulary knowledge to be a stronger predictor of reading comprehension than most other variables, even cognitive ability.

When researchers study successful students, they often find that vocabulary knowledge is an important factor in student learning (Martino & Hoffman 2002). Teachers must ensure that their students develop the specialized and technical vocabulary to discuss the discipline, as well as the generalized vocabulary to convey their thinking about the subjects they study.

Writing to Learn

Writing is an excellent way to learn. Did you know that we all clarify our thinking when we write? Students often say that they didn't know what they thought until they wrote it down. Writing not only helps students clarify their thinking but also provides the teacher with information about what students do and do not understand (Fisher & Frey 2004). However, the writing prompts must be constructed to ensure that students engage and think as they write.

Quality writing prompts remind students to do what good readers automatically do: summarize information, predict what's coming next, make connections between their lives and the text, question the information in the text and the author of the text, clarify information and ideas, visualize what the text has to say, and make inferences or draw conclusions from facts and ideas (Harvey & Goudvis 2000).

Summary

In short, learning is language based. To comprehend academic content, students must engage in a number of reading, writing, speaking, listening, and viewing activities. These activities must be grounded in well-developed content, and they must be accessible for students. Not all strategies are created equal. There are specific instructional strategies and techniques that enjoy a firm research base. The topics, ideas, approaches, and strategies outlined in this paper and in the references below will ensure that students become increasingly literate as they learn valuable content information.

Works Cited

Dochy, F., Segers, M., and Buehl, M. M. 1999. The relationship between assessment practices and outcomes of studies: The case of research on prior knowledge. *Review of Educational Research* 69:145–186.

Espin, C. A., and Foegen, A. 1996. Validity of general outcome measures for predicting secondary students' performance on content-area tasks. *Exceptional Children* 62:497–514.

Faber, J. E., Morris, J. D., and Lieberman, M. G. 2000. The effect of note taking on ninth grade students' comprehension. *Reading Psychology* 21:257–270.

Fisher, D. 2001. "We're moving on up": Creating a schoolwide literacy effort in an urban high school. *Journal of Adolescent & Adult Literacy* 45:92–101.

Fisher, D., and Frey, N. 2004. *Improving adolescent literacy: Strategies at work.* Upper Saddle River, NJ: Merrill Prentice Hall.

Fisher, D., Frey, N., and Williams, D. 2002. Seven literacy strategies that work. *Educational Leadership* 60(3):70–73.

Harvey, S., and Goudvis, A. 2000. *Strategies That Work: Teaching comprehension to enhance understanding.* York, ME: Stenhouse.

Irwin-DeVitis, L., and Pease, D. 1995. Using graphic organizers for learning and assessment in middle level classrooms. *Middle School Journal* 26(5):57–64.

Martino, N. L., and Hoffman, P. R. 2002. An investigation of reading and language abilities of college freshmen. *Journal of Research in Reading* 25:310–318.

Pauk, W. 1974. *How to study in college.* Boston: Houghton Mifflin.

Peverly, S. T., Brobst, K. E., Graham, M., and Shaw, R. 2003. College adults are not good at self-regulation: A study on the relationship of self-regulation, note taking, and test taking. *Journal of Educational Psychology* 95:335–346.

Wilson, E. 2002. Literature and literacy in the social studies classroom: Strategies to enhance social studies instruction. *Southern Social Studies Journal* 28(1):45–57.

Vocabulary Development

Teaching and Learning Vocabulary in *The Reader's Choice* Program

by Sharon F. O'Neal, PhD
Associate Professor, Texas State University

What Is Vocabulary?

At first, this question seems simple. Vocabulary is our knowledge of words and their corresponding meanings. These are the words we use when we speak and write. These are the words we understand when we listen and read. Our job as teachers is simply to decide which words are important and help our students learn them.

However, the question becomes more complicated when we begin to think about the gradations of understanding our students bring to the printed page. Sometimes a student just barely knows a word, and she may or may not be able to figure out the meaning of the word in context. Another student may know the meaning of a word only in a single context. Finally, another student may have a full and rich understanding of a vocabulary word in multiple contexts. This student can even use the context to figure out the definition of a word that she is not sure about.

As teachers of the language arts, we want our students to build that base of established, known words in multiple contexts. Current research has shed light on the essential importance of vocabulary knowledge and vocabulary strategies across content areas and throughout life.

Why Is Vocabulary Instruction Important?

Vocabulary is the first key connection to literacy. All of the oral language that surrounds young children will play a part in their understanding of words when they begin to read. Middle and high school students also make connections between and among their experiences and knowledge and the words on a page. The talk that surrounds that text may be critical to understanding text. Reading vocabulary is crucial for understanding texts at all levels. But what about the student who speaks a language other than English? How can we build his vocabulary so that he can comprehend the selections in a literature text?

In some classrooms, it is common to have students who speak other languages in the home. Understandably, students who are learning English while simultaneously trying to learn content often lag behind in English reading success. Such struggles are frequently due to lack of word knowledge. In addition, studies have shown that vocabulary instruction may be more important to test performance than prior knowledge of content is (Jimenez et al., 1996). Studies indicate that English language learners (ELL's) make gains in vocabulary development and reading comprehension if they receive an enriched program in vocabulary development (August, et al., 2006).

Yet students who struggle with reading usually avoid reading and therefore encounter fewer words in context. If reading skills are stalled at earlier grade levels, vocabulary growth may stop altogether. Such students may be stuck in a vicious cycle. They read less because they know fewer words, and they know fewer words because they read less. The goal of *The Reader's Choice* is to entice all readers to come to the page: those who scarcely know the language of literature, those who may know the meanings of words in limited contexts, and those who have a full and rich understanding of what the English language has to offer.

How Does *The Reader's Choice* Address Vocabulary Instruction?

The average student's reading vocabulary increases by between 3,000 and 5,000 words per year. Such acquisition results in a reading vocabulary of 25,000 words by the end of middle school and 50,000 words by the end of high school for the successful student (Graves 2000). If students are to flourish in school, they must acquire 4,000 new words per year. Many words can be learned through wide and varied reading experiences, but some words must be learned through direct instruction. *The Reader's Choice* offers teachers and students both short- and long-term strategies.

Short-term strategies include providing the teacher with key words prior to reading the selection. Glencoe has mined both the fiction and nonfiction selections for those vocabulary words that are most critical for understanding the reading passage. Students are pre-taught words through discussions and activities such as categorizing words and making personal connections to the unique words found in the text.

In addition to offering instruction that leads to the immediate understanding of the selected text, *The Reader's Choice* also values the importance of providing students with strategies they can use on their own. Such long-term goals include direct instruction in the meaning of prefixes and suffixes and how the addition of such word parts alters the meaning of the base words. Precise directions for using context and reference materials are emphasized as well. In other words, it is not enough just to teach a list of words. Readers need to know the structure of text and the relationship among words.

Students must understand the larger concepts related to selected vocabulary words. In *The Reader's Choice,* students' background knowledge is continually tapped and built so that they are better prepared for reading. Students must know many things about words—their literal meanings, their various connotations, and their semantic associates (synonyms and antonyms, for example). Both depth and breadth of word knowledge are examined. Teachers can assess word knowledge through a variety of products including journal entries, word maps, and word banks. These provide practice for the learner and inform the teacher about the progress of the learner.

Throughout the program, *The Reader's Choice* is sensitive to the importance of wide exposure to vocabulary. As a result, multiple opportunities are provided to read related texts in varied content areas. Teachers and students will find bibliographies of additional readings related to the text provided throughout the program.

Works Cited

August, D., Carlo, M., Lively, T., McLaughlin, B., and Snow, C. 2006. Promoting the vocabulary growth of English learners. In T. Young and M. Hadaway (Eds.) *Supporting the Development of English Learners: Increasing success in all classrooms.* Newark, DE: International Reading Association.

Graves, M. F. 2000. A vocabulary program to complement and bolster a middle grade comprehension program. In B. Taylor, M. Graves, and P. van den Broek (Eds.) *Reading for Meaning: Fostering comprehension in the middle grades.* Newark, DE: International Reading Association.

Jimenez, R., Garcia, G., and Pearson, P. 1996. The reading strategies of Latino/a students who are successful English readers: Opportunities and obstacles. *Reading Research Quarterly* 31:31–61.

Writing

by Jacqueline Jones Royster, DA
*Professor of English and Senior Vice Provost and
Executive Dean of the College of Arts and Sciences,
The Ohio State University*

As both art and artifact, writing is a flexible tool that can work dynamically with other elements of instruction to enhance both learning and performance. The collection of texts and activities in *Glencoe Literature: The Reader's Choice* offers a theoretically and pedagogically sound way to address the challenges of developing the writing and related skills of students in the classroom. Writing activities are generously incorporated throughout each thematic unit for a variety of purposes. The series takes into account contemporary trends in both scholarship and practice and sets forth features that offer much potential for success.

Writing to Make Personal Connections with Reading Selections

Through journaling and other writing activities in *The Reader's Choice*, students have a mechanism for responding to whatever they read and making sense of the details. Writing can help students express personal connections with ideas, images, and experiences; discover ways to go beyond their own connections toward broader implications; and note critical distinctions between their own experiences and the content of the reading selections.

Writing to Experiment as Creative Thinkers

We as teachers accomplish an important cultural task when we help students move from viewing themselves as just consumers of other people's writing to seeing themselves as producers of writing. The creative writing activities in *The Reader's Choice* encourage students to write in many genres and to compose and present their work through various media. With these writing activities, students can explore varied roles and diverse points of view as a way to think seriously about what it means to produce literature.

Writing to Understand Form and Function

Through the **Writing Workshops** in *The Reader's Choice*, students gain direct experience producing various forms and genres of writing. The genre knowledge students build helps them to see writing as having structure and organization as shaped by audience, purpose, and context. Throughout *The Reader's Choice*, writing activities reinforce students' understanding of form and function by asking them to try their own hand at writing reflective essays, literary analyses, historical investigations, autobiographical sketches, persuasive speeches, short stories, and other distinctive forms.

Writing to Develop Thinking Skills

Writing helps students think about what a text says and does and whether it is successful. Students can sort through ideas, weigh the impact and consequences of language choices, and use these assessments to make informed judgments about what works in written expression and why.

The writing activities in *The Reader's Choice* foster students' abilities to think like literary critics. The **Literary Criticism, You're the Critic,** and **Primary Source Quotation** activities, for example, use scholarly quotations to prompt students to write thoughtful analyses of the selections. Through writing, students can express what appeals to them as readers and explain how authors achieve particular effects, justifying their interpretations by providing examples and evidence from the text. Students may also investigate the broader meaning of texts through research and writing. By gathering and synthesizing information from primary and secondary sources, students can discover the historical, political, or cultural context of a literary work.

Writing to Communicate Effectively

The act of writing itself—writing frequently for many purposes and in various genres—hones students' abilities as writers and communicators. Through activities, workshops, and assessments, *The Reader's Choice* provides ample practice for developing writing skills. For example, the Writing Workshops at the end of each theme guide students through the writing process and focus on particular moments of engagement—

prewriting, drafting, revising, editing/proofreading, and publishing/presenting.

In addition, complete annotated **Writing Models**—both student workshop models and professional models—help teachers and students focus on these **Traits of Strong Writing:**

- **Ideas** The message or the theme and the details that develop it
- **Organization** The arrangement of main ideas and supporting details
- **Voice** A writer's unique way of using tone and style
- **Word Choice** The vocabulary a writer uses to convey meaning
- **Sentence Fluency** The smooth rhythm and flow of sentences in length and style
- **Conventions** Correct spelling, grammar, usage, and mechanics
- **Presentation** The way words and design elements look on a page

Writing to Master Standard English Conventions

The Reader's Choice provides two paths for achieving mastery of grammar, usage, and mechanics:

- **Point-of-Use Approach** In both the Student and Teacher Wraparound editions, **Grammar Workshops** and **Author's Language and Style** activities help teachers review a skill in grammar, usage, or mechanics while linking that skill to an author's

application of it in a literary work, thus giving students a "real-world" example from which to learn.

- **Systematic Approach** Teachers may use the *Language Handbook* in the **Reference Section** of *The Reader's Choice* to study English language conventions systematically, moving methodically through instruction in skills such as identifying parts of speech, using modifiers correctly, and enhancing sentence fluency through sentence combining.

Writing to Prepare for the Real World

Many writing activities in *The Reader's Choice* ask students to draft career-related or public documents in response to literature. For example, students might write a brochure about a poetic setting, an interview with a character from a short story, or a news broadcast on an author's life. The *Business Writing Handbook* focuses on business and technical documents, such as résumés, memos, and business e-mails. In addition, students are regularly asked to conduct research for informal essays and formal research reports and to use widely accepted conventions for citing and documenting sources.

To prepare students for the **Advanced Placement** examination and for college work, activities such as **Literary Analysis** and **Writing About Literature** require students to write analyses of works of literature and the literary elements that shape them. These kinds of writing help sharpen students' understandings of audience and purpose and enhance their abilities to write clearly and coherently for situations they will encounter beyond high school.

Recommended Readings

Benson, C., and Christian, S., (Eds.) 2002. *Writing to Make a Difference: Classroom projects for community change.* New York: Teachers College Press.

Branscombe, N. A., Goswami, D., and Schwartz, J., (Eds.) 1992. *Students Teaching, Teachers Learning.* Portsmouth, NH: Boynton/Cook.

Dean, D. 2006. *Strategic Writing: The writing process and beyond in the secondary English classroom.* Urbana, IL: NCTE.

Golub, J. N. 2000. *Making Learning Happen: Strategies for an interactive classroom.* Urbana, IL: NCTE.

Mitchell, D., and Christenbury, L. 2000. *Both Art and Craft: Teaching ideas that spark learning.* Urbana, IL: NCTE.

The National Commission on Writing in America's Schools and Colleges. 2003. *The Neglected "R."* New York: The College Entrance Examination Board.

Shanahan, T. (Ed.) 1994. *Teachers Thinking, Teachers Knowing: Reflections on literacy and language education.* Urbana, IL: NCTE.

English Language Learners

by Mary A. Avalos, PhD
Assistant Department Chair and Research Assistant Professor,
Department of Teaching and Learning, University of Miami

English language learners are a growing population in our schools. During the 2000–2001 academic year, more than 4.5 million English language learners were enrolled in U.S. public schools (McREL 2003). The growth of culturally and linguistically diverse populations is expected to continue through this decade. Immigrants come to the United States for various reasons—some to escape political or economic oppression, others to seek higher-paying wages or provide a higher standard of living for their families. Although shifting demographics have a greater impact on certain regions of the United States, all teachers should be prepared to teach all students.

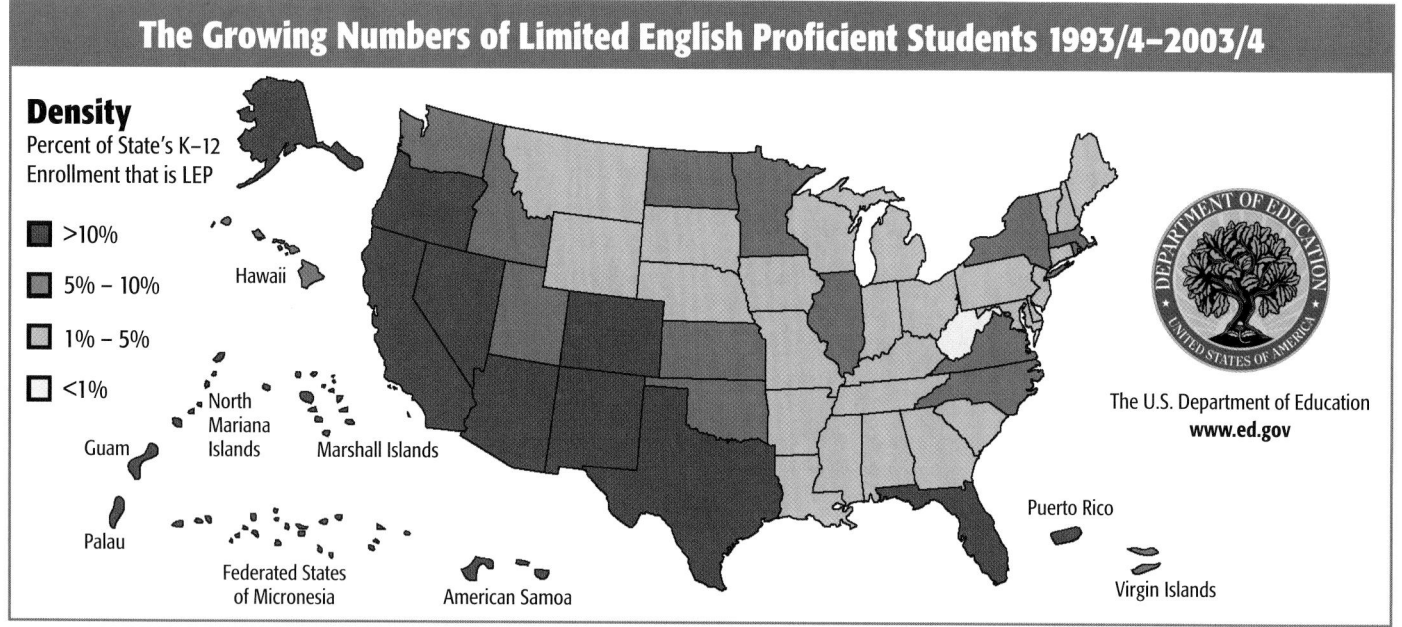

The Growing Numbers of Limited English Proficient Students 1993/4–2003/4

Density
Percent of State's K–12 Enrollment that is LEP

- ■ >10%
- ■ 5% – 10%
- ■ 1% – 5%
- □ <1%

Hawaii

North Mariana Islands
Guam
Marshall Islands

Palau

Federated States of Micronesia
American Samoa

Puerto Rico
Virgin Islands

The U.S. Department of Education
www.ed.gov

Meeting the Challenge

There are challenges specific to teaching English language learners, who must learn content while learning to read, write, and speak a new language. English language learners' literacy proficiency in their first language, or L1, will impact their literacy acquisition of a second language, or L2. (Au 1993; Cummins 2003; Hudelson 1984; Snow 1990), particularly if the L1 is similar to the L2.

English language learners make an easier transition between L1 and L2 if both languages share a similar writing system.

Writing System	Example
Alphabetic	English, French, Spanish, Italian
Syllabic	Cherokee
Logographic	Chinese

To provide effective instruction, teachers should build upon what English language learners know about language and literacy knowledge. Teachers should also consider English language learners' cultural traits, such as those related to celebration and mourning rituals, child-rearing practices, and food. Try to incorporate the students' cultural experiences into your teaching.

Gauging Levels of Language Proficiency

A common misconception is that English language learners are ready to proceed to mainstream instruction with little or no support once they are able to converse using everyday language. In reality, there are three levels of language proficiency as labeled by Cummins (2003).

Level of Language Proficiency	Example
Basic Interpersonal Conversation Skills (BICS)	ability to talk about daily activities, make requests, and retell a personal story or event
Discrete Language Skills	knowledge of phonological awareness, grammar rules, or conventions of writing in the learner's first language
Cognitive Academic Language Proficiency (CALP)	the ability to read and understand technical or subject area texts with low frequency words of Latin or Greek origin

By learning about language-acquisition processes, teachers can better meet the needs of English language learners.

Several instructional features of *Glencoe Literature: The Reader's Choice* help English language learners develop higher levels of language proficiency. Note the following examples.

1. analyzing the reading selections to facilitate comprehension of low frequency vocabulary, as well as identified vocabulary words for study

2. prompting students to activate prior knowledge before/while reading to make connections between the reader and the text

3. integrating literary elements throughout the selections to provide meaningful prompts in context

4. setting objectives to ensure that all students receive high quality, standards-based instruction

5. contextualizing writing, grammar, and spelling instruction throughout the program

All of these aides increase teacher awareness of text- and reader-based features as teachers instruct English language learners. This approach to instruction, in turn, better meets the unique needs of English language learners as they learn content and language together.

Works Cited

Au, K. H. 1993. *Literacy Instruction in Multicultural Settings.* Orlando, FL: Harcourt Brace College Publishers.

Cummins, J. 2003. Reading and the bilingual student: Fact and friction. In G. G. Garcia (Ed.) *English Learners: Reaching the highest level of English literacy.* Newark, DE: International Reading Association.

Hudelson, S. 1984. "Kan yu ret an rayt en ingles": Children become literate in English as a second language. *TESOL Quarterly* 18:221–238.

Mid-continent Research for Education and Learning. Fall 2003. English language learners and the No Child Left Behind Act. *Changing Schools: A newsletter from the Central Region Educational Laboratory* Retrieved from the Internet on February 17, 2006:

http://www.mcrel.org/PDF/ChangingSchools/5032NL_CSfall2003.pdf#search='percentage%20of%20English%20language%20learners%20in%20U.S.%20schools

Snow, C.E. 1990. Rationales for native language instruction in the education of language minority children: Evidence from research. In A. Padilla, H. Fairchild, and C. Valadez (Eds.) *Bilingual education: Issues and strategies.* pp. 60-74. Newbury Park, CA: Sage.

Jamestown Education

Support for All Readers

For over 35 years, Jamestown Education has made its primary focus helping all readers become better readers. The Jamestown programs shown here are based on the latest research in adolescent literacy and on over 35 years of experience reaching adolescent readers. Each of these programs can help you build a comprehensive and well-coordinated literary program.

Jamestown Literature: An Adapted Reader

- Grade Levels 6–10
- Reading Levels 3–8
- Instructional Support:
  This series provides grade-specific collections of literature adapted to lower reading levels. Providing struggling readers with alternative versions of canon literature offers an additional opportunity to differentiate instruction. Look for the image of *Jamestown Literature: An Adapted Reader* in the Teacher's Wraparound Edition. This reference means you can find the same selection in both *Glencoe Literature: The Reader's Choice* and *Jamestown Literature*.

In the Spotlight™

- Reading Levels 2–10
- Instructional Support:
  This eight-book series provides your students with engaging and motivating biographies to read while building their reading skills and vocabulary development. In each graduated unit, students are guided before, during, and after reading, with comprehension, skill, and vocabulary reinforcement, as well as writing exercises.

Timed Readings, Timed Readings Plus, Timed Readings in Literature

- Reading Levels 1–13+
- Instructional Support:
  Each series (ten books in each) helps your students increase both reading rate and comprehension. The fiction and nonfiction passages of uniform length are designed for systematic classroom practice to improve reading rate and comprehension of text.

Reading Fluency

- Reading Levels 1–10
- Instructional Support:
  This seven-book series helps your students read smoothly, accurately, and expressively. Students work in pairs to provide immediate feedback and self-assessment. Author Camille Blachowicz states that "the ability to read fluently is highly correlated with many other measures of reading competence."

Jamestown Reading Improvement

- Reading Levels 4–10
- Instructional Support:
  Authored by renowned reading expert Edward Fry, this eight-book series focuses on helping build your students' comprehension, vocabulary, and study skills. Repeated practice with targeted exercises ensures mastery of valuable reading skills.

Critical Reading Series

- Reading Levels 2–8
- Instructional Support:
  This 27-book, high-interest series, written at three reading spans, encourages your reluctant readers to build a love for nonfiction and focuses on critical reading skills. Topics ranging from *Fateful Journeys* to *Weird Science* to *Heroes* draw students in and give them ample opportunities to master the important skills found on both state and national tests.

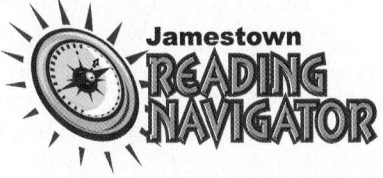

Jamestown Reading Navigator

Jamestown Reading Navigator is an online and print-based intervention program built upon the latest research in adolescent literacy, *Reading Next*. Here are the key objectives of the online version, available to students 24 hours a day from anywhere they can connect to the Web.

- Increase student achievement through direct, explicit instruction in comprehension strategies and modeling of good reading practices.
- Motivate and engage reluctant readers with a student-directed, self-paced learning environment enriched with interactive activities and media.
- Provide built-in formative and summative assessment to help teachers track student progress and make instructional decisions.

Assessment

by Beverly Ann Chin, PhD
Professor of English, Director of English Teaching Program,
University of Montana

What Is Assessment?

Assessment is the process of gathering information about student learning. The purpose of assessment is to provide evidence on what and how well students are learning in the English language arts. The best assessments clearly reflect learning objectives, instructional strategies, and curriculum standards.

Formative assessments—or assessments *for* learning— are ongoing opportunities for students to gain information about themselves and their learning processes. Teachers use formative assessments during the instructional units to help students discover their own areas of strength and areas for improvement in the English language arts.

Summative assessments—or assessments *of* learning— occur at the end of a unit of study and summarize what students have learned and how well they have met the learning objectives. Summative assessments are more formal, culminating experiences and often include student demonstrations or performances of their learning.

How Does *The Reader's Choice* Integrate Assessment?

Glencoe Literature: The Reader's Choice carefully weaves assessment *for* learning and assessment *of* learning throughout the instructional units.

We provide numerous opportunities to help students access information about their learning progress. Formative assessments, such as **Selection and Unit**

Assessments and **Interactive Tutor Self-Assessments,** give information about what students are learning and help teachers differentiate or modify their instruction. These assessments *for* learning are diagnostic and enable teachers to provide more support and resources for students during the instructional unit.

The Reader's Choice also provides multiple methods of summative and performance assessments, including:

■ assessment by learning objectives
■ rubrics for assessing student writing, listening, and speaking

Each of these assessments *of* learning gives teachers and students a clear summary of what students have learned and how well they have met the learning objectives for the unit.

In addition, *The Reader's Choice* provides students with many opportunities to practice for large-scale, standardized tests. **Test Preparation and Practice** and the *Exam***View** *Pro Assessment Suite* **CD** enable students to become familiar with different test formats and help students demonstrate their knowledge and abilities in formal testing environments.

Through formative and summative assessments, English language arts teachers gain valuable information and insight into their students' understandings of and appreciations for literature. By using assessments that align with the learning objectives and curriculum standards, we empower our students to become learners who are able to set goals, monitor their learning processes, and reflect on their growth as readers, writers, speakers, and listeners.

References

Marzano, R. J., Pickering, D. J., & McTighe, J. (1993). *Assessing Student Outcomes.* Alexandria, VA: Association for Supervision and Curriculum Development.

Nave, G., & Bellamy, P. (2005). *Improving Student Learning Through Integrated Assessment and Instruction: A Training Manual for Guided Professional Development.* Portland, OR: Northwest Regional Educational Laboratory.

Stiggins, R. J. (2001). *Student-involved Classroom Assessment* (3rd ed.). Upper Saddle River, NJ: Prentice-Hall.

Stiggins, R. J., Arter, J. A., Chappuis, J., & Chappuis, S. (2004). *Classroom Assessment for Student Learning: Doing It Right— Using It Well.* Portland, OR: Assessment Training Institute.

Wiggins, G., & McTighe, J. (1998). *Understanding by Design.* Alexandria, VA: Association of Supervision and Curriculum Development.

Technology Use

Electronic Technologies: *Everything* to Do with Literacy

by Jeffrey D. Wilhelm, PhD, Professor of English Education, Boise State University

What Is Technology?

A technology can be defined as any tool that extends our human abilities—that helps us accomplish our work more effectively. Literacy is the ability to use the most powerful tools to exchange information and to communicate, which humans do in a variety of deep and complex ways.

Neil Postman (1992) cautions that we must learn how best to use technology for our purposes or we are doomed to be used by the technology. Many critics of computers in schools argue that this is what happens: Computers are often used as expensive ways to implement old and ineffective ways of teaching. Further, students often lose sight of the nature of technology as a tool, using it instead for its own sake.

However, there is an alternative—the kind of technology use offered in *Glencoe Literature: The Reader's Choice.* By using technological applications in our inquiry-based program, students find information, organize data, develop new data and understandings, and design and represent new understandings.

The rewards of this kind of technological instruction are great. First, the purposeful use of such technologies motivates students. It fosters engagement, collaboration, and substantive learning (Smith and Wilhelm 2002, 2006; Wilhelm, 2006). Students learn to use the Internet, hypermedia, and other applications in a meaningful context. The technology also supports traditional ways of reading and composing as students converse through Web logs and e-mail, find information on the Internet, organize and analyze data electronically, and use video and computers to construct documents that can be shared through other electronic means. This kind of curriculum has been shown to have many positive effects, particularly for students often considered reluctant or "at-risk" (Wilhelm and Friedemann 1998).

How Does *The Reader's Choice* Integrate Technology?

In *The Reader's Choice,* technology is used to improve reading, composing, and learning. Technology features, such as *Skills Arcade,* **Interactive Tutor Self-Assessments, Vocabulary PuzzleMakers,** and **eWorkbooks,** reflect these principles, fostering inquiry and deep understanding.

Seymour Papert (1996), the world's foremost authority on computers and learning, writes that "the computer is the world's greatest construction kit." He agrees that literacy is intimately involved in technology and its critical use. He argues that schools that do not make meaningful use of the computer are failing our kids. Critical use, he tells us, can occur only if students find and design knowledge with technology. This kind of work is what Papert calls "hard fun," and it leads to powerful and exciting forms of learning. We have provided the context and support for this kind of learning in the text you hold in your hands. Turn the page and get ready for some "hard fun" of your own.

Works Cited

Beck, C., and Kosnick, C. 2004. Constructivist accounts of learning. In K. Leithwood, et al. (Eds.) *Teaching for Deep Understanding.* pp.13–21. Toronto: EFTP/OISE.

Papert, S. 1996. *The Connected Family.* Atlanta, GA: Longstreet Press.

Postman, N. 1992. *Technopoly: The surrender of culture to technology.* New York: Vintage.

Smith, M. W., and Wilhelm, J. D. 2002 *Reading Don't Fix No Chevys: Literacy in the lives of young men.* Portsmouth, NH: Heinemann.

Smith, M. W., and Wilhelm, J. D. 2006 *Going with the Flow: How to engage boys (and girls) in their literacy learning.* Portsmouth, NH: Heinemann.

Wilhelm, J. D. 2006. *Inquiring Minds Learn to Read and Write: Inquiry, questioning and discussion strategies to improve reading and writing.* New York: Scholastic.

Wilhelm, J. D., and Friedemann, P. 1998. *Hyperlearning: Where projects, inquiry, and technology meet.* York, ME: Stenhouse.

Project CRISS

by Carol M. Santa, PhD
Original developer of Project CRISS,
Director of Education at the Montana Academy

What Is CRISS?

CRISS stands for Creating Independence through Student-owned Strategies. It is a staff development program that I created in collaboration with middle and high school teachers in Kalispell, Montana.

The CRISS Philosophy

Project CRISS is more than a collection of learning strategies. Its underlying power rests not on the individual strategies but on the teaching philosophy behind them. This philosophy integrates work from cognitive psychology, social learning theory, and neurological research about how the brain learns. It includes the overlapping principles in the chart below.

A Systematic Approach

Project CRISS is a valuable basis for instruction. It provides a systematic approach for using what we now know about teaching and learning. The following chart lists questions we continually need to ask ourselves while we are teaching. Use this chart to monitor your efforts to incorporate CRISS principles into your teaching.

CRISS Principles	The CRISS Philosophy	Yes	No	Somewhat
Background knowledge	Did I assist students in thinking about what they already knew about the topic before beginning the unit? Did I develop necessary concepts before students read?			
Purpose setting	Did my students have a clear purpose about what they were going to learn before beginning the lesson?			
Author's craft	Can my students use the author's style of presentation to facilitate their understanding?			
Active involvement	Were my students engaged in the topic? Did I help students become actively involved in their learning?			
Discussion	Did my students have opportunities to talk about what they were learning?			
Organization	Did my students organize information in a variety of ways?			
Writing	Did my students write about what they were learning?			
Teacher modeling	Did I do enough teacher modeling of learning strategies so that students could begin using them on their own?			

Guide to Readability

Throughout the teacher materials in your Teacher Wraparound Edition, you will encounter DRP readability measures assigned to the reading selections in *The Reader's Choice*. You will also find readability scores based on the Lexile Framework® for Reading and the Dale-Chall Readability Formula. You can use these scores to select reading materials that are suitable for your entire class or for individual students.

Degrees of Reading Power® (DRP)

DRP values indicate the readability of prose text. The higher the value, the more difficult the text. The scale ranges from 1 to 100; commonly encountered English text tends to fall somewhere between 25 and 85. Although middle school texts have an average difficulty of 56, and high school texts have an average difficulty of 62, no single readability level is appropriate for each grade level. Rather, a typical classroom has materials with a range of readability levels available for use—some intended for less proficient readers, some for average readers, and some for stronger readers. The following chart shows the average DRP readability range for materials widely available for use at each grade. Some materials you might use, however, will certainly fall outside of the range for your particular grade.

Grade	DRP Readability Ranges
6	51–61
7	52–62
8	53–64
9	53–65
10	51–68
11	56–67
12	57–68

The Lexile® Framework

A Lexile measure assigned to a text is the specific number that describes the reading demands of the text. The typical Lexile Scale ranges from 200 to 1700 Lexiles. As with the DRP measures, there is not a direct translation from a specific Lexile measure to a specific grade level. Within any classroom, there will be a range of readers and a range of materials to be read. The levels shown on the following chart indicate the approximate range of Lexile scores for 50 percent of the materials found in a typical grade-level classroom. For example, the middle half of the instructional materials typically found in a sixth-grade classroom ranges in difficulty from about 850L to 1050L.

Grade	Text Measures (from Lexile Framework Map)
6	850L to 1050L
7	950L to 1075L
8	1000L to 1100L
9	1050L to 1150L
10	1100L to 1200L
11 and 12	1100L to 1300L

Dale-Chall Readability Formula

The idea behind this formula is that readers typically find it easier to read, process, and recall a passage if the words and sentences are familiar and grade appropriate. The Dale-Chall Formula assesses the difficulty of a passage by computing two different values from the text. The first measure is the average number of words per sentence. The second measure is the percentage of words in the passage not found on the grade-appropriate Dale Word List. The following chart shows the average Dale-Chall readability scores for grades 5 through 12.

Grade	Dale-Chall Readability Ranges
5–6	5.0 to 5.9
7–8	6.0 to 6.9
9–10	7.0 to 7.9
11–12	8.0 to 8.9

* Degrees of Reading Power, DRP, and TASA are registered trademarks of Touchstone Applied Science Associates, Inc. (TASA). Lexile is a registered trademark of MetaMetrics, Inc.

SCOPE AND SEQUENCE

The charts on these and the following two pages provide an overview of the scope and sequence for *Glencoe Literature: The Reader's Choice—Course 5.* For a detailed scope and sequence of skills, see the chart preceding the numbered part of each unit in the Teacher Wraparound Edition. Refer also to the Index of Skills (pages R85–R94) for a comprehensive listing of all skills and concepts taught in *The Reader's Choice—Course 5.*

● = Introduce/Teach   ● = Review

	UNIT 1	UNIT 2	UNIT 3	UNIT 4	UNIT 5	UNIT 6
Literary Criticism						
Analayzing Literature in Context						
Historical Approach	●	●	●	●	●	●
Artistic Approach		●	●	●	●	
Biographical Approach	●	●				
Literary Genres						
Oral Tradition Forms						
Song					●	
Myth, Folklore, and Legend					●	
Fiction						
Short Story	●			●		●
Novel Excerpt					●	
Nonfiction						
Autobiography or Memoir		●				
Biography		●	●			
Magazine Article	●	●	●	●	●	●
Newspaper Article		●				●
Speech		●		●		
Informational Text	●	●	●	●	●	●
Public Document		●		●		
Journal or Diary			●			
Letter	●		●			

● = Introduce/Teach ● = Review

	UNIT 1	UNIT 2	UNIT 3	UNIT 4	UNIT 5	UNIT 6
Poetry						
Narrative poem			●			●
Ballad			●		●	
Epic			●			
Drama						
Comedy				●		
Tragedy				●		
Literary Elements						
Literary Structure						
Plot	●			●	●	●
Setting	●	●	●	●	●	●
Characters	●	●	●	●	●	●
Point of View	●		●			●
Theme	●	●	●	●	●	●
Voice and Tone	●	●	●		●	●
Author's Purpose		●	●	●		●
Literary Language						
Imagery	●	●	●	●		●
Symbolism	●		●			●
Figures of Speech				●	●	●
Sound Devices			●			
Diction	●		●			●
Rhetorical Strategies		●	●	●	●	

● = Introduce/Teach   ● = Review

	UNIT 1	UNIT 2	UNIT 3	UNIT 4	UNIT 5	UNIT 6
Reading Skills						
Strategies						
Analyzing	●	●	●	●	●	●
Clarifying			●		●	
Drawing Conclusions		●	●			
Making Inferences	●		●	●	●	●
Making Predictions				●		●
Monitoring Comprehension			●			
Paraphrasing			●			
Previewing	●	●	●	●	●	●
Questioning	●	●	●			
Recognizing Bias		●		●		
Summarizing		●			●	
Synthesizing	●	●	●	●	●	●
Vocabulary Development						
Analogies	●	●	●	●	●	●
Antonyms	●	●	●	●	●	●
Context Clues	●	●	●	●	●	●
Denotation and Connotation	●		●	●		●
Multiple-Meaning Words	●		●			
Prefixes and Suffixes					●	
Synonyms	●	●	●		●	●
Word Roots	●	●		●	●	●

○ = Introduce/Teach   ● = Review

	UNIT 1	UNIT 2	UNIT 3	UNIT 4	UNIT 5	UNIT 6
Writing and Grammar						
Types of Writing						
Literary Criticism: Biographical or Historical Approach	○	●	●	●	●	●
Biographical Narrative	○	○				
Reflective Essay		○	●			
Persuasive Speech				○		
Research Report		●			●	
Short Story						○
Writing Process						
Prewriting, Drafting, Revising, Editing and Proofreading, Presenting	●	●	●	●	●	●
Traits of Strong Writing	●	●	●	●	●	●
Grammar, Usage, and Mechanics						
Parts of Speech	●	●	●	●	●	●
Capitalization and Punctuation	●	●	●	●	●	●
Sentence Structure	●	●	●	●	●	●
Listening, Speaking, and Viewing						
Presenting Literary Criticism	●					
Photo Essay		●				
Reflective Presentation			●			
Persuasive Speech				●		
Expository Presentation					●	
Oral Interpretation of a Short Story						●

To Teachers

Welcome to the Teacher Wraparound Edition of *Glencoe Literature: The Reader's Choice—Course 5.* We have created this teacher edition based on input from experienced teachers and educational consultants. Teaching suggestions, background information, point-of-use strategies, leveled activities for differentiated instruction, and more—all are conveniently "wrapped" around every page of the reduced student text.

Teaching Support The point-of-use strategies, learning objectives, activities, and informative notes in the side columns support and guide your approach to standards-based instruction.

INTRODUCING UNIT ONE

Focus

BELLRINGER

Bellringer Options
Literature Launcher Video
Daily Language Transparency 1
Or bring to class a bottle of syrup. **Say:** The flavor in this syrup is intense because it is compressed into a more compact form. How do you think the same thing is true of a short story? Have students discuss how being a more compressed type of fiction can make a short story "sweeter," such as with more focused action, fewer characters, and limited setting. Point out that since a short story writer must convey a lot in a short space, each detail is important.

Objectives for the Unit Introduction
- To identify and interpret various literary elements used in the short story (SE)
- To analyze the effect that these literary elements have upon the reader (SE)
- To analyze short stories for the ways in which authors inspire the reader to share emotions (TWE)

Ta Matete (We Shall Not Go to Market Today), 1882. Paul Gauguin. Gouache on canvas, 73 x 92 cm. Kunstmuseum, Basel, Switzerland. ★

UNIT 1 THE SHORT STORY

Unit Introduction Skills

Reading Skills
- Identifying Sequence (SE pp. 2, 6)
- Literary Response (TWE p. 6)

The Short Story

Listening/Speaking/Viewing Skills
- Discussing Theme (SE p. 8)
- Discussion (TWE p. 8)

Literary Elements
- Plot (SE pp. 2, 5)
- Character (SE pp. 3, 4)
- Setting (SE pp. 2, 4)
- Conflict and Plot (TWE p. 2)
- Diction (TWE p. 4)

Writing Skills/Grammar
- Character Analysis (SE p. 8)

Unit Introduction Skills The web diagram summarizes the skills of a major literary genre taught in the Student Edition and the Teacher Wraparound Edition.

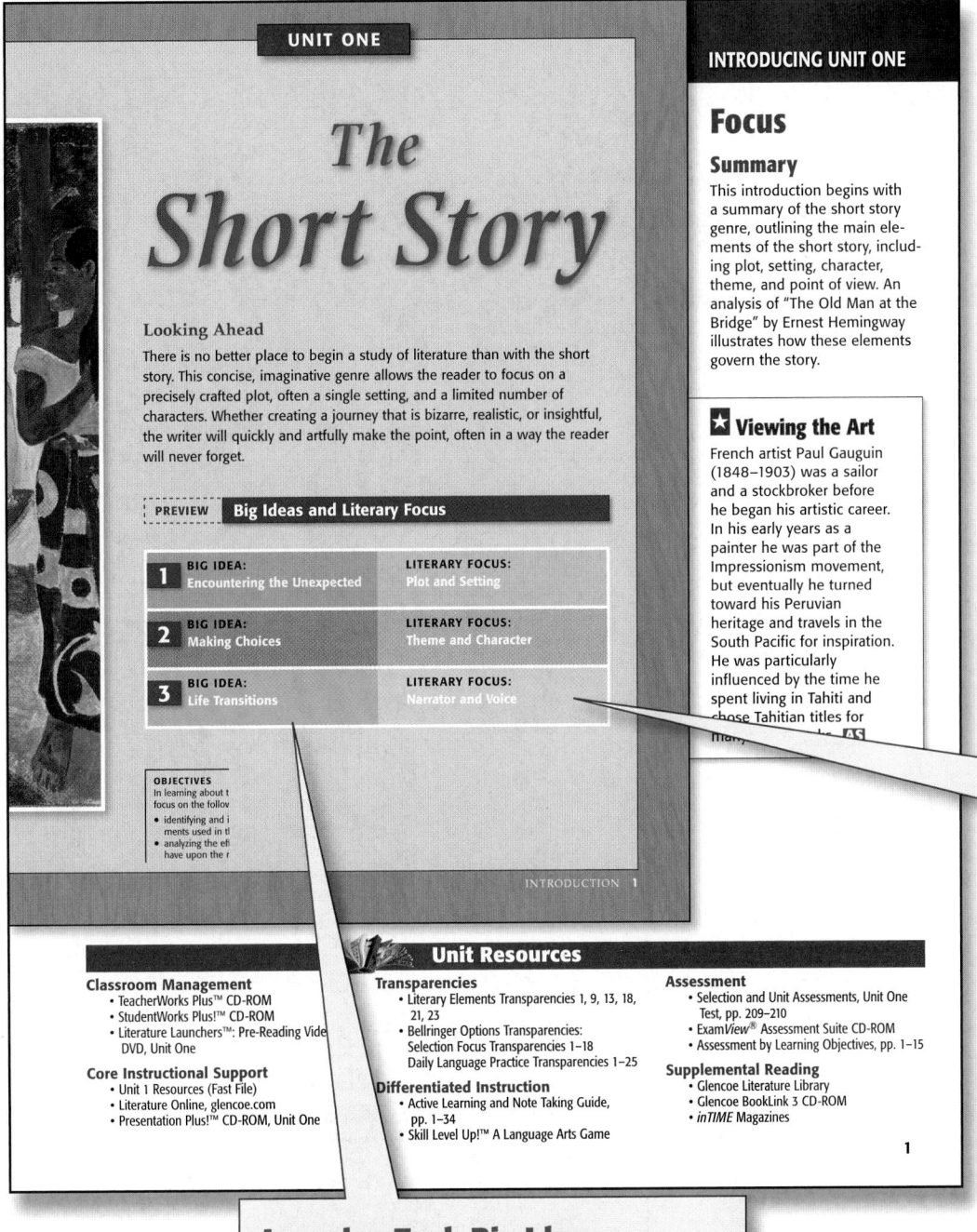

UNIT ONE

The Short Story

Looking Ahead

There is no better place to begin a study of literature than with the short story. This concise, imaginative genre allows the reader to focus on a precisely crafted plot, often a single setting, and a limited number of characters. Whether creating a journey that is bizarre, realistic, or insightful, the writer will quickly and artfully make the point, often in a way the reader will never forget.

PREVIEW **Big Ideas and Literary Focus**

1	**BIG IDEA:** Encountering the Unexpected	**LITERARY FOCUS:** Plot and Setting
2	**BIG IDEA:** Making Choices	**LITERARY FOCUS:** Theme and Character
3	**BIG IDEA:** Life Transitions	**LITERARY FOCUS:** Narrator and Voice

OBJECTIVES
In learning about t
focus on the follov
• identifying and i
ments used in tl
• analyzing the ef
have upon the r

INTRODUCTION 1

INTRODUCING UNIT ONE

Focus

Summary
This introduction begins with a summary of the short story genre, outlining the main elements of the short story, including plot, setting, character, theme, and point of view. An analysis of "The Old Man at the Bridge" by Ernest Hemingway illustrates how these elements govern the story.

★ Viewing the Art
French artist Paul Gauguin (1848–1903) was a sailor and a stockbroker before he began his artistic career. In his early years as a painter he was part of the Impressionism movement, but eventually he turned toward his Peruvian heritage and travels in the South Pacific for inspiration. He was particularly influenced by the time he spent living in Tahiti and chose Tahitian titles for ma...

Unit Resources

Classroom Management
• TeacherWorks Plus™ CD-ROM
• StudentWorks Plus!™ CD-ROM
• Literature Launchers™: Pre-Reading Vide
  DVD, Unit One

Core Instructional Support
• Unit 1 Resources (Fast File)
• Literature Online, glencoe.com
• Presentation Plus!™ CD-ROM, Unit One

Transparencies
• Literary Elements Transparencies 1, 9, 13, 18, 21, 23
• Bellringer Options Transparencies:
  Selection Focus Transparencies 1–18
  Daily Language Practice Transparencies 1–25

Differentiated Instruction
• Active Learning and Note Taking Guide, pp. 1–34
• Skill Level Up!™ A Language Arts Game

Assessment
• Selection and Unit Assessments, Unit One Test, pp. 209–210
• ExamView® Assessment Suite CD-ROM
• Assessment by Learning Objectives, pp. 1–15

Supplemental Reading
• Glencoe Literature Library
• Glencoe BookLink 3 CD-ROM
• inTIME Magazines

1

Literary Focus
The **Literary Focus** helps students analyze characteristics of a particular genre. Each part within a unit features one or two key literary elements.

Learning Tool: Big Ideas
The **Big Ideas** target thought-provoking concepts that your students can trace as they read the literary selections in the unit. Each part within a unit focuses on one Big Idea.

Lesson Support:
Structure of Reading Selections

The Teacher Wraparound Edition for reading selections in *Glencoe Literature: The Reader's Choice* is organized in a three-part structure—*Focus, Teach,* and *Assess.*

Focus A Bellringer activity and other teaching strategies engage your students in the reading selection.

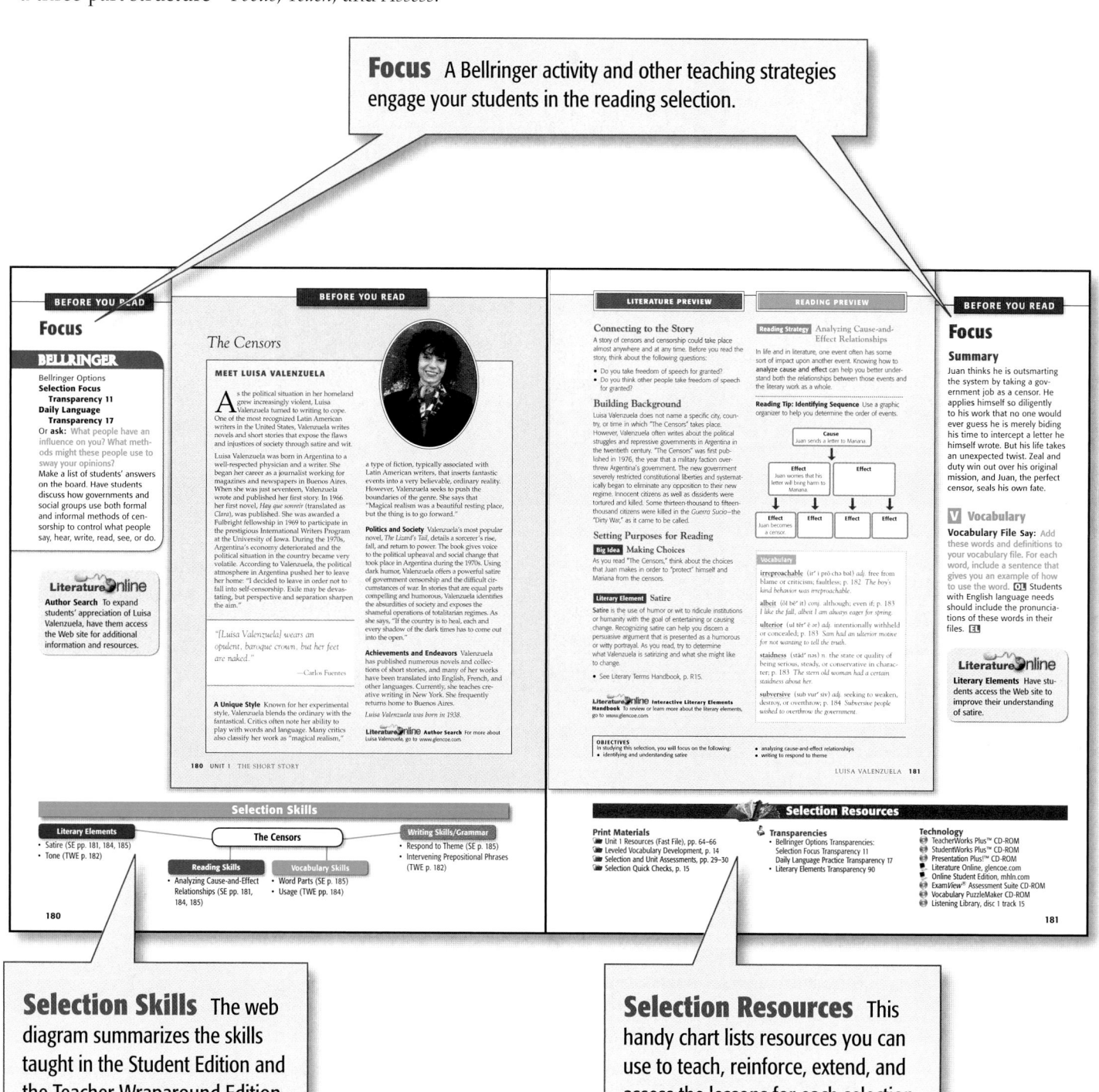

Selection Skills The web diagram summarizes the skills taught in the Student Edition and the Teacher Wraparound Edition.

Selection Resources This handy chart lists resources you can use to teach, reinforce, extend, and assess the lessons for each selection.

Teach Leveled activities stimulate learning and motivation.

The Big Idea Thought-provoking statements prompt students to explore the Big Idea in context to the reading selection.

Assess Answers to questions and activities are provided.

Teach

Big Idea

Making Choices
Say: Think about the following question as you read. What is Juan's initial attitude toward the censors? *(At first, Juan believes the censors employed by the government try so hard to find treachery that they find what does not exist. In an attempt to sabotage the system, he becomes a censor.)* **OL**

L Literary Element

Tone Remind students that tone is the writer's attitude toward the subject. One way that a writer communicates tone is through word choice and descriptive language. **Ask:** What phrases create an ominous tone? *("Poor Juan!" "they caught him with his guard down"; "one of fate's dirty tricks"; "a feeling you can't trust"; "without thinking twice")* **OL**

Readability Scores
Dale-Chall: 6.0
DRP: 62
Lexile: 1170

THE **CENSORS**

Luisa Valenzuela

Postal Montage. Natalie Racioppa.

Poor Juan! One day they caught him with his guard down before he could even realize that what he had taken as a stroke of luck was really one of fate's dirty tricks. These things happen the minute you're careless, as one often is. Juancito¹ let happiness—a feeling you can't trust—get the better of him when he received from a confidential source Mariana's new address in Paris and knew that she hadn't forgotten him. Without thinking twice, he sat down at his table and wrote her a letter. *The* letter that now keeps his mind off his job during the day and won't let him sleep at night (what had he scrawled, what had he put on that sheet of paper he sent to Mariana?).

Juan knows there won't be a problem with the letter's contents, that it's *irreproachable*, harmless. But what about the rest? He knows that they examine, sniff, feel, and read between the lines of each and every letter, and check its tiniest comma and most accidental stain. He knows that all letters pass from hand to hand and go through all sorts of tests in the huge censorship offices and that, in the end, very few continue on their way. Usually it takes months, even years, if there aren't any snags; all this time the freedom, maybe even the life, of both sender and receiver is in jeopardy. And that's why Juan's so troubled: thinking that something might happen to Mariana because of his letters. Of all people, Mariana, who must finally feel safe there where she always dreamt she'd live. But he knows that the *Censor's Secret*

1. *Juancito* (wän sē′ tō)

Big Idea **Making Choices** Considering the title of the story, why do you think Juan's choice to write a letter might be significant? **B1**

Vocabulary
irreproachable (ir′ i prōō cha bal) adj. free from blame or criticism; faultless

182 UNIT 1 THE SHORT STORY

182

Additional Support

REAL **Leveled Reading** An adapted version of this selection is available on page 36 of *Jamestown Literature: An Adapted Reader*, grade 10.

Skills Practice

GRAMMAR: Intervening Prepositional Phrases A verb must agree with its subject. If a prepositional phrase appears between the subject and the verb, the verb must still agree with its subject, not the object of the preposition. Have students rewrite each sentence, underlining the simple subject and the verb and enclosing the intervening prepositional phrase in parentheses.
1. Juan's passion for censoring letters takes over his life. *(Juan's passion (for censoring letters) takes over his life.)*
2. His goal in the early weeks is to help Mariana reach his goal *(during the early weeks) to help Mariana.)* **OL**

AFTER YOU READ

RESPONDING AND THINKING CRITICALLY

Respond
1. (a)What feelings did you have about Juan at the end of the story? (b)Did your feelings about him change during the course of the story? Explain.

Recall and Interpret
2. (a)What does Juan fear will happen to Mariana as a result of his letter? (b)What does this tell you about the kind of government Juan lives under?
3. (a)What is Juan's "unoriginal idea"? (b)Why are "more and more censors" needed, making it easy for Juan to get hired?

Analyze and Evaluate
4. (a)What parts of this story seem logical and believable to you? (b)Are there any parts that are unbelievable? Use details from the story to support your answer.
5. What does Valenzuela achieve by keeping the tone of the story light and casual?

Connect
6. **Big Idea** **Making Choices** Whose choices, Juan's or the government's, do you think had a greater impact on the outcome of the story? Explain.

LITERARY ANALYSIS

Literary Element **Satire**
Humor—a common element of *satire*—can often be persuasive as well as entertaining because it is less likely to alienate people who might initially disagree.
1. How does Juan's transformation into the perfect censor become the "punch line" for this satire? Explain.
2. Is the author's satire aimed more at the government or at individuals like Juan?

Writing About Literature
Respond to Theme Valenzuela uses satire to make a statement about a government's control over the lives of its citizens. Write a brief essay in which you identify and discuss the theme of "The Censors." Include elements from the story that are related to the theme, as well as any impressions or ideas that struck you as you read.

After you complete a draft of your essay, meet with a peer reviewer to evaluate each other's work and suggest revisions. Then proofread and edit your draft for errors in spelling, grammar, and punctuation.

Literature Online **Web Activities** For eFlashcards, Selection Quick Checks, and other Web activities, go to www.glencoe.com.

READING AND VOCABULARY

Reading Strategy Analyzing Cause-and-Effect Relationships
When authors do not tell their stories chronologically, the reader must pay close attention in order to determine the actual sequence of events and the **cause-and-effect relationships** of those events to one another.
1. Describe how the story is organized.
2. How would the impact of the story change if events were ordered differently?

Vocabulary Practice
Practice with Word Parts Read the roots and definitions below. Then pick the best definition for each of the boldfaced vocabulary words.
Latin root: *ulter*—"farther, beyond"
Old French root: *reprochier*—"to blame, accuse"
Latin root: *subvertere*—"to turn upside down, overthrow"
1. Her *ulterior* purpose was to meet with friends.
 a. cruel **b.** concealed **c.** necessary
2. The *irreproachable* candidate got the job.
 a. historical **b.** experienced **c.** faultless
3. The *subversive* group overthrew the government.
 a. rebellious **b.** powerful **c.** evil

LUISA VALENZUELA **185**

Reading Strategy
1. Begins with a reference to Juan's fate and then is told chronologically
2. Answers will vary.

Vocabulary
1. b 2. c 3. a

CheckPoint
Use the CheckPoint questions on Presentation Plus! to check students' mastery of the selection. These questions can be used with interactive response keypads for immediate student feedback.

AFTER YOU READ

Assess

1. (a) Students may not sympathize because Juan causes his own death. (b) Feelings may change from sympathy to contempt.
2. (a) Juan fears that the censors will go after Mariana. (b) The government is totalitarian.
3. (a) To get a job as a censor and retrieve his letter (b) The government wants to exert more and more control over citizens' private messages.
4. (a) Censorship, fear of censors, and executions seem believable. (b) Students may find it unbelievable that Juan would convict himself.
5. It keeps the story from being somber and supports the author's wish to mock the government's absurdities.
6. Some may say Juan's choice to change; others, the government's choice to remove freedom

Literary Element

1. Juan becomes such a perfect censor that he censors his own letter.
2. Students may say that it is aimed at the government, with the *Censor's Secret Command*, the dehumanizing nature of the censor's job, and the building's outwardly "festive air."

Writing About Literature

Students should consider how satire points out the absurdities of bureaucracy, the impact of people's decisions on their lives, and the importance of personal liberties.

185

Color-Coded Highlighting The legend below explains the kinds of color coding.

- **Big Idea**
- **Literary Element**
- **Reading Strategy**
- **Vocabulary**

Informational Text

The wide range of informational text in *Glencoe Literature: The Reader's Choice* broadens students' reading to include more than just poetry, short stories, and plays.

Perspectives Award-winning book excerpts provide students with the in-depth information they need to explore the cultural, political, historical, and literary contexts of a reading selection.

LITERARY PERSPECTIVE on *Mark Twain*
Informational Text

Storytelling Is As Old As Mankind

Joyce Carol Oates

Storm In A Teacup. Cathy McKinty.

Building Background

Author Joyce Carol Oates won the National Book Award in 1969 for her novel *Them*. A contemporary short story is a fictional narrative in prose containing the elements of plot, character, setting, theme, and point of view. In this excerpt from the introduction to the *Oxford Book of American Short Stories*, Oates traces the history of the short story and how it has evolved with the voices of such writers as Mark Twain.

Set a Purpose for Reading

Read to discover the history of the short story and elements of fiction used by writers such as Mark Twain.

Reading Strategy

Evaluating Historical Influences

When you examine the social influences of a historical period on a literary work or genre you are **evaluating historical influences**. As you read, take notes on how history has influenced the short story. Use a timeline like the one below.

Egyptians write on papyri → Canterbury Tales → Mark Twain achieves popularity as an American writer

The "literary" short story, the meticulously constructed short story, descends to us by way of the phenomenon of magazine publication, beginning in the nineteenth century, but has as its ancestor the oral tale.

We must assume that storytelling is as old as mankind, at least as old as spoken language. Reality is not enough for us—we crave the imagination's embellishments upon it. *In the beginning. Once upon a time. A long time ago there lived a princess who.* How the pulse quickens, hearing such beginnings! such promises of something new, strange, unexpected! . . .

Like a river fed by countless small streams, the modern short story derives from a multiplicity of sources. Historically, the earliest literary documents of which we have knowledge are Egyptian papyri[1] dating from 4000–3000 B.C., containing a work called, most intriguingly, *Tales of the Magicians.* The Middle Ages revered such secular works as fabliaux,[2]

1. *Papyri* are papers made from the stems or pith of the papyrus, which is a tall aquatic plant.
2. *Fabliaux* are medieval verse tales with comic themes about life.

JOYCE CAROL OATES **31**

English Language Coach

Clarifying Meaning Explain that the root of the word *embellishment* is *bel,* which means "beautiful" in Middle French. The prefix *em-* means "to cause to be." An embellishment is something that decorates or causes something to be beautiful. **EL**

Reading in the Real World

Career The study of Egyptian papyri is called *papyrology.* For over 100 years, literature scholars have studied papyrus documents. Have students use library or Internet research to explore what these writings reveal about Egyptian culture. **OL**

LITERARY PERSPECTIVE
Informational Text

Focus

Summary
In this excerpt, Joyce Carol Oates traces the literary short story from oral tradition to nineteenth-century American magazines. She argues that Mark Twain and other American writers infused written stories with the vernacular of oral tradition.

Teach

R Reading Strategy

Evaluating Historical Influences Before students read, ask them to consider what effect the invention of the printing press might have had on the short story. Have them include this cultural event on their time lines.
Ask: How does the author support her claim that storytelling is "as old as mankind"? (*Oates argues that the human imagination demands that reality be embellished with stories. Human cultural history is filled with folktales and stories written thousands of years ago.*) **OL**

Readability Scores
Dale-Chall: 12.9
DRP: 74
Lexile: 1520

See also Active Learning and Note Taking Guide, pp. 15–19.

Objectives
- To evaluate historical influences on literary works (SE)
- To understand the origins of a literary genre (SE)

31

Teaching Support Leveled activities and options for differentiated instruction in the bottom channel help meet the needs of all your students, including English language learners.

TIME articles
Linked to a Big Idea, an author, or a reading selection, these articles deliver the facts on topical issues.

Informational Text

TIME

Focus

Summary

The article begins with Carl Safina's wrenching description of an albatross mother feeding her young chick, hindered by a green toothbrush stuck in her gullet. Safina details the many ways in which the oceans around the world are being polluted, overfished, and overfarmed. He suggests ways in which governments can work together to address these problems.

Teach

Big Idea

Making Choices

Say: Consider the following question as you read. What are some other choices you can make to help preserve wildlife and the environment? *(Students may mention using alternative energy sources, recycling, consuming less, and disposing of trash properly.)* **OL**

Informational Text

Media Link to Making Choices

Preview the Article

In "Cry of the Ancient Mariner," the writer and environmentalist Carl Safina examines the reasons why marine life is being destroyed and provides some possible solutions.

1. From the title, what words would you use to describe what the tone of the article might be?

2. Skim the article. What do you think it will be about?

Set Purpose for Reading

Read to discover an environmental concern and the writer's viewpoint on saving ocean life.

Reading Strategy

Determining the Main Idea and Supporting Details

Determining the **main idea** involves finding the most important thought the writer is trying to convey about his or her subject. The main idea is not always obvious, so use the supporting details in the text to guide you. As you read, create and complete a graphic organizer like the one shown below.

Main Idea:

Supporting Detail 1: Fishing destroys over eighty million sea creatures each year.

Supporting Detail 2:

Supporting Detail 3:

OBJECTIVES
- Determine the main idea and supporting details.
- Skim text for an overall impression and particular information.
- Distinguish fact from opinion.

186 UNIT 1 THE SHORT STORY

TIME

Cry of the Ancient
Mariner

"Even in the middle of the deep blue sea, the albatross feels the hard hand of humanity"

By CARL SAFINA

AT THE LONELY CENTER OF THE NORTH PACIFIC OCEAN, farther from just about everything than just about anywhere, lies Midway Atoll, a coral reef enclosed by a lagoon. I've come with Canadian writer and zoologist Nancy Baron to the world's largest Laysan albatross colony—400,000 exquisite masters of the air—a feathered nation gathered to breed, cramming an isle a mile by two.

Ravenous, goose-size chicks so jam the landscape that it resembles a poultry farm. Many have waited more than a week for a meal, while both parents forage the ocean's vast expanse. An adult glides in on 7-ft. wings. After flying perhaps 2,000 miles nonstop to return here, in 10 minutes she will be gone again, searching for more food. She surveys the scene through lovely dark pastel-shadowed eyes, then calls, "Eh-eh-eh." Every nearby chick answers, but she recognizes her own chick's voice and weaves toward it.

Aggressive with hunger, the whining chick bites its parent's bill to stimulate her into throwing up her payload. The adult hunches, vomiting, pumping out fish eggs and several squid. The chick swallows in seconds what its parent logged 4,000 miles to get. The chick begs for more. The adult arches her neck and vomits again. Nothing comes. We whisper, "What's wrong?"

Slowly comes the surreal sight of a green plastic toothbrush emerging from the bird's gullet. With her neck arched, the mother cannot fully pass the straight brush. She tries several times to disgorge it, but can't. Nancy and I can hardly bear this. The albatross reswallows and, with the brush stuck inside, wanders away.

Message from the Albatross
In the world in which albatrosses came from, the birds swallowed pieces of floating pumice, or lightweight, vocanic glass,

---

Additional Support

See Also
Active Learning and Note Taking Guide, pages 24–30.

186

Skills Practice

WRITING: Persuasion Encourage students to brainstorm a topic for a persuasive essay on an environmental issue. Remind them that good persuasive writing includes the following elements: clear thesis statements; strong, reliable evidence; and convincing reasoning. Reinforce the importance of using a logical argument, supported by credible and relevant facts. Have students continue with research and an outline for their topic. **OL**

Teaching Support
Skills Practice in the bottom channel targets content areas for building your students' proficiency and provides strategies to introduce, teach, and reinforce concepts.

Unit Resources

These well-organized, easy-to-read pages, preceding each unit of the Teacher Wraparound Edition, provide resources you need to plan and present the selections and features.

Additional Instructional Support

Literature and Reading

- Active Learning and Note Taking Guide, pp. 145–177
- *inTIME* Magazines
- Glencoe Literature Library
- Literature Launchers: Pre-Reading Videos
- Literature Classics

English Language Learner

- English Language Coach, Unit Resources (Fast File)
- *inTIME* Magazines (Spanish)
- Spanish Listening Library

Writing, Grammar, and Spelling

- REAL Success in Writing: Research and Reports
- Writing Constructed Responses
- Spelling Power eWorkbook
- Revising with Style eWorkbook
- Sentence Diagraming eWorkbook
- Glencoe Grammar and Composition Handbook
- Grammar and Language Workbook
- Grammar and Language eWorkbook

PROFESSIONAL DEVELOPMENT

- Professional Development Package

Technology

- TeacherWorks Plus™
- StudentWorks Plus™
- Literature Launchers: Pre-Reading Videos
- Vocabulary PuzzleMaker
- Literature Library Vocabulary PuzzleMaker
- Skill Level Up!™ A Language Arts Game
- glencoe.com
- Presentation Plus! ™
- ExamView® Assessment Suite
- Literature Library ExamView® Assessment Suite
- Listening Library Audio CD, disc 2, tracks 16–29
- Interactive Tutor: Self-Assessment
- Glencoe BookLink 3
- Online Student Edition, mhln.com
- Glencoe Online Essay Grader
- Grammar and Language eWorkbook
- Revising with Style eWorkbook
- Sentence Diagraming eWorkbook
- Spelling Power eWorkbook
- Literature Classics
- Spanish Listening Library

Transparencies

- Read Aloud, Think Aloud Transparencies 26–31
- Bellringer Options Transparencies
  - Selection Focus Transparencies 39–43
  - Daily Language Practice Transparencies 82–91
- Grammar and Language Transparencies 16, 41, 57
- Writing Workshop Transparencies 26–30
- Visual Literacy/Fine Art Transparencies

Unit Resources

Glencoe Literature: The Reader's Choice offers a comprehensive package of tools to optimize student learning and the teaching experience. Each resource has been designed to assist students in specific areas and to offer instructional support for teachers. While all of these areas are covered in the core textbook, some students may need extra practice or additional help in specific areas. The resource package is designed so that you, the teacher, can choose which items will best assist your students. You may also use these resources as homework assignments and for assessment purposes. The following are resources recommended for use with Unit five.

Key for Unit Resource

- Blackline Master
- Workbook
- Supplemental Text
- CD-ROM
- DVD
- Transparency
- Web-based

Essential Instructional Support

FAST FILE Unit 5 Resources

Reading and Literature
- Unit Introduction, pp. 1–2
- The Big Idea Foldable, pp. 3–4
- The Big Idea School-Home Connection, p. 5
- The Big Idea School-Home Connection (Spanish), p. 6
- Challenge Planner, pp. 7–10
- Academic Vocabulary Development, pp. 11–12
- Comparing Literature Graphic Organizer, p. 47
- Literary Elements, pp. 17, 21, 24, 28, 35, 37, 40, 44, 48
- Reading Strategies, pp. 18, 22, 25, 27, 29, 31, 36, 38, 41, 43, 45, 49
- Active Reading Graphic Organizers, pp. 54 –63
- Selection Vocabulary Practice, pp. 19, 23, 26, 30, 39, 42, 46, 50
- Literary Focus, pp. 15, 33

Writing, Grammar, and Spelling
- Spelling Practice, p. 51
- Grammar Workshop, p. 20
- Writing Workshop Graphic Organizer, p. 52

Speaking, Listening, and Viewing
- Speaking, Listening, and Viewing Activity, p. 53

English Language Learners
- English Language Coach, pp. 16, 34

Differentiated Instruction

- Active Learning and Note Taking Guide pp. 145–177
- Leveled Vocabulary Development, pp. 69–76
- Skill Level Up!™ A Language Arts Game
- Listening Library Audio CD, disc 2, tracks 16–29
- Glencoe BookLink 3
- Vocabulary PuzzleMaker
- Literature Library Vocabulary PuzzleMaker

ASSESSMENT — GLENCOE'S ADVANTAGE

- Selection and Unit Assessment, pp. 163–186, 217–218
- Selection Quick Checks, pp. 82–93
- Selection Quick Checks (Spanish), pp. 82–93
- Assessment by Learning Objectives, pp. 54–60
- Rubrics for Assessing Student Writing, Listening, and Speaking, pp. 14–15, 36–37
- Standardized Test Preparation and Practice
- Glencoe Online Essay Grader
- Interactive Tutor: Self-Assessment
- ExamView® Assessment Suite
- Literature Library ExamView® Assessment

UNIT FIVE RESOURCES

 REAL Success: Reading Excellence at All Levels

Glencoe REAL Success is a suite of new reading and language arts products designed to foster reading excellence at all levels. Look for TWE point-of-use references for these specific products that will help your students succeed in reading this Unit.

- *Jamestown Literature, An Adapted Reader*
- REAL Success in Writing: Research and Reports
- Skill Level Up!™ A Language Arts Game
- CheckPoint PowerPoint™ slides
- Literature/Reading support at Glencoe Web site

inTIME

A lively collection of articles drawn from issues of the TIME family of magazines helps students develop the skills they need to interact with informational text in a meaningful way. Each of the news stories, feature articles, reviews, profiles, and essays in the magazine connect to an author, work, or theme in *Glencoe Literature: The Reader's Choice*. See the *inTIME* Teacher's Guide for specific connections to each unit and for reproducible student worksheets designed to develop students' reading and critical thinking skills.

Literature Launchers

Set the scene with Glencoe's Literature Launchers, engaging pre-reading video segments that introduce each unit. Each Unit Launcher brings the literature to life, featuring expert testimony and archival stills and footage from the time.

Insert your Glencoe Literature Launchers into your DVD player. Select the Unit 1 Launcher from the menu to introduce Legends and Myths.

Teacher Wraparound Edition Key

Level Appropriate Code

AL = Activities for students working above grade level
OL = Activities for students working at grade level
BL = Activities for students working below grade level
EL = Activities for English language learners
AS = Information for all students

Teacher Wraparound Prompts

R **Reading Skill** These activities help you teach reading ...ry.

Vocabulary These activities help students comprehend ...rate them into reading.

BI **Big Idea** These activities and questions prompt students to explore the Big Idea.

L **Literary Element** These activities and questions help students comprehend selections and learn more about each genre.

★ **Enrichment** Additional activities and information involving art appreciation and history.

957F

Additional Glencoe Resources

FOLDABLES™ Study Organizer — Dinah Zike's Foldables™

Foldables™ are three-dimensional, interactive graphic organizers that help students practice basic writing skills, review key vocabulary terms, and answer Big Ideas. Every unit contains a Foldable activity. You can find the pattern and directions for the Unit 5 Foldable in the Unit 5 Resources Fast File booklet. You can use the foldables as they are presented or modify them to suit the needs of your students.

Glencoe Literature Library

The collection of hardcover books includes full-length novels, novellas, plays, and works of nonfiction. Each volume consists of at least one complete extended-length reading accompanied by several related readings from a broad range of genres. A separate Study Guide for each *Glencoe Literature Library* book provides teaching notes and reproducible activity pages for students. Glencoe Literature Library titles that complement this unit include:

- *The Red Badge of Courage with Related Readings* by Stephen Crane
- *Beowulf with Related Readings*

Literature Online

For a wealth of online resources that support the instruction in Unit 5, students and teachers can visit our Web site at glencoe.com. Students will find additional learning, practice, and assessment opportunities such as these, which are noted in the student text:

- Author Search
- Big Idea Overview and Activity
- Interactive Literary Elements Handbook
- Study Central
- Unit Assessment
- Web Activities
- Writing Models

Teachers will find planning and instructional tools that include the following:

- Book Lesson Plans
- Web Activity Lesson Plans
- Teacher Forum
- Professional Resources
  Go to glencoe.com to see the entire selection of *Glencoe Literature* online resources.

Glencoe BOOKLINK

Use the Glencoe BookLink 3 CD-ROM, a database of more than 26,700 titles, to *create customized reading lists* for your students.

- Search for award-winning titles (e.g., Newbery Award winners, Coretta Scott King Award winners, and Caldecott Medal winners) and for books on several state recommended reading lists.
- Find Degrees of Reading Power™ (DRP) and Lexile™ readability scores for all selections.
- Organize reading lists by students' reading level, author, genre, theme, or area of interest.
- Get a brief summary of each selection.

You can find recommended leveled readings for this unit with Independent Reading (see pages 1100 and 1101).

Presentation Plus! / CheckPoint

Glencoe's Presentation Plus!™, a multimedia teaching tool, lets you present dynamic lessons that will engage your students. Using Microsoft PowerPoint®, you can customize the presentations to create your own personalized lessons. Use CheckPoint questions with interactive response keypads to get immediate student feedback during lessons, to increase student participation, and to assess student comprehension.

Online Essay

Use Glencoe's online essay grader powered by SkillWriter™ to score your students' writing and to provide individualized feedback to each student automatically.

You and your students can visit glencoe.com to link to the essay grader. *Students* can enter their essays and receive feedback on demand. *You* can manage demographic data, assign tests and generate individual student and aggregated reports. The essay grader can help you

- save time with automatic scoring and individualized feedback
- supplement in-class writing instruction using guided writing practice

957E

Classroom Resources

Unit Resources

Fast Files Booklets

These blackline master booklets provide all the teaching materials you need to reinforce the content in each unit of *Glencoe Literature: The Reader's Choice.* One to two pages of each booklet focus on the following topics or skills:

- Unit Introduction
- The Big Idea Foldables™
- The Big Idea: School-Home Connection (English and Spanish versions)
- Unit Challenge: Planner and Rubrics
- Academic Vocabulary Practice
- Literary History
- Comparing Literature Graphic Organizers
- Literary Focus
- Literary Elements
- Key Reading Skills Practice
- Spelling Practice
- Selection Vocabulary Development
- English Language Coach
- Grammar Practice
- Writing Workshop Graphic Organizers
- Active Reading Graphic Organizers
- Listening, Speaking, and Viewing Activities

Literature and Reading

Active Learning and Note Taking Guide SE

This set of consumable workbooks provides structured outline support for students to use before, during, and after reading and helps them focus on key concepts and information. Activities include interactive exercises on literary elements and vocabulary for writing about literature. The workbooks are offered in four versions:

- **Grade-Level Active Learning and Note Taking Guide** Addresses students who are reading at grade level.
- **Enriched Active Learning and Note Taking Guide** Challenges students to develop a basic understanding of the skills.
- **Adapted Active Learning and Note Taking Guide** Helps students who are reading one or two grades below grade level.
- **ELL Active Learning and Note Taking Guide** Coaches English language learners to master the content.

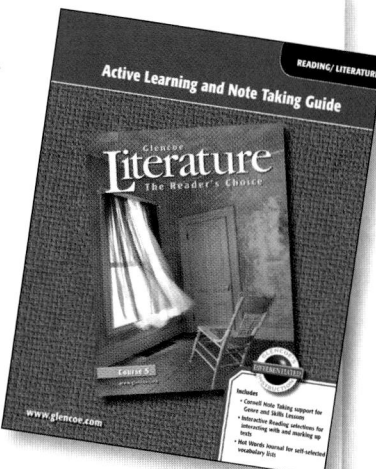

Literature Library

Glencoe Literature Library offers an extensive collection of hardcover books that help you encourage your students to read independently. Choose from among the more than 120 full-length literary works—novels, novellas, plays, and nonfiction. Each book includes related readings from a broad range of genres. Support your teaching with these technology products:

- *Literature Library ExamView Assessment Suite* **CD** Offers you the flexibility to create customized tests for all the literary works included in the *Glencoe Literature Library* collection.
- **Literature Library Vocabulary PuzzleMaker** Allows you to create crossword puzzles, word-search puzzles, and jumble puzzles based on vocabulary selected from the *Glencoe Literature Library* collection.

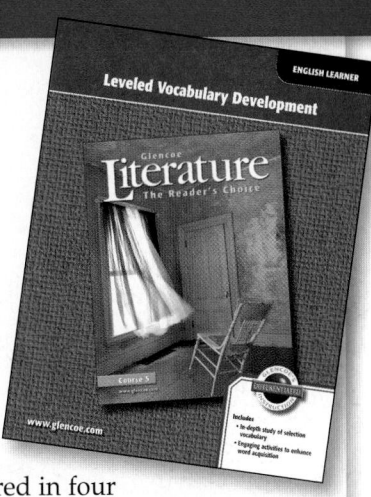

Ethnic Anthologies

This collection of anthologies with teacher guides broadens students' reading and understanding of American literature. Encourage your students to study classic and contemporary authors from diverse ethnic and cultural backgrounds.

- African American Literature
- Asian American Literature
- Hispanic American Literature
- Native American Literature

inTIME Magazine

These high-interest collections of articles drawn from issues of *TIME* magazine and other Time, Inc., publications help students develop reading strategies to interact with informational text. The *inTIME* magazines are available in both English and Spanish and include teacher guides.

Literature Launchers: Pre-Reading Videos/DVD

Each of the engaging video segments on this DVD brings the literature to life, providing both visual and historical context for every unit.

Literature Classics CD-ROM

Glencoe Literature Classics CD-ROM brings a collection of more than 1,100 additional classic literature selections directly to your classroom—accessible by author, title, date, genre, country, course/grade level, and Big Idea. Genre Focus Lesson Plans with blackline masters are also provided.

Writing

REAL Success in Writing: Research and Reports

These blackline masters reinforce and extend the coverage of research presented in the Student Edition.

Writing Constructed Responses

This sourcebook with blackline masters helps students effectively respond to short-essay questions.

Differentiated Instruction

Leveled Vocabulary Development

These blackline masters provide practice on selection vocabulary. The booklet is offered in four versions:

- Leveled Vocabulary Grade Level
- Leveled Vocabulary Enriched
- Leveled Vocabulary Adapted
- Leveled Vocabulary English Language Learner

Vocabulary PuzzleMaker

This easy-to-use program lets you create crossword puzzles, word search puzzles, and jumble puzzles in an instant. To generate your puzzles, choose from selection and academic vocabulary (in both English and Spanish) and any of the terms included in the Literary Terms Handbook.

Listening Library Audio CD

The *Listening Library* Audio CD contains engaging recordings of all the selections in *Glencoe Literature: The Reader's Choice.* These will help students improve overall comprehension and reading fluency.

Spanish Listening Library Audio CD

Provide valuable support to your English language learners with the *Spanish Listening Library* Audio CD. This CD includes Spanish translations of key selections and Spanish summaries of virtually all selections.

Skill Level Up!™ A Language Arts Game CD-ROM

Skill Level Up! A Language Arts Game offers an innovative approach to language arts and reading skills practice, assessment, and remediation.

Glencoe BookLink 3 CD-ROM

Use the *Glencoe BookLink 3* CD-ROM, a database of more than 26,700 titles, to create customized reading lists for your students. Search for award-winning titles and for books on several state-recommended reading lists.

Assessment

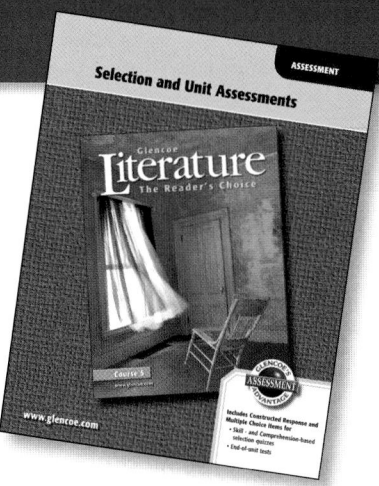

Selection and Unit Assessments

This assessment tool contains comprehensive tests and answer keys for all selections and units.

Exam*View*® Assessment Suite

With the Test Generator you can quickly create customized unit- or selection-based assessments. Use the unit exams or the selection-specific exams provided in both English and Spanish on this CD-ROM, or create your own questions.

Selection Quick Check

These short-answer questions serve as a quick way to assess students' basic comprehension of a selection. (Spanish and English)

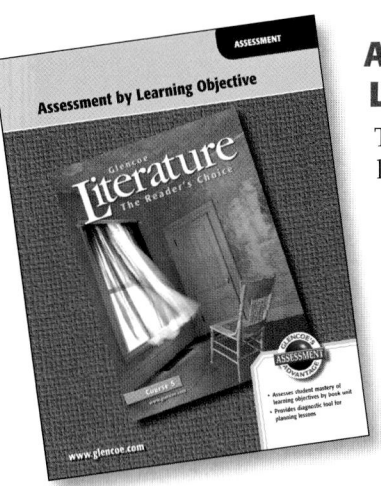

Assessment by Learning Objective

These booklets help you assess learning objectives related to reading strategy, literary element, genre, or literary period or movement.

Rubrics for Assessing Student Writing, Listening, and Speaking

In structured assessment activities with evaluation rubrics, students apply their understanding of book selections to real-world situations.

Standardized Test Prep and Practice

This assessment tool contains exercises and activities that get students ready for the high-stakes standardized exams.

Interactive Tutor: Self-Assessment

This software allows students to review unit-based skills at their own pace and provides immediate prescriptive feedback. You can monitor student progress using the software's reporting system.

Technology Resources

StudentWorks™ Plus CD-ROM

StudentWorks™ Plus contains everything that your students need on one easy-to-use CD-ROM—the complete Student Edition, text in audio, access to all student workbooks, links to online activities and resources, and unit-based PowerPoint projects.

Online Student Edition

Showcasing the interactive versions of McGraw-Hill textbooks, mhln.com offers the same content as the printed text, with multimedia-enhanced content. Games, interactivities, and other items are correlated directly to each page.

TeacherWorks™ Plus CD-ROM

TeacherWorks™ Plus contains a suite of easy-to-use and effective tools designed to help you develop lesson plans, manage daily activities, access all textbook materials, and utilize resources on the Internet.

Exam*View*® Assessment Suite

With the Test Generator you can quickly create customized unit- or selection-based assessments. Use the unit exams or the selection-specific exams provided in both English and Spanish on this CD-ROM, or create your own questions.

Skill Level Up!™ A Language Arts Game CD-ROM

Skill Level Up!™ A Language Arts Game offers an innovative approach to language arts and reading skills practice, assessment, and remediation.

Presentation Plus!™ CD-ROM

This multimedia application enables teachers to present dynamic lessons for every unit and selection in *Glencoe Literature*. The PowerPoint multimedia presentations can be edited and customized for teacher lesson planning.

Vocabulary PuzzleMaker CD-ROM

This easy-to-use program lets you create crossword puzzles, word-search puzzles, and jumble puzzles in an instant. To generate your puzzles, choose from selection and academic vocabulary (in both English and Spanish), and any of the terms included in the Literary Terms Handbook.

Literature Classics CD-ROM

Glencoe Literature Classics CD-ROM brings a collection of more than 1,100 additional classic literature selections directly to your classroom—accessible by author, title, date, genre, country, course/grade level, and Big Idea. Genre Focus Lesson Plans with blackline masters are also provided.

Literature Library ExamView® Assessment Suite CD-ROM

This software offers you the flexibility to create customized tests for all the literary works included in the *Glencoe Literature Library* collection.

Literature Library PuzzleMaker CD-ROM

This easy-to-use software allows you to create crossword puzzles, word-search puzzles, and jumble puzzles based on vocabulary selected from the *Glencoe Literature Library* collection.

Literature Launchers: Pre-Reading Videos DVD

Each of the engaging video segments on this DVD brings the literature to life, providing both visual and historical context for every unit.

Listening Library Audio CD

The *Listening Library* Audio CD contains engaging recordings of all the selections in *Glencoe Literature: The Reader's Choice*. These recordings will help students improve overall comprehension and reading fluency.

Spanish Listening Library Audio CD

Provide valuable support to your English language learners with the *Spanish Listening Library* Audio CD. This CD includes Spanish translations of key selections and Spanish summaries of virtually all selections.

Glencoe BookLink 3 CD-ROM

Use the *Glencoe BookLink 3* CD-ROM, a database of more than 26,700 titles, to create customized reading lists for your students. Search for award-winning titles and for books on several state-recommended reading lists.

Glencoe Online Essay Grader

Improve student writing and save time with Glencoe's Online Essay Grader, powered by SkillWriter™. Glencoe's Online Essay Grader will score your students' Writing Workshop assignments and provide individualized feedback automatically.

Internet Resources (glencoe.com)

For online resources that support the instruction in *Glencoe Literature*, students and teachers can visit our Web site at **glencoe.com**. Students will find additional learning, practice, and assessment opportunities.

Transparencies

- **Read Aloud, Think Aloud Transparencies** model active reading.
- **Bellringer Option Transparencies** include warm-up exercises to engage students and provide a quick review of previously taught activities.
- **Literary Analysis Transparencies** help reinforce literary elements that are the focus of each lesson.
- **Grammar and Writing Workshop Transparencies** help reinforce the skills taught in the Grammar and Writing workshops in the Student Edition.
- **Visual Literacy Arts Transparencies** enhance a strong humanities approach to literature and help students analyze visual representations of literary concepts and characters.

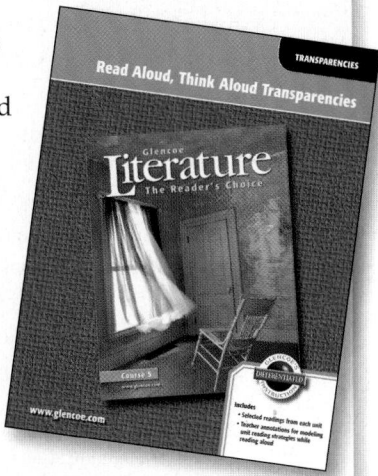

Glencoe Resources for Independent Reading

Foster a lifelong love of reading by encouraging your students to read independently. The following resources can help students improve their critical thinking skills, vocabulary, and ability to connect with literature. Have your students maintain reading lists to keep track of their progress. Parents or guardians can review the lists to help students set manageable goals.

Glencoe Literature Library

Below is a sampling from our collection of hardcover books, which includes full-length novels, novellas, plays, and works of nonfiction. Each *Glencoe Literature Library* volume consists of at least one complete extended-length reading accompanied by several related readings from a broad range of genres. Works include short stories, poems, essays, and informational articles. In addition, a separate Study Guide for each *Glencoe Literature Library* book provides teaching notes and reproducible activity pages for students. Students may also find these activity pages at **www.glencoe.com**.

The Adventures of Huckleberry Finn
    by Mark Twain **DRP 54***
All Quiet on the Western Front
    by Erich Maria Remarque **DRP 52**
. . . And the Earth Did Not Devour Him
    by Tomas Rivera **DRP 52**
Animal Farm by George Orwell **DRP 60**
The Autobiography of Benjamin Franklin
    by Benjamin Franklin **DRP 64**
The Autobiography of Miss Jane Pittman
    by Ernest J. Gaines **DRP 49**
The Awakening by Kate Chopin **DRP 58**
Beowulf
Billy Budd by Herman Melville **DRP 68**
The Bridge of San Luis Rey by Thornton Wilder **DRP 55**
The Brothers Karamazov by Fyodor Dostoevsky **DRP 55**
The Canterbury Tales by Geoffrey Chaucer **DRP 59**
The Chosen by Chaim Potok **DRP 56**
A Country Doctor by Sarah Orne Jewett **DRP 59**
Cyrano de Bergerac by Edmond Rostand
Ethan Frome by Edith Wharton **DRP 59**

Fallen Angels by Walter Dean Myers **DRP 47**
Frankenstein by Mary Shelley **DRP 64**
Great Expectations by Charles Dickens **DRP 60**
Gulliver's Travels by Jonathan Swift **DRP 67**
Hamlet by William Shakespeare
Heart of Darkness and *The Secret Sharer*
    by Joseph Conrad **DRP 58**
A House for Mr Biswas by V. S. Naipaul **DRP 58**
The House of the Seven Gables
    by Nathaniel Hawthorne **DRP 65**
The Importance of Being Earnest by Oscar Wilde
Invisible Man by Ralph Ellison **DRP 57**
Jane Eyre by Charlotte Brontë **DRP 61**
Julius Caesar by William Shakespeare
The Jungle by Upton Sinclair **DRP 59**
The Mayor of Casterbridge by Thomas Hardy **DRP 60**
The Metamorphosis by Franz Kafka **DRP 57**
A Midsummer Night's Dream by William Shakespeare
My Ántonia by Willa Cather **DRP 57**
Narrative of the Life of Frederick Douglass
    by Frederick Douglass **DRP 62**
Nectar in a Sieve by Kamala Markandaya **DRP 56**
Night by Elie Wiesel **DRP 51**
One Day in the Life of Ivan Denisovich
    by Aleksandr Solzhenitsyn **DRP 56**

Degrees of Reading Power DRP values indicate the readability of prose text. The higher the value, the more difficult the text. Though the scale ranges from 0 to 100, texts widely available for use at grades nine through twelve typically range from 53 to 68. Some materials, however, may certainly fall outside of this range.

Anthologies for Independent Reading

The following anthologies offer students introductions to the richness and variety of literature written by African, Asian, Hispanic, and Native Americans. A Teacher's Guide for each anthology suggests answers to questions accompanying each selection to help further student discussion.

- *Glencoe African American Literature*
- *Glencoe Asian American Literature*
- *Glencoe Hispanic American Literature*
- *Glencoe Native American Literature*

Our Town by Thornton Wilder
Picture Bride by Yoshiko Uchida **DRP 55**
Pride and Prejudice by Jane Austen **DRP 61**
A Raisin in the Sun by Lorraine Hansberry
The Red Badge of Courage by Stephen Crane **DRP 60**
The Return of the Native by Thomas Hardy **DRP 61**
The Scarlet Letter by Nathaniel Hawthorne **DRP 67**
Sense and Sensibility by Jane Austen **DRP 63**
A Separate Peace by John Knowles **DRP 59**
Silas Marner by George Eliot **DRP 55**
The Souls of Black Folk by W. E. B. Du Bois **DRP 66**
The Story of My Life by Helen Keller **DRP 59**
The Strange Case of Dr Jekyll and Mr Hyde
   by Robert Louis Stevenson **DRP 63**
A Tale of Two Cities by Charles Dickens **DRP 62**
The Tempest by William Shakespeare
Things Fall Apart by Chinua Achebe **DRP 56**
The Time Machine and *The War of the Worlds*
   by H. G. Wells **DRP 59**
To Kill a Mockingbird by Harper Lee **DRP 51**
Walden by Henry David Thoreau **DRP 62**
The Way to Rainy Mountain
   by N. Scott Momaday **DRP 55**
Wuthering Heights by Emily Brontë **DRP 61**
The Yearling by Marjorie Kinnan Rawlings **DRP 53**

inTIME magazine

This lively collection of articles drawn from issues of *TIME* helps students develop the skills they need to interact with informational text in a meaningful way. Each of the news stories, feature articles, reviews, profiles, and essays connects to an author, a reading selection, or a Big Idea in *Glencoe Literature: The Reader's Choice.* The magazines are available in both English and Spanish editions. In addition, a separate Teacher Guide, including lessons and reproducible student worksheets designed to develop students' reading and critical thinking skills, accompanies each magazine.

Unit at a Glance
THE SHORT STORY

About the Unit

Unit One covers the short story and focuses on literary elements such as plot, setting, theme, character, narrator, and voice.

Unit Introduction
Building Background
2–3 days

Genre Focus: Short Story
pp. 2–3

Literary Analysis Model: Ernest Hemingway, "Old Man at the Bridge"
pp. 4–5

Writers on Reading
pp. 6–7

Unit Introduction Wrap-Up
p. 8

Part 1: Encountering the Unexpected
7–10 days

Part 1 covers plot and setting within the short story. A chart showing the core skills taught in this Part appears on pages 9A–9B.

SELECTIONS AND FEATURES

LITERARY FOCUS: Plot and Setting
pp. 10–11

Saki, "The Open Window"
pp. 12–19

Mark Twain, "The Californian's Tale"
pp. 20–30

LITERARY PERSPECTIVE: Joyce Carol Oates, "Storytelling Is As Old As Mankind"
pp. 31–34

Shirley Jackson, "The Summer People"
pp. 35–48

Vocabulary Workshop: Denotation and Connotation
p. 49

Edwidge Danticat, "The Book of the Dead"
pp. 50–63

R. K. Narayan, "An Astrologer's Day"
pp. 64–71

Grammar Workshop: Mechanics
p. 72

Chinua Achebe, "Civil Peace"
pp. 73–81

Edgar Allan Poe, "The Masque of the Red Death"
pp. 82–92

Part 2: Making Choices
7–9 Days

Part 2 covers character and theme in the short story. A chart showing the core skills taught in this Part appears on pages 93A–93B.

SELECTIONS AND FEATURES

Part 3: Life Transitions
8–10 Days

Part 3 covers narrator and voice in the short story. A chart showing the core skills taught in this Part appears on pages 191A–191B.

SELECTIONS AND FEATURES

End-of-Unit Features
5–6 Days

Unit Resources

Glencoe Literature: The Reader's Choice offers a comprehensive package of tools to optimize student learning and the teaching experience. Each resource has been designed to assist students in specific areas and to offer instructional support for teachers. While all of these areas are covered in the core textbook, some students may need extra practice or additional help in specific areas. The resource package is designed so that you, the teacher, can choose which items will best assist your students. You may also use these resources as homework assignments and for assessment purposes. The following are resources recommended for use with Unit One.

Key for Unit Resource

- 📁 Blackline Master
- 📙 Workbook
- 📖 Supplemental Text
- 💿 CD-ROM
- 💾 DVD
- 🔬 Transparency
- 💻 Web-based

Essential Instructional Support

FAST FILE Unit 1 Resources

Reading and Literature

- Unit Introduction, pp. 1–2
- The Big Idea Foldable, pp. 3–4
- The Big Idea School-Home Connection, p. 5
- The Big Idea School-Home Connection (Spanish), p. 6
- Challenge Planner, pp. 7–10
- Academic Vocabulary Development, pp. 11–16
- Comparing Literature Graphic Organizers, p. 74
- Literary Elements, pp. 20, 23, 27, 30, 33, 37, 40, 46, 49, 52, 55, 58, 61, 64, 71, 75, 78, 82, 85, 88, 91
- Reading Strategies, pp. 21, 24, 26, 28, 31, 34, 38, 41, 47, 50, 53, 56, 59, 62, 65, 67, 72, 76, 79, 83, 86, 89, 92
- Active Reading Graphic Organizers, pp. 97–106
- Selection Vocabulary Practice, pp. 22, 25, 29, 32, 35, 39, 42, 48, 51, 54, 57, 60, 63, 66, 73, 77, 80, 84, 87, 90, 93
- Literary Focus, pp. 18, 44, 69

Writing, Grammar, and Spelling

- Spelling Practice, p. 94
- Grammar Practice, pp. 36, 81
- Writing Workshop Graphic Organizer, p. 95

Speaking, Listening and Viewing

- Speaking, Listening, and Viewing Activities, p. 96

English Language Learners

- English Language Coach, pp. 19, 45, 70

Differentiated Instruction

- 📙 Active Learning and Note Taking Guide, pp. 1–34
- 📁 Leveled Vocabulary Development, pp. 1–21
- 💿 Skill Level Up!™ A Language Arts Game
- 💿 Listening Library Audio CD, disc 1, tracks 1–25
- 💿 Glencoe BookLink 3
- 💿 Vocabulary PuzzleMaker
- 💿 Literature Library Vocabulary PuzzleMaker

ASSESSMENT

- 📁 Selection and Unit Assessments, Unit One Test, pp. 209–210
- 📁 Selection Quick Checks, pp. 1–23
- 📁 Selection Quick Checks (Spanish), pp. 1–23
- 📁 Assessment by Learning Objectives, pp. 1–15
- 📁 Rubrics for Assessing Student Writing, Listening, and Speaking, p. 12
- 📁 Standardized Test Preparation and Practice
- 💻 Glencoe Online Essay Grader
- 💿 Interactive Tutor: Self-Assessment
- 💿 ExamView® Assessment Suite
- 💿 Literature Library ExamView® Assessment

Additional Instructional Support

Literature and Reading

- Active Learning and Note Taking Guide, pp. 1–34
- *inTIME* Magazines
- Glencoe Literature Library
- Literature Launchers: Pre-Reading Videos
- Literature Classics

Writing, Grammar, and Spelling

- REAL Success in Writing: Research and Reports
- Writing Constructed Responses
- Spelling Power eWorkbook
- Revising with Style eWorkbook
- Sentence Diagraming eWorkbook
- Glencoe Grammar and Composition Handbook
- Grammar and Language Workbook
- Grammar and Language eWorkbook

PROFESSIONAL DEVELOPMENT

- Professional Development Package

Transparencies

- Read Aloud, Think Aloud Transparencies 1–8
- Bellringer Options Transparencies
  - Selection Focus Transparencies 1–18
  - Daily Language Practice Transparencies 1–25
- Grammar and Language Transparencies 11, 24, 35
- Writing Workshop Transparencies 6–10
- Visual Literacy/Fine Art Transparencies

English Language Learner

- English Language Coach, Unit Resources (Fast File)
- *inTIME* Magazines (Spanish)
- Spanish Listening Library

Technology

- TeacherWorks Plus™
- StudentWorks Plus™
- Literature Launchers: Pre-Reading Videos
- Vocabulary PuzzleMaker
- Literature Library Vocabulary PuzzleMaker
- glencoe.com
- Presentation Plus!™
- ExamView TM Assessment Suite
- Literature Library ExamView™ Assessment Suite
- Listening Library, disc 1, tracks 1–25
- Interactive Tutor: Self-Assessment
- Glencoe BookLink 3
- Online Student Edition, mhln.com
- Glencoe Online Essay Grader
- Grammar and Language eWorkbook
- Revising with Style eWorkbook
- Sentence Diagraming eWorkbook
- Spelling Power eWorkbook
- Literature Classics
- Spanish Listening Library

Additional Glencoe Resources

Dinah Zike's Foldables™

Foldables™ are three-dimensional, interactive graphic organizers that help students practice basic writing skills, review key vocabulary terms, and answer Big Ideas. Every unit contains a Foldable™ activity. You can find the pattern and directions for the Unit 1 Foldable in the Unit 1 Resources Fast Files booklet. You can use the foldables as they are presented or modify them to suit the needs of your students.

For a wealth of online resources that support the instruction in Unit 1, students and teachers can visit our Web site at glencoe.com. Students will find additional learning, practice, and assessment opportunities such as these, which are noted in the student text:

- Author Search
- Big Idea Overview and Activity
- Interactive Literary Elements Handbook
- Study Central
- Unit Assessment
- Web Activities
- Writing Models

Teachers will find planning and instructional tools that include the following:

- Book Lesson Plans
- Web Activity Lesson Plans
- Teacher Forum
- Professional Resources

Go to glencoe.com to see the entire selection of *Glencoe Literature* online resources.

PRESENTATION Plus! CheckPoint

Glencoe's Presentation Plus!™, a multimedia teaching tool, lets you present dynamic lessons that will engage your students. Using Microsoft PowerPoint®, you can customize the presentations to create your own personalized lessons. Use CheckPoint questions with interactive response keypads to get immediate student feedback during lessons, to increase student participation, and to assess student comprehension.

Glencoe Literature Library

This collection of hardcover books includes full-length novels, novellas, plays and works of nonfiction. Each volume consists of at least one complete extended-length reading accompanied by several related readings from a broad range of genres. A separate Study Guide for each *Glencoe Literature Library* book provides teaching notes and reproducible activity pages for students. Glencoe Literature Library titles that complement this unit include:

- *The Friends with Related Readings* by Rosa Guy
- *Nectar in a Sieve with Related Readings* by Kamala Markaudaya
- *My Ántonia with Related Readings* by Willa Cather

GLENCOE BOOKLINK

Use the Glencoe BookLink 3 CD-ROM, a database of more than 26,700 titles, to *create customized reading lists* for your students.

- Search for award-winning titles, (e.g., Newbery Award winners, Coretta Scott King Award winners, and Caldecott Medal winners) and for books on several state recommended reading lists.
- Find Degrees of Reading Power™ (DRP) and Lexile™ readability scores for all selections.
- Organize reading lists by students' reading level, author, genre, theme, or area of interest.
- Get a brief summary of each selection.

You can find recommended leveled readings for this unit with Independent Reading (see pages 300 and 301).

Online Essay Grader

Use Glencoe's online essay grader powered by SkillWriter™ to score your students' writing and to provide individualized feedback to each student automatically.

You and your students can visit glencoe.com to link to the essay grader. *Students* can enter their essays and receive feedback on demand. *You* can manage demographic data, assign tests and generate individual student and aggregated reports. The essay grader can help you

- Save time with automatic scoring and individualized feedback.
- Supplement in-class writing instruction using guided writing practice.

REAL Success: Reading Excellence at All Levels

Glencoe REAL Success is a suite of new reading and language arts products designed to foster reading excellence at all levels. Look for TWE point-of-use references for these specific products that will help your students succeed in reading this Unit.

- *Jamestown Literature: An Adapted Reader*
- REAL Success in Writing: Research and Reports
- Skill Level Up!™ A Language Arts Game
- CheckPoint PowerPoint™ slides
- Literature/Reading support at Glencoe Web site

A lively collection of articles drawn from issues of the TIME family of magazines helps students develop the skills they need to interact with informational text in a meaningful way. Each of the news stories, feature articles, reviews, profiles, and essays in the magazine connects to an author, work, or theme in *Glencoe Literature: The Reader's Choice.* See the *inTIME* Teacher's Guide for specific connections to each unit and for reproducible student worksheets designed to develop students' reading and critical thinking skills.

Literature Launchers

Set the scene with Glencoe's Literature Launchers, engaging pre-reading video segments that introduce each unit. Each Unit Launcher brings the literature to life, featuring expert testimony and archival stills and footage from the time.

Insert your Glencoe Literature Launchers into your DVD player. Select the Unit 1 Launcher from the menu to introduce The Short Story.

Teacher Wraparound Edition Key

Level Appropriate Code

AL = Activities for students working above grade level

OL = Activities for students working at grade level

BL = Activities for students working below grade level

EL = Activities for English language learners

AS = Information for all students

Teacher Wraparound Prompts

R **Reading Skill** These activities help you teach reading skills and vocabulary.

V **Vocabulary** These activities help students comprehend words and incorporate them into reading.

BI **Big Idea** These activities and questions prompt students to prepare to answer the Big Idea.

L **Literary Element** These activities and questions help students comprehend selections and learn more about each genre.

★ **Enrichment** Additional activities and information involving art appreciation and history.

Professional Development Center

From Your Authors:

Teaching Literary Analysis: Short Story

Make Personal Connections For a text to matter, students must connect what they read to ideas, events, and situations in their own lives. These connections provide motivation for reading and allow readers to better understand what they are reading. Pre-reading activities can also activate and build prior knowledge. Create activities and ask questions that encourage students to connect to the short story text. For example, before students read "Two Kinds" by Amy Tan, ask them to discuss what their parents expect from young people their age. After students name some expectations, ask them if these expectations are realistic or not. Ask students to describe how parents' expectations influence them and their view of themselves. Then tell students that they are about to read a story about a mother who has unrealistic expectations of her daughter.

Develop Historical Perspective Reading short stories allows students to understand and appreciate the experiences of others, including those who live in another time and place. As they read, students can keep a log of different characters and their perspectives—either as stated by the author or inferred by the reader—as these characters interact with one another or with the events in the story. While reading "When Mr. Pirzada Came to Dine" by Jhumpa Lahiri, for example,

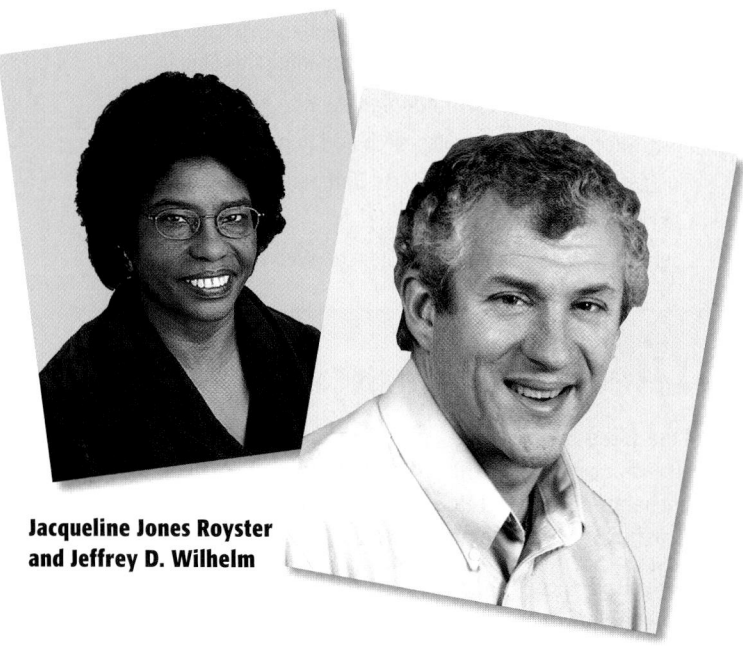

**Jacqueline Jones Royster
and Jeffrey D. Wilhelm**

ask students to keep a log of what the narrator thinks and feels, how she interacts with other characters, and how she reacts to the historical events that occur. Ask students to think about how they would react in a similar situation.

Teacher to Teacher

Every student has a story to tell. To make it easier for students to talk about themselves, I tell them about my life. Next, I use a writing prompt and ask students to write a story. I may give a list of character descriptions and have students create sentences about characters. This preliminary exercise gives them a tool to fall back on when describing characters in their story. Using a list of writing tips I've put together, students correct their own papers and then break into peer groups to edit each other's work. The writing tips and corrections are progressive, so we edit only for those things we are working on that week or have worked on previously. In addition to writing their stories, students might write and perform rap songs about one of the short stories in the unit, or they might perform a skit based on one of the stories we have read.

**Jelani Khalid
N. P. Moss Middle School
Carencro, Louisiana**

Teacher Chat Room

Making Literature Come Alive

Before you begin this unit or sometime during the unit, talk with other teachers about ways they have taught short stories. Have a lunch-time discussion group or an after-school hour for professional development and discuss the following questions:

How can I help make short stories interesting to students?

- Before reading a story, relate a part of the narrative to something that matters personally or socially to students.

- Work to help students connect to a reading before they read by activating their prior knowledge on the general topic of the story. Before reading "The Censors" by Luisa Valenzuela, ask students to discuss what they know about censorship. Encourage students to discuss their knowledge of censorship on a personal level, national level, and worldwide level. Discussing censorship and allowing students to express their opinions on the subject will activate their prior knowledge and help them to connect to the story.

How do I help students embrace the process of literary analysis?

- Ask students to consider the role of the author and the author's purpose for writing.

- Share your own reactions to the mood and tone of the story with students. Ask students which words the author uses to establish the mood or tone.

How can visual texts help students better understand the structure and elements of a story?

- Give students pictures related to the story or the unit to be studied. Ask them to group the pictures, to tell what they know about the pictures, and to use the pictures to predict what the story will be about. For example, before reading Dylan Thomas's "A Child's Christmas in Wales," show pictures depicting a winter landscape, a family celebrating the holiday around the table, children opening presents, and so on. Have students discuss what all the pictures have in common and what they think the story will be about.

- Famous photographs and paintings can be used to teach various literary elements. For example, the painting *American Gothic* could be studied before a unit on relationships or to explore how a setting might affect or constrain a character's development.

- Picture books and cartoons exhibit elements and structures similar to more sophisticated texts. They can be used to introduce ideas like irony or story structure in ways that are easier to access and understand.

Focus

BELLRINGER

Bellringer Options
Literature Launcher Video
Daily Language Transparency 1
Or bring to class a bottle of syrup. **Say:** The flavor in this syrup is intense because it is compressed into a more compact form. How do you think the same thing is true of a short story? Have students discuss how being a more compressed type of fiction can make a short story "sweeter," such as with more focused action, fewer characters, and limited setting. Point out that since a short story writer must convey a lot in a short space, each detail is important.

Objectives for the Unit Introduction

• To identify and interpret various literary elements used in the short story (SE)
• To analyze the effect that these literary elements have upon the reader (SE)
• To analyze short stories for the ways in which authors inspire the reader to share emotions (TWE)

Ta Matete (We Shall Not Go to Market Today), 1882. Paul Gauguin. Gouache on canvas, 73 x 92 cm. Kunstmuseum, Basel, Switzerland. ★

UNIT 1   THE SHORT STORY

Unit Introduction Skills

Reading Skills

• Identifying Sequence (SE pp. 2, 6)
• Literary Response (TWE p. 6)

The Short Story

Listening/Speaking/Viewing Skills

• Discussing Theme (SE p. 8)
• Discussion (TWE p. 8)

Literary Elements

• Plot (SE pp. 2, 5)
• Character (SE pp. 3, 4)
• Setting (SE pp. 2, 4)
• Conflict and Plot (TWE p. 2)
• Diction (TWE p. 4)

Writing Skills/Grammar

• Character Analysis (SE p. 8)

The *Short Story*

Looking Ahead

There is no better place to begin a study of literature than with the short story. This concise, imaginative genre allows the reader to focus on a precisely crafted plot, often a single setting, and a limited number of characters. Whether creating a journey that is bizarre, realistic, or insightful, the writer will quickly and artfully make the point, often in a way the reader will never forget.

PREVIEW   **Big Ideas and Literary Focus**

1	**BIG IDEA:** Encountering the Unexpected	**LITERARY FOCUS:** Plot and Setting
2	**BIG IDEA:** Making Choices	**LITERARY FOCUS:** Theme and Character
3	**BIG IDEA:** Life Transitions	**LITERARY FOCUS:** Narrator and Voice

OBJECTIVES
In learning about the genre of short stories, you will focus on the following:

- identifying and interpreting various literary elements used in the short story
- analyzing the effect that these literary elements have upon the reader

- analyzing short stories for the ways in which authors inspire the reader to share emotions

INTRODUCTION **1**

Focus

Summary

This introduction begins with a summary of the short story genre, outlining the main elements of the short story, including plot, setting, character, theme, and point of view. An analysis of "The Old Man at the Bridge" by Ernest Hemingway illustrates how these elements govern the story.

★ Viewing the Art

French artist Paul Gauguin (1848–1903) was a sailor and a stockbroker before he began his artistic career. In his early years as a painter he was part of the Impressionism movement, but eventually he turned toward his Peruvian heritage and travels in the South Pacific for inspiration. He was particularly influenced by the time he spent living in Tahiti and chose Tahitian titles for many of his works. **AS**

Unit Resources

Classroom Management
- TeacherWorks Plus™ CD-ROM
- StudentWorks Plus!™ CD-ROM
- Literature Launchers™: Pre-Reading Videos DVD, Unit One

Core Instructional Support
- Unit 1 Resources (Fast File)
- Literature Online, glencoe.com
- Presentation Plus!™ CD-ROM, Unit One

Transparencies
- Literary Elements Transparencies 1, 9, 13, 18, 21, 23
- Bellringer Options Transparencies: Selection Focus Transparencies 1–18 Daily Language Practice Transparencies 1–25

Differentiated Instruction
- Active Learning and Note Taking Guide, pp. 1–34
- Skill Level Up!™ A Language Arts Game

Assessment
- Selection and Unit Assessments, Unit One Test, pp. 209–210
- Exam*View*® Assessment Suite CD-ROM
- Assessment by Learning Objectives, pp. 1–15

Supplemental Reading
- Glencoe Literature Library
- Glencoe BookLink 3 CD-ROM
- *inTIME* Magazines

Teach

L1 Literary Element

Setting Ask: What is the setting of the Finney excerpt? *(a ledge outside a tall city building)* Contrast this setting with the settings of the Twain, Saki, and Poe stories. Point out the importance of details in determining setting. **OL**

L2 Literary Element

Plot Ask: What makes the quotation from "The Open Window" part of the exposition? *(The sentence introduces the setting, as well as the open window, a key to the plot.)* **OL**

★ Writer's Technique

Local Color Writing When setting dominates in a short story, it may be called a local color story. This type of story is written mainly to depict the way of life in a certain region. In the late nineteenth century, a local color movement arose in the United States. Discus the local color elements in these Twain excerpts about the West. **AS**

Genre Focus

What are the elements that shape a short story?

Katherine Anne Porter, one of the great American short-story writers, said, "Human life itself may be almost pure chaos, but the work of the artist is to take these handfuls of confusion and disparate things, things that seem to be irreconcilable, and put them together in a frame to give them some kind of shape and meaning." Consciously or unconsciously, writers make choices. The writer chooses who will be the star of the story, who will tell the story, where the story will take place, and most importantly—what happens! In short story writing, authors make very precise and focused choices about these elements of fiction.

Plot and Setting in Short Stories

Where, When, and How

Setting is the time and place in which a story happens. The setting includes not only physical surroundings but also can include ideas, customs, values, and beliefs of that period.

> Now, balanced easily and firmly, he stood on the ledge outside in the slight, chill breeze, eleven stories above the street, staring into his own lighted apartment, odd and different-seeming now.
>
> —Jack Finney, **from "Contents of the Dead Man's Pockets"**

Sequence of Events

Plot is the sequence of events in a story. Most plots begin with the **exposition,** which introduces the characters, setting, and conflicts. **Rising action** develops the conflict with complications and leads to the **climax,** when the story reaches its emotional high point. The **falling action** is the logical result of the climax, and the **resolution** presents the final outcome. The plot diagram below gives an example of plot development from the fairy tale "Cinderella."

> "'You may wonder why we keep that window wide open on an October afternoon," said the niece, indicating a large French window that opened on to a lawn.
>
> —Saki (H. H. Munro), **from "The Open Window"** **L2**

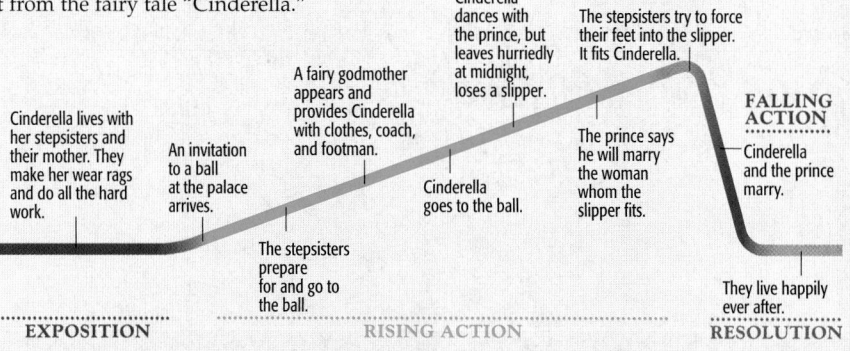

Additional Support

Skills Practice

LITERARY ELEMENT: Conflict and Plot Identify the types of conflict that advance the plot of a short story. These may be with nature, society, another character, or oneself. Review with students that a plot usually presents complications of one or more conflicts that reach a climax, and then after a turning point the falling action and resolution follow. Using these terms, have students predict what the conflict will be in stories excerpted on these pages. Also ask them to analyze the conflicts in familiar fairy tales and diagram their plot elements on the board, as was done with the Cinderella story. **OL**

Theme and Character in Short Stories

Protagonist and Antagonist

The main character in a story is the **protagonist.** The protagonist faces the main conflict of the story. In many stories, an **antagonist** works against the protagonist in overcoming the conflict. The antagonist is usually a character the reader does not like.

> Thirty-five years ago I was out prospecting on the Stanislaus, tramping all day long with pick and pan and horn, and washing a hatful of dirt here and there, always expecting to make a rich strike, and never doing it.
>
> —Mark Twain, **from "The Californian's Tale"** ★

Implied and Stated Themes

The central message of a story is its **theme.** For example, a theme might give an insight into human nature or a perception about life. Sometimes authors state their themes directly. More often, a theme is implied through elements in the story, such as what happens to the main character or what the character learns.

> Luis thought that maybe if they ate together once in a while things might get better between them, but he always had something to do around dinnertime and ended up at a hamburger joint. Tonight was the first time in months they had sat down at the table together.
>
> —Judith Ortiz Cofer, **from "Catch the Moon"**

Narrator and Voice in Short Stories

Point of View

The person telling a story is the **narrator.** Stories are usually told from a **first-** or **third-person point of view.** Stories told from a first-person point of view have narrators inside the story that use "I" in telling the story. Stories told from a third-person point of view have narrators outside the story, using "she" or "he" to tell the story.

> The young man was daring and brave, eager to go up to the mountaintop. He had been brought up by good, honest people who were wise in the ancient ways and who prayed for him.
>
> —Lame Deer, **from "The Vision Quest"**

Language Choices

Every narrator, whether speaking from a first-person or third-person point of view, has a **voice.** The narrator's voice tells us who the narrator is. Authors are careful to make the narrator's vocabulary and syntax consistent. The narrator cannot sound like an eighty-year-old widow in one sentence and a fourteen-year-old orphan in the next sentence. Often, authors choose an objective and calm voice, so that the reader will see the narrator as a qualified authority who "knows" what is happening in the tale.

> It was toward the close of the fifth or sixth month of his seclusion, and while the pestilence raged most furiously abroad, that the Prince Prospero entertained his thousand friends at a masked ball of the most unusual magnificence.
>
> —Edgar Allan Poe, **from "The Masque of the Red Death"**

 Study Central Visit www.glencoe. com to review the elements that shape a short story.

Teach

L3 Literary Element

Character and Theme Ask: Who is the protagonist in the Mark Twain excerpt? *(An unsuccessful gold miner)* What theme, or insight into human nature, does the second excerpt from the Twain tale suggest? *(It points out that some things cannot be fully understood; this theme may be developed further in the story.)* OL

R Reading Strategy

Analyzing Point of View and Language Ask: How do the points of view and narrators' voice differ in the selections by Lame Deer and Edgar Allan Poe? What can you tell from language choice? *(Both use third-person narration, but Poe's intricate vocabulary indicates a narrator who is educated and sophisticated, whereas Lame Deer's narrator appears plain-spoken and sincere.)* OL

Literature Online

Study Central Have students access the Web site for resources that will help them to review the short story.

English Language Coach

Pronouns Review pronoun identification with English language learners. Have students create a chart of the English pronouns of first person (I, we), second person (you), and third person (he, she, it, they). Have them practice identifying how these pronouns reveal point of view. EL

Differentiated Instruction

Vocabulary Assist less proficient readers with difficult vocabulary in the Poe excerpt: *seclusion, pestilence, magnificence.* As they read, remind students to use context, word origins, and word parts such as suffixes and prefixes to determine meaning. Also advise looking up unfamiliar words in a dictionary. BL

Objectives
- To identify and interpret literary elements in the short story (SE)
- To analyze conflict and plot (TWE)

3

Teach

R1 **Reading Strategy**

Analyzing Point of View

Ask: What point of view does the story use, and what can you tell about the narrator? *(The narrator is a reporter who takes interest in the old man but leaves to resume his duties. He is sympathetic)* What does the narrator's attention to the "far bank" explain? *(He is worried about the impending attack by the Fascists.)* What is the author's tone toward the narrator? *(Sensitivity but harshness that the narrator doesn't help.)* **OL**

★ Writer's Technique

Minimalism Point out Ernest Hemingway's minimalist style. Tell students that Hemingway was a reporter in the Spanish Civil War, and ask how his experiences might have affected this story. **AS**

R2 **Reading Strategy**

Predicting Reread the last paragraph. **Ask:** What do you predict will happen to the old man? *(He will die.)* What do you predict will happen to the narrator? *(He will probably be scarred.)* Discuss students' responses to the story. **OL**

Additional Support

Literary Analysis Model
How do literary elements shape a short story?

Ernest Hemingway (1899–1961), the twentieth-century master of minimalism, had a significant influence on the fiction of his time and after. In "Old Man at the Bridge," he succinctly captures the effects of the Spanish Civil War on civilians.

Old Man at the Bridge
by Ernest Hemingway

**APPLYING
Literary Elements**

Narrator

The story is told from the first-person point of view.

Setting

The story takes place at a bridge in northeastern Spain during the Spanish Civil War (1936–1939).

Character

As you learn more about the old man, the story's protagonist, you may begin to care about him.

Voice

In the dialogue, the characters' speech is brief. This is characteristic of Hemingway's style.

R1 An old man with steel rimmed spectacles and very dusty clothes sat by the side of the road. There was a pontoon bridge across the river and carts, trucks, and men, women and children were crossing it. The mule-drawn carts staggered up the steep bank from the bridge with soldiers helping push
5 against the spokes of the wheels. The trucks ground up and away heading out of it all and the peasants plodded along in the ankle deep dust. But the old man sat there without moving. He was too tired to go any further.

It was my business to cross the bridge, explore the bridgehead beyond and find out to what point the enemy had advanced. I did this and
10 returned over the bridge. There were not so many carts now and very few people on foot, but the old man was still there.

"Where do you come from?" I asked him.

"From San Carlos," he said, and smiled.

That was his native town and so it gave him pleasure to mention it and he smiled.
15 "I was taking care of animals," he explained.

"Oh," I said, not quite understanding.

"Yes," he said, "I stayed, you see, taking care of animals. I was the last one to leave the town of San Carlos."

He did not look like a shepherd nor a herdsman and I looked at his black
20 dusty clothes and his gray dusty face and his steel rimmed spectacles and said, "What animals were they?"

"Various animals," he said, and shook his head. "I had to leave them."

I was watching the bridge and the African looking country of the Ebro Delta and wondering how long now it would be before we would see the
25 enemy, and listening all the while for the first noises that would signal that ever mysterious event called contact, and the old man still sat there.

"What animals were they?" I asked.

"There were three animals altogether," he explained. "There were two goats and a cat and then there were four pairs of pigeons."

Skills Practice

LITERARY ELEMENT: Diction Note that this story uses personal language to focus on the human drama of war. **Ask:** What is the effect of the words *dusty, gray, blankly, tiredly,* and *dully* in describing the old man? *(The diction arouses the reader's sympathy.)* Point out that Hemingway describes the man as smiling and thanking. **Ask:** What do the old man's concerns and actions show about him? *(The old man is kind and gentle, in contrast with the brutality of war.)* Contrast the language of the story with language usually associated with war. **OL**

30   "And you had to leave them?" I asked.

"Yes. Because of the artillery. The captain told me to go because of the artillery."

"And you have no family?" I asked, watching the far end of the bridge where a few last carts were hurrying down the slope of the bank.

35   "No," he said, "only the animals I stated. The cat, of course, will be all right. A cat can look out for itself, but I cannot think what will become of the others."

"What politics have you?" I asked.

"I am without politics," he said. "I am seventy-six years old. I have

40 come twelve kilometers now and I think now I can go no further."

"This is not a good place to stop," I said. "If you can make it, there are trucks up the road where it forks for Tortosa."

"I will wait a while," he said, "and then I will go. Where do the trucks go?"

"Towards Barcelona," I told him.

45   "I know no one in that direction," he said, "but thank you very much. Thank you again very much."

He looked at me very blankly and tiredly, then said, having to share his worry with some one, "The cat will be all right, I am sure. There is no need to be unquiet about the cat. But the others. Now what do you think

50 about the others?"

"Why they'll probably come through it all right."

"You think so?"

"Why not," I said, watching the far bank where now there were no carts.

"But what will they do under the artillery when I was told to leave

55 because of the artillery?"

"Did you leave the dove cage unlocked?" I asked.

"Yes."

"Then they'll fly."

"Yes, certainly they'll fly. But the others. It's better not to think about

60 the others," he said.

  "If you are rested I would go," I urged. "Get up and try to walk now."

"Thank you," he said and got to his feet, swayed from side to side and then sat down backwards in the dust.

"I was taking care of animals," he said dully, but no longer to me. **L**

65 "I was only taking care of animals."

There was nothing to do about him. It was Easter Sunday and the Fascists were advancing toward the Ebro. It was a gray overcast day with a low ceiling so their planes were not up. That and the fact that cats know how to look after themselves was all the good luck that old man would ever have. **R2**

Plot

You may hope that the old man will be able to flee with the others, but, in the climax of the story, he is too tired to stand.

Theme

The implication is that war is unlucky for the civilians whose lives it touches.

Reading Check

Analyzing How does the story reach its climax and how is it resolved?

Teach

Reading Check

Answer: The man is about to flee, but feels too tired. He can only sit back down and await his fate.

L Literary Element

Theme Ask: What is ironic about the old man's evacuation? *(Although he is near death, the old man is most concerned about his animals. In addition, it is ironic that the old man who is so worried about leaving his animals is himself left to die by the narrator.)* How does the narrator's callousness to the old man illustrate the theme? *(It shows what war does to people psychologically.)* **OL**

★ Political History

Spanish Civil War Explain that the Spanish Civil War from 1936–39 is considered to be a prelude to World War II. The forces of Francisco Franco, backed by Fascist Italy and Nazi Germany, defeated the republican government. Discuss the story's setting, Spain's Ebro Delta in the late 1930s during the Spanish Civil War, as Fascist forces are advancing. **AS**

Reading in the Real World

Citizenship Encourage students to read newspaper articles about the impact of international conflicts on ordinary citizens. After students report on their stories and draw comparisons with "Old Man at the Bridge," post the news articles on a classroom bulletin board. **OL**

Building Reading Fluency

Irony Help students identify irony by reading relevant passages aloud. Diagram the contrast between what readers would expect a dying man to worry about and what the old man worries about, as well as how they would expect the narrator to help and what he actually does. Probe students' reactions. **BL**

Objectives
- To identify and interpret literary elements in a short story (SE)
- To analyze diction (TWE)

5

Teach

R1 Reading Strategy

Evaluating Viewpoints
Point out that writers have different approaches to telling stories. **Ask:** What kind of storytelling do the fiction writers Eudora Welty, Raymond Carver, John Gardner, and Margaret Atwood appreciate? *(Welty appreciates how fiction can illuminate cause-and-effect relationships. Carver prefers a straightforward plot and realistic characters. Gardner appreciates the art of building to a climax, and Margaret Atwood appreciates a sense of urgency in telling a story.)*
Invite students to tell whether they agree or disagree with each author and to explain why. Encourage them to provide examples from stories they have read or heard. **OL**

R2 Reading Strategy

Interpreting Meaning Ask:
What does Calvino mean by "the ear" driving a story? *(The reader's response is the determining factor.)* What does Atwood mean by "urgency"? *(the sense of the importance of a story)*
Ask students to summarize the reader's role in responding to a short story. **OL**

Writers on Reading

What do writers say about short stories?

Reading the Short Story R1

Identifying Sequence

Writing a story or a novel is one way of discovering *sequence* in experience, of stumbling upon cause and effect in the happenings of a writer's own life. This has been the case with me. Connections slowly emerge. Like distant landmarks you are approaching, cause and effect begin to align themselves, draw closer together. Experiences too indefinite of outline in themselves to be recognized for themselves connect and are identified as a larger shape. And suddenly a light is thrown back, as when your train makes a curve, showing that there has been a mountain of meaning rising behind you on the way you've come, is rising there still, proven now through retrospect. . . .

Writing fiction has developed in me an abiding respect for the unknown in a human lifetime and a sense of where to look for the threads, how to follow, how to connect, find in the thick of the tangle what clear line persists. The strands are all there: to the memory nothing is ever really lost.

—Eudora Welty, **from** *One Writer's Beginnings* ★

Appreciating Realistic Characters

I lean toward realistic, "life-like" characters—that is to say, people—in realistically detailed situations. I'm drawn toward the traditional (some would call it old-fashioned) methods of storytelling: one layer of reality unfolding and giving way to another, perhaps richer layer; the gradual accretion of meaningful detail; dialogue that not only reveals something about character but advances the story. I'm not very interested, finally, in haphazard revelations, attenuated characters, stories where method or technique is all—stories, in short, where nothing much happens or where what *does* happen merely confirms

one's sour view of a world gone out of control. Too, I distrust the inflated language that some people pile on when they write fiction. I believe in the efficacy of the concrete word, be it noun or verb, as opposed to the abstract or arbitrary or slippery word—or phrase or sentence.

—Raymond Carver, **from the Introduction to** *The Best American Short Stories* 1986

> *"It is not the voice that commands the story: it is the ear."*
> —Italo Calvino   R2

Enjoying Suspense

All good fiction contains suspense, different kinds of suspense in different kinds of fiction. Take the simplest kind first.

Anyone can write "A shot rang out" or "There lay the body of Mrs. Uldridge." What is harder to write is the moment leading up to such a climax. When the writing is successful, the reader senses that the climax is coming and feels a strong urge to skip to it directly, but cannot quite tear himself from the paragraph he's on. Ideally, every element in the lead-in passage should be a relevant distraction that heightens the reader's anticipation and at the same time holds, itself, such interest—through richness of literal or metaphoric language, through startling accuracy of perception, or through the deepening thematic and emotional effect of significant earlier moments recalled—that the reader is reluctant to dash on.

—John Gardner, **from** *The Art of Fiction*

Additional Support

Skills Practice

READING: Literary Response Tell students that any time they share their thoughts or feelings about something they read, they are responding to a text. Invite students to respond to the writings on these pages in a range of ways:

• **discussion**—Discussion elicits meaning through sharing of ideas. Ask students

which writer they think best captures their idea of a good story, and make sure they back up what they say with specifics.

• **journal**—Encourage students to keep a reading journal where they jot down their reactions to what they read. In this case, suggest that they write out

On the Way to the Market, Bahamas, 1885. Watercolor. Winslow Homer. Brooklyn Musem of Art.

Storytelling with Urgency

Anyone who has ever told, or tried to tell, a story to children will know that there is one thing without which none of the rest is any good. Young children have little sense of dutifulness or of delaying anticipation. They are longing to hear a story, but only if you are longing to tell one. They will not put up with your lassitude or of boredom: if you want their full attention, you must give them yours. You must hold them with your glittering eye or suffer the pinches and whispering. You need . . . a sense of urgency. *This is the story I must tell; this is the story you must hear.*

Urgency does not mean frenzy. The story can be a quiet story, a story about dismay or missed chances or a wordless revelation. But it must be urgently told. It must be told with as much intentness as if the teller's life depended on it. . . .

Is all this too much to ask? Not really; because many stories . . . do it superbly.

—Margaret Atwood, **from the Introduction to** *The Best American Short Stories* **1989**

Literature Online **InterActive Reading Practice**
Visit www.glencoe.com for more practice reading a short story.

Reading Check

Responding From your own reading experiences, which passage do you identify with most closely? Explain.

Teach

Reading Check

Students' responses will vary. Students should explain their choices.

L Literary Element

Style and Meaning Ask:
What point does Welty make through her journey metaphors of "distant landmarks," "light thrown back," and "mountain of meaning"? *(She clarifies how writing is a process of self-discovery, leading to understanding of causes, connections, and sequence.)* What effect does Welty's writing have on you? *(Students may find it inspiring.)* **OL**

★ Viewing the Art

Although Winslow Homer (1836–1910) has had to depict gruesome scenes as a Civil War illustrator, he has also produced a body of work consisting of more light-hearted subjects such as women and children in realistic and natural scenes. Ask students to reflect on what they believe the woman in the painting is doing or where she is going. **AS**

Differentiated Instruction

their reactions to Welty's, Carver's, Gardner's, Calvino's, and Atwood's comments.

• **oral interpretation or dramatization**—Tell students that another way to respond to what they read is through dramatic reading or acting out what they have read. **OL**

Figurative Language Point out the rich figurative language Welty and Carver use to make their points about fiction. Have students visualize Carver's description of a story unfolding in layers and forming an accretion, or gradual accumulation, of detail. **BL**

Objectives
• To identify and interpret literary elements in the short story (SE)
• To respond to literature (TWE)

7

Assess/Close

Guide to Reading Short Stories

Discuss what is unique about reading short stories. Point out that short stories are microcosms for all fiction since they contain the same elements and provide excellent material for learning to analyze literature.

Elements of Short Stories

Review the elements of the short story. Apply each element to "The Old Man at the Bridge."

Activities

1. **Literary Analysis** Diagram the plot movement that arises from these two characters' interactions. Students should recognize the exposition, the rising action, the climax, and the falling action and resolution implied by the last paragraph.

2. **Listening / Speaking** Build students' awareness of the skills needed for a good discussion.

FOLDABLES™
Study Organizer

Have students make and label the Foldables Study Organizer. Then have them write notes about each literary element under each heading.

Additional Support

Wrap-Up

Guide to Reading Short Stories

- Short stories often allow readers to focus on one setting and a small number of characters.

- Plot development in short stories tends to be very compact, especially the exposition, falling action, and resolution.

- Reading a short story well involves determining the theme, often by paying attention to what befalls the main character.

- Notice whether the narrator is inside the story (first-person point of view) or outside the story (third-person point of view).

- To help you stay engaged as you read a story, think of your own adjectives to describe the characters and the narrator.

Elements of Short Stories

- **Plot** is what happens in a story.
- **Setting** is where the story takes place.
- **Characters** are the actors in a story.
- The **narrator** tells the story.
- **Voice** refers to the kind of language the narrator uses to tell the story.
- The **theme** is the story's most meaningful message.

Activities

Use what you have learned about reading and analyzing short stories to complete one of the following activities.

1. Literary Analysis Write about the relationship between the narrator and the old man in "Old Man at the Bridge." How did their interactions affect the plot?

2. Listening/Speaking In a small group, discuss the theme of "Old Man at the Bridge." Give each group member a chance to choose a line from the story that contributes to the theme and to explain how the line contributes to the story's meaning.

3. Note Taking Try using this study organizer to keep track of literary elements in the stories in Unit 1.

FOLDABLES
Study Organizer

FOLDABLES STUDY ORGANIZER

| Plot |
| Setting |
| Theme |
| Character |
| Narrator |
| Voice |

OBJECTIVES
- Analyze interactions between characters in a literary text.
- Use effective strategies for informal and formal discussions.
- Identify theme, setting, characters, and point of view.

Skills Practice

SPEAKING AND LISTENING:
Discussion Review the following good discussion skills:

- Listen to other people's ideas carefully.
- State your ideas succinctly and clearly.
- Stay on target with the topic.

- Pose questions that are interpretive rather than factual.
- Wrap up a discussion with a summary.
- Practice with a mock discussion in which students monitor the use of these skills. **OL**

PART 1

Encountering the Unexpected

Accident in the Hall of Mirrors, 1999. Graeme Wilcox. Acrylic on canvas, 128 x 158 cm. ★

BI   BIG IDEA

People never know exactly what their futures will bring. Many people expect that tomorrow will be much like today. In the short stories in Part 1, you will encounter people and events that are not always what they initially seem to be. As you read these stories, ask yourself: How do people cope when they suddenly encounter the unexpected?

9

UNIT ONE: PART 1

Analyzing and Extending

BI   Big Idea

Encountering the Unexpected Ask students to consider their reactions to unexpected occurrences in their own lives, and suggest that they predict how the fictional characters might experience surprising happenings. Part 1 will deepen their understanding of the experience of encountering the unexpected. Encourage students to contemplate this "big idea." **OL**

★ Viewing the Art

The Scottish painter Graeme Wilcox has studied at the Glasgow School of Art and at the Brighton College of Art. His paintings, realistic in nature, invite the viewer to ponder what may happen next to the subjects. Ask students to study the painting, and discuss their reactions. **AS**

English Language Coach

Building Background Help students to connect with and better understand the literature in Part 1 by considering their experiences coming to the United States. Ask students what was most unexpected, what their reactions were, and how they learned to cope with the unexpected. **EL**

Differentiated Instruction

Establishing a Purpose for Reading Tell less proficient readers that they will gain more from their reading if they establish a purpose beforehand. Explain that some purposes for reading include to enjoy, discover information, interpret, follow directions, and find models for their own writing. **BL**

Objectives for Part 1
• To analyze literary elements (SE)
• To develop skill in diagramming plot (SE)

9

Part 1: Encountering the Unexpected

Readability Scores Key
Dale-Chall/DRP/Lexile

PACING (DAYS)		SELECTIONS AND FEATURES	LITERARY ELEMENTS
STANDARD	BLOCK		
1 class session	1	LITERARY FOCUS: Plot and Setting, pp. 10-11	Plot and Setting, SE pp. 10–11
		"The Open Window" by Saki **6.5/61/1070**, pp. 12-19	Flashback, SE pp. 13, 14, 18 Plot, SE p. 18
1–2 class sessions	1	**"The Californian's Tale"** by Mark Twain **4.0/61/1050**, pp. 20-30	Foreshadowing, SE pp. 21, 24, 27, 29 Plot, SE p. 29
		LITERARY PERSPECTIVE on Mark Twain: "Storytelling is as Old as Mankind" by Joyce Carol Oates **12.9/74/1520**, pp. 31-34	
1–2 class sessions	1	**"The Summer People"** by Shirley Jackson **6.2/63/1200**, pp. 35-48	Conflict, SE pp. 36, 38, 40, 42, 43, 46, 47 Foreshadowing, SE p. 47 Characterization, TWE p. 42
1–2 class sessions	1	Vocabulary Workshop: Denotation and Connotation, p. 49	
		"The Book of the Dead" by Edwidge Danticat **5.9/56/920**, pp. 50-63	Irony, SE pp. 51, 53-60, 62 Conflict, SE p. 62 Dialect, TWE p. 56
1 class session	1	**"An Astrologer's Day"** by R. K. Narayan **9.2/62/940**, pp. 64-71	Description, SE pp. 65, 67-70 Irony, SE p. 70
		Grammar Workshop: Mechanics, p. 72	
1 class session	1	**"Civil Peace"** by Chinua Achebe **6.8/61/1150**, pp. 73-81	Dialect, SE pp. 74, 78-80 Conflict, SE p. 80
1 class session		**"The Masque of the Red Death"** by Edgar Allan Poe **9.5/66/1240**, pp. 82-92	Mood, SE pp. 83, 85, 86, 89, 91 Description, SE p. 91

About the Part

Part 1 covers plot and setting within the short story.

READING AND CRITICAL THINKING	VOCABULARY	WRITING AND GRAMMAR	SPEAKING, LISTENING, AND VIEWING
Analyzing Plot, TWE p. 10		Quickwrite, SE p. 11	
Identifying Sequence, SE pp. 13, 14, 15, 18 Visualizing, TWE p. 16	Context Clues, SE p. 18 Academic Vocabulary, SE p. 18 Compound Words, TWE p. 14	Setting and Plot, SE p. 19 Using Parenthetical Phrases, SE p. 19	Analyzing Art, SE p. 16 Group Activity, SE p. 17 Literary Criticism, SE p. 19
Analyzing Cause and Effect, SE pp. 21–30 Predicting, TWE p. 22 Identifying Spatial Relationships, TWE p. 24	Word Parts, SE p. 30 Academic Vocabulary, SE p. 30	Evaluate Author's Craft, SE p. 30	Analyzing Art, TWE pp. 22, 26 Contrasting Viewpoints, TWE p. 26
Evaluating Historical Influences, SE p. 31; TWE p. 33			Analyzing Art, TWE pp. 32, 34
Responding to Plot, SE pp. 36-46, 48 Analyzing Details, TWE p. 38 Activating Prior Knowledge, TWE p. 40	Context Clues, SE p. 48; TWE p. 42 Academic Vocabulary, SE p. 48	Analyze Setting, SE p. 48 Persuasive Writing, TWE p. 44	Analyzing Art, SE p. 45; TWE p. 41 Role-Play, SE p. 48
	Using a Semantic Chart, SE p. 49		
Comparing and Contrasting, SE pp. 51, 53-60, 62 Visualizing, TWE p. 54	Context Clues, SE pp. 51, 62 Academic Vocabulary, SE p. 62	Analyze Plot, SE p. 63 Handling Dialogue, SE p. 63 Quotation Marks, SE p. 63 Literary Response, TWE p. 52	Analyzing Art, SE p. 59; TWE pp. 54, 57 Literature Groups, SE p. 63 Reciting Dialogue, TWE p. 58
Analyzing Cultural Context, SE pp. 65-67, 71	Word Origins, SE pp. 65, 71 Academic Vocabulary, SE p. 71	Analyze Conflict, SE p. 71 Creating Dialogue, TWE p. 68	Connecting, TWE p. 69
		Using Apostrophes in Possessives, SE p. 72	
Analyzing Historical Context, SE pp. 74-76, 78, 79, 81 Varying Reading Rate, TWE p. 76	Word Origins, SE pp. 74, 81 Academic Vocabulary, SE p. 81	Respond to Plot, SE p. 81 Personal Pronouns, TWE p. 78	Analyzing Art, SE p. 78 Interviewing, SE p. 81
Interpreting Imagery, SE pp. 83, 86, 88, 91	Analogies, SE pp. 83, 91 Academic Vocabulary, SE p. 91	Analyze Plot, SE p. 92 Sentence Structure, SE p. 92	Analyzing Art, SE p. 87 Literature Groups, SE p. 92

Focus

BELLRINGER

Bellringer Options
Daily Language Transparency 2
Or when students arrive at class, have the room set up differently, such as with the lights off, the desks upside-down or rearranged, and art images projected on the walls. **Say:** Think about how you respond when you encounter something unexpected in your life. How do you cope with new challenges? Discuss student responses.

Teach

L Literary Element

Plot and Setting Ask: Based on the details in the passage, what kind of setting does Shirley Jackson portray? *(a quiet rustic setting.)* What expectation does that setting set up for what will happen? *(It sets up the expectation for peaceful and pleasant events.)* **OL**

Literary Elements Have students access the Web site to improve their understanding of plot and setting.

Additional Support

Plot and Setting

How do short stories create events and places?

Think of a favorite story. Where does it take place? Can you imagine the same people, events, and themes happening somewhere else? Especially in a short story, where there is often only one setting, the setting can be an essential component of the tale being told. In Shirley Jackson's short stories, the bucolic, small-town settings she so often uses are an integral part of her stories' characteristic twists and turns.

Secluded Little House by Water. Connie Hayes.

The Allisons' country cottage, seven miles from the nearest town, was set prettily on a hill; from three sides it looked down on soft trees and grass that seldom, even at mid-summer, lay still and dry. On the fourth side was the lake, which touched against the wooden pier the Allisons had to keep repairing, and which looked equally well from the Allisons' front porch, their side porch or any spot on the wooden staircase leading from the porch down to the water. Although the Allisons loved their summer cottage, looked forward to arriving in early summer and hated to leave in the fall, they had not troubled themselves to put in any improvements, regarding the cottage itself and the lake as improvement enough for the life left to them. The cottage had no heat, no running water except the precarious supply from the backyard pump, and no electricity.

—Shirley Jackson, *from* "The Summer People"

Setting

Setting is the time and the place of a story. It also includes the customs, beliefs, and values of that time and place. An author can use the setting to create expectations in a reader. Then, the author can use those expectations to create a mood such as surprise, disappointment, or shock. Consider the setting of "The Summer People":

Detail	Aspect of Setting
"summer cottage"	custom of vacationing
"no running water"	rural place; modern time
"seven miles from the nearest town"	isolated place

Skills Practice

READING: Analyzing Plot Ask students to label each of the elements in a plot diagram with the appropriate incident from "The Open Window." **Ask:** What does the exposition introduce in "The Open Window"? *(It introduces the character of Framton Nuttel and his situation.)*

What story the niece tells is part of the rising action? *(The story of the men not returning from hunting is a major plot complication.)*
What makes the return of the men the climax of the story? *(It is intensely emotional because the niece makes Nuttel think he is seeing ghosts.)*

Plot

Plot is the sequence of events in a story. A good plot has a clear beginning, middle, and ending. Plots often begin with a character or characters and a situation or a conflict.

Plot includes the story's exposition, rising action, climax, falling action, and resolution.

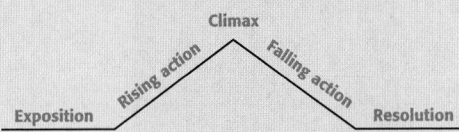

Exposition In the beginning of a story, novel, or play, you will meet the main characters, learn about their situations, and uncover the story's setting. This part of the story is called the **exposition**. The following passage of exposition introduces Framton Nuttel, a man in need of a "nerve cure" who is a stranger in the home of an aunt and her niece.

> Privately [Framton Nuttel] doubted more than ever whether these formal visits on a succession of total strangers would do much towards helping the nerve cure which he was supposed to be undergoing.
>
> —Saki, *from "The Open Window"* **R**

Rising Action After the reader is introduced to the conflict, the story may become more complicated, and the reader becomes more interested and engaged. This is called the **rising action.** Now, the reader wants to know, what happens next? Mr. Nuttel is about to hear a ghost story from the niece whose home he is visiting. The reader must wonder how he will handle the excitement.

> Out through that window, three years ago to a day, her husband and her two young brothers went off for their day's shooting. They never came back.

Climax The most exciting moment in a story is called the **climax**. This moment is the most emotionally intense, interesting, or suspenseful one. For better or for worse, the character's conflict is resolved.

> The child was staring out through the open window with dazed horror in her eyes. . . . In the deepening twilight three figures were walking across the lawn towards the window; they all carried guns under their arms.

Falling Action After the excitement of the climax, the **falling action** shows what happens as a result of the climax.

> "A most extraordinary man, a Mr. Nuttel," said Mrs. Sappleton; "could only talk about his illnesses, and dashed off without a word of good-bye or apology when you arrived. One would think he had seen a ghost."

Resolution The **resolution** is sometimes considered a part of the falling action, or *denouement*. It may reveal or suggest the final outcome of the conflict. "The Open Window" reveals in a sentence that the niece has tricked Mr. Nuttell.

> "I expect it was the spaniel," said the niece calmly; "he told me he had a horror of dogs."

OBJECTIVES
- Analyze complex elements of plot, such as major events, problems, conflicts, and resolutions.
- Trace the development of a familiar plot.

Teach

R Reading Strategy

Making Inferences Ask: What can you infer about Framton Nuttel and his situation from the exposition in "The Open Window"? *(Framton Nuttel, who is anxious and suffering from a mental disorder, is visiting relatives as part of a rehabilitation program.)* **OL**

★ Viewing the Art

The concept of setting directly relates to Maine artist Connie Hayes's work. Hayes describes the act of painting as "a response to a specific environment," and says that "a sense of place is important." **Ask:** What mood does the setting of this painting evoke in you? Explain. *(Students' answers will vary.)* **AS**

Assess

Quickwrite

Suggest that students use widely known stories, such as fairy tales, for creating their plot diagrams.

Differentiated Instruction

What is the result in the falling action? *(Nuttel flees the house in horror.)*
How is the story wrapped up in the resolution? *(The resolution reveals the devious niece hides the trick she plays on Nuttel.)*
Have students practice diagramming plots of favorite movies and TV programs. **OL**

Vocabulary To prepare less proficient readers for the textbook's explanation of "The Summer People" excerpt, point out the word *bucolic*, and see if students can explain its meaning: "quiet, rustic, pastoral." To help students remember, note its origins from Greek *boukolos*, meaning "herdsman," and *bous*, meaning "ox." **BL**

Objectives
- To make inferences about setting (SE)
- To develop skill in diagramming plot (SE)
- To identify and analyze elements of plot (TWE)

11

Focus

BELLRINGER

Bellringer Options
Selection Focus Transparency 1
Daily Language Transparency 3
Or ask: What are some synonyms for the word *lying?*
Write students' responses on the board, and discuss.
Ask: What is the difference between lying and tricking? *(Tricking sounds less serious than lying, as in a joke.)* What is the difference between lying and storytelling? *(Storytelling is meant to entertain, while lying is meant to deceive.)*

Literature Online

Author Search To expand students' appreciation of Saki, have them access the Web site for additional information and resources.

The Open Window

MEET SAKI

What if, as a child, you were locked away in a country house with two strict, bickering aunts as your guardians? How would you satisfy your desire for diversion? If you possessed the satiric humor, wit, and writing talents of Saki, you might have found satisfaction as he did, by writing stories.

Childhood Trials Hector Hugh Munro (Saki's real name) was the third child in an upper-class English family. He was born in the former British colony of Burma. When his mother was pregnant with her fourth child, the family returned to England, but she was killed in a tragic accident before giving birth. Saki's father decided to return to Burma. He sent his three young children to live with his mother and two unmarried sisters in a small English village.

Saki's aunts were not at all suited to caring for children. They imposed strict rules and constantly quarreled with each other. Saki eventually found relief when he went off to school, but he clearly never forgot his childhood experiences. Many of Saki's stories would have tyrannical aunts and young children who wreaked havoc on adults.

From Burma to London When Saki was twenty-three, he took a position with the military police in Burma. While he did not enjoy the heat of the Far East, he was enthralled by the region's exotic landscape, especially the wild animals. Munro's fascination with and respect for animals emerges as another repeated feature of his stories.

When he contracted malaria, Saki returned to England. When he was well, he moved to London to pursue his literary career. In 1900

Literature Online Author Search For more about Saki, go to www.glencoe.com.

"The best stories of Munro are all of childhood, its humor and its comedy as well its cruelty and unhappiness."
—Graham Greene, from *The Best of Saki*

his first work, *The Rise of the Russian Empire,* was published. Reviewers said Munro's work was sarcastic and lacked seriousness. Fortunately for the literary world, Munro did not give up his aspirations to be a writer. He simply learned to redirect this sarcasm, along with his wit and sharp observations of society, into short stories.

Finding Success Also in 1900, Saki began writing captions for political cartoons. It was at this time that he took his rather surprising pen name, the single name Saki, an allusion to the *Rubáiyát of Omar Khayyám,* a famous epic poem.

By 1909 Saki was able to focus solely on writing short stories. However, in 1914 he joined the army to fight in World War I. He said that he was glad to be in the trenches, so far from "all the thousand and one horrors of civilization." Saki was mortally wounded on a French battlefield. However, his literature lives on. Saki's stories and three novels have been published in the volume *The Complete Works of Saki,* and they continue to delight readers today.

Saki was born in 1870 and died in 1916.

Selection Skills

Literary Elements
• Flashback (SE pp. 13, 14, 18)
• Plot (SE p. 18)

The Open Window

Reading Skills
• Identifying Sequence (SE pp. 13, 14, 15, 18)
• Visualizing (TWE p. 16)

Vocabulary Skills
• Context Clues (SE p. 18)
• Academic Vocabulary (SE p. 18)
• Compound Words (TWE p. 14)

Listening/Speaking/Viewing Skills
• Analyzing Art (SE p. 16)
• Literary Criticism (SE p. 19)

Writing Skills/Grammar
• Setting and Plot Analysis (SE p. 19)
• Parenthetical Phrases (SE p. 19)

Connecting to the Short Story

In Saki's "The Open Window," two characters act on their first impressions of each other. Before you read the short story, think about the following questions:

- Think about a time when you first met someone. What assumptions did you make about him or her?
- Has your first impression of someone ever turned out to be wrong?

Building Background

"The Open Window" takes place at the country manor of the Sappletons, a typical upper-class English family. Wealthy families such as the Sappletons often lived in the city but maintained a second residence in the English countryside, where the pace of life was less stressful. It was not unusual for upper-class families to welcome into their homes strangers who brought with them a letter of introduction from a mutual acquaintance.

At the time of this story, hunting was a popular amusement among the upper classes. In "The Open Window," the men are hunting snipe, which are wetland game birds. Bird dogs, such as spaniels, were brought along on a hunt to flush out birds resting in the brush and then to retrieve the felled birds.

Setting Purposes for Reading

Big Idea **Encountering the Unexpected**

As you read, pay attention to how Saki uses the twists and turns in the story to manipulate not only the story characters, but his readers as well.

Literary Element **Flashback**

A **flashback** is an interruption of the chronological order of the story to show an event that happened earlier. Authors use flashback to give readers information that may help explain the main events of the story.

- See Literary Terms Handbook, p. R6.

Literature Online **Interactive Literary Elements Handbook** To review or learn more about the literary elements, go to www.glencoe.com.

OBJECTIVES

In studying this selection, you will focus on the following:
- understanding flashback
- identifying sequence of events
- analyzing the effectiveness of elements of plot
- writing to analyze the relevance of setting and time frame

Reading Strategy Identifying Sequence

To **identify sequence** is to recognize the order in which the most important events in a literary work happen. In a fictional story such as "The Open Window," we can look for clues or signal words that point to the chronological, or time, order of events.

Reading Tip: Organize Events Use a sequence chart to put important events in the story in chronological order.

SEQUENCE OF EVENTS

The first thing that happens is:
Framton Nuttel waits for Mrs. Sappleton with her niece Vera.

⬇

After that:
Vera asks Nuttel if he knows anything about her aunt, and he says, "Only her name and address."

⬇

Next:
Vera tells Nuttel about her aunt's "great tragedy."

Vocabulary

self-possessed (self′ pə zest′) *adj.* in control of oneself; composed; p. 14 *Many people were nervous, but she was completely self-possessed.*

duly (dōō′ le) *adv.* rightfully; suitably; p. 14 *He was duly impressed with the grand house.*

moor (moor) *n.* a tract of open, rolling, wild land, often having marshes; p. 15 *He pulled on a good pair of boots before hiking across the moor.*

infirmity (in fur′ mə tē) *n.* a weakness or ailment; p. 16 *He once was a vibrant, energetic man, but age and infirmity had slowed him down.*

imminent (im′ ə nənt) *adj.* likely to happen soon; p. 16 *Dark, thick clouds are gathering, and rain seems imminent.*

Focus

Summary

Framton Nuttel calls on Mrs. Sappleton. As he awaits Mrs. Sappleton, her niece tells him that it is the third anniversary of the disappearance of a hunting party led by Mrs. Sappleton's husband and that the distraught Mrs. Sappleton refuses to accept the loss and keeps the French window open for the party's return. Nuttel flees in fear when he sees the supposedly long-missing hunting party approach the house.

V Vocabulary

Vocabulary File Say: Add these words and definitions to your vocabulary file. For each word, include a sentence that gives you an example of how to use the word. **OL** Students with English language needs should include the pronunciations of these words in their files. **EL**

Literary Elements Have students access the Web site to improve their understanding of flashback.

Selection Resources

Print Materials
- 📁 Unit 1 Resources (Fast File), pp. 20–22
- 📁 Leveled Vocabulary Development, p. 1
- 📁 Selection and Unit Assessments, pp. 1–2
- 📁 Selection Quick Checks, p. 1

Transparencies
- Bellringer Options Transparencies:
  Selection Focus Transparency 1
  Daily Language Practice Transparency 3
- Literary Elements Transparency 37

Technology
- 💿 TeacherWorks Plus™ CD-ROM
- 💿 StudentWorks Plus™ CD-ROM
- 💿 Presentation Plus!™ CD-ROM
- 💻 Literature Online, glencoe.com
- 💻 Online Student Edition, mhln.com
- 💿 ExamView® Assessment Suite CD-ROM
- 💿 Vocabulary PuzzleMaker CD-ROM
- 💿 Listening Library, disc 1 track 1

L Literary Element

Flashback Answer: *Nuttel is in the country. His sister has encouraged him to visit people to help his nerves.*
Ask: Based on this flashback, do you believe this visit will help Nuttel's nerves? *(Answers will vary. Some will say that it is better to be around people; others will say that it will make him more nervous.)* **OL**

R1 Reading Strategy

Identifying Sequence
Answer: *This is after Framton's arrival at their home. He is sitting with the niece, thinking of the conversation in the flashback.* **OL**

Readability Scores
Dale-Chall: 6.5
DRP: 61
Lexile: 1070

The Open Window

Saki ★

My aunt will be down presently, Mr. Nuttel," said a very **self-possessed** young lady of fifteen; "in the meantime you must try and put up with me."

Framton Nuttel endeavored to say the correct something which should **duly** flatter the niece of the moment without unduly discounting the aunt that was to come. Privately he doubted more than ever whether these formal visits on a succession of total strangers would do much towards helping the nerve cure which he was supposed to be undergoing.

"I know how it will be," his sister had said when he was preparing to migrate to this rural retreat; "you will bury yourself down there and not speak to a living soul, and your nerves will be worse than ever from moping. I shall just give you letters of introduction to all the people I know there. Some of them, as far as I can remember, were quite nice."

Framton wondered whether Mrs. Sappleton, the lady to whom he was presenting one of the letters of introduction, came into the nice division.

"Do you know many of the people round here?" asked the niece, when she judged that they had had sufficient silent communion.

Literary Element Flashback *What background information does this flashback provide?* **L**

Reading Strategy Identifying Sequence *Is this taking place before or after Framton Nuttel's arrival at the Sappletons' home? Explain how it relates to the flashback that precedes it.* **R1**

Vocabulary

self-possessed (self′ pə zest′) *adj.* in control of oneself; composed
duly (dōō′ lē) *adv.* rightfully; suitably

14 UNIT 1 THE SHORT STORY

Additional Support

VOCABULARY: Compound Words
Tell students that the word *chalkboard* is a compound word, a word made up of two other words with separate and distinct meanings. You probably know what the compound means because you know the meanings of its parts. Explain that they can determine the meanings of many compound words by thinking about the meanings of their parts. For example, a person who is self-possessed possesses (and therefore controls) himself or herself. Have students brainstorm a list of other compound words. **OL**

"Hardly a soul," said Framton. "My sister was staying here, at the rectory,[1] you know, some four years ago, and she gave me letters of introduction to some of the people here."

He made the last statement in a tone of distinct regret.

"Then you know practically nothing about my aunt?" pursued the self-possessed young lady.

"Only her name and address," admitted the caller. He was wondering whether Mrs. Sappleton was in the married or widowed state. An undefinable something about the room seemed to suggest masculine habitation.

"Her great tragedy happened just three years ago," said the child; "that would be since your sister's time."

"Her tragedy?" asked Framton; somehow in this restful country spot tragedies seemed out of place.

"You may wonder why we keep that window wide open on an October afternoon," said the niece, indicating a large French window[2] that opened on to a lawn.

"It is quite warm for the time of the year," said Framton; "but has that window got anything to do with the tragedy?"

"Out through that window, three years ago to a day, her husband and her two young brothers went off for their day's shooting. They never came back. In crossing the **moor** to their favorite snipe-shooting ground they were all three engulfed in a treacherous piece of bog. It had been that dreadful wet summer, you know, and places that were safe in other years gave way suddenly without warning. Their bodies were never recovered. That was the dreadful part of it." Here the child's voice lost its self-possessed note and became fal-

---

1. A *rectory* is the house in which a priest or minister lives.
2. A *French window* is a pair of door-like windows hinged at opposite sides and opening in the middle.

Big Idea Encountering the Unexpected *Why might the reader be as surprised by the mention of tragedy as Nuttel is?* **BI**

Vocabulary

moor (moor) *n.* a tract of open, rolling, wild land, often having marshes

teringly human. "Poor aunt always thinks that they will come back some day, they and the little brown spaniel that was lost with them, and walk in at that window just as they used to do. That is why the window is kept open every evening till it is quite dusk. Poor dear aunt, she has often told me how they went out, her husband with his white waterproof coat over his arm, and Ronnie, her youngest brother, singing, 'Bertie, why do you bound?' as he always did to tease her, because she said it got on her nerves. Do you know, sometimes on still, quiet evenings like this, I almost get a creepy feeling that they will all walk in through that window—"

She broke off with a little shudder. It was a relief to Framton when the aunt bustled into the room with a whirl of apologies for being late in making her appearance.

"I hope Vera has been amusing you?" she said.

"She has been very interesting," said Framton.

"I hope you don't mind the open window," said Mrs. Sappleton briskly; "my husband and brothers will be home directly from shooting, and they always come in this way. They've been out for snipe in the marshes today, so they'll make a fine mess over my poor carpets. So like you men-folk, isn't it?"

She rattled on cheerfully about the shooting and the scarcity of birds, and the prospects for duck in the winter. To Framton it was all purely horrible. He made a desperate but only partially successful effort to turn the talk on to a less ghastly topic; he was conscious that his hostess was giving him only a fragment of her attention, and her eyes were constantly straying past him to the open window and the lawn beyond. It was certainly an unfortunate coincidence that he should have paid his visit on this tragic anniversary.

"The doctors agree in ordering me complete rest, an absence of mental excitement, and avoidance of anything in the nature of

Reading Strategy Identifying Sequence *What is the sequence of events that leads up to Nuttel wanting to change the topic?* **R2**

SAKI **15**

English Language Coach

Setting the Tone Point out to English language learners that the niece is telling a scary story. The author uses several descriptive words to emphasize the scary tone. On the board, write the words *tragedies, dreadful, creepy, shudder, horrible,* and *ghastly*. Discuss what part of speech each is and how the words help set the tone of the story.

As students read, ask them to look for additional examples of words that set the tone for this scary story and invite them to add new words to their vocabulary notebooks. **EL**

BI₁ **Big Idea**

Encountering the Unexpected **Answer:** *If the husband and brothers are dead, no one should be "here at last."* **OL**

BI₂ **Big Idea**

Encountering the Unexpected **Answer:** *If readers knew ahead of time that she made up tales, there would be no surprises in the story. The story becomes entertaining when the reader does not quite know what is going on until the end.* **OL**

⭐ **Viewing the Art**

Answer: *The girl's expression conveys a feeling of boredom and dissatisfaction. This may be how the niece feels about her life and why she makes up stories.* **AS**

✓**CheckPoint**

Use the CheckPoint questions on Presentation Plus! to check students' mastery of the selection. These questions can be used with interactive response keypads for immediate student feedback.

At the Window, 1894. William Merritt Chase. Pastel and paper, 18.5 x 11 in. Brooklyn Museum of Art, NY. Gift of Mrs. Henry Wolf, Austin M. Wolf, and Hamilton A. Wolf.

Viewing the Art: What does this girl's facial expression convey? What qualities might the girl in this painting share with the niece in the story? ⭐

violent physical exercise," announced Framton, who labored under the tolerably wide-spread delusion that total strangers and chance acquaintances are hungry for the least detail of one's ailments and **infirmities,** their cause and cure. "On the matter of diet they are not so much in agreement," he continued.

"No?" said Mrs. Sappleton, in a voice which only replaced a yawn at the last moment. Then she suddenly brightened into alert attention— but not to what Framton was saying.

"Here they are at last!" she cried. "Just in time for tea, and don't they look as if they were muddy up to the eyes!"

Framton shivered slightly and turned towards the niece with a look intended to

convey sympathetic comprehension. The child was staring out through the open window with dazed horror in her eyes. In a chill shock of nameless fear Framton swung round in his seat and looked in the same direction.

In the deepening twilight three figures were walking across the lawn towards the window; they all carried guns under their arms, and one of them was additionally burdened with a white coat hung over his shoulders. A tired brown spaniel kept close at their heels. Noiselessly they neared the house, and then a hoarse young voice chanted out of the dusk: "I said, Bertie, why do you bound?"

Framton grabbed wildly at his stick and hat; the hall door, the gravel drive, and the front gate were dimly noted stages in his headlong retreat. A cyclist coming along the road had to run into the hedge to avoid **imminent** collision.

"Here we are, my dear," said the bearer of the white mackintosh,[3] coming in through the window; "fairly muddy, but most of it's dry. Who was that who bolted out as we came up?"

"A most extraordinary man, a Mr. Nuttel," said Mrs. Sappleton; "could only talk about his illnesses, and dashed off without a word of good-bye or apology when you arrived. One would think he had seen a ghost."

"I expect it was the spaniel," said the niece calmly; "he told me he had a horror of dogs. He was once hunted into a cemetery somewhere on the banks of the Ganges by a pack of pariah[4] dogs, and had to spend the night in a newly dug grave with the creatures snarling and grinning and foaming just above him. Enough to make any one lose their nerve." Romance[5] at short notice was her specialty.ᔕ

---

3. A *mackintosh* is a heavy-duty raincoat.
4. The *Ganges* is a river in northern India. A *pariah* is one who is shunned or despised by others. In India, where dogs are not highly regarded, packs of wild dogs are considered pariahs.
5. Here, *romance* means "tales of extraordinary or mysterious events."

Big Idea Encountering the Unexpected *Why is this exclamation unexpected?* **BI₁**

Vocabulary
infirmity (in fur′ mə tē) *n.* a weakness or ailment

Big Idea Encountering the Unexpected *Why does Saki wait until the last line of the story to tell readers that telling tales was Vera's specialty?* **BI₂**

Vocabulary
imminent (im′ ə nənt) *adj.* likely to happen soon

Additional Support

Skills Practice

READING: Visualizing Explain that visualizing what you read is like creating mental pictures using the details and descriptions provided by the author. If you can visualize the story it becomes much more interesting. **Ask:** What details and descriptions help you create a mental picture of the last scene in the story in which Mrs. Sappleton sees the hunting party returning home?

Write students' responses on the board. Then have them close their eyes and form a mental picture of the scene. After a few moments of quiet thought, have students sketch a picture that resembles their mental picture. **OL**

RESPONDING AND THINKING CRITICALLY

Respond

1. What was your reaction to Vera and Framton Nuttel?

Recall and Interpret

2. (a)Why does Framton Nuttel visit Mrs. Sappleton? (b)What do you think Vera notices as they sit in silence and wait for Mrs. Sappleton?

3. (a)What does Vera ask Framton Nuttel to break the silence? (b)Do you think that she asks this question because she is curious, or do you think she has another motive? Explain.

4. (a)What is Vera's reaction to the appearance of the three men returning from the moor? (b)How do you think this contributed to Nuttel's reaction?

Analyze and Evaluate

5. (a) How might Vera's poise and self-confidence contribute to her being believed? (b)In analyzing Vera's behavior, what might you conclude about Vera's motives?

6. Saki is often described as a master of wit and humor. Would you describe this story as witty or humorous? Explain.

7. The author subtly plays with the theme of hunting in this story. How is Vera like a hunter and Framton Nuttel like her prey?

Connect

8. Would you like to be friends with Vera? Why or why not? Use details from the story to support your opinion.

9. **Big Idea** **Encountering the Unexpected** A surprise reversal of events is a common theme in Saki's stories. (a)How does Saki employ this theme in "The Open Window"? (b)What was your reaction to this reversal? Explain.

PRIMARY VISUAL ARTIFACT

Viewing a Painting

Examine the painting. Notice how the contrast of light and dark draws the eye to the animals in the picture. As you continue to view the painting, consider how its subject matter and tone evoke the topic and tone of Saki's story, "The Open Window."

A Spaniel Frightening Ducks, 1821. James Ward. Oil on canvas, 122 x 182 cm. Tate Gallery, London.

Group Activity Discuss the following questions with classmates. Refer to the painting and cite evidence from "The Open Window" for support.

1. (a)What event does this painting show? (b)What does this event have to do with the story Vera tells Framton Nuttel?

2. (a)What story does Vera tell to explain why Framton Nuttel bolts from the house? (b)How does the mood of the painting compare to the mood of Vera's story about Nuttel?

Group Activity

1. (a) The painting shows a spaniel flushing birds out of the brush. (b) Vera tells Nuttel that a spaniel accompanied the three men on their hunting expedition.

2. (a) Vera says that Nuttel was once chased into a cemetery by dogs and had to spend the night there with the dogs growling at him. (b) The painting is warm and ordinary as it reflects a common experience of the times. Vera's story is horrific and bizarre.

Assess

1. Students may dislike Vera for fabricating stories to frighten Mr. Nuttel. Others may admire her creativity and imagination. Some may not like Nuttel because he is nervous and gullible. Others may sympathize with him.

2. (a) Nuttel is taking a vacation to improve his nerves. His sister gives him a letter of introduction encouraging him. (b) Nuttel's discomfort and nervousness

3. (a) If Nuttel knows anyone in the area (b) She has another motive. She must make sure that Nuttel does not know about her uncle or her brothers, or he will know that the story is not true.

4. (a) Vera stares in horror out the open window. (b) It makes her story more believable.

5. (a) She probably seems mature and unlikely to tell childish tales. (b) She is mischievous; she is mean.

6. Mr. Nuttel's quick exit and Mrs. Sappleton's response to it are told in an amused tone, and Vera's final tale is so absurd as to be humorous.

7. Vera senses Nuttel's weaknesses and attacks him.

8. Some students might enjoy Vera's imagination. Others may fear her guile. It might depend on whether or not they knew Vera told tales or if they were her victims.

9. (a) There are several reversals: from humor (nervous Nuttel) to tragedy (the three deaths) to horror (the "ghosts" appear) to humor (Nuttel departs and Vera tells an outrageous story). (b) Students may be surprised that Nuttel found Vera's outrageous story believable.

Assess

Literary Element

1. Waiting for Mrs. Sappleton's appearance
2. Visiting did not help his nerves

Review: Plot

Exposition: Nuttel pays a visit to the Sappletons. Vera questions Nuttel.

Rising Action: Vera relates "the tragedy." It is the reason for the open window. Mrs. Sappleton is waiting for the hunting party's return—confirming her apparent delusion.

Climax: Nuttel sees the hunting party returning and thinks they are ghosts.

Falling Action: Nuttel bolts from the house. Vera says it is because he is afraid of dogs.

Resolution: Invention was Vera's specialty.

Reading Strategy

1. Nervous Nuttel visits Mrs. Sappleton. In her absence, her niece tells of a missing hunting party. The aunt clearly expects her husband's return. The party appears, and Nuttel runs away in horror. Vera invents an explanation.

Literary Element Flashback

Authors frequently use **flashback** to help readers understand a character's current attitude and behavior. It gives the reader more information than would be gained from simply watching the events of the story unfold. In a movie, a flashback is often easier to identify, because characters are dressed differently, are younger, or are in different places. In literature, the reader must rely on elements in the story for clues, such as a change of scene or someone talking who is not present before the flashback begins. Flashback allows a writer to explain the past in a dramatic, creative fashion.

1. How does the setting provide an opportunity for the author to use flashback in the story?

2. Explain how the flashback makes the outcome of the story ironic.

Review: Plot

As you learned on page 10, **plot** refers to the sequence of events from the beginning to the end of a story.

Partner Activity Meet with another classmate and work together to identify the plot elements of "The Open Window." Working with your partner, create a plot diagram like the one below. Then fill it in with specific events from the story.

START

Exposition

Rising Action

Climax

Falling Action

Resolution

FINISH

Reading Strategy Identifying Sequence

"The Open Window" tells the story of what happens when Framton Nuttel pays a visit to the country home of the Sappletons. Within this story is a second narrative. That is the story that Vera tells Nuttel about her uncle's death while hunting on the moors. Review the **sequence** chart you created to recall how the main events in the story are connected.

1. Use your sequence chart to summarize the story.

2. When the author used a flashback at the beginning of the story, what helped you recognize that?

Vocabulary Practice

Practice with Context Clues Read each of the following sentences and identify the word or words that provide a context clue for the word in bold.

1. The younger daughter was always **self-possessed,** unlike her nervous older sister.
   a. The younger daughter
   b. unlike her nervous

2. He always did the right thing, and he was **duly** polite in addressing the young woman.
   a. always did right thing
   b. addressing the young woman

3. We stood at the edge of the **moor** and gazed out at the wide stretch of wet, marshy land.
   a. stood at the edge
   b. wet, marshy land

Academic Vocabulary

Here are two vocabulary words from the list on page R82. These words will help you think, write, and talk about the selection.

deduce (di dōōs′) *v.* to use logic to draw a conclusion about someone or something

mental (ment′əl) *adj.* related to the mind; often used to describe disorders of the mind

Practice and Apply
1. What can you **deduce** about Vera's personality?
2. How does Framton Nuttel's **mental** state affect his behavior and the outcome of this story?

18 UNIT 1 THE SHORT STORY

---

2. He converses with his absent sister. The flashback explains why Nuttel is visiting Mrs. Sappleton; this must come before the actual visit.

Vocabulary

1. b **2.** a **3.** b

Academic Vocabulary

1. Creative, spontaneous, mischievous
2. Nervous and gullible, he runs from the horror.

Writing About Literature

Analyze Setting and Plot Think about the setting for "The Open Window." Could this story have taken place at any other time or in any other place? Write a brief essay in which you analyze Saki's choice of setting and explain how the setting impacts the main events in the plot. Use evidence from the story to support your analysis.

As you draft, write from start to finish. Follow the writing pattern shown here to help you organize your essay and keep you on track.

START

Introduction ▸ Describe the setting. Tell where the action takes place, the time of day, and the social status of the characters.

Body Paragraph(s) ▸ Explain how different elements of the setting affect the development of the plot.

Conclusion ▸ Briefly summarize your analysis of the setting and its impact on the plot.

FINISH

After you complete your draft, meet with a peer reviewer to evaluate each other's work and to suggest revisions. Then proofread and edit your draft for errors in spelling, grammar, and punctuation.

Literary Criticism

"The cruelty is certainly there," writes critic Elizabeth Drew about Saki's stories, "but it has nothing perverted or pathological about it. . . . It is the genial heartlessness of the normal child, whose fantasies take no account of adult standards of human behavior." Write a short response in which you state whether you agree or disagree that this statement applies to "The Open Window" and to Vera. Include evidence from the story to support your opinion. Then use your response to debate this issue with your group.

Saki's Language and Style

Using Parenthetical Phrases In "The Open Window," Saki makes use of parenthetical phrases to expand, explain, or digress from a thought within a sentence and within the narrative. Most people's thought patterns follow this style, so by using parenthetical phrases Saki creates more natural, casual sounding dialogue and prose. Notice how the use of the parenthetical phrase, set off by commas in the following sentence, makes Nuttel's sister sound like a real person.

> "Some of them, as far as I can remember, were quite nice."

Consider the use of parenthetical phrases in these other sentences from the story and the information that they add.

> "Framton wondered whether Mrs. Sappleton, the lady to whom he was presenting one of the letters of introduction, came into the nice division."

> "My sister was staying here, at the rectory, you know, some four years ago, and she gave me letters of introduction to some of the people here."

Activity Find two other examples of sentences with parenthetical phrases in the story, and think about whether they expand, explain, or digress from the thoughts in the sentence. Then write two sentences of your own with parenthetical phrases. Remember to use commas to set off the parenthetical phrases in the sentences.

Revising Check

Parenthetical Phrases Adding information through the use of parenthetical phrases is something to consider when revising your own writing. With a partner, go through your setting and plot analysis and note places where you could expand or explain an idea more clearly with a parenthetical phrase. Revise your draft to include parenthetical phrases, and check that you have used commas correctly to set them off.

 Web Activities For eFlashcards, Selection Quick Checks, and other Web activities, go to www.glencoe.com.

SAKI **19**

Assess

Writing About Literature

Use these criteria when evaluating students' writing:

- Does the introduction identify the setting details that directly affect the main events in the plot, such as the country setting, the upper-class home, and the twilight?
- Do the body paragraphs discuss how the setting details cause the characters to act as they do?
- Does the conclusion summarize the impact of setting on overall plot?

Literary Criticism

Students may find the story cruel both in its description of Nuttel and in Vera's attitude toward him. But Vera tells a ghastly story not only to Nuttel but also to her aunt, suggesting that she is not out to inflict harm but simply to indulge her childish taste for the macabre.

Saki's Language and Style

Possible examples: "It had been that dreadful wet summer, you know, and places that were safe in other years gave way suddenly without warning"; ". . . and Ronnie, her youngest brother, singing 'Bertie, why do you bound?' as he always did to tease her, because she said it got on her nerves."

Revising Check

Remind students that parenthetical phrases expand, explain, or digress from a thought within a sentence. They should identify places in their essay that could use further explanation.

Web Activities Have students access the Web site for interactive activities that will help them assess their understanding of the selection.

Focus

BELLRINGER

Bellringer Options
Selection Focus Transparency 2
Daily Language Transparency 4
Or ask: Do you or your family members have stories you tell over and over? Invite several students to share their stories. What characteristics make these stories worth telling repeatedly? *(Such stories often teach a lesson or have a strange or shocking twist.)*

Literature Online

Author Search To expand students' appreciation of Mark Twain, have them access the Web site for additional information and resources.

The Californian's Tale

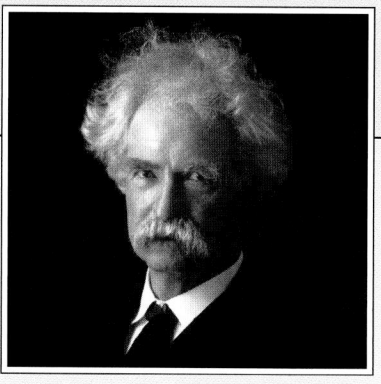

MEET MARK TWAIN

Mark Twain is the pen name of one of America's best-known and most beloved authors. Born Samuel Langhorne Clemens, he first used the name Mark Twain—a nautical term meaning "two fathoms deep"—when he wrote humorous pieces for a Nevada newspaper.

Twain lost his father when he was eleven. Within a few years he was helping to support his family. At age thirteen, he apprenticed to a local printer. Soon he was working at the local newspaper, which was established by his brother Orion. Twain's primary job was to set type, but he also wrote humorous articles.

During his late teens and early twenties, Twain moved from his home in Hannibal, Missouri, to St. Louis, then to several East Coast cities, and finally back to the Midwest. Eventually, he met a pilot who took him on as an apprentice. Twain loved being on the Mississippi. He gained his pilot's license and worked steering riverboats for several years until the Civil War interrupted the boat traffic.

> *"The human race has one really effective weapon, and that is laughter."*
>
> —Mark Twain

Western Adventures In 1861 Twain traveled west with Orion to Nevada. Twain tried to prospect for gold and silver and speculated in mines and timber, but he was unsuccessful. And so he returned to newspaper writing. Twain wrote a mix of biting political commentaries and humorous stories that earned him notice and respect. In 1866, on another travel-writing assignment, he took a steamboat trip

from San Francisco, California, to Honolulu, Hawaii. The next year, Twain took an even longer trip, sailing from California to Central America, traveling by land across Panama, sailing to New York, and then across the Atlantic Ocean to Europe and Southwest Asia. He published accounts of his travels as his first book, *Innocents Abroad*.

Worldwide Popularity From that time forward, Twain gained both national and international acclaim as a writer and lecturer, and wrote the books for which he is best known today: *The Adventures of Tom Sawyer* (1876), *The Prince and the Pauper* (1881), and *The Adventures of Huckleberry Finn* (1885). A brilliant storyteller, Twain's lectures were even more popular and lucrative than his books. Audiences all over the world loved his witty anecdotes, told in an exaggerated drawl with well-placed pauses that heightened dramatic tension and humor.

Twain penned "The Californian's Tale" in 1892, while living in Europe with his family. His wife Olivia, who had been having health problems for more than ten years, seemed to be regaining her strength and vitality. The love and devotion shown by the main character of "The Californian's Tale" toward his wife may have reflected Twain's own feelings toward Olivia.

Mark Twain was born in 1835 and died in 1910.

Literature Online **Author Search** For more about Mark Twain, go to www.glencoe.com.

Selection Skills

Literary Elements
- Foreshadowing (SE pp. 21, 24, 27, 29)
- Plot (SE p. 29)

The Californian's Tale

Reading Skills
- Analyzing Cause-and-Effect Relationships (SE pp. 21–30)
- Predicting (TWE p. 22)
- Identifying Spatial Relationships (TWE p. 24)

Vocabulary Skills
- Word Parts (SE p. 30)
- Academic Vocabulary (SE p. 30)

Listening/Speaking/Viewing Skills
- Contrasting Viewpoints (TWE p. 26)
- Dialogue (TWE p. 28)

Writing Skills/Grammar
- Evaluating Author's Craft (SE p. 30)

Connecting to the Story

What makes a dwelling feel like home? In Twain's short story "The Californian's Tale," the narrator visits a dwelling that gives him great comfort. Before you read the story, think about the following questions:

- What kinds of things make a home a comfortable place?
- How important is it to have people that care about you, whether they are relatives, friends, or neighbors, live near you?

Building Background

This story takes place in central California. Gold was first discovered there in 1848 near what is now Sacramento. Within the next year, almost 100,000 people, most of them young men, had moved to California, trying to strike it rich by prospecting for gold. They were called the "forty-niners," referring to the year that they came to California. Only a few of the forty-niners made a fortune during the gold rush. Most of them had little luck finding gold. In many places where gold was discovered in the early 1850s, the mineral was not very plentiful. Such areas underwent a quick boom and a just-as-rapid bust; Twain's story takes place in one such deserted mining area in the late 1860s or the early 1870s.

Setting Purposes for Reading

Big Idea Encountering the Unexpected

As you read "The Californian's Tale," examine how the unexpected affects the events of the story and the lives of the characters.

Literary Element Foreshadowing

Foreshadowing is a writer's use of clues to hint at events that will happen later in a story. As you read, look for clues that suggest that all is not necessarily as it seems.

- See Literary Terms Handbook, p. R7.

Literature Online Interactive Literary Elements Handbook To review or learn more about the literary elements, go to www.glencoe.com.

Reading Strategy Analyzing Cause-and-Effect Relationships

A cause is something that makes something else happen; an effect is what happens as a result of a cause. Fiction writers include **cause-and-effect relationships** to further the action of a plot.

Reading Tip: Taking Notes Use diagrams like the one below to analyze some of the causes and effects in this short story.

Cause
Narrator is prospecting for gold in a region where mining has been abandoned.

↓

Effect
Narrator spends a lot of time by himself.

Vocabulary

predecessor (pred′ ə ses′ ər) *n.* one who comes, or has come before in another time; p. 23 *Groups of Native Americans were the predecessors of the miners who settled in central California.*

solace (sol′ is) *n.* relief from sorrow or disappointment; comfort; p. 23 *Homey touches in a hotel room may give solace to weary travelers.*

sedate (si dāt′) *adj.* quiet and restrained in style or manner; calm; p. 25 *Dominique felt so sedate while reading that she promptly fell asleep.*

imploring (im plôr′ ing) *adj.* asking earnestly; begging; p. 26 *He gave an imploring glance, as if to ask, "Did you bring me a gift for my birthday?"*

boding (bōd′ ing) *n.* a warning or indication, especially of evil; p. 27 *Their boding about the theft was a result of the disorder.*

OBJECTIVES
In studying this selection, you will focus on the following:
- understanding foreshadowing
- analyzing cause-and-effect relationships
- writing to evaluate the author's craft

MARK TWAIN **21**

Focus

Summary

In an area of California that used to be populated by gold miners, the narrator meets a man, Henry, who urges him to stay and meet his wife. Henry's miner friends visit and discuss the wife's homecoming. When Henry becomes increasingly agitated about his wife's return, his friends give him a specially made drink. After he falls asleep, the friends explain to the narrator that the wife died nineteen years before and Henry has been insane with grief ever since. They conduct the annual charade on the anniversary of her death.

V Vocabulary

Vocabulary File Say: Add these words and definitions to your vocabulary file. For each word, include a sentence that gives you an example of how to use the word. **OL** Students with English language needs should include the pronunciations of these words in their files. **EL**

Literary Elements Have students access the Web site to improve their understanding of foreshadowing.

Selection Resources

Print Materials
- Unit 1 Resources (Fast File), pp. 23–25
- Leveled Vocabulary Development, p. 2
- Selection and Unit Assessments, pp. 3–4
- Selection Quick Checks, p. 2

Transparencies
- Bellringer Options Transparencies: Selection Focus Transparency 2
  Daily Language Practice Transparency 4
- Literary Elements Transparency 6

Technology
- TeacherWorks Plus™ CD-ROM
- StudentWorks Plus™ CD-ROM
- Presentation Plus!™ CD-ROM
- Literature Online, glencoe.com
- Online Student Edition, mhln.com
- Exam*View*® Assessment Suite CD-ROM
- Vocabulary PuzzleMaker CD-ROM
- Listening Library, disc 1 track 2

Encountering the Unexpected Say: Keep these questions in mind as you read: Why does Henry's house seem unusual to the narrator? *(Similar cottages were abandoned.)* How does the house affect the narrator? *(First he wants to run away; later he anticipates Henry's wife's return.)* **OL**

R1 Reading Strategy

Analyzing Cause-and-Effect Relationships
Answer: *People have moved away because there is no more gold to be mined there.* **OL**

★ Viewing the Art

American painter Grant Wood was a pioneer in regionalist art, incorporating farm scenes from his homeland of rural Iowa **Ask:** How does Wood's regional painting compare to Twain's writing style? *(Students may mention that both Wood and Twain combine popular [or "folk"] themes with the forms of so-called high art.)* **AS**

Readability Scores
Dale-Chall: 4.0
DRP: 61
Lexile: 1050

THE CALIFORNIAN'S TALE

Old House with Tree Shadows, 1916. Grant Wood. Oil on composition board, 13 x 15 inches. Cedar Rapids Museum of Art, Iowa ★

Mark Twain

Thirty-five years ago I was out prospecting on the Stanislaus, tramping all day long with pick and pan and horn, and washing a hatful of dirt here and there, always expecting to make a rich strike, and never doing it. It was a lovely region, woodsy, balmy, delicious, and had once been populous, long years before, but now the people had vanished and the charming paradise was a solitude.[1]

They went away when the surface diggings gave out. In one place, where a busy little city with banks and newspapers and fire companies and a mayor and aldermen had been, was nothing but a wide expanse of emerald turf, with not even the faintest sign that human life had ever been present there. This was down toward Tuttletown.[2] In the country neighborhood thereabouts, along the dusty roads, one found at intervals the prettiest little cottage homes, snug and cozy, and so cobwebbed with vines snowed thick with roses that the doors and windows were wholly hidden from sight—sign that these were deserted homes, forsaken years ago by defeated and disappointed families who could neither sell them nor give them away. Now and then, half an hour apart, one came across solitary log cabins of the earliest mining

---

1. The narrator was exploring for gold *(prospecting)* along the Stanislaus River in central California. Here, *solitude* refers to a lonely, isolated place.

Reading Strategy Analyzing Cause-and-Effect Relationships *Why are there no longer many people living along the Stanislaus River in this part of California?* **R1**

---

2. *Tuttletown* was a mining town near the Stanislaus.

Skills Practice

READING: Predicting Tell students that as they read a story, they make predictions about the characters and plot based on prior knowledge and on what they learned while previewing the selection. Have students preview the story, read the first page, and list their predictions. Then draw attention to the first sentence of the story. **Ask:** Why do you think the narrator is still telling this story 35 years later? *(It must be a striking or surprising story.)* Instruct students to verify and adjust their predictions as they read the selection. **OL**

days, built by the first gold-miners, the **predecessors** of the cottage-builders. In some few cases these cabins were still occupied; and when this was so, you could depend upon it that the occupant was the very pioneer who had built the cabin; and you could depend on another thing, too—that he was there because he had once had his opportunity to go home to the States rich, and had not done it; had rather lost his wealth, and had then in his humiliation resolved to sever[3] all communication with his home relatives and friends, and be to them thenceforth as one dead. Round about California in that day were scattered a host of these living dead men—pride-smitten[4] poor fellows, grizzled[5] and old at forty, whose secret thoughts were made all of regrets and longings—regrets for their wasted lives, and longings to be out of the struggle and done with it all.

It was a lonesome land! Not a sound in all those peaceful expanses of grass and woods but the drowsy hum of insects; no glimpse of man or beast; nothing to keep up your spirits and make you glad to be alive. And so, at last, in the early part of the afternoon, when I caught sight of a human creature, I felt a most grateful uplift. This person was a man about forty-five years old, and he was standing at the gate of one of those cozy little rose-clad cottages of the sort already referred to. However, this one hadn't a deserted look; it had the look of

being lived in and petted and cared for and looked after; and so had its front yard, which was a garden of flowers, abundant, gay, and flourishing. I was invited in, of course, and required to make myself at home—it was the custom of the country.

It was delightful to be in such a place, after long weeks of daily and nightly familiarity with miners' cabins—with all which this implies of dirt floor, never-made beds, tin plates and cups, bacon and beans and black coffee, and nothing of ornament but war pictures from the Eastern illustrated papers tacked to the log walls. That was all hard, cheerless, materialistic[6] desolation, but here was a nest which had aspects to rest the tired eye and refresh that something in one's nature which, after long fasting, recognizes, when confronted by the belongings of art, howsoever cheap and modest they may be, that it has unconsciously been famishing and now has found nourishment. I could not have believed that a rag carpet could feast me so, and so content me; or that there could be such **solace** to the soul in wallpaper and framed lithographs,[7] and bright-colored tidies[8] and lamp-mats, and Windsor chairs, and varnished what-nots,[9] with sea-shells and books and china vases on them, and the score of little unclassifiable tricks

Visual Vocabulary
A *Windsor chair* has a high, spoked back, slanting legs, and a slightly curving seat. It is named for the city in England where this style of chair was first designed and built.

---

3. To *sever* means to "break off."
4. Someone who is *smitten* is strongly affected by some powerful feeling.
5. *Grizzled* means "gray or mixed with gray."

Reading Strategy Analyzing Cause-and-Effect Relationships *Summarize the circumstances that have caused these men to end up pride-smitten, poor, and alone.* **R2**

Big Idea Encountering the Unexpected *How does the mood of the story here differ from the mood evoked in the first paragraph?* **B1**

Vocabulary

predecessor (pred´ ə ses´ ər) *n.* one who comes, or has come before in another time

---

6. *Materialistic* means "having a strong focus on material wants and needs."
7. *Lithographs* are pictures printed by a process in which a flat surface is treated either to retain or to repel ink.
8. *Tidies* are small, decorative coverings placed over the back or arms of a chair or sofa to keep them from being soiled or worn.
9. *What-nots* are open shelves for displaying objects.

Vocabulary

solace (sol´ is) *n.* relief from sorrow or disappointment; comfort

MARK TWAIN **23**

L Literary Element

Foreshadowing Answer:
This detail suggests that the home is almost too perfect and that the woman must be extremely fastidious. **OL**

BI Big Idea

Encountering the Unexpected Answer: *The man hopes that the narrator will find his beloved's picture. The guessing game creates mystery, intrigue, and fun, but it makes the narrator uncomfortable.* **OL**

---

and touches that a woman's hand distributes about a home, which one sees without knowing he sees them, yet would miss in a moment if they were taken away. The delight that was in my heart showed in my face, and the man saw it and was pleased; saw it so plainly that he answered it as if it had been spoken.

"All her work," he said, caressingly; "she did it all herself—every bit," and he took the room in with a glance which was full of affectionate worship. One of those soft Japanese fabrics with which women drape with careful negligence the upper part of a picture-frame was out of adjustment. He noticed it, and rearranged it with cautious pains, stepping back several times to gauge the effect before he got it to suit him. Then he gave it a light finishing pat or two with his hand, and said: "She always does that. You can't tell just what it lacks, but it does lack something until you've done that—you can see it yourself after it's done, but that is all you know; you can't find out the law of it. It's like the finishing pats a mother gives the child's hair after she's got it combed and brushed, I reckon. I've seen her fix all these things so much that I can do them all just her way, though I don't know the law of any of them. But she knows the law. She knows the why and the how both; but I don't know the why; I only know the how."

He took me into a bedroom so that I might wash my hands; such a bedroom as I had not seen for years: white counterpane,[10] white pillows, carpeted floor, papered walls, pictures, dressing-table, with mirror and pincushion and dainty toilet things; and in the corner a washstand, with real chinaware bowl and pitcher, and with soap in a china dish, and on a rack more than a dozen tow-

---

10. A *counterpane* is a quilt or bedspread.

els—towels too clean and white for one out of practice to use without some vague sense of profanation.[11] So my face spoke again, and he answered with gratified words:

"All her work; she did it all herself—every bit. Nothing here that hasn't felt the touch of her hand. Now you would think—But I mustn't talk so much."

By this time I was wiping my hands and glancing from detail to detail of the room's belongings, as one is apt to do when he is in a new place, where everything he sees is a comfort to his eye and his spirit; and I became conscious, in one of those unaccountable ways, you know, that there was something there somewhere that the man wanted me to discover for myself. I knew it perfectly, and I knew he was trying to help me by furtive[12] indications with his eye, so I tried hard to get on the right track, being eager to gratify him. I failed several times, as I could see out of the corner of my eye without being told; but at last I knew I must be looking straight at the thing—knew it from the pleasure issuing in invisible waves from him. He broke into a happy laugh, and rubbed his hands together, and cried out:

"That's it! You've found it. I knew you would. It's her picture."

I went to the little black-walnut bracket on the farther wall, and did find there what I had not yet noticed—a daguerreotype-case.[13]

> **"That second glimpse broke down my good resolution."**

---

11. *Profanation* is the act of making something impure through unworthy use.
12. Here, *furtive* means "stealthy."
13. A *daguerreotype* (də ger´ ə tīp´) is a photograph produced by exposing light to a silver-coated copper plate, a process invented by Louis Daguerre in France in the mid-1800s.

Literary Element Foreshadowing *What idea or feeling does this detail give you about the home? About the woman?* **L**

Big Idea Encountering the Unexpected *What do you think the man hopes the narrator will discover? What mood does this guessing game help create?* **BI**

Additional Support

Skills Practice

READING: Identifying Spatial Relationships Being able to follow and visualize what an author is describing is an important reading skill. Have students in groups or in pairs create poster montages illustrating the interior of the cottage based on the abundant details in Mark Twain's story. Point out that the interior Twain describes is of the typical Victorian style, which would have been popular in England and the United States in the mid-1800s. Students may want to use the library or the Internet to locate books that illustrate the houses

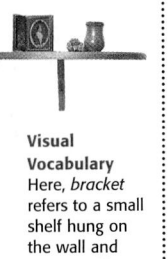

It contained the sweetest girlish face, and the most beautiful, as it seemed to me, that I had ever seen. The man drank the admiration from my face, and was fully satisfied.

"Nineteen her last birthday," he said, as he put the picture back; "and that was the day we were married. When you see her—ah, just wait till you see her!"

"Where is she? When will she be in?"

"Oh, she's away now. She's gone to see her people. They live forty or fifty miles from here. She's been gone two weeks today."

"When do you expect her back?"

"This is Wednesday. She'll be back Saturday, in the evening—about nine o'clock, likely."

I felt a sharp sense of disappointment.

"I'm sorry, because I'll be gone then," I said, regretfully.

"Gone? No—why should you go? Don't go. She'll be so disappointed."

She would be disappointed—that beautiful creature! If she had said the words herself they could hardly have blessed me more. I was feeling a deep, strong longing to see her—a longing so supplicating,[14] so insistent, that it made me afraid. I said to myself: "I will go straight away from this place, for my peace of mind's sake."

"You see, she likes to have people come and stop with us—people who know things, and can talk—people like you. She delights in it; for she knows—oh, she knows nearly everything herself, and can talk, oh, like a bird—and the books she reads, why, you would be astonished. Don't go; it's only a little while, you know, and she'll be so disappointed."

I heard the words, but hardly noticed them, I was so deep in my thinkings and strugglings. He left me, but I didn't know. Presently he was back, with the picture-case in his hand, and he held it open before me and said:

"There, now, tell her to her face you could have stayed to see her, and you wouldn't."

That second glimpse broke down my good resolution. I would stay and take the risk. That night we smoked the tranquil pipe, and talked till late about various things, but mainly about her; and certainly I had had no such pleasant and restful time for many a day. The Thursday followed and slipped comfortably away. Toward twilight a big miner from three miles away came—one of the grizzled, stranded pioneers—and gave us warm salutation,[15] clothed in grave and sober speech. Then he said:

"I only just dropped over to ask about the little madam, and when is she coming home. Any news from her?"

"Oh yes, a letter. Would you like to hear it, Tom?"

"Well, I should think I would, if you don't mind, Henry!"

Henry got the letter out of his wallet, and said he would skip some of the private phrases, if we were willing; then he went on and read the bulk of it—a loving, **sedate,** and altogether charming and gracious piece of handiwork, with a postscript full of affectionate regards and messages to Tom, and Joe, and Charley, and other close friends and neighbors.

As the reader finished, he glanced at Tom, and cried out:

"Oho, you're at it again! Take your hands away, and let me see your eyes. You always do that when I read a letter from her. I will write and tell her."

---

15. A *salutation* is an expression of greeting.

Reading Strategy Analyzing Cause-and-Effect Relationships *In staying, what risk does the narrator decide he will face?* **R1**

Reading Strategy Analyzing Cause-and-Effect Relationships *What does Tom do when he hears the woman's letter read aloud?* **R2**

Vocabulary

sedate (si dāt´) *adj.* quiet and restrained in style or manner; calm

---

14. *Supplicating* means "asking for in a humble or earnest manner; beseeching."

Teach

R1 Reading Strategy

Analyzing Cause-and-Effect Relationships
Answer: *The narrator decides he will face the risk of falling in love with the woman and having his heart broken. There is also the subtle implication that the narrator fears that the woman will fall in love with him, and that he will destroy a marriage, another man, and a beautiful home.* **OL**

R2 Reading Strategy

Analyzing Cause-and-Effect Relationships
Answer: *He breaks into tears.* **OL**

Differentiated Instruction

and furniture of this period. Suggest that students look through decorating magazines and cut out pictures of furniture and accessories similar to those described in the story. Finally, have them use the pictures they have collected to create poster montages of the cottage. **OL**

Less Proficient Readers Some students may find the long narrative passages in this story difficult. Have pairs of students choose a two- to three-paragraph section to read silently. Then have them collaborate on a short summary of each paragraph. **BL**

Objectives
• To understand foreshadowing (SE)
• To analyze cause-and-effect relationships (SE)
• To visualize spatial relationships as described in text (TWE)

25

BI₁ Big Idea

Encountering the Unexpected Answer: *Students might wonder what Tom means by "getting ready for her" and what Henry knows about the plans. They might also wonder at Tom's strange lapses in memory and changes in mood.* **OL**

R Reading Strategy

Analyzing Cause-and-Effect Relationships
Answer: *Henry becomes uneasy because the narrator keeps looking at his watch.* **OL**

⭐ **Viewing the Photo**

Daguerreotyping Daguerreotypes were popular in the 1840s and 1850s because they produced more detailed images than previous photography methods. However, the subject might have to sit still for as long as fifteen minutes before the image could be fixed onto a piece of silver-plated copper. **AS**

Portrait of Martha Pickman Rogers in her Wedding Gown, 19th century. Photographer unknown. Daguerreotype, 4¼ x 5½ in. Bequest of Maxim Karolik, Courtesy Museum of Fine Arts, Boston. ⭐

"Oh no, you mustn't, Henry. I'm getting old, you know, and any little disappointment makes me want to cry. I thought she'd be here herself, and now you've got only a letter."

"Well, now, what put that in your head? I thought everybody knew she wasn't coming till Saturday."

"Saturday! Why, come to think, I did know it. I wonder what's the matter with me lately? Certainly I knew it. Ain't we all getting ready for her? Well, I must be going now. But I'll be on hand when she comes, old man!"

Late Friday afternoon another gray veteran tramped over from his cabin a mile or so away, and said the boys wanted to have a little gaiety and a good time Saturday night,

> **Big Idea** Encountering the Unexpected *What questions do you have about this comment?* **BI₁**

26 UNIT 1 THE SHORT STORY

if Henry thought she wouldn't be too tired after her journey to be kept up.

"Tired? She tired! Oh, hear the man! Joe, *you* know she'd sit up six weeks to please any one of you!"

When Joe heard that there was a letter, he asked to have it read, and the loving messages in it for him broke the old fellow all up; but he said he was such an old wreck that *that* would happen to him if she only just mentioned his name. "Lord, we miss her so!" he said.

Saturday afternoon I found I was taking out my watch pretty often. Henry noticed it, and said, with a startled look:

"You don't think she ought to be here so soon, do you?"

I felt caught, and a little embarrassed; but I laughed, and said it was a habit of mine when I was in a state of expectancy. But he didn't seem quite satisfied; and from that time on he began to show uneasiness. Four times he walked me up the road to a point whence we could see a long distance; and there he would stand, shading his eyes with his hand, and looking. Several times he said:

"I'm getting worried, I'm getting right down worried. I know she's not due till about nine o'clock, and yet something seems to be trying to warn me that something's happened. You don't think anything has happened, do you?"

I began to get pretty thoroughly ashamed of him for his childishness; and at last, when he repeated that **imploring** question still another time, I lost my patience for the moment, and spoke pretty brutally to him. It seemed to shrivel him up and cow[16] him; and he looked so wounded and so humble after that, that I detested myself for having done the cruel and unnecessary thing. And

---

16. To *cow* is to frighten with threats.

Reading Strategy Analyzing Cause-and-Effect Relationships *Why does Henry become uneasy in this situation?* **R**

Vocabulary

imploring (im plôr′ ing) *adj.* asking earnestly; begging

Additional Support

Skills Practice

VIEWING: Contrasting Viewpoints
The skill—or lack thereof—of Depression-era painter Grant Wood (1891–1942) was hotly debated during his lifetime. While his paintings of Midwestern people and settings were popular with the public, one art critic described them as "sen-timental" and "cheap." Group students on the basis of their opinions of the Wood painting on page 22. Have each group brainstorm a list of reasons supporting their opinion. Then conduct a class debate on the artistic merit of the painting. **OL**

so I was glad when Charley, another veteran, arrived toward the edge of the evening, and nestled up to Henry to hear the letter read, and talked over the preparations for the welcome. Charley fetched out one hearty speech after another, and did his best to drive away his friend's **bodings** and apprehensions.[17]

"Anything *happened* to her? Henry, that's pure nonsense. There isn't anything going to happen to her; just make your mind easy as to that. What did the letter say? Said she was well, didn't it? And said she'd be here by nine o'clock, didn't it? Did you ever know her to fail of her word? Why, you know you never did. Well, then, don't you fret; she'll *be* here, and that's absolutely certain, and as sure as you are born. Come, now, let's get to decorating—not much time left."

Pretty soon Tom and Joe arrived, and then all hands set about adorning the house with flowers. Toward nine the three miners said that as they had brought their instruments they might as well tune up, for the boys and girls would soon be arriving now, and hungry for a good, old-fashioned breakdown.[18] A fiddle, a banjo, and a clarinet—these were the instruments. The trio took their places side by side, and began to play some rattling dance-music, and beat time with their big boots.

It was getting very close to nine. Henry was standing in the door with his eyes directed up the road, his body swaying to the torture of his mental distress.

> ## "Anything *happened* to her? Henry, that's pure nonsense."

He had been made to drink his wife's health and safety several times, and now Tom shouted:

"All hands stand by! One more drink, and she's here!"

Joe brought the glasses on a waiter,[19] and served the party. I reached for one of the two remaining glasses, but Joe growled, under his breath:

"Drop that! Take the other."

Which I did. Henry was served last. He had hardly swallowed his drink when the clock began to strike. He listened till it finished, his face growing pale and paler; then he said:

"Boys, I'm sick with fear. Help me—I want to lie down!"

They helped him to the sofa. He began to nestle and drowse, but presently spoke like one talking in his sleep, and said: "Did I hear horses' feet? Have they come?"

One of the veterans answered, close to his ear: "It was Jimmy Parrish come to say the party got delayed, but they're right up the road a piece, and coming along. Her horse is lame, but she'll be here in half an hour."

"Oh, I'm *so* thankful nothing has happened!"

He was asleep almost before the words were out of his mouth. In a moment those handy men had his clothes off, and had tucked him into his bed in the chamber where I had washed my hands. They closed the door and came back. Then they seemed preparing to leave; but I said: "Please don't go, gentlemen. She won't know me; I am a stranger."

They glanced at each other. Then Joe said:

"She? Poor thing, she's been dead nineteen years!"

"Dead?"

---

17. *Apprehensions* are fears or anxieties about what might happen.
18. Here, *breakdown* refers to a fast, lively country dance.

Literary Element Foreshadowing *What hint does this image give you about what might happen?* **L**

Vocabulary

boding (bōd´ ing) n. a warning or indication, especially of evil

19. The *waiter*, in this case, is a small tray.

Big Idea Encountering the Unexpected *Why do you think Joe says this to the narrator?* **BI₂**

MARK TWAIN **27**

Teach

L Literary Element

Foreshadowing Answer: *This detail heightens the tension in the story and makes it seem more likely that the woman will not be coming home.* **OL**

BI₂ Big Idea

Encountering the Unexpected
Answer: *The drink is spiked with a drug and is intended only for Henry.* **OL**

★ Writer's Technique

Dialect Twain's diction and use of dialect convey the speech patterns of the forty-niners. **Ask:** What words and phrases communicate that these characters are of a different time and place? *(Words like "cow," "bodings," and "fret"; phrases like "right down worried" and "fetched out.")* **AS**

Differentiated Instruction

Parts of Speech Identifying the part of speech of an unfamiliar word can help students decode it. **Write on the board:** The dog came to the window in the rain and gave its master an imploring look. **Ask:** What part of speech is *imploring* here? *(It is an adjective modifying "look.")* What kind of look might a dog give its master if it is outside in the rain? *(a look begging to come in)* **Say:** *Imploring* means "begging." Have students working in pairs decode several unfamiliar words from the story using this method. **BL**

Objectives
• To analyze cause-and-effect relationships (SE)
• To contrast viewpoints (TWE)

Teach

⭐ Cultural History

Sierra Nevada Miwok
Before the gold rush, this area was inhabited by the Miwok Native Americans. The Miwok hunted deer and ground acorns into meal on *Chaw'se*, or grinding rocks. Miners often barred Native Americans from their hunting and fishing grounds. Native groups began raiding mining settlements for food and supplies. **AS**

CheckPoint

Use the CheckPoint questions on Presentation Plus! to check students' mastery of the selection. These questions can be used with interactive response keypads for immediate student feedback.

Prospector pans for gold in Northern California, c. 1890. Hand-tinted photograph.

⭐ "That or worse. She went to see her folks half a year after she was married, and on her way back, on a Saturday evening, the Indians captured her within five miles of this place, and she's never been heard of since."

"And he lost his mind in consequence?"

"Never has been sane an hour since. But he only gets bad when that time of the year comes round. Then we begin to drop in here, three days before she's due, to encourage him up, and ask if he's heard from her, and Saturday we all come and fix up the house with flowers, and get everything ready for a dance. We've done it every year for nineteen years. The first Saturday there was twenty-seven of us, without counting the girls; there's only three of us now, and the girls are all gone. We drug him to sleep, or he would go wild; then he's all right for another year—thinks she's with him till the last three or four days come round; then he begins to look for her, and gets out his poor old letter, and we come and ask him to read it to us. Lord, she was a darling!" ✑

28   UNIT 1   THE SHORT STORY

Additional Support

Skills Practice

LISTENING AND SPEAKING:

Dialogue Review ways to communicate meaning while performing a dialogue. Speakers can vary the tone, volume, and emphasis of their voices. Point out that facial expression is also an effective means of communication, especially in response to someone else's speech. Have students work in small groups to practice and perform the final passage of the story. Encourage students to use tone and facial expressions to communicate the characters' emotions. **OL**

RESPONDING AND THINKING CRITICALLY

Respond

1. Did the ending of the story surprise you? Why or why not?

Recall and Interpret

2. (a)Describe how the narrator comes upon Henry's cottage. How is his cottage different from other dwellings that the narrator has seen in the area so far? (b)Why is this difference surprising?

3. (a)Summarize what happens at the cottage on Saturday night before Henry falls asleep. (b)What might Henry's state of mind indicate about him and about the action of the story?

4. (a)Explain what the narrator learns at the end of the story about the woman. (b)Why do Henry's friends wait so long to reveal the truth to the narrator?

Analyze and Evaluate

5. What is the narrator's attitude toward the men who live in the log cabins? Support your answer with evidence from the story.

6. (a)Identify three or more ways that Twain builds suspense. (b)Which do you think was most effective?

7. (a)Why do you think Twain decided not to reveal Henry's wife's name? (b)Do you think this made the story more effective? Explain.

Connect

8. **Big Idea** **Encountering the Unexpected** (a)In what ways does the final twist in the plot change the way you think about the characters? (b)Do you think Twain intended you to change your ideas about the character? Why or why not?

9. Do you think Henry's friends have been doing the right thing? Explain your answer.

LITERARY ANALYSIS

Literary Element Foreshadowing

Although the ending of the story "The Californian's Tale" proves to be a surprise for most readers, Twain uses **foreshadowing** to hint at the ending. Foreshadowing can be conveyed by mood or mood shifts, by details of the setting or the characters that are strange or jarring, or by plot events that serve as clues as to how the story will be resolved.

1. Which details related to the setting and the characters foreshadow the ending of the story? Explain how each detail you mention provides a hint about the ending.

2. Which plot events help foreshadow the ending of the story? Explain how each event hints at this ending.

Review: Plot

As you learned on page 10–11, writers use exposition to introduce the setting, the characters, and the **plot** of a story. In "The Californian's Tale," the exposition helps readers picture the land along the Stanislaus River, the cottage, and Henry. The exposition also helps readers enter into the events witnessed by the narrator once he enters the cottage. Turn to the beginning of "The Californian's Tale" and reread Twain's exposition.

Partner Activity Work with another classmate to fill in a graphic organizer like the one shown. In the graphic organizer, record details of the story that help readers gain their first impressions of the setting, characters, and plot. Share your organizer with the class.

Exposition

| Setting | | Characters
The narrator,
a prospector
for gold | | Plot |

MARK TWAIN **29**

Literary Element

1. The miners are in their forties, and Henry's wife is nineteen, which is unlikely. The immaculate cleanliness of the home seems too perfect. The region is both peaceful and desolate, raising questions about what a woman might face on a journey home.

2. Answers will vary. Students might mention Tom's and Joe's weeping when they hear the letters or the rising tension as Henry's wife does not arrive.

Review: Plot

Encourage students to identify the mood that Twain conveys through the details of plot and setting.

Assess

1. Answers will vary.
2. (a) He is prospecting when he finds Henry's cozy, well-kept cottage. Miners' cottages are dirty and uncomfortable. (b) Other cottages are deserted and overgrown.
3. (a) Henry worries that something has happened to his wife. Friends arrive and decorate the house, play music, toast his wife's health, and give Henry a sedating drink. (b) Henry's nervous and frantic behavior foreshadow the tragic ending and indicate that Henry may know his wife is not coming home.
4. (a) Henry's wife is dead. (b) They may be afraid that the narrator will tell Henry and upset him.
5. The narrator pities them, calling them "living dead men" and "poor fellows."
6. (a) Descriptions of the cottage, the woman, and Henry; the narrator's desire to see her; Henry's awaiting; and Tom's statement, "One more drink and she'll be here." (b) Students should give one example of suspense.
7. (a)To increase the suspense, or to make her a symbol for women (b) Students may respond to her universality, or say that a named character would make Henry's grief more poignant.
8. (a) The miners are kind and sensitive. (b) Answers will vary.
9. Students may think that it is right because it is done out of kindness. Others may think that the lack of truth harms Henry.

Assess

Reading Strategy

1. Answers should discuss questions raised by the surprise ending and whether the causes presented in the story have multiple effects.

2. Students may find it implausible that Henry's friends have maintained their deception for nineteen years.

Vocabulary

1. a **2.** b **3.** b **4.** c **5.** a

Academic Vocabulary

1. All of the preparations that Henry's friends perform are annual events.

2. They convene at his house to fool Henry into thinking that his wife is on her way home.

Writing About Literature

Details that characterize Henry's wife include the following:

"can talk like a bird"
"loving sedate, and altogether charming and gracious"
"sweet, girlish face"

Students' essays should

• cite specific details from the story

• explain how these details create a clear image of Henry's wife

---

Reading Strategy Analyzing Cause-and-Effect Relationships

The ending of "The Californian's Tale" is a series of events that form a **cause-and-effect** chain. Review the diagrams you made as you read the story, and add additional causes and effects that you notice.

1. What questions do you have about the ending of the story and the cause-and-effect chains that you made?

2. Based on the ending and the questions you came up with, how believable is this story? Explain.

Vocabulary Practice

Practice Word Parts Read the roots and definitions below. Then choose the best definition for each vocabulary word.

Latin root: *decedere*—"to depart"
Latin root: *solari*—"to console"
Latin root: *sedere*—"to sit"
Latin root: *implorare*—"to call for help"
Old English root: *bodian*—"to proclaim"

1. predecessor
   a. ancestor   **b.** offspring   **c.** superior
2. solace
   a. sunshine   **b.** comfort   **c.** cruelty
3. sedate
   a. anxious   **b.** calm   **c.** wise
4. imploring
   a. arguing   **b.** desiring   **c.** begging
5. boding
   a. warning   **b.** evidence   **c.** home

Academic Vocabulary

Here are two words from the vocabulary list on page R82. These words will help you think, write, and talk about the selection.

annual (an′ ū əl) *adj.* occurring once a year

convene (kən vēn′) *v.* to assemble or to cause to assemble

Practice and Apply
1. Which events of the story are **annual**?
2. Why do Henry's friends **convene** at his house?

Writing About Literature

Evaluate Author's Craft Although Henry's wife is absent from the story, a detailed image of her emerges. Write a five-paragraph essay in which you explain how Twain is able to create such a clear image of a character who never appears in the story.

Begin by going back through the story and finding specific ways in which Twain characterizes Henry's wife. Record these details on a web like the one shown.

In your essay, discuss specific details of the story and explain how they help to create a clear image of the wife. Refer to your graphic organizer as you write your essay. After you complete your draft, meet with a peer reviewer to evaluate each other's work and to suggest revisions. Then proofread and edit your draft for errors in spelling, grammar, and punctuation.

Interdisciplinary Activity

Research the gold deposits that lured forty-niners to California in the mid-1800s. You might focus on what geological forces created such gold deposits or on how miners extracted the gold from the land. Make a model or a drawing to illustrate your findings and share it with the class.

 Web Activities For eFlashcards, Selection Quick Checks, and other Web activities, go to www.glencoe.com.

Interdisciplinary Activity

Encourage students to use both print and online resources to research the gold deposits.

Literature Online

Web Activities Have students access the Web site for interactive activities that will help them assess their understanding of the selection.

LITERARY PERSPECTIVE on *Mark Twain*
Informational Text

Storytelling Is As Old As Mankind

Joyce Carol Oates

Storm In A Teacup. Cathy McKinty.

Building Background

Author Joyce Carol Oates won the National Book Award in 1969 for her novel *Them*.

A contemporary short story is a fictional narrative in prose containing the elements of plot, character, setting, theme, and point of view. In this excerpt from the introduction to the *Oxford Book of American Short Stories*, Oates traces the history of the short story and how it has evolved with the voices of such writers as Mark Twain.

Set a Purpose for Reading

Read to discover the history of the short story and elements of fiction used by writers such as Mark Twain.

Reading Strategy

Evaluating Historical Influences

When you examine the social influences of a historical period on a literary work or genre you are **evaluating historical influences**. As you read, take notes on how history has influenced the short story. Use a timeline like the one below.

| Egyptians write on papyri | Canterbury Tales | Mark Twain achieves popularity as an American writer |

The "literary" short story, the meticulously constructed short story, descends to us by way of the phenomenon of magazine publication, beginning in the nineteenth century, but has as its ancestor the oral tale.

We must assume that storytelling is as old as mankind, at least as old as spoken language. Reality is not enough for us—we crave the imagination's embellishments upon it. *In the beginning. Once upon a time. A long time ago there lived a princess who.* How the pulse quickens, hearing such beginnings! such promises of something new, strange, unexpected! . . .

Like a river fed by countless small streams, the modern short story derives from a multiplicity of sources. Historically, the earliest literary documents of which we have knowledge are Egyptian papyri[1] dating from 4000–3000 B.C., containing a work called, most intriguingly, *Tales of the Magicians*. The Middle Ages revered such secular works as fabliaux,[2]

1. *Papyri* are papers made from the stems or pith of the papyrus, which is a tall aquatic plant.
2. *Fabliaux* are medieval verse tales with comic themes about life.

JOYCE CAROL OATES **31**

English Language Coach

Clarifying Meaning Explain that the root of the word *embellishment* is *bel,* which means "beautiful" in Middle French. The prefix *em-* means "to cause to be." An embellishment is something that decorates or causes something to be beautiful. **EL**

Reading in the Real World

Career The study of Egyptian papyri is called *papyrology.* For over 100 years, literature scholars have studied papyrus documents. Have students use library or Internet research to explore what these writings reveal about Egyptian culture. **OL**

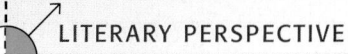

Focus

Summary

In this excerpt, Joyce Carol Oates traces the literary short story from oral tradition to nineteenth-century American magazines. She argues that Mark Twain and other American writers infused written stories with the vernacular of oral tradition.

Teach

R Reading Strategy

Evaluating Historical Influences Before students read, ask them to consider what effect the invention of the printing press might have had on the short story. Have them include this cultural event on their time lines.

Ask: How does the author support her claim that storytelling is "as old as mankind"? *(Oates argues that the human imagination demands that reality be embellished with stories. Human cultural history is filled with folktales and stories written thousands of years ago.)* **OL**

Readability Scores
Dale-Chall: 12.9
DRP: 74
Lexile: 1520

See also Active Learning and Note Taking Guide, pp. 15–19.

Objectives
• To evaluate historical influences on literary works (SE)
• To understand the origins of a literary genre (SE)

Teach

Big Idea

Encountering the Unexpected **Say:** Keep the following questions in mind as you read: What assumptions does the author make about the short story? *(It is an ancient form that comes naturally with language and once existed mainly as a folktale or ballad. The "flavor" of the oral tale makes a written story better.)* What characteristics make Mark Twain's writing unique in American literature, according to the author? *(He brought the vernacular flavor to written stories. His stories were read by people at all levels of culture.)* **OL**

★ Viewing the Art

Egyptian Pictographs In addition to writing on papyrus, Egyptians also told stories by painting words and pictures on stone walls. Their written language, hieroglyphics, began as pictures but evolved into a system in which certain images stood for certain sounds. This language system is the ancestor of our own phonetic alphabet. **AS**

Informational Text

Book of the Dead: Four Rudders of Heaven, Offerings to Osiris. ★
Egyptian Art. Papyrus. British Museum, London.

---

ballads,[3] and verse romances; the Arabian *Thousand and One Nights*[4] and the Latin tales and anecdotes of the *Gesta Romanorum,*[5] collected before the end of the thirteenth century, as well as the one hundred tales of Boccaccio's *The Decameron,*[6] and Chaucer's *Canterbury Tales,*[7] were enormously popular for centuries. Storytelling as an oral art, like the folk ballad, was, or is, characteristic of non-literate cultures, for obvious reasons. Even the prolongation of light (by artificial means) had an effect upon the storytelling

tradition of our ancestors. The rise in literacy marked the ebbing of interest in old fairy tales and ballads, as did the gradual stabilization of languages and the cessation[8] of local dialects in which the tales and ballads had been told most effectively. (The Brothers Grimm[9] noted this phenomenon: if, in High German, a fairy tale gained in superficial clarity, it "lost in flavor, and no longer had such a firm hold on the kernel of meaning.")

One of the signal accomplishments of American literature, most famously exemplified by the great commercial and critical success of Samuel Clemens, is the reclamation of that "lost" flavor—the use, as style, of dialect, regional, and strongly (often comically) vernacular[10] language. Of course, before Samuel Clemens cultivated the ingenuous-

---

3. *Ballads* are short narrative poems that are supposed to be sung. They have simple stanzas and a refrain, and are often folk in origin.
4. *The Thousand and One Nights* is a collection of tales about Aladdin, Ali Baba, and Sinbad the Sailor. Their author and the date when they were written are unknown.
5. *Gesta Romanorum* is a collection of anecdotes and tales in Latin.
6. *Giovanni Boccacio* (1313–1375) was an Italian poet and scholar. He most likely wrote *The Decameron* from 1348–1353. *The Decameron,* which means "Ten Days' Work," contains one hundred stories.
7. *Geoffrey Chaucer* (1342/43–1400) was a famous English poet. *The Canterbury Tales,* his seminal work, tells the story of about thirty pilgrims who convene at a London Inn to travel to and from Thomas à Becket of Canterbury's shrine.

8. *Cessation* means "the act of coming to a stop."
9. *The Brothers Grimm* was the nickname for Jacob Ludwig Carl Grimm (1785–1863) and Wilhelm Carl Grimm (1786–1859), who wrote collections of folktales, including *Kinder- und Hausmärchen,* which is commonly known as *Grimm's Fairy Tales.*
10. *Vernacular* means "the everyday speech of a country or region."

Additional Support

Skills Practice

TEST PREPARATION: Vocabulary
Explain that aptitude tests require a broad knowledge of words and their meanings. **Ask:** What is the definition of the word *ascend*? Write the following answer selections on the board: "a. movement upward; b. to rise; c. a position of power." *(b)* Follow the same process to find synonyms *(climb, rise)* and antonyms *(descend, fall)* for *ascend.* Then have students choose an unfamiliar word from the selection and use a dictionary and thesaurus to write three similar test questions for a partner. **OL**

ironic persona of "Mark Twain," there were dialect writers and tale-tellers in America (for instance, Joel Chandler Harris, creator of the popular "Uncle Remus" stories[11]); but Mark Twain was a phenomenon of a kind previously unknown here—our first American writer to be avidly read, coast to coast, by all classes of Americans, from the most high-born to the least cultured and minimally literate. The development of mass-market newspapers and subscription book sales made this success possible, but it was the brilliant reclamation of the vernacular in Twain's work (the early "The Celebrated Jumping Frog of Calaveras County,"[12] for instance) that made him into so uniquely *American* a writer, our counterpart to Dickens.

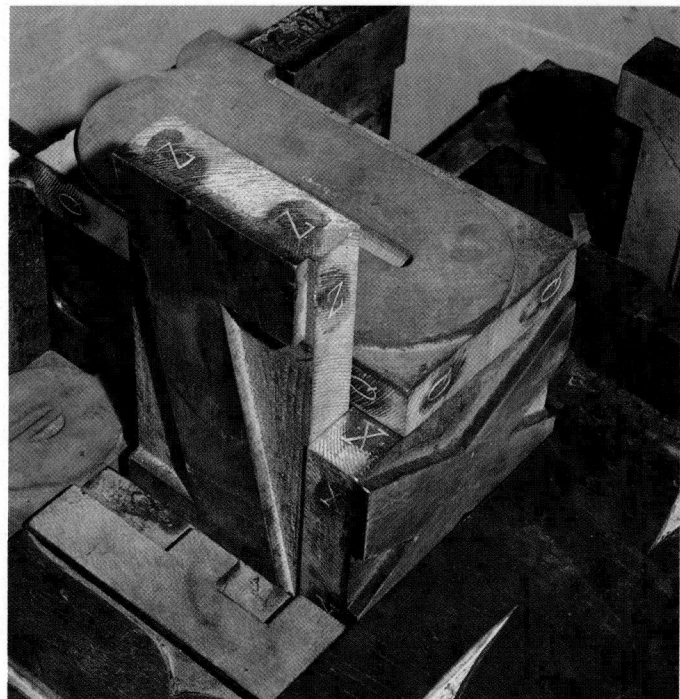

Wooden Type Block. Marco Prozzo.

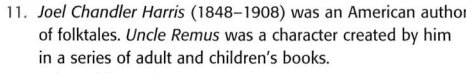 Twain's rapid ascent was by way of popular newspapers, which syndicated features coast to coast, and his crowd-pleasing public performances, but the more typical outlet for a short story writer, particularly of self-consciously "literary" work, was the magazine. Virtually every writer, from Washington Irving[13] and Nathaniel Hawthorne[14] onward,

began his or her career publishing short fiction in magazines before moving on to book publication; in the nineteenth century, such highly regarded, and, in some cases, high-paying magazines as *The North American Review, Harper's Monthly, Atlantic Monthly, Scribner's Monthly* (later *The Century*), *The Dial*, and *Graham's Magazine* (briefly edited by Edgar Allan Poe[15]) advanced the careers of writers who would otherwise have had financial difficulties in establishing themselves. In post-World War II America, the majority of short story writers publish in small-circulation "literary" magazines throughout their careers. It is all but unknown for a writer to publish a book of short stories without having published most of them in magazines beforehand. ～

---

11. *Joel Chandler Harris* (1848–1908) was an American author of folktales. *Uncle Remus* was a character created by him in a series of adult and children's books.
12. *"The Celebrated Jumping Frog of Calaveras County"* is a tall tale that tells of a narrator who goes to the gold mining town of Angel's Camp and meets Simon Wheeler, who tells him the story of a pet frog that competed in jumping races.
13. *Washington Irving* (1783–1859) was an American novelist and short story writer.
14. *Nathaniel Hawthorne* (1804–1864) was a well-known American novelist and short-story writer.

15. *Edgar Allan Poe* (1809–1849) was an American short story writer and poet.

JOYCE CAROL OATES **33**

Teach

★ Viewing the Art

In the Western hemisphere, the invention of the printing press by Johannes Gutenberg (c. 1395–c. 1468) changed literature. Before, texts had to be handwritten or stamped with carved wooden blocks. **AS**

Assess

1. Answers will vary. Short stories fit well in magazines.
2. (a) An oral tale (b) Narrator, dialect and vernacular
3. (a) Regional dialect and comic vernacular (b) A conversational, humorous tone
4. (a) Short stories can be read quickly, and often complement a magazine's theme. (b) Answers will vary. Literature in magazines is not less significant, but it may be perceived as less valuable.

For additional assessment, see 📁 Selection and Unit Assessment, pp. 5–6.

The Printer, 1875. Adrien Ferdinand de Braekeleer. Oil on canvas, 78 x 68 cm. Koninklijk Museum voor Schone Kunsten, Antwerp, Belgium.

RESPONDING AND THINKING CRITICALLY

Respond

1. Were you surprised to learn that contemporary short story writers most often begin their careers with magazine publications? Why or why not?

Recall and Interpret

2. (a)What is the earliest "ancestor" of the contemporary short story? (b)How is this heritage apparent in modern short stories you have read?

3. (a)What are some facets of Mark Twain's writing that recapture, as Oates writes, "that lost flavor" of American writing? (b)What do you think these elements of writing add to a literary work?

Analyze and Extend

4. (a)Why do you think short stories became popular selections for contemporary magazines? (b)Do you think that literature printed in magazines is any less significant than literature printed in books? Explain.

5. (a)Joyce Carol Oates is a prolific writer of fiction, including novels and short stories. What biases might she have about the craft of short story writing? (b)Do you think her biases affect her point of view in this excerpt? Why or why not?

Connect

6. (a)What did Oates claim made Mark Twain a "uniquely American writer"? (b)How is this trait represented in "The Californian's Tale"?

> **OBJECTIVES**
> • Evaluate the philosophical, political, religious, ethical, and social influence of a historical period.
> • Read to enhance the understanding of history of U.S. culture.
> • Interpret the influences of historical context on literary works.
> • Understand the origins of a literary genre.

---

5. (a) She may think the short story form is superior. (b) Answers will vary. Her experience provides a writer's insight.

6. (a) His use of vernacular (b) A casual, conversational tone, with many contractions, fragments, and interjections

The Summer People

MEET SHIRLEY JACKSON

It takes a special talent to make readers shiver in horror with one story, then make them laugh out loud with the next. Shirley Jackson had such a talent. She was an original, and her devoted readers consider her one of the best-kept secrets of literature.

Jackson was born and raised in a comfortable and happy California home. During her college years at Syracuse University, Jackson published a magazine, *The Spectre,* that offered witty essays and biting editorials. The magazine created controversy among the college staff and delight among the students. After graduation, Jackson married fellow *Spectre* writer Stanley Edgar Hyman and moved to Vermont. There, Jackson and Hyman started a family, lived modestly, and wrote furiously.

Jackson was a casual, down-to-earth person with an irrepressible sense of humor. Strictly disciplined, she maintained a rigorous schedule of writing amidst the duties of motherhood.

> "I delight in what I fear."
>
> —Shirley Jackson

Tales of Humor and Horror As her children grew, Jackson found the time to write light-hearted books celebrating ordinary domestic life. During the same period, she also wrote dark, macabre stories about perfectly normal people doing perfectly terrible things. These disturbing tales created a sensation. When the frightening tale "The Lottery" appeared in the literary magazine *The New Yorker,* the magazine was deluged with complaints from angry readers. Even Jackson's mother asked her why she couldn't write something more pleasant. Jackson replied that readers were misunderstanding the purpose of her work. She refused to soften the impact of her stories, continuing instead to craft frighteningly realistic tales of everyday people performing stunning acts of cruelty.

A Writer of Rare Skill Jackson possessed a remarkable eye for detail and an ability to create a cinematic experience for the reader. In her stories, nothing happens by accident. Every character and every description provides important information and tantalizes the reader with a glimpse of what is not being shown. According to Jackson, "There must be some furthering of the story in every sentence, and even the most fleeting background characters must partake of the story in some way; they must be characters peculiar to *this* story and no other."

Jackson's rich life ended with her sudden death at the age of forty-five. According to her husband, her stories were intended to do more than simply entertain or scare. They were calculated to awaken readers to an important truth: the people who do terrible things in this world are "ordinary" people, much like you and I. Maybe they *are* you and I. Jackson's husband called her work "a sensitive and faithful anatomy of our times, fitting symbols for our distressing world of the concentration camp and The Bomb."

Shirley Jackson was born in 1919 and died in 1965.

 Author Search For more about Shirley Jackson, go to www.glencoe.com.

SHIRLEY JACKSON **35**

Focus

BELLRINGER

Bellringer Options
Daily Language Transparency 5
Or write the words "summer cottage" on the board. **Ask:** What words come to mind when you hear the term, "summer cottage"?
Have students brainstorm words, phrases, or descriptions that they associate with a summer cottage. Prompt students' thinking by encouraging them to consider where a summer cottage might be located and the types of people who might live there.

Literature Online

Author Search To expand students' appreciation of Shirley Jackson, have them access the Web site for additional information and resources.

Selection Skills

The Summer People

Literary Elements
- Conflict (SE pp. 36–47)
- Foreshadowing (SE p. 47)
- Characterization (TWE p. 42)

Reading Skills
- Responding to Plot (SE pp. 36–46, 48)
- Activating Prior Knowledge (TWE p. 40)
- Making Inferences (TWE p. 46)

Vocabulary Skills
- Context Clues (SE p. 48)
- Academic Vocbulary (SE p. 48)

Listening/Speaking/Viewing Skills
- Analyzing Art (SE p. 45; TWE p. 41)
- Role-Play (SE p. 48)

Writing Skills/Grammar
- Analysis of Setting (SE p. 48)
- Persuasive Writing (TWE p. 44)

Focus

Summary

Mr. and Mrs. Allison have spent many wonderful summers at their cottage near the lake. At the end of each summer, they have gone home to New York, leaving the friendly neighbors and the small-town atmosphere behind. But this year is different. The Allison's have decided to stay past Labor Day—something "summer people" never do.

V Vocabulary

Vocabulary File Say: Add these words and definitions to your vocabulary file. For each word, include a sentence that gives you an example of how to use the word. **OL** Students with English language needs should include the pronunciations of these words in their files. **EL**

Literary Elements Have students access the Web site to improve their understanding of conflict.

Connecting to the Story

We all have places where we feel that we belong. Sometimes, however, it is good to vary our routine a little and get to know other people and places better. Before you read the story, think about these questions:

- What makes you feel like you belong in a place?
- How do you treat outsiders—people who come from somewhere else?

Building Background

"The Summer People" takes place during the late 1940s or 1950s in rural New England. It tells the story of a couple that lives in New York City during the winter and in a cabin near a small country town during the summer. The couple's home in the country lacks modern conveniences such as central heat, electricity, and indoor plumbing. The couple normally leaves the country for the city around Labor Day, a holiday that occurs on the first Monday of September. At the time the story is set in, cellular phones did not exist.

Setting Purposes for Reading

Big Idea **Encountering the Unexpected**
Have you ever heard the saying "expect the unexpected"? Everyone responds differently to surprises. As you read, notice how the characters in the story respond to unexpected events.

Literary Element **Conflict**
Most stories revolve around a **conflict**, or struggle between opposing forces. A conflict can be external or internal. An **external conflict** is one between a character and an outside force, such as another character, nature, society, or fate. An **internal conflict** takes place within the mind of a character who is torn between different courses of action. As you read, try to determine what conflicts lie at the heart of the story.

- See Literary Terms Handbook, p. R4.

Literature Online **Interactive Literary Elements Handbook** To review or learn more about the literary elements, go to www.glencoe.com.

OBJECTIVES
In studying this selection, you will focus on the following:
- analyzing conflict
- responding to plot
- understanding foreshadowing
- writing to analyze local color

36   UNIT 1   THE SHORT STORY

Responding is identifying and expressing what you like, dislike, or find surprising in a selection. When you react in a personal way to what you read, you enjoy your reading more and remember it better. As you read the story, think about your reactions. How do you feel about what is happening? What attracts your attention as you read?

Reading Tip: Making a Chart Use a chart like the one shown below to record notable or striking details of the story's plot and the responses you have to those details.

Notable Details	My Response
The Allisons stay in a summer home that lacks conveniences.	The summer home seems pleasant and safe.

Vocabulary

precarious (pri kār′ ē əs) *adj.* uncertain or unpredictable; p. 37 *Due to problems with this year's crops, the store's supply of vegetables is precarious.*

vague (vāg) *adj.* unclear or undetermined; p. 38 *When she questioned Robert, he was vague; his mind seemed to be somewhere else.*

acutely (a kūt′ lē) *adv.* very perceptively or discerningly; p. 39 *The expert was acutely aware of the differences between the two species.*

erratically (ər rat′ i ka lē) *adv.* in an irregular or unpredictable way; p. 40 *I don't see my aged aunt very often; I visit her part of the country erratically.*

improvident (im prov′ ə dent) *adj.* wasteful or unthrifty; p. 41 *His refusal to recycle bottles or cardboard was improvident.*

Selection Resources

Print Materials
- Unit 1 Resources (Fast File), pp. 27–29
- Leveled Vocabulary Development, p. 3
- Selection and Unit Assessments, pp. 7–8
- Selection Quick Checks, p. 4

Transparencies
- Bellringer Option Transparencies: Daily Language Practice Transparency 5
- Literary Elements Transparency 3

Technology
- TeacherWorks Plus™ CD-ROM
- StudentWorks Plus™ CD-ROM
- Presentation Plus!™ CD-ROM
- Literature Online, glencoe.com
- Online Student Edition, mhln.com
- ExamView® Assessment Suite CD-ROM
- Vocabulary PuzzleMaker CD-ROM
- Listening Library, disc 1 track 4

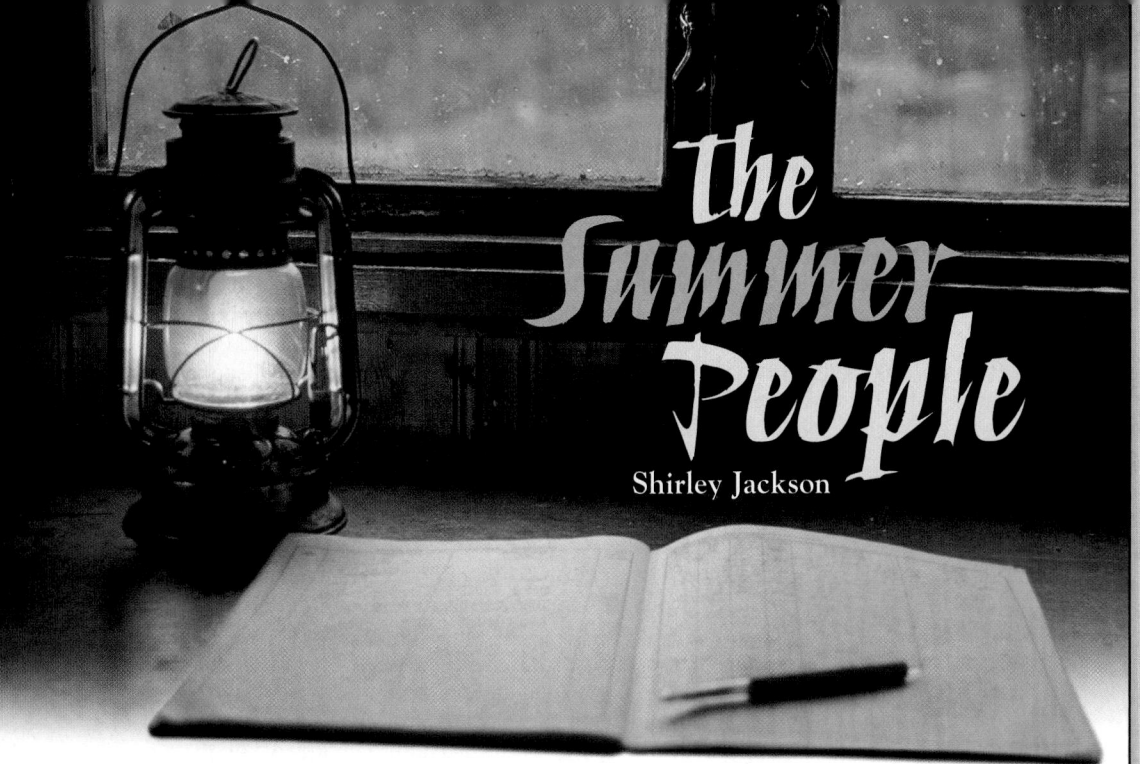

The Summer People

Shirley Jackson

The Allisons' country cottage, seven miles from the nearest town, was set prettily on a hill; from three sides it looked down on soft trees and grass that seldom, even at midsummer, lay still and dry. On the fourth side was the lake, which touched against the wooden pier the Allisons had to keep repairing, and which looked equally well from the Allisons' front porch, their side porch or any spot on the wooden staircase leading from the porch down to the water. Although the Allisons loved their summer cottage, looked forward to arriving in the early summer and hated to leave in the fall, they had not troubled themselves to put in any improvements, regarding the cottage itself and the lake as improvement enough for the life left to them. The cottage had no heat, no running water except the **precarious** supply from the backyard pump, and no electricity.

For seventeen summers, Janet Allison had cooked on a kerosene[1] stove, heating all their water; Robert Allison had brought buckets full of water daily from the pump and read his paper by kerosene light in the evenings; and they had both, sanitary city people, become stolid and matter-of-fact about their backhouse.[2] In the first two years they had gone through all the standard vaudeville and magazine jokes about backhouses and by now, when they no longer had frequent guests to impress, they had subsided to a comfortable security which made the backhouse, as well as the pump and the kerosene, an indefinable asset to their summer life.

---

1. *Kerosene* is a kind of fuel made by distilling petroleum and is often used in camp stoves.
2. A *backhouse* (also called an *outhouse*) is a small building used as a bathroom in houses that lack plumbing.

Reading Strategy Responding to Plot *What are your first impressions of the Allisons' summer home?* **R**

Vocabulary

precarious (pri kār′ e əs) *adj.* uncertain or unpredictable

SHIRLEY JACKSON **37**

Teach

R Reading Strategy

Responding to Plot Answer: *Answers will vary. Students may say the passage creates a sense of an idyllic rural home.* **OL**

Use the CheckPoint questions on Presentation Plus! to monitor students' comprehension. These questions can be used with interactive response keypads for immediate student feedback.

Readability Scores
Dale-Chall: 6.2
DRP: 63
Lexile: 1200

Differentiated Instruction

Analyzing Details Creating a "setting web" will enable less proficient readers to understand important details about the story's setting. Draw a web on the board and fill it in as students share what they know so far about the setting. **Ask:** What are some things we know about the setting in this story? Think about where the cottage is, what it looks like, and how the Allisons live there. *(The setting is near a small rural town; the people are from New York, and they come to the summer cottage each year.)* **BL**

Objective
• To respond to plot (SE)

Encountering the Unexpected Say: *Observations help us form ideas about what will happen. Sometimes, though, we encounter the unexpected. Think of an event you would not expect to happen at the Allisons' summer cottage.* (*Possible answer: Wild parties and violence are things that would seem extraordinary in this setting.*) **OL**

R **Reading Strategy**

Responding to Plot Answer: *Answers will vary. Students may say that good weather and nice surroundings would be good reasons to stay.* **OL**

L **Literary Element**

Conflict Answer: *The Allisons experienced conflict about staying at the cottage longer; conflict between Mrs. Allison's and Mr. Babcock's point of view.* **Ask:** *What are some ways a writer shows conflict in a character?* (*Through conversation, actions, body language. Mrs. Allison's movements show conflict.*) **OL**

In themselves, the Allisons were ordinary people. Mrs. Allison was fifty-eight years old and Mr. Allison sixty; they had seen their children outgrow the summer cottage and go on to families of their own and seashore resorts; their friends were either dead or settled in comfortable year-round houses, their nieces and nephews **vague.** In the winter they told one another they could stand their New York apartment while waiting for the summer; in the summer they told one another that the winter was well worth while, waiting to get to the country.

Since they were old enough not to be ashamed of regular habits, the Allisons invariably left their summer cottage the Tuesday after Labor Day, and were as invariably sorry when the months of September and early October turned out to be pleasant and almost insufferably barren in the city; each year they recognized that there was nothing to bring them back to New York, but it was not until this year that they overcame their traditional inertia³ enough to decide to stay in the cottage after Labor Day.

"There isn't really anything to take us back to the city," Mrs. Allison told her husband seriously, as though it were a new idea, and he told her, as though neither of them had ever considered it, "We might as well enjoy the country as long as possible."

Consequently, with much pleasure and a slight feeling of adventure, Mrs. Allison went into their village the day after Labor Day and told those natives with whom she had dealings, with a pretty air of breaking away from tradition, that she and her husband had decided to stay at least a month longer at their cottage.

---

3. *Inertia* (i nur′ shə) is a resistance to change.

Reading Strategy Responding to Plot *What is your response to the Allisons' decision?* **R**

Vocabulary

vague (vāg) *adj.* unclear or undetermined

"It isn't as though we had anything to take us back to the city," she said to Mr. Babcock, her grocer. "We might as well enjoy the country while we can."

"Nobody ever stayed at the lake past Labor Day before," Mr. Babcock said. He was putting Mrs. Allison's groceries into a large cardboard carton, and he stopped for a minute to look reflectively into a bag of cookies. "Nobody," he added.

"But the city!" Mrs. Allison always spoke of the city to Mr. Babcock as though it were Mr. Babcock's dream to go there. "It's so hot—you've really no idea. We're always sorry when we leave."

"Hate to leave," Mr. Babcock said. One of the most irritating native tricks Mrs. Allison had noticed was that of taking a trivial statement and rephrasing it downward, into an even more trite⁴ statement. "I'd hate to leave myself," Mr. Babcock said, after deliberation, and both he and Mrs. Allison smiled. "But I never heard of anyone ever staying out at the lake after Labor Day before."

"Well, we're going to give it a try," Mrs. Allison said, and Mr. Babcock replied gravely, "Never know till you try."

Physically, Mrs. Allison decided, as she always did when leaving the grocery after one of her inconclusive conversations with Mr. Babcock, physically, Mr. Babcock could model for a statue of Daniel Webster,⁵ but mentally . . . it was horrible to think into what old New England Yankee stock had degenerated. She said as much to Mr. Allison when she got into the car, and he said, "It's generations of inbreeding. That and the bad land."

Since this was their big trip into town, which they made only once every two weeks to buy things they could not have delivered, they spent all day at it, stopping to have a sandwich in the newspaper and soda shop, and leaving packages heaped in the back of

---

4. Here, *trite* means "even more ordinary and unoriginal."
5. *Daniel Webster* (1782-1852) was a famous New England lawyer, statesman, and public speaker.

Literary Element Conflict *What possible conflicts have you identified so far?* **L**

Additional Support

READING: Analyzing Details
Mr. and Mrs. Allison take a trip into town for groceries and other supplies. **Ask:** *What does this shopping trip tell you* about the Allisons' summer cottage? (*It is in a remote location, where shops are not nearby.*) **OL**

the car. Although Mrs. Allison was able to order groceries delivered regularly, she was never able to form any accurate idea of Mr. Babcock's current stock by telephone, and her lists of odds and ends that might be procured[6] was always supplemented, almost beyond their need, by the new and fresh local vegetables Mr. Babcock was selling temporarily, or the packaged candy which had just come in. This trip Mrs. Allison was tempted, too, by the set of glass baking dishes that had found themselves completely by chance in the hardware and clothing and general store, and which had seemingly been waiting there for no one but Mrs. Allison, since the country people, with their instinctive distrust of anything that did not look as permanent as trees and rocks and sky, had only recently begun to experiment in aluminum baking dishes instead of ironware, and had, apparently within the memory of local inhabitants, discarded stoneware in favor of iron.

Mrs. Allison had the glass baking dishes carefully wrapped, to endure the uncomfortable ride home over the rocky road that led up to the Allisons' cottage, and while Mr. Charley Walpole, who, with his younger brother Albert, ran the hardware-clothing-general store (the store itself was called Johnson's, because it stood on the site of the old Johnson cabin, burned fifty years before Charley Walpole was born), laboriously unfolded newspapers to wrap around the dishes, Mrs. Allison said, informally, "Course, I *could* have waited and gotten those dishes in New York, but we're not going back so soon this year."

"Heard you was staying on," Mr. Charley Walpole said. His old fingers fumbled maddeningly with the thin sheets of newspaper, carefully trying to isolate only one sheet at a time, and he did not look up at Mrs. Allison

"Don't know about staying on up there to the lake. Not after Labor Day."

as he went on, "Don't know about staying on up there to the lake. Not after Labor Day."

"Well, you know," Mrs. Allison said, quite as though he deserved an explanation, "it just seemed to us that we've been hurrying back to New York every year, and there just wasn't any need for it. You know what the city's like in the fall." And she smiled confidingly up at Mr. Charley Walpole.

Rhythmically he wound string around the package. He's giving me a piece long enough to save, Mrs. Allison thought, and she looked away quickly to avoid giving any sign of impatience. "I feel sort of like we belong here, more," she said. "Staying on after everyone else has left." To prove this, she smiled brightly across the store at a woman with a familiar face, who might have been the woman who sold berries to the Allisons one year, or the woman who occasionally helped in the grocery and was probably Mr. Babcock's aunt.

"Well," Mr. Charley Walpole said. He shoved the package a little across the counter, to show that it was finished and that for a sale well made, a package well wrapped, he was willing to accept pay. "Well," he said again. "Never been summer people before, at the lake after Labor Day."

Mrs. Allison gave him a five-dollar bill, and he made change methodically, giving great weight even to the pennies. "Never after Labor Day," he said, and nodded at Mrs. Allison, and went soberly along the store to deal with two women who were looking at cotton house dresses.

As Mrs. Allison passed on her way out she heard one of the women say **acutely**, "Why is

---

Big Idea Encountering the Unexpected *How does Mr. Walpole respond to the Allisons' unexpected news?* **BI₂**

Vocabulary

acutely (a kūt´ lē) *adv.* very perceptively or discerningly

---

6. *Procure* means "to get or acquire."

39

Teach

BI₂ Big Idea

Encountering the Unexpected Answer: *Students may say that Mr. Walpole is not encouraging and is reserved about the news that the couple is staying. Students may be struck by Mr. Walpole's repetition of the fact that summer people never stay after Labor Day.*
Ask: How do Mr. Walpole's actions indicate his reaction to the news? *(Answers will vary but may reflect the idea that Mr. Walpole seemed distracted or preoccupied by the news. He fumbled with the sheets of paper and appeared to be concentrating on the string, taking a long time to wrap Mrs. Allison's package.)* **OL**

★ Writer's Technique

Description A writer helps readers learn about characters by using particular words. **Say:** The author describes the country people as having an "instinctive distrust" of things that do not seem permanent. **Ask:** What does this tell you about the people of the town? *(The people are skeptical and do not easily trust other people or things they do not know.)* **AS**

Reading in the Real World

Career Point out to students that in later life they may find themselves working with many different types of people. Invite students to imagine they are working with someone like Mr. Walpole. Ask them to identify ways that they might communicate effectively with this person in a collaborative team environment. Suggest students conduct library research on workplace communications. They might access trade journals, like the *Journal of Business Communications,* or recent books on this topic. Have students compile their findings and share them with the class. **OL**

Objectives
• To respond to plot (SE)
• To analyze conflict (SE)
• To analyze details (TWE)

Teach

L Literary Element

Conflict Answer: *Towns-people have established routines and seem to share common viewpoint; newcomers regarded suspiciously.*
Ask: How long does it seem to take to become accepted as a citizen of the town? *(A long time; Mrs. Martin is still considered relative newcomer, and Allisons have been summer visitors for 17 years.)* `OL`

R1 Reading Strategy

Responding to Plot Answer: *Students may be struck by how townspeople repeat the point that summer people do not extend their stays; their lack of encouragement for Allisons' plans.* **Ask:** Why do you think summer visitors in this town have never stayed past Labor Day? *(Answers will vary. It may be that people had to return to jobs or children to school; or that people expected weather to worsen.)* `OL`

BI Big Idea

Encountering the Unexpected Answer: *She plans to decorate the cabin, possibly bake, and continue to enjoy the rural lifestyle.* `OL`

one of them dresses one dollar and thirty-nine cents and this one here is only ninety-eight?"

"They're great people," Mrs. Allison told her husband as they went together down the sidewalk after meeting at the door of the hardware store. "They're so solid, and so reasonable, and so *honest.*"

"Makes you feel good, knowing there are still towns like this," Mr. Allison said.

"You know, in New York," Mrs. Allison said, "I might have paid a few cents less for these dishes, but there wouldn't have been anything sort of personal in the transaction."

"Staying on to the lake?" Mrs. Martin, in the newspaper and sandwich shop, asked the Allisons. "Heard you was staying on."

"Thought we'd take advantage of the lovely weather this year," Mr. Allison said.

Mrs. Martin was a comparative newcomer to the town; she had married into the newspaper and sandwich shop from a neighboring farm, and had stayed on after her husband's death. She served bottled soft drinks, and fried egg and onion sandwiches on thick bread, which she made on her own stove at the back of the store. Occasionally when Mrs. Martin served a sandwich it would carry with it the rich fragrance of the stew or the pork chops cooking alongside for Mrs. Martin's dinner.

"I don't guess anyone's ever stayed out there so long before," Mrs. Martin said. "Not after Labor Day, anyway."

"I guess Labor Day is when they usually leave," Mr. Hall, the Allisons' nearest neighbor, told them later, in front of Mr. Babcock's store, where the Allisons were getting into their car to go home. "Surprised you're staying on."

"It seemed a shame to go so soon," Mrs. Allison said. Mr. Hall lived three miles away; he supplied the Allisons with butter and eggs, and occasionally, from the top of their hill, the Allisons could see the lights in his house in the early evening before the Halls went to bed.

Literary Element Conflict *What sets newcomers apart from townspeople? How long does it seem to take to become accepted as a citizen of the town?* `L`

"They usually leave Labor Day," Mr. Hall said.

The ride home was long and rough; it was beginning to get dark, and Mr. Allison had to drive very carefully over the dirt road by the lake. Mrs. Allison lay back against the seat, pleasantly relaxed after a day of what seemed whirlwind shopping compared with their day-to-day existence; the new glass baking dishes lurked agreeably in her mind, and the half bushel of red eating apples, and the package of colored thumbtacks with which she was going to put up new shelf edging in the kitchen. "Good to get home," she said softly as they came in sight of their cottage, silhouetted above them against the sky.

"Glad we decided to stay on," Mr. Allison agreed.

Mrs. Allison spent the next morning lovingly washing her baking dishes, although in his innocence Charley Walpole had neglected to notice the chip in the edge of one; she decided, wastefully, to use some of the red eating apples in a pie for dinner, and, while the pie was in the oven and Mr. Allison was down getting the mail, she sat out on the little lawn the Allisons had made at the top of the hill, and watched the changing lights on the lake, alternating gray and blue as clouds moved quickly across the sun.

Mr. Allison came back a little out of sorts; it always irritated him to walk the mile to the mailbox on the state road and come back with nothing, even though he assumed that the walk was good for his health. This morning there was nothing but a circular from a New York department store, and their New York paper, which arrived **erratically** by

Reading Strategy Responding to Plot *What do you find most striking about the townspeople's responses to the Allisons?* `R1`

Big Idea Encountering the Unexpected *What are Mrs. Allison's expectations about the coming weeks?* `BI`

Vocabulary

erratically (ər rat′ i ka lē) *adv.* in an irregular or unpredictable way

40 UNIT 1 THE SHORT STORY

Additional Support

Skills Practice

READING: Activating Prior Knowledge Have students think about a time that they have been in a situation similar to that of the Allisons. They may have been summer visitors, tourists in a new town, or going out with friends in a different neighborhood. **Ask:** Think of a time that you were in a neighbor-

hood different from your own. Did you feel "at home" there? *(Answers will vary. Students should be able to express how their ability to feel comfortable in a new place was, at least in part, dependent on their interaction with people around them.)* `OL`

40

Reeds at the Starnberg Lake [near Munich], 1866. Christian Morgenstern (Ernst Bernhard). Oil on canvas, 32 x 40.8 cm. Hamburger Kunsthalle, Hamburg, Germany. ★

mail from one to four days later than it should, so that some days the Allisons might have three papers and frequently none. Mrs. Allison, although she shared with her husband the annoyance of not having mail when they so anticipated it, pored[7] affectionately over the department store circular, and made a mental note to drop in at the store when she finally went back to New York, and check on the sale of wool blankets; it was hard to find good ones in pretty colors nowadays. She debated saving the circular to remind herself, but after thinking about getting up and getting into the cottage to put it away safely somewhere, she dropped it into the grass beside her chair and lay back, her eyes half closed.

"Looks like we might have some rain," Mr. Allison said, squinting at the sky.

"Good for the crops," Mrs. Allison said laconically,[8] and they both laughed.

---

7. *Pore* means "to read or study carefully."
8. *Laconically* means "concisely or with few words."

Reading Strategy Responding to Plot *What is your reaction to the Allisons' attitudes about the townspeople and country living?* **R2**

The kerosene man came the next morning while Mr. Allison was down getting the mail; they were getting low on kerosene and Mrs. Allison greeted the man warmly; he sold kerosene and ice, and, during the summer, hauled garbage away for the summer people. A garbage man was only necessary for **improvident** city folk; country people had no garbage.

"I'm glad to see you," Mrs. Allison told him. "We were getting pretty low."

The kerosene man, whose name Mrs. Allison had never learned, used a hose attachment to fill the twenty-gallon tank which supplied light and heat and cooking facilities for the Allisons; but today, instead of swinging down from his truck and unhooking the hose from where it coiled affectionately around the cab of the truck, the man stared uncomfortably at Mrs. Allison, his truck motor still going.

"Thought you folks'd be leaving," he said.

"We're staying on another month," Mrs. Allison said brightly. "The weather was so nice, and it seemed like—"

Vocabulary

improvident (im prov′ ə dent) *adj.* wasteful or unthrifty

SHIRLEY JACKSON **41**

Teach

R2 **Reading Strategy**

Responding to Plot **Answer:**
Students may indicate that the Allisons enjoy living at their cottage. They have not added amenities, indicating that they don't mind a certain degree of rustic living, which students may admire. The Allisons exhibit a degree of disrespect for the townspeople, to which students may react negatively.) **OL**

★ **Viewing the Art**

Ask: Does the painting reflect your idea of what the area surrounding the Allisons' cottage looks like? *(Students may say that this image is desolate and unfriendly, similar to the countryside after the summer is over.)* **AS**

English Language Coach

Idioms Idioms are difficult for English Language learners to understand because there is no direct translation. Help students understand idioms by encouraging them to think of common examples they might use. **Say:** Notice the term "out of sorts" in the story. "Out of sorts" means "irritated" or "unhappy." This is an example of an idiom. An idiom has a special meaning that is different from the individual words themselves. Think of some idioms we use today. *(Possible answers: "under the weather," "out of touch")* **EL**

Objectives
• To analyze conflict (SE)
• To respond to plot (SE)
• To activate prior knowledge (TWE)

Teach

R1 Reading Strategy

Responding to Plot Answer: *Answers will vary. Students may be surprised, or they may think that their unpleasant suspicions are being confirmed.*
Ask: What do you expect the kerosene man to do about helping the Allisons? *(Answers should indicate an understanding of the man's intent, which is to not supply the Allisons with fuel.)* OL

L1 Literary Element

Conflict Answer: *Mrs. Allison needs to have kerosene delivered so she and her husband can stay in their cottage past Labor Day, while the kerosene man says he cannot provide something for which he has not planned. Both parties cannot meet their goals.)* OL

V Vocabulary

Ask: How do the context clues help you to understand the meaning of *placatingly*? *(Clearly Mrs. Allison was trying to make her husband feel better; therefore, placatingly must have something to do with making people feel better.)* OL

"That's what they told me," the man said. "Can't give you no oil, though."

"What do you mean?" Mrs. Allison raised her eyebrows. "We're just going to keep on with our regular—"

"After Labor Day," the man said. "I don't get so much oil myself after Labor Day."

Mrs. Allison reminded herself, as she had frequently to do when in disagreement with her neighbors, that city manners were no good with country people; you could not expect to overrule a country employee as you could a city worker, and Mrs. Allison smiled engagingly as she said, "But can't you get extra oil, at least while we stay?"

"You see," the man said. He tapped his finger exasperatedly against the car wheel as he spoke. "You see," he said slowly, "I order this oil. I order it down from maybe fifty, fifty-five miles away. I order back in June, how much I'll need for the summer. Then I order again . . . oh, about November. Round about now it's starting to get pretty short." As though the subject were closed, he stopped tapping his finger and tightened his hands on the wheel in preparation for departure.

"But can't you give us *some?*" Mrs. Allison said. "Isn't there anyone else?"

"Don't know as you could get oil any-wheres else right now," the man said consideringly. "*I can't give you none.*" Before Mrs. Allison could speak, the truck began to move; then it stopped for a minute and he looked at her through the back window of the cab. "Ice?" he called. "I could let you have some ice."

Mrs. Allison shook her head; they were not terribly low on ice, and she was angry. She ran a few steps to catch up with the truck, calling, "Will you try to get us some? Next week?"

"Don't see's I can," the man said. "After Labor Day, it's harder." The truck drove away, and Mrs. Allison, only comforted by the thought that she could probably get ker-

Reading Strategy Responding to Plot *What is your reaction to the kerosene man's words?* **R1**

42 UNIT 1 THE SHORT STORY

osene from Mr. Babcock, or, at worst, the Halls, watched it go with anger. "Next summer," she told herself. "Just let him try coming around next summer!"

There was no mail again, only the paper, which seemed to be coming doggedly on time, and Mr. Allison was openly cross when he returned. When Mrs. Allison told him about the kerosene man he was not particularly impressed.

"Probably keeping it all for a high price during the winter," he commented. "What's happened to Anne and Jerry, do you think?"

Anne and Jerry were their son and daughter, both married, one living in Chicago, one in the Far West; their dutiful weekly letters were late; so late, in fact, that Mr. Allison's annoyance at the lack of mail was able to settle on a legitimate grievance. "Ought to realize how we wait for their letters," he said. "Thoughtless, selfish children. Ought to know better."

"Well, dear," Mrs. Allison said placatingly.[9] Anger at Anne and Jerry would not relieve her emotions toward the kerosene man. After a few minutes she said, "Wishing won't bring the mail, dear. I'm going to go call Mr. Babcock and tell him to send up some kerosene with my order." **V**

"At least a postcard," Mr. Allison said as she left.

As with most of the cottage's inconveniences, the Allisons no longer noticed the phone particularly, but yielded to its eccentricities without conscious complaint. It was a wall phone, of a type still seen in only few communities; in order to get the operator, Mrs. Allison had first to turn the sidecrank and ring once. Usually it took two or three tries to force the operator to answer, and Mrs. Allison, making any kind of telephone call, approached the phone with resignation and a sort of desperate patience. She had to crank the phone three times this morning

---

9. To *placate* is to reduce the anger of, or to calm.

Literary Element Conflict *What conflict occurs between Mrs. Allison and the kerosene man?* **L1**

Additional Support

Skills Practice

LITERARY ELEMENT:

Characterization Explain that characterization is a tool a writer uses to reveal the personality of characters in a story or play. Knowing Mrs. Allison's thoughts helps readers understand more about her character. **Say:** What did Mrs. Allison mean by "city manners were no good with country people"? *(In her opinion, city people and country people are very different. Her frequent arguments with her neighbors may indicate that she feels superior to them.)* OL before the operator answered, and then it was still longer before Mr. Babcock picked up the receiver at his phone in the corner of the grocery behind the meat table. He said, "Store?" with the rising inflection that seemed to indicate suspicion of anyone who tried to communicate with him by means of this unreliable instrument.

"This is Mrs. Allison, Mr. Babcock. I thought I'd give you my order a day early because I wanted to be sure and get some—"

"What say, Mrs. Allison?"

Mrs. Allison raised her voice a little; she saw Mr. Allison, out on the lawn, turn in his chair and regard her sympathetically. "I said, Mr. Babcock, I thought I'd call in my order early so you could send me—"

"Mrs. Allison?" Mr. Babcock said. "You'll come and pick it up?"

"Pick it up?" In her surprise Mrs. Allison let her voice drop back to its normal tone and Mr. Babcock said loudly, "What's that, Mrs. Allison?"

"I thought I'd have you send it out as usual," Mrs. Allison said.

"Well, Mrs. Allison," Mr. Babcock said, and there was a pause while Mrs. Allison waited, staring past the phone over her husband's head out into the sky. "Mrs. Allison," Mr. Babcock went on finally, "I'll tell you, my boy's been working for me went back to school yesterday and now I got no one to deliver. I only got a boy delivering summers, you see."

"I thought you *always* delivered," Mrs. Allison said.

"Not after Labor Day, Mrs. Allison," Mr. Babcock said firmly. "You never been here after Labor Day before, so's you wouldn't know, of course."

"Well," Mrs. Allison said helplessly. Far inside her mind she was saying, over and over, can't use city manners on country folk, no use getting mad.

"Are you sure?" she asked finally. "Couldn't you just send out an order today, Mr. Babcock?"

"Matter of fact," Mr. Babcock said, "I guess I couldn't, Mrs. Allison. It wouldn't hardly pay, delivering, with no one else out at the lake."

"What about Mr. Hall?" Mrs. Allison asked suddenly, "the people who live about three miles away from us out here? Mr. Hall could bring it out when he comes."

"Hall?" Mr. Babcock said. "John Hall? They've gone to visit her folks upstate, Mrs. Allison."

"But they bring all our butter and eggs," Mrs. Allison said, appalled.

"Left yesterday," Mr. Babcock said. "Probably didn't think you folks would stay on up there."

"But I told Mr. Hall . . ." Mrs. Allison started to say, and then stopped. "I'll send Mr. Allison in after some groceries tomorrow," she said.

"You got all you need till then," Mr. Babcock said, satisfied; it was not a question, but a confirmation.

After she hung up, Mrs. Allison went slowly out to sit again in her chair next to her husband. "He won't deliver," she said. "You'll have to go in tomorrow. We've got just enough kerosene to last till you get back."

"He should have told us sooner," Mr. Allison said.

It was not possible to remain troubled long in the face of the day; the country had never seemed more inviting, and the lake moved quietly below them, among the trees, with the almost incredible softness of a summer picture. Mrs. Allison sighed deeply, in the pleasure of possessing for themselves that sight of the lake, with the distant green hills beyond, the gentleness of the small wind through the trees.

Literary Element Conflict *How is Mrs. Allison's attitude toward her problems beginning to shift?* **L2**

Big Idea Encountering the Unexpected *How well-prepared for the unexpected are the Allisons?* **BI**

SHIRLEY JACKSON **43**

Reading Strategy Responding to Plot *Are you surprised by Mr. Babcock's refusal to deliver groceries? What are your inferences about the townspeople?* **R2**

Teach

R2 Reading Strategy

Responding to Plot Answer: *Answers will vary. Students may not be surprised because of Mrs. Allison's conflict with the kerosene man. Students may say that the townspeople do not want the Allisons to stay in the town.* **OL**

L2 Literary Element

Conflict Answer: *Students may say that Mrs. Allison is beginning to be worried by her transactions with the townspeople. She suspects that they do not want her in the town.* **OL**

BI Big Idea

Encountering the Unexpected Answer: *The Allisons are unprepared for the problems besetting them. They lack basic provisions and friends whom they can call on for help.* **OL**

★ Cultural History

Telephones Early telephones were very different from the phones used today. Often, families shared telephone lines with people they did not even know. Sometimes it was necessary to call an operator to get in touch with someone else. **AS**

Differentiated Instruction

Creating Dialogue Creating dialogue is a way for students to enhance their understanding of a story's plot and the interactions among its characters. Have students create a new dialogue between Mrs. Allison and Mr. Babcock. **Say:** Mrs. Allison has a dialogue with Mr. Babcock about having supplies delivered. With a classmate, create new dialogue for these two characters. Remember that your dialogue should reflect the personalities of the characters and should help the reader learn something about the plot. **AL**

Objectives
• To respond to plot (SE)
• To analyze conflict (SE)
• To understand characterization (TWE)

43

Teach

BI₁ Big Idea

Encountering the Unexpected Ask: Do you think it unexpected that the Allisons' car will not start? Why or why not? *(Answers will vary. Students may say it is not unexpected, since the car is old. They also may cite the many other things that seem to be going wrong in the Allisons' life, so therefore the car trouble is expected.)* **OL**

R₁ Reading Strategy

Responding to Plot Answer: *Students may say that they notice the increasingly negative mood in the story.*
Ask: Do you think this story could have taken place in another setting? Why? *(Answers should reflect the idea that the plot is dependent on a setting that is isolated; however, the action could have taken place in many other remote areas.)* **OL**

R₂ Reading Strategy

Responding to Plot Answer: *Answers should indicate students' perception that Mr. Allison is growing older and his health is not as good as it once was. Mrs. Allison is concerned about this.* **OL**

The weather continued fair; the next morning Mr. Allison, duly armed with a list of groceries, with "kerosene" in large letters at the top, went down the path to the garage, and Mrs. Allison began another pie in her new baking dishes. She had mixed the crust and was starting to pare the apples when Mr. Allison came rapidly up the path and flung open the screen door into the kitchen.

BI₁ "Damn car won't start," he announced, with the end-of-the-tether[10] voice of a man who depends on a car as he depends on his right arm.

"What's wrong with it?" Mrs. Allison demanded, stopping with the paring knife in one hand and an apple in the other. "It was all right on Tuesday."

"Well," Mr. Allison said between his teeth, "it's not all right on Friday."

"Can you fix it?" Mrs. Allison asked.

"No," Mr. Allison said, "I can not. Got to call someone, I guess."

"Who?" Mrs. Allison asked.

"Man runs the filling station, I guess." Mr. Allison moved purposefully toward the phone. "He fixed it last summer one time."

A little apprehensive, Mrs. Allison went on paring apples absentmindedly, while she listened to Mr. Allison with the phone, ringing, waiting, finally giving the number to the operator, then waiting again and giving the number again, giving the number a third time, and then slamming down the receiver.

"No one there," he announced as he came into the kitchen.

"He's probably gone out for a minute," Mrs. Allison said nervously; she was not quite sure what made her so nervous, unless it was the probability of her husband's losing his temper completely. "He's there alone, I imagine, so if he goes out there's no one to answer the phone."

"That must be it," Mr. Allison said with heavy irony. He slumped into one of the kitchen chairs and watched Mrs. Allison paring apples. After a minute, Mrs. Allison said

soothingly, "Why don't you go down and get the mail and then call him again?"

Mr. Allison debated and then said, "Guess I might as well." He rose heavily and when he got to the kitchen door he turned and said, "But if there's no mail—" and leaving an awful silence behind him, he went off down the path.

Mrs. Allison hurried with her pie. Twice she went to the window to glance at the sky to see if there were clouds coming up. The room seemed unexpectedly dark, and she herself felt in the state of tension that preceded a thunderstorm, but both times when she looked the sky was clear and serene, smiling indifferently down on the Allisons' summer cottage as well as on the rest of the world. When Mrs. Allison, her pie ready for the oven, went a third time to look outside, she saw her husband coming up the path; he seemed more cheerful, and when he saw her, he waved eagerly and held a letter in the air.

"From Jerry," he called as soon as he was close enough for her to hear him, "at last—a letter!" Mrs. Allison noticed with concern that he was no longer able to get up the gentle slope of the path without breathing heavily; but then he was in the doorway, holding out the letter. "I saved it till I got here," he said.

Mrs. Allison looked with an eagerness that surprised her on the familiar handwriting of her son; she could not imagine why the letter excited her so, except that it was the first they had received in so long; it would be a pleasant, dutiful letter, full of the doings of Alice and the children, reporting progress with his job, commenting on the recent weather in Chicago, closing with love from all; both Mr. and Mrs. Allison could, if they wished, recite a pattern letter from either of their children.

Mr. Allison slit the letter open with great deliberation, and then he spread it out on

---

Reading Strategy Responding to Plot *What aspects of this scene grab your attention?* **R₁**

Reading Strategy Responding to Plot *What are your feelings about this detail?* **R₂**

---

10. To be at the *end-of-the-tether* is to exhaust all patience.

UNIT 1 THE SHORT STORY

Additional Support

Skills Practice

WRITING: Persuasive Writing Have students write a letter to the editor of the Allisons' local newspaper, calling for a change in the town's rescue operations. **Say:** The Allisons might remind us of many people who find themselves alone in a difficult situation. Think of some ways that might be available for someone who cannot reach the outside world. Put your ideas into a letter to the editor. Attempt to persuade the editor to put your ideas into practice. When you have finished your letter, exchange papers with a partner for review. **OL**

Variety 2, 1997. Mary Iverson.
Viewing the Art: How does the mood in this painting reflect the mood in the story? ⭐

the kitchen table and they leaned down and read it together.

"Dear Mother and Dad," it began, in Jerry's familiar, rather childish handwriting, *"Am glad this goes to the lake as usual, we always thought you came back too soon and ought to stay up there as long as you could. Alice says that now that you're not as young as you used to be and have no demands on your time, fewer friends, etc., in the city, you ought to get what fun you can while you can. Since you two are both happy up there, it's a good idea for you to stay."*

Uneasily Mrs. Allison glanced sideways at her husband; he was reading intently, and she reached out and picked up the empty envelope, not knowing exactly what she wanted from it. It was addressed quite as usual, in Jerry's handwriting, and was postmarked "Chicago." Of course it's postmarked Chicago, she thought quickly, why

would they want to postmark it anywhere else? When she looked back down at the letter, her husband had turned the page, and she read on with him: *"—and of course if they get measles, etc., now, they will be better off later. Alice is well, of course; me too. Been playing a lot of bridge lately with some people you don't know, named Carruthers. Nice young couple, about our age. Well, will close now as I guess it bores you to hear about things so far away. Tell Dad old Dickson, in our Chicago office, died. He used to ask about Dad a lot. Have a good time up at the lake, and don't bother about hurrying back. Love from all of us, Jerry."*

"Funny," Mr. Allison commented.

"It doesn't sound like Jerry," Mrs. Allison said in a small voice. "He never wrote anything like . . ." She stopped.

"Like what?" Mr. Allison demanded. "Never wrote anything like what?"

Mrs. Allison turned the letter over, frowning. It was impossible to find any sentence, any word, even, that did not sound like Jerry's regular letters. Perhaps it was only that the letter was so late, or the unusual number of dirty fingerprints on the envelope.

"I don't know," she said impatiently.

"Going to try that phone call again," Mr. Allison said.

Mrs. Allison read the letter twice more, trying to find a phrase that sounded wrong.

Big Idea Encountering the Unexpected *What is unexpected or unusual about Jerry's letter?* **BI₂**

SHIRLEY JACKSON **45**

Differentiated Instruction

Making Predictions Help less proficient readers to understand the connection between making predictions and encountering the unexpected. **Say:** Mr. and Mrs. Allison know what to expect in letters from their children. Why was this letter unexpected? Pair up with a partner to compare the letter that the Allisons received with the type of letter they expected. **BL**

Teach

BI₂ Big Idea

Encountering the Unexpected Answer: *Students may say that Jerry's letter is later than expected and that the letter itself seems insensitive, even cruel. The Allisons are used to receiving pleasant letters from their children.*
Ask: How do you think Mr. and Mrs. Allison feel after reading Jerry's letter? *(Answers should reflect the idea that the letter appeared to be unsettling for them; their actions suggest that they may be feeling apprehensive.)* **OL**

⭐ Viewing the Art

Answer: *Answers will vary. Students may say that the lonely and empty mood in the painting is similar to the cool cruelty of the town.* **AS**

Objectives
• To respond to plot (SE)
• To write persuasively (TWE)

R **Reading Strategy**

Responding to Plot **Answer:** *Answers will vary. Students may be horrified to realize what is happening to the Allisons.* **OL**

L **Literary Element**

Conflict **Answer:** *Someone who wants to harm the Allisons would do such things. This could be anyone in the town who does not want the summer visitors to stay past Labor Day.* **OL**

BI **Big Idea**

Encountering the Unexpected **Answer:** *The light at the Hall place was unexpected because Mr. Babcock, the grocer, had claimed that the Halls had left town to visit relatives.* **OL**

CheckPoint

Use the CheckPoint questions on Presentation Plus! to check students' mastery of the selection. These questions can be used with interactive response keypads for immediate student feedback.

Then Mr. Allison came back and said, very quietly, "Phone's dead."

"What?" Mrs. Allison said, dropping the letter.

"Phone's dead," Mr. Allison said.

The rest of the day went quickly; after a lunch of crackers and milk, the Allisons went to sit outside on the lawn, but their afternoon was cut short by the gradually increasing storm clouds that came up over the lake to the cottage, so that it was as dark as evening by four o'clock. The storm delayed, however, as though in loving anticipation of the moment it would break over the summer cottage, and there was an occasional flash of lightning, but no rain. In the evening Mr. and Mrs. Allison, sitting close together inside their cottage, turned on the battery radio they had brought with them from New York. There were no lamps lighted in the cottage, and the only light came from the lightning outside and the small square glow from the dial of the radio.

The slight framework of the cottage was not strong enough to withstand the city noises, the music and the voices, from the radio, and the Allisons could hear them far off echoing across the lake, the saxophones in the New York dance band wailing over the water, the flat voice of the girl vocalist going inexorably out into the clean country air. Even the announcer, speaking glowingly of the virtues of razor blades, was no more than an inhuman voice sounding out from the Allisons' cottage and echoing back, as though the lake and the hills and the trees were returning it unwanted.

During one pause between commercials, Mrs. Allison turned and smiled weakly at her husband. "I wonder if we're supposed to … *do* anything," she said.

"No," Mr. Allison said consideringly. "I don't think so. Just wait."

Reading Strategy Responding to Plot *What is your response to this news?* **R**

Mrs. Allison caught her breath quickly, and Mr. Allison said, under the trivial melody of the dance band beginning again, "The car had been tampered[11] with, you know. Even I could see that."

Mrs. Allison hesitated a minute and then said very softly, "I suppose the phone wires were cut."

"I imagine so," Mr. Allison said.

After a while, the dance music stopped and they listened attentively to a news broadcast, the announcer's rich voice telling them breathlessly of a marriage in Hollywood, the latest baseball scores, the estimated rise in food prices during the coming week. He spoke to them, in the summer cottage, quite as though they still deserved to hear news of a world that no longer reached them except through the fallible batteries on the radio, which were already beginning to fade, almost as though they still belonged, however tenuously, to the rest of the world.

Mrs. Allison glanced out the window at the smooth surface of the lake, the black masses of the trees, and the waiting storm, and said conversationally, "I feel better about that letter of Jerry's."

"I knew when I saw the light down at the Hall place last night," Mr. Allison said.

The wind, coming up suddenly over the lake, swept around the summer cottage and slapped hard at the windows. Mr. and Mrs. Allison involuntarily moved closer together, and with the first sudden crash of thunder, Mr. Allison reached out and took his wife's hand. And then, while the lightning flashed outside, and the radio faded and sputtered, the two old people huddled together in their summer cottage and waited.

---

11. To *tamper with* is to damage or alter something.

Literary Element Conflict *Who might want to tamper with the Allisons' car and phone wires?* **L**

Big Idea Encountering the Unexpected *Why was the light at the Hall place unexpected?* **BI**

Additional Support

Skills Practice

READING: Making Inferences

Explain: The Allisons shared few words toward the end yet seemed to understand each other well. When Mrs. Allison said, "I wonder if we're supposed to . . . *do* anything," Mr. Allison knew what she meant. **Ask:** Was his response the best reply? How might Mr. Allison have responded to encourage his wife to take action? *(He might have encouraged his wife to consider the negative consequences of doing nothing; he might have suggested walking to a telephone, or flagging down help on the road.)* Have students write a paragraph to answer. **OL**

RESPONDING AND THINKING CRITICALLY

Respond

1. In your opinion, what was the most frightening or disturbing moment of the story? Explain.

Recall and Interpret

2. (a)What decision do the Allisons make at the beginning of the story? Why? (b)How do they expect to spend autumn as a result of their decision?

3. (a)What happens when the Allisons go into town? (b)How do the townspeople learn of the Allisons's decision? How do they react?

4. (a)For what goods and services do the Allisons rely on the townspeople? Why? (b)What happens when they try to obtain these goods and services after Labor Day?

5. (a)Why is Mr. Allison anxious about the mail? (b)How would you describe the letter the Allisons receive from their son Jerry?

6. (a)At the end of the story, what do the Allisons realize? (b)In the closing scene, what do you think the Allisons are waiting for? Explain.

Analyze and Evaluate

7. (a)From the story, what ideas did you form about the town and its inhabitants? (b)What do you infer about the townspeoples' attitudes toward outsiders?

8. (a)What attitudes does Mrs. Allison display toward the townspeople? (b)Were there points in the story when you felt sympathy for the townspeople? Explain.

9. **Suspense** is the increasing feeling of interest and excitement that readers experience as the plot of a story builds. In your opinion, what elements—such as descriptions of character, setting, or plot—helped make this story suspenseful? Support your answer with examples from the story.

Connect

10. **Big Idea** **Encountering the Unexpected** (a)How do the townspeople seem to react to the unexpected? (b)In your opinion, what **theme**, or overall message, about human nature does Shirley Jackson express in this story? Explain.

LITERARY ANALYSIS

Literary Element **Conflict**

Most stories are based on a problem, or **conflict**, that gets resolved over the course of the story. **External conflicts** exist when a character struggles with an outside force, such as another person, society, fate, or nature. An **internal conflict** exists in a character's mind, when he or she is torn between different feelings and goals. Many stories have more than one conflict. Typically, the conflicts are related in some way.

1. What is the main external conflict in "The Summer People"?

2. Identify another external conflict in the story. How does this conflict get resolved?

3. Describe an internal conflict that Mr. Allison or Mrs. Allison might have. How does it relate to the main conflict you identified in question 1 above? Explain.

Review: Foreshadowing

As you learned on page 21, **foreshadowing** is the author's use of clues to prepare readers for events that will happen later in a story.

Partner Activity Meet with a partner to discuss Jackson's use of foreshadowing. What details throughout the story provide clues that the Allisons are in trouble? With your partner, go back and review the story, looking for clues that help suggest what will happen to the Allisons. Use a chart like the one shown to list the clues and to explain their significance.

Foreshadowing	Significance of Foreshadowing
Mr. Babcock repeats that nobody, "nobody," has ever stayed at the lake past Labor Day.	The Allisons will not succeed in staying past Labor Day. Perhaps bad things have happened to people who tried before.

SHIRLEY JACKSON **47**

Assess

1. Students may say the cruelty of the townspeople.

2. (a) They won't return to the city; the weather is nice. (b) By having a peaceful and pleasant time

3. (a) They buy provisions, discuss decision with townspeople. (b) They tell Mr. Babcock, news travels fast throughout town. Townspeople tell Allisons summer people never stay past Labor Day.

4. (a) Heating fuel and food; Cottage lacks basic plumbing, electricity. (b) Townspeople refuse to help them.

5. (a) Children's letters may help him feel he is in contact with outside world. (b) Letter seems insensitive.

6. (a) Townspeople have conspired against them. (b) They might be waiting for death or help.

7. (a) Townspeople seem unfriendly and narrow-minded. (b) They are hostile toward outsiders.

8. (a) Friendly but condescending (b) Answers will vary.

9. Students may cite townspeople's eerie responses when Allisons first announced they were staying, the strange letters, etc.

10. (a) The townspeople seem unable to adjust to the unexpected presence of visitors after Labor Day. (b) People can cause great cruelty.

Literary Element

1. The Allisons' staying and townspeople wanting them to leave

2. Broken car and cut phone lines; Allisons decide to wait it out.

3. Mrs. Allison might be struggling with feelings of uselessness and wondering if she caused people to turn against her.

Review: Foreshadowing

To identify instances of foreshadowing, students should review the plot to determine when they felt impelled to make a prediction about how the story would turn out.

Assess

Reading Strategy

1. Students should provide a brief summary of the main events of the story, support their answers, and explain what parts they found surprising or disturbing.

2. (a) Answers will vary. Students may say they began to realize the Allisons' fate when the car wouldn't start and they didn't have the necessary oil. (b) Answers will vary. Students may say that the end was creepy but appropriate for such a gloomy tale.

Vocabulary

1. a **2.** b **3.** a **4.** c

Academic Vocabulary

1. She begins the story by creating a setting that appears warm and inviting and creates an increasingly threatening atmosphere.

2. He tells Mrs. Allison that the boy he hires for delivery only works during the summer; therefore, the Allisons will need to pick up their groceries themselves.

Reading Strategy Responding to Plot

By **responding** to the events of a story as you read, you build awareness of the story's meaning. You also enjoy your reading more.

1. Summarize the story's **plot**—the sequence of events in the story. What aspects of the plot did you find most disturbing or surprising?

2. (a)At what point in the story did you begin to realize what might happen to the Allisons? (b)What was your reaction to the ending of the story? Explain.

Vocabulary Practice

Practice with Context Clues Use context clues to choose the correct definitions for the boldfaced vocabulary words.

1. Despite her **precarious** grip, she did not drop the vase.
   a. uncertain **b.** solid **c.** mandatory

2. The politician's answer was **vague** and unspecific.
   a. exact **b.** imprecise **c.** unknowing

3. I can tell when my cat is **acutely** alert; her ears perk up.
   a. intensely **b.** intermittently **c.** suddenly

4. My parents encourage me not to be an **improvident** spender.
   a. ungrateful **b.** careful **c.** wasteful

Academic Vocabulary

Here are two words from the vocabulary list on page R82.

vary (vār′ ē) *v.* to change in form or appearance; alter

shift (shift) *v.* to move or transfer something from one place or person to another

Practice and Apply
1. How does Jackson **vary** the mood of the story?
2. How does Mr. Babcock **shift** the burden of getting groceries to the Allisons after Labor Day?

Writing About Literature

Analyze Setting Authors use local color when they use specific details in their writing to evoke a particular region. For example, details about the way people speak, the traditions they keep, and the way in which they live and work may help authors to suggest truths about characters and to create a strong feeling of place.

How does Shirley Jackson use local color to create a convincing portrait of her story's **setting**—a small New England town during the 1940s or 1950s? Write a brief essay discussing the details of local color that help characterize the people in the town. You might organize your essay like this:

After you complete your draft, meet with a peer reviewer to evaluate each other's work and to suggest revisions. Then proofread and edit your draft for errors in spelling, grammar, and punctuation.

Listening and Speaking

Think about Mr. and Mrs. Allison sitting in their cottage, waiting for something to happen. What might they discuss as they wait? With a partner, role-play a conversation between Mr. and Mrs. Allison. In your conversation, review what has happened so far, why it happened, and what you think might happen next. Share your conversation with the class.

Literature Online **Web Activities** For eFlashcards, Selection Quick Checks, and other Web activities, go to www.glencoe.com.

Web Activities Have students access the Web site for interactive activities that will help them assess their understanding of the selection.

Writing About Literature
Students' essays should

- include specific examples from the text that characterize the country town and its people
- include an explanation as to why Jackson portrayed the town as she did and what that portrayal contributed to the story

Listening and Speaking
To ensure students stay on task, have groups write their conversations down and turn them in.

Vocabulary Workshop

Denotation and Connotation

Using a Semantic Chart

"Consequently, with much pleasure and a slight feeling of adventure, Mrs. Allison went into their village the day after Labor Day and told those natives with whom she had dealings, with a pretty air of breaking away from tradition, that she and her husband had decided to stay at least a month longer at their cottage."

—Shirley Jackson, from "The Summer People"

Connecting to Literature In Shirley Jackson's short story "The Summer People," the local residents never say or do anything overtly mean to the Allisons. However, Jackson uses the **connotations** of the words she selects to suggest the residents' rather sinister reaction to the Allisons' decision to stay. When Mrs. Allison says that they are simply giving it a try, "Mr. Babcock replie[s] gravely, 'Never know till you try.'" Jackson could have used *seriously*, or *ominously*, but she chooses *gravely* to hint at disturbing implications in Mr. Babcock's words.

A chart like the one below can help you analyze, or look more closely at, words—at their similarities, their differences, and their shades of meaning. Follow these instructions to create the chart:

- In the left-hand column of the chart, place the words you will analyze.
- Consult a dictionary to find definitions, or denotations, for them.
- In the second column of the chart, enter the definition for each term.
- In the third column of the chart, record ideas, images, or feelings that you associate with each word. Such associations are the word's connotations.

A semantic features chart has been started below.

Word	Denotation	Connotation
Seriously	to a serious degree	consequences; heaviness

Exercise

On a separate sheet of paper, copy and complete the chart. With your classmates, discuss the denotations and the connotations of the words you have chosen. Below the chart, explain briefly how words such as *gravely* contribute to the mood of the story and foreshadow its ending.

▶ **Vocabulary Terms**

The **denotation** of a word is its literal meaning; the **connotation** of a word is its implied meaning.

▶ **Test-Taking Tip**

If, during a test, you are asked about the denotation of a word, think about how you would define the word for someone else. To describe the word's connotation, think about the images and ideas the word brings to mind.

▶ **Reading Handbook**

For more about denotation and connotation, see the Reading Handbook, p. R20.

Literature Online
eFlashcards Visit www.glencoe.com for eFlashcards and other vocabulary activities.

OBJECTIVES
- Analyze denotation and connotation.
- Create graphic organizers to understand text.

Vocabulary Workshop
Denotation and Connotation

Focus

Ask: What feelings and ideas do you associate with these words: *cloudy, chains, bluebirds,* and *Halloween*? *(Students may suggest negative or positive feelings for each.)* Explain the difference between the denotations and connotations. **OL**

Teach

Recognizing Connotations Ask students to suggest words with similar denotations but different connotations, such as *slender, slim, skinny,* and *bony*. Discuss how an author can select connotative words to contribute to a certain mood, tone, characterization, or purpose. **OL**

Assess

Exercise Students' charts will vary. Students should understand and demonstrate the difference between denotation and connotation in their discussions.

eFlashcards Have students access the Web site for more practice with denotation and connotation.

Objectives
- To analyze denotation and connotation (SE)
- To create graphic organizers to understand text (SE)

English Language Coach

Connotations Students new to the United States may be unfamiliar with the secondary denotations of words used in "The Summer People" passage. For example, in "pretty air," *air* means "a person's manner or bearing," and *pretty* means "pleasing." Review with students the connotations of these words: *pleasure, adventure,* and *breaking*

away. **Ask:** Considering these words, what impression do you get of Mrs. Allison? *(She seems free, happy, and pleasant.)* On another note, for students unfamiliar with Labor Day, mention that this holiday celebrating the American worker traditionally marks the end of summer. **EL**

Focus

BELLRINGER

Bellringer Options
Daily Language Transparency 6
Or draw a T-chart on the board. Title the left side of the chart "Before Parenthood." Title the right side "After Parenthood."
Ask: How much do you know about the early lives of your parents. List some interesting things.

Have students discuss their parents' lives. If they do not know much about their lives, have them guess at the kinds of people their parents were.

Literature Online

Author Search To expand students' appreciation of Edwidge Danticat, have them access the Web site for additional information and resources.

The Book of the Dead

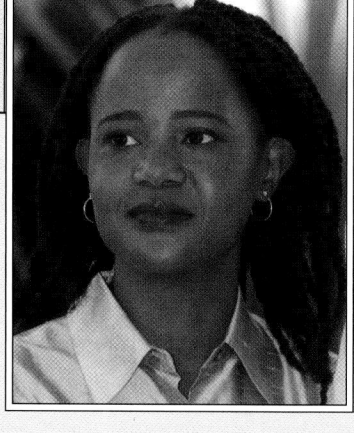

MEET EDWIDGE DANTICAT

The Haitian storyteller calls out "Krik?" This means, roughly, "Want to hear a story?" "Krak," the listeners answer, saying more or less, "We do." The scene takes place in Haiti, and the words are spoken in Haitian Creole, a language that evolved from French. This is the storytelling culture into which Edwidge Danticat (ed wēdj´ dän tə kah´) was born.

Living in Two Worlds Edwidge Danticat grew up in Port-au-Prince, a large port city that is the capital of Haiti. When she was very young, her parents left their home for the United States. Danticat remained behind, in the care of an aunt and uncle. She joined her parents in Brooklyn, New York, when she was twelve. Fitting in was not easy for Danticat; she spoke only Haitian Creole and reflected Haitian culture in her dress and hairstyle. One way she coped with the experience of being an outsider was by keeping journals in Haitian Creole, French, and English. When she began to write for an audience, one of her goals was to explain the experience of leaving one land for another.

> "One of [my] most important themes is migration, the separation of families, and how much that affects the parents and children who live through that experience."
>
> —Edwidge Danticat

Always a Writer Although Danticat always had an interest in writing—she had begun by the age of nine—her parents wanted her to prepare for a practical occupation, preferably in medicine. Danticat attempted to follow this route in high school, but she also never stopped writing. In fact, she produced some of the materials for her first novel while she was still a teenager.

Danticat became a rising star in American fiction at a young age. Her first novel, *Breath, Eyes, Memory,* written when she was a graduate student, was a selection for Oprah Winfrey's popular television book club. This was just the beginning of a rich and rapid outpouring of books, which has included several more novels, a work of fiction for young adults, and a collection of short stories called *Krik? Krak!* Danticat has also edited a collection of writing about Haitian immigration and written a travel book.

A finalist for the National Book Award, Danticat won the prestigious PEN/Faulkner Award for fiction in 2005 for her novel *The Dew Breaker.* Although originally written as a short story, "The Book of the Dead" became the first chapter of this novel.

Edwidge Danticat was born in 1969.

Literature Online **Author Search** For more about Edwidge Danticat, go to www.glencoe.com.

Selection Skills

The Book of the Dead

Literary Elements
- Irony (SE pp. 51, 53–60, 62)
- Conflict (SE p. 62)
- Dialect (TWE p. 56)

Reading Skills
- Comparing and Contrasting (SE pp. 51, 53–60, 62)

Vocabulary Skills
- Context Clues (SE pp. 51, 62)
- Academic Vocabulary (SE p. 62)

Listening/Speaking/Viewing Skills
- Analyzing Art (SE p. 59)
- Reciting Dialogue (TWE p. 58)

Writing Skills/Grammar
- Plot Analysis (SE p. 63)
- Dialogue (SE p. 63)
- Literary Response (TWE p. 52)

Study Skills/Research/Assessment
- Proverbs (TWE p. 60)

Connecting to the Story

Children often do not know everything there is to know about their parents. Before you read "The Book of the Dead," think about the following questions:

- What kinds of secrets might you keep from a child if you were a parent?
- What kinds of facts about a parent's past are important for a child to know?

Building Background

This selection takes place in contemporary times but also refers to dark days in the history of Haiti. From 1957 to 1971, the country was ruled by the brutal dictator François "Papa Doc" Duvalier. During this time, thugs employed by his government terrorized citizens, arresting, torturing, and beating Duvalier's opponents. Illiterate, poor, and desperate, many of these torturers and murderers did their jobs just to feed their families.

The title of the story is an allusion to the Egyptian Book of the Dead, which is a collection of texts related to funeral ceremonies of ancient Egypt. These texts were considered important for helping the dead undergo trials, or tests, before reaching happiness in the afterlife.

Setting Purposes for Reading

Big Idea Encountering the Unexpected

As you read, notice all of the unexpected occurrences in this story, both in the present and in the past.

Literary Element Irony

Irony is a contrast between what is expected and what actually happens. In **situational irony**, the outcome of a situation is the opposite of a character's expectations. In **dramatic irony**, the reader has information that characters do not have. As you read, think about how and why Danticat uses irony in this story.

- See Literary Terms Handbook, p. R9.

Literature Online **Interactive Literary Elements Handbook** To review or learn more about the literary elements, go to www.glencoe.com.

Reading Strategy Comparing and Contrasting

Comparing and contrasting is exploring the similarities and differences between two or more subjects. One way to deepen your understanding of this story is to compare and contrast the actions of the two families it portrays.

Reading Tip: Make a Diagram Use a Venn diagram to compare information about the narrator's family with information about the Fonteneau family.

Bienaime family | Fonteneau family

Vocabulary

interject (in´ tər jekt´) v. to cut into with a comment; p. 53 *Lily likes to interject her own comments into other people's conversations.*

mesmerize (mez´ mə rīz´) v. to hypnotize; p. 56 *Diego was so mesmerized by the flow of the water over the falls that he could not leave.*

vulnerability (vul´ nər ə bil´ ə tē) n. a state of being open to harm, damage, or illness; p. 56 *The buyers understood the vulnerability of the small cottage by the sea, but they bought it anyway.*

eradicate (i rad´ ə kāt´) v. to do away with completely; p. 56 *The thief tried to eradicate all traces of his presence from the crime scene.*

testament (tes´ tə mənt) n. proof of or tribute to; p. 57 *Winning the race after her injury was a testament to Rosa's determination.*

Vocabulary Tip: Context Clues Words and phrases that surround an unfamiliar word can give clues to its meaning.

Focus

Summary

A two-foot-high sculpture of Annie's father is the reason for her trip to Tampa. Accompanied by her father, the artist is traveling to Florida to sell the statue to the television star Gabrielle Fonteneau who, like Annie, is Haitian. The story begins in a Lakeland hotel where Annie has discovered that both her father and sculpture are missing. Through this discovery, Annie unearths a troublesome secret that not only costs her the sale of her first sculpture but changes her life forever.

V Vocabulary

Vocabulary File Say: Add these words and definitions to your vocabulary file. For each word, include a sentence that gives you an example of how to use the word. **OL** Students with English language needs should include the pronunciations of these words in their files. **EL**

Literature Online

Literary Elements Have students access the Web site to improve their understanding of irony.

EDWIDGE DANTICAT **51**

Selection Resources

Print Materials
- 📁 Unit 1 Resources (Fast File), pp. 30–32
- 📁 Leveled Vocabulary Development, p. 4
- 📁 Selection and Unit Assessments, pp. 9–10
- 📁 Selection Quick Checks, p. 5

Transparencies
- Bellringer Options Transparencies: Daily Language Practice Transparency 6
- Literary Elements Transparency 8

Technology
- TeacherWorks Plus™ CD-ROM
- StudentWorks Plus™ CD-ROM
- Presentation Plus!™ CD-ROM
- Literature Online, glencoe.com
- Online Student Edition, mhln.com
- ExamView® Assessment Suite CD-ROM
- Vocabulary PuzzleMaker CD-ROM
- Listening Library, disc 1 track 5

Encountering the Unexpected

Say: Keep the following question in mind as you read. How does Annie's view of her father change? *(Initially, she regards him highly; later she reevaluates her feelings; at the conclusion she has come to terms with his behaviors and sees his scars as wounds she must bear with him.)* **OL**

BI **Big Idea**

Encountering the Unexpected

Answer: *She does not tell the truth to the police.*
Annie's dishonesty may catch the reader by surprise. **Ask:** Does Annie sustain the reader's trust? *(Yes, though Annie lies to the police, she confides in the reader.)* **OL**

Readability Scores
Dale-Chall: 5.9
DRP: 56
Lexile: 920

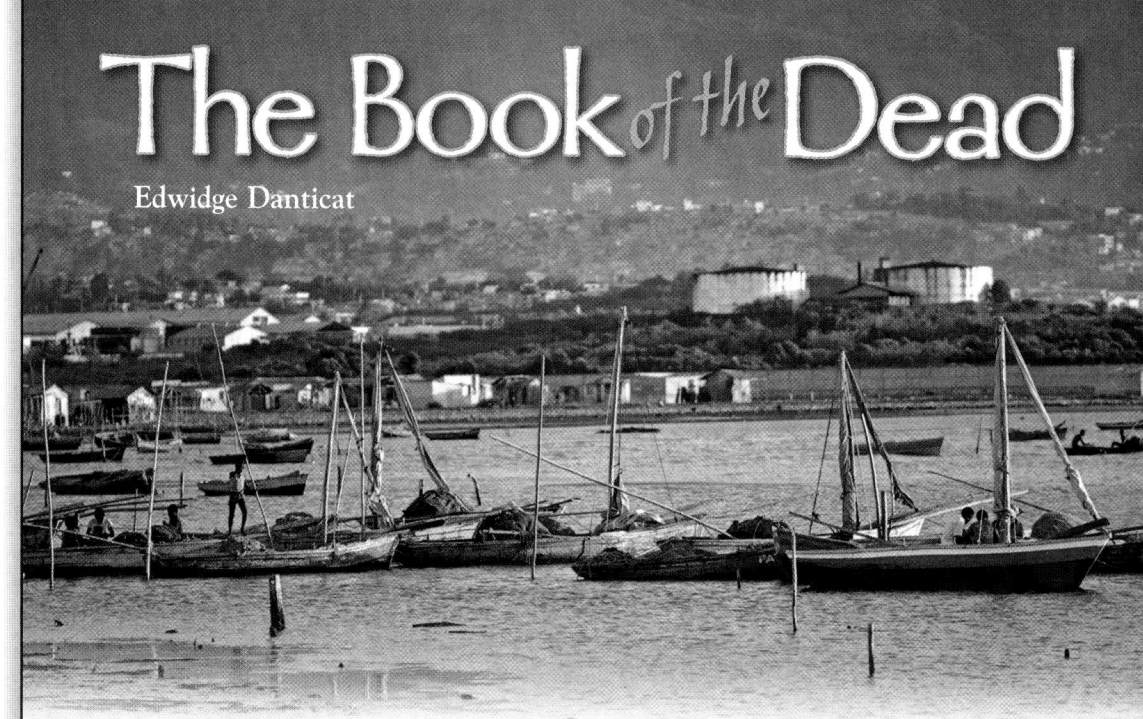

The Book of the Dead

Edwidge Danticat

My father is gone. I am slouched in a cast-aluminum chair across from two men, one the manager of the hotel where we're staying and the other a policeman. They are waiting for me to explain what has become of him, my father.

The manager—"Mr. Flavio Salinas," the plaque on his office door reads—has the most striking pair of chartreuse[1] eyes I have ever seen on a man with an island-Spanish lilt[2] to his voice.

The officer is a baby-faced, short white Floridian with a pot belly.

"Where are you and your daddy from, Ms. Bienaime?" he asks.

I answer "Haiti" even though I was born and raised in East Flatbush, Brooklyn, and have never visited my parents' birthplace. I do this because it is one more thing I have longed to have in common with my parents.

The officer plows forward. "You down here in Lakeland from Haiti?"

"We live in New York. We were on our way to Tampa."

I find Manager Salinas's office gaudy. The walls are covered with orange-and-green wallpaper, briefly interrupted by a giant gold-leaf-bordered print of a Victorian cottage that somehow resembles the building we're in. Patting his light-green tie, he whispers reassuringly, "Officer Bo and I will do the best we can to help you find your father."

We start out with a brief description: "Sixty-four, five feet eight inches, two hundred and twenty pounds, moon-faced, with thinning salt-and-pepper hair. Velvet-brown eyes—"

"Velvet-brown?" says Officer Bo.

"Deep brown—same color as his complexion."

---

1. *Chartreuse* (shär trōōz′) is a brilliant yellow-green.
2. A *lilt* is a rhythmic flow of speech.

Big Idea Encountering the Unexpected *How are the narrator's actions different from what you might expect?* **BI**

52 UNIT 1 THE SHORT STORY

Skills Practice

WRITING: Literary Response

Explain that responses to literature can be intellectual or emotional. To respond intellectually, readers explore the logical features of a text; to respond emotionally, readers examine their feelings about a text. Have students record intellectual and emotional responses in a journal.

(For intellectual responses, ideas about the legitimacy of the father's disappearance, or the manager's reaction to his disappearance may be expressed. Emotional responses should effectively express some feeling about the story's beginning.) **OL**

My father has had partial frontal dentures for ten years, since he fell off his and my mother's bed when his prison nightmares began. I mention that, too. Just the dentures, not the nightmares. I also bring up the claw-shaped marks that run from his left ear down along his cheek to the corner of his mouth—the only visible reminder of the year he spent at Fort Dimanche, the Port-au-Prince prison ironically named after the Lord's Day.[3]

"Does your daddy have any kind of mental illness, senility?" asks Officer Bo.

"No."

"Do you have any pictures of your daddy?"

I feel like less of a daughter because I'm not carrying a photograph in my wallet. I had hoped to take some pictures of him on our trip. At one of the rest stops I bought a disposable camera and pointed it at my father. No, no, he had protested, covering his face with both hands like a little boy protecting his cheeks from a slap. He did not want any more pictures taken of him for the rest of his life. He was feeling too ugly.

"That's too bad," says Officer Bo. "Does he speak English, your daddy? He can ask for directions, et cetera?"

"Yes."

"Is there anything that might make your father run away from you—particularly here in Lakeland?" Manager Salinas **interjects.** "Did you two have a fight?"

I had never tried to tell my father's story in words before now, but my first sculpture of him was the reason for our trip: a two-foot-high mahogany figure of my father, naked, crouching on the floor, his back arched like the curve of a crescent moon, his down-cast eyes fixed on his short stubby fingers and the wide palms of his hands. It was

___

3. In French, *dimanche* means "Sunday."

Literary Element Irony *What is ironic about the prison's name?* **L**

Vocabulary

interject (in´ tər jekt´) *v.* to cut into with a comment

___

hardly revolutionary, minimalist[4] at best, but it was my favorite of all my attempted representations of him. It was the way I had imagined him in prison.

The last time I had seen my father? The previous night, before falling asleep. When we pulled into the pebbled driveway, densely lined with palm and banana trees, it was almost midnight. All the restaurants in the area were closed. There was nothing to do but shower and go to bed.

"It is like a paradise here," my father said when he saw the room. It had the same orange-and-green wallpaper as Salinas's office, and the plush green carpet matched the walls. "Look, Annie," he said, "it is like grass under our feet." He was always searching for a glimpse of paradise, my father.

He picked the bed closest to the bathroom, removed the top of his gray jogging suit, and unpacked his toiletries. Soon after, I heard him humming, as he always did, in the shower.

After he got into bed, I took a bath, pulled my hair back in a ponytail, and checked on the sculpture—just felt it a little bit through the bubble padding and carton wrapping to make sure it wasn't broken. Then I slipped under the covers, closed my eyes, and tried to sleep.

I pictured the client to whom I was delivering the sculpture: Gabrielle Fonteneau, a young woman about my age, an actress on a nationally syndicated[5] television series. My friend Jonas, the principal at the East Flatbush elementary school where I teach drawing to fifth graders, had shown her a picture of my "Father" sculpture, and, the way Jonas told it, Gabrielle Fonteneau had fallen in love with it and wished to offer it as a gift to her father on his birthday.

Since this was my first big sale, I wanted to make sure that the piece got there safely. Besides, I needed a weekend away, and both

___

4. A *minimalist* work of art is simple and spare.
5. A *nationally syndicated* television show is one that is shown nationwide.

Reading Strategy Comparing and Contrasting *How do the father and daughter react differently to the hotel decor?* **R**

EDWIDGE DANTICAT **53**

Answer: *Students may predict that the father has taken the sculpture.* **OL**

⭐ Viewing the Art

Pam Ingall's first art teacher was her father, who started Gonzaga University's Art Department. She later studied in Italy, at Gonzaga University itself, New York, and Seattle to perfect her technique. Ingalls often paints uncomplicated scenes and subjects, such as simple kitchen furniture or a bowl of fruit, but pours bold color and emotion into them. Ingalls has won over 60 awards for her art so far in her career, and is an active artist today. **AS**

---

my mother and I figured that my father, who watched a lot of television, both in his barbershop and at home, would enjoy meeting Gabrielle, too. But when I woke up the next morning my father was gone.

I showered, put on my driving jeans and a T-shirt, and waited. I watched a half hour of midmorning local news, smoked three mentholated cigarettes even though we were in a nonsmoking room, and waited some more. By noon, four hours had gone by. And it was only then that I noticed that the car was still there but the sculpture was gone.

I decided to start looking for my father: in the east garden, the west garden, the dining room, the exercise room, and in the few guest rooms cracked open while the maid changed the sheets; in the little convenience store at the Amoco gas station nearby; even in the Salvation Army thrift shop that from a distance seemed to blend into the interstate. All that waiting and looking actually took six hours, and I felt guilty for having held back so long before going to the front desk to ask, "Have you seen my father?"

I feel Officer Bo's fingers gently stroking my wrist. Up close he smells like fried eggs and gasoline, like breakfast at the Amoco. "I'll put the word out with the other boys," he says. "Salinas here will be in his office. Why don't you go back to your room in case he shows up there?"

Room with a View, 1999. Pam Ingalls.

I return to the room and lie in the unmade bed, jumping up when I hear the click from the electronic key in the door. It's only the housekeeper. I turn down the late-afternoon cleaning and call my mother at the beauty salon where she perms, presses, and braids hair, next door to my father's barbershop. But she isn't there. So I call my parents' house and leave the hotel number on their machine. "Please call me as soon as you can, Manman. It's about Papi."[6]

Once, when I was twelve, I overheard my mother telling a young woman who was about to get married how she and my father had first

---

Big Idea Encountering the Unexpected *Were you surprised that the sculpture is also missing?* **BI**

6. *Manman* and *Papi* are Haitian Creole words for "Mom" and "Dad."

Additional Support

Skills Practice

READING: Visualizing Have students read the scene describing the evening Annie's parents met. **Say:** Use sensory clues to form a mental picture of this scene. (Allow students time to practice.) Now, read the scene aloud without the sensory details. **Ask:** How does the elimination of sensory details affect your visualization of the scene? *(Students should note that they cannot tell what the father's face looks like nor can they imagine how he falls into the mother's arms. The scene has a different meaning without these descriptions.)* **OL**

met on the sidewalk in front of Fort Dimanche the evening that my father was released from jail. (At a dance, my father had fought with a soldier out of uniform who had him arrested and thrown in prison for a year.) That night, my mother was returning home from a sewing class when he stumbled out of the prison gates and collapsed into her arms, his face still bleeding from his last beating. They married and left for New York a year later. "We were like two seeds planted in a rock," my mother had told the young woman, "but somehow when our daughter, Annie, came we took root."

My mother soon calls me back, her voice staccato[7] with worry:

"Where is Papi?"

"I lost him."

"How you lost him?"

"He got up before I did and disappeared."

"How long he been gone?"

"Eight hours," I say, almost not believing myself that it's been that long. My mother is clicking her tongue and humming. I can see her sitting at the kitchen table, her eyes closed, her fingers sliding up and down her flesh-colored stockinged legs.

"You call police?"

"Yes."

"What they say?"

"To wait, that he'll come back."

My mother is thumping her fingers against the phone's mouthpiece, which is giving me a slight ache in my right ear.

"Tell me where you are," she says. "Two more hours and he's not there, call me, I come."

I dial Gabrielle Fonteneau's cellular-phone number. When she answers, her voice sounds just as it does on television, but more silken and seductive without the sitcom laugh track.

---

7. *Staccato* means "short and clipped."

Literary Element Irony *What is ironic about this situation?* **L1**

Reading Strategy Comparing and Contrasting *Compare and contrast the mother's and daughter's reactions to the disappearance.* **R**

"To think," my father once said while watching her show, "Haitian-born actresses on American television."

"And one of them wants to buy my stuff," I'd added.

When she speaks, Gabrielle Fonteneau sounds as if she's in a place with cicadas,[8] waterfalls, palm trees, and citronella candles to keep the mosquitoes away. I realize that I, too, am in such a place, but I can't appreciate it.

"So nice of you to come all this way to deliver the sculpture," she says. "Jonas tell you why I like it so much? My papa was a journalist in Port-au-Prince. In 1975,[9] he wrote a story criticizing the dictatorship, and he was arrested and put in jail."

"Fort Dimanche?"

"No, another one," she says. "Caserne. Papa kept track of days there by scraping lines with his fingernails on the walls of his cell. One of the guards didn't like this, so he pulled out all his fingernails with pliers."

I think of the photo spread I saw in the *Haitian Times* of Gabrielle Fonteneau and her parents in their living room in Tampa. Her father was described as a lawyer, his daughter's manager; her mother a court stenographer.[10] There was no hint in that photograph of what had once happened to the father. Perhaps people don't see anything in my father's face, either, in spite of his scars.

"We celebrate his birthday on the day he was released from prison," she says. "It's the hands I love so much in your sculpture. ⭐ They're so strong."

I am drifting away from Gabrielle Fonteneau when I hear her say, "So when will you get here? You have instruction from

---

8. *Cicadas* are large-winged insects that make a loud buzzing sound.
9. The year *1975* reveals a difference between the two fathers: although both lived during horrible political times, the narrator's father experienced the more brutal regime of "Papa Doc" Duvalier while Fonteneau's father was imprisoned under the regime of his son, "Baby Doc."
10. A *court stenographer* is a person who writes or types legal proceedings word for word.

Literary Element Irony *How is this information about Fonteneau's father an example of situational irony?* **L2**

EDWIDGE DANTICAT **55**

Teach

L1 Literary Element

Irony Answer: *A bleeding stranger stumbles out of a prison into the arms of a woman—and yet she marries him.* **OL**

R Reading Strategy

Comparing and Contrasting Answer: *The mother seems to feel a greater sense of urgency than does the daughter. She is ready to get on a plane if the father hasn't returned in two hours.* **OL**

L2 Literary Element

Irony Answer: *Based on the photo spread, the narrator had not expected that Fonteneau's father, a well-to-do lawyer, had a history of being tortured.* **OL**

⭐ Writer's Technique

Revealing Information A writer can reveal information through a story's exposition or through its dialogue. Have students examine Annie's telephone conversation with Gabrielle Fonteneau. **Ask:** Is this the most effective way for the author to reveal information about Gabrielle Fonteneau's father? (*For some, this may be a clever way of revealing necessary information. Others may find it heavy-handed. They may feel manipulated by the writer.*) **AS**

Objectives

- To analyze irony (SE)
- To compare and contrast (SE p. 51)
- To visualize a scene (TWE)

English Language Coach

Nonnative Speakers Explain to nonnative speakers that the dialogue shared between Annie and her mother does not reflect Standard English. Quotes like "How you lost him?" and "How long he been gone?" are included to capture the true speech of the character, and to heighten the story's believability. Have students point out examples of informal speech, and then ask them to rephrase the statements or questions using Standard English. **EL**

Teach

BI₁ **Big Idea**

Encountering the Unexpected Answer: *Her father is not with her at that moment. She has no way of knowing if he will be able to join her for the appointment at noon the next day.* **OL**

BI₂ **Big Idea**

Encountering the Unexpected Answer: *Her father's unusual behavior is making him seem vulnerable to her, so she remembers a time from long ago when she first realized that a parent could die.* **OL**

Jonas, right? Maybe we can make you lunch. My mother makes great *lanbi*."[11]

"I'll be there at twelve tomorrow," I say. "My father is with me. We are making a little weekend vacation of this."

My father loves museums. When he isn't working in his barbershop, he's often at the Brooklyn Museum. The ancient Egyptian rooms are his favorites.

"The Egyptians, they was like us," he likes to say. The Egyptians worshipped their gods in many forms and were often ruled by foreigners. The pharaohs were like the dictators he had fled. But what he admires most about the Egyptians is the way they mourned.

"Yes, they grieve," he'll say. He marvels at the mummification that went on for weeks, resulting in bodies that survived thousands of years.

My whole adult life, I have struggled to find the proper manner of sculpting my father, a man who learned about art by standing with me most of the Saturday mornings of my childhood, **mesmerized** by the golden masks, the shawabtis,[12] and Osiris, ruler of the underworld.

When my father finally appears in the hotel-room doorway, I am awed by him. Smiling, he looks like a much younger man, further bronzed after a long day at the beach.

"Annie, let your father talk to you." He walks over to my bed, bends down to unlace his sneakers. "*On ti koze*, a little chat."

"Where were you? Where is the sculpture, Papi?" I feel my eyes twitching, a nervous reaction I inherited from my mother.

---

11. *Lanbi* is a Creole dish made from conch, a mollusk that lives in a shell. (The shell is also called a conch.)
12. In ancient Egyptian belief, *shawabtis* are guardian spirits—miniature figures that would be placed in a coffin with the deceased and perform work for the person through the afterlife.

Big Idea Encountering the Unexpected *How is this different from what you might expect the narrator to say?* **BI₁**

Vocabulary

mesmerize (mez′ mə rīz′) *v.* to hypnotize

"That's why we need to chat," he says. "I have objections with your statue."

He pulls off his sneakers and rubs his feet with both hands.

"I don't want you to sell that statue," he says. Then he picks up the phone and calls my mother.

"I know she called you," he says to her in Creole. "Her head is so hot. She panics so easily: I was just out walking, thinking."

I hear my mother lovingly scolding him and telling him not to leave me again. When he hangs up the phone, he picks up his sneakers and puts them back on.

"Where is the sculpture?" My eyes are twitching so hard now that I can barely see.

"Let us go," he says. "I will take you to it."

As my father maneuvers the car out of the parking lot, I tell myself he might be ill, mentally ill, even though I have never detected anything wrong beyond his prison nightmares. I am trying to piece it together, this sudden yet familiar picture of a parent's **vulnerability.** When I was ten years old and my father had the chicken pox, I overheard him say to a friend on the phone, "The doctor tells me that at my age chicken pox can kill a man." This was the first time I realized that my father could die. I looked up the word "kill" in every dictionary and encyclopedia at school, trying to comprehend what it meant, that my father could be **eradicated** from my life.

My father stops the car on the side of the highway near a man-made lake, one of those artificial creations of the modern tropical city, with curved stone benches surrounding stagnant water. There is little light to see by except a half-moon. He heads toward one of the benches, and I sit down next to him, letting my hands dangle between my legs.

"Is this where the sculpture is?" I ask.

Big Idea Encountering the Unexpected *Why do you think the narrator has this memory at this particular moment?* **BI₂**

Vocabulary

vulnerability (vul′ nər ə bil′ ə tē) *n.* state of being open to harm, damage, or illness
eradicate (i rad′ ə kāt′) *v.* to do away with completely

Additional Support

Skills Practice

LITERARY ELEMENT: Dialect Point out this sentiment expressed by Annie's father: "The Egyptians, they was like us." **Ask:** Is this statement grammatically correct? (*No; "was" should be "were."*) **Ask:** Why would the author include a grammatically incorrect statement here?

(*The author wants to accurately portray the character.*) Explain that the father's speech is a dialect. Have students pair up and list examples of the dialect they use in everyday life. (*Students may list examples of intimate sayings or slang.*) **OL**

"In the water," he says.

"O.K.," I say. "But please know this about yourself. You are an especially harsh critic."

My father tries to smother a smile.

"Why?" I ask.

He scratches his chin. Anger is a wasted emotion, I've always thought. My parents got angry at unfair politics in New York or Port-au-Prince, but they never got angry at my grades—at all the B's I got in everything but art classes—or at my not eating vegetables or occasionally vomiting my daily spoonful of cod-liver oil. Ordinary anger, I thought, was a weakness. But now I am angry. I want to hit my father, beat the craziness out of his head.

"Annie," he says. "When I first saw your statue, I wanted to be buried with it, to take it with me into the other world."

"Like the ancient Egyptians," I say.

He smiles, grateful, I think, that I still recall his passions.

"Annie," he asks, "do you remember when I read to you from *The Book of the Dead?*"

"Are you dying?" I say to my father. "Because I can only forgive you for this if you are. You can't take this back."

He is silent for a moment too long.

I think I hear crickets, though I cannot imagine where they might be. There is the highway, the cars racing by, the half-moon, the lake dug up from the depths of the ground, the allee[13] of royal palms beyond. And there is me and my father.

"You remember the judgment of the dead," my father says, "when the heart of a person is put on a scale. If it is heavy, then this person cannot enter the other world."

It is a **testament** to my upbringing that I am not yelling at him.

"I don't deserve a statue," he says, even while looking like one: the Madonna of

---

13. An *allee* is a tree-lined walkway.

Literary Element Irony *Relate the narrator's anger to situational irony. Remember that her father has information that she does not.* **L**

Vocabulary

testament (tes′ tə mənt) n. proof of or tribute to

Palm Trees, 1997. Patti Mollica. Oil on canvas. Collection of the Artist. ★

Humility,[14] for example, contemplating[15] her losses in the dust.

"Annie, your father was the hunter," he says. "He was not the prey."

"What are you saying?" I ask.

"We have a proverb," he says. "'One day for the hunter, one day for the prey.' Your father was the hunter. He was not the prey." Each word is hard won as it leaves my father's mouth, balanced like those hearts on the Egyptian scale.

---

14. The *Madonna of Humility* refers to a particular representation of the Virgin Mary, the mother of Christ, in a humble attitude.

15. Here *contemplating* means "thoughtfully considering."

EDWIDGE DANTICAT **57**

Teach

L Literary Element

Irony Answer: *The narrator expected to take a nice vacation with her father and sell a sculpture to a famous TV actress. Instead, events have taken a peculiar and frustrating turn. Her frustration over her father's unusual behavior has changed into anger because she can't understand his motives.* **OL**

★ Viewing the Art

Ask students to think about the relationship between the narrator's father and tropical settings, like the one depicted in the painting. Have students discuss whether or not the father would have come to terms with his feelings and discarded the statue if the story were to take place in Brooklyn, where the characters live currently. **Ask:** How might this environment unlock the father's deep-seated feelings? *(Students may say that it reminds him of his homeland of Haiti and what life was like when he was younger. in doing so, he is able to reflect on his life as a whole and the purpose of it.)* **AS**

Differentiated Instruction

Gifted and Talented The narrator's comprehension of her father's mortality at age ten affected her understanding of her own life. Proficient readers will understand that this memory's significance is closely tied to the plot. Have students explore this in a short paragraph. *(Possible answers: Annie discovered at a young age that her father was capable of dying. She was uncomfortable with the thought and probably pushed the thought away. His strange behavior forces her to reconsider his mortality.)* **AL**

Objectives
• To understand irony (SE)
• To identify dialect (TWE)

Encountering the Unexpected Answer: *He is not who she once thought he was. His prison story is a lie. He was a torturer, not a prisoner.* **OL**

R1 **Reading Strategy**

Comparing and Contrasting Answer: *He feels deep remorse for what he did in the past.* **OL**

R2 **Reading Strategy**

Comparing and Contrasting Answer: *The Fonteneau family is well to do. The parents are a lawyer and a court stenographer. They live in an elegant home and visit oceanfront property in Haiti each year. In contrast, the narrator's parents are a barber and a hairdresser.* **OL**

"Annie, when I saw your mother the first time, I was not just out of prison. I was a guard in the prison. One of the prisoners I was questioning had scratched me with a piece of tin. I went out to the street in a rage, blood all over my face. I was about to go back and do something bad, very bad. But instead comes your mother. I smash into her, and she asks me what I am doing there. I told her I was just let go from prison and she held my face and cried in my hair."

"And the nightmares, what are they?"

"Of what I, your father, did to others."

"Does Manman know?"

"I told her, Annie, before we married."

I am the one who drives back to the hotel. In the car, he says, "Annie, I am still your father, still your mother's husband. I would not do these things now."

When we get back to the hotel room, I leave a message for Officer Bo, and another for Manager Salinas, telling them that I have found my father. He has slipped into the bathroom, and now he runs the shower at full force. When it seems that he is never coming out, I call my mother at home in Brooklyn.

"How do you love him?" I whisper into the phone.

My mother is tapping her fingers against the mouthpiece.

"I don't know, Annie," she whispers back, as though there is a chance that she might also be overheard by him. "I feel only that you and me, we saved him. When I met him, it made him stop hurting the people. This is how I see it. He was a seed thrown into a rock, and you and me, Annie, we helped push a flower out of a rock."

When I get up the next morning, my father is already dressed. He is sitting on the edge of his bed with his back to me, his head bowed, his face buried in his hands. If I were sculpting him, I would make him a praying mantis,[16] crouching motionless, seeming to pray while waiting to strike.

With his back still turned, my father says, "Will you call those people and tell them you have it no more, the statue?"

"We were invited to lunch there. I believe we should go."

He raises his shoulders and shrugs. It is up to me.

The drive to Gabrielle Fonteneau's house seems longer than the twenty-four hours it took to drive from New York: the ocean, the palms along the road, the highway so imposingly neat. My father fills in the silence in the car by saying, "So now you know, Annie, why your mother and me, we have never returned home."

The Fonteneaus' house is made of bricks of white coral, on a cul-de-sac with a row of banyans[17] separating the two sides of the street.

Silently, we get out of the car and follow a concrete path to the front door. Before we can knock, an older woman walks out. Like Gabrielle, she has stunning midnight-black eyes and skin the color of sorrel,[18] with spiralling curls brushing the sides of her face. When Gabrielle's father joins her, I realize where Gabrielle Fonteneau gets her height. He is more than six feet tall.

Mr. Fonteneau extends his hands, first to my father and then to me. They're large, twice the

> "Your father was the hunter. He was not the prey."

---

16. A *praying mantis* is a large green insect that feeds on other insects. It carries its forelegs in a position that resembles hands in prayer.
17. *Banyans* are fig trees.
18. *Sorrel* is brown-orange.

Reading Strategy Comparing and Contrasting *How does this image contrast with how the father is actually feeling?* **R1**

Big Idea Encountering the Unexpected *What is the narrator learning about her father?* **BI**

Reading Strategy Comparing and Contrasting *What contrasts are there between the Fonteneau and Bienaime families?* **R2**

Additional Support

Skills Practice

SPEAKING: Reciting Dialogue A literary experience can be enhanced by hearing the words in a story spoken aloud. When a story is verbalized the emotion found in its exposition or dialogue is internalized differently. Place students in pairs. Have them recite the dialogue between the father and daughter. Require students to relay a written or oral comment about the effects of oral reading. (*Possible responses: I was able to better understand the father because I felt his feeling through my voice; I felt even worse for the daughter after having to ask "why?"*) **OL**

The Garden, Giverny, 1902. Claude Monet. Oil on canvas, 89.5 x 92.3 cm. Oesterreichische Galerie im Belvedere, Vienna.

Viewing the Art: How does the place shown here suit the description of the Fonteneau's home? ★

size of my father's. The fingernails have grown black, thick, densely dark, as though the past had nestled itself there in black ink.

We move slowly through the living room, which has a cathedral ceiling and walls covered with Haitian paintings—Obin, Hyppolite, Tiga, Duval-Carrié.[19] Out on the back terrace, which towers over a nursery of orchids and red dracaenas,[20] a table is set for lunch.

Mr. Fonteneau asks my father where his family is from in Haiti, and my father lies. In the past, I thought he always said a different province because he had lived in all those places, but I realize now that he says this to keep anyone from tracing him, even though twenty-six years and eighty more pounds shield him from the threat of immediate recognition.

When Gabrielle Fonteneau makes her entrance, in an off-the-shoulder ruby dress, my father and I stand up.

"Gabrielle," she says, when she shakes hands with my father, who blurts out spontaneously, "You are one of the flowers of Haiti."

---

19. *Obin, Hyppolite, Tiga,* and *Duval-Carrié* are Haitian artists.
20. *Dracaenas* are tropical shrubs, trees, or houseplants.

Gabrielle Fonteneau tilts her head coyly.

"We eat now," Mrs. Fonteneau announces, leading me and my father to a bathroom to wash up before the meal. Standing before a pink seashell-shaped sink, my father and I dip our hands under the faucet flow.

"Annie," my father says, "we always thought, your mother and me, that children could raise their parents higher. Look at what this girl has done for her parents."

During the meal of conch, plantains,[21] and mushroom rice, Mr. Fonteneau tried to draw my father into conversation. He asks when my father was last in Haiti.

"Twenty-six years," my father replies.

"No going back for you?" asks Mrs. Fonteneau.

"I have not had the opportunity," my father says.

---

21. *Plantains,* a type of banana, are a staple food of the tropics.

Reading Strategy Comparing and Contrasting *What similarities and differences are there between Gabrielle and the narrator?* R₃

Literary Element Irony *What is ironic about this statement?* L

Teach

R₃ Reading Strategy

Comparing and Contrasting Answer: *Gabrielle is a movie actress; the narrator is a drawing teacher and artist. Each is an only daughter. Gabrielle has apparently raised her parents' standard of living, while Annie has not had great financial success. Both are concerned about the facts of their fathers' pasts.* **OL**

L Literary Element

Irony Answer: *The father knows he cannot return to Haiti. He is known as a torturer. Others in the room (except his daughter) don't know this.* **OL**

★ Viewing the Art

Answer: *The painting shows a place that is secluded and private. It appears that the person who owns the garden must be well-off in order to maintain such a property. The Fonteneaus' home also appears to be surrounded by a lush landscape in a private place.* **AS**

Differentiated Instruction

Understanding Sequence In a few paragraphs, the story moves from the hotel room to Gabrielle Fonteneau's house. Some readers may be baffled by such quick transitions. Explain that words like "then" and "next" might signal changes in time, but that they are not always necessary. When the author jumps ahead without giving much detail, readers must use their own experiences to fill in missing events. Have students fill in possible events between the hotel scene and the car ride. (*Annie and her father argue; Annie calls her mother to talk.*) **BL**

Objectives
• To compare and contrast (SE)
• To recite dialogue (TWE)

R **Reading Strategy**

Comparing and Contrasting Answer: *Both see sculpture as way to please their fathers. Each sees it as way to show understanding of her father's past.* **OL**

BI **Big Idea**

Encountering the Unexpected Answer: *Students may say it is not surprising that the truth came out eventually.* **OL**

CheckPoint

Use the CheckPoint questions on Presentation Plus! to check students' mastery of the selection. These questions can be used with interactive response keypads for immediate student feedback.

"We go back every year to a beautiful place overlooking the ocean in the mountains in Jacmel," says Mrs. Fonteneau.

"Have you ever been to Jacmel?"[22] Gabrielle Fonteneau asks me.

I shake my head no.

"We are fortunate," Mrs. Fonteneau says, "that we have another place to go where we can say our rain is sweeter, our dust is lighter, our beach is prettier."

"So now we are tasting rain and weighing dust," Mr. Fonteneau says, and laughs.

"There is nothing like drinking the sweet juice from a green coconut you fetched yourself from your own tree, or sinking your hand in sand from the beach in your own country," Mrs. Fonteneau says.

"When did you ever climb a coconut tree?" Mr. Fonteneau says, teasing his wife.

I am imagining what my father's nightmares might be. Maybe he dreams of dipping his hands in the sand on a beach in his own country and finds that what he comes up with is a fist full of blood.

After lunch, my father asks if he can have a closer look at the Fonteneaus' back-yard garden. While he's taking the tour, I confess to Gabrielle Fonteneau that I don't have the sculpture.

"My father threw it away," I say.

Gabrielle Fonteneau frowns.

"I don't know," she says. "Was there even a sculpture at all? I trust Jonas, but maybe you fooled him, too. Is this some scam, to get into our home?"

"There was a sculpture," I say. "Jonas will tell you that. My father just didn't like it, so he threw it away."

She raises her perfectly arched eyebrows, perhaps out of concern for my father's sanity or my own.

"I'm really disappointed," she says. "I wanted it for a reason. My father goes home

---

22. *Jacmel* is a small, picturesque beach town on Haiti's southern peninsula.

when he looks at a piece of art. He goes home deep inside himself. For a long time he used to hide his fingers from people. It's like he was making a fist all the time. I wanted to give him this thing so that he knows we understand what happened to him."

"I am truly sorry," I say.

Over her shoulders, I see her parents guiding my father through rows of lemongrass. I want to promise her that I will make her another sculpture, one especially modeled on her father. But I don't know when I will be able to work on anything again. I have lost my subject, the father I loved as well as pitied.

In the garden, I watch my father snap a white orchid from its stem and hold it out toward Mrs. Fonteneau, who accepts it with a nod of thanks.

"I don't understand," Gabrielle Fonteneau says. "You did all this for nothing."

I wave to my father to signal that we should perhaps leave now, and he comes toward me, the Fonteneaus trailing slowly behind him.

With each step he rubs the scars on the side of his face.

Perhaps the last person my father harmed had dreamed this moment into my father's future—his daughter seeing those marks, like chunks of warm plaster still clinging to a cast, and questioning him about them, giving him a chance to either lie or tell the truth. After all, we have the proverb, as my father would say: "Those who give the blows may try to forget, but those who carry the scars must remember." ❧

Reading Strategy Comparing and Contrasting *When it comes to the sculpture, how are Gabrielle's motives and the narrator's motives alike?* **R**

Big Idea Encountering the Unexpected *Is the narrator saying that what happened in this story is a surprise—or no surprise at all?* **BI**

Additional Support

Skills Practice

RESEARCH: Proverbs Note that all cultures have proverbs that express common sentiments. Recite the story's concluding proverb. Ask students to analyze its meaning. *(People left unscarred have an easier time forgetting than those who bear a permanent reminder.)* **Ask:** Does your family have a saying that expresses a similar idea? Ask students who say "yes" to state the proverb. Assign students the task of researching proverbs. Ask them to find a proverb that several cultures share. Have them report their findings to the class. **OL**

RESPONDING AND THINKING CRITICALLY

Respond

1. Do you feel more sympathy for the narrator or her father? Explain.

Recall and Interpret

2. (a)Why are the narrator and her father going to Florida? (b)Name two or more reasons why this is such an important trip for the narrator.

3. (a)What happens to the narrator's father after they reach the hotel? (b)What are the father's motives for his actions?

4. (a)In your own words, tell what the sculpture of the father looks like. (b)Explain how the pose in which the narrator has depicted her father unexpectedly shows him as he is now, rather than as he was in his prison days.

Analyze and Evaluate

5. (a)Why do you think the father never told his daughter the truth before? (b)What is the effect of telling the truth now?

6. Once the sculpture is gone, there is no reason to go to the Fonteneau home. Why do you think the author includes this scene?

7. How do the references to the ancient Egyptians and the Book of the Dead make the story richer?

Connect

8. **Big Idea** Encountering the Unexpected
What do you think prompted the father's unexpected confession?

YOU'RE THE CRITIC: Different Viewpoints

Style and Substance

Critics have applauded Edwidge Danticat both for what she says and how well she says it. Read the two excerpts of literary criticism below. The first quotation is about Danticat's style: the choices she makes about words, sentences, paragraphs, and more that make her writing all her own. The second quotation is about her style as well as her underlying themes.

> *The slow accumulation of details pinpointing the past's effects on the present make for powerful reading . . . and Danticat is a crafter of subtle, gorgeous sentences and scenes.*
> —Publishers Weekly

> *Danticat allows her characters (and readers) no answers, no resolutions. She's a master at capturing the inarticulate sorrow and bafflement that evil inspires.*
> —Ron Charles, The Christian Science Monitor

Group Activity Work with classmates to discuss and answer the following questions.

1. (a)Restate the quotation from *Publishers Weekly* in your own words. (b)Find two or more sentences or scenes from the story that support or rebut the critic's comment. Explain the reasons for your choices.

2. Discuss the quotation from Ron Charles. Then talk about the ending of "The Book of the Dead" to determine whether there are any answers or resolutions. Reach a group consensus of agreement or disagreement with the critic. Give reasons for your opinion.

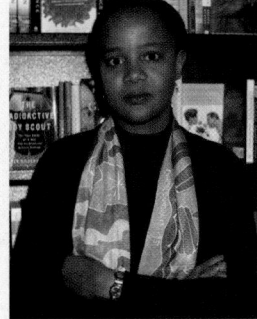

EDWIDGE DANTICAT **61**

Assess

1. The daughter has learned something terrible about her father, but her father has lived with a horrible truth for years.

2. (a) To transport a sculpture the narrator made (b) It is her first major sale and is being sold to a famous client. Also, trip is opportunity to spend time with father.

3. (a) He disappears. (b) The sculpture caused a crisis; he realizes he must confess his past to daughter and wants to get rid of the sculpture.

4. (a)Shows father crouching on the ground, looking down at his hands (b) The blood might show someone who cannot erase his bad deeds.

5. (a) He was ashamed and spared her the truth. (b) Daughter feels lied to all her life.

6. Contrasts the Fonteneau family with narrator's. Also shows ambiguity by daughter accepting hospitality without revealing entire truth.

7. Father's interest in Egyptian art and texts creates complexity; not just cardboard villain.

8. Answers will vary. A long journey gives people time for reflection. The sculpture honored the father; it was being sold, which extended the lie beyond the boundaries of the Bienaime family. This pushed the father to confess.

Group Activity

1. (a) Danticat builds up details slowly to show how the past affects the present. She creates well-written sentences and believable scenes. (b) The first scene with the hotel manager and police officer is powerful. "When she speaks, Gabrielle Fonteneau sounds as if she's in a place with cicadas, waterfalls, palm trees, and citronella candles to keep the mosquitoes away" might be a "gorgeous" sentence.

2. Students will likely agree that the story does not have a clear-cut resolution. It is clear that guilt will probably haunt the father for the rest of his life, but perhaps he will achieve some salvation through his daughter's forgiveness.

Assess

Literary Element

1. Even relationships between family members can hold shocking and unexpected surprises.

2. Answers will vary. The sculpture's fate at the bottom of the lake might be seen as ironic. However, it may be considered a fitting place, with the sculpture representing father's past deeds submerged beneath his heavy heart.

Review: Conflict

Conflicts for the narrator: telling the officer about her father's past in prison (internal), reacting to the news of the sculpture (external and internal), reacting to the truth about her father (internal), what to do about the Fonteneaus (external). Conflicts for the father: hiding his past from everyone but his wife (internal), his feelings about the sculpture (internal), how to prevent the sculpture from getting into the Fonteneaus' hands (external). Critique student charts based on the following criteria:

- Do students include at least four examples of conflict?
- Do students cite the type of conflict being demonstrated?

Literary Element Irony

Writers sometimes use **irony** to express an idea without having to spell it out for readers or add a moral to the story. For example, Danticat sets up a situation in which both her narrator and the readers are in the dark about the father's past. The **situational irony** is that a trip to sell a sculpture that honors the father's past leads to a revelation that the father's past is not at all honorable.

1. What do the ironies in the story suggest about relationships between individuals?

2. Would you describe the fate of the sculpture as ironic? Explain your answer.

Review: Conflict

As you learned on page 36, there are two basic types of **conflict**—internal and external. An **internal conflict** takes place within the mind of a character who is torn between opposing feelings, desires, or goals. An **external conflict** exists when a character struggles against some outside force, such as another person, nature, society, or fate.

Partner Activity Meet with a partner to discuss the conflict in the story. Make a chart like the one below to list two or more conflicts that the narrator faces in the story. Then list two or more conflicts that the father faces.

Conflict	Internal	External
Not reporting her father's disappearance right away	X	

Reading Strategy Comparing and Contrasting

Review the Venn diagram you made to compare the two families in this story. Focus on any details you recorded about each father's actions.

1. How were the situations that the fathers faced in Haiti alike and different?

2. Does the author imply any reasons why one father might have acted differently from the other?

Vocabulary Practice

Practice with Context Clues Determine the best meaning for each boldfaced word.

1. That's not how I see it!" Rob **interjected**.
   a. replied   b. interrupted   c. agreed

2. **Mesmerized** by her actions, the children stared at the clown.
   a. hypnotized   b. frightened   c. disturbed

3. Aisha had to miss the party because of her **vulnerability** to infection.
   a. likeness   b. willingness   c. openness

4. Scientists hope to **eradicate** the disease by 2020.
   a. get   b. wipe out   c. study

5. The new clinic was a **testament** to determination and hard work.
   a. barrier   b. tribute   c. disappointment

Academic Vocabulary

Here are two words from the vocabulary list on page R82.

vision (vizh′ ən) n. a thought or idea created by one's imagination

diminish (di min′ ish) v. to become less over time

Practice and Apply
1. What **visions** might the narrator's father have of future encounters with his past?
2. Do you think the narrator's shock over what her father has told her will **diminish** over time? Explain.

Reading Strategy

1. Both were victims of cruel dictators, but Bienaime became a tool of the dictatorship.

2. Bienaime may have been poorer, less educated, and more desperate. He became a barber in the U.S. Fonteneau became a lawyer.

Vocabulary

1. b   2. a   3. c   4. b   5. b

Academic Vocabulary

1. Annie's father may have visions of meeting his victims.

2. It might diminish, just as the impact of any horrible thing diminishes over time.

Writing About Literature

Analyze Plot The plot of "The Book of the Dead" does not begin at the earliest event and go neatly forward in time to reach the most recent event. Instead, it uses flashbacks to return the reader to the past and to explain events in the present. Write a brief essay in which you identify the flashbacks and explain how they enrich the story, explain events, or give insights into the characters.

Begin your prewriting by creating a working thesis that gives one or more reasons for the flashbacks, such as "Danticat uses flashbacks in 'The Book of the Dead' in order to <reason 1> and <reason 2>." Include your thesis in your introduction. Then, as you draft, structure your body paragraphs in this way:

> - *Topic Sentence with Reason:* _____
>   _____
> - *Support from Story:* _____
>   _____
> - *Explanation:* _____
>   _____

Conclude your essay by restating your main points, but do not repeat them word for word. If you wish, you can also add a fresh concluding thought.

After you complete your draft, have a peer read it and suggest revisions. Then proofread and edit your work for errors in spelling, grammar, and punctuation.

Literature Groups

Will Annie and her father ever resolve their conflict? As a group, map that conflict by discussing all the ways it has already separated them in this story and by speculating on all the ways in which it will affect their daily lives in the future. Then examine the relationship between the father and daughter that appeared to exist before he revealed the truth about his past. Use this information to make a prediction about how and when the characters might resolve the conflict or why they are doomed never to resolve it.

Danticat's Language and Style

Handling Dialogue Much of "The Book of the Dead" is told through dialogue. The dialogue tells what is happening, and it also provides a great deal of insight into the characters and their world. As you read this passage, note how the use of quotation marks, paragraphing, and speaker tags helps you understand who is speaking and follow the conversation.

> "How you lost him?"
>
> "He got up before I did and disappeared."
>
> "How long he been gone?"
>
> "Eight hours," I say. . . .

The words "I say" are a speaker tag. A speaker tag identifies who is speaking, often by providing a pronoun or noun and a verb, such as "he added," "she whispered," or "Annie replied." As you can see from the passage, however, not all dialogue requires a speaker tag to identify it. When there is no speaker tag, a reader must carefully watch for quotation marks and paragraph changes to identify changing speakers.

Activity List five or more examples of dialogue from the story. For each one, identify all the clues (quotation marks, paragraphing, and speaker tags) that help the reader know who is speaking.

Revising Check

Dialogue The most common error writers make when they quote dialogue in essays is forgetting the quotation marks, especially the final or end quotation mark. Be sure to proofread your analysis of the use of flashbacks for this easy-to-fix error.

 Web Activities For eFlashcards, Selection Quick Checks, and other Web activities, go to www.glencoe.com.

EDWIDGE DANTICAT **63**

Assess

Writing About Literature

Use these criteria when evaluating students' writing:
- Does the essay identify the flashbacks in the story?
- Does the essay explain how flashbacks add or detract from the story?

Literature Groups

Accept all reasonable answers. Students may say that the conflict will separate Annie and her father because
- Annie will resent that he destroyed her sculpture.
- Annie will not trust her father because he was dishonest.
- Annie will feel pity toward her father.
- Annie's father will feel guilty and ashamed of his past actions.

Danticat's Language and Style

Students might offer these examples and clues:
"Where are you and your daddy from, Ms. Bienaime?" he asks. (quotation marks, new paragraph, speaker tag)
"It is like a paradise here," my father said. . . . (quotation marks, new paragraph, speaker tag)
"Yes." (quotation marks, new paragraph)
"And one of them wants to buy my stuff," I'd added. (quotation marks, new paragraph, speaker tag)
"Of what I, your father, did to others." (quotation marks, new paragraph)

Revising Check

Encourage students to identify all clues to who is speaking in Danticat's story. This will help them to better understand how to handle dialogue and quotation marks. Ask students to properly identify the terms "speaking tags," "quotation marks," and "paraphrasing."

Literature Online

Web Activities Have students access the Web site for interactive activities that will help them assess their understanding of the selection.

Focus

BELLRINGER

Bellringer Options
Selection Focus Transparency 3
Daily Language Transparency 7
Or write the word *astrologer* on the chalkboard. **Ask:** What does an astrologer do? Write students' responses on the chalkboard. Discuss what type of person might work as an astrologer. Have students consider this astrologer's character as they read.

Author Search To expand students' appreciation of R. K. Narayan, have them access the Web site for additional information and resources.

An Astrologer's Day

MEET R. K. NARAYAN

As a young boy, R. K. Narayan (nä rä′ yan) had absolutely no use for school. "Going to school seemed to be a never-ending nuisance each day," he once wrote. Narayan much preferred spending time with his pet monkey, who liked to hang by its tail from the roof, and his pet peacock, who acted as the family watchdog. Despite his aversion to school, Narayan's family placed a high value on education. But Narayan never changed his opinion that school was too serious. Today, Narayan's stories are regularly assigned to students in schools around the world. Considering his unenthusiastic view of formal education, Narayan may have enjoyed this irony.

"I want a story to be entertaining, enjoyable, and illuminating in some way."

—R. K. Narayan

The Decision to be a Writer Rasipuram Krishnaswami Narayan was born in Madras, India, and raised by his grandmother. After graduating from college, he turned to fiction writing as a career. He chose to write in English, a language that he was fond of and knew well. "English is a very adaptable language. And it's so transparent it can take on the tint of any country." Narayan did not find immediate success as a writer and once said that writing "was all frustration and struggle for more than fifteen years." His first novel, *Swami and Friends*, was finally published in 1935 with the help of British writer Graham Greene. Narayan went on to publish numerous other novels, several short story collections, and other works.

A Literary Voice of India Narayan is probably best known as the creator of Malgudi, a fictional South Indian village that has been called a "zany, eccentric and, at the same time, true to life world." It is the setting for almost all of Narayan's novels and short stories, including "An Astrologer's Day." Of his invented village, Narayan remarked, "Malgudi was an earth-shaking discovery for me, because I had no mind for facts and things like that, which would be necessary in writing about . . . any real place." Narayan's stories about Malgudi are often comic considerations of individuals trying to find peace in a turbulent world.

Reviewers consistently use the adjectives *simple*, *elegant*, *natural*, *graceful*, *sympathetic*, *funny*, and *ironic* to describe Narayan's writing. Critic Judith Freeman writes that Narayan "takes a Western reader into the very heart of an Indian village. . . . The foreignness of the setting, rituals and traditions may seem to us exotic, but the underlying humanity of Narayan's dramas can't fail to strike a familiar chord."

R. K. Narayan was born in 1906 and died in 2001.

LiteratureOnline Author Search For more about R. K. Narayan, go to www.glencoe.com.

64 UNIT 1 THE SHORT STORY

Selection Skills

Literary Elements
• Description (SE pp. 65, 67–70)
• Irony (SE p. 70)
• Characterization (TWE p. 66)

An Astrologer's Day

Reading Skills
• Analyzing Cultural Context (SE pp. 65–67, 71)

Vocabulary Skills
• Word Origins (SE pp. 65, 71)
• Academic Vocabulary (SE p. 71)

Writing Skills/Grammar
• Analysis of Conflict (SE p. 71)
• Creating Dialogue (TWE p. 68)

Connecting to the Short Story

If you could, would you want to know your future? In Narayan's short story, a man asks to have his future told. Before you read the story, think about the following questions:

- Why might people want to know their futures?
- In your opinion, how much of one's future is decided by the choices one makes, by fate, or by coincidence?

Building Background

Astrology is a form of fortune telling. It originated in ancient Babylonia and has been practiced in many cultures, including those of ancient Rome, Greece, India, and China. Some astrologers claim the ability to foretell an individual's future by drawing and studying a chart called a *horoscope*. A horoscope shows the configuration of the planets and stars at the moment of an individual's birth. This configuration supposedly influences that person's life. Those who believe in astrology may rely on their astrologers to counsel them on major decisions. Astronomers and other scientists, however, maintain that the configuration of heavenly bodies has nothing to do with human destiny.

Setting Purposes for Reading

Big Idea Encountering the Unexpected

As you read, think about what is revealed when a man asks about his future.

Literary Element Description

Description is writing that gives a carefully detailed portrayal of a person, place, thing, or event. Writers often use details that appeal to the five senses—hearing, sight, taste, touch, and smell—to help the reader experience what the characters are experiencing. Good descriptive writing helps the reader to understand what is being described and to imagine the characters. As you read the story, use the descriptive details to visualize the setting and the characters.

- See Literary Terms Handbook, p. R4.

Literature Online **Interactive Literary Elements Handbook** To review or learn more about the literary elements, go to www.glencoe.com.

OBJECTIVES
In studying this selection, you will focus on the following:
- understanding description
- analyzing cultural context
- writing to analyze conflict

Reading Strategy Analyzing Cultural Context

When you **analyze cultural context,** you pay attention to the details that reveal the setting, dress, speech, mannerisms, and behaviors characteristic of a particular culture at a particular time in history. As you read the short story, look for details that help you better understand the customs of India and its people in the 1940s, which is when this story probably takes place. Read the footnotes for help in understanding some of the cultural references in the story.

....

Reading Tip: Taking Notes As you read, take notes about cultural details that relate to the setting, characters, and main events in the plot.

....

Vocabulary

enhance (en hans´) *v.* to make greater, as in beauty or value; p. 66 *Wearing too much makeup may detract from your beauty, not enhance it.*

impetuous (im pech´ o͞o əs) *adj.* rushing headlong into things; rash; p. 68 *It was an impetuous decision, made without any thought.*

paraphernalia (par´ ə fər nāl´ yə) *n.* things used in a particular activity; equipment; p. 68 *The traveling chef carried his own pots, pans, and other cooking paraphernalia.*

piqued (pēkt) *adj.* aroused in anger or resentment; offended; p. 68 *The director was piqued by the play's disastrous reviews.*

incantation (in´ kan tā´ shən) *n.* words spoken in casting a spell; p. 69 *In Shakespeare's Macbeth, witches utter an eerie incantation.*

Vocabulary Tip: Word Origins The origin, or history, of most words can be found in a dictionary.

Focus

Summary

An astrologer who knows little about fortune-telling is about to end an ordinary day. After leaving his village under mysterious circumstances, he has managed to earn a living by telling his customers what they want to hear. When he tries to lure in one last customer, he makes a wager with a man who suspects that he is a fake.

V Vocabulary

Vocabulary File Say: Add these words and definitions to your vocabulary file. For each word, include a sentence that gives you an example of how to use the word. **OL** Students with English language needs should include the pronunciations of these words in their files. **EL**

Literary Elements Have students access the Web site to improve their understanding of description.

R. K. NARAYAN **65**

Selection Resources

Print Materials
- Unit 1 Resources (Fast File), pp. 33–35
- Leveled Vocabulary Development, p. 5
- Selection and Unit Assessments, pp. 11–12
- Selection Quick Checks, p. 6

Transparencies
- Bellringer Options Transparencies:
  Selection Focus Transparency 3
  Daily Language Practice Transparency 7
- Literary Elements Transparency 11

Technology
- TeacherWorks Plus™ CD-ROM
- StudentWorks Plus™ CD-ROM
- Presentation Plus!™ CD-ROM
- Literature Online, glencoe.com
- Online Student Edition, mhln.com
- Exam*View*® Assessment Suite CD-ROM
- Vocabulary PuzzleMaker CD-ROM
- Listening Library, disc 1 track 6

Encountering the Unexpected Answer: *The astrologer gives advice based on what his customers reveal about themselves and on his knowledge of what troubles most people. He tricks his customers into believing he has a special ability to read their future.* **OL**

R1 **Reading Strategy**

Analyzing Cultural Context
Answer: *He chooses a bright, saffron-colored turban, which is a traditional Indian headdress but in a flashy color, to attract attention, appear unconventional, and fit people's expectations of how an astrologer should look.*
Ask: What would have happened to the astrologer's business if he had worn a suit or dressed in more common attire? *(His customers would have doubted his authenticity and probably would not have done business with him.)* **OL**

Readability Scores
Dale-Chall: 9.2
DRP: 62
Lexile: 940

An Astrologer's Day

R. K. Narayan

Indian Star Chart, ca. 1840
By permission of the British Library

Punctually at midday he opened his bag and spread out his professional equipment, which consisted of a dozen cowrie[1] shells, a square piece of cloth with obscure mystic charts on it, a notebook and a bundle of palmyra writing. His forehead was resplendent with sacred ash and vermilion,[2] and his eyes sparkled with a sharp abnormal gleam which was really an outcome of a continual searching look for customers, but which his simple clients took to be a prophetic light and felt comforted. The power of his eyes was considerably **enhanced** by their position—placed as they were between the painted forehead and the dark whiskers which streamed down his cheeks: even a half-wit's eyes would sparkle in such a setting. To crown the effect he wound a saffron-colored[3] turban around his head. This color scheme never failed. People were attracted to him as bees are attracted to cosmos or dahlia stalks. He sat under the boughs of a spreading tamarind tree which flanked a path running through the Town Hall Park. It was a remarkable place in many ways: a surging crowd was always moving up and down this narrow road morning till night. A variety of trades and occupations was represented all along its way: medicine-sellers, sellers of stolen hardware and junk, magicians and, above all, an auctioneer of cheap cloth, who created enough din all day to attract the whole town. Next to him in vociferousness[4] came a vendor of fried groundnuts, who gave his ware a fancy name each day, calling it Bombay Ice-Cream one

---

1. A *cowrie* (kau′rē) is a small snail commonly found in warm, shallow waters of the Pacific and Indian Oceans.
2. Here, *obscure* means "difficult to understand" and *mystic* means "having hidden or secret meanings." *Palmyra* (pal mī′ ra) refers to paper made from the leaves of the palmyra tree. The man's forehead is full of splendor *(resplendent)* in that it is painted with dark ash and a red pigment called *vermilion.*

Big Idea Encountering the Unexpected *What do customers misunderstand about the astrologer?* **BI**

Vocabulary

enhance (en hans′) *v.* to make greater, as in beauty or value

---

3. *Saffron* is an orange-yellow color.
4. *Vociferousness* (vō sif′ ər əs nəs) means "noisy outcrying."

Reading Strategy Analyzing Cultural Context *How does the astrologer's manner of dress suit his character?* **R1**

Additional Support

Skills Practice

LITERARY ELEMENT:

Characterization This first page contains many details about the astrologer's physical appearance and his environment. Read some of this description out loud. Ask students how this description helps readers understand the story. *(It paints a picture in readers' minds and helps make the setting and the astrologer seem real.)* Ask what students would think of someone dressed in an outfit like the astrologer's. *(Possible responses: He is a fake. He is a fortune-teller. He is from a foreign country.)* **OL**

day, and on the next Delhi Almond, and on the third Raja's Delicacy, and so on and so forth, and people flocked to him. A considerable portion of this crowd dallied before the astrologer too. The astrologer transacted his business by the light of a flare which crackled and smoked up above the groundnut heap nearby. Half the enchantment of the place was due to the fact that it did not have the benefit of municipal lighting. The place was lit up by shop lights. One or two had hissing gaslights, some had naked flares stuck on poles, some were lit up by old cycle lamps and one or two, like the astrologer's, managed without lights of their own. It was a bewildering criss-cross of light rays and moving shadows. This suited the astrologer very well, for the simple reason that he had not in the least intended to be an astrologer when he began life; and he knew no more of what was going to happen to others than he knew what was going to happen to himself next minute. He was as much a stranger to the stars as were his innocent customers. Yet he said things which pleased and astonished everyone: that was more a matter of study, practice and shrewd guesswork. All the same, it was as much an honest man's labor as any other, and he deserved the wages he carried home at the end of a day.

He had left his village without any previous thought or plan. If he had continued there he would have carried on the work of his forefathers—namely, tilling the land, living, marrying and ripening in his cornfield and ancestral home. But that was not to be. He had to leave home without telling anyone, and he could not rest till he left it behind a couple of hundred miles. To a villager it is a great deal, as if an ocean flowed between.

He had a working analysis of mankind's troubles: marriage, money and the tangles of human ties. Long practice had sharpened his perception. Within five minutes he understood what was wrong. He charged three pice[5] per question and never opened his mouth till the other had spoken for at least ten minutes, which provided him enough stuff for a dozen answers and advices. When he told the person before him, gazing at his palm, "In many ways you are not getting the fullest results for your efforts," nine out of ten were disposed to agree with him. Or he questioned: "Is there any woman in your family, maybe even a distant relative, who is not well disposed[6] towards you?" Or he gave an analysis of character: "Most of your troubles are due to your nature. How can you be otherwise with Saturn where he is? You have an **impetuous** nature and a rough exterior." This endeared him to their hearts immediately, for even the mildest of us loves to think that he has a forbidding exterior.

The nuts-vendor blew out his flare and rose to go home. This was a signal for the astrologer to bundle up too, since it left him in darkness except for a little shaft of green light which strayed in from somewhere and touched the ground before him. He picked up his cowrie shells and **paraphernalia** and was putting them back into his bag when the green shaft of light was blotted out; he looked up and saw a man standing before him. He sensed a possible client and said: "You look so careworn. It will do you good to sit down for a while and chat with me." The other grumbled some vague reply. The astrologer pressed his invitation; whereupon the other thrust his palm under his nose, saying: "You call yourself an astrologer?" The astrologer

---

5. A *pice* is a coin of India of very small value.
6. In this paragraph, *disposed* is used twice with slightly different meanings. The first time, you might substitute *likely* or *inclined*. The second time, substitute *favorable* for the phrase "well disposed."

Vocabulary

impetuous (im pech′ ōō əs) *adj.* rushing headlong into things; rash

paraphernalia (par′ ə fər nāl′ yə) *n.* things used in a particular activity; equipment

Literary Element Description *What does this description of lights add to the mood—the feeling—of the story?* **L**

Reading Strategy Analyzing Cultural Context *What can you infer about the customs of people in the astrologer's village?* **R₂**

R. K. NARAYAN **67**

Teach

Description Answer:
Vivid words include "hooted," "swore," and "agitated."
Discuss why these vivid words are a better choice than more commonly used words, such as *cried*, *yelled*, or *upset*, which have similar meanings. *(They create a more precise visual and auditory impression of the scene.)* **OL**

★ Cultural History

The rupee is the basic unit of India's currency. It has been used in India since the sixteenth century. The coins are either copper-nickel or silver, and the banknotes display the likeness of Mohandas Gandhi, who helped free the country from the British in the twentieth century. Like American currency, Indian currency comes in a variety of denominations. The word *rupee* comes from the word for silver in Sanskrit, an ancient Indian language. **AS**

---

felt challenged and said, tilting the other's palm towards the green shaft of light: "Yours is a nature . . ." "Oh, stop that," the other said. "Tell me something worthwhile. . . ."

Our friend felt **piqued.** "I charge only three pice per question, and what you get ought to be good enough for your money. . . ." At this the other withdrew his arm, took out an anna and flung it out to him, saying, "I have some questions to ask. If I prove you are bluffing, you must return that anna to me with interest."

"If you find my answers satisfactory, will you give me five rupees?"[7]

"No."

"Or will you give me eight annas?"

"All right, provided you give me twice as much if you are wrong," said the stranger. This pact was accepted after a little further argument. The astrologer sent up a prayer to heaven as the other lit a cheroot.[8] The astrologer caught a glimpse of his face by the matchlight. There was a pause as cars hooted on the road, jutka[9] drivers swore at their horses and the babble of the crowd agitated the semi-darkness of the park. The other sat down, sucking his cheroot, puffing out, sat there ruthlessly. The astrologer felt very uncomfortable. "Here, take your anna back. I am not used to such challenges. It is late for me today. . . ." He made preparations to bundle up. The other held his wrist and said, "You can't get out of it now. You dragged me in while I was passing." The astrologer shivered in his grip; and his voice shook and became faint. "Leave me

today. I will speak to you tomorrow." The other thrust his palm in his face and said, "Challenge is challenge. Go on." The astrologer proceeded with his throat drying up. "There is a woman . . ."

"Stop," said the other. "I don't want all that. Shall I succeed in my present search or not? Answer this and go. Otherwise I will not let you go till you disgorge[10] all your coins." The astrologer muttered a few **incantations** and replied, "All right. I will speak. But will you give me a rupee if what I say is convincing? Otherwise I will not open my mouth, and you may do what you like." After a good deal of haggling the other agreed. The astrologer said, "You were left for dead. Am I right?"

"Ah, tell me more."

"A knife has passed through you once?" said the astrologer.

"Good fellow!" He bared his chest to show the scar. "What else?"

"And then you were pushed into a well nearby in the field. You were left for dead."

"I should have been dead if some passerby had not chanced to peep into the well," exclaimed the other, overwhelmed by enthusiasm. "When shall I get at him?" he asked, clenching his fist.

"In the next world," answered the astrologer. "He died four months ago in a far-off town. You will never see any more of him." The other groaned on hearing it. The astrologer proceeded.

"Guru Nayak—"

"You know my name!" the other said, taken aback.[11]

---

7. The *anna* is a former coin of India that was equal to four pice. The *rupee* is a coin of India (and other countries) equal to sixteen annas.
8. A *cheroot* (shə rōōt') is a cigar cut square at both ends.
9. A *jutka* (jōōt' kə) is a two-wheeled, horse-drawn vehicle.

Literary Element Description *Identify the vivid words the author uses in this sentence to describe the street scene surrounding the astrologer and his client.* **L1**

Vocabulary

piqued (pēkt) *adj.* aroused in anger or resentment; offended

---

10. Here, *disgorge* means "to give up or hand over."
11. The expression *taken aback* means "suddenly surprised or startled."

Big Idea Encountering the Unexpected *Did it surprise you when the astrologer called his client by the correct name? Explain.* **BI**

Vocabulary

incantation (in' kan tā' shən) *n.* words spoken in casting a spell

---

Additional Support

Skills Practice

WRITING: Creating Dialogue
Discuss with students some of the phrases the astrologer uses with his ordinary customers. Pair off students and have them write an exchange between the astrologer and one of these customers. Students can use the phrases mentioned in the story as a starting point. Each pair should perform their dialogue for the rest of the class. **OL**

"As I know all other things. Guru Nayak, listen carefully to what I have to say. Your village is two days' journey due north of this town. Take the next train and be gone. I see once again great danger to your life if you go from home." He took out a pinch of sacred ash and held it out to him. "Rub it on your forehead and go home. Never travel southward again, and you will live to be a hundred."

"Why should I leave home again?" the other said reflectively.[12] "I was only going away now and then to look for him and to choke out his life if I met him." He shook his head regretfully. "He has escaped my hands. I hope at least he died as he deserved." "Yes," said the astrologer. "He was crushed under a lorry."[13] The other looked gratified to hear it.

---

12. Here, *reflectively* (ri flek′ tiv lē) means "in a way that shows serious and careful consideration."
13. Here, a *lorry* is a long, flat, horse-drawn wagon.

The place was deserted by the time the astrologer picked up his articles and put them into his bag. The green shaft was also gone, leaving the place in darkness and silence. The stranger had gone off into the night, after giving the astrologer a handful of coins.

It was nearly midnight when the astrologer reached home. His wife was waiting for him at the door and demanded an explanation. He flung the coins at her and said, "Count them. One man gave all that."

"Twelve and a half annas," she said, counting. She was overjoyed. "I can buy some *jaggery*[14] and coconut tomorrow. The child has been asking for sweets for so many days now. I will prepare some nice stuff for her."

"The swine has cheated me! ★ He promised me a rupee," said the astrologer. She looked up at him. "You look worried. What is wrong?"

"Nothing."

After dinner, sitting on the *pyol*,[15] he told her, "Do you know a great load is gone from me today? I thought I had the blood of a man on my hands all these years. That was the reason why I ran away from home, settled here and married you. He is alive."

She gasped, "You tried to kill!"

"Yes, in our village, when I was a silly youngster. We drank, gambled and quarreled badly one day—why think of it now? Time to sleep," he said, yawning, and stretched himself on the *pyol.* ❧

---

14. *Jaggery* is unrefined sugar made from palm tree sap.
15. A *pyol* (pī′ ōl) is a low bench.

Literary Element Description *What details in this sentence and the previous one describe the street scene? How has the action on the street changed since the beginning of the story?* **L₂**

R. K. NARAYAN **69**

Teach

BI Big Idea

Encountering the Unexpected **Answer:** *Some students may be surprised because the astrologer has no extraordinary powers. Other's might have predicted that the astrologer recognized the client.* **OL**

L₂ Literary Element

Description Answer: *The street is deserted, dark, and silent. Earlier it was crowded, well lit, and noisy.*
Discuss how the change in the description contributes to the mood of the story. **OL**

★ Writer's Technique

Dramatic Irony Say: Dramatic irony occurs when the reader recognizes something that a character does not. **Ask:** What example of dramatic irony do you see in the conclusion? *(The astrologer is annoyed because he was robbed of a few cents, but he almost robbed the other man of his life.)* **AS**

✓ CheckPoint

Use the CheckPoint questions on Presentation Plus! to check students' mastery of the selection. These questions can be used with interactive response keypads for immediate student feedback.

Objectives
• To understand description (SE)
• To create dialogue (TWE)

Differentiated Instruction

Connecting In the story, the astrologer lies to Guru Nayak about his skills as an astrologer and about the fate of his attacker. Although students may initially judge the astrologer harshly for lying, they, too, may have told a lie in the past. Tell students to think about one time when they told a lie. Have the students write down everything that comes to mind about that experience. After five minutes, have the students read over what they have written down. Go around the room and ask each student to share his or her experience with the class. **BL**

69

Assess

1. Students' answers will vary.

2. (a) He looks unusual and otherworldly. (b) He listens to them and tells them what they want to hear.

3. (a) He is poor. He sits under a tree every day, telling people's fortunes. (b) He expected to get married in his home village and farm there for his entire life.

4. (a) The stranger had been stabbed, pushed into a well, and left for dead. (b) The astrologer does not want the man to recognize him and get revenge.

5. (a) In the dark, the stranger cannot recognize the astrologer. (b) The stranger might have killed the astrologer; the astrologer would not have been able to trick him.

6. (a) The astrologer calls the stranger a cheat, but his words mask his fear of a man who could have killed him. (b) He was ashamed.

7. He might say he analyzes people and tells them pleasing things about the future. Most people want assurance that the future will be better than the present.

8. Students may mention the hints of the astrologer's past or the mood of mystery.

RESPONDING AND THINKING CRITICALLY

Respond

1. (a) What was your reaction to the conversation between the astrologer and his wife? (b) Does this new knowledge reinforce or change your opinion of the astrologer? Explain.

Recall and Interpret

2. (a) According to the narrator, how does the astrologer's appearance help him attract customers? (b) In your opinion, how does the astrologer help the customers and satisfy their needs?

3. (a) Describe the astrologer's current life. (b) How does this differ from the life he expected to live?

4. (a) What details does the astrologer give the stranger about his past? (b) Why does he advise the stranger to go home immediately?

Analyze and Evaluate

5. (a) Why is it important that this story takes place in the evening? (b) How would the story have been different if it had taken place earlier in the day?

6. (a) How would you characterize the astrologer's attitude toward the stranger after their encounter? (b) What attitude did the astrologer seem to have about the incident from his past?

7. How do you think the astrologer would respond to these questions: What makes you such a successful astrologer? Why do most people want to know the future?

Connect

8. **Big Idea** **Encountering the Unexpected** Suspense is the feeling of anticipation you may have as you read. In this story, what details contributed to your feelings of suspense and surprise? Explain.

LITERARY ANALYSIS

Literary Element Description

Description helps readers visualize what is happening in a story. Notice the vivid description in this passage from "An Astrologer's Day": "The astrologer caught a glimpse of [the stranger's] face by the matchlight. There was a pause as cars hooted on the road, *jutka* drivers swore at their horses and the babble of the crowd agitated the semidarkness of the park." Descriptive language can help bring a character to life. Description also can help build suspense or provide clues about what might happen next.

1. List descriptive details that help you visualize the marketplace in which the astrologer conducts his business.

2. What details and techniques does Narayan use to describe the astrologer?

Review: Irony

As you learned on page 51, **irony** is a contrast or discrepancy between appearances and reality. **Situational irony** exists when what occurs is the opposite of expectations.

Partner Activity Meet with another classmate and discuss the use of situational irony in Narayan's story. In your opinion, what is ironic about Guru Nayak's meeting with the astrologer? To answer, go back through the story and find three details that you consider especially ironic. Record them in a graphic organizer like the one shown. Then share your thoughts about these details with the class.

Irony in "An Astrologer's Day"

Detail	Detail	Detail

Literary Element

1. Details include the other vendors and their wares, the vendors' lights, and the noises of the traffic and people.

2. His physical appearance, his techniques, his words, and his actions.

Review: Irony

Possible example of situational irony: Guru Nayak doubts that the astrologer can tell him anything about his life, while other customers expect the astrologer to tell them the truth.

Reading Strategy Analyzing Cultural Context

The cultural details that relate to setting, characters, and plot in "An Astrologer's Day" add authenticity to the story and make the characters and events believable.

1. How does the author's depiction of the street where the astrologer works compare to other open markets you have visited or seen in pictures?

2. The astrologer attracts many customers who are pleased and astonished by what he tells them. What does this tell you about the people of the town?

Vocabulary Practice

Word Origins Choose the language from which each word originated. Use a dictionary if you need help.

1. enhance	a. Middle English	b. Greek
2. impetuous	a. Sanskrit	b. Latin
3. paraphernalia	a. Norse	b. Greek
4. piqued	a. French	b. Algonquin
5. incantation	a. Spanish	b. Latin

Academic Vocabulary

Here are two words from the vocabulary list on page R82. These words will help you think, write, and talk about the selection.

subsequent (sub′sə kwənt) *adj.* happening after something else; following

negate (ni gāt′) *v.* to declare something false or invalid

Practice and Apply

1. What do you think would happen if Guru Nayak paid a **subsequent** visit to the astrologer?

2. Does the fact that the astrologer was a "silly youngster" when he stabbed Guru Nayak **negate** his crime or his guilt?

Writing About Literature

Analyze Conflict Think about the external and internal conflicts in "An Astrologer's Day." Write a brief essay in which you analyze these conflicts. Explain how the conflicts are resolved and what they reveal about the characters involved. Use evidence from the story to support your analysis.

As you draft, write from start to finish. Follow the writing path shown here to help you organize your essay and keep you on track.

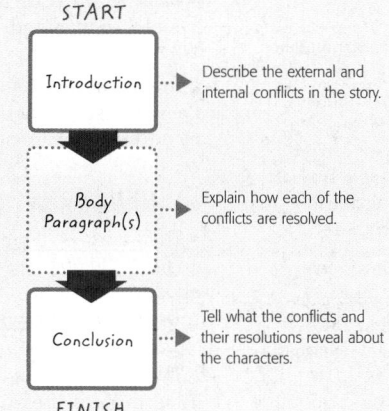

START

Introduction → Describe the external and internal conflicts in the story.

Body Paragraph(s) → Explain how each of the conflicts are resolved.

Conclusion → Tell what the conflicts and their resolutions reveal about the characters.

FINISH

After you complete your draft, meet with a peer reviewer to evaluate each other's work and to suggest revisions. Then proofread and edit your draft for errors in spelling, grammar, and punctuation.

Literary Criticism

William Walsh writes about the Indian village where Narayan set many of his stories: "Whatever happens in India happens in Malgudi, and whatever happens in Malgudi happens everywhere." With a partner, consider how this quotation applies to "An Astrologer's Day." What story elements are universal? Which are unique to the time and place in which the story is set?

Literature Online Web Activities For eFlashcards, Selection Quick Checks, and other Web activities, go to www.glencoe.com.

R. K. NARAYAN **71**

Assess

Reading Strategy

1. It is similar to a stereotypical market, with different stalls selling a variety of goods and foods, crowds of people shopping, and vendors calling out to potential clients. The groundnuts and the astrologer's appearance are specifically Indian. The gaslights and flares would be replaced by electric lights today.

2. They believe in the powers of astrology, and they trust the astrologer. They are willing to confide in strangers.

Vocabulary

1. a 2. b 3. b 4. a 5. b

Academic Vocabulary

1. He would probably recognize the astrologer as his attacker and be even more enraged that the astrologer tried to trick him to avoid punishment.

2. Most students will probably say that the astrologer is still guilty of the crime and deserves to be punished.

Writing About Literature

Use these criteria when evaluating students' writing:

- Does the introduction clearly identify each conflict, including specific details?

- Do the body paragraphs explain how the conflicts are resolved?

- Do the body paragraphs use evidence from the story to support explanations and opinions?

Literary Criticism

Students may say that charlatans, drunken brawls, and chance encounters between people who have been separated for a long time are universalities. Guilt over a past crime and relief to find that a crime has not actually been committed can be considered universal sentiments as well. The setting of Town Hall Park, the astrologer's particular rituals, and the occupations of the others at the market are unique to the setting.

Literature Online

Web Activities Have students access the Web site for interactive activities that will help them assess their understanding of the selection.

Focus

Write the following on the board:
- the children's playground
- the year's gone by

Ask: Which uses an apostrophe correctly? *(The first phrase uses an apostrophe correctly in a possessive, while the second uses an apostrophe incorrectly in a plural.)* Make sure that students can distinguish between plurals and possessives. `OL`

Teach

Possessives On the board, list: singular noun, plural noun ending in *s*, plural noun not ending in *s*, and indefinite pronoun.
Have students give examples of how to make possessives for each. `OL`

Assess

Exercise

1. The fishermen's catch was brought to the market each morning.
2. Other vendors' stalls were clean and bright.
3. C

Grammar Workshop
Mechanics

▶ **Vocabulary Terms**

A **possessive** noun shows possession, ownership, or a relationship between two nouns that is similar to ownership.

▶ **Test-Taking Tip**

To decide whether a noun needs an apostrophe alone or an apostrophe and *s*, consider the number of the noun. A plural noun that ends in *s* needs only an apostrophe to make it possessive.

▶ **Language Handbook**

For more on using apostrophes to form possessives, see the Language Handbook p. R56.

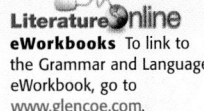
Literature Online
eWorkbooks To link to the Grammar and Language eWorkbook, go to www.glencoe.com.

OBJECTIVES
- Understand usage of possessive apostrophes.
- Recognize and correct errors in grammar.

Using Apostrophes in Possessives

"He had a working analysis of mankind's troubles: marriage, money and the tangles of human ties."

— R. K. Narayan, from "An Astrologer's Day"

In the quotation above, the possessive case of the singular noun *mankind* is *mankind's*. The literal meaning of the phrase *mankind's troubles* is "the troubles of mankind."

Connecting to Literature An important use of the apostrophe is to form the possessive of nouns and indefinite pronouns. The possessive is formed by adding either an apostrophe alone or an apostrophe and *s*.

Examples

- *The heroism of the witness saved the man in the well.*
To form the possessive of a singular noun that ends in *s*, add an apostrophe and *s*.
  The witness's heroism saved the man in the well.

- *The astrologer answered the questions of the clients.*
To form the possessive of a plural noun that ends in *s*, add only an apostrophe.
  The astrologer answered the clients' questions.

- *The honking of the geese woke up the teacher.*
To form the possessive of a plural noun that does not end in *s*, add an apostrophe and *s*.
  The geese's honking woke up the teacher.

- *The astrologer earned his money by answering the questions of everybody.*
To form the possessive of an indefinite pronoun (such as *somebody*), add an apostrophe and *s*. Apostrophes are not used with possessive pronouns.
  The astrologer earned his money answering everybody's questions.

Exercise

Revise for Clarity If the sentence is correct, write *C*. If the sentence is incorrect, rewrite it correctly.

1. The fishermens catch was brought to market each morning.
2. Other vendors's stalls were clean and bright.
3. Each day the astrologer told everyone's fortune.

Additional Support

Literature Online

eWorkbooks Have students access the Web site for more practice with using apostrophes in possessives.

Skills Practice

GRAMMAR: Possessives of Compound Nouns Write these nouns on the board and discuss their possessives: *sergeant-at-arms, Mom and Dad.* Tell students that compound nouns, such as *sister-in-law* and *Secretary of State*, form possessives with only the last word (*sister-in-law's, Secretary of State's*).

Explain that two nouns joined by *and* form the possessive with only the last word to show joint possession, but with both words to show individual possession (*Jake and Kim's project, Jake's and Kim's smiles*). After students practice with more examples, have them teach this lesson to the class. `OL`

Civil Peace

MEET CHINUA ACHEBE

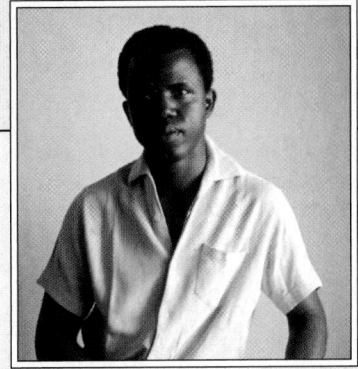

T he story is our escort; without it, we are blind." Chinua Achebe (ə chā´ bā) wrote these words to stress the importance of keeping Africa's precolonial stories and culture alive.

Achebe was born in Ogidi, Nigeria. His family was Ibo and Christian. While growing up, Achebe experienced traditional village life. After graduating from University College in Ibadan, he worked for more than ten years for the Nigerian Broadcasting Company. Achebe left this job in 1966 partly because of political problems that led to civil war in Nigeria in 1967. The Ibo, one of Nigeria's largest ethnic groups, tried to separate from Nigeria to form the independent Republic of Biafra. Achebe worked for the Ibo cause and represented Biafra as a diplomat. He has since taught in universities in Nigeria, Massachusetts, and Connecticut. Throughout his career, he has authored five novels, as well as many essays, poems, and children's stories. He was also the director of Heinemann Education Books Ltd. (now called the Heinemann African Writers Series) and helped develop series to foster publication of African and Caribbean writers.

"It is the story that outlives the sound of war-drums and the exploits of brave fighters."

—Chinua Achebe, from *Anthills of the Savannah*

The African Voice Achebe writes in English so that his stories will have a wider audience. However, his themes revolve around the people of Africa, their struggles under colonial rule, and their fight for independence. Achebe combines the rhythms and speech patterns of the

Ibo with the English language so that English readers will gain a sense of the African people and culture. In "Civil Peace," his characters speak English but with an African dialect. Achebe has said that "People create stories create people; or rather stories create people create stories." Achebe writes about his people honestly, detailing both the good and the bad. By communicating his messages about life, Achebe has preserved the African storytelling tradition.

Civil War and Civil Peace Achebe wrote radio programs that supported the Biafrans during the Civil War, but he could not bring himself to write novels during the war. He did, however, write three short stories about the war. "Civil Peace" is one of those stories. Many readers find the story to have an optimistic point of view, even though Achebe provides a true-to-life description of the region after the war.

The title of Achebe's most popular novel, *Things Fall Apart*, is an allusion to the William Butler Yeats poem "The Second Coming." Achebe's novel, a powerful account of a "strong" man whose life is dominated by fear and anger, is recognized as a masterpiece of modern African literature. Through his literature and his roles as a teacher and the creator of the Heinemann African Writers Series, Achebe has inspired a new generation of writers.

Chinua Achebe was born in 1930.

Literature Online Author Search For more about Chinua Achebe, go to www.glencoe.com.

CHINUA ACHEBE **73**

Focus

BELLRINGER

Bellringer Options
Selection Focus Transparency 4
Daily Language Transparency 8
Or ask: What kinds of things are important to you in your own life? What would you be willing to leave behind in order to save those things that are most important to you?

Literature Online

Author Search To expand students' appreciation of Chinua Achebe, have them access the Web site for additional information and resources.

Selection Skills

Literary Elements
- Dialect (SE pp. 74, 78–80)
- Conflict (SE p. 80)

Civil Peace

Listening/Speaking/Viewing Skills
- Analyzing Art (SE p. 78)
- Interviewing (SE p. 81)

Reading Skills
- Analyzing Historical Context (SE pp. 74–76, 78, 79, 81)
- Varying Reading Rate (TWE p. 76)

Vocabulary Skills
- Word Origins (SE pp. 74, 81)
- Academic Vocabulary (SE p. 81)

Writing Skills/Grammar
- Response to Plot (SE p. 81)
- Personal Pronouns (TWE p. 78)

Focus

Summary

At the end of the Biafran Civil War, Jonathan Iwegbu feels fortunate to be left with his family, a bicycle, and the shell of his house. The Iwegbus set to work getting back on their feet and finally trade in their hard-earned Biafran money for 20 Nigerian pounds. That same night, a gang of armed thieves demands the money, and Jonathan fearfully gives up all his worldly wealth. The next morning, however, the family is back at work without complaint. Money does not bring happiness, Jonathan explains to his neighbors.

V Vocabulary

Vocabulary File Say: Add these words and definitions to your vocabulary file. For each word, include a sentence that gives you an example of how to use the word. **OL** Students with English language needs should include the pronunciations of these words in their files. **EL**

Literary Elements Have students access the Web site to improve their understanding of dialect.

Connecting to the Story

Jonathan Iwegbu is proud of his "Happy survival!" He has very few possessions, but what he does have is of great value to him. Achebe shows the reader what he thinks the most important things in life are and what people should be grateful for. Before you read the story, think about the following questions:

- If a disaster occurred today, what would you save to ensure your "happy survival"?
- If you had very few possessions and someone stole something from you, how would you feel? Would you accept the loss, or would you get angry?

Building Background

This story takes place in Nigeria, probably in 1970, shortly after the end of the Nigerian Civil War.

Nigeria, located on the western coast of Africa, is the most densely populated country on the continent. Once a British colony, it became an independent nation in 1960. The Nigerian Civil War began in 1967 when the Ibo tried to separate from Nigeria to form the independent Republic of Biafra. After enduring years of bloody battles, the Ibo were forced to surrender in 1970, ending the war. In connection with the war, Biafrans suffered a severe famine, in which nearly a million people died of starvation.

Setting Purposes for Reading

Big Idea Encountering the Unexpected

As you read, notice how Jonathan Iwegbu experiences both joy and sorrow in encountering the unexpected.

Literary Element Dialect

A **dialect** is a variation of a language spoken by a particular region or class. Understanding a writer's use of dialect will give you a richer sense of a scene or character. As you read, examine how Achebe uses dialect to illustrate both British and African elements in Nigeria.

- See Literary Terms Handbook, p. R4–R5.

Literature Online Interactive Literary Elements Handbook To review or learn more about the literary elements, go to www.glencoe.com.

OBJECTIVES
In studying this selection, you will focus on the following:
- understanding dialect
- analyzing historical context
- analyzing conflict and how it develops the plot of a story
- writing to respond to plot

Reading Strategy Analyzing Historical Context

When you **analyze a story's historical context**, you think of how the characters and events in the story are affected by what is taking place at the time the story is set. Understanding the experiences of the characters during a certain period helps you comprehend why they feel or act as they do. As you read, notice how living through the Nigerian civil war affects Jonathan Iwegbu's life.

Reading Tip: Analyzing Effects Use a web diagram like the one below to list the effects of the Nigerian civil war on Jonathan Iwegbu's life.

Vocabulary

commandeer (kom′ ən dēr′) v. to seize for use by the military or government; p. 75 *The general commandeered the commercial airplane for the battle.*

amenable (ə mē′ nə bəl) *adj.* responsive; able to be controlled; p. 76 *After being sedated, the animal was amenable to being treated by the veterinarian.*

retail (rē′ tāl) v. to sell directly to consumers. p. 76 *The farmer retailed his produce door to door.*

fortnight (fôrt′ nīt′) n. two weeks; p. 76 *The festival lasted for a fortnight, not just the usual week.*

edifice (ed′ ə fis) n. a building, especially a large, important-looking one; p. 76 *The castle was an impressive edifice.*

Vocabulary Tip: Word Origins Among English words adapted from other languages is *edifice*—from the Latin word *aedificium,* for "a building."

Selection Resources

Print Materials
- Unit 1 Resources (Fast File), pp. 37–39
- Leveled Vocabulary Development, p. 6
- Selection and Unit Assessments, pp. 13–14
- Selection Quick Checks, p. 7

Transparencies
- Bellringer Options Transparencies: Selection Focus Transparency 4 Daily Language Practice Transparency 8
- Literary Elements Transparency 12

Technology
- TeacherWorks Plus™ CD-ROM
- StudentWorks Plus™ CD-ROM
- Presentation Plus!™ CD-ROM
- Literature Online, glencoe.com
- Online Student Edition, mhln.com
- ExamView® Assessment Suite CD-ROM
- Vocabulary PuzzleMaker CD-ROM
- Listening Library, disc 1 track 7

Civil Peace

Chinua Achebe R1

Jonathan Iwegbu counted himself extraordinarily lucky. "Happy survival!" meant so much more to him than just a current fashion of greeting old friends in the first hazy days of peace. It went deep to his heart. He had come out of the war with five inestimable blessings—his head, his wife Maria's head and the heads of three out of their four children. As a bonus he also had his old bicycle—a miracle too but naturally not to be compared to the safety of five human heads.

The bicycle had a little history of its own. One day at the height of the war it was **commandeered** "for urgent military action." Hard as its loss would have been to him he

would still have let it go without a thought had he not had some doubts about the genuineness of the officer. It wasn't his disreputable rags, nor the toes peeping out of one blue and one brown canvas shoes, nor yet the two stars of his rank done obviously in a hurry in biro,[1] that troubled Jonathan; many good and heroic soldiers looked the same or worse. It was rather a certain lack of grip and firmness in his manner.

Visual Vocabulary
A *raffia* bag is one woven from the fibers of the raffia palm tree.

---

1. The stars signifying the officer's rank had been hand-drawn in ink. *Biro* (bī′ rō) is a British term for a ballpoint pen.

Vocabulary

commandeer (kom′ ən dēr′) *v*. to seize for use by the military or government

Reading Strategy Analyzing Historical Context *Why would Jonathan have let his bicycle go "without a thought"? Why did he think of himself as "extraordinarily lucky"?* R2

CHINUA ACHEBE **75**

Encountering the Unexpected Say: Consider this question as you read: Why is Jonathan's happiness unexpected? *(He has experienced great loss and the death of one child.)* **OL**

BL₁ **Big Idea**

Encountering the Unexpected Answer: *The bicycle needed only some lubricating. It is surprising that Jonathan could have come out of the war with something in such good condition.* **OL**

R **Reading Strategy**

Analyzing Historical Context Answer: *They are resuming life after the war.* **OL**

★ **Writer's Technique**

Word Choice A writer's choice of words influences the reader's perceptions. **Ask:** Why has Achebe used the phrase "of course" to begin the second sentence describing Jonathan's house? *(If Jonathan is lucky to have a house without doors and windows, what must the city look like?)* **AS**

So Jonathan, suspecting he might be **amenable** to influence, rummaged in his raffia bag and produced the two pounds with which he had been going to buy firewood which his wife, Maria, **retailed** to camp officials for extra stock-fish and corn meal, and got his bicycle back. That night he buried it in the little clearing in the bush where the dead of the camp, including his own youngest son, were buried. When he dug it up again a year later after the surrender all it needed was a little palm-oil greasing. "Nothing puzzles God," he said in wonder.

He put it to immediate use as a taxi and accumulated a small pile of Biafran money ferrying camp officials and their families across the four-mile stretch to the nearest tarred road. His standard charge per trip was six pounds and those who had the money were only glad to be rid of some of it in this way. At the end of a **fortnight** he had made a small fortune of one hundred and fifteen pounds.

Then he made the journey to Enugu² and found another miracle waiting for him. It was unbelievable. He rubbed his eyes and looked again and it was still standing there before him. But, needless to say, even that monumental blessing must be accounted also totally inferior to the five heads in the family. This newest miracle was his little house in Ogui Overside. Indeed nothing puzzles God! Only two houses away a huge concrete

> *"Of course the doors and windows were missing and five sheets off the roof. But what was that!"*

edifice some wealthy contractor had put up just before the war was a mountain of rubble. And here was Jonathan's little zinc house³ of no regrets built with mud blocks quite intact! Of course the doors and windows were missing and five sheets off the roof. But what was that? And anyhow he had returned to Enugu early enough to pick up bits of old zinc and wood and soggy sheets of cardboard lying around the neighborhood before thousands more came out of their forest holes looking for the same things. He got a destitute carpenter with one old hammer, a blunt plane and a few bent and rusty nails in his tool bag to turn this assortment of wood, paper and metal into door and window shutters for five Nigerian shillings or fifty Biafran pounds. He paid the pounds, and moved in with his overjoyed family carrying five heads on their shoulders. ★

His children picked mangoes near the military cemetery and sold them to soldiers' wives for a few pennies—real pennies this time—and his wife started making breakfast akara balls⁴ for neighbors in a hurry to start life again. With his family earnings he took his bicycle to the villages around and bought fresh palm wine which he mixed generously in his rooms with the water which had recently started running again in the public tap down the road, and opened up a bar for soldiers and other lucky people with good money.

---

2. *Enugu* (ā nōō´ gōō) is a city in southeastern Nigeria.

Big Idea Encountering the Unexpected *Why was Jonathan surprised by the condition of his bicycle?* **BL₁**

Vocabulary

amenable (ə mē´ nə bəl) *adj.* responsive; able to be controlled
retail (rē´tāl) *v.* to sell directly to the consumer
fortnight (fôrt´ nīt´) *n.* two weeks

---

3. A *zinc house* is one with a zinc-coated metal roof.
4. *Akara balls* are ball-shaped bean cakes.

Reading Strategy Analyzing Historical Context *What do the actions of Jonathan's family members show?* **R**

Vocabulary

edifice (ed´ ə fis) *n.* a building, especially a large, important-looking one

---

Additional Support

Skills Practice

READING: Varying Reading Rate Readers naturally read different texts at different paces. **Ask:** For what reasons might you slow your reading rate? *(Possible responses: to comprehend a text with many facts; to understand difficult words or sentence structure; to appreciate text with interesting literary effects.)* Have students time each other as they read two paragraphs. Tell them to read a paragraph that is made up of dialect and a paragraph that is written in plain English. Then have students discuss why the paragraph written in dialect took longer to read. **OL**

At first he went daily, then every other day and finally once a week, to the offices of the Coal Corporation where he used to be a miner, to find out what was what. The only thing he did find out in the end was that that little house of his was even a greater blessing than he had thought. Some of his fellow ex-miners who had nowhere to return at the end of the day's waiting just slept outside the doors of the offices and cooked what meal they could scrounge together in Bournvita tins. As the weeks lengthened and still nobody could say what was what Jonathan discontinued his weekly visits altogether and faced his palm wine bar.

But nothing puzzles God. Came the day of the windfall when after five days of endless scuffles in queues and counter queues in the sun outside the Treasury he had twenty pounds counted into his palms as ex gratia[5] award for the rebel money he had turned in. It was like Christmas for him and for many others like him when the payments began. They called it (since few could manage its proper official name) *egg rasher*.

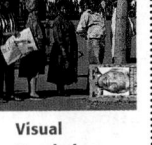

Visual Vocabulary
Here a queue (kyū) means a line of people.

As soon as the pound notes were placed in his palm Jonathan simply closed it tight over them and buried fist and money inside his trouser pocket. He had to be extra careful because he had seen a man a couple of days earlier collapse into near madness in an instant before that oceanic crowd because no sooner had he got his twenty pounds than some heartless ruffian picked it off him. Though it was not right that a man in such an extremity of agony should be blamed yet many in the queues that day were able to remark quietly on the victim's carelessness, especially after he pulled out the innards of his pocket and revealed a hole in it big enough to pass a thief's head. But of course he had insisted that the money had been in the other pocket, pulling it out too to show its comparative wholeness. So one had to be careful.

Jonathan soon transferred the money to his left hand and pocket so as to leave his right free for shaking hands should the need arise, though by fixing his gaze at such an elevation as to miss all approaching human faces he made sure that the need did not arise, until he got home.

He was normally a heavy sleeper but that night he heard all the neighborhood noises die down one after another. Even the night watchman who knocked the hour on some metal somewhere in the distance had fallen silent after knocking one o'clock. That must have been the last thought in Jonathan's mind before he was finally carried away himself. He couldn't have been gone for long, though, when he was violently awakened again.

"Who is knocking?" whispered his wife lying beside him on the floor.

"I don't know," he whispered back breathlessly.

The second time the knocking came it was so loud and imperious that the rickety old door could have fallen down.

"Who is knocking?" he asked then, his voice parched and trembling.

"Na tief-man and him people," came the cool reply. "Make you hopen de door." This was followed by the heaviest knocking of all.

Maria was the first to raise the alarm, then he followed and all their children.

"Police-o! Thieves-o! Neighbors-o! Police-o! We are lost! We are dead! Neighbors, are you asleep? Wake up! Police-o!"

This went on for a long time and then stopped suddenly. Perhaps they had scared the thief away. There was total silence. But only for a short while.

"You done finish?" asked the voice outside. "Make we help you small. Oya, everybody!"

---

5. Something that is awarded *ex gratia* (eks gräsh' ē ə) is given as a favor rather than as a legal right. The Latin word *gratia* means "kindness."

Big Idea Encountering the Unexpected *What visitors might be at the door? Are Jonathan and his wife completely surprised? Explain.* **BI₂**

CHINUA ACHEBE **77**

Teach

BI₂ **Big Idea**

Encountering the Unexpected Answer: *Students may say that thieves, soldiers, or the police are at the door. Jonathan was wary when he went to sleep.* **OL**

Differentiated Instruction

Less Proficient Readers An African country in the aftermath of a brutal war is far removed from the experiences of most students. Some students may not understand the situation and its impact on people. Discuss what human beings, whatever their circumstances, have in common. **Say:** Even though your lives may seem different from those of the characters in the story, physical differences are often superficial. **Ask:** What similarities and differences do you see between your life and Jonathan's life? *(Possible responses: Similarity—he loves his family. Difference—he lived through a civil war.)* **BL**

Objectives
• To analyze historical context (SE)
• To vary reading rates (TWE)

77

Teach

R1 Reading Strategy

Analyzing Historical Context Answer: *The neighbors are either scared or used to such activities in their region. The thieves call for the police because they know that no one will come.* **OL**

L1 Literary Element

Dialect Answer: Soja *means "soldier." This word and others such as* sometaim *and* dem *show how the dialect sounds. The characters are not saying English words with a British pronunciation.* **OL**

⭐ Viewing the Art

Robert Gwathmey (1903–1988) was an American artist of the social realist school that flourished in the 1930s and 1940s. He was one of the first white artists to portray the dignity of African American life.

Answer: *The parents create a warm, nurturing atmosphere for their children. Like Jonathan, they value and protect their children.* **AS**

Children Dancing, c. 1948. Robert Gwathmey. Oil on canvas, 30 x 40 in. The Butler Institute of American Art, Youngstown, OH.

Viewing the Art: How does the atmosphere these parents are creating for their children ⭐ reflect the way Jonathan cares for his family?

© Estate of Robert Gwathmey/Licensed by VAGA, New York, NY.

"*Police-o! Tief-man-o! Neighbors-o! we done loss-o! Police-o! . . .*"

There were at least five other voices besides the leader's.

Jonathan and his family were now completely paralyzed by terror. Maria and the children sobbed inaudibly like lost souls. Jonathan groaned continuously.

The silence that followed the thieves' alarm vibrated horribly. Jonathan all but begged their leader to speak again and be done with it.

"My frien," said he at long last, "we don try our best for call dem but I tink say dem all done sleep-o . . . So wetin we go do now? Sometaim you wan call soja? Or you wan make we call dem for you? Soja better pass police. No be so?"

"Na so!" replied his men. Jonathan thought he heard even more voices now than before and groaned heavily. His legs were sagging under him and his throat felt like sandpaper.

"My frien, why you no de talk again. I de ask you say you wan make we call soja?"

Reading Strategy Analyzing Historical Context

Why does no one in the neighborhood respond when the thieves pound on Jonathan's door? Why do the thieves call for the police? **R1**

Literary Element Dialect *What does the term "soja" mean? Why is this word and others presented here with unusual spellings?* **L1**

78 UNIT 1 THE SHORT STORY

Additional Support

Skills Practice

GRAMMAR: Personal Pronouns

Write the following sentence on the board: *I tink say dem all done sleep-o.* Underline *dem* (them) and point out that it is the subject of a clause. It would be *they* in Standard English. (*I would say they are all asleep.*) Write these pronouns on the board: *me, you, her, him,* and *it; us, you,* and *them.* Point out that objective pronouns are used as direct objects, indirect objects, or objects of a preposition. Have students pair up and compose four sentences using the following phrases correctly: *Jonathan and her; the thieves and them; you and me; them and us.* Have students check each other's sentences. **OL**

"No."

"Awrighto. Now make we talk business. We no be bad tief. We no like for make trouble. Trouble done finish. War done finish and all the katakata[6] wey de for inside. No Civil War again. This time na Civil Peace. No be so?"

"Na so!" answered the horrible chorus.

"What do you want from me? I am a poor man. Everything I had went with this war. Why do you come to me? You know people who have money. We . . ."

"Awright! We know say we you no get plenty money. But we sef no get even anini.[7] So derefore make you open dis window and give us one hundred pound and we go commot. Orderwise we de come for inside now to show you guitar-boy like dis . . ."

A volley of automatic fire rang through the sky. Maria and the children began to weep aloud again.

"Ah, missisi de cry again. No need for dat. We done talk say we we na good tief. We just take our small money and go nwayorly. No molest. Abi we de molest?"

"At all!" sang the chorus.

"My friends," began Jonathan hoarsely. "I hear what you say and I thank you. If I had one hundred pounds . . ."

"Lookia my frien, no be play we come play for your house. If we make mistake and step for inside you no go like am-o. So derefore . . ."

"To God who made me; if you come inside and find one hundred pounds, take it and shoot me and shoot my wife and children. I swear to God. The only money I have in this life is this twenty-pounds *egg rasher* they gave me today . . ."

"OK. Time de go. Make you open dis window and bring the twenty pound. We go manage am like dat."

There were now loud murmurs of dissent among the chorus: "Na lie de man de lie; e get plenty money . . . Make we go inside and search properly well . . . Wetin be twenty pound? . . ."

"Shurrup!" rang the leader's voice like a lone shot in the sky and silenced the murmuring at once. "Are you dere? Bring the money quick!"

"I am coming," said Jonathan fumbling in the darkness with the key of the small wooden box he kept by his side on the mat.

Visual Vocabulary
A *demijohn* is a large earthenware or glass bottle, encased in wicker.

At the first sign of light as neighbors and others assembled to commiserate with him he was already strapping his five-gallon demijohn to his bicycle carrier and his wife, sweating in the open fire, was turning over akara balls in a wide clay bowl of boiling oil. In the corner his eldest son was rinsing out dregs of yesterday's palm wine from old beer bottles.

"I count it as nothing," he told his sympathizers, his eyes on the rope he was tying. "What is *egg rasher*? Did I depend on it last week? Or is it greater than other things that went with the war? I say, let *egg rasher* perish in the flames! Let it go where everything else has gone. Nothing puzzles God." ◞

---

6. The word *katakata* may be meant to imitate the sound of gunfire. The rest of the phrase is Nigerian dialect for "that went with it."

7. An *anini* (ä nē′nē) is a small Nigerian coin worth less than one cent.

Literary Element Dialect *What does the author's use of dialect here add to the story?* **L₂**

Reading Strategy Analyzing Historical Context *Why does Jonathan tell the thieves that he has this money?* **R₂**

Big Idea Encountering the Unexpected *Why might Jonathan's neighbors have been surprised by his response to the robbery?* **BI**

CHINUA ACHEBE **79**

Reading in the Real World

Citizenship Explain to students that people in countries around the world often experience oppression and upheaval as a result of civil wars and political revolutions. Have students search for newspaper and magazine articles that discuss the impact of political or social issues in countries other than their own. Have them read the articles and discuss their findings with the class. **OL**

Assess

1. (a) Students may say his attitude is grateful. (b) Answers will vary.

2. (a) He did not appear or act official. (b) Nigeria was lawless.

3. (a) Jonathan starts a bar; his wife makes akara balls; his children sell mangoes. He trades in his Biafran money for Nigerian pounds. (b) He works hard and does not take his luck for granted.

4. (a) They may have known of Jonathan's *egg rasher.* (b) People steal from fellow citizens instead of working to improve conditions.

5. Telling about the robbery through the voices of the participants helps the reader experience it more clearly.

6. (a) Everything happens for a reason. (b) He accepts both good fortune and misfortune with simple trust.

7. Answers will vary. Even though the peace is full of hardship and lawlessness, Jonathan is at peace in the midst of the trouble.

8. Security, prosperity, and well-being are not related to status or possessions. Jonathan's attitude of acceptance enables him to experience life gratefully.

RESPONDING AND THINKING CRITICALLY

Respond

1. (a) What is Jonathan Iwegbu's attitude toward life? (b) What kind of attitude do you think you would have if your situation was similar to Jonathan's?

Recall and Interpret

2. (a) Why did Jonathan mistrust the officer who wanted to take his bicycle? (b) What does this tell you about the situation in Nigeria?

3. (a) In what ways does Jonathan begin to rebuild his life after the war? (b) What does this suggest about Jonathan's character?

4. (a) Why do the thieves come to Jonathan's house? (b) What does this reveal about life in Nigeria after the war?

Analyze and Evaluate

5. How does Achebe's transition from narrating the events to using dialogue between characters contribute to this story?

6. (a) What does Jonathan mean by his statement, "Nothing puzzles God"? (b) What does this statement reveal about Jonathan's character?

7. Do you think that the title of this story is appropriate, or would "Civil War" have been a better title? Explain.

Connect

8. **Big Idea** Encountering the Unexpected What message do you think emerges from Jonathan's unexpected, but repeated, good fortune? How does his unexpected attitude in the midst of misfortune affect the way he experiences life?

LITERARY ANALYSIS

Literary Element Dialect

Dialect is a regional variation of a language. In Africa, approximately two thousand languages are spoken, and possibly as many or more dialects exist. Africa consists of many different groups of people, and it has been colonized by different groups of Europeans. Dialect, therefore, identifies a group of people and tells something about their history.

1. What words in the text show the British influence on the Ibo's language?

2. Why do you think the thieves who come to rob Jonathan speak English with a heavier African accent than Jonathan does?

3. Why do you think Achebe had Jonathan speak English rather than the Ibo language?

Review: Conflict

As you learned on page 36, **conflict** is the central struggle between two opposing forces in a story or play. An **external conflict** exists when a character struggles against some outside force, such as another person, nature, society or fate. An **internal conflict** is a struggle between opposing thoughts or desires within the mind of a character.

Partner Activity Pair up with another student and identify various conflicts in the story. Using a chart like the one below, list the conflicts in the first column and the outcomes of each conflict in the second column.

Civil Peace	
Conflicts	Outcomes

Literary Element

1. biro, fortnight

2. They are from a different region and speak a different dialect.

3. This may serve to set Jonathan apart from the rampant violence and destruction that surround him.

Review: Conflict

Possible answers:
Conflict: Jonathan vs. the thieves
Outcome: Jonathan gives the thieves his money but escapes with his life.
Conflict: Jonathan's family vs. poverty
Outcome: Jonathan starts a taxi service and sells food.

READING AND VOCABULARY

Reading Strategy Analyzing Historical Context

Through **historical context**, one can clearly picture the lawless, war-torn setting of Nigeria. Such context makes Jonathan's attitude toward life seem all the more remarkable.

1. How would you describe the civil peace in Nigeria?

2. How does Jonathan feel about the changes that the war has inflicted on him and his family?

Vocabulary Practice

Word Origins Match the following vocabulary words from "Civil Peace" with their word origins. Use a dictionary if you need help.

1. retail   2. commandeer

3. amenable   4. fortnight

a. from the French verb *retaillier* meaning "to cut up"

b. originally from the Latin verb *minare*, meaning "to drive cattle"

c. from the Latin *com-* ("very much") and *mando* ("hand" plus "to give")

d. Old English word that means "fourteen nights"

Academic Vocabulary

Here are two words from the vocabulary list on page R82.

sufficient (sə fish′ ənt) *adj.* enough to meet the needs of a particular purpose

involve (in volv′) *v.* to engage someone in an activity

Practice and Apply

1. Why did Jonathan Iwegbu think that his blessings were **sufficient**?

2. Why did the neighbors in Jonathan's village not **involve** themselves in the robbery?

WRITING AND EXTENDING

Writing About Literature

Respond to Plot Early in the story, Achebe introduces Jonathan Iwegbu and reveals why Jonathan considers himself "extraordinarily lucky" after the Nigerian civil war. Jonathan, however, encounters misfortune too. In a brief essay, describe your reactions to the various threats Jonathan faces when thieves invade his home. State which threat you found most frightening and explain why you think that it endangers Jonathan and his family most. Use evidence from the story for support.

As you write, use the writing path shown here to help you organize your essay and keep you on track.

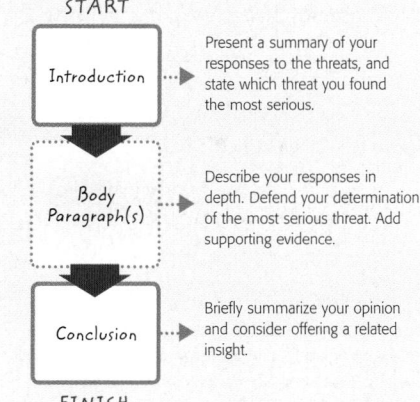

START

Introduction → Present a summary of your responses to the threats, and state which threat you found the most serious.

Body Paragraph(s) → Describe your responses in depth. Defend your determination of the most serious threat. Add supporting evidence.

Conclusion → Briefly summarize your opinion and consider offering a related insight.

FINISH

After you complete a draft of your essay, ask a classmate to read it and suggest revisions. Then proofread and edit your work for errors in spelling, grammar, and punctuation.

Learning for Life

Imagine that you are a police officer in Nigeria interviewing the Iwegbu family and their neighbors after the robbery. Write out a few interview questions and some possible replies. Then have students act out your dialogue. Consider the following: Why would robbers want to steal from their own people? Why did they want to cause trouble in a recently troubled region? Why did neighbors not respond to the robbers' yelling?

 Web Activities For eFlashcards, Selection Quick Checks, and other Web activities, go to www.glencoe.com.

CHINUA ACHEBE **81**

AFTER YOU READ

Assess

Reading Strategy

1. People are poor and sometimes desperate; there is no effective police force; the conditions are still dangerous.

2. Jonathan not only accepts the negative repercussions of war but considers himself blessed to have so much to call his own.

Vocabulary

1. a   **2.** c   **3.** b   **4.** d

Academic Vocabulary

1. Jonathan did not have many things after the war, but what he had was very important to him, namely his family and a few possessions.

2. The neighbors did not want to get involved in the robbery because they were either afraid or used to conflict in their region.

Writing About Literature

Use these criteria when evaluating students' writing:

• Does the introduction describe their personal responses to the threats that Jonathan and his family face?

• Do the body paragraphs determine which threat they think is the most severe, and provide evidence to support their determinations?

Learning for Life

Students' interviews should simulate a real-life police investigation and include specific details from Achebe's story. Remind students to create a recognizable portrait of Jonathan.

Web Activities Have students access the Web site for interactive activities that will help them assess their understanding of the selection.

81

Focus

BELLRINGER

Bellringer Options
Selection Focus Transparency 5
Daily Language Transparency 9
Or say: Imagine that a serious contagious illness is spreading across the country. Hospitals desperately need volunteers to help care for the sick. But you have an isolated cabin deep in the woods where you could go with a few friends or family members. What would you do? Have students discuss the risks involved in each option and explain their decisions.

Literature Online

Author Search To expand students' appreciation of Edgar Allan Poe, have them access the Web site for additional information and resources.

The Masque of the Red Death

MEET EDGAR ALLAN POE

With his dark, deep-set eyes and intense gaze, Edgar Allan Poe looked the part of a Romantic poet. The rhythms of his poetry fascinated readers. His mystery and horror stories, with chilling plots and memorable characters, set a standard for subsequent writers. Despite his talent, Poe constantly struggled to earn a living.

*"All that we see or seem
Is but a dream within a dream."*

—Edgar Allan Poe
from "A Dream Within a Dream"

Early Struggles Edgar Poe was born in Boston, Massachusetts, to traveling actors. His father disappeared a year later; his mother died when Poe was about two years old. John and Frances Allan of Richmond, Virginia, became foster parents to Poe but never legally adopted him. Poe took the Allans' surname as his middle name.

Poe attended the University of Virginia. He was an excellent student but also a gambler, accumulating debts he could not repay. Many times, his foster father grudgingly helped him. A gifted writer, Poe published his first book of poems at age eighteen. However, he made no money from the book.

Poe served in the army for two years, then entered the military academy at West Point, which dismissed him for skipping all his classes and drills for a week. Finally, he moved to New York City and turned to writing full-time. His short story "MS. Found in a Bottle" won a writing prize, which led to a job at the *Southern Literary Messenger* in Richmond. The magazine published many of his reviews, poems, essays, and stories—a boost both to Poe's reputation and the magazine's circulation.

Terrifying Tales By 1836 Poe had a family to support. He had married Virginia Clemm, his teenage cousin, and lived with her and her mother. Poe held a succession of jobs while continuing to produce a steady stream of poetry and fiction, including his only full-length novel, *The Narrative of Arthur Gordon Pym;* the haunting horror tales "The Fall of the House of Usher" and "The Masque of the Red Death"; and "The Murders in the Rue Morgue," considered to be the first modern detective story.

By 1844 Poe's melodic poem "The Raven" had become a great success. However, in 1847 the settled life that had always eluded him turned tragic when his cherished young wife became desperately ill and died of tuberculosis.

Although Ralph Waldo Emerson, Poe's contemporary, dismissed him as the "the jingle man," Poe's reputation as a writer grew. In 1849 he went to Richmond to give a lecture, and was expected later in Philadelphia for an editing job. But he was found unconscious on a street in Baltimore and died several days later. The cause of his death remains unknown. The writer whose work was obsessed with death and murder became himself the main character in an unsolved mystery.

Edgar Allan Poe was born in 1809 and died in 1849.

Literature Online Author Search For more about Edgar Allan Poe, go to www.glencoe.com.

82 UNIT 1 THE SHORT STORY

Selection Skills

The Masque of the Red Death

Literary Elements
• Mood (SE pp. 83, 85, 86, 89, 91)
• Description (SE p. 91)
• Point of View (TWE p. 84)

Reading Skills
• Interpreting Imagery (SE pp. 83, 86, 88, 91)
• Monitoring Understanding (TWE p. 86)

Vocabulary Skills
• Analogies (SE pp. 83, 91)
• Academic Vocabulary (SE p. 91)

Listening/Speaking/Viewing Skills
• Analyzing Art (SE p. 87)
• Creating Dialogue (TWE p. 88)

Writing Skills/Grammar
• Analysis of Plot (SE p. 92)
• Varying Sentence Structure (SE p. 92)

Connecting to the Story

"The Masque of the Red Death" is about a group of people who hope to escape the inevitable. Through elaborate efforts, they try to avoid a plague that threatens to decimate their country. The plot follows their struggles with events that are beyond their control. Before you read the story, think about the following questions:

- What events in your life do you think you can control?
- What events do you perceive as beyond your control?

Building Background

In the 1300s, an epidemic of a disease called plague caused an estimated twenty-five million deaths when it swept across Europe. At that time, the disease was known as the Black Death.

"The Masque of the Red Death" is an **allegory,** a literary work with two levels of meaning—the literal and the symbolic. All or most of the characters, settings, and events in an allegory are **symbols**—that is, they stand for ideas or qualities beyond themselves. The overall purpose of an allegory is to teach a moral lesson.

Setting Purposes for Reading

Big Idea Encountering the Unexpected

As you read "The Masque of the Red Death," notice how Poe uses sinister settings and plot twists to introduce unexpected events.

Literary Element Mood

Mood is the emotional quality or atmosphere of a literary work. A writer's choice of language, subject matter, setting, and tone, as well as such sound devices as rhyme and rhythm, contribute to the mood of a work. As you read "The Masque of the Red Death," analyze which elements of the story contribute to the story's mood. What, in your opinion, is the mood that Poe conveys?

- See Literary Terms Handbook, p. R11.

Literature Online Interactive Literary Elements Handbook To review or learn more about the literary elements, go to www.glencoe.com.

OBJECTIVES
In studying this selection, you will focus on the following:
- understanding mood
- interpreting imagery
- analyzing descriptions
- writing to analyze plot

Reading Strategy Interpreting Imagery

Writers often use **imagery,** which is language that appeals to one or more of the five senses. Imagery utilizes "word pictures" to evoke an emotional response and help readers understand a story's meaning and mood. As you read, notice how Poe includes rich sensory details to generate suspense.

Reading Tip: Taking Notes Create a chart that lists images from the story and their emotional impact.

Imagery	Emotional Response
"Blood was its Avatar and its seal—the redness and the horror of blood."	The Red Death is a horrible disease.

Vocabulary

profuse (prə fūs´) *adj.* great in amount, plentiful; p. 84 *A profuse rain often leads to flooding.*

countenance (koun´ tə nəns) *n.* the face; p. 86 *Her smiling countenance revealed her happiness.*

wanton (wont´ ən) *adj.* shamelessly unrestrained, immoral; p. 86 *Sometimes, wild dancing makes dancers seem wanton.*

spectral (spek´ trəl) *adj.* ghostlike; p. 89 *The gleaming snow gave the scene a spectral quality.*

blasphemous (blas´ fə məs) *adj.* showing disrespect or scorn for God or anything sacred; p. 89 *As she grew angrier, her words became increasingly blasphemous.*

Vocabulary Tip: Analogies An analogy is a comparison that shows similarities between two things that are dissimilar. In analogy exercises, you will determine the relationship between one pair of words and then identify the same relationship in a second pair.

Focus

Summary

The "Red Death" is raging. People are dying. Prince Prospero invites 1,000 friends into his abbey and locks out the world. There he and his friends live, believing that they are safe from the fate that has killed so many. One night the prince holds a special masked ball. The costumed revelers party until the stroke of midnight. As the clock chimes, an unusual guest appears dressed in red. The prince pursues the guest through the chambers of his home until at last he comes face to face with—the Red Death.

V Vocabulary

Vocabulary File Say: Add these words and definitions to your vocabulary file. For each word, include a sentence that gives you an example of how to use the word. **OL** Students with English language needs should include the pronunciations of these words in their files. **EL**

Literature Online

Literary Elements Have students access the Web site to improve their understanding of mood.

EDGAR ALLAN POE **83**

Selection Resources

Print Materials
- Unit 1 Resources (Fast File), pp. 40–42
- Leveled Vocabulary Development, p. 7
- Selection and Unit Assessments, pp. 15–16
- Selection Quick Checks, p. 8

Transparencies
- Bellringer Options Transparencies:
  Selection Focus Transparency 5
  Daily Language Practice Transparency 9
- Literary Elements Transparency 10

Technology
- TeacherWorks Plus™ CD-ROM
- StudentWorks Plus™ CD-ROM
- Presentation Plus!™ CD-ROM
- Literature Online, glencoe.com
- Online Student Edition, mhln.com
- Exam*View*® Assessment Suite CD-ROM
- Vocabulary PuzzleMaker CD-ROM
- Listening Library, disc 1 track 8

Teach

Big Idea

Encountering the Unexpected Say: As you read, keep the following questions in mind: What does Prince Prospero expect will happen as a result of his plan? *(He expects that he and his friends will be safe from the Red Death.)* What do you think will happen to frustrate his expectations? *(Answers may include speculations on how the prince's safety might be threatened by an enemy locked inside the abbey.)* **OL**

BI₁ Big Idea

Encountering the Unexpected Answer: *The prince and his friends may think they are healthy enough to avoid the disease or are protected from it.* **OL**

★ Writer's Technique

Repetition In the opening paragraph of "The Masque of the Red Death," Poe repeats variations on the words *blood* and *red* several times. Have students discuss the effects of such repetition. **AS**

Readability Scores
Dale-Chall: 9.5
DRP: 66
Lexile: 1240

Bodiam Castle, 1906. Wilfred Ball.

☙ The Masque of the Red Death ☙

Bodiam Castle, 1906. Wilfred Ball.

Edgar Allan Poe

The "Red Death" had long devastated the country. No pestilence had ever been so fatal, or so hideous. Blood was its Avatar[1] and its seal—the redness and the horror of blood. There were sharp pains, and sudden dizziness, and then **profuse** bleeding at the pores, with dissolution.[2] The scarlet stains upon the body and especially upon the face of the victim, were the pest ban[3] which shut him out from the aid and from the sympathy of his fellow-men. And the whole seizure, progress, and termination of the disease, were the incidents of half an hour.

But the Prince Prospero was happy and dauntless[4] and sagacious.[5] When his dominions[6] were half depopulated, he summoned to his presence a thousand hale and light-hearted friends from among the knights and dames of his court, and with these retired to the deep seclusion of one of his castellated abbeys.[7] This was an extensive

---

1. In Hinduism, an *Avatar* is a god that takes on human form. Here, the word means a visible form, or embodiment, of the disease.
2. Here, *dissolution* is death.
3. A *pest ban* is an official declaration that a person has been stricken with plague. Here, the blood stains on the victim's body became his or her own pest ban.

Vocabulary

profuse (prə fūs′) *adj.* great in amount, plentiful

4. *Dauntless* means "fearless" or "courageous."
5. *Sagacious* means "wise."
6. The prince's *dominions* are the territories he rules.
7. A *castellated abbey* is a fortified structure originally built as a monastery or intended, as the prince's was, to resemble one.

Big Idea Encountering the Unexpected *From the grim description of the Red Death, why do you suppose Prince Prospero and his friends seem so light-hearted?* **BI₁**

84 UNIT 1 THE SHORT STORY

Additional Support

Skills Practice

LITERARY ELEMENT: Point of View
Explain that "The Masque of the Red Death" is told from a third-person point of view. **Say:** There are two types of third-person point of view. A third-person limited point of view reveals only one character's perspective. A third-person omniscient narrator knows everything. Have students read the first page of the story and define the point of view. *(third-person omniscient)* Have them support their claims with evidence from the story. *(The narrator knows that "no pestilence had ever been so fatal.")* **OL**

and magnificent structure, the creation of the prince's own eccentric yet august taste. A strong and lofty wall girdled it in. This wall had gates of iron. The courtiers, having entered, brought furnaces and massy hammers and welded the bolts. They resolved to leave means neither of ingress nor egress[8] to the sudden impulses of despair or of frenzy from within. The abbey was amply provisioned. With such precautions the courtiers might bid defiance to contagion. The external world could take care of itself. In the meantime it was folly to grieve, or to think. The prince had provided all the appliances of pleasure. There were buffoons, there were improvisatori,[9] there were ballet-dancers, there were musicians, there was Beauty, there was wine. All these and security were within. Without was the "Red Death."

It was toward the close of the fifth or sixth month of his seclusion, and while the pestilence raged most furiously abroad, that the Prince Prospero entertained his thousand friends at a masked ball of the most unusual magnificence.

It was a voluptuous[10] scene, that masquerade. But first let me tell of the rooms in which it was held. There were seven—an imperial suite. In many palaces, however, such suites form a long and straight vista, while the folding doors slide back nearly to the walls on either hand, so that the view of the whole extent is scarcely impeded. Here the case was very different; as might have been expected from the duke's love of the *bizarre.* The apartments were so irregularly disposed[11] that the vision embraced but little more than one at

a time. There was a sharp turn at every twenty or thirty yards, and at each turn a novel effect. To the right and left, in the middle of each wall, a tall and narrow Gothic window looked out upon a closed corridor which pursued the windings of the suite. These windows were of stained glass whose color varied in accordance with the prevailing hue of the decorations of the chamber into which it opened. That at the eastern extremity was hung, for example, in blue—and vividly blue were its windows. The second chamber was purple in its ornaments and tapestries, and here the panes were purple. The third was green throughout, and so were the casements.[12] The fourth was furnished and lighted with orange—the fifth with white—the sixth with violet. The seventh apartment was closely shrouded in black velvet tapestries that hung all over the ceiling and down the walls, falling in heavy folds upon a carpet of the same material and hue. But in this chamber only, the color of the windows failed to correspond with the decorations. The panes here were scarlet—a deep blood color. Now in no one of the seven apartments was there any lamp or candelabrum, amid the profusion of golden ornaments that lay scattered to and fro or depended from the roof. There was no light of any kind emanating from lamp or candle within the suite of chambers. But in the corridors that followed the

Visual Vocabulary
Gothic architecture developed in Europe between the twelfth and sixteenth centuries. A Gothic window has a pointed arch and many small panes of stained or clear glass.

---

8. With *means neither of ingress nor egress,* there is no way in and no way out.
9. *Buffoons* are clowns or comedians, and *improvisatori* (im prov′ ə zə tôr′ ē) are poets who improvise, or make up, verses as they perform.
10. Here, *voluptuous* (və lup′ chŏō əs) means "giving great pleasure to the senses."
11. *Bizarre* means "that which is extremely strange or odd." A bizarre feature of Prospero's abbey is the way the rooms (*apartments*) are arranged (*disposed*) so that only one is visible at a time.

12. *Casements* are windows.

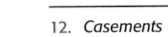
Big Idea Encountering the Unexpected *How does the description of the layout of the rooms highlight the atmosphere in the story?* **BI₂**

Literary Element Mood *What is special about the rooms in which the party is held? How do the rooms add to the mood of the story?* **L**

EDGAR ALLAN POE **85**

Teach

R Reading Strategy

Interpreting Imagery
Answer: *They feel uneasy, and everything stops. Students may say that the chiming means that death is near and life is passing.* **OL**

L Literary Element

Mood Answer: *Poe uses these words to create a mood of wanton excess—a party thrown by a madman.*

Ask: *What additional adjectives would you use to describe the masquerade? (Possible answers include* dreamlike, nightmarish, weird, *and* scary.*)* **OL**

---

suite, there stood, opposite to each window, a heavy tripod, bearing a brazier[13] of fire, that projected its rays through the tinted glass and so glaringly illumined the room. And thus were produced a multitude of gaudy and fantastic appearances. But in the western or black chamber the effect of the fire-light that streamed upon the dark hangings through the blood-tinted panes was ghastly in the extreme, and produced so wild a look upon the **countenances** of those who entered, that there were few of the company bold enough to set foot within its precincts at all.

It was in this apartment, also, that there stood against the western wall, a gigantic clock of ebony. Its pendulum swung to and fro with a dull, heavy, monotonous clang; and when the minute-hand made the circuit of the face, and the hour was to be stricken, there came from the brazen[14] lungs of the clock a sound which was clear and loud and deep and exceedingly musical, but of so peculiar a note and emphasis that, at each lapse of an hour, the musicians of the orchestra were constrained to pause, momentarily, in their performance, to hearken to the sound; and thus the waltzers perforce ceased their evolutions; and there was a brief disconcert[15] of the whole gay company; and, while the chimes of the clock yet rang, it was observed that the giddiest grew pale, and the more aged and sedate passed their hands over their brows as if in confused revery or meditation. But when the echoes had fully ceased, a light laughter

at once pervaded the assembly; the musicians looked at each other and smiled as if at their own nervousness and folly, and made whispering vows, each to the other, that the next chiming of the clock should produce in them no similar emotion; and then, after the lapse of sixty minutes (which embrace three thousand and six hundred seconds of the Time that flies), there came yet another chiming of the clock, and then were the same disconcert and tremulousness and meditation as before.

But, in spite of these things, it was a gay and magnificent revel. The tastes of the duke were peculiar. He had a fine eye for colors and effects. He disregarded the *decora* of mere fashion. His plans were bold and fiery, and his conceptions glowed with barbaric lustre. There are some who would have thought him mad. His followers felt that he was not. It was necessary to hear and see and touch him to be *sure* that he was not.

He had directed, in great part, the movable embellishments of the seven chambers, upon occasion of this great *fête;*[16] and it was his own guiding taste which had given character to the masqueraders. Be sure they were grotesque. There were much glare and glitter and piquancy and phantasm—much of what has been since seen in "Hernani."[17] There were arabesque figures with unsuited limbs and appointments. There were delirious fancies such as the madman fashions. There were much of the beautiful, much of the **wanton,** much of the *bizarre,* something of the terrible, and not a little of that which might have excited disgust. To and fro in the seven cham-

---

13. A *brazier* (brā′ zhər) is a metal pan used to hold burning coal or charcoal, as a source of heat and light.
14. The clock's outer parts are *ebony,* a black wood; its inner workings are brass *(brazen).*
15. The musicians feel obliged *(constrained)* to stop playing, the waltzers halt their complex patterns of movement *(evolutions),* and everyone experiences temporary confusion and disorder *(disconcert).*

16. A *fête* (fāt) is a large, elaborate party.
17. Here, *piquancy* (pē′ kən sē) refers to what is charming, and *phantasm* to what is fantastic and unreal. *Hernani,* an 1830 drama and, especially, an opera based on the drama, is notable for its use of colorful, imaginative spectacle.

Reading Strategy Interpreting Imagery *How do people react to the sound of the chimes? What do you think the chiming means?* **R**

Vocabulary

countenance (koun′ tə nəns) *n.* the face

Literary Element Mood *How do these words help convey the mood of the story at this point?* **L**

Vocabulary

wanton (wont′ ən) *adj.* shamelessly unrestrained; immoral

Additional Support

Skills Practice

READING: Monitoring Understanding Explain that stopping occasionally to summarize what they have read so far can help students deepen their understanding of a text. Have students write short summaries of the story so far. Invite several to share their summaries with the rest of the class. **Ask:** What is confusing or unclear about the story so far? What questions do you have about what might happen in the rest of the story? Have students write down their questions. Instruct them to jot down the answers to these questions as they continue to read. **OL**

bers there stalked, in fact, a multitude of dreams. And these—the dreams—writhed in and about, taking hue from the rooms, and causing the wild music of the orchestra to seem as the echo of their steps. And, anon, there strikes the ebony clock which stands in the hall of the velvet. And then, for a moment, all is still, and all is silent save the voice of the clock. The dreams are stiff-frozen as they stand. But the echoes of the chime die away—they have endured but an instant—and a light, half-subdued laughter floats after them as they depart. And now again the music swells, and the dreams live, and writhe to and fro more merrily than ever, taking hue from the many-tinted windows through which stream the rays from the tripods. But to the chamber which lies most westwardly of the seven there are now none of the maskers

who venture; for the night is waning away; and there flows a ruddier light through the blood-colored panes; and the blackness of the sable drapery appals[18]; and to him whose foot falls upon the sable carpet, there comes from the near clock of ebony a muffled peal more solemnly emphatic than any which reaches *their* ears who indulge in the more remote gaieties of the other apartments.

But these other apartments were densely crowded, and in them beat feverishly the heart of life. And the revel went whirlingly on, until at length there commenced the sounding of midnight upon the clock. And

---

18. To *appal* means "to horrify, dismay, or shock."

Big Idea Encountering the Unexpected *What clues does the author give that something is about to happen?* BI

Teach

BI Big Idea
Encountering the Unexpected Answer: *The chiming of the clock; the "uneasy cessation" of the music and the dancing*
Ask students to compare Poe's story with others in which a clock strikes twelve or in which time is an important factor. *(Possible examples include "Cinderella" and "Rip Van Winkle." In each of these stories, time has a magical quality that affects the characters' lives.)* OL

★ Viewing the Art
Jean Baptiste Carpeaux (1827–1875) was a French sculptor and painter. The Tuileries mentioned in the title of the painting was a royal palace in Paris, France. Napoleon III, shown in the painting, ruled France from 1852 to 1870. He was the nephew of Napoleon Bonaparte.
Answer: *Like the story, this painting depicts a costume ball in grand surroundings, possibly a castle or an abbey.* AS

Reading in the Real World

Career Virologists study viruses and the diseases they cause. **Ask:** What type of education and training would you need to become a virologist? What path might a virologist's career follow? Have students use the library and the Internet to answer these questions. OL

Differentiated Instruction

Synonyms as Context Clues Explain that synonyms can often help students decode unfamiliar words. **Ask:** Which words on this page are synonyms for the word *black*? (sable *and* ebony) Which word has a similar meaning to the verb *peal*? (chime) BL

Objectives
• To understand mood (SE)
• To interpret imagery (SE)
• To summarize a text to monitor understanding (TWE)

Encountering the Unexpected

Ask: Who might this guest be? *(Answers will vary but might include a disgruntled guest who is tired of being locked away or who wants to punish the prince for his immoral behavior.)* **OL**

R Reading Strategy

Interpreting Imagery
Answer: *He causes a stir because his costume is bright red, draws attention, and is deemed inappropriate by the other guests. He is dressed as the Red Death, something no one finds funny.* **OL**

★ Viewing the Art

Ask: What type of mood or emotion does this image evoke in you? *(Students' answers will vary. Possible responses include dangerous, evil, suspenseful, unknown, and foreboding.)* **AS**

Eyes in Darkness. Artist Unknown.

then the music ceased, as I have told; and the evolutions of the waltzers were quieted; and there was an uneasy cessation of all things as before. But now there were twelve strokes to be sounded by the bell of the clock; and thus it happened, perhaps that more of thought crept, with more of time, into the meditations of the thoughtful among those who revelled. And thus too, it happened, perhaps, that before the last echoes of the last chime had utterly sunk into silence, there were many individuals in the crowd who had found leisure to become aware of the presence of a masked figure which had arrested the attention of no single individual before. And the rumor of this new presence having spread itself whisperingly around, there arose at length from the whole company a buzz, or murmur, expressive of disapprobation[19] and

---

19. *Disapprobation* means "disapproval."

surprise—then, finally, of terror, of horror, and of disgust.

In an assembly of phantasms such as I have painted, it may well be supposed that no ordinary appearance could have excited such sensation. In truth the masquerade license of the night was nearly unlimited; but the figure in question had out-Heroded Herod,[20] and gone beyond the bounds of even the prince's indefinite decorum. There are chords in the hearts of the most reckless which cannot be touched without emotion. Even with the utterly lost, to whom life and death are equally jests, there are matters of which no jest can be made. The whole company, indeed, seemed now deeply to feel that in the costume and bearing of the stranger neither wit nor propriety existed. The figure was tall and gaunt, and shrouded from head to foot in the habiliments[21] of the grave. The mask which concealed the visage was made so nearly to resemble the countenance of a stiffened corpse that the closest scrutiny must have had difficulty in detecting the cheat. And yet all this might have been endured, if not approved, by the mad revellers around. But the mummer had gone so far as to assume the type of the Red Death. His vesture[22] was dabbled in *blood*—and his broad brow, with all the features of the face, was besprinkled with the scarlet horror.

---

20. To have *out-Heroded Herod,* the mysterious figure has done something even more outrageous than Herod the Great, the tyrant who, in an effort to kill the baby Jesus, ordered the murder of all male infants in Bethlehem.
21. *Habiliments* are clothes.
22. A *mummer* is a person dressed in a mask and costume for a party or play, and *vesture* is clothing.

Reading Strategy Interpreting Imagery *In a room full of bizarrely costumed people, why does this new figure cause such a stir?* **R**

Additional Support

Skills Practice

SPEAKING AND LISTENING:
Creating Dialogue Poe's story has little dialogue. Help students brainstorm guidelines for adding dialogue. Possible guidelines might include the following:

• Use language appropriate to the character, time, and setting.

• Provide information about what is happening, as well as reactions to it, or questions about it.

• Use voice inflections appropriate to the mood and tone.

Have small groups of students write a dialogue to go with the appearance of

When the eyes of Prince Prospero fell upon this **spectral** image (which, with a slow and solemn movement, as if more fully to sustain its *rôle*, stalked to and fro among the waltzers) he was seen to be convulsed, in the first moment with a strong shudder either of terror or distaste; but, in the next, his brow reddened with rage.

"Who dares"—he demanded hoarsely of the courtiers who stood near him—"who dares insult us with this **blasphemous** mockery? Seize him and unmask him—that we may know whom we have to hang, at sunrise, from the battlements!"

It was in the eastern or blue chamber in which stood the Prince Prospero as he uttered these words. They rang throughout the seven rooms loudly and clearly, for the prince was a bold and robust man, and the music had become hushed at the waving of his hand.

It was in the blue room where stood the prince, with a group of pale courtiers by his side. At first, as he spoke, there was a slight rushing movement of this group in the direction of the intruder, who, at the moment was also near at hand, and now, with deliberate and stately step, made closer approach to the speaker. But from a certain nameless awe with which the mad assumptions of the mummer had inspired the whole party, there were found none who put forth hand to seize him; so that, unimpeded, he passed within a yard of the prince's person; and, while the vast assembly, as if with one impulse, shrank from the centres of the rooms to the walls, he made his way uninterruptedly, but with the same solemn and measured step which had distinguished him from the first, through the blue chamber to the purple—through the purple to the green—through the green to the orange—through this again to the white—and even thence to the violet, ere a decided movement had been made to arrest him. It was then, however, that the Prince Prospero, maddening with rage and the shame of his own momentary cowardice, rushed hurriedly through the six chambers, while none followed him on account of a deadly terror that had seized upon all. He bore aloft a drawn dagger, and had approached, in rapid impetuosity, to within three or four feet of the retreating figure, when the latter, having attained the extremity of the velvet apartment, turned suddenly and confronted his pursuer. There was a sharp cry—and the dagger dropped gleaming upon the sable carpet, upon which, instantly afterward, fell prostrate in death the Prince Prospero. Then, summoning the wild courage of despair, a throng of the revellers at once threw themselves into the black apartment, and, seizing the mummer, whose tall figure stood erect and motionless within the shadow of the ebony clock, gasped in unutterable horror at finding the grave cerements[23] and corpse-like mask, which they handled with so violent a rudeness, untenanted[24] by any tangible form.

And now was acknowledged the presence **BI3** of the Red Death. He had come like a thief in the night. And one by one dropped the revellers in the blood-bedewed halls of their revel, and died each in the despairing posture of his fall. And the life of the ebony clock went out with that of the last of the gay. And the flames of the tripods expired. And Darkness and Decay and the Red Death held illimitable[25] dominion over all. ❧

Big Idea Encountering the Unexpected *Why do you think the figure is able to walk from room to room without anyone stopping him?* **BI2**

Vocabulary

spectral (spek´ trəl) *adj.* ghostlike

blasphemous (blas´ fə məs) *adj.* showing disrespect or scorn for God or anything sacred

---

23. *Cerements* are strips of cloth used to wrap a dead body.
24. *Untenanted* means "unoccupied" or "uninhabited."
25. *Illimitable* means "limitless" or "incapable of being bounded."

Literary Element Mood *How has the mood changed over the course of the story?* **L**

EDGAR ALLAN POE **89**

Teach

BI2 **Big Idea**

Encountering the Unexpected Answer: *Everyone is afraid and repulsed. He reminds them of something they do not want to think about.* **OL**

BI3 **Big Idea**

Encountering the Unexpected Ask: What surprises you about the identity of the mysterious guest? *(Students might be surprised that the guest is not a person but the Red Death itself.)* **OL**

L **Literary Element**

Mood Answer: *The mood has changed from grim to strange and disturbing.* **OL**

CheckPoint

Use the CheckPoint questions on Presentation Plus! to check students' mastery of the selection. These questions can be used with interactive response keypads for immediate student feedback.

Differentiated Instruction

the mysterious guest. Suggest that they write the dialogue, practice it, and present it to the class. **OL**

Less Proficient Readers Poe's writing is often difficult to decode. Instruct students to choose a difficult passage and rewrite it in their own words. Remind students to preserve the author's meaning, tone, and mood. **BL**

Objectives
• To interpret imagery (SE)
• To understand mood (SE)
• To create dialogue (TWE)

Assess

1. (a) Students may say it is selfish and uncaring to host a ball during such great suffering. (b) Students may express compassion for the guests' rising desperation in spite of the atmosphere of gaiety.

2. (a) It is contagious, deadly, sudden, painful, bloody, and disfiguring. (b) The sudden onset, profuse bleeding, and quick death

3. (a) The room is black with red windows and has a ghoulish appearance. (b) It suggests that time is running out.

4. (a) Outraged, he commands his men to capture the man. (b) The prince thinks he can escape death.

5. (a) He may regard these things as safeguards against the death that is claiming the common people. (b) The unusual colors of the seven chambers, the opulent trappings, the frenzied tempo, and other such details

6. The end of life's journey: death

7. (a) The prince is afraid of the disease. He wants to kill the one who reminds him of its power. (b) The gloomy chamber, the row of colored rooms, and the massive clock highlight the power of darkness and death.

RESPONDING AND THINKING CRITICALLY

Respond

1. (a) How did you first react to the idea of the masked ball? (b) How did your feelings about the ball develop as the story progressed?

Recall and Interpret

2. (a) Why is the "Red Death" such a terrible and feared disease? (b) What aspect of the "Red Death" does the story portray as especially sinister? Explain.

3. (a) How is the seventh room different from the other rooms? (b) Why do you think the clock is housed in this room?

4. (a) How does Prince Prospero respond to the costume and behavior of the uninvited guest? (b) What does his response reveal about his attitude toward death in general?

Analyze and Evaluate

5. (a) Why might the prince be so drawn to excessive luxury and constant merriment? (b) What details does Poe use to portray the prince's obsessive nature?

6. "The Masque of the Red Death" is an **allegory**, a literary work with both a literal and a symbolic meaning. What does the abbey's seventh chamber represent in an allegorical reading of the story?

7. (a) Why do you think the prince is so determined to kill the intruder? (b) How does the author weave images from the story together to build the sense of hopelessness in the scene leading up to the prince's death?

Connect

8. **Big Idea** Encountering the Unexpected Does the author prepare you for the ending, or is it unexpected? Explain.

PRIMARY VISUAL ARTIFACT

Behind a Mask

The word *masque* has a number of meanings: "a form of entertainment popular in the sixteenth and seventeenth centuries, often using masks and based on allegory"; "a masquerade"; and "a mask." Poe uses all three meanings in "The Masque of the Red Death." Masks have been used throughout the world since the Stone Age as a form of disguise and as a part of folk festivals and religious ceremonies. Some masks worn at modern-day Carnival and Mardi Gras celebrations are of grotesque or fanciful faces.

Discuss the following questions with your classmates.

1. How does Poe use all three meanings of *masque* in his short story?

2. Why do you think people sometimes wear grotesque, rather than beautiful, masks at Halloween and during Carnival and Mardi Gras?

3. What do the masks in "The Masque of the Red Death" symbolize?

Tragic Theater Mask, 3rd–2nd century. Bronze. The Lowe Art Museum, The University of Miami, FL.

8. Students may expect the ending because of the people's dread, or they may express surprise that the guest is actually Death.

Primary Visual Artifact

1. The party was a masquerade, to which the people wore masks. The partygoers' joy is not real—another masque.

2. To change into something they are not and to feel free to act differently.

3. The masks represent an attempt to escape from the reality of the plague.

LITERARY ANALYSIS

Literary Element Mood

The **mood** of "The Masque of the Red Death" is always dark, but it shifts as the story develops. In the exposition of the story—the first paragraph in which Poe sets the scene—the mood is macabre and grotesque. The images, which are explicit and even gory, evoke the atmosphere outside the abbey walls, where the Red Death is ravaging the people in the countryside. The mood inside the abbey, after the prince has gathered his friends inside its walls, is markedly different.

1. Create a list of adjectives that describe the mood of the story at different points in its development. Where are the mood shifts in the story?

2. Poe gives a detailed description of how Prince Prospero decorated the seven rooms in which the masked ball was held. Reread the description, and then write a sentence describing the mood evoked by one of the rooms.

Review: Description

As you learned on page 65, **description** is a detailed portrayal of a person, a place, an object, or an event.

Partner Activity Poe includes almost no dialogue in "The Masque of the Red Death." Instead, he uses description to drive the narrative, to reveal the characters to the reader, and to evoke various moods. Meet with a classmate to discuss the rhetorical devices and sound devices that Poe uses in his descriptions. With your partner, create a two-column chart like the one below. In the left column, list rhetorical devices and sound devices. In the right column, give short examples from the story.

Rhetorical and Sound Devices	Example
Alliteration	p. 86 "There were much glare and glitter and piquancy and phantasm"

READING AND VOCABULARY

Reading Strategy Interpreting Imagery

"The Masque of the Red Death" is filled with word pictures that appeal to one or more of the five senses.

1. Name three details used in the story that appeal to the sense of sight.

2. Find two examples of details that appeal to other senses.

3. Which detail in the story did you find the most frightening? Explain.

Vocabulary Practice

Practice with Analogies Choose the word that best completes each analogy.

1. nose : countenance :: finger :
   a. thumb   **b.** knuckle   **c.** hand

2. generous : stingy :: profuse :
   a. sufficient   **b.** meager   **c.** abundant

3. blasphemous : reverent :: healthy :
   a. robust   **b.** sickly   **c.** hale

4. jealous : possessive :: spectral :
   a. grisly   **b.** gruesome   **c.** ghostly

5. bizarre : ordinary :: wanton :
   a. restrained   **b.** immoral   **c.** cruel

Academic Vocabulary

Here are two vocabulary words from the list on page R82. These words will help you think, write, and talk about the selection.

isolate (ī'sə lāt') v. to separate from others

entity (en'tə tē) n. someone or something having an independent existence

Practice and Apply
1. Why did the partygoers **isolate** themselves from the general population?
2. In what way was the seventh room a separate **entity**?

EDGAR ALLAN POE **91**

Assess

Literary Element

1. Answers will vary. Students' adjectives might include *hideous, light-hearted, voluptuous, gaudy, fantastic, gay, peculiar, barbaric, mad, bizarre, terrible,* and *spectral.* The exposition is macabre and grotesque. The initial months of seclusion are claustrophobic but also festive and decadent. When the uninvited guest enters, the mood is one of foreboding and mystery. The mood at the end is of grim death.

2. Students should write an original sentence that conveys the mood evoked by one of the story's rooms.

Review: Description

Possible responses:

Rhetorical and Sound Devices	Example
Personification	"there was Beauty, there was wine. All these and security were within. Without was the 'Red Death.'"
Allegory	"while the chimes of the clock yet rang, it was observed that the giddiest grew pale, and the more aged and sedate passed their hands over their brows"

Reading Strategy

1. Examples include the scarlet blood, the colors of the rooms, the ebony clock.

2. Examples include the chiming of the clock, music, people laughing and whispering, and the feel of velvet.

3. Most students will cite the figure at the end of the story because of its mystery and grotesque appearance.

Vocabulary

1. c 2. b 3. b 4. c 5. a

Academic Vocabulary

1. They were trying to escape the plague.

2. It looked different from the other rooms.

Assess

Writing About Literature

Use these criteria when evaluating students' writing:

- Does the introduction describe the clock and its role in Poe's story?
- Do the body paragraphs offer insight into how the people in the story react to the chimes of the clock?
- Does the conclusion analyze the meaning of the clock in everyday life and in the story?

Literature Groups

Use these criteria when evaluating students' web diagrams:

- Is the center of the web labeled "Essential Elements of Horror Stories"?
- Are the primary elements that branch from the center of the web general characteristics, such as "suspense" and "gothic atmosphere"?
- Does the web also include support of the primary elements, such as titles of particular stories or movies?

Web Activities Have students access the Web site for interactive activities that will help them assess their understanding of the selection.

Writing About Literature

Analyze Plot In this story, Poe's use of the huge clock heightens the suspense. Suspense is a feeling of uncertainty or dread about what is going to happen next.

Write a brief essay that describes the clock and how it contributes to the story's suspense. Use examples from the story. You might ask yourself these questions:

- What does a clock do—in the story and in real life?
- How do people in the story react to the chimes?
- What is special about the sound of the chimes?
- What happens when the clock chimes? When it stops?
- What do you think the chiming means?

Follow the writing path shown here to help you organize your essay and keep on track.

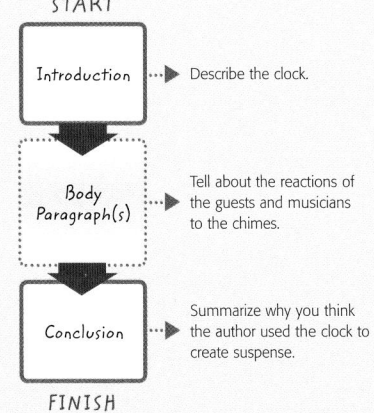

START

Introduction → Describe the clock.

Body Paragraph(s) → Tell about the reactions of the guests and musicians to the chimes.

Conclusion → Summarize why you think the author used the clock to create suspense.

FINISH

After you complete your draft, meet with a peer reviewer to evaluate each other's work and to suggest revisions. Then proofread and edit your draft for errors in spelling, grammar, and punctuation.

Literature Groups

Create a horror story web diagram using words and phrases that describe essential elements of a good horror story. Use "The Masque of the Red Death" and other horror stories you know as a guide. Refer to your web as you debate this question in your group: *What are the essential elements of a good horror story?* Share your ideas with the class.

92 UNIT 1 THE SHORT STORY

Poe's Language and Style

Varying Sentence Structure In "The Masque of the Red Death," Poe uses a variety of sentence structures to help create vivid and emotional scenes. To emphasize a point, he often uses short, simple sentences. When the story becomes more frenzied and exciting, he presents longer, more involved sentences with many clauses.

A **simple sentence** has one main clause and no subordinate clauses.

The "Red Death" had long devastated the country.

A **complex sentence** has one main clause and one or more subordinate clauses. A main clause can stand on its own; subordinate clauses cannot.

[main clause] But in the western or black chamber the effect of the fire-light that streamed upon the dark hangings through the blood-tinted panes was ghastly in the extreme, [subordinate clause] and produced so wild a look upon the countenances of those who entered, that there were few of the company bold enough to set foot within its precincts at all.

A **compound-complex sentence** has more than one main clause and at least one subordinate clause.

[main clause] In truth the masquerade license of the night was nearly unlimited; [main clause] but the figure in question had out-Heroded Herod, [subordinate clause] and gone beyond the bounds of even the prince's indefinite decorum.

Activity Make a three-column chart that lists the three types of sentence structures described above. Scan the story for other examples of the three sentence structures and add them to your chart.

Revising Check

Sentence Structure It is important to remember to vary your sentences when you revise your own writing. With a partner, go through your essay about the clock as a symbol of suspense. Note places where varied sentence structures would make your essay more engaging. Revise your draft to improve your sentences.

Poe's Language and Style

Possible examples:
Simple: But the Prince Prospero was happy and dauntless and sagacious.
Complex: And the revel went whirlingly on, until at length there commenced the sounding of midnight upon the clock.

Compound-complex: He had directed, in great part, the movable embellishments of the seven chambers, upon occasion of this great *fête*; and it was his own guiding taste which had given character to the masqueraders.

Making Choices

Girl with Red Gloves, 2001. Lizzie Riches. Oil on canvas, 29.92 X 22.83 in. Private collection. ★

BIG IDEA

Morning to night, people are faced with choices. Some of those choices have the power to change who we are. In the short stories in Part 2, you will read about difficult choices and surprising consequences. As you read these stories, ask yourself: How do the choices you make change who you are?

93

Analyzing and Extending

R Reading Strategy

Evaluate Direct students to read the Big Idea for Part 2. Have students think about why it sometimes is difficult to make a choice. Explain that a dilemma is a situation usually involving an undesirable choice. **Ask:** How does this painting relate to the Big Idea? *(The subject of the painting is in the process of making a choice.)* OL

★ Viewing the Art

Lizzie Riches (1950–) grew up in London and moved to the English countryside to pursue her career. Her style went against the trends of the 1960s, so she preferred to paint pieces relating humans and their natural surroundings. **Ask:** In what way does the painting *Girl with Red Gloves* represent the choices people make? *(The girl appears to be reconsidering her choice of red gloves instead of black ones.)* AS

English Language Coach

Building Background Discuss memorable characters who make choices in television shows, films, and books. Help students to become familiar with the types of choices characters make, their motivation in making them, and the consequences they experience as a result. EL

Differentiated Instruction

Deriving Meaning Prompt less proficient readers to consider the theme and its application to their lives. Suggest that students keep journals of choices they make and the feelings they have before and after making their decisions. Calling upon their own experiences may help them connect to the literature. BL

Objectives for Part 2
- To analyze theme and character (SE)
- To develop skill in writing characterization (SE)
- To respond to a literary theme (TWE)

93

Part 2: Making Choices

Readability Scores Key
Dale-Chall/DRP/Lexile

PACING (DAYS)		SELECTIONS AND FEATURES	LITERARY ELEMENTS
STANDARD	BLOCK		
2 class sessions	1	LITERARY FOCUS: Theme and Character, pp. 94-95	Theme and character, SE pp. 94–95
		"Two Kinds" by Amy Tan **4.5/54/860**, pp. 96-109	Motivation, SE pp. 97-99, 103–104, 106-108 Theme, SE p. 108
		"The Car We Had to Push" by James Thurber **7.3/60/1080**, pp. 110-119	Dialogue, SE pp. 111, 113, 114, 116, 118 Dialect, SE p. 118
2–3 class sessions	1–2	**"Tuesday Siesta"** by Gabriel García Márquez **4.5/55/860**, pp. 120-129	Implied Theme, SE pp. 121, 123, 126, 128 Flat and Round Characters, SE p. 128
		Vocabulary Workshop: Multiple-Meaning Words, p. 130	
		"When Mr. Pirzada Came to Dine" by Jhumpa Lahiri **8.7/60/1170**, pp. 131-147	Theme, SE pp. 132-146 Conflict, SE p. 146
2 class sessions	1	**"To Da-duh, in Memoriam"** by Paule Marshall **6.5/59/1220**, pp. 148-161	Characterization, SE pp. 149-160 Setting, SE p. 160
		"Contents of the Dead Man's Pocket" by Jack Finney **6.7/59/1190**, pp. 162-179	Symbol, SE pp. 163, 166, 172, 175, 176, 178 Motivation, SE p. 178 Point of View, TWE p. 174
1–2 class sessions	1	**"The Censors"** by Luisa Valenzuela **6.0/62/1170**, pp. 180-185	Satire, SE pp. 181, 184, 185 Tone, TWE p. 182
		TIME magazine, **"Cry of the Ancient Mariner"** by Carl Safina **12.3/67/1180**, pp. 186-190	Irony, TWE p. 188

About the Part

Part 2 covers character and theme in the short story.

READING AND CRITICAL THINKING	VOCABULARY	WRITING AND GRAMMAR	SPEAKING, LISTENING, AND VIEWING
Making Inferences about Character, TWE p. 95		Quickwrite, SE p. 95	
Connecting, SE pp. 97, 99, 101-103, 105, 109 Generalizing, TWE p. 104	Analogies, SE pp. 97, 109 Academic Vocabulary, SE p. 109	Analyze Character, SE p. 109 Personal Essay, TWE p. 100	Literature Groups, SE p. 109 Analyzing Art, SE p. 105; TWE pp. 102, 106
Making Generalizations About Characters, SE pp. 111, 112, 114–116, 118	Word Origins, SE pp. 111, 118 Academic Vocabulary, SE p. 118	Analyze Humor, SE p. 119 Using Colons, SE p. 119	Analyzing Art, SE p. 117; TWE pp. 113, 115 News Story, SE p. 119
Making Inferences About Theme, SE pp. 121, 122, 125, 126, 129	Word Parts, SE p. 129 Academic Vocabulary, SE p. 129	Summarize Flashback, SE p. 129	Analyzing Art, SE pp. 124, 127 Literature Groups, SE p. 129
	Distinguishing Definitions, SE p. 130	Parts of Speech, TWE p. 130	
Comparing and Contrasting Characters, SE pp. 132-147	Context Clues, SE p. 147 Academic Vocabulary, SE p. 147	Evaluate Author's Craft, SE p. 147	Analyzing Art, TWE pp. 133, 136, 139, 142, 144
Making Inferences About Characters, SE pp. 149-161 Visualizing, TWE p. 158	Synonyms, SE p. 161 Academic Vocabulary, SE p. 161	Analyze Character, SE p. 161 Travel Brochure, SE p. 161 Participles, TWE p. 152	Analyzing Art, SE p. 150; TWE pp. 153, 156
Responding to Characters, SE pp. 163, 165, 167, 169, 171, 173-176, 178 Predicting, TWE p. 164	Analogies, SE pp. 163, 178 Academic Vocabulary, SE p. 178	Essay on Theme, SE p. 179 Using Introductory Phrases, SE p. 179	Group Activity, SE p. 177 Performing, SE p. 179 Analyzing Art, TWE pp. 164, 168, 170
Analyzing Cause-and-Effect Relationships, SE pp. 181, 184, 185	Word Parts, SE p. 185 Usage, TWE p. 184	Respond to Theme, SE p. 185	Analyzing Art, TWE p. 183
Determining the Main Idea and Supporting Details, SE p. 186–187		Persuasion, TWE p. 186	Viewing the Photograph, TWE pp. 187–188

Teach

Big Idea

Making Choices Ask students to name the roles they play, such as student, athlete, sibling, etc. Have them consider choices they have made in each of those roles that have had consequences. Tell students that the selections in Part 2 will deepen their understanding of making choices, and encourage students to consider this Big Idea. **OL**

L Literary Element

Theme Ask: In "Two Kinds" why are the narrator and her mother opposed? *(The narrator wants to be free and independent, and her mother wants her to obey traditions.)* Discuss the regrets the narrator experiences as a result of her choice to use spiteful and rebellious words. **Ask:** What lesson could the narrator learn, which might express the theme? *(She may learn the need for understanding an opposing viewpoint.)* **OL**

Theme and Character

How do short stories develop themes and create characters?

Have you ever been so angry that you said something you later regretted? Perhaps, like many teenagers, you have argued with a parent or guardian and later regretted the fight. How is it sometimes hard for people who are feeling strong emotions to make choices about what they say? How do your feelings affect the choices you make?

"Only two kinds of daughters," she shouted in Chinese. "Those who are obedient and those who follow their own mind! Only one kind of daughter can live in this house. Obedient daughter!"

"Then I wish I weren't your daughter. I wish you weren't my mother," I shouted. As I said these things I got scared. It felt like worms and toads and slimy things crawling out of my chest, but it also felt good, that this awful side of me had surfaced, at last.

"Too late to change this," my mother said shrilly.

And I could sense her anger rising to its breaking point. I wanted to see it spill over.

—Amy Tan, *from* "Two Kinds"

Theme L

The **theme** of a story is its message about life. Sometimes a theme is expressed directly. This is called a **stated theme.** More commonly, a reader must look closely at the experiences of the main character and the lessons he or she learns to discover the theme. This is called an **implied theme.** The theme of "Two Kinds" is implied. What lessons might the narrator of "Two Kinds" learn? How might those lessons relate to the theme?

Additional Support

Skills Practice

LITERARY ELEMENT:

Characterization Discuss the methods of characterization in the passages on these pages:

- **dialogue**—Amy Tan uses dialogue to characterize. The daughter's words illustrate her rebellious nature.

- **narration**—R. K. Narayan's narration indirectly characterizes the astrologer.

- **direct characterization**—Narayan directly states that the astrologer was "as much a stranger to the stars as were his innocent customers." Have students find one other example of each method from Unit One stories. **OL**

Author's Purpose The **author's purpose** will affect the delivery and impact of a story's theme. An author generally writes to inform, entertain, persuade, tell a story, or express an opinion. An author writing to inform, persuade or express an opinion is more likely to state a theme. An author writing to entertain or tell a story usually implies the theme through lessons the important characters learn.

> A vision comes as a gift born of humility, of wisdom, and of patience. If from your vision quest you have learned nothing but this, then you have already learned much.
>
> —Lame Deer, **from "The Vision Quest"**

Character

A person in a literary work is called a **character.** Main characters are the most important. Secondary characters are less important and are also called minor characters. There are other ways to describe characters. A **round character** reveals more than one personality trait. A **flat character** reveals only one personality trait throughout the story. Finally, a **static character** will not change in the course of a story, while a **dynamic character** will.

> He was as much a stranger to the stars as were his innocent customers. Yet he said things which pleased and astonished everyone: that was more a matter of study, practice and shrewd guesswork.
>
> —R. K. Narayan, **from "An Astrologer's Day"**

Characterization The way in which an author lets the reader know about a character is called **characterization.** Methods of characterization fall into two basic categories: direct and indirect. In **direct characterization,** a writer makes clear and direct statements about a character's personality. For example, in "The Masque of the Red Death" Edgar Allen Poe describes Prince Prospero as "happy and dauntless and sagacious." In **indirect characterization,** the writer uses a character's words and actions as well as other character's thoughts and statements to reveal a character's personality. In the excerpt from "An Astrologer's Day," Narayan uses the character's thoughts to tell the reader that the man does not see the future, but does possess insight into his customers.

Quickwrite

Make up your own fictional character using a graphic organizer like the one below. In the center oval, write your character's name. In each of the eight circles, write an adjective that describes your character. Then use each adjective in a sentence that could appear in your story. You may write sentences of dialogue, direct characterization, or indirect characterization. Try to suggest whether your character is flat or round, as well as static or dynamic, through the sentences you write. Finally, write a theme that a story about that character might convey.

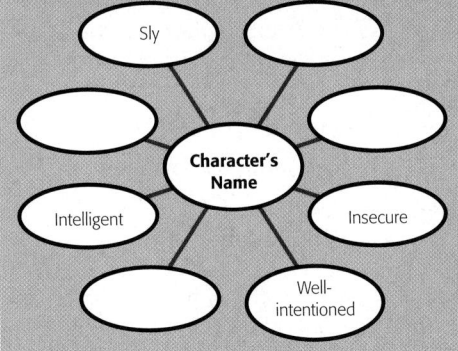

OBJECTIVES
- Understand characters' traits through narration, dialogue, dramatic monologue, and soliloquy.
- Understand themes (general observations about life or human nature) in a short story.

LITERARY FOCUS **95**

Teach

R **Reading Strategy**

Making Inferences About Character **Ask:** What can you infer about the astrologer in "An Astrologer's Day"? *(He is a fraud when it concerns knowing the future, but he is talented at satisfying his customers.)* **OL**

Assess

Quickwrite

Brainstorm with students for adjectives and character traits, such as *trusting, domineering,* and *deceitful.* Students' characterizations should be fleshed out with specific details through description, dialogue, dramatic soliloquy, monologue, or narration.

English Language Coach

Figurative Language Assist English language learners with identifying the figurative language in the Amy Tan excerpt, and discuss why it is used. **Ask:** What feelings are associated with "worms and toads and slimy things"? *(Repulsive, disgusting, and loathsome feelings.)* **EL**

Differentiated Instruction

Author's Purpose Review with less proficient readers the excerpt from "The Vision Quest" and discuss the author's purpose. *(to inform)* **Ask:** How does this purpose affect the statement of theme? *(The theme is stated directly in the first sentence.)* Contrast this with Amy Tan's implied theme. **BL**

Objectives
- To understand characters' traits through narration, dialogue, dramatic monologue, and soliloquy (SE)
- To understand themes in a short story (SE)
- To compare and contrast characterization (TWE)

Focus

BELLRINGER

Bellringer Options
Selection Focus Transparency 6
Daily Language Transparency 11
Or write on the blackboard several different careers, such as doctor, athlete, writer, and actress.
Ask: Are you interested in any of these careers? What other career paths are you interested in pursuing?
Have students discuss their dream jobs or ideal career paths and what they would like to achieve in these jobs.

Literature Online

Author Search To expand students' appreciation of Amy Tan, have them access the Web site for additional information and resources.

Two Kinds

MEET AMY TAN

Writing always has been Amy Tan's passion. In fact, she published her first essay, "What the Library Means to Me," when she was just eight years old. Though Tan went on to become an award-winning author, her fame did not come easily.

Troubled Years Amy Tan was born in Oakland, California. Her parents had immigrated to the United States from China. When Tan was a teenager, her father and her older brother both died of brain tumors within the space of a few months. Tan's mother, who began to worry that toxic chemicals in the environment were responsible, moved the family first to Holland, then to Germany, and later to Switzerland. These were difficult years for Tan. She escaped by diving into the world of books. "Reading for me was a refuge," she says.

Tan describes herself at that time as "a horrible child. I was angry. I was numb. Teenagers are already cynical at that age. But I also had this layer of grief that came out in anger." Conflicts arose between mother and daughter, which lasted for years. Some of the issues were cultural, some were generational, and others were purely personal.

"I have a life that inspires me with a lot of stories."

—Amy Tan

Fact and Fiction Later, Tan incorporated this tension into several novels, the first of which was *The Joy Luck Club,* published in 1989. This novel detailed the many differences between a young Chinese woman and her late mother's Chinese friends. The novel earned a great deal of praise for Tan and has since been turned into an audiotape, a play, and a successful film. The story "Two Kinds" comes from that book.

Although Tan incorporates her real life and its conflicts into her fiction, she adapts and reshapes the details in her work. One advantage to being a writer, she says, is that she can imagine the things she dreams of doing, like trekking in Nepal or raising Yorkshire terriers, and put them in her stories.

Tan eventually resolved her differences with her mother, who encouraged her to tell the truth about painful details of their family's past. Many of these details found their way into Tan's next novel, *The Kitchen God's Wife,* as well as later works. Tan has now written five novels, a screenplay of *The Joy Luck Club,* and a book of essays titled *The Opposite of Fate: A Book of Musings.*

In these essays, Tan explores her own cultural heritage. As a young person, Tan has said, she tried to distance herself from her Chinese origins. However, her writing helped her discover how much her Chinese mother had influenced her. "My books have amounted to taking her stories—a gift to me—and giving them back to her."

Amy Tan was born in 1952.

Literature Online **Author Search** For more about Amy Tan, go to www.glencoe.com.

Selection Skills

Two Kinds

Literary Elements
• Motivation (SE pp. 97–99, 103–104, 106–108)
• Theme (SE p. 108)

Reading Skills
• Connecting (SE pp. 97–109)
• Generalizing (TWE p. 104)
• Sequencing (TWE p. 106)

Vocabulary Skills
• Analogies (SE pp. 97, 109)
• Academic Vocabulary (SE p. 109)
• Context Clues (TWE p. 102)

Listening/Speaking/ Viewing Skills
• Small-Group Discussion (SE p. 109)
• Analyzing Art (SE p. 105)

Writing Skills/Grammar
• Analyzing Character (SE p. 109)
• Personal Essay (TWE p. 100)

Study Skills/Research/Assessment
• Internet Resources (TWE p. 98)

Connecting to the Story

Would you like to be an acclaimed artist or musician? Before you read the story, think about the following questions:

- What experiences truly motivate people to achieve?
- Can anyone achieve greatness by sheer determination and effort, or is greatness inborn?

Building Background

The story is set in San Francisco's Chinatown, which is one of the largest Chinese communities outside of Asia. The neighborhood—with its fascinating mix of restaurants, shops, businesses, and religious and cultural institutions—is a crowded and bustling place. The area was settled by Chinese immigrants who arrived during the Gold Rush of 1849. Chinatown continues to grow and change, as immigrants arrive to begin new lives, just as the mother in "Two Kinds" had done in 1949.

Big Idea | Making Choices

As you read this story, notice the different choices the narrator and her mother make.

Literary Element | Motivation

Motivation is the reason or cause for a character's actions. Knowing a character's motivation for acting a certain way can help you understand his or her behavior more fully. Sometimes an author will state a character's motivation directly, while other times the motivation will be implied, leaving the reader to interpret the underlying reasons for a character's actions. As you read "Two Kinds," pay attention to how the author communicates the motivations behind the characters' behavior.

- See Literary Terms Handbook, p. R11.

Literature Online Interactive Literary Elements Handbook To review or learn more about the literary elements, go to www.glencoe.com.

Reading Strategy | Connecting to Personal Experience

Connecting is linking what you read to events and situations in your life or in other selections that you have read. When you make a **personal connection** to a story, you may identify more closely with the characters' experiences as well as the story's central theme.

Reading Tip: Consciously Connect Look for connections between story details and your life. Use a simple chart to note the connections that you find.

Story Detail	Personal Connection
narrator is child of immigrants	my parents were once immigrants

Vocabulary

prodigy (prod′ə jē) n. an extraordinarily gifted or talented person, especially a child; p. 98 *The child prodigy played the difficult piece well.*

reproach (ri prōch′) n. blame; disgrace; discredit; p. 99 *My aunt did not criticize me aloud, but her look was filled with reproach and anger.*

reverie (rev′ər ē) n. fanciful thinking, daydream; p. 102 *The teacher's abrupt question snapped me out of my reverie.*

discordant (dis kôrd′ənt) adj. not in agreement or harmony; p. 102 *While some violinists make beautiful music, I produce only discordant sounds.*

fiasco (fē as′ kō) n. a complete or humiliating failure; p. 104 *None of the actors knew their lines, so the play was a fiasco.*

Vocabulary Tip: Analogies Analogies show the relationship between words. Completing analogies helps you understand words more completely.

Focus

Summary

Jing-mei's mother, a Chinese immigrant, wants her American-born daughter to become a prodigy. Jing-mei shows no particular promise. Jing-mei takes lessons with a deaf teacher who cannot hear how poorly she plays. At a talent show, she embarrasses herself and her family. Afterward, her mother accuses her of disobedience; Jing-mei counters that her mother wants her to be someone she is not. Years later, Jing-mei understands that the obedient daughter and the disobedient daughter are complementary parts of herself.

V Vocabulary

Vocabulary File Say: Add these words and definitions to your vocabulary file. For each word, include a sentence that gives you an example of how to use the word. **OL** Students with English language needs should include the pronunciations of these words in their files. **EL**

Literature Online

Literary Elements Have students access the Web site to improve their understanding of motivation.

AMY TAN **97**

Selection Resources

Print Materials
- 📁 Unit 1 Resources (Fast File), pp. 46–48
- 📁 Leveled Vocabulary Development, p. 8
- 📁 Selection and Unit Assessments, pp. 17–18
- 📁 Selection Quick Checks, p. 9

Transparencies
- Bellringer Options Transparencies: Selection Focus Transparency 6
  Daily Language Practice Transparency 11
- Literary Elements Transparency 16

Technology
- 💿 TeacherWorks Plus™ CD-ROM
- 💿 StudentWorks Plus™ CD-ROM
- 💿 Presentation Plus!™ CD-ROM
- 💻 Literature Online, glencoe.com
- 💻 Online Student Edition, mhln.com
- 💿 ExamView® Assessment Suite CD-ROM
- 💿 Vocabulary PuzzleMaker CD-ROM
- 💿 Listening Library, disc 1 track 9

Big Idea

Making Choices

Say: Keep the following questions in mind as you read. What choices does Jing-mei make that affect her relationship with her mother? *(She plays a game to see how long it will take her mother to give up on the nightly tests; she doesn't try very hard to learn piano; she says that she wishes she'd never been born.)* Why do you think she makes these choices? *(She is determined to be herself and not to strive to be more.)* **OL**

L1 Literary Element

Motivation Answer: *The mother may feel this way because she lost everything in China and views the United States as a land of opportunity.* **OL**

Readability Scores
Dale-Chall: 4.5
DRP: 54
Lexile: 860

Two Kinds

Amy Tan

Sign in Chinatown Section of San Francisco.

My mother believed you could be anything you wanted to be in America. You could open a restaurant. You could work for the government and get good retirement. You could buy a house with almost no money down. You could become rich. You could become instantly famous.

"Of course, you can be **prodigy,** too," my mother told me when I was nine. "You can be best anything. What does Auntie Lindo know? Her daughter, she is only best tricky."

America was where all my mother's hopes lay. She had come to San Francisco in 1949 after losing everything in China: her mother and father, her family home, her first hus-band, and two daughters, twin baby girls. But she never looked back with regret. Things could get better in so many ways.

We didn't immediately pick the right kind of prodigy. At first my mother thought I could be a Chinese Shirley Temple.[1] We'd watch Shirley's old movies on TV as though they were training films. My mother would poke my arm and say, "*Ni kan.* You watch." And I would see Shirley tapping her feet, or singing a sailor song, or pursing her lips into a very round O while saying "Oh, my goodness."

"*Ni kan,*" my mother said, as Shirley's eyes flooded with tears. "You already know how. Don't need talent for crying!"

Vocabulary

prodigy (prod′ə jē) n. an extraordinarily gifted or talented person, especially a child

1. *Shirley Temple* was a popular child movie star of the 1930s.

Literary Element Motivation *What reasons might the mother have for her optimism about the United States?* **L1**

98 UNIT 1 SHORT STORY

Additional Support

Skills Practice

RESEARCH: Internet Resources

Shirley Temple is most famous for her many movie roles as a young child, beginning in 1932 with *Merrily Yours* and *What's to Do?* Temple was barely four years old when she started acting, and, other than a few television appearances, left the silver screen in the late 1940s. Have students use Internet resources to find out more about Temple's life—before, during, and after her acting career—and her films while making sure to evaluate the reliability of the Web sites they use. **OL**

Soon after my mother got this idea about Shirley Temple, she took me to the beauty training school in the Mission District[2] and put me in the hands of a student who could barely hold the scissors without shaking. Instead of getting big fat curls, I emerged with an uneven mass of crinkly black fuzz. My mother dragged me off to the bathroom and tried to wet down my hair.

"You look like Negro Chinese," she lamented, as if I had done this on purpose.

The instructor of the beauty training school had to lop off these soggy clumps to make my hair even again. "Peter Pan is very popular these days," the instructor assured my mother. I now had hair the length of a boy's, with curly bangs that hung at a slant two inches above my eyebrows. I liked the haircut, and it made me actually look forward to my future fame.

In fact, in the beginning I was just as excited as my mother, maybe even more so. I pictured this prodigy part of me as many different images, and I tried each one on for size. I was a dainty ballerina girl standing by the curtain, waiting to hear the music that would send me floating on my tiptoes. I was like the Christ child lifted out of the straw manger, crying with holy indignity. I was Cinderella stepping from her pumpkin carriage with sparkly cartoon music filling the air.

In all of my imaginings I was filled with a sense that I would soon become perfect. My mother and father would adore me. I would be beyond **reproach.** I would never feel the need to sulk, or to clamor for anything.

But sometimes the prodigy in me became impatient. "If you don't hurry up and get me out of here, I'm disappearing for good," it warned. "And then you'll always be nothing."

Every night after dinner my mother and I would sit at the Formica-topped[3] kitchen table. She would present new tests, taking her examples from stories of amazing children that she had read in Ripley's Believe It or Not or Good Housekeeping, Reader's Digest, or any of a dozen other magazines she kept in a pile in our bathroom. My mother got these magazines from people whose houses she cleaned. And since she cleaned many houses each week, we had a great assortment. She would look through them all, searching for stories about remarkable children.

The first night she brought out a story about a three-year-old boy who knew the capitals of all the states and even of most of the European countries. A teacher was quoted as saying that the little boy could also pronounce the names of the foreign cities correctly. "What's the capital of Finland?" my mother asked me, looking at the story.

All I knew was the capital of California, because Sacramento was the name of the street we lived on in Chinatown. "Nairobi!"[4] I guessed, saying the most foreign word I could think of. She checked to see if that might be one way to pronounce *Helsinki* before showing me the answer.

The tests got harder—multiplying numbers in my head, finding the queen of hearts in a deck of cards, trying to stand on my head without using my hands, predicting the daily temperatures in Los Angeles, New York, and London. One night I had to look at a page from the Bible for three minutes and then report everything I could remember. "Now

---

2. The *Mission District* is a residential neighborhood in San Francisco.

Reading Strategy Connecting to Personal Experience
What kinds of daydreams about success are common today? R

Vocabulary

reproach (ri prōch´) n. blame, disgrace, discredit

3. *Formica* (fôr mī´ kə) is a plastic substance used to cover kitchen and bathroom surfaces because it is resistant to heat and water.
4. *Nairobi* (nī rō´ bē) is the capital of Kenya in east central Africa.

Literary Element Motivation *What motivates the mother to ask her daughter this question?* L2

AMY TAN **99**

Teach

R Reading Strategy

Connecting to Personal Experience Answer: *Becoming a rock star, professional athlete, movie star.* OL

L2 Literary Element

Motivation Answer: *The mother wants her daughter to be like the boy in the story.* OL

★ Cultural History

Cartoon Allusions Tan alludes to two famous fictional and fairy-tale figures on this page: Cinderella and Peter Pan. Disney released its feature-length film *Cinderella* in 1950 and *Peter Pan* in 1953. Tan's use of these allusions reflects the young age of her narrator. AS

✓ CheckPoint

Use the CheckPoint questions on Presentation Plus! to monitor students' comprehension. These questions can be used with interactive response keypads for immediate student feedback.

English Language Coach

Dialect Clarify for students that English is the second language for the narrator's mother. She often leaves out words or uses incorrect syntax. Have them keep a log of statements by the mother that they believe are grammatically incorrect. Then have partners work together to try to correct the statements. At the end of the selection, ask partners to share their work with the class. EL

Objectives
• To analyze motivation (SE)
• To connect to personal experience (SE)
• To conduct Internet research (TWE)

Making Choices Answer:
Students may say that the narrator's choice reveals that she underestimates her mother's desire for her to be a prodigy. **Ask:** What does this imply about Jing-mei's interest in becoming a prodigy? *(This implies that Jing-mei has no deep-rooted desire to become the prodigy her mother wants her to be.)* **OL**

★ Language History

Eponyms Point out that F. A. Mesmer (1734–1815) an Austrian doctor and specialist in hypnotism, gave his name to the language with the verb *mesmerize.* Rudolf Diesel, Daniel Fahrenheit, and James Watt are also eponyms, people whose names have become part of our vocabulary. Ask students to find the origins of some other eponymous words: *maverick, boycott, chauvinist, guy,* and *leotard.* **AS**

Jehoshaphat[5] had riches and honor in abundance and . . . that's all I remember, Ma," I said.

And after seeing, once again, my mother's disappointed face, something inside me began to die. I hated the tests, the raised hopes and failed expectations. Before going to bed that night I looked in the mirror above the bathroom sink, and when I saw only my face staring back—and understood that it would always be this ordinary face—I began to cry. Such a sad, ugly girl! I made high-pitched noises like a crazed animal, trying to scratch out the face in the mirror.

And then I saw what seemed to be the prodigy side of me—a face I had never seen before. I looked at my reflection, blinking so that I could see more clearly. The girl staring back at me was angry, powerful. She and I were the same. I had new thoughts, willful thoughts—or, rather, thoughts filled with lots of won'ts. I won't let her change me, I promised myself. I won't be what I'm not. So now when my mother presented her tests, I performed listlessly, my head propped on one arm. I pretended to be bored. And I was. I got so bored that I started counting the bellows of the foghorns out on the bay while my mother drilled me in other areas. The sound was comforting and reminded me of the cow jumping over the moon. And the next day I played a game with myself, seeing if my mother would give up on me before eight bellows. After a while I usually counted only one bellow, maybe two at most. At last she was beginning to give up hope.

Two or three months went by without any mention of my being a prodigy. And then

"I won't let her change me, I promised myself."

one day my mother was watching the *Ed Sullivan Show*[6] on TV. The TV was old and the sound kept shorting out. Every time my mother got halfway up from the sofa to adjust the set, the sound would come back on and Sullivan would be talking. As soon as she sat down, Sullivan would go silent again. She got up—the TV broke into loud piano music. She sat down—silence. Up and down, back and forth, quiet and loud. It was like a stiff, embraceless dance between her and the TV set. Finally, she stood by the set with her hand on the sound dial.

She seemed entranced by the music, a frenzied little piano piece with a mesmerizing quality, which alternated between quick, playful passages and teasing, lilting[7] ones.

"*Ni kan,*" my mother said, calling me over with hurried hand gestures. "Look here."

I could see why my mother was fascinated by the music. It was being pounded out by a little Chinese girl, about nine years old, with a Peter Pan haircut. The girl had the sauciness[8] of a Shirley Temple. She was proudly modest, like a proper Chinese child. And she also did a fancy sweep of a curtsy, so that the fluffy skirt of her white dress cascaded to the floor like the petals of a large carnation.

In spite of these warning signs, I wasn't worried. Our family had no piano and we couldn't afford to buy one, let alone reams of sheet music and piano lessons. So I could be generous in my comments when my mother bad-mouthed the little girl on TV.

---

6. The *Ed Sullivan Show* was a popular weekly variety show on TV in the 1950s and 1960s.
7. *Lilting* means "light and lively."
8. *Sauciness* means "boldness that is playful and lighthearted."

Big Idea Making Choices *What might the narrator's choice to ignore the "warning signs" reveal about her?* **BI₁**

---

5. *Jehoshaphat* (ji hosh′ ə fat′) was a king of Judah in the ninth century BC.

Additional Support

Skills Practice

WRITING: Personal Essay Suggest to students that our personalities are multifaceted. Like the narrator, we are not always what we appear to be or would like to be. One way to understand who we are is through writing. Have students write two paragraphs under the general heading *Myself.* The first paragraph should be entitled *What Other People See,* the second one *What I See.* For the first paragraph, have students write a physical description; for the second, have them write about the "face" that may not be visible to others. **OL**

"Play note right, but doesn't sound good!" my mother complained. "No singing sound." "What are you picking on her for?" I said carelessly. "She's pretty good. Maybe she's not the best, but she's trying hard." I knew almost immediately that I would be sorry I had said that.

"Just like you," she said. "Not the best. Because you not trying." She gave a little huff as she let go of the sound dial and sat down on the sofa.

Visual Vocabulary
Edvard *Grieg* (grēg), 1843–1907, was a Norwegian composer.

The little Chinese girl sat down also, to play an encore of "Anitra's Tanz," by Grieg. I remember the song, because later on I had to learn how to play it.

Three days after watching the *Ed Sullivan Show* my mother told me what my schedule would be for piano lessons and piano practice. She had talked to Mr. Chong, who lived on the first floor of our apartment building. Mr. Chong was a retired piano teacher, and my mother had traded house-cleaning services for weekly lessons and a piano for me to practice on every day, two hours a day, from four until six.

When my mother told me this, I felt as though I had been sent to hell. I whined, and then kicked my foot a little when I couldn't stand it anymore.

"Why don't you like me the way I am?" I cried, "I'm *not* a genius! I can't play the piano. And even if I could, I wouldn't go on TV if you paid me a million dollars!"

My mother slapped me. "Who ask you to be genius?" she shouted. "Only ask you be your best. For you sake. You think I want you to be genius! Hnnh! What for! Who ask you!"

"So ungrateful," I heard her mutter in Chinese. "If she had as much talent as she has temper, she'd be famous now."

> **Reading Strategy** Connecting to Personal Experience
> *Can you recall a situation in which you felt similarly about a decision you did not like?* **R**

Mr. Chong, whom I secretly nicknamed Old Chong, was very strange, always tapping his fingers to the silent music of an invisible orchestra. He looked ancient in my eyes. He had lost most of the hair on the top of his head, and he wore thick glasses and had eyes that always looked tired. But he must have been younger than I thought, since he lived with his mother and was not yet married.

I met Old Lady Chong once, and that was enough. She had a peculiar smell, like a baby that had done something in its pants, and her fingers felt like a dead person's, like an old peach I once found in the back of the refrigerator; its skin just slid off the flesh when I picked it up.

I soon found out why Old Chong had retired from teaching piano. He was deaf. "Like Beethoven!" he shouted to me. "We're both listening only in our head!" And he would start to conduct his frantic silent sonatas.[9]

Our lessons went like this. He would open the book and point to different things, explaining their purpose: "Key! Treble! Bass! No sharps or flats! So this is C major! Listen now and play after me!"

And then he would play the C scale a few times, a simple chord, and then, as if inspired by an old unreachable itch, he would gradually add more notes and running trills and a pounding bass until the music was really something quite grand.

I would play after him, the simple scale, the simple chord, and then just play some nonsense that sounded like a cat running up and down on top of garbage cans. Old Chong **BI₂** would smile and applaud and say, "Very good! But now you must learn to keep time!"

So that's how I discovered that Old Chong's eyes were too slow to keep up with the wrong

Visual Vocabulary
Ludwig van *Beethoven* (bā′ tō vən), 1770–1827, was a German composer.

---

9. *Sonatas* are instrumental compositions, commonly written for piano.

Teach

R **Reading Strategy**

Connecting to Personal Experience Answer: *Students' answers will vary. Many will recall with similar frustration a decision a parent made.* **OL**

BI₂ Big Idea

Making Choices Ask: How do you think Jing-mei's decision to play haphazardly will make her mother feel? *(It will probably make her mother angry that Jing-mei does not take her piano lessons very seriously.)* **OL**

★ Cultural History

Ed Sullivan From 1948 to 1971, Sullivan hosted a popular television variety show. Some of the performers who appeared on the show went on to become among the best-known names in entertainment, from Elvis Presley to the Beatles. **Ask:** What TV shows do we have today that compare to *The Ed Sullivan Show*? **Answer:** *Students may cite* American Idol, Star Search, *and various late-night talk shows.* **AS**

Differentiated Instruction

Reviewing Characters This is a good point in "Two Kinds" to pause and review what readers know about the principal characters. Have students write *Daughter Thinks* and *Mother Thinks* on a piece of paper. **Say:** Beneath each heading write sentences or phrases you believe are going through the minds of these characters. While they write, draw on the board large outlines of two human heads. Label one *Jing-mei* and the other *Mother*. Ask for volunteers to write their best thoughts within the appropriate heads. Discuss these thoughts with the class. **BL**

Objectives
• To connect what you read to personal experience (SE)
• To write a personal essay (TWE)

101

Teach

R1 Reading Strategy

Connecting to Personal Experience **Answer:** *Students might mention reading traditional stories, such as "Cinderella" or other stories with competitive siblings. They might also mention family rivalries.* OL

★ Viewing the Art

Have students study this statue of a ballerina by Edgar Degas. Guide them to notice her posture, her stance, and her facial expression. Then have them picture in their minds Jing-mei and her cousin Waverly. **Ask:** Does this picture make you think of Jing-mei or Waverly? Why? *(Most students will probably be reminded of Waverly, who sounds more like the "ideal," pleasing, and perhaps smug daughter.)* AS

Little Dancer of Fourteen Years, 1880–1881. Edgar Degas. Philadelphia Museum of Art. ★

notes I was playing. He went through the motions in half time. To help me keep rhythm, he stood behind me and pushed down on my right shoulder for every beat. He balanced pennies on top of my wrists so that I would keep them still as I slowly played scales and arpeggios.[10] He had me curve my hand around an apple and keep that shape when playing chords. He marched stiffly to show me how to make each finger dance up and down, staccato,[11] like an obedient little soldier.

He taught me all these things, and that was how I also learned I could be lazy and get away with mistakes, lots of mistakes. If I hit the wrong notes because I hadn't practiced enough, I never corrected myself. I just kept

---

10. *Arpeggios* (är pej′ ē ōz) are chords in which the notes are played in succession instead of all at the same time.
11. To play music *staccato* (stə kä′ tō) is to produce sharp, distinct breaks between successive tones.

Big Idea Making Choices *What choice has the narrator made about her piano playing?* BI

playing in rhythm. And Old Chong kept conducting his own private **reverie.**

So maybe I never really gave myself a fair chance. I did pick up the basics pretty quickly, and I might have become a good pianist at that young age. But I was so determined not to try, not to be anybody different, that I learned to play only the most ear-splitting preludes, the most **discordant** hymns.

Over the next year I practiced like this, dutifully in my own way. And then one day I heard my mother and her friend Lindo Jong both talking in a loud, bragging tone of voice so that others could hear. It was after church, and I was leaning against a brick wall, wearing a dress with stiff white petticoats. Auntie Lindo's daughter, Waverly, who was my age, was standing farther down the wall, about five feet away. We had grown up together and shared all the closeness of two sisters, squabbling over crayons and dolls. In other words, for the most part, we hated each other. I thought she was snotty. Waverly Jong had gained a certain amount of fame as "Chinatown's Littlest Chinese Chess Champion."

"She bring home too many trophy," Auntie Lindo lamented that Sunday. "All day she play chess. All day I have no time do nothing but dust off her winnings." She threw a scolding look at Waverly, who pretended not to see her.

"You lucky you don't have this problem," Auntie Lindo said with a sigh to my mother.

And my mother squared her shoulders and bragged: "Our problem worser than yours. If we ask Jing-mei[12] wash dish, she

---

12. *Jing-mei* (jing′ mā)

Reading Strategy Connecting to Personal Experience
In what situations have you experienced the type of relationship described here? R1

Vocabulary

reverie (rev′ər ē) *n.* fanciful thinking, daydream
discordant (dis kôrd′ənt) *adj.* not in agreement or harmony

Additional Support

Skills Practice

VOCABULARY: Context Clues **Say:** When reading on your own, you can often figure out the meanings of new words by looking at their context— the other words and sentences that surround them. Have students look at the highlighted word *discordant.* **Ask:** What context clues could you use to determine the meaning of this word? *("Ear-splitting preludes" is the best clue because it describes the sound of something discordant. Jing-mei's determination "not to try" implies that she doesn't play well and produces an ugly sound.)* OL hear nothing but music. It's like you can't stop this natural talent."

And right then I was determined to put a stop to her foolish pride.

A few weeks later Old Chong and my mother conspired to have me play in a talent

Visual Vocabulary
A *spinet* (spin' it) is a small, upright piano.

show that was to be held in the church hall. By then my parents had saved up enough to buy me a sec- ondhand piano, a black Wurlitzer spinet with a scarred bench. It was the showpiece of our living room.

For the talent show I was to play a piece called "Pleading Child," from Schumann's[13] *Scenes From Childhood*. It was a simple, moody piece that sounded more difficult than it was. I was supposed to memorize the whole thing. But I dawdled over it, playing a few bars and then cheating, looking up to see what notes followed. I never really listened to what I was playing. I daydreamed about being somewhere else, about being someone else.

The part I liked to practice best was the fancy curtsy: right foot out, touch the rose on the carpet with a pointed foot, sweep to the side, bend left leg, look up, and smile.

My parents invited all the couples from their social club to witness my debut. Auntie Lindo and Uncle Tin were there. Waverly and her two older brothers had also come. The first two rows were filled with children either younger or older than I was. The littlest ones got to go first. They recited simple nursery rhymes, squawked out tunes on miniature violins, and twirled hula hoops in

---

13. Robert *Schumann* (shōō' män), 1810–1856, was a German composer.

Literary Element Motivation *What do you think motivated the narrator's decision here?* **L1**

Reading Strategy Connecting to Personal Experience *Everyone has daydreamed at some time or other about being someone else. Why do you think people do this?* **R2**

pink ballet tutus, and when they bowed or curtsied, the audience would sigh in unison, "*Awww*," and then clap enthusiastically.

When my turn came, I was very confident. I remember my childish excitement. It was as if I knew, without a doubt, that the prodigy side of me really did exist. I had no fear whatsoever, no nervousness. I remember thinking, This is it! This is it! I looked out over the audience, at my mother's blank face, my father's yawn, Auntie Lindo's stiff- lipped smile, Waverly's sulky expression. I had on a white dress, layered with sheets of lace, and a pink bow in my Peter Pan haircut. As I sat down, I envisioned people jumping to their feet and Ed Sullivan rushing up to introduce me to everyone on TV.

And I started to play. Everything was so beautiful. I was so caught up in how lovely I looked that I wasn't worried about how I would sound. So I was surprised when I hit the first wrong note. And then I hit another, and another. A chill started at the top of my head and began to trickle down. Yet I couldn't stop playing, as though my hands were bewitched. I kept thinking my fingers would adjust themselves back, like a train switching to the right track. I played this strange jumble through to the end, the sour notes staying with me all the way.

When I stood up, I discovered my legs were shaking. Maybe I had just been nervous, and the audience, like Old Chong, had seen me go through the right motions and had not heard anything wrong at all. I swept my right foot out, went down on my knee, looked up, and smiled. The room was quiet, except for Old Chong, who was beaming and shouting, "Bravo! Bravo! Well done!" But then I saw my mother's face, her stricken face. The audience clapped weakly, and as I walked back to my chair, with my whole face quivering as I tried not to cry, I heard a little boy whisper loudly to his

Literary Element Motivation *What desire motivates the narrator here?* **L2**

Teach

L1 Literary Element

Motivation Answer: *The nar- rator was motivated by a dis- like for the falsehoods that her mother communicated.* **OL**

R2 Reading Strategy

Connecting to Personal Experience Answer: *Students might suggest the desire to escape from reality or to improve upon it.* **OL**

L2 Literary Element

Motivation Answer: *The narrator is motivated by a desire for fame and glory.* **Ask:** Considering what you know about Jing-mei's piano prac- tice habits, how do you think her performance will turn out? *(Students will probably agree that her performance will go very poorly.)* **OL**

Reading in the Real World

Career The arts pages of magazines and newspapers carry stories about musicians who are performing in upcom- ing concerts. These are not critical reviews, but feature stories and inter- views. Have students bring to class fea- ture stories on musicians. Let them read and discuss these in groups. Have them discuss questions: *Is this a well-rounded picture of the artist? Is the author tell- ing me what to think? Does the article persuade me that the artist is worth hearing?* **OL**

Objectives
• To connect what you read to per- sonal experience (SE)
• To analyze motivation (SE)
• To use context clues to under- stand vocabulary (TWE)

Teach

L Literary Element

Motivation Answer: *The mother was probably crushed by her daughter's public humiliation.* **OL**

BI Big Idea

Making Choices Answer: *Until now, the narrator has been difficult but obedient. Deciding not to be obedient is a significant change and is sure to cause trouble.* **OL**

★ Writer's Technique

Figurative Meanings Ask students what they would usually associate with the word *anchor*. Point out that here it is used figuratively, instead of literally: the parents are not ships and there is no heavy weight restraining them. Encourage students to think of other verbs that can be used figuratively. **AS**

---

mother, "That was awful," and the mother whispered back, "Well, she certainly tried."

And now I realized how many people were in the audience—the whole world, it seemed. I was aware of eyes burning into my back. I felt the shame of my mother and father as they sat stiffly through the rest of the show.

We could have escaped during intermission. Pride and some strange sense of honor must have anchored my parents to their ★ chairs. And so we watched it all: The eighteen-year-old boy with a fake moustache who did a magic show and juggled flaming hoops while riding a unicycle. The breasted girl with white makeup who sang an aria[14] from *Madame Butterfly* and got an honorable mention. And the eleven-year-old boy who won first prize playing a tricky violin song that sounded like a busy bee.

Visual Vocabulary
Madame Butterfly is a famous opera by Italian composer Giacomo Puccini.

After the show the Hsus, the Jongs, and the St. Clairs, from the Joy Luck Club, came up to my mother and father.

"Lots of talented kids," Auntie Lindo said vaguely, smiling broadly.

"That was somethin' else," my father said, and I wondered if he was referring to me in a humorous way, or whether he even remembered what I had done.

Waverly looked at me and shrugged her shoulders. "You aren't a genius like me," she said matter-of-factly. And if I hadn't felt so bad, I would have pulled her braids and punched her stomach.

But my mother's expression was what devastated me: a quiet, blank look that said she had lost everything. I felt the same way, and everybody seemed now to be coming up, like gawkers at the scene of an accident, to see what parts were actually missing.

When we got on the bus to go home, my father was humming the busy-bee tune and my mother was silent. I kept thinking she

wanted to wait until we got home before shouting at me. But when my father unlocked the door to our apartment, my mother walked in and went straight to the back, into the bedroom. No accusations. No blame. And in a way, I felt disappointed. I had been waiting for her to start shouting, so that I could shout back and cry and blame her for all my misery.

I had assumed that my talent-show **fiasco** meant that I would never have to play the piano again. But two days later, after school, my mother came out of the kitchen and saw me watching TV.

"Four clock," she reminded me, as if it were any other day. I was stunned, as though she were asking me to go through the talent-show torture again. I planted myself more squarely in front of the TV.

"Turn off TV," she called from the kitchen five minutes later.

I didn't budge. And then I decided. I didn't have to do what my mother said anymore. I wasn't her slave. This wasn't China. I had listened to her before, and look what happened. She was the stupid one.

She came out from the kitchen and stood in the arched entryway of the living room. "Four clock," she said once again, louder.

"I'm not going to play anymore," I said nonchalantly. "Why should I? I'm not a genius."

She stood in front of the TV. I saw that her chest was heaving up and down in an angry way.

"No!" I said, and I now felt stronger, as if my true self had finally emerged. So this was what had been inside me all along. "No! I won't!" I screamed.

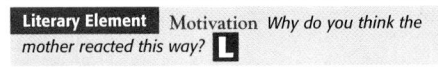

Literary Element Motivation *Why do you think the mother reacted this way?* **L**

Big Idea Making Choices *Why is this a serious choice?* **BI**

Vocabulary
fiasco (fē as′kō) n. a complete or humiliating failure

---

14. An *aria* (är′ ē ə) is an elaborate composition for solo voice.

104 UNIT 1   THE SHORT STORY

Additional Support

Skills Practice

READING: Generalizing Point out that reading about fictional characters often enables readers to understand the behavior of people in general. For example, analyzing the characters in "Two Kinds" can lead to generalizations about relationships between parents and children. **Say:** Formulate a generalization about parent-child relationships based on the mother and daughter in "Two Kinds." Have students state their generalization and the textual evidence upon which it is based. Have the class decide whether each generalization is valid. **OL**

Young Girl at a Grand Piano, 1904. Carl Larsson.
Viewing the Art: Compare and contrast the attitude of the girl in this painting with that of Jing-mei.

She snapped off the TV, yanked me by the arm and pulled me off the floor. She was frighteningly strong, half pulling, half carrying me toward the piano as I kicked the throw rugs under my feet. She lifted me up and onto the hard bench. I was sobbing by now, looking at her bitterly. Her chest was heaving even more and her mouth was open, smiling crazily as if she were pleased that I was crying.

"You want me to be someone that I'm not!" I sobbed. "I'll never be the kind of daughter you want me to be!"

"Only two kinds of daughters," she shouted in Chinese. "Those who are obedient and those who follow their own mind! Only one kind of daughter can live in this house. Obedient daughter!"

"Then I wish I weren't your daughter. I wish you weren't my mother," I shouted. As I said these things I got scared. It felt like worms and toads and slimy things crawling

---

Reading Strategy Connecting to Personal Experience
Think of a time when you said something you regretted. How did your reaction compare to the narrator's? **R**

AMY TAN **105**

Teach

R Reading Strategy

Connecting to Personal Experience Answer:
Students' answers will vary, but should include whether they reacted with fear or some other emotion. **OL**

★ Viewing the Art

Answer: *The piano eclipses all but the player's eyes, implying that music is a very significant part of the musician's life. The guitar hanging on the wall is another clue to the significance of music to the pianist's life. This is very unlike Jing-mei. Jing-mei does not care about the music or perfecting her ability to play it well.* **Ask:** *What would a picture of Jing-mei playing the piano look like? (Answers will vary. Students will probably say that the picture would be Jing-mei staring forlornly at the piano or playing listlessly.)* **AS**

Differentiated Instruction

Visual Learning Jing-mei feels as though she is two people: the obedient daughter and the rebel trying to break free. Some students will find this internal conflict easier to understand if they visualize Jing-mei's opposing personae. Have students find or create visual symbols for the two sides of Jing-mei's personality. These could be sketches of her two "faces," abstract designs, or symbolic objects. Ask them to present their creations to the class with a brief explanation of their significance. **BL**

Objectives
• To analyze motivation (SE)
• To connect to personal experience (SE)
• To make generalizations about character (TWE)

Teach

L1 **Literary Element**

Motivation Answer: *Perhaps she wants her mother to feel the same intensity of negative emotion that she herself feels.* **OL**

⭐ Viewing the Art

Don Jacot (1949–) is a photorealist painter who was born in Chicago and lives in Michigan. Students may be surprised to learn that the image is a painting. Point out to them the way that the artist shows reflections in the window. **AS**

Storefront Window, Chinatown, NY, 1993.
Don Jacot.

out of my chest, but it also felt good, that this awful side of me had surfaced, at last.

"Too late change this," my mother said shrilly.

And I could sense her anger rising to its breaking point. I wanted to see it spill over. And that's when I remembered the babies she had lost in China, the ones we never talked about. "Then I wish I'd never been born!" I shouted. "I wish I were dead! Like them."

It was as if I had said magic words. Alakazam!—her face went blank, her mouth closed, her arms went slack, and she backed out of the room, stunned, as if she were blowing away like a small brown leaf, thin, brittle, lifeless.

Literary Element Motivation *Why do you think the narrator had this desire?* **L1**

106 UNIT 1   THE SHORT STORY

It was not the only disappointment my mother felt in me. In the years that followed, I failed her many times, each time asserting my will, my right to fall short of expectations. I didn't get straight *A*s. I didn't become class president. I didn't get into Stanford. I dropped out of college.

Unlike my mother, I did not believe I could be anything I wanted to be. I could only be me.

And for all those years we never talked about the disaster at the recital or my terrible declarations afterward at the piano bench. Neither of us talked about it again, as if it were a betrayal that was now unspeakable. So I never found a way to ask her why she had hoped for something so large that failure was inevitable.

Additional Support

Skills Practice

READING: Sequencing Say: The order in which thoughts are arranged is called sequence. Three common forms of sequencing are chronological order, spatial order, and order of importance. Write on the board *I didn't get into Stanford. I played horribly at the talent show. I didn't become high school class president. I dropped out of college.* Then write *Chronological Order* and *Order of Importance* on the board and have the students create the two different sequences. **OL**

And even worse, I never asked her about what frightened me the most: Why had she given up hope? For after our struggle at the piano, she never mentioned my playing again. The lessons stopped. The lid to the piano was closed, shutting out the dust, my misery, and her dreams.

So she surprised me. A few years ago she offered to give me the piano, for my thirtieth birthday. I had not played in all those years. I saw the offer as a sign of forgiveness, a tremendous burden removed.

"Are you sure?" I asked shyly. "I mean, won't you and Dad miss it?"

"No, this your piano," she said firmly. "Always your piano. You only one can play."

"Well, I probably can't play anymore," I said. "It's been years."

"You pick up fast," my mother said, as if she knew this was certain. "You have natural talent. You could be genius if you want to."

"No, I couldn't."

"You just not trying," my mother said. And she was neither angry nor sad. She said it as if announcing a fact that could never be disproved. "Take it," she said.

But I didn't, at first. It was enough that she had offered it to me. And after that, every time I saw it in my parents' living room, standing in front of the bay window, it made me feel proud, as if it were a shiny trophy that I had won back.

"You could be genius if you want to."

Big Idea Making Choices *Do you think the mother's choice here is consistent with how she has been portrayed thus far? Explain.* **BI**

Literary Element Motivation *Do you think the narrator is correct about the motivation behind her mother's offer?* **L₂**

Last week I sent a tuner over to my parents' apartment and had the piano reconditioned, for purely sentimental reasons. My mother had died a few months before, and I had been getting things in order for my father, a little bit at a time. I put the jewelry in special silk pouches. The sweaters she had knitted in yellow, pink, bright orange—all the colors I hated—I put in mothproof boxes. I found some old Chinese silk dresses, the kind with little slits up the sides. I rubbed the old silk against my skin, and then wrapped them in tissue and decided to take them home with me.

After I had the piano tuned, I opened the lid and touched the keys. It sounded even richer than I remembered. Really, it was a very good piano. Inside the bench were the same exercise notes with handwritten scales, the same secondhand music books with their covers held together with yellow tape.

I opened up the Schumann book to the dark little piece I had played at the recital. It was on the left-hand page, "Pleading Child." It looked more difficult than I remembered. I played a few bars, surprised at how easily the notes came back to me.

And for the first time, or so it seemed, I noticed the piece on the right-hand side. It was called "Perfectly Contented." I tried to play this one as well. It had a lighter melody but with the same flowing rhythm and turned out to be quite easy. "Pleading Child" was shorter but slower; "Perfectly Contented" was longer but faster. And after I had played them both a few times, I realized they were two halves of the same song. ❧

AMY TAN **107**

Teach

BI Big Idea

Making Choices Answer: *Students may say that her choice is surprising, given her previous insistence that her daughter excel.* **OL**

L₂ Literary Element

Motivation Answer: *Students' responses will vary. Some may say it showed what her mother felt all along—that she was in fact capable of anything she set her mind to.* **OL**

★ Cultural History

Classical Music Robert Schumann (1810–1856) was one of the great composers for piano. Apart from his virtuoso keyboard compositions, he wrote a number of beautiful and delightfully simple pieces for beginning students, such as *Spinning Song* and *The Happy Farmer.* Have students research Schumann and his contemporaries. **AS**

✓ CheckPoint

Use the CheckPoint questions on Presentation Plus! to check students' mastery of the selection. These questions can be used with interactive response keypads for immediate student feedback.

English Language Coach

Past Perfect Tense Write on the board: *I opened the book to the piece I had played at the recital.* Point out that this is an example of the past perfect tense. It refers to past actions that ended before another past action began.

Explain that Jing-mei opened the book in the past, but Jing-mei played the piece at the talent show even further in the past. Have students use the past perfect tense of the verbs *open, play, die, knit,* and *offer* in sentences of their own. **EL**

Objectives
- To analyze motivation (SE)
- To understand sequencing (TWE)

Assess

1. Answers will vary.

2. (a) Her ordinary face and her "angry, powerful" prodigy face (b) It takes hard work and a dedication that she does not have.

3. (a) Confident and excited (b) They had expected a splendid performance.

4. (a) Jing-mei says she wishes that she were dead, like her mother's twins. (b) Her mother never discusses the twins, probably because this memory is so painful.

5. (a) Jing-mei is the only one who can play the piano. (b) Answers should include evidence from the text.

6. (a) Jing-mei wants to be appreciated for who she is; her mother wants her to excel. (b) The author describes the girl's inner reactions to her mother, building the tension.

7. (a) Jing-mei's mother may base her own worth on her daughter's achievements. (b) Jing-mei shows a strong personality.

8. (a) Jing-mei accepts her ambivalence and that she does have some musical skill. (b) Mother seems more accepting of and complimentary toward her daughter.

RESPONDING AND THINKING CRITICALLY

Respond

1. (a)What was your reaction to the conflict between Jing-mei and her mother? (b)Do you think that one person was more at fault than the other?

Recall and Interpret

2. (a)What two faces does Jing-mei see when she looks in the mirror after another failed prodigy training session? (b)Why does Jing-mei decide to stop trying to become a prodigy?

3. (a)How does Jing-mei feel when it is her turn to perform at the recital? (b)Why do she and her parents feel so humiliated by her performance?

4. (a)What hurtful remark does Jing-Mei say to her mother after their big argument? (b)In your opinion, what makes her comments so brutal?

5. (a)What reasons does Jing-mei's mother give for offering Jing-mei the piano for her thirtieth birthday? (b)Do you think Jing-mei's mother finally forgives her daughter for her hurtful comment?

Analyze and Evaluate

6. (a)What do you think is the underlying issue of Jing-mei and her mother's final argument? (b)How does the author illustrate the mounting tension between them?

7. (a)Why do you think Jing-mei's mother set unrealistic goals for her daughter? (b)What do Jing-mei's responses tell you about her?

8. (a)In what ways had Jing-mei changed by the end of the story? (b)How had Jing-mei's mother changed by the end of the story?

Connect

9. **Big Idea** Making Choices Which choice do you think is most central to the outcome of this story? Explain.

LITERARY ANALYSIS

Literary Element Motivation

In literature, a character's **motivation** is not always perfectly clear. At times, a character's motivation may be weak or mixed, making it difficult to discern or understand. Think about the characters in "Two Kinds." Was it easy or difficult to determine the motivation for their actions?

1. Although the mother says that she only wants Jing-mei to "be [her] best. For [her] sake," what else might motivate her? Use details from the text to support your answer.

2. Jing-mei decides to thwart her mother's "foolish pride," but she does prepare for the talent show, including practicing her fancy curtsy. Why do you think she does this?

Review: Theme

As you learned on page 94, the **theme** is the central message of a story that readers can apply to life.

Partner Activity Meet with another classmate and review the title and main events in the story. Then determine how they contribute to the story's theme. You might note the main events and other important details on a web like the one shown here.

---

9. When Jing-mei refused to make a real effort to learn to play or when she decided not to correct her mistakes

Literary Element

1. The desire for status, as shown in the Shirley Temple incident, or competitiveness, as shown in the discussion with Waverly Jong's mother

2. Students may say that the girl gets caught up in the excitement of appearing in public and being a star.

Review: Theme

Students' responses might include these themes: People are who they are; people do things that have lasting consequences; parents and children see the world differently.

Assess

Reading Strategy Connecting to Personal Experience

As you read, try to **connect** to the story by looking beyond the specific characters and events and focusing on the emotions, situations, or concepts.

1. List feelings, situations, or concepts from this story that are familiar to you from other literary works, films, or television shows.

2. Meet with your classmates to identify entries that appeared on a majority of your lists and discuss why certain concepts, situations, or feelings are common in literature, film, and television.

Vocabulary Practice

Practice with Analogies

Choose the word that best completes each analogy.

1. reverie : daydream :: nap
   a. wake   **b.** sadden   **c.** doze

2. harmonious : discordant :: mesmerizing
   a. magical   **b.** boring   **c.** clashing

3. failure : fiasco :: meal
   a. feast   **b.** snack   **c.** hunger

4. prodigy : talented :: giant
   a. bold   **b.** tall   **c.** frightening

5. reproach : praise :: knowledge
   a. learning   **b.** criticism   **c.** ignorance

Academic Vocabulary

Here are two words from the vocabulary list on page R82. These words will help you think, write, and talk about the selection.

proportion (prə pôr′shən) *n.* a balanced or proper share or relationship

compensate (kom′pən sāt′) *v.* to counterbalance something or make up for it

Practice and Apply

1. Was the mother's desire for a prodigy in **proportion** to her daughter's ability? Explain.

2. What did Old Chong do to **compensate** for his inability to hear?

Writing About Literature

Analyze Character Write a paragraph or two evaluating Jing-mei's actions. A good evaluation is based on certain criteria, so consider what these should be. Do you think that Jing-mei's actions seem appropriate for her age and her situation? What do you think of the way she reacts to her mother? What does she think her mother wants? What does Jing-mei want for herself?

Begin by identifying and briefly describing Jing-mei, using details from the story. You might want to make a chart like the one below to organize details that support your opinion.

Details	Conclusions
Jing-mei learns to "be lazy and get away with mistakes, lots of mistakes." p. 102	This seems appropriate for Jing-mei's age. I was lazy about practicing to play the violin when I was young too.
"And right then I was determined to put a stop to her foolish pride." p. 103	Jing-mei thinks that her mother is foolish for wanting her to be a genius or prodigy.

Review the details you have selected from the text. Then write your evaluation, supporting your main idea with those examples as well as facts and perhaps comparisons. To focus attention on your ideas, try to keep your tone neutral.

When you have completed a draft, exchange it with a peer reviewer. Then edit your evaluation and correct any errors in spelling, grammar, and punctuation.

Literature Groups

Should parents ever require their children to take music lessons, as Jing-mei's mother did, or to play a sport, or participate in any activity? With a small group, look back at "Two Kinds" and list the reasons why the mother's requirements of Jing-mei were beneficial and why they were not. Cite specific examples from the story as you develop your list. Then, compare your group's list with that of another group, and discuss your opinions together.

Literature Online Web Activities For eFlashcards, Selection Quick Checks, and other Web activities, go to www.glencoe.com.

Reading Strategy

1. Students might identify family conflicts, the desire for fame and glory, the shame of public failure, or the immigrant experience.

2. Students may suggest that some stories are widely read because they deal with issues that are universal and recognizable by many readers.

Vocabulary

1. c **2.** b **3.** a **4.** b **5.** c

Academic Vocabulary

1. No, because the mother expected her daughter to be a prodigy but her daughter had only average talent.

2. Old Chong watched his students and paid close attention to their rhythm.

Writing About Literature

Students' paragraphs should

- make a judgment and state reasons for it
- include details from the story to support their judgments

Literature Groups

Students' responses should

- indicate an opinion that relates to the topic of parents' choosing activities for their children
- include details from the story
- discuss whether children's personality should be a factor

Literature Online

Web Activities Have students access the Web site for interactive activities that will help them assess their understanding of the selection.

Focus

BELLRINGER

Bellringer Options
Selection Focus Transparency 7
Daily Language
Transparency 12
Or **ask:** What kinds of silly situations have occurred in your family or a friend's family?
Have students share anecdotes and provide amusing details of funny family situations.

Author Search To expand students' appreciation of James Thurber, have them access the Web site for additional information and resources.

The Car We Had to Push

MEET JAMES THURBER

Although known as a humorist and a lover of pranks, James Thurber has also been called a "complicated and tormented man." He enjoyed vast success as a writer for much of his life, but his later years were marred by unhappiness and ill health.

Thurber was born at the end of the nineteenth century, and he died at the dawning of the Space Age. He saw many social changes, yet his most widely read stories are set in the years of his youth. Thurber was born in Columbus, Ohio, where he lived with his parents and brothers until he left for college. His family and home appear in modified form in many of his best works.

***The New Yorker* Years** Thurber lost an eye in a childhood accident, and this injury kept him out of the service during World War I. He spent a year in Paris working for the State Department and later worked as a reporter. In 1927 he joined the staff of a new magazine: *The New Yorker*. The magazine and its staff changed his life.

> *"If I couldn't write, I couldn't breathe."*
>
> —James Thurber

The magazine became famous, and Thurber was one of its best-known writers. He was also a constant doodler and sketcher, sometimes even drawing on office walls. His officemate E. B. White, also a respected author, urged Thurber to submit drawings to the magazine's art department. Thurber refused, so one day the frustrated White snatched drawings from the trash and submitted them. To Thurber's surprise, they were accepted, and soon his cartoons as well as his stories graced *The New Yorker's* pages.

Later Works Thurber's *My Life and Hard Times* (1933), a collection that contains "The Car We Had to Push," has been described as "a special kind of autobiography, existing somewhere between the world of fact and the world of fantasy." Many consider it to be among Thurber's finest writings.

From 1929 through 1967, Thurber wrote one new book every year or two. In 1942 he published a collection of stories that included "The Secret Life of Walter Mitty." The title character was a timid man who daydreamed about taking part in heroic adventures. The story became a classic that was turned into several movies and has formed the basis for innumerable television plots.

In the 1940s, Thurber began writing fables, plays, and children's books as well as essays. These were difficult years for Thurber; he had numerous health problems and lost the sight in his remaining eye. He continued to work, however, by dictating his books.

In 1959 he published *The Years with Ross*, a biography of editor Harold Ross and an account of Thurber's years at *The New Yorker*. Thurber published only one major work after that, *A Thurber Carnival*, which was a series of skits.

People still read Thurber's works for their humor and vitality. His humor, wrote one critic, "has a timeless quality that should guarantee him a readership far into the future."

James Thurber was born in 1894 and died in 1961.

Literature Online Author Search For more about James Thurber, go to www.glencoe.com.

Selection Skills

Literary Elements
• Dialogue (SE pp. 111, 113, 114, 116, 118)
• Dialect (SE p. 118)

Reading Skills
• Making Generalizations About Characters (SE pp. 111–118)
• Previewing (TWE p. 112)
• Using Graphic Organizers (TWE p. 116)

The Car We Had to Push

Vocabulary Skills
• Word Origins (SE pp. 111, 118)
• Academic Vocabulary (SE p. 118)

Listening/Speaking/Viewing Skills
• Analyzing Illustrations (SE p. 117)
• Presenting a News Story (SE p. 119)

Writing Skills/Grammar
• Analyzing Humor (SE p. 119)
• Using Colons (SE p. 119)

Connecting to the Story

Does everyone embrace new technologies with open arms? In Thurber's story, cars and electricity are relatively new technologies. Before you read the story, think about the following questions:

- Why might people fear a force or machine that they do not fully understand?
- What technologies have been introduced in your lifetime?

Building Background

In the early twentieth century, cars were viewed as exotic and unpredictable machines. Early cars ran on steam and inspired fears about explosions. Later cars had to be started manually, using a crank that the motorist inserted into the front of the engine and turned forcefully until the engine started. If the car backfired, the crank could kick back with enough force to break bones. In addition, early cars regularly got flat tires and lacked automatic transmissions, which allows the driver to simply put the car into *drive*. Early cars were so unreliable that many people made jokes about them, and numerous laws required drivers to signal warnings to others on the roads.

Setting Purposes for Reading

Big Idea Making Choices

As you read this selection, think about why some of the characters choose to try to trick another character rather than deal with issues directly.

Literary Element Dialogue

Dialogue is conversation between characters in a literary work. Besides adding interest, dialogue can contribute to characterization by revealing aspects of a character's personality. As you read "The Car We Had to Push," notice how the characters' dialogue reveals aspects of his or her personality and attitudes.

- See Literary Terms Handbook, p. R5.

Literature Online **Interactive Literary Elements Handbook** To review or learn more about the literary elements, go to www.glencoe.com.

OBJECTIVES
In studying this selection, you will focus on the following:
- making inferences from dialogue
- making generalizations about characters
- analyzing dialect
- writing to analyze humor

Reading Strategy *Making Generalizations About Characters*

When you **generalize about a character**, you draw upon various details to make a general statement about that character. Such conclusions can enhance the richness and meaning of a story. As you read, pay attention to details that lead you to make generalizations about characters.

Reading Tip: Chart Clues Use a graphic organizer to record details that provide clues to make a generalization about the character.

Vocabulary

repercussion (rē′ pər kush′ ən) *n.* an effect or result of some action; p. 112 *The repercussions of cheating can be very serious.*

exhortation (eg′ zôr tā′ shən) *n.* a strong appeal or warning; p. 113 *The exhortations of the crowd spurred on the runners.*

contend (kən tend′) *v.* to declare or maintain as a fact; argue; p. 114 *My mother contends that I ate raw turnips as a child.*

lucid (lōō′ sid) *adj.* clear-headed, mentally alert; p. 116 *My father is lucid even when half-asleep.*

Vocabulary Tip: Word Origins Knowing word histories can help you when you encounter an unfamiliar word with a familiar root.

JAMES THURBER **111**

Focus

Summary

The narrator describes his family's coming to terms with various technological advances. His mother was superstitious of telephones, and his grandmother thought electricity leaked into the house. His family had a car that had to be pushed. One day his brother rigged the car so that a bundle of kitchen items would fall out and told his father the engine had fallen out. The car was finally destroyed when a streetcar ran into it.

V Vocabulary

Vocabulary File Say: Add these words and definitions to your vocabulary file. For each word, include a sentence that gives you an example of how to use the word. **OL** Students with English language needs should include the pronunciations of these words in their files. **EL**

Literary Elements Have students access the Web site to improve their understanding of dialogue.

Selection Resources

Print Materials
- Unit 1 Resources (Fast File), pp. 49–51
- Leveled Vocabulary Development, p. 9
- Selection and Unit Assessments, pp. 19–20
- Selection Quick Checks, p. 10

Transparencies
- Bellringer Options Transparencies:
  Selection Focus Transparency 7
  Daily Language Practice Transparency 12
- Literary Elements Transparency 17

Technology
- TeacherWorks Plus™ CD-ROM
- StudentWorks Plus™ CD-ROM
- Presentation Plus!™ CD-ROM
- Literature Online, glencoe.com
- Online Student Edition, mhln.com
- Exam*View*® Assessment Suite CD-ROM
- Vocabulary PuzzleMaker CD-ROM
- Listening Library, disc 1 track 10

Big Idea

Making Choices

Say: Keep the following question in mind as you read. How do choices that the characters make add to the humor of the story? *(The parents' choice not to learn about new technologies results in funny misunderstandings. The family's choice to fake Zenas's return adds humor and absurdity.)* **OL**

R Reading Strategy

Making Generalizations About Characters **Answer:** *His feelings may not always be informed by experience or knowledge.* **OL**

★ Cultural History

Reo The Reo Motor Car Company was started in 1904 by Ransom Eli Olds, who previously had created the Oldsmobile line. The name *Reo* came from his initials. Among the most well-known Reos were the Royale and the Speed Wagon. **AS**

Readability Scores

Dale-Chall: 7.3
DRP: 60
Lexile: 1080

THE CAR WE HAD TO PUSH

James Thurber

It took sometimes as many as five or six. James Thurber. Illustration from *My Life and Hard Times*, 1933.

Many autobiographers, among them Lincoln Steffens and Gertrude Atherton,[1] describe earthquakes their families have been in. I am unable to do this because my family was never in an earthquake, but we went through a number of things in Columbus that were a great deal like earthquakes. I remember in particular some of the **repercussions** of an old Reo we had that ★ wouldn't go unless you pushed it for quite a way and suddenly let your clutch out. Once, we had been able to start the engine easily by cranking it, but we had had the car for so many years that finally it wouldn't go unless you pushed it and let your clutch out. Of course, it took more than one person to do this; it took sometimes as many as five or six, depending on the grade of the roadway

and conditions underfoot. The car was unusual in that the clutch and brake were on the same pedal, making it quite easy to stall the engine after it got started, so that the car would have to be pushed again.

My father used to get sick at his stomach pushing the car, and very often was unable to go to work. He had never liked the machine, even when it was good, sharing my ignorance and suspicion of all automobiles of twenty years ago and longer. The boys I went to school with used to be able to identify every car as it passed by: Thomas Flyer, Firestone-Columbus, Stevens Duryea, Rambler, Winton, White Steamer, etc. I never could. The only car I was really interested in was one that the Get-Ready Man, as we called him, rode around town in: a big Red Devil with a door in the back. The Get-Ready Man was a lank unkempt elderly gentleman with

---

1. Besides their autobiographies, *Steffens* wrote nonfiction books and articles; *Atherton* wrote novels. Their major works were published between 1898 and 1936.

Vocabulary

repercussion (rē´ pər kush´ ən) *n.* an effect or result of some action

Reading Strategy Making Generalizations About Characters *From this statement, what sort of generalization could be made about father?* **R**

112 UNIT 1   THE SHORT STORY

Additional Support

Skills Practice

READING: Previewing Point out that Thurber's story focuses on humorous encounters and misconceptions about the technology of the time. Discuss the differences between life today and life in the 1910s and 1920s with regard to technology. Ask students to brainstorm

a list of inventions that were new at the time this story takes place, such as electric lights, refrigerators, telephones, cars, phonographs, and airplanes. Have students share stories they have heard from their grandparents or other people they know who remember this time. **OL** wild eyes and a deep voice who used to go about shouting at people through a megaphone to prepare for the end of the world. "get ready! get read-y!" he would bellow. "the worllld is coming to an end!" His startling **exhortations** would come up, like summer thunder, at the most unexpected times and in the most surprising places. I remember once during Mantell's production of "King Lear" at the Colonial Theatre, that the Get-Ready Man added his bawlings to the squealing of Edgar and the ranting of the King and the mouthing of the Fool, rising from somewhere in the balcony to join in. The theatre was in absolute darkness and there were rumblings of thunder and flashes of lightning offstage. Neither father nor I, who were there, ever completely got over the scene, which went something like this:

EDGAR: Tom's a-cold.—O, do de, do de, do de!—Bless thee from whirlwinds, starblasting, and taking . . . the foul fiend vexes!

[Thunder off.]

Vocabulary

exhortation (eg´ zôr tā´ shən) n. a strong appeal or warning

LEAR: What! Have his daughters brought him to this pass?—

GET-READY MAN: Get ready! Get ready!

EDGAR: Pillicock sat on Pillicock-hill:—
          Halloo, halloo, loo, loo!

[Lightning flashes.]

GET-READY MAN: The Worllld is com-ing to an End!

FOOL: This cold night will turn us all to fools and madmen!

EDGAR: Take heed o' the foul fiend: obey thy paren—

GET-READY MAN: Get *Rea*-dy!

EDGAR: Tom's *a-cold!*

GET-READY MAN: The *Worr*-uld is coming to an end! . . .

They found him finally, and ejected him, still shouting. The Theatre, in our time, has known few such moments.

Literary Element Dialogue *What do the Get-Ready Man's interjected warnings reveal about his personality?* **L**

The Get-Ready Man. James Thurber. Illustration from *My Life and Hard Times*, 1933. ★

Teach

L Literary Element

Dialogue Answer: *The Get-Ready Man is obsessed with the end of the world and feels compelled to warn others about it, often doing so in inappropriate ways. He is unable to restrain himself from issuing his warnings even during a play.* **OL**

★ Viewing the Illustration

James Thurber published drawings such as this one in *The New Yorker*, a magazine that is still published weekly.

Ask: What does this illustration add to the story? Why do you suppose Thurber chose to represent the people in this way? *(Thurber does not describe how people reacted to the Get-Ready Man in his story, but in the cartoon he depicts them responding with confusion and fear.)* **AS**

✓ CheckPoint

Use the CheckPoint questions on Presentation Plus! to monitor students' comprehension. These questions can be used with interactive response keypads for immediate student feedback.

Differentiated Instruction

Parody Point out that Thurber quotes actual lines from a climactic scene in Act Three of *King Lear*, one of Shakespeare's greatest tragedies. In this scene Edgar pretends to be a madman. Explain to students that in parody, an author imitates the style of a literary work for a humorous effect.

Ask: How does Thurber's incorporation of quotes from *King Lear* add to the humor of the scene? *(Thurber shows how the Get-Ready Man's bellowing adds to the scene's theme of madness and chaos. Structuring the dialogue in the formal manner of a play heightens this effect.)* **BL**

Objectives
• To make generalizations about characters (SE)
• To make inferences from dialogue (SE)
• To preview literature by analyzing the historical context (TWE)

Teach

R1 **Reading Strategy**

Making Generalizations About Characters Answer: *Students might suggest that Roy is a practical joker.* **OL**

L **Literary Element**

Dialogue Answer: *Father is a bit gullible in that he fell for the trick.* **OL**

BI **Big Idea**

Making Choices
Answer: *The narrator's mother is able to feel in control of the telephone by removing the receiver from the hook during storms. This action tells you that she did not grow up with modern inventions such as the telephone. It also tells you that she knows little about how the telephone actually works and that she is superstitious.* **OL**

But to get back to the automobile. One of my happiest memories of it was when, in its eighth year, my brother Roy got together a great many articles from the kitchen, placed them in a square of canvas, and swung this under the car with a string attached to it so that, at a twitch, the canvas would give way and the steel and tin things would clatter to the street. This was a little scheme of Roy's to frighten father, who had always expected the car might explode. It worked perfectly. That was twenty-five years ago, but it is one of the few things in my life I would like to live over again if I could. I don't suppose that I can, now. Roy twitched the string in the middle of a lovely afternoon, on Bryden Road, near Eighteenth Street. Father had closed his eyes and, with his hat off, was enjoying a cool breeze. The clatter on the asphalt was tremendously effective: knives, forks, can-openers, pie pans, pot lids, biscuit-cutters, ladles, eggbeaters fell, beautifully together, in a lingering, clamant[2] crash. "Stop the *car*!" shouted father. "I can't," Roy said. "The engine fell out." "God Almighty!" said father, who knew what *that* meant, or knew what it sounded as if it might mean.

It ended unhappily, of course, because we finally had to drive back and pick up the stuff and even father knew the difference between the works of an automobile and the equipment of a pantry. My mother wouldn't have known, however, nor *her* mother. My mother, for instance, thought—or, rather, knew—that it was dangerous to drive an automobile without gasoline: it fried the valves, or something. "Now don't you dare drive all over town without gasoline!" she would say to us when we started off. Gas-oline, oil, and water were much the same to her, a fact that made her life both confusing and perilous. Her greatest dread, however, was the Victrola—we had a very early one, back in the "Come Josephine in My Flying Machine" days. She had an idea that the Victrola might blow up. It alarmed her, rather than reassured her, to explain that the phonograph was run neither by gasoline nor by electricity. She could only suppose that it was propelled by some newfangled and untested apparatus which was likely to let go at any minute, making us all the victims and martyrs of the wild-eyed Edison's dangerous experiments.[3] The telephone she was comparatively at peace with, except, of course, during storms, when for some reason or other she always took the receiver off the hook and let it hang. She came naturally by her confused and groundless fears, for her own mother lived the latter years of her life in the horrible suspicion that electricity was dripping invisibly all over the house. It leaked, she **contended,** out of empty sockets if the wall switch had been left on. She would go around screwing in bulbs, and if they lighted up she would hastily and fearfully turn off the wall switch and

Visual Vocabulary
Victrola is the trademark name of a record player; early models were hand-cranked, just as wind-up toys are. Electric phonographs were first produced in the 1920s.

---

2. Anything *clamant* (klā′ mənt) is noisy and demanding of attention.

Reading Strategy Making Generalizations About Characters *What does this incident suggest about Roy's personality?* **R1**

Literary Element Dialogue *What do you learn about father from his response to the "clamant crash"?* **L**

---

3. *Martyrs* are those who suffer or die for a cause. The *dangerous experiments* of Thomas A. *Edison* produced inventions that changed the world, including the light bulb, the first practical phonograph (1877), and important improvements to the telephone.

Big Idea Making Choices *Why does the narrator's mother choose to remove the telephone from the hook during storms? What does this action tell you about the mother?* **BI**

Vocabulary

contend (kən tend′) *v.* to declare or maintain as a fact; argue

Additional Support

Skills Practice

READING: Visualizing Encourage students to visualize the scenes described on this page, particularly the trick that Roy plays on his father and to imagine the kitchen items falling onto the road.

Ask: Which details make the scene particularly vivid? *(Students may mention the father calmly enjoying the ride before hearing the noise of the kitchen utensils falling onto the road.)* **OL**

Electricity was leaking all over the house. James Thurber. Illustration from *My Life and Hard Times*, 1933.

go back to her *Pearson's* or *Everybody's*,[4] happy in the satisfaction that she had stopped not only a costly but a dangerous leakage. Nothing could ever clear this up for her.

Our poor old Reo came to a horrible end, finally. We had parked it too far from the curb on a street with a car line. It was late at night and the street was dark. The first streetcar[5]

that came along couldn't get by. It picked up the tired old automobile as a terrier might seize a rabbit and drubbed it unmercifully, losing its hold now and then but catching a new grip a second later. Tires booped and whooshed, the fenders queeled and graked, the steering wheel rose up like a spectre and disappeared in the direction of Franklin Avenue with a melancholy whistling sound, bolts and gadgets flew like sparks from a Catherine wheel.[6] It was a splendid spectacle but, of course, saddening to everybody

---

4. These were popular magazines of the early 1900s.
5. Since a *streetcar* runs on rails, it cannot avoid things in its path.

Reading Strategy Making Generalizations About Characters *What generalization about the grandmother could you logically make from this passage?* **R2**

---

6. A *spectre* is a ghost or ghostly vision. The *Catherine wheel* is a firework that, when lighted, spins like a pinwheel and spouts colorful sparks and flames.

JAMES THURBER **115**

Teach

R2 Reading Strategy

Making Generalizations About Characters Answer: *She is given to obsessive fears about dangers that are not real.* **OL**

⭐ **Viewing the Illustration**

Thurber drew simple, expressive faces that captured a range of human emotions.
Ask: Do you find the story about the grandmother funnier after viewing the drawing? Why or why not? *(Students may say that the drawing adds humor to the story because of the expression on the grandmother's face and its emphasis on her absurd worry.)* **AS**

Differentiated Instruction

Imagery Point out the vivid aural and visual imagery that Thurber uses to describe the demise of the family car. Discuss with students how the author's word choice creates this imagery and the effect that his colorful similes give to the overall scene. Also remind students that words that imitate the sounds they describe are examples of onomatopoeia, such as the made-up words *booped*, *queeled*, and *graked*. **AL**

Objectives
• To make generalizations about characters (SE)
• To make inferences from dialogue (SE)
• To visualize scenes (TWE)

Teach

(except the motorman of the streetcar, who was sore). I think some of us broke down and wept. It must have been the weeping that caused grandfather to take on so terribly. Time was all mixed up in his mind; automobiles and the like he never remembered having seen. He apparently gathered, from the talk and excitement and weeping, that somebody had died. Nor did he let go of this delusion. He insisted, in fact, after almost a week in which we strove mightily to divert him, that it was a sin and a shame and a disgrace on the family to put the funeral off any longer. "Nobody is dead! The automobile is smashed!" shouted my father, trying for the thirtieth time to explain the situation to the old man. "Was he drunk?" demanded grandfather, sternly. "Was who drunk?" asked father. "Zenas," said grandfather. He had a name for the corpse now: it was his brother Zenas, who, as it happened, *was* dead, but not from driving an automobile while intoxicated. Zenas had died in 1866. A sensitive, rather poetical boy of twenty-one when the Civil War broke out, Zenas had gone to South America—"just," as he wrote back, "until it blows over." Returning after the war had blown over, he caught the same disease that was killing off the chestnut trees in those years, and passed away. It was the only case in history where a tree doctor had to be called in to spray a person, and our family had felt it very keenly; nobody else in the United States caught the blight. Some of us have looked upon Zenas' fate as a kind of poetic justice.

Now that grandfather knew, so to speak, who was dead, it became increasingly awkward to go on living in the same house with him as if nothing had happened. He would go into towering rages in which he threatened to write to the Board of Health unless the funeral were held at once. We realized that something had to be done. Eventually, we persuaded a friend of father's, named

---

Reading Strategy Making Generalizations About Characters *How might you expect grandfather to act based on this statement?* **R**

116 UNIT 1   THE SHORT STORY

George Martin, to dress up in the manner and costume of the eighteen-sixties and pretend to be Uncle Zenas, in order to set grandfather's mind at rest. The impostor looked fine and impressive in sideburns and a high beaver hat, and not unlike the daguerreotypes of Zenas in our album. I shall never forget the night, just after dinner, when this Zenas walked into the living room. Grandfather was stomping up and down, tall, hawk-nosed, round-oathed. The newcomer held out both his hands. "Clem!" he cried to grandfather. Grandfather turned slowly, looked at the intruder, and snorted. "Who air *you*?" he demanded in his deep, resonant voice. "I'm Zenas!" cried Martin. "Your brother Zenas, fit as a fiddle and sound as a dollar!" "Zenas, my foot!" said grandfather. "Zenas died of the chestnut blight in '66!"

Grandfather was given to these sudden, unexpected, and extremely **lucid** moments; they were generally more embarrassing than his other moments. He comprehended before he went to bed that night that the old automobile had been destroyed and that its destruction had caused all the turmoil in the house. "It flew all to pieces, Pa," my mother told him, in graphically describing the accident. "I knew 'twould," growled grandfather. "I allus told ye to git a Pope-Toledo." ∾

Visual Vocabulary
Daguerreotypes (də ger′ ə tīps′) are photographs made by exposing light to silver-coated copper plates; Louis Daguerre invented the process in France in the mid-1800s.

Big Idea Making Choices *Why do you think the narrator's family chooses to stage an impersonation as a way of setting "grandfather's mind at rest"?* **BI**

Literary Element Dialogue *How does this exclamation contrast with grandfather's earlier dialogue?* **L**

Vocabulary

lucid (lōō′ sid) *adj.* clear-headed; mentally alert

Skills Practice

READING: Using Graphic Organizers Point out that part of the humor of Thurber's story comes from his frequent digressions from his main topic: his family's automobile. Thurber describes the Get-Ready Man, Father, Mother, Grandfather, and Zenas. Showing these characters and ideas graphically can help students understand the humor and organization of Thurber's story. Have students create a graphic such as a chart or cluster map that shows the characters in the selection and the relationship of each to the automobile. Ask volunteers to put their graphic aids on the board. **OL**

RESPONDING AND THINKING CRITICALLY

Respond

1. (a)Which character or situation did you find funniest? (b)Why? Give details.

Recall and Interpret

2. (a)Who is the narrator, and what is his relationship to the story? (b)What is the narrator's tone, or attitude, toward the people and events? Use details from the story to support your response.

3. (a)Who owned the car, and why did it have to be pushed? (b)What does the car symbolize in this story? Support your answer with details from the story.

4. (a)What confusion does grandfather have about his brother Zenas? (b)Why might the narrator consider grandfather's lucid moments to be "more embarrassing than his other moments"?

Analyze and Evaluate

5. Why do you think Thurber includes the Get-Ready Man in the story? What effect does this part of the story create?

6. How does the car's demise match the overall mood, or atmosphere, of the story?

7. What qualities of this story do you think helped lead to Thurber's enormous popular success during his lifetime? Cite examples from the story to support your opinion.

Connect

8. People in the narrator's childhood were often suspicious of technology, but nevertheless chose to use it. What kinds of similar choices do people make today?

9. **Big Idea** Making Choices Why do you think Thurber chose to remember the episodes in this story as humorous? How else might he have portrayed them?

PRIMARY VISUAL ARTIFACT

Thurber's Cartoons

Thurber's drawings were so beloved that when *The New Yorker* moved from its original location to larger offices, they carved his cartoons off his office walls. They brought these sections of wall to the new location, where they could be displayed.

Look at the drawings Thurber made to illustrate his story. Choose your favorite and find a partner who chose the same drawing.

Partner Activity Discuss the following questions with your partner. Refer back to the drawing and cite specific details to use as support.

1. Whether you like or dislike Thurber's drawings in general, what is it about the drawing you chose that appeals to you?

2. How effective is the drawing at capturing both the story's details and mood? Explain.

3. What are some distinguishing characteristics of the drawing?

The Get-Ready Man. James Thurber.
Illustration from *My Life and Hard Times,* 1933.

JAMES THURBER **117**

Thurber's Cartoons

1. Answers will vary. Students should discuss specific qualities of the drawings such as the sense of movement they convey or the facial expressions of the characters.

2. Most students may think that Thurber's loose, cartoonish drawings capture the details and light-hearted mood of the story.

3. Students should identify specifics, such as a lack of background or shading, the emphasis on gesture, or the befuddled expressions on characters' faces.

Assess

1. (a)Students should correctly identify a character or situation and indicate why they thought this character or situation was funniest.

2. (a)James Thurber is the narrator, and he is recounting events that happened to him and his family. (b)Thurber has a tone of amused tolerance for life's absurdities. Details from the story will vary.

3. (a)The family owned the car, which had to be pushed due to its poor condition. (b)The car symbolizes technological advancement. Details will vary.

4. (a)Grandfather is confused about when Zenas died. (b)The lucid moments make it harder to explain Grandfather's confusion.

5. The episode foreshadows later absurdities in the study.

6. The car's demise is as wacky as the rest of the story.

7. Thurber's gentle humor, his love of the absurd, and the vivid imagery all contributed to his success. Students should give specific examples from the story.

8. Students might mention people who use computers despite fears of viruses or hacking, or people who worry about cell phone safety yet continue to use the phones.

9. Thurber had learned to react to his family's eccentricities with humor. If he had not done so, his memories might have been hurtful.

Assess

Literary Element

1. The dialogue allows readers to "hear" what is happening, thereby illustrating the hilarity. Students may note the lightning, the doomsday tone of the Get-Ready Man, and such Shakespearean phrases as "the foul fiend vexes" and "fools and madmen."

2. The father's shouting reveals his frustration; Grandfather thinks the corpse is his late brother.

3. Students might mention "fit as a fiddle and sound as a dollar" or "Zenas, my foot!"

Review: Dialect

Students may point to the Get-Ready Man's speeches or to mother's statement that the car "flew all to pieces."

Reading Strategy

1. They are all confused and somewhat frightened by technology. Father worries the car will explode; mother worries that the car will run without gas and be dangerous; grandmother worries about electricity dripping all over the house.

2. Students might respond with *zany, eccentric,* or *funny.* Supporting details will vary.

Literary Element Dialogue

Dialogue is one technique of introducing a character to the reader. Good dialogue sounds natural, so it often contains sentence fragments or pauses. Used effectively, dialogue not only helps to reveal a character's personality but also contains details that help readers understand the events of the story and predict what might happen next. Dialogue can also add drama or humor to a story.

1. Thurber weaves together dialogue from Shakespeare's "King Lear," with the Get-Ready Man's warnings. Note the interplay between the dialogue in the play, the scenic elements, and the Get-Ready Man's warnings. Why is this more humorous than merely describing what happened during the play?

2. Reread the dialogue between grandfather and the narrator's father when the father tries to explain that no one has died. List two details that you learn from that dialogue.

3. Reread the scene between George Martin and grandfather that takes place near the end of the story. What language do the characters use that shows the absurdity of this scheme?

Review: Dialect

As you learned on page 74, **dialect** is a variation of a language that is spoken in a particular region or by a certain group of people. Dialects often differ from the standard form of a language in vocabulary, pronunciation, or grammatical form. In "The Car We Had to Push," the grandfather uses dialect when he says "I knew 'twould . . . . I allus told ye to git a Pope-Toledo."

Partner Activity Meet with another classmate and find another example of dialect in the story. Rewrite the dialect using Standard English. Afterwards, compare the two versions and draw conclusions about why Thurber chose to use dialect rather than Standard English.

Reading Strategy Making Generalizations About Characters

A **generalization** is a statement about people, places or ideas that is based on some type of evidence. A reader looks at specific details and tries to identify patterns or trends within them. Then the reader tries to create a statement that identifies that trend.

1. What attitude does the narrator's family have toward technology? List at least three details that support your generalization.

2. What word or words would you use to describe this family? Provide several details to support this generalization.

Vocabulary Practice

Practice with Word Origins Use a dictionary to find the origin of each vocabulary word.

1. repercussion   **a.** Latin   **b.** Dutch

2. exhortation   **a.** Greek   **b.** Middle English

3. contend   **a.** Spanish   **b.** Middle English

4. lucid   **a.** Latin   **b.** French

Academic Vocabulary

Here are two words from the vocabulary list on page R82. These words will help you think, write, and talk about the selection.

technology (tek no′ lə jē) *n.* applied or practical knowledge used to solve problems

series (sēr′ ēz) *n.* a group of related items or events that follow one another

Practice and Apply
1. Why did the narrator's parents view **technology** as dangerous?
2. Why does the narrator explain the entire **series** of events that finally destroyed the car?

Vocabulary

1. a
2. b
3. b
4. a

Academic Vocabulary

1. The family did not understand technology.

2. The series of events is absurd; each detail adds humor to the story.

Writing About Literature

Analyze Humor How does Thurber use the car as the "vehicle" for holding this story together? The story contains many separate elements of humor, including the following: anecdotes, or brief stories, about the car to present details about character and events; parody, in which an author imitates the style of a literary work for humorous effect, as Thurber did in the scene in the theater; and hyperbole, or exaggeration.

Write a brief essay explaining how Thurber combines these elements to present characters and events and to make his readers laugh.

After drafting, meet with a peer reviewer to evaluate each other's work and suggest revisions. Then edit and proofread your draft for errors in spelling, grammar, or punctuation.

Listening and Speaking

Choose a passage or anecdote from the story, and prepare it as a news story that might be broadcast on radio or television. Include the facts that answer *who? what? where? when? why?* and *how?* Rehearse your presentation and present it to the class in a reportorial style.

Thurber's Language and Style

Using Colons Many people are unsure how to use colons, but Thurber clearly understood this form of punctuation. In "The Car We Had to Push," he uses colons in several different ways: to introduce a list after an independent clause; to introduce a long or formal quotation; to introduce material that explains, illustrates, or restates previous material; and to indicate which character is speaking during the play.

In each instance, the colon is the proper and most efficient mark of punctuation. Here are two examples from the story:

> *The clatter on the asphalt was tremendously effective: knives, forks, can-openers, pie pans, pot lids, biscuit-cutters, ladles, eggbeaters fell, beautifully together, in a lingering, clamant crash.*

> *He had a name for the corpse now: it was his brother Zenas, who, as it happened, was dead, but not from driving an automobile while intoxicated.*

Activity Find two other sentences in the story in which Thurber uses a colon. Rewrite each sentence without colons. As you tinker with form, try to retain as much of Thurber's original meaning as possible. Then write a sentence or two explaining how the versions differ in meaning and in their effect on the reader.

Revising Check

Colons Reread your analysis of Thurber's humor and see if you can find any lists or explanations that might be better introduced by a colon. Revise your draft as necessary.

Literature Online Web Activities For eFlashcards, Selection Quick Checks, and other Web activities, go to www.glencoe.com.

Assess

Writing About Literature

Students' essays should

- explain how the car motif holds the story together
- give examples of Thurber's use of anecdotes or parody

Listening and Speaking

Students should accurately relate information from the story in their news stories, including the 5Ws and H.

Thurber's Language and Style

Students' writing should include two sentences from the story that include colons. Their rewrites should not alter the meaning of the sentences. The two sets of sentences should be compared.

Literature Online

Web Activities Have students access the Web site for interactive activities that will help them assess their understanding of the selection.

Focus

BELLRINGER

Bellringer Options
Selection Focus Transparency 8
Daily Language
 Transparency 13
Or display photographs of
different climates (such
as alpine, grassland, and
tropical). **Ask:** What is life
like in each of these climates? How are people's lives
affected by climate? Have
students consider as they
read how a very warm climate
affects people's lives.

Author Search To expand
students' appreciation of
Gabriel García Márquez, have
them access the Web site for
additinal information and
resources.

Tuesday Siesta

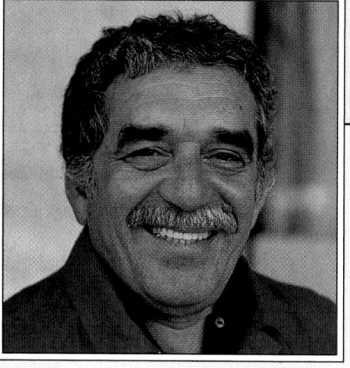

MEET GABRIEL GARCÍA MÁRQUEZ

Born in Aracataca, Colombia, Gabriel García Márquez lived with his grandparents in "an enormous house, full of ghosts." His grandparents loved telling imaginative folktales, filled with omens, premonitions, and spirits. His grandfather also told stories about his war experiences, the triumphs of the South American revolutionary hero Simón Bolívar, and the plight of impoverished local farmers under an oppressive government. It is only natural then that García Márquez's literature is often built of realistic themes and plots related to the culture and people of his childhood village, fantastic elements from his grandmother's tales, and new magical details from his imagination. He once said that the goal of all his writing is to tap "the magic in commonplace events." This style of writing has come to be known as magical realism.

"There's not a single line in all my work that does not have a basis in reality. The problem is that Caribbean reality resembles the wildest imagination."

—Gabriel García Márquez

Education and Early Writing When García Márquez was eight years old, he was sent to a boarding school in the port city of Barran-quilla, where his classmates nicknamed him "the Old Man" because he seemed so shy and serious. At twelve, he won a scholarship to a Jesuit school for gifted students, where he developed an avid love of reading and writing stories. Although the focus of his college studies was the writing of nonfiction, he continued to write fiction as well. In 1946, when he was

nineteen, he published his first short story, "The Third Resignation," in the Bogotá newspaper, *El Espectador*. He also received his first rave review, when the editor of the paper called him "the new genius of Colombian letters!"

For the next ten years, García Márquez worked primarily as a contributing writer for *El Espectador*. In 1955, after he wrote a news story exposing government corruption in Colombia, Gustavo Rojas Pinilla, the Colombian dictator, shut down the newspaper. García Márquez then returned to fiction writing.

International Fame In 1958 García Márquez married Mercedes Barcha Pardo. Two years later, after the birth of their son, the couple moved to Mexico City, where García Márquez gained fame as a screenwriter, journalist, novelist, and publicist. In 1967 he published his most famous work, the novel *One Hundred Years of Solitude*, which has been translated into many different languages and has sold millions of copies.

In 1982 García Márquez received the highest international award for writing—the Nobel Prize in Literature. The Nobel selection committee celebrated his novels and short stories,"where the miraculous and the real converge . . . [and reflect] a continent and its human riches and poverty."

Gabriel García Márquez was born in 1928.

Author Search For more about Gabriel García Márquez, go to www.glencoe.com.

Selection Skills

Literary Elements

- Implied Theme (SE pp. 121, 123, 126, 128)
- Flat and Round Characters (SE p. 128)

Tuesday Siesta

Reading Skills

- Making Inferences About Theme (SE pp. 121–129)
- Establishing a Purpose for Reading (TWE p. 122)

Vocabulary Skills

- Word Parts (SE p. 129)
- Academic Vocabulary (SE p. 129)
- Dictionary Skills (TWE p. 124)

Listening/Speaking/Viewing Skills

- Analyzing Art (SE pp. 124, 127)
- Literature Groups (SE p. 129)
- Proverbs (TWE p. 126)

Writing Skills/Grammar

- Summarize Flashback (SE p. 129)

LITERATURE PREVIEW

Connecting to the Story

Gabriel García Márquez sets most of his stories in the Latin American villages and cities that he has known throughout his life. Living conditions that reflect the underlying struggle of poverty and the enduring, unforgiving hot climate are common aspects of his settings. Before you read, think about these questions:

- How might extreme temperatures affect your moods, actions, and choices?
- What advice have you gleaned from people or books that has helped you make better choices?

Building Background

"Tuesday Siesta" takes place in a Latin American country, probably in the 1930s or 1940s. During the hottest part of the day in such tropical climates, many people avoid heatstroke and sunstroke by taking *siestas,* or naps. Siesta time usually begins around noon. Schools, shops, and even post offices often close so that people can go home, have a meal, and then rest for several hours. Later in the day, when the heat of the sun has diminished, activities resume.

Setting Purposes for Reading

Big Idea Making Choices

As you read this story, think about the circumstances that lead a young man to make a tragic choice.

Literary Element Implied Theme

The theme of a piece of literature is a central understanding, or truth, about life. Most often, authors do not state the theme directly. Instead, they offer an **implied theme,** which they reveal gradually through details in the setting, plot events, dialogue, and action. As you read, note the details concerning time and place (setting) and characters' actions that García Márquez uses to imply the underlying theme of this story.

- See Literary Terms Handbook, p. R18.

Literature Online Interactive Literary Elements **Handbook** To review or learn more about the literary elements, go to www.glencoe.com.

OBJECTIVES
In studying this selection, you will focus on the following:
- recognizing and understanding implied theme
- making inferences about a theme
- analyzing flat and round characters
- writing to summarize flashback

READING PREVIEW

Reading Strategy Making Inferences About Theme

To **infer** is to make a reasonable guess about the meaning of a literary work based on what the author implies. While reading this story, note details in the setting, plot events, and character dialogues and actions that give hints about García Márquez's implied theme.

Reading Tip: Taking Notes Use a diagram like the one below to record your inferences about the theme. One detail has been given as an example.

Inferences from setting ex. humid air, stifling smoke	Inferences from plot	Inferences from characters

Implied Theme

Vocabulary

interminable (in tur′ mi nə bəl) *adj.* lasting or seeming to last, forever; endless; p. 122 *We tried to be patient, but the rainstorm seemed interminable.*

serenity (sə ren′ə tē) *n.* calmness; peacefulness; p. 123 *The serenity of the deep, silent forest calmed my jittery nerves.*

scrutinize (skroot′ ən īz′) *v.* to look at closely; to inspect carefully; p. 125 *I'm not sure I will recognize Sally, so I'll scrutinize the face of each woman who gets off the train.*

inscrutable (in skroo′ tə bəl) *adj.* mysterious; p. 126 *His face was inscrutable as he scanned the group—it was impossible to guess his opinion.*

skeptical (skep′ ti kəl) *adj.* having or showing doubt or suspicion; questioning; disbelieving; p. 126 *Roger is extremely forgetful, so I'm skeptical that he will remember to call.*

GABRIEL GARCÍA MÁRQUEZ **121**

Focus

Summary

A mother and her twelve-year-old daughter in a Latin American country ride a train on a hot August day to a distant village, arriving during siesta. The mother leads her daughter to the parish house and insists on seeing the priest because she needs the keys to the cemetery. The priest is shocked to learn that a thief recently killed in the town was her son. The woman maintains her dignity and does not cry. By the time she and her daughter are ready to visit the grave, a curious crowd has gathered.

V Vocabulary

Vocabulary File **Say:** Add these words and definitions to your vocabulary file. For each word, include a sentence that gives you an example of how to use the word. **OL** Students with English language needs should include the pronunciations of these words in their files. **EL**

Literature Online

Literary Elements Have students access the Web site to improve their understanding of implied theme.

Selection Resources

Print Materials
- Unit 1 Resources (Fast File), pp. 52–54
- Leveled Vocabulary Development, p. 10
- Selection and Unit Assessments, pp. 21–22
- Selection Quick Checks, p. 11

Transparencies
- Bellringer Options Transparencies: Selection Focus Transparency 8 Daily Language Practice Transparency 13
- Literary Elements Transparency 18

Technology
- TeacherWorks Plus™ CD-ROM
- StudentWorks Plus™ CD-ROM
- Presentation Plus!™ CD-ROM
- Literature Online, glencoe.com
- Online Student Edition, mhln.com
- ExamView® Assessment Suite CD-ROM
- Vocabulary PuzzleMaker CD-ROM
- Listening Library, disc 1 track 11

Teach

Big Idea

Making Choices

Say: Keep this question in mind as you read: What choices has the woman made in making this journey? *(She has chosen to arrive during siesta, when people in the town will be sleeping. She has chosen to visit her son's grave in spite of the scorn she might face.)* **OL**

R Reading Strategy

Making Inferences About Theme

Answer: *The mother and daughter wear "severe and poor mourning clothes" and this is the girl's first train ride. These details suggest that they have little money and are in mourning. The theme will concern poverty and loss.* **OL**

Readability Scores

Dale-Chall: 4.5
DRP: 55
Lexile: 860

Tuesday Siesta

Gabriel García Márquez
Translated by J. S. Bernstein

The train emerged from the quivering tunnel of sandy rocks, began to cross the symmetrical, **interminable** banana plantations, and the air became humid and they couldn't feel the sea breeze any more. A stifling blast of smoke came in the car window. On the narrow road parallel to the railway there were oxcarts loaded with green bunches of bananas. Beyond the road, in uncultivated spaces set at odd intervals there were offices with electric fans, red-brick buildings, and residences with chairs and little white tables on the terraces among dusty palm trees and rosebushes. It was eleven in the morning, and the heat had not yet begun.

"You'd better close the window," the woman said. "Your hair will get full of soot."

The girl tried to, but the shade wouldn't move because of the rust.

They were the only passengers in the lone third-class car. Since the smoke of the locomotive kept coming through the window, the girl left her seat and put down the only things they had with them: a plastic sack with some things to eat and a bouquet of flowers wrapped in newspaper. She sat on the opposite seat, away from the window, facing her mother. They were both in severe and poor mourning clothes.

Vocabulary

interminable (in tur′ mi nə bəl) *adj.* lasting, or seeming to last, forever; endless

Reading Strategy Making Inferences About Theme
What does this passage suggest about the characters' economic and emotional situation? How might these details reveal the author's implied theme? **R**

Additional Support

Skills Practice

READING: Establishing a Purpose for Reading Have students brainstorm a list of different types of writing (such as poems, short stories, articles, recipes, and instructions). **Ask:** What is your purpose for reading a textbook? a novel? *(Students may say that they read textbooks to learn and read novels for fun.)*

Help students identify purposes for each of the reading materials listed. Purposes should include the following:

- entertain
- inform
- persuade
- teach   **OL**

The girl was twelve years old, and it was the first time she'd ever been on a train. The woman seemed too old to be her mother, because of the blue veins on her eyelids and her small, soft, and shapeless body, in a dress cut like a cassock. She was riding with her spinal column braced firmly against the back of the seat, and held a peeling patent-leather handbag in her lap with both hands. She bore the conscientious **serenity** of someone accustomed to poverty.

By twelve the heat had begun. The train stopped for ten minutes to take on water at a station where there was no town. Outside, in the mysterious silence of the plantations, the shadows seemed clean. But the still air inside the car smelled like untanned leather. The train did not pick up speed. It stopped at two identical towns with wooden houses painted bright colors. The woman's head nodded and she sank into sleep. The girl took off her shoes. Then she went to the washroom to put the bouquet of flowers in some water.

When she came back to her seat, her mother was waiting to eat. She gave her a piece of cheese, half a corn-meal pancake, and a cookie, and took an equal portion out of the plastic sack for herself. While they ate, the train crossed an iron bridge very slowly and passed a town just like the ones before, except that in this one there was a crowd in the plaza. A band was playing a lively tune under the oppressive sun. At the other side of town the plantations ended in a plain which was cracked from the drought.

The woman stopped eating.

"Put on your shoes," she said.

The girl looked outside. She saw nothing but the deserted plain, where the train began to pick up speed again, but she put the last

"The town was floating in the heat."

piece of cookie into the sack and quickly put on her shoes. The woman gave her a comb.

"Comb your hair," she said.

The train whistle began to blow while the girl was combing her hair. The woman dried the sweat from her neck and wiped the oil from her face with her fingers. When the girl stopped combing, the train was passing the outlying houses of a town larger but sadder than the earlier ones.

"If you feel like doing anything, do it now," said the woman. "Later, don't take a drink anywhere even if you're dying of thirst. Above all, no crying."

The girl nodded her head. A dry, burning wind came in the window, together with the locomotive's whistle and the clatter of the old cars. The woman folded the plastic bag with the rest of the food and put it in the handbag. For a moment a complete picture of the town, on that bright August Tuesday, shone in the window. The girl wrapped the flowers in the soaking-wet newspapers, moved a little farther away from the window, and stared at her mother. She received a pleasant expression in return. The train began to whistle and slowed down. A moment later it stopped.

There was no one at the station. On the other side of the street, on the sidewalk shaded by the almond trees, only the pool hall was open. The town was floating in the heat. The woman and the girl got off the train and crossed the abandoned station—the tiles split apart by the grass growing up between—and over to the shady side of the street.

It was almost two. At that hour, weighted down by drowsiness, the town was taking a siesta. The stores, the town offices, the public school were closed at eleven, and didn't reopen until a little before four, when the

Literary Element Implied Theme *What do the mother's words and tone to her daughter suggest about their situation?* **L**

GABRIEL GARCÍA MÁRQUEZ **123**

Teach

L Literary Element

Implied Theme Answer: *The mother's instructions suggest she chooses to be self-sufficient, to show others that she and her daughter can take care of themselves and do not want pity.* **OL**

★ Writer's Technique

Figurative Language
Point out examples of figurative language in the story, such as "the shadows seemed clean," "a town larger but sadder than the earlier ones," and "The town was floating in the heat." Discuss how Márquez's use of figurative language enhances his description. **AS**

✓ CheckPoint

Use the CheckPoint questions on Presentation Plus! to monitor students' comprehension. These questions can be used with interactive response keypads for immediate student feedback.

Reading in the Real World

Citizenship Have students use the phone book and the Internet to research organizations in their community that provide the poor and indigent with food, clothing, shelter, and other necessities. Consider inviting a representative of one of the organizations to be a guest speaker. **OL**

Objectives
• To make inferences about a theme (SE)
• To recognize and understand implied theme (SE)
• To establish a purpose for reading (TWE)

Teach

Making Choices Answer:
Yes. She comes from that region and knows the customs. She most did not want to draw attention to their visit. **OL**

BI₂ Big Idea

Making Choices Answer:
She is determined to get her way. She says it is an emergency because no other response would motivate the priest to see her right away. **OL**

★ Viewing the Art

Joaquín Torres-García (1874–1949) was born in Uruguay and moved with his family to Barcelona, Spain, when he was a teenager. He attended art school and later designed windows for Antoni Gaudi for Gaudi's famous Barcelona cathedrals. In his paintings, he strove to temper instinct with reason, creating an intellectual framework for his art. *Campanario* is the Spanish word for "bell tower"; this painting shows a South American Catholic church.
Answer: *The scene captures the emptiness of a village during siesta.* **AS**

Campanario, c. 1947. Joaquín Torres-García. Oil on board laid down on panel, 13¼ x 16½ in. Private collection.
Viewing the Art: How does this scene help you envision the town during siesta?

train went back. Only the hotel across from the station, with its bar and pool hall, and the telegraph office at one side of the plaza stayed open. The houses, most of them built on the banana company's model, had their doors locked from inside and their blinds drawn. In some of them it was so hot that the residents ate lunch in the patio. Others leaned a chair against the wall, in the shade of the almond trees, and took their siesta right out in the street.

Keeping to the protective shade of the almond trees, the woman and the girl entered the town without disturbing the siesta. They went directly to the parish house.[1] The woman scratched the metal grating on the door with her fingernail, waited a moment, and scratched again. An electric fan was humming inside. They did not hear the steps. They hardly heard the slight creaking of a door, and immediately a cautious voice, right next to the metal grating: "Who is it?" The woman tried to see through the grating.

"I need the priest," she said.

"He's sleeping now."

"It's an emergency," the woman insisted. Her voice showed a calm determination.

The door was opened a little way, noiselessly, and a plump, older woman appeared, with very pale skin and hair the color of iron. Her eyes seemed too small behind her thick eyeglasses.

"Come in," she said, and opened the door all the way.

They entered a room permeated with an old smell of flowers. The woman of the house led them to a wooden bench and signaled them to sit down. The girl did so, but her mother remained standing, absent-mindedly, with both hands clutching the handbag. No noise could be heard above the electric fan.

The woman of the house reappeared at the door at the far end of the room. "He says you should come back after three," she

---

1. A *parish house* is the home of the priest of a local church district.

Big Idea Making Choices *Do you think the mother chooses to arrive when most people are inside? Explain?* **BI₁**

Big Idea Making Choices *Why does the woman use that tone of voice? Why does the woman say that it is an emergency?* **BI₂**

Additional Support

Skills Practice

VOCABULARY: Dictionary Skills
Use words from the vocabulary list or create an alternative list from the selection for practicing dictionary skills. Have students choose two words from the list and use their dictionaries to identify the following for each word:

- part of speech
- origin or etymology
- definitions
- synonyms
- idioms that use this word **OL**

said in a very low voice. "He just lay down five minutes ago."

"The train leaves at three-thirty," said the woman.

It was a brief and self-assured reply, but her voice remained pleasant, full of undertones.[2] The woman of the house smiled for the first time.

"All right," she said.

When the far door closed again, the woman sat down next to her daughter. The narrow waiting room was poor, neat, and clean. On the other side of the wooden railing which divided the room, there was a worktable, a plain one with an oilcloth cover, and on top of the table a primitive typewriter next to a vase of flowers. The parish records were beyond. You could see that it was an office kept in order by a spinster.[3]

The far door opened and this time the priest appeared, cleaning his glasses with a handkerchief. Only when he put them on was it evident that he was the brother of the woman who had opened the door.

"How can I help you?" he asked.

"The keys to the cemetery," said the woman.

The girl was seated with the flowers in her lap and her feet crossed under the bench. The priest looked at her, then looked at the woman, and then through the wire mesh of the window at the bright, cloudless sky.

"In this heat," he said. "You could have waited until the sun went down."

The woman moved her head silently. The priest crossed to the other side of the railing, took out of the cabinet a notebook covered in oilcloth, a wooden penholder, and an inkwell, and sat down at the table. There was more than enough hair on his hands to account for what was missing on his head.

"Which grave are you going to visit?" he asked.

"Carlos Centeno's," said the woman.

"Who?"

"Carlos Centeno," the woman repeated.

The priest still did not understand.

"He's the thief who was killed here last week," said the woman in the same tone of voice. "I am his mother."

The priest **scrutinized** her. She stared at him with quiet self-control, and the Father blushed. He lowered his head and began to write. As he filled the page, he asked the woman to identify herself, and she replied unhesitatingly, with precise details, as if she were reading them. The Father began to sweat. The girl unhooked the buckle of her left shoe, slipped her heel out of it, and rested it on the bench rail. She did the same with the right one.

It had all started the Monday of the previous week, at three in the morning, a few blocks from there. Rebecca, a lonely widow who lived in a house full of odds and ends, heard above the sound of the drizzling rain someone trying to force the front door from outside. She got up, rummaged around in her closet for an ancient revolver that no one had fired since the days of Colonel Aureliano Buendía,[4] and went into the living room without turning on the lights. Orienting herself not so much by the noise at the lock as by a terror developed in her by twenty-eight years of loneliness, she fixed in her imagination not only the spot where the door was but also the exact height of the lock. She clutched the weapon with both hands, closed her eyes, and squeezed the trigger. It was the first time in her life that she had fired a gun. Immediately after the explosion, she could hear nothing except the murmur of the drizzle on the galvanized roof. Then she heard a little metallic bump on the cement porch, and a very low voice, pleasant but terribly exhausted: "Ah, Mother." The man they found dead in front of the house in the morn-

4. *Aureleano Buendía* (ou′ rā lyä′ nō bwän dē′ ä)

Reading Strategy Making Inferences About Theme
Why does the priest blush after finding out that he is talking with the thief's mother? **R**

Vocabulary

scrutinize (skro̅o̅t′ ən īz) *v.* to look at closely; inspect carefully

GABRIEL GARCÍA MÁRQUEZ **125**

---

2. *Undertones* are underlying or implied meanings.
3. *Spinster* usually refers to an older woman who has never been married.

Teach

L Literary Element

Implied Theme Answer: *His "pleasant but terribly exhausted" voice indicates he was probably not a hardened criminal. His poverty is implied from his clothing. He wore pants with a rope for a belt and was barefoot. He may have been planning to steal valuables and sell them for food.* **OL**

R Reading Strategy

Making Inferences About Theme Answer: *She probably wants the priest to know how hard her son worked to help feed his family and of the extreme sacrifices he made.* **OL**

★ Cultural History

Spanish Names In Spanish-speaking countries, a person's surname is sometimes joined to the mother's maiden name using *y*, the Spanish word for *and*. In some cases, a woman takes her husband's name in the following manner: Luz Chavez-Izguerra de Luna, where Luna is the husband's surname. **AS**

---

ing, his nose blown to bits, wore a flannel shirt with colored stripes, everyday pants with a rope for a belt, and was barefoot. No one in town knew him.

"So his name was Carlos Centeno," murmured the Father when he finished writing.

"Centeno Ayala,"[5] said the woman. "He was my only boy." ★

The priest went back to the cabinet. Two big rusty keys hung on the inside of the door; the girl imagined, as her mother had when she was a girl and as the priest himself must have imagined at some time, that they were Saint Peter's keys.[6] He took them down, put them on the open notebook on the railing, and pointed with his forefinger to a place on the page he had just written, looking at the woman.

"Sign here."

The woman scribbled her name, holding the handbag under her arm. The girl picked up the flowers, came to the railing shuffling her feet, and watched her mother attentively.

The priest sighed.

"Didn't you ever try to get him on the right track?"

The woman answered when she finished signing.

"He was a very good man."

The priest looked first at the woman and then at the girl, and realized with a kind of pious[7] amazement that they were not about to cry. The woman continued in the same tone:

---

5. *[Ayala]* The young man's full name was Carlos *Centeno Ayala* (sen tā' nō   ä yä' lə). In Spanish-speaking countries, one's first name and surname are, by custom, followed by the mother's maiden name.
6. *Saint Peter's keys* refers to the traditional belief of some Christians that Saint Peter is in charge of the keys to the gates of heaven.
7. The word *pious* (pī' əs) may mean *either* having genuine reverence for God *or* having a false or hypocritical religious devotion.

Literary Element Implied Theme *What might these details say about the thief's motive? What might his motive say about the theme?* **L**

"I told him never to steal anything that anyone needed to eat, and he minded me. On the other hand, before, when he used to box, he used to spend three days in bed, exhausted from being punched."

"All his teeth had to be pulled out," interrupted the girl.

"That's right," the woman agreed. "Every mouthful I ate those days tasted of the beatings my son got on Saturday nights."

"God's will is **inscrutable**," said the Father.

But he said it without much conviction, partly because experience had made him a little **skeptical** and partly because of the heat. He suggested that they cover their heads to guard against sunstroke. Yawning, and now almost completely asleep, he gave them instructions about how to find Carlos Centeno's grave. When they came back, they didn't have to knock. They should put the key under the door; and in the same place, if they could, they should put an offering for the Church. The woman listened to his directions with great attention, but thanked him without smiling.

The Father had noticed that there was someone looking inside, his nose pressed against the metal grating, even before he opened the door to the street. Outside was a group of children. When the door was opened wide, the children scattered. Ordinarily, at that hour there was no one in the street. Now there were not only children. There were groups of people under the almond trees. The Father scanned the street swimming in the heat and then he understood. Softly, he closed the door again.

> "The man they found dead in front of the house..."

Reading Strategy Making Inferences About Theme
Why does the mother share this memory? **R**

Vocabulary

inscrutable (in skroot' tə bəl) *adj.* mysterious
skeptical (skep' ti kəl) *adj.* having or showing doubt or suspicion; questioning; disbelieving

126 UNIT 1 THE SHORT STORY

Additional Support

Skills Practice

LISTENING AND SPEAKING:

Proverbs Divide the class into small discussion groups. Have each group choose a chairperson to keep the discussion focused, a recorder to take notes, and an evaluator to gauge how well the group interacts. Then write the following proverb on the board: "Never judge a person until you have walked a mile in his or her shoes." Have students discuss how the proverb applies to the story "Tuesday Siesta." After fifteen minutes, group evaluators should rate how well the group interacted. **OL**

126

Landscape with Figures (Paisaje con Figura).
Arturo Gordon Vargas (1853–1933). Oil on canvas, 43 x 54 cm.

Viewing the Art: In your opinion, how are the characters in the painting similar to the woman and the girl in the story?

"Wait a moment," he said without looking at the woman.

His sister appeared at the far door with a black jacket over her nightshirt and her hair down over her shoulders. She looked silently at the Father.

"What was it?" he asked.

"The people have noticed," murmured his sister.

"You'd better go out by the door to the patio," said the Father.

"It's the same there," said his sister. "Everybody is at the windows."

The woman seemed not to have understood until then. She tried to look into the street through the metal grating. Then she took the bouquet of flowers from the girl and began to move toward the door. The girl followed her.

"Wait until the sun goes down," said the Father.

"You'll melt," said his sister, motionless at the back of the room. "Wait and I'll lend you a parasol."

"Thank you," replied the woman. "We're all right this way.

She took the girl by the hand and went into the street. ❧

Big Idea Making Choices *Why might the mother have chosen not to accept the woman's parasol?* **BI**

GABRIEL GARCÍA MÁRQUEZ **127**

Teach

BI Big Idea
Making Choices
Answer: *Students may say the mother was not ashamed of her son, so she did not want to appear to be hiding. Others may say she is a proud woman and did not want to take something from the woman and thereby be obligated to her. She may also be modeling behavior for her daughter not to accept charity from others.* **OL**

★ Viewing the Art
Arturo Gordon Vargas spent his entire life in Chile. He spent much of his career as an art professor, painting on the side. His work is known for his emphasis on light and on colored shadows. His themes included the life of the poor as well as religious and cultural events.
Answer: *The people in the painting seem to be mother and daughter. As in the story, they seem to be lonely and poor.* **AS**

✓ CheckPoint
Use the CheckPoint questions on Presentation Plus! to check students' mastery of the selection. These questions can be used with interactive response keypads for immediate student feedback.

Objectives
• To recognize and understand implied theme (SE)
• To make inferences about a theme (SE)
• To use effective speaking and listening strategies in group discussion (TWE)

Differentiated Instruction

Prepositional Phrases Of the ten most frequently used words in the English language, three are the prepositions *of, to,* and *in.* Prepositional phrases can modify either verbs or nouns. Have students copy three sentences from the last page of "Tuesday Siesta" that contain prepositional phrases. Instruct them to underline the prepositional phrases and label them adverbial (modifying an action verb) or adjectival (modifying a noun). *Possible answer: "She looked silently <u>at the Father</u>"* (adverbial). **BL**

127

Assess

1. Students may sympathize with the mother because she is going to mourn at her son's grave.

2. (a) The streets are empty. (b) To avoid being noticed

3. (a) To pay their final respects to Carlos; to get the key to the cemetery (b) She remains devoted to her son.

4. (a) The woman's only son; killed while trying to break into a house (b) She taught him never to steal other people's food. She wants to convey that he was not just a common criminal.

5. (a) The hot day emphasizes the difficulty of the situation. (b) The mother and daughter's journey on such a hot day shows the mother's determination; heat adds to the priest's discomfort. The oppressive heat suggests the oppression of poverty.

6. (a) They share things and take care of one another. (b) A larger role for the daughter might detract from the role of the mother.

7. (a) Grief, shame, and anger (b) It helped her preserve her dignity.

8. Robbing the house would be permissible if he didn't take food. Students should say whether he is a criminal, a victim, or both, and explain why.

RESPONDING AND THINKING CRITICALLY

Respond

1. For which character in this story do you feel the most sympathy? Explain.

Recall and Interpret

2. (a) What do the mother and daughter see as they walk from the train station to the parish house? (b) Why might the mother have decided to arrive in town during the afternoon siesta?

3. (a) What is the purpose of the mother and daughter's trip, and why do they go to the parish house? (b) What might lead the mother to act and speak the way she does while with the priest?

4. (a) Who was Carlos Centeno, and what happened to him the week before? (b) Carlos's mother refers to him as a thief but also tells the priest that he was "a very good man." What might she mean by this? Use details from the story to support your opinion.

Analyze and Evaluate

5. (a) Why might the author have chosen such an oppressively hot day for the setting of the story? (b) Do you feel that the heat of the day adds to the drama and theme of the story? Explain.

6. (a) How would you describe the relationship between the mother and the daughter? (b) Do you think the story would have been more interesting if the daughter had played a larger role? Explain.

7. (a) What feelings might the mother have chosen to hide from others? (b) Do you think that hiding her feelings was an effective defense?

Connect

8. **Big Idea** **Making Choices** How would you reconcile the moral code that Carlos' mother taught him with the fact that he tried to rob the house? In your opinion, who is at fault for Carlos's death: Carlos, his mother, the widow who shot him, society, or some combination of factors?

LITERARY ANALYSIS

Literary Element Implied Theme

The **theme** of a piece of literature is a central understanding, or truth, it offers about life. Some themes are universal, meaning that they are widely held ideas about life. Themes and topics are different. The *topic* of a work might be poverty; the *theme* would be what the writer says about poverty. An **implied theme** is not stated directly. Think back upon details that provide hints about the theme that Gabriel García Márquez implies in this story.

1. (a) From the details of the story, what kind of a life do you think the Centeno Ayala family leads before the robbery? (b) What does the story imply about Carlos Centeno's motives for trying to rob the widow?

2. (a) Why do the townspeople gather around the priest's house? (b) What does the mother's response to their presence tell you about her?

3. What theme, or insight into life or human nature, does the story express? Explain how the details of the story help to imply the theme.

Review: Flat and Round Characters

As you learned on pages 94–95, a **flat** character reveals only one personality trait. By contrast, a **round** character shows varied, and sometimes, contradictory traits, like the "main characters" in your own life.

Partner Activity With a partner, use a chart like the one below to classify the characters in this story as flat or round. Then meet with the class to discuss the characters' traits that led to your classifications.

Flat Characters	Round Characters

Additional Support

Literary Element

1. (a) Impoverished (b) He wanted to steal valuables he could sell to buy food.

2. (a) To see the thief's relatives (b) She will not let others' opinions affect her.

3. A mother will honor the memory of her son regardless of the type of person he is. The mother makes a difficult journey to pay tribute to her son.

Review: Flat and Round Characters

Mother and priest are round characters; daughter and priest's sister are flat.

Reading Strategy — Making Inferences About Theme

"Tuesday Siesta" has an implied theme. García Márquez offers many hints about the theme in the setting, plot events, dialogue, and actions. What specific inferences can you draw about this theme due to:

1. details in the **setting**;
2. details in the **plot events**;
3. details in the **dialogue**;
4. details in the characters' **actions**?

Vocabulary Practice

Practice with Word Parts Use the information about suffixes below to choose the best definition for each vocabulary word.

Suffix: *al*—changes nouns or verbs to adjectives
Suffix: *able*—adjective suffix meaning "able"
Suffix: *ity*—noun suffix meaning "quality"
Suffix: *ize*—verb suffix meaning "to make like"

1. interminable   **a.** endless   **b.** finite
2. serenity   **a.** calmness   **b.** to make serene
3. scrutinize   **a.** cleaned   **b.** inspect
4. inscrutable   **a.** to know   **b.** mysterious
5. skeptical   **a.** disbelieving   **b.** disbeliever

Academic Vocabulary

Here are two words from the vocabulary list on page R82.

legal (lē′ gəl) *adj.* according to the law

locate (lō′ kāt) *v.* to find; to determine the position of an object or place

Practice and Apply
1. How was Carlos's actual fate different from the customary **legal** punishment for stealing?
2. Why was it necessary for the mother to visit the priest in order to **locate** her son's grave?

Writing About Literature

Summarize Flashback A flashback is an interruption in the regular, chronological order of the events in the plot. It takes the reader back to an event that happened earlier, before the story began. García Márquez uses a flashback in this story. In it, he introduces a new character and describes something that happened a week before the story takes place. Write a brief essay summarizing the information provided in this flashback. Then explain how the flashback helps readers better understand the actions of the characters and how it helps to imply a theme. You might format your essay as shown.

> **Introduction**
> A statement of your main idea about what flashback added to the story.
>
> ↓
>
> **Body**
> A summary of the details of the flashback, along with an explanation of what the flashback contributed to the plot and theme
>
> ↓
>
> **Conclusion**
> A brief recap of the details you discussed and a final thought about what flashback added to the story

When you are finished with your draft, meet with a partner to evaluate each other's work and suggest revisions. Then proofread and edit your draft for errors in spelling, grammar, and punctuation.

Literature Groups

In your opinion, was Carlos more honorable for trying to support his family or more dishonorable for stealing? Let each member of your group give an opinion about this question, and feel free to challenge your fellow group members to support their opinions with evidence from the story. Finally, tally up the group's response and share the results with your class.

 Literature Online   **Web Activities** For eFlashcards, Selection Quick Checks, and othe Web activities, go to www.glencoe.com.

GABRIEL GARCÍA MÁRQUEZ **129**

Assess

Reading Strategy

1. Oppressive heat, third-class train car, dusty town: poverty and discomfort
2. The mother comes to town to place flowers on her son's grave, who has been killed while trying to rob a house; the priest expresses disapproval; the mother remains determined: dignity in the face of difficulty.
3. The priest speaks with condescension; she responds with coolness and determination; she reveals her moral code, and she refers to her son as both a "thief" and "a very good man": poverty and difficult circumstances.
4. Mother and daughter undertake the journey despite the heat; mother refuses to wait until nightfall to visit the grave, and walks out to face the crowd: dignity under difficult circumstances.

Vocabulary

1. a   2. a   3. b   4. b   5. a

Academic Vocabulary

1. If the police had apprehended Carlos, he likely would have gone to jail.
2. The priest had the key to the cemetery; he knew the location of the grave.

Writing About Literature

Students' essays should:
- summarize the events of the attempted burglary
- evaluate the role of the flashback in the implied theme

Literature Groups

Students should support their opinions with evidence from the story.

Literature Online

Web Activities Have students access the Web site for interactive activities that will help them assess their understanding of the selection.

129

Focus

Write this sentence on the board: "Tears began." **Ask:** What different meanings could this sentence have, depending on the definition of the multiple-meaning word? *(The sentence could refer to crying or to a rip starting.)* **Say:** In this lesson you will explore how to determine the intended meaning of a word. **OL**

Teach

Identifying Multiple Meanings
Guide students to notice the context of a sentence or passage that helps to identify the definition of each multiple-meaning word. List other multiple-meaning words (e.g., *sweep, fair, track*), and ask students to write sentences using each word with two different meanings. **OL**

Assess

1. b **2.** a **3.** a **4.** a **5.** b

eFlashcards Have students access the Web site for more practice with multiple-meaning words.

Additional Support

130

► **Test-Taking Tip**

To determine the intended meaning of a multiple-meaning word, use context clues. Remember that the right meaning will be the correct part of speech.

► **Reading Handbook**

For more about multiple-meaning words, see the Reading Handbook, p. R20.

Literature Online
eFlashcards Visit www.glencoe.com for eFlashcards and other vocabulary activities.

OBJECTIVES
• Recognize multiple-meaning words.
• Use context clues to determine the intended meaning of a word.

Vocabulary Workshop

Multiple-Meaning Words

Distinguishing Definitions

"She sat on the opposite seat, away from the window, facing her mother. They were both in severe and poor mourning clothes."

—Gabriel García Márquez, from "Tuesday Siesta"

Connecting to Literature The second sentence in this quotation from "Tuesday Siesta" includes two **multiple-meaning words:** *severe* and *poor*. *Severe* can mean either "plain" or "harshly judgmental"; and *poor* can mean either "humble" or "poverty-stricken." From the context, readers realize that the women's clothes were plain and humble.

English is full of multiple-meaning words. Here are some common ones:

Word	Meaning	Example
plain	*n.* flat, treeless land	The **plain** stretched, unbroken, into the distance.
	adj. simple and unadorned	They were **plain** and simple people.
	adj. evident	The priest's embarrassment was **plain** to them.
still	*adv.* yet	They **still** had not reached the station.
	adj. quiet and unmoving	During the siesta, the whole town was **still**.
	v. to calm	The rabbi **stilled** the woman's fears.
train	*n.* connected line of railroad cars	The women took a **train** to visit her aunt.
	n. trailing part of a dress	The bride's gown had a long, intricate **train**.
	v. to teach or instruct	She **trained** her puppy to be obedient.

Exercise

Choose the correct definition for the multiple-meaning word in each sentence. Consult a dictionary if you need help.

1. After softball practice, the girl went shopping for a new *bat*.
　a. winged mammal 　　**b.** wooden sports implement

2. He used *tape* to close the box.
　a. sticky fastening strip 　**b.** to record

3. To land, the plane must *bank* steeply.
　a. to follow a curve 　　**b.** ridge

4. He waited to start work until the sun *rose*.
　a. to move upward 　　**b.** aromatic flower

5. *Nail* the sides of the box securely.
　a. metal fastener 　　**b.** to secure

130 UNIT 1　THE SHORT STORY

Skills Practice

GRAMMAR: Parts of Speech
Review with students the parts of speech and how they are indicated in a dictionary. Explain how nouns are used to name people, places, and things, while verbs express action or states of being, and adjectives modify nouns, while adverbs modify verbs or adjectives. Provide sentences from the stories containing multiple-meaning words (e.g., "It picked up the tired old automobile, ... losing its <u>hold</u> now and then"). Based on their understanding of parts of speech, have students identify which definition of the word applies (e.g, *hold* as a noun means "a grip"). **OL**

When Mr. Pirzada Came to Dine

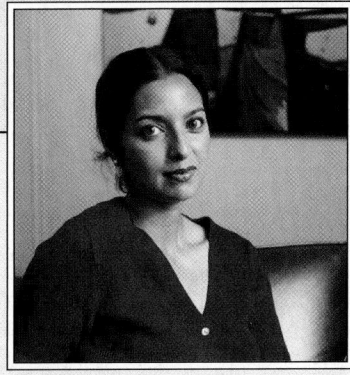

MEET JHUMPA LAHIRI

Jhumpa (joom' pa) Lahiri began her writing career when she was a child. In elementary school, she and her best friend composed stories during recess, thinking them aloud "sentence by sentence." Many sentences later, in 2000, Lahiri won the Pulitzer Prize for fiction for *Interpreter of Maladies,* her collection of short stories about people in India and Indian immigrants in the United States. "It's been the happiest possible ending," she says.

> *"The question of identity is always a difficult one, but especially so for those who are culturally displaced."*
>
> —Jhumpa Lahiri

The Interpreter of Maladies Jhumpa Lahiri was born in London, but her Bengali parents, a librarian and a teacher, emigrated to Rhode Island, where she grew up. As a child, Lahiri often spent time with her extended family in Calcutta, India, as well. She received her bachelor's degree from Barnard College, and then three master's degrees and a doctorate in Renaissance Studies from Boston University. Within a year of completing her dissertation, Lahiri had hired a literary agent, sold a book, and published a story in *The New Yorker.* The story in *The New Yorker* and those published by other magazines formed the basis for *The Interpreter of Maladies.*

Lahiri's work often deals with the difficulties that dislocated and homesick Indian immigrants face in trying to cope with a new culture. Lahiri notes that her work reflects the sense of displacement she experienced as a

child of immigrants. As she says, "For immigrants, the challenges of exile, the loneliness, the constant sense of alienation, the knowledge of and longing for a lost world, are more explicit and distressing than for their children. On the other hand, the problem for the children of immigrants, those with strong ties to their country of origin, is that they feel neither one thing nor the other. The feeling that there was no single place to which I fully belonged bothered me growing up."

Her First Novel In 2003 Lahiri published *The Namesake.* The novel deals with a rebellious son who is learning how to juggle both Indian and U. S. identities and come to terms with the significance of his strange first name, "Gogol." Lahiri says, "I had always been aware of having an unusual name and the difficulties one faces living with a name in a place where it doesn't make sense." The novel, unlike her short stories, allows Lahiri to develop her characters and explore their lives at a slower pace. In her *New York Times* review, Michiko Kakutani called it ". . . a debut novel that is as assured and eloquent as the work of a longtime master of the craft."

Jhumpa Lahiri was born in 1967.

 Author Search For more about Jhumpa Lahiri, go to www.glencoe.com.

Focus

BELLRINGER

Bellringer Options
Daily Language
   Transparency 14
Or **say:** Think about a time when you had to be apart from someone or something you cared about.
Have students share some of their experiences. Ask them to describe their feelings during that time.

Literature Online

Author Search To expand students' appreciation of Jhumpa Lahiri, have them access the Web site for additional information and resources.

Selection Skills

When Mr. Pirzada Came to Dine

Literary Elements
• Theme (SE pp. 132–146)
• Conflict (SE p. 146)
• Point of View (TWE p. 142)

Reading Skills
• Comparing and Contrasting Characters (SE pp. 132–147)
• Drawing Conclusions (TWE p. 140)

Vocabulary Skills
• Context Clues (SE p. 147)
• Academic Vocabulary (SE p. 147)

Writing Skills/Grammar
• Evaluate the Author's Craft (SE p. 147)
• Describing a Character (TWE p. 136)

Study Skills/Research/Assessment
• South Asian Recipes (TWE p. 138)

Focus

Summary

A young girl named Lilia remembers Mr. Pirzada's evening visits to her home. Mr. Pirzada had left his family in East Pakistan to write a book on foliage in the United States. While he was gone, a war started in his country, so he feared for the safety of his wife and seven daughters. Through his visits, Lilia learns what it means to miss someone.

V Vocabulary

Vocabulary File Say: Add these words and definitions to your vocabulary file. For each word, include a sentence that gives you an example of how to use the word. **OL** Students with English language needs should include the pronunciations of these words in their files. **EL**

Literary Elements Have students access the Web site to improve their understanding of theme.

Connecting to the Story

Imagine being safe and secure with friends while your family endures a crisis thousands of miles away. Before you read the story, think about the following questions:

- How would you react in this kind of situation?
- How would you interact with friends who know how worried you are about your family?

Building Background

In 1947 British rule came to an end in India, and the region was divided along religious lines into two countries, India and Pakistan. Muslim Pakistan consisted of two geographical regions, West Pakistan and East Pakistan, divided by the large Hindu country of India. In 1971, when this story takes place, West Pakistan and East Pakistan were engaged in conflict as a result of East Pakistan's demand for independence from West Pakistan. West Pakistan invaded East Pakistan, causing millions of East Pakistanis to take refuge in India. India soon got involved, bringing a rapid end to the war, and the independent state of Bangladesh was declared in East Pakistan.

Setting Purposes for Reading

Big Idea Making Choices

As you read, think about the circumstances that lead Mr. Pirzada to make the difficult choice to stay in the United States rather than return to his family.

Literary Element Theme

A **theme** is a central message of a written work that readers can apply to life. Some works have a **stated theme** that is expressed directly. More commonly, works have an **implied theme** which is revealed gradually. Literary works often have one or more themes. As you read, try to determine the themes in Lahiri's story.

- See Literary Terms Handbook, p. R18.

Literature Online **Interactive Literary Elements Handbook** To review or learn more about the literary elements, go to www.glencoe.com.

Reading Strategy Comparing and Contrasting Characters

To **compare and contrast characters** is to determine similarities and differences between them. Comparing and contrasting characters can help you better understand who the characters are and why they act in certain ways. Notice how Lahiri describes the characters and how they are like and unlike one another.

Reading Tip: Taking Notes Use a chart to record various similarities and differences between characters.

Mr. Pirzada	from Dacca, is Muslim, speaks Bengali and English
Lilia's father	from Calcutta, is Hindu, speaks Bengali and English
Lilia's mother	
Lilia	
Dora	

Vocabulary

ascertaining (as′ər tān′ ing) v. finding out definitely; p. 133 *The police were ascertaining who had robbed the bank.*

austere (ôs tēr′) adj. without ornament, very simple; p. 135 *Her dress was austere, lacking any embroidery or decoration.*

impeccably (im pek′ə blē) adv. without error or flaw; p. 136 *His manners were impeccably polite.*

imperceptible (im′pər sep′tə bəl) adj. slight, barely capable of being seen or sensed; p. 137 *The movement in the grass was so imperceptible that we did not see the snake.*

intimidation (in tim′ə dā shən) n. act of making one feel afraid or discouraged; p. 141 *The opposing team used intimidation to threaten the soccer players.*

OBJECTIVES
In studying this selection, you will focus on the following:
- understanding theme
- comparing and contrasting characters
- analyzing conflict
- writing to evaluate the author's craft

132 UNIT 1 THE SHORT STORY

Selection Resources

Print Materials
- 📁 Unit 1 Resources (Fast File), pp. 55–57
- 📁 Leveled Vocabulary Development, p. 11
- 📁 Selection and Unit Assessments, pp. 23–24
- 📁 Selection Quick Checks, p. 12

Transparencies
- Bellringer Options Transparencies: Daily Language Practice Transparency 14
- Literary Elements Transparency 18

Technology
- 💿 TeacherWorks Plus™ CD-ROM
- 💿 StudentWorks Plus™ CD-ROM
- 💿 Presentation Plus!™ CD-ROM
- 💻 Literature Online, glencoe.com
- 💻 Online Student Edition, mhln.com
- 💿 ExamView® Assessment Suite CD-ROM
- 💿 Vocabulary PuzzleMaker CD-ROM
- 💿 Listening Library, disc 1 track 12

When Mr. Pirzada Came to Dine

Jhumpa Lahiri

Avenue of the Elysian Fields, 1888.
Vincent van Gogh. Oil on canvas.

In the autumn of 1971 a man used to come to our house, bearing confections[1] in his pocket and hopes of **ascertaining** the life or death of his family. His name was Mr. Pirzada, and he came from Dacca, now the capital of Bangladesh, but then a part of Pakistan. That year Pakistan was engaged in civil war. The eastern frontier, where Dacca was located, was fighting for autonomy[2] from the ruling regime[3] in the west. In March, Dacca had been invaded, torched, and shelled by the Pakistani army. Teachers were dragged onto streets and shot, women dragged into barracks and raped. By the end of the summer, three hundred thousand people were said to have died. In Dacca Mr. Pirzada had a three-story home, a lectureship in botany at the university, a wife of twenty years, and seven daughters between the ages of six and sixteen whose names all began with the letter A. "Their mother's idea," he explained one day, producing from his wallet a black-and-white picture of seven girls at a picnic, their braids tied with ribbons, sitting cross-legged in a row, eating chicken curry[4] off of banana leaves. "How

---

1. *Confections* are sweets, such as candy or preserves.
2. To have *autonomy* is to have the right to self-rule.
3. A *regime* (rə zhēm′) is a system of government.

Vocabulary

ascertaining (as′ər tān′ ing) *v.* finding out definitely

---

4. *Chicken curry* is chicken cooked with various spices including curry powder, ginger, and turmeric.

Literary Element Theme *A theme of a story can often develop out of contrasts in setting. How would you describe life in Dacca?* **L**

JHUMPA LAHIRI **133**

Teach

L Literary Element

Theme Answer: *Life in Dacca appears to be chaotic and violent.* **OL**

★ Viewing the Art

The title of this Vincent van Gogh painting refers to the mythical land of Elysium, which is a paradise or heaven. **Ask:** Why do you think van Gogh chose this title? *(Van Gogh possibly saw the setting as an earthly example of paradise.)* **AS**

✓CheckPoint

Use the CheckPoint questions on Presentation Plus! to monitor students' comprehension. These questions can be used with interactive response keypads for immediate student feedback.

Readability Scores
Dale-Chall: 8.7
DRP: 60
Lexile: 1170

Differentiated Instruction

Gathering Background Because the story deals with a different culture, students may have trouble overcoming their own lack of experience with other cultures. Divide the class into groups and assign each group a different topic related to the culture and history of the Indian region. Food, music, and clothing are three possible topics. Each group should do some research on their topic and present their findings to the class. **BL**

Objectives
• To understand theme (SE)

133

Teach

Making Choices Say: *As you read, think about the choices each character makes or has made. (Mr. Pirzada chooses to finish his book before going home, Lilia chooses to throw away her Halloween candy and to pray for Mr. Pirzada's family, Lilia's parents chose to leave India and come to America.)* **OL**

B1₁ **Big Idea**

Making Choices Answer: *Some students may say that living in the United States is preferable to returning to Dacca. Others may think that he values his career more than his family.* **OL**

⭐ Political History

India and Pakistan

Between 1876 and 1947, the areas now known as India and Pakistan were under British rule as a single territory called India. When the people of the region finally gained independence from Britain, the area was divided so the Muslims would be in Pakistan and the Hindus would be in India. However, people of both religions remained in both regions, which led to unrest. **AS**

---

am I to distinguish? Ayesha, Amira, Amina, Aziza, you see the difficulty."

Each week Mr. Pirzada wrote letters to his wife, and sent comic books to each of his seven daughters, but the postal system, along with most everything else in Dacca, had collapsed, and he had not heard word of them in over six months. Mr. Pirzada, meanwhile, was in America for the year, for he had been awarded a grant from the government of Pakistan to study the foliage[5] of New England. In spring and summer he had gathered data in Vermont and Maine, and in autumn he moved to a university north of Boston, where we lived, to write a short book about his discoveries. The grant was a great honor, but when converted into dollars it was not generous. As a result, Mr. Pirzada lived in a room in a graduate dormitory,[6] and did not own a proper stove or a television set of his own. And so he came to our house to eat dinner and watch the evening news.

At first I knew nothing of the reason for his visits. I was ten years old, and was not surprised that my parents, who were from India, and had a number of Indian acquaintances at the university, should ask Mr. Pirzada to share our meals. It was a small campus, with narrow brick walkways and white pillared buildings, located on the fringes of what seemed to be an even smaller town. The supermarket did not carry mustard oil,[7] doctors did not make house calls, neighbors never dropped by without an invitation, and of these things,

> **"One moment we were free and then we were sliced up."**

every so often, my parents complained. In search of compatriots,[8] they used to trail their fingers, at the start of each new semester, through the columns of the university directory, circling surnames[9] familiar to their part of the world. It was in this manner that they discovered Mr. Pirzada, and phoned him, and invited him to our home.

I have no memory of his first visit, or of his second or his third, but by the end of September I had grown so accustomed to Mr. Pirzada's presence in our living room that one evening, as I was dropping ice cubes into the water pitcher, I asked my mother to hand me a fourth glass from a cupboard still out of my reach. She was busy at the stove, presiding over a skillet of fried spinach with radishes, and could not hear me because of the drone of the exhaust fan and the fierce scrapes of her spatula.[10] I turned to my father, who was leaning against the refrigerator, eating spiced cashews[11] from a cupped fist.

"What is it, Lilia?"

"A glass for the Indian man."

"Mr. Pirzada won't be coming today. More importantly, Mr. Pirzada is no longer considered Indian," my father announced, brushing salt from the cashews out of his trim black beard. "Not since Partition.[12] Our country was divided. 1947." ⭐

When I said I thought that was the date of India's independence from Britain, my father said, "That too. One moment we were free and then we were sliced up," he explained,

---

5. *Foliage* (fō′lē ij) is clusters of leaves or branches.
6. A *dormitory* is a residence building with private rooms, typically for college students.
7. *Mustard oil* is made from mustard seeds and is used in cooking Indian foods.

Big Idea **Making Choices** *Why do you think Mr. Pirzada decides to stay in the United States instead of going home?* **B1₁**

8. *Compatriots* are people from one's home country.
9. A *surname* is a person's family name.
10. A *spatula* is a cooking utensil with a broad flexible blade used to spread or mix food.
11. *Cashews* are roasted nuts from the cashew tree.
12. *Partition* refers to the creation of independent countries out of parts of the British Empire. Partition created India and Pakistan.

Additional Support

Skills Practice

LITERARY ELEMENTS: Simile Lilia's father describes India as being "sliced up . . . like a pie." **Say:** Similes are comparisons between two unlike things using the word *as* or *like*. Writers use similes to help readers see or understand part of the story better. Have students write five similes to describe something in the classroom or outside. Each student should share a simile with the rest of the class. **OL**

drawing an X with his finger on the counter-top, "like a pie. Hindus here, Muslims there. Dacca no longer belongs to us." He told me that during Partition Hindus and Muslims had set fire to each other's homes. For many, the idea of eating in the other's company was still unthinkable.

It made no sense to me. Mr. Pirzada and my parents spoke the same language, laughed at the same jokes, looked more or less the same. They ate pickled mangoes[13] with their meals, ate rice every night for supper with their hands. Like my parents, Mr. Pirzada took off his shoes before entering a room, chewed fennel[14] seeds after meals as a digestive, drank no alcohol, for dessert dipped **austere** biscuits into successive cups of tea. Nevertheless my father insisted that I understand the difference, and he led me to a map of the world taped to the wall over his desk. He seemed concerned that Mr. Pirzada might take offense if I accidentally referred to him as an Indian, though I could not really imagine Mr. Pirzada being offended by much of anything. "Mr. Pirzada is Bengali, but he is a Muslim," my father informed me. "Therefore he lives in East Pakistan, not India." His finger trailed across the Atlantic, through Europe, the Mediterranean, the Middle East, and finally to the sprawling orange diamond that my mother once told me resembled a woman wearing a sari[15] with her left arm extended. Various cities had been circled with lines drawn between them to indicate my parents' travels, and the place of their birth, Calcutta,

was signified by a small silver star. I had been there only once and had no memory of the trip. "As you see, Lilia, it is a different country, a different color," my father said. Pakistan was yellow, not orange. I noticed that there were two distinct parts to it, one much larger than the other, separated by an expanse of Indian territory; it was as if California and Connecticut constituted a nation apart from the U.S.

My father rapped his knuckles on top of my head. "You are, of course, aware of the current situation? Aware of East Pakistan's fight for sovereignty?"

I nodded, unaware of the situation.

We returned to the kitchen, where my mother was draining a pot of boiled rice into a colander.[16] My father opened up the can on the counter and eyed me sharply over the frames of his glasses as he ate some more cashews. "What exactly do they teach you at school? Do you study history? Geography?"

"Lilia has plenty to learn at school," my mother said. "We live here now, she was born here." She seemed genuinely proud of the fact, as if it were a reflection of my character. In her estimation, I knew, I was assured a safe life, an easy life, a fine education, every opportunity. I would never have to eat rationed food, or obey curfews, or watch riots from my rooftop, or hide neighbors in water tanks to prevent them from being shot, as she and my father had. "Imagine having to place her in a decent school. Imagine her having to read during power failures by the light of kerosene lamps. Imagine the pressures, the tutors, the constant exams." She ran a hand through her hair, bobbed[17] to a suitable length for her part-time job as a bank teller. "How can you possibly expect her to know about Partition? Put those nuts away."

---

13. *Mangoes* are the sweet fruit from the tropical mango tree.
14. *Fennel* is a plant with aromatic seeds used to flavor foods.
15. A *sari* (sär′ē) is a garment worn by Hindu women consisting of a long piece of cloth; one end is wrapped around the waist to form a skirt and the other end is thrown over the shoulder or head.

Reading Strategy Comparing and Contrasting Characters *Why does Lilia think that Mr. Pirzada is an Indian man?* **R**

Vocabulary

austere (ôs tēr′) *adj.* without ornament, very simple

---

16. A *colander* is a bowl-shaped utensil with holes in the bottom for draining liquids.
17. *Bobbed* means "cut short."

Big Idea Making Choices *Why do you think Lilia's mother seems proud of this fact?* **BI₂**

JHUMPA LAHIRI **135**

Teach

R **Reading Strategy**
Comparing and Contrasting Characters
Answer: *Mr. Pirzada has a similar appearance, speaks the same language, has the same sense of humor, and has the same eating and drinking habits as her parents, who are Indian.* **Ask:** Why do so many similarities exist between Mr. Pirzada and Lilia's parents, even though they are not from the same country? *(Even though the countries are now separate, that was not the case when they were born. Overlap between the two cultures of the two nations would remain.)* **OL**

BI₂ **Big Idea**
Making Choices
Answer: *Perhaps Lilia's mother seems proud that Lilia was born in the United States because she originally made the choice to live and raise a child here.* **OL**

Differentiated Instruction

Geography Students may have difficulty with the story because they are unfamiliar with the geographic areas being discussed by the characters. Have a map or a globe in your classroom, print maps of the area from the Internet, or view an atlas in the library. Give each student a chance to point out India, Pakistan, Bangladesh, and the United States on the map so they can see the location and understand the distance separating Mr. Pirzada from his family. Alternatively, give each student a blank map of the world and have them label the four countries themselves. **BL**

Objectives
• To compare and contrast characters (SE)
• To understand simile (TWE)

L1 Literary Element

Theme Answer: *This detail emphasizes how well Lilia knows the history of the United States, but not what is happening in the country where her parents were born.* **OL**

★ Viewing the Art

This silk head cover illustrates two of the popular crafts in Gujarat, one of India's states. in Gujarat, *bandhani* is a tie-and-dye technique, which creates the color and texture of the head cover pictured here. The other craft from the area is *patola*, which involves fine silk fabric. **Ask:** What might these two craft examples suggest about Gujarat's culture? *(The culture emphasized an attention to intricate details and beautiful things.)* **AS**

"But what does she learn about the world?" My father rattled the cashew can in his hand. "What is she learning?"

We learned American history, of course, and American geography. That year, and every year, it seemed, we began by studying the Revolutionary War. We were taken in school buses on field trips to visit Plymouth Rock, and to walk the Freedom Trail, and to climb to the top of the Bunker Hill Monument. We made dioramas[18] out of colored construction paper depicting George Washington crossing the choppy waters of the Delaware River, and we made puppets of King George wearing white tights and a black bow in his hair. During tests we were given blank maps of the thirteen colonies, and asked to fill in names, dates, capitals. I could do it with my eyes closed.

The next evening Mr. Pirzada arrived, as usual, at six o'clock. Though they were no longer strangers, upon first greeting each other, he and my father maintained the habit of shaking hands.

"Come in, sir. Lilia, Mr. Pirzada's coat, please."

He stepped into the foyer,[19] **impeccably** suited and scarved, with a silk tie knotted at his collar. Each evening he appeared in ensembles[20] of plums, olives, and chocolate browns. He was a compact man, and though his feet were perpetually splayed,[21] and his belly slightly wide, he nevertheless maintained an efficient posture, as if balancing in either hand two suitcases of equal weight. His ears were insulated by tufts[22]

Woman's head cover (detail), 19th century. Gujarat. c. 1860–1870. Silk, printed in imitation of tie-dye. ★ Victoria and Albert Museum, London.

of graying hair that seemed to block out the unpleasant traffic of life. He had thickly lashed eyes shaded with a trace of camphor, a generous mustache that turned up playfully at the ends, and a mole shaped like a flattened raisin in the very center of his left cheek. On his head he wore a black fez[23] made from the wool of Persian lambs, secured by bobby pins, without which I was never to see him. Though my father always offered to fetch him in our car, Mr. Pirzada preferred to walk from his dormitory to our neighborhood, a distance of about twenty minutes on foot, studying trees and shrubs on his way, and when he entered our house his knuckles were pink with the effects of crisp autumn air.

---

18. *Dioramas* are three-dimensional miniature scenes.
19. A *foyer* (foi′ər) is an entrance hall.
20. Here, *ensembles* (än säm′bəls) are clothes of matching colors.
21. *Splayed* feet are spread out awkwardly.
22. *Tufts* are short clumps or clusters.

Literary Element Theme *Why do you think Lahiri includes this detail?* **L1**

Vocabulary

impeccably (im pek′ə blē) *adv.* without error or flaw

23. A *fez* is a tall felt hat, usually red, with a black tassel hanging from the crown.

Additional Support

Skills Practice

WRITING: Describing a Character
Lahiri devotes a significant portion of this scene to describing Mr. Pirzada. **Say:** Character description is important because it allows you to picture this person in your mind. A vivid description, like the one in the story, makes the character seem more real. Have students close their eyes and picture someone they know. While the image is still fresh in their minds, have them write down every detail about the person's appearance. Have them turn those details into a brief descriptive paragraph. **OL**

"Another refugee, I am afraid, on Indian territory."

"They are estimating nine million at the last count," my father said.

Mr. Pirzada handed me his coat, for it was my job to hang it on the rack at the bottom of the stairs. It was made of finely checkered gray-and-blue wool, with a striped lining and horn buttons, and carried in its weave the faint smell of limes. There were no recognizable tags inside, only a hand-stitched label with the phrase "Z. Sayeed, Suitors" embroidered on it in cursive with glossy black thread. On certain days a birch or maple leaf was tucked into a pocket. He unlaced his shoes and lined them against the baseboard; a golden paste clung to the toes and heels, the result of walking through our damp, unraked lawn. Relieved of his trappings, he grazed my throat with his short, restless fingers, the way a person feels for solidity behind a wall before driving in a nail. Then he followed my father to the living room, where the television was tuned to the local news. As soon as they were seated my mother appeared from the kitchen with a plate of mincemeat kebabs with coriander chutney.[24] Mr. Pirzada popped one into his mouth.

"One can only hope," he said, reaching for another, "that Dacca's refugees are as heartily fed. Which reminds me." He reached into his suit pocket and gave me a small plastic egg filled with cinnamon hearts. "For the lady of the house," he said with an almost **imperceptible** splay-footed bow.

"Really, Mr. Pirzada," my mother protested. "Night after night. You spoil her."

---

24. *Mincemeat . . . chutney* is a mixture of chopped apples, raisins, and meat skewered and broiled, served with a relish made with the aromatic herb coriander.

Reading Strategy Comparing and Contrasting Characters *Why does Mr. Pirzada call himself a "refugee . . . on Indian territory"?* **R**

Vocabulary

imperceptible (im´pər sep´tə bəl) *adj.* slight, barely capable of being seen or sensed

---

"I only spoil children who are incapable of spoiling."

It was an awkward moment for me, one which I awaited in part with dread, in part with delight. I was charmed by the presence of Mr. Pirzada's rotund[25] elegance, and flattered by the faint theatricality of his attentions, yet unsettled by the superb ease of his gestures, which made me feel, for an instant, like a stranger in my own home. It had become our ritual, and for several weeks, before we grew more comfortable with one another, it was the only time he spoke to me directly. I had no response, offered no comment, betrayed no visible reaction to the steady stream of honey-filled lozenges, the raspberry truffles, the slender rolls of sour pastilles. I could not even thank him, for once, when I did, for an especially spectacular peppermint lollipop wrapped in a spray[26] of purple cellophane, he had demanded, "What is this thank-you? The lady at the bank thanks me, the cashier at the shop thanks me, the librarian thanks me when I return an overdue book, the overseas operator thanks me as she tries to connect me to Dacca and fails. If I am buried in this country I will be thanked, no doubt, at my funeral."

It was inappropriate, in my opinion, to consume the candy Mr. Pirzada gave me in a casual manner. I coveted each evening's treasure as I would a jewel, or a coin from a buried kingdom, and I would place it in a small keepsake box made of carved sandalwood beside my bed, in which, long ago in India, my father's mother used to store the ground areca[27] nuts she ate after her morning bath. It was my only memento of a grandmother I had never known, and until Mr. Pirzada came to our lives I could find nothing to put

---

25. *Rotund* means "plump."
26. Here, *spray* means that the cellophane has been shaped or twisted to look like a flower.
27. *Areca* nuts come from the betel palm, a type of tall palm tree.

Literary Element Theme *Why do you think Mr. Pirzada makes such an outburst when Lilia thanks him for the candy?* **L₂**

JHUMPA LAHIRI **137**

Teach

Comparing and Contrasting Characters

Answer: *Mr. Pirzada keeps the watch set to the local time in Dacca; he is constantly aware of life in two different time zones, unlike Lilia's family.* **Ask:** What realization does Lilia have because of Mr. Pirzada's watch? *(Lilia realizes that life is going on elsewhere.)* **OL**

R2 Reading Strategy

Comparing and Contrasting Characters

Answer: *Unlike Mr. Pirzada and her parents, Lilia has not lived in the areas now engaged in war; further, she is not familiar with the politics and geographic details involved.* **OL**

---

inside it. Every so often before brushing my teeth and laying out my clothes for school the next day, I opened the lid of the box and ate one of his treats.

That night, like every night, we did not eat at the dining table, because it did not provide an unobstructed view of the television set. Instead we huddled around the coffee table, without conversing, our plates perched on the edges of our knees. From the kitchen my mother brought forth the succession of dishes: lentils with fried onions, green beans with coconut, fish cooked with raisins in a yogurt sauce. I followed with the water glasses, and the plate of lemon wedges, and the chili peppers, purchased on monthly trips to Chinatown and stored by the pound in the freezer, which they liked to snap open and crush into their food.

Before eating Mr. Pirzada always did a curious thing. He took out a plain silver watch without a band, which he kept in his breast pocket, held it briefly to one of his tufted ears, and wound it with three swift flicks of his thumb and forefinger. Unlike the watch on his wrist, the pocket watch, he had explained to me, was set to the local time in Dacca, eleven hours ahead. For the duration of the meal the watch rested on his folded paper napkin on the coffee table. He never seemed to consult it.

Now that I had learned Mr. Pirzada was not an Indian, I began to study him with extra care, to try to figure out what made him different. I decided that the pocket watch was one of those things. When I saw it that night, as he wound it and arranged it on the coffee table, an uneasiness possessed me; life, I realized, was being lived in Dacca first. I imagined Mr. Pirzada's daughters ris-

> " . . . life, I realized, was being lived in Dacca first."

ing from sleep, tying ribbons in their hair, anticipating breakfast, preparing for school. Our meals, our actions, were only a shadow of what had already happened there, a lagging ghost of where Mr. Pirzada really belonged.

At six-thirty, which was when the national news began, my father raised the volume and adjusted the antennas. Usually I occupied myself with a book, but that night my father insisted that I pay attention. On the screen I saw tanks rolling through dusty streets, and fallen buildings, and forests of unfamiliar trees into which East Pakistani refugees had fled, seeking safety over the Indian border. I saw boats with fan-shaped sails floating on wide coffee-colored rivers, a barricaded university, newspaper offices burnt to the ground. I turned to look at Mr. Pirzada; the images flashed in miniature across his eyes. As he watched he had an immovable expression on his face, composed but alert, as if someone were giving him directions to an unknown destination.

During the commercial my mother went to the kitchen to get more rice, and my father and Mr. Pirzada deplored the policies of a general named Yahyah Khan.[28] They discussed intrigues I did not know, a catastrophe I could not comprehend. "See, children your age, what they do to survive," my father said as he served me another piece of fish. But I could no longer eat. I could only steal glances at Mr. Pirzada, sitting beside me in his olive green jacket, calmly creating a well in his rice to make room for a second helping of lentils. He was not my notion of a man burdened by such grave concerns.

---

28. *Yahyah Khan,* or Agha Mohammad Yahya Khan, was a West Pakistan general who led troops into East Pakistan.

Reading Strategy Comparing and Contrasting Characters *How does winding the pocket watch make Mr. Pirzada different from Lilia's family?* **R1**

Reading Strategy Comparing and Contrasting Characters *Why do you think Lilia cannot comprehend the scope and complexities of the war?* **R2**

Additional Support

Skills Practice

RESEARCH: Recipes Lahiri uses Indian food as a symbol for comfort in the story. Several Indian dishes are mentioned in the story, but most students will be unfamiliar with the difference between Indian and American cuisines. Have students pair up and find recipes for Indian dishes. Each pair should share their recipe with the class. **Ask:** What differences do you see between Indian food and American food? *(Students may comment on the heavy use of herbs and spices, the emphasis on rice, or the lack of certain types of meat.)* **OL**

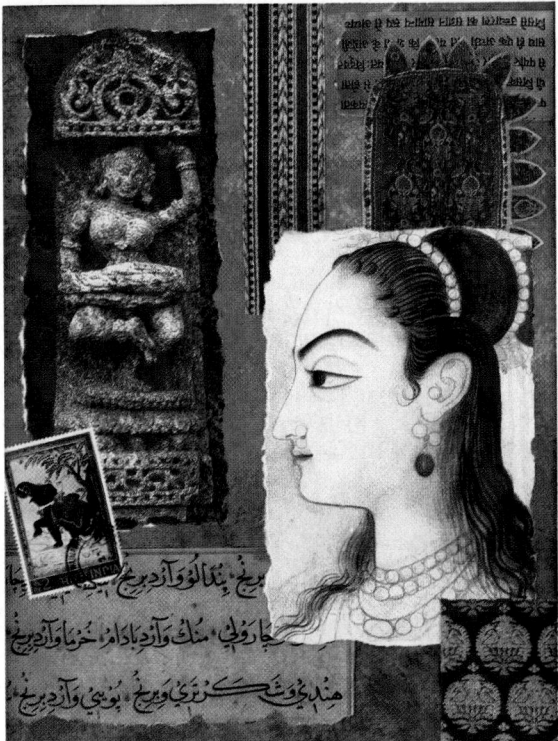

Romantic India I, 2000.
Gerry Charm. Collage. ★

I wondered if the reason he was always so smartly dressed was in preparation to endure with dignity whatever news assailed[29] him, perhaps even to attend a funeral at a moment's notice. I wondered, too, what would happen if suddenly his seven daughters were to appear on television, smiling and waving and blowing kisses to Mr. Pirzada from a balcony. I imagined how relieved he would be. But this never happened.

That night when I placed the plastic egg filled with cinnamon hearts in the box beside my bed, I did not feel the ceremonious satisfaction I normally did. I tried not to think about Mr. Pirzada, in his lime-scented overcoat, connected to the unruly, sweltering world we had viewed a few hours ago in our bright, carpeted living room. And yet for several moments that was all I could think about. My stomach tightened as I worried whether his wife and seven daughters were now members of the drifting, clamoring crowd that had flashed at intervals on the screen. In an effort to banish[30] the image I looked around my room, at the yellow canopied[31] bed with matching flounced[32] curtains, at framed class pictures mounted on white and violet papered walls, at the penciled inscriptions by the closet door where my father recorded my height on each of my birthdays. But the more I tried to distract myself, the more I began to convince myself that Mr. Pirzada's family was in all likelihood dead. Eventually I took a square of white chocolate out of the box, and unwrapped it, and then I did something I had never done before. I put the chocolate in my mouth, letting it soften until the last possible moment, and then as I chewed it slowly, I prayed that Mr. Pirzada's family was safe and sound. I had never prayed for anything before, had never been taught or told to, but I decided, given the circumstances, that it was something I should do. That night, when I went to the bathroom I only pretended to brush my teeth, for I feared that I would somehow rinse the prayer out as well. I wet the brush and rearranged the tube of paste to prevent my parents from asking any questions, and fell asleep with sugar on my tongue.

No one at school talked about the war followed so faithfully in my living room.

---

29. *Assailed* means "attacked" or "assaulted."

30. *Banish* means "to drive away" or "force to leave."
31. A *canopy* is a cloth covering fastened above a bed.
32. *Flounced* means "gathered" or "pleated."

Big Idea Making Choices *Why do you think Lilia decides to pray for Mr. Pirzada's family?* **BI**

JHUMPA LAHIRI **139**

Teach

BI Big Idea
Making Choices
Answer: *Lilia's concern over Mr. Pirzada and his family has become so intense that she has trouble thinking of anything else. Praying for Mr. Pirzada's family seems like the only thing she can do to help them—or to relieve her own anxiety.* **OL**

★ Viewing the Art
Romantic India I is an example of a collage, which is a combination of various pictures or items to create a new piece of art. The central focus of this collage is a depiction of Indra, who was an important god in Hinduism. Indra was considered war-like and used thunderbolts as weapons.
Ask: Why would this collage be called *Romantic India*? *(The term* romantic *doesn't necessarily refer to examples of love; it can also refer to feelings of nostalgia. The elements of this collage are from a past period in Indian culture, so perhaps* romantic *reflects a yearning for returning to the past.)* **AS**

Differentiated Instruction

Characterization Students may not understand why Lilia has a sudden urge to pray for Mr. Pirzada's family after she looks around her room. **Ask:** What feelings do you think Lilia has when she is looking around her room and thinking about Mr. Pirzada's family? *(Lilia probably feels guilty because she is safe and secure in her own nice room while his daughters' lives may be in danger.)* **BL**

Objectives
• To compare and contrast characters (SE)
• To gain insight into a culture by researching recipes (TWE)

139

Teach

Theme Answer: *Lahiri may have chosen to include this scene to show the limitations of Lilia's education; her history class focuses only on U.S. history, not global events.* **OL**

R Reading Strategy

Comparing and Contrasting Characters

Answer: *Mr. Pirzada and Lilia's parents are drawn together because of their similar interests, and they enjoy the familiarity of each other as they live in a foreign country.* **OL**

★ Cultural History

Scrabble The board game Scrabble was created by an architect named Alfred Butts in 1931. His inspiration came from crossword puzzles, and the game was called Criss-Cross Words prior to being trademarked Scrabble in 1948. By 1952, Scrabble's popularity in the United States had grown, and it was introduced in England in 1954. Soon it became known throughout the Western world. **AS**

We continued to study the American Revolution, and learned about the injustices of taxation without representation, and memorized passages from the Declaration of Independence. During recess the boys would divide in two groups, chasing each other wildly around the swings and seesaws, Redcoats against the colonies. In the classroom our teacher, Mrs. Kenyon, pointed frequently to a map that emerged like a movie screen from the top of the chalkboard, charting the route of the *Mayflower,* or showing us the location of the Liberty Bell. Each week two members of the class gave a report on a particular aspect of the Revolution, and so one day I was sent to the school library with my friend Dora to learn about the surrender at Yorktown. Mrs. Kenyon handed us a slip of paper with the names of three books to look up in the card catalogue. We found them right away, and sat down at a low round table to read and take notes. But I could not concentrate. I returned to the blond-wood shelves, to a section I had noticed labeled "Asia." I saw books about China, India, Indonesia, Korea. Eventually I found a book titled *Pakistan: A Land and Its People.* I sat on a footstool and opened the book. The laminated jacket crackled in my grip. I began turning the pages, filled with photos of rivers and rice fields and men in military uniforms. There was a chapter about Dacca, and I began to read about its rainfall, and its jute[33] production. I was studying a population chart when Dora appeared in the aisle.

"What are you doing back here? Mrs. Kenyon's in the library. She came to check up on us."

I slammed the book shut, too loudly. Mrs. Kenyon emerged, the aroma of her perfume filling up the tiny aisle, and lifted the book by the tip of its spine as if it were a hair clinging to my sweater. She glanced at the cover, then at me.

"Is this book a part of your report, Lilia?"

---

33. *Jute* is a fiber from the jute plant that is used to make rope, burlap, or sacks.

---

140 UNIT 1   THE SHORT STORY

"No, Mrs. Kenyon."

"Then I see no reason to consult[34] it," she said, replacing it in the slim gap on the shelf. "Do you?"

As weeks passed it grew more and more rare to see any footage[35] from Dacca on the news. The report came after the first set of commercials, sometimes the second. The press had been censored, removed, restricted, rerouted. Some days, many days, only a death toll was announced, prefaced by a reiteration[36] of the general situation. More poets were executed, more villages set ablaze. In spite of it all, night after night, my parents and Mr. Pirzada enjoyed long, leisurely meals. After the television was shut off, and the dishes washed and dried, they joked, and told stories, and dipped biscuits in their tea. When they tired of discussing political matters they discussed, instead, the progress of Mr. Pirzada's book about the deciduous[37] trees of New England, and my father's nomination for tenure, and the peculiar eating habits of my mother's American coworkers at the bank. Eventually I was sent upstairs to do my homework, but through the carpet I heard them as they drank more tea, and listened to cassettes of Kishore Kumar,[38] and played Scrabble on the coffee table, laughing and arguing long into the night about the spellings of English words. I wanted to join them, wanted, above all, to console Mr. Pirzada somehow. But apart from eating a piece of candy for the sake of his family and praying for their safety, there was nothing I could do. They played Scrabble until the eleven o'clock news, and ★

---

34. Here, *consult* means "to get information from."
35. *Footage* refers to a segment of newsreel film.
36. *Reiteration* is repeating or saying over again.
37. *Deciduous* trees lose their leaves each year.
38. *Kishore Kumar* was a famous actor and singer in Indian films.

Literary Element Theme *Why do you think Lahiri chose to include this scene?* **L1**

Reading Strategy Comparing and Contrasting Characters *What draws Mr. Pirzada and Lilia's parents together?* **R**

Additional Support

Skills Practice

READING: Drawing Conclusions
When Lilia looks through the library book about Dacca, her teacher reprimands her because the book has nothing to do with her assignment. Although this scene is short, it allows the reader to draw some conclusions about American education in the early 1970s. **Ask:** What can we conclude about Lilia's education as described so far? *(The focus of social studies classes was the United States. The social studies curriculum was not as multicultural as it is today.)* **OL**

then, sometime around midnight, Mr. Pirzada walked back to his dormitory. For this reason I never saw him leave, but each night as I drifted off to sleep I would hear them, anticipating the birth of a nation on the other side of the world.

One day in October Mr. Pirzada asked upon arrival, "What are these large orange vegetables on people's doorsteps? A type of squash?"

"Pumpkins," my mother replied. "Lilia, remind me to pick one up at the supermarket."

"And the purpose? It indicates what?"

"You make a jack-o'-lantern," I said, grinning ferociously. "Like this. To scare people away."

"I see," Mr. Pirzada said, grinning back. "Very useful."

The next day my mother bought a ten-pound pumpkin, fat and round, and placed it on the dining table. Before supper, while my father and Mr. Pirzada were watching the local news, she told me to decorate it with markers, but I wanted to carve it properly like others I had noticed in the neighborhood.

"Yes, let's carve it," Mr. Pirzada agreed, and rose from the sofa. "Hang the news tonight." Asking no questions, he walked into the kitchen, opened a drawer, and returned, bearing a long serrated[39] knife. He glanced at me for approval. "Shall I?"

I nodded. For the first time we all gathered around the dining table, my mother, my father, Mr. Pirzada, and I. While the television aired unattended we covered the tabletop with newspapers. Mr. Pirzada draped his jacket over the chair behind him, removed a pair of opal[40] cuff links, and rolled up the starched sleeves of his shirt.

"First go around the top, like this," I instructed, demonstrating with my index finger.

He made an initial incision[41] and drew the knife around. When he had come full circle he lifted the cap by the stem; it loosened effortlessly, and Mr. Pirzada leaned over the pumpkin for a moment to inspect and inhale its contents. My mother gave him a long metal spoon with which he gutted the interior until the last bits of string and seeds were gone. My father, meanwhile, separated the seeds from the pulp and set them out to dry on a cookie sheet, so that we could roast them later on. I drew two triangles against the ridged surface for the eyes, which Mr. Pirzada dutifully carved, and crescents for eyebrows, and another triangle for the nose. The mouth was all that remained, and the teeth posed a challenge. I hesitated.

"Smile or frown?" I asked.

"You choose," Mr. Pirzada said.

As a compromise I drew a kind of grimace,[42] straight across, neither mournful nor friendly. Mr. Pirzada began carving, without the least bit of **intimidation,** as if he had been carving jack-o'-lanterns his whole life. He had nearly finished when the national

> " . . .each night as I drifted off to sleep I would hear them, anticipating the birth of a nation on the other side of the world. "

---

40. *Opal* is a type of mineral used as a gemstone.
41. *Initial incision* means the "first cut."
42. A *grimace* (grim′ is) is a twisting of the face into an ugly or painful smile.

Vocabulary

intimidation (in tim′ ə dā shən) n. act of making one feel afraid or discouraged

---

39. *Serrated* means having a sawlike edge.

Literary Element Theme *Why does Mr. Pirzada decide not to watch the news?* **L₂**

JHUMPA LAHIRI **141**

Teach

L₂ Literary Element

Theme Answer: *He chooses to participate in a uniquely American tradition: carving pumpkins for Halloween. He may also feel relieved to have some distraction from the news.* **Ask:** Why does Mr. Pirzada not know about jack-o'-lanterns? *(Halloween is not celebrated in his country, so the traditions associated with the holiday would be unfamiliar to him.)* **OL**

Building Reading Fluency

Readers Theater Reading the same passage several times can help students improve their understanding of the material and their reading skills. Divide students into small groups. Each group will practice reading a scene from the story in order to increase their fluency. The students should each pick a speaking part, read their sections, then switch parts so that everyone in the group gets a chance to be each character. The group should then prepare to present their reading of the scene in front of the class. **BL**

Objectives
• To understand theme (SE)
• To compare and contrast characters (SE)
• To draw conclusions (TWE)

Teach

L Literary Element

Theme Answer: *He may feel sorry for making a gash in the pumpkin. More importantly, after hearing the news that India may go to war with Pakistan, he may also feel guilty for not paying attention to the news, as though he were betraying his family.* **OL**

R1 Reading Strategy

Comparing and Contrasting Characters

Answer: *Lilia's parents allow them to leave the house at night because they think it is safe; in East Pakistan, it is likely that many children are not safe, no matter where they are.* **OL**

★ Viewing the Art

Shanti Panchal's work was inspired by his homesickness for his native India. Panchal left India in 1978 and moved to Britain. Like the rest of his art, the colors he uses represent the colors of the Gujarat, an area of India north of Bombay. **Ask:** How does this piece seem inspired by Panchal's homesickness?

(The piece depicts someone returning home, probably to India, after being gone a long time.) **AS**

news began. The reporter mentioned Dacca, and we all turned to listen: An Indian official announced that unless the world helped to relieve the burden of East Pakistani refugees, India would have to go to war against Pakistan. The reporter's face dripped with sweat as he relayed the information. He did not wear a tie or a jacket, dressed instead as if he himself were about to take part in the battle. He shielded his scorched face as he hollered things to the cameraman. The knife slipped from Mr. Pirzada's hand and made a gash dipping toward the base of the pumpkin.

"Please forgive me." He raised a hand to one side of his face, as if someone had slapped him there. "I am—it is terrible. I will buy another. We will try again."

"Not at all, not at all," my father said. He took the knife from Mr. Pirzada, and carved around the gash, evening it out, dispensing altogether with[43] the teeth I had drawn. What resulted was a disproportionately large hole the size of a lemon, so that our jack-o'-lantern wore an expression of placid[44] astonishment, the eyebrows no longer fierce, floating in frozen surprise above a vacant, geometric gaze.

For Halloween I was a witch. Dora, my trick-or-treating partner, was a witch too. We wore black capes fashioned from dyed pillowcases and conical hats with wide cardboard brims. We shaded our faces green with a broken eye shadow that belonged to Dora's mother, and my mother gave us two burlap sacks that had once contained basmati rice,[45]

Home Coming—After a Long Absence, 1998. Shanti Panchal. Watercolor on paper, 98 x 79 cm. Private collection.

for collecting candy. That year our parents decided that we were old enough to roam the neighborhood unattended. Our plan was to walk from my house to Dora's, from where I was to call to say I had arrived safely, and then Dora's mother would drive me home. My father equipped us with flashlights, and I had to wear my watch and synchronize it with his. We were to return no later than nine o'clock.

When Mr. Pirzada arrived that evening he presented me with a box of chocolate-covered mints.

"In here," I told him, and opened up the burlap sack. "Trick or treat!"

---

43. *Dispensing . . . with* means "getting rid of."
44. *Placid* means "calm, undisturbed."
45. *Basmati rice* is a kind of long-grain rice grown in India.

Literary Element Theme *Is there more than one reason for which Mr. Pirzada feels he needs to be forgiven? Explain.* **L**

Reading Strategy Comparing and Contrasting Characters *How does this detail emphasize the differences between children's lives in Boston and in East Pakistan?* **R1**

Additional Support

Skills Practice

LITERARY ELEMENT: Point of View Lahiri chooses to write this story from the first-person point of view with Lilia as the narrator. **Say:** The first-person point of view lets you get inside Lilia's head and allows you to view events from her perspective only. The author could have chosen a third-person point of view for her story instead. **Explain the difference between first- and third-person points of view. Ask students to pick one of the two Halloween-related scenes in the story and rewrite it using a third-person point of view. OL**

"I understand that you don't really need my contribution this evening," he said, depositing the box. He gazed at my green face, and the hat secured by a string under my chin. Gingerly he lifted the hem of the cape, under which I was wearing a sweater and a zipped fleece jacket. "Will you be warm enough?"

I nodded, causing the hat to tip to one side. He set it right. "Perhaps it is best to stand still."

The bottom of our staircase was lined with baskets of miniature candy, and when Mr. Pirzada removed his shoes he did not place them there as he normally did, but inside the closet instead. He began to unbutton his coat, and I waited to take it from him, but Dora called me from the bathroom to say that she needed my help drawing a mole on her chin. When we were finally ready my mother took a picture of us in front of the fireplace, and then I opened the front door to leave. Mr. Pirzada and my father, who had not gone into the living room yet, hovered in the foyer. Outside it was already dark. The air smelled of wet leaves, and our carved jack-o'-lantern flickered impressively against the shrubbery by the door. In the distance came the sounds of scampering feet, and the howls of the older boys who wore no costume at all other than a rubber mask, and the rustling apparel of the youngest children, some so young that they were carried from door to door in the arms of their parents.

"Don't go into any of the houses you don't know," my father warned.

Mr. Pirzada knit his brows together. "Is there any danger?'

"No, no," my mother assured him. "All the children will be out. It's a tradition."

Big Idea **Making Choices** *How does Mr. Pirzada's comment reflect his own actions?* BI₁

Reading Strategy *Comparing and Contrasting Characters* *Why is Mr. Pirzada so worried about the girls, while Lilia's mother does not seem concerned about their safety?* R₂

"Perhaps I should accompany them?" Mr. Pirzada suggested. He looked suddenly tired and small, standing there in his splayed, stockinged feet, and his eyes contained a panic I had never seen before. In spite of the cold I began to sweat inside my pillowcase.

"Really, Mr. Pirzada," my mother said, "Lilia will be perfectly safe with her friend."

"But if it rains? If they lose their way?"

"Don't worry," I said. It was the first time I had uttered those words to Mr. Pirzada, two simple words I had tried but failed to tell him for weeks, had said only in my prayers. It shamed me now that I had said them for my own sake.

He placed one of his stocky fingers on my cheek, then pressed it to the back of his own hand, leaving a faint green smear. "If the lady insists," he conceded, and offered a small bow.

We left, stumbling slightly in our black pointy thrift-store shoes, and when we turned at the end of the driveway to wave good-bye, Mr. Pirzada was standing in the frame of the doorway, a short figure between my parents, waving back.

"Why did that man want to come with us?" Dora asked.

"His daughters are missing." As soon as I said it, I wished I had not. I felt that my saying it made it true, that Mr. Pirzada's daughters really were missing, and that he would never see them again.

"You mean they were kidnapped?" Dora continued. "From a park or something?"

"I didn't mean they were missing. I meant, he misses them. They live in a different country, and he hasn't seen them in a while, that's all."

We went from house to house, walking along pathways and pressing doorbells. Some people had switched off all their lights for effect, or strung rubber bats in their windows. At the McIntyres' a coffin was placed in front of the door, and Mr. McIntyre rose

Big Idea **Making Choices** *Why does Lilia choose to tell Mr. Pirzada not to worry at this point, instead of earlier in the story?* BI₂

Teach

BI₁ Big Idea
Making Choices
Answer: *Mr. Pirzada has chosen to stay in the United States rather than return to his family in East Pakistan. He may believe that this is the best option, just as it may be best for Lilia to stand still in her costume.* OL

R₂ Reading Strategy
Comparing and Contrasting Characters
Answer: *Unlike Lilia's mother, he is unfamiliar with the trick-or-treating custom. He is also probably thinking about the safety of his own daughters, who are in a dangerous place.* OL

BI₂ Big Idea
Making Choices
Answer: *Lilia may feel hesitant to tell Mr. Pirzada not to worry about his family because she does not know what will happen to them; it is much easier for Lilia to tell him not to worry about her because she knows that she will be safe.* OL

English Language Coach

Using a Thesaurus Students may encounter a number of unfamiliar words in this story. **Say:** Sometimes you'll run across a word you don't know. When that happens, you should look the word up in a dictionary. Sometimes the definition from a dictionary will be difficult to understand, so you need another way of finding word meanings. Explain to students what a thesaurus is. **Say:** Use a thesaurus to look up the word you don't know, and then look at the list of synonyms for the word. Have students select ten unfamiliar words from the selection and look them up using a thesaurus. EL

Objectives
- To understand theme (SE)
- To compare and contrast characters (SE)
- To analyze point of view (TWE)

Teach

Comparing and Contrasting Characters

Answer: *Unlike Lilia's parents and Mr. Pirzada, they have no ties to India or Pakistan and therefore have no personal or cultural reason to watch reports of the events occurring there.* **OL**

★ Viewing the Art

In the sixth century, a South Asian book called *Visnudharmottara* classified the paintings found in the region. Based on these classifications, this particular piece would be considered natural because it depicts three girls in a nature setting. **Ask:** *What feeling do you get from this painting? (The painting seems joyful. The girls appear to be enjoying themselves in a beautiful, natural setting.)* **AS**

Additional Support

---

from it in silence, his face covered with chalk, and deposited a fistful of candy corns into our sacks. Several people told me that they had never seen an Indian witch before. Others performed the transaction without comment. As we paved our way with the parallel beams of our flashlights we saw eggs cracked in the middle of the road, and cars covered with shaving cream, and toilet paper garlanding[46] the branches of trees. By the time we reached Dora's house our hands were chapped from carrying our bulging burlap bags, and our feet were sore and swollen. Her mother gave us bandages for our blisters and served us warm cider and caramel popcorn. She reminded me to call my parents to tell them I had arrived safely, and when I did I could hear the television in the background. My mother did not seem particularly relieved to hear from me. When I replaced the phone on the receiver it occurred to me that the television wasn't on at Dora's house at all. Her father was lying on the couch, reading a magazine, with a glass of wine on the coffee table, and there was saxophone music playing on the stereo.

After Dora and I had sorted through our plunder, and counted and sampled and traded until we were satisfied, her mother drove me back to my house. I thanked her for the ride, and she waited in the driveway until I made it to the door. In the glare of her headlights I saw that our pumpkin had been shattered, its thick shell strewn in chunks across the grass. I felt the sting of tears in my eyes, and a sudden pain in my throat, as if it had been stuffed with the sharp tiny pebbles that crunched with each step under my aching feet. I opened the door, expecting the three of them to be standing in the foyer, waiting to receive me, and to grieve for our ruined pumpkin, but there was no one. In the living room Mr. Pirzada, my father, and mother were sitting side by side on the sofa.

The television was turned off, and Mr. Pirzada had his head in his hands.

What they heard that evening, and for many evenings after that, was that India and Pakistan were drawing closer and closer to war. Troops from both sides lined the border, and Dacca was insisting on nothing short of independence. The war was to be waged on East Pakistani soil. The United States was siding with West Pakistan, the Soviet Union with India and what was soon to be Bangladesh. War was declared officially on December 4, and twelve days later, the Pakistani army, weakened by having to fight three thousand miles from their source of supplies, surrendered in Dacca. All of these facts I know only now, for they are available to me in any history book, in any library. But then it remained, for the most part, a remote mystery with haphazard[47] clues. What I remember during those twelve days of the war was that my father no longer asked me to watch the news with them, and that Mr. Pirzada stopped bringing me candy, and that my mother refused to serve anything other than boiled eggs with rice for dinner. I remember some nights helping my mother spread a sheet and blankets on the couch so that Mr. Pirzada could sleep there, and high-pitched voices hollering in the middle of the night when my parents called our relatives in Calcutta to learn more details about the situation. Most of all I remember the three of them operating during that time as if they were a single person, sharing a single meal, a single body, a single silence, and a single fear.

In January, Mr. Pirzada flew back to his three-story home in Dacca, to discover what was left of it. We did not see much of him in those final weeks of the year; he was busy finishing his manuscript, and we went to Philadelphia to spend Christmas with friends of my parents. Just as I have no memory of

---

46. A *garland* is a wreath, usually of flowers or leaves. Here, the garland is toilet paper strewn through the branches.

Reading Strategy Comparing and Contrasting Characters *Why are Dora's parents not watching the news?* **R1**

47. *Haphazard* means "random, occurring by chance."

Reading Strategy Comparing and Contrasting Characters *What has finally given all the adults the same single-minded sense of fear?* **R2**

Skills Practice

LITERARY ELEMENT: Climax

Say: A story's climax occurs when it reaches the highest point of the action. It's the moment everything else is building toward. In small groups, have students list the different events that make up the plot of this story. Have them circle the event that represents the story's climax. **OL**

his first visit, I have no memory of his last. My father drove him to the airport one afternoon while I was at school. For a long time we did not hear from him. Our evenings went on as usual, with dinners in front of the news. The only difference was that Mr. Pirzada and his extra watch were not there to accompany us. According to reports Dacca was repairing itself slowly, with a newly formed parliamentary government. The new leader, Sheikh Mujib Rahman, recently released from prison, asked countries for building materials to replace more than one million houses that had been destroyed in the war. Countless refugees returned from India, greeted, we learned, by unemployment and the threat of famine.[48] Every now and then I studied the map above my father's desk and pictured Mr. Pirzada on that small patch of yellow, perspiring heavily, I imagined, in one of his suits, searching for his family. Of course, the map was outdated by then.

Finally, several months later, we received a card from Mr. Pirzada commemorating[49] the Muslim New Year, along with a short letter. He was reunited, he wrote, with his wife and children. All were well, having survived the events of the past year at an estate belonging to his wife's grandparents in the mountains of Shillong.[50] His seven daughters were a bit taller, he wrote, but otherwise they were the same, and he still could not keep their names in order. At the end of the letter he thanked us for our hospitality, adding that although he now understood the meaning of the words "thank you" they still were not adequate to express his gratitude. To celebrate the good news my mother prepared a special dinner that evening, and when we sat down to eat at the coffee table we toasted our water glasses, but I did not

Girls in a Wood.
Indian Art.

feel like celebrating. Though I had not seen him for months, it was only then that I felt Mr. Pirzada's absence. It was only then, raising my water glass in his name, that I knew what it meant to miss someone who was so many miles and hours away, just as he had missed his wife and daughters for so many months. He had no reason to return to us, and my parents predicted, correctly, that we would never see him again. Since January, each night before bed, I had continued to eat, for the sake of Mr. Pirzada's family, a piece of candy I had saved from Halloween. That night there was no need to. Eventually, I threw them away. ✷

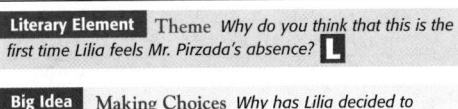

Literary Element Theme *Why do you think that this is the first time Lilia feels Mr. Pirzada's absence?* **L**

Big Idea Making Choices *Why has Lilia decided to throw the candy away?* **BI**

---

48. *Famine* is an extreme lack of food, leading to starvation.
49. *Commemorating* means "honoring the memory of."
50. *Shillong* is a part of India north of East Pakistan.

JHUMPA LAHIRI **145**

Assess

1. Answers will vary.

2. (a) He enjoys the familiar food and the conversation. (b) Lilia reminds him of his daughters.

3. (a) Fears for the girls' safety (b) Thinks about his own daughters' safety in Dacca

4. (a) They survived and live with relatives. (b) Mr. Pirzada has completed his studies in the United States, and a return trip would be expensive.

5. (a) Other countries can be less politically stable, and warfare and violence more of a threat. (b) Since Mr. Pirzada is the main character and concerned about the war, the situation in East Pakistan must be described accurately.

6. (a) Food helps comfort Mr. Pirzada and reminds him of his culture; candy triggers Lilia's empathy for his family. (b) Lahiri effectively uses food to represent the warmth and connection between the characters.

7. Mr. Pirzada made the difficult choice of staying in the United States when his family was in danger.

RESPONDING AND THINKING CLEARLY

Respond

1. (a) What was your reaction when you realized that Mr. Pirzada decided to stay in the United States instead of returning to Dacca and to his family? (b) Do you think that he regretted his decision?

Recall and Interpret

2. (a) Why does Mr. Pirzada come to dinner at Lilia's house? (b) Why do you think he gives Lilia candy?

3. (a) How does Mr. Pirzada react when Dora and Lilia go trick-or-treating on Halloween? (b) Why do you think he reacts in this way?

4. (a) What does Mr. Pirzada discover about his family when he gets back to Dacca? (b) Why do you think Lilia's parents predict that they will never see Mr. Pirzada again?

Analyze and Evaluate

5. (a) Explain what Lilia has learned about life in other countries and how it differs from life in the United States. (b) Lahiri vividly describes the war and political situation in East Pakistan. How accurate do you think a writer should be in a fictional story? Explain.

6. (a) Analyze Lahiri's use of food in the story. In your analysis, consider the food Lilia's mother serves and the candy Mr. Pirzada brings Lilia. (b) In your opinion, how effective is Lahiri's use of food in the story?

Connect

7. **Big Idea** **Making Choices** Who do you think has made the most difficult choice in the story? Explain.

LITERARY ANALYSIS

Literary Element Theme

In some stories a **theme** is stated directly, but more often a theme is implied, as in "When Mr. Pirzada Came to Dine." To discover an implied theme, you might look at the experiences of the main characters and ask what message about life the story communicates.

1. Cultural belonging is an important element in the story. How attached is Lilia to U.S. culture? How attached is Mr. Pirzada to U.S. culture? Explain.

2. What message, or theme, does Lahiri portray through the experiences of Lilia and Mr. Pirzada?

Try making web diagrams to record their experiences. Then assess the experiences as a whole to determine Lahiri's message.

Review: Conflict

As you learned on page 36, **conflict** is a struggle between opposing forces in a story.

Partner Activity Meet with another classmate and discuss the various kinds of conflicts in the story. For example, there is a major external conflict between West Pakistan and East Pakistan. Working with your partner, create a chart like the one below in which you list the kinds of conflicts (external and internal) in the story in one column and their resolutions in the other column.

Kinds of Conflict	Resolution
External: War in East Pakistan	India enters war and defeats West Pakistan; Bangladesh becomes an independent nation.

Literary Element

1. Lilia was born and raised in the United States and understands much more about U.S. culture than Indian culture. Mr. Pirzada is not very connected to U.S. culture.

2. The story examines how immigrants search for a sense of belonging in a new culture.

Review: Conflict

Partners should create charts that show both external and internal conflicts in the story.

READING AND VOCABULARY

Reading Strategy Comparing and Contrasting Characters

Now that you have recorded various similarities and differences between **characters** in the story, you should have enough information to answer the following questions.

1. Which characters are most similar? Explain.

2. Which characters are most different? Explain.

3. What do you think Lahiri's purpose is in showing contrasting characters?

Vocabulary Practice

Practice with Context Clues For each boldfaced vocabulary word, use context clues to select the best definition.

1. **ascertaining** the value of the used car
   a. writing   b. finding out   c. refuting

2. an **austere** meal of carrots and bread
   a. simple   b. delicious   c. extravagant

3. navigated the obstacle course **impeccably**
   a. hesitantly   b. arrogantly   c. flawlessly

4. a nearly **imperceptible** shift from blue-green to green
   a. undetectable   b. blinding   c. masterful

5. the bully often relied on **intimidation**
   a. bribery   b. scare tactics   c. compliments

Academic Vocabulary

Here are two words from the vocabulary list on page R82. These words will help you think, write, and talk about the selection.

restore (ri stôr′) v. to bring back to an original condition

intense (in tens′) adj. extreme or excessive

Practice and Apply

1. What did India hope to **restore** by entering the war against West Pakistan?

2. At what point in the story do Lilia's parents and Mr. Pirzada show the most **intense** emotion?

WRITING AND EXTENDING

Writing About Literature

Evaluate Author's Craft When you **evaluate**, you determine how well a writer has achieved his or her purpose. Writers often weave aspects of culture or history into the plot of a story to create effects, such as realism or suspense, or to reveal theme and conflict. Write a brief essay evaluating Lahiri's use of culture and history in her plot to create particular effects in the story.

Follow the writing path shown here to help you organize your essay and stay on track.

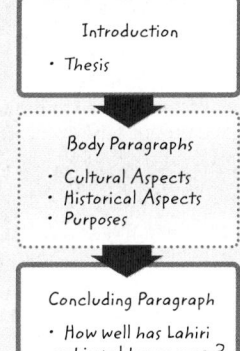

Introduction
• Thesis

Body Paragraphs
• Cultural Aspects
• Historical Aspects
• Purposes

Concluding Paragraph
• How well has Lahiri achieved her purpose?

After you complete your draft, meet with a peer reviewer to evaluate each other's work and to suggest revisions. Then proofread and edit your draft for errors in spelling, grammar, and punctuation.

Reading Further

You may enjoy reading other stories in Lahiri's *Interpreter of Maladies*. For example, "Mrs. Sen's" portrays a lonely Indian woman trying to survive in the United States. "A Blessed House" deals with two newlyweds trying to understand each other's point of view. "The Third and Final Continent" is about a young Indian man in Boston who is preparing to send for his wife, who is still in India. Lastly, "The Treatment of Bibi Haldar" is about an ailing woman in India who searches for a husband in her town.

Literature Online **Web Activities** For eFlashcards, Selection Quick Checks, and other Web activities, go to www.glencoe.com.

AFTER YOU READ

Assess

Reading Strategy

1. Lilia's family and Mr. Pirzada are the most similar, given their cultural backgrounds and habits.

2. Mrs. Kenyon and Dora's father are most different from Lilia's family and Mr. Pirzada. They have a different cultural background and spend their time differently than Lilia's family or Mr. Pirzada.

3. It emphasizes different concerns or lack of concern in characters. For example, Mrs. Kenyon and Dora's father are unconcerned about the war in East Pakistan because it does not directly affect them.

Vocabulary

1. b 2. a 3. c 4. a 5. b

Academic Vocabulary

1. India hoped to restore peace to the region.

2. They show the most intense emotion when India invades East Pakistan.

Literature Online

Web Activities Have students access the Web site for interactive activities that will help them assess their understanding of the selection.

Writing About Literature

Students' essays should:

• note that Lahiri uses the East Pakistan war as background to help create suspense about the fate of Mr. Pirzada's family and to develop reasons for the growing rapport between him and Lilia's family.

• show that the physical conflict between nations creates an inner conflict in Mr. Pirzada.

• discuss how cultural connections, such as food, are shown to comfort Mr. Pirzada and link him to Lilia and her family.

Focus

BELLRINGER

Bellringer Options
Selection Focus Transparency 9
Daily Language
 Transparency 15
Or **ask:** How would you describe your city or town to someone who has never been there? Have students identify the most recognizable features of their cities or towns. Encourage them to think about unique features, special buildings, climate, and vegetation.

Author Search To expand students' appreciation of Paule Marshall, have them access the Web site for additional information and resources.

To Da-duh, in Memoriam

MEET PAULE MARSHALL

A basement kitchen may sound like an unlikely place for a writer to find her inspiration, but that is where the award-winning African American writer Paule Marshall found hers.

Homegrown Inspiration "I grew up among poets," Marshall wrote in her autobiographical essay, "From the Poets in the Kitchen." Each afternoon, these "poets," who, in reality, were ordinary housewives, gathered around the kitchen table of the brownstone home in the close-knit, West-Indian community of 1930s Brooklyn, New York, where Marshall was born and raised. Marshall sat in the corner and listened as the women, including her mother, talked "endlessly, passionately, poetically, and with impressive range." During these late afternoon conversations, Marshall learned about the "old country," the small Caribbean island of Barbados, the homeland of Marshall's parents. Her ear became attuned to their idiomatic, rhythmic language that was a combination of English words, Barbadian syntax, and African sounds. These women were to become Marshall's primary writing teachers. "They taught me my first lessons in the narrative art. They trained my ear. They set a standard of excellence." While Marshall also credits both white and African American "literary giants" with helping her find her literary voice, she attributes the best of her work to these women. It is a "testimony to the rich legacy of language and culture they so freely passed on to me in the wordshop of the kitchen."

"My work asks that you become involved, that you think."

—Paule Marshall

Finding the Writer's Path Marshall was around eight or nine years old when she "graduated" from the corner of her kitchen to the neighborhood library. There, she became immersed in the written word. She was a voracious reader, consuming volumes by Austen, Thackeray, Fielding, and Dickens. One day she picked up a book by Paul Laurence Dunbar. Until then, she had been unaware that there was an African American voice in literature. Nor had she been conscious of her need to read about the history of her race. It was around this time, she says, that she "began harboring the dangerous thought of someday trying to write myself." Her discovery of Dunbar inspired her to explore that dream.

In 1953 Marshall graduated with honors from Brooklyn College with a degree in English Literature. In 1954 she published her first short story, "The Valley Between." Today, Marshall is widely read and recognized as, according to critic Carol Field, a "highly gifted writer." Her first book, *Brown Girl, Brownstones,* which was mostly ignored by readers at the time of its publication in 1959, now is considered a classic coming-of-age novel.

Paule Marshall was born in 1929.

Author Search For more about Paule Marshall, go to www.glencoe.com.

148 UNIT 1   THE SHORT STORY

Selection Skills

Literary Elements

- Characterization (SE pp. 149–160)
- Setting (SE p. 160)

To Da-duh, in Memoriam

Reading Skills

- Making Inferences About Characters (SE pp. 149–161)
- Visualizing (TWE p. 158)

Vocabulary Skills

- Synonyms (SE p. 161)
- Academic Vocabulary (SE p. 161)

Listening/Speaking/Viewing Skills

- Analyzing Art (SE p. 150)
- Connecting Images with Text (TWE p. 156)

Writing Skills/Grammar

- Analyze Character Development (SE p. 161)
- Participles (TWE p. 152)
- Literary Response (TWE p. 154)

Connecting to the Story

Have you ever felt the need to compete with someone? In Paule Marshall's short story, a young girl from New York City and her grandmother from Barbados become embroiled in a clash of cultures and a contest of one-upmanship. Before you read, think about the following questions:

- Is it ever acceptable to argue with a grandparent or older relative?
- How important is it for you to prove that your life is better than someone else's?

Building Background

"To Da-duh, in Memoriam" takes place in Barbados in the 1930s. Barbados is a tiny Caribbean island with mostly flat terrain. Its highest point, Mount Hillaby, is shorter than New York City's Empire State Building. The stalks of sugar cane referred to in the story can grow from seven to thirty feet high. Although the people of Barbados speak English, the folk culture is of African origin. The island became an independent state in 1966 after being under British colonial rule for more than three centuries.

Setting Purposes for Reading

Big Idea Making Choices

As you read, consider how the narrator's relationship with her grandmother affects her later in life.

Literary Element Characterization

Characterization is the method a writer uses to reveal a character's personality. A writer may use direct statements, or **direct characterization,** to describe a character. The writer may also choose to reveal the character's personality through **indirect characterization,** or through his or her words, thoughts, and actions or through what other characters think and say about the character. As you read the story, examine how Marshall uses characterization to reveal the personalities of the narrator and her grandmother.

- See Literary Terms Handbook, p. R3.

OBJECTIVES
In studying this selection, you will focus on the following:
- understanding characterization
- making inferences about characters
- analyzing the author's use of setting
- writing to analyze character development

Reading Strategy Making Inferences About Characters

To **infer** is to make a reasonable guess about some element of a story from what a writer implies. In a short story such as "To Da-duh, in Memoriam," we must observe details to make inferences about the characters.

Reading Tip: Taking Notes Use a chart to record the inferences you draw about the narrator and Da-duh.

Detail	Inference
"intense, unrelenting struggle between her back . . . and the rest of her"	Da-duh is proud, strong, and determined.

Vocabulary

formidable (fôr´ mi də bəl) *adj.* causing fear, dread, or awe by reason of size, strength, or power; p. 151 *Defeat was almost guaranteed against such a formidable opponent.*

decrepit (di krep´ it) *adj.* broken down by long use or old age; p. 153 *A strong wind would surely blow down the decrepit wooden shack.*

hurtle (hurt´ əl) *v.* to move rapidly, especially with much force or noise; p. 154 *They hurtle toward the finish line on their homemade scooters.*

arrogant (ar´ ə gənt) *adj.* full of self-importance; haughty; p. 154 *She spoke in an arrogant tone, as if the rest of us were inferior to her.*

malicious (mə lish´ əs) *adj.* having or showing a desire to harm another; p. 158 *His malicious actions resulted in injuries to several bystanders.*

Literature Online Interactive Literary Elements Handbook To review or learn more about the literary elements, go to www.glencoe.com.

PAULE MARSHALL **149**

Focus

Summary

A girl from New York visits her grandmother in Barbados. Each tries to top the other with examples of how grand their homes and neighborhoods are. Finally, the grandmother shows the child a high hill and the child counters with a description of the Empire State Building. With this, the grandmother appears to lose all interest in life. The child returns to New York and soon learns that her grandmother has died. But the memories of that summer live on, bringing richness and beauty to the girl's life and art.

V Vocabulary

Vocabulary File Say: Add these words and definitions to your vocabulary file. For each word, include a sentence that gives you an example of how to use the word. **OL** Students with English language needs should include the pronunciations of these words in their files. **EL**

Literary Elements Have students access the Web site to improve their understanding of characterization.

Selection Resources

Print Materials
📁 Unit 1 Resources (Fast File), pp. 58–60
📁 Leveled Vocabulary Development, p. 12
📁 Selection and Unit Assessments, pp. 25–26
📁 Selection Quick Checks, p. 13

Transparencies
- Bellringer Options Transparencies: Selection Focus Transparency 9
  Daily Language Practice Transparency 15
- Literary Elements Transparency 15

Technology
- TeacherWorks Plus™ CD-ROM
- StudentWorks Plus™ CD-ROM
- Presentation Plus!™ CD-ROM
- Literature Online, glencoe.com
- Online Student Edition, mhln.com
- ExamView® Assessment Suite CD-ROM
- Vocabulary PuzzleMaker CD-ROM
- Listening Library, disc 1 track 13

Teach

Making Choices Say: Keep the following questions in mind as you read. What are some ways that the author and her grandmother are different? In what ways are they similar? *(They were born and raised in different places; they have different histories and have experienced different types of events; their cultural frames of reference are very different. On the other hand, they share a family tie; they are both strong and determined; they have affection for each other.)* **OL**

⭐ **Viewing the Art**

Answer: *Like Da-duh's, the house in the painting is a weathered wonder structure. The grounds are remarkable for dense, lush, and sloping terrain.* **AS**

Readability Scores

Dale-Chall: 6.5
DRP: 59
Lexile: 1220

To Da-duh, in Memoriam

Paule Marshall

Good Old Days, 1993. Shakito. Private collection.
⭐ **Viewing the Art:** How is this house similar to Da-duh's? How do the grounds reflect the island in the story?

> "... Oh Nana! all of you
> is not involved in this
> evil business Death,
> Nor all of us in life."
>
> —*from* "At My
> Grandmother's Grave,"
> by Lebert Bethune

Additional Support

Skills Practice

READING: Making Inferences About Characters Ask: What clues can you find on the first two pages that tell you something about Da-duh's personality? *(She has eyes that are unnervingly alive with the appearance of someone who embodies many contradictory things. She has a personality that is intimidating, even to the author's strong mother.)* Have students use what they know about Da-duh to make predictions about the role she might play in the story. *(Possible answer: she will be a strong character and will be significant in the life of the young girl.)* **OL**

I did not see her at first I remember. For not only was it dark inside the crowded disembarkation[1] shed in spite of the daylight flooding in from outside, but standing there waiting for her with my mother and sister I was still somewhat blinded from the sheen of tropical sunlight on the water of the bay which we had just crossed in the landing boat, leaving behind us the ship that had brought us from New York lying in the offing.[2] Besides, being only nine years of age at the time and knowing nothing of islands I was busy attending to the alien sights and sounds of Barbados, the unfamiliar smells.

I did not see her, but I was alerted to her approach by my mother's hand which suddenly tightened around mine, and looking up I traced her gaze through the gloom in the shed until I finally made out the small, purposeful, painfully erect figure of the old woman headed our way.

Her face was drowned in the shadow of an ugly rolled-brim brown felt hat, but the details of her slight body and of the struggle taking place within it were clear enough—an intense, unrelenting[3] struggle between her back which was beginning to bend ever so slightly under the weight of her eighty-odd years and the rest of her which sought to deny those years and hold that back straight, keep it in line. Moving swiftly toward us (so swiftly it seemed she did not intend stopping when she reached us but would sweep past us out the doorway which opened onto the sea and like Christ walk upon the water!), she was caught between the sunlight at her end of the building and the darkness inside—and

for a moment she appeared to contain them both: the light in the long severe old-fashioned white dress she wore which brought the sense of a past that was still alive into our bustling present and in the snatch of white at her eye; the darkness in her black high-top shoes and in her face which was visible now that she was closer.

It was as stark and fleshless as a death mask, that face. The maggots might have already done their work, leaving only the framework of bone beneath the ruined skin and deep wells at the temple and jaw. But her eyes were alive, unnervingly so for one so old, with a sharp light that flicked out of the dim clouded depths like a lizard's tongue to snap up all in her view. ★ Those eyes betrayed a child's curiosity about the world, and I wondered vaguely seeing them, and seeing the way the bodice of her ancient dress had collapsed in on her flat chest (what had happened to her breasts?), whether she might not be some kind of child at the same time that she was a woman, with fourteen children, my mother included, to prove it. Perhaps she was both, both child and woman, darkness and light, past and present, life and death—all the opposites contained and reconciled in her.

"My Da-duh," my mother said formally and stepped forward. The name sounded like thunder fading softly in the distance.

"Child," Da-duh said, and her tone, her quick scrutiny of my mother, the brief embrace in which they appeared to shy from each other rather than touch, wiped out the fifteen years my mother had been away and restored the old relationship. My mother, who was such a **formidable** figure

---

1. To *disembark* is to get off a ship or plane.
2. In this context, *in the offing* means "just in view from the shore."
3. An *unrelenting* (un´ri len´ ting) struggle is one that does not ease or lessen in intensity.

Literary Element Characterization *What does the description reveal here about this old woman?* **L**

Reading Strategy Making Inferences About Characters **R**
What can you infer about Da-duh from how she is dressed?

Vocabulary
formidable (fôr´ mi də bəl) *adj.* causing fear, dread, or awe by reason of size, strength, or power

PAULE MARSHALL **151**

Teach

Characterization Answer:
She wants readers to realize that the narrator is an independent, feisty, defiant child, and a worthy opponent for her headstrong grandmother.

Ask: Do you think the narrator has a high degree of self-confidence in relating to her grandmother? Explain. *(Students should note that the narrator describes her sister as the prettier one, perhaps indicating a lack of confidence in her appearance; however, she seems to exhibit independence and to be a match for her grandmother in will and strength.)* **OL**

★ Viewing the Art

Say: Compare and contrast this painting of a Central Park skyline in New York City with the painting of a tropical scene on page 153.

(Students may note that in the first painting the buildings dwarf the trees, but the opposite occurs in the second painting.) **AS**

Central Park Skyline, 1999. ★
Mary Iverson.

in my eyes, had suddenly with a word been reduced to my status.

"Yes, God is good," Da-duh said with a nod that was like a tic.[4] "He has spared me to see my child again."

We were led forward then, apologetically because not only did Da-duh prefer boys but she also liked her grandchildren to be "white," that is, fair-skinned; and we had, I was to discover, a number of cousins, the outside children of white estate managers and the like, who qualified. We, though, were as black as she.

My sister being the oldest was presented first. "This one takes after the father," my mother said and waited to be reproved.

Frowning, Da-duh tilted my sister's face toward the light. But her frown soon gave

way to a grudging smile, for my sister with her large mild eyes and little broad winged nose, with our father's high-cheeked Barbadian cast to her face, was pretty.

"She's goin' be lucky," Da-duh said and patted her once on the cheek. "Any girl child that takes after the father does be lucky."

She turned then to me. But oddly enough she did not touch me. Instead leaning close, she peered hard at me, and then quickly drew back. I thought I saw her hand start up as though to shield her eyes. It was almost as if she saw not only me, a thin truculent[5] child who it was said took after no one but myself, but something in me

---

5. To be *truculent* is to be fierce and ready to fight.

Literary Element Characterization *Why do you think Marshall has the narrator describe herself in this way?* **L1**

---

4. Here, a *tic* is an involuntary twitching.

152 UNIT 1 THE SHORT STORY

Additional Support

Skills Practice

GRAMMAR: Participles Understanding participles can enable students to write creatively and to have a greater understanding of literature. Have students identify participles in the text and incorporate them into their own creative writing. **Say:** Da-duh gave a "grudging" smile. *Grudging* is a participle, or a verbal adjective. Present participles end in *-ing.* Identify in this story other participles. Then compose a paragraph using these words. **OL**

Tropical Scene. Albert Bierstadt (1830–1902). Oil on paper laid on board. Private Collection. ★

which for some reason she found disturbing, even threatening. We looked silently at each other for a long time there in the noisy shed, our gaze locked. She was the first to look away.

"But Adry," she said to my mother and her laugh was cracked, thin, apprehensive. "Where did you get this one here with this fierce look?"

"We don't know where she came out of, my Da-duh," my mother said, laughing also. Even I smiled to myself. After all I had won the encounter. Da-duh had recognized my small strength—and this was all I ever asked of the adults in my life then.

Visual Vocabulary *Lorry* is what the British call a truck.

"Come, soul," Da-duh said and took my hand. "You must be one of those New York terrors you hear so much about."

She led us, me at her side and my sister and mother behind, out of the shed into the sunlight that was like a bright driving summer rain and over to a group of people clustered beside a **decrepit** lorry. They were our relatives, most of them from St. Andrews

although Da-duh herself lived in St. Thomas, the women wearing bright print dresses, the colors vivid against their darkness, the men rusty black suits that encased them like strait-jackets. Da-duh, holding fast to my hand, became my anchor as they circled round us like a nervous sea, exclaiming, touching us with their calloused hands, embracing us shyly. They laughed in awed bursts: "But look Adry got big-big children!" / "And see the nice things they wearing, wristwatch and all!" / "I tell you, Adry has done all right for sheself in New York. . . ."

Da-duh, ashamed at their wonder, embarrassed for them, admonished them the while. . . . "Why you all got to get on like you never saw people from 'Away' before? You would think New York is the only place in the world to hear wunna.[6] That's why I don't like to go anyplace with you St. Andrews people, you know. You all ain't been colonized."

6. *To hear wunna* may be Da-duh's way of saying "to have wonders."

Literary Element Characterization *What does this detail tell you about Da-duh?* L2

PAULE MARSHALL **153**

Teach

Making Inferences About Characters Answer: *While Da-duh sees the cane as "pretty enough," her granddaughter seems intimidated by it. She may be more accustomed to nature kept at a distance.* **OL**

BI Big Idea

Making Choices
Answer: *Da-duh seems proud of her land and wants the child, with whom she feels a special kinship, to appreciate the land and to know that New York does not have everything.* **OL**

We were in the back of the lorry finally, packed in among the barrels of ham, flour, cornmeal and rice and the trunks of clothes that my mother had brought as gifts. We made our way slowly through Bridgetown's clogged streets, part of a funereal[7] procession of cars and open-sided buses, bicycles and donkey carts. The dim little limestone shops and offices along the way marched with us, at the same mournful pace, toward the same grave ceremony—as did the people, the women balancing huge baskets on top their heads as if they were no more than hats they wore to shade them from the sun. Looking over the edge of the lorry I watched as their feet slurred the dust. I listened, and their voices, raw and loud and dissonant in the heat, seemed to be grappling with each other high overhead.

Da-duh sat on a trunk in our midst, a monarch amid her court. She still held my hand, but it was different now. I had suddenly become her anchor, for I felt her fear of the lorry with its asthmatic motor (a fear and distrust, I later learned, she held of all machines) beating like a pulse in her rough palm.

As soon as we left Bridgetown behind though, she relaxed, and while the others around us talked she gazed at the canes standing tall on either side of the winding marl[8] road. "C'dear," she said softly to herself after a time. "The canes this side are pretty enough."

They were too much for me. I thought of them as giant weeds that had overrun the island, leaving scarcely any room for the small tottering houses of sunbleached pine we passed or the people, dark streaks as our lorry **hurtled** by. I suddenly feared that

we were journeying, unaware that we were, toward some dangerous place where the canes, grown as high and thick as a forest, would close in on us and run us through with their stiletto blades. I longed then for the familiar: for the street in Brooklyn[9] where I lived, for my father who had refused to accompany us ("Blowing out good money on foolishness," he had said of the trip), for a game of tag with my friends under the chestnut tree outside our aging brownstone house.

"Yes, but wait till you see St. Thomas canes," Da-duh was saying to me. "They's canes father, bo," she gave a proud **arrogant** nod. "Tomorrow, God willing, I goin' take you out in the ground and show them to you."

True to her word Da-duh took me with her the following day out into the ground. It was a fairly large plot adjoining her weathered board and shingle house and consisting of a small orchard, a good-sized canepiece and behind the canes, where the land sloped abruptly down, a gully. She had purchased it with Panama money sent her by her eldest son, my uncle Joseph, who had died working on the canal. We entered the ground along a trail no wider than her body and as devious and complex as her reasons for showing me her land. Da-duh strode briskly ahead, her slight form filled out this morning by the layers of sacking petticoats she wore under her working dress to protect her against the damp. A fresh white cloth, elaborately arranged around her head, added to her height, and lent her a vain, almost roguish air.

Her pace slowed once we reached the orchard, and glancing back at me occasionally over her shoulder, she pointed out the various trees.

---

7. *Funereal* means "like, or suitable to, a funeral."
8. A *marl* road is paved with crumbly clay of the sort used to make cement.

Reading Strategy   Making Inferences About Characters
What kind of inference could you make about the narrator from this detail? **R1**

Vocabulary

hurtle (hurt′ əl) *v.* to move rapidly, especially with much force or noise

---

9. *Brooklyn* is one of New York City's five boroughs, or districts.

Big Idea   Making Choices *Based on what you already know about Da-duh, why do you think she wants to show her land to her granddaughter?* **BI**

Vocabulary

arrogant (ar′ ə gənt) *adj.* full of self-importance; haughty

---

Additional Support

Skills Practice

WRITING: Literary Response
Students may develop creative writing skills by writing about their reactions to the writing of others. Have students reread the passages describing sugarcane fields. Then have them write a paragraph describing their reactions to the author's description. **Say:** A good writer can make a reader feel as if he or she were part of a scene. Reread the passages in which the author describes the sugarcane fields. Then, write about how this description makes you feel. **OL**

"This here is a breadfruit," she said. "That one yonder is a papaw. Here's a guava. This is a mango. I know you don't have anything like these in New York. Here's a sugar apple." (The fruit looked more like artichokes than apples to me.) "This one bears limes. . . ." She went on for some time, intoning the names of the trees as though they were those of her gods. Finally, turning to me, she said, "I know you don't have anything this nice where you come from." Then, as I hesitated: "I said I know you don't have anything this nice where you come from. . . ."

"No," I said and my world did seem suddenly lacking.

Da-duh nodded and passed on. The orchard ended and we were on the narrow cart road that led through the canepiece, the canes clashing like swords above my cowering head. Again she turned and her thin muscular arms spread wide, her dim gaze embracing the small field of canes, she said—and her voice almost broke under the weight of her pride, "Tell me, have you got anything like these in that place where you were born?"

"No."

"I din' think so. I bet you don't even know that these canes here and the sugar you eat is one and the same thing. That they does throw the canes into some damn machine at the factory and squeeze out all the little life in them to make sugar for you all so in New York to eat. I bet you don't know that."

"I've got two cavities and I'm not allowed to eat a lot of sugar."

But Da-duh didn't hear me. She had turned with an inexplicably angry motion and was making her way rapidly out of the canes and down the slope at the edge of the field which led to the gully below. Following her apprehensively down the incline amid a stand of banana plants whose leaves flapped like elephants' ears in the wind, I found myself in the middle of a small tropical wood—a place dense and damp and gloomy and tremulous with the fitful play of light and shadow as the leaves high above moved against the sun that was almost hidden from view. It was a violent place, the tangled foliage fighting each other for a chance at the sunlight, the branches of the trees locked in what seemed an immemorial[10] struggle, one both necessary and inevitable. But despite the violence, it was pleasant, almost peaceful in the gully, and beneath the thick undergrowth the earth smelled like spring.

This time Da-duh didn't even bother to ask her usual question, but simply turned and waited for me to speak.

"No," I said, my head bowed. "We don't have anything like this in New York."

"Ah," she cried, her triumph complete. "I din' think so. Why, I've heard that's a place where you can walk till you near drop and never see a tree."

"We've got a chestnut tree in front of our house," I said.

"Does it bear?" She waited. "I ask you, does it bear?"

"Not anymore," I muttered. "It used to, but not anymore."

She gave the nod that was like a nervous twitch. "You see," she said. "Nothing can bear there." Then, secure behind her scorn, she added, "But tell me, what's this snow like that you hear so much about?"

"It was a violent place, the tangled foliage fighting each other for a chance at the sunlight. . . ."

---

10. An *immemorial* struggle would be one that extended back beyond memory or record.

Reading Strategy Making Inferences About Characters
Why does the child make a negative comment about sugar? **R2**

Reading Strategy Making Inferences About Characters
Why does the grandmother show the child all of these wonderful places? **R3**

PAULE MARSHALL **155**

Teach

Making Choices

Answer: *She may want to show her grandmother that life in Barbados has not prepared her grandmother for life in what the child thinks is the real world.* **OL**

⭐ **Viewing the Art**

Victor Collector is an artist from Barbados known for his realistic paintings of life there. He has said that "learning and sharing with my fellow man is what inspires me the most." **AS**

Wash Day. Victor Collector. Oil on canvas. Private Collection.

Looking up, I studied her closely, sensing my chance, and then I told her, describing at length and with as much drama as I could summon not only what snow in the city was like, but what it would be like here, in her perennial summer kingdom.

". . . And you see all these trees you got here," I said. "Well, they'd be bare. No leaves, no fruit, nothing. They'd be covered in snow. You see your canes. They'd be buried under tons of snow. The snow would be higher than your head, higher than your house, and you wouldn't be able to come down into this here gully because it would be snowed under. . . ."

She searched my face for the lie, still scornful but intrigued. "What a thing, huh?" she said finally, whispering it softly to herself.

"And when it snows you couldn't dress like you are now," I said. "Oh no, you'd freeze to death. You'd have to wear a hat and gloves and galoshes and ear muffs so your ears

wouldn't freeze and drop off, and a heavy coat. I've got a Shirley Temple[11] coat with fur on the collar. I can dance. You wanna see?"

Before she could answer I began, with a dance called the Truck which was popular back then in the 1930s. My right forefinger waving, I trucked around the nearby trees and around Da-duh's awed and rigid form. After the Truck I did the Suzy-Q, my lean hips swishing, my sneakers sidling zigzag over the ground. "I can sing," I said and did so, starting with "I'm Gonna Sit Right Down and Write Myself a Letter," then without pausing, "Tea For Two," and ending with "I Found a Million Dollar Baby in a Five and Ten Cent Store."

For long moments afterwards Da-duh stared at me as if I were a creature from Mars, an emissary from some world she did not know but which intrigued her and whose power she both felt and feared. Yet something about my performance must have pleased her, because bending down she slowly lifted her long skirt and then, one by one, the layers

---

Big Idea Making Choices *Why does the child choose to respond to her grandmother's question in this way?* **BI₁**

11. *Shirley Temple* was a popular child movie star of the 1930s.

Additional Support

Skills Practice

VIEWING: Connecting Images with Text Encourage students to enhance their appreciation of the ways in which art and text can work together. Have them work in small groups to express their response to the painting on this page. **Say:** Art can help us to see things in unique and interesting ways. Often, our perceptions of art are different from the perceptions of those around us. Share your response with other members of your group. Note your differences and similarities. **OL**

of petticoats until she came to a drawstring purse dangling at the end of a long strip of cloth tied round her waist. Opening the purse she handed me a penny. "Here," she said half-smiling against her will. "Take this to buy yourself a sweet at the shop up the road. There's nothing to be done with you, soul."

From then on, whenever I wasn't taken to visit relatives, I accompanied Da-duh out into the ground, and alone with her amid the canes or down in the gully I told her about New York. It always began with some slighting remark on her part: "I know they don't have anything this nice where you come from," or "Tell me, I hear those foolish people in New York does do such and such. . . ." But as I answered, recreating my towering world of steel and concrete and machines for her, building the city out of words, I would feel her give way. I came to know the signs of her surrender: the total stillness that would come over the little hard dry form, the probing gaze that like a surgeon's knife sought to cut through my skull to get at the images there, to see if I were lying; above all, her fear, a fear nameless and profound, the same one I had felt beating in the palm of her hand that day in the lorry.

Over the weeks I told her about refrigerators, radios, gas stoves, elevators, trolley cars, wringer washing machines, movies, airplanes, the cyclone at Coney Island,[12] subways, toasters, electric lights: "At night, see, all you have to do is flip this little switch on the wall and all the lights in the house go on. Just like that. Like magic. It's like turning on the sun at night."

"But tell me," she said to me once with a faint mocking smile, "do the white people have all these things too or it's only the people looking like us?"

I laughed. "What d'ya mean," I said. "The white people have even better." Then: "I beat up a white girl in my class last term."

"Beating up white people!" Her tone was incredulous.

"How you mean!" I said, using an expression of hers. "She called me a name."

For some reason Da-duh could not quite get over this and repeated in the same hushed, shocked voice, "Beating up white people now! Oh, the lord, the world's changing up so I can scarce recognize it anymore."

One morning toward the end of our stay, Da-duh led me into a part of the gully that we had never visited before, an area darker and more thickly overgrown than the rest, almost impenetrable. There in a small clearing amid the dense bush, she stopped before an incredibly tall royal palm which rose cleanly out of the ground, and drawing the eye up with it, soared high above the trees around it into the sky. It appeared to be touching the blue dome of sky, to be flaunting its dark crown of fronds right in the blinding white face of the late morning sun.

Da-duh watched me a long time before she spoke, and then she said, very quietly, "All right, now, tell me if you've got anything this tall in that place you're from."

I almost wished, seeing her face, that I could have said no. "Yes," I said. "We've got buildings hundreds of times this tall in New York. There's one called the Empire State Building that's the tallest in the world. My class visited it last year and I went all the way to the top. It's got over a hundred floors. I can't describe how tall it is. Wait a minute. What's the name of that hill I went to visit the other day, where they have the police station?"

"You mean Bissex?"

"Yes, Bissex. Well, the Empire State Building is way taller than that."

---

12. *Coney Island* is an amusement park and beach in Brooklyn, and the *Cyclone* was a popular thrill ride.

Big Idea Making Choices *Why do you think Da-duh chooses to take the child with her, instead of someone else?* **BI₂**

Reading Strategy Making Inferences About Characters *Why does Da-duh have this reaction when the child talks about New York City?* **R₁**

Reading Strategy Making Inferences About Characters *What does this comment tell you about the relationship between the child and Da-duh?* **R₂**

Big Idea Making Choices *Why does the girl choose to answer as she does?* **BI₃**

PAULE MARSHALL **157**

Teach

BI₂ Big Idea

Making Choices
Answer: *She enjoys her granddaughter's free spirit, and she also wants her granddaughter to appreciate her land.* **OL**

R₁ Reading Strategy

Making Inferences About Characters Answer: *Da-duh seems threatened by her granddaughter's description. She may question her own ability to survive in a place like New York City.* **OL**

R₂ Reading Strategy

Making Inferences About Characters Answer: *The narrator seems to feel more protective of her grandmother at this point, but she still agitates Da-duh by describing New York City. She is torn between wanting to shield Da-duh from the realities of modern life and wanting to boast about the skyscrapers in her city.* **OL**

BI₃ Big Idea

Making Choices Answer: *The urge to top her grandmother overcomes her, and she brags about the height of the buildings in New York City.* **OL**

Objectives
- To make inferences about characters (SE)
- To connect images with text (TWE)

Reading in the Real World

Citizenship Say: Da-duh is surprised that her granddaughter's lifestyle includes social interaction with "white folks." Do some research to learn about the history of race relations in Barbados. Share your findings with the class.

(Students' findings should include: Slaves worked British plantations until the end of slavery in 1834; the island population today is 90% black, 4% white, and 6% racially mixed.) **OL**

Teach

L1 Literary Element

Characterization Answer:
Da-duh's strong will seems to be failing. OL

★ Political History

Barbados Labor Unrest The 1930s represented a time of political and racial unrest in Barbados. In 1934, white sugar planters took steps to weaken the emerging black labor movement. The resulting strike of 1937 brought about strong resistance and violence. AS

"You're lying now!" she shouted, trembling with rage. Her hand lifted to strike me.

"No, I'm not," I said. "It really is, if you don't believe me I'll send you a picture postcard of it soon as I get back home so you can see for yourself. But it's way taller than Bissex."

All the fight went out of her at that. The hand poised to strike me fell limp to her side, and as she stared at me, seeing not me but the building that was taller than the highest hill she knew, the small stubborn light in her eyes (it was the same amber as the flame in the kerosene lamp she lit at dusk) began to fail. Finally, with a vague gesture that even in the midst of her defeat still tried to dismiss me and my world, she turned and started back through the gully, walking slowly, her steps groping and uncertain, as if she were suddenly no longer sure of the way, while I followed triumphant yet strangely saddened behind.

The next morning I found her dressed for our morning walk but stretched out on the Berbice chair in the tiny drawing room where she sometimes napped during the afternoon heat, her face turned to the window beside her. She appeared thinner and suddenly indescribably old.

"My Da-duh," I said.

"Yes, nuh," she said. Her voice was listless and the face she slowly turned my way was, now that I think back on it, like a Benin mask, the features drawn and almost distorted by an ancient abstract sorrow.

"Don't you feel well?" I asked.

"Girl, I don't know."

"My Da-duh, I goin' boil you some bush tea," my aunt, Da-duh's youngest child, who lived with her, called from the shed roof kitchen.

"Who tell you I need bush tea?" she cried, her voice assuming for a moment its old authority. "You can't even rest nowadays without some **malicious** person looking for

> **Vocabulary**
> malicious (mə lish′ əs) *adj.* having or showing a desire to harm another

> **Literary Element** Characterization *How does the light in Da-duh's eyes help to characterize her in this scene?* L1

158 UNIT 1 THE SHORT STORY

---

you to be dead. Come girl," she motioned me to a place beside her on the old-fashioned lounge chair, "give us a tune."

I sang for her until breakfast at eleven, all my brash irreverent Tin Pan Alley[13] songs, and then just before noon we went out into the ground. But it was a short, dispirited walk. Da-duh didn't even notice that the mangoes were beginning to ripen and would have to be picked before the village boys got to them. And when she paused occasionally and looked out across the canes or up at her trees it wasn't as if she were seeing them but something else. Some huge, monolithic[14] shape had imposed itself, it seemed, between her and the land, obstructing her vision. Returning to the house she slept the entire afternoon on the Berbice chair.

She remained like this until we left, languishing away the mornings on the chair at the window gazing out at the land as if it were already doomed; then, at noon, taking the brief stroll with me through the ground during which she seldom spoke, and afterwards returning home to sleep till almost dusk sometimes.

On the day of our departure she put on the austere, ankle length white dress, the black shoes and brown felt hat (her town clothes she called them), but she did not go with us to town. She saw us off on the road outside her house and in the midst of my mother's tearful protracted[15] farewell, she leaned down and whispered in my ear, "Girl, you're not to forget now to send me the picture of that building, you hear."

By the time I mailed her the large colored picture postcard of the Empire State Building she was dead. She died during the famous '37 strike which began shortly after we left. On the day of her death England sent planes flying low over the island in a ★

---

13. *Tin Pan Alley* was a district in New York City associated with composers and publishers of popular music. These pop songs were bright and lively, often treating their subjects with rude and disrespectful (*brash, irreverent*) mockery.
14. A *monolithic* shape would resemble a monument or other structure formed from a single, giant block of stone.
15. A *protracted* (prō trak′ təd) farewell would be one that takes a lot of time.

Additional Support

Skills Practice

READING: Visualizing Encourage students to create mental images of the setting for this story by learning about the words used to describe the setting. **Say:** Da-duh is sitting in a "Berbice" chair. A Berbice chair, named for a former Caribbean colony, has large arms, and is for relaxing. **Ask:** How does this information help you to visualize the scene created by the author? (*Students should indicate that details like this help them to understand the setting and to imagine what is happening.*) OL

158

Forsaken Treasures. Victor Collector. Oil on canvas. Private Collection.

show of force—so low, according to my aunt's letter, that the downdraft from them shook the ripened mangoes from the trees in Da-duh's orchard. Frightened, everyone in the village fled into the canes. Except Da-duh. She remained in the house at the window so my aunt said, watching as the planes came swooping and screaming like monstrous birds down over the village, over her house, rattling her trees and flattening the young canes in her field. It must have seemed to her lying there that they did not intend pulling out of their dive, but like the hardback beetles which hurled themselves with suicidal force against the walls of the house at night, those menacing silver shapes would hurl themselves in an ecstasy of self-immolation[16] onto the land, destroying it utterly.

When the planes finally left and the villagers returned they found her dead on the Berbice chair at the window.

She died and I lived, but always, to this day even, within the shadow of her death. For a brief period after I was grown I went to live alone, like one doing penance,[17] in a loft above a noisy factory in downtown New York and there painted seas of sugarcane and huge swirling Van Gogh[18] suns and palm trees striding like brightly-plumed Tutsi[19] warriors across a tropical landscape, while the thunderous tread of the machines downstairs jarred the floor beneath my easel, mocking my efforts. ✎

16. *Self-immolation* is the act of setting oneself on fire.

17. *Penance* (pen′ əns) is a punishment one undergoes, usually voluntarily, to show sorrow for having committed a sin or offense.
18. *Van Gogh* was a nineteenth-century Dutch painter famous for his swirling brush strokes and for the dramatic effects they produced.
19. The *Tutsi* are a people in central Africa.

Reading Strategy Making Inferences About Characters
What does the narrator mean when she says she lives within the shadow of her grandmother's death? **R**

Literary Element Characterization *How does the author reveal that the narrator remains troubled by the conflict with her grandmother?* **L2**

PAULE MARSHALL **159**

Differentiated Instruction

Assess

1. There was no "winner." The narrator appears to win, but because of the child's triumph, her grandmother becomes dispirited.

2. (a) A formidable and mysterious person (b) To assert herself

3. (a) Grandmother shows off her favorite places. Granddaughter tells her about snow, sings, and dances. (b) Da-duh is not familiar with anything outside of Barbados, her point of reference.

4. (a) Initially, she doubts the child's claims, but ultimately she is awed. (b) Da-duh has experienced little of the world outside of Barbados.

5. (a) After her granddaughter says New York City has buildings taller than Bissex hill, Da-duh's health begins to fail. (b) The grandmother realizes that her world seems insignificant.

6. The modern, urban world

7. "Birds of a feather flock together"; although they are from different worlds, their personalities are similar.

8. She stood up to her grandmother. Most students will probably wish that the narrator had acted differently out of respect.

RESPONDING AND THINKING CRITICALLY

Respond

1. Do you think that either Da-duh or the child "won" their battle of wills? Explain.

Recall and Interpret

2. (a) Describe the narrator's initial impression of Da-duh. (b) Why do you think the narrator tries to "win" the initial encounter between Da-duh and herself?

3. (a) Summarize what happens the first time Da-duh takes her granddaughter "out into the ground." (b) In your opinion, why does Da-duh compare Barbados with New York City?

4. (a) How does Da-duh react to her granddaughter's descriptions of New York City? (b) What conclusions can you draw about Da-duh based on her reaction to the girl's descriptions?

Analyze and Evaluate

5. (a) At what point in the story do Da-duh's appearance and behavior abruptly change? Describe this change. (b) What do you think causes this change, and what does it signify?

6. In your opinion, what does the Empire State Building symbolize, or represent, in this story?

7. Which of these aphorisms best describes the relationship between the narrator and Da-duh: "Birds of a feather flock together" or "Opposites attract"? Explain.

Connect

8. **Big Idea** Making Choices How did the narrator choose to treat Da-duh? Do you approve of this decision? Explain.

LITERARY ANALYSIS

Literary Element Characterization

The two basic methods that a writer uses to reveal the personality of a character are **direct** and **indirect** characterization. For example, Marshall uses the method of direct characterization when the narrator describes Da-duh's face as "stark and fleshless as a death mask." She uses indirect characterization when Da-duh describes her granddaughter as "one of those New York terrors."

1. Give another example of direct characterization that describes the narrator.

2. Find another example of indirect characterization in the story. What does it show about the character?

3. What method of characterization does the author use to show how Da-duh has changed by the end of the story? Use evidence from the story to support your response.

Review: Setting

As you learned on pages 10–11, **setting** is where and when a story takes place. Setting includes not only the physical surroundings, but also the ideas, customs, values, and beliefs of the people in that place and time.

Partner Activity Meet with a classmate and discuss the details that Paule Marshall used to re-create Barbados in the 1930s. Think about how the setting influences the characters and events. Working with your partner, create a web diagram like the one below. Fill it in with specific examples and details that evoke the setting and help you understand its importance to the story.

Literary Element

1. Da-duh says the narrator has a "fierce look."

2. When Da-duh describes some trees and says, "I know you don't have anything this nice where you come from."

3. Direct: "thinner and suddenly indescribably old," "listless," "the features drawn and almost distorted."

Review: Setting

speech: "has done all right for sheself"; *lorry*

dress: black high-top shoes, "fresh white cloth, elaborately arranged around her head"

landscape: open-sided buses, bicycles and donkey carts, limestone shops, "women balancing huge baskets on top of their heads," fields of cane

READING AND VOCABULARY

Reading Strategy Making Inferences About Characters

Paule Marshall does not tell you everything about the narrator and Da-duh. Instead, she provides specific and vivid details to help you **make inferences** about their personalities. Review the inference chart you created for clues about the narrator and her grandmother.

1. In your opinion, how are the personalities of the narrator and Da-duh alike? How are they different?

2. List at least two important details that helped you form each opinion.

Vocabulary Practice

Practice with Synonyms Each word on the left is a vocabulary word from "To Da-duh, in Memoriam." Find the synonym for each vocabulary word listed in the first column.

1. malicious   **a.** toxic   **b.** evil
2. decrepit   **a.** dilapidated   **b.** depressed
3. arrogant   **a.** haughty   **b.** gallant
4. hurtle   **a.** loud noise   **b.** propel
5. formidable   **a.** fearsome   **b.** gentle

Academic Vocabulary

Here are two words from the vocabulary list on page R82.

instance (in′ stəns) *n.* an example or illustration of an event or thing

correspond (kôr′ ə spond′) *v.* to be the same as something else; to match

Practice and Apply
1. What **instance** from the story do you think best captures the conflict between Da-duh and the girl?
2. How do the values of Da-duh **correspond** with those of her granddaughter?

WRITING AND EXTENDING

Writing About Literature

Analyze Character A character who grows or changes during a story is called a **dynamic character**. Write an essay in which you analyze how the narrator of "To Da-duh, in Memoriam" grows and changes as a result of her visit to Barbados. Use specific details from the story to support your ideas.

As you draft, write from start to finish. Follow the writing chart shown here to help you organize your essay.

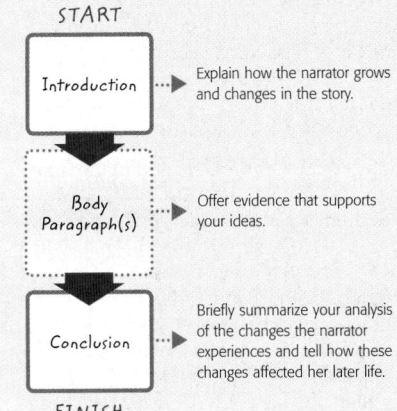

START

Introduction → Explain how the narrator grows and changes in the story.

Body Paragraph(s) → Offer evidence that supports your ideas.

Conclusion → Briefly summarize your analysis of the changes the narrator experiences and tell how these changes affected her later life.

FINISH

After you complete your draft, meet with a peer reviewer to evaluate each other's work and to suggest revisions. Then proofread and edit your draft for errors in spelling, grammar, and punctuation.

Internet Connection

Work with a partner to create a tourist brochure about Barbados. Use the Internet to locate information about the sights, sounds, and tastes of this West Indian island. Include in your brochure key attractions, up-to-date travel information, and brief advice on what to do, where to eat, and where to stay. Illustrate your brochure, if you wish.

Literature Online **Web Activities** For eFlashcards, Selection Quick Checks, and other Web activities, go to www.glencoe.com.

PAULE MARSHALL   **161**

AFTER YOU READ

Assess

Reading Strategy

1. They are alike in that they are proud, stubborn, and determined. They are different in that Da-duh is comfortable, appreciative, and at peace in the natural world, while the narrator appreciates the liveliness of the city.

2. At the beginning of the story, the two characters stare each other down. The grandmother shows off her trees and orchard. The narrator thinks of the canes as giant weeds and considers the gully violent. Da-duh speaks about the city with scorn, while the narrator dances and sings to tell about her home.

Vocabulary

1. b   **2.** a   **3.** a   **4.** b   **5.** a

Academic Vocabulary

1. Examples: the child describes snow; Da-duh shows her royal palm.
2. Da-duh values nature; granddaughter values the modern world.

Writing About Literature

Students' essays should:
- identify the changes the narrator experiences
- offer specific details as evidence

Internet Connection

Make sure students use reliable Web sites to gather their information.

Literature Online

Web Activities Have students access the Web site for interactive activities that will help them assess their understanding of the selection.

Focus

BEFORE YOU READ

Contents of the Dead Man's Pocket

BELLRINGER

Bellringer Options
Selection Focus Transparency 10
Daily Language
 Transparency 16
Or **write on the board:** When is it worth the risk? **Ask:** How far would you go to protect a possession that is very important to you? Then have students discuss the kinds of things they think they or others might risk their lives for. Why would this be worth it?

Author Search To expand students' appreciation of Jack Finney, have them access the Web site for additional information and resources.

MEET JACK FINNEY

The author of novels, short stories, and television screenplays, Jack Finney is most famous as a science-fiction writer. Perhaps his best-known work is the novel *The Body Snatchers*, which he published in 1955. Renamed and reissued a year later as *Invasion of the Body Snatchers*, this science-fiction thriller was adapted three times as a movie, and each version became a cult classic.

When the novel was first released in the mid-1950s, the age of McCarthyism, critics were quick to interpret it as an allegory based on the real fears of a Communist takeover in the United States at that time. Finney scoffed at that interpretation, claiming that his novel was nothing more than popular entertainment. "It was just a story meant to entertain, and with no more meaning than that," Finney once stated, adding that "the idea of writing a whole book in order to say that it's not really a good thing for us all to be alike . . . makes me laugh."

"One should never use the word 'fun' as an adjective except when referring to the writings of Jack Finney."

—*The San Francisco Examiner*

Born in Milwaukee, Wisconsin, Finney grew up in suburban Chicago. After graduation from Knox College in Galesburg, Illinois, Finney moved to New York City, where he worked as a writer for an advertising agency.

In 1946 he published his first short story, "The Widow's Walk," which won a special prize in an *Ellery Queen's Mystery Magazine* contest. After that breakthrough, he continued to write and publish short stories in many popular magazines, including *The Saturday Evening Post, Collier's,* and *McCall's.*

In the early 1950s, Finney, his wife, and their two children moved from New York City to Marin County, California. In 1954, he published his first novel, *5 Against the House.* That novel, *Assault on a Queen* (1959), and *Good Neighbor Sam* (1963) were all adapted into popular films.

After the success of *Invasion of the Body Snatchers* in 1956, Finney continued to write more science fiction, although he resisted classification as a science-fiction author, considering himself a fantasy writer who was most interested in ordinary people's responses to extraordinary situations. In 1957 he published a short-story collection entitled *The Third Level,* which contains the story you are about to read, "Contents of the Dead Man's Pocket."

Finney wrote a time-travel novel, *Time and Again,* in 1970; many critics believe that it was Finney's masterpiece. Its main character works as an advertising writer in New York City before being recruited by the government for a secret time-travel project. In 1995, just months before his death, Finney published a long-awaited sequel to this novel.

Jack Finney was born in 1911 and died in 1995.

Literature Online **Author Search** For more about Jack Finney, go to www.glencoe.com.

Selection Skills

Literary Elements
• Symbol (SE pp. 163–178)
• Motivation (SE p. 178)

Reading Skills
• Responding to Characters (SE pp. 163–178)
• Predicting (TWE p. 164)

Contents of the Dead Man's Pocket

Vocabulary Skills
• Analogies (SE pp. 163, 178)
• Academic Vocabulary (SE p. 178)

Listening/Speaking/ Viewing Skills
• Performing Monologues (SE p. 179)

Writing Skills/Grammar
• Essay on Theme (SE p. 179)
• Using Introductory Phrases (SE p. 179)
• Summarizing (TWE p. 170)
• Compatibility of Tenses (TWE p. 172)
• Creating Suspense (TWE p. 176)

Connecting to the Story

It is often easy to take for granted what we value most in our lives. Other things can consume our attention, making it difficult to maintain our priorities. Before you read "Contents of the Dead Man's Pocket," think about the following questions:

- What are your priorities in life?
- How well do you divide your attention among your priorities?
- When have you regretted neglecting your priorities?

Building Background

This story takes place in New York City, probably during the 1950s—a time before personal computers and widespread use of photocopying machines. Therefore, you will note that the main character types documents on a portable typewriter and uses carbon paper—thin, ink-coated sheets of paper placed between two pieces of writing paper—to make a copy of a typewritten document. You will also note that the change in his pocket includes, among other pieces, a fifty-cent piece, known as a "half-dollar."

Setting Purposes for Reading

Big Idea Making Choices

As you read, think about the choice that leads the main character to thrust himself into deadly circumstances.

Literary Element Symbol

A **symbol** is any object, person, place, or experience that exists on a literal level but also represents, or stands for, something else, usually an abstract concept. For example, a dove is literally a bird, but it is also often used figuratively as a symbol of the abstract concept of peace. Understanding the author's use of symbols can help you better comprehend the story. As you read "Contents of the Dead Man's Pocket," look for a literal expression or object that also represents an abstract concept.

- See Literary Terms Handbook, p. R17.

Reading Strategy Responding to Characters

When you respond to what you are reading, you interact with the text in an important way. To **respond to characters** in a literary work, ask yourself questions about what you like, what you do not like, what surprises you, and how you feel about the characters in a story. As you read "Contents of the Dead Man's Pockets," think about how the main character, Tom Benecke, makes you feel.

....

Reading Tip: Taking Notes To better understand your responses to characters, take notes about them as you read.

Vocabulary

convoluted (kon′ və lōō ′ təd) *adj.* turned in or wound up upon itself; coiled; twisted; p. 166 *Instead of a flat piece of wood, the ornate, antique railing was convoluted.*

improvised (im′ prə vīzd′) *adj.* invented, composed, or done without preparation; p. 166 *Because I was unprepared for John's strange question, I had to offer him an improvised answer.*

taut (tôt) *adj.* tense; tight; p. 169 *The leash grew taut and straight when the dog leaped forward.*

pent-up (pent′ up) *adj.* not expressed or released; held in; p. 171 *I remained calm until I hung up the phone, but then my pent-up sadness made me burst into tears.*

reveling (rev′ əl ing) *adj.* taking great pleasure; p. 172 *Reveling in delight, the little boy ran up and down the aisle of toys.*

Vocabulary Tip: Analogies An analogy is a type of comparison that is based on the relationships between things or ideas. Some analogies involve synonyms or antonyms.

Literature Online Interactive Literary Elements Handbook To review or learn more about the literary elements, go to www.glencoe.com.

OBJECTIVES
In studying this selection, you will focus on the following:
- understanding and identifying symbols
- responding to characters
- analyzing the main character's motivation
- writing to explore how theme and title are related

JACK FINNEY **163**

Focus
Summary

Tom, an ambitious young professional, plans to work late at home on an important project while his wife goes off alone to the movies. A gust of wind snatches up the only copy of his notes and whisks it out the window. The paper settles on a ledge about fifteen feet from the window of Tom's eleventh-floor apartment. Not willing to let weeks of research be lost so easily, Tom goes out on the ledge to get the paper. Tom's near-death experience causes him to rethink his priorities in life.

V Vocabulary

Vocabulary File Say: Add these words and definitions to your vocabulary file. For each word, include a sentence that gives you an example of how to use the word. **OL** Students with English language needs should include the pronunciations of these words in their files. **EL**

Literature Online

Literary Elements Have students access the Web site to improve their understanding of symbol.

Selection Resources

Print Materials
- Unit 1 Resources (Fast File), pp. 61–63
- Leveled Vocabulary Development, p. 13
- Selection and Unit Assessments, pp. 27–28
- Selection Quick Checks, p. 14

Transparencies
- Bellringer Options Transparencies: Selection Focus Transparency 10 Daily Language Practice Transparency 16
- Literary Elements Transparency 20

Technology
- TeacherWorks Plus™ CD-ROM
- StudentWorks Plus™ CD-ROM
- Presentation Plus!™ CD-ROM
- Literature Online, glencoe.com
- Online Student Edition, mhln.com
- ExamView® Assessment Suite CD-ROM
- Vocabulary PuzzleMaker CD-ROM
- Listening Library, disc 1 track 14

Big Idea

Making Choices

Say: Keep these questions in mind as you read: What are the consequences of the main character's choices? How do his choices lead to a change in what he considers most important? (*His choice to dedicate himself to his work means that he doesn't spend much time with his wife. His choice to retrieve his important paper puts his life in danger. This danger causes him to re-evaluate his priorities.*) **OL**

★ Viewing the Art

Have students study the painting on this page. **Ask:** What does this painting suggest about the relationship between the man and the woman? (*Students may say that the man is ignoring the woman and that she looks sad or lonely.*) **AS**

Readability Scores

Dale-Chall: 6.7
DRP: 59
Lexile: 1190

Room in New York, 1932. Edward Hopper. Oil on canvas, 29 x 36 in. Sheldon Memorial Art Gallery, University of Nebraska–Lincoln, F. M. Hall Collection. 1936.H-166. ★

Contents of the Dead Man's Pocket

Jack Finney

At the little living-room desk Tom Benecke rolled two sheets of flimsy and a heavier top sheet, carbon paper sandwiched between them, into his portable.[1] *Inter-office Memo*, the top sheet was headed, and he typed tomorrow's date just below this; then he glanced at a creased yellow sheet, covered with his own handwriting, beside the typewriter. "Hot in here," he muttered to himself. Then, from the short hallway at his back, he heard the muffled clang of wire coat hangers in the bedroom closet, and at this reminder of what his wife was doing he thought: Hot, hell—guilty conscience.

He got up, shoving his hands into the back pockets of his gray wash slacks,[2] stepped to the living-room window beside the desk and stood breathing on the glass, watching the expanding circlet of mist, staring down through the autumn night at Lexington Avenue, eleven stories below. He was a tall, lean, dark-haired young man in a pullover sweater, who looked as though he had played not football, probably, but bas-

---

1. Before the laptop computer, one might type on a compact, fairly lightweight typewriter called a *portable*.

2. *Wash slacks* are pants that, because they are cotton, can be washed instead of dry-cleaned.

Additional Support

Skills Practice

READING: Predicting Ask students to read the first paragraph and then make predictions about what will happen in the story. **Ask:** Based on this paragraph, what kinds of conflicts do you expect might develop in the story? (*Students may expect conflicts between Tom and his wife, possibly related to the work that he is doing.*) **Ask:** What mood does the setting create, and how do you think this might relate to events to follow? (*Students may answer that the setting creates a stifling atmosphere and a feeling of tension.*) Remind students to revise their predictions as they read. **OL**

ketball in college. Now he placed the heels of his hands against the top edge of the lower window frame and shoved upward. But as usual the window didn't budge, and he had to lower his hands and then shoot them hard upward to jolt the window open a few inches. He dusted his hands, muttering.

But still he didn't begin his work. He crossed the room to the hallway entrance and, leaning against the doorjamb, hands shoved into his back pockets again, he called, "Clare?" When his wife answered, he said, "Sure you don't mind going alone?"

"No." Her voice was muffled, and he knew her head and shoulders were in the bedroom closet. Then the tap of her high heels sounded on the wood floor and she appeared at the end of the little hallway, wearing a slip, both hands raised to one ear, clipping on an earring. She smiled at him—a slender, very pretty girl with light brown, almost blonde, hair—her prettiness emphasized by the pleasant nature that showed in her face. "It's just that I hate you to miss this movie; you wanted to see it too." "Yeah, I know." He ran his fingers through his hair. "Got to get this done though."

She nodded, accepting this. Then, glancing at the desk across the living room, she said, "You work too much, though, Tom—and too hard."

He smiled. "You won't mind though, will you, when the money comes rolling in and I'm known as the Boy Wizard of Wholesale Groceries?"

"I guess not." She smiled and turned back toward the bedroom.

> "he saw the yellow sheet drop to the window ledge and slide over out of sight."

Reading Strategy Responding to Characters *What is Tom's attitude toward his wife?* **R1**

Reading Strategy Responding to Characters *How do you feel about Tom's decision to miss the movie? Would you have made the same choice?* **R2**

At his desk again, Tom lighted a cigarette; then a few moments later as Clare appeared, dressed and ready to leave, he set it on the rim of the ash tray. "Just after seven," she said. "I can make the beginning of the first feature."

He walked to the front-door closet to help her on with her coat. He kissed her then and, for an instant, holding her close, smelling the perfume she had used, he was tempted to go with her; it was not actually true that he had to work tonight, though he very much wanted to. This was his own project, unannounced as yet in his office, and it could be postponed. But then they won't see it till Monday, he thought once again, and if I give it to the boss tomorrow he might read it over the weekend . . . "Have a good time," he said aloud. He gave his wife a little swat and opened the door for her, feeling the air from the building hallway, smelling faintly of floor wax, stream gently past his face.

He watched her walk down the hall, flicked a hand in response as she waved, and then he started to close the door, but it resisted for a moment. As the door opening narrowed, the current of warm air from the hallway, channeled through this smaller opening now, suddenly rushed past him with accelerated force. Behind him he heard the slap of the window curtains against the wall and the sound of paper fluttering from his desk, and he had to push to close the door.

Turning, he saw a sheet of white paper drifting to the floor in a series of arcs, and another sheet, yellow, moving toward the window, caught in the dying current flowing through the narrow opening. As he watched, the paper struck the bottom edge of the window and hung there for an instant, plastered against the glass and wood. Then as the mov-

---

Big Idea Making Choices *Why does Tom choose to work on his special project?* **B1**

JACK FINNEY **165**

Teach

R1 Reading Strategy
Responding to Characters
Answer: *Tom regards his wife with tender concern tinged with feelings of guilt for letting her go to the movies alone.* **OL**

R2 Reading Strategy
Responding to Characters
Answer: *Some students will disapprove of Tom's decision to work instead of spending time with his wife.* **OL**

B1 Big Idea
Making Choices
Answer: *Tom has fierce career ambitions and a strong sense of purpose to succeed at his job.* **OL**

★ Writer's Technique

Setting Finney's meticulous attention to detail and his colorful descriptions create a vivid setting for his story. From the opening scene and through the most dramatic moments, the focus on a detailed and realistic portrayal of Tom's world contributes to the story's powerful suspense. **AS**

✓ CheckPoint

Use the CheckPoint questions on Presentation Plus! to monitor students' comprehension. These questions can be used with interactive response keypads for immediate student feedback.

Objectives
- To respond to characters (SE)
- To make predictions (TWE)

Differentiated Instruction

Detailed Description The dense visual descriptions in this story may cause confusion for less proficient readers. Ask these students to focus on mental images as they read and to use sketching to record these mental pictures. **BL** Students with strong spatial abilities who create detailed mental images as they read will also benefit from this activity. Encourage students to sketch the most important images from the story in a notebook. Have them make sketches quickly and then return to make their favorites into finished drawings later on. **AL**

Teach

L Literary Element

Symbol Answer: *To Tom, the yellow sheet of paper represents a significant portion of his past and the possibility of future success.* **OL**

BI₁ Big Idea

Making Choices
Answer: *He will either go out on the ledge to retrieve the paper or redo his research.* **OL**

ing air stilled completely the curtains swinging back from the wall to hang free again, he saw the yellow sheet drop to the window ledge and slide over out of sight.

He ran across the room, grasped the bottom edge of the window and tugged, staring through the glass. He saw the yellow sheet, dimly now in the darkness outside, lying on the ornamental ledge a yard below the window. Even as he watched, it was moving, scraping slowly along the ledge, pushed by the breeze that pressed steadily against the building wall. He heaved on the window with all his strength and it shot open with a bang, the window weight rattling in the casing. But the paper was past his reach and, leaning out into the night, he watched it scud[3] steadily along the ledge to the south, half plastered against the building wall. Above the muffled sound of the street traffic far below, he could hear the dry scrape of its movement, like a leaf on the pavement.

The living room of the next apartment to the south projected a yard or more farther out toward the street than this one; because of this the Beneckes paid seven and a half dollars less rent than their neighbors. And now the yellow sheet, sliding along the stone ledge, nearly invisible in the night, was stopped by the projecting blank wall of the next apartment. It lay motionless, then, in the corner formed by the two walls—a good five yards away, pressed firmly against the ornate corner ornament of the ledge, by the breeze that moved past Tom Benecke's face.

He knelt at the window and stared at the yellow paper for a full minute or more, waiting for it to move, to slide off the ledge and fall, hoping he could follow its course to the street, and then hurry down in the elevator and retrieve it. But it didn't move, and then he saw that the paper was caught firmly between a projection of the **convoluted** corner

ornament and the ledge. He thought about the poker from the fireplace, then the broom, then the mop—discarding each thought as it occurred to him. There was nothing in the apartment long enough to reach that paper.

It was hard for him to understand that he actually had to abandon it—it was ridiculous—and he began to curse. Of all the papers on his desk, why did it have to be this one in particular! On four long Saturday afternoons he had stood in supermarkets counting the people who passed certain displays, and the results were scribbled on that yellow sheet. From stacks of trade publications, gone over page by page in snatched half hours at work and during evenings at home, he had copied facts, quotations and figures onto that sheet. And he had carried it with him to the Public Library on Fifth Avenue, where he'd spent a dozen lunch hours and early evenings adding more. All were needed to support and lend authority to his idea for a new grocery-store display method; without them his idea was a mere opinion. And there they all lay, in his own **improvised** shorthand—countless hours of work—out there on the ledge.

For many seconds he believed he was going to abandon the yellow sheet, that there was nothing else to do. The work could be duplicated. But it would take two months, and the time to present this idea, was *now*, for use in the spring displays. He struck his fist on the window ledge. Then he shrugged. Even though his plan were adopted, he told himself, it wouldn't bring him a raise in pay—not immediately, anyway, or as a direct result. It won't bring me a promotion either, he argued—not of itself.

Literary Element Symbol *What does the yellow sheet of paper represent to Tom?* **L**

Big Idea Making Choices *How might you summarize the two choices that Tom is weighing about how to solve this problem?* **BI₁**

---

3. To *scud* is to run or move swiftly.

Vocabulary

convoluted (kon′ və loo′ təd) *adj.* turned in or wound up upon itself; coiled; twisted

Vocabulary

improvised (im′ prə vīzd′) *adj.* invented, composed, or done without preparing beforehand

Additional Support

Skills Practice

READING: Using Logical Reasoning Tom has a choice in this story: to painstakingly duplicate two months of work or attempt to retrieve his paper. His career ambitions spur him to go after the paper, but is this a logical choice? What kinds of considerations does Tom make before deciding to go

out on the ledge? Have small groups of students make a chart in which they compare the advantages of each option with the possible consequences. As a class, discuss this question: Did Tom make a logical choice? What choice would students have made? **OL**

But just the same, and he couldn't escape the thought, this and other independent projects, some already done and others planned for the future, would gradually mark him out from the score of other young men in his company. They were the way to change from a name on the payroll to a name in the minds of the company officials. They were the beginning of the long, long climb to where he was determined to be, at the very top. And he knew he was going out there in the darkness, after the yellow sheet fifteen feet beyond his reach.

By a kind of instinct, he instantly began making his intention acceptable to himself by laughing at it. The mental picture of himself sidling along the ledge outside was absurd—it was actually comical—and he smiled. He imagined himself describing it; it would make a good story at the office and, it occurred to him, would add a special interest and importance to his memorandum, which would do it no harm at all.

To simply go out and get his paper was an easy task—he could be back here with it in less than two minutes—and he knew he wasn't deceiving himself. The ledge, he saw, measuring it with his eye, was about as wide as the length of his shoe, and perfectly flat. And every fifth row of brick in the face of the building, he remembered—leaning out, he verified this—was indented half an inch, enough for the tips of his fingers, enough to maintain balance easily. It occurred to him that if this ledge and wall were only a yard aboveground—as he knelt at the window staring out, this thought was the final confirmation of his intention—he could move along the ledge indefinitely.

Reference, 1991. Jeremy Annett. Oil on canvas. Private collection. ★

On a sudden impulse, he got to his feet, walked to the front closet and took out an old tweed jacket, it would be cold outside. He put it on and buttoned it as he crossed the room rapidly toward the open window. In the back of his mind he knew he'd better hurry and get this over with before he thought too much, and at the window he didn't allow himself to hesitate. He swung a leg over the sill, then felt for and found the ledge a yard below the window with his foot. Gripping the bottom of the window frame very tightly and carefully, he slowly ducked his head under it, feeling on his face the sudden change from the warm air of the room to the chill outside. With infinite care he brought out his other leg, his mind concentrating on what he was doing. Then he slowly stood erect. Most of the putty, dried out and brittle, had dropped off the bottom edging of the window frame,

---

Reading Strategy Responding to Characters *What do you think is Tom's highest priority? How do you feel about his priorities?* **R**

Big Idea Making Choices *Now that Tom has made his choice, why does he act "on a sudden impulse," "before he thought too much"?* **BI₂**

Teach

R Reading Strategy

Responding to Characters
Answer: *Tom's career goals are his highest priority. Students may say that Tom should value time with his wife more.* **OL**

BI₂ Big Idea

Making Choices
Answer: *Students will probably say that he is trying to avoid becoming paralyzed by fear or to trick himself into thinking that he is safe.* **OL**

★ Viewing the Art

Ask: Does this desk look like your visualization of Tom's "little living-room desk"? Explain.
(Students' answers will vary. Accept all reasonable responses.)

Reading in the Real World

Career Tom's long-term goals are important to this story because his ambition to work his way up in his company is a major factor in his decision to retrieve the paper.

Have students think about what long-term goals they consider important for themselves. Ask them to pick one goal to focus on that could be academic, work-related, or personal. Then have them do research in a library or on the Internet to find advice about achieving goals. Have them present their findings to the class. **OL**

Objectives
- To understand and identify symbols (SE)
- To respond to characters (SE)
- To use logical reasoning (TWE)

Teach

Responding to Characters
Answer: *Most students will empathize with Tom as he struggles to control his fear. Some students might feel worried about his fate.* **OL**

⭐ Viewing the Art

Richard Haas is well known for his 1970s trompe l'oeil paintings on a monumental scale. He painted illusionist architectural facades on the flat exteriors of buildings. Discuss the appearance of the building in the painting. Ask students to relate this painting to Tom's predicament. *(Students may say that the steep, stark buildings in the painting emphasize the danger of Tom's undertaking.)* **AS**

William Street at Night, 1981. Richard Haas.
Watercolor, 33 ¼ x 23 in.

Additional Support

Skills Practice

READING: Sequencing To monitor students' comprehension, review key events every few pages. Write events, including but not limited to the following, on a set of note cards:

• Tom's wife leaves for the movie.

• The paper blows out the window.

• Tom steps onto the ledge.

• Tom bends down to grasp the paper.

• Terror overcomes him when he sees the street below.

Review the story by choosing cards naming events that students have already read about. Also, shuffle the cards and have students arrange them in chronological order. **OL** he found, and the flat wooden edging provided a good gripping surface, a half inch or more deep, for the tips of his fingers.

Now, balanced easily and firmly, he stood on the ledge outside in the slight, chill breeze, eleven stories above the street, staring into his own lighted apartment, odd and different-seeming now.

First his right hand, then his left, he carefully shifted his finger-tip grip from the puttyless window edging to an indented row of bricks directly to his right. It was hard to take the first shuffling sideways step then—to make himself move—and the fear stirred in his stomach, but he did it, again by not allowing himself time to think. And now—with his chest, stomach, and the left side of his face pressed against the rough cold brick—his lighted apartment was suddenly gone, and it was much darker out here than he had thought.

Without pause he continued—right foot, left foot, right foot, left—his shoe soles shuffling and scraping along the rough stone, never lifting from it, fingers sliding along the exposed edging of brick. He moved on the balls of his feet, heels lifted slightly; the ledge was not quite as wide as he'd expected. But leaning slightly inward toward the face of the building and pressed against it, he could feel his balance firm and secure, and moving along the ledge was quite as easy as he had thought it would be. He could hear the buttons of his jacket scraping steadily along the rough bricks and feel them catch momentarily, tugging a little, at each mortared crack. He simply did not permit himself to look down, though the compulsion to do so never left him; nor did he allow himself actually to think. Mechanically—right foot, left foot, over and again—he shuffled along crabwise, watching the projecting wall ahead loom steadily closer. . . .

Then he reached it and, at the corner—he'd decided how he was going to pick up the paper—he lifted his right foot and placed it carefully on the ledge that ran along the projecting wall at a right angle to the ledge on which his other foot rested. And now, facing the building, he stood in the corner formed by the two walls, one foot on the ledging of each, a hand on the shoulder-high indentation of each wall. His forehead was pressed directly into the corner against the cold bricks, and now he carefully lowered first one hand, then the other, perhaps a foot farther down, to the next indentation in the rows of bricks.

Very slowly, sliding his forehead down the trough of the brick corner and bending his knees, he lowered his body toward the paper lying between his outstretched feet. Again he lowered his fingerholds another foot and bent his knees still more, thigh muscles **taut**, his forehead sliding and bumping down the brick V. Half squatting now, he dropped his left hand to the next indentation and then slowly reached with his right hand toward the paper between his feet.

He couldn't quite touch it, and his knees now were pressed against the wall; he could bend them no farther. But by ducking his head another inch lower, the top of his head now pressed against the bricks, he lowered his right shoulder and his fingers had the paper by a corner, pulling it loose. At the same instant he saw, between his legs and far below, Lexington Avenue stretched out for miles ahead.

He saw, in that instant, the Loew's theater sign, blocks ahead past Fiftieth Street; the miles of traffic signals, all green now; the lights of cars and street lamps; countless neon signs; and the moving black dots of people. And a violent instantaneous explosion of absolute terror roared through him. ⭐ For a motionless instant he saw himself externally—bent practically double, bal-

Reading Strategy Responding to Characters *Why does Tom feel a surge of terror when he actually grasps the yellow paper?* **R2**

Vocabulary

taut (tôt) *adj.* tense; tight

Reading Strategy Responding to Characters *What is your reaction to Tom's current situation?* **R1**

Teach

R2 Reading Strategy

Responding to Characters
Answer: *Tom gets his first glimpse of Lexington Avenue, eleven stories below, with its throbbing vitality from which Tom has excluded himself.* **OL**

★ Writer's Technique

Metaphor Say: A metaphor is a figure of speech that compares or equates two seemingly unlike things. Point out the sentence "And a violent instantaneous explosion of absolute terror roared through him." **Ask:** What purpose do these metaphors serve? (*The image of a violent explosion coupled with the word* roared *vividly conveys the suddenness and power of Tom's fear.*) **AS**

English Language Coach

Vivid Verbs Help English language learners understand the ways that Tom moves and reacts while on the window ledge. Write these phrases on the board: *he shuffled along crab-wise; he began to tremble violently;* (p. 169). *his body swayed outward;* (p. 170). *he slid his left foot;* (p. 171). *he saw himself striding, he stumbled; he staggered sideways;* (p. 172). For each of the verbs, ask one student to read the sentence aloud in which the verb appears, and another student to act it out. **EL**

Objectives
- To respond to characters (SE)
- To sequence events in a story (TWE)

Teach

⭐ Viewing the Art

Yvonne Jacquette was among a group of American painters who questioned the role of realism in the modern world and struggled to find worthwhile content. John L. Ward explains in his book *American Realist Painting 1945–1980* that in the late 1960s artists such as Jacquette chose objects for their formal possibilities and painted them in a neutral style. The interaction of large shapes and movements was stressed. Students may find the perspective a bit dizzying or frightening if they imagine looking down from the window ledge of a tall building as Tom does in the story. **AS**

"Flatiron Intersection", 1975. Yvonne Jacquette. Oil on canvas, 60 x 80 in. Private collection Courtesy Brooke Alexander, Inc., New York City.

anced on this narrow ledge, nearly half his body projecting out above the street far below—and he began to tremble violently, panic flaring through his mind and muscles, and he felt the blood rush from the surface of his skin.

In the fractional moment before horror paralyzed him, as he stared between his legs at that terrible length of street far beneath him, a fragment of his mind raised his body in a spasmodic jerk to an upright position again, but so violently that his head scraped hard against the wall, bouncing off it, and his body swayed outward to the knife edge of balance, and he very nearly plunged backward and fell. Then he was leaning far into the corner again, squeezing and pushing into it, not only his face but his chest and stomach, his back arching; and his

fingertips clung with all the pressure of his pulling arms to the shoulder-high half-inch indentation in the bricks.

He was more than trembling now; his whole body was racked with a violent shuddering beyond control, his eyes squeezed so tightly shut it was painful, though he was past awareness of that. His teeth were exposed in a frozen grimace, the strength draining like water from his knees and calves. It was extremely likely, he knew, that he would faint, to slump down along the wall, his face scraping, and then drop backward, a limp weight, out into nothing. And to save his life he concentrated on holding onto consciousness, drawing deliberate deep breaths of cold air into his lungs, fighting to keep his senses aware.

170 UNIT 1   THE SHORT STORY

Additional Support

Skills Practice

WRITING: Summarizing Most students will be familiar with the brief, enticing summaries on the backs of books, the purpose of which is to capture the interest of readers browsing through shelves and convince them to purchase the book. "Contents of the Dead Man's Pocket" is a suspenseful story with a powerful message about human values. Challenge students to write a suspenseful summary of the story to this point. Encourage students to look at summaries on the backs of books for models to use for their own summaries. **OL**

Then he knew that he would not faint, but he could not stop shaking nor open his eyes. He stood where he was, breathing deeply, trying to hold back the terror of the glimpse he had of what lay below him; and he knew he had made a mistake in not making himself stare down at the street, getting used to it and accepting it, when he had first stepped out onto the ledge.

It was impossible to walk back. He simply could not do it. He couldn't bring himself to make the slightest movement. The strength was gone from his legs; his shivering hands—numb, cold and desperately rigid—had lost all deftness; his easy ability to move and balance was gone. Within a step or two, if he tried to move, he knew that he would stumble clumsily and fall.

Seconds passed, with the chill faint wind pressing the side of his face, and he could hear the toned-down volume of the street traffic far beneath him. Again and again he slowed and then stopped, almost to silence; then presently, even this high, he would hear the click of the traffic signals and the subdued roar of the cars starting up again. During a lull in the street sounds, he called out. Then he was shouting *"Help!"* so loudly it rasped his throat. But he felt the steady pressure of the wind, moving between his face and the blank wall, snatch up his cries as he uttered them, and he knew they must sound directionless and distant. And he remembered how habitually, here in New York, he himself heard and ignored shouts in the night. If anyone heard him, there was no sign of it, and presently Tom Benecke knew he had to try moving; there was nothing else he could do.

Eyes squeezed shut, he watched scenes in his mind like scraps of motion-picture film—he could not stop them. He saw himself stumbling suddenly sideways as he crept along the ledge and saw his upper body arc outward, arms flailing. He saw a dangling shoestring caught between the ledge and the sole of his other shoe, saw a foot start to move, to be stopped with a jerk, and felt his balance leaving him. He saw himself falling with a terrible speed as his body revolved in the air, knees clutched tight to his chest, eyes squeezed shut, moaning softly.

Out of utter necessity, knowing that any of these thoughts might be reality in the very next seconds, he was slowly able to shut his mind against every thought but what he now began to do. With fear-soaked slowness, he slid his left foot an inch or two toward his own impossibly distant window. Then he slid the fingers of his shivering left hand a corresponding distance. For a moment he could not bring himself to lift his right foot from one ledge to the other; then he did it, and became aware of the harsh exhalation of air from his throat and realized that he was panting. As his right hand, then, began to slide along the brick edging, he was astonished to feel the yellow paper pressed to the bricks underneath his stiff fingers, and he uttered a terrible, abrupt bark that might have been a laugh or a moan. He opened his mouth and took the paper in his teeth, pulling it out from under his fingers.

By a kind of trick—by concentrating his entire mind on first his left foot, then his left hand, then the other foot, then the other hand—he was able to move, almost imperceptibly, trembling steadily, very nearly without thought. But he could feel the terrible strength of the **pent-up** horror on just the other side of the flimsy barrier he had erected in his mind; and he knew that if it broke through he would lose this thin artificial control of his body.

During one slow step he tried keeping his eyes closed; it made him feel safer, shutting him off a little from the fearful reality of where he was. Then a sudden rush of giddiness swept over him and he had to open his eyes wide, staring sideways at the cold rough brick and

---

Reading Strategy Responding to Characters *How does Tom try to cope with his fear?* **R**

Vocabulary

pent-up (pent′ up) *adj.* not expressed or released; held in

Big Idea Making Choices *What leads Tom to realize that he has no other choice but to "try moving"?* **BI**

JACK FINNEY **171**

Teach

L1 Literary Element

Symbol Answer: *Security and simple happiness* **OL**

L2 Literary Element

Symbol Answer: *The glass window symbolizes a barrier separating the safe, domestic world of the past from the dangerous, isolated one of the present.* **OL**

★ Writer's Technique

Portrayal of Time When Tom first glances back into his apartment and sees that his cigarette is still burning, he is shocked to realize how little time has actually passed since he stepped out onto the ledge. **Ask:** As you read this selection, what sense do you get of the passage of time in the story? What techniques contribute to the way that time seems to pass? *(Students may say that the dense and detailed descriptions of Tom's every movement and panicked thought give the impression that much time has gone by. They may point out that this selection is surprisingly long for portraying only a few minutes of a man's life.)* **AS**

---

angled lines of mortar, his cheek tight against the building. He kept his eyes open then, knowing that if he once let them flick outward, to stare for an instant at the lighted windows across the street, he would be past help.

He didn't know how many dozens of tiny sidling steps he had taken, his chest, belly and face pressed to the wall; but he knew the slender hold he was keeping on his mind and body was going to break. He had a sudden mental picture of his apartment on just the other side of this wall—warm, cheerful, incredibly spacious. And he saw himself striding through it, lying down on the floor on his back, arms spread wide, **reveling** in its unbelievable security. The impossible remoteness of this utter safety, the contrast between it and where he now stood, was more than he could bear. And the barrier broke then, and the fear of the awful height he stood on coursed through his nerves and muscles. A fraction of his mind knew he was going to fall, and he began taking rapid blind steps with no feeling of what he was doing, sidling with a clumsy desperate swiftness, fingers scrabbling along the brick, almost hopelessly resigned to the sudden backward pull and swift motion outward and down. Then his moving left hand slid onto not brick but sheer emptiness, an impossible gap in the face of the wall, and he stumbled.

His right foot smashed into his left ankle-bone; he staggered sideways, began falling, and the claw of his hand cracked against glass and wood, slid down it, and his finger tips were pressed hard on the puttyless edging of his window. His right hand smacked gropingly beside it as he fell to his knees; and, under the full weight and direct downward pull of his sagging body, the open window dropped shudderingly in its frame till it closed and his wrists struck the sill and were jarred off.

> **Literary Element** Symbol *As Tom thinks about his apartment, what does the apartment suddenly symbolize to him?* **L1**

> **Vocabulary**
> **reveling** (rev′ əl ing) *adj.* taking great pleasure

172 UNIT 1 THE SHORT STORY

For a single moment he knelt, knee bones against stone on the very edge of the ledge, body swaying and touching nowhere else, fighting for balance. Then he lost it, his shoulders plunging backward, and he flung his arms forward, his hands smashing against the window casing on either side; and—his body moving backward—his fingers clutched the narrow wood stripping of the upper pane.

For an instant he hung suspended between balance and falling, his finger tips pressed onto the quarter-inch wood strips. Then, with utmost delicacy, with a focused concentration of all his senses, he increased even further the strain on his finger tips hooked to these slim edgings of wood. Elbows slowly bending, he began to draw the full weight of his upper body forward, knowing that the instant his fingers slipped off these quarter-inch strips he'd plunge backward and be falling. Elbows imperceptibly bending, body shaking with the strain, the sweat starting from his forehead in great sudden drops, he pulled, his entire being and thought concentrated in his finger tips. Then suddenly, the strain slackened and ended, his chest touching the window sill, and he was kneeling on the ledge, his forehead pressed to the glass of the closed window.

Dropping his palms to the sill, he stared into his living room—at the red-brown davenport across the room, and a magazine he had left there; at the pictures on the walls and the gray rug; the entrance to the hallway; and at his papers, typewriter and desk, not two feet from his nose. A movement from his desk caught his eye and he saw that it was a thin curl of blue smoke; his cigarette, the ash long, was still burning in the ash tray where he'd left it—this was past all belief—only a few minutes before. ★

His head moved, and in faint reflection from the glass before him he saw the yellow paper clenched in his front teeth. Lifting a hand from the sill he took it from his mouth;

> **Literary Element** Symbol *What might the glass window symbolize?* **L2**

Additional Support

Skills Practice

GRAMMAR: Compatibility of Tenses Occasionally, a writer may have to shift tenses to show that one event precedes or follows another. Ask students to write sentences using compatible tenses of verbs, for example:

1. called, had heard *(I called to warn him, but they had already heard the alarm.)*

2. thawed, had frozen *(Although the water had frozen, it thawed quickly once the sun came out.)* **OL**

the moistened corner parted from the paper, and he spat it out.

For a moment, in the light from the living room, he stared wonderingly at the yellow sheet in his hand and then crushed it into the side pocket of his jacket.

He couldn't open the window. It had been pulled not completely closed, but its lower edge was below the level of the outside sill; there was no room to get his fingers underneath it. Between the upper sash and the lower was a gap not wide enough—reaching up, he tried—to get his fingers into; he couldn't push it open. The upper window panel, he knew from long experience, was impossible to move, frozen tight with dried paint.

Very carefully observing his balance, the finger tips of his left hand again hooked to the narrow stripping of the window casing, he drew back his right hand, palm facing the glass, and then struck the glass with the heel of his hand.

His arm rebounded from the pane, his body tottering, and he knew he didn't dare strike a harder blow. ★

But in the security and relief of his new position, he simply smiled; with only a sheet of glass between him and the room just before him, it was not possible that there wasn't a way past it. Eyes narrowing, he thought for a few moments about what to do. Then his eyes widened, for nothing occurred to him. But still he felt calm: the trembling, he realized, had stopped. At the back of his mind there still lay the thought that once he was again in his home, he could give release to his feelings. He actually would lie on the floor, rolling, clenching tufts of the rug in his hands. He would literally run across the room, free to move as he liked, jumping on the floor, testing and reveling in its absolute security, letting the relief flood through him, draining the fear from his mind and

> "he drew back his right hand, palm facing the glass, and then struck the glass with the heel of his hand."

body. His yearning for this was astonishingly intense, and somehow he understood that he had better keep this feeling at bay.

He took a half dollar from his pocket and struck it against the pane, but without any hope that the glass would break and with very little disappointment when it did not. After a few moments of thought he drew his leg up onto the ledge and picked loose the knot of his shoelace. He slipped off the shoe and, holding it across the instep, drew back his arm as far as he dared and struck the leather heel against the glass. The pane rattled, but he knew he'd been a long way from breaking it. His foot was cold and he slipped the shoe back on. He shouted again, experimentally, and then once more, but there was no answer.

The realization suddenly struck him that he might have to wait here till Clare came home, and for a moment the thought was funny. He could see Clare opening the front door, withdrawing her key from the lock, closing the door behind her and then glancing up to see him crouched on the other side of the window. He could see her rush across the room, face astounded and frightened, and hear himself shouting instructions: "Never mind how I got here! Just open the wind—" She couldn't open it, he remembered, she'd never been able to; she'd always had to call him. She'd have to get the building superintendent or a neighbor, and he pictured himself smiling and answering their questions as he climbed in. "I just wanted to get a breath of fresh air, so—"

> **Reading Strategy** Responding to Characters *How have your feelings toward Tom changed? Explain.* **R**

> **Big Idea** Making Choices *Why might Tom imagine himself downplaying the severity of his choice while speaking to Clare?* **BI**

JACK FINNEY **173**

R1 Reading Strategy

Responding to Characters
Answer: *Compared with the life-threatening situation Tom is in, a little burn scarcely matters. He probably is so charged with adrenaline that he may not even feel the burn.* **OL**

R2 Reading Strategy

Responding to Characters
Ask: What do you predict that Tom will do next, after he fails to attract attention by burning the letters? *(Answers will vary. Some students may say that Tom will try to gain people's attention some other way before giving up completely.)* **OL**

He couldn't possibly wait here till Clare came home. It was the second feature she'd wanted to see, and she'd left in time to see the first. She'd be another three hours or—He glanced at his watch; Clare had been gone eight minutes. It wasn't possible, but only eight minutes ago he had kissed his wife good-by. She wasn't even at the theater yet!

It would be four hours before she could possibly be home, and he tried to picture himself kneeling out here, finger tips hooked to these narrow strippings, while first one movie, preceded by a slow listing of credits, began, developed, reached its climax and then finally ended. There'd be a newsreel next, maybe, and then an animated cartoon, and then interminable scenes from coming pictures. And then, once more, the beginning of a full-length picture—while all the time he hung out here in the night.

He might possibly get to his feet, but he was afraid to try. Already his legs were cramped, his thigh muscles tired; his knees hurt, his feet felt numb and his hands were stiff. He couldn't possibly stay out here for four hours, or anywhere near it. Long before that his legs and arms would give out; he would be forced to try changing his position often—stiffly, clumsily, his coordination and strength gone—and he would fall. Quite realistically, he knew that he would fall; no one could stay out here on this ledge for four hours.

A dozen windows in the apartment building across the street were lighted. Looking over his shoulder, he could see the top of a man's head behind the newspaper he was reading; in another window he saw the blue-gray flicker of a television screen. No more than twenty-odd yards from his back were scores of people, and if just one of them would walk idly to his window and glance out. . . . For some moments he stared over his shoulder at the lighted rectangles, waiting. But no one appeared. The man reading his paper turned a page and then continued his reading. A figure passed another of the windows and was immediately gone.

In the inside pocket of his jacket he found a little sheaf of papers, and he pulled one out

and looked at it in the light from the living room. It was an old letter, an advertisement of some sort; his name and address, in purple ink, were on a label pasted to the envelope. Gripping one end of the envelope in his teeth, he twisted it into a tight curl. From his shirt pocket he brought out a book of matches. He didn't dare let go the casing with both hands but, with the twist of paper in his teeth, he opened the matchbook with his free hand; then he bent one of the matches in two without tearing it from the folder, its red-tipped end now touching the striking surface. With his thumb, he rubbed the red tip across the striking area.

He did it again, then again, and still again, pressing harder each time, and the match suddenly flared, burning his thumb. But he kept it alight, cupping the matchbook in his hand and shielding it with his body. He held the flame to the paper in his mouth till it caught. Then he snuffed out the match flame with his thumb and forefinger, careless of the burn, and replaced the book in his pocket. Taking the paper twist in his hand, he held it flame down, watching the flame crawl up the paper, till it flared bright. Then he held it behind him over the street, moving it from side to side, watching it over his shoulder, the flame flickering and guttering in the wind.

There were three letters in his pocket and he lighted each of them, holding each till the flame touched his hand and then dropping it to the street below. At one point, watching over his shoulder while the last of the letters burned, he saw the man across the street put down his paper and stand—even seeming, to Tom, to glance toward his window. But when he moved, it was only to walk across the room and disappear from sight. **R2**

There were a dozen coins in Tom Benecke's pocket and he dropped them, three or four at a time. But if they struck anyone, or if anyone noticed their falling, no one connected them with their source, and no one glanced upward.

Reading Strategy Responding to Characters *What does this action suggest about Tom's state?* **R1**

Additional Support

Skills Practice

LITERARY ELEMENT: Point of View Point of view is an important element in this story. Because the events are related by a narrator who describes all of Tom's thoughts and feelings as they occur, the readers exist in the moment with him and feel the strong suspense of not knowing what will happen next or whether or not Tom will make it to safety. Have students write a short piece after reading to the end of page 174, imagining that the man in the apartment across the street looks out of his window and sees Tom on the ledge. Ask students to write an ending for the story told from the point of view of this man. **OL**

His arms had begun to tremble from the steady strain of clinging to this narrow perch, and he did not know what to do now and was terribly frightened. Clinging to the window stripping with one hand, he again searched his pockets. But now—he had left his wallet on his dresser when he'd changed clothes—there was nothing left but the yellow sheet. It occurred to him irrelevantly that his death on the sidewalk below would be an eternal mystery; the window closed—why, how, and from where could he have fallen? No one would be able to identify his body for a time, either—the thought was somehow unbearable and increased his fear. All they'd find in his pockets would be the yellow sheet. Contents of the dead man's pockets, he thought, *one sheet of paper bearing penciled notations—incomprehensible.*

He understood fully that he might actually be going to die; his arms, maintaining his balance on the ledge, were trembling steadily now. And it occurred to him then with all the force of a revelation that, if he fell, all he was ever going to have out of life he would then, abruptly, have had. Nothing, then, could ever be changed; and nothing more—no least experience or pleasure—could ever be added to his life. He wished, then, that he had not allowed his wife to go off by herself tonight—and on similar nights. He thought of all the evenings he had spent away from her, working; and he regretted them. He thought wonderingly of his fierce ambition and of the direction his life had taken; he thought of the hours he'd spent by himself, filling the yellow sheet that had brought him out here. *Contents of the dead man's pockets,* he thought with sudden fierce anger, *a wasted life.*

He was simply not going to cling here till he slipped and fell; he told himself that now. There was one last thing he could try; he had been aware of it for some moments, refusing to think about it, but now he faced it. Kneeling here on the ledge, the finger tips of one hand pressed to the narrow strip of wood, he could, he knew, draw his other hand back a yard perhaps, fist clenched tight, doing it very slowly till he sensed the outer limit of balance, then, as hard as he was able from the distance, he could drive his fist forward against the glass. If it broke, his fist smashing through, he was safe; he might cut himself badly, and probably would, but with his arm inside the room, he would be secure. But if the glass did not break, the rebound, flinging his arm back, would topple him off the ledge. He was certain of that.

He tested his plan. The fingers of his left hand clawlike on the little stripping, he drew back his other fist until his body began teetering backward. But he had no leverage now— he could feel that there would be no force to

Paper Falling, 2003. ⭐
Chris Rogers.

JACK FINNEY **175**

Teach

B1 Big Idea

Making Choices
Answer: *He figures that a few more guaranteed seconds of life are better than immediate death.* **OL**

R Reading Strategy

Responding to Characters
Answer: *Tom's wife and marriage are most important to him. For most students, this will cause them to have a positive opinion of Tom.* **OL**

L Literary Element

Symbol Answer: *The yellow paper may symbolize concerns that are less important than his marriage and the pleasant company of his wife.* **OL**

CheckPoint

Use the CheckPoint questions on Presentation Plus! to check students' mastery of the selection. These questions can be used with interactive response keypads for immediate student feedback.

---

his swing—and he moved his fist slowly forward till he rocked forward on his knees again and could sense that his swing would carry its greatest force. Glancing down, however, measuring the distance from his fist to the glass, he saw that it was less than two feet.

It occurred to him that he could raise his arm over his head, to bring it down against the glass. But, experimenting in slow motion, he knew it would be an awkward girl-like blow without the force of a driving punch, and not nearly enough to break the glass.

Facing the window, he had to drive a blow from the shoulder, he knew now, at a distance of less than two feet; and he did not know whether it would break through the heavy glass. It might; he could picture it happening, he could feel it in the nerves of his arm. And it might not; he could feel that too—feel his fist striking this glass and being instantaneously flung back by the unbreaking pane, feel the fingers of his other hand breaking loose, nails scraping along the casing as he fell.

He waited, arm drawn back, fist balled, but in no hurry to strike; this pause, he knew, might be an extension of his life. And to live even a few seconds longer, he felt, even out here on this ledge in the night, was infinitely better than to die a moment earlier than he had to. His arm grew tired, and he brought it down and rested it.

Then he knew that it was time to make the attempt. He could not kneel here hesitating indefinitely till he lost all courage to act, waiting till he slipped off the ledge. Again he drew back his arm, knowing this time that he would not bring it down till he struck. His elbow protruding over Lexington Avenue far below, the fingers of his other hand pressed down bloodlessly tight against the narrow stripping, he waited, feeling the sick tenseness and terrible excitement building. It grew and swelled toward the moment of action, his nerves tautening.

> **Big Idea** Making Choices *Express in your own words why Tom chooses to pause before striking the glass with his fist.* **B1**

He thought of Clare—just a wordless, yearning thought—and then drew his arm back just a bit more, fist so tight his fingers pained him, and knowing he was going to do it. Then with full power, with every last scrap of strength he could bring to bear, he shot his arm forward toward the glass, and he said, *"Clare!"*

He heard the sound, felt the blow, felt himself falling forward, and his hand closed on the living-room curtains, the shards and fragments of glass showering onto the floor. And then, kneeling there on the ledge, an arm thrust into the room up to the shoulder, he began picking away the protruding slivers and great wedges of glass from the window frame, tossing them in onto the rug. And, as he grasped the edges of the empty window frame and climbed into his home, he was grinning in triumph.

He did not lie down on the floor or run through the apartment, as he had promised himself; even in the first few moments it seemed to him natural and normal that he should be where he was. He simply turned to his desk, pulled the crumpled yellow sheet from his pocket and laid it down where it had been, smoothing it out; then he absently laid a pencil across it to weight it down. He shook his head wonderingly, and turned to walk toward the closet.

There he got out his topcoat and hat and, without waiting to put them on, opened the front door and stepped out, to go find his wife. He turned to pull the door closed and warm air from the hall rushed through the narrow opening again. As he saw the yellow paper, the pencil flying, scooped off the desk and, unimpeded by the glassless window, sail out into the night and out of his life, Tom Benecke burst into laughter and then closed the door behind him. ∾

> **Reading Strategy** Responding to Characters *What do you think is most important to Tom? How does this affect your opinion of him?* **R**

> **Literary Element** Symbol *What do you think that piece of paper has come to symbolize to Tom?* **L**

Additional Support

Skills Practice

WRITING: Creating Suspense

Finney uses chronological order throughout this story. This helps the reader understand precisely what is happening when and is an excellent way to create suspense. Have students choose a topic that contains an element of suspense and write a few paragraphs describing the sequence of events. Suggest that they use words that denote time order, such as *before, then, next, after, meanwhile, yesterday, later, now,* and *soon.* **OL**

RESPONDING AND THINKING CRITICALLY

Respond

1. Which part of the story did you react to most strongly? Explain.

Recall and Interpret

2. (a)Why does Tom decide not to go to the movies with Clare? (b)What do you learn about Tom from this decision?

3. (a)After Tom begins work, what happens to interrupt him, and what does he decide to do? (b)What rules does he make up for himself, and why?

4. (a)Briefly summarize Tom's risky adventure. (b)What lesson do you think this adventure teaches him?

Analyze and Evaluate

5. (a)At the beginning of the story, what did Tom do that might lead someone to judge him as untruthful? b)What might he have done to be more honest and fair?

6. (a)What inferences can you draw about Tom, based on his decision to retrieve the paper? (b)Do you think his decision is realistic or does the author create an unbelievable situation? Explain.

7. (a)For about how long was Tom out on the ledge? (b)Do you think that the author does a good job of holding the reader's attention and making that amount of time seem much longer, due to suspense? Explain.

Connect

8. **Big Idea** **Making Choices** What message is the author presenting about the choices people sometimes make regarding priorities in life? Do you agree with the message? Explain.

YOU'RE THE CRITIC: Point/Counterpoint

Allegory or Fantasy?

People often disagree about Finney's purpose for writing. Read these two summaries of the opposing viewpoints.

Many critics of Finney's novel The Body Snatchers *interpreted the work as an allegory, a symbolic literary work in which the characters, settings, and events stand for things that are larger than themselves. The purpose of such an allegory is to teach a moral lesson.*

Some critics and readers scoff at the idea of deep, allegorical intent in Finney's work. They say that Finney's stories are just fun reading—suspenseful, thought-provoking fantasies. Finney was quite modest about his stories, saying that he just wanted to write about ordinary people's responses to extraordinary situations. Furthermore, he promoted the view that his story was meant purely as entertainment.

Group Activity Discuss the following questions. Refer to the critics' viewpoints and cite evidence from "Contents of the Dead Man's Pocket."

1. Do you think that Finney intended his story to be an allegory or is it simply entertainment? Explain.

2. Do you think that "Contents of the Dead Man's Pocket" fits the description of Finney's writing as an ordinary person's reaction to an extraordinary situation?

JACK FINNEY **177**

Assess

1. Students may say that they reacted most strongly to Tom's terror on the ledge.

2. (a) He wants to work on his project. (b) He is ambitious and determined to succeed.

3. (a) The piece of paper flies out the window, and he decides to retrieve it. (b) He tells himself not to look down or think too much. He is trying to keep calm.

4. (a) He edges along the ledge, almost falling. He tries to draw people's attention, but has no luck. When he gets back to the window, he cannot open it and must smash it. When he gets back inside, the yellow paper flies away again. (b) Not to risk his life for his career

5. (a) He tells his wife that he has to work, when he really does not have to finish his project that night. (b) He might have explained to her why the project was so important.

6. (a) He is confident, ambitious, and willing to take risks. He is unwise in weighing risks with benefits and in judging what is most important. (b) Some might think that it is realistic that an ambitious person might fool himself into taking such a terrible risk.

7. (a) The action lasts for about eight minutes. (b) Students will probably say that the author built suspense effectively.

8. People sometimes give greater value than necessary to work and other pursuits; their priorities get mixed up. The real value in Tom's life is his marriage. Students will probably agree.

You're the Critic

1. Students should choose a viewpoint and support it with evidence from the story.

2. Students will probably say that it fits Finney's description. Tom, an ordinary man, faces an extraordinary situation when he ventures out on the window ledge.

Assess

Literary Element

1. The research he needs to get ahead; his "ticket"

2. The ordinary comforts of the life that he risked

3. Evidence of his wasted life and mixed-up priorities

4. Something that can easily be replaced; something of far less value than his marriage and his wife

Review: Motivation

1. To enjoy his wife's company

2. To complete his project and get ahead at work

3. To get his project to his boss as soon as possible

4. He did not want to have to redo all of his research.

5. To stay calm

6. To enjoy a few more seconds of guaranteed life

Reading Strategy

1. Some will disapprove of his apparent priorities. Some may see him as normal.

2. Many will say they were not surprised, because Tom was so determined to move ahead in the company.

3. Many will say that they felt better about Tom after he re-evaluated his priorities.

Literary Element Symbol

A **symbol** is an object, person or idea that represents something else, usually an abstract concept. For example, on the literal level, a flag is a piece of cloth. However, a flag can also be the symbol of a nation. In this story, several objects are used as symbols. Write a brief description of what the following items symbolized in this story.

1. the yellow piece of paper (at the beginning of the story)

2. the burning cigarette, as Tom saw it through the window

3. the contents of the dead man's pocket, as envisioned by Tom in a police report about his death

4. the yellow piece of paper (at the end of the story)

Review: Motivation

As you learned on page 97, a character's **motivation** is the stated or implied reason or cause for that character's actions.

Partner Activity Meet with another classmate to discuss what motivates Tom at different stages within the story. Use a "clock" diagram like the one below to jot down your thoughts.

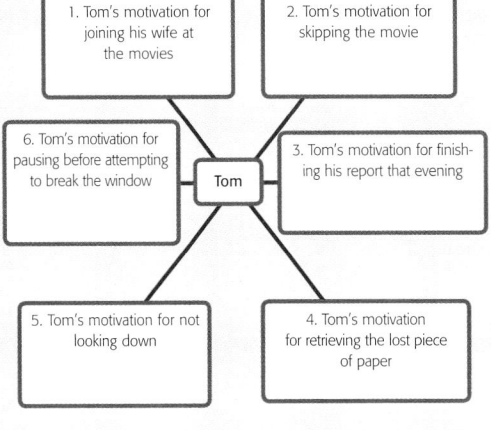

1. Tom's motivation for joining his wife at the movies

2. Tom's motivation for skipping the movie

3. Tom's motivation for finishing his report that evening

4. Tom's motivation for retrieving the lost piece of paper

5. Tom's motivation for not looking down

6. Tom's motivation for pausing before attempting to break the window

Tom

Reading Strategy Responding to Characters

When you **respond to characters** as you read, you are likely to get more from your reading. By paying attention to how characters make you feel, what questions they create for you, and how they might surprise you as you read, you become more engaged in your reading. Refer to the notes that you took about the characters as you read to answer the following questions.

1. How did you feel about Tom Benecke at the beginning of the story?

2. Were you surprised by Tom Benecke's decision to go after the yellow piece of paper? Explain.

3. How did you feel about Tom Benecke at the end of the story? Did your opinion of him change?

Vocabulary Practice

Practice with Analogies Choose the word that best completes each analogy.

1. knot : convoluted :: noose :
   a. tight b. looped c. stretched

2. tightrope : taut :: noodle :
   a. safe b. delicate c. slack

3. improvised : rehearsed :: temporary :
   a. voluntary b. permanent c. brief

4. pent-up : held in :: soldier :
   a. warrior b. war c. weapon

5. reveling : pleasure :: weeping :
   a. sadness b. crying c. tears

Academic Vocabulary

Here are two vocabulary words from the list on page R82.

document (dok′yə mənt) *n.* a printed record

estimate (es′tə mit) *n.* an educated guess, based on approximated numbers or volumes

Practice and Apply

1. Why was Tom's **document** so important to him?

2. What types of **estimates** appeared on it?

Vocabulary

1. b **2.** c **3.** b **4.** a **5.** a

Academic Vocabulary

1. It represented hours of research, and he felt that it would help him get ahead at work.

2. Estimates of types of customers, buying habits, and related information

Writing About Literature

Analyze Title Authors often give hints about the theme, or message about life, that they want to communicate in their written work. What hints about the theme appear in the title of this story? Write a brief essay exploring how the theme and title of this story are related.

To organize your thoughts for the essay, use a cluster web like the one shown below.

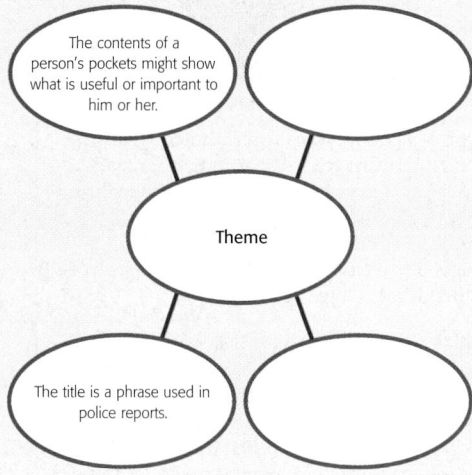

After you complete your draft, have a peer read it and suggest revisions. Then proofread and edit your work for errors in spelling, grammar, and punctuation.

Performing

To let the reader understand Tom's predicament and his character, Finney writes what Tom is thinking as he gropes his way along the ledge. However, if this story, like many of Finney's other works, was adapted into a movie, the character playing Tom would have to speak his thoughts aloud for the audience to gain the same insight. Write a first-person monologue for Tom, based on part of the story. Deliver it to the class, using facial expressions and a tone of voice appropriate to Tom's precarious situation on the ledge. Remember: Don't look down!!

Literature Online **Web Activities** For eFlashcards, Selection Quick Checks, and other Web activities, go to www.glencoe.com.

Finney's Language and Style

Using Introductory Phrases In this story, Jack Finney uses many introductory prepositional and participial phrases to describe Tom's actions and emotions. An **introductory phrase** is a phrase at the beginning of a sentence. A **prepositional phrase** consists of a preposition, its object, and any modifiers of the object. A prepositional phrase can function as an adjective or an adverb, depending on what it modifies. A **participial phrase** contains a participle and any complements or modifiers necessary to complete its meaning. For example:

> **Introductory Prepositional Phrase:** *For many seconds* he believed he was going to abandon the yellow sheet, that there was nothing else to do.

> **Introductory Participial Phrase:** *Dropping his palms to the sill,* he stared into his living room. . . .

Introductory Phrase	Type
At the little living-room desk . . .	Prepositional
Turning, he saw . . .	Participial
At his desk again, . . .	Prepositional
By a kind of instinct, . . .	Prepositional
Half squatting now, . . .	Participial

Activity On a sheet of paper, combine each of the following sentence pairs by changing one of the sentences into an introductory prepositional or participial phrase.

1. Tom waved to Clare. He wished he could go with her.

2. Tom sidled across the ledge. His heart was in his mouth.

3. Tom took deep breaths. He was afraid that he would faint.

4. Tom felt the rough bricks. He pressed his face to the wall.

5. A man was reading. He was in a nearby apartment.

Revising Check

Introductory Phrases Revise the essay that you wrote regarding the title of this story. Alter some of the sentences by changing them to include an introductory prepositional or participial phrase.

JACK FINNEY **179**

Assess

Writing About Literature

Students' essays should:

• identify the title of the story

• identify the phrase as one that Tom thinks about and that often appears on police accident reports

• relate the phrase to Tom's revelation of his "wasted life" or mixed-up priorities

• relate Tom's revelation to Finney's message about the important values in life

• contain at least one sentence beginning with a prepositional or participial phrase

Performing

Students' monologues should:

• reflect story details accurately

• be "in character" relative to Tom's background, motivation, traits, and situation

• use appropriate facial expressions and tone of voice

Finney's Language and Style

Possible responses:

1. Wishing that he could go with her, Tom waved to Clare.

2. With his heart in his mouth, Tom sidled across the ledge.

3. Afraid that he would faint, Tom took deep breaths.

4. Pressing his face to the wall, Tom felt the rough bricks.

5. In a nearby apartment, a man was reading.

Literature Online

Web Activities Have students access the Web site for interactive activities that will help them assess their understanding of the selection.

Focus

Author Search To expand students' appreciation of Luisa Valenzuela, have them access the Web site for additional information and resources.

The Censors

MEET LUISA VALENZUELA

As the political situation in her homeland grew increasingly violent, Luisa Valenzuela turned to writing to cope. One of the most recognized Latin American writers in the United States, Valenzuela writes novels and short stories that expose the flaws and injustices of society through satire and wit.

Luisa Valenzuela was born in Argentina to a well-respected physician and a writer. She began her career as a journalist working for magazines and newspapers in Buenos Aires. When she was just seventeen, Valenzuela wrote and published her first story. In 1966 her first novel, *Hay que sonreír* (translated as *Clara*), was published. She was awarded a Fulbright fellowship in 1969 to participate in the prestigious International Writers Program at the University of Iowa. During the 1970s, Argentina's economy deteriorated and the political situation in the country became very volatile. According to Valenzuela, the political atmosphere in Argentina pushed her to leave her home: "I decided to leave in order not to fall into self-censorship. Exile may be devastating, but perspective and separation sharpen the aim."

> "[Luisa Valenzuela] wears an opulent, baroque crown, but her feet are naked."
>
> —Carlos Fuentes

A Unique Style Known for her experimental style, Valenzuela blends the ordinary with the fantastical. Critics often note her ability to play with words and language. Many critics also classify her work as "magical realism,"

a type of fiction, typically associated with Latin American writers, that inserts fantastic events into a very believable, ordinary reality. However, Valenzuela seeks to push the boundaries of the genre. She says that "Magical realism was a beautiful resting place, but the thing is to go forward."

Politics and Society Valenzuela's most popular novel, *The Lizard's Tail*, details a sorcerer's rise, fall, and return to power. The book gives voice to the political upheaval and social change that took place in Argentina during the 1970s. Using dark humor, Valenzuela offers a powerful satire of government censorship and the difficult circumstances of war. In stories that are equal parts compelling and humorous, Valenzuela identifies the absurdities of society and exposes the shameful operations of totalitarian regimes. As she says, "If the country is to heal, each and every shadow of the dark times has to come out into the open."

Achievements and Endeavors Valenzuela has published numerous novels and collections of short stories, and many of her works have been translated into English, French, and other languages. Currently, she teaches creative writing in New York. She frequently returns home to Buenos Aires.

Luisa Valenzuela was born in 1938.

Author Search For more about Luisa Valenzuela, go to www.glencoe.com.

180 UNIT 1   THE SHORT STORY

Selection Skills

Literary Elements

The Censors

Writing Skills/Grammar

• Satire (SE pp. 181, 184, 185)
• Tone (TWE p. 182)

Reading Skills

Vocabulary Skills

• Respond to Theme (SE p. 185)
• Intervening Prepositional Phrases (TWE p. 182)

• Analyzing Cause-and-Effect Relationships (SE pp. 181, 184, 185)

• Word Parts (SE p. 185)
• Usage (TWE pp. 184)

Connecting to the Story

A story of censors and censorship could take place almost anywhere and at any time. Before you read the story, think about the following questions:

- Do you take freedom of speech for granted?
- Do you think other people take freedom of speech for granted?

Building Background

Luisa Valenzuela does not name a specific city, country, or time in which "The Censors" takes place. However, Valenzuela often writes about the political struggles and repressive governments in Argentina in the twentieth century. "The Censors" was first published in 1976, the year that a military faction overthrew Argentina's government. The new government severely restricted constitutional liberties and systematically began to eliminate any opposition to their new regime. Innocent citizens as well as dissidents were tortured and killed. Some thirteen-thousand to fifteen-thousand citizens were killed in the *Guerra Sucia*—the "Dirty War," as it came to be called.

Setting Purposes for Reading

Big Idea Making Choices

As you read "The Censors," think about the choices that Juan makes in order to "protect" himself and Mariana from the censors.

Literary Element Satire

Satire is the use of humor or wit to ridicule institutions or humanity with the goal of entertaining or causing change. Recognizing satire can help you discern a persuasive argument that is presented as a humorous or witty portrayal. As you read, try to determine what Valenzuela is satirizing and what she might like to change.

- See Literary Terms Handbook, p. R15.

Literature Online **Interactive Literary Elements Handbook** To review or learn more about the literary elements, go to www.glencoe.com.

Reading Strategy Analyzing Cause-and-Effect Relationships

In life and in literature, one event often has some sort of impact upon another event. Knowing how to **analyze cause and effect** can help you better understand both the relationships between those events and the literary work as a whole.

....

Reading Tip: Identifying Sequence Use a graphic organizer to help you determine the order of events.

Cause
Juan sends a letter to Mariana.

↓

Effect
Juan worries that his letter will bring harm to Mariana.

Effect

↓   ↓   ↓   ↓

Effect
Juan becomes a censor.

Effect

Effect

Effect

Vocabulary

irreproachable (ir′ i prō chə bəl) *adj.* free from blame or criticism; faultless; p. 182 *The boy's kind behavior was irreproachable.*

albeit (ôl bē′ it) *conj.* although; even if; p. 183 *I like the fall, albeit I am always eager for spring.*

ulterior (ul tēr′ ē ər) *adj.* intentionally withheld or concealed; p. 183 *Sam had an ulterior motive for not wanting to tell the truth.*

staidness (stād′ nəs) *n.* the state or quality of being serious, steady, or conservative in character; p. 183 *The stern old woman had a certain staidness about her.*

subversive (sub vur′ siv) *adj.* seeking to weaken, destroy, or overthrow; p. 184 *Subversive people wished to overthrow the government.*

Focus

Summary

Juan thinks he is outsmarting the system by taking a government job as a censor. He applies himself so diligently to his work that no one would ever guess he is merely biding his time to intercept a letter he himself wrote. But his life takes an unexpected twist. Zeal and duty win out over his original mission, and Juan, the perfect censor, seals his own fate.

V Vocabulary

Vocabulary File Say: Add these words and definitions to your vocabulary file. For each word, include a sentence that gives you an example of how to use the word. **OL** Students with English language needs should include the pronunciations of these words in their files. **EL**

Literary Elements Have students access the Web site to improve their understanding of satire.

OBJECTIVES
In studying this selection, you will focus on the following:
- identifying and understanding satire

- analyzing cause-and-effect relationships
- writing to respond to theme

Selection Resources

Print Materials
- Unit 1 Resources (Fast File), pp. 64–66
- Leveled Vocabulary Development, p. 14
- Selection and Unit Assessments, pp. 29–30
- Selection Quick Checks, p. 15

Transparencies
- Bellringer Options Transparencies:
  Selection Focus Transparency 11
  Daily Language Practice Transparency 17
- Literary Elements Transparency 90

Technology
- TeacherWorks Plus™ CD-ROM
- StudentWorks Plus™ CD-ROM
- Presentation Plus!™ CD-ROM
- Literature Online, glencoe.com
- Online Student Edition, mhln.com
- ExamView® Assessment Suite CD-ROM
- Vocabulary PuzzleMaker CD-ROM
- Listening Library, disc 1 track 15

Teach

Big Idea

Making Choices

Say: Think about the following question as you read. What is Juan's initial attitude toward the censors? *(At first, Juan believes the censors employed by the government try so hard to find treachery that they find what does not exist. In an attempt to sabotage the system, he becomes a censor.)* **OL**

L Literary Element

Tone Remind students that tone is the writer's attitude toward the subject. One way that a writer communicates tone is through word choice and descriptive language. **Ask:** What phrases create an ominous tone? *("Poor Juan!" "they caught him with his guard down"; "one of fate's dirty tricks"; "a feeling you can't trust"; "without thinking twice")* **OL**

Readability Scores

Dale-Chall: 6.0
DRP: 62
Lexile: 1170

THE CENSORS

Luisa Valenzuela

Postal Montage. Natalie Racioppa.

Poor Juan! One day they caught him with his guard down before he could even realize that what he had taken as a stroke of luck was really one of fate's dirty tricks. These things happen the minute you're careless, as one often is. Juancito[1] let happiness—a feeling you can't trust—get the better of him when he received from a confidential source Mariana's new address in Paris and knew that she hadn't forgotten him. Without thinking twice, he sat down at his table and wrote her a letter. *The* letter that now keeps his mind off his job during the day and won't let him sleep at night (what had he scrawled, what had he put on that sheet of paper he sent to Mariana?).

Juan knows there won't be a problem with the letter's contents, that it's **irreproachable**, harmless. But what about the rest? He knows that they examine, sniff, feel, and read between the lines of each and every letter, and check its tiniest comma and most accidental stain. He knows that all letters pass from hand to hand and go through all sorts of tests in the huge censorship offices and that, in the end, very few continue on their way. Usually it takes months, even years, if there aren't any snags; all this time the freedom, maybe even the life, of both sender and receiver is in jeopardy. And that's why Juan's so troubled: thinking that something might happen to Mariana because of his letters. Of all people, Mariana, who must finally feel safe there where she always dreamt she'd live. But he knows that the *Censor's Secret*

---

1. *Juancito* (wan sē′ tō)

Big Idea Making Choices *Considering the title of the story, why do you think Juan's choice to write a letter might be significant?* **BI**

182 UNIT 1 THE SHORT STORY

Vocabulary

irreproachable (ir′ i prō chə bəl) *adj.* free from blame or criticism; faultless

---

Additional Support

Leveled Reading An adapted version of this selection is available on page 36 of *Jamestown Literature: An Adapted Reader*, grade 10.

Skills Practice

GRAMMAR: Intervening Prepositional Phrases A verb must agree with its subject. If a prepositional phrase appears between the subject and the verb, the verb must still agree with its subject, not the object of the preposition. Have students rewrite each sentence, underlining the simple subject and the verb and enclosing the intervening prepositional phrase in parentheses.

1. Juan's passion for censoring letters takes over his life. (*Juan's passion (for censoring letters) takes over his life.*)

2. His goal during the early weeks is to help Mariana. (*His goal (during the early weeks) is to help Mariana.*) **OL**

Businessmen Reading the Fine Print.
Bruno Budrovic.

Command operates all over the world and cashes in on the discount in air fares; there's nothing to stop them from going as far as that hidden Paris neighborhood, kidnapping Mariana, and returning to their cozy homes, certain of having fulfilled their noble mission.

Well, you've got to beat them to the punch, do what everyone tries to do: sabotage the machinery, throw sand in its gears, get to the bottom of the problem so as to stop it.

This was Juan's sound plan when he, like many others, applied for a censor's job—not because he had a calling or needed a job: no, he applied simply to intercept his own letter, a consoling **albeit** unoriginal idea. He was hired immediately, for each day more and more censors are needed and no one would bother to check on his references.

Ulterior motives couldn't be overlooked by the *Censorship Division*, but they needn't be too strict with those who applied. They knew how hard it would be for the poor guys to find the letter they wanted and even if they did, what's a letter or two when the new censor would snap up so many others? That's how Juan managed to join the *Post Office's Censorship Division*, with a certain goal in mind.

The building had a festive air on the outside that contrasted with its inner **staidness**.

LUISA VALENZUELA **183**

183

Teach

L1 Literary Element

Satire Answer: *Valenzuela ridicules the corruption of the government by showing how the Post Office's Censorship Division rewards employees for currying favor with a repressive authority.* **OL**

R Reading Strategy

Analyzing Cause-and-Effect Relationships

Answer: *Juan's superiors reward him for censoring the most harmless of letters, even though his actions will bring his fellow citizens great harm.* **OL**

L2 Literary Element

Satire Answer: *In reality, Juan's work is not that demanding. Instances that require him to be truly discerning are rare, and he often detects threatening material when it actually is not present.* **OL**

BI Big Idea

Making Choices

Answer: *By the time Juan and his letter cross paths again, the job of finding hidden messages has so changed him that he does not even think twice about censoring his own innocent letter.* **OL**

Little by little, Juan was absorbed by his job, and he felt at peace since he was doing everything he could to get his letter for Mariana. He didn't even worry when, in his first month, he was sent to *Section K* where envelopes are very carefully screened for explosives.

It's true that on the third day, a fellow worker had his right hand blown off by a letter, but the division chief claimed it was sheer negligence on the victim's part. Juan and the other employees were allowed to go back to their work, though feeling less secure. After work, one of them tried to organize a strike to demand higher wages for unhealthy work, but Juan didn't join in; after thinking it over, he reported the man to his superiors and thus got promoted.

You don't form a habit by doing something once, he told himself as he left his boss's office. And when he was transferred to *Section J*, where letters are carefully checked for poison dust, he felt he had climbed a rung in the ladder.

By working hard, he quickly reached *Section E* where the job became more interesting, for he could now read and analyze the letters' contents. Here he could even hope to get hold of his letter, which, judging by the time that had elapsed, had gone through the other sections and was probably floating around in this one.

Soon his work became so absorbing that his noble mission blurred in his mind. Day after day he crossed out whole paragraphs in red ink, pitilessly chucking many letters into the censored basket. These were horrible days when he was shocked by the subtle and conniving ways employed by people to pass on **subversive** messages; his

---

| **Literary Element** | Satire *How does Valenzuela use satire here?* **L1** |

| **Vocabulary** |

subversive (sub vur′ siv) *adj.* seeking to weaken, destroy, or overthrow

---

instincts were so sharp that he found behind a simple "the weather's unsettled" or "prices continue to soar" the wavering hand of someone secretly scheming to overthrow the Government.

His zeal brought him swift promotion. We don't know if this made him happy. Very few letters reached him in *Section B*—only a handful passed the other hurdles—so he read them over and over again, passed them under a magnifying glass, searched for microprint with an electronic microscope, and tuned his sense of smell so that he was beat by the time he made it home. He'd barely manage to warm up his soup, eat some fruit, and fall into bed, satisfied with having done his duty. Only his darling mother worried, but she couldn't get him back on the right track. She'd say, though it wasn't always true: Lola called, she's at the bar with the girls, they miss you, they're waiting for you. Or else she'd leave a bottle of red wine on the table. But Juan wouldn't overdo it: any distraction could make him lose his edge and the perfect censor had to be alert, keen, attentive, and sharp to nab cheats. He had a truly patriotic task, both self-denying and uplifting.

His basket for censored letters became the best fed as well as the most cunning basket in the whole *Censorship Division*. He was about to congratulate himself for having finally discovered his true mission, when his letter to Mariana reached his hands. Naturally, he censored it without regret. And just as naturally, he couldn't stop them from executing him the following morning, another victim of his devotion to his work. ✎

| **Reading Strategy** | Analyzing Cause-and-Effect Relationships *What do the cause and effect in this sentence reveal about Juan's superiors?* **R** |

| **Literary Element** | Satire *Explain what is satirical in this passage.* **L2** |

| **Big Idea** | Making Choices *How does Juan's choice affect his final outcome?* **BI** |

Additional Support

Skills Practice

VOCABULARY: Usage Tell students that by reading and writing they will learn how to use words extensively in the right context. The word *ulterior*, for example, may be defined as "intentionally withheld or concealed; hidden," but a person playing hide-and-seek is not ulterior. In "The Censors," *ulterior* modifies *motive*, or intention, and this is its most common use. Another word from "The Censors" is *irreproachable*. A painter's work habits may be irreproachable (faultless); a perfectly painted wall is not. Have students use the words *ulterior*, *irreproachable*, and *subversive* correctly in sentences. **OL**

RESPONDING AND THINKING CRITICALLY

Respond

1. (a)What feelings did you have about Juan at the end of the story? (b)Did your feelings about him change during the course of the story? Explain.

Recall and Interpret

2. (a)What does Juan fear will happen to Mariana as a result of his letter? (b)What does this tell you about the kind of government Juan lives under?

3. (a)What is Juan's "unoriginal idea"? (b)Why are "more and more censors" needed, making it easy for Juan to get hired?

Analyze and Evaluate

4. (a)What parts of this story seem logical and believable to you? (b)Are there any parts that are unbelievable? Use details from the story to support your answer.

5. What does Valenzuela achieve by keeping the tone of the story light and casual?

Connect

6. | Big Idea | **Making Choices** Whose choices, Juan's or the government's, do you think had a greater impact on the outcome of the story? Explain.

LITERARY ANALYSIS

Literary Element Satire

Humor—a common element of **satire**—can often be persuasive as well as entertaining because it is less likely to alienate people who might initially disagree.

1. How does Juan's transformation into the perfect censor become the "punch line" for this satire? Explain.

2. Is the author's satire aimed more at the government or at individuals like Juan?

Writing About Literature

Respond to Theme Valenzuela uses satire to make a statement about a government's control over the lives of its citizens. Write a brief essay in which you identify and discuss the theme of "The Censors." Include elements from the story that are related to the theme, as well as any impressions or ideas that struck you as you read.

After you complete a draft of your essay, meet with a peer reviewer to evaluate each other's work and suggest revisions. Then proofread and edit your draft for errors in spelling, grammar, and punctuation.

 Web Activities For eFlashcards, Selection Quick Checks, and other Web activities, go to www.glencoe.com.

READING AND VOCABULARY

Reading Strategy Analyzing Cause-and-Effect Relationships

When authors do not tell their stories chronologically, the reader must pay close attention in order to determine the actual sequence of events and the **cause-and-effect relationships** of those events to one another.

1. Describe how the story is organized.

2. How would the impact of the story change if events were ordered differently?

Vocabulary Practice

Practice with Word Parts Read the roots and definitions below. Then pick the best definition for each of the boldfaced vocabulary words.

Latin root: *ulter*—"farther, beyond"
Old French root: *reprochier*—"to blame, accuse"
Latin root: *subvertere*—"to turn upside down, overthrow"

1. Her **ulterior** purpose was to meet with friends.
   a. cruel   **b.** concealed   **c.** necessary

2. The **irreproachable** candidate got the job.
   a. historical   **b.** experienced   **c.** faultless

3. The **subversive** group overthrew the government.
   a. rebellious   **b.** powerful   **c.** evil

LUISA VALENZUELA **185**

Assess

1. (a) Students may not sympathize because Juan causes his own death. (b) Feelings may change from sympathy to contempt.

2. (a) Juan fears that the censors will go after Mariana. (b) The government is totalitarian.

3. (a) To get a job as a censor and retrieve his letter (b) The government wants to exert more and more control over citizens' private messages.

4. (a) Censorship, fear of censors, and executions seem believable. (b) Students may find it unbelievable that Juan would convict himself.

5. It keeps the story from being somber and supports the author's wish to mock the government's absurdities.

6. Some may say Juan's choice to change; others, the government's choice to remove freedom

Literary Element

1. Juan becomes such a perfect censor that he censors his own letter.

2. Students may say that it is aimed at the government, with the *Censor's Secret Command,* the dehumanizing nature of the censor's job, and the building's outwardly "festive air."

Writing About Literature

Students should consider how satire points out the absurdities of bureaucracy, the impact of people's decisions on their lives, and the importance of personal liberties.

Reading Strategy

1. Begins with a reference to Juan's fate and then is told chronologically

2. Answers will vary.

Vocabulary

1. b **2.** c **3.** a

✓CheckPoint

Use the CheckPoint questions on Presentation Plus! to check students' mastery of the selection. These questions can be used with interactive response keypads for immediate student feedback.

Focus

Summary

The article begins with Carl Safina's wrenching description of an albatross mother feeding her young chick, hindered by a green toothbrush stuck in her gullet. Safina details the many ways in which the oceans around the world are being polluted, overfished, and over-farmed. He suggests ways in which governments can work together to address these problems.

Teach

Big Idea

Making Choices

Say: Consider the following question as you read. What are some other choices you can make to help preserve wildlife and the environment? *(Students may mention using alternative energy sources, recycling, consuming less, and disposing of trash properly.)* **OL**

Media Link to Making Choices

Preview the Article

In "Cry of the Ancient Mariner," the writer and environmentalist Carl Safina examines the reasons why marine life is being destroyed and provides some possible solutions.

1. From the title, what words would you use to describe what the tone of the article might be?

2. Skim the article. What do you think it will be about?

Set Purpose for Reading

Read to discover an environmental concern and the writer's viewpoint on saving ocean life.

Reading Strategy

Determining the Main Idea and Supporting Details
Determining the **main idea** involves finding the most important thought the writer is trying to convey about his or her subject. The main idea is not always obvious, so use the **supporting details** in the text to guide you. As you read, create and complete a graphic organizer like the one shown below.

Main Idea:

Supporting Detail 1: Fishing destroys over eighty million sea creatures each year.

Supporting Detail 2:

Supporting Detail 3:

OBJECTIVES
- Determine the main idea and supporting details.
- Skim text for an overall impression and particular information
- Distinguish fact from opinion.

186 UNIT 1 THE SHORT STORY

Cry of the Ancient Mariner

"Even in the middle of the deep blue sea, the albatross feels the hard hand of humanity"

By CARL SAFINA

AT THE LONELY CENTER OF THE NORTH PACIFIC OCEAN, farther from just about everything than just about anywhere, lies Midway Atoll, a coral reef enclosed by a lagoon. I've come with Canadian writer and zoologist Nancy Baron to the world's largest Laysan albatross colony—400,000 exquisite masters of the air—a feathered nation gathered to breed, cramming an isle a mile by two.

Ravenous, goose-size chicks so jam the landscape that it resembles a poultry farm. Many have waited more than a week for a meal, while both parents forage the ocean's vast expanse. An adult glides in on 7-ft. wings. After flying perhaps 2,000 miles nonstop to return here, in 10 minutes she will be gone again, searching for more food. She surveys the scene through lovely dark pastel-shadowed eyes, then calls, "Eh-eh-eh." Every nearby chick answers, but she recognizes her own chick's voice and weaves toward it.

Aggressive with hunger, the whining chick bites its parent's bill to stimulate her into throwing up her payload. The adult hunches, vomiting, pumping out fish eggs and several squid. The chick swallows in seconds what its parent logged 4,000 miles to get. The chick begs for more. The adult arches her neck and vomits again. Nothing comes. We whisper, "What's wrong?"

Slowly comes the surreal sight of a green plastic toothbrush emerging from the bird's gullet. With her neck arched, the mother cannot fully pass the straight brush. She tries several times to disgorge it, but can't. Nancy and I can hardly bear this. The albatross reswallows and, with the brush stuck inside, wanders away.

Message from the Albatross
In the world in which albatrosses came from, the birds swallowed pieces of floating pumice, or lightweight, vocanic glass,

---

Additional Support

See Also 📖
Active Learning and Note Taking Guide, pages 24–30.

Skills Practice

WRITING: Persuasion Encourage students to brainstorm a topic for a persuasive essay on an environmental issue. Remind them that good persuasive writing includes the following elements: clear thesis statements; strong, reliable evidence; and convincing reasoning. Reinforce the importance of using a logical argument, supported by credible and relevant facts. Have students continue with research and an outline for their topic. **OL**

for the fish eggs stuck to them. Albatrosses transferred this survival strategy to toothbrushes, bottle caps, nylon netting, toys, and other floating junk. Where chicks die, a pile of colorful plastic particles that used to be in their stomachs often marks their graves.

Through the intimate bond between parent and offspring flows the continuity of life itself. That our human trash stream crosses even this sacred bond is evidence of a wounded world, its relationships disfigured. The albatross's message: Consumer culture has reached every watery point on the compass. From sun-bleached coral reefs to icy polar waters, no place, no creature, remains apart.

Set the Record Straight

If albatrosses' eating plastic seems surprising, so do many of the oceans' problems. The facts often defy common perceptions. Examples:

• Most people think oil spills cause the most harm to ocean life. They don't. Fishing does. When a tanker wrecks, news crews flock to film gooey beaches and dying animals. Journalists rush right past the picturesque fishing boats whose huge nets and 1,000-hook longlines cause far more havoc on the marine world than spilled oil.

Fishing annually extracts more than 80 million tons of sea creatures worldwide. An additional 20 million tons of unwanted fish, seabirds, marine mammals, and turtles get thrown overboard, dead. Overfishing has seriously reduced major populations of cod, swordfish, tuna, snapper, grouper, and sharks. Instead of sensibly living off nature's interest, many fisheries have mined the wild capital, and

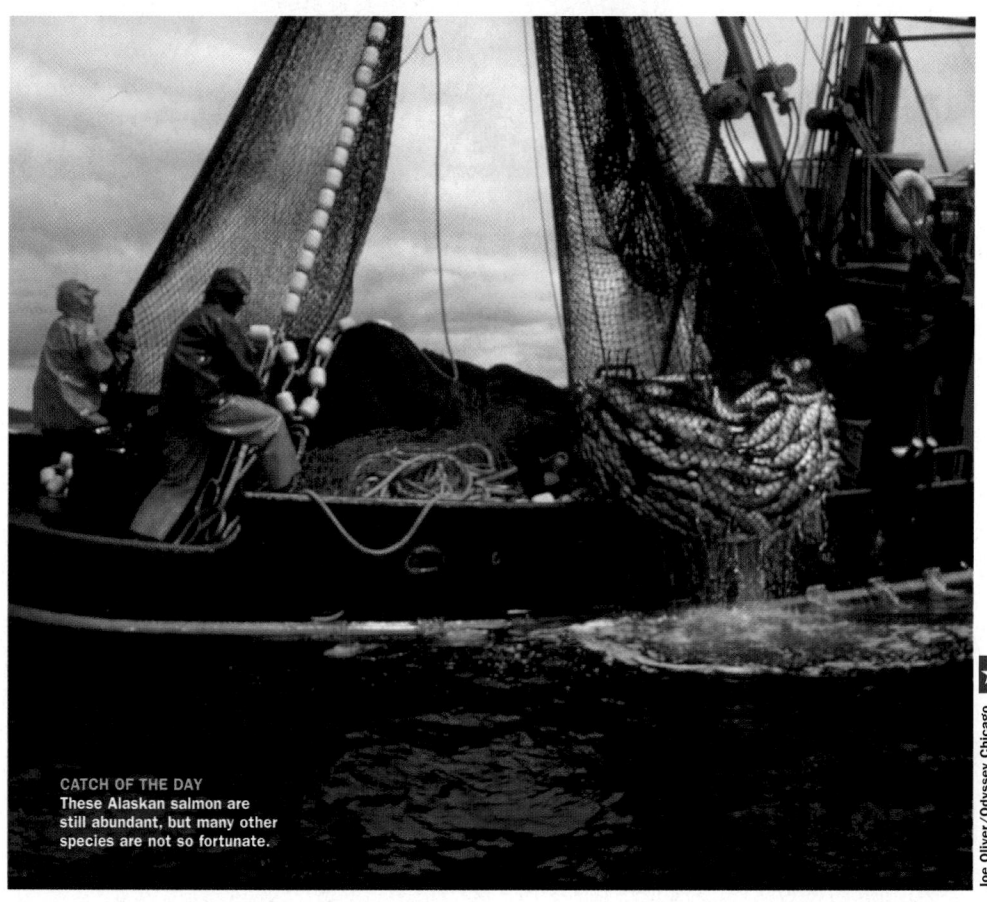

CATCH OF THE DAY
These Alaskan salmon are still abundant, but many other species are not so fortunate.

Joe Oliver/Odyssey Chicago

CRY OF THE ANCIENT MARINER **187**

Informational Text
TIME

Teach

R Reading Strategy

Determining Main Idea and Supporting Details

Ask: What is the main idea of Safina's essay? *(The destruction of marine life can and should be prevented.)* **Ask:** What are some of the supporting details you found when reading? *(Fishing captures more than 80 million tons of sea creatures each year; sewage and other waste runoff from the land has made entire areas of the sea uninhabitable; commercial and recreational fishing and shipping fleets damage sea-floor habitats.)* **OL**

★ Viewing the Photograph

Have students examine the photograph and share their reactions. Then ask them whether the jobs and revenue created by the fishing industry are worth the effects on the environment. **AS**

Reading in the Real World

Citizenship Encourage students to read the newspaper and local publications, looking for articles about environmental problems in their own states, cities, and neighborhoods. Ask students how those readings compare with Safina's essay, in terms of persuasive tone or style. **OL**

Objectives
• To determine main idea and supporting details (SE)
• To review the elements of good persuasive writing (TWE)

Teach

★ Viewing the Photograph

Have students respond to the emotional impact of the photograph and its caption. Ask students to share other examples of pollution's effect on wildlife. **AS**

famous fishing banks lie bankrupt, including the revered cod grounds of New England and Atlantic Canada.

Enforcing fishing limits—to give the most devastated fish populations a chance to rebuild—could ultimately enable us to catch at least 10 million more tons of sea life than we do now. Government-subsidized shipbuilders and fleets drive much of the overfishing. Ending those subsidies—as New Zealand has already done—would mean paying less to get more in the long run.

• Most ocean pollution doesn't come from ships. It comes from land. Gravity is the sea's enemy. Silt running off dirt roads and clear-cut forest land ruins coral reefs and U.S. salmon rivers. Pesticides and other poisons sprayed into the air and washed into rivers find the ocean. (Midway's albatrosses have in their tissues as much of the industrial chemicals called PCBs as do Great Lakes bald eagles.) The biggest sources of coastal pollution are waste from farm animals, fertilizers, and human sewage. They can spawn red tides and other harmful algae blooms that rob oxygen from the water, killing sea life. The Mississippi River, whose fine heartland silt once built fertile delta wetlands, now builds in the Gulf of Mexico a spreading dead zone—almost empty of marine life—the size

VIOLATING A SACRED BOND
Because of humankind's endless trash stream, the seabirds feed plastic to their young.

Kevin Schafer ★

of New Jersey. Improving sewage treatment and cleaning up the runoff from farms will be increasingly vital to preserving coastal water quality.

• Fish farming—aquaculture—doesn't take pressure off wild fish. Many farms use large numbers of cheap, wild-caught fish as feed to raise fewer shrimp and fish of more profitable varieties. And industrial-scale fish- and shrimp-aquaculture operations sometimes damage the coastlines where the facilities are located. The farms can foul

the water, destroy mangroves and marshes, drive local fishers out of business, and serve as breeding grounds for fish diseases. In places such as Bangladesh, Thailand, and India, which grow shrimp mainly for export to richer countries, diseases and pollution usually limit a farm's life to 10 years. The companies then move and start again.

To avoid becoming just another environmental headache, aquaculture needs standards. Raising fish species foreign to the local habitat should be discouraged, since

> **❝Heartland silt from the Mississippi River is creating a spreading dead zone in the Gulf of Mexico.❞**

Additional Support

Skills Practice

LITERARY ELEMENT: Irony In nonfiction as well as in fiction, irony can occur. For example, on this page, the author places the word *sanctuary* in quotation marks, indicating that the word means the opposite of its usual definition—an example of verbal irony. Situational irony occurs when the actual outcome of a situation is different from someone's expectations. Have students find examples of situational irony in this article. (*The albatross feeding its chick a toothbrush; the harmful effects of fish farming supposedly a conservation measure*) **OL**

escapees can drive out native fish or infect them with disease. Penning fish in open waterways is also problematic. Even when the impact on the environment is minimized—as it is with well-run Maine salmon farms—rows of large fish corrals in natural waterways can be eyesores. Fish farming is best done in indoor, onshore facilities. The fish rarely escape, and the wastewater can be treated before being released. Growing vegetarian species such as tilapia is ideal, since they don't have to be fed wild fish.

• The biologically richest stretches of ocean are more disrupted than the richest places on land. Continents still have roadless wilderness areas where motorized vehicles have never gone. But on the world's continental shelves, it is hard to find places where boats dragging nets haven't etched tracks into sea-floor habitats. In Europe's North Sea and along New England's Georges Bank and Australia's Queensland coast, trawlers, boats used for catching fish in large nets, may scour the bottom four to eight times every year. And the U.S. National Marine Sanctuaries hardly deserve the name. Commercial and recreational fishing with lines, traps, or nets is allowed almost everywhere in these "sanctuaries."

New Zealand and the Philippines are among the countries that have set up reserves in which fish are actually left alone. Marine life tends to recover in these areas, then spread beyond them, providing cheap insurance against overfishing outside the reserves.

WHAT YOU CAN DO

AVOID EATING SEAFOOD FROM ENDANGERED POPULATIONS

Like fish but don't want to help wipe out a species? The Monterey Bay Aquarium in California has published a menu of dos and don'ts. Some excerpts:

BEST CHOICES

Dungeness crab
Halibut (Alaska)
Mahi-mahi
Salmon (Alaska, wild caught)
Tilapia
Striped bass

BAD CHOICES

Atlantic cod
Orange roughy
Chilean sea bass
Shark
Shrimp
Swordfish

Though the oceans' problems can seem overwhelming, solutions are emerging and attitudes are changing. Most people have shed the fantasy that the sea can provide food forever, lessen endless pollution, and accept unlimited trash. In 1996, the U.S. passed the Sustainable Fisheries Act, which set up rules against overfishing—a recognition that protecting sea life is good business. Some fish, such as striped bass and redfish, are recovering because of catch limits. Alaskan,

Falkland, Australian, and New Zealand longline boats are taking care not to kill albatrosses. Turtles are being saved by trapdoors in shrimp nets so they can escape. **BI**

Joining Together to Help the Seas

The oceans' future depends most of all on international cooperation. Working through the U.N., the world's nations have outlawed giant drift nets. Other treaties to protect the seas and the fish in them are in the works, though not all nations are enthusiastic about signing them. Among top fishing nations, Japan relies heavily on seafood and yet is exceptionally disrespectful toward the ocean. It has disagreed with international limits on catches of southern bluefin tuna and used "scientific research" as a phony justification for hunting whales in the International Whaling Commission's Antarctic Sanctuary. A world leader in so many ways, Japan would greatly improve its moral position by helping to heal the seas.

A good place to start that healing would be to give albatrosses a future with more food and less plastic trash to swallow. A U.N. marine-pollution treaty makes dumping plastics illegal, but policing at sea is impractical. Nonetheless, ships could be required to carry up-to-date equipment for handling garbage and storing liquid waste that might otherwise be dumped into the water. Routine discharges put more oil into the sea than major spills.

We should expand our idea of zoning from land to sea. Instead of an ocean free-for-all, we should mark some areas for fishing only with traps and hooks and lines, and others

Teach

BI Big Idea

Making Choices Ask: Do you believe enough time, energy, and funding is being directed toward solving the problems plaguing the oceans? Have students support their responses with details from this article. **OL**

English Language Coach

Environmental Issues Students from other countries may not be familiar with the environmental movement in the U.S. Encourage these students to research environmental issues and compare their findings to what they know about environmental concerns in their native countries. **OL**

Assess

1. Some students may already have had ideas about preventing pollution and saving wildlife. Others may say that the article persuaded them to see conservation as an urgent cause.

2. (a) Setting fishing limits or eliminating government subsidies (b) He said eventually we could catch 10 million more tons of sea life.

3. (a) Students may say that the writer believes fish farming causes more problems than it solves. (b) Most students will say they had never considered fish farming as harmful to sea life prior to reading the article.

4. (a) The writer says that the ocean's future depends on international cooperation. (b) He identifies several laws and treaties that have been created to protect the oceans, but they are not effective when some countries fail to abide by them.

5. (a) The third main idea (b) The writer discusses the harm done to the oceans and marine life due to overfishing, fish farming, and environmental pollution. He then provides possible solutions to these problems and argues that action must be taken.

6. (a) When the writer speaks of the future or what he believes will happen, he is expressing opinions, because

For additional assessment, see ✏ Selection and Unit Assessment, pp. 31–32.

as wildlife sanctuaries. As we've seen with once rich cod grounds, if we don't declare some areas closed by foresight, they will declare themselves closed by collapse. The map of the land has many colors, while in most minds the sea is still the blank space between continents. Let's start coloring in that blue expanse and map a more sensible future for the sea.

Four centuries ago, poet John Donne wrote that no man is an island entire to himself. On Midway an albatross gagging on a toothbrush taught me that no island is an island. In the oceans, less is truly more: less trash, less habitat destruction, and catching fewer fish now will mean more food later on for both people and wildlife. The oceans make our planet habitable, and the wealth of oceans spans nutritional, climatological, biological, aesthetic, spiritual, emotional, and ethical areas. Like the albatross, we need the seas more than the seas need us. Will we understand this well enough to reap all the riches that a little restraint, cooperation, and compassion could bring?

— Updated 2005, from TIME, Special Earth Day Issue, Spring 2000

Carl Safina, founder of the National Audubon Society's Living Oceans Program, is author of Song for the Blue Ocean.

RESPONDING AND THINKING CRITICALLY

Respond

1. How did you feel about the importance of preventing the destruction of marine life before and after you read the article?

Recall and Interpret

2. (a) What is one solution to the problem of overfishing that the writer provided? (b) Did he provide substantial evidence as to why this solution would work?

3. (a) What was the writer's opinion of aquaculture, or fish farming? (b) How did this article affect your views of fish farming?

4. (a) On what, in the writer's opinion, does the ocean's future depend? (b) How did the writer support his opinion on this concern?

Analyze and Evaluate

5. (a) Choose the sentence that best describes the main idea of the reading selection.

   i   Saving the environment is a necessity for humankind.

   ii Marine life can only continue to survive if immediate action is taken.

   iii Overfishing, fish farming, and pollution must be curbed and/or prevented in order to save the oceans and marine life.

6. (a) How can you tell which of the writer's claims are facts and which are opinions? (b) How do you think this affects the validity of his claims?

7. The writer is the founder of the National Audubon Society's Living Oceans Program. The National Audubon Society is a network of community-based centers as well as scientific and educational programs geared toward sustaining the life of birds and promoting conservation. How do you think the writer's background influences his opinions and writing style?

Connect

8. (a) Restate the choices that the writer provides as a solution for preserving ocean life. (b) Which of these choices do you think would be the easiest to achieve and why?

we do not know the future. These statements are not verifiable. (b) It leaves room for disagreement, but the facts he does include still make his opinions look reasonable.

7. He is probably well informed about harm done to the environment and the steps to conserve it.

8. (a) We need to enforce fishing limits, end fishing subsidies, improve sewage treatment, create standards for aquaculture, create marine sanctuaries, get all countries to cooperate, and create fishing zones. (b) Students may say creating sanctuaries would be easiest, because countries can do it in their own waters.

PART 3

Life Transitions

All the Days of My Life No. 2, 1999. Evelyn Williams. Oil on canvas, 48.03 X 59.84 in. Private collection. ⭐

BI BIG IDEA

Life transitions are universal, prevalent in all cultures. Some cultures mark transitions with ceremony, while others simply observe a gradual shift in perspective and worldview. In the short stories in Part 3, you will encounter various rites of passage. As you read these stories, ask yourself: How do you, your family, and your friends mark transitions in your lives?

191

Analyzing and Extending

BI Big Idea

Life Transitions Direct students to read the Big Idea for Part 3. Explain that a rite of passage refers to an event that changes a person significantly, often marking a transition from innocence to experience. **Ask:** How does this painting relate to the Big Idea? *(The subject of the painting is portrayed as looking back at earlier stages of her life.)* **OL**

⭐ Viewing the Art

British artist Evelyn Williams (1929–) began painting when she was fourteen. Ask students to notice the details in her arresting painting *All the Days of My Life No. 2.* **Ask:** What does it suggest about a life passage? *(A life passage is a transition from one stage of life to the next.)* **AS**

English Language Coach

Building Background Help students new to the United States to connect with and understand the literature in Part 3 by considering reactions their family members have had to life transitions such as births, deaths, and other major life events. Discuss how some people cope better than others. **EL**

Differentiated Instruction

Activate Prior Knowledge Less proficient readers will gain more from their reading if they draw on personal experience with a subject. Encourage students to consider their knowledge of life's transitions as they read Part 3. Also, have them draw up questions beforehand. **BL**

Objectives for Part 3
• To analyze a writing style (SE)
• To use different styles to achieve different purposes (SE)

Part 3: Life Transitions

Readability Scores Key
Dale-Chall/DRP/Lexile

PACING (DAYS)		SELECTIONS AND FEATURES	LITERARY ELEMENTS
STANDARD	BLOCK		
1-2 class sessions	1	LITERARY FOCUS: Narrator and Voice, pp. 192-193	Narrator and Voice, SE p. 192 Analyzing Style, TWE p. 192
		"Everyday Use" by Alice Walker **5.5/53/810**, pp. 194-206	Reliable/Unreliable Narrator, SE pp. 195-205 Dialogue, SE p. 205
2 class sessions	1	COMPARING LITERATURE Theme Across Genres **"Through the Tunnel"** by Doris Lessing **6.6/54/860**, pp. 208-220 **"The Vision Quest"** by Lame Deer **6.4/55/890**, pp. 221-223 **"Dear Pie"** from *Rules to Live By* by F. Scott Fitzgerald **8.4/54/1040**, pp. 224-226	Point of View, SE pp. 209-212, 215, 216, 220 Conflict, TWE p. 216
1 class session	1	**"Catch the Moon"** by Judith Ortiz Cofer **7.5/59/930**, pp. 227-237	Point of View, SE pp. 228, 230, 231, 233, 235, 236 Plot, SE p. 236
		Grammar Workshop: Sentence Structure, p. 238	
2-3 class sessions	1-2	**"A Child's Christmas in Wales"** by Dylan Thomas **6.5/58/1200**, pp. 239-250	Diction, SE pp. 240, 241, 243-247, 249 Voice, SE p. 249
		"Winter Night" by Kay Boyle **4.3/57/1200**, pp. 251-263	Tone, SE pp. 252, 253, 255, 256, 258, 260-262 Theme, SE p. 262
1 class session	1	**"And of Clay Are We Created"** by Isabel Allende **6.8/64/1240**, pp. 264-277	Persona, SE pp. 265, 267, 268, 270–272, 274, 276 Plot and Setting, SE p. 276
2 class session	1	**"Lullaby"** by Leslie Marmon Silko **5.6/56/900**, pp. 278-289	Style, SE pp. 279, 281–282, 284, 286, 288 Narrator, SE p. 288
2-3 class session		Writing Workshop: Literary Criticism, pp. 290-297	
1 class session	2-3	Speaking, Listening, and Viewing Workshop: Delivering an Oral Report, pp. 298–299	
2 class sessions		Test Preparation and Practice, pp. 302-307	

About the Part

Part 3 covers narrator and voice in the short story.

READING AND CRITICAL THINKING	VOCABULARY	WRITING AND GRAMMAR	LISTENING, SPEAKING, AND VIEWING
Analyzing Voice, TWE p. 193			
Questioning, SE pp. 195–206 Comparing and Contrasting, TWE p. 202	Word Parts, SE pp. 195, 206 Academic Vocabulary, SE p. 206	Evaluate Author's Craft, SE p. 206 Describing Characters, TWE p. 196	Interview, SE p. 206 Analyzing Art, SE pp. 199, 203; TWE p. 201
Visualizing, SE pp. 209, 211–213, 217, 220 Previewing, TWE p. 208 Predicting, TWE p. 210 Identifying Cause-and-Effect Relationships, TWE p. 218 Summarizing, TWE p. 226	Antonyms, SE pp. 209, 220	Quickwrite, SE p. 225 Spatial Order, TWE p. 212 Infinitive and Prepositional Phrases, TWE p. 222 Prewriting, TWE p. 224	Analyzing Art, SE p. 218; TWE pp. 210, 213, 214, 217, 223 Art Activity, SE p. 220 Discussion Starter, SE p. 223 Comparing Author's Culture, SE p. 226
Interpreting Imagery, SE pp. 228, 229, 231, 234, 235, 237	Denotations and Connotations, SE p. 237	Analyze Point of View, SE p. 237	Analyzing Art, SE p. 232 Literature Groups, SE p. 237
		Avoiding Sentence Fragments, SE p. 238	
Connecting to Personal Experience, SE pp. 240, 242, 244, 246, 247, 249	Analogies, SE p. 249 Academic Vocabulary, SE p. 249	Evaluate Author's Craft, SE p. 250	Analyzing Art, SE pp. 244, 247; TWE p. 242
Activating Prior Knowledge, SE pp. 252, 253, 254, 257–260, 263	Word Origins, SE pp. 252, 263 Academic Vocabulary, SE p. 263	Compare and Contrast Characters, SE p. 263	Analyzing Art, SE p. 255; TWE pp. 256, 258, 260
Analyzing Sensory Details, SE pp. 265, 266, 268–274, 276	Analogies, SE p. 276 Academic Vocabulary, SE p. 276	Applying Point of View, SE p. 277	Group Activity, SE p. 275 Dramatization, TWE p. 270
Evaluating Characters, SE pp. 279, 281–283, 286, 287, 289	Word Origins, SE p. 289 Academic Vocabulary, SE p. 289	Analyze Setting and Mood, SE p. 289	Analyzing Art, TWE pp. 280, 284, 286
Recognizing Figurative Language, TWE p. 296	Word Origins, TWE p. 292	Organization, TWE p. 294	
	Transitions, TWE p. 298		
Visualizing, TWE p. 302		Comma Splices, TWE p. 306	

Teach

Big Idea

Life Transitions

Ask students to consider their reactions to life transitions they have experienced. Tell students that Part 3 will deepen their understanding of human responses to life's transitions. Encourage students to contemplate this "big idea" and its relation to the artwork. **OL**

L Literary Element

Narrator and Voice

Ask: What can you tell about the narrator and point of view of "A Child's Christmas in Wales"? *(The narrator is an adult looking back on being a fun-loving child. The story is told in first-person point of view.)* **OL**

Narrator and Voice

How are stories told?

Who will tell the story? This is an important question for anyone who is writing a short story. Choosing a narrator is a decision that shapes the style of a story. A narrator can speak from within the story, providing first-person narration, or from outside the story. There, it is possible to view the thoughts and feelings of all the characters. Based on who is telling it, a story can be told in vastly different ways.

Snowballing, c. 1917. Dame Laura Knight. Watercolor heightened with bodycolor over pencil, 52 x 75 cm. Private collection. ★

It was on the afternoon of the day of Christmas Eve, and I was in Mrs. Prothero's garden, waiting for cats, with her son Jim. It was snowing. It was always snowing at Christmas. December, in my memory, is white as Lapland, although there were no reindeers. But there were cats. Patient, cold, and callous, our hands wrapped in socks, we waited to snowball the cats. Sleek and long as jaguars and horrible-whiskered, spitting and snarling, they would slink and sidle over the white back-garden walls, and the lynx-eyed hunters, Jim and I, fur-capped and moccasined trappers from Hudson Bay, off Mumbles Road, would hurl our deadly snowballs at the green of their eyes.

The wise cats never appeared. We were so still, Eskimo-footed arctic marksmen in the muffling silence of the eternal snows—eternal, ever since Wednesday—that we never heard Mrs. Prothero's first cry from her igloo at the bottom of the garden. Or, if we heard it at all, it was, to us, like the far-off challenge of our enemy and prey, the neighbor's polar cat. But soon the voice grew louder. "Fire!" cried Mrs. Prothero, and she beat the dinner-gong.

—Dylan Thomas, **from "A Child's Christmas in Wales"** **L**

Point of View

A story with a **first-person point of view** is told by a character, referred to as "I." The reader sees people and events through the eyes of one character, and the reader cannot know more than this character knows. For example, the reader cannot know what another character thinks. **Limited third-person point of view** is similar. The narrator is outside the story, but only reveals the thoughts of one character, referred to as "he" or "she." A **third-person omniscient point of view** differs greatly from the first two: The narrator is outside the story but knows everything about the characters and events.

Additional Support

Skills Practice

LITERATURE: Analyzing Style
Discuss the style of these selections.
Ask: How does the choice of first-person narrator affect "A Child's Christmas in Wales"? *(Through a first-person narrator, Thomas presents charming "inside" details from a child's imagination.)* How does this choice of narrator affect the tone? *(Since the narrator is an adult looking back on childhood, the tone is formal.)* What is the style of "A Child's Christmas in Wales"? *(Thomas's sophisticated style uses vivid diction, flowing sentences, imaginative figures of speech, and vibrant sensory images.)* Encourage students to pay attention to style. **OL**

Voice

Voice is the distinctive use of language that conveys the author's personality to the reader Sentence structure, word choice, and tone are elements that contribute to an author's voice. When reading other works by the same author, a reader can recognize the author's voice by his or her unique use of language.

A narrator has a voice too, because the author gives the narrator a particular way of speaking and using language, which contributes to the overall emotional quality of the story. The tone of the narrator's voice also contributes to the setting, plot, and theme.

> It was a lonesome land! Not a sound in all those peaceful expanses of grass and woods but the drowsy hum of insects; no glimpse of man or beast; nothing to keep up your spirits and make you glad to be alive.
>
> —Mark Twain, **from "The Californian's Tale"** R

Diction Good writers choose words carefully. **Diction** refers to an author's choice of words. Authors choose their words to give the reader a specific feeling or to convey a particular meaning. Consider the difference in diction between these two examples:

> Constance hates lap swimming.
> Constance loathes repetitive lap swimming.

Tone Diction also helps communicate the **tone** of a story. Tone is the author's attitude toward the subject. An author's tone might be sympathetic, objective, serious, ironic, sad, bitter, or humorous.

For example, even the title of Isabel Allende's story "And of Clay Are We Created," incorporates the story's tone. Notice that she did not call her story "We Are Created of Clay." The title she wrote immediately communicates the story's solemn tone to the reader. On the other hand, James Thurber uses an amused, affectionate tone in "The Car We Had to Push."

Style

The sum total of language choices an author makes is his or her **style**. How sophisticated is the narrator's vocabulary? Does he or she speak in long, flowing sentences or short, choppy ones? Is the language formal or informal? It makes a difference whether the author writes about an *automobile* or a *car*. Like tone, style can tell a reader about the author's purpose in writing and his or her attitude toward the subject and audience.

> You've no doubt seen those TV shows where the child who has 'made it' is confronted, as a surprise, by her own mother and father, tottering in weakly from backstage. (A pleasant surprise, of course: what would they do if parent and child came on the show only to curse out and insult each other?) On TV mother and child embrace and smile into each other's faces.
>   Sometimes the mother and father weep, the child wraps them in her arms and leans across the table to tell how she would not have made it without their help. I have seen these programs.
>
> —Alice Walker, **from "Everyday Use"**

Quickwrite

Write a few sentences describing your classroom, or some other room, in your own style. Do not worry about trying to sound like a writer; write the way you talk. After you write your sentences, use the checklist below to analyze your style. Think about your choices, then rewrite your description for a different purpose. Write as if you were trying to sell the room. Then analyze your style in the second description.

- ☐ Words: long or short?
- ☐ Sentences: long or short?
- ☐ Language: formal or informal?
- ☐ How would you describe the tone?
- ☐ How would you describe the voice?

OBJECTIVES
- Analyze a writing style.
- Use different styles to achieve different purposes.

LITERARY FOCUS

Teach

R Reading Strategy

Analyzing Voice Ask: What can you infer about the narrator of "The Californian's Tale"? (*The narrator, a gold prospector, is lonely and downcast.*) **OL**

★ Viewing the Art

Ask: What story does this painting tell? (*Answers will vary.*) **AS**

Assess

Quickwrite

Check for a contrast between the two styles. The first description should be more conversational with shorter words, more informal language, and a friendlier, more personal tone. The second passage should be more formal with an enthusiastic, positive tone and correct usage.

English Language Coach

Paraphrasing Since the Thomas passage will be difficult for students new to the United States, have them reread it aloud and define unfamiliar words until they can paraphrase successfully. Help students with vocabulary such as *slink, sidle, callous,* and *moccasined.* **EL**

Differentiated Instruction

Visualizing Details Encourage less proficient readers to visualize details in these passages, especially the extended metaphor in "A Child's Christmas in Wales" of the boys being arctic fur trappers. Visualizing *jaguars* and *lynx-eyed,* adds to the enjoyment. **BL**

Objectives
- To analyze a writing style (SE)
- To use different styles to achieve different purposes (SE)
- To analyze style (TWE)

Focus

BELLRINGER

Bellringer Options
**Selection Focus
    Transparency 12**
**Daily Language
    Transparency 19**
Or tell students that they will be reading a short story that emphasizes the varying personalities and attitudes of each member of a household and the effects these attributes have on the family unit.

Ask: What are some of the different personalities present in your household? How are some family members different from others? In what ways are they all alike?

Have students think of one adjective for each person in the family unit.

Author Search To expand students' appreciation of Alice Walker, have them access the Web site for additional information and resources.

Everyday Use

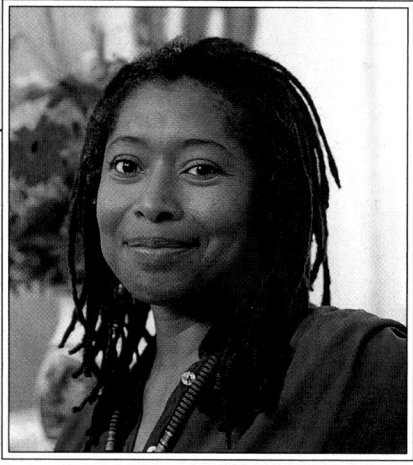

MEET ALICE WALKER

If Alice Walker's brother had not accidentally shot her in the eye with a BB gun when she was eight, she might not have become a writer. After children at school made fun of her, she "retreated into solitude, and read stories and began to write poems." Her great love for the written word had begun.

Early Years Walker grew up in Eatonton, Georgia, a small town where her parents farmed. They were sharecroppers—people who rented other people's land to grow crops. Sharecroppers made just enough money to survive and viewed education as the means to a better life for their children. Walker received a scholarship to Spelman College in Atlanta, the nation's oldest college for African American women. At Spelman during some of the most important years of the Civil Rights Movement, Walker was lured into political activism.

> "We will be ourselves and free, or die in the attempt. Harriet Tubman was not our great-grandmother for nothing."
>
> —Alice Walker

A Child of the Civil Rights Movement

Walker was ten years old when the Supreme Court ruled that "separate but equal" was unconstitutional in schools. Her parents in the rural South knew only the days of segregation and racism, but Walker came to know a different way of life. Walker saw people beaten and battered for protesting for their rights, yet she also experienced what it was like to live in a world that was not completely segregated.

Walker knew that the changes she went through in the 1960s and onward were difficult for the previous generation. She wrote, "In the Sixties many of us scared our parents profoundly when we showed up dressed in our 'African' . . . clothes. We shocked them. . . ." In "Everyday Use," Walker portrays the clash between generations that sometimes resulted from this rapid change.

An African American Woman's Voice Walker has published many volumes of fiction, nonfiction, and poetry. Her most famous book, *The Color Purple,* won the Pulitzer Prize and the American Book Award. Steven Spielberg's movie version garnered numerous Academy Award nominations.

One of Walker's greatest influences was Zora Neale Hurston, whom Walker praised for portraying African American people as "complete, complex, *undiminished* human beings." Walker's own work reflects a similar commitment to portraying the beauty and complexity of the African American experience.

Alice Walker was born in 1944.

Literature Online Author Search For more about Alice Walker, go to www.glencoe.com.

Selection Skills

Literary Elements
- Reliable/Unreliable Narrator (SE pp. 195–205)
- Dialogue (SE p. 205)

Reading Skills
- Questioning (SE pp. 195–206)

Vocabulary Skills
- Word Parts (SE pp. 195, 206)
- Academic Vocabulary (SE p. 206)

Everyday Use

**Listening/Speaking/
Viewing Skills**
- Analyzing Art (SE pp. 199, 203; TWE p. 201)

Writing Skills/Grammar
- Evaluate Author's Craft (SE p. 206)
- Describing Characters (TWE p. 196)
- Usage (TWE p. 198)
- Possessive Pronouns (TWE p. 200)
- Historical Research (TWE p. 204)

Connecting to the Story

In this story, you will meet a daughter who thinks that her mother's and sister's lives should look more like her own. But the mother, who tells the story, rejects her daughter's new way of life. Before you read the story, ask yourself:

- When have I watched grown children disapprove of how their parents live?
- How do most parents deal with such a situation?

Building Background

"Everyday Use" takes place in the rural South in the 1970s. At that time, there was often a great contrast between African Americans living in cities, especially in the North, and African Americans who had never left the rural South. These differences were caused in part by the embrace by some African Americans of the cultural identity movement of the 1970s. The cultural identity movement advocated a return to African ways and emphasized that "black is beautiful." Many people wore traditional African clothing and an "Afro" hairstyle. Others took new names, followed Muslim dietary guidelines, and adopted other customs and language related to their new identity.

Setting Purposes for Reading

Big Idea Life Transitions

As you read, think about how the selection addresses change: who changes, who does not change, and why.

Literary Element Reliable/Unreliable Narrator

The **narrator** is the person who tells the story. The narrator may be a **reliable,** or trustworthy, source of information and interpretation. A narrator might also be **unreliable,** or unable to be trusted. Determining if the narrator of a story is reliable or unreliable will help you assess whether aspects of the story are true and unbiased. As you read "Everyday Use," identify the narrator and consider whether and why her version of events is likely to be true or objective.

- See Literary Terms Handbook, p. R11.

OBJECTIVES
In studying this selection, you will focus on the following:
- analyzing a reliable/unreliable narrator
- analyzing dialogue

Reading Strategy Questioning

Questioning is asking yourself whether specific information in a selection is important, as well as whether you understand what you have read. Questioning helps you focus on and comprehend essential aspects of a selection. As you read, ask yourself what the story's many details say about Mama and her daughters.

Reading Tip: Making a Chart Use a chart like the one shown to record details and your questions.

Detail	My Question
"When the hard clay is swept clean"	Why is this detail here?

Vocabulary

sidle (sīd′əl) v. to move sideways, especially in a way that does not attract attention or cause disturbance; p. 197 *The shy child quietly sidled up to me.*

furtive (fur′tiv) adj. secret; shifty; sly; p. 198 *The guilty man wore a furtive smile while maintaining his innocence.*

oppress (ə pres′) v. to control or govern by the cruel or unjust use of force or authority; p. 200 *Some governments further oppress people living in poverty.*

doctrine (dok′trin) n. particular principle or position that is taught or supported, as of a religion; p. 201 *They believe in the doctrine of original sin.*

Vocabulary Tip: Word Parts Word parts are prefixes, suffixes, and base words, or roots.

 Literature Online **Interactive Literary Elements Handbook** To review or learn more about the literary elements, go to www.glencoe.com.

- questioning
- writing an evaluation of the author's craft

ALICE WALKER **195**

Focus

Summary

Mama and her daughter Maggie await the arrival of Dee, Maggie's older sister, who has broken away from their rural poverty. Dee arrives with a boyfriend named Asalamalakim. Dee has taken to calling herself Wangero. She is as condescending and assertive as Mama remembers. After dinner, Dee discovers two quilts and demands to have them. Mama defies Dee and explains that the quilts are for Maggie. Dee leaves in a rage, but Mama and Maggie enjoy the evening with a newfound respect for each other.

V Vocabulary

Vocabulary File
Say: Add these words and definitions to your vocabulary file. For each word, include a sentence that gives you an example of how to use the word. **OL** Students with English language needs should include the pronunciations of these words in their files. **EL**

Literature Online

Literary Elements Have students access the Web site to improve their understanding of reliable/unreliable narrator.

Teach

Big Idea

Life Transitions Say: Keep this question in mind as you read. What changes do Maggie and Mama undergo as a result of Dee's visit? *(Mama learns to stand up to her overbearing and demanding daughter, Dee, in order to protect her weaker daughter, Maggie. As a result, Mama is pleased with herself, and Maggie no longer fears her older sister.)* **OL**

L1 Literary Element

Reliable/Unreliable Narrator Answer: *She is waiting in the yard for Maggie's sister; she is proud of her clean, swept yard.* **OL**

R1 Reading Strategy

Questioning Answer: *The narrator wishes that she had a warm relationship with Dee. Based on this passage, have students predict what might happen later in story. (It sounds as if Mama and her daughter do not get along well, so there may be some confrontation later in the story.)* **OL**

Readability Scores
Dale-Chall: 5.5
DRP: 53
Lexile: 810

EVERYDAY USE

Alice Walker

Fog over Rural Road in Great Smoky Mountains.
William Manning.

I will wait for her in the yard that Maggie and I made so clean and wavy yesterday afternoon. A yard like this is more comfortable than most people know. It is not just a yard. It is like an extended living room. When the hard clay is swept clean as a floor and the fine sand around the edges lined with tiny, irregular grooves, anyone can come and sit and look up into the elm tree and wait for the breezes that never come inside the house.

Maggie will be nervous until after her sister goes: she will stand hopelessly in corners, homely and ashamed of the burn scars down her arms and legs, eying her sister with a mixture of envy and awe. She thinks her sister has held life always in the palm of one hand, that "no" is a word the world never learned to say to her.

You've no doubt seen those TV shows where the child who has "made it" is confronted, as a surprise, by her own mother and father, tottering in weakly from backstage. (A pleasant surprise, of course: What would they do if parent and child came on the show only to curse out and insult each other?) On TV mother and child embrace and smile into each other's faces. Sometimes the mother and father weep, the child wraps them in her arms and leans across the table to tell how she would not have made it without

Literary Element Reliable/Unreliable Narrator *What have you learned about the narrator so far?* **L1**

Additional Support

Skills Practice

WRITING: Describing Characters
The picture of Mama that emerges on page 197 is created by a catalog of what she does (wears overalls, slaughters hogs, washes in ice water). Point out that character is only superficially defined by appearance. Have students write the following sentence:

"_____ is the sort of person who . . ." Then ask them to think of someone they know well, fill in the blank, and complete the sentence several times with an action characteristic of that person. Finally, have them write a paragraph describing the subject. **OL** their help. I have seen these programs.

Sometimes I dream a dream in which Dee and I are suddenly brought together on a TV program of this sort. Out of a dark and soft-seated limousine I am ushered into a bright room filled with many people. There I meet a smiling, gray, sporty man like Johnny Carson who shakes my hand and tells me what a fine girl I have. Then we are on the stage and Dee is embracing me with tears in her eyes. She pins on my dress a large orchid, even though she has told me once that she thinks orchids are tacky flowers.

In real life I am a large, big-boned woman with rough, man-working hands. In the winter I wear flannel nightgowns to bed and overalls during the day. I can kill and clean a hog as mercilessly as a man. My fat keeps me hot in zero weather. I can work outside all day, breaking ice to get water for washing; I can eat pork liver cooked over the open fire minutes after it comes steaming from the hog. One winter I knocked a bull calf straight in the brain between the eyes with a sledge hammer and had the meat hung up to chill before nightfall. But of course all this does not show on television. I am the way my daughter would want me to be: a hundred pounds lighter, my skin like an uncooked barley pancake. My hair glistens in the hot bright lights. Johnny Carson has much to do to keep up with my quick and witty tongue.

But that is a mistake. I know even before I wake up. Who ever knew a Johnson with a quick tongue? Who can even imagine me

looking a strange white man in the eye? It seems to me I have talked to them always with one foot raised in flight, with my head turned in whichever way is farthest from them. Dee, though. She would always look anyone in the eye. Hesitation was no part of her nature.

"How do I look, Mama?" Maggie says, showing just enough of her thin body enveloped in pink skirt and red blouse for me to know she's there, almost hidden by the door.

"Come out into the yard," I say.

Have you ever seen a lame animal, perhaps a dog run over by some careless person rich enough to own a car, **sidle** up to someone who is ignorant enough to be kind to him? That is the way my Maggie walks. She has been like this, chin on chest, eyes on ground, feet in shuffle, ever since the fire that burned the other house to the ground.

Dee is lighter than Maggie, with nicer hair and a fuller figure. She's a woman now, though sometimes I forget. How long ago was it that the other house burned? Ten, twelve years? Sometimes I can still hear the flames and feel Maggie's arms sticking to me, her hair smoking and her dress falling off her in little black papery flakes. Her eyes seemed stretched open, blazed open by the flames reflected in them. And Dee. I see her standing off under the sweet gum tree she used to dig gum out of; a look of concentration on her face as she watched the last dingy gray board of the house fall in toward the red-hot brick chimney. Why don't you do a dance around the ashes? I'd wanted to ask her. She had hated the house that much.

ALICE WALKER **197**

Reliable/Unreliable

Narrator Answer: *She resents Dee's education and new ideas because she thinks that Dee feels superior as a result and because Dee forces her ideas on her and Maggie.* **OL**

BI1 Big Idea

Life Transitions Answer:
When Mama was young, children received little or no education. Now children go to school, and Dee even went to college. **OL**

L2 Literary Element

Reliable/Unreliable

Narrator Answer: *The narrator is probably offended that Dee hates her house. This likely affects the way the narrator's visit with Dee is recounted in the story.* **OL**

I used to think she hated Maggie, too. But that was before we raised the money, the church and me, to send her to Augusta[1] to school. She used to read to us without pity; forcing words, lies, other folks' habits, whole lives upon us two, sitting trapped and ignorant underneath her voice. She washed us in a river of make-believe, burned us with a lot of knowledge we didn't necessarily need to know. Pressed us to her with the serious way she read, to shove us away at just the moment, like dimwits, we seemed about to understand.

Dee wanted nice things. A yellow organdy[2] dress to wear to her graduation from high school; black pumps to match a green suit she'd made from an old suit somebody gave me. She was determined to stare down any disaster in her efforts. Her eyelids would not flicker for minutes at a time. Often I fought off the temptation to shake her. At sixteen she had a style of her own: and knew what style was.

I never had an education myself. After second grade the school was closed down. Don't ask me why: in 1927 colored asked fewer questions than they do now. Sometimes Maggie reads to me. She stumbles along good-naturedly but can't see well. She knows she is not bright. Like good looks and money, quickness passed her by. She will marry John Thomas (who has mossy teeth in an earnest face) and then I'll be free to sit here and I guess just sing church songs to myself. Although I never was a good singer. Never could carry a tune. I was always better at a man's job. I used to love to milk till I was hooked in the side in '49. Cows are soothing and slow

and don't bother you, unless you try to milk them the wrong way.

I have deliberately turned my back on the house. It is three rooms, just like the one that burned, except the roof is tin; they don't make shingle roofs any more. There are no real windows, just some holes cut in the sides, like the portholes in a ship, but not round and not square, with rawhide holding the shutters up on the outside. This house is in a pasture, too, like the other one. No doubt when Dee sees it she will want to tear it down. She wrote me once that no matter where we "choose" to live, she will manage to come see us. But she will never bring her friends. Maggie and I thought about this and Maggie asked me, "Mama, when did Dee ever *have* any friends?"

She had a few. **Furtive** boys in pink shirts hanging about on washday after school. Nervous girls who never laughed. Impressed with her they worshiped the well-turned phrase, the cute shape, the scalding humor that erupted like bubbles in lye. She read to them.

When she was courting Jimmy T she didn't have much time to pay to us, but turned all her faultfinding power on him. He *flew* to marry a cheap city girl from a family of ignorant flashy people. She hardly had time to recompose herself.

When she comes I will meet—but there they are!

Maggie attempts to make a dash for the house, in her shuffling way, but I stay her with my hand. "Come back here," I say. And she stops and tries to dig a well in the sand with her toe.

It is hard to see them clearly through the strong sun. But even the first glimpse of leg

---

1. *Augusta* is a city in Georgia.
2. *Organdy* is a lightweight fabric, usually made of cotton.

Literary Element Reliable/Unreliable Narrator *How does Mama feel about her daughter's education and new ideas?* **L1**

Big Idea Life Transitions *How have things changed since Mama was young?* **BI1**

Literary Element Reliable/Unreliable Narrator *How do you think it makes the narrator feel that Dee hates her house? Do you think this affects how she tells her story? Explain.* **L2**

Vocabulary

furtive (fur' tiv) *adj.* secret; shifty; sly

Additional Support

Skills Practice

GRAMMAR AND LANGUAGE:

Usage Write the following sentences on the board:
She looked at her sister with something <u>like</u> *fear.*
She gasped <u>like</u> *a bee had stung her.*
In each sentence, underline *like*. Point out that in the first case the word is

employed before a noun as a preposition, which is conventional Standard English. In the second example, *like* is used as a conjunction, connecting two clauses. This usage is common in everyday speech, but in more formal, written English the word *as* or the phrase *as if* is preferred.

Girl in a Green Dress, 1930. William H. Johnson. Oil on canvas, 24¼ x 19 ½ in. National Museum of American Art, Washington, DC.

Viewing the Art: Which of the two sisters might be more like the girl in this portrait? Explain. ⭐

my eyes. There are yellows and oranges enough to throw back the light of the sun. I feel my whole face warming from the heat waves it throws out. Earrings gold, too, and hanging down to her shoulders. Bracelets dangling and making noises when she moves her arm up to shake the folds of the dress out of her armpits. The dress is loose and flows, and as she walks closer, I like it. I hear Maggie go "Uhnnnh" again. It is her sister's hair. It stands straight up like the wool on a sheep. It is black as night and around the edges are two long pigtails that rope about like small lizards disappearing behind her ears.

"Wa-su-zo-Tean-o!" she says, coming on in that gliding way the dress makes her move. The short stocky fellow with the hair to his navel is all grinning and follows up with "Asalam-alakim,[3] my mother and sister!" He moves to hug Maggie but she falls back, right up against the back of my chair. I feel her trembling there and when I look up I see the perspiration falling off her chin.

"Don't get up," says Dee. Since I am stout it takes something of a push. You can see me trying to move a second or two before I make it. She turns, showing white heels through her sandals, and goes back to the car. Out she peeks next with a Polaroid. She stoops down quickly and lines up picture after picture of me sitting there in front of

out of the car tells me it is Dee. Her feet were always neat-looking, as if God himself had shaped them with a certain style. From the other side of the car comes a short, stocky man. Hair is all over his head a foot long and hanging from his chin like a kinky mule tail. I hear Maggie suck in her breath. "Uhnnnh," is what it sounds like. Like when you see the wriggling end of a snake just in front of your foot on the road. "Uhnnnh."

Dee next. A dress down to the ground, in this hot weather. A dress so loud it hurts

---

Big Idea Life Transitions *Why do the man's hair and beard signify change to Mama?* **BI₂**

3. *Wa-su-zo-Tean-o!* (wä sōō′ zō tēn′o) and *Asalamalakim* (ä säl ä mä′ lä kēm) are greetings.

ALICE WALKER **199**

Teach

R1 **Reading Strategy**

Evaluating Ask: Does it make sense for Dee to take pictures of a place she hates so much? *(Dee's life is now is so different from her upbringing that she is like a tourist in a foreign country, taking snapshots of the strange world she is passing though. Dee may also want to amaze her new friends with images of primitive country life.)* **OL**

R2 **Reading Strategy**

Questioning Answer: *She may feel that her intelligence is being undermined.* **OL**

L1 **Literary Element**

Reliable/Unreliable Narrator Answer: *Mama feels that Asalamalakim is looking down on her as if she were some impossibly out-dated person. Asalamalakim is amused.* **OL**

R3 **Reading Strategy**

Questioning Answer: *Most students will say that Mama did know from the beginning. In her own way, she is making fun of Hakim-a-barber.* **OL**

---

the house with Maggie cowering behind me. She never takes a shot without making sure the house is included. When a cow comes nibbling around the edge of the yard she snaps it and me and Maggie *and* the house. Then she puts the Polaroid in the back seat of the car, and comes up and kisses me on the forehead.

Meanwhile Asalamalakim is going through motions with Maggie's hand. Maggie's hand is as limp as a fish, and probably as cold, despite the sweat, and she keeps trying to pull it back. It looks like Asalamalakim wants to shake hands but wants to do it fancy. Or maybe he don't know how people shake hands. Anyhow, he soon gives up on Maggie.

"Well," I say. "Dee."

"No, Mama," she says. "Not 'Dee,' Wangero Leewanika Kemanjo!"[4]

"What happened to 'Dee'?" I wanted to know.

"She's dead," Wangero said. "I couldn't bear it any longer, being named after the people who **oppress** me."

"You know as well as me you was named after your aunt Dicie," I said. Dicie is my sister. She named Dee. We called her "Big Dee" after Dee was born.

"But who was *she* named after?" asked Wangero.

"I guess after Grandma Dee," I said.

"And who was she named after?" asked Wangero.

"Her mother," I said, and saw Wangero was getting tired. "That's about as far back as I can trace it," I said. Though, in fact, I probably could have carried it back beyond the Civil War through the branches.

"Well," said Asalamalakim, "there you are."

"Uhnnnh," I heard Maggie say.

"There I was not," I said, "before 'Dicie' cropped up in our family, so why should I try to trace it that far back?"

He just stood there grinning, looking down on me like somebody inspecting a Model A car. Every once in a while he and Wangero sent eye signals over my head.

"How do you pronounce this name?" I asked.

"You don't have to call me by it if you don't want to," said Wangero.

"Why shouldn't I?" I asked. "If that's what you want us to call you, we'll call you."

"I know it might sound awkward at first," said Wangero.

"I'll get used to it," I said. "Ream it out again."

Well, soon we got the name out of the way. Asalamalakim had a name twice as long and three times as hard. After I tripped over it two or three times he told me to just call him Hakim-a-barber.[5] I wanted to ask him was he a barber, but I didn't really think he was, so I didn't ask.

"You must belong to those beef cattle peoples down the road," I said. They said "Asalamalakim" when they met you, too, but they didn't shake hands. Always too busy: feeding the cattle, fixing the fences, putting up salt-lick shelters, throwing down hay. When the white folks poisoned some of the herd the men stayed up all night with

---

Visual Vocabulary The *Model A* was manufactured by the Ford Motor Company from 1927 to 1931.

---

4. *Wangero Leewanika Kemanjo* (wän gãr′ ō lē wä′ nē kə ke män′jō)

Reading Strategy Questioning *How do you think Asalamalakim's comment makes Mama feel?* **R2**

Vocabulary

oppress (ə pres′) *v.* to control or govern by the cruel and unjust use of force or authority

---

5. *Hakim-a-barber* (hä kēm′ ä bär′ bər)

Literary Element Reliable/Unreliable Narrator *What is Mama's view of this conversation? What do you think Asalamalakim's view might be?* **L1**

Reading Strategy Questioning *Do you think that Mama knew all along that Asalamalakim was a greeting, not a name? Explain.* **R3**

Additional Support

Skills Practice

GRAMMAR AND LANGUAGE:
Possessive Pronouns Write the following sentences on the board and underline the words *hers* and *your:*
Dee acted as if the quilts were already <u>hers</u>.
Dee said, "You don't understand <u>your</u> heritage."

Say: Possessive pronouns are pronouns that show ownership. Other common possessive pronouns include *my, mine, his, its, our,* and *their.* Remember that apostrophes are not used with possessive pronouns. Therefore, always write *its* (not *it's*) and *your* (not *you're*) to show possession. **OL**

Giving Thanks, 1942, Horace Pippin.
The Barnes Foundation, Merion Station, PA. ★

rifles in their hands. I walked a mile and a half just to see the sight.

Hakim-a-barber said, "I accept some of their **doctrines**, but farming and raising cattle is not my style." (They didn't tell me, and I didn't ask, whether Wangero (Dee) had really gone and married him.)

We sat down to eat and right away he said he didn't eat collards and pork was unclean. Wangero, though, went on through the chitlins and corn bread, the greens and everything else. She talked a blue streak over the sweet potatoes. Everything delighted her. Even the fact that we still used the benches her daddy made for the table when we couldn't afford to buy chairs.

"Oh, Mama!" she cried. Then turned to Hakim-a-barber. "I never knew how lovely these benches are. You can feel the rump prints," she said, running her hands underneath her and along the bench. Then she gave a sigh and her hand closed over Grandma Dee's butter dish. "That's it!" she said. "I knew there was something I wanted to ask you if I could have." She jumped up from the table and went over in the corner where the churn stood, the milk in it clabber[6] by now. She looked at the churn and looked at it.

"This churn top is what I need," she said. "Didn't Uncle Buddy whittle it out of a tree you all used to have?"

"Yes," I said.

"Uh huh," she said happily. "And I want the dasher, too."

"Uncle Buddy whittle that, too?" asked the barber.

Dee (Wangero) looked up at me.

---

6. *Clabber* is the thick, clotted part of sour milk.

Literary Element Reliable/Unreliable Narrator *From this narration of events, what impressions are you gaining of Asalamalakim? Explain.* **L2**

Vocabulary

doctrine (dok′ trin) n. a particular principle or position that is taught or supported, as of a religion

Big Idea Life Transitions *Why is Dee so interested in these everyday objects?* **BI**

Literary Element Reliable/Unreliable Narrator *Mama calls Hakim-a-barber "the barber." What does this reveal about her attitude toward him?* **L3**

ALICE WALKER **201**

Differentiated Instruction

Clarifying The exposition of "Everyday Use" is long and fragmented, as Mama's narrative spans the decades with the speed of thought. It may be useful to review what the reader knows and does not know. Have students write three headings at the top of a sheet of paper: *What I Know, What I Think I Know,* and *What I Don't Know.* Give them a few minutes to list as many items as they can under each of these headings. Then have them share information with a partner. Create a master list on the board. Point out that early in any story some confusion is common. **BL**

Teach

R1 Reading Strategy

Questioning Answer:
Maggie overheard the discussion about the quilts. She is upset because they have been promised to her. **OL**

L Literary Element

Reliable/Unreliable

Narrator Answer: *Dee would likely describe things differently. Mama's interpretation of Dee's action may reflect her frustration with Dee, rather than Dee's actual motivation for coming back.* **OL**

BI1 Big Idea

Life Transitions

Answer: *Dee is cruel enough to say "backward," and thinks "everyday use" is inappropriate. Mama and Maggie find "everyday use" for everything.* **OL**

"Aunt Dee's first husband whittled the dash," said Maggie so low you almost couldn't hear her. "His name was Henry, but they called him Stash."

"Maggie's brain is like an elephant's," Wangero said, laughing. "I can use the churn top as a centerpiece for the alcove[7] table," she said, sliding a plate over the churn, "and I'll think of something artistic to do with the dasher."

When she finished wrapping the dasher[8] the handle stuck out. I took it for a moment in my hands. You didn't even have to look close to see where hands pushing the dasher up and down to make butter had left a kind of sink in the wood. In fact, there were a lot of small sinks; you could see where thumbs and fingers had sunk into the wood. It was beautiful light yellow wood, from a tree that grew in the yard where Big Dee and Stash had lived.

After dinner Dee (Wangero) went to the trunk at the foot of my bed and started rifling through it. Maggie hung back in the kitchen over the dishpan. Out came Wangero with two quilts. They had been pieced by Grandma Dee and then Big Dee and me had hung them on the quilt frames on the front porch and quilted them. One was in the Lone Star pattern. The other was Walk Around the Mountain. In both of them were scraps of dresses Grandma Dee had worn fifty and more years ago. Bits and pieces of Grandpa Jarrell's Paisley shirts. And one teeny faded blue piece, about the size of a penny matchbox, that was from Great Grandpa Ezra's uniform that he wore in the Civil War.

"Mama," Wangero said sweet as a bird. "Can I have these old quilts?"

I heard something fall in the kitchen, and a minute later the kitchen door slammed.

---

7. An *alcove* (al′ kōv) is a small room or recessed opening off of a larger room.

8. A *dasher* is part of a churn, an old-fashioned device for making butter.

Reading Strategy Questioning *Why might Maggie have slammed the kitchen door?* **R1**

"Why don't you take one or two of the others?" I asked. "These old things was just done by me and Big Dee from some tops your grandma pieced before she died."

"No," said Wangero. "I don't want those. They are stitched around the borders by machine."

"That'll make them last better," I said.

"That's not the point," said Wangero. "These are all pieces of dresses Grandma used to wear. She did all this stitching by hand. Imagine!" She held the quilts securely in her arms, stroking them.

"Some of the pieces, like those lavender ones, come from old clothes her mother handed down to her," I said, moving up to touch the quilts. Dee (Wangero) moved back just enough so that I couldn't reach the quilts. They already belonged to her.

"Imagine!" she breathed again, clutching them closely to her bosom.

"The truth is," I said, "I promised to give them quilts to Maggie, for when she marries John Thomas."

She gasped like a bee had stung her.

"Maggie can't appreciate these quilts!" she said. "She'd probably be backward enough to put them to everyday use."

"I reckon she would," I said. "God knows I been saving 'em for long enough with nobody using 'em. I hope she will!" I didn't want to bring up how I had offered Dee (Wangero) a quilt when she went away to college. Then she had told me they were old-fashioned, out of style.

"But they're *priceless*!" she was saying now, furiously; for she has a temper. "Maggie would put them on the bed

---

Literary Element Reliable/Unreliable Narrator *Would Dee explain her action the same way that Mama does? Do you judge Mama to be a reliable narrator at this point? Explain.* **L**

Big Idea Life Transitions *How does this passage suggest a fundamental difference in values between Dee, Mama, and Maggie?* **BI1**

Reading Strategy Questioning *Why does Dee want the quilts now, when she did not want to take one to college?* **R2**

Additional Support

Skills Practice

READING: Comparing and Contrasting Conducting a detailed comparison of the two sisters in the story can help students draw conclusions about the story's theme and about the narrator's character traits. Have students create a chart contrasting Maggie and Dee. Suggest that they begin with superficial traits, such as physical appearance and style of dress, progress to discernible traits, such as speaking styles, and end with traits they infer from the characters' dialogue and actions, such as kindness and generosity. Have volunteers contribute items for a chart on the board. **OL**

Quilts on the Line, 1994. Anna Belle Lee Washington. Oil on canvas, 20 x 30 in.

Viewing the Art: Compare and contrast the family and the setting of this painting with those in the story. What are the most striking differences? Similarities?

and in five years they'd be in rags. Less than that!"

"She can always make some more," I said. "Maggie knows how to quilt."

Dee (Wangero) looked at me with hatred. "You just will not understand. The point is these quilts, *these* quilts!"

"Well," I said, stumped. "What would *you* do with them?"

"Hang them," she said. As if that was the only thing you *could* do with quilts.

Maggie by now was standing in the door. I could almost hear the sound her feet made as they scraped over each other.

"She can have them, Mama," she said, like somebody used to never winning anything, or having anything reserved for her. "I can 'member Grandma Dee without the quilts."

I looked at her hard. She had filled her bottom lip with checkerberry snuff and it gave her face a kind of dopey, hangdog look. It was Grandma Dee and Big Dee who taught her how to quilt herself. She stood there with her scarred hands hidden in the folds of her skirt. She looked at her sister with something like fear but she wasn't mad at her. This was Maggie's portion. This was the way she knew God to work.

When I looked at her like that something hit me in the top of my head and ran down to the soles of my feet. Just like when I'm in church and the spirit of God touches me and I get happy and shout. I did something I never had done before: hugged Maggie to me, then dragged her on into the room, snatched the quilts out of Miss Wangero's hands and dumped them into Maggie's lap. Maggie just sat there on my bed with her mouth open.

"Take one or two of the others," I said to Dee.

But she turned without a word and went out to Hakim-a-barber.

Big Idea Life Transitions *Why do you think Mama reacts this way?* **BI₂**

ALICE WALKER **203**

Reading in the Real World

Careers Dee's way of life is a far cry from the rural poverty in which she was raised. Have students think of real-life examples of men or women whose present careers have little in common with their backgrounds—people who have risen to prominence from deprivation or from different cultures. Ask students to cut out newspaper or magazine articles about their subjects and to share their findings with others in groups. Have them consider such questions as these: How did the person transform his or her life? Is he or she happier as a result? **OL**

Teach

R₂ Reading Strategy

Questioning Answer: *Dee's perspective has changed; she now sees the quilts as works of art or valuable artifacts of her former life.* **OL**

BI₂ Big Idea

Life Transitions
Answer: *Mama cannot accept the new Dee. Dee represents new ideas. Maggie represents Mama's way of life. Mama's choice to give Maggie the quilts is an assertion of her preference and her own ideals.* **OL**

★ Viewing the Art

Answer: *Students may mention that the scene in the painting is far more serene than what is depicted in the story or that none of the characters in the painting is dressed as outlandishly as Dee (Wangero). Similarities may include the rural setting, the prominence of women and girls, the African American characters, and the importance of the quilts.* **AS**

Objectives
• To analyze a reliable/unreliable narrator (SE)
• To question (SE)
• To analyze art (SE)
• To compare and contrast (TWE)

Teach

 Literary Element

Point of View Ask students to consider what the story would be like if it had been told from Maggie's point of view. How would she tell about the scene in which Mama snatches the quilts from Dee? *(Students may mention fear of Dee and surprise at Mama's actions.)* **OL**

L2 Literary Element

Reliable/Unreliable Narrator Answer: *Mama feels satisfied at the end of Dee's visit: she sits there "just enjoying." If Dee had told the story, she might have portrayed her mother as being upset, resentful, or spiteful.* **OL**

CheckPoint

Use the CheckPoint questions on Presentation Plus! to check students' mastery of the selection. These questions can be used with interactive response keypads for immediate student feedback.

★ Viewing the Art

The term *appliqué* comes from the French word *appliquer,* meaning "to put on." Appliqué is a type of quilting in which fabric patches, often decorative ones, are sewn onto a larger piece of material. **AS**

Biblical quilt, Virginia, 19th Century. American School. Cotton with applique. Private Collection.

"You just don't understand," she said, as Maggie and I came out to the car.

"What don't I understand?" I wanted to know.

"Your heritage," she said. And then she turned to Maggie, kissed her, and said, "You ought to try to make something of yourself, too, Maggie. It's really a new day for us. But from the way you and Mama still live you'd never know it."

She put on some sunglasses that hid everything above the tip of her nose and her chin.

Maggie smiled; maybe at the sunglasses. But a real smile, not scared. After we watched the car dust settle I asked Maggie to bring me a dip of snuff. And then the two of us sat there just enjoying, until it was time to go in the house and go to bed. ⌁

> **Literary Element** Reliable/Unreliable Narrator *How does Mama feel about the way Dee's visit ended? If Dee had been the narrator, how might the story have ended differently?* **L2**

204 UNIT 1 THE SHORT STORY

Additional Support

Skills Practice

RESEARCH: Political and Social History Have students use Internet and library resources to learn more about the United States during the time period of this story. Tell students to research some of the major events of the 1960s and 1970s and then have them share their research with the rest of the class. Challenge students to create a multimedia presentation. **OL**

RESPONDING AND THINKING CRITICALLY

Respond

1. To whom would you have given the quilts? Explain.

Recall and Interpret

2. (a)How does Mama describe each daughter before Dee's arrival? (b)How do you think Mama feels about Maggie and Dee based on these descriptions?

3. (a)What is special about the two quilts Dee wants? (b)How does the origin of the quilts affect Maggie's and Dee's feelings about them?

4. (a)Why does Dee leave the house so abruptly? (b)Before Dee leaves, she tells Mama, "You just don't understand." Do you think that Mama understands? Explain.

Analyze and Evaluate

5. Why does the author begin the story with a description of the yard and a daydream about being on a television show?

6. (a)How important is the setting in this story? (b)How might the story be different if the characters lived in another time and place?

7. (a)Why do you think Hakim-a-barber (also called Asalamalakim) is in the story? (b)How does the character of Hakim-a-barber make the story richer and more interesting?

Connect

8. **Big Idea** **Life Transitions** Mama does not like many of the ways that Dee has changed since leaving home. What is your opinion of the changes that Dee has undergone? Explain.

LITERARY ANALYSIS

Literary Element Reliable/Unreliable Narrator

In "Everyday Use," Alice Walker tells her story through Mama's eyes. Mama is the **narrator**, and everything the reader learns is from her point of view.

1. The author might have told this story from the point of view of Dee or Maggie. Why do you think she chose Mama as the narrator?

2. Do you think the story would be different if Mama was not the narrator? Try writing a summary of the story's events through the eyes of another character. You might chose Dee, Maggie, or Hakim-a-barber (Asalamalakim). Before you begin writing your summary, make a list of ways in which your character is different from and similar to Mama. These qualities will help you determine how your character's retelling will vary with that of Mama.

3. The reader must decide whether the narrator is reliable; that is, whether to trust what the narrator says. Do you trust Mama's version of events? In what ways is she reliable? In what ways might she be unreliable?

Review: Dialogue

As you learned on page 111, **dialogue** is conversation between characters in a literary work. Dialogue can contribute to characterization, create mood, advance the plot, and develop theme.

Partner Activity Work with a classmate to analyze sections of dialogue. Decide what each section contributes to the story.

Dialogue	What It Contributes
"Wa-su-zo-Tean-o!"	Helps show how Dee has changed; helps contrast Dee's world and way of life with Mama's
"What happened to 'Dee'?"	Helps show that Mama does not readily accept Dee's new ways

ALICE WALKER **205**

Literary Element

1. Mama can see the virtues and flaws of both daughters. Maggie might have been too weak, and Dee too overwhelming, as a narrator.

2. Summaries should show a different perspective.

3. Mama knows the truth from her point of view, but she does not have a wide experience of the world.

Review: Dialogue

Dialogue	"How do I look, Mama?"	"There I was not."
What It Contributes	Helps show that Maggie is insecure	Helps show that Mama is witty

---

Assess

1. Students may give both quilts to Dee, since she asked for them, or one to Dee and one to Maggie.

2. (a) Maggie is homely, envious, timid, and "not bright." Dee is bold, aggressive, and stylish. (b) Mama feels that Dee is overconfident and cruel; Mama identifies most with Maggie.

3. (a) Grandma Dee pieced them from scraps of old clothing. (b) Maggie sees them both as useful and a connection to her grandmother; Dee is interested in their aesthetic and cultural value.

4. (a) Dee is angry that she was not given the quilts. (b) Mama understands Dee's selfishness and Maggie's appreciation for the quilts, but not the Dee's new values.

5. To contrast Dee's view of Mama with how Mama wishes she were viewed and to show that Mama longs for positive interaction

6. (a) The setting emphasizes how life changed radically for some African Americans who moved from rural simplicity to urban centers. (b) The clash of values might not be as intense.

7. (a) Hakim-a-barber helps portray the new world Dee inhabits and the values she has embraced. (b) He underscores the conflict between Dee and her mother.

8. Students may say that Dee has changed with the times, whereas Mama lives in the past, or that Dee fails to respect tradition.

Assess

Reading Strategy

1. Students may say that the characters and the situation are complex, and complexity always raises questions. When change happens fast (in one generation), old ways and new ways clash.

2. Change is complicated. It is clear from the story that none of the characters is entirely right or wrong.

Vocabulary

1. a **2.** c **3.** b **4.** a

Academic Vocabulary

1. Dee's attributes include self-confidence, a desire to do better than her own family did, and a lack of respect for her mother and sister's home and values.

2. Students may say yes because Mama is wise enough to keep the quilts at home and give them to Maggie. Others may say that there was no single right thing to do.

Writing About Literature

Use these criteria when evaluating students' writing:

• Does the introduction contain a thesis statement that addresses the topic?

Reading Strategy Questioning

Mama's limited point of view is not entirely reliable. This puts the burden on the reader to ask questions throughout the reading of "Everyday Use."

1. Why does Walker present a story with so many open questions? What are Walker's ideas about change and the clash between old and new ways?

2. Do you think Walker's goal was to give us a story with predictable answers, or was she showing us how complicated change can be? Explain.

Vocabulary Practice

Practice with Word Parts For each of the following questions, select the best answer.

1. Which of the following words has a root word that means "teach"?
   a. doctrine   **b.** oppress   **c.** furtive

2. Which of the following words contains a suffix that suggests an adjective?
   a. sidle   **b.** initiate   **c.** furtive

3. Which of the following words has a root word that means "side"?
   a. distress   **b.** sidle   **c.** doctrine

4. Which of the following words has a prefix that can mean "against"?
   a. restrict   **b.** oppress   **c.** prescribe

Academic Vocabulary

Here are two words from the vocabulary list on page R82.

attribute (a′trə byut) *n.* a characteristic or quality of a person, place, thing, or idea

credit (kre′dit) *v.* to consider someone or something, usually in a positive way, as the source, possessor, or agent of a quality

Practice and Apply
1. What are Dee's main **attributes**?
2. Do you **credit** Mama with doing the right thing?

Writing About Literature

Evaluate Author's Craft When Walker chose Mama as the narrator of this story, she knew that Mama would tell the story in a particular way. She also knew that Mama's limited life experience would be reflected in her point of view. Why do you think Walker chose to use a partially reliable narrator?

Develop an answer to this question and turn it into a thesis statement for your paper. A thesis statement describes the main idea you will support. Then gather evidence from the story that supports your thesis and present it in three body paragraphs. One way to relate your thesis to your body paragraphs in both content and structure is shown below.

Walker chose an unreliable narrator because reason 1,   reason 2,   and reason 3

| Body Paragraph 1 Reason 1 | Body Paragraph 2 Reason 2 | Body Paragraph 3 Reason 3 |

After you complete a draft of your paper, have a peer read it and suggest revisions. Then proofread and edit your work for errors in spelling, grammar, and punctuation.

Learning For Life

Talk to older relatives or friends about their childhoods or about the way things used to be when they were young. Use questions like these to get started:

• When you think of your childhood, what memories stand out most clearly?

• What special objects do you remember from your past? Why were they important to you?

• What was the best thing about the "good old days?" What was the worst thing?

Record your interviews or take notes. Share the information you have gathered with the rest of your class.

 Web Activities For eFlashcards, Selection Quick Checks, and other Web activities, go to www.glencoe.com.

• Do the body paragraphs provide evidence supporting the thesis statement?

Learning For Life

Have students compare the world in the "good old days" with today's world.

Literature Online

Web Activities Have students access the Web site for interactive activities that will help them assess their understanding of the selection.

Comparing Literature Across Genres

Connecting to the Reading Selections

How do writers and storytellers pass along lessons they have learned about life? The three literary works compared here—a short story, a legend, and a personal letter—each share wisdom.

COMPARING THE [Big Idea] Life Transitions

Young people setting off on their own, even for a short time, face challenges. They find strength from their families, their cultures, and their own inner resources. The three selections you are about to read treat this theme in different ways. In the short story, an English boy endures an ordeal of his own making that initiates him into adulthood. In the legend, a young Native American man attempts a quest that teaches him a lesson in humility. In the letter, a famous American author gives whimsical advice in practical living to his twelve-year-old daughter, who is attending a summer camp.

COMPARING Narrators

The relationship between the narrator to the literary work is the **narrative point of view.** In a letter or personal essay, the narrator always speaks in the first-person point of view. In fiction, the narrator can be inside or outside the story. A first-person narrator is a character who has access only to his or her own thoughts and feelings. A third-person narrator speaks to the reader from outside the story. Some third-person narrators are omniscient, which means that they know everything about all the characters in the story. Some third-person narrators have limited access to the thoughts and feelings of one character, and the reader views the story through that character's eyes.

COMPARING Author's Cultures

The writers featured here share rites of passage within their cultures—rituals associated with a change in status for an individual. In the three selections you are about to read, the rite of passage takes different forms: the first involves an individual, internal conflict within a young boy; the second involves the relation between an individual and his community; and the third involves fatherly advice to a teenage girl.

COMPARING LITERATURE **207**

Focus

BELLRINGER

Bellringer Options
Selection Focus
   Transparency 13
Daily Language
   Transparency 20
Or write on the board some common challenges students face every day, such as "standing up to a bully," "studying hard for a test," and "making new friends." **Ask:** What are some challenges you've faced in your life?
Have students discuss difficult challenges they've wanted to overcome in order to fulfill a need (to impress others, to accomplish a task).

Connecting to the Reading Selections

Allow students to share their responses to the opening question. Then have students discuss what they already know about Doris Lessing, Native American legends, and F. Scott Fitzgerald.

Selection Skills

Comparing Literature

Literary Elements
- Point of View (SE pp. 209–212, 215, 216, 220)
- Conflict (TWE p. 216)

Vocabulary Skills
- Antonyms (SE pp. 209, 220)

Reading Skills
- Visualizing (SE pp. 209, 211–213, 217, 220)
- Summarizing (TWE p. 226)

Listening/Speaking/ Viewing Skills
- Analyzing Art (SE p. 218; TWE pp. 210, 213, 214, 217, 223)

Writing Skills/Grammar
- Quickwrite (SE p. 225)
- Infinitive Phrases (TWE p. 222)
- Prewriting (TWE p. 224)

Life Skills
- Goal Setting (TWE p. 214)

Focus

COMPARING LITERATURE

BEFORE YOU READ

★ Literary History

Lessing's "Space Fiction"
Doris Lessing is the author of a science fiction series called *Canopus in Argos: Archives.* One of these books, *The Making of the Representative for Planet 8,* is about the inhabitants of a paradisaical planet. They are saved from annihilation by merging themselves into one indestructible soul. Lessing and composer Philip Glass wrote an opera based on the book. **AS**

Author Search To expand students' appreciation of Doris Lessing, have them access the Web site for additional information and resources.

Through the Tunnel

MEET DORIS LESSING

A theme of Lessing's life, starting fresh, took roots early. At the age of four, Lessing traveled with her parents on a transcontinental journey by train, leaving their home in Persia (now Iran) and traversing Russia, Europe, and England. From there, her family began their quest for a new life in Southern Rhodesia (now Zimbabwe).

Adjusting to Africa Doris's world as an energetic child was the African bush. She reveled in the land's wildlife, spaciousness, and smells. As was customary at the time for expatriates, Lessing was sent to boarding schools—first a convent, and then to a British girls' school. There, the young teenager developed pinkeye. Even when she was fully recovered, Lessing insisted that her eyesight was ruined: her mother came and got her, and "that was the end of [her] life at school." Educating herself at home, Lessing developed her writing skills. Soon after, she sold her first story to a magazine. Her career was launched.

Her first novel, *The Grass Is Singing,* was published in 1950. Her early work heavily draws from her years in Africa. *Martha Quest,* her second novel, depicts a white woman in Africa who escapes farm life by fleeing to the city, marries, divorces, and joins the Communist party—all parallels to Lessing's experience.

Unaffected by Criticism Lessing grew as a writer throughout her career. Never unduly influenced by social or political fashions of the day, Lessing has been difficult to categorize for the critics who review her work. Her books have received mixed reviews. Critics have characterized her style as being "blunt," having "analytical purity," and possessing "frankness and clarity."

"That is what learning is. You suddenly understand something you've understood all your life, but in a new way."

—Doris Lessing

The range of literary forms Lessing has tackled is impressive: short stories, fiction, nonfiction, "space fiction," essays, and plays. In 1962 Lessing published the controversial feminist novel *The Golden Notebook.* It quickly became a best seller. Her nonfiction books include *The Wind Blows away Our Words,* concerning the wars in Afghanistan during the 1980s, and *African Laughter: Four Visits to Zimbabwe,* an honest account of the new nation. She has also begun a series of autobiographies.

Critic William Peden summed up Lessing's strengths as a writer: "She tells a story which can be read with delight and wonder . . . a meaningful commentary on one or another phase of the endlessly varied human experience."

Doris Lessing was born in 1919.

LiteratureOnline Author Search For more about Doris Lessing, go to www.glencoe.com.

Additional Support

Skills Practice

READING: Previewing Students may find it beneficial to preview the selections that are about to read. Have students read through the titles of the selections, look at the art, skim the selections, and predict each author's purpose. Have them write down their ideas of what each selection is about. This can help students to derive more meaning and enjoyment from the text. **OL**

Connecting to the Story

Have you ever watched someone your age perform a difficult or challenging physical feat? Then have you asked yourself, "Could I do that?" In Lessing's story a young boy challenges himself to a feat where failure could mean death. Before you read, think about the following questions.

- Why do you think people challenge themselves to accomplish dangerous goals?
- What sorts of challenges have you given yourself?

Building Background

The story takes place at the seashore, probably on the Mediterranean coast during the 1940s or 1950s. Here, native boys could dive off rocks into the sea and practice breath-hold diving. This type of diving uses no equipment other than goggles or a facemask. Breath-hold diving can be very dangerous because of the great force of water pressure: water is more than a thousand times denser than air. Most breath-hold divers can remain submerged for less than one minute, although with training, some divers can stay underwater for several minutes.

Setting Purposes for Reading

Big Idea Life Transitions

As you read, identify Jerry's personal challenge and think about why this transition might be so important to him at this time in his life.

Literary Element Point of View

Point of View is the relationship of the narrator to the story. When a narrator in the third-person who is all-knowing tells a story, it is called **third-person omniscient point of view**. But although an all-knowing narrator knows everything about the characters and events, he or she may choose not to tell readers everything, leaving some aspects of human nature up to readers to ponder.

- See Literary Terms Handbook, p. R13.

Literature Online Interactive Literary Elements Handbook To review or learn more about the literary elements, go to www.glencoe.com.

Reading Strategy Visualizing

Readers **visualize** or form a mental image of events and places in a story through the descriptive words that the writer uses to appeal to senses of sight, hearing, touch, taste, and smell. Visualizing a scene is a useful and effective way to remember and understand what you read.

Reading Tip: Identifying Sensory Descriptions Use a chart like the one below to record Jerry's description of his tunnel experience and the corresponding senses.

Descriptive Phrases	Sense
"hot roughness"	touch
"fanged and angry boulders"	sight

Vocabulary

conscientiously (kon′ shē en′ shəs lē) adv. thoughtfully and carefully, p. 210 Slowly and conscientiously, the jury examined the evidence.

contrition (kən trish′ ən) n. sorrow for one's sin or wrongdoing; repentance; p. 210 A thief who shows contrition is on his way to being reformed.

supplication (səp′ lə kā′shən) n. an earnest and humble request; p. 211 After numerous supplications, the downtrodden man was finally given a job.

beseeching (bi sēch′ing) adj. begging; asking earnestly; p. 213 The homeless woman raised beseeching hands to all who passed by.

incredulous (in krej′ə ləs) adj. unwilling or unable to believe; p. 216 We were incredulous at the child's story of the candy-stealing ghost.

Vocabulary Tip: Some words have an exact opposite, or **antonym**, such as hot and cold. Some words have several antonyms—for example, courageous and valiant are antonyms of cowardly. Some words, such as dog, have no true antonym.

Focus

Summary

Jerry, a young English boy on vacation at a beach resort, is amazed as he watches a group of local boys perform daring dives from high rocks. When the boys reject him, apparently because he cannot duplicate their feat, he challenges himself to swim the tunnel and prove himself. His plan for accomplishing this goal includes learning to hold his breath for longer and longer periods of time. Finally, he successfully swims the tunnel and, in the process, makes an important discovery about himself.

V Vocabulary

Vocabulary File

Say: Add these words and definitions to your vocabulary file. For each word, include a sentence that gives you an example of how to use the word. **OL** Students with English language needs should include the pronunciations of these words in their files. **EL**

Literary Elements Have students access the Web site to improve their understanding of point of view.

OBJECTIVES
In studying this selection, you will focus on the following:
- analyzing third-person omniscient point of view
- visualizing sensory details in setting
- illustrating a scene from a literary text

DORIS LESSING **209**

Selection Resources

Print Materials
- Unit 1 Resources (Fast File), pp. 75–77
- Leveled Vocabulary Development, p. 16
- Selection and Unit Assessments, pp. 35–36
- Selection Quick Checks, p. 18

Transparencies
- Bellringer Options Transparencies:
  Selection Focus Transparency 13
  Daily Language Practice Transparency 20
- Literary Elements Transparency 22

Technology
- TeacherWorks Plus™ CD-ROM
- StudentWorks Plus™ CD-ROM
- Presentation Plus!™ CD-ROM
- Literature Online, glencoe.com
- Online Student Edition, mhln.com
- ExamView® Assessment Suite CD-ROM
- Vocabulary PuzzleMaker CD-ROM
- Listening Library, disc 1 tracks 18, 19, 20

COMPARING LITERATURE

Teach

Big Idea

Life Transitions

Say: Keep the following questions in mind as you read. Why does Jerry want to go off on his own? Why does Jerry want to impress the older boys so much? How does Jerry change over the course of the story? *(He hungers for an adventure. He wants to be accepted by the older boys. He goes from immature to self-confident.)* **OL**

L1 Literary Element

Point of View Answer: *Her thoughts reveal that she is concerned that she has not been paying enough attention to Jerry. Jerry recognizes this response, suggesting that she is usually thoughtful and concerned.* **OL**

★ Viewing the Art

A Lonely Beach Composition is one factor responsible for how a viewer responds to the image. **Ask:** How does the placement of the path and the vegetation influence your perception of the beach? *(Students might say that the placement of the path on the right edge of the image makes the beach seem isolated).* **AS**

Through the Tunnel

Doris Lessing

Beach. Bobbi Tull. ★

Going to the shore on the first morning of the vacation, the young English boy stopped at a turning of the path and looked down at a wild and rocky bay, and then over to the crowded beach he knew so well from other years. His mother walked on in front of him, carrying a bright striped bag in one hand. Her other arm, swinging loose, was very white in the sun. The boy watched that white, naked arm, and turned his eyes, which had a frown behind them, toward the bay and back again to his mother. When she felt he was not with her, she swung around. "Oh, there you are, Jerry!" she said. She looked impatient, then smiled. "Why, darling, would you rather not come with me? Would you rather—" She frowned, **conscientiously** worrying over what

amusements he might secretly be longing for, which she had been too busy or too careless to imagine. He was very familiar with that anxious, apologetic smile. **Contrition** sent him running after her. And yet, as he ran, he looked back over his shoulder at the wild bay; and all morning, as he played on the safe beach, he was thinking of it.

Next morning, when it was time for the routine of swimming and sunbathing, his mother said, "Are you tired of the usual beach, Jerry? Would you like to go somewhere else?"

> **Literary Element** Point of View By expressing Jerry's and his mother's perspectives here, how does the narrator help you understand the mother's character? **L1**

> **Vocabulary**
>
> **conscientiously** (kon′ shē en′ shəs lē) *adv.* thoughtfully and carefully

> **Vocabulary**
>
> **contrition** (kən trish′ ən) *n.* sorrow for one's sin or wrongdoing; repentance

210 UNIT 1 THE SHORT STORY

Additional Support

Leveled Reading An adapted version of this selection is available on page 114 of *Jamestown Literature: An Adapted Reader* grade 10.

210

Skills Practice

READING: Predicting Using prior knowledge and the information they've gathered in the first few paragraphs of reading, students can predict what they will learn in reading a selection or what event might happen next in a selection. **Say:** Use the title and text clues from the first page to predict what you think the conflict in the story might be. Suggest that students periodically revisit their prediction as they're reading to verify or revise it. *(Students should realize that there will probably be some sort of tunnel Jerry will contend with in the bay.)* **OL**

"Oh, no!" he said quickly, smiling at her out of that unfailing impulse of contrition—a sort of chivalry.[1] Yet, walking down the path with her, he blurted out, "I'd like to go and have a look at those rocks down there."

She gave the idea her attention. It was a wild looking place, and there was no one there; but she said, "Of course, Jerry. When you've had enough, come to the big beach. Or just go straight back to the villa,[2] if you like." She walked away, that bare arm, now slightly reddened from yesterday's sun, swinging. And he almost ran after her again, feeling it unbearable that she should go by herself, but he did not.

She was thinking, Of course he's old enough to be safe without me. Have I been keeping him too close? He mustn't feel he ought to be with me. I must be careful.

He was an only child, eleven years old. She was a widow. She was determined to be neither possessive nor lacking in devotion. She went worrying off to her beach.

As for Jerry, once he saw that his mother had gained her beach, he began the steep descent to the bay. From where he was, high up among red-brown rocks, it was a scoop of moving bluish green fringed with white. As he went lower, he saw that it spread among small promontories and inlets of rough, sharp rock, and the crisping, lapping surface showed stains of purple and darker blue. Finally, as he ran sliding and scraping down the last few yards, he saw an edge of white surf and the shallow, luminous movement of water over white sand, and, beyond that, a solid, heavy blue.

He ran straight into the water and began swimming. He was a good swimmer. He went out fast over the gleaming sand, over a middle region where rocks lay like discolored monsters under the surface, and then he was in the real sea—a warm sea where irregular cold currents from the deep water shocked his limbs.

When he was so far out that he could look back not only on the little bay but past the promontory that was between it and the big beach, he floated on the buoyant surface and looked for his mother. There she was, a speck of yellow under an umbrella that looked like a slice of orange peel. He swam back to shore, relieved at being sure she was there, but all at once very lonely.

On the edge of a small cape that marked the side of the bay away from the promontory was a loose scatter of rocks. Above them, some boys were stripping off their clothes. They came running, naked, down to the rocks. The English boy swam toward them, but kept his distance at a stone's throw. They were of that coast; all of them were burned smooth dark brown and speaking a language he did not understand. To be with them, of them, was a craving that filled his whole body. He swam a little closer; they turned and watched him with narrowed, alert dark eyes. Then one smiled and waved. It was enough. In a minute, he had swum in and was on the rocks beside them, smiling with a desperate, nervous **supplication**. They shouted cheerful greetings at him; and then, as he preserved

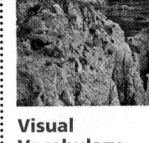

Visual Vocabulary
Promontories are high points of land or rock overlooking the water.

---

1. Here, *chivalry* (shiv′ əl rē) means "an act of courtesy or politeness."
2. *Villa*, from the Italian word, means "house," usually one in the country or at the seashore.

Reading Strategy Visualizing *What mental picture does the word "wild" provoke? How does it contrast with the beach where the characters swim and sunbathe?* **R**

Literary Element Point of View *Here, the omniscient narrator reveals the mother's concerns. What internal conflict might she be experiencing?* **L2**

Literary Element Point of View *Why do you think the urge to be with the boys is so strong in Jerry?* **L3**

Vocabulary

supplication (səp′ lə kā′shən) n. an earnest and humble request

DORIS LESSING **211**

Teach

R Reading Strategy

Visualizing Answer: *"Wild" elicits a vision of an untamed, perhaps dangerous place—not the safe, familiar beach.* **OL**

L2 Literary Element

Point of View

Answer: *Her son is growing up. She wants to give him independence, but finds it difficult.* **OL**

L3 Literary Element

Point of View

Answer: *Their company would make him feel less lonely and isolated.* **OL**

CheckPoint

Use the CheckPoint questions on Presentation Plus! to monitor students' comprehension. These questions can be used with interactive response keypads for immediate student feedback.

Readability Scores
Dale-Chall: 6.6
DRP: 54
Lexile: 860

English Language Coach

Prefixes Write *impatient, careless, unbearable,* and *darker* on the board. Help English language learners analyze the words. Point out that the prefix *im-*, which means "not," may also be spelled *ir-, in-,* or *il-,* depending on the spelling of its root word. Add that not all words that begin with *im-* and *in-*, such as *imagine,* contain prefixes. Have students find other words with prefixes and suffixes in the story. Then have partners discuss what the root words mean and how the prefixes and suffixes change its meaning. **EL**

Objectives
• To analyze third-person omniscient point of view (SE)
• To visualize sensory details in a setting (SE)
• To make predictions (TWE)

Teach

BI Big Idea

Life Transitions
Answer: *For Jerry, being accepted by peers is important.* **OL**

L Literary Element

Point of View Answer: *His plea to be accepted despite failure is an innate, unchangeable part of his immaturity or insecurity.* **OL**

R1 Reading Strategy

Visualizing
Answer: *The tanned boys with heads back spouting water up into the air look like brown whales surfacing to breathe.* **OL**

---

his nervous, uncomprehending smile, they understood that he was a foreigner strayed from his own beach, and they proceeded to forget him. But he was happy. He was with them.

They began diving again and again from a high point into a well of blue sea between rough, pointed rocks. After they had dived and come up, they swam around, hauled themselves up, and waited their turn to dive again. They were big boys—men, to Jerry. He dived, and they watched him; and when he swam around to take his place, they made way for him. He felt he was accepted, and he dived again, carefully, proud of himself.

Soon the biggest of the boys poised himself, shot down into the water, and did not come up. The others stood about, watching. Jerry, after waiting for the sleek brown head to appear, let out a yell of warning; they looked at him idly and turned their eyes back toward the water. After a long time, the boy came up on the other side of a big dark rock, letting the air out of his lungs in a sputtering gasp and a shout of triumph. Immediately the rest of them dived in. One moment, the morning seemed full of chattering boys; the next, the air and the surface of the water were empty. But through the heavy blue, dark shapes could be seen moving and groping.

Jerry dived, shot past the school of underwater swimmers, saw a black wall of rock looming at him, touched it, and bobbed up at once to the surface, where the wall was a low barrier he could see across. There was no one visible; under him, in the water, the dim shapes of the swimmers had disappeared. Then one, and then another of the boys came up on the far side of the barrier of rock, and he understood that they had swum through some gap or hole in it. He plunged down again. He could see nothing through the stinging salt water but the blank rock. When he came up the boys were all on the

---

Big Idea Life Transitions *Why might Jerry value the boys' acceptance so much?* **BI**

---

diving rock, preparing to attempt the feat again. And now, in a panic of failure, he yelled up, in English, "Look at me! Look!" and he began splashing and kicking in the water like a foolish dog.

They looked down gravely, frowning. He knew the frown. At moments of failure, when he clowned to claim his mother's attention, it was with just this grave, embarrassed inspection that she rewarded him. Through his hot shame, feeling the pleading grin on his face like a scar that he could never remove, he looked up at the group of big brown boys on the rock and shouted, *"Bonjour! Merci! Au revoir! Monsieur, monsieur!"*[3] while he hooked his fingers round his ears and waggled them.

Water surged into his mouth; he choked, sank, came up. The rock, lately weighted with boys, seemed to rear up out of the water as their weight was removed. They were flying down past him, now, into the water; the air was full of falling bodies. Then the rock was empty in the hot sunlight. He counted one, two, three. . . .

At fifty, he was terrified. They must all be drowning beneath him, in the watery caves of the rock! At a hundred, he stared around him at the empty hillside, wondering if he should yell for help. He counted faster, faster, to hurry them up, to bring them to the surface quickly, to drown them quickly—anything rather than the terror of counting on and on into the blue emptiness of the morning. And then, at a hundred and sixty, the water beyond the rock was full of boys blowing like brown whales. They swam back to the shore without a look at him.

---

3. *"Bonjour! . . . monsieur!"* These words are French for "Hello! Thanks! Good-bye! Sir, sir!"

Literary Element Point of View *The narrator explains Jerry's response to failure with a simile. What does this figure of speech imply about Jerry?* **L**

Reading Strategy Visualizing *What mental image do you have of "boys blowing like brown whales"?* **R1**

Additional Support

Skills Practice

WRITING: Spatial Order Writers can organize details of a setting in spatial order, presenting details from left to right, far to near, top to bottom, clockwise, etc. Read aloud the description of the setting, beginning in the fifth paragraph on page 211. Have students determine the kind of spatial order Lessing uses *(top to bottom)*. Ask them to note phrases used to present that order, such as *to the bay* and *over white sand*. Have students write a short descriptive paragraph about a favorite scene or setting using phrases that convey spatial order. **OL**

Cap Ferrat, 1965. Mikhail Trufanov.
Oil on card, 22.9 x 33 cm. Private Collection. ⭐

He climbed back to the diving rock and sat down, feeling the hot roughness of it under his thighs. The boys were gathering up their bits of clothing and running off along the shore to another promontory. They were leaving to get away from him. He cried openly, fists in his eyes. There was no one to see him, and he cried himself out.

It seemed to him that a long time had passed, and he swam out to where he could see his mother. Yes, she was still there, a yellow spot under an orange umbrella. He swam back to the big rock, climbed up, and dived into the blue pool among the fanged and angry boulders. Down he went, until he touched the wall of rock again. But

the salt was so painful in his eyes that he could not see.

He came to the surface, swam to shore, and went back to the villa to wait for his mother. Soon she walked slowly up the path, swinging her striped bag, the flushed, naked arm dangling beside her. "I want some swimming goggles," he panted, defiant and **beseeching**.

She gave him a patient, inquisitive look as she said casually, "Well, of course, darling."

But now, now, now! He must have them this minute, and no other time. He nagged and pestered until she went with him to a shop. As soon as she had bought the goggles, he grabbed them from her hand as if

Reading Strategy Visualizing *What mental image does "fanged and angry" help you create?* **R₂**

Vocabulary

beseeching (bi sēch′ ing) *adj.* begging; asking earnestly

DORIS LESSING **213**

Teach

R₂ Reading Strategy

Visualizing
Answer: *The blue pool with the fanged boulders looks like an angry mouth swallowing Jerry. "Fanged" suggests sharp, pointed rocks and "angry" suggests the possibility of a dangerous attack.*
Ask: Why would the author use these particular words to describe the rocks? *(It makes the rocks sound like living, violent animals for Jerry to defeat. The sea and earth themselves are his adversaries.)* **OL**

⭐ **Viewing the Art**

Mikhail Trufanov, a Russian artist who died in the late 1980s, painted a number of portraits of laborers at work and at rest. **Ask:** What would Jerry think of this swimmer? Explain your answer. *(The swimmer looks fairly professional and skilled, so Jerry would probably admire him. Jerry might also be envious of his skill.)* **AS**

Reading in the Real World

Career In recent years, improvements in digital camera technology have simplified and made more efficient some aspects of photography. Many professional photographers have switched from film-based cameras to high-end digital cameras, which record images onto an electronic medium, usually memory cards of one type or another. Have students research additional information about professional digital cameras, such as size, cost, quality of image, and ease of use. **OL**

Objectives
• To analyze third-person omniscient point of view (SE)
• To visualize sensory details in setting (SE)
• To write using spatial order (TWE)

Teach

R **Reading Strategy**

Visualizing Ask: How would you characterize this description, in terms of visual image and physical sensation? *(The fish are bright and shiny like silver. They are tiny and soft and feel like light flakes on the skin as they swim past.)* **OL**

★ Viewing the Art

John Bunker has had his art collected by a number of museums, including the Jacksonville Museum of Modern Art and the Cummer Museum of Art and Gardens. His work often features flowers, sea shells, and fish. **Ask:** How does the painting show the change in Jerry's underwater world after he has gotten the goggles? *(It shows that the underwater world is no longer a dark, completely alien place for Jerry now that he can open his eyes to see it. It is a world filled with life and color, showing that he is taking a step toward enlightenment.)* **AS**

School of Fish, 1991.
John Bunker. Mixed media. ★

she were going to claim them for herself, and was off, running down the steep path to the bay.

Jerry swam out to the big barrier rock, adjusted the goggles, and dived. The impact of the water broke the rubber-enclosed vacuum, and the goggles came loose. He understood that he must swim down to the base of the rock from the surface of the water. He fixed the goggles tight and firm, filled his lungs, and floated, face down, on the water. Now, he could see. It was as if he had eyes of a different kind—fish eyes that showed everything clear and delicate and wavering in the bright water.

Under him, six or seven feet down, was a floor of perfectly clean, shining white sand, rippled firm and hard by the tides. Two grayish shapes steered there, like long, rounded pieces of wood or slate. They were fish. He saw them nose toward each other, poise motionless, make a dart forward, swerve off, and come around again. It was like a water dance. A few inches above them the water sparkled as if sequins were dropping through it. Fish again—myriads of minute fish, the length of his fingernail, were drifting through the water, and in a moment he could feel the innumerable tiny touches of them against his limbs. It was like swimming in flaked silver. The great rock the big boys had swum through rose sheer out of the white sand—black, tufted lightly with greenish weed. He could see no gap in it. He swam down to its base.

Again and again he rose, took a big chestful of air, and went down. Again and again he groped over the surface of the rock, feeling it, almost hugging it in the desperate need to find the entrance. And then, once, while he was clinging to the black wall, his knees came up, and he shot his feet out forward and they met no obstacle. He had found the hole.

R

Additional Support

Skills Practice

LIFE SKILLS: Goal Setting Jerry's goal is to swim the tunnel. He is likely to accomplish his goal if he forms a plan: (1) get the equipment he needs (goggles); (2) locate and explore the tunnel entrance; (3) teach himself to hold his breath; (4) practice diving and holding his breath for long periods of time. Have students think about and set a realistic goal for themselves, such as raising a grade one or two letters or saving a certain amount of money. They should outline a plan that includes what they need to do to accomplish their goal. **OL**

He gained the surface, clambered about the stones that littered the barrier rock until he found a big one, and, with this in his arms, let himself down over the side of the rock. He dropped, with the weight, straight to the sandy floor.

Clinging tight to the anchor of stone, he lay on his side and looked in under the dark shelf at the place where his feet had gone. He could see the hole. It was an irregular, dark gap; but he could not see deep into it. He let go of his anchor, clung with his hands to the edges of the hole, and tried to push himself in.

He got his head in, found his shoulders jammed, moved them in sidewise, and was inside as far as his waist. He could see nothing ahead. Something soft and clammy touched his mouth; he saw a dark frond[4] moving against the grayish rock, and panic filled him. He thought of octopuses, of cling-

ing weed. He pushed himself out backward and caught a glimpse, as he retreated, of a harmless tentacle[5] of seaweed drifting in the mouth of the tunnel. But it was enough. He reached the sunlight, swam to shore, and lay on the diving rock. He looked down into the blue well of water. He knew he must find his way through that cave, or hole, or tunnel, and out the other side.

First, he thought, he must learn to control his breathing. He let himself down into the water with another big stone in his arms, so that he could lie effortlessly on the bottom of the sea. He counted. One, two, three. He counted steadily. He could hear the move-

---

4. A *frond* is a large leaf with many divisions, or a leaf-like part of a plant such as seaweed.

5. A *tentacle* is a long, flexible limb that could belong to a plant or to a creature such as an octopus.

Big Idea Life Transition *In what ways will this feat be a transition for Jerry?* **BI**

Literary Element Point of View *What sort of change in Jerry's character is the narrator describing here?* **L**

DORIS LESSING **215**

Teach

BI Big Idea

Life Transitions

Answer: *It will be both a physical transition and a mental or emotional transition from frustration to a sense of accomplishment.* **OL**

L Literary Element

Point of View Answer: *Jerry's adoption of a rational, methodical plan shows that he is becoming more logical and mature and less impulsive and childlike.* **Ask:** If the narrator were not omniscient, how might the author's description of Jerry's plan differ? *(The description would probably not show Jerry's counting. It would probably not describe his inner feelings or thoughts. The description would focus more on what was going on around Jerry and what an outsider could observe of Jerry's behavior.)* **OL**

English Language Coach

Less Proficient Readers For less proficient readers, it can often be difficult to visualize the story and relate to the characters. A simple drama strategy called *tableau* or *frozen pictures* can help these readers connect with characters.

Have students act out a scene from the story, such as Jerry's clowning around, freezing the action at its climax. Then tap students in the frozen picture to come to life and talk about the character's feelings or motivations. **EL**

Objectives
- To analyze third-person omniscient point of view (SE)
- To visualize details in setting (SE)
- To develop and plan goals (TWE)

Teach

L Literary Element

Point of View **Answer:**
Jerry's internal conflict is very real. He is scared not to attempt to swim through the tunnel, but horrified at what could happen to him once inside. **AL**

⭐ Writer's Technique

Scientific Backup
Although Lessing does not explain Jerry's nosebleeds, she shows that she has researched the science behind free diving and air pressure. Research helps writers to realistically portray characters and their actions. Nosebleeds are often caused by changes in air pressure. In practicing, Jerry subjects himself to the pressure of the water for long periods of time. This greater pressure makes his heart beat faster. Then, when he makes an abrupt return to the lesser pressure of the air, blood vessels close to the surface of the nasal membrane rupture and cause bleeding. **AS**

---

ment of blood in his chest. Fifty-one, fifty-two. . . . His chest was hurting. He let go of the rock and went up into the air. He saw that the sun was low. He rushed to the villa and found his mother at her supper. She said only, "Did you enjoy yourself?" and he said, "Yes."

All night the boy dreamed of the water-filled cave in the rock, and as soon as breakfast was over he went to the bay.

That night, his nose bled badly. For hours he had been underwater, learning to hold his breath, and now he felt weak and dizzy. His mother said, "I shouldn't overdo things, darling, if I were you."

That day and the next, Jerry exercised his lungs as if everything, the whole of his life, all that he would become, depended upon it. Again his nose bled at night, and his mother insisted on his coming with her the next day. It was a torment to him to waste a day of his careful self training, but he stayed with her on that other beach, which now seemed a place for small children, a place where his mother might lie safe in the sun. It was not his beach.

He did not ask for permission, on the following day, to go to his beach. He went, before his mother could consider the complicated rights and wrongs of the matter. A day's rest, he discovered, had improved his count by ten. The big boys had made the passage while he counted a hundred and sixty. He had been counting fast, in his fright. Probably now, if he tried, he could get through that long tunnel, but he was not going to try yet. A curious, most unchildlike persistence, a controlled impatience, made him wait. In the meantime, he lay underwater on the white sand, littered now by stones he had brought down from the upper air, and studied the entrance to the tunnel. He knew every jut and corner of it, as far as it was possible to see. It was as if he already felt its sharpness about his shoulders.

He sat by the clock in the villa, when his mother was not near, and checked his time.

He was **incredulous** and then proud to find he could hold his breath without strain for two minutes. The words "two minutes," authorized by the clock, brought close the adventure that was so necessary to him.

In another four days, his mother said casually one morning, they must go home. On the day before they left, he would do it. He would do it if it killed him, he said defiantly to himself. But two days before they were to leave—a day of triumph when he increased his count by fifteen—his nose bled so badly that he turned dizzy and had to lie limply over the big rock like a bit of seaweed, watching the thick red blood flow on to the rock and trickle slowly down to the sea. He was frightened. Supposing he turned dizzy in the tunnel? Supposing he died there, trapped? Supposing—his head went around, in the hot sun, and he almost gave up. He thought he would return to the house and lie down, and next summer, perhaps, when he had another year's growth in him—*then* he would go through the hole.

But even after he had made the decision, or thought he had, he found himself sitting up on the rock and looking down into the water; and he knew that now, this moment, when his nose had only just stopped bleeding, when his head was still sore and throbbing—this was the moment when he would try. If he did not do it now, he never would. He was trembling with fear that he would not go; and he was trembling with horror at that long, long tunnel under the rock, under the sea. Even in the open sunlight, the barrier rock seemed very wide and very heavy; tons of rock pressed down on where he would go. If he died there, he would lie until one day—perhaps not before next year—those big boys would swim into it and find it blocked.

Literary Element Point of View *How realistic and convincing is Jerry's internal conflict?* **L**

Vocabulary

incredulous (in krej′ ə ləs) *adj.* unwilling or unable to believe.

Additional Support

Skills Practice

LITERARY ELEMENT: Conflict
External conflict exists when a character struggles against an outside force such as another character or nature itself. Internal conflict exists when the character struggles with his or her feelings or opposing goals. **Ask:** What types of con-flicts are found in "Through the Tunnel"? *(There are both internal and external conflicts in the story. Jerry's attempts to swim through the tunnel involve an external conflict with nature. Jerry's struggle with his fear and insecurity is an internal conflict.)* **OL**

Figure In Water. Kari Van Tine. ⭐

He put on his goggles, fitted them tight, tested the vacuum. His hands were shaking. Then he chose the biggest stone he could carry and slipped over the edge of the rock until half of him was in the cool, enclosing water and half in the hot sun. He looked up once at the empty sky, filled his lungs once, twice, and then sank fast to the bottom with the stone. He let it go and began to count. He took the edges of the hole in his hands and drew himself into it, wriggling his shoulders in sidewise as he remembered he must, kicking himself along with his feet.

Soon he was clear inside. He was in a small rock-bound hole filled with yellow-

Reading Strategy Visualizing *To what senses do the words and images in this sentence appeal?* **R**

DORIS LESSING **217**

Teach

R Reading Strategy

Visualizing Answer: *They appeal to sight and touch.* **OL**

⭐ Viewing the Art

Kari Van Tine's art often features feminine figures, angels, and lithely rendered animals. **Ask:** How does the artist make the water seem more significant than the swimmer? How might this idea connect to the story? *(The artist makes the water take up most of the image, dwarfing the swimmer. Also, the swimmer's head is lost to the edge of the picture, making the water and the act of swimming more important. In the story, the water is one of Jerry's antagonists, something that dwarfs him with its great power and depth.)* **AS**

Differentiated Instruction

Spatial Learners Students with strong spatial abilities may respond to their reading more readily through visual images than through words. These students can use sketching to help themselves and other students visualize settings, characters, and key story events. As students read the story, have them stop whenever they form a strong visual impression and make a quick sketch of that impression. They may also choose to add captions or labels to their sketches. Spatial learners may find these sketches useful references when answering questions about the story. **BL**

Objectives
- To analyze third-person omniscient point of view (SE)
- To visualize sensory details in setting
- To analyze art (TWE)
- To analyze conflict (TWE)

Teach

⭐ Viewing the Art

Edward Hopper (1882–1967) painted this picture early in his career. It suggests the simple, realistic style reflected in his later urban paintings. **Answer:** *The painting emphasizes the desolation of the diving area, underscoring the dangers of Jerry's undertaking.* **AS**

Rocky Sea Shore, 1916–1919. Edward Hopper. Oil on canvas panel, 9½ x 12¹⁵⁄₁₆ in. Collection of Whitney Museum of American Art, New York. Josephine N. Hopper Bequest. 70.166.

Viewing the Art: How does the scene portrayed here affect your understanding of the beach that Jerry goes to?

ish-gray water. The water was pushing him up against the roof. The roof was sharp and pained his back. He pulled himself along with his hands—fast, fast—and used his legs as levers. His head knocked against something; a sharp pain dizzied him. Fifty, fifty-one, fifty-two. . . . He was without light, and the water seemed to press upon him with the weight of rock. Seventy-one, seventy-two. . . . There was no strain on his lungs. He felt like an inflated balloon, his lungs were so light and easy, but his head was pulsing.

He was being continually pressed against the sharp roof, which felt slimy as well as sharp. Again he thought of octopuses, and wondered if the tunnel might

be filled with weed that could tangle him. He gave himself a panicky, convulsive kick forward, ducked his head, and swam. His feet and hands moved freely, as if in open water. The hole must have widened out. He thought he must be swimming fast, and he was frightened of banging his head if the tunnel narrowed.

A hundred, a hundred and one. . . . The water paled. Victory filled him. His lungs were beginning to hurt. A few more strokes and he would be out. He was counting wildly; he said a hundred and fifteen, and then, a long time later, a hundred and fifteen again. The water was a clear jewel-green all around him. Then he saw, above his head, a crack running up

218 UNIT 1 THE SHORT STORY

Additional Support

Skills Practice

READING: Identifying Cause-and-Effect Relationships Point out that when a reader asks "Why?" he or she is analyzing cause and effect. Explain that there is often more than one cause for an effect or more than one effect produced by a cause. Have students create a cluster map showing the causes of Jerry's

dive through the tunnel. Suggest that they write the effect—"Jerry's Dive"—in the center and connect each cause to it with a line. Encourage students to look beyond the obvious cause—Jerry's admiration of the older boys—to subtle causes such as his loneliness or desire for challenge. **OL**

Visual Vocabulary
A *mussel* is a kind of shellfish. Mussels are in the same scientific classification as clams, oysters, and scallops.

through the rock. Sunlight was falling through it, showing the clean, dark rock of the tunnel, a single mussel shell, and darkness ahead.

He was at the end of what he could do. He looked up at the crack as if it were filled with air and not water, as if he could put his mouth to it to draw in air. A hundred and fifteen, he heard himself say inside his head—but he had said that long ago. He must go on into the blackness ahead, or he would drown. His head was swelling, his lungs cracking. A hundred and fifteen, a hundred and fifteen pounded through his head, and he feebly clutched at rocks in the dark, pulling himself forward, leaving the brief space of sunlit water behind. He felt he was dying. He was no longer quite conscious. He struggled on in the darkness between lapses into unconsciousness. An immense, swelling pain filled his head, and then the darkness cracked with an explosion of green light. His hands, groping forward, met nothing; and his feet, kicking back, propelled him out into the open sea.

He drifted to the surface, his face turned up to the air. He was gasping like a fish. He felt he would sink now and drown; he could not swim the few feet back to the rock. Then he was clutching it and pulling himself up on to it. He lay face down, gasping. He could see nothing but a red-veined, clotted dark. His eyes must have burst, he thought; they were full of blood. He tore off his goggles and a gout[6] of blood went into the sea. His nose was bleeding, and the blood had filled the goggles.

He scooped up handfuls of water from the cool, salty sea, to splash on his face, and did not know whether it was blood or salt water he tasted. After a time, his heart quieted, his eyes cleared, and he sat up. He could see the local boys diving and playing half a mile away. He did not want them. He wanted nothing but to get back home and lie down.

In a short while, Jerry swam to shore and climbed slowly up the path to the villa. He flung himself on his bed and slept, waking at the sound of feet on the path outside. His mother was coming back. He rushed to the bathroom, thinking she must not see his face with bloodstains, or tearstains, on it. He came out of the bathroom and met her as she walked into the villa, smiling, her eyes lighting up.

"Have a nice morning?" she asked, laying her hand on his warm brown shoulder a moment.

"Oh, yes, thank you," he said.

"You look a bit pale." And then, sharp and anxious, "How did you bang your head?"

"Oh, just banged it," he told her.

She looked at him closely. He was strained; his eyes were glazed-looking. She was worried. And then she said to herself, Oh, don't fuss! Nothing can happen. He can swim like a fish.

They sat down to lunch together.

"Mummy," he said, "I can stay under water for two minutes—three minutes, at least." It came bursting out of him.

"Can you, darling?" she said. "Well, I shouldn't overdo it. I don't think you ought to swim any more today."

She was ready for a battle of wills, but he gave in at once. It was no longer of the least importance to go to the bay. ❧

Big Idea Life Transitions *Why is Jerry no longer interested in the local boys?* **BI₁**

Big Idea Life Transitions *Why do you think Jerry kept his triumph of swimming through the tunnel to himself?* **BI₂**

6. Here, *gout* refers to a mass of fluid that gushes or bursts forth.

DORIS LESSING **219**

Teach

BI₁ Big Idea
Life Transitions
Answer: *He has learned that preparing for and accomplishing a goal is more important than impressing others. His identity is more secure and clear; he is able to affirm himself.* **OL**

BI₂ Big Idea
Life Transitions
Answer: *He may realize how dangerous it was and that it would worry his mother. In his newfound maturity, he may no longer feel the need to tell her about all of his triumphs.* **OL**

CheckPoint

Use the CheckPoint questions on Presentation Plus! to monitor students' mastery of the selection. These questions can be used with interactive response keypads to get immediate student feedback.

Differentiated Instruction

Oral Reading Jerry's swim through the tunnel is described with mounting tension and suspense. Less-proficient readers may find it difficult to visualize the diving scene and to feel the suspense that Lessing weaves into the narrative. Have students take turns reading aloud the entirety of Jerry's dive. Guide them to increase the urgency in their reading the farther into the passage they read. Have them emphasize Jerry's counting—"Fifty, fifty-one, fifty-two . . ."—and the pain he feels as he scrapes his way through the tunnel. **BL**

Objectives
• To analyze art (SE)
• To identify cause-and-effect relationships (TWE)

Assess

1. (a) Students may say they would have been more cautious. (b) Answers will vary.

2. They are "burned smooth dark brown," and they speak a different language. They are initially friendly; when Jerry acts childishly, they leave.

3. (a) He uses a large rock as a weight and lowers himself to the cave. Then he explores the first few feet. (b) To prove that he equals the other boys

4. (a) Not underwater for full length of time; never in any real danger (b) He must exceed his practice time to escape drowning.

5. (a) Protective, but knows he needs some freedom (b) Students may say it is implausible to let an eleven-year-old go alone to an isolated beach.

6. (a) Other boys do it, so it is physically possible. (b) Yes, he knows she worries about him.

7. (a) Narrow, dark, sharp, longer than anticipated, and has entangling seaweed (b) Jerry gains self-confidence but takes a big risk.

8. Her seemingly confident release of him encourages him to strike out on his own.

Web Activities Have students access the Web site for interactive activities that will help them assess their understanding of the selection.

RESPONDING AND THINKING CRITICALLY

Respond

1. (a)How would you have challenged yourself if you had been in Jerry's place? (b)With whom would you have shared your experience?

Recall and Interpret

2. Describe the boys Jerry encounters, and trace the change in their attitudes toward him.

3. (a)Summarize what Jerry does when he goes to the beach the second time. (b)Why do you think Jerry decides that he must go through the tunnel?

4. (a)How is Jerry's preparation unlike the real test? (b)In your opinion, what is the most dramatic moment of Jerry's actual test? Explain.

Analyze and Evaluate

5. (a)How would you describe the mother's feelings toward Jerry? (b)Do you think Lessing makes the mother a realistic character, or do some of her actions seem implausible or unbelievable?

6. (a)How has Lessing made Jerry's decision to go through the tunnel seem credible or genuine? (b)Does it seem believable that Jerry does not tell his mother what he has accomplished?

7. (a)Explain how Lessing has made the tunnel seem sinister and dangerous. (b)Evaluate how successfully Lessing has shown the benefits of pushing oneself beyond one's limits.

Connect

8. **Big Idea** **Life Transitions** Both Jerry and his mother go through a major transition in this story How is each character's response to the other helpful to these transitions?

LITERARY ANALYSIS

Literary Element Point of View

A **third-person omniscient narrator** can give us insight into all characters in a story by revealing and interpreting their deepest thoughts and feelings. The omniscient narrator is usually objective and is therefore more reliable than a first-person narrator, who may be prone to misjudge or allow emotion to cloud his or her perception of events.

1. In the story's first paragraph, how does Lessing use the third-person omniscient point of view?

2. How did Lessing's use of the third-person omniscient point of view in this story make its telling more effective?

Interdisciplinary Activity: Art

Illustrate one of the underwater scenes that is described in the story. Be sure to include all of the details depicted in that scene.

Literature Online **Web Activities** For eFlashcards, Selection Quick Checks, and other Web activities, go to www.glencoe.com.

READING AND VOCABULARY

Reading Strategy Visualizing

Visualizing the scenes and events in the story can help increase your understanding of their meaning.

1. When Jerry starts to explore the entrance to the tunnel, the narrator says, "He could see nothing ahead. Something soft and clammy touched his mouth. . . ." What do you imagine that "something" is, and how does it make you feel?

2. (a)The narrator never describes Jerry's physical appearance. How do you visualize Jerry? (b)Does your visualization of Jerry make his accomplishment seem more or less remarkable?

Vocabulary Practice

Practice with Antonyms Find the antonym for each vocabulary word listed in the first column.

1. conscientiously   **a.** calmly   **b.** carelessly
2. contrition   **a.** unremorseful   **b.** joy
3. supplication   **a.** plea   **b.** demand
4. beseeching   **a.** ordering   **b.** begging
5. incredulous   **a.** gullible   **b.** doubtful

Literary Element

1. The narrator reveals the thoughts and feelings of Jerry and his mother, using the words "contrition" and "conscientiously" to give insight.

2. Jerry and his mother change over the course of the story. The use of this point of view allows the reader to see the growth.

Reading Strategy

1. Seaweed or a fish. This creates fear.

2. (a) Students may say short and slim. (b) More

Vocabulary

1. b   2. a   3. b   4. a   5. a

THE VISION QUEST

Told by Lame Deer
Recorded by Richard Erdoes

Mountain Spirit. Stephan Daige.

A brash young Native American, is determined to have a vision that will enable him to become a medicine man. Two elders take him to a hilltop and prepare the traditional pit and sweat lodge. The young man has only angered the spirits, who order him to leave and chase him with a boulder. Feeling failure, the youth returns to his village. His uncle reminds him that humility is an important lesson.

Author Search To expand students' appreciation of Lame Deer, have them access the Web site for additional information and resources.

✓CheckPoint

Use the CheckPoint questions on Presentation Plus! to monitor students' comprehension. These questions can be used with interactive response keypads for immediate student feedback.

BEFORE YOU READ

Building Background

Recalling his own vision quest, Lame Deer once said, "I thought of my forefathers who had crouched here before . . . I felt their presence." Lame Deer is a spiritual name that has been handed down from father to son in one Sioux family. The Lame Deer who told the story "Vision Quest" is also called John Fire. He was born in the late 1800s on the Rosebud Reservation in South Dakota. He spent much of his youth in schools run by the Bureau of Indian Affairs, where Native American children were encouraged to leave their native language and culture behind.

Nevertheless, Lame Deer became a medicine man, one who upholds the ancient traditions of his people.

Richard Erdoes was born in the early 1900s in what is now Austria. He came to New York in the 1940s. As an artist and writer on assignment in the United States, Erdoes met many Native Americans and became involved in their civil rights struggle. In 1967 he met John Fire Lame Deer and recorded this story.

Literature Online Author Search For more about Lame Deer, go to www.glencoe.com.

A young man wanted to go on a *hanbleceya,* or vision seeking, to try for a dream that would give him the power to be a great medicine man. Having a high opinion of himself, he felt sure that he had been created

to become great among his people and that the only thing lacking was a vision.

The young man was daring and brave, eager to go up to the mountaintop. He had been brought up by good, honest people who were wise in the ancient ways and who

LAME DEER **221**

Readability Scores
Dale-Chall: 6.4
DRP: 55
Lexile: 890

English Language Coach

Legends and Myths All cultures have their own legends and myths that are passed down from generation to generation to teach lessons about life. Students from other cultures may know some of the legends and myths commonly told in their society. Have these students share their stories, and have other students

share some of the legends and myths they've read or heard. In addition, families have their own traditions and stories that are often embellished. Encourage students to share a family story and examine how this kind of story relates to myths and legends. **EL**

Teach

Big Idea

Life Transitions

Ask: Based on what you've read, do you think the young man will succeed on his quest? Explain. *(Students may say that the man will succeed because most quest stories are stories of success. Others might point out that the young man's arrogance may cause him trouble.)* **OL**

L Literary Element

Point of View

Ask: Is the young man a fool, a hero, or a little of both? *(Students may say he is a little of both. He is persistent as a hero but stubborn as a fool.)* **OL**

★ Literary History

The Boulder in Myth

Boulders appear in legends and myths as objects of power, obstacles, and even punishments. In a Greek myth, Sisyphus was punished in Tartarus (the mythical underworld) with the eternal task of rolling a boulder up a hill. Every time he reached the top, the boulder rolled back down and Sisyphus had to start over. **AS**

---

prayed for him. All through the winter they were busy getting him ready, feeding him wasna,[1] corn, and plenty of good meat to make him strong. At every meal they set aside something for the spirits so that they would help him to get a great vision. His relatives thought he had the power even before he went up, but that was putting the cart before the horse, or rather the travois[2] before the horse, as this is an Indian legend.

When at last he started on his quest, it was a beautiful morning in late spring. The grass was up, the leaves were out, nature was at its best. Two medicine men accompanied him. They put up a sweat lodge[3] to purify him in the hot, white breath of the sacred steam. They sanctified him with the incense of sweet grass, rubbing his body with sage, fanning it with an eagle's wing. They went to the hilltop with him to prepare the vision pit and make an offering of tobacco bundles. Then they told the young man to cry, to humble himself, to ask for holiness, to cry for power, for a sign from the Great Spirit, for a gift which would make him into a medicine man. After they had done all they could, they left him there.

He spent the first night in the hole the medicine men had dug for him, trembling and crying out loudly. Fear kept him awake, yet he was cocky, ready to wrestle with the spirits for the vision, the power he wanted. But no dreams came to ease his mind. Toward morning before the sun came up, he heard a voice in the swirling white mists of dawn. Speaking from no particular direction, as if it came from different places, it said: "See here, young man, there are other spots you could have picked; there are other hills

around here. Why don't you go there to cry for a dream? You disturbed us all night, all us creatures and birds; you even kept the trees awake. We couldn't sleep. Why should you cry here? You're a brash young man, not yet ready or worthy to receive a vision."

But the young man clenched his teeth, determined to stick it out, resolved to force that vision to come. He spent another day in the pit, begging for enlightenment which would not come, and then another night of fear and cold and hunger.

When dawn arrived once more, he heard the voice again: "Stop disturbing us; go away!" The same thing happened the third morning. By this time he was faint with hunger, thirst, and anxiety. Even the air seemed to oppress him, to fight him. He was panting. His stomach felt shriveled up, shrunk tight against his backbone. But he was determined to endure one more night, the fourth and last. Surely the vision would come. But again he cried for it out of the dark and loneliness until he was hoarse, and still he had no dream. **L**

Just before daybreak he heard the same voice again, very angry: "Why are you still here?" He knew then that he had suffered in vain; now he would have to go back to his people and confess that he had gained no knowledge and no power. The only thing he could tell them was that he got bawled out every morning. Sad and cross, he replied, "I can't help myself; this is my last day, and I'm crying my eyes out. I know you told me to go home, but who are you to give me orders? I don't know you. I'm going to stay until my uncles come to fetch me, whether you like it or not."

All at once there was a rumble from a larger mountain that stood behind the hill. It became a mighty roar, and the whole hill trembled. The wind started to blow. The ★ young man looked up and saw a boulder poised on the mountain's summit. He saw lightning hit it, saw it sway. Slowly the boulder moved. Slowly at first, then faster and faster, it came tumbling down the mountainside, churning up earth, snapping huge trees

---

1. *Wasna* is a high-energy food made of meat, fat, and berries pounded together.
2. A *travois* (trə voi´) is a V-shaped sled made of hide or netting supported by two long poles that are harnessed to a horse or dog.
3. A *sweat lodge* is a hut made of branches bent and tied to form a framework, which is covered by hides or blankets. Inside, steam is produced by pouring or sprinkling water over red-hot rocks contained in a central pit.

Additional Support

Skills Practice

GRAMMAR: Infinitive and Prepositional Phrases Write the following sentences on the board, underlining the phrases beginning with the word *to* in each sentence:
He wanted <u>to endure</u> one more night.
He stumbled back <u>to his village</u>.
Point out that the word *to* is used to introduce both infinitive and prepositional phrases. In the first case, *to* is followed by the base form of a verb and in the second by a noun or pronoun. Ask students to read the first page of the story again, locate all the phrases beginning with the word *to,* and identify each phrase as infinitive or prepositional. **OL**

as if they were little twigs. And the boulder was coming right down on him!

The young man cried out in terror. He was paralyzed with fear, unable to move. The boulder dwarfed everything in view; it towered over the vision pit. But just as it was an arm's length away and about to crush him, it stopped. Then, as the young man stared open-mouthed, his hair standing up, his eyes starting out of his head, the boulder *rolled up the mountain,* all the way to the top. He could hardly believe what he saw. He was still cowering motionless when he heard the roar and rumble again and saw that immense boulder coming down at him once more. This time he managed to jump out of his vision pit at the last moment. The boulder crushed it, obliterated it, grinding the young man's pipe and gourd rattle into dust.

Again the boulder rolled up the mountain, and again it came down. "I'm leaving, I'm leaving!" hollered the young man. Regaining his power of motion, he scrambled down the hill as fast as he could. This time the boulder actually leap-frogged over him, bouncing down the slope, crushing and pulverizing everything in its way. He ran unseeingly, stumbling, falling, getting up again. He did not even notice the boulder rolling up once more and coming down for the fourth time. On this last and most fearful descent, it flew through the air in a giant leap, landing right in front of him and embedding itself so deeply in the earth that only its top was visible. The ground shook itself like a wet dog coming out of a

The Navajo. Maynard Dixon (1875–1946). Oil on canvas. Private Collection.

stream and flung the young man this way and that.

Gaunt, bruised, and shaken, he stumbled back to his village. To the medicine men he said: "I have received no vision and gained no knowledge. I have made the spirits angry. It was all for nothing."

"Well, you did find out one thing," said the older of the two, who was his uncle. "You went after your vision like a hunter after buffalo, or a warrior after scalps. You were fighting the spirits. You thought they owed you a vision. Suffering alone brings no vision nor does courage, nor does sheer will power. A vision comes as a gift born of humility, of wisdom, and of patience. If from your vision quest you have learned nothing but this, then you have already learned much. Think about it." ✎

Discussion Starter

Can an experience be useful even if you fail to reach your goal? Discuss this question in a small group. List some benefits a person might get from an experience even if the original goal is not reached. Use specific details from the legend to support your opinions. Then share your conclusions with the rest of the class.

LAME DEER **223**

COMPARING LITERATURE

Teach

Discussion Starter

Students will likely conclude that an experience can be useful even if a goal is not reached. They should point out that although the young man in the legend does not achieve his goal, he learns valuable lessons about humility, patience, and respect.

⭐ Viewing the Art

Painter Maynard Dixon went on numerous excursions—some lasting as long as a month—into the rugged, undeveloped American West, which ultimately became his home. He combined his accurate, unromanticized observations there with the techniques of European modernism **Ask:** How do Dixon's artistic journeys mirror the young man's vision quest? *(Both suggest that one cannot truly see the outer world without knowing oneself.)* **AS**

CheckPoint

Use the CheckPoint questions on Presentation Plus! to check students' mastery of the selection. These questions can be used with interactive response keypads for immediate student feedback.

Objectives
- To visualize sensory details in setting (TWE)
- To analyze third-person omniscient point of view (SE)
- To identify infinitive and prepositional phrases (TWE)

English Language Coach

The Oral Tradition "The Vision Quest" has some qualities of a legend. Although now in written form, it likely originated as an oral story, passed down through the generations. Remind students that people still love to hear stories. (Many comedians incorporate humorous stories into their acts. Songs often tell stories.) Have students think of some stories that they could tell aloud. Then have students pair up and each tell one story to his or her partner. Invite students to recite their partner's story to the class. **EL**

Teach

Summary

F. Scott Fitzgerald writes a letter to Scottie, his twelve-year-old daughter who is at camp for the summer. He discusses what he believes or doesn't believe, what is and is not worth worrying about, and provides a short list of things to think about.

Author Search To expand students' appreciation of F. Scott Fitzgerald, have them access the Web site for additional information and resources.

CheckPoint

Use the CheckPoint questions on Presentation Plus! to monitor students' comprehension. These questions with interactive response keypads for immediate student feedback.

Readability Scores
Dale-Chall: 8.4
DRP: 54
Lexile: 1040

Dear Pie

F. Scott Fitzgerald to
Frances Scott "Scottie" Fitzgerald

BEFORE YOU READ

Building Background

F. Scott Fitzgerald achieved success early as a writer, publishing the novel *This Side of Paradise* in 1920 when he was only twenty-four years old. It was followed quickly by *The Beautiful and Damned* in 1922 and *The Great Gatsby* in 1925. Fitzgerald and his wife, Zelda, lived lavishly, both in the United States and abroad, and spent most of the money he earned from his writing. They regularly moved between Paris and various cities on the French Riviera. Despite Fitzgerald's success as a writer, the couple consistently lived beyond their means and experienced financial struggles as a result. In 1930 Zelda Fitzgerald suffered a nervous breakdown and was hospitalized.

In the summer of 1933, Fitzgerald was in Maryland working on his novel *Tender Is the Night*. His wife was being treated for the mental illness that would last the rest of her life. During that time he wrote the following letter to their beloved daughter, Scottie, who was twelve years old and away at summer camp.

Author Search For more about F. Scott Fitzgerald, go to www.glencoe.com.

La Paix, Rodgers' Forge,
Towson, Maryland,
August 8, 1933.

Dear Pie:

I feel very strongly about you doing duty. Would you give me a little more documentation about your reading in French? I am glad you are happy—but I never believe much in happiness. I never believe in misery either. Those are things you see on the stage or the screen or the printed page, they never really happen to you in life.

All I believe in in life is the rewards for virtue (according to your talents) and the *punishments* for not fulfilling your duties, which are doubly costly. If there is such a volume in the camp library, will you ask Mrs. Tyson to let you look up a sonnet of Shakespeare's in which the line occurs *"Lilies that fester smell far worse than weeds."*

Have had no thoughts today, life seems composed of getting up a *Saturday Evening Post* story. I think of you, and always pleasantly; but if you call me "Pappy" again I am going to take the White Cat out and beat his bottom *hard, six times for every time you are impertinent.* Do you react to that?

I will arrange the camp bill.
Halfwit, I will conclude. Things to worry about:

224 UNIT 1   THE SHORT STORY

Additional Support

Skills Practice

WRITING: Prewriting In the prewriting stage, students explore topics, gather information, and begin to organize their material. Have students employ prewriting strategies for a letter that they will write. Use the following questions to help them prewrite:

- What is the purpose of the letter?

- To whom should I write the letter?

- What do my purpose and audience determine about the length of the letter? Appropriate topics? Tone and language of the writing?

- What will I write about?

When students are finished prewriting, have them draft their letters. **OL**

American novelist F. Scott Fitzgerald, his wife Zelda, and daughter, Scottie, go for a motor jaunt in Italy.

Worry about courage
Worry about cleanliness
Worry about efficiency
Worry about horsemanship
Worry about . . .

Things not to worry about:

Don't worry about popular opinion
Don't worry about dolls
Don't worry about the past
Don't worry about the future
Don't worry about growing up
Don't worry about anybody getting ahead of you
Don't worry about triumph
Don't worry about failures unless it comes through your own fault
Don't worry about mosquitoes
Don't worry about flies
Don't worry about insects in general
Don't worry about parents
Don't worry about boys
Don't worry about disappointments
Don't worry about pleasures
Don't worry about satisfactions **L**

Things to think about:

What am I really aiming at?
How good am I really in comparison to my contemporaries in regard to:
(a) Scholarship

(b) Do I really understand about people and am I able to get along with them?
(c) Am I trying to make my body a useful instrument or am I neglecting it?

With dearest love,

P.S. My come-back to your calling me Pappy is christening you by the word Egg, which implies that you belong to a very rudimentary state of life and that I could break you up and crack you open at my will and I think it would be a word that would hang on if I ever told it to your contemporaries. "Egg Fitzgerald." How would you like that to go through life with "Eggie Fitzgerald" or "Bad Egg Fitzgerald" or any form that might occur to fertile minds? Try it once more and I swear to God I will hang it on you and it will be up to you to shake it off. Why borrow trouble? **BI**

Love anyhow.

> **Quickwrite**
>
> Fitzgerald writes that he does not believe much in happiness or misery, only in rewards and punishments. Do you agree or disagree with his opinion? Reread the first two paragraphs of the letter and write a paragraph explaining your views.

F. SCOTT FITZGERALD **225**

Teach

L Literary Element

Point of View

Ask: How would you characterize Fitzgerald as a narrator? *(Some students will say that Fitzgerald sounds independent and confident. His list of things not to worry about demonstrates disregard for typical concerns.)* **OL**

BI Big Idea

Life Transitions

Ask: Through what stage of life is Fitzgerald trying to guide his daughter? Why does he choose the nickname "Egg"? *(He is trying to guide her through her adolescent years, in which she is beginning to worry about social acceptance. Fitzgerald believes this to be "a very rudimentary state of life," and he seems determined that she be respectful.)* **OL**

Quickwrite

Students may say that Fitzgerald is writing about rewards and punishments because that is how parents often talk to their children. Students should back up their opinions with valid reasoning.

CheckPoint

Use the CheckPoint questions on Presentation Plus! to check students' mastery of the selection. These questions can be used with interactive response keypads for immediate student feedback.

Objectives
• To analyze point of view (TWE)
• To develop prewriting strategies (TWE)

English Language Coach

Parenting Parenting styles differ from culture to culture, society to society. Students from other cultures may be raised with different parenting styles. Have these students discuss common parental styles in their cultures and compare them to Fitzgerald's, as expressed in this letter. **EL**

Reading in the Real World

Citizenship Have students think about local, political, and community issues. Have them create their own lists of things to worry about and things not to worry about in their country and their own communities. **OL**

Assess

Comparing The Big Idea

Students should work in small groups to compose lists. They can refer to Fitzgerald's lists for ideas, but they should draw upon their own experiences in compiling their list for each character.

Comparing Narrator

1. Readers would not know the mother's thoughts and fears about her son.

2. Students should support their answers with details from the letter.

3. The account would be written from a first-person point of view. Students will likely say that the story would be very different. For example, the main character would not have felt so isolated and frightened.

Comparing Author's Culture

Students' analyses should compare the initiation event in one story with the initiation customs of a society or group they have researched.

- *Through the Tunnel*
  by Doris Lessing
- *The Vision Quest*
  by Lame Deer
- *"Dear Pie"*
  by F. Scott Fitzgerald

COMPARING THE Big Idea Life Transitions

Writing Make two three-column charts with the following headings: Things to Worry About, Things Not to Worry About, Things to Think About. Then fill in one chart to give to the boy in "Through the Tunnel" and the other to give to the young man in "The Vision Quest." What wisdom can you share with each to help them through their life transitions?

COMPARING Narrator

Group Activity "Through the Tunnel" is told from a **third-person omniscient,** or all-knowing, **point of view.** "The Vision Quest," in which the narrator reveals the thoughts and feelings of only one character, has a **third-person limited point of view.** "Dear Pie," a personal letter, has a **first-person point of view.** In a group, discuss the following questions. Cite evidence from the selections to support your points.

1. How would "Through the Tunnel" be different if it had a first-person point of view?
2. Even though the narrator of "Dear Pie" is writing about his daughter, what do you learn about him? Do you think he is a good parent?
3. Suppose that someone else had accompanied the young man on his vision quest and had written about it. From what point of view would the account be written? How would the story be different?

COMPARING Author's Culture

Speaking and Listening The boys in "Through the Tunnel" and "The Vision Quest" experienced rites of passage along the road from childhood to adulthood. Most cultures have initiation rituals to mark that transition. Investigate the initiation customs of a society or a group, such as a club or service organization. Then, based on your findings, write an analysis that compares the initiation customs of the society or group you studied with those of the culture in one of these stories. Before you write your analysis, use a chart similar to the one below to help you organize your main points. Describe or demonstrate these customs for your class.

Initiation Customs of (society or group)	Initiation Customs in ("The Tunnel" or "The Vision Quest")	Comparison of Initiation Customs

Additional Support

Skills Practice

READING: Summarizing
Summarizing a selection or series of selections can help students to assemble what they have learned into brief and coherent structures that can be useful for later study and review. Have students summarize this Comparing Literature section. In their summaries, they should include answers to the questions *Who? What? Why?* and *How?* Students should make sure to exclude extraneous information or details. **OL**

Catch the Moon

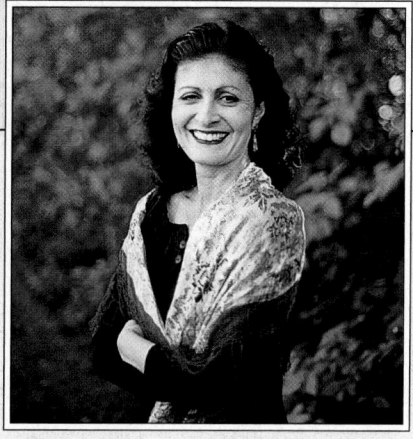

MEET JUDITH ORTIZ COFER

"Latina wherever I am," is the way Judith Ortiz Cofer sees herself. When she was a child, her family moved from her birthplace of Puerto Rico to Paterson, New Jersey. However, they made frequent trips back to Puerto Rico, so she always felt close to her cultural roots. She has a childhood memory of sitting in her grandmother's living room, which was furnished with mahogany rocking chairs. "It was on these rockers that my mother, her sisters and my grandmother sat on these afternoons of my childhood to tell their stories, teaching each other and my cousin and me what it was like to be a woman, more specifically, a Puerto Rican woman."

"I write in English, yet I write obsessively about my Puerto Rican experience."

—Judith Ortiz Cofer

Bilingual Advantage Early on, Cofer experienced a disadvantage of the family's frequent moving. Cofer was teased for having "a Spanish accent when [she] spoke English; and, when [she] spoke Spanish, [she] was told that [she] sounded like a 'Gringa.'" Cofer transformed this into an advantage when she began writing fiction and poetry. Writer Marian C. Gonsior says that Cofer deals with "the effect on Puerto Rican Americans of living in a world split between the island culture of their homeland and the teeming tenement life of the United States." After receiving her bachelor's degree from Augusta College in Georgia, Cofer began her long teaching career, first as a bilingual teacher in Florida public schools and then as an English and Spanish teacher at colleges and universities. She is currently the Franklin Professor of English and Creative Writing at the University of Georgia, Athens.

Writer of Poetry and Fiction In graduate school Cofer began writing poetry in order to express the concerns of Latina women. Cofer believes that "poetry has made me more disciplined. . . . Poetry taught me about economizing in language and about the power of language." Ten years later, Cofer began writing fiction, and her first novel, *The Line of the Sun,* was nominated for a Pulitzer Prize in 1989. Cofer has also written *An Island Like You: Stories of the Barrio,* a book of short stories for young adults. The stories are set in Paterson, New Jersey, and deal with the problems facing Puerto Rican teenagers. Chicana author Sandra Cisneros says, "In these stories, both hilarious and tragic, [Cofer] has captured the isolated lives of those wobbling between two clashing cultures—childhood and adulthood." "Catch the Moon" is one of the stories in *An Island Like You.*

Judith Ortiz Cofer was born in 1952.

 Author Search For more about Judith Ortiz Cofer, go to www.glencoe.com.

Focus

BELLRINGER

Bellringer Options
Selection Focus
    Transparency 14
Daily Language
    Transparency 21
Or write the following quotation on the board: "All learning has an emotional base."–*Plato*
Ask: Who in your life has helped you to learn something new? Who has helped you become a better person? Have students discuss how they've learned their most important lessons. **Ask:** Do you agree or disagree with Plato's quotation?

Author Search To expand students' appreciation of Judith Ortiz Cofer, have them access the Web site for additional information and resources.

Selection Skills

Literary Elements

Catch the Moon

Listening/Speaking/Viewing Skills

- Point of View (SE pp. 228, 230, 231, 233, 235, 236)
- Plot (SE p. 236)

- Analyzing Art (SE p. 232; TWE p. 234)
- Literature Groups (SE p. 237)

Reading Skills

Vocabulary Skills

Writing Skills/Grammar

- Interpreting Imagery (SE pp. 228, 229, 231, 234, 235, 237)
- Verifying Predictions (TWE p. 230)
- Making Inferences (TWE p. 232)

- Denotations and Connotations (SE p. 237)
- Academic Vocabulary (SE p. 237)

- Analytical Essay (SE p. 237)
- Adjective Clauses (TWE p. 234)

Focus

Summary

Luis Cintrón has been released from juvenile detention on the condition that he work in his father's junkyard for six months. Gloomy at his prospects and still depressed by his mother's death three years earlier, Luis encounters a young woman who comes to the yard looking for a hubcap. Moved by both her beauty and her kindness, Luis experiences a flood of emotions that allow him to grieve, love, and learn self-respect.

V Vocabulary

Vocabulary File Say: Add these words and definitions to your vocabulary file. For each word, include a sentence that gives you an example of how to use the word. **OL** Students with English language needs should include the pronunciations of these words in their files. **EL**

Literary Elements Have students access the Web site to improve their understanding of point of view.

Connecting to the Story

When was the last time you gave someone a special gift or did something really nice for another person without asking for or expecting anything in return? Before you read the story, think about these questions:

- Why might someone suddenly do something special for another person?
- Why does gift giving make the giver feel good?

Building Background

A *barrio* is an urban neighborhood where most of the people are of Hispanic heritage. People in a *barrio* may have been born in the United States or have come from Spanish-speaking countries such as Mexico, Puerto Rico, the Dominican Republic, or Cuba.

Hubcaps, or wheel covers, come in thousands of different styles. While they are mostly for show, hubcaps do keep dirt and moisture away from the wheel nuts and bearings in a car's wheel assembly. The flashiest hubcaps were made during the 1950s and 1960s. Some antique hubcaps have become collectors' items. Trying to find a replacement for a lost hubcap on an old or classic car can be a time-consuming chore, taking a person from one junkyard to the next.

Setting Purposes for Reading

Big Idea Life Transitions

As you read, notice how a self-centered young man begins to mature and learns the value of giving selflessly.

Literary Element Point of View

Point of view is the standpoint from which a story is told. In a story told from a **third-person limited point of view**, the narrator describes events as only one character perceives them. This enables readers to learn a lot about this particular character's thoughts and feelings, though the information about other characters is much more limited. As you read, think about why Cofer chose to tell the story from the third-person limited point of view.

- See Literary Terms Handbook, p. R13.

OBJECTIVES
In studying this selection, you will focus on the following:
- analyzing point of view
- interpreting imagery
- understanding plot exposition
- writing to analyze different points of view

Reading Strategy Interpreting Imagery

Writers use **imagery**, details that appeal to the senses, to help readers see, hear, smell, taste, or feel what the writer is describing. As you read, identify imagery and consider its meaning or significance.

Reading Tip: Taking Notes Use a chart like the one below to record instances of imagery and your interpretation of them.

Imagery	Interpretation
p. 229 "steel jungle of his car junkyard"	Here "steel jungle" is used figuratively to suggest a place that is hard, cold, and dense with debris.

Vocabulary

harass (hə ras´) *v.* to bother or annoy repeatedly; p. 230 *Several times a day the bully would harass the children.*

makeshift (māk´ shift) *adj.* suitable as a temporary substitute for the proper or desired thing; p. 231 *He used a tent as his makeshift home.*

vintage (vin´ tij) *adj.* characterized by enduring appeal; classic; p. 231 *He drove a vintage Model T car.*

decapitate (di kap´ ə tāt) *v.* to cut off the head of; p. 232 *We watched the hunter decapitate the elk he had shot.*

relic (rel´ ik) *n.* an object that has survived decay, destruction, or the passage of time and is valued for its historic interest; p. 233 *We saw a knight's armor and other relics at the museum.*

Literature Online Interactive Literary Elements Handbook To review or learn more about the literary elements, go to www.glencoe.com.

Selection Resources

Print Materials
- Unit 1 Resources (Fast File), pp. 78–80
- Leveled Vocabulary Development, p. 17
- Selection and Unit Assessments, pp. 37–38
- Selection Quick Checks, p. 19

Transparencies
- Bellringer Options Transparencies:
  Selection Focus Transparency 14
  Daily Language Practice Transparency 21
- Literary Elements Transparency 22

Technology
- TeacherWorks Plus™ CD-ROM
- StudentWorks Plus™ CD-ROM
- Presentation Plus!™ CD-ROM
- Literature Online, glencoe.com
- Online Student Edition, mhln.com
- ExamView® Assessment Suite CD-ROM
- Vocabulary PuzzleMaker CD-ROM
- Listening Library, disc 1 track 21

Catch the Moon

Judith Ortiz Cofer

Luis Cintrón sits on top of a six-foot pile of hubcaps and watches his father walk away into the steel jungle of his car junk-yard. Released into his old man's custody after six months in juvenile hall—for break-ing and entering—and he didn't even take anything. He did it on a dare.

But the old lady with the million cats was a light sleeper, and good with her aluminum cane. He has a scar on his head to prove it.

Now Luis is wondering whether he should have stayed in and done his full time. Jorge Cintrón of Jorge Cintrón & Son, Auto Parts and Salvage, has decided that Luis should wash and polish every hubcap in the yard. The hill he is sitting on is only the lat-est couple of hundred wheel covers that have come in. Luis grunts and stands up on top of his silver mountain. He yells at no one, "Someday, son, all this will be yours," and sweeps his arms like the Pope blessing a crowd over the piles of car sandwiches and mounds of metal parts that cover this acre of land outside the city. He is the "Son" of Jorge Cintrón & Son, and so far his father has had more than one reason to wish it was plain Jorge Cintrón on the sign.

Luis has been getting in trouble since he started high school two years ago, mainly because of the "social group" he organized—

Reading Strategy Interpreting Imagery *What does this image tell you about Luis?*

English Language Coach

Understanding Tense Writers may use a shift in tense between paragraphs to affect tone. A shift in tense within a sentence signals when one event comes before or after another event. When reading and writing, remember the fol-lowing two rules:

- When two or more events occur at the same time, writers use the same verb tense to describe each event.
- When two events have occurred at dif-ferent times in the past, writers shift tense to indicate that one action ends before another action begins. **EL**

Teach

L₁ Literary Element
Point of View
Answer: *Luis's opinion of* West Side Story *tells you that he does not feel connected to the culture portrayed in the movie. He also is not afraid to express his opinion.* **OL**

BI Big Idea
Life Transitions
Answer: *Luis agrees to put on a cultural activity only to save his club, not because he thinks that the club should change its ways.* **OL**

L₂ Literary Element
Point of View
Answer: *Even though Luis may seem like a troublemaker, he can also be insightful and thoughtful.* **OL**

---

a bunch of guys who were into **harassing** the local authorities. Their thing was taking something to the limit on a dare or, better still, doing something dangerous, like breaking into a house, not to steal, just to prove that they could do it. That was Luis's specialty, coming up with very complicated plans, like military strategies, and assigning the "jobs" to guys who wanted to join the Tiburones.[1]

Tiburón means "shark," and Luis had gotten the name from watching an old movie[2] about a Puerto Rican gang called the Sharks with his father. Luis thought it was one of the dumbest films he had ever seen. Everybody sang their lines, and the guys all pointed their toes and leaped in the air when they were supposed to be slaughtering each other. But he liked their name, the Sharks, so he made it Spanish and had it air-painted on his black T-shirt with a killer shark under it, jaws opened wide and dripping with blood. It didn't take long for other guys in the barrio to ask about it.

Man, had they had a good time. The girls were interested too. Luis outsmarted everybody by calling his organization a social club and registering it at Central High. That meant they were legal, even let out of last-period class on Fridays for their "club" meetings. It was just this year, after a couple of botched[3] jobs, that the teachers

> "It didn't take long for other guys in the barrio to ask about it."

had started getting suspicious. The first one to go wrong was when he sent Kenny Matoa to *borrow* some "souvenirs" out of Anita Robles's locker. He got caught. It seems that Matoa had been reading Anita's diary and didn't hear her coming down the hall. Anita was supposed to be in the gym at that time but had copped out with the usual female excuse of cramps. You could hear her screams all the way to Market Street.

She told the principal all she knew about the Tiburones, and Luis had to talk fast to convince old Mr. Williams that the club did put on cultural activities such as the Save the Animals talent show. What Mr. Williams didn't know was that the animal that was being "saved" with the ticket sales was Luis's pet boa, which needed quite a few live mice to stay healthy and happy. They kept E.S. (which stood for "Endangered Species") in Luis's room, but she belonged to the club and it was the members' responsibility to raise the money to feed their mascot. So last year they had sponsored their first annual Save the Animals talent show, and it had been a great success. The Tiburones had come dressed as Latino Elvises and did a grand finale to "All Shook Up" that made the audience go wild. Mr. Williams had smiled while Luis talked, maybe remembering how the math teacher, Mrs. Laguna, had dragged him out in the aisle to rock-and-roll with her. Luis had gotten out of that one, but barely.

His father was a problem too. He objected to the T-shirt logo, calling it disgusting and vulgar. Mr. Cintrón prided himself on his own neat, elegant style of dressing after work, and on his manners and large vocabulary, which he picked up by taking correspondence courses in just

---

1. Tiburones (tē′ boo rō′ nās)
2. *[old movie…]* The narrator is describing the feature film *West Side Story*, a 1961 musical based on Shakespeare's play *Romeo and Juliet*, set in the youth gang atmosphere of New York City in the late 1950s.
3. *Botched* means "badly or clumsily done."

Literary Element Point of View *The narrator reveals Luis's opinion of* West Side Story. *What does this tell you about him?* **L₁**

Vocabulary

harass (hə ras′) *v.* to bother or annoy repeatedly

Big Idea Life Transitions *Do you think that Luis feels any remorse for the actions of the Tiburones at this point? Explain.* **BI**

Additional Support

Leveled Reading
An adapted version of this selection is available on page 70 of *Jamestown Literature: An Adapted Reader* grade 10.

Skills Practice

READING: Verifying Predictions
Point out that readers make predictions about what will happen in a story based on information and understanding people's behavior. After students have read the story through page 230, have them write what will happen to Luis next; for example, he may get into trouble again. After students have read through page 231, have them predict the role Naomi will play in the story. When students have finished reading the story, have them meet with a partner and discuss the accuracy of their predictions. **OL**

about everything. Luis thought that it was just his way of staying busy since Luis's mother had died, almost three years ago, of cancer. He had never gotten over it.

All this was going through Luis's head as he slid down the hill of hubcaps. The tub full of soapy water, the can of polish, and the bag of rags had been neatly placed in front of a **makeshift** table made from two car seats and a piece of plywood. Luis heard a car drive up and someone honk their horn. His father emerged from inside a new red Mustang that had been totaled. He usually dismantled every small feature by hand before sending the vehicle into the *cementerio*,[4] as he called the lot. Luis watched as the most beautiful girl he had ever seen climbed out of a **vintage** white Volkswagen Bug. She stood in the sunlight in her white sundress waiting for his father, while Luis stared. She was like a smooth wood carving. Her skin was mahogany, almost black, and her arms and legs were long and thin, but curved in places so that she did not look bony and hard— more like a ballerina. And her ebony hair was braided close to her head. Luis let his breath out,

Visual Vocabulary Many people consider the *Volkswagen Beetle*, also nicknamed "VW" or "Bug," to be a classic car. Compact, durable, and affordable, the Bug was extremely popular in the 1960s and early 1970s.

---

4. *Cementerio* (se men tā′ rē ō) is Spanish for "cemetery."

Literary Element Point of View *What does this sentence tell you about Luis?* **L₂**

Reading Strategy Interpreting Imagery *How would you interpret the description of the beautiful girl in the midst of the junkyard?* **R₁**

Vocabulary

makeshift (māk′ shift′) *adj.* suitable as a temporary substitute for the proper or desired thing
vintage (vin′ tij) *adj.* characterized by enduring appeal; classic

---

feeling a little dizzy. He had forgotten to breathe. Both the girl and his father heard him. Mr. Cintrón waved him over.

"Luis, the señorita here has lost a wheel cover. Her car is twenty-five years old, so it will not be an easy match. Come look on this side."

Luis tossed a wrench he'd been holding into a toolbox like he was annoyed, just to make a point about slave labor. Then he followed his father, who knelt on the gravel and began to point out every detail of the hubcap. Luis was hardly listening. He watched the girl take a piece of paper from her handbag.

"Señor Cintrón, I have drawn the hubcap for you, since I will have to leave soon. My home address and telephone number are here, and also my parents' office number." She handed the paper to Mr. Cintrón, who nodded.

"Sí, señorita, very good. This will help my son look for it. Perhaps there is one in that stack there." He pointed to the pile of caps that Luis was supposed to wash and polish. "Yes, I'm almost certain that there is a match there. Of course, I do not know if it's near the top or the bottom. You will give us a few days, yes?"

Luis just stared at his father like he was crazy. But he didn't say anything because the girl was smiling at him with a funny expression on her face. Maybe she thought he had X-ray eyes like Superman, or maybe she was mocking him.

"Please call me Naomi, Señor Cintrón. You know my mother. She is the director of the funeral home. . . ." Mr. Cintrón seemed surprised at first; he prided himself on having a great memory. Then his friendly expression changed to one of sadness as he recalled the day of his wife's burial. Naomi did not finish her sentence. She reached over and placed her hand on Mr. Cintrón's arm for a moment. Then she said "Adiós" softly, and got in her

---

Literary Element Point of View *Why do you think Luis reacts this way?* **L₃**

Reading Strategy Interpreting Imagery *Why does Naomi touch Mr. Cintrón's arm?* **R₂**

JUDITH ORTIZ COFER **231**

Teach

R₁ Reading Strategy

Interpreting Imagery
Answer: *Her beauty is a stark contrast to the pile of wrecked cars.* **OL**

L₃ Literary Element

Point of View
Answer: *Luis probably thinks that his father is asking him to do the impossible.* **OL**

R₂ Reading Strategy

Interpreting Imagery
Answer: *She is showing sympathy toward him for his loss.* **Ask:** How does this image help you understand Naomi's character? *(This small action shows that Naomi is a caring and gentle person while also illustrating her respect for Mr. Cintrón's feelings.)* **OL**

Reading in the Real World

Career Jorge Cintrón, a hard-working Puerto Rican immigrant, will never be featured in the national press, but many of his compatriots and fellow Latinos have achieved stardom in their adopted countries. Have students locate magazine or newspaper articles celebrating the accomplishments of Latino Americans. Ask students to give brief oral reports about their subjects. **OL**

Objectives
• To interpret imagery (SE)
• To analyze point of view (SE)
• To verify predictions (TWE)

Teach

BI Big Idea

Life Transitions

Answer: *The way Luis throws the hubcaps, heedless of where they might end up, demonstrates his immaturity and lack of focus. On the other hand, his growing pride in his work and desire to please his father reflect an increasing maturity.* **OL**

★ Viewing the Art

René Magritte (1890–1967), a Belgian artist, is remembered for surreal images that hover between comedy and nightmare, such as a fish with human legs. **Answer:** *The tree appears to have caught the moon in its branches. The painting conveys a romantic and magical mood.* **AS**

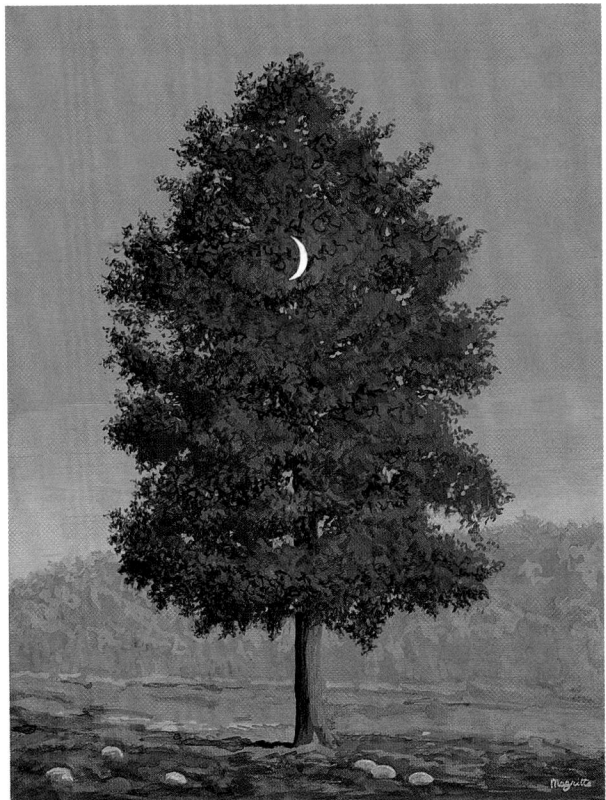

September 16, c. 1955. René Magritte. Oil on canvas, 14 x 10⅞ in. The Minneapolis Institute of Arts.

Viewing the Art: In what ways does this painting express the title and mood of the story?

shiny white car. She waved to them as she left, and her gold bracelets flashing in the sun nearly blinded Luis.

Mr. Cintrón shook his head. "How about that," he said as if to himself. "They are the Dominican owners of Ramirez Funeral Home." And, with a sigh, "She seems like such a nice young woman. Reminds me of your mother when she was her age."

Hearing the funeral parlor's name, Luis remembered too. The day his mother died, he had been in her room at the hospital while his father had gone for coffee. The alarm had gone off on her monitor and nurses had come running in, pushing him outside. After that, all he recalled was the anger that had made him punch a hole in his bedroom wall. And after-

ward he had refused to talk to anyone at the funeral. Strange, he did see a black girl there who didn't try like the others to talk to him, but actually ignored him as she escorted family members to the viewing room and brought flowers in. Could it be that the skinny girl in a frilly white dress had been Naomi? She didn't act like she had recognized him today, though. Or maybe she thought that he was a jerk.

Luis grabbed the drawing from his father. The old man looked like he wanted to walk down memory lane. But Luis was in no mood to listen to the old stories about his falling in love on a tropical island. The world they'd lived in before he was born wasn't his world. No beaches and palm trees here. Only junk as far as he could see. He climbed back up his hill and studied Naomi's sketch. It had obviously been done very carefully. It was signed "Naomi Ramirez" in the lower right-hand corner. He memorized the telephone number.

Luis washed hubcaps all day until his hands were red and raw, but he did not come across the small silver bowl that would fit the VW. After work he took a few practice Frisbee shots across the yard before showing his rows and rows of shiny rings drying in the sun. His father nodded and showed him the bump on his temple where one of Luis's flying saucers had gotten him. "Practice makes perfect, you know. Next time you'll probably **decapitate** me." Luis heard him struggle with the word

---

Big Idea Life Transitions *Does this passage show a change in Luis's attitude? Explain.* **BI**

Vocabulary

decapitate (di kap′ ə tāt′) *v.* to cut off the head of

Additional Support

Skills Practice

READING: Making Inferences

Explain that writers don't always directly state what they want you to understand. By providing clues, they can imply certain information. Readers must combine those clues with their own background and knowledge to infer what the writer

means. **Ask:** Why does Luis suddenly notice that his father has "turned into an old man"? Encourage students to base their conclusions on the clues the author has given them about the relationship between Luis and his father. **OL** *decapitate*, which Mr. Cintrón pronounced in syllables. Showing off his big vocabulary again, Luis thought. He looked closely at the bump, though. He felt bad about it.

"They look good, hijo."[5] Mr. Cintrón made a sweeping gesture with his arms over the yard. "You know, all this will have to be classified. My dream is to have all the parts divided by year, make of car, and condition. Maybe now that you are here to help me, this will happen."

"Pop . . ." Luis put his hand on his father's shoulder. They were the same height and build, about five foot six and muscular. "The judge said six months of free labor for you, not life, okay?" Mr. Cintrón nodded, looking distracted. It was then that Luis suddenly noticed how gray his hair had turned—it used to be shiny black like his own—and that there were deep lines in his face. His father had turned into an old man and he hadn't even noticed.

"Son, you must follow the judge's instructions. Like she said, next time you get in trouble, she's going to treat you like an adult, and I think you know what that means. Hard time, no breaks."

"Yeah, yeah. That's what I'm doing, right? Working my hands to the bone instead of enjoying my summer. But listen, she didn't put me under house arrest, right? I'm going out tonight."

"Home by ten. She did say something about a curfew, Luis." Mr. Cintrón had stopped smiling and was looking upset. It had always been hard for them to talk more than a minute or two before his father got offended at something Luis said, or at his sarcastic tone. He was always doing something wrong.

Luis threw the rag down on the table and went to sit in his father's ancient Buick, which was in mint condition. They drove home in silence.

After sitting down at the kitchen table with his father to eat a pizza they had picked up

on the way home, Luis asked to borrow the car. He didn't get an answer then, just a look that meant "Don't bother me right now."

Before bringing up the subject again, Luis put some ice cubes in a Baggie and handed it to Mr. Cintrón, who had made the little bump on his head worse by rubbing it. It had GUILTY written on it, Luis thought.

"Gracias, hijo." His father placed the bag on the bump and made a face as the ice touched his skin.

They ate in silence for a few minutes more; then Luis decided to ask about the car again.

"I really need some fresh air, Pop. Can I borrow the car for a couple of hours?"

"You don't get enough fresh air at the yard? We're lucky that we don't have to sit in a smelly old factory all day. You know that?"

"Yeah, Pop. We're real lucky." Luis always felt irritated that his father was so grateful to own a junkyard, but he held his anger back and just waited to see if he'd get the keys without having to get in an argument.

"Where are you going?"

"For a ride. Not going anywhere. Just out for a while. Is that okay?"

His father didn't answer, just handed him a set of keys, as shiny as the day they were manufactured. His father polished everything that could be polished: doorknobs, coins, keys, spoons, knives, and forks, like he was King Midas counting his silver and gold. Luis thought his father must be really lonely to polish utensils only he used anymore. They had been picked out by his wife, though, so they were like **relics.** Nothing she had ever owned could be

Visual Vocabulary
A *plantain* (plant′ ən) is a tropical fruit similar to a banana that must be cooked before eating.

---

5. *Hijo* (ē′ hō) is Spanish for "son."

Literary Element Point of View *Do you think Mr. Cintrón would agree with Luis's perception?* **L**

Vocabulary

relic (rel′ ik) n. an object that has survived decay, destruction, or the passage of time and is valued for its historic interest

JUDITH ORTIZ COFER **233**

Teach

R1 Reading Strategy

Interpreting Imagery
Answer: *It is his way of honoring her and keeping her alive in his memory.* `OL`

BI1 Big Idea

Life Transitions
Answer: *Luis misses the distractions that living in the apartment building provided. He feels nostalgic about his experiences there.* `OL`

R2 Reading Strategy

Interpreting Imagery
Answer: *Luis releases his grief, and it comes as an overwhelming torrent, like a flood.* `OL`

 Viewing the Art

Reginald Ainsley Cartwright (b. 1938) uses the abstract form of cubism to emphasize qualities in his subject matter. **Ask:** What stands out when you look at this painting? *(Students may note that the scrap merchant appears small and almost hidden behind the variety of vehicles and parts in his yard.)* `AS`

Scrap Merchant, 1983. Reg Cartwright.
Oil on canvas, 91.4 x 76.2 cm. Private Collection.

thrown away. Only now the dishes, forks, and spoons were not used to eat the yellow rice and red beans, the fried chicken, or the mouth-watering sweet plantains that his mother had cooked for them. They were just kept in the cabinets that his father had turned into a museum for her. Mr. Cintrón could cook as well as his wife, but he didn't have the heart to do it anymore. Luis thought that maybe if they ate together once in a while things might get better between them, but he always had something to do around dinnertime and ended up at a hamburger joint. Tonight was the first time in months they had sat down at the table together.

Luis took the keys. "Thanks," he said, walking out to take his shower. His father kept looking at him with those sad, patient eyes. "Okay. I'll be back by ten, and keep the ice on that egg," Luis said without looking back.

He had just meant to ride around his old barrio, see if any of the Tiburones were hanging out at El Building, where most of them lived. It wasn't far from the single-family home his father had bought when the business started paying off: a house that his mother lived in for three months before she took up residence at St. Joseph's Hospital. She never came home again. These days Luis wished he still lived in that tiny apartment where there was always something to do, somebody to talk to.

Instead Luis found himself parked in front of the last place his mother had gone to: Ramirez Funeral Home. In the front yard was a huge oak tree that Luis remembered having climbed during the funeral to get away from people. The tree looked different now, not like a skeleton, as it had then, but green with leaves. The branches reached to the second floor of the house, where the family lived.

For a while Luis sat in the car allowing the memories to flood back into his brain. He remembered his mother before the illness changed her. She had not been beautiful, as his father told everyone; she had been a sweet lady, not pretty but not ugly. To him, she had been the person who always told him that she was proud of him and loved him. She did that every night when she came to his bedroom door to say good-night. As a joke he would sometimes ask her,

---

Reading Strategy Interpreting Imagery *Why do you think Mr. Cintrón takes such good care of his wife's belongings?* **R1**

Big Idea Life Transitions *How does Luis feel about the apartment where he used to live?* **BI1**

Additional Support

Skills Practice

GRAMMAR: Adjective Clauses
Write the following sentence on the board: *In the front yard was an oak tree that Luis remembered having climbed.* Underline the section from the word *that* to the end. Ask students how these five words function. (*They modify the noun oak.*) Point out that clauses beginning with *that, which, who, whom, whose,* *where,* and *when* often function as adjectives, modifying the nouns or pronouns they follow.
Have students locate adjective clauses on this page and identify the noun that each clause modifies. (*Examples: where most of them lived, El Building; his father had bought, home*) `OL`

"Proud of what? I haven't done anything." And she'd always say, "I'm just proud that you are my son." She wasn't perfect or anything. She had bad days when nothing he did could make her smile, especially after she got sick. But he never heard her say anything negative about anyone. She always blamed *el destino*, fate, for what went wrong. He missed her. He missed her so much. Suddenly a flood of tears that had been building up for almost three years started pouring from his eyes. Luis sat in his father's car, with his head on the steering wheel, and cried, "Mami, I miss you."

When he finally looked up, he saw that he was being watched. Sitting at a large window with a pad and a pencil on her lap was Naomi. At first Luis felt angry and embarrassed, but she wasn't laughing at him. Then she told him with her dark eyes that it was okay to come closer. He walked to the window, and she held up the sketch pad on which she had drawn him, not crying like a baby, but sitting on top of a mountain of silver disks, holding one up over his head. He had to smile.

The plate-glass window was locked. It had a security bolt on it. An alarm system, he figured, so nobody would steal the princess. He asked her if he could come in. It was soundproof too. He mouthed the words slowly for her to read his lips. She wrote on the pad, "I can't let you in. My mother is not home tonight." So they looked at each other and talked through the window for a little while. Then Luis got an idea. He signed to her that he'd be back, and drove to the junkyard.

Luis climbed up on his mountain of hubcaps. For hours he sorted the wheel covers by make, size, and condition, stopping only to call his father and tell him where he was and what he was doing. The old man did

not ask him for explanations, and Luis was grateful for that. By lamppost light, Luis worked and worked, beginning to understand a little why his father kept busy all the time. Doing something that had a beginning, a middle, and an end did something to your head. It was like the satisfaction Luis got out of planning "adventures" for his Tiburones, but there was another element involved here that had nothing to do with showing off for others. This was a treasure hunt. And he knew what he was looking for.

Finally, when it seemed that it was a hopeless search, when it was almost midnight and Luis's hands were cut and bruised from his work, he found it. It was the perfect match for Naomi's drawing, the moon-shaped wheel cover for her car, Cinderella's shoe. Luis jumped off the small mound of disks left under him and shouted, "Yes!" He looked around and saw neat stacks of hubcaps that he would wash the next day. He would build a display wall for his father. People would be able to come into the yard and point to whatever they wanted.

Luis washed the VW hubcap and polished it until he could see himself in it. He used it as a mirror as he washed his face and combed his hair. Then he drove to the Ramirez Funeral Home. It was almost pitch-black, since it was a moonless night. As quietly as possible, Luis put some gravel in his pocket and climbed the oak tree to the second floor. He knew he was in front of Naomi's window—he could see her shadow through the curtains. She was at a table, apparently writing or drawing, maybe waiting for him. Luis hung the silver disk carefully on a branch near the window, then threw the gravel at the glass. Naomi ran to the window and drew the curtains aside while Luis held on to the thick branch and waited to give her the first good thing he had given anyone in a long time. ✎

Reading Strategy Interpreting Imagery *What does the imagery of a flood suggest about Luis's emotional response?* **R₂**

Literary Element Point of View *How does this passage demonstrate the third-person limited point of view?* **L**

Big Idea Life Transitions *What do you think the last sentence of the story means?* **BI₂**

Teach

L Literary Element

Point of View Answer: *The passage grants the reader access to some of Luis's thoughts. It does not tell the reader what is going on inside the heads of other characters.* **OL**

BI₂ Big Idea

Life Transitions
Answer: *Luis has come to realize how his behavior has affected those around him.* **OL**

★ Cultural History

Cinderella If any students are unfamiliar with the story of Cinderella, give a brief synopsis of the plot. Luis uses Naomi's drawing to find the right hubcap as the prince in "Cinderella" uses Cinderella's shoe to find the right woman. **AS**

✓ CheckPoint

Use the CheckPoint questions on Presentation Plus! to check students' mastery of the selection. These questions can be used with interactive response keypads for immediate student feedback.

Differentiated Instruction

Creative Writing Although "Catch the Moon" has a gritty, urban setting, its happy conclusion is like those in fairy tales. Have students create their own nontraditional "fairy tales" by taking a classic plot they know well, such as that in "Cinderella," and transposing it to a modern setting. Have students write summaries of the updated versions. Challenge students to expand their summaries into full–length short stories. **AL**

Objectives
• To analyze point of view (SE)
• To interpret imagery (SE)
• To understand adjective clauses (TWE)

Assess

1. (a) Yes, because Luis has rarely shown such selfless effort. (b) Students may grow to like Luis more as he matured and acted more respectfully.

2. (a) It is a condition of his release. (b) Luis is angry and complains. He does not respect his father's business.

3. (a) Luis and his father have trouble communicating. They both miss Luis's mother. (b) Yes. Luis separates the hubcaps into piles and plans a display wall. He better understands his father.

4. (a) He leaves a hubcap. (b) That giving is rewarding

5. She is loving and kind.

6. He organizes the hubcaps.

7. It suggests hopefulness, optimism, magic, and romance. Finding the hubcap represents Luis's catching the moon—a beautiful, elusive gift.

8. From defiant and self-absorbed to hardworking and sacrificing

Literary Element

1. Naomi was friendly and smiling. She would not be so if he were a jerk.

2. Luis is proud of his actions; students may say that he is

RESPONDING AND THINKING CRITICALLY

Respond

1. (a) Were you surprised by Luis's actions at the end of the story? Explain. (b) How did your feelings about Luis change as you read the story?

Recall and Interpret

2. (a) Why does Luis work at his father's junkyard? (b) What do you think Luis's feelings are about his job at the junkyard? Support your answer with details from the story.

3. (a) Describe the relationship between Luis and his father. (b) Do you think there is a chance for Luis and his father to build a better relationship? Use details from the story to support your answer.

4. (a) What does Luis leave in the tree for Naomi? (b) What do you think Luis discovers about himself as he searches for his gift to Naomi?

Analyze and Evaluate

5. In what ways can Naomi be compared with Luis's mother?

6. Explain how Luis also gives a gift to his father as he searches for the hubcap.

7. Evaluate the title of the story and explain why you do or do not think it is a good one.

Connect

8. **Big Idea** **Life Transitions** The story begins with Luis sitting on a pile of hubcaps and ends with him hanging a hubcap in a tree. Trace the kind of character transition Luis has made by the end of the story.

LITERARY ANALYSIS

Literary Element Point of View

The third-person limited narrator of "Catch the Moon" describes events only as Luis perceives them. Readers hear Luis's thoughts as he describes his gang activities and as he comments on his father or Naomi. Readers have to judge whether Luis's comments are accurate or fair and infer what his thoughts reveal about his character. Readers also should be alert to dramatic irony in the story: a contrast between what Luis thinks and what the reader knows is true.

1. The narrator does not reveal Naomi's opinion of Luis. After she leaves the junkyard, Luis worries if "maybe she thought that he was a jerk." Judge how accurate Luis's concern is.

2. The narrator reveals Luis's pride in his gang activities. Contrast Luis's feelings about his gang activities with your own perspective on gangs. What dramatic irony do you notice?

3. Evaluate Cofer's decision to use third-person limited point of view. What advantages and disadvantages might this point of view have?

Review: Plot

As you learned on pages 10–11, a key feature of **plot** is exposition, which introduces the story's characters, setting, and situation. A successful exposition will grab the reader's attention.

Partner Activity Meet with another classmate and talk about what the exposition of the story reveals about Luis, specifically with regard to where he is and why. Working with your partner, create a chart like the one below. Then fill it in with details about Luis, the setting, and the situation.

Details About Luis	Details About Setting	Details About Situation

immature and deceitful.

3. Readers receive information about one character's thoughts, but have to judge reliability. Readers must infer other characters' thoughts.

Review: Plot

About Luis: gang leader; designed T-shirts with sharks logo; deceives teachers; arrested and now on a six-month probation
About setting: junkyard; piles of metal parts and hubcaps.
About situation: released into custody of father to work in junkyard; Luis must wash and polish hubcaps.

READING AND VOCABULARY

Reading Strategy — Interpreting Imagery

Writers make their work come alive by using **imagery** to lend meaning to a scene or situation and help readers understand the relationships between characters.

1. Which images do you think are the most meaningful in the story? Explain.

2. Look back at the images of food that Luis's mother once prepared and contrast it with what Luis and his father eat now. What meaning lies behind the contrasting images?

Vocabulary — Practice

Practice with Denotations and Connotations For each word below, decide whether it has a positive, negative, or neutral connotation.

1. harass
   a. negative **b.** positive **c.** neutral
2. makeshift
   a. negative **b.** positive **c.** neutral
3. vintage
   a. negative **b.** positive **c.** neutral
4. decapitate
   a. negative **b.** positive **c.** neutral
5. relic
   a. negative **b.** positive **c.** neutral

Academic Vocabulary

Here are two words from the vocabulary list on page R82. These words will help you think, write, and talk about the selection.

alternative (ôl tûr′ nə tiv) *n.* a choice between two or more things

demonstrate (dem′ ən strāt) *v.* to explain or make clear by using examples

Practice and Apply

1. What **alternative** does Luis have if he chooses not to work for his father?
2. Does Luis **demonstrate** his feelings for Naomi?

WRITING AND EXTENDING

Writing About Literature

Analyze Point of View How would "Catch the Moon" be different if it were told from the first-person point of view? Write a brief essay analyzing how Luis, his father, and Naomi might have told this story from his or her own point of view. What would each character know about the others? How accurate would their perceptions be?

As you draft, write from start to finish. Use the following chart to help you organize your essay.

Details that Luis reveals	Details that Mr. Cintrón reveals	Details that Naomi reveals

After you complete your draft, meet with a peer reviewer to evaluate each other's work and suggest revisions. Then proofread and edit your draft for errors in spelling, grammar, and punctuation.

Literature Groups

Does Cofer suggest that Luis's association with the Tiburones is productive or harmful for him? Debate this question. Form two debate groups and one panel, who will vote after the groups' arguments are made. Find evidence from the story to support your group's view; panelists should note evidence for both sides. After each group presents its case, the panel should vote. Do you agree with the decision?

 Web Activities For eFlashcards, Selection Quick Checks, and other Web activities, go to www.glencoe.com.

JUDITH ORTIZ COFER **237**

Assess

Reading Strategy

1. (a) Most students will say that the image of the hubcap recurs in the story as a connection between Luis and his father and Luis and Naomi. The hubcap also reflects the moon in the title of the story; both are elusive and seemingly impossible to grasp.

2. Luis and his father rarely eat together at home; Luis's father doesn't cook anymore; Luis eats in fast food restaurants. The change reflects a loss of intimacy in the family since Luis's mother died.

Vocabulary

1. a 2. a 3. b 4. a 5. b

Academic Vocabulary

1. Luis can choose to serve six more months in juvenile hall.

2. Luis does when he hangs the VW hubcap in a tree outside Naomi's room.

Writing About Literature

Use these criteria when evaluating students' writing:

- Does the essay identify the details that each character might have contributed to the story?

- Does the essay discuss how each character would describe and perceive other characters?

- Does the conclusion summarize how the story would change if written from these alternate viewpoints?

Literature Groups

Students may state that Luis's association with the Tiburones was harmful because Luis ended up in juvenile detention. Students on the pro side of the debate may argue that the consequences of being involved with the Tiburones allowed Luis to release some agonizing emotions and come to terms with the loss of his mother.

Literature Online

Web Activities Have students access the Web site for interactive activities that will help them assess their understanding of the selection.

Focus

Write the following on the board: Gave an unusual gift. A runner on the team. Because he delayed. **Ask:** What makes these sentence fragments? Have students supply a subject for the first fragment, a verb for the second, and an independent clause to complete the third. **OL**

Teach

Subordinate Clause
Have students list the conjunctions that begin subordinate clauses, such as *although, since,* and *when.* **OL**

Assess

Exercise
Luis and his father had not gotten along since his mother's death. Often Luis got into trouble and was punished. Luis saw Naomi at the junkyard. He thought she was the most beautiful girl in the world. Luis worked hard to find a match for her missing hubcap. He memorized her telephone number, which she had written on the paper with her drawing of the hubcap.

▶ **Vocabulary Terms**

A sentence is a group of words that expresses a complete thought. A **sentence fragment** does not express a complete thought, and often lacks a subject and/or a verb.

▶ **Test-Taking Tip**

When writing for a test, check carefully to make sure that each sentence has a subject and a verb and conveys a complete thought.

▶ **Language Handbook**

For more on sentence fragments, see the Language Handbook pp. R50–R51.

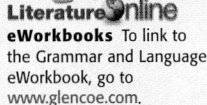

Literature Online

eWorkbooks To link to the Grammar and Language eWorkbook, go to www.glencoe.com.

OBJECTIVES
- Identify and correct sentence fragments.
- Rewrite sentences to clarify meaning.

Grammar Workshop
Sentence Structure

Avoiding Sentence Fragments

"'Home by ten. She did say something about a curfew, Luis.' Mr. Cintron had stopped smiling and was looking upset."

—Judith Ortiz Cofer, from "Catch the Moon"

Connecting to Literature A fragment is an incomplete part of something. A **sentence fragment** is a word or group of words that is only part of a sentence. People often use sentence fragments in conversation, as in the quotation from "Catch the Moon." The fragment "Home by ten" lacks both a verb and a subject. Although it could mean either the time Luis should be home or when the speaker will be home, Luis understands that Mr. Cintron is reminding him of his curfew. In writing, however, a fragment that leaves out important information can be confusing.

Problem 1   **Word group missing a subject, a verb, or both**
Needs a new hubcap. [lacks a subject]
Only three hubcaps on the car. [lacks a verb]

Solution   **Add the missing subject and/or verb.**
The Bug needs a new hubcap.
The Bug only has three hubcaps.

Problem 2   **Subordinate clause that does not express a complete thought**
Because the judge sentenced him to work in the junkyard.

Solution A   **Join the subordinate clause to a main clause.**
Luis was helping his father because the judge sentenced him to work in the junkyard.

Solution B   **Remove the subordinating conjunction at the beginning of the clause.**
The judge sentenced him to work in the junkyard.

Exercise

Proofreading: Use the strategies shown above to correct the sentence fragments in this paragraph.

Luis and his father had not gotten along. Since his mother's death. Often got into trouble and was punished. Luis saw Naomi at the junkyard. The most beautiful girl in the world. Worked hard to find a match for her missing hubcap. He memorized her telephone number. Had written on the paper with her drawing of the hubcap.

Additional Support

eWorkbooks Have students access the Web site for more practice with sentence fragments.

238

English Language Coach

Types of Clauses Looking at the prefix *sub-*, which means "lesser," may help English language learners remember that a subordinate (or dependent) clause is less than a sentence. Using similar word analysis, explain that *independent* uses the prefix *in-*, meaning "not." Therefore, independent clauses do not depend on other clauses, and may stand alone. **EL**

Differentiated Instruction

Recognizing Sentence Fragments
Tell students that advertising copy often contains sentence fragments to make it seem more conversational. Have students identify fragments in ads. Discuss levels of language and why sentence fragments are not acceptable in formal writing, even though they may be common in everyday speech. **AL**

A Child's Christmas in Wales

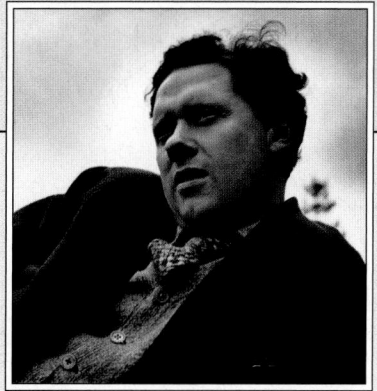

MEET DYLAN THOMAS

From the time he first listened to child-hood nursery rhymes, Dylan Thomas loved language. That love is reflected in his poetry, for which he is best known. But Thomas was also a skilled writer of prose, as attested by his famous short story "A Child's Christmas in Wales."

Early Life Dylan Thomas was born on the coast of Wales in Swansea, a place he later called an "ugly, lovely town." His father was an English teacher at the grammar school there. Thomas attended his father's school and even became the editor of the school newspaper, but he did not do well in classes that he did not like. He reveled in literature, however, and published his first poem when he was seventeen. By that time, Thomas had already left school to become a reporter for the *South Wales Evening Post*. Thomas's first book of poetry, *18 Poems*, was published when he was twenty.

> "I hold a beast, an angel, and a madman in me, and my enquiry is as to their working."
>
> —Dylan Thomas

An Individual Voice Dylan's poems were not like those of British poets of the period, who often found their voice in a grim, social realism. Thomas's poems expressed poignant emotions in a whimsical style. They relied heavily on sound and rhythm. His work blended comedic elements with the deeper pathos that shaped his literary vision and life. Thomas dealt with themes of birth, decay, sin, and redemption.

Success and Hardship In 1937 Thomas married an Irishwoman, Caitlin Macnamara, and started a family. Though Thomas was becoming known for his literary prowess, his lack of financial sense led to serious monetary troubles. During World War II, he turned to script writing for film and radio, thinking this would result in more lucrative returns. He also wrote humorous prose, such as his *Portrait of the Artist as a Young Dog* (1940), a collection of stories about his younger days.

Thomas continued to write great poems into the 1940s, but as the decade progressed, depression and exhaustion lessened his creative output. To keep up with expenses, he began giving poetry readings throughout the United States. Audiences were thrilled by his dynamic reading style, boyish looks, and personal charm.

In 1952 Dylan's *Collected Poems* was published and became an immediate success. A year later, during his third U.S. tour, Thomas died suddenly in New York City. He was thirty-nine.

Dylan Thomas was born in 1914 and died in 1953.

 Author Search For more about Dylan Thomas, go to www.glencoe.com.

DYLAN THOMAS **239**

Selection Skills

A Child's Christmas in Wales

Literary Elements
• Diction (SE pp. 240, 241, 243–247, 249)
• Voice (SE p. 249)

Reading Skills
• Connecting to Personal Experience (SE pp. 240, 242, 244, 246, 247, 249)
• Sequence of Events (TWE p. 246)

Vocabulary Skills
• Academic Vocabulary (SE p. 249)
• Analogies (SE p. 249)
• Synonyms and Antonyms (TWE p. 244)

Listening/Speaking/Viewing Skills
• Analyzing Art (SE pp. 244, 247; TWE p. 242)
• Listening to Author's Reading (SE p. 250)

Writing Skills/Grammar
• Evaluate Author's Craft (SE p. 250)
• Using Proper Nouns (SE p. 250)

Focus

Summary

Thomas recalls his boyhood memories of Christmases spent in Wales. He shifts from past to present and from real details to imagined events. Beginning with a humorous description of a fire in a neighbor's house, Thomas's narrative is interrupted by a boy who is listening to his stories. The boy asks Thomas questions about his past, and Thomas tells him the details. Thomas then shifts to recollections of adventures and conversations with friends.

Literary Elements Have students access the Web site to improve their understanding of diction.

V Vocabulary

Vocabulary File Say: Add these words and definitions to your vocabulary file. For each word, include a sentence that gives you an example of how to use the word. **OL** Students with English language needs should include the pronunciations of these words in their files. **EL**

Connecting to the Short Story

In the following story, Dylan Thomas describes a typical Christmas holiday in Wales in the early 1900s, in part inspired by his experiences as a child. With wry humor and near reverential fondness for the past, Thomas describes a typical family, traditional food, and even a house fire in lyrically descriptive detail. Before you read the short story, think about the following questions:

- What memories do you have of holidays or celebrations when you were younger?
- How are your family's holiday traditions like those described in this story? How are they different?

Building Background

The events described in this selection take place in the town of Swansea, Wales. Although Wales has been part of Great Britain for more than 450 years, the Welsh people have maintained their own traditions, literature, and even language (although the people of Wales primarily speak English, about one-fifth speak Welsh, an ancient Celtic language). The Welsh have always loved poetry and song.

In this selection, Thomas uses an unusual literary device that springs from oral traditions. At one point in the story, a boy who has apparently been listening to the speaker interrupts his narration—as if the speaker were orally telling the story. The narrator and the boy continue a conversation for pages with you, the reader, listening in.

Big Idea Life Transitions

As you read this short story, notice how the narrator fondly remembers a childhood holiday. As he describes his Christmas celebrations, he blends both real details with mythical, memory-enhanced events. As you read, think about how you recall memories from your past.

Literary Element Diction

Diction is a writer's choice of words and their arrangement in phrases, sentences, or lines. Diction is an important element of a writer's style. As you read, note Thomas's choice of words and their effect on your understanding and ability to imagine what he is writing about.

- See Literary Terms Handbook, p. R5.

OBJECTIVES
In studying this selection, you will focus on the following:
- evaluating the impact of diction

Reading Strategy Connecting to Personal Experience

When you **connect to personal experience,** you relate what you read to what you have experienced in your own life. Connecting in this way can strengthen your appreciation of literature. As you read this story, connect the narrator's retelling of his childhood holiday with memories of your own childhood celebrations.

Reading Tip: Comparing and Contrasting As you read, ask yourself: How are the details similar to what I remember about my childhood holidays? How are they different? Record your responses in a chart like the one below.

Similar	Different

Vocabulary

daft (daft) *adj.* without sense or reason; crazy; silly; p. 243 *Your idea to swim home is daft.*

judiciously (jōō dish′ əs lē) *adv.* in a way that shows good judgment; sensibly; p. 245 *He spent his money judiciously and bought only what he needed.*

hale (hāl) *adj.* in good physical condition; healthy; p. 245 *The doctor pronounced the newborn baby hale and of normal length and weight.*

stridently (strīd′ ənt lē) *adv.* in a loud, harsh manner; shrilly; p. 245 *The dissatisfied customer stridently insisted on talking to the manager.*

lurk (lurk) *v.* to stay hidden, ready to attack; p. 246 *The hungry lions lurk in the tall grass.*

Literature Online **Interactive Literary Elements Handbook** To review or learn more about the literary elements, go to www.glencoe.com.

- connecting what is read to personal experiences
- writing an evaluation of the author's craft

240 UNIT 1 THE SHORT STORY

Selection Resources

Print Materials
- Unit 1 Resources (Fast File), pp. 82–84
- Leveled Vocabulary Development, p. 18
- Selection and Unit Assessments, pp. 39–40
- Selection Quick Checks, p. 20

Transparencies
- Bellringer Options Transparencies:
  Selection Focus Transparency 15
  Daily Language Practice Transparency 22
- Literary Elements Transparency 26

Technology
- TeacherWorks Plus™ CD-ROM
- StudentWorks Plus™ CD-ROM
- Presentation Plus!™ CD-ROM
- Literature Online, glencoe.com
- Online Student Edition, mhln.com
- ExamView® Assessment Suite CD-ROM
- Vocabulary PuzzleMaker CD-ROM
- Listening Library, disc 1 track 22

A Child's Christmas in Wales

Dylan Thomas

Winter in Wales, c. 1954. Fred Uhlman. Oil on canvas, 46 x 61 cm. Private collection.

One Christmas was so much like another, in those years around the sea-town corner[1] now and out of all sound except the distant speaking of the voices I sometimes hear a moment before sleep, that I can never remember whether it snowed for six days and six nights when I was twelve or whether it snowed for twelve days and twelve nights when I was six.

All the Christmases roll down toward the two-tongued sea, like a cold and headlong moon bundling down the sky that was our street; and they stop at the rim of the ice-edged, fish-freezing waves, and I plunge my hands in the snow and bring out whatever I can find. In goes my hand into that wool-white bell-tongued ball of holidays resting at the rim of the carol-singing sea, and out come Mrs. Prothero and the firemen.

It was on the afternoon of the day of Christmas Eve, and I was in Mrs. Prothero's garden, waiting for cats, with her son Jim.

---

1. The expression *around the sea-town corner* means "out of sight" or "long gone."

Literary Element Diction *What effect do Thomas's choice of words and use of alliteration create?* **L**

DYLAN THOMAS **241**

R Reading Strategy

Connecting to Personal Experience
Answer: *Students' responses should include details as to why their experiences are similar to or different from the narrator's.)* **OL**

BI₁ Big Idea

Life Transitions
Answer: *The narrator describes the boys imagining themselves as Arctic Eskimo hunters, so Mrs. Prothero's first cry fits their fantasy; then he switches to describing reality when it becomes clear that she is really shouting, "Fire!"* **OL**

★ Viewing the Art

Explain to students that this painting is of a dinner table set to celebrate the Jewish holiday of Rosh Hashana. Ask students why the painting may be an appropriate visual for this story about Christmas celebrations. **AS**

The Table, 1995. Elizabeth Barakah Hodges. Oil on canvas. ★

It was snowing. It was always snowing at Christmas. December, in my memory, is white as Lapland, though there were no reindeers. But there were cats. Patient, cold, and callous, our hands wrapped in socks, we waited to snowball the cats. Sleek and long as jaguars and horrible-whiskered, spitting and snarling, they would slink and sidle over the white back-garden walls, and the lynx-eyed² hunters, Jim and I, fur-capped and moccasined trappers from Hudson Bay, off Mumbles Road, would hurl our deadly snowballs at the green of their eyes.

The wise cats never appeared. We were so still, Eskimo-footed arctic marksmen in the muffling silence of the eternal snows—eternal, ever since Wednesday—that we never heard Mrs. Prothero's first cry from her igloo at the

bottom of the garden. Or, if we heard it at all, it was, to us, like the far-off challenge of our enemy and prey, the neighbour's polar cat. But soon the voice grew louder. "Fire!" cried Mrs. Prothero, and she beat the dinner-gong.

And we ran down the garden, with the snowballs in our arms, toward the house; and smoke, indeed, was pouring out of the dining-room, and the gong was bombilating, and Mrs. Prothero was announcing ruin like a town crier in Pompeii.³ This was better than all the cats in Wales standing on the wall in a row. We bounded into the house, laden with snowballs, and stopped at the open door of the smoke-filled room.

Something was burning all right; perhaps it was Mr. Prothero, who always slept there after midday dinner with a newspaper over his face. But he was standing in the middle of the room, saying, "A fine Christmas!" and smacking at the smoke with a slipper. "Call the fire brigade," cried Mrs. Prothero as she beat the gong.

"They won't be there," said Mr. Prothero, "it's Christmas."

There was no fire to be seen, only clouds of smoke and Mr. Prothero standing in the middle of them, waving his slipper as though he were conducting.

"Do something," he said.

And we threw all our snowballs into the smoke—I think we missed Mr. Prothero—and ran out of the house to the telephone box.

"Let's call the police as well," Jim said.

"And the ambulance."

"And Ernie Jenkins, he likes fires."

---

2. The *lynx-eyed* hunters have sharp vision like the lynx, a wildcat of Europe and Asia.

Reading Strategy Connecting to Personal Experience
How do having snow and throwing snowballs relate to your experiences of or ideas about wintertime? **R**

Big Idea Life Transitions *How does the narrator connect the world of childhood to the adult world in this passage?* **BI₁**

---

3. *Pompeii* (pom pā′) was a Roman city destroyed and buried by a volcanic eruption in AD 79.

Additional Support

RESEARCH: Wales Remind students that Dylan Thomas grew up in Wales, a country that is part of Great Britain. In "A Child's Christmas in Wales," Thomas mentions chasing with jawbones "the English and the bears," reflecting long-standing resentment toward the English among non-English British citizens. Have students research the political history of Wales and its relationship to England. Ask them to determine how Thomas would have felt about the English, as well as how the Welsh feel about the English today. **OL**

But we only called the fire brigade, and soon the fire engine came and three tall men in helmets brought a hose into the house and Mr. Prothero got out just in time before they turned it on. Nobody could have had a noisier Christmas Eve. And when the firemen turned off the hose and were standing in the wet, smoky room, Jim's aunt, Miss Prothero, came downstairs and peered in at them. Jim and I waited, very quietly, to hear what she would say to them. She said the right thing, always. She looked at the three tall firemen in their shining helmets, standing among the smoke and cinders and dissolving snowballs, and she said: "Would you like anything to read?"

Years and years and years ago, when I was a boy, when there were wolves in Wales, and birds the color of red-flannel petticoats whisked past the harp-shaped hills, when we sang and wallowed all night and day in caves that smelt like Sunday afternoons in damp front farmhouse parlors, and we chased, with the jawbones of deacons, the English and the bears, before the motor-car, before the wheel, before the duchess-faced horse, when we rode the **daft** and happy hills bareback, it snowed and it snowed. But here a small boy says: "It snowed last year, too. I made a snowman and my brother knocked it down and I knocked my brother down and then we had tea."

"But that was not the same snow," I say. "Our snow was not only shaken from whitewash buckets down the sky, it came shawling[4] out of the ground and swam and drifted out of the arms and hands and bodies of the trees; snow grew overnight on the roofs of the houses like a pure and grandfather moss, minutely white-ivied the walls and settled on the postman, opening the gate, like a dumb, numb thunderstorm of white, torn Christmas cards."

---

4. Snow that is *shawling* is rising up like a shawl that is pulled up over the shoulders.

Big Idea Life Transitions *From this description, how do you think the narrator now feels about his childhood?* **BI₂**

Vocabulary

daft (daft) *adj.* without sense or reason; crazy; silly

"Were there postmen then, too?"

"With sprinkling eyes and wind-cherried noses, on spread, frozen feet they crunched up to the doors and mittened on them manfully. But all that the children could hear was a ringing of bells."

"You mean that the postman went rat-a-tat-tat and the doors rang?"

"I mean that the bells that the children could hear were inside them."

"I only hear thunder sometimes, never bells."

"There were church bells, too."

"Inside them?"

"No, no, no, in the bat-black, snow-white belfries, tugged by bishops and storks. And they rang their tidings over the band-aged town, over the frozen foam of the powder and ice-cream hills, over the crackling sea. It seemed that all the churches boomed for joy under my window; and the weathercocks crew for Christmas, on our fence."

"Get back to the postmen."

"They were just ordinary postmen, fond of walking and dogs and Christmas and the snow. They knocked on the doors with blue knuckles. . . ."

"Ours has got a black knocker. . . ."

"And then they stood on the white Welcome mat in the little, drifted porches and huffed and puffed, making ghosts with their breath, and jogged from foot to foot like small boys wanting to go out."

"And then the Presents?"

"And then the Presents, after the Christmas box.[5] And the cold postman, with a rose on his button-nose, tingled down the tea-tray-slithered run of the chilly glinting hill. He went in his ice-bound boots like a man on fishmonger's slabs.[6] He wagged his bag like a frozen camel's hump, dizzily turned the corner on one foot, and, by God, he was gone."

"Get back to the Presents."

---

5. A *Christmas box* is a present for the postman.
6. The blocks or trays of ice on which fish are displayed at a market are *fishmonger's slabs*.

Literary Element Diction *How does the author's diction and description of the postmen and the children in these two sentences help convey a vivid voice?* **L**

DYLAN THOMAS **243**

Teach

BI₂ Big Idea
Life Transitions
Answer: *The narrator's tone in this description is one of fondness and nostalgia. Presumably, the narrator's memories of childhood are happy. He may feel bittersweet now recalling something so pleasant that no longer exists for him.* **OL**

L Literary Element
Diction
Answer: *Words such as* cherried, *meaning "red," and phrases such as "mittened on them manfully" for "knocked" suggest an appreciative, playful voice and an author who values life's everyday moments.* Explain that the narrator's voice is closely tied to the words he uses. Recite the passage beginning "With sprinkling eyes . . . ." Replace "cherried" with "red" and "mittened on them manfully" with "knocked." Discuss how this changes the voice. **OL**

★ Writer's Technique

Personification Thomas uses personification to cleverly convey his narrative. **Ask:** Can snow swim? Explain that Thomas lends this human characteristic to the snow to better demonstrate its movement. **AS**

Differentiated Instruction

Multiple Modes of Expression
Interpersonal, or social, learners thrive when given the opportunity to interact with fellow students. In addition, they can help motivate classmates with their energy and enthusiasm. Harness this positive energy by having the social learners in your class do role-playing activities. Students can work in small groups to perform two or three scenes from "A Child's Christmas in Wales." After students select and practice their scenes, invite them to present them to the class. Use these performances to assess their comprehension of the text. **BL**

Objectives
- To connect what is read to personal experiences
- To evaluate the impact of diction (SE)
- To research political history (TWE)

Teach

L1 Literary Element

Diction

Answer: *Possible answers include* engulfing, *"made for giant sloths,"* blinding, *"for victims of headshrinking tribes,"* rasping, pictureless, *and* drowned. **OL**

R Reading Strategy

Connecting to Personal Experience Answer: *Students' answers will vary.* **Say:** A reader will not always be able to make a personal connection with a text. Explain that writers and readers cannot always find common ground. **Ask:** How can a reader connect to a text in instances where no *personal* connection is possible? *(While readers may not always find familiarity in a text, they can connect with it by admiring or loathing the characters, by identifying a universal theme, or learning a valuable lesson.)* **OL**

★ Viewing the Art

Answer: *Children in the scene and the story are having a snowball fight. Also the town's buildings and streets are covered in snow.* **AS**

"There were the Useful Presents: engulfing mufflers of the old coach days, and mittens made for giant sloths; zebra scarfs of a substance like silky gum that could be tug-o'-warred down to the galoshes; blinding tam-o'-shanters like patchwork tea cosies and bunny-suited busbies and balaclavas[7] for victims of headshrinking tribes; from aunts who always wore wool next to the skin there were moustached and rasping vests that made you wonder why the aunts had any skin left at all; and once I had a little crocheted nose bag from an aunt now, alas, no longer whinnying with us. And pictureless books in which small boys, though warned with quotations not to, would skate on Farmer Giles' pond and did and drowned; and books that told me everything about the wasp, except why."

"Go on to the Useless Presents."

"Bags of moist and many-coloured jelly babies and a folded flag and a false nose and a tram[8] conductor's cap and a machine that punched tickets and rang a bell; never a catapult; once, by mistake that no one could explain, a little hatchet; and a celluloid[9] duck that made, when you pressed it, a most unducklike sound, a mewing moo that an ambitious cat might make who wished to be a cow; and a painting book in which I could make the grass, the trees, the sea and the animals any color I pleased, and still the dazzling sky-blue sheep are grazing in the red field under the rainbow-billed and pea-green birds.

Hardboileds, toffee, fudge and allsorts, crunches, cracknels, humbugs, glaciers, marzipan, and butterwelsh for the Welsh. And troops of bright tin soldiers who, if they could not fight, could always run. And Snakes-and-Families and Happy Ladders. And Easy Hobbi-Games for Little Engineers, complete with instructions.

Oh, easy for Leonardo! And a whistle to make the dogs bark to wake up the old man next door to make him beat on the wall with his stick to shake our picture off the wall.

And a packet of cigarettes: you put one in your mouth and you stood at the corner of the street and you waited for hours, in vain, for an old lady to scold you for smoking a cigarette, and then with a smirk you ate it. And then it was breakfast under the balloons."

"Were there Uncles, like in our house?"

"There are always Uncles at Christmas.

Snowballing, c. 1917. Dame Laura Knight. Watercolor heightened with bodycolor over pencil, 52 x 75 cm. Private collection.
Viewing the Art: What similarities do you find between the scene in this painting and the winter memories that Thomas describes?
★

---

7. *Busbies* and *balaclavas* are different types of hats made of wool or fur.
8. In Britain, a streetcar is called a *tram.*

Literary Element Diction What words does Thomas use to describe the Useful Presents to make you think that the narrator did not particularly care for them? **L1**

Reading Strategy Connecting to Personal Experience
Did you sort presents into "useful" and "useless," or make similar classifications of gifts, when you were a young child? Explain. **R**

9. *Celluloid* is a kind of plastic.

Additional Support

Skills Practice

VOCABULARY: Synonyms and Antonyms Students demonstrate mastery of a word's meaning when they can replace it with another, similar word and especially when they can determine the word's opposite. Select ten words from the page above. Instruct students to replace these words with synonyms. **Say:** Be sure that your synonyms effectively replace the original words. You can check by plugging the synonyms into the original sentences. Encourage students to use dictionaries and thesauri. Next, have students repeat the activity, this time using antonyms. **OL**

The same Uncles. And on Christmas mornings, with dog-disturbing whistle and sugar fags[10] I would scour the swatched[11] town for the news of the little world, and find always a dead bird by the white Post Office or by the deserted swings; perhaps a robin, all but one of his fires out. Men and women wading or scooping back from chapel, with taproom noses and wind-bussed cheeks, all albinos, huddled their stiff black jarring feathers against the irreligious snow.

Mistletoe hung from the gas brackets[12] in all the front parlours; there was sherry and walnuts and bottled beer and crackers by the dessertspoons; and cats in their fur-abouts watched the fires; and the high-heaped fire spat, all ready for the chestnuts and the mulling pokers.[13]

Some few large men sat in the front parlours, without their collars, Uncles almost certainly, trying their new cigars, holding them out **judiciously** at arms' length, returning them to their mouths, coughing, then holding them out again as though waiting for the explosion; and some few small Aunts, not wanted in the kitchen, nor anywhere else for that matter, sat on the very edges of their chairs, poised and brittle, afraid to break, like faded cups and saucers."

Not many those mornings trod the piling streets: an old man always, fawn-bowlered,[14] yellow-gloved and, at this time of year, with spats[15] of snow, would take his constitutional to the white bowling green[16] and back, as he would take it wet or fine on Christmas Day or Doomsday; sometimes two **hale** young men, with big pipes blazing, no overcoats, and wind-blown scarfs, would trudge, unspeaking, down to the forlorn sea, to work up an appetite, to blow away the fumes, who knows, to walk into the waves until nothing of them was left but the two curling smoke clouds of their inextinguishable briars. Then I would be slap-dashing home, the gravy smell of the dinners of others, the bird smell, the brandy, the pudding and mince, coiling up to my nostrils, when out of a snow-clogged side lane would come a boy the spit of myself, with a pink-tipped cigarette and the violet past of a black eye, cocky as a bullfinch, leering all to himself.

I hated him on sight and sound, and would be about to put my dog whistle to my lips and blow him off the face of Christmas when suddenly he, with a violet wink, put *his* whistle to *his* lips and blew so **stridently,** so high, so exquisitely loud, that gobbling faces, their cheeks bulged with goose, would press against their tinselled windows, the whole length of the white echoing street. For dinner we had turkey and blazing pudding,[17] and after dinner the Uncles sat in front of the fire, loosened all buttons, put

---

10. *Sugar fags* are candy cigarettes.
11. *Swatched* is a variation of the word *swathed* and means "bound" or "wrapped."
12. *Gas brackets* are wall-mounted gas lamps that are fed by gas piped through the walls.
13. *Mulling pokers* are fireplace pokers used to heat and stir *mull*, a hot, spiced wine.

14. The man who is *fawn-bowlered* is wearing a fawn-colored *bowler*, a round, narrow-brimmed hat.
15. *Spats* are short coverings made of cloth or leather, worn over the tops of the shoes and around the ankles.
16. The old man took his *constitutional*, or walk, every day, regardless of the weather. A *bowling green* is the lawn used in a bowling game.
17. *Blazing pudding* is a fancy pudding that is doused with brandy and served flaming.

Literary Element Diction *What do you picture here? What does this description tell you about the robin?* **L2**

Vocabulary

judiciously (jōō dish′ əs lē) *adv.* in a way that shows good judgment; sensibly

Vocabulary

hale (hāl) *adj.* in good physical condition; healthy
stridently (strīd′ ənt lē) *adv.* in a loud, harsh manner; shrilly

DYLAN THOMAS **245**

Teach

R1 Reading Strategy

Connecting to Personal Experience Answer: *The adult narrator is describing holiday scenes from his own childhood with a child's perspective.* **OL**

L1 Literary Element

Diction Answer: *The family has eaten a large holiday dinner—"rich and heavy" describes the food and the way the family must now be feeling. The dinner is also rich with the presence of family members.* **OL**

BI Big Idea

Life Transitions Answer: *The narrator remembers his childhood fondly, viewing it as a time of imagination and exploration.* **OL**

★ Writer's Technique

Listing An effective way of shaping a scene is to list its elements. Read aloud the sentence beginning "Mothers, aunts, and sisters . . ." and continue to the paragraph's end. **Ask:** How many images are offered here? *(Between eight and eleven.)* Discuss the effectiveness of Thomas's listing. **AS**

Visual Vocabulary
Tureens are deep dishes used for serving food at the table.

their large moist hands over their watch chains, groaned a little and slept. Mothers, aunts, and sisters scuttled to and fro, bearing tureens. Auntie Bessie, who had already been frightened, twice, by a clock-work mouse, whimpered at the sideboard and had some elderberry wine. The dog was sick. Auntie Dosie had to have three aspirins, but Auntie Hannah, who liked port, stood in the middle of the snowbound backyard, singing like a big-bosomed thrush. I would blow up balloons to see how big they would blow up to; and, when they burst, which they all did, the Uncles jumped and rumbled. In the rich and heavy afternoon, the Uncles breathing like dolphins and the snow descending, I would sit among festoons and Chinese lanterns and nibble dates and try to make a model man-o'-war, following the Instructions for Little Engineers, and produce what might be mistaken for a sea-going tramcar.

Or I would go out, my bright new boots squeaking, into the white world, on to the seaward hill, to call on Jim and Dan and Jack and to pad through the still streets, leaving huge deep footprints on the hidden pavements.

"I bet people will think there's been hippos."

"What would you do if you saw a hippo coming down our street?"

"I'd go like this, bang! I'd throw him over the railings and roll him down the hill and then I'd tickle him under the ear and he'd wag his tail."

"What would you do if you saw *two* hippos?"

Iron-flanked and bellowing he-hippos clanked and battered through the scudding snow toward us as we passed Mr. Daniel's house.

"Let's post Mr. Daniel a snowball through his letter box."

"Let's write things in the snow."

"Let's write, 'Mr. Daniel looks like a spaniel' all over his lawn."

Or we walked on the white shore.

"Can the fishes see it's snowing?"

The silent one-clouded heavens drifted on to the sea. Now we were snow-blind travellers lost on the north hills, and vast dew-lapped[18] dogs, with flasks round their necks, ambled and shambled up to us, baying "Excelsior."[19] We returned home through the poor streets where only a few children fumbled with bare red fingers in the wheel-rutted snow and catcalled after us, their voices fading away, as we trudged uphill, into the cries of the dock birds and the hooting of ships out in the whirling bay. And then, at tea the recovered Uncles would be jolly; and the ice cake loomed in the center of the table like a marble grave. Auntie Hannah laced her tea with rum, because it was only once a year.

Bring out the tall tales now that we told by the fire as the gaslight bubbled like a diver. Ghosts whooed like owls in the long nights when I dared not look over my shoulder; animals **lurked** in the cubbyhole under the stairs where the gas meter ticked. And I remember that we went singing carols once, when there wasn't the shaving of a moon to light the flying streets. At the end of a long road was a

Visual Vocabulary
Festoons are decorations that hang in loops or curves.

---

18. *Dewlapped* dogs have a loose fold of skin under the throat.
19. *Baying* means "howling." *Excelsior* is a Latin word meaning "still higher; ever upward." It is often used as an inspirational motto.

Reading Strategy Connecting to Personal Experience *Do you think the description in this paragraph is written from a child's or an adult's perspective? Explain.* **R1**

Literary Element Diction *Why does Thomas describe the afternoon as "rich and heavy"?* **L1**

Big Idea Life Transitions *What can you infer about the narrator's attitude toward his childhood from the details in this story?* **BI**

Vocabulary

lurk (lurk) *v.* to stay hidden, ready to attack

246 UNIT 1 THE SHORT STORY

Additional Support

Skills Practice

READING: Sequence of Events

Although the author merges several Christmases, a sequence of events exists. The narrative is ordered from the afternoon on Christmas Eve to Christmas night. Analyzing the sequence can help students understand the story. Have students chart the narrative's main events on a timeline. For example, on Christmas afternoon, the aunts do the dishes while the uncles smoke cigars. Use this example to illustrate that the time when an event occurs can be determined by its context. Facilitate discussions as students develop their timelines. **OL**

Home Sweet Home. Walter Dendy Sadler (1854–1923).
Oil on canvas. Private collection.
Viewing the Art: What images or scenes from the story does this painting bring to mind? ★

drive that led to a large house, and we stumbled up the darkness of the drive that night, each one of us afraid, each one holding a stone in his hand in case, and all of us too brave to say a word. The wind through the trees made noises as of old and unpleasant and maybe webfooted men wheezing in caves. We reached the black bulk of the house.

"What shall we give them? 'Hark the Herald'?"

"No," Jack said, " 'Good King Wenceslas.' I'll count three."

One, two, three, and we began to sing, our voices high and seemingly distant in the snow-felted darkness round the house that was occupied by nobody we knew. We stood close together, near the dark door.

> *Good King Wenceslas looked out*
> *On the Feast of Stephen . . .*

And then a small, dry voice, like the voice of someone who has not spoken for a long time, joined our singing: a small dry, egg-shell voice from the other side of the door: a small dry voice through the keyhole. And when we stopped running we were outside *our* house; the front room was lovely; balloons floated under the hot-water-bottle-gulping gas; everything was good again and shone over the town.

"Perhaps it was a ghost," Jim said.

"Perhaps it was trolls," Dan said, who was always reading.

"Let's go in and see if there's any jelly left," Jack said. And we did that.

Always on Christmas night there was music. An uncle played the fiddle, a cousin

sang "Cherry Ripe," and another uncle sang "Drake's Drum." It was very warm in the little house.

Auntie Hannah, who had got on to the parsnip wine, sang a song about Bleeding Hearts and Death, and then another in which she said her heart was like a Bird's Nest; and then everybody laughed again; and then I went to bed. Looking through my bedroom window, out into the moonlight and the unending smoke-coloured snow, I could see the lights in the windows of all the other houses on our hill and hear the music rising from them up the long, steadily falling night. I turned the gas down, I got into bed. I said some words to the close and holy darkness, and then I slept. ❧

Literary Element Diction How does the narrator's specific language enhance the mood in this passage? **L₂**

Reading Strategy Connecting to Personal Experience
How have you felt at the end of a long holiday? Describe what you did after your festivities ended. **R₂**

DYLAN THOMAS **247**

Differentiated Instruction

247

Assess

1. Answers will vary.

2. (a) The boys hear the call, "Fire!", race over, and call the fire brigade. (b) Excited and amused. Phrases: "Do something," "announcing ruin like a town crier in Pompeii," and "would you like anything to read?"

3. (a) Useful: mufflers, mittens, tam-o'-shanters; Useless: fudge, painting book, tin soldiers (b) Stable, comfortable and generous

4. (a) They nap, clean, and play. These details provide realism. These "boring" details help to authenticate the memory. (b) The children walking outside in new boots; then they are hippos and become lost travelers in the hills.

5. Sample answers: snow; light; music

6. Happy and pleasant, remembered as an idyllic time

7. Family-oriented, traditional, music loving

8. To convey the playful and creative nature of childhood, or how children themselves move between the real and the imaginary

RESPONDING AND THINKING CRITICALLY

Respond

1. Which event from Thomas's short story made the strongest impression on you?

Recall and Interpret

2. (a) Summarize what happens at the Prothero home on Christmas Eve. (b) How does the narrator seem to feel about this event and about the Protheros? Use words from the passage to help explain.

3. (a) What categories of presents does the speaker describe? Give at least three examples from each category. (b) What might you infer about the narrator's childhood from the presents he describes?

4. (a) What do the adults and children do after Christmas dinner? Why does the narrator include these details? (b) In his accounts of what the children do, when does the narrator mix elements of reality and fantasy?

Analyze and Evaluate

5. Select two examples of **imagery** in the story. Evaluate how effective each example is in helping you see, hear, smell, feel, or taste what Thomas describes.

6. What kinds of memories does the narrator recall from his childhood Christmases? Why do you think he does this?

7. What conclusions might you draw about the culture in which the narrator grew up? Support your conclusions with evidence from the story.

Connect

8. **Big Idea** Life Transitions Although this selection is fiction and contains imagined incidents, Thomas seamlessly imbued it with realistic details, perhaps inspired by his own experiences as a child in Wales. Why do you think he did this?

DAILY LIFE AND CULTURE

Turn-of-the-Century Wales

The setting of "A Child's Christmas in Wales"—Dylan Thomas's childhood hometown—was the town of Swansea, Wales, in the early 1900s. At that time, many of the Welsh living there were coal miners. Others, especially in industrial southern Wales, where Swansea was located, worked in factories. Swansea prospered as a coastal town located near coalfields.

In the early 1900s automobiles were still rare. People did not own private telephones (hence, the boys run out of the Prothero house to the "telephone box" to report a fire), and gas lamps, not electricity, were used to light homes.

Although Wales was united politically with England in 1536, the Welsh people tried to preserve their Welsh identity and cultural traditions. Even so, in the early 1900s it became culturally fashionable not to teach children Welsh. Dylan Thomas was raised in an English-speaking home.

1. What would daily communication have been like in a community like Swansea, where there were no telephones in the home?

2. How is language important in preserving a culture? What problems might result when a native language is no longer taught?

Daily Life and Culture

1. Students might suggest that immediate communication would be more difficult, especially in emergencies such as fires. On the other hand, people might be friendlier to each other since they would often talk face-to-face.

2. Sample answers: Because language is a very important part of a people's culture, much of a culture's character is lost when the language is not preserved. Children who are no longer taught the language grow up lacking a part of their cultural identity.

Literary Element Diction

Diction refers to a writer's choice of words; it is an important element of the writer's voice and style. Skilled writers, such as Dylan Thomas, choose their words carefully to convey a particular tone and meaning. For example, Thomas specifically chooses fantastic words and phrases, such as "two-tongued sea," "eternal snows," and "ice-cream hills," that add a dream-like quality to the narrator's descriptions.

1. Rewrite this sentence in contemporary, informal diction: "Bring out the tall tales now that we told by the fire as the gaslight bubbled like a diver."

2. Why might Thomas have chosen the specific language he used in this story?

3. Identify three examples of word choice that you think convey the tone or meaning of the story particularly well.

Review: Voice

As you learned on pages 192–193, **voice** is the author's distinctive use of language that conveys the author's or narrator's personality and tone. Voice depends in part on diction.

Partner Activity Meet with another classmate and together offer three examples of writing with a distinctive voice in "A Child's Christmas in Wales." For each example, write a couple of sentences explaining what makes its language so effective. Make a chart like the one below.

Example	Why It Is Distinctive
"All the Christmases roll down toward the two-tongued sea, like a cold and headlong moon bundling down the sky that was our street…"	The author uses creative, vivid, and unconventional figurative language, such as the simile "like a cold and headlong moon…."

Reading Strategy Connecting to Personal Experience

Comparing and contrasting your experiences with those of the narrator can help you understand what you have read.

Go back now to some questions posed before you read the selection. How would you answer them?

1. How are your family's holiday traditions or celebrations like the narrator's?

2. How are they different?

Vocabulary Practice

Practice with Analogies Choose the word pair that best completes the analogy.

1. screech: stridently::
   a. murmur: quietly
   b. look: sneakily
   c. scold: unfairly
   d. giggle: uncontrollably
   e. sing: sweetly

2. hale: disease::
   a. tall: strength
   b. wise: advice
   c. jealous: love
   d. fair: bias
   e. warm: fever

3. lurk: retreat::
   a. stomp: tiptoe
   b. whistle: shout
   c. parade: march
   d. teach: illustrate
   e. march: amble

4. composed: daft::
   a. troubled: perturbed
   b. ready: unprepared
   c. distrustful: wise
   d. elegant: expensive
   e. patient: hesitant

Academic Vocabulary

Here is a word from the vocabulary list on page R82.

domestic (də mes′ tik) *adj.* having to do with the home

Practice and Apply
1. How did the narrator describe the **domestic** scene after Christmas dinner?

Assess

Literary Element

1. Sample: We told stories by the fire, while the gaslights made noise.

2. Thomas chose words for sound as well as meaning to create a rich setting, portray the sights, sound, smells and tastes of Wales at Christmas, and to communicate a child's active imagination.

3. Examples: "snow-felted darkness," "hot-water-bottle-gulping gas," "a small dry, eggshell voice," "he wagged his bag like a frozen camel's hump"

Review: Voice

Example	Why it is Distinctive
—"I think we missed Mr. Prothero"—	In context, this statement is humorous.
"Always on Christmas night there was music . . . It was very warm in the little house."	This statement captures the nostalgia of youth
"I would blow up balloons to see how big they would blow up to."	This statement portrays the boyish attitude and exuberance of the narrator.

Reading Strategy

1-2. Students' responses will depend on their personal experiences. They should include specific examples of how their experiences are similar to or different from the narrator's.

Vocabulary

1. a **2.** d **3.** a **4.** b

Academic Vocabulary

After Christmas dinner, the uncles slept while the women cleaned up. Then they all played music and sang.

Assess

Writing About Literature

Use these criteria when evaluating students' writing:

- Does the essay identify the advantages and disadvantages of the narrative approach?
- Does the essay explore reasons why Thomas combined real and imagined memories?
- Does the essay express an opinion?

Listening and Speaking

Point out to students that an effective oral reading strategy focuses on the language and tries to express the emotion of the text.

Thomas's Language and Style

Possible answers: (1) "There are always Uncles . . . ." Thomas was trying to show that uncles are special. (2) "Useful Presents" and "Useless Presents" shows the importance of presents in a child's life.

Activity

1. the afternoon of the day of Christmas Eve
2. Mrs. Prothero and the firemen
3. there were wolves in Wales
4. trappers from Hudson Bay, off Mumbles Road

Writing About Literature

Evaluate Author's Craft In this short story, Dylan Thomas merges the real and imagined recollections of a Christmas in Wales. In an essay, evaluate this approach. Consider these questions:

What are the advantages and disadvantages of combining plausible and clearly fictional situations into one story?

- Why do you think Thomas chose this approach?
- Do you think that his approach was successful?

Use evidence and examples from the selection—as well as from your own life, if applicable—to support your ideas.

Before you begin drafting, list the advantages and the disadvantages of Thomas's approach. Then organize your ideas into five paragraphs:

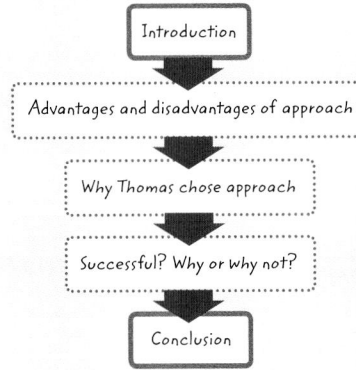

Introduction

↓

Advantages and disadvantages of approach

↓

Why Thomas chose approach

↓

Successful? Why or why not?

↓

Conclusion

After completing your draft, meet with a peer reviewer to evaluate each other's work and suggest revisions. Then proofread and edit your draft for errors in spelling, grammar, and punctuation.

Listening and Speaking

In addition to being a writer, Dylan Thomas was a gifted and popular speaker who read from his works with a forceful, distinctive voice. Find and listen to a recording of Thomas reading his work. You can find these recordings on the Internet as well as in many libraries. After listening, take turns with classmates reading some of Thomas's poetry or prose aloud, first modeling his speaking style, then reading as you would normally. Give feedback to one another and discuss the differences.

Thomas's Language and Style

Using Proper Nouns In "A Child's Christmas in Wales," Dylan Thomas creates a rich description of the narrator's childhood holidays by using proper nouns. Proper nouns are the names of particular persons, places, things, or ideas. A proper noun may consist of more than one word. Proper nouns always begin with capital letters. Consider, for example, how much less effective Thomas's description of presents might be without the proper nouns in this passage:

> And troops of bright tin soldiers who, if they could not fight, could always run. And Snakes-and-Families and Happy Ladders. And Easy Hobbi-Games for Little Engineers, complete with instructions.

Notice some of the proper nouns and regular nouns used in the story:

Proper Noun	Regular Noun
Ernie Jenkins	postmen
Hudson Bay	farmhouse
Christmas	marzipan

Sometimes a writer will deliberately capitalize a noun that is not proper. Find at least two examples of words in "A Child's Christmas in Wales" that technically should not be capitalized. Why do you think Thomas capitalized these words?

Activity Rewrite the following phrases from "A Child's Christmas in Wales," capitalizing proper nouns as appropriate.

1. the afternoon of the day of christmas eve
2. mrs. prothero and the firemen
3. there were wolves in wales
4. trappers from hudson bay, off mumbles road

Revising Check

Proper Nouns With a partner, review your essay on Dylan Thomas's craft. Check for correct capitalization of nouns and proper nouns.

Literature Online **Web Activities** For eFlashcards, Selection Quick Checks, and other Web activities, go to www.glencoe.com.

Literature Online

Web Activities Have students access the Web site for interactive activities that will help them assess their understanding of the selection.

Winter Night

MEET KAY BOYLE

When the first reports of Nazi atrocities made their way out of Europe during World War II, many people could not believe that they were true. Even after the end of the war, many refused to believe that the Holocaust had actually occurred. Kay Boyle not only believed it, but she chose to write about it.

Literary Activism Kay Boyle's social consciousness was formed early in life. She was born in St. Paul, Minnesota, but spent much of her childhood in Europe. By the age of seventeen, she had already written a novel, short stories, and a great deal of poetry.

After marrying a Frenchman, Boyle moved to France. She had formed a friendship with poet William Carlos Williams and published her first poems. Her most productive years as a writer, however, occurred during the 1920s and 1930s, when she was part of a group of expatriate writers and artists living in Paris.

Boyle visited Germany several times during the 1930s. By 1941, however, she left Europe for the United States and lived in New York for the duration of World War II. After the war, Boyle returned to Europe, where she published the short story "Winter Night" in 1946. In Germany she listened to the stories of people who had been displaced by the war. Boyle also wrote about the trials of Nazi war criminals and the lingering suffering of the people who had experienced the war. She reflected on how ordinary people had been scarred forever by political events: "They dwell on their separate islands of pain, each waiting for a hand to reach out to him, for the word of explanation to be given." Boyle re-creates these "islands of pain" in much of her finest fiction, including "Winter Night."

> "The decision to speak out is the vocation and lifelong peril by which the intellectual must live."
>
> —Kay Boyle

A Long and Prolific Life During a life that spanned almost the entire twentieth century, Boyle wrote more than thirty-five books, including novels and short story collections. She also wrote numerous essays and worked as a translator. While many of Boyle's works are about love and other affairs of the human heart, she also showed how the lives of individuals are influenced by the political world in which they live.

Just as Boyle felt a moral responsibility to tell the story of what had happened to the Jews in Nazi Germany, she also considered it her duty to speak up on issues ranging from the Civil Rights Movement to the war in Vietnam. A large part of her writing in later life was devoted to such causes. Among Boyle's many awards and honors were two O. Henry prizes for short fiction and a Guggenheim Fellowship. She was also elected to the Academy of Arts and Letters.

Kay Boyle was born in 1902 and died in 1992.

 Author Search For more about Kay Boyle, go to www.glencoe.com.

KAY BOYLE **251**

Focus

BELLRINGER

Bellringer Options
Selection Focus
    Transparency 16
Daily Language
    Transparency 23
Or ask students to recall when they were little children.
Ask: How did you feel when something happened to interrupt the pattern of your life, such as a parent's going away? *(Students may reveal feelings of disquiet, fear, and insecurity, especially at night.)* Have students role-play a conversation between a child and a babysitter after a parent leaves.

Literature Online

Author Search To expand students' appreciation of Kay Boyle, have them access the Web site for additional information and resources.

Selection Skills

Winter Night

Literary Elements
- Tone (SE pp. 252, 253, 255, 256, 258, 260–262)
- Theme (SE p. 262)
- Irony (TWE p. 258)
- Point of View (TWE p. 256)

Reading Skills
- Activating Prior Knowledge (SE pp. 252–254, 257–260, 263)
- Making Inferences (TWE p. 254)
- Compare and Contrast (TWE p. 260)

Vocabulary Skills
- Word Origins (SE pp. 252, 263)
- Academic Vocabulary (SE p. 263)

Listening/Speaking/Viewing Skills
- Analyzing Art (SE p. 255; TWE pp. 256, 258, 260)

Writing Skills/Grammar
- Compare and Contrast Characters (SE p. 263)

Focus

Summary

As night falls, seven-year-old Felicia anxiously awaits her mother but is told that she will once again be left in the care of a sitter. This sitter turns out to be different from the others, because she is especially fond of Felicia, who reminds her of another little girl she cared for in a Nazi concentration camp. Throughout the evening, the woman shares the little girl's story with Felicia. By the end of the evening the woman and Felicia, share a special bond and cling to each other.

V Vocabulary

Vocabulary File Say: Add these words and definitions to your vocabulary file. For each word, include a sentence that gives you an example of how to use the word. **OL** Students with English language needs should include the pronunciations of these words in their files. **EL**

Literary Elements Have students access the Web site to improve their understanding of tone.

Connecting to the Story

In "Winter Night," a chance meeting occurs between a child who misses her mother and a woman who misses a child. Before you read the selection, think about the following questions:

- Have you ever felt a connection with someone you were meeting for the first time?
- What could you do to help someone who is grieving the loss of a loved one?

Building Background

This story takes place in New York City, probably around the mid-1940s, near the end of World War II (1939–1945). At that time, the horrors of Nazi concentration camps began to come to light. In these camps, Nazi dictator Adolf Hitler carried out his plan to "purify" Europe by killing millions of Jews, Gypsies, and members of other ethnic groups.

On the U.S. home front during the war, women played a key role in the war effort by working in defense plants and in other businesses, replacing the millions of men who had gone off to war. Some women worked in professional capacities that had traditionally been reserved for men.

Setting Purposes for Reading

Big Idea Life Transitions

As you read this story, think about how the child and the woman who comes to care for her experience and cope with change.

Literary Element Tone

The **tone** of a story is the attitude the writer takes toward his or her subject matter. A writer's tone may convey a variety of attitudes, including sympathy, objectivity, seriousness, irony, sadness, bitterness, or humor. As you read "Winter Night," notice the tone of the story.

• See Literary Terms Handbook, p. R18.

Literature Online Interactive Literary Elements Handbook To review or learn more about the literary elements, go to www.glencoe.com.

Reading Strategy Activating Prior Knowledge

Activating prior knowledge is considering what you already know about the world and using that knowledge to deepen your understanding of the literary work you are reading.

Reading Tip: Recording What You Know Use a chart to record details from the story about which you have prior knowledge.

Detail	My Prior Knowledge
p. 253 "New York apartment"	Even if people are all around, the child may feel very alone in this setting.

Vocabulary

abeyance (ə bā′ əns) n. a state of temporary inactivity; p. 253 *All our work was held in abeyance until Martin told us to continue working.*

reprieve (ri prēv′) v. to give temporary relief, as from something unpleasant or difficult; p. 253 *Lily was reprieved from watching the toddler for five minutes, and then she resumed her job.*

obscurity (əb skyoor′ ə tē) n. darkness; dimness; p. 254 *It was hard to see anyone in the obscurity of the dimly lit park at night.*

derision (di rizh′ən) n. mockery; ridicule; p. 254 *Lee's derision included nasty comments about Angela's work habits.*

singular (sing′ gyə lər) adj. unusual or remarkable; p. 256 *Clarence had a singular ability to say the right thing at the right time.*

Vocabulary Tip: Word Origins Many English words come from Latin, Greek, and earlier forms of the English language we speak today.

OBJECTIVES

In studying this selection, you will focus on the following:
- identifying tone
- writing to compare and contrast characters
- activating prior knowledge
- analyzing theme

Selection Resources

Print Materials
- Unit 1 Resources (Fast File), pp. 85–87
- Leveled Vocabulary Development, p. 19
- Selection and Unit Assessments, pp. 41–42
- Selection Quick Checks, p. 21

Transparencies
- Bellringer Options Transparencies:
  Selection Focus Transparency 16
  Daily Language Practice Transparency 23
- Literary Elements Transparency 25

Technology
- TeacherWorks Plus™ CD-ROM
- StudentWorks Plus™ CD-ROM
- Presentation Plus!™ CD-ROM
- Literature Online, glencoe.com
- Online Student Edition, mhln.com
- Exam*View*® Assessment Suite CD-ROM
- Vocabulary PuzzleMaker CD-ROM
- Listening Library, disc 1 track 23

Winter Night

Kay Boyle

Soho in Winter, New York. Angelo Cavalli.

T here is a time of apprehension which begins with the beginning of darkness, and to which only the speech of love can lend security. It is there, in **abeyance,** at the end of every day, not urgent enough to be given the name of fear but rather of concern for how the hours are to be **reprieved** from fear, and those who have forgotten how it was when they were children can remember nothing of this. It may begin around five o'clock on a winter afternoon when the light outside is dying in the windows. At that hour the New York apartment in which Felicia lived was filled with shadows, and the little girl would wait alone in the living room, looking out at the winter-stripped trees that stood black in the park against the isolated ovals of unclean snow. Now it was January, and the day had been a cold one; the

water of the artificial lake was frozen fast, but because of the cold and the coming darkness, the skaters had ceased to move across its surface. The street that lay between the park and the apartment house was wide, and the two-way streams of cars and busses, some with their headlamps already shining, advanced and halted, halted and poured swiftly on to the tempo of the traffic signals' altering lights. The time of apprehension had set in, and Felicia, who was seven, stood at the window in the evening and waited before she asked the question. When the signals below would change from red to green again, or when the double-decker bus would turn the corner below, she would ask it. The words of it were

Literary Element Tone *What tone is conveyed by the description of the late winter afternoon, both inside and outside the apartment?* **L**

Reading Strategy Activating Prior Knowledge *Why is the child feeling apprehensive? What is she reluctant to ask?* **R**

Vocabulary

abeyance (ə bā′ əns) *n.* a state of temporary inactivity

reprieve (ri prēv′) *v.* to give temporary relief, as from something unpleasant or difficult

KAY BOYLE **253**

Teach

Visual Vocabulary
A *double-decker bus* has two decks, or floors, each containing passenger seats. Often, the upper deck is roofless and has low walls.

already there, tentative in her mouth, when the answer came from the far end of the hall.

"Your mother," said the voice among the sound of kitchen things, "she telephoned up before you came in from nursery school. She won't be back in time for supper. I was to tell you a sitter was coming in from the sitting parents' place."[1]

Felicia turned back from the window into the **obscurity** of the living room, and she looked toward the open door, and into the hall beyond it where the light from the kitchen fell in a clear yellow angle across the wall and onto the strip of carpet. Her hands were cold, and she put them in her jacket pockets as she walked carefully across the living-room rug and stopped at the edge of light.

"Will she be home late?" she said.

For a moment there was the sound of water running in the kitchen, a long way away, and then the sound of the water ceased, and the high, Southern voice went on:

"She'll come home when she gets ready to come home. That's all I have to say. If she wants to spend two dollars and fifty cents and ten cents' carfare on top of that three or four nights out of the week for a sitting parent to come in here and sit, it's her own business. It certainly ain't nothing to do with you or me. She makes her money, just like the rest of us does. She works all day down there in the office, or whatever it is, just like the rest of us works, and she's entitled to spend her money like she wants to spend it. There's no law in the world against buying your own freedom. Your mother and me, we're just buying our own freedom, that's

1. Today, a *sitting parents' place* would be called a "babysitters' agency" or "child-care agency."

Vocabulary

obscurity (əb sky͞oor′ ə tē) *n.* darkness; dimness

all we're doing. And we're not doing nobody no harm."

"Do you know who she's having supper with?" said Felicia from the edge of dark. There was one more step to take, and then she would be standing in the light that fell on the strip of carpet, but she did not take the step.

"Do I know who she's having supper with?" the voice cried out in what might have been **derision,** and there was the sound of dishes striking the metal ribs of the drainboard by the sink. "Maybe it's Mr. Van Johnson, or Mr. Frank Sinatra,[2] or maybe it's just the Duke of Wincers[3] for the evening. All I know is you're having soft-boiled egg and spinach and applesauce for supper, and you're going to have it quick now because the time is getting away."

The voice from the kitchen had no name. It was as variable as the faces and figures of the women who came and sat in the evenings. Month by month the voice in the kitchen altered to another voice, and the sitting parents were no more than lonely aunts of an evening or two who sometimes returned and sometimes did not to this apartment in which they had sat before. Nobody stayed anywhere very long any more, Felicia's mother told her. It was part of the time in which you lived, and part of the life of the city, but when the fathers came back, all this would be miraculously changed. Perhaps you would live in a house again, a small one, with fir trees on either side of the short brick walk, and Father would drive up every night from the station just after darkness

2. *Van Johnson* and *Frank Sinatra* were popular movie stars in the 1940s.
3. *Wincers* is the character's pronunciation of "Windsor." In 1936, King Edward VIII gave up the British throne to marry an American divorcee. He was then given the title Duke of Windsor.

Big Idea Life Transitions *What does this detail tell you about Felicia's life?* **B1**

Reading Strategy Activating Prior Knowledge *Where are the fathers? How do you know?* **R**

Vocabulary

derision (di rizh′ ən) *n.* mockery; ridicule

Additional Support

Skills Practice

READING: Making Inferences
Explain the importance of reading between the lines and making inferences from details. Write the following quotations from the story on the board: "There's no harm in the world against buying your freedom" and "We're not doin' nobody no harm." **Ask:** What can you infer about the mother from the idea that she is "buying her freedom"? *(The mother is paying sitters so she can have time for herself. She may be trying to escape her troubles by working and socializing.)* **Ask:** Are these statements literal or ironic? *(Both are ironic because the mother may be trading one form of slavery for another.)* **OL**

Portrait of Madame Benard, 1928-1929. Edward Vuillard. Oil on canvas, 114.5 x 102.5 cm. Musee d'Orsay, Paris.

Viewing the Art: How would you describe this woman's attitude? What similarities or differences do you find with the attitude of the babysitter in the story? ⭐

set in. When Felicia thought of this, she stepped quickly into the clear angle of light, and she left the dark of the living room behind her and ran softly down the hall.

The drop-leaf table[4] stood in the kitchen between the refrigerator and the sink, and Felicia sat down at the place that was set. The voice at the sink was speaking still, and while Felicia ate it did not cease to speak until the bell of the front door rang abruptly. The girl walked around the table and went down the hall, wiping her dark palms in her apron, and, from the drop-leaf table, Felicia watched her step from the angle of light into darkness and open the door.

---

4. A *drop-leaf table* has hinged sections that can be folded down when not in use.

Literary Element Tone *What is the author's attitude toward the housekeeper?* **L**

"You put in an early appearance," the girl said, and the woman who had rung the bell came into the hall. The door closed behind her, and the girl showed her into the living room, and lit the lamp on the bookcase, and the shadows were suddenly bleached away. But when the girl turned, the woman turned from the living room too and followed her, humbly and in silence, to the threshold of the kitchen. "Sometimes they keep me standing around waiting after it's time for me to be getting on home, the sitting parents do," the girl said, and she picked up the last two dishes from the table and put them in the sink. The woman who stood in the doorway was a small woman, and when she undid the white silk scarf from around her head, Felicia saw that her hair was black. She wore it parted in the middle, and it had not been cut, but was drawn back loosely into a knot behind her head. She had very

KAY BOYLE **255**

Teach

L Literary Element

Tone Answer: *Such a description clues the reader that this person is going to be important to the story. She will not be one of the "variable" babysitters.* Have students list words and actions that indicate the babysitter has suffered great sadness. *(She is described as unsmiling and having "unspeakable grief.")* Ask students whether they think tragedy makes people stronger or more sensitive. Point out the patterns of light and dark and how they correspond to the characters. **OL**

BI Big Idea

Life Transitions

Answer: *Answers will vary. The woman might explain why she is sad and how a child figures into her story.* **OL**

★ Viewing the Art

William Adolphe Bouguereau (1825–1905) was a prolific artist. Over his career, he painted hundreds of paintings and was well-known for his work. Bouguereau took his time with his work, making sure no stroke was without purpose. **AS**

---

clean white gloves on, and her face was pale, and there was a look of sorrow in her soft black eyes. "Sometimes I have to stand out there in the hall with my hat and coat on, waiting for the sitting parents to turn up," the girl said, and, as she turned on the water in the sink, the contempt she had for them hung on the kitchen air. "But you're ahead of time," she said, and she held the dishes, first one and then the other, under the flow of steaming water.

The woman in the doorway wore a neat black coat, not a new-looking coat, and it had no fur on it, but it had a smooth velvet collar and velvet lapels. She did not move, or smile, and she gave no sign that she had heard the girl speaking above the sound of water at the sink. She simply stood looking at Felicia, who sat at the table with the milk in her glass not finished yet.

"Are you the child?" she said at last, and her voice was low, and the pronunciation of the words a little strange.

"Yes, this here's Felicia," the girl said, and the dark hands dried the dishes and put them away. "You drink up your milk quick now, Felicia, so's I can rinse your glass."

"I will wash the glass," said the woman. "I would like to wash the glass for her," and Felicia sat looking across the table at the face in the doorway that was filled with such unspoken grief. "I will wash the glass for her and clean off the table," the woman was saying quietly. "When the child is finished, she will show me where her night things are."

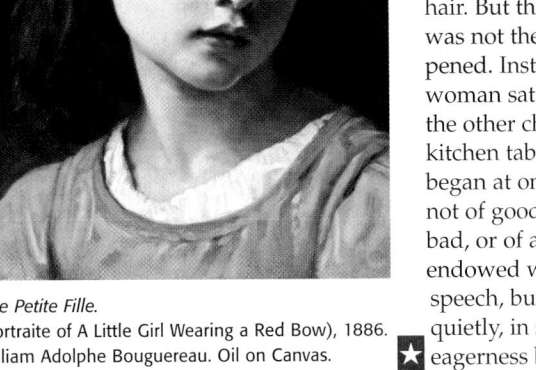

Une Petite Fille.
(Portraite of A Little Girl Wearing a Red Bow), 1886.
William Adolphe Bouguereau. Oil on Canvas.

"The others, they wouldn't do anything like that," the girl said, and she hung the dishcloth over the rack. "They wouldn't put their hand to housework, the sitting parents. That's where they got the name for them," she said.

Whenever the front door closed behind the girl in the evening, it would usually be that the sitting parent who was there would take up a book of fairy stories and read aloud for a while to Felicia; or else would settle herself in the big chair in the living room and begin to tell the words of a story in drowsiness to her, while Felicia took off her clothes in the bedroom, and folded them, and put her pajamas on, and brushed her teeth, and did her hair. But this time, that was not the way it happened. Instead, the woman sat down on the other chair at the kitchen table, and she began at once to speak, not of good fairies or bad, or of animals endowed with human speech, but to speak quietly, in spite of the eagerness behind her words, of a thing that seemed of **singular** importance to her.

"It is strange that I should have been sent here tonight," she said, her eyes moving slowly from feature to feature of Felicia's face, "for you look like a child that I knew once, and this is the anniversary of that child."

"Did she have hair like mine?" Felicia asked quickly, and she did not keep her

---

Big Idea Life Transitions *How do you think this evening will be different for Felicia?* **BI**

Vocabulary

singular (sing´ gyə lər) *adj.* unusual or remarkable

Literary Element Tone *Why do you think the author chose to describe the babysitter in such great detail?* **L**

Additional Support

Skills Practice

LITERARY ELEMENT: Point of View
Have students identify the story's point of view. Note that the narrator does not usually divulge the characters' thoughts but is simply a vigilant observer. Point out the following observations to students and ask what they reveal: "She simply stood looking at Felicia . . .," "the eagerness behind her words," "her eyes moving slowly from feature to feature of Felicia's face."
Ask: How does the sitter's attentiveness affect Felicia? *(Felicia changes from being shy to curious, responding to the woman with more emotion than she has shown before.)* **OL**

eyes fixed on the unfinished glass of milk in shyness any more.

"Yes, she did. She had hair like yours," said the woman, and her glance paused for a moment on the locks which fell straight and thick on the shoulders of Felicia's dress. It may have been that she thought to stretch out her hand and touch the ends of Felicia's hair, for her fingers stirred as they lay clasped together on the table, and then they relapsed into passivity again. "But it is not the hair alone, it is the delicacy of your face, too, and your eyes the same, filled with the same spring lilac color," the woman said, pronouncing the words carefully. "She had little coats of golden fur on her arms and legs," she said, "and when we were closed up there, the lot of us in the cold, I used to make her laugh when I told her that the fur that was so pretty, like a little fawn's skin on her arms, would always help to keep her warm."

"And did it keep her warm?" asked Felicia, and she gave a little jerk of laughter as she looked down at her own legs hanging under the table, with the bare calves thin and covered with a down of hair.

"It did not keep her warm enough," the woman said, and now the mask of grief had come back upon her face. "So we used to take everything we could spare from ourselves, and we would sew them into cloaks and other kinds of garments for her and for the other children. . . ."

"Was it a school?" said Felicia when the woman's voice had ceased to speak.

"No," said the woman softly, "it was not a school, but still there were a lot of children there. It was a camp—that was the name the place had; it was a camp. It was a place where they put people until they could decide what was to be done with them." She sat with her hands clasped, silent a moment, looking at Felicia. "That

little dress you have on," she said, not saying the words to anybody, scarcely saying them aloud. "Oh, she would have liked that little dress, the little buttons shaped like hearts, and the white collar—"

"I have four school dresses," Felicia said. "I'll show them to you. How many dresses did she have?"

"Well, there, you see, there in the camp," said the woman, "she did not have any dresses except the little skirt and the pull-over. That was all she had. She had brought just a handkerchief of her belongings with her, like everybody else—just enough for three days away from home was what they told us, so she did not have enough to last the winter. But she had her ballet slippers," the woman said, and her clasped fingers did not move. "She had brought them because she thought during her three days away from home she would have the time to practice her ballet."

"I've been to the ballet," Felicia said suddenly, and she said it so eagerly that she stuttered a little as the words came out of her mouth. She slipped quickly down from the chair and went around the table to where the woman sat. Then she took one of the woman's hands away from the other that held it fast, and she pulled her toward the door. "Come into the living room and I'll do a pirouette[5] for you," she said, and then she stopped speaking, her eyes halted on the woman's face. "Did she—did the little girl—could she do a pirouette very well?" she said.

"Yes, she could. At first she could," said the woman, and Felicia felt uneasy now at the sound of sorrow in her words. "But after that she was hungry. She was hungry all winter," she said in a low voice. "We were all hungry, but the children were the hungriest. Even now," she said, and her voice went suddenly savage, "when I see milk like that, clean, fresh milk standing in a glass, I want to cry out loud,

Reading Strategy Activating Prior Knowledge *From what you know about World War II, what do you think happened to the child?* **R**

5. A *pirouette* (pir´ o͞o et´) is a rapid full turn done while standing on the toes of one foot.

KAY BOYLE **257**

Teach

R Reading Strategy

Activating Prior Knowledge Answer: *The child may have died in a concentration camp.* Ask: What parallels are drawn between Felicia and the little girl? *(Their hair, face, clothes, and ballet dancing are compared.)* Ask students what they can infer from their differences, including Felicia's four dresses and her trips to the ballet. *(Felicia has material comforts.)* Explain that despite her more fortunate circumstances, Felicia is still sad and lonely. **OL**

★ **Political History**

Concentration Camps
The babysitter is referring to the Nazi concentration camps during World War II. Millions of people died in concentration camps during the Holocaust, including children, as Nazi dictator Adolf Hitler carried out his plan to "purify" Europe by killing Jews, Gypsies, homosexuals, and members of other ethnic groups. During the end of the war, the horrors of the camps came to light. Have students generate questions they would like to have answered about the camps, then do research and share their knowledge. **AS**

English Language Coach

Connotation Advise students that many words have implied meanings that go beyond their dictionary definitions. Point out the repetition of the word *clasped*. Ask what connotation the word has and when it is used. In addition, point out the figurative language in "mask of grief." **EL**

Differentiated Instruction

Compare and Contrast is a way of showing how two things or events are different. Have students make a two-column chart to contrast Felicia's nightly routine with what she does on this winter night. Remind them to continue adding to the chart as they finish reading the story. **BL**

Objectives
- To identify tone (SE)
- To activate prior knowledge (SE)
- To analyze point of view (TWE)

Tone Answer: *The milk reminds her of how deprived and hungry the child was. This memory makes her angry.* **Ask:** How does Boyle show that the babysitter still struggles with grief? *(She shows her withdrawing from Felicia, then returning to the present.)* **OL**

R1 Reading Strategy

Activating Prior Knowledge Answer: *The women and children were in a Nazi concentration camp and probably Jewish. They were most frequently put into death camps.* **Ask:** How do you think the woman feels describing this experience? *(She wants to forget this period in her life, but she cannot.)* **OL**

★ Viewing the Art

Susan Ryder is a British artist who paints cheery scenes of beautiful rooms or portraits of people both famous and not. She has had several exhibitions at London galleries and also produces commissioned pieces for clients. **AS**

The Drum Table, 2004. Susan Ryder. Oil on canvas, 101.6 x 91.4 cm. ★ Private Collection.

I want to beat my hands on the table, because it did not have to be . . .” She had drawn her fingers abruptly away from Felicia now, and Felicia stood before her, cast off, forlorn, alone again in the time of apprehension. “That was three years ago,” the woman was saying, and one hand was lifted, as in weariness, to shade her face. “It was somewhere else, it was in another country,” she said, and behind her hand her eyes were turned upon the substance of a world in which Felicia had played no part.

“Did—did the little girl cry when she was hungry?” Felicia asked, and the woman shook her head.

“Sometimes she cried,” she said, “but not very much. She was very quiet. One night when she heard the other children crying, she said to me, ‘You know, they are not crying because they want something to eat. They are crying because their mothers have gone away.’”

“Did the mothers have to go out to supper?” Felicia asked, and she watched the woman’s face for the answer.

“No,” said the woman. She stood up from her chair, and now that she put her hand on the little girl’s shoulder, Felicia was taken into the sphere of love and intimacy again. “Shall we go into the other room, and you will do your pirouette for me?” the woman said, and they went from the kitchen and down the strip of carpet on which the clear light fell. In the front room, they paused hand in hand in the glow of the shaded lamp, and the woman looked about her, at the books, the low tables with the magazines and ash trays on them, the vase of roses on the piano, looking with dark, scarcely seeing eyes at these things that had no reality at all.

Literary Element   Tone   *Why do you think the woman’s tone changes so abruptly?* **L**

Reading Strategy   Activating Prior Knowledge   *Where were the mothers and children? Why were they there?* **R1**

Additional Support

Skills Practice

LITERARY ELEMENT: Types of Irony
Explain the three types of irony. Situational irony is a contrast between what is expected and what actually occurs. Verbal irony is the contrast between what a character says and what is meant. In dramatic irony, the reader has information that a character does not have. Ask students how Boyle uses dramatic irony in this story. Challenge them to contrast what the reader understands about the mothers that “have gone away” and what Felicia understands. Have students point out details that reveal Felicia’s level of understanding. **OL**

It was only when she saw the little white clock on the mantelpiece that she gave any sign, and then she said quickly: "What time does your mother put you to bed?"

Felicia waited a moment, and in the interval of waiting the woman lifted one hand and, as if in reverence, touched Felicia's hair.

"What time did the little girl you knew in the other place go to bed?" Felicia asked.

"Ah, God, I do not know, I do not remember," the woman said.

"Was she your little girl?" said Felicia softly, stubbornly.

"No," said the woman. "She was not mine. At least, at first she was not mine. She had a mother, a real mother, but the mother had to go away."

"Did she come back late?" asked Felicia.

"No, ah, no, she could not come back, she never came back," the woman said, and now she turned, her arm around Felicia's shoulders, and she sat down in the low soft chair. "Why am I saying all this to you, why am I doing it?" she cried out in grief, and she held Felicia close against her. "I had thought to speak of the anniversary to you, and that was all, and now I am saying these other things to you. Three years ago today, exactly, the little girl became my little girl because her mother went away. That is all there is to it. There is nothing more."

Felicia waited another moment, held close against the woman, and listening to the swift, strong heartbeats in the woman's breast.

"But the mother," she said then in a small, persistent voice, "did she take a taxi when she went?"

"And then she tied her ballet slippers up in the handkerchief again, and she went up to the guard standing at the door."

"This is the way it used to happen," said the woman, speaking in hopelessness and bitterness in the softly lighted room. "Every week they used to come into the place where we were and they would read a list of names out. Sometimes it would be the names of children they would read out, and then a little later they would have to go away. And sometimes it would be the grown people's names, the names of the mothers or big sisters, or other women's names. The men were not with us. The fathers were somewhere else, in another place."

"Yes," Felicia said. "I know."

"We had been there only a little while, maybe ten days or maybe not so long," the woman went on, holding Felicia against her still, "when they read the name of the little girl's mother out, and that afternoon they took her away."

"What did the little girl do?" Felicia said.

"She wanted to think up the best way of getting out so that she could go find her mother," said the woman, "but she could not think of anything good enough until the third or fourth day. And then she tied her ballet slippers up in the handkerchief again, and she went up to the guard standing at the door." The woman's voice was gentle, controlled now. "She asked the guard please to open the door so that she could go out. 'This is Thursday,' she said, 'and every Tuesday and Thursday I have my ballet lessons. If I miss a ballet lesson, they do not count the money off, so my mother would be just paying for nothing, and she cannot afford to pay for nothing. I missed my ballet lesson on Tuesday,' she said to the guard, 'and I must not miss it again today.'"

Reading Strategy Activating Prior Knowledge *What do you think happened to the little girl's mother?* **R2**

Big Idea Life Transitions *How does Felicia relate the little girl's story to her own life?* **BI**

KAY BOYLE **259**

Teach

R2 Reading Strategy

Activating Prior Knowledge Answer: *She most likely died in an extermination camp.* **Ask:** Why doesn't the sitter explain what happened to the little girl's mother? *(She may realize that Felicia is too young to hear such things, or she may realize that the child may fear that her own mother will never come back.)* **OL**

BI Big Idea

Life Transitions

Answer: *When the woman tells Felicia that the little girl's mother went away, Felicia relates to her situation because her own mother is not home. Felicia assumes the little girl's father was away fighting in the war, like her own father, when in reality the little girl's father was probably a prisoner in another camp.* **Ask:** How is Felicia's comment, "I know," ironic? *(When Felicia says "I know," she doesn't really know.)* **OL**

English Language Coach

Dialogue The author uses dialogue to tell the reader what is being said. Have students read the dialogue aloud to practice using language in a way that reflects the characters and mood of the story. Note the importance of facial expressions, gestures, pacing, and tone of voice. **BL**

Differentiated Instruction

Drawing Conclusions A conclusion is a judgment formed from specific facts. Have students use the details in the story to draw conclusions about what happened at the camp and why the people were there. Have them support their conclusions with specific facts. **OL**

Objectives
- To identify tone (SE)
- To activate prior knowledge (SE)
- To recognize irony (TWE)

Teach

L1 Literary Element

Tone Answer: *Students should note that the words* smiling, love, *and* contentment, *as well as the* dancing, *create the liveliest, happiest tone in the story so far.* **Ask:** What accounts for the change in tone? *(Felicia and the sitter are responding to each other and enjoying their bond.)* **OL**

R Reading Strategy

Activating Prior Knowledge Answer: *Students should say that most caretakers would insist on basic hygiene or maintaining everyday rules.* **Ask:** Why doesn't the sitter require Felicia to wash and brush her teeth? *(Perhaps the woman wisely realizes that it would break the mood, or she wants to extend kindness to Felicia to compensate for the little girl's suffering.)* **OL**

★ Viewing the Art

Have students study the painting and keep this visual in mind as they read this section of the story. **Ask:** Why do you think the sitter would tell the little girl about the ballets? *(She probably wanted to get her mind off of her real life and the tragedies she had experienced.)* **AS**

Felicia lifted her head from the woman's shoulder, and she shook her hair back and looked in question and wonder at the woman's face.

"And did the man let her go?" she said.

"No, he did not. He could not do that," said the woman. "He was a soldier and he had to do what he was told. So every evening after her mother went, I used to brush the little girl's hair for her," the woman went on saying. "And while I brushed it, I used to tell her the stories of the ballets. Sometimes I would begin with *Narcissus*,"[6] the woman said, and she parted Felicia's locks with her fingers, "so if you will go and get your brush now, I will tell it while I brush your hair."

"Oh, yes," said Felicia, and she made two whirls as she went quickly to the bedroom. On the way back, she stopped and held on to the piano with the fingers of one hand while she went up on her toes. "Did you see me? Did you see me standing on my toes?" she called to the woman, and the woman sat smiling in love and contentment at her.

"Yes, wonderful, really wonderful," she said. "I am sure I have never seen anyone do it so well." Felicia came spinning toward her, whirling in pirouette after pirouette, and she flung herself down in the chair close to her, with her thin bones pressed against the woman's soft, wide hip. The woman took the silver-backed, monogrammed brush and the tortoise-shell comb in her hands, and now she began to brush Felicia's hair. "We did not have any soap at all and not very much water to wash in, so I never could fix her as nicely and prettily as I wanted to," she said, and the brush stroked regularly, carefully down, caressing the shape of Felicia's head.

"If there wasn't very much water, then how did she do her teeth?" Felicia said.

"She did not do her teeth," said the woman, and she drew the comb through

---

6. *Narcissus* is a ballet based on the Greek myth of Narcissus, who scorns all women, believing he is more beautiful than they. The goddess of love punishes him by making him fall in love with his own reflection in a pool.

Literary Element Tone *How does the tone of the story change here?* **L1**

260 UNIT 1   THE SHORT STORY

Felicia's hair. "There were not any toothbrushes or tooth paste, or anything like that."

Felicia waited a moment, constructing the unfamiliar scene of it in silence, and then she asked the tentative question.

"Do I have to do my teeth tonight?" she said.

"No," said the woman, and she was thinking of something else, "you do not have to do your teeth."

"If I am your little girl tonight, can I pretend there isn't enough water to wash?" said Felicia.

"Yes," said the woman, "you can pretend that if you like. You do not have to wash," she said, and the comb passed lightly through Felicia's hair.

"Will you tell me the story of the ballet?" said Felicia, and the rhythm of the brushing was like the soft, slow rocking of sleep.

"Yes," said the woman. "In the first one, the place is a forest glade with little pale birches growing in it, and they have green veils over their faces and green veils drifting from their fingers, because it is the springtime. There is the music of a flute," said the woman's voice softly, softly, "and creatures of the wood are dancing—"

"But the mother," Felicia said as suddenly as if she had been awaked from sleep. "What did the little girl's mother say when she didn't do her teeth and didn't wash at night?"

"The mother was not there, you remember," said the woman, and the brush moved steadily in her hand. "But she did send one little letter back. Sometimes the people who went away were able to do that. The mother wrote it in a train, standing up in a car that had no seats," she said, and she might have been telling the story of the ballet still, for her voice was gentle and the brush did not falter on Felicia's hair. "There were perhaps a great many other people standing up in the train with her, perhaps all trying to write their little letters on the bits of paper they

Reading Strategy Activating Prior Knowledge *How is the woman unlike a typical babysitter?* **R**

Big Idea Life Transitions *What is the new relationship between the woman and Felicia?* **BI**

Additional Support

Skills Practice

READING: Compare and Contrast

Felicia is intrigued by the babysitter because she is different from other sitters. She is also different from Felicia's mother in terms of how she treats Felicia. Have students list the characteristics, appearance, and actions of the babysitter and compare and contrast them to other characters in the

story. **Ask:** What do you know about her? What inferences can you draw about her? *(The sitter has dark hair, an accent, worn clothes, a kind manner, a grief-stricken face, and familiarity with the ballet. She has suffered, as the reader learns, from being in a concentration camp in Europe.)* **OL** had managed to hide on them, or that they had found in forgotten corners as they traveled. When they had written their letters, then they must try to slip them out through the boards of the car in which they journeyed, standing up," said the woman, "and these letters fell down on the tracks under the train, or they were blown into the fields or onto the country roads, and if it was a kind person who picked them up, he would seal them in envelopes and send them to where they were addressed to go. So a letter came back like this from the little girl's mother," the woman said, and the brush followed the comb, the comb the brush in steady pursuit through Felicia's hair. "It said good-by to the little girl, and it said please to take care of her. It said: 'Whoever reads this letter in the camp, please take good care of my little girl for me, and please have her tonsils looked at by a doctor if this is possible to do.'"

"And then," said Felicia softly, persistently, "what happened to the little girl?"

"I do not know. I cannot say," the woman said. But now the brush and comb had ceased to move, and in the silence Felicia turned her thin, small body on the chair, and she and the woman suddenly put their arms around each other. "They must all be asleep now, all of them," the woman said, and in the silence that fell on them again, they held each other closer. "They must be quietly asleep somewhere, and not crying all night because they are hungry and because they are cold. For three years I have been saying 'They must all be asleep, and the cold and the hunger and the seasons or night or day or nothing matters to them—'"

It was after midnight when Felicia's mother put her key in the lock of the front door, and

The Star, c. 1878. Edgar Degas. Pastel on paper, 38 x 28 in. Philadelphia Museum of Art.

pushed it open, and stepped into the hallway. She walked quickly to the living room, and just across the threshold she slipped the three blue foxskins from her shoulders and dropped them, with her little velvet bag, upon the chair. The room was quiet, so quiet that she could hear the sound of breathing in it, and no one spoke to her in greeting as she crossed toward the bedroom door. And then, as startling as a slap across her delicately tinted face, she saw the woman lying sleeping on the divan, and Felicia, in her school dress still, asleep within the woman's arms.

Literary Element Tone *How does the tone change at the end of the story?* **L2**

KAY BOYLE **261**

BI **Big Idea**

Life Transitions Answer: *Felicia has become "her little girl," and the woman replaces Felicia's mother—at least for the night. Both are content with this turn of events.* **OL**

L2 **Literary Element**

Tone Answer: *The final image is peaceful, but there is also a sense of bitterness. Boyle uses the simile "as startling as a slap across her delicately tinted face" to show that the mother is shocked and upset by her discovery.* **Ask:** What can you infer about the author's attitude toward the mother from the last sentence of the story? *(The author seems to disapprove of the mother's neglect of her daughter. Felicia had to seek comfort with another sorrowful soul because her mother was unavailable to her.)* **OL**

CheckPoint

Use the CheckPoint questions on Presentation Plus! to check students' mastery of the selection. These questions can be used with interactive response keypads for immediate student feedback.

English Language Coach

Euphemisms Explain that sometimes words like *asleep* and *rest* are euphemisms for death. Note that euphemisms are less direct but less offensive than the words they replace. Help students with limited English to compile a list of euphemisms and define them. **EL**

Differentiated Instruction

Irregular Verbs Write on the board "The notes were ____ into the fields," and ask for the correct form of *blow*. Refer to irregular verb forms such *as written, found, were,* and *said.* Review with students the past and past participle forms of several irregular verbs. **BL**

Objectives
• To identify tone (SE)
• To activate prior knowledge (SE)
• To compare and contrast characters (TWE)

Assess

1. Students may say they do not approve, but may note extenuating circumstances.

2. (a) Housekeepers and baby-sitters (b) She wishes her mother were home more.

3. (a) She has dark hair, sad eyes. She takes an interest in her. (b) Felicia likes the woman. She might be first person who pays attention.

4. (a) There was little food or clothing and mothers were often taken away. The little girl liked ballet. (b) About same age, missed their mothers, and liked ballet. However, Felicia is well off and safe. The other girl was a prisoner.

5. She may realize that Felicia is too young to hear such things. It is possible that she does not know what happened to the little girl.

6. Love fails in the form of the mother and the house-keeper, and when the woman cannot continue to take care of the girl in the camp. Love succeeds, however, in the bond between Felicia and the babysitter.

7. To start paying more attention to Felicia

8. Yes, war has changed the lives of Felicia, her parents, the babysitter, and the little girl.

RESPONDING AND THINKING CRITICALLY

Respond

1. Do you approve of the way in which Felicia's mother is raising her daughter? Why or why not?

Recall and Interpret

2. (a)Who takes care of Felicia when her mother is away? (b)How does Felicia feel about her mother's frequent absences? Support your answer with evidence from the story.

3. (a)Describe the woman who comes to take care of Felicia for the evening. How is she different from the other sitting parents? (b)How does Felicia react to the woman? In your opinion, why does Felicia react this way?

4. (a)Summarize what the woman tells Felicia about the camp and the little girl she met there. (b)Compare and contrast Felicia and the little girl. How are they alike? How are they different?

Analyze and Evaluate

5. Why does the woman not simply tell Felicia what happened to the little girl in the camp?

6. It has been said that Kay Boyle's stories provide a catalog of the ways in which love can fail. Do you think this story demonstrates the failure of love? Explain your answer.

7. What advice would you like to give to Felicia's mother?

Connect

8. **Big Idea** **Life Transitions** Have political events affected the lives of all the characters in the story? Explain.

LITERARY ANALYSIS

Literary Element Tone

An author conveys **tone** through elements of the story such as word choice, punctuation, sentence structure, and figures of speech. For example, short, clipped sentences can create a fast-paced or urgent tone. The use of slang and informal language can create a carefree or light tone. Figures of speech, depending on their content and meaning, can show everything from despair to humor.

1. What words would you use to describe the house-keeper's attitude toward Felicia? What specific details help create this attitude, or tone?

2. What words would you use to describe the babysit-ter's attitude toward Felicia? What specific details help create this attitude, or tone?

3. Boyle begins the story by saying it was a time of apprehension. Here, *apprehension* means "suspi-cion or fear; foreboding." When does the tone change during the story? Does apprehension return? Explain.

Review: Theme

As you learned on page 94, **theme** is the central idea about life conveyed by a literary work. Some works have a stated theme, which is expressed directly. Most short stories have an implied theme, which is revealed through events, dialogue, or descriptions.

Partner Activity With a partner, make a web to show the parallel relationships between Felicia and the little girl in the camp. What theme, or idea about life, does the story convey about relationships?

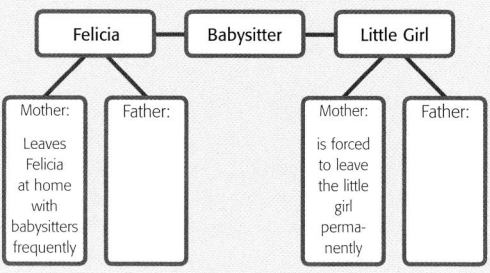

Literary Element

1. Words include *condescend-ing, cold,* and *dismissive.* Details include: the house-keeper's impatience with the girl when she asks about her mother and when she is finishing her milk.

2. Words include *gentle, attentive, sad,* and *reverent.* Details include: the woman watches Felicia intently and lapses into stories about the little girl she cared for during the war.

3. Felicia loses her feelings of apprehen-sion when she warms up to the baby-sitter. The reader, however, continues to feel apprehension throughout the story—for the fate of the little girl in the camp and for Felicia's mother's imminent return.

Review: Theme

Students should discuss the way in which the sitter attempts to create a feel-ing of parental comfort with both the children.

Reading Strategy Activating Prior Knowledge

The woman tells Felicia a lot about the little girl in her past—but not everything. As a result, the reader has to fill in the blanks in the story by using **prior knowledge.** Review the chart you made as you read, and think about the prior knowledge you used that Felicia does not have.

1. Give three examples of events that were implied in the story but not stated, and for which you had to supply prior knowledge.

2. Explain how your prior knowledge added to your understanding of each event.

Vocabulary Practice

Practice with Word Origins Use a dictionary to look up the origin of each of the following words. Explain the connection between the origin of each word and its current meaning.

1. derision   **a.** Latin   **b.** Greek
2. reprieve   **a.** Latin   **b.** Middle English
3. singular   **a.** Latin   **b.** Old English
4. obscurity   **a.** Middle English   **b.** Greek
5. abeyance   **a.** Latin   **b.** Old French

Academic Vocabulary

Here are two words from the vocabulary list on page R82.

parallel (par′ə lel′) *n.* similarity

regime (rə zhēm′) *n.* government in power

Practice and Apply
1. What **parallels** do you find between Felicia and the woman who comes to babysit?
2. What purpose did the Nazi **regime** have for creating camps?

Literature Online **Web Activities** For eFlashcards, Selection Quick Checks, and other Web activities, go to www.glencoe.com.

Writing About Literature

Compare and Contrast Characters "Winter Night" implies a world of contrast between Felicia's mother and the woman who arrives to care for Felicia. Write an essay in which you compare and contrast these two characters.

Prewrite by listing details about each character on an organizer like the one below. Consider what you learn—or do not learn—about the women's jobs, life experiences, and attitudes toward Felicia.

Mother

Babysitter

Use your organizer to develop a thesis that states two or more main points of comparison or contrast. In separate body paragraphs, use details from the story to support each main point. Conclude by restating your thesis in a fresh way.

When your draft is complete, meet with a peer reviewer to evaluate each other's work and suggest revisions. Then proofread and edit your draft for errors in spelling, grammar, and punctuation.

Internet Connection

Like the woman in "Winter Night," many survivors of Nazi concentration camps have told others about their experiences in the camps. Search the Internet to find one or two such accounts to share with the class.

You should also be able to find magazine and newspaper articles and transcripts from television news shows and films in which survivors tell of their experiences. Compare and contrast the way the stories are reported by different types of media.

KAY BOYLE **263**

Assess

Reading Strategy

1. Students might list the little girl's death, her mother's death during the war, and the woman's release or escape from the camp.

2. Students may discuss their previous knowledge of the Holocaust or their experiences with the death of a family member or friend and how they coped.

Vocabulary

1. a; *derision* comes from the Latin words *de-,* meaning "down," and *ridere,* meaning "to laugh"; the noun *derision* means "mockery" or "ridicule"

2. b; *reprieve* comes from Middle English *repreven,* form of *reproven* meaning "to reprove," literally meaning "to test again"

3. a; *singular* comes from Latin *singularis,* meaning "separate" or "extraordinary"

4. a; *obscurity* comes from Middle English

5. b; *abeyance* comes from Old French

Academic Vocabulary

1. Both Felicia and the woman are lonely. In some ways, both are victims of political circumstances.

2. They used the camps to detain and kill people in a plan to "purify" Europe.

Internet Connection

Make sure that students use reliable Web sites as sources.

Writing About Literature

Use these criteria when evaluating students' writing:

• Does the essay compare and contrast the two characters?

• Does the essay include a logical thesis and adequate support and development of each main point?

Literature Online

Web Activities Have students access the Web site for interactive activities that will help them assess their understanding of the selection.

Focus

BELLRINGER

Bellringer Options
**Selection Focus
    Transparency 17
Daily Language
    Transparency 24**
Or have students define *natural disaster* and create a list of natural disasters. *(Responses: tornadoes, earthquakes, tsunamis, etc.)* **Ask:** What natural disasters have you experienced or heard about? Have students discuss impact of natural disasters. Ask them to consider public's reaction to disasters.

Literature Online

Author Search To expand students' appreciation of Isabel Allende, have them access the Web site for additional information and resources.

And of Clay Are We Created

MEET ISABEL ALLENDE

For most of her life, Isabel Allende (ēs′ äbel ä yen′ dä) has felt like a wanderer. Although she is Chilean, she was born in Lima, Peru, where her father held a diplomatic post. Her parents divorced when she was young, and she lived with her grandparents for several years in Santiago, Chile. When her mother remarried, Allende moved with her mother and stepfather, also a diplomat, to La Paz, Bolivia.

Life in Chile From Bolivia, the family was next stationed in Beirut, Lebanon, and then moved on to Europe. The threat of war in the Middle East returned Allende back to her grandfather's house in Chile. She was fifteen years old and wanted to put down roots. Her grandfather provided Allende with an intensive education in Chilean history and geography, which deepened her love for her country. Trips that she and her grandfather took to different parts of Chile fueled this love, as did her reading of great Chilean poets, including Pablo Neruda and Gabriela Mistral.

"I write to preserve memory. I write what should not be forgotten."

—Isabel Allende

Allende's grandfather also gave her gifts that she would later call upon as a writer. He entertained her with folk tales and admonished her with proverbs. He told her fascinating accounts of strange characters in their family and recited lengthy poems from memory.

In 1959 Allende started working for the United Nations Food and Agricultural Organization in Santiago, first as a secretary, then as an editor and a press officer. She later became a broadcast journalist and wrote for and edited a feminist magazine.

Exile Isabel Allende's life changed forever on September 11, 1973, when the president of Chile, Salvador Allende, was killed and a brutal military dictatorship took over. The murdered president had been Isabel's beloved uncle. Within a few years, it was no longer safe for Allende and her family to stay in Chile, so they went into exile in Venezuela.

Allende could not find a job in journalism in Venezuela and worked as a teacher for several years. One January night in 1981, she began writing a letter to her grandfather, who was almost 100 years old and in poor health, and continued working on it for an entire year. The letter became the manuscript for her first novel, *The House of the Spirits.* This book was translated from Spanish into many other languages and became a bestseller in several countries.

Since 1982 Allende has written nearly a dozen books, most of them novels. In 1988 she moved yet again—this time, to the United States. The story "And of Clay Are We Created" was first published in 1991 in *The Stories of Eva Luna.*

Isabel Allende was born in 1942.

Literature Online Author Search For more about Isabel Allende, go to www.glencoe.com.

Selection Skills

And of Clay Are We Created

Literary Elements
• Persona (SE pp. 265–268, 270–272, 274, 276)
• Plot and Setting (SE p. 276)
• Allusion (TWE p. 274)

Reading Skills
• Analyzing Sensory Details (SE pp. 265, 266, 268–274, 276)
• Identifying Cause and Effect (TWE p. 266)

Vocabulary Skills
• Analogies (SE p. 276)
• Academic Vocabulary (SE p. 276)

Listening/Speaking/Viewing Skills
• Analyzing Art (TWE pp. 267, 268, 273)
• Dramatization (TWE p. 270)

Writing Skills/Grammar
• Apply Point of View (SE p. 277)
• Compound Subjects (TWE p. 272)
• Responding to Mood (TWE p. 268)

Connecting to the Story

Would you try to save the life of a total stranger? In Allende's story, a natural disaster has killed and wounded thousands of people. Before you read the story, think about the following questions:

- How do you generally respond when you learn about such events?
- What are some different factors that influence how you respond? Try to list four or more things.

Building Background

"And of Clay Are We Created" is fiction and the characters in it are fictional. However, the story is based on an actual event that occurred in the South American country of Colombia in 1985. A snow-covered volcano, Nevado del Ruiz, had been active for at least several hundred years, although it had been fairly quiet for more than a century. In 1984 it started to show warning signs of activity and erupted in November 1985. Heat from the eruption melted snow and ice on the mountain and sent a monstrous mudslide crashing into the valley below. Nearly two thousand people died in the village of Chinchina; in the town of Amero, more than twenty-three thousand perished, along with fifteen thousand animals, smothered under a blanket of mud and debris. Thousands more were injured and left homeless.

Setting Purposes for Reading

Big Idea Life Transitions

As you read, notice how Allende uses the mud as a device to hold the lives of the three main characters in suspension for three days.

Literary Element Persona

The **persona** is the voice an author creates to tell a story. Even if the story is told from a first-person point of view, as is "And of Clay Are We Created," the narrator is not the author. As you read, identify characteristics of the persona Allende created to tell this story.

- See Literary Terms Handbook, p. R12.

Reading Strategy Analyzing Sensory Details

Sensory details are highly descriptive words and phrases that appeal to one or more of the senses: hearing, sight, smell, taste, and touch.

Reading Tip: Taking Notes Use a chart to record sensory details in this story.

Sense	Detail from the story
touch	p. 272 "her silk hair against his cheek"

Vocabulary

presentiment (pri zen′ tə mənt) n. a feeling that something is about to happen; p. 267 *Although the scientists had no monitoring equipment, they had a presentiment that the volcano would soon erupt.*

equanimity (ēk′ wə nim′ ə tē) n. the ability to remain calm and assured; p. 267 *The equanimity of the mayor helped calm the hurricane survivors.*

fortitude (fôr′ tə tōōd′) n. firm courage or strength of mind in the face of pain or danger; p. 267 *Relief workers often show fortitude when they aid people during a disaster.*

pandemonium (pan′ də mō′ nē əm) n. wild disorder and uproar; p. 269 *Pandemonium broke out as looters smashed grocery store windows.*

tribulation (trib′ yə lā′ shən) n. great misery or distress; suffering; p. 273 *A natural disaster nearly always brings tribulation, but it sometimes brings people together as well.*

Literature Online **Interactive Literary Elements Handbook** To review or learn more about the literary elements, go to www.glencoe.com.

Focus

Summary

After a volcanic eruption, a mudslide kills many people. Television crews are sent to the scene. A reporter films volunteers who have discovered a young girl alive but trapped. The reporter struggles to free the girl and must face his own past.

V1 Vocabulary

Vocabulary File Say: Add these words and definitions to your vocabulary file. For each word, include a sentence that gives you an example of how to use the word. OL Students with English language needs should include the pronunciations of these words in their files. EL

Literary Elements Have students access the Web site to improve their understanding of persona.

OBJECTIVES

In studying this selection, you will focus on the following:
- understanding persona
- analyzing sensory details
- understanding plot and setting
- writing a letter to understand point of view

ISABEL ALLENDE **265**

Selection Resources

Print Materials
- 📁 Unit 1 Resources (Fast File), pp. 88–90
- 📁 Leveled Vocabulary Development, p. 20
- 📁 Selection and Unit Assessments, pp. 43–44
- 📁 Selection Quick Checks, p. 22

Transparencies
- Bellringer Options Transparencies:
  Selection Focus Transparency 17
  Daily Language Practice Transparency 24
- Literary Elements Transparency 23

Technology
- TeacherWorks Plus™ CD-ROM
- StudentWorks Plus™ CD-ROM
- Presentation Plus!™ CD-ROM
- Literature Online, glencoe.com
- Online Student Edition, mhln.com
- Exam*View*® Assessment Suite CD-ROM
- Vocabulary PuzzleMaker CD-ROM
- Listening Library, disc 1 track 24

Teach

And of Clay Are We Created

Isabel Allende
Translated by
Margaret Sayers Peden

Volcano, 1999. Sally Elliott.
Watercolor on paper, 27.9 x 38.1cm. Private Collection. ★

They discovered the girl's head protruding from the mudpit, eyes wide open, calling soundlessly. She had a First Communion name, Azucena.[1] Lily. In that vast cemetery where the odor of death was already attracting vultures from far away, and where the weeping of orphans and wails of the injured filled the air, the little girl obstinately clinging to life became the symbol of the tragedy.

The television cameras transmitted so often the unbearable image of the head budding like a black squash from the clay that there was no one who did not recognize her and know her name. And every time we saw her on the screen, right behind her was Rolf Carlé,[2] who had gone there on assignment, never suspecting that he would find a fragment of his past, lost thirty years before.

First a subterranean[3] sob rocked the cotton fields, curling them like waves of foam. Geologists had set up their seismographs[4]

---

1. *Azucena* (à zōō kē´nà)

2. *Rolf Carlé* (rälf cär lā´)
3. Something *subterranean* is beneath the earth's surface.
4. *Seismographs* are scientific instruments that record the intensity and duration of earthquakes.

Big Idea Life Transitions *What questions does this passage prompt for you?* **BI**

Reading Strategy Analyzing Sensory Details *Which senses do these details appeal to?* **R1**

Reading Strategy Analyzing Sensory Details *What feeling do these details help establish?* **R2**

Skills Practice

weeks before and knew that the mountain had awakened again. For some time they had predicted that the heat of the eruption could detach the eternal ice from the slopes of the volcano, but no one heeded their warnings; they sounded like the tales of frightened old women. The towns in the valley went about their daily life, deaf to the moaning of the earth, until that fateful Wednesday night in November when a prolonged roar announced the end of the world, and walls of snow broke loose, rolling in an avalanche of clay, stones, and water that descended on the villages and buried them beneath unfathomable[5] meters of telluric[6] vomit. As soon as the survivors emerged from the paralysis of that first awful terror, they could see that houses, plazas, churches, white cotton plantations, dark coffee forests, cattle pastures—all had disappeared. Much later, after soldiers and volunteers had arrived to rescue the living and try to assess the magnitude of the cataclysm, it was calculated that beneath the mud lay more than twenty thousand human beings and an indefinite number of animals putrefying in a viscous soup. Forests and rivers had also been swept away, and there was nothing to be seen but an immense desert of mire.[7]

When the station called before dawn, Rolf Carlé and I were together. I crawled out of bed, dazed with sleep, and went to prepare coffee while he hurriedly dressed. He stuffed his gear in the green canvas backpack he always carried, and we said goodbye, as we had so many times before. I had no **presentiments**. I sat in the kitchen, sipping my coffee and planning the long hours without him, sure that he would be back the next day.

He was one of the first to reach the scene, because while other reporters were fighting their way to the edges of that morass[8] in jeeps, bicycles, or on foot, each getting there however he could, Rolf Carlé had the advantage of the television helicopter, which flew him over the avalanche. We watched on our screens the footage captured by his assistant's camera, in which he was up to his knees in muck, a microphone in his hand, in the midst of a bedlam[9] of lost children, wounded survivors, corpses, and devastation. The story came to us in his calm voice. For years he had been a familiar figure in newscasts, reporting live at the scene of battles and catastrophes with awesome tenacity. Nothing could stop him, and I was always amazed at his **equanimity** in the face of danger and suffering; it seemed as if nothing could shake his **fortitude** or deter his curiosity. Fear seemed never to touch him, although he had confessed to me that he was not a courageous man, far from it. I believe that the lens of the camera had a strange effect on him; it was as if it transported him to a different time from which he could watch events without actually participating in them. When I knew him better, I came to realize that this fictive distance seemed to protect him from his own emotions.

Rolf Carlé was in on the story of Azucena from the beginning. He filmed the volunteers who discovered her, and the first persons who tried to reach her; his camera zoomed in on the girl, her dark face, her large desolate eyes, the

---

5. Here, *unfathomable* (un fath′ əm ə bəl) means "immeasurable."
6. *Telluric* (te loor′ ik) means "coming or rising from the earth."
7. The decaying (*putrefying*) corpses are buried in the muddy slime, a thick, syrupy (*viscous*) soup; the landscape has become a wasteland of mud (*mire*).

Literary Element Persona Summarize what you learn about the narrator from this excerpt. **L1**

Vocabulary

presentiment (pri zen′ tə mənt) n. a feeling that something is about to happen

---

8. A *morass* (mə ras′) is any difficult, confused, or entangling condition or situation.
9. Here, *bedlam* refers to the noisy uproar and confusion of the situation.

Literary Element Persona *From what you already know about the narrator, why is she qualified to give this information?* **L2**

Vocabulary

equanimity (ēk′ wə nim′ ə tē) n. the ability to remain calm and assured
fortitude (fôr′ tə tōōd′) n. firm courage or strength of mind in the face of pain or danger

---

Teach

L1 Literary Element

Persona Answer: *The narrator and Rolf Carlé are married or lovers.* OL

L2 Literary Element

Persona Answer: *The narrator has a close, emotional connection to Rolf.* OL

★ Viewing the Art

Sally Elliot, a contemporary American painter, uses her dreams and surroundings to create symbolism. Contemporary art embodies many artistic practices that connect the natural world to social perception. **Ask:** In what way does Elliot's art reflect the agony of letting a loved one go? *(The volcano symbolizes the explosive power of love and heartache and liberation from self-obsession.)* AS

✓ CheckPoint

Use the CheckPoint questions on Presentation Plus! to monitor students' comprehension. These questions can be used with interactive response keypads for immediate student feedback.

Readability Scores
Dale-Chall: 6.8
DRP: 64
Lexile: 1240

Objectives
- To analyze sensory details (SE)
- To understand persona (SE)
- To determine cause and effect (TWE)

English Language Coach

Offering Comfort In the story, government officials, the armed forces, the media, and religious leaders come together to offer aid, provide information, and look for solutions. Ask English language learners to discuss what kinds of aid and comfort would be offered and by whom if a natural disaster occurred in their native countries. EL

Teach

**Analyzing Sensory
Details Answer:** *He seems
somewhat detached about the
entire situation, given that he
can discuss the smell of corpses
as easily as he describes the
temperature. At first, Rolf
treats the girl as he would any
important story he needed to
report.* **OL**

L **Literary Element**

Persona Answer: *The narrator shows an affection-
ate, admiring, and loving
attitude.* **OL**

⭐ Viewing the Art

Arthur Bowen Davies, an
American painter and lithog-
rapher, was born in Utica,
New York, and studied at
the Art Students League in
New York City and at the
Art Institute of Chicago. He
is considered a romantic
artist. **AS**

Landscape (Camaldoli), 1928. Arthur Bowen Davies.
Albright-Knox Art Gallery, Buffalo, NY.

plastered-down tangle of her hair. The mud
was like quicksand around her, and anyone
attempting to reach her was in danger of sinking. They threw a rope to her that she made no
effort to grasp until they shouted to her to
catch it; then she pulled a hand from the mire
and tried to move, but immediately sank a little deeper. Rolf threw down his knapsack and
the rest of his equipment and waded into the
quagmire, commenting for his assistant's
microphone that it was cold and that one
could begin to smell the stench of corpses.

"What's your name?" he asked the girl,
and she told him her flower name. "Don't
move, Azucena," Rolf Carlé directed, and

kept talking to her, without a thought for
what he was saying, just to distract her,
while slowly he worked his way forward in
mud up to his waist. The air around him
seemed as murky as the mud.

It was impossible to reach her from the
approach he was attempting, so he retreated
and circled around where there seemed to
be firmer footing. When finally he was close
enough, he took the rope and tied it beneath
her arms, so they could pull her out. He
smiled at her with that smile that crinkles his
eyes and makes him look like a little boy; he
told her that everything was fine, that he was
here with her now, that soon they would have
her out. He signaled the others to pull, but as

Reading Strategy Analyzing Sensory Details *At this point
in the story, what is Rolf Carlé's attitude about the mudslide?
What is his attitude about the young girl he is approaching?* **R1**

Literary Element Persona *What is the narrator's attitude
toward Rolf here?* **L**

Additional Support

Skills Practice

WRITING: Responding to Mood
Point out to students that personal opinions and reactions to literature should
always be supported by examples from
the text. Have students write a brief
description of the mood at the point
in the story when the doctor arrives to
examine the girl. Remind students that

mood refers to the emotion created in
the reader by a literary work. After students describe the mood, direct them to
find examples in the literature that support their descriptions. Have students follow up by writing a paragraph using their
textual evidence to support their descriptions of mood. **OL**

soon as the cord tensed, the girl screamed. They tried again, and her shoulders and arms appeared, but they could move her no farther; she was trapped. Someone suggested that her legs might be caught in the collapsed walls of her house, but she said it was not just rubble, that she was also held by the bodies of her brothers and sisters clinging to her legs.

"Don't worry, we'll get you out of here," Rolf promised. Despite the quality of the transmission, I could hear his voice break, and I loved him more than ever. Azucena looked at him, but said nothing.

During those first hours Rolf Carlé exhausted all the resources of his ingenuity to rescue her. He struggled with poles and ropes, but every tug was an intolerable torture for the imprisoned girl. It occurred to him to use one of the poles as a lever but got no result and had to abandon the idea. He talked a couple of soldiers into working with him for a while, but they had to leave because so many other victims were calling for help. The girl could not move, she barely could breathe, but she did not seem desperate, as if an ancestral resignation allowed her to accept her fate. The reporter, on the other hand, was determined to snatch her from death. Someone brought him a tire, which he placed beneath her arms like a life buoy, and then laid a plank near the hole to hold his weight and allow him to stay closer to her. As it was impossible to remove the rubble blindly, he tried once or twice to dive toward her feet, but emerged frustrated, covered with mud, and spitting gravel. He concluded that

> *The girl could not move, she barely could breathe, but she did not seem desperate . . .*

he would have to have a pump to drain the water, and radioed a request for one, but received in return a message that there was no available transport and it could not be sent until the next morning.

"We can't wait that long!" Rolf Carlé shouted, but in the **pandemonium** no one stopped to commiserate.[10] Many more hours would go by before he accepted that time had stagnated and reality had been irreparably distorted.

A military doctor came to examine the girl, and observed that her heart was functioning well and that if she did not get too cold she could survive the night.

"Hang on, Azucena, we'll have the pump tomorrow," Rolf Carlé tried to console her.

"Don't leave me alone," she begged.

"No, of course I won't leave you."

Someone brought him coffee, and he helped the girl drink it, sip by sip. The warm liquid revived her and she began telling him about her small life, about her family and her school, about how things were in that little bit of world before the volcano had erupted. She was thirteen, and she had never been outside her village. Rolf Carlé, buoyed by a premature optimism, was convinced that everything would end well: the pump would arrive, they would drain the water, move the rubble, and Azucena would be transported by helicopter to a hospital where she would recover rapidly and where he

---

10. No one stopped to show or express sympathy—to *commiserate* (kə miz′ ə rāt′).

Big Idea Life Transitions *What does Azucena's idea about why she cannot move tell you about her feelings concerning the situation?* **BI₁**

Reading Strategy Analyzing Sensory Details *What do you learn about the disaster scene from these sensory details?* **R₂**

Big Idea Life Transitions *What is the mood at this point in the story? What hint does the author give that things are likely to change?* **BI₂**

Vocabulary

pandemonium (pan′ də mō′ nē əm) n. wild disorder and uproar

ISABEL ALLENDE **269**

Teach

BI₁ **Big Idea**

Life Transitions
Answer: *Azucena's idea may reveal the level of grief, and possibly guilt, she is experiencing because she has survived the mudslide while her siblings have died.* **OL**

R₂ **Reading Strategy**

Analyzing Sensory Details
Answer: *The disaster scene is noisy, hectic, and chaotic.* **OL**

BI₂ **Big Idea**

Life Transitions
Answer: *The mood appears upbeat given that Azucena's heart is functioning well, that she is revived by a warm beverage, and that Rolf thinks things will end well. However, the word* premature *indicates that things might not actually end so well.* **OL**

Differentiated Instruction

Multiple Modes of Expression
Interpersonal learners are sensitive to and supportive of other people. The narrator knows Rolf, loves him, and understands him better as the story progresses. She admires some things about him. She knows he has problems, but she is nonjudgmental about them.

Draw a pyramid of boxes on the board and write the title "Showing Support for Others." *Ask students to list ways one person can show support for another person. (Possible answers include praising them, encouraging them, being nonjudgmental, defending them, and listening to them.)* **BL**

Objectives
• To understand persona (SE)
• To respond to mood (TWE)

L1 Literary Element

Persona

Answer: *The narrator has become emotionally connected to Azucena, just as Rolf has, and feels united with him in this concern.* **OL**

R1 Reading Strategy

Analyzing Sensory Details

Answer: *They give a sense of the desperate activity of the rescue workers, the appearance and attitude of the survivors, and their dire need.*

Say: Natural disasters often bring out the best in people.

Ask: Why do you think strangers would be so willing to help people in desperate need? **OL**

BI Big Idea

Life Transitions

Answer: *Bureaucratic obstacles that are slowing the delivery of medicines to hospitals will also slow the delivery of the pump to the site where Azucena is trapped. She may die as a result.* **OL**

---

could visit her and bring her gifts. He thought, She's already too old for dolls, and I don't know what would please her; maybe a dress. I don't know much about women, he concluded, amused, reflecting that although he had known many women in his lifetime, none had taught him these details. To pass the hours he began to tell Azucena about his travels and adventures as a newshound, and when he exhausted his memory, he called upon imagination, inventing things he thought might entertain her. From time to time she dozed, but he kept talking in the darkness, to assure her that he was still there and to overcome the menace of uncertainty.

That was a long night.

Many miles away, I watched Rolf Carlé and the girl on a television screen. I could not bear the wait at home, so I went to National Television, where I often spent entire nights with Rolf editing programs. There, I was near his world, and I could at least get a feeling of what he lived through during those three decisive days. I called all the important people in the city, senators, commanders of the armed forces, the North American ambassador, and the president of National Petroleum, begging them for a pump to remove the silt, but obtained only vague promises. I began to ask for urgent help on radio and television, to see if there wasn't *someone* who could help us. Between calls I would run to the newsroom to monitor the satellite transmissions that periodically brought new details of the catastrophe. While reporters selected scenes with most impact for the news report, I searched for footage that featured Azucena's mudpit. The screen reduced the disaster to a single plane and accentuated the tremendous distance that separated me from Rolf Carlé; nonetheless, I was there with him. The child's every suffering hurt me as it did him; I felt his frustration, his impotence. Faced with the impossibility of communicating with him, the fantastic idea came to me that if I tried, I

> **Literary Element** Persona *What do these actions tell you about the narrator and her connection to Rolf?* **L1**

could reach him by force of mind and in that way give him encouragement. I concentrated until I was dizzy—a frenzied and futile activity. At times I would be overcome with compassion and burst out crying; at other times, I was so drained I felt as if I were staring through a telescope at the light of a star dead for a million years.

I watched that hell on the first morning broadcast, cadavers of people and animals awash in the current of new rivers formed overnight from the melted snow. Above the mud rose the tops of trees and the bell towers of a church where several people had taken refuge and were patiently awaiting rescue teams. Hundreds of soldiers and volunteers from the Civil Defense were clawing through rubble searching for survivors, while long rows of ragged specters awaited their turn for a cup of hot broth. Radio networks announced that their phones were jammed with calls from families offering shelter to orphaned children. Drinking water was in scarce supply, along with gasoline and food. Doctors, resigned to amputating arms and legs without anesthesia, pled that at least they be sent serum and painkillers and antibiotics; most of the roads, however, were impassable, and worse were the bureaucratic obstacles that stood in the way. To top it all, the clay contaminated by decomposing bodies threatened the living with an outbreak of epidemics.

Azucena was shivering inside the tire that held her above the surface. Immobility and tension had greatly weakened her, but she was conscious and could still be heard when a microphone was held out to her. Her tone was humble, as if apologizing for all the fuss. Rolf Carlé had a growth of beard, and dark circles beneath his eyes; he looked near exhaustion. Even from that enormous dis-

> **Reading Strategy** Analyzing Sensory Details *How do these sensory details enliven the activities of the disaster area?* **R1**

> **Big Idea** Life Transitions *What hint does this give you about the pump that Rolf and the narrator had been requesting? How will this affect Azucena?* **BI**

Additional Support

Skills Practice

LISTENING AND SPEAKING:

Dramatization Discuss tips and suggestions for presenting a dramatization of a story event. Possible tips and suggestions include:

- Decide how many people will speak.
- Write dialogue for each person or choose dialogue from the story to read.
- Practice reading the dialogue as the characters would say it.
- Decide what props, if any, are needed. Ask students to work in groups to dramatize a scene from the story. Provide time for students to prepare and practice their scenes. Then ask them to present their dramatizations to the class. **OL**

tance I could sense the quality of his weariness, so different from the fatigue of other adventures. He had completely forgotten the camera; he could not look at the girl through a lens any longer. The pictures we were receiving were not his assistant's but those of other reporters who had appropriated Azucena, bestowing on her the pathetic responsibility of embodying the horror[11] of what had happened in that place. With the first light Rolf tried again to dislodge the obstacles that held the girl in her tomb, but he had only his hands to work with; he did not dare use a tool for fear of injuring her. He fed Azucena a cup of the cornmeal mush and bananas the Army was distributing, but she immediately vomited it up. A doctor stated that she had a fever, but added that there was little he could do: antibiotics were being reserved for cases of gangrene. A priest also passed by and blessed her, hanging a medal of the Virgin around her neck. By evening a gentle, persistent drizzle began to fall.

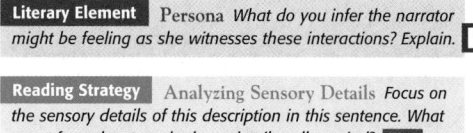

"The sky is weeping," Azucena murmured . . .

"The sky is weeping," Azucena murmured, and she, too, began to cry. ★

"Don't be afraid," Rolf begged. "You have to keep your strength up and be calm. Everything will be fine. I'm with you, and I'll get you out somehow."

Reporters returned to photograph Azucena and ask her the same questions, which she no longer tried to answer. In the meanwhile, more television and movie teams arrived with spools of cable, tapes, film, videos, precision lenses, recorders, sound consoles, lights, reflecting screens, auxiliary motors, cartons of supplies, electricians, sound technicians, and cameramen: Azucena's face was beamed to millions of screens around the world. And all the while Rolf Carlé kept pleading for a pump. The improved technical facilities bore results, and National Television began receiving sharper pictures and clearer sound; the distance seemed suddenly compressed, and I had the horrible sensation that Azucena and Rolf were by my side, separated from me by impenetrable glass. I was able to follow events hour by hour; I knew everything my love did to wrest the girl from her prison and help her endure her suffering; I overheard fragments of what they said to one another and could guess the rest; I was present when she taught Rolf to pray, and when he distracted her with the stories I had told him in a thousand and one nights beneath the white mosquito netting of our bed.

When darkness came on the second day, Rolf tried to sing Azucena to sleep with old Austrian folk songs he had learned from his mother, but she was far beyond sleep. They spent most of the night talking, each in a stupor of exhaustion and hunger, and shaking with cold. That night, imperceptibly, the unyielding floodgates that had contained Rolf Carlé's past for so many years began to open, and the torrent of all that had lain hidden in the deepest and most secret layers of memory poured out, leveling before it the obstacles that had blocked his consciousness for so long. He could not tell it all to Azucena;

---

11. [appropriated . . . horror] In other words, the reporters are using televised images of Azucena's situation, making her a living symbol of the tragedy.

Literary Element Persona *Based on what you know about Rolf, why would his decision not to use the camera be significant?* **L2**

Literary Element Persona *What do you infer the narrator might be feeling as she witnesses these interactions? Explain.* **L3**

Reading Strategy Analyzing Sensory Details *Focus on the sensory details of this description in this sentence. What event from the story do these details call to mind?* **R2**

ISABEL ALLENDE **271**

BI **Big Idea**

Life Transitions
Answer: *Both are trapped—Azucena in the mud, Rolf in the terror of the past. Both are facing their fears and are in a time of transition in their lives.* **OL**

R1 **Reading Strategy**

Analyzing Sensory Details
Answer: *He is remembering Katherina's scent and the kitchen smells. He may be either remembering or perceiving the smell of his own sweat, but he perceives the smell of the putrefying clay in the present.* **OL**

L **Literary Element**

Persona
Answer: *Since these are Rolf's own visions, he must have shared them with the narrator at some later time; or she infers that this is what was happening to him.* **OL**

she perhaps did not know there was a world beyond the sea or time previous to her own; she was not capable of imagining Europe in the years of the war. So he could not tell her of defeat, nor of the afternoon the Russians had led them to the concentration camp to bury prisoners dead from starvation. Why should he describe to her how the naked bodies piled like a mountain of firewood resembled fragile china? How could he tell this dying child about ovens and gallows? Nor did he mention the night that he had seen his mother naked, shod in stiletto-heeled red boots, sobbing with humiliation. There was much he did not tell, but in those hours he relived for the first time all the things his mind had tried to erase. Azucena had surrendered her fear to him and so, without wishing it, had obliged Rolf to confront his own. There, beside that hellhole of mud, it was impossible for Rolf to flee from himself any longer, and the visceral[12] terror he had lived as a boy suddenly invaded him. He reverted to the years when he was the age of Azucena, and younger, and, like her, found himself trapped in a pit without escape, buried in life, his head barely above ground; he saw before his eyes the boots and legs of his father, who had removed his belt and was whipping it in the air with the never-forgotten hiss of a viper coiled to strike. Sorrow flooded through him, intact and precise, as if it had lain always in his mind, waiting. He was once again in the armoire where his father locked him to punish him for imagined misbehavior, there where for eternal hours he had crouched with his eyes closed, not to see the darkness, with his hands over his ears, to shut out the beating of his heart, trembling, huddled like a cornered animal. Wandering in the mist of his memories he found his sister Katherina, a sweet, retarded child who spent her life

hiding, with the hope that her father would forget the disgrace of her having been born. With Katherina, Rolf crawled beneath the dining room table, and with her hid there under the long white tablecloth, two children forever embraced, alert to footsteps and voices. Katherina's scent melded with his own sweat, with aromas of cooking, garlic, soup, freshly baked bread, and the unexpected odor of putrescent clay. His sister's hand in his, her frightened breathing, her silk hair against his cheek, the candid gaze of her eyes. Katherina . . . Katherina materialized before him, floating on the air like a flag, clothed in the white tablecloth, now a winding sheet, and at last he could weep for her death and for the guilt of having abandoned her. He understood then that all his exploits as a reporter, the feats that had won him such recognition and fame, were merely an attempt to keep his most ancient fears at bay, a stratagem[13] for taking refuge behind a lens to test whether reality was more tolerable from that perspective. He took excessive risks as an exercise of courage, training by day to conquer the monsters that tormented him by night. But he had come face to face with the moment of truth; he could not continue to escape his past. He was Azucena; he was buried in the clayey mud; his terror was not the distant emotion of an almost forgotten childhood, it was a claw sunk in his throat. In the flush of his tears he saw his mother, dressed in black and clutching her imitation-crocodile pocketbook to her bosom, just as he had last seen her on the dock when she had come to put him on the boat to South America. She had not come to dry his tears, but to tell him to pick up a

---

13. A *stratagem* is a trick or scheme for achieving some purpose.

Reading Strategy Analyzing Sensory Details *Which sensory details is Rolf remembering? Which does he actually perceive from the present setting?* **R1**

Literary Element Persona *The narrator is not present with Rolf on the second night that he stays with Azucena. How do you think the narrator gained this information about what Rolf was remembering?* **L**

---

12. Here, *visceral* means "emotional or instinctive rather than intellectual."

Big Idea Life Transitions *How are Rolf and Azucena now in a similar situation?* **BI**

Skills Practice

GRAMMAR: Compound Subjects
Write this sentence on the board, underlining the words shown: *Immobility and tension had taken their toll on the girl.* Explain that the underlined words are an example of a compound subject (two or more simple subjects joined with a conjunction). Write each sentence on the board. Ask students to expand each sentence by using a compound subject. Possible answers are shown.

1. Water *(and clay)* raced into the valley.
2. Medicines *(and food)* were needed.
3. Azucena *(and Rolf)* endured the chilly night. **OL**

Muddy Road through the Field. Alexei Savrasovi. ⭐
Tretyakov Gallery, Moscow, Russia.

shovel: the war was over and now they must bury the dead.

"Don't cry. I don't hurt anymore. I'm fine," Azucena said when dawn came.

"I'm not crying for you," Rolf Carlé smiled. "I'm crying for myself. I hurt all over."

The third day in the valley of the cataclysm began with a pale light filtering through storm clouds. The President of the Republic visited the area in his tailored safari jacket to confirm that this was the worst catastrophe of the century; the country was in mourning; sister nations had offered aid; he had ordered a state of siege; the Armed Forces would be merciless, anyone caught stealing or committing other offenses would be shot on sight. He added that it was impossible to remove all the corpses or count the thousands who had disappeared; the entire valley would be declared holy ground, and bishops would come to celebrate a solemn mass for the souls of the victims. He went to the Army field tents to offer relief in the form of vague promises to crowds of the rescued, then to the improvised hospital to offer a word of encouragement to doctors and nurses worn down from so many hours of **tribulations.** Then he asked to be taken to see Azucena, the little girl the whole world

Reading Strategy Analyzing Sensory Details *What point is the writer making by including this detail about how the president was dressed?* **R2**

Vocabulary

tribulation (trib´ yə lā´ shən) n. great misery or distress; suffering

ISABEL ALLENDE **273**

Teach

R2 Reading Strategy

Analyzing Sensory Details
Answer: *The narrator gives this detail to show that the president's visit is staged. His clothes are carefully considered to fit the circumstances; but they are tailored, indicating that they are not really meant for emergency, hands-on recovery, or expedition work.* **OL**

⭐ Viewing the Art

Many Russian landscape artists of the nineteenth century created images of a road or path as metaphors for the difficult choices people have to make in life. Alexei Savrasov used the theme of the road to reflect his emotions towards nature and people and their interconnection with each other. **Ask:** What is the connection between Savrasov's landscape and the themes in "And of Clay Are We Created"? *(Some students might say Savrasov's muddy road depicts Rolf's struggle to let go. Others might reflect on how Rolf felt upon his first encounter with Azucena.)* **AS**

English Language Coach

Contrasting Conjunctions Ask a volunteer to locate a sentence with the conjunction *and* and one with the conjunction *but.* Have students describe what the difference is in meaning between *and* and *but.* Provide or have students provide several example sentences with each word. Discuss the added sense of hopelessness and failure that Allende's repeated choice of *but* rather than *and* conveys. **EL**

Objectives
• To understand persona (SE)
• To analyze sensory details (SE)
• To recognize and correctly use compound subjects (TWE)

Teach

B1 Big Idea

Life Transitions

Answer: *Azucena's simple innocence may have reminded Rolf of his sister. Her acceptance may have set an example for him as he knew he must deal with his own past.* **OL**

L Literary Element

Persona Answer: Possible answers might include the idea that Rolf and the narrator were not simply lovers, but life-long companions. The narrator has very strong empathy for both Rolf and Azucena. **OL**

R1 Reading Strategy

Analyzing Sensory Details
Answer: *Both Rolf and Azucena may have felt stuck in the "clay" of sorrow and hopelessness but are freed by love and hope. Azucena's death frees her from further fear and pain.* **OL**

CheckPoint

Use the CheckPoint questions on Presentation Plus! to check students' mastery of the selection. These questions can be used with interactive response keypads for immediate student feedback.

had seen. He waved to her with a limp statesman's hand, and microphones recorded his emotional voice and paternal[14] tone as he told her that her courage had served as an example to the nation. Rolf Carlé interrupted to ask for a pump, and the President assured him that he personally would attend to the matter. I caught a glimpse of Rolf for a few seconds kneeling beside the mudpit. On the evening news broadcast, he was still in the same position; and I, glued to the screen like a fortuneteller to her crystal ball, could tell that something fundamental had changed in him. I knew somehow that during the night his defenses had crumbled and he had given in to grief; finally he was vulnerable. The girl had touched a part of him that he himself had no access to, a part he had never shared with me. Rolf had wanted to console her, but it was Azucena who had given him consolation.

I recognized the precise moment at which Rolf gave up the fight and surrendered to the torture of watching the girl die. I was with them, three days and two nights, spying on them from the other side of life. I was there when she told him that in all her thirteen years no boy had ever loved her and that it was a pity to leave this world without knowing love. Rolf assured her that he loved her more than he could ever love anyone, more than he loved his mother, more than his sister, more than all the women who had slept in his arms, more than he loved me, his life companion, who would have given anything to be trapped in that well in her place,

who would have exchanged her life for Azucena's, and I watched as he leaned down to kiss her poor forehead, consumed by a sweet, sad emotion he could not name. I felt how in that instant both were saved from despair, how they were freed from the clay, how they rose above the vultures and helicopters, how together they flew above the vast swamp of corruption and laments. How, finally, they were able to accept death. Rolf Carlé prayed in silence that she would die quickly, because such pain cannot be borne.

By then I had obtained a pump and was in touch with a general who had agreed to ship it the next morning on a military cargo plane. But on the night of that third day, beneath the unblinking focus of quartz lamps and the lens of a hundred cameras, Azucena gave up, her eyes locked with those of the friend who had sustained her to the end. Rolf Carlé removed the life buoy, closed her eyelids, held her to his chest for a few moments, and then let her go. She sank slowly, a flower in the mud.

You are back with me, but you are not the same man. I often accompany you to the station and we watch the videos of Azucena again; you study them intently, looking for something you could have done to save her, something you did not think of in time. Or maybe you study them to see yourself as if in a mirror, naked. Your cameras lie forgotten in a closet; you do not write or sing; you sit long hours before the window, staring at the mountains. Beside you, I wait for you to complete the voyage into yourself, for the old wounds to heal. I know that when you return from your nightmares, we shall again walk hand in hand, as before. ∾

---

14. Here, *paternal* means "fatherly."

Big Idea **Life Transitions** *From what you have learned about Azucena, how might she have helped Rolf make this transition?* **B1**

Literary Element **Persona** *What do you learn about the narrator here? Does this detail surprise you? Why or why not?* **L**

Reading Strategy Analyzing Sensory Details *In what ways were Azucena and Rolf stuck in, then freed from, the clay? Explain.* **R**

274 UNIT 1 THE SHORT STORY

Additional Support

Skills Practice

LITERARY ELEMENT: Allusions
Point out to students that an allusion is a reference to a well-known character, place, or situation from history, music, art, or other literature. Explain that in some creation stories, the first human was made from the dust of the ground. Point out the title of the story and relate it to the words sometimes used in Christian funeral services: "Ashes to ashes. Dust to dust." Ask students what the expression means. *(We all die and ultimately return to the earth, usually by being buried.)* Also help students see that the title emphasizes our shared humanity. **OL**

274

RESPONDING AND THINKING CRITICALLY

Respond

1. Which character in the story do you admire the most? Why?

Recall and Interpret

2. (a)What are Azucena's circumstances at the beginning of the story? (b)What did she come to symbolize as the story progressed?

3. (a)What attitude did you notice among the people who survived the disaster? (b)What does this indicate about their culture?

4. (a)Summarize what happens to Azucena and to Rolf. (b)In what way is each of them "saved from despair" and "freed from the clay"?

Analyze and Evaluate

5. **Irony** is a contrast between appearance and reality. (a)What ironic situations did you notice in this story? (b)How do you think these ironies furthered the main message of the story? Explain.

6. What do you think the title of this story means? In your opinion, is it an appropriate title? Why or why not?

7. One critic wrote that Allende is capable of moving "between the personal and the political, between reality and fantasy." Do these observations apply to this story? Why or why not?

Connect

8. **Big Idea** Life Transitions In what ways do Rolf and Azucena exchange roles in this story?

9. At what point in the story did you sense that Azucena's situation was hopeless?

YOU'RE THE CRITIC: Visual Literacy

Putting Events in Time Order

Make a timeline like the one below. Reread "And of Clay Are We Created," filling in the timeline as you read. Above the timeline, include external events relating to the mudslide and the rescue operation. Below the timeline, include what is happening to Rolf Carlé internally as he participates in the disaster.

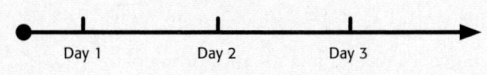

External Events

Day 1   Day 2   Day 3

Internal Events (for Rolf)

Group Activity Share your timeline with your classmates. Then discuss the following questions, referring to your timelines. Look back at the story to resolve any disagreements about the sequence of events.

1. Summarize the different efforts Rolf makes to save Azucena.

2. How does Rolf's attitude toward Azucena change as the story progresses? Find specific evidence from the story to support your answer.

3. Why do you think Rolf tries so hard to save Azucena? Support your answer with two or more reasons.

ISABEL ALLENDE **275**

---

9. Possible answer: when Allende calls the image of Azucena "unbearable"

Group Activity

1. He tries to pull Azucena out with ropes and poles, then with a lever; he works with soldiers to free her; he dives down to remove rubble and begs for a pump.

2. First, he sees her as a victim of the disaster; then as an innocent young girl; finally, as a friend who has helped him face difficulties and whom he wants to comfort.

3. Rolf is a newshound and knows what makes a good story. He also comes to care for Azucena as a human being. He may be grateful to her for helping him face his past.

Assess

1. Students may cite Azucena, Rolf, or the narrator. Their reasons will vary.

2. (a) Azucena is trapped in the mud. (b) Courage and patience

3. (a) The survivors were patient and undemanding. (b) Fatalism or acceptance

4. (a) Azucena waits for rescue but dies. Rolf has flashbacks of a traumatic childhood while trying to help free her. (b) Azucena's death frees her from further fear and pain, while Rolf is freed to confront his past and to resolve some of its trauma.

5. (a) Television stations could get equipment to the spot where Azucena was trapped, but no one could get a pump to the scene to rescue the girl. (b) The irony might show that there are greater ways to help people than simply by saving lives. If the message is about the cruelty of fate, the irony might indicate that government action (or inaction) is a part of life that must be accepted.

6. We all die and return to the earth. It is appropriate because the word *clay* has several meanings, including the clay in which the girl is trapped and the earth to which we all return.

7. This story is personal and focuses on what happens between Azucena and Rolf. The inept behavior of the government in responding to the disaster makes it a political statement as well. The story includes realistic and fantastic situations.

8. She begins to console him.

Assess

Literary Element

1. Like Allende, the narrator is well traveled; is a woman of action (for example, she goes to the news station and makes phone calls to government officials); is a journalist and lives in Europe.

2. Readers get a personal and empathetic view of Rolf. This viewpoint is similar to watching events unfold on television—which is an important part of the story. If Rolf had been the narrator, readers might not have seen the larger picture of the disaster—only the scene close to Azucena.

3. The narrator loses her closeness with Rolf. He is "not the same man" at the end of the story.

Review: Plot and Setting

Students' Venn diagrams may vary. The setting circle may contain these phrases: *Colombia, 1985, fatalism of culture.* The plot circle may contain these phrases: *volcano erupt; girl is trapped in mud; 200,000 people die.* Where the circles intersect, students might write *mudslide.*

Literary Element Persona

A **persona** is the person created by the author to tell a story. In Latin, a *persona* was a mask worn by an actor. In a similar way, adopting a persona allows an author to distance himself or herself from the reader. It is like slipping on a mask, or a different personality. The attitudes and beliefs expressed by the narrator may not be the same as those of the author.

1. Reread the information about Isabel Allende on p. 264. What do the unnamed narrator and Allende have in common? How might Allende have drawn on her own life to create both the narrator and Rolf?

2. Why do you think Allende chose the persona of someone not at the scene of the action? How would the story have been different if Rolf Carlé had been the narrator?

3. Even though Allende distances herself from the reader through a persona, her narrator is nevertheless affected by the action of the story. What consequences does the narrator face as a result of Rolf's attempt to save Azucena?

Review: Plot and Setting

As you learned on pages 10–11, the **plot** is the series of events that make up a story, and the **setting** is the time and place of a story. The setting also includes the ideas, customs, values, and beliefs of a particular time and place.

Partner Activity Meet with a classmate and talk about the plot and setting of this story. Reread sections from the story as necessary. Make a Venn diagram to show how the plot and setting interact. Your diagram should indicate how the setting is essential to the story's plot and how the plot contributes to at least one key detail of the story's setting. Share your diagram with the class.

Reading Strategy Analyzing Sensory Details

Allende uses **sensory details** to make the setting and characters more vivid and to evoke a strong emotional reaction in the reader. Refer to the chart of sensory details that you began on page 265.

1. Of the details you listed, which do you think are the strongest? Do some appeal to more than one sense?

2. Skim the story for more sensory details to add to your chart. Try to add at least one more to each row. Explain why you think each one evokes an emotional reaction.

Vocabulary Practice

Practice with Analogies Choose the word that best completes each analogy.

1. ecstasy : happiness :: tribulation :
   a. discomfort   **b.** faith   **c.** risk
2. hostility : unfriendliness :: pandemonium :
   a. simplicity   **b.** insecurity   **c.** confusion
3. fortitude : weakness :: bedlam :
   a. peace   **b.** cruelty   **c.** uproar
4. equanimity : calmness :: presentiment :
   a. insensitivity   **b.** uneasiness   **c.** anger

Academic Vocabulary

Here are two words from the vocabulary list on page R82. These words will help you think, write, and talk about the selection.

link (lingk) *n.* a connecting element

remove (ri mōōv′) *n.* a distance or interval separating one person or thing from another

Practice and Apply

1. How did Azucena serve as a **link** between people in the disaster zone and the rest of the world?
2. How did Rolf Carlé usually put himself at a safe **remove** from his journalistic subjects?

Reading Strategy

1. Students should choose the sensory details they find the strongest and identify those that appeal to more than one sense.
2. Answers will vary. Students should focus on the emotion evoked by each detail, such as fear or tenderness.

Vocabulary

1. a 2. c 3. a 4. b

Academic Vocabulary

1. Her image was broadcast on television; she helped people understand the terrible suffering people there faced.
2. He did not get emotionally involved in their plights.

WRITING AND EXTENDING

Writing About Literature

Apply Point of View Imagine that you are Rolf Carlé. Write a personal letter to the narrator, giving your own account of some or all of the events described in "And of Clay Are We Created." Use a graphic organizer like the one below to help you decide on elements to include in the draft of your letter. As you work on your draft, look back at the story to review what Rolf says and does, so you can write more precisely from his point of view.

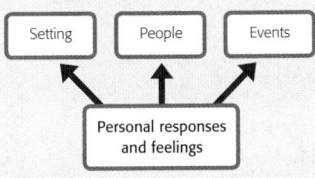

After completing your draft, meet with a peer reviewer to evaluate each other's work and to suggest revisions. Then proofread and edit your draft to correct any errors in spelling, grammar, and punctuation.

Literature Groups

The emotional quality or atmosphere that an author creates in a story is the **mood**. Meet with several of your classmates to discuss how Allende creates and shifts the mood of "And of Clay Are We Created." Discuss the following questions.

- What adjectives would you use to describe the mood at the very beginning of the story?

- What images and sensory details does Allende use to help create this mood?

- Find two or more places where you think the mood of the story shifts. How does Allende create these mood shifts?

Literature**Online** **Web Activities** For eFlashcards, Selection Quick Checks, and other Web activities, go to www.glencoe.com.

GRAMMAR AND STYLE

Allende's Language and Style

Comparing by Degrees Most adjectives and adverbs have three degrees with which to express comparison: positive, comparative, and superlative. In "And of Clay Are We Created," Allende builds tension by using adjectives and adverbs with different degrees of comparison. Consider, for example, some of these parts of sentences from the story:

"She pulled a hand from the mire and tried to move, but immediately sank a little <u>deeper</u>."

"The President of the Republic visited the area . . . to confirm that this was the <u>worst</u> catastrophe of the century."

"All that had lain hidden in the deepest and <u>most secret</u> layers of memory poured out."

Here is one way to list the adjectives and adverbs underlined above in their three degrees of comparison.

Positive	Comparative	Superlative
deep	deeper	deepest
bad	worse	worst
secret	more secret	most secret

Activity Find more adjectives and adverbs in the story. Create a chart of your own, listing the three comparison forms for each adjective and adverb. Notice how Allende's choice of adjectives and adverbs and their degrees of comparison add to the mood of the story.

Revising Check

Comparisons With a partner, go through your personal letter to the narrator and note places where different degrees of adjectives or adverbs would make your writing clearer and more vivid. Revise your draft to make improvements. Use a dictionary if you need to.

ISABEL ALLENDE **277**

Assess

Writing About Literature

Use these criteria when evaluating students' writing:

- Is the letter written from Rolf's point of view?

- Does the letter offer a personal account of the events that took place following the volcanic eruption?

Literature Groups

Students may note that the fearful and desperate mood at the beginning of the story is created by adjectives such as "unbearable" and "frightened," and images such as "head budding like a black squash." They may note the shift to a sense of calm on p. 269, and to a feeling of distance on p. 270.

Allende's Language and Style

Ask students why they think Allende uses so many superlative adjectives and adverbs in her descriptions. *(Students may say that Allende is trying to convey the dire situation of the characters.)*

Revising Check

Note that the superlative degree is used only when comparing three or more items. The comparative form can be used when comparing two items.

Literature**Online**

Web Activities Have students access the Web site for interactive activities that will help them assess their understanding of the selection.

Focus

BELLRINGER

Bellringer Options
Selection Focus Transparency 18
Daily Language Transparency 25
Or write *comforts* on the chalkboard.
Ask: What are some things that comfort you when you're feeling down?
Have students discuss some of the things that comfort them when they're feeling sad. Some possibilities: a favorite movie, a particular song, a fun activity. Write these on the board.

Author Search To expand students' appreciation of Leslie Marmon Silko, have them access the Web site for additional information and resources.

Lullaby

MEET LESLIE MARMON SILKO

I suppose at the core of my writing is the attempt to identify what it is . . . to grow up neither white nor fully traditional Indian," Leslie Marmon Silko has written. Silko, descended from a Laguna Indian woman who had married a white man, grew up enduring the pain of being accepted by neither white people nor Native Americans. Although her writing focuses on Native American identity, Silko does not claim to represent Native Americans in general. Silko has written, "I am only one human being, one Laguna woman."

"I was never afraid or lonely though I was high in the hills, many miles from home—because I carried with me the feeling I'd acquired from listening to the old stories."

—Leslie Marmon Silko

Steeped in Tradition Leslie Marmon Silko was born in Albuquerque, New Mexico. Her father was a professional photographer and manager of the Marmon Trading Post in Old Laguna, the small village where Leslie and her two sisters grew up. Silko's extended family contributed to the rich culture and historical legacy of Old Laguna. Silko credits her family's love of books and storytelling as instrumental to the development of her own creativity and interest in literature. She also notes that the physical and social landscape surrounding her hometown—including the San José River, the hunting grounds of Mt. Taylor, and the Cañoncito Navajo Reservation that appears in "Lullaby"—provided the setting and background for much of her writing.

Silko attended the University of New Mexico, where she studied English and creative writing. While there, her first short story, "The Man to Send Rain Clouds," was published. In 1974 she went on to publish several additional short stories in a Native American anthology, as well as *Laguna Woman,* a collection of poetry. After moving to Ketchikan, Alaska, Silko began writing the novel *Ceremony,* which was published in 1977. Since her return to the Southwest, she has published novels, poetry, and short stories.

Other Artistic Pursuits Silko's artistic endeavors have not been confined to literature. She has been involved in the visual arts of filmmaking and photography, and has published photographs in acclaimed arts magazines as well as in her own literary works. Her fiction and poetry collection *Storyteller,* published in 1981, features photos of her family and childhood environment. Silko founded the Laguna Film Project and, with support from the National Endowment for the Humanities, filmed *Arrowboy and the Witches,* an hour-long version of her story "Estoy-eh-moot and the Kunideeyahs."

Leslie Marmon Silko was born in 1948.

LiteratureOnline Author Search For more about Leslie Marmon Silko, go to www.glencoe.com.

Selection Skills

Lullaby

Literary Elements
- Style (SE pp. 279, 281, 282, 284, 286, 288)
- Narrator (SE p. 288)
- Flashback (TWE p. 282)

Reading Skills
- Evaluating Characters (SE pp. 279, 281–283, 286, 287, 289)
- Questioning (TWE p. 280)
- Evaluating (TWE p. 286)

Vocabulary Skills
- Word Origins (SE p. 289)
- Academic Vocabulary (SE p. 289)

Listening/Speaking/Viewing Skills
- Analyzing Art (TWE pp. 280, 284, 286)
- Dialogue (TWE p. 284)

Writing Skills/Grammar
- Analyzing Setting and Mood (SE p. 289)

Connecting to the Story

In Silko's short story, an elderly woman remembers her past as her life nears its end. Most of her memories revolve around children she loved dearly and lost. Before you read the story, think about the following questions:

- When you are feeling troubled or discouraged, do you ever think back to a happier time in the past?
- Why do you think memories are so powerful?

Building Background

"Lullaby" takes place in west central New Mexico, near the Cañoncito (Navajo) Reservation; parts of the story may actually take place on the reservation. The time of the story is probably the late 1960s or the 1970s.

Pulmonary tuberculosis, also known as TB, is a contagious lung disease that can lead to death if left untreated. The first antibiotic treatment for TB was not discovered until 1943. By the mid-1950s, chest X-rays were used to test millions of people in the United States for TB; infected people were then treated for the disease. But large numbers of infected people remained undiagnosed and thus continued to infect others. Included in this group were thousands of Navajos, many of whom mistrusted white doctors. In the 1950s, U.S. government health agencies began testing Navajos for TB. Infected people were sent away—sometimes against their will—to special hospitals, called sanatoriums, for long-term care.

Setting Purposes for Reading

Big Idea Life Transitions

As you read, notice how Silko uses the experiences of death, loss, and change to portray life in transition.

Literary Element Style

The author's choice and arrangement of words make up the **style** of a literary work. Style can reveal the author's purpose in writing and the attitude toward his or her subject, characters, and audience.

- See Literary Terms Handbook, p. R17.

OBJECTIVES

In studying this selection, you will focus on the following:
- understanding style
- evaluating characters
- determining the role of a narrator in a story
- writing to analyze setting and mood

Reading Strategy Evaluating Characters

Characters are the people portrayed in a literary work. When you evaluate characters, you make judgments or form opinions about them. Such evaluations help the reader develop a framework for explaining a character's actions, statements, thoughts, and feelings. As you read this story, notice how Silko provides opportunities for the reader to evaluate different characters.

Reading Tip: Asking Questions Use a chart like the one shown to record details from the story that help you form opinions about Ayah.

Detail	Opinion About Ayah
"She smiled at the snow which was trying to cover her little by little."	She is at home in nature.

Vocabulary

arroyo (ə roi′ ō) n. a dry gully or stream bed; p. 281 *The thirsty horse did not find water as it cantered along the arroyo.*

crevice (krev′ is) n. a narrow crack into or through something; p. 283 *Mark watched his father fill in the crevice in the wall.*

sparse (spärs) adj. thinly spread or distributed; p. 286 *The berries were so sparse that we could not gather enough to make a pie.*

distortion (dis tôr′ shən) n. an appearance of being twisted or bent out of shape; p. 287 *The crack in the mirror caused a distortion in my image.*

Literature**Online** **Interactive Literary Elements Handbook** To review or learn more about the literary elements, go to www.glencoe.com.

LESLIE MARMON SILKO **279**

Focus

Summary

An elderly Navajo woman remembers her happy childhood, and the loss of her children to war and poverty. She thinks about the difficulties of her present life. When her husband dies, she sings a song for all her losses.

V Vocabulary

Vocabulary File Say: Add these words and definitions to your vocabulary file. For each word, include a sentence that gives you an example of how to use the word. **OL** Students with English language needs should include the pronunciations of these words in their files. **EL**

Literary Elements Have students access the Web site to improve their understanding of style.

Selection Resources

Print Materials
- Unit 1 Resources (Fast File), pp. 91–93
- Leveled Vocabulary Development, p. 21
- Selection and Unit Assessments, pp. 45–46
- Selection Quick Checks, p. 23

Transparencies
- Bellringer Options Transparencies: Selection Focus Transparency 18 Daily Language Practice Transparency 25
- Literary Elements Transparency 24

Technology
- TeacherWorks Plus™ CD-ROM
- StudentWorks Plus™ CD-ROM
- Presentation Plus!™ CD-ROM
- Literature Online, glencoe.com
- Online Student Edition, mhln.com
- ExamView® Assessment Suite CD-ROM
- Vocabulary PuzzleMaker CD-ROM
- Listening Library, disc 1 track 25

Teach

Big Idea

Life Transitions

Say: Keep the following questions in mind as you read. How is loss an important part of the narrator's life? What life changes are illustrated by the narrator's memories? *(The loss of Ella and Danny is important because she ended up blaming her husband for their departure. Jimmie's death is important because his life represented happiness to the narrator. Her memories illustrate the narrator's transition from a young, vibrant woman to an elderly, embittered woman.)* **OL**

★ Viewing the Art

Stephan Daigle, a Canadian painter and illustrator, uses geometric patterns and images of nature to create allegories. **Ask:** What story might this picture be telling? *(Students might point out the animals and the giant owl in the sun, as well as the series of moon-like objects arching across the sky. Perhaps the story is about how the sun nurtures life on Earth.)* **AS**

Readability Scores
Dale-Chall: 5.6
DRP: 56
Lexile: 900

Additional Support

Lullaby
Leslie Marmon Silko

Owl Watching Over Wildlife. Stephan Daigle. ★

280 UNIT 1   THE SHORT STORY

Skills Practice

READING: Questioning Have students read the first eighteen lines of the story. Encourage students to think about where Ayah is and what she is doing. **Ask:** Where is the elderly woman? Why do you think she is there?

(She is sitting outside in the snow. There is no explanation at this point, but clearly the woman is in a reflective mood. She may have gone out to get away from something or someone.) **OL**

The sun had gone down but the snow in the wind gave off its own light. It came in thick tufts like new wool—washed before the weaver spins it. Ayah[1] reached out for it like her own babies had, and she smiled when she remembered how she had laughed at them. She was an old woman now, and her life had become memories. She sat down with her back against the wide cottonwood tree, feeling the rough bark on her back bones; she faced east and listened to the wind and snow sing a high-pitched Yeibechei[2] song. Out of the wind she felt warmer, and she could watch the wide fluffy snow fill in her tracks, steadily, until the direction she had come from was gone. By the light of the snow she could see the dark outline of the big **arroyo** a few feet away. She was sitting on the edge of Cebolleta[3] Creek, where in the springtime the thin cows would graze on grass already chewed flat to the ground. In the wide deep creek bed where only a trickle of water flowed in the summer, the skinny cows would wander, looking for new grass along winding paths splashed with manure.

Ayah pulled the old Army blanket over her head like a shawl. Jimmie's blanket—the one he had sent to her. That was a long time ago and the green wool was faded, and it was unraveling on the edges. She did not want to think about Jimmie. So she thought about the weaving and the way her mother had done it. On the tall wooden loom set into the sand under a tamarack[4] tree for shade. She could see it clearly. She had been only a little girl when her grandma gave her the wooden combs to pull the twigs and burrs from the raw, freshly washed wool. And while she combed the wool, her grandma sat beside her, spinning a silvery strand of yarn around the smooth cedar spindle. Her mother worked at the loom with yarns dyed bright yellow and red and gold. She watched them dye the yarn in boiling black pots full of beeweed petals, juniper berries, and sage. The blankets her mother made were soft and woven so tight that rain rolled off them like birds' feathers. Ayah remembered sleeping warm on cold windy nights, wrapped in her mother's blankets on the hogan's[5] sandy floor.

Visual Vocabulary
In yarn-making, the *spindle* is a round, tapered stick that is turned by hand to twist wool fibers into a thread of yarn. **L**

The snow drifted now, with the northwest wind hurling it in gusts. It drifted up around her black overshoes—old ones with little metal buckles. She smiled at the snow which was trying to cover her little by little. She could remember when they had no black rubber overshoes; only the high buckskin leggings that they wrapped over their elkhide moccasins. If the snow was dry or frozen, a person could walk all day and not get wet; and in the evenings the beams of the ceiling would hang with lengths of pale buckskin leggings, drying out slowly.

She felt peaceful remembering. She didn't feel cold any more. Jimmie's blanket seemed warmer than it had ever been. And she could remember the morning he was born. She could remember whispering to her

---

1. *Ayah* (ä′ yə)
2. The *Yeibechei* (yā′ bə chā) are masked Navajo dancers who sing in high-pitched voices.
3. *Cebolleta* (se′ bō yā′ tä) is also the name of a town in the story.

Big Idea Life Transitions *What does this sentence tell you about how the woman's life has changed?* **BI**

Reading Strategy Evaluating Characters *What does this sentence reveal about Ayah?* **R**

Vocabulary
arroyo (ə roi′ ō) *n.* a dry gully or stream bed

---

4. *Tamarack* is another name for the larch, a tree in the pine family.
5. Traditionally, a *hogan* is a Navajo dwelling made of wood and covered with earth.

LESLIE MARMON SILKO **281**

Teach

Evaluating Characters

Answer: *Chato is educated, or he wants to share his skills with his wife.* **Ask:** *In what kind of position or role does this put Chato in relation to Ayah? (It puts him in a care-giving role when it comes to their dealings with the white people. It also puts him in a position of great responsibility and power—he is Ayah's sole representative in the white world.)* **OL**

L Literary Element

Style Answer: *Lizards eat flies. She is frightened by the predatory way in which they look at her children. Silko uses this simile to convey Ayah's fear of losing her children.* **OL**

---

mother, who was sleeping on the other side of the hogan, to tell her it was time now. She did not want to wake the others. The second time she called to her, her mother stood up and pulled on her shoes; she knew. They walked to the old stone hogan together, Ayah walking a step behind her mother. She waited alone, learning the rhythms of the pains while her mother went to call the old woman to help them. The morning was already warm even before dawn and Ayah smelled the bee flowers blooming and the young willow growing at the springs. She could remember that so clearly, but his birth merged into the births of the other children and to her it became all the same birth. They named him for the summer morning and in English they called him Jimmie.

It wasn't like Jimmie died. He just never came back, and one day a dark blue sedan with white writing on its doors pulled up in front of the boxcar shack where the rancher let the Indians live. A man in a khaki uniform trimmed in gold gave them a yellow piece of paper and told them that Jimmie was dead. He said the Army would try to get the body back and then it would be shipped to them; but it wasn't likely because the helicopter had burned after it crashed. All of this was told to Chato[6] because he could understand English. She stood inside the doorway holding the baby while Chato listened. Chato spoke English like a white man and he spoke Spanish too. He was taller than the white man and he stood straighter too. Chato didn't explain why; he just told the military man they could keep the body if they found it. The white man looked bewildered; he nodded his head and he left. Then Chato looked at her and shook his head, and then he told her, "Jimmie isn't coming home anymore," and when he spoke, he used the words to speak of the dead. She didn't cry then, but she hurt inside with anger. And she mourned him as the years passed, when a horse fell with Chato

---

6. *Chato* (chä´tō)

Reading Strategy Evaluating Characters *What does this detail tell you about Chato?* **R1**

---

and broke his leg, and the white rancher told them he wouldn't pay Chato until he could work again. She mourned Jimmie because he would have worked for his father then; he would have saddled the big bay[7] horse and ridden the fence lines each day, with wire cutters and heavy gloves, fixing the breaks in the barbed wire and putting the stray cattle back inside again.

She mourned him after the white doctors came to take Danny and Ella away. She was at the shack alone that day they came. It was back in the days before they hired Navajo women to go with them as interpreters. She recognized one of the doctors. She had seen him at the children's clinic at Cañoncito[8] about a month ago. They were wearing khaki uniforms and they waved papers at her and a black ball-point pen, trying to make her understand their English words. She was frightened by the way they looked at the children, like the lizard watches the fly. Danny was swinging on the tire swing on the elm tree behind the rancher's house, and Ella was toddling around the front door, dragging the broomstick horse Chato made for her. Ayah could see they wanted her to sign the papers, and Chato had taught her to sign her name. It was something she was proud of. She only wanted them to go, and to take their eyes away from her children.

She took the pen from the man without looking at his face and she signed the papers in three different places he pointed to. She stared at the ground by their feet and waited for them to leave. But they stood there and began to point and gesture at the children. Danny stopped swinging. Ayah could see his fear. She moved suddenly and grabbed Ella into her arms; the child squirmed, trying to get back to her toys. Ayah ran with the baby toward Danny; she screamed for him to run and then she grabbed him around his chest and

---

7. Here, *bay* is the horse's color—a reddish brown.
8. *Cañoncito* (kan´ yən sē´ tō) is the name of the Navajo reservation located in west central New Mexico.

Literary Element Style *Explain what this simile means.* **L**

Additional Support

Skills Practice

LITERARY ELEMENT: Flashback
Review with students that a flashback is a shift back in time to a memory of an event or events from the past, usually before the story's beginning. It interrupts the chronological sequence of the story,

but gives readers information or background that may help explain particular events. **Ask:** *Where does the flashback begin on this page? (It begins with Ayah remembering the birth of Jimmie.)* **OL** carried him too. She ran south into the foot-hills of juniper trees and black lava rock. Behind her she heard the doctors running, but they had been taken by surprise, and as the hills became steeper and the cholla cactus were thicker, they stopped. When she reached the top of the hill, she stopped to listen in case they were circling around her. But in a few minutes she heard a car engine start and they drove away. The children had been too surprised to cry while she ran with them Danny was shaking and Ella's little fingers were gripping Ayah's blouse.

Visual Vocabulary
A *cholla* (choi´ə) is a spiny, shrubby, or treelike cactus.

She stayed up in the hills for the rest of the day, sitting on a black lava boulder in the sunshine where she could see for miles all around her. The sky was light blue and cloudless, and it was warm for late April. The sun warmth relaxed her and took the fear and anger away. She lay back on the rock and watched the sky. It seemed to her that she could walk into the sky, stepping through clouds endlessly. Danny played with little pebbles and stones, pretending they were birds' eggs and then little rabbits. Ella sat at her feet and dropped fistfuls of dirt into the breeze, watching the dust and particles of sand intently. Ayah watched a hawk soar high above them, dark wings gliding; hunting or only watching, she did not know. The hawk was patient and he circled all afternoon before he disappeared around the high volcanic peak the Mexicans called Guadalupe.[9]

Late in the afternoon, Ayah looked down at the gray boxcar shack with the paint all peeled from the wood; the stove pipe on the roof was rusted and crooked. The fire she had built that morning in the oil drum stove had burned out. Ella was asleep in her lap now and Danny sat close to her, complaining that he was hungry; he asked when they would go to the house. "We will stay up here until your father comes," she told him, "because those white men were chasing us." The boy remembered then and he nodded at her silently.

If Jimmie had been there he could have read those papers and explained to her what they said. Ayah would have known then, never to sign them. The doctors came back the next day and they brought a BIA[10] ★ policeman with them. They told Chato they had her signature and that was all they needed. Except for the kids. She listened to Chato sullenly; she hated him when he told her it was the old woman who died in the winter, spitting blood; it was her old grandma who had given the children this disease. "They don't spit blood," she said coldly. "The whites lie." She held Ella and Danny close to her, ready to run to the hills again. "I want a medicine man first," she said to Chato, not looking at him. He shook his head. "It's too late now. The policeman is with them. You signed the paper." His voice was gentle.

It was worse than if they had died: to lose the children and to know that somewhere, in a place called Colorado, in a place full of sick and dying strangers, her children were without her. There had been babies that died soon after they were born, and one that died before he could walk. She had carried them herself, up to the boulders and great pieces of the cliff that long ago crashed down from Long Mesa; she laid them in the **crevices** of sandstone and buried them in fine brown

10. The Bureau of Indian Affairs, or *BIA*, is the federal agency in charge of administering government policies toward Native Americans.

Reading Strategy Evaluating Characters *What does this detail tell you about Chato's personality?* **R₂**

Vocabulary

crevice (krev´ is) n. a narrow crack into or through something

9. *Guadalupe* (gwä´ də lōō´ pā)

Big Idea Life Transitions *Why do you think Ayah remembers even the smallest details of this day?* **BI**

LESLIE MARMON SILKO **283**

Teach

BI₁ Big Idea

Life Transitions

Answer: *Because her other children are buried near her, she feels as though they are with her; Danny and Ella are being raised by strangers.* **Ask:** How is the pain she feels over Danny and Ella's absence different from her feelings about Jimmie's death? *(Jimmie left and never came back; there was nothing she could do about his death. In a way, he is still alive in her mind. She feels she might have kept Danny and Ella but failed.)* **OL**

L Literary Element

Style Answer: *Ayah feels a pain in her belly that is made worse by things that remind her of the children. She feels as if she can't eat or breathe.* **OL**

⭐ Viewing the Art

Ask: How does the mood of the painting compare with the mood of the story? *(Both have an ominous mood.)* **AS**

Monument Valley at Sunset.
Robert McIntosh.

sand with round quartz pebbles that washed down the hills in the rain. She had endured it because they had been with her. But she could not bear this pain. She did not sleep for a long time after they took her children. She stayed on the hill where they had fled the first time, and she slept rolled up in the blanket Jimmie had sent her. She carried the pain in her belly and it was fed by everything she saw: the blue sky of their last day together and the dust and pebbles they played with; the swing in the elm tree and broomstick horse choked life from her. The pain filled her stomach and there was no room for food or for her lungs to fill with air. The air and the food would have been theirs.

She hated Chato, not because he let the policeman and doctors put the screaming children in the government car, but because he had taught her to sign her name. Because it was like the old ones always told her about learning their language or any of their

ways: it endangered you. She slept alone on the hill until the middle of November when the first snows came. Then she made a bed for herself where the children had slept. She did not lie down beside Chato again until many years later, when he was sick and shivering and only her body could keep him warm. The illness came after the white rancher told Chato he was too old to work for him anymore, and Chato and his old woman should be out of the shack by the next afternoon because the rancher had hired new people to work there. That had satisfied her. To see how the white man repaid Chato's years of loyalty and work. All of Chato's fine-sounding English talk didn't change things.

It snowed steadily and the luminous light from the snow gradually diminished into the darkness. Somewhere in Cebolleta a dog barked and other village dogs joined with it. Ayah looked in the direction she had come, from the bar where Chato was buying the wine. Sometimes he told her to go on ahead and wait; and then he never came. And when she finally went back looking for him, she would find him passed out at the bottom of the wooden steps to Azzie's Bar. All the wine would be gone and most of the money too, from the pale blue check that came to them once a month in a government envelope. It was then that she would look at his face and his hands, scarred by ropes and the barbed wire of all those years, and she

---

Big Idea Life Transitions *Why is the absence of Danny and Ella more upsetting to Ayah than the deaths of her other children?* **BI₁**

Literary Element Style *How does the author describe Ayah's feelings after losing her children?* **L**

284 UNIT 1 THE SHORT STORY

Additional Support

Skills Practice

LISTENING AND SPEAKING:

Dialogue Authors use dialogue many ways, to: tell what has happened or is happening, let the reader know what the character is like or is thinking. Here the author uses little dialogue. **Ask:** Why does Silko use so little dialogue? *(Most of the story takes place in Ayah's*

memory.) Have students select a scene such as when the couple is told about Jimmie's death (see p. 282). Ask them to write dialogue and indicate what might have been said. Remind students to use correct paragraphing, punctuation, and capitalization. Allow time for groups to present their dialogues. **OL** would think, this man is a stranger; for forty years she had smiled at him and cooked his food, but he remained a stranger. She stood up again, with the snow almost to her knees, and she walked back to find Chato.

It was hard to walk in the deep snow and she felt the air burn in her lungs. She stopped a short distance from the bar to rest and readjust the blanket. But this time he wasn't waiting for her on the bottom step with his old Stetson hat pulled down and his shoulders hunched up in his long wool overcoat.

She was careful not to slip on the wooden steps. When she pushed the door open, warm air and cigarette smoke hit her face. She looked around slowly and deliberately, in every corner, in every dark place that the old man might find to sleep. The bar owner didn't like Indians in there, especially Navajos, but he let Chato come in because he could talk Spanish like he was one of them. The men at the bar stared at her, and the bartender saw that she left the door open wide. Snowflakes were flying inside like moths and melting into a puddle on the oiled wood floor. He motioned to her to close the door, but she did not see him. She held herself straight and walked across the room slowly, searching the room with every step. The snow in her hair melted and she could feel it on her forehead. At the far corner of the room, she saw red flames at the mica window of the old stove door; she looked behind the stove just to make sure. The bar got quiet except for the Spanish polka music playing on the jukebox. She stood by the stove and shook the snow from her blanket and held it near the stove to dry. The wet wool smell reminded her of new-born goats in early March, brought inside to warm near the fire. She felt calm. ★

Visual Vocabulary
Mica is a mineral (abundant in New Mexico) that can be split into thin, strong, flexible sheets. A sheet of colorless mica makes a decent, inexpensive substitute for glass.

In past years they would have told her to get out. But her hair was white now and her face was wrinkled. They looked at her like she was a spider crawling slowly across the room. They were afraid; she could feel the **R** fear. She looked at their faces steadily. They reminded her of the first time the white people brought her children back to her that winter. Danny had been shy and hid behind the thin white woman who brought them. And the baby had not known her until Ayah took her into her arms, and then Ella had nuzzled close to her as she had when she was nursing. The blonde woman was nervous and kept looking at a dainty gold watch on her wrist. She sat on the bench near the small window and watched the dark snow clouds gather around the mountains; she was worrying about the unpaved road. She was frightened by what she saw inside too: the strips of venison drying on a rope across the ceiling and the children jabbering excitedly in a language she did not know. So they stayed for only a few hours. Ayah watched the government car disappear down the road and she knew they were already being weaned from these lava hills and from this sky. The last time they came was in early June, and Ella stared at her the way the men in the bar were now staring. Ayah did not try to pick her up; she smiled at her instead and spoke cheerfully to Danny. When he tried to answer her, he could not seem to remember and he spoke English words with the Navajo. But he gave her a scrap of paper that he had found somewhere and carried in his pocket; it was folded in half, and he shyly looked up at her and said it was a bird. She asked Chato if they were home for good this time. He spoke to the white woman and she shook her head. "How much longer?" he asked, and she said she didn't know; but Chato saw how she stared at the boxcar shack. Ayah turned away then. She did not say good-bye.

Big Idea Life Transitions *What does the author mean by this statement?* **BI₂**

LESLIE MARMON SILKO **285**

Teach

ⓡ Reading Strategy
Evaluating Characters Say: What about Ayah might frighten the people in the bar? (*She is an elderly woman, probably not the type of person who usually frequents bars. They don't know how to act around her or what to think of her. Also, the bar owner usually doesn't allow Navajos into the bar.*) **OL**

BI₂ **Big Idea**
Life Transitions
Answer: *The children were losing their memories of their parents and their home.* **OL**

★ Writer's Technique
Sensory Descriptions
Say: The author uses sensory descriptions to enhance the reading experience. What senses does she appeal to in this section? (*Touch/feeling (snow melting on her forehead), vision (red flames in the stove), sound (Spanish polka music), smell (wet wool).*) **AS**

Reading in the Real World

College and Career Ayah and Chato have several language and cultural misunderstandings involving white people. Point out that students may find themselves in similar situations. **Ask:** What steps could you take to prepare for these situations? To handle situations like these? (*To prepare: learn a foreign language; study the customs of other cultures; converse with people from other cultures. To handle situations: be patient; use universal body language; use words that are similar in many languages (yes, no).*) **OL**

Objectives
• To understand style (SE)
• To evaluate characters (SE)
• To write dialogue (TWE)

Teach

Evaluating Characters
Answer: *She is used to feeling powerless, so she enjoys this role reversal.* **OL**

L Literary Element

Style Answer: *Ayah's and Chato's lives are silent, dry, and empty, like the caves.* **OL**

★ Viewing the Art

John Newcomb's acrylic paintings often feature landscapes rendered on large canvasses, some as large as 3 feet by 4 feet. Many Native American groups believe in the vision quest, a traditional search for spiritual guidance in other worldly forces. **Ask:** How might Ayah's remembering be a type of vision quest? *(It could be a vision quest in that she seems to be seeking understanding and enlightenment by thinking back on her life.)* **AS**

Vision Quest, 1999. John Newcomb.
Acrylic on canvas. Private Collection.

She felt satisfied that the men in the bar feared her. Maybe it was her face and the way she held her mouth with teeth clenched tight, like there was nothing anyone could do to her now. She walked north down the road, searching for the old man. She did this because she had the blanket, and there would be no place for him except with her and the blanket in the old adobe barn near the arroyo. They always slept there when they came to Cebolleta. If the money and the wine were gone, she would be relieved because then they could go home again: back to the old hogan with a dirt roof and rock walls where she herself had been born. And the next day the old man could go back to the few sheep they still had, to follow along behind them, guiding them, into dry sandy arroyos where **sparse** grass grew. She knew he did not like walking behind old ewes when for so many years he rode big

quarter horses and worked with cattle. But she wasn't sorry for him; he should have known all along what would happen.

There had not been enough rain for their garden in five years; and that was when Chato finally hitched a ride into the town and brought back brown boxes of rice and sugar and big tin cans of welfare[11] peaches. After that, at the first of the month they went to Cebolleta to ask the postmaster for the check; and then Chato would go to the bar and cash it. They did this as they planted the garden every May, not because anything would survive the summer dust, but because it was time to do this. The journey passed the days that smelled silent and dry like the caves above the canyon with yellow painted buffaloes on their walls.

He was walking along the pavement when she found him. He did not stop or turn around when he heard her behind him. She walked beside him and she noticed how slowly he moved now. He smelled strong of woodsmoke and urine. Lately he had been forgetting. Sometimes he called her by his sister's name and she had been gone for a long time. Once she had found him wandering on the road to the white man's ranch, and she asked him why he was going that way; he laughed at her and said, "You know they can't run that ranch without me," and he walked on determined, limping on the leg that had been crushed many years before. Now he looked at her curiously, as if

Reading Strategy Evaluating Characters *Why do you think Ayah would want the men to fear her?* **R1**

Vocabulary

sparse (spärs) *adj.* thinly spread or distributed

11. The canned peaches came from a government *welfare* program to help needy people.

Literary Element Style *How does this description echo the mood of the story at this point?* **L**

Additional Support

Skills Practice

READING: Evaluating Throughout a selection, readers make evaluations about many things—the characters and the plot, for example. In "Lullaby," the reader forms opinions or judgments about Ayah. Sometimes those opinions or judgments will change. Have students discuss how they felt about Ayah at the beginning of the story. Encourage them to compare their evaluation of the woman with those of the white people she encountered throughout her life. Have students discuss how and why their opinions about Ayah changed by the end of the story. **OL**

for the first time, but he kept shuffling along, moving slowly along the side of the highway. His gray hair had grown long and spread out on the shoulders of the long overcoat. He wore the old felt hat pulled down over his ears. His boots were worn out at the toes and he had stuffed pieces of an old red shirt in the holes. The rags made his feet look like little animals up to their ears in snow. She laughed at his feet; the snow muffled the sound of her laugh. He stopped and looked at her again. The wind had quit blowing and the snow was falling straight down; the southeast sky was beginning to clear and Ayah could see a star.

"Let's rest awhile," she said to him. They walked away from the road and up the slope to the giant boulders that had tumbled down from the red sandrock mesa throughout the centuries of rainstorms and earth tremors. In a place where the boulders shut out the wind, they sat down with their backs against the rock. She offered half of the blanket to him and they sat wrapped together.

The storm passed swiftly. The clouds moved east. They were massive and full, crowding together across the sky. She watched them with the feeling of horses—steely blue-gray horses startled across the sky. The powerful haunches pushed into the distances and the tail hairs streamed white mist behind them. The sky cleared. Ayah saw that there was nothing between her and the stars. The light was crystalline.[12] There was no shimmer, no **distortion** through earth haze. She breathed the clarity of the night sky; she smelled the purity of the half moon and the stars. He was lying on his side with his knees pulled up near his belly for warmth. His eyes were closed

---

12. Here, *crystalline* means "clear and pure as a crystal."

Reading Strategy Evaluating Characters *Do Ayah's actions indicate that she has forgiven Chato?* **R2**

now, and in the light from the stars and the moon, he looked young again.

She could see it descend out of the night sky: an icy stillness from the edge of the thin moon. She recognized the freezing. It came gradually, sinking snowflake by snowflake until the crust was heavy and deep. It had the strength of the stars in Orion, and its journey was endless. Ayah knew that with the wine he would sleep. He would not feel it. She tucked the blanket around him, remembering how it was when Ella had been with her; and she felt the rush so big inside her heart for the babies. And she sang the only song she knew to sing for babies. She could not remember if she had ever sung it to her children, but she knew that her grandmother had sung it and her mother had sung it:

> The earth is your mother,
>   she holds you.
> The sky is your father,
>   he protects you.
> Sleep,
> sleep.
> Rainbow is your sister,
>   she loves you.
> The winds are your brothers,
>   they sing to you.
> Sleep,
> sleep.
> We are together always
> We are together always
> There never was a time
> when this
> was not so. ☙

Visual Vocabulary
The constellation *Orion* contains two of the brightest stars in the sky. In Greek mythology, Orion is traditionally depicted as a hunter wearing a belt with a sword at his side.

Big Idea Life Transitions *Why do you think Ayah finds the lullaby comforting?* **BI**

Teach

R2 **Reading Strategy**

Evaluating Characters
Answer: *Students may say that she has relented somewhat now that he is old and ill. She has always taken care of him, even when she was angriest about losing the children.* **OL**

BI **Big Idea**

Life Transitions **Answer:** *The lullaby seems to say that family will remain. Also, it was sung by her mother and grandmother.* **OL**

✓**CheckPoint**

Use the CheckPoint questions on Presentation Plus! to check students' mastery of the selection. These questions can be used with interactive response keypads for immediate student feedback.

Differentiated Instruction

Musical Students Some students have a special ability to create or perform music. They can help other students in creating musical presentations. At the end of the story, Ayah sings a lullaby. The reader knows the words, but not the tune. Invite students to create a melody to go with the words of the lullaby. Remind students that the melody will need to fit the rhythm of the words. Students might present the song by singing it or by accompanying the singing with a piano, guitar, violin, or other instrument. **AL**

Objectives
• To understand style (SE)
• To evaluate characters (SE)

Assess

1. (a) Ayah is portrayed as having suffered the most. (b) Possibly Chato, since he is depicted as a hard worker who got fired after years of loyalty

2. (a) Snow reminds her of her babies; blanket reminds her of Jimmie; black shoes remind her of buckskin leggings. (b) She finds happiness in remembering.

3. (a) He looks confused and dirty. (b) He has grown old and distant.

4. (a) She offers half her blanket. (b) She knows he is dying.

5. The lullaby represents her greatest loves, her children.

6. (a) He knows that he cannot fight the system. (b) They could have not signed the documents.

7. (a) Ayah lives in the past; Chato is an alcoholic. (b) They have grown distant but are still very dependent upon each other.

8. They have endured the adversity and, in that way, triumphed over it. But students may claim their attitudes have defeated them.

Literary Element

1. Ayah remembers her mother and grandmother weaving

RESPONDING AND THINKING CRITICALLY

Respond

1. (a) For which character did you have more sympathy, Ayah or Chato? Explain. (b) For whom did you have more respect or admiration? Give reasons.

Recall and Interpret

2. (a) In the first three paragraphs of the story, what reminds Ayah of events in the past? (b) Why might Ayah's thoughts turn so often to the past?

3. (a) When Ayah finally finds Chato near the end of the story, how does he look and act? (b) What do Chato's appearance and actions reveal about him?

4. (a) How does Ayah care for Chato after they find shelter among the boulders? (b) What do you think motivates Ayah to treat Chato this way?

Analyze and Evaluate

5. Why do you think the author chose to title this story "Lullaby"?

6. (a) Why does Chato react as he does when the white doctors come to take Danny and Ella? (b) Could Chato and Ayah have done anything to prevent the doctors from taking their children? Explain.

7. (a) How have Ayah and Chato learned to cope with the hardships they have experienced? (b) How have their ways of coping affected their relationship?

Connect

8. **Big Idea** **Life Transitions** Think about the many obstacles and tragedies that have shaped Ayah and Chato's lives. In your opinion, have they triumphed over adversity, or has it defeated them? Explain.

Literary Element Style

Style is the author's choice and arrangement of words and sentences in a literary work. Style is related to the author's **voice**, or the distinctive use of language to convey the author's, narrator's, or main character's personality to the reader.

Consider this passage from the beginning of the story: "The sun had gone down but the snow in the wind gave off its own light. It came in thick tufts like new wool—washed before the weaver spins it. Ayah reached out for it like her own babies had, and she smiled when she remembered how she had laughed at them."

1. How does Silko use the idea of weaving and blankets throughout the story? Why do you think she chose this idea?

2. How is Ayah's personality revealed in the passage above?

3. Find another example in the story in which Silko's style and voice reveal something about a character.

Review: Narrator

As you learned on pages 192–193, the narrator is the person who tells a story. The narrator might be a character in the story or stand outside the story and comment on the action.

Partner Activity Meet with a classmate to discuss the narrator's role in this story. Draw a chart like the one below to help you think about the narrator's relationship to the main characters. Then answer the questions.

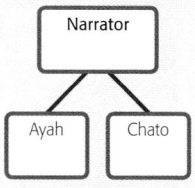

1. What is the narrator's relationship to the characters in the story? Give reasons for your answer.

2. How would the story be different if Ayah were the narrator? If Chato were the narrator? Do you think Silko made the best choice of narrator for this story? Explain.

---

blankets. She wraps herself in her son's blanket. She wraps her husband in a blanket. Silko probably chose this idea because Navajos are known for their blankets and blankets are symbols of security and comfort.

2. She loves her children.

3. Examples include descriptions of the day Ayah hid her children and Chato's appearance later in life.

Review: Narrator

1. The narrator stands outside the story. She knows the characters' thoughts and feelings.

2. Silko made the best choice for telling this story. No other narrator would have been as impartial.

READING AND VOCABULARY

Reading Strategy Evaluating Characters

When you **evaluate characters**, you form opinions and make judgments about them. By evaluating the characters in Silko's story, you can better explain the characters' actions, statements, thoughts, and feelings.

1. What is your opinion of Ayah? Give three details from the story to provide support for your answer.

2. How does your opinion of Ayah affect your enjoyment of the story? Explain.

Vocabulary Practice

Practice with Word Origins Knowing the origin of a word can help you determine its meaning in English. The first step is to identify the language from which the word came. Use a dictionary to determine the origins of the following vocabulary words.

1. arroyo   **a.** French   **b.** Spanish
             c. Greek   **d.** Latin

2. crevice   **a.** French   **b.** Spanish
             c. Greek   **d.** Latin

3. sparse   **a.** French   **b.** Latin
            c. Greek   **d.** Spanish

4. distortion   **a.** Latin   **b.** Spanish
             c. Greek   **d.** French

Academic Vocabulary

Here are two words from the vocabulary list on page R82.

federal (fed′ ər əl) *adj.* relating to a government in which a group of states with individual powers is governed by a central authority

contact (kon′ takt) *n.* a touching or coming together; communication

Practice and Apply

1. Where does an agency of the **federal** government appear in the story and what does it do?

2. How does Ayah feel when the white people come in **contact** with her family?

WRITING AND EXTENDING

Writing About Literature

Analyze Setting and Mood The narrator of "Lullaby" describes a variety of settings in which present and past events take place. Choose one of those settings and identify details the narrator uses to describe the setting. Then write an analysis of how the setting helps to create a particular atmosphere, or mood, in that part of the story. Incorporate examples from the story to support your main points.

Use a table like the one below to help plan your analysis.

Details About Setting	Mood Created
The snow is falling like new wool. Ayah is reaching out for it like her babies once had.	nostalgia

When you finish writing, meet with a small group of classmates to share your analysis. Check your work for errors in spelling, grammar, and punctuation.

Learning for Life

Imagine that you are Ayah's friend and she has come to you, confused and frightened about what the doctors want and what they intend to do. Write a letter of inquiry, asking the doctors to explain the situation. Be polite and businesslike in your approach. Use the proper form for a business letter.

 Literature Online Web Activities For eFlashcards, Selection Quick Checks, and other Web activities, go to www.glencoe.com.

LESLIE MARMON SILKO **289**

Assess

Reading Strategy

1. Students may have a negative opinion of Ayah because she did not do more to keep her children and did not support Chato enough. Others may say that Ayah did the best that she could, given the circumstances.

2. Some students may say that, as a result of their opinion, they enjoyed the story more. Others will disagree.

Vocabulary

1. b   2. d   3. b   4. a

Academic Vocabulary

1. The doctors bring a police officer from the Bureau of Indian Affairs, or BIA.

2. She cannot understand them, and she feels that her children's lives are out of her control.

Writing About Literature

Use these criteria when evaluating students' writing:

• Does the essay clearly identify the setting and use details to describe it?

• Does the essay identify the atmosphere, or mood, created?

• Does the essay explain how the setting helps create atmosphere?

Learning for Life

Review the parts of a business letter. Then suggest that students make a list of key questions to be asked in the letter.

Literature Online

Web Activities Have students access the Web site for interactive activities that will help them assess their understanding of the selection.

Focus

BELLRINGER

Bring a globe to class and set it spinning. Have students point to spots and identify them. **Say:** What you read may have special connections to certain places in the world and certain times in history. It may also reveal something about a person's life. Refer to a place on the globe and ask students to think of stories or movies that offer a historical perspective on that place, as Greek myths do about the ancient Greek world.

Summary

In this workshop, students will write literary criticism from a historical or biographical perspective. Students will follow the stages of the writing process, including prewriting, drafting, revising, and editing. Two lessons, on varying sentence openings and correcting run-on sentences, are provided.

Writing Models Have students access the Web site for interactive writing models and writing guides.

Additional Support

The Writing Process

In this workshop, you will follow the stages of the writing process. At any stage, you may think of new ideas to include and better ways to express them. Feel free to return to earlier stages as you write.

Prewriting
- - - - - - - - - - -
Drafting
- - - - - - - - - - -
Revising

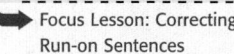 Focus Lesson: Varying Sentence Openers

Editing & Proofreading

 Focus Lesson: Correcting Run-on Sentences

Presenting
- - - - - - - - - - -

Literature Online
Writing Models For models and other writing activities, go to www.glencoe.com.

OBJECTIVES
- Write literary criticism that analyzes the way in which a work is related to an individual life or its historical period.
- Present and support a thesis.

Writing Workshop

Literary Criticism

 Taking a Biographical or Historical Approach

"Thirty-five years ago I was out prospecting on the Stanislaus, tramping all day long with pick and pan and horn, and washing a hatful of dirt here and there, always expecting to make a rich strike, and never doing it."

—Mark Twain, from "A Californian's Tale"

Connecting to Literature In "A Californian's Tale," Mark Twain does more than tell an entertaining story: he also presents historical facts. He recreates a real time and place and provides details about what happened there. A writer of **literary criticism** can use those details in analyzing the story from a historical perspective. Study the rubric below to learn about writing literary criticism based on biographical or historical details.

Rubric: Features of Literary Criticism

Goals	Strategies
To comment on how a work is related to a particular place or time (history) or to an individual life (biography)	☑ Present a thesis that summarizes the insight ☑ Present main ideas and details that support the thesis
To explain and develop ideas	☑ Provide evidence from the text and explain how it relates to main points and the thesis
To maintain a consistent focus and tone	☑ Use a formal tone throughout the paper ☑ Relate everything to the thesis
To present organized, linked, and fluid ideas to the reader	☑ Create a clear introduction, body, and conclusion ☑ Use each body paragraph to present and develop one main idea ☑ Use transitions

290 UNIT 1 THE SHORT STORY

Workshop Resources

Print Materials
📁 Unit 1 Resources (Fast File), pp. 94–96
📁 REAL Success in Writing
📁 Writing Constructed Responses, pp. 36–41
📖 Glencoe Literature Library

Transparencies
- Grammar and Language Transparencies 11, 24, 35
- Writing Workshop Transparencies 6–10
- Visual Literacy/Fine Art Transparencies

Technology
- Grammar & Language eWorkbook
- Revising with Style eWorkbook
- Sentence Diagraming eWorkbook
- Spelling Power eWorkbook
- Online Essay Grading, glencoe.com
- Literature Library Exam*View*™ Assessment Suite CD-ROM
- Literature Library Vocabulary PuzzleMaker CD-ROM

> ▶ **Assignment**
>
> Write an essay of literary criticism. Use your essay to show how a literary work is related to themes and issues of its historical period or to an individual's life. As you move through the stages of the writing process, keep your audience and purpose in mind.
>
> **Audience:** your teacher
>
> **Purpose:** to explain and inform by analyzing how a work of literature is related to a real time, place, or person

Analyzing a Professional Model

In the literary criticism that follows, Paule Marshall presents biographical details that shed light on her short story, "To Da-duh, In Memoriam." The reader learns not only that Da-duh was a real person but also that she appears throughout Marshall's works. As you read the criticism, identify the features that it consists of. Pay close attention to the comments in the margin: they point out features that you may want to include in your own literary criticism.

Real-Life Story Behind "To Da-duh, In Memoriam"
by Paule Marshall ★

This is the most autobiographical of stories, a reminiscence largely of a visit I paid to my grandmother (whose nickname was Da-duh) on the island of Barbados when I was nine. Ours was a complex relationship—close, affectionate yet rivalrous. During the year I spent with her a subtle kind of power struggle went on between us. It was as if we both knew, at a level beyond words, that I had come into the world not only to love her and to continue her line but to take her very life in order that I might live.

Wash Day.
Victor Collector.
Oil on canvas.
Private Collection.

> **Real World Connection**
>
> For many literature courses, you may need to write literary criticism essays. As you will see in this Writing Workshop assignment, the key to success is creating a clear, insightful thesis and supporting it with details from the text.

> **Focus**
>
> Create—and maintain—a biographical or historical focus.
>
> **Formal Tone**
>
> Maintain a formal tone throughout your paper.

Writing Workshop

Literary Criticsm

Teach

Big Idea

Life Transitions
Point out that fiction frequently explores how people, places, and events change. **Ask:** How can literary criticism relate to life transitions? *(Writers of literary criticism can comment on the historical and biographical perspectives in the literature. Writers can analyze what the fiction reveals about a person, place, or time.)* In preparation for writing literary criticism, advise students to reread the selection they will write about, noting what it conveys about a specific time, place, or person. **OL**

★ Literary History

Paule Marshall Remind students that Paule Marshall (1929–) is an award-winning author of poems, short stories, and novels. **Ask:** What new biographical perspective does this essay give you on "To Da-duh, in Memoriam" on pages 150–159? *(It reveals that the character of Da-duh is based on Marshall's grandmother, and it illuminates that relationship.)* **AS**

English Language Coach

Mode of Writing To clarify the definition of *literary criticism,* call for volunteers to look up the term. Elicit two main points: (a) it is writing about literature; and (b) it is analytical in nature. Ask students to distinguish between fact, analysis, and evaluation, providing examples of each. **EL**

Differentiated Instruction

Critical Response Encourage gifted and advanced students to extend their understanding of literary criticism by reading book reviews in reputable publications such as *New York Times Book Review, New York Review of Books,* and *Booklist.* Direct students to publications suitable to their reading level. **AL**

Objectives
- To write literary criticism that analyzes the way in which a work is related to an individual life or its historical period (SE)
- To analyze a literary model (TWE)

291

Teach

Writing Skills

Analyzing Biographical Context

Ask: In this piece, what does Paule Marshall reveal about her grandmother that informs her fiction? *(She reveals that many characters in her fiction were drawn from her real-life complex and competitive relationship with her grandmother. Marshall describes her respect for her grandmother, which carries over into symbolic figures in her writing.)* Have students make a list of the biographical details presented. **OL**

Transitions

Use transition words and phrases to connect ideas, sentences, and paragraphs smoothly.

Main Ideas/Details

Present your main ideas in topic sentences and support them in the body of each paragraph.

Evidence

Use examples as evidence and to support the points you make.

Organization

Make sure to follow a logical pattern of organization, such as introduction, body, and conclusion.

Conclusion

Conclude by summarizing ideas, but do not repeat them word for word.

Years later, when I got around to writing the story, I tried giving the contest I had sensed between us a wider meaning. I wanted the basic theme of youth and old age to suggest rivalries, dichotomies of a cultural and political nature, having to do with the relationship of western civilization and the Third World.

Apart from this story, Da-duh also appears in one form or another in my other work as well. She's the old hairdresser, Mrs. Thompson, in *Brown Girl, Brownstones*, who offers Selina total, unquestioning love. She's Leesy Walkes and the silent cook, Carrington, in *The Chosen Place, the Timeless People*. She's Aunt Vi in "Reena" and Medford, the old family retainer in "British Guiana" from *Soul Clap Hands and Sing*. And she's Avey Johnson's Great-aunt Cuney in *Praisesong for the Widow*. Da-duh turns up everywhere.

She's an ancestor figure, symbolic for me of the long line of black women and men—African and New World—who made my being possible, and whose spirit I believe continues to animate my life and work. I wish to acknowledge and celebrate them. I am, in a word, an unabashed ancestor worshipper.

Reading-Writing Connection Think about the writing techniques that you have just encountered and try them out in the literary criticism you write.

Forsaken Treasures. Victor Collector. Oil on canvas. Private Collection.

Additional Support

Skills Practice

VOCABULARY: Word Origins Paule Marshall pays tribute to her grandmother, "whose spirit I believe continues to animate my life." *Animate* comes from the Latin word *anima* for "life." *Animate* means "to bring to life." Ask students for examples of other words that derive from *anima*, such as *animal, animosity,* and *animated.* Tell them to pay attention to Latin and Greek roots when they encounter new words. As practice, have them determine how word origins can help them understand these words from the student essay they will read: *indignities, endured, graphic.* **OL**

Prewriting

Find the Work and Decide Your Approach The work of literature you choose must contain enough biographical or historical details for a successful essay. Always "test" the work before you begin writing to see whether it will work for a biographical or historical approach.

▶ If you want to write a **biographical criticism**, begin by identifying the person whose life you will focus on. Then find details in the story that illustrate his or her life. List details or make a cluster diagram.

▶ If you want to take a **historical approach to literary criticism**, begin by identifying the time, the place, and the culture. Then find details in the story that show this historical world. You can use a cluster diagram or simply make a list.

Develop a Thesis Review your list of ideas or your cluster. Decide on a focus. That is, write a sentence or two that provides an overview of what the details seem to say. This is your working thesis, which you can revise as you go along.

Working Thesis: Details in "Lullaby" show Navajo culture.

Develop an Organizational Plan Your next step is to decide on the main points to make in your essay. You can either revise your thesis to show those main points and base your paragraph plan on it, or you can begin mapping out your body paragraphs and then revise your thesis. Either way, follow these steps to create a plan for each body paragraph.

▶ Think of a main idea for the body paragraph.

▶ List details, quotations, or examples from the story that illustrate or support that main idea.

▶ Add thoughts of your own about the main idea.

▶ Make a paragraph plan like this one for each body paragraph.

Body Paragraph Plan

Main Idea: Because she is Navajo and speaks a different language, Ayah is suspicious of the English-speaking doctors.

Details from the Story: The doctors looked at the children "like the lizard watches the fly."

My Thoughts: This is a good simile. It shows Ayah's fear. It shows how alien the doctors are to her. Ayah goes to the foothills to find comfort. Nature helps her feel better.

Talk About Your Ideas Meet with a partner. Refer to your working theses and paragraph plans as you discuss the focus of your papers so far and the main ideas you will present to support them. Ask your partner for suggestions on how to revise your thesis and make sure that your main ideas relate to it. Then talk about your writing voice. For this assignment, you want to sound objective, not personal. Ask your partner to comment on how objective, formal, and impersonal your plan is so far.

A Working Thesis

You need not worry if you cannot come up with a perfect thesis during the prewriting stage. As you develop your draft, the focus of your paper will become clearer to you. You can improve your thesis at any time during the writing process.

Test Prep

If you are asked in a test to show how history or biography shapes a work, remember that you do not have to be an expert in this area. Instead, focus on how the details in the work tell you about a time, a place, or a person.

Teach

Writing Skills

Thesis Point out that a thesis must be narrow enough to be supported well. **Ask:** *What keeps Marshall's thesis narrow?* *(It is restricted to one story and one relationship.)* Ask students to write three possible theses for their literary criticism and to consult with a peer partner about which is best. Make sure that each student's thesis is approved as the writing process continues. **OL**

Writing Skills

Supporting Evidence Emphasize that each paragraph of an essay should present details to support the main point of that paragraph. Discuss how Marshall develops her thesis. **Ask:** *How does Marshall support her thesis? (Her main points are that "To Da-duh, in Memoriam" is about her grandmother and that others of her stories expand upon this relationship and present similar characters. These characters symbolize Marshall's respect for her elders.)* **OL**

Differentiated Instruction

Organization An essay should be well organized, with a beginning, middle, and end. Help less proficient writers focus on organization by creating diagrams to outline the model essays. Suggest that they use outlines to plan a good organization for their writing as well. **EL**

English Language Coach

Levels of Usage Explain that the formal tone of literary criticism requires precise, correct language and grammar. In contrast, an informal tone is more relaxed in its use of language and may even use slang. Help students practice different levels of language and identify when each is appropriate. **BL**

Objectives

• To present and support a thesis (SE)
• To analyze biographical context (TWE)
• To understand word origins (TWE)

Teach

Writing Skills

Tone Answer: *The tone of the essay, with an absence of slang and contractions, is formal.* `OL`

Writing Skills

Thesis Answer: *The thesis—"Silko reflects Navajo culture in her story"—is related to history through its descriptions of Navajo culture and traditions.* `OL`

Writing Skills

Evidence Answer: *Ayah sees the world symbolically through the tradition of weaving. The examples dealing with traditional crafts relate to Navajo history.* `OL`

Writing Skills

Historical Focus Answer: *The author analyzes how skills were once passed down—not through formal education but from generation to generation.* `OL`

Drafting

Use Transitions As you get your ideas down on paper, remember to connect your ideas with transitions. Transitions are links that help the reader follow thoughts. One very useful transition in any literary analysis begins with the phrase *For example.* You can use this transition phrase to introduce evidence from the text or to connect a detail to a main idea.

Analyzing a Workshop Model

Here is a final draft of an essay that takes a historical approach to literary criticism. Read the essay and answer the questions in the margin. Use the answers to these questions to guide you as you write.

Lullaby

Tone

What is the author's tone? Give examples of choices the writer makes to create the tone.

The short story "Lullaby" by Leslie Marmon Silko, is about Ayah, an aging Navajo woman who waits for, looks for, and finally takes care of her husband, Chato. While she waits for and then searches for Chato, Ayah reflects on her memories, both happy and painful. She remembers her childhood and her children. She recalls how one child died and two were taken from her because they had tuberculosis. She thinks about the difficulties and indignities that her husband, Chato endured while working for the white men. In "Lullaby" Silko conveys aspects of Navajo culture—a deep connection with nature, strong ties to family, reliance on tradition—and demonstrates how these cultural elements affect Ayah. Silko reflects Navajo culture in her story through unusual similes and through beautifully crafted descriptions.

Thesis

What is the thesis? How is it related to history?

For example, in the story's first sentence, Silko uses a simile to show how Ayah sees the world symbolically through the tradition of weaving: "the snow in the wind gave off its own light. It came in thick tufts like new wool—washed before the weaver spins it."

Evidence

What main idea does this evidence support? How does the evidence relate to the thesis of the paper?

Silko then uses description to show how the tradition of weaving is handed down from one generation to the next. Ayah thinks "about the weaving and the way her mother [did] it. . . . She could see it clearly. She had been only a little girl. . . . And while she combed the wool, her grandma sat beside her, spinning, . . . her mother worked at the loom. . . . " These lines show that strong family ties are important to Ayah. She comforts herself with pleasant family memories such as this when she does not want to think about more painful memories, such as those of her dead son, Jimmie.

Historical Focus

How does this analysis shed light on a time or place?

Additional Support

Skills Practice

WRITING: Organization Point out that an effective introduction grabs readers' attention and makes them want to continue reading. In literary criticism, an effective introduction also states the thesis—the author's main idea. A lively quotation, a well-chosen anecdote, or a thought-provoking question can engage readers in an introduction. Ask students to write two alternative introductions for their literary criticisms and to consult with their peers about which is more effective. `OL`

Details about the natural world provide insights into Ayah's life. For example, the yarn for weaving is dyed in "boiling black pots full of beeweed petals, juniper berries, and sage." This detail is followed by a beautiful, haunting simile: "The blankets her mother made were soft and woven so tight that rain rolled off them like birds' feathers."

The vivid details that Silko uses to describe Ayah's memories reflect Ayah's connection to nature and tradition. Ayah remembers the "high buckskin leggings that they wrapped over their elkhide moccasins" when she was young. She recalls how she walked "a step behind her mother" when they "walked to the old stone hogan together" when Ayah was ready to give birth. In her house, strips of venison are hung up to dry.

Later, Silko uses a graphic simile to illustrate Ayah's past fears of what the English-speaking doctors would do to her children: "She was frightened by the way they looked at the children, like the lizard watches the fly." Seeking comfort, Ayah fled with her children into nature, into the "foothills of juniper trees and black lava rock" where "the sun warmth relaxed her and took the fear and anger away."

Through description, the author also shows the reader how Ayah and her family face the challenges and consequences of generations of poverty. Their cows are "skinny." Their house is a "boxcar shack." Ayah grew up in an "old hogan with a dirt roof and rock walls." They live in an area of "dry sandy arroyos where sparse grass grew."

At the end of the story, Ayah sings Chato a traditional lullaby that likens earth, sky, rainbow, and wind to mother, father, sister, and brother. Thus, Silko's ending reinforces her use of beautiful descriptive and figurative language to reflect the deep connection with nature, family, and tradition that characterizes Navajo culture. Despite the many deep troubles that Ayah has endured, she—like many Navajo—is able to take comfort in her cultural heritage and to derive strength from it.

Monument Valley at Sunset. Robert McIntosh.

Exposition

Main Idea/Details

What is main idea of this paragraph? How do the details explain and support it?

Consistent Focus

Explain how the essay has a consistent focus so far.

Transitions

List three transitions that the author has used so far to link ideas, sentences, or paragraphs.

Organization

How does the organization of the essay help you follow the main ideas?

Conclusion

How does this essay end? Why is this an effective conclusion?

Writing Workshop

Literary Criticism

Teach

Writing Skills

Main Idea/Details Answer:
The main idea is that the natural world provides insights into the woman that Ayah became. The detail about natural dyes confirms that those who live close to nature depend on it. **OL**

Writing Skills

Consistent Focus Answer:
The details throughout the essay show Ayah's connection to nature and ancient traditions. **OL**

Writing Skills

Transitions Answer: For example, then, *and* later **OL**

Writing Skills

Organization Answer:
The essay is organized chronologically: from Ayah's early life close to nature to her moving away from it into the modern world. **OL**

Writing Skills

Conclusion Answer:
Restatement of the original thesis shows that Ayah's life even now is connected to history and her early traditions. **OL**

Differentiated Instruction

Conclusion Point out that this model essay has an effective conclusion. It ties all the threads of the literary analysis together and draws the essay to a close. The second sentence of the concluding paragraph also restates the thesis in a new and interesting way. Finally, the conclusion leaves the reader with a thought-provoking idea: "she—like many Navajo—is able to take comfort in her cultural heritage." Ask students to brainstorm to create a list of dos and don'ts for a conclusion. Have them apply these pointers to their own writing. **BL**

Objectives
- To present and support a thesis (SE)
- To identify supporting evidence for a thesis (TWE)
- To write an effective introduction (TWE)

Teach

Writing Process

Revising Remind students that asking these questions both before and after they write will help them write a more thorough analysis. **OL**

Writing Process

Editing and Proofreading

After students edit and proofread their own work, have them trade papers with a partner. Partners should check each other's writing for errors in grammar, punctuation, and mechanics. Have students prepare a checklist for this purpose. **OL**

Traits of Strong Writing

Ideas message or theme and the details that develop it

Organization arrangement of main ideas and supporting details

Voice writer's unique way of using tone and style

Word Choice vocabulary a writer uses to convey meaning

Sentence Fluency rhythm and flow of sentences

Conventions correct spelling, grammar, usage, and mechanics

Presentation the way words and design elements look on a page

For more information on using the Traits of Strong Writing, see pages R33–R34 of the Writing Handbook.

Revising

Peer Review Ask a classmate to read your draft to identify your thesis and the main ideas that support it. Ask your reviewer to review the traits of strong writing too; then think about how they apply to your work. Use any comments to guide you as you revise.

Use the rubric below to help you evaluate your writing.

Rubric: Writing Effective Literary Criticism

- ☑ Do you show how a work is related to a time, a place, a culture, or a life?
- ☑ Do you present a clear thesis?
- ☑ Do you maintain a consistent focus and tone?
- ☑ Do you present a clear introduction, body, and conclusion?
- ☑ Do your body paragraphs present main ideas and evidence?
- ☑ Do you link ideas with transitions?

▶ **Focus Lesson**

Varying Sentence Openers

Avoid beginning consecutive sentences with *it, the,* or a noun or pronoun. Instead, vary your openers. You can begin with a descriptive word (such as *suddenly* or *inside*); a phrase (such as *in the shadows* or *having seen enough*); or a clause (such as *when the man spoke* or *because it was Saturday*).

Draft:

Silko uses a graphic simile to illustrate Ayah's past fears of what the English-speaking doctors would do to her children: "She was frightened by the way they looked at the children, like the lizard watches the fly." Ayah fled with her children in to the comfort of nature, into the "foothills of juniper trees and black lava rock" where "the sun warmth relaxed her and took the fear and anger away."

Revision:

Later,[1] Silko uses a graphic simile to illustrate Ayah's past fears of what the English-speaking doctors would do to her children: "She was frightened by the way they looked at the children, like the lizard watches the fly." Seeking comfort,[2] Ayah fled with her children into nature, into the "foothills of juniper trees and black lava rock" where "the sun warmth relaxed her and took the fear and anger away."

1: Opens with a Descriptive Word   2: Opens with a Phrase

Additional Support

Skills Practice

READING: Recognizing Figurative Language The essay refers to Silko's use of figurative language. Help students to recognize language that is not literal. Give examples of familiar idioms that express a truth beyond the literal level (for example, "catch one's eye"). **OL**

Then have students practice using figurative language by creating their own idioms. **AL**

Editing and Proofreading

Get It Right When you have completed the final draft of your story, proofread it for errors in grammar, usage, mechanics, and spelling. Refer to the Language Handbook, pages R46–R60, as a guide.

► **Focus Lesson**

Correcting Run-on Sentences

Be sure that all the sentences in your essay are complete. Avoid run-on sentences, which present two or more independent clauses (groups of words that could stand alone as sentences) without the correct punctuation. Below is an example of a problem with run-on sentences and possible solutions from the Workshop Model.

Problem: The following is a run-on sentence.

Their cows are "skinny," their house is a "boxcar shack."

Solution A: Create two sentences.

Their cows are "skinny." Their house is a "boxcar shack."

Solution B: Use a semicolon to separate the two independent clauses.

Their cows are "skinny"; their house is a "boxcar shack."

Solution C: Use a comma and a coordinating conjunction to join the independent clauses.

Their cows are "skinny," and their house is a "boxcar shack."

Tense Consistency

Did you remember to write about literature in the present tense? Did you maintain a consistent use of the present tense wherever it made sense? Check for verb tense as a separate proofreading step.

Reading Aloud

Ask a classmate or a family member to read your essay aloud to you. If the reader stumbles anywhere, you may have left out a word, made a typographical error, or created another problem that should be remedied.

Presenting

Following Conventional Style Do not strive to give your analysis an original or creative look. Instead, be sure to follow the guidelines your teacher sets for page formats, fonts, and spacing. Also eliminate underlining and exclamation marks used only for emphasis. Your words, not your formatting, should create all the emphasis you need.

Writer's Portfolio

Place a copy of your literary criticism in your portfolio to review later.

Writing Workshop

Literary Criticism

Teach

Writing Process

Presenting Encourage students to view their finished work as publishable. They may present their analyses in different ways. A student who wishes to make a copy for the library or for class circulation, for instance, might select a cover that is both suited to the topic and likely to attract readers. Illustrations in an analysis related to Navajo culture could feature colors, patterns, or symbols associated with the Southwest. On the back of the booklet might be a brief synopsis of the work or bulleted questions on the topic to arouse interest.
Suggest that students do library or online research to gather information about their subjects. **OL**

Differentiated Instruction

Peer Review For students who need the most help in writing, increase opportunities for peer review. Students benefit from the feedback of readers telling them what they understood, saying what parts they liked most and least, and offering suggestions for improvement. **BL**

English Language Coach

Grammar Provide extra grammar practice in students' areas of highest need. Refer them to online grammar practice Web sites and skills exercises in textbooks. Also encourage them to practice points of English usage through e-mail and messaging. **EL**

Objectives

- To write literary criticism that analyses the way in which a work is related to an individual life or its historical period (SE)
- To present and support a thesis (SE)
- To recognize figurative language (TWE)

Focus

Summary

In this workshop, students will learn techniques for planning and rehearsing an oral literary criticism and presenting it to the class.

Teach

Speaking Skills

Using Visual Aids Give students time to rehearse their presentations with their visual aids so that they become confident about incorporating the visual elements into their speeches. Students should test computer slides or overhead transparencies ahead of time. **OL**

Speaking Skills

Avoiding Stage Fright Help students ease nervousness about speaking in front of the class by providing the following tips:

- Be well prepared and familiar with your content.
- Have note cards as reminders.
- Imagine yourself speaking to supportive friends.
- Take your time and make eye contact. **OL**

Think Big

In an oral presentation, your main points are most important. As you turn your writing into an oral presentation, streamline your essay by eliminating any unnecessary details and emphasizing the main ideas.

Give Verbal Cues

Listeners sometimes have a harder time following ideas than readers do. To help your readers follow your organization, use signal words and phrases such as *my thesis is* and *in conclusion*.

Speaking, Listening, and Viewing Workshop

Literary Criticism

Delivering an Oral Report

Connecting to Literature Leslie Marmon Silko, the author of "Lullaby," was reared in a culture in which all knowledge was once passed along orally. In this culture, she says, "All information, scientific, technological, historical, religious, is put into narrative form. It is easier to remember that way." In this workshop, you will deliver your literary criticism, as an oral report, to an audience of listeners.

> **Assignment** Adapt your literary criticism to create an oral report and present it to the class.

Planning Your Presentation

Your goal is to present your literary criticism in an interesting and informative way. Follow these guidelines to plan your presentation.

- Focus on your thesis. This is the most important idea in your presentation: be sure that you make it clear. Plan to state it and to restate it.
- Create a clear and engaging introduction that includes your thesis, a body that presents your main ideas, and a conclusion that restates or summarizes your most important points.
- Support each main idea you present with details from the literature. Add your own explanations to link those details to your thesis.

Getting Started

- Work with a classmate to identify main ideas in your literary criticism. Discuss which details belong in your presentation and which can be omitted.
- Discuss ways to make the introduction and the conclusion more interesting or lively for listeners.
- Work alone to create an outline or other plan for your presentation.

Additional Support

Skills Practice

VOCABULARY: Transitions Remind students of the importance of transitions in a speech to help listeners identify the main points. Have the class brainstorm effective transitional words, such as *first, second, more important,* and *in conclu-* *sion.* Tell students to make sure that they include transitions in their speeches to signal new ideas or the connections between ideas. Advise them to circle the transitions in their speeches. **OL**

Creating Slides or Posters

What kinds of visual aids will help your listeners follow your presentation? The most effective thing you can do is create slides on the computer or posters that present or telegraph your thesis and main points. An alternative is to create overhead transparencies or posters. Whatever you create, they should be easy to view, created in the same readable font or handwriting, and spaced for maximum legibility. Notice how the slides below match; notice, too, how easy they are to read.

<table>
<tr>
<td>

The tradition of weaving is handed down.

Descriptive details and story evidence

- "she combed the wool"
- "her grandma sat beside her spinning"

</td>
<td>

Ayah is connected to nature and tradition.

- "their elk hide moccasins"
- hanging up strips of venison to dry

</td>
</tr>
</table>

Rehearsing

Rehearse your presentation several times by yourself, making sure that your words and your graphic aids are working together perfectly. Then try making your complete presentation in front of a family member or a classmate. Ask for comments, as well as for any questions your listener might have. This will help you anticipate questions your audience might ask later.

Finally, keep these verbal and nonverbal techniques in mind.

Techniques for Delivering a Presentation

Verbal Techniques	Nonverbal Techniques
☑ **Volume** Speak loudly enough that everyone can hear you.	☑ **Display** Be sure that your audience can see your slides or posters. Consider using an easel for posters.
☑ **Repetition** Some repetition is fine in an oral report. For example, you might remind your listeners of your thesis as you state each main point.	☑ **Eye Contact** As you point out your posters or slides, look at them. As you make other points, look at your audience.
☑ **Tone** This is a formal presentation, so your tone should be consistently formal.	☑ **Gestures** Use natural hand gestures as you speak. Do your best to avoid nervous fidgeting.
☑ **Pronunciation** Speak each word clearly.	☑ **Posture** Stand up straight and hold your head up.

Make Visual Connections

Be sure that your visuals and your oral presentation work together. As you deliver your thesis and your main points, point to them on your visuals.

Use Visuals to Convey Importance

Present main ideas in type or writing that is bigger or bolder than you use for supporting details. Present the big ideas first and list the details below. You can also indent supporting details.

Be a Listener Too

Volunteer to listen to and evaluate a classmate's presentation. Draw conclusions, for your own use, about what makes a presentation effective or ineffective.

OBJECTIVES
- Share your literary criticism in an oral presentation.
- Use visuals, electronic media, or both to enhance the oral presentation.

Speaking, Listening, and Viewing Workshop

Literary Criticism

Teach

Viewing Skills

Viewing Visual Aids Remind students to pay special attention to the ideas presented on slides, posters, or overhead sheets, as these are usually key points in an oral presentation. At the same time, advise students to keep in mind how the visual elements relate to what a presenter is saying. **OL**

Listening Skills

Note Taking Ask students to take notes on other students' presentations. Suggest that they sharpen their listening skills by writing the presenters' theses prominently and listing supporting points underneath. At the same time, ask them to jot down questions they have about each student's ideas. These will come in handy for postpresentation discussion. **OL**

English Language Coach

Speaking Practice Have students to practice their speeches for you ahead of time, outside class. Coach students on pronunciations of words they hesitate over and suggest that they mark these pronunciations on their note cards. **EL**

Differentiated Instruction

Visual Cues Advise readers to use highlighters to mark up their written speeches, indicating main points and words to emphasize. Encourage them to use these visual cues as reminders of what to stress as they repeatedly rehearse their speech. **BL**

Objectives
- To share literary criticism in an oral presentation (SE)
- To use visual aids, electronic media, or both to enhance the oral presentation (SE)
- To use transitions effectively (TWE)
- To take notes on an oral presentation (TWE)

Focus

Summary

The purpose of this feature is to interest students in reading additional short stories by writers represented in this unit or about the Big Ideas of this unit: Encountering the Unexpected, Making Choices, and Life Transitions. The diversity and history of the short story are represented by this sampling of grade-appropriate short story anthologies.

Teach

Additional Support

Short Stories and Novels

In only a few pages, short stories do it all: they introduce characters, setting, and the first events of the plot; they build up tension or suspense and rise to a climax; they develop characters; they present a theme; and they deliver a satisfying ending. For more short stories with a variety of themes, try the first three suggestions below. For novels that incorporate the Big Ideas of encountering the unexpected, making choices, and life transitions, try the titles from the Glencoe Literature Library on the next page.

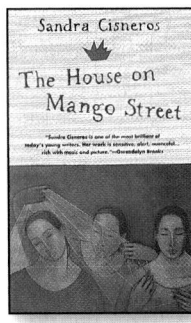

The House on Mango Street

by Sandra Cisneros ★

This collection of related short stories details the life of Esperanza, a Mexican American girl. Like Sandra Cisneros, who often uses her life experiences as subjects in both her fiction and nonfiction, Esperanza Cordero lives in a Spanish-speaking community in Chicago. Esperanza's hopes, joys, and fears are explored in a series of short vignettes, each of which focuses on a seemingly minor incident, such as an interaction with a mean boy or a troubling episode at school. The stories in *The House on Mango Street* can stand individually, or the book can be read as a novel.

Calling the Wind: Twentieth Century African-American Short Stories

edited by Clarence Major

This collection of fifty-nine short stories begins with a tale written by Charles Chestnutt in 1899 and ends with Terry McMillan's short story, "Quilting on the Rebound," written in 1991. In between are stories by some of the greatest authors of the twentieth century, including Richard Wright, Ralph Ellison, Langston Hughes, James Baldwin, Ernest Gaines, Toni Morrison, and Jamaica Kincaid. About two-thirds of the collection is devoted to stories written after 1962. In his introduction, Major explains that the collection sets out, among other things, to deny readers the chance for racial stereotyping. "To gather a group of stories that offer a wide range of workable metaphors for the ways we live" is just one of Major's purposes for the anthology.

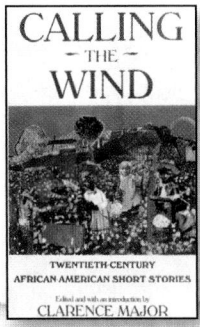

Skills Practice

READING: Literary Response The editor of *Calling the Wind* promises "a wide range of metaphors for the way we live." Remind students that a metaphor is an implied comparison between two or more things. **Ask:** How can a story be a metaphor for a way of living? *(A story can provide a vivid and colorful way of understanding everyday life.)* Encourage students to respond to what they read and to the way in which stories provide "metaphors" for their own lives. Encourage students to keep journals of their responses to their independent reading. **OL**

CRITICS' CORNER

"Poe assumed in his tales one crucial condition: every mind is either half-mad or capable of slipping easily into madness. He was not so much concerned with precisely what madness was but with the conditions and stages whereby madness came to exist and evidenced itself in otherwise average, commonplace human beings."

—Edward H. Davidson, *Selected Writings of Edgar Allan Poe*

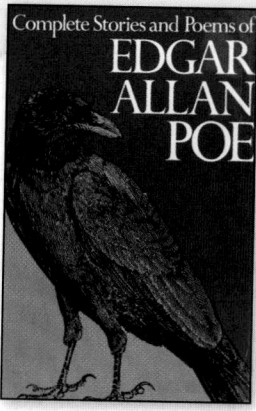

Complete Stories and Poems of Edgar Allan Poe ★

by Edgar Allan Poe

For more thrilling tales from one of the earliest and greatest masters of horror and suspense, try this collection of his complete works. Popular tales include "The Tell-Tale Heart," the story of a heart that goes on beating after death, as well as "The Murders in the Rue Morgue," a forerunner of the detective story genre. For a trip through an underground cemetery and the horrors of being buried alive, read "The Cask of Amontillado." For a journey into the world's most famous haunted house, open to "The Fall of the House of Usher."

From the Glencoe Literature Library

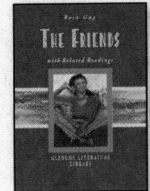

The Friends

by Rosa Guy

Encountering the Unexpected, the main character tries to understand the problems that develop between her and her best friend.

Nectar in a Sieve

by Kamala Markandaya

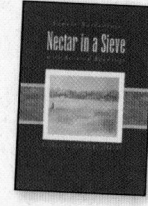

The process of *Making Choices* to adapt to life's ordeals are recorded through the eyes of a woman from a small village in India.

My Ántonia

by Willa Cather

A novel about the struggles and rewards and *Life Transitions* of pioneer life on the Great Plains in the nineteenth century.

Teach

★ Literary History

Anthologies Say: Anthologies, collections of writings by various authors, have been important in literary history. *Anthology* comes from a Greek word meaning "a gathering of flowers." One of the historical purposes of creating anthologies is to introduce writers to the public. A famous early anthology known as the Greek Anthology contains thousands of Greek poems written between the sixth century B.C. and the tenth century A.D. The Bible is considered an anthology because it contains various authors' writings. **AS**

Glencoe Literature Library

Glencoe Literature Library offers an extensive collection of hardcover books that help you encourage your students to read independently. Choose among the more than 120 full-length literary works—novels, novellas, plays, and nonfiction. Each book includes related readings from a broad range of genres. Go to www.Glencoe.com for more information.

Objectives
- To encourage independent reading of short stories and novels (SE)
- To recognize a historical perspective for literary anthologies (TWE)
- To encourage literary response to independent reading (TWE)

Reading in the Real World

Reading Across Texts and Cultures
Emphasize the importance of reading widely to integrate ideas from different sources. A range of classical and contemporary texts, along with a scope of many cultures, brings valuable new understanding of the world. **Ask:** What are some differences in the fiction of world cultures?

What common elements appear in fiction from different world cultures? *(Cultures have different worldviews and characteristics but common themes about human nature.)* Urge students to read widely, drawing on the literature of many world cultures and many times in history. **AS**

Test Preparation and Practice

Focus

BELLRINGER

Say: The best way to succeed on a test is to prepare. Being prepared means not only being familiar with the subject matter but also mastering an arsenal of effective test-taking strategies. Have students brainstorm effective strategies for test taking and invite them to share their most successful tips.

Teach

Assessment Explain to students that this Test Preparation and Practice lesson is designed to develop test-taking strategies as well as to test their mastery of the skills and vocabulary covered in this unit. Students will read two fiction selections and answer context, comprehension, and inference questions. Then they will complete ten vocabulary sentences and answer ten paragraph-improvement questions. Finally they will write a short essay. **OL**

Reading: Fiction

Carefully read the following passages. Use context clues to help you define any words with which you are unfamiliar. Pay close attention to story elements such as theme, voice, and tone. Then, on a separate sheet of paper, answer the questions on page 304.

from "When the Buffalo Climbed a Tree" by Mark Twain

line

"Your *saddle*? Did you take your saddle up in the tree with you?"

"Take it up in the tree with me? Why, how you talk. Of course I didn't. No man could do that. It fell in the tree when it came down."

"Oh—exactly."

5 "Certainly. I unwound the lariat, and fastened one end of it to the limb. It was the very best green raw-hide, and capable of sustaining tons. I made a slip-noose in the other end, and then hung it down to see the length. It reached down twenty-two feet—half way to the ground. I then loaded every barrel of the Allen with a double charge. I felt satisfied. I said to myself, if he never thinks of that one thing that I dread, all right—but if he does, all right anyhow—I am fixed for him. But don't you know

10 that the very thing a man dreads is the thing that always happens? Indeed it is so. I watched the bull, now, with anxiety—anxiety which no one can conceive of who has not been in such a situation and felt that at any moment death might come. Presently a thought came into the bull's eye. I knew it! Said I—if my nerve fails now, I am lost. Sure enough, it was just as I had dreaded, he started in to climb the tree—

15 "What, the bull?"

"Of course—who else?"

"But a bull can't climb a tree."

He can't, can't he? Since you know so much about it, did you ever see a bull try?"

"No! I never dreamt of such a thing."

20 "Well, then, what is the use of your talking that way, then? Because you never saw a thing done, is that any reason why it can't be done?"

"Well, all right—go on. What did you do?"

"The bull started up, and got along well for about ten feet, then slipped and slid back. I breathed easier. He tried it again—got up a little higher—slipped again. But he came at it once more, and this

25 time he was careful. He got gradually higher and higher, and my spirits went down more and more. Up he came—an inch at a time—with his eyes hot, and his tongue hanging out. Higher and higher—hitched his foot over the stump of a limb, and looked up, as much as to say, 'You are my meat, friend.' Up again—higher and higher, and getting more excited the closer he got. He was within ten

Additional Support

Skills Practice

READING: Visualizing Advise students that before they take a test on a piece of fiction, they must make sure they understand it. Explain that a good way to comprehend the Mark Twain excerpt is to visualize it. Guide students to visualize the way the rope supposedly hangs from the tree, for example. Tell students that when they visualize, they should create a picture in their mind's eye. **Say:** Visualizing is one of the best ways to comprehend information in fiction. **OL**

feet of me! I took a long breath,—and then said I, 'It is now or never.' I had the coil of the lariat all
30 ready; I paid it out slowly, till it hung right over his head; all of a sudden I let go of the slack, and the
slip-noose fell fairly round his neck! Quicker than lightning I out with the Allen and let him have it in
the face. It was an awful roar, and must have scared the bull out of his senses. When the smoke
cleared away, there he was dangling in the air, twenty foot from the ground, and going out of one
convulsion into another faster than you could count! I didn't stop to count, anyhow I shinned down
35 the tree and shot for home."

"Bemis, is all that true, just as you have stated it?"

"I wish I may rot in my tracks and die the death of a dog if it isn't."

"The Unicorn in the Garden" by James Thurber

line
Once upon a sunny morning a man who sat in a breakfast nook looked up from his scrambled
eggs to see a white unicorn with a golden horn quietly cropping the rose in the garden. The man
went up to the bedroom where his wife was still asleep and woke her. "There's a unicorn in the
garden," he said. "Eating roses." She opened one unfriendly eye and looked at him. "The unicorn is a
5 mythical beast," she said, and turned her back on him. The man walked slowly downstairs and out
into the garden. The unicorn was still there; he was now browsing among the tulips. "Here, unicorn,"
said the man, and pulled up a lily and gave it to him. The unicorn ate it gravely. With a high heart,
because there was a unicorn in his garden, the man went upstairs and roused his wife again. "The
unicorn," he said, "ate a lily." His wife sat up in bed and looked at him, coldly. "You are a booby," she
10 said, "and I am going to have you put in the booby-hatch." The man, who had never liked the words
"booby" and "booby-hatch," and who liked them even less on a shining morning when there was a
unicorn in the garden, thought for a moment. "We'll see about that," he said. He walked over to the
door. "He has a golden horn in the middle of his forehead," he told her. Then he went back to the
garden to watch the unicorn; but the unicorn had gone away. The man sat among the roses and went
15 to sleep.
And as soon as the husband had gone out of the house, the wife got up and dressed as fast as
she could. She was very excited and there was a gloat in her eye. She telephoned the police and she
telephoned the psychiatrist; she told them to hurry to her house and bring a strait-jacket. When the
police and the psychiatrist arrived, they sat down in chairs and looked at her, with great interest. "My
20 husband," she said, "saw a unicorn this morning." The police looked at the psychiatrist and the
psychiatrist looked at the police. "He told me it ate a lily," she said. The psychiatrist looked at the
police and the police looked at the psychiatrist. "He told me it had a golden horn in the middle of its
forehead," she said. At a solemn signal from the psychiatrist, the police leaped from their chairs and
seized the wife. They had a hard time subduing her, for she put up a terrific struggle, but they finally
25 subdued her. Just as they got her into the strait-jacket, the husband came into the house.
"Did you tell your wife you saw a unicorn?" asked the police. "Of course not," said the husband.
"The unicorn is a mythical beast." "That's all I wanted to know," said the psychiatrist. "Take her away.
I'm sorry sir, but your wife is as crazy as a jay bird." So they took her away, cursing and screaming, and
shut her up in an institution. The husband lived happily ever after.
30 *Moral: don't count your boobies until they are hatched.*

Teach

R Reading Strategy

Verb Tenses Draw students' attention to the mixture of past and present tenses in "The Unicorn in the Garden." **Say:** James Thurber's verbs in this story are not really inconsistent, even though both the present tense and the past tense appear throughout. Why do you think that this is so? *(The story as a whole is told in the past tense, but the ongoing dialogue within the story is in the present tense.)* Explain that certain combinations of verb tenses are compatible, or work correctly together: the past and past perfect tenses, for example, or present and present perfect tenses. **OL**

Differentiated Instruction

Taking Notes Encourage less proficient readers to take notes on the passages they read for a test. One good technique is to outline or "map" a passage, noting the main points and sequence of events. Then, when questions are asked about a specific topic, the student will know where to look. **BL**

English Language Coach

Vocabulary English language learners may be unfamiliar with Twain's Western terms: *lariat* (rope), *raw-hide* (untanned cattle hide), *slip-noose* (rope loop tied so it tightens when pulled), *Allen* (type of gun), *double-charge* (amount of gunpowder), and *shinned* (climbed). Before students begin the test, explain them. **EL**

Objectives
- To draw inferences (SE)
- To analyze fiction (SE)
- To practice visualizing (TWE)
- To develop test-taking strategies (TWE)

Assess

1. **B** is the correct answer. Bemis is clearly relating the story of a recent event, although it is humorous and not entirely true.

2. **D** is the correct answer. Bemis states that the lariat extended halfway down.

3. **C** is the correct answer. The listener interrupts Bemis several times to point out the fantastic nature of the story.

4. **A** is the correct answer. Bemis tells his story with apparent sincerity. Nothing suggests that he is joking. *Experience* and *calmness* are only partly relevant to the question.

5. **C** is the correct answer. The story is a discussion between Bemis and his listener.

6. **B** is the correct answer. The listener's reaction and common sense make clear that Bemis is stretching the truth.

7. **D** is the correct answer. The other answers could all apply, but the designation *tall tale* best characterizes the story.

8. **B** is the correct answer. Both options **A** and **B** relate to tone, but the humor in the tale makes *comic* the correct choice.

Literature Online

Unit Assessment Have students access the Web site to prepare for the Unit 1 test.

Items 1–7 apply to "When the Buffalo Climbed a Tree"

1. Which best describes the setting of Twain's story?
   A Bemis is sitting in a tree.
   B Bemis is relating a recent event.
   C Bemis is telling a joke.
   D Bemis is lying to his friend.

2. How far down did the lariat hang?
   A twenty feet
   B thirty feet
   C to the ground
   D halfway to the ground

3. Which of the following best describes the mood of the listener in Twain's story?
   A jealous
   B deceived
   C doubtful
   D sincere

4. In what manner does Bemis tell his story?
   A with certainty
   B with humor
   C with experience
   D with calmness

5. How many voices appear in Twain's story?
   A three—Bemis's, his listener's, the bull's
   B one—Bemis's
   C two—Bemis's and his listener's
   D one—the narrator's

6. How would you best describe the character of Bemis in the selection by Twain?
   A He is untrustworthy.
   B He is given to exaggeration.
   C He is believable.
   D He is truthful.

7. Which best describes the selection by Twain?
   A narration
   B fiction
   C drama
   D a tall tale

Items 8–14 apply to "The Unicorn in the Garden"

8. Which best describes the tone of Thurber's story?
   A tragic
   B comic
   C mythical
   D fictional

9. How many voices appear in Thurber's story?
   A one—the husband's
   B one—the wife's
   C four—the husband's, the wife's, the unicorn's, and the psychiatrist's
   D four—the husband's, the wife's, the police officer's, and the psychiatrist's

10. How many times does the husband go upstairs to tell his wife about the unicorn?
    A twice
    B once
    C three times
    D none

11. What does the word *gloat*, in line 17, suggest about the wife's character?
    A Locking her husband up would please her.
    B Unicorns excite her too.
    C She cannot understand her husband.
    D Confrontations between the two are common.

12. From the ending, what do you conclude that the husband, in line 12, is thinking about?
    A He decides to return to watch the unicorn.
    B He becomes intent on proving his sanity.
    C He plans to turn the tables on his wife.
    D He is determined to ignore his wife.

13. Irony relates to a difference between what is expected and what occurs. Which of the following situations in Thurber's story is ironic?
    A There was a unicorn in the garden.
    B The wife, not the husband, is insane.
    C The wife is committed to an institution.
    D The authorities believe the husband.

14. What does the moral of the story mean?
    A Humor makes things more interesting.
    B Outcomes are often unexpected.
    C A husband is always in control.
    D Life is ironic and confusing.

9. **D** is the correct answer. These four characters in the story speak at least once.

10. **A** is the correct answer. We learn that he went upstairs "again" and no more.

11. **A** is the correct answer. The wife clearly enjoys tormenting her husband.

12. **C** is the correct answer. The husband remarks, "We'll see about that"; later he denies having seen the unicorn.

13. **C** is the correct answer. The irony is that the wife, not the husband, is locked up.

14. **B** is the correct answer. No other option literally interprets the figurative moral.

Vocabulary Skills: Sentence Completion

For each question, choose the word or words that best complete the sentence.

1. The courtroom anxiously awaited the jury's _____ verdict after hours of deliberation.
  A imminent
  B dire
  C cautious
  D self-possessed

2. The mayor, as a(n) _____ elected official, worked comfortably with the support of the entire community.
  A impeccably
  B vaguely
  C duly
  D amiably

3. Rosa Parks, a famous civil rights figure, carried herself with strength and determination, and this _____ served as a model of courage for others.
  A infirmity
  B equanimity
  C vulnerability
  D fortitude

4. Unlike those who followed him, George Washington had no _____ when he was elected the first president.
  A doctrine
  B predecessor
  C obscurity
  D prodigy

5. Hiking alongside the _____ ensured that the traveler would always have water in this desert area.
  A solace
  B derision
  C arroyo
  D moor

Literature Online **Unit Assessment** To prepare for the Unit test, go to www.glencoe.com.

6. The mountains presented a _____ barrier to a disabled hiker.
  A convoluted
  B decrepit
  C imperceptible
  D formidable

7. The couple believed that counseling could only _____ their already-close relationship.
  A eradicate
  B assuage
  C contend
  D enhance

8. The principal had a _____ quality that conveyed dignity and calm.
  A sedate
  B furtive
  C droll
  D wanton

9. The crisis demanded swift attention, so the bystander _____ passersby for help.
  A ascertained
  B implored
  C harassed
  D oppressed

10. Investors who watch the stock market with _____ fear that their investments will not do well.
  A credulity
  B infirmity
  C pandemonium
  D presentiments

Differentiated Instruction

Synonyms Point out that occasionally synonyms used in context can provide clues to the meaning of unfamiliar words. Examples are item 3, where *strength* is a synonym of *fortitude*, and item 8, where *calm* is a synonym of *sedate*. Provide similar sentences for practice. **BL**

English Language Coach

Sound-Alike Words English language learners may confuse words that sound alike. For example, *imminent* may be confused with *eminent*. Help students to distinguish between sound-alike words with different meanings, such as *effect/affect, officious/official, equanimity/equality.* **EL**

Assess

1. **A** is the correct answer. The context suggests an immediate verdict.

2. **C** is the correct answer. The words *comfortably* and *support* lend credibility to the mayor's having been rightfully elected.

3. **D** is the correct answer. The key words *strength* and *determination* convey the meaning of bravery.

4. **B** is the correct answer. Washington, as the first U.S. president, could have had no predecessor.

5. **C** is the correct answer. A moor is not a "desert area." Neither of the other options makes sense here.

6. **D** is the correct answer. Option **A** is beside the point. Option **B** makes no sense. Option **C** conveys a meaning opposite to that intended.

7. **D** is the correct answer. To "eradicate" or "assuage" an "already-close" relationship would be illogical. Option **C** makes no sense.

8. **A** is the correct answer. *Furtive, droll,* and *wanton* would all be out of place in a dignified personality.

9. **B** is the correct answer. No other option makes sense.

10. **D** is the correct answer. Only option **D** conveys anxiety and uncertainty, the main impressions created.

305

Assess

1. **D** is the correct answer. There are no punctuation errors in the sentence.

2. **B** is the correct answer. Two independent clauses are separated by a comma.

3. **D** is the correct answer. Options **A** and **C** contain grammatical errors. Option **B** is verbose and unclear.

Grammar and Writing Skills: Paragraph Improvement

Read carefully through the following draft of a student's essay. Pay close attention to word choice, content, and grammar, especially run-on and comma-splice errors. Also watch verb tense and punctuation. Then, on a separate sheet of paper, answer the questions on pages 306–307.

(1) *Mark Twain, a great humorist of the American nineteenth century, is widely recognized as one of the greatest American writers.* (2) *His stories are often humorous, the serious side of them makes them more interesting.* (3) *He sometimes used darker humor, relying on satire and irony to make his points.* (4) *Often critical about human nature.*

(5) *His most famous novel The Adventures of Huckleberry Finn condemn the ethical practices, such as slavery, in the South.* (6) *It is about a boy named Huck and his friend Jim a slave.* (7) *The two are friends during their adventures.*

(8) *When Huck rejects society an important event for the story.* (9) *He is confused between what he's been taught and what he feels for Jim.* (10) *His friend Jim is a slave according to the rules of society.* (11) *As a friend Huck has a problem with that.* (12) *He sees the human side of Jim.*

(13) *Twain tried to make people to look at themselves and change for the better.* (14) *It is ironic that the people he made fun of were among his most devoted readers.* (15) *Twains cynical view of human nature more seen in his later writing.* (16) *He influenced many other writers, like James Thurber, who also went on to become a popular humorist.*

1. Which is the best way to revise sentence 1?
   A Insert a colon after *is*.
   B Delete the comma after *Twain*.
   C Insert a comma after *recognized*.
   D Make no change.

2. Which of the following grammatical errors appears in sentence 2?
   A sentence fragment
   B comma splice
   C misplaced modifier
   D incorrect verb tense

3. Which of the following is the best revision of sentence 2?
   A His stories, which are often humorous, the serious side of them makes them more interesting.
   B Although his stories are often humorous, there is a serious side to them that makes them more interesting.
   C Although his stories, which are often humorous, the serious side of them makes them more interesting.
   D His stories, though often humorous, have a serious side, which makes them more interesting.

Additional Support

Skills Practice

GRAMMAR: Avoiding Comma Splices **Write on the board:** Twain's writing is humorous, Thurber's writing is funny too. Ask students what is wrong with the sentence. Tell them that a comma splice is the incorrect joining of independent clauses (clauses that can stand alone) with only a comma and no conjunction. Point out that a comma splice can be corrected by inserting a conjunction such as *and,* by replacing the comma with a semicolon, or by making two sentences. Show students these corrections and provide additional examples to correct. **OL**

4. Which of the following grammatical errors appears in sentence 4?
  A sentence fragment
  B run-on sentence
  C comma splice (fused sentence)
  D incorrect verb tense

5. Which of the following revisions is the best way to combine sentences 3 and 4?
  A His humor sometimes used satire and irony to make his points, often critical about human nature.
  B He sometimes used a darker humor, using satire and irony to make his points critical about human nature.
  C His humor was sometimes dark, relying on satire and irony to make points often critical of human nature.
  D His humor was sometimes dark relying on satire and irony to make points often critical of human nature.

6. Which of the following is the best revision of sentence 5?
  A His most famous novel, *The Adventures of Huckleberry Finn*, condemns unethical practices, such as slavery, in the South.
  B His most famous novel *The Adventures of Huckleberry Finn* condemns unethical practices, such as slavery, in the South.
  C His most famous *The Adventures of Huckleberry Finn* condemns the ethical practices, such as slavery, in the South.
  D His most famous book, *The Adventures of Huckleberry Finn*, condemns the ethical practices, such as slavery, in the South.

7. Which of the following revisions is the best way to combine sentences 6 and 7?
  A It is about a boy named Huck and his friend Jim, a slave, and about how the two are friends during their adventures.
  B It is about a boy named Huck and his friend Jim a slave, the two become friends during their adventures.
  C It is a story about a boy named Huck and a slave named Jim, who become friends through their adventures.
  D It is a story about a boy named Huck and his friend, a slave, Jim, who become friends through their adventures.

8. Which of the following grammatical errors appears in sentence 8?
  A incorrect verb tense
  B run-on sentence
  C comma splice (fused sentence)
  D sentence fragment

9. Which of the following is the best revision for sentence 15?
  A Twain's view of human nature increased in his later writing.
  B Twain's cynical view of human nature is saw more and more in his later writing.
  C Twain's cynical view of human nature seen more in his later writing.
  D Twain's cynical view of human nature increased in his later writing.

10. Which sentence in the last paragraph is least relevant to the essay as a whole?
  A 13
  B 14
  C 15
  D 16

Essay

Compare and contrast the two stories by Twain and Thurber. Discuss how the use of humor, irony, or satire contributes to the meaning of each story. What effect do these have on the reader? As you write, keep in mind that your essay will be checked for **ideas, organization, voice, word choice, sentence fluency, conventions,** and **presentation.**

Assess

4. **A** is the correct answer. Sentence 4 has neither a subject nor a verb.

5. **C** is the correct answer. In option **A**, humor is said to do what only a writer can. In option **B**, the verb forms *used* and *using* appear redundantly. Option **D** lacks a comma to set off a non-essential phrase.

6. **A** is the correct answer. The book title should be italicized and set off with commas as a nonessential appositive.

7. **C** is the correct answer. Option **A** changes the punctuation but is still verbose. Option **D** is confusing because of the double appositive phrase. Option **B** contains a comma splice.

8. **D** is the correct answer. This "sentence" is only a modifying clause and a subject without a verb. It is, therefore, a sentence fragment.

9. **D** is the correct answer. Options **B** and **C** contain verb-tense errors. Option **A** is grammatically correct, but it lacks an important descriptive element present in the original.

10. **D** is the correct answer. Sentence 16 strays from the main idea in the paragraph by addressing Twain's influence on another writer.

Essay

Students' essays should

- compare and contrast the stories by Twain and Thurber

- discuss the use of humor, irony, and satire, with examples from both texts

- state and support a thesis

Differentiated Instruction

Organization Have writers begin with an outline. Instruct students to list their theses and at least three supporting ideas each. For each idea, have them list at least two supporting details. Tell students that following a logical outline will result in a well-organized essay. **EL**

307

Unit at a Glance
NONFICTION

About the Unit
Unit Two covers nonfiction and analyzes autobiography, biography, memoir, narrative, anecdote, essays, argument, and persuasion.

Unit Introduction
Building Background
2–3 days

Genre Focus: Nonfiction
pp. 310–311

Literary Analysis Model: Robert E. Hemenway, from *Zora Heale Hurston*
pp. 312–313

Writers on Reading
pp. 314–315

Unit Introduction Wrap-Up
p. 316

Part 1: The Power of Memory
7–9 days

Part 1 covers autobiography and biography. A chart showing the core skills taught in this Part appears on pages 317A–317B.

SELECTIONS AND FEATURES

LITERARY FOCUS: Narrative Nonfiction
pp. 318–319

Jeanne Wakatsuki Houston and James D. Houston, from *Farewell to Manzanar*
pp. 320–335

Grammar Workshop: Language Usage
p. 336

Mark Mathabane, from *Kaffir Boy*
pp. 337–352

Maya Angelou, "Living Well. Living Good."
pp. 353–359

Mark Stevens and Annalyn Swan, "First Impressions" from *De Kooning: An American Master*
pp. 360–371

Vocabulary Workshop: Technical Words
p. 372

Frank McCourt, "Typhoid Fever" from *Angela's Ashes*
pp. 373–383

Literary Perspective: Carolyn Hughes, from "Looking Forward to the Past: A Profile of Frank McCourt"
pp. 384–387

Annie Dillard, "Terwilliger Bunts One" from *An American Childhood*
pp. 388–398

Part 2: Quests and Encounters
4–6 days

Part 2 covers personal and expository essays. A chart showing the core skills taught in this Part appears on pages 399A–399B.

SELECTIONS AND FEATURES

LITERARY FOCUS: Expository and Personal Essay
pp. 400–401

Garrison Keillor, "How to Write a Letter"
pp. 402–410

Jewelle L. Gomez, "A Swimming Lesson"
pp. 411–417

Diane Ackerman, "Encounter in the Sea"
pp. 418–428

Lewis Thomas, "The Tucson Zoo"
pp. 429–434

Sandra Cisneros, "Straw into Gold: The Metamorphosis of the Everyday"
pp. 435–442

Part 3: Keeping Freedom Alive
6–8 days

Part 3 covers argument and persuasion. A chart showing the core skills taught in this Part appears on pages 443A–443B.

SELECTIONS AND FEATURES

LITERARY FOCUS: Persuasive Essay and Speech
pp. 444–445

Susan B. Anthony, "On Women's Right to Vote"
pp. 446–451

Martin Luther King Jr. "I've Been to the Mountaintop"
pp. 452–463

Comparing Literature: Different Viewpoints
Chester Brown, "Not Just Comics"
Charles McGrath, "How Cool Is Comics Lit?"
Teresa Méndez, "'Hamlet' too hard? Try a comic book"
Andrew Arnold, "The Graphic Novel Silver Anniversary"
pp. 464–482

Carl Sandburg, "Address on the Anniversary of Lincoln's Birth"
pp. 483–490

TIME magazine: "What I See in Lincoln's Eyes"
pp. 491–493

Toni Morrison, "Cinderella's Stepsisters"
pp. 494–499

End-of-Unit Features
5–6 days

Writing Workshop: Biographical Narrative
p. 500–507

Professional Model: Alice Jackson Baughn, from *Eudora Welty: 1909–2001*
pp. 501–502

Speaking, Listening, and Viewing Workshop: Presenting a Photoessay
pp. 508–509

INDEPENDENT READING
pp. 510–511

Test Preparation and Practice
pp. 512–517

Unit Resources

Glencoe Literature: The Reader's Choice offers a comprehensive package of tools to optimize student learning and the teaching experience. Each resource has been designed to assist students in specific areas and to offer instructional support for teachers. While all of these areas are covered in the core textbook, some students may need extra practice or additional help in specific areas. The resource package is designed so that you, the teacher, can choose which items will best assist your students. You may also use these resources as homework assignments and for assessment purposes. The following are resources recommended for use with Unit Two.

Key for Unit Resource

- 🗁 Blackline Master
- ▯ Workbook
- 📖 Supplemental Text
- 💿 CD-ROM
- 🔒 DVD
- 🖍 Transparency
- 💻 Web-based

Essential Instructional Support

FAST FILE — Unit 2 Resources

Reading and Literature

- Unit Introduction, pp. 1–2
- The Big Idea Foldable, pp. 3–4
- The Big Idea School-Home Connection, p. 5
- The Big Idea School-Home Connection (Spanish), p. 6
- Challenge Planner, pp. 7–10
- Academic Vocabulary Development, pp. 11–13
- Comparing Literature Graphic Organizers, p. 64
- Literary Elements, pp. 17, 21, 24, 27, 30, 34, 40, 43, 46, 49, 52, 58, 61, 65, 68, 72
- Reading Strategies, pp. 18, 22, 25, 28, 31, 33, 35, 41, 44, 47, 50, 53, 59, 62, 66, 69, 71, 73
- Active Reading Graphic Organizers, pp. 78–87
- Selection Vocabulary Practice, pp. 19, 23, 26, 29, 32, 36, 42, 45, 48, 51, 54, 60, 63, 67, 70, 74

Writing, Grammar, and Spelling

- Spelling Practice, p. 75
- Grammar Workshop, p. 20
- Writing Workshop Graphic Organizer, p. 76

Speaking, Listening, and Viewing

- Speaking, Listening, and Viewing Activities, p. 77

English Language Learners

- English Language Coach, pp. 16, 39, 57

Differentiated Instruction

- ▯ Active Learning and Note Taking Guide, pp. 35–69
- 🗁 Leveled Vocabulary Development, pp. 22–37
- 💿 Skill Level Up!™ A Language Arts Game
- 💿 Listening Library Audio CD, disc 1, tracks 26–45
- 💿 Glencoe BookLink 3
- 💿 Vocabulary PuzzleMaker
- 💿 Literature Library Vocabulary PuzzleMaker

ASSESSMENT

- 🗁 Selection and Unit Assessments, Unit Two, pp. 47–82, 211–212
- 🗁 Selection Quick Checks, pp. 24–41
- 🗁 Selection Quick Checks (Spanish), pp. 24–41
- 🗁 Assessment by Learning Objectives, pp. 16–27
- 🗁 Rubrics for Assessing Student Writing, Listening, and Speaking, pp. 8–9, 44–45
- 🗁 Standardized Test Preparation and Practice
- 💻 Glencoe Online Essay Grader
- 💿 Interactive Tutor: Self-Assessment
- 💿 Exam*View*® Assessment Suite
- 💿 Literature Library Exam*View*® Assessment

Additional Instructional Support

Literature and Reading

- Active Learning and Note Taking Guide, pp. 35–69
- *inTIME* Magazines
- Glencoe Literature Library
- Literature Launchers: Pre-Reading Videos
- Literature Classics

Writing, Grammar, and Spelling

- REAL Success in Writing: Research and Reports
- Writing Constructed Responses
- Spelling Power eWorkbook
- Revising with Style eWorkbook
- Sentence Diagraming eWorkbook
- Glencoe Grammar and Composition Handbook
- Grammar and Language Workbook
- Grammar & Language eWorkbook

PROFESSIONAL DEVELOPMENT

- Professional Development Package

Transparencies

- Read Aloud, Think Aloud Transparencies 10–17
- Bellringer Options Transparencies
  - Selection Focus Transparencies 19–25
  - Daily Language Practice Transparencies 26–45
- Grammar and Language Transparencies 12, 19, 43, 52, 69
- Writing Workshop Transparencies 11–15
- Visual Literacy/Fine Art Transparencies

English Language Learner

- English Language Coach, Unit Resources (Fast File)
- *inTIME* Magazines (Spanish)
- Spanish Listening Library

Technology

- TeacherWorks Plus™
- StudentWorks Plus™
- Literature Launchers: Pre-Reading Videos
- Vocabulary PuzzleMaker
- Literature Library Vocabulary PuzzleMaker
- Skill Level Up!™ A Language Arts Game
- glencoe.com
- Presentation Plus!™
- ExamView™ Assessment Suite
- Literature Library ExamView™ Assessment Suite
- Listening Library
- Interactive Tutor: Self-Assessment
- Glencoe BookLink 3
- Online Student Edition, mhln.com
- Glencoe Online Essay Grader
- Grammar and Language eWorkbook
- Revising with Style eWorkbook
- Sentence Diagraming eWorkbook
- Spelling Power eWorkbook
- Literature Classics
- Spanish Listening Library

Additional Glencoe Resources

Dinah Zike's Foldables™

Foldables™ are three-dimensional, interactive graphic organizers that help students practice basic writing skills, review key vocabulary terms, and answer Big Ideas. Every unit contains a Foldable activity. You can find the pattern and directions for the Unit 2 Foldable in the Unit 2 Resources Fast Files booklet. You can use the foldables as they are presented or modify them to suit the needs of your students.

For a wealth of online resources that support the instruction in Unit 2, students and teachers can visit our Web site at glencoe.com. Students will find additional learning, practice, and assessment opportunities such as these, which are noted in the student text:

- Author Search
- Big Idea Overview and Activity
- Interactive Literary Elements Handbook
- Study Central
- Unit Assessment
- Web Activities
- Writing Models

Teachers will find planning and instructional tools that include the following:

- Book Lesson Plans
- Web Activity Lesson Plans
- Teacher Forum
- Professional Resources

    Go to glencoe.com to see the entire selection of *Glencoe Literature* online resources.

Glencoe's Presentation Plus!, a multimedia teaching tool, lets you present dynamic lessons that will engage your students. Using Microsoft PowerPoint®, you can customize the presentations to create your own personalized lessons. Use CheckPoint questions with interactive response keypads to get immediate student feedback during lessons, to increase student participation, and to assess student comprehension.

Glencoe Literature Library

The collection of hardcover books include full-length novels, novellas, plays and works of nonfiction. Each volume consists of at least one complete extended-length reading accompanied by several related readings from a broad range of genres. A separate Study Guide for each *Glencoe Literature Library* book provides teaching notes and reproducible activity pages for students.
Glencoe Literature Library titles that complement this unit include:

- ***Night with Related Readings*** by Elie Wiesel
- ***Adventures of Huckleberry Finn with Related Readings*** by Mark Twain
- ***The Autobiography of Miss Jane Pittman*** by Ernest J. Gaines

GLENCOE BOOKLINK

Use the Glencoe BookLink 3 CD-ROM, a database of more than 26,700 titles, to *create customized reading lists* for your students.

- Search for award-winning titles (e.g., Newbery Award winners, Coretta Scott King Award winners, and Caldecott Medal winners) and for books on several state recommended reading lists.
- Find Degrees of Reading Power™ (DRP) and Lexile™ readability scores for all selections.
- Organize reading lists by students' reading level, author, genre, theme, or area of interest.
- Get a brief summary of each selection.

You can find recommended leveled readings for this unit with Independent Reading (see pages 510 and 511).

Online Essay Grader

Use Glencoe's online essay grader powered by SkillWriter™ to score your students' writing and to provide individualized feedback to each student automatically.

You and your students can visit glencoe.com to link to the essay grader. *Students* can enter their essays and receive feedback on demand. *You* can manage demographic data, assign tests, and generate individual student and aggregated reports. The essay grader can help you

- Save time with automatic scoring and individualized feedback.
- Supplement in-class writing instruction using guided writing practice.

REAL Success: Reading Excellence at All Levels

Glencoe REAL Success is a suite of new reading and language arts products designed to foster reading excellence at all levels. Look for TWE point-of-use references for these specific products that will help your students succeed in reading this Unit.

- *Jamestown Literature: An Adapted Reader,* grade 10
- REAL Success in Writing: Research and Reports
- Skill Level Up!™ A Language Arts Game
- CheckPoint PowerPoint™ slides
- Literature/Reading support at Glencoe Web site

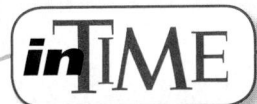

A lively collection of articles drawn from issues of the TIME family of magazines helps students develop the skills they need to interact with informational text in a meaningful way. Each of the news stories, feature articles, reviews, profiles, and essays in the magazine connect to an author, work, or theme in *Glencoe Literature: The Reader's Choice.* See the *inTIME* Teacher's Guide for specific connections to each unit and for reproducible student worksheets designed to develop students' reading and critical thinking skills.

Literature Launchers

Set the scene with Glencoe's Literature Launchers, engaging pre-reading video segments that introduce each unit. Each Unit Launcher brings the literature to life, featuring expert testimony and archival stills and footage from the time.

Insert your Glencoe Literature Launchers into your DVD player. Select the Unit 2 Launcher from the menu to introduce Nonfiction.

Teacher Wraparound Edition Key

Level Appropriate Code

AL = Activities for students working above grade level

OL = Activities for students working at grade level

BL = Activities for students working below grade level

EL = Activities for English language learners

AS = Information for all students

Teacher Wraparound Prompts

R **Reading Skill** These activities help you teach reading skills and vocabulary.

V **Vocabulary** These activities help students comprehend words and incorporate them into reading.

BI **Big Idea** These activities and questions prompt students to prepare to answer the Big Idea.

L **Literary Element** These activities and questions help students comprehend selections and learn more about each genre.

★ **Enrichment** Additional activities and information involving art appreciation and history.

Professional Development Center

From Your Authors:

Teaching Literary Analysis: Nonfiction

Make Real-World Connections Nonfiction—writing about real people, events, and ideas—can have a strong appeal for students. Nevertheless, it is important for teachers to frame readings with a purpose that connects to students' current lives. For example, teachers can prepare students to read Martin Luther King Jr.'s speech "I've Seen the Promised Land," by asking preliminary discussion questions. Teachers may ask questions like the following: What are civil rights? What threatens them? How can we protect them?

Build Background Help students understand that nonfiction is different from fiction in that the content is generally factually correct, and the author attempts to verify his or her account. Nonfiction takes several different forms, such as autobiographies, biographies, memoirs, diaries, speeches, news articles, and essays. Have students read and compare several nonfiction selections from the unit. For example, have students read the autobiographical excerpt from *Farewell to Manzanar* by Jeanne Wakatsuki Houston and James D. Houston as well as the biographical excerpt from *Zora Neale Hurston* by Robert E. Hemenway. Or have students read the speech "On Women's Right to Vote" by Susan B. Anthony and the speech given by Toni Morrison, "Cinderella's

**Beverly Ann Chin
and Douglas Fisher**

Stepsisters." As students read, ask them to take notes on how the two selections are similar and different, how the selections are representative of the nonfiction genre, and which selection they prefer and why.

**Jerry D. Stover
Clay County High School
Clay, West Virginia**

Teacher to Teacher

I introduce my students to nonfiction by having them write essays and create graphics focusing on our community with the goal of learning more about our heritage and the art forms of the Appalachian Mountains. After I introduced this activity, the students decided to publish their work in a book. The first one—a 100-page paperback—came out in 1976. Every year since then students have chosen to put together a new book. In its thirtieth volume, the book is now a hardcover edition and includes photos students have taken and their stories and essays about our people and their art. Since we are one of the poorest counties in the nation, students publish this book without school funds; it's all done with hard work and a few donations. I believe that this activity helps teach students that the classroom is an open window to the nature of human accomplishments, thoughts, beliefs, and values.

Teacher Chat Room

Making Literature Come Alive

Before you begin this unit or sometime during the unit, talk with other teachers about ways they have taught nonfiction. Have a lunch-time discussion group or an after-school hour for professional development and discuss the following questions and answers from our authors:

How can I encourage students to read nonfiction?

- When you are studying a unit, provide newspapers, magazines, and other nonfiction texts that relate to the unit topic. Have book carts of materials available to make your room a rich classroom library.

- Encourage students to find Internet sites or weblogs that comment on issues that come up in class.

- "Book talk" or read aloud from nonfiction texts. For example, have students take turns reading "Encounters in the Sea" by Diane Ackerman aloud in class.

In particular, how can I motivate students to read biographies?

- Help students recall facts they know about the subjects.

- Choose biographies of people or subjects students know.

- Before reading about an issue or inquiry topic, highlight some of the people who were involved. For example, before reading King's speech "I've Seen the Promised Land," discuss King, Ralph Abernathy, or the Freedom Riders' involvement in the Civil Rights Movement.

- Before reading a text by an author, instead of doing a long review of his or her life or work, highlight a few interesting things about him or her. Introducing a human connection to authors is a great way to encourage reading.

How can I help students discover biases in nonfiction texts?

- Tell students that just because a text is nonfiction does not mean they should believe everything in it.

- Have students tell a "two-sided story" about an event they experienced and how they reported it to their friends or parents.

- Help students figure out who the author is, what his or her purposes are, and whether or not they want to believe him or her. For example, while students read Frank McCourt's "Typhoid Fever" from *Angela's Ashes,* have them discuss the following questions: What do you know about Frank McCourt? What qualifies him to write about this subject? What do you think his purpose for writing is (to inform, to describe, to entertain, to persuade)? Do you think that this selection is accurate and believable?

Focus

BELLRINGER

Bellringer Options
Literature Launcher Video
Daily Language Practice
Transparency 26
Or mention recent movies and current television shows based on real life. **Ask:** If you see an exciting movie or television program, does it make it better to know it's a true story? Discuss the natural curiosity people have about other people's lives as well as the appeal of learning something new from nonfiction. Point out that nonfiction is "true" in two senses — true to observable facts and true to the human experience. Tell students that through this unit they will learn a great deal about reading nonfiction.

Objectives for the Unit Introduction
• To understand characteristics of different types of nonfiction (SE)
• To identify and explore literary elements significant to nonfiction (SE)
• To analyze the effect that these literary elements have upon the reader (SE)

Coming to America, 1985. Malcah Zeldis.

308   UNIT 2   NONFICTION

Unit Introduction Skills

Reading Skills
• Analyzing Text Structure (SE pp. 312–313)
• Evaluating Characterization (TWE p. 312)
• Asking Questions (TWE p. 316)

Nonfiction

Literary Elements
• Genres of Nonfiction (SE pp. 308–316)
• Tone (TWE p. 314)
• Analyzing Humor (TWE p. 310)

Listening/Speaking/Viewing Skills
• Discussing a Text (SE p. 316)

Writing Skills/Grammar
• Analyze Motivation (SE p. 316)

NONFICTION

Looking Ahead

Nonfiction—writing about real people, events, and ideas—includes autobiographies, memoirs, biographies, diaries, letters, essays, news articles, and speeches. Reading nonfiction helps us feel we are not alone. Through reading nonfiction, we find others who share our experiences, feelings, passions, and values. Our ideas, ideals, and causes are articulated and defended by the nonfiction writer.

> PREVIEW **Big Ideas and Literary Focus**

1 **BIG IDEA:** The Power of Memory	**LITERARY FOCUS:** Narrative Nonfiction: Autobiography and Biography
2 **BIG IDEA:** Quests and Encounters	**LITERARY FOCUS:** Expository and Personal Essay
3 **BIG IDEA:** Keeping Freedom Alive	**LITERARY FOCUS:** Persuasive Essay and Speeches

OBJECTIVES
In learning about the genre of nonfiction, you will focus on the following:
- understanding characteristics of different types of nonfiction
- identifying and exploring literary elements significant to nonfiction
- analyzing the effect that these literary elements have upon the reader

INTRODUCTION **309**

Focus

Summary

This introduction begins with descriptions of different types of nonfiction. An analysis of an excerpt from *Zora Neale Hurston* presents the genre of biography and shows how its elements work together to achieve the author's purpose. Authors' comments on the genre of nonfiction are also included.

★ Viewing the Art

Malcah Zeldis (1931–) is a self-taught folk artist who creates exuberant paintings with bold colors and a flat style. **Ask:** How does this painting capture the theme "Quests and Encounters"? *(The subject matter and folk style convey the journey of immigrants as they seek a new life in the United States.)* **AS**

Unit Resources

Classroom Management
- TeacherWorks Plus™ CD-ROM
- StudentWorks Plus™ CD-ROM
- Literature Launchers™: Pre-Reading Videos DVD, Unit Two

Core Instructional Support
- Unit 2 Resources (Fast File)
- Literature Online, glencoe.com
- Presentation Plus!™ CD-ROM, Unit Two

Transparencies
- Literary Elements Transparencies 18, 23, 27, 31, 32, 34, 35, 42, 59, 94, 95
- Bellringer Options Transparencies: Selection Focus Transparencies 19–25 Daily Language Practice Transparencies 26–45

Differentiated Instruction
- Active Learning and Note Taking Guide, pp. 35–69
- Skill Level Up!™ A Language Arts Game

Assessment
- Selection and Unit Assessments, Unit Two, pp. 47–82, 211–212
- Exam*View*® Assessment Suite CD-ROM
- Assessment by Learning Objectives, pp. 16–27

Supplemental Reading
- Glencoe Literature Library
- Glencoe BookLink 3 CD-ROM
- *inTIME* Magazines

Teach

Analyzing Genre Ask: Why is "An American Childhood" autobiography? *(It is a true narrative that tells the story of Annie Dillard's experiences, and it is told in the first person.)* **OL**

Drawing Conclusions Ask: What can you tell from details in the passage about de Kooning's profession and character traits? *(The portfolio of drawings indicates he might be an artist, and his desire to "give one that I'll miss" indicates generosity.)* **OL**

GENRE FOCUS
What forms make up the nonfiction genre?

The motivations for writing and reading nonfiction are as many as the writers and readers of nonfiction. Some writers seek to share the lives of others with readers to illustrate a lesson or share insight into a particular time and place. Others look within and share their own experiences.

Narrative Nonfiction: Autobiography and Biography

Writing About Oneself

A literary work telling the story of one's own experiences can be called an autobiography or a memoir. **Autobiography** usually refers to a work that attempts to tell a person's entire life. **Memoir** usually refers to a work that focuses on the author's personal experience during a particular event or period.

> Our father kept in his breast pocket a little black notebook. There he noted jokes he wanted to remember. Remembering jokes was a moral obligation. People who said, "I can never remember jokes," were like people who said, obliviously, "I can never remember names," or "I don't bathe."
>
> —Annie Dillard, from "An American Childhood" **L**

Writing About Another

An account of another person's life is called a **biography** whether it is long or short. People are curious about the lives of famous, successful, or inspiring people, from royalty, such as Queen Elizabeth, to media stars, such as Oprah Winfrey.

> De Kooning brought over a portfolio of drawings and began leafing through them. At last, he seemed to settle on one. He looked at it. But then he slipped the drawing back into the portfolio. "No," he said, "I want to give one that I'll miss."
>
> —Mark Stevens and Annalyn Swan, **from** *De Kooning: An American Master* **R1**

Additional Support

Skills Practice

LITERARY ELEMENT: Humor Use the Keillor excerpt to analyze techniques of humor: "In an envelope that is not a bill" is understatement, language that makes something seem less than what it is. It's humorous to value a friend's letter merely for not being a bill. *Wahoos* is a silly-sounding word, playing on the definition "an exuberant cry" to call up images of wildness. "A long day spent among wahoos and savages" is an ironic comparison between work and a jungle since it expresses a contrast between what is expected and what occurs. Have students identify and explain two other examples of humor from the essay. **OL**

ository and Personal Essay

Formal or Informal Essays

Essays are written to communicate ideas or opinions. They are short works of nonfiction that focus on a single topic. **Formal essays** are serious in tone, and their purpose is either to explain (expository) or to persuade. **Informal,** or **personal, essays** are conversational in tone, and are written on any topic that the writer wishes to share with the reader. Generally, their content relates to an experience in the writer's life.

> Such a sweet gift–a piece of handmade writing, in an envelope that is not a bill, sitting in our friend's path when she trudges home from a long day spent among wahoos and savages, a day our words will help repair. They don't need to be immortal, just sincere. ★
>
> —Garrison Keillor, **from "How to Write a Letter"**

Persuasive Essay and Speeches

Writing for Change

One type of **formal essay** is the persuasive essay. Letters may be written by organizations to encourage readers to donate money. Advertisements are written by corporations to encourage readers to purchase products. Essays and articles are sometimes written to change the way readers think on subjects from letter writing to space travel. Speeches are usually written to encourage a certain behavior, or to win over the listener to a cause.

One type of persuasion is **argument,** which relies on logic, reason, and evidence to convince the reader. Notice that the excerpt from King's speech contains both argument and sarcasm, which is a type of emotional appeal.

> Secondly, let us keep the issues where they are. The issue is injustice. The issue is the refusal of Memphis to be fair and honest in its dealings with its public servants, who happen to be sanitation workers. Now, we've got to keep attention on that. That's always the problem with a little violence. You know what happened the other day, and the press dealt only with the window-breaking. I read the articles. They very seldom got around to mentioning the fact that one thousand, three hundred sanitation workers were on strike, and that Memphis is not being fair to them, and that Mayor Loeb is in dire need of a doctor. They didn't get around to that.
>
> Now we're going to march again, and we've got to march again, in order to put the issue where it is supposed to be. And force everybody to see that there are thirteen hundred of God's children here suffering, sometimes going hungry, going through dark and dreary nights wondering how this thing is going to come out. That's the issue. And we've got to say to the nation: we know it's coming out. For when people get caught up with that which is right and they are willing to sacrifice for it, there is no stopping point short of victory.
>
> —Martin Luther King Jr., **from "I've Been to the Mountaintop"**

R2

 Study Central Visit www.glencoe.com to review the different types of nonfiction.

INTRODUCTION **311**

INTRODUCING UNIT TWO

Teach

R2 Reading Strategy

Recognizing Author's Purpose Ask: What is the purpose of Martin Luther King Jr.'s speech? *(His goal is to persuade his audience to avoid violence and focus on the issue of injustice.)* **Ask:** What logical reasons does King give? *(The press will focus on any violence, which will distract from the primary issue.)* **OL**

★ Writer's Technique

Informal Essay Ask: What personal elements appear in "How to Write a Letter"? *(The references to a friend and personal experiences, the casual words such as* wahoo, *and the conversational style make the essay personal.)* Discuss what the essay would have been like if it had been written as a formal essay. **AS**

Literature Online

Study Central Have students visit the Web site for resources that will help them to review nonfiction.

English Language Coach

Multiple-Meaning Words Students may be confused by multiple-meaning words such as *argument*. Encourage them to use the context to understand that *argument* in this section means "the offering of reasons" rather than "a disagreement." Have them use context with other multiple-meaning words. **EL**

Differentiated Instruction

Categorizing Nonfiction Provide less proficient readers with a blank chart to fill in. Under the heading "Nonfiction" one branch has two boxes for "True Life Stories" (biography and autobiography) and the other has two boxes for "Explanation/Persuasion" (informal and formal essays). **BL**

Objectives

- To understand characteristics of different types of nonfiction (SE)
- To identify and explore literary elements significant to nonfiction (SE)
- To analyze humor in an informal essay (TWE)

311

Teach

L1 Literary Element

Biography Ask: How does Robert Hemenway's purpose differ from an essayist's? *(He wants to tell readers a person's life story whereas an essayist's purpose is to explain or persuade.)* Discuss why Hemenway's biography is termed a "literary biography." **OL**

L2 Literary Element

Analyzing Character Ask: How does Hemenway portray Zora Neale Hurston? *(As a determined, talented person.)* **Ask:** What details show these traits? *(Hemenway tells how Hurston left her job to go to New York and describes her as "confident" and "much praised" for her writing.)* **OL**

★ Writer's Technique

Description Examine Hemenway's descriptive style. Point out the last sentence in the first paragraph, and ask students to identify sensory language that helps them to visualize Hurston's appearance. **AS**

LITERARY ANALYSIS MODEL
How will literary elements help readers analyze nonfiction?

Robert E. Hemenway (1941–) has been a professor of English and American Studies and a University Dean and Chancellor. His literary biography *Zora* *Neale Hurston* was a "Best Books" pick by *The New York Times* in 1978.

APPLYING Literary Elements

Nonfiction
Nonfiction is writing about real people and events.

Nonfiction
In trying to determine which category of nonfiction the excerpt belongs to, you can rule out the **L1 essay** because the author is narrating events in the life of a person, not expressing ideas and opinions. You can also rule out **speech.**

Biography
Hurston is referred to as "she" rather than "I," so you can rule out **autobiography** and **memoir** and determine that the kind of nonfiction you have just read is **biography.**

from *Zora Neale Hurston*
by Robert E. Hemenway

In the first week of January, 1925, Zora Neale Hurston arrived in New York City with one dollar and fifty cents in her purse, no job, no friends, but filled with "a lot of hope." She came from Washington, leaving a steady job as a manicurist in a Seventh Avenue barbershop to explore
5 the opportunities for a career as a writer. As a part-time student at Howard University for the previous five years, she had been an aspiring English major, much praised for her short stories and poems, and she had a vague idea of studying writing in one of Manhattan's many colleges. She carried most of her belongings in her bag, including a number of
10 manuscripts that she hoped would impress. Even if they did not, she was confident of her ability to survive in the big city; she had been on her own since the age of fourteen. Brown skinned, big boned, with freckles and high cheekbones, she was a striking woman; her dark brown eyes were both impish and intelligent, her voice was rich and black—with
15 the map of Florida on her tongue.   ★

She went first to the offices of the National Urban League on East Twenty-third Street, where she asked to be introduced to Charles S. Johnson, editor of the Urban League's magazine, *Opportunity: A Journal of Negro Life.* A month earlier he had published one of her short stories,
20 and since September he had been encouraging her to submit material to the literary contest his magazine currently sponsored. Johnson, director of research for the league, had single-handedly turned *Opportunity* into an expression of "New Negro" thought. "New Negroes" were black people who made clear that they would not accept a subordinate role in
25 American society, and Johnson believed that young writers like Zora Neale Hurston would help prove the cultural parity of the races. He urged her to stay in New York, and as she settled in, he helped her find a series of odd jobs. Mrs. Johnson often gave Zora carfare to make sure she could accept the frequent dinner invitations at the Johnson house.   **L2**

Additional Support

Skills Practice

READING: Evaluating Characterization Point out that biographers use the same techniques of characterization as fiction writers, portraying people by what they say and do as well as describing them directly. As students read biographies, suggest that they answer these questions to help them evaluate the characterization: How much interpretation does the author include? Are the author's interpretations confirmed by fact? How credible and knowledgeable is the author about the subject? What seems to be the author's purpose for writing the biography? **OL**

30 For a young girl from rural Florida and provincial Washington who had been working for ten years to secure an education, this interest and help must have made all the sacrifice seem worthwhile. She had arrived at a hard-won sense of self built around the knowledge that because she was black her life had been graced in unusual ways, and she had confidence
35 that she could express that grace in fiction. The story Johnson had printed a month earlier, "Drenched in Light," embodied this personal vision she brought to New York; it was her initial contribution to the cultural uprising that Johnson and others were calling a "Harlem Renaissance." ★

"Drenched in Light" was Hurston's calling card on literary New York, the
40 tangible evidence she could point to that she was indeed a serious writer. It is also a statement of personal identity. It tells of a day in the life of Isie Watts, a "little brown figure perched upon the gate-post" in front of her Eatonville, Florida, home. Isie likes
45 to race up and down the road to Orlando, "hailing gleefully all travelers." As a result, "everybody in the country" knows "Isie Watts, the joyful," and how she likes to laugh and play, beg rides in cars, and live to the fullest
50 every minute of her young life. Isie gets into various scrapes, including an impish attempt to shave her sleeping grandmother, and eventually is given a ride by a passing white motorist, despite her grandmother's disapproval. There is
55 no building toward a dramatic climax, and very little plot. The structure of the story is thematic. The point is that Isie, poor and black, is far from tragic; rather, she is "drenched in light," a condition which endears her to everyone,
60 although it presents her grandmother with a discipline problem. Isie is persistently happy, and the implication is that whites suffer from an absence of such joy. Isie's white benefactor ends the story, "I want a little of her sunshine
65 to soak into my soul. I need it."

Hurston may have been manipulating white stereotypes of black people here, but it is not a matter of satire. She remembered Eatonville as a place of great peace and happiness, identify-
70 ing that happiness as a function of her family and communal existence. **R**

Biography

Biographies can be short or long. This excerpt is from a book-length biography.

Writer Zora Neale Hurston

Reading Check

Interpreting What would you expect the rest of this book to be about?

Teach

Reading Check

Students may expect the rest of the book to be about Zora Neale Hurston's subsequent career as a writer.

R Reading Strategy

Articulating Personal Response Discuss how different people will have different responses to the Zora Neale Hurston biography, depending on their points of view. Consider how an aspiring writer, a young African American, and a cultural historian might respond differently. Ask students to explain their own personal responses and reasons for them. **OL**

★ Literary History

Harlem Renaissance The cultural flowering of African American literature and arts during the 1920s and 1930s is known as the Harlem Renaissance. Major artists of this movement, largely based in New York City's Harlem, included writers Zora Neale Hurston, Langston Hughes, Claude McKay, and Countee Cullen, as well as painters, dancers, singers, and musicians. **AS**

Reading in the Real World

Career Have students read nonfiction about a career of interest to them. Suggest that they read and summarize three articles or one book explaining the goals, responsibilities, environment, and expectations for the career they choose. Have them share what they learned. **OL**

Building Reading Fluency

Diction Tell students that the words *provincial* and *rural* are synonymous. Have them contrast these words with other terms describing Hurston in the final paragraph. Invite students to read that paragraph aloud, noticing how the contrast contributes to the characterization of Hurston. **BL**

Objectives

- To understand characteristics of different types of nonfiction (SE)
- To learn that people respond differently to texts based on their point of view (TWE)
- To evaluate characterization (TWE)

Teach

R1 Reading Strategy

Interpreting Nonfiction
Discuss the main point each author makes about nonfiction. **Ask:** What insightful observations does Epstein make about the personal essay? *(It has a confessional element and conveys individuality.)* **Ask:** What drawback of autobiography does Norris reveal? *(Autobiography writers usually show themselves in a positive light and are not honest.)* **Ask:** What makes the Norris passage humorous? (The quotation she chooses illustrates Twain's self-deprecating humor.) **Ask:** What idea do both Lopate and Norris emphasize? (They comment on the honesty of the narrator, Norris saying it is impossible and Lopate not.)* **OL**

★ Literary History

Essayists Joseph Epstein, former editor of *The American Scholar* magazine, has written numerous books. Kathleen Norris is a poet and author of nonfiction books including the award-winning *Dakota*. New Yorker Philip Lopate is the author of essay collections and novels. **AS**

Additional Support

WRITERS ON READING
What do writers say about nonfiction?

Reading Nonfiction

The Individual Perspective

R1 An element of confession resides in the personal essay, but, in my view, it ought not to dominate. . . . The etiquette for confession in the essay, again in my view, ought to be the same as that for confession in religion: be brief, be blunt, be gone.

What the essayist confronting a subject usually has to confess is that he or she is not quite like other men or women—but then, it turns out, neither are most men and women like other men and women. That seems to me perhaps the chief value of personal essayists: by displaying their individuality, they remind readers of their own individuality.

—Joseph Epstein, *from The Introduction to The Personal Essay: A Form Of Discovery*

> *"Biography is: a system in which the contradictions of a human life are unified."*
>
> —José Ortega Y Gasset

The Challenge of Honesty **R1**

The most interesting autobiography ever conceived, I think, must be Mark Twain's. Partially written, partially dictated, never published in its entirety, and never according to his intentions, in many ways a colossal failure of a book, Twain's autobiography grappled with every psychological and compositional difficulty characteristic of the genre. Twain knew how easy it was to exhibit ourselves in "creditable attitudes exclusively" and tried to display himself as honestly as he could. It was a noble experiment but it proved impossible: "I have been dictating this autobiography of mine," he wrote, "for three months; I have thought of fifteen hundred or two thousand incidents in my life which I am ashamed of but I have not gotten one of them to consent to go on paper yet."

—Kathleen Norris, *from The Best American Essays 2001*

Piccadilly Line, 1998. Hilary Rosen. Watercolor on paper, 35.43 x 27.56 in. Private collection.

Skills Practice

LITERARY ELEMENT: Tone Point out that the authors on these pages employ different tones, or attitudes toward their subject matter, even though all are discussing the same topic. **Ask:** How does Joseph Epstein's tone differ from Kathleen Norris's? *(Kathleen Norris uses a more humorous tone, as seen in her choice of anecdotes.)* **Ask:** What is Philip Lopate's tone, and why does he use it? (He uses an authoritative tone, as seen in his quoting of E. B. White and his listing of what an essayist "must" do.)* **OL**

7th Avenue Subway, 1931. James Wilfrid Kerr. Oil on panel, 91.44 x 55.8 in. Museum of the City of New York. ⭐

A Reliable Narrator

The spectacle of baring the naked soul is meant to awaken the sympathy of the reader, who is apt to forgive the essayist's self-absorption in return for the warmth of his or her candor. Some vulnerability is essential to the personal essay. Unproblematically self-assured, self-contained, self-satisfied types will not make good essayists. There is, of course, such a thing as a rhetoric of sincerity, and the skilled essayist can fake a vulnerable tone. But if this is done too often, the skilled reader will turn away in disgust. "There is one thing the essayist cannot do—he cannot indulge himself in deceit or in concealment, for he will be found out in no time," wrote E. B. White.

The personal essayist must above all be a reliable narrator; we must trust his or her core of sincerity. We must also feel secure that the essayist has done a fair amount of introspective homework already, is grounded in reality, and is trying to give us the maximum understanding and intelligence of which he or she is capable. A dunderhead and a psychotic killer may be sincere, but that would not sufficiently recommend them for the genre.

—Phillip Lopate, **from** *The Art of the Personal Essay*

Literature Online InterActive Reading Practice
Visit www.glencoe.com for more practice reading nonfiction.

Reading Check

Responding From your own reading experiences, which passage do you identify with most closely? Explain.

INTRODUCTION **315**

Differentiated Instruction

Colon Point out to students the two uses of the colon in the Epstein passage: preceding a list and preceding an explanatory statement. Have students find other examples of correct colon usage and write sentences of their own. **BL**

English Language Coach

Paradox Students new to the English language may not be familiar with the term *paradox*, meaning "a contradiction." **Ask:** Why does Lopate say personal essays are a paradox? *(Because confessions of essayists undermine readers' trust in them)* **EL**

Teach

Reading Check

Answer: *Students should explain their choices.*

R₂ Reading Strategy

Determining Main

Idea Encourage students to decide each author's main point about reading nonfiction. Note that Lopate emphasizes the value of what the writer has to offer. **Ask:** What makes an essayist reliable, according to Lopate? *(Research, background, intelligent analysis)* **OL**

InterActive Reading Have students access the Web site for more practice with reading strategies.

⭐ Viewing the Art

The first underground subway line opened in New York City on October 27, 1904. In the early years of the city's subway system, it was made up of privately owned, separate systems that eventually competed with each other for development and business. By 1968, the Metropolitan Transit Authority took control of the entire system. **AS**

Objectives
• To understand characteristics of different types of nonfiction (SE)
• To compare and contrast tone (TWE)

315

Assess/Close

Guide to Reading Nonfiction Have students outline the types of nonfiction and explain what new insights they gained into techniques for reading nonfiction.

Activities

1. Have students identify historical and biographical elements of the excerpt that they would like to learn more about.

2. To get students started, ask what Hemenway seems to admire about Hurston and what she represents to him. Encourage students to connect with what would motivate them to write various types of nonfiction.

3. Emphasize the value of the Foldables™ study organizer for review and for reference while reading the selections in the unit.

FOLDABLES™
Study Organizer

Have students make and label the Three-Tab Book Foldable. Then have them write notes under each tab of their Foldables.

WRAP-UP

Guide to Reading Nonfiction

- When reading nonfiction, first determine what type of work you are reading.

- Try to identify the author's purpose. Is he or she writing to explain, to entertain, or to persuade you?

- If the author's purpose is to inform or explain, look for a thesis statement and support for the thesis.

- If the author's purpose is to entertain, look for literary elements, such as figurative language, dialogue, and suspense.

- If the author's purpose is to persuade, determine whether the author is presenting an argument, emotional appeals, or a combination of both.

Elements of Nonfiction

- **Nonfiction** is writing about real people and real events.

- An **autobiography** tells the story of the writer's own life.

- A **memoir** tells about an event in the writer's own life.

- A **biography** tells the story of another person's life.

- An **essay** is a short work of nonfiction on a single topic. An essay can be **formal** or **informal**.

- Informal, or **personal**, essays are meant primarily to entertain. Formal essays may be intended to explain or persuade.

- **Persuasive** essays and speeches are intended to change the way people act and think. Persuasive writing contains argument that persuades through logic, reason, and evidence.

Activities

Use what you have learned about reading and analyzing nonfiction to complete one of these activities.

1. Comprehension/Analysis In small groups, discuss the excerpt from *Zora Neale Hurston* and list three questions you could research that are suggested by the text.

2. Inquiry/Research Analyze the author's motivation for writing about Zora Neale Hurston. Use your analysis as the first entry in a chart that shows your ideas about the kinds of motivations writers might have for writing autobiographies, memoirs, essays, or speeches.

3. Note Taking Try using this study organizer to practice identifying forms of nonfiction. For each selection, write clues you used to determine the form.

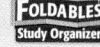
FOLDABLES Study Organizer **THREE-TAB BOOK**

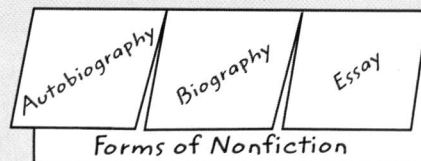

OBJECTIVES
- Generate relevant questions about readings on issues that can be researched.
- Organize and convert information into different forms such as charts and graphs.
- Identify the characteristics that distinguish literary forms.

Additional Support

Skills Practice

READING: Asking Questions
Students may wonder about Zora Neale Hurston's family, why she had been on her own since fourteen, and why she was determined to be a writer. Suggest that they generate relevant questions for research in these ways:

- Jot down things that puzzle them.

- Brainstorm for questions related to topics of interest.

- Pose two or three specific questions that can be answered by research.

- Focus in on a single relevant question that is narrow enough to be researched adequately. **OL**

THE POWER OF MEMORY

Souvenir, 1891. Émile Friant. Oil on canvas. Musée de la Ville de Paris, Musée du Petit-Palais, France. ★

BIG IDEA

Shared personal memories have the power to create a bond between the writer and reader. Historical memories have the power to shape national identities. In the nonfiction works in Part 1, you will read excerpts from life stories that could change the way you view the world. As you read these texts, ask yourself: When someone shares a personal memory with me, do I feel closer to them or understand them better? Why might that be?

317

Analyzing and Extending

Big Idea

The Power of Memory
Ask students to consider their most powerful memories and the effect that sharing memories has on themselves and others. Also discuss how personal memories can enlighten us about a time in history. Tell students that Part 1 will deepen their understanding of the power of memory. Encourage students to contemplate this "big idea" and its relation to the artwork. **OL**

★ Viewing the Art

Émile Friant (1863–1932) was a French Realist painter who studied under Alexandre Cabanel and painted mainly portraits and common people from everyday life. Ask students to look carefully at his painting *Souvenir* and ask whether the woman seems to be lost in her memories. **AS**

English Language Coach

Building Background Help students new to the United States to connect with and understand the literature in Part 1 by considering their family history. Ask if students have relatives who relate memories in an interesting way. Ask students about their reactions to these shared memories. **EL**

Differentiated Instruction

Activate Prior Knowledge Less proficient readers will benefit from drawing on personal experience. Encourage them to tell what biographies or autobiographies have impressed them and why. Point out that some people find that real-life experiences have greater impact than fiction. **BL**

Objectives for Part 1
- To understand the literary forms and the terms *biography* and *autobiography* (SE)
- To identify the characteristics that distinguish biography from autobiography
- To write a journal entry (SE)
- To draw inferences about author's purpose (TWE)

Part 1: The Power of Memory

Readability Scores Key
Dale-Chall/DRP/Lexile

PACING (DAYS)		SELECTIONS AND FEATURES	LITERARY ELEMENTS
STANDARD	BLOCK		
2 class sessions	1	LITERARY FOCUS: Narrative Nonfiction, pp. 318-319	Autobiography and Biography, SE pp. 318, 319
		from *Farewell to Manzanar* by Jeanne Wakatsuki Houston and James D. Houston **5.9/57/1020**, pp. 320-335	Historical Narrative, SE pp. 321-323, 326, 330, 332, 334 Autobiography, SE p. 334; TWE pp. 322, 327, 328
		Grammar Workshop: Language Usage, p. 336	
2 class sessions	1	From *Kaffir Boy* by Mark Mathabane **6.4/53/910**, pp. 337-352	Theme, SE pp. 338, 340, 343, 345, 346, 351 Conflict, SE p. 351
		"Living Well. Living Good." by Maya Angelou **7.7/59/1110**, pp. 353-359	Memoir, SE pp. 354, 355, 358 Theme, SE p. 358
1–2 class sessions	1	"First Impressions" from *De Kooning: An American Master* by Mark Stevens and Annalyn Swan **6.4/66/1160**, pp. 360-371	Author's Purpose, SE pp. 361, 363, 367, 370 Biography, SE p. 370
		Vocabulary Workshop: Technical Words, p. 372	
2–3 class sessions	1–2	"Typhoid Fever" from *Angela's Ashes* by Frank McCourt **6.4/66/1160**, pp. 373-383	Voice, SE pp. 374, 376, 378–380, 382 Memoir, SE p. 382
		HISTORICAL PERSPECTIVE on *Angela's Ashes:* from *Looking Forward to the Past* by Carolyn T. Hughes **5.8/61/1050**, pp. 384-387	
		"Terwilliger Bunts One" from *An American Childhood* by Annie Dillard **6.3/59/1040**, pp. 388-398	Anecdote, SE pp. 389, 390, 393, 394, 397 Voice, SE p. 397

About the Part

Part 1 covers autobiography and biography.

READING AND CRITICAL THINKING	VOCABULARY	WRITING AND GRAMMAR	LISTENING, SPEAKING, AND VIEWING
Analyzing Style, TWE p. 319		Quickwrite, SE p. 319	
Summarizing, SE pp. 321, 323, 324, 325, 327, 328, 333, 335 Evaluating, TWE p. 328	Word Parts, SE pp. 321, 335; TWE p. 324 Academic Vocabulary, SE p. 335	Compare and Contrast Setting, SE p. 335 Dash, TWE p. 332	Analyzing Art, SE pp. 329, 331; TWE pp. 325, 332 Interviewing, TWE p. 326
		Making Subjects and Verbs Agree, SE p. 336	
Analyzing Cause-and-Effect Relationships, SE pp. 338, 339, 342, 344, 347, 348, 351	Analogies, SE p. 351 Academic Vocabulary, SE p. 351	Evaluate Author's Craft, SE p. 352 Quotation Marks, SE p. 352	Analyzing Art, SE pp. 341, 343, 348; TWE p. 345 Analyze Conflict, SE p. 351
Drawing Conclusions, SE pp. 354, 357, 359	Analogies, SE p. 359 Academic Vocabulary, SE p. 359	Evaluate Author's Craft, SE p. 359	Connecting to Personal Experience, SE p. 359
Making Generalizations, SE pp. 361, 363, 364, 369, 371 Previewing, TWE p. 362	Analogies, SE pp. 361, 371 Academic Vocabulary, SE p. 371 Using Context, TWE p. 364	Respond to Mood, SE p. 371 Coordinating Conjunctions, TWE p. 366	Analyzing Art, SE pp. 365, 368, 369, 371; TWE pp. 362, 366
	Jargon, SE p. 372		
Analyzing Style, SE pp. 374, 375, 376, 382 Drawing Conclusions, TWE p. 380	Word Origins, SE pp. 374, 382 Academic Vocabulary, SE p. 382	Respond to Plot, Se p. 383 Narrating in the Present Tense, SE p. 383	Group Activity, SE p. 381 Research Activity, SE p. 383 Analyzing Art, TWE pp. 375
Recognizing Author's Purpose, SE p. 384; TWE pp. 385, 387 Creating New Knowledge, TWE p. 386			
Connecting to Personal Experience, SE pp. 389, 391, 393, 395, 397	Word Parts, SE pp. 389, 397 Academic Vocabulary, SE p. 397	Comic Devices, SE p. 398 Subject and Object Pronouns, SE p. 398	Analyzing Art, SE p. 392 Discuss Criticism, SE p. 396 Humorous Stories, SE p. 398

Focus

Bellringer Options
Daily Language Practice
Transparency 27
Or show photojournalistic images of people at different times in history and invite students to bring to class snapshots of favorite memories. Discuss the value of sharing memories and what would inspire students to share their memories with others. **Ask:** What makes a person's memories powerful to others? *(Students may say when others could learn from them or when they can make a personal connection with others.)*

Teach

L Literary Element

Biography and Autobiography Help students see that Maya Angelou's excerpt is biographical, since it tells about another person's life. **Ask:** What is effective about Maya Angelou's selection of facts for her biography of Aunt Tee? *(Angelou arouses suspense by saying the couple's words "won Aunt Tee's sympathy forever.")* **OL**

Additional Support

NARRATIVE NONFICTION: AUTOBIOGRAPHY AND BIOGRAPHY

How do you write about a real person, including yourself?

Nonfiction writing is meant to be factual, and a biography should tell the facts of the life of its subject. But which facts should be told? To write down all the facts of any life, or even of one day, is inconceivable. The art of biography is in choosing the facts to tell and identifying a way of telling them that captures the reader's interest.

Victorian Parlor II, 1945. Horace Pippin. Oil on canvas, 25¼ x 30 in. Metropolitan Museum of Art, New York. Arthur Hoppock Hearn Fund, 1958.

Aunt Tee said that what occurred during every Saturday party startled her and her friends the first time it happened. They had been playing cards, and Aunt Tee, who had just won the bid, held a handful of trumps. She felt a cool breeze on her back and sat upright and turned around. Her employers had cracked her door open and beckoned to her. Aunt Tee, a little peeved, laid down her cards and went to the door. The couple backed away and asked her to come into the hall, and there they both spoke and won Aunt Tee's sympathy forever.

—Maya Angelou, *from* **"Living Well. Living Good."** **L**

Skills Practice

LITERARY ELEMENT: Analyzing Author's Purpose Discuss the purpose an author might have for writing nonfiction about powerful memories; for example, to convey a historical experience or to entertain with amusing details. **Ask:** For the excerpts on these pages, how do the authors' purposes differ? *(Dillard writes to entertain and connect with readers while Angelou writes to help people live more satisfying lives. Like Langston Hughes, Jeanne Wakatsuki Houston and James D. Houston write to portray a haunting cultural experience.)* **OL**

Biography

The word *biography* comes from the Greek *bio-* meaning "life," and *-graphy* meaning "writing." In **biography** the author gives the reader an account of another person's life. The author will use the pronouns "he" or "she" to refer to the subject. Biographies can be book-length, but they can also be short pieces.

Biography does not need to limit itself to discussing a single person. Poet Langston Hughes refused to differentiate between his personal experience and the common experience of African Americans in the United States. For him, one man's experience was the experience of everyone. In this way, a writer may explore a group's experience through that of an individual or several individuals.

Autobiography

When a person writes about his or her own life, it is called **autobiography.** *Auto-* is from the Greek word meaning "self." In an autobiography, the pronoun "I" refers to the subject—the author him- or herself. Authors have many purposes for sharing the stories of their lives. Some, like Martin Luther King Jr., write to help others live satisfying and meaningful lives. Others, like Jeanne Wakatsuki Houston and James D. Houston, write to give readers a personal glimpse of an event in United States history.

> None of these kids ever actually attacked. It was the threat that frightened us, their fearful looks, and the noises they would make, like miniature Samurai, in a language we couldn't understand.
>
> —Jeanne Wakatsuki Houston and James D. Houston, from *Farewell to Manzanar*

Memoir The term **memoir** is sometimes used as a synonym for **autobiography** or the label can be applied to a particular kind of autobiography— autobiographical writing that focuses on a specific period or event in the writer's life. It can also refer to an autobiographical style that is more story-like. Annie Dillard's memoir captures her mother's unusual personality.

> "Spell 'poinsettia,'" Mother would throw out at me, smiling with pleasure. "Spell 'sherbet.'" The idea was not to make us whizzes, but, quite the contrary, to remind us—and I, especially, needed reminding—that we didn't know it all just yet.
>
> —Annie Dillard, **from "Terwilliger Bunts One"** R

Woman in Blue, 1995. Leslie Braddock. Acrylic on canvas, 60 X 48 in. Private collection.

Quickwrite

Writing a Journal Entry Write a private journal entry about an event in your life that you would like to remember. Write it just for yourself without worrying about spelling, grammar, or punctuation. You do not have to show it to anyone. Later, you can rewrite it using the "five Ws" (who, what, where, when, why) and share it with someone else.

OBJECTIVES
- Understand the literary forms and terms *biography* and *autobiography.*
- Identify the characteristics that distinguish biography from autobiography.
- Write a journal entry.

Teach

R Reading Strategy

Analyzing Style Ask: What makes Annie Dillard's style that of a memoir? *(Use of first person for telling about Annie Dillard's own life makes it auto-biographical. It is written like a story with dialogue and narrative details, which makes it a memoir.)* **OL**

Quickwrite

Encourage students to make a habit of writing down details about events they would like to remember. Advise them to jot down specific details about what they see, hear, feel, and think. Note that many authors use their journals as source material for their writing. **OL**

★ Viewing the Art

Horace Pippin (1888–1946) is famous for his folk art. Folk art generally refers to art made by people who have not received formal artistic training; some consider it the "art of the people," or a less elite form of artistic expression. **AS**

English Language Coach

Cultural Allusions Students new to the United States may not understand cultural allusions in some of the excerpts, such as the references to playing the card game whist *(bid, trumps)* in the Angelou excerpt, and the word *Samurai,* meaning "a member of the military in feudal Japan," in the Houston excerpt. **EL**

Differentiated Instruction

Visualizing Details Encourage less proficient readers to visualize descriptive details, such as the "fearful looks" and incomprehensible noises "like miniature Samurai." **Ask:** Why do the authors retell this episode? *(It was frightening, and the authors make readers feel closer by sharing it.)* **BL**

Focus

BEFORE YOU READ

BELLRINGER

Bellringer Options
**Selection Focus
    Transparency 19**
**Daily Language Practice
    Transparency 28**
Or **on the board, write:** *evacuate.*
Ask: What would you be most concerned about if you were suddenly forced to evacuate your home? *(Students may worry about leaving friends and neighbors, being uprooted from school, being separated from family, leaving pets and possessions, and facing an uncertain future.)* Advise students to keep those reactions in mind as they read this narrative about a young girl evacuated from her home.

Author Search To expand students' appreciation of Jeanne Wakatsuki Houston and James D. Houston, have them access the Web site for additional information and resources.

---

from *Farewell to Manzanar*

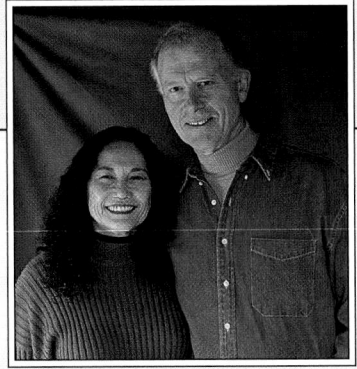

MEET JEANNE WAKATSUKI HOUSTON AND JAMES D. HOUSTON

Jeanne Wakatsuki Houston was only seven years old when her family, just for being Japanese, was relocated to an internment camp during World War II. It took her nearly twenty-five years to talk about her life in the Manzanar internment camp, but when she did, she broached the subject in the form of an award-winning book, *Farewell to Manzanar*, co-authored by her husband, James D. Houston.

The United States at War When Japan attacked a United States fleet at Pearl Harbor in 1941, the U.S. was drawn into World War II. Many people unfairly blamed Japanese Americans. Despite the fact that many of them had U.S. citizenship, they were distrusted and systematically discriminated against. For example, Japanese American people in the fishing industry were seen as threats to national security because in theory, they could smuggle oil to the Japanese navy. Wakatsuki Houston's father was arrested because he was a fisherman.

Memories of Internment Wakatsuki Houston was born in Inglewood, California. When the war began, Wakatsuki Houston's family was sent to the Manzanar internment camp, where the conditions were very harsh. Manzanar was built very quickly, so no modern conveniences existed. Approximately eleven-thousand people of Japanese ancestry lived there in a one-square-mile block of wooden barracks, surrounded by barbed wire and posted guards. The people there worked hard to build a community by planting gardens, painting, and forming schools and churches. Many were full-fledged U.S. citizens and many did not even speak Japanese. Despite their loyalty to the United States, however, they were treated as if they were the enemy. For Wakatsuki Houston, the memory of Manzanar changed her life.

After her family's release in 1945, Wakatsuki Houston continued to struggle to overcome prejudice and the shame of being punished simply for being Japanese. During her college years, she met and married James D. Houston. She went back to visit Manzanar in 1972, a visit she says helped her come to terms with the experience. According to Wakatsuki Houston, "Papa's life ended at Manzanar, though he lived for twelve more years after getting out. Until this trip I had not been able to admit that my own life really began there."

> *"[Writing was] a way of coming to terms with the impact these years have had on my life."*
>
> —Jeanne Wakatsuki Houston

Preventing Injustice By writing about her experience in the internment camp, Wakatsuki Houston has helped to educate people in the United States about an important, and tragic, episode in U.S. history. She hopes her work will help inspire Americans to ensure that such injustice is never repeated.

Jeanne Wakatsuki Houston was born in 1934. James D. Houston was born in 1933.

Literature Online Author Search For more about Jeanne Wakatsuki Houston and James D. Houston, go to www.glencoe.com.

320 UNIT 2 NONFICTION

Selection Skills

from Farewell to Manzanar

Literary Elements

- Historical Narrative (SE pp. 321, 322, 323, 326, 330, 332, 334)
- Autobiography (SE p. 334, TWE pp. 322, 327, 328)

Reading Skills

- Summarizing (SE pp. 321, 323, 324, 325, 327, 328, 333, 335)
- Evaluating (TWE p. 328)
- Research (TWE p. 330)

Vocabulary Skills

- Word Parts (SE pp. 321, 335, TWE p. 324)
- Academic Vocabulary (SE p. 335)

Listening/Speaking/Viewing Skills

- Analyzing Art (SE pp. 329, 331; TWE pp. 325, 332)
- Interviewing (TWE p. 326)

Writing Skills/Grammar

- Compare and Contrast Setting (SE p. 335)
- Dash (TWE p. 332)

LITERATURE PREVIEW

Connecting to the Historical Narrative

Under the influence of war or economic crises, people sometimes make unwise decisions. The decision to intern Japanese Americans was both unfair and unnecessary. Think about the following questions before you read "Farewell to Manzanar":

- How would you feel if you were given forty-eight hours to pack only a few of your belongings and leave your home?
- How would you feel about the government if they relocated your family because of your nationality or ancestry?

Building Background

After Japan's surprise attack on Pearl Harbor, many people in the United States were suspicious of people of Japanese ancestry living in the United States. Japanese Americans were punished regardless of their citizenship status or views on the war. In February 1942, President Franklin D. Roosevelt issued Executive Order 9066, which essentially gave the U.S. War Department the authority to move Japanese Americans from their homes on the West Coast and confine them to special camps for the duration of the war. Some 110,000 Japanese Americans, two-thirds of them U.S. citizens, were relocated by the military to ten remotely situated, prison-like camps.

Setting Purposes for Reading

Big Idea The Power of Memory

As you read the story, think about how sharing memories helps people learn more about themselves and make connections to other people.

Literary Element Historical Narrative

A **historical narrative** is a nonfiction account that tells about important historical events. As you read, notice what real-life details Wakatsuki Houston uses to tell the story of Japanese Americans in an internment camp.

- See Literary Terms Handbook, p. R8.

Literature Online Interactive Literary Elements Handbook To review or learn more about the literary elements, go to www.glencoe.com.

OBJECTIVES
In studying this selection, you will focus on the following:
- understanding historical narratives
- using summarizing to increase comprehension
- writing an essay to compare and contrast settings
- identifying and analyzing autobiography

READING PREVIEW

Reading Strategy Summarizing

When you **summarize,** you determine the most important ideas in a selection and then restate them concisely in your own words. Summarizing can help you better remember and understand what you read.

Reading Tip: Summarizing Details As you read, use a graphic organizer like the one below to help you list details from a paragraph. Then write one or two sentences to sum up the main idea of the paragraph.

Detail	Detail	Detail
When I was born [Papa] was farming near Inglewood.	When he started fishing, we moved to Ocean Park, near Santa Monica, and until they picked him up, that's where we lived.	But with him gone and no way of knowing what to expect, my mother moved all of us down to Terminal Island.

Conclusion

Papa used to be a farmer, but he became a fisher and was arrested near our home in Ocean Park, near Santa Monica. My mother moved us to Terminal Island so we could be near other Japanese.

Vocabulary

patriarch (pā'trē ärk´) n. the male head of a family or group; p. 324 *My brother became the patriarch of our family after my father died.*

designation (des´ig nā´shən) n. a distinguishing name or mark; p. 326 *The scientist gave the seeds that were not watered the designation "test group."*

alleviate (ə lē´vē āt´) v. to make easier to bear; relieve; lessen; p. 328 *The medicine promised to alleviate his suffering.*

subordinate (sə bôr´də nāt´) v. to cause to be, or treat as, secondary, inferior, or less important; p. 333 *A mother subordinates her own needs to care for the needs of her children.*

Vocabulary Tip: Word Parts Word parts can help you determine the meaning of unfamiliar words.

JEANNE WAKATSUKI HOUSTON AND JAMES D. HOUSTON   **321**

BEFORE YOU READ

Focus

Summary

In this excerpt from *Farewell to Manzanar,* Jeanne Wakatsuki Houston recalls her experience as a child during World War II. After the narrator's father is arrested by the U.S. government, her mother moves the family to two different Japanese American ghettos. Then they are forced to relocate to Manzanar, a Japanese American internment camp in California, where the living conditions are inadequate and the residents lack privacy.

V Vocabulary

Vocabulary File Say: Add these words and definitions to your vocabulary file. For each word, include a sentence that gives you an example of how to use the word. **OL** Students with English language needs should include the pronunciations of these words in their files. **EL**

Literature Online

Literary Elements Have students access the Web site to improve their understanding of historical narrative.

Selection Resources

Print Materials
- Unit 2 Resources (Fast File), pp. 17–19
- Leveled Vocabulary Development, p. 22
- Selection and Unit Assessments, pp. 47–48
- Selection Quick Checks, p. 24

Transparencies
- Bellringer Options Transparencies: Selection Focus Transparency 19 Daily Language Practice Transparency 28
- Literary Elements Transparency 31

Technology
- TeacherWorks Plus™ CD-ROM
- StudentWorks Plus™ CD-ROM
- Presentation Plus!™ CD-ROM
- Literature Online, glencoe.com
- Online Student Edition, mhln.com
- ExamView® Assessment Suite CD-ROM
- Vocabulary PuzzleMaker CD-ROM
- Listening Library, disc 1 track 26

Teach

BI₁ Big Idea

The Power of Memory Say: Keep the following questions in mind as you read: What is the effect of the author's memories on the reader? What purpose does sharing her memories serve? (*Wakatsuki Houston presents a child's-eye view of disturbing events. Her recollections arouse empathy and indignation.*) **OL**

L₁ Literary Element

Historical Narrative

Answer: *Because of the attack on Pearl Harbor by the Japanese, people were hostile to Japanese Americans. Mama felt safer in an area with other Japanese people rather than being the only Japanese family in the old neighborhood.* Emphasize that this historical narrative tells a true story set in a specific historical period. **OL**

BI₂ Big Idea

The Power of Memory
Answer: *She remembers her father telling her that he would sell her to the "Chinaman." It is ironic that she does not think of herself as Asian.* **OL**

> *Readability Scores*
> Dale-Chall: 5.9
> DRP: 57
> Lexile: 1020

Farewell to Manzanar

School Children Say Pledge of Allegiance in San Francisco, April 16, 1942. Dorothea Lange. Silver Gelatin Photograph.

Jeanne Wakatsuki Houston
and James D. Houston

BI₁ In December of 1941 Papa's disappearance didn't bother me nearly so much as the world I soon found myself in.

He had been a jack-of-all-trades. When I was born he was farming near Inglewood. Later, when he started fishing, we moved to Ocean Park, near Santa Monica, and until they picked him up, that's where we lived, in a big frame house with a brick fireplace, a block back from the beach. We were the only Japanese family in the neighborhood. Papa liked it that way. He didn't want to be labeled or grouped by anyone. But with him gone and no way of knowing what to expect, my mother moved all of us down to Terminal Island.[1]

Woody already lived there, and one of my older sisters had married a Terminal Island boy. Mama's first concern now was to keep the family together; and once the war began, she felt safer there than isolated racially in Ocean Park. But for me, at age seven, the island was a country as foreign as India or Arabia would have been. It was the first time I had lived among other Japanese, or gone to school with them, and I was terrified all the time.

This was partly Papa's fault. One of his threats to keep us younger kids in line was "I'm going to sell you to the Chinaman." When I had entered kindergarten two years earlier, I was the only Oriental in the class.

---

1. *Terminal Island,* part of the Port of Los Angeles, is at the city's southern tip.

> **Literary Element** Historical Narrative *Why does Mama feel safer in Terminal Island?* **L₁**

322 UNIT 2 NONFICTION

Additional Support

Leveled Reading
An adapted version of this selection is available on page 282 of *Jamestown Literature: An Adapted Reader,* grade 10.

322

Skills Practice

LITERARY ELEMENT:

Autobiography Call students' attention to the first-person point of view used in this autobiographical historical narrative. As an adult, Wakatsuki Houston is recalling events that occurred when she was seven years old. **Ask:** How does the point of view influence what read-

ers discover? (*Experiences and thoughts are filtered through one person's eyes. Readers should remain aware of Wakatsuki Houston's age, experiences, and interests at the time the events occurred.*) Have students give an example that shows the child's-eye view. (*An example on page 322 is the incident in kindergarten.*) **OL** earlier, I was the only Oriental in the class. They sat me next to a Caucasian girl who happened to have very slanted eyes. I looked at her and began to scream, certain Papa had sold me out at last. My fear of her ran so deep I could not speak of it, even to Mama, couldn't explain why I was screaming. For two weeks I had nightmares about this girl, until the teachers finally moved me to the other side of the room. And it was still with me, this fear of Oriental faces, when we moved to Terminal Island.

In those days it was a company town, a ghetto owned and controlled by the canneries. The men went after fish, and whenever the boats came back—day or night—the women would be called to process the catch while it was fresh. One in the afternoon or four in the morning, it made no difference. My mother had to go to work right after we moved there. I can still hear the whistle— two toots for French's, three for Van Camp's—and she and Chizu would be out of bed in the middle of the night, heading for the cannery.

The house we lived in was nothing more than a shack, a barracks with single plank walls and rough wooden floors, like the cheapest kind of migrant workers' housing. The people around us were hardworking, boisterous, a little proud of their nickname, *yo-go-re*, which meant literally *uncouth one*, or roughneck, or dead-end kid. They not only spoke Japanese exclusively, they spoke a dialect peculiar to Kyushu,[2] where their families had come from in Japan, a rough, fisherman's language, full of oaths and insults. Instead of saying *ba-ka-ta-re*, a common insult meaning *stupid*, Terminal Islanders would say *ba-ka-ya-*

ro, a coarser and exclusively masculine use of the word, which implies gross stupidity. They would swagger and pick on outsiders and persecute anyone who didn't speak as they did. That was what made my own time there so hateful. I had never spoken anything but English, and the other kids in the second grade despised me for it. They were tough and mean, like ghetto kids anywhere. Each day after school I dreaded their ambush. My brother Kiyo, three years older, would wait for me at the door, where we would decide whether to run straight home together, or split up, or try a new and unexpected route.

None of these kids ever actually attacked. It was the threat that frightened us, their fearful looks, and the noises they would make, like miniature Samurai, in a language we couldn't understand.

At the time it seemed we had been living under this reign of fear for years. In fact, we lived there about two months. Late in February the navy decided to clear Terminal Island completely. Even though most of us were American-born, it was dangerous having that many Orientals so close to the Long Beach Naval Station, on the opposite end of the island. We had known something like this was coming. But, like Papa's arrest, not much could be done ahead of time. There were four of us kids still young enough to be living with Mama, plus Granny, her mother, sixty-five then, speaking no English, and nearly blind. Mama didn't know where else she could get work, and we had nowhere else to move *to*. On February 25 the choice was made for us. We were given forty-eight hours to clear out.

The secondhand dealers had been prowling around for weeks, like wolves, offering

Visual Vocabulary
For centuries, the *Samurai* (sam' oo rī') were a class of fearsome warriors. Japan abolished its class system in the 1860s.

2. *Kyushu* is the southernmost of Japan's four main islands.

Big Idea The Power of Memory *Why does Wakatsuki Houston remember being afraid of the little girl with slanted eyes?* **BI2**

Big Idea The Power of Memory *Why would a small thing like the sound of a whistle be important to the author?* **BI3**

Reading Strategy Summarizing *How does Wakatsuki Houston describe the other Japanese at Terminal Island?* **R**

Literary Element Historical Narrative *Why did the navy think it was dangerous to have Asian Americans close to the Long Beach Naval Station?* **L2**

JEANNE WAKATSUKI HOUSTON AND JAMES D. HOUSTON **323**

Differentiated Instruction

Predicting Have students contrast the Wakatsukis' lifestyles in Ocean Park and on Terminal Island. For example, read aloud the descriptions of the two houses: "a big frame house with a brick fireplace, a block back from the beach" and "a shack, a barracks, with single plank walls and rough wooden floors." **Ask:** What would be your prediction of the mother's reaction to the new surroundings, the absence of her husband, and the odd work hours? *(She was probably unsettled and distressed by the new and difficult way of life. The family's lifestyle in Ocean Park had been much more comfortable.)* **OL**

Teach

R1 Reading Strategy

Summarizing Answer:
Executive Order 9066 gave the War Department the authority to move Japanese Americans, who were perceived as threats, to military areas in the western states. **OL**

B1 Big Idea

The Power of Memory
Answer: *It is an old Japanese phrase meaning "it cannot be helped." The author understands how the words apply to internment camps. The Japanese Americans were powerless to change their internment, but they made the best of what they had to endure.* **OL**

★ Political History

Terminal Island In 1942 the island was a fishing village of about 3,000 people, mainly Japanese Americans. After the Pearl Harbor attack in 1941, many of the men were taken away, and the other residents were the first group forced into internment camps. The town no longer exists. **AS**

humiliating prices for goods and furniture they knew many of us would have to sell sooner or later. Mama had left all but her most valuable possessions in Ocean Park, simply because she had nowhere to put them. She had brought along her pottery, her silver, heirlooms like the kimonos Granny had brought from Japan, tea sets, lacquered tables, and one fine old set of china, blue and white porcelain, almost translucent.[3] On the day we were leaving, Woody's car was so crammed with boxes and luggage and kids we had just run out of room. Mama had to sell this china.

Visual Vocabulary
A *kimono* (ki mō′ nō) is a loose robe or gown tied with a sash, traditionally worn as an outer garment by Japanese men and women.

One of the dealers offered her fifteen dollars for it. She said it was a full setting for twelve and worth at least two hundred. He said fifteen was his top price. Mama started to quiver. Her eyes blazed up at him. She had been packing all night and trying to calm down Granny, who didn't understand why we were moving again and what all the rush was about. Mama's nerves were shot, and now navy jeeps were patrolling the streets. She didn't say another word. She just glared at this man, all the rage and frustration channeled at him through her eyes.

He watched her for a moment and said he was sure he couldn't pay more than seventeen fifty for that china. She reached into the red velvet case, took out a dinner plate and hurled it at the floor right in front of his feet.

The man leaped back shouting, "Hey! Hey, don't do that! Those are valuable dishes!"

Mama took out another dinner plate and hurled it at the floor, then another and another, never moving, never opening her mouth, just quivering and glaring at the retreating dealer, with tears streaming down her cheeks. He finally turned and scuttled

out the door, heading for the next house. When he was gone she stood there smashing cups and bowls and platters until the whole set lay in scattered blue and white fragments across the wooden floor.

The American Friends Service[4] helped us find a small house in Boyle Heights, another minority ghetto, in downtown Los Angeles, now inhabited briefly by a few hundred Terminal Island refugees. Executive Order 9066 had been signed by President Roosevelt, giving the War Department authority to define military areas in the western states and to exclude from them anyone who might threaten the war effort. There was a lot of talk about internment, or moving inland, or something like that in store for all Japanese Americans. I remember my brothers sitting around the table talking very intently about what we were going to do, how we would keep the family together. They had seen how quickly Papa was removed, and they knew now that he would not be back for quite a while. Just before leaving Terminal Island Mama had received her first letter, from Bismarck, North Dakota. He had been imprisoned at Fort Lincoln, in an all-male camp for enemy aliens.

Papa had been the **patriarch**. He had always decided everything in the family. With him gone, my brothers, like councilors in the absence of a chief, worried about what should be done. The ironic thing is, there wasn't much left to decide. These were mainly days of quiet, desperate waiting for what seemed at the time to be inevitable. There is a phrase the Japanese use in such situations, when something difficult must be endured. You would hear the

---

3. A material that is *translucent*, such as frosted glass, allows light to pass through but does not permit objects on the other side to be clearly distinguished.

4. The *American Friends Service* is a Quaker charity that provides assistance to political and religious refugees and other displaced persons.

Reading Strategy Summarizing *Summarize the information Wakatsuki Houston provides about the factors that affected Japanese Americans as the war progressed.* **R1**

Vocabulary

patriarch (pā′trē ärk′) n. the male head of a family or group

---

Additional Support

Skills Practice

VOCABULARY: Word Parts On the board write: *Papa was the <u>patriarch</u>, a new and <u>unexpected</u> route,* and *their <u>fearful</u> looks.* Ask students how they can use word parts to decode the meaning of *patriarch, fearful,* and *unexpected.* Remind them that the suffix *–arch* indicates a kind of ruler; the suffix *–ful* means "full of" or "having"; and the prefix *un-* means "not." Using their knowledge of word parts, have them explain the meaning of the words *matriarch, unhelpful, unsuccessful,* and *unhealthful.* Remind them to use context clues as well as word parts. **OL**

Dust Storm at Manzanar (California), July 3, 1942. Dorothea Lange. Silver Gelatin Photograph.

older heads, the Issei,[5] telling others very quietly, *"Shikata ga nai"* (It cannot be helped). *"Shikata ga nai"* (It must be done).

Mama and Woody went to work packing celery for a Japanese produce dealer. Kiyo and my sister May and I enrolled in the local school, and what sticks in my memory from those few weeks is the teacher—not her looks, her remoteness. In Ocean Park my teacher had been a kind, grandmotherly woman who used to sail with us in Papa's boat from time to time and who wept the day we had to leave. In Boyle Heights the teacher felt cold and distant. I was confused by all the moving and was having trouble with the classwork,

but she would never help me out. She would have nothing to do with me.

This was the first time I had felt outright hostility from a Caucasian. Looking back, it is easy enough to explain. Public attitudes toward the Japanese in California were shifting rapidly. In the first few months of the Pacific war, America was on the run. Tolerance had turned to distrust and irrational fear. The hundred-year-old tradition of anti-Orientalism on the west coast soon resurfaced, more vicious than ever. Its result became clear about a month later, when we were told to make our third and final move.

The name Manzanar meant nothing to us when we left Boyle Heights. We didn't know

---

5. *Issei* (ēs´ sā´) literally means "first generation" and refers to Japanese natives who immigrated to the United States.

Big Idea The Power of Memory Why does the author remember the Issei saying Shikata ga nai? **BI**

Reading Strategy Summarizing How does the author summarize the prejudice against the Japanese in America at this time? **R2**

JEANNE WAKATSUKI HOUSTON AND JAMES D. HOUSTON **325**

Teach

L1 Literary Element

Historical Narrative

Answer: *Ignorance and prejudice frequently lead people to suspect the innocent of treason and to exert violence against them.* Explain that political factors such as the desire to win popular support and eliminate business competition also influenced the decision to intern Japanese Americans. **OL**

BI Big Idea

The Power of Memory

Answer: *The passengers were relieved to have the journey's tense silence broken by the narrator's innocent enthusiasm. Even the greeters outside laughed, temporarily bridging a gap between the greeters and the arriving group.* **OL**

★ Political History

Manzanar Manzanar was the first internment camp run by the War Relocation Authority. It was constructed within six weeks on the site of a former farming community. Construction began in March of 1942, and by July its population was 10,000. **AS**

★ where it was or what it was. We went because the government ordered us to. And, in the case of my older brothers and sisters, we went with a certain amount of relief. They had all heard stories of Japanese homes being attacked, of beatings in the streets of California towns. They were as frightened of the Caucasians as Caucasians were of us. Moving, under what appeared to be government protection, to an area less directly threatened by the war seemed not such a bad idea at all. For some it actually sounded like a fine adventure.

Our pickup point was a Buddhist church in Los Angeles. It was very early, and misty, when we got there with our luggage. Mama had bought heavy coats for all of us. She grew up in eastern Washington and knew that anywhere inland in early April would be cold. I was proud of my new coat, and I remember sitting on a duffel bag trying to be friendly with the Greyhound driver. I smiled at him. He didn't smile back. He was befriending no one. Someone tied a numbered tag to my collar and to the duffel bag (each family was given a number, and that became our official **designation** until the camps were closed), someone else passed out box lunches for the trip, and we climbed aboard.

I had never been outside Los Angeles County, never traveled more than ten miles from the coast, had never even ridden on a bus. I was full of excitement, the way any kid would be, and wanted to look out the window. But for the first few hours the shades were drawn. Around me other people played cards, read magazines, dozed, waiting. I settled back, waiting too, and finally fell asleep. The bus felt very secure to me. Almost half its passengers were immediate relatives. Mama and my older

---

brothers had succeeded in keeping most of us together, on the same bus, headed for the same camp. I didn't realize until much later what a job that was. The strategy had been, first, to have everyone living in the same district when the evacuation began, and then to get all of us included under the same family number, even though names had been changed by marriage. Many families weren't as lucky as ours and suffered months of anguish while trying to arrange transfers from one camp to another.

We rode all day. By the time we reached our destination, the shades were up. It was late afternoon. The first thing I saw was a yellow swirl across a blurred, reddish setting sun. The bus was being pelted by what sounded like splattering rain. It wasn't rain. This was my first look at something I would soon know very well, a billowing flurry of dust and sand churned up by the wind through Owens Valley.[6]

We drove past a barbed-wire fence, through a gate, and into an open space where trunks and sacks and packages had been dumped from the baggage trucks that drove out ahead of us. I could see a few tents set up, the first rows of black barracks, and beyond them, blurred by sand, rows of barracks that seemed to spread for miles across this plain. People were sitting on cartons or milling around, with their backs to the wind, waiting to see which friends or relatives might be on this bus. As we approached, they turned or stood up, and some moved toward us expectantly. But inside the bus no one stirred. No one waved or spoke. They just stared out the windows, ominously silent. I didn't understand this. Hadn't we finally arrived, our whole family intact? I opened a window, leaned out, and yelled happily. "Hey! This whole bus is full of Wakatsukis!"

Outside, the greeters smiled. Inside there was an explosion of laughter, hysterical,

---

Literary Element Historical Narrative *What do these details suggest about the dangers of scapegoating a group of people?* **L1**

Vocabulary

designation (des´ig nā´shən) *n.* a distinguishing name or mark

---

6. Manzanar was built in *Owens Valley*, near Death Valley, about two hundred miles north of Los Angeles.

Big Idea The Power of Memory *Why does the author remember the people in the bus and the greeters laughing?* **BI**

Additional Support

Skills Practice

SPEAKING: Interviewing Tell students that many historical narratives are based on interviews. Review the basics of interviewing with students:

- Explain the purpose of the interview and arrange a convenient time.
- Ask open-ended questions.
- Listen carefully and take notes.

- Be respectful and polite.
- Ask follow-up questions.
- Thank the person.

Have students interview someone whose grandparents experienced the World War II era about his or her reactions to Pearl Harbor and the internment camps. **OL**

Visual Vocabulary
A soldier in the field eats from a *mess kit,* which is a metal container that holds eating utensils and opens into a plate with two compartments.

tension-breaking laughter that left my brothers choking and whacking each other across the shoulders.

We had pulled up just in time for dinner. The mess halls[7] weren't completed yet. An outdoor chow line snaked around a half-finished building that broke a good part of the wind. They issued us army mess kits, the round metal kind that fold over, and plopped in scoops of canned Vienna sausage, canned string beans, steamed rice that had been cooked too long, and on top of the rice a serving of canned apricots. The Caucasian servers were thinking that the fruit poured over rice would make a good dessert. Among the Japanese, of course, rice is never eaten with sweet foods, only with salty or savory foods. Few of us could eat such a mixture. But at this point no one dared protest. It would have been impolite. I was horrified when I saw the apricot syrup seeping through my little mound of rice. I opened my mouth to complain. My mother jabbed me in the back to keep quiet. We moved on through the line and joined the others squatting in the lee[8] of half-raised walls, dabbing courteously at what was, for almost everyone there, an inedible concoction.

After dinner we were taken to Block 16, a cluster of fifteen barracks that had just been finished a day or so earlier—although finished was hardly the word for it. The shacks were built of one thickness of pine planking covered with tarpaper. They sat on concrete footings, with about two feet of open space between the floorboards and the ground. Gaps showed between the planks, and as the weeks passed and the green wood dried out, the gaps widened. Knotholes gaped in the uncovered floor.

Each barracks was divided into six units, sixteen by twenty feet, about the size of a living room, with one bare bulb hanging from the ceiling and an oil stove for heat. We were assigned two of these for the twelve people in our family group; and our official family "number" was enlarged by three digits—16 plus the number of this barracks. We were issued steel army cots, two brown army blankets each, and some mattress covers, which my brothers stuffed with straw.

The first task was to divide up what space we had for sleeping. Bill and Woody contributed a blanket each and partitioned off the first room: one side for Bill and Tomi, one side for Woody and Chizu and their baby girl. Woody also got the stove, for heating formulas.

The people who had it hardest during the first few months were young couples like these, many of whom had married just before the evacuation began, in order not to be separated and sent to different camps. Our two rooms were crowded, but at least it was all in the family. My oldest sister and her husband were shoved into one of those sixteen-by-twenty-foot compartments with six people they had never seen before—two other couples, one recently married like themselves, the other with two teenage boys. Partitioning off a room like that wasn't easy. It was bitter cold when we arrived, and the wind did not abate.[9] All they had to use for room dividers were those army blankets, two of which were barely enough to keep one person warm. They argued over whose blanket should be sacrificed and later argued about noise at night—the parents wanted their boys asleep by 9:00 P.M.—and they continued arguing over matters like that for six months, until my

---

7. In the army, a *mess hall* is the place where meals are eaten.
8. *Lee* is shelter or protection, especially on the side of something facing away from the wind.

Reading Strategy Summarizing *Summarize the information given in this passage about the food at Manzanar. What point is the author making here?* **R**

---

9. The fact that the wind did not *abate* means that it did not lessen in force or intensity.

JEANNE WAKATSUKI HOUSTON AND JAMES D. HOUSTON **327**

Teach

R Reading Strategy
Summarizing
Answer: *The author is showing that the Caucasian food servers lacked an understanding of traditional Japanese cuisine. The author also shows that almost every aspect of life at Manzanar was difficult for the residents to deal with: even the food they ate was poorly planned.* **OL**

L₂ Literary Element
Autobiography Point out the description of the barracks, and discuss how the narrator's point of view is evident. **Ask:** How does the description of the barracks differ from one that would be found in an encyclopedia? *(Details such as the poor construction, barren appearance, and people's reactions are more descriptive and personal.)* **OL**

★ Political History

Restitution Explain that Japanese Americans who were interned during World War II lost an estimated $500 million in real estate property (houses, farms, and businesses) and other possessions, jobs, and civil rights. In 1988 President Ronald Reagan signed Public Law 100-383, which offered about $20,000 in restitution to each internee. **AS**

English Language Coach

Unfamiliar Words Since English language learners may not recognize context clues, they may need help to make sense of unfamiliar words. Have them create a chart with these headings: Place Names, People Names, Japanese Words, Other Terms. Ask them to list unfamiliar words and their definitions. **EL**

Differentiated Instruction

Descriptive Verbs Write the words *pelted, snaked,* and *whacked* on the board. Explain that vivid verbs help the reader to picture scenes and events. Ask students to point out other expressive verbs, and remind them to use precise and vivid action verbs in their own writing. **OL**

Objectives
• To understand a historical narrative
• To use summarizing to increase comprehension (SE)
• To identify and analyze autobiography (TWE)
• To use interviewing to evoke a historical narrative (TWE)

Teach

R **Reading Strategy**

Summarizing Answer: *They had to share a compartment with strangers, who complained when someone stayed up past 9 p.m. They left to harvest sugar beets in Idaho for poor wages so they could have a room of their own.* **OL**

L1 **Literary Element**

Autobiography Remind students that Wakatsuki Houston's point of view colors this historical narrative. **Ask:** How does the child's point of view come across in the narrator's response to the barracks? *(She doesn't mind the barracks because she can sleep with her mother, and she enjoys joking about the dustiness with her siblings.)* **OL**

BI **Big Idea**

The Power of Memory
Answer: *Humor relieves tension and depression and keeps people connected. By giggling at the dust and heaps of clothes, Kiyo and the author have fun and bond in an otherwise depressing situation.* Discuss how children might view the internment experience differently from adults, as well as what role humor would play in this kind of situation. **OL**

sister and her husband left to harvest sugar beets in Idaho. It was grueling[10] work up there, and wages were pitiful, but when the call came through camp for workers to **alleviate** the wartime labor shortage, it sounded better than their life at Manzanar. They knew they'd have, if nothing else, a room, perhaps a cabin of their own.

That first night in Block 16, the rest of us squeezed into the second room—Granny, Lillian, age fourteen, Ray, thirteen, May, eleven, Kiyo, ten, Mama, and me. I didn't mind this at all at the time. Being youngest meant I got to sleep with Mama. And before we went to bed I had a great time jumping up and down on the mattress. The boys had stuffed so much straw into hers, we had to **L1** flatten it some so we wouldn't slide off. I slept with her every night after that until Papa came back.

We woke early, shivering and coated with dust that had blown up through the knotholes and in through the slits around the doorway. During the night Mama had unpacked all our clothes and heaped them on our beds for warmth. Now our cubicle looked as if a great laundry bag had exploded and then been sprayed with fine dust. A skin of sand covered the floor. I looked over Mama's shoulder at Kiyo, on top of his fat mattress, buried under jeans and overcoats and sweaters. His eyebrows were gray, and he was starting to giggle. He was looking at me, at my gray eyebrows and coated hair, and pretty soon we were both giggling. I looked at Mama's face to see if she thought Kiyo was funny. She lay very still next to me on our mattress, her eyes scanning everything—bare rafters, walls, dusty kids—scanning slowly, and I

---

10. Grueling work is very difficult, exhausting work.

Reading Strategy Summarizing *Summarize what happened to the author's sister and brother-in-law.* **R**

Vocabulary
alleviate (ə lē′vē āt′) *v.* to make easier to bear; relieve; lessen

think the mask of her face would have cracked had not Woody's voice just then come at us through the wall. He was rapping on the planks as if testing to see if they were hollow.

"Hey!" he yelled. "You guys fall into the same flour barrel as us?"

"No," Kiyo yelled back. "Ours is full of Japs." All of us laughed at this.

"Well, tell 'em it's time to get up," Woody said. "If we're gonna live in this place, we better get to work."

He gave us ten minutes to dress, then he came in carrying a broom, a hammer, and a sack full of tin can lids he had scrounged somewhere. Woody would be our leader for a while now, short, stocky, grinning behind his mustache. He had just turned twenty-four. In later years he would tour the country with Mr. Moto, the Japanese tag-team wrestler, as his sinister assistant Suki—karate chops through the ropes from outside the ring, a chunky leg reaching from under his kimono to trip up Mr. Moto's foe. In the ring Woody's smile looked sly and crafty; he hammed it up. Offstage it was whimsical, as if some joke were bursting to be told.

"Hey, brother Ray, Kiyo," he said. "You see these tin can lids?"

"Yeah, yeah," the boys said drowsily, as if going back to sleep. They were both young versions of Woody.

"You see all them knotholes in the floor and in the walls?"

They looked around. You could see about a dozen.

Woody said, "You get those covered up before breakfast time. Any more sand comes in here through one of them knotholes, you have to eat it off the floor with ketchup."

"What about sand that comes in through the cracks?" Kiyo said.

Woody stood up very straight, which in itself was funny, since he was only about five-foot-six.

Big Idea The Power of Memory *Why does the author remember moments of humor during her stay at Manzanar?* **BI**

Additional Support

Skills Practice

READING: Evaluating According to the narrator's evaluation of the situation, young couples such as Bill and Tomi had it the worst at the camp because of the lack of privacy at a time when they were just getting used to being a couple. Discuss what is most important to people at different stages of life and how people at various stages would be affected differently by the internment. (For example, it was important to the narrator to be with her family.) Finally, ask students to evaluate which age group they think suffered most at the camp and to support their evaluations. **OL**

"Don't worry about the cracks," he said. "Different kind of sand comes in through the cracks."

He put his hands on his hips and gave Kiyo a sternly comic look, squinting at him through one eye the way Papa would when he was asserting his authority. Woody mimicked Papa's voice: "And I can tell the difference. So be careful."

The boys laughed and went to work nailing down lids. May started sweeping out the sand. I was helping Mama fold the clothes we'd used for cover, when Woody came over and put his arm around her shoulder. He was short; she was even shorter, under five feet.

He said softly, "You okay, Mama?"

She didn't look at him, she just kept folding clothes and said, "Can we get the cracks covered too, Woody?"

L2 Outside the sky was clear, but icy gusts of wind were buffeting our barracks every few minutes, sending fresh dust puffs up through the floorboards. May's broom could barely keep up with it, and our oil heater could scarcely hold its own against the drafts.

"We'll get this whole place as tight as a barrel, Mama. I already met a guy who told me where they pile all the scrap lumber."

"Scrap?"

"That's all they got. I mean, they're still building the camp, you know. Sixteen blocks left to go. After that, they say maybe we'll get some stuff to fix the insides a little bit."

Her eyes blazed then, her voice quietly furious. "Woody, we can't live like this. Animals live like this."

It was hard to get Woody down. He'd keep smiling when everybody else was ready to explode. Grief flickered in his eyes. He blinked it away and hugged her tighter. "We'll make it better, Mama. You **BI** watch."

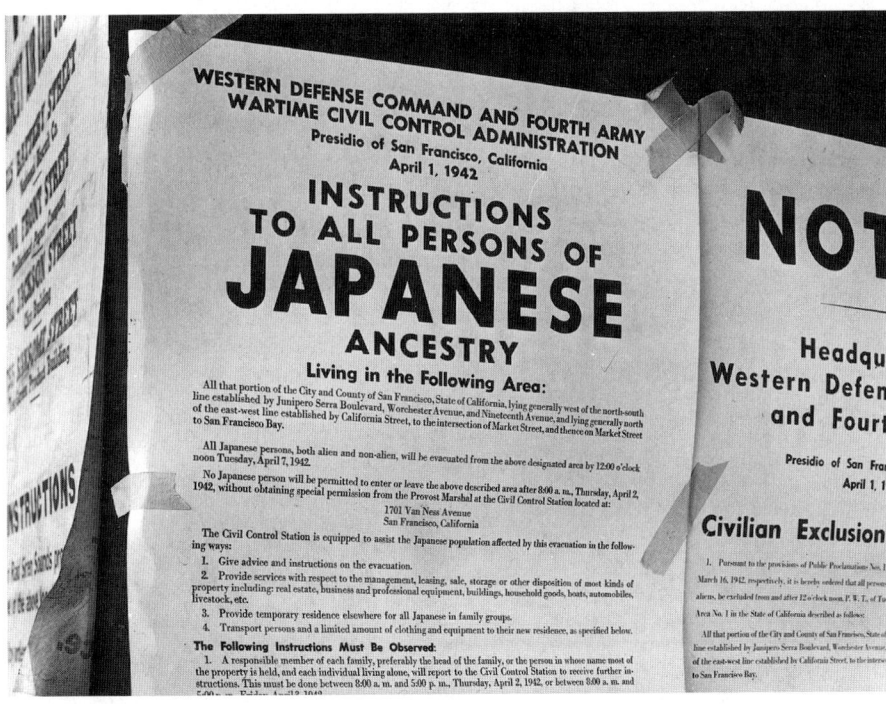

Posted notice informing people of Japanese ancestry of imminent relocation rules due to fears of treason and spying during early years of WWII, April 11, 1942. Dorothea Lange. Silver Gelatin Photograph.

Viewing the Art: If you saw a sign like this posted today, how would it make you feel? Explain. ⭐

JEANNE WAKATSUKI HOUSTON AND JAMES D. HOUSTON **329**

Teach

L2 **Literary Element**

Setting Note that the setting makes a major impression on the narrator. Have students describe the environment at Manzanar. **Ask:** What does the narrator emphasize about the climate and weather in this location? *(The wind, cold, and dust.)* **OL**

BI **Big Idea**

The Power of Memory Ask: What stands out about the author's memories of Woody? *(Woody was a humorous and optimistic leader. He tried to give hope to those around him.)* **OL**

⭐ **Viewing the Art**

Answer: *Students might feel shocked, confused, outraged, or afraid.*
With this evacuation order, General John DeWitt informed families such as the narrator's that they had less than a week to leave San Francisco. **AS**

English Language Coach

Figurative Language Students may need some help with figurative language, as in "a skin of sand" and "the mask of her face." Explain that the metaphors are not to be taken literally; instead, their implied comparisons create vivid images. Ask students to write metaphors of their own. **EL**

Differentiated Instruction

Visualizing Spatial concepts are important to understanding the internment camp. Ask students to draw aerial views of the camp itself, of Block 16 with its barracks, and of a building divided into six 16-by-20-foot units. Encourage students to visualize the camp and imagine themselves there. **OL**

Objectives
- To use summarizing to increase comprehension (SE)
- To identify and analyze autobiography (TWE)
- To use evaluating to analyze characters (TWE)

L Literary Element

Historical Narrative

Answer: *People knew that Japanese Americans ate rice and used soy sauce but did not know that Japanese Americans found fruit poured over rice repulsive. This shows the lack of understanding many people had of Japanese culture.* **OL**

BI Big Idea

The Power of Memory

Answer: *The seamstresses adapting World War I army clothes is an example of the Japanese Americans making the best of their situation. It helped fill their time and make the situation a little more bearable.* **OL**

★ Writer's Technique

Description Ask students to notice the description of the internees' clothing: "We were a band of Charlie Chaplins marooned in the California desert." Have them explain the figurative language and sensory images that create a vivid picture of the internees' appearances. *(Sensory details such as the oversize clothing, pea coats, and Mama's earmuffs help create a vivid portrait.)* **AS**

We could hear voices in other cubicles now. Beyond the wall Woody's baby girl started to cry.

"I have to go over to the kitchen," he said, "see if those guys got a pot for heating bottles. That oil stove takes too long—something wrong with the fuel line. I'll find out what they're giving us for breakfast."

"Probably hotcakes with soy sauce," Kiyo said, on his hands and knees between the bunks.

"No." Woody grinned, heading out the door. "Rice. With Log Cabin Syrup and melted butter."

I don't remember what we ate that first morning. I know we stood for half an hour in cutting wind waiting to get our food. Then we took it back to the cubicle and ate huddled around the stove. Inside, it was warmer than when we left, because Woody was already making good his promise to Mama, tacking up some ends of lath[11] he'd found, stuffing rolled paper around the door frame.

Trouble was, he had almost nothing to work with. Beyond this temporary weather stripping, there was little else he could do. Months went by, in fact, before our "home" changed much at all from what it was the day we moved in—bare floors, blanket partitions, one bulb in each compartment dangling from a roof beam, and open ceilings overhead so that mischievous boys like Ray and Kiyo could climb up into the rafters and peek into anyone's life.

The simple truth is the camp was no more ready for us when we got there than we were ready for it. We had only the dimmest ideas of what to expect. Most of the families, like us, had moved out from southern California with as much luggage as each person could carry. Some old men left Los Angeles wearing Hawaiian shirts and Panama hats and stepped off the bus at an altitude of 4000 feet, with nothing available but sagebrush and tarpaper to stop the April winds pouring down off the back side of the Sierras.[12]

The War Department was in charge of all the camps at this point. They began to issue military surplus from the First World War—olive-drab knit caps, earmuffs, peacoats, canvas leggings. Later on, sewing machines were shipped in, and one barracks was turned into a clothing factory. An old seamstress took a peacoat of mine, tore the lining out, opened and flattened the sleeves, added a collar, put arm holes in and handed me back a beautiful cape. By fall dozens of seamstresses were working full-time transforming thousands of these old army clothes into capes, slacks and stylish coats. But until that factory got going and packages from friends outside began to fill out our wardrobes, warmth was more important than style. I couldn't help laughing at Mama walking around in army earmuffs and a pair of wide-cuffed, khaki-colored wool trousers several sizes too big for her. Japanese are generally smaller than Caucasians, and almost all these clothes were oversize. They flopped, they dangled, they hung.

It seems comical, looking back; we were a band of Charlie Chaplins marooned in the California desert. But at the time, it was pure chaos. That's the only way to

Visual Vocabulary
A *peacoat* is a double-breasted jacket of thick woolen cloth, worn especially by sailors.

Visual Vocabulary
The great actor and director *Charlie Chaplin* gained fame for his role as a tramp in baggy pants in a series of movies in the 1920s. ★

---

11. In construction, *lath* is any of the thin, narrow strips of wood used as a foundation for plaster or tiles.

Literary Element Historical Narrative *How does Kiyo's comment reflect the misperceptions many people in the United States had about Japanese Americans?* **L**

12. The *Sierras,* or Sierra Nevada Mountains, run through eastern California. Manzanar was between these mountains and Death Valley.

Big Idea The Power of Memory *What was significant about the author's memory of the seamstresses?* **BI**

Additional Support

Skills Practice

RESEARCH: Internment Camps

The narrator describes Woody's efforts to improve the construction of the barracks, and later she expresses admiration for the seamstresses in the camp. Have students conduct research to find out more about how Japanese Americans in internment camps created culture and meaning in their lives. To give students some focus areas, have them create a chart with these columns: Schools, Arts, Communication, Activities, and Homemaking. Suggest that students refer to the Internet and printed resources for information; have them report their findings. **AL**

Children Awaiting Relocation (Assembly Center, Turlock, California), May 2, 1942. Dorothea Lange. Silver Gelatin Photograph.
Viewing the Art: What does this photograph suggest about life in the internment camp? ★

JEANNE WAKATSUKI HOUSTON AND JAMES D. HOUSTON **331**

Teach

R Reading Strategy

Summarizing On the board write: *The simple truth is the camp was no more ready for us when we got there than we were ready for it.* Ask students to supply details that show the truth of this summary. In addition, request that students summarize Woody's responsibilities. (*He is responsible for taking care of his family, as well as helping his mother and siblings.*) **OL**

★ Viewing the Art

More than 10,000 people were interned at Manzanar, with families living together in cramped quarters. **Answer:** *The kids look unhappy, tired, despondent; they huddle close together perhaps for warmth or from insecurity or fear. The kids' ill-fitting, adult clothes and hats and crammed suitcases imply unpreparedness and confusion.* **AS**

English Language Coach

Making Inferences Students new to the United States may need coaching to make inferences as they read. **Ask:** What inferences can you draw about Woody and Mama's relationship? (*She depends on him for help and support, and he is caring toward her.*) Point out details that show this relationship. **EL**

Differentiated Instruction

Evaluating Narration Invite students to brainstorm about what indicates a credible nonfiction account, such as specific details and historical accuracy. Ask students to evaluate the narrator's recollections about her internment experience. Encourage them to supply evidence to support their evaluations. **AL**

Objectives
- To understand historical narratives (SE)
- To use summarizing to increase comprehension (TWE)
- To conduct research to learn more about historical setting (TWE)

331

Teach

Group of evacuees of Japanese ancestry lined up outside train after arriving at Santa Anita Assembly Center from San Pedro as row of US soldiers face them, March 31, 1942. Dorothea Lange. Silver Gelatin Photograph. **★**

describe it. The evacuation had been so hurriedly planned, the camps so hastily thrown together, nothing was completed when we got there, and almost nothing worked.

I was sick continually, with stomach cramps and diarrhea. At first it was from the shots they gave us for typhoid, in very heavy doses and in assembly-line fashion: swab, jab, swab, *Move along now,* swab, jab, swab, *Keep it moving.* That knocked all of us younger kids down at once, with fevers and vomiting. Later, it was the food that made us sick, young and old alike. The kitchens were too small and badly ventilated. Food would spoil from being left out too long. That summer, when the heat got fierce, it would spoil faster. The refrigeration kept breaking down. The cooks, in many cases, had never cooked before. Each block had to provide its own volunteers. Some were lucky and had a professional or two in their midst.

But the first chef in our block had been a gardener all his life and suddenly found himself preparing three meals a day for 250 people.

"The Manzanar runs" became a condition of life, and you only hoped that when you rushed to the latrine, one would be in working order.

That first morning, on our way to the chow line, Mama and I tried to use the women's latrine in our block. The smell of it spoiled what little appetite we had. Outside, men were working in an open trench, up to their knees in muck—a common sight in the months to come. Inside, the floor was covered with excrement, and all twelve bowls were erupting like a row of tiny volcanoes.

Mama stopped a kimono-wrapped woman stepping past us with her sleeve pushed up against her nose and asked, "What do you do?"

"Try Block Twelve," the woman said, grimacing. "They have just finished repairing the pipes."

It was about two city blocks away. We followed her over there and found a line of

---

Literary Element Historical Narrative *What does this information tell you about living conditions at Manzanar?* **L**

Skills Practice

GRAMMAR: Dash On the board write: *They were up to their knees in muck—a common sight.* Point out the dash and explain that a dash is a punctuation mark used for two specific purposes:

- to indicate an abrupt change in a sentence

- to set off explanatory matter

Guide students to see that the dash in the above sentence is used to show an abrupt shift. Then ask students to find examples of dashes used in both ways. **OL** women waiting in the wind outside the latrine. We had no choice but to join the line and wait with them.

Inside it was like all the other latrines. Each block was built to the same design, just as each of the ten camps, from California to Arkansas, was built to a common master plan. It was an open room, over a concrete slab. The sink was a long metal trough against one wall, with a row of spigots for hot and cold water. Down the center of the room twelve toilet bowls were arranged in six pairs, back to back, with no partitions. My mother was a very modest person, and this was going to be agony for her, sitting down in public, among strangers.

One old woman had already solved the problem for herself by dragging in a large cardboard carton. She set it up around one of the bowls, like a three-sided screen. OXYDOL was printed in large black letters down the front. I remember this well, because that was the soap we were issued for laundry; later on, the smell of it would permeate these rooms. The upended carton was about four feet high. The old woman behind it wasn't much taller. When she stood, only her head showed over the top.

She was about Granny's age. With great effort she was trying to fold the sides of the screen together. Mama happened to be at the head of the line now. As she approached the vacant bowl, she and the old woman bowed to each other from the waist. Mama then moved to help her with the carton, and the old woman said very graciously, in Japanese, "Would you like to use it?"

Happily, gratefully, Mama bowed again and said, "Arigato" (Thank you). "Arigato gozaimas" (Thank you very much). "I will return it to your barracks."

"Oh, no. It is not necessary. I will be glad to wait."

The old woman unfolded one side of the cardboard, while Mama opened the other; then she bowed again and scurried out the door.

Those big cartons were a common sight in the spring of 1942. Eventually sturdier partitions appeared, one or two at a time. The first were built of scrap lumber. Word would get around that Block such and such had partitions now, and Mama and my older sisters would walk halfway across the camp to use them. Even after every latrine in camp was screened, this quest for privacy continued. Many would wait until late at night. Ironically, because of this, midnight was often the most crowded time of all. Like so many of the women there, Mama never did get used to the latrines. It was a humiliation she just learned to endure: *shikata ga nai*, this cannot be helped. She would quickly **subordinate** her own desires to those of the family or the community, because she knew cooperation was the only way to survive. At the same time she placed a high premium on personal privacy, respected it in others and insisted upon it for herself. Almost everyone at Manzanar had inherited this pair of traits from the generations before them who had learned to live in a small, crowded country like Japan. Because of the first they were able to take a desolate stretch of wasteland and gradually make it livable. But the entire situation there, especially in the beginning—the packed sleeping quarters, the communal mess halls, the open toilets—all this was an open insult to that other, private self, a slap in the face you were powerless to challenge. ❧

shikata ga nai, this cannot be helped

Big Idea The Power of Memory *How would it affect you to see friends or family members endure humiliations such as the ones Mama endured?* **BI**

Reading Strategy Summarizing *What does this summary of conditions at Manzanar show the reader? What might have been the author's purpose in including it here?* **R**

Vocabulary

subordinate (sə bôr′də nāt′) *v.* to cause to be, or treat as, secondary, inferior, or less important

JEANNE WAKATSUKI HOUSTON AND JAMES D. HOUSTON **333**

Assess

1. Answers will vary; students may say that the camp's conditions were disturbing.

2. (a) As if she had moved to another country (b) Everything was unfamiliar; she had grown up among Caucasians.

3. Mama broke all the dishes.

4. (a) Coldly (b) The Ocean Park teacher was kind and grandmotherly.

5. (a) To provide historical context for the story (b) Most students will say yes.

6. (a) To contrast her brick frame house with the poor living conditions at the camp, to show that her family was respectable before they were segregated and persecuted (b) Students may say the comparison shows how much the narrator's life changed and how greatly her mother suffered.

7. The small barracks had no insulation or furnishings. Internees came from warm climates, wearing light clothing and whatever clothes they could carry. They were not emotionally prepared for life in the camps.

8. Students' answers will vary.

RESPONDING AND THINKING CRITICALLY

Respond

1. What detail of Manzanar affected you the most? Explain.

Recall and Interpret

2. (a)How did the author feel about moving to Terminal Island? (b)Why do you think the author felt this way?

3. What did Mama do when the secondhand dealer offered her a low price for her valuable dishes?

4. (a)How did the teacher at Boyle Heights treat the author? (b)Compare and contrast that teacher to the teacher from Ocean Park.

Analyze and Evaluate

5. (a)Why does the author mention various events in U.S. history throughout the selection? (b)Do you think this makes her story more effective?

6. (a)Why does the author offer descriptions of her houses throughout this time period? (b)Do the comparisons of the houses achieve an important purpose within the selection? Explain.

7. What does the author mean when she says "The camp was no more ready for us when we got there than we were ready for it"? Explain.

Connect

8. **Big Idea** **The Power of Memory** Jeanne Wakatsuki Houston said that going back to visit Manzanar made her realize that her life began there. Discuss the lessons you learned about U.S. internment of Japanese Americans from reading about Wakatsuki Houston's memories.

LITERARY ANALYSIS

Literary Element **Historical Narrative**

A **historical narrative** can blend elements of objectivity and subjectivity. For instance, some facts mentioned by Wakatsuki Houston are verifiable and recounted in numerous other sources. Other details described by Wakatsuki Houston are anecdotal, deal with feelings and perceptions, and come from her personal memories. Both kinds of details—the objective and the subjective—have much to teach the reader about what happened to many Japanese Americans during World War II.

1. How would this story be different if someone who had no personal experiences related to Manzanar had written it? Do you think it would be as effective?

2. Does Wakatsuki Houston give enough objective details about the historical period to help the reader understand the context of the narrative?

Review: Autobiography

As you learned on pages 318-319, an **autobiography** is a person's account of his or her own life. In most autobiographies, the writer tells the story from the first-person point of view, using the pronoun *I*. The use of this point of view makes most autobiographies very personal and subjective.

Partner Activity Meet with another student and list some details from the selection that you would not find in a more objective source, such as an encyclopedia. How do these details help you better understand this episode in U.S. history?

Details	Evaluation
Mama breaks her valuable china.	gives a personal account; offers a perspective that a strictly factual account wouldn't
Children waking up in barracks with dust on their eyebrows	

Literary Element

1. Most students will say that a version by someone who had not experienced Manzanar would not be as visceral or compelling.

2. Most students will say that she provided enough information for them to grasp the historical context.

Review: Autobiography

Students' lists should contain specific details from the selection and an explanation of how each affected their interpretation of this historical event.

Reading Strategy — Summarizing

When you **summarize**, you describe the main ideas and events of a selection in your own words and in a logical sequence.

1. Summarize events in the life of Wakatsuki Houston's family before and after their internment at Manzanar.

2. What were the most important points or insights conveyed by the family's story? Explain.

Vocabulary — Practice

Practice with Word Parts Use your knowledge of suffixes to choose the best definition for each vocabulary word.

1. patriarch
   a. a male ruler of a group
   b. a male who is part of a group
   c. a male who is excluded from a group

2. designation
   a. resignation
   b. to name something
   c. an instance of naming something

3. alleviate
   a. to cause pain to lessen
   b. to cause pain
   c. painful

4. subordinate
   a. the act of being inferior
   b. to make inferior or secondary
   c. second

Academic Vocabulary

Here are two words from the vocabulary list on page R82.

implicate (im′plə kāt′) *v.* to involve or connect

modify (mod′ə fī′) *v.* to change

Practice and Apply
1. Why was Papa **implicated** as a spy?
2. Why did the people in the camp **modify** their barracks?

Writing About Literature

Compare and Contrast Setting In *Farewell to Manzanar,* the narrator describes the different settings in which the events of the selection occur. Write a brief essay comparing and contrasting these settings. Which place does the narrator seem to like best? Why? Use evidence from the text to support your opinion. Before you write your essay, use the following graphic organizer to help you organize your ideas.

| Introductory paragraph–thesis |

| First body paragraph–first point in support of thesis |
| Examples and reasons to support your first point |

| Second body paragraph–second point in support of thesis |
| Examples and reasons to support your second point |

| Concluding paragraph–summary and thesis |

When you are finished writing, meet with another student to read each other's essays and to suggest revisions. Then proofread and edit your essay for errors in spelling, punctuation, and grammar.

Reading Further

If you would like to read more about Japanese Americans during World War II, you might enjoy this nonfiction work:

Behind Barbed Wire: The Imprisonment of Japanese Americans during World War II, by Daniel S. Davis, looks at the factors that led to the internment of Japanese Americans.

Literature Online Web Activities For eFlashcards, Selection Quick Checks, and other Web activities, go to www.glencoe.com.

JEANNE WAKATSUKI HOUSTON AND JAMES D. HOUSTON **335**

Assess

Reading Strategy

1. Students' answers should describe the most important events in the family's life, including the difficult experience of living at Terminal Island and the humiliation and want experienced at Manzanar.

2. Students may say that the story indicates that Japanese Americans were no different than other immigrants and that their internment was unwarranted and humiliating.

Vocabulary

1. a
2. c
3. a
4. b

Academic Vocabulary

1. As a fisherman, he had the means to bring oil to the Japanese navy.

2. Conditions were terrible; they had to work hard to make them livable.

Writing About Literature

Use these criteria when evaluating students' writing:

- Does the essay compare and contrast the settings in which the narrator lived?

- Does the essay evaluate which setting they think the narrator liked best?

Literature Online

Web Activities Have students access the Web site for interactive activities that will help them assess their understanding of the selection.

Focus

Say: In many cases it is not clear whether you should use a singular or plural verb. This lesson will help you to make the correct decision.

Teach

Recognizing Predicate Nominatives
Describe predicate nominatives as words equated with the subject by the use of linking verbs. Give examples, such as "The cook is a former <u>gardener</u>" and "Voting rights and laws are the <u>topic</u> of my book." Draw arrows from the subject to the predicate nominative. Point out that subject-verb agreement questions arise when the subject is plural and the predicate nominative is singular, or vice versa. **Say:** Regardless of the predicate nominative, the verb should always agree with the subject. Point out how the verbs in the sample sentences agree with the subjects. **OL**

Assess

1. tries
2. don't
3. stop
4. are
5. was

▶ **Agreement**

A **verb** is the action word in a sentence and the **subject** is who or what does the action. **Subject-verb** agreement occurs when the subject and verb match in person and number.

▶ **Test-Taking Tip**

To help ensure subject-verb agreement when writing for a test, identify each subject as singular or plural and use an appropriate verb.

▶ **Language Handbook**

For more on subject-verb agreement, see the Language Handbook, pp. R46–R60.

Literature Online
eWorkbooks To link to the Grammar and Language eWorkbook, go to www.glencoe.com.

OBJECTIVES
• Understand subject-verb agreement.
• Recognize singular and plural subjects.

Grammar Workshop

Language Usage

Making Subjects and Verbs Agree

"Each barracks was divided into six units, sixteen by twenty feet, about the size of a living room. . . ."

—Jeanne Wakatsuki Houston and James D. Houston, from "Farewell to Manzanar"

Connecting to Literature In every sentence, the **verb**—or action word—must agree with the **subject**—or actor—in both person and number. In the sentence above, although the subject, *barracks*, looks plural, it functions as a unit and takes the singular auxiliary verb *was*. You can avoid subject-verb agreement errors in your own writing by following these guidelines:

• **With a compound subject that is joined by** *and* . . .
Use a singular verb if the parts of the subject make up a single unit or if they refer to the same person or thing.
Rice and fruit is an unheard-of combination for Japanese people.
Use a plural verb if the parts of the subject refer to separate people or things.
The neighborhood bully and his friend were frightening.
• **With a compound subject that is joined by** *or* or *nor* . . .
Use a verb that agrees with the subject closest to it.
Either their homework or their chores keep the children inside.
Neither below-zero temperatures nor a blizzard prevents him from sledding.
• **With a subject that is a collective noun** . . .
Use a singular verb if the noun refers to a group as a whole.
The committee has to come to a decision by noon.
Use a plural verb if the parts of the subject refer to separate individuals.
The committee discuss their responses to the new regulations.
• **With a subject that differs in number from its predicate nominative** . . .
Use a verb that agrees in number with the subject.
The floor is slats of scrap lumber.
Army blankets become a room divider.

Exercise

For each sentence below, write out the correct form of the verb.

1. The family (tries, try) to stick together and support each other.
2. The children (doesn't, don't) learn to speak Japanese.
3. Neither Mother nor other parents (stops, stop) worrying about their children.
4. Manzanar and many other camps (is, are) located on the west coast.
5. Harvesting beets in Idaho (were, was) hard work, but better than life in Manzanar.

Additional Support

eWorkbooks Have students access the Web site for more practice with subject-verb agreement.

Skills Practice

GRAMMAR: Compound Subjects
Subject-verb agreement can be more difficult when compound subjects are involved, and students may benefit from extra practice with this topic. **Write the following sentences on the board:**

• Bacon and eggs make a good breakfast.

• Either Ms. Simpson or the scouts found the fossil.

• Melinda and Kim were winners.

• Neither presents nor ice cream pleases Teal.

Then have students work in pairs to identify whether each contains a singular or plural verb and explain why. **OL**

from *Kaffir Boy*

MEET MARK MATHABANE

What was it like to grow up in South Africa under the system of apartheid? For Mark Mathabane (mä tä bä′ne) "it meant hate, bitterness, hunger, pain, terror, violence, fear, dashed hopes and dreams."

Dark Childhood Mathabane spent his early years living in poverty and fear under the apartheid government, which separated black South Africans in ghettos and treated them as inferior people. Constant police raids and relocation to worthless parcels of land where work and education were scarce made life unbearable for black South Africans.

Mathabane's family lived in Alexandra township, in a square-mile ghetto packed with 200,000 black South Africans. Barely subsisting on the ten dollars that Mathabane's father made each week, life in the Alexandra township for them was already brutal and harsh. But when Mathabane's father was arrested for being unemployed, the family fell into even deeper poverty.

> "*Books aren't written with the comfort of readers in mind. I know I didn't write* Kaffir Boy *that way. I wrote it to reflect reality, to show the world the inhumanity of the apartheid system.*"
>
> —Mark Mathabane

Escape from Oppression Although illiterate, Mathabane's mother understood the importance of education and insisted that her son attend school. Mathabane made up his mind to master English, which black South Africans were forbidden to learn. At the age of thirteen, he took up tennis and just five years later won a tennis scholarship to an American college; he later called this scholarship "my passport to freedom."

In 1986 Mathabane published his first book, *Kaffir Boy,* an honest portrayal of the horrors of growing up under apartheid. Despite being banned by the South African government for its powerful anti-apartheid sentiment, this autobiography was hugely successful.

A New Life *Kaffir Boy in America,* an account of Mathabane's arrival and first years in the United States, followed in 1989. This sequel relates Mathabane's difficulties in adapting to a new culture and lifestyle in a land that was wonderfully different from, but possessed unfortunate similarities to, the apartheid system.

In 1992 Mathabane and his wife, Gail, published *Love in Black and White,* a book about their emotional struggle to maintain an interracial relationship against social conventions. Mathabane followed this book with *African Women: Three Generations,* the novel *Ubuntu* and, most recently, *Miriam's Song.* Mathabane's other accomplishments include appearances on national television shows such as *The Oprah Winfrey Show* and *Larry King,* articles in major newspapers and magazines such as *The New York Times* and *USA Today,* and a one-year stint as a White House Fellow.

Mark Mathabane was born in 1960.

 Author Search For more about Mark Mathabane, go to www.glencoe.com.

MARK MATHABANE **337**

Selection Skills

Reading Skills
- Analyzing Cause–and–Effect Relationships (SE pp. 338, 339, 342, 344, 347, 348, 351)
- Responding (TWE p. 342)
- Drawing Conclusions (TWE p. 346)
- Problem and Solution (TWE p. 348)

from Kaffir Boy

Literary Elements
- Theme (SE pp. 338, 340, 343, 345, 346, 351)
- Conflict (SE p. 351)

Vocabulary Skills
- Analogies (SE p. 351)
- Academic Vocabulary (SE p. 351)

Listening/Speaking/Viewing Skills
- Analyze Conflict (SE p. 351)

Writing Skills/Grammar
- Quotation Marks (SE p. 352)
- Evaluate Author's Craft (SE p. 352)

Focus

Summary

In this excerpt from *Kaffir Boy*, Mark Mathabane recalls the events that propelled him into school at age seven. At first, the young Mathabane agrees with a gang of older street kids that school is a waste of time. Early one morning, Mama practically drags him to school. On the way, they meet a woman who tells them about her oldest son who joined a gang and was stabbed to death. After Mama is beaten up for putting him in school, Mathabane begins to comprehend the importance of an education.

V Vocabulary

Vocabulary File Say: Add these words and definitions to your vocabulary file. For each word, include a sentence that gives you an example of how to use the word. **OL** Students with English language needs should include the pronunciations of these words in their files. **EL**

Literary Elements Have students access the Web site to improve their understanding of theme.

Connecting to the Autobiography

In this excerpt from *Kaffir Boy*, Mark Mathabane recalls the events that showed him the value of education. Before you read the selection, think about the following questions:

- How does education affect your life?
- How does education change the way in which you see the world?

Building Background

Apartheid, which means "separateness," was a policy of racial discrimination that was officially adopted in 1948 by South Africa's white government. Under apartheid, black South Africans, who made up more than seventy-five percent of the population, and other nonwhite people were forced to live and work under a system of strict racial segregation. The separate and unequal conditions under which nonwhites lived extended to every facet of life, including education.

Apartheid sparked strong opposition in South Africa and in many other parts of the world, and came to a definitive end in 1994 with the electoral victory of Nelson Mandela's African National Congress. Mandela then became the first black president of South Africa.

Setting Purposes for Reading

Big Idea The Power of Memory

As you read, notice how Mathabane shows the power of memory to change one's life for the better.

Literary Element Theme

Theme is the central message of a work of literature that readers can apply to life. Finding the theme of a story helps you better connect with the author's purpose in writing. As you read, try to determine the central theme of this selection from Mathabane's *Kaffir Boy*.

- See Literary Terms Handbook, p. R18.

Literature Online **Interactive Literary Elements Handbook** To review or learn more about the literary elements, go to www.glencoe.com.

OBJECTIVES

In studying this selection, you will focus on the following:
- analyzing theme
- examining cause-and-effect relationships
- understanding internal and external conflict
- writing to evaluate an author's craft

Reading Strategy Analyzing Cause-and-Effect Relationships

A **cause-and-effect relationship** is a connection between the reason for an occurrence and the occurrence itself. **Analyzing** these relationships helps to explain why things happen and why a character or person makes the decisions he or she makes.

Reading Tip: Making Connections Use a chart like the one below to make connections between causes and effects in the selection.

Cause	Effect
His gang refuses to go to school.	Narrator decides not to go to school.

Vocabulary

coterie (kō′tər ē) *n.* a small group of people who share a particular interest and often meet socially; p. 342 *Janelle and her airplane-loving coterie crafted model airplanes.*

admonish (ad mon′ish) *v.* to warn, as against a specific action; p. 342 *José's parents admonished him to stay out of the canyon.*

peruse (pə rōōz′) *v.* to read through or examine carefully; p. 344 *The doctor perused the medical journals for detailed information.*

credence (krēd′əns) *n.* trustworthiness, especially in the reports or statements of others; p. 346 *The lawyer's argument had more credence than the accounts of bystanders.*

vehemently (vē′ə mənt lē) *adv.* strongly; intensely; passionately; p. 347 *The peace activists argued vehemently against the war.*

Selection Resources

Print Materials
- Unit 2 Resources (Fast File), pp. 21–23
- Leveled Vocabulary Development, p. 23
- Selection and Unit Assessments, pp. 49–50
- Selection Quick Checks, p. 25

Transparencies
- Bellringer Options Transparencies:
  Selection Focus Transparency 20
  Daily Language Practice Transparency 29
- Literary Elements Transparency 18

Technology
- TeacherWorks Plus™ CD-ROM
- StudentWorks Plus™ CD-ROM
- Presentation Plus!™ CD-ROM
- Literature Online, glencoe.com
- Online Student Edition, mhln.com
- ExamView® Assessment Suite CD-ROM
- Vocabulary PuzzleMaker CD-ROM
- Listening Library, disc 1 track 27

from

Kaffir Boy

Mark Mathabane

South African boys play soccer with an undersized ball in Soweto. 1990, Soweto, South Africa.

"Education will open doors where none seem to exist."

When my mother began dropping hints that I would soon be going to school, I vowed never to go because school was a waste of time. She laughed and said, "We'll see. You don't know what you're talking about." My philosophy on school was that of a gang of ten-, eleven-, and twelve-year-olds whom I so revered that their every word seemed that of an oracle.[1]

These boys had long left their homes and were now living in various neighborhood junkyards, making it on their own. They slept in abandoned cars, smoked glue and benzene,[2] ate pilchards and brown bread, sneaked into the white world to caddy and, if unsuccessful, came back to the township to steal beer and soda bottles from she-beens,[3] or goods from the Indian traders on First Avenue. Their life style was exciting, adventurous, and full of surprises; and I was attracted to it. My mother told me that they were no-gooders, that they would amount to nothing, that I should not associate with them, but I paid no heed. What does she know? I used to tell myself. One thing she did not know was that the gang's way of life had captivated me wholly, particularly their philosophy on school: they hated it and considered an education a waste of time.

They, like myself, had grown up in an environment where the value of an education was never emphasized, where the first thing a child learned was not how to read and write

---

1. In Greek mythology, the gods sometimes spoke through an *oracle*, or a person such as a priestess.
2. The boys are taking a risk with *benzene,* a poisonous liquid obtained from coal.
3. *Shebeens* are taverns operating without government license or approval.

Reading Strategy Analyzing Cause-and-Effect Relationships *Why do you think the gang has such appeal for Mathabane compared to the life his mother wants for him?* **R**

MARK MATHABANE **339**

English Language Coach

Sharing Prior Knowledge Having students from other cultures share what they know can help draw them out socially while benefiting others in the class by teaching them about cultural differences. Invite students who have lived or traveled in South Africa or other countries to share their knowledge about and experiences with the schools and/or the culture of those countries. When possible, have students who have traveled or lived abroad bring in photos, music, books, or clothing that reflect each culture. Invite them to share these objects with the class. **EL**

L1 Literary Element

Theme Answer: *He seems to be somewhat passive; he feels that he is under the gang's influence.* **OL**

L2 Literary Element

Theme Answer: *Students should note that the gang life was a dirty and corrupting influence on Mathabane.* **OL**

★ Writer's Technique

Dialogue Dialogue often serves to tell the reader about the characters and to create drama in a story. **Ask:** What does the dialogue on this page tell you about each character?

Answer: *The narrator's words show that he is a defiant, head-strong, disrespectful youth. The mother's words show that she is a determined, commanding woman. Granny's words show that she is a little gentler than the mother.* **AS**

Readability Scores

Dale-Chall: 6.4
DRP: 53
Lexile: 910

---

and spell, but how to fight and steal and rebel; where the money to send children to school was grossly[4] lacking, for survival was first priority. I kept my membership in the gang, knowing that for as long as I was under its influence, I would never go to school.

One day my mother woke me up at four in the morning.

★ "Are they here? I didn't hear any noises," I asked in the usual way.

"No," my mother said. "I want you to get into that washtub over there."

"What!" I balked, upon hearing the word washtub. I feared taking baths like one feared the plague. Throughout seven years of hectic living the number of baths I had taken could be counted on one hand with several fingers missing. I simply had no natural inclination for water; cleanliness was a trait I still had to acquire. Besides, we had only one bathtub in the house, and it constantly sprung a leak.

"I said get into that tub!" My mother shook a finger in my face.

Reluctantly, I obeyed, yet wondered why all of a sudden I had to take a bath. My mother, armed with a scrubbrush and a piece of Lifebuoy soap, purged[5] me of years and years of grime till I ached and bled. As I howled, feeling pain shoot through my limbs as the thistles of the brush encountered stubborn calluses, there was a loud knock at the door.

Instantly my mother leaped away from the tub and headed, on tiptoe, toward the bedroom. Fear seized me as I, too, thought of the police. I sat frozen in the bathtub, not knowing what to do.

"Open up, Mujaji [my mother's maiden name]," Granny's voice came shrilling through the door. "It's me."

4. Here, *grossly* means "totally; entirely."
5. To *purge* is to cleanse or get rid of whatever is unclean or undesirable.

Literary Element Theme *Do you think the author has strong convictions of his own at this point? Explain.* **L1**

Literary Element Theme *What do you think is the connection between cleanliness and Mathabane's life in the gang?* **L2**

My mother heaved a sigh of relief; her tense limbs relaxed. She turned and headed to the kitchen door, unlatched it, and in came Granny and Aunt Bushy.

"You scared me half to death," my mother said to Granny. "I had forgotten all about your coming."

"Are you ready?" Granny asked my mother.

"Yes—just about," my mother said, beckoning me to get out of the washtub.

She handed me a piece of cloth to dry myself. As I dried myself, questions raced through my mind: What's going on? What's Granny doing at our house this ungodly[6] hour of the morning? And why did she ask my mother, "Are you ready?" While I stood debating, my mother went into the bedroom and came out with a stained white shirt and a pair of faded black shorts.

"Here," she said, handing me the togs, "put these on."

"Why?" I asked.

"Put them on I said!"

I put the shirt on; it was grossly loose-fitting. It reached all the way down to my ankles. Then I saw the reason why: it was my father's shirt!

"But this is Papa's shirt," I complained. "It don't fit me."

"Put it on," my mother insisted. "I'll make it fit."

"The pants don't fit me either," I said. "Whose are they anyway?"

"Put them on," my mother said. "I'll make them fit."

Moments later I had the garments on; I looked ridiculous. My mother started working on the pants and shirt to make them fit. She folded the shirt in so many intricate ways and stashed it inside the pants, they too having been folded several times at the waist. She then choked the pants at the waist with a piece of sisal rope to hold them up. She then lavishly smeared my face, arms, and legs with a mixture of pig's fat and vaseline. "This will insulate you from the cold," she said. My skin

6. In this context, *ungodly* means "outrageous; shocking."

Additional Support

Skills Practice

RESEARCH: Outlining Apartheid, a legalized system of racial segregation and oppression of blacks, was formally instituted in South Africa in 1948. Black Africans were forced into nine separate "nations" and restricted to small rural areas of infertile land. Have students use various resources to find out more about apartheid. After they've taken notes on their findings, have them organize their notes into either chronological or conceptual outlines. **OL**

Children in Alexandra Township.

Viewing the Art: What does the background in this photograph tell you about these children's daily lives? How might the older three react to being enrolled in school like the author?

gleamed like the morning star, and I felt as hot as the center of the sun, and I smelled God knows like what. After embalming me, she headed to the bedroom.

"Where are we going, Gran'ma?" I said, hoping that she would tell me what my mother refused to tell me. I still had no idea I was about to be taken to school.

"Didn't your mother tell you?" Granny said with a smile. "You're going to start school."

"What!" I gasped, leaping from the chair where I was sitting as if it were made of hot lead. "I am not going to school!" I blurted out and raced toward the kitchen door.

My mother had just reappeared from the bedroom and guessing what I was up to, she yelled, "Someone get the door!"

Aunt Bushy immediately barred the door. I turned and headed for the window. As I leaped for the windowsill, my mother lunged at me and brought me down. I tussled, "Let

go of me! I don't want to go to school! Let me go!" but my mother held fast onto me.

"It's no use now," she said, grinning triumphantly as she pinned me down. Turning her head in Granny's direction, she shouted, "Granny! Get a rope quickly!"

Granny grabbed a piece of rope nearby and came to my mother's aid. I bit and clawed every hand that grabbed me, and howled protestations against going to school; however, I was no match for the two determined matriarchs.[7] In a jiffy they had me bound, hands and feet.

"What's the matter with him?" Granny, bewildered, asked my mother. "Why did he suddenly turn into an imp[8] when I told him you're taking him to school?"

"You shouldn't have told him that he's being taken to school," my mother said. "He doesn't want to go there. That's why I requested you come today, to help me take him there. Those boys in the streets have been a bad influence on him."

---

7. *Matriarchs* (mā′trē ärks′) are women who head families or who have great authority in other groups.
8. Here, *imp* means "a mischievous child."

MARK MATHABANE **341**

The Power of Memory
Answer: *The day became very significant to him and affected the path he followed in life, so it is understandable that he would have strong memories of it.* **OL**

L **Literary Element**

Theme Ask: What does it say about growing up in South Africa that children as young as the narrator are carrying around infants and looking for food? *(It shows that children must grow up faster than they would in the United States. They must take on at an early age the responsibilities of adults.)* **OL**

R **Reading Strategy**

Analyzing Cause-and-Effect Relationships
Answer: *Life on the streets, and involvement with gangs probably caused him to become a tsotsi.* **OL**

BI₂ **Big Idea**

The Power of Memory
Answer: *The woman wants to save the lives of other boys if she can.* **OL**

Additional Support

As the two matriarchs hauled me through the door, they told Aunt Bushy not to go to school but stay behind and mind the house and the children.

The sun was beginning to rise from beyond the veld[9] when Granny and my mother dragged me to school. The streets were beginning to fill with their everyday traffic: old men and women, wizened,[10] bent, and ragged, were beginning their rambling; workless men and women were beginning to assemble in their usual **coteries** and head for shebeens in the backyards where they discussed how they escaped the morning pass raids[11] and contemplated the conditions of life amidst intense beer drinking and vacant, uneasy laughter; young boys and girls, some as young as myself, were beginning their aimless wanderings along the narrow, dusty streets in search of food, carrying bawling infants piggyback.

As we went along some of the streets, boys and girls who shared the same fears about school as I were making their feelings known in a variety of ways. They were howling their protests and trying to escape. A few managed to break loose and make a mad dash for freedom, only to be recaptured in no time, **admonished** or whipped, or both, and ordered to march again.

As we made a turn into Sixteenth Avenue, the street leading to the tribal school I was being taken to, a short, chubby black woman came along from the opposite direction. She

---

9. In South Africa, the *veld* (velt) is a rolling grassland with scattered trees or bushes.
10. When the elderly become *wizened* (wiz´ ənd), they are shriveled or withered due to age.
11. *Pass raids* refers to the practice whereby police periodically stopped black South Africans to see that they had the proper papers authorizing them to be in specific areas.

Big Idea The Power of Memory *Why might Mathabane remember so vividly the details of that day later in life?* **BI₁**

Vocabulary

coterie (kō´tər ē) *n.* a small group of people who share a particular interest and often meet socially
admonish (ad mon´ish) *v.* to warn, as against a specific action

---

had a scuttle[12] overflowing with coal on her *doek*-covered (cloth-covered) head. An infant, bawling deafeningly, was loosely swathed with a piece of sheepskin onto her back. Following closely behind the woman, and picking up pieces of coal as they fell from the scuttle and placing them in a small plastic bag, was a half-naked, potbellied, and thumb-sucking boy of about four. The woman stopped abreast.[13] For some reason we stopped too.

"I wish I had done the same to my oldest son," the strange woman said in a regretful voice, gazing at me. I was confounded[14] by her stopping and offering her unsolicited opinion.

"I wish I had done that to my oldest son," she repeated, and suddenly burst into tears; amidst sobs, she continued, "before . . . the street claimed him . . . and . . . turned him into a *tsotsi*."[15]

Granny and my mother offered consolatory remarks to the strange woman.

"But it's too late now," the strange woman continued, tears now streaming freely down her puffy cheeks. She made no attempt to dry them. "It's too late now," she said for the second time, "he's beyond any help. I can't help him even if I wanted to. *Uswile*[16] [He is dead]."

"How did he die?" my mother asked in a sympathetic voice.

"He shunned school and, instead, grew up to live by the knife. And the same knife he lived by ended his life. That's why whenever I see a boy-child refuse to go to school, I stop and tell the story of my dear little *mbitsini*[17] [heartbreak]."

---

12. Here, a *scuttle* is a coal container.
13. *Abreast* means "alongside the others."
14. To be *confounded* is to be confused or bewildered.
15. A *tsotsi* (tsot sē) is an armed street hoodlum or gangster.
16. *Uswile* (ōō swēl ā)
17. *mbitsini* (əm bit sē´ nē)

Reading Strategy Analyzing Cause-and-Effect Relationships *What does the woman think caused her son to become a tsotsi?* **R**

Big Idea The Power of Memory *Why does the woman's memory of her son make her want to tell the story to other boys?* **BI₂**

Skills Practice

READING: Responding Say: How you respond to a selection can take different forms. Responses to reading can include discussions, journals, oral interpretations, and dramatizations. Form a reader's theater. Have students choose characters from the selection to read aloud. Have the remaining students take turns reading for the narrator. Begin the dramatic reading with Mathabane's mother waking him for school, and end with the end of the school scene on the next page. **OL**

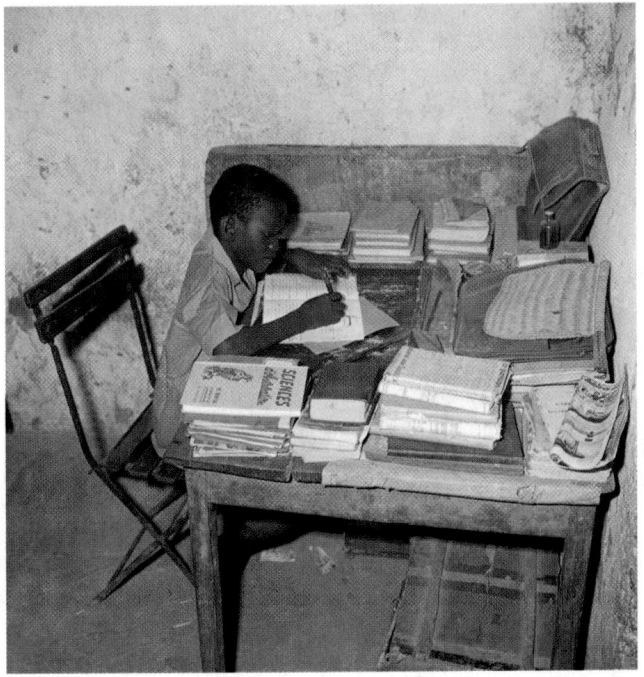

Schoolboy in Mali. A schoolboy does homework at his desk, Mali. 1960, Mali.
Viewing the Art: How does this child's attitude and activities reflect the theme of Mathabane's tale?

Having said that, the strange woman left as mysteriously as she had arrived.

"Did you hear what that woman said!" my mother screamed into my ears. "Do you want the same to happen to you?"

I dropped my eyes. I was confused.

"Poor woman," Granny said ruefully. "She must have truly loved her son."

Finally, we reached the school and I was ushered into the principal's office, a tiny cubicle facing a row of privies[18] and a patch of yellowed grass.

"So this is the rascal we'd been talking about," the principal, a tall, wiry man, foppishly[19] dressed in a black pin-striped suit, said to my mother as we entered. His austere,[20] shiny face, inscrutable and imposing, reminded me of my father. He was sitting behind a brown table upon which stood piles of dust and cobweb-covered books and papers. In one upper pocket of his jacket was arrayed a variety of pens and pencils; in the other nestled a lily-white handkerchief whose presence was more decorative than utilitarian.[21] Alongside him stood a disproportionately portly[22] black woman, fashionably dressed in a black skirt and a white blouse. She had but one pen, and this she held in her hand. The room was hot and stuffy and buzzing with flies.

"Yes, Principal," my mother answered, "this is he."

"I see he's living up to his notoriety," remarked the principal, noticing that I had been bound. "Did he give you too much trouble?"

"Principal," my mother sighed. "He was like an imp."

---

18. *Privies* (priv′ēz) are outhouses, or toilets.
19. The man surely would not think that he dressed *foppishly*—in the style of one who pays too much attention to his or her clothes.
20. *Austere* means "serious, strict, or severe."

Literary Element Theme *Why is it significant that Mathabane encounters this woman?* **L**

21. Something that is *utilitarian* is functional or practical.
22. A *portly* person has a heavy or stout but dignified appearance.

MARK MATHABANE **343**

Teach

L Literary Element

Theme Answer: *This woman warns Mathabane of his future if he continues his life on the street and does not pursue education.* **OL**

⭐ Viewing the Art

Children in Alexandra Township Answer: *The crude school room and stacks of outdated materials show that it was difficult for children to receive a contemporary education, but dedicated study, as indicated here in the boy's intense expression, can help one to achieve a life outside of such poverty.*

Explain to students that most photographs taken by professionals have a purpose. If the focus is on a person or a group of people, that is what will be featured. If the photographer wants to tell a story or provide information, background information will be included. **AS**

English Language Coach

Sharing Prior Knowledge Explain to the class that different cultures have different attitudes toward education. In addition, teaching and learning occur in different ways depending on the culture in which it takes place. Invite English language learners from other cultures to explain their cultures' attitudes toward education. Ask them also to describe details about schools in their cultures: such as teaching strategies, amount of homework, subjects studied, and interactions between teachers and students. **EL**

Objectives
• To examine cause-and-effect relationships (SE)
• To analyze theme (SE)
• To respond to literature by reading aloud (TWE)

Teach

R Reading Strategy

Analyzing Cause-and-Effect Relationships

Answer: *Some students may say that he will be frightened into attending school, and others may think that the threat makes it more likely that he will run away and join the gang.*
Say: Read the next paragraph. Why do Mama and Granny smile? *(Students should realize that the women are glad to see that the young Mathabane is frightened of the canes because that will make him more likely to not run away and to stay in school.)* **OL**

★ Writer's Technique

Paradox Explain to students that Granny's comment is a paradox—a statement with two parts that are both true, yet seem to contradict each other. **Ask:** How is her comment contradictory but also true? *(She understands the regulations but doesn't understand their justice or sense.)* **AS**

"He's just like the rest of them, Principal," Granny sighed. "Once they get out into the streets, they become wild. They take to the many vices of the streets like an infant takes to its mother's milk. They begin to think that there's no other life but the one shown them by the *tsotsis*. They come to hate school and forget about the future."

"Well," the principal said. "We'll soon remedy all that. Untie him."

"He'll run away," my mother cried.

"I don't think he's that foolish to attempt that with all of us here."

"He *is* that foolish, Principal," my mother said as she and Granny began untying me. "He's tried it before. Getting him here was an ordeal in itself."

The principal rose from his seat, took two steps to the door and closed it. As the door swung closed, I spotted a row of canes of different lengths and thicknesses hanging behind it. The principal, seeing me staring at the canes, grinned and said, in a manner suggesting that he had wanted me to see them, "As long as you behave, I won't have to use any of those on you."

Use those canes on me? I gasped. I stared at my mother—she smiled; at Granny—she smiled too. That made me abandon any inkling of escaping.

"So they finally gave you the birth certificate and the papers," the principal addressed my mother as he returned to his chair.

"Yes, Principal," my mother said, "they finally did. But what a battle it was. It took me nearly a year to get all them papers together." She took out of her handbag a neatly wrapped package and handed it to the principal. "They've been running us around for so long that there were times when I thought he would never attend school, Principal," she said.

> **Reading Strategy** Analyzing Cause-and-Effect Relationships *What effect do you think the principal's statement will have on Mathabane's commitment to attending school?* **R**

344 UNIT 2 NONFICTION

"That's pretty much standard procedure, Mrs. Mathabane," the principal said, unwrapping the package. "But you now have the papers and that's what's important.

"As long as we have the papers," he continued, minutely **perusing** the contents of the package, "we won't be breaking the law in admitting your son to this school, for we'll be in full compliance with the requirements set by the authorities in Pretoria."[23]

"Sometimes I don't understand the laws from Pitori,"[24] Granny said. "They did the same to me with my Piet and Bushy. Why, Principal, should our children not be allowed to learn because of some piece of paper?"

"The piece of paper you're referring to, Mrs. Mabaso [Granny's maiden name]," the principal said to Granny, "is as important to our children as a pass is to us adults. We all hate passes; therefore, it's only natural we should hate the regulations our children are subjected to. But as we have to live with passes, so our children have to live with the regulations, Mrs. Mabaso. I hope you understand, that is the law of the country. We would have admitted your grandson a long time ago, as you well know, had it not been for the papers. I hope you understand."

"I understand, Principal," Granny said, ★ "but I don't understand," she added paradoxically.

One of the papers caught the principal's eye and he turned to my mother and asked, "Is your husband a Shangaan, Mrs. Mathabane?"

"No, he's not Principal," my mother said. "Is there anything wrong? He's Venda and I'm Shangaan."[25]

---

23. The rules come from South Africa's capital, *Pretoria*.
24. *Pitori* is Granny's pronunciation of "Pretoria."
25. The people of South Africa belong to many different ethnic groups, including *Venda* and *Shangaan,* each with its own language.

> **Vocabulary**
> **peruse** (pə rōōz') *v.* to read through or examine carefully

---

Additional Support

Skills Practice

RESEARCH: Using a Search Engine Knowing the correct way to use a search engine is an important skill in Internet research. Have students search the Internet to find out more about South African ethnic groups and their languages, history, and customs. In particular, students should look for informa-tion about the two groups the narrator belongs to, Shangaan and Venda, as well as the others that have been mentioned, Zulu and Sisotho. Have students use the same key words in several differ-ent search engines to see what kinds of results each engine will find. **OL**

South African man with passbook.

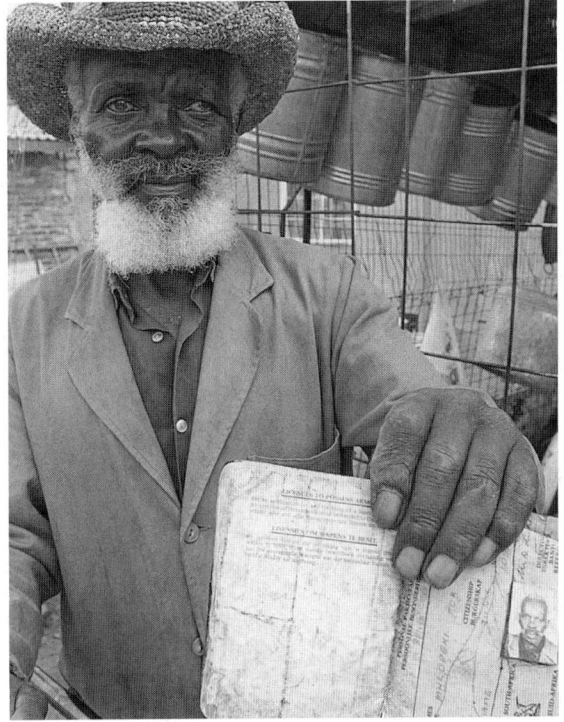

The principal reflected for a moment or so and then said, concernedly, "No, there's nothing seriously wrong. Nothing that we can't take care of. You see, Mrs. Mathabane, technically, the fact that your child's father is a Venda makes him ineligible to attend this tribal school because it is only for children whose parents are of the Shangaan tribe. May I ask what language the children speak at home?"

"Both languages," my mother said worriedly, "Venda and Shangaan. Is there anything wrong?"

The principal coughed, clearing his throat, then said, "I mean which language do they speak more?"

"It depends, Principal," my mother said, swallowing hard. "When their father is around, he wants them to speak only Venda. And when he's not, they speak Shangaan. And when they are out at play, they speak Zulu and Sisotho."[26]

"Well," the principal said, heaving a sigh of relief. "In that case, I think an exception can be made. The reason for such an exception is that there's currently no school for Vendas in Alexandra. And should the authorities come asking why we took in your son, we can tell them that. Anyway, your child is half-half."

Everyone broke into a nervous laugh, except me. I was bewildered by the whole thing. I looked at my mother, and she seemed greatly relieved as she watched the principal register me; a broad smile broke across her face. It was as if some enormously heavy burden had finally been lifted from her shoulders and her conscience.

"Bring him back two weeks from today," the principal said as he saw us to the door. "There're so many children registering today that classes won't begin until two weeks hence. Also, the school needs repair and cleaning up after the holidays. If he refuses to come, simply notify us, and we'll send a couple of big boys to come fetch him, and he'll be very sorry if it ever comes to that."

As we left the principal's office and headed home, my mind was still against going to school. I was thinking of running away from home and joining my friends in the junkyard.

I didn't want to go to school for three reasons: I was reluctant to surrender my freedom and independence over to what I heard

---

26. *Zulu* and *Sisotho* are ethnic groups as well as languages.

Big Idea The Power of Memory *What detail of her own life might Mathabane's mother be remembering or thinking about at this moment?* **BI**

Literary Element Theme *How does this passage contribute to a recurring theme in the story?* **L**

MARK MATHABANE **345**

Teach

L **Literary Element**

Theme **Answer:** *Students may note that it is another example of how disadvantaged the author is and how things are stacked against him.* **OL**

BI **Big Idea**

The Power of Memory
Answer: *Mathabane's mother recalls how her own lack of education has adversely affected her life.* **Ask:** How might education make Mathabane's life different from his mother's life? *He will be able to make intelligent, informed decisions in his life. He will be able to think beyond the limiting scope of his personal experience.* **OL**

★ Viewing the Art

Under apartheid, black Africans had to carry identification papers whenever they left their communities. Even though most of them worked their entire lives outside their communities, they could get in trouble if they did not have their papers. **Ask:** What evidence is there in the photograph that this man has lived for a long time under apartheid? *(Students may note that the papers are tattered and stained and that the photograph on his document looks younger than the old man does now.)* **AS**

Reading in the Real World

Citizenship Point out that oppressive governments still exist in many places. Have students research to find out what life is like in countries where certain groups suffer political oppression. **AL**

English Language Coach

Pronunciation Students for whom reading does not come easily are likely to have difficulty pronouncing the African words in this selection. Encourage them to read footnotes. As they look at the pronunciation of each word, pronounce it for them, and then have them repeat the word. **EL**

Objectives
• To analyze theme (SE)
• To use search engine to conduct research (TWE)

345

Teach

L Literary Element

Theme Answer: *Students should note that the contrast between the two worlds highlights the author's development of a theme of a crossroads or a place of difficult choices; others may point out a theme of awakening or hope.* **OL**

★ Cultural History

Marriage A *lobola*, or bride price, is a part of Zulu marriage arrangements. A price is determined to make up for the "loss" of a daughter. Ten head of cattle is usually the price paid by the future husband of the bride. In ancient and medieval Europe and many other parts of the world, there was a similar marriage tradition called the dowry, which is still common in some modern countries. Have students look up the definition of *dowry*.

Ask: How does the dowry differ from the lobola? *(The dowry is the money or property brought to the marriage by the wife.)* **AS**

---

every school-going child call "tyrannous discipline." I had heard many bad things about life in tribal school—from daily beatings by teachers and mistresses who worked you like a mule to long school hours—and the sight of those canes in the principal's office gave ample **credence** to rumors that school was nothing but a torture chamber. And there was my allegiance to the gang.

But the thought of the strange woman's lamentations over her dead son presented a somewhat strong case for going to school: I didn't want to end up dead in the streets. A more compelling argument for going to school, however, was the vivid recollection of all that humiliation and pain my mother had gone through to get me the papers and the birth certificate so I could enroll in school. What should I do? I was torn between two worlds.

But later that evening something happened to force me to go to school.

I was returning home from playing soccer when a neighbor accosted[27] me by the gate and told me that there had been a bloody fight at my home.

"Your mother and father have been at it again," the neighbor, a woman, said.

"And your mother left."

I was stunned.

"Was she hurt badly?"

"A little bit," the woman said. "But she'll be all right. We took her to your grandma's place."

I became hot with anger.

"Is anyone in the house?" I stammered, trying to control my rage.

"Yes, your father is. But I don't think you should go near the house. He's raving mad. He's armed with a meat cleaver. He's chased

---

27. In this case, to *accost* is to approach and speak to, often in a pushy way.

> **Literary Element** Theme *What does the contrast between these two different worlds have to do with the themes of the story?* **L**

> **Vocabulary**
>
> **credence** (krēd´əns) *n.* trustworthiness, especially in the reports or statements of others

---

out your brother and sisters, also. And some of the neighbors who tried to intervene he's threatened to carve them to pieces. I have never seen him this mad before."

I brushed aside the woman's warnings and went. Shattered windows convinced me that there had indeed been a skirmish of some sort. Several pieces of broken bricks, evidently broken after being thrown at the door, were lying about the door. I tried opening the door; it was locked from the inside. I knocked. No one answered. I knocked again. Still no one answered, until, as I turned to leave:

"Who's out there?" my father's voice came growling from inside.

"It's me, Johannes,"[28] I said.

"Go away, . . . !" he bellowed. "I don't want you or that . . . mother of yours setting foot in this house. Go away before I come out there and kill you!"

"Let me in!" I cried. "Dammit, let me in! I want my things!"

"What things? Go away, you black swine!"

I went to the broken window and screamed obscenities at my father, daring him to come out, hoping that if he as much as ever stuck his black face out, I would pelt him with the half-a-loaf brick in my hand. He didn't come out. He continued launching a tirade[29] of obscenities at my mother and her mother. . . . He was drunk, but I wondered where he had gotten the money to buy beer because it was still the middle of the week and he was dead broke. He had lost his entire wage for the past week in dice and had had to borrow bus fare.

"What happened, Mama?" I asked, fighting to hold back the tears at the sight of her disfigured face.

"Nothing, child, nothing," she mumbled, almost apologetically, between swollen lips. "Your papa simply lost his temper, that's all."

"But why did he beat you up like this, Mama?" Tears came down my face. "He's never beaten you like this before."

---

28. The author's name was *Johannes* (yō hä´ nis) before he changed it to Mark.
29. A *tirade* (tī rād´) is a long, angry, or scolding speech.

Additional Support

Skills Practice

READING: Drawing Conclusions

Have students reread the paragraph that begins "Granny did not reply; she knew well not to" on page 347. **Say:** This paragraph reveals a lot about Mama. From what you have learned so far, what kind of person is Mama? *(She is an independent-minded, strong-willed, intelligent woman who does not believe in the gender restrictions of her culture and wants more from life than most people in her community.)* **OL**

My mother appeared reluctant to answer me. She looked searchingly at Granny, who was pounding millet with pestle and mortar and mixing it with sorghum[30] and nuts for an African delicacy. Granny said, "Tell him, child, tell him. He's got a right to know. Anyway, he's the cause of it all."

"Your father and I fought because I took you to school this morning," my mother began. "He had told me not to, and when I told him that I had, he became very upset. He was drunk. We started arguing, and one thing led to another."

"Why doesn't he want me to go to school?"

"He says he doesn't have money to waste paying for you to get what he calls a useless white man's education," my mother replied. "But I told him that if he won't pay for your schooling, I would try and look for a job and pay, but he didn't want to hear that, also. 'There are better things for you to work for,' he said. 'Besides, I don't want you to work. How would I look to other men if you, a woman I owned, were to start working?' When I asked him why shouldn't I take you to school, seeing that you were now of age, he replied that he doesn't believe in schools. I told him that school would keep you off the streets and out of trouble, but still he was belligerent."

"Is that why he beat you up?"

"Yes, he said I disobeyed his orders."

"He's right, child," Granny interjected. "He paid *lobola* [bride price] for you. And your father ate it all up before he left me."

To which my mother replied, "But I desperately want to leave this beast of a man. But with his *lobola* gone I can't do it. ★ That worthless thing you call your husband shouldn't have sold Jackson's scrawny cattle and left you penniless."

"Don't talk like that about your father, child," Granny said. "Despite all, he's still your father, you know. Anyway, he asked for *lobola* only because he had to get back what he spent raising you. And you know it would have been taboo for him to let you or any of your sisters go without asking for *lobola*."

"You and Papa seemed to forget that my sisters and I have minds of our own," my mother said. "We didn't need you to tell us whom to marry, and why, and how. If it hadn't been for your interference, I could have married that schoolteacher."

Granny did not reply; she knew well not to. When it came to the act of "selling" women as marriage partners, my mother was **vehemently** opposed to it. Not only was she opposed to this one aspect of tribal culture, but to others as well, particularly those involving relations between men and women and the upbringing of children. But my mother's sharply differing opinion was an exception rather than the rule among tribal women. Most times, many tribal women questioned her sanity in daring to question well-established mores.[31] But my mother did not seem to care; she would always scoff at her opponents and call them fools in letting their husbands enslave them completely.

Though I disliked school, largely because I knew nothing about what actually went on

---

30. *Millet* is a grain similar to wheat, and *sorghum* is a syrup made from a tropical grass.

---

31. The customs and moral standards followed by most people in a given society are called *mores* (môr´āz).

Teach

Analyzing Cause-and-Effect Relationships

Answer: *It helps Mathabane to realize why his father acts abusively. He realizes that life on the streets without an education would turn him into his father.* **Ask:** *Do you think the statement would have affected Mathabane as much had his father not acted abusively earlier that day? (The statement probably would not have been as powerful had his father's behavior not taken a turn for the worse that day.)* **OL**

⭐ Viewing the Art

Answer: *The photo shows that even in the segregated communities, some people are poorer than others.* Explain to students that equality did not exist even within the black African communities. Differences in eduction, background, and tribal group created differences in status—and often led to conflict. In addition, despite apartheid, thousands of black Africans flooded into South Africa every year from other African countries, because there were more jobs in South Africa than elsewhere. **AS**

⭐ Alexandra Township, South Africa.
Viewing the Art: What does this photograph tell you about life under apartheid?

there, and the little I knew had painted a dreadful picture, the fact that a father would not want his son to go to school, especially a father who didn't go to school, seemed hard to understand.

"Why do you want me to go to school, Mama?" I asked, hoping that she might, somehow, clear up some of the confusion that was building in my mind.

"I want you to have a future, child," my mother said. "And, contrary to what your father says, school is the only means to a future. I don't want you growing up to be like your father."

The latter statement hit me like a bolt of lightning. It just about shattered every defense mechanism and every pretext[32] I had against going to school.

---

32. A *pretext* is a false reason or excuse one gives to hide a true reason or motive.

Reading Strategy Analyzing Cause-and-Effect Relationships *Why do you think the statement had such a strong effect on Mathabane?* **R**

348 UNIT 2 NONFICTION

"Your father didn't go to school," she continued, dabbing her puffed eyes to reduce the swelling with a piece of cloth dipped in warm water, "that's why he's doing some of the bad things he's doing. Things like drinking, gambling, and neglecting his family. He didn't learn how to read and write; therefore, he can't find a decent job. Lack of any education has narrowly focused his life. He sees nothing beyond himself. He still thinks in the old, tribal way, and still believes that things should be as they were back in the old days when he was growing up as a tribal boy in Louis Trichardt. Though he's my husband, and your father, he doesn't see any of that."

"Why didn't he go to school, Mama?"

"He refused to go to school because his father led him to believe that an education was a tool through which white people were going to take things away from him, like they did black people in the old days. And that a white man's education was

---

Additional Support

READING: Problem and Solution

Point out that the selection deals with education as a solution to a major problem and to the conflicts among the characters. Have students make a chart illustrating various problems and solutions in the story. At the top, they should write the headings *Problem* and *Solution*. Down the left side, they should write *Mathabane*, *Mathabane's Mother*, *Mathabane's Father*, and *Position of Blacks in South Africa*. After students have completed their charts, have them discuss the various problems and solutions. **OL**

348

worthless insofar as black people were concerned because it prepared them for jobs they can't have. But I know it isn't totally so, child, because times have changed somewhat. Though our lot isn't any better today, an education will get you a decent job. If you can read or write you'll be better off than those of us who can't. Take my situation: I can't find a job because I don't have papers, and I can't get papers because white people mainly want to register people who can read and write. But I want things to be different for you, child. For you and your brother and sisters. I want you to go to school, because I believe that an education is the key you need to open up a new world and a new life for yourself, a world and life different from that of either your father's or mine. It is the only key that can do that, and only those who seek it earnestly and perseveringly will get anywhere in the white man's world. Education will open doors where none seem to exist. It'll make people talk to you, listen to you, and help you; people who otherwise wouldn't bother. It will make you soar, like a bird lifting up into the endless blue sky, and leave poverty, hunger, and suffering behind. It'll teach you to learn to embrace what's good and shun what's bad and evil. Above all, it'll make you a somebody in this world. It'll make you grow up to be a good and proud person. That's why I want you to go to school, child, so that education can do all that, and more, for you."

A long, awkward silence followed, during which I reflected upon the significance of my mother's lengthy speech. I looked at my mother; she looked at me.

Finally, I asked, "How come you know so much about school, Mama? You didn't go to school, did you?"

"No, child," my mother replied. "Just like your father, I never went to school." For the second time that evening, a mere statement of fact had a thunderous impact on me. All ★ the confusion I had about school seemed to leave my mind, like darkness giving way to light. And what had previously been a dark, yawning void in my mind was suddenly transformed into a beacon of light that began to grow larger and larger, until it had swallowed up, blotted out, all the blackness. That beacon of light seemed to reveal things and facts, which, though they must have always existed in me, I hadn't been aware of up until now.

"But unlike your father," my mother went on, "I've always wanted to go to school, but couldn't because my father, under the sway of tribal traditions, thought it unnecessary to educate females. That's why I so much want you to go, child, for if you do, I know that someday I too would come to go, old as I would be then. Promise me, therefore, that no matter what, you'll go back to school. And I, in turn, promise that I'll do everything in my power to keep you there."

With tears streaming down my cheeks and falling upon my mother's bosom, I promised her that I would go to school **L** "forever." That night, at seven and a half years of my life, the battlelines in the family were drawn. My mother on the one side, illiterate but determined to have me drink, for better or for worse, from the well of knowledge. On the other side, my father, he too illiterate, yet determined to have me drink from the well of ignorance. Scarcely aware of the magnitude of the decision I was making or, rather, the decision which was being emotionally thrust upon me, I chose to fight on my mother's side, and thus my destiny was forever altered. ∾

> **Big Idea** The Power of Memory *How do you think his mother's statements might change Mathabane's feelings now and later in his life?* **BI**

English Language Coach

Multilingualism Point out to less proficient readers that the narrator speaks four different languages, depending on whom he is with and where he is. Explain that speaking more than one language is common in many parts of the world. Discuss the advantages of being multilingual, such as being able to converse with people from other cultures. Invite multilingual students to tell what languages they speak and in what situations they speak them. Invite them to say a few words or sentences in those languages. **EL**

Assess

1. (a) Answers will vary. Students may choose the scene in which the narrator's mother and Granny tie him up or the scene in which Mathabane screams at his father. (b) Students may point to each scene's emotional impact and suspense.

2. (a) It is a waste of time. (b) It is the attitude of the gang members he admires.

3. (a) He becomes enraged and abuses his wife. (b) It reveals the father's hopelessness about the future and his mother's belief that her children can have better lives.

4. (a) She does not want him to face the same limitations she faced. (b) It steers him away from a dangerous life as a gang member.

5. Students may say that his use of South African words makes the narrative more authentic and interesting.

6. The setting is essential because it was this specific time and place that forced Mathabane into facing the decision he faced.

7. It shows the problems that result from ignorance.

8. Her lack of education and abusive treatment at the hands of her society and husband made her an angry

---

RESPONDING AND THINKING CRITICALLY

Respond

1. (a) What scene from this selection lingers in your mind? (b) What about this scene is memorable?

Recall and Interpret

2. (a) As this excerpt begins, what is Mathabane's attitude toward school and where did this attitude come from? (b) Why has he adopted this attitude?

3. (a) How does Mathabane's father react to the day's events? (b) How does the conflict between Mathabane's parents reflect their different outlooks on his life?

4. (a) What goal does Mathabane's mother have for him? (b) How does this goal change Mathabane's life?

Analyze and Evaluate

5. Mathabane uses South African words throughout the text. In your opinion, do these words enhance or detract from the reading experience? Explain.

6. How important is the setting—the time and place—of this autobiographical story? How does it influence the events that occur?

7. Consider Mathabane's use of cultural details such as the treatment of women. How do these details illuminate Mathabane's purpose in this selection?

Connect

8. **Big Idea** The Power of Memory Mathabane tells this story with the benefit of hindsight. How can he now see that his mother's past altered her son's life?

DAILY LIFE AND CULTURE

A Life Apart

Apartheid refers to the policy the South African government used to legally segregate the white minority from the nonwhite majority. Apartheid originated with the Population Registration Act of 1950, which classified South Africans into one of three categories: the Bantu, or black citizens, the "Coloured," or biracial citizens, and white citizens.

Under apartheid the Bantu group was separated and divided into powerless tribal "homelands" called Bantustans. These areas were typically very poor and economically deprived, with jobs scarce and opportunities for education limited. Once they had been ousted from urban areas, Bantu access to cities was strictly regulated. Nonwhite South Africans were required to carry a "pass," or documents that allowed their presence in otherwise restricted areas. Social interaction between the races was also strictly limited.

Resistance to apartheid grew in the second half of the twentieth century. Anti-apartheid groups, formed by nonwhite Africans with the

support of some white citizens, held protests, demonstrations and strikes. The most famous incident of resistance was the Soweto riots in 1976, which occurred after the government enacted language requirements and restrictions in the schools.

- What are some ways in which people can try to change oppressive policies like apartheid?

- What similarities and differences do you see between South Africa's apartheid and the United States' segregation policies in the nineteenth and early to mid twentieth centuries?

---

and rebellious person. This led her to fight for a better life for her son.

A Life Apart

- Students may suggest organizing protests or promoting education among the oppressed people.

- Students may cite the "separate but equal" policies: having separate schools for African Americans and having African Americans sit in the back of buses.

LITERARY ANALYSIS

Literary Element Theme

Some works of literature have a **stated theme**, which is expressed directly. More works have an **implied theme**, which is revealed gradually through events, dialogue, or description. A literary work may have more than one theme.

1. What is the central theme in this selection from *Kaffir Boy*? Is this theme stated or implied? Explain.

2. What other themes can you identify from this selection? Are they connected to the central theme? Explain.

Review: Conflict

As you learned on page 36, **conflict** is the central struggle between two opposing forces in a story or drama. An external conflict exists when a character struggles against some outside force, such as another person, nature, society, or fate. An internal conflict is a struggle that takes place within the mind of a character who is torn between opposing feelings, desires, or goals.

Partner Activity With a classmate, discuss the conflicts in this selection from *Kaffir Boy*. Working with your partner, create two charts similar to the ones below. Fill in the first chart with examples from the text that demonstrate an internal conflict. Fill in the second chart with examples from the text that demonstrate external conflicts.

Internal Conflicts
Mathabane is torn between going to school and joining his friends.

External Conflicts
Mathabane doesn't want to take a bath.

READING AND VOCABULARY

Reading Strategy Analyzing Cause-and-Effect Relationships

Authors use **cause-and-effect relationships** to show why events occur and why characters make decisions.

1. What do you think is the most significant cause-and-effect relationship in this selection?

2. How is this relationship connected to the main theme of the selection?

Vocabulary Practice

Practice with Analogies Analogies can illustrate many different relationships: synonym-antonym, part to whole, and object to function, to name a few. Circle the word that best completes the analogy.

1. coterie : individual :: sports team :
   a. player   b. referee   c. football

2. admonish : warn :: sprint :
   a. stroll   b. walk   c. run

3. peruse : read :: scrutinize :
   a. ignore   b. watch   c. run

4. credence : trust :: optimism :
   a. truth   b. hope   c. belief

5. vehemently : passionate :: lethargically :
   a. sadden   b. angrily   c. indifferent

Academic Vocabulary

Here are two words from the vocabulary list on page R82. These words will help you think, write, and talk about the selection.

facilitate (fə sil′ə tāt′) *v.* to make easier; to help bring about

whereas (wār az′) *adj.* while at the same time; although

Practice and Apply

1. How does Granny **facilitate** Mathabane's finally going to school?

2. Mathabane's mother believes that education is valuable, **whereas** Mathabane's father thinks that education is useless. What accounts for this difference in opinion?

MARK MATHABANE **351**

Vocabulary

1. a 2. c 3. b 4. b 5. c

Academic Vocabulary

1. Granny helps Mama tie him up and walk him to school. She also urges Mama to explain the reasons for a good education.

2. Mathabane's mother believes that lack of education is responsible for her and her family's poor situation. His father is angry at his life's outcome and was taught that education was useless.

Assess

Literary Element

1. The central theme is the saving power of education as exemplified by the choice Mathabane had to make between the streets and education. It was Mathabane's decision, and it was a decision that probably saved his life. The theme is stated in his mother's monologue and Mathabane's thoughts.

2. The themes of violence, drug abuse, and the cultural treatment of women as property, or the *lobola*. The themes of violence and drug abuse are connected to the central theme; they represent one path that Mathabane could follow. The theme of *lobola* is related; it shows the oppression that Mathabane's mother wants her son to leave behind.

Review: Conflict

Students should be able to explain how each conflict they list is or is not resolved.

Reading Strategy

1. Students may say that Mathabane's mother's comment about her not wanting him to end up like his father is the most significant cause-effect relationship, because it affected him deeply.

2. Answers should support the relationship the student identified as most significant.

Assess

Writing About Literature

Use these criteria when evaluating students' writing:

- Does the essay cite Mathabane's mother's monologue at the end of the selection?

- Does the essay show that his mother's monologue is important because it states the theme of the selection?

- Does the essay explain that Mathabane uses monologue to explain and emphasize the importance of the decision he had to make?

- Does the essay express an opinion about the effectiveness of Mathabane's use of monologue?

Internet Connection

Make sure that students use reliable Web sites as their sources. Encourage students to use Web sites operated by academic and research institutions, government Web sites, and online encyclopedias.

Mathabane's Language and Style

1. "Why do you want me to go to school, Mama?"
2. "I said, 'get into that tub!'"

Writing About Literature

Evaluate Author's Craft A monologue is a long speech by a character in a literary work. Write a one- or two-page analysis of Mathabane's use of monologue. Who delivers a monologue in this selection? Why is monologue a crucial part of this selection? For what purposes does Mathabane use monologue? Is Mathabane's use of monologue effective? Why or why not?

Before you begin drafting, take notes on Mathabane's use of monologue in a two-column chart.

Example	Evaluation	Purpose
"I believe that an education is the key you need to open up a new world and a new life for yourself," p. 349	Very effective because it states Mother's exact belief	Illustrates theme of education as a means to improve life

Include quotes from the text related to Mathabane's use of monologue, as well as any impressions or ideas that strike you as you read. Once you have completed the chart, begin drafting.

After completing your draft, meet with a peer reviewer to assess each other's writing and suggest revisions. Then proofread and edit your writing for errors in spelling, grammar, and punctuation.

Internet Connection

Use the Internet to learn about the political situation in South Africa today. Make a list of questions, such as: What form of government does South Africa have? What are the most pressing political and social issues? What progress has been made in healing the wounds caused by decades of apartheid? Share your findings with the class.

Mathabane's Language and Style

Using Quotation Marks Throughout *Kaffir Boy*, Mathabane uses quotation marks to include vivid dialogue. Notice how the quotation marks and dialogue in the excerpt below add action and characterization:

> "Didn't your mother tell you?" Granny said with a smile. "You're going to start school."
> "What!" I gasped, leaping from the chair where I was sitting as if it were made of hot lead. "I am not going to school!"

Quotation marks are used to enclose a direct quotation. Quotation marks should be placed outside periods and commas; outside exclamation points and question marks when the quoted matter is an exclamation or question; and inside exclamation points and question marks when the quoted matter is not an exclamation or question.

Notice Mathabane's effective use of quotation marks:

Example	Placement of Quotation Marks
"Put them on I said!"	outside exclamation point
"I'll make it fit."	outside period
"You scared me half to death,"	outside comma

Activity Correct the punctuation in the following sentences as needed.

1. "Why do you want me to go to school, Mama"?
2. "I said get into that tub"!

Revising Check

Quotation Marks Correct punctuation is an important part of effective and professional writing. With a partner, go through your essay about Mathabane's use of monologue and correct errors in your usage of quotation marks.

Literature Online **Web Activities** For eFlashcards, Selection Quick Checks, and other Web activities, go to www.glencoe.com.

Literature Online

Web Activities Have students access the Web site for interactive activities that will help them assess their understanding of the selection.

Revising Check

Remind students that when quoting a passage that already contains double quotation marks one should substitute single quotations for them.

Living Well. Living Good.

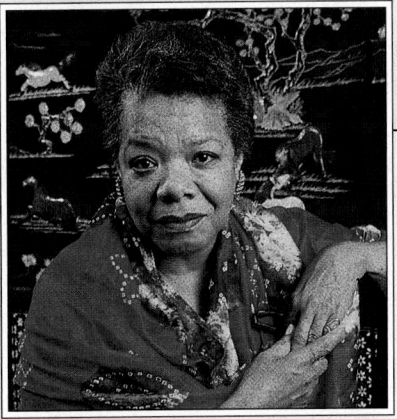

MEET MAYA ANGELOU

Maya Angelou had a difficult early life, but she overcame her obstacles to become a successful performer and writer. She is considered one of the most influential African American women of her time.

Angelou was born Marguerite Johnson in St. Louis, Missouri. She spent most of her childhood in Stamps, Arkansas, with her paternal grandmother. As a young girl, she spent a lot of time reading books. She developed a love of literature, including the works of Langston Hughes and William Shakespeare.

"In all my work, what I try to say is that as human beings we are more alike than we are unalike."

—Maya Angelou

In 1940 Angelou and her brother were taken to San Francisco, California. Five years later, at the age of seventeen, Angelou graduated from high school and gave birth to a son. To support herself and her son, she held odd jobs, working as a waitress, cook, and dancer. During the 1950s, she performed professionally using the stage name of Maya Angelou.

Her Literary Career Begins After touring twenty-two countries performing in a production of *Porgy and Bess*, Angelou left the United States. For a few years she lived in Cairo, Egypt, where she worked as an associate editor for the *Arab Observer*. In 1962 she moved to Ghana. There she wrote for the *African Review* and worked at the University of Ghana's School of Music and Drama.

When Angelou returned to the United States, James Baldwin, whom she had met through the Harlem Writers Guild several years earlier, encouraged her to write an autobiography. At first she rejected the idea, but later she reconsidered and decided to write *I Know Why the Caged Bird Sings*. This autobiography details her life from her childhood in Stamps to the birth of her son.

Continued Success After the success of her first autobiography, Angelou published four more. In addition to her autobiographies, Angelou wrote several collections of poetry, including *Just Give Me a Cool Drink of Water 'fore I Diiie*, which was nominated for a Pulitzer Prize in 1972.

Angelou wrote and presented a poem called "On the Pulse of Morning" for the 1993 inauguration of President Bill Clinton. Later that year she published a collection of essays called *Wouldn't Take Nothing for My Journey Now*, from which this essay was taken.

Maya Angelou was born in 1928.

 Author Search For more about Maya Angelou, go to www.glencoe.com.

MAYA ANGELOU **353**

Focus

BELLRINGER

Bellringer Options
Selection Focus
Transparency 21
Daily Language Practice
Transparency 30
Or on the board write: *Money Can't Buy Happiness* **Ask:**
Do you agree or disagree with this statement? Have students discuss their responses in class.

Literature Online

Author Search To expand students' appreciation of Maya Angelou, have them access the Web site for additional information and resources.

Selection Skills

Living Well. Living Good.

Literary Elements
- Memoir (SE pp. 354, 355, 358)
- Theme (SE p. 358)

Reading Skills
- Drawing Conclusions (SE pp. 354, 357, 359)

Vocabulary Skills
- Analogies (SE p. 359)
- Academic Vocabulary (SE p. 359)

Listening/Speaking/Viewing Skills
- Connection to Personal Experience (SE p. 359)
- Analyzing Art (TWE p. 355, 357)

Writing Skills/Grammar
- Author's Craft Analysis (SE p. 359)
- Personal Narrative (TWE p. 356)

Focus

Summary

Maya Angelou shares a story told to her by her Aunt Tee, who worked as a maid for a rich family in Bel Air. Her employers ate poorly, did little entertaining, and seemed unhappy. Aunt Tee threw parties regularly for her friends, ate rich food, and had a good time. During one of the parties, her employers ask to join her. Aunt Tee's experience with the family taught Angelou that money does not buy happiness.

Literary Elements Have students access the Web site to improve their understanding of memoir.

V Vocabulary

Vocabulary File Say: Add these words and definitions to your vocabulary file. For each word, include a sentence that gives you an example of how to use the word. **OL** Students with English language needs should include the pronunciations of these words in their files. **EL**

LITERATURE PREVIEW

Connecting to the Essay

Angelou uses the essay "Living Well. Living Good." to illustrate her idea of what the phrase "living well" really means. Everyone seems to have a different opinion about the meaning of that phrase. Before you read, think about the following questions:

- What does "living well" mean to you?
- If you had all the money you wanted, what would you still need to live a good life?

Building Background

This selection includes a reference to meals consisting of pigs' feet, greens, and fried chicken. These and similar foods are sometimes called "soul food." They belong to the tradition of African American cuisine. This culinary tradition began when Africans became enslaved people in the South. They combined African and European cooking methods into a new style of cooking. They used many plants for ingredients, eating cornmeal, sweet potatoes and hominy (made from corn). Enslaved people also cooked meat parts the plantation owners typically would not eat, like pigs' feet or chitlins (pig intestines). Today African Americans continue to enjoy this traditional cuisine. As a testament to this tradition's enduring popularity, soul food restaurants can be found throughout the country.

Setting Purposes for Reading

Big Idea The Power of Memory

As you read, think about why Angelou's memory of this anecdote has stayed with her.

Literary Element Memoir

Memoir is a nonfiction narrative illustrating some event or memory from the author's life. As you read, try to determine why Angelou remembered and chose to tell this story in her essay.

- See Literary Terms Handbook, p. R10.

Literature Online **Interactive Literary Elements Handbook** To review or learn more about the literary elements, go to www.glencoe.com.

OBJECTIVES

In studying this selection, you will focus on the following:
- understanding memoir as a literary form
- analyzing the author's implicit and explicit beliefs about a topic
- analyzing implied and stated theme
- writing a critique to evaluate the author's craft

READING PREVIEW

Reading Strategy Drawing Conclusions About Author's Beliefs

Authors often include clues to their own beliefs in their writing. By looking for these clues, you can **draw conclusions about the author's beliefs** and gain a deeper appreciation for the work itself. While reading this piece, determine what this essay says about Angelou's beliefs.

Reading Tip: Looking at Details When you are trying to draw conclusions, look at the details the author has included in the essay. They can provide you with the information you need to make your conclusions.

Details	Conclusion
Sofas and chairs were tautly upholstered.	Angelou respects Aunt Tee's neatness.

Vocabulary

meticulous (mi tik′yə ləs) adj. characterized by great or excessive concern about details; p. 355 *Proofreaders are meticulous when they are reading.*

commodious (kə mō′dē əs) adj. having or containing ample room; spacious; p. 356 *The house was commodious for a family of four.*

convivial (kən viv′ē əl) adj. fond of merriment and parties with good company; sociable; p. 357 *Everyone agreed she was a convivial person.*

scenario (si nār′ē ō′) n. an outline or model of an expected or imagined series of events; p. 357 *The worst-case scenario is that it will rain.*

inhibit (in hib′it) v. to hold back one's natural impulses; restrain p. 357 *A lack of encouragement can inhibit a child's talents.*

354 UNIT 2 NONFICTION

Selection Resources

Print Materials
- 📁 Unit 2 Resources (Fast File), pp. 24–26
- 📁 Leveled Vocabulary Development, p. 24
- 📁 Selection and Unit Assessments, pp. 51–52
- 📁 Selection Quick Checks, p. 26

Transparencies
- Bellringer Options Transparencies:
  Selection Focus Transparency 21
  Daily Language Practice Transparency 30
- Literary Elements Transparency 27

Technology
- TeacherWorks Plus™ CD-ROM
- StudentWorks Plus™ CD-ROM
- Presentation Plus!™ CD-ROM
- Literature Online, glencoe.com
- Online Student Edition, mhln.com
- ExamView® Assessment Suite CD-ROM
- Vocabulary PuzzleMaker CD-ROM
- Listening Library, disc 1 track 28

354

Living Well. Living Good.

Victorian Parlor II, 1945. Horace Pippin. Oil on canvas, 25¼ x 30 in. Metropolitan Museum of Art, New York. Arthur Hoppock Hearn Fund, 1958.

Maya Angelou

Aunt Tee was a Los Angeles member of our extended family.[1] She was seventy-nine when I met her, sinewy,[2] strong, and the color of old lemons. She wore her coarse, straight hair, which was slightly streaked with gray, in a long braided rope across the top of her head. With her high cheekbones, old gold skin, and almond eyes, she looked more like an Indian chief than an old black woman. (Aunt Tee described herself and any favored member of her race as Negroes. *Black* was saved for those who had incurred her disapproval.)

She had retired and lived alone in a dead, neat ground-floor apartment. Wax flowers and china figurines sat on elaborately embroidered and heavily starched doilies. Sofas and chairs were tautly upholstered. The only thing at ease in Aunt Tee's apartment was Aunt Tee.

I used to visit her often and perch on her uncomfortable sofa just to hear her stories. She was proud that after working thirty years as a maid, she spent the next thirty years as a live-in housekeeper, carrying the keys to rich houses and keeping **meticulous** accounts.

"Living in lets the white folks know Negroes are as neat and clean as they are,

---

> **Literary Element** Memoir *How does this passage suggest that the essay is an example of a memoir and not an autobiography?* **L**

> **Vocabulary**
>
> **meticulous** (mi tik′yə ləs) *adj.* characterized by great or excessive concern about details

---

1. Parents and their children make up what is called the nuclear family. One's *extended family* includes other relatives who are related by blood or marriage.
2. Here, *sinewy* (sin′ ū ē) could mean "physically powerful" or "vigorously healthy."

MAYA ANGELOU **355**

BI₁ **Big Idea**

The Power of Memory
Answer: *Aunt Tee is making a point about the value of joy compared to the value of possession.* **OL**

BI₂ **Big Idea**

The Power of Memory
Answer: *Remembering the past can be a way to learn life lessons or understand how to improve one's present life.* **OL**

★ **Writer's Technique**

Compare and Contrast
Angelou sets up a comparison between the life of Aunt Tee's employers and that of Aunt Tee's friends on Saturdays. **Ask:** What can you learn from this comparison? **Answer:** *Aunt Tee's employers have lost the excitement in their lives. Their food and evenings are dull. Aunt Tee and her friends, however, can still have a good time even though their lives are hard.* **AS**

Readability Scores
Dale-Chall: 7.7
DRP: 59
Lexile: 1110

---

sometimes more so. And it gives the Negro maid a chance to see white folks ain't no smarter than Negroes. Just luckier. Sometimes."

Aunt Tee told me that once she was housekeeper for a couple in Bel Air,[3] California, lived with them in a fourteen-room ranch house. There was a day maid who cleaned, and a gardener who daily tended the lush gardens. Aunt Tee oversaw the workers. When she had begun the job, she had cooked and served a light breakfast, a good lunch, and a full three- or four-course dinner to her employers and their guests. Aunt Tee said she watched them grow older and leaner. After a few years they stopped entertaining and ate dinner hardly seeing each other at the table. Finally, they sat in a dry silence as they ate evening meals of soft scrambled eggs, melba toast, and weak tea. Aunt Tee said she saw them growing old but didn't see herself aging at all.

She became the social maven.[4] She started "keeping company" (her phrase) with a chauffeur down the street. Her best friend and her friend's husband worked in service[5] only a few blocks away.

On Saturdays Aunt Tee would cook a pot of pigs' feet, a pot of greens, fry chicken, make potato salad, and bake a banana pudding. Then, that evening, her friends—the chauffeur, the other housekeeper, and her husband—would come to Aunt Tee's **commodious** live-in quarters. There the four would eat and drink, play records and dance. As the evening wore on, they would settle down to a serious game of bid whist.[6]

---

3. *Bel Air* is one of the wealthiest, most fashionable communities in Los Angeles.
4. A *maven* is one who has special knowledge or experience and is an expert in a given field.
5. Aunt Tee's two friends *in service* are servants in another household.
6. *Bid whist* is a card game, somewhat like bridge, for two players or two teams of two players.

Vocabulary

commodious (kə mō′dē əs) *adj.* having or containing ample room; spacious

---

Naturally, during this revelry jokes were told, fingers snapped, feet were patted, and there was a great deal of laughter.

Aunt Tee said that what occurred during every Saturday party startled her and her friends the first time it happened. They had been playing cards, and Aunt Tee, who had just won the bid, held a handful of trumps. She felt a cool breeze on her back and sat upright and turned around. Her employers had cracked her door open and beckoned to her. Aunt Tee, a little peeved, laid down her cards and went to the door. The couple backed away and asked her to come into the hall, and there they both spoke and won Aunt Tee's sympathy forever.

"Theresa, we don't mean to disturb you . . ." the man whispered, "but you all seem to be having such a good time . . ."

The woman added, "We hear you and your friends laughing every Saturday night, and we'd just like to watch you. We don't want to bother you. We'll be quiet and just watch."

The man said, "If you'll just leave your door ajar, your friends don't need to know. We'll never make a sound." Aunt Tee said she saw no harm in agreeing, and she talked it over with her company. They said it was OK with them, but it was sad that the employers owned the gracious house, the swimming pool, three cars, and numberless palm trees, but had no joy. Aunt Tee told me that laughter and relaxation had left the ★ house; she agreed it was sad.

That story has stayed with me for nearly thirty years, and when a tale remains fresh in my mind, it almost always contains a lesson which will benefit me.

My dears, I draw the picture of the wealthy couple standing in a darkened hallway, peering into a lighted room where black servants were lifting their voices in

---

Big Idea The Power of Memory *Why would Aunt Tee feel that it was especially meaningful to share this memory with Angelou?* **BI₁**

Big Idea The Power of Memory *What does Angelou seem to imply that one should do with personal memories?* **BI₂**

WRITING: Narrative While the essay is an example of a memoir, Aunt Tee's story is an example of a narrative. **Say:** A narrative is a story, usually focusing on one particular day or moment in a person's life. Most narratives include a moral or a lesson. Have each student write a narrative about an event in his or her life that taught him or her an important lesson. **OL**

merriment and comradery, and I realize that living well is an art which can be developed. Of course, you will need the basic talents to build upon: They are a love of life and ability to take great pleasure from small offerings, an assurance that the world owes you nothing and that every gift is exactly that, a gift. That people who may differ from you in political stance, sexual persuasion, and racial inheritance can be founts of fun, and if you are lucky, they can become even **convivial** comrades.

Living life as art requires a readiness to forgive. I do not mean that you should suffer fools gladly, but rather remember your own shortcomings, and when you encounter another with flaws, don't be eager to righteously seal yourself away from the offender forever. Take a few breaths and imagine yourself having just committed the action which has set you at odds.

Because of the routines we follow, we often forget that life is an ongoing adventure. We leave our homes for work, acting and even believing that we will reach our destinations with no unusual event startling

us out of our set expectations. The truth is we know nothing, not where our cars will fail or when our buses will stall, whether our places of employment will be there when we arrive, or whether, in fact, we ourselves will arrive whole and alive at the end of our journeys. Life is pure adventure, and the sooner we realize that, the quicker we will be able to treat life as art: to bring all our energies to each encounter, to remain flexible enough to notice and admit when what we expected to happen did not happen. We need to remember that we are created creative and can invent new **scenarios** as frequently as they are needed. Life seems to love the liver of it. Money and power can liberate only if they are used to do so. They can imprison and **inhibit** more finally than barred windows and iron chains. ◐

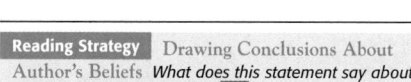

When I Get that Feeling, 2000. Colin Bootman. Oil on board. Private Collection. ★

Reading Strategy Drawing Conclusions About Author's Beliefs *What does this statement say about Angelou's beliefs about life?* **R**

Vocabulary

scenario (si năr′ ē ō′) *n.* an outline or model of an expected or imagined series of events

inhibit (in hib′ it) *v.* to hold back one's natural impulses; restrain

Vocabulary

convivial (kən viv′ ē əl) *adj.* fond of merriment and parties with good company; sociable

MAYA ANGELOU **357**

Assess

1. (a) Some reasons are boredom, curiosity, or envy. (b) Aunt Tee felt sorry for their joyless lives.

2. (a) Fun-loving, organized, strong-willed, and compassionate (b) Neat because most of her life was spent cleaning; tough because she had to face life as a servant

3. (a) Her parties consisted of dancing, jokes, and games. (b) The employers are unhappy and bored; Aunt Tee and her guests love life, enjoy a good meal and each other.

4. (a) Because one never knows whether a job will be there tomorrow, how long life will last, or whether a destination will be reached (b) Answers will vary.

5. Her story reinforces Angelou's idea of living well and makes her lesson more memorable.

6. Money and power can improve life but can also inhibit success and happiness.

7. Students should support their opinions with facts and reasons.

8. (a) Memories helped Aunt Tee to realize that she was happy without wealth or power. (b) For Angelou, the memory may have helped her focus on life's adventures and its possibilities.

RESPONDING AND THINKING CRITICALLY

Respond

1. (a) What reasons can explain why Aunt Tee's employers wanted to watch her parties? (b) What does Aunt Tee's cooperation with her employers say about her attitude toward them?

Recall and Interpret

2. (a) How would you describe Aunt Tee's personality? (b) How do these traits reflect the life Aunt Tee has led?

3. (a) Describe the parties of Aunt Tee and the routines of the employers. (b) What do these differences suggest about the level of happiness of Aunt Tee and the employers?

4. (a) What are Angelou's reasons for saying that "life is pure adventure"? (b) Do you agree with that definition of life? Explain.

Analyze and Evaluate

5. Why did Angelou choose to include the story of her Aunt Tee in this essay, instead of only explaining her idea of "living well"?

6. At the end of the essay, Angelou comments about the effects of money and power. What can you conclude about Angelou's true feelings about their value?

7. Assess Angelou's suggestions about "living well." Is it possible to live the way she suggests? Why or why not?

Connect

8. **Big Idea** The Power of Memory Memory can influence our lives in many ways. (a) Did memories influence Aunt Tee? Explain. (b) How might the memory of Aunt Tee have influenced Angelou's life? Explain.

LITERARY ANALYSIS

Literary Element Memoir

A **memoir** is a personal account of events from the author's past. It is usually written from the first-person point of view, using the pronoun *I*; this point of view allows the reader to see events as the author did. While an autobiography usually tells the story of a person's entire life, a memoir—like "Living Well. Living Good."—typically focuses on a single incident or a particular period in a person's life. Unlike a historical account, which is objective and emphasizes facts, a memoir usually includes the author's personal observations and responses to people and events.

1. Why is "Living Well. Living Good." classified as a memoir?

2. What role does Angelou play in the essay?

3. Could Angelou have converted this essay into an autobiography? Explain.

Review: Theme

As you learned on page 132, **theme** is the central idea of a piece of literature. The theme can be stated directly, meaning that the author points out the main idea of the work for the reader. The theme can also be implied, meaning that the reader must use context clues to determine the central idea.

Partner Activity Pair up with a classmate and discuss the theme of "Living Well. Living Good." First, write down the theme. Next, decide if the theme is stated directly or implied in the content. Support your decision by listing specific examples from the content. Use a web like the one below to organize your ideas.

Literary Element

1. It includes personal observations and responses to people and events; it is not the story of her life but the story of one incident.

2. Angelou is an observer.

3. It could be included as part of an autobiography.

Review: Theme

The partner activity responses should be as follows:

- The theme is enjoying life.
- Support includes the comparison of Aunt Tee's parties and her employer's lives, Angelou's own conclusions, and the examples near the end of the selection.

READING AND VOCABULARY

Reading Strategy Drawing Conclusions About Author's Beliefs

Authors regularly incorporate their beliefs into their works. Recognizing those beliefs usually requires readers to evaluate the details in the text and then to **draw a conclusion** from those specific clues. One way to find those conclusions is to consider the author's use of details and what they suggest about the author.

1. What conclusions can you draw from the text about Angelou's beliefs about "living well"?

2. Support your opinion by listing two details.

Vocabulary Practice

Practice with Analogies Choose the word pair that best completes each analogy:

1. meticulous : perfectionist ::
   a. tiny : housekeeper **b.** irritable : grouch

2. commodious : space ::
   a. large : gigantic **b.** luxurious : comfort

3. convivial : socialite ::
   a. victorious : winner **b.** careless : child

4. outline : scenario ::
   a. describe : description **b.** deceive : truth

5. inhibit : restraint ::
   a. love : spouse **b.** imagine : visualization

Academic Vocabulary

Here are two words from the vocabulary list on page R82.

apparent (ə par′ənt) *adj.* real, obvious, simple to recognize

promote (prə mōt′) *v.* to assist in growth or development

Practice and Apply
1. What was **apparent** about Aunt Tee's employers?
2. What idea did Angelou **promote** in this memoir?

WRITING AND EXTENDING

Writing About Literature

Evaluate the Author's Craft After telling Aunt Tee's story, Angelou concludes her essay with comments about living as a form of art. What is your opinion of this conclusion? Does it add to your understanding and appreciation of the selection, or does it simply repeat the ideas expressed in Aunt Tee's story? Write a critique in which you answer these questions. Support your ideas using specific details from the selection.

Before you begin writing, read through the selection again. This time, think about your opinion of Angelou's conclusion. Make a list of passages from the text that can be used to support your opinion.

When your draft is finished, ask another student to read and evaluate your work. Make changes to your draft based on the evaluation.

Passage	How it Supports My Opinion
"the employers owned the gracious house ... but had no joy." p. 354	This supports my opinion that the conclusion gives a powerful life lesson. It shows that material wealth did not make the couple happy.

Literature Groups

Think about your friends and relatives who are elderly. Are they more like Aunt Tee and her friends or more like Aunt Tee's employers? Why? With your group, discuss what the essay reveals about how elderly people live, and what can be done to improve the lives of elderly people you know.

Literature Online **Web Activities** For eFlashcards, Selection Quick Checks, and other Web activities, go to www.glencoe.com.

MAYA ANGELOU **359**

Assess

Reading Strategy

1. Angelou believes that money cannot buy happiness, that appreciating the unpredictability of life is important to having a good life, and that enjoying friends is more important than being wealthy or powerful.

2. Answers may include the bland meals the employers ate and Aunt Tee's lively parties.

Vocabulary

1. b **2.** b **3.** a **4.** a **5.** b

Academic Vocabulary

1. Student answers may state that the employers are rich, unhappy, or envious of Aunt Tee.

2. Students should explain that Angelou wanted to promote the idea that life should be enjoyed every day.

Writing About Literature

Use these criteria when evaluating students' writing:

- Does the essay include an opinion of Angelou's conclusion?
- Does the essay include support from the text for that opinion?

Literature Groups

Students should discuss their own experiences with elderly people.

Literature Online

Web Activities Have students access the Web site for interactive activities that will help them assess their understanding of the selection.

Focus

BELLRINGER

Bellringer Options
Daily Language Practice
Transparency 31
Or on the board, write: *I didn't think there were any artists in America.* **Ask:** Why might a person who has never visited the United States think this is true? Have students share their opinions and discuss the various misconceptions that exist about life in the United States. If students have personal immigration stories, ask them to share those as well.

Author Search To expand students' appreciation of Mark Stevens and Annalyn Swan, have them access the Web site for additional information and resources.

First Impressions
from De Kooning: An American Master

MEET MARK STEVENS AND ANNALYN SWAN

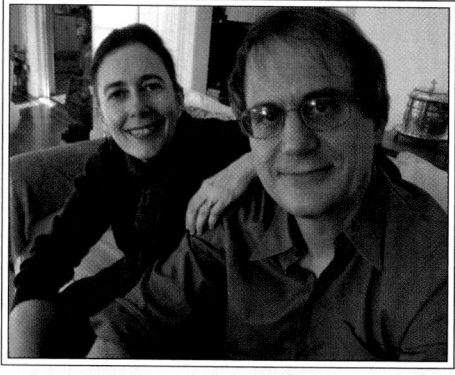

Mark Stevens, an art critic for the magazine *New York*, has written about a wide variety of artists. His subjects range from masters like Vincent van Gogh and Willem de Kooning to folk and outsider artists. Stevens's wife and coauthor, Annalyn Swan, is an award-winning music critic who has written for magazines including *Time, The New Republic, The Atlantic Monthly*, and *New York*. She has also been a senior arts editor at *Newsweek*.

A Long Time Coming Swan and Stevens dedicated ten years of their lives to researching and writing their biography of Willem de Kooning. While one conducted research and interviews exploring the first half of de Kooning's life, the other did research about the second half. Then the couple worked together to shape their material into a coherent whole.

"We were lucky. We had a subject that never bored us. . . . we really liked de Kooning."

—Annalyn Swan

Writing About a Life The art of biography—writing about someone's life—writing has developed as times and literary traditions have changed. Many authors today see biography as the creation of art from fact; to be successful, a biographer can fail neither art nor truth.

Over the many years of their research and writing, Stevens and Swan found that their respect and admiration for de Kooning deepened. They were keen to do justice to this original and complex man. Swan said, "That de Kooning was an immigrant colored everything in his life. He was forever caught between Europe and the New World, suffused with private longings, regret, loneliness and joy. . . . For a biographer, exploring such a complicated subject is fascinating."

Stevens and Swans's years of labor were validated when they were awarded a Pulitzer Prize in 2005. One reviewer had this to say about their work: "When we get the chance to look at the whole life and work of Willem de Kooning, the upheaval in American art in the middle of the 20th century comes into clearer focus. That alone makes *De Kooning: An American Master* . . . an important book."

Mark Stevens and Annalyn Swan live in New York.

Literature Online Author Search For more about Mark Stevens and Annalyn Swan, go to www.glencoe.com.

Selection Skills

First Impressions

Literary Elements
- Author's Purpose (SE pp. 361, 363, 367, 370)
- Biography (SE p. 370)

Reading Skills
- Making Generalizations (SE pp. 361, 363, 364, 369, 371)
- Previewing (TWE p. 362)

Vocabulary Skills
- Analogies (SE pp. 361, 371)
- Academic Vocabulary (SE p. 371)
- Using Context (TWE p. 364)

Listening/Speaking/Viewing Skills
- Analyzing Art (SE pp. 365, 368, 369, 371; TWE pp. 362, 366)
- Interviewing (TWE p. 368)

Writing Skills/Grammar
- Respond to Mood (SE p. 371)
- Coordinating Conjunctions (TWE p. 366)

Connecting to the Biography

The following biography excerpt relates an immigrant's first impressions upon arrival in the United States. De Kooning spoke no English and arrived with only the desire to create a better life for himself. He eventually became one of the foremost painters in the United States. Before you read, think about the following questions:

- How do you handle new experiences?
- How would you feel and how would you handle the challenges of everyday life if no one around you spoke your language?

Building Background

Willem de Kooning was born in the Netherlands in 1904. He eventually became a leader in an artistic movement called Abstract Expressionism. Abstract artists make no attempt to re-create the world as it really exists. The major abstract movements at work in the early twentieth century included Expressionism, Cubism, Futurism, and Fauvism. All of these movements emphasized the gap between art and natural appearances.

Setting Purposes for Reading

Big Idea The Power of Memory

As you read this selection from *De Kooning: An American Master,* notice how Stevens and Swan emphasize de Kooning's recollections of his arrival in the United States.

Literary Element Author's Purpose

The **author's purpose** is the author's reason for writing a literary work. Understanding the author's purpose enables you to grasp why the author presents certain events and characters as he or she does. As you read, try to determine what Stevens and Swan hope to accomplish by sharing de Kooning's first impressions of America with the reader.

- See Literary Terms Handbook, p. R2.

Literature Online **Interactive Literary Elements Handbook** To review or learn more about the literary elements, go to www.glencoe.com.

Reading Strategy Making Generalizations About Events

When you base conclusions about a text on specific examples, ideas, or anecdotes, you are **making generalizations**, observations that may relate universal themes and ideas to a text. As you read, make generalizations about the **events** in this biography by asking yourself: Why are these events occurring as they are? How do they relate to my background information? What do they say about the people involved?

Reading Tip: Taking Notes As you read, record specific examples in the text and then generalize.

Passage	Generalization
De Kooning first lived with other Dutch immigrants in the United States.	This made him feel comfortable, since his surroundings were new.

Vocabulary

obligatory (ə blig´ə tôr´ē) *adj.* required or necessary; p. 362 *The student went to class regularly because the teacher said attendance was obligatory.*

artisan (är´tə zən) *n.* a skilled craftsman; p. 364 *Fine details reveal the cabinetmaker as an artisan.*

belie (bi lī´) *v.* to misrepresent; to give a false impression of; p. 366 *The warm loving light in the small child's eyes belied her refusal to hug her mother.*

torrential (tô ren´chəl) *adj.* flowing rapidly and abundantly; p. 366 *Walking in the torrential rain left us completely soaked.*

Vocabulary Tip: Analogies An analogy is a comparison between things or ideas.

MARK STEVENS AND ANNALYN SWAN **361**

Focus

Summary

In this excerpt from *De Kooning: An American Master,* the authors record Willem de Kooning's first impressions of the United States upon arrival as a Dutch immigrant. Beginning with de Kooning's first—and rather disappointing—sighting of the American coastline and his first American home in Hoboken, New Jersey, the reader learns of de Kooning's experiences and choices that eventually lead him to the artist and poet hangouts in Greenwich Village and the world of experimental art.

Vocabulary

Vocabulary File Say: Add these words and definitions to your vocabulary file. For each word, include a sentence that gives you an example of how to use the word. **OL** Students with English language needs should include the pronunciations of these words in their files. **EL**

Literature Online

Literary Elements Have students access the Web site to improve their understanding of author's purpose.

 Selection Resources

Teach

BI₁ Big Idea

The Power of Memory
Say: Think about the following as you read: The authors intertwine anecdotes, description, and quotations to piece together a narrative of de Kooning's life. How does their use of de Kooning's recollections help the reader understand the man? *(They offer the reader a glimpse into the man's hopes, dreams, and desires.)* **OL**

BI₂ Big Idea

The Power of Memory
Answer: *He expected to see things that were exciting and new—not a place that was like home.* **OL**

⭐ **Viewing the Art**

Francis Hopkinson Smith (1838–1915) was a self-taught American watercolorist who viewed his art as a hobby. Smith worked as an engineer. He helped construct the foundations for the Statue of Liberty, which he also painted. **AS**

Readability Scores
Dale-Chall: 6.4
DRP: 66
Lexile: 1160

The Statue of Liberty. Francis Hopkinson Smith (ca. 1851–1915). ⭐

First Impressions

from *DeKooning: An American Master*

Mark Stevens and Annalyn Swan

BI₁ I didn't think there were any artists in America.

"Look Bill, America!" With that shout from the sailors, de Kooning looked out over the water—and looked again. He saw "a sort of Holland, lowlands, just like back home," as he remembered it. No skyscrapers with glittering lights. No beckoning Statue of Liberty. Not only was he disappointed at his first glimpse of America, he was also apprehensive as the ship steamed into the Virginia port of Newport News on July 30. The voyage itself had been stressful. He found the English ship filthy and,

for much of the trip, was forced to hide in the hot, dark engine room where the sailors—while never officially acknowledging his presence—gave him lots of work. . . .

What sort of country, de Kooning wondered, was this America? He felt particularly uneasy because he knew no English, which forced him to rely completely upon friends. Cohan, as cheerful and optimistic as ever, proved a resourceful companion who helped steer de Kooning to New York without passing through the usual entry point for immigrants on Ellis Island—the **obligatory** first step for legal entrance into the United States

Big Idea The Power of Memory *Why was de Kooning disappointed when he first saw America?* **BI₂**

Vocabulary
obligatory (ə blig′ə tôr′ē) *adj.* required or necessary

362 UNIT 2 NONFICTION

Additional Support

Skills Practice

READING: Previewing This excerpt occurs several chapters into *De Kooning: An American Master*. Have students look at the title, the quotation that acts as a subtitle, and the first few sentences to gain perspective about what is happening. **Ask:** What do these clues tell the reader about the selection? *(The subject will experience something for the first time. Art and the United States are both somehow involved. The subject is arriving in the United States from Holland, and is disappointed by what he sees.)* Have students use this information to predict what will happen to de Kooning. **OL**

by way of Manhattan. The passage of the Immigration Act of 1924 had sharply curtailed the flow of immigrants into America, and, while the new quotas were less restrictive for northern Europeans than for others, illegal immigrants like Cohan and de Kooning faced certain deportation from Ellis Island. Calling upon his network of Dutch friends, Cohan arranged to board a coast vessel carrying goods from Newport News to Boston.

Throughout the next week, as they steamed up the eastern seaboard, de Kooning and Cohan stoked the engines and worked as firemen. Disembarking in Boston, they proceeded by train to Rhode Island, where, with a group of Dutch sailors, they boarded another coast vessel bound for the old South Street port at the tip of Manhattan. Although South Street had been the center of the city's harbor life from the colonial era through the nineteenth century, the shipping business had mostly moved by the 1920s to docks along the Hudson River on the West Side of Manhattan. South Street was a quiet back door into the city for those who wanted to avoid scrutiny.

"We had enough money to buy a ticket on a passenger boat," de Kooning remembered of the trip from Rhode Island, "with music and dancing, and early one morning I just walked off the ship and I couldn't believe it—I was free on the streets of New York." As at Newport News, he was not overwhelmed by his first impressions. De Kooning, who always relished the debunking[1] observation, said about his first view of New York: "This I remember: no skyscrapers. They had disappeared in the fog." Their few possessions in hand, the group of Dutchmen headed purposefully uptown to Barclay Street, where they boarded one of the ferries connecting Manhattan to Hoboken, New Jersey, the town across the river where they planned to stay. This is probably when de Kooning saw the counterman recklessly pouring coffee into the row of cups and was suddenly seized by the difference between Holland and America—the first slow and deliberate, the other driven, haphazard, profligate.

Like most immigrants, de Kooning spent his early months in America swaddled among his own countrymen. Hoboken was the logical place for a Dutch stowaway to live during the first unsettling days, as Cohan, the impresario of their emigration, recognized. Once a sleepy river town and leafy retreat for New Yorkers eager to escape the summer heat, Hoboken had become by the 1920s an important shipping town with a population of about seventy thousand. Four ferries connected it with its huge neighbor. The ships of nine big oceangoing lines docked at its piers, including the Netherlands-American Steam Navigation Company, which attracted a number of Dutch settlers. By the time de Kooning arrived, the traditionally German flavor of Hoboken had almost disappeared, owing in part to a huge wave of Italian immigrants around the turn of the century. There remained a northern European overlay to the city, however, along with a liberal sprinkling of Dutch inhabitants. The first Dutch Reformed Church had been founded in 1850 and maintained a high profile in the local community, and the Holland Seaman's Home provided a welcoming refuge for Dutch, German, and Scandinavian sailors and immigrants. "My sailor friends knew the Dutch settlement there, and they brought me to the Dutch Seaman's Home, a sort of boarding house," de Kooning said. "Thanks to them the landlady gave me three weeks' credit. It was a nice, very clean little house. I liked it quite well."

Located at 332 River Street, the Holland Seaman's Home was across the road from the

---

1. Debunking means exposing a myth.

Reading Strategy Making Generalizations About Events *Why do de Kooning and his friend avoid the more traditional points of entry into the United States?* **R**

Literary Element Author's Purpose *What does this observation reveal about the place de Kooning has come from? What does it help you understand about de Kooning?* **L₁**

Literary Element Author's Purpose *Why do the authors describe Hoboken, New Jersey, at length and in such detail?* **L₂**

MARK STEVENS AND ANNALYN SWAN **363**

Teach

R Reading Strategy

Making Generalizations About Events Answer: *They were entering illegally and wanted to avoid discovery.* **OL**

L₁ Literary Element

Author's Purpose Answer: *In Holland, life is slower. The United States is much faster-paced. De Kooning is used to paying close attention to details and quality of life.* **OL**

L₂ Literary Element

Author's Purpose Answer: *They are illustrating the time and the setting, and explaining why so many Dutch immigrants like de Kooning settled there.* **OL**

★ Cultural History

Ellis Island Ellis Island, in Upper New York Bay, is most famous for its role as a major point of entry for immigrants to the United States. Over 17 million immigrants entered through Ellis Island between 1892 and 1924. **AS**

✓CheckPoint

Use the CheckPoint questions on Presentation Plus! to monitor students' comprehension. These questions can be used with interactive response keypads for immediate student feedback.

Objectives
• To understand the author's purpose (SE)
• To make generalizations (SE)
• To preview a literary selection (TWE)

Reading in the Real World

Citizenship Have students find articles in newspapers or magazines that discuss immigration today. Have students discuss how life for immigrants has changed and how it has remained the same. **OL**

R1 Reading Strategy

Making Generalizations About Events Answer: *He is ambivalent about his relocation to America. He embraces his new identity with an American name. However, he feels more comfortable around things that remind him of home.* **OL**

BI Big Idea

The Power of Memory

Answer: *By wearing fine clothing, de Kooning demonstrated his success and newfound American identity. Clothing became a kind of currency to de Kooning, who calculated his earnings in clothes he could purchase.* **OL**

R2 Reading Strategy

Making Generalizations About Events Answer: *Immigrants are often confronted with significant language barriers in their new homes. They may be unable to fully express themselves. Their lack of knowledge can make them self-conscious and less willing to interact.* **OL**

docks lining the river and near the Lutheran Seaman's Mission. Just down River Street were the Holland bakery, the Holland Hotel, and a restaurant called Holland. Despite his desire to leave the Old World, de Kooning—who instantly dropped his Dutch name, Willem, in favor of the all-American "Bill"—found the traces of home comforting. Plenty of work was available. More than thirty painters and decorators worked in Hoboken in 1926, a number of them either German or Dutch immigrants. Their establishments bore such names as Braue and Schermerhorn, Otto Burckhardt and Son, and Fred Schlegel. "Three days later I was a housepainter," de Kooning said, "and got nine dollars a day, a nice salary for that time."

For someone who with a few notable exceptions paid little attention to how he dressed, de Kooning showed a particular preoccupation with clothes during his early days in America: they represented both a badge of success and a symbol of a new identity. After only one week of work, de Kooning proudly remembered, "I could buy a new suit, black for Sundays, low-belt trousers, nice workmen's clothes, for I didn't want to be different. . . . I do like a fine suit and a nice tie." If in one week he could afford a suit, "In three weeks I could pay off my rent and had new underwear and socks." Like many immigrants, de Kooning also wanted to demonstrate his success to his family and maintain the legend of a land of riches. A photograph taken in 1926, and no doubt sent home to Holland, shows de Kooning and a Dutch friend on the ferry between New York and Hoboken. De Kooning is lolling back against the railing, clearly at ease with the camera, the world, and his relative prosperity. In contrast to his

Reading Strategy Making Generalizations About Events *What does de Kooning have in common with many people who visit a foreign country?* **R1**

Big Idea The Power of Memory *In what ways did clothing become meaningful to de Kooning as he began his life in America?* **BI**

364 UNIT 2 NONFICTION

Dutch companion, who is dressed in a poorly fitting jacket and workingman's cap, de Kooning is handsomely turned out. His three-piece suit is elegant, his shirt collar starchily correct. On his head is a fedora, raked jauntily over his forehead and all but hiding his eyes.

De Kooning could get by without much English, though it was not always easy. In the beginning, he knew how to order only one thing in restaurants—a hamburger. (When he finally tried to order something else at the local restaurant, the waiter said, "Hamburger, right?" de Kooning meekly nodded.) On the job, he found he had much to learn about the way his new country operated, which often differed from the careful, **artisanal** manners of Holland. "I was impressed by the workers' efficiency and their tools," he said. "We worked without stopping for eight hours and used much larger and better brushes than those we had in Holland. I learned a great deal on how to mix pigment with water and oil." He was struck by the American willingness simply to slap new paint over old; in Holland, housepainters would strip a window down to the wood before repainting. He also tried his hand at sign painting, and came away with a high regard for the veterans with whom he worked. "Sign painting was difficult for me because they used other letters here," he said. "How those old guys smoking their pipes did it, I don't know."

De Kooning soon found helpful and congenial Dutch friends. Leo Cohan, who worked as a cook in a restaurant in Hoboken, sometimes arranged for de Kooning to get free meals; between lodgings, de Kooning occasionally stayed in Cohan's rented room. A man

Reading Strategy Making Generalizations About Events *What general conclusions can you draw from this exchange?* **R2**

Reading Strategy Making Generalizations About Events *What insights into Holland and America did de Kooning gain from working as a house painter in Hoboken?* **R3**

Vocabulary

artisan (är´tə zən) n. a skilled craftsman

Additional Support

Skills Practice

VOCABULARY: Using Context

Explain: Readers can often determine the meanings of unfamiliar words by using the context—or the situation—created by other words in the sentence. Tell students to use context to determine the meaning of unfamiliar words in this selection. Have students make a list of unfamiliar words, and then have them analyze the context to determine the meanings of the words on their lists. **OL**

Greenwich Village. Frances Treanor. Pastel on paper, 53.3 x 81.2 cm. Private Collection.

Viewing the Art: What scene in this biography does this painting resemble?

named Wimpy Deruyter—a ship's mechanic who befriended de Kooning on the voyage to America—visited whenever he was back in town. De Kooning's keenest friendship, however, was with a Dutch singer named Bart van der Schelling. Well known for never keeping a job or having any money, Bart was big, charming, and exceedingly attractive. (He would later fight in the Spanish Civil War and eventually became a naïve,[2] or "primitive" painter.) Like Leo Cohan, he remained close to de Kooning for years: in the early thirties Bill and Bart spent so much time together they seemed like brothers.

On Sundays, de Kooning would go sightseeing with friends. Little remained of the

rustic charm that had once brought New Yorkers across the river to Hoboken. Its main allure in the Prohibition[3] era was its great number of speakeasies;[4] a local poll taken in 1930 named Hoboken the "wettest"[5] city in New Jersey. But there was some greenery in the area. Only steps from the Holland Seaman's Home was Hudson Square, which looked over the river. Just beyond lay the Stevens Institute of

2. *Naïve painters* usually have no formal artistic training and are known for painting directly on a canvas without preliminary drawings.

3. The *Prohibition era* officially began in 1919 with the 18th Amendment to the Constitution, which prohibited the sale or consumption of alcoholic beverages anywhere in the U.S. The 18th Amendment was repealed in 1933 with the 21st Amendment.

4. *Speakeasies* were places that existed during the Prohibition era where people could go to purchase illegal alcohol.

5. *Wet* means that alcohol was available for purchase, so the reference to Hoboken being the *"wettest" city in New Jersey* means that one could find a lot of places to obtain alcohol.

MARK STEVENS AND ANNALYN SWAN **365**

Teach

BI Big Idea

The Power of Memory
Answer: *De Kooning's memory of the multiplicity of cultures around the seaport of Rotterdam made him feel comfortable in New York, a city with a diverse and vibrant population. Some students may note the irony of feeling "at home" among people who are separated from their homes and, culturally, from one another.* **OL**

★ Viewing the Photograph

Tony Vaccaro's photograph of de Kooning portrays him as a robust, almost giantlike figure. Encourage students to discuss the physical and mental challenges many immigrants endured during the Great Depression. Remind students that de Kooning supported himself by commercial jobs that required hard labor with little pay. **AS**

Technology, which was housed in a mansion on a promontory known as Castle Point. De Kooning went there often to look across the water at the city. With friends like Bart, Wimpy, and Leo—who sounded like a troupe of comics—de Kooning also began to explore New York. He felt comfortable with its kaleidoscopic jumble of ethnic groups, which recalled the mixing of Dutch and foreigners around the Rotterdam[6] docks. He saw the poverty, too, which **belied** the myth of easy riches: the slums on the Lower East Side;[7] the tenements with windowless inner rooms and public toilets on every other floor; the two-bit flophouses[8] on the Bowery. (One day, he would come to love the photographs of Weegee[9]—the great chronicler of the city's meaner streets.) But that was not the New York that caught his eye. The Roaring Twenties were one of the city's great decades. It thrived on too much money, not enough sleep, and worried cries from the rest of the country about "decadence."[10] The WPA[11] guide to the city, compiled as part of the 1930s Federal Writers'

Willem de Kooning, 1953. Tony Vaccaro.

★

---

6. *Rotterdam* is a city in the southwestern portion of the Netherlands.
7. The *Lower East Side* of New York City's Manhattan borough attracted many immigrants because of the availability of cheap housing.
8. *Flophouses* were cheap hotels or rooming houses that could be found in a section of New York City called *the Bowery*.
9. *Weegee* is the professional name of photographer Arthur Fellig, who became famous for his crime-scene photos.
10. *Decadence* is the process of falling into decay or decline.
11. The *WPA* is the Works Progress Administration Federal Arts Project. The program started in the 1930s and was known for hiring artists who ranged in experience and style.

Big Idea The Power of Memory *How does the memory of Holland affect de Kooning's experience of New York City?* **BI**

Vocabulary

belie (bi lī´) *v.* to misrepresent; to give a false impression of

---

Project, perfectly captured the proudly self-conscious, rhetorical flair of the period:

> All through the 1920s New York had been not only the symbol of America but the symbol of the modern—the fortunate giant in his youth, the world city whose past weighed least heavily upon its future. . . . It was a city infallible in finance, **torrential** in pace, unlimited in resource, hard as infrangible diamonds, forever leaping upon the moment beyond. "You can get away with anything," said Ellen Thatcher in John Dos

Vocabulary

torrential (tô ren´chəl) *adj.* flowing rapidly and abundantly

---

Additional Support

Skills Practice

GRAMMAR AND LANGUAGE:
Coordinating Conjunctions On the board, write these coordinating conjunctions: *and, but, or, nor, for, yet.* Remind students that coordinating conjunctions connect phrases and other words that are equal in grammatical value. Examples: *Jorge <u>and</u> Joe are fin-* *ishing their homework together; Natalia is writing her essay, <u>but</u> Lisa is reading her novel.* Point out that a coordinating conjunction between two independent clauses usually requires a comma before the conjunction. Have students write five sentences that contain coordinating conjunctions and proper punctuation. **OL**

Passos' *Manhattan Transfer*, "if you do it quick enough." Speed—with its dividend, sensation—became the master formula in every human activity and technique: Wall Street, dancing, crime, the theater, construction, even death. ★

What de Kooning thrilled to was the pop energy of the city, which was exotic to a Dutchman who grew up in the subdued culture of northern Europe. Here was freedom from the constraints of class, taste, and disapproving looks; here was a new kind of openness, an invitation to wonder. One of the first places he visited was Coney Island, a masterpiece of rhinestone splendor that provided entertainment for New York's lower and middle classes. Cecil Beaton described it this way during the 1930s:

> Every Saturday and Sunday a million people go to bathe at Coney Island, reached by subway in half an hour. They stay until the electric bulbs silhouette the minarets, domes and turrets, illumine the skeletons of roller-coasters and the magnificent pleasure-palace of George C. Tilyou (the Barnum of Coney Island), which with its many columns and electrical splendour, resembles something from the Pan-American exposition of 1900. The passengers on the Cyclone rend the air with their concerted screams.

"I liked the sentimental side of the people," de Kooning said, "the girls, the houses on the avenues, and the skyscrapers." Not surprisingly, he relished Times Square. Perhaps it reminded him of the square at the foot of the Coolsingel[12] in Rotterdam, where he had whiled away time with the Randolfis. Except it was bigger, more extravagant, cra-

zier. Like the harbor of Rotterdam, Times Square was a crossroads populated by . . . just about everyone. Times Square in 1926 was lined with movie houses, shooting galleries, and amusement arcades. At night, it shimmered with thousands of brightly colored electric lights. De Kooning had himself photographed amid the bustle of Times Square. He looked like a man at home. Once de Kooning found his footing in America, Hoboken seemed too much like North Rotterdam. Crowded tenements, cold-water walk-ups, and communal backyard toilets or privies were the realities of working-class life in Hoboken; he had not left Rotterdam to move to a similarly depressed city across the ocean. More important, he missed living in a bohemian milieu. It was one thing to be a workingman living among artists or people like the Randolfis who flourished on the margins of society. It was quite another to be a workingman among workers. On Sundays, a friend with an old car sometimes drove him to Storm King, a high promontory of land up the Hudson with sweeping views down the river. "We would stand by the parapet and look at the view of the city," de Kooning said. "It used to scare me to death. I would say to myself, 'There's no art here. You came to the wrong place.'" Although he visited the galleries on Fifty-seventh Street, they mostly showed plummy European paintings intended for conservative apartments on the Upper East Side. He saw nothing like Mondrian.[13]

Leo Cohan urged de Kooning to move across the river. "I said to him, 'Bill, you mustn't hang around in Hoboken. You must go to Manhattan. There you'll find other artists.'" In Hoboken, de Kooning began to hear about a community in the city called Greenwich Village, where poets and painters were said to live. He determined its location—south of Fourteenth Street and

---

12. *Coolsingel* is a main street in the old part of Rotterdam.

Literary Element Author's Purpose *What insights into de Kooning's artistic sensibilities do the authors suggest by including these observations?* **L1**

---

13. Piet *Mondrian* was a Dutch abstract painter.

Literary Element Author's Purpose *Why do you think de Kooning is ready for a change?* **L2**

MARK STEVENS AND ANNALYN SWAN **367**

Teach

American John Wenger (1887–1976) displayed artistic talent at the age of three. He eventually became a designer of stage settings who also created colorful outdoor scenes. **Answer:** *Students may note the seaside setting for swimming, the colorful structures, the Ferris wheel.* **AS**

BI₁ **Big Idea**

The Power of Memory
Answer: *He was reminded of his early interest in art. This recollection helped move him toward the success he eventually achieved.* **OL**

⭐ *Coney Island,* 1931. John Wenger. Watercolor and tempera over pencil on paperboard, 55.1 x 71.1 cm. Brooklyn Museum of Art, New York.

Viewing the Art: What does this painting help viewers understand about Coney Island's appeal?

north of Canal Street—and one day found himself amid the oddly angled streets and old brownstones. But he could not find "the Village" he had heard about. "There were just lots of Italians standing around on corners. Inside, you know, the Village was nice, but from the outside, you couldn't tell it was there—it was so quiet." Then, while still living in Hoboken, de Kooning met a Sicilian artist named Mirabaggo, who lived in the Village. When a barber whom Mirabaggo knew retired, he bought the empty barbershop and opened a coffeehouse decorated with plaster copies of Greek and Roman sculpture. De Kooning began to spend time there on weekends. Soon he was also going to Café Rienzi, another coffeehouse that opened shortly

after Mirabaggo's. He began to discover old Village hangouts, such as the Pepper Pot, the MacDougal Tavern, and the Jumble Shop. All of them had been in varying degrees haunts of writers and artists since the 1890s. Of greatest importance to de Kooning, however, was the living presence of painters. "Here in Greenwich Village there was a strong tradition of painting and poetry," he said. "I had not known this, and it brought back memories of my interests when I was 14, 15 or 16 years old."

Now that he had located an American art world, de Kooning naturally wanted to join

---

Big Idea The Power of Memory *Why do you think this recollection is signifcant for de Kooning?* **BI₁**

Additional Support

Skills Practice

RESEARCH: Interviewing Say:
Books, periodicals, and the Internet are sources of information. Sometimes, however, writers must use other sources. Stevens and Swan could not rely solely on library and electronic research. They had to interview people who knew de Kooning to develop a sense of who he

was and what he became. Have students interview an adult family member or friend about someone who lived a generation earlier. For example, students might interview a grandparent about a great-grandparent or a parent about a grandparent. Tell them to prepare questions in advance. The answers should help it. He made some drawings and illustrations to replace the portfolio that he had left behind in Belgium, and began to read the Help Wanted ads for commercial artists in the Manhattan newspapers, just as he had in Brussels. When one ran in the *New York World* he dropped off his portfolio at the stated address. To his dismay, the place was mobbed with applicants for the job. He had all but given up hope when a man appeared holding aloft a portfolio and shouting, "Where's de Kooning?" The American's pronunciation was jarring. In Dutch, de Kooning was pronounced with a hard "o"—as in Koning. In American, he was de Kooning.

The job was his. De Kooning was so pleased—his first triumph in America!—that he signed up immediately, no questions asked. "I didn't even ask them the salary because I thought if I made twelve dollars a day as a house painter [de Kooning variously described his Hoboken wages as nine or twelve dollars a day] I would make at least twenty dollars a day being an artist." The elation abruptly ended after a week when he was handed twenty-five dollars. "I was so astonished I asked him if that was a day's pay," said de Kooning. "He said, 'No, that's for the whole week.'" De Kooning had learned the hard way that less skilled labor could pay more than an arts-related job and that life in America was not going to be easy. "It turned out to be quite different from what I thought," de Kooning said of America. "Nowhere near as luxurious as I imagined it."

Disgruntled, de Kooning spent the weekend wondering whether or not to return to

Door to the River, 1960. Willem de Kooning. The Willem de Kooning Foundation.

Viewing the Art: In your opinion, what elements of this painting most vividly demonstrate de Kooning's originality? ⭐

housepainting in Hoboken. Cohan and other Dutch friends urged him to keep the new job. As Cohan sensed, art and the company of artists would finally prove far more important to his friend than a fatter paycheck. Although de Kooning by no means considered himself a serious painter—that would only come years later—he made an essential decision that weekend: he must at least live in the neighborhood of art. His hopes of making a fortune waned, but his interest in an American art world strengthened. A little more than a year after his arrival in Hoboken, de Kooning packed his few possessions, said good-bye to his sailor friends, and took the ferry into Manhattan. ∽

Reading Strategy Making Generalizations About Events *What does this story illustrate about the experiences of many immigrants to America?* **R**

Big Idea The Power of Memory *What do you think changed for de Kooning?* **BI₂**

MARK STEVENS AND ANNALYN SWAN **369**

students understand what life was like in the time and place in which the subject lived. **OL** Have talented students write a compare-and-contrast essay, comparing de Kooning's experiences to those of their interview subjects. **AL**

Building Reading Fluency

Reading with Inflection The last four paragraphs of the selection contain direct quotations and descriptive observation. Have students pair up and take turns reading these paragraphs aloud. Suggest that they use vocal inflection—as if they were acting—to add meaning to their reading. **BL**

Assess

1. Answers will vary.

2. (a) The Statue of Liberty and Ellis Island (b) He was disappointed.

3. (a) While people in the United States did not take as much time with their crafts as in Holland, they were freer to express themselves. (b) The freedom to express himself allowed him to develop as an acclaimed artist.

4. (a) He no longer needed or wanted to be among his countrymen. (b) It introduced him to a community of artists.

5. Most students will say the authors show the foundation that led to de Kooning's success.

6. Students might note how the authors intersperse de Kooning's quotations throughout the selection, providing a personal touch.

7. De Kooning loved the idea of being free to express himself. The only way to pursue this type of success was to delve into the American art world.

8. Students may say the differences in attitude between these countries were what most likely gave rise to de Kooning's artistic endeavors and sensibilities.

370

RESPONDING AND THINKING CRITICALLY

Respond

1. What did you consider most interesting or surprising about de Kooning's experiences? Explain.

Recall and Interpret

2. (a)What was missing from de Kooning's first glimpse of the United States? (b)How did his first impressions affect him?

3. (a)What differences did de Kooning notice between life in Holland and life in the United States? (b)What impact did these differences have on de Kooning?

4. (a)What reasons do Stevens and Swan cite for de Kooning's departure from Hoboken? (b)Why might the move have helped his career as an artist? Explain.

Analyze and Evaluate

5. De Kooning eventually becomes an influential and innovative abstract painter. Do you believe that the biographers' description of de Kooning's arrival in the United States helps you understand his eventual success? Explain.

6. To be successful, a biographer must provide facts about a person's life and must also capture the essence of that person. Do you believe that Stevens and Swan accomplish this goal? Explain why or why not.

7. At first, de Kooning viewed success in the United States in terms of income. Later, his views of success shifted. Analyze de Kooning's transition and determine what brought about the change in his attitude.

Connect

8. **Big Idea** The Power of Memory From the comparisons between Holland and the United States, do you believe that de Kooning would have achieved the same artistic success had he remained in Holland? Explain.

LITERARY ANALYSIS

Literary Element Author's Purpose

Authors often write to achieve one or more of the following **purposes**: to persuade, to inform, to explain, to entertain, or to describe. One might attribute several of these purposes to Stevens and Swan's biography of Willem de Kooning.

1. Which purpose do you think most applies to this selection? Explain.

2. Cite several passages that support your claim.

Review: Biography

As you learned on pages 318–319, a **biography** is an account of someone's life written by someone else. In addition to describing a person's life, a biography provides insight into the time and place in which the person lived.

Partner Activity Pair up with a classmate and examine the selection you just read. Determine how the authors'

use of quotations helps provide a historical and cultural context. Working with your partner, create a two-column chart similar to the one below. Fill in the left-hand column with examples from the text that demonstrate the author's use of quotations from other sources. In the right-hand column, explain how each example provides a historical or cultural context.

Examples of Quotations from Other Sources	Explanation of Historical or Cultural Context
"Every Saturday and Sunday, a million people go to bathe at Coney Island," quoted on page 367.	It was an inexpensive and appealing form of entertainment, so it attracted a lot of people from the lower and middle classes.

Literary Element

1. To persuade readers that the seeds of de Kooning's artistic sensibilities were sown in his early impressions of the United States

2. Students may cite passages in which the authors quote or paraphrase de Kooning, as well as the details—the counterman, the exchange over the hamburger, de Kooning's vain attention to his appearance—about his early experiences in the U.S.

Review: Biography

You may want to present students with more information in the form of a video or photographs regarding this time period. This will help students visualize the references in the text.

Reading Strategy Making Generalizations About Events

Making generalizations helps readers understand the main points and implications of a work. For example, considering de Kooning's experiences enables us to generalize about other immigrants' lives at the time.

1. (a) What generalizations can you make about de Kooning's reasons for coming to the United States? (b) What does the selection suggest about how the United States could both confound and reward the expectations of immigrants?

2. Find three examples from the text that support your ideas. Explain.

Vocabulary Practice

Practice with Analogies Choose the word pair that best completes each of the following analogies.

1. fallacy : truth ::
   a. honesty : policy
   b. cowardice : bravery
   c. delusion : deception

2. artisan : craft ::
   a. craftsman : trade
   b. wood : carpenter
   c. artist : paint

3. promise : obliged ::
   a. marriage : divorced
   b. pledge : committed
   c. vow : uncertain

Academic Vocabulary

Here are two words from the vocabulary list on page R82.

overseas (ō´vər sēz´) *adj.* relating to travel over the seas

migrate (mī´grāt) *v.* to move to another place

Practice and Apply
1. Describe de Kooning's **overseas** route.
2. Why did he **migrate** to the United States?

Writing About Literature

Respond to Mood Mood is the emotional quality or ambiance of a literary work. Many elements come together to create mood, including diction, syntax, setting, tone, rhetorical devices such as imagery, and sound devices such as rhythm. Write a brief essay in which you identify and respond to the mood in "First Impressions." In your response, remember to refer to specific elements that create mood.

Before you begin drafting, take notes using a graphic organizer like the one below.

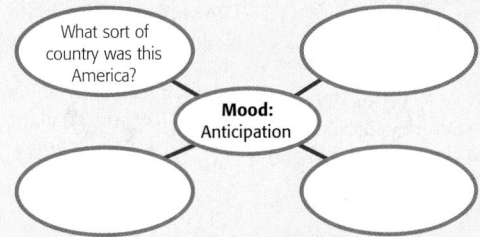

What sort of country was this America?

Mood: Anticipation

Include quotations that exemplify the mood of the piece. Once you have completed your diagram, begin drafting.

After you complete your draft, meet with a peer reviewer. Evaluate each other's work and suggest revisions. Then proofread and edit your draft for errors in spelling, grammar, and punctuation.

Interdisciplinary Activity

With a partner, do research about de Kooning and his fellow New York "rebel artists" who helped develop Abstract Expressionism. Who were they? How did they become friends? What made their art so groundbreaking? Use your research to create a multimedia presentation about the Abstract Expressionists. You may include elements such as photographs, art reproductions, and music. Share your presentation with the class.

Literature Online Web Activities For eFlashcards, Selection Quick Checks, and other Web activities, go to www.glencoe.com.

MARK STEVENS AND ANNALYN SWAN **371**

Assess

Reading Strategy

1. (a) Students may say that de Kooning wanted to experience the American Dream or that he wanted to experience the feeling of being completely free to express himself. (b) It suggests that although immigrants might have to change their previous ways, they would experience a freedom without parallel.

2. Answers could include "Here was a new kind of openness, an invitation to wonder" or "It was quite another to be a workingman among workers."

Vocabulary

1. b
2. a
3. b

Academic Vocabulary

1. De Kooning traveled from Europe to Newport News, Virginia, on an English ship. He worked on board the ship to pay his way.

2. Artistic freedom

Writing About Literature

Use these criteria when evaluating students' writing:

- Does the essay identify and describe the mood of the selection?

- Does the essay refer to specific elements that create mood, including diction, syntax, setting, tone, rhetorical devices, and sound devices?

Interdisciplinary Activity

Other prominent artists of the Abstract Expressionism movement include: Jackson Pollock, Mark Rothko, Franz Kline, Elaine de Kooning, and Helen Frankenthaler.

Literature Online

Web Activities Have students access the Web site for interactive activities that will help them assess their understanding of the selection.

Focus

Ask: What jargon or technical terms do you know from sports or music? *(Students may suggest terms such as designated hitter or reprise.)* You may also wish to discuss when it is or is not appropriate to use jargon in students' own writing.

Teach

Defining Jargon **Say:** Clues for defining jargon are word parts, subject matter, and context. Write this sentence from *De Kooning: An American Master* on the board: "He . . . eventually became a naïve, or 'primitive,' painter." **Ask:** Which strategies can you use to define the jargon in this sentence? *(Context and subject matter help to define naïve as "primitive.")* Provide other examples of sentences with jargon for students to define. **OL**

Assess

1. pigment—coloring substance

2. strip—to remove paint

3. portfolio—collection of an artist's work

4. bohemian—unconventional, devoted to art

▶ **Vocabulary Terms**

Jargon is the specialized or technical language of a trade such as law, medicine, art, and sports.

▶ **Test-Taking Tip**

When you encounter unfamiliar jargon in a reading selection, look for word parts you already know. Then consider the subject of the selection and the context of the sentence to determine the meaning of the word.

Literature Online
eFlashcards Visit www.glencoe.com for eFlashcards and other vocabulary activities.

OBJECTIVES
- Use context clues and word-part analysis to understand unfamiliar words.
- Verify word meanings by using a dictionary.
- Identify jargon.

Vocabulary Workshop
Technical Words

Understanding Jargon

"On the job, he found he had much to learn about the way his new country operated, which often differed from the careful, artisanal manners of Holland."

—Mark Stevens and Annalyn Swan, from "First Impressions" from
De Kooning, An American Master

Connecting to Literature Unless you are a painter or have read a good deal about art, you probably are not familiar with the word *artisanal* used in the quotation above. You may, however, have read or heard the word *artisan*, meaning "a skilled worker," and know many words with the suffix –*al*, which means "like" or "characterized by." The context, or setting in which the word appears, also gives you a clue that *artisanal* means "skillfully crafted."

Words like *artisanal*, which are related to a specific field or trade, are called **jargon**. This specialized language also includes specific meanings given to common words. For example, in "First Impressions," a painter is described as *naïve*, which generally means "lacking experience and understanding." In its use as jargon, though, it refers to a painting style characterized by a lack of formal training. Likewise, reference to a *brush* in this selection most likely indicates a paintbrush, not a hairbrush. See the chart below for some common examples of jargon.

Jargon	Specific field or trade	Meaning when used as jargon
anomaly	medicine	defect
bug	computers and technology	error, especially in a program
czar	politics	person who is in charge of a policy or agenda

Exercise

Identify the jargon in each of the following sentences related to "First Impressions." Then use the context to write a definition for the jargon you found. Check your answers using a dictionary.

1. De Kooning learned about how to mix pigments with oil and water while painting houses.

2. In Holland, housepainters always stripped windows down to the wood before repainting them.

3. De Kooning created new paintings and illustrations for his portfolio to show employers.

4. Hoboken was very much like North Rotterdam, and not the bohemian setting he had expected.

Additional Support

eFlashcards Have students access the Web site for more practice with technical words.

Skills Practice

VOCABULARY: Context Clues For less proficient readers, review types of context clues that help define jargon:

- examples
- explanation
- synonym or antonym
- contrast

Give students practice with sentences such as "He preferred *plein air* painting to painting indoors." *(A contrast defines "plein air" as "outdoor.")* **OL**

Typhoid Fever
from *Angela's Ashes*

MEET FRANK McCOURT

"When I look back on my childhood I wonder how I survived at all. It was, of course, a miserable childhood: the happy childhood is hardly worth your while." Thus begins Frank McCourt's powerful memoir, *Angela's Ashes*.

Frank McCourt was born in Brooklyn, New York, to recently immigrated Irish parents. His father, Malachy McCourt, struggled with alcoholism and unemployment. His mother, Angela Sheehan, bore the grim task of raising young children in the face of unrelenting poverty. In the mid-1930s, the McCourts moved back to Limerick, Ireland, to better their lives.

An Irish Childhood In Ireland, however, the McCourts fared no better, given the country's economic depression, unstable employment, and wretched living conditions. Angela tried to sustain the family by scrimping and saving, and by soliciting help from Catholic charities and the government. She also endured the deaths of three of her children.

Breaking Free When he was nineteen, McCourt decided to go to the United States to begin a new life. After working a series of jobs, McCourt served in the Korean War, which entitled him to benefits under the GI Bill and

funded his education at New York University. He became a teacher and taught in New York City public schools for twenty-seven years.

A Story to Tell McCourt knew he had a story to tell and struggled for years trying tell it. "All along I wanted to do this book badly. I would have to do it or I would have died howling." In 1996, at the age of sixty-six, he finally published *Angela's Ashes*.

> "*I learned the significance of my own insignificant life.*"
>
> —Frank McCourt

McCourt's gritty story gripped readers almost immediately. When he wrote *Angela's Ashes*, McCourt did not want to write something "charming or lyrical." Instead, he wanted to offer a description of his poverty-stricken Irish childhood that was real and honest. He won several prestigious awards for the book, including the Pulitzer Prize.

Two years later, McCourt followed *Angela's Ashes* with *'Tis*, the second work in his memoir series. *'Tis* chronicles his adventures in the United States, including his first job, his time in the military, his college education, and his profession as a teacher. McCourt published another book in 2005, *Teacher Man*. It is based on his own unique experience of teaching in the U.S. public school system.

Frank McCourt was born in 1930.

 Author Search For more about Frank McCourt, go to www.glencoe.com.

FRANK McCOURT **373**

Focus

BELLRINGER

Bellringer Options
Daily Language Practice Transparency 32
Or write on the board two excerpts from the selection: *I do believe, induced by potent circumstances / that thou art mine enemy* and *The wind was a torrent of darkness among the gusty trees, / The moon was a ghostly galleon tossed upon cloudy seas.* **Ask:** Which lines of poetry do you like more? What are some of your favorite poems or lines of poetry? Have students discuss their favorite poems and state why these are their favorites.

Literature Online

Author Search To expand students' appreciation of Frank McCourt, have them access the Web site for additional information and resources.

Selection Skills

Literary Elements
- Voice (SE pp. 374, 376, 378–380, 382)
- Memoir (SE p. 382)

Reading Skills
- Analyzing Style (SE pp. 374–376, 382)
- Drawing Conclusions (TWE p. 380)

Typhoid Fever

Vocabulary Skills
- Word Origins (SE pp. 374, 382)
- Academic Vocabulary (SE p. 382)

Study Skills/Research/ Assessment
- Small-Group Research (SE p. 383)

Writing Skills/Grammar
- Respond to Plot (SE p. 383)
- Present Tense (SE p. 383)
- Quotation Marks (TWE p. 376)
- Run-On Sentences (TWE p. 378)

Focus

Summary

Author Frank McCourt recalls his childhood experience as a typhoid fever patient in a Fever Hospital. One day Patricia Madigan, the girl in the room next to his, starts up a conversation with him. The two develop a sweet friendship against the wishes of Sister Rita, one of the hospital's nuns. Frank recites Shakespeare to Patricia, and she reads poetry to him. Eventually, Sister Rita banishes Frank to an empty ward. Patricia dies soon afterward.

V Vocabulary

Vocabulary File Say: Add these words and definitions to your vocabulary file. For each word, include a sentence that gives you an example of how to use the word. **OL** Students with English language needs should include the pronunciations of these words in their files. **EL**

Literary Elements Have students access the Web site to improve their understanding of voice.

Connecting to the Memoir

The following selection tells of the author's early experiences with love while bedridden in a hospital. Before you read, think about the following questions:

- When you are sick, what do you do to keep your mind occupied?
- When was the first time that something made you realize part of your childhood had vanished?

Building Background

Typhoid fever (tī′foid fē′vər) is an infection spread via food, water, and milk contaminated with the *Salmonella typhi* bacteria. If not treated effectively, typhoid can cause widespread damage to the body and can be fatal. Today typhoid is common in disaster-struck regions and impoverished areas with inadequate sanitary systems. It can be prevented by vaccine and treated with antibiotics.

Diphtheria (dif thēr′ē ə) is a disease caused by bacteria that have been infected by certain viruses. If left untreated, death can result from inflammation of the heart or suffocation brought about by a buildup of dead tissue in the throat. The disease is treated with antibiotics and can be prevented by vaccination.

Setting Purposes for Reading

Big Idea The Power of Memory

As you read this selection from *Angela's Ashes,* think about how McCourt portrays his childhood decades after he lived it.

Literary Element Voice

Voice is the distinctive use of language that conveys the author's or narrator's personality to the reader. Voice is determined by elements of style such as word choice and tone. Noting an author's voice can help you understand his or her perspective.

- See Literary Terms Handbook, p. R18.

Literature Online Interactive Literary Elements Handbook To review or learn more about the literary elements, go to www.glencoe.com.

OBJECTIVES
In studying this selection, you will focus on the following:
- analyzing style and voice
- understanding memoir
- expressing personal responses

374 UNIT 2 NONFICTION

Reading Strategy Analyzing Style

Style consists of the expressive qualities that distinguish an author's work, including word choice and the length and arrangement of sentences, as well as the use of figurative language and imagery. **Analyzing style** can reveal an author's attitude and purpose.

Reading Tip: Asking Questions Ask yourself questions about style as you read and record them in a chart like the one shown below:

Question	Answer	Example
What kinds of imagery does McCourt use?	He uses fantastical and nonsensical imagery to create an air of innocence or childhood.	"a poem about an owl and a pussy-cat that went to sea in a green boat with honey and money"
What kinds of words does McCourt use?		

Vocabulary

induce (in dōōs′) *v.* to lead or move by persuasion; to bring about; p. 377 *The physicians decided to induce labor.*

potent (pōt′ənt) *adj.* having strength or authority; powerful; p. 377 *The black widow spider injects a potent poison into its victims.*

rapier (rā′pē ər) *n.* a narrow, long-bladed, two-edged sword; p. 379 *The pirates drew their rapiers and dueled on deck.*

Vocabulary Tip: Word Origins Many English words are derived from Latin and the languages that developed from it, including Italian, Spanish, and French.

Selection Resources

Print Materials
- Unit 2 Resources (Fast File), pp. 30–32
- Leveled Vocabulary Development, p. 26
- Selection and Unit Assessments, pp. 55–56
- Selection Quick Checks, p. 28

Transparencies
- Bellringer Options Transparencies: Daily Language Practice Transparency 32
- Literary Elements Transparency 23

Technology
- TeacherWorks Plus™ CD-ROM
- StudentWorks Plus™ CD-ROM
- Presentation Plus!™ CD-ROM
- Literature Online, glencoe.com
- Online Student Edition, mhln.com
- Exam*View*® Assessment Suite CD-ROM
- Vocabulary PuzzleMaker CD-ROM
- Listening Library, disc 1 track 30

A Sick Ward at the Salpetriere. Mabel Henrietta May. Oil on canvas. Musée de l'Assistance Publique, Hopitaux de Paris, France.

Typhoid Fever

from *Angela's Ashes*   Frank McCourt

The other two beds in my room are empty. The nurse says I'm the only typhoid patient and I'm a miracle for getting over the crisis.

The room next to me is empty till one morning a girl's voice says, Yoo hoo, who's there?

I'm not sure if she's talking to me or someone in the room beyond.

Yoo hoo, boy with the typhoid, are you awake?

I am.

Are you better?

I am.

Well, why are you here?

I don't know. I'm still in the bed. They stick needles in me and give me medicine.

What do you look like?

I wonder. What kind of a question is that? I don't know what to tell her.

Yoo hoo, are you there, typhoid boy?

I am.

What's your name?

Frank.

That's a good name. My name is Patricia Madigan. How old are you?

Ten.

> **Reading Strategy** Analyzing Style *McCourt does not use quotation marks to set off dialogue. What effect does this style have?* **R**

FRANK McCOURT **375**

Teach

Big Idea

The Power of Memory
Say: Keep the following in mind as you read: which parts of the selection seem like genuine memories and which seem fictional? (*Answers will vary. The dialogue is probably somewhat fictionalized.*) **OL**

R Reading Strategy

Analyzing Style Answer:
Students may say that at first it is confusing but that it then actually makes the narrative flow, like a conversation. **OL**

★ Viewing the Art

The hospital in this painting, Salpêtrière, is in Paris. Originally an arsenal where saltpeter, used in making gunpowder, was stored, the building was converted to a hospital and shelter for poor, disabled, and mentally ill people. Today, the hospital continues to provide care for people in need. **AS**

CheckPoint

Use the CheckPoint questions on Presentation Plus! to monitor students' comprehension. These questions can be used with interactive response keypads for immediate student feedback.

Differentiated Instruction

Spatial Learners Looking at and creating visual representations are good ways to engage students with spatial intelligence and to develop the spatial skills of others in the class. Have students find Ireland and England on a world map or globe. Have them notice that Ireland is actually two countries, Ireland and Northern Ireland. Also have them notice Ireland's proximity to England, the primary reason the countries' histories are so intertwined. Then have students create their own maps that include the places in the story. **BL**

Objective
• To analyze style (SE)

L Literary Element

Voice Answer: *Students may say that McCourt's use of voice helps to portray Patricia as straightforward and clever.* **OL**

R Reading Strategy

Analyzing Style Answer: *His writing style mimics the way a child speaks and thinks.* **OL**

★ Cultural History

Religion in Ireland *The Little Messenger of the Sacred Heart* was a Catholic magazine founded in the mid-1870s by German-born Arnold Janssen, a Catholic priest and former teacher. The magazine shows up in the Fever Hospital because of the hospital's Catholic ownership and staff. **AS**

Readability Scores

Dale-Chall: 4.1
DRP: 48
Lexile: 1200

Oh. She sounds disappointed.

But I'll be eleven in August, next month.

Well, that's better than ten. I'll be fourteen in September. Do you want to know why I'm in the Fever Hospital?

I do.

I have diphtheria and something else.

What's something else?

They don't know. They think I have a disease from foreign parts because my father used to be in Africa. I nearly died. Are you going to tell me what you look like?

I have black hair.

You and millions.

I have brown eyes with bits of green that's called hazel.

You and thousands.

I have stitches on the back of my right hand and my two feet where they put in the soldier's blood.

Oh, God, did they?

They did.

You won't be able to stop marching and saluting.

There's a swish of habit and click of beads and then Sister Rita's voice. Now, now, what's this? There's to be no talking between two rooms especially when it's a boy and a girl. Do you hear me, Patricia?

I do, Sister.

Do you hear me, Francis?

I do, Sister.

You could be giving thanks for your two remarkable recoveries. You could be saying the rosary. You could be reading *The Little Messenger of the Sacred Heart* that's beside your beds. Don't let me come back and find you talking.

She comes into my room and wags her finger at me. Especially you, Francis, after thousands of boys prayed for you at the Confraternity.[1] Give thanks, Francis, give thanks.

---

1. A *confraternity* is a group of people dedicated to a religious cause.

Literary Element Voice *What does McCourt's use of voice convey about Patricia's personality?* **L**

She leaves and there's silence for awhile. Then Patricia whispers, Give thanks, Francis, give thanks, and say your rosary, Francis, and I laugh so hard a nurse runs in to see if I'm all right. She's a very stern nurse from the County Kerry and she frightens me. What's this, Francis? Laughing? What is there to laugh about? Are you and that Madigan girl talking? I'll report you to Sister Rita. There's to be no laughing for you could be doing serious damage to your internal apparatus.

She plods out and Patricia whispers again in a heavy Kerry accent, No laughing, Francis, you could be doin' serious damage to your internal apparatus. Say your rosary, Francis, and pray for your internal apparatus.

Mam visits me on Thursdays. I'd like to see my father, too, but I'm out of danger, crisis time is over, and I'm allowed only one visitor. Besides, she says, he's back at work at Rank's Flour Mills and please God this job will last a while with the war on and the English desperate for flour. She brings me a chocolate bar and that proves Dad is working. She could never afford it on the dole. He sends me notes. He tells me my brothers are all praying for me, that I should be a good boy, obey the doctors, the nuns, the nurses, and don't forget to say my prayers. He's sure St. Jude pulled me through the crisis because he's the patron saint[2] of desperate cases and I was indeed a desperate case.

Patricia says she has two books by her bed. One is a poetry book and that's the one she loves. The other is a short history of England and do I want it? She gives it to Seamus,[3] the man who mops the floors every day, and he brings it to me. He says, I'm not supposed to be bringing anything from a dipteria room to a typhoid room with all the germs flying around and hiding between the pages and if

---

2. A *patron saint* is a saint to whom a craft, activity, or the protection of a person or place is dedicated.
3. *Seamus* (shā´mus)

Reading Strategy Analyzing Style *McCourt blends narration and dialogue here. What is the effect of this stylistic technique?* **R**

Additional Support

GRAMMAR AND LANGUAGE:

Quotation Marks Quotation marks are used to separate direct quotations and dialogue from the rest of the narrative. Part of Frank McCourt's writing style is to exclude quotation marks, a style that demands greater vigilance on the reader's part. Make a copy of the first page of text from the selection for each student. Then have students insert quotation marks in the correct places. **OL**

you ever catch dipteria on top of the typhoid they'll know and I'll lose my good job and be out on the street singing patriotic songs with a tin cup in my hand, which I could easily do because there isn't a song ever written about Ireland's sufferings I don't know.

Oh, yes, he knows Roddy McCorley. He'll sing it for me right enough but he's barely into the first verse when the Kerry nurse rushes in. What's this, Seamus? Singing? Of all the people in this hospital you should know the rules against singing. I have a good mind to report you to Sister Rita.

Ah, God, don't do that, nurse.

Very well, Seamus. I'll let it go this one time. You know the singing could lead to a relapse in these patients.

When she leaves he whispers he'll teach me a few songs because singing is good for passing the time when you're by yourself in a typhoid room. He says Patricia is a lovely girl the way she often gives him sweets from the parcel her mother sends every fortnight. He stops mopping the floor and calls to Patricia in the next room, I was telling Frankie you're a lovely girl, Patricia, and she says, You're a lovely man, Seamus. He smiles because he's an old man of forty and he never had children but the ones he can talk to here in the Fever Hospital. He says, Here's the book, Frankie. Isn't it a great pity you have to be reading all about England after all they did to us, that there isn't a history of Ireland to be had in this hospital.

The book tells me all about King Alfred and William the Conqueror and all the kings and queens down to Edward, who had to wait forever for his mother, Victoria, to die

before he could be king. The book has the first bit of Shakespeare I ever read.

*I do believe, **induced** by **potent** circumstances*
That thou art mine enemy.

The history writer says this is what Catherine, who is a wife of Henry the Eighth, says to Cardinal Wolsey, who is trying to have her head cut off. I don't know

---

Big Idea The Power of Memory *Why might McCourt remember this so many years later?* **BI**

Vocabulary

induce (in dōōs′) *v.* to lead or move by persuasion; to bring about

potent (pōt′ənt) *adj.* having strength or authority; powerful

Teach

BI Big Idea

The Power of Memory
Answer: *Perhaps McCourt grew to admire and appreciate Shakespeare, and therefore his first exposure to Shakespeare's writing became a significant event in his life.* **OL**

★ Viewing the Art

Answer: *Like Sister Rita, this woman appears to be stern and pious. She is also holding a rosary, to which Sister Rita refers. Bernadette Soubirous was fourteen in 1858 when she reported seeing the vision of the Virgin Mary in Lourdes, France. Waters from the spring where the Virgin is said to have appeared are believed to have miraculous healing powers, and tens of thousands of people make pilgrimages to Lourdes every year. Bernadette died in 1879 and was named a saint in 1933.* **AS**

Reading in the Real World

Career: Musical Therapy The nurses and nuns in the selection discourage communication between patients, the recitation of poetry, and singing. Today, by contrast, medical therapy comes in many forms, including musical therapy. Professional musical therapists evaluate and treat physical and mental illnesses through musical activities, which may include playing music for patients or getting patients involved in musical activities. Have students conduct research on the career of musical therapy, including training, methods, and results, and have them share their findings with the class. **OL**

Objectives
• To analyze style and voice (SE)
• To understand the use of quotation marks (TWE)

Teach

Voice Answer: *Young Frank loves to read, even when he does not understand all of the words. The words seem magical to him, and he is impressed by Shakespeare. He is straightforward about what he feels.* **OL**

★ Viewing the Art

The earliest stained glass dates back to ancient Rome, when it was used to decorate homes. The brilliant colors are made when metal oxides are added to molten glass. In the twelfth and thirteenth centuries, stained glass became a fine art, with richly detailed panels that allowed light to stream in. Stained glass fell out of favor during the Reformation, and many stained-glass panels were ordered destroyed. The art form was revived in the nineteenth and twentieth centuries by artists such as Louis Comfort Tiffany and Marc Chagall. **AS**

★ Stained glass window of Saint Elizabeth Healing the Sick. Gothic, 13th Century. St. Elizabeth, Marburg, Germany.

what it means and I don't care because it's Shakespeare and it's like having jewels in my mouth when I say the words. If I had a whole book of Shakespeare they could keep me in the hospital for a year.

Patricia says she doesn't know what induced means or potent circumstances and she doesn't care about Shakespeare, she has her poetry book and she reads to me from beyond the wall a poem about an owl and a pussycat that went to sea in a green boat with honey and money and it makes no sense and when I say that Patricia gets huffy and says that's the last poem she'll ever read to me. She says I'm always reciting the lines from Shakespeare and they make no sense either. Seamus stops mopping again and tells us we shouldn't be fighting over poetry because we'll have enough to fight about when we grow up and get married. Patricia says she's sorry and I'm sorry too so she reads me part of another poem which I have to remember so I can say it back to her early in the morning or late at night when there are no nuns or nurses about,

The wind was a torrent of darkness among the gusty trees,

Literary Element **Voice** *What does McCourt's use of voice in this sentence tell you about his personality as a child?* **L1**

378 UNIT 2 NONFICTION

Additional Support

Skills Practice

GRAMMAR AND LANGUAGE:
Run-On Sentences Although run-on sentences can be a stylistic choice, as in McCourt's writing, it is best in most cases to fix these grammatically incorrect sentences. Make copies of the run-on sentence on page 378 that begins "Patricia says she doesn't know what induced means" and give each student a copy. Have them correct the run-on sentence by breaking it into multiple sentences, separating its sections with semicolons, or any other correct means. **OL**

*The moon was a ghostly galleon tossed upon
cloudy seas,*

*The road was a ribbon of moonlight over the
purple moor,*[4]

And the highwayman came riding

Riding riding

*The highwayman came riding, up to the old
inn-door.*

He'd a French cocked-hat[5] *on his forehead, a
bunch of lace at his chin,*

A coat of the claret[6] *velvet, and breeches*[7]
of brown doe-skin,

*They fitted with never a wrinkle, his boots
were up to the thigh.*

*And he rode with a
jewelled twinkle,*

His pistol butts a-twinkle,

His **rapier** *hilt a-twinkle, under the jewelled sky.*

Every day I can't wait for the doctors and
nurses to leave me alone so I can learn a
new verse from Patricia and find out what's
happening to the highwayman and the landlord's red-lipped daughter. I love the poem
because it's exciting and almost as good as
my two lines of Shakespeare. The redcoats
are after the highwayman because they
know he told her, I'll come to thee by moonlight, though hell should bar the way.

I'd love to do that myself, come by moonlight for Patricia in the next room, though
hell should bar the way. She's ready to read
the last few verses when in comes the nurse
from Kerry shouting at her, shouting at me, I

---

4. A *moor* is a wide, boggy expanse of land.
5. A *French cocked-hat* is a triangular hat with its brim turned
   upward in three places.
6. *Claret*, also the name of a red wine, is a dark, purplish red
   color.
7. *Breeches* are an old term for pants.

Literary Element Voice *What does this statement tell you
about the narrator's personality?* **L₂**

Vocabulary

rapier (rā′pē ər) *n.* a narrow, long-bladed, two-edged
sword

---

told ye there was to be no talking between
rooms. Dipthteria is never allowed to talk to
typhoid and visa versa. I warned ye. And
she calls out, Seamus, take this one. Take the
by. Sister Rita said one more word out of
him and upstairs with him. We gave ye a
warning to stop the blathering but ye
wouldn't. Take the by, Seamus, take him.

Ah, now, nurse, sure isn't he harmless. 'Tis
only a bit o' poetry.

Take that by, Seamus, take him at once.

He bends over me and whispers, Ah, God,
I'm sorry, Frankie. Here's your English history book. He slips the book under my shirt
and lifts me from the bed. He whispers that
I'm a feather. I try to see Patricia when we
pass through her room but all I can make
out is a blur of dark head on a pillow.

Sister Rita stops us in the hall to tell me
I'm a great disappointment to her, that she
expected me to be a good boy after what God
had done for me, after all the prayers said by
hundreds of boys at the Confraternity, after
all the care from the nuns and nurses of the
Fever Hospital, after the way they let my
mother and father in to see me, a thing rarely
allowed, and this is how I repaid them lying
in the bed reciting silly poetry back and forth
with Patricia Madigan knowing very well
there was a ban on all talk between typhoid
and diphtheria. She says I'll have plenty of
time to reflect on my sins in the big ward
upstairs and I should beg God's forgiveness
for my disobedience reciting a pagan English
poem about a thief on a horse and a maiden
with red lips who commits a terrible sin
when I could have been praying or reading
the life of a saint. She made it her business to
read that poem so she did and I'd be well
advised to tell the priest in confession.

The Kerry nurse follows us upstairs
gasping and holding on to the banister. She
tells me I better not get the notion she'll be
running up to this part of the world every
time I have a little pain or a twinge.

Big Idea The Power of Memory *Why do you think
McCourt remembers and is able to re-create details like this?* **BI**

FRANK McCOURT **379**

Voice Answer: *He is
young, somewhat naive, and
romantic.* **OL**

BI **Big Idea**

The Power of Memory
Answer: *The experience in the
hospital must have affected
McCourt deeply for him to
remember it in such detail.
Other students may argue that
McCourt probably has embellished some of the details in
order to create a more effective story.* **Ask:** *If, in reality,
McCourt did see Patricia on his
way past, why do you think he
would have changed it in this
memoir? (In not revealing what
she looks like, McCourt maintains the mystery and romance
surrounding the friendship. In
being faceless, Patricia comes
to represent the concept of
unattainable love.)* **OL**

English Language Coach

Vernacular Speech Students for
whom reading does not come easily are
likely to have difficulty with Seamus's
vernacular speech. Consider writing on
the board some of his unusual contractions, such as *'twas, 'tis,* and *'twould,*
followed by their two-word counterparts:
it was, it is, and *it would.* Other difficult
phrases may include "never heard the
likes of it," "has a good mind to," and
"lovely in yourself." Have the class discuss the meanings of these phrases to
make sure everyone understands. **BL**

Objectives
• To analyze voice (SE)
• To understand run-on sentences
  (TWE)

Teach

L Literary Element

Voice Answer: *The narrator seems very mature for his age; he knows exactly what the adults are trying to shield him from.* **OL**

BI Big Idea

The Power of Memory
Answer: *Students will probably say that he was very sad after her death. Possibly he felt badly that he was not in the room next to hers when she died.* **Ask:** *Do you think McCourt thinks he could have saved or rescued her, like the highwayman in the poem?* *(The romantic part of him probably thinks he could have rescued her, but the mature part of him knows that there was nothing he could have done.)* **OL**

CheckPoint

Use the CheckPoint questions on Presentation Plus! to check students' mastery of the selection. These questions can be used with interactive response keypads for immediate student feedback.

There are twenty beds in the ward, all white, all empty. The nurse tells Seamus put me at the far end of the ward against the wall to make sure I don't talk to anyone who might be passing the door, which is very unlikely since there isn't another soul on this whole floor. She tells Seamus this was the fever ward during the Great Famine[8] long ago and only God knows how many died here brought in too late for anything but a wash before they were buried and there are stories of cries and moans in the far reaches of the night. She says 'twould break your heart to think of what the English did to us, that if they didn't put the blight on the potato they didn't do much to take it off. No pity. No feeling at all for the people that died in this very ward, children suffering and dying here while the English feasted on roast beef and guzzled the best of wine in their big houses, little children with their mouths all green from trying to eat the grass in the fields beyond, God bless us and save us and guard us from future famines.

Seamus says 'twas a terrible thing indeed and he wouldn't want to be walking these halls in the dark with all the little green mouths gaping at him. The nurse takes my temperature, 'Tis up a bit, have a good sleep for yourself now that you're away from the chatter with Patricia Madigan below who will never know a gray hair.

She shakes her head at Seamus and he gives her a sad shake back.

Nurses and nuns never think you know what they're talking about. If you're ten going on eleven you're supposed to be simple like my uncle Pat Sheehan who was dropped on his head. You can't ask questions. You can't show you understand what the nurse said about Patricia Madigan, that she's going to die, and you can't show you want to cry over this girl who taught you a lovely poem which the nun says is bad.

The nurse tells Seamus she has to go and he's to sweep the lint from under my bed and mop up a bit around the ward. Seamus tells me she's a right oul' witch for running to Sister Rita and complaining about the poem going between the two rooms, that you can't catch a disease from a poem . . . . He never heard the likes of it, a little fella shifted upstairs for saying a poem and he has a good mind to go to the *Limerick Leader*[9] and tell them print the whole thing except he has this job and he'd lose it if ever Sister Rita found out. Anyway, Frankie, you'll be outa here one of these fine days and you can read all the poetry you want though I don't know about Patricia below, I don't know about Patricia, God help us.

He knows about Patricia in two days because she got out of the bed to go to the lavatory when she was supposed to use a bedpan and collapsed and died in the lavatory. Seamus is mopping the floor and there are tears on his cheeks and he's saying, 'Tis a dirty rotten thing to die in a lavatory when you're lovely in yourself. She told me she was sorry she had you reciting that poem and getting you shifted from the room, Frankie. She said 'twas all her fault.

It wasn't, Seamus.

I know and didn't I tell her that. ❧

> *"...have a good sleep for yourself now that you're away from the chatter with Patricia Madigan below who will never know a gray hair."*

---

8. The *Great Famine* refers to the Irish potato famine of the 1840s, during which many Irish citizens died from starvation and disease.

9. *Limerick* is the town in Ireland in which the story takes place. The *Limerick Leader* is a local publication, probably a newspaper.

Literary Element **Voice** *What does this tell you about the narrator's level of maturity?* **L**

Big Idea **The Power of Memory** *How do you think Patricia's death and her sorrow over McCourt's departure affected McCourt?* **BI**

Additional Support

Skills Practice

RESEARCH: Drawing Conclusions

The Irish Potato Famine of the 1840s was caused by the spread of a parasitic, moldlike organism. Because this major source of nourishment and income disappeared, many Irish citizens emigrated to the United States and England. Those who could not afford to travel were left behind to die from disease and starvation. Have students use various resources to research the Potato Famine and other places in the world now stricken by famine. Have them analyze the information and compare their notes. Tell them to make a comparative graph or chart and present their findings to the class. **OL**

RESPONDING AND THINKING CRITICALLY

Respond

1. (a)How did you feel after reading the selection? (b)What specifically about the selection made you feel this way? Explain.

Recall and Interpret

2. (a)What is the first reason Sister Rita gives for telling Frank and Patricia not to talk to each other? (b)What does this tell you about the time period and setting in which this selection takes place?

3. (a)What are the subjects of McCourt's and Patricia's poetry? (b)What does their love for these written passages tell you about their different tastes in literature?

4. (a)Which patients had Frankie's new ward previously housed? (b)How does this knowledge affect the mood of the selection?

Analyze and Evaluate

5. Does Frank and Patricia's dialogue sound like the dialogue of a ten-year-old and a fourteen-year-old? Illustrate your answer with examples from the text.

6. Describe the adults who appear in the excerpt. What kind of effect do you think the portrayal of the adults has on the excerpt as a whole?

Connect

7. **Big Idea** The Power of Memory In memoirs, authors have the chance to present their past using a narrative style and structure. Do you think this selection reads more like fiction or nonfiction? Explain.

A Child's Perspective

McCourt waited many years to write *Angela's Ashes* because he needed time to understand his painful childhood. As he says, "I couldn't have written this book fifteen years ago because I was carrying a lot of baggage around. . . . and I had attitudes and these attitudes had to be softened. I had to get rid of them, I had to become, as it says in the Bible, as a child. . . . The child started to speak in this book. And that was the only way to do it, without judging."

Group Activity Discuss the following questions with classmates. Refer back to the question and cite evidence from the selection for support.

1. Why do you think it was important for McCourt to become "as a child" in *Angela's Ashes?*

2. What are some ways in which the excerpt reflects the perspective of a child? Be specific in your answer.

FRANK McCOURT **381**

A Child's Perspective

1. Students may say that McCourt suffered injustices as a child, and he needed to take on a more innocent, childlike perspective in order to judge his childhood fairly.

2. Students may note the diction, the sense of limited perspective, and the sense of innocence.

Assess

1. (a) Students will probably say that they were sad after reading the selection. (b) Students will probably refer to Patricia's death as the cause of their emotional response.

2. (a) There should be no talking between rooms, "especially when it's a boy and a girl." (b) The story takes place in a very strict and rigid setting and time period in which girls and boys are kept separate.

3. (a) Frank reads about English history, while Patricia reads about an owl and a pussycat and also about a highwayman's romantic rescue of a red-lipped woman. (b) McCourt likes the serious and dramatic. Patricia likes the fanciful and playful. Both like the highwayman, a poem of love and conflict.

4. (a) Victims of the Great Famine (b) It creates a somber, oppressive, or depressing mood.

5. Students will probably think that the dialogue sounds authentic. They should support their opinions with excerpts.

6. The nuns do not sympathize with the children; Seamus is a comforting and kind figure. This conveys that most adults do not want to connect with or understand children.

7. Students might say that the selection reads like fiction because of the author's use of a child narrator and because it may seem so different from their lives.

Assess

Literary Element

1. Students will probably say that the voice sounds like that of a young boy using mostly easy words without adding his own thoughts.

2. Students should note that McCourt uses short, clipped sentences, such as his replies to Patricia; run-on sentences with simple vocabulary and images; and picked-up adult expressions.

Review: Memoir

Students' charts may include old-fashioned ideas about disease, which lead to scoldings from the adults; and the current war, which keeps McCourt's father from visiting.

Reading Strategy

1. McCourt uses casual or everyday speech. His poetic style may remind some students of oral storytelling.

2. To show that young people can experience wonderful but also unjust events and both have the power to shape the adults that they will become is his purpose. Students should note McCourt's use of imagery, humor, and wistful thoughts.

Literary Element Voice

An author uses **voice** to communicate his personality or opinions to the reader. The voice in an autobiographical work such as *Angela's Ashes* is the voice of the author's younger self as perceived by his adult self. When analyzing a writer's voice, look at how the writer uses elements such as sentence structure, word choice, and tone.

1. Does the voice in this selection sound like that of a young boy or that of an adult? Explain.

2. What stylistic devices does McCourt use to create his narrator's voice?

Review: Memoir

As you learned on page 354, **memoir** is a type of narrative nonfiction that presents the story of a period in the writer's life. It is usually written from the first-person point of view and emphasizes the narrator's own experience of this period. It may also reveal the impact of significant historical events on his or her life.

Partner Activity With a classmate, discuss "Typhoid Fever" as a memoir. Working with your partner, create a two-column chart similar to the one below. Fill in the left-hand column with examples of historical details or events referenced in the text. In the right-hand column, describe each example's effect on the author's life.

Historical Detail or Event	Effect on Author
old-fashioned medicine	had to stay isolated in the Fever Hospital

Reading Strategy Analyzing Style

An author's **style** affects how a reader responds to a piece of writing. Long sentences are often characteristic of a fluid, poetic style that connects many ideas. Simple word choice can reflect the voice of the narrator or can be a way to communicate ideas in an easy-to-understand manner. Use of imagery and figurative language is a common technique of poetic writers. Style can also be a clue to the author's purpose.

1. From this selection, how would you characterize McCourt's style of writing?

2. What do you think might be McCourt's purpose in writing this piece? What elements of McCourt's style hint at this purpose?

Vocabulary Practice

Practice with Word Origins A word's origins often give clues to its meaning. Match each vocabulary word with its corresponding root word. Use a dictionary for assistance. Then write a sentence using each word.

1. induce   a. *rapiere*, sword

2. potent   b. *inducere*, to lead in

3. rapier   c. *potens*, powerful

Academic Vocabulary

Here are two words from the vocabulary list on page R82. These words will help you think, write, and talk about the selection.

expose (iks pōz´) *v.* to make known or visible; to make vulnerable

medical (med´i kəl) *adj.* of or relating to treatment by physicians; relating to medicine

Practice and Apply

1. How was Patricia **exposed** to an unknown disease?

2. What **medical** procedures do the doctors and nurses administer to Frank?

Vocabulary

1. b **2.** c **3.** a

Academic Vocabulary

1. Her father's experiences in Africa may have resulted in her exposure to the unknown sickness.

2. They give injections and dispense medicine to him.

Writing About Literature

Respond to Plot McCourt describes a number of events from his childhood in this selection, such as his and Patricia's trading of poetry, Seamus's attempts to help them, punishment at the hands of the nurses and nuns, and Patricia's death. In your opinion, is Frankie and Patricia's relationship romantic? Did you find Seamus's character humorous? How did you feel after the author tells of Patricia's death? Write a one- or two-page analysis in which you explore your personal responses to these events. Use evidence from the text to help explain your responses.

Before you begin writing your first draft, take notes on your reactions to the events in the selection in a two-column chart, such as the one below:

Event	Response
trading of poetry	I found this childish and silly.

Include quotes from the text related to the events, as well as any impressions or ideas that strike you as you read. Once you have completed the chart, begin drafting.

After finishing your first draft, trade essays with a peer reviewer. Evaluate each other's work and suggest ways to improve each other's essays. Then proofread and edit your work for mistakes in spelling, grammar, and punctuation.

Interdisciplinary Activity

In a small group, gather facts about the historical and scientific context of "Typhoid Fever." What was happening in Ireland and the rest of the world in the early 1940s? What was the state of medical research just before and during this time? Then analyze how these scientific and historical facts influenced the events of "Typhoid Fever."

McCourt's Language and Style

Narrating in the Present Tense McCourt narrates "Typhoid Fever" in the present tense, even though he experienced these events fifty years prior to writing *Angela's Ashes.* The most common writing tense is actually past tense, especially when writing about the past. Note McCourt's use of tense in the following passage:

> She leaves and there's silence for awhile. Then Patricia whispers, Give thanks, Francis, give thanks, and say your rosary, Francis, and I laugh so hard a nurse runs in to see if I'm all right. She's a very stern nurse from the County Kerry and she frightens me.

Here is the same passage written in the past tense. Read and compare it to McCourt's original passage:

> She left and there was silence for awhile. Then Patricia whispered, Give thanks, Francis, give thanks, and say your rosary, Francis, and I laughed so hard a nurse ran in to see if I was all right. She was a very stern nurse from the County Kerry and she frightened me.

Did the past tense version make you feel differently than the first? How did it affect the narrator's voice? By writing in the present tense, McCourt makes his memories seem active and alive. Also, because he frequently combines narration and dialogue, writing in the present tense maintains tense consistency and thus prevents confusion.

Activity Change these sentences to present tense.

1. She shook her head at Seamus and he gave her a sad shake back.

2. The nurse said I was the only typhoid patient and I was a miracle for getting over the crisis.

3. I would have liked to have seen my father, too, but I was out of danger, crisis time was over, and I was allowed only one visitor.

Revising Check

The Present Tense Consistency of tense is an important element of writing. With a partner, go through your essay about your response to the events in "Typhoid Fever" and make sure you use tense correctly and consistently.

 Web Activities For eFlashcards, Selection Quick Checks, and other Web activities, go to www.glencoe.com.

Assess

Writing About Literature

Use these criteria when evaluating students' writing:

- Does the essay explore their responses to several events from the text?

- Does the essay provide examples from the text to help explain their responses?

Interdisciplinary Activity

Make sure students use valid sources to conduct their research. Have them submit a bibliography with their factual information.

McCourt's Language and Style

1. She shakes her head at Seamus, and he gives her a sad shake back.

2. The nurse says I am the only typhoid patient and I am a miracle for getting over the crisis.

3. I would like to see my father, too, but I am out of danger, crisis time is over, and I am allowed only one visitor.

Revising Check

Ask students to compile a class list of errors related to consistency of tense. Review a few of the errors with the whole class.

Literature Online

Web Activities Have students access the Web site for interactive activities that will help them assess their understanding of the selection.

Focus

Summary

This article is an examination of Frank McCourt, the author of *Angela's Ashes*. The article outlines the worldwide success of the memoir, and McCourt comments on the pervasive bleakness of the book. He discusses the value of personal experiences to a writer. He talks about his long teaching career and his experience writing *Angela's Ashes*.

Teach

BI₁ **Big Idea**

The Power of Memory

Say: Keep the following questions in mind as you read: What does McCourt believe is the best writing inspiration or subject matter? How does writing affect his well-being? *(He believes personal experiences are the best inspiration or subject matter for writing. Writing gives him a great sense of accomplishment. He feels that he was born to be a writer.)* **OL**

Readability Scores
Dale-Chall: 5.8
DRP: 61
Lexile: 1050

Additional Support

See also ▨ Active Learning and Note Taking Guide, pp. 49–55.

HISTORICAL PERSPECTIVES on *Angela's Ashes*
Informational Text

Frank McCourt, 1998. New York.

from

Looking Forward to the Past

A Profile of Frank McCourt

Carolyn T. Hughes

BI₁

Building Background

Author Frank McCourt, who spent his childhood in Limerick, Ireland, revisits his early years in *Angela's Ashes*. In this selection, Hughes discusses why McCourt was inspired to write a memoir of his childhood in Limerick.

Set a Purpose for Reading

Read to learn about McCourt's personal journey in writing *Angela's Ashes*.

Reading Strategy

Recognizing Author's Purpose

Recognizing the author's purpose involves identifying the author's intent for writing a literary work. Authors may write for any or all of the following purposes: to persuade, inform, explain, entertain, or describe. As you read, use a web diagram like the one below to take notes on the details of the interview.

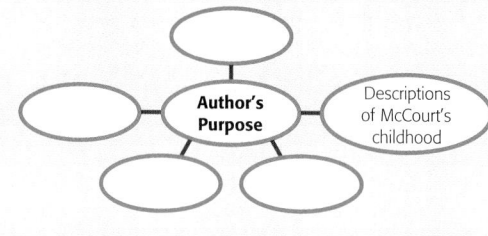

Author's Purpose · Descriptions of McCourt's childhood

384 UNIT 2 NONFICTION

Angela's Ashes is McCourt's attempt to come to terms with his childhood—one so beset by tragedy and misfortune that he has called his work simply an "epic of woe." In 1930 McCourt was born in Brooklyn, to Irish immigrants Malachy and Angela. His parents, crushed by the recent death of their daughter and by the alcoholic Malachy's inability to hold a job, moved the family back to Ireland—but bad luck followed them. McCourt's twin brothers died shortly after the family returned to Limerick, and he himself almost perished from typhoid fever. But the greatest challenge for McCourt to contend with was his father's continued drinking and eventual abandonment of the family. In 1941 Malachy McCourt, Sr., left for England, ostensibly to get a factory job. He was supposed to send home money. It never happened. He disappeared, leaving his family to fend for themselves.

At times, the landscape of *Angela's Ashes* is so bleak it's downright depressing. But McCourt's use of a child narrator (an idea that came to him "in a dream") works to soften the tragedy of the story. Instead of being delivered

---

Skills Practice

RESEARCH AND STUDY SKILLS:
Locating Information Using the appropriate resources is important when researching a paper. Research materials present different types of information and present information in different ways. For example, a book index may list books of similar subject matter but probably will not provide much specific information about the individual books. Have students locate different types of resources to find biographical information about McCourt, a list of his books, summaries of his books, and the publications that contain his other writings. **OL**

through an adult's jaded vision, the events are relayed from an innocent, even lighthearted perspective, without judgment, which makes room for the poignancy and humor so celebrated by readers and critics.

Much of *Angela's Ashes* is devoted to the depiction of McCourt's educational experience at Leamy National School in Limerick, where, he says, his teachers had about as light a touch as the Marquis de Sade.[1] When McCourt became a teacher himself, he was determined to provide a creative, productive environment for his students. He began his career in 1959 at McKee Vocational and Technical High School on Staten Island, and after 13 years went on to Stuyvesant High, where he became the kind of teacher students dream of. Claire Costello, a Stuyvesant alumna who now works as a Manhattan attorney, says that McCourt was so popular that students who were not assigned to his classes would audit them (now not many teachers can claim *that* kind of approbation).[2] In class McCourt was known to play Irish records, and even to break out his harmonica and play a tune or two himself. While his approachability endeared him to his students, McCourt insists he learned more from his students than they did from him.

"I found that in the beginning of my teaching career, just like everybody else, I would put on an act and try to be what I wasn't: the teacher who knows *everything*. Sometimes I felt I was saying things that I really didn't mean. 'Oh, yeah, I understand *The Waste Land*,[3] I understand Shakespeare,' when I might not. But one of the things I discovered in the classroom was honesty. I don't mean it from any moral or ethical sense. It's a powerful tool to tell the truth."

R The practice of telling the truth was an exercise that would prove important for McCourt. And in having to articulate to his students lessons on how to write, he was formulating the strategies that he would eventually put to use

---

1. The *Marquis de Sade* (1740–1814) was a French nobleman and writer condemned for his abusive behavior.
2. *Approbation* means "praise."
3. *The Waste Land* is a famous poem by American writer T. S. Eliot.

himself. "I told them, 'If you write, it's like having a Geiger counter[4] you can run over your life. There will be hot spots—when you had your first fight with your brother, when you fell in love, your first kiss, and all that—then you look for conflict.' The ol' conflict dilemma. I also told them to get the stories of their fathers and mothers and grandparents. There are grandparents sitting at home now who are mines of information and stories. They want to tell them, but most people cast them aside. I told my students, 'There's your material; get out the tape recorder, take notes.'"   **BI₂**

McCourt acknowledges being an avid note taker himself and says it helped him with the writing of his book. "I've been keeping journals for forty years, and there were things I discovered in my notebooks that I had forgotten about—like how my mother was attracted to my father and his hangdog look. Well, one of the reasons why he had a hangdog look then was because he had just been released from three months in prison for hijacking a truck. He thought it was full of cans of pork and beans, but it turned out to be buttons." McCourt laughs. "I had forgotten about that completely."

Although McCourt has spent much of his life teaching writing, he admits he's suspicious of today's writing programs. "It depends on the person, but I think you'd be better off falling in love, you'd be better off getting rejected by someone. These are valuable experiences!" McCourt says. "My point is, anything is worth writing about. I gave my students an assignment. I said, 'Look, pick somebody in this class, don't look at them right now, but you are going to write about this person. You are going to observe them for a month and then write.' It forced them, encouraged them, to observe another human being and perhaps realize the significance of insignificance."

One of the major reasons it took McCourt so long to write *Angela's Ashes* was that he didn't understand the truth of his own lesson. He marginalized the significance of his early

---

4. A *Geiger counter*, an instrument with a tube and electronic equipment, is used to detect particles of radiation.

CAROLYN T. HUGHES **385**

Teach

Big Idea

The Power of Memory

Ask: How can negative memories affect the present? *(Bad memories, like those of McCourt's difficult, impoverished upbringing, can affect a person's emotional well-being and make that person feel negatively toward himself or herself. They can also affect how a person views the world and create a pessimistic attitude toward life.)* **OL**

★ Literary History

The Village Voice The *Voice* is a popular weekly newspaper based in New York City. Founded in 1955 by Ed Fancher, Dan Wolf, and noted writer Norman Mailer, the *Voice* is known for its hard-hitting and lively journalistic style and its relentless investigations into the sometimes lurid politics of Manhattan. The paper has won a number of awards over the years, including three Pulitzer prizes, and is considered by the people of New York to be a first-rate source of information on the local cultural scene. **AS**

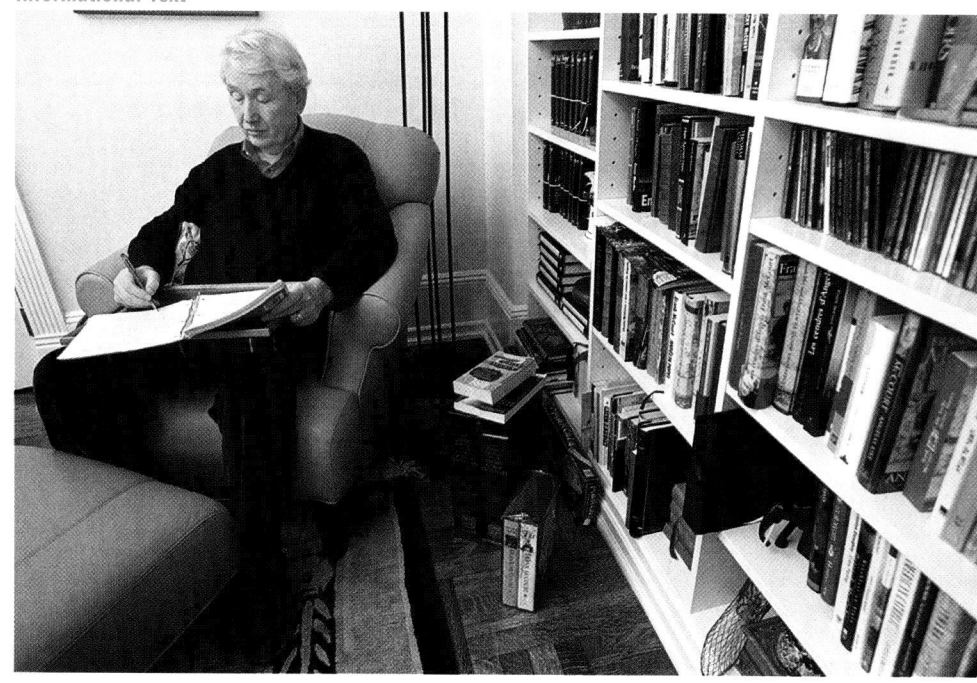

Frank McCourt in New York. January 4, 2000. Tore Bergsake.

life, believing that his family's crushing poverty rendered their story inconsequential. His background, in fact, was a source of embarrassment: "In my twenties and thirties, I didn't want to write about being poor. I had to overcome a lot of fear—overcome the shame. I guess you could say I was suffering from low self-esteem."

In 1969, McCourt did attempt to write a book about his life. "I think I called it *If You Were in the Lane*. It was completely derivative. I was imitating everybody, even Evelyn Waugh.[5] Imagine me writing like Evelyn Waugh!"

Although he didn't give up writing completely, it was 25 years before McCourt would try to tackle his own story again. In the meantime he wrote the occasional article—he published a piece about a Jewish cemetery in Limerick in the *Village Voice* and

a series of articles about New York for the *Manhattan Spirit*. McCourt even tried his hand as an entertainer. In 1984, he starred with brother Malachy, an actor, Manhattan bar owner, and renowned bon vivant,[6] in a cabaret show called *A Couple of Blaguards*. The show premiered in New York and went on to Chicago, San Francisco, and Ireland. The brothers McCourt sang Irish songs and told stories about their family. (The play, directed by Howard Platt, is now enjoying a successful run at New York's Triad Theater.)

When McCourt retired from teaching and finally turned to the writing of *Angela's Ashes,* it didn't take long for him to finish it. He wrote most of the book at his home in Pennsylvania. "I started it in October 1994. The actual writing took a year—actually, less than a year because I was distracted by various events and people visiting, so maybe it took ten months of

---

5. *Evelyn Waugh* (1903–1966) was a British writer, known for his satiric portrayals of the British upper classes.

6. *Bon vivant* means "a person with sophisticated tastes, especially of food and drink."

Additional Support

Skills Practice

READING ACROSS TEXTS AND CULTURES: Creating New Knowledge An important student task is to read widely and to integrate information from different sources. The memoir is a popular form of literature. In addition to McCourt's follow-up memoirs, *'Tis* and *Teacher Man*, sug-

gest to students some memoirs by other authors, such as *The Diary of a Young Girl* by Anne Frank, *The Story of My Life* by Helen Keller, and *Night* by Elie Wiesel. Have students read another memoir and compare it to the selection in terms of subject matter and style. Ask students to present their analysis to the class. **OL** straight writing. I just got up every morning and I wrote. What was it Red Smith[7] said? 'You sit at the desk and you open a vein.' That was my routine. I wrote on the right-hand page of my notebook, and on the left-hand side I jotted down notes about what I needed to dig deeper into." McCourt didn't have any set schedule for how many hours a day he would work: "I didn't push. . . . When it came, it came." Having his wife as a sounding board helped. "I would read passages to Ellen—and she thought it was fine."

McCourt showed the first 159 pages to Molly Friedrich, a New York City neighbor who also happens to be a literary agent. She agreed to work with McCourt, and passed the manuscript on to Nan Graham, editor in chief at Scribner. Graham, no easy sell, loved it: "I edited *The Liar's Club*,"[8] Graham says. "I've seen a lot of memoirs, but from the beginning I thought the work and voice in *Angela's Ashes* was extraordinary. I bought the book within a

week. There really was so little to do as far as editing. This man is a stunning writer."

McCourt handed in his final draft to Graham on November 30, 1995, the 328th anniversary of the birth of Jonathan Swift,[9] one of McCourt's favorite writers (he has a thing for significant dates). Although working on the book was emotionally draining, McCourt felt an overwhelming sense of accomplishment when he finished it. "I would have been very unhappy if I had died without writing it. I would have begged for another year. 'Jesus, give me another year!' I would have died howling. So I did it, and I'm glad it's out of the way. You see, it's a great thing to know why you were put on this earth. I was a teacher, but teaching was my second occupation. All the time I was a writer not writing, just jotting things down in notebooks and so on. But all the time the book was developing in my head as I taught the kids at Stuyvesant. It was forming and waiting to be born." ✿ R

---

7. *Red Smith* (1905–1982) was an American sports columnist.
8. *Liar's Club* was author Mary Karr's popular 1995 memoir.

9. *Jonathan Swift* (1667–1745) was an Irish author celebrated for his satiric prose in such works as *Gulliver's Travels*.

RESPONDING AND THINKING CRITICALLY

Respond

1. What is your opinion of McCourt's claim that "anything is worth writing about"?

Recall and Interpret

2. (a)For what reason(s) did McCourt decide to use a child's point of view to narrate *Angela's Ashes*? (b)What might this say about his perspective on childhood?

3. (a)What was the most important quality that McCourt realized he must have in order to be a good teacher? (b)How did he apply what he learned as a teacher to his work as a writer?

Analyze and Extend

4. (a)Hughes delves into McCourt's upbringing, his offbeat methods of teaching, and his brief stint as an actor. Why do you think she includes these details of McCourt's life? (b)Do these details support McCourt's message about writing? Why or why not?

5. (a)Hughes says that "one of the major reasons it took McCourt so long to write *Angela's Ashes* was that he didn't understand the truth of his own lesson." What do you think Hughes means by this comment? (b)What do you think Hughes believes the act of writing can teach a person?

Connect

6. McCourt attempted to write a book about his life in 1969. It took another twenty-five years before he wrote *Angela's Ashes*. Do you think the passing of time distanced him from or made him more aware of his memories of the past? How do you think the passage of time colors your memories?

OBJECTIVES
- Determine the author's purpose and point of view and their effects on the text.
- Evaluate the text's organization and content to determine the author's purpose, reasoning, and effectiveness.

CAROLYN T. HUGHES **387**

Focus

BELLRINGER

Bellringer Options
**Selection Focus
Transparency 22
Daily Language Practice
Transparency 33
Or on the board, write:**
Humor is emotional chaos remembered in tranquility.
—James Thurber
A sense of humor . . . is the ability to understand a joke—and that the joke is oneself.
—Clifton Fadiman
Ask: Do you agree with these quotations? Which is more accurate? Have students discuss their reactions in small groups.

Author Search To expand students' appreciation of Annie Dillard, have them access the Web site for additional information and resources.

Terwilliger Bunts One from *An American Childhood*

MEET ANNIE DILLARD

As a child, Annie Dillard was encouraged by her parents to investigate the world around her. That keen attention to detail and fascination for living things is reflected in Dillard's writing, whether she is describing a grasshopper on her window or discussing her family's idiosyncrasies.

> *"The dedicated life is worth living. You must give with your whole heart."*
>
> —Annie Dillard

An American Childhood Annie Dillard, the oldest of three daughters, had an unusual childhood. Her parents, the Doaks, were creative thinkers who encouraged and inspired creativity in Dillard and her sisters. The world was open to the Doak sisters to explore, question, and discover. During adolescence, Dillard began experimenting with writing poetry. She read poets of all kinds and particularly admired the works of Ralph Waldo Emerson. Dillard wrote poetry in her own style as well as in the style of her favorite poets. She was also a voracious reader; she notes that, at the age of thirteen, "I was reading books on drawing, painting, rocks, criminology, birds, moths, beetles, stamps, ponds and streams, medicine." In fact, Dillard reread her favorite book—*The Field Book of Ponds and Streams*—every year.

Tinker Creek and Beyond Dillard received both her bachelor's and master's degrees in English from Hollins College near Roanoke, Virginia. She enjoyed reading such authors as Henry James, Thomas Hardy, and Ernest Hemingway. Dillard wrote a 40-page paper in college about Henry David Thoreau, and her book, *Pilgrim at Tinker Creek*, is often compared to Thoreau's *Walden; or Life in the Woods.* Like Thoreau, Dillard spent time living in nature next to Tinker Creek in Virginia's Roanoke Valley. Just as Thoreau described life in the woods in *Walden,* in *Pilgrim at Tinker Creek,* Dillard examines the beautiful and sometimes brutal natural world. Dillard, like Thoreau, uses her observations to reflect on identity and her place in the world. *Pilgrim at Tinker Creek* won the Pulitzer Prize for Nonfiction in 1975, when Dillard was only thirty years old.

After writing a novel and several books about writing, Dillard was inspired by the birth of her first daughter to complete a memoir, entitled *An American Childhood.* Dillard describes growing up with eccentric parents: a father who quit his lucrative job to mimic Mark Twain's journey down the Mississippi River and a mother who encouraged her daughters to explore the world outside the family home as soon as they could remember their phone number. Dillard's mother, who was allowed to edit the manuscript for the book, wryly observed that "Annie loves us very dearly, but she doesn't particularly like us."

According to Michael J. Farrell, "Dillard urges us not to turn away, coaxes us instead to look Life in the eye." Whether writing about the natural world or the human one, Dillard observes with an unflinching gaze.

Annie Dillard was born in 1945.

Literature Online **Author Search** For more about Annie Dillard, go to www.glencoe.com.

388 UNIT 2 NONFICTION

Selection Skills

Literary Elements
- Anecdote (SE pp. 389, 390, 393, 394, 397)
- Voice (SE p. 397)

Terwilliger Bunts One

Reading Skills
- Connecting to Personal Experience (SE pp. 389–397)
- Reading for Main Idea and Supporting Details (TWE p. 390)

Vocabulary Skills
- Word Parts (SE pp. 389, 397)
- Academic Vocabulary (SE p. 397)

Listening/Speaking/Viewing Skills
- Telling Humorous Stories (SE p. 398)

Writing Skills/Grammar
- Analyze Comic Devices (SE p. 398)
- Subject and Object Pronouns (SE p. 398)
- Conducting Research (TWE p. 392)
- Dialogue (TWE p. 394)

Connecting to the Memoir

In *An American Childhood*, Dillard recounts stories about her childhood. The author's intent in this excerpt is to reveal her mother's depth and wit through a series of humorous family memories. Before you read, think of someone in your life who reminds you of Dillard's mother.

- How do you use humor in your daily life?
- How does humor affect your mood and how you go about your day?

Building Background

An American Childhood is set in Pittsburgh, Pennsylvania, in the 1950s. At that time, most middle-class married women did not work outside the home or pursue their own careers. Women who were fortunate or wealthy enough to attend college were generally assumed to be looking for a husband. Even a well-educated married woman of the 1950s was expected to be content to take care of her husband and children.

Setting Purposes for Reading

Big Idea The Power of Memory

As you read this selection, notice how Dillard links her humorous memories of her mother to incidents in childhood that helped her to develop her insights as a writer.

Literary Element Anecdote

An **anecdote** is a brief account of an interesting occurrence. Anecdotes add depth and variety to the flow of text and help the reader to better visualize the characters and events. As you read the story, notice how Dillard uses anecdotes to deepen our understanding of her mother's approach to life.

- See Literary Terms Handbook, p. R1.

Literature Online **Interactive Literary Elements Handbook** To review or learn more about the literary elements, go to www.glencoe.com.

Reading Strategy Connecting to Personal Experience

Often authors write about situations, settings, or characters to which or whom the reader can relate. **Connecting to personal experience** can help you better understand the author's message. As you read, find situations in the text that remind you of instances in your own life.

....

Reading Tip: Making a Chart You might choose events, characters, or something else from the excerpt that seems familiar to compare to your personal experiences. Record your thoughts on a chart like the one below.

Situations in the text	Reminds me of...
Mother rolled down the hill at the beach.	I have an aunt who was like that when she was younger.

Vocabulary

tremulously (trem′ yə ləs lē) *adv.* in a trembling or vibrating way; p. 391 *After he heard the knock at the door, he tremulously asked, "Who's there?"*

eschew (es chōō′) *v.* to keep apart from something disliked or harmful; avoid; p. 391 *Because I dislike music with violent lyrics, I eschew it.*

advocate (ad′ və kāt′) *v.* to publicly support; p. 393 *I advocate the passing of that law, and I will be sure to vote for it.*

stolid (stol′ id) *adj.* showing little or no emotion; p. 394 *Her face was stolid after hearing the bad news; we never knew how sad she was.*

....

Vocabulary Tip: Word Parts Word parts are prefixes, suffixes, and base words or roots.

Focus

Summary

In this memoir, the author describes her mother's sense of humor. She loved wordplay and practical jokes. Although she had the capacity to run New York City, she had to be content to run her own household, so she thought up clever inventions to make housework easier. Her odd sense of humor taught the author and her sisters to take a stand.

V Vocabulary

Vocabulary File Say: Add these words and definitions to your vocabulary file. For each word, include a sentence that gives you an example of how to use the word. **OL** Students with English language needs should include the pronunciations of these words in their files. **EL**

Literature Online

Literary Elements Have students access the Web site to improve their understanding of anecdote.

OBJECTIVES
In studying this selection, you will focus on the following:
- analyzing the author's use of anecdote
- connecting literature to personal experience
- analyzing the author's use of voice
- writing an essay analyzing comic devices

ANNIE DILLARD **389**

Selection Resources

Print Materials
- 📁 Unit 2 Resources (Fast File), pp. 34–36
- 📁 Leveled Vocabulary Development, p. 27
- 📁 Selection and Unit Assessments, pp. 59–60
- 📁 Selection Quick Checks, p. 30

Transparencies
- Bellringer Options Transparencies: Selection Focus Transparency 22
  Daily Language Practice Transparency 33
- Literary Elements Transparency 32

Technology
- 🔘 TeacherWorks Plus™ CD-ROM
- 🔘 StudentWorks Plus™ CD-ROM
- 🔘 Presentation Plus!™ CD-ROM
- 💻 Literature Online, glencoe.com
- 💻 Online Student Edition, mhln.com
- 🔘 Exam*View*® Assessment Suite CD-ROM
- 🔘 Vocabulary PuzzleMaker CD-ROM
- 🔘 Listening Library, disc 1 track 31

Teach

BI₁ **Big Idea**

The Power of Memory
Say: Keep the following questions in mind as you read: How did the author feel about her mother's antics while she was growing up? How have her attitudes changed? (*While growing up, the author was embarrassed by her mother's unusual behavior. The author now respects her mother's intellect and ingenuity.*) **OL**

L **Literary Element**

Anecdote Answer: *It introduces the author's mother*

★ Viewing the Art

American artist Andy Warhol (1928–1987) used images of popular culture to comment on U.S. society. His work often repeated images such as S&H Green Stamps on a single canvas to reflect how the media saturates society with visuals that influence consumerism. **AS**

Readability Scores
Dale-Chall: 6.3
DRP: 59
Lexile: 1040

Additional Support

Leveled Reading
An adapted version of this selection is available on page 248 of *Jamestown Literature: An Adapted Reader*, grade 10.

390

Terwilliger Bunts One

from An American Childhood

Annie Dillard

S&H Green Stamps, 1965. Andy Warhol.
The Andy Warhol Foundation for the Visual Arts.

BI₁

One Sunday afternoon Mother wandered through our kitchen, where Father was making a sandwich and listening to the ball game. The Pirates were playing the New York Giants at Forbes Field. In those days, the Giants had a utility infielder[1] named Wayne Terwilliger. Just as Mother passed through, the radio announcer cried—with undue drama—"Terwilliger bunts one!"

"Terwilliger bunts one?" Mother cried back, stopped short. She turned. "Is that English?"

"The player's name is Terwilliger," Father said. "He bunted."

"That's marvelous," Mother said. "'Terwilliger bunts one.' No wonder you listen to baseball. 'Terwilliger bunts one.'"

For the next seven or eight years, Mother made this surprising string of syllables her own. Testing a microphone, she repeated, "Terwilliger bunts one"; testing a pen or a typewriter, she wrote it. If, as happened surprisingly often in the course of various improvised gags, she pretended to whisper something else in my ear, she actually whispered, "Terwilliger bunts one." Whenever someone used a French phrase, or a Latin one, she answered solemnly, "Terwilliger bunts one." If Mother had had, like Andrew

---

1. In this context, *utility* means "useful generally rather than in a specialized function." So, a *utility infielder* is capable of playing shortstop or first, second, or third base.

390 UNIT 2 NONFICTION

Literary Element Anecdote *How does this opening anecdote draw the reader in?* **L**

Skills Practice

READING: Main Idea and Supporting Details Identifying the main idea and supporting details of an essay is crucial to students' understanding of an essay. Have students write a sentence that summarizes the main idea of Dillard's essay. Then have them list five details from the essay that support that main idea. Ask volunteers to read their main ideas and details. **OL**

Carnegie,[2] the opportunity to cook up a motto for a coat of arms,[3] hers would have read simply and tellingly, "Terwilliger bunts one." (Carnegie's was "Death to Privilege.")

She served us with other words and phrases. On a Florida trip, she repeated **tremulously**, "That . . . is a royal poinciana." I don't remember the tree; I remember the thrill in her voice. She pronounced it carefully, and spelled it. She also liked to say "portulaca."[4]

The drama of the words "Tamiami Trail" stirred her, we learned on the same Florida trip. People built Tampa on one coast, and they built Miami on another. Then—the height of visionary[5] ambition and folly— they piled a slow, tremendous road through the terrible Everglades to connect them. To build the road, men stood sunk in muck to their armpits. They fought off cottonmouth moccasins and six-foot alligators. They slept in boats, wet. They blasted muck with dynamite, cut jungle with machetes; they laid logs, dragged drilling machines, hauled dredges, heaped limestone. The road took fourteen years to build up by the shovelful, a Panama Canal in reverse, and cost hundreds of lives from tropical, mosquito-carried diseases. Then, capping it all, some genius thought of the word Tamiami: they called the road from Tampa to Miami, this very road under our spinning wheels, the Tamiami Trail. Some called it Alligator

Alley. Anyone could drive over this road without a thought.

Hearing this, moved, I thought all the suffering of road building was worth it (it wasn't my suffering), now that we had this new thing to hang these new words on— Alligator Alley for those who like things cute, and, for connoisseurs like Mother, for lovers of the human drama in all its boldness and terror, the Tamiami Trail.

Back home, Mother cut clips from reels of talk, as it were, and played them back at leisure. She noticed that many Pittsburghers confuse "leave" and "let." One kind relative brightened our morning by mentioning why she'd brought her son to visit: "He wanted to come with me, so I left him." Mother filled in Amy and me on locutions we missed. "I can't do it on Friday," her pretty sister told a crowded dinner party, "because Friday's the day I lay in the stores."[6]

(All unconsciously, though, we ourselves used some pure Pittsburghisms. We said "tele pole," pronounced "telly pole," for that splintery sidewalk post I loved to climb. We said "slippy"—the sidewalks are "slippy." We said, "That's all the farther I could go." And we said, as Pittsburghers do say, "This glass needs washed," or "The dog needs walked"—a usage our father **eschewed**; he knew it was not standard English, nor even comprehensible English, but he never let on.)

"Spell 'poinsettia,'" Mother would throw out at me, smiling with pleasure. "Spell 'sherbet.'" The idea was not to make us whizzes, but, quite the contrary, to remind us—and I, especially, needed reminding— that we didn't know it all just yet. "There's a

---

2. Based in Pittsburgh, *Andrew Carnegie* (1835–1919) made a fortune in the steel industry and donated $350 million to social and educational institutions.

3. A *coat of arms* is an arrangement of symbols on a shield that, along with a motto, represents one's ancestry.

4. Both the *royal poinciana* and the *portulaca* (pôr´chə la´ kə) are native to the tropics and bear bright flowers.

5. Here, *visionary* refers to imagining something in perfect but unrealistic form. People had foreseen the benefits of connecting the two cities but overlooked practical considerations involved in constructing the road.

6. *Locutions* are forms or styles of verbal expression. Where this woman said she had to *lay in the stores,* Mother might have said she had to go grocery shopping.

Reading Strategy Connecting to Personal Experience
What does the author reveal here about her mother's personality? **R**

Big Idea The Power of Memory *Why do you think her mother is trying to remind the author that she does not "know it all just yet"?* **BI₂**

Vocabulary

tremulously (trem´ yə ləs lē) *adv.* in a trembling or vibrating way

Vocabulary

eschew (es chōō´) *v.* to keep apart from something disliked or harmful; avoid

ANNIE DILLARD **391**

English Language Coach

391

Teach

⭐ **Viewing the Art**

Answer: *This advertisement helps illustrate the importance of marketing through the use of attractive graphics and exciting, sensationalized language. The author's mother would feel impressed by the circusman's boldness and confidence, much as she was impressed by the Ivory soap adman.*

Showman P. T. Barnum (1810–1891) is sometimes called the Shakespeare of Advertising. In partnership with James A. Bailey (1847–1906), Barnum launched "The Greatest Show on Earth," a spectacle that appealed to opera lovers and curiosity seekers alike. **AS**

deer standing in the front hall," she told me one quiet evening in the country.

"Really?"

"No. I just wanted to tell you something once without your saying, 'I know.'"

Supermarkets in the middle 1950s began luring, or bothering, customers by giving out Top Value Stamps or Green Stamps.[7] When, shopping with Mother, we got to the head of the checkout line, the checker, always a young man, asked, "Save stamps?"

"No," Mother replied genially, week after week, "I build model airplanes." I believe she originated this line. It took me years to determine where the joke lay.

---

7. *[Top Value . . . Stamps]* Stores gave customers a certain number of stamps per dollar spent. These stamps were saved up and later exchanged for merchandise.

Anyone who met her verbal challenges she adored. She had surgery on one of her eyes. On the operating table, just before she conked out, she appealed feelingly to the surgeon, saying, as she had been planning to say for weeks, "Will I be able to play the piano?" "Not on me," the surgeon said. "You won't pull that old one on me."

It was, indeed, an old one. The surgeon was supposed to answer, "Yes, my dear, brave woman, you will be able to play the piano after this operation," to which Mother intended to reply, "Oh, good, I've always wanted to play the piano." This pat scenario bored her; she loved having it interrupted. It must have galled[8] her that usually her acquaintances were so predictably unalert; it must have galled her that, for the length of her life, she could surprise everyone so continually, so easily, when

---

8. Here, *galled* means "irritated."

Ringling Brothers and Barnum & Bailey—Trains. Artist unknown.
Viewing the Art: What idea in the selection does this advertisement help illustrate? ⭐

Additional Support

Skills Practice

RESEARCH: Library and Internet Skills Have students choose a commercial product that Mother mentions and find a description and the history of the product using either library or Internet sources. Suggest that students might find advertisements for the product in old periodicals housed in the library and that they might use the Internet to find the manufacturer's Web site. When students have finished their research, have them pretend that they are Mother and write a letter to the manufacturer explaining what they liked and disliked about the product and whether they would use the product again. **OL**

she had been the same all along. At any rate, she loved anyone who, as she put it, saw it coming, and called her on it.

She regarded the instructions on bureaucratic forms as straight lines.[9] "Do you

Visual Vocabulary
Swee'pea is the baby in "Popeye" cartoons.

advocate the overthrow of the United States government by force or violence?" After some thought she wrote, "Force." She regarded children, even babies, as straight men.[10] When Molly learned to crawl, Mother delighted in buying her gowns with drawstrings at the bottom, like Swee'pea's, because, as she explained energetically, you could easily step on the drawstring without the baby's noticing, so that she crawled and crawled and crawled and never got anywhere except into a small ball at the gown's top.

When we children were young, she mothered us tenderly and dependably; as we got older, she resumed her career of anarchism.[11] She collared us into her gags. If she answered the phone on a wrong number, she told the caller, "Just a minute," and dragged the receiver to Amy or me, saying, "Here, take this, your name is Cecile," or, worse, just, "It's for you." You had to think on your feet. But did you want to perform well as Cecile, or did you want to take pity on the wretched caller?

---

9. *Bureaucratic* refers to the rigidly formal paperwork and procedures involved in dealing with government officials and agencies. For Mother, these things were setups for jokes—the *straight lines* that led to punch lines.
10. *Straight men* are people who assist comedians by feeding them straight lines or serving as objects of fun.
11. Here, *anarchism* refers to active resistance against what is oppressive and undesirable.

Literary Element Anecdote *What does the exchange with the surgeon reveal about what Dillard's mother values in life?* **L**

Reading Strategy Connecting to Personal Experience *Which option do you think the author might have chosen in this situation? Why?* **R**

Vocabulary
advocate (ad′ və kāt′) *v.* to support publicly

During a family trip to the Highland Park Zoo, Mother and I were alone for a minute. She approached a young couple holding hands on a bench by the seals, and addressed the young man in dripping[12] tones: "Where have you been? Still got those baby-blue eyes; always did slay me. And this"—a swift nod at the dumbstruck young woman, who had removed her hand from the man's—"must be the one you were telling me about. She's not so bad, really, as you used to make out. But listen, you know how I miss you, you know where to reach me, same old place. And there's Ann over there—see how she's grown? See the blue eyes?"

And off she sashayed,[13] taking me firmly by the hand, and leading us around briskly past the monkey house and away. She cocked an ear back, and both of us heard the desperate man begin, in a high-pitched wail, "I swear, I never saw her before in my life. . . ."

On a long, sloping beach by the ocean, she lay stretched out sunning with Father and friends, until the conversation gradually grew tedious, when without forethought she gave a little push with her heel and rolled away. People were stunned. She rolled deadpan and apparently effortlessly, arms and legs extended and tidy, down the beach to the distant water's edge, where she lay at ease just as she had been, but half in the surf, and well out of earshot.

She dearly loved to fluster people by throwing out a game's rules at whim[14]—when she was getting bored, losing in a dull sort of way, and when everybody else was taking it too seriously. If you turned your back, she moved the checkers around on the board. When you got them all straightened out, she denied she'd touched them; the next time you turned your back, she lined them up on the rug or hid them under your chair. In a betting rummy game called *Michigan*, she routinely played out of turn, or called

---

12. *Dripping* here refers to using excessive charm or appeal.
13. She *sashayed* or walked in a way that showed a seeming lack of interest.
14. The phrase *at whim* means "suddenly and unexpectedly."

ANNIE DILLARD **393**

Teach

L **Literary Element**

Anecdote Answer: *She appreciates people who can think outside the box or who can challenge her intellect.* **OL**

R **Reading Strategy**

Connecting to Personal Experience Answer: T*he author would have chosen to act out the part of Cecile to please her mother, or she would have told the caller it was a wrong number because she was embarrassed.* Have students discuss how they would feel if they were witnesses to or objects of Mother's practical jokes. **OL**

⭐ **Cultural History**

Cartoon Characters Elzie Crisler Segar introduced the cartoon character Popeye, a sailor who develops superhuman strength after eating spinach, in comic strip form in 1928. Popeye cartoons were made for American television in the 1960s and 70s. Swee'pea is Popeye's adopted baby. **AS**

Reading in the Real World

Career Have students locate an article about some aspect of the English language, such as complaints about the ways people misuse it. Have students check the *Index to Periodical Literature* in the library in order to find an article. Have students share their articles and discuss them in small groups, focusing on questions such as these: *What is the topic of the article? What point is the author trying to make? What facts or examples are used to support this point?* **OL**

Objectives
• To analyze the author's use of anecdote (SE)
• To connect literature to personal experience
• To conduct research, using the library or the Internet (TWE)

Teach

Anecdote Answer: *They may have felt their intelligence and abilities were going to waste as housewives, since there were not many opportunities for them outside the home.* **OL**

★ Viewing the Art

Answer: *Although this advertisement is from 1898, Ivory soap remained popular in the era in which Dillard grew up. The advertisement touts the soap's versatility and affordability—attractive qualities for households in the 1950s.*

Ivory Soap is one of many inventions that resulted from a mistake or accident. Other such inventions include the chocolate chip cookie, created when the baker ran out of baker's chocolate and substituted semisweet chocolate bits that didn't quite melt. The Frisbee® was originally a pie tin, and Velcro® came to be when the inventor returned from a walk with burrs stuck to his pants and decided to examine the structure of burrs under a microscope. **AS**

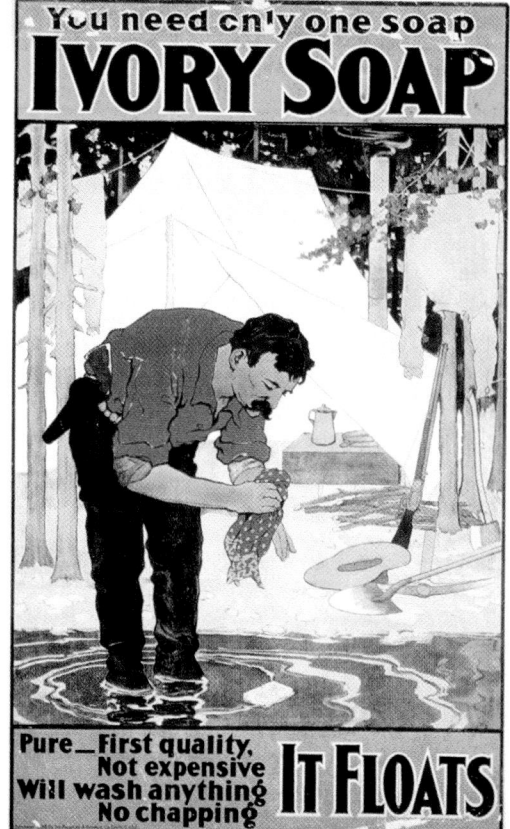

Ivory Soap Advertising Poster, 1898. Artist unknown.
Viewing the Art: What details in this reproduction evoke the era in which Dillard grew up? ★

them, or showed her hand, or tossed her cards in a handful behind her back in a characteristic swift motion accompanied by a vibrantly innocent look. It drove our **stolid** father crazy. The hand was over before it began, and the guests were appalled. How do you score it, who deals now, what do you do with a crazy person who is having so much fun? Or they were down seven, and the guests were appalled. "Pam!" "Dammit, Pam!" He groaned. What ails such people? What on earth possesses them? He rubbed his face.

She was an unstoppable force; she never let go. When we moved across town, she persuaded the U.S. Post Office to let her keep her old address—forever—because she'd had stationery printed. I don't know how she did it. Every new post office worker, over decades, needed to learn that although the Doaks' mail is addressed to here, it is delivered to there.

Mother's energy and intelligence suited her for a greater role in a larger arena—mayor of New York, say—than the one she had. She followed American politics closely; she had been known to vote for Democrats. She saw how things should be run, but she had nothing to run but our household. Even there, small minds bugged her; she was smarter than the people who designed the things she had to use all day for the length of her life.

"Look," she said. "Whoever designed this corkscrew never used one. Why would anyone sell it without trying it out?" So she invented a better one. She showed me a drawing of it. The spirit of American enterprise never faded in

out a card she didn't hold, or counted backward, simply to amuse herself by causing an uproar and watching the rest of us do double takes and have fits. (Much later, when serious suitors came to call, Mother subjected them to this fast card game as a trial by ordeal; she used it as an intelligence test and a measure of spirit. If the poor man could stay a round without breaking down or running out, he got to marry one of us, if he still wanted to.)

She excelled at bridge, playing fast and boldly, but when the stakes were low and the hands dull, she bid slams[15] for the devilment of it, or raised her opponents' suit to bug

---

15. When she *bid slams,* Mother "went for broke," betting that she would win every or all but one of the tricks in a round of play.

| Literary Element | Anecdote What does this sentence reveal about how some women of that generation may have felt? **L** |

| Vocabulary |

stolid (stol´ id) *adj.* showing little or no emotion

Additional Support

Skills Practice

WRITING: Dialogue Dillard says that her mother challenged her daughters' dates to ridiculous card games to test their intelligence and measure their spirit. Help students develop a deeper understanding of the text by having them imagine the conversation that might have taken place between Mother and her daughters' boyfriends. Suggest that students consider how the young men might have felt and how her daughters might have reacted. Then have them write the dialogue that might have taken place between Mother, Annie as a teenager, and one of Annie's boyfriends. **OL**

Mother. If capitalizing and tooling up[16] had been as interesting as theorizing and thinking up, she would have fired up a new factory every week, and chaired several hundred corporations.

"It grieves me," she would say, "it grieves my heart," that the company that made one superior product packaged it poorly, or took the wrong tack[17] in its advertising. She knew, as she held the thing mournfully in her two hands, that she'd never find another. She was right. We children wholly sympathized, and so did Father; what could she do, what could anyone do, about it? She was Samson[18] in chains. She paced.

She didn't like the taste of stamps so she didn't lick stamps; she licked the corner of the envelope instead. She glued sandpaper to the sides of kitchen drawers, and under kitchen cabinets, so she always had a handy place to strike a match. She designed, and hounded workmen to build against all norms,[19] doubly wide kitchen counters and elevated bathroom sinks. . . . She drew plans for an over-the-finger toothbrush for babies, an oven rack that slid up and down, and—the family favorite—Lendalarm. Lendalarm was a beeper you attached to books (or tools) you loaned friends. After ten days, the beeper sounded. Only the rightful owner could silence it.

she was smarter than the people who designed the things she had to use all day

She repeatedly reminded us of P. T. Barnum's dictum:[20] You could sell anything to anybody if you marketed it right. The adman who thought of making Americans believe they needed underarm deodorant was a visionary. So, too, was the hero who made a success of a new product, Ivory soap. The executives were horrified, Mother told me, that a cake of this stuff floated. Soap wasn't supposed to float. Anyone would be able to tell it was mostly whipped-up air. Then some inspired adman made a leap: Advertise that it floats. Flaunt it. The rest is history.

She respected the rare few who broke through to new ways. "Look," she'd say, "here's an intelligent apron." She called upon us to admire intelligent control knobs and intelligent pan handles, intelligent andirons and picture frames and knife sharpeners. She questioned everything, every pair of scissors, every knitting needle, gardening glove, tape dispenser. Hers was a restless mental vigor that just about ignited the dumb household objects with its force.

Torpid[21] conformity was a kind of sin; it was stupidity itself, the mighty stream against which Mother would never cease to struggle. If you held no minority opinions, or if you failed to risk total ostracism for them daily, the world would be a better place without you. . . .

She simply tried to keep us all awake. And in fact it was always clear to Amy and me, and to Molly when she grew old enough to listen, that if our classmates came to cruelty, just as much as if the neighborhood or the nation came to madness, we were expected to take, and would be each separately capable of taking, a stand. ◦◦

---

16. *Capitalizing* and *tooling up* has to do with providing the finances and equipment necessary to start up a new business or factory.

17. The company took the wrong course of action or *tack*.

18. In the Bible, *Samson* is powerful and mighty until an enemy tricks him. Soon Samson is chained up in prison.

19. Here, the *norms* are rules, standards, and accepted practices.

20. In the 1800s, *Barnum* presented many popular entertainments, including what is now the Ringling Brothers and Barnum & Bailey Circus. The actual words of his famous saying (*dictum*) were "There's a sucker born every minute."

21. Something that's *torpid* is dull and lifeless.

Reading Strategy Connecting to Personal Experience *Why do you think people like Dillard's mother may prefer theorizing and inventing to running a business?* **R**

Big Idea The Power of Memory *Why do you think the author used the words "and would be each separately capable of taking" here?* **BI**

ANNIE DILLARD **395**

Teach

R Reading Strategy

Connecting to Personal Experience Answer: *Students may point out that independent thinkers like Dillard's mother are happiest when they can develop new ideas and be free from routines.* **OL**

BI Big Idea

The Power of Memory Answer: *She is making the point that her mother taught them to think for themselves and stand for what they believed to be right, even if they had to do it alone.* **OL** Have students consider the ways in which the author has incorporated her memories of her mother into her life as demonstrated by this selection. (*She has used her mother's example to become a better writer and an independent woman.*) **AL**

CheckPoint

Use the CheckPoint questions on Presentation Plus! to check students' mastery of the selection. These questions can be used with interactive response keypads for immediate student feedback.

Building Reading Fluency

Using a Dictionary for Pronunciation Tell students to pair up and select a passage that presents difficulty for them. Have them make a list of words from the passage that are difficult to decode, and then use a dictionary to find the pronunciations and meanings of the words. Suggest that students repeat the words aloud several times. Once they have gained some confidence, have students read the selection to each other paying particular attention to the pronunciation of the words on their lists. **BL**

Objectives
• To analyze the author's use of anecdote (SE)
• To make personal connections to the literature (SE)
• To use dialogue to better understand the text (TWE)

Assess

1. Students' responses will vary.

2. (a) The phrase may seem absurd, or she may like the combination of sounds. (b) A whimsical sense of humor; enjoys the absurdities of language and life

3. (a) Finds humor in bureaucratic forms, answers the questions literally (b) Life should not be taken too seriously.

4. (a) Pretends to know a young man sitting with his girlfriend; purposely misplays a bridge hand (b) She does not seem to care about the couple and she seems to try to upset her bridge partners.

5. Dillard's mother continually thinks of ways to improve products and invents new and useful ones.

6. (a) Details of the Tamiami Trail; "Pittsburghisms"; and card game antics (b) Details add humor and affection and enliven scenes.

7. (a) Most people would disapprove of causing strife for entertainment. (b) Some may respect her fearlessness; others may disapprove of her cruelty.

8. Her humor and zest for life would make her an ideal mother for some; others would not want a quirky, restless mother.

RESPONDING AND THINKING CRITICALLY

Respond

1. What questions would you like to ask the author about her mother?

Recall and Interpret

2. (a) Why does Dillard's mother enjoy the phrase "Terwilliger bunts one"? (b) What does her mother's reaction to and use of this phrase suggest about her personality?

3. (a) Dillard's mother finds humor in situations that ordinarily would not be considered funny. Give an example and explain why the situation is comical. (b) What can you infer about her mother's philosophy of life from the way she responds to rules and regulations?

4. (a) Describe two incidents that illustrate how her mother's unexpected behavior flusters people. (b) Do you think the author's mother cares about the consequences of her actions?

Analyze and Evaluate

5. Explain what Dillard means when she says that the "spirit of American enterprise never faded in Mother."

6. (a) Identify places in the selection that illustrate the author's attention to detail. (b) How do these details enhance your appreciation of the selection?

7. (a) How do you think most people would react to the mother's treatment of the young couple at the zoo? (b) Does this incident make you respect Dillard's mother more, or less?

Connect

8. **Big Idea** The Power of Memory How does the author's mother compare with your mental picture of an ideal mother? Explain.

YOU'RE THE CRITIC: Different Viewpoints

How Successfull is Dillard's Memoir?

Some critics have compared Dillard to Henry David Thoreau, since both authored detailed accounts of their time spent observing nature. Read the following two excerpts of literary criticism. As you read, compare and contrast the opinions of the two critics.

"Ms. Dillard has written. . . . an exceptionally interesting account. She is one of those people who seem to be more fully alive than most of us. . . . She is a stunning observer. . . . And yet, An American Childhood is not quite as good as it at first promised to be. By choosing to make the book an account of the growth of her mind, an inner rather than an outer narrative, Ms. Dillard almost necessarily forfeited plot. Except at the end, the book does not build; there is no continuous narrative. And though scores of people appear, only two of them are real characters: Annie Dillard herself and, for one wonderful chapter, her mother."

—Noel Perrin

"[Annie Dillard] preaches Thoreau's doctrine and her own—"Do what you love"—and like Thoreau she takes pains to clarify how that is done, how passionately she loves what she is about. . . . The principle is the same for all, though it would take enormous energy and curiosity as well as clear thinking to live as Annie Dillard does. She makes it sound like a profitable enterprise."

—Helen Bevington

Group Activity Discuss the following questions with your classmates. Consider the two excerpts and use evidence from An American Childhood to support your answers.

1. (a) How do Perrin's and Bevington's assessments differ? (b) What do their assessments have in common?

2. Bevington writes that Dillard preaches Thoreau's doctrine as her own: "Do what you love." How is this doctrine demonstrated in An American Childhood?

Different Viewpoints

1. (a) Perrin believes the book does not live up to its own expectations and is weak in both plot and character development, while Bevington thoroughly approves of it. (b) Both critics compare Dillard to Thoreau and comment on her zest for life and keen powers of observation.

2. Answers may vary, but students should note the author's desire to live life to its fullest.

Literary Element Anecdote

If you wanted to explain a friend's personality to someone who had never met him or her, you might tell an **anecdote** about your friend, such as a funny story that revealed your friend's sense of humor. Anecdotes can be used for many different purposes within a work of literature. Essayists often use anecdotes to support their opinions, clarify their ideas, get a reader's attention, or entertain. Biographers often use anecdotes to illustrate a point about their subjects.

1. What main point do you think Dillard wanted to make through the anecdotes about her mother?

2. When you read how Dillard's mother subjected hopeful suitors to a fast and furious card game to test their merits, what insight did you have into the mother-daughter relationship?

Review: Voice

As you learned on page 374, **voice** is the distinctive use of language that conveys the author's or narrator's personality to the reader. Voice is determined by elements of style such as word choice and tone.

Partner Activity Pair up with a classmate and discuss Dillard's use of voice in *An American Childhood*.

1. Make a list of passages from the text that reveal Dillard's voice as she describes her memories of her mother.

2. Explain how each passage illustrates the author's personality.

Author's Voice	Personality Traits
"I don't remember the tree; I remember the thrill in her voice," page 391	receptive, open
"Alligator Alley for those who like things cute," page 391	sarcastic, funny

Reading Strategy Connecting to Personal Experience

Readers bring **personal experiences** to what they read. These experiences guide readers toward insightful analysis of the text.

1. Which of your personal experiences most helped you relate to Dillard's stories about her mother?

2. Do you think most readers would be able to connect to these stories? Why or why not?

Vocabulary Practice

Practice with Word Parts Read the roots and definitions below. Then pick the best definition for each of the boldface vocabulary words.

Latin Root: *tremulus*—"trembling"
Old French Root: *eschiver*—"to shun"
Latin Root: *advocare*—"to call for"
Latin Root: *stolidus*—"firm"

1. She approached the door **tremulously**, for she did not know what awaited her.
   a. bravely **b.** constantly **c.** timidly

2. She **eschewed** taking the train and instead called a taxi cab.
   a. looked forward to **b.** enjoyed **c.** avoided

3. The doctor did not **advocate** taking massive doses of vitamins.
   a. recommend **b.** refuse **c.** oppose

4. His face remained **stolid** even when he found out that his mother had died.
   a. uncertain **b.** sad **c.** emotionless

Academic Vocabulary

Here are two words from the vocabulary list on page R82.

intelligence (in tel′e jəns) *n.* the ability to learn

rational (rash′ən əl) *adj.* having the ability to reason or understand clearly

Practice and Apply
1. How would Dillard's mother define **intelligence**?
2. Was her mother's behavior **rational**? Explain.

ANNIE DILLARD **397**

Assess

Literary Element

1. She wanted to portray her mother's complexity, uniqueness, and significant influence as a role model.

2. Their mother cared about the quality and character of men who wanted to marry her daughters, but she was also very controlling to want to judge their worth by her rules.

Review: Voice

Students may also compare and contrast the author's voice to her mother's voice.

Reading Strategy

1. Student experiences should include mother, parental, or family relationships.

2. Students may say that it is difficult to relate to this story since the mother was unique. Other students may find that their familial relationships were similiar.

Vocabulary

1. c
2. c
3. a
4. c

Academic Vocabulary

1. Students should recognize the type of person her mother holds in esteem—someone who can think for himself or herself and avoid conformity.

2. Answers will vary. Students should recognize the motives behind many of her mother's actions.

Assess

Writing About Literature

Use these criteria when evaluating students' writing:

- Does the essay identify and analyze one example of hyperbole from the story?

- Does the essay explain how hyperbole operates in a humorous way?

Examples of hyperbole include the following:

- "She was Samson in chains."—Mother was a strong person whose power had been taken away. The author is referring to Mother's frustration with poorly designed products.

- "Hers was a restless mental vigor . . ."—Mother's active intelligence made household objects more useful. Her mental vigor is directed toward these objects.

- "Torpid conformity was a kind of sin . . . the mighty stream . . ."—Mother never wanted to be like everyone else.

Listening and Speaking

Encourage students to write down their jokes or anecdotes and to keep them appropriate for their audience.

Writing About Literature

Analyze Comic Devices Dillard makes use of hyperbole as a comic device. **Hyperbole** is an extreme exaggeration used to emphasize a point or to create a certain effect. Hyperbole is a figure of speech, and it is not meant to be taken literally. For example, when Dillard says, "Mother's energy and intelligence suited her for a greater role in a larger arena—mayor of New York, say," she does not actually mean that her mother should have been mayor of New York City. She is using hyperbole. Because New York City is one of the largest, most complex cities of the world to govern, Dillard wants her readers to imagine what it would be like to live with someone who has the energy to run a city like New York.

Find another example of hyperbole in the story and analyze its use as a comic device. Then write a brief essay explaining your analysis. Include an introduction, body paragraph(s), and a conclusion.

After completing your first draft, exchange essays with another student. Evaluate each other's work and make suggestions for improvement. Make sure you proofread your own essay for errors in spelling, punctuation, and grammar.

Listening and Speaking

Spoken humor can range from joke telling to relating amusing anecdotes. With a small group, discuss performances by comedians or humorists whom you admire. Then prepare a joke or humorous anecdote and practice telling it with your group. Some anecdotes may cause your classmates to laugh, while other anecdotes may evoke amused recognition. In your group, discuss what makes a joke or anecdote effective. Then tell your group's best story or joke to the class.

Literature Online Web Activities For eFlashcards, Selection Quick Checks, and other Web activities, go to www.glencoe.com.

Dillard's Language and Style

Using Subject and Object Pronouns Pronouns such as *I, he,* and *they* are used as subjects and predicate nominatives in sentences. Object pronouns such as *me, her,* and *them* are used as objects of verbs or prepositions. Note how Dillard uses a variety of subject and object pronouns in the following passage:

> She dearly loved to fluster people by throwing out a game's rules at whim—when she was getting bored, losing in a dull sort of way, and when everybody else was taking it too seriously. If you turned your back, she moved the checkers around on the board. When you got them all straightened out, she denied she'd touched them; the next time you turned your back she lined them up on the rug or hid them under your chair.

Do you think that Dillard's use of the second person—the subject pronoun *you*—is an effective method for describing the checkers game to the reader? Why or why not?

Activity Meet with a partner and complete the following exercise. Choose the correct subject or object pronouns.

1. (We, Us) children wholly sympathized and so did Father.

2. If she answered the phone on a wrong number, she dragged the receiver to Amy or (I, me).

3. During a family trip to the Highland Park Zoo, Mother and (me, I) were alone for a minute.

Revising Check

Pronouns Review the essay you wrote about Dillard's use of comic devices. Make sure that you used pronouns correctly. Are there places that are better suited to another pronoun? In the future, as you check your essays for errors in spelling, punctuation, and grammar, make sure that your subject and object pronouns are correct.

Dillard's Language and Style

1. We **2.** me **3.** I

Revising Check

Students can also exchange their essays with classmates to check for proper use of pronouns.

Literature Online

Web Activities Have students access the Web site for interactive activities that will help them assess their understanding of the selection.

QUESTS AND ENCOUNTERS

Analyzing and Extending

BI Big Idea

Quests and Encounters

Ask students to consider what makes something a quest or an encounter. Bring out the idea that these experiences are unforgettable because they are elevated beyond the realm of ordinary experience. In that way, they might seem "heroic," as the introductory paragraph describes. Tell students that Part 2 will deepen their understanding of quests and encounters, as well as the emotions and motives surrounding the sharing of these experiences. Encourage students to contemplate this "big idea" and its relation to the artwork. **OL**

Le Château des Pyrénées, 1959. René Magritte. Oil on canvas, 100 x 140 cm. Israel Museum, Jerusalem.

⭐ Viewing the Art

René Magritte (1898–1967) was a famous surrealist painter from Belgium. *The Castle of the Pyrénées* shows Magritte's affection for the wide open sky—an affection that began in his childhood years—as well as his ability to convey the depths of imagination. **AS**

BI BIG IDEA

Sometimes what seems like an ordinary day is transformed into something extraordinary. Unexpectedly, your routine is turned into a quest or a meeting is elevated to an encounter. In the nonfiction works in Part 2, you will read essays about ordinary and extraordinary quests and encounters. As you read these texts, ask yourself: In which moments in my life have I been asked to take on the role of the hero?

399

English Language Coach

Connotations Make sure that students understand that *quest* means "a search," and *encounter* means "a direct meeting." Discuss the connotations of these words, such as the association of quest with a journey searching for adventure, as by medieval knights. **EL**

Differentiated Instruction

Drawing on Personal Background
Guide less proficient readers to connect with the literature in Part 2 by relating their own quests and encounters. Have them jot down quests or encounters that stand out in their memories. Prompt them with ideas such as quests for grades and friendships. **BL**

Objectives for Part 2
• To identify the characteristics that distinguish essays from other literary forms (SE)
• To understand the different types of essays
• To determine a writer's motives (SE)
• To write about an experience using freewriting (SE)

Part 2: Quests and Encounters

Readability Scores Key
Dale-Chall/DRP/Lexile

PACING (DAYS)		SELECTIONS AND FEATURES	LITERARY ELEMENTS
STANDARD	BLOCK		
2–3 class sessions	1–2	LITERARY FOCUS: Expository and Personal Essays, pp. 400-401	Expository and Personal Essays, SE p. 401; TWE p. 400 Determining Authors' Motives, TWE p. 400
		"How to Write a Letter" by Garrison Keillor **5.2/55/1040**, pp. 402-410	Thesis, SE pp. 403, 404, 409 Essay, SE p. 409 Analogy, TWE p. 404
		"A Swimming Lesson" by Jewelle L. Gomez **8.4/62/1190**, pp. 411-417	Narrative Essay, SE pp. 412, 413, 414, 416 Anecdote, SE p. 416
1 class session	1–2	**"Encounter in the Sea"** by Diane Ackerman **9.8/61/1140**, pp. 418-428	Descriptive Essay, SE pp. 419, 421, 423, 427 Mood, SE p. 427
1–2 class sessions		**"The Tucson Zoo"** by Lewis Thomas **9.8/64/1030**, pp. 429-434	Structure, SE pp. 430, 431, 434
		"Straw into Gold: The Metamorphosis of the Everyday" by Sandra Cisneros **6.8/57/930**, pp. 435-442	Reflective Essay, SE pp. 436, 438, 440, 441 Thesis, SE p. 441

About the Part

Part 2 covers personal and expository essays.

READING AND CRITICAL THINKING	VOCABULARY	WRITING AND GRAMMAR	LISTENING, SPEAKING, AND VIEWING
		Quickwrite, SE p. 401	
Analyzing Style, SE pp. 403, 404, 407, 409, 410 Identifying Figurative Language, SE p. 403 Understanding Idioms, TWE p. 406	Synonyms, SE pp. 403, 409 Academic Vocabulary, SE p. 409	Apply Thesis, SE p. 410 Using Idioms, SE p. 410, TWE p.406	Visual Literacy, SE p. 408 Group Discussion, SE p. 410 Analyzing Art, TWE pp. 405, 406
Connecting to Personal Experience, SE pp. 412, 414, 417	Context Clues, SE pp. 412, 417	Explore Author's Purpose, SE p. 417 Descriptive Writing, TWE p. 414	Group Discussion, SE p. 417
Recognizing Author's Purpose, SE pp. 419, 422, 425, 427 Establishing a Purpose, TWE p. 420 Silent Reading, TWE p. 424	Word Origins, SE pp. 419, 427 Academic Vocabulary, SE p. 427	Analyze Thesis, SE p. 428 Describing Sequence of Events, SE p. 428	Group Activity, SE p. 426 Panel Discussion, SE p. 428 Analyzing Art, TWE pp. 420, 423, 424
Drawing Conclusions About Meaning, SE pp. 430, 432-434	Antonyms, SE p. 434	Semicolons, TWE p. 432	Debating, SE p. 434
Analyzing Text Structure, SE pp. 436, 438, 439, 442	Analogies, SE pp. 436, 442 Academic Vocabulary, SE p. 442 Context Clues, TWE p. 438	Apply Form, SE p. 442 Noun Phrases, TWE p. 440	Analyzing Art, TWE pp. 437, 439

Teach

Big Idea

Quests and Encounters Show students photos of an Olympic gold medal, an Oscar, a sports trophy, and world leaders shaking hands. **Ask:** In what ways are these symbols of quests and encounters? *(Students may suggest that people work hard in search of these signs of accomplishment.)* Why might authors write of their quests and encounters? *(Quests usually require significant effort and can bring immense satisfaction, while encounters may be with unforgettable characters.)* Discuss student responses. **OL**

L Literary Element

Expository and Personal Essays **Ask:** What makes Lewis Thomas's excerpt an essay? *(It is an expression of his viewpoint.)* **Ask:** What feelings does Thomas share about his encounter with otters and beavers? *(Joyfulness and gratitude)* **Ask:** Why does Thomas share this experience? *(To explain a transformation that happened for him)* **OL**

EXPOSITORY AND PERSONAL ESSAYS

Why write an essay?

Essayists write for many reasons. They may wish to make their readers think about a new idea or to share an experience with their audience. Others are motivated by a passion for truth or by a political purpose. In "The Tucson Zoo," Lewis Thomas seeks to share an experience with his readers.

L I was transfixed. As I now recall it, there was only one sensation in my head: pure elation mixed with amazement at such perfection. Swept off my feet, I floated from one side to the other, swiveling my brain, staring astounded at the beavers, then at the otters. I could hear shouts across my corpus callosum, from one hemisphere to the other. I remember thinking, with what was left in charge of my consciousness, that I wanted no part of the science of beavers and otters; I wanted never to know how they performed their marvels; I wished for no news about the physiology of their breathing, the coordination of their muscles, their vision, their endocrine systems, their digestive tracts. I hoped never to have to think of them as collections of cells. All I asked for was the full hairy complexity, then in front of my eyes, of whole, intact beavers and otters in motion.

It lasted, I regret to say, for only a few minutes, and then I was back in the late twentieth century, reductionist as ever, wondering about the details by force of habit, but not, this time, the details of otters and beavers. Instead, me. Something worth remembering had happened in my mind, I was certain of that; I would have put it somewhere in the brain stem; maybe this was my limbic system at work. I became a behavioral scientist, an experimental psychologist, an ethologist, and in the instant I lost all the wonder and the sense of being overwhelmed. I was flattened.

—Lewis Thomas, **from "The Tucson Zoo"**

Additional Support

Skills Practice

LITERARY ELEMENT:
Determining Authors' Motives
Encourage students to consider authors' motives for writing essays. Bring up these questions about the excerpts on these pages:

• What is Lewis Thomas's purpose? *(To share his viewpoint about animals.)*

• What is Garrison Keillor's purpose? *(To encourage letter writing.)*

• What is Jewelle L. Gomez's purpose? *(To describe an influential person.)*

Point out that, to a certain extent, personal essays are often motivated by a desire to entertain, and have students cite illustrative examples. **OL**

The Essay

An **essay** is a short work of nonfiction that focuses on a single topic. The essays in this part were written to inform or to share experiences with the reader. The excerpt on the previous page by Lewis Thomas is an example of a **personal** essay because he shares his feelings about beavers and otters. Essays are generally categorized as **expository, personal,** and **persuasive.**

Expository Essays

The word *expository* is a derivative of the word *expose*, which means "to make known or to explain." Whenever you write to inform, to give directions, to explain an idea, or to make something clear, you are writing **exposition.**

Sit for a few minutes with the blank sheet in front of you, and meditate on the person you will write to, let your friend come to mind until you can almost see her or him in the room with you. Remember the last time you saw each other and how your friend looked and what you said and what perhaps was unsaid between you, and when your friend becomes real to you, start to write.

—Garrison Keillor, **from "How to Write a Letter"**

Personal Essays

Personal essays are usually informal in their language and tone, and they often contain passages of expository writing. A personal essay often reflects on an incident in the writer's life. The writer may share a life lesson with the reader or perhaps shed light on a time or place long gone. Other personal essays can be written to please oneself or an audience of like-minded readers.

But a personal essay can also be a kind of writing that is common on applications, such as those for college admissions. These essays should be more formal in language and tone. When you write a personal essay for a college application, your audience will be a selection committee.

None of the social issues of 1957 had a chance of catching my attention that year. All that existed for me was my grandmother, rising from the surf like a Dahomean queen, shaking her head free of her torturous rubber cap, beaming down at me when I finally took the first strokes on my own.

—Jewelle L. Gomez, **from "A Swimming Lesson"**

Persuasive Essays

In **persuasive** writing, the writer attempts to influence the reader to accept an idea, adopt a point of view, or perform an action. Persuasive writing may appeal to the reader's emotions. However, a type of persuasive writing called **argument** relies solely on reason, logic, and evidence. Many persuasive essays and speeches use a combination of argument and appeal to the emotions. You will encounter persuasive writing and speaking in Part 3.

Quickwrite

Describing a Quest Think of quests and encounters from your own life. Remember times when you were afraid or discouraged but still persevered. Think of meetings that changed you, even if they were with beings as simple as a mouse. Choose one of the prompts from the list below and then write about your quest or encounter for ten minutes without stopping. Write as fast as you can, no matter what, even if what you are writing does not make sense. This writing approach is called "freewriting."

Prompts

Listen...I remember...

I want to tell you...

OBJECTIVES
- Identify the characteristics that distinguish essays from other literary forms.
- Understand the different types of essays.
- Determine a writer's motives.
- Write about an experience using freewriting.

Teach

R Reading Strategy

Analyzing Essays Ask: What makes the Keillor passage expository? *(He explains how to get inspiration to write a letter to a friend.)* **Ask:** What indicates that the passage by Jewelle L. Gomez is part of a personal essay? *(It tells the impact of a personal experience, her swimming lesson with her grandmother.)* **OL**

Quickwrite

Encourage fluency rather than organization or correct usage. The idea is to get words on paper and edit later. See that students express their personal experiences, feelings, or opinions.

English Language Coach

Cultural Allusion Review with students new to the United States the term "Dahomean queen" in "A Swimming Lesson." Point out that Dahomey was a kingdom in west Africa that was located in what is now Benin. Discuss the connotations of this allusion, which portrays Gomez's grandmother as regal. **EL**

Differentiated Instruction

Analyzing Theme Review with less proficient readers how each excerpt reflects the Big Idea. **Ask:** What makes Gomez's experience a quest? *(Gomez is on a quest for approval from her grandmother.)* Comment on Keillor's quest to write a letter and Thomas's encounter with animals. **BL**

Focus

BELLRINGER

Bellringer Options
Daily Language Practice Transparency 35
Or poll students about how often they write or receive letters. Discuss how letters differ from e-mails and phone calls, as well as what may prevent students from writing letters more frequently. Then read a few short passages from a memorable letter. **Ask:** Have you received any letters that made an impression on you? Have students discuss letters that were special to them. Ask them why they liked these letters.

Author Search To expand students' appreciation of Garrison Keillor, have them access the Web site for additional information and resources.

How to Write a Letter

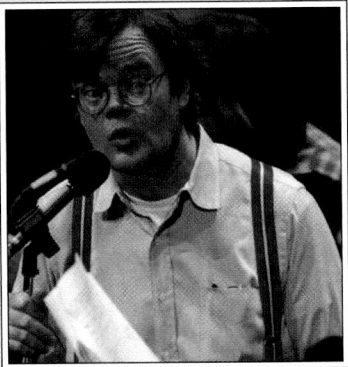

MEET GARRISON KEILLOR

At an early age, Garrison Keillor felt that a name change was in order if he were to fulfill his dream of becoming a professional writer. Born Gary Edward Keillor in Anoka, Minnesota, Keillor grew up in a conservative religious household. His parents disapproved of activities such as drinking, dancing, and singing; their six children were forbidden to watch television. Radio was permitted because, according to Keillor, "I don't think people smoked as much on radio." Keillor aspired to follow in the footsteps of Mark Twain. He started his own newspaper, called *The Sunnyvale Star*, at the age of eleven and submitted poems for his middle school paper under the pseudonym "Garrison Edwards," which had a distinguishing quality that "Gary" lacked. After high school, Keillor pursued his interest in literature at the University of Minnesota, graduating in 1966 with a bachelor's degree in English.

> "*Some luck lies in not getting what you thought you wanted but getting what you have.*"
>
> —Garrison Keillor

After college, Keillor hitchhiked to the East Coast in pursuit of a job with a magazine or book publisher. He realized that he wanted to write for a Midwestern audience, and returned to Minnesota. In 1969 Keillor found employment with Minnesota Public Radio. It was there he began writing and hosting the radio show for which he is best known, *A Prairie Home Companion*. The show

first aired in 1974. It featured music and comedy, including imaginary commercials, and stories told by Keillor. These stories captured the warmth and idiosyncrasies of small-town America. Keillor's tales from the quiet, fictional town of Lake Wobegon, Minnesota, became widely popular. By 1980, *A Prairie Home Companion* was broadcast nationally to an audience of two to three million listeners.

Dual Passions: Writing and Talking In interviews, Keillor has confessed that he never imagined staying in radio. However, his monologues for *A Prairie Home Companion* developed and honed his storyteller's voice. In 1970 *The New Yorker* magazine published one of his stories. Subsequently, he became a regular contributor to the magazine, a realization of a lifelong dream. Keillor once said, "I have written for *The New Yorker* since high school, though they weren't aware of it at the time."

In 1985 his radio characters' voices as well as their stories became Keillor's bestselling novel, *Lake Wobegon Days*. He continues to write, and has published several more works, including *Leaving Home* and *We Are Still Married.*

Garrison Keillor was born in 1942.

Author Search For more about Garrison Keillor, go to www.glencoe.com.

Selection Skills

How to Write a Letter

Literary Elements
- Thesis (SE pp. 403, 404, 409)
- Essay (SE p. 409)
- Analogy (TWE p. 404)

Reading Skills
- Analyzing Style (SE pp. 403, 404, 407, 409, 410)
- Understanding Idioms (TWE p. 406)

Vocabulary Skills
- Synonyms (SE pp. 403, 409)
- Academic Vocabulary (SE p. 409)

Listening/Speaking/Viewing Skills
- Visual Literacy (SE p. 408)

Writing Skills/Grammar
- Write a Letter (SE p. 410)
- Using Idioms (SE p. 410; TWE p. 406)

Connecting to the Essay

One of life's small joys is writing and receiving letters. A letter may call to mind a familiar face, a forgotten incident, or a memorable moment. Before you read, think about the following questions:

- What opportunities for personal expression does writing a letter have over talking on the phone?
- What do you discover about yourself in the process of writing a letter?

Building Background

Like his revered predecessor Mark Twain, Garrison Keillor is an American humorist. Although "How to Write a Letter" is nonfiction, it reflects the definition of a "humorous story" found in Twain's essay "How to Tell a Story."

The humorist, Twain says, is one who has mastered the art of *telling*, not just storytelling. In the following essay, Keillor's *telling* involves informing his audience about themselves and others. "How to Write a Letter" provides instruction to readers on their own needs, behaviors, and assumptions. As he reinforces the importance of communicating on an intimate and memorable level, Keillor provides humorous revelations that remind us not to take ourselves too seriously and not to take ourselves—and others—for granted.

Setting Purposes for Reading

Big Idea Quests and Encounters

As you read, notice how Keillor encourages his readers to think about the different kinds of encounters writing a letter creates.

Literary Element Thesis

A **thesis** is the main idea of a work of nonfiction. The thesis may be stated directly or implied. Recognizing a writer's thesis helps the reader understand and evaluate the text within a larger framework.

- See Literary Terms Handbook, p. R18.

Literature Online **Interactive Literary Elements Handbook** To review or learn more about the literary elements, go to www.glencoe.com.

Reading Strategy Analyzing Style

Analyzing style entails looking critically at the author's word choice, length and arrangement of sentences, as well as the use of figurative language and imagery. Close examination of style can reveal the author's attitude and purpose.

⋯⋯⋯⋯⋯⋯⋯⋯⋯⋯⋯⋯⋯⋯⋯⋯

Reading Tip: Identifying Figurative Language It is useful to identify examples of figurative language, imagery, and idioms to analyze style as you read.

Metaphors	Similes	Idioms
shy people are compared to leaves	paper is as big as Montana	out of the woods

Vocabulary

immortal (i môrt′ əl) *adj.* lasting or living forever; everlasting; p. 404 *The Greeks believed that their deities were immortal.*

vague (vāg) *adj.* uncertain; unclear; not precisely expressed; p. 404 *We got lost because her directions were too vague.*

anonymity (an′ə nim′ ətē) *n.* being unknown; having no name; unrecognized; p. 404 *The famous actor used a different name to preserve his anonymity.*

obligatory (ə blig′ə tôr′ē) *adj.* legally or morally binding; required; p. 404 *The teacher let her students know that homework was obligatory.*

declarative (di klar′ə tiv) *adj.* a type of sentence or expression that makes a simple statement; p. 406 *The toddler only said declarative statements.*

Vocabulary Tip: Synonyms Synonyms are words that have the same or similar meanings.

Focus

Summary

Writing a letter is the best way to communicate with people, according to Keillor. Not only does it reveal who a person is, but it also acts as a process of self-discovery. In addition, letters leave a long-lasting impression. Garrison Keillor defends the importance of writing letters and provides insightful tips for overcoming possible obstacles to writing letters.

V Vocabulary

Vocabulary File Say: Add these words and definitions to your vocabulary file. For each word, include a sentence that gives you an example of how to use the word. **OL** Students with English language needs should include the pronunciations of these words in their files. **EL**

Literary Elements Have students access the Web site to improve their understanding of thesis.

OBJECTIVES
In studying this selection, you will focus on the following:
- identifying and evaluating thesis
- analyzing style and figurative language
- analyzing the use of humor in an essay
- writing letters

GARRISON KEILLOR   **403**

Selection Resources

Print Materials
- 📁 Unit 2 Resources (Fast File), pp. 40–42
- 📁 Leveled Vocabulary Development, p. 28
- 📁 Selection and Unit Assessments, pp. 61–62
- 📁 Selection Quick Checks, p. 31

Transparencies
- Bellringer Options Transparencies: Daily Language Practice Transparency 35
- Literary Elements Transparency 34

Technology
- TeacherWorks Plus™ CD-ROM
- StudentWorks Plus™ CD-ROM
- Presentation Plus!™ CD-ROM
- Literature Online, glencoe.com
- Online Student Edition, mhln.com
- Exam*View*® Assessment Suite CD-ROM
- Vocabulary PuzzleMaker CD-ROM
- Listening Library, disc 1 track 32

Teach

How to Write a Letter

Garrison Keillor

We shy persons need to write a letter now and then, or else we'll dry up and blow away. It's true. And I speak as one who loves to reach for the phone, dial the number, and talk. I say, "Big Bopper here— what's shakin', babes?" The telephone is to shyness what Hawaii is to February, it's a way out of the woods, *and yet:* a letter is better.

Such a sweet gift—a piece of handmade writing, in an envelope that is not a bill, sitting in our friend's path when she trudges home from a long day spent among wahoos[1] and savages, a day our words will help repair. They don't need to be **immortal**, just sincere. She can read them twice and again tomorrow: *You're*

someone I care about, Corinne, and think of often and every time I do you make me smile.

We need to write, otherwise nobody will know who we are. They will have only a **vague** impression of us as A Nice Person, because, frankly, we don't shine at conversation, we lack the confidence to thrust our faces forward and say, "Hi, I'm Heather Hooten; let me tell you about my week." Mostly we say "Uh-huh" and "Oh, really." People smile and look over our shoulder, looking for someone else to meet.

So a shy person sits down and writes a letter. To be known by another person— to meet and talk freely on the page—to be close despite distance. To escape from **anonymity** and be our own sweet selves and express the music of our souls.

---

1. *Wahoos* here most likely refers to loud and annoying people who get on one's nerves.

Reading Strategy Analyzing Style *What does Keillor achieve by beginning his essay with "we"?* **R**

Vocabulary

immortal (i môrt′ əl) *adj.* lasting or living forever; everlasting

Literary Element Thesis *At this point in the essay, how do you think this statement might relate to Keillor's main idea?* **L₁**

Vocabulary

vague (vāg) *adj.* uncertain; unclear; not precisely expressed
anonymity (an′ə nim′ ətē) *n.* being unknown; having no name; unrecognized

404 UNIT 2 NONFICTION

Same thing that moves a giant rock star to sing his heart out in front of 123,000 people moves us to take ballpoint in hand and write a few lines to our dear Aunt Eleanor. *We want to be known.* We want her to know that we have fallen in love, that we quit our job, that we're moving to New York, and we want to say a few things that might not get said in casual conversation: *Thank you for what you've meant to me, I am very happy right now.*

The first step in writing letters is to get over the guilt of not writing. You don't "owe" anybody a letter. Letters are a gift. The burning shame you feel when you see unanswered mail makes it harder to pick up a pen and makes for a cheerless letter when you finally do. *I feel bad about not writing, but I've been so busy,* etc. Skip this. Few letters are **obligatory**, and they are

Thanks for the wonderful gift and I am terribly sorry to hear about George's death and *Yes, you're welcome to stay with us next month,* and not many more than that. Write those promptly if you want to keep your friends. Don't worry about the others, except love letters, of course. When your true love writes, *Dear Light of My Life, Joy of My Heart, O Lovely Pulsating Core of My Sensate Life,* some response is called for.

Literary Element

Thesis *How does this "first step" reveal an element of Keillor's thesis?* **L2**

Vocabulary

obligatory (ə blig′ə tôr′ē) *adj.* legally or morally binding; required

Letter on Table. Michele Warner. ★

GARRISON KEILLOR **405**

Teach

★ Viewing the Art

Have students read the letter in the painting. **Ask:** What clues in the letter provide information about the writer's situation? *(Students might say that the date and the reference to fighting suggest that the writer is a soldier in World War II.)* Then, have them identify parts of the letter that Keillor might like, and explain their answers. *(Students might point out examples of the letter's sincerity or its conversational style.)* **AS**

✓CheckPoint

Use the CheckPoint questions on Presentation Plus! to monitor students' comprehension. These questions can be used with interactive response keypads for immediate student feedback.

Differentiated Instruction

Humor Humor can be difficult to recognize. Define exaggeration and verbal irony as techniques of humor; verbal irony is saying one thing and meaning another. Have students provide examples of exaggeration and verbal irony as well as odd juxtapositions or unexpected language. **Ask:** What do you find humorous in Keillor's essay and why? *(Students will cite different passages, but one good example is "We need to write. Otherwise nobody will know who we are." This is humorous because it uses exaggeration to make a point.)* **BL**

Objectives
• To analyze style and figurative language (SE)
• To identify and evaluate thesis (SE)
• To understand the use of analogy (TWE)

405

Teach

⭐ Viewing the Art

The French Impressionist artist Edgar Degas (1834–1917) is probably best known for his paintings of the variety of life in Paris. The subject of this painting, Edmond Duranty, was a French critic who proclaimed that novels should be written in a simple and easily understood style. **Ask:** What do you think Duranty would think about Keillor's stylistic advice? *(Students might say that he would support it, since Keillor emphasizes the importance of keeping the style simple and casual.)* **AS**

Edmond Duranty, 1879. Edgar Degas. Pastel. Glasgow City Art Museum and Galleries, Scotland. ⭐

Some of the best letters are tossed off in a burst of inspiration, so keep your writing stuff in one place where you can sit down for a few minutes and (*Dear Roy, I am in the middle of a book entitled* We Are Still Married *but thought I'd drop you a line. Hi to your sweetie, too.*) dash off a note to a pal. Envelopes, stamps, address book, everything in a drawer so you can write fast when the pen is hot.

A blank white eight-by-eleven sheet can look as big as Montana if the pen's not so hot—try a smaller page and write boldly. Or use a note card with a piece of fine art on the front; if your letter ain't good, at least they get the Matisse. Get a pen that makes a sensuous line, get a comfortable typewriter, a friendly word processor—whichever feels easy to the hand.

Sit for a few minutes with the blank sheet in front of you, and meditate on the person you will write to, let your friend come to mind until you can almost see her or him in the room with you. Remember the last time you saw each other and how your friend looked and what you said and what perhaps was unsaid between you, and when your friend becomes real to you, start to write.

Additional Support

Skills Practice

WRITING: Idioms Write the following phrase on the board: *when the pen is hot.* Ask students if this expression is meant to be taken literally. Help them to recognize it as an idiom and to offer explanations for why such figurative language is effective. *(Idioms are imaginative and colorful. They connect with concrete experience and draw the reader in.)* Remind students to look for other examples of figurative language as they read. **OL**

Write the salutation—*Dear* You—and take a deep breath and plunge in. A simple **declarative** sentence will do, followed by another and another and another. Tell us what you're doing and tell it like you were talking to us. Don't think about grammar, don't think about lit'ry[2] style, don't try to write dramatically, just give us your news. Where did you go, who did you see, what did they say, what do you think?

If you don't know where to begin, start with the present moment: *I'm sitting at the kitchen table on a rainy Saturday morning. Everyone is gone and the house is quiet.* Let your simple description of the present moment lead to something else, let the letter drift gently along.

The toughest letter to crank out is one that is meant to impress, as we all know from writing job applications; if it's hard work to slip off a letter to a friend, maybe you're trying too hard to be terrific. A letter is only a report to someone who already likes you for reasons other than your brilliance. Take it easy.

Don't worry about form. It's not a term paper. When you come to the end of one episode, just start a new paragraph. You can go from a few lines about the sad state of pro football to the fight with your mother to your fond memories of Mexico to your

cat's urinary-tract infection[3] to a few thoughts on personal indebtedness and on to the kitchen sink and what's in it. The more you write, the easier it gets and when you have a True True Friend to write to, a *compadre*,[4] a soul sibling, then it's like driving a car down a country road, you just get behind the keyboard and press on the gas.

Don't tear up the page and start over when you write a bad line—try to write your way out of it. Make mistakes and plunge on. Let the letter cook along and let yourself be bold. Outrage, confusion, love—whatever is in your mind, let it find a way to the page. Writing is a means of discovery, always, and when you come to the end and write *Yours ever* or *Hugs and kisses,* you'll know something you didn't when you wrote *Dear Pal.*

> *Let the letter cook along and let yourself be bold.*

Probably your friend will put your letter away, and it'll be read again a few years from now—and it will improve with age. And forty years from now, your friend's grandkids will dig it out of the attic and read it, a sweet and precious relic of the ancient eighties that gives them a sudden clear glimpse of you and her and the world we old-timers knew. You will then have created an object of art. Your simple lines about where you went, who you saw, what they said, will speak to those children and they will feel in their hearts the humanity of our times.

You can't pick up a phone and call the future and tell them about our times. You have to pick up a piece of paper. ✎

---

2. *Lit'ry* is short for "literary." Keillor is poking fun at the idea of trying to make one's letter a great work of literature.

Big Idea Quests and Encounters *How does allowing a letter to "drift gently along" create the opportunity for writers to encounter themselves?* **BI₁**

Reading Strategy Analyzing Style *Sometimes Keillor inserts sentences composed of two or three words throughout the essay. What effect do these shorter sentences have?* **R**

Vocabulary

declarative (di klar′ə tiv) *adj.* a type of sentence or expression that makes a simple statement; an explanatory statement

---

3. *Urinary tract infection* occurs anywhere along the urinary tract, for example, the kidneys or bladder.
4. A *compadre* is a close friend or pal.

Big Idea Quests and Encounters *Reread the last two sentences of this essay. What kind of encounter does Keillor fear we will fail to have if people stop writing to each other?* **BI₂**

GARRISON KEILLOR **407**

Assess

1. (a) Students may not see letters as more self-revealing than other communication. (b) People may write letters to be vague or impersonal or to impress.

2. (a) Examples: a pen that "makes a sensuous line," a "comfortable typewriter," and a "friendly word processor" (b) The instruments used to write are as important as the environment.

3. (a) Recalling what the recipient looks like, your last conversation, and the things left unsaid will help the writer. (b) Thinking of the person closes the physical distance.

4. Some students might say he uses familiar images. Others might say both the letter writer and the rock star want recognition.

5. Students might say yes, explaining that Keillor's conversational tone is inviting and does not try to impress.

6. Keillor sees letter writing as joyous, creative, and insightful, not stressful.

7. Answers will vary.

8. Students should explain their motivation for writing letters, such as the desire for self-discovery or the pleasure of mentally encountering a person who is far away.

RESPONDING AND THINKING CRITICALLY

Respond

1. (a) Do you agree with Keillor that people need to write letters "to be known"? (b) What other reasons would someone have for writing a letter?

Recall and Interpret

2. (a) Describe the adjectives Keillor uses when naming the kinds of instruments that are useful to have when writing a letter. (b) What do you feel Keillor tries to capture about writing in these descriptions?

3. (a) How does thinking about the letter's recipient aid in the writing process? (b) Why does Keillor feel it is important to mentally conjure up this person?

4. Why do you think Keillor compares writing letters to the performance of a rock musician?

Analyze and Evaluate

5. Do you think that Keillor exemplifies the kind of writing that he encourages in his essay? Explain why or why not.

6. Why does Keillor give the advice, "Don't tear up the page and start over when you write a bad line—try to write your way out of it"?

7. Did you find "How to Write a Letter" humorous? Explain your answer using examples from the text.

Connect

8. **Big Idea** **Quests and Encounters** What kind of quest do you, personally, embark upon when writing a letter? Explain.

VISUAL LITERACY

Step-by-Step Directions

In his essay, Keillor gives detailed instructions explaining how to write a letter. As you reread the essay, write out his step-by-step directions in your own words. You can make a flow chart like the one shown, design instructional note cards, or make a detailed outline. When listing each step, you may want to list or refer to some of the specific details or suggestions that Keillor includes in his essay. Remember to number each step.

1. Looking over Keillor's set of directions, which directives address a person's attitude or approach to writing?

2. Which address the mechanics of writing?

HOW TO WRITE A LETTER

Step 1: Get over the guilt of not writing before or more often.

↓

Step 2: Meditate about the person to whom you will write the letter.

↓

Step 3: Write the salutation: "Dear _____,"

↓

Step 4: Take a deep breath, then "plunge in" to your writing, start with the present.

↓

Step 5: Do not worry about form; ignore grammar and style. If you make mistakes, keep on writing.

↓

Step 6: End your letter with "Yours ever" or "Hugs and Kisses."

Visual Literacy

1. Get over the guilt of not writing. Write letters of obligation promptly. Write when you are most inspired. Think about the person to whom you are writing. Focus on the specifics.

2. Write in simple sentences, without regard to form, grammar, style. Keep the contents simple. If you make a mistake, just keep writing.

Literary Element Thesis

The **thesis** is the main idea of a work of nonfiction. While some essays state the thesis directly, others imply the main idea through hints and suggestions. Writers may use an implied thesis when they want the reader to come to his or her own conclusions.

1. What is the thesis in "How to Write a Letter"? Is it a direct or an implied thesis? Explain.

2. If you could write a different title for the essay, what would that be?

Review: Essay

As you learned on pages 400–401, an **essay** is a short piece of nonfiction writing on any topic. The purpose of an essay is to communicate an idea or opinion. Formal essays generally have serious and impersonal tones, and their purpose is to instruct (expository essays) or persuade. Typically, in a formal essay, the author develops a main idea in a logical, highly organized way. An informal, or personal, essay entertains while it informs, usually with a light, conversational style. Notice how Keillor's essay is a combination of an expository and a personal essay, in that it seeks to explain the letter-writing process while entertaining the reader. Keillor uses humor—which can be in the form of sarcasm, exaggeration, and irony—to point out human failings and explain the more general irony found in many interpersonal situations.

Partner Activity Pair up with a classmate to discuss the author's informal use of humor. Find examples of the different types of humor Keillor uses: exaggeration, sarcasm, and irony.

Type of Humor	Examples
Exaggeration	Dear Light of My Life; Joy of My Heart; O Lovely Pulsating Core of My Sensate Life

Reading Strategy Analyzing Style

Literary analysis requires you to look separately at different elements of a writer's style—word choice, syntax, figurative language, rhetorical devices, sound devices, and organization of main ideas. Analyzing style helps you look at the text more critically, allowing you to better understand the author's purpose for writing.

1. Does Keillor conclude with the same point with which he begins the essay? If not, why might he end on a different note? Does this conclusion strengthen or weaken his thesis? Explain.

2. Do his arguments throughout the essay support the thesis stated in the introduction? Explain.

Vocabulary Practice

Practice with Synonyms Find the synonym for each vocabulary word from "How to Write a Letter."

1. immortal
   a. fleeting **b.** eternal **c.** profound
2. vague
   a. definite **b.** undefined **c.** transparent
3. anonymity
   a. secrecy **b.** fame **c.** celebrity
4. obligatory
   a. requisite **b.** voluntary **c.** willing
5. declarative
   a. inquisitive **b.** affirmative **c.** relative

Academic Vocabulary

Here are two words from the vocabulary list on page R82.

topic (top´ik) *n.* the subject of a book, conversation, essay, speech, etc.

edit (ed´it) *v.* to reorganize, prepare, or change a text for publication

Practice and Apply
1. What **topic** does Keillor suggest in this essay?
2. According to Keillor, how should a person **edit** the letter that he or she is writing?

Assess

Literary Element

1. Students may point to the direct thesis, explicitly stated by Keillor, that people should write letters in order to be known. Other students may point out other big ideas—writing as a way of encountering yourself and as a method of leaving personal testament to future generations—but these are versions of the above-stated thesis.

2. Responses will vary, but they should focus on the act of writing a letter.

Review: Essay

Students' charts should include humorous lines that are examples of exaggeration, sarcasm, and irony. Some charts may include the following: Exaggeration: sheet can look as big as Montana; Sarcasm: day spent among wahoos and savages; at least they get the Matisse; Irony: lit'ry

Reading Strategy

1. He concludes with a slightly different point, emphasizing the importance of letter writing as a way of speaking to future generations. Keillor's conclusion strengthens his essay because he assumes that his readers would like future generations to know them as well.

2. Keillor's arguments support his thesis. Some may argue that the how-to directives are what makes his essay particularly strong—his readers think he is merely giving directions when he is arguing for something more.

Vocabulary

1. b
2. b
3. a
4. a
5. b

Academic Vocabulary

1. Keillor suggests that in writing letters, one should begin with the present. He also encourages the writer to move from one topic to another without heavy thought or deliberation.

2. Keillor suggests that the writer edit minimally because a letter is not a formal document.

Assess

Writing About Literature

Students' letters should

- reveal aspects of themselves
- show a connection with the person addressed

Literature Groups

1. Responses may vary. Some students may state that the impromptu nature of e-mails leads people to spend less time thinking about form and grammar. Others may argue that the same hesitations or difficulties people may have about handwritten letters apply to electronic messages.

2. Students' answers may vary. Most will say that the essay is just as applicable today; some may say that a similar effect could be achieved by writing e-mails.

Keillor's Language and Style

Students' charts may include the following idioms:
music of our souls—the good qualities that make us who we are
sing his heart out—sing enthusiastically
let the letter cook along—to keep going without hesitation
when the pen is hot—writer is inspired

Writing About Literature

Apply Thesis Write a one-to-two page letter to someone following the guidelines Keillor provides in his essay. Remember to "meditate upon" the person to whom you are writing before starting the letter. You may want to use a web diagram like the one shown below to organize your thoughts about your subject.

After you complete your first draft, meet with a peer reviewer to read over each other's letters and to suggest revisions. Then proofread and edit your draft for errors in spelling, grammar, and punctuation.

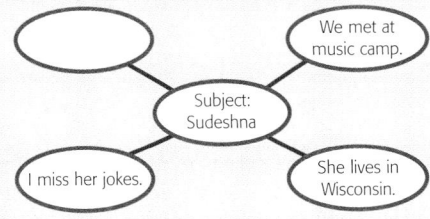

Literature Groups

In today's technologically advanced culture, people increasingly correspond through electronic messaging. Chat rooms and instant messaging seem to have combined the telephone and the letter. Some may argue that people feel closer to whomever they are writing because e-mails are instantaneous mediums of communication. Others may argue that the exact opposite is true because electronic messaging does not encourage face-to-face interactions.

Group Activity Discuss this issue in your group, using evidence from the "How to Write a Letter" to support your position. Share your conclusions with the rest of your class.

1. How have e-mails and the Internet changed the kind of communication that takes place in a handwritten letter?

2. Do you feel Keillor's essay is more applicable today than when it was first published in 1982? Explain your response.

Keillor's Language and Style

Using Idioms In "How to Write a Letter," Keillor peppers his essay with a variety of idiomatic expressions that make his writing more conversational and personal. An idiom is a saying or group of words that takes on a special meaning, different from the usual meaning of the words that make it up. Phrases such as "catch his eye," "turn the tables," "over the hill," and "keep tabs on" are idiomatic expressions understood by native speakers of English. They are often puzzling to non-native speakers.

Activity Work with a partner to identify and translate the idioms contained in Keillor's essay. Create a two-column chart. In the left column, copy idioms from Keillor's essay. In the right column, explain what these idioms mean.

Idioms	Meaning
out of the woods	out of trouble, out of an uncomfortable or difficult situation

Revising Check

Idioms Work with a partner to revise the letter you wrote following Keillor's guidelines. See if you can include idioms you use in everyday conversation and find a place to incorporate an idiom into the letter you have written.

Literature Online **Web Activities** For eFlashcards, Selection Quick Checks, and other Web activities, go to www.glencoe.com.

Literature Online

Web Activities Have students access the Web site for interactive activities that will help them assess their understanding of the selection.

Revising Check

When students add idioms to their letters, encourage them to limit their use of clichés and instead incorporate unique or clever sayings.

A Swimming Lesson

MEET JEWELLE L. GOMEZ

What do I hope to achieve by writing? Changing the world!" Award-winning writer and social activist Jewelle L. Gomez attributes much of her success to her great-grandmother. "My great-grandmother . . . was born on an Indian reservation in Iowa and had been a widow for fifty years. She maintained an intellectual curiosity and graciousness that no amount of education could have created. She formed the basis of much of my intellectual yearnings."

"My writing flows directly out of the great storytelling that runs in my family."

—Jewelle L. Gomez

In Her Blood Gomez was born in Boston to parents of African American, Native American, and Portuguese ancestry. She lived with her great-grandmother until she was twenty-two years old. Although she lived in poverty as a child and young adult, Gomez was able to attend college. She earned a bachelor's degree from Northeastern University and a master's degree from Columbia University School of Journalism. Before becoming a published writer, Gomez worked as a television production assistant in Boston and as a stage manager for plays in New York City.

Growing up in a family of storytellers, Gomez always knew she wanted to be a writer. But she struggled for many years before discovering a subject that inspired her. A play written by African American poet Ntozake Shange changed her life. The play celebrated ordinary African American women, portraying them as strong and beautiful. Until that point, Gomez

had never seen or read anything that described African American women as heroes. Watching Shange's play, she found herself thinking of her grandmother and great-grandmother. What if she wrote about them and other women like them? At that moment, she discovered a subject she wanted to write about for the rest of her life.

Fact and Imagination Growing up during the Civil Rights Movement and the Black Power Movement of the 1960s taught Gomez about social activism. It seemed everyone she knew was trying to make U.S. society a better place for people of color. Since then, Gomez's strong belief in equality—for minorities, women, and other groups—has been the guiding force in her writing and her life. "All oppressions are interconnected," she once said. Themes of equality, power, and responsibility are evident in her essays, plays, poetry, novels, and short stories.

All of Gomez's writing contains tidbits from her own life—even her fiction. In her novel *The Gilda Stories*, Gomez created a female African American vampire. Gilda is not a typical vampire, however, because she uses her power to help others rather than harm them. Gomez gave Gilda's character some of the traits of her own African American and Native American female ancestors. *The Gilda Stories* won two Lambda Literary Awards in 1991.

Jewelle L. Gomez was born in 1948.

 Author Search For more about Jewelle L. Gomez, go to www.glencoe.com.

Focus

Summary

Jewelle L. Gomez recounts her childhood trips in the late 1950s with her grandmother, Lydia, to a mostly white beach in Revere, Massachusetts. Ignoring the racial tension at the beach, Lydia teaches her granddaughter to swim, modeling self-confidence, athleticism, and a fearless love of the sea. Later, Gomez discovers that her grandmother could not swim very well, but by teaching her granddaughter to swim, Lydia also taught her to be proud of her accomplishments, her appearance, and her heritage.

V Vocabulary

Vocabulary File Say: Add these words and definitions to your vocabulary file. For each word, include a sentence that gives you an example of how to use the word. **OL** Students with English language needs should include the pronunciations of these words in their files. **EL**

Literary Elements Have students access the Web site to improve their understanding of narrative essay.

Connecting to the Narrative Essay

In the following narrative essay, Jewelle L. Gomez recalls how her grandmother, Lydia, taught her to swim. Before you read the essay, think about the following questions:

- What skill do you possess that you learned from a family member or other adult?
- What methods did that person use to teach you?

Building Background

This story takes place in the summer of 1957 at Revere Beach in Revere, Massachusetts, five miles north of Boston. It was the first public U.S. beach, established in 1896. Until the late 1980s, the sandy, crescent-shaped beach was flanked by amusement rides, restaurants and food stands, dance pavilions, and arcades. People from the entire Boston metropolitan area were able to reach Revere Beach by public transportation, and they flocked there during the summer months.

Setting Purposes for Reading

Big Idea Quests and Encounters

Gomez's encounter with the beach and the ocean teaches her more than just swimming.

Literary Element Narrative Essay

A **narrative essay** is a short nonfiction story. Written in the first person, narrative essays usually relate events drawn from the writer's own life, allowing the reader to directly experience the author's perspective. Compared with a formal essay, a narrative essay differs by the use of a light, conversational tone. As you read, think about why Gomez chose the narrative essay form for this essay.

- See Literary Terms Handbook, p. R11.

Literature Online Interactive Literary Elements Handbook To review or learn more about the literary elements, go to www.glencoe.com.

OBJECTIVES

In studying this selection, you will focus on the following:
- understanding the narrative essay form
- connecting to personal experience
- understanding anecdote
- writing to explore author's purpose

Reading Strategy Connecting to Personal Experience

Connecting to personal experience means linking what you read to events or experiences in your own life. Making this type of connection can help you better understand a story and its characters.

Reading Tip: Make a Diagram As you read "A Swimming Lesson," write down details about the author's experiences that are similar to yours where the two circles of the Venn diagram intersect.

Vocabulary

benevolence (bə nev′ ə ləns) n. kindness; generosity; p. 414 *Gabriel's benevolence was apparent in his tireless work for the poor.*

vulnerable (vul′ nər ə bəl) adj. easily damaged or hurt; p. 414 *Children are vulnerable to injuries.*

mainstream (mān′ strēm′) adj. representing the most widespread attitudes and values of a society or group; p. 414 *The play was very popular because it appealed to mainstream audiences.*

superfluous (soo pur′ floo əs) adj. not needed; unnecessary; p. 414 *The student's research paper contained a great deal of superfluous information.*

invaluable (in val′ ū ə bəl) adj. very great in value; p. 415 *I probably would not have found the building without my father's invaluable directions.*

Vocabulary Tip: Using Context Clues
Context clues surround an unfamiliar word in a sentence and can help you define it.

Selection Resources

Print Materials
- 📁 Unit 2 Resources (Fast File), pp. 43–45
- 📁 Leveled Vocabulary Development, p. 29
- 📁 Selection and Unit Assessments, pp. 63–64
- 📁 Selection Quick Checks, p. 32

Transparencies
- Bellringer Options Transparencies:
  Selection Focus Transparency 23
  Daily Language Practice Transparency 36
- Literary Elements Transparency 34

Technology
- 💿 TeacherWorks Plus™ CD-ROM
- 💿 StudentWorks Plus™ CD-ROM
- 💿 Presentation Plus!™ CD-ROM
- 💻 Literature Online, glencoe.com
- 💻 Online Student Edition, mhln.com
- 💿 ExamView® Assessment Suite CD-ROM
- 💿 Vocabulary PuzzleMaker CD-ROM
- 💿 Listening Library, disc 1 track 33

A Swimming Lesson

Jewelle L. Gomez BI₁

At nine years old I didn't realize my grandmother, Lydia, and I were doing an extraordinary thing by packing a picnic lunch and riding the elevated train from Roxbury[1] to Revere Beach. It seemed part of the natural rhythm of summer to me. I didn't notice how the subway cars slowly emptied of most of their Black passengers as the train left Boston's urban center and made its way into the Italian and Irish suburban neighborhoods to the north. It didn't seem odd that all of the Black families stayed in one section of the beach and never ventured onto the boardwalk to the concession stands or the rides except in groups.

I do remember Black women perched cautiously on their blankets, tugging desperately at bathing suits rising too high in the rear and complaining about their hair "going back." Not my grandmother, though. She glowed with unashamed athleticism as she waded out, just inside the reach of the waves, and moved along the riptide[2] parallel to the shore. Once submerged, she would load me onto her back and begin her long, tireless strokes. With the waves partially covering us, I followed her rhythm with my short, chubby arms, taking my cues from the powerful movement of her back muscles. We did this again and again until I'd fall off, and she'd catch me and set me upright in the strong New England surf. I was thrilled by the wildness of the ocean and my grandmother's fearless relationship to it. I loved the way she never consulted her mirror after her swim, but always looked as if she had been born to the sea, a kind of aquatic heiress.

None of the social issues of 1957 had a chance of catching my attention that year. All that existed for me was my grand-

---

1. Boston's *Roxbury* neighborhood is southwest of downtown

Literary Element Narrative Essay *From this sentence, what do you learn about the relationship between white and African American people at Revere Beach?* **L**

---

2. The *riptide* is the strong surface current that flows rapidly away from shore, returning to sea the water carried landward by waves.

Big Idea Quests and Encounters *How does the author's grandmother seem to feel about the ocean?* **BI₂**

JEWELLE L. GOMEZ **413**

Teach

BI₁ Big Idea

Quests and Encounters
Say: As you read, consider this question: How does Gomez's quest change as the essay progresses? *(It becomes one for understanding—of her grandmother's motives and her ancestor's history.)* **OL**

L Literary Element

Narrative Essay Answer:
The African American people and the white people stay in separate areas. The African American people feel safe only in groups. **OL**

BI₂ Big Idea

Quests and Encounters
Answer: *She seems happy and confident in the water.* **OL**

CheckPoint

Use the CheckPoint questions on Presentation Plus! to monitor students' comprehension. These questions can be used with interactive response keypads for immediate student feedback.

Readability Scores
Dale-Chall: 8.4
DRP: 62
Lexile: 1190

English Language Coach

Complex Sentences Gomez's essay contains many long, complex sentences. Help English language learners decode meaning by breaking sample sentences into phrases and clauses and having students paraphrase each part. **EL**

Differentiated Instruction

Research Researching race relations in cities on the east coast of the United States in the 1950s and 1960s will help less proficient readers place Gomez's essay in its historical context. **BL**

Objective
• To understand the narrative essay form (SE)

Connecting to Personal Experience Answer: *Like Gomez, students might admire certain adults for their confidence, courage, dignity, or kindness.* **OL**

L **Literary Element**

Narrative Essay

Answer: *The author apparently wants to link her early childhood experiences with Lydia to the knowledge she gained as a college student.* **Ask:** In what ways do you predict that the author's earlier experience with Lydia will affect her as an adult? (*Students might predict the author will try to learn new skills, confident she will succeed.*) **OL**

---

mother, rising from the surf like a Dahomean[3] queen, shaking her head free of her torturous rubber cap, beaming down at me when I finally took the first strokes on my own. She towered above me in the sun with a **benevolence** that made simply dwelling in her presence a reward in itself. Under her gaze I felt part of a long line of royalty. I was certain that everyone around us—Black and white—saw and respected her magnificence.

Although I sensed her power, I didn't know the real significance of our summers together as Black females in a white part of town. Unlike winter, when we were protected by the cover of coats, boots and hats, summer left us **vulnerable** and at odds with the expectations for women's bodies—the narrow hips, straight hair, flat stomachs, small feet—handed down from the **mainstream** culture and media. But Lydia never noticed. Her long chorus-girl legs ended in size-nine shoes, and she dared to make herself even bigger as she stretched her broad back and became a woman with a purpose: teaching her granddaughter to swim.

My swimming may have seemed a **superfluous** skill to those who watched

I was thrilled by the wildness of the ocean and my grandmother's fearless relationship to it.

our lessons. After all, it was obvious that I wouldn't be doing the backstroke on the Riviera[4] or in the pool of a penthouse spa. Certainly nothing in the popular media at that time made the "great outdoors" seem a hospitable place for Black people. It was a place in which we were meant to feel comfortable at best and hunted at worst. But my prospects for utilizing my skill were irrelevant to me, and when I finally got it right I felt as if I had learned some **invaluable** life secret.

When I reached college and learned the specifics of slavery and the Middle Passage,[5] the magnitude of that "peculiar institution"[6] was almost beyond my comprehension; it was like nothing I'd learned before about the history of my people. It was difficult making a connection with those Africans who had been set adrift from their own land. My initial reaction was "Why didn't the slaves simply jump from the ships while they were still close to shore, and swim home?" The child in me who had learned to survive in water was crushed to find that my ancestors had not necessarily shared this skill. Years later when I visited West Africa and learned of the poisonous, spiny fish that inhabit most of the coastal

---

3. *Dahomean* (də hō′mā ən) *n.* refers to Dahomey, a country in western Africa now called Benin (ben in′). Several kingdoms flourished in this region from the 1300s to the 1600s.

Reading Strategy Connecting to Personal Experience *Think about an adult whom you admire. How do you identify with the author's feelings here?* **R1**

Vocabulary

benevolence (bə nev′ ə ləns) *n.* kindness; generosity

vulnerable (vul′ nər ə bəl) *adj.* easily damaged or hurt

mainstream (mān′ strēm′) *adj.* representing the most widespread attitudes and values of a society or group

superfluous (soo pur′ floo əs) *adj.* not needed; unnecessary

4. A popular resort area, the *Riviera* lies along the Mediterranean coasts of Italy and France.
5. The *Middle Passage* was the route followed by slave traders from Africa to the Americas. Through the months-long voyage, slaves suffered filth, disease, abuse, and death.
6. Prior to the Civil War, Southerners referred to slavery as their *peculiar institution*, meaning that they considered it to be vital to their economy and way of life.

Literary Element Narrative Essay *Why does the author move ahead in time from her childhood to her college days at this point in the essay?* **L**

Vocabulary

invaluable (in val′ ū ə bəl) *adj.* very great in value

Additional Support

Skills Practice

WRITING: Descriptive Writing Narrative essays often contain writing that appeals to the senses, which helps readers relate to the writer's experience. Have students write short narrative essays that use descriptive writing to draw readers in. Have them use the following checklist as a guide.

☐ Descriptive details reinforce subject matter and theme(s) of the essay.
☐ Sensory images are varied, clear, and striking.
☐ Verbs are lively and exact.
☐ Details are carefully organized. **OL**

waters, I understood why swimming was not the local sport there that it was in New England. And now when I take to the surf, I think of those ancestors and of Lydia.

The sea has been a fearful place for us. It swallowed us whole when there was no escape from the holds of slave ships. For me, to whom the dark fathoms of a tenement hallway were the most unknowable thing so far encountered in my nine years, the ocean was a mystery of terrifying proportions. In teaching me to swim, my grandmother took away my fear. I began to understand something outside myself—the sea—and consequently something about myself as well. I was no longer simply a fat little girl: My body had become a sea vessel—sturdy, enduring, graceful. I had the means to be safe.

Before she died last summer I learned that Lydia herself couldn't really swim that well. As I was splashing, desperately trying to learn the right rhythm—face down, eyes closed, air out, reach, face up, eyes open, air in, reach—Lydia was brushing the ocean's floor with her feet, keeping us both afloat. When she told me, I was stunned. I reached into my memory trying to combine this new information with the Olympic vision I'd always kept of her. At first I'd felt disappointed, tricked, the way I used to feel when I'd learn that a favorite movie star was only five feet tall. But then I quickly realized what an incredible act of bravery it was for her to pass on to me a skill she herself had not quite mastered—a skill that she knew would always bring me a sense of accomplishment. And it was more than just the swimming. It was the ability to stand on any beach anywhere and be proud of my large body, my African hair. It was not fearing the strong muscles in my own back; it was gaining control over my own life. ❧

Southwold, July Morning. Hugo Grenville (b. 1958). Oil on canvas, 71.1 x 91.4 cm. Private Collection.

JEWELLE L. GOMEZ **415**

Teach

R2 **Reading Strategy**

Connecting to Personal Experience Ask: What fears have you been able to overcome? Did anyone help you overcome your fears? (*Students might have overcome fear of water, certain animals, or the dark. They may have been encouraged or comforted by family or friends.*) **OL**

★ **Viewing the Art**

British artist Hugo Grenville (1958–) has attended school at Eton, joined the Coldstream Guards as an officer, traveled to and lived in Africa and India, and worked in advertising and as an art dealer. Since 1989 Grenville has been a full-time painter, creating works that he feels "express the joy of life in light and color" and communicate "our longing for a better world." **AS**

CheckPoint

Use the CheckPoint questions on Presentation Plus! to check students' mastery of the selection. These questions can be used with interactive response keypads for immediate student feedback.

Differentiated Instruction

Small-Group Presentations Families frequently have stories of ancestors' suffering and coping with hardships. Have students collect representative stories to present in small groups, using methods that best suit their different learning styles. Options for presenting might include the following:

- Visual Aid (time lines, dioramas, computer animation)
- Performance (storytelling, monologues, skits)
- Writing (personal essays, journal entries)
- Interaction (interviews) **AL**

Objectives
- To connect to personal experience (SE)
- To understand the narrative essay form (SE)
- To write descriptively (TWE)

415

Assess

1. (a) It might have shaken her confidence. (b) Some may say that Lydia should have been honest, but others may say that she deceived in order to help.

2. (a) She likes the sea and is not self-conscious. (b) Gomez admires her fearlessness and self-confidence.

3. (a) An African American's lifestyle was not thought to include swimming pools. (b) The young Gomez is not aware that her future could be limited.

4. (a) The poisonous fish explained why her ancestors were not swimmers. (b) For Gomez, swimming is liberating; for them, dangerous.

5. (a) She is a positive role model. (b) Role models provide guidance and encourage confidence.

6. (a) Racism, segregation, and sexism. (b) The young Gomez was not aware of the issues but the adult Gomez recognizes how courageous the trips were given the issues of the time.

7. Role models help build self-confidence and teach how to face and overcome conflict.

8. Answers will vary.

RESPONDING AND THINKING CRITICALLY

Respond

1. (a)Why do you think Lydia hid the fact that she was walking on the ocean floor from her granddaughter? (b)What is your reaction to Lydia's deception?

Recall and Interpret

2. (a)What is Lydia's attitude toward the sea and toward her own body? (b)How does this attitude seem to affect the author's feelings for her grandmother?

3. (a)According to Gomez, why might observers have considered her swimming lessons a waste of time? (b)Why do you think Gomez views the lessons differently than what she speculates the observers think?

4. (a)What historical information has helped Gomez understand her ancestors' attitude toward the sea? (b)Compare Gomez's own attitude with that of her ancestors.

Analyze and Evaluate

5. (a)Assess whether or not Lydia is a positive role model for her granddaughter. (b)Are role models important for young people? Explain your opinion.

6. (a)What are the "social issues of 1957" to which Gomez refers in this essay? (b)How does her adult view of these issues differ from her childhood view of them?

7. What is the theme, or main idea, of this essay? Explain.

Connect

8. **Big Idea** **Quests and Encounters** Have you ever conquered a fear, as Gomez did with Lydia's help? Describe your experience.

LITERARY ANALYSIS

Literary Element **Narrative Essay**

A good narrative essay, or nonfiction story, contains all the elements of any good narrative: characters, setting, and plot. Like short stories, most narrative essays include a central conflict or problem and have a climax and resolution. Many narrative essays are autobiographical, and the author's purpose is to tell about life experiences and life lessons.

1. Compare and contrast Gomez's essay with a short story. Use details from the essay to support your answer.

2. Authors typically write for one or more of the following purposes: to inform, to persuade, to describe, to explain, to entertain. What do you think Gomez's purpose was in writing her essay? Explain.

Review: Anecdote

As you learned on page 389, an **anecdote** is a brief, personal account of a remarkable incident or event. Essayists often use anecdotes to support their opinions, to clarify their ideas, to entertain, or to get the reader's attention.

Group Activity With two other students, share anecdotes from your own lives. After each student has shared an anecdote, discuss what opinions or ideas the anecdote could be used to support in a narrative essay. Use the chart from "A Swimming Lesson" as a model for your personal examples. Then make a chart using your own anecdotes.

Anecdote	Ideas and Opinions
I loved the way she never consulted her mirror after her swim.	Lydia was comfortable with her appearance.

Literary Element

1. Both have setting, plot, and sharply drawn characters. But the essay is factual; the story, fictional.

2. To describe her grandmother and to tell of the lessons learned from Lydia

Review: Anecdote

Students should share anecdotes and explain what ideas or opinions the anecdotes support. Encourage students to focus on times when they learned something new or confronted a challenge.

Reading Strategy Connecting to Personal Experience

Even when a piece of narrative writing describes unfamiliar places and events, it is often easy to connect with the universal emotions an author evokes.

1. Find a passage that evokes a particular emotion. How does the narrator feel at that moment? What do you feel?

2. Which parts of the sentence or passage helped to create your emotional reaction?

Vocabulary Practice

Practice with Context Clues Read each of the following sentences and determine which words provide context clues for the vocabulary word.

1. The book described the benefits of **benevolence**. Being kind and generous, it said, has its own rewards.
   a. described the benefits
   b. Being kind and generous
   c. its own rewards

2. Homes built on shorelines and cliffs are often **vulnerable** to damage during storms.
   a. built on shorelines
   b. to damage
   c. storms

3. The teacher made a list of **mainstream** newspapers that included the widely read *Chicago Tribune* and the *New York Times*.
   a. made a list
   b. widely read
   c. *New York Times*

4. While shooting the movie, the director decided that the fourth camera was **superfluous**. She could make do with three instead.
   a. fourth camera
   b. make do with three
   c. instead

5. He wondered if the letter was an **invaluable** piece of history, or a fake forged by someone trying to make a buck.
   a. or a fake
   b. piece of history
   c. make a buck

Writing About Literature

Explore Author's Purpose "A Swimming Lesson" is an informal essay that tells a story. Write a short essay explaining why Gomez might have chosen to write a narrative essay rather than a more formal essay. Use evidence from the essay and examples from your own experience for support.

Before you begin drafting, establish at least two of Gomez's purposes by creating graphic organizers like the one shown here:

Once you have completed your draft, exchange it with a peer. When you have read each other's work, meet to evaluate the drafts and suggest revisions. Edit your draft, using your peer's comments and your own judgment to improve the writing. Finally, proofread for errors in spelling, grammar, and punctuation.

Literature Groups

Do you think children can become respectable adults without good role models? Would author Jewelle L. Gomez have grown into a confident, caring, responsible, politically active woman without the influence of her grandmother? Why or why not? Discuss these questions in a group of four to six students. Cite specific evidence from "A Swimming Lesson" and from your personal experience to support your argument.

Literature Online **Web Activities** For eFlashcards, Selection Quick Checks, and other Web activities, go to www.glencoe.com.

JEWELLE L. GOMEZ **417**

Assess

Reading Strategy

1. Possible passages include the moment when Lydia stands over the author and Gomez feels great admiration for her grandmother, or the moment when Gomez discovers the truth about what happened to her African ancestors during the Middle Passage. These passages might evoke feelings of love, admiration, confusion, or horror in the reader.

2. Students might cite words such as *royalty, respected,* and *magnificence,* or phrases such as *beyond my comprehension* and *I was crushed.*

Vocabulary

1. b
2. b
3. b
4. b
5. a

Literature Online

Web Activities Have students access the Web site for interactive activities that will help them assess their understanding of the selection.

Writing About Literature

Students' essays should

- analyze Gomez's reasons for presenting her subject in the format of a narrative essay

- use specific examples from Gomez's essay and personal experience to support their analyses

Literature Groups

Some students might argue that children without good role models will grow up to be irresponsible. Others might say that even without good role models, a child has a chance to grow up to be a responsible adult. Students should refer to the essay and their own experience to support their argument.

Focus

BELLRINGER

Bellringer Options
**Daily Language Practice
Transparency 37**
Or ask: Do you believe that animals are intellectually or emotionally complex creatures? Explain. *(Affirmative or negative responses should be supported with details.)* Explain that many people believe that domestic animals are more sophisticated because personal relationships are forged with them more often. Wild animals generally are not afforded this belief, however. Have students discuss this difference in view. Then ask them to consider the possibility of "cultured" wild animals.

Literature Online

Author Search To expand students' appreciation of Diane Ackerman, have them access the Web site for additional information and resources.

Encounter in the Sea

MEET DIANE ACKERMAN

Diane Ackerman possesses a wonder about the natural world that informs and shapes her writing. Winner of numerous awards for poetry and nonfiction, in her work Ackerman creates a distinctive fusion of art, journalism, and science.

Writer in Training Fascinated with nature at a young age, Ackerman studied both science and literature at college. In her career, she has taught at several prestigious universities, been a writer-in-residence at various writing programs, and hosted a PBS series entitled *Mystery of the Senses*, based on her book *A Natural History of the Senses* (1990), a blend of anthropology, folklore, history, and poetry. In her books, Ackerman has explored nature, flying, astronomy, gardening, travel, and love. Ackerman finds interest in both the fantastic and the mundane.

> "The charm of language is that, though it's human made, it can on rare occasions capture emotions and sensations [that] aren't."
>
> —Diane Ackerman

Fusion of Science and Art Ackerman publishes both prose and poetry but asserts that "poetry continues to be the real source of my creativity." Of her first book of poetry, *The Planets* (1976), astronomer Carl Sagan said, "One of the triumphs of Ackerman's [poetry] is the demonstration of how closely compatible planetary exploration and poetry, science and art really are."

Ackerman is a keen observer. Whether she is discussing how human beings relate to each other, watching dolphins swim and play, or examining tree frogs in a swamp, she notices everything—and then writes about it. In Ackerman's vision, human life is intimately tied to science, technology, and the natural world.

Love of Language Above all, Ackerman loves language. She has written, "All language is poetry. Each word is a small story, a thicket of meanings. . . . We clarify life's confusing blur with words. We cage flooding emotions with words. We coax elusive memories with words. We educate with words. We don't really know what we think, how we feel, what we want, or even who we are until we struggle to find the right words." Ackerman's work invites readers to revel in the beauty and power of language.

Diane Ackerman was born in 1948.

Literature Online **Author Search** For more about Diane Ackerman, go to www.glencoe.com.

Selection Skills

Reading Skills

- Recognizing Author's Purpose (SE pp. 419, 422, 425, 427)
- Establishing a Purpose (TWE p. 420)
- Sustained Silent Reading (TWE p. 424)

Encounter in the Sea

Literary Elements

- Descriptive Essay (SE pp. 419, 421, 423, 427)
- Mood (SE p. 427)

Vocabulary Skills

- Word Origins (SE pp. 419, 427)
- Academic Vocabulary (SE p. 427)

Listening/Speaking/Viewing Skills

- Panel Discussions (SE p. 428)

Writing Skills/Grammar

- Analyze Thesis (SE p. 428)
- Describing Sequence of Events (SE p. 428)
- Conduct Research (TWE p. 422)

Connecting to the Essay

How do humans communicate with animals? What makes humans and animals different—or similar? In this essay, Ackerman recounts meeting with dolphins in the wild. Before you read the essay, think about the following questions:

- How would you react in an encounter with an unfamiliar or wild animal?
- How would you compare your interactions with animals to your interactions with people?

Building Background

Like humans, dolphins are warm-blooded mammals. The spotted dolphins described in this essay usually grow to six to seven feet in length and weigh two hundred to three hundred pounds. They live in groups of five to fifteen individuals. Dolphins are social and intelligent and have sophisticated navigation ability. Swimming with dolphins has become a popular activity, both in the United States and elsewhere. The following essay combines characteristics of science reporting and nature writing while also remaining a personal account. Like a science reporter, Ackerman conveys facts and explanations; like a nature writer, she describes natural surroundings.

Setting Purposes for Reading

Big Idea Quests and Encounters

As you read, notice what Ackerman finds strange and familiar in her new acquaintances.

Literary Element Descriptive Essay

An essay is a short work of nonfiction written on a single topic with the purpose of communicating an idea or opinion. There are various types of essays, including the **descriptive essay.** A descriptive essay is characterized by writing that uses carefully selected details to help the reader visualize settings, events, and characters. As you read, notice the descriptive details Ackerman uses.

- See Literary Terms Handbook, p. R4.

OBJECTIVES
In studying this selection, you will focus on the following:
- identifying the characteristics of a descriptive essay
- recognizing and analyzing the author's purpose
- understanding mood
- writing to analyze thesis

Reading Strategy Recognizing Author's Purpose

The **author's purpose** is the author's intent in writing a literary work. Authors typically write for one or more of the following purposes: to persuade, to inform, to explain, to describe, or to entertain. While reading this essay, try to determine Ackerman's purpose.

Reading Tip: Asking Questions By asking questions, you can become more aware of the author's purpose. When you notice an episode, detail, or fact, ask yourself how it might relate to the purposes listed above.

> **Vocabulary**
>
> **indelible** (in del′ ə bəl) adj. unable to be erased or removed; permanent; p. 420 *His boating accident left an indelible scar on his right knee.*
>
> **intermittent** (in′ tər mit′ ənt) adj. occurring at intervals; not steady and continuous; p. 422 *The intermittent rain continued throughout the night.*
>
> **gregarious** (gri gār′ ē əs) adj. one who is fond of company; social; p. 423 *Tom was a popular boy because of his gregarious personality.*
>
> **ingenuity** (in′ jə nōō′ ə tē) n. ability to devise or contrive; cleverness; skillfulness; p. 423 *Raj's ingenuity helped him survive alone in the wilderness.*
>
> **Vocabulary Tip: Word Origins** The origin, or history, of most words, can be found in a dictionary. Usually, the language and root from which the word originated reveal the word's history.

Literature Online Interactive Literary Elements Handbook To review or learn more about the literary elements, go to www.glencoe.com.

Focus

Summary

"Encounter in the Sea" is a descriptive essay about a researcher's visit with the spotted dolphins of Little Bahama Bank. Rumored to communicate with humans, the dolphins draw Ackerman to their home. She finds the wonderful creatures, and, to her amazement, they welcome the researchers. The humans and dolphins play, trust, and recognize the compassion in one another.

V Vocabulary

Vocabulary File Say: Add these words and definitions to your vocabulary file. For each word, include a sentence that gives you an example of how to use the word. **OL** Students with English language needs should include the pronunciations of these words in their files. **EL**

Literary Elements Have students access the Web site to improve their understanding of descriptive essay.

Selection Resources

Print Materials
- 📁 Unit 2 Resources (Fast File), pp. 46–48
- 📁 Leveled Vocabulary Development, p. 30
- 📁 Selection and Unit Assessments, pp. 65–66
- 📁 Selection Quick Checks, p. 33

Transparencies
- Bellringer Options Transparencies: Daily Language Practice Transparency 37
- Literary Elements Transparency 34

Technology
- TeacherWorks Plus™ CD-ROM
- StudentWorks Plus™ CD-ROM
- Presentation Plus!™ CD-ROM
- Literature Online, glencoe.com
- Online Student Edition, mhln.com
- Exam*View*® Assessment Suite CD-ROM
- Vocabulary PuzzleMaker CD-ROM
- Listening Library, disc 1 track 34

Teach

BI1 **Big Idea**

Quests and Encounters
Say: Keep the following question in mind as you read: How is Ackerman changed by her encounter with the spotted dolphins? (*She is humbled by the realization that the dolphins exist intelligently and compassionately.*) **OL**

BI2 **Big Idea**

Quests and Encounters
Answer: *Students may respond that she wants to experience the "purity of exchange" that is "magical in its intensity," characteristics that she says are part of the dolphins' play, and as a researcher, she can chronicle their history and habits.* **OL**

⭐ Viewing the Art

Joan Grout, a native of Washington state, is a watercolor artist known mainly for her landscape and seascape paintings of the Pacific Northwest. **AS**

Readability Scores
Dale-Chall: 9.8
DRP: 61
Lexile: 1140

Encounter in the Sea

Diane Ackerman

Sailing. Joan Grout. ⭐

BI1

Wild creatures have lessons to teach about trust and play.

Humans love playing with other animals, and sometimes this leads to a purity of exchange almost magical in its intensity, deep play at its best. For instance, I once heard about a friendly group of spotted dolphins that are drawn to music played underwater and readily swim with divers in the warm currents of the Bahamas. Research teams visit yearly to chronicle their history and habits. Villagers in the sea, the dolphins form a community that changes as couples mate, young are born, the aged die, and new alliances[1] are forged. There is nothing like the **indelible**

thrill of meeting a wild animal on its own terms in its own element, so I decided to join a week-long trip. One morning I flew to Grand Bahama, took a cab to the West End, and boarded a two-masted schooner[2] along with eight other researchers. We were hoping to encounter spotted dolphins often enough during the week at sea to be able to identify and catalog individuals.

At 6:30 the following morning, we left the West End behind and cruised toward the Little Bahama Bank, a shallow area that spotted dolphins seem to prefer. After a few minutes, we hoisted[3] the mainsail, from which two rows of short ties hung

---

1. An *alliance* is a union or an agreement to cooperate.

Vocabulary

indelible (in del′ə bəl) *adj.* unable to be erased or removed; permanent

2. A *schooner* is a ship with two or more masts in which the front mast is smaller than the other masts.
3. *Hoisted* means "raised by using ropes or pulleys."

Big Idea Quests and Encounters *Summarize the factors that helped Ackerman decide to join a research team to study spotted dolphins.* **BI2**

420 UNIT 2 NONFICTION

Additional Support

Skills Practice

READING: Establishing a Purpose
Students often spend a great deal of time discovering an author's purpose for writing. Although this is time well spent and often essential to the comprehension of a text, they should also establish their own purpose—a purpose for reading. Have students preview the selection before they begin. Provide a list of purposes and ask students to establish personal goals. Explain that a reader can have several objectives when approaching a text and that while the teacher may provide one or more, a student should have a few of his or her own. **OL**

like fringe. Then we sat on benches or low deck chairs, finding shade under a large blue canopy[4] stretched over the center of the boat and attached by a web of ropes over the boom. The ocean poured blue-black all around us with rose-gold shimmers from the sun. Gradually, the water mellowed to navy blue, then indigo,[5] and finally azure,[6] as we drew closer to the shallows.[7] Clumps of turtle grass[8] looked like cloud shadows on the floor. After three hours, a pale-blue ribbon appeared on the horizon and we headed toward it. Flying fish leaped near the bow and hurled themselves through the air a dozen yards at a time, like rocks skipping over the water.

Soon we entered the dreamtime of the aqua shallows. This area rises like a stage or platform in the ocean, without coral or large schools of fish. It appears to be a desert, a barren[9] pan;[10] but there are few places on earth without life of some sort. Here there is a bustling plant community, from simple blue-green algae to more complicated plants with stems and leaves. Plankton,[11] the first step of the food chain, thrives on the banks, even though the waters look quite empty to the casual observer.

A bottlenosed dolphin leaped near the boat, then zoomed in and lined up with the bow, swinging back and forth like a surfer finding the sweetest spot of a wave. Soon it was joined by a second. Hobos[12] hitching a ride, the dolphins weren't moving their tails at all, but were carried along at speed by the bow wave. They seemed to relish the sport. Beautiful as these dolphins were, we were on the lookout for their cousins, the spotted ones.

A Concorde[13] sailed overhead, making a double *boom!* as it passed. What is speed to the passengers on that supersonic,[14] I wondered, or to the dolphins surfing on the bow wave?

"More dolphins!" the captain cried, pointing west.

As seven spotted dolphins homed in[15] on the boat, we donned snorkeling gear and jumped into the water with them. A mother and baby accompanied by another female arrived first, swam straight up to us and started playing. A dolphin went close to one woman, waited for her to follow, then started turning tight circles with her. Like dervishes, dolphin and human spun together. Meanwhile, two other dolphins dived down to the bottom, about forty feet below, and made fast passes at me. I turned to follow them. Slowing, they allowed me to swim with them in formation, only inches away. By now the dolphins were all over us, swirling and diving, coasting close and wiggling away to see if we'd follow. If I dived, they dived, and they often accompanied me back to the surface, eye to eye. At first it was startling how close they came. We have an invisible no-man's-land around our bodies that others don't enter unless they mean to romance or harm us. To have a wild animal enter that dangerous realm, knowing that you could hurt it or it could hurt you, but that neither of you will, produces instantaneous trust. After it happens once, all fear vanishes. Somehow, they managed to keep their slender distance—as little as two or three inches—without actually making physical contact.

---

13. A *Concorde* is the name of a type of airplane that can travel at twice the speed of sound.
14. *Supersonic* means "having a speed greater than that of sound."
15. Here, *homed in* refers to being guided toward an object or target by sounds.

---

4. A *canopy* is a covering hung or held up over a throne, bed, person, or other object.
5. *Indigo* is a color between blue and violet.
6. *Azure* is a deep, sky-blue color.
7. *Shallows* refers to a shallow place in a body of water.
8. *Turtle grass* is a type of underwater plant.
9. *Barren* means "unable to produce fruit or vegetation."
10. Here, a *pan* is a natural basin or depression in land.
11. *Plankton* are small, microscopic organisms that drift or float in sea or fresh water.
12. Here, *hobo* refers to a wandering person.

DIANE ACKERMAN **421**

R **Reading Strategy**

Recognizing Author's Purpose Answer: *She wants the reader to recognize that a dolphin's communication mechanism is unlike a human's. She also wants the reader to recognize that it may serve some of the same purposes: investigating, categorizing, and bonding with others.* **OL**

⭐ **Cultural History**

Echolocation Echolocation is a normal physiological process of the dolphins. Sound waves that they emit are reflected by invisible or distant objects, allowing the dolphins to detect them. The process is used to avoid obstacles and procure food, and can also be used for social interaction. **AS**

But they were touching in another sense, with their X-ray-like sonar,[16] patting our skin, reaching deep inside us to our bones and soft tissues. At times, I could feel their streaming clicks. They seemed especially interested in one woman's belly. Could they tell she was pregnant? Probably. I wonder how the fetus showed up on their sonar. Could they echolocate[17] our stomachs and know what we ate for lunch? Could they detect broken bones and tumors? Could they diagnose some diseases in us and in themselves? Hard to say. Because we couldn't touch them, they seemed aloof. But they were touching us constantly. For them, the contact was intimate, sensuous, if one-sided. What do dolphins feel when they echolocate one another?

⭐ At least we know *how* dolphins echolocate: they produce narrow streams of clicks (**intermittent** bursts of sound that last less than a thousandth of a second each) by blowing air back and forth through nasal passages. When the sound enters a fat-filled cavity in the head, it's focused into a single beam that can be directed wherever the dolphin wishes. First the dolphin sends out a general click, then it refines the signal to identify the object, which usually takes about six clicks, each one adjusting the picture so subtly that only chaos theory[18] can explain it. At lightning speed, the dolphin sends out a signal, waits for the echo, decides what pulse to send next, waits for that one's echo, and so on, until it detects the object and classifies it. Some likely categories are: edible,[19] dangerous, sexy, inani-

mate, useful, human, never-before-encountered, none of the above.

For an hour, the dolphins played exhausting, puppyish chase-and-tumble games. Meanwhile, we tried to study their markings. Each had a distinctive pattern of spots, tail notches, blazes. Often they darted to the sandy bottom and found silvery sand dabs that they chased and ate. They were like hyperactive children, easily bored, full of swerve[20] and spunk. And we were their big bathtub toys. Taking a striped, pink-and-purple ribbon from the end of my long braid, I let it float within eyeshot of a dolphin. In a flash, the dolphin grabbed the ribbon, then tossed it up, caught it with a flipper, tossed it backward, kicked it with its tail, caught it with the other flipper, spun around, slid it over its nose, swam away with it, then returned a moment later and let it fall through the water like a cast-off toy. A clear invitation. Taking a lungful of air, I dived after the ribbon, grabbed it with one hand, tossed it back to my fins and flicked it with a clumsy kick. By this time I needed to resurface to breathe, so I let the ribbon drift down, undulating[21] like a piece of kelp.[22] The dolphin collected it at speed over the pyramid of one flipper, let it slide back to the tail, whisked it up and tossed it with the other flipper. I knew the rules of the game, but I didn't have the breath to play it. Even if I were a pearl diver[23] and could hold my breath for over five minutes, I would still have been out of my league. After a few more of my clumsy lunges for the ribbon, the dolphin swam away,

---

16. *Sonar* is a method for underwater detection by the use of reflected or emitted sound.
17. To *echolocate* is to locate objects by reflected sounds, especially ultrasound. Echolocation is used by bats and many marine mammals.
18. *Chaos theory* is the mathematical study of complex systems that are highly sensitive to slight changes in conditions, such that small events can give rise to strikingly great consequences.
19. *Edible* means "suitable for eating."

Vocabulary

intermittent (in´ tər mit´ ənt) *adj.* occurring at intervals; not steady and continuous

---

20. Here, *swerve* refers to movements that change direction abruptly.
21. *Undulating* means "waving or moving up and down, in or out."
22. *Kelp* is a large, brown, broad-leafed seaweed.
23. *Pearl diving* is an old-fashioned way of harvesting oysters to get pearls. Divers sometimes go one hundred feet underwater without air equipment.

Reading Strategy Recognizing Author's Purpose
What is Ackerman's purpose in explaining—and speculating about—how dolphins use echolocation? **R**

Skills Practice

RESEARCH: Researching Points of Interest Many students will be impressed by Diane Ackerman's encounter with spotted dolphins. Channel this enthusiasm by having students experience their own virtual encounter with spotted dolphins through online research and, perhaps, through trips to local aquariums. They should then organize their experiences into descriptive essays to be shared with classmates. As students prepare to compile their research, remind them that quoted phrases and sentences must appear in quotation marks and that ellipses indicate omissions. **OL**

Dolphins, Joy Baer. Fresco. Private collection.

turning its attention to a human who could stay underwater longer, a man taking still photographs with a flash camera.

When at last they veered off toward the horizon, we gathered under the blue canopy to fill in sketch sheets and record the details of each animal. These rough sketches would be compared to photos of known animals, and become part of the researchers' catalog. You'd think nine observers might supply the same facts, but we didn't all agree on what we saw. Indeed, we sounded like people comparing different versions of an accident. As I filled out sketch sheets, I scanned my memory for head, tail, and flank markings.

Literary Element Descriptive Essay *How do the details in this sentence help portray Ackerman's experience?* **L**

Living mainly in the tropics,[24] spotted dolphins have long, narrow beaks, and can be heavily freckled. Like reverse fawns, the young begin life solid colored, usually gray, and only develop white spots as they age. By the time they're elderly, they're covered in swirls of spots and splotches. They grow to about eight feet long, have teeth, and are **gregarious**. They love to play, which they do with endless **ingenuity** and zest.[25] Athletic, acrobatic swimmers, they leap into

---

24. The *tropics* refers to the area of the earth near the equator.
25. Here, *zest* means "excitement."

Vocabulary

gregarious (gri gār′ ē əs) *adj.* one who is fond of company; social

ingenuity (in′jə nōo′ ə tē) *n.* ability to devise or contrive; cleverness; skillfulness

DIANE ACKERMAN **423**

Teach

⭐ Viewing the Art

Thomas Moran (1837–1926) is considered one of America's greatest landscape artists. His paintings so majestically captured the American geography that they helped stir Congress to create the National Park System, specifically Yellowstone National Park. **Ask:** How does the painting reflect Ackerman's view of nature? *(The painting depicts nature as beautiful, but there is also a wild quality about it that sets it apart.)* **AS**

Fiercely the Red Sun Descending Burned His Way Across the Heavens, 1875. Thomas Moran. North Carolina Museum of Art.

aerial pirouettes,[26] cartwheels, and what seem like attempts to see how long they can hover in the air.

Over the next week, we encountered spotted dolphins every day, the longest session lasting three hours, so long in fact that we were the first to give up out of exhaustion, only to find the dolphins racing after us and trying to tempt us back to romp.[27] Mother dolphins often brought the sleek little surprise of their babies, which appeared perfect and unmarked by life. Sometimes a baby would swim tucked underneath its mother, making a crescent shape, so that it looked as if the baby were still being carried inside. We grew to know them as individuals, a rare privilege. In our travels across the banks, we played with dolphins nine times. The most frequent visitor was a particularly rambunctious[28] five-year-old female called "Nicky," and she became a special favorite. Often, the dolphins arrived like a visitation. Long hours of waiting, in a slow-motion of heat, glare, and water, were suddenly broken by the wild and delicious turmoil of incoming dolphins. When they left, everything fell calm again and we waited once more, at a low ebb,[29] under the harrowing[30] sun.

On our last day, after a particularly exhausting afternoon with Nicky and her friends, we gathered on the deck to watch the sunset. These were some of the most dramatic moments in each day, when the soft aqua of the water fanned through rainbow blues and was washed away in the molten lava of the setting sun. Night fell heavily, in

---

26. A *pirouette* is a dancer's spin on one foot.
27. To *romp* means "to engage in high-spirited, carefree play."

28. *Rambunctious* means "behaving loudly and wildly."
29. Here, *ebb* is the flowing away of the tide from the shore.
30. *Harrowing* means "distressing or very upsetting."

424 UNIT 2 NONFICTION

Additional Support

Skills Practice

READING: Sustained Silent Reading Students may be surprised to learn that reading silently is a skill requiring practice. **Ask:** Do you lose track when you read silently? Do you ever get distracted? Can you read with noise, or must you have silence? *(Answers will vary.)* Have students answer the questions to determine their ideal reading conditions. Give these tips for silent reading: Get comfortable, but not too comfortable; maintain comprehension by asking yourself questions as you read; take breaks; adjust your reading rate to the demands of the text. **OL**

thick black drapes. Retreating to the galley[31] downstairs, we sat and talked about the week. Despite the mild discomforts of ocean sailing, everyone was sad the voyage was over, and all felt nourished by a week of such intimate play with wild animals. I was especially surprised by how eager the dolphins were to make eye contact. Their wildness disappears on one level and is enhanced on another when you stare straight into their eyes, realizing that these are wild creatures and there is some-thing special happening inside their minds. At the very least, there is a willing gentleness and an awareness that draws you in. One reason the plight of the dolphin touches us is because we fear they may be self-aware, not just meaty animals but intelligent life-forms. Suppose, like us, they have inner universes? Suppose they are not like elk[32] or salmon, but animals with a culture of sorts, animals that can judge us?

During the night, the winds kicked up and four-foot seas rolled in from the southwest. Sleeping on deck, I awakened to find that I had slid off my air mattress and my legs were suspended over the side of the boat. Hands folded on my chest, I looked set for burial at sea. So I retreated below, wedged myself into a narrow bunk, and tried to sleep, which was nearly impossible given the lurching and shuddering of the boat. My thoughts turned frequently to the dolphins. Where were they now? What were they doing in that incomprehensible darkness of sea and greater darkness of night? I was stricken[33] both by our kinship[34] with them and by the huge rift[35] between us evolution has created. They were minds in the ocean long before we were minds on the land. They abide by[36] rhythms older than we know or can invent. We pretend we can outsmart and ignore such rhythms, but in our hearts we know we're steered by them. ∿

---

31. A *galley* here refers to the kitchen on a ship.
32. An *elk* is a type of large deer.

33. *Stricken* means "overwhelmed by something unpleasant."
34. *Kinship* refers to a close relationship, as if related by family.
35. Here, a *rift* is a breach or split between friendly relations.
36. To *abide by* is to obey or follow a given set of rules.

Reading Strategy Recognizing Author's Purpose
What is Ackerman asking you, the reader, to think about in this sentence? **R**

Dolphin Jumping. Lina Chesak.

DIANE ACKERMAN **425**

Assess

1. Answers will vary.

2. (a) They approach, swim close, and mimic them. (b) Humans would not get as close to strange animals.

3. (a) They use echolocation—bursts of sound that echo back. (b) Students might say that the categories represent information for survival or that these human categories do not apply.

4. (a) Sketch sheets with head, tail, and flank markings. (b) For identification, to track their history and habits

5. (a) Dervishes, wiggling, exhausting, puppyish, chase-and-tumble, hyperactive, rambunctious, ingenuity, zest (b) Answers will vary, but some students might say the dolphins sound fun and playful.

6. She compares the dolphins to bored children; mentions one individual by name, Nicky; and refers to Nicky as having "friends."

7. People don't acknowledge intelligence in other life-forms—it would jeopardize the uniqueness of humans.

8. (a) An adventure or a thrill, the sense of play described in the first paragraph, or wildness (b) She found a sense of play, but she also found an unexpected alien quality.

RESPONDING AND THINKING CRITICALLY

Respond

1. What detail or episode in the essay did you find most intriguing? Why?

Recall and Interpret

2. (a) In their first meeting, how do the dolphins react to the new humans? (b) How does this reaction illustrate some differences and similarities between humans and dolphins?

3. (a) How do dolphins sense the world around them? (b) Do you think the ideas Ackerman proposes about dolphin perception make sense? Why or why not?

4. (a) What kind of data did the research team collect? (b) Why are they interested in such data?

Analyze and Evaluate

5. (a) What descriptive words does Ackerman use to depict the dolphins' behavior? (b) Does she succeed in making their kind of play sound appealing for adult humans? Why or why not?

6. How does Ackerman anthropomorphize—that is, assign human characteristics to—the spotted dolphins?

7. What are Ackerman's views and feelings about intelligence in other life-forms? Cite evidence from the essay.

Connect

8. **Big Idea** Quests and Encounters (a) What do you think Ackerman is searching for at sea with the dolphins? (b) Ultimately, does she find what she is looking for? Explain.

YOU'RE THE CRITIC: DIFFERENT VIEWPOINTS

Eloquent exploration or self-indulgent journal?

Read the following two excerpts of literary criticism on Ackerman's book *Deep Play*. Notice the different reactions of each critic to Ackerman's work.

"Ackerman writes best when she balances her impressions with objective knowledge, like research on the functions of play. . . . When she maintains a reporter's outward focus, she can deliver the sharp, unexpected details that make a scene come alive. . . . Such particular observations, however, are outnumbered by the overly personalized, picturesque and predictable. . . . [The] book's meandering tone suggests a personal journal rather than a work of journalism. . . . It is as if Ackerman sometimes becomes so enthralled by chunks of her luxuriant language that she loses track of their cumulative effect. . . . Ackerman's often patronizing, self-indulgent tone does not encourage the reader's patience."

—Winifred Gallagher, the *New York Times*

"Diane Ackerman's perspective is a gift. . . . Her passions bubble up through her sincere words, bursting against her readers, infecting them with her love of life. . . . [The phenomenon of deep play] is a subject that Ackerman, a rapt and eloquent student of the world, is clearly an expert of: As a poet, prose-writer, and documentarian of scientific phenomena, she has a childlike sense of wonder. . . . and a poet's gift for expressing it."

—Meredith Phillips, the *Austin Chronicle*

Group Activity Discuss the following questions with classmates.

1. (a) What are the differences between these two critical views? (b) From your reading of "Encounter in the Sea," which critic do you agree with more? Support your opinion.

2. (a) What objections does Gallagher raise about Ackerman's writing? (b) What suggestions do you think Gallagher would give?

Different Viewpoints

1. (a) Gallagher responds negatively to *Deep Play*, while Phillips praises it. (b) Responses will vary.

2. (a) Gallagher thinks that Ackerman's book is "self-indulgent," "overly personalized," and short on "objective knowledge." (b) She might encourage Ackerman to find a balance between personal, emotional responses and objective, scientific information.

LITERARY ANALYSIS

Literary Element Descriptive Essay

A **descriptive essay** is a short piece of nonfiction writing that gives a detailed portrayal of a person, a place, an object, or an event. In the essay "Encounter in the Sea," Ackerman uses sensory details, or descriptions that appeal to one or more of the five senses, to communicate the unique experience of encountering wild spotted dolphins in the ocean. The details she uses may evoke an emotional response in the reader.

1. Identify two examples of sensory details that Ackerman includes in her essay. How do those details help describe her experience?

2. How would this essay be different if it were written as a formal essay, which is characterized by a serious and impersonal tone, or a persuasive essay, which is written with the purpose of convincing a reader to accept an opinion or idea? Do you think that one of those forms of essays would communicate Ackerman's experience better?

Review: Mood

As you learned on page 83, **mood** refers to the emotional quality or atmosphere of a piece of writing. A writer's choice of language, subject matter, setting, and tone, as well as sound devices and imagery, contribute to creating mood.

Partner Activity With a classmate, discuss the mood of this essay. Working with your partner, create a web diagram to show which elements of the essay contribute to the mood of the essay. In the center of your diagram, describe the overall mood.

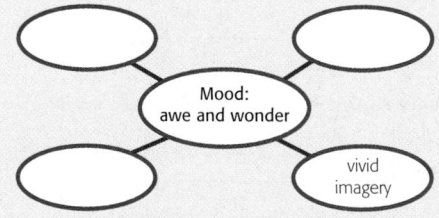

Mood: awe and wonder

vivid imagery

READING AND VOCABULARY

Reading Strategy Recognizing Author's Purpose

Sometimes an **author** will have more than one **purpose** for writing. Look for details in the essay and think about the purposes they serve. Record this information in a diagram like the one below.

to explain: Ackerman explains echolocation to show how dolphins perceive their surroundings.

Author's Purpose

to describe:

to entertain:

to persuade:

to inform:

1. Why do you think Ackerman wrote this essay?

2. What descriptions in the essay support Ackerman's purposes? Explain.

Vocabulary Practice

Word Origins Choose the language from which each word originated. Use a dictionary for help.

1. indelible
   a. Middle English **b.** Spanish

2. intermittent
   a. Sanskrit **b.** Latin

3. gregarious
   a. Norse **b.** Latin

4. ingenuity
   a. Latin **b.** Greek

Academic Vocabulary

Here is a word from the vocabulary list on page R82. This word will help you think, write, and talk about the selection.

flexible (flek′ sə bəl) *adj.* able to adjust easily

Practice and Apply
Why are dolphins **flexible** about whom they choose to play with?

DIANE ACKERMAN **427**

AFTER YOU READ

Assess

Literary Element

1. Answers will vary. Possible examples include "I could feel their streaming clicks"; "Taking a lungful of air, I dived after the ribbon . . ."; and "Night fell heavily, in thick black drapes."

2. Students' answers will vary according to how they respond to Ackerman's writing style. Some might think that her descriptions are essential for communicating her deeply personal experiences with nature. Others might prefer a more objective style.

Review: Mood

Students' web diagrams might include word choice describing the dolphins, the underwater setting, and the author's personal feelings about the experience.

Reading Strategy

1. Some students may think that Ackerman wrote the essay to advocate for animal rights; others might think that she wrote it to express her wonder at the natural world.

2. Ackerman's detailed descriptions draw the reader into the fascinating world of dolphins—their playfulness and their apparent ability to communicate and perhaps to think. Ackerman arouses within the reader a desire to experience her encounter with spotted dolphins and, in doing so, makes the reader sympathetic to her views of recognizing intelligence in other life-forms and affording them the same respect that we give people.

Vocabulary

1. a **2.** b **3.** b **4.** a

Academic Vocabulary

In interacting with humans, they appear to be more interested in playful interaction than in any particular individual.

427

Assess

Writing About Literature

Students' essays should

- analyze Ackerman's thesis and how she supports it
- include a clear thesis statement
- use correct grammar, spelling, and punctuation

Ackerman's Language and Style

Students' examples may include expressions such as "the following morning," "Soon it was joined by others," "Meanwhile, we tried to study their markings," and "Over the next week." How and in what order the events occurred would not be clear with the expressions of sequence.

Revising Check

Tell students that a good way of indicating sequence in their work is to use introductory words or phrases like *next, then, before, the following day, the previous night,* and so on.

Web Activities Have students access the Web site for interactive activities that will help them assess their understanding of the selection.

Writing About Literature

Analyze Thesis The thesis of an essay is its main idea. A thesis may be stated directly or implied. To make a thesis seem logical and convincing, the writer must support the thesis with anecdotes, descriptions, and other details. In your opinion, what is the thesis of Ackerman's essay? What anecdotes, descriptions, or other details does she use to support her thesis?

Write a brief essay analyzing Ackerman's thesis and the details she uses to support it. To help you organize your essay, write an outline of the main points in the selection. Include a discussion of Ackerman's thesis and her supporting evidence.

I. Paraphrase Thesis

   A.

   B.

II. Describe Details and Support the Thesis

   A.

   B.

III. Give Conclusions about Ackerman's Thesis and Supporting Details

   A.

   B.

After you complete your draft, meet with a peer reviewer to evaluate each other's work and to suggest revisions. Then proofread and edit your draft for errors.

Interdisciplinary Activity: Science

In your class, hold panel discussions by having groups of two or three students research topics related to dolphin interactions with humans, such as human-dolphin therapy, recreation, or casualties suffered by dolphins as a result of tuna fishing. Some questions your group may want to consider are:

1. How do interactions with dolphins enhance physical therapy? What specific benefits do they bring to people of all ages?

2. How can a community raise greater local and global awareness for marine life? Discuss the damaging effects of pollution and overfishing.

Ackerman's Language and Style

Describing the Sequence of Events Throughout the essay, Ackerman gives a detailed account of her time spent with spotted dolphins. She describes the experience in chronological order and with extreme attention to detail. Consider, for example, how much less effective her description would be without this detailed sequence of events:

> At 6:30 the following morning, we left the West End behind and cruised toward the Little Bahama Bank, a shallow area that spotted dolphins seem to prefer. After a few minutes, we hoisted the mainsail, from which two rows of short ties hung like fringe. Then we sat on benches or low deck chairs, finding shade under a large blue canopy. . . .

Notice some of Ackerman's effective indications of the sequence of events:

Details that show sequence
"Soon we entered the dreamtime . . ."
"Meanwhile, two other dolphins dived . . ."
"For an hour, the dolphins played . . ."
"By this time I needed to resurface . . ."

Activity Create a chart of your own, listing more examples of details that show the sequence of events in Ackerman's encounter. Think about how each example would be different without the information provided about sequence.

Revising Check

Sequence of Events It is important to consider sequence when revising your own writing. With a partner, go through your essay about Ackerman's essay on dolphins. Note places where describing the sequence of events would make your observations clearer. Revise your draft as necessary.

Literature Online **Web Activities** For eFlashcards, Selection Quick Checks, and other Web activities, go to www.glencoe.com.

Interdisciplinary Activity: Science

1. Some theories suggest that dolphins' echolocation can stimulate healing properties in the body and reduce hard-to-find, hard-to-treat physical damage. Studies also suggest dolphin therapy helps children with autism and learning disorders.

2. A community can spread the word about how we rely on marine life. Pollution and overfishing drastically decrease the populations of marine life that we depend on and benefit from.

428

The Tucson Zoo

MEET LEWIS THOMAS

Award-winning author Lewis Thomas was a renowned physician and research biologist. He taught at some of the top medical schools in the United States. As a writer, he established a reputation as a master of the short essay. In his inquisitive musings on nature, science, technology, and other subjects, he celebrated the mystery and marvel of life.

> *"We are built to make mistakes, coded for error."*
>
> —Lewis Thomas

Medical Background The son of a doctor and a nurse, Thomas had an early interest in the medical profession. He enrolled at Princeton University at fifteen and graduated when he was only nineteen years old. He entered Harvard Medical School at an exciting and dynamic time for the field of medicine—clinical science and antibiotics were both in the early stages of development. He graduated from medical school at the age of twenty-three.

During the course of his medical career, he worked at many U.S. universities, including

New York University, Yale, Johns Hopkins, Tulane, and the University of Minnesota. His roles at these institutions varied. Over the years, he worked as a researcher, teacher, administrator, and pediatrician, among other specialties. He also served in the U.S. Navy Medical Corps.

Writer and Researcher Thomas's interest in writing began almost as early as his interest in science and medicine. He developed an interest in poetry while at Princeton, and after medical school, during his internship at Boston City Hospital, supported himself in part by publishing poems in various magazines, including *Harper's Bazaar* and the *Saturday Evening Post*. Before becoming a respected prose writer, he began writing his essays simply "for fun."

Popular Appeal The interest and wonder that Thomas brought to both science and life was at the heart of his appeal to a wide audience. He combined common sense, daily observations, and detailed scientific knowledge in his writing. Thomas's philosophy of life and science could be symbolized by the concept of symbiosis, a relationship between organisms that benefits both. As one writer explained, "Thomas's scientific training enabled him to show how human biology is . . . linked to the biology of the planet as a whole."

Thomas's first book, *The Lives of a Cell: Notes of a Biology Watcher*, is a collection of essays originally published in his column in the *New England Journal of Medicine*. In 1975 *The Lives of a Cell: Notes of a Biology Watcher* won a National Book Award. Thomas's other works include *The Medusa and the Snail* (1979), *The Youngest Science* (1983), *Late Night Thoughts on Listening to Mahler's Ninth Symphony* (1983), and *The Fragile Species* (1992).

Lewis Thomas was born in 1913 and died in 1993.

 Author Search For more about Lewis Thomas, go to www.glencoe.com.

LEWIS THOMAS **429**

Focus

BELLRINGER

Bellringer Options
**Selection Focus Transparency 24
Daily Language Practice
Transparency 38**
Or write the word *altruism* on the board. Explain that the word means unselfish concern for others. It also refers to behavior exhibited by some animals that does not benefit the individual animal but does benefit the group. **Ask:** Can you think of animals that exhibit altruism? Have students discuss the ways in which these animals display altruism, and then have them discuss ways in which human beings can be altruistic.

Literature Online

Author Search To expand students' appreciation of Lewis Thomas, have them access the Web site for additional information and resources.

Selection Skills

Literary Elements
- Structure (SE pp. 430, 431, 434)

The Tucson Zoo

Listening/Speaking/Viewing Skills
- Debating Issues (SE p. 434)

Reading Skills
- Drawing Conclusions About Meaning (SE pp. 430, 432, 433, 434)

Vocabulary Skills
- Antonyms (SE p. 434)

Writing Skills/Grammar
- Semicolons (TWE p. 432)

Focus

Summary

On a visit to the Tucson Zoo, the narrator views a tank of otters and beavers from an underwater perspective. He is fascinated and realizes that some kind of positive response mechanism has been triggered in his brain. In analyzing the experience, the narrator concludes that "we hanker for friends" and that usefulness may be more important to civilization than individuality and solitary selfishness.

V Vocabulary

Vocabulary File Say: Add these words and definitions to your vocabulary file. For each word, include a sentence that gives you an example of how to use the word. **OL** Students with English language needs should include the pronunciations of these words in their files. **EL**

Literary Elements Have students access the Web site to improve their understanding of structure.

Connecting to the Essay

Thomas's personal reaction to some lively beavers and otters at the Tucson Zoo in Arizona reminds him that a scientist can miss the wonder of the whole when focusing only on the parts. Thomas realizes that his fascination with the animals has triggered some kind of positive response mechanism in his brain. Before you read the essay, think about the following questions:

- Do you like to analyze the component parts of things, or would you rather step back and look at the whole?
- Do you act on your instincts, or do you analyze your reactions and emotions?

Building Background

The cortex of the brain has two cerebral hemispheres, or sides. The left side is analytical; it allows one to recognize the parts, or details, of a whole. It cannot, however, combine the parts to let one see the whole. The right hemisphere is creative. It allows one to see the whole of something from its parts. The right side also allows one to be in a good mood while the left side controls darker moods. The *corpus callosum,* which Thomas refers to in his essay, is an arch of nervous tissue that bridges the two hemispheres and allows them to communicate with each other.

Setting Purposes for Reading

Big Idea Quests and Encounters

As you read Thomas's essay, notice how he explores his personal encounter and interprets it as a journey of human discovery.

Literary Element Structure

Structure refers to the particular order or pattern a writer uses to present ideas. Narratives commonly follow a chronological order, while the structure of persuasive or expository writing may vary. As you read, pay attention to how Thomas structures his essay.

- See Literary Terms Handbook, p. R17.

Literature Online Interactive Literary Elements Handbook To review or learn more about the literary elements, go to www.glencoe.com.

OBJECTIVES
In studying this selection, you will focus on the following:
- understanding the structure of an essay

Reading Preview

Reading Strategy Drawing Conclusions About Meaning

When readers **draw conclusions about meaning,** they are actively thinking about and interpreting content while they are reading.

Reading Tip: Asking and Answering Questions
Asking and then answering questions while you read can help you draw conclusions.

Question	Answer
Why does Thomas say that he "wanted no part of the science of beavers and otters"?	He is so enthralled by their antics that he does not want to analyze their behaviors.

Vocabulary

elation (i lā´shən) n. a feeling of great joy; ecstasy; p. 431 *The whole team experienced elation when Mara scored the winning goal.*

intact (in takt´) adj. entire; untouched, uninjured, and having all parts; p. 432 *She dropped the egg, but somehow it remained intact.*

exultation (eg´ zul tā´shən) n. joy; jubilation; p. 432 *The woman experienced exultation when her lost child was found.*

debasement (di bās´mənt) n. the state of being lowered in quality, value, or character; degradation; p. 433 *Those collectibles have suffered a debasement in their value recently.*

attribute (at´rə būt) n. a quality or characteristic of a person or thing; p. 433 *Honesty is a good attribute to possess.*

- drawing conclusions to develop different levels of meaning
- preparing and conducting a debate

Selection Resources

Print Materials
- Unit 2 Resources (Fast File), pp. 49–51
- Leveled Vocabulary Development, p. 31
- Selection and Unit Assessments, pp. 67–68
- Selection Quick Checks, p. 34

Transparencies
- Bellringer Options Transparencies:
  Selection Focus Transparency 24
  Daily Language Practice Transparency 38
- Literary Elements Transparency 59

Technology
- TeacherWorks Plus™ CD-ROM
- StudentWorks Plus™ CD-ROM
- Presentation Plus!™ CD-ROM
- Literature Online, glencoe.com
- Online Student Edition, mhln.com
- ExamView® Assessment Suite CD-ROM
- Vocabulary PuzzleMaker CD-ROM
- Listening Library, disc 1 track 35

The Tucson Zoo

Lewis Thomas

Science gets most of its information by the process of reductionism,[1] exploring the details, then the details of the details, until all the smallest bits of the structure, or the smallest parts of the mechanism, are laid out for counting and scrutiny. Only when this is done can the investigation be extended to encompass the whole organism or the entire system. So we say.

Sometimes it seems that we take a loss, working this way. Much of today's public anxiety about science is the apprehension that we may forever be overlooking the whole by an endless, obsessive preoccupation with the parts. I had a brief, personal experience of this misgiving one afternoon in Tucson, where I had time on my hands and visited the zoo, just outside the city. The designers there have cut a deep pathway between two small artificial ponds, walled by clear glass, so when you stand in the center of the path you can look into the depths of each pool, and at the same time you can regard the surface. In one pool, on the right side of the path, is a family of otters; on the other side, a family of beavers. Within just a few feet from your face, on either side, beavers and otters are at play, underwater and on the surface, swimming toward your face and then away, more filled with life than any creatures I have ever seen before, in all my days. Except for the glass, you could reach across and touch them.

I was transfixed. As I now recall it, there was only one sensation in my head: pure **elation** mixed with amazement at such perfection. Swept off my feet, I floated from one side to the other, swiveling my brain, staring astounded at the beavers, then at the otters. I could hear shouts across my corpus callosum, from one hemisphere to the other. I remember

---

1. *Reductionism* is a method of explaining complex processes or structures by reducing them to more basic principles or units.

Literary Element Structure *How does this sentence change the essay's structure?* **L**

Vocabulary

elation (i lā´shən) *n.* a feeling of great joy; ecstasy

LEWIS THOMAS **431**

English Language Coach

Individuals or Groups Discuss with English-language learners how their native cultures view the role of the individual; for example, what happens when a person does not act as expected in that culture? Sometimes change comes when an individual or a group decides to act in ways different from what is expected and encourages others to do the same. Ask groups of students to discuss what the result may be. Have each group write a report about a country where individuals or groups brought about change. **EL**

Objectives
• To understand the structure of an essay (SE)

431

Teach

R1 **Reading Strategy**

Drawing Conclusions
About Meaning Answer:
He cannot escape his habit of reductionist thinking. **OL**

R2 **Reading Strategy**

Drawing Conclusions
About Meaning Answer: *He has turned his reductionist thinking upon himself and has reduced himself to parts.* **OL**

★ **Writer's Technique**

Voice Explain that *voice* in writing is how an author uses language to reveal his or her personality. Lewis uses words and phrases that allow the reader to see him as a rational scientist and as a human being awed by animals. Encourage students to look for words and phrases as they read that display voice. **AS**

---

thinking, with what was left in charge of my consciousness, that I wanted no part of the science of beavers and otters; I wanted never to know how they performed their marvels; I wished for no news about the physiology[2] of their breathing, the coordination of their muscles, their vision, their endocrine systems,[3] their digestive tracts. I hoped never to have to think of them as collections of cells. All I asked for was the full hairy complexity, then ★ in front of my eyes, of whole, **intact** beavers and otters in motion.

It lasted, I regret to say, for only a few minutes, and then I was back in the late twentieth century, reductionist as ever, wondering about the details by force of habit, but not, this time, the details of otters and beavers. Instead, me. Something worth remembering had happened in my mind, I was certain of that; I would

have put it somewhere in the brain stem; maybe this was my limbic system[4] at work. I became a behavioral scientist, an experimental psychologist, an ethologist,[5] and in the instant I lost all the wonder and the sense of being overwhelmed. I was flattened.

But I came away from the zoo with something, a piece of news about myself: I am coded, somehow, for otters and beavers. I exhibit instinctive behavior in their presence, when they are displayed close at hand behind glass, simultaneously below water and at the surface. I have receptors[6] for this display. Beavers and otters possess a "releaser" for me, in the terminology of ethology, and the releasing was my experience. What was released? Behavior. What behavior? Standing, swiveling flabbergasted, feeling **exultation**

---

2. *Physiology* is the branch of biology that studies the functions of living organisms and their parts.
3. The *endocrine system* consists of glands that secrete hormones into the bloodstream, affecting such bodily processes as growth and sexual development.

Reading Strategy Drawing Conclusions About Meaning
What does Thomas come to realize by this statement? **R1**

Vocabulary

intact (in takt´) *adj.* entire; untouched, uninjured, and having all parts

4. The *limbic system* is a region of the brain involved in the control of emotions and some types of behavior.
5. *Ethology* (eth ol´ə jē) is the study of animal behavior, including instinctive, or inherited, behavior.
6. *Receptor* refers to a sensory nerve cell that responds to a stimulus in the environment and sends a message to the brain.

Reading Strategy Drawing Conclusions About Meaning
Why does Thomas feel flattened at this moment? **R2**

Vocabulary

exultation (eg´ zul tā´shən) *n.* joy; jubilation

432 UNIT 2 NONFICTION

Additional Support

Skills Practice

GRAMMAR: Semicolons Write on the board: *Something worth remembering had happened in my mind, I was certain of that; I would have put it somewhere in the brain stem; maybe this was my limbic system at work.* Circle the semicolons and ask why they are used in this sentence. Point out that a semicolon

is used to join main clauses that are not joined by a coordinating conjunction. Ask students to rewrite the following, using semicolons: *On the other side of the glass were beavers and otters at play. These animals dove beneath the surface, played underwater, and swam toward us.* **OL** Have more advanced students and a rush of friendship. I could not, as the result of the transaction, tell you anything more about beavers and otters than you already know. I learned nothing new about them. Only about me, and I suspect also about you, maybe about human beings at large: we are endowed with genes which code out our reaction to beavers and otters, maybe our reaction to each other as well. We are stamped with stereotyped, unalterable patterns of response, ready to be released. And the behavior released in us, by such confrontations, is, essentially, a surprised affection. It is compulsory behavior and we can avoid it only by straining with the full power of our conscious minds, making up conscious excuses all the way. Left to ourselves, mechanistic and autonomic,[7] we hanker for friends.

Everyone says, stay away from ants. They have no lessons for us; they are crazy little instruments, inhuman, incapable of controlling themselves, lacking manners, lacking souls. When they are massed together, all touching, exchanging bits of information held in their jaws like memoranda, they become a single animal. Look out for that. It is a **debasement**, a loss of individuality, a violation of human nature, an unnatural act.

Sometimes people argue this point of view seriously and with deep thought. Be individuals, solitary and selfish, is the message. Altruism,[8] a jargon word for what used to be called love, is worse than weakness, it is sin, a violation of nature. Be separate. Do not be a social animal. But this is a hard argument to make convincingly when you have to depend on language to make it. You have to print up leaflets or publish books and get them bought and sent around, you have to turn up on television and catch the attention of millions of other human beings all at once, and then you have to say to all of them, all at once, all collected and paying attention: be solitary; do not depend on each other. You can't do this and keep a straight face.

Maybe altruism is our most primitive **attribute,** out of reach, beyond our control. Or perhaps it is immediately at hand, waiting to be released, disguised now, in our kind of civilization, as affection or friendship or attachment. I don't see why it should be unreasonable for all human beings to have strands of DNA coiled up in chromosomes, coding out instincts for usefulness and helpfulness. Usefulness may turn out to be the hardest test of fitness for survival, more important than aggression, more effective, in the long run, than grabbiness. If this is the sort of information biological science holds for the future, applying to us as well as to ants, then I am all for science.

One thing I'd like to know most of all: when those ants have made the Hill, and are all there, touching and exchanging, and the whole mass begins to behave like a single huge creature, and *thinks*, what on earth is that thought? And while you're at it, I'd like to know a second thing: when it happens, does any single ant know about it? Does his hair stand on end? ∾

Visual Vocabulary
Chromosomes are strands of DNA and proteins in the nucleus of cells. DNA carries the genes that pass on hereditary information from parent to child.

---

7. In psychology, *compulsory* means "arising from an irresistible, illogical urge." Here, *mechanistic* means physically or biologically determined, and *autonomic* means involuntary and spontaneous.
8. In ethology, *altruism* is an animal's self-sacrificing behavior that benefits another animal or group of animals. Similarly, in humans, the term means "unselfish concern for others."

Big Idea Quests and Encounters *How does the encounter with beavers and otters lead Thomas to this conclusion?* **BI**

Reading Strategy Drawing Conclusions About Meaning *Explain what you think the author means in this sentence.* **R₃**

Vocabulary
debasement (di bās′mənt) *n.* the state of being lowered in quality, value, or character; degradation

Vocabulary
attribute (at′rə būt) *n.* a quality or characteristic of a person or thing

LEWIS THOMAS **433**

Assess

1. Answers will vary.

2. (a) Only after its parts have been studied in detail (b) He is fascinated by their whole behavior.

3. (a) Because they act collectively and are not individuals (b) How to work together for the good of all

4. (a) It may be our most primitive and important instinct (b) He wonders if any one ant is aware of what is happening

5. To be useful and value love and friendship within a group

6. Many people have felt the need for friendship and love.

7. Thomas concludes that the whole is more important than the details, yet points to the individual's role and reaction.

8. (a) New encounters can help you learn about yourself and others. (b) Some students might say that Thomas is on a quest for understanding of himself or the world.

Literary Element

1. The essay uses cause and effect: the author's zoo trip triggers his meditations.

2. Students should support their answers with textual evidence.

Web Activities Have students access the Web site for interactive activities that will help them assess their understanding of the selection.

RESPONDING AND THINKING CRITICALLY

Respond

1. Were you surprised by Thomas's conclusions about people? Why or why not?

Recall and Interpret

2. (a) According to the process of reductionism, when can an entire organism be investigated? (b) How does this process contrast with the author's experience with the beavers and otters?

3. (a) According to Thomas, why does everyone say to "stay away from ants"? (b) What message do some people learn from ants?

4. (a) What ideas does Thomas present about altruism? (b) What do you think Thomas means in his final reference to ants?

Analyze and Evaluate

5. In your opinion, what was Thomas's purpose?

6. Do you agree with the conclusions that Thomas draws about instinctive behavior in people? Explain.

7. In your opinion, is Thomas a reductionist? Explain your answer.

Connect

8. **Big Idea** **Quests and Encounters** (a) What does this essay suggest that new encounters can do for a person? (b) Would you say that Thomas is on a quest? If so, what is his quest?

LITERARY ANALYSIS

Literary Element **Structure**

There is a variety of ways in which writers can order their ideas in expository writing. For example, the **structure** can follow a pattern of cause and effect, or describe a problem and offer a solution.

1. How would you describe the essay's structure?

2. Can you think of an alternative structure for this essay? Do you think your proposed alternative would be more or less effective? Explain.

Debating

In this essay, Thomas expresses some doubt about using reductionism as the main process for gaining information. He shows concern that by focusing on the smallest details, we might lose sight of the whole of what we study. With a partner, prepare a debate in which one person argues for using reductionism as the primary method and the other argues for using the "big picture" method. Once you have prepared and practiced debating, present your debate to the rest of your class.

Literature Online **Web Activities** For eFlashcards, Selection Quick Checks, and other Web activities, go to www.glencoe.com.

READING AND VOCABULARY

Reading Strategy **Drawing Conclusions About Meaning**

Readers **draw conclusions** at different points in the reading experience in order to create different levels of **meaning.**

1. What conclusions about himself and other people does Thomas draw from his experience?

2. List three details from the essay that helped you draw a conclusion about whether Thomas is a reductionist.

Vocabulary Practice

Practice with Antonyms Find the antonym for each vocabulary word.

1. debasement
   a. improvement   **b.** lapse
2. intact
   a. apart   **b.** selective
3. elation
   a. joy   **b.** sorrow
4. exultation
   a. understanding   **b.** depression

Reading Strategy

1. That we all long for friends

2. Possible answers: "I exhibit instinctive behavior," "instincts for usefulness and helpfulness," "never to have to think about . . . collections of cells," "no news about the physiology."

Debating

Review the rules and etiquette for debating with the class before students present their debates.

Vocabulary

1. a 2. a 3. b 4. b

Straw into Gold: The Metamorphosis of the Everyday

MEET SANDRA CISNEROS

Sandra Cisneros is one of the most distinctive voices in American literature today. Born in Chicago to a Mexican American mother and a Mexican father, Cisneros spent her childhood living uncomfortably between two worlds. The family frequently traveled back and forth to Mexico for extended periods of time. Each time they returned to the United States, the family would settle in a new location and at a new school within Chicago's *barrios.* The numerous moves made it difficult for Cisneros to make friends. Being the only girl in a family of brothers did not help either, as she was often left out and overlooked.

Because she was shy, she was often lonely. But, Cisneros writes, "that loneliness . . . was good for a would-be writer—it allowed me time to think and think, to imagine, to read and prepare myself." In high school, a teacher helped Cisneros nurture her love of writing. After high school, Cisneros received a scholarship to Loyola University in Chicago. She graduated in 1976 with a bachelor's degree in English, and went on to the prestigious University of Iowa Writers' Workshop. At the Writer's Workshop, Cisneros felt keenly aware of her outsider status.

> "You can't erase what you know. You can't forget who you are."
>
> —Sandra Cisneros

Finding Her Voice Yet, it was at the Iowa Writers' Workshop that Cisneros found her voice. She realized that the very thing she had tried to escape—the shame and separation of being different—made her unique in a sea of sameness. She knew then that her role as a writer was to depict the loneliness, isolation, tragedies, and triumphs of the outsider.

Mango Street In 1982 Cisneros received her first National Endowment for the Arts grant, which allowed her to write full-time. Two years later, she published her breakthrough work, *The House on Mango Street.* It was wildly successful with critics and readers alike.

The House on Mango Street is a series of vignettes about a young girl, Esperanza, growing up in a Chicago barrio. The stories, a blend of fiction and poetry, echo Cisneros's own youth and her yearning to make sense of her life in relation to her surroundings. Like the author, Esperanza is painfully aware of her status as an outsider.

After the success of her first work, Cisneros went on to publish other works of fiction: *Woman Hollering Creek* (1991) and *Caramelo* (2002). She has also published two collections of poetry, including *My Wicked, Wicked Ways* (1987) and *Loose Woman* (1992).

In 1995 Cisneros received a MacArthur Fellowship—a prestigious monetary award known as the "genius grant." The award is an official acknowledgement of her permanent status in the American literary world.

Sandra Cisneros was born in 1954.

Literature Online **Author Search** For more about Sandra Cisneros, go to www.glencoe.com.

Focus

BELLRINGER

Bellringer Options
Daily Language Practice Transparency 39
Or write *Experiences* on the board. **Ask:** What personal experiences could you write about? Have students discuss some experiences and how they could become stories or parts of stories.

Literature Online

Author Search To expand students' appreciation of Sandra Cisneros, have them access the Web site for additional information and resources.

Selection Skills

Literary Elements
- Reflective Essay (SE pp. 436, 438, 440, 441)
- Thesis (SE p. 441)

Straw into Gold

Reading Skills
- Analyzing Text Structure (SE pp. 436, 438, 439, 442)

Vocabulary Skills
- Analogies (SE pp. 436, 442)
- Academic Vocabulary (SE p. 442)
- Context Clues (TWE p. 438)

Listening/Speaking/Viewing Skills
- Analyzing Art (TWE pp. 437, 449)

Writing Skills/Grammar
- Applying Form (SE p. 442)
- Noun Phrases (TWE p. 440)

Focus

Summary

After relating a challenging, but inspiring, experience making tortillas in France, Sandra Cisneros describes her development as a writer. She describes how her childhood experiences and observations have fueled the characters and ideas in her writing. Cisneros talks about the influence of her family life on her identity and art. She concludes by saying that she has picked straw from her life and spun it into gold through her writing.

V Vocabulary

Vocabulary File Say: Add these words and definitions to your vocabulary file. For each word, include a sentence that gives you an example of how to use the word. **OL** Students with English language needs should include the pronunciations of these words in their files. **EL**

Literary Elements Have students access the Web site to improve their understanding of reflective essays.

Connecting to the Essay

"Straw into Gold: The Metamorphosis of the Everyday" is an essay in which the author reflects on how her life sculpted her into the writer she is today. Before you read the essay, think about the following questions:

- What elements of your past have transformed your life?
- Does thinking about the past help you understand the person you are today?

Building Background

In this selection, you will read about how Cisneros lived in Europe with the aid of a grant awarded by the National Endowment for the Arts (NEA). The NEA is a public agency designed to support the arts financially, to expose all people in the United States to art, and to provide arts education. The NEA was created by Congress in 1965 and is an independent part of the federal government. Artists of every medium, from dance to literature, apply to the NEA for grant money they can use to support themselves while pursuing artistic endeavors. The NEA is the largest funder of the arts in the United States.

Setting Purposes for Reading

Big Idea Quests and Encounters

As you read this essay, notice how Cisneros connects everyday life to the idea of the heroic quest.

Literary Element Reflective Essay

A **reflective essay** is a type of personal essay in which the author thinks back on events or themes in her or his life and connects them to the present. A reflective essay is usually written in a light, conversational style and, while entertaining the reader, it also provides insight into the author's personal experiences and how those experiences are reflected in the author's work.

- See Literary Terms Handbook, p. R14.

Literature Online Interactive Literary Elements Handbook To review or learn more about the literary elements, go to www.glencoe.com.

OBJECTIVES
In studying this selection, you will focus on the following:
- understanding reflective essays
- analyzing text structure
- analyzing an author's thesis
- writing to apply form

436 UNIT 2 NONFICTION

Reading Strategy Analyzing Text Structure

Text structure is the particular order or pattern a writer uses to present ideas. A reflective essay is an example of narrative writing. Narratives commonly follow a chronological order, while the structure of persuasive or expository writing may vary. Listing detailed information, using cause and effect, or describing a problem and then offering a solution are some other ways in which a writer can present a topic.

Reading Tip: Asking Questions To analyze text structure, it might be useful to ask yourself questions as you read. Use a chart to record your questions and the answers you uncover as you read.

Question	Answer
Are the ideas presented in chronological order?	No, they are not in time order.

Vocabulary

intuitively (in tōō´ ə tiv lē) adv. knowing, sensing, understanding; instinctively; p. 438 *The stand-up comedian intuitively knew what not to joke about.*

taboo (tə bōō´) n. a cultural or social rule forbidding something; p. 438 *Speaking disrespectfully to one's elders is taboo.*

nomadic (nō mad´ik) adj. moving from place to place; wandering; p. 438 *After she finished college, my sister was nomadic, traveling the world.*

nostalgia (nos tal´jə) n. a longing for things or people of the past; p. 439 *Seeing my old friends created feelings of nostalgia for my college days.*

Vocabulary Tip: Analogies An analogy is a comparison that shows the relationship between two words or ideas that are otherwise dissimilar or unrelated.

Selection Resources

Print Materials
- Unit 2 Resources (Fast File), pp. 52–54
- Leveled Vocabulary Development, p. 32
- Selection and Unit Assessments, pp. 69–70
- Selection Quick Checks, p. 35

Transparencies
- Bellringer Options Transparencies: Daily Language Practice Transparency 39
- Literary Elements Transparency 34

Technology
- TeacherWorks Plus™ CD-ROM
- StudentWorks Plus™ CD-ROM
- Presentation Plus!™ CD-ROM
- Literature Online, glencoe.com
- Online Student Edition, mhln.com
- Exam*View*® Assessment Suite CD-ROM
- Vocabulary PuzzleMaker CD-ROM
- Listening Library, disc 1 track 36

STRAW INTO GOLD

The Metamorphosis of the Everyday

Sandra Cisneros

Women Making Tortilla Dough. Diego Rivera. Fresco. Court of Labour. Ministry of Public Information, Mexico.

Teach

L Literary Element

Reflective Essay Ask: What details hint that this is a reflective essay? *(It's a personal experience; the style is conversational.)* **OL**

★ Viewing the Art

Diego Rivera (1886–1957) was one of Mexico's greatest artists. Rivera created and displayed his works in public places, so they could be viewed by his favorite subjects—common workers. **AS**

✓ CheckPoint

Use the CheckPoint questions on Presentation Plus! to monitor students' comprehension. These questions can be used with interactive response keypads for immediate student feedback.

When I was living in an artists' colony in the south of France, some fellow Latin-Americans who taught at the university in Aix-en-Provence invited me to share a home-cooked meal with them. I had been living abroad almost a year then on an NEA[1] grant, subsisting mainly on French bread and lentils so that my money could last longer. So when the invitation to dinner arrived, I accepted without hesitation. Especially since they had promised Mexican food.

What I didn't realize when they made this invitation was that I was supposed to be involved in preparing the meal. I guess they assumed I knew how to cook Mexican food because I am Mexican. They wanted specifically tortillas, though I'd never made a tortilla in my life.

It's true I had witnessed my mother rolling the little armies of dough into perfect circles, but my mother's family is from Guanajuato; they are *provincianos*, country folk. They only know how to make flour tortillas. My father's family, on the other hand, is *chilango*[2] from Mexico City. We ate corn tortillas but we didn't make them. Someone was sent to the corner tortilleria to buy some. I'd never seen anybody make corn tortillas. Ever.

Somehow my Latino hosts had gotten a hold of a packet of corn flour, and this is what they tossed my way with orders to

---

1. The *NEA* is the National Endowment for the Arts—a federal agency that funds artistic projects of organizations and individuals.

2. *Chilango* (chē län´ gō) is a Mexican slang term that means "native to Mexico City."

SANDRA CISNEROS **437**

Readability Scores
Dale-Chall: 6.8
DRP: 57
Lexile: 930

Differentiated Instruction

Pronunciation Students for whom reading does not come easily are likely to have difficulty pronouncing the Spanish words in this selection. Write some of the Spanish words and terms and their pronunciations on the board. Guide the class to pronounce these words and terms correctly. **EL**

Reading in the Real World

College The selection mentions the author's MFA degree and the grant she received from the National Endowment for the Arts. Have students do some research on different MFA programs and the various grants available through the NEA. **OL**

Objective
• To understand reflective essays (SE)

437

Quests and Encounters

Answer: *Cisneros felt that she was faced with an impossible task. She did not want to disappoint her friends, who assumed that because she was of Mexican descent, she could make tortillas.* **OL**

R1 **Reading Strategy**

Analyzing Text Structure

Answer: *Answers may vary. Students may say that it begins with an incident that happens in France and then develops chronologically to show how the author triumphed over adversity.* **Ask:** Why might the author have begun the essay with the incident in France? *(The incident sets up the theme of the essay and connects it to the title. The incident is also an interesting story that captures the reader's attention.)* **OL**

L **Literary Element**

Reflective Essay **Answer:**
Students should note that culture, heritage, and upbringing are woven into her writing. **OL**

produce tortillas. *Así como sea.* Any ol' way, they said and went back to their cooking.

Why did I feel like the woman in the fairy tale who was locked in a room and ordered to spin straw into gold? I had the same sick feeling when I was required to write my critical essay for the MFA[3] exam—the only piece of noncreative writing necessary in order to get my graduate degree. How was I to start? There were rules involved here, unlike writing a poem or story, which I did **intuitively**. There was a step by step process needed and I had better know it. I felt as if making tortillas—or writing a critical paper, for that matter—were tasks so impossible I wanted to break down into tears.

Somehow though, I managed to make tortillas—crooked and burnt, but edible nonetheless. My hosts were absolutely ignorant when it came to Mexican food; they thought my tortillas were delicious. (I'm glad my mama wasn't there.) Thinking back and looking at an old photograph documenting the three of us consuming those lopsided circles I am amazed. Just as I am amazed I could finish my MFA exam.

I've managed to do a lot of things in my life I didn't think I was capable of and which many others didn't think I was capable of either. Especially because I am a woman, a Latina, an only daughter in a family of six men. My father would've liked to have seen me married long ago. In our culture men and women don't leave their father's house except by way of marriage. I crossed my father's threshold with

nothing carrying me but my own two feet. A woman whom no one came for and no one chased away.

To make matters worse, I left before any of my six brothers had ventured away from home. I broke a terrible **taboo**. Somehow, looking back at photos of myself as a child, I wonder if I was aware of having begun already my own quiet war.

I like to think that somehow my family, my Mexicanness, my poverty, all had something to do with shaping me into a writer. I like to think my parents were preparing me all along for my life as an artist even though they didn't know it. From my father I inherited a love of wandering. He was born in Mexico City but as a young man he traveled into the U.S. vagabonding. He eventually was drafted and thus became a citizen. Some of the stories he has told about his first months in the U.S. with little or no English surface in my stories in *The House on Mango Street* as well as others I have in mind to write in the future. From him I inherited a sappy heart. (He still cries when he watches Mexican soaps—especially if they deal with children who have forsaken their parents.)

My mother was born like me—in Chicago but of Mexican descent. It would be her tough streetwise voice that would haunt all my stories and poems. An amazing woman who loves to draw and read books and can sing an opera. A smart cookie.

When I was a little girl we traveled to Mexico City so much I thought my grandparents' house on La Fortuna, number 12, was home. It was the only constant in our **nomadic** ramblings from one Chicago flat to another. The house on Destiny Street, number 12, in the colonia Tepeyac would be

---

3. *MFA* stands for Master of Fine Arts—an academic degree.

Big Idea Quests and Encounters *Why does Cisneros use this particular analogy?* **BI**

Reading Strategy Analyzing Text Structure *Explain how the essay has been structured so far.* **R1**

Vocabulary

intuitively (in tōō′ə tiv lē) *adv.* knowing, sensing, understanding; instinctively

Literary Element Reflective Essay *How has Cisneros's family become a source for her writing?* **L**

Vocabulary

taboo (tə bōō′) *n.* a cultural or social rule forbidding something

nomadic (nō mad′ik) *adj.* moving from place to place; wandering

Additional Support

VOCABULARY: Context Clues

Say: You can often figure out the meanings of words by looking at their context, the surrounding words and sentences.

Have students look at the sentences that contain the words *intuitively, taboo,* and *nomadic.* Have them find context

clues that give hints to their definitions. *(Don't need to know "rules" to do something* intuitively; *a* taboo *is something "terrible" (a rule) that can be broken;* nomadic *is "rambling" from one place to another.)* **OL**

South Side Street, Franklin McMahon. ⭐

perhaps the only home I knew, and that **nostalgia** for a home would be a theme that would obsess me.

My brothers also figured greatly in my art. Especially the older two; I grew up in their shadows. Henry, the second oldest and my favorite, appears often in poems I have written and in stories which at times only borrow his nickname, Kiki. He played a major role in my childhood. We were bunk-bed mates. We were co-conspirators. We were pals. Until my oldest brother came back from studying in Mexico and left me odd woman out for always.

What would my teachers say if they knew I was a writer now? Who would've guessed it? I wasn't a very bright student. I didn't much like school because we moved so much and I was always new and funny looking. In my fifth-grade report card I have nothing but an avalanche of C's and D's, but I don't remember being that stupid. I was good at art and I read plenty of library books and Kiki laughed at all my jokes. At home I was fine, but at school I never opened my mouth except when the teacher called on me.

When I think of how I see myself it would have to be at age eleven. I know I'm thirty-two on the outside, but inside I'm eleven. I'm the girl in the picture with skinny arms and a crumpled skirt and

Vocabulary

nostalgia (nos tal´jə) a longing for things or people of the past

Reading Strategy Analyzing Text Structure *How does the essay's middle section differ from the beginning?* **R2**

SANDRA CISNEROS **439**

Teach

Quests and Encounters

Answer: *Texas has a large population of people of Mexican descent. Cisneros mentions a mayor with the same last name as hers and other Chicanas and Chicanos as artists, writers, and politicians.* **Ask:** What phase of the author's quest does Texas represent? *(Texas seems to represent a type of returning home, a completion of the quest and her soul-searching. Because she is a wanderer at heart who feels only a mild sense of true home, however, the return home is mostly metaphorical.)* **OL**

L Literary Element

Reflective Essay

Answer: *Students may say that the straw represents her life experiences that she has turned into gold through her writing.* **OL**

✓CheckPoint

Use the CheckPoint questions on Presentation Plus! to check students' mastery of the selection. These questions can be used with interactive response keypads for immediate student feedback.

---

crooked hair. I didn't like school because all they saw was the outside me. School was lots of rules and sitting with your hands folded and being very afraid all the time. I liked looking out the window and thinking. I liked staring at the girl across the way writing her name over and over again in red ink. I wondered why the boy with the dirty collar in front of me didn't have a mama who took better care of him.

I think my mama and papa did the best they could to keep us warm and clean and never hungry. We had birthday and graduation parties and things like that, but there was another hunger that had to be fed. There was a hunger I didn't even have a name for. Was this when I began writing?

In 1966 we moved into a house, a real one, our first real home. This meant we didn't have to change schools and be the new kids on the block every couple of years. We could make friends and not be afraid we'd have to say goodbye to them and start all over. My brothers and the flock of boys they brought home would become important characters eventually for my stories—Louie and his cousins, Meme Ortiz and his dog with two names, one in English and one in Spanish.

My mother flourished in her own home. She took books out of the library and taught herself to garden—to grow flowers so envied we had to put a lock on the gate to keep out the midnight flower thieves. My mother has never quit gardening.

This was the period in my life, that slippery age when you are both child and woman and neither, I was to record in *The House on Mango Street*. I was still shy. I was a girl who couldn't come out of her shell.

How was I to know I would be recording and documenting the women who sat their sadness on an elbow and stared out a window? It would be the city streets of Chicago I would later record, as seen through a child's eyes.

I've done all kinds of things I didn't think I could do since then. I've gone to a prestigious university, studied with famous writers, and taken an MFA degree. I've taught poetry in schools in Illinois and Texas. I've gotten an NEA grant and run away with it as far as my courage would take me. I've seen the bleached and bitter mountains of the Peloponnesus.[4] I've lived on an island. I've been to Venice twice. I've lived in Yugoslavia. I've been to the famous Nice[5] flower market behind the opera house. I've lived in a village in the pre-Alps and witnessed the daily parade of promenaders.

I've moved since Europe to the strange and wonderful country of Texas, land of Polaroid-blue skies and big bugs. I met a mayor with my last name. I met famous Chicana and Chicano artists and writers and *políticos.*[6]

Texas is another chapter in my life. It brought with it the Dobie-Paisano Fellowship, a six-month residency on a 265-acre ranch. But most important, Texas brought Mexico back to me.

In the days when I would sit at my favorite people-watching spot, the snakey Woolworth's counter across the street from the Alamo[7] (the Woolworth's which has since been torn down to make way for progress), I couldn't think of anything else I'd rather be than a writer. I've traveled and lectured from Cape Cod to San Francisco, to Spain, Yugoslavia, Greece, Mexico, France, Italy, and now today to Texas. Along the way there has been straw for the taking. With a little imagination, it can be spun into gold. ∾

---

4. *Peloponnesus* (pĕl´ə pə nē´ səs) is the peninsula forming the southern part of mainland Greece.
5. *Nice* (nēs) is a port city in southern France.
6. *Políticos* (pô lē´ tē kôs) means "politicians."
7. The *Alamo* is a mission chapel in San Antonio, Texas. It was the site of a famous battle in Texas's war for independence from Mexico.

Big Idea Quests and Encounters *In what ways does Texas bring Mexico back to Cisneros?* **BI**

Literary Element Reflective Essay *What do straw and gold represent for Cisneros?* **L**

Additional Support

Skills Practice

GRAMMAR: Noun Phrases **Say:** A noun phrase consists of a noun and its modifiers but functions as a single unit, such as "burnt, crooked tortillas" and "her parents' expectations." Write the following examples on the board and have students identify the noun phrases in each sentence (answers are italicized):

1. *Her favorite brother of all* influenced her writing.

2. *The dislocated child in the family* felt connected when she visited *her grandparents' welcoming home.* **OL**

RESPONDING AND THINKING CRITICALLY

Respond

1. (a)How does Cisneros show that her childhood relates to her experiences as a writer? (b)What things in Cisneros's experience of life are similar to your own?

Recall and Interpret

2. (a)How was Cisneros's departure from her family home atypical of her culture? (b)What does this suggest about Cisneros as a person?

3. (a)How does Cisneros describe her mother? (b)What does this description suggest about how Cisneros feels about her mother?

4. (a)Why did Cisneros not enjoy school? (b)What do her memories of school reveal about the kind of child Cisneros was?

Analyze and Evaluate

5. How is Cisneros's difficult experience trying to make corn tortillas an effective analogy for her life?

6. (a)How would you describe Cisneros's narrative style? (b)Did her style capture your attention? Why?

7. Explain how Cisneros succeeds in creating a nostalgic atmosphere in her essay.

Connect

8. **Big Idea** **Quests and Encounters** Cisneros goes on a quest to trace her own origins as a writer. In what ways does her essay help her succeed on this quest?

LITERARY ANALYSIS

Literary Element **Reflective Essay**

The purpose of a **reflective essay** is to show how the past is relevant to the present. Like other types of personal essays, the reflective essay uses informal language and tone, and often reflects an incident or experience in the writer's life. The author's purpose for writing a reflective essay may be to share an insight with his or her audience about a significant personal event, or simply to entertain them. In this reflective essay, Cisneros describes and evaluates how her experiences as a child and in early adulthood helped shape her writing style and her role as a writer.

1. How is Cisneros's past relevant to her present life?

2. What are some examples of informal tone or language in Cisneros's essay?

3. In your opinion, why does Cisneros want to share her reflections with readers?

Review: Thesis

As you learned on page 403, the **thesis** is the main idea in a nonfiction selection. The thesis may be stated or implied. Some writers may use an implied thesis when they want a reader to draw his or her own conclusions.

Partner Activity Pair up with a classmate and discuss the thesis of "Straw into Gold." Working with your partner, create a graphic organizer similar to the one below. Fill in what you think might be the thesis of the essay. Then fill in the boxes with supporting details.

SANDRA CISNEROS **441**

Literary Element

1. Her past is used as the basis for her present life as a writer.

2. The tone is conversational, blending dialogue and narration— "Any ol' way, they said and went back to their cooking"—and using slang and colloquial expressions, such as "mama and papa" and "people watching."

3. Perhaps to show that people can learn and grow from their past.

Review: Thesis

Students may say the thesis is that obstacles can be surmounted through hard work and determination. Details: Earning an MFA; awarded an NEA grant; studied with famous writers

---

Assess

1. (a) Childhood experiences are essential to how she sees and writes about life. (b) Answers will vary.

2. (a) Most women in traditional Latino culture leave home only to marry. (b) Indicates Cisneros's independent personality.

3. (a) Cisneros describes her mother as an "amazing woman who loves to draw and read books and can sing an opera." (b) She has great respect for her mother.

4. (a) Her family traveled so much that she was always in a new school and always felt "funny looking." (b) She was a shy, withdrawn, and possibly lonely child.

5. It represents one of the many seemingly impossible tasks that she manages to perform successfully.

6. (a) Some students may say that her style is casual and conversational. (b) Students may say that Cisneros' style captures their attention because they feel she is speaking directly to them.

7. Students may say that she succeeds because she describes the past in such poignant detail.

8. She succeeds on this quest because she concludes that she can overcome difficult obstacles and weave her many life experiences into her writing.

Assess

Reading Strategy

1. Cisneros organizes the essay into four sections: the opening anecdote; reflections about her parents; reflections about her childhood; and a conclusion about the amazing things she has done, the places she has visited, and how all of her experience is reflected in her writing.

2. Some students may disagree and say that the straw represents Cisneros's experiences; the gold, her success; and the text structure, her personality.

Vocabulary

1. a 2. c 3. c 4. c

Academic Vocabulary

1. Students may agree that Cisneros wrote the essay to confirm her identity as an artist, because a reflective essay is a way for a writer to reveal personal things about themselves.

2. Details could include Cisneros's leaving home unmarried, and becoming a successful writer despite poor grades.

Reading Strategy Analyzing Text Structure

Text structure is a crucial component of a piece of writing because it helps the author guide readers through a story or essay. The text structure can help writers convey their messages. Think about what Cisneros's message is in this essay, and how the text structure she created helps convey her message.

1. How does Cisneros organize "Straw into Gold: The Metamorphosis of the Everyday"?

2. One could describe the essay the following way: "The words are the straw, the essay is the gold, and the text structure is the loom." Do you agree or disagree with this analysis of the essay?

Vocabulary Practice

Practice with Analogies Choose the word that completes the analogy.

1. exit : leave :: intuitively :
   a. instinctively **b.** slowly **c.** sadly

2. requirement : allows :: taboo :
   a. describes **b.** recommends **c.** forbids

3. chronic : repeating :: nomadic :
   a. airplane **b.** couch **c.** roaming

4. anticipation : future :: nostalgia :
   a. present **b.** sadness **c.** past

Academic Vocabulary

Here are two words from the vocabulary list on page R82. These words will help you think, write, and talk about the selection.

confirm (kən furm´) v. to strengthen; to validate

nevertheless (nev´ər thə les´) adv. despite; however

Practice and Apply
1. Do you think that Cisneros wrote this essay to **confirm** her identity as an artist? Explain.
2. What details show that Cisneros experienced difficulties but **nevertheless** overcame them?

Literature Online **Web Activities** For eFlashcards, Selection Quick Checks, and other Web activities, go to www.glencoe.com.

Writing About Literature

Apply Form An anecdote is a brief account of an interesting happening. Cisneros compares her anecdotal experience of making tortillas to the fairy tale "Rumpelstiltskin," in which a girl must spin straw into gold. Cisneros then applies this metaphor to her life.

Think of a fairy tale or fable you can use as a basis for writing about a personal experience from your own life. Why did you choose this fairy tale or fable? How does it relate to the experience you chose? How does this anecdote relate to your life as a whole?

Before you begin drafting, take notes on your choices of anecdote, fairy tale, or fable in a chart like the one below:

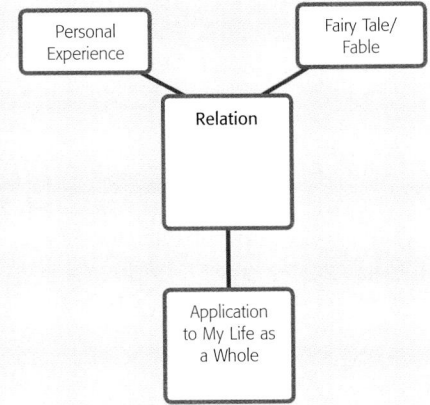

Include details from your own life and from the fairy tale or fable. Once you have completed the diagram, begin drafting.

After completing your reflective essay, meet with a peer reviewer to assess each other's work and suggest revisions. Then proofread and edit your writing for errors in spelling, grammar, and punctuation.

Reading Further

Consider reading Sandra Cisneros's other works, such as *The House on Mango Street*, a novelistic collection of short stories about a girl's childhood in Chicago, and *Caramelo*, the saga of a family's wanderings between Mexico and the United States. For additional biographical information about Cisneros, consider Virginia Brackett's *A Home in the Heart: The Story of Sandra Cisneros.*

Literature Online

Web Activities Have students access the Web site for interactive activities that will help them assess their understanding of the selection.

Writing About Literature

Students' essays should

• choose a fairy tale or fable, or a detail from a fairy tale or fable, relevant to a personal experience

• explain why the particular fairy tale or fable was chosen

• apply an anecdotal experience to a theme in their lives

KEEPING FREEDOM ALIVE

Lift Up Thy Voice and Sing, ca. 1942–44. William H. Johnson, Oil on paperboard, 25.55 x 21.26 in. Smithsonian American Art Museum, Washington, DC.

BIG IDEA

Freedom can mean many things. There is freedom to express yourself. There is also the freedom to pursue your dreams, even if that means making sacrifices along the way. In the nonfiction works in Part 3, you will read speeches, articles, and essays from people who have reached out for freedom. As you read these selections, ask yourself: What does freedom mean to me, and what would I give up to keep it? **BI**

English Language Coach

Building Background Guide students new to the United States to connect with the literature in Part 3 by reviewing some historical issues related to freedom. For example, review freedoms that resulted from the Revolutionary War, Bill of Rights, Nineteenth Amendment, and Civil Rights Act. **EL**

Differentiated Instruction

Metaphor Guide less proficient readers to notice that the theme of Part 3, "Keeping Freedom Alive," is a metaphor comparing freedom to a living thing. Have students suggest other metaphors for freedom, and point them to other metaphors in this introduction, such as Toni Morrison's "rainbow journey." **BL**

Analyzing and Extending

BI Big Idea

Keeping Freedom Alive

Ask: Which types of freedom do you consider essential? *(Students may mention freedom of expression, freedom to vote, or others.)* Stimulate discussion based on student responses. Tell students that Part 3 will deepen their understanding of the idea of keeping freedom alive. Encourage students to contemplate this "big idea" and its relation to the artwork. **OL**

★ Viewing the Art

This painting by African American artist William H. Johnson (1910–) has a title reminiscent of the song known as the African American national anthem, "Lift Every Voice and Sing." **Ask:** What aspect of freedom does the painting portray? *(Its depiction of the joyful patriotic singing recalls the movement to achieve freedom and equality for African Americans.)* **AS**

Objectives for Part 3

• To analyze persuasive texts and to evaluate logical arguments (SE)
• To evaluate the way in which the author's intent affects the structure and tone of a text (SE)
• To recognize that people respond differently to texts based on their points of view (SE)

Part 3: Keeping Freedom Alive

Readability Scores Key
Dale-Chall/DRP/Lexile

PACING (DAYS)		SELECTIONS AND FEATURES	LITERARY ELEMENTS
STANDARD	BLOCK		
2–3 class sessions	1–2	LITERARY FOCUS: Persuasive Essay and Speech, pp. 444–445	Argument and Persuasion, SE p. 445 Author's Intent, TWE p. 444
		"On Women's Right to Vote" by Susan B. Anthony **8.8/67/1110**, pp. 446–451	Rhetorical Devices, SE pp. 447-450 Argument, SE p. 450
		"I've Been to the Mountaintop" by Martin Luther King Jr. **6.3/56/900**, pp. 452–463	Allusion, SE pp. 453, 455, 456, 457, 458, 460, 462, 463
2 class sessions	1	Comparing Literature Different Viewpoints **"Not Just Comics"** by Chester Brown, pp. 464–469 **"How Cool Is Comics Lit?"** by Charles McGrath **12.2/69/1410**, pp. 470–473 **"'Hamlet' too hard? Try a comic book"** by Teresa Méndez **11.1/69/1280**, pp. 474–477 **"The Graphic Novel Silver Anniversary"** by Andrew Arnold **9.9/68/1250**, pp. 478–482	Rhetorical Devices, SE pp. 466–481 Humor, TWE p. 468 Analogies, TWE p. 470 Style, TWE p. 472
2–3 class sessions	1–2	**"Address on the Anniversary of Lincoln's Birth"** by Carl Sandburg **10.1/62/1290**, pp. 483–490	Understanding Quotations, SE pp. 484, 486, 487, 489 Persuasion, SE p. 489
		TIME magazine, **"What I See in Lincoln's Eyes"** by Barack Obama **8.0/64/1220**, pp. 491–494	
		"Cinderella's Stepsisters" by Toni Morrison **9.3/62/970**, pp. 495–499	Author's Purpose, SE pp. 495–498 Analogy, SE p. 498
2–3 class sessions	2–3	Writing Workshop: Biographical Narrative, pp. 500–507	
1 class session		Speaking, Listening, and Viewing Workshop: Presenting a Photoessay, pp. 508–509	
2 class sessions		Test Preparation and Practice, pp. 512–517	

About the Part

Part 3 covers argument and persuasion.

READING AND CRITICAL THINKING	VOCABULARY	WRITING AND GRAMMAR	LISTENING, SPEAKING, AND VIEWING
Analyzing Persuasive Writing, TWE p. 445			
Recognizing Bias, SE pp. 447, 449, 451	Word Parts, SE pp. 447, 451 Academic Vocabulary, SE p. 451	Compare and Contrast Arguments, SE p. 451	Debate, TWE p. 448 Analyzing Art, TWE p. 448
Identifying Problem and Solution, SE pp. 453, 455, 456, 458, 459, 463	Synonyms, SE p. 463	Analyze Rhetorical Devices, SE p. 463	Analyzing Art, TWE pp. 456–462
Comparing Persuasive Appeals, SE pp. 464, 465, 482; TWE p. 466 Comparing Authors' Viewpoints, SE pp. 464, 482 Identifying Assumptions and Ambiguities, SE pp. 466-481 Researching Cultural Context, TWE p. 474	Synonyms, SE pp. 466, 481	Quickwrite, SE pp. 473, 480 Tone, TWE p. 478	Performing, SE p. 481 Group Activity, SE p. 482 Analyzing Art, TWE pp. 468–480
Distinguishing Fact and Opinion, SE pp. 484-486, 489	Analogies, SE pp. 487, 489 Academic Vocabulary, SE p. 489	Evaluate Author's Craft, SE p. 490 Displaying Poetic Style, SE p. 490	Literary Criticism, SE p. 490 Analyzing Art, TWE pp. 485, 487
Analyzing a Visual Image, SE p. 491; TWE pp. 492, 493		Vivid Verbs, TWE p. 492	
Analyzing Text Structure, SE pp. 495, 497, 499 Connotation, TWE p. 496	Word Parts, SE pp. 495, 499 Academic Vocabulary, SE p. 499	Analyze Genre Elements, SE p. 499	Discuss Analogies, SE p. 498

Teach

Big Idea

Keeping Freedom Alive

Raise a school issue related to freedom, such as dress codes or closed campus, and ask for students' opinions. Then refer to a national or international issue in the news about a group struggling for independence. **Ask:** What makes people fight for freedom? *(Students may raise ideas such as that freedom is a natural desire or a compelling motive for action.)* Discuss student responses. **OL**

L Literary Element

Argument and Persuasion

Diagram on the board the two types of persuasion: argument and emotion. **Ask:** What type of persuasion does Anthony use in "On Women's Right to Vote"? *(She uses argument by appealing solely to reason.)* **Ask:** What logical arguments does Anthony make? *(Anthony argues logically that since citizens are entitled to rights and women are citizens, women are entitled to rights.)* Note that this is an example of deductive reasoning. **OL**

PERSUASIVE ESSAY AND SPEECH

What makes writing convincing?

There are varying methods for convincing a person to change his or her ideas or actions. You can use emotional appeals, which encourage your audience to respond to its desire for pleasure, happiness, security, or satisfaction. Or you can appeal to a listener's reason. If you can use logic to prove that your idea is correct, then you can often persuade others to think and act accordingly.

Webster, Worcester, and Bouvier all define a citizen to be a person in the United States, entitled to vote and hold office. The only question left to be settled now is: Are women persons? And I hardly believe any of our opponents will have the hardihood to say they are not. Being persons, then, women are citizens; and no state has a right to make any law, or to enforce any old law, that shall abridge their privileges or immunities. Hence, every discrimination against women in the constitutions and laws of the several states is today null and void, precisely as is every one against Negroes.

—Susan B. Anthony, **from "On Women's Right to Vote"**

Portrait of American woman suffrage leader Susan B. Anthony (1820-1906). She is shown in profile, seated at her desk. Photograph, 1900. ★

Additional Support

Skills Practice

LITERARY ELEMENTS: Author's Intent

Encourage students to assess how an author's intent affects the structure and tone of a piece of persuasive writing. Discuss the excerpts on these pages with the following questions:

- What is Martin Luther King Jr.'s intent? *(King intends to rally African Americans to fight for equal rights.)* How does his speech reflect that intent? *(His tone is inspiring and insistent, using emphatic sentences and repetition to reinforce it.)*

- What is Teresa Méndez's intent? *(Méndez intends to expand the use of graphic novels and comic books in schools.)* How does her writing reflect that intent? *(Her tone is reasonable*

Persuasion

Persuasion is writing that attempts to convince readers to think or act in a particular way. Writers of persuasive essays may appeal to logic, as in argument, but they might also appeal to emotion. Consider the combination of logic and emotion in this argument in favor of comic books and graphic novels.

For the reluctant reader, they are absorbing. For the struggling reader or the reader still learning English, they offer accessibility: pictures for context, and possibly an alternate path into classroom discussions of higher-level texts. They expand vocabulary and introduce the ideas of plot, pacing, and sequence.

—Teresa Méndez, **from "'Hamlet' too hard? Try a comic book"**

One of the important skills persuasive writers must develop is that of anticipating the opposition and confronting their arguments. Below, Toni Morrison anticipates the argument that to be successful, people must be concerned only with their own best interests.

In your rainbow journey toward the realization of personal goals, don't make choices based only on your security and your safety. Nothing is safe. That is not to say that anything ever was, or that anything worth achieving ever should be. . . . But in pursuing your highest ambitions, don't let your personal safety diminish the safety of your stepsister. In wielding the power that is deservedly yours, don't permit it to enslave your stepsisters.

—Toni Morrison, **from "Cinderella's Stepsisters"**

Argument

Argument is a specific type of persuasive writing or speaking in which logic and evidence is used to appeal to the reader's or listener's reason. Notice in the excerpt on the previous page how Anthony ignores emotional appeals and tries to persuade the reader through reason and logic. This may be the more difficult path to changing people's thoughts and actions, but it also may lead to permanent change. Anthony died before women won the right to vote, but her argument prodded a nation toward a change in its constitution. Martin Luther King Jr. also used logical argument in his many speeches. King wished to convince people that African Americans deserved to enjoy the same rights and privileges that other people in the United States enjoyed.

We aren't engaged in any negative protest and in any negative arguments with anybody. We are saying that we are determined to be men. We are determined to be people. We are saying that we are God's children. And that we don't have to live like we are forced to live.

—Martin Luther King Jr., **from "I've Been to the Mountaintop"** **R**

Quickwrite

Anticipating Arguments Think of a local issue and choose a position. Practice anticipating the argument of your opposition by listing three arguments you are likely to encounter.
Issue: Build a new municipal pool
Position: The city should build the pool

The Other Side

1. Municipal pools are too expensive to maintain.

2.

3.

OBJECTIVES
- Analyze persuasive texts to evaluate logical arguments.
- Evaluate the way in which the author's intent affects the structure and tone of a text.

- Recognize that people respond differently to texts based on their points of view.

---

and intelligent, and she uses the jargon of educators.)
- **What is Toni Morrison's intent?** *(Morrison intends to persuade women in power to support other women, not abuse them.)* How does her tone reflect that intent? *(Her tone is cautionary and personal.)* **OL**

English Language Coach

Cultural Allusions Explain to students new to the United States the reference in Susan B. Anthony's speech to Webster, Worcester, and Bouvier. Tell students that Anthony gave her speech after being arrested for illegally casting a vote in the 1872 Presidential election and refusing to pay a fine. **EL**

Teach

R Reading Strategy

Analyzing Persuasive Writing Ask: What makes King's speech argument? *(King uses the logic that African Americans are working positively and are equal.)* **Ask:** What makes Mendez's writing persuasion? *(She uses emotional words such as* absorbing *and* struggling *with logical arguments about accessibility of graphic novels.)* **Ask:** What makes Morrison's writing persuasion? *(It appeals to the mind and the heart.)* **OL**

★ Viewing the Art

Although best known for her tireless efforts for the women's suffrage movement, Susan B. Anthony's first worked in support of the temperance movement, which promoted the prohibition of alcoholic beverages. **AS**

Assess

Quickwrite

To help focus an argument, encourage students to develop counterarguments. Evaluate these for logic and clarity.

Objectives
- To analyze persuasive texts and to evaluate logical arguments (SE)
- To recognize that people respond differently to texts based on their points of view (SE)
- To evaluate the way in which the author's intent affects the structure and tone of a text (TWE)

Focus

BELLRINGER

Bellringer Options
Daily Language Practice Transparency 41
Or **Ask:** Is voting important in our society? Have students discuss their opinions and their reasons for those opinions. **Ask:** How would you feel if you didn't have the right to vote? Have students discuss the implications of not being able to vote.

Author Search To expand students' appreciation of Susan B. Anthony, have them access the Web site for additional information and resources.

On Women's Right to Vote

MEET SUSAN B. ANTHONY

It seems unbelievable today, but picture an adult woman (and U.S. citizen) going to a local polling place to vote—and getting arrested! That is what happened to Susan B. Anthony when she attempted to cast her ballot for a presidential candidate in 1872. Unjustly convicted of the "crime" (the judge had decided that she was guilty before the trial began) and fined $100, she refused to pay the fee. Luckily, no further penalties resulted. Anthony's choice to act on her belief that women should have the same voting rights as men was a risky one at that time. Yet Anthony was a bold and determined woman, and such brave actions characterized her life, work, and writing.

An Early Achiever Anthony was born into a Massachusetts Quaker family whose religious values encouraged her independent spirit and ensured that she could express herself freely. Anthony was three when she began to read and write, and she received an excellent education, unlike many women of her time. She began teaching in 1840 and eventually became the respected headmistress at a school in upstate New York.

> *"The fight must not cease; you must see that it does not stop. . . . Failure is impossible."*
>
> —Susan B. Anthony

A Lasting Partnership A decisive career and life change for Anthony came in 1851 when she met Elizabeth Cady Stanton. Stanton was already active in the women's rights movement when Anthony joined the cause. The two women became lifelong friends and colleagues.

Although Stanton was the principal speechwriter, both women lectured and published articles and books, including the first volumes of *History of Woman Suffrage.* Many recognized Anthony's determined spirit and organizational skills as the human engine that propelled the women's rights movement forward.

Women's Rights Leader Anthony had always been involved in social causes. She had begun her activist career as a temperance reformer, helping those who suffered from the effects of alcoholism. Later she had joined leading abolitionists in the struggle to end slavery. However, she spent the majority of her time in bringing about the passage of the Nineteenth Amendment—the addition to the Constitution that gave women the right to vote. Unfortunately, Anthony did not live to see this crucial legal victory, one that suffragists had worked for five decades to enact. The Nineteenth Amendment became law on August 26, 1920, fourteen years after Anthony's death. In 1979 Anthony's contributions were recognized when her image became the first female historical figure to be put on a U.S. coin—the Susan B. Anthony dollar. It is a fitting tribute to a woman who devoted much of her life to protecting the rights of all U.S. women.

Susan B. Anthony was born in 1820 and died in 1906.

Literature Online Author Search For more about Susan B. Anthony, go to www.glencoe.com.

Selection Skills

Literary Elements
- Rhetorical Devices (SE pp. 447–450)
- Argument (SE p. 450)

On Women's Right to Vote

Reading Skills
- Recognizing Bias (SE pp. 447, 449, 451)

Vocabulary Skills
- Word Parts (SE pp. 447, 451)
- Academic Vocabulary (SE p. 451)

Listening/Speaking/Viewing Skills
- Debating (TWE p. 448)
- Analyzing Art (TWE p. 448)

Writing Skills/Grammar
- Compare and Contrast Arguments (SE p. 451)

Connecting to the Speech

In her speech, Anthony discusses why she felt that women deserved the right to vote in the United States. Before you read, think about the following questions:

- What actions would you take if you felt that your rights were being violated?
- Would you be willing to join a movement or an organization to help secure your rights?

Building Background

In 1873, when Anthony delivered this speech, many people in the United States were fighting for women's suffrage. *Suffrage* means "the right to vote." After becoming involved in the antislavery movement, some women came to believe that their rights were being violated because they were not allowed to vote or hold office. The first convention discussing women's rights was held in Seneca Falls, New York, in 1848.

In 1890 two women's suffrage groups merged to form the National American Woman Suffrage Association. For years, the group fought for voting rights for women. By 1918 fifteen states had granted women voting rights equal to men's. Two years later, the Nineteenth Amendment was added to the Constitution, and all U.S. women were finally able to vote.

Setting Purposes for Reading

Big Idea Keeping Freedom Alive

As you read Anthony's speech, think about how she defines freedom.

Literary Element Rhetorical Devices

Rhetorical devices are tools of persuasion, such as appeals to logic, emotion, ethics, or authority, used by an author or speaker. Noting an author's rhetorical devices may provide clues about his or her objective. As you read, identify the rhetorical devices Anthony uses.

- See Literary Terms Handbook, p. R14.

Literature Online Interactive Literary Elements Handbook To review or learn more about the literary elements, go to www.glencoe.com.

OBJECTIVES
In studying this selection, you will focus on the following:
- identifying and evaluating rhetorical devices
- recognizing bias and its effects on a text

Reading Strategy Recognizing Bias

Bias is an author's inclination toward a particular opinion or position. Look for examples of bias in Anthony's reasons for why women should get the right to vote.

Reading Tip: Looking for Bias Identifying bias can help you understand an author's motivation and identify when bias may affect his or her credibility or logic. Use a chart to keep track of any examples of bias.

Example	Why It Shows Bias
"I not only committed no crime . . ."	The judge found Anthony guilty before the trial started.

Vocabulary

domestic (də mes′ tik) *adj.* relating to a country, especially one's own; p. 448 *We must mind our domestic policy, while not ignoring global strategy.*

ordain (ôr dān′) *v.* to order or establish; to appoint; p. 448 *The king did ordain that food would not be taxed.*

odious (ō′ dē əs) *adj.* disgusting or offensive; p. 449 *An odious smell was coming from the piles of garbage.*

aristocracy (ar′ is tok′ rə sē) *n.* type of government in which a minority of upper-class individuals rule; p. 449 *The country was governed by an aristocracy, even though most of civilians were not wealthy.*

dissension (di sen′ shən) *n.* disagreement within a group; p. 449 *Dissension among the committee members made it difficult for them to make decisions.*

Vocabulary Tip: Word Parts Many words are made up of separate parts, such as roots, prefixes (which come before the root word), and suffixes (which come after the root word). If you encounter a word you do not know, examining its parts can help you determine the meaning of the entire word.

- evaluating the effectiveness of the author's arguments
- writing an essay to compare and contrast speakers' arguments

SUSAN B. ANTHONY **447**

Focus

Summary

After being arrested for illegally voting in a presidential election, Susan B. Anthony gave this speech to win support for women's suffrage. The main point of her speech is that all the people in the country are part of the democracy. She posits that if women are people, then they do indeed have the right to participate in electing government leaders.

V Vocabulary

Vocabulary File

Say: Add these words and definitions to your vocabulary file. For each word, include a sentence that gives you an example of how to use the word. **OL** Students with English language needs should include the pronunciations of these words in their files. **EL**

Literary Elements Have students access the Web site to improve their understanding of rhetorical devices.

Selection Resources

Print Materials
- Unit 2 Resources (Fast File), pp. 58–60
- Leveled Vocabulary Development, p. 33
- Selection and Unit Assessments, pp. 71–72
- Selection Quick Checks, p. 36

Transparencies
- Bellringer Options Transparencies: Daily Language Practice Transparency 41
- Literary Elements Transparency 42

Technology
- TeacherWorks Plus™ CD-ROM
- StudentWorks Plus™ CD-ROM
- Presentation Plus!™ CD-ROM
- Literature Online, glencoe.com
- Online Student Edition, mhln.com
- ExamView® Assessment Suite CD-ROM
- Vocabulary PuzzleMaker CD-ROM
- Listening Library, disc 1 track 37

Keeping Freedom Alive

Say: *While you read, keep the following question in mind: Why is the right to vote necessary for freedom?* (Being able to vote allows people to select their leaders. Leaders who try to take away voters' freedoms can be elected out of office.) **OL**

BI **Big Idea**

Keeping Freedom Alive

Answer: *Without the right to vote, women have few means to protect their legal interests.* **OL**

L1 **Literary Element**

Rhetorical Devices Answer: *Anthony is appealing to their ethics and emotions, their sense of fairness, their love of liberty, and their anger at injustice.* **OL**

⭐ Viewing the Art

Marches and parades were effective and popular tools for the women's suffrage movement because they drew considerable public attention. **AS**

Readability Scores

Dale-Chall: 8.8
DRP: 67
Lexile: 1110

On Woman's Right to Vote

Susan B. Anthony

Friends and fellow citizens: I stand before you tonight under indictment[1] for the alleged crime of having voted at the last presidential election, without having a lawful right to vote. It shall be my work this evening to prove to you that in thus voting, I not only committed no crime, but, instead, simply exercised[2] my citizen's rights, guaranteed to me and all United States citizens by the National Constitution, beyond the power of any state to deny.

The preamble of the Federal Constitution says: "We, the people of the United States, in order to form a more perfect union, establish justice, insure **domestic** tranquility, provide for the common defense, promote the general welfare,[3] and secure the blessings of liberty to ourselves and our posterity,[4] do **ordain** and establish this Constitution for the United States of America."

It was we, the people; not we, the white male citizens; nor yet we, the male citizens; but we, the whole people, who formed the Union. And we formed it, not to give the blessings of liberty, but to secure them; not to the half of ourselves and the half of our posterity, but to the whole people—women as well as men. And it is a downright mockery to talk to women of their enjoyment of the blessings of liberty while they are denied the use of the only means of securing them provided by this democratic republican government—the ballot.

For any state to make sex a qualification that must ever result in the disfranchisement[5] of one entire half of the people is to

---

1. An *indictment* is a statement that charges someone with committing a crime.
2. Here, *exercised* means "used or practiced."
3. Here, *welfare* refers to well-being.
4. Posterity means "future generations."

5. Disfranchisement means the taking away of someone's rights as a citizen.

Literary Element Rhetorical Devices *What type of reaction is Anthony trying to evoke in listeners with this statement?* **L1**

Big Idea Keeping Freedom Alive *Why does Anthony believe that women need the right to vote in order to secure their liberties?* **BI**

Vocabulary

domestic (də mes′ tik) *adj.* relating to one's own country
ordain (ôr dān′) *v.* to order or establish; to appoint

Additional Support

Skills Practice

SPEAKING: Debate Say: *Susan B. Anthony was passionate about women's suffrage and was able to convey that passion in her speech.* Divide the class into two teams and have them prepare to debate a legal topic affecting their lives, such as raising or lowering the voting age. Give the teams time to plan their arguments. Have four or five members of each team debate the topic in front of the class. **AL**

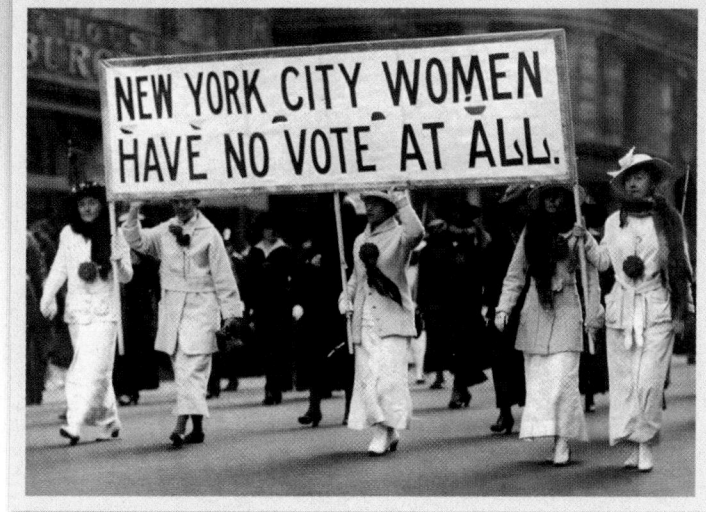

Women marching for woman suffrage in New York City. c.1910. ★

pass a bill of attainder,[6] or an *ex post facto* law,[7] and is therefore a violation of the supreme law of the land. By it the blessings of liberty are forever withheld from women and their female posterity.

To them this government has no just powers derived from the consent of the governed. To them this government is not a democracy. It is not a republic. It is an **odious aristocracy**; a hateful oligarchy[8] of sex; the most hateful zaristocracy ever established on the face of the globe; an oligarchy of wealth, where the rich govern the poor. An oligarchy of learning, where the educated govern the ignorant, or even an oligarchy of race, where the Saxon rules the African, might be endured; but this oligarchy of sex, which makes father, brother, husband, sons, the oligarchs over the mother and sisters, the wife and daughters, of every household—which ordains all men sovereigns,[9] all women subjects, carries **dissension**, discord, and rebellion into every home of the nation.

Webster, Worcester, and Bouvier[10] all define a citizen to be a person in the United States, entitled to vote and hold office. The only question left to be settled now is: Are women persons? And I hardly believe any of our opponents will have the hardihood to say they are not. Being persons, then, women are citizens; and no state has a right to make any law, or to enforce any old law, that shall abridge their privileges or immunities.[11] Hence, every discrimination against women in the constitutions and laws of the several states is today null and void, precisely as is every one against Negroes. ∾

---

6. A bill of attainder is an act of the legislature in which someone is declared guilty of a serious crime without a trial.
7. An ex post facto law is a law that punishes an individual for committing a crime even though the act was not considered criminal when the person committed it.
8. An *oligarchy* is a government in which a small group has authority.

9. Sovereigns are individuals invested with supreme authority.
10. Webster, Worcester, and Bouvier refers to Noah Webster, Joseph Emerson Worcester, and John Bouvier, who all published dictionaries.
11. Here, *immunities* means "protection from penalties or prosecution."

Reading Strategy Recognizing Bias *Explain how Anthony's bias is present in this statement.* **R**

Vocabulary

odious (ō′dē əs) *adj.* disgusting or offensive
aristocracy (ar′is tok′rə sē) *n.* a type of government in which a minority of upper-class individuals rule

Literary Element Rhetorical Devices *How does Anthony attempt to persuade her audience of the legitimacy of her view here? Is she successful? Explain.* **L₂**

Vocabulary

dissension (di sen′shən) *n.* disagreement within a group

SUSAN B. ANTHONY **449**

Teach

R **Reading Strategy**

Recognizing Bias
Answer: *Anthony's statement is biased because she uses hyperbole and emotionally charged language to convey her point. Her opinion is that the government is not a democracy when women are denied the right to vote; she promotes this opinion by using forceful and emotional language instead of facts and logic.* **OL**

L₂ **Literary Element**

Rhetorical Devices **Answer:** *Anthony appeals to logic. She argues that if the only requirement for voting is being a "person," women should not be denied the right to vote unless they are not considered "persons." Students' answers regarding Anthony's success in persuading the audience will vary, and their comments should be supported by evidence from the text.* **OL**

✓CheckPoint

Use the CheckPoint questions on Presentation Plus! to check students' mastery of the selection. These questions can be used with interactive response keypads for immediate student feedback.

Building Reading Fluency

Previewing Say: Before you read material that may contain some difficult or unfamiliar words, skim through the passage and identify words you don't know. Look up their meanings in a dictionary so you'll know the word when you encounter it in the passage. Have students preview the speech and select at least five words. They should look up the meanings of the words and write a sentence for each of them to help reinforce the meaning. **BL**

Objectives
• To identify and evaluate rhetorical devices (SE)
• To recognize bias and its effects on a text (SE)
• To present an argument (TWE)

449

Assess

1. Answers will vary. Anthony made a good argument because she used the Constitution to show how women were unfairly discriminated against.

2. (a) Women are citizens worthy of all rights guaranteed by the Constitution; women contributed to the founding of the United States; not allowing women to vote is illegal. (b) Cultural opinions and beliefs differed at that time.

3. (a) Bill of attainder, or an *ex post facto law.* (b) Yes, those laws, too, are unconstitutional and unjust.

4. (a) Citizenship requires only that a person be born in the United States. If women are persons, they should not be denied any of the rights offered to citizens, including the right to vote. (b) Answers should be supported by textual examples.

5. Anthony compares the plight of women to African Americans, who also were denied many rights, including the right to vote. They won that right in 1870.

6. (a) It might have angered some people because it criticized the country, or it may have saddened some because the United States was not living up to its dem-

RESPONDING AND THINKING CRITICALLY

Respond

1. Do you agree with Anthony's arguments regarding women's right to vote? Which of Anthony's points made the strongest impact on you? Explain.

Recall and Interpret

2. (a) What are two reasons Anthony gives for why women should be allowed to vote? (b) Why do you think it took so long for the laws to finally change? Explain.

3. (a) To what does Anthony compare laws forbidding women to vote? (b) Is her comparison a valid one? Explain.

4. (a) Why does Anthony ask "Are women persons?" (b) Do you agree with her logic? Explain.

Analyze and Evaluate

5. Why does Anthony close her speech with a reference to "Negroes"?

6. In her speech, Anthony argues that for women who are not allowed to vote "this government is not a democracy." (a) What effect do you think this statement might have had on her listeners? (b) Is her statement a valid one? Explain.

7. In this speech, Anthony is trying to persuade her listeners. If you were listening to her speech in 1873, would you have been persuaded to support her cause? Explain.

Connect

8. **Big Idea** Keeping Freedom Alive (a) Why does Anthony believe that freedom requires giving all citizens the right to vote? (b) Do you agree with Anthony's opinion? Explain.

LITERARY ANALYSIS

Literary Element Rhetorical Devices

Authors use **rhetorical devices** to persuade readers. These devices can include appeals to logic, which present facts and reasoning; appeals to ethics, which focus on authority and credibility; or appeals to emotions, which can be attempts to scare, entertain, or anger an audience. Although authors may use all three of these approaches, one type is often used more than the others in a piece of writing.

1. Which rhetorical device in this speech does Anthony use most effectively to persuade her audience?

2. Which specific example of a rhetorical device from the speech do you think is most effective? Explain.

3. One rhetorical device Anthony uses in her speech is the analogy, a comparison based on a similarity between things that are otherwise unlike. What does she compare to a "hateful oligarchy of sex"? Do you think that this is an effective use of a rhetorical device?

She compares the United States government to an oligarchy. Some students may agree that the analogy is apt; others may think that it is overblown.

450 UNIT 2 NONFICTION

Review: Argument

As you learned on pages 444–445, **argument** refers to statements, reasons, and facts that support or oppose a point. Many persuasive techniques and rhetorical devices can be used to bolster an argument.

Partner Activity With a classmate, discuss Anthony's argument for allowing women to vote. Create a two-column chart similar to the one below. In one column, list one of the logical points Anthony makes to support her argument. In the second column, brainstorm about some of the possible responses that people arguing against Anthony may have had.

Anthony's Argument	Critics' Responses
Women played a role in establishing the United States.	Women had not played any role in the government previously.

---

ocratic ideals. (b) Responses should include textual support.

7. Answers should be supported by textual evidence and should discuss the impact of the rhetorical devices.

8. (a) Anthony believes that one who is unable to influence politics can easily lose all rights. (b) Answers should be supported by textual examples.

Literary Element

1. Appeals to logic, ethics, or emotions

2. Answers should cite a rhetorical device from the speech.

3. She compares the United States government to an oligarchy. Students may feel the analogy is apt or overblown.

Reading Strategy · Recognizing Bias

To detect **bias** in a written work, use strategies such as looking for oversimplification, analyzing the writer's reasoning, and identifying emotionally charged language.

1. Identify two examples of bias in Anthony's speech. Which strategies helped you identify them?

2. In your opinion, did the bias in Anthony's speech affect her credibility? Explain.

Vocabulary · Practice

Practice with Word Parts Read the roots and definitions, then pick the best definition for each word.

Greek Root: *aristos*—"best"
Latin Root: *dissentire*—"disagree"
Latin Root: *domus*—"house"
Latin Root: *odiosus*—"hateful"
Latin Root: *ordinare*—"appoint"

1. **aristocracy** is a government ruled by
   a. the elite   **b.** the poor   **c.** a group

2. **dissension**
   a. laziness   **b.** disorganization
   c. disagreement

3. **domestic**
   a. relating to one's home country
   b. foreign   **c.** shaped like a dome

4. **odious**
   a. pleasant   **b.** disgusting   **c.** strong

5. **ordained**
   a. called   **b.** appointed   **c.** trained

Academic Vocabulary

Here is a word from the vocabulary list on page R82. This word will help you think, write, and talk about the selection.

institute (in′stə toot′) *v.* to establish or initiate

Practice and Apply
How did Anthony help **institute** change?

Writing About Literature

Compare and Contrast Arguments Anthony was not the only speaker who voiced an opinion about women's right to vote. Find and read one or two other speeches on the same topic. In an essay, **compare or contrast the arguments** made in these different speeches. Pay close attention to the speakers' use of logic. Be sure to use specific evidence from each of the speeches, including Anthony's, to support your ideas.

Before you begin writing, you should make an outline of the similarities and differences between the speeches. Your outline should look similar to the example below.

> I. Anthony's "On Women's Right to Vote"
>
>   A. Anthony believes not allowing women to vote is similar to passing a bill of attainder.
>
> II. Other Speeches' Titles
>
>   A. List one of the other writers' arguments.

After completing your draft, exchange essays with another classmate to evaluate each other's work and to suggest revisions. Then proofread and edit your draft for errors in spelling, grammar, and punctuation.

Learning for Life

Research a law that restricts or guarantees the rights of individuals younger than eighteen years old. Some examples include laws related to making legal contracts or freedom of the student press. After you complete your research, write your own speech, discussing the causes and effects of the law that you have chosen. Deliver the speech to your class.

Literature Online **Web Activities** For eFlashcards, Selection Quick Checks, and other Web activities, go to www.glencoe.com.

SUSAN B. ANTHONY   **451**

Assess

Review: Argument

Anthony's arguments are that women are citizens worthy of all constitutional rights; women helped create the United States; and not allowing women to vote is illegal. Responses should address each of her arguments.

Reading Strategy

1. She refers to her voting as an alleged crime, compares men to slaveholders and oligarchs, and presents one side of the issue. Students can find examples of bias by watching for oversimplification, emotionally charged language, or one-sided arguments.

2. Student answers will vary but should provide support for their responses.

Vocabulary

1. a **2.** c **3.** a **4.** b **5.** b

Academic Vocabulary

Students should explain that through the efforts of Anthony and others, women eventually gained the right to vote.

Writing About Literature

Use these criteria when evaluating student's writing:

- Does the essay compare and contrast two speeches?
- Does the essay analyze the use of logic in each speech?
- Does the essay demonstrate correct grammar and punctuation?

Learning for Life

Speeches will vary, but should include

- mention of a specific law
- discussion of the causes and effects of this law

Literature Online

Web Activities Have students access the Web site for interactive activities that will help them assess their understanding of the selection.

451

Focus

BELLRINGER

Bellringer Options
Daily Language Practice Transparency 42
Or write the Martin Luther King Jr. quotation on the board.
Ask: What makes King's words inspiring? Are there any issues today that you feel this strongly about?

Have students discuss individuals and groups that face discrimination in the United States today and the ways that this discrimination is similar to or different from the injustices King was fighting. Ask them to describe what causes they would support and why.

Author Search To expand students' appreciation of Martin Luther King Jr., have them access the Web site for additional information and resources.

I've Been to the Mountaintop

MEET MARTIN LUTHER KING JR.

During the historic March on Washington in 1963, Martin Luther King Jr. set the moral tone for the civil rights movement with his famous "I Have a Dream" speech. In 1964 he was awarded the Nobel Peace Prize for leading nonviolent demonstrations to help African Americans gain their civil rights. With great courage and insight, King inspired Americans of all backgrounds to come together to work for a more just, equitable, and compassionate society.

"I have a dream my four little children will one day live in a nation where they will not be judged by the color of their skin but by the content of their character. I have a dream today!"

—Martin Luther King Jr.

Launching the Civil Rights Movement Born the son of a minister in Atlanta, Georgia, King began his rise to leadership by entering Morehouse College at the age of fifteen. After receiving a PhD in theology from Boston University, King became a minister in a Montgomery, Alabama, church. Shortly after moving there, King became a leader of the first major nonviolent protest of the civil rights movement. Inspired by the life and teachings of Mohandas Gandhi, whose doctrine of passive resistance was to become his own guiding principle, King began the Montgomery bus boycott. The African American citizens of Montgomery, tired of being forced to give up

their seats for whites, stayed off the buses for more than a year to force an end to segregation. Their peaceful protest was successful, and the outstanding public speaking and leadership skills King displayed drew national attention.

Expanding the Struggle After the boycott, King served as president of the Southern Christian Leadership Conference and helped to spread the civil rights struggle throughout the South and the nation. In 1963, when the center of the struggle shifted to Birmingham, Alabama, King was there. He and other demonstrators were jailed, and violence exploded in the streets, but King's stance on nonviolent resistance remained firm. While behind bars, King wrote his famous document, *Letter from a Birmingham Jail*, in which he answered his critics and galvanized support for his program of civil disobedience.

In the mid to late 1960s, King expanded his agenda to include protests against the rapidly escalating war in Vietnam. In 1968, at the age of thirty-nine, King fell victim to an assassin's bullet. The world mourned. At his funeral, over a thousand people, including political leaders and foreign dignitaries, crowded into King's church, Ebenezer Baptist Church in Atlanta, Georgia. Outside, almost one hundred thousand more paid tribute. King's message of respect, for democracy and for the dignity of all people, still lives.

Martin Luther King Jr. was born in 1929 and died in 1968.

Literature Online Author Search For more about Martin Luther King Jr., go to www.glencoe.com.

Selection Skills

Literary Elements
- Allusion (SE pp. 453, 455, 456, 457, 458, 460, 462, 463)

I've Been to the Mountaintop

Reading Skills
- Identifying Problem and Solution (SE pp. 453, 455, 456, 458, 459, 463)
- Distinguishing Fact and Opinion (TWE p. 462)
- Previewing (TWE p. 454)

Vocabulary Skills
- Synonyms (SE p. 463)

Listening/Speaking/Viewing Skills
- Analyzing Art (TWE pp. 456–462)

Writing Skills/Grammar
- Analyze Rhetorical Devices (SE p. 463)
- Simple Subjects and Predicates (TWE p. 460)

Connecting to the Speech

In this speech, King stresses that nonviolence is the best way to protest injustice, even when it means enduring the physical attacks of opponents. Before you read the speech, think about the following questions:

- Would you be willing to dedicate your life to a cause in which you strongly believed?
- Would you be willing to stand up for the rights of other people even though you might be harmed in the process?

Building Background

In April 1968, Martin Luther King Jr. traveled to Memphis, Tennessee, to lend his support to African American sanitation workers who were on strike against the city. Memphis Mayor Henry Loeb had refused to recognize and negotiate with the nearly all-African American union organization that had called the strike. To dramatize the workers' plight, King had already led one march, and had plans to lead another. On the evening of April 3, he spoke to a crowd of about two thousand people. The speech he gave is the one you are about to read. The next evening, King was assassinated as he stood on the balcony outside his motel room.

Setting Purposes for Reading

Big Idea Keeping Freedom Alive

In this speech, King argues that freedom and equality belong to everyone. As you read, notice what arguments King gives to support his ideas.

Literary Element Allusion

An **allusion** is a reference to a character, a place, or a situation from history, music, art, or literature. In his speeches, King uses allusions to make his points clear. As you read, pay close attention whenever King brings up well-known quotations and examples from history.

- See Literary Terms Handbook, p. R1.

Literature Online Interactive Literary Elements Handbook To review or learn more about the literary elements, go to www.glencoe.com.

OBJECTIVES

In studying this selection, you will focus on the following:
- analyzing allusion
- identifying problem and solution
- writing an essay to analyze the use of parallelism and repetition as rhetorical devices

---

Reading Strategy Identifying Problem and Solution

One purpose of persuasive speeches is to **identify** a **problem** and suggest a **solution** or solutions for that problem. While reading this speech, try to determine the problems King discusses and the solutions he proposes.

Reading Tip: Asking Questions It might be useful to ask yourself questions as you read, such as: What are the problems? What details about the problems does King provide? What solutions does King suggest? What support does he give for his solutions? As you read, fill in a chart like the one shown.

Problems	Solutions

Vocabulary

grapple (grap′ əl) v. to struggle, as though wrestling; to come to terms with; p. 455 *The city council is meeting tonight to discuss how best to grapple with town budget issues.*

relevant (rel′ ə vənt) adj. related to the issue at hand; p. 458 *Though pollution is an important issue, it is not relevant to our discussion of the need for a new library.*

agenda (ə jen′ də) n. an outline of tasks to be accomplished; p. 458 *The agenda lists what we need to discuss during this meeting.*

compassionate (kəm pash′ ə nit) adj. having or showing sympathy for another's misfortune, combined with a desire to help; p. 459 *A variety of compassionate organizations work to help victims of disasters.*

Focus

Summary

It is April 1968, and the African American sanitation workers of Memphis, Tennessee, have been on strike. Martin Luther King Jr. comes to the city to organize another march in their support, and he gives a speech stressing the need to stand together. In an ironic twist of fate, he ends the speech with a comment that he may not get to the "promised land" with the others because of threats on his life but that he has seen what the future holds—freedom and equality that will be won. King is killed while in Memphis.

V Vocabulary

Vocabulary File

Say: Add these words and definitions to your vocabulary file. For each word, include a sentence that gives you an example of how to use the word. **OL** Students with English language needs should include the pronunciations of these words in their files. **EL**

Literature Online

Literary Elements Have students access the Web site to improve their understanding of allusion.

MARTIN LUTHER KING JR. **453**

Keeping Freedom Alive

Say: Keep the following questions in mind as you read: What is necessary to the achievement of freedom and equality, according to King? How does he say that people should work toward these goals? *(King believes that to achieve freedom and equality, people must remain determined, be willing to endure hardship, and stick together and help each other. He stresses that people should fight for these goals in nonviolent ways, such as by withdrawing economic support from racist institutions.)* **OL**

L1 Literary Element

Allusion Make sure that students understand the Biblical allusion used in the title.
Ask: In the Bible, who was promised a land? By whom? *(God promised the Israelites a land of their own. This land is referred to as the promised land.)* **OL**

Readability Scores
Dale-Chall: 6.3
DRP: 56
Lexile: 900

I've Been to the Mountaintop

Martin Luther King Jr.

Segregation Protest March

Thank you very kindly, my friends. As I listened to Ralph Abernathy[1] in his eloquent and generous introduction and then thought about myself, I wondered who he was talking about. It's always good to have your closest friend and associate say something good about you. And Ralph is the best friend that I have in the world.

I'm delighted to see each of you here tonight in spite of a storm warning. You reveal that you are determined to go on anyhow. Something is happening in Memphis, something is happening in our world.

As you know, if I were standing at the beginning of time, with the possibility of general and panoramic view of the whole human history up to now, and the Almighty said to me, "Martin Luther King, which age would you like to live in?" —I would take my mental flight by Egypt through, or rather across the Red Sea, through the wilderness on toward the promised land. **L1** And in spite of its magnificence, I wouldn't stop there. I would move on by Greece, and take my mind to Mount Olympus. And I would see Plato, Aristotle, Socrates, Euripides and Aristophanes[2] assembled around the Parthenon as they discussed the great and eternal issues of reality.

But I wouldn't stop there. I would go on, even to the great heyday of the Roman Empire. And I would see developments

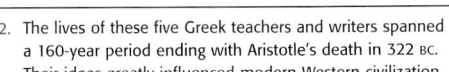

Visual Vocabulary
The *Parthenon*, a temple built in the fifth century BC, still stands in Athens, Greece.

---

1. With King and other African American ministers, *Ralph Abernathy* founded the Southern Christian Leadership Conference (SCLC), an organization devoted to the nonviolent struggle against racism and discrimination.

2. The lives of these five Greek teachers and writers spanned a 160-year period ending with Aristotle's death in 322 BC. Their ideas greatly influenced modern Western civilization.

Additional Support

Skills Practice

READING: Previewing Have students read the title and the first page and ask for their reactions to King's opening comments.
Ask: What does the introduction to his speech tell you about King? *(Students may say that King's introduction shows him to be modest and generous.)* Then have students discuss what they know about the purpose of King's speech or what they predict its purpose might be. Ask them to pay attention to his various purposes as they read and then to determine whether their predictions were correct. **OL**

Visual Vocabulary
Martin Luther (1483–1546) was a German theologian whose arguments challenging certain teachings of the Roman Catholic Church led to the Protestant Reformation.

around there, through various emperors and leaders. But I wouldn't stop there. I would even come up to the day of the Renaissance, and get a quick picture of all that the Renaissance did for the cultural and esthetic life of man. But I wouldn't stop there. I would even go by the way that the man for whom I'm named had his habitat. And I would watch Martin Luther as he tacked his ninety-five theses[3] on the door at the church in Wittenberg.

But I wouldn't stop there. I would come on up even to 1863, and watch a vacillating president by the name of Abraham Lincoln finally come to the conclusion that he had to sign the Emancipation Proclamation. But I wouldn't stop there. I would even come up to the early thirties, and see a man grappling with the problems of the bankruptcy of his nation. And come with an eloquent cry that we have nothing to fear but fear itself.[4]

But I wouldn't stop there. Strangely enough, I would turn to the Almighty, and say, "If you allow me to live just a few years in the second half of the twentieth century, I will be happy." Now that's a strange statement to make, because the world is all messed up. The nation is sick. Trouble is in the land. Confusion all around. That's a strange statement. But I know, somehow, that only when it is dark enough, can you see the stars. And I see God working in this period of the twentieth century in a way that men, in some strange way, are responding—

something is happening in our world. The masses of people are rising up. And wherever they are assembled today, whether they are in Johannesburg, South Africa; Nairobi, Kenya; Accra, Ghana; New York City; Atlanta, Georgia; Jackson, Mississippi; or Memphis, Tennessee—the cry is always the same —"We want to be free."

And another reason that I'm happy to live in this period is that we have been forced to a point where we're going to have to **grapple** with the problems that men have been trying to grapple with through history, but the demands didn't force them to do it. Survival demands that we grapple with them. Men, for years now, have been talking about war and peace. But now, no longer can they just talk about it. It is no longer a choice between violence and nonviolence in this world; it's nonviolence or nonexistence.

That is where we are today. And also in the human rights revolution, if something isn't done, and in a hurry, to bring the colored peoples of the world out of their long years of poverty, their long years of hurt and neglect, the whole world is doomed. Now, I'm just happy that God has allowed me to live in this period, to see what is unfolding. And I'm happy that he's allowed me to be in Memphis.

I can remember, I can remember when Negroes were just going around as Ralph has said, so often, scratching where they didn't itch, and laughing when they were not tickled. But that day is all over. We mean business now, and we are determined to gain our rightful place in God's world.

And that's all this whole thing is about. We aren't engaged in any negative protest and in

---

3. Here, *theses* means "arguments."
4. In these two sentences, King is referring to President Franklin D. Roosevelt, who led the United States during the Great Depression of the 1930s.

Literary Element Allusion *How would you characterize the kinds of people and events that King is alluding to?* **L2**

Big Idea Keeping Freedom Alive *What issues do you think the people in these places have in common?* **BI**

Reading Strategy Identifying Problem and Solution *What problems has King identified?* **R**

Vocabulary
grapple (grap′əl) *v.* to struggle, as though wrestling; to come to terms with

MARTIN LUTHER KING JR.   **455**

Teach

L2 Literary Element
Allusion Answer: *King alludes to great and notable people from many eras.* **OL**

BI Big Idea
Keeping Freedom Alive
Answer: *People in these places suffer injustice and oppression. Like King's audience, the people who suffer the most in these places are people of color.* **OL**

R Reading Strategy
Identifying Problem and Solution Answer: *King alludes to the racial injustice plaguing the United States, the poverty, hurt, and neglect suffered by people of color around the world, and war.* **OL**

★ Political History
The Emancipation Proclamation This proclamation was issued by Abraham Lincoln on January 1, 1863, during the Civil War. It freed all slaves in the areas of the Confederacy still rebelling against the Union. **AS**

CheckPoint
Use the CheckPoint questions on Presentation Plus! to monitor students' comprehension. These questions can be used with interactive response keypads for immediate student feedback.

Objectives
- To analyze allusion (SE)
- To identify problem and solution (SE)
- To make predictions (TWE)

English Language Coach

World Leaders Discuss Martin Luther King Jr. as one of many leaders who have led struggles for freedom and equality. Ask English-language learners to describe similar leaders from their cultures and to compare them to King. Mention expressions that are associated with the American Civil Rights Movement, such as *boycott, sit-in,* and *I have a dream.* Make sure English-language learners understand these terms. Have them list expressions associated with important leaders and movements in their native countries to share with the class. **EL**

Teach

L1 Literary Element

Allusion Answer: *Students may say that by reminding listeners that Pharaoh was able to keep the slaves subjected only until they unified, King is helping his listeners understand that they need to unify also.* **OL**

R Reading Strategy

Identifying Problem and Solution Answer: *King explains that minor incidents of violence, such as window-breaking, are distracting people from the real issue behind the strike: the suffering of hard-working people. King encourages people to march in order to support the strikers and to remind people of the real reasons for the strike.* **OL**

⭐ Viewing the Photograph

Flip Schulke, an award-winning photojournalist, received his first Kodak "Brownie" camera at age fifteen and has been taking photographs ever since. He pioneered the field of underwater photography, covered the Civil Rights Movement extensively, and has received numerous awards and honors. **AS**

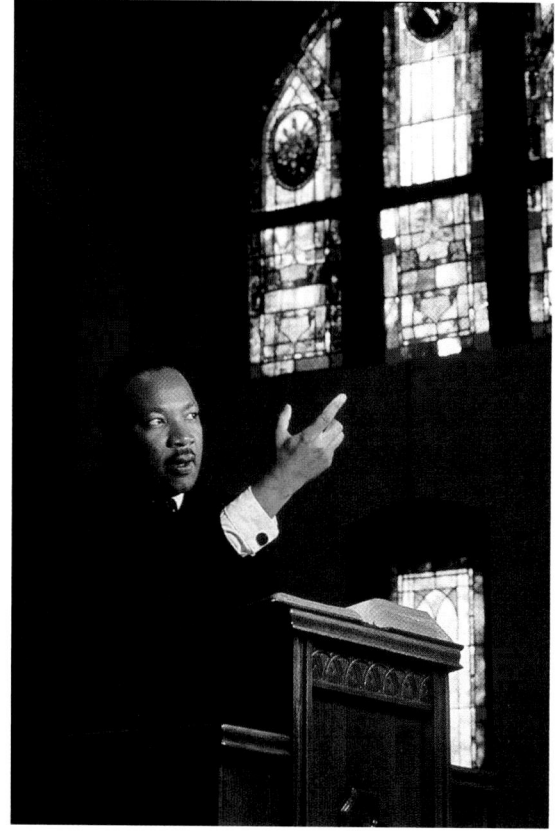

Portrait of Martin Luther King Jr. Flip Schulke.

any negative arguments with anybody. We are saying that we are determined to be men. We are determined to be people. We are saying that we are God's children. And that we don't have to live like we are forced to live.

Now, what does all of this mean in this great period of history? It means that we've got to stay together. We've got to stay together and maintain unity. You know, whenever Pharaoh[5] wanted to prolong the period of slavery in Egypt, he had a favorite, favorite formula for doing it. What was that? He kept the slaves fighting among themselves. But whenever the slaves get together,

---

5. In the Bible, the *Pharaoh* (ruler) of ancient Egypt enslaved the Israelites until Moses led them out of Egypt and into Canaan, which they called the "promised land."

456 UNIT 2 NONFICTION

---

something happens in Pharaoh's court, and he cannot hold the slaves in slavery. When the slaves get together, that's the beginning of getting out of slavery. Now let us maintain unity.

Secondly, let us keep the issues where they are. The issue is injustice. The issue is the refusal of Memphis to be fair and honest in its dealings with its public servants, who happen to be sanitation workers. Now, we've got to keep attention on that. That's always the problem with a little violence. You know what happened the other day, and the press dealt only with the window-breaking. I read the articles. They very seldom got around to mentioning the fact that one thousand, three hundred sanitation workers were on strike, and that Memphis is not being fair to them, and that Mayor Loeb is in dire[6] need of a doctor. They didn't get around to that.

Now we're going to march again, and we've got to march again, in order to put the issue where it is supposed to be. And force everybody to see that there are thirteen hundred of God's children here suffering, sometimes going hungry, going through dark and dreary nights wondering how this thing is going to come out. That's the issue. And we've got to say to the nation: we know it's coming out. For when people get caught up with that which is right and they are willing to sacrifice for it, there is no stopping point short of victory.

We aren't going to let any mace stop us. We are masters in our nonviolent movement in disarming police forces; they don't

---

6. *Dire* means "dreadful" or "terrible."

Literary Element Allusion *What point does the allusion to Pharaoh's court help bring home to King's listeners?* **L1**

Reading Strategy Identifying Problem and Solution *What problem does King explain in this sentence? What does he encourage people to do to address this problem?* **R**

Additional Support

Skills Practice

RESEARCH: Greek Philosophers In his speech, King names several ancient Greek philosophers and writers. These men contributed ideas about government that Americans consider important. Ask each student to research the ideas of one of these philosophers or writers.

Have students look especially for connections between their subjects' ideas and American concepts of government, equality, and democracy. Ask the students to write brief reports about their findings to share with the class. **OL** know what to do. I've seen them so often. I remember in Birmingham, Alabama, when we were in that majestic struggle there we would move out of the 16th Street Baptist Church day after day; by the hundreds we would move out. And Bull Connor[7] would tell them to send the dogs forth and they did come; but we just went before the dogs singing, "Ain't gonna let nobody turn me round." Bull Connor next would say, "Turn the fire hoses on." And as I said to you the other night, Bull Connor didn't know history. He knew a kind of physics that somehow didn't relate to the transphysics[8] that we knew about. And that was the fact that there was a certain kind of fire that no water could put out. And we went before the fire hoses; we had known water. If we were Baptist or some other denomination, we had been immersed. If we were Methodist, and some others, we had been sprinkled, but we knew water.[9]

That couldn't stop us. And we just went on before the dogs and we would look at them; and we'd go on before the water hoses and we would look at it, and we'd just go on singing "Over my head I see freedom in the air." And then we would be thrown in the paddy wagons, and sometimes we were stacked in there like sardines in a can. And they would throw us in, and old Bull would say, "Take them off," and they did; and we would just go in the paddy wagon singing, "We Shall Overcome." And every now and then we'd get in the jail, and we'd see the jailers looking through the windows being moved by our prayers, and being moved by

our words and our songs. And there was a power there which Bull Connor couldn't adjust to; and so we ended up transforming Bull into a steer, and we won our struggle in Birmingham.

Now we've got to go on to Memphis just like that. I call upon you to be with us Monday. Now about injunctions: We have an injunction[10] and we're going into court tomorrow morning to fight this illegal, unconstitutional injunction. All we say to America is, "Be true to what you said on paper." If I lived in China or even Russia, or any totalitarian country, maybe I could understand the denial of certain basic First Amendment privileges, because they hadn't committed themselves to that over there. But somewhere I read of the freedom of assembly. Somewhere I read of the freedom of speech. Somewhere I read of the freedom of the press. Somewhere I read that the greatness of America is the right to protest for right. And so just as I say, we aren't going to let any injunction turn us around. We are going on.

We need all of you. And you know what's beautiful to me, is to see all of these ministers of the Gospel. It's a marvelous picture. Who is it that is supposed to articulate the longings and aspirations of the people more than the preacher? Somehow the preacher must be an Amos,[11] and say, "Let justice roll ★ down like waters and righteousness like a mighty stream." Somehow, the preacher must say with Jesus, "The spirit of the Lord is upon me, because he hath anointed me to deal with the problems of the poor."[12]

And I want to commend the preachers, under the leadership of these noble men: James Lawson, one who has been in this struggle for many years; he's been to jail for struggling; but he's still going on, fighting for

---

7. *Bull Connor*, whose given name was Eugene, was Birmingham's Commissioner of Public Safety and a candidate for mayor in the 1964 election.
8. *Physics* is the study of the physical properties of light, heat, electricity, magnetism, and so on. With the invented word *transphysics,* King refers to things that transcend, or go beyond, the physical, such as morality and philosophy.
9. King is referring to the Christian ritual of baptism, which may involve immersion in water or the sprinkling or pouring of water over a person's head.

---

10. An *injunction* is a court order barring a specific action, such as a march, demonstration, or strike.
11. The Hebrew prophet *Amos* lived in the eighth century BC.
12. Here, King has freely paraphrased the words that Jesus was reading from the prophet Isaiah.

Literary Element   Allusion *Why does King make these allusions in these two sentences?* **L2**

Big Idea   Keeping Freedom Alive *What arguments does King make against the court injunction?* **B1**

MARTIN LUTHER KING JR.   **457**

Teach

L2 Literary Element

Allusion Answer: *Students may say that these allusions are friendly ways of connecting with the audience and, possibly, of reminding them of the commitments that come with religious faith.* **OL**

B1 Big Idea

Keeping Freedom Alive Answer: *King refers to the founding ideas of the United States and of the rights guaranteed in the Constitution, which would seem to permit the march despite the court's injunction: freedom of assembly, freedom of speech, and freedom of the press.* **OL**

★ Literary History

Amos Amos, a prophet of the Israelites, denounced Israel's sins, particularly those of injustice, corruption, and greed. The Bible verse that King quotes is Amos 5:24: "I want to see a mighty flood of justice—a torrent of doing good." **AS**

Differentiated Instruction

Paraphrasing Some students may have trouble following King's arguments and main ideas. Point out that one of his rhetorical techniques is to use allegories and stories as lead-ins to his main ideas. Explain that this type of passage can be simplified and paraphrased in one sentence. An example is King's reference to different periods of human history. Ask less proficient readers to condense several such passages into single sentences. Then ask them to explain what important arguments these passages support. **BL**

Objectives
- To analyze allusion (SE)
- To identify problem and solution (SE)
- To research historical content (TWE)

L Literary Element

Allusion Answer: *King says that these ideas of the afterlife are well and fine but that it is not enough for ministers and others to comfort the poor and suffering with these ideas. They must also care about what happens to the poor and suffering while they are alive; they must work to make the country more compassionate and fair.* **OL**

R1 Reading Strategy

Identifying Problem and Solution Answer:
According to King, African Americans would be able to pressure businesses to adopt fairer practices toward their workers. **OL**

the rights of his people. Rev. Ralph Jackson, Billy Kiles; I could just go right on down the list, but time will not permit. But I want to thank them all. And I want you to thank them, because so often, preachers aren't concerned about anything but themselves. And I'm always happy to see a **relevant** ministry.

It's alright to talk about "long white robes over yonder," in all of its symbolism. But ultimately people want some suits and dresses and shoes to wear down here. It's alright to talk about "streets flowing with milk and honey," but God has commanded us to be concerned about the slums down here, and his children who can't eat three square meals a day. It's alright to talk about the new Jerusalem, but one day, God's preacher must talk about the New York, the new Atlanta, the new Philadelphia, the new Los Angeles, the new Memphis, Tennessee. This is what we have to do.

Now the other thing we'll have to do is this: Always anchor our external direct action with the power of economic withdrawal. Now, we are poor people, individually, we are poor when you compare us with white society in America. We are poor. Never stop and forget that collectively, that means all of us together, collectively we are richer than all the nations in the world, with the exception of nine. Did you ever think about that? After you leave[13] the United States,

> ### "And we've come by here to ask you to make the first item on your agenda—fair treatment, where God's children are concerned."

Soviet Russia, Great Britain, West Germany, France, and I could name the others, the Negro collectively is richer than most nations of the world. We have an annual income of more than thirty billion dollars a year, which is more than all of the exports of the United States, and more than the national budget of Canada. Did you know that? That's power right there, if we know how to pool it.

We don't have to argue with anybody. We don't have to curse and go around acting bad with our words. We don't need any bricks and bottles, we don't need any Molotov cocktails, we just need to go around to these stores, and to these massive industries in our country, and say, "God sent us by here, to say to you that you're not treating his children right. And we've come by here to ask you to make the first item on your **agenda**—fair treatment, where God's children are concerned. Now, if you are not prepared to do that, we do have an agenda that we must follow. And our agenda calls for withdrawing economic support from you . . ."

But not only that, we've got to strengthen black institutions. I call upon you to take your money out of the banks downtown and deposit your money in Tri-State Bank—we want a "bank-in" movement in Memphis. So go by the savings and loan association. I'm not asking you something that we don't do ourselves at SCLC. Judge Hooks and others

---

13. Here, the expression *after you leave* means "not counting" or "apart from."

> **Literary Element** Allusion *In this paragraph, King alludes to common ideas of heaven and the afterlife. What point does he make about these ideas?* **L**

> **Vocabulary**
> **relevant** (rel´ ə vənt) *adj.* related to the issue at hand

> **Reading Strategy** Identifying Problem and Solution *What good outcomes could be obtained by pooling economic resources, according to King?* **R1**

> **Vocabulary**
> **agenda** (ə jen´ də) *n.* an outline of tasks to be accomplished

Additional Support

Skills Practice

WRITING: Organizing a Persuasive Speech King's speech aims at motivating and persuading his followers. A persuasive speech must include reasons why the listeners should do something or believe something. The writer lists arguments and organizes them according to what will be most persuasive, sometimes putting the strongest argument first and sometimes building up to the strongest argument. Have students work in pairs to develop an outline for a persuasive speech, with emphasis on organization. Have them brainstorm for arguments to support their points of view. **OL**

will tell you that we have an account here in the savings and loan association from the Southern Christian Leadership Conference. We're just telling you to follow what we're doing. Put your money there. You have six or seven black insurance companies in Memphis. Take out your insurance there. We want to have an "insurance-in."

Now these are some practical things we can do. We begin the process of building a greater economic base. And at the same time, we are putting pressure where it really hurts. I ask you to follow through here.

Now, let me say as I move to my conclusion that we've got to give ourselves to this struggle until the end. Nothing would be more tragic than to stop at this point, in Memphis. We've got to see it through. And when we have our march, you need to be there. Be concerned about your brother. You may not be on strike. But either we go up together, or we go down together.

Let us develop a kind of dangerous unselfishness. One day a man came to Jesus; and he wanted to raise some questions about some vital matters in life. At points, he wanted to trick Jesus, and show him that he knew a little more than Jesus knew, and through this, throw him off base. Now that question could have easily ended up in a philosophical and theological debate. But Jesus immediately pulled that question from mid-air, and placed it on a dangerous curve between Jerusalem and Jericho. And he talked about a certain man, who fell among thieves. You remember that a Levite and a priest passed by on the other side. They didn't stop to help him. And finally a man of

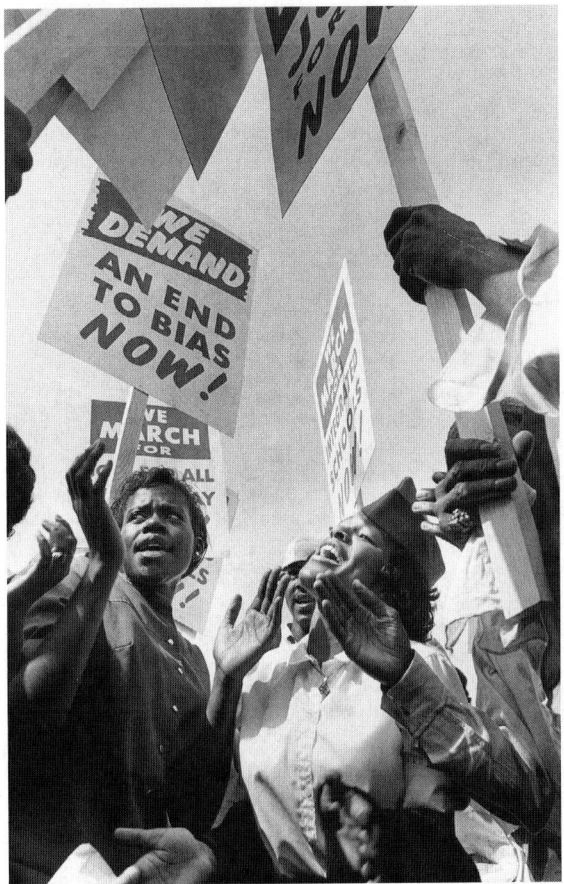
Civil rights marchers in Washington. Marching for equality ★

another race came by. He got down from his beast, decided not to be **compassionate** by proxy.[14] But with him, administered first aid, and helped the man in need. Jesus ended up saying, this was the good man, this was the great man, because he had the capacity to project the "I" into the "thou," and to be

14. In ancient Israel, men of the *Levite* tribe were temple priests or assistants. One might expect the two religious men to help, especially since the victim is also Jewish. Instead, it is *a man of another race* who decides not to leave it to someone else—a *proxy*, or substitute—to help.

Reading Strategy Identifying Problem and Solution
What argument does King make for attending the march? **R2**

MARTIN LUTHER KING JR. **459**

Teach

R2 Reading Strategy

Identifying Problem and Solution
Answer: *King argues that if the strikers fail, African Americans throughout Memphis will be the losers.* **OL**

★ **Viewing the Photograph**

Ask: How do you think the people in the photograph feel? *(Student responses may include: joyful, serious, animated, passionate, or united.)* **AS**

Reading in the Real World

Citizenship King's powerful words persuaded many people to join the Civil Rights Movement despite fierce opposition and danger. What are important issues of today that lead people to take sides? Ask students to choose a current issue on which people have strong views and to find two persuasive articles expressing opposite opinions in magazines, newspapers, or on the Internet. Ask them to summarize the articles for the class and then to express their own opinions on the subject and what led them to take a particular stand. **OL**

Objectives
• To analyze allusion (SE)
• To analyze problem and solution
• To organize a persuasive speech (TWE)

Teach

L1 Literary Element

Allusion Answer: *Excuses include those used by people who emphasize their busy schedules—even their involvement in worthy activities—to get out of helping others. People may also use technicalities, such as religious laws, to get out of helping others.* **OL**

BI Big Idea

Keeping Freedom Alive Answer: *Students may say that King encourages attitudes of responsibility, generosity, caring, and solidarity.* **OL**

★ Writer's Technique

Irony Mention that irony is when an event happens that is the opposite of what is expected. Point out that King uses irony in describing the circumstances in which he was stabbed and almost died. **Ask:** What is ironic about the attack? *(It is ironic that it was committed by an African American woman.)* **AS**

concerned about his brother. Now you know, we use our imagination a great deal to try to determine why the priest and the Levite didn't stop. At times we say they were busy going to church meetings—an ecclesiastical gathering—and they had to get on down to Jerusalem so they wouldn't be late for their meeting. At other times we would speculate that there was a religious law that "One who was engaged in religious ceremonials was not to touch a human body twenty-four hours before the ceremony." And every now and then we begin to wonder whether maybe they were not going down to Jerusalem, or down to Jericho, rather to organize a "Jericho Road Improvement Association." That's a possibility. Maybe they felt that it was better to deal with the problem from the causal root, rather than to get bogged down with an individual effort.

But I'm going to tell you what my imagination tells me. It's possible that these men were afraid. You see, the Jericho road is a dangerous road. I remember when Mrs. King and I were first in Jerusalem. We rented a car and drove from Jerusalem down to Jericho. And as soon as we got on that road, I said to my wife, "I can see why Jesus used this as a setting for his parable."[15] It's a winding, meandering road. It's really conducive for ambushing. You start out in Jerusalem, which is about 1200 miles, or rather 1200 feet above sea level. And by the time you get down to Jericho, fifteen or twenty minutes later, you're about 2200 feet

> "And let us move on in these powerful days, these days of challenge to make America what it ought to be."

below sea level. That's a dangerous road. In the days of Jesus it came to be known as the "Bloody Pass." And you know, it's possible that the priest and the Levite looked over that man on the ground and wondered if the robbers were still around. Or it's possible that they felt that the man on the ground was merely faking. And he was acting like he had been robbed and hurt, in order to seize them over there, lure them there for quick and easy seizure. And so the first question that the Levite asked was, "If I stop to help this man, what will happen to me?" But then the Good Samaritan came by. And he reversed the question: "If I do not stop to help this man, what will happen to him?"

That's the question before you tonight. Not, "If I stop to help the sanitation workers, what will happen to all of the hours that I usually spend in my office every day and every week as a pastor?" The question is not, "If I stop to help this man in need, what will happen to me?" "If I do not stop to help the sanitation workers, what will happen to them?" That's the question.

Let us rise up tonight with a greater readiness. Let us stand with a greater determination. And let us move on in these powerful days, these days of challenge to make America what it ought to be. We have an opportunity to make America a better nation. And I want to thank God, once more, for allowing me to be here with you.

You know, several years ago, I was in New York City autographing the first book that I had written. And while sitting there autographing books, a demented[16] black woman

---

15. A *parable* is a brief story intended to illustrate some truth or moral lesson.

Literary Element Allusion *According to King, what kinds of excuses do people make for not stopping to help one another?* **L1**

---

16. *Demented* means "insane."

Big Idea Keeping Freedom Alive *What attitude or spirit does King encourage his listeners to adopt?* **BI**

460 UNIT 2 NONFICTION

Additional Support

Skills Practice

GRAMMAR: Simple Subjects and Simple Predicates King uses many simple subjects and predicates to make his speeches clear and direct. Write these sentences on the board: The issue is injustice. *(issue; is)* The priest was going to Jericho. *(priest; was going)*

Discuss each simple subject and simple predicate. Have students name the simple subject and the simple predicate in the following: (1) Now these are some practical things. *(these; are)* (2) We can develop a kind of dangerous unselfishness. *(We; can develop)* **OL** came up. The only question I heard from her was, "Are you Martin Luther King?"

And I was looking down writing, and I said yes. And the next minute I felt something beating on my chest. Before I knew it I had been stabbed by this demented woman.

I was rushed to Harlem Hospital. It was a dark Saturday afternoon. And that blade had gone through, and the X rays revealed that the tip of the blade was on the edge of my aorta, the main artery. And once that's punctured, you drown in your own blood—that's the end of you.

It came out in the *New York Times* the next morning, that if I had sneezed, I would have died. Well, about four days later, they allowed me, after the operation, after my chest had been opened, and the blade had been taken out, to move around in the wheel chair in the hospital. They allowed me to read some of the mail that came in, and from all over the states, and the world, kind letters came in. I read a few, but one of them I will never forget. I had received one from the President and the Vice-President. I've forgotten what those telegrams said. I'd received a visit and a letter from the Governor of New York, but I've forgotten what the letter said. But there was another letter that came from a little girl, a young girl who was a student at the White Plains High School. And I looked at that letter, and

Dr. Martin Luther King, Jr. hugs his wife Coretta after learning he had been awarded the Nobel Prize for Peace

I'll never forget it. It said simply, "Dear Dr. King: I am a ninth-grade student at the White Plains High School." She said, "While it should not matter, I would like to mention that I am a white girl. I read in the paper of your misfortune, and of your suffering. And I read that if you had sneezed, you would have died. And I'm simply writing you to say that I'm so happy that you didn't sneeze."

And I want to say tonight, I want to say that I am happy that I didn't sneeze. Because if I had sneezed, I wouldn't have been around here in 1960, when students all over the South started sitting in at lunch counters. And I knew that as they were sitting in, they were really standing up for the best in the American dream. And taking the whole nation back to those great walls of democracy which were dug deep by the Founding Fathers in the Declaration of Independence and the Constitution. If I had sneezed, I wouldn't have been around in 1962, when Negroes in Albany, Georgia,[17] decided to straighten their backs up. And whenever men and women straighten their backs up, they are going somewhere, because a man can't ride your back unless it is bent. If I had sneezed, I wouldn't have been here in 1963, when the black people of Birmingham, Alabama,

---

17. In 1962 King took part in demonstrations in *Albany, Georgia,* protesting the segregation of public facilities.

MARTIN LUTHER KING JR.   **461**

Teach

L2 Literary Element

Allusion Ask: What purposes might be served by King's allusion to the letter from the high school student? **Answer:** *King may be attempting to remind his audience of the support and good will of some white people. He may also be attempting to interject a little light-heartedness and entertainment while illustrating his point.* **OL**

★ Viewing the Photograph

Martin Luther King Jr. was awarded the Nobel Peace Prize for 1964. The youngest male recipient of the Peace Prize at that time, King donated all of the prize money to the Civil Rights Movement. **Ask:** What emotions does this photograph stir in you? *(Students may feel pride for King's accomplishment or perhaps sadness, knowing that his mission would end abruptly with his assassination four years later.)* **AS**

English Language Coach

Pronunciation English-language learners may have difficulty pronouncing some of the long, multisyllabic words in this selection. Write words such as *panoramic, magnificence, emancipation, nonexistence, sanitation, immersed, unconstitutional,* and *meandering* on the board and review their correct pronunciation with students.

Have students write the words they find challenging on flash cards with the definitions on the back of the cards. Have students work in pairs to practice pronouncing and defining the words. **EL**

Objectives
• To analyze allusion(SE)
• To understand simple subjects and simple predicates (TWE)

461

Teach

Keeping Freedom Alive
Answer: *King was reminding his listeners of the many victories the Civil Rights Movement had achieved thus far.* **OL**

L Literary Element

Allusion Answer: *Students may say that King thinks that he has been blessed to be a part of the struggle. He does not feel the need to actually witness the final victory of justice and freedom in person; he feels privileged enough just knowing that it will happen.* **OL**

⭐ **Viewing the Photograph**

Sit-ins were used extensively as a form of direct-action, nonviolent protest during the Civil Rights Movement. The first publicized sit-in of the movement occurred at a Woolworth's store in Greensboro, North Carolina, on February 1, 1960. **Ask:** Why might a sit-in be an effective form of protest? *(Sit-ins draw public attention while remaining nonviolent. In addition to promoting a message, they also arouse sympathy from bystanders.)* **AS**

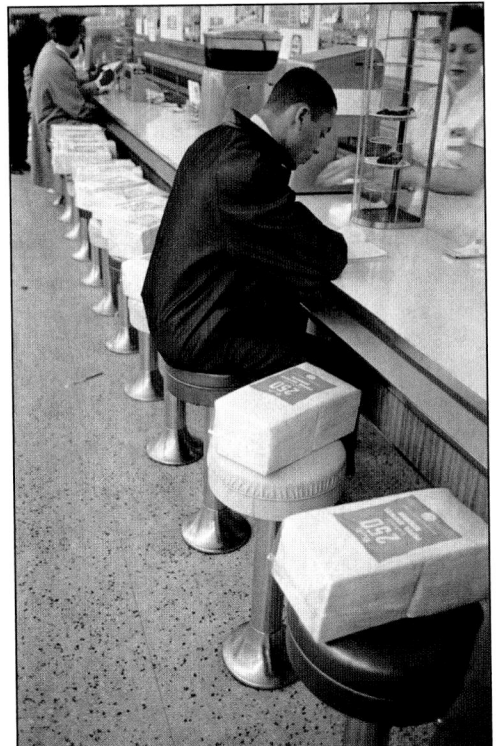

An African American student sits at a lunch counter reserved for white customers during a sit-in to protest segregation. Packages of napkins have been placed on nearby stools to discourage other protesters from joining the sit-in. ⭐

aroused the conscience of this nation, and brought into being the Civil Rights Bill. If I had sneezed, I wouldn't have had a chance later that year, in August, to try to tell America about a dream that I had had. If I had sneezed, I wouldn't have been down in Selma, Alabama,[18] to see the great movement there. If I had sneezed, I wouldn't have been in Memphis to see a community rally around those brothers and sisters who are suffering. I'm so happy that I didn't sneeze.

And they were telling me, now it doesn't matter now. It really doesn't matter what happens now. I left Atlanta this morning, and as we got started on the plane, there

---

18. In *Selma, Alabama*, in 1965, King led a march to protest restrictions on African American voting rights. Soon afterward, the Voting Rights Act of 1965 was passed.

Big Idea Keeping Freedom Alive *What does King hope to illustrate by mentioning these events?* **BI**

462 UNIT 2 NONFICTION

were six of us, the pilot said over the public address system, "We are sorry for the delay, but we have Dr. Martin Luther King on the plane. And to be sure that all of the bags were checked, and to be sure that nothing would be wrong with the plane, we had to check out everything carefully. And we've had the plane protected and guarded all night."

And then I got into Memphis. And some began to say the threats, or talk about the threats that were out. What would happen to me from some of our sick white brothers?

Well, I don't know what will happen now. We've got some difficult days ahead. But it doesn't matter with me now. Because I've been to the mountaintop. And I don't mind. Like anybody, I would like to live a long life. Longevity has its place. But I'm not concerned about that now. I just want to do God's will. And He's allowed me to go up to the mountain. And I've looked over. And I've seen the promised land. I may not get there with you. But I want you to know tonight, that we, as a people will get to the promised land. And I'm happy, tonight. I'm not worried about anything. I'm not fearing any man. Mine eyes have seen the glory of the coming of the Lord. ∾

Literary Element Allusion *In this final passage, King alludes to the "promised land" and ends by quoting the patriotic American song "The Battle Hymn of the Republic." What is the meaning of the passage?* **L**

Additional Support

CheckPoint

Use the CheckPoint questions on Presentation Plus! to check students' mastery of the selection. These questions can be used with interactive response keypads for student feedback.

Skills Practice

READING: Distinguishing Fact and Opinion To persuade his audience that marching and nonviolent protesting are the necessary means to achieve freedom and equality, King presents many arguments and much information. When does he use facts as evidence, and when does he give his opinions? Ask students to determine what is fact and what is opinion.

Ask: Which technique do you find more persuasive and why? *(Answers will vary. Students should support their responses with examples from the text.)* **OL**

RESPONDING AND THINKING CRITICALLY

Respond

1. Which sentence or passage made the greatest impression on you? Why?

Recall and Interpret

2. (a)Summarize King's mental journey through history. In which age does he want to live? (b)What might you infer about King's character and beliefs on the basis of the age he chooses?

3. (a)What plan of action does King outline for African American people in Memphis? (b)What is the purpose of King's plan of action?

4. What feelings does King express about the dangers he faces? What reasons does he give for his feelings?

Analyze and Evaluate

5. What is your opinion of King's nonviolent approach to instituting political and social change?

6. How did the prophetic aspects of this speech affect your reaction to it? Explain.

Connect

7. **Big Idea** **Keeping Freedom Alive** If King were alive today, what issues do you think he might be addressing? Why?

Literary Element Allusion

In this speech, King uses both historical and biblical **allusions**. For example, King says, "I would take my mental flight by Egypt through, or rather across the Red Sea, through the wilderness toward the promised land." He is alluding to the biblical story in which Moses leads the Israelites out of slavery in Egypt to the promised land of Canaan.

1. Why do you think King alludes to the Israelites' flight from Egypt?

2. Locate two more examples of historical allusions in the speech, and explain why they are included.

Writing About Literature

Analyze Rhetorical Devices The use of a series of words, phrases, clauses, or sentences that have a similar grammatical structure is called **parallelism**. Speakers and writers often use parallelism to emphasize ideas and to create a rhythmic flow to the language. An example of parallelism occurs when King says, "But either we go up together, or we go down together." Another rhetorical device used by speakers and writers is **repetition**. King repeats sounds, words, and phrases to create emphasis and to increase the unity of his speech. Write a brief essay discussing one example of parallelism and one example of repetition in the speech.

Reading Strategy **Identifying Problem and Solution**

Persuasive speeches often focus on a specific **problem** and suggest **solutions** to that problem.

1. What is the main problem King discusses in his speech?

2. What solutions does King suggest? Do these seem like effective solutions to you? Explain.

Vocabulary Practice

Practice with Synonyms Find the synonym for each vocabulary word.

1. grapple
  a. push **b.** struggle **c.** lasso
2. relevant
  a. applicable **b.** unfit **c.** wrong
3. agenda
  a. pamphlet **b.** essay **c.** outline
4. compassionate
  a. kindhearted **b.** cruel **c.** right

Literature Online **Web Activities** For eFlashcards, Selection Quick Checks, and other Web activities, go to www.glencoe.com.

MARTIN LUTHER KING JR. **463**

Assess

1. Answers will vary.

2. (a) Students should summarize King's journey through Egypt, Greece, the Roman Empire, the Renaissance, the Protestant Reformation, the Civil War, the Great Depression, and the present. He wants to live in the present. (b) King understands how people can change the present.

3. (a) They must stay united and focused on the issue, remain peaceful, and march for their brothers. (b) To get people to support the strikers and to march

4. King is happy and not worried. He knows that things will turn out right. He has seen a positive future.

5. King's nonviolent approach was successful. Its result was social and political change.

6. Students may indicate that they were amazed by how prophetic his words were.

7. Students might mention unemployment, unequal opportunity, and racism.

Reading Strategy

1. Inequality between whites and blacks

2. Economic boycotts, unity, and persistence. These seem effective.

Literature Online

Web Activities Have students access the Web site for interactive activities that will help them assess their understanding of the selection.

Literary Element

1. The struggle of the Israelites, also slaves, is comparable to the African American journey toward equality.

2. Lincoln's signing of the Emancipation Proclamation and Martin Luther and the Protestant Reformation; King compares the current struggle for equality to these momentous events.

Writing About Literature

Make sure that students discuss the effects of repetition and parallelism, especially on the persuasiveness of King's essay, in their essays.

Vocabulary

1. b **2.** a **3.** c **4.** a

463

Focus

BELLRINGER

Bellringer Options
Daily Language Practice Transparency 43
Or pass out copies of a comic strip—or an excerpt from a comic book or a graphic novel—in which the text has been removed from the dialogue bubbles.
Ask: What are these characters saying? Have students discuss what the characters might be saying. Have them notice the characters' expressions and body language. Ask them to write in their own dialogue. Then pass out copies of the comic with the original dialogue.

Connecting to the Reading Selections

Allow students to share their responses to the opening question. Then have students discuss what they already know about comic books and graphic novels.

Comparing Literature: *Different Viewpoints*

Connecting to the Reading Selections

Who should read comic books? When should they be read? Where should they be read? Should they be read at all? Answers to these questions depend upon the perspective of the person who is answering them. The four works compared here—by Chester Brown, Charles McGrath, Teresa Méndez, and Andrew Arnold—each explore the development of the comic book and the related graphic novel from a different perspective.

COMPARING THE Big Idea **Keeping Freedom Alive**

Freedom of expression remains one of the cornerstones upon which the United States was built. Without the ability to speak, create, and think freely, freedom itself would cease to exist. These works by Brown, McGrath, Méndez, and Arnold suggest that the graphic novel may eventually earn a place of respect in the literary world.

COMPARING Persuasive Appeals

Persuasive appeals are attempts on the part of authors to influence their readers. These writers use persuasion to express their thoughts about the graphic novel's place in modern culture.

COMPARING Authors' Viewpoints

Each of these authors explores the graphic novel from a slightly different perspective and for a different purpose. Popular culture plays an important role in determining what people read, and a generation raised on the graphic images found on television and in video games seems to be drawn naturally to an art form that combines words and images to tell a story.

464 UNIT 2 NONFICTION

Selection Skills

Reading Skills
- Comparing Persuasive Appeals (SE pp. 464, 465, 482; TWE p. 466)
- Comparing Authors' Viewpoints (SE pp. 464, 482)
- Identifying Assumptions and Ambiguities (SE pp. 466–481)

Comparing Literature

Literary Elements
- Rhetorical Devices (SE pp. 466–481)
- Analogies (TWE p. 470)

Vocabulary Skills
- Synonyms (SE pp. 466, 481)

Listening/Speaking/Viewing Skills
- Performing (SE p. 481)
- Analyzing Art (TWE pp. 468–480

Writing Skills/Grammar
- Quickwrite (SE pp. 473, 480)
- Tone (TWE p. 478)

Persuasive Text

READING AND ANALYZING PERSUASIVE TEXT

An **argument** is a reason given to prove or support a point. It is often used in persuasive speaking or writing. In order to recognize when a writer or speaker is attempting to persuade, it is important for the audience to understand the structure of an argument and the appeals that are likely to be made.

The Structure of an Argument At its most basic, an argument consists of a specific position plus evidence supporting that position. The strongest argument is a logical one, which means that the argument is structured in such a way that it makes sense. An argument can be structured logically by using either inductive or deductive reasoning.

Inductive reasoning involves drawing a general conclusion from a series of specific facts. The chart below shows how inductive reasoning led the Health Department of ABCville to test fifteen ill people to determine what caused an illness for one hundred people. If the sample is selected randomly from the entire hundred, it will be fairly representative of the population.

> **Sample:** fifteen of one hundred people
>
> ↓
>
> **Facts:** All fifteen of the sample suffer nausea and dizziness Thursday evening. All one hundred ate lunch at Ye Olde XYZ Shoppe on Thursday.
>
> ↓
>
> **Generalization:** One hundred got food poisoning at Ye Olde XYZ Shoppe.

Deductive reasoning involves drawing a specific conclusion from general facts. When you use deductive reasoning, begin with a generalization, state a related fact, and draw a conclusion based on the generalization and the fact.

> **Generalization:** Food poisoning is caused by bacteria that grow in cooked food left at room temperature for six hours.
>
> ↓
>
> **Fact:** At Ye Olde XYZ Shoppe, Juanita ate food that had been left out all day.
>
> ↓
>
> **Conclusion:** It is likely that Juanita will get food poisoning.

Persuasive Appeals and Problems with Arguments A **persuasive appeal** is an attempt to convince someone of something by creating a sympathetic response. There are several different types of appeals, including logical, emotional, and ethical appeals. Logical appeals contain solid evidence, such as facts, examples, statistics, or testimony, that appeals to the intellect. Emotional appeals contain information or ideas that target emotions. Ethical appeals address the reader's morals and values.

Sometimes **fallacies**, or errors in reasoning, can weaken an argument. A **deductive fallacy** is an invalid deductive argument. For example, you know that all European countries have U.N. ambassadors, and you know that Sierra Leone has a U.N. ambassador. However, you cannot conclude then that Sierra Leone is therefore a European country. An **inductive fallacy** is when arguments appear to be inductive arguments, but they in fact do not provide adequate support to draw a generalization. For example, imagine that you know that the water in a certain lake is toxic, and you also know that factory spilloff causes high levels of toxic chemicals. If you assume that the toxic chemicals in the lake are therefore due to factory spilloff, then you are making an inductive fallacy.

COMPARING LITERATURE **465**

Focus

Reading and Analyzing Persuasive Text

Ask students for examples of inductive and deductive appeals in advertising. *(An inductive ad might present a series of car reviews to conclude that a given sedan is the best on the market. A deductive ad might suggest that people who excel at sports drink a certain juice, so you should too.)*
Ask: Why might a writer choose to use a logical appeal instead of an emotional appeal, or vice versa? *(Answers will vary. Students may say that a logical appeal is a better choice for an argument that deals with abstract concepts, while an emotional appeal is better suited to "human interest" arguments, or issues in which there is no clear right and wrong.)*

Selection Resources

Print Materials
- 📁 Unit 2 Resources (Fast File), pp. 64–67
- 📁 Leveled Vocabulary Development, p. 35
- 📁 Selection and Unit Assessments, pp. 75–76
- 📁 Selection Quick Checks, p. 38

Transparencies
- Bellringer Options Transparencies: Daily Language Practice Transparency 43
- Literary Elements Transparency 42

Technology
- 💿 TeacherWorks Plus™ CD-ROM
- 💿 StudentWorks Plus™ CD-ROM
- 💿 Presentation Plus!™ CD-ROM
- 💻 Literature Online, glencoe.com
- 💻 Online Student Edition, mhln.com
- 💿 ExamView® Assessment Suite CD-ROM
- 💿 Vocabulary PuzzleMaker CD-ROM
- 💿 Listening Library, disc 1 tracks 39–42

COMPARING LITERATURE

BEFORE YOU READ

Focus

Summary

This is a comic strip in the form of a graphic novel, set on the front of *The New York Times Magazine.* An interviewer, talking to an artist, asserts that graphic novels are just comics with more pages. After the artist responds, the interviewer says that they must continue the interview inside the magazine. Inside, the interviewer has been replaced by a duck. Much to the duck's chagrin, the artist feels that he and his medium are being ridiculed.

V Vocabulary

Vocabulary File Say: Add these words and definitions to your vocabulary file. For each word, include a sentence that gives you an example of how to use the word. **OL** Students with English language needs should include the pronunciations of these words in their files. **EL**

Literary Elements Have students access the Web site to improve their understanding of rhetorical devices.

Additional Support

LITERATURE PREVIEW

Connecting to the Selections

The following selections debate the issue of the graphic novel's place in modern culture. Two authors see it as a new genre, while one sees it as a mode of learning. Before you read the selections, think about the following questions:

- What is your opinion of the graphic novel format?
- Do you think the graphic novel format has educational value?

Building Background

Popular culture, also known as pop culture, consists of movies, books, TV, sports, music, and anything else that has mass appeal. Some artistic movements can even be classified as pop culture. The work of artists Andy Warhol and Roy Lichtenstein, who painted with comic-strip themes, was easily mass-produced, contributing to their mass appeal and pop-culture status in the 1960s. Much of the mass appeal associated with pop culture is largely due to the influence of the media. Magazines, television programs, and advertising influence the public's attitudes toward goods and services, and even contribute to consumers' tastes. Ironically, even some commercials have managed to attain pop-culture status.

Setting Purposes for Reading

Big Idea Keeping Freedom Alive

As you read the following selections, notice how the authors promote the graphic novel as a literary form. One author promotes the graphic novel as a way to educate reluctant readers, struggling learners, and students whose first language is not English. This idea raises the issue of the role education plays in preserving freedom of expression.

Literary Element Rhetorical Devices

Rhetoric is the effective use of language in order to persuade, so **rhetorical devices** are techniques of persuasive writing. These techniques include repetition, parallelism, analogy, and logic. As you read, watch for the authors' uses of these devices.

- See Literary Terms Handbook, p. R14.

Literature Online Interactive Literary Elements Handbook To review or learn more about the literary elements, go to www.glencoe.com.

READING PREVIEW

Reading Strategy Identifying Assumptions and Ambiguities

A writer may assume that a point is true, rather than prove that it is. Or his or her writing may be ambiguous, having several meanings. Learning how to **identify assumptions and ambiguities** can help readers develop their own conclusions by distinguishing fact and opinion. While reading the following selections, try to recognize any assumptions and ambiguities.

....

Reading Tip: Making Inferences Using logic to evaluate the evidence in the selection will allow you to arrive at a conclusion or to infer the meaning of passages that contain assumptions or ambiguities. Use a chart like the one below to help you organize your thoughts.

Assumption or Ambiguity	Inference
"Once kids know how to read, there is no good reason to continue to use dumbed-down materials."	The speaker of the quote has assumed that all writing in a graphic novel format is dumbed down.

Vocabulary

vernacular (vər nak′ yə lər) *adj.* a form of language particular to a certain group of people; jargon; p. 470 *The vernacular used by lawyers can be very confusing to their clients.*

renaissance (ren′ə säns′) *n.* rebirth or comeback; p. 470 *Once shuttered and silent, the opera house is now in the midst of a renaissance and a revival of its long-lost glory.*

savvy (sav′ē) *adj.* having practical knowledge or understanding; p. 472 *Children today seem to be born computer-savvy.*

Vocabulary Tip: Synonyms Words that have the same or nearly the same meaning are called synonyms. The words *same* and *equal,* for example, are synonyms. Note that synonyms are always the same part of speech.

Skills Practice

READING: Analyzing Persuasive Appeals Say:
Chester Brown is using a graphic novel format to argue that graphic novels should be taken seriously. **Ask:** What is unusual about this approach? *(Arguments usually come in the form of persuasive essays or articles.)* Why might Brown have chosen this approach? *(Students may say that this format tests Brown's argument: If readers think about his points, Brown has proved that the graphic novel is capable of presenting serious subjects.)* Have students think of other nontraditional approaches that could augment a persuasive appeal. **OL**

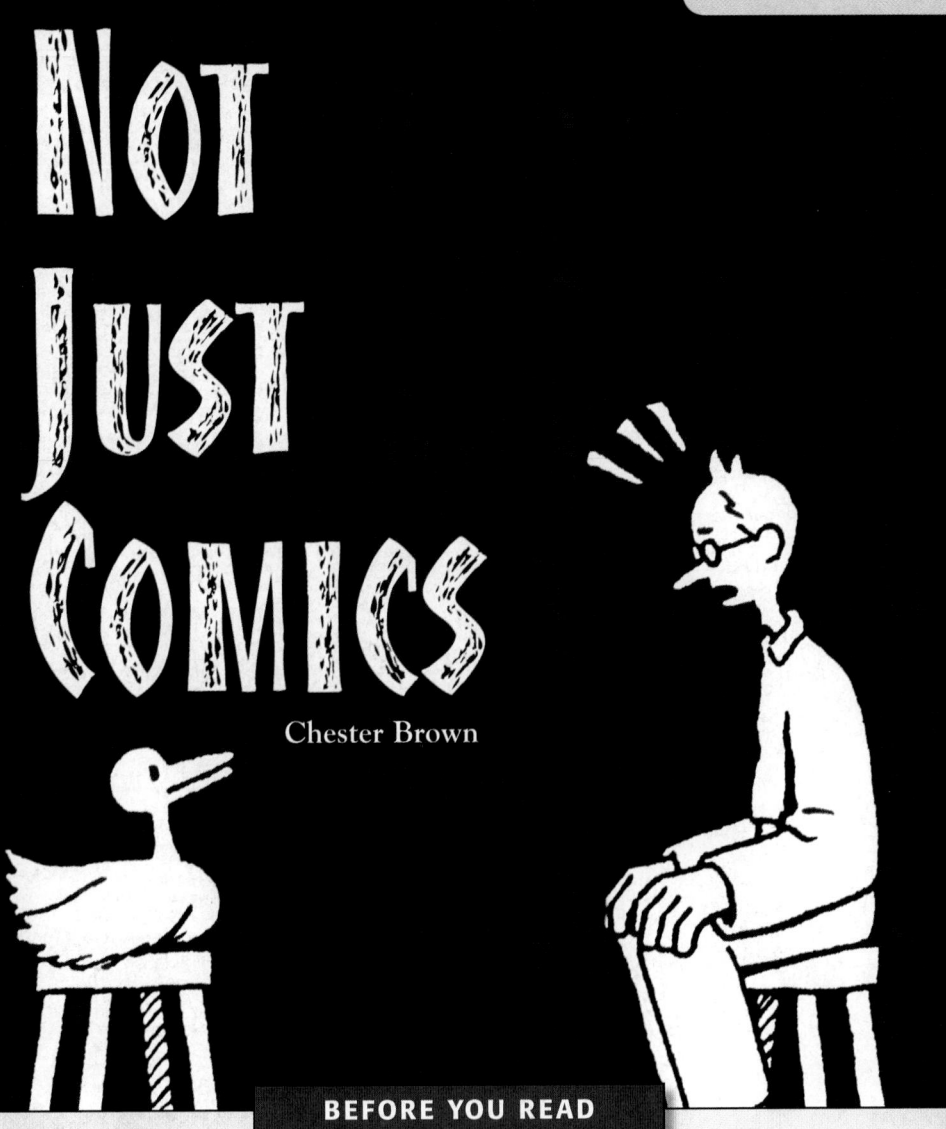

Not Just Comics

Chester Brown

BEFORE YOU READ

Building Background

What is the nearly universal appeal of a comic strip, a series of pictorial panels wherein characters' words and thoughts are indicated by means of "balloons" containing speech? Cartoons with word balloons were popular as far back as the eighteenth century, especially in political caricatures. It can even be argued that the first comic strip was a tapestry that showed the events of the Trojan War. Throughout the years,

this popular art form has continued to reinvent itself—and in the process find more fans. Chester Brown is one of Canada's best known cartoonists. When questioned about the future of comics in an interview with *TIME*, Brown replied, "I certainly think that this is the most exciting time in terms of the work coming out. There has never been better work being published." ★

CHESTER BROWN **467**

Focus

★ Literary History

Comics and Graphic Novels Graphic storytelling has existed in various forms for centuries: morality tales, political satires and caricatures, historical broadsheets, and romanticized crime stories. The modern concept of the newspaper comic strip began in 1894 with *The Yellow Kid* by Richard Outcault and grew in popularity with such strips as *The Katzenjammer Kids* and, slightly later, *Krazy Kat*. Have students find examples of such early comics and compare them to the newspaper comics of today. **Ask:** What similarities do early comics share with graphic novels? *(Answers will include such standardized devices as the framed panel, speech and thought balloons, chronological progression from left to right and top to bottom, and motion lines.)* **AS**

CheckPoint

Use the CheckPoint questions on Presentation Plus! to monitor students' comprehension. These questions can be used with interactive response keypads for immediate student feedback.

Objectives
• To identify an author's use of persuasive techniques (SE)
• To analyze persuasive appeals (TWE)

English Language Coach

Analyzing Audience Discuss with students that writers of written material and speeches consider the audience for which they are writing. For example, a speech at a pep rally has a different style from one given by a diplomat at the United Nations. **Ask:** *Do you think the same type of language adjustment*

would be true for artists of comics? Have students analyze the language of several comics and possibly a few graphic novels. Ask them to determine what audience is most likely targeted by each and explain whether they find a difference in the vocabulary used by the artists. **EL**

Teach

R1 Reading Strategy

Identifying Assumptions and Ambiguities

Ask: What assumption is the interviewer making when he says that comic books only represent more pages and better paper? *(He is assuming that there is no significant or noteworthy difference between comic books and graphic novels.)* **OL**

⭐ Viewing the Art

Ask: How does the interviewee's body language express his emotions? *(When he makes the important statement about the scope of graphic novels, his hands reach out to emphasize his point. He looks indignant when the interviewer interrupts to stop the interview. He looks downright offended when the interviewer says they must continue the interview inside.)* **AS**

Additional Support

Skills Practice

LITERARY ELEMENT: Humor Humor is the quality that makes characters and their situations amusing. Help students to understand how an author makes something funny and also to find meaning behind the humor. Have students discuss this comic strip—why it's funny and what its hidden meanings might be. *(It is treated like a TV interview with a "commercial break" so that the reader can open the magazine. One meaning: comic books are usually about talking animals and fantastical beings, and now, despite these lowly origins, graphic novels are trying to take themselves seriously as well as to be taken seriously.)* **OL**

Teach

BI Big Idea

Keeping Freedom Alive

Ask: Do you think the artist feels that his freedom of expression is threatened? *(Mostly he feels ridiculed and that his medium is not taken seriously. He probably doesn't feel that his freedom of expression is being violated.)* **OL**

R2 Reading Strategy

Identifying Assumptions and Ambiguities

Ask: What assumption is the interviewee making here by not sitting with the duck? *(He is assuming that he is the victim of a practical joke, that the duck couldn't possibly be a real interviewer.)* **OL**

CheckPoint

Use the Check Point questions on Presentation Plus! to check students' mastery of the selection. These questions can be used with interactive response keypads for immediate student feedback.

CHESTER BROWN **469**

Building Reading Fluency

Dramatic Reading Dramatic readings can help students read more quickly and efficiently by giving them a sense of how language flows. Have three students volunteer for the roles of the interviewer, the interviewee, and the duck. Have them stage the interview in front of the class, making sure to act out the gestures and actions of the illustrated characters. After they have finished, have three other students volunteer for the parts. When they stage the interview, have them perform different actions from the ones illustrated in the comic strip. **BL**

Objectives
- To analyze and evaluate arguments (SE)
- To analyze humor (TWE)

469

Teach

Big Idea

Keeping Freedom Alive

Say: Keep the following questions in mind as you read. What is the difference between a comic book and a graphic novel? Do graphic novels deserve to be taken seriously as a form of literature and art? *(Students who enjoy graphic novels and comics will probably be outspoken in their support of the form. Others will disagree.)* **OL**

L Literary Element

Rhetorical Devices **Answer:**
The author compares graphic novels to past novels that were accessible to many people and part of mass culture. He suggests a link between interest in graphic novels and stereotypes of young people as lacking attention spans.

Ask: Do you think that comics are a dumbed-down form of literature? *(Students who enjoy comics will disagree; students who don't enjoy comics will probably agree.)* **OL**

Readability Scores
Dale-Chall: 12.2
DRP: 69
Lexile: 1410

Charles McGrath

BEFORE YOU READ

Building Background

A definitive definition for the graphic novel does not exist. In simple terms, a graphic novel is an illustrated story. Often it is a longer form of a comic book, with more complex story lines and aimed at a more mature audience. The term is also used for collections of illustrated short stories or previously published comic books. Charles McGrath is the former editor of the *New York Times Book Review*, and was also an editor at *The New Yorker*. He currently is a writer for the *New York Times*. McGrath was not a comic-book fan as a child, so he says he had to train himself to read graphic novels as an adult—then realized he was "having a huge amount of fun." How is reading a graphic novel different from reading a conventional novel? The writer of a literary work uses imagery, or "word pictures," to evoke an emotional response in the reader. A graphic novelist uses actual pictures, along with words. For this reason, as McGrath points out, good graphic novels are "virtually unskimmable."

The most innovative novels being published now just may be those of some seriously strange cartoonists.

Comic books are what novels used to be—an accessible, **vernacular** form with mass appeal—and if the highbrows are right, they're a form perfectly suited to our dumbed-down culture and collective attention deficit. Comics are also enjoying a **renaissance** and a new-found respectability right now. In fact, the fastest-growing section of your local bookstore these days is apt to be the one devoted to comics and so-called graphic novels. It is the over-crowded space way in the back—next to sci-fi probably, or between New Age and hobbies—and unless your store is staffed by someone unusually devoted, this section is likely to be a mess. "Peanuts" anthologies, and fat, catalog-size collections of "Garfield" and "Broom

Literary Element Rhetorical Devices *Explain the analogy used in this passage. What comparisons are being made?* **L**

Vocabulary

vernacular (vər nak′yə lər) *adj.* a form of language particular to a certain group of people; jargon

Vocabulary

renaissance (ren′ə säns′) *n.* rebirth or comeback

Additional Support

Skills Practice

LITERARY ELEMENT: Analogy

Ask: How is "renaissance" an effective analogy for this persuasive text? *("Renaissance" makes comic books sound more respectable and higher-quality. The word refers back to a time of great artistic innovation and skill, thus making comic writers sound like more commonly accepted artists.)* **OL**

BAM! Dynamic Duo Studio. ★

Hilda." Shelf loads of manga—those Japanese comic books that feature slender, wide-eyed teenage girls who seem to have a special fondness for sailor suits. Superheroes, of course, still churned out in installments by the busy factories at Marvel and D.C. Also, newer sci-fi and fantasy series like "Y: The Last Man," about literally the last man on earth (the rest died in a plague).

You can ignore all this stuff—though it's worth noting that manga sells like crazy, especially among women. What you're looking for is shelved upside down and sideways sometimes—comic books of another sort, substantial single volumes (as opposed to the slender series installments), often in hard cover, with titles that sound just like the titles of "real" books: "Palestine," "Persepolis,"

"Blankets" (this one tips in at 582 pages, which must make it the longest single-volume comic book ever), "David Chelsea in Love," "Summer Blonde," "The Beauty Supply District," "The Boulevard of Broken Dreams." Some of these books have titles that have become familiar from recent movies: "Ghost World," "American Splendor," "Road to Perdition." Others, like Chris Ware's "Jimmy Corrigan: The Smartest Kid on Earth" (unpaged, but a good inch and a quarter thick) and Daniel Clowes's "David Boring," have achieved cult status on many campuses.

These are the graphic novels—the equivalent of "literary novels" in the mainstream publishing world—and they are beginning to be taken seriously by the critical establishment. "Jimmy Corrigan" even won the 2001

Reading Strategy Identifying Assumptions and Ambiguities *What assumption is the author implying that most people make about graphic novels?* **R**

Big Idea Keeping Freedom Alive *Why do you think there has been some resistance to graphic novels in the "mainstream publishing world"?* **BI**

CHARLES McGRATH **471**

Teach

R Reading Strategy

Identifying Assumptions and Ambiguities
Answer: *McGrath is assuming that most readers believe that graphic novels are easy to read because they contain pictures.* **OL**

BI Big Idea

Keeping Freedom Alive
Answer: *The author/artists who create graphic novels have gone beyond traditional writing to create something new. New, experimental forms frequently meet with resistance at first.* **OL**

★ Viewing the Art

Point out that "Bam!" is an example of onomatopoeia, or a word whose sound imitates what it describes. Here, the motion lines, explosive cloud, and central blast reinforce the word's meaning with visual details. Have students name other examples of onomatopoeia and illustrate the words. **AS**

✓ CheckPoint

Use the CheckPoint questions on Presentation Plus! to monitor students' comprehension. These questions can be used with interactive response keypads for immediate student feedback.

Objectives
• To analyze rhetorical devices (SE)
• To understand analogies (TWE)

471

English Language Coach

Comic World Students from other cultures may not be familiar with some American comics, such as "Broom Hilda" and "Garfield." Consider bringing in the comics section from a newspaper or obtaining some comic collections from the library to help these students. **EL**

Differentiated Instruction

Discourse Have students discuss their favorite comic strips or comic books. Encourage them to explain why those particular comics or characters are their favorites. Ask where else these comics have appeared, such as on television, in commercials, and in movies. **BL**

Teach

R1 Reading Strategy

Identifying Assumptions and Ambiguities Answer: *Students may agree or disagree with the assumed truth in the ideas of the "critical mass" and the "new generation of readers" with short attention spans. Words like "something like" and "perhaps" are hints to these assumptions.* OL

BI1 Big Idea

Keeping Freedom Alive
Answer: *Graphic novels may make it easier to discuss serious themes in a nonthreatening format. Also, drawings have no language barrier, and may cross cultural divides more easily than traditional writing.* OL

★ Political History

The 1978–79 Islamic Revolution in Iran resulted in the overthrow of the ruling shah. The exiled Ayatollah Khomeini returned to Iran and created an interim regime, which in a mere five years executed 5,000 government officials who had worked for the shah. **AS**

Guardian Prize[1] for best first book, a prize that in other years has gone to authors like Zadie Smith, Jonathan Safran Foer and Philip Gourevitch.

The notion of telling stories with pictures goes back to the cavemen. Comic-book scholars make a big deal of Rodolphe Töpffer, a 19th-century Swiss artist who drew stories in the form of satiric pictures with captions underneath.

There was a minor flowering of serious comic books in the mid-80's, with the almost simultaneous appearance of Art Spiegelman's groundbreaking "Maus"; of the "Love and Rockets" series, by two California brothers, Gilbert and Jaime Hernandez; and of two exceptionally smart and ambitious superhero-based books, "Watchmen," by Alan Moore and Dave Gibbons, and "Batman: The Dark Knight Returns," by Frank Miller. Newspapers and magazines ran articles with virtually the same headline: "Crash! Zap! Pow! Comics Aren't Just for Kids Anymore!" But the movement failed to take hold, in large part because there weren't enough other books on the same level.

The difference this time is that there is something like a critical mass of artists, young and old, uncovering new possibilities in this once-marginal form, and a new generation of readers, perhaps, who have grown up staring at cartoon images on their computer screens and in their video games, not to mention the **savvy** librarians and teachers who now cater to their interests and short attention spans. The publicity that has spilled over from movies like "Ghost World," originally a graphic novel by Dan

---

1. The *Guardian Prize* is awarded to first books. The *Guardian* is a British newspaper.

Reading Strategy Identifying Assumptions and Ambiguities *Is the author making a valid assumption about the attention spans of modern-day readers? How does this generalization tie in with the point of his article?* **R1**

Vocabulary

savvy (sav′ē) *adj.* one who has practical knowledge or understanding

472 UNIT 2 NONFICTION

Clowes, has certainly not hurt. And there is much better distribution of high-end comics now, thanks in part to two enterprising publishers, Drawn and Quarterly in Montreal and Fantagraphics Books in Seattle, which have managed to get their wares into traditional bookstores, not just the comics specialty shops. Some of the better-known graphic novels are published not by comics companies at all but by mainstream publishing houses and have put up mainstream sales numbers. "Persepolis," for example, Marjane Satrapi's charming, poignant story, drawn in small black-and-white panels that evoke Persian miniatures, about a young girl growing up in Iran and her family's suffering following the 1979 Islamic revolution, ★ has sold 450,000 copies worldwide so far; "Jimmy Corrigan" sold 100,000 in hardback, and the newly released paperback is also moving briskly.

These are not top best-seller figures, exactly, but they are sales that any publisher would be happy with, and several are now trying to hop on the graphic-novel bandwagon. Meanwhile, *McSweeney's Quarterly*, a key barometer of the literary climate, especially among the young and hip, has devoted its entire new issue to comics and graphic novels, and the contents are virtually a state-of-the-art anthology, edited and designed by Chris Ware. Dave Eggers, the editor of *McSweeney's*, told me, "I'm just trying to show how hard it is to do this stuff well and to give it a little dignity."

The term "graphic novel" is actually a misnomer. Satrapi's "Persepolis" books are nonfiction, and so, for that matter, is "Maus," once you accept the conceit that human beings are played, so to speak, by cats, dogs, mice and frogs. The newest book by Chester Brown (who drew the cover for this issue of the *Times Magazine*) is a full-scale, 200-plus-page comic-book biography (which took five

---

Big Idea Keeping Freedom Alive *How do you think graphic novels might help spread ideas of freedom?* **BI1**

Additional Support

Skills Practice

LITERARY ELEMENT: Style The author uses a number of stylish phrases in this article. Have students discuss the following phrases, specifically how it reveals the author's purpose or attitude.

1. "State-of-the-art" *(Gives the subject a high-tech, fancy sound. Some students may notice the double meaning—the word "art" can refer to the art form of the graphic novel.)*

2. "Key barometer" *(Gives the subject a scientific sound—it is something that can be gauged and measured.)* OL

years to research and draw) of Louis Riel, who in Brown's native Canada occupies roughly the position that John Brown[2] does here. Nor are all these books necessarily "graphic" in the sense of being realistic or explicit. . . .

But for want of a universally agreed-on alternative, the graphic-novel tag has stuck, and it received something like official sanction a year and a half ago when Spiegelman and Chris Oliveros, the publisher of *Drawn and Quarterly*, persuaded the book-industry committee that decides on subject headings to adopt a graphic-novel category with several subsections: graphic novel/literature, graphic novel/humor, graphic novel/science fiction and so on.

The graphic novel is not just like the old *Classics Illustrated* series, an illustrated version of something else. It is its own thing: an integrated whole, of words and images both, where the pictures don't just depict the story; they're part of the telling.

In certain ways, graphic novels are an almost primitive medium and require a huge amount of manual labor: drawing, inking, coloring and lettering, most of it done by hand (though a few artists have begun to experiment with computer drawing). It's as if a traditional novelist took his printout and then had to copy it over, word by word, like a quill-wielding monk in a medieval monastery. For some graphic novelists, just four or five panels is a good day's work, and even a modest-size book can take years to complete.

---

2. *John Brown* (1800–1859) was a U.S. abolitionist who was tried for treason, convicted, and executed.

Literary Element Rhetorical Devices *What analogy is used to persuade the book industry to accept graphic novels?* **L**

Big Idea Keeping Freedom Alive *In what ways does this literary form represent freedom of expression?* **BI₂**

Like a lot of graphic novelists, Marjane Satrapi begins with a prose script and then begins to sketch it out, lightly and loosely, in pencil. "When I've done that, then in my brain my book is finished," she said from Paris, where she lives now. "The problem is that only I know what it looks like. For you to see it, then I have to drudge. It's a very, very long process."

Such labor demands a certain obsessional personality and sometimes results in obsessional storytelling. What all graphic novelists aspire to, however—whether they start with words or with an image or two—is a sense of motion, of action unfolding in the blank spaces between their stop-action frames. They spend a lot of time thinking about how the panels are arranged and the number of panels it takes (or doesn't) to depict a given amount of narrative. Most of these effects are meant to work on us, the readers, almost subconsciously, but they require a certain effort nonetheless. You have to be able to read and look at the same time, a trick not easily mastered, especially if you're someone who is used to reading fast. Graphic novels, or the good ones anyway, are virtually unskimmable. And until you get the hang of their particular rhythm and way of storytelling, they may require more, not less, concentration than traditional books. ☙

Reading Strategy Identifying Assumptions and Ambiguities *In this sentence, McGrath is referring to an assumption on the part of the reader. What do you think he assumes that many readers believe about the graphic novel format?* **R₂**

Quickwrite

In this selection, Charles McGrath defends the graphic novel as an up-and-coming literary form, citing the artistry and skill required to meld words and images effectively. Write a paragraph in which you respond to McGrath's position.

CHARLES McGRATH **473**

Differentiated Instruction

Visual Learners Students who find visual learning beneficial might find it easier to grasp the views expressed in the article by planning and/or creating their own comic strips or short graphic stories. Have students form small groups.

Ask each group to write a short, simple storyline that could be illustrated in a single page of illustrations. Encourage artistic students to sketch the panels for each story. **BL**

Focus

Summary

This article discusses the increasingly popular choice by teachers to teach comics in the classroom. These teachers claim that with decreasing proficiency in reading at the high school level the use of comics has enabled them to inspire unmotivated high school students to read not only comic books but everything else assigned to them—and more. Detractors say comics are dumbed-down materials that should not be used and may actually decrease readers' interest in nongraphic literature.

Teach

⭐ Viewing the Art

The Marvel Comics character Spider-man, created by Stan Lee and Steve Ditko, first appeared in 1962 and since has appeared in daily comic strips, an animated series, and several motion pictures. **AS**

Readability Scores
Dale-Chall: 11.1
DRP: 69
Lexile: 1280

Additional Support

"HAMLET"
Too Hard?
Try a Comic Book

Teresa Méndez

474 UNIT 2 NONFICTION

Building Background

At a time when fewer young people read for pleasure, and music videos and video games dominate as entertainment for teens, the graphic novel is becoming one of the most popular literary formats. In 2004 estimated total retail sales of graphic novels reached approximately $205 million. Some libraries report that graphic novels and comics are their best circulating items.

The following article debates the value of the graphic novel in the classroom, especially when used as a tool to connect with students.

Teresa Méndez is a staff writer for the *Christian Science Monitor*. Many of her articles focus on the status of education in the United States.

It may be a shocking dilution of academics—or an ingenious way to hook reluctant readers.

At Oneida High School in upstate New York, Diane Roy teaches the students who failed ninth-grade English the first time around. Last year, on the heels of "Hamlet," she presented her class with a graphic novel—essentially a variety of comic book.

Comic books have long been deemed inappropriate classroom reading material. If they appeared at all, they were smuggled in, disguised within the pages of a physics textbook or a volume of Shakespeare.

It's this image—of comic book as contraband[1]—that has endured in the popular imagination at least since the 1950s, when the Senate Judiciary Committee investigated the comic book's sinister influence and potential to inspire juvenile delinquency.

---

1. *Contraband* items are illegal or prohibited. Here, the term refers to reading material not considered appropriate for the classroom.

Spider-Man Reading Daily Bugle Newspaper, 2005. Mike Mayhew Marvel Comics.

Skills Practice

READING: Researching Cultural Context Ask: What other cultural references in Méndez's article pique your curiosity? *(Answers may include the Senate Judiciary Committee investigation,* traditional books about the Holocaust, and the high school literary crisis.) Have students use the library or the Internet to gain a fuller understanding of one of these topics. **OL**

But now the books are turning up on some classroom bookshelves—especially in classes where teachers are desperate to engage struggling and reluctant adolescent readers. For a certain type of student—particularly those who are visually oriented and bright but may lack the motivation or maturity to succeed in freshman English—the graphic novel can become a "bridge to other things," explains Ms. Roy.

Today, the comic book—and its lengthier sibling, the graphic novel—are growing in scope and popularity. In 2002, the theme of the annual Teen Read Week sponsored by YALSA, the youth branch of the American Library Association, was "Get Graphic." Graphic novels can be found in public and school libraries, as well as bookstores, where entire shelves are often devoted to the genre. Manga, the Japanese graphic novels, have swept up teen readers.

And in July, the *New York Times Magazine* ran a cover story positing that the comic book could become the next "new literary form."

Roy's experiment with the graphic novel as text struck gold when she assigned Art Spiegelman's "Maus," the story of his parents' experience in the Holocaust told as a cat and mouse allegory—a highly regarded work that won the Pulitzer Prize. From there, some students moved to graphic novels about Hitler, and finally made their way to traditional books about the Holocaust.

Each student was required to read five graphic novels. But "there wasn't a single student in this class of kids—nonreaders who don't enjoy reading—who didn't read double that number," Roy says. "They would read them overnight . . . they were reading them at lunch, in the hallway."

Roy adapted her curriculum on graphic novels from a series developed for teachers by the New York City Comic Book Museum.

Literacy efforts have traditionally focused not on adolescents, but on younger students.

And some reading experts are worried that with most reform efforts being directed at students in the third grade or lower, another crisis is being ignored.

Even as elementary student scores on federal tests are increasing slightly, high school scores are declining. Only about one third of 12th-graders were reading at a proficient level in 2002, down from 40 percent in 1992.

Adolescent readers face a host of complicated problems, ranging from general reluctance to pick up a book to aliteracy, an inability to fully grasp the meaning of words. Proponents suggest that comic books and graphic novels can help.

For the reluctant reader, they are absorbing. For the struggling reader or the reader still learning English, they offer accessibility: pictures for context, and possibly an alternate path into classroom discussions of higher-level texts. They expand vocabulary, and introduce the ideas of plot, pacing, and sequence.

But such arguments remain unconvincing to many other educators who firmly believe this form of pop culture has no place in the classroom.

"Once kids know how to read, there is no good reason to continue to use dumbed-down materials," writes Diane Ravitch, a professor of education at New York University, in an e-mail. "They should be able to read poems, novels, essays, books that inform them, enlighten them, broaden their horizons."

And there is always a concern about the appropriateness of content.

But just getting reluctant adolescents to read—anything—can be a boon to their discovery of the joy of reading, says Marilyn Reynolds, author of "I Won't Read and You

---

Reading Strategy Identifying Assumptions and Ambiguities *What assumption is made here about the value of graphic novels in the classroom?* **R**

Big Idea Keeping Freedom Alive *How do you think graphic novels might help struggling readers feel freer to join in class discussions?* **BI**

TERESA MÉNDEZ **475**

Teach

L Literary Element

Rhetorical Devices

Ask: Why does the author claim that comic books may become the "next new literary form"? *(It is a quote from a respected source, the* New York Times Magazine. *It supports the idea that the graphic novel is becoming a serious form of art. It lends credence to the author's article.)* **OL**

R Reading Strategy

Identifying Assumptions and Ambiguities

Answer: *The author assumes that graphic novels are still secondary to traditional novels in the classroom.* **OL**

BI Big Idea

Keeping Freedom Alive

Answer: *The visual components of graphic novels may serve as a gateway to comprehension for struggling readers.* **OL**

✔CheckPoint

Use the CheckPoint questions on Presentation Plus! to monitor students' comprehension. These questions can be used with interactive response keypads for immediate student feedback.

English Language Coach

Cultural Differences Students from other cultures may not be familiar with the concept of comic books as "contraband" or of students' former crafty procedure of hiding comic books between the pages of school textbooks. Have these students discuss the attitude towards comic books in their own cultures: positive, negative, or neutral. Have all the students compare the American and non-American attitudes. **EL**

Objectives
- To identify assumptions and ambiguities (SE)
- To analyze cultural differences (TWE)

Teach

L Literary Element

Rhetorical Devices

Answer: *Students may say that the parallels between comics and mythology may actually give readers greater respect for both forms.* **OL**

★ Viewing the Art

Have students notice the elements of fantasy in the painting. *(the face in the smoke, the moonrise, the shadowy forest, the hanging moss)* As a class, discuss what the artist may be suggesting about the book in the painting, or about books in general. *(Stories can have a seemingly mystical power to conjure visions.)* **AS**

Dream Book, 1995. Christian Pierre. Acrylic. Private collection. ★

Can't Make Me: Reaching Reluctant Teen Readers."

Ms. Reynolds, who worked for decades at an alternative high school for struggling students in a Los Angeles suburb, tells the story of a girl "steeped" in graphic novels whom she met at a library.

"That's probably all she will read in high school," says Reynolds. "She's a rebel. She's probably failing English . . . because she doesn't conform, but she's got this fervor for that kind of expression. How much better that than not having any fervor at all."

Reynolds may be extreme in her belief that reading a comic book or graphic novel is a worthy end in itself. Most educators hold that the genre is best used as a bridge to more complex material.

For example, Wonder Woman comics could interest students in Greek mythology, says Philip Charles Crawford, the library director at Essex High School, in Essex Junction, VT.

"The subject matter leads you other places and I think the majority of readers are going to read other things," says Mr. Crawford, who has written "Graphic Novels 101: Selecting and Using Graphic Novels to Promote Literacy for Children and Young Adults."

And graphic novels like Marjane Satrapi's memoirs, "Persepolis" and "Persepolis 2,"

> **Literary Element** Rhetorical Devices *Do you think that readers of comics about mythical heroes will indeed be interested in literary mythology? Is this a valid argument for letting children read comic books?* **L**

476 UNIT 2 NONFICTION

Additional Support

Skills Practice

READING: Text Structures Writers organize their work according to its topic and purpose. Structure may be based on comparison and contrast, cause and effect, chronological order, or problem and solution. **Ask:** How is this text structured? Explain. *(The text has a problem-and-solution structure. The problem is that some students are not motivated or have difficulty reading traditional literary texts. The solution presented is the teaching of these materials through comic books and graphic novels, an approach that has had success in motivating students who are uninterested or have difficulty.)* **OL**

Pilot Giving Thumbs up Signal.
Steve and Ghy Sampson.

⭐

have exposed readers to life in Iran in the wake of the Islamic Revolution. Ms. Satrapi recently spoke at Edwin G. Foreman High School in Chicago, where students read "Persepolis" for class.

But others worry that the comics versions of classics like "Frankenstein" or "The Odyssey" may come to replace the originals. Carol Jago, an English teacher at Santa Monica High School in California, believes this raises questions of equity in the classroom. "If we end up giving the real thing to our honors students and the comic books to everyone else, we're actually demeaning the nature of public education," she says.

Yet defenders of the comic book point out that many adolescent aficionados of the genre have gone on to excel at the written word.

> **Reading Strategy** Identifying Assumptions and Ambiguities *What is ambiguous about the phrase "the nature of public education"?* **R**

For his book "Give Our Regards to the Atomsmashers!" editor Sean Howe collected essays in which established writers like Jonathan Lethem and Aimee Bender divulge their longtime love of comics.

Even Edward P. Jones, who won this year's Pulitzer Prize for his novel "The Known World," recently admitted that he was weaned on comic books. Until he was 13, he says, he'd never read a book without a picture. ∽

> **Discussion Starter**
>
> Méndez presents both arguments for and against using graphic novels as teaching tools. Meet with a small group to discuss your opinion about the place of the graphic novel in a school setting. Do you believe that graphic novels should be used in the classroom? If so, what uses are appropriate? Should graphic novels be used as a bridge to other material? Should they be used to teach all students or only certain students? Summarize your discussion for the rest of your class.

TERESA MÉNDEZ **477**

English Language Coach

Visual Context Non-native English speakers may find it easier to learn to read with the help of illustrations. Have these students share their experiences in trying to learn English and discuss whether they have found visual aids helpful. **EL**

Reading in the Real World

College Some students may be interested in becoming artists, writers, graphic designers, or even graphic novelists. Have them conduct research on the Internet to find colleges with undergraduate programs in creative writing, art, and graphic design. **OL**

Focus

Summary

This article discusses the state of the graphic novel on the twenty-fifth anniversary of its inception. The author addresses whether the term *graphic novel* is really appropriate and lists a few alternatives suggested by graphic novel writers. The author says that these books must be celebrated as a fundamentally unique form of literature and not just an offshoot of the prose novel. He discusses a publisher's desire to see graphic novels categorized with other literature and not relegated to their own section in bookstores. The article concludes with projections about the future of the medium.

Readability Scores
Dale-Chall: 9.9
DRP: 68
Lexile: 1250

Additional Support

The GRAPHIC NOVEL
Silver Anniversary
Andrew Arnold

Young Woman Doing a Martial Arts Kick in Front of a Robot Steve and Ghy Sampson.

BEFORE YOU READ

Building Background

While still popular, the superheroes and super-villains that most people associate with comic books have given way to a new type of content. Any topic is now fair game for the graphic novel. Graphic novels cover anything from current and historical events to biographical and autobiographical accounts. Their vast popularity has earned the graphic novel pop-culture status. Andrew Arnold began reading comic books as a child. He started writing about alternative comic book releases before eventually writing a column about the genre for Time.com. Arnold is a graduate of New York University's Graduate School of Journalism.

Japanese manga, superhero collections, non-fiction, autobiography—all of these are "graphic novels," a term that now applies to any square-bound book with a story told in comics format. "The problem with the word 'graphic novel' is that it is an arguably misguided bid for respectability where graphics are respectable and novels are respectable so you get double respectability," Spiegelman[1] says. Eisner[2] himself dislikes the phrase, calling it a "limited term," and prefers "graphic literature or graphic story."

Either of those terms seems preferable to the striving, mostly-inaccurate "graphic novel." But some would argue against any such terminology. Chip Kidd, book designer and "graphic novel" editor at Pantheon, an imprint of the giant trade publisher

---

1. Art Spiegelman is the author of *Maus* (1986), a Holocaust memoir in graphic novel form.

2. Will Eisner's *A Contract with God, and Other Tenement Stories*, published in 1978, is an admired, early graphic novel.

Skills Practice

WRITING: Tone Have students rewrite the paragraph that begins "As a critic, though" to achieve a variety of different tones: satirical, earnest, pleading, militant, self-deprecating, or others. As a class, discuss what words remain the same regardless of tone, what words change, and how tone helps readers understand a writer's meaning. **OL**

Random House, loathes the ghettoizing of such books, starting with their name. "What I don't like is when we have to categorize everything in order to appreciate or understand it," he wrote in an email. "At Pantheon, we do not see these books as part of a 'line,' or a 'program' any more than we would books by Ha Jin or Stanley Crouch.[3] They are simply books we want to publish that happen to use the form of visual narrative."

As a critic, though, I would argue that these types of books are fundamentally different from prose. Blurring the line between them would be charmingly quixotic[4] at best and harmful at worst. That which distinguishes drawn books from prose is what we love about them. The Artistry is different—way beyond mere genre—and must be celebrated. In order to talk about the unique pleasures of drawn books we necessarily distinguish them from their text-only relatives.

But categorizing graphic novels goes beyond artistic semantics[5] to the real bottom line—dollars and cents. Most big bookstores put all the graphic novels together in one place. Trade bookstores have become an increasingly important outlet for comic publishers so the strategy for selling them on the floor has become critical. Should Superman, manga and "Maus," sit side by side? Chip Kidd, among many others, can't stand this. "I truly believe that Spiegelman's 'Maus' should be shelved next to Elie Wiesel and Primo Levi,[6] not next to the X-Men. Maus is a

Holocaust memoir first and a comic book second." Micha Hershman, the graphic novel buyer for a bookstore chain has no such doubts. "The graphic novel is a format," he says. "We would not segment the category by splitting up the graphic novel section." According to Hershman, research shows the "demographics for 'Maus' overlap with the ones for Spider-Man," so that it is theoretically easier to lure the reader of one to the other than it is to lure a reader of Elie Wiesel to "Maus."

Something seems to be working because graphic novels have finally reached a point of critical mass in both popular consciousness and sales.

Could graphic novels eventually make the traditional comic book disappear? Frank Miller, author of "The Dark Knight Returns," recently shocked a comics industry crowd at the annual Eisner awards by pronouncing the format to be a goner, declaring, "Our future is not in pamphlets." Nick Purpura disputes this, saying, "the serialized versions pay for the trades. That way publishers get to sell it twice—once to comics fans and again to people who only buy collections." Even so, he says, "books that sold marginally as comics sell better as graphic novels." Additionally, there have been an increasing number of "original graphic novels," as Purpura calls them, which never appeared in serialized form. The most impressive example of these is DC comics' October release of "Sandman: Endless Nights," by Neil Gaiman, which reached number 20 on the New York Times bestseller list.

The future of the graphic novel seems both sunny and dim. As a term for a kind of

---

3. *Ha Jin* is an award-winning Chinese American author. *Stanley Crouch* is an American journalist and critic.
4. *Quixotic* means "foolishly impractical."
5. *Semantics* is the branch of linguistics that deals with the meanings of words, as well as their historical development.
6. *Elie Wiesel* and *Primo Levi* are both Jewish writers who survived Nazi concentration camps.

Literary Element Rhetorical Devices *A ghetto is a section of a city where a minority group lives due to economic pressure. How does this analogy describe the perception of graphic novels by many publishers?* **L1**

Reading Strategy Identifying Assumptions and Ambiguities *Is this statement an assumption, an ambiguity, or neither? Explain.* **R**

Big Idea Keeping Freedom Alive *Why do individual bookstores in a chain usually not have the freedom to organize books as they wish?* **BI**

Literary Element Rhetorical Devices *Here the writer uses sensory words to create a mental image. If this article were part of a graphic novel, how might this imagery be shown?* **L2**

ANDREW ARNOLD **479**

Teach

L1 **Literary Element**
Rhetorical Devices
Answer: *The word means "the separation or isolation into a ghetto." The use of this word implies that the author feels very strongly that there is widespread discrimination against graphic novels as a literary form.* **OL**

R **Reading Strategy**
Identifying Assumptions and Ambiguities
Answer: *Neither. Arnold is stating an unambiguous opinion that he intends to back up with examples.* **OL**

BI **Big Idea**
Keeping Freedom Alive
Answer: *The chain, not the individual store, usually controls inventory and display.*
Ask: What effect might chain bookstores have on our reading tastes as a society? *(Students may say that reading tastes will become more uniform, or that chain bookstores expose readers to books they might otherwise not have encountered.)* **OL**

L2 **Literary Element**
Rhetorical Devices
Answer: *Students may suggest images of sun breaking through heavy clouds.* **OL**

Objectives
• To identify an author's use of persuasive techniques (SE)
• To analyze and evaluate arguments (SE)
• To analyze tone (TWE)

English Language Coach

Pronunciation Non-native English speakers may find some of the words in this selection difficult. Write on the board the following words and their pronunciations: *arguably, loathes, ghettoizing, quixotic, theoretically.* Help students to pronounce these words as they come to them. **EL**

Reading in the Real World

College College classes tend to assign many papers, so it is important for students to learn the academic value of the resources available in libraries. Discuss with students the resources available in libraries: reference books, audio and visual resources, periodicals, and so forth. **OL**

Teach

BI Big Idea

Keeping Freedom Alive

Answer: *Graphic novels have allowed writers the freedom to explore new means of expression and to tell stories in new ways.* OL

⭐ Viewing the Art

Superman is not the only pop-culture icon that Andy Warhol incorporated in his "myth series." The series also includes works inspired by Mickey Mouse, Uncle Sam, and Santa Claus. AS

Quickwrite

Make sure that students' paragraphs accurately state Arnold's definition of the graphic novel and of "Artistry." Also, check that students' interpretations of Arnold's assertions are supported by evidence from the text.

CheckPoint

Use the CheckPoint questions on Presentation Plus! to check students' mastery of the selection. These questions can be used with interactive response keypads for immediate student feedback.

---

book, "graphic novel" has become increasingly dissatisfying. "Maybe for a short window it was enough to say 'graphic novel' but soon it won't be," says Art Spiegelman, "because if you talk about [Chris Ware's] 'Jimmy Corrigan' as a graphic novel you'll have to explain that it's not manga or Marvel. Then you are left saying, 'well it's got a seriousness of purpose' that the phrase 'graphic novel' alone won't offer." On the positive side, the public awareness of these

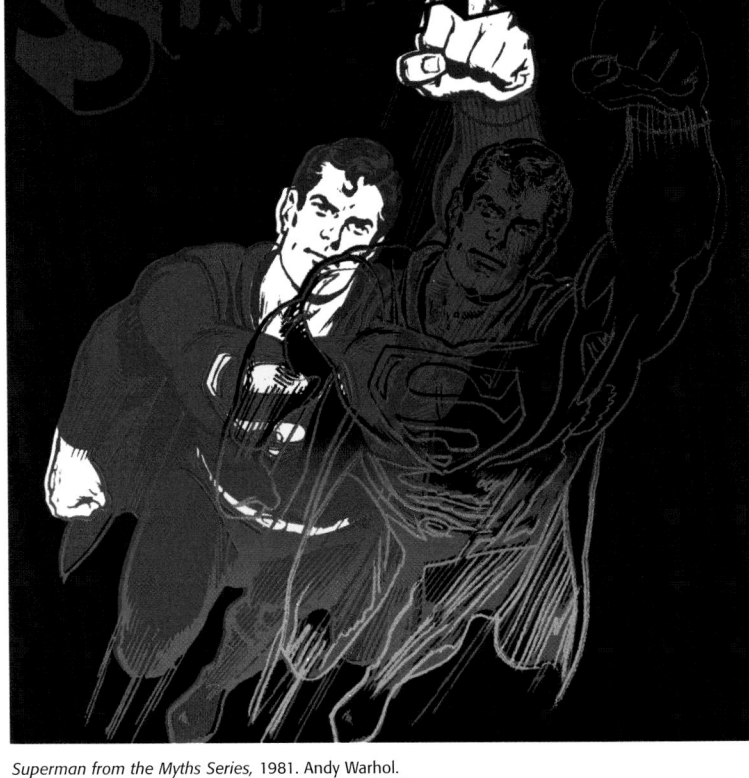

Superman from the Myths Series, 1981. Andy Warhol. The Andy Warhol Foundation for the Visual Arts. ⭐

books has vastly increased, creating a kind of renaissance era of intense creativity and quality. Says Spiegelman, "Ultimately the future of the graphic novel is dependent on how much great work gets produced against all odds. I'm much more optimistic than I was that there's room for something and I know that right now there's more genuinely interesting comic art than there's been for decades and decades." ∾

Big Idea Keeping Freedom Alive *In what ways have graphic novels spurred artistic freedom among writers and artists?* BI

Quickwrite

In this selection, Andrew Arnold says of the graphic novel: "That which distinguishes drawn books from prose is what we love about them. The Artistry is different—way beyond mere genre—and must be celebrated." Write two to three paragraphs addressing this comment. Consider the following in your response: How does Arnold define the graphic novel as opposed to regular literature? How might he define "Artistry" and why did he capitalize that word? What does he mean when he refers to "mere genre" and asserts that the artistry "must be celebrated"?

Additional Support

Literature Online

Web Activities Have students access the Web site for interactive activities that will help them assess their understanding of the selection.

Skills Practice

READING: Scanning Say: Skimming and scanning a text are good ways to refresh your memory about a passage you've read or to get a general overview of new material. When the students have finished reading the selection, have them scan the selection quickly and underline key words and important information. Then have them share their results and evaluate the key words and information they chose. OL

RESPONDING AND THINKING CRITICALLY

Respond

1. (a)With which of these authors do you agree most? (b)With which do you disagree? Explain.

Recall and Interpret

2. (a)What examples does McGrath offer of picture stories that predate comics and graphic novels? (b)Why do you think he mentions these examples?

3. What reasons does Méndez give that support using graphic novels in the classroom? Do you believe that her evidence is valid? Explain.

4. (a)What does Arnold say about the term "graphic novel"? (b)Why do you think he believes that the topic is important enough to be discussed in his column?

Analyze and Evaluate

5. McGrath describes the artistic process and the painstaking efforts involved in creating a graphic novel. Analyze his argument and decide if you believe that his appeal is successful.

6. Evaluate Méndez's use of rhetorical devices. Consider whether her argument is valid and whether she incorporates any fallacies into her argument.

7. Arnold describes the marketing approach used by many bookstores to sell graphic novels. Decide whether he uses similar techniques in his column to promote the graphic novel as a literary form.

Connect

8. **Big Idea** **Keeping Freedom Alive** Méndez writes that graphic novels reach all students. In what ways does educational opportunity relate to keeping freedom alive? Explain.

LITERARY ANALYSIS

Literary Element **Rhetorical Devices**

Writers who wish to persuade their readers employ **rhetorical devices** to sway their readers' opinions.

Effective rhetoric appeals to logic, emotion, morality, or authority. A common rhetorical device is the **analogy**, which is a comparison based on a relationship between things that are otherwise dissimilar or unrelated.

1. What analogy does Brown make in his comic? Explain.

2. When Méndez writes about using graphic novels in the classroom, do you think she is appealing to logic, emotion, morality, or authority? Explain.

Performing

With a partner, write and perform a skit in which two students argue about the value of graphic novels and try to persuade the other of his or her opinion. One student should be a fan of graphic novels and the other student should be scornful of them. When you have finished, present your skit to the class.

Literature Online **Web Activities** For eFlashcards, Selection Quick Checks, and other Web activities, go to www.glencoe.com.

READING AND VOCABULARY

Reading Strategy **Identifying Assumptions and Ambiguities**

Sometimes authors try to influence readers by presenting their personal assumptions as facts, or by making statements that are ambiguous. **Identifying assumptions and ambiguities** will help you determine whether you agree with the author's opinions.

1. What assumption is Brown's comic based upon?

2. See Brown's graphic-novel defender as he protests: "I don't have to put up with this sort of juvenile nonsense." How is this statement ambiguous?

Vocabulary *Practice*

Practice with Synonyms Find the synonym for each vocabulary word listed below.

1. vernacular	a. jargon	b. difference
2. renaissance	a. rebirth	b. falter
3. savvy	a. cruel	b. expert

Assess

1. Answers will vary.

2. (a) Cave drawings and a satirical Swiss artist (b) He is probably offering them as evidence that the graphic novel is worthy of recognition.

3. (a) Graphic novels encourage nonreaders to read and can be used as a bridge to other subject matter. Students' opinions will vary.

4. (a) The term is inaccurate and too broad. (b) Defining the form could influence public attitudes toward it.

5. Students should determine whether McGrath is making a logical or an emotional appeal and whether his evidence makes it valid.

6. Méndez uses causation to argue that because students are willing to read comic books, comic books should be used in school. She introduces a fallacy when she mentions the *New York Times Magazine* article.

7. Arnold organizes his arguments logically, writing for a specific type of reader, just as the bookstores understand their buyers.

8. Students should recognize the relationship between education and future opportunities.

Literary Element

1. He compares the graphic novel to an interview in which the questions are longer than the response.

2. Logic, with numerous balanced opinions from each side

Reading Strategy

1. The graphic novel must be defended as a legitimate form.

2. "Juvenile nonsense" could refer to the duck, to the public attitude toward graphic novels, or to comic books in general.

Vocabulary

1. a 2. a 3. b

Performing

Encourage students to expand on the ideas presented in this lesson and offer personal anecdotes as evidence in their skits.

Assess

Comparing the Big Idea

Students may say that people must continually exercise their freedoms in order to preserve them. They may also say that the fact that some people disagree emphasizes the right to think and create freely.

Comparing Persuasive Appeals

1. Brown, McGrath, and Arnold all say that the graphic novel is a legitimate literary form that deserves recognition and respect. Méndez says the graphic novel has potential as an educational resource.

2. All the authors use logical appeals by presenting facts as evidence. Méndez also uses an emotional appeal when she emphasizes the plight of nonreaders who benefit from graphic novels in the classroom.

3. Answers will vary according to students' personal inclinations. Students should support their answers with passages from the selections.

Comparing Authors' Viewpoints

- All four authors recognize the vast appeal of the graphic novel. They all seem to support the format as a legitimate literary format.

- Méndez focuses specifically on the reading habits of young people. She uses the interest that young people have in comics as support for her argument that the format should be used in educational settings. McGrath and Arnold recognize the influence of the graphic novel on all age groups. Brown does not address the issue, but would probably agree that the graphic novel has influenced reading habits.

- Méndez is the only author who mentions this issue. She seems to support the use of the graphic-novel format in schools. The other authors do not discuss the issue, although they do support the graphic novel as a legitimate literary form.

Wrap-Up: Comparing Literature *Different Viewpoints*

- *Not Just Comic Books* by Chester Brown
- *How Cool Is Comics Lit?* by Charles McGrath
- *"Hamlet" too hard? Try a comic book* by Teresa Méndez
- *The Graphic Novel Silver Anniversary* by Andrew Arnold

COMPARING THE **Big Idea** Keeping Freedom Alive

Writing The authors of "How Cool Is Comics Lit?" and "The Graphic Novel Silver Anniversary" both present the graphic novel as a new form of expression worthy of literary and artistic merit. Think beyond the creative importance of these works and consider what literary and artistic thought mean in terms of freedom of expression. Write a brief essay in which you consider the contributions by graphic novelists to the continuation of a free society. Also consider how negative public opinion toward the genre might affect it.

COMPARING Persuasive Appeals

Group Activity As an attempt to influence, a persuasive appeal can be very powerful. It is important for readers to identify these appeals so that they can draw informed conclusions. Although each of the selections compared here has a different purpose, they all use persuasive appeals to communicate the authors' positions. With a small group, discuss the following questions:

1. What is each author trying to communicate about the graphic novel format?
2. What persuasive appeals does each author use to influence the reader?
3. Which of the selections, in your opinion, presents the strongest argument about the role of the graphic novel in modern culture? Support your answer with passages from the selections.

COMPARING Authors' Viewpoints

Partner Activity Chester Brown, Charles McGrath, Teresa Méndez, and Andrew Arnold each have a different purpose in discussing the format of the graphic novel. What do their varying purposes reveal about their beliefs? With a partner, make inferences about each author's beliefs about the following topics:

- the role of the graphic novel in modern or pop culture
- the influence of pop culture on the reading habits of young people
- the effectiveness of the graphic novel when used in an educational setting

Support your inferences with details from the selections. Use a graphic organizer like the one below to organize your ideas. Then share your thoughts with your classmates.

OBJECTIVES
- Identify an author's use of persuasive techniques.
- Analyze and evaluate arguments.
- Compare and contrast authors' messages and beliefs.

Address on the Anniversary of Lincoln's Birth

MEET CARL SANDBURG

Few people would have predicted that Carl Sandburg would grow up and become a noteworthy writer of his generation. The son of working-class Swedish immigrants, Sandburg was born in Galesburg, Illinois. He left school after eighth grade in order to work at a variety of jobs that included washing dishes, shining shoes, selling newspapers, and driving a milk truck.

Early Books Sandburg enlisted in the army during the Spanish-American war and later returned to Galesburg, where he enrolled at Lombard College. Sandburg then worked as a journalist in Milwaukee and later moved to Chicago, where he continued to pursue a career in journalism. He began writing poetry, and soon he had enough poems to publish a book, *Chicago Poems*. This work was controversial because Sandburg wrote about the working class and used colloquial, as opposed to literary, language. To some critics, using "the language of factory and sidewalk" was almost an insult; to others, it was a bold and distinguishing characteristic.

"Slang is a language that rolls up its sleeves, spits on its hands and goes to work."

—Carl Sandburg

Sandburg began to travel around the country, collecting poems, folk stories, and songs. He made a series of public appearances, at which he recited his own poems and sang some of the folk songs that he had collected. Later, Sandburg published a book of several hundred songs that he had collected over time, called *American Songbag*.

The Lincoln Books From an early age, Sandburg had an interest in Abraham Lincoln. In the mid 1920s, Sandburg began collecting information about Abraham Lincoln for a biography. Originally, he envisioned it to be a children's book, but it gradually grew into a large, two-volume work called *Abraham Lincoln: The Prairie Years*. The book covered the period of time between Lincoln's birth and his move to Washington, D.C., when he became president.

The book was a popular success that presented a portrait of Lincoln that few had seen before; Sandburg's Lincoln was a complex individual, not a legend. Some critics felt that Sandburg mixed fact and fiction in this volume, but Sandburg was not discouraged. He later produced a four-volume biography about Lincoln's later life called *Abraham Lincoln: The War Years*. This book silenced his critics and earned him a Pulitzer Prize in 1939.

Sandburg was a prolific writer. A friend once commented that "trying to write briefly about Carl Sandburg is like trying to picture the Grand Canyon in one black and white snapshot." Penelope Niven, a biographer of Sandburg, wrote that "he helped the American people discover their national identity through songs, poems, and that mythical national hero, Abraham Lincoln."

Carl Sandburg was born in 1878 and died in 1967.

 Author Search For more about Carl Sandburg, go to www.glencoe.com.

CARL SANDBURG **483**

Focus

BELLRINGER

Bellringer Options
Daily Language Practice Transparency 44
Or write the word *Freedom* on the board. **Ask:** What does freedom mean to you? Jot down student responses. Explain that freedom means different things to different people. Then have students write a paragraph explaining what freedom means to them.

Literature Online

Author Search To expand students' appreciation of Carl Sandburg, have them access the Web site for additional information and resources.

Selection Skills

Address on the Anniversary of Lincoln's Birth

Literary Elements
- Understanding Quotations (SE pp. 484, 486, 487, 489)
- Persuasion (SE p. 489)

Reading Skills
- Distinguishing Fact and Opinion (SE pp. 484, 485, 486, 489)

Vocabulary Skills
- Analogies (SE pp. 484, 489)
- Academic Vocabulary (SE p. 489)

Listening/Speaking/Viewing Skills
- Presenting an Oral Report (TWE p. 486)

Writing Skills/Grammar
- Evaluate Author's Craft (SE p. 490)
- Write a Blurb (SE p. 490)

Focus

Summary

In celebrating President Lincoln's birth, the U.S. Congress acknowledged one of America's beloved leaders and the great influence he had on his country. Abraham Lincoln was born in 1809 and died in 1865, just a few days after the end of America's long and divisive Civil War. In honoring Lincoln, poet Carl Sandburg helped Americans remember the strength, character, and convictions of the sixteenth president of the United States.

V Vocabulary

Vocabulary File

Say: Add these words and definitions to your vocabulary file. For each word, include a sentence that gives you an example of how to use the word. **OL** Students with English language needs should include the pronunciations of these words in their files. **EL**

Literary Elements Have students access the Web site to improve their understanding of quotations.

Connecting to the Address

Carl Sandburg honored Abraham Lincoln in a speech before the U.S. Congress in 1959. Before you read, think about the following questions:

- Why might the remembrance of outstanding historical figures be useful to a nation?
- What would cause you to admire a national leader?

Building Background

The Confederate States of America had formed by the time Abraham Lincoln was sworn in as the nation's sixteenth president in 1861. In his first inaugural address, Lincoln tried unsuccessfully to bring the South back into the Union. After the bombardment of Fort Sumter, he declared a blockade of Southern ports. After the Civil War began, he called Congress to meet on July 4, 1861, in a special session.

Lincoln accepted the fact that only a vigorous war effort would restore the Union. He had a will to win despite enormous battle casualties and political opposition—much of it coming from within his own cabinet. The history of Lincoln's administration followed the course of the Civil War.

Setting Purposes for Reading

Big Idea Keeping Freedom Alive

As you read, notice how Sandburg relates his impressions of Lincoln to the preservation of freedom and national unity.

Literary Element Quotation

A **quotation** is a passage taken from another author's text and inserted word for word into a speech or work of literature. The use of quotations can provide insights about a writer's character or message. As you read the speech, notice how Sandburg incorporates Lincoln's words into his own, original text.

- See Literary Terms Handbook, p. R14.

Literature Online Interactive Literary Elements Handbook To review or learn more about the literary elements, go to www.glencoe.com.

OBJECTIVES
In studying this selection, you will focus on the following:
- understanding quotations
- distinguishing between fact and opinion
- recognizing an author's use of persuasion
- writing to evaluate an author's craft

Reading Strategy Distinguishing Fact and Opinion

A **fact** is a statement that can be proven true beyond a reasonable doubt. An **opinion** is a personal interpretation or belief. Determining whether what you read is rooted in fact or opinion can help you evaluate an author's message and purpose.

Reading Tip: Identifying Facts and Opinions Use a chart to list facts and opinions as you read.

Fact	Opinion
"He enforced conscription of soldiers for the first time in American history." p. 485	Lincoln is described as a man "who is both steel and velvet." p. 485

Vocabulary

paradox (par′ə doks′) n. a statement that seems contradictory and yet may be true; p. 485 *They were puzzled by the paradox in the song lyrics.*

imperative (im per′ə tiv) adj. expressing a command or order; p. 486 *Their mother said it was imperative to come straight home after school.*

turbulent (tur′byə lənt) adj. causing unrest, violent action, or disturbance; p. 486 *Turbulent seas caused the captain to seek calmer waters.*

emancipation (i man′ sə pā′ shən) n. the process of becoming free from control or the power of another; p. 486 *After their emancipation, the former slaves were no longer considered property.*

valor (val′ər) n. courageous spirit; personal bravery; p. 486 *The soldiers showed valor when they did not flee from the enemy's gunfire.*

Vocabulary Tip: Analogies An **analogy** conveys a logical relationship between words or sets of words.

Selection Resources

Print Materials
- Unit 2 Resources (Fast File), pp. 68–70
- Leveled Vocabulary Development, p. 36
- Selection and Unit Assessments, pp. 77–78
- Selection Quick Checks, p. 39

Transparencies
- Bellringer Options Transparencies: Daily Language Practice Transparency 44
- Literary Elements Transparency 95

Technology
- TeacherWorks Plus™ CD-ROM
- StudentWorks Plus™ CD-ROM
- Presentation Plus!™ CD-ROM
- Literature Online, glencoe.com
- Online Student Edition, mhln.com
- ExamView® Assessment Suite CD-ROM
- Vocabulary PuzzleMaker CD-ROM
- Listening Library, disc 1 track 4

Address on the Anniversary of Lincoln's Birth

CARL SANDBURG

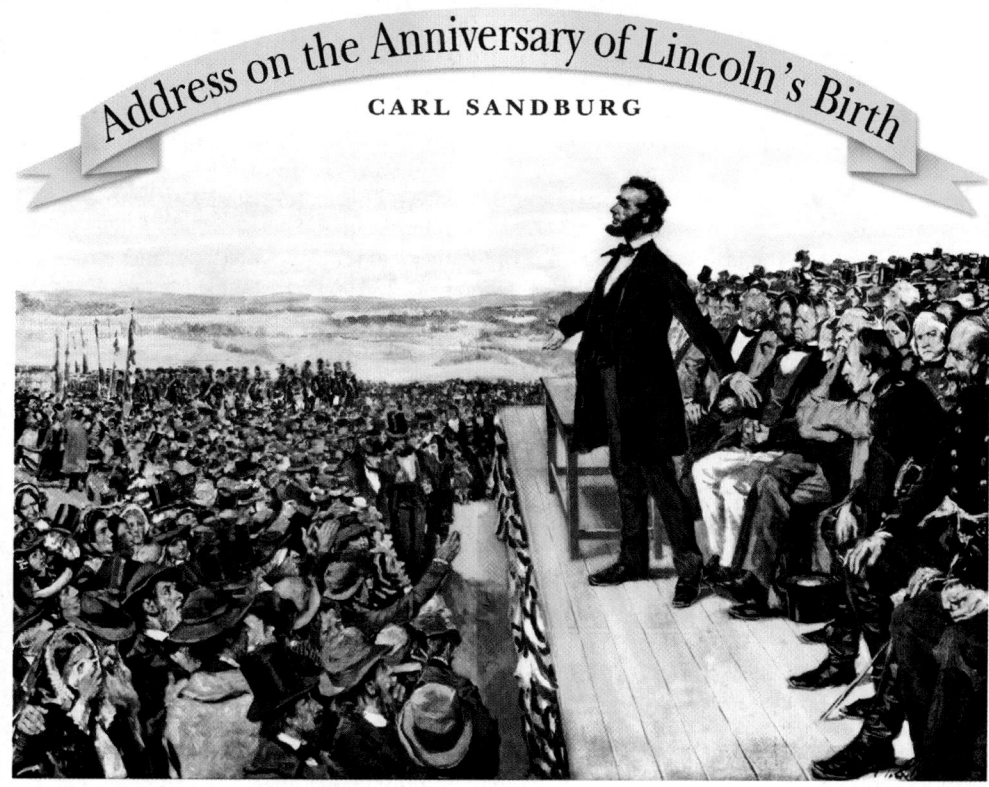

President Lincoln's Address at Gettysburg.
Artist unknown. Hand colored halftone.

Not often in the story of mankind does a man arrive on earth who is both steel and velvet, who is as hard as rock and soft as drifting fog, who holds in his heart and mind the **paradox** of terrible storm and peace unspeakable and perfect. Here and there across centuries come reports of men alleged to have these contrasts. And the incomparable Abraham Lincoln, born 150 years ago this day, is an approach if not a perfect realization of this character.

In the time of the April lilacs in the year 1865, on his death, the casket with his body was carried north and west a thousand miles, and the American people wept as never before. Bells sobbed, cities wore crepe, people stood in tears and with hats off as the railroad burial car paused in the leading cities of seven states, ending its journey at Springfield, Illinois, the home town.

During the four years he was president, he at times, especially in the first three months, took to himself the powers of a dictator. He commanded the most powerful armies till then assembled in modern warfare. He enforced conscription of soldiers for the first

Reading Strategy Distinguishing Fact and Opinion
Does the phrase "powers of a dictator" reflect an opinion or a fact about Lincoln's presidency? **R**

Reading in the Real World

Keeping Freedom Alive
Answer: *Students should conclude that Lincoln was decisive—he was willing to overturn a three-hundred-year-old tradition in order to do what was right.* **OL**

L1 **Literary Element**

Quotation Answer: *Students may suggest that Lincoln's own words support the points that Sandburg is trying to make— that Lincoln is honest, compassionate, and humble.* **OL**

R **Reading Strategy**

Distinguishing Fact and Opinion Answer: *It is factual that Lincoln occasionally expressed intense emotional behavior, such as weeping. However, the statement that his weeping "made weeping appropriate, decent, [and] majestic" cannot be proven and thus is an opinion.* **OL**

Readability Scores
Dale-Chall: 10.1
DRP: 62
Lexile: 1290

---

time in American history. Under **imperative** necessity he abolished the right of habeas corpus. He directed politically and spiritually the wild, massive, **turbulent** forces let loose in civil war.

He argued and pleaded for compensated **emancipation** of the slaves. The slaves were property, they were on the tax books along with horses and cattle, the valuation of each slave next to his name on the tax assessor's books. Failing to get action on compensated emancipation, as a chief executive having war powers, he issued the paper by which he declared the slaves to be free under "military necessity." In the end nearly $4 million worth of property was taken away from those who were legal owners of it, property confiscated, wiped out as by fire and turned to ashes, at his instigation and executive direction. Chattel property recognized and lawful for 300 years was expropriated, seized without payment.

In the month the war began he told his secretary, John Hay,[1] "My policy is to have no policy." Three years later in a letter to a Kentucky friend made public, he confessed plainly, "I have been controlled by events." His words at Gettysburg were sacred, yet strange with a color of the familiar: "We cannot consecrate—we cannot hallow—this ground. The brave men, living and dead, who struggled here, have consecrated it, far beyond our poor power to add or detract."

---

1. *John Milton Hay*, President Lincoln's secretary, became Secretary of State in 1898.

Big Idea Keeping Freedom Alive *What does this statement reveal about Lincoln's character and values?* **BI**

Literary Element Quotation *How do the quotations in this paragraph help the reader understand Lincoln?* **L1**

Vocabulary

imperative (im per′ə tiv) *adj.* expressing a command or order

turbulent (tur′byə lənt) *adj.* causing unrest, violent action, or disturbance

emancipation (i man′sə pā′shən) *n.* the process of becoming free from control or the power of another

486 UNIT 2 NONFICTION

He could have said "the brave Union men." Did he have a purpose in omitting the word *Union*? Was he keeping himself and his utterance clear of the passion that would not be good to look at when the time came for peace and reconciliation? Did he mean to leave an implication that there were brave Union men, and brave Confederate men, living and dead, who had struggled there? We do not know of a certainty. Was he thinking of the Kentucky father whose two sons died in battle, one in Union blue, the other in Confederate gray, the father inscribing on the stone over their double grave, "God knows which was right"? We do not know. . . .

While the war winds howled, he insisted that the Mississippi was one river meant to belong to one country, that railroad connection from coast to coast must be pushed through and the Union Pacific Railroad[2] made a reality. While the luck of war wavered and broke and came again, as generals failed and campaigns were lost, he held enough forces of the North together to raise new armies and supply them, until generals were found who made war as victorious war has always been made—with terror, frightfulness, destruction, and on both sides, North and South, **valor** and sacrifice past words of man to tell.

In the mixed shame and blame of the immense wrongs of two crashing civilizations, often with nothing to say, he said nothing, slept not at all, and on occasions he was seen to weep in a way that made weeping appropriate, decent, majestic. . . .

The people of many other countries take Lincoln now for their own. He belongs to them. He stands for decency, honest dealing,

---

2. *The Union Pacific Railroad* came into being when President Lincoln signed the Pacific Railway Act, which directed the Union Pacific and the Central Pacific companies to construct a transcontinental railroad.

Reading Strategy Distinguishing Fact and Opinion *What in this statement is factual? What cannot be proved?* **R**

Vocabulary

valor (val′ər) *n.* courageous spirit; personal bravery

Additional Support

Skills Practice

RESEARCH: Historical Context
Explain that President Lincoln's Gettysburg Address is considered one of the greatest speeches in American history. Have students conduct research to learn more about this famous speech, such as when and where it took place and how it affected people. Also ask students to research the events leading up to the Gettysburg Address. Have them determine whether Lincoln's speech is worthy of the praise it received. Then have students present their findings in an oral report. **OL**

The Death of Lincoln (1809–65), 1868. Alonzo Chappel. Oil on canvas.
Chicago Historical Society.

plain talk, and funny stories. "Look where he came from. Don't he know all us strugglers, and wasn't he a kind of tough struggler all his life right up to the finish?" Something like that you can hear in any nearby neighborhood and across the seas.

Millions there are who take him as a personal treasure. He had something they would like to see spread everywhere over the world. Democracy? We can't find words to say exactly what it is, but he had it. In his blood and bones he carried it. In the breath of his speeches and writings it is there. Popular government? Republican institution? Government where the people have the say-so, one way or another telling their elected leaders what they want? He had the idea. It's there in the lights and shadows of his personality, a mystery that can be lived but never fully spoken in words.

Our good friend the poet and playwright Mark Van Doren[3] tells us, "To me, Lincoln seems, in some ways, the most interesting man who ever lived. He was gentle, but his gentleness was combined with a terrific toughness, an iron strength."

How did Lincoln say he would like to be remembered? His beloved friend, Representative Owen Lovejoy[4] of Illinois, had died in May of 1864 and friends wrote to Lincoln and he replied that the pressure of duties kept him from joining them in efforts for a marble monument to Lovejoy, the last sentence of his letter saying, "Let him have the marble monument along with the well-assured and more enduring one in the hearts of those who love liberty, unselfishly, for all men."

So perhaps we may say that the well-assured and most enduring memorial to Lincoln is invisibly there, today, tomorrow, and for a long time yet to come in the hearts of lovers of liberty, men and women who understand that wherever there is freedom there have been those who fought, toiled, and sacrificed for it. ✎

---

3. *Mark Van Doren* (1894–1973) was an American poet and teacher who is known for his verse play *The Last Days of Lincoln* (1959).

4. *Owen Lovejoy* was elected to the House of Representatives from the state of Illinois in 1856 and served five terms.

Literary Element Quotation *What does Sandburg hope to accomplish by quoting Mark Van Doren here?* **L2**

Teach

L2 Literary Element

Quotation Answer: *Students should conclude that this quotation acts as a second opinion, showing that Sandburg is not alone in his conclusions about Lincoln. It also supplies yet another vivid description of Lincoln.* **OL**

★ Viewing the Art

Not just a talented artist, Alonzo Chappel (1828–1887) was also a history buff. Inspired by what he read, he painted many famous scenes of American history, including this painting, which depicts Lincoln's death. **Ask:** Does the mood of this painting reflect the mood of Lincoln's mourners? *(Students likely will respond that the mood of the painting is somber, respectful, and mournful, much like that of Lincoln's supporters after his death.)* **AS**

CheckPoint

Use the CheckPoint questions on PresentationPlus! to check students' mastery of the selection. These questions can be used with interactive response keypads for immediate student response.

English Language Coach

Terminology Help students understand the terminology used to describe the North and the South during the Civil War. **Say:** The American Civil War came about because of very different ideas held by states in the North and South. Northern states wanted to keep all the states together in one union. These were known as the Union states. Southern states chose instead to break away and form their own group, or confederacy. Southern states became known as the Confederate states. **EL**

Objectives
• To distinguish between fact and opinion (SE)
• To understand quotations (SE)
• To conduct research about historical context (TWE)

Assess

1. Answers will vary but should reference the text.

2. (a) Lincoln has qualities that appeal to people around the world: decency, honesty, plain talk, and humor.
(b) Sandburg believed life for all people involved struggle.

3. (a) Lincoln claimed that he was controlled by events.
(b) Lincoln could adjust his policy to the needs of the moment.

4. (a) Sandburg defined democracy as the people having "say-so" with their leaders.
(b) Democracy must be lived to be understood.

5. The surprising contrast draws the reader into the text.

6. Sandburg's claim encourages further study.

7. It reflects Lincoln's own struggle for freedom.

8. Lincoln's actions resulted in freedom for many.

RESPONDING AND THINKING CRITICALLY

Respond

1. How did you react to Sandburg's claim that "the most enduring monument to Lincoln is invisibly there, today, tomorrow, and for a long time yet to come in the hearts of lovers of liberty"?

Recall and Interpret

2. (a) According to Sandburg, what makes people everywhere feel that Lincoln is "their own"? (b) What does this comment suggest about how Sandburg viewed the lives of people everywhere?

3. (a) From the quotations, what was Lincoln's opinion about the way in which he conducted the Civil War? (b) What might these comments reveal about his state of mind and his personal ability?

4. (a) According to Sandburg, what is the essence of democracy? (b) What might Sandburg mean by saying that democracy is "a mystery that can be lived but never fully spoken in words"?

Analyze and Evaluate

5. In the first paragraph, Sandburg portrays Lincoln in terms of metaphorical contrasts, such as "steel and velvet." Is this an effective introduction? Explain.

6. Sandburg twice claims that "we do not know" when he speculates about Lincoln's thoughts. By doing this, does he help or hinder his reader's understanding of Lincoln? Explain.

7. The speech ends with the phrase "wherever there is freedom there have been those who fought, toiled, and sacrificed for it." How does this conclusion fit into Sandburg's discussion of Lincoln?

Connect

8. **Big Idea** Keeping Freedom Alive Lincoln is often referred to as "the great emancipator." How does this speech support this view?

PRIMARY VISUAL ARTIFACT

Lincoln's Funeral Procession

Sandburg's words generate emotion. View this photograph of the hearse that carried the President's body and determine how the photo complements points in the speech.

1. What does the design and detailing of the hearse tell you about the person it carried?
2. What does it tell you about the time period?
3. Does the photo reveal anything that the speech does not address? Explain.

Primary Visual Artifact

1. That it was an important person
2. That it was during the 19th century
3. Answers will vary.

LITERARY ANALYSIS

Literary Element Quotation

Authors use **quotations** for various purposes. For example, a quotation may provide the reader with greater insight into an author's or another person's life or philosophy. Quotations can also make nonfiction texts, which generally do not contain much dialogue, "come alive."

1. Why does Sandburg include quotations in his speech?

2. Explain how the following Lincoln quotation contributes to Sandburg's purpose: "Let him have the marble monument along with the well-assured and more enduring one in the hearts of those who love liberty, unselfishly, for all men."

Review: Persuasion

As you learned on pages 444–445, **persuasion** is a type of writing that attempts to convince readers to think or act in a particular way. Among other techniques, writers of persuasive works appeal to reason or emotion to sway readers.

Partner Activity Pair up with a classmate and discuss Sandburg's use of persuasion in his speech. Create a two-column chart similar to the one below to help you identify the types of appeals used to persuade. Fill in the left-hand column with examples from the text that demonstrate persuasion. In the right-hand column, identify the type of appeal that is used.

Examples of Persuasion	Type of Appeal
"Bells sobbed, cities wore crepe, people stood in tears."	emotional appeal

READING AND VOCABULARY

Reading Strategy Distinguishing Fact and Opinion

In his speech, Sandburg combines fact and opinion in an attempt to make an appeal that is both emotional and logical.

1. Do you think Sandburg succeeds in his attempt to persuade by combining fact and opinion? Explain.

2. To support your opinion, list three details from the speech.

Vocabulary Practice

Practice with Analogies Choose the word that best completes each of the following analogies.

1. paradox : contradictory :: lie :
   a. meanspirited   c. dastardly
   b. accurate   d. untrue

2. cowardice : valor :: ignorance :
   a. fight   c. knowledge
   b. test   d. school

3. calm : turbulent :: relaxed :
   a. fretful   c. terrible
   b. hateful   d. peaceful

4. emancipation : free :: bondage :
   a. tight   c. freedom
   b. captive   d. monetary

5. imperative : command :: hopeful :
   a. wish   c. approximation
   b. fear   d. order

Academic Vocabulary

Here are two words from the vocabulary list on page R82.

exceed (ik sēd′) v. to go beyond a set limit

infer (in fur′) v. to draw a reasonable conclusion; guess; surmise

Practice and Apply
1. In what ways does Sandburg's speech **exceed** the mere listing of facts about Lincoln?
2. What can you **infer** about Sandburg from the speech?

CARL SANDBURG **489**

AFTER YOU READ

Assess

Literary Element

1. The quotations emphasize Lincoln's humanity and help readers grasp his ideas.

2. Lincoln believed that an abstract ideal—liberty—was a more enduring and worthwhile memorial than any marble monument. Some students may say that Lincoln was more concerned with freedom than with recognition.

Review: Persuasion

When students finish, have them evaluate Sandburg's appeals and determine which are most effective, and why.

Reading Strategy

1. Answers will vary.

2. Students might select passages such as: "The casket with his body was carried north and west a thousand miles, and the American people wept as never before"; "In the mixed shame and blame . . . [he] slept not at all, and on occasions he was seen to weep in a way that made weeping appropriate."

Vocabulary

1. d 2. c 3. a 4. b 5. a

Academic Vocabulary

1. Students may note Sandburg's inclusion of personal opinions, quotations, thoughts on democracy and freedom, and speculation about Lincoln's thoughts.

2. Sandburg greatly admired Lincoln for his approach to the war and for his personal qualities. Like Lincoln, Sandburg saw life as a struggle and cared deeply about democracy and liberty for all people.

Assess

Writing About Literature

Students' essays should

- examine the use of juxtaposition in the selection
- include details from the text
- include relevant personal responses to the selection

Literary Criticism

Encourage students to write blurbs not only from their own perspective but from a variety of perspectives. For example, they may write from the point of view of an academic journal editor, a poetry magazine editor, or a reviewer whose ancestors were freed from slavery by Lincoln's Emancipation Proclamation.

Sandburg's Language and Style

Make sure students understand that inverted word order, such as Sandburg's, should be used judiciously. It often creates a lofty tone, as in "Millions there are who take him as a personal treasure." Therefore, students may want to avoid it in a piece with a casual tone, or when writing dialogue spoken by a character who uses language in a more ordinary or conversational way.

Writing About Literature

Evaluate Author's Craft Sandburg uses juxtaposition—the placement of two or more distinct ideas or events side by side for the purposes of comparison and contrast—to describe characters and events. Write a brief essay in which you examine Sandburg's use of juxtaposition. Make sure you include details from the text as well as any personal responses you feel are relevant.

Use a graphic organizer like the one below to help organize your thoughts and support your main points.

After completing your draft, meet with a peer reviewer to evaluate each other's work and suggest revisions. Then proofread and edit your draft for errors in spelling, grammar, and punctuation.

Literary Criticism

In a February 14, 1926, review of *Abraham Lincoln: The Prairie Years,* the *New York Times* praised the biography and heralded it as innovative.

"A new experience awaits the reader of Carl Sandburg's book on Lincoln. There has never been biography quite like this before. . . . There is no question here of a new school of biographical writing. The thing Mr. Sandburg has done cannot well be repeated; his achievement is an intensely individual one, suffused by the qualities which are peculiarly his own as a poet. As those who have read him know, they are not qualities of conventional poetry, nor is this new book of his a merely emotional rendering of the Lincoln story. It is as full of facts as Jack Horner's pie was full of plums."

Meet with a few of your classmates to collaborate on writing five blurbs—short descriptions from reviews that might appear on the front of a magazine containing Sandburg's speech about Lincoln. As you write your blurbs, take the *New York Times* reviewer's comments into consideration, as well as what you have already discussed about Sandburg.

Sandburg's Language and Style

Displaying Poetic Style Sandburg creates a poetic tone in "Address on the Anniversary of Lincoln's Birth" by using vivid imagery and by inverting word order for emphasis and variety. Note his use of imagery and inversion in the following examples:

Imagery: "Not often in the story of mankind does a man arrive on earth who is both steel and velvet, who is as hard as rock and soft as drifting fog, who holds in his heart and mind the paradox of terrible storm and peace unspeakable and perfect."

Inversion: "In his blood and bones he carried it." (A more conventional way to phrase this sentence would be: *He carried it in his blood and bones.*)

Activity Find examples of Sandburg's use of imagery and inversion. Use a chart like the one below to record your examples.

Inversion	Imagery
"Millions there are who take him as a personal treasure."	"with terror, frightfulness, destruction, and on both sides, North and South, valor and sacrifice past words of man to tell"

Revising Check

Poetic Style Revise the essay you wrote analyzing Sandburg's use of juxtaposition to include imagery and inverted word order where appropriate.

Literature Online **Web Activities** For eFlashcards, Selection Quick Checks, and other Web activities, go to www.glencoe.com.

Literature Online

Web Activities Have students access the Web site for interactive activities that will help them assess their understanding of the selection.

Revising Check

Remind students that when using inverted word order they should still strive to make their writing clear and grammatically correct.

Visual Image "Lincoln's face is as finely lined as a pressed flower." → **Emotional Response**

TIME

What I See in Lincoln's Eyes

He never won Illinois' Senate seat. But in many ways, he paved the way for me.

By BARACK OBAMA

MY FAVORITE PORTRAIT OF ABRAHAM LINCOLN comes from the end of his life. In it, Lincoln's face is as finely lined as a pressed flower. He appears frail, almost broken; his eyes, averted from the camera's lens, seem to contain a heartbreaking melancholy, as if he sees before him what the nation had so recently endured.

It would be a sorrowful picture except for the fact that Lincoln's mouth is turned ever so slightly into a smile. The smile doesn't negate the sorrow. But it alters tragedy into grace. It's as if this rough-faced, aging man has cast his gaze toward eternity and yet still cherishes his memories—of an imperfect world and its fleeting, sometimes terrible beauty. On trying days, the portrait, a reproduction of which hangs in my office, soothes me; it always asks me questions.

What is it about this man that can move us so profoundly? Some of it has to do with Lincoln's humble beginnings, which often speak to our own. When I moved to Illinois 20 years ago to work as a community organizer, I had no money in my pockets and didn't know a single soul. During my first six years in the state legislature, Democrats were in the minority, and I couldn't get a bill heard, much less passed. In my first race for Congress, I had my head handed to me. So when I, an African American man with a funny name, born in Hawaii of a father from Kenya and a mother from Kansas, announced my candidacy for the United States Senate, it was hard to imagine a less likely scenario than that I would win—except, perhaps, for the one that allowed a child born in the backwoods of Kentucky with less than a year of formal education to end up as Illinois' greatest citizen and our nation's greatest President.

In Lincoln's rise from poverty, his ultimate mastery of language and law, his capacity to overcome personal loss and remain determined in the face of repeated defeat—in all this, he reminded me not just of my own struggles. He also reminded me of a larger, fundamental element of American life—the

---

Teach

Analyzing a Visual Image
Obama says he "cannot swallow whole the view of Lincoln as the Great Emancipator." **Ask:** How does this image reinforce Obama's argument? *(Students may say that his skepticism—the idea that views must be "chewed" and should not be accepted blindly—prevents his essay from being mere hero worship, letting the reader know that he has carefully considered his argument.)* **OL**

Readability Scores
Dale-Chall: 8.0
DRP: 64
Lexile: 1220

enduring belief that we can constantly remake ourselves to fit our larger dreams.

A connected idea attracts us to Lincoln: As we remake ourselves, we remake our surroundings. He didn't just talk or write or theorize. He split rail, fired rifles, tried cases, and pushed for new bridges and roads and waterways. In his sheer energy, Lincoln captures a hunger in us to build and to innovate. It's a quality that can get us in trouble; we may be blind at times to the costs of progress. And yet, when I travel to other parts of the world, I remember that it is precisely such energy that sets us apart, a sense that there are no limits to the heights our nation might reach.

R1 Still, as I look at his picture, it is the man and not the icon that speaks to me. I cannot swallow whole the view of Lincoln as the Great Emancipator. As a law professor and civil rights lawyer and as an African American, I am fully aware of his limited views on race. Anyone who actually reads the Emancipation Proclamation knows it was more a military document than a clarion call for justice. Scholars tell us too that Lincoln wasn't immune from political considerations and that his temperament could be indecisive and morose.

But it is precisely those imperfections— and the painful self-awareness of those failings etched in every crease of his face and reflected in those haunted eyes—that

April 10, 1865

Collection of Keya Morgan/Keya Gallery

make him so compelling. For when the time came to confront the greatest moral challenge this nation has ever faced, this all too human man did not pass the challenge on to future generations. He neither demonized the fathers and sons who did battle on the other side nor sought to diminish the

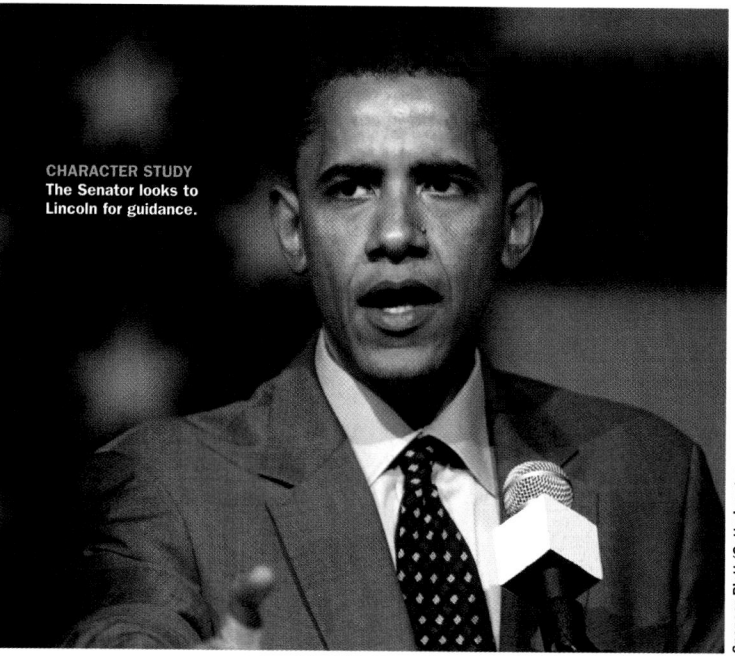

CHARACTER STUDY
The Senator looks to Lincoln for guidance.

Spencer Platt/Getty Images

terrible costs of his war. In the midst of slavery's dark storm and the complexities of governing a house divided, he somehow kept his moral compass pointed firm and true.

What I marvel at, what gives me such hope, is that this man could overcome depression, self-doubt, and the constraints of biography and not only act decisively but retain his humanity. Like a figure from the Old Testament, he wandered the earth, making mistakes, loving his family but causing them pain, despairing over the course of events, trying to divine God's will. He did not know how things would turn out, but he did his best.

A few weeks ago, I spoke at the commencement at Knox College in Galesburg, Illinois. I stood in view of the spot where Lincoln and Stephen Douglas

Additional Support

Skills Practice

WRITING: Vivid Verbs Throughout his essay, Obama uses vivid verbs in his descriptions. Well-chosen action verbs express ideas clearly and forcefully. Have students work in pairs to locate several vivid verbs in the selection. *(Answers might be "split," "fired," "captures," "etched," and "squeeze.")* **Say:** Now think of a person to describe and list active and vivid verbs that describe this person. Remember to use verbs that are relevant for your particular subjects. **OL**

held one of their famous debates during their race in 1858 for the U.S. Senate. The only way for Lincoln to get onto the podium was to squeeze his lanky frame through a window, whereupon he reportedly remarked, "At last I have finally gone through college." Waiting for the soon-to-be graduates to assemble, I thought that even as Lincoln lost that Senate race, his arguments that day would result, centuries later, in my occupying the same seat that he coveted. He may not have dreamed of that exact outcome. But I like to believe he would have appreciated the irony. Humor, ambiguity, complexity, compassion—all were part of his character. And as Lincoln called once upon the better angels of our nature, I believe that he is calling still, across the ages, to summon some measure of that character, the American character, in each of us today.

—From TIME, July 4, 2005

RESPONDING AND THINKING CRITICALLY

Respond

1. How did you react to Obama opening the article by describing the portrait of Lincoln?

Recall and Interpret

2. (a)What was Obama's career background prior to becoming a senator? (b)Do you agree with Obama that his early experiences were similar to President Lincoln's? Explain.

3. Why does Obama say that he "cannot swallow whole the view of Lincoln as the Great Emancipator"?

4. What qualities does Obama say defined "the American character"? Restate them in your own words.

Analyze and Evaluate

5. (a)Choose the sentence that best describes the main idea of the reading selection:

   i Lincoln could be "indecisive and morose," contrary to most people's perceptions of him.

   ii Barack Obama gives Lincoln direct credit for his political success.

   iii Lincoln remains a profound source of inspiration to many people in the United States, largely due to the story of his success and his actions as president.

   (b)Explain why you think that your choice is the best possible answer.

6. When Obama describes the portrait of Lincoln, he uses specific word choices, including vivid verbs and adjectives, and figurative language. Choose three examples of his specific word choice and explain why each example works well.

7. Obama says that Lincoln's portrait "always asks me questions." From the topics covered in this article, what might those questions be?

8. Good persuasive writing presents and refutes counterarguments to its thesis. Do you think that Obama's article is an example of good persuasive writing? Why or why not?

Connect

9. Obama draws a comparison between his own journey to the U.S. Senate and Lincoln's path from being "a child born in the backwoods of Kentucky with less than a year of formal education . . . [to] our nation's greatest President." In what ways do both of their lives and accomplishments represent the U.S. ideals of freedom and liberty and the achievement of the "American dream"?

WHAT I SEE IN LINCOLN'S EYES   **493**

Teach

R2 **Reading Strategy**

Analyzing a Visual Image
Ask: What are some of the ways in which Obama describes Lincoln? *(splitting rail, trying cases, and struggling with depression and self-doubt)* **Ask:** How do these images lead to a deeper understanding of Lincoln, the man, and Lincoln, the politician? *(They humanize the man and realistically show his political motivations.)* **OL**

See also ▌Active Learning and Note Taking Guide, pp. 64–69.

Assess

1. Most students will agree that it was an effective tool for opening the article.

2. (a) He was a community organizer and then served in the Illinois legislature. (b) Most students will agree that both men began humbly and then entered politics in Illinois.

3. He believes that the Emancipation Proclamation was more a "military document" than a treatise of justice.

4. The abilities to endure, to invent, to act with compassion, and to prevail despite adversity

5. (a) iii (b) Options i and ii are too narrow. Option ii also misinterprets Obama's opinion: He seems to believe that Lincoln "paved the way" for him in a symbolic sense, not necessarily causing his political success.

6. Students may mention "frail, almost broken," "this rough-faced, aging man," "finely lined as a pressed flower," or other details. They should note that the precision of these images evokes the complicated emotions Obama feels for his subject.

7. Questions might include *How did Lincoln shape the American spirit?* *How has he influenced my choices today?*

8. Some students will say that Obama effectively points out Lincoln's flaws. Others may say that Obama seems biased.

9. Both men rose from humble beginnings to prestigious positions.

493

Focus

BELLRINGER

Bellringer Options
Daily Language Practice Transparency 45
Or ask students to recall the Cinderella fairy tale and have them retell it in their own words or act it out for the class.
Ask: What lesson do you think the Cinderella story teaches women today? *(Students may mention that women should be independent and kind.)* **Say:** Author Toni Morrison finds a very original message in "Cinderella."

Author Search To expand students' appreciation of Toni Morrison, have them access the Web site for additional information and resources.

✓CheckPoint

Use the CheckPoint questions on Presentation Plus! to monitor students' comprehension. These questions can be used with interactive response keypads for immediate student feedback.

Cinderella's Stepsisters

MEET TONI MORRISON

In 1993 Toni Morrison became the first African American woman to be awarded the Nobel Prize in Literature. This prestigious prize, given to one outstanding writer every year, recognizes a variety of literature and authors. This recognition of Morrison solidified her standing as an internationally renowned and respected author.

Beginnings Toni Morrison was born Chloe Anthony Wofford in Lorain, Ohio. She later changed her first name to "Toni" because she grew tired of people mispronouncing "Chloe." As a child, Morrison read constantly. She also enjoyed listening to her community's folktales, which her father related to her. She began her studies at Howard University, where she received a bachelor's degree in English. She went on to earn a master's degree from Cornell University. After graduating, she taught English at Texas Southern University and Howard University. She became a textbook editor and later a senior editor at a major publishing house in New York City. Morrison published her first novel, *The Bluest Eye*, in 1970. *The Bluest Eye* is set in 1941 in Ohio and tells the story of a young African American girl who is consumed with wanting to achieve a white ideal of beauty: blonde hair and blue eyes.

> "At some point in life the world's beauty becomes enough."
>
> —Toni Morrison

Style Morrison's work is praised for its examination of the experience of being an African American woman in the United States at various historical times. Her characters tend to be strong and realistic. Morrison also has a unique narrative style; she does not necessarily use straightforward narrative to tell her stories in a clear, logical order. She sometimes changes scenes or point of view abruptly. Morrison also incorporates elements such as myth and superstition to advance her narratives.

Continued Success Morrison's successes include the novels *Sula* (1973), *Song of Solomon* (1977), *Tar Baby* (1981), *Jazz* (1992), *Paradise* (1998), and *Love* (2003). *Beloved* (1987), won a Pulitzer Prize for fiction. In addition to her novels, Morrison has written short stories, plays, speeches, essays, and nonfiction, including *Playing in the Dark: Whiteness and Literary Imagination* (1992) and *Remember: The Journey to School Integration* (2004).

Morrison writes to communicate the female African American experience. She claims that one of her goals in writing is to encourage other African American women to "repossess, re-name [and] re-own." Yet ultimately her books are popular with a wide variety of readers and, as a result, Morrison has been called one of the best American writers of her time.

Toni Morrison was born in 1931.

Author Search For more about Toni Morrison, go to www.glencoe.com.

Selection Skills

Literary Elements
Cinderella's Stepsisters
Listening/Speaking/Viewing Skills
- Author's Purpose (SE pp. 495–498)
- Analogy (SE p. 498)
- Discussing Analogies (SE p. 498)

Reading Skills
Vocabulary Skills
- Analyzing Text Structure (SE pp. 495, 497, 499)
- Connotation (TWE p. 496)
- Word Parts (SE pp. 495, 499)
- Academic Vocabulary (SE p. 499)

Writing Skills/Grammar
- Analyzing Genre Elements (SE p. 499)

Connecting to the Speech

In her speech, Toni Morrison reminds us to be mindful of everyone we come in contact with as we seek to reach our goals. Before you read the speech, think about the following questions:

- When is a time when you were responsible for others?
- How did you remain concerned about and compassionate towards others as you carried out your duties?

Building Background

Because of her fame as a writer and prestigious award winner, Toni Morrison was asked to speak at graduation at Barnard College, a women's college affiliated with Columbia University in New York City.

In her speech to the graduating women of Barnard, Morrison uses the well-known fairy tale of Cinderella to make the point that women in positions of power should still look out for their fellow females in the world. Her speech, "Cinderella's Stepsisters," uses the Cinderella story to show how women in power sometimes treat women in positions beneath them unfairly.

Setting Purposes for Reading

Big Idea Keeping Freedom Alive

As you read this speech by Toni Morrison, notice how she is able to use a widely known fairy tale to achieve her ultimate goal: taking a stand against cruel and selfish behavior and maintaining freedom for women in the process.

Literary Element Author's Purpose

An **author's purpose** is his or her intent in writing a literary work, such as a speech. An author's purpose is dependent in part on his or her audience. For example, the author may intend to inform, persuade, entertain, tell a story, or express an opinion.

- See Literary Terms Handbook, p. R2.

Literature Online **Interactive Literary Elements Handbook** To review or learn more about the literary elements, go to www.glencoe.com.

Reading Strategy Analyzing Text Structure

Text structure is the way a piece of writing is organized. By **analyzing the text structure**, you can use a text's organizational pattern to better understand the main ideas or the author's message.

.....

Reading Tip: Finding Examples To determine how the speech is organized, identify the main idea and then look for examples where it is emphasized. Use a web like the one below.

Main Idea of Speech: Taking a stand

Vocabulary

fetish (fet′ ish) n. abnormally obsessive preoccupation or attachment; a fixation; p. 496 *She has a fetish for books; she buys them constantly.*

dominion (də min′ yən) n. control or the exercise of control; p. 496 *The king's dominion spans the entire country.*

deflect (di flekt′) v. to cause to turn aside; to bend or deviate; p. 497 *The police officer's vest is able to deflect gunshots directed at him.*

emanate (em′ə nāt′) v. to come or set forth, as from a source; p. 497 *The campfire emanated so much heat that we had to move our chairs back.*

abstraction (ab strak′ shən) n. theoretical concept isolated from real application; p. 497 *An idea is an abstraction, while an action is not.*

.....

Vocabulary Tip: Word Parts Understanding the parts of a word is the first step to understanding the meaning of the word.

Focus

Summary

Toni Morrison's speech to Barnard College graduates spins off from the story of Cinderella's selfish stepsisters to urge young women to have concern for other women as they act in positions of responsibility. She counsels them to avoid oppressing other women and instead concentrate on nurturing them.

V Vocabulary

Vocabulary File

Say: Add these words and definitions to your vocabulary file. For each word, include a sentence that gives you an example of how to use the word. **OL** Students with English language needs should include the pronunciations of these words in their files. **EL**

Literature Online

Literary Elements Have students access the Web site for interactive activities that will improve their understanding of author's purpose.

OBJECTIVES

In studying this selection, you will focus on the following:
- determining author's purpose
- analyzing text structure
- writing to analyze genre elements
- evaluating analogy

TONI MORRISON **495**

Selection Resources

Print Materials
- 📁 Unit 2 Resources (Fast File), pp. 72–74
- 📁 Leveled Vocabulary Development, p. 37
- 📁 Selection and Unit Assessments, pp. 81–82
- 📁 Selection Quick Checks, p. 41

Transparencies
- Bellringer Options Transparencies: Daily Language Practice Transparency 45
- Literary Elements Transparency 35

Technology
- TeacherWorks Plus™ CD-ROM
- StudentWorks Plus™ CD-ROM
- Presentation Plus!™ CD-ROM
- Literature Online, glencoe.com
- Online Student Edition, mhln.com
- ExamView® Assessment Suite CD-ROM
- Vocabulary PuzzleMaker CD-ROM
- Listening Library, disc 1 track 45

Teach

L1 Literary Element

Author's Purpose Answer:
Because Morrison is speaking to a graduating college class, this statement helps to clarify to the audience that she will be focusing not only on their present but also on their past. **OL**

BI1 Big Idea

Taking a Stand
Answer: *She is concerned that though women gather together, they may do so to harm rather than help each other.* **OL**

★ Literary History

Cinderella Folktale Many cultures have variations of the Cinderella folktale, a traditional story passed down orally before it was written down. During the nineteenth century, the tale was written by Charles Perrault in France and by Jacob and Wilhelm Grimm in Germany. **AS**

Readability Scores
Dale-Chall: 9.3
DRP: 62
Lexile: 970

Two Young Girls from Finland, 1907. Sonia Delaunay Coll. Henri Nannen, Emden, Germany.

Cinderella's Stepsisters
Toni Morrison

L et me begin by taking you back a little. Back before the days at college. To nursery school, probably, to a once-upon-a-time time when you first heard, or read, or, I suspect, even saw "Cinderella." Because it is Cinderella that I want to talk about; because it is Cinderella who causes me a feeling of urgency. What is unsettling about that fairy tale is that it is essentially the story of household—a world, if you please—of women gathered together and held together in order to abuse another woman. There is, of course, a rather vague absent father and a nick-of-time prince with a foot **fetish**. But neither has much personality. And there are the surrogate "mothers," of course (god- and step-), who contribute both to Cinderella's grief and to her release and happiness. But it is her stepsisters who interest me. How crippling it must have been for those young girls to grow up with a mother, to watch and imitate that mother, enslaving another girl.

I am curious about their fortunes after the story ends. For contrary to recent adaptations,[1] the stepsisters were not ugly, clumsy, stupid girls with outsize feet. The Grimm collection describes them as "beautiful and fair in appearance." When we are introduced to them they are beautiful, elegant, women of status, and clearly women of power. Having watched and participated in the violent **dominion** of another woman, will they be any less cruel when it comes their turn to enslave other children, or even when they are required to take care of their own mother?

> **Literary Element** Author's Purpose *How does this statement help Morrison engage her audience's attention?* **L1**

> **Big Idea** Keeping Freedom Alive *What concerns might Morrison have regarding the freedom of women?* **BI1**

Vocabulary

fetish (fet′ ish) n. abnormally obsessive preoccupation or attachment; a fixation

Vocabulary

dominion (də min′ yən) n. control or the exercise of control

1. *Adaptations* are compositions that are written in a new form.

Additional Support

Skills Practice

READING: Connotation Point out that Morrison chooses her words carefully, selecting words with powerful connotations, or implied meanings, such as *abuse, crippling,* and *outsize.* **Ask:** What is the effect of these highly connotative words? *(They spark negative attitudes toward oppressing women and therefore reinforce Morrison's purpose of urging women to support each other.)* Ask students to find other examples of words with highly positive or negative connotations. **OL**

It is not a wholly medieval problem. It is quite a contemporary[2] one: feminine power when directed at other women has historically been wielded in what has been described as a "masculine" manner. Soon you will be in a position to do the very same thing. Whatever your background—rich or poor—whatever the history of education in your family—five generations or one—you have taken advantage of what has been available to you at Barnard and you will therefore have both the economic and social status of the stepsisters *and* you will have their power.

I want not to *ask* you but to *tell* you not to participate in the oppression of your sisters. . . . Women who stop the promotion of other women in careers are women, and another woman must come to the victim's aid. Social and welfare workers who humiliate their clients may be women, and other women colleagues have to **deflect** their anger.

I am alarmed by the violence that women do to each other: professional violence, competitive violence, emotional violence. I am alarmed by the willingness of women to enslave other women. I am alarmed by a growing absence of decency on the killing floor of professional women's worlds. You are the women who will take your place in the world where *you* can decide who shall flourish and who shall wither; you will make distinctions between the deserving poor and the undeserving poor; where you can yourself determine which life is expendable[3] and which is indispensable. Since you

will have the power to do it, you may also be persuaded that you have the right to do it. As educated women the distinction between the two is first-order business.

I am suggesting that we pay as much attention to our nurturing sensibilities as to our ambition. You are moving in the direction of freedom and the function of freedom is to free somebody else. You are moving toward self-fulfillment, and the consequences of that fulfillment should be to discover that there is something just as important as you are and that just-as-important thing may be Cinderella—or your stepsister.

In your rainbow journey toward the realization of personal goals, don't make choices based only on your security and your safety. Nothing is safe. That is not to say that anything ever was, or that anything worth achieving ever should be. Things of value seldom are. It is not safe to have a child. It is not safe to challenge the status quo.[4] It is not safe to choose work that has not been done before. Or to do old work in a new way. There will always be someone there to stop you. But in pursuing your highest ambitions, don't let your personal safety diminish the safety of your stepsister. In wielding the power that is deservedly yours, don't permit it to enslave your stepsisters. Let your might and your power **emanate** from that place in you that is nurturing and caring.

Women's rights is not only an **abstraction**, a cause; it is also a personal affair. It is not only about "us"; it is also about me and you. Just the two of us. ❧

---

2. *Contemporary* means "current" or "modern."
3. *Expendable* means "easily replaced."

Reading Strategy Analyzing Text Structure *How does Morrison move away from discussing the Cinderella tale here?* **R**

Literary Element Author's Purpose *How does Morrison make this plea to her audience effective?* **L₂**

Vocabulary

deflect (di flekt′) *v.* to cause to turn aside; to bend or deviate

---

4. *Status quo* means "the existing condition."

Big Idea Keeping Freedom Alive *What is Morrison asking the audience to do to protect freedom for themselves and for women in general?* **BI₂**

Vocabulary

emanate (em′ə nāt′) *v.* to come or set forth, as from a source

abstraction (ab strak′ shən) *n.* theoretical concept isolated from real application

TONI MORRISON **497**

English Language Coach

Parallelism Morrison uses two effective rhetorical devices: parallelism and repetition. Point out the sentence "I am alarmed by the violence . . . emotional violence." Note the repetition of "I am alarmed" in the next two sentences. Also point out the parallelism of "professional violence, competitive violence, emotional violence." **Ask:** What is the effect of these devices? *(They call attention to important ideas and give the speech a cadence that makes the ideas memorable.)* Have students find other examples of parallelism and repetition. **EL**

Teach

R Reading Strategy

Analyzing Text Structure
Answer: *Morrison began her speech by reinterpreting a traditional fairy tale, but now she tells her listeners that abuse among women is not just an ancient problem. With this statement, she connects that past, fictional story with the present.* **OL**

L₂ Literary Element

Author's Purpose Answer: *She constructs her plea as a demand, not a question. She strongly admonishes her audience to influence positively the women they may encounter in the workplace and the world outside their college experience.* **OL**

BI₂ Big Idea

Taking a Stand
Answer: *Morrison asks the women to make the distinction between having the power to oppress and using it. She warns them to keep their power in check. They should strive to treat others fairly and not take advantage of anyone.* **OL**

CheckPoint

Use the CheckPoint questions on Presentation Plus! to check students' mastery of the selection. These questions can be used with interactive response keypads for immediate student feedback.

Objectives
- To determine author's purpose (SE)
- To analyze text structure (SE)
- To evaluate analogy (SE)

Assess

1. (a) That women harm one another instead of nurturing one another. (b) Many students would have agreed with her. Some might have been unaware of this type of behavior.

2. (a) They "enslave other women" to gain power and prestige. (b) Because these graduates may eventually wield power, she warns them not to abuse that power.

3. (a) With fairness and kindness. (b) They know right from wrong and should act accordingly.

4. (a) That women's rights are not simply a case of "us" but rather are "about me and you." They become personal because they are about women's relationships. (b) By being a positive and nurturing example at work and in relationships.

5. (a) By referring to the enslavement of women, women who stop the promotion of other women, and women who humiliate other women, she persuades her listeners that small positive actions can effect great changes. (b) It strengthens her argument by eliciting an instinctive response that the stepsisters' cruelty was undeserved and unjust. She

RESPONDING AND THINKING CRITICALLY

Respond

1. (a) What do you think are the main points Morrison made in her speech? (b) If you were a Barnard graduate and could have interacted with Morrison afterward, what comments might you have offered in response to her speech?

Recall and Interpret

2. (a) According to Morrison, how do women in power often treat one another? (b) How might this affect the graduates to whom she is speaking?

3. (a) From Morrison's view, how should those in power treat one another? (b) How should the students' education distinguish them from others in power?

4. (a) What does Morrison mean by saying that women's rights are "a personal affair"? (b) How might a listener seek to make a difference?

Analyze and Evaluate

5. (a) How does Morrison persuade her listeners to take action? (b) How does Morrison's alignment with Cinderella's stepsisters strengthen or weaken her argument?

6. Is this speech appropriate for men as well as women? Explain your position.

7. (a) Morrison claims that women often oppress other women. What evidence does she use to support this statement?

Connect

8. **Big Idea** Keeping Freedom Alive Morrison takes a stand against women oppressing women in this speech. In what ways do you find her argument to be valid?

LITERARY ANALYSIS

Literary Element Author's Purpose

When Toni Morrison crafted the speech "Cinderella's Stepsisters," you can be sure that her purpose was shaped by her audience. She knew that she would be speaking to graduates of a prestigious women's college, many of whom would likely be going on to high-paying positions in the world of business. In this case, the intended audience had an effect on the topic and purpose of the literary work, because Morrison wished to convey a specific message to this particular group of people.

1. An author's purpose may be to inform, to entertain, to persuade, to tell a story, or to express an opinion. How would you characterize Morrison's purpose or purposes in this speech? Explain.

2. Morrison says, "I am alarmed by the growing absence of decency on the killing floor of professional women's worlds." However, she does not give any examples to back up her observations. Do you think her purpose would be better served by including specific examples of the oppression she abhors? Why or why not?

498 UNIT 2 NONFICTION

Review: Analogy

As you learned on pages 444–445, an **analogy** is a comparison that shows the relationship between two things that are otherwise dissimilar. Writers often use an analogy to explain something unfamiliar by comparing it to a familiar concept.

Partner Activity With a classmate, discuss how Morrison uses something familiar (the Cinderella story) to make a point to her listeners. Make a web like the one below to organize your thoughts about the analogy. Then, evaluate whether you think that this analogy is successful and why.

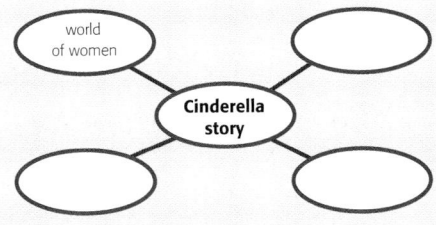

world of women — Cinderella story

connects their behavior to similar oppression taking place today.

6. Students should note and cite examples of unjust and cruel behavior by men in the workplace.

7. She says that women do professional, competitive, and emotional violence to each other.

8. Students may agree or disagree with Morrison's points.

Literary Element

1. To persuade. Students should refer to textual examples.

2. Some will say that the speech is persuasive without examples, which might affect the flow of the powerful language. Others may feel examples are useful.

Reading Strategy Analyzing Text Structure

When writing a speech, authors frequently use an interesting, unconventional or thought-provoking beginning, also called a "hook," to capture their audience's attention early on. Consider how the **structure** of the speech helps get and maintain the audience's attention.

1. Why does Morrison remind her listeners about the concept of the familiar story?

2. Evaluate how well you think the structure of the speech helped keep your attention.

Vocabulary Practice

Practice with Word Parts Use your knowledge of roots, as well as prefixes and suffixes, to pick the best definition for each of the boldfaced vocabulary words.

1. She tried to **deflect** her friend's questions.
   a. tolerate   **b.** redirect   **c.** answer

2. The powerful speaker held **dominion** over the mesmerized audience.
   a. control   **b.** discussion   **c.** necessity

3. A stench **emanates** from the garbage cans.
   a. ceases   **b.** increases   **c.** comes out

4. She had a **fetish** for trinkets, which were displayed all over her house.
   a. preoccupation **b.** dislike   **c.** sympathy

5. While world peace seemed like an **abstraction**, he felt like there were concrete ways to move toward making it a reality.
   a. possibility   **b.** action   **c.** idea

Academic Vocabulary

Here are two words from the vocabulary list on page R82.

inhibit (in hib′it) v. to prohibit, restrain, forbid

trend (trend) n. the general direction in which something tends to move.

Practice and Apply

1. How do some women **inhibit** the progress of other women?

2. How might Morrison's speech reverse the **trend** of the oppression of women?

Writing About Literature

Analyze Genre Elements Morrison's goal in writing is to persuade her audience to accept her argument that women need to make a conscious effort to support other women. In her speech, Morrison uses several elements common to the genre of persuasive speeches. To strengthen both her argument and her writing, Morrison relies on parallelism of sentences, repetition of key words, and juxtaposition of ideas to make her speech compelling and ultimately convincing. Do you think that Morrison does an effective job of persuading her audience? Write a one-page response in which you persuade your audience to accept your viewpoint. Use examples from Morrison's speech as evidence for your argument.

Before you begin writing, create a list of literary devices or genre elements you think Morrison uses effectively. Also identify possible areas of improvement in her speech. Create a chart like the one below to organize your ideas. Use these ideas to help you write your persuasive essay.

Genre Element	Example	Effective?
Juxtaposition	Morrison compares a real-world problem, women oppressing other women, with descriptions of a fictional fairy tale.	

Reading Further

Toni Morrison's novels offer a unique look into the African American experience. Read *Beloved* to learn more about slavery and its haunting effects. Additionally, *Conversations with Toni Morrison* offers interesting insight about her feelings on contemporary black literature.

Literature Online **Web Activities** For eFlashcards, Selection Quick Checks, and other Web activities, go to www.glencoe.com.

TONI MORRISON **499**

Reading Further

Morrison's novel *Beloved* was adapted into a 1998 film version starring Oprah Winfrey.

Literature Online

Web Activities Have students access the Web site for interactive activities that will help them assess their understanding of the selection.

Assess

Review: Analogy

Students should refer to specific textual examples.

Reading Strategy

1. Although most listeners are already familiar with the story, they may not recall the characters and specific details. By summarizing the story at the beginning, Morrison will not confuse or alienate any listeners.

2. Answers will vary. Some students may suggest that the speech would not have captured the listeners' attention without the Cinderella story, a familiar reference, at the beginning.

Vocabulary

1. b 2. a 3. c 4. a 5. c

Academic Vocabulary

1. Women can stop other women from being promoted and from succeeding at certain jobs.

2. It brings the topic to the attention of those just entering the workforce.

Writing About Literature

Students' essays should

- argue whether they thought Morrison's use of genre elements was effective and whether her speech was persuasive

- give textual examples of genre elements that Morrison used in her speech, including repetition, juxtaposition, and parallelism

Focus

BELLRINGER

Have students list the names of their best friend, a favorite teacher, and a famous person on a piece of paper. Then ask students to list adjectives that describe these people, and to write down some important events in their lives.

Summary

Students will write and present biographical sketches. They will follow the stages of the writing process, including prewriting, drafting, revising, and editing. Two mini-lessons on using action verbs and correcting verb tense are provided.

Writing Models Have students access the Web site for interactive writing models and writing guides.

The Writing Process

In this workshop, you will follow the stages of the writing process. At any stage, you may think of new ideas to include and better ways to express them. Feel free to return to earlier stages as you write.

Prewriting

Drafting

Revising

➡ Focus Lesson: Using Action Verbs

Editing & Proofreading

➡ Focus Lesson: Correcting Verb Tense

Presenting

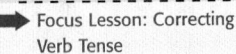
Writing Models For models and other writing activities, go to www.glencoe.com.

OBJECTIVES
- Write a biographical sketch that narrates, explains, or does both.
- Use verb tenses consistently and correctly.

Writing Workshop

Biographical Narrative

 ### Writing a Biographical Sketch

"De Kooning had learned the hard way . . . that life in America was not going to be easy. 'It turned out to be quite different from what I thought,' de Kooning said of America. 'Nowhere near as luxurious as I imagined it.'"

—Mark Stevens and Annalyn Swan, "First Impressions"
from *De Kooning: An American Master*

Connecting to the Literature A biographical sketch does not tell a whole life story; instead, it concentrates on an interesting experience in the life of its subject. Whether the sketches are narrated or explained, they contain specific and descriptive details that create interest, support ideas, and supply background information. The rubric below highlights the goals and strategies for writing a successful biographical sketch.

Rubric: Features of Biographical Sketches

Goals	Strategies
To present several main ideas or events that reveal a person's life, character, or both.	☑ Present main ideas and details about events, personalities, and actions
To use specific details to make the biographical subject convincing	☑ Research the subject to find interesting information ☑ Use precise nouns, action verbs, and concrete details
To narrate events or describe qualities in a logical order	☑ Use chronological order for events
To provide readers with necessary background information	☑ Explain specific references that might be unfamiliar to the audience ☑ Link the subject's actions to details of his or her life

---

Additional Support

 ## Workshop Resources

Print Materials
- 📁 Unit 2 Resources (Fast File), pp. 75–77
- 📁 REAL Success in Writing: Research and Reports
- 📁 Writing Constructed Responses, pp. 1–26, 54–60
- 📖 Glencoe Literature Library

🖥 Transparencies
- Grammar and Language Transparency 51
- Writing Workshop Transparencies 11–15
- Visual Literacy/Fine Art Transparencies

Technology
- Grammar & Language eWorkbook
- Revising with Style eWorkbook
- Sentence Diagraming eWorkbook
- Spelling Power eWorkbook
- Online Essay Grader, glencoe.com
- Literature Library ExamView™ Assessment Suite CD-ROM
- Literature Library Vocabulary PuzzleMaker CD-ROM

▶ Assignment

Write a biographical sketch. As you move through the stages of the writing process, keep your audience and purpose in mind.

Audience: classmates and peers

Purpose: to present a brief, focused sketch of a person by narrating selected events or presenting selected main ideas that make the person seem real to your audience

Analyzing a Professional Model

In the biographical sketch that follows, Alice Jackson Baughn presents a brief look at the author Eudora Welty. As you read the sketch, notice how Baughn selects just a few important main ideas to tell her audience about Welty, presenting each in a well-developed paragraph. Pay close attention to the comments in the margin. They point out features that you may want to include in your biographical sketch.

from *Eudora Welty: 1909–2001* by Alice Jackson Baughn

In Mississippi, to hear Eudora Welty read from her works was as prized as a pair of tickets to the state's Egg Bowl, the annual gridiron classic between the University of Mississippi and Mississippi State University. That strong Southern accent delivered with her unique inflections drew her audience to a special place. The grande dame of American literature died Monday in a Jackson, Miss., hospital near the family home where she had lived for almost all of her 92 years. She was hospitalized with pneumonia on Saturday.

Considered by many literary critics to be America's greatest living writer, Welty's many honors included the Pulitzer Prize in 1973 for *The Optimist's Daughter*. The recipient of numerous honorary degrees, including ones from Harvard and Yale, Welty was also recognized internationally. In 1987, France knighted her. Welty's autobiography, *One Writer's Beginnings*, became the longest-running book on *The New York Times'* best-seller list in 1984. It described how the daughter of a Mississippi insurance salesman grew into an astute observer of human nature with a keen sense of place in story-telling. Welty translated that knowledge into essays, short stories, novels and photography over eight decades. Her first published story, "Death of a Traveling

Real-World Connection

You may be required to use nonfiction narrative skills to tell facts about your own life when you apply to college or for a job. The main points you present about your experiences and your character, along with the details that support them, may be used to judge your merits as a future student or an employee.

Introduction
Introduce your subject and create interest in him or her.

Main Ideas/Details
Present main ideas about the person and support them with details.

Background Information
Provide background information to help your reader come to know your subject.

Teach

Big Idea

Keeping Freedom Alive

Say: Keep the following idea in mind as you read. Social and political change occurs not only at the national level, but at the grassroots level as well. Encourage students to think about people in their own families and communities who may have compelling stories of their own to share. Remind students that material for fascinating biographical sketches is all around them. **Ask:** What family member or community activist could you interview for a biographical sketch? *(Answers will vary.)* **OL**

★ Writer's Technique

Introductions Point out to students that successful biographical sketches start with a "hook," or an attention-getting device. **Ask:** What is the attention-getting device in the Baughn piece? *(the first sentence of the essay)* Why does Baughn open her sketch with a reference to the Egg Bowl? *(Welty lived her entire life in Mississippi, and its people and places provided the foundation for her literary work.)* **AS**

Differentiated Instruction

Descriptive Details Help less proficient readers identify descriptive details. Have students list some the particular details Baughn uses in her description of Welty, her life, and her home. **Ask:** How is your impression of the grocery store where Welty shopped enriched by knowing it was a "Jitney-Jungle"? *(Students may suggest that these grocery stores are common in the South, and so this tells the reader that this is a story about the South.)* **BL**

Objectives
• To write a biographical sketch that narrates, explains, or does both (SE)
• To recognize effective introductions (TWE)

Writing Workshop

Biographical Narrative

Teach

Writing Skills

Outlining Explain to students that there are many ways to outline their ideas for their essays. Some students have more success with formal, linear outlines, and others are better able to organize their ideas with idea mapping—writing the main idea in a center circle, with spokes leading to supporting details in smaller circles. Encourage students to work with different forms of outlining to find the one that best suits their thinking style. **OL**

⭐ Language History

Narration and Exposition

Ask for student volunteers to look up *narration* and *exposition* in the dictionary. **Ask:** What is the definition of *narration*? *(Narration, whether fiction or nonfiction, tells a story. Narratives usually include a setting, plot, characters, and a problem to be resolved.)* What is the definition of *exposition*? *(Exposition explains a topic, process, or problem in detail. Sometimes expository writing compares and contrasts.)* **AS**

Main Ideas

Present several main ideas in your sketch, devoting a full paragraph to each.

Specific Details

Present specific details to add interest and help bring the person to life.

Focus

Stay focused on your subject and the details and events that make the subject interesting or memorable.

Supporting Details

Add interest and depth to a biographical sketch with a variety of supporting details.

Salesman," came in 1936. Her last book was *Church Courtyards*, published by the University Press of Mississippi last year.

Welty's love of photography began during the 1930s. She was working for the Works Progress Administration, a job that took her across Mississippi, and she took her camera along. Besides photographing people, Welty snapped images of a Mississippi that no longer exists, except in her stories. Some of Welty's photos were exhibited in small New York galleries in 1936 and 1937. Today, they are highly valued collector's items.

Welty never married and lived alone—until several years ago when failing health demanded that she hire nurses and a caretaker—in the house she had occupied with her parents and siblings in the historic Belhaven section of Jackson, the state's capital. Nothing about the Tudor-styled house on the oak-canopied street alerted passersby to the status of Welty's literary existence. An oak tree planted by Welty's mother decades ago still stands in the front yard.

Welty shopped almost daily at the old Jitney-Jungle grocery story only a few blocks from her home. Fans too timid to knock on her front door often went to the store and waited for her to appear. But Welty was always gracious to her adoring fans, particularly young writers. As her health declined, her doctors ordered her to post a sign at the entrance of her home forbidding visitors without an appointment. But Welty, always the gracious southern lady, thought the message was too curt. Beneath the warning, in a spiderly script, she had scrawled a penciled note of apology.

The Mississippi writers Welty mentored and befriended reads like a "Who's Who" of American literature. Forty-eight-year-old Carolyn Haines, author of the critically acclaimed novels *Summer of the Redeemers* and *Touched*, said Welty's work played a tremendous role in her decision to become a writer:

> "I was sitting in my eighth-grade English class, reading 'The Wide Net' with it hidden behind my English grammar book. I was supposed to be diagramming sentences, but Miss Welty had my mind millions of miles away. I remember it so well because it was the first time in my life that I realized a person could write about people who talked like me, and that realization changed my life."

Reading-Writing Connection Think about the writing techniques that you have just encountered and try them out in the biographical sketch you write.

Additional Support

Skills Practice

RESEARCH: Research Questions

After students choose a subject, they will need to focus their questions in order to research the necessary background information. The questions students ask and research will shape their final essays. Encourage students to think of questions that are relevant to their subjects, as well as questions that are neither too broad nor too narrow. Have students generate a list of possible research questions for their subjects. Then have students arrange the questions by category. Students may find that categorizing their questions leads to discovering other questions they would like to pursue. **OL**

Prewriting

Choose Your Subject Make a list of people who interest you. For each one, jot down facts you already know about the person or reasons to choose that person as a subject. Study your list and choose your best idea.

Research and Read Find out more about your subject by using the Internet, library databases, or books. Take notes that paraphrase and summarize the information you find.

Identify Your Main Ideas To bring your character "to life" in a biographical sketch, you will need to make main points about the person and narrate events in the person's life. Many biographical sketches do both. In a two-column chart, list important events (in the first column) and main ideas about the person (in the second column). Circle ideas that could serve as topics for two to four body paragraphs in your biographical sketch.

Make a Plan There are several ways to make a plan for writing.

▶ **Make a formal outline.** A formal outline shows your main points in order as well as the details or subtopics that support or develop the main points.

▶ **Make an informal outline.** An informal outline shows your main points in order, as well as prewriting notes related to each main point.

▶ **Make an introduction-body-conclusion map** like this one.

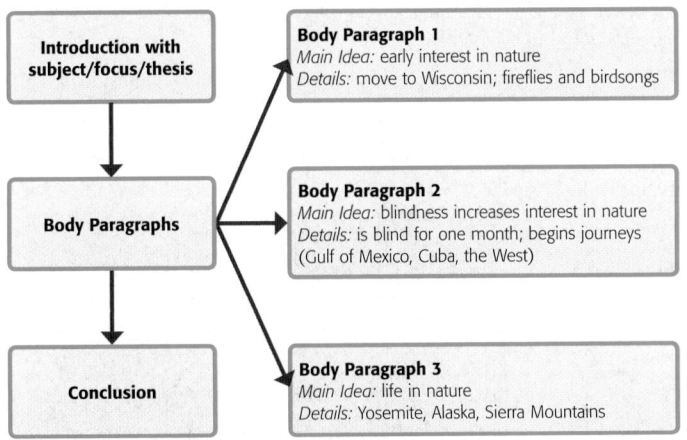

Discuss Your Ideas Consult your writing plan as you tell a partner about your ideas so far. To develop your writing voice, listen to your own speaking voice as you talk about your subject. Ask your partner to identify words and phrases that convey your enthusiasm, wonder, or other emotions and attitudes toward your subject. Jot down those words and phrases.

> **A Sketch, Not a Life Story**
>
> Did you notice how the model does *not* begin with *She was born* and end with *She died*? Instead, it presents main ideas such as *Welty was a great writer; Welty loved photography;* and *Welty lived alone.* Your sketch should do the same.

> **Test Prep**
>
> If you have to write a biographical sketch for a test, choose a subject you know well. As a prewriting test of how suitable your topic is, see whether you can list three main events in the person's life or three important ideas about the person, as well as a few details to support the main idea.

Teach

Writing Process

Prewriting Have students interview each other about their subjects. Suggest that they work through a list of "wh" questions to flesh out their ideas for their essays. **Say:** Interview each other about your subjects by asking the following questions: Who is this person? What did this person accomplish or achieve? Where did this person live? When did this person live? Why is this person significant? **OL**

Writing Process

Drafting Remind students that chronological order offers an effective pattern of organization to use when summarizing major events in a person's life. Ask students to locate on a rough timeline when specific events occurred in their subject's life. **Ask:** What words and phrases can you use to indicate chronological order? *(Some suggestions might be "soon followed," " years later," " until," "before," "when," "meanwhile.")* **OL**

Differentiated Instruction

Comparative Reading Challenge gifted learners to seek out a subject who has written his or her autobiography or memoir *and* about whom biographies have also been written. Have them compare and contrast what they learn from each different accounts of their subject's life. Suggest students research fairly famous people, whether historical political leaders, modern activists or even entertainment figures. General questions that would guide the comparative reading include "What is this person's self-perception?" and "How is this person described by others?" **AL**

Objectives
- To write a biographical sketch that narrates, explains, or does both (SE)
- To ask focused and relevant research questions (TWE)

503

Teach

Writing Skills

Using Quotations Encourage students to gather and use quotes by their subjects, if possible. **Say:** One way of engaging your readers is by including the words of your subjects. Well-chosen quotations reveal much about your subjects. If your subject is particularly funny, or wise, you can communicate those qualities by using their own words. **OL**

Writing Skills

Taking Careful Notes Remind students of the importance of taking careful notes when doing their research. Encourage students to keep track of their sources and notes with note cards and a working bibliography. Students should place direct quotes in quotation marks on their note cards, and keep track of where they find their information. **Say:** If you are directly quoting from a source, you must document it. If you are using the ideas from a source, you must document them. Using a source's words or ideas as your own, even if unintentional, is called plagiarism, and is a serious offense. **OL**

Drafting

Creating Unified, Focused Paragraphs As you write, remember that each of your body paragraphs should be about one main idea or event. If the paragraph retells an event, arrange your details in chronological order. Use transition expressions such as *first, next,* and *then* to connect ideas. Do not stray from retelling the story of the event. If the paragraph presents a main idea, such as the person's sense of humor, all details in the paragraph must relate to that topic. You should either present a topic sentence or clearly imply one. To link ideas in a main-idea-and-details paragraph, use transition words or phrases such as "for example."

Analyzing a Workshop Model

Here is a final draft of a biographical sketch. Read the sketch and answer the questions in the margin. Use the answers to these questions to guide you as you write.

John Muir, Nature Observer

Introduction
How does the writer introduce the subject and create interest?

Focus
What will the focus of the essay be?

Main Idea
What is the main idea of the second paragraph?

When I go hiking in Muir Woods near San Francisco, I think about John Muir, a famous person in U.S. history. Like me, John Muir loved the outdoors and had fun exploring wild places. He inspired many people, including students my age, to learn more about nature and to protect the environment. Last year my friend and I worked on a project titled "Speaking Out for Nature: John Muir's Legacy." Here are a few significant events from his life that I studied.

John Muir was born in Scotland sometime in the 1830s. When Muir was a young boy, he and his family left their homeland and came to the United States. They settled in Wisconsin, an area filled with spectacular scenery and wildlife. At an early age, Muir became very curious about the world of nature and enjoyed observing plants and animals. For example, the sight of fireflies filled

Meadow of Daisies and Wildflowers. Walter Geiersperger.

Additional Support

Skills Practice

WRITING: Sentence Style and Variety Point out to students that effective writing is composed of varied sentences. While different writers have different styles, sentences that vary in length and complexity provide for more engaging reading. Write these sen-

tences on the board: *John Muir loved nature. John Muir wrote about the Sierra Mountains. He traveled around the world. He liked to observe wildlife.* Have students think of different ways to combine the sentences. Discuss the effects of the rewriting. **OL**

The early morning moon sets above a Sierra Nevada mountain at Mono Lake. Phil Schermeister.

him with wonder. He found the songs of robins during springtime enchanting. The beautiful Wisconsin flowers that grew in the meadows fascinated him. Throughout his life, Muir continued this habit of closely watching nature.

In the late 1860s, after the Civil War had ended, another experience had a major influence on Muir's view of nature and the course of his life. While working in a carriage shop, he injured his eyes and, as a result, became blind for a month. This unfortunate accident changed Muir's outlook forever, making him appreciate the value of his eyesight. When he regained his ability to see, he determined to devote himself to observing nature. Soon afterward he began an extended journey on foot from the Midwest to the Gulf of Mexico. Next he sailed to Cuba, crossed over to Panama, and then sailed up the West Coast to San Francisco, the city where I live today. Then Muir began to explore the Sierra Nevada and the Yosemite regions of California.

Over the next several years, Muir divided his time between living in a small cabin in Yosemite and traveling across the mountains of the western United States. Picture a tall, thin man carrying a backpack, hiking alone as he stops to examine gigantic trees and colossal mountains. Muir discovered glaciers in Alaska and wrote a series of articles about the Sierra Mountains. He became well known for his views on nature and conservation. ★

Specific Details

List three specific details that the writer uses to support the main idea of the second paragraph.

Background Information

What background information does this paragraph supply? How does it help the reader understand the subject, John Muir?

Precise Words and Details

How do precise words make the writing more interesting? Consider nouns, adjectives, and action verbs.

Descriptive Details

How do descriptive details help bring the subject "to life"?

Main Idea

What is the main idea of the final paragraph?

Teach

Writing Skills

Sentence Fluency Draw students' attention to the variety of types of sentences in the professional models. Ask the students to comment on the "sound" of the writing. **Ask:** Does the writing sound repetitive, with the same rhythm over and over? Do you hear choppy, short sentences? Do you hear a variety of long, short, complex, and simple sentences? Encourage students to read their paragraphs aloud to check for sentence fluency. **OL**

★ Cultural History

Sierra Club John Muir (1838–1914) was one of the founding fathers of the modern natural conservation movement. In 1892, he helped found the Sierra Club, an organization devoted to natural preserves and wildlife conservation. He was the club's first president, and remained so until his death in 1914. **AS**

Narration/Description

1. By creating a link between himself and John Muir

2. Muir's love of nature

3. Nature interested Muir from an early age in Wisconsin.

4. Fireflies filled him with wonder; birdsongs enchanted him; the flowers in the meadows fascinated him.

5. It explains how Muir's temporary

blindness made him appreciate his eyesight.

6. Vivid verbs (*sailed, determined*) and specific place names (nouns)

7. They enable the reader to visualize the subject and his surroundings.

8. Muir divided his time between Yosemite and mountains in the West.

Objectives
• To write a biographical sketch that narrates, explains, or does both (SE)
• To write varied sentences (TWE)

Teach

Writing Process

Revising After students finish writing their biographical sketches, tell them to wait a couple of days before revising. They will approach their work with renewed vision and clarity after some time away from it. **OL**

Writing Skills

Avoiding Empty Phrases

One skill students should focus on is using precise and concise language. **Say:** Be careful to avoid using empty phrases. Often, one word does the work of several. For example, instead of writing "at this point in time," write "now"; instead of "for the reason that," use "because."

Have students examine their biographical sketches to cull empty phrases. **OL**

Traits of Strong Writing

Ideas message or theme and the details that develop it

Organization arrangement of main ideas and supporting details

Voice writer's unique way of using tone and style

Word Choice vocabulary a writer uses to convey meaning

Sentence Fluency rhythm and flow of sentences

Conventions correct spelling, grammar, usage, and mechanics

Presentation the way words and design elements look on a page

For more information on using the Traits of Strong Writing, see pages R33–R34 of the Writing Handbook.

Revising

Peer Review Ask a classmate to read your draft and to identify the subject and three main points you make about the subject or events you narrate about the person's life. If your classmate cannot identify the points or events, revise your work, perhaps by adding topic sentences. As you revise, refer to the traits of strong writing.

Use the rubric below to help you evaluate your writing.

Rubric: Writing an Effective Biographical Sketch

☑ Do you present a few important events in your subject's life or a few main points about your subject?

☑ Do you use specific details to support your main points or tell your events?

☑ Do you narrate events in chronological order and/or tell main ideas in a logical order?

☑ Do you use descriptive details and other precise language to bring your subject to life?

☑ Do you supply any necessary background information so that readers can follow your writing?

▶ **Focus Lesson**

Using Action Verbs

Action verbs, such as *thought*, *begged*, and *climbed*, are always preferable to state-of-being verbs, such as *were*, *is*, and *would be*. Action verbs show what is happening; they also often make a sentence tighter, or more concise, as well as clearer. Notice how action verbs improve the passage from the Workshop Model below.

Draft:

While working in a carriage shop, he was not careful and was, as a result, blind for a month. This unfortunate accident is what changed Muir forever and is what made him value his eyesight. When he was able to see again, he was sure that he was a "nature" person.

Revision:

While working in a carriage shop, he <u>injured his eyes</u>[1] and, as a result, became blind for a month. This unfortunate accident <u>changed Muir's outlook forever, making him value</u>[2] his eyesight. When <u>he regained his ability to see, he determined to devote himself to observing nature.</u>[3]

1: Shows Action   **2: Tightens Sentence**   **3: Makes Meaning Clearer**

Additional Support

Skills Practice

VOCABULARY: Word Choice Like action verbs, precise adjectives communicate ideas and images much more effectively than vague words. Have students write a list of adjectives that describe their subjects. **Ask:** What adjectives have you used to describe your subjects? *(Answers will vary.)* Have students compare their lists of adjectives with each other. Often, seeing other students' ideas can trigger new ways of thinking about their own subjects. **OL**

Editing and Proofreading

Get It Right When you have completed the final draft of your sketch, proofread it for errors in grammar, usage, mechanics, and spelling. Refer to the Language Handbook, pages R46–R60, as a guide.

Teach

Writing Process

Editing and Proofreading
After students edit and proofread their own work, have them trade their biographical sketches with a partner. Have partners check each other's sketches for errors in grammar, punctuation, and mechanics. Then, encourage students to review their comments with their partners. **OL**

▶ **Focus Lesson**

Correcting Verb Tense

The tense of a verb shows whether the action takes place in the present, the past, or the future. When you edit, always check to see that you have used the correct form of each verb. Also be sure that you have maintained or changed verb tenses to reflect the time of the action.

Peer Review

Sometimes you are so involved with your work that you cannot see typographical or other errors. Ask a peer to proofread your work and to suggest places to review. Make any corrections that seem warranted on your own.

Problem: The verb ending is missing or incorrect.

He decide to devote himself to observing nature.

Solution: Use the *-ed* form of a regular verb for the past tense.

He decided to devote himself to observing nature.

Problem: The tense of the sentence is shifted incorrectly.

Muir discovered glaciers in Alaska and writes articles.

Solution: Use the past tense for two or more events that both occurred and ended in the past.

Muir discovered glaciers in Alaska and wrote articles.

Problem: The tense of the sentence is not shifted to show that events occurred at different times.

Here are a few significant events from his life that I study.

Solution: Shift from the present to the past to show an event that occurred before the present action.

Here are a few significant events from his life that I studied.

Writing Process

Presenting While doing research for these essays, students may discover interesting photographs or portraits of their subjects. Encourage students to include copies of these with their final biographical sketches. **OL**

Writer's Portfolio

Place a copy of your biographical sketch in your portfolio to review later.

Presenting

Maximum Readability Be sure that you present your work in the most readable way. That means using neat handwriting or a font that can be read easily. It also means double-spacing word-processed copy, creating one-inch margins, and indenting paragraphs five spaces.

Reading in the Real World

Citizenship Encourage students to use their new understanding of biographical sketches by scouting out biographical features in newspaper and magazine articles, and new biographies in bookstores and libraries. Reading about others' lives often gives students a wider sense of understanding of the world and of their communities. Suggest that students look for articles about local people in the newspaper, and bring them in to share with their classmates. **OL**

Objectives
• To use verb tenses consistently and correctly (SE)
• To use precise and descriptive adjectives (TWE)

507

Focus

Summary

In this workshop, students will learn techniques for planning, rehearsing, and presenting a photo-essay to the class.

Teach

Speaking Skills

Considering Your Audience An effective oral presentation is aimed at a specific audience. Good speakers adapt their tone, language, and subject matter to their audience, whether it is a group of small children or an auditorium full of adults. Tell students to take these aspects of an audience into consideration:

- age
- education and experience
- familiarity with the subject
- motive for listening
- occasion for the gathering
- size of the group **OL**

Keep Your Options Open

After you have gathered images, reevaluate your choice for presenting. For example, certain groups of images may lend themselves better to a montage than to a time line.

Speaking, Listening, and Viewing Workshop

Photoessay

Presenting a Photoessay

Connecting to Literature When authors present life stories, they convey not only facts and observations about lives but also images that help the reader envision the subject. For example, in "First Impressions," the reader can visualize de Kooning's first glimpse of New York City— skyscrapers hidden by thick fog. Throughout the excerpt, images help show the reader de Kooning's life and world.

> **Assignment** Present a photoessay to show the life and world of the subject you wrote about in your biographical sketch.

Planning Your Presentation

Consider which photoessay form best lends itself to your biographical subject, the details in your sketch, and your audience's interests:

- Time Line: The form of an illustrated time line is a good choice for representing a narrative essay with a clear sequence of events.
- Biopic: The form of a biopic, a series of images that tell a life story, is a great choice if you are using technology such as slides or a video.
- Montage: The form of a montage, a series of images that communicates main ideas about a person, is a good choice for representing an expository essay about a person.

The illustration below shows part of a montage of the life of John Muir.

Muir began observing plants and animals at an early age.

Additional Support

Skills Practice

SPEAKING: Body Language In preparation for giving presentations, remind students of the importance of effective body language. **Say:**

- Look directly at your audience, except when you are glancing at a photograph that you are describing.

- Stand up tall but in a relaxed and comfortable way.

- Use relaxed, natural gestures to emphasize important points or point out photographs.

Advise students to practice their presentation in front of a mirror. **OL**

Creating Your Visual Media

First, do research to find your images. Consider these options:

- Concentrate on the general category of images you need, such as nature, construction, a particular sport or hobby, or government. Look for general-interest books on these topics for possible photos.
- Search the Internet for free downloadable images of your subject or your subject's world.

Next, prepare and assemble the images. You may want to mount them on the same color poster board or digitize them for a slide presentation. Consider ways to group, label, and organize the images that will show the main ideas or events most effectively.

Coordinating Your Words and Images

Photographs do not speak for themselves. It is up to you to create the narrative that links the images and tells the story.

In part, you can tell the story through labels you attach to your images. You want to go beyond that, however, to introduce your subject, create interest, and provide important background information that the images may not convey. Most of all, you want your listeners and viewers to see and appreciate what you find in the images. Plan a narrative with a clear introduction, main ideas or events and details, and a conclusion.

Remind Listeners of the Main Ideas and Events

Be sure that you link your photographs to the events or main ideas in your biographical subject. You cannot assume that your listeners and viewers will make these connections themselves.

Techniques for Presenting a Photoessay

Verbal Techniques	Nonverbal Techniques
☑ **Tone** Convey your interest in your subject through your tone of voice.	☑ **Facial Expression** Convey your interest in your subject through your facial expressions.
☑ **Pace** Take time with each photograph. Consider allowing time for listeners and viewers to understand and absorb everything you say.	☑ **Display** Be sure that your images can be seen. Consider using an easel or a chalkboard tray for display. Do not stand in front of your images.
☑ **Enunciation** Avoid rushing through your points and running your words together. Be sure that everyone can hear and understand you.	☑ **Focus** When you are talking about your photos, look at and point out the photos. The rest of the time, make eye contact with your audience.
☑ **Volume** Be sure to speak loudly enough that everyone can hear you.	☑ **Posture** Stand up straight and hold your head up but try not to look stiff.

OBJECTIVES
- Deliver expository and narrative presentations. Include visual aids that organize and display information.
- Analyze the interests of the audience; choose effective verbal and nonverbal techniques for presentations.

Teach

Listening Skills

Being a Good Listener
Before a presentation begins, students should make sure they are in a good position to hear the speech and see the photographs. They should also be prepared to listen attentively. During the presentation, they should stay quiet and give the speaker their full attention. To reinforce their learning, they may want to take notes and ask questions at the close of the presentation. **OL**

Viewing Skills

Viewing Photographs
A good photograph tells a story. Tell students that as audience members their job is to seek to understand the story that each photograph tells. Encourage students to pay attention to the biographical or cultural information that each of the photographs reveals. **OL**

English Language Coach

Speaking Cues Have students with minimal English speaking abilities use speaking aids such as captions on the back of each photograph. The captions may be read as the photographs are displayed. Have these students practice their presentations for you ahead of time, and coach them on pronunciation. **EL**

Differentiated Instruction

Introduction Remind students that the introduction to their presentation should grab the audience's attention. Suggest these possibilities: a striking fact, a humorous anecdote, a quotation, or an explanation of the title. Encourage students to select an attention-getter that is appropriate for their subject. **AL**

509

Focus

Summary

The purpose of this feature is to interest students in reading additional nonfiction and fiction related to the themes of this unit. Powerful and inspiring nonfiction, along with classic and contemporary novels by outstanding writers are recommended.

Teach

★ Literary History

Nature Writing Nature has been the subject of a great deal of literature throughout the ages. Neoclassicists saw nature as a source of order in the world, while Romantics saw nature as a source of freedom and originality. In the twentieth century Rachel Carson, like Annie Dillard, was a superb nature writer who combined scientific knowledge with emotional response to nature. **AS**

Nonfiction and Novels

PEOPLE HAVE BEEN WRITING nonfiction ever since they scratched into stone the first records of loans and trades, births and deaths, and suns and moons. Nonfiction writing encompasses everything from history to data analyses. For more nonfiction with a variety of themes, try the first three suggestions below. For novels that incorporate the Big Ideas of *The Power of Memory, Quests and Encounters,* and *Keeping Freedom Alive,* try the titles from the Glencoe Literature Library on the next page.

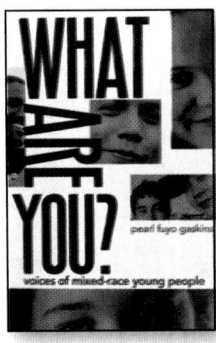

What Are You? Voices of Mixed-Race Young People

by Pearl Fuyo Gaskins

Gaskins, whose mother was Japanese and whose father was American, spent years gathering reflections from students with parents of mixed race. They reflect on the issues of appearing not to belong to any one group, of being categorized inaccurately, and of never being able to check the correct "box" about race because more than one box applies. Many affirm their own identities with statements such as "I know who I am," while some focus on the assumptions others make about them.

The Edge of the Sea ★

by Rachel Carson

How do small sea creatures hold onto rocks while strong waves wash over them? How does the arctic jellyfish survive "being solidly frozen for hours"? Carson, a keen observer of nature and an early environmentalist, reveals the dramatic and varied communities of plant and animal life along the rocky shores, sandy beaches, and coral reefs of the Atlantic Ocean. Delicate drawings depict the rich variety of life forms.

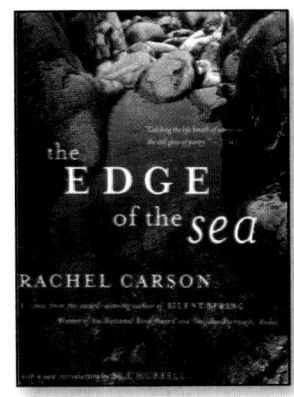

510 UNIT 2 NONFICTION

Additional Support

Skills Practice

READING: Connecting Encourage students to see connections between the independent reading and the unit's nonfiction. Point out that *What Are You?* and *Farewell to Manzanar,* reflect similar themes of prejudice and identity, as does *Kaffir Boy.* Also, Tracy Kidder's biography of Paul Farmer, like the biographies of Lincoln and Gandhi, extols an extraor-

dinary life. Discuss other connections between the recommended reading and the unit selections, such as the similarity between *The Edge of the Sea* and "Encounter in the Sea." Also discuss the novels' connections to the themes of the unit. **OL**

"Mountains Beyond Mountains *is inspiring, disturbing, and completely* absorbing. It will rattle our complacency; it will prick our conscience. One senses that Farmer's life and work has affected Kidder, and it is a measure of Kidder's honesty that he is willing to reveal this to the reader. . . . I had the . . . feeling after reading Mountains Beyond Mountains *that . . .* something had changed in me and it was impossible not to become involved."

—Abraham Verghese, the *New York Times Book Review*

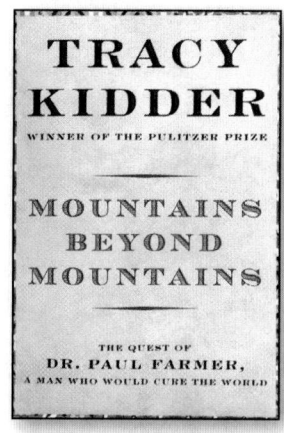

Mountains Beyond Mountains

by Tracy Kidder

This Pulitzer-Prize-winning biography chronicles the career of Dr. Paul Farmer, an American doctor who has spent much of his life solving health care problems for the people of Haiti and other nations. Committed to the ideal of equality in health care, Farmer and many other dedicated volunteers devote their considerable talents and energy to controlling diseases and saving lives by taking measures that others have found too difficult or expensive. An inspirational book, this story encourages thinking beyond traditional boundaries.

From the Glencoe Literature Library

Night ★

by Elie Wiesel

This autobiographical novel shows the *Power of Memory* and brings the brutal reality of the Holocaust to life.

Adventures of Huckleberry Finn

by Mark Twain

Embarking on a series of *Quests and Encounters*, Huck sails down the Mississippi River with Jim, who has escaped from slavery.

The Autobiography of Miss Jane Pittman

by Ernest J. Gaines

The strength and courage of Jane Pittman, a formerly enslaved woman, are an inspiration and a testament to the concept of *Keeping Freedom Alive*.

Teach

★ Literary History

Autobiography

Say: An autobiography is the story of a person's life written by that person. While memoirs often deal with public events and well-known people, an autobiography focuses strictly on the story of the author's own life and contains self-analysis. As with Elie Wiesel's *Night*, fiction can be autobiographical when an author draws upon their life story to write a novel. Also, authors can simulate autobiography in a novel, such as *The Autobiography of Miss Jane Pittman*. In many ways, the genre of autobiography has changed throughout the centuries. **AS**

Reading in the Real World

Citizenship Ask: What perspectives do these books provide on the issue "What does it mean to be an American?" Point out that African American identity is central to *The Autobiography of Miss Jane Pittman* and *The Adventures of Huckleberry Finn,* while mixed-race identity is the focus of *What Are You?* and

Night is an exploration of Jewish identity. Have students write down what makes them feel like U.S. citizens and also what makes them feel different from others in the United States. Encourage them to probe these questions of American identity as they read the recommended literature. **OL**

Objectives

- To encourage independent reading of nonfiction and novels (SE)
- To encourage making connections to independent reading (TWE)

511

Focus

BELLRINGER

Say: Knowing test-taking strategies can help you succeed in school as well as in other real-life situations, such as gaining entrance to a post-secondary school or earning credentials for a career. Review with students effective strategies for test taking, and invite students to share their most successful tips for test preparation.

✎ Or use **Bellringer Option Transparency.**

Teach

Assessment Explain to students that this Test Preparation and Practice lesson helps them to practice and master the skills and vocabulary taught in the unit. First they will read an autobiographical selection and answer comprehension questions about it. Then they will use their knowledge of vocabulary to complete sentences. They will also use grammar and writing skills to improve a writing passage, and finally they will write a short essay. **OL**

Test Preparation and Practice

English–Language Arts

Reading: Nonfiction

Carefully read the following passages. Use context clues to help you define any words with which you are unfamiliar. Pay close attention to story elements such as theme, voice, and tone. Then, on a separate sheet of paper, answer the questions on pages 513–514.

---

from *Wouldn't Take Nothing for My Journey Now* by Maya Angelou

line

When my son was six and I twenty-two, he told me quite solemnly that he had to talk to me. We both sat down at the kitchen table, and he asked with an old man's eyes and a young boy's voice, "Mother, do you have any sweaters that match?" I was puzzled at first. I said, "No," and then I understood he was talking about the pullover and cardigan sets which were popular with white
5 women. And I said, "No, I don't," maybe a little huffily. And he said, "Oh, I wish you did. So that you could wear them to school when you come to see me."

I was tickled but I am glad I didn't laugh because he continued, "Mother, could you please only come to school when they call you?" Then I realized that my attire, which delighted my heart and certainly activated my creativity, was an embarrassment to him.
10 When people are young, they desperately need to conform, and no one can embarrass a young person in public so much as an adult to whom he or she is related. Any outré action or wearing of "getups" can make a young person burn with self-consciousness.

I learned to be a little more discreet to avoid causing him displeasure. As he grew older and more confident, I gradually returned to what friends thought of as my eccentric way of dressing. I was
15 happier when I chose and created my own fashion.

I have lived in this body all my life and know it much better than any fashion designer. I think I know what looks good on me, and I certainly know what feels good on me.

I appreciate the creativity which is employed in the design of fabric and the design of clothes, and when something does fit my body and personality, I rush to it, buy it quickly, and wear it
20 frequently. But I must not lie to myself for fashion's sake. I am only willing to purchase the item which becomes me and to wear that which enhances my image of myself to myself.

If I am comfortable inside my skin, I have the ability to make other people comfortable inside their skins although their feelings are not my primary reason for making my fashion choice. If I feel good inside my skin and clothes, I am thus free to allow my body its sway, its natural grace, its natural
25 gesture. Then I am so comfortable that whatever I wear looks good on me even to the external fashion arbiters.

Additional Support

Skills Practice

READING: Determining Main Idea Tell students that identifying the main idea of a nonfiction passage will help them to answer questions about it accurately. To determine the main idea, suggest that students pay special attention to the introduction and conclusion.

Advise them to notice what larger idea all of the ideas and details in the passage support. In some cases, the main idea of a passage will be stated directly, but in other cases it will not. Before students answer the comprehension questions, discuss the main idea of the passage. **OL**

1 What does the son find embarrassing about his mother?
A. She has very little money.
B. She feels comfortable in her skin.
C. She comes to school in unusual outfits.
D. She does not dress like the white mothers.

2 From what point of view is the selection written?
F. first person
G. second person
H. third person omniscient
I. third person limited

3 Beginning in line 10, the mother states that young people "desperately need to conform." Which of the following best explains what she means by this statement?
A. They do not want to be individuals.
B. They do not like independence.
C. They are needy and insecure.
D. They face pressure to fit in with the crowd.

4 From the context in line 11, what do you conclude that the word *outré* means?
F. immodest
G. unconventional
H. feverish
I. shameful

5 Which of the following best defines the phrase *burn with self-consciousness*, as it is used in line 12?
A. be aware of one's self
B. be aware of others
C. be ill at ease socially
D. be angry at others

6 How does Angelou reveal the personality of her son?
F. through indirect characterization
G. through direct characterization
H. through the words of another person
I. through the use of metaphor

7 From the context, what do you conclude that the word *arbiters*, in the last line, means?
A. enforcers
B. contemporaries
C. critics
D. onlookers

8 Which of the following best describes the mother's personality?
F. controversial
G. passionate
H. passive
I. conformist

9 What is the overall tone of the reading selection?
A. sarcastic
B. tense
C. ironic
D. confident

10 From the context, which of the following do you think is the best synonym for the word *eccentric*, in line 14?
F. unusual
G. absurd
H. energetic
I. casual

Assess

1. **C** is the correct answer. In the second paragraph the mother states that it was her "attire" that embarrassed him. Option **D** implies a conclusion about her fashion options.

2. **F** is the correct answer. The selection is written from the mother's perspective.

3. **D** is the correct answer. The derived answer comes from the context.

4. **G** is the correct answer. No other option is suggested in the context.

5. **C** is the correct answer. All of the other options fall short of the author's image of social uneasiness.

6. **F** is the correct answer. The son's character is revealed by what he says.

7. **C** is the correct answer. None of the other answers correspond to the fashion judgment the author alludes to throughout.

8. **G** is the correct answer. The mother expresses her creativity through fashion. Options **H** and **I** in no way reflect her personality. Nowhere do we read about general controversy, so option **F** is incorrect.

9. **D** is the correct answer. The mother portrays herself as confident that what she wears suits her personality.

10. **F** is the correct answer. Option **G** suggests that there was no reason for her style, and option **I** implies that she did not dress up. Option **H** is vague.

Differentiated Instruction

Predicting Tell less proficient readers that an effective strategy for test taking is to predict the answer before reading the multiple-choice options. Being able to make an educated guess as to the correct response shows comprehension of the reading and the question. Once students have made a prediction, sug-gest that they choose the answer that best matches the prediction. If students find they cannot predict the answer to the question, they may need to reread the passage to improve their comprehension. Use one of the questions to help students practice predicting the correct answer. **BL**

Assess

11. **A** is the correct answer. The selection is about personal experience that the author relates in her own words.

12. **H** is the correct answer. The selection is about a personal experience written for an audience.

13. **D** is the correct answer. No process is described here, so option **A** is incorrect. The author never exactly explains what her fashion taste *is*, so option **B** is incorrect. The selection goes beyond being strictly entertaining, so option **C** is incorrect.

14. **G** is the correct answer. Options **F** and **I** are too superficial. Option **H** makes little sense in this context.

Unit Assessment Have students access the Web site to prepare for the Unit Two test.

---

⑪ The selection is from an autobiography. Which of the following best defines this genre, or style of writing?
 A. personal experience told through that person's words
 B. personal experience told through the words of another
 C. fictional account of a personal experience
 D. narration that is largely unreliable because of its limited perspective

⑫ From the selection, which of the following do you conclude is a characteristic of autobiography?
 F. personal experience meant to be private
 G. personal experience meant to impress others
 H. personal experience meant to be shared
 I. personal experience meant to enhance the truth

⑬ Which of the following best describes the author's purpose in writing the passage?
 A. to explain a process
 B. to describe her fashion taste
 C. to entertain an audience
 D. to express herself

⑭ Which of the following best describes the main idea of this selection from Angelou's continuing autobiography?
 F. Clothes make the woman.
 G. Security comes from within.
 H. Life is full of prejudice.
 I. If you've got it, flaunt it.

Literature Online **Unit Assessment** To prepare for the Unit test, go to www.glencoe.com.

Additional Support

Skills Practice

VOCABULARY: Context Clues Write on the board: Like a ruler of any kind, a patriarch has authority. See if students can determine the definition of *patriarch*. Remind them that context clues can help them to define unfamiliar words. Explain the following types of context clues:

- a synonym or explanation of an unknown word
- a reference to what a word is not
- an example or association with the word
- a general topic linked to the word **OL**

Vocabulary Skills: Sentence Completion

For each item in the Vocabulary Skills section, choose the word that best completes the sentence.

1 The student set an hour aside to _____ his notes before tomorrow's test.
A. peruse
B. ordain
C. induce
D. advocate

2 The warrior used his shield to _____ a storm of arrows.
F. inhibit
G. deflect
H. ordain
I. debase

3 The scientist, a _____ man, attended to every detail of his work himself.
A. meticulous
B. nomadic
C. abstract
D. vague

4 Before the championship, the coach tried to imagine all possible _____ in which his team could win.
F. advocates
G. scenarios
H. agenda
I. dominions

5 Her unwillingness to help _____ her expressions of concern.
A. emanated
B. belied
C. admonished
D. eschewed

6 As he thought over the problem, the old chief wore a/an _____ expression that betrayed no emotion.
F. stolid
G. potent
H. indelible
I. infallible

7 Because the safety report contained too much _____ information, it was difficult to determine what was essential.
A. obligatory
B. superfluous
C. tremulous
D. indelible

8 The teacher spoke in short, _____ sentences that were clear and to the point.
F. vague
G. relevant
H. declarative
I. compassionate

9 The directions contained _____ information that was essential for completing the project.
A. commodious
B. intermittent
C. invaluable
D. mainstream

10 The most _____ people are usually good listeners.
F. superfluous
G. intact
H. convivial
I. compassionate

Assess

1. **A** is the correct answer. The statement implies an examination. *Ordain* means "to establish," so option **B** is incorrect. *Induce* means "to bring about," so option **C** is incorrect. *Advocate* means "to increase," so option **D** is incorrect.

2. **G** is the correct answer. *Inhibit* means "to restrain," so option **F** is incorrect. *Ordain* means "to order or establish," so option **H** is incorrect. *Debase* means "to lower or humiliate," so option **I** is incorrect.

3. **A** is the correct answer. It relates to the scientist's attentiveness to detail.

4. **G** is the correct answer. *Imagine* is the key word. No other option makes sense in the context.

5. **B** is the correct answer. The contradiction between *unwillingness* and *concern* is key. No other option makes sense in this context.

6. **F** is the correct answer. The phrase *betrayed no emotion* is the clue. *Potent* means "powerful," so option **G** is incorrect. *Indelible* means "permanent," so option **H** is incorrect. *Infallible* means "always correct," so option **I** is incorrect.

7. **B** is the correct answer. The sentence draws a comparison between essential and nonessential information. Option **A** conveys the opposite meaning. Options **C** and **D** make no sense in the context.

8. **H** is the correct answer. *Declarative* conveys simple statements. Option **F** is an antonym. Option **G** might make sense, but the description of the type of sentences the teacher uses makes option **H** the correct option. Option **I** makes no sense in the context.

9. **C** is the correct answer. The information is essential to complete the project, so it is highly valued. *Mainstream* information may not be essential. Options **A** and **B** make no sense in the context.

10. **I** is the correct answer. *Listeners* is the operative word here. *Convivial* suggests someone who speaks more than listens, so option **H** is an unlikely option. Options **F** and **G** make no sense in context.

Assess

1. **C** is the correct answer. A complete sentence must contain a subject and a predicate. The sentence is a fragment, because it lacks a predicate.

2. **F** is the correct answer. **G** and **I** still contain fragment errors. **H** contains a comma error.

3. **D** is the correct answer. The other three options all contain punctuation errors, and all three still contain fragment errors.

Grammar and Writing Skills: Paragraph Improvement

Read carefully through the following first draft of a student's essay. Pay close attention to the content and organization. Watch for grammatical errors (such as sentence fragments, run-on sentences, and lack of subject-verb agreement) and punctuation errors, such as misplaced or missing commas. Then, on a separate sheet of paper, answer the questions on pages 516–517.

(1) Native American writers of autobiographical literature continue to reach a wide audience. (2) These writers oral traditions with modern literary forms. (3) There are; however, differences between this literature and traditional Western autobiographies. (4) Are the most notable.

(5) Autobiography in Western tradition commonly tells the story of an individual's rise. (6) Through personal achievements. (7) Western culture praises the individual he or she overcomes adversity. (8) Benjamin Franklin's autobiography is well known for this approach. (9) When he outlines his accomplishments, he instructs us in how to be better people.

(10) Conversely American Indian cultures tends to downplay the individual's importance. (11) In their worldview—the people, land, universe, are all of equal importance. (12) The individual are just a small part of something larger not the center of everything. (13) Black Elk and Lame Deer are two of the best known Native American authors of autobiographies.

1 What grammatical error occurs in sentence 2?
   A. comma splice
   B. fused sentence
   C. sentence fragment
   D. misplaced modifier

2 Which of the following is the best revision for sentence 2?
   F. These writers combine oral tradition with modern literary forms.
   G. These writers combine oral tradition; with modern literary forms.
   H. These writers combine oral traditions with, modern literary forms.
   I. These writers combine oral traditions. With modern literary forms.

3 Which of the following is the best revision for sentence 3?
   A. There are; however, differences between this literature, and traditional Western autobiographies.
   B. There are however; differences between this literature and traditional Western autobiographies.
   C. There are, however, differences between this literature; and traditional Western autobiographies.
   D. There are, however, differences between this literature and traditional Western autobiographies.

Additional Support

Skills Practice

LISTENING: Functional Material Explain to students that instructors often give test directions orally. Ask students to listen carefully as you read aloud the test directions at the top of page 516. Ask students who clearly understand the directions to restate them. Tell students that restating or paraphrasing information is a listening strategy for checking comprehension. **OL**

4 What part of speech is necessary to transform sentence 4 from a sentence fragment to a complete sentence?

  F. verb
  G. subject
  H. adjective
  I. adverb

5 What would be the best way to revise sentence 6?

  A. Make no change.
  B. Delete the sentence.
  C. Combine it with sentence 7.
  D. Combine it with sentence 5.

6 Which of the following errors occurs in sentence 7?

  F. run-on sentence
  G. fragment
  H. lack of subject-verb agreement
  I. misplaced modifier

7 Sentence 9 contains two clauses separated by a comma. Which of the following choices represents the sentence structure?

  A. independent clause, independent clause
  B. independent clause, dependent clause
  C. dependent clause, independent clause
  D. dependent clause, complete sentence

8 Which of the following is the best revision for sentence 10?

  F. Conversely: American Indian cultures tend to downplay the individual's importance.
  G. Conversely, American Indian cultures tends to downplay the individual's importance.
  H. American Indian cultures tend to conversely downplay the individual's importance.
  I. Conversely, American Indian cultures tend to downplay the individual's importance.

9 Which of the following is the best revision for sentence 11?

  A. In their worldview: the people, land, universe, are all of equal importance.
  B. In their worldview, the people, the land, and everything else in the universe are of equal importance.
  C. In their worldview, all—the people, the land, and the universe—are of equal importance.
  D. In their worldview; the people, the land, and the universe, are all of equal importance.

10 Which of the following would be the best addition to the essay?

  F. an introduction about several tribal nations.
  G. a bibliography
  H. background about the student writer
  I. elaboration on the authors mentioned in the closing sentence

Essay

Discuss a few characteristics of the autobiographical genre. Consider the following points: How does this literary form differ from fiction? Why might a writer choose to write about his or her life? Can the writer be as creative in writing autobiography as in writing fiction? As you write, keep in mind that your essay will be evaluated for **ideas, organization, voice, word choice, sentence fluency, conventions,** and **presentation.**

Assess

4. **G** is the correct answer. Sentence **4** is a fragment with a linking verb (*are*) and a predicate adjective (*notable*) but no subject.

5. **D** is the correct answer. Sentence **6** could be made a dependent clause of sentence **5**: *Autobiography in Western tradition commonly tells the story of an individual's rise through personal achievements.*

6. **F** is the correct answer. The clause beginning with *he or she* could be a sentence in its own right.

7. **C** is the correct answer. The first clause in the sentence is dependent (it has a subject and a predicate but cannot stand alone); the second clause is independent.

8. **I** is the correct answer. Sentence **10** needs a comma after the transitional word that begins the sentence, and it lacks subject-verb agreement. Only option **I** corrects both of these errors.

9. **B** is the correct answer. Only this option contains the correct use of definite articles and puncuation.

10. **I** is the correct answer. Sentence **13** seems "tacked on" without explanation. It could begin a short paragraph that would tell what contributions make their autobiographies valuable.

Essay

Students' essays should

- state and support a thesis
- compare and contrast autobiography and fiction
- identify at least three characteristics of the autobiographical genre

Unit at a Glance
POETRY

About the Unit

Unit Three covers poetry and poetic elements such as form and structure, language, and sound devices.

Unit Introduction
Building Background
2–3 days

Genre Focus: Poetry
pp. 520–521

Literary Analysis Model:
Walt Whitman, "O Captain! My Captain!"
pp. 522–523

Writers on Reading
pp. 524–525

Wrap-Up
p. 526

Part 1: The Energy of the Everyday
6–9 days

Part 1 covers form and structure. A chart showing the core skills taught in this Part appears on pages 527A–527B.

SELECTIONS AND FEATURES

LITERARY FOCUS: Form and Structure
pp. 528–529

Robert Hayden, "Those Winter Sundays"
pp. 530–533

Vocabulary Workshop: Context Clues
p. 534

Billy Collins, "Creatures"
pp. 535–539

Theodore Roethke, "The Waking"
pp. 540–545

Jean Toomer, "Reapers"
pp. 546–549

Pablo Neruda, "Ode to My Socks"
pp. 550–556

Aleksandr Solzhenitsyn, "A Storm in the Mountains"
pp. 557–561

Grammar Workshop: Language Usage
p. 562

N. Scott Momaday, "The Print of the Paw" and "To an Aged Bear"
pp. 563–568

Matsuo Bashō, Three Haiku
pp. 569–572

Lady Ise, Two Tanka
pp. 573–576

Chitra Banerjee Divakaruni, "Woman with Kite"
pp. 577–582

Part 2: Loves and Losses
6–8 days

Part 2 covers poetic language. A chart showing the core skills taught in this Part appears on pages 583A–583B.

SELECTIONS AND FEATURES

Part 3: Issues of Identity
4–6 days

Part 3 covers poetic sound devices. A chart showing the core skills taught in this Part appears on pages 645A–645B.

SELECTIONS AND FEATURES

End-of-Unit Features
5–6 days

Unit Resources

Glencoe Literature: The Reader's Choice offers a comprehensive package of tools to optimize student learning and the teaching experience. Each resource has been designed to assist students in specific areas and to offer instructional support for teachers. While all of these areas are covered in the core textbook, some students may need extra practice or additional help in specific areas. The resource package is designed so that you, the teacher, can choose which items will best assist your students. You may also use these resources as homework assignments and for assessment purposes. The following are resources recommended for use with Unit Three.

Key for Unit Resource

- 📁 Blackline Master
- 📄 Workbook
- 📖 Supplemental Text
- 💿 CD-ROM
- 💽 DVD
- 🖌 Transparency
- 💻 Web-based

Essential Instructional Support

FAST FILE Unit 3 Resources

Reading and Literature

- Unit Introduction, pp. 1–2
- The Big Idea Foldable, pp. 3–4
- The Big Idea School-Home Connection, p. 5
- The Big Idea School-Home Connection (Spanish), p. 6
- Challenge Planner, pp. 7–10
- Academic Vocabulary Development, pp. 11–13
- Comparing Literature Graphic Organizer, p. 91
- Literary Elements, pp. 17, 20, 23, 25, 28, 31, 35, 38, 40, 42, 48, 51, 54, 58, 61, 64, 67, 70, 73, 76, 82, 84, 87, 92
- Reading Strategies, pp. 18, 21, 24, 26, 29, 32, 36, 39, 43, 49, 52, 55, 57, 59, 62, 65, 68, 71, 74, 77, 78, 83, 85, 88, 93
- Active Reading Graphic Organizers, pp. 98–107
- Selection Vocabulary Practice, pp. 19, 22, 27, 30, 33, 37, 44, 50, 53, 56, 60, 63, 66, 69, 72, 75, 86, 89, 94
- Literary Focus, pp. 15, 46, 80

Writing, Grammar, and Spelling

- Spelling Practice, p. 95
- Grammar Workshop, p. 34
- Writing Workshop Graphic Organizer, p. 96

Speaking, Listening, and Viewing

- Speaking, Listening, and Viewing Activity, p. 97

English Language Learners

- English Language Coach, pp. 16, 47, 81

Differentiated Instruction

- 📄 Active Learning and Note Taking Guide pp. 70–105
- 📁 Leveled Vocabulary Development, pp. 38–57
- 💿 Skill Level Up!™ A Language Arts Game
- 💿 Listening Library Audio CD, disc 1, tracks 46–80
- 💿 Glencoe BookLink 3
- 💿 Vocabulary PuzzleMaker
- 💿 Literature Library Vocabulary PuzzleMaker

ASSESSMENT

- 📁 Selection and Unit Assessments, Unit Three, pp. 83–136, 213–214
- 📁 Selection Quick Checks, pp. 42–68
- 📁 Selection Quick Checks (Spanish), pp. 42–68
- 📁 Assessment by Learning Objectives, pp. 28–44
- 📁 Rubrics for Assessing Student Writing, Listening and Speaking, pp. 10–11, 30–31
- 📁 Standardized Test Preparation and Practice
- 💻 Glencoe Online Essay Grading
- 💿 Interactive Tutor: Self-Assessment
- 💿 Exam*View*® Assessment Suite
- 💿 Literature Library Exam*View*® Assessment

Additional Instructional Support

Literature and Reading

- Active Learning and Note Taking Guide, pp. 70–105
- *inTIME* Magazines
- Glencoe Literature Library
- Literature Launchers: Pre-Reading Videos
- Literature Classics

Writing, Grammar, and Spelling

- REAL Success in Writing: Research and Reports
- Writing Constructed Responses
- Spelling Power eWorkbook
- Revising with Style eWorkbook
- Sentence Diagraming eWorkbook
- Glencoe Grammar and Composition Handbook
- Grammar and Language Workbook
- Grammar & Language eWorkbook

PROFESSIONAL DEVELOPMENT

- Professional Development Package

Transparencies

- Read Aloud, Think Aloud Transparencies 18–19
- Bellringer Options Transparencies
  - Selection Focus Transparencies 26–34
  - Daily Language Practice Transparencies 46–72
- Grammar and Language Transparencies 3, 28, 34, 71
- Writing Workshop Transparencies 16–20
- Visual Literacy/Fine Art Transparencies

English Language Learner

- English Language Coach
- *inTIME* Magazines (Spanish)
- Spanish Listening Library

Technology

- TeacherWorks Plus™
- StudentWorks Plus™
- Literature Launchers: Pre-Reading Videos
- Vocabulary PuzzleMaker
- Literature Library Vocabulary PuzzleMaker
- Skill Level Up!™ A Language Arts Game
- glencoe.com
- Presentation Plus! ™
- Exam*View*® Assessment Suite
- Literature Library Exam*View*® Assessment Suite
- Listening Library
- Interactive Tutor: Self-Assessment
- Glencoe BookLink 3
- Online Student Edition, mhln.com
- Glencoe Online Essay Grading
- Grammar and Language eWorkbook
- Revising with Style eWorkbook
- Sentence Diagraming eWorkbook
- Spelling Power eWorkbook
- Literature Classics
- Spanish Listening Library

Additional Glencoe Resources

Dinah Zike's Foldables™

Foldables™ are three-dimensional, interactive graphic organizers that help students practice basic writing skills, review key vocabulary terms, and answer Big Ideas. Every unit contains a Foldable activity. You can find the pattern and directions for the Unit 3 Foldable in the Unit 3 Resources Fast Files booklet. You can use the foldables as they are presented or modify them to suit the needs of your students.

For a wealth of online resources that support the instruction in Unit 3, students and teachers can visit our Web site at glencoe.com. Students will find additional learning, practice, and assessment opportunities such as these, which are noted in the student text:

- Author Search
- Big Idea Overview and Activity
- Interactive Literary Elements Handbook
- Study Central
- Unit Assessment
- Web Activities
- Writing Models

Teachers will find planning and instructional tools that include the following:

- Book Lesson Plans
- Web Activity Lesson Plans
- Teacher Forum
- Professional Resources

  Go to glencoe.com to see the entire selection of *Glencoe Literature* online resources.

Glencoe's Presentation Plus!™, a multimedia teaching tool, lets you present dynamic lessons that will engage your students. Using Microsoft PowerPoint®, you can customize the presentations to create your own personalized lessons. Use CheckPoint questions with interactive response keypads to get immediate student feedback during lessons, to increase student participation, and to assess student comprehension.

Glencoe Literature Library

The collection of hardcover books include full-length novels, novellas, plays, and works of nonfiction. Each volume consists of at least one complete extended-length reading accompanied by several related readings from a broad range of genres. A separate Study Guide for each *Glencoe Literature Library* book provides teaching notes and reproducible activity pages for students.
Glencoe Literature Library titles that complement this unit include:

- ***Nothing But the Truth with Related Readings*** by Avi
- ***Cyrano de Bergerac with Related Readings*** by Edmond Rostand
- ***Picture Bride with Related Readings*** by Yoshiko Uchida

GLENCOE
BOOKLINK

Use the Glencoe BookLink 3 CD-ROM, a database of more than 26,700 titles, to *create customized reading lists* for your students.

- Search for award-winning titles, (e.g., Newbery Award winners, Coretta Scott King Award winners, and Caldecott Medal winners) and for books on several state recommended reading lists.
- Find Degrees of Reading Power™ (DRP) and Lexile™ readability scores for all selections.
- Organize reading lists by students' reading level, author, genre, theme, or area of interest.
- Get a brief summary of each selection.

You can find recommended leveled readings for this unit with Independent Reading (see pages 696 and 697).

Online Essay Grading

Use Glencoe's online essay grader powered by SkillWriter™ to score your students' writing and to provide individualized feedback to each student automatically.

You and your students can visit glencoe.com to link to the essay grader. *Students* can enter their essays and receive feedback on demand. *You* can manage demographic data, assign tests, and generate individual student and aggregated reports. The essay grader can help you

- Save time with automatic scoring and individualized feedback.
- Supplement in-class writing instruction using guided writing practice.

REAL Success: Reading Excellence at All Levels

Glencoe REAL Success is a suite of new reading and language arts products designed to foster reading excellence at all levels. Look for TWE point-of-use references for these specific products that will help your students succeed in reading this Unit.

- *Jamestown Literature: An Adapted Reader,* Grade 10
- REAL Success in Writing: Research and Reports
- Skill Level Up!™ A Language Arts Game
- CheckPoint PowerPoint™ slides
- Literature/Reading support at Glencoe Web site

A lively collection of articles drawn from issues of the TIME family of magazines helps students develop the skills they need to interact with informational text in a meaningful way. Each of the news stories, feature articles, reviews, profiles, and essays in the magazine connects to an author, work, or theme in *Glencoe Literature: The Reader's Choice.* See the *inTIME* Teacher's Guide for specific connections to each unit and for reproducible student worksheets designed to develop students' reading and critical thinking skills.

Literature Launchers

Set the scene with Glencoe's Literature Launchers, engaging pre-reading video segments that introduce each unit. Each Unit Launcher brings the literature to life, featuring expert testimony and archival stills and footage from the time.

Insert your Glencoe Literature Launchers into your DVD player. Select the Unit 3 Launcher from the menu to introduce Poetry.

Teacher Wraparound Edition Key

Level Appropriate Code

AL = Activities for students working above grade level

OL = Activities for students working at grade level

BL = Activities for students working below grade level

EL = Activities for English language learners

AS = Information for all students

Teacher Wraparound Prompts

R **Reading Skill** These activities help you teach reading skills and vocabulary.

V **Vocabulary** These activities help students comprehend words and incorporate them into reading.

BI **Big Idea** These activities and questions prompt students to prepare to answer the Big Idea.

L **Literary Element** These activities and questions help students comprehend selections and learn more about each genre.

★ **Enrichment** Additional activities and information involving art appreciation and history.

Professional Development Center

From Your Authors:

Teaching Literary Analysis: Poetry

Make Media Connections It is a rare student who gets excited about reading a poem. One way to get students excited about poetry is to show them that many poems discuss ideas that are important to them. For example, most students like music. Most of the music they listen to addresses a particular issue or human problem through lyrics that are basically narrative poems, lyric poems, forms of plainsong, or oratorical poems. A lot of song lyrics are about love or relationships, others deal with social protest or social action, and still others deal with emotions like grief or joy. Before reading poetry, invite students into a conversation about what poems mean, their value, and how we can use them to think about our lives. As students read William Shakespeare's sonnet "Shall I Compare Thee to a Summer's Day," introduce the poem as a love note from Shakespeare to a woman. Before reading, have students discuss what ideas or words they might include in a love note to someone today. As they read, have them compare what Shakespeare is saying to what a modern day love note might say.

Make Personal Connections Any connection you can make between a particular poem and student experiences will motivate students to read and understand the poem. For example, before students read "Those Winter Sundays" by Robert Hayden, ask them to brainstorm a list of the daily things their parents do for them (like driving them places, washing their clothes, and helping them with their home-

Jacqueline Jones Royster and Beverly Ann Chin

work). Point out to students that people often forget to show appreciation for the small things their parents do and that parents often show how much they love and care for their children in small gestures. Then have students read the poem and discuss how the speaker didn't notice his father's small acts of love until he became an adult.

**Melodie Garcia Wick
Gallup Catholic High School
Gallup, New Mexico**

Teacher to Teacher

My students are Zuni and Navaho, so I have their grandfathers and grandmothers come to class on separate days and tell stories of their traditions. Grandparents teach students how to fine-tune their listening skills using stories passed down through great oral storytelling traditions. Then when we begin the poetry unit, I first give students an overview of a poet, before reading his or her work aloud. Students are better prepared to listen to the images and sensory descriptions they hear in the poetry. Then I ask students to watch a sunrise or sunset. I remind them that this is the same sun that shone on their grandparents and that will shine on their children and their children's children. Students then write a poem about their experiences, and they write a reflection on their poems.

Teacher Chat Room

Making Literature Come Alive

Before you begin this unit or sometime during the unit, talk with other teachers about ways they have taught poetry. Have a lunch-time discussion group or an after-school hour for professional development and discuss the following questions and answers from our authors:

How can I help students enjoy poetry?

- Make poetry more about life and less about school. For example, as students read "miss rosie" by Lucille Clifton, have them discuss different heroes in their own lives. Ask students to describe why they look up to their heroes and how they would react if their heroes fell from status. Help students to relate to the speaker's feelings about Miss Rosie by asking them to describe their own feelings towards people whom they respect.

- Focus on students' personal experiences and how their experiences connect to the poems.

- Make sure that students are not just reading poetry but considering the ideas that really matter in the poems.

- Make the study of poetry playful and fun by using limericks, riddles, and metaphor poems.

How can I help students understand figurative language?

- Encourage students to use the poems presented in this unit as models for writing their own creative and fun poetry. Help students write limericks, play with words, and try out new and different poetic forms. For example, have students read haiku poetry by Matsuo Bashō and tanka poetry by Lady Ise. Then have students play with the poetic forms of haiku and tanka by creating their own poems.

- Have students create advertisements or satires that use various forms of figurative language.

- Study a poem that uses personification and then have students write their own poetry that incorporates personification. For example, have students read "Horses Graze" by Gwendolyn Brooks. Ask them to identify the author's use of personification and explain what human qualities are given to the horses. Once students understand the author's model, have them create their own poems to show their understanding of the device.

How can I help students to understand various poetic devices?

- Have students create poster exhibits or glossaries of poetic terms and devices. Divide the poetic terms and devices among the students. Then, have students define the term, cite a poem or passage in which the device is used, and explain how the device worked to create and communicate meaning within the poem. Have students work in groups to compile their information into a creative presentation. In groups, students should teach the rest of the class about their poetic terms.

Focus

BELLRINGER

Bellringer Options
Literature Launcher Video
Daily Language Practice
 Transparency 46
Or write on the board:

- "rhythmical creation of beauty"—Poe

- "musical thought"—Carlyle

- "imaginative expression of strong feeling"—Wordsworth

- "the record of the best and happiest moments of the best and happiest minds"—Shelley

- "painting with the gift of speech"—Simonides

- "the lava of the imagination" —Byron

Ask: What do you think is being described? *(Poetry.)* **Ask:** What do these quotes say about poetry, and how true do you think they are? *(They portray poetry as colorful, inventive, and beautiful.)* Point out that in this unit, students will come to understand and appreciate poetry better.

Objectives for the Unit Introduction

- To identify and interpret literary elements used in poetry (SE)
- To analyze the effect that poetic elements have upon the reader (SE)
- To analyze poetry for the ways in which poets inspire the reader to share emotion (SE)

Orpheus, 1969. Marc Chagall. Oil on canvas, 97 x 130 cm. Private collection. ★

518 UNIT 3 POETRY

Unit Introduction Skills

Reading Skills

- Reading Poetry (SE pp. 522–523)
- Responding (SE p. 525)
- Activating Prior Knowledge (TWE p. 524)

Poetry

Literature Skills

- Poetic Form and Structure (SE p. 520)
- Poetic Language (SE pp. 520–521)
- Analyzing Sound Techniques (SE p. 521)

Listening/Speaking/Viewing Skills

- Dramatic Reading (SE p. 526)

Poetry

Looking Ahead

Like other forms of literature, poetry concerns real life, but it distills that life to its essence. Poetry is the most concentrated form of literature: It makes every word and even every syllable count. All good poems allow the reader to experience the power and magic of words in a way that no other form of literature can.

PREVIEW | **Big Ideas and Literary Focus**

1	**BIG IDEA:** The Energy of the Everyday	**LITERARY FOCUS:** Form and Structure
2	**BIG IDEA:** Loves and Losses	**LITERARY FOCUS:** Language
3	**BIG IDEA:** Issues of Identity	**LITERARY FOCUS:** Sound Devices

OBJECTIVES

In learning about the genre of poetry, you will focus on the following:

- identifying and interpreting various literary elements used in poetry
- analyzing the effect that poetic elements have upon the reader
- analyzing poetry for the ways in which poets inspire the reader to share emotion

INTRODUCTION **519**

Focus

Summary

This introduction begins with examples of the elements of poetry. An analysis of Walt Whitman's "O Captain! My Captain!" reveals the elements of poetry working together to create a desired effect. Finally, authors comment on the genre of poetry.

★ Viewing the Art

Ask: What elements of this painting seem poetic? *(Students may note elements such as the colors, the soft lines, and musical elements such as the women dancing.)* **AS**

Unit Resources

Classroom Management
- TeacherWorks Plus™ CD-ROM
- StudentWorks Plus™ CD-ROM
- Literature Launchers™: Pre-Reading Videos DVD, Unit Three

Core Instructional Support
- Unit 3 Resources (Fast File)
- Literature Online, glencoe.com
- Presentation Plus!™ CD-ROM, Unit Three

Transparencies
- Literary Elements Transparencies 45, 46, 59, 60, 61, 62, 68, 69, 70, 71, 72, 73, 74
- Bellringer Options Transparencies: Selection Focus Transparencies 26–34 Daily Language Practice Transparencies 46–72

Differentiated Instruction
- Active Learning and Note Taking Guide, pp. 70–105
- Skill Level Up!™ A Language Arts Game

Assessment
- Selection and Unit Assessments, Unit Three, pp. 83–136, 213–214
- Exam*View*® Assessment Suite CD-ROM
- Assessment by Learning Objectives, pp. 28–44

Supplemental Reading
- Glencoe Literature Library
- Glencoe BookLink 3 CD-ROM
- *inTIME* Magazines

519

Teach

R Reading Strategy

Visualizing Imagery

Invite students to visualize the sensory images in "Night Clouds" and to explain what feelings they evoke. *("Milky dust" and "vermilion tongue" are vibrant visual images that evoke a magical feeling.)* Likewise, in "Those Winter Sundays," ask students what feeling "blueblack cold" suggests. *(It creates an image of pain and suffering.)* **OL**

★ Literary History

Poetic Conventions Tell students that the conventions of poetry are customary style devices that have become accepted because of their habitual use. However, throughout history, poetic conventions have changed. Poets such as Hughes choose to use certain fresh techniques, but these too with habitual use could become poetic conventions. Discuss the conventions that Hughes uses in "Harlem" *(lines, simile)* and how he diverges from tradition *(capitalization).* **AS**

Genre Focus

What distinguishes poetry from prose?

Mexican poet Octavio Paz believes that "to create among people the possibility of wonder, admiration, enthusiasm, mystery, the sense that life is marvelous . . . to *make* life a marvel—that is the role of poetry."

How does poetry give a sense of the mystery and marvel of life? It uses what African American poet Quincy Troupe calls "the music of language." Says Troupe, "I want the words to sing." The elements of poetry, while they may be found in other genres, are essential to the art of poetry.

The Form and Structure of Poetry

Lines and Stanzas

Poetry does not look like prose. Poetry is arranged in lines and stanzas. A **line** is a horizontal row of words, which may or may not form a complete sentence. A **stanza** is a group of lines forming a unit and separated from the next stanza by a line of space.

> The mother smiled to know her child
> Was in a sacred place,
> But that smile was the last smile
>   To come upon her face.
>
> —Dudley Randall, **from "Ballad of Birmingham"**

Speaker

The **speaker** is the voice that communicates with the reader of a poem. A speaker can be the voice of a person, an animal, or even a thing.

> Sundays too my father got up early
> And put his clothes on in the blueblack cold,
>
> —Robert Hayden, **from "Those Winter Sundays"**

The Language of Poetry

Figurative Language

A **figure of speech** is a word or expression that is not meant to be taken literally.

- A **simile** uses the word *like* or *as* to compare two seemingly unlike things.

- A **metaphor** compares two or more different things by stating or implying that one thing *is* another.

- **Personification** involves giving human characteristics to an animal, object, or idea.

simile
> Maybe it just sags like
>   a heavy load.
>
> —Langston Hughes, **from "Harlem"**

metaphor
★
> the spring rain
>   is a
>   thread of pearls
>
> —Lady Ise, **from a tanka**

personification
> Sometime too hot the eye of heaven shines,
>   And often is his gold complexion dimmed;
>
> —William Shakespeare, **from "Shall I Compare Thee to a Summer's Day?"**

Additional Support

Skills Practice

LITERARY ELEMENT: Figurative Language Review the types of figurative language. Make sure that students can explain these figures of speech and their emotional connotations:

- **simile:** Ferlinghetti's "the poet like an acrobat" is a simile comparing a poet to a performer.

- **metaphor:** Lady Ise's "thread of pearls" is a metaphor for spring rains that has connotations of beauty and precious value.

- **personification:** Shakespeare's "the eye of heaven" and "his gold complexion" personify heaven. Discuss the feelings these figures of speech elicit. **OL**

Imagery

Imagery is descriptive language used to represent objects, feelings, and thoughts. It often appeals to one or more of the five senses: sight, hearing, touch, taste, and smell.

> Scatter the milky dust of stars,
> Or the tiger sun will leap upon you and destroy you
> With one lick of his vermilion tongue.
>
> —Amy Lowell, **from "Night Clouds"**

The Sound of Poetry

Rhyme

Rhyme is the repetition of a final stressed vowel and succeeding sounds in two or more words. **Internal rhyme** occurs within lines of poetry. **End rhyme** occurs at the ends of lines. **Rhyme scheme,** the pattern formed by end rhymes, is shown by a row of letters (*a b a b*) in which a different letter of the alphabet signals each new rhyme.

> Why is it no one ever sent me yet   a
>   One perfect limousine, do you suppose?   b
> Ah no, it's always just my luck to get   a
>   One perfect rose.   b
>
> —Dorothy Parker, **from "One Perfect Rose"**

Rhythm and Meter

A poet chooses words and arranges them to create **rhythm,** the pattern of stressed and unstressed syllables in a line. Rhythm can be regular or irregular. **Meter** is a regular rhythm. The basic unit in measuring rhythm is the **foot,** which usually contains one stressed syllable marked with (ˊ) and one or more unstressed syllables marked with (˘).

> If I / had loved / you less / or played / you slyly
> I might / have held / you for / a sum / mer more,
>
> —Edna St. Vincent Millay, **from "Well, I Have Lost You; and I Lost you Fairly"**

Other Sound Devices

- **Alliteration** is the repetition of consonant sounds at the beginnings of words.
- **Consonance** is the repetition of consonant sounds within words or at the ends of words.
- **Assonance** is the repetition of vowel sounds within non-rhyming words.
- **Onomatopoeia** is the use of a word or phrase, such as *swoosh* or *clank,* that imitates or suggests the sound of what it describes.

alliteration
Flew home with Hamp
Shuffled in Dexter's Deck

—Jayne Cortez, **from "Jazz Fan Looks Back"**

consonance
And kisses are a better fate

—E. E. Cummings, **from "since feeling is first"**

assonance
So long lives this, and this gives life to thee.

—William Shakespeare, **from "Shall I Compare Thee to a Summer's Day?"**

Literature Online Study Central Visit www.glencoe.com to review distinguishing poetry from prose.

INTRODUCTION **521**

Teach

R Reading Strategy

Identifying Speaker Ask: Who is the speaker in "Those Winter Sundays"? *(The speaker is someone looking back on childhood days.)* **Ask:** Who is the speaker in "One Perfect Rose"? *(The speaker is a woman who is sarcastic about wanting luxurious gifts.)* **OL**

L Literary Element

Analyzing Sound Devices Show students how to identify end rhyme patterns. **Ask:** Why is the rhyme scheme in "One Perfect Rose" *abab*? *(The first and third lines rhyme, as do the second and fourth.)* Review the definitions of alliteration, assonance, and consonance. **Ask:** How does "So long lives this" use both alliteration and assonance? *(The repetition of the initial l sound is alliteration, and the repetition of the short i sound is assonance.)* Have students give more examples of these devices that shape sound in poetry. **OL**

Literature Online

Study Central Have students visit the Web site for resources that will help them to review poetry.

English Language Coach

Poetic Language Point out to English language learners that classical poetry may contain poetic language or archaic usages, such as Shakespeare's "give life to thee," with *thee* meaning "you." Give other examples of poetic diction, such as *o'er* for "over," and encourage students to use a dictionary for definitions. **EL**

Differentiated Instruction

Rhythm Invite students to read the lines from Edna St. Vincent Millay's poem aloud, paying attention to the rhythm. Encourage them to notice the "beat" in the lines that is similar to the beat in music. Suggest that students tap out the rhythm for these lines on their desks. **BL**

Objectives
- To identify and interpret literary elements used in poetry (SE)
- To analyze the effect that poetic elements have upon the reader (SE)
- To understand and respond to figurative language (TWE)

521

Teach

R Reading Strategy

Analyzing Contrasts Ask:
What contrasting images stand out in this poem? *(Images of a cheering and adoring crowd contrast with the Captain's dead body.)* **Ask:** What impression do the images create? *(They emphasize the sadness of the Captain's death.)* **OL**

★ Writer's Technique

Ode and Elegy Two types of lyric poems, poems that express a poet's emotions, are ode and elegy. An ode is an elaborate lyric poem with a lofty style and a dignified purpose; an elegy is a formal treatment of the subject of death in a sad and dignified way. Discuss "O Captain! My Captain!" as an ode and an elegy. Have students compare the poem with Whitman's acclaimed Lincoln elegy "When Lilacs Last in the Dooryard Bloomed." **AS**

Literary Analysis Model
How do literary elements create meaning in a poem?

Abraham Lincoln is the subject of "O Captain! My Captain!" In the poem, Walt Whitman captures his emotions after the assassination of President Lincoln. Walt Whitman (1819–1892) is one of the pioneers of modern poetry.

O Captain! My Captain! ★
by Walt Whitman

APPLYING Literary Elements

Stanza (lines 1–4)
The first half of each stanza, or major division, focuses on the crowd.

Speaker (lines 5–8)
The second half of each stanza focuses on the speaker's sadness.

Imagery (lines 3 and 6)
The sound of bells and the sight of blood are vivid sensory details.

Repetition (line 9)
The repeated use of words such as *Captain* and phrases such as "fallen cold and dead" helps create a musical and emotional effect.

Alliteration (lines 10–11)
The repeated initial consonant sounds in phrases such as *"flag is flung"* and *"ribbon'd wreaths"* produce musical effects as well.

O Captain! my Captain! our fearful trip is done;
The ship has weather'd every rack, the prize we sought is won;
The port is near, the bells I hear, the people all exulting,
While follow eyes the steady keel, the vessel grim and daring:
    But O heart! heart! heart!
5   O the bleeding drops of red,
        Where on the deck my Captain lies,
          Fallen cold and dead.

  O Captain! my Captain! rise up and hear the bells;
10 Rise up—for you the flag is flung—for you the bugle trills,
For you bouquets and ribbon'd wreaths—for you the shores a-crowding,
For you they call, the swaying mass, their eager faces turning;
    Here Captain! dear father!
      This arm beneath your head;
15   It is some dream that on the deck,
        You've fallen cold and dead.

R

522 UNIT 3 POETRY

Additional Support

Skills Practice

LITERARY ELEMENT: Analyzing Sound Techniques Encourage students to read "O Captain! My Captain!" aloud to appreciate its musical effects. **Ask:** What do you notice about the poem's sound when you hear it read? *(repetition, rhythm, alliteration, rhyme)* Discuss what techniques are used in these phrases:

- "done . . . won" (rhyme)
- "O Captain! My Captain!" (repetition)
- "safe and sound" (alliteration)
- "victor ship" (assonance)
- "pale and still" (consonance)

Have students point out other examples of these techniques in the poem. **OL**

My Captain does not answer, his lips are pale and still;
My father does not feel my arm, he has no pulse nor will;
The ship is anchor'd safe and sound, its voyage closed and done;
20 From fearful trip, the victor ship, comes in with object won;
   Exult, O shores, and ring, O bells!
      But I, with mournful tread,
         Walk the deck my Captain lies, **L**
            Fallen cold and dead.

Figurative Language
(lines 17–18)

The speaker uses metaphor in comparing Lincoln to a captain and a father.

Rhythm (lines 21–24)

The pattern of stressed and unstressed syllables produces a regular rhythm.

The draft above shows Whitman's early attempts to write "O Captain! My Captain!" At this stage, the repetition of the final poem is already in place, as well as the metaphor of Lincoln as the captain and father to the country. Whitman uses specific words to create imagery that is powerful and packed with meaning. What emotions do these stanzas capture?

Reading Check

Evaluating In your opinion, which of the literary elements did Whitman use most successfully in "O Captain! My Captain!"? Explain your choice.

INTRODUCTION **523**

Teach

Reading Check

Answer: *Students may appreciate the extended metaphor, imagery, or sound techniques.* **OL**

L Literary Element

Rhythm and Rhyme Ask students to identify the stanza form in "O Captain! My Captain!" *(four long lines followed by four shorter lines),* as well as the poem's rhyme scheme *(aabbcded).* **OL**

★ Writer's Technique

Extended Metaphor Tell students that an extended metaphor is an indirect comparison that continues beyond a single mention and becomes more elaborate throughout a poem. Discuss the extended metaphor of "O Captain! My Captain!" comparing President Lincoln to the captain of a ship and how the metaphor is elaborated with words such as *keel, vessel, shores,* and *voyage.* Invite students to notice the secondary extended metaphor comparing the president to a father. **AS**

Building Reading Fluency

Sound Techniques Read the poem aloud, and discuss its musical sound. Review sound devices, and have students point out what contributes to the pleasant sound of the poem, such as alliteration, rhyme, and rhythm. Make sure students can give examples. **OL**

Differentiated Instruction

Poetic Diction Explain to less proficient readers that poets choose words not only for their connotation and denotation but also for their sound. Point out the highly apt words *trills* and *mournful* as examples. Discuss why Whitman might have chosen these words and how their sound suggests their meaning. **BL**

Objectives

- To identify and interpret literary elements used in poetry (SE)
- To analyze the effect that poetic elements have upon the reader (SE)
- To analyze sound techniques in poetry (TWE)

523

Teach

Reading Strategy

Comparing and Contrasting Point out that the two passages by Kenneth Koch and Kate Farrell provide tips for reading poetry by comparing and contrasting poetry with other activities. **Ask:** With what do Koch and Farrell contrast reading poetry? *(Reading a newspaper, as well as sitting in the sun or watching television.)* **Ask:** What points do they make with these contrasts? *(Reading poetry calls for more emotional response than reading a newspaper and is more active than sitting in the sun or watching television.)* **OL**

★ Literary History

Origins of Poetry Poetry predates written language, and the earliest poems were composed as verses for songs. Early bards, or singer-poets, passed on this poetry through an oral tradition. The first recorded poems were long narratives called epics. Sometime after the ancient Greek poet Homer, poetry became separate from music. **AS**

Writers on Reading
What do writers say about poetry?

Reading Poetry ★

Responding to a Poem

It doesn't make sense to read poetry the way you read a newspaper article. It is good, in general, to read a poem with the kind of freedom, openness and sensitive attentiveness to your own thoughts and feelings that you have when you write a poem yourself or when you listen to a friend talking, or when you hear music. You understand the meaning of the words in the poem with your intellect, but you also respond to the poem with a part of your intelligence that includes your feelings and imagination and experience.

—Kenneth Koch and Kate Farrell, **from** *Sleeping on the Wing*

The Fiddler, 1911. Marc Chagall. Oil on canvas. Kunstsammlung Nordrhein-Westfalen, Duesseldorf, Germany.

Poetry in Context

A poem is best read in the light of all other poems ever written. We read A the better to read B (we have to start somewhere; we may get very little out of A). We read B the better to read C, C the better to read D, D the better to go back and get something more out of A. Progress is not the aim, but circulation. The thing is to get among the poems where they hold each other apart in their places as the stars do.

—Robert Frost, **from "The Prerequisites"**

> *"Poetry is above all a concentration of the power of language."*
>
> —Adrienne Rich

Being an Active Reader

Reading poetry is not a completely passive pleasure, as is sitting in the sun or watching television. It is more like the pleasure you get from playing tennis or listening to music. There is a difference between what you feel the first time you play tennis and the fiftieth time. Or between the first time you go to a concert and later on, when you know more about the music and are used to concerts. Poetry is like that. The more you know about it and the more you read it, the more at ease you'll feel with it, the better you'll get at reading it, and the more you'll like it. When you read a poem, the poet's experience becomes, in a way, your own, so you see things and think things you wouldn't see and think otherwise.

—Kenneth Koch and Kate Farrell, **from** *Sleeping on the Wing*

Additional Support

Skills Practice

READING: Activating Prior Knowledge Invite students to share their past experiences with reading poetry and relate their experiences to the comments the authors make on these pages. **Ask:** Do these authors speak to any of your concerns about reading poetry? *(Students may say they have* found reading poetry difficult and have been frustrated by trying to find hidden meanings. The authors give them strategies for approaching poetry.) Discuss new insights students have learned from these authors that will help them to approach poetry differently and perhaps appreciate it more. **OL**

A Russian Folk Tale, 1967–72. Leonid Tikhomrov. Oil on canvas. Private collection.

Appreciating Poetry

Anyone who feels poetry is an alien or ominous form should consider the style in which human beings think. "How do you think?" I ask my students. "Do you think in complete, elaborate sentences? In fully developed paragraphs with careful footnotes? Or in flashes and bursts of images, snatches of lines leaping one to the next, descriptive fragments, sensory details?" We think in poetry. But some people pretend poetry is far away.

—Naomi Shihab Nye, **from "Lights in the Windows"**

Literature Online **InterActive Reading Practice**
Visit www.glencoe.com for more practice reading poetry.

Understanding Poems

When you are at a loss to understand a poem, following the images (which means tracking the nouns) will often bring you a clarity you can use to make sense of the rest of the poem.

L

—Molly Peacock, **from "The Three Systems of a Poem"**

Reading Check

Responding From your own reading experiences, which passage do you identify with most closely? Explain.

INTRODUCTION **525**

Teach

Reading Check

Answer: *Students should explain their choices.* **OL**

L Literary Element

Imagery Have students explain the main point that Molly Peacock makes. *(Notice the imagery to understand poetry better.)* **Ask:** How does Peacock's approach make sense if you think of poetry as Rich and Nye define it? *(Imagery reflects the concentrated language and thought-like form of poetry.)* **OL**

Literature Online

InterActive Reading Have students access the Web site for more practice with reading strategies.

Objectives

- To analyze the effect that poetic elements have upon the reader (SE)
- To analyze poetry for the ways in which poets inspire the reader to share emotion (SE)
- To activate prior knowledge about poetry (TWE)

Differentiated Instruction

Synthesizing Less proficient readers may have difficulty integrating all of the recommendations from these authors. Have them first summarize all six recommendations and then synthesize them with their own observations. Finally, help students apply the strategies to reading a poem. **BL**

Reading in the Real World

Citizenship After discussing the strategies that the authors provide for reading poetry, have students compile similar guidelines for reading newspapers, magazines, campaign literature, and other resources for good citizenship. Remind them of the importance of critical thinking. **OL**

525

Assess/Close

Guide to Reading Poetry
Review the guide, and ask students what new insights they gained from reading poetry. **OL**

Elements of Poetry
Review the definitions and apply them to a poem. **OL**

Activities

1. Suggest that students pay attention to tone of voice, facial expressions, and gestures to convey emotion. Encourage students to be creative.

2. See if students have questions about the function of any of the elements of poetry. Check webs for completeness.

3. Emphasize the value of the foldables study organizer for review and for reference while reading the selections in the unit.

FOLDABLES™
Study Organizer

Have students make and label the Three-Pocket Foldable. Then have them write notes about each literary element on note cards to insert in the pockets of their Foldables.

Additional Support

Wrap-Up

Guide to Reading Poetry

- Poets use words differently than do writers of prose.

- Reading poetry well involves using your emotions, experiences, and imagination as well as your intelligence.

- Read a poem from beginning to end several times.

- Focus on what the words of the poem are actually saying.

- Respond to the poem as a whole before analyzing it.

Elements of Poetry

- **Imagery** is descriptive language that appeals to the five senses.

- **Figurative language** compares unlike things in imaginative ways.

- The pattern of stressed and unstressed syllables in a line of poetry creates **rhythm.**

- **Rhyme** and other sound devices repeat certain sounds to create musical effects.

- The **speaker** is the voice in the poem that talks to the reader.

- A **line** is a row of words; a **stanza** is a group of lines that form a unit.

Activities ➤

Use what you have learned about reading and analyzing poetry to do one of these activities.

1. Speaking/Listening How would you present the poem "O Captain! My Captain!" to convey the speaker's intense emotions? Record a dramatic reading of Whitman's poem to play for the class.

2. Visual Literacy Create a concept web illustrating the elements that work together to create meaning in a poem.

3. Note Taking You might try using this graphic organizer to keep track of the main kinds of literary elements in this unit.

 FOLDABLES Study Organizer **THREE-POCKET BOOK**

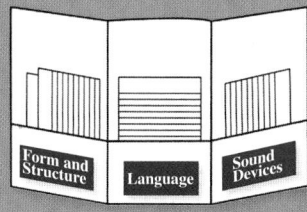

Form and Structure | Language | Sound Devices

OBJECTIVES
- Identify and interpret various elements used in poetry.
- Analyze the effect that poetic elements have upon the reader.

- Analyze poetry for the ways in which poets inspire the reader to share emotion.

Skills Practice

WRITING: Literary Response
Invite students to keep journals in which they jot down their personal responses as they read each poem in the unit. **Say:** To monitor your emotional response, ask yourself how you feel when you read a certain poem. To respond intellectually, think about what the poem says. Suggest that students read the poems aloud so that they can experience each poem's sound. Also suggest that they use their journals to compare and evaluate the poems they read. Encourage them to share their journal responses with other students and with you. **OL**

The Energy of the Everyday

The Girl with Paddleboat, 1865. Gustave Courbet. ★

BIG IDEA

We sometimes hear people say, "If I had it to do over again, I would take time to stop and smell the roses." We are constantly surrounded with opportunities to take in the wonder of life. The poems in Part 3 find wonder in everyday experiences. As you read the poems, ask yourself: What are some of my favorite memories of everyday experiences? What made those times special? **BI**

527

Analyzing and Extending

BI Big Idea

The Energy of the Everyday Ask: What does "take time to stop and smell the roses" mean to you? *(Appreciating the here and now)* **Ask:** How can poetry help you take time to smell the roses? (*The poet observes ordinary things closely and looks at them in fresh ways.*) Encourage students to contemplate the Big Idea and its relation to the artwork as they read the poems in Part 1. **OL**

★ Viewing the Art

French realist painter Gustave Courbet (1819–1877) began a movement toward Realism in French painting by truthfully painting everyday people and scenes. Courbet's work exhibited a departure from Romanticism in that the everyday people he portrayed were not idealized but rather realistically presented. **AS**

English Language Coach

Building Background Have students new to the United States explain the theme "Energy of the Everyday." Guide students to connect with the literature by discussing how they see energy in everyday occurrences. Prepare students for poetic terms; suggest that they make a chart for future reference. **EL**

Differentiated Instruction

Connotations Guide less proficient readers to notice that the Big Idea "The Energy of the Everyday" contrasts the word *energy,* which has connotations of excitement, with *everyday,* which has connotations of dullness. Have students conjecture why the title emphasizes this contrast. **BL**

Objectives for Part 1
- To analyze how rhythm inspires readers' emotions (SE)
- To understand structure in poetry (SE)
- To recognize the significance of various literary devices (SE)

527

Part 1: The Energy of the Everyday

Readability Scores Key
Dale-Chall/DRP/Lexile

PACING (DAYS)		SELECTIONS AND FEATURES	LITERARY ELEMENTS
STANDARD	**BLOCK**		
1–2 class sessions	1	LITERARY FOCUS: Form and Structure, pp. 528–529	Form and Structure, SE pp. 528-529 Poetic Forms, TWE p. 528
		"Those Winter Sundays" by Robert Hayden, pp. 530–533	Line and Stanza, SE pp. 531-533 Alliteration, Assonance, and Consonance, TWE p. 532
		Vocabulary Workshop: Recognizing Homonyms and Homophones, p. 534	
2–3 class sessions	1–2	**"Creatures"** by Billy Collins, pp. 535–539	Enjambment, SE pp. 536, 538, 539 Assonance, TWE p. 538
		"The Waking" by Theodore Roethke, pp. 540–545	Meter and Rhythm, SE pp. 541, 544 Stanza, SE p. 544
		"Reapers" by Jean Toomer, pp. 546–549	Rhyme and Rhyme Scheme, SE pp. 547, 549 Alliteration, TWE p. 548
		"Ode to My Socks" by Pablo Neruda, pp. 550–556	Free Verse, SE pp. 551, 553, 555 Structure, SE p. 555
2 class sessions	1	**"A Storm in the Mountains"** by Aleksandr Solzhenitsyn, pp. 557–561	Prose Poetry, SE pp. 558, 561
		Grammar Workshop: Language Usage, p. 562	
		"The Print of the Paw" and **"To An Aged Bear"** by N. Scott Momaday, pp. 563–568	Speaker, SE pp. 564, 566, 567 Prose Poetry, SE p. 567
1–2 class sessions	1	**"Three Haiku"** by Matsuo Bashō, pp. 569–572	Haiku, SE pp. 570, 572
		"Two Tanka" by Lady Ise, pp. 573–576	Tanka, SE pp. 574, 576
		"Woman with Kite" by Chitra Banerjee Divakaruni, pp. 577–582	Verse Paragraph, SE pp. 578, 580, 581 Enjambment, SE p. 581

About the Part

Part 1 covers form and structure.

READING AND CRITICAL THINKING	VOCABULARY	WRITING AND GRAMMAR	LISTENING, SPEAKING, AND VIEWING
Analyzing Rhythm, TWE p. 529		Quickwrite, SE p. 529	
Analyzing Tone, SE pp. 531-533 Sound Techniques, TWE p. 532	Context Clues, SE pp. 533	Apply Theme, SE p. 533	Analyzing Art, SE p. 532 Reading Aloud, TWE p. 532
	Homophones, TWE p. 534		
Analyzing Structure, SE pp. 536, 539	Word Parts, SE pp. 536, 539	Respond to Style, SE p. 539	Analyzing Art, TWE p. 537
Analyzing Mood, SE pp. 541–542, 544	Academic Vocabulary, SE p. 544	Author's Purpose, SE p. 545 Using Infinitives, SE p. 545	Analyze Photograph, SE p. 543
Analyzing Meter and Rhythm, SE pp. 547, 549 Visualizing a Poem's Images, SE p. 547	Synonyms, SE p. 549	Analyze Criticism, SE p. 549	
Monitoring Comprehension, SE pp. 551, 553, 555	Word Parts, pp. 551, 555 Academic Vocabulary, SE p. 555	Genre Elements, SE p. 556 Using Adjectives, SE p. 556	Performing, SE p. 556 Analyzing Art, TWE p. 552
Visualizing, SE pp. 558, 560, 561	Analogies, SE pp. 558, 561	Song Writing, SE p. 561	Music Activity, SE p. 561 Analyzing Art, TWE p. 559
		Avoiding Incorrect Pronoun Reference, SE p. 562	
Applying Background Knowledge, SE pp. 564, 568	Word Parts, SE p. 568 Academic Vocabulary, SE p. 568	Evaluate Author's Craft, SE p. 568	Literature Groups, SE p. 568 Brief Speech, TWE p. 566
Interpreting Imagery, SE pp. 570, 572 Visualizing, SE p. 570	Academic Vocabulary, SE p. 572	Writing Haiku, SE p. 572	Analyzing Art, TWE p. 571
Comparing and Contrasting Imagery, SE pp. 574, 576	Academic Vocabulary, SE p. 576		
Making Inferences About the Speaker, SE pp. 578, 582	Context Clues, SE pp. 578, 582 Academic Vocabulary, SE p. 582	Analyze Cultural Context, SE p. 582	Literary Criticism, SE p. 582 Analyzing Art, TWE p. 579

Focus

BELLRINGER

Bellringer Options
**Daily Language Practice
Transparency 47
Or ask:** What do you see in
your everyday life that is truly
wonderful? *(Students may raise
ideas such as the beauty of
nature or the joys of friendship.)*
Discuss student responses to
this question, and follow up
by asking students about favorite memories of everyday experiences.

Teach

L Literary Element

Form and Structure Diagram
poem structures on the board
to illustrate stanzas, lines, and
rhyme schemes. **Ask:** Do you
prefer poems that rhyme to
those that don't? Why or why
not? *(Answers will vary.)* **OL**

Literary Elements Have students access the Web site to
improve their understanding
of form and structure.

Form and Structure

How does a poem fit together?

What is a poem? What are its parts? While many
poems at first appear to be simply collections of
rhymed lines, their structure can be far more
complex. The structure of prose is a relatively
simple matter of proper sentences grouped into
paragraphs. The structure of poetry offers many
more possibilities to explore. In the following
cartoon, Calvin writes an ode.

Form

A **line** of poetry is a word or row of words that
may or may not form a complete sentence. A
stanza is a group of lines followed by a line of
space. You can think of lines as roughly equivalent
to sentences in prose and stanzas as paragraphs.
Some poetic forms have rules about how many
stanzas, how many lines, and even how many
end rhymes are included. Haiku, tanka, and sonnet
are examples of poetic forms.

Types of Stanzas A stanza of two lines that
rhyme is a **couplet**. The rhyme scheme is aa. Stanzas
of four, six, and eight lines are respectively called
quatrains, sestets, and **octaves.** In English poetry,
quatrains with *abab* rhyme scheme are common.

Rhyme scheme The term **rhyme scheme** refers
to the rhyming pattern of a poem. Lowercase
letters are used to show rhyme schemes. Each
end sound is assigned its own letter. Study the
abab rhyme scheme in this stanza. **L**

If I had loved you less or played you slyly	a
I might have held you for a summer more,	b
But at the cost of words I value highly,	a
And no such summer as the one before.	b

—Edna St. Vincent Millay, **from "Well, I Have Lost
You; and I Lost You Fairly"**

R Rhythm Stressed and unstressed syllables create
a pattern in poetry, called **rhythm.** When the
pattern is predictable it is called **meter,** but it
does not have to be predictable. Rhythm can
create a musical quality, but it can also draw
attention to certain words or ideas. Langston
Hughes uses rhythm in this way in "A Dream
Deferred," when in the last line he asks, "Or
does it explode?"

528 UNIT 3 POETRY

Additional Support

Skills Practice

**LITERARY ELEMENT: Poetic

Forms** Tell students that rhythm, rhyme,
sound, and structure can reinforce the
poet's intent. Ask students if they notice
ways that sound reinforces meaning in
the excerpts on pp. 528–529. Finally,

introduce poetic devices that convey
emotion and meaning in poetry:
personification—Personification gives non-
humans human traits.
simile—A simile compares two unlike
things using *like* or *as.*

Meter Predictable rhythms are called **meter.** Different meters are named for how many feet are in each line. **Trimeter** has three feet, **tetrameter** has four feet, **pentameter** has five feet, and **hexameter** has six feet. Iambic pentameter appears in many English poems. An **iamb** is a foot that has an unstressed syllable followed by a stressed syllable, and pentameter means there are five of them in a line.

˘ ´ ˘ ´ ˘ ´ ˘ ´ ˘ ´
Shall I compare thee to a summer's day?

˘ ´ ˘ ´ ˘ ´ ˘ ´ ˘ ´
Thou art more lovely and more temperate.

—William Shakespeare, **from "Shall I Compare Thee to a Summer's Day?"**

Foot The **foot** is the basic unit of stressed and unstressed syllables used to describe rhythm in poetry. A foot usually has two or three syllables.

Scansion In addition to paying close attention to the sounds of letters and words in poems, poets pay attention to each syllable and whether it is stressed or unstressed. Stressed and unstressed syllables create **rhythms.** Each rhythmical unit is called a **foot,** and a regular pattern of stressed and unstressed syllables is called **meter.** Stressed syllables are marked with (´) and unstressed syllables are marked with (˘).

˘ ´ ˘ ´ ˘ ´ ˘ ´ ˘ ´
Give warning to the world that I am fled

˘ ´ ˘ ´ ˘ ´ ˘ ´ ˘ ´
From this vile world, with vilest worms to dwell:

—William Shakespeare, **from "Sonnet 71"**

Structure

Poets build structure into their poems in several ways. They may use rhythm and rhyme to connect ideas. They may use repetition to emphasize main ideas or images. And they may use stanzas to separate the poem into distinct parts, in much the same way that paragraphs separate ideas in an essay. Each stanza within a poem may serve a different purpose. For example, one stanza could describe a problem, one stanza could explore solutions, and one stanza could re-create a time before the problem existed.

Lyric Poem Lyric poems are short poems by one speaker who expresses thoughts and feelings to create a single, unified impression. Jimmy Santiago Baca's poem "I Am Offering This Poem" is an example of a lyric poem.

It's all I have to give,
and all anyone needs to live,
and to go on living inside,
when the world outside
no longer cares if you live or die;
remember,
                    I love you

—Jimmy Santiago Baca, **from "I Am Offering This Poem"**

Free Verse Poetry without a fixed pattern of meter and rhyme is called **free verse.** Some free verse uses sound devices and a rhythm similar to speaking patterns.

What did I know, what did I know
of love's austere and lonely offices?

—Robert Hayden, **from "Those Winter Sundays"**

Quickwrite

Choose a form from the examples above and write a poem, paying special attention to the form, stanzas, lines, and rhyme scheme.

OBJECTIVES
• Recognize the significance of various literary devices.
• Understand structure in poetry.

• Analyze poetry for the methods used by poets, such as rhythm, to inspire the reader and to share emotion.

LITERARY FOCUS **529**

Focus

BELLRINGER

Bellringer Options
**Selection Focus
Transparency 26
Daily Language Practice
Transparency 48
Or on the board, write:** Sundays too my father got up early
Ask: What are some different ways that parents demonstrate love for their children?

Then have students discuss the different ways that children react to the love shown by their parents or other family members, and what they might appreciate and what they might take for granted.

CheckPoint

Use the CheckPoint questions on Presentation Plus! to monitor students' comprehension. These questions can be used with interactive response keypads for immediate student feedback.

Author Search To expand students' appreciation of Robert Hayden, have them access the Web site for additional information and resources.

Those Winter Sundays

MEET ROBERT HAYDEN

Ever wonder what will happen to your classmates, those burrowing bookworms, who enjoy reading for reading's sake? Well, they just might grow up to be famous authors and poets. Robert Hayden was one of those bookish students, and he went on to become a poet and professor, earning a living through the written word.

> "I loved those books, partly because they took me completely out of the environment I lived in, and they appealed to my imagination. . . ."
>
> —Robert Hayden

A Life with Books Hayden was born in Detroit, Michigan. Growing up, he was too nearsighted to play sports with his friends, so he found companionship in books. After high school, he read many contemporary poets including those of the Harlem Renaissance—which he discovered by accident, stumbling upon the famous anthology *The New Negro* at a time when he could not afford to go to college. Later he won a scholarship to Detroit City College (now called Wayne State University) where he majored in foreign languages and minored in English.

After receiving a master's degree in 1944, Hayden began his academic career. He spent twenty-three years at Fisk University, where he eventually became a professor of English. He ended his academic career at the University of Michigan, teaching there for eleven years. Hayden once said that he considered himself to be "a poet who teaches in order to earn a living so that he can write a poem or two now and then."

Politics, Poetry, and Faith Hayden's poetry was deeply influenced by the poetry of his mentor and graduate school professor, W. H. Auden. Hayden creates stanza structures that are creative and original, even when they appear in traditional forms. In this way, his poetry balances free verse and traditional forms. Hayden's poetry is usually arranged into even stanzas with lines in regular patterns. Another main feature of Hayden's verse is that he avoids full rhyme; in some cases, he substitutes assonance or consonance.

The subject matter of Hayden's poetry tends to focus on historical themes and events. Hayden learned all he could about other African American writers and poets. Hayden was also influenced by the politics of the times. He experienced discrimination and segregation while he lived in Nashville. However, he refrained from writing aggressively about the injustices he witnessed. Instead, he strove to approach subjects such as civil rights as "an artist and not a propagandist."

Hayden's poetry was equally inspired by his faith. Hayden and his wife were followers of Baha'i, a religion that believes in the unity of all religions and people. His belief may have inspired Hayden to say "I don't believe that races are important; I believe that people are important."

Robert Hayden was born in 1913 and died in 1980.

Literature Online **Author Search** For more about Robert Hayden, go to www.glencoe.com.

Selection Skills

Literary Elements
- Line and Stanza (SE pp. 531, 533)

Those Winter Sundays

Writing Skills/Grammar
- Apply Theme (SE p. 533)

Reading Skills
- Analyzing Tone (SE pp. 531–533)
- Analyzing Sound Techniques (TWE p. 532)

Vocabulary Skills
- Context Clues (SE p. 533)

Listening/Speaking/Viewing Skills
- Analyzing Art (SE p. 532)

Connecting to the Poem

In this poem, you meet a son remembering his father. In his recollection, the son gains a newfound understanding of his father's love. Before you read the poem, think about the following questions:

- How often do you reflect on what your parents or family members do to show their love for you?
- How do you interpret and respond to their everyday gestures and manners?

Building Background

Poet and teacher Robert Hayden dedicated his life to his craft and to working "closely with young people" in order "to encourage creative writing." He researched and celebrated his heritage in his poetry. Hayden said, "I believe in the essential oneness of all people," and his poems portray universal human concerns of loss and love. Hayden won many awards for his work and was the first African American to be named as the Library of Congress consultant in poetry, a position now called poet laureate.

Setting Purposes for Reading

Big Idea The Energy of the Everyday

As you read this poem, notice how Hayden captures the different moods and actions of his characters through vivid imagery.

Literary Element Line and Stanza

A **line** in a poem usually consists of a single word or row of words. A **stanza** is a group of lines forming a unit in a poem or song, and is similar to the paragraph unit in prose. Typically, stanzas are separated by a line of space. In this poem, note how the poet uses lines and stanzas to help convey ideas. As you read, try to determine the author's focus and thematic intent of each stanza.

- See Literary Terms Handbook, pp. R9 and R16.

Literature Online **Interactive Literary Elements Handbook** To review or learn more about the literary elements, go to www.glencoe.com.

OBJECTIVES
In studying this selection, you will focus on the following:
- understanding the genre elements of poetry, such as line and stanza
- analyzing tone to comprehend a poem's meaning
- writing a conversation to express a poem's theme

Reading Strategy Analyzing Tone

Tone refers to an author's attitude toward his or her subject matter. A writer's tone might project a variety of attitudes such as sympathy, objectivity, or humor. It may be conveyed through elements such as word choice, punctuation, sentence structure, and figures of speech. When you analyze the tone of a selection, you deepen your understanding of the author's message. Try to determine the speaker's tone as you read Hayden's poem.

....

Reading Tip: Asking Questions Use a chart like the one below to identify how the speaker uses description to achieve a certain tone. Fill in the circles with descriptions from the poem and note the tone conveyed.

Vocabulary

chronic (kron′ik) *adj.* persistent; ongoing, especially of sickness or pain; p. 532 *Chronic backaches made it difficult for my mom to garden.*

indifferently (in dif′ər ənt lē) *adv.* not concerned about someone or something; without a preference; p. 532 *When Mr. Tate spoke, his children listened indifferently, as they were not interested.*

austere (ôs tēr′) *adj.* stern; severe in appearance; p. 532 *Micky's austere expression let us know that he was pretty disappointed.*

Focus

Summary

The speaker of this poem remembers his father's loving sacrifices. He appeared indifferent and ungrateful toward his father as a child, but now regrets this, appreciating the actions that represent "love's austere and lonely offices."

V Vocabulary

Vocabulary File Say: Add these words and definitions to your vocabulary file. For each word, include a sentence that gives you an example of how to use the word. **OL** Students with English language needs should include the pronunciations of these words in their files. **EL**

Literary Elements Have students access the Web site to improve their understanding of line and stanza.

ROBERT HAYDEN **531**

Selection Resources

Print Materials
- Unit 3 Resources (Fast File), pp. 17–19
- Leveled Vocabulary Development, p. 38
- Selection and Unit Assessments, pp. 83–84
- Selection Quick Checks, p. 42

Transparencies
- Bellringer Options Transparencies: Daily Language Practice Transparency 48
- Literary Elements Transparency 59

Technology
- TeacherWorks Plus™ CD-ROM
- StudentWorks Plus™ CD-ROM
- Presentation Plus!™ CD-ROM
- Literature Online, glencoe.com
- Online Student Edition, mhln.com
- ExamView® Assessment Suite CD-ROM
- Vocabulary PuzzleMaker CD-ROM
- Listening Library, disc 1 track 46

Teach

BI Big Idea

The Energy of the Everyday Ask: What details make the everyday actions described in the poem particularly vivid? (*Students may mention imagery such as "the blueblack cold," or "cracked hands that ached" as particularly vivid.*) **OL**

R Reading Strategy

Analyzing Tone Answer: *Some may say that this suggests a sad, regretful tone. Others may say that it shows the true nature of love: do something kind without getting anything in return.* **OL**

★ Viewing the Art

Answer: *Observational and stoic. It reflects the speaker's melancholic revelation of his father's love.* **AS**

▶ CheckPoint

Use the CheckPoint questions on Presentation Plus! to check students' mastery of the selection. These questions can be used with interactive response keypads for immediate student feedback.

Those Winter Sundays

Robert Hayden

Sundays too my father got up early
and put his clothes on in the blueblack cold,
then with cracked hands that ached
from labor in the weekday weather made
5 banked fires[1] blaze. No one ever thanked him.

I'd wake and hear the cold splintering, breaking.
When the rooms were warm, he'd call,
and slowly I would rise and dress,
fearing the **chronic** angers of that house,

10 Speaking **indifferently** to him,
who had driven out the cold
and polished my good shoes as well.
What did I know, what did I know
of love's **austere** and lonely offices?[2]

BI

Lynford, 1969. Karen Armitage. Oil on canvas. Private collection.
Viewing the Art: How would you describe this man's expression and mood? Compare and contrast them to the personal qualities conveyed by the speaker of the poem. ★

---

1. *Banked fires* are ones that have been covered with ashes to keep them burning at a very low level.
2. *Offices* can mean both "duties and responsibilities" or "favors and kindness."

Reading Strategy Analyzing Tone *How do these five words from the speaker contribute to the tone of the poem?* **R**

Vocabulary

chronic (kron′ik) *adj.* persistent; ongoing, especially of sickness or pain
indifferently (in dif′ər ənt lē) *adv.* not concerned about someone or something; without a preference
austere (ôs tēr′) *adj.* stern; severe in appearance

532 UNIT 3 POETRY

Additional Support

Skills Practice

READING: Sound Techniques
Remind students of the definitions of alliteration, assonance, and consonance and point out that Hayden uses several examples of these techniques in his poem. Ask students to point out examples of each, and explain the effect(s) that they have on the poem after reading it silently. Then ask volunteers to read the poem aloud, and have students discuss the different ways that the alliteration, assonance, and consonance strike them after experiencing them this way. **OL**

532

RESPONDING AND THINKING CRITICALLY

Respond

1. Which one line or image from "Those Winter Sundays" most resonated with you? Explain.

Recall and Interpret

2. (a)What did the speaker's father do on Sunday mornings in the winter? (b)As a child, did the speaker appreciate his father's efforts? How do you know?

3. (a)Why do you think the speaker spoke indifferently to his father? (b)In the third stanza, how has the father "driven out the cold"?

4. What does the speaker now understand that he did not understand before?

Analyze and Evaluate

5. (a)How does the speaker personify the cold? (b)How does this reflect the son's feelings?

6. (a)What do you think was Robert Hayden's motive in writing this poem? (b)Who do you think he would most like to reach with this poem?

Connect

7. **Big Idea** The Energy of the Everyday In what ways does Hayden bring greater significance to the daily responsibilities a parent performs? Explain.

LITERARY ANALYSIS

Literary Element Line and Stanza

Examining the contribution each **line** and **stanza** makes to the overall movement and thematic development of the poem can help you better understand the poet's purpose and intention.

1. What is the specific focus of each separate stanza? How might the focus of the third stanza incorporate those of the first two?

2. How does each line in the poem trace the speaker's development as a person?

Writing About Literature

Apply Theme In many of his poems, Hayden revisits the settings of his working-class Detroit childhood. Imagine a conversation between a child and his or her parent or guardian on such a winter morning. In your conversation, the two can either bring up or avoid issues of gratitude and fear of anger. Write down this imagined conversation, including words, phrases, or images from the poem that made an impression upon you.

Literature Online Web Activities For eFlashcards, Selection Quick Checks, and other Web activities, go to www.glencoe.com.

READING AND VOCABULARY

Reading Strategy Analyzing Tone

Analyzing tone helps you better understand the message the poet tries to convey and the response the poet strives to elicit. Pay attention to word choice, repetition, and imagery used to convey a particular feeling. Review the descriptions in your chart to help you answer the following questions.

1. How do the speaker's descriptions of the cold house mirror his attitude toward his father?

2. Examine the speaker's word choice. What does it tell you about the speaker and his father's love?

Vocabulary Practice

Practice with Context Clues For each vocabulary word, use context clues to figure out its meaning. Think about which type of context clue helped you.

1. Every time Jane fidgeted, Grandmother gave her an **austere**, disapproving look.
   a. nervous **b.** stern **c.** warm
2. Mary suffered from **chronic** allergies until she finally got a prescription for a new medication.
   a. ongoing **b.** extreme **c.** occasional
3. Shipra did not care which movie we saw, so she reacted **indifferently** when I picked one.
   a. sadly **b.** happily **c.** without a preference

ROBERT HAYDEN **533**

Assess

1. Answers will vary.
2. (a) He stoked the furnace to warm the room before waking his children. (b) No; he spoke indifferently to him.
3. (a) He took his father for granted. (b) The father provides warmth as well as love.
4. Love is expressed in common, everyday gestures.
5. (a) By giving it shape and sound (b) Reflects the son's indifferent, ungrateful feelings toward his father
6. (a) To point out the limited perspective children have of their parents (b) Children and adults who remember being children
7. The poem asks readers to examine the small, daily things people do for others.

Literary Element

1. First: father; second: speaker; third: interaction between the two
2. The second and third stanzas trace his realization of his father's love and his regret over not appreciating it.

Writing About Literature

Students' essays should

• use vivid details to describe the conversation.

• focus on the relationship between a child and his or her parent or guardian.

• apply the theme of "Those Winter Sundays" to their writing.

Vocabulary

1. b **2.** a **3.** c

Reading Strategy

1. They reveal his lack of sympathy for his father.

2. Love isn't always demonstrative but sometimes subtle and quietly expressed.

Literature Online

Web Activities Have students access the Web site for interactive activities that will help them assess their understanding of the selection.

Focus

On the board, write the following homophones: *principle/ principal.* Ask students to distinguish between the two words. Then see if students can give the meanings of homonyms such as *lean* ("thin") and *lean* ("to bend").

Teach

Identifying Homonyms and Homophones Review the definitions of homonym and homophone, and review the meanings of the listed homophones. Provide sentences for students to complete with one of the listed homophones. Also provide homonyms (e.g., *mean, run*) for students to use in sentences. **OL**

Assess

1. passed 2. weather
3. heal 4. night 5. know

eFlashcards Have students access the Web site for more practice with homonyms and homophones.

▶ **Test-Taking Tip**

To help you understand the meaning of a **homonym** you come across in a reading passage, carefully examine the sentence in which the word appears and the surrounding sentences. The context should provide clues to the word's meaning.

▶ **Reading Handbook**

For more about using context to discover meaning, see the Reading Handbook, p. R20.

eFlashcards Visit www.glencoe .com for eFlashcards and other vocabulary activities.

OBJECTIVES
- Use context clues to understand homophones and homonyms.
- Recognize the multiple meanings of homonyms.

534 UNIT 3 POETRY

Recognizing Homonyms and Homophones

". . . with cracked hands that ached / from labor in the weekday weather made / banked fires blaze."

—Robert Hayden, from "Those Winter Sundays"

Connecting to Literature In this excerpt from his poem about his father, Robert Hayden uses the word *banked*, meaning not "stored for safekeeping" nor "steeply inclined," but rather, "covered with ashes to burn slowly." Words like *banked* that sound and are spelled alike but have different meanings are called **homonyms.** Words like *weather* and *whether*, which sound alike but are spelled differently, are called **homophones.** Although homonyms and homophones can be confusing, the context, or setting, in which the word appears usually provides clues to the word's meaning. From Hayden's use of *banked* to describe fires and our own knowledge of them, we can determine which definition he means.

Part of the reason why English is difficult for many non-native speakers to learn is because of its many homophones. Here is a list of some common ones:

ate/eight	right/rite/write
for/for/four	row/roe
here/hear	scent/sent/cent
higher/hire	site/sight/cite
its/it's	some/sum
morning/mourning	their/there/they're
none/nun	to/too/two
one/won	wholly/holy/holey

Exercise

Use context clues to decide which homonym or homophone belongs in each sentence below. Use a dictionary if you need help.

1. Father (passed/past) him a pair of freshly shined shoes.
2. The fire kept out the cold (whether/weather).
3. The warmth helped (heel/heal) their chilled bodies.
4. It counteracted the loneliness of the (night/knight).
5. He did not (know, no) how to express his feelings to his father.

Additional Support

Skills Practice

VOCABULARY: Homophones
Discuss with less proficient readers the following types of context clues that help to identify homophones or homonyms:

- synonyms—words that mean the same
- antonyms—words that mean the opposite

- examples—signaled by words such as *like, such as, for example*
- comparisons—signaled by words such as *like, similar, as*
- contrasts—signaled by words such as *instead, rather, although*
- cause-effect relationships—signaled by words such as *since* and *because* **OL**

Creatures

MEET BILLY COLLINS

Billy Collins has managed a most unusual feat for a contemporary poet: popular and critical acclaim. Whether musing about the three blind mice or a museum painting, Collins writes with a wry humor that gently ushers the reader into his poem and reveals truths about the human experience using twists of language and thought. Collins says that he envisions the beginning of a poem as "a kind of welcome mat where I invite the reader inside."

Beginnings Collins is a native of New York City, the son of a nurse and an electrician. After high school, he attended the College of the Holy Cross in Worchester, Massachusetts. Collins then earned a doctorate in Romantic Poetry from the University of California at Riverside in 1971. He returned to New York, where he met and married his wife, Diane. Collins then began teaching in the English Department at Lehman College, City University of New York.

> "I believe poetry belongs in unexpected places—in elevators and on buses and subways."
>
> —Billy Collins

During the 1970s, Collins's poetry began to appear in many literary publications, including the *American Poetry Review,* the *Paris Review,* and the *New Yorker.* In 1977 Collins published his first book of poetry, *Pokerface,* followed by his second collection, *Video Poems,* in 1980. Eight years later, Collins published *The Apple that Astonished Paris.* His next book, *Questions about Angels,* was included in the 1990 National Poetry Series.

A National Reputation With the publication of *Questions about Angels,* Collins's popularity reached the national level. The New York Public Library named him a "Literary Lion" in 1992, and the following year he was awarded the Bess Hokin Prize by the prestigious *Poetry* magazine. His poems appeared in the *Best American Poetry* anthologies in 1992, 1993, and 1997. He continued to publish and also edited two anthologies of poetry and released *The Best Cigarette,* a CD of Collins reading thirty-three of his poems. His other accolades include various literary prizes and fellowships from the Guggenheim Foundation and the National Endowment for the Arts.

Collins was named Poet Laureate of the United States in 2001, a position he held for two years. During that time, he created a jazz/poetry channel for Delta Airlines in-flight entertainment. He also developed *Poetry 180: A Poem a Day for High Schools.* Collins selected 180 poems, one to be read aloud each morning along with the school announcements. He described the project as a "jukebox of poems" and emphasized that the students were not to analyze the poetry—they were to simply experience the language. Collins also was named Poet Laureate of the State of New York.

Billy Collins was born in 1941.

 Author Search For more about Billy Collins, go to www.glencoe.com.

BILLY COLLINS **535**

Focus

BELLRINGER

Bellringer Options
Daily Language Practice Transparency 49
Or initiate a class discussion about childhood fears.
Ask: What fears did you have as a child? How did these fears change as you grew older? How can you explain these changes? Prompt students to consider the power of imagination. **Ask:** Is losing the power to imagine a necessary hazard of growing up? Prompt students to support their answers with examples

✓CheckPoint

Use the CheckPoint questions on Presentation Plus! to monitor students' comprehension. These questions can be used with interactive response keypads for immediate student feedback.

Author Search To expand students' appreciation of Billy Collins, have them access the Web site for additional information and resources.

Selection Skills

Literary Elements
- Enjambment (SE pp. 536, 538, 539)
- Assonance (TWE p. 538)

Creatures

Writing Skills/Grammar
- Responding to Style (SE p. 539)

Reading Skills
- Analyzing Structure (SE pp. 536, 539)

Vocabulary Skills
- Practice with Word Parts (SE pp. 536, 539)

Listening/Speaking/Viewing Skills
- Analyzing Art (TWE p. 537)

BEFORE YOU READ

Focus

Summary

The speaker of the poem describes how—as Hamlet saw the shapes of creatures in clouds—as a child he saw haunted faces trapped in inanimate objects: the grain of wood on furniture, the pattern of wallpaper, the carpet nap. As an adult, the speaker's companion shows him the face in a rock, and he responds by throwing the rock far away, into the sea.

Literary Elements Have students access the Web site to improve their understanding of enjambment.

V Vocabulary

Vocabulary File

Say: Add these words and definitions to your vocabulary file. For each word, include a sentence that gives you an example of how to use the word. **OL** Students with English language needs should include the pronunciations of these words in their files. **EL**

Connecting to the Poem

The following poem talks about seeing creatures in everyday objects. Before you read the poem, think about the following questions:

- What do you see when you look at clouds?
- Do you expect age or experience to change what you see?

Building Background

Hamlet tells the story of the sensitive young prince of Denmark in the months after his father, the king, is murdered by his uncle Claudius. Hamlet resolves to murder Claudius as retribution. However, he spends much of the play thinking and soliloquizing rather than acting on his resolution. As a result of his reputation as a thinker, and not a doer, Hamlet has often been reimagined as the archetypal pensive, tormented male artist.

Setting Purposes for Reading

Big Idea The Energy of the Everyday

As you read this poem, pay attention to how creatures are seen in everyday objects and how the speaker reacts to them.

Literary Element Enjambment

Enjambment is the continuation of the sense of a sentence or phrase from one line of a poem to the next without a pause between the lines. The first line below is an example of enjambment:

> Many times I would be daydreaming
> on the carpet and one would appear next to me,

Enjambment contrasts with end-stopped lines, in which the sense and the grammatical structure reach completion at the end of a line. Enjambment can occur in both metered and free-verse poetry.

- See Literary Terms Handbook, p. R5.

Literature Online Interactive Literary Elements Handbook To review or learn more about the literary elements, go to www.glencoe.com.

OBJECTIVES
In studying this selection, you will focus on the following:
- analyzing the author's use of enjambment
- analyzing the structure
- recognizing and understanding word parts
- writing to respond to the author's style

Reading Strategy Analyzing Structure

Analyzing text structure involves identifying the order or pattern an author uses to present his or her ideas. Many elements help to form the structure of a poem or literary work, including cause-and-effect relationships, chronological order, problem and solution, the repetition of certain rhetorical devices, and lists. As you read, identify the various ways in which Collins structures this poem.

Reading Tip: Noting Descriptive Words As you read the poem, note the words that Collins uses to describe the creatures he sees and the locations where he sees them.

Creature Location	Description
"in the furniture of childhood"	"trapped under surfaces of wood"

Vocabulary

submerged (səb murjd´) *adj.* hard to see; sunken p. 537 *The real plan was submerged in a mass of detail.*

bureau (byoor´ō) *n.* a chest of drawers for the bedroom; p. 537 *Please put the clothes back in the bureau.*

melancholy (mel´ən kol´ē) *adj.* depressed; dejected; p. 538 *The dark and rainy day created a melancholy mood in the school.*

grimace (gri mās´ing) *v.* to make a face expressing disgust, disapproval, or pain; p. 538 *The boy grimaced at his mother when she scolded.*

fissure (fish´ər) *n.* a narrow crack; p. 538 *The earthquake caused a fissure in the earth.*

Vocabulary Tip: Word Parts Many English words can be divided into parts: prefix, base word or root, and suffix.

Selection Resources

Print Materials
- 📁 Unit 3 Resources (Fast File), pp. 20–22
- 📁 Leveled Vocabulary Development, p. 39
- 📁 Selection and Unit Assessments, pp. 85–86
- 📁 Selection Quick Checks, p. 43

Transparencies
- Bellringer Options Transparencies: Daily Language Practice Transparency 49
- Literary Elements Transparency 65

Technology
- 💿 TeacherWorks Plus™ CD-ROM
- 💿 StudentWorks Plus™ CD-ROM
- 💿 Presentation Plus!™ CD-ROM
- 💻 Literature Online, glencoe.com
- 💻 Online Student Edition, mhln.com
- 💿 ExamView® Assessment Suite CD-ROM
- 💿 Vocabulary PuzzleMaker CD-ROM
- 💿 Listening Library, disc 1 track 47

Creatures

Billy Collins

Hamlet[1] noticed them in the shapes of clouds,
but I saw them in the furniture of childhood,
creatures trapped under surfaces of wood,

one **submerged** in a polished sideboard,
5 one frowning from a chair-back,
another howling from my mother's silent **bureau,**
locked in the grain of maple, frozen in oak.

1. *Hamlet.* In Shakespeare's
   Hamlet, Act III, Scene II, Hamlet
   compares the shape of a cloud
   to a camel, a weasel, and
   a whale.

Vocabulary

submerged (səb murjd′) *adj.* hard to see; sunken
bureau (byoor′ō) *n.* a chest of drawers for the bedroom

BILLY COLLINS **537**

Teach

Big Idea

The Energy of the Everyday Say: Keep the following questions in mind as you read: What is the speaker's perception of the everyday objects he describes? Does his perception change as the poem progresses? *(The objects seem to him to have life trapped inside them that is trying to escape. This perception seems to frighten or disturb him, even as an adult.)* **OL**

★ Viewing the Art

Spanish painter Salvador Dalí (1904–1989) is best known as one of the founders of Surrealism. Surrealism emphasizes the powerful influence of the subconscious in creating visuals. In many of Dalí's works, everday objects are juxtaposed and transformed to produce unusual and fantastic images. **Ask:** In what ways is the painting similar to and different from the way the speaker in the poem "sees" creatures? *(In both works, faces or creatures are seen where they really do not exist. Students may say that in the painting, many different objects function together to form a face, while in the poem, the speaker usually sees creatures in individual objects.)* **AS**

English Language Coach

Participles Help English language learners understand the role of participles in this poem. **Ask:** What is described as trapped (submerged, frowning, howling, locked, etc.)? **Answer:** *The creatures are trapped.* Trapped *is an adjective that modifies* creatures. **EL**

Differentiated Instruction

Less Proficient Readers Pair less proficient readers with other students and have them take turns reading the poem aloud. Afterward, students should list and define any unfamiliar words in the poem using a dictionary and a thesaurus. **BL**

Objective
• To establish a purpose for reading (TWE)

537

Teach

L Literary Element

Enjambment Answer: *These lines exemplify enjambment because one line flows into the next without a pause.* **OL**

BI Big Idea

The Energy of the Everyday Answer: *Students should say that the stone reminds the speaker of his fears as a child. The stone evokes memories and feelings, even though it is a lifeless object.* **OL**

CheckPoint

Use the CheckPoint questions on Presentation Plus! to check students' mastery of the selection. These questions can be used with interactive response keypads for immediate student feedback.

I would see these presences, too,
in a swirling pattern of wallpaper
10   or in the various greens of a porcelain lamp,
each looking so **melancholy,** so damned,
some peering out at me as if they knew
all the secrets of a secretive boy.

Many times I would be daydreaming
15   on the carpet and one would appear next to me,
the oversize nose, the hollow look.

So you will understand my reaction
this morning at the beach
when you opened your hand to show me
20   a stone you had picked up from the shoreline.

"Do you see the face?" you asked
as the cold surf circled our bare ankles.
"There's the eye and the line of the mouth,
like it's **grimacing,** like it's in pain."

25   "Well, maybe that's because it has a **fissure**
running down the length of its forehead
not to mention a kind of twisted beak," I said,

taking the thing from you and flinging it out
over the sparkle of blue waves
30   so it could live out its freakish existence
on the dark bottom of the sea

and stop bothering innocent beachgoers like us,
stop ruining everyone's summer.

Literary Element   Enjambment *How do these lines exemplify enjambment? Explain.* **L**

Big Idea   The Energy of the Everyday *Why does the stone, an ordinary object, bother the speaker so much?* **BI**

Vocabulary

melancholy (mel′ ən kol′ ē) *adj.* depressed; dejected
grimace (gri mās′ ing) *v.* to make a face expressing disgust, disapproval, or pain
fissure (fish′ ər) *n.* a narrow crack

538   UNIT 3   POETRY

Additional Support

Skills Practice

LITERARY ELEMENT: Assonance
Explain: Assonance is the repetition of vowel sounds in a poem. The technique is often used as a way to unify a poem without using rhyme. Have groups of students copy two stanzas from the poem onto sheets of paper and follow the steps below:

1. Choose one student to read the stanzas aloud while others note similar vowel sounds by underlining them and connecting them with lines.

2. Evaluate how well assonance unifies these stanzas.

3. Present your findings to the class. **OL**

538

RESPONDING AND THINKING CRITICALLY

Respond

1. Describe your feelings about the creatures after reading the poem.

Recall and Interpret

2. (a)How does the speaker describe the "creatures" in the furniture? (b)Why do you think the speaker sees creatures in the furniture?

3. (a)How does the speaker react to the stone his companion finds on the beach? (b)Why do you think the speaker reacts in this way?

Analyze and Evaluate

4. Does the speaker's reaction to the stone seem rational? Explain.

5. (a)Can you identify with the speaker's reaction in the poem? (b)How does Collins help you to identify with the experience?

6. (a)Why do you think the speaker directly addresses his companion in the fifth stanza? (b)Is this technique effective? Explain your answer.

Connect

7. **Big Idea** **The Energy of the Everyday** The everyday is usually considered non-threatening. In what ways has Collins made the everyday threatening? Explain.

LITERARY ANALYSIS

Literary Element Enjambment

Poets use **enjambment** to create a conversational tone and flow in their poems. Collins uses this technique in many lines in this poem.

1. Where does the poet use enjambment in the poem?

2. How effective is the author's use of enjambment? Explain.

Writing About Literature

Respond to Style Write a personal response to "Creatures." In your essay, discuss what you liked or disliked about the poem. Also discuss your response to the style of the poem, including the first-person point of view, the word choice, and the effect of the last stanza. Be sure to give examples from the poem to support your opinions.

When you are finished with your draft, have your peer reviewer critique your essay and offer suggestions. Then, with these suggestions in mind, make revisions to your work. Finally, proofread your essay and edit it for mistakes in spelling, grammar, and punctuation.

Literature Online Web Activities For eFlashcards, Selection Quick Checks, and other Web activities, go to www.glencoe.com.

READING AND VOCABULARY

Reading Strategy Analyzing Structure

Structure is the order or pattern an author uses to present ideas. Cause and effect, chronological order, describing a problem and offering a solution, or listing information are all types of structures that Collins could have chosen.

1. Describe the structure that Collins uses to organize the poem. Support your answer with examples.

2. How does the structure of the poem help you better understand its message?

Vocabulary Practice

Practice with Word Parts Use your knowledge of roots, as well as your knowledge of prefixes and suffixes, to pick the best definition for each of the boldfaced vocabulary words.

1. She **submerged** herself in the pool very slowly.
   a. swam   b. washed   c. immersed

2. Yao felt **melancholy** for weeks after the fight.
   a. angry   b. gloomy   c. unkind

3. Erin **grimaced** while taking out the trash.
   a. made a face   b. grinned   c. flexed

4. The dropped plate had a small **fissure**.
   a. dent   b. stain   c. crack

BILLY COLLINS **539**

Assess

1. Students' responses will vary.

2. (a) As *trapped, frowning,* and *melancholy* (b) The speaker imagines them because of the reflections or designs.

3. (a) The speaker throws the stone into the water. (b) It reminds him of his childhood fears.

4. The speaker's reaction is purely emotional, not rational.

5. Responses will vary.

6. (a) Because he understands exactly what his companion sees (b) Yes, because it emphasizes the emotional reaction and helps show that the speaker's past influences the present.

7. Collins has made the everyday frightening by describing ordinary objects with words such as *howling, twisted,* and *freakish*.

Literary Element

1. In stanzas 3, 4, 5, 6, 7, and 8.

2. It creates a conversational tone.

Writing About Literature

Students' essays should
- evaluate point of view.
- analyze effects of specific words.
- use examples from the poem to support main ideas.

Literature Online

Web Activites Have students access the Web site for interactive activities that will help them assess their understanding of the selection.

Reading Strategy

1. Students may say that it is chronological, moving from the speaker's childhood to an incident that occurs when he is an adult.

2. The structure emphasizes the poem's themes by illustrating how the childhood fears in the first part of the poem affect the speaker's adult behavior.

Vocabulary

1. c   2. b   3. a   4. c

Focus

BELLRINGER

Bellringer Options
Daily Language Practice Transparency 50
Or on the board, write: *Let the wind take you where it will* and *Look before you leap.*
Ask: What is the difference in philosophy between these two sayings? With which one do you agree? Have students discuss the difference between the sayings and with which one they agree. Have them discuss other sayings or life philosophies they follow.

Author Search To expand students' appreciation of Theodore Roethke, have them access the Web site for additional information and resources.

Use the CheckPoint questions on Presentation Plus! to monitor students' comprehension. These questions can be used with interactive response keypads for immediate student feedback.

The Waking

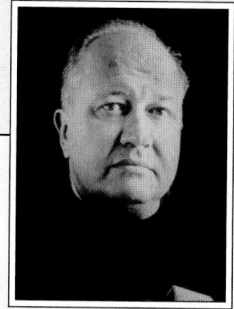

MEET THEODORE ROETHKE

In his book *Teacher Man*, author Frank McCourt recounts searching for poems that his restless high school students would enjoy. No other poem touched his students as deeply as Theodore Roethke's poem "My Papa's Waltz." Students from a variety of backgrounds saw their lives and complicated feelings about their families captured perfectly by Roethke's words.

A Rare Gift Roethke was a much loved and honored poet during his lifetime, winning the Pulitzer Prize and the National Book Award. His poems are closely observed lyrics that detail the processes of the natural world. Roethke was also a master of strict forms of poetry. In "The Waking," he puts thoroughly modern ideas into an old-fashioned poetic form called the villanelle.

> *"Any serious writer uses the imagery he saw and heard and felt about him as a youth. This is the imagery most vivid to him. It becomes symbolic."*
>
> —Theodore Roethke

Memory and Poetry Roethke fashioned his poems from strong memories about his childhood in Saginaw, Michigan. Roethke's father and grandfather were florists, and Roethke grew up in a world of flowers, plants, and large commercial greenhouses. Like Emerson and Whitman, Roethke almost mystically identified with nature: "In my veins, in my bones I feel it." Throughout his life, Roethke spent abundant time in nature.

During Roethke's sophomore year of high school, his father died from lung cancer. Roethke was devastated by the loss. At seventeen, he entered the University of Michigan, the first in his family to attend college. He went on to graduate studies at Harvard University. At Harvard, he gave three of his poems to poet and professor Robert Hillyer. Hillyer said, "Any editor who wouldn't buy these is a fool!" Encouraged, Roethke turned to poetry as a career.

Teacher and Writer As Roethke developed his poetry, he also began to teach, eventually serving as professor at Michigan State College, Pennsylvania State University, Bennington College, and the University of Washington. Over the years, Roethke mentored many important poets, including Richard Hugo, James Wright, and David Wagoner. Roethke challenged these students even as he immersed them in literature. According to Hugo, Roethke was "an outrageous man who would take outrageous stances and create something beautiful out of them. . . . That gave me a faith that you could be a pretty ridiculous person and still do something worthwhile or beautiful."

While Roethke's professional life thrived, his personal life was troubled. He suffered from depression, for which he was often hospitalized. Roethke died of a heart attack when he was only fifty-five. He left behind grateful students and many classic poems.

Theodore Roethke was born in 1908 and died in 1963.

Author Search For more about Theodore Roethke, go to www.glencoe.com.

540 UNIT 3 POETRY

Selection Skills

Literary Elements

- Meter and Rhythm (SE pp. 541, 544)
- Stanza (SE p. 544)
- Sound Devices (TWE p. 542)

Reading Skills

- Analyzing Mood (SE pp. 541, 542, 544)

The Waking

Vocabulary Skills

- Academic Vocabulary (SE p. 544)

Writing Skills/Grammar

- Analyzing Author's Purpose (SE p. 545)
- Using Infinitives (SE p. 545)

Connecting to the Poem

In "The Waking," the speaker expresses ideas about life, death, knowledge, and self-awareness. Before you read the poem, think about the following questions:

- Do you have a personal philosophy of life that you believe in or follow?
- What reminds you of the connection between human beings and nature?

Building Background

The form of poetry known as the *villanelle* derives its name from a type of Italian rustic song. The shape of the villanelle was established by the work of the French poet Jean Passerat, who died in 1602. Critics compare the popularity once enjoyed by Passerat's villanelles to that of popular songs today.

Villanelles are nineteen lines long. They have five stanzas of three lines each, followed by one stanza of four lines. The first line of the first stanza is repeated as the last line of the second and fourth stanzas. The third line of the first stanza is repeated as the last line of the third and fifth stanzas. These two repeated lines are repeated once more at the end of the poem.

Setting Purposes for Reading

Big Idea The Energy of the Everyday

As you read "The Waking," notice what Roethke suggests about the value of everyday life.

Literary Element Meter and Rhythm

Meter is a regular pattern of stressed and unstressed syllables that gives a line of poetry a predictable rhythm. **Rhythm** gives poetry a musical quality, adds emphasis to certain words, and helps convey a poem's meaning. Examining meter and rhythm can help you understand a poem's meaning and appreciate its aural quality. As you read the poem, try to determine its meter and the effect of its rhythm.

- See Literary Terms Handbook, pp. R10 and R14.

Reading Strategy — Analyzing Mood

The **mood** is the emotional quality of a literary work. A writer's choice of language, subject matter, setting, and tone—as well as sound devices such as rhyme and rhythm—contribute to creating mood. Understanding the mood will help you appreciate a writer's state of mind. While reading this poem, try to determine the mood of the individual lines and of the poem as a whole to help you better understand the poet's meaning.

Reading Tip: Finding Examples Use a chart to record examples of language, subject matter, setting, tone, and sound devices that create a strong mood.

Types	Examples	Mood
Language	alliteration: fate, fear, feeling	dark; mysterious
Subject matter		
Setting		
Tone		
Sound devices		

Flying the Kite. Lucy Raverat. RONA Gallery, London.

Literature Online **Interactive Literary Elements Handbook** To review or learn more about the literary elements, go to www.glencoe.com.

OBJECTIVES

In studying this selection, you will focus on the following:
- understanding meter and rhythm
- analyzing mood
- writing an analysis of an author's purpose
- determining stanza structure

Focus

Summary

The speaker narrates his philosophy of living by actively living, by going where he is drawn and must inevitably go. He expresses his love of the natural way of things, of the holiness of the earth and light. He urges the reader to live as he does— by experiencing life.

Literary Elements Have students access the Web site to improve their understanding of meter and rhythm.

THEODORE ROETHKE **541**

Selection Resources

Print Materials
- Unit 3 Resources (Fast File), pp. 23–24
- Selection and Unit Assessments, pp. 87–88
- Selection Quick Checks, p. 44

Transparencies
- Bellringer Options Transparencies: Daily Language Practice Transparency 50
- Literary Elements Transparencies 60, 61

Technology
- TeacherWorks Plus™ CD-ROM
- StudentWorks Plus™ CD-ROM
- Presentation Plus!™ CD-ROM
- Literature Online, glencoe.com
- Online Student Edition, mhln.com
- ExamView® Assessment Suite CD-ROM
- Vocabulary PuzzleMaker CD-ROM
- Listening Library, disc 1 track 48

Teach

BI₁ Big Idea

The Energy of the Everyday Say: Keep the following questions in mind as you read: What is your place in nature? Is nature a guiding principle in your life? *(Answers will vary. Most students will probably not think of nature as a guiding principle in their life, more as something external that should be respected and conserved.)* **OL**

R Reading Strategy

Analyzing Mood Answer: *Students may say happiness or joy.* **OL**

BI₂ Big Idea

The Energy of the Everyday Answer: *He capitalizes* ground. *He makes it seem sacred.* **OL**

✓ CheckPoint

Use the CheckPoint questions on Presentation Plus! to check students' mastery of the selection. These questions can be used with interactive response keypads for immediate student feedback.

The WAKING BI₁

Theodore Roethke

I wake to sleep, and take my waking slow.
I feel my fate in what I cannot fear.
I learn by going where I have to go.

We think by feeling. What is there to know?
5   I hear my being dance from ear to ear.
I wake to sleep, and take my waking slow.

Of those so close beside me, which are you?
God bless the Ground! I shall walk softly there,
And learn by going where I have to go.

10   Light takes the Tree; but who can tell us how?
The lowly worm climbs up a winding stair;
I wake to sleep, and take my waking slow.

Great Nature has another thing to do
To you and me; so take the lively air,
15   And, lovely, learn by going where to go.

This shaking keeps me steady. I should know.
What falls away is always. And is near.
I wake to sleep, and take my waking slow.
I learn by going where I have to go.

The Sun Rises While the Moon Sleeps, 1990. Peter Davidson. Mixed media on paper, 27.3 x 20.3 cm. Private Collection.

Reading Strategy Analyzing Mood *What emotion is conveyed by this image?* **R**

Big Idea The Energy of the Everyday *How does Roethke make the ground seem important?* **BI₂**

Additional Support

Skills Practice

LITERARY ELEMENT: Sound Devices Poets use sound devices to emphasize certain words and create rhythm. "The Waking" uses a number of sound devices to create an auditory foundation for the natural philosophy it promotes. Have volunteers read the poem aloud so that students can get a sense of what the poem sounds like. Then have students identify the sound devices Roethke employs in the poem, such as assonance, consonance, rhyme, and alliteration. **OL**

RESPONDING AND THINKING CRITICALLY

Respond

1. (a)Is this an uplifting poem? Explain. (b)How can you apply this poem to your own life?

Recall and Interpret

2. (a)How does the speaker "take" his waking? (b)What do you think the speaker means by this recurring phrase?

3. (a)Identify two lines that address learning or thinking. (b)What ideas about knowledge do these lines express?

4. (a)What climbs up a winding stair? (b)In your opinion, why did the poet include this image?

Analyze and Evaluate

5. (a)What is "another thing" that nature has to do "to you and me," according to stanza 5? (b)Explain the advice we are given in line 14. How is it related to the refrain "I learn by going where I have to go"?

6. In your opinion, what attitude does the speaker express toward nature?

7. "What falls away is always." Do you agree with this statement? Explain.

Connect

8. **Big Idea** **The Energy of the Everyday** (a)Roethke seems to be expressing a philosophy of how people should live their lives. What is this philosophy? (b)Would you follow this philosophy? Explain.

VISUAL LITERACY: Photograph

Leaning Toward the Light

Study the image of the tree reaching toward the sun. Think about how it might apply to the line "Light takes the Tree." This is an example of a phenomenon called *tropism,* in which a plant or certain animals respond to a stimulus more from one direction than from another. Specifically, this picture shows *phototropism,* or a response to light. As you can see in the image, the tree leans toward the sunlight as it grows because it is attracted to the source of the stimulus. With a partner, do research to learn more about the natural processes that cause trees to grow toward light and other reflex-like activities of plants.

1. What do trees depend on for their survival?

2. Explain in your own words why a tree might lean toward light.

3. Do you think the tree knows that it needs what the light provides? Explain.

4. (a)In what ways are people like trees? (b)Specifically, how is the speaker of this poem like the poem's tree?

THEODORE ROETHKE **543**

Assess

1. (a) Students may say that it is uplifting because it talks about living life freely and intuitively. (b) Students might say that they could take life more slowly, noticing the sanctity of things as simple as the ground and a tree.

2. (a) Slowly (b) He lives life slowly but purposefully, noticing beauty in the simplicity of nature.

3. (a) "We think by feeling. What is there to know?" and "I learn by going where I have to go." (b) Thought is a product of emotion and knowledge is gained through living, instead of theorizing.

4. (a) The lowly worm (b) It conveys humility.

5. (a) Naturally we will die. (b) Appreciate the world around us and learn from it.

6. The speaker shows respect for nature and its mystery and ability to teach us.

7. Some students may agree because we always remember what we've lost. Other students may disagree because once something is gone, it leaves our memory.

8. (a) Life should be taken slowly so that we notice the importance of mundane things. We should live by feeling, and learn by living. (b) Some students might like its guidelines for living, while others might not like its emphasis on emotion over thought.

Visual Literacy

1. Light and water

2. The tree goes toward what it needs.

3. It instinctively "knows" that it needs the light; obviously it does not consciously know.

4. (a) People tend toward what they need to stay alive. (b) The speaker gravitates toward what is sustaining.

Assess

Literary Element

1. Students should copy the stanza and mark it using iambic pentameter.

2. They are consistent, like a heartbeat. This promotes living by feeling the rhythms of nature.

Review: Stanza

1. The first and third lines of the first stanza are repeated alternately at the end of each succeeding stanza.

2. (a) Its rhythmic, musical form is appealing. (b) Its rustic tradition is fitting for promoting appreciation for everyday things.

Reading Strategy

1. The words are dark and mysterious, but the line conjures the image of someone facing darkness triumphantly.

2. The mood varies a little.

   stanza 3: joyful, respectful

   stanza 4: mysterious

   stanza 5: humble, encouraging

   stanza 6: hopeful

Literary Element Meter and Rhythm

The basic unit of **meter** is the foot. The length of a metrical line can be expressed in terms of the number of feet it contains (see Literary Handbook). The meter in "The Waking" is iambic pentameter, the most common meter in English poetry. In iambic pentameter, the predominant foot, or unit of rhythm, is the iamb. An iamb is an unstressed syllable followed by a stressed syllable. There are five feet in each line of iambic pentameter. The following lines from "The Waking" are an example of iambic pentameter:

⏑ ´ ⏑ ´ ⏑ ´ ⏑ ´ ⏑ ´
I wake to sleep, and take my waking slow.

⏑ ´ ⏑ ´ ⏑ ´ ⏑ ´ ⏑ ´
I feel my fate in what I cannot fear.

⏑ ´ ⏑ ´ ⏑ ´ ⏑ ´ ⏑ ´
I learn by going where I have to go.

1. Copy the next stanza in the poem and mark the meter as modeled above.

2. How might the meter and rhythm be important to the meaning of the poem?

Review: Stanza

As you learned on page 531, a **stanza** is a group of lines that form a unit in a poem or song. A stanza in a poem is similar to a paragraph in prose. The stanzas in "The Waking" form a villanelle, a 19-line structure divided into five tercets, or three-line stanzas, and one quatrain. (The quatrain is the last stanza.) The most unusual characteristic of the villanelle is its use of refrains, or repeated lines.

While Roethke adheres to the demands of the villanelle, he varies the form slightly to avoid stiffness. For instance, in places he uses slant rhyme, rhyme in which the words rhymed sound similar but do not rhyme exactly (as in *jackal* and *buckle*).

Partner Activity Meet with a partner to discuss the stanzas and refrains of "The Waking." With your partner, answer these questions.

1. How does Roethke vary the refrains in "The Waking"? Provide an example.

2. (a)Why would modern poets choose to write in so limited and demanding a form as the villanelle? (b)Why is the villanelle form appropriate to the subject of "The Waking"?

544 UNIT 3 POETRY

Reading Strategy Analyzing Mood

Mood is a broader term than tone, which refers to the attitude of a speaker or author toward the subject matter of a work. Mood also differs from atmosphere, which is concerned mainly with the physical qualities that contribute to a mood, such as time, place, and weather. Mood is the emotional quality that the work conveys to the reader. The mood of a literary work can be consistent or can change over the course of the piece.

1. "I feel my fate in what I cannot fear." What mood is created by this line?

2. Over the course of the poem, does the mood shift? Chart the mood in each stanza of the poem to determine your answer. Use the chart below as a guide.

Stanza	Mood
1	dark; mysterious; proud
2	happier; shows uncertainty
3	
4	

Academic Vocabulary

Here are two words from the vocabulary list on page R82.

hypothesis (hī poth′ə sis) *n.* a statement or guess made for the purpose of testing and evaluating

simulate (sim′ yə lāt′) *adj.* to imitate the look and/or feel of something

Practice and Apply

1. From this poem, do you think Roethke would support the composing and testing of **hypotheses** as a means of learning? Explain.

2. According to the poem, can humans **simulate** their own reality, or are they dependent on the world as it is? Explain.

Academic Vocabulary

1. He would not support hypothesizing as a way to learn. He believes in learning by living.

2. Humans cannot simulate reality; they are dependent on what nature gives them.

Writing About Literature

Explore Author's Purpose An author's purpose in writing a piece of literature can usually be found in the poem's meaning or message. Write a one- or two-page analysis of Roethke's purpose in writing "The Waking." Use evidence from the poem to defend your position.

Before you begin your draft, use a web like the one below to gather the supporting evidence. In the center oval, write a phrase that describes the author's purpose. In the ovals above the author's purpose, write down individual quotes that relate to the purpose, taking care to write them down accurately. In the ovals below the author's purpose, write down any impressions or ideas that strike you as you read. Once you have completed the web, begin your draft.

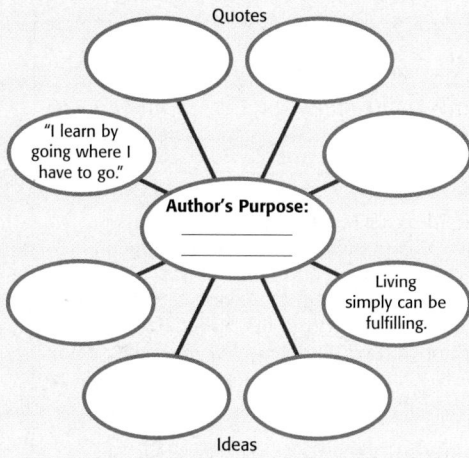

Quotes

"I learn by going where I have to go."

Author's Purpose:
_____

Living simply can be fulfilling.

Ideas

After you complete your draft, meet with a peer reviewer to assess each other's work and to provide constructive criticism. Then proofread and edit your draft for errors in spelling, grammar, and punctuation.

Learning for Life

Start a journal to collect advice you come across about living a happy life. Include poems, quotations, anecdotes, and advice you've heard from friends, family, and people who inspire you. For each bit of advice, be sure to include details about the source as well as the date you discovered the advice.

Roethke's Language and Style

Using Infinitives In "The Waking," Roethke uses simple verb forms, called **infinitives,** to express the simplicity of his philosophy of life. In particular Roethke uses the infinitive form: the root of a verb plus the word *to*. Infinitives generally express the idea of action. Notice Roethke's repeated use of infinitives throughout the poem:

"I wake *to sleep,* and take my waking slow.
I feel my fate in what I cannot fear.
I learn by going where I have *to go.*"

Also notice that Roethke takes care not to "split" his infinitives, or put a word or phrase between *to* and the root of the verb. For example, the sentence *I wanted to not go home* contains a split infinitive. The sentence could be corrected by writing it as *I wanted not to go home.* Whenever possible, you should avoid using split infinitives in your writing.

Activity Make a list of Roethke's infinitives. What do these verbs have in common? Which are repeated? What clues do these words give you to Roethke's purpose and the meaning of the poem?

Revising Check

Infinitives The correct use of infinitives is important to consider when revising your writing. With a partner, go through your analysis of Roethke's purpose and make sure you have correctly used infinitives. Where possible, simplify your verb constructions by using infinitives. When using infinitives, try to avoid splitting them.

Literature Online Web Activities For eFlashcards, Selection Quick Checks, and other Web activities, go to www.glencoe.com.

THEODORE ROETHKE **545**

Assess

Writing About Literature

Students' essays should

- form a thesis about Roethke's purpose in "The Waking."
- support the thesis with quotations from the poem.
- clearly and thoughtfully analyze the supporting quotations.

Learning for Life

Journal entries should include

- dated entries.
- sources of information or ideas.

Roethke's Language and Style

- Roethke uses these infinitives: *to sleep, to go, to do, to know.*
- These verbs are basic and monosyllabic.
- The infinitives *to sleep* and *to go* are repeated, suggesting the speaker's continual process of waking.
- They express Roethke's simple, direct philosophy of life.

Revising Check

Students should

- locate infinitives in their analyses.
- determine whether infinitives were used correctly.
- simplify verb constructions by using infinitives.
- avoid splitting infinitives.

Literature Online

Web Activities Have students access the Web site for interactive activities that will help them assess their understanding of the selection.

Focus

Reapers

BELLRINGER

Bellringer Options
**Selection Focus
Transparency 27
Daily Language Practice
Transparency 51
Or ask:** Where do poets get their ideas? Have students talk about their opinions about how poets generate ideas. Students should mention that poets often get their ideas from everyday experiences.

Author Search To expand students' appreciation of Jean Toomer, have them access the Web site for additional information and resources.

Use the CheckPoint questions on Presentation Plus! to monitor students' comprehension. These questions can be used with interactive response keypads for immediate student feedback.

MEET JEAN TOOMER

Jean Toomer envisioned a new American identity, forged from many races. "Here in America we are in the process of forming a new race," Toomer once said. "I had seen the divisions, the separatisms and antagonisms . . . [yet] a new type of man was arising in this country—not European, not African, not Asiatic—but American. And in this American I saw the divisions mended, the differences reconciled."

A Divided Identity Born in Washington, D.C., Toomer spent most of his childhood living in white neighborhoods while attending African American schools. As a child, he lived with his mother and his grandfather, who was the first governor of African American descent in U.S. history. Even as a child, Toomer was deeply aware of racial divisions in his society. Toomer had both European and African ancestry, and strangers often misidentified him as belonging to one race or another. By the time he graduated from high school, Toomer began to deny any racial identity, instead preferring to classify himself as an American.

After high school, Toomer completed courses in a variety of subjects at several universities, but he never received a degree. Instead, he pursued his literary studies on his own. He attended lectures and read the works of William Shakespeare and Leo Tolstoy. Between 1918 and 1923, Toomer wrote a number of short stories, poems, and plays. He drew his inspiration from the poetry of Walt Whitman and Charles Baudelaire. He also became part of a vibrant literary circle that included novelist Hart Crane and Sherwood Anderson.

Finding His Heritage In 1921 Toomer took a teaching job in Georgia, which turned out to be a life-changing experience. Toomer viewed his time in Georgia as a return to his African American roots. As a result, Toomer wrote

Cane, an experimental novel combining short stories, poems, and a play. The book, published in 1923, inspired authors of the Harlem Renaissance, a great flourishing of African American arts from the 1920s through the 1940s.

> *"We learn the rope of life by untying its knots."*
> —Jean Toomer

Searching for Meaning Toomer was also committed to philosophical enlightenment, which he pursued through yoga and meditation. He also joined the Quakers, attracted by the idea that all people are unified by the spirit of God within them. By 1950 he began to devote himself solely to the pursuit of philosophical teachings.

Toomer's Legacy Despite his early literary success, Toomer's writing was nearly forgotten after his death. Gradually, the significance of his work gained recognition. In 1969 critic Robert Bone wrote: "It was Jean Toomer's genius to discover and to celebrate the qualities of 'soul,' and thereby to inaugurate the Negro Renaissance. For this alone he will be enshrined as a major figure in the canon of American Negro letters."

Jean Toomer was born in 1894 and died in 1967.

Literature Online Author Search For more about Jean Toomer, go to www.glencoe.com.

546 UNIT 3 POETRY

Selection Skills

Literary Elements
- Rhyme and Rhyme Scheme (SE pp. 547, 549)
- Alliteration (TWE p. 548)

Reading Skills
- Analyzing Meter and Rhythm (SE pp. 547, 549)
- Visualizing (SE p. 547)

Reapers

Vocabulary Skills
- Synonyms (SE p. 549)

Writing Skills/Grammar
- Poem Analysis (SE p. 549)

546

Connecting to the Poem

How do you feel about the possibility of machines performing human jobs? Before you read the poem, think about the following questions:

- Do you think that machines and technology have diminished the need for human contact? Explain.
- How do feelings and compassion differentiate people from machines?

Building Background

The Harlem Renaissance, also known as the "New Negro Movement," was a period of great creativity and artistic output among African Americans. Harlem, an African American community in New York City, provided a location for this unprecedented artistic movement to flourish. Artists and writers of the movement often focused on the African American experience in the United States. Writers such as James Weldon Johnson and Langston Hughes were among several African Americans from this period whose works became popular within the mainstream culture.

Setting Purposes for Reading

Big Idea The Energy of the Everyday

As you read "Reapers," notice how Toomer endows a seemingly ordinary event with new energy and emotion.

Literary Element Rhyme and Rhyme Scheme

Rhyme is the repetition of the same stressed vowel sounds and any succeeding sounds in two or more words. End rhyme occurs at the ends of lines of poetry, while internal rhyme occurs within lines. Slant rhymes occur when words include sounds that are similar but do not rhyme exactly. **Rhyme scheme** is the pattern that end rhymes form in a stanza or in a poem. As you read, try to determine the effect of the rhyme and the rhyme scheme found in Toomer's poem.

- See Literary Terms Handbook, p. R14.

Literature Online **Interactive Literary Elements Handbook** To review or learn more about the literary elements, go to www.glencoe.com.

OBJECTIVES
In studying this selection, you will focus on the following:
- understanding rhyme and rhyme scheme
- analyzing a poem's rhythm and meter

Reading Strategy Analyzing Rhythm and Meter

Poets utilize **rhythm and meter** to enhance the musical quality and meaning of their work. While reading "Reapers," **analyze** the meter, the regular pattern of stressed and unstressed syllables, and rhythm, which can be either regular (with a predictable pattern of meter) or irregular, in order to understand what the poet wants to express. For example, the repetitive beat of the poem illustrates the image of the workers swinging the scythes in a consistent rhythm.

Reading Tip: Visualizing Listen to the "beat" of the poem while it is being read aloud. Visualize the images that the author is trying to portray through the rhythm. Use a graphic organizer like the one below to help you determine what images you visualize and how they affect your understanding of the poem.

Line: "And start their silent swinging, one by one."

Images from meter and rhyme: regular motion of people working in the fields; people working in a synchronized way

Effect on mood: somber, tedious, repetitive—makes me think of tiring and dull work

Vocabulary

reapers (rē ′pərs) n. machines or people that cut grain for harvesting; p. 548 *The reapers worked in the fields all day.*

scythes (sīths) n. cutting implements made of a long, curved single-edged blade; p. 548 *The men used scythes to cut through the long wheat in the fields.*

hones (hōnz) n. whetstones or similar tools used to sharpen knives and other types of blades; p. 548 *They used hones to make the knives razor-sharp.*

- visualizing a poem's images
- analyzing criticism by rewriting a poem

JEAN TOOMER **547**

Focus

Summary

The poem's narrator watches farmers harvesting their crops using reaping equipment. The mower runs over a rat but keeps going, illustrating the inhumanity of machines.

V Vocabulary

Vocabulary File Say: Add these words and definitions to your vocabulary file. For each word, include a sentence that gives you an example of how to use the word. **OL** Students with English language needs should include the pronunciations of these words in their files. **EL**

Literary Elements Have students access the Web site to improve their understanding of rhyme and rhyme scheme.

Selection Resources

Print Materials
- 📁 Unit 3 Resources (Fast File), pp. 25–27
- 📁 Selection and Unit Assessments, pp. 89–90
- 📁 Selection Quick Checks, p. 45

Transparencies
- Bellringer Options Transparencies: Daily Language Practice Transparency 51
- Literary Elements Transparency 60

Technology
- 🔘 TeacherWorks Plus™ CD-ROM
- 🔘 StudentWorks Plus™ CD-ROM
- 🔘 Presentation Plus!™ CD-ROM
- 💻 Literature Online, glencoe.com
- 💻 Online Student Edition, mhln.com
- 🔘 ExamView® Assessment Suite CD-ROM
- 🔘 Vocabulary PuzzleMaker CD-ROM
- 🔘 Listening Library, disc 1 track 49

Teach

The Energy of the Everyday Say: While you read the poem, keep the following question in mind: Why would a poet write about such an ordinary event? *(Poets see the unusual in usual activities. They use activities that readers can easily picture to explore more abstract themes.)* **OL**

BI₂ Big Idea

The Energy of the Everyday Answer: *Students may say that Toomer is showing how machines lack the control and sensitivity that humans have. The machine continues cutting, even after injuring the rat, while humans may have shown awareness of or even sympathy for an injured living creature.* **OL**

 CheckPoint

Use the CheckPoint questions on Presentation Plus! to check students' mastery of the selection. These questions can be used with interactive response keypads for immediate student feedback.

Harvesting, 19th Century. Adolphe Joseph Thomas Monticelli. Oil on canvas, 121 x 92.5 cm. Ciurlionis State Art Museum. Kaunas, Lithuania.

Reapers

Jean Toomer

BI₁

Black **reapers** with the sound of steel on stones
Are sharpening **scythes**. I see them place the **hones**
In their hip-pockets as a thing that's done,
And start their silent swinging, one by one.

5 Black horses drive a mower through the weeds,
And there, a field rat, startled, squealing bleeds.
His belly close to ground. I see the blade,
Blood-stained, continue cutting weeds and shade.

Big Idea The Energy of the Everyday *How do these lines add meaning to an otherwise ordinary object?* **BI₂**

Vocabulary

reapers (rē ′pərs) *n.* machines or people that cut grain for harvesting
scythes (sīths) *n.* cutting implements made of a long, curved single-edged blade
hones (hōnz) *n.* whetstones or similar tools used to sharpen knives and other types of blades

548 UNIT 3 POETRY

Additional Support

Skills Practice

LITERARY ELEMENT: Alliteration
Say: Alliteration means that an initial sound is repeated in two or more nearby words. The phrase "happy holidays" is an example because the "h" sound starts both words. Have students identify examples of alliteration in the poem. **Ask:** Why do poets use alliteration? *(Students should answer that alliteration helps create the poem's rhythm.)* **OL**

RESPONDING AND THINKING CRITICALLY

Respond

1. What are your feelings about farm machinery after reading the poem?

Recall and Interpret

2. (a)Describe in your own words what the reapers do. (b)What attitude do the reapers seem to have toward their work?

3. (a)What happens to the field rat in the poem? (b)Why do you think Toomer includes this incident?

4. (a)What sound does the injured rat make? (b)What effect does this sound have as you read the poem?

Analyze and Evaluate

5. (a)What connections do you see between the reapers and the horses? (b)Why do you think Toomer links the reapers and the horses in this way?

6. (a)How does the rhythm of this poem reflect its content? (b)If the poem did not have this kind of rhythm, would it have the same impact? Explain.

7. (a)What do you think is Toomer's purpose in writing this poem? (b)Do you think Toomer accomplishes his purpose in the poem? Explain.

Connect

8. **Big Idea** **The Energy of the Everyday** How does the meter of "Reapers" add to the reader's sensory experience of "the everyday"?

Literary Element Rhyme and Rhyme Scheme

Toomer uses a particular rhyme and rhyme scheme to achieve a certain purpose. **Rhyme scheme** is designated by the assignment of a different letter of the alphabet to each new rhyme. For example, in the first four lines of Toomer's poem "Georgia Dusk," the rhyme scheme is *abba:*

The sky, lazily disdaining to pursue	*a*
The setting sun, too indolent to hold	*b*
A lengthened tournament for flashing gold,	*b*
Passively darkens for night's barbeque[.]	*a*

These lines also contain **end rhyme** ("hold," "gold") and **internal rhyme** ("tournament," "indolent").

1. What kind of rhyme does "Reapers" have? Explain.

2. What is the rhyme scheme of "Reapers"? How is it important to the poem?

Literary Criticism

Critic Motley Deakin remarks that "the general effect of [Toomer's] poetry is a loosening of poetic structures, a movement towards prose." Evaluate this idea by rewriting "Reapers" as prose. When you are finished, decide whether you agree with this critic's analysis. Why or why not?

Reading Strategy Analyzing Meter and Rhythm

Poets often try to convey meaning through meter and rhythm.

1. Describe the rhythm of "Reapers."

2. How do you think the rhythm is important to the meaning of the poem?

3. Try reading the poem with a different rhythm. Does this change the poem's effect? Explain.

Vocabulary Practice

Practice with Synonyms Choose the synonym for each vocabulary word from "Reapers."

1. reapers
 a. harvesters   **b.** slaves

2. scythes
 a. knives   **b.** machines

3. hones
 a. whetstones   **b.** steel

Literature Online **Web Activities** For eFlashcards, Selection Quick Checks, and other Web activities, go to www.glencoe.com.

JEAN TOOMER **549**

Assess

1. Answers will vary.

2. (a) Use scythes to cut down weeds (b) Matter-of-fact and deliberate

3. (a) The mower runs over it. (b) To show that the machines lack human sensitivity

4. (a) It squeals. (b) It makes the reader uncomfortable, feeling the rat's suffering.

5. (a) Both are black. (b) To show how the field work dehumanizes the men

6. (a) The rhythm reflects the swinging of the reapers' scythes. (b) No, because the poem would lose the sense of tedious routine that the reapers face each day.

7. (a) To contrast humans and machines to show that machines are a poor substitute for human labor (b) Some students may say yes because of how he structured the poem as comparison.

8. The meter simulates the rhythm of the workers' scythes swinging motion. Toomer also uses meter and rhythm to copy the sound that a machine might make through a repeated pattern of sounds.

Literary Element

1. End rhyme

2. *aabbccdd;* it creates a consistent sense of rhythm, like the reapers' labor.

Literary Criticism

Students should
- rewrite poem using prose
- present an opinion regarding critic's analysis
- explain reasoning

Reading Strategy

1. The rhythm is plodding and repetitive.
2. It reflects the nature of farm work.
3. Answers will vary.

Literature Online

Web Activities Have students access the Web site for interactive activities that will help them assess their understanding of the selection.

Vocabulary

1. a   **2.** a   **3.** a

Focus

BELLRINGER

Bellringer Options
**Selection Focus
Transparency 28
Daily Language Practice
Transparency 52**
Or show students any number of "ordinary" things—a belt, a piece of fruit, or a mug, for example.
Ask: What makes these items special? Instruct students to list the exceptional qualities of the objects. Then ask students to note any personal connection to them. Explain that everyday things can represent meaningful times, events, or people in our lives.

Literature Online

Author Search To expand students' appreciation of Pablo Neruda, have them access the Web site for additional information and resources.

CheckPoint

Use the CheckPoint questions on Presentation Plus! to monitor students' comprehension. These questions can be used with interactive response keypads for immediate student feedback.

Ode to My Socks

MEET PABLO NERUDA

Equally enchanted with a pair of socks, an artichoke, or olive oil, the poet Pablo Neruda (pä´blō nä rōō´dä) could transform any ordinary object into a rich treasure. He was a master of the ode, a poem that praises its subject matter, and collected these poems in a book called *Elemental Odes.* These odes were full of celebration for the objects and circumstances of everyday life, a reflection of Neruda's desire to write for the common person rather than an exclusive or esoteric audience.

Neruda was born Neftalí Ricardo Reyes Basoalto in rural Chile. His father was a railway worker and his mother was a teacher. Neruda began writing poetry at the age of ten and published his first book of poems at age nineteen, under the pen name "Pablo Neruda." He later legally changed his name.

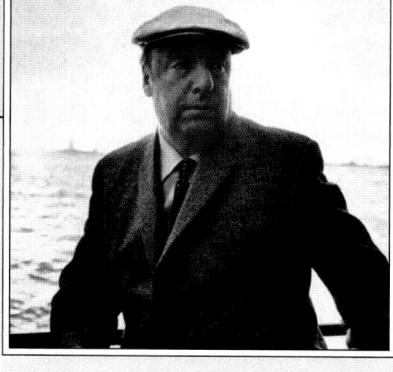

"I could not live separated from nature."

—Pablo Neruda

A Life of Poetry and Passion His second book, *Twenty Love Poems and a Song of Despair,* was an instant success, and Neruda was well on his way to becoming a world-renowned poet. However, despite his early success with poetry, he did not reject his other passions, namely his interest in politics and social causes. Shortly after the publication of his first two books, he went to Asia as Chile's honorary consul. This was the first of many positions in his consular career, which would take him to Spain, France, and Mexico.

Love, Nature, and Social Concerns Neruda is widely known for his poetry featuring

passionate and poignant expressions of love. However, his works cover a broad range of subjects. Many of his odes focus their attention on simple subjects such as those found in nature, a beloved theme of Neruda's.

Neruda also desired to make his poems accessible; he did not believe in poetry as an elitist art form. His major work, *Canto General,* was a book of 340 poems that celebrated the history of Latin America from ancient times. He was equally passionate regarding social justice for the people of his native Chile and was involved in political causes there throughout his life. Neruda's controversial communist beliefs led to his exile from his native country for a number of years. He returned to his beloved Chile in 1952 and lived there until his death in 1973, twelve days after the defeat of Chile's democratic leadership by the dictator General Augusto Pinochet. His works were banned under the oppressive Pinochet regime until 1990.

Neruda's poetry was celebrated throughout his life. Chile awarded him the National Literature Prize in 1945. In 1971 he received the Nobel Prize in Literature "for poetry that with action of an elemental force brings alive a continent's destiny and dreams."

Pablo Neruda was born in 1904 and died in 1973.

Literature Online **Interactive Literary Elements Handbook** To review or learn more about the literary elements, go to www.glencoe.com.

Selection Skills

Literary Elements

Ode to My Socks

- Free Verse (SE pp. 551, 553, 555)
- Structure (SE p. 555)

Reading Skills

- Monitoring Comprehension (SE pp. 551, 553, 555)
- Activating Prior Knowledge (TWE p. 552)

Vocabulary Skills

- Practice with Word Parts (SE pp. 551, 555)
- Academic Vocabulary (SE p. 555)

Listening/Speaking/Viewing Skills

- Performing (SE p. 556)
- Analyzing Art (TWE p. 552)

Writing Skills/Grammar

- Analyze Genre Elements (SE p. 556)
- Using Adjectives (SE p. 556)

Connecting to the Poem

The following poem pays homage to a pair of socks that Pablo Neruda treasures. Before you read the poem, think about the following questions:

- How do material objects in your possession become important to you?
- Of your prized possessions, which is most valuable to you? Why?

Building Background

Traditionally, odes are long, lyrical poems that often use seven- and eleven-syllable rhythms. Odes are categorized by their expression of noble and dignified feelings. They also typically exalt their subject matter. Pablo Neruda, who once said, "My poetry became clear and happy when it branched off towards humbler subjects and things," satisfied only part of this definition. While Neruda's odes do famously celebrate their subjects, they do not flaunt the lofty style characterized by traditional odes. Rather, they sing the praises of the ordinary, the fundamental, and the essential.

Setting Purposes for Reading

Big Idea The Energy of the Everyday

As you read "Ode to My Socks," try to appreciate the narrator's reverence for his socks, an everyday item. Focus, too, on the significance of the ideas and images flanking the ode's subject.

Literary Element Free Verse

Free verse is poetry without a fixed pattern of rhyme, meter, line length, or stanza arrangement. Traditional rules of form are often replaced with techniques such as repetition and alliteration to generate the poem's musical configurations. As you read, notice how the unrestrained feel of the free verse form affects the way in which Neruda communicates his ideas.

- See Literary Terms Handbook, p. R7.

Literature Online Interactive Literary Elements Handbook To review or learn more about the literary elements, go to www.glencoe.com.

OBJECTIVES
In studying this selection, you will focus on the following:
- understanding free verse
- using paraphrasing and questioning to monitor comprehension

Reading Strategy Monitoring Comprehension

When you **paraphrase**, you restate a text's meaning in your own words. **Questioning** a text involves asking yourself about the relevance of a given selection. **Monitoring comprehension** by paraphrasing and questioning can help you better understand a work.

Reading Tip: Keeping Track of Your Understanding
After reading "Ode to My Socks" once, revisit each stanza individually. As you complete a stanza, paraphrase it and ask yourself questions about its meaning. Use a chart to record your use of paraphrasing and questioning.

Stanza	Maru Mori brought me / a pair / of socks / which she knitted herself / with her sheepherder's hands, / two socks as soft / as rabbits.
Paraphrase	A loved one or friend knitted, with her own hands, a delicate pair of socks.
Question	Why has the author described Maru Mori's hands as "sheepherder's hands"?
Answer	Sheepherders, by trade, protect and care for flocks of sheep. This image is a metaphor for his friend's loving ways.

Vocabulary

immense (i mens´) *adj.* immeasurable; vast; huge; p. 553 *I felt immense pleasure in presenting the student with the scholarship.*

decrepit (di krep´it) *adj.* ruined with age; depleted; p. 553 *The decrepit bus did not look safe.*

sacred (sā´krid) *adj.* worthy of reverence; p. 553 *The archaeologist eagerly uncovered the sacred texts.*

remorse (ri môrs´) *n.* distress stemming from the guilt of past wrongs; p. 553 *The sobbing prisoner showed remorse in court.*

Vocabulary Tip: Word Parts The main part of a word is its *root*. Additional word parts such as *prefixes* or *suffixes* can be added to the root to form new words.

- analyzing structure and its effects on a text
- writing to analyze genre elements

PABLO NERUDA **551**

Focus

Summary

The narrator has been given a simple pair of socks. He treasures the gift immensely, and through a string of beautiful descriptions and metaphors, convinces the reader of their significance.

V Vocabulary

Vocabulary File Say: Add these words and definitions to your vocabulary file. For each word, include a sentence that gives you an example of how to use the word. **OL** Students with English language needs should include the pronunciations of these words in their files. **EL**

Literary Elements Have students access the Web site to improve their understanding of free verse.

Selection Resources

Print Materials
- 📂 Unit 3 Resources (Fast File), pp. 28–30
- 📂 Leveled Vocabulary Development, p. 41
- 📂 Selection and Unit Assessments, pp. 91–92
- 📂 Selection Quick Checks, p. 46

Transparencies
- Bellringer Options Transparencies: Daily Language Practice Transparency 52
- Literary Elements Transparency 49

Technology
- 🔘 TeacherWorks Plus™ CD-ROM
- 🔘 StudentWorks Plus™ CD-ROM
- 🔘 Presentation Plus!™ CD-ROM
- 💻 Literature Online, glencoe.com
- 💻 Online Student Edition, mhln.com
- 🔘 ExamView® Assessment Suite CD-ROM
- 🔘 Vocabulary PuzzleMaker CD-ROM
- 🔘 Listening Library, disc 1 track 50

Big Idea

The Energy of the Everyday Say: Think about the following questions while reading: How does the narrator convince the reader of his socks' importance? Why might he be interested in exalting a pair of socks? *(He describes their softness, beauty, and usefulness. He appreciates simplicity and encourages the reverence of ordinary things.)* **OL**

★ Viewing the Art

Pablo Picasso (1881–1973) was one of the most influential artists of the 20th century. He is one of the founders of the Cubist art movement, which emphasizes that it is necessary to look at something from several points of view in order to truly understand it. At an early age, Picasso showed an amazing ability to draw, as exhibited in the sketch *Foot*. Picasso's father helped him put on his first exhibition when Picasso was thirteen. **AS**

Foot, 1894. Pablo Picasso. Charcoal and conte crayon on paper, 33.2 x 49.7 cm. Museu Picasso, Barcelona, Spain.

Ode to My Socks

Pablo Neruda
Translated by Robert Bly

Additional Support

READING: Activating Prior Knowledge Students will enhance their understanding of this selection by drawing on prior knowledge. They can use the events in Neruda's poem to recall similar experiences of their own, thereby improving their comprehension of the text. **Ask:** What objects hold sincere meaning in your life? *(Examples: sweaters, jewelry boxes, baseballs)* Help students expand prior knowledge by asking them to recall a specific story that endeared them to the object. Share these events aloud. **OL**

Maru Mori brought me
a pair
of socks
which she knitted herself
5 with her sheepherder's hands,
two socks as soft
as rabbits.
I slipped my feet
into them
10 as though into
two
cases
knitted
with threads of
15 twilight
and sheepskin.

Violent socks,
my feet were
two fish made
20 of wool,
two long sharks
sea-blue, shot
through
by one golden thread,
25 two **immense** blackbirds,
two cannons:
my feet
were honored
in this way
30 by
these
heavenly
socks.
They were
35 so handsome
for the first time
my feet seemed to me
unacceptable
like two **decrepit**
40 firemen, firemen
unworthy
of that woven
fire,
of those glowing
45 socks.

Nevertheless
I resisted
the sharp temptation
to save them somewhere
50 as schoolboys
keep
fireflies,
as learned men
collect
55 **sacred** texts,
I resisted
the mad impulse
to put them
into a golden
60 cage
and each day give them
birdseed
and pieces of pink melon.
Like explorers
65 in the jungle who hand
over the very rare
green deer
to the spit[1]
and eat it
70 with **remorse**,
I stretched out
my feet
and pulled on
the magnificent
75 socks
and then my shoes.

The moral
of my ode is this:
beauty is twice
80 beauty
and what is good is doubly
good
when it is a matter of two socks
made of wool
85 in winter.

---

1. A *spit* is a rod on which meat is roasted.

Big Idea The Energy of the Everyday *What kind of schoolboy impulse is the author trying to convey here?* **BI**

Literary Element Free Verse *What elements of free verse does the writer use here?* **L**

Vocabulary

sacred (sāʹkrid) *adj.* worthy of reverence
remorse (ri môrsʹ) *n.* distress stemming from the guilt of past wrongs

---

Reading Strategy Monitoring Comprehension *How might you paraphrase this line?* **R**

Vocabulary

immense (i mensʹ) *adj.* immeasurable; vast; huge
decrepit (di krepʹit) *adj.* ruined with age; depleted

R Reading Strategy

Monitoring Comprehension Answer: *Answers will vary, but may be similar to "extremely colorful socks."* OL

BI Big Idea

The Energy of the Everyday Answer: *The hunting or seizing impulse that schoolboys seem to have with objects that fascinate them* OL

L Literary Element

Free Verse Answer: *Varied line length, no set meter, and use of alliteration* OL

CheckPoint

Use the CheckPoint questions on Presentation Plus! to check students' mastery of the selection. These questions can be used with interactive response keypads for immediate student feedback.

Differentiated Instruction

Peer Tutoring Proficient readers can offer less proficient readers intensive one-on-one instruction and bolster their confidence. Pair advanced readers with less proficient readers to model proper decoding skills and fluency. Use questions like the following: How does the narrator's reverence for his socks relate to materialism? How does it differ? *(Materialism denotes an unhealthy love of "things." The narrator's preoccupation with his socks might be seen as materialistic. The narrator's love of his socks does not suggest that he covets other things with the same passion.)* **BL**

Objectives
• To use paraphrasing and questioning to monitor comprehension (SE)
• To understand free verse (SE)
• To activate prior knowledge (TWE)

Assess

1. Students might say that sentimental value is greater than materialistic value.

2. (a) Fish; sharks; blackbirds; cannons; decrepit firemen (b) The images are not beautiful and contrast with the beautiful socks.

3. (a) As cold and uninviting, like fish or sharks (b) Decrepit firemen are ineffective against a blaze, and the narrator's feet aren't up to facing "that woven fire" of the socks.

4. (a) Schoolboys with fireflies and learned men with sacred texts (b) The temptation seems to be innate and universal, since these two examples are of vastly different groups: carefree schoolboys and learned men. The author might suggest that concealing beautiful things is a natural impulse.

5. Students should refer to Neruda's reverential descriptions of the socks using content from the poem.

6. (a) Students may cite such straightforward examples as "my feet were two fish made of wool" or "two socks as soft as rabbits." (b) To relay ideas in a more natural, accessible way

7. The summary increases reader confidence in interpreting the poem.

554

RESPONDING AND THINKING CRITICALLY

Respond

1. Has Neruda's tribute to his socks affected how you feel about your socks? How has it affected your feelings about material possessions in general?

Recall and Interpret

2. (a) What has the speaker called his feet? (b) Why might the speaker choose to represent feet in so many ways?

3. (a) In lines 18–24, how does the speaker perceive his feet? (b) In lines 39–40, why do you think the speaker compares his feet to "two decrepit firemen"?

4. (a) According to the speaker, which two types of people hoard things? (b) From where might this temptation to hoard come?

Analyze and Evaluate

5. How well has Neruda expressed the meaningfulness of these socks? Explain.

6. (a) Using specific examples, explain how Neruda has veered from the traditional form of an ode. (b) Why do you think Neruda chose to break with tradition in writing this ode?

7. How might Neruda's decision to summarize his ode in the last stanza affect the reader's interpretation of its ideas?

Connect

8. **Big Idea** The Energy of the Everyday Neruda is known for his praise of the ordinary. What examples best illustrate this characteristic in "Ode to My Socks?" Explain.

YOU'RE THE CRITIC: Different Viewpoints

Ode to the Elementary

Pablo Neruda's odes differ greatly from the traditional form. Although some traditionalists might prefer the conventional form, most readers and critics respond favorably to Neruda's innovative approach. Read the following literary criticism excerpt and answer the questions that follow.

"The 'Elemental Odes'. . . were like nothing else people had seen. With them, Neruda hoped to reach a wider audience than he already had, and his hope was realized. The 'Odes' gained immediate and universal praise. They are about the things of everyday life: a lemon, a dead carob tree, a boy with a hare, a stamp album. And they were read by people who had never before paid attention to poetry. Written in very short lines, some as short as a single word, the 'Odes' tumble effortlessly down the page in chainlike sentences. Everything is seen in its best light, everything has value, everything deserves to be the subject of a poem."

—Mark Strand, the *New Yorker*

The Magician, 1992. Maria Angelica Ruiz-Tagle. Oil on canvas, 130 x 97 cm.

1. How do you think someone who prefers traditional odes, which have an elevated style, would respond to Strand's comments?

2. Which opinion do you agree with more: that Neruda created a valuable and accessible new kind of ode, or that his modifications degraded the form? Support your opinion.

3. What changes might a traditionalist make to Neruda's poem "Ode to My Socks"?

---

8. The poem's subject, socks, is a celebration of the ordinary, as are other objects present in the ode, like a friend knitting socks and twilight.

You're the Critic

1. They might disagree with him, saying Neruda should have followed the form's conventions.

2. Most students will respond favorably to Neruda's odes, citing their accessibility and cleverness; however, some students might find ordinary subjects unworthy of praiseful poetry.

3. Structure the poem like classic verse (in seven- and eleven-syllable rhythms), use an elevated style, and choose a worthy subject.

Literary Element Free Verse

With **free verse**, a writer is not bound by form or arrangement. An author may embark upon the subject matter with less regard for traditional form. Rather, the writer has freedom to arrange the lines and stanzas according to sound, the importance of ideas, appearances, or any other criteria the author personally chooses. The free verse Neruda uses in his odes has been praised for creating "a river of print flowing down the page."

1. Which lines in "Ode to My Socks" would you say are the most unconventional? Explain.

2. How do the varied line lengths affect the recitation of the poem?

Review: Structure

As you learned on pages 528–529, **structure** is the distinct order or arrangement used to present a writer's ideas. Ideas may be presented in a variety of ways, including chronologically, according to relevancy, or in order of importance.

Group Activity With a group of two or three classmates, analyze the structure of "Ode to My Socks." Assign one stanza to each student for evaluation. Once all group members have examined a stanza, record your group's findings in a chart similar to the one below. Use the left-hand column to indicate the stanza number. Use the right-hand column to describe the stanza's structure.

Stanza	Structure
Maru Mori brought me / a pair / of socks / which she knitted herself / with her sheepherder's hands, / two socks as soft / as rabbits. / I slipped my feet / into them / as though into / two / cases / knitted / with threads of / twilight / and sheepskin.	This stanza is ordered sequentially.

Reading Strategy Monitoring Comprehension

Monitoring comprehension can help you gain a deeper understanding of a poem and its meaning, especially in an unconventional poem like this Neruda ode. Use the strategies of paraphrasing and questioning to help you uncover meaning. A good way to monitor your comprehension is to paraphrase the entire selection and then ask yourself questions about what elements are most important.

1. Paraphrase the events in "Ode to My Socks."

2. What, do you think, is the most important aspect of this poem?

Vocabulary Practice

Practice with Word Parts Identify the correct word part for each vocabulary word. Use a dictionary if you need help.

1. What is the prefix in **immense**?
   a. -se   **b.** mens   **c.** im-

2. What part of **decrepit** is a prefix that usually means "out of" or "away from"?
   a. crep   **b.** -it   **c.** de-

3. What is the root of **sacred**?
   a. -red   **b.** acre   **c.** sacr

4. What is the root of **remorse**?
   a. mors   **b.** re-   **c.** -se

Academic Vocabulary

Here are two words from the vocabulary list on page R82. These words will help you think, write, and talk about the selection.

compatible (kəm pat′ə bəl) *adj.* able to exist together amicably

fluctuate (fluk′ chōō āt′) *v.* to waver; to move backward and forward or up and down

Practice and Apply
1. How does Neruda make the stanzas of "Ode to My Socks" **compatible**?
2. How does Neruda make the lines **fluctuate**?

PABLO NERUDA **555**

Assess

Literary Element

1. Students should cite very short lines and lines that use very simple diction, since this is a key difference between Neruda's odes and conventional ones.

2. It causes the reader to pause in the middle of thoughts that would usually require no pause.

Review: Structure

Students charts might show the following:
Stanza 2: a series of metaphors for his feet, reflecting decreasing worthiness
Stanza 3: chronologically from resisting each temptation to putting on the socks
Stanza 4: a summary of this theme, going from abstract to concrete

Reading Strategy

1. A friend brought the narrator a pair of knitted socks, sewn with her own hands. When he slipped the socks on, he could not believe how soft they were. After this, the narrator started comparing them to a lot of different things, including his own feet. He was tempted to hide the socks but decides not to, figuring that he has been doubly blessed with something both beautiful and useful.

2. Students might say the simplicity of style and tone—as well as that of the subject matter—is the most important aspect because it makes it more accessible and widens the audience for poetry.

Vocabulary

1. c   2. c   3. c   4. a

Academic Vocabulary

1. The stanzas adhere to a free verse form that brings out a musical quality of the words.

2. With varying lengths

Assess

Writing About Literature

Students' essays should

- identify which genre elements Neruda used in his ode and which he rejected.

- give specific examples from the text to support their ideas.

- use correct spelling, grammar, and punctuation.

Performing

Students' performances should

- relay the events in the poem.

- mimic the emotional quality of the poem.

- demonstrate creativity.

Neruda's Language and Style

Students' analyses should

- list the adjectives in each stanza.

- classify the importance of each adjective.

Writing About Literature

Analyze Genre Elements "I confess that to write with simplicity has been my most difficult undertaking." These sentiments, expressed by Neruda, seem to contradict the nature of a traditional ode, which has four general qualities: an ode uses and describes exalted, intensified emotions; it elevates its subject matter in a noble manner; it uses complex stanza forms; and it embodies the musical qualities of lyric poetry. Write a one- to two-page essay that analyzes Neruda's use of genre elements in "Ode to My Socks."

Before you draft your essay, record on the chart below examples in which Neruda uses the genre elements and those where he does not.

Genre Element	Used?	Examples
Exalted, intensified emotion	Yes and No	The poem overall is not very emotional, but Neruda does say that he resists "sharp temptations" and "wild impulses," which suggest strong feelings.
Elevated subject		
Complex stanza forms		
Musical qualities/ Lyric poetry		

Once your draft is complete, ask a peer reviewer to evaluate your work. Then proofread and edit your draft for errors in spelling, grammar, and punctuation.

Performing

With a classmate, deliver a performance of "Ode to My Socks." Through pantomiming and recitation, relay the events and emotions illustrated in the poem to your classmates. Decide who will read the poem and who will act out the speaker's words. Demonstrate your creativity by adding lighting, music, and slides to your performance, or present a simple pantomime version with just words and meaningful movement.

Neruda's Language and Style

Using Adjectives Throughout "Ode to My Socks," Neruda uses adjectives efficiently and eloquently to express the qualities of his socks. Consider his use of adjectives in the following example:

> I resisted
> the mad impulse
> to put them
> into a golden
> cage . . .

Neruda strikes a balance between using enough adjectives for the reader to appreciate his subject and not crowding his poem with description. Consider how the poem would be different without any adjectives.

> I resisted
> the impulse
> to put them
> into a
> cage . . .

Then think about how the poem would be different if Neruda had overused adjectives.

> I, wise, resisted
> the mad impulse
> to put them
> into a gilded, golden
> cage . . .

In each example, under- or overusing adjectives alters the desired image.

Activity Create a two-column chart to analyze the adjectives in "Ode to My Socks." In the first column, list the adjective. In the second column, determine how important you think each adjective is: low, medium, or high.

Revising Check

Adjectives Choosing appropriate adjectives to describe nouns will help you clarify your writing. Review your essay about genre elements in "Ode to My Socks." Determine the relevance of each adjective you used in your essay and make any changes that you deem necessary.

Literature Online Web Activities For eFlashcards, Selection Quick Checks, and other Web activities, go to www.glencoe.com.

Revising Check

Students should

- locate adjectives in their essays.

- review relevance of each adjective and make necessary changes.

Web Activities Have students access the Web site for interactive activities that will help them assess their understanding of the selection.

A Storm in the Mountains

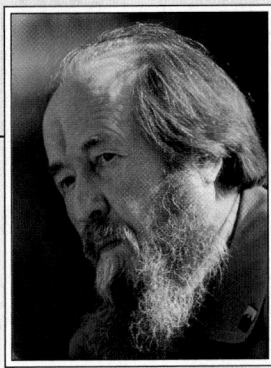

MEET ALEKSANDR SOLZHENITSYN

In a life rendered chaotic—personally, professionally and politically—Aleksandr Isayevich Solzhenitsyn created order through his writing.

Born to a widowed mother, who worked as a typist to support her only child, Solzhenitsyn sacrificed his literary ambitions to pursue degrees in mathematics and physics. Yet he still loved literature, so much that he enrolled in correspondence courses in literature at Moscow State University.

Solzhenitsyn served in the Russian army during World War II. However, in 1945 he was arrested and charged with treason for writing a personal letter in which he criticized Soviet ruler Joseph Stalin. The government sentenced Solzhenitsyn, without a fair trial, to eight years in a camp for political prisoners.

"Own only what you can carry with you; know language, know countries, know people. Let your memory be your travel bag."

—Aleksandr Solzhenitsyn

During his imprisonment, Solzhenitsyn worked as a mathematician and physicist. He was later transferred to a forced-labor camp, where he contracted intestinal cancer. It was not treated until he was near death. Eventually, he was sent to Khazakhstan for treatment and survived. Finally, in 1956, he was freed from exile.

Memory as Inspiration Throughout his entire ordeal, Solzhenitsyn wrote in secret. The experiences of his forced imprisonment and illness served as the basis for his writing. Eventually, Solzhenitsyn decided to take his secret writing public. He published his first work, *One Day in the Life of Ivan Denisovich*, a widely read tale of an "everyman" dealing with the horrors of a single day in a forced labor camp. The book sparked political attention and activity in both the Soviet Union and abroad.

The Line That Shifts Though he suffered government retaliation for his publications, Solzhenitsyn continued to publish his politically-charged fiction. Awarded the Nobel Prize for Literature in 1970, Solzhenitsyn did not accept his prize in person, fearing that the Soviet government would not allow him to reenter the country.

The Gulag Archipelago (1973)—a catalogue of Soviet abuses detailing the harsh labor camps called the "Gulag"—established Solzhenitsyn as a chronicler of modern Russian history. The controversial publication, however, led to another exile in 1974.

Solzhenitsyn lived and wrote in the United States until the *glasnost*—a political openness that allowed for criticism of the government—brought Russians a renewed interest and wider accessibility to his writing, prompting a return to his homeland in 1994.

Aleksandr Solzhenitsyn was born in 1918.

Literature Online **Author Search** For more about Aleksandr Solzhenitsyn, go to www.glencoe.com.

ALEKSANDR SOLZHENITSYN **557**

Focus

BELLRINGER

Bellringer Options
Daily Language Practice Transparency 53
Or have students write a paragraph to describe their perceptions of a storm in the mountains. **Say:** Think about encountering a storm in the mountains. Write a paragraph to describe what you might think, feel, and do. Select words carefully to help your readers understand your meaning.

Literature Online

Author Search To expand students' appreciation of Aleksandr Solzhenitsyn, have them access the Web site for additional information and resources.

CheckPoint

Use the CheckPoint questions on Presentation Plus! to monitor students' comprehension. These questions can be used with interactive response keypads for immediate student feedback.

Selection Skills

Literary Elements
- Prose Poetry (SE pp. 558, 561)

A Storm in the Mountains

Listening/Speaking/Viewing Skills
- Analyzing Art (TWE p. 559)

Reading Skills
- Visualizing (SE pp. 558, 560, 561)

Vocabulary Skills
- Analogies (SE pp. 558, 561)

Writing Skills/Grammar
- Songwriting (SE p. 561)

Study Skills/Research/Assessment
- Nature in Poetry (TWE p. 560)

Focus

Summary

A thunderstorm might bring welcome rain and relief to hopeful farmers facing drought. Or it might create a frightening scenario in which people are forced to fight for their lives. Whatever the situation, a thunderstorm shows nature at its most powerful and majestic. In a storm, common objects often seem to be something they are not, and imagination can run to unexpected places.

V Vocabulary

Vocabulary File Say: Add these words and definitions to your vocabulary file. For each word, include a sentence that gives you an example of how to use the word. **OL** Students with English language needs should include the pronunciations of these words in their files. **EL**

Literary Elements Have students access the Web site to improve their understanding of prose poetry.

Connecting to the Poem

The speaker of this poem describes his sense of awe at the power of an intense thunderstorm. Using vivid language, Solzhenitsyn shows the reader how inspiring nature can be. Before you read the poem, think about the following questions:

- How would you react if you had no shelter and were caught in a sudden thunderstorm?
- Recall a time when you witnessed severe weather. How did it make you feel?

Building Background

The former Soviet Union, also known as the Union of Soviet Socialist Republics, or U.S.S.R., was vast in size. It spanned from the Pacific Ocean to the Baltic and Black seas, over 6,800 miles from east to west. From north to south it stretched 2,800 miles. It consisted of 8,650,000 total square miles; the equivalent of over two times the area of the United States. The climate of the Soviet Union varied greatly. Its northern latitude and the southern mountain barriers ensured that the majority of the region had a cold climate. Extreme weather was common; only winter and summer existed as distinct seasons. The milder temperatures of spring and fall were typically short-lived points during periods of rapid weather change.

Setting Purposes for Reading

Big Idea The Energy of the Everyday

As you read, note the descriptive language Solzhenitsyn uses to describe an event as common as a storm.

Literary Element Prose Poetry

An alternative to verse form, **prose poetry** avoids line breaks and uses sentence and paragraph form instead. As you read, notice how prose poetry relies largely on imagery to convey ideas and emotions.

- See Literary Terms Handbook, p. R13.

Literature Online **Interactive Literary Elements Handbook** To review or learn more about the literary elements, go to www.glencoe.com.

OBJECTIVES
In studying this selection, you will focus on the following:
- understanding and analyzing prose poetry

Reading Strategy Visualizing

Visualizing is using words to create a mental picture. Authors often use imagery to help readers put themselves into the environment or mood of a poem or story. Visualizing is not limited to visual images; it encompasses perceptions from all five senses. While reading this poem, create a mental representation of the sensations described.

Reading Tip: Creating a List Use a chart like the one below to list examples of words or phrases from the poem that appeal to your senses.

Words/Expressions	Sense
"Everything was black—no peaks, no valleys, no horizon to be seen."	Sight

Vocabulary

searing (sēr´ing) *adj.* extremely hot or bright; p. 560 *The searing sunlight woke me up before my alarm clock went off.*

chaos (kā´os) *n.* a state of disorder and confusion; p. 560 *After the tornado hit, the town was filled with chaos.*

gorge (gôrj) *n.* the passageway between two higher land areas, such as a narrow valley; p. 560 *The Grand Canyon is one of the United States' most famous gorges.*

serpentine (sur´pən tēn´) *adj.* snake-like, twisting, winding; p. 560 *He had to pay attention as he drove on the serpentine mountain road.*

primal (prī´məl) *adj.* a basic, original state of being; p. 560 *One primal instinct is survival.*

Vocabulary Tip: Practice with Analogies Analogies show the relationship between words or ideas. You can use analogies to better understand difficult or unfamiliar words.

- using visualizing to better understand a text
- writing song lyrics to express a poem's theme

558 UNIT 3 POETRY

Selection Resources

Print Materials
- Unit 3 Resources (Fast File), pp. 31–33
- Leveled Vocabulary Development, p. 42
- Selection and Unit Assessments, pp. 93–94
- Selection Quick Checks, p. 47

Transparencies
- Bellringer Options Transparencies: Daily Language Practice Transparency 53
- Literary Elements Transparency 51

Technology
- TeacherWorks Plus™ CD-ROM
- StudentWorks Plus™ CD-ROM
- Presentation Plus!™ CD-ROM
- Literature Online, glencoe.com
- Online Student Edition, mhln.com
- ExamView® Assessment Suite CD-ROM
- Vocabulary PuzzleMaker CD-ROM
- Listening Library, disc 1 track 51

Before the Separation, 1999. Brenda Chrystie.

A Storm in the Mountains

Aleksandr Isayevich Solzhenitsyn
Translated by Michael Glenny

Big Idea

The Energy of the Everyday **Say:** Keep the following questions in mind as you read. **Ask:** How do the author's words help you to visualize the energy of the storm in the mountains? How do you think the author feels about the storm he describes? *(Students should identify words like "plunged" and "bursting" as conveying energy. Words like "awe" and "hugeness" show how the author feels about the magnitude of the storm.)* **OL**

Differentiated Instruction

Critical Response Encourage gifted and talented readers to write a response to the poem. **Say:** Solzhenitsyn writes about the power and turbulence of an unexpected mountain thunderstorm. In the end, though, instead of panic or fear, he describes an atmosphere of tranquility. Write a short essay describing your feelings about the poem and why you agree or disagree with the conclusions the author has drawn. *(Students should note that words like "primal" and "insignificant" indicate that the author sees himself and others as part of a "grand plan." Students should express and support their opinions.)* **AL**

Objective
• To establish a purpose for reading (TWE)

R Reading Strategy

Visualization *Students may say that the description of the landscape springing back helps them picture the surroundings as they are brightened suddenly from the lightning and then go back to darkness.* **OL**

★ Language History

Sabaoth The word "Sabaoth" is a reference to the Judeo-Christian God of the Old Testament in the role of warrior, or leader of armies. Historically, Russian folklore incorporates the idea of a cosmic battle between good and evil, or light and dark. Early Russian literature develops this theme, as well, with many references to lightning and thunder as weapons against the forces of evil. **AS**

✓ CheckPoint

Use the CheckPoint questions on Presentation Plus! to check students' mastery of the selection. These questions can be used with interactive response keypads for immediate student feedback.

It caught us one pitch-black night at the foot of the pass. We crawled out of our tents and ran for shelter as it came towards us over the ridge.

Everything was black—no peaks, no valleys, no horizon to be seen, only the **searing** flashes of lightning separating darkness from light, and the gigantic peaks of Belaya-Kaya and Djuguturlyuchat[1] looming up out of the night. The huge black pine trees around us seemed as high as the mountains themselves. For a split second we felt ourselves on terra firma;[2] then once more everything would be plunged into darkness and **chaos**.

The lightning moved on, brilliant light alternating with pitch blackness, flashing white, then pink, then violet, the mountains and pines always springing back in the same place, the hugeness filling us with awe;[3] yet when they disappeared, we could not believe that they had ever existed.

The voice of the thunder filled the **gorge**, drowning the ceaseless roar of the rivers. Like the arrows of Sabaoth,[4] the lightning flashes ★ rained down on the peaks, then split up into **serpentine** streams as though bursting into spray against the rock face, or striking and then shattering like a living thing.

As for us, we forgot to be afraid of the lightning, the thunder, and the downpour, just as a droplet in the ocean has no fear of a hurricane. Insignificant yet grateful, we became part of this world—a **primal** world in creation before our eyes.

---

1. *Belaya-Kaya* and *Djuguturlyuchat* are mountains in the western Caucasus mountain range in Russia.
2. *Terra firma* means "solid ground."
3. *Awe* is a feeling of wonderment or amazement.
4. *Sabaoth,* a Biblical reference, means "armies."

Reading Strategy Visualizing *How does Solzhenitsyn's imagery help you imagine the setting of the poem?* **R**

Vocabulary

searing (sîr´ing) *adj.* extremely hot or bright
chaos (kā´os) *n.* a state of disorder and confusion
gorge (gôrj) *n.* the passageway between two higher land areas, such as a narrow valley
serpentine (sur´pən tēn´) *adj.* snake-like, twisting, winding
primal (prī´məl) *adj.* a basic, original state of being

Additional Support

Skills Practice

RESEARCH: Nature in Poetry Have students work in small groups to conduct research. **Say:** This poem uses vivid imagery to captivate the reader and deliver a message about all people and our place in the universe. Other poems incorporate scenes from nature as well. Conduct research to learn how different authors use nature in their poetry. Encourage students to use online sources as well as library resources. Have groups share their findings with the class. **OL**

RESPONDING AND THINKING CRITICALLY

Respond

1. What example of imagery in the poem did you find most striking? Explain.

Recall and Interpret

2. (a)How does the speaker describe the lightning in the fourth paragraph? (b)What does this comparison suggest about his view of nature?

3. (a)What does the speaker compare himself and his group to at the end of the poem? (b)What does the speaker's changing feelings about the storm indicate about people's place in nature?

Analyze and Evaluate

4. Why, in your opinion, does the speaker think he can report on others' feelings and thoughts?

5. How can the storm make the speaker feel that one moment he is firmly on the ground, yet the very next he is plunged into chaos? Explain.

6. Why do the speaker and his companions forget to be afraid of the powerful storm?

Connect

7. **Big Idea** **The Energy of the Everyday** How would you explain the author's view of the relationship between people and nature?

LITERARY ANALYSIS

Literary Element Prose Poetry

Unlike poems that use verses and stanzas, **prose poetry** follows the narrative style with sentences and paragraphs but also maintains rhythm.

1. Read aloud the following phrase, "Everything was black—no peaks, no valleys, no horizon to be seen. . . ." Explain how this line blends poetic elements with prose format.

2. Read aloud the following phrase, ". . . then split up into serpentine streams as though bursting into spray against the rock face, or striking and then shattering. . . ." What about this phrase makes it poetic?

Interdisciplinary Activity: Music

The rhythm and flow of the words in a poem can be very similar to the lyrics in a song or the steady rhythm and tone of a piece of music. Music or song can also convey many of the same emotions and thoughts as a poem. Think of what kind of song and style of music would best depict the action and feeling of "A Storm in the Mountains." Write song lyrics using your own words to express what the poem says. Then describe what type of music would best suit your song.

READING AND VOCABULARY

Reading Strategy Visualizing

Using **visualizing** allows the reader to connect to the poem and understand its tone and meaning.

1. Which sensory details particularly helped you understand or connect to the poem? Explain.

2. Which sensory details do you think best communicated the tone and meaning of the poem?

Vocabulary Practice

Practice with Analogies Complete the following analogies. Use a dictionary if you need help.

1. searing : hot :: freezing :
   a. cold   b. temperature

2. chaos : disorder :: boisterous :
   a. male   b. noise

3. gorge : land :: channel :
   a. television   b. sea

4. serpentine : twisting :: circuitous :
   a. circus-like   b. circular

5. primal : civilized :: puerile :
   a. infant   b. adult

Literature Online **Web Activities** For eFlashcards, Selection Quick Checks, and other Web activities, go to www.glencoe.com.

ALEKSANDR SOLZHENITSYN **561**

Assess

1. Answers will vary.

2. (a) As arrow-like, then compared to a serpent; and finally it is said to be "like a living thing." (b) Nature may not be separate from humans, but instead something of which we are a part.

3. (a) Droplets of water in an ocean (b) Humans may fear and feel removed from nature, but we are still small elements of a much larger world.

4. Students may say that the speaker expresses this as a universal experience.

5. The abrupt switches between light and dark make things seem unstable.

6. The storm was so beautiful and amazing that the observers forgot that it might be a threat to them.

7. Students may say that human beings and nature are not unrelated but exist parallel to each other.

Literary Element

1. The sentence form shows prose format, but the rhythmic pattern makes it poetic.

2. This phrase uses the poetic device of alliteration, giving the line musical and onomatopoetic effects.

Literature Online

Web Activities Have students access the Web site for interactive activities that will help them assess their understanding of the selection.

Interdisciplinary Activity: Music

Students' songs should include figurative language and be original. Students should explain their choice of style.

Reading Strategy

1. Students should cite specific passages and identify which details they visualized.

2. Students may cite the phrases "shattering like a living thing" or "the hugeness filling us with awe."

Vocabulary

1. a 2. b 3. b 4. b 5. b

Focus

On the board, write: dogs and its owners **Ask:** Does the pronoun agree with its antecedent? *(No, the antecedent is plural and the pronoun is singular.)* **OL**

Teach

Pronoun Reference On the board, list these rules and review them with the class:

- Pronouns need antecedents.
- Pronouns must agree with antecedents.

Give students sentences for practicing pronoun reference. **OL**

Assess

Possible Rewrites:

1. Aleksandr Solzhenitsyn had to work as a mathematician because he had little money.
2. Solzhenitsyn was born in Russia during a time when writers had to censor their ideas.
3. I think that writers should be able to write about any topic.
4. When you read Solzhenitsyn's poetry, you find striking imagery.
5. I enjoy Solzhenitsyn's writing because it keeps me interested.

▶ **Vocabulary Terms**

Incorrect **pronoun reference** is the use of a pronoun that has no antecedent in the sentence or does not agree with its antecedent in person and number.

▶ **Test-Taking Tip**

To identify incorrect pronoun reference on a test, find the antecedent for each pronoun. If there is not one, replace the pronoun with an appropriate noun. If the antecedent differs in person and/or number from the pronoun, change the pronoun to agree with the antecedent.

▶ **Language Handbook**

For more on pronoun reference, see the Language Handbook, pp. R46–R60.

Literature Online
eWorkbooks To link to the Grammar and Language eWorkbook, go to www.glencoe.com.

OBJECTIVES
- Understand pronoun reference.
- Recognize and correct incorrect pronoun reference.

Avoiding Incorrect Pronoun Reference

"We crawled out of our tents and ran for shelter as it came towards us over the ridge."

— Aleksandr Solzhenitsyn, from "A Storm in the Mountains"

Connecting to Literature In this line from "A Storm in the Mountains," Aleksandr Solzhenitsyn describes the speaker's experience in the first person plural. The quotation is an example of correct **pronoun reference** because the pronouns *our* and *us* are the same person and number as the subject of the sentence, *we*. Incorrect pronoun reference is the use of a pronoun that has no antecedent or does not agree with its antecedent in person and number.

Problem	A pronoun has no antecedent in the sentence. *She carefully protected hers.* *It required many revisions because of its complexity.*
Solution	Replace the pronoun with an appropriate noun. *Anna carefully protected her papier-mâché box.* *The term paper required many revisions because of its complexity.*
Problem	A pronoun does not agree with its antecedent in person and number. *A writer must carefully choose what to include in their work.* *Kim wrote slowly to give its ideas time to develop.*
Solution	Replace the pronoun with one that agrees with its antecedent in person and number. *A writer must carefully choose what to include in his or her work.* *Kim wrote slowly to give her ideas time to develop.*

Exercise

Rewrite the following sentences to correct any incorrect pronoun references.

1. Aleksandr Solzhenitsyn had to work as a mathematician because one had little money.
2. Solzhenitsyn was born in Russia during a time when you had to censor their ideas.
3. I think that they should be able to write about any topic.
4. When one reads Solzhenitsyn's poetry, you find striking imagery.
5. I enjoy his writing because it keeps us interested.

Additional Support

eWorkbooks Have students access the Web site for more practice with pronoun reference.

Skills Practice

GRAMMAR: Pronoun Reference

For students who are less practiced writers, provide instruction on avoiding vague and ambiguous pronoun references. Explain these examples:

- "I like playing bridge. This is unusual." (*This* does not have a clear antecedent.

Tell students to avoid vague references with words such as *this, that,* and *it.*)

- "Cody asked Brad if his ride had arrived." (This sentence has an ambiguous reference because *his* could refer to Cody or Brad. Warn students to word their sentences so that the antecedent is clear.) **OL**

The Print of the Paw, To An Aged Bear

MEET N. SCOTT MOMADAY

Poet and novelist Navarre Scott Momaday absorbed the storytelling culture of American Indians throughout his youth. His father, a member of the Kiowa tribe, was a talented painter. His mother, of mixed English and Cherokee heritage, wrote children's books. Both of his parents taught literature and art on reservations throughout the southwestern United States.

A Teaching Heritage As they moved among tribes such as the Apache, the Navajo, and the Pueblo, Momaday developed his creative writing skills. His parents encouraged his love of classic literature as much as they cultivated his love of traditional Native American storytelling. After earning a degree from the University of New Mexico, Momaday followed in his parents' footsteps by teaching on the Jicarilla Apache Reservation in New Mexico.

Others spotted his unique combination of talent, skill, and heritage. Stanford University offered Momaday a poetry fellowship to its creative writing program. He spent the next five years studying under poet and critic Yvor Winters. In 1963 Momaday left Stanford with a PhD in English literature.

Next, he moved to Santa Barbara for a teaching position at the University of California. Over the next five years, he channeled his ideas of conflict between nature and the modern world into his first novel, *House Made of Dawn.*

Lifestyles in Conflict Still his best-known work, the book tells the story of a conflicted Army veteran, Abel, who returns to his Kiowa pueblo. Having seen the world and all of its technological wonders, Abel struggles with his people's traditions and lifestyle.

> *"If you are really compelled to write, that's where happiness is. It's in doing what you can do, and being the best you can be at it."*
>
> —N. Scott Momaday

House Made of Dawn earned Momaday a Pulitzer Prize in Fiction in 1969. Few authors have earned this major recognition; fewer still have earned it for their debut work. The book revitalized interest in the plight and the heritage of American Indians. Soon after, Momaday moved to Berkeley, California. He used the prestige of his award to help launch a course in American Indian oral tradition.

Rekindling Tradition Momaday spent the next three decades of his career teaching that course at several prestigious universities. Meanwhile, he published a string of books that showcase the American Indian style of storytelling. From a collection of traditional folktales illustrated by his father, to volumes of poetry and a memoir, Momaday has contributed much to modern Native American literature.

N. Scott Momaday was born in 1934.

 Author Search For more about N. Scott Momaday, go to www.glencoe.com.

N. SCOTT MOMADAY **563**

Focus

BELLRINGER

Bellringer Options
Daily Language Practice Transparency 54
Or tell students that many poets focus on their awe of the natural world and that this sense of awe inspires their work.
Ask: What aspects of nature do you find awe-inspiring? Have students discuss the animals, natural wonders, or natural phenomena by which they are awed. Students should identify the characteristics that make their choices awe-inspiring.

Literature Online

Author Search To expand students' appreciation of N. Scott Momaday, have them access the Web site for additional information and resources.

CheckPoint

Use the CheckPoint questions on Presentation Plus! to monitor students' comprehension. These questions can be used with interactive response keypads for immediate student feedback.

Selection Skills

Literary Elements
- Speaker (SE pp. 564, 566, 567)
- Prose Poetry (SE p. 567)

Listening/Speaking/Viewing Skills
- Debating an Issue (SE p. 568)
- Giving a Speech (TWE p. 566)
- Analyzing Art (TWE p. 566)

The Print of the Paw / To an Aged Bear

Reading Skills
- Applying Background Knowledge (SE pp. 564, 568)
- Using Rhythm (TWE p. 565)

Vocabulary Skills
- Word Parts (SE p. 568)
- Academic Vocabulary (SE p. 568)

Writing Skills/Grammar
- Evaluating Author's Craft (SE p. 568)
- Writing Poetry (TWE p. 566)

Focus

Summary

Both of the following poems glorify and pay homage to bears and the natural world that they inhabit. The speaker's love for the colossal creatures he describes is evident in every carefully chosen word and every crisply turned phrase. In the first poem, "The Print of the Paw," the speaker happens upon a paw print and envisions the bear that left the print. In the second poem, "To An Aged Bear," the speaker seemingly guides an old bear through the highlights of his life to his final resting place.

V Vocabulary

Vocabulary File Say: Add these words and definitions to your vocabulary file. For each word, include a sentence that gives you an example of how to use the word. **OL** Students with English language needs should include the pronunciations of these words in their files. **EL**

Literary Elements Have students access the Web site to improve their understanding of the speaker in poetry.

Connecting to the Poems

The following two poems express a deep appreciation for animals, including animals that most people would be afraid of. Looking at creatures with an unconventional or different perspective can change the way in which you relate to nature. Before you read these poems, think about the following questions:

- How do you normally interact with animals?
- How does thinking about an old animal change the way you feel about a species?

Building Background

Like some other Native American authors, Momaday challenges us to disconnect ourselves from the bustle of modern living. By emphasizing ancient relationships between humans and other creatures, the poet encourages us to awaken or reawaken our love of nature.

Momaday reminds us that American Indians hold bears in high regard. His language evokes the strength, wisdom, and nobility of these creatures that American Indians have honored for centuries.

Setting Purposes for Reading

Big Idea The Energy of the Everyday

As you read these selections, observe how the poet links animals, humans, and the natural world.

Literary Element Speaker

The **speaker** is the person whose "voice" we "hear" in a poem, much like the narrator who tells the story in a work of prose. The speaker may be the poet, or a character created to represent a specific point of view. Knowing something about the speaker and his or her point of view can help you grasp the meaning of a poem at a deeper level. As you read, try to determine the voice and what it conveys about the speaker.

- See Literary Terms Handbook, p. R16.

Literature Online Interactive Literary Elements Handbook To review or learn more about the literary elements, go to www.glencoe.com.

OBJECTIVES
In studying this selection, you will focus on the following:
- identifying the speaker in a poem
- applying background knowledge to better understand a text
- understanding the construction of prose poetry
- writing an essay to evaluate an author's craft

Reading Strategy Applying Background Knowledge

Applying background knowledge to your reading can help you recognize different perspectives. Sometimes a poet will deliberately have the speaker reflect an attitude different from that of the poet, to exaggerate an opposing view.

Reading Tip: Using Perspective Descriptions may point out the differences in perspective between American Indian-held beliefs and those of non-American Indians. In the graphic organizer below, list a word that the author uses to describe the bear on the left side, and write a synonym for that characteristic in the box to the right.

Author's Description of Bear	Synonym for Description Word
mythic	legendary

Vocabulary

meticulous (mi tik′yə ləs) *adj.* precise; careful; worried about details; p. 565 *Sondra, meticulous about her stamp collection, kept it in cabinets.*

cipher (sī′fər) *n.* a signifying figure; a number or symbol; p. 565 *A zero is a cipher representing a numberless quantity.*

glyph (glif) *n.* an engraved, symbolic figure; p. 565 *Scientists study ancient glyphs to learn secrets from, and clues about, the past.*

infirmity (in fur′mə tē) *n.* weakness; frailty; failing; p. 566 *Mrs. Palltuck's infirmity prevented her from doing errands by herself.*

conflagration (kon′flə grā′shən) *n.* a huge fire; p. 566 *Even veteran firefighters rarely witnessed this kind of conflagration.*

Selection Resources

Print Materials
- Unit 3 Resources (Fast File), pp. 35–37
- Leveled Vocabulary Development, p. 43
- Selection and Unit Assessments, pp. 95–96
- Selection Quick Checks, p. 48

Transparencies
- Bellringer Options Transparencies: Daily Language Practice Transparency 54
- Literary Elements Transparency 21

Technology
- TeacherWorks Plus™ CD-ROM
- StudentWorks Plus™ CD-ROM
- Presentation Plus!™ CD-ROM
- Literature Online, glencoe.com
- Online Student Edition, mhln.com
- ExamView® Assessment Suite CD-ROM
- Vocabulary PuzzleMaker CD-ROM
- Listening Library, disc 1 tracks 52–53

The Print of the Paw

N. Scott Momaday

BI₁ It lies among leaves. Indeed, a leaf, fast and broken, is impressed in the heel's deep hollow. The leaf is yellow and brown, and brittle at the edges. The
5 edges have been crushed; there is a fine dust of color, like pollen, in the mold. Deeper than the heel's hollow are the claw's piercings. They are precisely placed in the earth as if the great beast
10 moved with **meticulous** grace. The toes turn inward, perhaps to describe like a keel[1] the center of gravity upon which a great weight is balanced. Were I to construct a model of this bear, based
15 upon this single print, it would turn out to be a mythic and wondrous thing.

It would be a **cipher**, a **glyph**, a huge shape emergent on the wall of a cave, a full figure in polychrome[2]—splotches
20 of red and yellow in black outline. And I would be an artist of the first rank on this occasion, if on no other, for I should proceed directly, in the disinterested manner of a child, from
25 this nearly perfect print of the paw. And all who should lay eyes upon my work would know, beyond any shadow of a doubt, how much I love the bear whose print this is.

Jemez Springs, 1997

---

2. *Polychrome* means "decorated in many colors."

Big Idea The Energy of the Everyday *What effect does the "nearly perfect" paw print have on the speaker?* **BI₂**

---

1. A *keel* is the long piece of wood or steel along the bottom of a boat or ship that helps keep it stable.

Vocabulary

meticulous (mi tik′yə ləs) *adj.* precise; careful; worried about details

Vocabulary

cipher (si′fər) *n.* a signifying figure; a number or symbol
glyph (glif) *n.* an engraved, symbolic figure

N. SCOTT MOMADAY **565**

Building Reading Fluency

Finding the Beat Help students improve their reading fluency by pointing out the rhythmic pattern of this prose poem. Read "The Print of the Paw" aloud to the class, first telling students to listen for the natural rise and fall of your voice. Tell students that your vocal variation results from pausing at logical points in the poem and from making your voice higher or lower. Pair students and have them take turns reading the poem aloud. Tell them to use punctuation to determine when and for how long they should pause, and suggest that they model their vocal inflection on an animated lunchroom conversation. **BL**

Teach

L1 Literary Element

Speaker Answer: *Students' answers will vary. They may interpret the speaker as wise and powerful. They may also suggest that the speaker has a deep understanding of and respect for the natural world.* **OL**

L2 Literary Element

Alliteration Have students find examples of alliteration in the poem. *(hold hard; setting sun; shadow shade; singing soil)* **OL**

★ Viewing the Art

George Catlin (1796–1872) gave up a career as a lawyer to paint and write about Native Americans and their cause. His goal was to document the Native American culture before it was destroyed by westward expansion. **Ask:** Why might the bear be lying down and have such a fierce expression? *(Students may say that the bear has been injured or may be protecting a cub.)* **AS**

 CheckPoint

Use the CheckPoint questions on Presentation Plus! to check students' mastery of the selections. These questions can be used with interactive response keypads for immediate student feedback.

To An Aged Bear

Weapons and Physiognomy of the Grizzly Bear, 1846. George Catlin. Oil on canvas. Smithsonian American Art Museum, Washington, DC. ★

N. Scott Momaday

Hold hard this **infirmity**.
It defines you. You are old.

Now fix yourself in summer,
In thickets of ripe berries,

5   And venture toward the ridge
Where you were born. Await there

The setting sun. Be alive
To that old **conflagration**

One more time. Mortality
10   Is your shadow and your shade.

Translate yourself to spirit;
Be present on your journey.

Keep to the trees and waters.
Be the singing of the soil.

Santa Fe, 1995

> **Literary Element** Speaker *What are your impressions of this poem's speaker?* **L1**
>
> **Vocabulary**
> **infirmity** (in fur′mə tē) n. weakness; frailty; failing
> **conflagration** (kon′flə grā′shən) n. a huge fire

566 UNIT 3 POETRY

Additional Support

Skills Practice

WRITING: Poetry Have students rewrite "To An Aged Bear" using a prose poetry format like that of "The Print of the Paw" on page 565. Then have students compare and contrast their versions of the poem with the original and determine what was gained and what was lost by the change in format. **OL**

RESEARCH: Native American Cultures Have students research Native American cultures in order to develop a deeper understanding of Momaday's interest in and relationship to nature. Have students share their work with the class by preparing a brief speech using visual effects. **OL**

RESPONDING AND THINKING CRITICALLY

Respond

1. (a)How did you feel about bears before you read the poems? (b)What do you think about bears now?

Recall and Interpret

2. (a)To what type of vessel does the speaker compare the bear's claws in "The Print of the Paw"? (b)What impression does this analogy evoke?

3. (a)In "To An Aged Bear," what does the speaker tell the bear to "await"? (b)In the context of the poem, to what else might this phrase refer?

4. (a)In "To An Aged Bear," what two words does the speaker use to describe mortality? (b)By using these words, what is the speaker saying about the bear's relationship to mortality?

Analyze and Evaluate

5. (a)How would you classify the tone of the first half of "The Print of the Paw"? (b)How is this tone an effective choice in relation to the rest of the poem? Explain.

6. (a)In "To An Aged Bear," what natural images are used? (b)Are these images effective in creating a setting for the poem? Why or why not?

7. (a)In "To An Aged Bear," the speaker tells the bear, "you are old." What might be another way to interpret this statement? (b)What images reinforce this reading?

Connect

8. **Big Idea** **The Energy of the Everyday** From the ideas expressed in these two poems, how does the energy of a creature like a bear resonate throughout our world? Explain.

LITERARY ANALYSIS

Literary Element Speaker

The **speaker** in each of Momaday's poems expresses poignant feelings for nature and for animals. Yet each speaker expresses his or her feelings and ideas in a different style and form. How did you respond to each speaker? Review these poems, paying careful attention to each speaker. Then answer the following questions:

1. What clues are given to help you identify each speaker?

2. Is it your impression that you are hearing from the same speaker in both poems? Support your answer with details from the texts.

Review: Prose Poetry

As you learned on page 558, **prose poetry** uses imagery, rhythm, and other poetic devices to express ideas and emotions. Instead of using line breaks, the author of a prose poem writes in sentences and paragraphs.

Partner Activity With a classmate, discuss the advantages and disadvantages of writing a prose poem, compared to writing a poem in a more traditional form. Working with your partner, create a two-column chart similar to the one below. Fill in the left-hand column with advantages of prose poems and the right-hand column with disadvantages.

Pro	Con
Uses imagery and sensory details to create vivid descriptions	Often, there is not a rhyme scheme or regular meter

N. SCOTT MOMADAY **567**

Literary Element

1. In "The Print of the Paw," specific references to art and creativity suggest an artist is speaking. In "To An Aged Bear," the tone of the speaker is teaching or instructing the bear.

2. The speaker in "To An Aged Bear" uses language that suggests an omniscience that differs from the grounded, more human point of view in "The Print of the Paw." One might argue that the aged bear is personified and speaking to itself in "To An Aged Bear."

Review: Prose Poetry

Students should be able to explain the reasoning behind their charts.

Assess

1. (a) Students may say scary or dangerous. (b) Students may say that the poems prompted them to view bears as noble and gentle.

2. (a) The keel of a ship (b) It evokes a sense of something massive yet graceful.

3. (a) The setting sun (b) The bear's impending death

4. (a) Shadow and shade (b) Like one's shadow, death is always close. Death can also be a relief, like shade on a sunny day.

5. (a) Literal and clinical-sounding, as though the speaker is taking notes for biology class. (b) The speaker's tone is effective because its focus is the creative impetus for envisioning a symbolic model of the bear, exhibiting a deep admiration that proceeds "directly, in the disinterested manner of a child."

6. (a) Summer, thickets of berries, a ridge, sunset, trees and water, and soil (b) Students may say that the images effectively evoke clear pictures in their imaginations.

7. (a) The bear is nearing death. (b) Students may point out the setting seen and the reference to mortality.

8. Bears are mythic animals. They spur art and creativity and provide a model for solidity and balance.

Assess

Reading Strategy

1. Momaday's concerns about nature and creativity are reflected consistently in each of the texts.

2. For "The Print of the Paw," knowing this background information helps the reader understand the almost praiseful tone of the second half of the poem. For "To An Aged Bear," it helps the reader understand the last two stanzas, which emphasize the existence of the spirit and its unity with the natural world.

Vocabulary

1. a **2.** a **3.** b **4.** b **5.** b

Academic Vocabulary

1. To get an impression of the bear

2. *Mythic, wondrous, huge,* and *polychrome*

Web Activities Have students access the Web site for interactive activities that will help them assess their understanding of the selection.

Reading Strategy Applying Background Knowledge

You read about Momaday's American Indian heritage on page 563. By **applying background knowledge** to your reading of the poems, you can better understand their context.

1. Do you think that the speaker in each poem represents Momaday's own point of view? Explain.

2. How does knowing that the author has strong roots in American Indian traditions, specifically those related to nature, help you understand the poems?

Vocabulary Practice

Practice with Word Parts Using the information below, choose the best definition for each word.

Latin root: *meticulosus*—"fearful"
Latin root: *conflagrare*—"to burn up"
Latin root: *infirmus*—"weak, frail"
Arabic root: *sifr*—"empty"
Greek root: *glyph*—"carved work"

1. meticulous
   a. worried about details   **b.** unaware
2. cipher
   a. signifying zero   **b.** signifying full
3. glyph
   a. glib   **b.** symbolic figure
4. infirmity
   a. hale   **b.** frailty
5. conflagration
   a. whipping   **b.** huge fire

Academic Vocabulary

Here are two words from the vocabulary list on page R82. These words will help you think, write, and talk about the selection.

inspect (in spekt´) *v.* to review or examine

bulk (bulk) *n.* a large portion of matter

Practice and Apply
1. Why does the speaker **inspect** the paw print?
2. How does the speaker describe the bear's **bulk**?

Writing About Literature

Evaluate Author's Craft Scholars praise Momaday for the way in which he selects words with more than one meaning to describe his subjects. Using these words allows him to change the tone of a poem or to evoke compelling images in the reader's mind.

Choose five words from the selections and then write a brief essay explaining how their multiple meanings create an even richer experience for the reader. You may want to consult a dictionary to explore additional meanings of everyday words.

Before you begin drafting, construct a chart like the one below, listing the possible meanings of key words.

Word	Usual Meaning	Deeper Meaning or Image
fix	repair	stay in one place

Include quotes from the poems that support your ideas. Once you have completed the chart, begin drafting.

After completing your draft, meet with a peer reviewer to evaluate each other's work and to suggest revisions. Then proofread and edit your draft for errors in spelling, grammar, and punctuation.

Literature Groups

Together with your peers, discuss the legitimacy of prose poetry as a literary form. In your opinion, which of the two poems is more effective? Does the prose poetry in "The Print of the Paw" effectively convey Momaday's message? How well does he get his message across in the more traditional "To An Aged Bear"?

Literature **Online** **Web Activities** For eFlashcards, Selection Quick Checks, and other Web activities, go to www.glencoe.com.

Writing About Literature

Students might select *fast* (quick, resistant); *fine* (superior, small); *hard* (tough, difficult); *fix* (repair, stay still); *ripe* (mature, decaying); and *keep* (remain, celebrate).

Literature Groups

Discussions should include
- opinions of group members
- responses to the literature
- responses to the poet

Three Haiku

MEET MATSUO BASHŌ

Japanese poet Matsuo Bashō devoted his life to perfecting the haiku. The shortest poetic form in the world, the haiku contains just seventeen syllables, in three lines of five, seven, and five syllables. The haiku evolved from the Japanese *renga*—a sequence of linked verses usually written by a group of poets. The opening line of the *renga* evolved into the *hokku*, now known as the haiku. The shortening of the form represented a new spiritual development for seventeenth-century Japanese poets like Bashō. Inspired by the teachings of Zen Buddhism, which emphasized surpassing logical, everyday thought, they turned their attention to capturing the small details of life, especially focusing on nature.

Rarely did Bashō and his contemporaries think of themselves as poets, but rather as guides. The early writers of haiku strove to place the reader within an experience in nature—such as observing a misty rain, or listening closely to a bird's call. Writing as specifically and simply as they could about the details of such an experience, they hoped the poem might lead their reader to enlightenment. "What is important," Bashō wrote, "is . . . returning to daily experience, seek therein the true and the beautiful."

"Every day is a journey, and the journey itself is home."

—Matsuo Bashō

From Samurai Son to Master Poet Born in 1644 to a family of samurai warriors in the province of Iga, Bashō spent most of his youth in service to a feudal lord. During the first half of his life, a new era of Japanese culture unfolded, when a drastic policy caused the country to close itself to foreigners. This resulted in a new interest in Japanese art, ethics, history, and poetry. Bashō and the young lord he served, Todo Yoshitada, became close companions, sharing a passion for poetry. When Yoshitada died in his early twenties, it is believed Bashō's grief inspired him to leave Iga and set out for a life committed to poetry, traveling, and following a Zen ideology.

A Hunger for Travel The details of Bashō's life after his departure from Iga are obscure, though it is certain that he became a master of haiku by his early thirties and gained many disciples. One such disciple built him a cottage near Edo (now Tokyo), where another student planted a banana plant as a gift. The Japanese name for banana plant is *bashō,* which the poet playfully adopted as his name.

During the remainder of his life, Bashō continued to produce elegant haiku that explored themes of beauty, loneliness, and suffering. He eventually became a Zen priest, giving up all possessions and wandering on pilgrimages with fellow priests and poets. He spent the last ten years of his life traveling through Japan; one such journey to the northern interior of Japan is captured in his most famous work, *Narrow Road to the Deep North,* a kind of travel diary in *haiban* form, or prose alternating with haiku.

Matsuo Bashō was born in 1644 and died in 1694.

 Author Search For more about Matsuo Bashō, go to **www.glencoe.com.**

MATSUO BASHŌ **569**

Selection Skills

Three Haiku

Literary Elements
• Haiku (SE pp. 570, 572)

Reading Skills
• Interpreting Imagery (SE pp. 570, 572)
• Visualizing (SE p. 570)

Vocabulary Skills
• Academic Vocabulary (SE p. 572)

Writing Skills/Grammar
• Apply Form (SE p. 572)

Focus

Summary

The first haiku begins with melted frost resting in the speaker's hand. This image is a signal of spring's approach, but it is also a signal of autumn's end. It is this thought—this contemplation of the death of things—that sits with the speaker for the other haiku. The final haiku subtly calls spring "nameless," is nostalgic, and further contemplates themes of rebirth and loss.

Literary Elements Have students access the Web site to improve their understanding of haiku.

Connecting to the Haiku

The haiku that follow articulate both themes of dying and rebirth, yet the author paints these opposing ideas with beautiful images. Before you read the poems, think about the following questions:

• What are some beautiful images of rebirth?
• Can you identify any beautiful images related to death?

Building Background

Matsuo Bashō's sentiments—"Don't follow in the footsteps of the old poets, seek what they sought"—urged poets to honor the writers who came before them, but also to search for growth, and perhaps perfection in their own works. These thoughts were reflective of the standards he held for himself. By setting such high standards for his writing, the haiku master assured that the lifelong cultivation of his craft would be a diligent and progressive process.

Setting Purposes for Reading

Big Idea The Energy of the Everyday

As you read the three haiku, observe Bashō's attention to the intricate details of a changing season.

Literary Element Haiku

Haiku is an unrhymed Japanese verse form consisting of seventeen syllables that are arranged in three lines. The first and third lines have five syllables each; the second line has seven syllables. While some translations of haiku lose the poet's original syllable count when translated into English, the traditional goal of haiku—to suggest large ideas, using the simplest and fewest words—remains.

Although they leave much to the reader's imagination, haiku poets use explicit and evocative words to lead readers in the right direction. Matsuo Bashō, perhaps the greatest haiku poet of all time, said that a good poem should "seem light as a shallow river flowing over its sandy bed."

As you read the haiku, notice the images and ideas that Bashō's words bring to your mind.

• See Literary Terms Handbook, p. R7.

OBJECTIVES
In studying this selection, you will focus on the following:
• understanding and analyzing haiku as a literary form

Reading Strategy Interpreting Imagery

Imagery refers to the pictures, created through descriptions and sensory details, that writers use to evoke emotional responses from their readers. By stimulating the five senses, authors present more vivid scenes and inspire readers to better understand what is being described. When you **interpret imagery**, you use your own knowledge of the world and your understanding of the text to create meaning for the images present.

....

Reading Tip: Visualizing As a reader, you can better prepare yourself to receive imagery by trying to picture what the writer has depicted. Use the writer's clues, such as the color, texture, and position of things to imagine the scene set before you. As you read the three haiku, try to visualize the author's accounts of nature. Record your imagined pictures in a graphic organizer like the one below, and then expand these recordings to illustrate a full scene incorporating the author's description.

Line	Visualization	Expansion
It would melt in my hand.	A hand cupped and holding a lump of frost.	I see a young man in a jacket with a scarf leaning down to gather a chunk of frost between his fingers.

Literature Online Interactive Literary Elements **Handbook** To review or learn more about the literary elements, go to www.glencoe.com.

• understanding and interpreting imagery
• applying the haiku form to your own creative writing

570 UNIT 3 POETRY

Selection Resources

Print Materials
📁 Unit 3 Resources (Fast File), pp. 38–39
📁 Selection and Unit Assessments, pp. 97–98
📁 Selection Quick Checks, p. 49

Transparencies
• Bellringer Options Transparencies: Daily Language Practice Transparency 55
• Literary Elements Transparency 48

Technology
💿 TeacherWorks Plus™ CD-ROM
💿 StudentWorks Plus™ CD-ROM
💿 Presentation Plus!™ CD-ROM
💻 Literature Online, glencoe.com
💻 Online Student Edition, mhln.com
💿 ExamView® Assessment Suite CD-ROM
💿 Vocabulary PuzzleMaker CD-ROM
💿 Listening Library, disc 1 track 54

Autumn Tree.
Japanese School
17th century. Silk
painting. Private
collection. ★

Three Haiku

Matsuo Bashō
Translated by Robert Hass **BI₁**

It would melt
in my hand—
     the autumn frost.

    First day of spring—
I keep thinking about
    the end of autumn.

    Spring!
a nameless hill
    in the haze.

Big Idea   The Energy of the Everyday *Why do you think, despite spring's arrival, the speaker continues to deliberate autumn's end?* **BI₂**

MATSUO BASHŌ **571**

Assess

1. Answers will vary.

2. (a) Frost (b) The melting frost is also a distinct sensation used to draw the reader to the scene.

3. (a) Autumn's end (b) The speaker may not adjust well to change.

4. (a) A nameless hill in the haze (b) It suggests spring's lack of clarity or distinction.

5. By describing frost melting in the narrator's hand (touch) and a blurred hill (sight)

6. Melting frost; the narrator's hand; a hill; and haze. Answers about effectiveness will vary.

7. Answers will vary.

8. Powerful elements: autumn's death and spring's birth. Gentle elements: melting frost in a hand, a hill in the haze.

Literary Element

1. (a) The birth of one season and the death of another (b) The contrast inspires contemplation in the reader. This allows a larger idea to be expressed concisely.

2. The death of one thing is followed by the birth of another.

RESPONDING AND THINKING CRITICALLY

Respond

1. Are the images in the three haiku familiar to you? Describe your feelings about the changing seasons.

Recall and Interpret

2. (a) What substance melts in the speaker's hand? (b) Why might the author have chosen to include this kind of sensory detail here?

3. (a) What is the speaker reminded of on spring's first day? (b) Draw inferences about the speaker's life from his feelings about the end of autumn.

4. (a) How does the speaker describe spring in the third haiku? (b) Analyze the author's decision to identify spring using this image.

Analyze and Evaluate

5. How does the author appeal to the reader's senses? Cite specific examples from the text.

6. How many images of or ideas about nature are presented in these three haiku? Which do you think is most effective? Explain.

7. How well has Bashō disclosed the wonder of changing seasons in these short poems? Could he have done a better job with longer poems?

Connect

8. **Big Idea** **The Energy of the Everyday** Nature is often described as both a powerful and gentle force. What powerful elements do you see in the three haiku? What gentle elements do you see?

LITERARY ANALYSIS

Literary Element Haiku

Haiku generally address some subject in nature and simultaneously attempt to tackle grand ideas in a very limited amount of space. Such strict features make the form a challenge to create, but Bashō's work is a firm demonstration of how beauty can be both encompassing and concise. Think about the following questions:

1. (a) What conflicting elements are present in the haiku? (b) How do these elements help the author communicate a "big idea" in only three lines?

2. What striking idea about the relationship between birth and death in nature is addressed by the author?

Writing About Literature

Apply Form Conveying effective imagery within the restrictions of the haiku form can be mastered through practice. With persistence, a beginning writer can start to evoke the form's signature beauty. Using Bashō's three haiku as a guide, write a haiku of your own and then explain how it meets the criteria of the traditional form. Recall the three-line structure and the required number of syllables per line.

Literature Online **Web Activities** For eFlashcards, Selection Quick Checks, and other Web activities, go to www.glencoe.com.

572 UNIT 3 POETRY

READING AND VOCABULARY

Reading Strategy Interpreting Imagery

Imagery can be **interpreted** on more than one level. By analyzing and interpreting an author's use of imagery, you understand not only the image presented, but also the author's purpose for its inclusion.

1. Why do you think Bashō begins the first haiku with a sensory detail?

2. How might the author justify the absence of any distinct images in the second haiku?

Academic Vocabulary

Here are two words from the vocabulary list on page R82.

visual (vizh′ōō′əl) n. something appealing to sight that is used for illustration or demonstration

minimal (min′ə məl) adj. minimum; least

Practice and Apply

1. What **visual** clue is used to describe spring?

2. Explain how the author is able to express such thoughtful ideas using **minimal** words.

Additional Support

Web Activities Have students access the Web site for interactive activities that will help them assess their understanding of the selection.

Writing About Literature

Students' haiku should

• recall the three-line structure and the required number of syllables per line

Reading Strategy

1. It's a familiar tactile image that pulls the reader into the scene.

2. The absence emphasizes the image in the first haiku and encourages readers' contemplation.

Academic Vocabulary

1. Melting frost

2. Answers may state that sensory details can express large ideas.

Two Tanka

MEET LADY ISE

Considered one of the Thirty-six Poetic Geniuses of Japan, Lady Ise enjoyed the celebrity status and fame that accompanied literary accomplishment in ancient Japan. Her achievement is especially impressive considering that official poetry during that era was written primarily by men.

A Woman of the Court Lady Ise served in Emperor Uda's Kyoto court and was known there for her literary works. Ise was part of a court "salon," a place where women developed and enjoyed their own culture. In addition to her writing, Ise was also a talented musician.

Many of her poems were written for paintings on standing screens, which were often commissioned to recognize important occasions. The poems represented the words of a person pictured on the screen and were inserted at the top of the panel by a calligrapher. These compositions were an early step in the development of the culture's narrative literature.

> "... Why then do rumors /
> Like swirling pillars of dust /
> Rise as high as the heavens?"
>
> —Lady Ise

Ise's poetry is formal in style, the rigidity of its structure reflecting the formality of the court. It subtly critiques the political scene and the role of women, allowing her an opportunity for political and social maneuvering. Much of her work is found in a collection of Japanese poetry known as the *Kokin Wakashū*, or *Kokinshū*, published around the year 905. The first in a series of imperially commissioned collections of Japanese poetry, the *Kokinshū*

is also the first major work in *kana*, a Japanese writing system using syllable-based characters. In addition, Ise assembled the *Ise Shū*, a separate collection of her own work. The first thirty-two or thirty-three poems of this collection, usually referred to as her "diary," and their prose introductions are assumed to be autobiographical, but scholars question how much fiction they contain.

Murasaki Shikibu, c. 978–1014. Japanese court lady and author, who wrote *Genji Monogatari* (Tale of the *Genji*).

Not only was Ise well represented in official Japanese collections, but the placement of her entries at the beginning and ending of such books lent them additional prestige. She also participated in poetry contests, in which she often triumphed over leading male poets, and she was selected to write official accounts of two such contests.

Lady Ise's Life Many of the facts of Lady Ise's life are uncertain. Scholars believe that she was the daughter of Fujiwara no Tsugukage, a provincial governor of Ise. Earlier generations of the family had held high governmental posts, but in Tsugukage's era their ranking had declined, although they maintained a scholarly reputation. Ise entered the service of the consort of Emperor Uda at about the age of fifteen. After the emperor's death, Ise continued in service to the household until her death. Evidence suggests that her two children were of royal heritage. Her son died in infancy; however, her daughter, Nakatsukasa, lived to become an accomplished poet.

Lady Ise was born c. 875 and died in c. 938.

 Author Search For more about Lady Ise, go to www.glencoe.com.

LADY ISE **573**

Focus

BELLRINGER

Bellringer Options
Selection Focus Transparency 29
Daily Language Practice Transparency 56
Or tell students that tanka are poems meant to capture a brief moment in time. **Ask:** What moments in time do you think should be—or could be—captured in a poem? Create a list of student ideas, and then have them choose a few to discuss in small groups. Have students focus on why these moments in time deserve to be written about. Also ask students to consider whether these moments have added significance.

Author Search To expand students' appreciation of Lady Ise, have them access the Web site for additional information and resources.

CheckPoint

Use the CheckPoint questions on Presentation Plus! to monitor students' comprehension. These questions can be used with interactive response keypads for immediate student feedback.

Selection Skills

Literary Elements
• Tanka (SE pp. 574, 576)

Two Tanka

Vocabulary Skills
• Academic Vocabulary (SE p. 576)

Reading Skills
• Comparing and Contrasting Imagery (SE pp. 574, 576)
• Analyzing Tanka Mathematically (SE p. 576)

Focus

Summary

The first tanka captures drops of rain on a willow branch just before they fall to the ground. The poet vividly compares the rain drops to a string of pearls, as if the life-giving rain were adorning the tree.

The second tanka captures a flock of geese just as they are taking flight. The speaker wonders if the geese, who are beginning their migration just as spring arrives, will feel a sense of loss over never experiencing the new birth of spring.

Literary Elements Have students access the Web site to improve their understanding of tanka.

Connecting to the Tanka

Japanese poetry often attempts to capture a moment in time—the way a snapshot captures a single second out of the 86,400 seconds that occur in every day. The following poems communicate just such moments frozen in time. Before you read the two tanka, think about the following questions:

- When you recall a moment in time, do you remember that moment in words or in pictures?
- What types of "moments" are worth capturing?

Building Background

The Japanese language itself has much to do with the development of short poems such as tanka and haiku. English poetry often makes use of rhyme; however, it is typically not a feature of Japanese poetry because all Japanese words end in one of five vowels. English poetry also makes use of rhythm, or meter. However, Japanese words do not have stressed syllables, so rhythm is not a device used in Japanese poetry.

One of the few ways that Japanese poetry can be distinguished from Japanese prose is by the syllabic pattern for which traditional Japanese verse is known.

Setting Purposes for Reading

Big Idea The Energy of the Everyday

As you read the two tanka, notice how Ise, using words that capture the reader's emotion and imagination rather than intellect, paints a picture of the everyday.

Literary Element Tanka

Tanka is an unrhymed Japanese verse form. Most tanka focus on a single thought or idea related to love or to an appreciation of nature, common themes in Japanese poetry. Tanka adhere to a strict form that consists of five lines. The first and third lines have five syllables each; the other lines have seven syllables each. Keep in mind that the two tanka presented here are translated from Japanese to English. Therefore, the syllables per line may not always fit the prescribed structure.

- See Literary Terms Handbook, p. R17.

OBJECTIVES
In studying this selection, you will focus on the following:
- understanding tanka as a poetic form

Reading Strategy Comparing and Contrasting Imagery

When reading poetry, it helps to **compare and contrast images** created by different poems. Sometimes the simple act of thinking about the differences between images can help you grasp the poet's meaning.

Reading Tip: Visualizing the Images Try drawing pictures that resemble the images described in each of the poems. Look at your drawings and make a list of similarities and differences between the two images. Use a Venn diagram like the one below to help you organize your thoughts.

First Tanka   Second Tanka

There are bright shiny droplets of water. | These images suggest spring. | The geese spread wings as they prepare to take flight.

Deer Under a Maple Tree. Mori Sushin Tessan. Hand painted, ink and colour on paper. British Library, London.

Interactive Literary Elements Handbook To review or learn more about the literary elements, go to www.glencoe.com.

- comparing and contrasting imagery to deepen understanding of poetry
- analyzing tanka mathematically

Selection Resources

Print Materials
- Unit 3 Resources (Fast File), pp. 40–41
- Selection and Unit Assessments, pp. 99–100
- Selection Quick Checks, p. 50

Transparencies
- Bellringer Options Transparencies:
  Selection Focus Transparency 29
  Daily Language Practice Transparency 56
- Literary Elements Transparency 48

Technology
- TeacherWorks Plus™ CD-ROM
- StudentWorks Plus™ CD-ROM
- Presentation Plus!™ CD-ROM
- Literature Online, glencoe.com
- Online Student Edition, mhln.com
- ExamView® Assessment Suite CD-ROM
- Vocabulary PuzzleMaker CD-ROM
- Listening Library, disc 1 track 55

Print of a River Under Cherry Blossoms, 1833–1834.
Ando Hiroshige.

Two Tanka

Lady Ise
Translated by Willis Barnstone **BI₁**

Hanging from the branches of a green
willow tree,
R the spring rain
is a
thread of pearls.

Translated by Etsuko Terasaki
with Irma Brandeis

Lightly forsaking[1]
the Spring mist as it rises,
the wild geese are setting off.
Have they learned to live
in a flowerless country?

---

1 *Forsaking* means "turning away from" or
   "abandoning."

Big Idea The Energy of the Everyday *How
does this line evoke the energy of the everyday?* **BI₂**

LADY ISE **575**

Teach

BI₁ Big Idea

The Energy of the Everyday Say: Think about this question as you read: Why are everyday occurrences worth capturing in a poem? *(Small moments in time—especially those that may not last—are worth saving.)* **OL**

R Reading Strategy

Comparing and Contrasting Imagery Have students describe or sketch the structure of willow branches. **Ask:** Why is this effect like a necklace? *(The downward-curving branch and the drops of water clinging to it resemble pearls on a necklace.)* **OL**

BI₂ Big Idea

The Energy of the Everyday Answer: *It speaks of an everyday occurrence—the flight of geese—and evokes the energy of geese beginning their flight.* **OL**

CheckPoint

Use the CheckPoint questions on Presentation Plus! to check students' mastery of the selection. These questions can be used with interactive response keypads for immediate student feedback.

Objectives
• To establish a purpose for reading (TWE)
• To compare and contrast imagery (TWE)

Differentiated Instruction

Identifying Main Idea Less proficient readers may struggle with tanka because so much is expressed in few words. Since tanka focus on one thought, it might help students to identify the main idea of each poem. Have students identify key words, and then think about what the key words might represent.

They should try to develop a concrete meaning of the word as well as a symbolic meaning. For example, both poems mention spring, which might refer to the season but could also symbolize nature. After students have analyzed their key words, have them describe the main idea of each poem in their own words. **BL**

Assess

1. Answers will vary.
2. (a) Raindrops and pearls (b) The precious importance and beauty of rain
3. (a) Mist rising and geese flying (b) There is a sense of loss at the geese's departure.
4. (a) Have they learned to live in a flowerless country? (b) The cycle of migration means geese never experience spring.
5. Answers will vary.
6. Answers will vary.
7. Answers will vary.

Literary Element

1. The shortness of the poem encourages the reader to focus much more closely on the images and words to discover what the poet is saying.
2. Answers will vary, but students should pay careful attention to word choice.

Interdisciplinary Activity: Math

Answers may vary, but the simplest one that can be made is:
$3(2(5) + 3(7)) = 93$
(93 total syllables)

RESPONDING AND THINKING CRITICALLY

Respond

1. (a)What about these images seems familiar to you? (b)Describe the images in your own words.

Recall and Interpret

2. (a)What two things are compared in the first tanka? (b)What insights about these things does the comparison bring to mind?
3. (a)What natural events does the speaker present in the second tanka? (b)How do these events contribute to the mood, or atmosphere, of the tanka?
4. (a)What question does the speaker ask in the second tanka? (b)What might be its meaning?

Analyze and Evaluate

5. In what ways do the images of spring in the two tanka reflect your own observations of spring? Explain.
6. In your opinion, which tanka offers more for you to think about? Why?

Connect

7. **Big Idea** The Energy of the Everyday Do you agree or disagree that the language and imagery used in these two poems captures the reader's emotion rather than intellect? Support your answer with evidence from the poems.

LITERARY ANALYSIS

Literary Element Tanka

Because **tanka** are so short and simple, the tanka writer, like the haiku poet, must rely on precise, direct language to suggest ideas. A tanka can have different meanings for different readers, depending on the life experiences of each reader.

1. How does the length of the poem affect the impression it leaves upon the reader? Explain.
2. Choose one of the two tanka. For as many of the words in the tanka as you can, think of or look up a synonym. Rewrite the tanka using your synonyms. Analyze how the tanka's meaning or mood has changed as a result.

Interdisciplinary Activity: Math

Imagine traditional tanka as a mathematical expression or equation. Each syllable in one line of poetry stands for one number. So, a line with five syllables is the number 5; a line with seven syllables is the number 7. Write a mathematical expression or equation that represents the total number of syllables in three tanka, given the traditional number of syllables per line. Try to make it as simple as possible. What is the total number of syllables?

Literature Online Web Activities For eFlashcards, Selection Quick Checks, and other Web activities, go to www.glencoe.com.

READING AND VOCABULARY

Reading Strategy Comparing and Contrasting Imagery

The thought process involved in comparing and contrasting concepts takes place at a high critical thinking level. **Comparing and contrasting imagery** in poetic works—especially Japanese poetic works—guides readers toward a deeper and fuller understanding by helping them draw conclusions about themes.

1. Compare and contrast the images in the two tanka and determine the themes of each.
2. In support of your opinion, list details from each of the poems.

Academic Vocabulary

Here are two words from the vocabulary list on page R82. These words will help you think, write, and talk about the selection.

framework (frām′wurk′) n. a structure or a pattern

core (kôr) n. the central foundation or basis of something

Practice and Apply
1. Describe the **framework** of a traditional tanka.
2. What is the **core** theme of the two tanka?

Additional Support

Web Activities Have students access the Web site for interactive activities that will help them assess their understanding of the selection.

Reading Strategy

1. The first tanka compares raindrops on a branch to a string of pearls. The second tanka depicts geese departing as spring arrives. The first praises spring's beauty. The second laments those that never experience this beauty.
2. Students might list: thread of pearls, lightly forsaking, flowerless country.

Academic Vocabulary

1. Five lines with the first and third lines having five syllables and the remaining three lines having seven syllables
2. The precious quality of fleeting beauty

Woman with Kite

MEET CHITRA BANERJEE DIVAKARUNI

When Chitra Divakaruni arrived in the United States from India in 1976, the nineteen-year-old from Calcutta received a shock. As she walked with her family in Chicago, she was taunted by white teens who shouted racial slurs. At first, she kept quiet about the episode. Later she wrote, "I never talked to anyone about it; I felt ashamed. Writing was a way to go beyond the silence." When Divakaruni found her voice, she used it to speak for the marginalized and the silenced, namely women and immigrants. In her work, she tells of women caught between the traditions in India and contemporary life in the United States.

"Women in particular respond to my work because I'm writing about them, women in love, in difficulties, women in relationships."

—Chitra Banerjee Divakaruni

A New Awareness In the United States, Divakaruni found many new opportunities. She earned a PhD from the University of California at Berkeley. She also began to reevaluate the circumstances of women in India. She saw how women's options were limited by lack of education and oppressive marriages, and that these experiences continued even after the women came to the United States. "At Berkeley, I volunteered at the women's center," she says. "As I got more involved, I became interested in helping battered women." In 1991 she and her friends created Maitri, an organization that provides services to Indian American women. Her experiences working for Maitri deepened her understanding of the plight of immigrant women. "I saw that a lot of problems stemmed from issues of domestic violence," Divakaruni said.

Speaking for Women While at Maitri, Divakaruni also developed a desire to write. She says that the women at Maitri "made me think a lot more about the issues I was seeing and how it related to the lives of immigrants, and I wanted to write about it." She began to write poems about immigrant women trying to forge a new identity while retaining ties to tradition. She also wrote short stories about these women, which she collected in *Arranged Marriages*. Divakaruni has since won numerous awards for her poetry, short stories, and novels.

A noted author and activist, Divakaruni still pursues her goal of speaking for women. In addition to teaching at the University of Houston, she serves on the board of Maitri and the Advisory Board of Asians against Domestic Abuse in Houston. Through her writing, Divakaruni pursues a special breed of activism. "I want people to relate to my characters, to feel their joy and pain, because it will be harder to [be] prejudiced when they meet them in real life."

Chitra Banerjee Divakaruni was born in 1956.

 Author Search For more about Chitra Banerjee Divakaruni, go to www.glencoe.com.

CHITRA BANERJEE DIVAKARUNI **577**

Focus

BELLRINGER

Bellringer Options
**Daily Language Practice
Transparency 57
Or ask:** What do you think makes the president laugh? Discuss what adults find amusing. **Say:** What do you think amused these same people before adulthood and parenthood? *(Games, sports, playing outside, friendships)* Discuss the gains and losses that come with adulthood. Lead this discussion to the extreme losses and oppression felt by some Indian women.

Author Search To expand students' appreciation of Chitra Banerjee Divakaruni, have them access the Web site for additional information and resources.

✓CheckPoint

Use the CheckPoint questions on Presentation Plus! to monitor students' comprehension. These questions can be used with interactive response keypads for immediate student feedback.

Selection Skills

Literary Elements
- Verse Paragraph (SE pp. 578, 580, 581)
- Enjambment (SE p. 581)

Woman with Kite

Reading Skills
- Making Inferences About the Speaker (SE pp. 578, 582)

Vocabulary Skills
- Practicing with Context Clues (SE pp. 578, 582)
- Academic Vocabulary (SE p. 582)

Writing Skills/Grammar
- Analyzing Cultural Context (SE p. 582)
- Literary Criticism (SE p. 582)

Focus

Summary

An otherwise refined woman takes a grounded kite from her son's hands. As she works to put it in flight, she rediscovers a time before marriage and children—a time when she was nothing more than a child and could laugh and play freely without the limits of womanhood. Two nearby widows watch her in disdain, but nostalgia prevents her from acknowledging them, her needy children, or her restrictive Indian culture. She puts the kite into orbit.

V Vocabulary

Vocabulary File

Say: Add these words and definitions to your vocabulary file. For each word, include a sentence that gives you an example of how to use the word. **OL** Students with English language needs should include the pronunciations of these words in their files. **EL**

Literary Elements Have students access the Web site to improve their understanding of verse paragraphs.

Connecting to the Poem

In this poem, Divakaruni reminds us how a simple activity, like flying a kite, can help us put aside ordinary or troublesome issues. Before you read the poem, think about the following questions:

- What activities do you use to help forget everyday concerns?
- Do you ever set aside your inhibitions and act on impulse, regardless of the opinions of others?

Building Background

Many contemporary authors of Indian descent write about the conflict of their social traditions with those of Western society. Previous generations of immigrants to America—such as Polish, Irish, and Scandinavian families—struggled with similar conflicts. Today's immigrants face broader challenges involving not only language barriers, but also religious concerns and marked differences in the roles that women play in society. Immigrants and their children must wrestle with obligations to family and to religion while facing unexpected opportunities in their new home.

Setting Purposes for Reading

Big Idea The Energy of the Everyday

As you read this poem, notice how the poet infuses everyday objects and experiences with passion and energy.

Literary Element Verse Paragraph

Many contemporary poets use verse paragraphs to organize their poems into thoughts. A **verse paragraph** is a group of lines that forms a unit. Unlike a stanza, a verse paragraph does not have a fixed number of lines. As you read, observe how Divakaruni uses verse paragraphs to emphasize key thoughts in the poem.

- See Literary Terms Handbook, p. R18.

Literature Online **Interactive Literary Elements Handbook** To review or learn more about the literary elements, go to www.glencoe.com.

OBJECTIVES

In studying this selection, you will focus on the following:
- understanding verse paragraphs
- making inferences about the speaker of the poem
- analyzing the use of enjambment
- writing an essay to analyze cultural context

Reading Strategy Making Inferences About the Speaker

Some poems feature speakers who attempt to sway readers by using persuasive devices. Then readers must **make inferences about the speaker.** By being aware of the language and images a speaker uses, readers can infer hidden aspects of the speaker's personality and purpose.

Reading Tip: Look for Word Clues When reading poetry, watch for clues about the speaker's opinion or perspective. List the most powerful words, noting the speaker's feelings about the subject.

Words	Opinions
sure-footed (line 16)	shows her strength and confidence

Vocabulary

querulous (kwer′ ə ləs) adj. argumentative; uncooperative; p. 579 *Because of the actor's querulous nature, he is very difficult to work with.*

disgruntled (dis grun′tld) adj. in a state of sulky dissatisfaction; p. 579 *The disgruntled children spent the rainy day complaining about being stuck in the house.*

translucent (trans lōō′sənt) adj. allowing light to pass through; almost clear, see-through; p. 580 *She could make out the shapes of the performers through the translucent curtain.*

flecking (flek′ing) v. leaving spots or streaks; p. 580 *Mud from the road was flecking the windshield, making it difficult for the driver to see.*

Vocabulary Tip: Context Clues The way an author uses unfamiliar words in context can help you understand their meaning.

Selection Resources

Print Materials
- Unit 3 Resources (Fast File), pp. 42–44
- Leveled Vocabulary Development 44
- Selection and Unit Assessments, pp. 101–102
- Selection Quick Checks, p. 51

Transparencies
- Bellringer Options Transparencies: Daily Language Practice Transparency 57
- Literary Elements Transparency 49

Technology
- TeacherWorks Plus™ CD-ROM
- StudentWorks Plus™ CD-ROM
- Presentation Plus!™ CD-ROM
- Literature Online, glencoe.com
- Online Student Edition, mhln.com
- ExamView® Assessment Suite CD-ROM
- Vocabulary PuzzleMaker CD-ROM
- Listening Library, disc 1 track 56

Woman Flying a Kite, 1750. Indian. Book illumination painting, miniature painting. Sangaram Singh. ★

Woman with Kite

Chitra Banerjee Divakaruni

Meadow of crabgrass, faded dandelions,
querulous child-voices. She takes
from her son's **disgruntled** hands the spool
of a kite that will not fly.

> **Vocabulary**
>
> **querulous** (kwerʹə ləs) *adj.* argumentative; uncooperative
> **disgruntled** (dis grunʹtld) *adj.* in a state of sulky dissatisfaction

Teach

L Literary Element

Verse Paragraph Answer:
It emphasizes the ascent of the kite as well as the woman. Breaking here to start a new stanza signifies an important change in the woman. **OL**

BI Big Idea

The Energy of the Everyday Answer: *She is compared to fire and wild water. This shows that her reactions are elemental, or natural and uncontainable.* **OL**

 CheckPoint

Use the CheckPoint questions provided on Presentation Plus! to check students' mastery of the selection. These questions can be used with interactive response keypads for immediate student feedback.

---

5 Pulls on the heavy string, ground-glass rough
between her thumb and finger. Feels the kite,
translucent purple square, rise in a resistant arc,
flapping against the wind. Kicks off her *chappals*,[1]
tucks up her *kurta*[2] so she can run with it,
10 light **flecking** off her hair as when she was
sexless-young. Up, up

past the puff-cheeked clouds, she
follows it, her eyes slit-smiling at the sun.
She has forgotten her tugging children, their
15 *give me, give me* wails. She sprints
backwards, sure-footed, she cannot
fall, connected to the air, she
is flying, the wind blows through her, takes
her red *dupatta*,[3] mark of marriage.
20 And she laughs like a woman should never laugh

so the two widows on the park bench
stare and huddle their white-veiled heads
to gossip-whisper. The children have fallen,
breathless, in the grass behind.
25 She laughs like wild water, shaking
her braids loose, she laughs
like a fire, the spool a blur
between her hands,
the string unraveling all the way
30 to release it into space, her life,
into its bright, weightless orbit.

1. *Chappals* are traditional Indian sandals, resembling flip-flops.
2. A *kurta* is a loose shirt, often worn by both men and women in India and Pakistan.

3. A *dupatta* is a traditional headscarf worn by Indian women to emphasize their modesty.

Literary Element Verse Paragraph *What effect does the poet create by breaking after these words?* **L**

Big Idea The Energy of the Everyday *What do the similes, or comparisons, in lines 25–27 tell you about the woman?* **BI**

Vocabulary

translucent (trans lōō′sənt) *adj.* allowing light to pass through; almost clear, see-through

flecking (flek′ing) *v.* leaving spots or streaks

Additional Support

Skills Practice

RESEARCH: Indian Culture Have students research Indian culture and history in order to develop a deeper understanding of Divakaruni's poem. Students may want to focus their research on gender roles in Indian culture or women's history in India. Students may share their work with the class by preparing a brief presentation. **OL**

RESPONDING AND THINKING CRITICALLY

Respond

1. What is your opinion of the woman's behavior? Explain.

Recall and Interpret

2. (a)What three items of traditional Indian clothing does the poet mention? (b)Why does Divakaruni mention these items in the poem?

3. (a)What garment does the wind blow off the woman? (b)What significance does this incident have for her?

4. (a)What happens to the kite? (b)What conclusion about the character's future can you make from the poet's description?

5. (a)Which words does the poet choose to italicize? (b)What kinds of effects does the use of italics create?

Analyze and Evaluate

6. (a)What do "crabgrass" and "dandelions" contribute to the setting of "Woman with Kite"? (b)Explain how the poet uses them as metaphors for the main character's life.

7. (a)In line 12, how does Divakaruni personify nature? (b)What effect does this personification have on the character?

8. (a)Explain one of the similes the poet uses in the final verse paragraph to describe the main character. (b)What is the significance of these similes?

Connect

9. **Big Idea** The Energy of the Everyday Describe how Divakaruni uses images of everyday elements and combines them to transform the main character.

LITERARY ANALYSIS

Literary Element Verse Paragraph

Contemporary poets often use **verse paragraphs** to organize their ideas. Divakaruni uses three verse paragraphs in "Woman with Kite" to raise dramatic tension and to highlight conflict.

1. Explain how the author uses a transition between the first and second verse paragraphs to underscore a change in her character's attitude.

2. How does the transition between the second and third paragraphs mimic the first transition?

Review: Enjambment

As you learned on page 536, **enjambment**, also known as a run-on line, is the continuation of the sense of a sentence or phrase from one line of a poem to the next without a pause between the lines. Enjambments offer poets the opportunity to underscore the dramatic elements of their work.

Partner Activity Pair up with a classmate and look for six examples of enjambment in "Woman with Kite." Working with your partner, create a two-column chart similar to the one below. Fill in the left column with examples of enjambment. In the right column, describe how this device gives the words at the beginning or at the end of the line a deeper meaning or more dramatic effect.

Key words	Deeper meaning
"Kicks off her chappals, / tucks up her kurta"	Emphasizes abandoning traditional behavior

CHITRA BANERJEE DIVAKARUNI **581**

Review: Enjambment

Students' charts might include:

"She takes / from her son's": *Suggests the quick, smooth motion of the woman grabbing the spool*

"when she was / sexless-young": *Stresses how smoothly she transforms into a girl again*

"clouds, she / follows it,": *Suggests she never stops looking at the kite*

"she sprints / backwards,": *Emphasizes the speed and flow of her motion*

"through her, takes / her red dupatta,": *Represents wind flowing through her*

"all the way / to release into": *Represents the unwinding flow of the string*

Assess

1. Answers will vary.

2. (a) *Chappals, kurta,* and *dupatta* (b) They represent the burden of tradition that inhibits her freedom.

3. (a) Her *dupatta* (b) Although married, she can at this moment feel free.

4. (a) It flies away. (b) The woman has let go of some confining attitudes.

5. (a) Foreign words and her children's demands (b) Draws attention to the words that are confining

6. (a) They show how the meadow is infested and threatened. (b) The woman's life has been engulfed by her culture's expectations.

7. (a) By giving the clouds puffed cheeks (b) It makes her happy and frees her.

8. (a) The similes *like wild water* and *like a fire* show how she is free and unrestricted. (b) They are elemental, suggesting connection to nature.

9. The woman transforms from a person to an elemental force, like fire, light, and water.

Literary Element

1. The break shows a change from suffocating mother to blooming free spirit.

2. The character's change continues, but the mid-sentence break shows how abrupt the change becomes.

Assess

Reading Strategy

1. Admires and approves of the woman's actions
2. Positive descriptions of the woman: *slit-smiling, sure-footed, wild water*. Negative portrayals of other characters: *querulous* and *gossip-whisper*

Vocabulary

1. a **2.** b **3.** a

Academic Vocabulary

1. Her traditional clothing and her children
2. Never laugh and wear proper clothing.

Writing About Literature

Students may suggest that the character faces challenges with raising her children, with meeting expectations of her elders, and with choosing between Indian cultural norms and American openness.

Literary Criticism

Students may list: kicking off her *chappals;* tucking up her *kurta;* allowing her *dupatta* to float away; leaving her children in the grass behind her; and laughing in the presence of elders.

Reading Strategy Making Inferences About the Speaker

Many contemporary poets, like Divakaruni, use their work to comment on events or situations in society. By looking for word clues and understanding a speaker's point of view, you can **make inferences about the speaker.** This process can help you reveal the poet's agenda.

1. What does the speaker think of the woman's actions?

2. List three details from the poem that support your opinion.

Vocabulary Practice

Practice with Context Clues Use the context clues in each sentence to help you choose the meaning of the underlined word.

1. After months of being ignored, Jim felt <u>disgruntled</u> at work.
   a. unhappy   **b.** proud   **c.** eager

2. The painter shook her brush, <u>flecking</u> her canvas with color.
   a. dousing   **b.** spattering   **c.** filling

3. The audience could make out the shadows of the models through a <u>translucent</u> screen.
   a. gauzy   **b.** concrete   **c.** reflective

Academic Vocabulary

Here are two words from the vocabulary list on page R82. These words will help you think, write, and talk about the selection.

confine (kən fīn′) *v.* to keep within bounds; to restrict

mature (mə to͞or′) *adj.* reaching full physical or mental development

Practice and Apply
1. What people or things **confine** the main character, especially at the start of the poem?
2. In the poem, how should a traditional Indian woman demonstrate a **mature** manner?

Writing About Literature

Analyze Cultural Context Divakaruni has written extensively about Indian women who must learn to handle the conflicts and challenges of living in the United States. Using examples from "Woman with Kite," write a one- to two-page essay detailing challenges the main character is likely to have to cope with in her daily life.

Before you begin drafting, make a list of clues about the character's life, like this:

Clues	Challenges
tucks up her kurta	Maybe she must dress formally, even in the park.

Use quotes from the poem to support your argument as to what Divakaruni implies in "Woman with Kite." Once you have completed the list, begin drafting.

After completing your draft, meet with a peer reviewer to evaluate each other's work and to suggest revisions. Then proofread and edit your draft for errors in spelling, grammar, and punctuation.

Literary Criticism

When the collection in which this poem first appeared was released, *San Francisco Chronicle* journalist Reena Jana wrote that Divakaruni created characters who wanted to cultivate "the courage to confront the unknown in pursuit of a life of beauty, comfort, and joy." Meet with a few of your classmates and make a list of five ways that the main character in this poem shows this kind of courage.

 Literature Online **Web Activities** For eFlashcards, Selection Quick Checks, and other Web activities, go to www.glencoe.com.

Literature Online

Web Activities Have students access the Web site for interactive activities that will help them assess their understanding of the selection.

PART 2

Loves and Losses

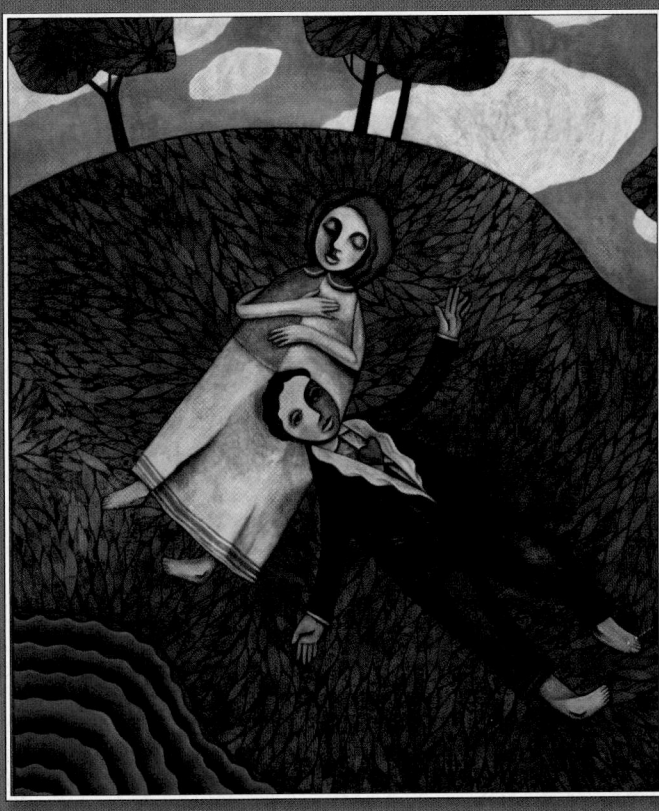

★ *River Diego, 1996.* Daniel Nevins. Oil, acrylic, and collage on wood. Private collection.

BIG IDEA

BI The poems in Part 2 express the joys and insights love can bring as well as the emptiness and ache of its loss. As you read the following poems, ask yourself: what elements of poetry work to express love and loss? What is the author's purpose in using these elements?

583

Analyzing and Extending

BI Big Idea

Loves and Losses

Explain to students that love and loss are common experiences, so they can be difficult to express in a unique and original way. Therefore, poets often turn to figurative language, such as simile and metaphor, to convey their emotions through creative comparisons. Encourage students to think about why the writers chose the specific comparisons they did as they read the poems in this part. **OL**

★ Viewing the Art

Daniel Nevins is an artist and illustrator who got a degree in fine arts from the University of Florida. **Ask:** What kind of love does the painting depict? *(Students might say that the painting depicts love as a place of refuge. The couple appears to be at peace with each other and their surroundings.)* **AS**

Objectives for Part 2
• To recognize and interpret imagery and figurative language, such as metaphor, simile, and personification (SE)
• To analyze the effect of imagery and figurative language and explain their appeal (SE)
• To analyze how poets inspire the reader to share emotions through the use of imagery and figurative language (SE)

English Language Coach

Syntax Students new to the English language may have difficulty with the often nontraditional syntax of poetry. Help them to "translate" lines into sentences with traditional word order. This will make it easier for them to recognize subjects, verbs, and modifiers—and therefore to comprehend meaning. **EL**

Differentiated Instruction

Intrapersonal Learning Before reading a poem, tell students about the poem's central emotion or idea. Then, allow them to journal about this topic so they can develop in-depth ideas about it. Later, when they read the poem, they can compare their thoughts on the topic with the poet's. **BL**

UNIT THREE

Part 2: Loves and Losses

Readability Scores Key
Dale-Chall/DRP/Lexile

PACING (DAYS)		SELECTIONS AND FEATURES	LITERARY ELEMENTS
STANDARD	BLOCK		
1–2 class sessions		LITERARY FOCUS: Language, pp. 584–585	Imagery and Figurative Language, SE p. 585 Onomatopoeia, TWE p. 584
	1	**"After Great Pain, A Formal Feeling Comes"** and **"Heart! We Will Forget Him!"** by Emily Dickinson, pp. 586–592	Personification, SE pp. 587, 591 Rhythm and Rhyme, SE p. 591
		"Well, I Have Lost You; and I Lost You Fairly" by Edna St. Vincent Millay, pp. 593–596	Sonnet, SE pp. 594, 596
2 class sessions		**"Shall I Compare Thee to a Summer's Day?"** by William Shakespeare, pp. 597–601	Metaphor, SE pp. 598, 600; TWE p. 599 Personification, SE p. 600
	1	VISUAL PERSPECTIVE on "Shall I Compare Thee to a Summer's Day?": **"Sonnet 18 By William Shakespeare"** by Dave Morice, pp. 602–609	Irony, TWE p. 602 Humor, TWE p. 604
		"Down by the Salley Gardens" and **"He Wishes for the Cloths of Heaven"** by William Butler Yeats, pp. 610–616	Lyric Poetry, SE pp. 611, 613, 615 Speaker, SE p. 615
1 class session		**"I Am Offering This Poem"** by Jimmy Santiago Baca, pp. 617–621	Metaphor and Simile, SE pp. 618, 619, 620 Lyric Poetry, SE p. 620
	1	**"since feeling is first"** by E. E. Cummings, pp. 622–625	Understanding Juxtaposition, SE pp. 623, 624, 625
1 class session		**"Horses Graze"** by Gwendolyn Brooks, pp. 626–629	Repetition, SE pp. 627, 628, 629 Sound Effects, TWE p. 628
		"Parlor" by Rita Dove, pp. 630–633	Imagery, SE pp. 631, 633
1–2 class sessions		**"Secondhand Grief"** by Sherman Alexie, pp. 634–637	Diction, SE pp. 635, 636, 637
	1	**"Ballad of Birmingham"** by Dudley Randall, pp. 638–641	Narrative Poetry, SE pp. 639, 640, 641
		HISTORICAL PERSPECTIVE on "Ballad of Birmingham": Review of **"4 Little Girls"** by Roger Ebert **6.6/61/1110**, pp. 642–644	

About the Part

Part 2 covers poetic language.

READING AND CRITICAL THINKING	VOCABULARY	WRITING AND GRAMMAR	LISTENING, SPEAKING, AND VIEWING
Analyzing Figurative Language, TWE p. 585		Quickwrite, SE p. 585	
Comparing and Contrasting Tune, SE pp. 587, 588, 591 Contrasting Point of View, SE p. 592	Antonyms, SE p. 591 Academic Vocabulary, SE p. 591	Compare and Contrast Point of View, SE p. 592 Capitalization, SE p. 592	Interpretive Reading, SE p. 592 Analyzing Art, TWE p. 589
Analyzing Diction, SE pp. 594, 596	Connotation and Denotation, SE pp. 594, 596	Writing a Letter, SE p. 596	
Analyzing Rhythm and Rhyme, SE pp. 598, 599, 601	Analogies, SE pp. 598, 601 Academic Vocabulary, SE p. 601	Writing Sonnets, SE p. 601	Dramatic Recitation, SE p. 601
Interpreting Graphic Representations of Literature, SE p. 602; TWE pp. 604-609			
Analyzing Repetition and Rhyme, SE pp. 611, 612, 615 Literary Response, TWE p. 612	Context Clues, SE pp. 611, 615 Academic Vocabulary, SE p. 615	Compare and Contrast Theme, SE p. 616 Compound Modifiers, SE p. 616	Group Discussion, SE p. 614 Music Activity, SE p. 616
Previewing and Reviewing, SE pp. 618, 619, 621	Connotation and Denotation, SE pp. 618, 621 Academic Vocabulary, SE p. 621	Lyric Poetry, SE p. 621	Literature Groups, SE p. 621
Paraphrasing, SE pp. 623, 625	Analogies, SE p. 625	Analyze Figurative Language, SE p. 625	Analyzing Art, TWE p. 624
Drawing Conclusions About Author's Meaning, SE pp. 627, 629	Denotation and Connotation, SE pp. 627, 629	Respond to Tone, SE p. 629	
Interpreting Imagery, SE pp. 631, 633	Context Clues, SE pp. 631, 633	Verb Tense, TWE p. 632	Role-Playing, SE p. 633
Visualizing, SE pp. 635, 637	Context Clues, SE pp. 635, 637	Analyze Rhythm, SE p. 637 Developing Ideas, TWE p. 636	
Applying Background Knowledge, SE pp. 639, 640, 641	Connotation and Denotation, SE p. 641	Analyze Structure, SE p. 641	
Evaluating Evidence, SE p. 642; TWE pp. 642, 643 Previewing, TWE p. 642			

The Language of Poetry

Focus

BELLRINGER

Bellringer Options
**Daily Language Practice
Transparency 58**
Or **say:** Many of the poems we
will read in this part use traditional poetic forms, such as the
sonnet, to express ideas of grief.
Why might a poet use a rigid
form to depict strong emotion?
*(Students may suggest that the
familiarity of the form offers
comfort and reminds us of the
universality of pain or that
elevating pain with heightened
language allows us to turn loss
into beauty.)*

Teach

L Literary Element

Figurative Language
Say: More than any other kind
of writing, poetry depends on
figurative language to re-create
the immediacy of experience.
How does Williams use language to mimic the sensation
of being passed by a rushing
truck? *(Students may mention
the enjambed lines, the discon-
certing absence of punctuation, or the flashes of color and
sound.)* **OL**

How does poetry appeal to the senses?

In his autobiography, William Carlos Williams
described writing "The Great Figure": "I heard a
great clatter of bells and the roar of a fire engine
passing the end of the street down Ninth Avenue.
I turned just in time to see the golden figure 5 on
a red background flash by. The impression was so

sudden and forceful that I took a piece of paper out
of my pocket and wrote a short poem." That poem
inspired Williams's friend, Charles Demuth, to paint
The Figure 5 in Gold. The artist used colors to
create visual images; the poet used words to create
images that appeal to a variety of senses.

> Among the rain
> and lights
> I saw the figure 5
> in gold
> on a red
> fire truck
> moving
> tense
> unheeded
> to gong clangs
> siren howls
> and wheels rumbling
> through the dark city

—William Carlos Williams, **"The
Great Figure"**

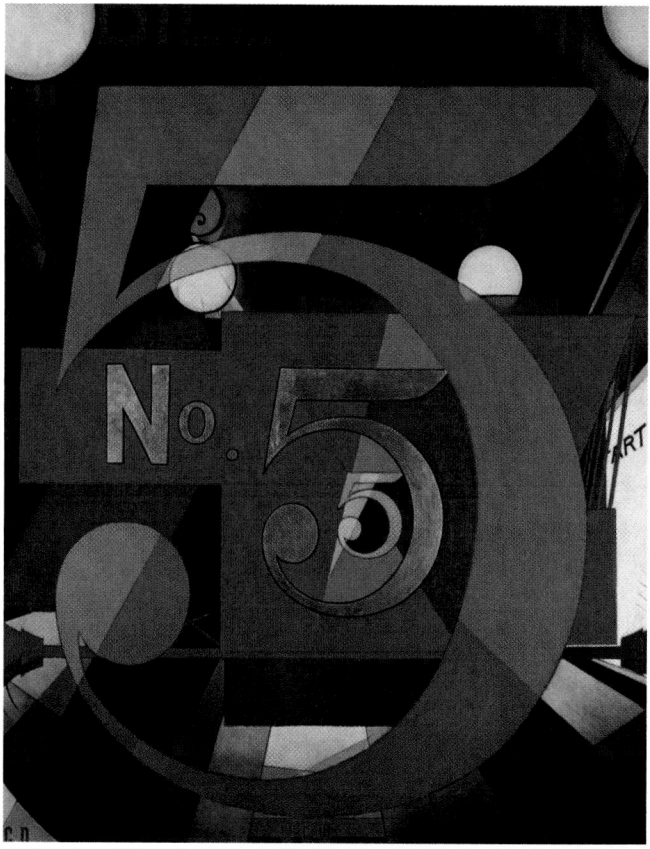

The Figure 5 in Gold, 1928. Charles Demuth. Oil on composition board, 91.4 x 75.6 cm.
Metropolitan Museum of Art, New York. ★

Additional Support

Skills Practice

LITERARY ELEMENT:

Onomatopoeia William Carlos
Williams uses a number of words that
evoke the noise of the passing fire truck:
"gong clangs"; "siren howls"; "rumbling."
Have a volunteer read the words out
loud. **Say:** Words that mimic the sounds
they describe are called onomatopoeia.

Ask students for other examples of
onomatopoeia. *(Students may suggest*
crack, whine, bang, ding, crash, *or other
words.)* Have students, working alone or
in groups, write short descriptive poems
that each contain at least two uses of
onomatopoeia. **OL**

Imagery

Imagery refers to the "word pictures" that writers create to represent a feeling, trigger a memory or idea, or evoke a sensory experience. To create effective images, writers use sensory details. Consider some of the images in "The Great Figure":

Images	Sensory Appeal
"Among the rain"	sight and touch
"the figure 5 / in gold/ on a red / fire truck"	sight
"gong clangs / siren howls / and wheels rumbling"	sight and hearing

Figurative Language

Figurative language conveys meaning beyond the literal meanings of words. Poets often make use of figurative language to convey fresh and original comparisons. Figures of speech are types of figurative language. Among the most common are simile, metaphor, personification, and hyperbole.

Simile Poets often make imaginative comparisons to convey ideas, feelings, and insights. One kind of comparison is called a **simile**. In this figure of speech, the writer uses such words as *like* or *as* or the phrase "as if" to make the comparison. For example, in the line "her eyes sparkled like diamonds," the comparison suggests the subject's eyes are radiant and glitter.

Metaphor In contrast to a simile, a **metaphor** implies a comparison instead of stating it directly; hence, there is no use of connectives such as *like* or *as*. An **extended metaphor** continues the comparison throughout a paragraph, a stanza, or an entire work.

No one lived there
but silence, a pale china gleam

—Rita Dove, **from "Parlor"**

In this metaphor, the speaker is comparing silence to a soft glimmer of light.

Personification This figure of speech gives human qualities to nonhuman things. William Shakespeare **personifies** death in this line from "Shall I Compare Thee to a Summer's Day?":

Nor shall Death brag thou wand'rest in his shade

Shakespeare compares death to a human who boasts that he has won a sought-after prize.

Hyperbole This figure of speech uses an obvious overstatement or exaggeration for either serious or comic effect. For example, when the speaker in "He Wishes for the Cloths of Heaven" says, "I have spread my dreams under your feet," the exaggeration conveys the passion and desire with which he loves.

Quickwrite

Rewriting Clichés A cliché refers to a figurative expression that has lost its freshness through overuse. Rewrite the following clichés so that they express fresh instead of stale comparisons.

1. "as slow as molasses"
2. "red as a rose"
3. "strong as an ox"

OBJECTIVES
- Recognize and interpret imagery and figurative language, such as metaphor, simile, and personification.
- Analyze the effect of imagery and figurative language and explain their appeal.

- Analyze how poets inspire the reader to share emotions through the use of imagery and figurative language.

Teach

R **Reading Strategy**

Analyzing Figurative Language

Say: Poets use figurative language to draw our attention to emotions. As you read the poems in this part, pay attention to how you would describe each emotion. Think of a time when you felt emotional about a similar person, place, or event. **Ask:** Does the poet's use of figurative language in these instances help you connect to the emotion? Why or why not? *(Some students will feel a strong connection to the language used by poets, while others may prefer different images or words.)* **OL**

★ Viewing the Art

The American Precisionists of the 1920s used hard edges and flat color to create formal, geometric landscapes. Charles Demuth also incorporated techniques of European cubism, abstracting forms and—in the case of *The Figure 5 in Gold*—abandoning traditional perspective. **AS**

Assess

Quickwrite

1. Student responses will vary. Answers should refer to the sticky and clingy quality of molasses.

2. Student responses will vary. Answers should refer to the color, intensity, or beauty of the rose.

3. Student responses will vary. Answers should refer to other strong, hard-working animals.

Focus

BELLRINGER

Bellringer Options
Daily Language Practice Transparency 59
Or **on the board, write:** *heart* and *mind*. **Ask:** What would your mind say to your heart if you were grieving a lost love? Have students write a brief dialogue between their heart and their mind. Have them discuss the different ways that people react to grief. Do they think minds and hearts react differently?

Or use **Bellringer Option Transparency.**

Author Search To expand students' appreciation of Emily Dickinson, have them access the Web site for additional information and resources.

Use the CheckPoint questions on Presentation Plus! to monitor students' comprehension. These questions can be used with interactive response keypads for immediate student feedback.

After Great Pain, A Formal Feeling Comes and *Heart! We Will Forget Him!*

MEET EMILY DICKINSON

Now considered one of the most important poets in American literature, Emily Dickinson saw her name in print only once: as second-place finisher for her entry in a bread contest. In fact, during her lifetime, her work remained largely private.

Emily Dickinson was born in Amherst, Massachusetts, to a prominent New England family. Her education included one year at Mount Holyoke Female Seminary, where she was greatly influenced by the Puritan religious tradition. Dickinson never married, and for nearly her entire life, she lived with her parents and her younger sister, Lavinia.

> *"The brain is wider than the sky."*
>
> —Emily Dickinson

A Private Life Dickinson began writing poems early in her life. However, as her life was private, so was her poetry. Of the nearly 1,800 poems she penned, Dickinson published only seven during her lifetime, and even then, she published them anonymously.

After Dickinson's death in 1886, her sister Lavinia discovered the enormity of Dickinson's work in her bedroom. Lavinia decided to reveal her sister's talent to the world. In 1890 and 1891, two collections of Dickinson's poetry were published, followed in later years by subsequent editions.

Throughout her life, Dickinson preferred solitude over socializing—a fact that has led to much speculation about her personal life. Despite many popular theories of loneliness or lovesickness, her self-imposed isolation may be viewed in another way. In the mid-nineteenth century, after completing their education, young women of Dickinson's social and economic standing were expected to marry and have children. Perhaps Dickinson desired something different for herself.

A Room of Her Own By not marrying, Dickinson carved out a space for herself to be able to write her poetry. Her retreat into her home, however, did not excuse her from domestic work entirely. Dickinson cared for her ailing mother and was much involved in the lives of her brothers' children. The domestic sphere is, in fact, one of the major themes of Dickinson's poetry.

A Daring New Voice Dickinson's poetic style was daring and unique. In her choice of topics, she departed from her female contemporaries by veering away from sentimentality and toward questioning life, death, God, and nature.

Emily Dickinson was born in 1830 and died in 1886.

Literature Online **Author Search** For more about Emily Dickinson, go to www.glencoe.com.

Selection Skills

Reading Skills
• Comparing and Contrasting Tone (SE pp. 587, 588, 591)

After Great Pain, A Formal Feeling Comes / Heart! We Will Forget Him!

Listening/Speaking/Viewing Skills
• Interpretive Reading (SE p. 592)
• Analyzing Art (TWE p. 589)

Literary Elements
• Personification (SE pp. 587, 591)
• Rhythm and Rhyme (SE p. 591)

Writing Skills/Grammar
• Contrasting Point of View (SE p. 592)

Vocabulary Skills
• Antonyms (SE p. 591)
• Academic Vocabulary (SE p. 591)

Connecting to the Poems

In both of the following poems, Emily Dickinson's speakers are dealing with emotional pain and grief. Before you read the poems, think about the following questions:

- How do people typically respond to emotionally painful events?
- How do you support others when they are grieving or emotionally upset?

Building Background

Emily Dickinson wrote many letters, some of which survived and give her readers insight into the events that may have inspired her poems. During the late 1850s, when she wrote "Heart! We Will Forget Him!", Dickinson's letters communicated a great love for a man. Many of her poems of this time portray great joy, but others reflect a great frustration with this love.

Dickinson wrote most of her poems (about eight hundred) during the Civil War (1861–1865), when wartime tension may have influenced her writing. She wrote "After Great Pain, A Formal Feeling Comes," in 1862, a year when the danger of the war threatened many of Dickinson's friends.

Setting Purposes for Reading

Big Idea Loves and Losses

As you read the poems, notice how Dickinson describes the themes of love and loss.

Literary Element Personification

Personification is a figure of speech in which inanimate objects are given human characteristics. Recognizing a poet's use of personification can help you understand what he or she intended to communicate. As you read, look for objects that Dickinson has personified.

- See Literary Terms Handbook, p. R12.

Literature Online **Interactive Literary Elements Handbook** To review or learn more about the literary elements, go to www.glencoe.com.

OBJECTIVES

In studying this selection, you will focus on the following:
- understanding personification
- comparing and contrasting tone
- understanding rhythm and rhyme
- writing to compare and contrast point of view

Reading Strategy Comparing and Contrasting Tone

A poet's **tone** is his or her attitude toward the subject matter. A poet's tone might convey several attitudes, including sympathy, objectivity, or humor. Dickinson often uses a playful tone in her poems. Understanding tone can help you determine a poet's meaning.

Reading Tip: Asking Questions Use a chart like the one below to help you ask questions about Dickinson's use of tone in the poems.

Questions	"After Great Pain, A Formal Feeling Comes"	"Heart! We Will Forget Him!"
Who is the speaker?	Someone who has suffered a painful loss	
Who does the speaker address?		The speaker's heart
What is the subject?		
What is the overall tone of poem?		

Vocabulary

ceremonious (ser´ ə mō´ nē əs) *adj.* carefully observant of the formal acts required by ritual, custom, or etiquette; p. 588 *Sam's graduation was a ceremonious occasion.*

recollect (rek´ ə lekt´) *v.* to remember; p. 588 *We used pictures to help Grandma recollect her childhood.*

stupor (stoo´ pər) *n.* a state of extreme lethargy; p. 588 *After twenty hours of traveling, Dan arrived in a stupor.*

lag (lag) *v.* to fall behind; p. 589 *If you continue to lag, we will be late for practice.*

EMILY DICKINSON **587**

Focus

Summary

In two short poems, Dickinson uses crisp, contemplative phrases to explore the pain of loss and grief. "After Great Pain, A Formal Feeling Comes" explores an individual's physical reactions to grief. "Heart! We Will Forget Him!" presents the mind's instructions to the heart while a person tries to forget a lost love.

V Vocabulary

Vocabulary File Say: Add these words and definitions to your vocabulary file. For each word, include a sentence that gives you an example of how to use the word. **OL** Students with English language needs should include the pronunciations of these words in their files. **EL**

Literature Online

Literary Elements Have students access the Web site to improve their understanding of personification.

Selection Resources

Print Materials
- 📁 Unit 3 Resources (Fast File), pp. 48–50
- 📁 Leveled Vocabulary Development 45
- 📁 Selection and Unit Assessments, pp. 103–104
- 📁 Selection Quick Checks, p. 52

Transparencies
- Bellringer Options Transparencies: Daily Language Practice Transparency 59
- Literary Elements Transparency 70

Technology
- TeacherWorks Plus™ CD-ROM
- StudentWorks Plus™ CD-ROM
- Presentation Plus!™ CD-ROM
- Literature Online, glencoe.com
- Online Student Edition, mhln.com
- Exam*View*® Assessment Suite CD-ROM
- Vocabulary PuzzleMaker CD-ROM
- Listening Library, disc 1 track 57

BI₁ **Big Idea**

Loves and Losses **Say:** Keep the following questions in mind as you read: What types of events would cause the pain and loss that Dickinson refers to in her poems? Is it important to know what specific events the author refers to in order to understand either of these poems? *(The specific cause of the suffering does not matter. Many events could cause a similar response, and it is the human response to loss that is important in understanding and identifying with these two poems.)* **OL**

R **Reading Strategy**

Comparing and Contrasting Tone **Answer:** *Students may note that the extra line makes this stanza feel longer and slower, conveying the sluggishness and apathy of the speaker.* Remind students that understanding tone directly relates to figuring out an author's purpose. Misreading the tone may lead to misinterpreting the message. **Ask:** How does the author's slow and formal tone help us understand the author's purpose? *(The formal tone complements Dickinson's attempt to show readers the stiff and removed way that people respond to pain.)* **OL**

Cotswold Park, Winter Woodland (Morning, December). Charles Neal. Oil on canvas.

After Great Pain, A Formal Feeling Comes

Emily Dickinson

BI₁ After great pain, a formal feeling comes —
The Nerves sit **ceremonious**, like Tombs —
The stiff Heart questions was it He, that bore,
And Yesterday, or Centuries before?

5   The Feet, mechanical, go round —
Of Ground, or Air, or Ought¹—
A Wooden way
Regardless grown,
A Quartz contentment, like a stone —

10 This is the Hour of Lead —
Remembered, if outlived,
As Freezing persons, **recollect** the Snow —
First — Chill — then **Stupor** — then the letting go —

---

1. Here, *Ought* means "anything," and is an archaic variant of *aught.*

Reading Strategy Comparing and Contrasting Tone *How does this stanza's extra line help convey the tone of the poem?* **R**

Vocabulary

ceremonious (ser´ə mō ´n əs) *adj.* carefully observant of the formal acts required by ritual, custom, or etiquette
recollect (rek´ə lekt´) *v.* to remember
stupor (stoo´pər) *n.* a state of extreme lethargy

588 UNIT 3 POETRY

Skills Practice

GRAMMAR AND LANGUAGE:

Adjectives Explain to students that writers use adjectives to limit the meanings of nouns and pronouns. Put up a transparency of "After Great Pain, A Formal Feeling Comes" and have volunteers underline the adjectives. *(great, for-mal, stiff, mechanical, Wooden, Quartz, Freezing)* **Say:** Name the noun modified by each of these adjectives. *(pain, feeling, Heart, Feet, way, contentment, persons)* Have students discuss how these adjectives affect the meaning of the poem. **BL**

Heart! We Will Forget Him!

Emily Dickinson

Ricordo di un dolore o Ritratto di Santina Negri (Memory of a Sorrow/Portrait of Santina Negri), 1889. Giuseppe Pellizza da Volpedo. Oil on canvas, 107 x 79 cm. Bergamo, Italy.

Heart! We will forget him!
You and I — tonight!
You may forget the warmth he gave —
I will forget the light!

When you have done, pray tell me
That I may straight begin!
Haste! lest[1] while you're **lagging**
I remember him!

---

1. Here, *lest* means "in order to prevent any possibility that."

> **Big Idea** Loves and Losses *Why do you think that Dickinson directly addresses the Heart?* **BI₂**

> **Vocabulary**
>
> **lag** (lag) *v.* to fall behind

Teach

BI₂ **Big Idea**

Loves and Losses Answer: *Students should conclude that Dickinson addresses the Heart to encourage herself to forget an unrequited love.* **OL**

★ Viewing the Art

Guiseppe Pellizza da Volpedo (1869–1907) was an Italian painter who came from a farming family. He began formal training as an artist at age sixteen and eventually studied under French and Italian masters. Volpedo is known primarily for portraits and landscapes. **AS**

✓CheckPoint

Use the CheckPoint questions on Presentation Plus! to check students' mastery of the selection. These questions can be used with interactive response keypads for immediate student feedback.

Differentiated Instruction

Research Students can use the Internet to learn more about Emily Dickinson. A good place to start is The Academy of American Poets, at http://www.poets.org/edick/. Remind students to evaluate carefully the credibility of Internet sources by looking for the Web site's source, recent updates, and evidence of careful text preparation. Allow time for students to share their findings. **OL** Challenge advanced students to create a multimedia presentation. **AL**

Objectives
- To compare and contrast tone (SE)
- To analyze adjectives and their effect on meaning (TWE)

Assess

1. Students should use examples in their responses.

2. (a) Tombs (b) It captures the feeling of numbness.

3. (a) The Hour of Lead (b) The image of lead reinforces the idea that every action feels sluggish, slow, and heavy.

4. (a) When the heart has forgotten him (b) So that the speaker can also forget him

5. (a) "Contentment, like a stone" and "as freezing persons" (b) The first reinforces the idea that the sufferer is not truly content; the second summarizes the steps of grief.

6. Some may say they add intensity; others may say they are distracting.

7. Students should note elements that make the poems concise or intense and explain how they strengthen or weaken the poems' messages.

RESPONDING AND THINKING CRITICALLY

Respond

1. Do you think "After Great Pain, A Formal Feeling Comes" and "Heart! We Will Forget Him!" express positive ideas about love and loss? Explain.

Recall and Interpret

2. (a)In "After Great Pain, A Formal Feeling Comes," to what are nerves compared? (b)What does this image suggest about the sufferer's physical feelings?

3. (a)What is being remembered in the third stanza of "After Great Pain, A Formal Feeling Comes"? (b)How does this image reinforce the ideas of the poem?

4. (a)What does the speaker in "Heart! We Will Forget Him!" want to be told? (b)Why does the speaker need this information?

Analyze and Evaluate

5. A **simile** is a figure of speech, using *like* or *as*, that is used to compare two things. (a)Identify two similes in "After Great Pain, A Formal Feeling Comes." (b)Discuss how Dickinson uses them to convey her grief in the poem.

6. Analyze Dickinson's use of exclamation marks in "Heart! We Will Forget Him!" Do you find them effective? Explain.

Connect

7. **Big Idea** **Loves and Losses** Dickinson is praised for the conciseness and intensity of her poems. How well do these qualities serve her ideas of love and loss?

DAILY LIFE AND CULTURE

Living Single

Before 1800, it was extremely uncommon and difficult to live as a single woman. This idea began to change during the nineteenth century, when the proportion of never-married women rose steadily. Emily Dickinson lived as a single, middle-class woman during a period marked by the emergence of the women's rights movement and vigorous debate over the proper roles for women.

Women in general, did not have many options or much real power. Single women, however, did retain certain civil rights that women who married did not have. Single women could, for example, make contracts and open bank accounts, and they often served as treasurers for the increasing number of women's organizations that developed during the prewar era. Many feminists debated the opportunities available to women and pushed for women's rights.

1. How do the lives of single, middle-class women of the 1800s compare to the lives of single, middle-class women of today?

2. Why do you think Emily Dickinson chose to live in relative seclusion? Explain.

Elizabeth Cady Stanton and Women's Rights

Daily Life and Culture

1. Students should list several qualities of life from the text and compare them to those of today's single, middle-class women.

2. Students may argue that she had a broken heart, that she had limited options as a nineteenth-century woman, or that she chose to dedicate herself to writing.

LITERARY ANALYSIS

Literary Element   Personification

Writers personify animals, objects, forces of nature, and ideas. Many human qualities, including emotions, physical gestures, and powers of speech, are attributed to personified items. **Personification** is used in both prose and poetry.

1. List the things personified in "After Great Pain, A Formal Feeling Comes" and "Heart! We Will Forget Him!"

2. Explain how the absence of personification would affect the poems.

Review: Rhythm and Rhyme

As you learned on page 541, **rhythm** is the pattern of beats created by the order of stressed and unstressed syllables. As you learned on page 547, **rhyme** is the repetition of the same stressed vowel sounds and any succeeding sounds in two or more words.

Partner Activity Pair up with a classmate and analyze the rhythm and rhyme of "After Great Pain, A Formal Feeling Comes" and "Heart! We Will Forget Him!" In most of Dickinson's early poems, the rhythm, or meter, models that of Puritan hymns. Common forms include quatrains (four lines) with steady six, eight, or ten iambs—unstressed and then stressed syllables, such as *da-DUM*.

Working with your partner, count the number of syllables in each line and use letters to label the basic rhyme scheme. Write your information in a chart like the one below.

"After Great Pain, A Formal Feeling Comes"		
Line Number	Number of Syllables	Rhyme Scheme
Stanza 1 1 2 3 4	10 10 10 10	
Stanza 2		
Stanza 3		A A B B

READING AND VOCABULARY

Reading Strategy   Comparing and Contrasting Tone

Writers use elements such as word choice, punctuation, sentence structure, and figures of speech to convey tone. Identifying these elements often helps readers clarify the tone in a piece of literature.

1. In "After Great Pain, A Formal Feeling Comes," which literary elements are used by Dickinson in the line "The Feet, mechanical, go round—"?

2. Do these elements seem to convey a tone of sympathy, humor, or objectivity? Explain.

Vocabulary   Practice

Practice with Antonyms Find the antonym for each vocabulary word from "After Great Pain, A Formal Feeling Comes" and "Heart! We Will Forget Him!" listed in the first column. Use a dictionary or a thesaurus if you need help.

1. ceremonious
   a. dignified   **b.** informal

2. recollect
   a. overlook   **b.** memorize

3. stupor
   a. dream   **b.** awareness

4. lag
   a. break   **b.** keep up

Academic Vocabulary

Here are two words from the vocabulary list on page R82. These words will help you think, write, and talk about the selection.

restrain (ri strān´) *v.* to hold back; to keep under control

collapse (kə laps´) *v.* to fall down; to give way

Practice and Apply
1. Does the speaker in "After Great Pain, A Formal Feeling Comes" **restrain** his or her feelings?
2. At what point does the speaker in "After Great Pain, A Formal Feeling Comes" **collapse**?

EMILY DICKINSON   **591**

AFTER YOU READ

Assess

Literary Element

1. The first poem personifies the sufferer's nerves, heart, and feet. The second poem personifies the heart and mind of someone who needs to forget an unrequited love.

2. Without personification, the poems would seem less descriptive and more traditional.

Review: Rhythm and Rhyme

Stanza 1: Rhyme Scheme: AABB; Stanza 2: lines 5,6,7,8,9; Number of syllables: 8,6,4,4,8; Rhyme Scheme: ABCDD; Stanza 3: lines 10,11,12,13; Number of syllables: 6,6,10,10

Reading Strategy

1. Personification and punctuation (the dash)

2. Personifying a body part helps express the pain felt by the sufferer, distancing the sufferer from the pain, and the dashes cause the reader to pause and slow down, reinforcing the solemn tone.

Vocabulary

1. b   **2.** a   **3.** b   **4.** b

Academic Vocabulary

1. Some students may say that the speaker's feelings are held in check by the somber, detached tone.

2. At the end of the poem

Assess

Writing About Literature

Students' essays should include:

- a personal response to the effect of point of view
- the similarities and differences of the two points of view
- evidence from the text

Listening and Speaking

Speakers should pause for dashes and other punctuation, speak clearly and with sufficient volume, and make eye contact. Listeners should complete a response sheet, noting one strength and one weakness for each speaker.

Dickinson's Language and Style

Following are sample answers:

Capitalized Word	Reason for capitalization
Tombs	connection to Nerves
The	beginning of a line
Heart	personification
He	reference to Christ
Yesterday	emphasis
Ground	Emphasis and connection

Writing About Literature

Compare and Contrast Point of View Dickinson uses third-person point of view in "After Great Pain, A Formal Feeling Comes" and first-person point of view in "Heart! We Will Forget Him!" How do these differing points of view affect your experience reading the poems? Write a one- or two-page analysis, in which you compare and contrast the points of view in these poems. Use evidence from Dickinson's poems to support your opinions.

Before you begin drafting, take notes on the similarities and differences of each poem's point of view in a Venn diagram, such as the one below.

"After Great Pain, A Formal Feeling Comes"
Speaker is standing outside the story

Both

"Heart! We Will Forget Him!"

Include point-of-view characteristics and quotes from the poems related to their points of view. Also, list any impressions or ideas that strike you as you read. Once you have completed the diagram, begin drafting.

After completing your draft, sit down with one of your peers to review each other's work and suggest revisions. Then proofread and edit your draft for errors in spelling, grammar, and punctuation.

Listening and Speaking

In small groups, choose one of Emily Dickinson's poems to read aloud. Review your poems silently and then take turns reading them aloud to the rest of the group, making sure to pause with the dashes. Take the time to speak clearly and make eye contact.

Once everyone has read, go around again, reading your poems without the pauses. Compare how the readings differ and discuss the functions of punctuation in poetry.

Literature Online **Web Activities** For eFlashcards, Selection Quick Checks, and other Web activities, go to www.glencoe.com.

Dickinson's Language and Style

Using Capitalization in Poetry The capitalization in Dickinson's poems has been called both sporadic and revolutionary. Poets in general often capitalize words for a variety of reasons. Capitalized words may occur at the beginning of lines, they may be first words of sentences, they may denote personified objects, or they may be proper nouns. Capitalization varies with a poet's style and the conventions of the historical period during which the poetry is written. Capitalization is used in prose writing for many of the same reasons.

Consider Dickinson's use of capitalization in the following example from "After Great Pain, A Formal Feeling Comes":

"The Nerves sit ceremonious like Tombs —
    The stiff Heart questions was it He, that bore,"

Notice that Dickinson uses capitalization at the beginning of lines and for personified objects (the Nerves, Tombs, and Heart are all given human characteristics in the poem).

Since most of Dickinson's poems were not published during her lifetime, readers do not always know if she intentionally capitalized a word or not. As you read her work, examine the capitalization and decide whether it adds to the meaning of the poems.

In the chart below, notice the first few capitalized words of "After Great Pain, A Formal Feeling Comes" and the reasons why each word was capitalized.

Capitalized Word	Reason for capitalization
After	beginning of a line
Nerves	personification

Activity Create a chart of your own, listing the rest of the capitalized words in "After Great Pain, A Formal Feeling Comes." Suggest reasons for capitalization.

Revising Check

Capitalization Review your essay on point of view again and make sure you have followed all of the basic capitalization rules in your own writing. Make any necessary revisions to correct capitalization errors.

Literature Online

Web Activities Have students access the Web site for interactive activities that will help them assess their understanding of the selection.

Well, I Have Lost You; and I Lost You Fairly

MEET EDNA ST. VINCENT MILLAY

Poet Edna St. Vincent Millay captured the youthful, liberated, and artistic spirit of New York City's Greenwich Village in the post-World War I period. In particular, one celebrated 1920 poem made her a symbol of her generation. The piece compared her passion for life to a flame burning brightly yet briefly.

Youthful Talent Millay's mother, Cora, moved her family to Camden, Maine, when Edna was a young girl. The single mother worked long hours to support her children while actively encouraging them to pursue artistic expression. Millay wrote her first poem at age five, and in 1917 she published her first volume of poetry. Her first notable poem, "Renascence," attracted a mentor who helped her obtain a scholarship to Vassar College.

> "My candle burns at both ends."
>
> —Edna St. Vincent Millay

Upon graduating in 1917, Millay moved to New York City. She temporarily supported herself with short stories and poems published in magazines under the pseudonym "Nancy Boyd." She also acted with the Provincetown Players, most notably writing and directing a one-act play in verse, *Aria da Capo*. She went on to win literary awards while publishing volumes of verse. Having written for *Vanity Fair*, Millay signed with the magazine to submit pieces from Europe. She spent two years in Europe as a correspondent.

In 1923 Millay married Eugen Jan Boissevain, a Dutch businessman. The pair bought a country home near Austerlitz, New York. From this base, she and her husband embarked on extensive reading tours. Boissevain was very supportive of Millay's creative projects and managed the household for her convenience. This gave Millay the personal freedom she desired and needed to write. Her success as a writer continued; she was the first woman awarded the Pulitzer Prize for poetry with "Ballad of the Harp-Weaver."

Political Activism While themes of love and nature dominated Millay's early writings, political and social concerns came to the forefront in the late 1920s. A socialist politically, she was even jailed once for her role in a public demonstration.

Later poems protested the brutality of repressive regimes. Much of this politically motivated poetry fell short of the poetic promise of her youth. However, "The Murder of Lidice" (1942) was exceptional for its moving account of Nazi brutality during World War II.

A year after the unsettling death of her husband in 1949, Millay died alone at her country home. She remains a poetic presence, remembered not only for her individualism and skill but also as a symbol of her time.

Edna St. Vincent Millay was born in 1892 and died in 1950.

 Author Search For more about Edna St. Vincent Millay, go to **www.glencoe.com**.

EDNA ST. VINCENT MILLAY **593**

Focus

BELLRINGER

Bellringer Options
Selection Focus Transparency 30
Daily Language Practice Transparency 60
Or **on the board write:** "Well, I Have Lost You; and I Lost You Fairly."
Ask: What do you think "I Lost You Fairly" might mean in the title of this poem? Have students discuss the kinds of situations in which a person might say this about breaking up with someone and the impression that such a statement gives them of the speaker of the poem.

Literature Online

Author Search To expand students' appreciation of Edna St. Vincent Millay, have them access the Web site for additional information and resources.

CheckPoint

Use the CheckPoint questions on Presentation Plus! to monitor students' comprehension. These questions can be used with interactive response keypads for immediate student feedback.

Selection Skills

Well, I Have Lost You; and I Lost You Fairly

Literary Elements
• Sonnet (SE pp. 594, 596)

Reading Skills
• Analyzing Diction (SE pp. 594, 596)

Vocabulary Skills
• Connotation and Denotation (SE pp. 594, 596)

Writing Skills/Grammar
• Letter writing (SE p. 596)

Focus

Summary

The speaker addresses a former lover. She mentions her sorrow at their parting, but her tone is proud and she stoically accepts the situation, implying that it is better to end things than to hold on to someone who no longer cares.

V Vocabulary

Vocabulary File Say: Add these words and definitions to your vocabulary file. For each word, include a sentence that gives you an example of how to use the word. **OL** Students with English language needs should include the pronunciations of these words in their files. **EL**

Literary Elements Have students access the Web site to improve their understanding of sonnets.

Connecting to the Poem

Think about the possible consequences of falling out of love. The following poem describes one perspective of lost love: reluctant acceptance of the situation. Before you read the poem, think about the following questions:

- Do couples who fall out of love always break up?
- Can couples who fall out of love remain friends?

Building Background

Edna St. Vincent Millay wrote this poem in the form of an English sonnet. The English sonnet is also called the Shakespearean sonnet because Shakespeare was the master of this sonnet form. English sonnets are divided into three quatrains, or groups of four lines, and one couplet, or pair of lines. The rhyme scheme is usually *abab, cdcd, efef, gg*. The English sonnet form allows for the presentation and development of a problem or question in the three quatrains, and a solution in the couplet.

Setting Purposes for Reading

Big Idea Loves and Losses

Love involves many conflicting emotions, perceived needs versus personal wants, and issues of trust. As you read this poem, pay attention to how the speaker expresses the pride and self-reliance of one who releases a lost love without petty games or ill feelings.

Literary Element Sonnet

A **sonnet** is a lyric poem of fourteen lines, usually written in iambic pentameter and typically following strict patterns of stanza divisions and rhymes. Knowing the elements of a sonnet will help you appreciate the beauty of this form of poetry. As you read the poem, notice the rhyming lines.

- See Literary Terms Handbook, p. R16.

Literature Online **Interactive Literary Elements Handbook** To review or learn more about the literary elements, go to www.glencoe.com.

OBJECTIVES

In studying this selection, you will focus on the following:
- understanding the sonnet form
- analyzing diction to better comprehend a text
- writing a letter in response to a poem's speaker

Reading Strategy Analyzing Diction

Diction includes the writer's choice of words, an important element in the writer's voice or style. Skilled writers choose their words carefully to convey a particular tone and meaning. Understanding why authors choose some words over others will help you understand tone and meaning. While reading this poem, pay attention to whether the poet uses abstract or concrete, general or specific, or formal or informal diction. By **analyzing diction**, you will gain a better understanding of what you are reading.

Reading Tip: Noting Words As you read the poem, note words Millay uses that you find particularly interesting or intriguing. Create a list of those words and think about other words the poet could have considered using instead.

Word from Poem	Possible Alternate Word
fairly	justly

Vocabulary

apprehension (ap´ri hen´shən) *n.* dread; fear of the future; p. 595 *Jean sensed her brother's apprehension about jumping off the high diving board.*

slyly (slī´lē) *adv.* cunningly; in an artful manner; p. 595 *Michael slyly hid the box of cookies so that no one would find and eat them.*

Vocabulary Tip: Connotation and Denotation The **connotation** of a word is the suggested or implied meanings associated with it beyond its dictionary definition, or **denotation**. A word can have a positive, negative, or neutral connotation. Words in poems are chosen to evoke certain connotations for the reader. Look beyond the denotation to get a glimpse of the poet's thoughts.

Well, I Have Lost You; and I Lost You Fairly

Edna St. Vincent Millay

The Invalid (Le Invalid). Georges Pierre Seurat (1859-1891). Private Collection, Paris.

Well, I have lost you; and I lost you fairly;
In my own way, and with my full consent.
Say what you will, kings in a tumbrel[1] rarely
Went to their deaths more proud than this one went.
5 Some nights of **apprehension** and hot weeping
I will confess; but that's permitted me;
Day dried my eyes; I was not one for keeping
Rubbed in a cage a wing that would be free.
If I had loved you less or played you **slyly**
10 I might have held you for a summer more,
But at the cost of words I value highly,
And no such summer as the one before.
Should I outlive this anguish—and men do—
I shall have only good to say of you.   ★

---

1. A *tumbrel* is a farmer's two-wheeled cart. During the French Revolution, such carts were used to carry condemned people—including King Louis XVI—to their executions.

Big Idea Loves and Losses *Why might the speaker consent to losing someone that she may, in fact, love?* **BI**

Vocabulary

apprehension (ap´ ri hen´shən) *n.* dread; fear of the future
slyly (slī´lē) *adv.* cunningly; in an artful manner

EDNA ST. VINCENT MILLAY **595**

Assess

1. Answers will vary.

2. (a) It is honest, proud, and independent. (b) She has not tried to manipulate her loved one or the situation, and they parted as equals.

3. (a) As hurt and suffering (b) She shows resilience, self-reliance, and acceptance.

4. (a) The lover who no longer loves is compared to a caged bird that wants its freedom. (b) Fear of entrapment by one and understanding by the other

5. (a) The speaker values honesty. (b) She refuses to lie or manipulate.

6. Answers will vary.

7. (a) The speaker's actions seem honorable and protect her from the self-hatred. (b) Answers will vary.

8. Answers will vary.

Literary Element

1. Fourteen lines, and a rhyme scheme typical of sonnets

2. Their different rhyming schemes act as an "independent" unit.

Writing About Literature

Students' letters should

- incorporate the theme.
- provide personal responses.

Literature Online

Web Activities Have students access the Web site for interactive activities that will help them assess their understanding of the selection.

RESPONDING AND THINKING CRITICALLY

Respond

1. Describe the mental image you formed after reading this poem.

Recall and Interpret

2. (a) Summarize the speaker's reaction and attitude toward the loss in lines 1–2. (b) What do you think the speaker means by losing "fairly" and "with my full consent"?

3. (a) How does the speaker describe her reaction to the loss in lines 5–7? (b) What does the tone of this description tell you about the speaker?

4. (a) What metaphor does the speaker use in lines 7–8? (b) What feeling does this comparison convey?

Analyze and Evaluate

5. (a) In your opinion, what does the speaker mean in lines 9–12? (b) What does this tell you about the speaker's values?

6. Do you think that the speaker will "outlive this anguish"? Give reasons for your answer.

7. (a) Do you think that the speaker acted wisely in the relationship described here? (b) Would you have acted the same way? Why or why not?

Connect

8. **Big Idea** Loves and Losses (a) How might you feel if a former boyfriend or girlfriend sent this poem to you? (b) After reading it, would you feel better about how the relationship ended? Explain.

LITERARY ANALYSIS

Literary Element Sonnet

This poem has a rhyming couplet, a characteristic of English, or Shakespearean **sonnets**. The rhyming couplet often presents a conclusion to the issues or questions discussed in the three quatrains. Examine again how "Well, I Have Lost You; and I Lost You Fairly" fits the sonnet form.

1. How does this poem fit the definition of a sonnet?

2. What makes the ending couplet sound like a conclusion?

Writing About Literature

Respond to the Speaker Imagine that the poem is addressed to you. Would you feel angry, sad, rejected, or relieved? Would you empathize with the speaker's point of view, especially with the lines "If I had loved you less or played you slyly / I might have held you for a summer more"? In a reply letter to the speaker, discuss love and loss from your perspective.

Literature Online **Web Activities** For eFlashcards, Selection Quick Checks, and other Web activities, go to www.glencoe.com.

READING AND VOCABULARY

Reading Strategy Analyzing Diction

The poet carefully uses words to convey the reasons why it was best to end her relationship. She also uses a casual but exacting tone as she directs the poem to a specific person, her lost love, and not to us, her readers.

1. How might you rephrase "played you slyly" in today's language?

2. Which words and phrases convey a matter-of-fact tone? Which ones imply passion?

Vocabulary Practice

Practice with Connotation and Denotation
Decide whether there is a positive, negative, or neutral connotation in the way that each vocabulary word is used in the sentences below. Use a dictionary or thesaurus if you need help.

1. Manuel's **apprehension** about singing ended after the audience applauded wildly.
   a. positive   **b.** negative   **c.** neutral

2. The boy **slyly** placed the gift for his mother's fortieth birthday on the front seat of her car.
   a. positive   **b.** negative   **c.** neutral

Reading Strategy

1. Possible answers: "string you along" or "play you for a fool"

2. Matter-of-fact: "lost you fairly," "full consent," "and men do"; Passion: "apprehension and hot weeping," "If I had loved you less," "And no such summer," and "anguish."

Vocabulary

1. b   2. a

Shall I Compare Thee to a Summer's Day?

MEET WILLIAM SHAKESPEARE

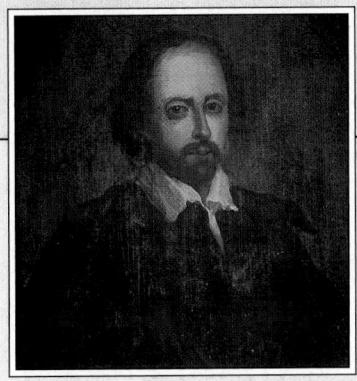

Over the years he has had many names. Some have called him "Gentle Will." Many are familiar with his most common nickname, "The Bard." And though the name Shakespeare brings to mind images of great onstage romance, horrific tragedy, and uproarious comedy, he was, before all else, "The Poet."

The Early Years Born to Mary Arden and John Shakespeare, William lived out his early years in Stratford-upon-Avon, England, where he most likely received an extensive education in Latin literature and grammar, history, and mythology. This immersion in the classics fuels much of the imagery and theme in Shakespeare's works.

Little else is known about his early life, but literary historians do know that in 1582 he married Anne Hathaway, with whom he had three children, Susanna, Hamnet, and Judith. By 1592, Shakespeare began showing up in the world of London theater, though there are conflicting stories as to how he arrived there.

> "[Shakespeare] was not of an age, but for all time!"
>
> —Ben Jonson

The Poet Shakespeare's first poems, *Venus and Adonis* and *The Rape of Lucrece,* were published in 1593 and 1594. Both were narrative works that demonstrated Shakespeare's education in ancient Roman history and mythology, specifically the mythical romance of the goddess Aphrodite and the mortal Adonis, and the tale of the rape of Lucrece—the daughter of an important ancient Roman family that supposedly incited a rebellion in Rome.

Although Shakespeare's canon features additional poetry, such as *The Phoenix and the Turtle* (1601), Shakespeare the Poet is best-known and regarded for his sonnets. Although probably written in the 1590s, Shakespeare's 154 sonnets were not published until 1609. These poems are noted for their universal theme of the power of love and beauty over nature and time.

Ghosts of Rhyme and Rhythm As might be expected with a literary figure as famous and enigmatic as Shakespeare, several mysteries surround this collection of sonnets. Whether the Poet himself or his publisher, Thomas Thorpe, is responsible for the mystery, someone dedicated the first 126 of the sonnets to a set of initials, a person who has been known to history only as W.H. A different oddity haunts sonnets 127–152, which are dedicated to a mysterious "dark lady." Theories abound on whom this person might be and to whom those initials might belong, but the world may never know the true answer.

Shakespeare lived to the age of fifty-two, a respectable age for the seventeenth century. Both his poetic drama and dramatic poetry live on today as some of the most quoted and esteemed literature of all time.

William Shakespeare was born in 1564 and died in 1616.

Literature Online **Author Search** For more about William Shakespeare, go to www.glencoe.com.

WILLIAM SHAKESPEARE **597**

Focus

BELLRINGER

Bellringer Options
Selection Focus Transparency 31
Daily Language Practice Transparency 61
Or **on the board write** common tokens of love, such as: *chocolates, flowers, love letter, poem.* **Ask:** Which is the best gift to give to express one's feelings for someone? The best to receive? The most meaningful? Have students discuss some tokens of love they've given or received. Have them talk about gifts they would like to give or receive.

Literature Online

Author Search To expand students' appreciation of William Shakespeare, have them access the Web site additional information and resources.

CheckPoint

Use the CheckPoint questions on Presentation Plus! to monitor students' comprehension. These questions can be used with interactive response keypads for immediate student feedback.

Selection Skills

Literary Elements	Shall I Compare Thee to a Summer's Day?	Listening/Speaking/Viewing Skills

Literary Elements
- Metaphor (SE pp. 598, 600; TWE p. 599)
- Personification (SE p. 600)

Shall I Compare Thee to a Summer's Day?

Listening/Speaking/Viewing Skills
- Dramatic Recitation (SE p. 601)

Reading Skills
- Analyzing Rhythm and Rhyme (SE pp. 598, 599, 601)

Vocabulary Skills
- Analogies (SE pp. 598, 601)
- Academic Vocabulary (SE p. 601)

Writing Skills/Grammar
- Writing Sonnets (SE p. 601)

Focus

Summary

Using an extended metaphor, the speaker compares his lover to a summer's day. He says that she is more lovely and more permanent than a summer's day and that her beauty will never fade but will be preserved in the beauty of the poem he writes.

V Vocabulary

Vocabulary File Say: Add these words and definitions to your vocabulary file. For each word, include a sentence that gives you an example of how to use the word. **OL** Students with English language needs should include the pronunciations of these words in their files. **EL**

Literary Elements Have students access the Web site to improve their understanding of metaphor.

Connecting to the Sonnet

The following sonnet is one of Shakespeare's most famous love poems. Shakespeare declares that his love's beauty will not fade as the summer fades and instead will live for all time. Before you read the poem, think about the following questions:

- To what would you compare someone you love or the emotion of love itself?
- Do you believe that love can last forever?

Building Background

Throughout history, people in love have expressed their feelings by giving tokens of their affection, such as flowers, poems, candy, jewelry, and locks of hair. Many of these items have symbolic meaning. A ring is a circle that may represent endless love. A lock of hair may be a cherished physical reminder of a beloved person. Flowers often represent ardent love in full bloom.

In each of Shakespeare's sonnets, the speaker presents his inner thoughts and feelings. Although each sonnet is a complete poem that stands on its own, all 154 of Shakespeare's sonnets together form a sonnet sequence—a series of sonnets on the same subject.

Setting Purposes for Reading

Big Idea Loves and Losses

As you read this poem, notice what Shakespeare says about love and think about why he feels that way.

Literary Element Metaphor

A **metaphor** is a figure of speech that compares or equates two seemingly unlike things to suggest an underlying similarity between the two. A metaphor does not use the words *like* or *as*. As you read, try to determine the overarching metaphor that binds the poem and its imagery together.

- See Literary Terms Handbook, p. R10.

Literature Online Interactive Literary Elements Handbook To review or learn more about the literary elements, go to www.glencoe.com.

OBJECTIVES
In studying this selection, you will focus on the following:
- identifying and analyzing author's use of metaphor and extended metaphor
- analyzing rhythm and rhyme in a sonnet
- identifying and analyzing author's use of personification
- writing to apply form

Reading Strategy Analyzing Rhythm and Rhyme

Rhythm is the pattern of beats created by the arrangement of stressed and unstressed syllables. **Rhyme** is the repetition of the same stressed vowel sounds and any succeeding sounds in two or more words. While reading this poem, take note of Shakespeare's use of rhythm and rhyme.

Reading Tip: Scanning and Scheming It might be useful to analyze the meter and rhyme scheme of the sonnet as you read. After determining the rhyme scheme, choose two lines from the poem and mark the meter with the appropriate stress symbols. Use the chart below as a guide.

Scansion	˘ / ˘ / ˘ / ˘ / ˘ /
Line	And often is his gold complexion dimmed
Scansion	
Line	

Vocabulary

temperate (tem′pər it) *adj.* calm and free from extremes of temperature; p. 599 *Most areas in the state of Virginia, which experiences few extreme temperatures, are considered temperate in climate.*

Vocabulary Tip: Analogy An analogy is a comparison that shows the relationship between words or ideas. You can use word analogies to master learning new vocabulary.

Selection Resources

Print Materials
- Unit 3 Resources (Fast File), pp. 54–56
- Leveled Vocabulary Development 47
- Selection and Unit Assessments, pp. 107–108
- Selection Quick Checks, p. 54

Transparencies
- Bellringer Options Transparencies: Daily Language Practice Transparency 61
- Literary Elements Transparency 69

Technology
- TeacherWorks Plus™ CD-ROM
- StudentWorks Plus™ CD-ROM
- Presentation Plus!™ CD-ROM
- Literature Online, glencoe.com
- Online Student Edition, mhln.com
- ExamView® Assessment Suite CD-ROM
- Vocabulary PuzzleMaker CD-ROM
- Listening Library, disc 1 track 59

Shall I Compare Thee to a Summer's Day?

William Shakespeare

The Great Oak, Moat Lawn with Rhododendrons & Azaleas—Morning, June, 2004. Charles Neal. Oil on canvas.

Shall I compare thee to a summer's day?
Thou art more lovely and more **temperate.**
Rough winds do shake the darling buds of May,
And summer's lease hath all too short a date.
5 Sometime too hot the eye of heaven shines,
And often is his gold complexion dimmed;
And every fair[1] from fair sometime declines,
By chance, or nature's changing course untrimmed:[2]
L But thy eternal summer shall not fade
10 Nor lose possession of that fair thou ow'st,[3]
Nor shall Death brag thou wand'rest in his shade,
When in eternal lines to time thou grow'st.
  So long as men can breathe or eyes can see,
  So long lives this, and this gives life to thee.

---

1. *Fair,* in this context, is a synonym for *beauty.*
2. Here, *untrimmed* means "stripped of beauty."
3. *[thou ow'st]* Read this poetic phrase as "you own" or "you possess."

Reading Strategy Analyzing Rhythm and Rhyme *How does the rhyme scheme of the last two lines differ from the rhyme scheme of the rest of the poem?* **R**

Vocabulary

temperate (tem′ par it) *adj.* calm and free from extremes of temperature

WILLIAM SHAKESPEARE **599**

599

Assess

1. (a) Answers will vary. (b) Some may say that a tangible gift, such as flowers, would be better. Others may prefer the permanence and power of a poem.

2. (a) A person in love (b) The person addressed is "lovely," "temperate" and in his or her prime ("summer").

3. (a) The beloved and a summer's day (b) The lover

4. (a) The poem will preserve the lover's beauty and grace. (b) The poet wants to give the gift of immortality.

5. By elevating her above such impressive things as summer, the sun, and death

6. (a) Some may say probably not, but others may say the speaker idealizes love and that it will fade. (b) The beauty seems to depend on love, so if the love vanishes, the beauty will vanish as well.

7. The poem recognizes the losses that time will bring, but it has found a way to keep love alive.

Literary Element

1. A comparison of the lover to a summer's day

2. Most people think of a summer's day as a lovely thing, so it makes a suitable object of comparison for a love poem.

RESPONDING AND THINKING CRITICALLY

Respond

1. (a) Does this poem reflect your personal views on love? Explain. (b) Do you think that a poem would make a good token of affection? Why or why not?

Recall and Interpret

2. (a) Who might the speaker of this poem be? (b) In your opinion, who is the speaker addressing? Use details from the poem to support your answers.

3. (a) What two things is the speaker comparing? (b) Which one does the speaker consider to be superior? How do you know this?

4. (a) According to the speaker, why will the subject of the poem have a summer that is eternal? (b) What might this tell you about the poet's reason for writing the poem?

Analyze and Evaluate

5. How does Shakespeare make the subject of the poem seem larger than life, like something elevated beyond the confines of nature?

6. (a) In your opinion, will the speaker's love ever fade? Explain. (b) If the speaker's love fades, will the subject's beauty fade along with the speaker's love? Explain your reasoning.

Connect

7. **Big Idea** Loves and Losses This poem is generally considered a powerful and fervently romantic love poem. How does this poem also connect to the idea of loss?

LITERARY ANALYSIS

Literary Element Metaphor

Some works of literature, such as "Shall I Compare Thee to a Summer's Day?", use an **extended metaphor**, or a metaphor that compares two unlike things in various ways throughout a paragraph, stanza, or an entire selection. Extended metaphors can deepen the meaning and detail of their comparisons more than singular metaphors are able to. Think about how the use of extended metaphor affects the sonnet you have read.

1. What is the extended metaphor in "Shall I Compare Thee to a Summer's Day?"

2. Why might Shakespeare have chosen to use this extended metaphor?

3. Why might Shakespeare have chosen something that was dissimilar and inferior to the subject being addressed in the poem?

Review: Personification

As you learned on page 587, **personification** is a figure of speech in which an animal, object, force of nature, or idea is given human characteristics.

Partner Activity Pair up with a classmate and discuss the use of personification in "Shall I Compare Thee to a Summer's Day?" Working with your partner, find three examples of personification. Why might Shakespeare have chosen to give human characteristics to these things? Use a chart like the one below to organize your discussion.

Example of Personification	Possible Reason
"Nor shall Death brag thou wand'rest in his shade"	Giving death human characteristics is a common, traditional device

3. As lovely as a summer's day is, Shakespeare sees faults in it. By choosing this metaphor, Shakespeare can elevate the beloved above something as beautiful and divine as a summer's day by exposing the faults in the summer. The lover becomes something beyond time and nature.

Review: Personification

The sun ("eye of heaven" with a "gold complexion"), a summer's day, and death (a braggart) are personified. By making these things human, Shakespeare magnifies the importance of the speaker's love.

Reading Strategy   Analyzing Rhythm and Rhyme

Rhythm and **rhyme** can give poetry a musical quality, add emphasis to certain words, and help convey the poem's meaning. Review the patterns of rhythm and rhyme in the sonnet, and then answer the following questions.

1. How is this sonnet structured? What meter does it use?

2. The rhymed couplet of a sonnet often presents a conclusion to the issues or questions discussed in the three quatrains preceding it. What is the effect of the couplet in the Shakespearean sonnet you have just read?

Vocabulary   Practice

Practice with Analogies Circle the word that best completes each analogy.

1. temperate : extreme :: quiet :
   a. mellow   **b.** loud   **c.** calm

2. rough : tree bark :: waxy :
   a. candle   **b.** glass   **c.** steel

3. possessions : purse :: textbooks :
   a. backpack   **b.** wallet   **c.** buy

Academic Vocabulary

Here are two words from the vocabulary list on page R82.

arbitrary (är´ bə trer´ ē) *adj.* decided or determined by impulse or personal preference and not by established logic or law

quote (kwōt) *v.* to repeat, in speaking or writing, the exact words spoken or written by another

Practice and Apply

1. Does Shakespeare's choice of extended metaphor seem like an **arbitrary** choice? Explain.

2. If you were to **quote** to your friends one line from this poem that holds a special meaning for you, which line would you choose?

Writing About Literature

Apply Form Write a sonnet about a beloved friend or family member, in which you compare him or her to something else. You may use an extended metaphor as a basis for the sonnet if you wish, but be sure to use the sonnet structure and rhyme scheme.

You might start your writing by listing some of the person's qualities. If you plan on using metaphors or an extended metaphor, it might help to identify things that have similar qualities as this person. For example, if your beloved is moody, you might compare him or her to unpredictable spring weather. Use a chart like the one below to organize potential subjects, their qualities, and possible comparisons.

Subject	Quality	Possible Comparison
My sister Beth	Wise and observant	An owl

Once you have finished listing qualities, and selected a subject and comparison, begin drafting your sonnet.

After completing your draft, meet with a peer reviewer to evaluate each other's poems and suggest revisions. Then proofread and edit your draft for errors in spelling, grammar, and punctuation.

When finished, write a paragraph explaining how your poem fits the criteria for the sonnet form.

Listening and Speaking

Use the Internet or a library to find recordings of Shakespearean sonnets read aloud. If recordings are not available, memorize "Shall I Compare Thee to a Summer's Day?" or another Shakespearean sonnet and practice reciting it aloud with a friend. When you feel that you have fine-tuned your recitation, perform the sonnet for your class.

Literature Online   Web Activities For eFlashcards, Selection Quick Checks, and other Web activities, go to www.glencoe.com.

Assess

Reading Strategy

1. Three quatrains and one couplet written in iambic pentameter

2. The speaker's final declaration summarizes his point: As long as people read his words, his love for the subject and his or her beauty will endure.

Vocabulary

1. b   2. a   3. a

Academic Vocabulary

1. No, it seems like a very thought-out and decisive choice.

2. Answers will vary. Students should explain the reasons for their decisions.

Writing About Literature

Students' poems should

- imitate sonnet meter, rhyme scheme, and format
- use metaphor or extended metaphor

Listening and Speaking

Students should

- select either "Shall I Compare Thee to a Summer's Day?" or another Shakespearean sonnet
- memorize the selected sonnet
- practice reading the sonnet aloud with a partner
- perform the sonnet for the class

Literature Online

Web Activities Have students access the Web site for interactive activities that will help them assess their understanding of the selection.

Focus

Summary

Artist Dave Morice reinterprets Shakespeare's Sonnet 18 ("Shall I Compare Thee to a Summer's Day?") with a recitation of the poem by illustrated monsters.

Teach

Big Idea

Loves and Losses Say: Keep the following questions in mind as you read: What is Morice's attitude toward Shakespeare's love poem? How does Morice express his own views on love through this reinterpretation of the sonnet? *(He seems to have a cynical or sarcastic attitude toward Shakespeare's poem. Morice's view of love could be that it goes beyond mere physical appearance—even his horrific monsters experience love for each other.)* **OL**

⊘ VISUAL PERSPECTIVE on "Shall I Compare Thee to a Summer's Day?"

Graphic Novel

William Shakespeare

Animated by Dave Morice

Building Background

Dave Morice is a poet and artist who has a PhD in Library Science from the University of Iowa. He began illustrating poems in 1979, and since then has completed many books on the subject, including *Poetry Comics: An Animated Anthology, How to Make Poetry Comics,* and *More Poetry Comics.* In his preface to *Poetry Comics, An Animated Anthology,* Morice explains his approach. "[My book] evolves from the close relationship that words and pictures have always had. Poetry and cartoonery are both art forms. Together, they can only enrich each other." In the following comic strip, Morice animates William Shakespeare's "Sonnet 18," which is also called "Shall I Compare Thee to a Summer's Day?"

Set a Purpose for Reading

Read to better appreciate the use of imagery and figurative language in poetry and to understand the relationship of visuals to text.

Reading Strategy

Interpreting Graphic Representations of Literature

One of the essential graphic elements of the comic book format is the panel. As you read Dave Morice's visual treatment of Shakespeare's "Sonnet 18," use a chart like the one below to record how he uses the panel format to represent the poem.

Page and position	Use
Page 604, top panels	Single line is illustrated by two linking panels

602 UNIT 3 POETRY

Additional Support

Skills Practice

LITERARY ELEMENT: Irony Irony is a contrast or discrepancy between appearance and reality, or between what is expected and what actually happens, this latter form known as situational irony. Discuss why the monsters' comments in the bottom two comic-strip panels are ironic. *(The comments are ironic because the wolflike creature is certainly not lovely. The dragon's comment seems to refer to itself. This is ironic because dragons are not known—in the Western world, at least—to be even remotely temperate creatures.)* **OL**

DAVE MORICE **603**

Teach

BI Big Idea

Loves and Losses **Ask:** How would you feel if one of these monsters had written you a love poem? How might this be a part of Morice's purpose? *(Students will probably say that they would feel awkward or strange receiving a poem from a monster. Morice's purpose could be to parody the fact that the sonnet is celebrated as a beautiful love poem, but no one ever considers that the speaker might be someone the subject is not very fond of.)* **OL**

★ Literary History

Classics in Comics

Morice's approach to retelling Shakespeare's sonnet is not without precedent. Two large comic book series, *Classics Illustrated* and *Classic Comics,* attempted to bring great classic novels and short stories to life in the colorful comic medium. *The Three Musketeers, The Last of the Mohicans,* and *Moby Dick* are just three of the literary works adapted by the two series, which ran from 1941 to 1971. **AS**

Differentiated Instruction

Role-Playing Less proficient readers may find Morice's illustrated version of Shakespeare's poem easier to follow than the nonillustrated original. Morice's interpretation turns the poem into a dialogue of monsters, a dramatic parody in which students may have fun participating. Have students take on the roles of the monsters to perform the poem. Students may find it fun to create monster masks for this performance. **BL**

Objectives
• To interpret graphic representations of literature (SE)
• To identify irony (TWE)

603

Teach

R1 Reading Strategy

Interpreting Graphic Representations of Literature Ask: What is the little monster holding in her claw? *(It appears she is holding the "summer's lease.")* **OL**

⭐ Literary History

Medusa The creature depicted in this panel is a humorous representation of Medusa, one of the more grisly of the Greek myths. Medusa, one of the three Gorgon sisters, was a beautiful woman who provoked Athena, the goddess of wisdom. Athena turned Medusa into a monster with snakes for hair and a face so repugnant that it turned to stone all who set eyes upon it. **AS**

Graphic Novel

604 UNIT 3 POETRY

Additional Support

Skills Practice

LITERARY ELEMENT: Humor This comic strip could be considered a parody of Shakespeare's sonnet because of its humorous presentation of what is considered a serious love poem. **Ask:** What makes this comic strip funny? *(Monsters reciting a love poem is the main joke. Also, the monsters are silly-looking and exaggerated. The fact that monsters are using such elevated language is quite humorous.)* **OL**

Graphic Novel

SOMETIMES TOO HOT

THE EYE OF HEAVEN SHINES,

HIS GOLD COMPLEXION

DIMMED;

AND OFTEN IS

R₃

DAVE MORICE **605**

Teach

R₂ **Reading Strategy**

Interpreting Graphic Representations of Literature Ask: What unpleasant feature of roses appears on this fire-breathing monster? *(There are thorns on the monster.)* **OL**

R₃ **Reading Strategy**

Interpreting Graphic Representations of Literature Ask: Why are black clouds drifting through these panels? *(The black clouds are in reference to the "gold complexion" of the sun being "dimmed." The poem refers to the overcast days of summer.)* **OL**

English Language Coach

Monsters Around the World
Students from different backgrounds may know stories about and images of monsters specific to their cultures. Have these students share stories they may have about these creatures or describe these monsters for the class. Also have students share common monster tales of the United States, such as the "monster under the bed" and the "monster in the closet" tales. Have students discuss the humorous aspects of monsters as well as their original, frightening aspects. **EL**

Objectives
- To interpret graphic representations of literature (SE)
- To understand literary devices such as personification (SE)
- To analyze humor (TWE)

Teach

R1 Reading Strategy

Interpreting Graphic Representations of Literature Ask: Why is this creature given the line "And every fair"? What might be the reason for her alarmed expression? *(She is given the line because she is grooming herself to enhance her beauty; "fair" means beauty. She might look alarmed because she is not as beautiful as she might have thought.)* OL

R2 Reading Strategy

Interpreting Graphic Representations of Literature Ask: How do the long necks of these creatures illustrate their words? *(Their necks wind around and get tangled with each other in "changing" courses. They are like "untrimmed" vines.)* OL

Graphic Novel

R1 AND EVERY FAIR

FROM FAIR   SOMETIMES DECLINES,

BY CHANCE

OR

NATURE'S CHANGING COURSE   UNTRIMMED;

606 UNIT 3 POETRY

Additional Support

Skills Practice

READING: Intended Audience The audience for whom Shakespeare wrote Sonnet 18 may not be the same audience for whom Morice illustrated the sonnet. Have students discuss Morice's intended audience. Have them consider the nature of the illustrations, the fact that they are an illustrated retelling, and that Morice has not changed the words of the sonnet, only the physical structure (line breaks and so forth). *(Although it is an illustrated rendition that may appeal to a younger audience, Morice's intended audience is probably one that is familiar with the original poem.)* OL

DAVE MORICE **607**

Teach

R3 Reading Strategy

Interpreting Graphic Representations of Literature Ask: How is the idea of "possession" communicated in the illustrations? *(In a sort of tug-of-war, the bearded creature is holding on to one leg of the sun-faced creature while the bespectacled monster grips the arm of the sun-faced creature.)* **OL**

BI Big Idea

Loves and Losses Ask: Why do you think Morice chose monsters as characters for his illustrations instead of humans? *(Students may point out the irony of using monsters as characters for a poem about love and eternal beauty; monsters are inherently repulsive or disturbing, making them unexpected candidates for an illustrated recitation of a Shakespearean poem. Students may also point out that monsters are an unusual choice of performer for Shakespeare.)* **OL**

Differentiated Instruction

Visual Learners Students with visual aptitude will probably find this lesson beneficial to their understanding of the sonnet. To further enhance their appreciation of the poem, have students discuss how they would illustrate this or another Shakespearean sonnet. Have the students divide into groups, choose a text, and plan an illustrated version of that text. Artistic students may help to draw sketches of these textual retellings. **OL**

Objectives

- To interpret graphic representations of literature (SE)
- To analyze the use of imagery to evoke readers' emotions (SE)
- To analyze audience (TWE)

Teach

R1 Reading Strategy

Interpreting Graphic Representations of Literature Ask: What has happened to the larger creature in the bottom panel? According to the illustration, how will the creature live on eternally? (*Apparently, the creature has died. The illustration makes it appear that the creature has sprouted stars into the night sky—these celestial objects will last throughout eternity.*) **OL**

⭐ Cultural History

Images of Death Death has been personified throughout history around the world. This panel portrays two common images of death: the raven, or blackbird, and the figure in the black robe, who also holds a staff topped with a skull. The hooded figure also sports horns, commonly associated in Western culture with demons, devils, and evil spirits. **AS**

608 UNIT 3 POETRY

Additional Support

Skills Practice

READING: Analyzing Tone Remind students that tone is a reflection of a writer's or speaker's attitude toward the subject. In this case, the illustrator's tone can be interpreted through his presentation. Have students discuss how Morice's illustrations might reflect his attitude toward Shakespeare's Sonnet 18. (*Morice treats the poem with exaggeration and humor, perhaps to parody the poem's place in literary history. His tone seems to be a bit sarcastic.*) **OL**

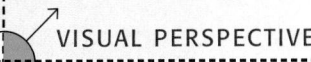
Teach

R₂ Reading Strategy

Interpreting Graphic Representations of Literature Ask: Why is the robed creature reaching out to the reader? How might this gesture change your interpretation of the poem? *(Students may say that the creature seems to be reaching out for an embrace. This gesture could imply that the speaker of the poem is speaking to the reader and not his lover.)* **OL**

Assess

1. Student answers will vary. Some students may think that they help bring Shakespeare's words to life.

2. (a) Morice broke up lines between and within panels. (b) Student answers will vary. Some may find that breaking up the lines made the poem lose some of its original rhythm. Others may find that having animated characters interact within lines of poetry helped them to understand the poem.

3. The different monsters present highly exaggerated versions of Shakespeare's images and metaphors.

4. No, sometimes the monsters address one another. In the last panel, the monsters address the reader.

For additional assessment, see 📁 Selection and Unit Assessment, pp. 109–110.

RESPONDING AND THINKING CRITICALLY

Respond

1. How did you react to the use of various creatures to narrate "Sonnet 18"?

Recall and Interpret

2. (a)How did Morice handle the line breaks in the sonnet? (b)Was this treatment effective? Why or why not?

3. How does Morice use graphic elements to represent Shakespeare's use of imagery and figurative laguage?

Analyze and Evaluate

4. Is it clear who is being addressed in Morice's "Sonnet 18"? Explain.

5. Writers from every generation have reinterpreted the work of writers who came before them. Writers may choose to pay tribute to the original work or make their own ironic or humorous statement about it. How does Morice's visual treatment of "Sonnet 18" reinterpret Shakespeare's work? Does Morice pay tribute to the poem or parody it? Cite evidence from the poem and the comic for support.

Connect

6. Did Morice's visual treatment of "Sonnet 18" enhance your understanding of the poem? Why or why not?

OBJECTIVES
- Interpret and evaluate the impact of graphic elements in a text.
- Analyze how poets use imagery to evoke readers' emotions.
- Understand literary terms, such as figurative language and personification.

DAVE MORICE **609**

---

5. Answers will vary. Some may feel that the animation of fire, "the eye of heaven," or the shading that indicates "his gold complexion dimmed" enhances a reader's appreciation of the sonnet and its language. Others may feel that using monsters to illustrate a poem about beauty parodies Shakespeare.

6. Students should indicate how the comic strip did or did not increase their understanding of the sonnet. Some may say it helped them visualize the images and actions described in the sonnet; others may say the illustrations were a distraction from Shakespeare's language.

Focus

BELLRINGER

Bellringer Options
Daily Language Practice Transparency 62
Or **say:** Think about a lesson you learned from a loved one.
Give students the opportunity to consider a lesson. **Say:** Now describe that lesson in two to four lines of rhyming poetry.
Ask students to share these with the class. Discuss the difficulty of articulating profound feelings with such rigid limitations.

Author Search To expand students' appreciation of William Butler Yeats, have them access the Web site for additional information and resources.

CheckPoint

Use the CheckPoint questions on Presentation Plus! to monitor students' comprehension. These questions may be used with interactive response keypads for immediate student feedback.

Down by the Salley Gardens and
He Wishes for the Cloths of Heaven

MEET WILLIAM BUTLER YEATS

When William Butler Yeats was fourteen years old, he could not spell and struggled with grammar. Today, however, Yeats is considered one of the most important and influential poets of the twentieth century.

A Voice of Ireland The oldest child of John Butler Yeats, a lawyer who later became a portrait painter, Yeats was born in Dublin, Ireland. His family moved to London when he was two, but he returned to Ireland often, spending holidays with his grandparents in the Irish countryside. He did not receive any formal schooling until he was twelve. A few years later, in 1880, his family returned to Dublin.

Yeats's mother helped him develop a love of Ireland and an interest in Irish folklore and legend that remained with him all his life. When he was in his early twenties, Yeats began to write poetry. Soon afterward, he met the Irish nationalist John O'Leary, who helped channel the young man's love of Irish literature and myths into the cause of preserving Irish identity. At the time, to make it easier to govern the Irish, the British were trying to eliminate Gaelic, the traditional language of Ireland. Yeats and others feared that Ireland's cultural heritage—especially its literature and folklore—would vanish with the outlawed language. In addition to interesting Yeats in politics, O'Leary helped him get his first poems published.

One way Yeats worked to preserve Irish literature and culture was through drama. In the late 1880s, he began writing plays, which were often based on Irish legends. In 1896 he met Lady Gregory, an aristocrat and fellow playwright. Yeats, Lady Gregory, and others helped found the Irish Literary Theatre in 1899, which in time grew into the renowned Abbey Theatre.

Love and Loss No biography of Yeats is complete without a mention of Maud Gonne. Yeats met Gonne when he was a young man in Dublin. She was an actress and a fiery and committed political activist, and they shared an interest in freeing Ireland from English domination. Yeats's attraction to Gonne lasted his entire life, and while the two were friends, his love for her was never returned as fully as he hoped. Not only did she refuse his marriage proposals, but she married another man. When her first husband died, she refused Yeats again. Still, Gonne always represented an ideal for Yeats, and she remained a source of poetic inspiration. When Yeats wrote about love and loss, he seared the pain of his own unrequited love onto the page.

Yeats's poetry varies greatly, and much of it is not as simple as the poems you are about to read. Nevertheless, he understood the value of simple, direct language in a poem and praised the ability to communicate concisely and clearly.

> *"Think like a wise man but express yourself like the common people."*
>
> —William Butler Yeats

Ironically, when Yeats won the Nobel Prize in Literature in 1923, it was awarded for his drama, which has not endured to the extent that his poetry has. Also, at the time, he had not yet written some of his best poetry, which is rich in symbolic content and modern in its images, style, and form.

William Butler Yeats was born in 1865 and died in 1939.

Literature Online **Author Search** For more about William Butler Yeats, go to www.glencoe.com.

Selection Skills

Down by the Salley Gardens
He Wishes for the Cloths of Heaven

Literary Elements
- Lyric Poetry (SE pp. 611, 613, 615)
- Speaker (SE p. 615)

Reading Skills
- Analyzing Repetition and Rhyme (SE pp. 611, 612, 615)
- Literary Response (TWE p. 612)

Vocabulary Skills
- Practice with Context Clues (SE pp. 611, 615)
- Academic Vocabulary (SE p. 615)

Writing Skills/Grammar
- Comparing and Contrasting Themes (SE p. 616)
- Compound Modifiers (SE p. 616)

Connecting to the Poems

Even great love can go wrong. Before you read these poems, think about the following questions:

- What mistakes do people make about love when they are young and foolish?
- How does love feel when it is not returned?

Building Background

As an Irish nationalist and lover of Irish folklore, Yeats was interested in preserving details of old Irish culture in his work. His poems frequently celebrate famous Celtic sites and Celtic legends and heroes. "Down by the Salley Gardens" is based on an old Irish popular song.

Both "Down by the Salley Gardens" and "He Wishes for the Cloths of Heaven" are full of the intense emotion of love. In the first poem, the speaker berates himself for getting love wrong. The second poem is a tribute to a love who has power over the speaker.

Setting Purposes for Reading

Big Idea Loves and Losses

As you read these poems, think about how Yeats expresses feelings of love, longing, and loss.

Literary Element Lyric Poetry

Lyric poetry expresses a speaker's personal thoughts and feelings and is typically short and musical. The word *lyric* comes from *lyre*, a stringed instrument used to accompany poetry in ancient Greece. While the subject of a lyric poem might be an object, a person, or an event, the emphasis of the poem is on the experience of emotion.

- See Literary Terms Handbook, p. R10.

Literature Online **Interactive Literary Elements Handbook** To review or learn more about the literary elements, go to www.glencoe.com.

OBJECTIVES

In studying these selections, you will focus on the following:
- understanding lyric poetry
- analyzing rhetorical devices, including repetition, parallelism, and juxtaposition
- examining the role and effect of the speaker in two poems
- writing to compare and contrast themes in two poems

WILLIAM BUTLER YEATS **611**

Reading Strategy Analyzing Repetition and Rhyme

Repetition and **rhyme** are techniques used to enhance a poem's sense of rhythm, to emphasize particular sounds, and to add to the musical quality of poetry. Repeating particular sounds, words, phrases, lines, or stanzas may help a poet to suggest particular emotions or ideas. Rhyme (as in the words *far* and *star*) may help to create unity within a poem.

Reading Tip: Taking Notes Use a graphic organizer to record examples of each device and your thoughts about why the author might have used them.

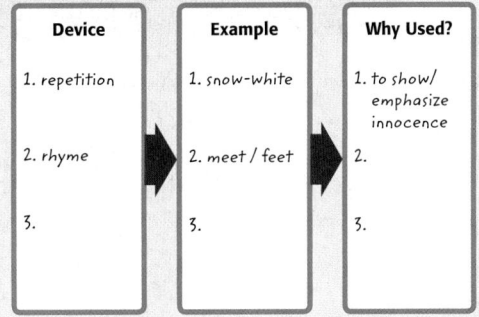

Device	Example	Why Used?
1. repetition	1. snow-white	1. to show/ emphasize innocence
2. rhyme	2. meet / feet	2.
3.	3.	3.

Vocabulary

embroidered (em broi′dərd) *adj.* decorated with needlework; p. 612 *The Guatemalan women wore colorful embroidered dresses to the fiesta.*

tread (tred) *v.* to step or walk on; p. 612 *We encourage our guests to tread lightly on the antique carpet.*

Vocabulary Tip: Context Clues Context clues are words and phrases near an unfamiliar word that can help you figure out its meaning. Common context clues are synonyms and examples.

Focus

Summary

The narrator in "Down by the Salley Gardens" has been instructed by his dearest to take love and life easy. He is young and foolish, though, and cannot heed her advice. His failure to do so leaves him heartbroken by the poem's end. The narrator of "He Wishes for the Cloths of Heaven" is poor but longs for "heavens' embroidered cloths" so that he may lay them at his love's feet. Unable to produce these cloths, he offers her his dreams and cautions her to be careful treading on them.

V Vocabulary

Vocabulary File Say: Add these words and definitions to your vocabulary file. For each word, include a sentence that gives you an example of how to use the word. **OL** Students with English language needs should include the pronunciations of these words in their files. **EL**

Literary Elements Have students access the Web site to improve their understanding of lyric poetry.

Selection Resources

Print Materials
- Unit 3 Resources (Fast File), pp. 58–60
- Leveled Vocabulary Development 48
- Selection and Unit Assessments, pp. 111–112
- Selection Quick Checks, p. 56

Transparencies
- Bellringer Options Transparencies: Daily Language Practice Transparency 62
- Literary Elements Transparency 52

Technology
- TeacherWorks Plus™ CD-ROM
- StudentWorks Plus™ CD-ROM
- Presentation Plus!™ CD-ROM
- Literature Online, glencoe.com
- Online Student Edition, mhln.com
- ExamView® Assessment Suite CD-ROM
- Vocabulary PuzzleMaker CD-ROM
- Listening Library, disc 1 tracks 61–62

Teach

BI₁ **Big Idea**

Loves and Losses
Say: Consider the following question as you read: How does the narrator of "He Wishes for the Cloths of Heaven" compare to the narrator of "Down by the Salley Gardens"? *(Both narrators are in compromising positions; they are unable to offer their loves what they need.)* **OL**

R **Reading Strategy**

Analyzing Repetition and Rhyme Answer: *The repetition emphasizes the message—take life and love easy.* **OL**

BI₂ **Big Idea**

Loves and Losses
Answer: *The speaker did not do what his love requested. As a result, the love is gone.* **OL**

★ Literary History

Feminine and Masculine Rhyme Rhyming words of two syllables, such as *mellow* and *yellow,* are called feminine rhymes. Masculine rhymes are categorized by monosyllables—as in *pair* and *chair.* "Down by the Salley Gardens" is an example of masculine rhyme. **AS**

The Artist's Garden at Giverny, 1900. Claude Monet. Oil on canvas. Musée d'Orsay, Paris.

Down by the Salley Gardens

William Butler Yeats

BI₁ Down by the salley¹ gardens my love and I did meet; **★**
She passed the salley gardens with little snow-white feet.
She bid me take love easy, as the leaves grow on the tree;
But I, being young and foolish, with her would not agree.
In a field by the river my love and I did stand,
And on my leaning shoulder she laid her snow-white hand.
She bid me take life easy, as the grass grows on the weirs;²
But I was young and foolish, and now am full of tears.

---

1. *Salley* is a variation of *sallow,* which is a type of willow tree.
2. Here, *weirs* are dams.

Reading Strategy Analyzing Repetition and Rhyme *What does the repetition of the word "grow(s)" in lines 3 and 7 suggest about the meaning of the poem?* **R**

Big Idea Loves and Losses *What cause and effect are suggested in this line?* **BI₂**

Additional Support

Skills Practice

READING: Literary Response Often the need to unlock a poem's meaning seems to supersede the pleasure of simply experiencing it. Explain to students that their personal interpretations of a poem are not only valid but just as important as any technical analyses. Allow them to simply read and enjoy the poems. Encourage them to share their visceral responses through journaling, oral explanations, or discussions. Note that although this approach may not feel very "literary," it actually is, and it mimics the habits of worldly readers and writers. **OL**

He Wishes for the Cloths of Heaven

William Butler Yeats

Lotto Tapestry from Ushak, Anatolia. Turkish. ★
Museo Nazionale del Bargello, Florence.

Had I the heavens' **embroidered** cloths,
Enwrought[1] with golden and silver light,
The blue and the dim and the dark cloths
Of night and light and the half light,
I would spread the cloths under your feet:
But I, being poor, have only my dreams;
I have spread my dreams under your feet;
Tread softly because you tread on my dreams.

---

1. *Enwrought* means "made with"; here, it means "embroidered with."

Literary Element Lyric Poetry *How do the repeated words at the ends of the lines tie in with the definition of lyric poetry?* **L**

Vocabulary

embroidered (em broi′ dərd) *adj.* decorated with needlework
tread (tred) *v.* to step or walk on

Teach

L Literary Element

Lyric Poetry Answer: *The repeated words make the poem sound like a song and also help emphasize the speaker's intense emotions.* **OL**

★ Viewing the Art

Tapestries are woven, decorative fabrics and are traditionally a luxury art. Just as the "cloths of heaven" that Yeats describes are unattainable in real life, for a majority of people a tapestry like the one shown here would not be acquired cheaply. **AS**

CheckPoint

Use the CheckPoint questions on Presentation Plus! to check students' mastery of the selection. These questions can be used with interactive response keypads for immediate student feedback.

Differentiated Instruction

Literary Decisions Reinforce the importance of a well-balanced approach to poetry—one that celebrates visceral responses but also observes intellectual ones. Divide students into two groups representing both types of response— "the emotional" and "the intellectual." Ask each group to develop arguments as to why its particular view is more beneficial to comprehension. Groups should choose one or two members to "argue" their point. Choose the group that more effectively presents its argument. Summarize by highlighting the importance of well-formed literary responses. **OL**

Objectives

- To understand lyric poetry (SE)
- To analyze the rhetorical device of repetition (SE)
- To respond to literature (TWE)

Assess

1. Students may say they cannot identify with being at an age where they felt "young and foolish" about love. They may have differing opinions on whether they could or could not be in love with a person who is capable of walking all over their dreams.

2. (a) To take love and life easy (b) Because leaves and grass grow naturally and slowly and cannot be rushed, perhaps as their love should grow

3. (a) Because he was young and foolish and in a hurry (b) Because he lost his love

4. (a) To spread them under his love's feet (b) She has the power to make the speaker either very happy or very unhappy.

5. (a) His dreams (b) He has nothing to offer but his dreams, and he asks that she respect them.

6. Students might say that the rest of the poem is sweet and charming.

7. Most will say that the speaker expresses intense emotion well, mainly through dramatic word choices—"cloths of heaven," gold and silver, light and night—and the repetition of "my dreams."

8. Support should be given for choices.

RESPONDING AND THINKING CRITICALLY

Respond

1. With which of the emotions in these poems do you identify most or least? Explain.

Recall and Interpret

2. (a) What advice did the speaker's love give him in "Down by the Salley Gardens"? (b) Why do you think she referred to the leaves and grass as examples?

3. (a) Why didn't the speaker agree with his love? (b) At the end of the poem, why is the speaker "full of tears"?

4. (a) In "He wishes for the Cloths of Heaven," what does the speaker want to do with the cloths of heaven? (b) What can you infer about the person who is addressed in the poem?

5. (a) What does the speaker in "He wishes for the Cloths of Heaven" say he has spread under his love's feet? (b) What can you infer about the treatment he hopes to receive from his love?

Analyze and Evaluate

6. The sadness in "Down by the Salley Gardens" is not suggested until the last line. Describe the mood of the poem's first seven lines.

7. How well does the speaker express intense emotion in "He wishes for the Cloths of Heaven"? Cite words and phrases from the poem to support your answer.

Connect

8. **Big Idea** Loves and Losses In which poem do you think the speaker conveys his sense of loss more effectively? Explain.

YOU'RE THE CRITIC: Different Viewpoints

Beautifully Simple or Simply Silly?

Read the two excerpts of literary criticism below. Both critics agree that Yeats was a man of genius. As you read the excerpts, notice the difference in tone between the two critics.

"[Yeats] has made for himself a poetical style which is much more simple, as it is much more concise, than any prose style; and, in the final perfecting of his form, he has made for himself a rhythm which is more natural, more precise in its slow and wandering cadence, than any prose rhythm. . . . Poetry, if it is to be of the finest quality, is bound to be simple, a mere breathing, in which individual words almost disappear into music."

—Arthur Symons

"[Yeats] hangs in the balance between genius and (to speak rudely) fool."

—Edward Dowden

Group Activity

With a small group, think about the two poems you just read and how you reacted to them. Which critic do you agree with more? Consider these questions in relation to the first quotation:

• Do you think that Yeats's poetry style is more simple than "any prose style"?

• Do you agree that the finest poetry "is bound to be simple"?

• Do you think Yeats's words "disappear into music"? If so, where? If not, why not?

Alternatively, you may want to focus on the second quotation and decide whether the poems seem both smart and silly to you. Then write a paragraph in which you agree or disagree with one of the critics and explain why.

Different Viewpoints

Students' essays should

• agree or disagree with one of the critics, or present original criticism.

• use evidence from the poems to support or contradict a critic, or to support original criticism.

LITERARY ANALYSIS

Literary Element Lyric Poetry

Often short and highly musical, **lyric poetry** expresses personal thoughts and emotions, rather than telling a story as narrative poetry does. Yeats is considered an outstanding lyric poet. What makes the poems you just read good examples of his art? What makes them good examples of lyric poetry in particular?

1. What overall emotion is expressed in each Yeats poem?

2. What qualities in "He Wishes for the Cloths of Heaven" identify it as a lyric poem? Cite evidence from the poem in your answer.

3. What elements of "Down by the Salley Gardens" make it possible to imagine the poem set to music?

Review: Speaker

As you learned on page 564, the speaker is the voice that communicates with the reader of a poem, similar to a narrator in a work of prose. The speaker's words convey a particular tone, or attitude, toward the subject of the poem.

Partner Activity Meet with a classmate and discuss the speaker in each poem. Create a chart like the one below to record information about the speakers. Decide whether the speakers are individuals in a specific time and place or whether each represents people who undergo a universal experience.

	Speaker in "Down by the Salley Gardens"	Speaker in "He Wishes for the Cloths of Heaven"
Clues to Identity	"I"	"I"
Facts About Speaker's Actions/Life	The speaker was once "young and foolish;" now, the speaker feels regret.	
Speaker's Attitude		

READING AND VOCABULARY

Reading Strategy Analyzing Repetition and Rhyme

Repetition is the recurrence of sounds, words, phrases, lines, or stanzas in a piece of writing. Writers use repetition to emphasize important ideas, to create rhythm, and to increase a feeling of unity in a work. **Rhyme** is the repetition of the same stressed vowel sounds and any succeeding sounds in two or more words. Rhyme is another device used by writers to emphasize ideas, to create rhythm, and to increase a work's unity.

1. Choose one of the poems and list three examples of repetition within it. How did these examples help to strengthen the work?

2. What was one example of rhyme in the poems that struck you as particularly effective? Explain.

Vocabulary Practice

Context Clues Use context clues to complete each sentence.

1. Colorful threads formed an intricate pattern on the ____ pillow.
   a. rustic **b.** complicated **c.** embroidered

2. The stairs are worn from the footsteps of people who ____ on them each day.
   a. canter **b.** tread **c.** soar

Academic Vocabulary

Here are two words from the vocabulary list on page R82.

reverse (ri vurs´) v. to turn completely around in direction, position, or thoughts

persist (pər sist´) v. to go on resolutely

Practice and Apply
1. In "Down by the Salley Gardens," how does the passage of time **reverse** the speaker's ideas about love?

2. What feelings does the speaker in "He Wishes for the Cloths of Heaven" express that will probably **persist** for some time?

WILLIAM BUTLER YEATS **615**

Assess

Literary Element

1. Sorrow over lost love in "Down by the Salley Gardens" and hope for reciprocated love in "He Wishes for the Cloths of Heaven."

2. Its musical qualities, resulting mainly from repetition, meter, and rhyme, and its intense emotion

3. The meter of the poem, the rhymes, and the repetition of phrases

Review: Speaker

Students' charts should include information about the speakers of both poems and indicate whether the speakers belong to a particular time and place or represent a universal experience.

Reading Strategy

1. In "Down by the Salley Gardens," lines 2 and 6, *snow-white feet* and *snow-white hand;* lines 3 and 7, "She bid me take easy"; lines 4 and 8, "But I [love/life] young and foolish."

2. Students should support their choices with examples from the poem.

Vocabulary

1. c **2.** b

Academic Vocabulary

1. When the speaker was young and foolish, he thought he could rush love and life; when he got older, he knew that he was wrong.

2. His great love

Assess

Writing About Literature

Students' analyses should

- include a thesis statement that clearly states comparisons or contrasts in theme
- include topic sentences in the body paragraphs that convey the main points of comparison and contrast
- use quoted evidence from the poems to support main points

Interdisciplinary Activity: Music

Students' performances should

- be supported by the relevant Web address/site
- reflect the basic melody of the online recording

Yeats's Language and Style

Students' hyphenated compounds should

- logically modify nouns
- be appropriate to the context

Writing About Literature

Compare and Contrast Themes The theme of a literary work is the central message about life expressed in the work. Both "Down by the Salley Gardens" and "He wishes for the Cloths of Heaven" deal with the topics of love and loss. What does each poem say specifically about this topic? Write a one- or two-page analysis in which you compare and contrast the themes of these poems. Include a thesis statement, which might be based on this model:

Both (Poem 1) and (Poem 2) are about _____, but (Poem 1) says _____, while (Poem 2) says _____ .

Consider using the following pattern of organization:

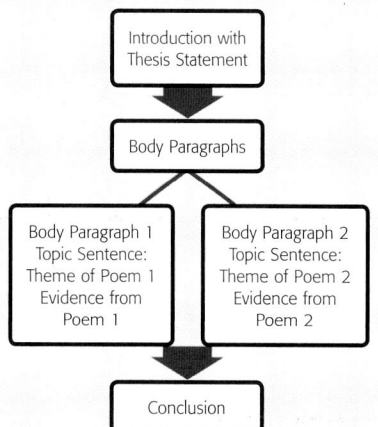

After completing your draft, meet with a peer reviewer. Evaluate each other's work and suggest revisions. Then proofread and edit your draft for errors in spelling, grammar, and punctuation.

Interdisciplinary Activity: Music

Yeats wrote "Down by the Salley Gardens" to be sung to an old melody, and many versions of the song are available online. Find a recording of the song on the Internet, and then prepare to perform it in class with several other students.

Literature Online **Web Activities** For eFlashcards, Selection Quick Checks, and other Web activities, go to www.glencoe.com.

Yeats's Language and Style

Using Hyphens for Compound Modifiers In "Down by the Salley Gardens," Yeats uses the term *snow-white* to modify the hand and feet of the speaker's love. He creates this compound modifier by hyphenating two words to create a single modifier. They work together to emphasize a pure but impermanent whiteness.

Compound modifiers enable the author to modify nouns vividly and concisely. You can join two words with a hyphen to form a compound modifier when it would not make sense, or would not be as effective, to join them with *and*. For example, consider the effect of not using a compound modifier in these examples:

"She passed the Salley gardens with little white feet."
"She passed the Salley gardens with little snow and white feet."

Activity Identify five nouns in Yeats's poems. Using language from the text, construct a compound modifier for each that is in keeping with the descriptions Yeats provides.

Noun	New Compound Modifier
grass	summer-green

Revising Check

Compound Modifiers With a partner, go through your compare-and-contrast essay and note places where compound modifiers might make your writing more vivid. Also be sure that you have hyphenated any two words you used that serve as a single modifier.

Literature Online

Web Activities Have students access the Web site for interactive activities that will help them assess their understanding of the selection.

I Am Offering This Poem

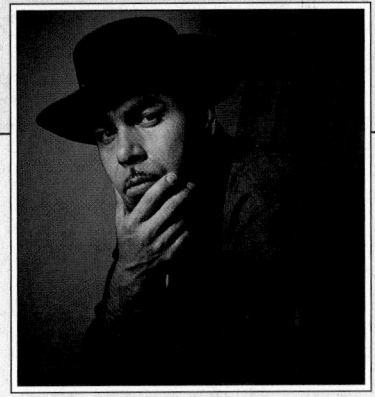

MEET JIMMY SANTIAGO BACA

Jimmy Santiago Baca, a self-described "child of the earth" and "Chicano," is today a famous poet and the author of several collections of poetry. Yet his path to literary success was neither conventional nor easy. Formerly illiterate, Baca did not learn to read and write under the guidance of a supportive teacher or by way of an encouraging parent. His discovery of language was solitary and did not occur until he reached adulthood. Baca was twenty-one and serving a prison term before he struggled to pull some meaning from a bilingual book given to him as a gift. Eventually, the words before him ceased to resemble a confusing mix of letters and transformed into decipherable, meaningful syllables and sentences. Asked to describe this experience of self-teaching, Baca explained the process as revolutionary.

> "I came upon poetry in much the same way that an infant first gasps for breath."
>
> —Jimmy Santiago Baca

A Deserted Poet Born in Santa Fe, New Mexico, Jimmy Santiago Baca has both Apache and Chicano heritage. He was deserted by his parents when he was only two years old; he then spent several years with his grandmother before being sent to an orphanage. Baca lived on the streets until he was faced with incarceration. Baca spent six years in prison, including four years in isolation, during which he taught himself to read and write. He began looking toward reformation.

Captive and nearly hopeless, Baca found a passion for poetry—"I was writing things that I remember doing as a kid and as an adult and

so forth. And what happened was that, in a place like prison where all sensory enjoyment was deprived, language became more real, more tangible than bars or concrete, than the structure of buildings in the landscape." Encouraged by a fellow prisoner, Baca submitted some of his poetry to *Mother Jones* magazine. Editor Denise Levertov printed Baca's poems and ultimately published his first major collection: *Immigrants in Our Own Land.*

Poet of the People Since the publication of his first book, Baca has produced many compositions, including novels and screenplays. In 2001, he published an award-winning memoir titled *A Place To Stand.* Currently, he travels across the United States facilitating writing workshops for adults and children. Despite international recognition, the self-described "poet of the people" finds time to teach at reservations, barrio community centers, housing projects, and correctional facilities. Wherever he goes, he carries a powerful message: "Poetry is what we speak to each other."

Baca is a recipient of the National Poetry Award, the American Book Award, the International Hispanic Heritage Award, and the Pushcart Prize.

Jimmy Santiago Baca was born in 1952.

 Author Search For more about Jimmy Santiago Baca, go to www.glencoe.com.

JIMMY SANTIAGO BACA **617**

Focus

BELLRINGER

Bellringer Options
Daily Language Practice Transparency 63
Or **ask:** Are material gifts necessary to indicate one's love for another person? (*Possible responses: No, love can be expressed in a variety of abstract ways; Yes, gifts are an important extension of one's feelings*). Guide students in a discussion that considers the pros and cons of all suggestions.

Author Search To expand students' appreciation of Jimmy Santiago Baca, have them access the Web site for additional information and resources.

CheckPoint

Use the CheckPoint questions on Presentation Plus! to monitor students' comprehension. These questions can be used with interactive response keypads for immediate student feedback.

Selection Skills

I Am Offering This Poem

Literary Elements
- Metaphor and Simile (SE pp. 618, 619, 620)
- Lyric Poetry (SE p. 620)

Reading Skills
- Previewing and Reviewing (SE pp. 618, 619, 621)

Vocabulary Skills
- Connotation and Denotation (SE pp. 618, 621)
- Academic Vocabulary (SE p. 621)

Listening/Speaking/Viewing Skills
- Group Discussion (SE p. 621)

Writing Skills/Grammar
- Writing Lyric Poetry (SE p. 621)

617

Focus

Summary

The narrator in Jimmy Santiago Baca's poem has but one thing to offer—his love. "I Am Offering This Poem" is an account of his feelings and of his determination to communicate them despite a lack of material wealth.

V Vocabulary

Vocabulary File Say: Add these words and definitions to your vocabulary file. For each word, include a sentence that gives you an example of how to use the word. **OL** Students with English language needs should include the pronunciations of these words in their files. **EL**

Literary Elements Have students access the Web site to improve their understanding of metaphor and simile.

Connecting to the Poem

The speaker in "I Am Offering This Poem" is a person of few possessions who compensates for a lack of material wealth with an intangible but powerful force: love. Before you read the poem, think about the following questions:

- What value do you place on material objects?
- How important is love when compared to these things?

Building Background

The traditional homes of Navajo Indians, called hogans, are most often built from logs and mud. Occasionally constructed from stone, the humble dwellings have no windows and frame a single entrance facing east. Usually covered by a blanket, this entrance is one of only two openings. The other opening, in the dome-shaped roof, allows smoke to pass from the fire within. With little or no furniture to border the fire, the residing family gathers and sleeps on sheepskins placed over the earthen floor.

Setting Purposes for Reading

Big Idea Loves and Losses

As you read "I Am Offering This Poem," observe the speaker's uncommon demonstrations of love.

Literary Element Metaphor and Simile

Simile is a figure of speech that makes a comparison between two otherwise dissimilar objects or ideas by connecting them with the words *like* or *as.* **Metaphor** is a figure of speech that compares two seemingly unlike things. Unlike simile, metaphor implies the comparison rather than stating it directly and does not use the connectives *like* or *as.* As you read, note the author's use of metaphor and simile and draw inferences from his decisions to use figurative language.

- See Literary Terms Handbook, pp. R10 and R16.

Literature Online Interactive Literary Elements Handbook To review or learn more about the literary elements, go to www.glencoe.com.

OBJECTIVES
In studying this selection, you will focus on the following:
- understanding metaphor and simile
- previewing and reviewing a poem
- analyzing lyric poetry
- applying the form and style of a poem by writing your own poem

618 UNIT 3 POETRY

Reading Strategy Previewing and Reviewing

Previewing is looking over a selection before you read it. It lets you begin to see what you already know and what you will need to know to understand the piece. It also helps you set a purpose for reading. **Reviewing** is going back over what you have read to remember what is important and to organize ideas so that you will recall them later. Reviewing is especially important when you have ideas and information to remember.

Reading Tip: Scanning Before reading Baca's poem in its entirety, quickly skim through it. Focus on the lines or stanzas that most interest you. Use a chart like the one below to jot down the things that attracted you to the words in the first place. Once you have recorded the lines and why you like them, take your previewing a step further and note the stylistic patterns of the author.

Line of Interest	Why I Like It	Author's Stylistic Choice
to warm your belly in winter	This is an interesting way to describe a full belly. Usually, fullness is illustrated through a sense of heaviness and not temperature.	The author's descriptions are unusual without using unfamiliar words.

Vocabulary

mature (mə choor′) *adj.* having reached a desired state; p. 619 *The seed has grown into a vast and mature tree.*

dense (dens) *adj.* thick; p. 619 *The girl's hair was dense with waves and curls.*

Vocabulary Tip: Connotation and Denotation Denotation refers to the dictionary meaning of a word while connotation refers to the suggested or implied meanings associated with a word.

Selection Resources

Print Materials
- Unit 3 Resources (Fast File), pp. 61–63
- Leveled Vocabulary Development 49
- Selection and Unit Assessments, pp. 113–114
- Selection Quick Checks, p. 57

Transparencies
- Bellringer Options Transparencies: Daily Language Practice Transparency 63
- Literary Elements Transparency 68, 69

Technology
- TeacherWorks Plus™ CD-ROM
- StudentWorks Plus™ CD-ROM
- Presentation Plus!™ CD-ROM
- Literature Online, glencoe.com
- Online Student Edition, mhln.com
- ExamView® Assessment Suite CD-ROM
- Vocabulary PuzzleMaker CD-ROM
- Listening Library, disc 1 track 63

I Am Offering This Poem

Jimmy Santiago Baca

I am offering this poem to you,
since I have nothing else to give.
Keep it like a warm coat
when winter comes to cover you,
5 or like a pair of thick socks
   the cold cannot bite through,

             I love you,

   I have nothing else to give you,
   so it is a pot full of yellow corn
10 to warm your belly in winter,
   it is a scarf for your head, to wear
   over your hair, to tie up around your face,

             I love you,

   Keep it, treasure this as you would
15 if you were lost, needing direction,
   in the wilderness life becomes when **mature**;
   and in the corner of your drawer,
   tucked away like a cabin or hogan
   in **dense** trees, come knocking,
20 and I will answer, give you directions,
   and let you warm yourself by this fire,
   rest by this fire, and make you feel safe,

             I love you,

   It's all I have to give,
25 and all anyone needs to live,
   and to go on living inside,
   when the world outside
   no longer cares if you live or die;
   remember,

30   I love you.

Angola's Dreams Grasp Finger Tips, 1973. Emilio Cruz.
Smithsonian American Art Museum, Washington, DC.

Literary Element Metaphor and Simile *What device has the poet employed here?* **L**

Reading Strategy Previewing and Reviewing *Besides expressing feelings for one person, what else is the speaker expressing in this poem?* **R**

Vocabulary

mature (mə choor′) *adj.* having reached a desired state
dense (dens) *adj.* thick

JIMMY SANTIAGO BACA **619**

Assess

1. (a) A family member or close friend or the narrator's girlfriend or wife (b) Most likely grateful for the narrator's commitment to love despite his inability to provide tangible examples of it

2. (a) Because he has nothing else to give (b) That he is courageous or foolish, honorable or impractical for offering only words

3. (a) That it serve as food, clothing, and shelter (b) Because it is a metaphor for love, and love is a powerful, encompassing energy

4. (a) The poem, which is a symbol for love (b) That he considers love a compelling and necessary force with great capabilities

5. (a) "I love you" is repeated and isolated, indicating its importance. (b) By including "I love you" in the existing stanzas or before each stanza

6. (a) Examples: financial status by an admission of possessing nothing, self-worth by a willingness to offer himself in place of material things (b) The message of love is communicated by being given a person's only and most valued possession.

RESPONDING AND THINKING CRITICALLY

Respond

1. (a) Who do you think this poem is intended for? Explain. (b) How would you expect the recipient to feel after reading the poem?

Recall and Interpret

2. (a) What reason does the speaker give for offering this poem? (b) What does this suggest about the speaker?

3. (a) What kinds of things does the speaker advise be done with the poem? (b) Why does the speaker believe that the poem can accomplish these things?

4. (a) What does the speaker propose is the one thing people require for existence? (b) What can you infer about the poet from this proposal?

Analyze and Evaluate

5. (a) How does the poem's structure help convey its message? (b) How else might the poem be structured and still communicate this message?

6. (a) How does Baca reveal characteristics of the speaker without directly showing his actions? (b) How do these characteristics help communicate the author's message?

7. (a) How does Baca divide the poem's stanzas? (b) How does the first stanza compare with the second? With the third and fourth stanzas?

Connect

8. **Big Idea** **Loves and Losses** Baca has experienced great loss in his life, including the loss of loved ones and his own freedom. How might these losses have inspired "I Am Offering This Poem"?

LITERARY ANALYSIS

Literary Element **Metaphor and Simile**

A **metaphor** compares two or more different things by stating or implying that one thing actually is another. A **simile** emphasizes a specific feature of something by comparing it to a separate object that is characteristic of that feature. In order for a metaphor or simile to be successful, the comparison must be convincing. When Sandra Cisneros writes, "I've been waiting patient as a spider all these years," the reader understands the simile because persistence is a quality attributed to spiders.

1. Identify two or three metaphors or similes in "I Am Offering This Poem." How does the use of these devices enhance the poem?

2. Change one of the poem's metaphors to a simile and then change one of its similes to a metaphor. How does the switch affect the descriptions?

Review: Lyric Poetry

As you learned on page 611, **lyric poetry** articulates the private thoughts and feelings of its speaker. Generally, lyric poetry is brief and melodic, yet packed with emotional intensity.

Partner Activity With a partner, read "I Am Offering This Poem" one stanza at a time. After completing a stanza, discuss the thoughts, feelings, and level of emotional intensity conveyed through its lines. Use a chart like the one below to track your discussion. Record the ideas and emotions you imagine the author experienced when writing the poem or record the ideas and emotions you experienced while reading it.

Stanza	Sentiment
1	Because the speaker has nothing but the poem to offer his or her loved one, he or she is sad. Modest means are replaced with creativity, though, and by offering a symbolic coat and scarf, he or she reveals a deep affection.
2	
3	
4	

7. (a) The first stanza addresses warmth; the second, nourishment; the third, security; the fourth, the poem's necessity. (b) The first and second stanzas address the specific qualities of clothing and food; the third, security and warmth; and the fourth, all encompassing.

8. Students may say that Baca's profound sense of loss and hardship gives him a better appreciation of love's worth.

Reading Strategy Previewing and Reviewing

By **previewing,** you can often find clues about the content of a selection before you begin reading. Similarly, **reviewing** the material will help you to remember important details.

1. The speaker compares his or her love to warming things. What does this tell you about the speaker's frame of mind?

2. Explain how the poem and the speaker are to be used like a compass through life.

Vocabulary Practice

Practice with Connotation and Denotation
Decide whether each sentence uses the vocabulary word with a positive or negative connotation.

1. The young man's **mature** demeanor impressed the interviewer.
   a. positive   **b.** negative

2. The correctional officers leapt into the **dense** crowd of riotous prisoners.
   a. positive   **b.** negative

Academic Vocabulary

Here are two words from the vocabulary list on page R82.

likewise (līk´wīz´) *adv.* in like manner

nonetheless (nun´<u>th</u>ə les´) *adv.* nevertheless

Practice and Apply

1. The first stanza of "I Am Offering This Poem" is comprised of six lines. **Likewise,** the last stanza contains six lines. Reexamine the stanzas and determine two additional structural similarities.

2. The speaker has little of material value; **nonetheless,** he or she is unselfish and benevolent. How might a person of modest means develop this generous spirit?

Literature Online Web Activities For eFlashcards, Selection Quick Checks, and other Web activities, go to www.glencoe.com.

Writing About Literature

Apply Form and Style At first glance, Baca's poem might appear to be a simple collection of love verses. Upon further examination, the poem becomes much more. A unique arrangement of words filled with emotion, the lyric poem highlights a very personal love story and simultaneously boasts the expert style of its author. Such creative writing is surely challenging, but begins to take shape with practice.

It is possible to strengthen your own creative writing skills through imitation. Write a lyric poem on love or loss that imitates Baca's style and uses the form displayed in "I Am Offering This Poem." Be sure to include a **refrain,** which is a line or set of lines that is repeated throughout a poem or song. "I love you" is the recurring refrain in "I Am Offering This Poem."

Before you begin drafting, create a Venn diagram like the one below that compares and contrasts Baca's style to your own. By separating the similarities and differences, your diagram should help you determine what stylistic features you share with Baca. Use this likeness to guide your imitation of his style.

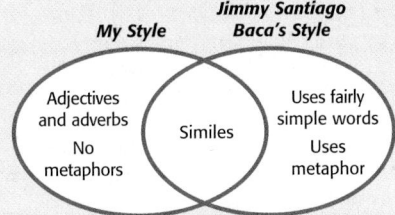

My Style — Adjectives and adverbs / No metaphors
Similes
Jimmy Santiago Baca's Style — Uses fairly simple words / Uses metaphor

Once your draft is complete, exchange poems with a peer reviewer and evaluate each other's work for style and form. Then edit your draft for errors in spelling, grammar, and punctuation.

Literature Groups

With a group of students, discuss the importance of communicating feelings to loved ones. Can love be truly expressed through gestures alone or are words needed? Support your views by drawing on your personal experiences.

Assess

Literary Element

1. Examples include: "like a warm coat," "like a pair of thick socks," "tucked away like a cabin or hogan." These devices increase the reader's understanding and enjoyment of a line or passage.

2. Examples: "Keep it like a warm coat" to "It is a warm coat"; "so it is a pot full of yellow corn" to "it is like a pot full of yellow corn" Students may notice that these slight changes seriously affect the author's style.

Review: Lyric Poetry

Students should fill in the chart after discussing the stanzas with their partners.

Reading Strategy

1. Responses should express the speaker's desire to have the person he loves feel comforted, secure, and safe.

2. Responses should include ". . . if you were lost, needing direction" and ". . . and I will answer, give you directions."

Vocabulary

1. a 2. b

Academic Vocabulary

1. Both stanzas contain lines of no more than eight words, and they consist of mainly nouns and verbs.

2. By giving him a less materialistic view of life

Writing About Literature

Students' lyric poems should
- model Baca's form and style
- include a refrain

2. be supported with examples

Literature Groups

Group discussions should
1. explore how feelings are communicated

Literature Online

Web Activities Have students access the Web site for interactive activities that will help them assess their understanding of the selection.

Focus

BELLRINGER

Bellringer Options
Daily Language Practice Transparency 64
Or **on the board write:** *since feeling is first.* **Ask:** What does this line mean to you? Have students write a poem starting with this line. Remind them that poetry may take many different forms and should reflect the feelings of the author.

Literature Online

Author Search To expand students' appreciation of E. E. Cummings, have them access the Web site for additional information and resources.

CheckPoint

Use the CheckPoint questions on Presentation Plus! to monitor students' comprehension. These questions can be used with interactive response keypads for immediate student feedback.

---

since feeling is first

MEET E. E. CUMMINGS

In his later poetry, E. E. Cummings experimented with poetic form and language to create a distinctive style. He also wrote essays, short stories, novels, plays, children's fiction, and a travel diary. But Cummings was not only a writer. He was a painter who had many solo exhibitions, a professor of poetry at Harvard University, and a prisoner of war during World War I.

Starting Out Edward Estlin Cummings was born in Cambridge, Massachusetts, home of Harvard University. His father, also named Edward, was a professor at the school, which Cummings later attended. While at Harvard, Cummings was influenced by the works of experimental writers such as Gertrude Stein and Ezra Pound. He graduated with a master's degree in 1916.

After leaving school, Cummings worked briefly for a mail-order book company. By April of 1917, World War I was raging in Europe, but the United States had not yet entered the war. Cummings volunteered to serve as an ambulance driver in France. Due to a misunderstanding, he was imprisoned on suspicion of treason for three months in a French detention camp.

> *"It takes courage to grow up and become who you really are."*
>
> —E. E. Cummings

A Champion of the Individual After the war, Cummings returned to Paris to study art. He turned his experiences in the French detention camp into his first book, *The Enormous Room*, published in 1922. This fictionalized account of his captivity depicted it as a time of personal growth. In 1923 he published a book of poetry, *Tulips and Chimneys*. While many of the poems are conventional in style, some show the playful form and punctuation that are hallmarks of Cummings's later work.

Cummings moved to New York City in 1924 and found himself regarded as a celebrity. *Vanity Fair* magazine gave him a long-term assignment as an essayist and portrait artist. This allowed him to set up his lifelong routine of painting after lunch and writing after dinner. Over the ensuing years, Cummings wrote twelve volumes of poems and won numerous awards.

Cummings wrote some of his poems in free verse, with no fixed meter or rhyme, but many have a rhyming sonnet structure. Other poems seem to spill across the page, reminding readers that the poet was also a painter who used his typography to create a visual image.

Despite the unusual form of many of Cummings's poems, his themes are often traditional: love, nature, childhood. At the same time, some of his writing is harshly critical of conventional thinking and of society's restrictions on freedom of expression. In one of his lectures at Harvard, Cummings said, "So far as I am concerned, poetry and every other art was, is, and forever will be strictly and distinctly a question of individuality."

E. E. Cummings was born in 1894 and died in 1962.

Literature Online **Author Search** For more about E. E. Cummings, go to www.glencoe.com.

Selection Skills

Literary Elements
- Understanding Juxtaposition (SE pp. 623, 624, 625)

since feeling is first

Reading Skills
- Paraphrasing (SE pp. 623, 625)

Vocabulary Skills
- Analogies (SE p. 625)

Writing Skills/Grammar
- Analyzing Figurative Language (SE p. 625)
- Conducting Background Research (TWE p. 624)

Connecting to the Poem

How important are our feelings? In this poem, Cummings reflects on the value of feeling. Before you read, think about the following questions:

- Is emotion, or feeling, valuable in other areas of life besides romantic relationships?
- Do you ever make a decision based on the way you feel?

Building Background

E. E. Cummings is known for manipulating syntax, or word order, in his poetry. As critic Richard P. Blackmur wrote, "Cummings has a fine talent for using familiar, even almost dead words, in such a context as to make them suddenly impervious to every ordinary sense; they become unable to speak, but with a great air of being bursting with something very important and precise to say." Cummings uses familiar words in unexpected places to surprise his readers and call their attention to the flexibility of language. As you read "since feeling is first," note places where Cummings arranges words in innovative ways.

Setting Purposes for Reading

Big Idea Loves and Losses

As you read the poem, notice what Cummings considers to be of lesser value than feeling.

Literary Element Juxtaposition

Juxtaposition is placing two or more distinct items or ideas side by side in order to compare or contrast them. Recognizing juxtaposition can help you understand the layers of meaning that an author intends to convey. As you read the poem, examine how Cummings uses juxtaposition to increase his reader's understanding of the power of feeling.

- See Literary Terms Handbook, p. R9.

Literature Online **Interactive Literary Elements Handbook** To review or learn more about the literary elements, go to www.glencoe.com.

Reading Strategy Paraphrasing

Paraphrasing is taking the author's exact meaning and putting it into your own words. Paraphrasing a poem can help you get past unusual phrasing and punctuation. This will be especially helpful for poems by Cummings since he is known for using an eccentric style. While reading "since feeling is first," try to paraphrase Cummings's ideas.

Reading Tip: Listing Important Words To get ready for paraphrasing, you may want to list words from the poem that seem particularly important to the author's meaning. Use a chart like the one below to list important words as you read. Note which part of speech each word represents—is the word a noun, a verb, an adjective, or an adverb? Be sure you understand the meaning of each word. Make the chart any length you need. Then try rewriting lines of the poem in your own words.

Word	Part of Speech	Meaning
feeling	noun	emotion

Vocabulary

syntax (sin′taks) n. ordered structure or systematic arrangement; the rules of language; p. 624 *Standard English syntax places the subject before the verb in a sentence.*

parenthesis (pə ren′ thə sis) n. digression or afterthought; disruption in continuity; p. 624 *No parenthesis marred the flow of main ideas in his argument.*

OBJECTIVES
In studying this selection, you will focus on the following:
- understanding juxtaposition
- paraphrasing a poem
- writing to analyze figurative language

E. E. CUMMINGS **623**

Loves and Losses Say: Keep the following question in mind as you read: How does Cummings feel about feelings, love, or romance? *(The poet believes feelings supersede logic or intellect.)* **OL**

L Literary Element

Juxtaposition Answer: *Students may note that "kisses" stand for an emotional response that Cummings sees as superior to intellect.)* **OL**

★ Viewing the Art

Poet and prominent Surrealist André Breton once described Catalan painter Joan Miró as "the most Surrealist of us all." Miró became internationally famous for his abstract and Surrealist art, joining the world of experience with that of dreams and fantasies. **AS**

✓ CheckPoint

Use the CheckPoint questions on Presentation Plus! to check students' mastery of the selection. These questions can be used with interactive response keypads for immediate student feedback.

since feeling is first

E. E. Cummings

Composition, 1933. Joan Miro. Oil on canvas, ★
1.66 x 1.33 m. Prague, Czech Republic.

since feeling is first
who pays any attention[1]
to the **syntax** of things
will never wholly kiss you;
5 wholly to be a fool
while Spring is in the world

my blood approves,
and kisses are a better fate
than wisdom
10 lady i swear by all flowers. Don't cry
—the best gesture of my brain is less than
your eyelids' flutter which says

we are for each other: then
laugh, leaning back in my arms
15 for life's not a paragraph

And death i think is no **parenthesis**

---

1. Here, *who pays any attention* is the subject of the statement rather than a question.

Literary Element Juxtaposition *Why does Cummings choose to compare kisses and wisdom?* **L**

Vocabulary

syntax (sin´taks) *n.* ordered structure or systematic arrangement; the rules of language

parenthesis (pə ren´thə sis) *n.* digression or afterthought; disruption in continuity

Additional Support

RESEARCH: Literature Imagery

Have students conduct research to learn more about the imagery of flowers in poetry. **Say:** Notice the line in which Cummings says, "lady i swear by all flowers." Poets from many cultures have incorporated the imagery of flowers into their work. In early Japanese poems, for example, emotions and ideas often were linked to natural objects like flowers. Research to find examples of flowers in poetry. *(Students may reference the work of poets such as Mibu no Tadamine or poems like "In the autumn fields" by an anonymous poet.)* **OL**

RESPONDING AND THINKING CRITICALLY

Respond

1. When you read "since feeling is first," did it seem like a love poem? Explain.

Recall and Interpret

2. (a)What kind of person does the poem's speaker say "will never wholly kiss you"? (b)What do you think Cummings means by this?

3. (a)In the poem, when is it acceptable to be a fool? (b)Why do you think the speaker limits being foolish to a particular time period?

4. (a)What does the speaker swear by when he addresses the lady in the second stanza? (b)Why would the speaker choose to swear by this particular image?

Analyze and Evaluate

5. Does the poem suggest that "feeling is first" only in a relationship of love? Explain.

6. Cummings ends the poem with "life's not a paragraph" and death "is no parenthesis." Does this ending fit the rest of the poem? Why or why not?

7. Cummings uses minimal capitalization in his poem. Does Cummings' disregard for rules of capitalization strengthen or weaken the poem? Explain.

Connect

8. **Big Idea** **Loves and Losses** What does the poem suggest to you about where feelings should rank in your own life? How much importance do you place on your emotions?

Literary Element Juxtaposition

Writers often use **juxtaposition** to compare unlike objects, actions, ideas, characters, settings, phrases, or words, creating a particular effect. In "since feeling is first," Cummings juxtaposes intellectual activity with emotional response.

1. Identify examples of juxtaposition in "since feeling is first." Explain how they support the theme.

2. How effective are these juxtapositions in conveying the speaker's meaning? Support your answer with details.

Writing About Literature

Analyze Figurative Language Poets often use metaphors to imply a comparison between two seemingly unlike things. Identify the metaphors Cummings uses for both emotion and reason in "since feeling is first." Write a short analysis in which you identify and explain the metaphors. Include examples from the poem and your personal experience.

Literature Online Web Activities For eFlashcards, Selection Quick Checks, and other Web activities, go to www.glencoe.com.

Reading Strategy Paraphrasing

What is the difference between **paraphrasing** and summarizing? When summarizing, you extract only the most essential ideas from the selection and you almost always end up with a shorter text. When paraphrasing, you completely restate the original text in your own words.

1. What main idea does Cummings try to communicate in "since feeling is first"?

2. Support your opinion by paraphrasing at least two quotations from the poem.

Vocabulary Practice

Practice with Analogies Choose the word that best completes each analogy.

1. syntax : language :: etiquette :
   a. eating   **b.** grammar   **c.** behavior

2. parenthesis : continuation :: acceptance :
   a. rejection   **b.** welcoming   **c.** punctuation

Vocabulary

1. c **2.** b

Writing About Literature

Students' essays should

- correctly identify metaphors
- explain the metaphors
- provide examples from the text

Literature Online

Web Activities Have students access the Web site for interactive activities that will help them assess their understanding of the selection.

Assess

1. Answers will vary.

2. (a) Someone who pays attention to the syntax (b) A person concerned with rules cannot fully experience feelings.

3. (a) In springtime (b) Spring is traditionally thought of as the season to be in love and of being foolish.

4. (a) "By all flowers" (b) Flowers have romantic and emotional connotations.

5. The poem suggests that emotion is of primary importance in all of life.

6. Some students may discuss life as an ongoing process, not constrained by "syntax" or logic.

7. Students should present their opinions, supported by examples.

8. Answers will vary.

Literary Element

1. Students should identify the comparisons of feeling to syntax and explain that in each, Cummings shows that the emotional is superior to the logical.

2. They clarify the poet's overall meaning and encourage readers to connect with the poem.

Reading Strategy

1. That a person cannot truly love if he or she is too focused on an intellectual response

2. Examples: "who pays any attention / to the syntax of things / will never wholly kiss you"

Focus

BELLRINGER

Bellringer Options
Daily Language Practice Transparency 65
Or point out that horses are often sources of literary inspiration.
Ask: What other animals are often featured in literary works? What qualities or characteristics do these animals have that inspire people to write about them? Have students discuss the inspirational value of animals and decide which animals they would choose to write about.

Author Search To expand students' appreciation of Gwendolyn Brooks, have them access the Web site for additional information and resources.

Use the CheckPoint questions on Presentation Plus! to monitor students' comprehension. These questions can be used with interactive response keypads for immediate student feedback.

Horses Graze

MEET GWENDOLYN BROOKS

"I want to write poems," said Gwendolyn Brooks, "that I could take . . . into the street, into the halls of a housing project." Witty, original, and sometimes outspoken, Brooks was one of the most respected American poets of the twentieth century. Brooks captured the hopes of urban African Americans, as well as their feelings of rage and despair in the face of racism and poverty.

An Early Love of Poetry Many characters in Brooks's poems are based on people who lived in her neighborhood on Chicago's South Side. Brooks knew the South Side intimately, having spent most of her life there. She was born to parents who had little money but who did have a deep love of literature and high expectations for their children. When Brooks, at age seven, brought her mother her first poems, her mother said, "You are going to be the lady Paul Laurence Dunbar," referring to a prominent African American poet.

By the time she was sixteen, Brooks had written more than seventy-five poems, and she had met two of the leading African American writers of her day, Langston Hughes and James Weldon Johnson. Both writers read and praised her poetry and encouraged her to continue writing. Hughes became her friend and mentor. With the publication of her second book, *Annie Allen,* Brooks became the first African American writer to win the Pulitzer Prize for poetry. Eventually Brooks was also named Poet Laureate of Illinois, poetry consultant to the Library of Congress, and a member of the National Women's Hall of Fame.

In her early books, Brooks chronicled the dreams and disappointments of everyday African Americans using traditional verse forms such as the ballad and the sonnet. In the 1960s, Brooks's poetry underwent an immense change in tone and content. Inspired by African American activism, Brooks began to write more overtly political poems that focused on social issues such as the need for unity within the African American community. She also began to incorporate colloquial speech and free verse into her work. "This is not time for sonnets," she once said, "but a time for raw, ragged free verse."

> *"If you love songs and rap, you love poetry."*
> —Gwendolyn Brooks

Although Brooks wrote primarily about urban African Americans, her poems, as Blyden Jackson notes, are brimming with "insights and revelations of universal application." They speak to the human condition and hence to all the citizens of the world.

Gwendolyn Brooks was born in 1917 and died in 2000.

Author Search For more about Gwendolyn Brooks, go to www.glencoe.com.

Selection Skills

Literary Elements
- Repetition (SE pp. 627, 628, 629)
- Sound Effects (TWE p. 628)

Horses Graze

Reading Skills
- Drawing Conclusions About Author's Meaning (SE pp. 627, 629)

Vocabulary Skills
- Denotation and Connotation (SE pp. 627, 629)

Writing Skills/Grammar
- Respond to Tone (SE p. 629)

Connecting to the Poem

Some people believe that animals have much to teach people if we pay attention. Before you read the poem, think about these questions:

- What have you learned from observing, interacting with, or hearing about an animal?
- How does the animal world different from the human world? How is it similar?

Building Background

Horses are hoofed, herbivorous (plant-eating) mammals related to the zebra. They are herd animals well adapted for living on the plains. Horses have wide, flat teeth designed for grinding grasses and other plants, and long foot bones that enable swift running. For centuries, horses were used extensively in warfare, agriculture, and transportation. They also played an important role in literature and art. In cave paintings from the Ice Age, wild horses and cattle were the most prominent images. In ancient Greek and Roman mythology, horses were associated with the sun and heavenly chariots.

Setting Purposes for Reading

Big Idea Loves and Losses

What is important in life? Do animals know better than we do? As you read, consider what the poem might be saying about human flaws and foibles.

Literary Element Repetition

Repetition is a literary device in which sounds, words, phrases, lines, or stanzas are repeated for emphasis. Writers use repetition to emphasize an important point, to expand an idea, or to help create rhythm. Repetition increases the unity of a work. As you read Brooks's poem, notice examples of repetition and think about what ideas they reinforce.

- See Literary Terms Handbook, p. R14.

Literature Online **Interactive Literary Elements Handbook** To review or learn more about the literary elements, go to www.glencoe.com.

Reading Strategy · Drawing Conclusions About Author's Meaning

When you draw conclusions, you use a number of pieces of information to make a general statement about people, places, events, and ideas. When you draw conclusions about an author's meaning, you look at details throughout the work and decide what the author wanted to say through these details.

....

Reading Tip: Record Details As you read, record details and use them to draw conclusions.

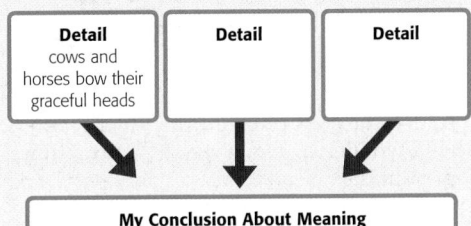

Vocabulary

oblivion (ə bli´v ən) *n.* a lack of awareness or memory; p. 628 *After the song's popularity passed, the group was consigned to oblivion.*

crest (krest) *n.* a peak, high point, or climax; p. 628 *Leah's joy was at its crest; she had never been happier.*

affirmation (a fər m´shən) *n.* positive agreement or judgment; p. 628 *As she bent down towards the child, the mother's face shone with affirmation.*

Vocabulary Tip: Connotation and Denotation The **connotation** of a word is its suggested or implied meaning. The **denotation** is its literal definition. For example, both *tenacious* and *stubborn* can mean "unwilling to be swayed," but *stubborn* has a more negative connotation.

Focus

Summary

The poet questions whether animals at pasture have a better understanding of the world than their human counterparts do. She says that they eat what they need, accept one another, and are content with the sky above them. It is almost as if they know that they share the sky with every other creature on the planet.

V Vocabulary

Vocabulary File Say: Add these words and definitions to your vocabulary file. For each word, include a sentence that gives you an example of how to use the word. **OL** Students with English language needs should include the pronunciations of these words in their files. **EL**

Literary Elements Have students access the Web site to improve their understanding of repetition.

OBJECTIVES
In studying this selection, you will focus on the following:
- understanding repetition as a literary device
- drawing conclusions about author's meaning
- writing an essay in response to a poem's tone

GWENDOLYN BROOKS **627**

Selection Resources

Print Materials
- 📁 Unit 3 Resources (Fast File), pp. 67–69
- 📁 Leveled Vocabulary Development 51
- 📁 Selection and Unit Assessments, pp. 117–118
- 📁 Selection Quick Checks, p. 59

Transparencies
- Bellringer Options Transparencies: Daily Language Practice Transparency 65
- Literary Elements Transparency 41

Technology
- ⚪ TeacherWorks Plus™ CD-ROM
- ⚪ StudentWorks Plus™ CD-ROM
- ⚪ Presentation Plus!™ CD-ROM
- 💻 Literature Online, glencoe.com
- 💻 Online Student Edition, mhln.com
- ⚪ ExamView® Assessment Suite CD-ROM
- ⚪ Vocabulary PuzzleMaker CD-ROM
- ⚪ Listening Library, disc 1 track 65

Big Idea

Loves and Losses Say:
Consider the following question as you read: Have we lost something valuable by moving away from our natural instincts? *(Students' answers will vary.)* **OL**

L1 Literary Element

Repetition Answer: *Students may say the repetition of these words helps to stress the steady single-mindedness of the horses and cows.* **OL**

L2 Literary Element

Personification Ask: What human quality is given to horses in line 24? *(speech)* **OL**

✓CheckPoint

Use the CheckPoint questions on Presentation Plus! to check students' mastery of the selection. These questions can be used with interactive response keypads for immediate student feedback.

Horses Graze

Gwendolyn Brooks

Cows graze.
Horses graze.
They
   eat
5   eat
   eat.
Their graceful heads
are bowed
bowed
10   bowed
in majestic[1] **oblivion**.
They are nobly oblivious
to your follies,
your inflation,[2]
15   the knocks and nettles[3] of administration.
They
   eat
   eat
   eat.
20   And at the **crest** of their brute satisfaction,
with wonderful gentleness, in **affirmation**,
they lift their clean calm eyes and they lie down
and love the world.
L2 They speak with their companions.
25   They do not wish that they were otherwhere.
Perhaps they know that creature feet may press
only a few earth inches at a time,
that earth is anywhere earth,
that an eye may see,
30   wherever it may be,
the Immediate arc, alone, of life, of love.
In Sweden,
China,
Afrika,
35   in India or Maine
the animals are sane;
they know and know and know
there's ground below
and sky
40   up high.

1. Here, *majestic* means "a quality of dignified greatness."
2. *Inflation* is an economic condition that occurs when consumer prices continuously rise or the purchasing power of money continuously declines; it can also mean "pomposity" or "empty pretentiousness."
3. A *knock* is a sharp blow or hit. A *nettle* is a weedy plant that releases a substance irritating to the skin; metaphorically, nettle can be anything that irritates.

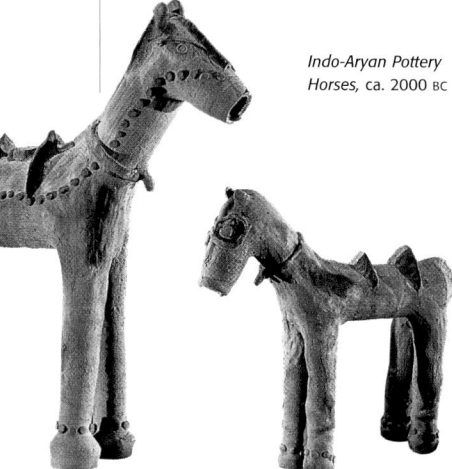

Indo-Aryan Pottery Horses, ca. 2000 BC

Literary Element Repetition *What does the repetition of eat and bowed help the author to stress?* **L1**

Vocabulary

oblivion (ə bliʹvē ən) n. a lack of awareness or memory
crest (krest) n. a peak, high point, or climax
affirmation (a fər māʹshən) n. positive agreement or judgment

Skills Practice

LITERARY ELEMENT: Sound Effects
Poetry is built with a mixture of sounds. Each word and each phrase is chosen carefully, not only for its meaning but also for its sound and its relationship to the next word and the next phrase. Have students reread the poem aloud and look for sound effects like repeated consonant and vowel sounds. *(Possibilities include the repetition of* f *and* n *sounds as well as long* o, *short* o, *and long* a *sounds.)* **OL**

RESPONDING AND THINKING CRITICALLY

Respond

1. What image or description in the poem did you find most striking? Explain.

Recall and Interpret

2. (a) What animals does the speaker describe in this poem? (b) To whom or what does the speaker compare them?

3. (a) How does the speaker describe the animals in lines 7–11? (b) Explain what you think the speaker means by "bowed / in majestic oblivion."

4. (a) How do the animals show their gentleness in lines 21–23? (b) What might the animals be affirming?

5. (a) According to the speaker, what do the animals "know," and in what way are they "sane"? (b) What might the poet be implying here about people?

Analyze and Evaluate

6. Brooks uses only a few words to describe people. Why, in your view, might she have chosen the word *inflation*? Explain its meaning in the context of the poem.

7. (a) What does the speaker think people could learn from animals? (b) Do you agree? Explain.

8. (a) Has this poem changed the way you see horses and cows? Explain. (b) Has it changed the way you see people? Explain.

Connect

9. **Big Idea** Loves and Losses (a) What does this poem suggest to you about what is truly important in life? (b) What does it suggest about the things that all people, and all creatures, have in common? Explain your answer.

LITERARY ANALYSIS

Literary Element Repetition

In poetry, **repetition** can emphasize words or ideas, and can add a musical quality.

1. Identify three examples of repetition in "Horses Graze."

2. For each example, explain what the repetition added to the poem. In your answer, consider these questions: What rhythmic or musical quality does the repetition have? How is it distributed throughout the poem? What ideas or meanings are reinforced by the repetition?

Writing About Literature

Respond to Tone The tone of a work is a reflection of the writer's attitude toward the subject. A writer's tone may convey a variety of attitudes, including sympathy, seriousness, sadness, or humor. What tone do you hear in "Horses Graze"? Write a brief essay in which you explain your ideas about the tone of the poem. Be sure to cite evidence from the poem in your answer.

Literature Online Web Activities For eFlashcards, Selection Quick Checks, and other Web activities, go to www.glencoe.com.

READING AND VOCABULARY

Reading Strategy Drawing Conclusions About Author's Meaning

One rewarding aspect of poetry is the conversation it invites between the poem and the reader. Your own experiences will help you to engage more deeply with the poem each time you read it.

1. Reread lines 24–31. What do you conclude about the meaning of these lines? Explain.

2. What point did Brooks wish to make in lines 32–40? To answer, consider details from lines 32–40.

Vocabulary Practice

Practice with Denotations and Connotations
Complete each sentence below.

1. The denotation of **oblivion** is ___.
   a. lack of awareness   **b.** infinity   **c.** sharpness

2. A connotation of **affirmation** is ___.
   a. agreement   **b.** belief   **c.** skepticism

3. The denotation of **crest** is ___.
   a. high point   **b.** achievement   **c.** downturn

GWENDOLYN BROOKS **629**

Assess

1. Answers will vary.

2. (a) Horses and cows (b) Humans

3. (a) Graceful, bowed (b) Bowing suggests humility and acceptance; the animals have greatness because they live in the here and now.

4. (a) "Clean calm eyes" and their lying down in ease (b) The goodness of life and the bounty of earth

5. (a) They know where they stand and are sane in their perspective (b) That humans have lost this intuition

6. *Inflation* relates to human pursuit of wealth and sense of self-importance.

7. (a) Humility, gentleness, a centered perspective, contentment (b) Answers will vary.

8. (a) Students may not have considered horses and cows capable of love. (b) Students may not have considered human ambition foolish.

9. (a) Answers will vary. (b) That all creatures rely on the earth and can be happy with what they have

Literary Element

1. *Graze, they, eat, bowed, oblivion/oblivious, earth, know*

2. Answers will vary but should be supported by examples.

Writing About Literature

Students' essays should
- identify the writer's attitude toward her subject
- explain the tone

Vocabulary

1. a **2.** a **3.** a

Reading Strategy

1. The animals seem to know that all creatures are equal and that life is much the same wherever one is.

2. Answers will vary. Students may say that these lines imply that animals—and people too—are the same everywhere.

Literature Online

Web Activities Have students access the Web site for interactive activities that will help them assess their understanding of the selection.

Focus

BELLRINGER

Bellringer Options
**Daily Language Practice
Transparency 66**
Or **ask:** Do you have a favorite possession that you don't like other people to touch? Why is it important to you that others keep their distance from this item? What is the significance of this possession in your life? If some students deny having a prized possession, prompt the class to analyze the differences between the two attitudes toward personal possessions.

Author Search To expand students' appreciation of Rita Dove, have them access the Web site for resources and bibliography.

CheckPoint

Use the CheckPoint questions on Presentation Plus! to monitor students' comprehension. These questions can be used with interactive response keypads for immediate student feedback.

Parlor

MEET RITA DOVE

"One can be a poet, but you have to have a life," poet Rita Dove says. "If you don't have a life, then I don't see where you're going to write your poems from." In order to inspire her own poetry, Dove devotes her time to many pursuits. She enjoys playing the viola de gamba, a seventeenth-century stringed instrument similar to the cello, and she has taken instruction in classical voice training and ballroom dancing. However, most people recognize Dove by her compassionate, intimate poems.

"All the moments that make up a human being have to be written about, talked about, painted, danced, in order to really talk about life."

—Rita Dove

Finding Her Voice Dove was born in the industrial city of Akron, Ohio, to a middle-class family. Her father was the first African American research chemist at a nationally prominent tire manufacturer. Dove's parents encouraged her to read, and as she says, "Going to the library was the one place we got to go without asking really for permission." Dove began writing at an early age, but she did not think she could have a career writing poetry. As she explains, "I didn't know writers could be real live people, because I never knew any writers." She also felt the pressure of her father, who wanted her to become a doctor or lawyer. Fortunately, Dove had a high school English teacher who noticed her talent and invited her to a writer's conference. There her deep interest in literary endeavors took hold, and Dove went on to study poetry in college and in Germany

on a prestigious Fulbright scholarship. She attended the highly esteemed University of Iowa Writers' Workshop, where she met her husband, the German writer Fred Viebahn.

A Champion for Poetry Many of Dove's poems revolve around trying to understand history, family, and a sense of one's place. Her most famous work, *Thomas and Beulah,* is a re-creation of her grandparents' lives from the 1920s to the 1960s. The book earned Dove a Pulitzer Prize.

Dove has enjoyed much success as a poet. She served as Poet Laureate of the United States from 1993 to 1995, the youngest person and the first African American to do so. This position of distinguished honor allowed Dove to introduce more poetry into the curricula of elementary school children. For Dove, the position "offers someone as a spokesperson for literature and poetry in this country. It means that one becomes an automatic role model." Dove's works have proven to appeal to a wide audience. She has read her poetry at a White House State dinner and also on the popular children's television show *Sesame Street.* Her last published book of poems—*On the Bus with Rosa Parks* (1999)—explores aspects of the life of the late civil rights activist.

Rita Dove was born in 1952.

Literature Online **Author Search** For more about Rita Dove, go to www.glencoe.com.

630 UNIT 3 POETRY

Selection Skills

Literary Elements
• Imagery (SE pp. 631, 633)

Parlor

Listening/Speaking/Viewing Skills
• Role-Playing (SE p. 633)

Reading Skills
• Interpreting Imagery (SE pp. 631, 633)
• Summarizing (SE p. 631)

Vocabulary Skills
• Content Clues (SE pp. 631, 633)

Writing Skills/Grammar
• Verb Tense (TWE p. 632)

Connecting to the Poem

The following poem is primarily about loss and the ways in which people react to loss. In this poem, the speaker's view of death is different from that of his or her family members. Before you read the poem, think about the following questions:

- Have you ever disagreed with family members about an important topic?
- How did you deal with this difference in opinion?

Building Background

A parlor is a formal room in a home, used primarily for conversation or the reception of guests.

The speaker of the poem listens to her transistor radio. Transistor radios were popular in the 1950s and 1960s. These lightweight radios ran on batteries and were small enough to hold in the hand or fit in a pocket. Teenagers plugged an earphone in one ear and tuned in to their favorite music.

Setting Purposes for Reading

Big Idea Loves and Losses

As you read this poem, ask yourself what lessons the speaker of the poem learned from his or her grandmother's life and death, and what message the poet conveys through her poem.

Literary Element Imagery

Imagery is descriptive language that appeals to one or more of the five senses: sight, hearing, touch, taste, and smell. This use of sensory detail helps create an emotional response in the reader. As you read "Parlor," pay close attention to Dove's imagery. Concentrating on it will help you grasp and retain the meaning as well as enhance your experience of the poem.

- See Literary Terms Handbook, p. R8.

Literature Online **Interactive Literary Elements Handbook** To review or learn more about the literary elements, go to www.glencoe.com.

OBJECTIVES
In studying this selection, you will focus on the following:
- analyzing the use of imagery and sensory details

Reading Strategy Interpreting Imagery

Writers use imagery to paint a picture with words in a way that helps the reader respond emotionally to what the writer has written. When you **interpret imagery,** you form a picture in your mind's eye of the images the writer has painted with words. While reading "Parlor," notice how the imagery that Dove uses helps you make sense of the poem.

Reading Tip: Summarizing Try visualizing the setting that Dove has created in the poem by summarizing each stanza using your own words and by drawing on the images created in your mind's eye. To help develop your thoughts use a graphic organizer like the one below for each stanza.

Stanza 1
We passed through
on the way to anywhere else.
No one lived there
but silence, a pale china gleam,

Summarize stanza's meaning:
_____
_____
_____

Summarize images within the stanza:
_____
_____
_____

Vocabulary

china (chī′nə) n. fine, glossy pottery used for tableware; p. 632 *I washed and dried the china after we ate dinner.*

aglow (ə glō′) adj. glowing; p. 632 *The house was so aglow with lights, she could see into every room.*

Vocabulary Tip: Context Clues When reading on your own, you can often figure out the meaning of an unfamiliar word by looking at its **context,** or the other words and sentences that surround it.

- understanding and interpreting imagery
- interpreting a poem orally

RITA DOVE **631**

Focus

Summary

The speaker of the poem describes her grandmother's parlor, an uninhabited room that contained many possessions that were only for show, not for use. The speaker's mother disagrees with the grandmother's philosophy; she thinks things should be used rather than merely displayed. After the grandmother's funeral, the speaker goes into the parlor. The feeling of loss she experiences there helps her to understand her grandmother's desire to keep the things she loved at a distance.

V Vocabulary

Vocabulary File Say: Add these words and definitions to your vocabulary file. For each word, include a sentence that gives you an example of how to use the word. **OL** Students with English language needs should include the pronunciations of these words in their files. **EL**

Literary Elements Have students access the Web site to improve their understanding of imagery.

Selection Resources

Print Materials
- 📁 Unit 3 Resources (Fast File), pp. 70–72
- 📁 Leveled Vocabulary Development 52
- 📁 Selection and Unit Assessments, pp. 119–120
- 📁 Selection Quick Checks, p. 60

Transparencies
- Bellringer Options Transparencies: Daily Language Practice Transparency 66
- Literary Elements Transparency 71

Technology
- 💿 TeacherWorks Plus™ CD-ROM
- 💿 StudentWorks Plus™ CD-ROM
- 💿 Presentation Plus!™ CD-ROM
- 💻 Literature Online, glencoe.com
- 💻 Online Student Edition, mhln.com
- 💿 Exam*View*® Assessment Suite CD-ROM
- 💿 Vocabulary PuzzleMaker CD-ROM
- 💿 Listening Library, disc 1 track 66

Teach

BI₁ **Big Idea**

Loves and Losses Say: Keep the following questions in mind as you read: What do the characters in the poem love? What have they lost? *(The speaker loves her grandmother and her transistor radio. Her grandmother loves her possessions and her family, but she keeps both at a distance. The mother loves life. The speaker and her mother have lost the grandmother.)* **OL**

BI₂ **Big Idea**

Loves and Losses Answer: *Answers will vary. It may show that the grandmother takes comfort in things she treasures, or she knew that eventually she would have to leave, so it was better not to become too close to things.* **OL**

Literature Online

Web Activities Have students access the Web site for interactive activities that will help them assess their understanding of the selection.

Two Tea Cups. Kari Van Tine.

Parlor

Rita Dove

BI₁

We passed through
on the way to anywhere else.
No one lived there
but silence, a pale **china** gleam,

5 and the tired eyes of saints
   aglow on velvet.

   Mom says things are made
   to be used. But Grandma insisted
   peace was in what wasn't there,
10 strength in what was unsaid.

   It would be nice to have a room
   you couldn't enter, except in your mind.
   I like to sit on my bed
   plugged into my transistor radio,
15 "Moon River" pouring through my head.

   How do you *use* life?
   How do you *feel* it? Mom says

   things harden with age; she says
   Grandma is happier now. After the
      funeral,
20 I slipped off while they stood around
   remembering—away from all
   the talking and eating and weeping

   to sneak a peek. She wasn't there.
   Then I understood why
25 she had kept them just so:

   so quiet and distant,
   the things that she loved.

Vocabulary

china (chī′ nə) *n.* fine, glossy pottery used for tableware
aglow (ə glō′) *adj.* glowing

Big Idea Loves and Losses *What does this statement tell you about the beliefs of the speaker's grandmother with regard to love and loss?* **BI₂**

632 UNIT 3 POETRY

Additional Support

CheckPoint

Use the CheckPoint questions on Presentation Plus! to check students' mastery of the selection. These questions can be used with interactive keypads for immediate feedback.

Skills Practice

GRAMMAR: Verb Tense Explain that Dove's use of verb tenses in "Parlor" offers clues to the poem's meaning. Instruct small groups of students to identify the verb tenses throughout the poem. Assign each group one of the following topics to present to the class:

- Verb tense and the sequence of events in the poem
- How present tense affects tone
- The effects of past tense
- Reasons for using several verb tenses in a poem **OL**

RESPONDING AND THINKING CRITICALLY

Respond

1. The speaker seems to think that it's best to keep the things you love at a distance. Do you agree? Why or why not?

Recall and Interpret

2. (a)What does the image of "tired eyes of saints / aglow on velvet" remind you of? (b)What can you infer about where the poem takes place based on this imagery?

3. (a)What do the speaker's mother and grandmother disagree about? (b)How would you characterize the speaker's grandmother? Be specific.

4. (a)How do you interpret the speaker's mother saying "things harden with age"? (b)What does the mother's view say about her?

Analyze and Evaluate

5. (a)The speaker states that he or she wishes for ". . . a room you couldn't enter, except in your mind." What do you think the speaker means? (b)Why do you think he or she wishes for this?

6. (a)How does Dove establish setting in this poem? (b)Do you think that her establishment of setting is effective?

7. Where does the ending of the poem take place? What clues lead you to think that this is the setting?

Connect

8. **Big Idea** Loves and Losses What does the speaker come to realize about loves and losses at the end of the poem? How does he or she come to realize this?

LITERARY ANALYSIS

Literary Element Imagery

Many writers use **imagery** to evoke an emotional response from their readers. Imagery often appeals to one or more of the five senses: sight, hearing, touch, taste, and smell.

1. How does the imagery in the poem appeal to your senses?

2. Is Dove's use of imagery effective in "Parlor"? Explain.

Listening and Speaking

With a partner, reread "Parlor" paying particular attention to stanzas three and five. Choose one person to be the mother and the other to be the grandmother. After rereading the poem, role-play a conversation between the two women. Center the discussion on whether things were made to be used or to be left alone.

Literature Online Web Activities For eFlashcards, Selection Quick Checks, and other Web activities, go to www.glencoe.com.

READING AND VOCABULARY

Reading Strategy Interpreting Imagery

Sometimes a poem has layers of meaning. For example, although this poem is about an event in the life of a child, the meaning of the poem is much deeper. When you **interpret imagery**, you determine the deeper meaning of images.

1. What main message do you think the poet is trying to convey in "Parlor"?

2. How does the imagery support the meaning of the poem?

Vocabulary Practice

Practice with Context Clues Use context clues to choose the correct definitions for the boldfaced vocabulary words.

1. They received a set of **china** for their wedding, and they used it every night for dinner.
   a. drapes   b. towels   c. tableware

2. The lights on the computer were **aglow**, so she knew it was on.
   a. dark   b. lit   c. beeping

RITA DOVE **633**

Assess

1. Students may prefer to keep things close to protect them.

2. (a) Some may say the things in the parlor are old and tired, but revered. (b) In Grandma's house

3. (a) How to live one's life, what things are important (b) Students may say wise, because she speaks of "peace" not being found in material things and "strength" in silence.

4. (a) That life simply gets more difficult, or that as people age they become cynical and stubborn (b) That she is pre-occupied with her own aging.

5. (a) That a private place, like a "room you couldn't enter," would be the safest place to keep things you love. (b) The speaker misses the grand-mother.

6. (a) "China gleam" and saints on velvet lend themselves to the image of an old parlor. (b) The setting, although iso-lated, has a deeper identity, much like the grandmother.

7. Perhaps in the dining room, near the parlor; Because she "slipped off to sneak a peek" at the place that she previously had "passed through"

8. She came to understand why Grandma had kept everything she loved at a distance.

Listening and Speaking

Students' role plays should identify the conflict in the poem and reflect the tone of each character.

Vocabulary

1. c   2. d

Literary Element

1. Students may mention hearing music and seeing beloved objects.

2. Answers will vary. Specific terms should be used in support of opinions

Reading Strategy

1. That some people are surrounded by things and people but don't get near physically or emotionally

2. Terms such as "silence," "tired," and "distant" evoke feelings of sadness.

Focus

BELLRINGER

Bellringer Options
Daily Language Practice
Transparency 67
Or **on the board write:** *alone.*
Ask: What does it mean to be alone? Have students discuss what being alone means to them. Suggest that they consider whether being alone is a positive or a negative experience or whether it varies depending upon the circumstances.

Literature Online

Author Search To expand students' appreciation of Sherman Alexie, have them access the Web site for additional information and resources.

CheckPoint

Use the CheckPoint questions on Presentation Plus! to monitor students' comprehension. These questions can be used with interactive response keypads for immediate student feedback.

Secondhand Grief

MEET SHERMAN ALEXIE

Sherman Alexie has overcome medical issues and the poverty of a reservation to become one of the preeminent Native American authors of our time.

An Early Love of Literature Sherman Alexie learned to read by the age of three. When he was only five years old, Alexie was reading tomes such as John Steinbeck's *Grapes of Wrath.* However, Alexie's love of literature isolated him from other children on the Spokane, Washington reservation where his family lived.

Alexie decided to attend high school away from the reservation, where he hoped to obtain a better education than his parents had received. While at Reardan High, he excelled in academics and became a basketball star. Additionally, he was the only American Indian to attend the school during his time there.

> *"If I were a doctor, nobody would be inviting me to talk to reservations. . . . Writers can influence more people."*
>
> —Sherman Alexie

Alexie attended Gonzaga University in Spokane on a scholarship. In his junior year, he transferred to Washington State University in Pullman. Alexie planned to become a doctor until he fainted several times in a human anatomy class and decided to switch majors. Alexie enrolled in a poetry workshop, and he excelled at writing. With his teacher's encouragement, he decided to make a career of it.

Same Passion, Different Forms Alexie has published twenty books; most recently, a collection of poems titled *Dangerous Astronomy.* In his work, Alexie draws on his experience and perspective to tell stories about modern American Indian life. He addresses themes of displacement, loss, and love, while challenging audiences to look past the clichéd portrayals of American Indians in the mass media. His characters strive for meaningful lives in the face of racism and economic disadvantage.

Alexie reaches out to audiences in a variety of media. He co-authored a screenplay based on one of his short stories, which became an award-winning, independent motion picture, *Smoke Signals.* The film is the first feature film entirely written, directed, produced, and acted by American Indians. Alexie followed an even more surprising career path by touring the United States as a stand-up comedian. Alexie also mentors young film writers through the Sundance Institute and judges a variety of writing contests.

Sherman Alexie was born in 1966.

Literature Online
Author Search For more about Sherman Alexie, go to www.glencoe.com.

Selection Skills

Secondhand Grief

Literary Elements
• Diction (SE pp. 635, 636, 637)

Reading Skills
• Visualizing (SE pp. 635, 637)

Vocabulary Skills
• Context Clues (SE pp. 635, 637)

Writing Skills/Grammar
• Analyzing Rhythm (SE p. 637)
• Developing Ideas (TWE p. 636)

Connecting to the Poem

In the following poem, Alexie addresses the challenges of growing up, dealing with the loss of a parent, and claiming our places as adults in society. Before you read the poem, think about the following questions:

- How do your parents or other family members link you to the past?
- How connected do you feel to other people in your community?

Building Background

Alexie uses his work to explore the challenges that American Indians face when trying to reconcile the need to contribute to modern society with the desire to honor historic traditions. As Alexie himself once said, "I . . . know that I live a happier, more adventurous life, by crossing borders. Of course, the crossings are always painful, as well." Drawing on his own experience of "crossing borders" by leaving the reservation on which he grew up, Alexie frequently writes about the conflicting desires and emotions felt by characters who leave their homes or societies to live in places where they at times may feel alienated and alone, yet may also have opportunities.

Setting Purposes for Reading

Big Idea Loves and Losses

As you read, notice how Alexie highlights the character's loneliness among a sea of people.

Literary Element Diction

Diction is a writer's choice of words. Diction is an important element in the writer's voice or style. Understanding why authors choose some words over others will help you understand the tone and meaning of a poem. As you read, notice how Alexie's careful choice of words affects the way in which you interpret the poem and its speaker.

- See Literary Terms Handbook, p. R5.

Literature Online **Interactive Literary Elements Handbook** To review or learn more about the literary elements, go to www.glencoe.com.

OBJECTIVES
In studying this selection, you will focus on the following:
- analyzing diction

Reading Strategy Visualizing

Visualizing is picturing a writer's ideas or descriptions in your mind's eye. Poets often illustrate actions without using typical cause-and-effect descriptions. Visualizing a poet's descriptions of a scene can help you understand the poem's sequence of events. As you read, identify five actions that the main character takes in the present. Because the poet does not always use verbs to describe those actions, look for words that evoke powerful images in your mind.

....

Reading Tip: Creating a Flow Chart Capture these images as a sequence of events, connected by arrows. For instance, if you were to capture the series of events that happened to the characters in the past, you might create a chart like this:

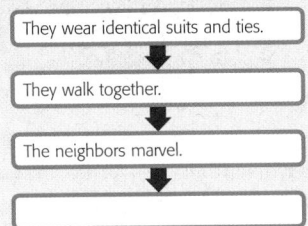

They wear identical suits and ties.

↓

They walk together.

↓

The neighbors marvel.

↓

Vocabulary

nostalgic (nos tal′jik) *adj.* longing for persons, things, or situations from the past; p. 636 *The old man was nostalgic for the music of his youth.*

marveled (mär′vəld) *v.* to become filled with wonder or astonishment; p. 636 *The young girl marveled at the toy store's selection of dolls.*

Vocabulary Tip: Context Clues When faced with an unfamiliar word, look to the context, or surrounding words and phrases, for clues to the unknown word's meaning. For example, in the lines "both of them wearing / identical suits and ties," the phrase "both of them" hints that *identical* means "being the same."

- using visualizing to interpret and understand a text
- writing to analyze rhythm

SHERMAN ALEXIE **635**

Focus

Summary

The speaker of the poem explores a son's grief over the loss of his father and the loss of his childhood home. The son takes up his father's clothes—and maybe even the threads of his father's life—as he finds his way in an unfamiliar world.

V Vocabulary

Vocabulary File Say: Add these words and definitions to your vocabulary file. For each word, include a sentence that gives you an example of how to use the word. **OL** Students with English language needs should include the pronunciations of these words in their files. **EL**

Literature Online

Literary Elements Have students access the Web site to improve their understanding of diction.

Selection Resources

Print Materials
📁 Unit 3 Resources (Fast File), pp. 73–75
📁 Leveled Vocabulary Development 53
📁 Selection and Unit Assessments, pp. 121–122
📁 Selection Quick Checks, p. 61

Transparencies
- Bellringer Options Transparencies: Daily Language Practice Transparency 67
- Literary Elements Transparency 26

Technology
🖥 TeacherWorks Plus™ CD-ROM
🖥 StudentWorks Plus™ CD-ROM
🖥 Presentation Plus!™ CD-ROM
💻 Literature Online, glencoe.com
💻 Online Student Edition, mhln.com
🖥 ExamView® Assessment Suite CD-ROM
🖥 Vocabulary PuzzleMaker CD-ROM
🖥 Listening Library, disc 1 track 67

Teach

BI₁ Big Idea

Loves and Losses **Say:** Keep the following question in mind as you read: Why does the character in the poem put on his father's clothes? *(He wears his father's clothes as a means of coping with his father's death, and possibly as a way of picking up where his father left off.)* **OL**

L Literary Element

Diction **Answer:** *Students should realize that a blazer is a lightweight sports jacket, contrasting with the more formal black shoes and wool pants. The father may have enjoyed dressing up, but not too formally.* **OL**

BI₂ Big Idea

Loves and Losses **Answer:** *Students might suggest that the speaker, far from his home, has lost his birthplace as well as his father.* **OL**

✔CheckPoint

Use the CheckPoint questions on Presentation Plus! to check students' mastery of the selection. These questions can be used with interactive response keypads for immediate student feedback.

Décalcomanie, 1966. René Magritte. Oil on canvas, 81 x 100 cm. Private collection.

Secondhand Grief

Sherman Alexie

BI₁ After his father dies
The son wears his clothes.

First, the black shoes
then the wool pants

5   and finally the blazer
with **nostalgic** lapels.

When he was a child
walking with his father

both of them wearing
10   identical suits and ties

the neighbors **marveled**
at how much they looked alike.

A thousand miles away
from his father's grave

15   He steps into his favorite overcoat
and then steps outside

to walk among fathers
and sons, strangers

strangers, strangers
20   strangers, strangers

strangers, strangers
strangers, all of them.

Literary Element **Diction** *What does the author's choice of "blazer" say about the father?* **L**

Vocabulary

nostalgic (nos tal′ jik) *adj.* longing for persons, things, or situations from the past
marveled (mär′ vəld) *v.* to become filled with wonder or astonishment

Big Idea **Loves and Losses** *Besides invoking the loss of a father, what other loss might the poet be referring to here?* **BI**

636 UNIT 3 POETRY

Additional Support

Skills Practice

WRITING: Developing Ideas

Explain that an opinion—whether in response to literature or about another issue—is always supported by evidence. Textual evidence is usually used when responding to literature. A writer must show how the example supports the point that is being made. Tell students to review their essays to determine whether they developed their ideas. Emphasize that all examples must relate to the opinion presented by the writer. **OL**

RESPONDING AND THINKING CRITICALLY

Respond

1. How do you feel about the idea of following in the footsteps of someone in your family?

Recall and Interpret

2. (a)Who does the son walk among? (b)How does the son feel about walking among these people?

3. (a)How far away from his family has the son moved? (b)What kind of environment does Alexie suggest the main character now lives in?

Analyze and Evaluate

4. How does Alexie use descriptions of clothing worn by the characters to suggest loss?

5. How does the author use images of clothing to suggest a change within the son?

6. How are secondhand clothes like "secondhand grief"?

Connect

7. **Big Idea** **Loves and Losses** Alexie suggests that the main character has lost not just his father, but also his connection to his heritage. Explain.

LITERARY ANALYSIS

Literary Element Diction

A careful choice of words can help authors create layers of meaning. Especially in poetry, where authors must convey much meaning in fewer words, **diction** can provide clues to attitude and meaning.

1. Without using verbs, Alexie paints a picture of a man getting dressed. What three transitions does he use to keep those images moving?

2. What shift in words does Alexie use to describe his character's change of location and his increasing isolation from other people?

Writing About Literature

Analyze Rhythm In "Secondhand Grief," Alexie uses words to create rhythm. How does his arrangement of lines on the page reflect the son's actions? What effect does Alexie create by repeating a key word? Write a brief analysis in which you examine the rhythm of this poem.

Before you begin drafting, read the poem aloud. Note the differences between the way the poem looks on paper and the way the poem sounds when spoken.

After completing your draft, meet with a peer reviewer to evaluate each other's work and suggest revisions. Be sure to proofread and edit your draft for errors in spelling, grammar, and punctuation.

READING AND VOCABULARY

Reading Strategy Visualizing

Especially when reading poetry, **visualizing** can help you better understand the action in a text. Visualizing can also help you remember information.

1. What kind of scene do you visualize when reading the last eight lines of the poem?

2. Does the repetition of "strangers" help you visualize them? Explain.

Vocabulary Practice

Practice with Context Clues Identify the context clues that help you define the boldfaced vocabulary words in the sentences below.

1. The old-fashioned diner made Grandma **nostalgic** for her youth.
   a. old-fashioned   **b.** Grandma   **c.** youth

2. Noah **marveled** at the astonishing results of his scientific experiment on magic.
   a. scientific   **b.** magic   **c.** astonishing

Literature Online Web Activities For eFlashcards, Selection Quick Checks, and other Web activities, go to www.glencoe.com.

SHERMAN ALEXIE **637**

Assess

1. Answers will vary.

2. (a) Strangers (b) Nostalgic in his father's clothing and isolated among strangers

3. (a) "A thousand miles away" (b) A cold, urban environment

4. Black shoes, suits, and ties suggest funeral attire.

5. As a child he wears clothes like his father's to emulate his father. Wearing his father's clothes as an adult shows he has adopted his father's habits or routines.

6. Secondhand clothing, like grief, represents a shared experience with anyone who has suffered loss.

7. He has moved a thousand miles away and is now surrounded by strangers.

Literary Element

1. "First," "then," "finally"

2. First he refers to "neighbors"; then to "a thousand miles away"; and finally to "strangers."

Reading Strategy

1. Students might suggest a crowded street in cool weather, in which the speaker is lost in a sea of people.

2. The repetition of "strangers" creates a monolithic image, reflecting the son's alienation.

Vocabulary

1. b   2. a

Writing About Literature

Students' essays should

- recognize that the two-line stanzas mimic the left-right motion of walking down a street
- notice that "strangers" creates a rhythm suggestive of footsteps

Literature Online

Web Activities Have students access the Web site for interactive activities that will help them assess their understanding of the selection.

637

Focus

Bellringer Options
Daily Language Practice Transparency 68
Or discuss the ballad as a narrative poem written to be sung, and often about a significant episode. **Ask:** If you were assigned to write a ballad, what episode would you write about? Have students discuss their ideas for ballads and explain why they would write about those topics or events. Have them consider what makes their events exciting or dramatic.

Author Search To expand students' appreciation of Dudley Randall, have them access the Web site for additional information and resources.

Use the CheckPoint questions on Presentation Plus! to monitor students' comprehension. These questions can be used with interactive response keypads for immediate student feedback.

Ballad of Birmingham

MEET DUDLEY RANDALL

A man whose first poem was published when he was only thirteen, Dudley Randall later started a publishing company with just twelve dollars. His tireless work and dedication brought recognition to a generation of African American writers.

The Broadside Dudley Randall is widely renowned for founding Broadside Press in 1965. This successful firm got its name from Randall's printing of his poem "Ballad of Birmingham" on a single sheet of paper, known in publishing lingo as a "broadside." Randall followed up that poem with another of his, "Dressed All in Pink," then continued the series with broadside printings of previously published work by Margaret Walker and Robert Hayden.

Broadside Press then began to publish poetry collections, like Randall's *Poem Counterpoem,* co-written with Margaret Esse Danner, *Cities Burning, Love You,* and *More to Remember.* By bringing into the literary spotlight such prominent writers as Alice Walker, Amiri Baraka, and Sonia Sanchez, Broadside Press proved itself to be an important and immensely valuable resource for a number of minority writers.

> *"A poet writes about what he feels, what agitates his heart and sets his pen in motion."*
>
> —Dudley Randall

Before Birmingham Born in Washington, D.C., Randall grew up in Detroit after a series of family migrations. Early in his career, he toiled as a foundry worker, served as a soldier in the South Pacific during World War II, and had a job as a postal worker. After studying English and Library Science in the late 1940s and early 1950s, Randall worked as a librarian in Missouri. He then returned home to Detroit in 1956 to work in the Wayne County Federated Library System.

The Mind of a Poet "The Ballad of Birmingham" is the most famous of Randall's poems, many of which were written during the tumultuous period of the civil rights movement in the United States. The collection *Cities Burning* is a response to the Detroit race riot of 1967. Brought about in part by police brutality toward African Americans, the chaos lasted for five days. Forty-three people died and more than seven thousand people were arrested.

His Legacy Randall's success as a poet grew while he was a poet in residence at the University of Detroit and during his later appointment as poet laureate of Detroit in 1981. The National Endowment for the Arts, a federal organization that provides funding for artistic endeavors by organizations and individuals, awarded Randall a Lifetime Achievement Award in 1996.

As both publisher and poet, Dudley Randall remains an important name in U.S. literary history.

Dudley Randall was born in 1914 and died in 2000.

Author Search For more about Dudley Randall, go to www.glencoe.com.

Selection Skills

Literary Elements
- Narrative Poetry (SE pp. 639, 640, 641)

Reading Skills
- Applying Background Knowledge (SE pp. 639, 640, 641)

Ballad of Birmingham

Vocabulary Skills
- Academic Vocabulary (SE p. 639)
- Connotation and Denotation (SE p. 641)

Writing Skills/Grammar
- Analyzing Structure (SE p. 641)

Study Skills/Research/Assessment
- Test Preparation (TWE p. 640)

Connecting to the Poem

The following poem is a poignant response to a tragic act of violence. Whether we experience it firsthand or hear about it on the news, violence, at some point, touches our lives. Before you read the poem, think about the following questions:

- Have you ever read or heard about a tragic event?
- Did you write or create something in response?

Building Background

Birmingham is the largest city in Alabama and one of the most economically important cities in the southern United States. A longtime home to the steel production industry, Birmingham was the site of much racial turbulence during the U.S. civil rights movement. "Ballad of Birmingham" is a response to the September 15, 1963, dynamite bombing of the Sixteenth Street Baptist Church, which killed four African American girls. The FBI investigation into the bombing continued off and on for decades, and resulted in the convictions of Robert Edward Chambliss in 1977 and former Ku Klux Klansmen Thomas Blanton Jr. and Bobby Frank Cherry in 2001 and 2002, respectively.

Setting Purposes for Reading

Big Idea Loves and Losses

As you read "Ballad of Birmingham," think about how Randall puts a human face on historical facts, particularly the loss of loved ones throughout the civil rights movement.

Literary Element Narrative Poetry

Narrative poetry is verse that tells a story. A literary ballad, such as "Ballad of Birmingham," usually recounts an exciting or dramatic episode. As you read, think about how Randall's choice of the ballad form helps him effectively tell this story.

- See Literary Terms Handbook, p. R11.

Reading Strategy Applying Background Knowledge

What you learn from what you read is connected in part to what you know. **Applying background knowledge** to your reading of a text can help you better understand and interpret it. As you read "Ballad of Birmingham," think about the information you read in the "Building Background" section and also use your prior knowledge.

....

Reading Tip: Taking Notes It might be useful to create a chart like the one below to keep track of what you know about the subject.

Detail	Background Knowledge
Birmingham	a city in Alabama; the site of activity during the civil rights movement

Academic Vocabulary

Here are two vocabulary words from the list on page R82. These words will help you think, write, and talk about the selection.

convince (kən vins′) v. to change someone's opinion; persuade

preliminary (pri lim′ə ner′ē) adj. introductory

Practice and Apply
1. What does the poet try to **convince** the lady?
2. What is the poem's **preliminary** idea?

OBJECTIVES
In studying this selection, you will focus on the following:
- understanding narrative poetry and ballad form
- applying background knowledge
- writing an analysis of a poem's structure

DUDLEY RANDALL **639**

Focus

Summary

The speaker of this narrative poem recounts a mother's fateful and ironic decision to send her daughter to church instead of a freedom march. Believing church to be a safe alternative to the streets of Birmingham, the mother refuses to allow her daughter to help "to make our country free."

Literary Elements Have students access the Web site to improve their understanding of narrative poetry.

Assess

Academic Vocabulary

1. By telling her that there is danger at the march—fierce dogs, clubs, hoses, and guns—and that at church she can sing in the children's choir

2. The preliminary idea is the poem's theme.

Selection Resources

Print Materials
- 📁 Unit 3 Resources (Fast File), pp. 76–77
- 📁 Leveled Vocabulary Development 54
- 📁 Selection and Unit Assessments, pp. 123–124
- 📁 Selection Quick Checks, p. 62

Transparencies
- Bellringer Options Transparencies: Daily Language Practice Transparency 68
- Literary Elements Transparency 53

Technology
- 💿 TeacherWorks Plus™ CD-ROM
- 💿 StudentWorks Plus™ CD-ROM
- 💿 Presentation Plus!™ CD-ROM
- 💻 Literature Online, glencoe.com
- 💻 Online Student Edition, mhln.com
- 💿 ExamView® Assessment Suite CD-ROM
- 💿 Vocabulary PuzzleMaker CD-ROM
- 💿 Listening Library, disc 1 track 68

Big Idea

Loves and Losses Say:
Think about these questions as you read: Why is the poem titled "Ballad of Birmingham" even though it describes one mother's loss? (This mother's loss is symbolic of everyone who lost loved ones during Birmingham's struggle to achieve civil liberties for all of its citizens.) **OL**

R Reading Strategy

Applying Background Knowledge Answer:
Students should note that there was a tragic bombing of a Birmingham church in 1963. **OL**

L Literary Element

Narrative Poetry Answer:
Randall's narration of the girl's preparation for church creates a calm and peaceful scene. **OL**

CheckPoint

Use the CheckPoint questions on Presentation Plus! to check students' mastery of the selection. These questions can be used with interactive response keypads for immediate student feedback.

Ballad of Birmingham
Dudley Randall

"Mother dear, may I go downtown
instead of out to play,
and march the streets of Birmingham
in a freedom march today?"

5   "No, baby, no, you may not go,
for the dogs are fierce and wild,
and clubs and hoses, guns[1] and jails
ain't good for a little child."

"But, mother, I won't be alone.
10 Other children will go with me,
and march the streets of Birmingham
to make our country free."

"No, baby, no, you may not go,
for I fear those guns will fire.
15 But you may go to church instead,
and sing in the children's choir."

She has combed and brushed her nightdark hair,
and bathed rose petal sweet,
and drawn white gloves on her small brown hands,
20 and white shoes on her feet.

The mother smiled to know her child
was in the sacred place,
but that smile was the last smile
to come upon her face.

25 For when she heard the explosion,
her eyes grew wet and wild.
She raced through the streets of Birmingham
calling for her child.

She clawed through bits of glass and brick,
30 then lifted out a shoe.
"O, here's the shoe my baby wore,
but, baby, where are you?"

1. *Clubs, hoses,* and *guns* were common weapons used by police and military troops to frighten and suppress demonstrators during peace and civil rights marches.

Reading Strategy Applying Background Knowledge *What information do you know about churches in Birmingham?* **R**

Literary Element Narrative Poetry *How does this stanza contribute to Randall's story-telling?* **L**

Additional Support

Web Activities Have students access the Web site for interactive activities that will help them assess their understanding of the selection.

Skills Practice

ASSESSMENT: Preparing for a Test
Remind students that preparing for a test begins long before the test is even scheduled. Test preparation involves listening carefully in class, taking good notes, and completing homework assignments that are intended to help students absorb the information. When the test has been announced, students should reread their notes, making sure that they understand any terms and concepts that may be covered on the test. Preparing and completing a study guide should also be part of the studying process. **OL**

RESPONDING AND THINKING CRITICALLY

Respond
1. (a)How did you feel at the end of the poem? (b)What about the poem made you feel this way?

Recall and Interpret
2. (a)What does the child want to do at the beginning of the poem? (b)Why is this a significant detail?
3. (a)What color are the child's shoes and gloves? (b)What do you think this color may mean or represent?
4. (a)Why does the mother smile? (b)How is this an ironic moment?

Analyze and Evaluate
5. In what way does the fifth stanza paint an effective picture of youth and innocence? Explain.
6. (a)How does the structure of the dialogue in the final stanza differ from the structure of the dialogue earlier in the poem? (b)How does this affect the emotional impact of the poem?

Connect
7. **Big Idea** **Loves and Losses** "Ballad of Birmingham" depicts a family tragedy against the backdrop of an important historical period. What might Randall be trying to say about the civil rights movement?

LITERARY ANALYSIS

Literary Element Narrative Poetry

Narrative poetry comes in many forms, including ballads, epics, and shorter works that focus on a specific event. "Ballad of Birmingham" takes the ballad form, which is usually made up of several ballad stanzas, a common four-line structure that is part of a long tradition in English poetry.

1. Read about ballad in the Literary Terms Handbook beginning on page R1. How does "Ballad of Birmingham" show ballad characteristics?
2. Does "Ballad of Birmingham" have a traditional narrative structure? Explain.

Writing About Literature

Analyze Structure Randall structures his poem in a particular way to make the largest possible impact. How does he use foreshadowing and irony to structure his ideas? How does he use **refrain** to structure the language and rhythm of his poem? Write a one- or two-page analysis of Randall's structural techniques. Use evidence from the poem for support.

Literature Online **Web Activities** For eFlashcards, Selection Quick Checks, and other Web activities, go to www.glencoe.com.

READING AND VOCABULARY

Reading Strategy Applying Background Knowledge

In a poem like "Ballad of Birmingham," which melds historical fact and fiction, being able to **apply background knowledge** to the text is essential to understanding its meaning.

1. Imagine that you did not know about the Birmingham church bombing prior to reading this poem. Would you have interpreted it differently? Explain.
2. How did your background knowledge of the Birmingham church bombing and the civil rights movement affect your response to this poem?

Vocabulary Practice

Practice with Connotation and Denotation
For each word from "Ballad of Birmingham" listed below, identify whether its connotation is positive, negative, or neutral.

1. freedom
   a. positive   b. negative   c. neutral
2. fierce
   a. positive   b. negative   c. neutral
3. nightdark
   a. positive   b. negative   c. neutral

DUDLEY RANDALL **641**

Assess

1. (a) Probably sad or angry (b) The mother's feelings of horror and the death
2. (a) Go to a freedom march (b) This establishes the setting and sets up the irony—violence not at a freedom march but at a church.
3. (a) White (b) White represents purity and innocence.
4. (a) Because she thinks her daughter is safe at church (b) Ironic because the church was the most dangerous place she could have been at that time
5. The white clothing, groomed hair, and smell of rose petals convey innocence.
6. (a) Stanzas 1–4 are entirely dialogue, but only half of the last stanza is dialogue. (b) It creates a stronger impact because the reader expects the child to answer.
7. Students may say that violence seeped into every aspect of life, including places that should be safe.

Literary Element

1. Students should mark the four stressed syllables in the first and third lines and the three stressed syllables in the second and fourth lines.
2. Yes, the opening four stanzas introduce the characters and set up the conflict (the mother believes the freedom march will be dangerous and thus sends her child to church). The action rises when the daughter leaves and the mother hears an explosion. The climax is when the mother pulls a shoe from the ruins. The resolution is the mother's final call to her child.

Reading Strategy
1. Students may say they would not have known it refers to a historical event.
2. Students may say it makes the poem more powerful and poignant.

Vocabulary
1. a 2. b 3. c

Writing About Literature
Students' essays should
- note the foreshadowing in "but that smile was the last smile/to come upon her face"
- note that foreshadowing is a structural device used to make events significant
- note the irony of a crime in a church

641

Focus

Summary

In this selection, film critic Roger Ebert reviews *4 Little Girls,* filmmaker Spike Lee's documentary about the 1963 church bombing in Birmingham, Alabama. Ebert describes the circumstances surrounding the bombing and its aftermath. He describes the bombing as "the catalyst for the civil rights movement."

Teach

R1 Reading Strategy

Evaluating Evidence Ask:
What did Walter Cronkite mean when he said that the church bombing "was the awakening"? *(The extreme violence convinced many Americans that racism and segregation were wrong.)* **OL**

Readability Scores
Dale-Chall: 6.6
DRP: 61
Lexile: 1110

---

4 Little Girls

Roger Ebert, *Chicago Sun-Times*, October 24, 1997

Pulitzer Prize Award-Winner

Birmingham Race Riot, 1964. Andy Warhol.

Building Background

Roger Ebert is a renowned film critic and recipient of the Pulitzer Prize for criticism in 1975. He has reviewed films in print for the *Chicago Sun-Times* since 1967, and on television for the former program *Siskel and Ebert* and currently on *Ebert and Roeper and the Movies.* In this review, Ebert praises Spike Lee's documentary film *4 Little Girls.*

Set a Purpose for Reading

Read to discover the plot of *4 Little Girls* and the history of the Birmingham, Alabama, church bombing.

Reading Strategy

Evaluating Evidence

Evaluating evidence is making a judgment or forming an opinion about the evidence an author uses to make a point or support an argument. Evaluating evidence also involves distinguishing between facts and opinions. Use a chart like the one below to track facts and opinions.

Fact	Opinion
Four girls were killed in the bombing.	Denise McNair was "filled with charisma."

Spike Lee's *4 Little Girls* tells the story of the infamous Birmingham, Ala., church bombing of September 15, 1963, when the lives of an 11-year-old and three 14-year-olds, members of the choir, were ended by an explosion. More than any other event, that was the catalyst for the civil rights movement, the moment when all of America could look away no longer from the face of racism. "It was the awakening," says Walter **R1** Cronkite[1] in the film.

The little girls had gone to church early for choir practice, and we can imagine them, dressed in their Sunday best, meeting their friends in the room destroyed by the bomb. We can fashion the picture in our minds because Lee has, in a way, brought them back to life, through photographs, through old home movies and especially through the memories of their families and friends.

---

1. *Walter Cronkite* (1916–) was a *CBS Evening News* anchor from 1962–1981.

Additional Support

Skills Practice

READING: Previewing As a movie review, this selection does not intend to provide the reader with every bit of information about the subject. Ask students to read the title and look at the illustrations and the organization of the selection to determine the author's purpose. *(The author's purpose is to convince his readers to see the movie he is reviewing.)* **OL** English language learners and reluctant readers might find it helpful to skim the entire selection before making a decision about author's purpose. **BL**

By coincidence, I was listening to the radio not long after seeing *4 Little Girls,* and I heard a report from Charlayne Hunter-Gault. In 1961, when she was 19, she was the first black woman to desegregate the University of Georgia. Today she is an NPR[2] correspondent. That is what happened to her. In 1963, Carole Robertson was 14, and her Girl Scout sash was covered with merit badges. Because she was killed that day, we will never know what would have happened in her life.

That thought keeps returning: The four little girls never got to grow up. Not only were their lives stolen, but so were their contributions to ours. I have a hunch that Denise McNair, who was 11 when she died, would have made her mark. In home movies, she comes across as poised and observant, filled with charisma. Among the many participants in the film, two of the most striking are her parents, Chris and Maxine McNair, who remember a special child.

Chris McNair talks of a day when he took Denise to downtown Birmingham, and the smell of onions frying at a store's lunch counter made her hungry. "That night I knew I had to tell her she couldn't have that sandwich because she was black," he recalls. "That couldn't have been any less painful than seeing her with a rock smashed into her head." Lee's film re-creates the day of the bombing through newsreel footage, photographs and eyewitness reports. He places it within a larger context of the Southern civil rights movement, and sit-ins and the arrests, the marches, the songs and the killings.

Birmingham was a tough case. Police commissioner Bull Connor is seen directing the resistance to marchers and traveling in an armored vehicle—painted white, of course. Gov. George Wallace makes his famous

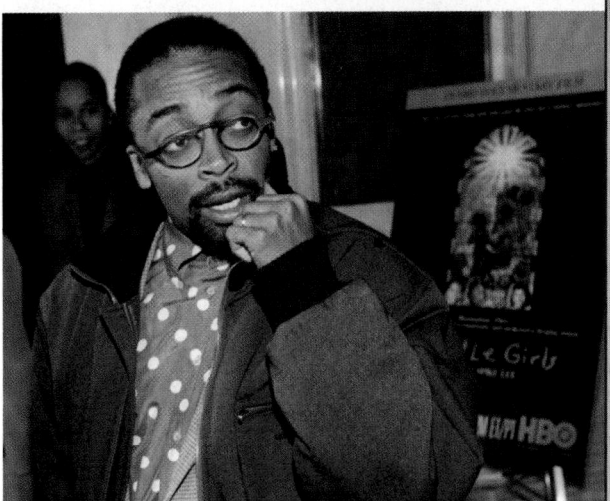

Film producer and director Spike Lee talks about his film, *4 Little Girls,* during a reception on Capitol Hill in Washington, DC, February 11, 1998.

vow to stand in the schoolhouse door and personally bar any black students from entering. Though they could not know it, their resistance was futile after September 15, 1963, because the hatred exposed by the bomb pulled all of their rhetoric[3] and rationalizations out from under them.

Spike Lee[4] says he has wanted to make this film since 1983, when he read a *New York Times Magazine* article by Howell Raines about the bombing. "He wrote me asking permission back then," Chris McNair told me in an interview. "That was before he had made any of his films." It is perhaps good that Lee waited, because he is more of a filmmaker now, and events have supplied him a dénouement[5] in the conviction of a man named Robert Chambliss ("Dynamite Bob") as the bomber. He was,

---

2. *NPR,* or *National Public Radio,* is a public radio network.

3. Here, *rhetoric* means "persuasive use of language."
4. *Spike Lee* (1957–) is a filmmaker known for his provocative films, including *Do the Right Thing, Malcolm X,* and *Summer of Sam.*
5. *Dénouement* means "the outcome of a series of events."

ROGER EBERT **643**

Teach

R2 Reading Strategy

Evaluating Evidence Ask:
What is Ebert's purpose in mentioning Charlayne Hunter-Gault? *(He is illustrating the accomplishments that could have been made by the four young girls.)* OL

R3 Reading Strategy

Evaluating Evidence Have students explain what the father meant by this statement. *(Telling his daughter that she wasn't good enough to eat in a restaurant was as painful as seeing her dead.)* OL

R4 Reading Strategy

Evaluating Evidence Have students explain what is meant by this passage. *(Until this violent incident, people accepted the reasoning of politicians and law enforcement officials.)* OL

★ Political History

Charlayne Hunter-Gault
In 1963 American journalist Charlayne Hunter-Gault became the first African American woman to graduate from the University of Georgia. **AS**

See also ◢ Active Learning and Note Taking Guide, pp. 88–93.

Objective
• To improve understanding by previewing a literary work (TWE)

English Language Coach

Segregation in the South English language learners may have difficulty understanding this selection because of the many historical and social references. Explain to students that segregation—the practice of separating blacks from whites—existed in the southern states until the passage of the Civil Rights Act in 1964. Blacks and whites had separate schools, parks, restaurants, restrooms, and even drinking fountains. Ask students to discuss their countries of origin and whether or not similar practices are or ever were in place. **EL**

Assess

1. Most students will say that the film sounds engaging, and that they would like to see it.

2. (a) The bombing of a Birmingham, Alabama, church on September 15, 1963, in which four young girls were killed. (b) Film can use actual footage of events and the reactions of the people who were affected by them.

3. (a) Through newsreels, home movies, photographs, and eyewitness reports (b) By the way film and television clips are juxtaposed

4. Some may argue that Ebert points out the tremendous effects of the event. Others may argue that he does not provide evidence to support the claim that the bombing sparked the Civil Rights Movement.

5. (a) He points out the comment of a Klansman—"I really didn't believe they would go this far"—as a way for the man to "disassociate" himself from the actions of the Ku Klux Klan. He also identifies the effort of Governor George Wallace, who favored racial segregation, to claim that his best friend was his

For additional assessment, see 📁 Selection and Unit Assessment, pp. 125–126.

644

---

said Raines, who met quite a few, "the most pathological[6] racist I've ever encountered." The other victims were Addie Mae Collins and Cynthia Wesley, both 14. In shots that are almost unbearable, we see the victims' bodies in the morgue. Why does Lee show them? To look full into the face of what was done, I think. To show racism its handiwork. There is a memory in the film of a burly white Birmingham policeman who after the bombing tells a black minister, "I really didn't believe they would go this far." The man was a Klansman,[7] the movie says, but in using the word "they" he unconsciously separates himself from his fellows. He wants to disassociate himself from the crime. So did

---

6. Here, *pathological* means "diseased."
7. A *Klansman* is a member of the white supremacist organization the Ku Klux Klan.

others. Before long even Wallace was apologizing for his behavior and trying to define himself in a different light. There is a scene in the film where the former governor, now old and infirm,[8] describes his black personal assistant, Eddie Holcey, as his best friend. "I couldn't live without him," Wallace says, dragging Holcey in front of the camera, insensitive to the feelings of the man he is tugging over for display.

Why is that scene there? It's sort of associated with the morgue photos, I think. There is mostly sadness and regret at the surface in *4 Little Girls,* but there is anger in the depths, as there should be.

---

8. Here, *infirm* means "feeble."

RESPONDING AND THINKING CRITICALLY

Respond

1. Would you be interested in seeing the film *4 Little Girls*? Why or why not?

Recall and Interpret

2. (a) What is the film *4 Little Girls* about? (b) What is different about documenting history on film versus other mediums?

3. (a) How does Spike Lee re-create the day of the Birmingham church bombing? (b) How does a documentary film director influence the message an audience receives from a film?

Analyze and Evaluate

4. Do you think Ebert supports his position that the Birmingham church bombing "was the catalyst for the civil rights movement"? What evidence does he present for his position?

5. (a) What images or moments in *4 Little Girls* does Ebert identify as ironic? (b) What does Ebert interpret Lee's message to be?

Connect

6. Both Dudley Randall's poem, "The Ballad of Birmingham," and Roger Ebert's film review of *4 Little Girls* make statements about the outcome of the Birmingham church bombing of 1963. What is similar about their messages? How are their messages different? In your opinion, which message is stronger? Explain.

OBJECTIVES
- Evaluate evidence presented in a text.
- Understand the historical and political context of a text.

African American personal assistant. (b) A record of racism in this country and the anger it fuels, among both the racists and those who suffer from racism's abuses.

6. Both authors comment on the tragedy of the Birmingham church bombing and have empathy for those involved.

Ebert's review dwells on the events and the victims. Randall's ballad focuses on two victims of the bombing. Both messages are strong, one creating a sense of sorrow by focusing on a slice of life and the other telling the story through a compassionate tone.

PART 3

Issues of Identity

Real Truth. Jerzy Kolacz. ★

BIG IDEA

Your identity is more than the clothes you wear, your interests, or your thoughts and emotions. Through all the changes of life, part of you does not change—that something by which you recognize yourself, no matter what. The poems in Part 3 deal with changing identity. As you read them, ask yourself: How have I changed in the last several years? What about me has not changed?

645

Analyzing and Extending

Big Idea

Issues of Identity
Offer this comment by psychologist Abraham Maslow: "Every person is, in part, 'his own project,' and makes himself." **Ask:** What is identity? How does a person create identity? *(Discuss student responses. Students may see personality, background, attitudes, interests, and abilities as part of identity.)* Tell students that poetry reminds readers of the uniqueness of each person and that Part 3 will deepen their understanding of identity. Encourage students to contemplate this "big idea" in relation to the artwork. **OL**

★ Viewing the Art

Ask: How does this painting reflect the theme of identity? *(Students may say that within all of us are other identities, sides, or faces. Also people often wear masks to hide their true selves.* **AS**

English Language Coach

Building Background Students new to the United States will be able to connect to the idea of identity. Discuss how the changes in their lives have affected them, and ask them to consider the importance of their cultural background to their identity. **EL**

Differentiated Instruction

Activating Prior Knowledge Guide less proficient students to consider what they know about issues of identity, and pose questions about what they would like to learn. Seeking answers to these questions can help students connect to the poetry they read. **BL**

Objectives for Part 3
• To recognize and interpret poetic elements like the effect of sound on meaning (SE)
• To understand the use of sounds to elicit the reader's emotions (SE)
• To evaluate the aesthetic qualities of style on tone, mood, and theme (SE)

645

Part 3: Issues of Identity

Readability Scores Key
Dale-Chall/DRP/Lexile

PACING (DAYS)		SELECTIONS AND FEATURES	LITERARY ELEMENTS
STANDARD	BLOCK		
1–2 class sessions	1–2	LITERARY FOCUS: Sound Devices, pp. 646–647	Sound Devices, SE pp. 646, 647 Style, TWE p. 646 Alliteration, TWE p. 647
		"miss rosie" by Lucille Clifton, pp. 648–651	Alliteration, SE pp. 649, 650, 651
		"After Apple-Picking" and **"Fire and Ice"** by Robert Frost, pp. 652–659	Assonance and Consonance, SE pp. 653, 655, 658 Alliteration, SE p. 658
1 class session	1	**"Arabic Coffee"** by Naomi Shihab Nye, pp. 660–663	Symbol, SE pp. 661, 663
		TIME magazine, **"We Are Family"** by Chang-rae Lee 7.1/58/1150, pp. 664–667	
2–3 class sessions	1	COMPARING LITERATURE Across Genres **"Dream Boogie," "Motto,"** and **"Harlem"** by Langston Hughes, pp. 668–674 **"Jazz Fan Looks Back"** by Jayne Cortez, pp. 675–676 **"Dizzy Gillespie, Explorer of New Sounds"** from *Giants of Jazz* by Studs Terkel 6.5/55/750, pp. 677–680 **"Playing Jazz"** by Wynton Marsalis 6.1/57/800, pp. 681–685	Rhyme and Rhyme Scheme, SE pp. 670, 672, 674 Scansion, TWE p. 672
2 class sessions	2	Writing Workshop: Reflective Essay, pp. 686–693	
		Speaking, Listening, and Viewing Workshop: Presenting a Reflective Essay, pp. 694–695	
		Test Preparation and Practice, pp. 698–703	Imagery and Theme, TWE p. 698

About the Part

Part 3 covers poetic sound devices.

READING AND CRITICAL THINKING	VOCABULARY	WRITING AND GRAMMAR	LISTENING, SPEAKING, AND VIEWING
Analyzing Sound Techniques, TWE p. 646		Quickwrite, SE p. 647	
Analyzing Sensory Details, SE pp. 649, 651	Connotation and Denotation, SE pp. 649, 651		Analyzing Art, SE p. 650 Literary Criticism, SE p. 651
Clarifying Meaning, SE pp. 653, 655, 658	Synonyms, SE pp. 653, 658 Academic Vocabulary, SE p. 658	Analyze Rhyme and Rhyme Scheme, SE p. 659	Comparing Written and Visual Imagery, SE p. 659
Analyzing Rhythm, SE pp. 661, 663 Figurative Language, TWE p. 662	Academic Vocabulary, SE p. 663	Respond to Figurative Language, SE p. 663	Analyzing Art, TWE p. 662
Analyzing Cultural Context, SE p. 664; TWE p. 665		Writing Letters, TWE p. 666	Analyzing Photographs, TWE pp. 664, 666
Making Inferences About Theme, SE pp. 670, 671, 674 Previewing, TWE p. 670 Analyzing Biography, TWE p. 678 Summarizing, TWE p. 684	Word Parts, SE p. 674 Context Clues, TWE p. 682	Quickwrite, SE pp. 676, 680 Comparison Essay, SE p. 685 Drafting a Letter, TWE p. 680 Types of Sentences, TWE p. 676	Discussion Starter, SE p. 684 Group Activity, SE p. 685 Analyzing Art, TWE pp. 672, 675, 679, 681
Identifying Transitions, TWE p. 688		Active versus Passive Voice, TWE p. 690	
			Reflections, SE pp. 694–695 Using Visual Aids, TWE p. 694
		Correct Use of Pronouns, TWE p. 702	

Teach

R Reading Strategy

Analyzing Sound Techniques **Ask:** What is the onomatopoeia in Emily Dickinson's poem? *(The word* buzz *mimics a fly.)* **Ask:** What type of rhyme do the "Fire and Ice" lines use? *(aa, a couplet)* **OL**

L1 Literary Element

Onomatopoeia **Ask:** What examples of onomatopoeia can you find in the cartoon? *(Some examples:* snip, snap, crack, whish, *and* krunch.) **Say:** Create a list of five other ono matopoeic words. Then write a stanza of poetry that includes two or more of these words. **OL**

Sound Devices

What makes poetry musical?

Most poems are written to be heard, like music, or to be imagined aloud in the reader's mind. The actor Ossie Davis said of Langston Hughes's work, "Langston Hughes belongs to whoever is listening. A possession in common, like the sights and sounds of a street corner hangout, or the barbershop debate over pretty girls, and baseball players: Open your ears and your heart if you've got one; Langston will walk right in and do the rest." As you read poetry, can you hear music in the words?

Onomatopoeia

Onomatopoeia is the use of a word or phrase that imitates or suggests the sound of what it describes, like the words *moan* and *thump.* Which word in the poem below is an example of onomatopoeia?

I heard a fly buzz—when I died—
The Stillness in the Room
Was like the Stillness in the Air—
Between the Heaves of Storm—

—Emily Dickinson, **from "I Heard a Fly Buzz When I Died"**

Rhyme

Rhyme is the repetition of stressed vowel sounds and all the sounds that follow in two or more words. For example, *cat* and *hat* rhyme, as do *willowier* and *billowier.* Rhymes at the ends of lines of poetry are called **end rhymes**.

From what I've tasted of desire
I hold with those who favor fire.

—Robert Frost, **from "Fire and Ice"**

Additional Support

Skills Practice

LITERARY ELEMENT: Style Discuss the effect of poetic style on tone, mood, and theme in "I Heard a Fly Buzz When I Died." **Ask:** What effect does the choice of speaker have on the poem? *(The speaker of the poem is someone who recalls the moment of his or her* death. This choice of speaker heightens the meaning and emotion of the poem.) **Ask:** What is the atmosphere in the room like? *(The atmosphere in the room is solemn and tense.)* **Ask:** What effect does the buzzing fly seem to have on the speaker? *(The fly distracts the*

Rhyming words within one line are called **internal rhyme:**

> Once upon a midnight <u>dreary</u>, while I
> pondered, weak and <u>weary</u>,
>
> —Edgar Allan Poe, **from "The Raven"**

Both end and internal rhymes can be **slant rhymes,** or rhymes that are close, but not exact.

Alliteration

Poets pay special attention to all the sounds in their lines. The term **alliteration** refers to sounds, usually consonants, that repeat, usually at the beginnings of words. Notice the use of alliteration, the repetition of *w, s,* and *p* sounds, in these lines:

> When I watch you
> wrapped up like garbage
> sitting, surrounded by the smell
> of too old potato peels
>
> —Lucille Clifton, **from "Miss Rosie"** **L2**

Assonance

When the repeated sound is a vowel sound rather than a consonant sound, the sound device is called **assonance.** Listen for three *oo* sounds in this line:

> No shutter'd room or school can commune with me,
>
> —Walt Whitman, **from "Song of Myself"**

Consonance

Alliteration, described above, is actually a special kind of **consonance,** the repetition of consonant sounds before and after different vowel sounds. Note the repetition of the *s* and *l* sounds in the following lines:

> She passed the salley gardens with little
>   snow-white feet.
> She bid me take love easy as the leaves
>   grow on the tree;
>
> —W. B. Yeats, **from "Down by the Salley Gardens"**

In the following two lines, note the repetition of *f, wh,* and *th* sounds:

> From what I've tasted of desire
> I hold with those who favor fire.
>
> —Robert Frost, **from "Fire and Ice"**

Quickwrite

Describing Feelings With Sounds Think about feelings and sounds. Choose one feeling, such as anger, greed, or pride. Use the graphic organizer to brainstorm words that you associate with the feeling you chose. Look closely at the words. Which words sound—not mean—the closest to your feeling? Do some letters sound the most like the feeling? Write a few phrases or lines with the right sound.

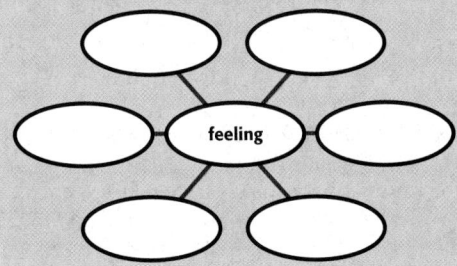

OBJECTIVES
- Recognize and interpret poetic elements like the effect of sound on meaning.
- Understand the use of sounds to elicit the reader's emotions.
- Evaluate the aesthetic qualities of style on tone, mood, and theme.

LITERARY FOCUS **647**

Teach

L2 Literary Element

Alliteration Ask: What are examples of alliteration in "miss rosie"? *(<u>w</u>hen and <u>w</u>atched; <u>s</u>itting, <u>s</u>urrounded, and <u>s</u>mell; <u>p</u>otato <u>p</u>eels)* **OL**

Assess

Quickwrite

Have students read the words aloud and think of them in terms of sound. Discuss what makes words sound like various feelings. Check students' phrases or lines for the attempt to capture a feeling with sound.

speaker from the heaviness of this moment, from dying; the fly is annoying and makes the speaker lose concentration.) **OL**

English Language Coach

Sound and Dialect Read the poetry aloud, emphasizing sound techniques, to help students new to the United States develop an ear for English. Ask them to experiment with different verbal interpretations of the lines. **EL**

Focus

BELLRINGER

Bellringer Options
**Selection Focus
Transparency 33
Daily Language Practice
Transparency 69**
Or have students make lists of words that describe who they are. **Ask:** Which of these words do you think will still describe you ten years from now? Twenty years from now? Have students circle the words that will still describe them in ten years and highlight the words that will describe them in twenty years. Have students share their lists in small groups and discuss why some words stayed and some did not.

Literature Online

Author Search To expand students' appreciation of Lucille Clifton, have them access the Web site for additional information and resources.

CheckPoint

Use the CheckPoint questions on Presentation Plus! to monitor students' comprehension. These questions can be used with interactive response keypads for immediate student feedback.

Miss Rosie

MEET LUCILLE CLIFTON

She may not be a household name, but Lucille Clifton has been compared to great poets such as Walt Whitman and Emily Dickinson. Her short poems reflect simplicity and a strong emphasis on celebrating the everyday and the ordinary. Clifton's poems powerfully reveal the complexities of life and also express optimism and the idea that things can get better.

In her poems, Clifton mainly focuses on the daily and often harsh realities of urban life. She realistically portrays the struggles of people in the inner city. Despite the gritty portrayals, Clifton's poems maintain a sense of hope and spiritual strength. She emphasizes "the qualities which have allowed us to survive." Clifton's own family history plays a large part in her ability to write about the pain of living while also offering a message about the ability to overcome: One of her female ancestors was kidnapped and brought to America against her will and another was the first African American female to be lynched in Virginia. Clifton confronts this tragic history while writing about the human experience.

"All of our stories become The Story. If mine is left out, something's missing."

—Lucille Clifton

Humble Beginnings Clifton was born during the Great Depression in New York. Her father was a steel mill worker, and her mother worked as a laundress and homemaker. Clifton's mother also enjoyed writing poetry, an ability passed on to her daughter. Even though neither of them had been formally educated, both of Clifton's parents passed on an appreciation for books and learning. Because of this, Clifton found herself prepared to enter college at the age of sixteen. She studied drama at Howard University and became an actor before seriously cultivating her interest in poetry.

Clifton's first book, a poetry collection titled *Good Times,* was published in 1969. It was hailed by the *New York Times* as one of the year's ten best books. Since then, Clifton has published several volumes of poetry. She has also written more than twenty children's books, including an award-winning fiction series about the life of a young African American boy named Everett Anderson.

Taking Her Place Today Clifton's many poems and stories have garnered her a rightful place among America's best writers. She has won many honors, including an Emmy Award, for her work. She was nominated for a Pulitzer Prize, becoming the first author to have two poetry books (*Next* and *Good Woman*) selected as finalists in the same year (1988).

Some of Clifton's major works of poetry include *Good News About the Earth, An Ordinary Woman, Quilting: Poems 1987–1990,* and *The Terrible Stories.* She also penned *Generations: A Memoir,* a work of prose focusing on her family's origins. Clifton has also been a Distinguished Professor of Humanities at St. Mary's College of Maryland since 1991.

Lucille Clifton was born in 1936.

Literature Online **Author Search** For more about Lucille Clifton, go to www.glencoe.com.

Selection Skills

Literary Elements
• Alliteration (SE pp. 649–651)

miss rosie

Vocabulary Skills
• Connotation and Denotation (SE pp. 649, 651)

Reading Skills
• Analyzing Sensory Details (SE pp. 649, 651)
• Reading Poetry (TWE p. 650)

Listening/Speaking/Viewing Skills
• Analyzing Art (SE p. 650)
• Group Discussion (SE p. 651)

Connecting to the Poem

The following poem by Lucille Clifton shows that we often identify people by how they look, not by what is inside them. Before you read the poem, think about the following questions:

- What visual clues do you use to judge a person?
- What makes you like or dislike a person when you first meet him or her?

Building Background

Many of Clifton's poems examine the varying roles of women in society. Our roles in life change with our age, marital status, children, and career. Our identity is often related to our roles. For example, you might have roles as child, friend, sibling, and student. You might also have roles as employee or volunteer. Some roles we choose, and some are chosen for us. For example, we choose to be a volunteer, but being the child of our parents is something we cannot choose. In this poem, poverty has given Miss Rosie a new role and a new identity.

Setting Purposes for Reading

Big Idea Issues of Identity

As you read this poem, notice how the identity of Miss Rosie has changed over time.

Literary Element Alliteration

Alliteration is the repetition of consonant sounds at the beginnings of words. The opening line of "Miss Rosie" is a good example of alliteration because it contains repeated *w* sounds.

"when i watch you"

Alliteration can help you vividly picture what an author is trying to portray. As you read, notice Clifton's use of alliteration and its effect on the text.

- See Literary Terms Handbook, p. R1.

Literature Online Interactive Literary Elements Handbook To review or learn more about the literary elements, go to www.glencoe.com.

Reading Strategy Analyzing Sensory Details

Sensory details are words that spark sense memories in the reader. These memories include details about the senses of taste, touch, sight, hearing, and smell. Recognizing these details can foster a deeper connection to a literary work. While reading this essay, note the sensory details that Clifton uses, as well as the senses to which they correspond.

Reading Tip: Finding Details Using a chart like the one below, record the sensory details in the poem and the senses they appeal to.

Sensory Detail	Sense
"wrapped up like garbage"	sight, smell
"you wet brown bag of a woman"	touch, sight

Vocabulary

Vocabulary Tip: Connotation and Denotation
Connotation is the suggested or implied meaning of a word or phrase that extends beyond the dictionary definition. Connotations can be positive, negative, or neutral. **Denotation** is the literal, or dictionary, meaning of a word or phrase. For example, the denotation of *timid* is "lacking in courage." The connotation of *timid*, however, is slightly negative—the word suggests cowardice or unassertiveness.

Focus

Summary

The poem's speaker reflects on the circumstances of a once-beautiful woman whose life has not turned out well. She thinks of Miss Rosie fondly as she was and is sad but honest about what Miss Rosie has become.

Literary Elements Have students access the Web site to improve their understanding of alliteration.

OBJECTIVES
In studying this selection, you will focus on the following:
- recognizing and understanding alliteration
- analyzing the use of sensory details
- understanding connotation and denotation
- responding to literary criticism

LUCILLE CLIFTON **649**

Selection Resources

Print Materials
- Unit 3 Resources (Fast File), pp. 82–83
- Selection and Unit Assessments, pp. 127–128
- Selection Quick Checks, p. 64

Transparencies
- Bellringer Options Transparencies: Daily Language Practice Transparency 69
- Literary Elements Transparency 72

Technology
- TeacherWorks Plus™ CD-ROM
- StudentWorks Plus™ CD-ROM
- Presentation Plus!™ CD-ROM
- Literature Online, glencoe.com
- Online Student Edition, mhln.com
- ExamView® Assessment Suite CD-ROM
- Vocabulary PuzzleMaker CD-ROM
- Listening Library, disc 1 track 70

Teach

L Literary Element

Alliteration

Answer: *It repeats the consonant s sound at the beginning of words.* **OL**

BI Big Idea

Issues of Identity

Answer: *It becomes positive, as she is depicted as a singularly beautiful woman.* **OL**

⭐ Viewing the Art

Answer: *The woman in the image could be a younger Miss Rosie, nicely dressed, pretty, well-groomed, confident. The older woman in the poem is sloppy, unattractive, poorly dressed, defeated.* **AS**

📽 CheckPoint

Use the CheckPoint questions on Presentation Plus! to check students' mastery of the selection. These questions can be used with interactive response keypads for immediate student feedback.

Yellow Hat, 1936. Norman Lewis. Oil on burlap, 36½ x 26 in. Collection of Loide Lewis and the late Reginald Lewis.

Viewing the Art: How does the woman in the painting compare with your image of the speaker in the poem? With your image of the young Miss Rosie? Which characteristics are the same and which are different? ⭐

miss rosie

Lucille Clifton

when i watch you
wrapped up like garbage
sitting, surrounded by the smell
of too old potato peels
5   or
when i watch you
in your old man's shoes
with the little toe cut out
sitting, waiting for your mind
10   like next week's grocery
i say
when i watch you
you wet brown bag of a woman
who used to be the best looking
        gal in georgia
15   used to be called the Georgia Rose
i stand up
through your destruction
i stand up

Literary Element Alliteration *How is this line a good example of alliteration?* **L**

Big Idea Issues of Identity *How does this description of Miss Rosie change her identity?* **BI**

650 UNIT 3 POETRY

Skills Practice

READING: Poetry Explain to students that reading poetry is different from reading prose. Have students take note of the absence of punctuation in "Miss Rosie." Tell them to try to figure out where the pauses—normally indicated by commas, periods, and other punctuation—belong. Have students read the poem silently several times, thinking about where they might pause naturally. Then have them take turns reading the poem aloud to a partner, experimenting with pauses in different places. **OL**

650

RESPONDING AND THINKING CRITICALLY

Respond

1. (a)How do you feel about Miss Rosie? (b)Did you feel differently about her at the end of the poem than you did at the beginning? Explain.

Recall and Interpret

2. a)How does Clifton describe Miss Rosie in lines 9–10? (b)What does this description imply about Miss Rosie?

3. (a)How does the speaker respond to Miss Rosie by the end of the poem? (b)In your opinion, what does the speaker think about Miss Rosie?

Analyze and Evaluate

4. (a)Write a short physical description of Miss Rosie, based on the details in the poem. (b)Do you think Clifton has given you enough details to go on?

5. In your opinion, does this poem present a stronger picture of Miss Rosie or of the speaker? Support your response with details from the poem.

Connect

6. **Big Idea** Issues of Identity In what ways does this poem relate to issues of identity?

LITERARY ANALYSIS

Literary Element Alliteration

Alliteration is often used by poets who like working with the sounds of words. Although we often think of poems as only being read silently, poetry is also an oral art. Many poems are read aloud, and poets often enjoy reading their own poems aloud. In these cases, the sounds of the words become very important to the overall reception of the poem by the audience.

1. Where does Clifton use alliteration in this poem? Give two examples.

2. How does Clifton's use of alliteration enhance the use of sensory details in the poem? Explain.

Literary Criticism

Ronald Baughman writes of "Miss Rosie" that "the poem . . . functions both as a lament for the woman destroyed and as a tribute to the new black woman who rises from the ashes of her predecessor's destruction."

With your classmates, discuss how the poem serves as both a lament and as a tribute. What do you learn about the woman who has been "destroyed"? How does the speaker "rise from the ashes"?

Literature Online Web Activities For eFlashcards, Selection Quick Checks, and other Web activities, go to www.glencoe.com.

READING AND VOCABULARY

Reading Strategy Analyzing Sensory Details

Often an author will use **sensory details** to help the reader envision what the author is describing. The selection of sensory words gives the reader a positive, negative, or neutral view of the person, object, or event being described.

1. What do you think Clifton's purpose was when she chose certain words to create sensory details?

2. In support of your opinion, list three sensory details from the poem.

Vocabulary Practice

Practice with Connotation and Denotation
Decide whether the connotation of each phrase below is positive, negative, or neutral. Use a dictionary or a thesaurus if you need help.

1. wrapped up like garbage
   a. positive   **b.** negative   **c.** neutral

2. smell of too old potato peels
   a. positive   **b.** negative   **c.** neutral

3. little toe cut out
   a. positive   **b.** negative   **c.** neutral

4. wet brown bag of a woman
   a. positive   **b.** negative   **c.** neutral

5. used to be called the Georgia Rose
   a. positive   **b.** negative   **c.** neutral

LUCILLE CLIFTON **651**

Assess

1. (a) Students may be sympathetic to her plight (b) Most students will likely think less of her before learning that she was beautiful.

2. (a) Miss Rosie sits and stares vacantly. (b) She has apparently lost touch with reality.

3. (a) The speaker pays tribute to Miss Rosie. (b) Compassionate and respectful

4. (a) Descriptions will vary. (b) The descriptions are not concrete, so it is difficult to write an accurate physical description.

5. Miss Rosie

6. With the identities of Miss Rosie: as a "bag lady" and as the Georgia Rose.

Literary Element

1. Lines 1–2 and 12–14

2. The alliteration and some of the sensory details are contained in the same phrases. The alliteration helps emphasize the sensory details.

Reading Strategy

1. She wanted to describe vividly the current condition of Miss Rosie.

2. Examples may include "wrapped up like garbage"; "surrounded by the smell/of too old potato peels"; "old man's shoes/with the little toe cut out"; "wet brown bag of a woman."

Vocabulary

1. b **2.** b **3.** b **4.** b **5.** a

Literature Online

Web Activities Have students access the Web site for interactive activities that will help them assess their understanding of the selection.

Literary Criticism

The woman who has been "destroyed" was once a renowned beauty. Her youthful potential has been defeated by life's hardships. The speaker takes notice of how life has treated the woman and vows to "stand up" to life.

Focus

BELLRINGER

Bellringer Options
Daily Language Practice Transparency 70
Or instruct students to write a paragraph addressing the following question: What is your favorite season and why? Encourage them to name specific memories, activities, or characteristics of the season that influence their answers. Invite a few volunteers to share their responses with the class.
Ask: What feelings or ideas does your favorite season symbolize to you? *(Answers will vary but might include spring symbolizing a sense of renewal.)*

Literature Online

Author Search To expand students' appreciation of Robert Frost, have them access the Web site for additional information and resources.

After Apple-Picking and *Fire and Ice*

MEET ROBERT FROST

Robert Frost won the highest admiration and respect from his many peers and readers throughout the twentieth century, and was asked by President John F. Kennedy to read a poem, "The Gift Outright," at his inauguration.

Frost wanted his poetry to appeal to the general book-buying public rather than just finding favor in literary circles. He wanted readers to dig at the roots of his poems and look beyond the realism of the natural environment, seeking deeper meaning and significance.

Frost led a remarkable life of the mind and spirit, one based in skepticism and deep thought driven by a desire to achieve success as a poet. Robert Frost was born in San Francisco, but moved to New England at the age of eleven. While still in high school he developed a love of poetry, a passion he shared with his future wife and fellow student, Elinor White. Frost published his first poem, "My Butterfly: An Elegy," at twenty. The next year, he and Elinor were married.

*"Poetry is a process
Poetry is the renewal of words
Poetry is the dawning of an idea"*

—Robert Frost

His Own Man True to his unconventional path to acclaim as a writer, Frost had abandoned his college studies. He once explained that organized education was "never [his] taste." Instead he worked on a farm and at a variety of blue-collar jobs. Nonetheless, he continued to pursue his literary goals and eventually returned to college, this time as a teacher. His tenacity and ambition, motivation, and hardiness provided the essential characteristics underlying his many literary accomplishments.

Cultural Connections Frost spent much of his life in New England and used its natural environment and culture as the basis for much of his poetry. Sly wit and understated expressions, attributable to the region, were common features in his poems. In his poetry, Frost used ordinary language that typically was easy to read, but beneath the surface revealed more complex feelings and undercurrents of doubt and uncertainty. Similarly, although Frost used traditional rhyme schemes, meter, and verse forms, his poems contain feelings and ideas linked typically to Modernist poets.

Frost received critical acclaim and numerous awards throughout his life and career. He was awarded Pulitzer Prizes for four books, including his *Collected Poems*. He was poet-in-residence for Harvard University, Amherst College, and Dartmouth University. Finally, he was the poetry consultant (now referred to as "poet laureate") to the Library of Congress from 1958 to 1959. The volume of awards he received, as well as his popularity, illustrates his importance as a poet.

Robert Frost was born in 1874 and died in 1963.

Literature Online **Author Search** For more about Robert Frost, go to www.glencoe.com.

Selection Skills

After Apple-Picking/ Fire and Ice

Reading Skills
- Clarifying Meaning (SE pp. 653, 655, 658)
- Interpreting Primary Source Material (SE p. 657)
- Making and Supporting Inferences (TWE p. 656)

Literary Elements
- Assonance and Consonance (SE pp. 653, 655, 658)
- Alliteration (SE p. 658)
- Enjambment (TWE p. 654)

Vocabulary Skills
- Synonyms (SE pp. 653, 658)
- Academic Vocabulary (SE p. 658)

Listening/Speaking/Viewing Skills
- Comparing Written and Visual Imagery (SE p. 659)

Writing Skills/Grammar
- Analyze Rhyme and Rhyme Scheme (SE p. 659)
- Inversion (SE p. 659)

Connecting to the Poems

Each of us struggles on occasion to decide upon a path to take in life. As we grow older, we may contemplate the decisions that have led to our present identities. Before you read the poems, think about the following questions:

● How have your thoughts shaped who you are?
● Where do you fit in society? In the world?

Building Background

"After Apple-Picking" and "Fire and Ice" were both written early in Frost's career. "After Apple-Picking" was written in 1914, before World War I began. Frost was living in England, where he was influenced by other poets living in the English countryside. Frost's own experience of living on farms, such as his family's Derry, New Hampshire, farm, is evident in his poetry.

"Fire and Ice" was written after the devastation wrought by World War I, and in the aftermath of the influenza pandemic of 1918, which took millions of lives. In his poems, he raises questions about existence and life issues affecting each of us.

Setting Purposes for Reading

Big Idea Issues of Identity

As you read the poems, notice the speaker in each. Decide whether the identity of the speaker changes from one poem to the next.

Literary Element Assonance and Consonance

Assonance is the repetition of the same or similar vowel sounds. **Consonance** is the repetition of consonant sounds, typically within or at the end of nonrhyming words and preceded by different vowel sounds. As you read the two poems, identify the use of assonance and consonance in each.

● See Literary Terms Handbook, pp. R2 and R4.

Literature Online Interactive Literary Elements Handbook To review or learn more about the literary elements, go to www.glencoe.com.

OBJECTIVES
In studying this selection, you will focus on the following:
● identifying assonance and consonance
● clarifying meaning
● recognizing and analyzing alliteration
● writing to analyze rhyme and rhyme scheme

Reading Strategy Clarifying Meaning

An author's meaning is not always obvious in a poem or literary work. **Clarifying meaning** can help you better understand what you are reading. Rereading any lines that you find confusing or challenging can help. Pay attention to end punctuation to track complete thoughts.

Reading Tip: Finding Alternative Meaning While reading, it might be useful to ask yourself what other meanings a phrase might contain. Create a chart like the following, writing the line or phrase from the poem in the first column and an alternative meaning in the second.

Complete Phrase	Alternative Meaning
"Toward heaven still"	trying unsuccessfully to climb to heaven

Vocabulary

bough (bou) n. a tree branch; p. 654 *Akim broke off a bough to chop for firewood, while Raman gathered smaller twigs for kindling.*

essence (es′əns) n. necessary characteristics of a thing; p. 654 *The essence of a democratic republic is having elected representatives.*

hoary (hor′ē) adj. white or gray with age; covered with frost; p. 654 *The old, dusty photographs had a hoary sheen.*

russet (rus′it) adj. a deep reddish-brown; p. 655 *The tree's russet-colored leaves were a definite sign that fall was approaching.*

Vocabulary Tip: Synonyms Words having the same or nearly the same meaning are called synonyms.

Focus

Summary

In "After Apple-Picking," the speaker is exhausted from picking apples all day. In this state, he sees the world as dreamlike and the season as representative of the end of life, leading into a long sleep. The speaker in "Fire and Ice" has heard people say that the world will end in either fire or ice. He argues for fire, comparing it to human desire, which he suggests is powerful enough to destroy the world. Then he compares ice to hatred and decides that it is also powerful enough to destroy the world.

V Vocabulary

Vocabulary File
Say: Add these words and definitions to your vocabulary file. For each word, include a sentence that gives you an example of how to use the word. **OL** Students with English language needs should include the pronunciations of these words in their files. **EL**

Literature Online

Literary Elements Have students access the Web site to improve their understanding of assonance and consonance.

ROBERT FROST **653**

Selection Resources

Print Materials
📁 Unit 3 Resources (Fast File), pp. 84–86
📁 Leveled Vocabulary Development 55
📁 Selection and Unit Assessments, pp. 129–130
📁 Selection Quick Checks, p. 65

Transparencies
● Bellringer Options Transparencies: Daily Language Practice Transparency 70
● Literary Elements Transparency 73, 74

Technology
● TeacherWorks Plus™ CD-ROM
● StudentWorks Plus™ CD-ROM
● Presentation Plus!™ CD-ROM
● Literature Online, glencoe.com
● Online Student Edition, mhln.com
● ExamView® Assessment Suite CD-ROM
● Vocabulary PuzzleMaker CD-ROM
● Listening Library, disc 1 tracks 71–72

Big Idea

Issues of Identity

Say: As you read, consider the following questions: What is the speaker's role in this poem? What does apple-picking make him feel and think about? (*He is a worker picking apples. He wants to pick them all but cannot. To him, apple-picking seems to symbolize both the promise of life—"the great harvest"—and the inevitability of death—the image of a ladder toward heaven; the necessity of sleeping before the job is completed.*) **OL**

⭐ Viewing the Art

Scrumping is a British term for stealing, specifically stealing apples from other people's orchards. **AS**

Scrumping Apples. Caroline Paterson (fl.1878–92). Watercolor on paper. Private collection.

After Apple-Picking

Robert Frost

My long two-pointed ladder's sticking through a tree
Toward heaven still,
And there's a barrel that I didn't fill
Beside it, and there may be two or three
5 Apples I didn't pick upon some **bough**.
But I am done with apple-picking now.
Essence of winter sleep is on the night,
The scent of apples: I am drowsing off.
I cannot rub the strangeness from my sight
10 I got from looking through a pane of glass
I skimmed this morning from the drinking trough
And held against the world of **hoary** grass.

> **Vocabulary**
>
> **bough** (bou) *n.* a tree branch
> **essence** (es′ əns) *n.* necessary characteristics of a thing
> **hoary** (hôr′) *adj.* white or gray with age; covered with frost

654 UNIT 3 POETRY

Additional Support

Skills Practice

LITERARY ELEMENT: Enjambment

Explain that enjambment occurs when a grammatical sentence in a poem takes up more than one line. Compare enjambed lines in "After Apple-Picking" with an end-stopped line, such as line 23. Have small groups write each line of the poem on a strip of paper. Instruct them to arrange the poem two different ways—first as Frost wrote it, and then as if each line were a complete sentence. Have them examine and read the poem aloud in each arrangement, and compare the effects in short presentations to the class. **OL**

It melted, and I let it fall and break.
But I was well
15 Upon my way to sleep before it fell,
And I could tell
What form my dreaming was about to take.
Magnified apples appear and disappear,
Stem end and blossom end,
20 And every fleck of **russet** showing clear.
My instep arch not only keeps the ache,
It keeps the pressure of a ladder-round.
I feel the ladder sway as the boughs bend.
And I keep hearing from the cellar bin
25 The rumbling sound
Of load on load of apples coming in.
For I have had too much
Of apple-picking: I am overtired
Of the great harvest I myself desired.
30 There were ten thousand thousand fruit to touch,
Cherish in hand, lift down, and not let fall.
For all
That struck the earth,
No matter if not bruised or spiked with stubble,
35 Went surely to the cider-apple heap
As of no worth.
One can see what will trouble
This sleep of mine, whatever sleep it is.
Were he not gone,
40 The woodchuck could say whether it's like his
Long sleep, as I describe its coming on,
Or just some human sleep.

> **Literary Element** Assonance and Consonance *What effect does this example of assonance create for you? Explain.* **L**
>
> **Big Idea** Issues of Identity *How might these lines help you identify the speaker's state of mind?* **BI**
>
> **Reading Strategy** Clarifying Meaning *How does this phrase evoke a darker, hidden meaning in Frost's poem?* **R**
>
> **Vocabulary**
>
> **russet** (rus′it) *adj.* a deep reddish-brown

Teach

L Literary Element

Assonance and Consonance
Answer: *The assonance softens the reading, which reinforces the sleepy, dreamlike quality the poet refers to.* **OL**

BI Big Idea

Issues of Identity
Answer: *These lines suggest a mental or emotional fatigue, a feeling of being overwhelmed by life that helps identify the speaker as a man of sorrow.* **OL**

R Reading Strategy

Clarifying Meaning Answer: *"The cider-apple heap" refers to the place where the seemingly damaged apples go, the ones deemed not good enough to be eaten. This phrase suggests that some people are cast aside as not being worthwhile; they are "damaged goods."* **OL**

CheckPoint

Use the CheckPoint questions on Presentation Plus! to monitor students' comprehension. These questions can be used with interactive response keypads for immediate student feedback.

Differentiated Instruction

Research Invite students to use the Internet to research where apples are grown and who harvests them in North America. **Ask:** What are some highlights and problems of the apple industry? **AL**

Differentiated Instruction

Symbolism List the words *tree, apple,* and *winter* on the board. **Ask:** What ideas and emotions do you associate with these words? How do these words add meaning to the poem? (*Students may suggest that* apple *and* tree *symbolize life, and* winter *symbolizes death.*) **BL**

Objectives
• To identify assonance and consonance (SE)
• To clarify meaning (SE)
• To evaluate the effects of enjambment (TWE)

Teach

L Literary Element

Assonance and Consonance Ask: Where does the first instance of assonance occur in the poem?
Answer: *The title: the long i sound in* fire *and* ice. **OL**

BI Big Idea

Issues of Identity
Answer: *Frost suggests that desire is part of our identity as humans.* **OL**

★ Cultural History

Myth and Science
Religious texts from many world cultures predict a fiery end to the world. Scientific evidence, however, suggests that the most destruction occurred during Earth's ice ages. **Ask:** Which argument would you side with, fire or ice? Why? **AS**

CheckPoint

Use the CheckPoint questions on Presentation Plus! to check students' mastery of the selection. These questions can be used with interactive response keypads for immediate student feedback.

Fire and Ice.

Robert Frost

Essay, Force. Frantisek Kupka, (1871–1957). Museum Moderner Kunst, Vienna, Austria.

Some say the world will end in fire,
Some say in ice.
From what I've tasted of desire
I hold with those who favor fire.
But if it had to perish twice,
I think I know enough of hate
To know that for destruction ice
Is also great
And would suffice.

Big Idea Issues of Identity *Poets often speak of the "human condition." To what aspect of the human condition, and, therefore, one's identity, does this line refer?* **BI**

Additional Support

Skills Practice

READING: Making and Supporting Inferences Say: When you infer something about a piece of writing, you use details from the text along with your own prior knowledge to come up with an idea not directly stated by the author. Have students choose one idea or image from each Frost poem to answer the questions below:

- What seems familiar or clear about the idea or image?
- What does the author suggest without saying directly?
- Which details from the text support your inferences? **OL**

RESPONDING AND THINKING CRITICALLY

Respond

1. What emotions did "After Apple-Picking" and "Fire and Ice" stir in you? Explain.

Recall and Interpret

2. (a)In "After Apple-Picking," what happens to the pane of glass that the speaker looks through? (b)What deeper meaning do you suppose Frost tries to convey with the "pane of glass" image?

3. (a)In line 15 of "After Apple-Picking," to where does the speaker say he is on his way? (b)What deeper meaning does the line suggest?

4. (a)According to the speaker in "Fire and Ice," what are the two ways in which some say the world will end? (b)What human events might trigger destruction by ice?

Analyze and Evaluate

5. (a)Do you think that Frost hints, in the first five lines of "After Apple-Picking," at a sense of frustration with apple-picking? Explain. (b)How do Frost's rural influences affect the literal reading of the poem?

6. According to many cultures, the world has been destroyed once by water. Why do you think the speaker in "Fire and Ice" sides with those who believe that the next destruction will occur by fire?

Connect

7. **Big Idea** Issues of Identity How does Frost identify the speaker in "After Apple-Picking"? Explain.

8. **Big Idea** Issues of Identity How does Frost identify the speaker in "Fire and Ice"? Explain.

PRIMARY SOURCE QUOTATION

The Meaning of Poetry

Robert Frost wrote many times about what poetry meant to him and how he personally interpreted it. Read the following quotes about poetry from Robert Frost, then answer the questions that follow.

"A poem begins in delight and ends in wisdom."

"A poem begins as a lump in the throat, a sense of wrong, a homesickness, a lovesickness."

"Poetry has got me indirectly or directly practically all the living I have had."

—Robert Frost

1. What might Frost mean when he says that a poem begins with "delight and ends in wisdom"? Have you had any personal experiences with delight or wisdom as a result of reading poetry?

2. What might a "lump in the throat," homesickness, lovesickness, and feelings that something is wrong have in common? Why might these things cause a poem to begin?

3. How can poetry "get" you life experiences? Do you agree with this statement? Explain.

4. Of these three quotations, which do you respond to the most? Explain your choice.

Assess

1. Answers will vary.

2. (a) It melts away. (b) It refers to a layer of ice that easily melts away like people or ideas.

3. (a) To sleep (b) Death

4. (a) Fire or ice (b) Actions motivated by hate

5. (a) It is endless. (b) The descriptions seem accurate.

6. Choices prompted by desire will lead to destruction.

7. He is an older, thoughtful male landowner, working the land at apple harvest. His thoughts turn toward the final years of life and curiosity about death's "long sleep."

8. The speaker is preoccupied with the faults of humanity and cavalierly contemplates the end of the world.

Primary Source Quotation

1. Frost might mean that at first glance, poems entertain, or delight, us. With further examination and contemplation, they can offer us wisdom and insight.

2. All those things are connected to strong, negative, or difficult emotions.

Frost suggests that poems are born out of feelings and emotions, particularly significant ones.

3. Answers will vary. Poetry can "get" you experiences by encouraging you to examine your relationship to the world around you.

4. Answers will vary.

Assess

Literary Element

1. An example: "Magnified apples" repeats the *a* sound, as in *cat*.

2. An example: "Essence of winter sleep is on the night, / The scent of apples: I am drowsing off," repeats the *s* sound, as in *scent*.

Review: Alliteration

"After Apple-Picking" "I was <u>w</u>ell upon my <u>w</u>ay"

"After Apple-Picking" "<u>b</u>oughs <u>b</u>end"

"Fire and Ice" "<u>w</u>orld <u>w</u>ill"

"Fire and Ice" "<u>f</u>avor <u>f</u>ire"

Reading Strategy

1. Punctuation helps readers understand where sentences end.

2. Answers might include: "For I have had too much / Of apple-picking: I am over-tired / Of the great harvest I myself desired."

Literary Element Assonance and Consonance

Many poets use **assonance** and **consonance** in their poems. These are sound devices that are more readily apparent to most of us when hearing a poem read aloud rather than reading it silently. Assonance and consonance can be used to enhance both the rhythm and imagery presented in a poem.

1. Identify an example of assonance in "After Apple-Picking." What vowel sound is repeated?

2. Identify an example of consonance in "After Apple-Picking." What consonant sound is repeated?

Review: Alliteration

As you learned on page 649, **alliteration** is the repetition of consonant sounds at the beginning of words. Alliteration can be used to emphasize words, reinforce meaning, or create a musical effect. An example of alliteration might be the phrase, "Later we located the laughing loons of Laredo."

Partner Activity Pair up with a classmate and discuss alliteration in "After Apple-Picking" and "Fire and Ice." Working with your partner, create a chart similar to the one below. Fill in the column with examples from the texts that demonstrate alliteration.

Poem	Alliteration
"After Apple-Picking"	"My long two-pointed ladder's"
"Fire and Ice"	"Some say"
"After Apple-Picking"	

After you have identified examples of alliteration in the poems, discuss with your partner the possible significance of each example.

Reading Strategy Clarifying Meaning

Frequently, poems do not include punctuation stops or might use them inconsistently. The poet depends on the readers to determine meaning in the text by rereading the poem and finding the punctuation stops for themselves. Identifying end punctuation is one way to clarify meaning as you read.

1. How might Frost's meaning in "After Apple-Picking" be clarified by finding the punctuation stops?

2. To support your opinion, list three details from the selection.

Vocabulary Practice

Practice with Synonyms Find the synonym for each vocabulary word. Use a dictionary or a thesaurus if you need help.

1. bough
   a. branch   b. creek

2. essence
   a. smell   b. core

3. hoary
   a. gentle   b. frosty

4. russet
   a. reddish   b. silver

Academic Vocabulary

Here are two words from the vocabulary list on page R82. These words will help you think, write, and talk about the selection.

potential (pə ten′shəl) *adj.* that which can be developed

consequent (kon′sə kwent′) *adj.* in a sequence

Practice and Apply

1. What is a **potential** meaning of "After Apple-Picking"?

2. In "Fire and Ice," what **consequent** action would destroy the world because of desire?

Vocabulary

1. a **2.** b **3.** b **4.** a

Academic Vocabulary

1. That a man who is tired after a life of hard work looks forward to the eternal sleep.

2. Destruction of the world by fire

WRITING AND EXTENDING

Writing About Literature

Analyze Rhyme and Rhyme Scheme In "After Apple-Picking" and "Fire and Ice," Frost utilizes unusual rhyme schemes. Write a short essay explaining the rhymes and rhyme scheme that Frost uses in these two poems. Explain how the patterns of rhyme affect each poem's meaning.

Before you begin drafting, take notes on the rhyme schemes and how rhyme is generally utilized in both poems. In your essay, use examples from each work to support your arguments. Use a web like the one shown below to brainstorm ideas and organize examples and evidence.

Meet with a peer reviewer after completing your draft. Edit each other's work and suggest revisions. Then proofread and edit your draft for errors in spelling, grammar, and punctuation.

Interdisciplinary Activity: Art

Find images (paintings or photographs) of either apple orchards and apple-picking or fire, ice, and world destruction. Using your visuals, compare and contrast them with the images in the respective poems. Do the images you found resemble how you visualize the poem's imagery? Present your findings to your class with a brief oral report.

Literature Online **Web Activities** For eFlashcards, Selection Quick Checks, and other Web activities, go to www.glencoe.com.

GRAMMAR AND STYLE

Frost's Language and Style

Using Inversion in Poetry In "After Apple-Picking" and "Fire and Ice," Frost uses inversion to create his rhyme scheme. Inversion is a reversal of the usual word order. Note the inversion present in the following example from Frost's poems:

> "And I keep hearing from the cellar bin
>
> The rumbling sound"

A more conventional way of writing that sentence, without inversion, would be:

> "And I keep hearing the rumbling sound
>
> from the cellar bin"

Notice how the emphasis and rhyme scheme changes in the second example.

Using the following organizer, find examples of inversion and then write the words in the order they would normally appear.

Inversion	Normal
"Toward heaven still"	still toward heaven

Activity Rewrite "After Apple-Picking" using the normal word order that you wrote for each inversion. Compare your revised version with Frost's version. What specific conclusions can you draw from the comparison? Explain.

Revising Check

Inversion Inversion can add rhythm and meaning to your writing. Review the essay you wrote analyzing Frost's use of rhyme and rhyme scheme, and look for places where you might be able to use inversion. Revise your draft to include any additions you wish to make.

ROBERT FROST **659**

Assess

Writing About Literature

Students' essays should

- identify rhyme patterns in each poem
- analyze rhyme and rhyme scheme in both poems
- cite examples to support ideas.

Interdisciplinary Activity

Students' presentations should

- include visual aids of either apple-picking or fire, ice, and world destruction.
- compare and contrast these images with images from either "After Apple-Picking" or "Fire and Ice".

Frost's Language and Style

Students' conclusions should

- note that the lack of inversion creates a conversational, proselike tone.
- note that the lack of inversion creates an irregular rhythm.

Revising Check

Point out to students that they should not overuse inversion when adding it to their drafts. Encourage them to locate places where inversion will enhance the rhythm or meaning of their essays.

Literature Online

Web Activities Have students access the Web site for interactive activities that will help them assess their understanding of the selection.

Focus

BELLRINGER

Bellringer Options
Daily Language Practice Transparency 71
Or **ask:** What do you think makes a successful social gathering? Have students talk about the activities that make a party or other get-together successful and enjoyable.

Author Search To expand students' appreciation of Naomi Shihab Nye, have them access the Web site for additional information and resources.

Use the CheckPoint questions on Presentation Plus! to monitor students' comprehension. These questions can be used with interactive response keypads for immediate student feedback.

Arabic Coffee

MEET NAOMI SHIHAB NYE

Naomi Shihab Nye published her first poem at the age of seven, in *Wee Wisdom*, a children's magazine. Nye loved reading and writing from a very young age. She writes, "I liked the portable, comfortable shape of poems. . . . And especially the way they took you to a deeper, quieter place."

Quiet Observer Indeed, Nye has been called a "quiet observer of the human condition." Of her own work, Nye writes, "I have always loved the gaps, the spaces between things, as much as the things. I love staring, pondering, mulling, puttering. I love the times when someone or something is late—there's that rich possibility of noticing more, in the meantime."

Born to an American mother and a Palestinian father in St. Louis, Missouri, Nye was a perceptive child. In the introduction to her collection of poems *19 Varieties of Gazelle*, she writes, "I got into the habit of writing little things down from the very beginning—not because they were more interesting than anyone else's 'little things,' but just so I could think about them."

> *"I want young people to be reminded, always, that voices are the best tools we have."*
>
> —Naomi Shihab Nye

Professional Poet Nye attended high school in a variety of exotic locales: Ramallah, Jordan; Old City, Jerusalem; and San Antonio, Texas. She earned a bachelor's degree from Trinity University in 1974, and began working as a writer-in-residence at various universities around the country. She has authored or edited over twenty volumes of poetry, essays, and fiction.

Nye is highly regarded as a poet, both for her original work and her edited anthologies for children and young adults. She has won several prestigious awards and fellowships, including four Pushcart Prizes and a Guggenheim Fellowship in 1997. She was also a finalist in 2002 for a National Book Award in young people's literature.

No Borders In her writing, Nye explores shared experiences and differences between cultures, as well as perspectives of people from countries around the world. She also writes about the tragedy of cultural and political conflicts, such as the Palestinian-Israeli conflict, and the power of strength in the face of adversity. One consistent theme of her poetry is how people are connected, whether they are neighbors, strangers, or enemies. Believing in the power of words to effect social change, she writes, "We have no borders when we read."

When speaking of her mission as a writer, Nye is forthright: "My goals have always been . . . to promote poems of humanity and intelligence that extend and connect us all as human beings."

Naomi Shihab Nye was born in 1952.

Literature Online Author Search For more about Naomi Shihab Nye, go to www.glencoe.com.

660 UNIT 3 POETRY

Selection Skills

Arabic Coffee

Literary Elements
• Symbol (SE pp. 661, 663)

Reading Skills
• Analyzing Rhythm (SE pp. 661, 663)
• Analyzing Figurative Language (TWE p. 662)

Vocabulary Skills
• Academic Vocabulary (SE p. 663)

Writing Skills/Grammar
• Respond to Figurative Language (SE p. 663)

Connecting to the Poem

In "Arabic Coffee," Nye shows the reader how even a simple act like making coffee for visitors represents caring. Before you read the poem, think about the following questions:

- When you spend time with loved ones, what gestures or actions do you use to show that you care for them?
- Why do you think the author uses coffee and clothing as symbols? What symbols are meaningful to you?

Building Background

In "Arabic Coffee," Nye alludes to the practice of tasseography, or fortune-telling with tea leaves. The practice of interpreting tea leaves to tell fortunes began centuries ago in China. The ritual continued through the centuries and, in parts of the Middle East, was adapted for Turkish (or Arabic) coffee as well as tea. In tasseography, one interprets the pattern of tea leaves or coffee grounds left in a cup or saucer after drinking the beverage. The reader may use certain symbols to interpret the pattern or may intuitively "read" the residue for deeper meaning.

Setting Purposes for Reading

Big Idea Issues of Identity

As you read, notice how the speaker describes the father and his treatment of the guests and explores the significance of people gathering together.

Literary Element Symbol

A **symbol** is any person, place, object, or experience that exists on a literal level within a work but also represents something on a figurative level. The symbol refers to or stands for someone or something else. Examining the use of symbols can help the reader understand the poet's intent. For example, recognizing that a road may symbolize a person's life could be critical to comprehending the message of a poem.

As you read "Arabic Coffee," examine how Nye uses the process of preparing and serving coffee as a symbol.

- See Literary Terms Handbook, p. R17.

Literature Online Interactive Literary Elements Handbook To review or learn more about the literary elements, go to www.glencoe.com.

OBJECTIVES
In studying this selection, you will focus on the following:
- interpreting literary symbols
- analyzing rhythm
- writing a letter responding to figurative language

Reading Strategy Analyzing Rhythm

Rhythm is the pattern of beats created by the arrangement of stressed and unstressed syllables in a line. When you **analyze rhythm** in an unrhymed poem, you pay attention to how structure, diction, and sound devices work together to create rhythm. Various elements of poetry, such as the length of words or lines, the flow of words from line to line, where thoughts begin or end, and word choice, all help create rhythm. While reading this poem, pay attention to the way Nye creates a flow and paces events and emotions.

Reading Tip: Noting Rhythm As you read the poem, note how the author creates rhythm using the elements listed above. Create a list of passages from the poem and explain how these passages convey rhythm.

Passage from Poem	Rhythm style
"small white cups"	Succession of using short words

Vocabulary

grounds (groundz) *n.* the remains of the coffee beans after water has been passed through them; sediment; p. 662 *When the filter tore, the wet coffee grounds made a mess on the countertop.*

offering (ô′ fər ing) *n.* something that is presented as a gift; p. 662 *An olive branch symbolizes a peace offering.*

Focus

Summary

The young narrator of the poem recalls the excitement of watching her father prepare coffee for their guests. The poem illustrates how common things, such as coffee and disappointment, bring people together.

V Vocabulary

Vocabulary File

Say: Add these words and definitions to your vocabulary file. For each word, include a sentence that gives you an example of how to use the word. **OL** Students with English language needs should include the pronunciations of these words in their files. **EL**

Literary Elements Have students access the Web site to improve their understanding of symbol.

NAOMI SHIHAB NYE **661**

Selection Resources

Print Materials
- Unit 3 Resources (Fast File), pp. 87–89
- Leveled Vocabulary Development 56
- Selection and Unit Assessments, pp. 131–132
- Selection Quick Checks, p. 66

Transparencies
- Bellringer Options Transparencies: Daily Language Practice Transparency 71
- Literary Elements Transparency 20

Technology
- TeacherWorks Plus™ CD-ROM
- StudentWorks Plus™ CD-ROM
- Presentation Plus!™ CD-ROM
- Literature Online, glencoe.com
- Online Student Edition, mhln.com
- ExamView® Assessment Suite CD-ROM
- Vocabulary PuzzleMaker CD-ROM
- Listening Library, disc 1 track 73

Teach

Issues of Identity

Answer: *Hospitality and generosity are important themes in this poem. Even though men and women do not usually sit together, all are welcome in this space.* **OL**

⭐ Viewing the Art

The artist Pam Ingalls once said, "I paint the beauty of everyday things." Ask students to identify how Ingalls uses this still life to elevate everyday things into objects of beauty. *(Students should note that the rich colors give the objects a sense of warmth and history. They look well-used, which suggests that they have brought comfort to their owners. By making ordinary creamers the object of a painting, the artist acknowledges their importance.)* **AS**

📽 CheckPoint

Use the CheckPoint questions on Presentation Plus! to check students' mastery of the selection. These questions can be used with interactive response keypads for immediate student feedback.

Arabic Coffee

Naomi Shihab Nye

Creamers, 2001. Pam Ingalls. ⭐

It was never too strong for us:
make it blacker, Papa, thick in the bottom,
tell again how years will gather
in small white cups,
5 how luck lives in a spot of **grounds.**

Leaning over the stove, he let it
boil to the top,[1] and down again.
Two times. No sugar in his pot.
And the place where men and women
10 break off from one another[2]
was not present in that room.
The hundred disappointments,
fire swallowing olive-wood beads[3]
at the warehouse, and the dreams
15 tucked like pocket handkerchiefs
into each day, took their places
on the table, near the half-empty
dish of corn. And none was
more important than the others,
20 and all were guests. When
he carried the tray into the room,
high and balanced in his hands,
it was an **offering** to all of them,
stay, be seated, follow the talk
25 wherever it goes. The coffee was
the center of the flower.
Like clothes on a line saying
You will live long enough to wear me,
a motion of faith. There is this,
30 and there is more.

1. *Boil to the top* refers to the preparation of coffee, which can be made by boiling ground coffee beans in hot water. The water boiling up captures the flavor and leaves the grounds at the bottom of the pot. Some of the grounds are transferred when the coffee is poured into a cup.
2. *The place where men and women break off from one another* refers to a practice that exists in many cultures, in which men and women stay separated from one another during public and social functions.
3. *Olive-wood beads* are wooden beads made from olive trees, often used for religious or ornamental jewelry.

Big Idea Issues of Identity *What does the speaker mean by this statement?* **BI**

Vocabulary

grounds (grounds) *n.* the remains of the coffee beans after water has been passed through them; sediment

offering (ô fər ing) *n.* something that is presented as a gift

662 UNIT 3 POETRY

Additional Support

Skills Practice

READING: Figurative Language
Remind students that figurative language is not literally true but expresses a truth beyond the literal level. **Ask:** What figure of speech is included in the line "The coffee was the center of the flower"? *(This line is a metaphor.)* What does the speaker mean by this phrase? *(Students will likely say that all activity was focused on the serving of the coffee.)* **OL**

RESPONDING AND THINKING CRITICALLY

Respond

1. Do you identify with the experience described in the poem? Explain why or why not.

Recall and Interpret

2. (a)How does the speaker like coffee prepared? (b)Why do you think the speaker first tells us her personal preference before explaining how Papa prepares it for others?

3. (a)What things are said to take their place at the table? (b)Why do you think the speaker chooses these images?

4. (a)As the talk flows wherever it goes, what does the coffee become? (b)What does this suggest about the importance of the coffee for this gathering?

Analyze and Evaluate

5. (a)Why might the speaker compare dark coffee grounds in the bottom of small white cups to luck and people gathering together? (b)Is this is an effective image? Explain.

6. (a)Why does the speaker compare dreams to pocket handkerchiefs? (b)Do you think this is an effective comparison? Why or why not?

7. (a)How do you interpret the following line: "You will live long enough to wear me"? (b)Why do you think Nye chose to italicize this line?

Connect

8. **Big Idea** Issues of Identity In what ways is this poem about identity? Explain.

LITERARY ANALYSIS

Literary Element Symbol

Nye uses symbols throughout "Arabic Coffee" to help the reader understand the meaning of the poem.

1. When the speaker explains in short sentences that her father boils the coffee two times, no sugar, and in preparation for guests, what do you think this act symbolizes? Explain.

2. How do "clothes on a line" symbolize hope and faith?

Writing About Literature

Respond to Figurative Language Figurative language is language or expressions that are not literally true but express some truth beyond the literal level. Types of figurative language include symbols, metaphors, and similes.

Read "Arabic Coffee" aloud, paying particular attention to Nye's use of figurative language. Think of a time when you were part of a gathering of friends or family. Write a letter describing that experience. Include figurative language in your letter. Draw upon Nye's use of figurative language and any shared experiences between her poem and your event.

Literature Online Web Activities For eFlashcards, Selection Quick Checks, and other Web activities, go to www.glencoe.com.

READING AND VOCABULARY

Reading Strategy Analyzing Rhythm

"Arabic Coffee" has a **rhythm** and pace that is established by the author's choice of words (diction) and where she chooses to start and end lines. A reader should be aware of the many elements an author uses to create and maintain rhythm in poetry.

1. What effect does the author create by making the first stanza one long sentence?

2. How does Nye's diction help create rhythm?

Academic Vocabulary

Here are two words from the vocabulary list on page R82.

assemble (ə sem′bəl) v. to gather as a group.

function (fungk′shən) n. a gathering of people for a specific purpose.

Practice and Apply

1. When people **assemble** for Papa's coffee, what do they bring with them?
2. Can the gathering described in "Arabic Coffee" be defined as a **function**? Explain.

NAOMI SHIHAB NYE **663**

Assess

1. Students should explain their answers.
2. (a) She likes it "strong" and "thick in the bottom." (b) It connects readers to both the speaker and her father.
3. (a) Disappointments and dreams (b) They are universal experiences.
4. (a) It becomes the center of the flower. (b) The coffee connects the guests.
5. (a) It shows how people can find luck and community in ordinary things. (b) The image helps the reader to understand the power of ordinary things.
6. (a) We keep both hidden, tucked away for a time when we need them. (b) Yes, by finding a meaningful similarity in two different things.
7. (a) The clothes show that tomorrow holds hope. (b) To call attention to the idea of a hopeful future
8. The poem emphasizes how community can define one's identity.

Literary Element

1. This act symbolizes the power of tradition and of hospitality.
2. The clothes are for future days.

Writing About Literature

Students' essays should:
- focus on one gathering.
- use figurative language specific to their own experiences.

Academic Vocabulary

1. Disappointments and dreams
2. Yes, people are gathered for a purpose.

663

Literature Online

Web Activities Have students access the Web site for interactive activities that will help them assess their understanding of the selection.

Reading Strategy

1. Without any breaks, the flow of words and thoughts evokes an excited child. The reader is drawn into the poem by the speaker's enthusiasm.

2. Repeating words with the same vowel sound creates a rhythm. For example, "it was an offering to all of them" repeats the *aw* sound, creating rhythm.

Focus

Summary

Chang-rae Lee, a Korean American writer, describes a trip he took to South Korea to visit his ailing grandmother. He reflects on themes of loss, belonging, and alienation. Although Lee's family immigrated to the United States when he was a toddler, and a language barrier exists between him and members of his family in South Korea, he feels at home when he is with them. He remarks, "Somehow all was fine. They were family."

Teach

⭐ Viewing the Photo

Have students study the people in the photograph. Ask them to imagine what Chang-rae Lee's parents might be thinking as they prepare to leave their homeland. **AS**

Readability Scores
Dale-Chall: 7.1
DRP: 58
Lexile: 1150

Media Link to Issues of Identity

Preview the Article

In "We Are Family," writer Chang-rae Lee comments on the unshakable bond between his relatives in Korea and himself.

1. From the title, what do you think the author values?

2. Skim the first paragraph. What mood do you think the author is trying to establish?

Set a Purpose for Reading

Read to discover Chang-rae Lee's identification with his Korean family and culture.

Reading Strategy

Analyzing Cultural Context
When you analyze cultural context, you consider the customs, beliefs, values, arts, and intellectual activities of a group of people and use this knowledge to better understand the theme or message of a literary work. To understand the cultural context of this selection, consider the cultural characteristics of the author's experiences in Korea and in the United States.

As you read, take notes using a two-column chart like the one below.

Korea	United States
Ties to distant relatives	Understanding Korean and responding in English to parents

OBJECTIVES
- Analyze the cultural context of a literary work.
- Connect literature to cultural contexts and to your own experiences.

664 UNIT 3 POETRY

TIME

We Are Family

During a visit to his native South Korea, novelist Chang-rae Lee learns that living abroad and losing his language are no barriers to belonging.

By CHANG-RAE LEE

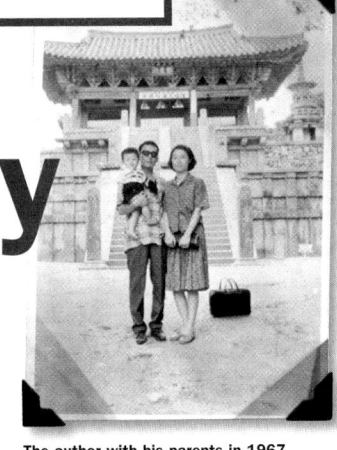

The author with his parents in 1967, before they emigrated from South Korea to the U.S. ⭐

THE LAST TIME I STOOD BEFORE MY GRANDFATHER'S GRAVE, IN the spring of 1989, it had been newly dug. My uncle had driven my father and me to Yong-In City, one hour south of Seoul, so that we could pay our respects. I remember the fog burning off to reveal the new season bursting forth in blooms of wild cherry and persimmon all around us on the hillside. And yet, there was a worn-out quality at the site. The burial ground was a three-meter-wide amphitheater carved out of the steep face of the hillside. The fresh earth was laid bare, roughly cut roots jutting out from the sheer wall of dirt. In the center of the dugout, the mound beneath which my grandfather was buried showed the first wispy strands of baby grass. There was no headstone as yet.

My father was on the verge of tears, finally seeing where his father lay. I wanted to feel the same pinch of loss, the same onrush of sadness. But I couldn't. Our family left Korea for America when I wasn't yet three, and since then I'd spent perhaps five hours total in my grandfather's presence. All I knew of him was that he'd lost his hardware business in Pyongyang to the communists on the eve of the Korean War. And when my father knelt low and bowed respectfully, the image I saw of my grandfather's face was drawn not from any memory of life but from the black-and-white picture of him that hung prominently in my childhood home.

I pictured that image once more when I visited his grave in May 2003. I was in Korea to visit my family, particularly to see my ailing maternal grandmother, and to do some research for my next novel. I had come once again with my uncle, a professor of business, but this time with his two sons as well, one of whom was just back from a year of language study in San Diego. Our mood as we climbed up the hill was expansive and lighthearted, and it seemed we were more on a picnicking

---

Additional Support

See also 📖 Active Learning and Note Taking Guide, pp. 98–105.

Skills Practice

RESEARCH: Immigration Patterns
Understanding patterns of immigration to the United States enriches students' awareness of the United States as a multicultural nation. Encourage each student to research a particular ethnic group or nationality and its pattern of immigration to the United States. Students should select a variety of recent immigrant groups as well as groups from the eighteenth, nineteenth, and twentieth centuries. Then have students compare their group with other students' groups. As a class project, create a large timeline on which each student locates his or her group. **OL**

hike than a dutiful visit to our ancestral dead. But as we ascended the path to the grave, the talk quieted.

Finally, at the end of a narrow deer path, there came an opening, and we emerged onto the same burial landing I had visited 14 years ago. To my surprise, there were two mounds instead of one and now a black granite headstone centered between, carved on the faces and sides with Chinese characters. I asked about the second mound and my uncle said that my grandmother and stepgrandmother had been unearthed from their resting places in Seoul and moved here some years before to join my grandfather.

"What is all the writing?" I asked. We were crouched by the black slab of rock.

"It's your grandfather's name. Your grandmothers' names are here," he said, pointing them out.

"And what about all these other characters?"

"These are his children. Here's your father. Here are your other uncles, then me, and your aunt. And here are the names of our spouses. This one is your mother's."

"My mother's?"

I touched the unfamiliar language sharply carved into the stone, almost saying her name aloud. She died a few years after my grandfather did, of stomach cancer.

"I didn't know it was done this way."

"Oh yes," my uncle said. "Everyone is here."

Learning to Belong

I kept thinking back on that phrase during the rest of my stay in Seoul: Everyone is here. As uttered by my uncle, it was a simple answer to a simple question, a matter of fact and a

literal record. And so it was. And yet, as I thought about the notion, it became more than just a straightforward record of my ancestors. For I realized how differently than I my uncle and his sons viewed that dark stone, how the names to them were just an ordinary fact of their lives,

> **"IN THEIR FIRST YEARS IN AMERICA, MY PARENTS DIDN'T ALWAYS ALLOW THEMSELVES THE FULL LEVEL OF EMOTIONS."**

like the ancient arrangement of the planets. To me, raised away in the States, the listing seemed more remarkable than that, a kind of supernatural alliance, extraordinary and wonderful.

For in our immigrant family of four, we were all we ever had. In the town where we lived (a small northern suburb of New York City), we were one of a handful of nonwhite families. Every great once in a while, there would be an uncle or aunt passing through New York, and they'd stay with us a few days or a week. In the evenings, my parents would chatter at the dinner table with special enthusiasm about all the reports from Seoul. My parents were generally happy, easygoing people, but in their first years in America, I would say they didn't always allow themselves to

experience many emotions, perhaps because they felt outside of and flustered by all the strangeness of their new world. And it was only when "home" made its return that they seemed to truly liven up. **R**

In later years, my parents considered America to be their only home, and although they possessed the means to do so by the time my mother died in 1991, our family had made only four visits to Korea in 23 years. Even as a serious teen, I didn't mind the summer trips we took as a family. Korea was a lot better than, say, a car trip to family friends, not so much because of any reconnecting with the family but for the food.

Best of all, were the grand meals we'd have at our relatives' cramped apartments or houses, the dozens of dishes completely covering the low tables they'd set out for us—the men sitting at the main table, the women lodged at one nearer the kitchen. In the fog of my jet-lagged mind, the only things that made sense to me amid the superfast talk, which I mostly couldn't understand, were all the bracing flavors, the radish kimchi and marinated raw crab and sesame-leaf pancakes. Even my father seemed somewhat overwhelmed by the rush of native language, occasionally asking people to repeat what they'd said.

And this is how I found myself on my recent trip, out with my father's side of the family at a popular barbecue restaurant, straining to understand everyone's questions about my family and work. I could say only a few words in response, my speaking ability in Korean not as developed as my aural comprehension. After the initial assurances that I could tolerate spicy food and a recounting of

WE ARE FAMILY **665**

Informational Text

TIME

Teach

Big Idea
Issues of Identity
Say: Consider the following idea as you read. As a Korean American, Lee lives in and experiences two cultures simultaneously. **Ask:** What are the ways in which Lee introduces his American readers to Korean culture? *(Lee makes several references to Korean food; he describes Korean burial practices; he refers to a "distinctive Korean mother–style scold.")* **OL**

R Reading Strategy
Analyzing Cultural Context In order to understand modern Korean culture and reasons why some people might emigrate, help students understand the Korean War. **Explain:** The Cold War, the political struggle between Communist and non-Communist systems in the years after World War II, provided the backdrop for the Korean War. The Korean War was fought from 1950 to 1953 between North Korea (Communist) and South Korea (non-Communist). Although limited to the Korean peninsula, it became an international war. The war was economically and socially destructive to both North Korea and South Korea. **OL**

English Language Coach

Cultural Experiences Stories like Lee's offer unique opportunities for students to have an open dialogue about their own experiences. Encourage students who have immigrated to this country to share their thoughts with other students about what it is like to live in two cultures. Questions to guide the discussion might include: What are some of the challenges of living in another country? *(Some students may refer to feelings of dislocation and isolation.)* In what ways do your two cultures conflict with each other? *(Some students may mention differences in customs, gender roles, or political ideas.)* **EL**

Objectives
- To analyze the cultural context of a literary work (SE)
- To conduct background research (TWE)

Teach

BI Big Idea

Issues of Identity

Explain: Issues of cultural identity are rarely simple. While Lee writes about and is immersed in his Korean culture, he is also aware of stereotypes that he encounters as an Asian American. **Ask:** In what ways might being around his family in South Korea be a relief to Lee? *(He implies that he does not have to explain himself "in customary ways" and that around his cousins, he did not feel like an "ethnic," or an outsider.)* OL

★ Viewing the Photo

Ask students to discuss if they believe it is important, as the author does, to keep ties to practically-unknown extended family members. Have students share any personal experiences they may have had regarding this. AS

BLOOD TIES Lee's ailing grandmother gave him a reason to journey home and reconnect with his mother's extended family. ★

the names and ages of my daughters, I naturally retreated into the customary table rituals of the barbecue. I attended to grilling the meat and whole cloves of garlic, readying the bean paste and the fragrant shoots of chrysanthemum, cupping the fresh lettuce leaf to wrap all of it in. While the others ate heartily and engaged in their lively conversations, I was happy for their company and just as pleased simply to sit there and eat, gleaning what talk I could.

There was no awkwardness due to the differences of our language or the brief time we'd spent together during our lives. Somehow all was fine. They were family. There was a certain ease in the gathering that I have rarely felt in my life. There was a level of comfort drawn, I think, from not having to explain myself in the customary ways. I wasn't defined by the cultural and personal stereotypes that are part of my "regular" existence as a teacher and writer and maybe (if there really is such a person) as an Asian American.

I kept thinking how plainly, deeply satisfying it was to be back among my cousins and aunts and uncles. With them, at least, I was not a provisional "I," not an ethnic, or outsider, or an artist or intellectual, but simply someone whose connections to others were clear and traceable and real. **BI**

Keep the Family Together

The next night, I went to my maternal aunt's house south of the Han River, where my grandmother Halmoni was staying. She was my only living grandparent, in her late 80s, and from recent reports, not doing terribly well. Her back was finally giving way, and she wasn't very mobile; my cousin told me she sometimes crawled to the bathroom rather than ask anyone for help.

I was nervous about seeing Halmoni in a bad state, not only for the sadness of such a sight but for the sake of her own pride. I almost wished I could have simply telephoned her my wishes of good health and love. When I rang the bell of my aunt's house, a young cousin greeted me and led me inside. My two aunts were busy back in the kitchen making final preparations for dinner. My cousin and I sat down in the living room. Before I could say anything, my aunts came out, both wiping their hands on their aprons. We all hugged each other, then my younger aunt asked her son where Halmoni was.

My cousin said he'd go look for our grandmother upstairs, but then Halmoni cleared her throat in the next room, effectively announcing herself. She came in, not crawling at all but walking with slowed, careful steps, her hunched back bent down almost to 90 degrees. She wrapped her arms around me, her face pressed into my chest, hardly taller now with her fallen posture than my six-year-old daughter. I could smell the faint almondy oiliness of her hair. And as much as I didn't want to think of her as frail, she most clearly was, her hold of me like the cling of someone straining to grab on more than to hug. Soon enough, we were sitting together on the sofa, her hands cupping mine,

> **"MY GRANDMOTHER WAS STARING RIGHT INTO MY EYES, GAZING, I'M SURE, AT THE REMNANTS OF HER FIRST CHILD."**

Additional Support

Skills Practice

CREATIVE WRITING: Letters Home

Say: Imagine that you are a recent immigrant to the United States. Write a letter to a family member or friend back home describing your new home and new experiences. Your letter should include a description of your surroundings, the new foods you have eaten, and your struggles with a new language. You might also mention things that you miss back home. OL

GENERATIONS **Author Lee with daughters Annika (left) and Eva, at their Princeton, New Jersey, house.**

gently kneading them just as she had often done to my sister and me as children.

"It's too far for you to come," she said. "It's good you didn't try to bring your family. You yourself shouldn't have bothered."

"It's no bother."

My cousin piped in, "Halmoni, he came over to see you, you know."

"Even more reason," she said, though half-smiling. She asked earnestly, "Are you tired?"

"I'm fine."

"You must be hungry."

"Not so much."

She called out to the kitchen, telling her daughters that I needed to eat right away. My younger aunt came out and said she could set the table, that we didn't have

to wait for the men to arrive (which was of course possible, though an impossibility).

"Really," I told her. "I want to wait."

She nodded and went back to the kitchen. Halmoni made a raspy sound in her throat at me, a distinctive Korean mother-style scold, the sound of which contains just the pitch to make one feel at once guilty and beloved.

"Are you feeling well these days?" I asked, having practiced the phrase (in Korean) on the subway ride.

"Sometimes I have a little trouble with my back. But not today. Your father is in good health?"

"Yes."

"You visit him regularly?"

"I try to."

"You must do so always," she said, tapping my hand for emphasis. "Keep the family together." She paused. "And your stepmother, she is well, too?"

"Yes."

Halmoni nodded.

"That's good," she said. "It's how it should be."

She was staring right into my eyes, gazing, I'm sure, at the remnants of her first child, my mother, the only one, with any mercy, who would precede her to the grave. I pictured my mother's black granite headstone back in New York, and then, too, my paternal grandfather's stone, and then Halmoni's and my father's and even my own, all the written names, cast wide.

—**Updated 2005, from TIME Asia, August 18/25, 2003**

RESPONDING AND THINKING CRITICALLY

Respond

1. Why do you think Lee opens his article with a description of his grandfather's gravesite?

Recall and Interpret

2. (a)How did Lee react to the names of his late family members on the black granite headstone? (b)Why do you think this reaction is significant?

3. (a)What might have made Lee feel like an outsider in the town in which he was raised? (b)How do you think being an outsider influenced Lee's perspective on family?

4. What were Lee's ties to his Korean heritage?

Analyze and Evaluate

5. (a)How does Lee approach the subject of loss in the article? (b)What does he learn or gain from his losses?

6. Lee does not follow a traditional structure in his writing. It is not chronological or sequential. What techniques does he use to organize the article? Support your answer with examples from the text.

Connect

7. Lee comments that he did not have to explain himself to his relatives "as a teacher and writer and maybe (if there really is such a person) as an Asian American." Why do you think he says this about the Asian American identity?

WE ARE FAMILY **667**

Assess

1. He is setting up the idea of family connections. He also introduces the topic of loss that is prevalent throughout the piece. He mentions the alienation he felt from knowing and not knowing his grandfather, which is similar to his relationships with many of his other relatives.

2. (a) Lee reacted in awe. He felt it was "remarkable" and "wonderful." (b) It contrasts with his Korean relatives, who think of the tradition as ordinary, and shows how an outsider may have a richer appreciation of cultural traditions. It also emphasizes the theme of family bonds.

3. (a) He was one of only a few Korean Americans in a mostly white American town. (b) It seemed to instill in him a greater longing to understand his heritage.

4. His ties included his family, a taste for spicy food, and being able to understand some Korean.

5. (a) He speaks of the loss of some of his Korean relatives as well as of his mother. He also experiences a sense of loss because he does not speak Korean well and is not able to visit his Korean relatives often. (b) He learns the importance of family and cultural connections. He gains a sense of his identity.

For additional assessment, see 📁 Selection and Unit Assessment, pp. 133–134.

6. He uses flashbacks—one is the memory of visiting his father's grave, and another is the memory of his family in the state of New York. He uses images, such as those of food. He also uses bits of conversation to transition from one thought to the next—for example, the phrase "everyone is here."

7. He discusses how he straddles both worlds of being an American and a Korean. His connection to his Korean heritage is strong, despite the small amount of time he has spent in Korea. He finds being an Asian American a difficult identity to inhabit because he straddles two cultures.

Focus

BELLRINGER

Bellringer Options
Selection Focus
Transparency 34
Daily Language Practice
Transparency 72

Or write some common mottoes on the board, such as "Be prepared," "Look before you leap," and so on. **Ask:** Do you agree with these mottoes? Do you have your own motto? Does having a motto help you make decisions?

Have students discuss mottoes they know as well as their own mottoes. Discuss whether a motto helps them make decisions or is simply a concise expression of their instinctive behavior.

Connecting to the Reading Selections

Allow students to share their responses to the opening question. Then have students discuss what they already know about Langston Hughes, Jayne Cortez, Studs Terkel, and Wynton Marsalis.

Comparing Literature *Across Genres*

Connecting to the Reading Selections

Jazz music is an essential part of African American culture. The selections compared here highlight the contributions of African Americans to literature, rhythm, and music.

United States, 1951

Langston Hughes
Dream Boogie..........................poem..........**669**
Even poetry can have a jazz-like feel

Langston Hughes
Motto...poem..........**672**
Hughes's personal motto may ring true for others

United States, 1951

United States, 1951

Langston Hughes
Harlem..poem..........**673**
What happens when we let our dreams go?

Jayne Cortez
Jazz Fan Looks Back.....................poem..........**675**
Cortez's memories of jazz greats still make her smile

United States, 1957

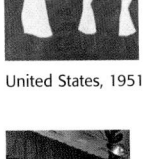
United States, 1951

Studs Terkel
Dizzy Gillespie, Explorer of New Sounds
from Giants of Jazz..............biography..........**677**
King of the trumpet

Wynton Marsalis
Playing Jazz...letter..........**681**
Marsalis shares his craft with a young musician

United States, 2002

United States, 2003

COMPARING THE Big Idea **Issues of Identity**

Identity may be defined as individuality or character. It is both who we are and what we are. Identity relates to our family histories, where we come from, and where we are now.

COMPARING Sound Devices

Sound devices are techniques used to appeal to the ear, especially in poetry. Writers use sound devices to create a sense of rhythm or a musical effect, and to emphasize particular sounds.

COMPARING Author's Purpose

An author's purpose can be described as his or her intent to create a literary work, and can be inspired by one or more of the following reasons: to persuade, to inform, to entertain, or to describe.

668 UNIT 3 POETRY

Selection Skills

Comparing Literature

Literary Elements
• Rhyme and Rhyme Scheme (SE pp. 670, 672, 674)
• Scansion (TWE p. 672)

Vocabulary Skills
• Word Parts (SE p. 674)
• Context Clues (TWE p. 682)

Writing Skills/Grammar
• Quickwrite (SE pp. 676, 680)
• Drafting a Letter (TWE p. 680)
• Types of Sentences (TWE p. 676)

Reading Skills
• Making Inferences about Theme (SE pp. 670, 671, 674)
• Analyzing Biography (TWE p. 678)
• Summarizing (TWE p. 684)

Dream Boogie, Motto, and Harlem

MEET LANGSTON HUGHES

African American writer Langston Hughes dedicated his life to improving race relations. His works linked prejudice and poverty to feelings of heartbreak and hopelessness among African Americans.

"I have discovered in life that there are ways of getting almost anywhere you want to go, if you really want to go."

—Langston Hughes

Early Wanderings Hughes was born in Joplin, Missouri, to parents who soon separated. His childhood consisted of living with either one parent or the other, or with a relative. Hughes turned to books for companionship and as an escape from feelings of loneliness and insecurity.

The love of reading created in Hughes a desire to write. The poetry of Walt Whitman and Carl Sandburg greatly influenced him toward the use of free verse and common speech patterns.

During the 1920s, Hughes held a variety of odd jobs in the Harlem neighborhood of New York City. Bothered by limited gains in race relations, he became a steward on a ship bound for West Africa. While abroad, Hughes learned about other cultures by traveling to Europe, Africa, Mexico, Russia, and Japan.

Speaking His Mind In 1921 Hughes published his first poem, "The Negro Speaks of Rivers," in the journal *Crisis,* edited by the noted African American author and civil rights leader W. E. B. Du Bois. Like Du Bois, Hughes believed that African Americans could find renewal by understanding and taking pride in their cultural roots.

In 1926 Hughes published his first book of verses, *The Weary Blues.* He blended African American and white rhythms and poetic forms. He became a major force in a growing African American cultural movement called the Harlem Renaissance. When Hughes graduated from Lincoln University in 1929, he became one of the first African Americans to earn a living solely through writing.

Hughes became a leader in integrating major forms of African American music—jazz, blues, and gospel—with his poetic lyrics. He believed that this form of expression helped to communicate the desperation of people in racial ghettos.

Bountiful Fruits Hughes grew more prosperous through his hard work. He became involved in such literary pursuits as prose writing, playwriting, journalism, and film projects.

In later life, Hughes received the Spingarn Medal from the NAACP for his many contributions to the betterment of African Americans. He was invited to join the National Institute of Arts and Letters in 1961. Hughes was known as the "Poet Laureate of the Negro Race" to many in the literary world, a title of which he was proud.

Langston Hughes was born in 1902 and died in 1967.

Literature Online **Author Search** For more about Langston Hughes, go to www.glencoe.com.

Focus

⭐ Cultural History

Walt Whitman (1819–1892) and Carl Sandburg (1878–1967) are among the most highly regarded of American poets. Whitman's *Leaves of Grass* was much maligned for its revolutionary use of free verse. Sandburg found inspiration in Whitman and adopted an even freer style of verse in his poetry on the splendor of everyday life. **AS**

Literature Online

Author Search To expand students' appreciation of Langston Hughes, have them access the Web site for additional information and resources.

 Selection Resources

Print Materials
- Unit 3 Resources (Fast File), pp. 92–94
- Leveled Vocabulary Development 57
- Selection and Unit Assessments, pp. 135–136
- Selection Quick Checks, p. 68

Transparencies
- Bellringer Options Transparencies: Daily Language Practice Transparency 72
- Literary Elements Transparency 60

Technology
- TeacherWorks Plus™ CD-ROM
- StudentWorks Plus™ CD-ROM
- Presentation Plus!™ CD-ROM
- Literature Online, glencoe.com
- Online Student Edition, mhln.com
- Exam*View*® Assessment Suite CD-ROM
- Vocabulary PuzzleMaker CD-ROM
- Listening Library, disc 1 tracks 75–77

Focus

Summary

"Dream Boogie" is an expression of the emotion evoked by deferred dreams underlying the beat of jazz music. "Motto" expresses Hughes's belief in an easygoing, nonconfrontational attitude toward life. "Harlem" is an angry hypothesis on the damage caused by deferring one's dreams.

V Vocabulary

Vocabulary File

Say: Add these words and definitions to your vocabulary file. For each word, include a sentence that gives you an example of how to use the word. **OL** Students with English language needs should include the pronunciations of these words in their files. **EL**

Literary Elements Have students access the Web site to improve their understanding of rhyme and rhyme scheme.

COMPARING LITERATURE

BEFORE YOU READ
Dream Boogie, Motto, and Harlem

Connecting to the Poems

Most of Hughes's poems are framed by his experiences of being an African American and a resident of Harlem during its cultural renaissance. Before you read the poems, think about the following questions:

- What does Hughes reveal about the African American experience during his time?
- How much power do published words have to bring about change in people's lives?

Building Background

Hughes was a champion at using language to convey his thoughts. In his poems, he portrayed the African American experience in the mid 1900s. During this time, many African Americans had dreams that went unrealized because of racism. Hughes used poetry to provoke awareness of the many frustrations felt by African Americans.

Setting Purposes for Reading

Big Idea Issues of Identity

As you read, notice how Hughes expresses his thoughts in a style that displays a distinctively African American musical quality, reminiscent of jazz music.

Literary Element Rhyme and Rhyme Scheme

Rhyme is the repetition of the same stressed vowel sounds and any succeeding sounds in two or more words. **Rhyme scheme** is the pattern that **end rhymes** (rhymes occurring at the ends of lines of poetry) form in a stanza or poem. Rhyme scheme is designated by the assignment of a different letter of the alphabet to each new rhyme. As you read the poems, examine how Hughes uses rhyme and rhyme scheme to help him convey his message.

- See Literary Terms Handbook, p. R14.

Literature Online **Interactive Literary Elements Handbook** To review or learn more about the literary elements, go to www.glencoe.com.

OBJECTIVES
In studying this selection, you will focus on the following:
- analyzing rhyme and rhyme scheme

Reading Strategy Making Inferences About Theme

To **make inferences about theme** is to draw a conclusion about the overall meaning of a literary work based on textual evidence and your background knowledge. Making inferences, or "reading between the lines," can increase your understanding of a poem's central meaning. As you read, ask yourself questions about the main points to help you find the poem's central meaning.

Reading Tip: Questioning Create a chart like the one below to organize your ideas through questioning as you read the poems.

Poem	Question	My Response
"Motto"	What message does this poem convey to its readers?	Your behavior toward others can affect how they treat you.
	What is your response after your initial reading of the poem?	

Vocabulary

deferred (di furd´) v. put off, postponed; p. 673 *Tom deferred his loan payment until he received a check from his employer.*

fester (fes´ tər) v. to become increasingly infected or inflamed, rot; p. 673 *The man let the cut on his leg fester until he developed a dangerous infection.*

- making inferences about theme
- evaluating an author's craft through writing

Additional Support

Skills Practice

READING: Previewing Before beginning a selection, students may find it beneficial to preview the selections they are about to read. Have students read through the titles of the selections, look at the art, skim the selections, and predict each author's purpose. Have them write down their ideas of what each selection is about. This can help students derive more meaning and enjoyment from the text. **OL**

Dream Boogie

Langston Hughes **BI₁**

Good morning, daddy!
Ain't you heard
The boogie-woogie rumble
Of a dream deferred?

5   Listen closely:
You'll hear their feet
Beating out and beating out a—

      You think
      It's a happy beat?

10   Listen to it closely:
Ain't you heard
something underneath
like a

      What did I say?

15   Sure,
I'm happy!
Take it away!

      Hey, pop!
      Re-bop![1]
20   *Mop!*

      Y-e-a-h!

Show Time (of the Blues), 20th century.
Romare Bearden.

---

1. *Re-bop* is another term for "bebop," a style of jazz characterized by a staccato two-note phrase that was the music's trademark.

Reading Strategy   Making Inferences About Theme *Why does the speaker ask if it's "a happy beat" and if "something underneath" is heard?* **R**

Big Idea Issues of Identity *What do you think Hughes suggests in the concluding lines beginning with "I'm happy"?* **BI₂**

LANGSTON HUGHES **671**

Teach

BI₁ Big Idea

Issues of Identity

Say: Keep the following questions in mind as you read. Who is the speaker in each poem? Where does the speaker search for identity? *(The speaker may be Hughes himself. He seems to be searching for identity within music and dreams.)* **OL**

R Reading Strategy

Making Inferences About Theme

Answer: *Because the beat is a blues for "a dream deferred"* **OL**

BI₂ Big Idea

Issues of Identity

Answer: *The speaker finds solace or happiness in the boogie beat of his people, or the group with whom he identifies.* **OL**

CheckPoint

Use the CheckPoint questions on Presentation Plus! to monitor students' comprehension. These questions can be used with interactive response keypads for immediate student feedback.

Building Reading Fluency

The feeling, intent, and style of a poem are much better communicated when the poem is read aloud. Have students take turns reading aloud "Dream Boogie" and the other poems in this lesson. Guide them to follow the emotional reading implied by the poem's language, structure, and punctuation. **BL**

Differentiated Instruction

Sensory Learners Students who learn best by experiencing subject matter may find it difficult to connect to reading selections about music. Consider bringing in jazz music from some of the musicians mentioned in these selections. Play the music for the class and have them discuss what feelings it evokes in them. **BL**

Objectives
- To make inferences about theme (SE)
- To preview reading selections (TWE)

COMPARING LITERATURE

Teach

L Literary Element
Rhyme and Rhyme Scheme
Answer: *The rhyme scheme is abcb. Students should notice that the second and fourth lines rhyme.* **OL**

BI Big Idea
Issues of Identity
Ask: If the speaker wants to fight against the plight of African Americans in his time, why might he have this motto? *(It sounds as if he believes in non-confrontational methods rather than direct protest.)* **OL**

★ Viewing the Art
Birdland is a famous New York City jazz club, opened in 1949 and named in honor of Charlie "Bird" Parker, a legendary saxophonist. About 1½ million people visited the club during its first five years, and it hosted many jazz greats, including Miles Davis, John Coltrane, Thelonius Monk, and Dizzy Gillespie. Originally located in Midtown Manhattan at Broadway and West 52nd Street, the club closed in 1965, reopened Uptown in 1986, and today is thriving again in Midtown on West 44th Street. **AS**

Bopping at Birdland (Stomp Time), 1979. Romare Bearden. Color lithograph on paper, 24 x 33¼ in. Smithsonian American Art Museum, Washington, DC. ★

MOTTO

Langston Hughes

I play it cool
And dig[1] all jive[2]
That's the reason
I stay alive.

5   My motto,
As I live and learn,
                    is:

Dig And Be Dug **BI**
In Return.

1. *Dig* is slang for "to like."
2. *Jive* may refer to swing music and the dancing performed to it, or the glib jargon of hipsters.

Literary Element Rhyme and Rhyme Scheme
What is the rhyme scheme in this stanza? **L**

672   UNIT 3   POETRY

Additional Support

Skills Practice

LITERARY ELEMENT: Scansion
Have students scan "Motto" to determine the poem's meter. *(The meter is irregular; it is mostly iambic dimeter, switching to trochaic in the third and last two lines.)*
I **play** / it **cool**
And **dig** / all **jive**

That's the / **rea**-son
I **stay** / a-**live**.
My **mott** / o
As I / **lived** and / **learn**,
is:
Dig and / **Be** Dug
In Re / **turn**. **OL**

Harlem

Langston Hughes

Dance, 1996. Francks Deceus. Mixed media on canvas, 76.2 x 101.6 cm. Private collection.

What happens to a dream **deferred?** **BI**

Does it dry up
like a raisin in the sun?
Or **fester** like a sore—
5 And then run?
Does it stink like rotten meat?
Or crust and sugar over—
like a syrupy sweet?

Maybe it just sags
10 like a heavy load.

Or does it explode? **R**

> **Vocabulary**
>
> **deferred** (di furd´) *v.* put off, postponed
> **fester** (fes´tər) *v.* to become increasingly infected or inflamed

LANGSTON HUGHES **673**

Teach

BI Big Idea

Issues of Identity
Ask: Why would the people of Harlem defer their dreams? *(They were forced into poor conditions by racial discrimination. They deferred their dreams to focus on day-to-day survival. There was neither time nor money to pursue their dreams.)* **OL**

R Reading Strategy

Making Inferences about Theme
Ask: How could an explosive dream be either positive or negative? *(It could be positive if it were an instigator of social improvement, such as a revolution against an oppressive system. It could be negative if it resulted in a senseless and regrettable act of violence.)* **OL**

CheckPoint

Use the CheckPoint questions on Presentation Plus! to check students' mastery of the selection. These questions can be used with interactive response keypads for immediate student feedback.

Differentiated Instruction

Spatial Learners Students with spatial aptitude may find it beneficial to place the poem's setting in a geographical context. Have students first locate New York City on a map. Then have them locate Harlem on a map of New York City. Have students locate important landmarks of the city, such as the Statue of Liberty and the Empire State Building. Guide them to notice that Harlem is located at one end of the island, away from the upscale Financial District and Tribeca area. **BL**

Objectives
- To analyze rhyme and rhyme scheme (SE)
- To make inferences about theme (SE)
- To analyze meter (TWE)

Assess

1. Students should reflect thoughtfully on the poems.

2. (a) He "plays it cool and digs all jive." (b) He does not lose his head and agrees with what people say.

3. (a) "Dig And Be Dug/In Return." (b) "Live and let live."

4. (a) "Or does it explode?" (b) Deferred dreams could result in violent action.

5. (a) "You think / "It's a happy beat?" and "What did I say?" (b) They suggest that the beat is not actually "happy."

6. The images are distasteful and therefore apt.

7. To hold the reader's attention and enhance the rhythm

8. Students should understand that Hughes is talking about the dreams of individuals, African American people, and the residents of Harlem.

Literary Element

1. Rhetorical questions rhyme and include similes.

2. They connect the reader to the sounds of Harlem.

Vocabulary

1. a   2. c

RESPONDING AND THINKING CRITICALLY

Respond

1. If you could ask Langston Hughes one question about his poetry, what would it be?

Recall and Interpret

2. (a)In "Motto," how does the speaker say that he stays alive? (b)What does this suggest to you about his situation in life?

3. (a)In "Motto," what are the speaker's actual words for the motto? (b)Rephrase the motto in your own words.

4. (a)What is the final question in "Harlem"? (b)What might this question mean?

Analyze and Evaluate

5. (a)In "Dream Boogie," what questions does the speaker ask the audience? (b)What is their effect on the poem? Explain.

6. In "Harlem," how effective are the images Hughes creates in conveying what happens to a "dream deferred"?

7. In "Dream Boogie," why does Hughes deviate from the rhyme scheme in some lines of the poem?

Connect

8. **Big Idea** **Issues of Identity** What does Hughes mean when he refers to a deferred dream? Explain.

LITERARY ANALYSIS

Literary Element **Rhyme and Rhyme Scheme**

Many different types of **rhyme schemes** exist in poetry. Established poets such as Hughes can take liberties with rhyme scheme for added meaning and innovation.

1. How is simile used as part of the rhyme scheme in "Harlem"?

2. How do you think the rhyme schemes affect the meanings of Hughes's poems?

Writing About Literature

Evaluate Author's Craft In these poems, Hughes conveys his ideas about African American life in a jazz-beat style. Write an essay describing this technique as Hughes applies it. Include your opinion of whether or not you think his presentation is effective. Refer to ideas, phrases, and lines from each of the three poems you have read.

When you have finished your draft, exchange it with another student. Evaluate each other's work and suggest revisions. Then proofread and edit your draft for errors in spelling, grammar, and punctuation.

Literature Online **Web Activities** For eFlashcards, Selection Quick Checks, and other Web activities, go to www.glencoe.com.

READING AND VOCABULARY

Reading Strategy **Making Inferences About Theme**

Looking at the words and phrases in a poem can help you **make inferences about theme.** A poet may convey his or her ideas in subtle ways. As you read, pay attention to the style of each poem. Think about meanings that are implied but not stated.

1. What theme is conveyed in this body of poetry?

2. In support of your opinion, list two details from the poems.

Vocabulary **Practice**

Word Parts Your knowledge of word roots can help you understand unfamiliar words. Read the roots and definitions below. Then use your knowledge of roots, prefixes, and suffixes to pick the best definition for each vocabulary word.
Latin Root: *deferre*—"to carry away" or "to transfer"
Latin Root: *fistula*—"pipe, ulcer"

1. Vijay **deferred** his plans of becoming a rock star until after he finished college.
   a. postponed   **b.** abandoned   **c.** followed

2. My mother put antibiotic cream on my cut to ensure that the wound would not **fester.**
   a. frighten   **b.** heal   **c.** become infected

Literature Online

Web Activities Have students access the Web site for interactive activities that will help them assess their understanding of the selection.

Writing About Literature

Students' essays should

- give examples of Hughes's technique
- clearly state and support an opinion about the effectiveness of the presentation

Reading Strategy

1. The deferred dreams of people, specifically African Americans confined because of racial prejudice.

2. Possible detail: *"Or does it explode?"*

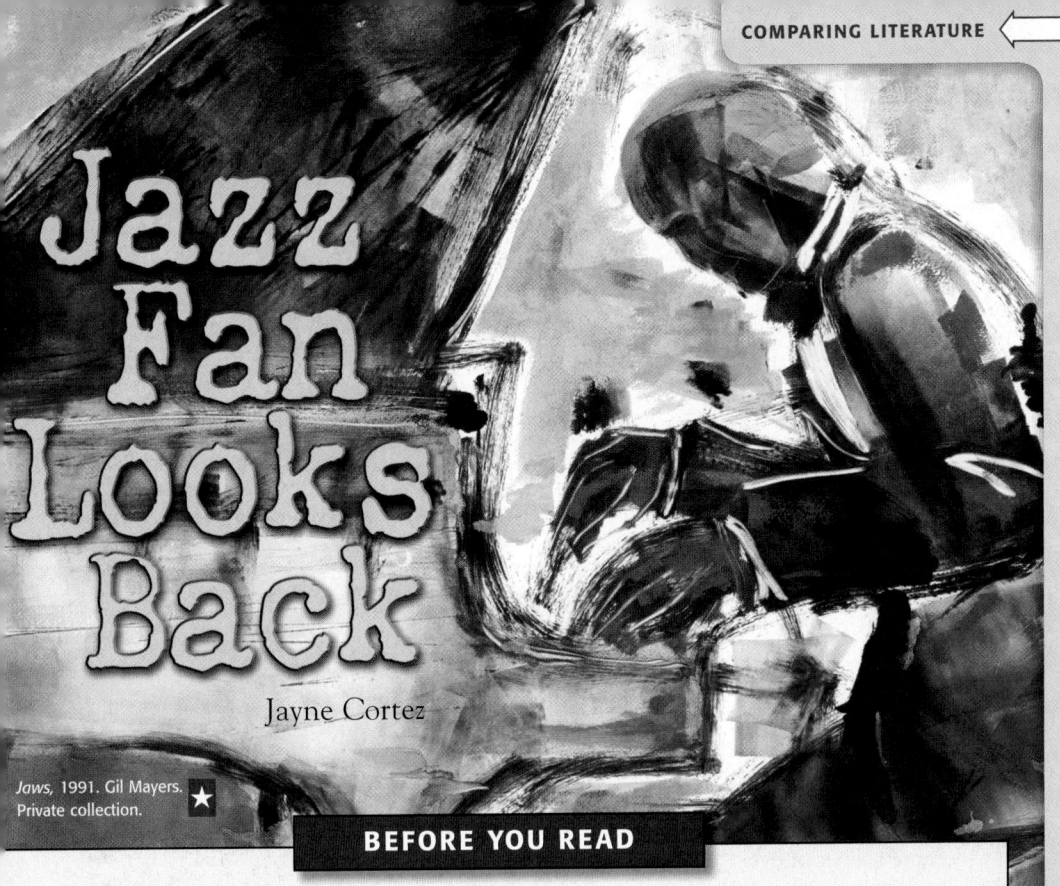

Jazz Fan Looks Back

Jayne Cortez

Jaws, 1991. Gil Mayers. Private collection. ⭐

Focus

Summary

This poem is a jazz fan's passionate reminiscence about her experiences listening to live jazz music by the greats, including Thelonious Monk, Charlie Parker, and Ella Fitzgerald.

⭐ Viewing the Art

Point out that jazz music is characterized by syncopated rhythms, improvisation, an African influence, and constant evolution. **Ask:** What elements of jazz do you see in this painting? *(Students might note that the painting has a strong sense of rhythm and movement. It appears somewhat abstract and improvised; it is unlike a realistic portrait. The bright and bold colors are reminiscent of the unique and daring uses of pitch and timbre in jazz music.)* **AS**

BEFORE YOU READ

Building Background

African American artists and writers, such as Maya Angelou, highly regard poet Jayne Cortez as a voice of her culture and era. Critics have praised Cortez because she "forged connections in her work that help us see how our histories are related." Much of her poetry addresses social problems in the United States and the world.

Cortez was born in Arizona, raised in California, and now lives in New York City. She has written ten books of poetry and her poems have been translated into twenty-eight languages. Additionally, she founded her own publishing company, Bola Press, in 1972. Cortez's many awards and honors include the American Book Award, the International African Festival Award, and fellowships from the National Endowment for the Arts and the New York Foundation for the Arts.

Music is part of both Cortez's personal and professional life. Her husband, Ornette Coleman, is a jazz musician.

Cortez herself is a member of a jazz and funk band, The Firespitters, whose other members include her son, Denardo. In fact, Cortez does not just write and publish her poetry: she also performs it with The Firespitters, with whom she has released nine recordings.

In "Jazz Fan Looks Back," Cortez displays her impressive knowledge of jazz music and history. In the poem, she cleverly associates several jazz musicians with some of their most popular compositions or tunes that they were known for playing. For example, the first line of the poem contains an allusion to jazz composer and pianist Thelonius Monk and his composition "Criss Cross." She also refers to jazz pianist Bud Powell and his compostion "Wail," saxophonist Sonny Stitt and his frequent tune "Count Every Star," and trumpeter Dizzy Gillespie and his composition "Groovin' High." In other lines, she skillfully relates musicians and their memorable personalities, behaviors, or talents: she references the gardenia flower

JAYNE CORTEZ **675**

✓CheckPoint

Use the CheckPoint questions on Presentation Plus! to monitor students' comprehension. These questions can be used with interactive response keypads for immediate student feedback.

English Language Coach

Jazz Musicians Students born in other countries, as well as students not versed in jazz history, may not be familiar with the names of the musicians mentioned in this poem. Have students conduct research to identify these musicians.

If time allows, have students find one unique characteristic for each musician. Have students from other cultures talk about famous musicians in their societies. **EL**

Teach

Big Idea

Issues of Identity

Say: Keep the following question in mind as you read. How is the speaker's identity intertwined with music? *(The speaker's identity seems wrapped up in music; the speaker is such a dedicated jazz fan that she feels as if she participates in the playing of the music with the musicians.)* OL

Quickwrite

Students' responses should express how they felt about the poem and state why they liked or disliked it. Students should compare their responses to this poem with their responses to "Dream Boogie."

Literature Online

Author Search To expand students' appreciation of Jayne Cortez, have them access the Web site for additional information and resources.

CheckPoint

Use the CheckPoint questions on Presentation Plus! to check students' mastery of the selection. These questions can be used with interactive response keypads for immediate student feedback.

that singer Billie Holiday was famous for wearing in her hair while performing and the wide vocal range that singer Dinah Washington could "scream." Finally, she clues her audience into the nicknames of other famous jazz artists: saxophonist and bandleader Charlie "Bird" Parker, tenor saxophonist Coleman "Hawk" Hawkins, and trumpeter "Fats" Navarro. To complete the mood of a jazz fan reminiscing, she mentions the Shrine Auditorium, a famous venue in Los Angeles.

Jayne Cortez was born in 1936.

Literature Online **Author Search** For more about Jayne Cortez, go to www.glencoe.com.

> I crisscrossed with Monk
> Wailed with Bud
> Counted every star with Stitt
> Sang "Don't Blame Me" with Sarah[1]
> 5   Wore a flower like Billie
> Screamed in the range of Dinah
> & scatted "How High the Moon" with Ella Fitzgerald
> as she blew roof off the Shrine Auditorium
>   Jazz at the Philharmonic
>
> 10   I cut my hair into a permanent tam
> Made my feet rebellious metronomes
> Embedded record needles in paint on paper
> Talked bopology[2] talk
> Laughed in high-pitched saxophone phrases
> 15   Became keeper of every Bird riff
> every Lester lick[3]
> as Hawk melodicized my ear of infatuated tongues
> & Blakey[4] drummed militant messages in
> soul of my applauding teeth
> 20   & Ray[5] hit bass notes to the last love seat in my bones
> I moved in triple time with Max[6]
> Grooved high with Diz
> Perdidoed with Pettiford[7]
> Flew home with Hamp[8]
> 25   Shuffled in Dexter's Deck[9]
> Squatty-rooed with Peterson[10]
> Dreamed a "52nd Street Theme" with Fats
> & scatted "Lady Be Good" with Ella Fitzgerald
> as she blew roof off the Shrine Auditorium
> 30   Jazz at the Philharmonic

1. *Sarah* refers to singer Sarah Vaughan.

2. *Bopology* is the study of *bop,* a style of jazz characterized by rhythmic and harmonic complexity, improvised solo performances, and brilliant playing.
3. *Lester* refers to tenor saxophonist Lester Young.
4. *Blakey* refers to jazz drummer and bandleader Art Blakey.
5. *Ray* refers to jazz bassist Ray Brown.
6. *Max* refers to jazz drummer and composer Max Roach.
7. *Pettiford* refers to jazz bassist Oscar Pettiford. "Perdida" is an old tune he liked to play.
8. *Hamp* refers to jazz vibraphonist Lionel Hampton. "Flying Home" is his most famous tune.
9. *Dexter* refers to Dexter Gordon, jazz saxophonist. "Clear the Dex" is one of his compositions.
10. *Peterson* refers to jazz pianist Oscar Peterson. "Squatty Roo" is one of his tunes.

Quickwrite

What are your feelings about the style of this poem? Explain why you like or dislike it. Write a paragraph to compare your feelings about this poem with your feelings about Hughes's "Dream Boogie."

Additional Support

Skills Practice

GRAMMAR: Types of Sentences
Write on the board:

- *He tooted into it a few times.*
- *Young Gillespie remembered his father as a brusque man, who never hesitated to administer a whacking whenever he felt it necessary.*
- *He had been diligently practicing on the trombone for months, but the trumpet was his favorite horn.*

Have students identify each type of sentence. *(in order: simple, complex, compound)* Then have students write a complex-compound sentence. OL

Dizzy Gillespie
Explorer of New Sounds

From *Giants of Jazz*   Studs Terkel

BEFORE YOU READ

Building Background

Studs Terkel is a New York City-born writer. After moving to Chicago, he began his career writing radio shows and ads, eventually hosting his own radio interview series. The show became a place for Terkel to highlight his love for all kinds of music, from jazz to blues to opera.

Giants of Jazz, from which this Dizzy Gillespie chapter is taken, was Terkel's first book. It contains biographies of thirteen jazz greats. *Giants of Jazz* was reprinted in 2002 and still sells well, fifty years after its initial publication. Studs Terkel continues to write, interview, and maintain a public presence.

Studs Terkel was born in 1912.

Literature Online Author Search For more about Studs Terkel, go to www.glencoe.com.

John Birks Gillespie was a lively, impish little boy.

"John Birks! John Birks!" his harried mother called out. "Where in the world is that child?" Of her nine children, this youngest one was the most irrepressible.

From the parlor came the sound of a pounding piano. She peered into the room, chuckled softly to herself, and shook her head. The four-year-old had clambered up on the high stool and was furiously stabbing at the keyboard with his pudgy little fingers. He gloried in the making of loud sounds.

All kinds of instruments were strewn about the Gillespie household, in Cheraw, South Carolina. The father was a bricklayer by day and an amateur musician by night. As leader of the local band, he was the guardian of the other members' instruments.

The small boy quickly tired of the piano and scurried toward a clarinet that lay upon the table. He tooted into it a few times. His large, luminous eyes wandered to the nearby mandolin. Curious, he plucked at the strings. Now a huge instrument loomed up before him. It rested in a corner, against the wall. It was a bass viol.[1] He approached it cautiously. With all his might, he plucked at a thick, taut string. The vibrating sound startled him. He jumped back. Soon he was at the piano again, blithely pounding away. Here he could make the most noise with the least effort. John Birks Gillespie was acquainting himself with musical instruments. All kinds. . . .

---

1. A *viol* is one of a family of stringed instruments with a flat back that is played with a curved bow.

STUDS TERKEL **677**

Focus

Summary

The biographical tale begins with Dizzy Gillespie's early years as he develops his unique voice, revolutionary style, and skills as a trumpet player. Eventually, he and sax player Charlie Parker develop a new form of jazz called bebop. Ultimately, Gillespie is hailed as a jazz great.

Literature Online

Author Search To expand students' appreciation of Studs Terkel, have them access the Web site for additional information and resources.

CheckPoint

Use the CheckPoint questions on Presentation Plus! to monitor students' comprehension. These questions can be used with interactive response keypads for immediate student feedback.

Readability Scores
Dale-Chall: 6.5
DRP: 55
Lexile: 750

English Language Coach

Instruments Students from other backgrounds may be unfamiliar with some of the musical instruments discussed in the selection. Have these students explain some of the instruments unique to their culture. Invite them to bring in one or two of these instruments, if possible. **EL**

Reading in the Real World

College The competition among professional musicians is fierce. Have students research some of the highly regarded schools for musical instruction. Have them discuss how pursuing a career in music might be different for musicians today than it was in Gillespie's day. **OL**

Teach

Big Idea

Issues of Identity

Say: Keep the following questions in mind as you read. What does it take to become a successful musician? How can innovation be difficult? *(Students might say it takes hard work, persistence, and spirit to become a successful musician. Innovation can be difficult because of rejection.)* **OL**

★ Cultural History

Roy Eldridge A professional jazz musician by age 16, Eldridge (1911–1989) led a long and distinguished career as a trumpeter and singer. Eldridge left Teddy Hill's band in 1935 to become lead trumpeter and occasional crooner for Fletcher Henderson's influential big band. He became one of the first African American members of a white big band when he joined Gene Krupa's troupe in 1941. **AS**

[At the age of fourteen, John's] idol was a trumpet player. There was a radio at the Harringtons. Each week it was a ritual to listen to the broadcast from New York's Savoy ★ Ball Room.[2] Roy Eldridge's trumpet was featured with the band of Teddy Hill. Young Gillespie listened intently to the solos of Eldridge. This man had his own special style; his horn had an amazingly wide range, rich colors, and a sharp bite.

"Little Jazz," as Eldridge was called, had gone beyond the New Orleans trumpet style as perfected by Louis Armstrong. He had discovered in the trumpet its own special quality. He added a new dimension to its playing. Young Gillespie sensed this and determined to simulate the style of Eldridge as closely as possible. He began to teach himself the technique of this horn with thoroughness and persistence. At times it was an ordeal for his mother in her search for peace and quiet. She was not the only one who moaned, "That noise is driving me crazy."

The members of the school band practiced wherever they could. As soon as they were kicked out of one home, they paraded into another. When the last weary mother cried, "Out, children. I can't hear myself think," they played in the open field. They blew loudly, joyously, and often off-key.

John Gillespie had a good ear. Soon he was considered the best trumpet player around. But he had one trouble. He could play in only one key: B-flat. It was his best-kept secret. That is, till the day Sonny Matthews returned to town. Sonny was Cheraw's best piano player. During his absence, Gillespie had gained his fine reputation as a trumpeter.

"Where's this John Birks I been hearin' about?" Sonny asked on his first day back. He invited Gillespie to his house for a two-man jam session.

"What do you wanna play, man?" asked the host.

---

2. The *Savoy Ball Room*, in the Harlem neighborhood of New York City, was where many big bands played.

"Anything. I don't care," replied the cocky young trumpeter.

"Okay, let's make it 'Nagasaki.'"

Sonny struck up a few chords on the piano. No sound came from the horn. John Birks Gillespie was mortified. Matthews was playing in the key of C!

From that moment on, an embarrassed young man with a horn vowed to learn every key. . . .

Lottie Gillespie moved her family to Philadelphia in 1935. Though it was a new world for John, he wasn't one bit afraid. He was confident and saucy. Hat cocked to one side, eyes twinkling mischievously, he was ready for any kind of prank. Here his fun-loving ways earned him the nickname of Dizzy. It stuck. . . .

In his constant quest for a new style on the trumpet, he heard a sound that intrigued him. It was 1939. He was working for Edgar Hayes at the World's Fair in New York. Hayes's clarinet player, Rudy Powell, was playing a riff, a repeated phrase, of changing chords. Dizzy rushed to the piano.

"I always go to the piano when I want to try out something new. You see, you can skip around on the piano so easily. You can pick out chords, skip notes, jump intervals. Then you transpose it for the trumpet."

He played the arrangement over and over. He was excited. An idea was taking form in his mind. "I realized there could be so much more in music than what everybody else was playing." Gillespie knew now there must be some new way of playing the trumpet.

Late in 1939, he joined the orchestra of Cab Calloway. There were some excellent musicians in the band. Among them were Chu Berry at the tenor sax, Hilton Jefferson at the alto, Cozy Cole at the drums, and Milt Hinton at the bass. During his two years with Calloway, Dizzy recorded more than fifty sides. More important, it was his period of groping for new ways to express himself. There were difficulties. Some of the band's veterans were irritated by Gillespie's unorthodoxies.

Additional Support

READING: Analyzing Biography
Remind students that a biography is an account of a person's life written by another person. **Ask:** How can you tell that Terkel based his writing on firsthand interviews? *(He uses quotations from the people involved and phrases such as "remembers Dizzy.")* How does Terkel bring his subject to life? *(He uses lively language and vivid details.)* **OL**

A portrait of trumpeter Dizzy Gillespie (1917–1993) in performance. He was known for his co-creation of the popular jazz bebop style.

"What's he trying to do anyway?"

"Why doesn't he stick to the arrangements?"

"The guy's a 'character.'"

Calloway himself was not too happy with Dizzy's didoes.[3] Occasionally during his musical explorations Dizzy would get lost. When he'd miss the final high note, after a long-range progression, the leader angrily muttered, "All right now! Enough of that! No more of that Chinese music!"

There were others in the band who sensed the pioneer in young Gillespie. Gently they encouraged him.

"Come here, kid," said Milt Hinton, the bass player, during an intermission. "Let's go on the roof and practice."

During the Calloway engagement at New York's Cotton Club, the two men were often on the roof, quietly working together. Hinton walked the bass, while Gillespie tried different chords and melodic patterns on his trumpet.

---

3. A *dido* is a mischievous prank.

"I like what you're trying to do," said Hinton. "Keep it up, kid."

Dizzy did keep it up, thanks to the opening of a little nightclub in Harlem. It was called Minton's Play House. Teddy Hill managed it. He encouraged young musicians to gather here after hours, to play exactly as they felt.

Gillespie became a regular habitué, together with Thelonious Monk, a pianist, and Kenny Clarke, a drummer. Clarke was experimenting as a drummer as Dizzy was as a trumpeter. His rhythm was implied rather than emphasized. He varied his punctuation, instead of steadily pounding away at the drum at four-to-the-bar. Here, too, Charlie Christian often came, after his regular stint with Goodman.

Another young musician seeking a new avenue in jazz frequented Minton's. He was an alto-sax player in the swing band of Jay McShann, recently arrived from Kansas City. His name was Charlie Parker. Later, Dizzy and he were to really cross paths and become the two major figures in the development of the jazz known as "bop."

STUDS TERKEL **679**

Differentiated Instruction

Geography Proficiency Musicians often go on tours to promote their music. For high-profile performers, these tours can span the globe. Have students mark on a map the many places around the world where Gillespie performed his music (*New York, Los Angeles,*

Scandinavia, India, Iraq, Turkey, Lebanon, and so on). Because Gillespie was based in New York, have students draw lines from New York City to these many locations to illustrate the great distances he traveled. **BL**

Teach

BI **Big Idea**

Issues of Identity

Ask: How might exposure to so many other artists help Gillespie form his own identity as a musician? (*He could bring a new sound and depth to a musical style steeped in tradition. By developing his own unique sound and influencing others, Gillespie's name could become associated with a style of music.*) **OL**

★ **Viewing the Art**

Have students share their impressions of Gillespie based on this portrait. **Ask:** Why might Gillespie's innovative style have irritated some musicians? (*They were surprised by his inventiveness. They were so rooted in tradition that they didn't like the sound of something new. Perhaps they thought he was showing off. Perhaps they were jealous of his ability.*) **AS**

Objectives
- To establish a purpose for reading (TWE)
- To analyze biography (TWE)

Teach

R Reading Strategy

Making Inferences about Theme

Ask: What can you infer about the theme based on Terkel's inclusion of this quotation? *(Terkel wants to make the point that Gillespie was a man of the people and a believer in the unifying powers of music.)* **OL**

Quickwrite

Students should respond to the effectiveness of the title "Explorer of New Sounds" and support an opinion as to whether Gillespie actually was an explorer of new sounds.

 CheckPoint

Use the CheckPoint questions on Presentation Plus! to check students' mastery of the selection. These questions can be used with interactive response keypads for immediate student feedback.

At Minton's, Dizzy's closest associate was Thelonious Monk.

"Monk and I would work on an idea," remembers Dizzy. "Then I'd try it out the next night with Calloway. Cab didn't like it. It was too strange for him."

The word spread quickly among musicians. Minton's was the place to visit for exciting jam sessions and new approaches. Soon the place was packed with players, many of whom had limited talents. The regulars had to find some way to keep the mediocre ones off the bandstand.

"What're we going to do about those cats who can't blow at all, but it takes them seven choruses to prove it?" asked the perplexed Gillespie. "By the time they get off, the night's shot."

"Let's practice in the afternoon," suggested Monk. "We'll work out variations so complex it'll scare 'em away."

That's how it began. Bewildered musicians of lesser talents shook their heads and walked off the stand. Gradually Dizzy and his colleagues became more and more interested in what they were doing. They explored more deeply. And a new jazz style was evolving. . . .

When Dizzy and Parker played, the music had drive and humor and warmth. Many of their imitators lacked this, because they lacked musicianship. These two artists were not seeking mimics, but colleagues. In the years that followed, numerous young musicians came into prominence. They were happily equipped with the attributes Gillespie and Bird sought—good craftsmanship, imagination, and daring. Hundreds of records were cut, originals as well as standards. Young musicians were developing new melodic lines based on chord sequences of popular jazz numbers. New recording companies came into being, scores of them.

Modern jazz was here to stay.

In Europe as in America the impact was felt. Though Gillespie's 1948 tour through Scandinavia was a financial flop, it was not due to the music. The band was mismanaged.

Dizzy's later appearances in Europe were enthusiastically received.

Perhaps the highlight of Dizzy Gillespie's career was his tour of the Middle East in 1956. Under the auspices of the U.S. State Department, he led a big band into such lands as India, Iraq, Turkey, and Lebanon. These were places where most people had never heard live jazz, let alone American artists. These concerts were divided into two parts. The first half dealt with origins, ranging from the African drums and spirituals to big band classics. The second half consisted of modern jazz.

Dizzy Gillespie was a wonderful ambassador of goodwill. He and his music won over these people immediately.

"I have never seen these people let themselves go like this," observed an American official at Damascus.[4] He himself had been suspicious of jazz.

In Ankara, Dizzy refused to play at an important gathering until the little ragamuffins outside the wall were let in.

"Man, we're here to play for the people." **R**

Dizzy called a young native trumpeter to the stage. The boy was so moved he could hardly speak. Gillespie handed him his cigarette case. Engraved on it were the words: "In token of the brotherhood of jazz."

Does it matter what label is given to jazz? Be it traditional or be it modern, if a talented man plays it with joy and love, that's all that matters.

Says Dizzy Gillespie: "I'm playing the same notes, but it comes out different. You can't teach the soul. You got to bring out your soul on those valves."

---

4. *Damascus* is the capital of Syria.

Quickwrite ....

Terkel chose "Explorer of New Sounds" for the title of his chapter on Dizzy Gillespie. Is this the best title for the chapter? Write a paragraph about the effectiveness of the title and whether you think, from the information in this excerpt, that Gillespie was an "explorer of sounds."

Skills Practice

WRITING: Drafting a Letter

Although largely supplanted by e-mail and instant messaging, letter writing is still an essential skill—especially in applying for jobs. Have students think of someone to whom they would like to write a personal letter. Remind them that their choice of audience determines the style and language appropriate for the letter. Have them decide on a topic for the letter. Then have them draft the letter. **OL**

Expression of Jazz, 1993. Maurice Faulk. Acrylic on canvas board.

Playing Jazz

Wynton Marsalis

BEFORE YOU READ

Building Background

Eight-time Grammy Award winner Wynton Marsalis is arguably one of the best jazz musicians and trumpeters today.

A classical musician as well, he has recorded the music of Bach, Beethoven, and Mozart to great critical acclaim. He has also played with some of the most highly regarded orchestras in the United States and the world.

Marsalis began publicly performing traditional New Orleans jazz when he was just eight years old. Marsalis describes his music as being the sound of democracy,

a concept he was introduced to by jazz great Art Blakey. According to Marsalis, "The jazz band works best when participation is shaped by intelligent communication." His jazz artistry continues to inspire budding musicians today.

Wynton Marsalis was born in 1961.

Literature Online **Author Search** For more about Wynton Marsalis, go to www.glencoe.com.

WYNTON MARSALIS **681**

Building Reading Fluency

Reading with Style Wynton Marsalis writes in an informal, conversational style. Have students take turns reading aloud paragraphs of the letter and try to capture the dramatic, conversational style of Marsalis's narrative voice. **BL**

Differentiated Instruction

Advanced Readers Marsalis provides four steps he believes are important in being a good jazz musician. Have students write lists of steps they believe are important in achieving goals in other disciplines, such as painting, basketball, or mathematics. **AL**

Focus

Summary

Jazz musician Wynton Marsalis writes to a young musician named Anthony. In the letter, Marsalis outlines his four components of successful jazz playing: developing musical vocabulary, infusing charisma, finding a personal goal, and swinging.

Literature Online

Author Search To expand students' appreciation of Wynton Marsalis, have them access the Web site for additional information and resources.

★ Viewing the Art

Tell students that Wynton Marsalis describes his music as "the sound of democracy." Then have them analyze this painting for signs of democracy, collaboration, communication, and participation. Encourage students to discuss how the democratic element of jazz makes jazz musicians similar to and different from other types of musicians or music groups, such as those in symphony orchestras or rock bands. **AS**

CheckPoint

Use the CheckPoint questions on Presentation Plus! to monitor students' comprehension. These questions can be used with interactive response keypads for immediate student feedback.

Teach

Big Idea

Issues of Identity

Say: Keep the following question in mind as you read: How can I apply Marsalis's "bases" to my own interests? *(Answers will vary. The "bases" are applicable to pretty much anything.)* **OL**

Readability Scores
Dale-Chall: 6.1
DRP: 57
Lexile: 800

July 18, 2003

Dear Anthony,

How are you, man? Glad to hear you got something from my last letter. Don't just read that stuff and lock it away in your head. Figure out how to apply it.

Tours go on and on. We just out here, from one city to the next. I just head where they tell me. So excuse the distance between these notes. I try to write when I can.

Man, last night we played a small, intimate club inside a Boston hotel. Can't complain at all; gig just felt good. Small places, man. The people all around you, making all kind of noise and grooving. It just inspires the band. Folks in the audience let the sound wash all over them, especially when our drummer, Herlin,[1] gets sanctified on the tambourine in 5/4.

After the gig, someone brought us a full-course meal—black-eyed peas, corn bread, barbecued ribs, mashed potatoes, even had the nerve to have some corn pudding. People cook for you when you sound good and have good manners. In all seriousness, though, no matter how often something like that happens, and it happens a lot, the love and generosity of spirit that we feel out here is always humbling. And it makes missing your family a bit more tolerable. But boy, if you don't like people, you'll have a lonely time out here.

I wanted to rap with you about playing. Yes, that simply, that essentially—what it takes to play jazz music. Playing covers four essential bases: the expansion of your musical vocabulary, employing charisma in your sound, locating your personal objective, and embracing swing. Let's spend some time chopping all four up.

First, the more vocabulary you know, the more you can play. It's just like talking. A person can know twenty words very well and communicate successfully. But there's gonna be a whole pile of things that he or she never talks about. You need to have vocabulary on all aspects of jazz—melodies, harmonies, rhythms, and personal effects. It's always best to start with what you should know—things from your region, then national things. In other words, if you're from Kansas City, you need to know what the Kansas City blues sounds like. Then you need to know American themes and tunes. And today you need to know more music, especially in the global sense. All over the world, styles of music have specific objectives. Learning those objectives will serve you well, allowing you to incorporate a greater breadth of material into your own vocabulary. Musicians in the Latin tradition always complain that the jazz musicians don't know any of their music. Study and learn whatever music catches your fancy from around the world with people who know it and can play it. The enhancement to your own music will be invaluable. Studying the vocabulary of music is like etymology.[2] If they're interested in romance languages, people will study Latin, from which all those languages descend. In the same manner, most groove music comes from the African 6/8 rhythm—the claves[3] in Cuban music to the shuffle of the Mississippi blues. But if you don't know your own language, your own vocabulary, forget about learning someone else's.

Second, always bring charisma to your sound. People want to *hear* some music. They don't come out to see robots toot horns. They want to be uplifted, amazed, and enlightened. Infuse your sound with charisma. What you do when playing for the public isn't much different from any stage-based performance. Imagine the actor who trots out onstage only to deliver lines in bland fashion with no regard to distinguishing his or her craft. Would that make you enthusiastic? You have to understand and locate your distinct approach to the music, and then infuse your playing with that sentiment. Whatever your approach turns out

---

1. *Herlin* is Wynton Marsalis's longtime drummer Herlin Riley.

2. *Etymology* means the history of a word.
3. *Claves* are a two-bar syncopated pattern of music.

Additional Support

Skills Practice

VOCABULARY: Context Clues
Explain that nonfiction writers often give direct context clues to the meaning of an unfamiliar word. Write these examples on the board and have students give the meaning of each underlined word.

- Swing is <u>quintessentially</u> American, or a perfect example of an American concept.

- Swing has a <u>hierarchy,</u> or organization by rank, just like a government.

- You can play any type of fun <u>syncopations</u>—stressing one or more normally unaccented beats in a measure. **OL**

Wynton Marsalis, 1999. New York City.

to be, deliver it with force, power, and conviction. With *fun,* man. This is *playing.*

But while you're up on that bandstand blowing with force and power, keep in mind that playing jazz is like anything else in life: When you start a thing off, you're much more enthusiastic than when you get to the middle. If you're running a race, you shoot out like Jesse Owens reborn. Playing ball? That enthusiasm might make you think you're Joe Montana.[4] Then after a couple of interceptions the thrill is gone. This happens in almost every activity in the world. So when you play, don't get carried away or burned out by the importance of your own effort. Start good. Finish good. Sound good. No more complicated than

that. And when I say sound good, I mean sounding good enough to get a job. Because when you sound good, people will hire you; when you sound good, people will be calling.

Of course, sounding good also goes beyond the marketplace; it goes right to the heart of your personal objectives—our third base of playing. Although objectives vary, depending on the individual, there exists a central, common point: What do you want to give to people? Let me lay this on you. Once I asked Sweets Edison,[5] "Why is it that you always sound good, from the first note that you play?"

"There's only one way to play, baby boy," Sweets answered. "There ain't but one way to do it."

Sweets means that you project your way with the ultimate feeling all the time, whether you're playing in a sad band, a great band, for elementary school students, at someone's birthday party at their house, or 'cause someone fixed a meal for you. When you pull your horn out, you should play as if that's the most important moment in your life. If it's not, make it be.

Remember when you were a kid and you really, really wanted something? It could have been the most trivial thing. Remember the way you begged and pleaded for it? Imagine playing with that passion, that desire, as if this was the most needed thing in your life. When we get older, we learn how to temper our wanting, our desire. Well, tap back into that childhood fervor and freedom of expression. That's what you have to have when you play. That thing you wanted the most and the way you were willing to sacrifice any speck of pride or dignity to obtain it. Remember how you wanted it; remember how you cried when you didn't get it? What about the girl who couldn't stand you? Or who liked you until Amos came around? Play with *that* passion.

Realize that the fundamentals of jazz help you develop your individuality, help you find that passion. Don't say, "I'm not going to really play blues," or "I'm not going

---

4. *Joe Montana* is a former professional football player.

5. *Sweets Edison* is the late jazz trumpeter Harry "Sweets" Edison.

WYNTON MARSALIS **683**

COMPARING LITERATURE

Teach

BI Big Idea

Issues of Identity

Ask: According to Marsalis, how is good music connected to identity? *(Music is made good by the player's unique approach to playing. This unique approach is the musician's identity.)* OL

R Reading Strategy

Making Inferences About Theme

Ask: What might Marsalis be trying to accomplish by corresponding with a young musician? *(Some students may say that Marsalis wants to tap into the uninhibited freedom of expression the younger musician may still have. Others may say that Marsalis wants to impart the valuable wisdom he has learned over the years.)* OL

English Language Coach

Casual Language Nonnative speakers may have difficulty adjusting to Marsalis's informal writing style. Point out examples of nonstandard words and constructions ("there's gonna be a whole pile of things," "Ain't but one way to do it"), slang ("Let me lay this on you"), and sentence fragments ("With *fun,* man"). Because Marsalis's written style is highly conversational, students may improve their comprehension by reading the piece out loud. To understand jazz idioms, students may want to research the terms in a dictionary of music history. EL

Objectives
• To make inferences about theme (SE)
• To write a letter (TWE)

Teach

BI Big Idea

Issues of Identity

Say: Marsalis calls swing "a democratic and *quintessentially* American concept." What might he mean by this? *(Swing involves individual and highly personal expression as well as maintaining identity in the face of change. Playing swing in an ensemble creates a constantly shifting balance of power to which all members contribute.)* **OL**

Discussion Starter

Students should discuss the author's purpose and why he talks about learning different types of music. They can discuss what Marsalis means by the "democracy" of swing.

CheckPoint

Use the CheckPoint questions on Presentation Plus! to check students' mastery of the selection. These questions can be used with interactive response keypads for immediate student feedback.

to address swing." Don't run from you. Running carries a cost. Have you ever noticed that when you hear a contemporary Latin band play and juxtapose it with a jazz band, the Latin music almost always sounds better? You wonder why that's the case? Just look at the bandstand. You'll see that the Latin musicians appear invested and involved; they believe in the integrity of their groove. Now look at the jazz band: not accepting the swing, trying to find some quasi-funk groove or, even worse, that sad jazz quasi-Latin groove. You can practically hear them muttering to themselves—"Swing is dead; let's try something else." They take detours to avoid sounding bad and run right into what they flee. The fourth and perhaps most important facet of playing jazz, *swing* and swinging.

You may hear about "quintessentially American" things. Well, what makes a thing quintessential is that it reflects the values of the thing it is supposed to be quintessentially about. In the case of an art form, it not only reflects the values, it embodies them, it ennobles them, and it emboldens them. That's why people study art forms with such intensity, because the artist channels the spirit of the nation. In the case of the swing, no one person created it; democracy is a collective experience. And swing is a demo-

BI cratic and *quintessentially* American concept.

Swing is supreme coordination under the duress of time. Swing is democracy made manifest; it makes you constantly adjust. At any given time, what's going to go on musically may not be to your liking. You have to know how to maintain your equilibrium and your balance, even if things are changing rapidly. Swing is designed for you to do that. Why? Each musician has a different concept of time. Sometimes I tell my students, "I want you all to stand up when a minute is over." And some people get up after twenty seconds. Some get up after a minute and a half. That shows the variance between

individual concepts of time. As a player you have to, of your own volition, come to a conclusion about how you approach time.

But swing has a hierarchy, like a government. The president of the swing is the drummer. The drummer has the loudest instrument and the cymbal is in the highest register. In African music it's called the bell rhythm. It's always the high rhythm, because you can hear that rhythm. In jazz, the bell rhythm is on the cymbal. You follow the bell rhythm.

But, like a government, swing also has checks and balances, because if the drummer rushes, the bass player might bring the time back. Sometimes the president of the swing is whoever has the best time. When Charlie Parker played, his time was so good that the bell rhythm would follow him. So you have that possibility. This is also a democratic proposition. If you have a weak president, man, you might need a strong legislative branch, or a stronger judiciary—checks and balances.

Swing ties in with the heart of the American experience: You make your way; you invent your way. In jazz, that means you challenge the time, and you determine the degree of difficulty of the rhythms you choose to play. You could play quarter notes, which are difficult to play in time. Or any type of impossible, fun syncopations. Or you could just play strings of eighth notes. You try to maintain your equilibrium with style, and work within the flow. That's what the swing offers.

Discussion Starter ....

Wynton Marsalis wrote this letter to a young boy who admired the jazz musician's talent. What is the author's purpose in writing what he did? Why does he discuss learning about different types of music? Why does he want the boy to understand the "democracy" of swing? Discuss your opinions in a small group.

Additional Support

Skills Practice

READING: Summarizing Have students summarize this Comparing Literature section. In their summaries, they should include answers to the questions *Who? What? Why?* and *How?* Students should make sure to exclude extraneous information or details. **OL**

Wrap-Up: Comparing Literature *Across Genres*

- *Dream Boogie, Motto, and Harlem*
  Langston Hughes
- *Jazz Fan Looks Back*
  Jayne Cortez
- from *Giants of Jazz*
  Studs Terkel
- *Playing Jazz*
  Wynton Marsalis

COMPARING THE Big Idea Issues of Identity

Writing Jazz may be the only major art form that truly originated in the United States. Jazz involves several forms of music—African rhythms and American band music—blended with some European influence. The best jazz music involves improvisation. Creating new music during a performance is what tends to separate the true jazz musician from those who can play only the notes written in a musical score. Many musicians, as well as aficionados, have found their identities in jazz. Think about the selections you have just read. Compare these writers in terms of the subjects they discuss. Are the writers alike in some ways? What makes each writer unique? How has music, specifically jazz, affected each writer?

Jump Up, 2000. Margie Livingston Campbell. Watercolor.

COMPARING Sound Devices

Group Activity Sound devices are techniques used by a writer to make a literary work more appealing to the ear. Form small groups to discuss the following questions:

1. What sound devices did you notice in the poetry you read? How do you feel about each poet's use of sound devices and rhyme schemes?
2. Which lines did you especially like in the poems you read? Which lines, if any, did you read more than once? In what ways were those lines especially pleasing to the ear?
3. In your opinion, which of the selections was the most appealing? Explain.

COMPARING Author's Purpose

Partner Activity Which of the authors, poems, and passages in this lesson had the greatest impact on you? With a partner, discuss your ideas about the following questions:

1. What will you remember from the readings in this section?
2. What did these readings teach you?
3. What further questions do you have about someone or something mentioned in these selections?

Support your answers with details from the texts. Then share them with your class.

OBJECTIVES
- Analyze works about the African American culture and experience.
- Understand ways in which music can affect people.
- Compare theme across genres.
- Compare and contrast authors' messages and beliefs.

COMPARING LITERATURE **685**

---

3. Students should offer specific questions about a subject or writer, such as how Wynton Marsalis began his letter-writing friendship with young Anthony, or what Dizzy Gillespie found most difficult about his success as a trumpeter.

Focus

Summary

In this workshop, students will write and present reflective essays in which they reflect upon personal experiences. Students will follow the stages of the writing process, including prewriting, drafting, revising, editing, and presenting. In addition, the workshop provides two mini-lessons, on using sensory details and correcting unclear pronoun reference.

Writing Models Have students access the Web site for interactive writing models and writing guides.

The Writing Process

In this workshop, you will follow the stages of the writing process. At any stage, you may think of new ideas to include and better ways to express them. Feel free to return to earlier stages as you write.

Prewriting
- - - - - - - - - - - - -
Drafting
- - - - - - - - - - - - -
Revising
- - - - - - - - - - - - -
 Focus Lesson:
  Using Sensory Details

Editing and Proofreading
- - - - - - - - - - - - -
Focus Lesson:
  Correcting Unclear
  Pronoun References

Presenting
- - - - - - - - - - - - -

Writing Models For models and other writing activities, go to www.glencoe.com.

OBJECTIVES
- Write a reflective essay that explores the meaning of a personal experience.
- Narrate the events, and describe the experience using sensory details.

Writing Workshop

Reflective Essay

 Reflecting on an Observation

"And at the crest of their brute satisfaction, with wonderful gentleness, in affirmation, they lift their clean calm eyes and they lie down and love the world."

—Gwendolyn Brooks, from "Horses Graze"

Connecting to Literature In Gwendolyn Brooks's poem, the speaker reflects on the lessons animals can teach us if we pay attention. Poems often present reflections—understandings and interpretations of experiences. Essays can do the same thing in paragraph form: look back, find significance, and present it in a meaningful and interesting way to an audience. In a reflective essay, you narrate and describe an experience or observation to show its effect on you. To write a successful reflective essay, begin by reading the goals and strategies below.

Rubric: Features of Reflective Essays

Goals	Strategies
To present a meaningful experience in your life	☑ Reflect, or look back on, a truly meaningful experience or observation
To present events, actions, or reactions in a logical order	☑ Present your experience as a narrative with a beginning, a middle, and an end
To make the experience seem real to the reader	☑ Include sensory details to help your reader imagine seeing, hearing, feeling, tasting, or smelling what you did
	☑ Use action verbs and precise nouns
To connect with an audience	☑ Use the first-person point of view
	☑ Use a tone that is as light or as serious as the experience or observation you narrate

---

Additional Support

Workshop Resources

Print Materials
- 📁 Unit 3 Resources (Fast File), pp. 95–97
- 📁 REAL Success in Writing: Research and Reports
- 📁 Writing Constructed Responses, pp. 1–26, 54
- 📖 Glencoe Literature Library

🖨 **Transparencies**
- Grammar and Language Transparencies 28
- Writing Workshop Transparencies 16–20
- Visual Literacy/Fine Art Transparencies

💻 **Technology**
- Grammar & Language eWorkbook
- Revising with Style eWorkbook
- Sentence Diagraming eWorkbook
- Spelling Power eWorkbook
- Online Essay Grading, glencoe.com
- Literature Library Exam*View*™ Assessment Suite CD-ROM
- Literature Library Vocabulary PuzzleMaker CD-ROM

Assignment

Write a reflection on an observation you have made or an experience you have had. As you move through the stages of the writing process, keep your audience and purpose in mind.

Audience: classmates and peers

Purpose: to explore the meaning and effect of a personal observation or experience

Analyzing a Professional Model

Joy Harjo finds her voice in both poetry and prose. As you read this reflection on the writer's deep, life-changing experience of hearing jazz for the first time, identify the narrative elements in the essay, as well as the ways in which descriptive details make the essay come alive. Pay close attention to the comments in the margin; they point out features that you might want to include in your own reflective essay.

"Suspended" by Joy Harjo ★

Once I was so small that I could barely peer over the top of the backseat of the black Cadillac my father polished and tuned daily; I wanted to see everything. It was around the time I acquired language, or even before that time, when something happened that changed my relationship to the spin of the world. My concept of language, of what was possible with music was changed by this revelatory moment. It changed even the way I looked at the sun. This suspended integer of time probably escaped ordinary notice in my parents' universe, which informed most of my vision in the ordinary world. They were still omnipresent gods. We were driving somewhere in Tulsa, the northern border of the Creek Nation. I don't know where we were going or where we had been, but I know the sun was boiling the asphalt, the car windows open for any breeze as I stood on tiptoes on the floorboard behind my father, a handsome god who smelled of Old Spice, whose slick black hair was always impeccably groomed, his clothes perfectly creased and ironed. The radio was on. I loved the radio, jukeboxes or any magic thing containing music even then.

Real-World Connection

For a job or college application, you might have to retell a personal experience—especially one that has had an important effect on your life or is related to the job or career you want.

First-Person Point of View

Write your reflection from the first-person point of view. Use the pronouns *I, we, me,* and *us,* and adjectives such as *my* and *our.*

Tone

Match your tone to your subject. You can also use your tone to invite your reader into the time, the place, and your experience or observation.

Narrative Elements

Include the elements you find in a story—setting, characters, and events.

Sensory Details

Help your reader imagine seeing, hearing, smelling, tasting, or touching what you experienced.

Teach

Big Idea

Issues of Identity
Say: People establish their identities in different ways. They may identify with aspects of their culture, their race, or their sex. Think about your own identity. **Ask:** How do you identify yourself? What experiences from your past have helped you establish your identity? *(Answers will vary.)* **OL**

★ Cultural History

Joy Harjo Inform students that Joy Harjo is also a musician—she sings and plays the saxophone. Her CD *Native Joy for Real* is a fusion of jazz, reggae, and tribal music mixed with singing, chanting, and poetry. Encourage students to listen to her music online or at a local music store. **AS**

Differentiated Instruction

Less Proficient Writers Less proficient writers may have difficulty pinpointing appropriate topics for their reflective essays. Answering the following questions might help them discover experiences to write about:

• Do you have a special pet? If so, do you remember the day your pet came to live with you?

• Is there a special accomplishment you would like to write about? For example, did you learn a new skill, win a game, or overcome a fear?

• Have you taken a trip to a special place? Could you write about your experiences in this place? **BL**

Objectives
• To write a reflective essay that explores the meaning of a personal experience (SE)
• To narrate the events and describe the experience using sensory details (SE)
• To identify an appropriate topic (TWE)

Writing Workshop

Teach

Writing Skills

Anecdotes Explain: An anecdote is a brief story about a past event. You can use an anecdote to illustrate a point, catch a reader's attention, or support an opinion or assertion. Encourage students to use an anecdote to introduce their reflective essay. Alternatively, they can use an anecdote to conclude their essay. The anecdote will leave the reader with one last impression of the student's experience. **OL**

⭐ Writer's Technique

Metaphor On page 687, Harjo refers to her parents as "omnipresent gods" and to her father as a "handsome god." **Ask:** What figure of speech is Harjo employing in these sentences? *(Harjo is using a metaphor, a figure of speech, to describe her parents as she saw them when she was a young girl.)* **Say:** Think about using metaphors in your own reflective essay. Metaphors can change the tone and direction of your writing in interesting ways. **AS**

Brass Section (Jamming at Minton's), From the Jazz Series, 1979. Romare Bearden. Color lithograph on paper, 24 x 32¾ in. Gift of Eugene Ivan Schuster. Smithsonian American Art Museum, Washington, DC.

Narrative Details
Tell the events in the order in which they occurred.

Descriptive Details
Use comparisons, precise nouns, and active verbs. Strive to show rather than just tell.

Narrative Structure
Make sure your essay has a beginning, middle, and end.

Conclusion
Be sure to tell the meaning of the observation or experience.

I wonder now what signaled this moment, a loop of time that on first glance could be any place in time. I became acutely aware of the line the jazz trumpeter was playing (a sound I later associated with Miles Davis). I didn't know the word *jazz* or *trumpet*, or the concepts. I don't know how to say it, with what sounds or words, but in that confluence of hot southern afternoon, in the breeze of aftershave and humidity, I followed that sound to the beginning, to the place of the birth of sound. I was suspended in whirling stars, a moon to which I'd traveled often by then. I grieved my parents' failings, my own life which I saw stretched the length of that rhapsody.

My rite of passage into the world of humanity occurred then, via jazz. The music made a startling bridge between familiar and strange lands, an appropriate vehicle, for though the music is predominantly west African in concept, with European associations, jazz was influenced by the Creek (or Muscogee) people, for we were there when jazz was born. I recognized it, that humid afternoon in my formative years, as a way to speak beyond the confines of ordinary language. I still hear it.

Reading-Writing Connection Think about the writing techniques that you have just encountered and try them out in the reflective essay you write.

Additional Support

Skills Practice

READING: Identifying Transitions
Using transitions effectively is an important skill in all types of writing. Students can begin learning how to use transitions by identifying them when reading. Ask students to select articles from magazines or journals, to photocopy them, and to bring them to class. As an in-class exercise, have students read through their articles, identifying transitional words and sentences by underlining or highlighting them. Encourage students to share their findings with the rest of the class. **OL**

Prewriting

Find a Topic You need to go back into your past to find a topic. Do this by thinking about different periods of your life. Record important experiences that occurred during each time frame. Be sure that you can find some meaning or significance in each event you list. Then choose the specific memory you like best.

List Details Once you have found a topic for writing, list details that seem to bring that experience or observation to life. You can use a cluster diagram for this purpose. Write your topic in the center and then list the associations, including sensory details, that you have with the experience.

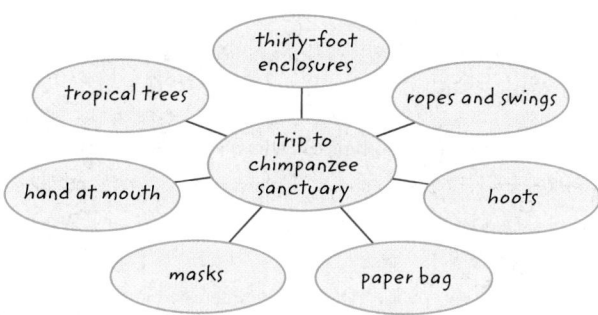

Make a Plan for Writing Your next step is to outline or organize your ideas for writing. One way to do this is by thinking out ideas for the beginning, middle, and end of your reflective essay. Draw a chart, or divide a piece of paper into three rows, and include the following information in each section:

▶ **Beginning**—The beginning of your reflective essay should accomplish the same goals that the beginning of any narrative accomplishes: it may provide important details about the time and place, introduce the characters or people who were important in the experience or observation, or start the action.

▶ **Middle**—The middle of your reflective essay should tell what happened. It may present a series of events or give the details of just one event.

▶ **End**—The end of your reflective essay should accomplish two goals: it should bring the action or events to a close in some way, and it should also state the meaning or significance of the experience.

Talk About Your Ideas Meet with a partner. Explain what your topic is and the significance of the experience you have chosen. Then review your organizational plan with your partner. To develop your writing voice, listen to your speaking voice now as you express the meaning of the experience or its effect on you. Work with your partner to identify words and phrases that reflect your voice and then jot them down.

The Writing Plan as a Test

If you have a topic but cannot develop it into a plan with a clear beginning, middle, and end, start over with a new topic. Prewriting is not a time for developing ideas only! It is also a time for finding out whether ideas for writing will work as essays.

Test Prep

If you have to write a reflective essay for a test, limit the prewriting stage to finding a topic and making a simple beginning-middle-end organizer before you begin your draft.

Differentiated Instruction

Current Articles Encourage students to look through magazines, newspapers, and books for examples of reflective essays. Reflective essays can be found in many sources, including autobiographies, creative nonfiction pieces, editorials, and anthologies. **BL** Challenge advanced students by having them find and analyze two reflective essays. Ask students to compare the essays and to note differences in tone, subject matter, and organization. **AL**

Teach

Writing Process

Prewriting As students gather ideas about an experience for their reflective essay, have them jot down sensory details that come to mind. **Say:** If you are writing about a particular time of year, remember the weather and temperature. If you are writing about a favorite meal or treat, think of words that describe how it tasted. If you are writing about playing a sport or an instrument, write down words that show how you felt when engaging in these activities. Remind students to include sensory details in the first draft of their reflective essay. **OL**

Writing Skills

Narrating Events When drafting their essay, some students might find it helpful to narrate orally to another student the experience they are writing about. Hearing their words aloud sometimes helps students focus on the tone and the direction they want to take in their essay.

Pair off students. Have one student in each pair take notes while the other narrates his or her essay. Then ask students to change places to repeat the activity. Have them check to ensure that their partner's essay has an introduction, a body, and a conclusion. **OL**

Objectives

• To analyze a professional model (SE)
• To identify transitions (TWE)

689

Teach

Writing Skills

Narrative Elements
Answers: *Students should mention setting, character, and perhaps dialogue.* **OL**

Writing Skills

First-Person Point of View
Answers: *The pronoun I shows that this essay is written from the first-person point of view.* **OL**

Writing Skills

Sensory Details **Answers:**
Possible responses: "glazed eyes"; "shifting from foot to foot"; "thirty-foot high domed enclosures"; "guava, banana, and other tropical trees" **OL**

Writing Skills

Narrative Details **Answers:**
Narrative details include the sequence of events (walking around, observing, and sketching), description of the setting, and characterization of the narrator and Tommy, in contrast to other students. **OL**

Drafting

Create a Structure As you write your ideas on paper in the form of sentences and paragraphs, remember that your essay should have a clear beginning, middle, and end. In some cases, you may be able to achieve this in just three paragraphs, one for each part of this essay. It is also fine to develop two or more paragraphs for the middle of your reflective essay and to add a full paragraph of reflection after the narrative.

Analyzing a Workshop Model

Here is a final draft of a reflective essay. Read the essay and answer the questions in the margin. Use the answers to these questions to guide you as you write.

Changed by a Chimp

"Tomorrow," Mrs. Dagostino announced enthusiastically, "we'll be visiting the Center for Great Apes." She continued brightly, "This is a very special opportunity for us. Not many people are allowed to visit, you know! I've waited two years to take a class there!"

"Who cares?" I thought. I wasn't the least bit interested in looking at a bunch of old chimps. Mrs. Dagostino then explained that this was a place for "retired" chimps—chimps that had been used in entertainment and research and were now no longer useful to the human beings that had kept them. "A retirement home for chimps," I groaned. "How ridiculous!"

Tommy and I were the last ones out of the school bus when we arrived at the sanctuary the next day. The guide was droning on about the "special enriching environment" and "complex primates." With glazed eyes, I shifted from foot to foot and thought about last night's soccer practice. The thirty-foot-high domed enclosures surrounded by guava, banana, and other tropical trees were about as interesting to me as twelve extra pages of math homework.

When we were finally allowed to walk around the perimeter of the chimps' enclosure, some students stopped to do what we had been instructed to do: observe the chimps' behaviors, take notes, and discuss what we saw. Chatting quietly, these students were noticing the separate daytime and nighttime areas for the chimps, as well as their ropes, swings, and hammocks. Some were also listening to the various hoots and calls, while others sketched the animals. Tommy and I talked about soccer.

Narrative Elements

What elements found in stories do you find in this paragraph?

First-Person Point of View

Which pronoun tells the reader that this essay is written from the first-person point of view?

Sensory Details

Which sensory details help you experience what the narrator experienced?

Narrative Details

What narrative, or story-telling, details do you find in this paragraph?

690 UNIT 3 POETRY

Skills Practice

WRITING: Active Versus Passive Voice Say: Strong writing is direct, and in nearly all cases active voice, rather than passive voice, creates more energy in your writing. Use passive voice only when you do not know the doer of the action or when you want to emphasize the receiver of an action or the action itself. Write the following sentence and similar ones on the board and have students convert them from passive to active voice: *Ahmed was sent by the teacher to the principal's office. (The teacher sent Ahmed to the principal's office.)* Encourage students to be aware of active and passive voice in their reading and writing. **OL**

When we were halfway around the perimeter, I noticed a chimp that seemed to be communicating with two adult visitors. I watched as the chimp picked up a brown bag that had been left in its enclosure. Using his hands, the chimp tore the bag into a piece of paper about six inches by eight inches. Then he tore an opening in one end. When he held the paper up to his face, I realized that he had created a mask. One of the visitors brought her hand to her mouth and closed her eyes. I knew that she saw and felt what I saw and felt at that moment: the animal behind the fence was, in some way, speaking to us.

The chimp handed the mask through the fence to the visitors and then made a second mask. In a few minutes, the visitors and the chimp were looking at each other through these torn bags. They were also, I understood, silently communicating. I just stood there thinking what it must be like for this "complex primate" to be used for research purposes or to live its life in any enclosure—even one as nice as the one provided by the Center for Great Apes.

The Center for Great Apes is not a zoo. Since few visitors are allowed in and visits are limited in duration, it was soon time to go. As we walked along the outside of the enclosure, the chimp companionably accompanied us as far as he could, trailing his right hand along the fence on his side. I felt as if he were saying goodbye to us.

I never said goodbye because, in fact, I never left that chimp behind. Three days later, it was my report about visiting the Center for Great Apes that Mrs. Dagostino read aloud to the class. The following summer, I enrolled in a special summer program that focused on chimpanzees and orangutans. And next year, when I apply to college, I am going to look for a school where I can study primates. Whatever chimps may have to tell us, I plan on finding out.

Descriptive Details
Explain how the writer shows, rather than tells, parts of his experience.

Tone
How would you describe the author's tone? How has it changed?

Narrative Structure
Identify the beginning, the middle, and the end of this essay.

Conclusion
What realization does the writer come to as a result of his observations and experiences?

Teach

Writing Skills

Descriptive Details

Answers: *To show the visitor's reaction to the mask, the writer might have stated directly that she was stunned. Instead, sensory details ("brought her hand to her mouth and closed her eyes" and "stood as if . . . wearing cement sneakers") convey the woman's astonishment.* **OL**

Writing Skills

Tone Answers: *Students might describe the tone as serious, full of awe, respectful, or reflective. This is a strong change from the earlier tone of indifference.* **OL**

Writing Skills

Narrative Structure

Answers: *Beginning: the announcement about the class visit to the sanctuary; middle: the negative attitude of the narrator and his friend; end: the series of events leading to the narrator's reversal of attitude* **OL**

Writing Skills

Conclusion Answers: *The narrator realizes how interesting chimpanzees are and decides to study primates.* **OL**

English Language Coach

Narration Because of the structure of the English language, English speakers tend to narrate stories in a linear fashion. It is important to explain that many cultures and languages do not have such linear tendencies and that this must be taken into account when teaching English language learners. Sometimes stories told by English language learners may seem rambling and disorganized. Remaining sensitive to different narrative strategies of various cultural groups will enhance both teaching and learning. **EL**

Objectives
• To analyze a workshop model (SE)
• To understand active and passive voice (TWE)

691

Teach

Writing Process

Revising Remind students that good writers take as much care in writing their conclusions as they do in writing their entire essays. Encourage students to pay careful attention to their concluding sentences, as readers remember best what they read last. **Say:** There are a number of ways you can effectively conclude your essay. For example, you might use an anecdote or close with a quotation. Whatever you choose, remember the importance of the last few sentences of your essay. **OL**

★ Writer's Technique

Reading Aloud Effective writers frequently read their writing aloud in the revising stage. Often, awkward phrases and confusing references come to light as the piece is read aloud. Students can practice this technique by reading the piece either to themselves or to others for comment. **AS**

Traits of Strong Writing

Ideas message or theme and the details that develop it

Organization arrangement of main ideas and supporting details

Voice writer's unique way of using tone and style

Word Choice vocabulary a writer uses to convey meaning

Sentence Fluency rhythm and flow of sentences

Conventions correct spelling, grammar, usage, and mechanics

Presentation the way words and design elements look on a page

For more information on using the Traits of Strong Writing, see pages R33–R34 of the Writing Handbook.

Revising

Peer Review When you finish your draft, have a peer reviewer read it. Ask him or her to identify narrative and descriptive elements in your writing. Then ask your reviewer to make suggestions about where to add background information, sensory details, or reflection. Also ask your reviewer to study the traits of strong writing, and to think about how they apply to your work.

Use the rubric below to help you evaluate your writing.

Rubric: Writing an Effective Reflective Essay

☑ Do you reflect, or look back on, a meaningful experience?

☑ Do you use the first-person point of view throughout your essay?

☑ Do you have a clear beginning, middle, and end?

☑ Do you use sensory details, precise nouns, and action verbs?

☑ Do you make the meaning of your experience clear to your reader?

☑ Is your tone appropriate for your subject?

▶ **Focus Lesson**

Using Sensory Details

Sensory details are words or phrases that appeal to one of the five senses. It is never necessary to use sensory details that appeal to all five senses—especially when they simply do not fit! Sensory details that are appropriate for the time, characters, place, and events enrich any narrative, however. Note how well-chosen sensory details improve the passage from the Workshop Model below.

Draft:

These students were doing everything we had been told to do.

Revision:

Chatting quietly,[1] these students were noticing the separate daytime and nighttime areas for the chimps, as well as their ropes, swings, and hammocks.[2] Some were also listening to the various hoots and calls,[3] while others sketched the animals.

1: Appeals to Hearing   **2:** Appeals to Sight   **3:** Appeals to Hearing

---

Additional Support

Skills Practice

WRITING: Punctuating Quotations Students may be using dialogue in their reflective essays. Remind them to correctly punctuate dialogue. Discuss the following rules:

- Use double quotation marks to enclose direct quotations from speakers or writers.

- Place commas and periods that follow quotations inside the quotation marks.

- If an exclamation or question mark belongs to a quotation, place it inside the quotation marks.

- Put colons and semicolons outside of quotation marks. **BL**

Editing and Proofreading

Get It Right When you have completed the final draft of your reflective essay, proofread it for errors in grammar, usage, mechanics, and spelling. Refer to the Language Handbook, pages R46–R60, as a guide.

> **Focus Lesson**

Correcting Unclear Pronoun References

A pronoun must refer to a noun or another pronoun. Often, it refers to a noun that appears earlier in the sentence. To be clear, it should refer to the closest noun or pronoun in the sentence or a previous sentence. Below are examples of unclear pronoun references and corrections.

Problem: Unclear Pronoun Reference

The pronoun *them* refers to the antecedent *the visitors and the chimp,* yet the writer intends the pronoun *them* to refer to the masks.

[He] then made a second mask. In a few minutes, the visitors and the chimp were looking at each other through them.

Solution A: Replace the pronoun with the exact noun to which it refers.

[He] then made a second mask. In a few minutes, the visitors and the chimp were looking at each other through these torn bags.

Solution B: Rewrite the sentence so that the pronoun clearly refers to a previous noun or pronoun.

He then made a second mask. In a few minutes, one visitor looked through it at the chimp while the chimp eyed the visitor through the first mask.

Problem: Unclear Pronoun Reference

The pronoun *They* does not refer to any specific person, place, or thing.

They say that chimps have a lot to tell us, so I plan on learning more about them.

Solution: Rewrite the sentence to eliminate the pronoun.

Whatever chimps may have to tell us, I plan on finding out.

Presenting

Do Not Rely on Your Spell-check Feature Never rely on a computer's spell-check feature to do the whole job of proofreading. A spell-checker has limited use, because it cannot distinguish certain kinds of errors, such as misused homonyms. After using the spell-checker, reread your paper to catch additional errors.

Look for Transitions

During the revising and proofreading stages, always add a separate step for checking transitions. Be sure that you have inserted words and phrases that help readers follow the order of events as well as the relationships between ideas.

Proofread for Common Errors

Some of the most common errors in writing include confusing *its* and *it's; they're, their,* and *there; who's* and *whose; your* and *you're; than* and *then;* and *effect* and *affect.* Check for and correct these common errors.

Writer's Portfolio

Place a copy of your reflective essay in your portfolio to review later.

Teach

Writing Process

Editing and Proofreading

While they are editing and proofreading their essays, have students look for and, if necessary, correct these common errors:

it's = it is
its = possessive pronoun
there = a place
their = possessive pronoun
effect = result (n.)
affect = influence (v.) **BL**

Writing Process

Presenting Before students turn in a final draft, encourage them to take the time to create a title that captures the essence of their essay, as well as the reader's attention. **Say:** Don't let your title be an afterthought. Good titles are brief but interesting. Sometimes writers use a phrase from the essay itself as the title. Try to create a title that is inviting to the reader. **OL**

Differentiated Instruction

Pronoun References Less proficient writers may have trouble recognizing cases of unclear pronoun reference in their own work. Have these students go through their reflective essays, circling each pronoun. Then have them circle, in a different color, the antecedent of each pronoun. Wherever there is a pronoun without an expressed antecedent or a pronoun whose relation to its antecedent is obscured by intervening words, they should revise their writing to eliminate the problem. **BL**

Objectives
- To use sensory details (SE)
- To correct unclear pronoun references (SE)
- To punctuate quotations (TWE)

693

Focus

Summary

In this workshop, students will learn techniques for planning and presenting a reflective essay to the class.

Teach

Speaking Skills

Organization Clear and logical organization is important for a speech. If students are telling about events, chronological organization may be logical. Provide these tips about organization:

- Keep your message clear.
- Keep your message simple.
- Make your presentation colorful.
- Have a strong opener and closer.
- Use clear transitions. **OL**

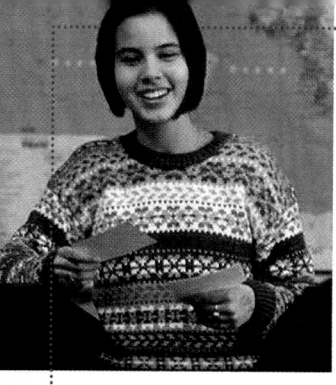

Choosing a Tone

If you are reflecting on a serious or sad experience, you will probably choose a formal tone. For less somber reflections, however, consider a conversational tone. You can include everyday expressions with a relaxed, person-to-person tone to draw your listeners in.

Speaking, Listening, and Viewing Workshop

Reflection

Presenting a Reflective Essay

Connecting to Literature Poet Joy Harjo expresses herself and her Cherokee and Creek heritage through music, art, and words. She has a band called Poetic Justice; she also paints and pursues other visual arts. According to Harjo, she approaches the art of poetry as a visual artist. In fact, any written work can be delivered, changed, or enhanced with the addition of visual aids and music. In this workshop, you will present a reflection that uses visuals to help express the events and their significance.

> **Assignment** Create an oral presentation of your reflective essay about an observation and deliver it to an audience.

Planning Your Presentation

Presenting an essay orally is not the same thing as simply reading it aloud. It is a chance to use your voice, body language, and visual aids to communicate meaning to an audience in a way that involves both listening and viewing.

- Begin by reading your essay aloud to yourself. As you read, think about your audience. Ask yourself which parts of your essay will be most interesting, which will be hardest to understand, and which might lend themselves to visual interpretation.
- Next, make notes. For example, circle or highlight the details, the dialogue, and the descriptions that you consider most effective and important. Underline anything that you think can be cut, needs more explanation, or will drag down your presentation. Jot down ideas for visuals in the margins.
- Revise your essay to make it a spoken script. In the script, retain all of your best details, dialogue, and descriptions. Expand them and enliven them. Omit details that contribute little to an overall impression or a theme. Add brief, interesting bits of explanation wherever they are needed.
- Finally, make note cards. After you rehearse and learn your presentation, these cards will serve as reminders or cues during your delivery.

— practice the gestures you will make during your presentation
— make eye contact with your audience members

Skills Practice

SPEAKING: Using Visual Aids
Discuss how to use visual aids most effectively in a presentation. Have students practice these techniques:

- Test your visual aids to make sure that everyone will be able to see them.
- Rehearse the timing of when to show the visual aids.

- Introduce visual aids before showing them.
- Keep talking as you show the visuals.
- Look at the audience, not the visuals.
- When a visual is not being used, keep it hidden from the audience so that they are not distracted. **OL**

Creating Your Visual Media

As you create your script and note cards, concentrate on the images you want to display or project. There are many options for visual aids—drawings, collages, photographs, and video. You can also incorporate colors, shapes, and designs into your project to represent a feeling or mood. Because you are telling a story, one way to plan your visuals is by sequencing images along a plot diagram.

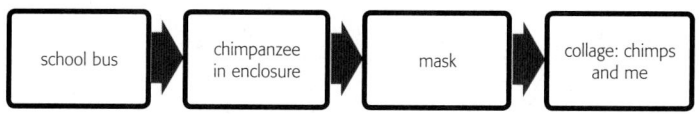

Once you have a plan, assemble your images in order and write brief prompts on your note cards that cue you to display each one at the right time.

Rehearsing

Never deliver an oral presentation without rehearsing it several times.

▶ You can rehearse your presentation the first few times by yourself. Get used to using your note cards as prompts and learn your presentation thoroughly. Be sure to practice the actual gestures you will use.

▶ Next, practice in front of a classmate or a family member. Ask your listener to comment on the effectiveness of each of the verbal and nonverbal techniques listed in the chart below. If possible, rehearse once more in front of the same person, incorporating his or her suggestions.

Verbal Techniques	Nonverbal Techniques
☑ **Tone** Whether your subject is light or serious, show your interest.	☑ **Visibility** Be sure that everyone can see your presentation.
☑ **Emphasis** Stress important words, details, and dialogue.	☑ **Eye Contact** Make eye contact with your audience.
☑ **Pronunciation** Make sure to pronounce each word distinctly.	☑ **Posture** Avoid leaning or slouching.
☑ **Volume** Be sure to speak loudly enough that everyone can hear you.	☑ **Gestures** Strike a balance between standing stiffly and making too many movements.
☑ **Emphasis** Stress important words and ideas.	☑ **Visual Aids** Use a photograph, collage, or computer presentation.

Videotape

Videotape your performance. Determine which areas need improvement.

Take Control

It is normal to be nervous during an oral presentation. Practice techniques that professionals use to overcome anxiety: being well prepared, dressing neatly and feeling good about their appearances, breathing deeply, and visualizing successful outcomes.

OBJECTIVES
- Orally narrate a series of events and communicate their significance to an audience.
- Produce concise notes for extemporaneous delivery.
- Enhance the presentation with visual aids.

English Language Coach

Speaking Practice Pair a student acquiring English with another student to practice giving presentations. Encourage students to rehearse repeatedly so that they are well prepared. Invite partners to offer constructive feedback. **EL**

Differentiated Instruction

Videotaping For students who need to build speaking skills, use a videotaping exercise in which students watch themselves deliver a speech and then set goals for improving their speaking. Make sure they pay attention to both the content of the speech and the delivery. **BL**

Teach

Speaking Skills

Using a Script Since reading a script without looking at the audience makes for a dull speech, help students learn to use a script as a guide, glancing at it only occasionally. Tell students it is essential to be well prepared and to know the speech thoroughly. Highlighting key words can help to provide reminders of main points, and note cards with key phrases can serve as cues. Both also help make students feel confident. **OL**

Listening Skills

Improve Listening Skills Advise students to practice good listening skills during other students' presentations. Provide these tips:

- Maintain eye contact with the speaker to stay involved.
- Stay focused and avoid distractions.
- Treat listening as an active, rather than a passive, process.
- Listen for main ideas.
- Ask yourself questions to stay involved, such as, What point is the speaker making?
- Sit up straight, pay attention, and give appropriate responses. **OL**

Objectives
- To orally narrate events (SE)
- To produce concise notes for extemporaneous delivery (SE)
- To enhance a presentation with visual aids (TWE)

695

Focus

Summary

The purpose of this feature is to interest students in reading more poetry or longer works related to the themes of this unit. Middle Eastern and Japanese haiku poets treat compelling topics, and a handbook encourages students to delve into writing poetry. A play and two novels range from classic to contemporary.

Teach

★ Literary History

Naomi Shihab Nye The child of an American mother and a Palestinian father, Naomi Shihab Nye lives with her family in Texas, where she graduated from Trinity University. She was a National Book Award finalist for *19 Varieties of Gazelle: Poems of the Middle East* and has won numerous other awards. She has edited seven highly praised poetry anthologies, and her poetry volumes include *Hugging the Jukebox, Fuel,* and *Red Suitcase.* **AS**

Poetry and Novels

POETRY IS THE MOST CONCENTRATED, abbreviated genre. In relatively few words, a poet may present the same themes that a novelist explores over hundreds of pages. As you have seen in this unit, poetry ranges from momentary glimpses of the natural world to longer, serious reflections on love and grief. For more poetry on a range of themes, as well as a book on how to write your own poetry, try the first three suggestions below. For novels and a play that incorporate the Big Ideas of *The Energy of the Everyday, Loves and Losses,* and *Issues of Identity,* try the titles from the Glencoe Literature Library on the next page.

The Space Between Our Footsteps: Poems and Paintings from the Middle East

selected by Naomi Shihab Nye

This collection of works from more than one hundred poets and artists from nineteen Middle Eastern countries explores themes that include family, childhood, journeys, war, peace, and joy. Award-winning poet and anthologist Naomi Shihab Nye pairs poems with full-color art from the countries represented. Nye's respect for and appreciation of Middle Eastern culture saturates the book. Yet, the overall effect of the anthology is one that emphasizes the similarities between people.

A Haiku Menagerie: Living Creatures in Poems and Prints

by Stephen Addiss with Fumiko and Akira Yamamoto

Showing how fascinating the smallest animal or insect can be, this collection of over one-hundred Japanese haiku features master poets' insights into the natural world. More than forty-eight woodblock prints illustrate the creatures described in the poems. The poems are presented both in English translations and the original Japanese.

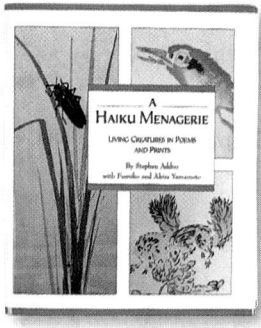

696 UNIT 3 POETRY

Additional Support

Skills Practice

WRITING: Poetry Encourage students to try their hands at writing poetry. One way to stimulate interest is to talk about song lyrics as poetry. Ask students to discuss high-impact or thought-provoking lines, as well as poetic devices. Then urge students to write their own lyrics or poems based on their observations, experiences, and journal entries. You might also provide some subject ideas, such as a winter day, a cafeteria scene, or a response to a poem in this unit. Read aloud passages from Mary Oliver's *A Poetry Handbook* to inspire and guide students in writing poetry. **OL**

CRITICS' CORNER

"Mary Oliver would probably never admit to anything so grandiose as an effort to connect the conscious mind and the heart (that's what she says poetry can do), but that is exactly what she accomplishes in this stunning little handbook, ostensibly written 'to empower the beginning writer. . . .' Oliver gives us tools for 'the listening mind,' tools we need to write poetry."

—Susan Salter Reynolds, the *Los Angeles Times Book Review*

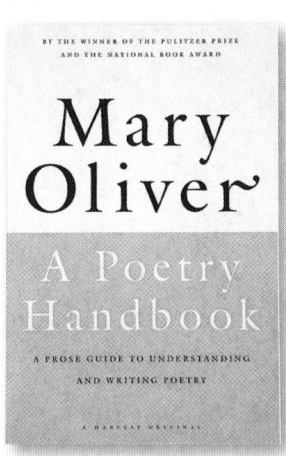

A Poetry Handbook

by Mary Oliver

In this highly readable handbook, Oliver reminds aspiring poets about sound, line, and diction and demonstrates that "out of writing, and the rewriting, beauty is born." Citing works from other poets, such as Elizabeth Bishop, T. S. Eliot, William Carlos Williams, and Lucille Clifton, Oliver reveals that writing good poetry is a craft. She urges would-be poets to take care of the special place within them that "houses the possibility of poems."

From the Glencoe Literature Library

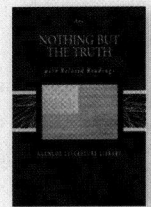

Nothing But the Truth: A Documentary Novel

By Avi

A simple action gives new meaning to *the energy of the everyday* and leads to a national scandal.

Cyrano de Bergerac

by Edmond Rostand ★

A poetic play about *loves and losses* features love, deception, and heartbreak.

Picture Bride

by Yoshiko Uchida

In this novel about *issues of identity*, a woman leaves Japan to marry a stranger in San Francisco.

Teach

★ Literary History

Cyrano de Bergerac

Written in 1897 by French playwright Edmond Rostand, this classic play portrays a tragic love story in keeping with the Big Idea of Loves and Losses. The play explores the theme of external and internal beauty as well. Ashamed of his unattractive appearance, Cyrano helps a friend woo Cyrano's own beloved, Roxane. Although less proficient readers may find this play difficult to understand, they may be motivated to make connections with the 1987 film *Roxanne,* a modern-day adaptation. **AS**

Glencoe Literature Library

Glencoe Literature Library offers an extensive collection of hardcover books that help you encourage your students to read independently. Choose among the more than 120 full-length literary works—novels, novellas, plays, and nonfiction. Each book includes related readings from a broad range of genres. Go to www.Glencoe.com for more information.

Objectives
- To encourage independent reading of poetry and novels (SE)
- To encourage students to write poetry (TWE)

Building Reading Fluency

Paired Reading Pair less proficient readers with more skilled readers to read poems aloud from one of the recommended anthologies. You might begin with both students reading together; the less skilled reader may start to read alone when he or she feels ready. The more skilled reader can correct misread words before continuing with the other student. Another strategy for building reading fluency is for the less skilled reader to practice reading the poem silently while listening to the other student and then to read the poem aloud. **BL**

Focus

BELLRINGER

Say: Practicing test-taking strategies is beneficial in many ways. It can help you in school and with real-world activities such as driving tests and job applications. Review study, time-management, and test-taking strategies students have learned. Invite students to comment on strategies that have been effective for them.

✎ Or use **Bellringer Option Transparency.**

Teach

Assessment Explain to students that Test Preparation and Practice helps them to practice and master the skills and vocabulary taught in the unit. First, they will read a poem and a prose selection and answer comprehension questions. Then they will use their vocabulary knowledge as they select words to complete sentences. They will also use grammar and writing skills as they rewrite a passage. Finally they will write a short essay comparing tone or voice in two poems. **OL**

Additional Support

698

Test Preparation and Practice

English–Language Arts

Reading: Poetry and Fiction

Carefully read the following two passages. Use context clues to help you define any words with which you are unfamiliar. Pay close attention to the themes, tones, and uses of literary and sound devices. Then, on a separate sheet of paper, answer the questions on pages 699–700.

"Daybreak in Alabama" by Langston Hughes

When I get to be a composer
I'm gonna write me some music about
Daybreak in Alabama
And I'm gonna put the purtiest songs in it
5 Rising out of the ground like a swamp mist
And falling out of heaven like soft dew.
I'm gonna put some tall tall trees in it
And the scent of pine needles
And the smell of red clay after rain
10 And long red necks
And poppy colored faces
And big brown arms
And the field daisy eyes
Of black and white black white black people
15 And I'm gonna put white hands
And black hands and brown and yellow hands
And red clay earth hands in it
Touching everybody with kind fingers
And touching each other natural as dew
20 In that dawn of music when I
Get to be a composer
And write about daybreak
In Alabama.

from "Red Velvet Dress" by Naomi Shihab Nye

In the next neighborhood over from their neighborhood lived the
Collins boys and the Parker boys that Lena knew from their jobs together
working on the berry-picking farm and the Emerson girls who spent
every Saturday morning at the library like Lena did and sometimes they
5 all traded favorite books and the big grandmother with the high hair that

Skills Practice

LITERARY ELEMENT: Imagery and Theme Emphasize that imagery shapes the theme of a poem or story. Have students point out the color imagery Hughes uses. **Ask:** What impression do the images convey? *(They suggest harmony and hopefulness about the future.)* Then discuss the images Naomi Shihab Nye uses. **Ask:** What effect do images about people such as Billy Collins and Annie's grandfather have? *(Details make both characters seem real and believable.)* **Ask:** How do images reveal the theme of the story? *(They show the need to see people as individuals, not just members of a group.)* **OL**

Lena's mother stared at once in the grocery checkout line. "I should have been her," she whispered to Lena, which Lena found very strange. How could anybody be anyone else? But Lena would never go to their houses and ask to see the Africans.

10 Because once you knew Billy Collins, you knew about his lizard collection and his turquoise stone that he kept in a pouch inside an egg carton with old pennies worth ten dollars each and the rusted key he dug out of the ground one day while they were plucking the berries. You knew his voice and shirts. You did not think A Group of Different People, 15 when you were thinking of friends.

Maybe the Robitailles weren't even like any other French-Canadians at all. Maybe Annie's grandfather who snapped his suspenders and brought them a fancy cold dessert called Tiramisu which he carried on ice cubes in his green car was just himself more than An Italian. In those 20 days not many people talked about being half-and-half, but years later Lena would know it was one of the richest kinds of milk.

So her father burned the dry leaves and a bat flew over him. Lena called out, "Bat! Daddy! Look, it's not a bird!" and he looked up. *"Ahlan wa sahlan,"* he called out, which meant "Welcome" in his own 25 first language of Arabic, and she laughed as the bat dipped and rose in graceful arcs. He did not say, Get away. He did not say, I wish you were something else. He said "Welcome" and the bat seemed to understand by circling close above his head.

Then she took a deep breath and called out to him. "Daddy, some 30 children came to the door. They wanted to see the Arab and I said we didn't have one. I never saw them on this street before. I never saw them at school either. But they might be from school. Are you mad at me?"

And her father came and sat beside her and took her hand in his own hand.

35 Her father said, "The world asks us all a lot of questions, doesn't it," and stared off into a strip of pink sky.

Then there was the clatter-bang muffler sound of Peter's father turning into his driveway next door.

Lena thought his feelings might be hurt. She said, "I'm sorry," and 40 her daddy laughed so loudly he startled her.

"You could have said Yes, but you were also right in saying No! All the questions have more than one good answer, don't you think? I could have put on my headdress for them! You could have pretended I didn't speak English. Maybe they'll come back and we can make them happy."

Questions 1–7 apply to "Daybreak in Alabama."

1 What literary device is used in "like a swamp mist," in line 5, and in "like soft dew," in line 6?
A simile
B personification
C metaphor
D hyperbole

2 What literary device is used in the poem's first six lines?
A end rhyme
B couplets
C enjambment
D alliteration

Assess

Reading

1. Option **A** is the correct answer. In each phrase, two essentially dissimilar things are compared by means of the word *like.*

2. Option **C** is the correct answer. The sense and grammatical construction of the thought extend beyond the ends of the lines.

Differentiated Instruction

Previewing Explain that an effective strategy for test taking is to preview a selection, gaining meaning from the title, text structure, and patterns. Have students preview "Daybreak in Alabama," noticing the title, the parallel beginning and ending, and the repetition of *and* at the beginning of lines. **BL**

Metaphor Review with less proficient readers the definition of *metaphor,* "an indirect comparison between two unlike things." Point out Hughes's metaphor "dawn of music" and Nye's metaphor "one of the richest kinds of milk." Ask students to explain the metaphors. **BL**

Assess

Reading

3. Option **A** is the correct answer. The speaker expresses his hopes for a better future.

4. Option **C** is the correct answer. The poem portrays someone who wants to change society.

5. Option **D** is the correct answer. A southern dialect characterizes much of the poem.

6. Option **B** is the correct answer. Option D does not suggest change or the image of newness. Options A and C are unrelated to the words *daybreak* and *dawn.*

7. Option **A** is the correct answer. The speaker describes people's intermingling. Options B and C are simplistic. Option D contradicts the poem's theme.

8. Option **C** is the correct answer. The narration is written according to Lena's perceptions of the world.

9. Option **B** is the correct answer. The fourth paragraph clearly states that Arabic is his first language.

3 What is the overall tone of the poem?
   A hopeful
   B tragic
   C comic
   D mysterious

4 Twice the speaker says, "when I get to be a composer." From the context, which of the following do you think best expresses the meaning of this statement?
   A The speaker wants to compose but doubts that this is possible.
   B The speaker has means, but little hope, of achieving his goals.
   C The speaker has high hopes for the future.
   D The speaker is an impractical dreamer.

5 What type of language is used in the poem? Consider the phrases "gonna write me," in line 2, and "purtiest songs," in line 4.
   A formal language
   B figurative language
   C grammatical language
   D dialect

6 What do the words *daybreak* and *dawn*, in Hughes's poem, evoke?
   A harmony in life
   B a new beginning
   C the end of an era
   D joyousness

7 Which of the following statements best describes the theme of the poem?
   A The speaker dreams of a world without divisions.
   B The landscape of Alabama stirs the speaker to write music.
   C The speaker anticipates living in a world of music.
   D The speaker despairs of racial unity.

Questions 8–15 apply to "Red Velvet Dress."

8 From what point of view is the selection written?
   A first person
   B second person
   C third-person limited
   D third-person omniscient

9 What is the first language of Lena's father?
   A English
   B Arabic
   C French
   D Italian

10 According to this passage, how many other members are in Lena's family?
   A one
   B two
   C three
   D four

11 What literary device is used in lines 27–28, in saying that the bat "seemed to understand"?
   A personification
   B metaphor
   C simile
   D literary comparison

12 What is the overall mood of this passage?
   A bitter
   B miserable
   C melancholy
   D comic

13 Which of the following sound devices is *clatter-bang*, in line 37?
   A alliteration
   B onomatopoeia
   C rhyme
   D consonance

14 What is the central problem that Lena struggles to overcome?
   A her confusion over her father's ideas
   B her fear of bats
   C her distress over people's prejudice
   D her fear of her father

15 What common theme appears in both the poem by Hughes and the passage by Nye?
   A Both passages have a negative message.
   B Both passages have optimistic narrators.
   C The writers of both passages use free verse.
   D Both passages relate to coping with inequality.

10. Option **B** is the correct answer. Lena's mother and father are the only other family members mentioned.

11. Option **A** is the correct answer. The father's statement attributes human qualities to a nonhuman being.

12. Option **C** is the correct answer. The young girl faces racism but seems neither bitter nor miserable. The overall mood is not comic.

13. Option **B** is the correct answer. *Clatter-bang* mimics a noisy, rattling sound.

14. Option **C** is the correct answer. It is evident from the passage that Lena does not understand why people are prejudiced.

15. Option **D** is the correct answer. Options A, B, and C do not express common themes.

Vocabulary Skills: Sentence Completion

For each item in the Vocabulary Skills section, choose the word that best completes the sentence.

1 The child soon learned that his _____ comments did not improve, but in fact worsened, his situation.
A embroidered
B meticulous
C querulous
D hoary

2 The _____ heat made it difficult for us to enjoy our summer vacation.
A dense
B hoary
C searing
D embroidered

3 Erin would no longer tolerate her employee's _____ tardiness.
A chronic
B disgruntled
C primal
D ceremonious

4 Walter could not _____ precisely when he had learned to read.
A marvel
B lag
C recollect
D tread

5 Although many in the crowd were quite _____ to the game's outcome, they cheered wildly anyway.
A austere
B melancholy
C indifferent
D serpentine

6 As the days passed into years, his memories of the farm faded into _____.
A conflagration
B oblivion
C essence
D stupor

7 The _____ on the cave wall was mysterious; its significance could not be determined.
A hones
B infirmity
C oblivion
D glyph

8 When Judy studied Chinese, she struggled with the differences in its _____ from that of English.
A syntax
B parenthesis
C fissure
D cipher

9 The house was _____ with dozens of candles, lit in celebration of the holiday.
A mature
B aglow
C submerged
D primal

10 When Aileen visited her parents, she became _____ about her childhood.
A ceremonious
B meticulous
C russet
D nostalgic

Literature Online **Unit Assessment** To prepare for the Unit test, go to www.glencoe.com.

TEST PREPARATION AND PRACTICE **701**

Assess

Vocabulary Skills

1. Option **C** is the correct answer. No other option makes sense here.

2. Option **C** is the correct answer. No other option can describe heat.

3. Option **A** is the correct answer. Option B makes some sense, but the words no longer suggest an ongoing problem. No other option makes sense here.

4. Option **C** is the correct answer. The past tense is the clue. No other option makes sense here.

5. Option **C** is the correct answer. The word *anyway* suggests contrast.

6. Option **B** is the correct answer. No other option makes sense.

7. Option **D** is the correct answer. No other option makes sense here.

8. Option **A** is the correct answer. No other option makes sense here.

9. Option **B** is the correct answer. No other option makes sense here.

10. Option **D** is the correct answer. The word *childhood* is the clue. Option A comes close, but nothing here suggests ceremony or ritual.

Unit Assessment Have students access the Web site to prepare for the Unit 3 test.

English Language Coach

Word Parts Tell students that word parts can help them define unfamiliar words. Point out the word *submerged*, for example. **Ask:** What does the prefix *sub-* reveal? (*Sub- means "below."*) Review other affixes from words in the poems, such as the prefix *un-* and the suffix *-less.* **EL**

Differentiated Instruction

Context Clues Point out the contrast in the fifth question, which distinguishes between the crowd's attitude and their enthusiastic cheering. Remind students that words such as *although, however, despite, but,* and *instead* indicate a contrast and provide clues for sentence completion tests. **BL**

701

Assess

Grammar and Writing Skills

1. Option **C** is the correct answer. In the relative clause describing the astronomer, the pronoun *whom* should be in the subjective case.

2. Option **B** is the correct answer. This option correctly inserts the subjective pronoun *who* as the subject of the clause.

3. Option **B** is the correct answer. The pronoun *which*, which refers to a thing, must be replaced with the pronoun *who* so that it correctly refers to the subject, *the narrator.*

4. Option **A** is the correct answer. The subject pronoun *He*, which is also the sentence subject, is singular; and the verb *seem* is plural.

Grammar and Writing Skills: Paragraph Improvement

Carefully read the following draft of a student's essay. Pay close attention to sentence structure and pronoun use. Then, on a separate sheet of paper, answer the questions on pages 702–703.

(1) *Walt Whitman's poem "When I Heard the Learn'd Astronomer" contrasts two distinct philosophies of life.* (2) *The astronomer, whom understands things by dissecting them, takes the scientific approach to life.* (3) *In opposition, the narrator, which represents the creative or poetic side, is a more romantic character.* (4) *He seem satisfied just to appreciate the world around him.*

(5) *As the poem begins, he describes the astronomer's lecture, in which he cites "proofs and figures" and "charts and diagrams."* (6) *The astronomer has gone to great lengths to understand and classify the information.* (7) *The narrator soon becomes bored with all the details and leaves: he "wandered off by himself" into the "night-air."* (8) *Once he's outside in the "mystical" night, he seems content as he looks up in "perfect silence at the stars."* (9) *The narrator, or poet, does not need the astronomer's charts and formulas to understand what he sees in the sky.*

(10) *Whitman shows us through the poem that life is mechanical and orderly just as its beautiful.* (11) *But as readers we learn only the narrator's point of view, so we are closer to that than to the astronomer.* (12) *In the end, personal experience is more to be valued than abstract and analytical theories.*

1 Which of the following errors occurs in sentence 2?
   A sentence fragment
   B verb tense error
   C incorrect pronoun
   D unclear antecedent

2 Which of the following is the best way to revise sentence 2?
   A Delete the nonessential interrupting clause.
   B Change *whom* to *who*.
   C Change the voice of the sentence.
   D Make no change.

3 Which of the following is the best way to revise sentence 3?
   A Change *which* to *whom*.
   B Change *which* to *who*.
   C Delete *in opposition*.
   D Make no change.

4 Which of the following errors appears in sentence 4?
   A lack of subject-verb agreement
   B sentence fragment
   C unclear antecedent
   D incorrect verb tense

Additional Support

Skills Practice

GRAMMAR: Pronouns Review with students the correct use of pronouns:

- All pronouns must have specific antecedents. Define *antecedent* as "the word a pronoun refers to," and give examples.

- Pronouns must agree in number and gender with their antecedents.

- *Who* is the subject form and *whom* is the object form.

- The pronoun *which* refers to objects, and the pronouns *whom* and *who* refer to people.

Write examples on the board to clarify each of these pronoun uses, and have students give additional examples. **OL**

5 Which noun in the previous sentences is the antecedent for the pronouns *He* and *him* in sentence 4?
  A poet
  B astronomer
  C Walt Whitman
  D narrator

6 Which of the following errors occurs in sentence 5?
  A lack of subject-verb agreement
  B unclear antecedent
  C incorrect verb tense
  D sentence fragment

7 Which of the following is the best revision for sentence 5?
  A As the poem begins, the narrator describes the astronomer's lecture, in which the astronomer cites "proofs and figures" and "charts and diagrams."
  B As the poem begins, which describes the astronomer's lecture, there are "proofs and figures" and "charts and diagrams."
  C As the poem begins, who describes the astronomer's lecture, where there are "proofs and figures" and "charts and diagrams."
  D As the poem begins, whom describes the astronomer's lecture, where there are "proofs and figures" and "charts and diagrams."

8 Which of the following is the best revision for sentence 10?
  A Whitman shows us through the poem that life is mechanical and orderly just as they are beautiful.
  B Whitman shows us, through the poem that life is mechanical and orderly just as its beautiful.
  C Whitman shows us, through the poem, that life is mechanical and orderly just as it is beautiful.
  D Whitman shows us through the poem that life is mechanical and orderly just as beautiful.

9 Which of the following is the best revision of sentence 11?
  A However, as readers we only get the narrator's point of view, so we are closer to his than to the astronomer.
  B As readers, however, we learn only the narrator's point of view, so we are closer to his view than to the astronomer's.
  C But as readers we only get the narrator's point of view, so we are closer to he than to the astronomer.
  D But as readers we only get the narrator's point of view, so we are closer to him than to the astronomer's.

10 Which of the following is the best way to revise sentence 12 for clarification?
  A Change the active voice to passive voice.
  B Change *In the end* to *In the final analysis*.
  C Rewrite the sentence to define *abstract*.
  D Make no change.

Essay

Choose any two works from this unit and write an essay that compares or contrasts the tone, or voice, in the two works. Consider how the tone contributes to the meaning of the poem or work. Explain how the tone affects the audience, or reader, of the work. As you write, keep in mind that your essay will be checked for **ideas, organization, voice, word choice, sentence fluency, conventions,** and **presentation.**

Assess

Grammar and Writing Skills

  5. Option **D** is the correct answer. From the context, it is clear that the pronouns refer to "the narrator," above.

  6. Option **B** is the correct answer. The antecedent of the pronoun *he* is unclear.

  7. Option **A** is the correct answer. Replacing *he* with *the narrator* corrects the unclear antecedent.

  8. Option **C** is the correct answer. This revision sets off the nonessential modifier *through the poem* and correctly replaces the possessive pronoun *its* with the contraction *it's.*

  9. Option **B** is the correct answer. This revision avoids beginning a sentence with a conjunction and eliminates the ambiguity of the demonstrative pronoun *that.*

  10. Option **D** is the correct answer. The sentence is correct as written.

Essay

Emphasize to students that their essays must focus on tone. Make sure they have a clear understanding of the term.

English Language Coach

Position of Adverbs Sentence order sometimes causes difficulty for English language learners. Point out that varying the location of adverbs can add interest to writing but that the adverb *only* must appear immediately before the word it modifies, as in "He requests only broccoli." **EL**

Differentiated Instruction

Active Voice **Write on the board:**
The driver was chased by the police.
Ask students to revise it to active voice. *(The police chased the driver.)* Remind students that active voice is preferable to passive voice. Provide practice sentences for distinguishing between the two. **BL**

Unit at a Glance
DRAMA

About the Unit

Unit Four covers drama and dramatic subgenres such as tragedy, comedy, and modern drama.

Part 1: Loyalty and Betrayal
11–12 days

Part 1 covers Greek and Renaissance tragedy. A chart showing the core skills taught in this Part appears on pages 713A–713B.

Part 2: Portraits of Real Life
7–9 days

Part 2 covers comedy and modern drama. A chart showing the core skills taught in this Part appears on pages 867A–867B.

SELECTIONS AND FEATURES

LITERARY FOCUS: Comedy and Modern Drama
pp. 868–869

Anton Chekhov, *A Marriage Proposal*
pp. 870–886

Grammar Workshop: Using Commas with Interjections and Parenthetical Expressions
p. 887

Harold Pinter, *That's Your Trouble*
pp. 888–892

LITERARY PERSPECTIVE: Harold Pinter, "Writing for the Theater"
pp. 893–895

Susan Glaspell, *Trifles*
pp. 896–912

Comparing Literature Across Genres
Josephina Niggli, *The Ring of General Macías*
Carmen Tafolla, "Marked"
Isak Dinesen, "The Ring"
pp. 913–939

End-of-Unit Features
5–6 days

Writing Workshop: Persuasive Speech
pp. 940–947

Professional Model: Everett Dirksen, "Why Marigolds Should Be the National Flower"
p. 941

Speaking, Listening, and Viewing Workshop: Delivering a Persuasive Speech
pp. 948–949

INDEPENDENT READING
pp. 950–951

Test Preparation and Practice
pp. 952–957

Unit Resources

Glencoe Literature: The Reader's Choice offers a comprehensive package of tools to optimize student learning and the teaching experience. Each resource has been designed to assist students in specific areas and to offer instructional support for teachers. While all of these areas are covered in the core textbook, some students may need extra practice or additional help in specific areas. The resource package is designed so that you, the teacher, can choose which items will best assist your students. You may also use these resources as homework assignments and for assessment purposes. The following are resources recommended for use with Unit Four.

Key for Unit Resources

- 🗀 Blackline Master
- ▯ Workbook
- 📖 Supplemental Text
- 💿 CD-ROM
- 📁 DVD
- 🔥 Transparency
- 💻 Web-based

Essential Instructional Support

FAST FILE — Unit 4 Resources

Reading and Literature

- Unit Introduction, pp. 1–2
- The Big Idea Foldable, pp. 3–4
- The Big Idea School-Home Connection, p. 5
- The Big Idea School-Home Connection (Spanish), p. 6
- Challenge Planner, pp. 7–10
- Academic Vocabulary Development, pp. 11–12
- Literary History, pp. 16–17, 25–26
- Comparing Literature Graphic Organizer, p. 56
- Literary Elements, pp. 18, 21, 27, 30, 33, 36, 39, 45, 49, 53, 57
- Reading Strategies, pp. 19, 22, 24, 28, 31, 34, 37, 40, 46, 50, 52, 54, 58
- Active Reading Graphic Organizers, pp. 63–72
- Selection Vocabulary Practice, pp. 20, 23, 29, 32, 35, 38, 41, 47, 51, 55, 59
- Literary Focus, pp. 14, 43

Writing, Grammar, and Spelling

- Spelling Practice, p. 60
- Grammar Workshop, p. 48
- Writing Workshop Graphic Organizer, p. 61

Speaking, Listening, and Viewing

- Speaking, Listening, and Viewing Activities, p. 62

English Language Learners

- English Language Coach, pp. 15, 44

Differentiated Instruction

- ▯ Active Learning and Note Taking Guide pp. 106–144
- 🗀 Leveled Vocabulary Development, pp. 58–68
- 💿 Skill Level Up!™ A Language Arts Game
- 💿 Listening Library Audio CD, disc 2, tracks 1–29
- 💿 Glencoe BookLink 3
- 💿 Vocabulary PuzzleMaker
- 💿 Literature Library Vocabulary PuzzleMaker

ASSESSMENT

- 🗀 Selection and Unit Assessments, Unit Three, pp. 137–162, 215–216
- 🗀 Selection Quick Checks, pp. 69–81
- 🗀 Selection Quick Checks (Spanish), pp. 69–81
- 🗀 Assessment by Learning Objectives, pp. 45–53
- 🗀 Rubrics for Assessing Student Writing, Listening, and Speaking, pp. 20–21, 42–43
- 🗀 Standardized Test Preparation and Practice
- 💻 Glencoe Online Essay Grader
- 💿 Interactive Tutor: Self-Assessment
- 💿 Exam*View*® Assessment Suite
- 💿 Literature Library Exam*View*® Assessment

Additional Instructional Support

Literature and Reading

- Active Learning and Note Taking Guide, pp. 106–144
- *inTIME* Magazines
- Glencoe Literature Library
- Literature Launchers: Pre-Reading Videos
- Literature Classics

Writing, Grammar, and Spelling

- REAL Success in Writing: Research and Reports
- Writing Constructed Responses
- Spelling Power eWorkbook
- Revising with Style eWorkbook
- Sentence Diagraming eWorkbook
- Glencoe Grammar and Composition Handbook
- Grammar and Language Workbook
- Grammar & Language eWorkbook

PROFESSIONAL DEVELOPMENT

- Professional Development Package

Transparencies

- Read Aloud, Think Aloud Transparencies 20–25
- Bellringer Options Transparencies
  - Selection Focus Transparencies 35–38
  - Daily Language Practice Transparencies 73–81
- Grammar and Language Transparencies 25, 55
- Writing Workshop Transparencies 21–25
- Visual Literacy/Fine Art Transparencies

English Language Learner

- English Language Coach
- *inTIME* Magazines (Spanish)
- Spanish Listening Library

Technology

- TeacherWorks Plus™
- StudentWorks Plus™
- Literature Launchers: Pre-Reading Videos
- Vocabulary PuzzleMaker
- Literature Library Vocabulary PuzzleMaker
- Skill Level Up!™ A Language Arts Game
- glencoe.com
- Presentation Plus!™
- ExamView® Assessment Suite
- Literature Library ExamView® Assessment Suite
- Listening Library
- Interactive Tutor: Self-Assessment
- Glencoe BookLink 3
- Online Student Edition, mhln.com
- Glencoe Online Essay Grader
- Grammar and Language eWorkbook
- Revising with Style eWorkbook
- Sentence Diagraming eWorkbook
- Spelling Power eWorkbook
- Literature Classics
- Spanish Listening Library

Additional Glencoe Resources

Dinah Zike's Foldables™

Foldables™ are three-dimensional, interactive graphic organizers that help students practice basic writing skills, review key vocabulary terms, and answer Big Ideas. Every unit contains a Foldable activity. You can find the pattern and directions for the Unit 4 Foldable in the Unit 4 Resources Fast Files booklet. You can use the foldables as they are presented or modify them to suit the needs of your students.

For a wealth of online resources that support the instruction in Unit 4, students and teachers can visit our Web site at glencoe.com. Students will find additional learning, practice, and assessment opportunities such as these, which are noted in the student text:

- Author Search
- Big Idea Overview and Activity
- Interactive Literary Elements Handbook
- Study Central
- Unit Assessment
- Web Activities
- Writing Models

Teachers will find planning and instructional tools that include the following:

- Book Lesson Plans
- Web Activity Lesson Plans
- Teacher Forum
- Professional Resources
  Go to glencoe.com to see the entire selection of *Glencoe Literature* online resources.

Presentation Plus! / CheckPoint

Glencoe's Presentation Plus!™, a multimedia teaching tool, lets you present dynamic lessons that will engage your students. Using Microsoft PowerPoint®, you can customize the presentations to create your own personalized lessons. Use CheckPoint questions with interactive response keypads to get immediate student feedback during lessons, to increase student participation, and to assess student comprehension.

Glencoe Literature Library

The collection of hardcover books includes full-length novels, novellas, plays, and works of nonfiction. Each volume consists of at least one complete extended-length reading accompanied by several related readings from a broad range of genres. A separate Study Guide for each *Glencoe Literature Library* book provides teaching notes and reproducible activity pages for students. Glencoe Literature Library titles that complement this unit include:

- ***Wuthering Heights with Related Readings***
  by Emily Brontë
- ***A House for Mr. Biswas with Related Readings***
  by V. S. Naipaul

GLENCOE BOOKLINK

Use the Glencoe **BookLink 3** CD-ROM, a database of more than 26,700 titles, to *create customized reading lists* for your students.

- Search for award-winning titles (e.g., Newbery Award winners, Coretta Scott King Award winners, and Caldecott Medal winners) and for books on several state-recommended reading lists.
- Find Degrees of Reading Power™ (DRP) and Lexile™ readability scores for all selections.
- Organize reading lists by students' reading level, author, genre, theme, or area of interest.
- Get a brief summary of each selection.

You can find recommended leveled readings for this unit with Independent Reading (see pages 950 and 951).

Online Essay Grader

Use Glencoe's online essay grader powered by SkillWriter™ to score your students' writing and to provide individualized feedback to each student automatically.

You and your students can visit glencoe.com to link to the essay grader. *Students* can enter their essays and receive feedback on demand. *You* can manage demographic data, assign tests, and generate individual student and aggregated reports. The essay grader can help you

- save time with automatic scoring and individualized feedback.
- supplement in-class writing instruction using guided writing practice.

REAL Success: Reading Excellence at All Levels

Glencoe REAL Success is a suite of new reading and language arts products designed to foster reading excellence at all levels. Look for TWE point-of-use references for these specific products that will help your students succeed in reading this Unit.

- *Jamestown Literature : An Adapted Reader,* Grade 10
- REAL Success in Writing: Research and Reports
- Skill Level Up! A Language Arts Game
- CheckPoint PowerPoint™ slides
- Literature/Reading support at Glencoe Web site

A lively collection of articles drawn from issues of the TIME family of magazines helps students develop the skills they need to interact with informational text in a meaningful way. Each of the news stories, feature articles, reviews, profiles, and essays in the magazine connect to an author, work, or theme in *Glencoe Literature: The Reader's Choice.* See the *inTIME* Teacher's Guide for specific connections to each unit and for reproducible student worksheets designed to develop students' reading and critical thinking skills.

Literature Launchers

Set the scene with Glencoe's Literature Launchers, engaging pre-reading video segments that introduce each unit. Each Unit Launcher brings the literature to life, featuring expert testimony and archival stills and footage from the time.

Insert your Glencoe Literature Launchers into your DVD player. Select the Unit 4 Launcher from the menu to introduce Drama.

Teacher Wraparound Edition Key

Level Appropriate Code

AL = Activities for students working above grade level
OL = Activities for students working at grade level
BL = Activities for students working below grade level
EL = Activities for English language learners
AS = Information for all students

Teacher Wraparound Prompts

R **Reading Skill** These activities help you teach reading skills and vocabulary.

V **Vocabulary** These activities help students comprehend words and incorporate them into reading.

BI **Big Idea** These activities and questions prompt students to prepare to answer the Big Idea.

L **Literary Element** These activities and questions help students comprehend selections and learn more about each genre.

★ **Enrichment** Additional activities and information involving art appreciation and history.

Professional Development Center

From Your Authors:

Teaching Literary Analysis: Drama

Make Real-World Connections Help students discover how the topics explored in this unit matter in the world today. Before students read a selection, ask a guiding or essential question. The question should identify a major topic or idea from a reading and express it as a question that is important to students and others in the world. Examples might include the following: what is worth fighting for? What is the human cost of war? What are the costs and benefits of non-conformity? Such questions not only address key issues, but they also give students an opportunity to discuss their beliefs. As students read *The Tragedy of Julius Caesar* by William Shakespeare, have them consider the following questions: What qualities do leaders from your country, state, or local government share with Julius Caesar? What makes someone an effective or ineffective leader? How does a leader's character affect the people he or she is leading?

Build Background To help students read and understand dramatic texts, identify the challenges that students may face in reading and assist them to meet those challenges. Before reading a drama such as *Antigone* by Sophocles, students should study the following aspects of the play: the title of the drama, which media is usually used to portray the drama (stage, television, or cinema), the names and descriptions of characters, where the action takes place and how this might

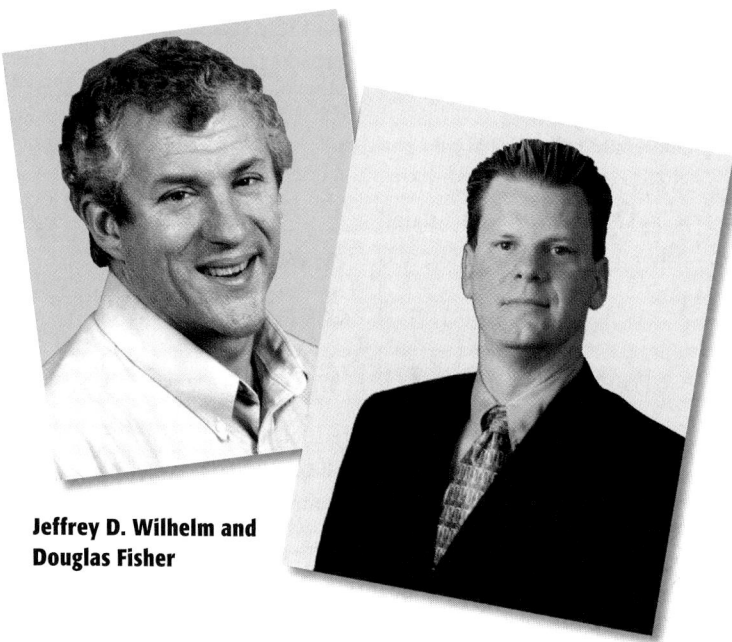

Jeffrey D. Wilhelm and Douglas Fisher

affect the characters, the type of people living in this environment, and the social and historical context of the drama. As students are reading the drama, they should read technical stage directions to better understand the actions and movements of characters, and they should also understand how dialogue is used to develop and portray characters.

Iraida C. Robledo
Palmer Trinity School
Miami, Florida

Teacher to Teacher

Many dramatic plays grow from some part of an author's life, so I first introduce the playwright. I ask students to think about what part of the playwright's life they might expect to see in a play he or she has written. Then I show excerpts of movies of the plays in the unit. I teach many English language learners, so reading the drama in class is important. Since I have a drama background, I act in the plays along with the students and read in different accents and dialects. This technique allows the students to see and hear the drama. I quite often interject explanations of different cultural experiences that arise from the play's text. I may also use an audio reading of a play. We always set the mood with music and different props. Students sit in a circle or semicircle. This class structure takes the attention away from me and puts it on the students to create a community of learners.

Teacher Chat Room

Making Literature Come Alive

Before you begin this unit or sometime during the unit, talk with other teachers about ways they have taught drama. Have a lunch-time discussion group or an after-school hour for professional development and discuss the following questions and answers from our authors:

 How can I help students learn to imagine a staged performance as they read a play?

- Before reading a dramatic script, help students understand how the conventions of drama help readers stage a play in their minds. Before reading a play like Anton Chekhov's *A Marriage Proposal,* ask students to read a short story, cartoon, or poem and translate it into a short skit for other students in class to perform. Students quickly learn that many things described through the narration of a story must be described through stage directions and dialogue in a script.

- Have students watch performances of a play, because playwrights intend for their work to be performed and not read. When teaching a play like *The Tragedy of Julius Caesar,* have students watch video segments of one or even multiple versions of the play.

- Watch major scenes in a play before reading the scene, since this provides background knowledge that assists in the reading. Then after reading the scene, discuss how the director used or ignored particular stage directions and cues in the script.

- Have students perform scenes directly from a drama like *Antigone* by Sophocles. Divide the students into groups and have each group take a scene from the drama. The groups practice and perform their scenes following the stage directions and saying the dialogue exactly as written in the text.

- Instead of having students perform the drama exactly as written in the script, have them perform their own version of a scene from the drama. Divide the class into groups and assign each group a scene from *Antigone* by Sophocles. Have students read and interpret the scene and then rewrite the scene into their own version. Encourage students to keep the main ideas and events from the scene but change the characters and setting to create their own unique version. Their versions could be set in their own school or another historical situation or setting.

- Have students create trailers for a drama and provide performed examples. After students have read *A Marriage Proposal* by Anton Chekhov, have small groups write trailers (like those created for movies) to advertise the drama. Allow students time to practice their trailers and then perform them for the rest of the class.

- Help students compose and perform their own short plays or skits that explore a major theme or issue from the unit but are based on their own experiences.

Focus

BELLRINGER

Bellringer Options
Literature Launcher Video
Daily Language Practice
Transparency 73
Or **ask:** How do you think reading a drama differs from seeing a drama? Discuss the special challenges of reading drama, such as the need to visualize scenes and construct action from dialogue. Students should note that seeing a play adds actors' interpretations, tone of voice, emphasis, emotions, actions, and gestures to the lines. It also brings the setting to life with stage sets, lights, and props. Tell students that in Unit 4, they will learn about classical and modern drama.

Objectives for the Unit Introduction

- To understand characteristics of different types of drama (SE)
- To identify and explore literary elements significant to drama (SE)
- To analyze the effect that these literary elements have upon the reader (SE)

Chorus Members, also called the *Extras*, 1877. Edgar Degas. Pastel on monotype. Louvre, Paris. ★

Unit Introduction Skills

Reading Skills

- Identifying Author's Purpose (SE pp. 706–712)
- Evaluating Characters (SE p. 712)
- Comparing and Contrasting (TWE p. 710)

Drama

Literary Elements

- Understanding Dramatic Conventions (SE pp. 706–712)
- Allusions (TWE p. 708)

Writing Skills/Grammar

- Presenting a Viewpoint (SE p. 712)

DRAMA

Looking Ahead

A drama, or play, is a story told mainly through the words and actions of characters. The story might unfold on a stage or on a movie or television screen. Readers of plays imagine actors speaking the dialogue and envision the setting, lighting, and actions described in the stage directions. Drama allows readers to see the story unfold before their very eyes.

PREVIEW **Big Ideas and Literary Focus**

| **1** | **BIG IDEA:** Loyalty and Betrayal | **LITERARY FOCUS:** Tragedy |
| **2** | **BIG IDEA:** Portraits of Real Life | **LITERARY FOCUS:** Comedy and Modern Drama |

OBJECTIVES
In learning about the genre of drama, you will focus on the following:

- understanding characteristics of different types of drama
- identifying and exploring literary elements significant to drama
- analyzing the effect that these literary elements have upon the reader

INTRODUCTION **705**

Focus

Summary

This introduction begins with a summary of the dramatic genre, outlining the characteristics of drama, including setting, plot, characters, dialogue, stage directions, tragedy, and comedy. An analysis of "The Janitor" by August Wilson illustrates how these elements contribute to the drama. Writers' reflections on various elements of drama are also included.

★ Viewing the Art

Say: Edgar Degas was a French Impressionist painter who lived from 1834–1917. He was known for his images of dancers and other figures in motion. **Ask:** What type of drama is probably being depicted in this painting? How can you tell? *(The painting probably depicts a musical. The chorus members seem to be mid-song, and their costumes and body positions reveal the larger-than-life emotion often conveyed by this genre.)* **AS**

Unit Resources

Classroom Management
- TeacherWorks Plus™ CD-ROM
- StudentWorks Plus™ CD-ROM
- Literature Launchers™: Pre-Reading Videos DVD, Unit Four

Core Instructional Support
- Unit 4 Resources (Fast File)
- Literature Online, glencoe.com
- Presentation Plus!™ CD-ROM, Unit Four

Transparencies
- Literary Elements Transparencies 1, 3, 13, 15, 50, 75, 77, 79, 80, 81
- Bellringer Options Transparencies: Selection Focus Transparencies 35–38 Daily Language Practice Transparencies 73–81

Differentiated Instruction
- Active Learning and Note Taking Guide, pp. 106–144
- Skill Level Up!™ A Language Arts Game

Assessment
- Selection and Unit Assessments, Unit Four, pp. 137–162, 215–216
- ExamView® Assessment Suite CD-ROM
- Assessment by Learning Objectives, pp. 45–53

Supplemental Reading
- Glencoe Literature Library
- Glencoe BookLink 3 CD-ROM
- *inTIME* Magazines

Teach

L₁ Literary Element

Analyzing Genre Have students compare and contrast short stories and dramas. *(Both have characters, plot, theme, and setting, but drama doesn't have point of view because characters speak directly.)* Also, compare and contrast comedy and tragedy. *(Tragedy deals seriously with sad or unfortunate events. Comedy traditionally ends with a happy event.)* **OL**

L₂ Literary Element

Analyzing Genre Have students determine which excerpts are tragedy and which are comedy. *(They may recognize the impending fall from power that Julius Caesar will experience, as well as his tragic flaw of egotism in thinking that "heaven and earth" reflect his fate. Students should also notice the suggestion of tragedy in* Trifles, *as well as the happy ending that makes* The Ring of General Macías *a comedy. They may recognize the humor in the characters of* A Marriage Proposal.*)* **OL**

GENRE FOCUS

L₁ What do fiction and drama have in common?

Playwright August Wilson said of his purpose, "I'm trying to take culture and put it onstage, demonstrate it is capable of sustaining you. There is no idea that can't be contained by life: Asian life, European life, certainly black life. My plays are about love, honor, duty, betrayal—things humans have written about since the beginning of time." Drama contains ideas in live action. Its characters, costumes, sets, and lighting combine to communicate the message, or theme, of the work.

Tragedy

Characters

The characters to be portrayed are listed at the beginning of a play. In tragedy, the main character is sometimes called the **tragic hero.** The tragic hero—and often other characters in a tragedy—is bound to take a terrible fall.

CHARACTERS

ANTIGONE: daughter of Oedipus
ISMENE: daughter of Oedipus
CREON: King of Thebes, uncle of Antigone and Ismene
EURIDICE: wife of Creon
HAEMON: son of Creon
TEIRESIAS: a blind prophet
A SENTRY:
A MESSENGER:
CHORUS: elders of Thebes
CHORAGOS: leader of the Chorus

—Sophocles, **from** *Antigone*

Tragic Plots

L₂ Tragic plots are driven by the hero's **tragic flaw,** or part of the character's personality that leads to his or her downfall, ruin, or death. During the rising action of the play, the audience often is aware of the flaw the hero cannot perceive. Tension mounts as the character takes the inevitable action that seals his or her fate. Then, in a frequently violent climax, the tragic outcome plays out.

SCENE 2. CAESAR'S house. A few hours later.
[Thunder and lightning. Enter JULIUS CAESAR in his nightgown.]
CAESAR. Nor heaven nor earth have been at peace tonight:
Thrice hath Calphurnia in her sleep cried out,
"Help, ho! they murther Caesar!" Who's within?

—William Shakespeare, **from** *The Tragedy of Julius Caesar*, **Act 2**

Literature**Online** **Study Central** Visit www.glencoe.com to review drama.

Additional Support

Skills Practice

LITERARY ELEMENT: Dramatic Conventions Point out some of the dramatic conventions used in the excerpts on these pages.

- **Cast of characters:** Note the list of characters for *Antigone.* Explain that previewing the character list helps in comprehending a play.

- **Lines:** In the Niggli excerpt, note the conventional way of indicating lines in a play. **Ask:** Who are the characters, and what can you tell about them? *(Raquel is a married woman, Andrés is a captain, and they are celebrating.)* **OL**

Dialogue

Plays consist mostly of **dialogue**, or conversation, among the characters. Through dialogue, the characters reveal themselves and the plot of the play moves forward. Unlike tragedies, comedies move toward a happy ending. In the script, the name of the character comes before the dialogue they will speak. Dialogue is sometimes referred to as **lines.**

Stage Directions

Stage directions can describe the setting of a play. They may also tell actors how they should appear and indicate some of the actions they should take on stage. They might describe sets, props, sound effects, or lighting, depending on the needs of the writer. Stage directions are set off from other text by being written in italics, or enclosed in parentheses or brackets.

Acts and Scenes

Plays usually have between one and five **acts**, but there is no rule about how many acts a play should have. Acts are further divided into **scenes.** Scene changes usually indicate a change in location or the passage of time. One-act plays often are not divided into scenes.

> RAQUEL. Yes. Tell me, captain, do you think it possible to love a person too much?
> ANDRÉS. Yes, señora, I do.
> RAQUEL. So do I. Let us drink a toast, captain—to honor. To bright and shining honor.
>
> —Josephina Niggli, **from** *The Ring of General Macías*

> SCENE: Chubukov's mansion—the living room *[LOMOV enters, formally dressed in evening jacket, white gloves, top hat. He is nervous from the start.]*
> CHUBUKOV. *[Rising.]* Well, look who's here! Ivan Vassilevitch! *[Shakes his hand warmly.]* What a surprise, old man! How are you?
>
> —Anton Chekhov, **from** *A Marriage Proposal*

> Scene: *The kitchen in the now abandoned farmhouse of John Wright, a gloomy kitchen, and left without having been put in order— . . . Unwashed pans under the sink, a loaf of bread outside the breadbox, a dish towel on the table—other signs of incompleted work. At the rear the shed door opens and the SHERIFF comes in followed by the COUNTY ATTORNEY and HALE.*
>
> —Susan Glaspell, **from** *Trifles*

R

HEY, MOM, I GOT A PART IN THE CLASS PLAY!

I GET TO SAY A LINE, AND EVERYTHING!

THAT'S WONDERFUL, CALVIN.

IT'S A GREAT DRAMATIC ROLE! MY CHARACTER WILL HAVE EVERYONE IN TEARS AT THE END OF THE SECOND ACT!

WHAT'S THE PLAY?

"NUTRITION AND THE FOUR FOOD GROUPS." I'M AN ONION.

©1986 Universal Press Syndicate

★

Building Reading Fluency

Using Stage Directions In the Chekhov excerpt, have pairs of students take the roles of Lomov and Chubukov. Ask them to read the dialogue aloud, following the stage directions and injecting emotion. Discuss the function of stage directions and how reading a play would change without them. **BL**

English Language Coach

Shakespearean English Assist English language learners with Elizabethan English, including such terms as *thrice* (three times), *ho* (exclamation), and *murther* (murder). Suggest comprehension techniques such as rereading, summarizing, and paraphrasing. Have students practice each. **EL**

Teach

R **Reading Strategy**

Drawing Inferences **Ask:** Based on details in the stage directions, where do you think the scene in *Trifles* will take place? *(It will take place in the kitchen of John Wright's house.)* **Ask:** What inferences can you draw about what has happened? *(Signs point to the fact that people left hurriedly. Something is amiss, and perhaps a crime has occurred.)* **OL**

★ **Viewing the Cartoon**

Say: Irony can be defined as the difference between what is expected and what actually occurs. **Say:** Identify the irony in this comic strip, and explain how it contributes to the humor. *(Calvin's last line is ironic. His mother and the reader expect him to be in a tragic play, but he is in a play about the four food groups. The crying arises not from tragic events, but from an onion. The humor arises from this revelation, as well.)* **AS**

Literature Online

Study Central Have students visit the Web site for resources that will help them to review drama.

Objectives

- To understand characteristics of different types of drama (SE)
- To identify and describe the conventions of dramatic literature (TWE)

Teach

R Reading Strategy

Recognizing Irony Ask:

What is ironic about the mono-logue of *The Janitor*? *(It is ironic that Sam may be more percep-tive than the conference speak-ers, that his boss interrupts him despite his wisdom, and that he is so wise despite his lack of formal education.)* **OL**

L1 Literary Element

Analyzing Genre Ask:

What do Sam's words tell you about him? *(They reveal Sam to be very wise and poetic, despite a lack of education.)* **Ask:** Why do you think Sam goes to the lectern and speaks? *(Sam may have been inspired by the sign, and he has considerable wis-dom to share.)* **OL**

★ Viewing the Art

Say: August Wilson says his characters remain "pointed toward the future." **Ask:** How might this artwork reflect the characters in Wilson's plays? *(The man in the picture is in control of his own fate; he creates a path that will take him to his destination.)* **AS**

Additional Support

708

LITERARY ANALYSIS MODEL
How do dramatists use literary elements?

August Wilson (1945–2005), a two-time Pulitzer prize winning dramatist, chronicled the African American experience in an epic series of ten plays.

"The Janitor," one of Wilson's earlier plays, may have been informed by growing up with a mother he admired who worked as a cleaning lady.

The Janitor
by August Wilson

APPLYING
Literary Elements

Characters

SAM and MR. COLLINS are the characters in *The Janitor.*

Setting

The story unfolds in the ballroom of a hotel.

Stage Directions

The italic text in brackets tells the actor what to do when he first comes onto the stage.

Dialogue

The words that come after the character's name are spoken by the actor on the stage. The ellipses suggest the manner in which the words should be spoken.

Monologue

A long speech by a character spoken either to others or as if alone is a monologue.

CHARACTERS
SAM
MR. COLLINS

SETTING: A hotel ballroom

5 *(SAM enters pushing a broom near the lectern. He stops and reads the sign hanging across the ballroom.)*

L1 **SAM.** National . . . Conference . . . on . . . Youth.

(He nods his approval and continues sweeping. He gets an idea, stops, and approaches the lectern. He clears his throat and begins to speak. His
10 *speech is delivered with the literacy of a janitor. He chooses his ideas care-fully. He is a man who has approached life honestly, with both eyes open.)*

SAM. I want to thank you all for inviting me here to speak about youth. See . . . I's fifty-six years old and I knows something about youth. The first thing I knows . . . is that youth is sweet before flight . . . its odor is rife
15 with speculation and its resilience . . . that's its bounce back . . . is remark-able. But it's that sweetness that we victims of. All of us. Its sweetness . . . and its flight. One of them fellows in that Shakespeare stuff said, "I am **R** not what I am." See. He wasn't like Popeye. This fellow had a different understanding. "I am not what I am." Well, neither are you. You are just
20 what you have been . . . whatever you are now. But what you are now ain't what you gonna become . . . even though it is with you now . . . it's inside you now this instant. Time . . . see, this how you get to this . . .

Skills Practice

LITERARY ELEMENT: Allusions
Students may need assistance interpret-ing the allusions in Sam's lines. Explain that allusions are references in literature to a character, place, or situation from history, literature, music, or art. Discuss Sam's allusions to Shakespeare, as well as these biblical allusions:

• Jacob's angel *(the angel of death that Jacob wrestles in Genesis)*

• Gabriel's horn *(herald of good news)*
Ask: How do these allusions reflect Sam's philosophy? *(They help Sam make the point that young people should make the most of their youth and appreciate the sweetness of youth.)* **OL**

Time ain't changed. It's just moved. Or maybe it ain't moved . . . maybe it just changed. It don't matter. We are all victims of the sweetness of **L2**
25 youth and the time of its flight. See . . . just like you I forgot who I am. I forgot what happened first. But I know the river I step into now . . . is not the same river I stepped into twenty years ago. See. I know that much. But I have forgotten the name of the river . . . I have forgotten the names of the gods . . . and like everybody else I have tried to fool them with my
30 dancing . . . and guess at their faces. It's the same with everybody. We don't have to mention no names. Ain't nobody innocent. We are all victims of ourselves. We have all had our hand in the soup . . . and made the music play just so. See, now . . . this what I call wrestling with Jacob's angel. You lay down at night and that angel come to wrestle with you.
35 When you wrestling with that angel you bargaining for you future. See. And what you need to bargain with is that sweetness of youth. So . . . to the youth of the United States I says . . . don't spend that sweetness too fast! 'Cause you gonna need it. See. I's fifty-six years old and I done found that out. But it's all the same. It all comes back on you . . . just like
40 reaping and sowing. Down and out ain't nothing but being caught up in the balance of what you put down. If you down and out and things ain't going right for you . . . you can bet you done put a down payment on your troubles. Now you got to pay up on the balance. That's as true as I'm standing here. Sometimes you can't see it like that. The last note on
45 Gabriel's horn always gets lost when you get to realizing you done heard the first. See, it's just like. . . .

R

MR. COLLINS. (*Entering.*) Come on, Sam . . . let's quit wasting time and get this floor swept. There's going to be a big important meeting here this afternoon.

50 **SAM.** Yessuh, Mr. Collins. Yessuh.
(*SAM goes back to sweeping as the lights go down to—*)
BLACK

Plot
The emotional height, or climax occurs when we experience the gap between Sam's wisdom and the way Mr. Collins treats him.

Reading Check
Analyzing Why might Wilson have set the play in a hotel ballroom?

INTRODUCING UNIT FOUR

Teach

Reading Check
Answer: *The setting magnifies the class differences between Sam and Mr. Collins. It is unlikely that Sam would attend a function in a hotel ballroom; his role is simply to clean it.* **OL**

L2 Literary Element
Analyzing Genre Ask: How does the theme of *The Janitor* relate to the message of Sam's speech? *(Both Sam's words and his life emphasize the fleeting nature of time: "We are all victims of the sweetness of youth and the time of its flight," he says.)* In addition, discuss Wilson's theme of the wisdom of the common man. Ask how Sam illustrates Wilson's comment about his characters being poor but not poor in spirit. **OL**

Differentiated Instruction

Dramatic Structure Review with less proficient students the definitions of tragedy and comedy, and discuss whether *The Janitor* is a tragedy or a comedy. In addition, have them review the dramatic conventions of the play. Finally, assist them with understanding the dialect. **BL**

Reading in the Real World

Careers *The Janitor* depicts a gap between the wisdom of the main character and his station in life. Have students read about careers to investigate how they can channel their talents and interests into a compatible career. Guide students to locate appropriate career resources in the library and online. **OL**

Objective
• To understand characteristics of different types of drama (SE)

Teach

R Reading Strategy

Determining Main Idea Ask students to summarize the author's main idea in each passage. *(Miller says that what sets tragedy apart from pathos is enlightenment. Norman contends that female playwrights are more likely to deal with creating order out of chaos, and Wilson maintains that his characters may be outwardly poor but not poor in spirit.)* Encourage students to state their responses to these comments. **OL**

★ Viewing the Art

Ask: How might a playwright determine the type of costume appropriate for a certain character? *(Playwrights often choose costumes that reflect a character's social class, economic status, or emotional state.)* **AS**

WRITERS ON READING

R What do writers say about drama?

Reading a Play

The Falling Piano

When Mr. B., while walking down the street, is struck on the head by a falling piano, the newspapers call this a tragedy. In fact, of course, this is only the pathetic end of Mr. B. Not only because of the accidental nature of his death; that is elementary. It is pathetic because it merely arouses our feelings of sympathy, sadness, and possibly of identification. What the death of Mr. B. does not arouse is the tragic feeling.

To my mind the essential difference, and the precise difference, between tragedy and pathos is that tragedy brings us not only sadness, sympathy, identification, and even fear; it also, unlike pathos, brings us knowledge or enlightenment.

But what sort of knowledge? In the largest sense, it is knowledge pertaining to the right way of living in the world. The manner of Mr. B.'s death was not such as to illustrate any principle of living. . . .

Tragedy arises when we are in the presence of a man who has missed accomplishing his joy. But the joy must be there, the promise of the right way of life must be there. Otherwise pathos reigns, and an endless, meaningless, and essen-

tially untrue picture of man is created—man helpless under the falling piano, man wholly lost in a universe which by its very nature is too hostile to be mastered.

—Arthur Miller, **from "The Nature of Tragedy"**

Looking Under the Bed

As women, our historical role has been to clean up the mess. Whether it's the mess left by war or death or children or sickness. I think the violence you see in plays by women is a direct reflection of that historical role. We are not afraid to look under the bed, or to wash the sheets; we know that life is messy. We know that somebody has to clean it up, and that only if it is cleaned up can we hope to start over, and get better. Just because you clean up one mess, that doesn't mean there won't be another one. There is no end to mess, really, but you can't stop cleaning. This fearless "looking under the bed" is what you see in so many plays by women, and it's exciting. It says, "There is order to be brought from this chaos, and I will not stop until I have it."

—Marsha Norman, **from** *Interviews with Contemporary Women Playwrights*

Procession of characters from Shakespeare, ca. 19th century. Irish School. Oil on board, ★ 12.24 x 54.25 in. Yale Center for British Art, Paul Mellon Fund, USA.

Additional Support

Skills Practice

READING: Comparing and Contrasting Point out that one of the techniques of literary criticism is comparison and contrast. Review how to recognize comparison and contrast and how it can help to clarify ideas. **Ask:** What do Miller, Wilson, and Norman compare and contrast? *(Miller compares and contrasts* pathos with tragedy; Wilson contrasts spiritual wealth with material wealth; Norman contrasts female dramatists with male dramatists.)* Encourage students to summarize what they learned about drama from these dramatists' comments. **OL**

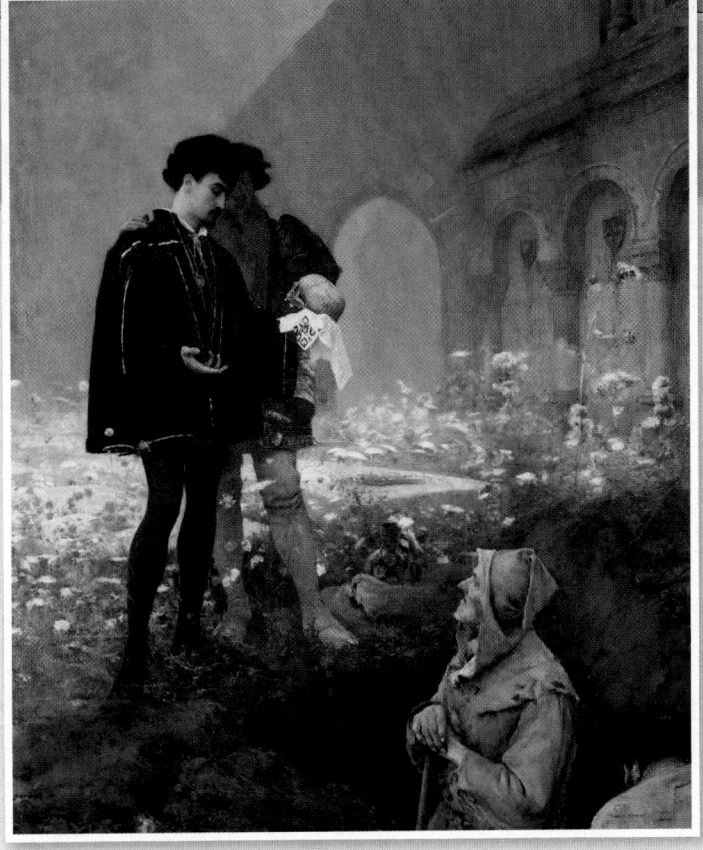

Hamlet and the Grave Digger, 1883. Pascal Adolphe Jean Dagnon-Bouveret. Oil on canvas, 33.5 x 40 in. Private collection.

Pockets Lined with Hope

[My characters] shout, they argue, they wrestle with love, honor, duty, betrayal; they have loud voices and big hearts; they demand justice, they love, they laugh, they cry, they murder, and they embrace life with zest and vigor. Despite the fact that the material conditions of their lives are meager. Despite the fact that they have no relationship with banking capital and their communities lack the twin pillars of commerce and industry. Despite the fact that their relationship to the larger society is one of servitude and marked neglect. In all the plays, the characters remain pointed toward the future, their pockets lined with fresh hope and an abiding faith in their own abilities and their own heroics.

—August Wilson, from "Aunt Ester's Children: A Century on Stage" **L**

"I don't consciously start writing a play that involves issues. After it's done, I sit back like everyone else and think about what it means."

—Suzan-Lori Parks

Literature Online **InterActive Reading Practice**
Visit www.glencoe.com for more practice reading drama.

Reading Check

Responding From your own reading experiences, which passage do you identify with most closely? Explain.

INTRODUCTION **711**

Teach

Reading Check

Answer: *Students should explain their answers by referring to plays they have seen or read.* **OL**

L Literary Element

Author's Style Discuss the tone of each passage on these pages. **Ask:** What are Miller's, Norman's, and Wilson's tones? *(Miller is optimistic; he says it is untrue that man is lost. Norman is enthusiastic; "it's exciting," she says. Wilson is exuberant while discussing his hopeful characters.)* **OL**

★ Viewing the Art

Explain that Dagnan-Bouveret, who lived from 1852–1929, was a French naturalist painter known for his highly precise and detailed paintings. **Ask:** Which of the three passages does this painting bring to mind and why? *(Students might choose the passage by Arthur Miller. The characters in the painting seem to be contemplating tragedy; they may be seeking, in Miller's words, "knowledge or enlightenment.")* **AS**

Interactive Reading Have students access the Web site for more practice with reading strategies.

Objective
• To understand characteristics of different types of drama (SE)

711

English Language Coach

Tragedy Students new to the English language may not understand the term *pathos*. Note that *pathos* means "the quality that arouses sympathy or pity" and has connotations of misery and sorrow. Distinguish other terms similar to tragedy, such as *sadness* and *misfortune*. **EL**

Differentiated Instruction

Fragments Point out that writers who are adept at using language may take liberties with sentence structure. Ask students to point out the fragments in Wilson's writing. *(The three fragments begin with "Despite.")* Discuss the purpose of Wilson's use of fragments. *(For emphasis)* **BL**

Assess/Close

Guide to Reading Drama
Advise students to use these suggestions as a checklist when they read plays.

Elements of Drama
Quiz students on these terms essential to understanding and commenting on dramatic literature.

Activities
1. Make sure that students identify the errors in subject-verb agreement, dropped verbs, pronoun mistakes, and double negatives.

2. Encourage students to use stage directions to guide their reading.

FOLDABLES™
Study Organizer

Have students make and label the Bound Book Foldable. Then have them use this study organizer to explore their personal responses to the plays they read in this unit.

Wrap-Up

Guide to Reading Drama

- Like fiction, drama has plot, setting, characters and theme.
- As you read drama, you may imagine the actors on a stage performing, or you may imagine the characters as real people.
- Preview the characters before you read.
- Read the stage directions as well as the dialogue.
- Pay special attention to what happens to the main character.

Elements of Drama

- A **tragedy** is a play in which the main character suffers a downfall.
- A **tragic hero** is the main character in a tragedy.
- A **comedy** is a play that deals with its subject in a light, familiar, or satirical manner.
- The **dialogue** is what the characters say to one another.
- The **stage directions** may describe the sets, props, sound effects, lighting, and the actions of the characters.
- Plays are divided into **acts** and **scenes**.

Activities

Use what you have learned about reading and analyzing drama to do one of these activities.

1. Writing/Evaluating Give August Wilson a grade for his use of language and grammar in "The Janitor." Base your grade on how effective his choices were in light of the character he is trying to portray. Support your grade in a written paragraph, citing examples from the play.

2. Listening/Speaking/Viewing Act out some of the lines from "The Janitor" in front of the class. Then, as a class, discuss how the lines express the message of the play.

3. Notetaking Try using this study organizer to explore your personal responses to the plays you read in this unit.

FOLDABLES Study Organizer **BOUND BOOK**

Reader-Response Journal

OBJECTIVES
- Evaluate writing for both mechanics and content.
- Determine main concept and supporting details in order to analyze and evaluate non-print media messages.
- Determine characters' traits by what the characters say about themselves in narration, dialogue, dramatic monologue, and soliloquy.

Skills Practice

READING: Characterization
Discuss how Wilson characterizes Sam through his own words as an uneducated but wise man.

- Discuss Wilson's use of dialect (e.g., *I's, 'cause, yessuh*) and what it shows about Sam's character.

- Discuss what ungrammatical usages such as *ain't* show about Sam's education.

- Discuss what the content of Sam's monologue reveals about his wisdom, experience, and empathy. **OL**

PART 1

Loyalty and Betrayal

Brutus and Portia, c. 1500–1550. Michelle da Verona (attr. to). Oil on canvas. Czartoryaski Museum, Poland. ★

BIG IDEA

It can be hard to know whom to trust. When people pursue wealth or power, they accumulate what other people are bound to desire. Even the most loyal ally can betray someone who possesses what his or her heart longs for. The selections in Part 1 deal with issues of loyalty and betrayal that have life-and-death consequences. As you read, ask yourself: What do I want most in the world, and what would I do or not do to get it? **BI**

713

Analyzing and Extending

BI Big Idea

Loyalty and Betrayal

Ask students the question posed in the epigraph: What do you want most, and would you be disloyal to friends or family to get it? *(Student answers will vary.)* Discuss the importance of loyalty to trust and friendship, as well as how other values can conflict with it. Tell students that Part 1 will deepen their understanding of loyalty and betrayal, and encourage students to consider this "big idea" in relation to the artwork. **OL**

★ Viewing the Art

Tell students that the painting depicts some of the characters in *Julius Caesar*, which they will read in this unit. Discuss with students what could be happening in this scene, referencing the facial expressions and body language of the subjects. **AS**

English Language Coach

Building Background Discuss with students what *loyalty* and *betrayal* mean. Give examples such as a double agent betraying his country or an athlete betraying his team by throwing a game. An example of loyalty might be defending a friend who is attacked. Have students give more examples. **EL**

Differentiated Instruction

Who* and *Whom Point out to students the phrase "whom to trust." Ask why *whom* is correct. *(As the object of the infinitive, the pronoun must be the object form.)* Provide sentences for students to complete with *who* or *whom,* such as "That is the person ____ he betrayed." *(whom)* **BL**

Objectives for Part 1

- To understand the literary form and the term *tragedy* (SE)
- To understand the characteristics of tragedy (SE)
- To articulate the relationship between the expressed purposes of tragedy and its characteristics (SE)

Part 1: Loyalty and Betrayal

Readability Scores Key
Dale-Chall/DRP/Lexile

PACING (DAYS)		SELECTIONS AND FEATURES	LITERARY ELEMENTS
STANDARD	BLOCK		
2–3 class sessions	1–2	LITERARY FOCUS: Tragedy, pp. 714–715	Tragedy, SE p. 714 Analyzing Tragedy, TWE p. 714
		LITERARY HISTORY: Greek Drama, p. 716–717	Drama, SE p. 716
		Antigone, **Scenes 1 and 2** by Sophocles, pp. 718–739	Protagonist and Antagonist, SE pp. 719–739
3 class sessions	1–2	*Antigone,* **Scenes 3, 4, and 5** by Sophocles, pp. 740–762	Tragic Flaw, SE pp. 740, 741, 743, 745, 748, 749, 752, 754, 758, 759, 761 Characterization, SE p. 761
		TIME magazine, "Ever Alluring" by Maryann Bird, **9.4/68/**1180, p. 763–766	
		Vocabulary Workshop: Denotation and Connotation, p. 767	
2 class sessions	1–2	LITERARY HISTORY: Elizabethan Drama, pp. 768–769	Drama, SE p. 768–769
		The Tragedy of Julius Caesar, **Act 1** by William Shakespeare, pp. 770–791	Blank Verse, SE pp. 771–791 Characterization, TWE p. 780
1 class session	1	*The Tragedy of Julius Caesar,* **Act 2** by William Shakespeare, pp. 792–811	Monologues, Soliloquies, and Asides, SE pp. 792–811
1 class session		*The Tragedy of Julius Caesar,* **Act 3** by William Shakespeare, pp. 812–833	Plot, SE pp. 812–833
1 class session	1	*The Tragedy of Julius Caesar,* **Act 4** by William Shakespeare, pp. 834–849	Foil, SE pp. 834–849
1 class session		*The Tragedy of Julius Caesar,* **Act 5** by William Shakespeare, pp. 850–866	Tragic Hero, SE pp. 850–865 Theme, SE p. 865

About the Part

Part 1 covers Greek and Renaissance tragedy.

READING AND CRITICAL THINKING	VOCABULARY	WRITING AND GRAMMAR	LISTENING, SPEAKING, AND VIEWING
Drawing Inferences About Heroes, TWE p. 715		Quickwrite, SE p. 715	Dramatic Reading, TWE p. 715
Introduction to Greek Drama, TWE p. 717			Outlining, TWE p. 716
Interpreting Imagery, SE pp. 719-739 Reading Verse, TWE p. 720 Summarizing, TWE p. 732	Context Clues, SE p. 719, 739	Internet Research, SE p. 739 Adjectives, TWE p. 730	Tone of Voice, TWE p. 722 Political Speeches, TWE p. 726
Recognizing Author's Purpose, SE pp. 740, 741, 744–757, 759, 761 Compare and Contrast, TWE p. 756	Antonyms, SE pp. 740, 761 Academic Vocabulary, SE p. 761 Prefixes, TWE p. 744	Analysis of Bias, SE p. 762 End Punctuation, TWE p. 758	Persuasive Techniques, TWE p. 746 Fables, TWE p. 750
Distinguishing Fact and Opinion, TWE p. 764			Analyzing Art, TWE p. 765
	Analyzing Loaded Language, TWE p. 767		
	Shakespeare's English Chart, TWE p. 768		
Making Inferences About Character, SE pp. 771–791	Synonyms, SE p. 791 Suffix -ous, TWE p. 788	Extended Metaphors, TWE p. 778	Analyzing Art, SE pp. 779, 782, 786, 789
Analyzing Cause and Effect, SE pp. 792–811	Word Parts, SE pp. 792, 811 Etymology, TWE p. 794	Analysis of Plot, SE p. 811 Parallel Sentence Structure, TWE p. 798	Analyzing Art, SE pp. 794, 796, 801, 805, 807, 810 Reading Aloud, TWE p. 796
Analyzing Figures of Speech, SE pp. 812–833	Context Clues, SE p. 833 Etymology, TWE p. 816	Simile, TWE p. 814 Blank Verse, TWE p. 826	Reading Maps, TWE p. 828 Analyzing Art, SE pp. 815
Making and Verifying Predictions, SE pp. 834–849	Antonyms, SE pp. 834, 849	Researching Background Information, TWE p. 840	Analyzing Art, SE pp. 835 Oral Reports, TWE p. 842
Evaluating Characters, SE p. 850–865	Analogies, SE pp. 850, 865	Writing a Review, SE p. 866 Vivid Verbs, SE p. 866	Analyzing Art, SE pp. 859, 862

Teach

L Literary Element

Tragedy Ask: What are Brutus's motives for betraying his friend Julius Caesar? *(For the good of Rome, to protect Rome from Caesar's growing power.)* Based on Brutus's speech, why might *Julius Caesar* be a tragedy, and why might Brutus be a tragic hero? *(Brutus is a respected leader of Rome trying to justify his murder of Caesar to the citizens of Rome. If he fails, he will experience a tragic downfall.)* **OL**

Tragedy

What makes a play a tragedy?

If you are interested in movie reviews, you might have noticed that comedies rarely receive more than two stars. The majority of "four star" movies are characterized as "dramas" and deal with serious themes and issues. Maybe you have asked yourself how it is possible that people enjoy being entertained by pain, loss, disappointment, and death. However, there is more to it than that. The human heart likes to be moved, and seeing how others deal with the pain and difficulties of the human experience can give a viewer insight into his or her own problems.

BRUTUS. Had you rather Caesar were living, and die all slaves, than that Caesar were dead, to live all free men? As Caesar lov'd me, I weep for him; as he was fortunate, I rejoice at it; as he was valiant, I honor him: but, as he was ambitious, I slew him. There is tears for his love; joy for his fortune; honor for his valor; and death for his ambition.

Who is here so base that would be a bondman? If any, speak, for him have I offended. Who is here so rude that would not be a Roman? If any, speak, for him have I offended. Who is here so vile that will not love his country? If any, speak, for him have I offended. I pause for a reply.

—William Shakespeare, from *Julius Caesar*, Act 3, Scene 2 **L**

The Death of Ceasar. Guillaume Lethiere (1760–1832). Oil on paper. 47.5 x 71.5 cm. Private Collection.

714 UNIT 4 DRAMA

Additional Support

Skills Practice

LITERARY ELEMENT: Tragedy
Discuss the purpose of classical tragedy to arouse pity and fear. **Ask:** In what sense can the story of a downfall arouse pity and fear? *(Empathy with an admirable character arouses pity, and concern that the same thing can happen to oneself accounts for the reaction of fear.)*

Use the excerpt from *Julius Caesar* to analyze how a tragedy fulfills the objective of arousing pity and fear. **Ask:** What makes Brutus admirable and sympathetic? *(Brutus is a reasonable, honorable, and sincere person, as his speech reveals.)* **Ask:** How does Brutus's tragic flaw lead to his downfall? *(His honor-*

Tragedy

A **tragedy** is a play in which the main character suffers a downfall. Heroes of tragedies are often royalty. In that way, they have a lot to lose. Tragedy is about loss. Sometimes the character's downfall is the result of outside forces. Other times, the character is undone by him- or herself.

The hero of a tragedy is sometimes called a **tragic hero.** If the hero's own character leads to his or her downfall, the tragic hero is said to have a **tragic flaw.**

"To be, or not to be: that is the question."

—William Shakespeare, **from** *Hamlet*

Hero

The **hero** is the main character of a literary work. He or she is usually someone with admirable traits or someone who performs noble deeds.

A tragic hero evokes both pity and fear in the audience. Often, the audience is aware of the hero's tragic flaw before the hero is. They may realize that the hero has made an irreversible mistake that will lead to a terrible fall or even death.

DUNCAN. No more that thane of Cawdor shall deceive
Our bosom interest: go pronounce his present death,
And with his former title greet Macbeth.
ROSS. I'll see it done.
DUNCAN. What he hath lost, noble Macbeth hath won.

—William Shakespeare, **from** *Macbeth*, **Act 1, Scene 2** [R]

Tragic Flaw The tragic flaw is the part of the hero's character that leads to his or her ruin or sorrow. The art of creating a tragic character is to create a tragic flaw that does not prevent the

audience from admiring the hero. The tragic flaw is not always a character defect. For example, Antigone faces a conflict between the human law and a higher law, not necessarily a flaw in her own character.

CREON. *[To ANTIGONE.]* Tell me, tell me briefly: Had you heard my proclamation touching this matter?
ANTIGONE. It was public. Could I help hearing it?
CREON. And yet you dared defy the law.
ANTIGONE. I dared.
It was not God's proclamation. That final Justice
That rules the world below makes no such laws.
Your edict, King, was strong,
But all your strength is weakness itself against
The immortal unrecorded laws of God.

—Sophocles, **from** *Antigone*, **Scene 2**

Quickwrite

Outline a character sketch for your own tragic hero. What will the character have to lose? What qualities will make him or her admirable so the audience will like him or her? What is the hero's tragic flaw? What will be the hero's downfall?

character's name

⬇

position or assets present at the opening that the character could lose

⬇

positive qualities

⬇

tragic flaw

⬇

downfall

LITERARY FOCUS **715**

Teach

[R] Reading Strategy

Drawing Inferences About Heroes **Ask:** Why do Duncan's lines suggest Macbeth is a hero? *(Macbeth is rising in power and is admired by Duncan. In the classical sense he is a hero, high in stature.)* What tragic flaw is revealed in Antigone? *(Her idealism and defiance in pursuit of a higher law may be her undoing.)* OL

Assess

Quickwrite

Have students create a similar graphic organizer to complete. Check that students outline traits that make sense for a tragic hero.

Differentiated Instruction

able intentions lead him to be disloyal to Caesar and set his downfall in motion.) Point out that Shakespeare's complex character portrayal makes the reader empathize with Brutus's conflict and achieves the desired aim of tragedy—pity and fear. OL

Dramatic Reading Help less proficient readers to understand the dramatic excerpts by having students take parts and read aloud. After an oral reading of Brutus's speech, review the meaning of unfamiliar terms and key phrases, such as "Not that I lov'd Caesar less, but that I lov'd Rome more." BL

LITERARY HISTORY

Focus

BELLRINGER

Bellringer Options
**Daily Language Practice
Transparency 74**
Or **write the following statement on the board:** Movies
have replaced theatrical drama.
Ask: Do you agree or disagree
with this statement? *(Students
may say that movies have taken
much of the audience from theater, but both still exist as distinct art forms.)* Have students
suggest similarities and differences between theater and
film. *(Similarities: players acting out a story; sets; dialogue.
Differences: drama is live; movies use music more extensively
and different camera angles)*

Teach

L Literary Element

Drama Ask: Which forms of
art are "told"? Which art forms
are "done"? *(Visual arts, literature, and music are "told" art
forms. Drama, dance, performance and interactive art are
"done." Film could be considered a fusion of the two.)* **OL**

See also █ Active Learning
and Note Taking Guide, pp.
120–123.

Additional Support

Literature Online

Literary History Have students access the Web site for
a summary, bibliography, and
other resources to enhance
their understanding of classical Greek drama.

Classical Greek Drama

> *"In every dramatic hero there is the
> idea of the Greek people, their fate,
> their will, and their destiny."*
> —Arthur Miller, from "On Social Plays"

THEATER WAS FAR MORE THAN ENTERTAINMENT
for the people of ancient Greece. It was
part of their religion, a way of displaying
loyalty to their city-state, and a method of
honoring local heroes. It was also a major social
event, a thrilling competition, and a place where
important philosophical issues could be aired.

In ancient Greece, plays grew out of religion and
myths. From the 6th century bc, religious festivals

Two statuettes of elderly comic actors. c. 375–350 b.c., Attica.

featured a chorus, or group of actors, that danced
and sang hymns to Dionysos, the god of wine. In
about 534 bc, the lyric poet Thespis introduced the
use of a single actor separate from the chorus. The
chorus voiced the attitudes of the community
while the actor delivered speeches, answered the
chorus, and performed the story. In the early fifth
century, the great dramatist Aeschylus (525–456 bc)
added a second actor to the stage; within a few
years, his rival Sophocles (496–406 bc) responded
by adding a third. With these changes, drama
(from the Greek word for *doing*, rather than *telling*)
was born, and actors today are still called thespians. **L**

At the Theater

What would you have seen from the benches of
an ancient Greek theater? Up to 15,000 spectators
could watch performances in the Theater of
Dionysos in Athens. Perched in the upper rows
of seats, a spectator was more than 55 yards from
the action below. The actors' gestures had to be
exaggerated and dramatic, for no one in the back
row could have interpreted slight movements.

Only men were allowed to perform. All the
actors wore masks made of wool, linen, wood,
or plaster. In the mid-fifth century, the time of
Sophocles, masks were fairly realistic
representations of human faces. In later
centuries, masks grew in size and became less
realistic, featuring deep eye sockets and wide,
gaping mouths, making actors appear larger
against the background. Typically, tragic actors
wore striking, richly decorated robes that set
them apart from the audience. Chorus members
wore more conventional costumes, which
identified the roles they were playing: soldiers,
priests, mourners, or even—in the case of
comedies—frogs, birds, or wasps.

Ancient Greek theaters were open-air, so the
lighting was natural. There were very few props.
A hunter might carry a bow; an old man, a stick;
a soldier, a sword and shield. These props served
more as symbols to identify the character's role
in the play than to provide an imitation of life.

716 UNIT 4 DRAMA

Skills Practice

**LISTENING, SPEAKING, AND
VIEWING: Outlining** As they read,
have students use note cards to take
notes on the history selection. Guide
them to look for significant   features and
ideas in the text, such as important playwrights and their contributions to Greek
drama as well as elements of classical

Greek dramatic performance. Have the
students group the note cards as they
classify and connect ideas. After they
take notes, have them write an outline of
the selection based on the information
in and the hierarchy/organization of their
note cards. **OL**

The violence—murder, suicide, and battles—almost always occurred offstage. Typically, a messenger would appear after the event and describe in gory detail what had just happened.

The Golden Age

During the fifth century bc, known as the golden age of Greek drama, drama grew to be a vital part of life in Athens. The festival of Dionysos, the most important Greek religious festival, introduced a drama competition. The four greatest Greek dramatists—Aeschylus, Sophocles, Euripides (480–406 bc), and Aristophanes (448–385 bc)— presented their plays at these festivals.

These dramatists—all from Athens—wrote plays in verse, based on themes familiar to their audiences. They retold myths, rewrote history, and ridiculed politicians. Aristophanes, the sole comic writer among the four Athenian masters, boldly and uproariously satirized society, politics, and even the gods, landing himself in legal trouble for doing so. However, his three great contemporaries were all tragic poets, whose plays captured humankind's timeless struggle to find the purpose of life and to achieve self-understanding.

Relief in honor of Euripides. Late Hellenistic period. Height: 60 cm. Archaeological Museum, Istanbul, Turkey.

Central to the tragedy is the fall of a great man (or woman, though her part would have been acted by a man). According to the Greek philosopher Aristotle, who wrote the first study of tragedy, the tragic hero should be neither very good nor very bad. The hero's fate is brought about by a flaw within his or her own character. In this way, the downfall of the tragic hero would encourage audiences to examine their own lives, to define their beliefs, and to cleanse their emotions of pity and terror through compassion for the character.

Literature Online Literary History For more about classical Greek drama, go to www.glencoe.com.

RESPONDING AND THINKING CRITICALLY

1. In your opinion, what is the most significant difference between ancient Greek theater and modern American theater?

2. How did the purposes of Greek comedy and tragedy differ?

3. Why do you think Aristotle argued that the tragic hero should be a person neither especially good nor especially bad?

OBJECTIVES
• Understand the characteristics of Greek drama.
• Connect to the historical context of literature.

LITERARY HISTORY **717**

English Language Coach

Introduction to Greek Drama
Students from non-Western cultures may not be familiar with the importance of Greek drama to the development of the dramatic tradition in the West. Have students locate Greece on a world map. Discuss some of the famous Greek myths of Hercules and the Cyclops. Have English language learners discuss the roots of dramatic and artistic performance in their own cultures and the importance of performance to their societies. **EL**

Teach

Big Idea

Loyalty and Betrayal
Say: Keep the following question in mind as you read: How might loyalty and betrayal figure into the fall of a tragic hero? *(A tragic hero's blind loyalty to a potentially damaging belief or to a once decent person turned bad could bring about the hero's fall. Betrayal could be incited by a flaw in the hero or naïveté.)* **OL**

Assess

1. Students' answers might focus on the ancient Greeks attending theater as a civic duty as the most significant difference; or they might point to the differences in performance style between ancient and modern theater.

2. Greek comedy was topical, satirizing contemporary issues; Greek tragedy addressed broader human issues.

3. The downfall of a very good person would be shocking and that of a very bad person would seem simply just. The audience will be much better able to identify with a person who possesses a mixture of good and bad qualities.

Focus

BELLRINGER

Bellringer Options
Selection Focus Transparency 35
Daily Language Practice
Transparency 75
Or write the word "bravery" on the board.
Say: Think of an example of someone who, in your opinion, acted bravely. Have students discuss their examples. As they describe the people in their examples, ask them to identify the decision each person had to make in order to act courageously.

Author Search To expand students' appreciation of Sophocles, have them access the Web site for additional information and resources.

Antigone, Scenes 1 and 2

MEET SOPHOCLES

The year is 468 BC, and everyone in Athens expects the upcoming festival to be thrilling. The streets are abuzz with talk about a newcomer to the competition. This young man is going to give the old champion a run for his money, people are saying. The authorities in charge know it too. They have appointed ten well-known generals to serve on the jury that declares the winner. It turns out that the event lives up to all expectations. The winner and new champion is twenty-eight-year-old Sophocles, whose plays—the first he has produced—are judged the best at the festival. For more than fifty years after this victory, Sophocles will be the reigning champion of Greek drama. To this day, he is revered as one of the greatest dramatists of all time.

Born to Succeed Sophocles was born to a wealthy family from Colonus, a village near Athens. Handsome, athletic, and skilled in music, the young man was groomed for stardom. At sixteen he was chosen to lead a chorus in honor of Greece's victory at the Battle of Salamis. He studied music under Lamprus, the most acclaimed musician of his time, and tragedy, musical composition, and choreography under Aeschylus, the great writer of tragedy. Sophocles would later dethrone Aeschylus in the 468 BC drama competition.

This period is called the Golden Age of Greece, and Sophocles was the golden superstar of the Greek stage. He acted and played the lyre (an instrument like the harp) in dramatic productions, retiring only when his voice became too weak to fill the enormous, open theaters of the day.

A Dramatist for the Ages As a writer, Sophocles was tireless, continuing to produce plays until the very end of his ninety-year life.

He brought new possibilities to drama by adding a third actor to the stage, and he is said to have introduced the art of "scene painting" to the theater. In all, he wrote 123 dramas, won twenty-four of thirty competitions, and never finished lower than second place. Only seven of his plays have survived in their entirety, but they are still studied and performed throughout the world.

> "The honor of life lies not in words but in deeds."
> —Sophocles

Sophocles the Citizen As a dramatist and poet, Sophocles took a realistic—and often grim—view of human existence. As a citizen, however, he was happy, patriotic, and conservative. He loved Athens and volunteered to serve in military campaigns and on embassies to foreign states. As a very old man, when his beloved city was beginning its fall from power, he was appointed to serve as one of ten *probouloi,* or chosen commissioners, to govern Athens. In his life, as in his art, Sophocles remained energetic and productive to the end.

Sophocles was born about 496 BC and died in 406 BC.

Literature Online Author Search For more about Sophocles, go to www.glencoe.com.

718   UNIT 4   DRAMA

Selection Skills

Reading Skills

- Interpreting Imagery (SE pp. 719–739)
- Reading Verse (TWE p. 720)
- Visualizing (TWE pp. 728)
- Summarizing (TWE p. 732)

Antigone, Scenes 1 and 2

Literary Element

- Protagonist and Antagonist (SE pp. 719–739)

Writing Skills/Grammar

- Internet Research (SE p. 739)
- Adjectives (TWE p. 730)
- Present Perfect Tense (TWE p. 736)

Listening/Speaking/Viewing Skills

- Viewing Art (SE p. 724)
- Tone of Voice (TWE p. 722)
- Political Speeches (TWE p. 726)

Vocabulary Skills

- Context Clues (SE pp. 719, 739)

Connecting to the Play

"Just do what you think is right." "Act according to your conscience." Advice like this is easy to give, but sometimes surprisingly difficult to carry out. Before you read *Antigone,* think about the following questions:

- When is doing the right thing difficult?
- When have you had a hard time deciding to do what was right?

Building Background

This play takes place in ancient Greece, in the city of Thebes, about thirty miles northwest of Athens. At the time, Thebes was one of the greatest cities of Greece. The Greeks of Sophocles' day believed that people had to do certain things to please the gods. If they fulfilled their duties, the gods would bring them good fortune. However, if they did not, the gods would bring famine, epidemics, and natural disasters. If a corpse was not buried or cremated according to a strict ritual, its soul might not get to Hades, the world of the dead. Instead, the soul would be forced to wander the earth, bringing shame upon relatives and angering the gods.

Setting Purposes for Reading

Big Idea Loyalty and Betrayal

Although we assume that loyalty is a good thing, loyalty to an unworthy cause may be even worse than betrayal. As you read *Antigone,* think about the complex relationship between loyalty and betrayal.

Literary Element Protagonist and Antagonist

The **conflict** in a work of literature is a struggle between opposing forces. The **protagonist** is the central character and the one who the reader is generally meant to sympathize with. The **antagonist** is the person or force that opposes the protagonist. As you read the play, think about who is the antagonist, who is the protagonist, and what their conflict consists of.

- See Literary Terms Handbook, pp. R1, R4, and R13.

Literature Online Interactive Literary Elements **Handbook** To review or learn more about the literary elements, go to www.glencoe.com.

Reading Strategy Interpreting Imagery

Writers create a rich world for their readers by the use of **imagery,** the "word pictures" that appeal to the senses and bring the written word to life. As you read *Antigone,* identify images and think about what feelings or meanings they suggest to you.

Reading Tip: Taking Notes Using a table like the one below can help you interpret imagery.

Image	Reason
"But his body must lie in the fields, a sweet treasure For carrion birds to find as they search for food."	This is a disgusting image that shows how cruel Creon's edict is and how much Antigone hates it.

Vocabulary

repulse (ri puls´) *n.* an act of beating back or driving away, as with force; p. 721 *A day of celebration followed the repulse of the invading army.*

famished (fam´isht) *adj.* intensely hungry; ravenous; p. 725 *Exhausted and famished, the missing hikers finally struggled out of the wilderness.*

comprehensive (kom´pri hen´siv) *adj.* including nearly everything; large in scope; complete; p. 728 *A comprehensive review of our safety procedures revealed many areas that are in need of improvement.*

pious (pī´əs) *adj.* devoutly religious; p. 729 *The streets of the holy city were crowded with pious pilgrims.*

arrogance (ar´ə gəns) *n.* overbearing pride; p. 738 *Her confidence seemed like arrogance to the judge.*

Vocabulary Tip: Context Clues Sometimes the meaning of a new word becomes clear through its surrounding words, or context.

Focus

Summary

Antigone is the daughter of Oedipus, former king of Thebes. Struggling for the throne, her brothers Eteocles and Polyneices prompt a civil war in which both are killed. Her uncle Creon is now king. Creon decrees that Polyneices was a traitor and may not be buried under penalty of death. Antigone asks her sister Ismene to help bury him, but Ismene refuses. Creon is told that someone has tried to bury Polyneices. When Antigone admits to it, Creon sentences her to death.

V Vocabulary

Vocabulary File

Say: Add these words and definitions to your vocabulary file. For each word, include a sentence that gives you an example of how to use the word. **OL** Students with English language needs should include the pronunciations of these words in their files. **EL**

Literary Elements Have students access the Web site to improve their understanding of protagonist and antagonist.

OBJECTIVES
In studying this selection, you will focus on the following:
- understanding the role of protagonist and antagonist
- interpreting imagery
- expanding on what you read through Internet research

ANTIGONE **719**

Selection Resources

Print Materials
- 📁 Unit 4 Resources (Fast File), pp. 18–23
- 📁 Leveled Vocabulary Development, p. 58–59
- 📁 Selection and Unit Assessments, pp. 137–140
- 📁 Selection Quick Checks, p. 69–70

Transparencies
- Bellringer Options Transparencies: Selection Focus Transparency 35 Daily Language Practice Transparency 75
- Literary Elements Transparencies 13, 75

Technology
- 💿 TeacherWorks Plus™ CD-ROM
- 💿 StudentWorks Plus™ CD-ROM
- 💿 Presentation Plus!™ CD-ROM
- 💻 Literature Online, glencoe.com
- 💻 Online Student Edition, mhln.com
- 💿 Exam*View*® Assessment Suite CD-ROM
- 💿 Vocabulary PuzzleMaker CD-ROM
- 💿 Listening Library, disc 2 tracks 1–2

Loyalty and Betrayal

Say: Keep the following questions in mind as you read. Which characters exhibit the truest form of loyalty? How many people are betrayed? (*Most students should note that Antigone's loyalty to her brother, and possibly Haimon's loyalty to Antigone, were the most unwavering and, therefore, the purest. Many people are betrayed: Eteocles, by Polyneices; Polyneices, by Ismene; Antigone, by Creon; and Haimon, by his father.*) **OL**

★ Political History

Argive Army The Argive army was the military force from Argos, a rival city-state of Thebes. **AS**

ANTIGONE

Sophocles
Translated by
Dudley Fitts and
Robert Fitzgerald

Additional Support

READING: Reading Verse Point out that *Antigone* is written in verse form and thus is divided into lines. Each line starts with a capital letter. Remind students that a capital letter at the beginning of a line does not necessarily indicate a new sentence. **Say:** To understand the lines' meaning, you must pay attention to the punctuation indicating the end of a sentence and read the play in sentence units. Help students identify the sentence units in the first speeches of Antigone and Ismene. Ask students to take turns reading the speeches aloud. **OL**

CHARACTERS

ANTIGONE: daughter of Oedipus

ISMENE: daughter of Oedipus

EURYDICE: wife of Creon

CREON: King of Thebes, uncle of Antigone and Ismene

HAIMON: son of Creon

TEIRESIAS: a blind prophet

A SENTRY

A MESSENGER

CHORUS: elders of Thebes

CHORAGOS: leader of the Chorus

SCENE: *Before the palace of Creon, King of Thebes. A central double door, and two lateral doors. A platform extends the length of the façade, and from this platform three steps lead down into the "orchestra," or chorus-ground.* TIME: *Dawn of the day after the **repulse** of the Argive army from the assault on Thebes.* ★

Vocabulary

repulse (ri puls′) *n.* an act of beating back or driving away, as with force

Antigone—Chorus. Artist unknown. Collection van Branteghem, Brussels. Reproduced in Le Theatre, 1899.

ANTIGONE, PROLOGUE **721**

Teach

L Literary Element

Protagonist and Antagonist

Ask: How much information is given about the characters at the beginning of the play? Can you use this list to predict who the protagonist and antagonist might be? *(Sophocles specifies family relationships. Antigone, the title character, is listed first and is probably the protagonist. Creon is the king and the play takes place in his palace; he may be the antagonist.)* **OL**

✔CheckPoint

Use the CheckPoint questions on Presentation Plus! to monitor students' comprehension. These questions can be used with interactive response keypads for immediate student feedback.

Differentiated Instruction

Spatial Learning A map of ancient Greece will help students recognize that the places mentioned in the play actually existed over 2,000 years ago. **Ask:** What do you already know about ancient Greece? *(Possible response: It is where the Olympics started; Greeks believed in many gods.)* Have students use an encyclopedia or other reference book to find a map of ancient Greece. Have them draw the map, including the cities of Thebes and Argos. Also have them include the two most powerful city-states, Athens and Sparta, and other places of interest such as Olympia, where the Olympic games were held. **BL**

Objectives
• To understand the role of protagonist and antagonist (SE)
• To read verse correctly (TWE)

721

Teach

L1 Literary Element

Protagonist and Antagonist Answer: *Antigone loves her brother and is outraged to think of his body treated as food for birds. She will do whatever it takes to honor him.* **OL**

L2 Literary Element

Protagonist and Antagonist Antigone is planning to bury her brother even though that action will put her in conflict with the law. Ismene must decide what she will do as well **Ask:** From the first page of the play, what have you learned about Antigone? *(She is strong, determined, decisive, and loyal to her family. She is active, not passive, in her reactions to events.)* How do these qualities help her as a protagonist? *(She will stand and fight for what she believes in against whatever or whoever threatens those beliefs.)* **OL**

⭐ Writer's technique

Exposition Point out that background information in a play, like other elements, might be communicated through dialogue. **AS**

ANTIGONE

Prologue

[ANTIGONE and ISMENE enter from the central door of the Palace.]

ANTIGONE.° Ismene,° dear sister,
You would think that we had already suffered enough
For the curse on Oedipus:°
I cannot imagine any grief
5   That you and I have not gone through. And now—
Have they told you of the new decree of our King Creon?

ISMENE. I have heard nothing: I know
That two sisters lost two brothers, a double death
In a single hour; and I know that the Argive army°
10 Fled in the night; but beyond this, nothing.

ANTIGONE. I thought so. And that is why I wanted you
To come out here with me. There is something we must do.

ISMENE. Why do you speak so strangely?

ANTIGONE. Listen, Ismene:
15 Creon buried our brother Eteocles
With military honors, gave him a soldier's funeral,
And it was right that he should; but Polyneices,
Who fought as bravely and died as miserably,—
They say that Creon has sworn
20 No one shall bury him, no one mourn for him,
But his body must lie in the fields, a sweet treasure
For carrion birds to find as they search for food.
That is what they say, and our good Creon is coming here
To announce it publicly; and the penalty—
25 Stoning to death in the public square!
                              There it is,
And now you can prove what you are:
A true sister, or a traitor to your family.

ISMENE. Antigone, you are mad! What could I possibly do?

ANTIGONE. You must decide whether you will help me or not.

30 **ISMENE.** I do not understand you. Help you in what?

ANTIGONE. Ismene, I am going to bury him. Will you come?

ISMENE. Bury him! You have just said the new law forbids it.

ANTIGONE. He is my brother. And he is your brother, too.

ISMENE. But think of the danger! Think what Creon will do!

35 **ANTIGONE.** Creon is not strong enough to stand in my way. **L2**

1 Antigone: (an tig′ ə nē). Ismene: (is mē′ nē).

3 Oedipus: (ed′ ə pəs).

8–9 two sisters . . . Argive army: After the death of Oedipus, King of Thebes (thēbz), his sons, Eteocles (ē tē′ ə klēz′) and Polyneices (pä′ lə nī′ sēz), struggled to gain the throne. Argos, a rival city-state, sent its army in support of Polyneices. Before the Argive (ar′ jīv) army was driven back, both Eteocles and Polyneices were killed in battle. Creon (krē′ on), their uncle and Oedipus's brother-in-law, became king.

Literary Element Protagonist and Antagonist *From what you have read so far, what conflict do you think may develop?* **L1**

722 UNIT 4 DRAMA

Additional Support

722

Skills Practice

LISTENING AND SPEAKING: Tone of Voice Much information is communicated not only through a speaker's words but also through his or her tone of voice. For example, in saying the words "I'm really mad at you," a person's tone may communicate anger, annoyance, or sarcasm. Have pairs of students practice reading the dialogue between Antigone and Ismene, lines 52–71. Encourage students to discuss each woman's tone and the emotions she is communicating with her voice. Have volunteers read selected lines of the dialogue. Ask other class members to identify the emotion being communicated through tone. **OL**

ISMENE. Ah sister!
Oedipus died, everyone hating him
For what his own search brought to light, his eyes
Ripped out by his own hand; and Jocasta died,
40   His mother and wife at once: she twisted the cords
That strangled her life;° and our two brothers died,
Each killed by the other's sword. And we are left:
But oh, Antigone,
Think how much more terrible than these
45   Our own death would be if we should go against Creon
And do what he has forbidden! We are only women,
We cannot fight with men, Antigone!
The law is strong, we must give in to the law
In this thing, and in worse. I beg the Dead
50   To forgive me, but I am helpless: I must yield
To those in authority. And I think it is dangerous business
To be always meddling.

ANTIGONE.   If that is what you think,
I should not want you, even if you asked to come.
You have made your choice, you can be what you
        want to be.
55   But I will bury him; and if I must die,
I say that this crime is holy: I shall lie down
With him in death, and I shall be as dear
To him as he to me.
                    It is the dead,
Not the living, who make the longest demands:
60   We die for ever . . .
                    You may do as you like,
Since apparently the laws of the gods mean nothing to you.

ISMENE. They mean a great deal to me; but I have no strength
To break laws that were made for the public good.

ANTIGONE. That must be your excuse, I suppose. But as for me,
65   I will bury the brother I love.

ISMENE.   Antigone,
I am so afraid for you!

ANTIGONE.   You need not be:
You have yourself to consider, after all.

ISMENE. But no one must hear of this, you must tell no one!
I will keep it a secret, I promise!

37–41 Oedipus died . . . her life:
Oedipus had killed Laïos (lī′ əs), the king of Thebes at the time, and married the queen, Jocasta (jō kas′ tə). Together, they had four children—Antigone, Ismene, and two sons. When it was revealed that Oedipus had, without realizing it, killed his own father and married his own mother, he blinded himself, was banished from Thebes, and died, and Jocasta hanged herself.

Running or fleeing maiden,
5th century BC. Artist unknown. Greek sculpture. Archaeological Museum, Eleusis, Greece.

Big Idea Loyalty and Betrayal *What is Antigone suggesting about her sister here?* BI

Differentiated Instruction

L Literary Element

L Literary Element

Protagonist and Antagonist

Answer: *Most students will think that Antigone is a protagonist because she displays bravery and loyalty. Some may say that by disobeying the law, she is acting like an antagonist.* Point out that in the prologue, Antigone is the protagonist and Ismene is the antagonist. Remind students that a protagonist is not necessarily good, and an antagonist is not necessarily evil. The antagonist is simply a person with whom the protagonist is in conflict. **OL**

★ Viewing the Art

Answer: *Antigone and Ismene are shown burying Polyneices. It shows Ismene accompanying her sister on her mission, though in the play she has said that she won't help her.*
Marie Spartali Stillman, (1844–1927) was an English painter and model, and associated with the Pre-Raphaelites, a group of artists whose Romantic works were set in the distant past. **AS**

Antigone. Marie Spartali Stillman. Oil on Canvas. Simon Carter Gallery, Woodbridge, Suffolk, England.
Viewing the Art: What characters are portrayed here? How does this image differ from the story line that you have read so far? ★

ANTIGONE.   Oh tell it! Tell everyone!
70   Think how they'll hate you when it all comes out
        If they learn that you knew about it all the time!

ISMENE. So fiery! You should be cold with fear.

ANTIGONE. Perhaps. But I am only doing what I must.

ISMENE. But can you do it? I say that you cannot.

75   ANTIGONE. Very well: when my strength gives out, I shall
        do no more.

ISMENE. Impossible things should not be tried at all.

ANTIGONE. Go away, Ismene:
        I shall be hating you soon, and the dead will too,
        For your words are hateful. Leave me my foolish plan:
80   I am not afraid of the danger; if it means death,
        It will not be the worst of deaths—death without honor.

ISMENE. Go then, if you feel that you must.
        You are unwise,
        But a loyal friend indeed to those who love you.

[Exit into the Palace. ANTIGONE *goes off,* L. *Enter the* CHORUS.]

Literary Element Protagonist and Antagonist *At this point, do you think Antigone is a protagonist or an antagonist? Explain.* **L**

724   UNIT 4   DRAMA

Additional Support

724

Skills Practice

RESEARCH: Ancient Burial Customs Explain that much of the action in *Antigone* is based on the significance in ancient Greek society of properly burying family members. This originated in the belief that the gods must be appeased or they would bring on disasters. **Say:** Other ancient civilizations also had characteristic funeral customs. For example, the Romans had elaborate funerals in which the deceased was carried atop a litter through the streets. Have students research ancient burial customs. Suggest that they find out about services, mummies and tombs, and memorials. **OL**

Parodos°

CHORUS.   Now the long blade of the sun, lying
      Level east to west, touches with glory
      Thebes of the Seven Gates. Open, unlidded
      Eye of golden day! O marching light
5   Across the eddy and rush of Dirce's stream,°
      Striking the white shields of the enemy
      Thrown headlong backward from the blaze of morning!

CHORAGOS.   Polyneices their commander
      Roused them with windy phrases,
10   He the wild eagle screaming
      Insults above our land,
      His wings their shields of snow,
      His crest their marshalled helms.

CHORUS.   Against our seven gates in a yawning ring
15   The **famished** spears came onward in the night;
      But before his jaws were sated with our blood,
      Or pinefire took the garland of our towers,
      He was thrown back; and as he turned, great Thebes—
      No tender victim for his noisy power—
20   Rose like a dragon behind him, shouting war.

CHORAGOS.   For God° hates utterly
      The bray of bragging tongues;
      And when he beheld their smiling,
      Their swagger of golden helms,
25   The frown of his thunder blasted
      Their first man from our walls.

CHORUS.   We heard his shout of triumph high in the air
      Turn to a scream; far out in a flaming arc
      He fell with his windy torch, and the earth struck him.
30   And others storming in fury no less than his
      Found shock of death in the dusty joy of battle.

CHORAGOS.   Seven captains at seven gates
      Yielded their clanging arms to the god
      That bends the battle-line and breaks it.°
35   These two only, brothers in blood,
      Face to face in matchless rage,

Parodos (pär′ ə dos): the first "song" of the Chorus.

5 Dirce's stream: This stream, which flows past Thebes, was named after a murdered queen.

21 God: Here, "God" refers to Zeus (zo͞os), the king of the gods, who used thunderbolts to strike down the invading Argives.

32–34 Seven captains . . . breaks it: The Thebans offered the captains' armor (arms) as a sacrifice to Ares (ā′ rēz), the god of war.

> **Reading Strategy** Interpreting Imagery *What is being described in this opening stanza?* **R1**

> **Reading Strategy** Interpreting Imagery *What does this image suggest about the two brothers?* **R2**

> **Vocabulary**
>
> **famished** (fam′ isht) *adj.* intensely hungry; ravenous

ANTIGONE, PROLOGUE   **725**

Teach

R1 Reading Strategy

Interpreting Imagery

Answer: *The description is of the morning sun shining on the enemy army.* **Ask:** What other images describing light can you find in the Parados? *(Other images of light include "long blade of the sun," "unlidded eye of golden day," and "marching light.")* Point out that writers use a variety of literary devices to enhance the imagery in their work. One such device is personification, a figure of speech in which an object or idea is given human charact eristics. **Say:** "The famished spears" (line 15) is an example of personification because it likens the army's weapons to a hungry person. Can you find another example of personification in the images listed above? *(The "unlidded/ Eye of golden day" is an example of personification.)* **OL**

R2 Reading Strategy

Interpreting Imagery

Answer: *The image suggests the fighting that the brothers engaged in against one another during the war.* **OL**

Objectives
• To understand the role of protagonist and antagonist (SE)
• To interpret imagery (SE)
• To analyze art (SE)
• To research ancient burial customs (TWE)

Teach

Mirroring each the other's death,
Clashed in long combat.

CHORUS. But now in the beautiful morning of victory
40   Let Thebes of the many chariots sing for joy!
With hearts for dancing we'll take leave of war:
Our temples shall be sweet with hymns of praise,
And the long night shall echo with our chorus.

SCENE 1

CHORAGOS. But now at last our new King is coming:
Creon of Thebes, Menoikeus'° son.
In this auspicious° dawn of his reign
What are the new complexities
5   That shifting Fate° has woven for him?
What is his counsel? Why has he summoned
The old men to hear him?

[Enter CREON from the Palace, C. He addresses the CHORUS from the top step.]

CREON. Gentlemen: I have the honor to inform you that our
Ship of State, which recent storms have threatened to
10   destroy, has come safely to harbor at last,° guided by the
merciful wisdom of Heaven. I have summoned you here this
morning because I know that I can depend upon you: your
devotion to King Laïos was absolute; you never hesitated in
your duty to our late ruler Oedipus; and when Oedipus
15   died, your loyalty was transferred to his children.
Unfortunately, as you know, his two sons, the princes
Eteocles and Polyneices, have killed each other in battle; and
I, as the next in blood, have succeeded to the full power of
the throne. I am aware, of course, that no Ruler can
20   expect complete loyalty from his subjects until he has been
tested in office. Nevertheless, I say to you at the very outset
that I have nothing but contempt for the kind of Governor
who is afraid, for whatever reason, to follow the course
that he knows is best for the State; and as for the man
25   who sets private friendship above the public welfare,—I
have no use for him, either. I call God to witness that if I
saw my country headed for ruin, I should not be afraid to
speak out plainly; and I need hardly remind you that I
would never have any dealings with an enemy of the

2 **Menoikeus** (me noi´ kē as)

3 **auspicious:** favorable, indicating good fortune.

5 **Fate:** The ancient Greeks believed that three sisters, called the Fates, controlled human destiny. The first sister was said to spin the thread of human life, the second decided its length, and the third cut it.

8–10 **Gentlemen . . . at last:** The expression "Ship of State" likens a nation to a ship under sail. In reassuring the citizens of Thebes that the "storms" are over, Creon is referring to the Argive invasion and the many troubles in the house of Oedipus.

Horseman and foot soldier fighting, 4th century BC. Artist unknown. Relief. National Archaeological Museum, Athens.

Reading Strategy   Interpreting Imagery *How does the imagery in the last stanza contrast with that of the previous stanzas?* **R**

Skills Practice

LISTENING: Political Speeches

Say: Creon's speech demonstrates the serious, formal style of political leaders. Discuss how Creon's speech is similar to and different from speeches by present-day government officials. *(Like modern leaders, Creon begins on a positive note uses formal language, and expresses* *his loyalty and patriotism. Students may find that Creon is more outspoken than modern leaders in expressing the value of loyalty to the State.)* Hand out a page with these questions:

- What is the speaker's overall tone: sincere, somber, concerned, sympathetic, or something else?

30   people. No one values friendship more highly than I; but
we must remember that friends made at the risk of wrecking
our Ship are not real friends at all.
    These are my principles, at any rate, and that is why I have
made the following decision concerning the sons of Oedipus:

35 Eteocles, who died as a man should die, fighting for his
country, is to be buried with full military honors, with all
the ceremony that is usual when the greatest heroes die;
but his brother Polyneices, who broke his exile to come
back with fire and sword against his native city and the

40 shrines of his fathers' gods, whose one idea was to spill the
blood of his blood and sell his own people into slavery—
Polyneices, I say, is to have no burial: no man is to touch
him or say the least prayer for him; he shall lie on the plain,
unburied; and the birds and the scavenging dogs can do

45 with him whatever they like.
    This is my command, and you can see the wisdom behind
it. As long as I am King, no traitor is going to be honored
with the loyal man. But whoever shows by word and deed
that he is on the side of the State,—he shall have my

50 respect while he is living, and my reverence when he is dead.

    CHORAGOS. If that is your will, Creon son of Menoikeus,
    You have the right to enforce it: we are yours.

    CREON. That is my will. Take care that you do your part.

    CHORAGOS. We are old men: let the younger ones carry it out.

55   CREON. I do not mean that: the sentries have been appointed.

    CHORAGOS. Then what is it that you would have us do?

    CREON. You will give no support to whoever breaks this law.

    CHORAGOS. Only a crazy man is in love with death!

    CREON. And death it is; yet money talks, and the wisest
60   Have sometimes been known to count a few coins too many.

[Enter SENTRY from L.]

    SENTRY. I'll not say that I'm out of breath from running, King,
    because every time I stopped to think about what I have to
    tell you, I felt like going back. And all the time a voice kept
    saying, "You fool, don't you know you're walking straight
65   into trouble?"; and then another voice: "Yes, but if you let

---

Literary Element   Protagonist and Antagonist *From his speech so far, how would you characterize Creon?* **L**

Big Idea   Loyalty and Betrayal *What does loyalty mean to Creon?* **BI₁**

Big Idea   Loyalty and Betrayal *Why does Creon believe that someone might be tempted to bury Polyneices?* **BI₂**

ANTIGONE, SCENE 1   **727**

Teach

L Literary Element

Protagonist and Antagonist
Answer: *Creon seems skilled in politics, strong-willed, religious, forthright, and patriotic. He seems to be a man of action. Others may point out that he will fight anyone who opposes him.* **OL**

BI₁ Big Idea

Loyalty and Betrayal
Answer: *Loyalty means obeying the laws of the state.* **OL**

BI₂ Big Idea

Loyalty and Betrayal
Answer: *Creon is suggesting that, despite the threat of the death penalty, someone could still be bribed to bury Polyneices.* **OL**

★ Language History

Sentry A *sentry* is a soldier standing guard. In this case, the sentry is guarding Polyneices' unburied body. **AS**

Differentiated Instruction

- What tone of voice, gestures, and facial expressions reinforce the tone?
- How appropriate is the speaker's tone to his or her message?

Show students a recorded speech by a political leader, and ask them to note the speaker's style. **OL**

Less Proficient Readers Ancient Greece may seem far removed from students' experiences. **Ask:** What similarities do you see between your life and Antigone's life? *(Possible responses: having brothers or sisters, getting in trouble for protecting a loved one, disagreeing with authority.)* **BL**

Objectives

- To understand the role of protagonist and antagonist (SE)
- To examine political speeches (TWE)

727

Teach

L1 Literary Element

Protagonist and Antagonist

Answer: *So far the sentry seems too weak, frightened, and confused to oppose anyone in the conflict. He is supposed to guard the body, and that is all he intended to do. He does feel an overwhelming duty to inform Creon of the news, but does not want to take any part in placing the blame on anyone.* **OL**

★ Writer's Technique

Stage Directions Call students' attention to the stage directions, which specifically describe Creon's attitude as the sentry speaks. Remind students that these directions help actors portray a play's characters. Have one or two volunteers demonstrate how they would follow the directions in playing the role of Creon. **AS**

---

somebody else get the news to Creon first, it will be even
worse than that for you!" But good sense won out, at least
I hope it was good sense, and here I am with a story that
makes no sense at all; but I'll tell it anyhow, because, as
70   they say, what's going to happen's going to happen, and—

CREON. Come to the point. What have you to say?

SENTRY. I did not do it. I did not see who did it. You must not
punish me for what someone else has done.

CREON. A **comprehensive** defense! More effective, perhaps,
75   If I knew its purpose. Come: what is it?

SENTRY. A dreadful thing . . . I don't know how to put it—

CREON. Out with it!

SENTRY.   Well, then;
    The dead man—

                Polyneices—

[Pause. The SENTRY *is overcome, fumbles for words.* CREON *waits impassively.]* ★

             out there—

                   someone,—
    New dust on the slimy flesh!

[Pause. No sign from CREON.*]*

80   Someone has given it burial that way, and
    Gone . . .

[Long pause. CREON *finally speaks with deadly control.]*

CREON. And the man who dared do this?

SENTRY.   I swear I
    Do not know! You must believe me!
                  Listen:
    The ground was dry, not a sign of digging, no,
85   Not a wheeltrack in the dust, no trace of anyone.
    It was when they relieved us this morning: and one of them,
    The corporal, pointed to it.
                 There it was,
    The strangest—
           Look:
    The body, just mounded over with light dust: you see?
90   Not buried really, but as if they'd covered it

Zeus and the eagle, 575 BC. Attributed to the Naukratis painter. Kylix (drinking cup). Museo Nazionale, Taranto, Italy.

Literary Element Protagonist and Antagonist *From what you have read so far, what stand does the sentry take in the conflict? Explain.* **L1**

Vocabulary

comprehensive (kom´pri hen´siv) *adj.* including nearly everything; large in scope; complete

---

Additional Support

Skills Practice

READING: Visualizing Remind students that in Greek drama, much action is described and not shown. Encourage students to visualize, as the original Greek audiences would have done, the scene of the sentries discovering the corpse of Polyneices partially covered with dirt. **Ask:** What images from the text are particularly vivid and help you see the scene? (*Answers will vary. Students may list "new dust on the slimy flesh" or "not a wheeltrack in the dust."*) **OL**

Just enough for the ghost's peace. And no sign
Of dogs or any wild animal that had been there.

And then what a scene there was! Every man of us
Accusing the other: we all proved the other man did it,
95   We all had proof that we could not have done it.
We were ready to take hot iron in our hands,
Walk through fire, swear by all the gods,
It was not I!
I do not know who it was, but it was not I!

[CREON's rage has been mounting steadily, but the SENTRY is too intent
upon his story to notice it.]

100   And then, when this came to nothing, someone said
A thing that silenced us and made us stare
Down at the ground: you had to be told the news,
And one of us had to do it! We threw the dice,
And the bad luck fell to me.° So here I am,
105   No happier to be here than you are to have me:
Nobody likes the man who brings bad news.

CHORAGOS. I have been wondering, King: can it be that the
gods have done this?

CREON. [*Furiously.*] Stop!
110   Must you doddering wrecks
Go out of your heads entirely? "The gods!"
Intolerable!
The gods favor this corpse? Why? How had he served them?
Tried to loot their temples, burn their images,
115   Yes, and the whole State, and its laws with it!
Is it your senile opinion that the gods love to honor bad
    men?
A **pious** thought!—
              No, from the very beginning
There have been those who have whispered together,
Stiff-necked anarchists, putting their heads together,
120   Scheming against me in alleys.° These are the men,
And they have bribed my own guard to do this thing.

103–104 We threw . . . to me: Like tossing a coin, throwing dice is a way to determine something randomly. In this case, it is who must do what no one wants to do.

117–120 A pious . . . in alleys: Anarchy is a state of disorder and confusion or lawlessness, often due to the absence of governmental authority. Anarchists believe that all forms of government are unjust and should be resisted. Here, Creon calls those who oppose him anarchists.

Big Idea   Loyalty and Betrayal *What makes the sentries so willing to betray each other?* **BI**

Literary Element   Protagonist and Antagonist *What new role has the chorus begun to assume in this conflict?* **L2**

Vocabulary

pious (pī′ əs) *adj.* devoutly religious

ANTIGONE, SCENE 1   **729**

Teach

BI Big Idea

Loyalty and Betrayal
Answer: *The sentries know someone will be held accountable, since there is no clear evidence pointing to the culprit. They realize that they must point their fingers at anyone but themselves in order to be spared.* **OL**

L2 Literary Element

Protagonist and Antagonist
Answer: *By suggesting that the gods are acting against Creon's wishes, the choragos is suggesting that Creon might be wrong. Until now, he has been completely supportive of him. The choragos is beginning to sound like the conscience Creon lacks.* **OL**

Reading in the Real World

Citizenship An obituary is a written notice of an individual's death usually accompanied by a brief account on the deceased's life. Obituaries can be found in most newspapers and are often a way to show honor or respect for the person who has died. Have students bring in some obituaries to share

with the class. **Ask:** What information is the same in each of the obituaries? *(Responses will include name, age, and date of death.)* What information is different? *(Responses may include hobbies, military service, personal details.)* Have students list both the practical and the emotional reasons for obituaries. **OL**

Objectives
• To understand the role of protagonist and antagonist (SE)
• To use visualization to better understand the text (TWE)

729

Big Idea

Loyalty and Betrayal
Answer: *Creon makes known that the man responsible will be punished severely. The people know that he is serious because he swears by God that this will occur.* **OL**

L Literary Element

Protagonist and Antagonist
Answer: *Creon is so stubborn that he would rather kill the wrong person than admit to his errors.* **Ask:** How has Creon treated the sentry in the lines leading up to this statement? *(Creon is rude, impatient, sarcastic, and accusatory.)* **Ask:** How is this consistent with his role as antagonist? *(We can tell that he is quick to judge and will oppose anyone who defies his orders.)* **OL**

ANTIGONE

[*Sententiously.*] Money!
There's nothing in the world so demoralizing as money.
Down go your cities,
125   Homes gone, men gone, honest hearts corrupted,
Crookedness of all kinds, and all for money!
[*To SENTRY.*]   But you—!
I swear by God and by the throne of God,
The man who has done this thing shall pay for it!
Find that man, bring him here to me, or your death
130   Will be the least of your problems: I'll string you up
Alive, and there will be certain ways to make you
Discover your employer before you die;
And the process may teach you a lesson you seem to
      have missed:
The dearest profit is sometimes all too dear:
135   That depends on the source. Do you understand me?
A fortune won is often misfortune.

SENTRY.   King, may I speak?

CREON.   Your very voice distresses me.

SENTRY.   Are you sure that it is my voice, and not your
      conscience?

CREON.   By God, he wants to analyze me now!

140   SENTRY.   It is not what I say, but what has been done, that
      hurts you.

CREON.   You talk too much.

SENTRY.   Maybe; but I've done nothing.

CREON.   Sold your soul for some silver: that's all you've done.

SENTRY.   How dreadful it is when the right judge judges wrong!

CREON.   Your figures of speech
145   May entertain you now; but unless you bring me the man,
You will get little profit from them in the end.

[*Exit CREON into the Palace.*]

SENTRY.   "Bring me the man"—!
I'd like nothing better than bringing him the man!
But bring him or not, you have seen the last of me here.
150   At any rate, I am safe!

[*Exit SENTRY.*]

Big Idea   Loyalty and Betrayal *How does Creon ensure the loyalty of his people?* **BI**

Literary Element   Protagonist and Antagonist *What insight about Creon does the sentry express here?* **L**

Additional Support

Skills Practice

WRITING: Adjectives in Poetry
Explain that Sophocles' ode includes vivid adjectives used in unusual contexts. **Say:** Sophocles describes the "shining furrows" of the earth, "the storm-gray sea," and "the sultry shoulders of the mountain bull." Challenge students to write a poem of at least four lines on any subject they wish. Encourage them to use interesting, unusual adjectives to make their images more compelling. Suggest that they get their ideas on paper first. During revision they can brainstorm for vivid descriptive words. Have students read their poems to the class. **OL**

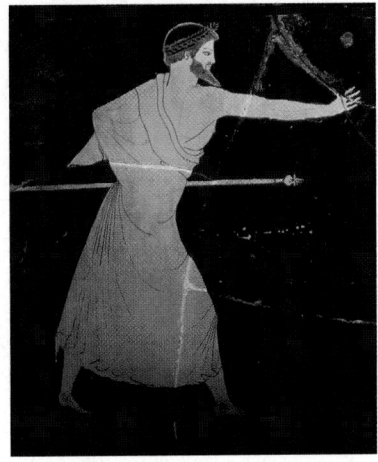

Zeus (detail), 500 BC. Attributed to the Berlin painter. Red-figure krater. Musée du Louvre, Paris.

Teach

R Reading Strategy

Interpreting Imagery
Answer: *People protect themselves against snow and rain, as they would against weapons in battle.* **OL**

ODE° 1

CHORUS. Numberless are the world's wonders, but none
    More wonderful than man; the stormgray sea
    Yields to his prows,° the huge crests bear him high;
    Earth, holy and inexhaustible, is graven°
5   With shining furrows where his plows have gone
    Year after year, the timeless labor of stallions.

    The lightboned birds and beasts that cling to cover,
    The lithe° fish lighting their reaches of dim water,
    All are taken, tamed in the net of his mind;
10   The lion on the hill, the wild horse windy-maned,
    Resign to him; and his blunt yoke has broken
    The sultry shoulders of the mountain bull.

    Words also, and thought as rapid as air,
    He fashions to his good use; statecraft is his,
15   And his the skill that deflects the arrows of snow,
    The spears of winter rain: from every wind
    He has made himself secure—from all but one:
    In the late wind of death he cannot stand.

    O clear intelligence, force beyond all measure!
20   O fate of man, working both good and evil!
    When the laws are kept, how proudly his city stands!
    When the laws are broken, what of his city then?
    Never may the anarchic man find rest at my hearth,
    Never be it said that my thoughts are his thoughts.

Ode: a song chanted by the Chorus.

3 **prows:** ships.
4 **graven:** formed or shaped with a chisel; sculpted.

8 **lithe:** easily bent; flexible.

Reading Strategy Interpreting Imagery *Why does the author refer to snow and rain in terms of "arrows" and "spears"?* **R**

ANTIGONE, SCENE 1 **731**

Differentiated Instruction

Clarifying Remind students that the chorus represents the townspeople of Thebes. **Say:** The chorus does not further the play's plot. Instead, it comments on various elements of the play. Have students write down the functions of the chorus. On the board, keep a running list of the chorus's function in each part of the play in which it appears. Have students refer to the Parados on page 725 and tell what its function is. *(It gives important background information.)* In the ode on page 731, the chorus affirms Creon's value system and brings up some themes of the play. **BL**

Objectives

- To interpret imagery (SE)
- To understand the role of protagonist and antagonist (SE)
- To use vivid adjectives to create effective poetry (TWE)

SCENE 2

Teach

BI₁ Big Idea

Loyalty and Betrayal
Answer: *She is his niece, the very last person he would suspect of disobeying him.* **OL**

[Re-enter SENTRY leading ANTIGONE.]

CHORAGOS. What does this mean? Surely this captive woman
    Is the Princess, Antigone? Why should she be taken?

SENTRY. Here is the one who did it! We caught her
    In the very act of burying him.—Where is Creon?

5   **CHORAGOS.** Just coming from the house.

[Enter CREON, C.]

CREON.   What has happened?
    Why have you come back so soon?

SENTRY. [*Expansively.*] O King,
    A man should never be too sure of anything:
    I would have sworn
    That you'd not see me here again: your anger
10   Frightened me so, and the things you threatened me with;
    But how could I tell then
    That I'd be able to solve the case so soon?

    No dice-throwing this time: I was only too glad to come!

    Here is this woman. She is the guilty one:
15   We found her trying to bury him.
    Take her, then; question her; judge her as you will.
    I am through with the whole thing now, and glad of it.

CREON. But this is Antigone! Why have you brought her here?

SENTRY. She was burying him, I tell you!

CREON. [*Severely.*]   Is this the truth?

20   **SENTRY.** I saw her with my own eyes. Can I say more?

CREON. The details: come, tell me quickly!

SENTRY.   It was like this:
    After those terrible threats of yours, King,
    We went back and brushed the dust away from the body.
    The flesh was soft by now, and stinking,
25   So we sat on a hill to windward and kept guard.
    No napping this time! We kept each other awake.
    But nothing happened until the white round sun
    Whirled in the center of the round sky over us:

Big Idea Loyalty and Betrayal *Why is Creon surprised that Antigone has been arrested?* **BI**

Additional Support

Skills Practice

READING: Summarizing Explain to students that to create an effective summary, they need to

- identify the main ideas
- create a logical sequence
- use your own words

Remind students not to include anything that is not essential to the basic message. **Say:** If you are unsure about a detail, take it out and see if your summary still sounds complete. Have students summarize the action of the play so far. Ask them to share their summary with someone who is not familiar with the story and see if it makes sense. **OL**

Then, suddenly,
30 A storm of dust roared up from the earth, and the sky
Went out, the plain vanished with all its trees
In the stinging dark. We closed our eyes and endured it.
The whirlwind lasted a long time, but it passed;
And then we looked, and there was Antigone!
35 I have seen
A mother bird come back to a stripped nest, heard
Her crying bitterly a broken note or two
For the young ones stolen. Just so, when this girl
Found the bare corpse, and all her love's work wasted,
40 She wept, and cried on heaven to damn the hands
That had done this thing.
                    And then she brought more dust
And sprinkled wine three times for her brother's ghost.

We ran and took her at once. She was not afraid,
Not even when we charged her with what she had done.
45 She denied nothing.
                    And this was a comfort to me,
And some uneasiness: for it is a good thing
To escape from death, but it is no great pleasure
To bring death to a friend.
                    Yet I always say
There is nothing so comfortable as your own safe skin!

50 CREON. [Slowly, dangerously.] And you, Antigone,
You with your head hanging,—do you confess this thing?

ANTIGONE. I do. I deny nothing.

CREON. [To SENTRY.]   You may go.

[Exit SENTRY.]

[To ANTIGONE.] Tell me, tell me briefly:
Had you heard my proclamation touching this matter?

55 ANTIGONE. It was public. Could I help hearing it?

CREON. And yet you dared defy the law.

ANTIGONE.   I dared.
It was not God's proclamation. That final Justice
That rules the world below makes no such laws.

Creon in Antigone. Artist unknown.
Musée Jatta-Ruro. Reproduced in
Le Theatre, 1899.

Reading Strategy Interpreting Imagery *What are some of the senses to which the images in the sentry's speech appeal so far?* **R**

Literary Element Protagonist and Antagonist *How do Antigone's actions as described by the sentry attract the reader's or audience's sympathy?* **L**

Big Idea Loyalty and Betrayal *Explain the sentry's philosophy about loyalty.* **BI₂**

ANTIGONE, SCENE 2 **733**

Differentiated Instruction

Contrasting Characters A graphic aid can help students clearly visualize the areas of conflict between Antigone and Creon. Draw a chart on the board similar to the one here. Have students contribute ideas. **BL**

Creon	Antigone
humanity	God
patriotism to state	loyalty to family

Objectives
• To interpret imagery (SE)
• To use summarizing as a strategy to better understand the text (TWE)

Teach

BI₁ Big Idea

Loyalty and Betrayal

Answer: *Here Antigone suggests that Creon's edict betrays religious laws—the "unrecorded laws of God."* **Ask:** What reasons does the choragos offer for Antigone's actions? *(He says she has inherited stubbornness from her father.)* **OL**

L₁ Literary Element

Protagonist and Antagonist

Answer: *In addition to the conflict between human law and God's law, Creon describes a conflict between men and women. He believes that men have authority over women and that women should not defy men.* **OL**

---

59 **edict:** an official order or decree issued by a person in authority.

	Your edict,° King, was strong,
60	But all your strength is weakness itself against
	The immortal unrecorded laws of God.
	They are not merely now: they were, and shall be,
	Operative for ever, beyond man utterly.

	I knew I must die, even without your decree:
65	I am only mortal. And if I must die
	Now, before it is my time to die,
	Surely this is no hardship: can anyone
	Living, as I live, with evil all about me,
	Think Death less than a friend? This death of mine
70	Is of no importance; but if I had left my brother
	Lying in death unburied, I should have suffered.
	Now I do not.
	You smile at me. Ah, Creon,
	Think me a fool, if you like; but it may well be
	That a fool convicts me of folly.

75 CHORAGOS. Like father, like daughter: both headstrong, deaf to reason!
She has never learned to yield.

CREON.   She has much to learn.
The inflexible heart breaks first, the toughest iron
Cracks first, and the wildest horses bend their necks
At the pull of the smallest curb.
                          Pride? In a slave?
80 This girl is guilty of a double insolence,
Breaking the given laws and boasting of it.
Who is the man here,
She or I, if this crime goes unpunished?
Sister's child, or more than sister's child,
85 Or closer yet in blood—she and her sister
Win bitter death for this!
[*To* SERVANTS.]   Go, some of you,
Arrest Ismene. I accuse her equally.
Bring her: you will find her sniffling in the house there.

90 Her mind's a traitor: crimes kept in the dark
Cry for light, and the guardian brain shudders;
But how much worse than this
Is brazen boasting of barefaced anarchy!

Big Idea Loyalty and Betrayal *What is Antigone saying about betrayal here? Who does she suggest is betraying whom?* **BI₁**

Literary Element Protagonist and Antagonist *What other conflict does Creon suggest may exist between him and Antigone?* **L₁**

Additional Support

Skills Practice

WRITING: Alliteration Point out Creon's use of alliteration (the repetition of initial consonant sounds) in line 92: "brazen boasting of barefaced anarchy." The repetition of the *b* sound emphasizes Creon's angry opinion of Antigone's behavior. Explain that alliteration can be effective in prose or poetry when used sparingly. If it is overused, it can have an unintentionally humorous effect. Have students write three sentences containing alliteration that describe any of the characters in *Antigone*. Point out that alliterative words do not have to be consecutive but are usually separated by one or two words at the most. **OL**

ANTIGONE. Creon, what more do you want than my death?

CREON.   Nothing.
That gives me everything.

ANTIGONE.   Then I beg you: kill me.
95 This talking is a great weariness: your words
Are distasteful to me, and I am sure that mine
Seem so to you. And yet they should not seem so:
I should have praise and honor for what I have done.
All these men here would praise me
100 Were their lips not frozen shut with fear of you.
[*Bitterly.*] Ah the good fortune of kings,
Licensed to say and do whatever they please!

CREON. You are alone here in that opinion.

ANTIGONE. No, they are with me. But they keep their tongues
in leash.

105 **CREON.** Maybe. But you are guilty, and they are not.

ANTIGONE. There is no guilt in reverence for the dead.

CREON. But Eteocles—was he not your brother too?

ANTIGONE. My brother too.

CREON.   And you insult his memory?

ANTIGONE. [*Softly.*] The dead man would not say that I insult it.

110 **CREON.** He would: for you honor a traitor as much as him.

ANTIGONE. His own brother, traitor or not, and equal in blood.

CREON. He made war on his country. Eteocles defended it.

ANTIGONE. Nevertheless, there are honors due all the dead.

CREON. But not the same for the wicked as for the just.

115 **ANTIGONE.** Ah Creon, Creon,
Which of us can say what the gods hold wicked?°

CREON. An enemy is an enemy, even dead.

ANTIGONE. It is my nature to join in love, not hate.

CREON. [*Finally, losing patience.*] Go join them, then; if you
must have your love,
120 Find it in hell!

CHORAGOS. But see, Ismene comes:

[*Enter ISMENE, guarded.*]

Those tears are sisterly, the cloud

116 Which . . . wicked: Note Antigone's belief that people cannot understand the thinking of the gods.

Big Idea Loyalty and Betrayal *What is Antigone suggesting about the loyalty of the chorus?* **BI₂**

Literary Element Protagonist and Antagonist *How is Creon trying to strengthen his position in this debate?* **L₂**

ANTIGONE, SCENE 2 **735**

ANTIGONE, SCENE 2 **735**

Teach

BI₂ Big Idea
Loyalty and Betrayal
Answer: *She claims that in their hearts they are on her side. They are only silent because they are afraid of Creon.* **OL**

L₂ Literary Element
Protagonist and Antagonist
Answer: *He points out that Polyneices was attacking Thebes. He was an enemy and could not be treated as an equal to his loyal brother.* **OL**

Building Reading Fluency

Decoding Meaning Have two volunteers read the conversation between Ismene and Antigone aloud (lines 130–147). **Ask:** What does Ismene mean when she says, "if she will let me say so. I am guilty"? (*She is saying that even though she did not actually try to bury Polyneices, she wants to accept guilt with Antigone, but she is not sure how Antigone is going to respond.*) Have students rewrite Ismene's line in their own words. Discuss the rest of the conversation line by line. Have students rewrite at least three more lines in their own words. **BL**

Objectives
- To interpret imagery (SE)
- To understand the role of protagonist and antagonist (SE)
- To use alliteration effectively (TWE)

Teach

R Reading Strategy

Interpreting Imagery

Answer: *He compares her to a snake, which is an ugly, negative image. He makes the comparison more negative with the image "sucking my blood" and the adverb "stealthily."* **OL**

L1 Literary Element

Protagonist and Antagonist

Answer: *Antigone is taunting her by claiming that Ismene does whatever Creon wants.* **Ask:** *How would you characterize Antigone and Ismene based on the surrounding conversation? (Ismene exhibits positive traits: she is courageous and unselfish. Antigone shows several negative traits: she is cold, sarcastic, and vengeful.)* **OL**

That shadows her eyes rains down gentle sorrow.

CREON. You too, Ismene,

125   Snake in my ordered house, sucking my blood
    Stealthily—and all the time I never knew
    That these two sisters were aiming at my throne!
                            Ismene,
    Do you confess your share in this crime, or deny it?
    Answer me.

130 ISMENE. Yes, if she will let me say so. I am guilty.

ANTIGONE. [*Coldly.*] No, Ismene. You have no right to say so.
    You would not help me, and I will not have you help me.

ISMENE. But now I know what you meant; and I am here
    To join you, to take my share of punishment.

135 ANTIGONE. The dead man and the gods who rule the dead
    Know whose act this was. Words are not friends.

ISMENE. Do you refuse me, Antigone? I want to die with you:
    I too have a duty that I must discharge to the dead.

ANTIGONE. You shall not lessen my death by sharing it.

140 ISMENE. What do I care for life when you are dead?

ANTIGONE. Ask Creon. You're always hanging on his opinions.

ISMENE. You are laughing at me. Why, Antigone?

ANTIGONE. It's a joyless laughter, Ismene.

ISMENE.   But can I do nothing?

ANTIGONE. Yes. Save yourself. I shall not envy you.

145   There are those who will praise you; I shall have honor, too.

ISMENE. But we are equally guilty!

ANTIGONE.   No more, Ismene.
    You are alive, but I belong to Death.

CREON. [*To the CHORUS.*] Gentlemen, I beg you to observe
    these girls:
    One has just now lost her mind; the other,

150   It seems, has never had a mind at all.

ISMENE. Grief teaches the steadiest minds to waver, King.

CREON. Yours certainly did, when you assumed guilt with
    the guilty!

ISMENE. But how could I go on living without her?

Reading Strategy   Interpreting Imagery *How does Creon use imagery to make Ismene seem guilty?* **R**

Literary Element   Protagonist and Antagonist *The word* antagonize *has the same root as* antagonist *and means "to provoke dislike or hostility." How is Antigone antagonizing Ismene here?* **L1**

Additional Support

Skills Practice

GRAMMAR: Present Perfect Tense Remind students that the present perfect verb tense is used to describe an action that was completed at some indefinite past time but still affects the present, or an action that started in the past and continues into the present. For example, in line 60 on page 727, Creon says, ". . . the wisest / Have sometimes been known to count a few coins too many." Have students find two additional examples of this tense on pages 727–728. (*line 55: "the sentries have been appointed" and line 73: "for what someone else has done."*) **OL**

L2 **Literary Element**
Protagonist and Antagonist
Ask: Has your opinion of Creon changed since the beginning of the play? If so, how? *(Some students may say that at the end of this scene Creon seems more cruel and ruthless than he did earlier. His treatment of Antigone may strike readers as a fair, though tragic, application of the law; however, he seems to callously disregard his son's happiness here.)* **OL**

The Sisters, 2004. Chris Gollon. Mixed media on canvas, 91.4 x 61 cm. Private Collection.

CREON.   You are.
    She is already dead.

ISMENE.   But your own son's bride!

155 CREON. There are places enough for him to push his plow.
    I want no wicked women for my sons!°

ISMENE. O dearest Haimon, how your father wrongs you!

CREON. I've had enough of your childish talk of marriage!

CHORAGOS. Do you really intend to steal this girl from
    your son?

160 CREON. No; Death will do that for me.

CHORAGOS.   Then she must die?

CREON. [*Ironically.*] You dazzle me.
                  —But enough of this talk!
  [*To GUARDS.*] You, there, take them away and guard
    them well:
  For they are but women, and even brave men run
  When they see Death coming. **L2**

[*Exit ISMENE, ANTIGONE, and GUARDS.*]

154–156 She is . . . sons: Here is a new complication: Antigone is engaged to marry Creon's son, Haimon. Thus, punishing her means punishing him, a fact that doesn't appear to bother Creon greatly.

Building Reading Fluency

Paraphrasing Students may wish to paraphrase when they read relatively difficult parts of *Antigone*, such as Ode 2 (page 738). **Say:** When you paraphrase, you must restate the text in your own words without omitting any important details. Have pairs or small groups of students read aloud the first stanza of the ode and then paraphrase it. **Say:** The first line may be paraphrased "People who have never experienced God's vengeance are lucky." Tell students to change difficult words to simpler ones and adjust the sentence structure if necessary. Have volunteers read their paraphrases line by line. **BL**

Objectives
• To interpret imagery (SE)
• To understand the role of protagonist and antagonist (SE)
• To identify and understand the uses of present perfect tense (TWE)

Teach

R **Reading Strategy**

Interpreting Imagery
Answer: *The chorus compares the rage to a powerful storm with a dangerous wave and "wind whipped sand."* **OL**

BI **Big Idea**

Loyalty and Betrayal
Answer: *Zeus never forgets sins of arrogance by humans, and he will eternally continue punishing those sins.* **OL**

⭐ **Language History**

Olympus Tell students that the modern Olympic games are a revival of the ancient Olympic games, which were held in Olympia to honor Zeus, the king of the gods on Mount Olympus. **AS**

✓**CheckPoint**

Use the CheckPoint questions on Presentation Plus! to check students' mastery of the selection. These questions can be used with interactive response keypads for immediate student feedback.

ANTIGONE

ODE 2

CHORUS. Fortunate is the man who has never tasted God's
        vengeance!
    Where once the anger of heaven has struck, that house is
        shaken
    For ever: damnation rises behind each child
    Like a wave cresting out of the black northeast,
5   When the long darkness under sea roars up
    And bursts drumming death upon the windwhipped sand.
    I have seen this gathering sorrow from time long past
    Loom upon Oedipus' children: generation from generation
    Takes the compulsive rage of the enemy god.
10 So lately this last flower of Oedipus' line
    Drank the sunlight! but now a passionate word
    And a handful of dust have closed up all its beauty.

        What mortal **arrogance**
        Transcends° the wrath of Zeus?
15 Sleep cannot lull him, nor the effortless long months
    Of the timeless gods: but he is young for ever,
    And his house is the shining day of high Olympos.°
        All that is and shall be,
        And all the past, is his.
20 No pride on earth is free of the curse of heaven.

        The straying dreams of men
        May bring them ghosts of joy:
    But as they drowse, the waking embers burn them;
    Or they walk with fixed eyes, as blind men walk.
25 But the ancient wisdom speaks for our own time:
        Fate works most for woe
        With Folly's fairest show.
    Man's little pleasure is the spring of sorrow.

14 **Transcends:** is greater or better than.

17 **Olympos:** Zeus and the other gods and goddesses were believed to live on Mount Olympus.

Reading Strategy | Interpreting Imagery *To what does the chorus compare the rage of the gods against Oedipus's children?* **R**

Big Idea | Loyalty and Betrayal *According to the chorus, what does Zeus consider to be the ultimate sin?* **BI**

Vocabulary

arrogance (ar′ə gəns) n. overbearing pride

738 UNIT 4 DRAMA

Additional Support

Skills Practice

READING: Visualizing The ode makes use of several extended metaphors, each of which conjures a visual image that reinforces the action and themes of the play. Have students discuss specific details of these images and how they contribute to the reader's understanding. *(Possible answers:*

Details like "the black northeast" and "the long darkness under the sea roars up" show the violence and size of Creon's fury. Antigone's unprotectedness and relative innocence are revealed in the image of her as a flower that "drank the sunlight.") **OL**

738

RESPONDING AND THINKING CRITICALLY

Respond

1. If you could have entered the action at any point in Scenes 1 and 2, when would you have done so, and what would you have said to Antigone? To Creon?

Recall and Interpret

2. (a)What new law has Creon just enacted, and what does Antigone propose doing about it? (b)In explaining her plans to Ismene, why does Antigone say that "this crime is holy"?

3. (a)What news does the sentry bring on his first visit to Creon? (b)What can you infer about Creon's personality from his reaction to this report?

4. (a)Why is Antigone brought to Creon? (b)Compare and contrast what Antigone believes to be important to what Creon values.

Analyze and Evaluate

5. (a)In what ways is the sentry different from the other characters? (b)What does he add to your appreciation of the play? Explain.

6. (a)What role does the chorus play in the drama? (b)How does their participation affect your understanding and enjoyment of the play?

7. (a) In what ways are Antigone and Creon different? How are they alike? (b)Did you think it was still possible for them to resolve their differences at any point before the end of Scene 2? Explain.

Connect

8. **Big Idea** Loyalty and Betrayal How does Sophocles demonstrate that the concepts of loyalty and betrayal are not as simple as they may seem?

LITERARY ANALYSIS

Literary Element Protagonist and Antagonist

The **protagonist** in a work of literature may well be in conflict with several **antagonists**, and the antagonists may not all be people. Conflicts can exist between a character and nature, between a character and society, or between ideas, values, or emotions within the protagonist's own mind. What conflicts can you identify in the play *Antigone*?

1. Which character did you sympathize with and why? Did your sympathies change over the course of the play? Explain.

2. In Scene 1, line 138, the sentry suggests that Creon may have an internal conflict. What is the sentry referring to specifically? Do you think that he has hit upon the truth? Explain.

Internet Connection

Generate several questions to research about ancient Greece. Then search the Internet for answers. You might narrow your search by using keywords such as Thebes, Oedipus, Acropolis, Sophocles, or Theatre of Dionysos. Prepare a report on any interesting findings and present it to your class.

READING AND VOCABULARY

Reading Strategy Interpreting Imagery

Authors use images not only to help a reader experience the world they are creating, but also to better communicate their ideas.

1. Look at *Ode 1* on page 731. What do the images in the second stanza have in common?

2. In line 12 of *Ode 2* on page 738, the chorus speaks of "a handful of dust." What does this image refer to?

Vocabulary Practice

Practice with Context Clues Identify the context clues that help you define each vocabulary word.

1. The **repulse**, or defeat, of the enemy was the one and only battle of that short war.
   a. defeat   b. enemy   c. short war

2. If you do not eat all day, you will be **famished**.
   a. do not eat   b. all day   c. will be

3. Our report was **comprehensive**, unlike yours, which contained little information.
   a. our report   c. information
   b. contained little

Assess

1. Responses should indicate an understanding of situation and character.

2. (a) Creon's law states that Eteocles will be buried and Polyneices left unburied. Antigone proposes to bury Polyneices anyway. (b) The gods require the burial.

3. (a) Someone has buried Polyneices. (b) Creon is arrogant, easily angered, and domineering.

4. (a) She has been caught reburying Polyneices. (b) She values loyalty to the gods and family. Creon values loyalty to the law and the state.

5. (a) He is hesitant, frightened, uneducated, or funny. (b) Many will appreciate the comic relief he provides.

6. (a) Discusses the action and themes of the play. (b) They provide a fairly objective viewpoint.

7. (a) They are proud, strong-minded, outspoken, and stubborn. Both are loyal, but to different things. (b) Many students will feel that these two characters were destined for a collision.

8. Loyalty to one ideal may involve betrayal of another.

Literary Element

1. Most students will side with Antigone. Some might agree with Creon.

2. The sentry is referring to Creon's conscience and his growing doubt. Creon might regret his decree, but to protect the State's best interests he must go ahead with his actions.

Internet Connection

Students' reports should
- identify aspects of ancient Greece
- present the information in an organized manner

Reading Strategy

1. Refer to living creatures and nature's wonders

2. Antigone tossed "a handful of dust" on her brother's corpse.

Vocabulary

1. a   2. a   3. b

Focus

Summary

Despite pleading from Haimon and warnings from Teiresias, Creon will not change his mind. He finally goes to the tomb to save Antigone but is too late. Antigone has hanged herself. Haimon then kills himself. When Creon returns, he finds that Eurydice has killed herself in grief. Creon, a broken man, admits that he has brought about his own downfall.

V Vocabulary

Vocabulary File

Say: Add these words and definitions to your vocabulary file. For each word, include a sentence that gives you an example of how to use the word. **OL** Students with English language needs should include the pronunciations of these words in their files. **EL**

Literary Element Have students access the Web site to improve their understanding of tragic flaw.

LITERATURE PREVIEW

Building Background

The ancient Greeks believed in life after death, but this was generally not an attractive prospect. The underworld—sometimes known as "Hades" after the god who reigned there—was literally far below the earth. The shadowy King Hades, brother of Zeus and Poseidon, lived in a palace with his queen, Persephone, whom he had kidnapped from the world above.

The newly dead first had to cross the river Acheron, ferried by the old boatman Charon. Next they encountered a fearsome three-headed dog, Cerberus, who would let them in, but would let no one escape. Finally they met the three judges who would decide their fates. The unfortunate were condemned to Tartarus, sometimes described as the deepest of hells, where they would be tortured by hideous women known as Furies. The virtuous were rewarded with a life of continual pleasure in Elysium, where flowers never stopped blooming. Most of the new arrivals, however, spent eternity as faded ghosts, wandering the cold, stony Asphodel Fields that surrounded the palace of Hades.

Literary Element Tragic Flaw

According to the Greek philosopher Aristotle (384–322 BC), the hero of a tragedy is a person of great ability who comes to grief because of a **tragic flaw:** a fault within his or her character. Pride, ambition, jealousy, self-doubt, and anger are among those human weaknesses that can defeat the tragic hero. Sometimes a tragic flaw can even be an excess of virtue, such as the love of honor or the pursuit of duty. *Antigone,* a play that Aristotle knew well, is one of the tragedies from which he derived his definition of a tragic flaw. As you read Scenes 3 to 5 of *Antigone,* note how internal forces determine the fate of the characters.

• See Literary Terms Handbook, p. R18.

Literature Online Interactive Literary Elements Handbook To review or learn more about the literary elements, go to www.glencoe.com.

OBJECTIVES

In studying this selection, you will focus on the following:
• understanding the concept of a tragic flaw
• recognizing the author's purpose
• analyzing characterization
• writing an essay to analyze bias

READING PREVIEW

Reading Strategy Recognizing Author's Purpose

Authors usually write fiction or drama with a **purpose:** to entertain, to inform or teach a lesson, to tell a story, or to persuade readers to accept an idea. As you read the conclusion of *Antigone,* try to determine why the author chose to tell this story in a particular manner.

Reading Tip: Recording Your Thoughts Using a table to record your responses to events in the play can help you determine the author's purpose.

Event	My Thoughts	Author's Purpose
The choragos's opinions slowly shift during the play.	He is feeling sorry for Antigone and begins to question Creon.	Sophocles is creating sympathy for Antigone.

Vocabulary

deference (def′ər əns) *n.* respect and honor due to another; p. 741 *My grandmother complains that kids today do not show any deference.*

perverse (pər vurs′) *adj.* determined to go against what is reasonable, expected, or desired; contrary; p. 745 *My dad tells me I am perverse when I say that I want to go winter camping!*

absolve (ab zolv′) *v.* to free from blame; p. 746 *The DNA results will absolve the suspect.*

prevail (pri vāl′) *v.* to be superior in power or influence; succeed; p. 748 *Cunning will often prevail over brute force.*

defile (di fīl′) *v.* to spoil the purity of; to make dirty or unclean; p. 752 *His horrible crime defiled his reputation forever.*

Vocabulary Tip: Antonyms Antonyms are words with opposite or nearly opposite meanings.

Selection Skills

Literary Elements
• Tragic Flaw (SE pp. 740, 741, 743, 745, 748, 749, 752, 754, 758, 759, 761)
• Characterization (SE p. 761)

Antigone, Scenes 3, 4, and 5

Reading Skills
• Recognizing Author's Purpose (SE pp. 740–761)
• Comparison and Contrast (TWE p. 756)

Vocabulary Skills
• Antonyms (SE pp. 740, 761)
• Academic Vocabulary (SE p. 761)
• Prefixes (TWE p. 744)

Listening/Speaking/Viewing Skills
• Viewing Art (SE p. 748)
• Persuasive Techniques (TWE p. 746)

Writing Skills/Grammar
• Analysis of Bias (SE p. 762)
• End Punctuation (TWE p. 758)

SCENE 3

CHORAGOS. But here is Haimon, King, the last of all your
    sons.
    Is it grief for Antigone that brings him here,
    And bitterness at being robbed of his bride?

[*Enter HAIMON.*]

    CREON. We shall soon see, and no need of diviners.°   —Son,
5   You have heard my final judgment on that girl:
    Have you come here hating me, or have you come
    With **deference** and with love, whatever I do?

    HAIMON. I am your son, father. You are my guide.
    You make things clear for me, and I obey you.
10   No marriage means more to me than your continuing
      wisdom.

    CREON. Good. That is the way to behave: subordinate
    Everything else, my son, to your father's will.
    This is what a man prays for, that he may get
    Sons attentive and dutiful in his house,
15   Each one hating his father's enemies,
    Honoring his father's friends. But if his sons
    Fail him, if they turn out unprofitably,
    What has he fathered but trouble for himself
    And amusement for the malicious?
                          So you are right
20   Not to lose your head over this woman.
    Your pleasure with her would soon grow cold, Haimon,
    And then you'd have a hellcat in bed and elsewhere.
    Let her find her husband in Hell!
    Of all the people in this city, only she
25   Has had contempt for my law and broken it.

    Do you want me to show myself weak before the people?
    Or to break my sworn word? No, and I will not.
    The woman dies.
    I suppose she'll plead "family ties." Well, let her.
30   If I permit my own family to rebel,
    How shall I earn the world's obedience?

4 **diviners:** people who predict the future.

Reading Strategy   Recognizing Author's Purpose *Why do you think Sophocles makes Haimon appear so calm and reasonable?* **R**

Literary Element   Tragic Flaw *How does Creon reveal his pride here?* **L**

Vocabulary

deference (def′ ər əns) *n.* respect and honor due to another

---

Teach

R Reading Strategy

Recognizing Author's Purpose Answer: *Students may suggest that Sophocles contrasts Haimon's even, calm temper with Creon's pride and fury.* **OL**

L Literary Element

Tragic Flaw Answer: *He seems as interested in his image as in the justice of the case. He is arguing already with Haimon, who has not disagreed with him yet.* **OL**

CheckPoint

Use the CheckPoint questions on Presentation Plus! to monitor students' comprehension. These questions can be used with interactive response keypads for immediate student feedback.

Differentiated Instruction

Research Ask students to use a search engine to find information about dictatorships or other oppressive forms of government. They may look for current situations or past governments that have been overthrown. Have students make a list of research questions and then research one topic that is of interest to them. Students might enter keywords such as *revolutions, dictatorships, French Revolution, American Revolution, Russian Revolution, Cuba, Libya,* or *Iraq.* Remind students to check the credibility of all Web sites. **AL**

Objectives
- To understand the concept of a tragic flaw (SE)
- To recognize the author's purpose (SE)

Teach

BI₁ Big Idea

Loyalty and Betrayal

Answer: *Creon wants the city to support his decisions.* **Ask:** What does Creon feel is the most important trait for a future leader to have? *(He feels the ability to obey is most important.)* **OL**

BI₂ Big Idea

Loyalty and Betrayal

Answer: *He suggests that there is considerable opposition to Creon but that people are afraid to speak out.* **OL**

Show me the man who keeps his house in hand,
He's fit for public authority.
                    I'll have no dealings
With law-breakers, critics of the government:

35   Whoever is chosen to govern should be obeyed—
Must be obeyed, in all things, great and small,
Just and unjust! O Haimon,
The man who knows how to obey, and that man only,
Knows how to give commands when the time comes.

40   You can depend on him, no matter how fast
The spears come: he's a good soldier, he'll stick it out.

Anarchy, anarchy! Show me a greater evil!
This is why cities tumble and the great houses rain down,
This is what scatters armies!

45   No, no: good lives are made so by discipline.
We keep the laws then, and the lawmakers,
And no woman shall seduce us. If we must lose,
Let's lose to a man, at least! Is a woman stronger than we?

CHORAGOS. Unless time has rusted my wits,
50   What you say, King, is said with point and dignity.

HAIMON. [*Boyishly earnest.*] Father:
Reason is God's crowning gift to man, and you are right
To warn me against losing mine. I cannot say—
I hope that I shall never want to say!—that you

55   Have reasoned badly. Yet there are other men
Who can reason, too; and their opinions might be helpful.
You are not in a position to know everything
That people say or do, or what they feel:
Your temper terrifies them—everyone

60   Will tell you only what you like to hear.
But I, at any rate, can listen; and I have heard them
Muttering and whispering in the dark about this girl.
They say no woman has ever, so unreasonably,
Died so shameful a death for a generous act:

65   "She covered her brother's body. Is this indecent?
She kept him from dogs and vultures. Is this a crime?
Death?—She should have all the honor that we can give
     her!"

Big Idea Loyalty and Betrayal *According to Creon, why is loyalty such an important trait?* **BI₁**

Big Idea Loyalty and Betrayal *What is Haimon suggesting about the loyalty of Creon's followers?* **BI₂**

Additional Support

Skills Practice

LISTENING: Tone of Voice

Encourage students to imagine Haimon's tone of voice as he talks to his father on page 742. **Ask:** What adjectives would you use to describe his tone? *(Possible responses: calm, reasonable, respectful.)* Remind students to look at the stage direction that states *"Boyishly earnest."* Ask for volunteers to read several of Haimon's lines in the tone they think he would use. Have students in the "audience" take notes describing the tone of voice they hear. **OL**

The *Armentum Rider*, c. 550 BC. Greek. Bronze, height: 23.6 cm. The British Museum, London. ⭐

This is the way they talk out there in the city.

You must believe me:
70 Nothing is closer to me than your happiness.
What could be closer? Must not any son
Value his father's fortune as his father does his?
I beg you, do not be unchangeable:
Do not believe that you alone can be right.
75 The man who thinks that,
The man who maintains that only he has the power
To reason correctly, the gift to speak, the soul—
A man like that, when you know him, turns out empty.

It is not reason never to yield to reason!

80 In flood time you can see how some trees bend,
And because they bend, even their twigs are safe,
While stubborn trees are torn up, roots and all.

Literary Element Tragic Flaw *How does Haimon manage to suggest that his father is flawed without directly criticizing him?* **L1**

Literary Element Tragic Flaw *What character fault does Haimon seem to think that his father has?* **L2**

ANTIGONE, SCENE 3 **743**

Teach

L1 Literary Element

Tragic Flaw
Answer: *Haimon mentions criticism and rumors among the people. He suggests that others are too frightened of Creon's temper to voice their suspicions, but that as a loyal and loving son he can mention them.* **OL**

L2 Literary Element

Tragic Flaw
Answer: *Haimon is suggesting that Creon is inflexible—unable to admit that someone besides himself may be right.* **OL**

⭐ Viewing the Art

Sophocles' rise to prominence coincided almost exactly with the flowering of classical Greek sculpture. This bronze horseman was created only a century or so before Sophocles wrote *Antigone*, yet it seems primitive in comparison with the fluid and highly realistic Parthenon sculptures, which were created in Sophocles' lifetime. Have students research other artistic developments of the Golden Age of Greece. **AS**

English Language Coach

Words Related to Government
Antigone has many references to law and government. Some words may be unfamiliar to English language learners or may have abstract meanings that are difficult to grasp. On the board, compile a list of government-related words used in the play. Creon's speech on pages 726–727 includes the words *State, throne, subjects, exile,* and *traitor.* Words on page 742 include *authority, govern, government, anarchy,* and *discipline.* Have volunteers use each word in a sentence. **BL**

Objectives
• To understand the concept of a tragic flaw (SE)
• To decipher meaning through tone of voice (TWE)

743

Teach

R Reading Strategy

Recognizing Author's Purpose Answer: *The choragos is politely suggesting that both father and son have good points, yet Creon is probably going to angrily explode. This observation emphasizes Creon's tragic flaw.* **Ask:** What additional flaw does Sophocles show with Creon's next lines? *(Creon assumes that the older a person is, the wiser he or she is—an invalid assumption.)* **OL**

BI Big Idea

Loyalty and Betrayal
Answer: *Haimon is accusing his father of disloyalty to the gods.* **OL**

And the same thing happens in sailing:
Make your sheet fast, never slacken,—and over you go,
85   Head over heels and under: and there's your voyage.
Forget you are angry! Let yourself be moved!
I know I am young; but please let me say this:
The ideal condition
Would be, I admit, that men should be right by instinct;
90   But since we are all too likely to go astray,
The reasonable thing is to learn from those who can teach.

CHORAGOS.   You will do well to listen to him, King,
If what he says is sensible. And you, Haimon,
Must listen to your father.—Both speak well.

95   CREON.   You consider it right for a man of my years and experience
To go to school to a boy?

HAIMON.   It is not right
If I am wrong. But if I am young, and right,
What does my age matter?

CREON.   You think it right to stand up for an anarchist?

100   HAIMON.   Not at all. I pay no respect to criminals.

CREON.   Then she is not a criminal?

HAIMON.   The City would deny it, to a man.

CREON.   And the City proposes to teach me how to rule?

HAIMON.   Ah. Who is it that's talking like a boy now?

105   CREON.   My voice is the one voice giving orders in this City!

HAIMON.   It is no City if it takes orders from one voice.

CREON.   The State is the King!

HAIMON.   Yes, if the State is a desert.

[*Pause.*]

CREON.   This boy, it seems, has sold out to a woman.

HAIMON.   If you are a woman: my concern is only for you.

110   CREON.   So? Your "concern"! In a public brawl with your father!

HAIMON.   How about you, in a public brawl with justice?

CREON.   With justice, when all that I do is within my rights?

HAIMON.   You have no right to trample on God's right.

Reading Strategy   Recognizing Author's Purpose *How does this observation by the choragos affect Creon? What point does Sophocles make by including this?* **R**

Big Idea   Loyalty and Betrayal *How has Haimon turned the argument to question his father's loyalty?* **BI**

Additional Support

Skills Practice

VOCABULARY: Prefixes Remind students that a prefix is added to a root or base word to change or add to its meaning. Put the words *anarchy* and *anarchist* on the board. **Say:** The root *arch*, "rule or government," comes from the Greek word *archein*, "to rule." Therefore, *anarchy*, with the prefix *an-*, "without," means "an absence of government." *Anarchist*, with the suffix *-ist*, "one that adheres to a doctrine," means "one who promotes anarchy." Have students give the definitions of *monarchy, squirearchy,* and *oligarchy.* **OL**

[CREON *interrupts impatiently.*]

CREON. If dirges and planned lamentations could put off death,
  Men would be singing for ever.
    [*To the* SERVANTS.]   Take her, go!
55   You know your orders: take her to the vault
  And leave her alone there. And if she lives or dies,
  That's her affair, not ours: our hands are clean.

ANTIGONE. O tomb, vaulted bride-bed in eternal rock,
  Soon I shall be with my own again
60   Where Persephone° welcomes the thin ghosts underground:
  And I shall see my father again, and you, mother,
  And dearest Polyneices—
                      dearest indeed
  To me, since it was my hand
  That washed him clean and poured the ritual wine:
65   And my reward is death before my time!

  And yet, as men's hearts know, I have done no wrong,
  I have not sinned before God. Or if I have,
  I shall know the truth in death. But if the guilt
  Lies upon Creon who judged me, then, I pray,
70   May his punishment equal my own.

CHORAGOS.   O passionate heart,
  Unyielding, tormented still by the same winds!

CREON. Her guards shall have good cause to regret their
  delaying.

ANTIGONE. Ah! That voice is like the voice of death!

CREON. I can give you no reason to think you are mistaken.

75   ANTIGONE. Thebes, and you my fathers' gods,
  And rulers of Thebes, you see me now, the last
  Unhappy daughter of a line of kings,
  Your kings, led away to death. You will remember
  What things I suffer, and at what men's hands,
80   Because I would not transgress° the laws of heaven.
  [*To the* GUARDS, *simply.*] Come: let us wait no longer.

[*Exit* ANTIGONE, L., *guarded.*]

60 **Persephone** (pər sef′ ə nē):
Persephone is the queen of the
underworld of the dead.

80 **transgress:** break or violate.

| Literary Element | Tragic Flaw *Why does Creon say this?* **L₂**

| Literary Element | Tragic Flaw *Antigone explains that she is being punished because
she "would not transgress the laws of heaven." Might there be other reasons for her
misfortune? Explain.* **L₃**

Teach

L₂ Literary Element

Tragic Flaw Answer: *Creon
is refusing to take responsibility
for his own actions. This suggests that either he is ignorant
of his flaws or else chooses to
ignore them.* **OL**

L₃ Literary Element

Tragic Flaw Answer: *Some
students may think that
Antigone's fate results from her
stubbornness and refusal to
acknowledge Creon's authority.
Others may suggest that her
death is an inescapable part of
her family's punishment.* **OL**

English Language Coach

Words Related to Death The play's
characters talk of death as the time for
Antigone's punishment nears. It may be
helpful to English language learners to
review some words related to death that
appear in the dialogue, such as *grave*,
tomb, and *dirge*s. Have students locate
such words in the text and keep track of
the lines in which they appear. Have students paraphrase these lines so that the
meanings of the words are clear. Have
students add to the list as they complete
the play. **EL**

Objectives
• To understand the concept of a
tragic flaw (SE)
• To research Greek mythology
(TWE)

Teach

R1 Reading Strategy

Recognizing Author's Purpose Answer: *No one "can prevail against untiring Destiny"; neither gods nor mortals, including Antigone, can avoid their fate once the gods have decreed it. Each legend tells of someone who was imprisoned and came to a tragic end because of Fate.* **OL**

⭐ **Writer's Technique**

Imagery Say: Sophocles uses imagery to paint vivid pictures in the minds of the readers. **Ask:** What examples of imagery can you find in Ode 4? (*"rain of gold," "sea-blackened ships," "cradled by gales"*) Discuss how the use of such images creates a specific mood. **AS**

ODE 4

CHORUS. All Danäe's beauty was locked away
    In a brazen cell where the sunlight could not come:
    A small room, still as any grave, enclosed her.
    Yet she was a princess too,
5   And Zeus in a rain of gold poured love upon her. ⭐
    O child, child,
    No power in wealth or war
    Or tough sea-blackened ships
    Can prevail against untiring Destiny!°

10   And Dryas' son also, that furious king,
    Bore the god's prisoning anger for his pride:
    Sealed up by Dionysos in deaf stone,
    His madness died among echoes.
    So at the last he learned what dreadful power
15   His tongue had mocked:
    For he had profaned the revels,
    And fired the wrath of the nine
    Implacable Sisters that love the sound of the flute.°

    And old men tell a half-remembered tale
20   Of horror done where a dark ledge splits the sea
    And a double surf beats on the gray shores:
    How a king's new woman, sick
    With hatred for the queen he had imprisoned,
    Ripped out his two sons' eyes with her bloody hands
25   While grinning Ares watched the shuttle plunge
    Four times: four blind wounds crying for revenge,

    Crying, tears and blood mingled.—Piteously born,
    Those sons whose mother was of heavenly birth!
    Her father was the god of the North Wind
30   And she was cradled by gales,
    She raced with young colts on the glittering hills
    And walked untrammeled in the open light:
    But in her marriage deathless Fate found means
    To build a tomb like yours for all her joy.°

1–9 All Danäe's . . . Destiny: The Chorus briefly relates three Greek legends. Danäe (dan′ ā ē′) was imprisoned by her father when it was foretold that she would bear a child who would kill him. After Zeus visited Danäe, she gave birth to Zeus's son, who did eventually kill his grandfather.

10–18 And Dryas' . . . flute: Dionysos (dī′ ə nī′ səs) is the god of wine and fertility, and the Implacable Sisters (also called the Muses) are the goddesses of the arts and sciences. After Dryas's son (King Lycurgus) objected to the worship of Dionysos, the Sisters imprisoned him and drove him mad.

19–34 And old men . . . all her joy: It was King Phineus who imprisoned his first wife (the queen) and allowed his jealous new wife to blind the queen's sons. This horrible act was done under the gleeful gaze of Ares, the war god.

Reading Strategy Recognizing Author's Purpose *How do the legends in Ode 4 relate to Antigone's situation? What moral is the chorus communicating here?* **R1**

Additional Support

Skills Practice

LISTENING AND SPEAKING:
Recounting Fables A fable is a simple tale that teaches a moral. In Ode 4, the chorus recounts three such stories to teach the lesson that a person cannot escape his or her fate. **Ask:** What other fables have you heard? (*Possible responses: "The Tortoise and the Hare," "The Lion and the Mouse."*) Have students create fables to illustrate important lessons they have learned. You may also suggest that students find a fable such as one by Aesop and retell it. Have students tell their fables to the class. **OL**

SCENE 5

[*Enter blind* TEIRESIAS, *led by a boy. The opening speeches of* TEIRESIAS *should be in singsong contrast to the realistic lines of* CREON.]

TEIRESIAS. This is the way the blind man comes, Princes,
    Princes, Lock-step, two heads lit by the eyes of one.

CREON. What new thing have you to tell us, old Teiresias?

TEIRESIAS. I have much to tell you: listen to the prophet, Creon.

5 CREON. I am not aware that I have ever failed to listen.

TEIRESIAS. Then you have done wisely, King, and ruled well.

CREON. I admit my debt to you. But what have you to say?

TEIRESIAS. This, Creon: you stand once more on the edge of
    fate.°

CREON. What do you mean? Your words are a kind of dread.

10 TEIRESIAS. Listen, Creon:
    I was sitting in my chair of augury, at the place
    Where birds gather about me. They were all a-chatter,
    As is their habit, when suddenly I heard
    A strange note in their jangling, a scream, a
15   Whirring fury; I knew that they were fighting,
    Tearing each other, dying
    In a whirlwind of wings clashing. And I was afraid.°
    I began the rites of burnt-offering at the altar,
    But Hephaistos failed me: instead of bright flame,
20   There was only the sputtering slime of the fat thighflesh
    Melting: the entrails dissolved in gray smoke,
    The bare bone burst from the welter. And no blaze!
    This was a sign from heaven. My boy described it,
    Seeing for me as I see for others.

25   I tell you, Creon, you yourself have brought
    This new calamity upon us. Our hearths and altars
    Are stained with the corruption of dogs and carrion birds
    That glut themselves on the corpse of Oedipus' son.
    The gods are deaf when we pray to them, their fire
30   Recoils from our offering, their birds of omen
    Have no cry of comfort, for they are gorged
    With the thick blood of the dead.°
               O my son,

Venus de Milo, detail of the back of the head, 100 BC. Greek artist. Marble. Musée du Louvre, Paris. ★

1–8 This is . . . of fate: The blind prophet serves as the gods' agent, or go-between, in their dealings with people.

11–17 I was sitting . . . afraid: Teiresias sits in his chair of augury to listen to the birds, whose sounds he interprets as messages from the gods, allowing him to foretell, or augur, the future. The birds' fighting is a very bad sign.

18–32 I began . . . of the dead: Another bad sign: Hephaistos (hi fes′ təs), the god of fire, is withholding fire. Teiresias says that the gods are rejecting the Thebans' sacrificial offerings because the animals have fed on Polyneices's corpse.

Reading Strategy   Recognizing Author's Purpose *How does Sophocles prepare us for the importance of Teiresias's prediction?* **R₂**

ANTIGONE, SCENE 5   **751**

Teach

L1 Literary Element

Tragic Flaw Answer:
Students should cite relevant events from the play in their answer. OL

BI Big Idea

Loyalty and Betrayal
Answer: *He is suggesting that someone has paid Teiresias to advise him to bury Polyneices.* OL

L2 Literary Element

Tragic Flaw Answer: *Brass can mean brashness, self-assurance and impudence, character traits Creon displays in this scene.* OL

★ Viewing the Art

Say: This painting depicts Athena, goddess of wisdom and patron of Athens. Compare this image to the image of Venus on the previous page. Do the goddesses share the same traits? *(Students will likely say that Athena is not merciless.)* **Ask:** Which character would you say is most strongly allied with Athena? *(Teiresias)* **AS**

These are no trifles! Think: all men make mistakes,
But a good man yields when he knows his course is wrong,
35 And repairs the evil. The only crime is pride.

Give in to the dead man, then: do not fight with a corpse—
What glory is it to kill a man who is dead?
Think, I beg you:
It is for your own good that I speak as I do.
40 You should be able to yield for your own good.

CREON. It seems that prophets have made me their especial province.
All my life long
I have been a kind of butt for the dull arrows
Of doddering fortune-tellers!
                    No, Teiresias:
45 If your birds—if the great eagles of God himself
Should carry him stinking bit by bit to heaven,
I would not yield. I am not afraid of pollution:
No man can **defile** the gods.
                    Do what you will,
Go into business, make money, speculate
50 In India gold or that synthetic gold from Sardis,°
Get rich otherwise than by my consent to bury him.
Teiresias, it is a sorry thing when a wise man
Sells his wisdom, lets out his words for hire!

TEIRESIAS. Ah Creon! Is there no man left in the world—

55 CREON. To do what?—Come, let's have the aphorism!°

TEIRESIAS. No man who knows that wisdom outweighs any wealth?

CREON. As surely as bribes are baser than any baseness.

TEIRESIAS. You are sick, Creon! You are deathly sick!

CREON. As you say: it is not my place to challenge a prophet.

60 TEIRESIAS. Yet you have said my prophecy is for sale.

CREON. This generation of prophets has always loved gold.

TEIRESIAS. The generation of kings has always loved brass.

Literary Element Tragic Flaw *From what you have read so far, is Teiresias's advice likely to be followed? Explain.* **L1**

Big Idea Loyalty and Betrayal *How does Creon question Teiresias's loyalty here?* **BI**

Literary Element Tragic Flaw *What is Teiresias accusing Creon of here?* **L2**

Vocabulary

defile (di fīl′) *v.* to spoil the purity of; to make dirty or unclean

---

50 **synthetic gold from Sardis:** The people of Sardis, the capital of ancient Lydia (in modern-day Turkey), invented metallic coinage, the "synthetic gold" that Creon speaks of.

55 **aphorism:** a concise statement of a general truth.

Pallas Athena, or *Armoured Figure,* 1664–65. Rembrandt Harmensz van Rijn. Oil on canvas, 118 x 81.1 cm. Museu Calouste Gulbenkian, Lisbon, Portugal.

Additional Support

Skills Practice

LISTENING AND SPEAKING:
Performing Dialogue Choosing and performing a portion of the play's dialogue can help students better appreciate and understand the play. Have students work in pairs and choose a portion of dialogue that they feel is particularly important to the play's themes. Encourage them to practice reading the dialogue, discussing the vocal tone, emphasis, facial expressions, and gestures that best communicate the dialogue's meaning. Have each pair perform their dialogue for the class, explaining why they think it is especially meaningful. **OL**

CREON. You forget yourself! You are speaking to your King.

TEIRESIAS. I know it. You are a king because of me.°

65 **CREON.** You have a certain skill; but you have sold out.

TEIRESIAS. King, you will drive me to words that—

CREON.   Say them, say them!
Only remember: I will not pay you for them.

TEIRESIAS. No, you will find them too costly.

CREON.   No doubt. Speak:
Whatever you say, you will not change my will.

70 **TEIRESIAS.** Then take this, and take it to heart!
The time is not far off when you shall pay back
Corpse for corpse, flesh of your own flesh.
You have thrust the child of this world into living night,
You have kept from the gods below the child that is theirs:
75 The one in a grave before her death, the other,
Dead, denied the grave. This is your crime:
And the Furies° and the dark gods of Hell
Are swift with terrible punishment for you.

Do you want to buy me now, Creon?

                              Not many days,
80 And your house will be full of men and women weeping,
And curses will be hurled at you from far
Cities grieving for sons unburied, left to rot
Before the walls of Thebes.

These are my arrows, Creon: they are all for you.

85 [*To* BOY.] But come, child: lead me home.
Let him waste his fine anger upon younger men.
Maybe he will learn at last
To control a wiser tongue in a better head.

[*Exit* TEIRESIAS.]

CHORAGOS. The old man has gone, King, but his words
90 Remain to plague us. I am old, too,
But I cannot remember that he was ever false.

CREON. That is true. . . . It troubles me.
Oh it is hard to give in! but it is worse
To risk everything for stubborn pride.

95 **CHORAGOS.** Creon: take my advice.

CREON.   What shall I do?

Reading Strategy Recognizing Author's Purpose *Why might Sophocles have Creon say these words?* **R**

64 **I know . . . me:** It was Teiresias who revealed the truth of Oedipus's relationship to Jocasta and thus set off the chain of events that led to Creon's becoming king.

77 **Furies:** three goddesses who avenge crimes. ★

ANTIGONE, SCENE 5   **753**

Teach

R Reading Strategy

Recognizing Author's Purpose Answer: *The argument with Teiresias has brought out the worst in Creon and antagonized the prophet, who clearly knows that something terrible is going to happen.* **OL**

★ Language History

Furies The Furies were goddesses who avenged criminal behavior. Ask students to discuss how the English word *fury* is connected to this mythology. **AS**

Differentiated Instruciton

Comparing Literature The French playwright Jean Anouilh wrote a modern version of *Antigone* in 1942, when the Nazis occupied Paris. Many people thought that Antigone represented the French resistance movement and Creon the German authority in Anouilh's play. Have students read Anouilh's play.

Encourage them to discuss, orally or in an essay, whether the moral issues in Sophocles' play transfer effectively to the twentieth century.
NOTE: Anouilh's work has adult themes. You may wish to review the play before recommending it to students. **AL**

Objectives
• To understand the concept of a tragic flaw (SE)
• To recognize the author's purpose (SE)
• To perform dialogue (TWE)

753

Teach

L Literary Element

Tragic Flaw Answer: *Some may argue that his determination is so strong that it will never waver. Others may suggest that his determination has been partly bluster and that he knows that Teiresias is speaking the truth.* **OL**

R1 Reading Strategy

Recognizing Author's Purpose Answer: *Creon is attempting to rescue Antigone from her tomb, but the audience fears he will be too late.* **OL**

BI Big Idea

Loyalty and Betrayal

Answer: *This statement shows significant change because previously he has claimed that human law is of primary importance.* **OL**

⭐ Viewing the Art

Ask: What do you know about Zeus? *(Students may mention his power, his temper, thunderbolts, or fondness for mortal women.)*

Ask: Given what you know of Zeus and the other gods, has Creon been wise to defy their laws? *(no)* **AS**

CHORAGOS. Go quickly: free Antigone from her vault
　And build a tomb for the body of Polyneices.

CREON. You would have me do this?

CHORAGOS.　　　　　　　　　　　　　　Creon, yes!
　And it must be done at once: God moves
100　Swiftly to cancel the folly of stubborn men.

CREON. It is hard to deny the heart! But I Will do it:
　I will not fight with destiny.

CHORAGOS. You must go yourself, you cannot leave it to
　others.

CREON. I will go.
　　　　　　　—Bring axes, servants:
105　Come with me to the tomb. I buried her, I
　Will set her free.
　　　　　　　Oh quickly!
　My mind misgives—
　The laws of the gods are mighty, and a man
　　must serve them
　To the last day of his life!

[*Exit* CREON.]

Paean°

CHORAGOS. God of many names

CHORUS.　　　　　　　　　　O Iacchos°
　　　　　　　　　　　　　　　　son
　of Kadmeian Semele
　　　　　　　　　O born of the Thunder!
　Guardian of the West
　　　　　　　　Regent
　of Eleusis' plain
　　　　　　　O Prince of maenad Thebes
5　and the Dragon Field by rippling Ismenos:°

CHORAGOS. God of many names

CHORUS.　　　　　　　　　the flame of torches
　flares on our hills
　　　　　　　the nymphs of Iacchos

Head of Zeus. Artist unknown. Bronze. National Archaeological Museum, Athens. ⭐

Paean (pē′ ən): a song of praise, joy, or thanksgiving. Here, the Chorus praises Dionysos.

3 Iacchos (yä′ kəs): considered Thebes's special protector because his mother had been a Theban princess. The Chorus begs Dionysos to come to Thebes and drive out evil.

1–5 God of . . . Ismenos: The names of Dionysos refer to people and places associated with him. His mother, **Kadmeian Semele** (sem′ ə lē), was the daughter of Kadmos, a king of Thebes. His father was Zeus, who controlled thunder. This plain was the site of religious ceremonies performed in honor of Dionysos, and the river **Ismenos** ran near Thebes. The **maenads** (mē′ nadz) were Dionysos's devoted priestesses.

Literary Element Tragic Flaw *Given what you know of Creon's character, is this change of heart likely?* **L**

Reading Strategy Recognizing Author's Purpose *How does Sophocles build up suspense in this passage?* **R1**

Big Idea Loyalty and Betrayal *How does this statement represent a significant change in Creon's attitude?* **BI**

754 UNIT 4 DRAMA

Additional Support

Skills Practice

LISTENING AND WRITING: Theater Review Have students attend a performance of *Antigone* or another play of your choice in your community. Encourage them to take along a notebook to the performance, and give them the assignment of writing a review of the performance. Tell them to look for the following characteristics: character movement (or blocking), tone of voice, facial expressions and gestures, and special effects. They may also wish to develop a rating system and assess the performance. You may wish to bring in copies of sample reviews from local newspapers for students to read. **OL**

dance at the spring of Castalia:

from the vine-close mountain
come ah come in ivy:°
10   *Evohé*° *evohé!* sings through the streets of Thebes
CHORAGOS.   God of many names
CHORUS.   Iacchos of Thebes
heavenly Child
of Semele bride of the Thunderer!
The shadow of plague is upon us:
come
with clement° feet
oh come from Parnasos
15   down the long slopes
across the lamenting water
CHORAGOS.   Io Fire! Chorister of the throbbing stars!
O purest among the voices of the night!
Thou son of God, blaze for us!

CHORUS.   Come with choric rapture of circling Maenads
20   Who cry *Io Iacche!*
God of many names!

Exodos°

[*Enter MESSENGER, L.*]

MESSENGER.   Men of the line of Kadmos, you who live
Near Amphion's citadel:°
I cannot say
Of any condition of human life "This is fixed,
This is clearly good, or bad." Fate raises up,
5   And Fate casts down the happy and unhappy alike:
No man can foretell his Fate.
Take the case of Creon:
Creon was happy once, as I count happiness:
Victorious in battle, sole governor of the land,
Fortunate father of children nobly born.
10   And now it has all gone from him! Who can say
That a man is still alive when his life's joy fails?
He is a walking dead man. Grant him rich,
Let him live like a king in his great house:
If his pleasure is gone, I would not give
15   So much as the shadow of smoke for all he owns.

Reading Strategy   Recognizing Author's Purpose *What is the effect of this line and that of the Paean as a whole?* **R₂**

Reading Strategy   Recognizing Author's Purpose *What point is the Messenger making here?* **R₃**

7–9 the nymphs . . . come in ivy:
Dionysos was raised by **nymphs**, long-lived women who were associated with trees and other parts of nature. The **spring of Castalia** is on Parnasos, a holy mountain. The grape **vine** and **ivy** were symbols of Dionysos.
10 *Evohé*: "Hallelujah."

14 clement: forgiving; merciful.

Exodos: the last part of the play.

2 Amphion's citadel: the wall around Thebes, which Amphion built by charming stones into place with music.

Differentiated Instruction

Music The music that accompanied Greek drama no longer exists, so there is no way to know exactly how the choral lines were sung. Songs such as the Paean may have been chanted as prayers like those in worship services. One such style of chanting is known as Gregorian chant or plainsong. Have students who are knowledgeable about music bring in a recording of Gregorian chants to class. Then have students work together to chant the Paean chorally in a similar way. **AL**

Teach

B1 **Big Idea**

Loyalty and Betrayal

Answer: *Immediately they perform a funeral ceremony for Polyneices. Then they go to rescue Antigone. This shows how completely Creon has altered his thinking about the gods—they are now of primary importance to him.* **OL**

★ Cultural History

Athena Athena, or Pallas, was the goddess of warfare and of wisdom and also the patroness of arts and crafts. A myth says that Athens was named for her after a contest between her and Poseidon. The town's citizens said they would name the city after the god or goddess who offered the most useful gift. Poseidon offered a horse and Athena offered an olive tree. The gods decided that Athena's gift was more valuable, and the city was named in her honor. **AS**

CHORAGOS. Your words hint at sorrow: what is your news
    for us?

MESSENGER. They are dead. The living are guilty of their death.

CHORAGOS. Who is guilty? Who is dead? Speak!

MESSENGER.   Haimon.
    Haimon is dead; and the hand that killed him
20   Is his own hand.

CHORAGOS.   His father's? or his own?

MESSENGER. His own, driven mad by the murder his father
    had done.

CHORAGOS. Teiresias, Teiresias, how clearly you saw it all!

MESSENGER. This is my news: you must draw what
    conclusions you can from it.

CHORAGOS. But look: Eurydice, our Queen:
25   Has she overheard us?

[*Enter EURYDICE from the Palace, C.*]

EURYDICE. I have heard something, friends:
    As I was unlocking the gate of Pallas'° shrine,
    For I needed her help today, I heard a voice
    Telling of some new sorrow. And I fainted
30   There at the temple with all my maidens about me.
    But speak again: whatever it is, I can bear it:
    Grief and I are no strangers.°

MESSENGER.   Dearest Lady,
    I will tell you plainly all that I have seen.
    I shall not try to comfort you: what is the use,
35   Since comfort could lie only in what is not true?
    The truth is always best.
                        I went with Creon
    To the outer plain where Polyneices was lying,
    No friend to pity him, his body shredded by dogs.
    We made our prayer in that place to Hecate°
40   And Pluto,° that they would be merciful. And we bathed
    The corpse with holy water, and we brought
    Fresh-broken branches to burn what was left of it,
    And upon the urn we heaped up a towering barrow
    Of the earth of his own land.
                   When we were done, we ran
45   To the vault where Antigone lay on her couch of stone.
    One of the servants had gone ahead,

27 Pallas: the goddess of wisdom; also known as Athena. ★

32 Grief and I . . . strangers: Eurydice (yoo rid′ i sē) is referring to the death of Megareus (me gàr′ ā ōōs), her older son, who died in the battle for Thebes.

39 Hecate (hek′ ə tē): another name for Persephone, the goddess of the underworld.
40 Pluto: another name for Hades, the god of the underworld.

Reading Strategy   Recognizing Author's Purpose *Why might Sophocles introduce Creon's wife at this late point in the play?* **R1**

Big Idea   Loyalty and Betrayal *What does the order in which Creon and the Messenger do their business tell you about Creon's new priorities?* **B1**

Additional Support

Skills Practice

READING: Comparison and Contrast Many of the conflicts of *Antigone* exist in the form of opposite or contrasting values. **Ask:** What examples of conflicting values have you noticed in the play? As students give answers, write the following conflicts on the board: *mortal vs. gods*

law vs. religion
man vs. woman
age vs. youth
state vs. family
Have students quote or summarize a portion of dialogue from *Antigone* that illustrates each set of contrasts. **OL**

And while he was yet far off he heard a voice
Grieving within the chamber, and he came back
And told Creon. And as the King went closer,
50 The air was full of wailing, the words lost,
And he begged us to make all haste. "Am I a prophet?"
He said, weeping, "And must I walk this road,
The saddest of all that I have gone before?
My son's voice calls me on. Oh quickly, quickly!
55 Look through the crevice there, and tell me
If it is Haimon, or some deception of the gods!"

We obeyed; and in the cavern's farthest corner
We saw her lying:
She had made a noose of her fine linen veil
60 And hanged herself. Haimon lay beside her,
His arms about her waist, lamenting her,
His love lost under ground, crying out
That his father had stolen her away from him.

When Creon saw him the tears rushed to his eyes
65 And he called to him: "What have you done, child? Speak
        to me.
What are you thinking that makes your eyes so strange?
O my son, my son, I come to you on my knees!"
But Haimon spat in his face. He said not a word,
Staring—
        And suddenly drew his sword
70 And lunged. Creon shrank back, the blade missed; and
        the boy,
Desperate against himself, drove it half its length
Into his own side, and fell. And as he died
He gathered Antigone close in his arms again,
Choking, his blood bright red on her white cheek.
75 And now he lies dead with the dead, and she is his
At last, his bride in the houses of the dead.

[Exit EURYDICE into the Palace.]

    CHORAGOS. She has left us without a word. What can this
        mean?

    MESSENGER. It troubles me, too; yet she knows what is best,
        Her grief is too great for public lamentation,
80 And doubtless she has gone to her chamber to weep
For her dead son, leading her maidens in his dirge.

Dionysos and his mother Semele,
6th century BC. Artist unknown.
Black-figured cup. Staatliche
Antikensammlung, Munich. ★

Reading Strategy Recognizing Author's Purpose *Why might Sophocles have
included this description?* R2

Reading Strategy Recognizing Author's Purpose *Do you think Sophocles
expected his audience to accept the Messenger's assumption that Eurydice has left to
grieve privately?* R3

Teach

L1 Literary Element

Tragic Flaw
Answer: *Some students may suggest that the choragos is finally able to speak the truth now that Creon is no longer a threat. Others may argue that the choragos's eyes, like Creon's, have been opened by the tragic events.* **OL**

★ Viewing the Art

Tell students that this mask is from a tomb in Mycenae, an important Bronze Age settlement in Greece. Mycenaean tombs show evidence of elaborate rites. The dead were buried with numerous precious ornaments, jewelry, formal weapons, and vases, cups, and other vessels. This man's beard shows him to be a powerful citizen.

Ask: What do such rites tell us about a civilization's relationship to death? How does this factor into the events of *Antigone?* *(The Mycenaeans likely believed in an afterlife that demanded extensive preparations. Students will likely find insight into the true significance of Creon's denying Polyneices a*

CHORAGOS. It may be so: but I fear this deep silence
[*Pause.*]

  MESSENGER. I will see what she is doing. I will go in.
[*Exit* MESSENGER *into the Palace.*]

[*Enter* CREON *with attendants, bearing* HAIMON's *body.*]

  CHORAGOS. But here is the King himself: oh look at him,
85   Bearing his own damnation in his arms.

  CREON. Nothing you say can touch me any more.
   My own blind heart has brought me
   From darkness to final darkness. Here you see
   The father murdering, the murdered son—
90   And all my civic wisdom!

   Haimon my son, so young, so young to die,
   I was the fool, not you; and you died for me.

  CHORAGOS. That is the truth; but you were late in learning it.

  CREON. This truth is hard to bear. Surely a god
95   Has crushed me beneath the hugest weight of heaven,
   And driven me headlong a barbaric way
   To trample out the thing I held most dear.

   The pains that men will take to come to pain!
[*Enter* MESSENGER *from the Palace.*]

  MESSENGER. The burden you carry in your hands is heavy,
100   But it is not all: you will find more in your house.

  CREON. What burden worse than this shall I find there?

  MESSENGER. The Queen is dead.

  CREON. O port of death, deaf world,
   Is there no pity for me? And you, Angel of evil,
105   I was dead, and your words are death again.
   Is it true, boy? Can it be true?
   Is my wife dead? Has death bred death?

  MESSENGER. You can see for yourself.

[*The doors are opened, and the body of* EURYDICE *is disclosed within.*]

  CREON. Oh pity!
110   All true, all true, and more than I can bear!
   O my wife, my son!

Literary Element Tragic Flaw *Why was Creon unable to come to this realization earlier?* **L1**

Additional Support

Skills Practice

WRITING: End Punctuation Review the three kinds of end punctuation:

- Period—at the end of declarative sentences and most imperative sentences.
- Question mark—at the end of interrogative sentences.
- Exclamation point—at the end of exclamatory sentences, strong interjec-

tions, and imperative sentences that express strong emotion.

Have students find at least three examples of each use of end punctuation in sentences from the play. Ask them to write the sentences and a brief explanation of why each is an example of a particular usage. **OL**

MESSENGER. She stood before the altar, and her heart
    Welcomed the knife her own hand guided,
    And a great cry burst from her lips for Megareus dead,
115   And for Haimon dead, her sons; and her last breath
    Was a curse for their father, the murderer of her sons.°
    And she fell, and the dark flowed in through her closing
      eyes.

CREON. O God, I am sick with fear.
    Are there no swords here? Has no one a blow for me?

120 MESSENGER. Her curse is upon you for the deaths of both.

CREON. It is right that it should be. I alone am guilty.
    I know it, and I say it. Lead me in,
    Quickly, friends.
    I have neither life nor substance. Lead me in.

125 CHORAGOS. You are right, if there can be right in so much
      wrong.
    The briefest way is best in a world of sorrow.

CREON. Let it come,
    Let death come quickly, and be kind to me.
    I would not ever see the sun again.

130 CHORAGOS. All that will come when it will; but we,
      meanwhile,
    Have much to do. Leave the future to itself.

CREON. All my heart was in that prayer!

CHORAGOS. Then do not pray any more: the sky is deaf.

CREON. Lead me away. I have been rash and foolish.
135   I have killed my son and my wife.
    I look for comfort; my comfort lies here dead.
    Whatever my hands have touched has come to nothing.
    Fate has brought all my pride to a thought of dust.

[*As CREON is being led into the house, the CHORAGOS advances and
speaks directly to the audience.*]

CHORAGOS. There is no happiness where there is no wisdom;
140   No wisdom but in submission to the gods.
    Big words are always punished,
    And proud men in old age learn to be wise.

116 **Was a curse . . . sons:** Note that even though Haimon stabbed himself and Megareus died in battle, Eurydice blames Creon for their deaths.

Funerary Mask, c. 1600 BC. Mycenaean.

Literary Element Tragic Flaw *Has your attitude toward Creon changed over the course of the play? In what way?* **L₂**

Reading Strategy Recognizing Author's Purpose *Why do you think Sophocles allows Creon's character to live on after those around him die?* **R**

Big Idea Loyalty and Betrayal *What is the play's final position on the issue of loyalty?* **BI**

Teach

L₂ Literary Element

Tragic Flaw Answer: *Creon's grief-stricken awareness of the harm he has caused may increase students' compassion for his tragedy.* **OL**

R Reading Strategy

Recognizing Author's Purpose Answer: *Students may point out that Creon's punishment is greater if he lives to see the consequences of his actions.* **OL**

BI Big Idea

Loyalty and Betrayal Answer: *People's first loyalty must be to the gods.* **OL**

✓CheckPoint

Use the CheckPoint questions on Presentation Plus! to check students' mastery of the selection. These questions can be used with interactive response keypads for immediate student feedback.

Differentiated Instruction

Monitoring Comprehension The poetic structure and sometimes unfamiliar words may make it difficult for some students to keep up with the action of the play. Because not understanding one passage might hinder a student's understanding of later sections, students should monitor their comprehension.

Encourage students to use the following techniques:

- Slow your reading rate. Reread to clarify.
- Ask yourself who, what, where, when, why, and how questions.
- Paraphrase difficult passages. **BL**

Objectives
- To understand the concept of a tragic flaw (SE)
- To recognize the author's purpose (SE)
- To identify and use the mechanics of end punctuation (TWE)

759

Assess

1. Students should show familiarity with the characters.

2. (a) To convince his father to spare Antigone's life. (b) It becomes an argument when Haimon suggests that Creon may be mistaken.

3. (a) Teiresias says Creon is bringing a plague upon Thebes and will suffer great tragedy. (b) Creon changes his mind because he is frightened by the prophecy, finally convinced he has wronged Antigone.

4. (a) Creon rushes to Antigone's tomb, stopping to bury Polyneices. He finds Antigone dead and witnesses Haimon's suicide. Eurydice kills herself. Creon repents his pride. (b) The message is that a person must listen to other people, or that the gods' law should be obeyed over human law.

5. Haimon is reasonable and diplomatic; Creon, proud, defensive, and volatile.

6. (a) At first Antigone is outraged and defiant. In Scene 4 she is depressed. (b) It may seem a natural response to the approach of death.

7. (a) Antigone, Oedipus' daughter, believes his family is paying for his sins. (b) Students may say that knowing allusions increases enjoyment.

RESPONDING AND THINKING CRITICALLY

Respond

1. Rank the main characters in order of how sympathetic you feel to them. Explain why you rank them this way.

Recall and Interpret

2. (a) Why does Haimon come to see his father? (b) How does their exchange of ideas evolve into a bitter argument?

3. (a) What does Teiresias tell Creon? (b) Why, do you think, does Creon change his mind?

4. (a) Summarize the events that occur after Teiresias leaves Creon. (b) What message, or lesson, does the audience take from these events?

Analyze and Evaluate

5. What differences in their personalities do Creon and Haimon reveal in their argument?

6. (a) Compare Antigone's demeanor in Scene 4 with her attitude in previous scenes. How has she changed? (b) Does her transformation seem believable to you?

7. (a) Explain how the house of Oedipus plays a role in *Antigone*. (b) Do these allusions affect your appreciation of the play? Explain.

Connect

8. **Big Idea** Loyalty and Betrayal Creon considers his opponents to be traitors. How loyal should citizens be to their national leaders? When does criticism become disloyalty? Support your answer with a reference to modern events.

VISUAL LITERACY

Determining Loyalty and Popularity

Much of the struggle in *Antigone* revolves around people's loyalty; specifically, whether they are loyal in general, and if so, where their loyalties lie. For example, Antigone is a very loyal character: her actions demonstrate loyalty to both her deceased brother and to religious law. However, she is not loyal to the king's law.

With a group of students, review the words and actions of the characters in *Antigone* to determine how loyal each one is in terms of religious law, the king's law, and family bonds. Use specific citations from the play to support your ideas. Then rank each character's position on line graphs like the ones below, with ten meaning "very much" and zero meaning "not at all." Share your group's results with the rest of the class and discuss any differences you find.

1. (a) Is one type of loyalty more important or valuable than the others? Explain. (b) Do you think Sophocles believed that one type of loyalty was the most noble? Explain your answer, using examples from the text.

2. What effect does a character's loyalty have on his or her popularity? Create new line graphs and rank the characters again, according to how much you like them. Tally the students' rankings and determine each character's average rank. Is there a correlation between a character's loyalty ranking and his or her popularity score? Discuss your findings as a class.

Religious Law

---

8. Students should show an understanding of the difference between criticism and treachery, and refer to a specific situation.

Visual Literacy

1. (a) Students should cite reasons for their rankings. (b) Answers will vary, but reasoning should be consistent with examples from the text.

2. Results will vary.

Literary Element: Tragic Flaw

Today we label people as heroes to acknowledge their bravery or hard work. To the writer of classical tragedies, however, a hero was a more complex character. A hero was a strong, often admirable person who failed to live up to his or her promise because of a **tragic flaw**. This might be a negative trait or a positive one that is inflexible or taken to excess.

1. Reread Teiresias's warning to Creon (Scene 5, lines 10–40). What flaw does the prophet specifically identify in the king's character? Do you believe that this weakness is sufficient to cause the tragedy that results? Explain.

2. How would you describe Antigone's personality? Does she have a trait that might qualify as a tragic flaw? Is she, too, a tragic hero, or is she an innocent victim of Creon? Explain.

Review: Characterization

As you learned on page 149, **characterization** refers to the way an author reveals the personality of a character. In drama we often learn about characters through **indirect characterization**, particularly by their words and actions.

Partner Activity Get together with a partner and create an organizer like the one below. In the left-hand boxes copy Creon's exact words. In the right-hand boxes describe things he does. Write your conclusion about Creon—based on these examples—in the bottom box. Then choose another character and create another graphic profile.

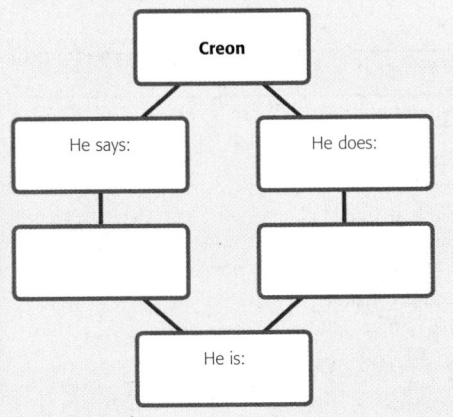

Creon

He says: He does:

He is:

Reading Strategy: Recognizing Author's Purpose

To identify an **author's purpose**, look carefully at the way a piece of literature is written, at your reactions to it, and at the message that comes across to you.

For each of the following statements concerning author's purpose, write a sentence saying why you agree or disagree.

1. Sophocles wrote *Antigone* to entertain the audiences at the Greek festivals.

2. *Antigone* was intended solely as a way of teaching the history of a famous family from Thebes.

Vocabulary Practice

Practice with Antonyms Choose the best antonym for each boldfaced vocabulary word.

1. The substitute teacher was amazed at the **deference** with which the students treated her.
   a. disrespect   **b.** cooperation   **c.** jokes

2. Surprisingly, the agreeable girl's sister was quite **perverse**.
   a. hilarious   **b.** acquiescent   **c.** contrary

3. Despite your accusations, the facts and evidence will **absolve** me.
   a. know   **b.** hate   **c.** blame

4. Grass stains **defiled** the girl's white dress.
   a. made clean   **b.** covered   **c.** decorated

Academic Vocabulary

Here are two words from the vocabulary list on page R82. These words will help you think, write, and talk about the selection.

code (kōd) *n.* a collection of principles or rules of conduct that instruct people in correct behavior

gender (jen′dər) *n.* the state of being of the male or female sex; sexual identity

Practice and Apply
1. What **code** of behavior is central to *Antigone*?
2. Did you detect any evidence of **gender** discrimination in the play? Explain.

ANTIGONE **761**

Literary Element

1. Teiresias says that Creon has the flaw of pride, a weakness sufficient to cause the tragedy; it prevents Creon from accepting that he is wrong and others are right.

2. Although Antigone is admirable in performing her duty, she is also stubborn and uncompromising. Students may see this as a tragic flaw and see Antigone as a tragic hero who contributes to her own demise.

Review: Characterization

Students' answers will vary. Students conclusions should be supported by textual references and characters' actions.

Reading Strategy

1. Students should agree: tragedies were considered a form of entertainment.

2. Students should disagree: teaching history was not the only purpose of the play.

Vocabulary

1. a **2.** b **3.** c **4.** a

Academic Vocabulary

1. The dead must be ritually washed and buried in order to enter the underworld.

2. Creon does not see women as equal to men. He assumes they will take subordinate roles.

Assess

Writing About Literature

Students' essays should

- identify possible bias in the play and analyze its effects.
- use specific quotations and details from the play to support their opinions.

Interdisciplinary Activity

Tell students to review the art on page 720 for a model to use in designing their masks.

Sophocles' Language and Style

Students' selections and explanations will vary. Have students read the examples they have chosen aloud, so that they can hear the rhythm of the lines and, thus, make logical conclusions as to why Sophocles has employed such punctuation.

Writing About Literature

Analyze Bias Would Antigone's fate have been different if she had been a man? Review the play for statements that reveal Creon's and other characters' attitudes toward women and their role in Thebes society. Then write two or three paragraphs summarizing these attitudes and stating whether or not, in your opinion, bias against women affected Creon's judgment and Antigone's fate. Support your analysis with specific quotations and other details from the play.

Using a table like the one below to record your own responses to events in the play can help you interpret bias.

Evidence from Play	My Interpretation
Creon: Fool, adolescent fool! Taken in by a woman!	Creon makes it clear that he would respect Haimon more if it had been a man who made him think this way.
Creon: Let's lose to a man, at least! Is a woman stronger than we?	Creon is asking a rhetorical question here: he believes that women are inherently weaker than men.

Interdisciplinary Activity

Greek drama was performed by actors wearing masks. Using cardboard, papier mâché, fabric, or other materials, make a mask that covers your entire face and expresses the dominant personality trait of one of the characters of *Antigone*. Use yarn for hair, and make sure to include eye holes and a substantial mouth opening.

 Literature Online **Web Activities** For eFlashcards, Selection Quick Checks, and other Web activities, go to www.glencoe.com.

Sophocles's Language and Style

Using Dashes Throughout *Antigone*, Sophocles punctuates lines with dashes. The dash is a form of punctuation that is often used when a comma is not quite strong enough. An author may use a dash to suggest hesitation in speech, to introduce an explanation, or to separate a phrase from the rest of a sentence, indicating a slight change of idea.

In the prologue of *Antigone*, for example, Antigone explains to Ismene, "It will not be the worst of deaths—death without honor." Here the dash sets apart a parenthetical phrase, or explanation.

In Scene 1 when the Sentry stammers, "The dead man—Polyneices—out there—someone,— / New dust on the slimy flesh!" the dashes show hesitation in his speech and also confusion in his thoughts.

In Scene 2, Creon says to the choragos, "You dazzle me. —But enough of this talk." Here the dash indicates a change of subject.

Activity Using a chart like the one below, copy several passages from *Antigone* that include dashes, and read them to a partner. Discuss and list what purpose you think the dash serves in each case.

Example from Play	Purpose of Dash
Haimon: Your temper terrifies them—everyone will tell you only what you like to hear.	Haimon hesitates here as he decides what is the politest way to make his point.

Revising Check

Dashes Go through your essay on analyzing bias in *Antigone*. Look for sentences in which you might have used a dash instead of a comma. Copy the sentences on a separate sheet of paper, using dashes. If you feel a revision is more effective, incorporate it into your essay.

Remember that a dash draws more attention to a phrase or thought than a comma does. Dashes are particularly useful when you wish to emphasize a passage.

Literature Online

Web Activities Have students access the Web site for interactive activities that will help them assess their understanding of the selection.

762

TIME

EVER ALLURING

Cleopatra could draw the crowds in ancient Rome. Now she's turning on her seductive charm in London.

By **MARYANN BIRD**

SHE IS ONE OF THE MOST FAMOUS FIGURES OF ANCIENT history, a name synonymous with beauty, yet no one knows what she really looked like. A Macedonian Greek, she ruled Egypt and was known for her relationships—political and romantic—with the two great Roman leaders of her time, Julius Caesar and Mark Antony. Her legend—wrapped in intrigue, conflict, and romance—lives on to this day. As Shakespeare wrote of Cleopatra in his play *Antony and Cleopatra:* "Age cannot wither her nor custom stale her infinite variety."

Although she has been dead since 30 B.C., Cleopatra VII, the last of the Ptolemaic rulers, still wields considerable power. The magic of her name drew big crowds to a 2001 exhibition called "Cleopatra of Egypt: From History to Myth" at the British Museum in London. For the show, which included new finds and interpretations, the museum attracted loans of many Cleopatra-related artifacts. Among them were sculptures, coins, paintings, ceramics, and jewelry from some 30 museums, libraries, and private collections around the world.

The Many Sides of Cleopatra

"Cleopatra's name is more evocative than any image of her," said co-curator Peter Higgs in an interview at the time of the exhibition's opening. He described the show as a "biographical study" that presented many different sides of Cleopatra, all of which contributed to the legend that she began building during her lifetime. Higgs acknowledged that not all classical scholars would concur with the museum's view of Cleopatra. "We know that not everyone is going to agree with us," he said. "We're not saying we're right about everything. This is our interpretation."

On the coins on display, *Cleopatra* appeared masculine and powerful. In the sculptures, some of which portrayed her as the goddess Isis, the divine mother whose cult she followed, she looked slim and serene. The

EVER ALLURING **763**

Teach

Big Idea

Loyalty and Betrayal

Say: Consider this question as you read: Why would loyalty and betrayal be so critical in Cleopatra's life and times? *(She was a ruler, and her political alliances were necessary to remain in power. Even one betrayal could signal the end of her reign and her life.)* **OL**

R Reading Strategy

Distinguishing Fact and Opinion

In determining fact and opinion in a descriptive essay such as Bird's, students may have to pull the facts out of the text to separate them from opinions, hearsay, or myths. **Ask:** What are the actual facts that you learn from this essay? *(Facts include the following: Cleopatra was an Egyptian pharaoh; she was Macedonian Greek; she died in 30 B.C.; she had political and personal relationships with Julius Caesar and Marc Antony; she was the last of the Ptolemaic rulers. Students may provide other facts as well.)* **OL**

HISTORY AND MYTH:
Bronze coins.

show also featured Renaissance paintings that portrayed her as a sensual and tragic figure. Modern representations of her came straight from Hollywood, embodied most famously by Elizabeth Taylor in the 1963 film *Cleopatra*. Taylor's famous off-screen affair with the film's Mark Antony, co-star Richard Burton, recalled the 14th century writer Giovanni Boccaccio's description of Cleopatra as a woman "who became an object of gossip for the whole world."

The star of the museum's exhibition, though, was a 40-inch black basalt statue on loan from the Hermitage Museum in St. Petersburg, Russia. One of the best-preserved representations of a Ptolemaic queen, it has been identified as Cleopatra VII. The striking figure holds a double horn of plenty and wears a headdress decorated with three cobras—symbols associated only with her.

A Bad Reputation

Not all the images in the exhibition were as flattering. Cleopatra's reputation in Rome declined after Octavian (later to become the emperor Augustus) defeated her and Antony at the Battle of Actium in 31 B.C. "Everything we know about Cleopatra comes from later Roman writers," explained Higgs, "and it's nearly all negative." He added that it was not surprising that "prudish and snobbish" Romans would have a low opinion of Egypt's queen, given that "she had taken away from them both Julius Caesar and Mark Antony." Still, said Higgs, even Cleopatra's critics acknowledged that she had some admirable qualities. Apart from her beauty, she is said to have been a humorous and charming conversationalist. Intelligent and savvy, she was a skilled diplomat who spoke several languages—and was clearly loved by Caesar and Antony, the fathers of her four children.

Like the pharaohs who came before her in the three centuries following Alexander the Great's conquest of Egypt in 332 B.C.,

Cleopatra had to appeal to both Greeks and Egyptians. She had to be seen as both a Greek monarch and an Egyptian pharaoh. She also needed to present herself as a powerful figure amid all the violence and chaos in the Mediterranean region at the time. Indeed, Cleopatra must have been ruthless in order to even gain the throne, given the bloodbaths that long characterized her family line.

Following Octavian's conquest of Egypt and Antony's death—he killed himself by falling on his sword—Cleopatra committed suicide, possibly with the help of a poisonous snake such as an asp or cobra. The new emperor then ordered that all statues of Cleopatra be destroyed. Most of the images of her that survived depict an attractive figure with a strong face, masculine in its features, emphasizing power. Old coins bearing her image, particularly rare Greek ones, have helped to identify Cleopatra in marble and limestone sculptures. So, too, did the tiniest item displayed at the museum—a half-inch piece of etched blue glass bearing Cleopatra's profile in a more realistic Greek style.

Cleopatra's Children

On public view for the first time was a 30-inch granite head believed to represent Ptolemy XV Caesar, Cleopatra's son by Julius Caesar. Also known as

---

Additional Support

See also ▨ Active Learning and Note Taking Guide, pp. 124–130.

Skills Practice

RESEARCH: Cleopatra VII Encourage students to learn more about Cleopatra VII. Direct them to appropriate online sources, encyclopedia entries, ancient history textbooks, classical texts, monographs, or even television documentaries. Tell students to consider themselves "fact-checkers." Questions they could pursue include: Did Cleopatra in fact commit suicide by snakebite? Who was Marc Antony? Who was Octavian? Why did Romans dislike her so, if they did? Suggest they keep notes on their findings, and bring them to share with the class. **OL**

Love and Power

**Basantite bust
of Caesar**

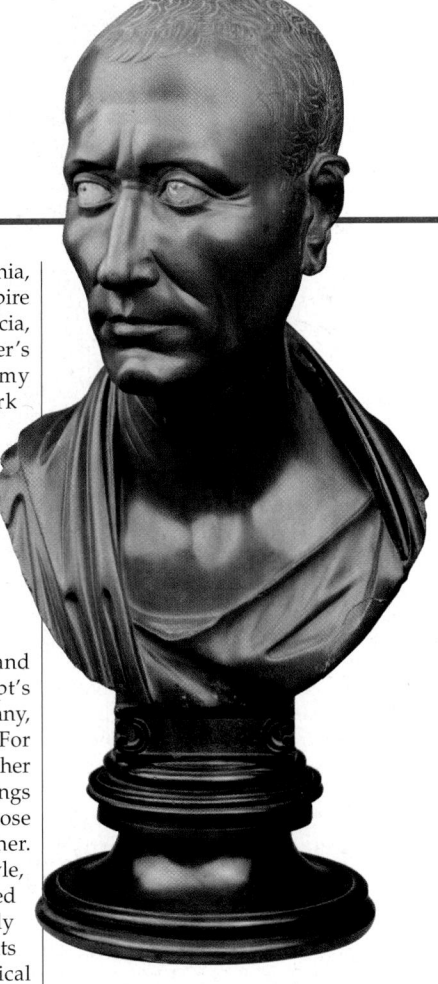

Caesarion, he co-ruled Egypt with his mother from 44 B.C. to 30 B.C. The sculpture was found in the harbor at Alexandria, Cleopatra's capital, by French archaeologists in 1997. The exhibition also included rare images of Cleopatra's other children. A marble statue of Cleopatra Selene—her daughter by Mark Antony—was lent by the Archaeological Museum in Cherchel, Algeria, where it was found. (Cherchel was the capital of the ancient kingdom of Mauretania, where Cleopatra Selene lived.) The statue had never been outside Algeria before. Another marble rendering of Cleopatra Selene, found near her husband's palace, showed her as a more mature woman, with a heavier face and "snail-shell" curls around her forehead.

Also on display was a bronze statuette which historians believe depicts Cleopatra's second son, Alexander Helios, as Prince of Armenia. According to the writings of the ancient Greek historian Plutarch, Mark Antony gave his sons by Cleopatra the title of kings, as well as many lands to rule. He gave Armenia, Media, and the Parthian Empire to Alexander. He gave Phoenicia, Syria, and Cilicia to Alexander's younger brother, Ptolemy Philadelphus. After Mark Anthony and Cleopatra died, though, their children were made to live out their lives in obscurity. Their half-brother Caesarion was not so fortunate. He was executed by Octavian.

Queen of the Silver Screen

Cleopatra's amazing life and dramatic death made Egypt's exotic queen an icon—to many, the first female superstar. For several hundred years after her death, Cleopatra and all things Egyptian intrigued even those Romans who demonized her. Her influence on Roman style, customs, and culture continued for a long time. By the early Renaissance in Europe, with its revival of interest in classical traditions, Cleopatra again became a subject of art, literature, and fashion. Many of the most famous events in her life—the luxurious banquet she held for Mark Antony, his death, her grief at his tomb, and her own death—were represented in paintings and sketches at the exhibition, as well as on other objects such as watches, fans, and vases.

> **❝**Everything we know about Cleopatra comes from later Roman writers, and it's nearly all negative.**❞**
>
> —PETER HIGGS,
> co-curator
> British Museum in London

EVER ALLURING **765**

Informational Text
TIME

Teach

⭐ Viewing the Art

Ask students to keep this image in mind as they read *Julius Caesar.* **Ask:** What character traits do you see reflected in this bust? Do you think they are accurate? *(Students will likely mention the stern, shrewd eyes and firm mouth, all indicating decisiveness. Some may suggest that the sculptor flattered Caesar or that a person's face does not always give an accurate picture of his or her character.)* **AS**

Reading in the Real World

Citizenship The political intrigue surrounding Cleopatra, Julius Caesar, and Marc Antony is not unique to them, nor to their time period. Encourage students to read current newspapers to look for other examples of alliances and betrayals among modern leaders—in both the nation and the world. Questions to guide students' reading could include the following: What do the leaders have to gain or lose in their alliances with each other? What are the results of betrayal? Have students write a mini-summary of their findings and share it with the class. **OL**

Objectives

• To distinguish fact from opinion (SE)
• To perform research outside class (TWE)

Assess

1. Most students will agree that Cleopatra seems like a fascinating person and historical icon.

2. (a) No one really knows what Cleopatra looked like. (b) Because she was a powerful female in history

3. (a) Sculptures, coins, paintings, ceramics, and jewelry (b) They can provide an idea of what Cleopatra looked like, how others perceived her, and what she valued, but likely not of her personality.

4. Writings of Roman historians (b) As powerful, manipulative, humorous, charming, intelligent, and a good communicator

5. "Famous," "synonymous with beauty," "a legend," "ruthless," "attractive," "Egypt's exotic queen," "icon," "first female superstar," "a tough and tragic seductress," and "a woman . . . for all time" (b) Her conclusions are drawn from others' and her own interpretations of Cleopatra. They are opinions supported by some factual information.

Cleopatra Dropping the Pearl into the Wine, c 1715. William Kent after Carlo Maratta. Red chalk drawing, 36.4 x 25.7 cm. The British Museum, London.

The Renaissance portrayal of the tough and tragic seductress—as derived from the early Romans—has trickled down to the current day.

Cleopatra found her way onto the silver screen even before movies had sound. In 1917, Theda Bara starred in a silent-film version of Cleopatra. Seventeen years later, Claudette Colbert played the Egyptian queen, and Hollywood waged an all-out publicity campaign to encourage female moviegoers to adopt the "Cleopatra look." Many copied Colbert's dark bangs after hearing the speech in which she described her feelings about Mark Antony: "I've seen a god come to life. I'm no longer a queen. I'm a woman."

A woman she was, and one for all time. With so much, yet so little, known about this queen without a face, this figure of history and myth, Cleopatra lives on in the "infinite variety" cited by Shakespeare. And like so many intrigued observers through the ages, visitors to the British Museum exhibition could draw their own picture of her.

—Updated 2005, from TIME, May 28, 2001

RESPONDING AND THINKING CRITICALLY

Respond

1. Did the article cause you to want to learn more about Cleopatra VII? Why or why not?

2. (a)Do historians know what Cleopatra looked like? (b)Why do you think there have been so many interpretations of her appearance?

3. (a)What are some of the artifacts of Cleopatra's time on exhibit at the British Museum? (b)How accurate a representation of history do you think can be derived from such artifacts?

4. (a)Where does most of the factual information about Cleopatra come from? (b)Generally, how is she characterized by historians?

Analyze and Evaluate

5. (a)What words does the author use to describe Cleopatra's image and character? (b)Do you think the author's conclusions are based on facts or opinions? Explain.

6. Does the author provide sufficient background information about Cleopatra for the reader? Why or why not?

7. The author calls Cleopatra "the first female superstar." How do you think movies have affected the legend of Cleopatra?

Connect

8. How are Antigone's and Cleopatra's characterizations similar and different?

6. The author seems to assume that the reader has some knowledge of Cleopatra. She does not explain who Julius Caesar or Mark Antony were, or Cleopatra's relationship to Ptolemaic rulers.

7. Movies have used beautiful actresses to play the role of Cleopatra, adding to her aura of glamour and attraction.

8. Both are characterized as headstrong, determined, and powerful. Antigone, however, tries to serve a noble cause. According to Peter Higgs, the Roman writers characterized Cleopatra as "nearly all negative."

Vocabulary Workshop

Denotation and Connotation

"For ever: damnation rises behind each child / Like a wave cresting out of the black northeast, /When the long darkness under sea roars up / And bursts drumming death upon the windwhipped sand."

—Sophocles, from *Antigone*

Recognizing Loaded Words

Connecting to Literature In the passage above, Sophocles uses words with strong negative denotations and connotations—*damnation, darkness,* and *death*—to describe the vengefulness of the gods. **Loaded words** such as these can make speech and writing powerful and persuasive. Loaded words can be powerful weapons, and it is important to recognize how and why a writer or speaker uses them.

Here are three types of loaded words:

- **Bias**—language that expresses an author's prejudice
  Antigone bravely wants to give her brother a proper burial.

The writer's use of the word *bravely* expresses her positive bias towards Antigone. A writer with a negative bias might have chosen a word like *recklessly* instead.

- **Hyperbole**—exaggerated language used to make a point
  The entire world was against Antigone.

The writer uses this broad overstatement to express extreme disapproval.

- **Propaganda**—language that often includes bias and hyperbole and may distort the truth to influence the public
  Anyone who does not agree with the logic of Creon must be an anarchist.

This exaggerated and distorted statement reveals the writer's positive bias towards Creon and attempt to influence people to feel and think similarly.

Exercise

Fill in each numbered space in the paragraph with the loaded word or phrase that best expresses the view of a writer who sides with Antigone.

Antigone is a woman who **1.** _____ stands up for the **2.** _____ principles she believes in. Being a **3.** _____ man, Creon **4.** _____ wants to allow his nephew to go unburied. The situation puts Antigone in **5.** _____.

1. a. courageously   **b.** stubbornly   **c.** foolishly

2. a. few   **b.** simple   **c.** worthy

3. a. respectable   **b.** cruel   **c.** gentle

4. a. strangely   **b.** generously   **c.** selfishly

5. a. power   **b.** a moral dilemma   **c.** grave danger

VOCABULARY WORKSHOP **767**

> ▶ **Vocabulary Terms**
>
> **Loaded words** express strong opinions or emotions. They can reveal **bias,** or prejudice; use **hyperbole,** or exaggeration; or be **propaganda,** which distorts the truth to be persuasive.

> ▶ **Test-Taking Tip**
>
> To identify loaded language in a reading passage, ask yourself, "Why did the writer write this? What is his or her point of view?" Then look for words or phrases with strong denotations and connotations that support that stance.

> ▶ **Reading Handbook**
>
> For more about loaded words, see the Reading Handbook, pp. R24–R25.

Literature Online
eFlashcards For eFlashcards and other vocabulary activities, go to www.glencoe.com.

OBJECTIVES
- Interpret denotations and connotations
- Identify the intended effects of persuasive language
- Recognize the influence of propaganda

Vocabulary Workshop

Denotation and Connotation

Focus

Read several advertisements to the class, and point out loaded words such as *best, premier, deluxe,* and *extraordinary.* **Ask:** What connotations do these words have? *(They have positive connotations.)* **Ask:** What is the effect of a series of these loaded words? *(They can sway a reader or listener.)*

Teach

Analyzing Loaded

Language Guide students to consider words with the same denotation but different connotations, such as *untidy, messy,* and *sloppy.* Have students create sentence strings, placing the words with the most positive connotations with *I,* neutral connotations with *you,* and negative connotations with *they.* An example would be "I am firm, you are strict, and they are harsh." **OL**

Assess

Exercise

1. a   **2.** c   **3.** b   **4.** c   **5.** b

eFlashcards Have students access the Web site for more practice with denotation and connotation.

Differentiated Instruction

Bias and Hyperbole Review with students the techniques of bias and hyperbole. Then ask students to identify bias and hyperbole in this passage from a letter to the editor: "Unfortunately the board is too cowardly to stand up for decent reforms. Instead they rubber-stamp every foolish proposal that comes their way." **Ask:** What is an example of hyperbole? *("They rubber-stamp every foolish proposal that comes their way" is exaggeration.)* **Ask:** What language is biased? *("unfortunately," "cowardly," "decent.")* Ask students to explain the effects of such loaded language. **BL**

Focus

BELLRINGER

Bellringer Options
Daily Language Practice Transparency 76
Or write the following question on the board: *Does the end justify the means?* Have students define "The end justifies the means." *(If the outcome is desirable, the methods used to achieve it are overlooked.)*
Ask: How would you answer this question?
Have students suggest scenarios in which a means to an end might be either acceptable or unacceptable.

Teach

L Literary Element

Drama Have students brainstorm ways in which Elizabethan actors might have communicated dramatic elements that are communicated by scenery, lighting, and other effects in modern theater. **OL**

See also ▓ Active Learning and Note Taking Guide, pp. 131–134.

Literature Online

Literary History Have students access the Web site for resources to enhance their understanding of Elizabethan drama.

Elizabethan Drama

"Every day at two o'clock in the afternoon in the city of London two or sometimes three comedies are performed, at separate places, . . . and whichever does best gets the greatest audience."
—Thomas Platter, diary entry from 1599

The Globe Theatre, 1616. Cornelius de Visscher. Engraving. British Library, London.

IN THE LATE 1500S, WHEN SHAKESPEARE BEGAN his career, English theater was going through major changes. For hundreds of years before this time, traveling actors, called "players," had toured the countryside, performing for audiences in towns and villages. They set up makeshift stages in public halls, marketplaces, and the courtyards of inns. Local officials, many of whom believed that "play-acting" violated biblical commandments, typically greeted acting companies with hostility.

Distrust of theater was so great that in 1574 the Common Council of London issued an order banishing players from London. To get around the order, actor James Burbage and his company of players built a playhouse in nearby Shorebridge. Completed in 1576, the building resembled the courtyard of an inn. Burbage's playhouse became the first public theater in England and was an immediate success, leading to the construction of other public theaters over the next few years.

Shakespeare's Globe

Shakespeare's theater company, the Lord Chamberlain's Men, performed at Burbage's theater until 1599, when they built their own playhouse, the Globe. Shakespeare referred to the Globe as "this wooden O," a term that has led historians to believe that it was a roughly circular building. The theater had three levels of galleries, covered by thatched roofs, overlooking an open courtyard. Projecting out into the yard was a platform stage about forty feet wide, with trapdoors for the entrance and exit of actors who played ghosts or other supernatural characters. At the back of the main stage was a small curtained inner stage used for indoor scenes. Above this stood a two-tiered gallery. The first tier was used to stage balcony and bedroom scenes; the second, to house musicians. Sound effects, such as the booming of thunder, were produced in a hut on top of the stage roof.

The globe could hold about three thousand spectators. Members of the middle class and nobility typically sat in the galleries after paying a twopence admission. For sixpence (what a skilled laborer earned in a day), wealthier members of the audience could sit in the "lords' room" directly over the stage. Less well-to-do-spectators, called

Skills Practice

STUDY SKILLS: Shakespeare's English Chart Have students create a chart in which they list unfamiliar words from the play. Have them create two columns with the headings *Word* and *Meaning.* Have students list words as they read. Suggest that they look up the meanings or write what they think the words mean. **OL**

"groundlings," could stand and watch from the courtyard for only a penny. Their close proximity to the stage created a noisy theatrical experience. Accounts of the time suggest that the groundlings did not hesitate to shout comments to the actors onstage. As theater became more profitable, its reputation improved. Eventually, Shakespeare's company received the support of Queen Elizabeth and her successor, King James.

The New Globe, London, interior.

Elizabethan Stagecraft

Because there was no artificial lighting, all performances at the Globe took place in the afternoon. There were few props and no movable scenery. Shakespeare made up for the lack of scenery by inviting audiences to visualize the scenes based on descriptive passages spoken by the characters. For example, a character's description of a raging storm would help Elizabethan audiences picture the fury of the weather. **L**

What the Elizabethan stage lacked in scenery, it made up for in costumes. Shakespeare's audiences considered clothing an important indication of social rank, so they demanded extravagant yet realistic costuming. An elaborate wardrobe was an Elizabethan theater company's biggest expense and most important asset.

In Shakespeare's time, audiences thought it immoral for women to appear on the stage, so boys performed the female roles. Very popular with Elizabethan theatergoers, these boy actors must have been highly skilled performers, who created convincing and moving portrayals of Shakespeare's great female roles, from Lady Macbeth and Cleopatra to Rosalind and Juliet.

Literature Online **Literary History** For more about Elizabethan drama, go to www.glencoe.com.

Literature Online **Literary History** For more about Elizabethan drama, go to www.glencoe.com.

RESPONDING AND THINKING CRITICALLY

1. What feature of Elizabethan stagecraft do you think a modern audience would have the most difficulty accepting?

2. What effects did the social values of Shakespeare's time have on Elizabethan theater?

3. How did the Globe's lack of scenery affect Shakespeare's plays?

OBJECTIVES
- Understand the characteristics of Elizabethan theater.
- Connect to the historical context of literature

LITERARY HISTORY **769**

Differentiated Instruction

Researching Roman Civilization
Julius Caesar tells the story of one momentous event in ancient Roman history. From the founding of Rome in 753 B.C.E. to the overthrow of the last emperor of the Western Roman Empire in C.E. 476, ancient Rome had a huge impact on Western civilization. Have groups of students research one aspect or accomplishment of ancient Roman culture, such as religion, architecture, engineering, art, literature, science, or political science. Have the groups report their findings, illustrated with maps, drawings, and photographs, to the class. **AL**

Focus

BELLRINGER

Bellringer Options
Selection Focus Transparency 36
Daily Language Practice
Transparency 77
Or write on the board:

• "Power will intoxicate the best hearts. No man is wise enough, nor good enough to be trusted with unlimited power" —Charles Caleb Colton

Ask: Do you agree or disagree with this quotation?
Students should explain what the quote means and then offer a personal response with their reasoning.

Author Search To expand students' appreciation of William Shakespeare, have them access the Web site for additional information and resources.

The Tragedy of Julius Caesar

MEET WILLIAM SHAKESPEARE

When the question "Who is the greatest writer that ever lived?" is asked, nine out of ten times the response is "William Shakespeare." Shakespeare's writings are more widely read and more often quoted than any other literary work, aside from the Bible. Unfortunately, there are no biographies of Shakespeare from his own time. The information we have comes from public records and comments by his rivals and admirers, such as the playwright Ben Jonson. "He was not of an age, but for all time," proclaimed Jonson shortly after Shakespeare's death.

"It seems to me most strange that men should fear, Seeing that death, a necessary end, Will come when it will come."

—William Shakespeare, from *Julius Caesar*

The Family Man Shakespeare was born in Stratford-upon-Avon, where his father was elected bailiff (the equivalent of a mayor). William was the third of at least eight children. He was the first boy and the first child to survive past childhood. Most likely, he attended the local grammar school, where he would have studied Latin and classical literature. At age eighteen, Shakespeare married twenty-six-year-old Anne Hathaway. The couple had three children: Susanna and twins Judith and Hamnet. Hamnet, their only son, died when he was eleven.

Success in the City Shakespeare moved to London sometime between 1585 and the early 1590s and worked as an actor and playwright.

Soon he was celebrated for his comedies and historical plays. By 1594 he had joined a company of players called the Lord Chamberlain's Men with whom he spent the remainder of his career. In 1599 the company built its own theater, the Globe.

In a time when writers received no royalties and most plays were never printed, Shakespeare grew wealthy from his share in the theater company's profits.

An Artist for All Time Shakespeare was a prolific writer and excelled at all forms of drama. His tragic masterpieces include *Hamlet, Romeo and Juliet, Othello, Macbeth,* and *King Lear.* His comedies are also classics. Modern audiences still respond to the antics and wordplay of *A Midsummer Night's Dream, Twelfth Night,* and *Much Ado About Nothing* as Shakespeare's own audiences did four centuries ago. In keeping with the standards of his time, Shakespeare borrowed nearly all of his plots from the works of others. With his rich language, superb theatrical skill, and an astonishing knowledge of human nature, he was able to transform these secondhand ideas into original and matchless works of art.

Seven years after Shakespeare's death, a group of friends brought out a collection of his works known as the *First Folio.* This volume played a crucial role in preserving his plays for future generations and—very possibly—"for all time."

William Shakespeare was born in 1564 and died in 1616.

Author Search For more about William Shakespeare, go to www.glencoe.com.

Selection Skills

The Tragedy of Julius Caesar, Act 1

Literary Element
• Blank Verse (SE pp. 771–791)
• Characterization (TWE p. 780)
• Foreshadowing (TWE p. 776)

Reading Skills
• Making Inferences About Characters (SE pp. 771–791)
• Understanding Shakespeare's Language (TWE p. 772)

Vocabulary Skills
• Synonyms (SE p. 791)
• Suffix -*ous* (TWE p. 788)
• Etymology (TWE p. 788)

Listening/Speaking/Viewing Skills
• Analyzing Art (SE pp. 779, 782, 786, 789)
• Expressing Emotions (TWE p. 784)

Writing Skills/Grammar
• Extended Metaphors (TWE p. 778)
• Description (TWE p. 786)

Connecting to the Play

You may hear people speak of "leadership qualities." What exactly are these qualities, and what makes a good leader? Before you read Act 1, think about the following questions:

- Who is the best leader you have ever known?
- What made him or her exceptional?

Building Background

Born in 100 BC, Julius Caesar was an immensely gifted military leader and politician. After conquering Gaul in western Europe, he defeated his rival Pompey and became dictator of Rome in 48 BC. Although he belonged to a noble family, he often looked for support from Rome's lower classes. Between military campaigns, he undertook popular social and political reforms. Caesar was a talented speaker and writer whose war commentaries are considered literary classics. Although he could be charming, Caesar's arrogance and ambition created enemies in the senate and a group of conspirators assassinated him in 44 BC.

Setting Purposes for Reading

Big Idea Loyalty and Betrayal

Society does not make it easy for a person to switch sides; that person may become known as a traitor. However, history is full of people who have turned against a cause or a person they once respected. As you read *Julius Caesar*, notice how Shakespeare depicts this change in his characters.

Literary Element Blank Verse

Much of *Julius Caesar* is written in a form of unrhymed poetry known as **blank verse**. Each line has a basic pattern of five iambic feet, or units of rhythm, with each foot made up of an unstressed syllable followed by a stressed syllable.

˘ ´ | ˘ ´ | ˘ ´ | ˘ ´ | ˘ ´
He had a fever when he was in Spain . . .

- See Literary Terms Handbook, p. R3.

Literature Online Interactive Literary Elements Handbook To review or learn more about the literary elements, go to www.glencoe.com.

OBJECTIVES
In studying this selection, you will focus on the following:
- analyzing the use of blank verse

Reading Strategy Making Inferences About Characters

In literature, as in life, a person's motivation, or reason for acting in a certain way, is not always clear. To find out what makes a **character** tick, the reader often has to **make inferences,** or use reason and knowledge of the situation to discover what the author is not telling.

Reading Tip: Examining the Evidence Use a chart like the one below to record details you are sure of. Then write the inferences you make based on those details.

I Know	I Infer
Brutus tells Cassius that he has been worried lately.	Brutus is afraid that Caesar is becoming too powerful.

Vocabulary

servile (sur´vil) *adj.* lacking self-respect; behaving as if other people are superior; p. 776 *The emperor's servile advisors bowed deeply in his presence.*

entreat (en trēt´) *v.* to ask earnestly; to beg; p. 781 *The charity entreated the public to help the many flood victims.*

infirmity (in fur´mə tē) *n.* a physical or mental weakness or disability; feebleness; p. 784 *After a year of therapy, she shows no signs of her former infirmity.*

enterprise (en´tər prīz´) *n.* an important project or undertaking; p. 785 *Sending human beings to Mars is an expensive and dangerous enterprise.*

incense (in sens´) *v.* to make very angry; p. 786 *Learning that three of his players had been suspended incensed the coach.*

- making inferences about characters
- discussing elements of memorable passages with a group

JULIUS CAESAR **771**

Focus

Summary

Flavius and Murellus are angered by workers rejoicing over Caesar's triumph over Pompey. Caesar is warned by a soothsayer to beware the ides of March. Cassius asks Brutus to participate in a plan to relieve Caesar of his power. Brutus won't commit himself. Casca returns from the festival and tells Brutus and Cassius that Mark Antony offered a crown to Caesar in front of the crowd, which he refused three times. Cassius plots to persuade Brutus to join his conspiracy.

V Vocabulary

Vocabulary File

Say: Add these words and definitions to your vocabulary file. For each word include a sentence that gives you an example of how to use the word. **OL** Students with English language needs should include the pronunciations of these words in their files. **EL**

Literature Online

Literary Elements Have students access the Web site for interactive activities to improve their understanding of blank verse.

Selection Resources

Print Materials
📁 Unit 4 Resources (Fast File), pp. 27–41
📁 Leveled Vocabulary Development, p. 60–64
📁 Selection and Unit Assessments, pp. 143–152
📁 Selection Quick Checks, p. 72–76

Transparencies
- Bellringer Options Transparencies: Selection Focus Transparency 36 Daily Language Practice Transparency 77
- Literary Elements Transparencies 1, 50, 75, 79, 80

Technology
🔘 TeacherWorks Plus™ CD-ROM
🔘 StudentWorks Plus™ CD-ROM
🔘 Presentation Plus!™ CD-ROM
💻 Literature Online, glencoe.com
💻 Online Student Edition, mhln.com
🔘 ExamView® Assessment Suite CD-ROM
🔘 Vocabulary PuzzleMaker CD-ROM
🔘 Listening Library, disc 2 tracks 4–8

Teach

Big Idea

Loyalty and Betrayal

Say: Keep the following question in mind as you read: Brutus feels loyalty to both Caesar and to the Roman people. How might this dual loyalty lead him to betrayal? *(Cassius's forged letters convince Brutus that the Roman people need him to save them from Caesar's tyranny. As a result, Brutus decides to join the conspiracy despite his loyalty to Caesar.)* **OL**

★ Viewing the Art

Julius Caesar's ambition and violent downfall have made him a fascinating historical figure for the ages. Here, we see an unknown medieval artist's impression of Caesar's triumph. **Say:** Although the artist presents the Romans in medieval garb, what elements of the painting are likely accurate? *(a sense of pomp and hubbub; men, weapons, and horses)* **AS**

THE TRAGEDY OF JULIUS CAESAR

William Shakespeare

The Triumph of Julius Caesar. Paolo Uccello. Tempera on panel. Musee des Arts Decoratifs, Paris. ★

772 UNIT 4 DRAMA

Additional Support

Skills Practice

READING: Understanding Shakespeare's Language

Shakespeare's language can be intimidating for many students. Help students demystify the language before reading. **Ask:** How many of you like Shakespeare? Have students share what they do not like about Shakespeare.

(Most will cite archaic language, inverted word order, and unusual usage.) Once these concerns are out in the open, explain that Shakespeare used language creatively to form the rhythm for which his plays are known. Once you start reading, have students find their own examples in the text. **OL**

CHARACTERS **R**

JULIUS CAESAR: ambitious military leader and politician; the most powerful man in Rome

CALPHURNIA: wife of Caesar

MARCUS BRUTUS: friend of Caesar, appointed by him to high office in the Roman government; a believer in the republic and member of the conspiracy against Caesar

PORTIA: wife of Brutus and daughter of a Roman patriot

CAIUS CASSIUS: brother-in-law of Brutus and member of the conspiracy against Caesar

MARK ANTONY: friend of Caesar, senator, and eloquent orator; member of the triumvirate, the three-man governing body that ruled Rome after Caesar's death

OCTAVIUS CAESAR: Caesar's great-nephew and official heir; member of the triumvirate

M. AEMILIUS LEPIDUS: military leader and member of the triumvirate

Conspirators Against Caesar

CASCA	METELLUS CIMBER	TREBONIUS
CINNA	DECIUS BRUTUS	CAIUS LIGARIUS

Senators

CICERO	PUBLIUS	POPILIUS LENA

Tribunes (Public Officials)

FLAVIUS	MURELLUS

Officers in the Armies of Brutus and Cassius

LUCILIUS	MESSALA	VOLUMNIUS
TITINIUS	YOUNG CATO	FLAVIUS

Servants of Brutus

LUCIUS	CLITUS	STRATO
VARRUS	CLAUDIO	DARDANIUS

Others

A SOOTHSAYER (one who predicts the future)

ARTEMIDORUS OF CNIDOS: teacher of rhetoric

CINNA: a poet

PINDARUS: servant of Cassius

ANOTHER POET

SERVANTS TO CAESAR, ANTONY, AND OCTAVIUS; CITIZENS, GUARDS, SOLDIERS

Teach

R Reading Strategy

Making Inferences About Characters Suggest that students read the cast of characters once and turn back and review it as necessary to identify a character who is speaking. **OL**

✓CheckPoint

Use the CheckPoint questions on Presentation Plus! to monitor students' comprehension. These questions can be used with interactive response keypads for immediate student feedback.

Differentiated Instruction

Learning Disabled Some students may benefit from a specific lesson on using the margin notes in the text. Explain that many of the students' questions can be answered by following along with the side notes, which are marked with a small superscript degree sign. Have a volunteer read aloud until he or she reaches a side note symbol. Encourage students to use their fingers, an index card, or a ruler to keep one finger on the text while reading the note so that they can refer back to the text. Have the volunteer demonstrate this technique and then reread the line and paraphrase it according to the side note. **BL**

Objective
• To understand Shakespeare's language (TWE)

L1 Literary Element

Blank Verse Answer: *The Cobbler is speaking in ordinary prose, not blank verse. There are no separate lines and no repeated rhythmic units.* **OL**

R Reading Strategy

Making Inferences About Characters Answer: *They believe the commoners to be inferior. They speak authoritatively and condescendingly, expecting obedience.* **OL**

★ Literary History

Shakespeare's Source
The background history for *Julius Caesar* came from essays on Brutus, Caesar, and Antony in *Lives of the Noble Grecians and Romans* by Plutarch (C.E. 46–120), a Greek biographer. This book was translated into English by Thomas North in 1579. **AS**

ACT 1

SCENE 1. Rome. A street.

[*Enter* FLAVIUS, MURELLUS, *and certain* COMMONERS *over the stage.*]

FLAVIUS. Hence! Home, you idle creatures, get you home!
  Is this a holiday? What, know you not,
  Being mechanical,° you ought not walk
  Upon a laboring day without the sign
5 Of your profession? Speak, what trade art thou?°

CARPENTER. Why, sir, a carpenter.

MURELLUS. Where is thy leather apron and thy rule?
  What dost thou with thy best apparel on?
  You, sir, what trade are you?

10 COBBLER. Truly, sir, in respect of° a fine workman, I am but, as
  you would say, a cobbler.°

MURELLUS. But what trade art thou? Answer me directly.

COBBLER. A trade, sir, that, I hope, I may use° with a safe
  conscience, which is indeed, sir, a mender of bad soles.

15 FLAVIUS. What trade, thou knave? Thou naughty knave,
  what trade?

COBBLER. Nay, I beseech you, sir, be not out° with me; yet, if
  you be out,° sir, I can mend you.

MURELLUS. What mean'st thou by that? Mend me, thou saucy
  fellow?

20 COBBLER. Why, sir, cobble you.

FLAVIUS. Thou art a cobbler, art thou?

COBBLER. Truly, sir, all that I live by is with the awl;° I meddle
  with no tradesman's matters, nor women's matters; but
  withal, I am indeed, sir, a surgeon to old shoes; when they
25 are in great danger, I recover them. As proper men as ever
  trod upon neat's leather° have gone upon my handiwork.

FLAVIUS. But wherefore art not in thy shop today?
  Why dost thou lead these men about the streets?

2–5 Is this a . . . art thou: Flavius and Murellus, public officials, remind the laborers that they should be dressed in their work outfits rather than their best clothes.
3 mechanical: manual laborers.

10 in respect of: in comparison with.

11 cobbler: "clumsy worker" or "shoemaker." The Cobbler plays on the word's double meaning. Murellus and Flavius fail to understand his pun at first and keep pressing him to reveal a trade he has already identified.
13 use: practice.

16 out: angry.
16–17 if you be out: if your shoes are worn out.

22 awl: a tool for making holes in leather. The Cobbler puns on the words *all, awl,* and *withal,* which means "nevertheless."

26 neat's leather: cowhide. The Cobbler claims that his shoes have been worn by as fine men as ever walked in shoes.

Literary Element Blank Verse *Is the Cobbler speaking in blank verse? How do you know?* **L1**

Reading Strategy Making Inferences About Characters *What attitude do Flavius and Murellus have toward commoners, such as the Carpenter and the Cobbler?* **R**

Additional Support

Skills Practice

RESEARCH: Roman Gods The ancient Romans worshipped gods related to the natural world. The feast of Lupercal, held on February 15, honored Lupercus, the god of the flocks, to ensure fertility for people, crops, and animals. Have students research other gods, beliefs, and festivals of the ancient Romans. Students can use the Internet or the library to gather information. For example, they may research Jupiter, god of the weather, or Ceres, goddess of the harvest. Have students present their material as an oral or written report, an illustration, or a diorama. **OL**

COBBLER. Truly, sir, to wear out their shoes, to get myself into
30 more work. But indeed, sir, we make holiday to see Caesar
and to rejoice in his triumph.°

MURELLUS. Wherefore rejoice? What conquest brings he home?
What tributaries° follow him to Rome,
To grace in captive bonds° his chariot wheels?
35 You blocks, you stones, you worse than senseless things!
O you hard hearts, you cruel men of Rome,
Knew you not Pompey? Many a time and oft
Have you climb'd up to walls and battlements,
To tow'rs and windows, yea, to chimney tops,
40 Your infants in your arms, and there have sate
The livelong day, with patient expectation,
To see great Pompey pass the streets of Rome;
And when you saw his chariot but° appear,
Have you not made an universal shout,
45 That Tiber° trembled underneath her banks
To hear the replication° of your sounds
Made in her concave shores?
And do you now put on your best attire?
And do you now cull out a holiday?°
50 And do you now strew flowers in his way,
That comes in triumph over Pompey's blood?°
Be gone!
Run to your houses, fall upon your knees,
Pray to the gods to intermit° the plague
55 That needs must light on this ingratitude.

FLAVIUS. Go, go, good countrymen, and, for this fault,
Assemble all the poor men of your sort;
Draw them to Tiber banks and weep your tears
Into the channel, till the lowest stream
60 Do kiss the most exalted shores of all.°

[Exit all the COMMONERS.]

See, whe'er their basest mettle be not mov'd;°
They vanish tongue-tied in their guiltiness.
Go you down that way towards the Capitol,
This way will I. Disrobe the images,
65 If you do find them deck'd with ceremonies.°

MURELLUS. May we do so?
You know it is the feast of Lupercal.°

---

31 **triumph:** triumphal celebration.
(The triumph was held to celebrate Julius
Caesar's defeat of two sons of Pompey
the Great, his former rival. Caesar gained
control over Rome when he defeated
Pompey in 48 BC)
33 **tributaries:** captured enemies who
pay tribute, or ransom money, for their
release.
34 **captive bonds:** the chains of prisoners.

43 **but:** only.

45 **Tiber:** a river running through Rome.
46 **replication:** echo.

49 **cull out a holiday:** pick out this day
as a holiday.

51 **Pompey's blood:** Pompey's sons.

54 **intermit:** hold back.

58–60 **Draw them to . . . of all:** Flavius
wants the commoners to weep into the
Tiber until the river's lowest water reaches
its highest banks.
61 **whe'er . . . mov'd:** whether their
humble spirits have not been touched.

64–65 **Disrobe the images . . .
ceremonies:** Flavius directs Murellus to
remove any decorations from the statues.
67 **feast of Lupercal:** religious festival
for a god worshiped by shepherds as a
protector of flocks.

Literary Element Blank Verse *Why is this line a perfect example of iambic*
pentameter? **L2**

Big Idea Loyalty and Betrayal *Why is Murellus so angry with the commoners?* **BI**

JULIUS CAESAR, ACT 1, SCENE 1 **775**

Teach

L2 Literary Element

Blank Verse

Answer: *The line has ten syllables, consisting of five metric feet, each with an unstressed syllable followed by a stressed syllable. Stresses fall clearly on the syllables* blocks, stones, worse, sense, *and* things. Have a volunteer read aloud the first four lines of Murellus's speech. Read line 35 and indicate on the board the pattern of stressed and unstressed syllables. Point out that the line is in perfect iambic pentameter. **Explain:** The entire speech is written in blank verse—unrhymed iambic pentameter—and Shakespeare uses blank verse for selected speeches. Have students finish reading the speech and characterize it. *(The speech is long, serious, and formal.)* **OL**

BI Big Idea

Loyalty and Betrayal

Answer: *Murellus accuses them of forgetting Pompey, who was once their hero.* **OL**

Differentiated Instruction

Drawing Maps The Tiber River, mentioned by Murellus, flowed along the western boundary of the ancient city of Rome. Have students locate a map of the ancient city of Rome in an encyclopedia or other reference book. Have them draw a copy of the map, including the Tiber River, the Appian Way, and the Forum. You might wish to make this an ongoing project by having students add any other landmarks mentioned in Shakespeare's dialogue as they continue reading the play. **BL**

Objectives
- To analyze the use of blank verse (SE)
- To make inferences about characters (SE)
- To research Roman gods (TWE)

775

FLAVIUS. It is no matter, let no images
Be hung with Caesar's trophies.° I'll about,
70   And drive away the vulgar° from the streets;
So do you too, where you perceive them thick.
These growing feathers pluck'd from Caesar's wing
Will make him fly an ordinary pitch,°
Who else would soar above the view of men
75   And keep us all in **servile** fearfulness.

[*They exit.*]

SCENE 2. Rome. A public place.

[*Enter* CAESAR, ANTONY *for the course,* CALPHURNIA,
PORTIA, DECIUS, CICERO, BRUTUS, CASSIUS, CASCA, CITIZENS,
and a SOOTHSAYER; *after them* MURELLUS *and* FLAVIUS.]

CAESAR. Calphurnia!

CASCA.   Peace, ho, Caesar speaks.

[*All fall silent as* CAESAR *calls for his wife.*]

CAESAR.   Calphurnia!

CALPHURNIA. Here, my lord.

CAESAR. Stand you directly in Antonio's way
When he doth run his course. Antonio!

5   ANTONY. Caesar, my lord?

CAESAR. Forget not in your speed, Antonio,
To touch Calphurnia; for our elders say,
The barren, touched in this holy chase,
Shake off their sterile curse.°

ANTONY.   I shall remember;
10   When Caesar says, "Do this," it is perform'd.

CAESAR. Set on, and leave no ceremony out.   [*Flourish.*]

SOOTHSAYER. Caesar!

CAESAR. Ha! Who calls?

CASCA. Bid every noise be still; peace yet again!

15   CAESAR. Who is it in the press° that calls on me?
I hear a tongue shriller than all the music,
Cry "Caesar!" Speak, Caesar is turn'd to hear.°

> **Reading Strategy** Making Inferences About Characters *How do Murellus and Flavius feel about Caesar?* **R1**

> **Reading Strategy** Making Inferences About Characters *How would you describe the relationship between Caesar and Antony?* **R2**

> **Vocabulary**
> servile (sur′vil) *adj.* lacking self-respect; behaving as if other people are superior

69 trophies: decorations honoring Caesar.
70 vulgar: common people.

72–73 These growing . . . pitch: Plucking feathers from a bird's wings prevents it from flying. Flavius uses this metaphor for his plan to keep Caesar's power at an ordinary **pitch**, or height.

Head of a woman, sometimes identified as Marciana, 1st quarter of the 2nd century AD Roman. Bronze. Louvre Museum, Paris.
Viewing the Art: Describe the woman portrayed here. How might she reflect Calphurnia's feelings at this point in the drama?

6–9 Forget not . . . curse: Caesar, who has no children, refers to a traditional belief that barren women could become fertile if they were struck by leather thongs carried by runners who passed through Rome on the feast of Lupercal.
15 press: crowd.
17 turn'd to hear: Caesar turns his good ear to the Soothsayer (he was deaf in one ear).

Teach

R1 Reading Strategy

Making Inferences About Characters Answer: *They scorn Caesar as one who makes himself too great. They believe he is a tyrant.* **OL**

R2 Reading Strategy

Making Inferences About Characters Answer: *Caesar trusts Antony and expects Antony to follow his orders; Antony is respectful and willing to take orders.* **OL**

★ Viewing the Art

Answer: *Students may say that the woman looks patient and enduring. Calphurnia may be patiently enduring Caesar's wish for children or feeling regret at not having had children.*

Additional Support

Skills Practice

LITERARY ELEMENT:

Foreshadowing Shakespeare uses foreshadowing to heighten suspense. Ask students how Shakespeare uses the soothsayer to make the foreshadowing more dramatic. (*Caesar and his friends are celebrating when the soothsayer dramatically interrupts with a cryptic message.*) **OL**

SOOTHSAYER. Beware the ides of March.°

CAESAR.   What man is that?

BRUTUS. A soothsayer bids you beware the ides of March.

20   CAESAR. Set him before me, let me see his face.

CASSIUS. Fellow, come from the throng, look upon Caesar.

CAESAR. What say'st thou to me now? Speak once again.

SOOTHSAYER. Beware the ides of March.

CAESAR. He is a dreamer, let us leave him. Pass.

[*They exit. BRUTUS and CASSIUS remain.*]

25   CASSIUS. Will you go see the order of the course?°

BRUTUS. Not I.

CASSIUS. I pray you do.

BRUTUS. I am not gamesome;° I do lack some part
    Of that quick spirit that is in Antony.
30   Let me not hinder, Cassius, your desires;
    I'll leave you.

CASSIUS. Brutus, I do observe you now of late;°
    I have not from your eyes that gentleness
    And show of love as I was wont to° have.
35   You bear too stubborn and too strange a hand
    Over your friend that loves you.°

BRUTUS.   Cassius,
    Be not deceiv'd: if I have veil'd my look,
    I turn the trouble of my countenance
    Merely upon myself.° Vexed I am
40   Of late with passions of some difference,°
    Conceptions only proper to myself,
    Which give some soil, perhaps, to my behaviors;°
    But let not therefore my good friends be griev'd
    (Among which number, Cassius, be you one),
45   Nor construe any further° my neglect,
    Than that poor Brutus, with himself at war,
    Forgets the shows of love to other men.

---

18 **ides of March:** March 15. In the Roman calendar, a day in the middle of every month was called the ides.

25 **order . . . course:** progress of the race.

28 **gamesome:** fond of games and sports.

32 **of late:** lately.

34 **was wont to:** used to.

35–36 **You bear . . . loves you:** Cassius uses the metaphor of a rider holding a tight rein on an unfamiliar horse to suggest Brutus's unfriendly behavior toward him.

37–39 **Be not . . . upon myself:** If I have seemed withdrawn, my displeased looks have been turned only on myself.
40 **passions of some difference:** conflicting emotions.
42 **Which give . . . behaviors:** Which might blemish my conduct.

45 **Nor . . . further:** Nor should you think any more of.

Literary Element   **Blank Verse** *How does Shakespeare maintain the rhythm of blank verse during dialogue?* **L**

Reading Strategy   Making Inferences About Characters *What does Caesar's behavior toward the soothsayer suggest about his character?* **R3**

Reading Strategy   Making Inferences About Characters *What do Brutus's words suggest about his personality and inner state?* **R4**

JULIUS CAESAR, ACT 1, SCENE 2   **777**

Teach

L Literary Element

Blank Verse Answer: *Shakespeare often breaks a single line of blank verse—ten syllables with five iambic feet—into two or more lines of dialogue spoken by different characters. Although the speaker changes, the rhythm and meter are maintained.* **OL**

R3 Reading Strategy

Making Inferences About Characters Answer: *Students may say that Caesar casually dismisses the soothsayer, showing self-assurance or even arrogance.* **OL**

R4 Reading Strategy

Making Inferences About Characters Answer: *Brutus's words suggest that he is thoughtful, even brooding; that he is serious and seems to have a quiet strength admired by others.* **OL**

★ Literary History

Blank Verse One reason for Shakespeare's use of blank verse was purely practical. Actors had to play several parts and learn many lines in a season. The regular rhythm of blank verse made the lines easier to memorize. **AS**

Differentiated Instruction

Paraphrasing Dialogue Paraphrasing speeches may help students better understand the dialogue. Have students write a paraphrase of each set of lines listed below. Suggest that they simplify sentence structure, sometimes by rearranging words or phrases, and replace difficult words with simpler ones.

1. lines 43–47 (*"My friends, including you, should not worry anymore about my neglecting them. I am simply preoccupied with personal problems."*)

2. lines 55–58 (*"Brutus, it is too bad you have no mirrors to let you see your own worthiness."*) **BL**

Objectives

• To analyze the use of blank verse (SE)
• To make inferences about characters (SE)
• To analyze foreshadowing (TWE)

Teach

BI₁ Big Idea

Loyalty and Betrayal

Answer: *Cassius is bitter about Caesar, sarcastically referring to him as "immortal"; he does not consider Caesar among the people of "best respect in Rome."* **OL**

BI₂ Big Idea

Loyalty and Betrayal

Answer: *Brutus apparently does not want Caesar to be crowned king, yet he considers himself Caesar's friend and supporter.* **OL**

CASSIUS. Then, Brutus, I have much mistook your passion,°
By means whereof this breast of mine hath buried
50   Thoughts of great value, worthy cogitations.°
Tell me, good Brutus, can you see your face?

BRUTUS. No, Cassius; for the eye sees not itself
But by reflection, by some other things.

CASSIUS. 'Tis just,
55   And it is very much lamented, Brutus,
That you have no such mirrors as will turn
Your hidden worthiness into your eye,
That you might see your shadow.° I have heard
Where many of the best respect in Rome
60   (Except immortal Caesar), speaking of Brutus
And groaning underneath this age's yoke,
Have wish'd that noble Brutus had his eyes.°

BRUTUS. Into what dangers would you lead me, Cassius,
That you would have me seek into myself
65   For that which is not in me?

CASSIUS. Therefore, good Brutus, be prepar'd to hear;
And since you know you cannot see yourself
So well as by reflection, I, your glass
Will modestly discover to yourself
70   That of yourself which you yet know not of.°
And be not jealous on° me, gentle Brutus;
Were I a common laughter, or did use
To stale with ordinary oaths my love
To every new protester; if you know
75   That I do fawn on men and hug them hard,
And after scandal them; or if you know
That I profess myself in banqueting
To all the rout, then hold me dangerous.°

[*Flourish and shout.*]

BRUTUS. What means this shouting? I do fear the people
80   Choose Caesar for their king.

CASSIUS.   Ay, do you fear it?
Then must I think you would not have it so.

BRUTUS. I would not, Cassius, yet I love him well.
But wherefore° do you hold me here so long?
What is it that you would impart to me?
85   If it be aught toward the general good,
Set honor in one eye and death i' th' other,
And I will look on both indifferently;°

48 mistook your passion: misunderstood your feelings.

49–50 By means . . . cogitations: Because of this I have kept important thoughts to myself.

58 shadow: reflection.

58–62 I have heard . . . eyes: Cassius claims that many highly respected Roman citizens, groaning under the oppression of Caesar's rule, wished that Brutus would recognize his own worth.

68–70 I, your . . . not of: I, your mirror, will reveal without exaggeration what you do not yet know about yourself.
71 jealous on: suspicious of.

72–78 Were I . . . dangerous: If I were a laughingstock or used to cheaply offering my affection to anyone, or if you know me to slander men after fawning on them, or if you know me to proclaim friendship to the common crowd while drinking, then consider me dangerous.

83 wherefore: why.

85–87 If it be aught . . . indifferently: If it is anything that concerns the public welfare, I will face honor and death impartially.

Big Idea Loyalty and Betrayal *What does Cassius reveal about his feelings here?* **BI₁**

Big Idea Loyalty and Betrayal *What is Brutus's dilemma?* **BI₂**

778 UNIT 4 DRAMA

Additional Support

Skills Practice

WRITING: Extended Metaphors On page 778 Cassius uses an extended metaphor. He says it is too bad Brutus does not have mirrors to reflect his inner goodness. In line 68, Cassius says that he himself will serve as Brutus's "glass," or mirror. Have students write a paragraph comparing two things with an extended metaphor. For example, they may decide to compare autumn to a woman ("Autumn in her wardrobe of yellow and orange . . ."). Encourage students to use words and images ("following on the heels of summer," "walking through the newly harvested fields") that extend the comparison. **OL**

The Flight of Aeneas from Troy.
Carle van Loo. 1705–1765.
Painting. Louvre, Paris.
Viewing the Art: What comparison does Cassius make between himself and Aeneas, as pictured here?

Teach

R **Reading Strategy**

Making Inferences About Characters
Answer: *Cassius seems to like and esteem Brutus sincerely, but he also spends considerable time flattering him. Cassius seems to have an ulterior motive for approaching Brutus in this way.* **OL**

★ **Viewing the Art**

Answer: *Just as Aeneas carried his frail father from burning Troy, so Cassius carried the nearly drowned Caesar from the Tiber River.* **AS**

For let the gods so speed° me, as I love
The name of honor more than I fear death.

90　CASSIUS. I know that virtue to be in you, Brutus,
　　As well as I do know your outward favor.°
　　Well, honor is the subject of my story:
　　I cannot tell what you and other men
　　Think of this life; but for my single self,
95　I had as lief not be as live to be
　　In awe of such a thing as I myself.°
　　I was born free as Caesar; so were you;
　　We both have fed as well, and we can both
　　Endure the winter's cold as well as he;
100　For once, upon a raw and gusty day,
　　The troubled Tiber chafing with her shores,°
　　Caesar said to me, "Dar'st thou,° Cassius, now
　　Leap in with me into this angry flood,
　　And swim to yonder point?" Upon the word,
105　Accoutred° as I was, I plunged in,
　　And bade him follow; so indeed he did.
　　The torrent roar'd, and we did buffet it
　　With lusty sinews,° throwing it aside
　　And stemming it with hearts of controversy;°
110　But ere we could arrive the point propos'd,
　　Caesar cried, "Help me, Cassius, or I sink!"
　　I, as Aeneas,° our great ancestor,
　　Did from the flames of Troy upon his shoulder
　　The old Anchises bear, so from the waves of Tiber

88　**speed:** favor.

91　**favor:** appearance.

94–96　**for my single . . . myself:**
Personally, I would rather not live than live in awe of another human being.

101　**chafing with her shores:** dashing into the shores (as if angry with them for their restraint).
102　**Dar'st thou:** Do you dare?

105　**Accoutred:** dressed in armor.

108　**sinews:** muscles.
109　**stemming . . . controversy:** making headway against the river's flow in a spirit of rivalry.

112　**Aeneas** (i nē′ əs): The legendary founder of Rome, who carried his father Anchises on his back as he fled the burning city of Troy after it was conquered by the Greeks.

Reading Strategy　Making Inferences About Characters　*How would you describe Cassius's attitude toward Brutus? Why might Cassius behave in this manner?* **R**

JULIUS CAESAR, ACT 1, SCENE 2　**779**

Differentiated Instruction

Performing Acting out scenes of the play by paraphrasing dialogue will help students understand both the dialogue and the characters' behavior and attitudes. Have pairs of students act out the discussion between Cassius and Brutus on pages 777–781 by paraphrasing each character's speeches. Suggest that students write brief summaries of each character's important speeches and discuss each one's motivation. Have volunteers act out their scenes. **BL**

Objectives
• To make inferences about characters (SE)
• To write an extended metaphor (TWE)

Teach

R1 **Reading Strategy**

Making Inferences About Characters Answer: *Caesar has probably been suggesting to the public that he is more than a mere man. Cassius is pointing out that Caesar is very human. He uses the term "god" ironically to make this point.* Explain to students that Cassius is describing an epileptic seizure and that this incident is one of several weaknesses that Shakespeare attributes to Caesar. **Ask:** Can you identify another weakness? *(Caesar almost drowns after challenging Cassius to a swimming competition, and Cassius has to save Caesar.)* **OL**

L1 **Literary Element**

Blank Verse Answer: *Lines 129 and 131 are regular. The others vary the pattern in some way.* **OL**

L2 **Literary Element**

Symbol Say: Cassius discusses Caesar's name at length and tells Brutus, "Yours is as fair a name." **Ask:** What do names symbolize in Cassius's speech? *(He uses a name to stand for the person and for accomplishments and abilities.)* **OL**

JULIUS CAESAR

115 Did I the tired Caesar. And this man
    Is now become a god, and Cassius is
    A wretched creature, and must bend his body°   **117** bend his body: bow.
    If Caesar carelessly but nod on him.
    He had a fever when he was in Spain,
120 And when the fit was on him, I did mark
    How he did shake—'tis true, this god did shake;
    His coward lips did from their color fly,
    And that same eye whose bend° doth awe the world   **123** bend: glance, look.
    Did lose his° luster; I did hear him groan;   **124** his: its.
125 Ay, and that tongue of his that bade the Romans
    Mark him, and write his speeches in their books,
    Alas, it cried, "Give me some drink, Titinius,"
    As a sick girl. Ye gods, it doth amaze me
    A man of such a feeble temper should
130 So get the start of the majestic world,   **130–131** So get the . . . alone: get ahead of all others and carry the victor's prize himself.
    And bear the palm alone.°

    [*Shout. Flourish.*]

    BRUTUS.   Another general shout?
        I do believe that these applauses are
        For some new honors that are heap'd on Caesar.

135 CASSIUS.   Why, man, he doth bestride the narrow world
        Like a Colossus,° and we petty men   **136** Colossus: The Colossus of Rhodes, a gigantic statue of the Greek god Apollo in the harbor of Rhodes, was said to be so tall that ships could sail through its legs.
        Walk under his huge legs, and peep about
        To find ourselves dishonorable graves.
        Men at some time are masters of their fates;
140   The fault, dear Brutus, is not in our stars,°   **140** stars: fate (believed to be determined by the position of the stars and planets at someone's birth).
        But in ourselves, that we are underlings.
        Brutus and Caesar; what should be in that "Caesar"?
        Why should that name be sounded more than yours?
        Write them together, yours is as fair a name;
145   Sound them,° it doth become the mouth as well;   **145** Sound them: say them.
        Weigh them, it is as heavy; conjure° with 'em,   **146** conjure: call up spirits.   **L2**
        "Brutus" will start a spirit as soon as "Caesar."
        Now, in the names of all the gods at once,
        Upon what meat doth this our Caesar feed,
150   That he is grown so great? Age,° thou art sham'd!   **150** Age: the present era.
        Rome, thou hast lost the breed of noble bloods!
        When went there by an age, since the great flood°   **152** great flood: a time, according to Roman mythology, when a god let loose a flood that drowned all but two people.
        But it was fam'd with more than with one man?°   **153** But it was . . . man: That was not celebrated for more than one great man.
        When could they say, till now, that talk'd of Rome,

Reading Strategy   Making Inferences About Characters *What is Cassius's attitude toward the idea that Caesar is a god?* **R1**

Literary Element   Blank Verse *Review lines 125 to 131. How many of these lines are regular iambic pentameter, and how many vary the pattern?* **L1**

Additional Support

Skills Practice

LITERARY ELEMENT:

Characterization The relationship between Brutus and Cassius spurs on the conflict throughout *Julius Caesar*. Have students characterize the relationship between Brutus and Cassius thus far in the play. *(They seem to know each other well. They share an obvious respect for one another and seem to recognize each other's strengths and weaknesses. Cassius knows that Brutus can be flattered and manipulated. Brutus seems to know that Cassius has an ulterior motive. Despite this awareness, Brutus seems to be succumbing to Cassius's flattery.)* **OL**

155 That her wide walks encompass'd but one man?
Now is it Rome indeed and room enough,°
When there is in it but one only man.
O! you and I have heard our fathers say
There was a Brutus once that would have brook'd
160 Th' eternal devil to keep his state in Rome
As easily as a king.°

BRUTUS. That you do love me, I am nothing jealous;°
What you would work me to, I have some aim.°
How I have thought of this, and of these times,
165 I shall recount hereafter. For this present,
I would not (so with love I might **entreat** you)
Be any further mov'd.° What you have said
I will consider; what you have to say
I will with patience hear, and find a time
170 Both meet° to hear and answer such high things.
Till then, my noble friend, chew° upon this;
Brutus had rather be a villager
Than to repute himself a son of Rome
Under these hard conditions as this time
175 Is like to lay upon us.

CASSIUS. I am glad that my weak words
Have struck but thus much show of fire from Brutus.

[*Enter* CAESAR *and his* TRAIN.]

BRUTUS. The games are done, and Caesar is returning.

CASSIUS. As they pass by, pluck Casca by the sleeve,
180 And he will (after his sour fashion) tell you
What hath proceeded worthy note today.°

BRUTUS. I will do so. But look you, Cassius,
The angry spot doth glow on Caesar's brow,
And all the rest look like a chidden train;°
185 Calphurnia's cheek is pale, and Cicero°
Looks with such ferret° and such fiery eyes
As we have seen him in the Capitol,
Being cross'd in conference by some senators.

CASSIUS. Casca will tell us what the matter is.

190 CAESAR. Antonio!

ANTONY. Caesar?

Big Idea Loyalty and Betrayal *What angers Cassius about Caesar's leadership?* **BI**

Reading Strategy Making Inferences About Characters *To what extent has Cassius succeeded in winning Brutus over to his side?* **R₂**

Vocabulary

entreat (en trēt′) *v.* to ask earnestly; to beg

Side notes (center column):

156 **Now is it . . . enough:** Cassius makes a pun on the words *Rome* and *room*, which were sometimes pronounced alike in Shakespeare's time.

159–161 **There was . . . king:** There once was a Brutus who would have accepted the devil ruling in Rome as easily as a king. (Cassius refers to Lucius Junius Brutus, who expelled the king and made Rome a republic in 509 BC Brutus claimed this hero as his ancestor.)

162 **am nothing jealous:** have no doubt.

163 **have some aim:** can guess.

167 **mov'd:** urged.

170 **meet:** suitable.

171 **chew:** ponder.

181 **What hath . . . today:** What noteworthy things have occurred today.

184 **chidden train:** scolded band of followers.

185 **Cicero:** a Roman senator famous for his oratory.

186 **ferret:** a weasel-like animal with red eyes.

Teach

BI **Big Idea**

Loyalty and Betrayal
Answer: *Cassius fears that Caesar wants to be a king. He argues that Rome must not be governed by one man.* **OL**

R₂ **Reading Strategy**

Making Inferences About Characters Answer: *Cassius has good reason to be confident that he has succeeded in winning over Brutus: Brutus is openly troubled by Caesar's ambitions. His last remark seems to indicate that some action is necessary.* **OL**

L₃ **Literary Element**

Foreshadowing Have students predict what lines 184–188 might foreshadow. (*Something unpleasant happened while Caesar was out in public, perhaps foreshadowing a complication in Caesar's leadership.*) **OL**

Objectives
• To make inferences about characters (SE)
• To analyze character relationships (TWE)

Differentiated Instruction

Classifying Quotations In reading *Julius Caesar*, students may find familiar quotations. For example, in line 194 Caesar says, "Yond Cassius has a lean and hungry look." Students may have heard "Beware the ides of March" and "he [Caesar] doth bestride the narrow world like a Colossus." Point out that people often use phrases and sentences first coined by Shakespeare. Suggest that students start a notebook of Shakespearean quotes as they complete the play, including phrases they have heard before and ones that strike them as particularly valid and original. **AL**

Teach

L1 Literary Element

Blank Verse Answer: *In both lines, the opening accents are reversed, so the stressed syllable is first.* **OL**

BI Big Idea

Loyalty and Betrayal

Answer: *Caesar implies that Cassius is too interested in what happens around him, is too quiet, and does not give himself over to enjoyment. He also implies that Cassius is jealous of powerful people and is dangerous to them.* **OL**

R1 Reading Strategy

Making Inferences About Characters Answer: *Answers will vary. Students may observe that Caesar spends more time talking about Cassius than he would if he were truly confident.* **OL**

★ Viewing the Art

Answer: *Students may say that the painting depicts a commanding, stern, decisive Caesar. They may argue that this is Caesar's outward image but that—thanks to Cassius—they now perceive Caesar as flawed and human.* **AS**

 JULIUS CAESAR

Gaius Julius Caesar; Roman statesman and general—"Caesar dictates his commentaries"—Painting (detail), 1812. Pelagio Palagi. Oil on canvas. Rome Palazzo del Quirinale.
Viewing the Art: What qualities of Caesar does this painting depict? Do you think they are accurate? Why or why not? ★

CAESAR. Let me have men about me that are fat,
Sleek-headed men, and such as sleep a-nights.
Yond Cassius has a lean and hungry look,
195   He thinks too much; such men are dangerous.

ANTONY. Fear him not, Caesar, he's not dangerous,
He is a noble Roman, and well given.°

CAESAR. Would he were fatter! But I fear him not.
Yet if my name were liable to fear,°
200   I do not know the man I should avoid
So soon as that spare Cassius. He reads much,
He is a great observer, and he looks
Quite through the deeds of men.° He loves no plays,
As thou dost, Antony; he hears no music;
205   Seldom he smiles, and smiles in such a sort
As if he mock'd himself, and scorn'd his spirit
That could be mov'd to smile at any thing.°
Such men as he be never at heart's ease
Whiles they behold a greater than themselves,
210   And therefore are they very dangerous.
I rather tell thee what is to be fear'd
Than what I fear; for always I am Caesar.

197 well given: favorably disposed (toward Caesar).

199 if my name . . . fear: if it were possible for me to fear anyone.

202–203 looks . . . of men: sees people's true motives in their actions.

206–207 scorn'd . . . any thing: scorned anyone who ever smiles.

Literary Element Blank Verse *Read these two lines to yourself. How do they vary the pattern of blank verse?* **L1**

Big Idea Loyalty and Betrayal *Why does Caesar think that Cassius is to be avoided?* **BI**

Reading Strategy Making Inferences About Characters *Is Caesar genuinely fearless as he claims? Explain.* **R1**

Additional Support

Skills Practice

WRITING: Commas with Introductory Words Remind students to use a comma after an introductory word or interjection. Point out line 224 on p. 783: "Why, for that too." Write the following sentences on the board, omitting the commas. Have students insert the commas.

- Why, saw you any thing more wonderful?
- Indeed, it is a strange-disposed time; . . .
- Ay, he spoke Greek.
- O, he sits high in all the people's hearts; . . . **OL**

Come on my right hand, for this ear is deaf,
And tell me truly what thou think'st of him.

[CAESAR *and his* TRAIN *exit.* CASCA *stays.*]

215   CASCA.   You pull'd me by the cloak, would you speak with me?

BRUTUS.   Ay, Casca; tell us what hath chanc'd° today,
That Caesar looks so sad.°

CASCA.   Why, you were with him, were you not?

BRUTUS.   I should not then ask Casca what had chanc'd.

220   CASCA.   Why, there was a crown offer'd him; and being offer'd
him, he put it by° with the back of his hand, thus, and then
the people fell a-shouting.

BRUTUS.   What was the second noise for?

CASCA.   Why, for that too.

225   CASSIUS.   They shouted thrice; what was the last cry for?

CASCA.   Why, for that too.

BRUTUS.   Was the crown offer'd him thrice?

CASCA.   Ay, marry, was't,° and he put it by thrice, every time
gentler than other; and at every putting-by mine honest
230   neighbors° shouted.

CASSIUS.   Who offer'd him the crown?

CASCA.   Why, Antony.

BRUTUS.   Tell us the manner of it, gentle Casca.

CASCA.   I can as well be hang'd as tell the manner of it; it was
235   mere foolery, I did not mark° it. I saw Mark Antony offer **L3**
him a crown—yet 'twas not a crown neither, 'twas one of
these coronets°—and as I told you, he put it by once; but
for all that, to my thinking, he would fain° have had it.
Then he offer'd it to him again; then he put it by again; but
240   to my thinking, he was very loath to lay his fingers off it.
And then he offer'd it the third time; he put it the third
time by; and still as he refus'd it, the rabblement hooted,
and clapp'd their chopp'd° hands, and threw up their
sweaty nightcaps, and utter'd such a deal of stinking
245   breath because Caesar refus'd the crown, that it had,
almost, chok'd Caesar; for he swounded,° and fell down at
it; and for mine own part, I durst not laugh, for fear of
opening my lips and receiving the bad air.

216   **chanc'd:** happened.
217   **sad:** serious.

221   **put it by:** pushed it aside.

228   **marry, was't:** indeed it was.

229–230   **mine honest neighbors:** Casca refers ironically to his "honest neighbors," for whom he has contempt.

235   **mark:** pay attention to.

237   **coronets:** small crowns.
238   **fain:** rather.

243   **chopp'd:** chapped.

246   **swounded:** fainted.

Literary Element   Blank Verse   *What difference do you notice between Casca's way of speaking and that of Caesar in this scene?* **L2**

Reading Strategy   Making Inferences About Characters   *Why does Caesar refuse the crown?* **R2**

JULIUS CAESAR, ACT 1, SCENE 2   **783**

Teach

L2 **Literary Element**

Blank Verse Answer: *Caesar uses blank verse; Casca speaks in prose.* **OL**

L3 **Literary Element**

Irony Remind students that in verbal irony, one thing is said and the opposite is true. Ask students to identify the irony in Casca's statement "It was mere foolery, I did not mark it" (lines 234–235). *(Casca says he hardly noticed the incident of Caesar's refusing the crown and then describes it in detail.)* **OL**

R2 **Reading Strategy**

Making Inferences About Characters Answer: *Students may conclude that Caesar's refusal is either genuine or for political reasons. Some may argue that he would like to accept the crown but puts on a show of modesty for the crowd.* **OL**

English Language Coach

Shakespearean English English language learners may be confused by English words they know that have different meanings in Shakespeare's play. On the board, start a list of known words that Shakespeare uses in unusual ways. For example, *and* can mean *if*, as in lines 263 and 277. *Soft* in line 249 means "wait," and *meet* in line 305 means "appropriate." Explain that students may never encounter these uses except in Shakespeare. Have students contribute additional words to the word list to make a glossary. **EL**

Objectives

- To analyze the use of blank verse (SE)
- To make inferences about characters (SE)
- To use commas correctly after introductory words (TWE)

783

Teach

R1 Reading Strategy

Making Inferences About Characters Answer: *Although he speaks with exaggerated, cruel humor, Casca implies that the poor, ignorant masses would follow Caesar under any circumstances. Casca's contempt for the poor seems genuine. He clearly loathes Caesar's popularity.* **OL**

BI Big Idea

Loyalty and Betrayal

Answer: *Caesar appears tyrannical in silencing those who disagree with him.* **OL**

★ Writer's Technique

Soliloquy A soliloquy is a convention of Shakespearean drama in which a character alone on stage delivers a speech explaining to the audience the character's feelings, plans, and motivations. Have students identify Cassius's soliloquy. *(lines 303–317)* **AS**

CASSIUS. But, soft,° I pray you; what, did Caesar swound?

250 CASCA. He fell down in the market place, and foam'd at mouth, and was speechless.

BRUTUS. 'Tis very like, he hath the falling sickness.°

CASSIUS. No, Caesar hath it not; but you, and I, And honest Casca, we have the falling sickness.

255 CASCA. I know not what you mean by that, but I am sure Caesar fell down. If the tag-rag people° did not clap him and hiss him, according as he pleas'd and displeas'd them, as they use to do the players in the theater, I am no true man.

BRUTUS. What said he when he came unto himself?

260 CASCA. Marry, before he fell down, when he perceiv'd the common herd was glad he refus'd the crown, he pluck'd me ope his doublet,° and offer'd them his throat to cut. And I had been a man of any occupation,° if I would not have taken him at a word,° I would I might go to hell
265 among the rogues. And so he fell. When he came to himself again, he said, if he had done or said anything amiss, he desir'd their worships to think it was his **infirmity**. Three or four wenches, where I stood, cried, "Alas, good soul!" and forgave him with all their hearts.
270 But there's no heed to be taken of them; if Caesar had stabb'd their mothers, they would have done no less.

BRUTUS. And after that, he came thus sad away?

CASCA. Ay.

CASSIUS. Did Cicero say anything?

275 CASCA. Ay, he spoke Greek.

CASSIUS. To what effect?

CASCA. Nay, and I tell you that, I'll ne'er look you i' th' face again. But those that understood him smil'd at one another, and shook their heads; but for mine own part, it was Greek
280 to me.° I could tell you more news too; Murellus and Flavius, for pulling scarfs off Caesar's images, are put to silence.° Fare you well. There was more foolery yet, if I could remember it.

CASSIUS. Will you sup with me tonight, Casca?

CASCA. No, I am promis'd forth.

249 soft: wait a minute.

252 'Tis very . . . falling sickness: It's very likely that he has epilepsy.

256 tag-rag people: ragged mob.

261–262 pluck'd . . . doublet: ripped open his short jacket.
263 And I . . . occupation: If I had been "a man of action" (or "a laborer").
264 a word: his word.

279–280 it was Greek to me: I couldn't understand a word of it.
281 put to silence: barred from speaking in public (or perhaps exiled or executed).

Reading Strategy Making Inferences About Characters *What does Casca mean by this remark? What is his attitude toward the mob?* **R1**

Big Idea Loyalty and Betrayal *What does the punishment of Murellus and Flavius indicate about Caesar and his rule?* **BI**

Vocabulary

infirmity (in fur′mə tē) *n.* a physical or mental weakness or disability; feebleness

784 UNIT 4 DRAMA

Additional Support

Skills Practice

LISTENING AND SPEAKING:

Expressing Emotions Point out that Casca expresses fear and wonder in his speech on page 784. Similarly, Caesar expresses pride and suspicion in his speech on page 782. Have students choose a speech of eight lines or more in which a character clearly expresses a specific emotion. Have them define the emotion and prepare a reading of the speech in which the emotion is evident. Encourage students to use facial expression, vocal speed and tone, and gestures to communicate emotion. Have students present their readings in small groups. **OL**

285 CASSIUS. Will you dine with me tomorrow?

CASCA. Ay, if I be alive, and your mind hold,° and your dinner
worth the eating.

CASSIUS. Good, I will expect you.

CASCA. Do so. Farewell, both. [*Exit.*]

290 BRUTUS. What a blunt fellow is this grown to be!
He was quick mettle° when he went to school.

CASSIUS. So is he now in execution
Of any bold or noble **enterprise**,
However he puts on this tardy form.°

295 This rudeness is a sauce to his good wit,
Which gives men stomach to disgest° his words
With better appetite.

BRUTUS. And so it is. For this time I will leave you.
Tomorrow, if you please to speak with me,

300 I will come home to you, or, if you will,
Come home to me, and I will wait for you.

CASSIUS. I will do so. Till then, think of the world.°

[*Exit BRUTUS.*]

Well, Brutus, thou art noble; yet I see
Thy honorable mettle may be wrought

305 From that it is dispos'd;° therefore it is meet°
That noble minds keep ever with their likes;
For who so firm that cannot be seduc'd?
Caesar doth bear me hard,° but he loves Brutus.
If I were Brutus now and he were Cassius,

310 He should not humor° me. I will this night,
In several hands, in at his windows throw,
As if they came from several citizens,
Writings, all tending to the great opinion
That Rome holds of his name; wherein obscurely

315 Caesar's ambition shall be glanced at.°
And after this, let Caesar seat him sure,°
For we will shake him, or worse days endure. [*Exit.*] ★

286 **your mind hold:** you don't change your mind.

291 **quick mettle:** lively, clever.

294 **However . . . form:** Although he puts on this dull manner.

296 **disgest:** digest.

302 **the world:** the present state of affairs.

304–305 **Thy honorable . . . dispos'd:** Your honorable nature can be manipulated to go against its normal inclinations.
305 **meet:** appropriate.
308 **doth bear me hard:** dislikes me.

310 **humor:** influence.

310–315 **I will . . . glanced at:** Tonight I will throw letters in different handwriting, as if they came from several citizens, into Brutus's windows. The letters will relate that Brutus is highly regarded in Rome and will subtly hint at Caesar's ambition.
316 **seat him sure:** seat himself securely.

Reading Strategy Making Inferences About Characters *Why does Cassius wish to meet with Casca?* **R2**

Reading Strategy Making Inferences About Characters *What aspect of Cassius's character now becomes clear? What are his true feelings about Brutus?* **R3**

Literary Element Blank Verse *In what way are these lines not blank verse? Why might Shakespeare have written them in this way?* **L**

Vocabulary

enterprise (en′tər priz′) *n.* an important project or undertaking

JULIUS CAESAR, ACT 1, SCENE 3 **785**

Differentiated Instruction

Creating Sound Effects The stage direction at the beginning of scene 3 specifies "thunder and lightning." Remind students that the Elizabethan theater had few resources available for special effects. Have pairs of students brainstorm ways in which they might have created thunder and lightning onstage in Shakespeare's time. Then have them think of ways they would do so now if they were producing the play without access to sophisticated lighting and equipment. Have students describe and discuss their ideas. **AL**

Objectives
• To analyze the use of blank verse (SE)
• To make inferences about characters (SE)
• To identify and interpret emotional expression in dramatic language (TWE)

785

Teach

SCENE 3. A Roman street. One month later.

[*Thunder and lightning. Enter (from opposite sides) CASCA (with his sword drawn) and CICERO.*]

CICERO. Good even,° Casca; brought you Caesar home?
Why are you breathless? And why stare you so?

CASCA. Are not you mov'd, when all the sway° of earth
Shakes like a thing unfirm? O Cicero,
5 I have seen tempests, when the scolding winds
Have riv'd° the knotty oaks, and I have seen
Th' ambitious ocean swell and rage and foam,
To be exalted with° the threat'ning clouds;
But never till tonight, never till now,
10 Did I go through a tempest dropping fire.
Either there is a civil strife in heaven,
Or else the world, too saucy° with the gods,
Incenses them to send destruction.

CICERO. Why, saw you any thing more wonderful?

15 CASCA. A common slave—you know him well by sight—
Held up his left hand, which did flame and burn
Like twenty torches join'd; and yet his hand,
Not sensible of° fire, remain'd unscorch'd.
Besides—I ha' not since put up my sword—
20 Against the Capitol I met a lion,
Who glaz'd° upon me and went surly by,
Without annoying me. And there were drawn
Upon a heap° a hundred ghastly women,
Transformed with their fear, who swore they saw
25 Men, all in fire, walk up and down the streets.
And yesterday the bird of night° did sit
Even at noonday upon the marketplace,
Hooting and shrieking. When these prodigies°
Do so conjointly meet,° let not men say,
30 "These are their reasons, they are natural";
For I believe they are portentous things
Unto the climate that they point upon.°

CICERO. Indeed, it is a strange-disposed time;
But men may construe things after their fashion,
35 Clean from the purpose of the things themselves.°
Comes Caesar to the Capitol tomorrow?

CASCA. He doth; for he did bid Antonio
Send word to you he would be there tomorrow.

1 even: evening.

3 sway: realm.

6 riv'd: split.

8 exalted with: raised as high as.

12 saucy: insolent.

18 sensible of: sensitive to.
21 glaz'd: stared.
22–23 drawn . . . heap: huddled together.
26 bird of night: screech owl.
28 prodigies: bizarre events.
29 conjointly meet: coincide.
31–32 portentous . . . point upon: bad omens for the place where they occur.
34–35 But men may . . . themselves: But people may interpret things in their own way, regardless of the real meaning of the things.

Big Idea Loyalty and Betrayal *What connection might there be between the unnatural events described by Casca and the events of previous scenes?* **BI₁**

Vocabulary

incense (in sens′) *v.* to make very angry

Owl, 20th century. Graham Sutherland. Oil on canvas. Private collection.
Viewing the Art: Can you infer a symbolic meaning from the presence of the "bird of night"? How does this detail affect the mood? ★

Additional Support

Skills Practice

WRITING: Description In scene 3, lines 5–10, Casca vividly describes a thunderstorm. Have students point out the elements that make the description compelling: personification (*"scolding winds"*), precise adjectives (*"knotty," "threatening"*), and vivid verbs (*"riv'd," "swell," "rage"*).

Have students write a paragraph describing a weather phenomenon. Encourage them to use the techniques used by Shakespeare, such as personification, precise adjectives, and vivid verbs. Have students exchange and read one another's descriptions. **OL**

CICERO. Good night then, Casca; this disturbed sky
40   Is not to walk in.

CASCA.   Farewell, Cicero.   [Exit CICERO.]

[Enter CASSIUS.]

CASSIUS. Who's there?

CASCA.   A Roman.

CASSIUS.   Casca, by your voice.

CASCA. Your ear is good. Cassius, what night is this!°

CASSIUS. A very pleasing night to honest men.

CASCA. Who ever knew the heavens menace so?

45   CASSIUS. Those that have known the earth so full of faults.
      For my part, I have walk'd about the streets,
      Submitting me° unto the perilous night;
      And thus unbraced,° Casca, as you see,
      Have bar'd my bosom to the thunder-stone;°
50   And when the cross blue lightning seem'd to open
      The breast of heaven, I did present myself
      Even in the aim° and very flash of it.

      CASCA. But wherefore did you so much tempt the heavens?
      It is the part of men to fear and tremble
55   When the most mighty gods by tokens° send
      Such dreadful heralds to astonish° us.

      CASSIUS. You are dull,° Casca; and those sparks of life
      That should be in a Roman you do want,°
      Or else you use not. You look pale, and gaze,
60   And put on fear, and cast yourself in wonder,
      To see the strange impatience of the heavens;
      But if you would consider the true cause
      Why all these fires, why all these gliding ghosts,
      Why birds and beasts from quality and kind,°
65   Why old men, fools, and children calculate,°
      Why all these things change from their ordinance,
      Their natures and preformed faculties,
      To monstrous quality—why, you shall find
      That heaven hath infus'd them with these spirits,
70   To make them instruments of fear and warning
      Unto some monstrous state.°
      Now could I, Casca, name to thee a man
      Most like this dreadful night,

42 **what night is this:** what a night this is!

47 **Submitting me:** exposing myself.
48 **unbraced:** with jacket open.
49 **thunder-stone:** thunderbolt.

52 **in the aim:** at the point where it was directed.

55 **tokens:** ominous signs.
56 **astonish:** stun with fear.

57 **dull:** stupid.
58 **want:** lack.

64 **from quality and kind:** act contrary to nature.
65 **calculate:** make prophecies.

66–71 **Why all these . . . state:** Cassius argues that things have changed from their normal behavior as a heavenly warning of some unnatural state of affairs.

Literary Element Blank Verse *These five syllables make up the end of a line of blank verse. Which syllables make up the beginning of the line?* **L**

Big Idea Loyalty and Betrayal *Cassius has been making an argument about Roman politics. Which side of the argument does he believe nature is taking?* **BI₂**

JULIUS CAESAR, ACT 1, SCENE 3   **787**

Reading in the Real World

Career Have students visit the library and research the various occupations that require knowledge of ancient history and ancient Latin or Greek. Students might read about high school or college teachers, archaeologists, historians, antique collectors, theologians, and museum curators. **OL**

College Have students visit the college and career department at school and visit university Web sites to learn more about college majors that involve ancient history and ancient Latin or Greek. **OL**

Teach

R1 Reading Strategy

Making Inferences About Characters Answer: *Cassius may be afraid of being overheard. He wants others to draw their own conclusions about Caesar, guided by his reasoning, but not forced. He is a manipulator.* **OL**

L Literary Element

Blank Verse

Answer: *You would have to pronounce the word* tower *as one syllable.* **OL**

R2 Reading Strategy

Making Inferences About Characters Answer: *Cassius reveals emotion and cunning, as he effectively uses this dramatic speech to convince Casca to support him.* **OL**

That thunders, lightens, opens graves, and roars
75   As doth the lion in the Capitol—
A man no mightier than thyself, or me,
In personal action, yet prodigious grown
And fearful,° as these strange eruptions are.

CASCA.   'Tis Caesar that you mean; is it not, Cassius?

80   CASSIUS.   Let it be who it is; for Romans now
Have thews° and limbs like to their ancestors;
But, woe the while,° our fathers' minds are dead,
And we are govern'd with our mothers' spirits;
Our yoke and sufferance° show us womanish.

85   CASCA.   Indeed, they say, the senators tomorrow
Mean to establish Caesar as a king;
And he shall wear his crown by sea and land,
In every place, save here in Italy.

CASSIUS.   I know where I will wear this dagger then;
90   Cassius from bondage will deliver Cassius.°
Therein,° ye gods, you make the weak most strong;
Therein, ye gods, you tyrants do defeat;
Nor stony tower, nor walls of beaten brass,
Nor airless dungeon, nor strong links of iron,
95   Can be retentive to the strength of spirit;
But life, being weary of these worldly bars,
Never lacks power to dismiss itself.
If I know this, know all the world besides,
That part of tyranny that I do bear
100   I can shake off at pleasure.

[*Thunder still.*]

CASCA.   So can I;
So every bondman in his own hand bears
The power to cancel his captivity.

CASSIUS.   And why should Caesar be a tyrant then?
Poor man, I know he would not be a wolf,
105   But that he sees the Romans are but sheep;
He were no lion, were not Romans hinds.°
Those that with haste will make a mighty fire
Begin it with weak straws. What trash° is Rome?
What rubbish and what offal?° when it serves

77–78 yet prodigious . . . fearful: yet has become ominous and threatening.

81 thews: muscles.
82 woe the while: alas for these times.

84 yoke and sufferance: servitude and patient submission.

89–90 I know . . . deliver Cassius: Cassius says that he would rather kill himself than submit to Caesar.
91 Therein: in that way (referring to suicide).

106 hinds: deer.

108 trash: "twigs" or "garbage."
109 offal: "chips of wood" or "garbage."

Reading Strategy Making Inferences About Characters *Why might Cassius not want to name Caesar directly?* **R1**

Literary Element Blank Verse *For this line to be in regular iambic pentameter, which word would you have to pronounce with just one syllable?* **L**

Reading Strategy Making Inferences About Characters *What does Cassius's speech about suicide indicate about his character?* **R2**

788 UNIT 4 DRAMA

Additional Support

788

Skills Practice

VOCABULARY: Suffix -ous Point out the words *dangerous* (p. 789), *monstrous*, and *prodigious*. The suffix *–ous* means "full of" or "possessing the qualities of." Have students look up the root word *prodigy* and explain the meaning of *prodigious* in line 77. *("portentous" or "exciting wonder")* **OL**

VOCABULARY: Etymology The word *tyrant* comes from the Latin *tyrannus*, which came from the Greek *tyrannos*. The meaning, "an absolute ruler," is unchanged. Have students name three other words with the same root. *(tyrannical, tyrannize, tyrannosaurus, tyranny)* **OL**

110   For the base matter° to illuminate
        So vile a thing as Caesar! But, O grief,
        Where hast thou led me? I, perhaps, speak this
        Before a willing bondman; then I know
        My answer must be made.° But I am arm'd,
115   And dangers are to me indifferent.

    CASCA.   You speak to Casca, and to such a man
        That is no fleering° tell-tale. Hold, my hand.
        Be factious for redress of all these griefs,°
        And I will set this foot of mine as far
120   As who goes farthest.

    CASSIUS.   There's a bargain made.
        Now know you, Casca, I have mov'd° already
        Some certain of the noblest-minded Romans
        To undergo with me an enterprise
        Of honorable-dangerous consequence;
125   And I do know, by this they stay for me
        In Pompey's Porch;° for now, this fearful night,
        There is no stir or walking in the streets;

110 **base matter:** kindling.

112–114 **I, perhaps . . . be made:**
Perhaps I am speaking to one who
accepts his slavery; if so, I shall have to
answer for my words (suggesting that
Casca might inform on him).
117 **fleering:** sneering.
118 **Be factious . . . griefs:** Form
a group to straighten out all these
problems.

121 **mov'd:** persuaded.

125–126 **by this . . . Porch:** By this
time they wait for me in the entrance to
the theater built by Pompey.

Reading Strategy   Making Inferences About Characters *From these remarks, who would you say Cassius disrespects more—Caesar or the people of Rome?* **R3**

Big Idea   Loyalty and Betrayal *What bargain has been made?* **BI**

Augustus and lictors, detail from the south frieze of the Ara Pacis Augustae, 13–9 BC Roman.
Museum of the Ara Pacis, Rome.
Viewing the Art: One of the duties of Roman officers called *lictors* was to accompany
officials like Caesar in public appearances. What does this image suggest to you about the
government of Rome in Caesar's time? ★

JULIUS CAESAR, ACT 1, SCENE 3   **789**

Teach

R3 **Reading Strategy**
**Making Inferences About
Characters Answer:** *Cassius
shows no respect for the people
of Rome, comparing them to
"weak straws," "trash," "rubbish," "offal," and "base matter." He hates them primarily for
submitting to what he views as
the tyranny of Caesar. He may
blame them even more than
Caesar for the current situation.*
Ask: What does this tell you
about Cassius's motivation?
*(Cassius is not motivated by
concern for the people, but
rather by his hatred for Caesar
and concern for himself.)* **OL**

BI **Big Idea**
Loyalty and Betrayal
Answer: *Casca has agreed to
keep Cassius's hatred of Caesar
secret and to help Cassius
in any plan to limit Caesar's
power.* **OL**

★ **Viewing the Art**
Answer: *The government
of Rome in Caesar's time
placed great emphasis on
the symbolism of office and
power.* **AS**

Building Reading Fluency

Paraphrasing Paraphrasing can be a
useful aid to comprehension. It requires
a close reading and ensures that a passage's meaning will be understood. Have
students paraphrase Cassius's speech in
lines 80–84 on page 788. Remind them
to replace difficult words with simpler
ones and to simplify sentence structure.

Have students read their renditions
aloud to a partner or small group. (*"We
are physically as strong as our fathers
were, but we are mentally weak. We are
submissive like our mothers."*) Suggest
that students paraphrase any difficulty
speeches. **BL**

Objectives
• To analyze the use of blank verse
  (SE)
• To make inferences about charac-
  ters (SE)
• To use root words to understand
  the meanings of unfamiliar words
  (TWE)

789

Teach

Big Idea

Loyalty and Betrayal

Answer: *Brutus is "noble" and highly respected by the people. If he is involved, Romans will believe that getting rid of Caesar is the right thing to do.* **OL**

⭐ Literary History

Shakespeare's Plots

Students may be surprised to learn that Shakespeare borrowed nearly every one of his plots from other sources. Plays such as *Julius Caesar* and *Henry V* are rooted in history. *Romeo and Juliet* is based on a poem written in 1562 and *Othello* on a story written by an Italian writer in 1565. **AS**

✓CheckPoint

Use the CheckPoint questions on Presentation Plus! to check students' mastery of the selection. These questions can be used with interactive response keypads to get immediate student feedback.

And the complexion of the element
[In] favor's like the work we have in hand,°
130   Most bloody, fiery, and most terrible.

[*Enter* CINNA.]

CASCA. Stand close awhile, for here comes one in haste.

CASSIUS. 'Tis Cinna, I do know him by his gait,
He is a friend. Cinna, where haste you so?

CINNA. To find out you. Who's that? Metellus Cimber?

135   CASSIUS. No, it is Casca, one incorporate°
To our attempts. Am I not stay'd for, Cinna?

CINNA. I am glad on't. What a fearful night is this!
There's two or three of us have seen strange sights.

CASSIUS. Am I not stay'd for? tell me.

CINNA.   Yes, you are.
140   O Cassius, if you could
But win the noble Brutus to our party—

CASSIUS. Be you content. Good Cinna, take this paper,
And look you lay it in the praetor's chair,
Where Brutus may but find it; and throw this
145   In at his window; set this up with wax
Upon old Brutus' statue.° All this done,
Repair° to Pompey's Porch, where you shall find us.
Is Decius Brutus and Trebonius there?

CINNA. All but Metellus Cimber, and he's gone
150   To seek you at your house. Well, I will hie,°
And so bestow these papers as you bade me.

CASSIUS. That done, repair to Pompey's theater.

[*Exit* CINNA.]

Come, Casca, you and I will yet ere day
See Brutus at his house. Three parts of him
155   Is ours already, and the man entire
Upon the next encounter yields him ours.°

CASCA. O, he sits high in all the people's hearts;
And that which would appear offense in us,
His countenance, like richest alchemy,
160   Will change to virtue and to worthiness.°

CASSIUS. Him, and his worth, and our great need of him,
You have right well conceited.° Let us go,
For it is after midnight, and ere day
We will awake him and be sure of him.

[*They exit.*] 🪙

Big Idea Loyalty and Betrayal *Why is it so important for the conspirators to have Brutus on their side?* **BI**

128–129 **the complexion . . . in hand:** The condition of the sky appears similar to the work we have to do.

135 **incorporate:** joined.

142–146 **Good Cinna . . . statue:** Marcus Brutus held the office of praetor, a high-ranking judge who settled disputes brought before him. Cassius directs Cinna to leave one letter on Brutus's chair, throw a second into his window, and fasten a third onto the statue of the hero Lucius Junius Brutus.
147 **Repair:** go.
150 **hie:** hurry.

155–156 **the man . . . ours:** When we next meet him, he will be entirely in our hands.

159–160 **His countenance . . . worthiness:** Alchemy was the "science" of trying to turn base metals into gold. Casca says that Brutus's noble reputation will change the public's attitude toward their plot from condemnation to admiration.
162 **conceited:** understood.

Additional Support

Skills Practice

READING: Problem and Solution It may be helpful for students to review act 1 in terms of problems and solutions. On the board, make a chart with the headings *Problem* and *Solution.* List the following problems and have students write the solutions seen so far: Cassius is jealous of Caesar's power; Roman citizens may object if Cassius and his friends kill Caesar; Brutus is a decent man and may not agree to killing Caesar. **OL**

RESPONDING AND THINKING CRITICALLY

Respond

1. Which character in Act 1 made the strongest impression on you? Why?

Recall and Interpret

2. (a)After seeing the public celebrating Caesar's triumph, what do Flavius and Murellus do? (b)Why do they respond this way?

3. (a)What stories about Caesar does Cassius tell Brutus? (b)What concerns Cassius the most?

4. (a)Whom do Cassius and Casca want to win over to their plan? (b)Why do they feel it is important for this person to join them?

Analyze and Evaluate

5. Do you think Shakespeare's portrayal of the commoners in Act 1 is realistic? Explain.

6. (a)What do Caesar's speech and actions tell you about his character? (b)Do you think that the conspirators have good reason for their reactions to Caesar? Why or why not?

7. How would you describe the overall **mood**, or feeling, of Act 1? Use specific details to support your description.

Connect

8. **Big Idea** **Loyalty and Betrayal** Act 1 establishes a choice facing Roman politicians between loyalty and betrayal. In what way does this choice remind you of present-day conflicts?

LITERARY ANALYSIS

Literary Element **Blank Verse**

Because **blank verse** is intended to sound like spoken language, its meter is often not perfectly regular. This line from *Julius Caesar* is an example of blank verse with regular iambic pentameter:

˘ ′ ˘ ′ ˘ ′
Upon / what meat / doth this /
˘ ′ ˘ ′
our Cae / sar feed

This line from the same speech is irregular:

˘ ′ ˘ ′ ˘ ′ ˘ ′
Brutus and / Caesar / ; what should be /
′ ˘ ′
in that / "Caesar?"

1. Find two lines with regular iambic pentameter. Indicate the stressed and unstressed syllables.

2. Find two lines with irregular iambic pentameter. Show the stressed and unstressed syllables.

Literature Groups

Form small groups to identify three passages of dialogue or monologue from Act 1 that seem particularly effective or descriptive. Discuss the elements that make each segment memorable. Compare your passages and analyses with those of other groups.

READING AND VOCABULARY

Reading Strategy **Making Inferences About Characters**

A character may have more than one reason—or even contradictory reasons—for acting in a certain way. Read the sentences below and identify at least two reasons why the characters in question behaved as they did.

1. Cassius wants Caesar out of power.

2. Caesar refuses to accept the crown from Antony.

3. Brutus does not announce his intentions.

Vocabulary **Practice**

Practice with Synonyms Find the synonym for each vocabulary word.

1. servile   a. injury
2. entreat   b. infuriate
3. infirmity   c. business
4. enterprise   d. implore
5. incense   e. obsequious

Literature Online **Web Activities** For eFlashcards, Selection Quick Checks, and other Web activities, go to www.glencoe.com.

JULIUS CAESAR **791**

Assess

1. Students should name a main character: Cassius, Brutus, or Caesar.

2. (a) They get angry. (b) In the past Romans honored Pompey.

3. (a) How he had to save Caesar from the river and how he once saw Caesar ill and helpless (b) He wants to show that Caesar is no stronger than anyone else.

4. (a) Brutus (b) The public trusts and respects him.

5. Students may find the portrayal realistic (the workers annoy their social betters) or unrealistic (the workers seem truly simple).

6. (a) Students might describe Caesar as arrogant, critical, tyrannical, fearful, or power-hungry. (b) Some may see these negative qualities as good reason for the conspirators' reactions.

7. The mood may be described as somber, dark, or angry based on Brutus's brooding, Cassius's plotting, and the thunderstorm.

8. Answers may mention that the cost of loyalty is the loss of freedom in a dictatorship, or that the cost of betrayal might be disorder or war.

Vocabulary

1. e 2. d 3. a 4. c 5. b

Web Activities Have students access the Web site for interactive activities that will help them assess their understanding of the selection.

Literary Element

1. Sample answers: *And do you now put on your best attire?* (Scene 1, line 48), *For who so firm that cannot be seduc'd?* (Scene 2, line 307).

2. Sample answers: *Either there is a civil strife in heaven* (Scene 3, line 11), *Even at noon day upon the market place* (Scene 3, line 27).

Reading Strategy

1. Cassius feels that Rome must stay a republic. He envies Caesar.

2. Caesar wants the commoners to believe that he does not want power. He wants the senators to crown him.

3. Brutus has not made up his mind. He feels loyalty toward Caesar.

Focus

Summary

Brutus agrees to kill Caesar. Calphurnia begs Caesar to stay home, but he goes to the Capitol anyway. Portia agonizes over Brutus's plan.

V Vocabulary

Vocabulary File Say: Add these words and definitions to your vocabulary file. For each word, include a sentence that gives you an example of how to use the word. **OL** Students with English language needs should include the pronunciations of these words in their files. **EL**

Literary Elements Have students access the Web site to improve their understanding of monologues, soliloquies, and asides.

LITERATURE PREVIEW

Connecting to the Play

You make decisions every day—most of these are no more important than what type of cereal to eat. Every so often, however, you have to make a decision that will have a major impact on your life. Before you read Act 2, think about the following questions:

- When you face an important decision, how do you select the best course of action?
- What was the most difficult decision you ever had to make? What was the result?

Building Background

Ancient Romans believed that observing the natural world could inform them about the future. Great storms, strange sights in the skies, and unusual behavior by animals were indications that not all was well. Powerful men, such as Caesar, might consult priests known as *augurs*, who were experts in detecting signs from nature. Less privileged Romans might simply observe the actions of large birds, such as owls, crows, and eagles. If they saw nothing out of the ordinary, they believed it was probably safe to proceed.

Setting Purposes for Reading

Big Idea Loyalty and Betrayal

As you read Act 2 of *Julius Caesar,* think about the motives of those who betray Caesar's trust. What causes their betrayal? What is the effect of their actions?

Literary Element Monologues, Soliloquies, and Asides

In a work of literature, a **monologue** is a long speech by one character. A **soliloquy** is a monologue delivered while a character is alone onstage. An **aside** is a comment that a character makes to the audience, which other characters onstage do not hear.

- See Literary Terms Handbook, pp. R1, R2, R10, and R16.

Literature Online **Interactive Literary Elements Handbook** To review or learn more about the literary elements, go to www.glencoe.com.

OBJECTIVES
In studying this selection, you will focus on the following:
- understanding the purpose of monologues, soliloquies, and asides

---

READING PREVIEW

Reading Strategy Analyzing Cause-and-Effect Relationships

One action often leads to another. Going to bed late may cause you to be sleepy the next day. This is an example of a **cause-and-effect relationship.** Being able to analyze *why* things happen (the cause) and *what* happens (the effect) is essential to fully understanding both works of literature and real-life experiences.

Reading Tip: Creating a Chain of Cause and Effect Use a graphic organizer like the one below to track cause-and-effect relationships.

Cause	Effect/Cause	Effect
Caesar may be crowned king.	Becoming king may go to Caesar's head.	Caesar may become a cruel dictator.

Vocabulary

interim (in′ tər im) *n.* the space of time that exists between events; p. 795 *We enjoyed the wedding and the reception, but there was nothing to do in the interim.*

commend (kə mend′) *v.* to speak highly of; to praise; p. 798 *The president commended the senator's service to the country.*

disperse (dis purs′) *v.* to break up and send in different directions; to scatter; p. 800 *It was hard for the mother dog to watch the vet disperse her litter.*

imminent (im′ ə nənt) *adj.* about to occur; p. 807 *With the sky so dark and cloudy, surely a thunderstorm is imminent.*

Vocabulary Tip: Word Parts Prefixes are affixes added to the beginning of words or bases to change their meaning.

- analyzing cause-and-effect relationships
- writing to analyze plot

Selection Skills

The Tragedy of Julius Caesar, Act 2

Literary Element
- Monologues, Soliloquies, and Asides (SE pp. 792–811)

Reading Skills
- Analyzing Cause and Effect (SE pp. 792–811)

Vocabulary Skills
- Word Parts (SE pp. 792, 811)
- Etymology (TWE p. 794)

Listening/Speaking/ Viewing Skills
- Analyzing Art (SE pp. 794, 796, 801, 805, 807, 810)

Writing Skills/Grammar
- Analysis of Plot (SE p. 811)
- Parallel Sentence Structure (TWE p. 798)

Study Skills
- Using Graphic Aids (TWE p. 810)

ACT 2

BI₁

SCENE 1. BRUTUS's garden. The ides of March.

[Enter BRUTUS in his orchard.]

BRUTUS. What, Lucius, ho!
   I cannot, by the progress° of the stars,
   Give guess how near to day. Lucius, I say!
   I would it were my fault° to sleep so soundly.
5   When, Lucius, when? Awake, I say! What, Lucius!

[Enter LUCIUS.]

LUCIUS. Call'd you, my lord?

BRUTUS. Get me a taper° in my study, Lucius.
   When it is lighted, come and call me here.

LUCIUS. I will, my lord.

[Exit LUCIUS.]

10   BRUTUS. It must be by his death;° and for my part,
   I know no personal cause to spurn° at him,
   But for the general.° He would be crown'd:
   How that might change his nature, there's the question.
   It is the bright day that brings forth the adder,°
15   And that craves° wary walking. Crown him that,°
   And then I grant we put a sting in him
   That at his will he may do danger with.
   Th' abuse of greatness is when it disjoins
   Remorse from power;° and, to speak truth of Caesar,
20   I have not known when his affections° sway'd
   More than his reason. But 'tis a common proof°
   That lowliness° is young ambition's ladder,
   Whereto the climber-upward turns his face;
   But when he once attains the upmost round,°
25   He then unto the ladder turns his back,
   Looks in the clouds, scorning the base degrees
   By which he did ascend. So Caesar may;
   Then lest he may, prevent.° And since the quarrel
   Will bear no color for the thing he is,

2 **progress:** position.

4 **I would . . . fault:** I wish it were my weakness.

7 **taper:** candle.

10 **his death:** Caesar's death.
11 **spurn:** strike out.
12 **the general:** the public good.

14 **adder:** poisonous snake.
15 **craves:** demands. **Crown him that:** If we crown him.

18–19 **Th' abuse . . . power:** Greatness is misused when it separates mercy from power.
20 **affections:** feelings, desires.
21 **a common proof:** a common occurrence.
22 **lowliness:** humility.
24 **upmost round:** top rung.

28 **Then lest . . . prevent:** Let us act in advance to prevent it.

Literary Element Monologues, Soliloquies, and Asides *What type of speech is this? How do you know?* **L**

Big Idea Loyalty and Betrayal *What prediction is Brutus making?* **BI₂**

JULIUS CAESAR, ACT 2, SCENE 1   **793**

English Language Coach

Figurative Language English language learners may become confused by Shakespeare's frequent use of figurative language. Explain that Shakespeare uses two extended figures of speech at the beginning of act 2. Brutus compares Caesar to an adder (a poisonous snake) in the danger he may pose to Rome. He compares the rise of Caesar to a person climbing a ladder. These comparisons help readers picture the play's characters. Begin a list of figures of speech from the play on the board, using keywords such as *adder.* Have students suggest additional items for the list as they complete the play. **EL**

793

Teach

L Literary Element

Metaphor Point out the conclusion of Brutus's extended metaphor. Have students explain how Caesar is like a serpent's egg. *(Like an unhatched snake, he is not dangerous now but he will become dangerous.)* **OL**

⭐ Viewing the Art

Answer: *Serpents are traditionally associated with cunning, deceit, guile, and treachery. Students may say that the conspirators (especially Cassius) display these qualities, or that Caesar is the most cunning and deceptive of all.* **AS**

JULIUS CAESAR

Two serpents, 1st century C.E. Artist unknown. Fresco painting (detail). Museo Archeologico Nazionale, Naples, Italy.
Viewing the Art: What qualities are generally associated with serpents? Which characters in the play display such qualities? Explain. ⭐

30   Fashion it thus: that what he is, augmented,
      Would run to these and these extremities;°
      And therefore think him as a serpent's egg,
 L Which hatch'd, would as his kind grow mischievous,
      And kill him in the shell.

[*Enter LUCIUS.*]

35   LUCIUS. The taper burneth in your closet,° sir.
      Searching the window for a flint, I found
      This paper thus seal'd up, and I am sure
      It did not lie there when I went to bed.

[*Gives him the letter.*]

      BRUTUS. Get you to bed again, it is not day.
40   Is not tomorrow, boy, the [ides] of March?

      LUCIUS. I know not, sir.

      BRUTUS. Look in the calendar, and bring me word.

      LUCIUS. I will, sir. [*Exit.*]

      BRUTUS. The exhalations° whizzing in the air
45   Give so much light that I may read by them.

[*Opens the letter and reads.*]

      "Brutus, thou sleep'st; awake, and see thyself!
      Shall Rome, etc. Speak, strike, redress!"°
      "Brutus, thou sleep'st; awake."

794 UNIT 4 DRAMA

**28–31 since the quarrel . . .
extremities:** Since our complaints are not supported by Caesar's present behavior, we will have to put our case the following way: if given more power, Caesar's nature would lead him to such and such extremes.

35 closet: small private room.

44 exhalations: meteors.

47 redress: correct a wrong.

Additional Support

794

Skills Practice

VOCABULARY: Etymology The Latin word *phantasma,* usually written in English as *phantasm,* can mean "an illusion" or "a ghost." It comes from the Greek word *phantazein,* "to present to the mind." Have students find other words with the same root, which include *fancy, fantasy,* and *phantom.* **OL**

VOCABULARY: Homophones Remind students that homophones are words that sound alike but are spelled differently. Write these homophones on the board: *bored, board; seam, seem; heard, herd; dear, deer; peace, piece.* Ask students what the words mean and how they fit into a sentence. **OL**

Such instigations° have been often dropp'd
50   Where I have took them up.
"Shall Rome, etc." Thus must I piece it out:°
Shall Rome stand under one man's awe? What, Rome?
My ancestors did from the streets of Rome
The Tarquin° drive when he was call'd a king.
55   "Speak, strike, redress!" Am I entreated
To speak and strike? O Rome, I make thee promise,
If the redress will follow, thou receivest
Thy full petition at the hand of Brutus!°

[Enter LUCIUS.]

LUCIUS. Sir, March is wasted fifteen days.

[Knock within.]

60   BRUTUS. 'Tis good. Go to the gate, somebody knocks.

[Exit LUCIUS.]

Since Cassius first did whet° me against Caesar,
I have not slept.
Between the acting of a dreadful thing
And the first motion,° all the **interim** is
65   Like a phantasma,° or a hideous dream.
The Genius and the mortal instruments°
Are then in council, and the state of a man,
Like to a little kingdom, suffers then
The nature of an insurrection.°

[Enter LUCIUS.]

70   LUCIUS. Sir, 'tis your brother° Cassius at the door,
Who doth desire to see you.

BRUTUS.   Is he alone?

LUCIUS. No, sir, there are moe° with him.

BRUTUS.   Do you know them?

LUCIUS. No, sir; their hats are pluck'd about their ears,
And half their faces buried in their cloaks,

Big Idea Loyalty and Betrayal *What does the audience know about the origin of these notes?* **BI**

Reading Strategy Analyzing Cause-and-Effect Relationships *What effect have the letters had on Brutus?* **R1**

Reading Strategy Analyzing Cause-and-Effect Relationships *What has caused Brutus's mind to be in such turmoil?* **R2**

Vocabulary

interim (in´ tər im) *n.* the space of time that exists between events

---

49 **instigations:** letters urging action.

51 **piece it out:** fill in the gaps in meaning.

54 **Tarquin** (tär´ kwin): the last king of Rome, driven out by Lucius Junius Brutus.

55–58 **Speak, strike . . . Brutus:** Brutus vows that Rome's petition for redress will be granted if it can be done through his words and actions.

61 **whet:** incite.

64 **motion:** prompting.
65 **phantasma:** nightmare.
66 **Genius . . . instruments:** the mental and physical powers that allow someone to take action.

67–69 **the state . . . insurrection:** Brutus compares his conflicted state of mind to a kingdom paralyzed by civil unrest.
70 **brother:** brother-in-law. (Cassius is married to Brutus's sister, Junia.)

72 **moe:** more.

JULIUS CAESAR, ACT 2, SCENE 1 **795**

Differentiated Instruction

Drawing Diagrams According to the stage direction at the beginning of scene 1, Brutus meets the conspirators in the garden of his house. The typical house of a wealthy Roman included a large walled garden in which fruits and vegetables were grown, thus the mention in the next stage direction of Brutus's "orchard." Have students research the design of a typical house of a well-to-do Roman. Have them draw diagrams or illustrations of the house and display them. **AL**

Teach

Teach

BI₁ Big Idea

Loyalty and Betrayal

Answer: *The visitors disguise themselves in case anyone should realize who they are and what they are plotting to do. The image of the cloaked visitors may suggest the shamefulness and sneakiness of betrayal.* **OL**

L₁ Literary Element

Monologues, Soliloquies, and Asides Answer: *Students may say that soliloquies are intended to express a character's inner thoughts and to impart nuance to the action of the plot.* Point out that Brutus personifies "Conspiracy." **Ask:** What does Brutus's personification of the conspiracy indicate about his attitude toward the undertaking? *(He despises its deceptive nature; he says it is too ugly to see the light of day and therefore must hide itself at night.)* **OL**

★ Viewing the Art

Answer: *Students may say the painting expresses somber resolve, contemplation, or brooding.* **AS**

---

75   That by no means I may discover° them
          By any mark of favor.°

BRUTUS.   Let 'em enter.

[*Exit LUCIUS.*]

          They are the faction. O Conspiracy,
          Sham'st thou° to show thy dang'rous brow by night,
          When evils are most free? O then, by day
80   Where wilt thou find a cavern dark enough
          To mask thy monstrous visage? Seek none, Conspiracy;
          Hide it in smiles and affability;
          For if thou path, thy native semblance° on,
          Not Erebus° itself were dim enough
85   To hide thee from prevention.°

[*Enter the CONSPIRATORS, CASSIUS, CASCA, DECIUS, CINNA, METELLUS, and TREBONIUS.*]

          CASSIUS. I think we are too bold upon° your rest.
          Good morrow,° Brutus, do we trouble you?

          BRUTUS. I have been up this hour, awake all night.
          Know I these men that come along with you?

90   CASSIUS. Yes, every man of them; and no man here
          But honors you; and every one doth wish
          You had but that opinion of yourself
          Which every noble Roman bears of you.
          This is Trebonius.

          BRUTUS.   He is welcome hither.

95   CASSIUS. This, Decius Brutus.

          BRUTUS.   He is welcome too.

          CASSIUS. This, Casca; this, Cinna; and this, Metellus Cimber.

          BRUTUS. They are all welcome.
          What watchful cares do interpose themselves
          Betwixt your eyes and night?°

100   CASSIUS. Shall I entreat a word?

[*They whisper.*]

          DECIUS. Here lies the east; doth not the day break here?

          CASCA. No.

          CINNA. O, pardon, sir, it doth; and yon gray lines
          That fret° the clouds are messengers of day.

---

75 **discover:** identify.
76 **favor:** appearance.

78 **Sham'st thou:** Are you ashamed?

83 **path . . . semblance:** go about undisguised.
84 **Erebus** (er′ ə bəs): in classical mythology, the dark place through which the dead pass on their way to Hades, the underworld.
85 **prevention:** discovery.

86 **too bold upon:** intruding upon.
87 **morrow:** morning.

Night. Simeon Solomon. Watercolour, ink and bodycolour on paper. Royal Albert Memorial Museum, Exeter, Devon, UK.

Viewing the Art: What mood or emotional quality is expressed by this painting? **★**

98–99 **What watchful . . . night:** What cares keep you awake?
104 **fret:** interlace.

Big Idea Loyalty and Betrayal *Why would the visitors not reveal their identity to Lucius? What does the image of the cloaked visitors suggest?* **BI₁**

Literary Element Monologues, Soliloquies, and Asides *From this passage, what impression do you have of the role of soliloquies in Shakespearean drama?* **L₁**

796 UNIT 4 DRAMA

Additional Support

Skills Practice

LISTENING AND SPEAKING:
Reading Verse Aloud Discuss guidelines for reading poetry aloud:

- Even though poetry is divided into lines, pay attention to sentence punctuation as you do when reading prose.
- Do not emphasize rhythm by reading in a singsong manner. Pronounce words with their normal stressed and unstressed syllables.

Have students choose a speech from *Julius Caesar* written in blank verse. Have them practice reading the speech with a partner, using the guidelines you have discussed. **OL**

105 CASCA. You shall confess that you are both deceiv'd.
       Here, as I point my sword, the sun arises,
       Which is a great way growing on the south,
       Weighing the youthful season of the year.
       Some two months hence, up higher toward the north
110   He first presents his fire, and the high east
       Stands, as the Capitol, directly here.°

     BRUTUS. Give me your hands all over,° one by one.

     CASSIUS. And let us swear our resolution.

     BRUTUS. No, not an oath. If not the face of men,
115   The sufferance of our souls, the time's abuse—
       If these be motives weak, break off betimes,°
       And every man hence to his idle bed.
       So let high-sighted° tyranny range on
       Till each man drop by lottery.° But if these
120   (As I am sure they do) bear fire° enough
       To kindle cowards and to steel with valor
       The melting spirits of women, then, countrymen,
       What need we any spur but our own cause
       To prick° us to redress? What other bond
125   Than secret Romans that have spoke the word
       And will not palter?° and what other oath
       Than honesty to honesty engag'd
       That this shall be, or we will fall for it?°
       Swear priests and cowards and men cautelous,°
130   Old feeble carrions,° and such suffering souls
       That welcome wrongs; unto bad causes swear
       Such creatures as men doubt; but do not stain
       The even virtue of our enterprise,
       Nor th' insuppressive mettle of our spirits,
135   To think that or our cause or our performance
       Did need an oath;° when every drop of blood
       That every Roman bears, and nobly bears,
       Is guilty of a several bastardy,°
       If he do break the smallest particle
140   Of any promise that hath pass'd from him.°

     CASSIUS. But what of Cicero? Shall we sound him?°
       I think he will stand very strong with us.

106–111 Here, as I . . . directly here: Casca insists that in the early spring the sun rises south of the spot pointed out by Decius and Cinna; it will rise farther north in about two months.
112 all over: all of you.

114–116 If not . . . betimes: The sadness in people's faces, the suffering of our souls, the corruption of our age—if these are weak motives, let's give up at once.
118 high-sighted: arrogant.
119 drop by lottery: die by chance (at Caesar's whim).
120 bear fire: are spirited.

124 prick: spur.

126 palter: waver; deceive.

126–128 what other oath . . . for it: What other oath is needed than that of honest men who have pledged to each other that they will prevail or die trying?
129 cautelous: wary; crafty.
130 carrions: men no better than corpses.

132–136 do not stain . . . oath: Do not insult the steadfast virtue of our undertaking or the indomitable courage of our spirits to think that either our cause or our actions require an oath.
136–140 every drop . . . from him: Brutus claims that no one of true Roman blood would break a promise.
138 Is guilty . . . bastardy: is illegitimate.
141 sound him: find out his feelings.

Reading Strategy Analyzing Cause-and-Effect Relationships *Why does Shakespeare insert this bit of dialogue among Decius, Casca, and Cinna about compass directions?* **R**

Literary Element Monologues, Soliloquies, and Asides *What argument does Brutus make against swearing an oath?* **L2**

Big Idea Loyalty and Betrayal *What does Brutus think is virtuous about their enterprise?* **BI2**

Teach

R Reading Strategy

Analyzing Cause-and-Effect Relationships
Answer: *Brutus and Cassius are conferring secretly about the assassination. The others are left to fill the time with awkward, unrelated chat.* **OL**

L2 Literary Element

Monologues, Soliloquies, and Asides **Answer:** *Brutus argues that the only motivation the plotters should have is the desire to rid Rome of Caesar's tyranny. That desire should make an oath superfluous.* **OL**

BI2 Big Idea

Loyalty and Betrayal
Answer: *Brutus believes that betraying Caesar's trust is their moral duty to end the tyranny and corruption that has led to the people's suffering.* **OL**

Differentiated Instruction

Paraphrasing Explain that working with a group to paraphrase parts of Shakespeare's text can help comprehension. Explain that to paraphrase is to put something into your own words. Have groups of students work with lines 114–140. Direct them to paraphrase the speech orally, helping each other. Then have them settle on one interpretation and write down the group's paraphrase. Have a volunteer from each group read their paragraphs aloud. **BL**

Objectives
• To understand the purpose of monologues, soliloquies, and asides (SE)
• To read verse aloud (TWE)

Teach

R Reading Strategy

Analyzing Cause-and-Effect Relationships

Answer: *Cassius thinks Mark Antony, as a friend of Caesar, would, if allowed to live, harm the plotters in some way.* **OL**

JULIUS CAESAR

CASCA. Let us not leave him out.

CINNA. No, by no means.

METELLUS. O, let us have him, for his silver hairs
145   Will purchase us a good opinion,
    And buy men's voices to **commend** our deeds.
    It shall be said his judgment rul'd our hands;
    Our youths and wildness shall no whit° appear,
    But all be buried in his gravity.°

150 **BRUTUS.** O, name him not! Let us not break with him,°
    For he will never follow anything
    That other men begin.

CASSIUS. Then leave him out.

CASCA. Indeed, he is not fit.

DECIUS. Shall no man else be touch'd but only Caesar?

155 **CASSIUS.** Decius, well urg'd. I think it is not meet
    Mark Antony, so well belov'd of Caesar,
    Should outlive Caesar; we shall find of him
    A shrewd contriver; and you know, his means,°
    If he improve them,° may well stretch so far
160   As to annoy us all; which to prevent,
    Let Antony and Caesar fall together.

BRUTUS. Our course will seem too bloody, Caius Cassius,
    To cut the head off and then hack the limbs—
    Like wrath in death and envy afterwards;°
165   For Antony is but a limb of Caesar.
    Let's be sacrificers, but not butchers, Caius.
    We all stand up against the spirit of Caesar,°
    And in the spirit of men there is no blood.
    O that we then could come by° Caesar's spirit,
170   And not dismember Caesar! But, alas,
    Caesar must bleed for it. And, gentle friends,
    Let's kill him boldly, but not wrathfully;
    Let's carve him as a dish fit for the gods,
    Not hew him as a carcass fit for hounds;
175   And let our hearts, as subtle masters do,
    Stir up their servants° to an act of rage,
    And after seem to chide 'em. This shall make
    Our purpose necessary, and not envious;
    Which so appearing to the common eyes,

148 no whit: not in the least.
149 gravity: dignity.
150 break with him: reveal our plot to him.

158 means: abilities.
159 improve them: uses them fully.

164 Like wrath . . . afterwards: as if the killings were motivated by anger and malice.

167 the spirit of Caesar: what Caesar represents.

169 come by: get possession of.

176 servants: hands.

Reading Strategy   Analyzing Cause-and-Effect Relationships *What does Cassius think would be the effect of letting Mark Antony live?* **R**

Vocabulary

commend (kə mend´) *v.* to speak highly of; to praise

Additional Support

Skills Practice

WRITING: Parallel Sentence Structure Using lines 172–174 in Brutus's speech, point out Shakespeare's use of parallel sentence structure and have students describe its effect. *(It has a pleasing, balanced effect that adds weight to the speaker's words.)* Have students write their own sentences using parallel structure. Tell them to use subjects, verbs, and other sentence parts in the same positions as in the original. For example, a sentence modeled on lines 173–174 might read *We can shout it like a cheer at a football game, not whisper it like a secret told to a friend.* Have volunteers read their sentences. **OL**

180 We shall be call'd purgers, not murderers.
And for Mark Antony, think not of him;
For he can do no more than Caesar's arm
When Caesar's head is off.

CASSIUS.   Yet I fear him,
For in the ingrafted° love he bears to Caesar—

185 BRUTUS. Alas, good Cassius, do not think of him.
If he love Caesar, all that he can do
Is to himself—take thought and die° for Caesar.
And that were much he should,° for he is given
To sports, to wildness, and much company.

190 TREBONIUS. There is no fear in him;° let him not die,
For he will live and laugh at this hereafter.

[*Clock strikes.*] ★

BRUTUS. Peace, count the clock.

CASSIUS.   The clock hath stricken three.

TREBONIUS. 'Tis time to part.

CASSIUS.   But it is doubtful yet
Whether Caesar will come forth today or no;
195 For he is superstitious grown of late,
Quite from the main opinion° he held once
Of fantasy, of dreams, and ceremonies.°
It may be these apparent prodigies,
The unaccustom'd terror of this night,
200 And the persuasion of his augurers°
May hold him from the Capitol today.

DECIUS. Never fear that. If he be so resolv'd,
I can o'ersway him; for he loves to hear
That unicorns may be betray'd with trees,
205 And bears with glasses, elephants with holes,
Lions with toils, and men with flatterers;°
But when I tell him he hates flatterers
He says he does, being then most flattered.
Let me work;
210 For I can give his humor the true bent,°
And I will bring him to the Capitol.

CASSIUS. Nay, we will all of us be there to fetch him.

BRUTUS. By the eight hour; is that the uttermost?°

---

184 **ingrafted:** deep-rooted.

187 **take thought and die:** die from grief.
188 **that were much he should:** It is unlikely that he would do such a thing.

190 **no fear in him:** nothing to fear from him.

196 **Quite from the main opinion:** contrary to the strong opinion.
197 **ceremonies:** omens.

200 **augurers:** religious officials who interpreted omens to predict future events.

203–206 **for he loves . . . flatterers:** Decius refers to legends that the mythical unicorn could be tricked into charging a tree and getting its horn stuck, and that bears can be lured by mirrors. He also refers to trapping elephants in pits and using nets to catch lions, and tricking men with flattery.
210 **give his . . . bent:** put him in the right mood.

213 **uttermost:** latest.

Big Idea Loyalty and Betrayal *What does Brutus mean in distinguishing between "purgers" and "murderers"? What do you think of this distinction?* **BI₁**

Big Idea Loyalty and Betrayal *Decius and the other conspirators seem to know Caesar well. How does this affect your attitude toward their plot?* **BI₂**

JULIUS CAESAR, ACT 2, SCENE 1 **799**

English Language Coach

Abstract Words Make sure English language learners understand the abstract terms *loyalty* and *betrayal.* If needed, have students look both words up in an English dictionary and say the words from their native languages that have the same meanings. Have both English language learners and English speakers give examples of ways in which people show loyalty to friends, family, and country. Then have them give examples of ways in which people betray friends, family, and country. **EL**

Objectives
• To analyze cause-and-effect relationships (SE)
• To write using parallel structure (TWE)

799

CINNA. Be that the uttermost, and fail not then.

215 METELLUS. Caius Ligarius doth bear Caesar hard,°
Who rated° him for speaking well of Pompey.
I wonder none of you have thought of him.

BRUTUS. Now, good Metellus, go along by him.
He loves me well, and I have given him reasons;
220 Send him but hither, and I'll fashion° him.

CASSIUS. The morning comes upon 's; we'll leave you, Brutus.
And, friends, **disperse** yourselves; but all remember
What you have said, and show yourselves true Romans.

BRUTUS. Good gentlemen, look fresh and merrily;
225 Let not our looks put on our purposes,
But bear it as our Roman actors do,
With untir'd spirits and formal constancy.°
And so good morrow to you every one.

[*They exit.* BRUTUS *remains.*]

Boy! Lucius! Fast asleep? It is no matter,
230 Enjoy the honey-heavy dew of slumber.
Thou hast no figures nor no fantasies,
Which busy care draws in the brains of men;
Therefore thou sleep'st so sound.

[*Enter* PORTIA.]

PORTIA.   Brutus, my lord!

BRUTUS. Portia! what mean you? wherefore rise you now?
235 It is not for your health thus to commit
Your weak condition to the raw cold morning.

PORTIA. Nor for yours neither. Y'have ungently,° Brutus,
Stole from my bed; and yesternight at supper
You suddenly arose and walk'd about,
240 Musing and sighing, with your arms across;°
And when I ask'd you what the matter was,
You star'd upon me with ungentle looks.
I urg'd you further; then you scratch'd your head,
And too impatiently stamp'd with your foot.
245 Yet I insisted, yet you answer'd not,
But with an angry wafter° of your hand
Gave sign for me to leave you. So I did,

Side notes:

215 **bear Caesar hard:** strongly resents Caesar.
216 **rated:** rebuked.

220 **fashion:** persuade.

224–227 **look fresh . . . constancy:** Brutus warns the others not to let their serious expressions show their intentions; they should carry out their plot appearing at ease and dignified.

237 **ungently:** discourteously.

240 **across:** folded.

R

246 **wafter:** waving.

Big Idea Loyalty and Betrayal *Why does Brutus make this request?* **BI₁**

Literary Element Monologues, Soliloquies, and Asides *What does this soliloquy reveal about Brutus?* **L**

Vocabulary

disperse (dis purs´) *v.* to break up and send in different directions; to scatter

800 UNIT 4 DRAMA

Teach

BI₁ Big Idea

Loyalty and Betrayal
Answer: *Brutus wishes to conceal the plot.* **OL**

L Literary Element

Monologues, Soliloquies, and Asides
Answer: *This soliloquy reveals Brutus's own inner tumult.* **OL**

R Reading Strategy

Visualizing Portia gives a detailed description of Brutus's actions. Encourage students to visualize Brutus based on her description. **Ask:** What emotions do the gestures and expressions indicate? *(worry, stress, preoccupation, impatience)* One or two students may wish to demonstrate. **OL**

Additional Support

Skills Practice

RESEARCH: Rights of Roman Women Women had some rights in ancient Rome. Although they were forbidden to enter politics, matrons of leading families sometimes wielded political influence. Women usually married at the age of 13 or 14, often to a boy chosen by their parents. Although many girls were educated at home or in private schools, few were allowed to pursue higher education. Have students research the everyday lives of women of various social classes in ancient Rome using the library or Internet sources. Encourage students to find out what rights women had and did not have. **OL**

250 Fearing to strengthen that impatience
Which seem'd too much enkindled, and withal°
Hoping it was but an effect of humor,°
Which sometimes hath his° hour with every man.
It will not let you eat, nor talk, nor sleep,
And could it work so much upon your shape
As it hath much prevail'd on your condition,
255 I should not know you Brutus.° Dear my lord,
Make me acquainted with your cause of grief.

BRUTUS. I am not well in health, and that is all.

PORTIA. Brutus is wise and, were he not in health,
He would embrace the means to come by it.

260 BRUTUS. Why, so I do. Good Portia, go to bed.

PORTIA. Is Brutus sick, and is it physical°
To walk unbraced and suck up the humors
Of the dank morning?° What, is Brutus sick,
And will he steal out of his wholesome bed,
265 To dare the vile contagion of the night,
And tempt the rheumy and unpurged air°

249 withal: also.
250 but an . . . humor: only a passing mood.
251 his: its.

253–255 And could . . . Brutus: And if it could change your appearance as much as it has changed your state of mind, I would not recognize you as Brutus.

261 physical: healthy.

262–263 humors . . . morning: damp morning mist.
266 tempt the . . . air: risk the damp and impure air. (It was believed that the night air was dangerous to breathe because it wasn't purified by the sun's rays.)

Big Idea Loyalty and Betrayal *What effect is thinking about the conspiracy having on Brutus?* **BI₂**

Statue of Julius Caesar.
Artist unknown. Museo Laternanense, Vatican Museums, Vatican State.
Viewing the Art: What words would you use to describe Caesar in this depiction? Explain. ★

JULIUS CAESAR, ACT 2, SCENE 1 **801**

Differentiated Instruction

Assassinations Explain that the assassination of Julius Caesar is one of several well-known political assassinations throughout history. Have students research and write a paper on other political assassinations, such as that of Archduke Francis Ferdinand of Austria in 1914, which was a contributing factor to World War I. They may also research the several attempts made to assassinate Adolf Hitler during World War II. Or they may choose to research one of the four American presidents who have been assassinated: Lincoln, Garfield, McKinley, and Kennedy. **AL**

Objectives
• To understand the purpose of monologues, soliloquies, and asides (SE)
• To develop understanding by researching background information (TWE)

Teach

R1 Reading Strategy

Analyzing Cause-and-Effect Relationships

Answer: *Brutus says that he is physically ill, but if he were truly ill, he would be resting in bed instead of pacing through the night.*

Ask: What can you tell about Portia and her feelings for Brutus? *(She seems devoted to Brutus. She is intuitive in realizing something is bothering him and is worried about him.)* **OL**

L Literary Element

Monologues, Soliloquies, and Asides

Answer: *Brutus makes this remark to the audience in an aside.* **OL**

To add unto his sickness? No, my Brutus;
You have some sick offense° within your mind,
Which by the right and virtue of my place,°
270   I ought to know of; and upon my knees
I charm you, by my once commended beauty,
By all your vows of love, and that great vow
Which did incorporate and make us one,
That you unfold to me, yourself, your half,
275   Why you are heavy, and what men tonight
Have had resort to you; for here have been
Some six or seven, who did hide their faces
Even from darkness.

BRUTUS.   Kneel not, gentle Portia.

PORTIA. I should not need, if you were gentle Brutus.
280   Within the bond of marriage, tell me, Brutus,
Is it excepted I should know no secrets
That appertain to you? Am I your self
But, as it were, in sort or limitation,°
To keep with you at meals, comfort your bed,
285   And talk to you sometimes? Dwell I but in the suburbs°
Of your good pleasure? If it be no more,
Portia is Brutus' harlot, not his wife.

BRUTUS. You are my true and honorable wife,
As dear to me as are the ruddy drops
290   That visit my sad heart.

PORTIA. If this were true, then should I know this secret.
I grant I am a woman; but withal
A woman that Lord Brutus took to wife.
I grant I am a woman; but withal
295   A woman well reputed, Cato's daughter.°
Think you I am no stronger than my sex,
Being so father'd and so husbanded?
Tell me your counsels, I will not disclose 'em.
I have made strong proof of my constancy,
300   Giving myself a voluntary wound
Here, in the thigh;° can I bear that with patience,
And not my husband's secrets?

BRUTUS.   O ye gods!
Render me worthy of this noble wife! [*Knock.*]
Hark, hark, one knocks. Portia, go in a while,
305   And by and by thy bosom shall partake

268 sick offense: harmful disorder.

269 by the right . . . place: as your wife.

283 in sort or limitation: after a fashion or within limits.

285 suburbs: outskirts.

295 Cato's daughter: Portia's father, Marcus Porcius Cato, killed himself rather than submit to Caesar's rule after Pompey was defeated.

299–301 I have made . . . thigh: Portia reveals that she intentionally cut her thigh before approaching Brutus to show her strong determination.

Reading Strategy Analyzing Cause-and-Effect Relationships *What causes Portia to distrust Brutus's explanation for his odd appearance?* **R1**

Literary Element Monologues, Soliloquies, and Asides *To whom does Brutus make this remark?* **L**

Additional Support

Skills Practice

WRITING: Commas After Adverb Clauses Point out line 291: "If this were true, then should I know this secret." **Say:** "If this were true" is an adverb clause. When an adverb clause begins a sentence, it is followed by a comma. Write the following sentences on the board. Have students punctuate them.

1. If he love Caesar all that he can do is to himself.

2. Since Cassius first did whet me against Caesar I have not slept.

3. If he be so resolv'd I can o'ersway him. **OL**

The secrets of my heart.
All my engagements I will construe° to thee,
All the charactery of my sad brows.°
Leave me with haste.

[*Exit* PORTIA.]

                    Lucius, who's that knocks?

[*Enter* LUCIUS *and* CAIUS LIGARIUS.]

310   LUCIUS. Here is a sick man that would speak with you.

    BRUTUS. Caius Ligarius, that Metellus spake of.
      Boy, stand aside. [*Exit* LUCIUS.] Caius Ligarius, how?°

    CAIUS. Vouchsafe° good morrow from a feeble tongue.

315   BRUTUS. O, what a time have you chose out, brave Caius,
      To wear a kerchief!° Would you were not sick!

    CAIUS. I am not sick, if Brutus have in hand
      Any exploit worthy the name of honor.

    BRUTUS. Such an exploit have I in hand, Ligarius,
      Had you a healthful ear to hear of it.

320   CAIUS. By all the gods that Romans bow before,
      I here discard my sickness!
                        Soul of Rome!
      Brave son, deriv'd from honorable loins!
      Thou, like an exorcist,° hast conjur'd up
      My mortified° spirit. Now bid me run,
325   And I will strive with things impossible,
      Yea, get the better of them. What's to do?

    BRUTUS. A piece of work that will make sick men whole.

    CAIUS. But are not some whole that we must make sick?

    BRUTUS. That must we also. What it is, my Caius,
330   I shall unfold to thee, as we are going
      To whom it must be done.°

    CAIUS.   Set on your foot.°
      And with a heart new-fir'd I follow you,
      To do I know not what; but it sufficeth
      That Brutus leads me on.

[*Thunder.*]

    BRUTUS.   Follow me, then. [*They exit.*]

---

307 **construe:** explain.
308 **charactery of . . . brows:** what is written in my sad brows (the reasons I am sad).

312 **how:** how are you?
313 **Vouchsafe:** Please accept.

315 **kerchief:** a scarf (wrapped around an ill person's head to protect against drafts).

323 **exorcist:** one who summons up spirits.
324 **mortified:** deadened.

330–331 **I shall . . . done:** They are going to Caesar's house to escort him to the Capitol.
331 **Set on your foot:** Go ahead.

Reading Strategy Analyzing Cause-and-Effect Relationships *Why is Brutus persuaded to reveal the secrets of his heart to Portia?* **R2**

Big Idea Loyalty and Betrayal *What does the trust and loyalty expressed by Caius suggest to you about Brutus?* **BI**

JULIUS CAESAR, ACT 2, SCENE 1   **803**

Teach

R2 Reading Strategy

Analyzing Cause-and-Effect Relationships
Answer: *Portia insists on her loyalty and trustworthiness, even proving it by wounding herself on the thigh.* **OL**

BI Big Idea

Loyalty and Betrayal
Answer: *Students may say it suggests that people around him regard Brutus as noble and wise.* **OL**

Differentiated Instruction

Performing Dialogue Point out that each conspirator plays a different role in the meeting. While Cassius is the leader, he is willing to defer to Brutus, whose support is badly needed. Brutus acts as the conscience of the group, urging a civilized assassination. The other men are followers and change their opin- ions quickly if their leaders do so. Have groups of students act out the conspiracy scene by paraphrasing the speeches. Suggest that each student prepare his or her part by writing notes to help para- phrase the dialogue. Have the groups perform their scenes for the class. **BL**

Objectives
- To analyze cause-and-effect rela- tionships (SE)
- To understand the purpose of monologues, soliloquies, and asides (SE)
- To use commas after adverb clauses (TWE)

803

Teach

L Literary Element

Monologues, Soliloquies, and Asides

Answer: *Students may say Shakespeare did this to foreshadow or provide hints of what might happen to Caesar.* **OL**

R₁ Reading Strategy

Analyzing Cause-and-Effect Relationships

Answer: *The events are otherworldly and inexplicable. She believes they may be portents of the death of a great man—perhaps Caesar.* **OL**

★ Cultural History

Roman Religion Caesar sends his servant to "bid the priests do present sacrifice." In ancient Rome, priests were government officials whose job was to win the favor of the gods for the good of the country. Have students find out more about the religious practices of the ancient Romans such as the duties of the priests and priestesses and the role of sacrifices and other ceremonies. **AS**

Additional Support

804

 JULIUS CAESAR

SCENE 2. CAESAR'S house. A few hours later.

[*Thunder and lightning. Enter JULIUS CAESAR in his nightgown.*]

    CAESAR. Nor heaven nor° earth have been at peace tonight.
      Thrice hath Calphurnia in her sleep cried out,
      "Help, ho! they murther° Caesar!" Who's within?

[*Enter a SERVANT.*]

    SERVANT. My lord?

5   CAESAR. Go bid the priests do present sacrifice,
      And bring me their opinions of success.°

    SERVANT. I will, my lord. [*Exit.*]

[*Enter CALPHURNIA.*]

    CALPHURNIA. What mean you, Caesar? Think you to walk forth?
      You shall not stir out of your house today.

10 CAESAR. Caesar shall forth; the things that threaten'd me
      Ne'er look'd but on my back; when they shall see
      The face of Caesar, they are vanished.

    CALPHURNIA. Caesar, I never stood on ceremonies,°
      Yet now they fright me. There is one within,
15   Besides the things that we have heard and seen,
      Recounts most horrid sights seen by the watch.°
      A lioness hath whelped° in the streets,
      And graves have yawn'd,° and yielded up their dead;
      Fierce fiery warriors fight upon the clouds
20   In ranks and squadrons and right form of war,°
      Which drizzled blood upon the Capitol;
      The noise of battle hurtled in the air;
      Horses did neigh, and dying men did groan,
      And ghosts did shriek and squeal about the streets.
25   O Caesar, these things are beyond all use,°
      And I do fear them.

    CAESAR.   What can be avoided
      Whose end is purpos'd by the mighty gods?
      Yet Caesar shall go forth; for these predictions
      Are to the world in general as to Caesar.°

30 CALPHURNIA. When beggars die, there are no comets seen;
      The heavens themselves blaze forth the death of princes.

Literary Element Monologues, Soliloquies, and Asides *Why did Shakespeare include this soliloquy?* **L**

Reading Strategy Analyzing Cause-and-Effect Relationships *Why does Calphurnia fear these strange events?* **R₁**

804 UNIT 4 DRAMA

Side notes

1 **Nor . . . nor:** neither . . . nor.

3 **murther:** murder.

5–6 **Go bid . . . success:** Tell the priests to make a sacrifice immediately, and bring me their interpretations of the results.

13 **stood on ceremonies:** believed in omens.

16 **watch:** night watchmen.

17 **whelped:** given birth.

18 **yawn'd:** opened.

20 **right form of war:** proper military formation.

25 **use:** normal experience.

29 **Are to the . . . Caesar:** apply to everyone as well as to me.

Skills Practice

INTERNET RESEARCH:

Shakespeare in Music Ask students to use a search engine to locate music that might allude to the works of Shakespeare. Students might enter the keyword *Shakespeare* in order to get a list of his works. Then they can try entering keywords including *Shakespeare music, Shakespeare lyrics,* and *Shakespeare songs.* Students should narrow their searches by adding titles of Shakespeare's plays to the aforementioned keywords. Also have students experiment with their own combinations of keywords. Have them print the lyrics to share with the class. **OL**

CAESAR. Cowards die many times before their deaths,
   The valiant never taste of death but once.
   Of all the wonders that I yet have heard,
35 It seems to me most strange that men should fear,
   Seeing that death, a necessary end,
   Will come when it will come.

[Enter a SERVANT.]

                                    What say the augurers?

SERVANT. They would not have you to stir forth today.
   Plucking the entrails of an offering forth,
40 They could not find a heart within the beast.°

CAESAR. The gods do this in shame of° cowardice;
   Caesar should be a beast without a heart
   If he should stay at home today for fear.
   No, Caesar shall not; Danger knows full well
45 That Caesar is more dangerous than he.

39–40 Plucking the . . . beast:
Augurers would examine the inner organs
of a sacrificed animal to predict the future.
The absence of a heart would be a
strange and unfavorable omen.
41 in shame of: to shame.

Caesar and his wife Calpurnia.
Fabio Canal, 1703-1767.
Palazzo Mangilli-Guion, Venice.
Viewing the Art: Is this artwork
effective at portraying Calphurnia's
character and emotions? Explain. ★

Differentiated Instruction

Designing Costumes Many people are familiar with the simple styles of Roman clothing. Ancient Romans wore long wool or linen tunics. Men wore a toga over their tunics. Men wore white clothing and women wore clothing of various colors. Caesar is said to have been a vain man who added fringed sleeves to his tunic. Have students design a costume for one of the characters in *Julius Caesar.* Have them find pictures of Roman clothing for men and women. Students may draw their costume designs or make them and model them for the class. **AL**

Electrotype copies of two lions from Rosenborg Castle, 17th century. Elkington & Co.
Electroplated copper, silvered, 98 x 165 x 64 cm and 98 x 165 x 60 cm. Victoria and Albert Museum, London.

Teach

R Reading Strategy

Analyzing Cause-and-Effect Relationships

Answer: *Students may say that Caesar will be put in danger.* **OL**

BI₁ Big Idea

Loyalty and Betrayal

Answer: *Answers will vary. Students may say that Caesar shows bravery, kindness, or cowardice.* **OL**

BI₂ Big Idea

Loyalty and Betrayal

Answer: *Answers will vary. Students may say that Decius's florid language seems insincere.* **OL**

We [are] two lions litter'd in one day,°
And I the elder and more terrible;
And Caesar shall go forth.

CALPHURNIA.   Alas, my lord,
Your wisdom is consum'd in confidence.
50 Do not go forth today; call it my fear
That keeps you in the house and not your own.
We'll send Mark Antony to the Senate House,
And he shall say you are not well today.
Let me, upon my knee, prevail in this.

55 CAESAR. Mark Antony shall say I am not well,
And for thy humor,° I will stay at home.

[*Enter* DECIUS.]

Here's Decius Brutus, he shall tell them so.

DECIUS. Caesar, all hail! good morrow, worthy Caesar,
I come to fetch you to the Senate House.

60 CAESAR. And you are come in very happy time°
To bear my greeting to the senators,
And tell them that I will not come today.
Cannot, is false; and that I dare not, falser;
I will not come today. Tell them so, Decius.

44–46 Danger knows . . . day: Caesar uses two figures of speech, first personifying danger and then using the metaphor that he and danger are lions born on the same day.

56 humor: whim.

60 in very happy time: at the right moment.

Reading Strategy Analyzing Cause-and-Effect Relationships *What do you think will happen because of Caesar's decision?* **R**

Big Idea Loyalty and Betrayal *From this scene, what ideas can you form about Caesar?* **BI₁**

Big Idea Loyalty and Betrayal *Does Decius seem sincere to you? Why or why not?* **BI₂**

806 UNIT 4 DRAMA

Additional Support

Skills Practice

READING: Identifying Author's Purpose Explain that in a play, the author has a purpose for each scene, such as to give background, show the nature of a character, further the plot, or increase suspense. Suggest that students define the author's purpose for each scene. Have students define

Shakespeare's purpose in each scene listed below.

1. Act 2, scene 1: Brutus and the conspirators in Brutus's garden *(To show character and advance plot)*

2. Act 2, scene 1: Brutus and Portia *(To show character and increase the audience's involvement)* **OL**

65 CALPHURNIA. Say he is sick.

CAESAR.   Shall Caesar send a lie?
Have I in conquest stretch'd mine arm so far
To be afeard to tell graybeards the truth?°
Decius, go tell them Caesar will not come.

DECIUS. Most mighty Caesar, let me know some cause,
70 Lest I be laugh'd at when I tell them so.

CAESAR. The cause is in my will, I will not come:
That is enough to satisfy the Senate.
But for your private satisfaction,
Because I love you, I will let you know.
75 Calphurnia here, my wife, stays° me at home:
She dreamt tonight° she saw my statue,
Which, like a fountain with an hundred spouts,
Did run pure blood, and many lusty Romans
Came smiling and did bathe their hands in it.
80 And these does she apply for° warnings and portents
And evils **imminent**, and on her knee
Hath begg'd that I will stay at home today.

DECIUS. This dream is all amiss interpreted,
It was a vision fair and fortunate.
85 Your statue spouting blood in many pipes,
In which so many smiling Romans bath'd,
Signifies that from you great Rome shall suck
Reviving blood, and that great men shall press
For tinctures, stains, relics, and cognizance.°
90 This by Calphurnia's dream is signified.

CAESAR. And this way have you well expounded it.

66–67 **Have I . . . truth:** Have I made such conquests to be afraid to tell old men the truth?

75 **stays:** keeps.
76 **tonight:** last night.

80 **apply for:** interpret as.

85–89 **Your statue . . . cognizance:** **Tinctures** are features added to a coat of arms; **relics** are the remains of saints; **cognizance** is a mark identifying one as a lord's follower. Decius interprets Calphurnia's dream as a sign of Caesar's prestige, with great men coming to him to show their political loyalty and reverence.

Big Idea Loyalty and Betrayal *What does this passage suggest about how the participants will behave as the plot unfolds?* **BI₃**

Vocabulary

imminent (im´ ə nənt) *adj.* about to occur

Grave relief of an Athenian married couple, C.E. 330. Artist unknown. Marble attic relief. Antikensammlung, Staatliche Museen zu Berlin.
Viewing the Art: How would you describe the scene featured in this relief? Which characters in *Julius Caesar* would best fit in your description? Why?
★

JULIUS CAESAR, ACT 2, SCENE 2   **807**

Reading in the Real World

Citizenship Much of the American system of government is based upon the ancient Roman system of government. Romans had a representative government, and even some of their terms have been adopted. Have students read about both systems of government and draw comparisons between the two. Suggest that students use scholarly journals, some of which can be accessed online by subscription services available at many school and public libraries. **OL** Have students write a report in which they compare and contrast the two systems of government. **AL**

Teach

R1 Reading Strategy

Analyzing Cause-and-Effect Relationships

Answer: *Decius's flattery, his appeals to Caesar's bravery, and his outright lying about the meaning of the portents convince Caesar to change his mind.* **OL**

R2 Reading Strategy

Questioning Ask: How does Caesar's greeting to Antony relate to what the reader knows about Antony's character? *(Caesar refers to Antony's reputation for enjoying socializing.)* **OL**

DECIUS. I have, when you have heard what I can say;
And know it now: the Senate have concluded
To give this day a crown to mighty Caesar.
95   If you shall send them word you will not come,
Their minds may change. Besides, it were a mock
Apt to be render'd,° for someone to say,
"Break up the Senate till another time,
When Caesar's wife shall meet with better dreams."
100 If Caesar hide himself, shall they not whisper,
"Lo, Caesar is afraid"?
Pardon me, Caesar, for my dear dear love
To your proceeding° bids me tell you this;
And reason to my love is liable.°
105 CAESAR. How foolish do your fears seem now, Calphurnia!
I am ashamed I did yield to them.
Give me my robe, for I will go.

[*Enter* BRUTUS, LIGARIUS, METELLUS CIMBER, CASCA, TREBONIUS,
CINNA, *and* PUBLIUS.]

And look where Publius is come to fetch me.

PUBLIUS. Good morrow, Caesar.

CAESAR.   Welcome, Publius.
110 What, Brutus, are you stirr'd so early too?
Good morrow, Casca. Caius Ligarius,
Caesar was ne'er so much your enemy°
As that same ague° which hath made you lean.
What is't o'clock?

BRUTUS.   Caesar, 'tis strucken eight.

115 CAESAR. I thank you for your pains and courtesy.

[*Enter* ANTONY.]

R2 See, Antony, that revels long a-nights,°
Is notwithstanding up. Good morrow, Antony.

ANTONY. So to most noble Caesar.

CAESAR.   Bid them prepare within;
I am to blame to be thus waited for.
120 Now, Cinna; now, Metellus; what, Trebonius,
I have an hour's talk in store for you;
Remember that you call on me today;
Be near me, that I may remember you.

TREBONIUS. Caesar, I will [*Aside.*] and so near will I be,
125 That your best friends shall wish I had been further.

CAESAR. Good friends, go in, and taste some wine with me,
And we, like friends, will straightway go together.

96–97 it were a . . . render'd: it would be a joke likely to be made.

102–103 my dear . . . proceeding: my very deep desire for your advancement.
104 liable: subservient. Decius says that his love for Caesar forces him to say this, even though he may be overstepping himself.

112 your enemy: Caesar had recently pardoned Ligarius for his support of Pompey during the civil war.
113 ague: sickness.

116 that revels long a-nights: who carouses late into the night.

Reading Strategy Analyzing Cause-and-Effect Relationships *What has caused Caesar to change his mind?* **R1**

Additional Support

Skills Practice

LISTENING AND SPEAKING: Asides
Remind students that the aside is a convention of Elizabethan drama, not necessarily realistic, but accepted by the audience. Point out that some asides can function as mini-soliloquies, ways for a character to share his or her inner state with the audience. Have students work in pairs and perform the asides of Trebonius and Brutus. Discuss ways to dramatize an aside, such as by turning away from certain characters or speaking directly to the audience. Have students invent and perform their own dramatic situations that involve one or more asides. **OL**

BRUTUS. [*Aside.*] That every like is not the same, O Caesar,
   The heart of Brutus earns to think upon.°

[*They exit.*]

SCENE 3.   A street near the Capitol. Shortly afterward.

[*Enter ARTEMIDORUS (reading a paper).*]

   ARTEMIDORUS.   "Caesar, beware of Brutus; take heed of Cassius;
   come not near Casca; have an eye to Cinna; trust not
   Trebonius; mark well Metellus Cimber; Decius Brutus loves
   thee not; thou hast wrong'd Caius Ligarius. There is but
5 one mind in all these men, and it is bent against Caesar. If
   thou beest not immortal, look about you; security gives
   way to conspiracy.° The mighty gods defend thee!
                  Thy lover,° Artemidorus."
   Here will I stand till Caesar pass along,
10 And as a suitor° will I give him this.
   My heart laments that virtue cannot live
   Out of the teeth of emulation.°
   If thou read this, O Caesar, thou mayest live;
   If not, the Fates with traitors do contrive.° [*Exit.*]

SCENE 4.   Another Roman street. Immediately after.

[*Enter PORTIA and LUCIUS.*]

   PORTIA.   I prithee, boy, run to the Senate House;
   Stay not to answer me, but get thee gone.
   Why dost thou stay?

   LUCIUS.   To know my errand, madam.

   PORTIA.   I would have had thee there and here again
5 Ere I can tell thee what thou shouldst do there°—
   O constancy,° be strong upon my side;
   Set a huge mountain 'tween my heart and tongue!
   I have a man's mind, but a woman's might.
   How hard it is for women to keep counsel!°— ★
10 Art thou here yet?

   LUCIUS.   Madam, what should I do?
   Run to the Capitol, and nothing else?
   And so return to you, and nothing else?

   PORTIA.   Yes, bring me word, boy, if thy lord look well,
   For he went sickly forth; and take good note

Literary Element   Monologues, Soliloquies, and Asides *What attitude towards the plot to murder Caesar does Brutus reveal here?* **L**

Reading Strategy   Analyzing Cause-and-Effect Relationships *What does Artemidorus decide to do as a result of the events that have already occured?* **R₃**

128–129 That every . . . upon: Brutus grieves to think that not everyone who appears to be a friend is a real friend.

6–7 security gives . . . conspiracy: overconfidence opens the way for enemy plots.
8 lover: devoted friend.
10 suitor: person presenting a special request to a ruler.
12 Out of . . . emulation: beyond the reach of envy.
14 contrive: conspire.

4–5 I would . . . do there: You could go there and return here before I could explain what you should do there.
6 constancy: firmness.
9 counsel: a secret.

Building Reading Fluency

Reading Aloud Shakespeare never intended for his plays to be read silently. Reading parts or even the whole play aloud as a class will help students understand the play better than independent reading. Assign parts to students on a volunteer basis, letting students know which parts are large and which are small. Suggest that students try to act out the play using their voices. You can even incorporate blocking—or stage position and movement—into key scenes, like the one in which the conspirators walk Caesar through the streets to the Capitol. **BL**

15   What Caesar doth, what suitors press to him.
        Hark, boy, what noise is that?

    LUCIUS. I hear none, madam.

     PORTIA.   Prithee, listen well.
       I heard a bustling rumor, like a fray,°
       And the wind brings it from the Capitol.

20   LUCIUS. Sooth,° madam, I hear nothing.

    [*Enter the* SOOTHSAYER.]

       PORTIA. Come hither, fellow; which way hast thou been?

       SOOTHSAYER. At mine own house, good lady.

       PORTIA. What is't a'clock?

       SOOTHSAYER.   About the ninth hour, lady.

       PORTIA. Is Caesar yet gone to the Capitol?

25   SOOTHSAYER. Madam, not yet; I go to take my stand,
       To see him pass on to the Capitol.

       PORTIA. Thou hast some suit to Caesar, hast thou not?

       SOOTHSAYER. That I have, lady, if it will please Caesar
       To be so good to Caesar as to hear me:
30   I shall beseech him to befriend himself.

       PORTIA. Why, know'st thou any harm's intended towards him?

       SOOTHSAYER. None that I know will be, much that I fear
         may chance.
       Good morrow to you. Here the street is narrow;
       The throng that follows Caesar at the heels,
35   Of senators, of praetors, common suitors,
       Will crowd a feeble man almost to death.
       I'll get me to a place more void,° and there
       Speak to great Caesar as he comes along.

    [*Exit.*]

       PORTIA. I must go in. Ay me! How weak a thing
40   The heart of woman is! O Brutus,
       The heavens speed thee in thine enterprise!
       Sure, the boy heard me—Brutus hath a suit
       That Caesar will not grant.°—O, I grow faint.—
       Run, Lucius, and commend me to my lord,°
45   Say I am merry. Come to me again,
       And bring me word what he doth say to thee. **L**

    [*They exit separately.*]

---

18 **bustling . . . fray:** noise of some activity such as a fight.

20 **Sooth:** truly.

37 **void:** empty.
42–43 **Brutus hath . . . grant:** Portia makes up this excuse about Brutus's petition to explain her nervousness to Lucius.
44 **commend me to my lord:** send my regards to my husband.

Portrait of a woman in encaustic on limewood with added gold leaf, c. AD 160–170, Roman period, Egypt. 44.3 x 20.4 cm. The British Museum, London.
Viewing the Art: What qualities do you think this woman possesses? Which of these qualities do you think Portia or Calphurnia shares? Explain.

810 UNIT 4 DRAMA

Teach

L Literary Element

Suspense Have students describe Portia's mood and attitude and explain how they increase the play's suspense. (*She is so worried and upset that she is almost physically ill. Her worry puts a human face on the political situation, increasing the reader's suspense.*) **OL**

★ Viewing the Art

Answer: *The woman seems to possess sensitivity, intelligence, and determination. Portia especially shares these qualities. Her sensitivity clashes with her determination as she struggles to conceal Brutus's dread secret.* **AS**

✓CheckPoint

Use the CheckPoint questions on Presentation Plus! to check students' mastery of the selection. These questions can be used with interactive response keypads for immediate student feedback.

Additional Support

Web Activities Have students access the Web site for interactive activities that will help them assess their understanding of the selection.

Skills Practice

STUDY SKILLS: Using Graphic Aids
Students may better understand and remember the sequence of events in *Julius Caesar* if they record the events graphically. Have students make a time line showing the major events of *Julius Caesar* through the first two acts. Point out that the time line should show only the most important events, so students must first decide what those events are. For example, they will probably want to list "A soothsayer warns Caesar about the ides of March," but they need not list "Casca speaks to Cicero." Encourage students to continue their time lines as they complete the play. **OL**

RESPONDING AND THINKING CRITICALLY

Respond

1. Which character are you most sympathetic toward? Why?

Recall and Interpret

2. (a)According to Brutus, why must Caesar be killed? (b)What can you infer about Cassius, Casca, and Brutus in Scene 1 as these conspirators make their plans?

3. (a)Why does Brutus want to spare Antony's life? (b)What opinion does Brutus seem to have of Antony?

4. (a)Why does Calphurnia want Caesar to remain at home? (b)In your opinion, why does Caesar eventually decide to go to the Capitol?

Analyze and Evaluate

5. If you were one of the conspirators, would you agree with Brutus or Cassius? Explain.

6. (a)Compare and contrast Portia and Calphurnia. (b)How do they compare with women you know or with contemporary female characters?

7. **Suspense** is the feeling of anticipation, even dread, which you experience as you read. What events or scenes in Act 2 contribute to its suspense? Explain.

Connect

8. **Big Idea** **Loyalty and Betrayal** (a)How do Brutus's intentions relate to the theme of loyalty and betrayal? (b)Do you accept Brutus's justification for killing Caesar? Why or why not?

LITERARY ANALYSIS

Literary Element Monologues, Soliloquies, and Asides

A **monologue** is a long speech given by one character. A **soliloquy** is a monologue delivered while a character is alone onstage. An **aside** is a comment that a character makes to the audience, which other characters onstage do not hear. All of these devices are used frequently in Shakespearean drama to provide information to the audience and to reveal the characters' thoughts.

1. What does Brutus reveal in his soliloquy at the beginning of Act 2?

2. What does Trebonius mean in Scene 2, lines 124–125? Why might Shakespeare have written these lines as an aside?

Writing About Literature

Analyze Plot Playwrights and other authors use foreshadowing to prepare readers for events that will happen later. Find examples of foreshadowing in Act 2. Then write a paragraph analyzing the examples and the plot events you think they foreshadow.

Literature Online **Web Activities** For eFlashcards, Selection Quick Checks, and other Web activities, go to www.glencoe.com.

READING AND VOCABULARY

Reading Strategy Analyzing Cause-and-Effect Relationships

In a play, one event may have an **effect** that becomes the **cause** of still another effect. This relationship leads to the formation of a chain of causes and effects.

1. What causes Caesar to have misgivings about going to the Capitol?

2. What causes Portia to send a servant to the Senate House?

Vocabulary Practice

Practice with Word Parts Use your knowledge of prefixes to choose the best definition for each word.

1. The start of the movie is **imminent**.
   a. elongated   b. momentary   c. delayed

2. In the **interim**, Tina had time to watch the news.
   a. period between   c. period after
   b. period before

3. The principal requested that the crowd **disperse** after the football game.
   a. gather   b. scatter   c. sit

4. I **commended** my son for taking out the trash.
   a. chided   b. praised   c. asked

JULIUS CAESAR **811**

Assess

1. Students should support their answers.

2. (a) To prevent tyranny (b) Students may say that Cassius seems forceful but bloodthirsty, Casca seems less forceful and more compliant, and Brutus seems principled.

3. (a) Antony will not be a threat once Caesar is killed. (b) That Antony is lighthearted and given to carousal

4. (a) Because of the strange happenings, she fears for Caesar's safety. (b) Vanity or bravery causes Caesar to go to the Capitol.

5. Students may agree with Brutus because he seems wiser than Cassius.

6. (a) Both Portia and Calphurnia are loyal and loving. Students may say that Portia seems all too willing to participate in her husband's plans, whereas Calphurnia is concerned with her husband's safety. (b) Students should support their answers.

7. Calphurnia's pleas, Artemidorus's and the soothsayer's plans to warn Caesar, and Portia's quest for information

8. (a) Brutus betrays his friend and leader, Caesar. (b) Students may not accept Brutus's justification because Caesar is not portrayed as tyrannical.

Writing About Literature

Students' paragraphs should explain the examples and the plot events that are foreshadowed.

Literary Element

1. He has no reason to dislike Caesar, and Caesar does not deserve assassination; but he thinks Caesar will misuse his power.

2. He will be close enough to stab Caesar. The aside emphasizes the irony of Caesar's closest colleagues turning on him.

Reading Strategy

1. The strange portents, the soothsayer's warnings, and Calphurnia's pleading

2. Brutus, looking unwell, leaves the house with a crowd of men.

Vocabulary

1. b 2. a 3. b 4. b

Focus

Summary

Caesar refuses to read a warning letter and goes to the Capitol. The conspirators stab Caesar. Antony reveals that he will get revenge. Antony speaks brilliantly of Caesar's glory and of the horrendous murder at Caesar's funeral. The crowd protests the assassination.

V Vocabulary

Vocabulary File

Say: Add these words and definitions to your vocabulary file. For each word, include a sentence that gives you an example of how to use the word. **OL** Students with English language needs should include the pronunciations of these words in their files. **EL**

Literary Elements Have students access the Web site to improve their understanding of plot.

LITERATURE PREVIEW

Connecting to the Play

What is the meaning of honor? To have honor is to act in a way that others respect and that brings credit to one's reputation. Before you read, think about these questions:

- What principles do you hold most dear?
- What would you do if a friend of yours betrayed or harmed another friend in the name of principle?

Building Background

Shakespeare closely followed *The Lives of the Noble Grecians and Romans,* and *The Life of Marcus Brutus,* written by Greek historian Plutarch. According to Plutarch, Caesar attempted to defend himself against the assassins, "but when he saw Brutus with his sword drawn in his hand, then he pulled his gown over his head, and made no more resistance. . . ." Plutarch also tells the tragic story of a poet named Cinna, who was among the angry mob after Caesar's death. Believing him to be a conspirator, the people attacked him and "slew him outright in the market place."

Setting Purposes for Reading

Big Idea Loyalty and Betrayal

Does Caesar deserve his fate? Are there wider principles that justify the betrayal by his friends?

Literary Element Plot

Plot is the sequence of events in a work. Conflicts are introduced in the **exposition,** the first stage of the plot. As a work progresses, **rising action** builds suspense and adds complications, which lead to the **climax,** or turning point. After the climax, which is the moment of highest emotional pitch or greatest suspense, comes the **falling action** and **resolution,** which reveal the logical results of the climax.

- See Literary Terms Handbook, p. R13.

Literature Online Interactive Literary Elements Handbook To review or learn more about the literary elements, go to www.glencoe.com.

OBJECTIVES

In studying this selection, you will focus on the following:
- understanding plot: rising action, climax, falling action, and resolution

READING PREVIEW

Reading Strategy Analyzing Figures of Speech

Figurative language is language that is not literally true, but that expresses some truth beyond the literal level. **Figures of speech** are a type of figurative language. They include:

- simile, a comparison that uses the words *like* or *as.*
- metaphor, a comparison that does not use the words *like* or *as.*
- personification, the giving of human characteristics to an animal, object, or idea.
- hyperbole, exaggeration that expresses strong emotion, makes a point, or evokes humor.

Reading Tip: Charting Memorable Language Use a chart to record striking or puzzling figures of speech and your ideas about what these figures of speech might mean.

Figure of Speech	Type of Figures of Speech	Meaning
"But I am constant as the northern star" p. 815	simile	Caesar is very steady and resolute.

Vocabulary

thrive (thrīv) *v.* to be successful; to grow well; p. 813 *My sister will thrive at college.*

misgiving (mis giv′ing) *n.* a feeling of doubt; apprehension p. 818 *My mom has misgivings about letting me go on the camping trip.*

malice (mal′is) *n.* a desire to hurt another person; p. 819 *My cousin sometimes acts with malice.*

vanquish (vang′kwish) *v.* to defeat; to overcome; p. 829 *The Greeks planned to vanquish the Trojans through a surprise attack on their city.*

orator (ôr′ə tər) *n.* a person skilled in public speaking; p. 829 *Martin Luther King Jr. was one of this country's most famous orators.*

- analyzing figures of speech: similes, metaphors, personification, and hyperbole
- writing to analyze rhetorical devices

Selection Skills

Literary Elements
- Plot (SE pp. 812–833)

Reading Skills
- Analyzing Figures of Speech (SE pp. 812–833)
- Identifying Main Idea and Supporting Details (TWE p. 822)

Vocabulary Skills
- Context Clues (SE p. 833)
- Etymology (TWE p. 816)

The Tragedy of Julius Caesar, Act 3

Listening/Speaking/Viewing Skills
- Analyzing Art (SE pp. 815, 820, 821, 824, 830)
- Reading Maps (TWE p. 828)

Writing Skills/Grammar
- Simile (TWE p. 814)
- Blank Verse (TWE p. 826)

ACT 3

BI₁

SCENE 1. The Capitol in Rome. The ides of March.

[*Flourish. Enter* CAESAR, BRUTUS, CASSIUS, CASCA, DECIUS, METELLUS, TREBONIUS, CINNA, ANTONY, PUBLIUS, POPILIUS, LEPIDUS, ARTEMIDORUS, *and the* SOOTHSAYER.]

    CAESAR. The ides of March are come.

    SOOTHSAYER. Ay, Caesar, but not gone.

    ARTEMIDORUS. Hail, Caesar! Read this schedule.°

    DECIUS. Trebonius doth desire you to o'er-read,
        (At your best leisure) this his humble suit.

5

    ARTEMIDORUS. O Caesar, read mine first; for mine's a suit
        That touches Caesar nearer. Read it, great Caesar.

    CAESAR. What touches us ourself shall be last serv'd.

    ARTEMIDORUS. Delay not, Caesar, read it instantly.

10   CAESAR. What, is the fellow mad?

    PUBLIUS.   Sirrah,° give place.

    CASSIUS. What, urge you your petitions in the street?
        Come to the Capitol.

[CAESAR *enters the Capitol, the rest following.*]

    POPILIUS. I wish your enterprise today may **thrive**.

    CASSIUS. What enterprise, Popilius?

    POPILIUS.   Fare you well. [*Leaves*
        him and joins CAESAR.]

15   BRUTUS. What said Popilius Lena?

    CASSIUS. He wish'd today our enterprise might thrive.
        I fear our purpose is discovered.

    BRUTUS. Look how he makes° to Caesar; mark him.

---

3 **schedule:** document.

10 **Sirrah:** an insulting form of address to an inferior.

18 **makes:** makes his way.

Big Idea Loyalty and Betrayal *From this remark, what do you infer about Caesar's character?* **BI₂**

Literary Element Plot *What might happen if the plotters are discovered?* **L**

Vocabulary

thrive (thriv) *v.* to be successful; to grow well

JULIUS CAESAR, ACT 3, SCENE 1 **813**

Teach

BI₁ Big Idea

Loyalty and Betrayal
Say: Consider the following as you read: To whom are the Romans loyal? *(The Romans seem fickle. They are loyal to the person who is nearest at the time.)* How does their nature contribute to the unfolding events? *(The Romans are easy to manipulate, so those in positions of power believe that they can have their way.)* **OL**

BI₂ Big Idea

Loyalty and Betrayal
Answer: *Answers will vary. Students may say that as a leader, Caesar appears to be upright and selfless.* **OL**

L Literary Element

Plot Answer: *Students may say that the plotters may be jailed or killed.* **OL**

CheckPoint

Use the CheckPoint questions on Presentation Plus! to monitor students' comprehension. These questions can be used with interactive response keypads for immediate student feedback.

English Language Coach

Shakespearean Word Order Point out that one unusual feature of Shakespeare's English is word order. Although English language learners may not have difficulty understanding meaning in phrases with unusual word order, they should also recognize that Shakespeare's phrasing is not standard today. Have students revise the following sentences to reflect today's standard English. Point out that revision may require adding a helping verb such as *do*.

1. Delay not, Caesar, read it instantly.
2. What mean you, Caesar? **EL**

Objective
• To understand plot (SE)

Teach

R1 Reading Strategy

Questioning Caesar refers to the request Metellus is making of him. Have students explain what it is. *(Caesar has banished Metellus's brother, and Metellus wants him recalled from exile.)* **OL**

R2 Reading Strategy

Analyzing Figures of Speech Answer: *Caesar's comments imply that Metellus's compliments are beneath him, Caesar. The compliments only serve to make Metellus appear servile, like a small dog.* **OL**

CASSIUS. Casca, be sudden, for we fear prevention.°
20   Brutus, what shall be done? If this be known,
   Cassius or Caesar never shall turn back,°
   For I will slay myself.

BRUTUS.   Cassius, be constant;°
   Popilius Lena speaks not of our purposes,
   For look he smiles, and Caesar doth not change.

25 CASSIUS. Trebonius knows his time; for look you, Brutus,
   He draws Mark Antony out of the way.

[ANTONY and TREBONIUS exit.]

DECIUS. Where is Metellus Cimber? Let him go
   And presently prefer° his suit to Caesar.

BRUTUS. He is address'd;° press near and second him.

30 CINNA. Casca, you are the first that rears your hand.

CAESAR. Are we all ready? What is now amiss
   That Caesar and his Senate must redress?

METELLUS. Most high, most mighty, and most puissant° Caesar,
   Metellus Cimber throws before thy seat
35   An humble heart. [*Kneeling.*]

CAESAR.   I must prevent thee, Cimber.
   These couchings and these lowly courtesies
   Might fire the blood of ordinary men,   **R1**
   And turn preordinance and first decree
   Into the [law] of children. Be not fond
40   To think that Caesar bears such rebel blood
   That will be thaw'd from the true quality
   With that which melteth fools—I mean sweet words,
   Low-crooked curtsies, and base spaniel fawning.°
   Thy brother by decree is banished;
45   If thou dost bend, and pray, and fawn for him,
   I spurn thee like a cur° out of my way.
   Know, Caesar doth not wrong, nor without cause
   Will he be satisfied.°

METELLUS. Is there no voice more worthy than my own,
50   To sound more sweetly in great Caesar's ear
   For the repealing of my banish'd brother?

BRUTUS. I kiss thy hand, but not in flattery, Caesar;
   Desiring thee that Publius Cimber may
   Have an immediate freedom of repeal.°

55 CAESAR. What, Brutus?

CASSIUS.   Pardon, Caesar! Caesar,
   pardon!

Reading Strategy   Analyzing Figures of Speech *What does Caesar mean when he says that Metellus's compliments are "base spaniel fawning"?* **R2**

814   UNIT 4   DRAMA

---

19 be sudden . . . prevention: be quick, for we fear that we will be stopped.

21 turn back: return alive.

22 constant: calm.

28 presently prefer: immediately present.
29 address'd: ready.

33 puissant: powerful.

36–43 These couchings . . . fawning: This kneeling and humble behavior might influence ordinary men and turn laws and decisions that have been firmly established into the whims of children. But don't be foolish enough to think that Caesar's emotions are so out of control that he will be swayed from the proper course with compliments, bowing, and fawning like a dog.
46 spurn thee . . . cur: kick you like a dog.
47–48 Know . . . satisfied: Caesar is not unjust, nor will he grant a pardon without good reason.

54 freedom of repeal: permission to be recalled from exile.

Additional Support

Skills Practice

WRITING: Simile Julius Caesar says that he is as determined and unchanging as the North Star. Encourage students to think of people they know whom they might compare to an astronomical body. Have students write a paragraph or poem in which they compare themselves or someone they know to the sun, the moon, the earth or other planet, a star, a meteor, or any other heavenly body. Point out that they must make their comparisons as clear as Caesar does in his speech. **OL**

The Death of Julius Caesar, 1793. Vincenzo Camuccini. Galleria d'Arte Moderna, Rome.
Viewing the Art: What emotions do you see expressed here? Do you think the same emotions are expressed in this scene? Explain. ★

As low as to thy foot doth Cassius fall,
To beg enfranchisement° for Publius Cimber.

CAESAR. I could be well mov'd, if I were as you;
If I could pray to move, prayers would move me;
60 But I am constant as the northern star,
Of whose true-fix'd and resting quality
There is no fellow in the firmament.°
The skies are painted with unnumb'red sparks,
They are all fire and every one doth shine;
65 But there's but one in all doth hold his place.
So in the world: 'tis furnish'd well with men,
And men are flesh and blood, and apprehensive;°
Yet in the number I do know but one
That unassailable holds on his rank,
70 Unshak'd of motion; and that I am he,
Let me a little show it, even in this—
That I was constant° Cimber should be banish'd,
And constant do remain to keep him so.

57 **enfranchisement:** restoration of his rights as a citizen.

62 **no fellow in the firmament:** no equal in the heavens. (Because the North Star appears directly above the North Pole, it seems to be stationary; the other stars seem to change position as the earth rotates.)

67 **apprehensive:** capable of reason.

72 **constant:** determined.

Big Idea Loyalty and Betrayal *In your opinion, why is Cassius behaving this way?* **BI₁**

Reading Strategy Analyzing Figures of Speech *What is Caesar suggesting by comparing himself to the North Star?* **R₃**

Big Idea Loyalty and Betrayal *Why might Caesar's speech have the effect of making the scheme seem justified?* **BI₂**

JULIUS CAESAR, ACT 3, SCENE 1 **815**

Teach

L1 Literary Element

Plot Answer: Students may say that the tension is high and still rising. **OL**

BI1 Big Idea

Loyalty and Betrayal
Answer: *Students may say that Caesar's last words are poignant, revealing his trust for Brutus until the very end.* **OL**

L2 Literary Element

Plot Answer: *The assassination is causing disorder and chaos.* **OL**

⭐ Political History

Julius Caesar Although *Julius Caesar* is based on historical figures and events, Shakespeare adapts history to fit his dramatic needs. While the play opens with Caesar's returning to Rome triumphantly after defeating Pompey, his actual return to Rome took place in 47 B.C.E., the year following Pompey's defeat. Caesar was actually assassinated in 44 B.C.E., three years after being named dictator. Shakespeare's version has Caesar killed before he has a chance to be named king. **AS**

JULIUS CAESAR

CINNA. O Caesar—

CAESAR.   Hence! Wilt thou lift up Olympus?°

75 DECIUS. Great Caesar—

CAESAR.   Doth not Brutus bootless° kneel?

CASCA. Speak hands for me!

[*They stab* CAESAR.]

CAESAR. Et tu, Brute?°—Then fall Caesar. [*Dies.*]

CINNA. Liberty! Freedom! Tyranny is dead!
    Run hence, proclaim, cry it about the streets.

80 CASSIUS. Some to the common pulpits,° and cry out
    "Liberty, freedom, and enfranchisement!"

BRUTUS. People, and senators, be not affrighted.
    Fly not; stand still; ambition's debt is paid.°

CASCA. Go to the pulpit, Brutus.

DECIUS.   And Cassius too.

85 BRUTUS. Where's Publius?

CINNA. Here, quite confounded with this mutiny.°

METELLUS. Stand fast together, lest some friend of Caesar's
    Should chance—

BRUTUS. Talk not of standing. Publius, good cheer,
90   There is no harm intended to your person,
    Nor to no Roman else. So tell them, Publius.

CASSIUS. And leave us, Publius, lest that the people,
    Rushing on us should do your age some mischief.

BRUTUS. Do so; and let no man abide° this deed,
95   But we the doers.

[*All but the* CONSPIRATORS *exit. Enter* TREBONIUS.]

CASSIUS. Where is Antony?

TREBONIUS.   Fled to his house amaz'd.°
    Men, wives, and children stare, cry out and run,
    As° it were doomsday.

BRUTUS.   Fates,° we will know your pleasures.
    That we shall die, we know, 'tis but the time,
100   And drawing days out, that men stand upon.°

74 lift up Olympus: try to do the impossible. (Olympus is a mountain in Greece; in classical mythology, it was the home of the gods.)
75 bootless: in vain.

77 *Et tu, Brute?*: Latin for, "And you, Brutus?" (He is shocked that even Brutus would betray him.)

80 pulpits: platforms for public speaking.

83 ambition's debt is paid: Ambition received what was due to it.

86 confounded with this mutiny: confused by this uproar.

94 abide: pay the penalty for.

96 amaz'd: stunned.

98 As: as if.

98 Fates: in classical mythology, three goddesses who determined human destiny.
99–100 'tis but . . . upon: It is only the time of death and prolonging of life that men care about.

Literary Element Plot *How would you describe the tension at this moment?* **L1**

Big Idea Loyalty and Betrayal *What do Caesar's dying words reveal?* **BI1**

Literary Element Plot *What effect is the assassination having on Rome?* **L2**

Additional Support

Skills Practice

VOCABULARY: Etymology Mark Antony calls Brutus *valiant.* Brutus calls Antony *valiant* in return. The word *valiant* comes from the Old French verb *valoir,* "to be of worth" and the Latin verb *valere,* "to be strong." Have students think of other words that come from the same word roots. (*valor, valid, validity, validate*) Have students find synonyms for *valiant.* (*courageous, brave, heroic, gallant, noble, chivalrous*) **OL**

The Three Fates, detail from the Month of March (upper portion). Francesco del Cossa, 1435–1478. Fresco painting. Palazzo Schifanoia, Ferrara, Italy.

CASCA. Why, he that cuts off twenty years of life
    Cuts off so many years of fearing death.

BRUTUS. Grant that, and then is death a benefit.
    So are we Caesar's friends, that have abridg'd
105   His time of fearing death. Stoop, Romans, stoop,
    And let us bathe our hands in Caesar's blood
    Up to the elbows, and besmear our swords.
    Then walk we forth, even to the marketplace,
    And waving our red weapons o'er our heads,
110   Let's all cry "Peace, freedom, and liberty!"

CASSIUS. Stoop then, and wash. How many ages hence
    Shall this our lofty scene be acted over
    In states unborn and accents yet unknown!

BRUTUS. How many times shall Caesar bleed in sport,°
115   That now on Pompey's basis° [lies] along
    No worthier than the dust!

CASSIUS.   So oft as that shall be,
    So often shall the knot of us be call'd
    The men that gave their country liberty. **R**

DECIUS. What, shall we forth?

CASSIUS.   Ay, every man away.
120   Brutus shall lead, and we will grace his heels
    With the most boldest and best hearts of Rome.

[*Enter a SERVANT.*]

BRUTUS. Soft, who comes here? A friend of Antony's.

SERVANT. Thus, Brutus, did my master bid me kneel;
    Thus did Mark Antony bid me fall down;
125   And, being prostrate, thus he bade me say;
    Brutus is noble, wise, valiant, and honest;°
    Caesar was mighty, bold, royal, and loving.
    Say, I love Brutus, and I honor him;
    Say, I fear'd Caesar, honor'd him, and lov'd him.
130   If Brutus will vouchsafe° that Antony
    May safely come to him, and be resolv'd°
    How Caesar hath deserv'd to lie in death,
    Mark Antony shall not love Caesar dead

114 in sport: for entertainment. (These prophecies–of reenacting Caesar's assassination in countries not yet founded and in languages not yet known–are fulfilled by the performance of Shakespeare's play.)
115 Pompey's basis: the base of Pompey's statue.

126 honest: honorable.

130 vouchsafe: allow.
131 be resolv'd: receive a satisfactory explanation.

Big Idea Loyalty and Betrayal *What does this remark suggest about how Brutus is feeling?* **BI₂**

JULIUS CAESAR, ACT 3, SCENE 1   **817**

BI₂ Big Idea

Loyalty and Betrayal
Answer: *Answers will vary. Students may say that there is regret and tenderness in Brutus's remark.* **OL**

R Reading Strategy

Predicting Have students predict whether Cassius's prophecy of fame and glory for the conspirators will be true at the end of the play. *(Answers will vary.)* **OL**

Differentiated Instruction

Describing Character Have a volunteer read aloud lines 126–127. Point out that although a list of words cannot truly characterize a person, the words have been chosen carefully to describe specific traits of each man. Have pairs of students choose four adjectives to describe another character in the play, such as Cassius, Antony, or Portia. They may wish to consult a dictionary or thesaurus, but remind them to double-check words found in a thesaurus by looking their meanings up in a dictionary. **BL**

Objectives
• To understand plot: rising action, climax, falling action, and resolution (SE)
• To develop vocabulary by understanding etymology (TWE)

Teach

L1 Literary Element

Plot Answer: *Students may say that Antony is still in doubt about whether the assassination of Caesar was the right thing to do.* **Ask:** What character traits prompt Brutus to accept Antony's offer to follow Brutus? *(Brutus is trusting of Mark Antony and idealistic about his own motives for killing Caesar.)* **OL**

L2 Literary Element

Imagery Have a volunteer read aloud line 158 of Antony's speech: "Now, whilst your purpled hands do reek and smoke." **Ask:** How does this line help characterize the assassins' deed? *(The vivid adjective and verbs emphasize the ugly, shocking murder.)* **OL**

R1 Reading Strategy

Analyzing Figures of Speech Answer: *Students may say that the conspirators have performed a wicked, violent action, and the consequences are visible. By saying he would not be more willing to die if he "lived a thousand years," Mark Antony emphasizes that he mourns for Caesar.* **OL**

818

So well as Brutus living; but will follow
135　The fortunes and affairs of noble Brutus
　　　Thorough the hazards of this untrod state°
　　　With all true faith. So says my master Antony.

　　BRUTUS.　Thy master is a wise and valiant Roman;
　　　I never thought him worse.
140　　　Tell him, so please him come unto this place,
　　　He shall be satisfied and, by my honor,
　　　Depart untouch'd.

　　SERVANT.　　　　　　I'll fetch him presently.° [*Exit SERVANT.*]

　　BRUTUS.　I know that we shall have him well to friend.°

　　CASSIUS.　I wish we may; but yet have I a mind
145　　That fears him much; and my **misgiving** still
　　　Falls shrewdly to the purpose.°

　　[*Enter ANTONY.*]

　　BRUTUS.　But here comes Antony. Welcome, Mark Antony.

　　ANTONY.　O mighty Caesar! dost thou lie so low?
　　　Are all thy conquests, glories, triumphs, spoils,
150　　Shrunk to this little measure? Fare thee well.
　　　I know not, gentlemen, what you intend,
　　　Who else must be let blood,° who else is rank.°
　　　If I myself, there is no hour so fit
　　　As Caesar's death's hour, nor no instrument
155　　Of half that worth as those your swords, made rich
　　　With the most noble blood of all this world.
　　　I do beseech ye, if you bear me hard,°
　　L2　Now, whilst your purpled° hands do reek and smoke,
　　　Fulfill your pleasure. Live a thousand years,
160　　I shall not find myself so apt° to die;
　　　No place will please me so, no mean of death,°
　　　As here by Caesar, and by you cut off,
　　　The choice and master spirits of this age.

　　BRUTUS.　O Antony! beg not your death of us.
165　　Though now we must appear bloody and cruel,

136 Thorough . . . state: through all the dangers of this new and uncertain state of affairs.

142 presently: immediately.

143 well to friend: as a good friend.

145–146 my misgiving . . . purpose: My suspicions always turn out to be close to the truth.

152 let blood: killed. **rank:** swollen with disease. In Antony's metaphor, political corruption is like a disease that must be treated by drawing blood from the patient.

157 bear me hard: have a grudge against me.
158 purpled: blood-stained.

160 apt: ready.

161 mean of death: way of dying.

Literary Element Plot *What position does Mark Antony take with regard to the killing of Caesar?* **L1**

Reading Strategy Analyzing Figures of Speech *What does Mark Antony mean when he says that the conspirators' hands "reek and smoke"? Why does he say he would not find himself so apt to die if he "lived a thousand years"?* **R1**

Vocabulary

misgiving (mis giv′ing) *n.* a feeling of doubt; apprehension

---

Additional Support

Skills Practice

GRAMMAR: Complete Subjects and Predicates Remind students that the complete subject of a sentence includes all the words that identify whom or what the sentence is about. The complete predicate includes all the words that tell what the subject is or does or what happens to it. Write this example:

The matter is answer'd directly. Point out that *The matter* is the complete subject and *is answer'd directly* is the complete predicate. Have students write each complete subject and predicate.

1. <u>I am going to Caesar's funeral</u>.
2. <u>Then I, and you, and all of us fell down</u>. **OL**

As by our hands and this our present act
You see we do, yet see you but our hands
And this the bleeding business they have done.
Our hearts you see not, they are pitiful;°
170 And pity to the general wrong of Rome—
As fire drives out fire, so pity pity—
Hath done this deed on Caesar.° For your part,
To you our swords have leaden° points, Mark Antony;
Our arms in strength of **malice,**° and our hearts
175 Of brothers' temper, do receive you in
With all kind love, good thoughts, and reverence.

CASSIUS. Your voice shall be as strong as any man's
In the disposing of new dignities.°

BRUTUS. Only be patient till we have appeas'd
180 The multitude, beside themselves with fear,
And then we will deliver you the cause°
Why I, that did love Caesar when I struck him,
Have thus proceeded.

ANTONY.   I doubt not of your wisdom.
Let each man render me his bloody hand. **R2**
185 First, Marcus Brutus, will I shake with you;
Next, Caius Cassius, do I take your hand;
Now, Decius Brutus, yours; now yours, Metellus;
Yours, Cinna; and, my valiant Casca, yours;
Though last, not least in love, yours, good Trebonius.
190 Gentlemen all—alas, what shall I say?
My credit° now stands on such slippery ground
That one of two bad ways you must conceit° me,
Either a coward or a flatterer.
That I did love thee, Caesar, O, 'tis true;
195 If then thy spirit look upon us now,
Shall it not grieve thee dearer than thy death,
To see thy Antony making his peace,
Shaking the bloody fingers of thy foes,
Most noble, in the presence of thy corse?°
200 Had I as many eyes as thou hast wounds,
Weeping as fast as they stream forth thy blood,
It would become me better than to close°
In terms of friendship with thine enemies.
Pardon me, Julius! Here wast thou bay'd,° brave hart,°
205 Here didst thou fall, and here thy hunters stand,
Sign'd in thy spoil,° and crimson'd in thy lethe.°

Big Idea Loyalty and Betrayal *Why is Brutus so eager to reassure Mark Antony?* **BI**

Vocabulary

malice (mal´is) n. a desire to hurt another person

---

169 pitiful: full of pity.

170–172 And pity . . . Caesar: Brutus says that just as one fire can extinguish another, their pity for Rome overcame their pity for Caesar.
173 leaden: blunt.
174 Our arms . . . malice: our arms seemingly full of malice (because still blood-stained).

177–178 Your voice . . . dignities: You will have equal say in deciding who will hold political office.

181 deliver you the cause: explain.

191 credit: reputation (because he was Caesar's friend).
192 conceit: judge, consider.

199 corse: corpse.

202 close: come to an agreement.

204 bay'd: cornered like a hunted animal. **hart:** male deer. Antony plays on the words *hart* and *heart* later in this speech.
206 Sign'd in thy spoil: marked with your slaughter. **lethe:** bloodstream. (In classical mythology, Lethe was a river in Hades, the underworld.)

Teach

BI **Big Idea**

Loyalty and Betrayal
Answer: *Answers will vary. Students may say that Brutus is afraid of Mark Antony. They may also say that he genuinely respects Mark Antony and wishes to impress him with the rightness of the murder.* **OL**

★ Cultural History

Architecture The Romans borrowed many features of Greek architecture such as columns and the portico (a sort of covered porch or walkway). Their important architectural innovations were arches and concrete. These enabled the Romans to build huge buildings such as public baths and amphitheaters and other structures such as bridges. **AS**

R2 **Reading Strategy**

Responding Say: Caesar seemed to think of Mark Antony as a son. In Act 2, Cassius describes both "the ingrafted love he bears to Caesar" and how he is "so well belov'd of Caesar." **Ask:** What is your reaction to Antony's shaking the hands of the conspirators? *(Students may say that they do not respect Antony for doing so, that he does so for political reasons, or that he is hiding his true feelings.)* **OL**

Differentiated Instruction

Paraphrasing Students may find the language and tone of Antony's speech difficult to comprehend. Starting with line 190, have students take turns paraphrasing a line of speech. If two or three lines fit together in meaning, sum up the meaning after the students' paraphrases. Be sure they understand that Antony is addressing the dead Caesar for several lines and that the final image of the hunted deer is a metaphor. After all lines have been paraphrased, ask students to describe Antony's emotional state. *(calm, then anguished and grief-stricken)* **BL**

Objectives
• To analyze figures of speech (SE)
• To write complete subjects and predicates (TWE)

O world! thou wast the forest to this hart,
And this indeed, O world, the heart of thee.
How like a deer, strooken by many princes,
210 Dost thou here lie!

CASSIUS. Mark Antony—

ANTONY.   Pardon me, Caius Cassius!
The enemies of Caesar shall say this:
Then, in a friend, it is cold modesty.°

CASSIUS. I blame you not for praising Caesar so,
215 But what compact mean you to have with us?

213 **modesty:** restraint.

Reading Strategy Analyzing Figures of Speech *To what things does Mark Antony compare Julius Caesar? How do these comparisons help to characterize Julius Caesar's death?* **R1**

*Bedroom From the Villa of
P. Fannius Sinistor* (detail of west
wall). 1st century BC, Roman.
Fresco on lime plaster, height:
(average) 8 ft. The Metropolitan
Museum of Art, New York. Rogers
Fund, 1903.
Viewing the Art: Do the details in
this fresco reinforce or alter the
images you have developed of
Brutus's and Caesar's homes?
Explain. ★

820 UNIT 4 DRAMA

Skills Practice

RESEARCH: Political Speeches In Act 3, Brutus and Antony give important political speeches that evoke a strong response in their audience. Have students research a famous political speech or speaker. Speakers they may want to focus on include Abraham Lincoln, Franklin Roosevelt, Winston Churchill, Martin Luther King, Jr., and John F. Kennedy. Encourage students to find information on the speaker's style and content and on the historical events for which they made their famous speeches. Also urge them to find excerpts or quotes from important speeches. **AL**

Will you be prick'd° in number of our friends,
Or shall we on,° and not depend on you?

ANTONY.   Therefore I took your hands, but was indeed
220   Sway'd from the point by looking down on Caesar.
Friends am I with you all, and love you all,
Upon this hope, that you shall give me reasons
Why, and wherein,° Caesar was dangerous.

BRUTUS.   Or else were this a savage spectacle. **R2**
Our reasons are so full of good regard°
225   That were you, Antony, the son of Caesar,
You should be satisfied.

ANTONY.   That's all I seek;
And am moreover suitor° that I may
Produce° his body to the marketplace,
And in the pulpit, as becomes a friend,
230   Speak in the order° of his funeral.

BRUTUS.   You shall, Mark Antony.

CASSIUS.   Brutus, a word with you.
[*Aside to BRUTUS.*] You know not what you do. Do not
        consent
That Antony speak in his funeral.
Know you how much the people may be mov'd
235   By that which he will utter?

BRUTUS.   By your pardon—
I will myself into the pulpit first,
And show the reason of our Caesar's death.
What Antony shall speak, I will protest°
He speaks by leave and by permission;
240   And that we are contented Caesar shall
Have all true rites and lawful ceremonies.
It shall advantage° more than do us wrong.

CASSIUS.   I know not what may fall,° I like it not.

BRUTUS.   Mark Antony, here, take you Caesar's body.
245   You shall not in your funeral speech blame us,
But speak all good you can devise of Caesar,
And say you do't by our permission;
Else shall you not have any hand at all
About his funeral. And you shall speak
250   In the same pulpit whereto I am going,
After my speech is ended.

ANTONY.   Be it so;
I do desire no more.

| **Literary Element** | Plot *What is Cassius's objection to Antony speaking at Caesar's funeral?* **L** |

216 **prick'd:** marked down; counted.
217 **on:** proceed.

222 **wherein:** in what way.

224 **good regard:** sound considerations.

227 **am moreover suitor:** furthermore I ask.
228 **Produce:** bring forth.

230 **order:** ceremony.

238 **protest:** declare.
242 **advantage:** benefit.
243 **fall:** happen.

The Fatal Hour: Fantastic Subject II,
19th century. Alexandre Evariste Fragonard.
Oil on canvas, 56 x 45.7 cm. Private collection.
Viewing the Art: What mood is expressed
by this painting? Does it correspond to the
mood in the play at this point? Explain.

JULIUS CAESAR, ACT 3, SCENE 1   **821**

Teach

BI Big Idea

Loyalty and Betrayal
Answer: *Antony may act as if he is willing to consider the conspirators' reasons for acting as they did, but in reality he is completely disgusted with them and opposed to them.* OL

R Reading Strategy

Analyzing Figures of Speech Answer: *This is a simile. Caesar's wounds are compared to mouths.* OL

L1 Literary Element

Soliloquy Say: With the use of a soliloquy, Shakespeare shows Antony's true feelings about the conspirators and the murder. Have students summarize Antony's feelings. *(He is furious and willing to make Rome and its citizens suffer to see that the conspirators are punished.)* OL

BRUTUS. Prepare the body then, and follow us.

[*They exit. ANTONY remains.*]

ANTONY. O pardon me, thou bleeding piece of earth,
255   That I am meek and gentle with these butchers!
    Thou art the ruins of the noblest man
    That ever lived in the tide of times.°
    Woe to the hand that shed this costly blood!
    Over thy wounds now do I prophesy
260   (Which like dumb mouths do ope their ruby lips
    To beg the voice and utterance of my tongue)
    A curse shall light° upon the limbs of men;
    Domestic fury and fierce civil strife
    Shall cumber° all the parts of Italy;
265   Blood and destruction shall be so in use,°
    And dreadful objects so familiar,
    That mothers shall but smile when they behold
    Their infants quartered° with the hands of war;
    All pity chok'd with custom of fell deeds;°
270   And Caesar's spirit, ranging° for revenge,
    With Ate° by his side come hot from hell,
    Shall in these confines with a monarch's voice
    Cry "Havoc!"° and let slip the dogs of war,
    That this foul deed shall smell above the earth
275   With carrion° men, groaning for burial. L1

[*Enter Octavius's SERVANT.*]

    You serve Octavius Caesar, do you not?

SERVANT. I do, Mark Antony.

ANTONY. Caesar did write for him to come to Rome.

SERVANT. He did receive his letters and is coming,
280   And bid me say to you by word of mouth—
    [*Seeing the body.*] O Caesar!—

ANTONY. Thy heart is big;° get thee apart and weep.
    Passion, I see, is catching, [for] mine eyes,
    Seeing those beads of sorrow stand in thine,
285   Began to water. Is thy master coming?

SERVANT. He lies tonight within seven leagues° of Rome.

ANTONY. Post° back with speed, and tell him what hath chanc'd.

---

257 **the tide of times:** all of history.

262 **light:** fall.

264 **cumber:** burden; harass.
265 **in use:** common.

268 **quartered:** cut to pieces.
269 **custom of fell deeds:** familiarity with cruel deeds.
270 **ranging:** roving (like an animal in search of prey).
271 **Ate:** goddess of vengeance and strife.
273 **Havoc:** a battle cry to kill without mercy. (Only a king could give this order.)
275 **carrion:** dead and rotting.

282 **big:** swollen with grief.

286 **seven leagues:** twenty-one miles.
287 **Post:** ride back quickly.

Big Idea Loyalty and Betrayal *What do these words reveal about Antony's true feelings regarding the conspirators?* BI

Reading Strategy Analyzing Figures of Speech *What figure of speech is this? What is being compared?* R

Additional Support

Skills Practice

READING: Identifying Main Idea and Supporting Details Point out that in their funeral speeches, Brutus and Antony each make one or more main points about Caesar and his murder. Have students state one main idea from each speech and the details used to support each idea. Point out that the main idea may not always be stated directly. For example, one of Antony's points is that Caesar was a great leader, which he never explicitly states. You may wish to have half the students work on one speech and half on the other. Then volunteers can write their main ideas and supporting details on the board. OL

290 Here is a mourning Rome, a dangerous Rome,
No Rome of safety for Octavius yet;
Hie hence,° and tell him so. Yet stay awhile,
Thou shalt not back till I have borne this corse
Into the marketplace. There shall I try,°
In my oration, how the people take
The cruel issue° of these bloody men,
295 According to the which thou shalt discourse
To young Octavius of the state of things.
Lend me your hand.

[*They exit (with* CAESAR's *body).*]

**SCENE 2. The Roman Forum, the city's great public square.
A few days later.**

[*Enter* BRUTUS *and* CASSIUS *with the* PLEBEIANS.]

PLEBEIANS. We will be satisfied!° Let us be satisfied!

BRUTUS. Then follow me, and give me audience, friends.
Cassius, go you into the other street,
And part the numbers.°
5   Those that will hear me speak, let 'em stay here;
Those that will follow Cassius, go with him;
And public reasons shall be rendered°
Of Caesar's death.

FIRST PLEBEIAN.   I will hear Brutus speak.

SECOND PLEBEIAN. I will hear Cassius, and compare
their reasons,
10 When severally° we hear them rendered.

[*Exit* CASSIUS *with some of the* PLEBEIANS. BRUTUS *goes into the pulpit.*]

THIRD PLEBEIAN. The noble Brutus is ascended; silence!

BRUTUS. Be patient till the last.°
Romans, countrymen, and lovers,° hear me for my cause,
and be silent, that you may hear. Believe me for mine
15 honor, and have respect to mine honor,° that you may
believe. Censure° me in your wisdom, and awake your
senses,° that you may the better judge. If there be any in
this assembly, any dear friend of Caesar's, to him I say,
that Brutus' love to Caesar was no less than his. If then
20 that friend demand why Brutus rose against Caesar, this
is my answer; Not that I lov'd Caesar less, but that I lov'd
Rome more. Had you rather Caesar were living, and die
all slaves, than that Caesar were dead, to live all free men?
As Caesar lov'd me, I weep for him; as he was fortunate, I

---

290 **Hie hence:** Go quickly from here.

292 **try:** test.

294 **cruel issue:** outcome of cruelty.

1 **satisfied:** The common people (plebeians) demand a full explanation of the assassination.

4 **part the numbers:** divide the crowd.

7 **rendered:** presented.

10 **severally:** separately.

12 **last:** end of the speech.
13 **lovers:** dear friends.

15 **have respect . . . honor:** remember that I am honorable.
16 **Censure:** judge.
17 **senses:** reason.

Literary Element   Plot *What are the Plebeians wanting?* **L2**

JULIUS CAESAR, ACT 3, SCENE 2   **823**

Teach

L2 Literary Element

Plot Answer: *An explanation of the murder, and justice* **OL**

L3 Literary Element

Prose Point out that Brutus's speech is written in prose. Have students explain how this form differs from blank verse. (*Prose is written in sentences and paragraphs with no regular rhythm. Blank verse is written with line divisions and in a pattern of stressed and unstressed syllables.*) **OL**

 Language History

Plebeian *Plebeian* is a Latin word meaning "common person." Forms of it are used today in the word *plebe*, a freshman at a military or naval academy, and in the word *plebiscite*, a special vote by all the people of a country or district for a ruler or a proposal. **AS**

Diffentiated Instruction

Diagramming the Forum The Forum was the section of ancient Rome that served as its center of law and government. It included the Senate House, temples, and Hall of Records. The Forum existed in this form from the mid-100s B.C.E. until after the fall of Rome in C.E. 476. Today the ruins of the Forum's buildings still stand in Rome. Have students research the Forum and make a diagram or drawing indicating the locations and identities of its buildings. Other students may wish to research the excavation of the Forum in modern times and the building parts that were recovered. **AL**

Objectives
• To understand plot (SE)
• To identify main idea and supporting details (TWE)

823

Teach

L1 Literary Element

Diction Brutus uses the word *honor* several times in his speech. Have students explain the meaning and connotations of the word. What effect does its use have on Brutus's speech? *(Brutus uses the word in respect to himself to mean "integrity" and in respect to Caesar to mean "respect" or "recognition." The positive connotation evokes emotional responses.)* **OL**

BI Big Idea

Loyalty and Betrayal

Answer: *Brutus is implying that Caesar was ambitious and therefore had to be killed to save Rome from tyranny. He says that anyone who "loves his country" will agree with this reasoning. Students may say that Brutus's conclusion is invalid, since it rests on what is possibly a false premise ("Caesar is ambitious").* **OL**

★ Viewing the Art

Answer: *This scene might depict the crowd assembling to hear Brutus and Antony speak about the slain Caesar.* **AS**

---

25 **L1** rejoice at it; as he was valiant, I honor him; but, as he was ambitious, I slew him. There is tears for his love; joy for his fortune; honor for his valor; and death for his ambition. Who is here so base that would be a bondman?° If any, speak, for him have I offended. Who is here so rude,° that

30 would not be a Roman? If any, speak, for him have I offended. Who is here so vile that will not love his country? If any, speak, for him have I offended. I pause for a reply.

ALL. None, Brutus, none.

BRUTUS. Then none have I offended. I have done no more to

35 Caesar than you shall do to Brutus. The question of his death is enroll'd in the Capitol;° his glory not extenuated,° wherein he was worthy; nor his offenses enforc'd,° for which he suffer'd death.

28 **bondman:** slave.
29 **rude:** uncivilized.

35–36 **The question . . . Capitol:** The reasons for his death are recorded in the public archives of the Capitol.
37 **extenuated:** diminished.
38 **enforc'd:** exaggerated.

Big Idea Loyalty and Betrayal *What is Brutus implying here? Is this a valid conclusion?* **BI**

The Roman Forum, 19th century. Francis Vyvyan Jago Arundale. Watercolour on paper, 64.5 x 100 cm. Private collection.
Viewing the Art: What events in the play might this scene depict? Explain. ★

824 UNIT 4 DRAMA

Skills Practice

LISTENING AND SPEAKING: Discussing Antony's Ideas In Antony's funeral speech lines 73–74, he says, "The evil that men do lives after them, The good is oft interred with their bones." Encourage students to consider this idea. Have students hold group discussions about Antony's statement. Have them think of people who are known for good and for evil. Encourage them to consider whether a person's evil deeds will overshadow his or her good ones. Is history always fair to the reputations of past leaders? **OL**

[*Enter* MARK ANTONY (*and others*) *with* CAESAR's *body.*]

40   Here comes his body, mourn'd by Mark Antony, who,
though he had no hand in his death, shall receive the
benefit of his dying, a place in the commonwealth,° as
which of you shall not? With this I depart, that, as I slew my
best lover for the good of Rome, I have the same dagger for
myself, when it shall please my country to need my death.

41 **a place in the commonwealth:** citizenship in a free republic.

45   ALL.   Live, Brutus, live, live!

     FIRST PLEBEIAN.   Bring him with triumph home unto his house.

     SECOND PLEBEIAN.   Give him a statue with his ancestors.

     THIRD PLEBEIAN.   Let him be Caesar.

     FOURTH PLEBEIAN.   Caesar's better parts°
     Shall be crown'd in Brutus.

48 **parts:** qualities.

     FIRST PLEBEIAN.   We'll bring him to his house
50   With shouts and clamors.

     BRUTUS.   My countrymen—

     SECOND PLEBEIAN.   Peace, silence! Brutus speaks.

     FIRST PLEBEIAN.   Peace, ho!

     BRUTUS.   Good countrymen, let me depart alone,
     And, for my sake, stay here with Antony.
55   Do grace to Caesar's corpse, and grace his speech
     Tending to Caesar's glories,° which Mark Antony
     (By our permission) is allow'd to make.
     I do entreat you, not a man depart,
     Save I alone, till Antony have spoke.

55–56 **Do grace . . . glories:** Pay respect to Caesar's body and listen respectfully to Antony's speech dealing with Caesar's glories.

60   FIRST PLEBEIAN.   Stay, ho, and let us hear Mark Antony.

     THIRD PLEBEIAN.   Let him go up into the public chair;°
     We'll hear him. Noble Antony, go up.

61 **public chair:** pulpit.

     ANTONY.   For Brutus' sake, I am beholding° to you.

63 **beholding:** indebted.

[*Goes into the pulpit.*]

     FOURTH PLEBEIAN.   What does he say of Brutus?

     THIRD PLEBEIAN.   He says, for Brutus' sake,
65   He finds himself beholding to us all.

     FOURTH PLEBEIAN.   'Twere best he speak no harm of Brutus
     here!

     FIRST PLEBEIAN.   This Caesar was a tyrant.

Literary Element   Plot *How do the people react to Brutus's speech? Why do they react in this way?* **L2**

Literary Element   Plot *What does the Plebeian mean by this remark?* **L3**

JULIUS CAESAR, ACT 3, SCENE 2   **825**

Teach

L2 Literary Element

Plot Answer: *The people react with approval. Brutus has appealed to their patriotism and their distrust of tyranny. He has convinced them that he, Brutus, is a patriot.* **OL**

L3 Literary Element

Plot Answer: *Students may say that the Plebeian is threatening Mark Antony.* **OL**

Differentiated Instruction

Oral Reading Students may enjoy reading aloud and listening to Antony's speech. Not only will this emphasize its masterly use of rhythm and repetition, but it will help students' comprehension of a pivotal event in the play. Have volunteers take turns reading lines 71–105 of Antony's speech. Encourage them to use vocal tone and speed to express the nobility of Antony's words without being overly dramatic. Have the rest of the class join in with a choral reading each time the speaker reaches the lines that Antony repeats: lines 84–85, 91–92, 96–97. **BL**

Objectives
• To understand plot (SE)
• To discuss ideas (TWE)

825

THIRD PLEBEIAN.   Nay, that's certain.
   We are blest that Rome is rid of him.

SECOND PLEBEIAN. Peace, let us hear what Antony can say.

70 **ANTONY.** You gentle Romans—

[*The noise continues.*]

   ALL.   Peace, ho, let us hear him.

   ANTONY. Friends, Romans, countrymen, lend me your ears!
   I come to bury Caesar, not to praise him.
   The evil that men do lives after them,
   The good is oft interred° with their bones;
75 So let it be with Caesar. The noble Brutus
   Hath told you Caesar was ambitious;
   If it were so, it was a grievous fault,
   And grievously hath Caesar answer'd° it.
   Here, under leave° of Brutus and the rest
80 (For Brutus is an honorable man,
   So are they all, all honorable men),
   Come I to speak in Caesar's funeral.
   He was my friend, faithful and just to me;
   But Brutus says he was ambitious,
85 And Brutus is an honorable man.
   He hath brought many captives home to Rome,
   Whose ransoms did the general coffers° fill;
   Did this in Caesar seem ambitious?
   When that the poor have cried, Caesar hath wept;
90 Ambition should be made of sterner stuff:
   Yet Brutus says he was ambitious;
   And Brutus is an honorable man.
   You all did see that on the Lupercal°
   I thrice presented him a kingly crown,
95 Which he did thrice refuse.° Was this ambition?
   Yet Brutus says he was ambitious;
   And sure he is an honorable man.
   I speak not to disprove what Brutus spoke,
   But here I am to speak what I do know.
100 You all did love him once, not without cause;
   What cause withholds you then to mourn for him?
   O judgment, thou art fled to brutish beasts,
   And men have lost their reason. Bear with me,
   My heart is in the coffin there with Caesar,
105 And I must pause till it come back to me.

74 interred: buried.

78 answer'd: paid the penalty for.
79 leave: permission.

87 general coffers: public treasury.

93 Lupercal: See Act 1, Scene 1, line 67.
95 Which he . . . refuse: the incident described by Casca in Act 1, Scene 2, lines 234–242.

Marcus Antonius (Mark Anthony) as Triumvirate. Artist unknown. Roman portrait bust. Vatican Museums, Vatican State.

Literary Element   Plot *What does Antony emphasize about Caesar here?* **L**

Reading Strategy   Analyzing Figures of Speech *What mood, or feeling, does Antony's language help to create?* **R**

Teach

L Literary Element

Plot Answer: *Antony emphasizes that Caesar was good, faithful, just, accomplished, and compassionate.* **OL**

R Reading Strategy

Analyzing Figures of Speech Answer: *Students may say that Antony's language helps to create a feeling of mourning, grief, and despair.* **OL**

★ Cultural History

The Art of Rhetoric The main subject of higher education in ancient Rome was *rhetoric,* the art of speaking and persuasion. Mark Antony proves to be skilled in rhetoric. Upper-class men studied rhetoric in order to enter law or politics. Cicero was known as the master orator at the time of Julius Caesar. His style of oratory—known as the "Asiatic"—was emotional, rhythmical, and ornate. **AS**

Additional Support

Skills Practice

WRITING: Blank Verse The funeral speeches of Brutus and Antony differ in emotional impact. This is partly because Brutus's speech is written in prose while Antony's is in blank verse. Review iambic pentameter by writing the scansion of a line from Antony's speech on the board. Have students write a paragraph about an issue they feel strongly about. Then challenge them to write the same ideas in blank verse. Have them discuss their writing experiences: What was challenging or satisfying about writing blank verse? How well did it fit their ideas? **OL**

FIRST PLEBEIAN. Methinks there is much reason in his sayings.

SECOND PLEBEIAN. If thou consider rightly of the matter,
   Caesar has had great wrong.

THIRD PLEBEIAN.   Has he, masters?
   I fear there will a worse come in his place.

110 **FOURTH PLEBEIAN.** Mark'd ye° his words? He would not take
      the crown,
   Therefore, 'tis certain he was not ambitious.

FIRST PLEBEIAN. If it be found so, some will dear abide it.°

SECOND PLEBEIAN. Poor soul, his eyes are red as fire with
   weeping.

THIRD PLEBEIAN. There's not a nobler man in Rome than
   Antony.

115 **FOURTH PLEBEIAN.** Now mark him, he begins again to speak.

ANTONY. But yesterday the word of Caesar might
   Have stood against the world; now lies he there,
   And none so poor to do him reverence.°
   O masters! if I were dispos'd to stir
120 Your hearts and minds to mutiny and rage,
   I should do Brutus wrong and Cassius wrong,
   Who (you all know) are honorable men.
   I will not do them wrong; I rather choose
   To wrong the dead, to wrong myself and you,
125 Than I will wrong such honorable men.
   But here's a parchment with the seal of Caesar;
   I found it in his closet, 'tis his will.
   Let but the commons° hear this testament—
   Which, pardon me, I do not mean to read—
130 And they would go and kiss dead Caesar's wounds,
   And dip their napkins° in his sacred blood;
   Yea, beg a hair of him for memory,
   And dying, mention it within their wills,
   Bequeathing it as a rich legacy
135 Unto their issue.°

FOURTH PLEBEIAN. We'll hear the will; read it, Mark Antony.

ALL. The will, the will! we will hear Caesar's will!

ANTONY. Have patience, gentle friends, I must not read it.
   It is not meet° you know how Caesar lov'd you:
140 You are not wood, you are not stones, but men;
   And being men, hearing the will of Caesar,
   It will inflame you, it will make you mad.

110 **Mark'd ye:** Did you listen to?

112 **dear abide it:** pay dearly for it.

118 **none . . . reverence:** No one is humble enough to honor him.

128 **commons:** common people.

131 **napkins:** handkerchiefs. (Antony refers to the custom of dipping cloths in the blood of martyrs.)

135 **issue:** children.

139 **meet:** proper.

Big Idea Loyalty and Betrayal *Why do the Plebeians call Antony noble?* **BI₁**

Big Idea Loyalty and Betrayal *Why does Antony flatter the Plebeians?* **BI₂**

JULIUS CAESAR, ACT 3, SCENE 2 **827**

Teach

BI₁ Big Idea

Loyalty and Betrayal
Answer: *Antony's apparently brave praise of his friend and his teary eyes convince the crowd that Antony is truthful and full of integrity and praise-worthy emotions.* **OL**

BI₂ Big Idea

Loyalty and Betrayal
Answer: *Students may say that Antony wishes to stir them up to rebellion against the assassins.* **OL**

Differentiated Instruction

Using Persuasion Role-play may help students understand Antony's clever manipulation of the people. Have students work in pairs. Partners are to pretend that each must convince the other to help him or her spend the next Saturday volunteering to clean the school. Suggest that students try any of the following techniques: 1. flattery, 2. bandwagon, 3. authority, 4. sincerity, 5. trickery, 6. emotion. After students have taken turns using various persuasive techniques, have them discuss which were most and least effective. **BL**

Objectives
• To analyze figures of speech (SE)
• To understand plot (SE)
• To write in blank verse and prose (TWE)

827

L Literary Element

Plot Answer: *The tension is rising as the crowd is growing passionate and violent. Questions may be growing in the reader's mind about what will happen to the plotters.* **OL**

R1 Reading Strategy

Analyzing Figures of Speech Answer: *Personification occurs when human qualities are attributed to the wound, which is treated as Brutus's neighbor answering a knock at the door. The figure of speech helps to portray Caesar as an innocent and Brutus as one who "unkindly" knocked, killing his friend.* **OL**

JULIUS CAESAR

'Tis good you know not that you are his heirs,
For if you should, O, what would come of it?

145   FOURTH PLEBEIAN. Read the will, we'll hear it, Antony.
You shall read us the will, Caesar's will.

ANTONY. Will you be patient? Will you stay awhile?
I have o'ershot myself° to tell you of it.
I fear I wrong the honorable men
150   Whose daggers have stabb'd Caesar; I do fear it.

FOURTH PLEBEIAN. They were traitors; honorable men!

ALL. The will! the testament!

SECOND PLEBEIAN. They were villains, murderers. The will, read the will!

ANTONY. You will compel me then to read the will?
155   Then make a ring about the corpse of Caesar,
And let me show you him that made the will.
Shall I descend? And will you give me leave?

ALL. Come down.

SECOND PLEBEIAN. Descend.

160   THIRD PLEBEIAN. You shall have leave.

[ANTONY comes down from the pulpit.]

FOURTH PLEBEIAN. A ring, stand round.

FIRST PLEBEIAN. Stand from the hearse, stand from the body.

SECOND PLEBEIAN. Room for Antony, most noble Antony.

ANTONY. Nay, press not so upon me; stand far° off.

165   ALL. Stand back; room, bear back.

ANTONY. If you have tears, prepare to shed them now.
You all do know this mantle.° I remember
The first time ever Caesar put it on;
'Twas on a summer's evening, in his tent,
170   That day he overcame the Nervii.°
Look, in this place ran Cassius' dagger through;
See what a rent° the envious Casca made;
Through this the well-beloved Brutus stabb'd,
And as he pluck'd his cursed steel away,
175   Mark how the blood of Caesar followed it,
As rushing out of doors, to be resolv'd
If Brutus so unkindly knock'd or no;°

148 o'ershot myself: gone further than I intended.

The Artemision with Artemis Ephesia. AD 117, Roman. Silver, diameter: 2.7 cm. Kunsthistorisches Museum, Muenzkabinett, Vienna, Austria.

164 far: farther.
167 mantle: cloak, toga.

170 Nervii: a fierce Gallic tribe defeated by Caesar in 57 BC.

172 rent: rip.

176–177 As rushing . . . no: as if rushing outside to learn for certain whether or not Brutus so cruelly and unnaturally "knocked."

Literary Element   Plot *How would you characterize the tension in this scene? What plot complications are developing?* **L**

Reading Strategy   Analyzing Figures of Speech *Where in these lines do you see an example of personification? Why does Antony's use of this figure of speech help to create sympathy for Caesar?* **R1**

Additional Support

Skills Practice

VIEWING: Maps Octavius's servant has ridden "seven leagues," or 21 miles, to deliver Octavius's message to Antony. One great accomplishment of the ancient Romans was an excellent system of roads. The Roman highway system spanned 50,000 miles reaching north to Britain, south to the Tigris and Euphrates Rivers, east to the Danube River, and west to Spain. Have students research the ancient Roman highway system and find maps that display all of the lands that were at one time part of the Roman Empire. **OL**

For Brutus, as you know, was Caesar's angel.°
Judge, O you gods, how dearly Caesar lov'd him!

180   This was the most unkindest cut of all;   **R2**
For when the noble Caesar saw him stab,
Ingratitude, more strong than traitors' arms,
Quite **vanquish'd** him. Then burst his mighty heart,
And, in his mantle muffling up his face,

185   Even at the base of Pompey's statue
(Which all the while ran blood) great Caesar fell.
O, what a fall was there, my countrymen!
Then I, and you, and all of us fell down,
Whilst bloody treason flourish'd° over us.

190   O now you weep, and I perceive you feel
The dint° of pity. These are gracious drops.
Kind souls, what weep you when you but behold
Our Caesar's vesture wounded? Look you here, [*Lifting
      CAESAR's mantle.*]
Here is himself, marr'd as you see with traitors.° **R3**

195   FIRST PLEBEIAN. O piteous spectacle!

SECOND PLEBEIAN. O noble Caesar!

THIRD PLEBEIAN. O woeful day!

FOURTH PLEBEIAN. O traitors, villains!

FIRST PLEBEIAN. O most bloody sight!

200   SECOND PLEBEIAN. We will be reveng'd.

ALL. Revenge! About! Seek! Burn! Fire! Kill! Slay!
      Let not a traitor live!

ANTONY. Stay, countrymen.

FIRST PLEBEIAN. Peace there, hear the noble Antony.

205   SECOND PLEBEIAN. We'll hear him, we'll follow him, we'll die
      with him.

ANTONY. Good friends, sweet friends, let me not stir you up
To such a sudden flood of mutiny.
They that have done this deed are honorable.
What private griefs° they have, alas, I know not,

210   That made them do it. They are wise and honorable,
And will, no doubt, with reasons answer you.
I come not, friends, to steal away your hearts.
I am no **orator**, as Brutus is;

Big Idea Loyalty and Betrayal *Antony emphasizes that he is not trying to turn the crowd against Brutus and the other plotters. Is he sincere?* **BI**

Vocabulary

vanquish (vang′kwish) *v.* to defeat; to overcome
orator (ôr′ə tər) *n.* a person skilled in public speaking

---

178 **angel:** favorite.

189 **flourish'd:** swaggered.

191 **dint:** force; blow.

192–194 **Kind souls . . . traitors:**
In a dramatic gesture, Antony uncovers Caesar's mutilated body after remarking how much the commoners weep when they gaze merely upon Caesar's mutilated clothing.

209 **private griefs:** personal grievances. Antony suggests that the conspirators killed Caesar not for the public reasons Brutus has declared but rather for personal, and therefore less worthy, motives.

Teach

R2 Reading Strategy

Interpreting Ask:
According to Antony, why was Brutus's "the unkindest cut of all"? (*Antony says Caesar dearly loved Brutus, and his betrayal broke Caesar's heart.*) **OL**

R3 Reading Strategy

Analyzing Arguments Have students describe the techniques Antony uses to gain the support of the people. (*He pretends that he does not want the people to know what was in Caesar's will; he predicts that they will be angered by what they hear; he plays on their emotions by having them look at Caesar's corpse; he points out each stab wound and tells which conspirator made it. His argument is based largely on emotional appeal.*) **OL**

BI Big Idea

Loyalty and Betrayal
Answer: *Answers will vary. Students should support their opinions.* **OL**

Differentiated Instruction

Using Music Point out that music is often used on stage and in film to accompany dramatic productions. It can add to the mood and heighten the drama of a play. Challenge students to find recorded music to accompany an important scene of the play. Have students play the music in class as they read the scene. Then they may explain the reasoning behind their choices. **BL**

Objectives
• To analyze figures of speech (SE)
• To understand plot (SE)
• To use maps to give context to literature (TWE)

But (as you know me all) a plain blunt man
215   That love my friend, and that they know full well
That gave me public leave to speak of him.
For I have neither wit, nor words, nor worth,
Action, nor utterance, nor the power of speech
To stir men's blood;° I only speak right on.
220   I tell you that which you yourselves do know,
Show you sweet Caesar's wounds, poor, poor, dumb
    mouths,
And bid them speak for me. But were I Brutus,
And Brutus Antony, there were an Antony
Would ruffle up° your spirits, and put a tongue
225   In every wound of Caesar, that should move
The stones of Rome to rise and mutiny.

ALL.   We'll mutiny.

FIRST PLEBEIAN.   We'll burn the house of Brutus.

THIRD PLEBEIAN.   Away then, come, seek the conspirators.

ANTONY.   Yet hear me, countrymen, yet hear me speak.

230   ALL.   Peace, ho, hear Antony, most noble Antony!

ANTONY.   Why, friends, you go to do you know not what.
Wherein hath Caesar thus deserv'd your loves?
Alas, you know not! I must tell you then;
You have forgot the will I told you of.

235   ALL.   Most true. The will! Let's stay and hear the will.

217–219 For I have . . . blood: Antony claims that he does not have the cleverness (wit), fluency (words), high personal standing or reputation (worth), gestures (action), and manner of speaking (utterance) of a skilled orator.

224 ruffle up: enrage.

Reading Strategy Analyzing Figures of Speech **Why does Antony again use this comparison?** **R1**

William Shakespeare: Julius Caesar–Forum–Stage design, 1914. Ludwig Sievert.
Viewing the Art: What feelings does this stage design stir in you? Do you think it is a good representation of the drama? ⭐

L SIEVERT 1914

830 UNIT 4 DRAMA

Skills Practice

WRITING: Compare and Contrast
The two funeral speeches contained in act 3 of *Julius Caesar* use persuasive techniques common to modern advertising, including emotional and intellectual appeals. Have students write an essay in which they compare and contrast Brutus's funeral speech with Antony's funeral speech. Tell students to reread the speeches and find lines that indicate whether the appeals are intellectual—aimed at the audience's intellect—or emotional—aimed at the audience's hearts. Then have them decide which speech—and which appeal—is ultimately more successful. **OL**

ANTONY. Here is the will, and under Caesar's seal:
   To every Roman citizen he gives,
   To every several° man, seventy-five drachmas.°

SECOND PLEBEIAN. Most noble Caesar! we'll revenge his death!

240 THIRD PLEBEIAN. O royal° Caesar!

ANTONY. Hear me with patience.

ALL. Peace, ho!

ANTONY. Moreover, he hath left you all his walks,
   His private arbors and new-planted orchards,°
245 On this side Tiber; he hath left them you,
   And to your heirs forever—common pleasures,°
   To walk abroad and recreate yourselves.
   Here was a Caesar! when comes such another?

FIRST PLEBEIAN. Never, never! Come, away, away!
250 We'll burn his body in the holy place,°
   And with the brands° fire the traitors' houses.
   Take up the body.

SECOND PLEBEIAN. Go fetch fire.

THIRD PLEBEIAN. Pluck down benches.

255 FOURTH PLEBEIAN. Pluck down forms,° windows,° anything.

[Exit PLEBEIANS with the body.]

ANTONY. Now let it work. Mischief, thou art afoot,
   Take thou what course thou wilt!

[Enter SERVANT.]

                              How now, fellow?

SERVANT. Sir, Octavius is already come to Rome.

ANTONY. Where is he?

260 SERVANT. He and Lepidus° are at Caesar's house.

ANTONY. And thither will I straight to visit him;°
   He comes upon a wish.° Fortune is merry,
   And in this mood will give us anything.

SERVANT. I heard him say, Brutus and Cassius
265 Are rid° like madmen through the gates of Rome.

ANTONY. Belike° they had some notice of the people,
   How I had mov'd them. Bring me to Octavius.

[They exit.]

238 **several:** individual. **drachmas:** silver coins.

240 **royal:** most generous.

244 **orchards:** gardens.

246 **common pleasures:** public recreation areas.

250 **the holy place:** the site of the most sacred Roman temples.
251 **brands:** pieces of burning wood.

255 **forms:** benches. **windows:** shutters.

260 **Lepidus:** one of Caesar's generals.

261 **thither will . . . him:** I will go there immediately to visit him.
262 **upon a wish:** just as I had wished.

265 **Are rid:** have ridden.

266 **Belike:** probably.

Big Idea Loyalty and Betrayal *What does this remark reveal about Antony?* **BI₁**

Reading Strategy Analyzing Figures of Speech *What does Antony mean when he says fortune is "merry" and will give him anything?* **R₂**

Literary Element Plot *How would you characterize the tension at this point in the act compared to what has come before?* **L**

JULIUS CAESAR, ACT 3, SCENE 2   **831**

Reading in the Real World

Citizenship Ancient Roman sculpture portrays Roman leaders as having physical and mental strength and strong character. Have students find newspapers or magazine articles and photographs of twentieth-century political leaders from all over the world. What character traits do the photographs seem to reflect? Does the information provided in the article match the appearance of the leader? How do contemporary leaders compare to Roman leaders in terms of character and inner strength? **OL**

Teach

B1 Big Idea

Loyalty and Betrayal

Answer: *Students may say that the mood of the crowd is unreasonable, violent, and ugly. The crowd is behaving this way because Mark Antony has stirred up their passions.* **OL**

R Reading Strategy

Connecting Encourage students to consider whether a scene similar to this riot could happen today. What events does it resemble? What truths about human nature does Shakespeare depict in the scene? *(Students may mention that riots resulting from protests against the government and racial issues have occurred in the United States. Shakespeare depicts an out-of-control crowd and the ability of a clever manipulator to provoke a crowd to violence.)* **OL**

 CheckPoint

Use the CheckPoint questions on Presentation Plus! to check students' mastery of the selection. These questions can be used with interactive response keypads for immediate student feedback.

 JULIUS CAESAR

SCENE 3. Shortly afterward. A street near the Forum.

[*Enter* CINNA *the poet, and after him the* PLEBEIANS.]

    CINNA.° I dreamt tonight° that I did feast with Caesar,
      And things unluckily charge my fantasy.°
      I have no will to wander forth of doors,
      Yet something leads me forth.

5 FIRST PLEBEIAN. What is your name?

    SECOND PLEBEIAN. Whither are you going?

    THIRD PLEBEIAN. Where do you dwell?

    FOURTH PLEBEIAN. Are you a married man or a bachelor?

    SECOND PLEBEIAN. Answer every man directly.

10 FIRST PLEBEIAN. Ay, and briefly.

    FOURTH PLEBEIAN. Ay, and wisely.

    THIRD PLEBEIAN. Ay, and truly, you were best.°

    CINNA. What is my name? Whither am I going? Where do I
      dwell? Am I a married man or a bachelor? Then, to answer
15   every man directly and briefly, wisely and truly: wisely I
      say, I am a bachelor.

    SECOND PLEBEIAN. That's as much as to say, they are fools that
      marry. You'll bear me a bang° for that, I fear. Proceed
      directly.

20 CINNA. Directly, I am going to Caesar's funeral.

    FIRST PLEBEIAN. As a friend or an enemy?

    CINNA. As a friend.

    SECOND PLEBEIAN. That matter is answer'd directly.

    FOURTH PLEBEIAN. For your dwelling—briefly.

25 CINNA. Briefly, I dwell by the Capitol.

    THIRD PLEBEIAN. Your name, sir, truly.

    CINNA. Truly, my name is Cinna.

    FIRST PLEBEIAN. Tear him to pieces, he's a conspirator.

    CINNA. I am Cinna the poet, I am Cinna the poet.

30 FOURTH PLEBEIAN. Tear him for his bad verses, tear him for his
      bad verses.

    CINNA. I am not Cinna the conspirator.

    FOURTH PLEBEIAN. It is no matter, his name's Cinna. Pluck but
      his name out of his heart, and turn him going.

35 THIRD PLEBEIAN. Tear him, tear him!
      Come, brands, ho, firebrands! To Brutus', to Cassius'; burn
      all! Some to Decius' house, and some to Casca's; some to
      Ligarius'. Away, go!

R [*All the* PLEBEIANS *exit (dragging off* CINNA).]

Big Idea Loyalty and Betrayal *How would you describe the mood of the crowd? Why are they behaving in this way?* **B1**

1 Cinna: a well-known poet, not the same Cinna who helped kill Caesar. **tonight:** last night.
2 things . . . fantasy: my imagination is burdened with bad omens.

12 you were best: you had better.

18 bear me a bang: get hit by me.

832 UNIT 4 DRAMA

Additional Support

Web Activities Have students access the Web site for interactive activities that will help them assess their understanding of the selection.

Skills Practice

READING: Identifying Cause-and-Effect Relationships Identifying the causes of several events in *Julius Caesar* can help students understand and review the play. List the following events from the play on the board. Have students write one or more causes for each event.

1. Brutus's joining the conspirators
2. Caesar's going to the Capitol on the ides of March
3. Caesar's assassination
4. Antony's anger at Brutus
5. The crowd's rioting **OL**

RESPONDING AND THINKING CRITICALLY

Respond

1. What was your reaction to Caesar's murder?

Recall and Interpret

2. (a)What most surprises Caesar when he is attacked? (b)What might Caesar have been thinking as he died? Explain.

3. (a)How does Antony respond to the conspirators immediately after Caesar's murder? (b)In your opinion, why does he behave this way?

4. (a)Summarize the crowd's reactions to Brutus's and Antony's funeral speeches. (b)What can you infer about the crowd from their reactions?

5. (a)What was the content of Caesar's will? (b)Why might Antony have read the will?

Analyze and Evaluate

6. How did Caesar's behavior outside the Capitol just before he died affect your reaction to his death?

7. (a)What is your opinion of Brutus? (b)Has it changed since Act 1? Explain.

8. (a)Why might Shakespeare have chosen to include the incident of the attack on Cinna the poet? (b)What contemporary incidents or events might you compare to that incident? Explain.

Connect

9. **Big Idea** **Loyalty and Betrayal** (a)Did Antony's soliloquy after his discussion with the conspirators surprise you? (b)As a friend to others, does Antony display loyalty, disloyalty, or both qualities? Explain your answer.

LITERARY ANALYSIS

Literary Element Plot

There are many points of suspense and high emotional pitch in Act 3. Which is the point of greatest emotional intensity, known in literature as the **climax**? In fact, critics do not all agree on this matter. Several places in Act 3 could plausibly be labeled the climax.

1. Summarize the exposition and rising action of Act 3. Which details help to contribute to the growing tension?

2. What, in your opinion, is the climax of Act 3? Explain.

3. Does the tension lessen after the climax? What questions are answered at the end of the act?

Writing About Literature

Analyze Rhetorical Devices Write a brief essay in which you analyze the techniques that Antony uses in his funeral speech. Does he portray Caesar's murder fairly, or does he distort the event? How does he use repetition, irony, and other rhetorical or persuasive techniques to make his point? What else does he do to win over his audience? Present to the class a list of techniques that Antony uses.

READING AND VOCABULARY

Reading Strategy Analyzing Figures of Speech

Figurative language often has the power to convey experiences more vividly than literal language.

1. (a)What figure of speech does Casca use when he stabs Caesar? (b)Explain its meaning.

2. For two other figures of speech in Act 3, identify the types and explain what you think the figure of speech was intended to convey.

Vocabulary Practice

Practice with Context Clues For each of the bold vocabulary words, use context clues to choose the best definition.

1. Most of our plants are **thriving** because we have treated them well.
   a. hibernating **b.** withering **c.** flourishing

2. Her expression was full of **malice**; her friend also gave me a hateful look.
   a. vengeance **b.** confusion **c.** kindness

JULIUS CAESAR **833**

Literary Element

1. The conspirators led Caesar to the Capitol and murdered him. Students should mention details that contributed to the rising tension.

2. Students may select Antony uncovering the body or the crowd rioting.

3. Answers will vary.

Reading Strategy

1. (a) Casca asks his hands to speak for him. (b) He means that his violent act will express his true feelings.

2. Answers will vary.

Vocabulary

1. c 2. a

Assess

1. Students should support their answers.

2. (a) Brutus's participation (b) He might have been experiencing shock at the betrayal of his friend.

3. (a) Antony acts conciliatory. (b) He is hiding his feelings until he can get support for revenge.

4. (a) The crowd agrees with Brutus but is later swayed by Antony's rhetoric. (b) They are emotional and easily swayed.

5. (a) Caesar's will specified that money, walks, and gardens be given to the Roman citizens. (b) To prove that Caesar loved the people, further inciting them to revenge

6. Caesar's behavior may reduce sympathy for him.

7. (a) Students may have less respect for Brutus. (b) He seems now to be rationalizing his part in the murder.

8. (a) To show the dangers of inciting a crowd to violence (b) Students may know of an incident of mob violence from recent history.

9. (a) Students may express surprise at Antony's feelings, because his conciliatory gestures were convincing. (b) Students may say that Antony is loyal to Caesar and that this requires him to deceive Brutus.

Writing About Literature

Essays should list and explain the various rhetorical devices used in Antony's speech.

833

Focus

Summary

After Caesar's murder, Rome is led by Antony and Octavius. Finding that Brutus and Cassius are raising an army, Antony and Octavius decide to go after them. Months later, Brutus and Cassius argue over administrative matters but make up and decide how best to fight Antony and Octavius. In his sleep Brutus meets the ghost of Caesar.

V Vocabulary

Vocabulary File

Say: Add these words and definitions to your vocabulary file. For each word, include a sentence that gives you an example of how to use the word. **OL** Students with English language needs should include the pronunciations of these words in their files. **EL**

Literary Elements Have students access the Web site to improve their understanding of foils.

LITERATURE PREVIEW

Connecting to the Play

Disagreements are a part of life. However, quarrelling can undermine cooperation and friendship. Before you read, think about these questions:

- Why do people quarrel?
- What does it take to be a good team player?

Building Background

After Brutus, Cassius, and the other conspirators fled Rome, Antony took charge of the city. He was soon joined by the eighteen-year-old Gaius Octavius, Caesar's great-nephew and adopted son. Octavius was intelligent, handsome, and skilled at oratory—easily a potential fellow leader with the forty-year-old Antony. Together with a governor named Lepidus, Octavius and Antony created a ruling triumvirate. To prevent internal opposition, the triumvirate began their reign by murdering two hundred of Rome's political leaders. Among these was the elderly senator and philosopher Cicero, a passionate defender of the Roman republic. Cassius and Brutus, meanwhile, assembled their armies in an area that is now northern Greece. There, they awaited the battle for the future of Rome.

Setting Purposes for Reading

Big Idea Loyalty and Betrayal

As you read, notice conflicts between characters. Consider what is revealed about various characters' desire for loyalty and fear of betrayal.

Literary Element Foil

A **foil** is a character who provides contrast with another character. A foil helps readers perceive strengths and weaknesses of another character. For instance, if a character is calm in a crisis, the foil's anxiety may help you perceive that calmness. As you read this Act 4, notice where one character serves as a foil for another.

- See Literary Terms Handbook, p. R7.

Literature Online **Interactive Literary Elements Handbook** To review or learn more about the literary elements, go to www.glencoe.com.

OBJECTIVES
In studying this selection, you will focus on the following:
- analyzing the role of a foil in literature

READING PREVIEW

Reading Strategy Making and Verifying Predictions

When you **make predictions** as you read, you make reasoned guesses about what will happen next based on clues the author provides together with your own understanding of characters and events. Then, as you continue reading, you **verify** the accuracy of the predictions, and modify your thinking and continue on.

Reading Tip: Charting Predictions As you read, write predictions in the first column of a chart like the one shown. Use the second column to give reasons for your thinking. Then use the third column to indicate what you discover as you read on.

I Predict	My Reason	The Outcome
Brutus and Cassius are going to argue and end their alliance.	They are very different. Brutus is thoughtful and honest. Cassius is emotional and cunning.	They fight but reconcile and resolve their differences.

Vocabulary

barren (bar′ən) *adj.* empty and dreary; without life; desolate; p. 836 *No one lives in the area surrounding the town; the land is barren.*

covert (kō′vərt) *adj.* secret; hidden; p. 837 *The reporter discovered a covert plan to escape.*

deceitful (di sēt′fəl) *adj.* untruthful and cunning; false; p. 838 *Some advertisements are honest; others are deceitful.*

rash (rash) *adj.* marked by haste and lack of caution or consideration; p. 842 *Meena's decision to end their friendship seemed rash to Laura.*

Vocabulary Tip: Antonyms Words that are antonyms have opposite meanings. Note that antonyms must be the same part of speech.

- making and verifying predictions
- performing independent research

834 UNIT 4 DRAMA

Selection Skills

Literary Elements
- Foil (SE pp. 834–849)

Reading Skills
- Making and Verifying Predictions (SE pp. 834–849)

The Tragedy of Julius Caesar, Act 4

Vocabulary Skills
- Antonyms (SE pp. 834, 849)

Listening/Speaking/Viewing Skills
- Analyzing Art (SE pp. 835, 843)
- Oral Reports (TWE p. 842)

Writing Skills/Grammar
- Researching Background Information (TWE p. 840)
- Commas in a Series (TWE p. 836)

Study Skills
- Collaborating (TWE p. 838)

ACT 4 B1

SCENE 1. Antony's house in Rome. A year and a half after Caesar's death.

[*Enter ANTONY, OCTAVIUS, and LEPIDUS.*]

ANTONY. These many then shall die, their names are prick'd.°

OCTAVIUS. Your brother too must die, consent you, Lepidus?°

LEPIDUS. I do consent—

OCTAVIUS.   Prick him down, Antony.

LEPIDUS. Upon condition Publius shall not live,
5   Who is your sister's son, Mark Antony.

1 **prick'd:** marked down on a list.

2 **Your brother . . . Lepidus:** Lepidus's brother was a prominent politician who sided with the conspirators after Caesar's assassination.

Ancient Romans. Artist unknown. Mosaic. Currier Gallery of Art, Manchester, NH.
Viewing the Art: What impressions of people in ancient Rome do you get from this mosaic? How do those impressions relate to characters in the play? ★

JULIUS CAESAR, ACT 4, SCENE 1 **835**

Teach

BI Big Idea

Loyalty and Betrayal
Answer: *Answers will vary. Students may say that Antony did not deal honestly with the Romans; he pretended to have their best interests at heart, but his motivations were political.* **OL**

L1 Literary Element

Dialogue Have students describe the relationship between Antony and Octavius. How might their dialogue be portrayed on stage? *(The two leaders seem to have a fragile relationship. Their dialogue on stage might appear as petty bickering.)* **OL**

L2 Literary Element

Foil Answer: *Octavius is honest and fair; Antony is dishonest and unfair.* **OL**

ANTONY. He shall not live; look, with a spot I damn him.
  But, Lepidus, go you to Caesar's house;
  Fetch the will hither, and we shall determine
  How to cut off some charge in legacies.°

10 LEPIDUS. What? shall I find you here?

OCTAVIUS. Or here or at the Capitol.

[*Exit LEPIDUS.*]

ANTONY. This is a slight unmeritable man,
  Meet° to be sent on errands; is it fit,
  The threefold world° divided, he should stand
15 One of the three to share it?

OCTAVIUS.   So you thought him,
  And took his voice who should be prick'd to die
  In our black sentence and proscription.° **L1**

ANTONY. Octavius, I have seen more days than you,
  And though we lay these honors on this man
20 To ease ourselves of divers sland'rous loads,°
  He shall but bear them as the ass bears gold,
  To groan and sweat under the business,
  Either led or driven, as we point the way;
  And having brought our treasure where we will,
25 Then take we down his load, and turn him off
  (Like to the empty ass) to shake his ears
  And graze in commons.°

OCTAVIUS.   You may do your will;
  But he's a tried and valiant soldier.

ANTONY. So is my horse, Octavius, and for that
30 I do appoint him store of provender.°
  It is a creature that I teach to fight,
  To wind,° to stop, to run directly on,
  His corporal° motion govern'd by my spirit;
  And in some taste° is Lepidus but so.
35 He must be taught, and train'd, and bid go forth;
  A **barren**-spirited fellow; one that feeds
  On objects, arts, and imitations,
  Which, out of use and stal'd by other men,

---

9 cut off . . . legacies: reduce the amount of money left to the people in Caesar's will.

13 Meet: fit.

14 threefold world: three parts of the Roman world. (In the autumn of 43 BC, Antony, Octavius Caesar, and Lepidus formed a triumvirate—a committee of three—to rule Rome. They divided up among themselves territory that the Romans had conquered.)

15–17 So you . . . proscription: Octavius wonders why Antony asked Lepidus to name people who should be sentenced to death if he had so poor an opinion of him.

20 divers sland'rous loads: the burden of accusations for our various actions.

24–27 And having . . . commons: When Lepidus has brought our treasure where we want it, we will send him off to shake his ears and graze on public land like an unburdened donkey.

30 appoint . . . provender: allot him a supply of food.

32 wind: turn.

33 corporal: bodily.

34 taste: degree.

Big Idea Loyalty and Betrayal *What does Antony's statement here suggest about him?* **BI**

Literary Element Foil *What does Octavius's statement indicate about the difference between Octavius and Antony?* **L2**

Vocabulary

barren (bar´ ən) *adj.* empty and dreary; without life; desolate

---

Additional Support

Skills Practice

GRAMMAR AND LANGUAGE:
Commas in a Series Write the following sentences adapted from Act 4 on the board. Omit the commas between the items in the series. Have students place the commas correctly.

1. Lepidus is a barren-spirited fellow, one that feeds on objects, arts, and imitations.

2. We, lying still, are full of rest, defense, and nimbleness. **OL**

40 Begin his fashion.° Do not talk of him
    But as a property.° And now, Octavius,
    Listen great things. Brutus and Cassius
    Are levying powers; we must straight make head;
    Therefore let our alliance be combin'd,
    Our best friends made, our means stretch'd;
45 And let us presently go sit in council,
    How **covert** matters may be best disclos'd,
    And open perils surest answered.°

    OCTAVIUS. Let us do so; for we are at the stake,
    And bay'd about with many enemies,°
50 And some that smile have in their hearts, I fear,
    Millions of mischiefs. [*They exit.*]

**SCENE 2. A military camp near Sardis in Asia Minor. Several
months later.**

[*Drum. Enter* BRUTUS, LUCILIUS, LUCIUS, *and the army.* TITINIUS *and*
PINDARUS *meet them.*]

    BRUTUS. Stand ho!

    LUCILIUS. Give the word ho! and stand.°

    BRUTUS. What now, Lucilius, is Cassius near?

    LUCILIUS. He is at hand, and Pindarus is come
5   To do you salutation from his master.

    BRUTUS. He greets me well. Your master, Pindarus,
      In his own change, or by ill officers,
      Hath given me some worthy cause to wish
      Things done undone,° but if he be at hand,
10   I shall be satisfied.°

    PINDARUS.   I do not doubt
      But that my noble master will appear
      Such as he is, full of regard and honor.

    BRUTUS. He is not doubted. A word, Lucilius.
      How he receiv'd you; let me be resolv'd.°

15 LUCILIUS. With courtesy and with respect enough,
      But not with such familiar instances,°
      Nor with such free and friendly conference,°
      As he hath us'd of old.

36–39 A barren-spirited . . . fashion:
a man with no originality, one who
indulges in curiosities, tricks, and fashions,
which he takes up only after they have
become outmoded.
40 a property: a mere tool.

41–47 Listen great . . . answered:
Listen to important matters. Brutus and
Cassius are raising armies; we must press
forward immediately. Therefore let us
become united, choose our allies, and
make the most of our resources. And let
us decide at once how hidden threats
may be uncovered and open dangers
most safely confronted.
48–49 we are . . . enemies: Octavius's
metaphor refers to bear-baiting, a popular
entertainment in which bears were tied to
stakes and surrounded by vicious dogs.

2 Give the . . . stand: Lucilius, one of
Brutus's officers, tells his subordinates to
pass on Brutus's command for the army
to halt (**stand**). He has returned from
Cassius's camp with Titinius, one of
Cassius's officers, and Pindarus, Cassius's
servant.

6–9 Your master . . . undone: Either a
change in Cassius or the misconduct of
his officers has given me good reason to
wish I could undo what I have done.
(Brutus is having some misgivings about
having participated in the conspiracy
because of incidents that have occurred in
Cassius's army.)
10 be satisfied: receive an explanation.
14 resolv'd: informed.

16 familiar instances: signs of
friendship.
17 conference: conversation.

Teach

R **Reading Strategy**

**Making and Verifying
Predictions Answer:** *Answers
will vary. Students should support their answers.* **OL**

⭐ **Political History**

Octavius Caesar Octavius
was the nephew of Julius
Caesar. After Caesar's death
in 44 B.C.E., Octavius, commanding Caesar's forces,
defeated Antony's army. He
forced Antony to accept him
as a chief officer. Octavius,
Antony, and Lepidus formed
the Second Triumvirate. This
is the situation at the beginning of act 4. In 27 B.C.E.,
several years later, Octavius
became the first Roman
emperor and became known
as Augustus. **AS**

Differentiated Instruction

Connecting Brutus describes an aspect
of friendship, starting with the vivid
image of "a hot friend cooling." Have
a volunteer read Brutus's speech, lines
18–27. Ask students to interpret Brutus's
simile. How is an insincere person like
certain horses? Point out that one reason
Shakespeare is still popular is his timeless understanding of people and relationships. Have students discuss whether
they have ever been treated by a friend
in the manner Brutus describes. **BL**

Objectives
• To analyze the role of a foil in lit-
  erature (SE)
• To use commas in a series (TWE)

837

Teach

BI₁ Big Idea

Loyalty and Betrayal
Answer: *Brutus is expressing a skeptical, critical attitude toward Cassius.* OL

R₁ Reading Strategy

Making and Verifying Predictions Answer: *Answers will vary. Students should support their answers.* OL

L₁ Literary Element

Foil Answer: *Cassius seems excitable; Brutus seems calmer and more reasonable.* OL

★ Political History

The Roman Army The Roman army was very strong, numbering about 300,000 men at its height. At first, only landed citizens could become soldiers, but the army later increased its ranks and developed a professional, well-trained army. In addition to fighting, soldiers built roads, aqueducts, bridges, and walls. Soldiers often developed a strong loyalty to their general, especially if they were rewarded with some of the spoils of battle. AS

BRUTUS.   Thou hast describ'd
    A hot friend cooling. Ever note, Lucilius,
20   When love begins to sicken and decay
    It useth an enforced ceremony.°
    There are no tricks in plain and simple faith;
    But hollow men, like horses hot at hand,
    Make gallant show and promise of their mettle;

[*Low march within.*]

25   But when they should endure the bloody spur,
    They fall their crests, and like **deceitful** jades
    Sink in the trial.° Comes his army on?

LUCILIUS.   They mean this night in Sardis to be quarter'd.
    The greater part, the horse in general,°
30   Are come with Cassius.

[*Enter CASSIUS and his POWERS.*]

BRUTUS.   Hark! He is arriv'd.
    March gently on to meet him.

CASSIUS.   Stand ho!

BRUTUS.   Stand ho! Speak the word along.

FIRST SOLDIER.   Stand!

35   SECOND SOLDIER.   Stand!

THIRD SOLDIER.   Stand!

CASSIUS.   Most noble brother, you have done me wrong.

BRUTUS.   Judge me, you gods! wrong I mine enemies?
    And if not so, how should I wrong a brother.

40   CASSIUS.   Brutus, this sober form° of yours hides wrongs,
    And when you do them—

BRUTUS.   Cassius, be content.
    Speak your griefs softly; I do know you well.
    Before the eyes of both our armies here
45   (Which should perceive nothing but love from us)
    Let us not wrangle. Bid them move away;
    Then in my tent, Cassius, enlarge your griefs,
    And I will give you audience.°

21 enforced ceremony: strained formality.
23–27 But hollow . . . trial: Brutus compares insincere men to horses that are spirited at the start but drop their proud necks as soon as they feel the spur, failing like nags (**jades**) when put to the test.
29 horse in general: main part of the cavalry.

A group of soldiers of the Praetorian guard, possibly from the Forum of Emperor Trajan, 1st–3rd century C.E. Artist unknown. Marble relief. Louvre, Paris.

40 sober form: dignified manner.

47–48 enlarge . . . audience: Explain your grievances, and I will listen.

Big Idea   Loyalty and Betrayal *What attitude toward Cassius is Brutus expressing?* **BI₁**

Reading Strategy   Making and Verifying Predictions *What do you predict will happen when Brutus and Cassius meet?* **R₁**

Literary Element   Foil *What contrast between Cassius and Brutus does this passage suggest?* **L₁**

Vocabulary

deceitful (di sēt′fəl) *adj.* untruthful and cunning; false

Additional Support

Skills Practice

STUDY SKILLS: Collaborating Have students consider the advantages and disadvantages of three men of equal power trying to run a country together. Point out that although students do not run a country, collaborating with others is an important life skill with which they have some experience. Have students work in small groups to begin a list of mistakes made by Antony, Octavius, and Lepidus in their political collaboration. For example, in the beginning of Act 4, Antony excludes one of their members, Lepidus, and then insults him behind his back; Octavius indulges in petty bickering with Antony; and Antony pulls rank

CASSIUS.   Pindarus,
50   Bid our commanders lead their charges off
      A little from this ground.

BRUTUS. Lucius, do you the like, and let no man
      Come to our tent till we have done our conference.
      Let Lucilius and Titinius guard our door.

[*They exit.* BRUTUS *and* CASSIUS *remain and withdraw into* BRUTUS'S
tent, while LUCILIUS *and* TITINIUS *mount guard without.*]

SCENE 3. BRUTUS'S tent. A few minutes later.

CASSIUS. That you wrong'd me doth appear in this;
      You have condemn'd and noted Lucius Pella
      For taking bribes here of the Sardians;
      Wherein my letters, praying on his side,
5   Because I knew the man, was slighted off.°

BRUTUS. You wrong'd yourself to write in such a case.

CASSIUS. In such a time as this it is not meet
      That every nice offense should bear his comment.°

BRUTUS. Let me tell you, Cassius, you yourself
10   Are much condemn'd to have an itching palm,°
      To sell and mart° your offices for gold
      To undeservers.

CASSIUS.   I, an itching palm?
      You know that you are Brutus that speaks this,
      Or, by the gods, this speech were else your last.

15 BRUTUS. The name of Cassius honors this corruption,
      And chastisement doth therefore hide his head.°

CASSIUS. Chastisement?

BRUTUS. Remember March, the ides of March remember:
      Did not great Julius bleed for justice' sake?
20   What villain touch'd his body, that did stab
      And not for justice? What? shall one of us,
      That struck the foremost man of all this world
      But for supporting robbers,° shall we now
      Contaminate our fingers with base bribes?
25   And sell the mighty space of our large honors
      For so much trash as may be grasped thus?
      I had rather be a dog, and bay the moon,
      Than such a Roman.

1–5 That you . . . off: Cassius complains that Brutus publicly disgraced (**noted**) a man for taking bribes, ignoring Cassius's request for leniency.

7–8 not meet . . . comment: not fitting that each minor offense should be criticized.

10 condemn'd to . . . palm: blamed for being greedy.

11 mart: trade.

15–16 The name . . . head: Because you have become associated with this corruption, the bribe-takers go unpunished.

23 supporting robbers: Brutus now suggests that one of Caesar's offenses was to protect corrupt officials.

Reading Strategy Making and Verifying Predictions *Do you think Brutus and Cassius will resolve their differences? Why or why not?* **R₂**

Literary Element Foil *What flaws in Cassius's personality are revealed by Brutus's comments?* **L₂**

Big Idea Loyalty and Betrayal *What point does Brutus make in these lines?* **BI₂**

JULIUS CAESAR, ACT 4, SCENE 3 **839**

Teach

R₂ Reading Strategy

Making and Verifying Predictions Answer: *Answers will vary. Students should support their answers.* **OL**

L₂ Literary Element

Foil Answer: *Students may say that Brutus's comments reveal Cassius's lack of scruples in exploiting the local people for their money.* **OL**

BI₂ Big Idea

Loyalty and Betrayal
Answer: *Brutus says that the conspirators killed Caesar, a great man, because he was associated with corruption. If the conspirators now become greedy and corrupt, they are just as hypocritical and evil as Caesar. Brutus would rather be a dog than such a Roman.* **OL**

Differentiated Instruction

on Octavius by saying: "I have seen more days than you." Have students continue their lists as they complete the play. Then discuss what students have learned about collaboration from their own experiences and from the play. **OL**

Evaluating In the course of their argument, Cassius says to Brutus, "A friend should bear his friend's infirmities." Have students discuss this idea. Ask them to what extent they agree or disagree with Cassius's statement. Have students offer examples from their own lives that support their opinions. **BL**

Objectives

- To analyze the role of a foil in literature (SE)
- To make and verify predictions (SE)
- To collaborate (TWE)

839

Teach

BI₁ Big Idea

Loyalty and Betrayal

Answer: *Brutus begins to behave as pettily as Cassius, falling into an "are too, are not" argument. He insults Cassius, saying, "Shall I be frighted when a madman stares?" He says that maybe lowly slaves will be moved by Cassius's bad temper, but that it only makes him, Brutus, laugh.* **OL**

R Reading Strategy

Making and Verifying Predictions Answer: *Answers will vary. Students should support their answers.* **OL**

CASSIUS.   Brutus, bait° not me,
    I'll not endure it. You forget yourself

30 To hedge me in.° I am a soldier, I,
    Older in practice, abler than yourself
    To make conditions.°

BRUTUS.   Go to; you are not, Cassius.

CASSIUS. I am.

BRUTUS. I say you are not.

35 **CASSIUS.** Urge me no more, I shall forget myself;
    Have mind upon your health; tempt me no farther.

BRUTUS. Away, slight man!

CASSIUS. Is't possible?

BRUTUS.   Hear me, for I will speak.
    Must I give way and room to your rash choler?°

40 Shall I be frighted when a madman stares?

CASSIUS. O ye gods, ye gods, must I endure all this?

BRUTUS. All this? ay, more. Fret till your proud heart break.
    Go show your slaves how choleric you are,
    And make your bondmen tremble. Must I budge?°

45 Must I observe you?° Must I stand and crouch
    Under your testy humor?° By the gods,
    You shall digest the venom of your spleen
    Though it do split you;° for, from his day forth,
    I'll use you for my mirth, yea, for my laughter,

50 When you are waspish.

CASSIUS.   Is it come to this?

BRUTUS. You say you are a better soldier;
    Let it appear so; make your vaunting° true,
    And it shall please me well. For mine own part,
    I shall be glad to learn of noble men.°

55 **CASSIUS.** You wrong me every way; you wrong me, Brutus;
    I said, an elder soldier, not a better.
    Did I say "better"?

BRUTUS.   If you did, I care not.

CASSIUS. When Caesar liv'd, he durst° not thus have
        mov'd° me.

BRUTUS. Peace, peace, you durst not so have tempted him.

60 **CASSIUS.** I durst not?

28 **bait:** provoke.

30 **hedge me in:** limit my freedom.

32 **conditions:** regulations.

39 **rash choler:** quick temper.

44 **budge:** flinch.
45 **observe you:** defer to you.
46 **testy humor:** irritable mood.

47–48 **digest . . . split you:** swallow the poison of your own anger, even if it makes you burst. (The spleen was thought to be the source of anger.)

52 **vaunting:** boasting.

54 **learn of noble men:** "learn from noble men" or "find out that you are noble."

58 **durst:** dared. **mov'd:** provoked.

Big Idea Loyalty and Betrayal *What details in this passage suggest that Brutus has lost his temper?* **BI₁**

Reading Strategy Making and Verifying Predictions *What do you predict will happen next?* **R**

Additional Support

Skills Practice

RESEARCH: Historical Background
As seen in the play, Caesar's assassination set off infighting and warfare in Rome. This climaxed in the crowning of Octavian as the first Roman emperor in 27 B.C.E. Have students choose a topic to research on the history of the Roman Empire from 27 B.C.E. until its fall in C.E.

476. Possible topics include the empire's height from C.E. 96 to 180, the rise of Christianity, the division of the empire in 284, and the final fall of the empire. They may also research some of the Roman Empire's most famous leaders, such as Augustus (Octavian), Marcus Aurelius, Diocletian, and Constantine. **OL**

BRUTUS. No.

CASSIUS. What? durst not tempt him?

BRUTUS.   For your life you
    durst not.

CASSIUS. Do not presume too much upon my love,
    I may do that° I shall be sorry for.

65 BRUTUS. You have done that you should be sorry for.
    There is no terror, Cassius, in your threats;
    For I am arm'd so strong in honesty
    That they pass by me as the idle wind,
    Which I respect not. I did send to you
70   For certain sums of gold, which you denied me;
    For I can raise no money by vile means.
    By heaven, I had rather coin my heart
    And drop my blood for drachmas than to wring
    From the hard hands of peasants their vile trash°
75   By any indirection.° I did send
    To you for gold to pay my legions,
    Which you denied me. Was that done like Cassius?
    Should I have answer'd Caius Cassius so?
    When Marcus Brutus grows so covetous
80   To lock such rascal counters° from his friends,
    Be ready, gods, with all your thunderbolts,
    Dash him to pieces!

CASSIUS.   I denied you not.

BRUTUS. You did.

CASSIUS. I did not. He was but a fool that brought
85   My answer back. Brutus hath riv'd° my heart.
    A friend should bear his friend's infirmities;°
    But Brutus makes mine greater than they are.

BRUTUS. I do not, till you practice them on me.

CASSIUS. You love me not.

BRUTUS.   I do not like your faults.

90 CASSIUS. A friendly eye could never see such faults.

BRUTUS. A flatterer's would not, though they do appear
    As huge as high Olympus.

64 **that:** something that.

74 **vile trash:** small sums of money.
75 **indirection:** dishonest means.
80 **rascal counters:** grubby coins.
85 **riv'd:** broken.
86 **bear . . . infirmities:** accept his friend's faults.

Big Idea Loyalty and Betrayal *Does the quarrel between Brutus and Cassius seem true to life? Why or why not?* **BI₂**

Literary Element Foil *What distinction does Brutus draw between himself and Cassius?* **L**

Big Idea Loyalty and Betrayal *What different ideas about loyalty and friendship are expressed here? With whose ideas do you agree?* **BI₃**

Jupiter Hurling a Flash of Lightning at the Titan, 17th century. Alessandro Algardi. Bronze sculpture. Louvre, Paris.

JULIUS CAESAR, ACT 4, SCENE 3 **841**

Differentiated Instruction

Analyzing Figurative Language In the course of the argument between Brutus and Cassius, Shakespeare uses several synonyms and figures of speech for *anger*. Help students find the various ways the two men refer to anger in their dialogue. List them on the board, explaining that many of them were commonly used in writings in Shakespeare's time. They include "rash choler," "choleric," "testy humor," "the venom of your spleen," and "waspish." **BL**

Teach

R1 Reading Strategy

Connecting Have students describe Cassius's mood in lines 93–107 and tell whether they have ever witnessed a person in such a mood. *(Cassius's attitude is one of self-pity and injured pride. Most students will say they have witnessed such an attitude in others.)* **OL**

BI Big Idea

Loyalty and Betrayal
Answer: *Brutus's attitude toward Cassius is softening. Brutus says that he will no longer be angered by Cassius's bad temper; he still believes Cassius is a good person.* **OL**

R2 Reading Strategy

Making and Verifying Predictions Answer: *Answers will vary. Students should support their answers.* **OL**

CASSIUS. Come, Antony, and young Octavius, come,
Revenge yourselves alone on Cassius,
95   For Cassius is aweary of the world;
Hated by one he loves, brav'd° by his brother,
Check'd like a bondman,° all his faults observ'd,
Set in a notebook, learn'd and conn'd by rote,°
To cast into my teeth. O, I could weep
100 **R1** My spirit from mine eyes! There is my dagger,
And here my naked breast; within, a heart
Dearer than Pluto's mine,° richer than gold:
If that thou be'st a Roman, take it forth.
I, that denied thee gold, will give my heart:
105   Strike as thou didst at Caesar; for I know,
When thou didst hate him worst, thou lovedst him better
Than ever thou lovedst Cassius.

BRUTUS.   Sheathe your dagger.
Be angry when you will, it shall have scope;
Do what you will, dishonor shall be humor.°
110   O Cassius, you are yoked° with a lamb
That carries anger as the flint bears fire,
Who, much enforced,° shows a hasty spark,
And straight° is cold again.

CASSIUS.   Hath Cassius liv'd
To be but mirth and laughter to his Brutus
115   When grief and blood ill-temper'd° vexeth him?

BRUTUS. When I spoke that, I was ill-temper'd too.

CASSIUS. Do you confess so much? Give me your hand.

BRUTUS. And my heart too.

CASSIUS.   O Brutus!

BRUTUS.   What's the matter?

CASSIUS. Have you not love enough to bear with me,
120   When that **rash** humor which my mother gave me
Makes me forgetful?°

BRUTUS.   Yes, Cassius, and from henceforth,
When you are over-earnest with your Brutus,
He'll think your mother chides, and leave you so.°

[*Enter a POET (to LUCILIUS and TITINIUS as they stand on guard).*]

96 brav'd: challenged.
97 Check'd like a bondman: scolded like a slave.
98 conn'd by rote: memorized.

102 Pluto's mine: all the riches in the earth. (Pluto, the Roman god of the underworld, was often confused with Plutus, the god of wealth.)

108–109 Be angry . . . humor: Brutus says that he will give Cassius's anger free play (**scope**) and will consider his insults merely the result of a bad mood.
110 yoked: allied.
112 enforced: struck hard; irritated.
113 straight: immediately.

115 blood ill-temper'd: moodiness.
121 forgetful: forget myself.
122–123 When you . . . so: When you are too difficult with me, I will attribute it to the quick temper you inherited from your mother, and leave it at that.

Statuette of Jupiter Dolichenus (standing on a bull) detail of the god, from a shrine, BC 200–250. Bronze, height 32 cm. Kunsthistorisches Museum, Vienna, Austria.

Big Idea Loyalty and Betrayal *How is Brutus's attitude shifting?* **BI**

Reading Strategy Making and Verifying Predictions *Is this how you predicted the argument would end? What will likely happen next?* **R2**

Vocabulary
rash (rash) *adj.* marked by haste and lack of caution or consideration

842 UNIT 4 DRAMA

Additional Support

Skills Practice

LISTENING AND SPEAKING:
Roman Stoicism The Roman philosophers Marcus Aurelius and Seneca carried on the Stoic philosophy created by the Greek philosopher Zeno. Seneca (4 B.C.E.–C.E. 65) focused on the disaster that would result if passions mastered reason. Marcus Aurelius (C.E. 121–180) focused on eliminating selfishness and forgiving others' offenses. Have students research one of the Roman Stoic philosophers. Ask them to summarize the philosopher's life and ideas and locate excerpts from his key works. Have them share their research in oral reports or in multimedia presentations. **OL**

POET. Let me go in to see the generals;
125   There is some grudge between 'em; 'tis not meet
      They be alone.

LUCILIUS. You shall not come to them.

POET. Nothing but death shall stay me.

[BRUTUS and CASSIUS step out of the tent.]

CASSIUS. How now. What's the matter?

130   POET. For shame, you generals! what do you mean?
      Love, and be friends, as two such men should be,
      For I have seen more years, I'm sure, than ye.

CASSIUS. Ha, ha! how vilely doth this cynic° rhyme!

BRUTUS. Get you hence, sirrah! saucy fellow, hence!

135   CASSIUS. Bear with him, Brutus, 'tis his fashion.

BRUTUS. I'll know his humor when he knows his time.°
      What should the wars do with these jigging° fools?
      Companion,° hence!

CASSIUS.   Away, away, be gone! [Exit POET.]

BRUTUS. Lucilius and Titinius, bid the commanders
140   Prepare to lodge their companies tonight.

CASSIUS. And come yourselves, and bring Messala with you
      Immediately to us.

[LUCILIUS and TITINIUS exit.]

BRUTUS. [To LUCIUS within.] Lucius, a bowl of wine!

[BRUTUS and CASSIUS return into the tent.]

CASSIUS. I did not think you could have been so angry.

BRUTUS. O Cassius, I am sick of many griefs.

145   CASSIUS. Of your philosophy you make no use,
      If you give place to accidental evils.°

BRUTUS. No man bears sorrow better. Portia is dead.

CASSIUS. Ha? Portia?

BRUTUS. She is dead.

150   CASSIUS. How scap'd I killing° when I cross'd you so?
      O insupportable and touching° loss!
      Upon what sickness?

133 cynic: rude fellow.

136 I'll know . . . time: I'll accept his quirks when he learns the proper time for them.
137 jigging: rhyming.
138 Companion: fellow (used here as a term of contempt).

145–146 Of your . . . evils: According to the philosophy Brutus studied, people should not accept chance misfortunes.
150 How scap'd I killing: How did I escape being killed?
151 touching: painful.

Literary Element Foil *How might the poet be said to act as a foil to Brutus and Cassius?* **L**

Brutus. c. 1539–1540. Michelangelo Buonarroti.
Marble, height: 29 1/8, in. Museo Nazionale del Bargello, Florence, Italy.
Viewing the Art: What traits of Brutus have been depicted here? How do they compare with the character you have read about? ⭐

JULIUS CAESAR, ACT 4, SCENE 3   **843**

Differentiated Instruction

Advanced Learners The scenes in which Cassius and Brutus argue and then make up after their argument might be acted in a humorous as well as a straightforward way. Have pairs of students volunteer to prepare a serious interpretation of the scene between Cassius and Brutus and others prepare a humorous interpretation. Have students focus on lines 83–107 and lines 107–122. Point out that by exaggerating the pettiness of the argument and the human weaknesses shown, students can gently satirize the characters and human nature. Have students perform their interpretations. **AL**

Teach

BI Big Idea

Loyalty and Betrayal
Answer: *Students may say that Portia's loyalty is great, even extreme.* **OL**

L Literary Element

Foil Answer: *Brutus reacts calmly and stoically to Portia's death.* Have students discuss Brutus's reaction in greater detail. Is it heartless and uncaring? *(Some students may say that Brutus's reaction is reasonable; others, that it is heartless; others, that he is denying his feelings of grief.)* **OL**

R1 Reading Strategy

Making and Verifying Predictions Answer: *Answers will vary. Students should support their answers.* **OL**

★ Literary History

Portia's Death According to Plutarch's history, Portia put "hot burning coals . . . into her mouth, and kept her mouth closed so that she choked herself." **AS**

JULIUS CAESAR

BRUTUS.   Impatient of° my absence,
And grief that young Octavius with Mark Antony
Have made themselves so strong—for with her death
155   That tidings came.° With this she fell distract,°
And (her attendants absent) swallow'd fire.°

CASSIUS. And died so?

BRUTUS.   Even so.

CASSIUS.   O ye immortal gods!

[*Enter Boy (LUCIUS) with wine and tapers.*]

BRUTUS. Speak no more of her. Give me a bowl of wine.
In this I bury all unkindness, Cassius. [*Drinks.*]

160   CASSIUS. My heart is thirsty for that noble pledge.
Fill, Lucius, till the wine o'erswell the cup;
I cannot drink too much of Brutus' love.

[*Drinks. Exit LUCIUS.*]

BRUTUS. Come in, Titinius. [*Enter TITINIUS and MESSALA.*]
Welcome, good Messala.
Now sit we close about this taper here,
165   And call in question our necessities.°

CASSIUS. Portia, art thou gone?

BRUTUS.   No more, I pray you.
Messala, I have here received letters
That young Octavius and Mark Antony
Come down upon us with a mighty power,°
170   Bending their expedition toward Philippi.°

MESSALA. Myself have letters of the selfsame tenure.°

BRUTUS. With what addition?

MESSALA. That by proscription° and bills of outlawry
Octavius, Antony, and Lepidus
175   Have put to death an hundred senators.

BRUTUS. Therein our letters do not well agree;
Mine speak of seventy senators that died
By their proscriptions, Cicero being one.

CASSIUS. Cicero one?

MESSALA.   Cicero is dead,
180   And by that order of proscription.
Had you your letters from your wife, my lord?

152 Impatient of: unable to endure.

154–155: with her death . . . came: I received news of her death and of their strength at the same time.
155 distract: insane.
156 fire: burning coals.

165 call . . . necessities: discuss what we must do.

169 power: army.
170 Bending . . . Philippi: Directing their march toward Philippi (an ancient town in northern Greece).
171 tenure: basic meaning.

173 proscription: condemning to death.

Big Idea Loyalty and Betrayal *How would you characterize Portia's loyalty to Brutus?* **BI**

Literary Element Foil *In comparison to Cassius, how does Brutus react to Portia's death?* **L**

Reading Strategy Making and Verifying Predictions *Considering this news, what do you predict might happen?* **R1**

844 UNIT 4 DRAMA

Additional Support

Skills Practice

LISTENING AND SPEAKING: Interpreting a Famous Speech
Brutus's speech in lines 218–224 is one of Shakespeare's often-quoted speeches. Reading the speech aloud can help students understand why this speech is widely admired. Have pairs of students practice reading the speech aloud. Encourage them to discuss the best ways to use vocal tone and emphasis. Then ask them why the speech may be popular. *(It uses a vivid extended metaphor; it describes a popular philosophy of life.)* **OL**

BRUTUS. No, Messala.

MESSALA. Nor nothing in your letters writ of her?

BRUTUS. Nothing, Messala.

MESSALA.   That methinks is strange.

185 BRUTUS. Why ask you? Hear you aught of her in yours?

MESSALA. No, my lord.

BRUTUS. Now as you are a Roman, tell me true.

MESSALA. Then like a Roman bear the truth I tell,
    For certain she is dead, and by strange manner. ★

190 BRUTUS. Why, farewell, Portia. We must die, Messala.
    With meditating that she must die once,°
    I have the patience to endure it now.

MESSALA. Even so great men great losses should endure.

CASSIUS. I have as much of this in art as you,
195   But yet my nature could not bear it so.°

BRUTUS. Well, to our work alive.° What do you think
    Of marching to Philippi presently?

CASSIUS. I do not think it good.

BRUTUS.   Your reason?

CASSIUS.   This it is;
    'Tis better that the enemy seek us;
200   So shall he waste his means,° weary his soldiers,
    Doing himself offense,° whilst we, lying still,
    Are full of rest, defense, and nimbleness.

BRUTUS. Good reasons must of force give place to better:
    The people 'twixt Philippi and this ground
205   Do stand but in a forc'd affection;°
    For they have grudg'd us contribution.
    The enemy, marching along by them,
    By them shall make a fuller number up,
    Come on refresh'd, new-added° and encourag'd;
210   From which advantage shall we cut him off
    If at Philippi we do face him there,
    These people at our back.

CASSIUS.   Here me, good brother.

BRUTUS. Under your pardon.° You must note beside
    That we have tried the utmost of our friends,°
215   Our legions are brimful,° our cause is ripe:
    The enemy increaseth every day;
    We, at the height, are ready to decline.
    There is a tide in the affairs of men,

---

191 **once:** at some time.

181–195 **Had you your . . . bear it so:** This passage contradicts lines 147–158, where Brutus tells Cassius of Portia's death. Many scholars believe that the second passage was mistakenly printed in a revised version of the play. According to this theory, Shakespeare originally emphasized Brutus's philosophical composure, but in rewriting the play, he decided to offer a warmer view of Brutus grieving for his wife.
194–195 **I have as . . . so:** Cassius says that although he shares Brutus's ideal of philosophical self-control, he could not practice it as Brutus does.
196 **alive:** "at hand" or "of the living."
200 **waste his means:** use up his supplies.
201 **Doing himself offense:** harming himself.
205 **Do stand . . . affection:** Are friendly toward us only because they have no choice.

209 **new-added:** reinforced.

213 **Under your pardon:** I beg your pardon (let me continue).
214 **tried . . . friends:** demanded from our allies all that they can give.
215 **brimful:** at full strength.

Reading Strategy Making and Verifying Predictions *How are the plans proposed by Brutus and Cassius different? What is the likely outcome?* **R2**

JULIUS CAESAR, ACT 4, SCENE 3 **845**

Teach

R2 **Reading Strategy**

Making and Verifying Predictions Answer: *The two leaders disagree on a clear way to win the conflict, indicating trouble ahead.* **OL**

Differentiated Instruction

Multiple Intelligences—Bodily-Kinesthetic Paraphrasing and acting out the quarrel between Brutus and Cassius can demonstrate the uneasy relationship between the two conspirators. Have students work in pairs and enact the dialogue between Brutus and Cassius on pages 843–844. Suggest that students define the emotions and attitudes of each character. Finally, have the two students act out the discussion, expressing the characters' emotions with voice, facial expressions, and gestures. **BL**

Objectives
• To analyze the role of a foil in literature (SE)
• To make and verify predictions (SE)
• To interpret a famous speech (TWE)

Teach

L Literary Element

Metaphor Have students identify the figure of speech in lines 218–224. *(It is a metaphor. Events in men's lives are compared to ocean currents.)* **OL**

R Reading Strategy

Making and Verifying Predictions Answer: *Answers will vary. Students should support their answers.*

Ask: Why do you think Cassius agrees to Brutus's plan? *(Students may say Brutus's speech was convincing, Cassius does not want to argue anymore, or he realizes he cannot win an argument with Brutus.)* **OL**

BI₁ Big Idea

Loyalty and Betrayal

Answer: *Cassius hopes that he and Brutus will never quarrel again. Students may say that Cassius's sincere request shows he can be softhearted.* **OL**

JULIUS CAESAR

220

Which, taken at the flood, leads on to fortune;
Omitted, all the voyage of their life
Is bound in shallows and in miseries.°
On such a full sea are we now afloat,
And we must take the current when it serves,
Or lose our ventures.

L

CASSIUS.   Then with your will° go on;

225   We'll along ourselves, and meet them at Philippi.

BRUTUS. The deep of night is crept upon our talk,
And nature must obey necessity,
Which we will niggard with a little rest.°
There is no more to say?

CASSIUS.   No more. Good night,

230   Early tomorrow will we rise, and hence.

BRUTUS. Lucius. [*Enter* LUCIUS.] My gown. [*Exit* LUCIUS.]
       Farewell, good Messala.
Good night, Titinius. Noble, noble Cassius,
Good night, and good repose.

CASSIUS.   O my dear brother!
This was an ill beginning of the night.

235   Never come such division 'tween our souls!
Let it not, Brutus.

[*Enter* LUCIUS *with the gown.*]

BRUTUS.   Everything is well.

CASSIUS. Good night, my lord.

BRUTUS.   Good night, good brother.

TITINIUS AND MESSALA. Good night, Lord Brutus.

BRUTUS.   Farewell
every one.

[*Exit (all but* BRUTUS *and* LUCIUS*).*]
     Give me the gown. Where is thy instrument?

240 **LUCIUS.** Here in the tent.

BRUTUS.   What, thou speak'st drowsily?
Poor knave,° I blame thee not; thou art o'erwatch'd.°
Call Claudius and some other of my men,
I'll have them sleep on cushions in my tent.

LUCIUS. Varrus and Claudio!

218–221 There is a . . . miseries: Brutus says that if men fail to act when the tide of fortune is flowing, they may never get another opportunity.

224 with your will: as you wish.

227–228 nature must . . . rest: Human nature has its needs, which we will grudgingly satisfy (**niggard**) by resting briefly.

241 knave: lad. **o'erwatch'd:** tired from staying awake too long.

Reading Strategy Making and Verifying Predictions *Whose ideas about strategy do you think will ultimately be proven correct, those of Cassius or those of Brutus?* **R**

Big Idea Loyalty and Betrayal *Why does Cassius make this request? What does it tell you about Cassius's character?* **BI₁**

846 UNIT 4 DRAMA

Additional Support

Skills Practice

LITERARY ELEMENT: Theme The theme of loyalty and betrayal has developed throughout the first four acts of *Julius Caesar.* As students prepare to read the final act of the play, have them review this theme in earlier acts. Have them consider which characters now feel loyalty and which now feel betrayal. How have the characters' feelings changed from earlier acts? How have relationships between characters changed as the play has progressed? **OL**

[*Enter* VARRUS *and* CLAUDIO.]

245   VARRUS.   Calls my lord?

      BRUTUS.   I pray you, sirs, lie in my tent and sleep;
         It may be I shall raise° you by and by
         On business to my brother Cassius.

      VARRUS.   So please you, we will stand and watch your
         pleasure.°

250   BRUTUS.   I will not have it so. Lie down, good sirs,
         It may be I shall otherwise bethink me.°

[VARRUS *and* CLAUDIO *lie down.*]

         Look, Lucius, here's the book I sought for so;
         I put it in the pocket of my gown.

      LUCIUS.   I was sure your lordship did not give it me.

255   BRUTUS.   Bear with me, good boy, I am much forgetful.
         Canst thou hold up thy heavy eyes awhile,
         And touch thy instrument a strain or two?°

      LUCIUS.   Ay, my lord, an't° please you.

      BRUTUS.   It does, my boy.
         I trouble thee too much, but thou are willing.

260   LUCIUS.   It is my duty, sir.

      BRUTUS.   I should not urge thy duty past thy might;
         I know young bloods look for a time of rest.

      LUCIUS.   I have slept, my lord, already.

      BRUTUS.   It was well done, and thou shalt sleep again;
265   I will not hold thee long. If I do live,
         I will be good to thee.

[*Music, and a song.*] ★

         This is a sleepy tune. O murd'rous slumber!
         Layest thou thy leaden mace° upon my boy,
         That plays thee music? Gentle knave, good night;
270   I will not do thee so much wrong to wake thee.
         If thou dost nod, thou break'st thy instrument;
         I'll take it from thee; and, good boy, good night.
         Let me see, let me see; is not the leaf turn'd down
         Where I left reading? Here it is, I think.

[*Enter the* GHOST OF CAESAR.]

275   How ill this taper burns!° Ha! who comes here?
         I think it is the weakness of mine eyes
         That shapes this monstrous apparition.

Big Idea   Loyalty and Betrayal   *What character traits does Brutus demonstrate in this scene?* **BI₂**

247 raise: awaken.

249 stand . . . pleasure: stay awake and be ready to serve you.
251 It may be . . . me: I might change my mind.

257 touch thy . . . two: play a song or two. (Lucius probably plays the lute, a stringed instrument.)
258 an't: if it.

267–268 O murd'rous . . . mace: Officers used to touch a rod (**mace**) to a person's shoulder as a sign of arrest. Brutus calls the mace of deathlike (**murd'rous**) sleep "leaden" because of its heaviness.
275 How ill . . . burns: It was believed that candles burn dimly when a ghost appears.

Young Boy Singing and Playing the Lute.
Michelangelo Merisi da Caravaggio, 1573–1610.
Hermitage, St. Petersburg, Russia.

JULIUS CAESAR, ACT 4, SCENE 3   **847**

Teach

BI₂ Big Idea

Loyalty and Betrayal
Answer: *Brutus demonstrates kindness and sensitivity toward others.* **OL**

★ Literary History

Music on Stage "Orpheus with his lute" from *Henry VIII* is traditionally sung in this scene when the play is staged. Shakespeare may have had in mind the song "Come, heavy sleep" from *First Book of Songs* by John Dowland, published in 1597. **AS**

Differentiated Instruction

Multiple Intelligences—Musical At the end of the act, Brutus's servant Lucius plays the lute, a stringed instrument popular during Shakespeare's time. Have musically inclined students produce a presentation including any of the following: an illustration and description of the lute, a demonstration of a lute and its music, a recording of Renaissance music that might have accompanied Shakespeare's production of *Julius Caesar,* or Renaissance music played on a guitar or other stringed instrument. Point out Brutus's description of the music as "a sleepy tone." **AL**

Objectives
• To make and verify predictions (SE)
• To analyze the development of theme (TWE)

R Reading Strategy

Making and Verifying Predictions Answer: *Answers will vary. Students should support their answers.*
Have students visualize the appearance of the ghost of Caesar. **Ask:** How might this scene be staged? Have them brainstorm ideas. **OL**

L Literary Element

Foreshadowing Ask students why the ghost is an effective device to foreshadow the end of Brutus's conflict. *(It is visually striking; a ghost is a supernatural symbol that has an emotional effect on people.)* **OL**

✓ CheckPoint

Use the CheckPoint questions on Presentation Plus! to check students' mastery of the selection. These questions can be used with interactive response keypads for immediate student feedback.

Web Activities Have students access the Web site for interactive activities that will help them assess their understanding of the selection.

 JULIUS CAESAR

> It comes upon me. Art thou anything?
> Art thou some god, some angel, or some devil,
> 280 That mak'st my blood cold, and my hair to stare?°
> Speak to me what thou art.

GHOST. Thy evil spirit, Brutus.

BRUTUS.   Why com'st thou?

GHOST. To tell thee thou shalt see me at Philippi.

BRUTUS. Well; then I shall see thee again?

285 GHOST. Ay, at Philippi.

BRUTUS. Why, I will see thee at Philippi then.

[*Exit* GHOST.]

> Now I have taken heart thou vanishest.
> Ill spirit, I would hold more talk with thee.
> **L** Boy! Lucius! Varrus! Claudio! Sirs, awake!
> 290 Claudio!

LUCIUS. The strings, my lord, are false.°

BRUTUS. He thinks he still is at his instrument.
Lucius, awake!

LUCIUS. My lord?

295 BRUTUS. Didst thou dream, Lucius, that thou so criedst out?

LUCIUS. My lord, I do not know that I did cry.

BRUTUS. Yes, that thou didst. Didst thou see anything?

LUCIUS. Nothing, my lord.

BRUTUS. Sleep again, Lucius. Sirrah Claudio!

300 [*To* CLAUDIO *and then* VARRUS.] Fellow thou, awake!

VARRUS. My lord?

CLAUDIO. My lord?

BRUTUS. Why did you so cry out, sirs, in your sleep?

BOTH. Did we, my lord?

BRUTUS.   Ay. Saw you anything?

305 VARRUS. No, my lord, I saw nothing.

CLAUDIO.   Nor I, my lord.

BRUTUS. Go and commend me° to my brother Cassius;
Bid him set on his pow'rs betimes before,°
And we will follow.

BOTH.   It shall be done, my lord.

[*They exit.*]

Reading Strategy Making and Verifying Predictions *What does the ghost's visit suggest to you? What do you think will happen at Philippi?* **R**

Julius Caesar, Act IV, Scene III, Brutus & The Ghost, 1906. Edwin Austin Abbey. Illustration created for Harper's Monthly.

280 **stare:** stand on end.
291 **false:** out of tune.

306 **commend me:** send my regards.
307 **set on . . . before:** start his troops moving early, at the lead.

Additional Support

Skills Practice

READING: Summarizing

Summarizing each act of *Julius Caesar* is a good way for students to make sure they understand the play's events and to review the play. Remind them that in summarizing, they state the text's main idea in their own words. Have students orally summarize each of the first four acts of the play. Tell students to keep their summaries brief—three to four sentences. Have them compare their summaries with a partner and discuss necessary details they omitted or unnecessary ones they included. **OL**

RESPONDING AND THINKING CRITICALLY

Respond

1. What do you think about the relationship between Brutus and Cassius?

Recall and Interpret

2. Compare the political situation in Rome after Caesar's murder with that under Caesar's rule.

3. (a)Describe the conflict between Brutus and Cassius in Act 4. (b)Who seems more to blame? Why?

4. (a)What battle plan does Cassius propose? (b)Why, do you think, does he agree to march to Philippi?

5. (a)What unexpected visitor comes to Brutus's tent? (b)How does Brutus react to this visitation? Explain.

Analyze and Evaluate

6. (a)What is your impression of Antony in Act 4? (b)Do his actions surprise you? Explain.

7. Why, do you think, did Shakespeare include the conflict between Cassius and Brutus?

8. In your opinion, what is the purpose of the exchange in Brutus's tent between Brutus and Lucius as Brutus prepares to sleep (Scene 3, lines 239–244)?

Connect

9. **Big Idea** **Loyalty and Betrayal** What examples of loyalty do you see in this act of the play? Explain.

LITERARY ANALYSIS

Literary Element Foil

In drama, the purpose of a **foil** is to highlight a particular quality of another character. One character's personality traits often become sharper when an individual with contrasting traits—a foil—is on stage.

1. (a)In Scene 1, which character serves as a foil to Antony? (b)What is the difference between that character and Antony? What flaws does Antony display?

2. In much of this act, Cassius could be said to serve as a foil to Brutus. What differences do you see between the two characters? What do these differences illustrate about Brutus? Explain.

Interdisciplinary Activity

Use library resources and the Internet to do research on armies in ancient Rome. How were armies organized? Who was in charge? Where were the armies stationed? How were funds raised to support them? Present your findings to the class in an oral report.

Literature Online **Web Activities** For eFlashcards, Selection Quick Checks, and other Web activities, go to www.glencoe.com.

READING AND VOCABULARY

Reading Strategy Making and Verifying Predictions

In making a prediction when you read, you generally look for evidence and then make an informed guess. To find evidence in dialogue, behavior, or unusual events you add your knowledge of life and human behavior. Your predictions increase your understanding and enjoyment of what you read.

1. What have you predicted correctly in the play so far? What has surprised you? Explain.

2. What will happen at Philippi? Why do you think so?

Vocabulary Practice

Practice with Antonyms For each bold vocabulary word, choose the best antonym.

1. **barren**
   a. overflowing   b. empty   c. quiet
2. **covert**
   a. secret   b. open   c. productive
3. **deceitful**
   a. honest   b. nervous   c. manipulative
4. **rash**
   a. humorous   b. hasty   c. cautious

JULIUS CAESAR **849**

Assess

1. Brutus and Cassius are close but have differing temperaments.

2. Instead of one ruler, Rome is led by the triumvirate, who take steps to kill many of their opponents. Students will likely agree that the city seems worse off without Caesar.

3. (a) Brutus has criticized Cassius's management and accused him of corruption. (b) Students may say that Cassius is more to blame, since his bribe taking was reprehensible.

4. (a) Cassius wants to wait for Antony and Octavius at Sardis. (b) Students may say that Cassius agrees to march to Philippi to stop the argument with Brutus.

5. (a) The ghost of Caesar (b) Brutus reacts with fright but also with curiosity.

6. (a)Students may say that he is a ruthless leader. (b) Students may be surprised at his coldness, or they may have been warned of his character by his soliloquy in Act 3.

7. Possibly to introduce the theme that illegal political actions result in conflict and chaos and that even the most powerful leaders have human failings

8. To set up the appearance of the ghost

9. Students may note that Brutus and Cassius are loyal to each other. Portia has demonstrated her loyalty to Brutus. Brutus and his servants are loyal to each other.

Literary Element

1. (a) Octavius (b) Octavius is honest and deals fairly with people. Antony displays greed and dishonesty.

2. Students may say that Cassius displays ruthlessness and greed. Brutus displays integrity and fairness. These differences illustrate that Brutus is admirable.

Reading Strategy

1. Students should give examples of a prediction that was correct and another that they need to modify.

2. Answers will vary.

Vocabulary

1. a   2. b   3. a   4. c

Focus

Summary

Antony and Octavius see the army of Brutus and Cassius coming to meet them. Cassius tells of bad omens of the battle's outcome. Cassius, mistakenly believing that Titinius has been captured, kills himself. Brutus also takes his own life. Antony and Octavius prepare to consolidate their own power.

V Vocabulary

Vocabulary File

Say: Add these words and definitions to your vocabulary file. For each word, include a sentence that gives you an example of how to use the word. **OL** Students with English language needs should include the pronunciations of these words in their files. **EL**

Literary Elements Have students access the Web site to improve their understanding of the tragic hero.

LITERATURE PREVIEW

Connecting to the Play

In *Julius Caesar*, Shakespeare confronts some difficult issues. One issue is what action should be taken when a monarch claims absolute power. Another is what effect violence has on its perpetrators. Before you read, think about the following questions:

- Can a person commit violence without being harmed by it in some way?
- How do people today view war, honor, and death?

Building Background

Julius Caesar portrays Rome's transition from a republic to an empire. The republic was governed by citizen assemblies: two elected consuls, who could serve for just one year, and a powerful Senate, which proposed laws and oversaw officials. In 48 BC Rome came under the control of the great general Julius Caesar, who seemed prepared to reestablish a strong monarchy. The defeat of the republicans who assassinated Caesar ended Rome's republican form of rule.

Setting Purposes for Reading

Big Idea Loyalty and Betrayal

As you read this act, think about how people display their loyalty to each other.

Literary Element Tragic Hero

A tragedy is a drama that ends in the downfall of its main character, or **tragic hero**. The tragic hero is usually a high-ranking or respected person who has a fatal weakness, or tragic flaw that causes his or her downfall. This flaw may be a good quality or virtue that is carried to excess or conflicts with other values.

- See Literary Terms Handbook, p. R18.

Literature Online **Interactive Literary Elements Handbook** To review or learn more about the literary elements, go to www.glencoe.com.

OBJECTIVES
In studying this selection, you will focus on the following:
- understanding the concept of the tragic hero
- evaluating characters
- analyzing theme
- writing to evaluate an author's craft

850 UNIT 4 DRAMA

READING PREVIEW

Reading Strategy Evaluating Characters

When you **evaluate** the actions of **characters** in your reading, you make judgments about them. If you consider why a character behaves in a certain way, you improve your understanding of the character and your judgment about the work as a whole.

Reading Tip: Making a Chart As you read, use a chart to list details of the characters' actions and speech and to record the significance of these details.

Character	Detail	Significance or Detail
Octavius	Says "I was not born to die on Brutus' sword."	Octavius is determined. He will be a formidable opponent.

Vocabulary

peevish (pē′vish) *adj.* irritable; bad-tempered; p. 853 *My reply was peevish due to lack of sleep.*

peril (per′əl) *n.* exposure to harm or danger; p. 854 *A mother elephant will always protect her offspring from peril.*

disconsolate (dis kon′sə lit) *adj.* dejected; mournful; unable to be comforted; p. 857 *Maria was disconsolate after missing a penalty shot in the playoffs.*

misconstrue (mis′kən strōō′) *v.* to misinterpret; to misunderstand; p. 858 *Diplomats choose their words carefully so they are not misconstrued.*

attain (ə tān′) *v.* to accomplish; to arrive at; p. 862 *If we work hard, we will attain our goal of graduating from high school.*

Vocabulary Tip: Analogies An analogy is a type of comparison based on the relationships between things or ideas. For example, the words *weak* and *illness* relate to each other in the same way as the words *strong* and *health*.

Selection Skills

Literary Elements
- Tragic Hero (SE pp. 850–865)
- Theme (SE p. 865)

Reading Skills
- Evaluating Characters (SE pp. 850–865)

The Tragedy of Julius Caesar, Act 5

Vocabulary Skills
- Analogies (SE pp. 850, 865)

Listening/Speaking/ Viewing Skills
- Analyzing Art (SE pp. 859, 862)
- Vocal Expression (TWE p. 860)

Writing Skills/Grammar
- Writing a Review (SE p. 866)
- Choosing Vivid Verbs (SE p. 866)

Study Skills
- Researching Background (TWE p. 852)

ACT 5

SCENE 1. **The Plains of Philippi in Greece. A few weeks later.**

[*Enter* OCTAVIUS, ANTONY, *and their* ARMY.]

    OCTAVIUS. Now, Antony, our hopes are answered.
      You said the enemy would not come down,
      But keep the hills and upper regions.
      It proves not so: their battles° are at hand;
5   They mean to warn° us at Philippi here,
      Answering before we do demand of them.°

    ANTONY. Tut, I am in their bosoms,° and I know
      Wherefore they do it. They could be content
      To visit other places, and come down
10   With fearful° bravery, thinking by this face
      To fasten in our thoughts that they have courage;°
      But 'tis not so.

[*Enter a* MESSENGER.]

    MESSENGER.   Prepare you, generals,
      The enemy comes on in gallant show;
      Their bloody sign° of battle is hung out,
15   And something to be done immediately.

    ANTONY. Octavius, lead your battle softly° on
      Upon the left hand of the even° field.

    OCTAVIUS. Upon the right hand I, keep thou the left. ★

    ANTONY. Why do you cross me in this exigent?°

20   OCTAVIUS. I do not cross you; but I will do so.° [*March.*]

[*Drum. Enter* BRUTUS, CASSIUS, *and their* ARMY; LUCILIUS, TITINIUS, MESSALA, *and others.*]

    BRUTUS. They stand, and would have parley.°

    CASSIUS. Stand fast, Titinius; we must out and talk.

    OCTAVIUS. Mark Antony, shall we give sign of battle?

    ANTONY. No, Caesar, we will answer on their charge.°
25   Make forth, the generals would have some words.

---

4 **battles:** armies.

5 **warn:** defy.

6 **Answering before . . . them:** responding hostilely before we even challenge them to fight.
7 **am in their bosoms:** know what is in their hearts.

8–11 **They could . . . courage:** Antony dismisses his enemy's bravery as a false show (**face**), saying that they would really prefer to be somewhere else.
10 **fearful:** "frightening" or "full of fear."

14 **bloody sign:** A red flag was flown from a Roman general's tent to signal the start of battle.
16 **softly:** slowly.
17 **even:** level.

19 **cross me in this exigent:** oppose me at this moment of crisis.
20 **I will do so:** I will do as I said. (Octavius insists on attacking from the right, which is usually the position of the most experienced general.)

21 **would have parley:** request a conference.

24 **answer on their charge:** respond when they attack.

Reading Strategy Evaluating Characters *In your opinion, what quality or qualities does Octavius display here?* **R**

English Language Coach

Vocabulary of War English language learners may be unfamiliar with some words used in Act 5 to describe the battle. Write the following words on the board: *general, charge, slaughter, soldier, sword, legions, troops.* Have students look up words they are unsure of in an English dictionary. Discuss their parts of speech. Call on students to pronounce the words; refer students to the dictionary pronunciation as needed. Suggest that students add the words to their vocabulary notebooks. **EL**

Teach

Big Idea

Loyalty and Betrayal
Say: Think about the following question as you read: Which character stands out as being the most honorable? *(Brutus is the most honorable—or the "noblest"—because he made choices based upon his perceived responsibility to others. Nothing he did was for his own good.)* **OL**

R Reading Strategy

Evaluating Characters
Answer: *Answers will vary. Students may say that Octavius displays confidence or arrogance.* **OL**

★ Political History

Octavius vs. Antony
Octavius's opposition to Antony's wishes may foreshadow a later battle between the two. In 31 B.C.E., Octavius defeated the joint forces of Antony and Cleopatra off the coast of Greece and became sole ruler of Rome. **AS**

✓ CheckPoint

Use the CheckPoint questions on Presentation Plus! to monitor students' comprehension. These questions can be used with interactive response keypads for immediate student feedback.

Objectives
• To understand the concept of the tragic hero (SE)
• To evaluate characters (SE)

OCTAVIUS. Stir not until the signal.

BRUTUS. Words before blows; is it so, countrymen?

OCTAVIUS. Not that we love words better, as you do.

BRUTUS. Good words are better than bad strokes, Octavius.

30 **ANTONY.** In your bad strokes, Brutus, you give good words;
Witness the hole you made in Caesar's heart,
Crying, "Long live! hail, Caesar!"

CASSIUS.   Antony,
The posture of your blows are yet unknown;°
But for your words, they rob the Hybla° bees,
35 And leave them honeyless.

ANTONY.   Not stingless too?

BRUTUS. O, yes, and soundless too;
For you have stol'n their buzzing, Antony,
And very wisely threat before you sting.

ANTONY. Villains! you did not so, when your vile daggers
40 Hack'd one another in the sides of Caesar.
You show'd your [teeth]° like apes, and fawn'd like hounds,
And bow'd like bondmen, kissing Caesar's feet;
Whilst damned Casca, like a cur, behind
Struck Caesar on the neck, O you flatterers!

45 **CASSIUS.** Flatterers? Now, Brutus, thank yourself;
This tongue had not offended so today,
If Cassius might have rul'd.°

OCTAVIUS. Come, come, the cause.° If arguing make us sweat,
The proof of it° will turn to redder drops.
50 Look,
I draw a sword against conspirators;
When think you that the sword goes up again?°
Never, till Caesar's three and thirty wounds
Be well aveng'd; or till another Caesar
55 Have added slaughter to the sword of traitors.°

BRUTUS. Caesar, thou canst not die by traitors' hands,
Unless thou bring'st them with thee.° **L2**

OCTAVIUS.   So I hope;
I was not born to die on Brutus' sword.

BRUTUS. O, if thou wert the noblest of thy strain,°
60 Young man, thou couldst not die more honorable.

33 **The posture . . . unknown:** We don't know what kind of blows you will strike.
34 **Hybla:** an area in Sicily noted for its honey. (Cassius is reminding Antony of his "sweet" words to the conspirators after the assassination.)

41 **show'd your [teeth]:** grinned.

47 **If Cassius . . . rul'd:** if Cassius had had his way (when he argued that Antony should be killed).
48 **cause:** business at hand.
49 **The proof of it:** deciding the argument in battle.

52 **goes up again:** goes back into its sheath.

54–55 **till another . . . traitors:** until the conspirators have killed another Caesar (that is, Octavius himself).
56–57 **Caesar . . . thee:** Brutus suggests that all the traitors are on the side of Octavius and Antony.

59 **strain:** family.

Big Idea Loyalty and Betrayal *Of what flaw does Antony accuse Brutus and Cassius?* **BI**

Literary Element Tragic Hero *What error on Brutus's part does Cassius allude to here?* **L1**

BI **Big Idea**

Loyalty and Betrayal
Answer: *Students may say he accuses them of hypocrisy or disloyalty.* **OL**

L1 **Literary Element**

Tragic Hero Answer: *Cassius alludes to Brutus's urging that the conspirators allow Mark Antony to live.*
Have students review the discussion between Brutus and Cassius in Act 2, scene 1, about whether Antony should be killed along with Caesar. **Say:** In light of the events in Act 5, consider Brutus's conviction that Antony should live. **OL**

L2 **Literary Element**

Dialogue Ask: Why do you think Shakespeare has four generals come together to exchange threats and insults? *(Since he cannot stage the battles, he brings the opponents together in other ways. It allows for exciting and colorful language and a review of events and alliances before the climactic battle.)* **OL**

Additional Support

Skills Practice

RESEARCH: Historical Background
Methods and weapons of warfare have evolved from the war chariots of the Sumerians and the battering rams of the Assyrians to the helicopters, jet fighters, and nuclear weapons of today. Have students research the battle methods, equipment, and weapons of the ancient Romans. Encourage them to show how the Romans improved earlier tactics and weaponry. Have them share their information with the class. **OL**

CASSIUS. A **peevish** schoolboy,° worthless of such honor,
Join'd with a masker and a reveler!°

ANTONY. Old Cassius still!

OCTAVIUS.   Come, Antony; away!
Defiance, traitors, hurl we in your teeth.
65 If you dare fight today, come to the field;
If not, when you have stomachs.°

[*Exit OCTAVIUS, ANTONY, and ARMY.*]

CASSIUS. Why, now blow wind, swell billow, and swim bark!
The storm is up, and all is on the hazard.°

BRUTUS. Ho, Lucilius, hark, a word with you.

[*LUCILIUS and (then) MESSALA stand forth.*]

LUCILIUS.   My lord?

[*BRUTUS and LUCILIUS converse apart.*]

CASSIUS. Messala!

70 MESSALA.   What says my general?

CASSIUS.   Messala,
This is my birthday; as this very day
Was Cassius born. Give me thy hand, Messala;
Be thou my witness that against my will
(As Pompey was)° am I compell'd to set
75 Upon one battle all our liberties.
You know that I held Epicurus strong,°   ⭐
And his opinion; now I change my mind,
And partly credit things that do presage.°
Coming from Sardis, on our former ensign°
80 Two mighty eagles fell, and there they perch'd,
Gorging and feeding from our soldiers' hands,
Who to Philippi here consorted° us.
This morning are they fled away and gone,
And in their steads do ravens, crows, and kites°
85 Fly o'er our heads, and downward look on us
As° we were sickly prey. Their shadows seem
A canopy most fatal, under which
Our army lies, ready to give up the ghost.

61 **schoolboy:** Octavius was twenty-one at the time of the battle.
62 **a masker and a reveler:** one who indulges in lavish entertainment and drunken feasts.

66 **stomachs:** appetite for battle.

68 **all is . . . hazard:** Everything is at stake.

74 **As Pompey was:** Pompey was persuaded against his better judgment to fight at Pharsalus, where he was defeated by Caesar.
76 **held Epicurus strong:** have been a firm believer of Epicurus (a Greek philosopher whose followers did not believe in omens).
78 **presage:** foretell the future.
79 **former ensign:** foremost banner.

82 **consorted:** accompanied.

84 **kites:** hawks. (All three birds are omens of death.)

86 **As:** As if.

| **Reading Strategy** | Evaluating Characters *What is Cassius's judgment of Antony? Do you agree?* **R** |

| **Literary Element** | Tragic Hero *How would you describe Cassius's feelings about the decision to approach Antony's army?* **L₃** |

| **Vocabulary** |

peevish (pē′vish) *adj.* irritable; bad-tempered

JULIUS CAESAR, ACT 5, SCENE 1   **853**

Differentiated Instruction

853

Teach

L Literary Element

Tragic Hero Answer: *Brutus does not believe in suicide and would not resort to it merely out of fear of the results of being captured. However, his pride is so great that he might be forced to kill himself rather than be sent as a bound prisoner through Rome.* **OL**

R1 Reading Strategy

Evaluating Characters

Answer: *They are determined to be optimistic about the day's events, even though they are also anxious. Their words demonstrate their respect and affection for one another.* **OL**

★ Political History

Legions and Phalanxes

The word *legion* refers to the army formation developed by the Romans in the early 300s B.C.E. In the 600s B.C.E. the Greeks introduced the *phalanx.* This was a formation in which spearmen wearing armor stood in a rectangle eight rows deep. The Romans improved on this formation by putting together three lines of small phalanxes, forming a legion. **AS**

 JULIUS CAESAR

MESSALA. Believe not so.

CASSIUS.   I but believe it partly,
90   For I am fresh of spirit, and resolv'd
        To meet all **perils** very constantly.°

BRUTUS. Even so, Lucilius.°

CASSIUS.   Now, most noble Brutus,
        The gods today stand friendly, that we may,
        Lovers in peace, lead on our days to age!°
95   But since the affairs of men rests still incertain,
        Let's reason with the worst that may befall.°
        If we do lose this battle, then is this
        The very last time we shall speak together:
        What are you then determined to do?

100 BRUTUS. Even by the rule of that philosophy
        By which I did blame Cato for the death
        Which he did give himself—I know not how,
        But I do find it cowardly and vile,
        For fear of what might fall, so to prevent
105   The time of life—arming myself with patience
        To stay the providence of some high powers
        That govern us below.°

CASSIUS.   Then, if we lose this battle,
        You are contented to be led in triumph
        Thorough the streets of Rome?

110 BRUTUS. No, Cassius, no. Think not, thou noble Roman,
        That ever Brutus will go bound to Rome;
        He bears too great a mind.° But this same day
        Must end that work the ides of March begun.
        And whether we shall meet again I know not;
115   Therefore our everlasting farewell take:
        Forever, and forever, farewell, Cassius!
        If we do meet again, why, we shall smile;
        If not, why then this parting was well made.

CASSIUS. Forever, and forever, farewell, Brutus!
120   If we do meet again, we'll smile indeed;

91 constantly: resolutely.

92 Even so, Lucilius: Brutus finishes his discussion with Lucilius.

93–94 The gods . . . age: May the gods remain friendly today, so that we, dear friends in peace with each other, may live to see old age.
96 Let's reason . . . befall: Let's consider the worst that can happen.

100–107 Even by the . . . below: Brutus says that according to his beliefs, suicide is cowardly (he refers to his father-in-law, Cato, who killed himself after Caesar's defeat of Pompey). He would endure his fate rather than cut short **(prevent)** his life because of what might happen.

110–112 Think not . . . mind: Brutus is suggesting that even though he rejects suicide, his pride would force him to commit such an act rather than allow himself to be paraded through the streets of Rome.

Literary Element Tragic Hero *What are Brutus's beliefs concerning honor?* **L**

Reading Strategy Evaluating Characters *How would you describe Brutus and Cassius as they say good-bye to each other?* **R1**

Vocabulary

peril (per′əl) *n.* exposure to harm or danger

Warrior on his death bed surrounded by mourners, 2nd century C.E. Artist unknown. Relief on a funeral stele. Museo Ostiense, Ostia, Italy.

Additional Support

GRAMMAR: Superlative Degree Point out the sentence "This was the noblest Roman of them all" in line 68 of scene 5. Explain that the modifier *noblest* is in the superlative degree: Brutus is being compared to all Romans.

The superlative degree is usually formed by adding *-est* or *most* to the modifier. Have students write five sentences describing characters in the play using the superlative degree. **OL**

If not 'tis true this parting was well made.

BRUTUS. Why then, lead on. O, that a man might know
The end of this day's business ere it come!
But it sufficeth that the day will end,
125   And then the end is known. Come, ho, away!

[BRUTUS, CASSIUS, and their ARMY withdraw to begin the battle.]

SCENE 2. The field of battle. Shortly afterward.

[Alarm. Enter BRUTUS and MESSALA.]

BRUTUS. Ride, ride, Messala, ride, and give these bills°   1 bills: written orders.
Unto the legions on the other side.°   2 legions on . . . side: other wing of
                                                                 troops (led by Cassius).

[Loud alarm.]

Let them set on at once; for I perceive
But cold demeanor° in Octavio's wing,   4 cold demeanor: lack of spirit.
5   And sudden push gives them the overthrow.
Ride, ride, Messala, let them all come down.

[They exit.]

SCENE 3. Another part of the battlefield. Several hours later.

[Alarms. Enter CASSIUS and TITINIUS.]

CASSIUS. O, look, Titinius, look, the villains° fly!   1 villains: Cassius's own troops (who are
Myself have to mine own turn'd enemy.°   retreating).
This ensign° here of mine was turning back;   2 Myself have . . . enemy: I have turned
I slew the coward, and did take it° from him.   to fighting my own men.
                                                               3 ensign: standard bearer.
                                                               4 it: the standard, or army flag.
5   TITINIUS. O Cassius, Brutus gave the word too early,
Who, having some advantage on Octavius,
Took it too eagerly. His soldiers fell to spoil,°   7 spoil: looting.
Whilst we by Antony are all enclos'd. [R2]

[Enter PINDARUS.]

PINDARUS. Fly further off, my lord, fly further off;
10   Mark Antony is in your tents,° my lord;   10 tents: camp.
Fly, therefore, noble Cassius, fly far off.

CASSIUS. This hill is far enough. Look, look, Titinius!
Are those my tents where I perceive the fire?

TITINIUS. They are, my lord.

CASSIUS.   Titinius, if thou lovest me,
15   Mount thou my horse, and hide° thy spurs in him   15 hide: dig.
Till he have brought thee up to yonder troops.
And here again, that I may rest assur'd
Whether yond troops are friend or enemy.

Big Idea Loyalty and Betrayal *Who has betrayed Cassius's army? What has Cassius done about it?* [B1]

JULIUS CAESAR, ACT 5, SCENES 2 AND 3   **855**

Teach

[B1] Big Idea

Loyalty and Betrayal
Answer: *A subordinate in Cassius's army was beginning to flee the battle. Cassius killed him and took the army flag from him.* **OL**

[R2] Reading Strategy

Reviewing Ask: What has happened since Brutus and Cassius parted? *(Brutus sent orders to Cassius to attack Antony while he attacks Octavius. Cassius's army has turned against him and retreated. Brutus's army has assumed victory over Octavius too soon and begun looting instead of helping Cassius fight Antony.)* **OL**

Reading in the Real World

Citizenship At its height, the Roman Empire included the majority of western Europe and a large portion of northern Africa. In addition to its military power, Roman contributions to future generations and future societies included its legal system; its architecture—especially roads, sewage systems, aqueducts, and dams; and its language and literature. Have students read current articles in magazines and newspapers and determine what contributions our society has made/is making toward future generations. Have students share their findings with the rest of the class. **OL**

Objectives
• To understand the concept of the tragic hero (SE)
• To evaluate characters (SE)
• To understand and use the superlative degree (TWE)

855

Teach

L1 Literary Element

Tragic Hero Answer: *That Brutus's men have suffered a disastrous loss.* **OL**

R1 Reading Strategy

Evaluating Characters

Answer: *Students may say that Cassius's remark indicates that he is a sensitive and affectionate friend.* **OL**

BI Big Idea

Loyalty and Betrayal

Answer: *Students may say that these words show that Romans honored what was brave and noble in their opponents. Cassius may have fatalistically believed that his own violence against Caesar destined Cassius for a violent death.* **OL**

TITINIUS. I will be here again, even with a thought.°

[*Exit.*]

20 **CASSIUS.** Go, Pindarus, get higher on that hill;
My sight was ever thick;° regard Titinius,
And tell me what thou not'st about the field.

[*PINDARUS goes up.*]

This day I breathed first: time is come round,
And where I did begin, there shall I end;
25 My life is run his compass.° Sirrah, what news?

PINDARUS. [*Above.*] O my lord!

CASSIUS. What news?

PINDARUS. Titinius is enclosed round about
With horsemen, that make to him on the spur,°
30 Yet he spurs on. Now they are almost on him.
Now, Titinius! Now some light.° O, he lights too!
He's ta'en!° [*Shout.*] And, hark, they shout for joy.

CASSIUS. Come down; behold no more.
O, coward that I am, to live so long,
35 To see my best friend ta'en before my face!

[*PINDARUS descends.*]

Come hither, sirrah.
In Parthia did I take thee prisoner,
And then I swore thee, saving of thy life,°
That whatsoever I did bid thee do,
40 Thou shouldst attempt it. Come now, keep thine oath;
Now be a freeman, and with this good sword,
That ran through Caesar's bowels, search° this bosom.
Stand not° to answer; here, take thou the hilts,°
And when my face is cover'd, as 'tis now,
45 Guide thou the sword. [*PINDARUS stabs him.*] Caesar, thou art reveng'd,
Even with the sword that kill'd thee. [*Dies.*]

PINDARUS. So, I am free; yet would not so have been,
Durst I have done my will. O Cassius,
Far from this country Pindarus shall run,
50 Where never Roman shall take note of him. [*Exit.*]

19 **even with a thought:** as quick as a thought.

21 **My sight . . . thick:** I have always been nearsighted.

25 **is run his compass:** has come full circle.

29 **make to . . . spur:** ride quickly toward him.

31 **some light:** some of them dismount.
32 **ta'en:** taken prisoner.

38 **swore thee . . . life:** made you swear when I saved your life.

42 **search:** penetrate.
43 **Stand not:** don't wait. **hilts:** sword handles.

Literary Element Tragic Hero *From the reports of Titinius and Pindarus, what does Cassius believe is happening?* **L1**

Reading Strategy Evaluating Characters *In your opinion, what does this remark indicate about the character of Cassius?* **R1**

Big Idea Loyalty and Betrayal *What Roman ideas about loyalty and destiny are suggested by this passage?* **BI**

856 UNIT 4 DRAMA

Additional Support

Skills Practice

WRITING: Vivid Verbs Messala pictures himself "thrusting" the report of Cassius's death into Brutus's ears. The vivid verb form (used as an adjective here) emphasizes the violent effect that the news will have. Have students locate three passages from Act 5 or other acts that use particularly vivid verbs. Have them write the sentences that include the verbs and then write sentences of their own using the verbs. Possible examples from Act 5 are scene 1, lines 39–40 ("Villains! you did not so, when your vile daggers *hack'd* one another

[*Enter* TITINIUS *and* MESSALA.]

MESSALA.   It is but change,° Titinius; for Octavius
    Is overthrown by noble Brutus' power,
    As Cassius' legions are by Antony.

TITINIUS.   These tidings will well comfort Cassius.

55   MESSALA.   Where did you leave him?

TITINIUS.   All **disconsolate**,
    With Pindarus his bondman, on this hill.

MESSALA.   Is not that he that lies upon the ground?

TITINIUS.   He lies not like the living. O my heart!

MESSALA.   Is not that he?

TITINIUS.   No, this was he, Messala,
60   But Cassius is no more. O setting sun,
    As in thy red rays thou dost sink tonight,
    So in his red blood Cassius' day is set! **L₂**
    The sun of Rome is set. Our day is gone,
    Clouds, dews,° and dangers come; our deeds are done!
65   Mistrust of my success° hath done this deed.

MESSALA.   Mistrust of good success° hath done this deed.
    O hateful error, melancholy's child,°
    Why dost thou show to the apt° thoughts of men
    The things that are not? O error, soon conceiv'd,
70   Thou never com'st unto a happy birth,
    But kill'st the mother that engend'red thee!°

TITINIUS.   What, Pindarus? Where art thou, Pindarus?

MESSALA.   Seek him, Titinius, whilst I go to meet
    The noble Brutus, thrusting this report
75   Into his ears; I may say "thrusting" it;
    For piercing steel and darts° envenomed
    Shall be as welcome to the ears of Brutus
    As tidings of this sight.

TITINIUS.   Hie you, Messala,
    And I will seek for Pindarus the while.

[*Exit* MESSALA.]

80   Why didst thou send me forth, brave Cassius?
    Did I not meet thy friends? and did not they
    Put on my brows this wreath of victory,
    And bid me give it thee? Didst thou not hear their shouts?

---

51 but change: only an exchange of fortune. (Pindarus was mistaken when he reported Titinius's capture—he had in fact come upon Brutus's troops.)

64 dews: Dews were considered unhealthy.
65 Mistrust of my success: Fear of my mission's outcome.
66 Mistrust of good success: Fear of how the battle would turn out.
67 O hateful . . . child: Messala suggests that Cassius's melancholy temperament caused him to misperceive events.
68 apt: ready (to be deceived).
71 the mother . . . thee: the mind that conceived the error.

76 darts: arrows.

Reading Strategy   Evaluating Characters   *What misunderstandings helped cause the death of Cassius? Who would you blame for his death?* **R₂**

Vocabulary

disconsolate   (dis kon′ sə lit) *adj.* dejected; mournful; unable to be comforted

---

Teach

L₂ Literary Element

Tragic Hero Ask: Could Cassius be considered a tragic hero? Why or why not? *(Even though Cassius was a high-ranking figure who fell from a great height, he was never presented as an admirable character. A true tragic hero has the potential for greatness, but fails due to some personal error or flaw.)* **OL**

R₂ Reading Strategy

Evaluating Characters
Answer: *Cassius mistakenly believed that Brutus's men had been routed and that his friend Titinius had been captured. Students may say they blame Pindarus and Titinius for providing bad information.* **OL**

---

in the sides of Caesar"); scene 1, line 64 ("Defiance, traitors, *hurl* we in your teeth"); scene 5, lines 24–25 ("It is more worthy to *leap* in ourselves than *tarry* till they push us"). **OL**

Reading in the Real World

Citizenship The last act of *Julius Caesar* illustrates the tragedy of war. Have students find articles about battles in the Civil War, World Wars I and II, and the Vietnam War. Have them compare what they read about real-life battles to the battle described in *Julius Caesar*. **OL**

Objectives
• To understand the concept of the tragic hero (SE)
• To evaluate characters (SE)
• To write using vivid verbs (TWE)

Teach

R1 Reading Strategy

Evaluating Characters
Answer: *Cassius is beloved by his soldiers, indicating that he was a good general.* **OL**

BI Big Idea

Loyalty and Betrayal
Answer: *Students may say that Brutus believes that his military setbacks are somehow being caused by Caesar.* **OL**

L Literary Element

Tragic Hero Answer:
Students may say that Brutus displays loyalty and affection for his friends, as well as determination and bravery in carrying on with battle. **Ask:** What is Brutus's major concern at this point in the play? *(Although he is grief-stricken by Cassius's death, he must focus on trying to win another battle.)* **OL**

Alas, thou hast **misconstrued** everything.
85 But hold thee, take this garland on thy brow;
Thy Brutus bid me give it thee, and I
Will do his bidding. Brutus, come apace,°
And see how I regarded° Caius Cassius.
By your leave, gods!—this is a Roman's part;°
90 Come, Cassius' sword, and find Titinius' heart. [*Dies.*]
[*Alarm. Enter* BRUTUS, MESSALA, LUCILIUS, VOLUMNIUS, YOUNG CATO, *and* STRATO.]

BRUTUS. Where, where, Messala, doth his body lie?

MESSALA. Lo, yonder, and Titinius mourning it.

BRUTUS. Titinius' face is upward.

CATO.°   He is slain.

BRUTUS. O Julius Caesar, thou art mighty yet!
95 Thy spirit walks abroad, and turns our swords
In our own proper° entrails. [*Low alarms.*]

CATO.   Brave Titinius!
Look, whe'er he have not crown'd° dead Cassius!

BRUTUS. Are yet two Romans living such as these?
The last of all the Romans, fare thee well!
100 It is impossible that ever Rome
Should breed thy fellow.° Friends, I owe moe° tears
To this dead man than you shall see me pay.
I shall find time, Cassius; I shall find time.
Come, therefore, and to Thasos° send his body;
105 His funerals shall not be in our camp,
Lest it discomfort° us. Lucilius, come,
And come, young Cato; let us to the field.
Labio and Flavio set our battles on.
'Tis three a'clock; and, Romans, yet ere night
110 We shall try fortune in a second fight.

[*They exit.*]

87 **apace:** quickly.

88 **regarded:** honored.

89 **By your . . . part:** Titinius asks the gods to pardon him because he is cutting his life short to fulfill a Roman's duty (part).

93 **Cato:** Brutus's brother-in-law, the son of Marcus Cato.

96 **our own proper:** our very own.

97 **Look . . . crown'd:** see how he has crowned.

101 **fellow:** equal. **moe:** more.

104 **Thasos:** an island near Philippi.

106 **discomfort:** dishearten.

Reading Strategy Evaluating Characters *What do you learn of Cassius's character from the reactions of Messala and Titinius to his death?* **R1**

Big Idea Loyalty and Betrayal *Why does Brutus invoke the name of Julius Caesar?* **BI**

Literary Element Tragic Hero *What admirable qualities does Brutus display in this scene?* **L**

Vocabulary

misconstrue (mis´kən strōō´) *v.* to misinterpret; to misunderstand

858 UNIT 4 DRAMA

Additional Support

Skills Practice

GRAMMAR AND LANGUAGE:
Affect* and *Effect Point out that *affect* is a verb meaning "to influence" or "to impress." *Effect* is a noun meaning "the result of an action" or a verb meaning "to accomplish." Have students use the correct word in each of the following sentences. This movie will (affect, effect) your emotions. *(affect)* The ultimate (affect, effect) of the law will be positive. *(effect)* **OL**

Base of the Column of Antoninus Pius, AD 138–161, Roman. Vatican State.
Viewing the Art: In what ways does this scene add to your understanding of the battles in this play? ★

SCENE 4. Another part of the battlefield. Shortly later.

[Alarm. Enter BRUTUS, MESSALA, (young) CATO, LUCILIUS, and FLAVIUS.]

> BRUTUS. Yet, countrymen, O, yet hold up your heads!°
>   *[They exit.]*
>
> CATO. What bastard doth not?° Who will go with me?
>   I will proclaim my name about the field.
>   I am the son of Marcus Cato,° ho!
> 5   A foe to tyrants, and my country's friend.
>   I am the son of Marcus Cato, ho!

[Enter SOLDIERS and fight.]

> LUCILIUS. And I am Brutus, Marcus Brutus, I;
>   Brutus, my country's friend; know me for Brutus!°

[YOUNG CATO is slain.]

1 Yet . . . heads: Brutus urges his troops to keep fighting.

2 What bastard doth not: Who among us was born so low that he doesn't?

4 Marcus Cato: Portia's father.

7–8 And I am . . . Brutus: Lucilius impersonates his leader to divert the enemy's attention from the real Brutus.

Reading Strategy   Evaluating Characters *What character traits does Shakespeare give the officers in the army of Cassius and Brutus?* **R2**

JULIUS CAESAR, ACT 5, SCENE 4   **859**

Differentiated Instruction

Multiple Intelligences—Bodily-Kinesthetic The stage directions in scene 4 read "Enter soldiers and fight" and "Young Cato is slain." Point out that sword fights in staged productions are carefully choreographed for effect and safety. Have students consult a drama instructor or a detailed book about stagecraft to research methods of choreographing battle scenes on the stage. Ask them to report their findings orally, including a demonstration if possible. **OL**

Objectives
• To understand the concept of the tragic hero (SE)
• To evaluate characters (SE)
• To distinguish between *affect* and *effect* (TWE)

Teach

R1 Reading Strategy

Evaluating Characters
Answer: *He shows that he is a shrewd and capable leader in realizing that a brave and resourceful soldier like Lucilius should be spared instead of being immediately punished for his deceit.* **OL**

★ Political History

Marcus Porcius Cato The character named Cato who dies in Act 5 is the son of Marcus Porcius Cato (95–46 B.C.E.), who was made praetor in 54 B.C.E. Marcus Cato supported Pompey in his quarrel against Julius Caesar. After Pompey's forces were defeated by Caesar, Cato committed suicide. He was considered a hero by those opposed to Julius Caesar's rule. This is probably the same Cato referenced earlier in the play as Portia's father. **AS**

O young and noble Cato, art thou down?
10   Why, now thou diest as bravely as Titinius,
    And mayst be honor'd, being Cato's son.

FIRST SOLDIER. Yield, or thou diest.

LUCILIUS.   Only I yield to die;
    There is so much that thou wilt kill me straight:°
    Kill Brutus, and be honor'd in his death.

15   **FIRST SOLDIER.** We must not. A noble prisoner!

[*Enter* ANTONY.]

    SECOND SOLDIER. Room, ho! Tell Antony, Brutus is ta'en.

    FIRST SOLDIER. I'll tell the news. Here comes the general.
    Brutus is ta'en. Brutus is ta'en, my lord.

    ANTONY. Where is he?

20   **LUCILIUS.** Safe, Antony, Brutus is safe enough.
    I dare assure thee that no enemy
    Shall ever take alive the noble Brutus;
    The gods defend him from so great a shame!
    When you do find him, or alive or° dead,
25   He will be found like Brutus, like himself.°

    ANTONY. This is not Brutus, friend, but, I assure you,
    A prize no less in worth. Keep this man safe,
    Give him all kindness; I had rather have
    Such men my friends than enemies. Go on,
30   And see whe'er Brutus be alive or dead,
    And bring us word unto Octavius' tent
    How everything is chanc'd.

    [*They exit.*]

SCENE 5. Another part of the field. Late in the day.

[*Enter* BRUTUS, CLITUS, DARDANIUS, VOLUMNIUS, *and* STRATO.]

    BRUTUS. Come, poor remains of friends, rest on this rock.

    CLITUS. Statilius show'd the torchlight,° but, my lord,
    He came not back. He is or ta'en or slain.

    BRUTUS. Sit thee down, Clitus; slaying is the word,
5   It is a deed in fashion.° Hark thee, Clitus. [*Whispering.*]

    CLITUS. What, I, my lord? No, not for all the world.

    BRUTUS. Peace then, no words.

13 There is . . . straight: You have good reason to kill me immediately.

24 or . . . or: either . . . or.
25 like himself: behaving like his noble self.

2 show'd the torchlight: signaled with a torch. (Statilius was sent out to see whether their camp was occupied by the enemy.)

5 It is . . . fashion: So many are being killed.

Reading Strategy Evaluating Characters *What traits does Antony show in his response to Lucilius's admission that he is not actually Brutus?* **R1**

Additional Support

Skills Practice

LISTENING AND SPEAKING: Vocal Expression Four great leaders have speeches near the end of *Julius Caesar.* Two are defeated and dying generals. The other two are victorious leaders who pay respects to the dead. Have groups of four students take turns reading the final speeches of Cassius (scene 3, lines 33–47), Brutus (lines 31–42 and 50–51), Antony (lines 68–75), and Octavius (lines 76–81). Encourage them to use their voices to express the characters' traits and attitudes at the end of the play. Then have them discuss what each speech says about its speaker. Which of the men seems noblest at the end? **OL**

CLITUS. I'll rather kill myself.

BRUTUS. Hark thee, Dardanius. [*Whispering.*]

DARDANIUS. Shall I do such a deed?

CLITUS. O Dardanius!

10 DARDANIUS. O Clitus!

CLITUS. What ill request did Brutus make to thee?

DARDANIUS. To kill him, Clitus. Look, he meditates.

CLITUS. Now is that noble vessel full of grief,
That it runs over even at his eyes.

15 BRUTUS. Come hither, good Volumnius; list° a word.

VOLUMNIUS. What says my lord?

BRUTUS. Why, this, Volumnius;
The ghost of Caesar hath appear'd to me
Two several° times by night; at Sardis once,
And this last night, here in Philippi fields.
20 I know my hour is come.

VOLUMNIUS. Not so, my lord.

BRUTUS. Nay, I am sure it is, Volumnius.
Thou seest the world, Volumnius, how it goes;°
Our enemies have beat us to the pit.°

[*Low alarms.*]

It is more worthy to leap in ourselves
25 Than tarry till they push us. Good Volumnius,
Thou know'st that we two went to school together;
Even for that our love of old, I prithee
Hold thou my sword-hilts, whilst I run on it.

VOLUMNIUS. That's not an office° for a friend, my lord.

[*Alarm still.*]

30 CLITUS. Fly, fly, my lord, there is no tarrying here.

BRUTUS. Farewell to you, and you, and you, Volumnius.
Strato, thou hast been all this while asleep;
Farewell to thee too, Strato. Countrymen,
My heart doth joy° that yet in all my life
35 I found no man but he was true to me.° **R₃**
I shall have glory by this losing day
More than Octavius and Mark Antony

---

15 **list:** hear.

18 **several:** separate.

22 **Thou seest . . . goes:** You see how things are going.
23 **pit:** a hole into which hunted animals are driven (also, a grave).

29 **office:** job.

34 **joy:** rejoice.
35 **no man . . . me:** no man to be unfaithful to me.

| **Literary Element** | Tragic Hero *What does Clitus think of Brutus?* **L** |

| **Reading Strategy** | Evaluating Characters *What judgments of Brutus might you form based on his request?* **R₂** |

JULIUS CAESAR, ACT 5, SCENE 5 **861**

Teach

L Literary Element

Tragic Hero Answer: *Clitus respects Brutus, calling him "noble" and "my lord." His refusal to kill Brutus may indicate he feels sorry for him.* **OL**

R₂ Reading Strategy

Evaluating Characters
Answer: *Answers will vary. Students should support their answers.* **OL**

R₃ Reading Strategy

Interpreting One of Brutus's last statements is "I found no man but he was true to me." Have students decide whether this is objectively true. If not, what does the statement say about Brutus? *(At least one person was not true to Brutus. Antony promised to support Brutus after Caesar's murder and then turned against Brutus. Students may say that Brutus is a very forgiving person if he chooses to ignore Antony's behavior. Or they might say he is naïve if he really does not recognize that this has occurred.)* **OL**

Differentiated Instruction

Research As indicated in the play, the defeat of Cassius and Brutus's army was mainly due to Mark Antony's military genius. After the victory, Antony claimed Rome's eastern provinces, leaving the western ones to Octavius. Have students research Antony's life after the defeat of Brutus and Cassius, including his political and romantic relationship with Cleopatra, Queen of Egypt. Suggest that they find out how Octavius eventually defeated Antony to become the first emperor of Rome. Have them present their research in oral or written reports or in a multimedia presentation. **AL**

Objectives
• To understand the concept of the tragic hero (SE)
• To evaluate characters (SE)
• To interpret and express literature vocally (TWE)

Teach

L1 Literary Element

Tragic Hero Answer: *Answers will vary. Students may say that Brutus's final speech reminds listeners that Brutus is admirable and had some good, honorable motivations for killing Caesar and fighting Antony. However, some error or flaw has ensured Brutus's downfall.* **OL**

⭐ Viewing the Art

Answer: *Students should name a scene from Act 5 and explain their choice, noting the dead on the ground and the soldiers watching—and perhaps fleeing—an unseen foe.* **AS**

By this vile conquest shall **attain** unto.°
So fare you well at once, for Brutus' tongue
40   Hath almost ended his life's history.
Night hangs upon mine eyes; my bones would rest,
That have but labor'd to attain this hour.

[*Alarm. Cry within, "Fly, fly, fly!"*]

CLITUS.   Fly, my lord, fly!

BRUTUS.   Hence! I will follow.

[*CLITUS, DARDANIUS, and VOLUMNIUS exit.*]

        I prithee, Strato, stay thou by thy lord,
45   Thou art a fellow of a good respect;°
        Thy life hath had some smatch° of honor in it.
        Hold then my sword, and turn away thy face,
        While I do run upon it. Wilt thou, Strato?

STRATO.   Give me your hand first. Fare you well, my lord.

36–38 I shall . . . unto: I shall have more glory from this defeat than Octavius and Antony will achieve from their ignoble victory.

45 respect: reputation.
46 smatch: taste.

Literary Element   Tragic Hero *What evidence in this scene suggests that Brutus is a tragic hero?* **L1**

Vocabulary

attain (ə tān´) *v.* to accomplish; to arrive at

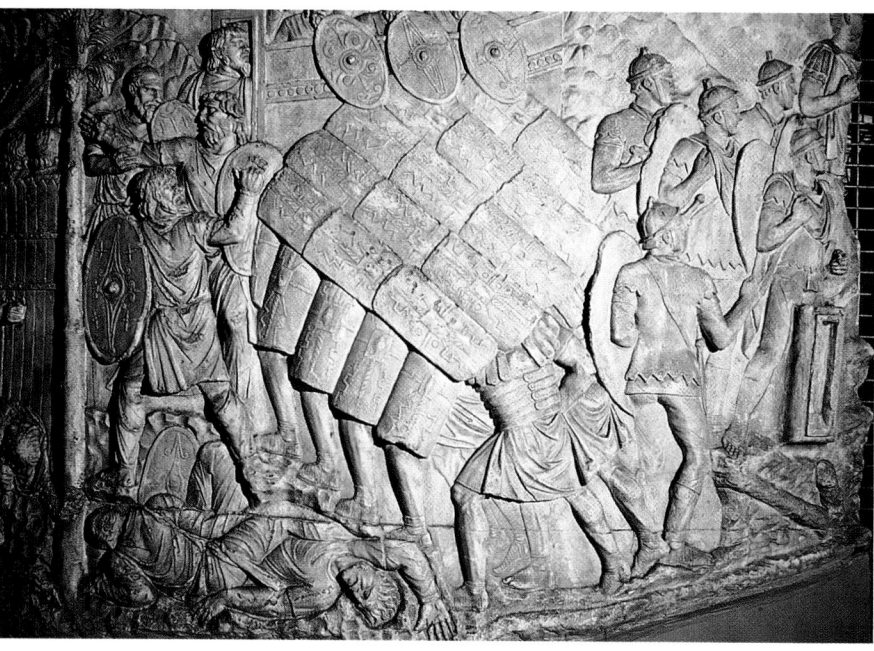

Trajan's Column, AD 112–113. Roman. Marble, approximately 68 m. Rome.
Viewing the Art: What scene from the play is depicted here? Why do you think so?

862   UNIT 4   DRAMA

Additional Support

Skills Practice

READING: Sequencing The important events of Act 5 occur rapidly and can be confusing when students try to recall the plot. Students can review the events of the battle in Act 5 by listing them in chronological order. Have students review Act 5 and summarize each event. Have them list the event summaries in numbered chronological order. For example, the first items on the list might be the following:

1. Brutus and Cassius come down from the hill and have an angry conference with Antony and Octavius.

50 BRUTUS. Farewell, good Strato. [*Runs on his sword.*] Caesar,
        now be still,
        I kill'd not thee with half so good a will.

[*Dies.*]

[*Alarm. Retreat. Enter* ANTONY, OCTAVIUS, MESSALA, LUCILIUS, *and
the* ARMY.]

    OCTAVIUS. What man is that?

    MESSALA. My master's man. Strato, where is thy master?

    STRATO. Free from the bondage you are in, Messala;
55   The conquerors can but make a fire of him;
        For Brutus only overcame himself,°
        And no man else hath honor by his death.

    LUCILIUS. So Brutus should be found. I thank thee, Brutus,
        That thou hast prov'd Lucilius' saying true.

60 OCTAVIUS. All that serv'd Brutus, I will entertain them.°
        Fellow, wilt thou bestow thy time with me?

    STRATO. Ay, if Messala will prefer° me to you.

    OCTAVIUS. Do so, good Messala.

    MESSALA. How died my master, Strato?

65 STRATO. I held the sword, and he did run on it.

    MESSALA. Octavius, then take him to follow thee,
        That did the latest° service to my master.

    ANTONY. This was the noblest Roman of them all;
        All the conspirators, save only he,
70   Did that they did in envy of great Caesar;
        He, only in a general honest thought
        And common good to all, made one of them.°
        His life was gentle,° and the elements
        So mix'd in him that Nature might stand up
75   And say to all the world, "This was a man!"°

    OCTAVIUS. According to his virtue let us use° him,
        With all respect and rites of burial.
        Within my tent his bones tonight shall lie,
        Most like a soldier, ordered honorably.°
80   So call the field to rest, and let's away,
        To part° the glories of this happy day. ✦

[*All exit.*]

Reading Strategy Evaluating Characters *Why are Brutus's dying words addressed to Caesar?* **R**

Big Idea Loyalty and Betrayal *Why does Octavius make this offer?* **BI**

Literary Element Tragic Hero *How does Antony claim that Brutus was different from the other conspirators? Do you agree with him? Explain.* **L₂**

---

56 **Brutus . . . himself:** only Brutus conquered himself.

60 **entertain them:** take them into my service.

62 **prefer:** recommend.

67 **latest:** last.

71–72 **He, only . . . them:** He joined them only with honorable intentions for the public good.
73 **gentle:** noble.
73–75 **His life . . . man:** The Elizabethans believed that four elements (earth, water, air, and fire) in the body determined a person's temperament. Antony says that in Brutus the elements were perfectly balanced.
76 **use:** treat.
79 **ordered honorably:** with all due honor.
81 **part:** divide.

Teach

R Reading Strategy

Evaluating Characters
Answer: *Brutus addresses Caesar's ghost, who appeared last night to signal Brutus's coming death and whose death is now avenged by Brutus's suicide.* **OL**

BI Big Idea

Loyalty and Betrayal
Answer: *Answers will vary. Students may say Octavius is honorable and recognizes Brutus's nobility and the nobility of the men's service to Brutus.* **OL**

L₂ Literary Element

Tragic Hero Answer: *Antony claims that the other conspirators attacked Caesar out of envy or greed, whereas Brutus did so out of a desire to improve the public good. Students may agree or disagree.* **OL**

✓CheckPoint

Use the CheckPoint questions on Presentation Plus! to check students' mastery of the selection. These questions can be used with interactive response keypads to get immediate student feedback.

---

2. Brutus and Cassius say good-bye to each other in case they are killed in battle.

3. The battle turns bad for Cassius when many of his soldiers abandon him and he sees Antony in his camp. **OL**

English Language Coach

Theme Have students discuss the four leaders who battle in Act 5, considering which of them has been loyal and which has betrayed others. Ask if it is possible to evaluate the leadership qualities of the characters based on this assessment. **EL**

Objectives
• To understand the concept of the tragic hero (SE)
• To improve reading comprehension by sequencing events (TWE)

Assess

1. Students may describe shock at the violence of war or sadness at the dying men.

2. (a) Cassius says that it is his birthday and that omen signals defeat for his army. (b) He may not want to dishearten Brutus or appear fearful.

3. (a) Cassius sends Titinius to check whether troops in the distance are friends or foes. Pindarus reports that Titinius has been taken prisoner. (b) The omens Cassius saw and his feeling that he would lose the battle

4. (a) that Caesar's spirit is mighty (b) Brutus believes that Caesar's spirit is defeating his army; he says his "spirit walks abroad, and turns our swords in our own proper entrails."

5. (a) Brutus commits suicide. (b) Octavius declares the battle ended, offers positions to Brutus's men, and prepares to divide the spoil with Antony. (c) Octavius's actions suggest that a good leader may be honorable in victory or defeat.

6. (a) In his funeral speech, Antony implied that Brutus was not honorable and had committed a crime in killing Caesar. Now he says Brutus is noble. (b) He realizes that Brutus acted unselfishly. He

RESPONDING AND THINKING CRITICALLY

Respond

1. What went through your mind as you finished reading this play? Explain.

Recall and Interpret

2. (a) What does Cassius confide to Messala before the battle? (b) Why do you think he refrains from making these remarks to Brutus?

3. (a) What event leads to Cassius's death? (b) What might have influenced Cassius to accept Pindarus's report?

4. (a) What does Brutus say about Caesar's spirit at Philippi? (b) In what way does Brutus believe that Caesar is affecting the events on the battlefield? Support your answer with evidence from Act 5.

5. (a) What happens to Brutus at the end of the play? (b) What actions does Octavius take at the end of the play? (c) What message do Octavius's actions suggest about honor and leadership?

Analyze and Evaluate

6. Compare Antony's speech at the end of the play with his discussion of Brutus at Caesar's funeral. (a) How have his views of Brutus changed? (b) Why have they changed?

7. Do you think that Antony and Octavius are motivated more by the desire for power or the wish to avenge Caesar's death? Explain, using evidence from the text.

8. What do you consider the most significant mistake committed at Philippi? Explain.

Connect

9. **Big Idea** Loyalty and Betrayal (a) What loyalties would you say are strongest in this play? (b) What betrayals seem the most damaging?

PRIMARY VISUAL ARTIFACT

Statues of Caesar

In the days before photography, how was the memory of a person's physical appearance kept alive? If you were a wealthy Roman, you very likely commissioned an artist to paint or sculpt the face of the person you wanted to remember. Artists also created busts, or sculpted representations of the upper part of the human figure. Julius Caesar understood the publicity value of a well-placed statue or bust. One figure of Caesar stood in a Roman temple with the inscription, "To the undefeated god." And to celebrate the opening of circus games, an ivory likeness of Caesar was carried through the streets. Many antique busts of Caesar survive.

1. What aspects of Caesar's character—as Shakespeare describes it—do you perceive in this bust?

2. Do you think that a piece of sculpture, such as this one, can convey certain human qualities better than a photograph can? Explain your answer in terms of this bust of Caesar.

Contemporary bust of Gaius Julius Caesar, c. 60–44 B.C. Capitoline Palace, Rome.

---

also has no more need to criticize Brutus; Brutus is dead.

7. Some students may see them as motivated by the desire for power, as seen in their struggles in Act 4 and on the battlefield. Others may say the men are motivated by the wish to avenge Caesar's death.

8. Students may mention Brutus and Cassius's coming to meet Antony and

Octavius; Brutus's claiming victory too soon; or Pindarus's telling Cassius that Titinius has been captured.

9. (a) Strong loyalties include that of Brutus to the people of Rome, Portia to Brutus, and Antony and Octavius to Caesar. (b) Damaging betrayals include Brutus's of Caesar and Antony's of Brutus.

LITERARY ANALYSIS

Literary Element Tragic Hero

Julius Caesar is an unusual tragedy because more than one character might be considered the **tragic hero.** Caesar is the title character, and his death is the central event in the play. However, the play focuses more on Brutus and ends with his death rather than Caesar's death.

1. (a)What is Caesar's tragic flaw? (b)What is Brutus's tragic flaw?

2. In your opinion, which character's fate is more tragic? Explain your choice.

Review: Theme

As you learned on page 338, the **theme** of a piece of literature is a dominant idea, often a universal message about life, that the writer communicates to the reader. Many works of literature have more than one theme.

Partner Activity Meet with a classmate to identify one important theme of *Julius Caesar*. Working with your partner, create a web diagram like the one below. First, write the theme in the central oval. Then fill in the outer ovals with evidence that supports the theme.

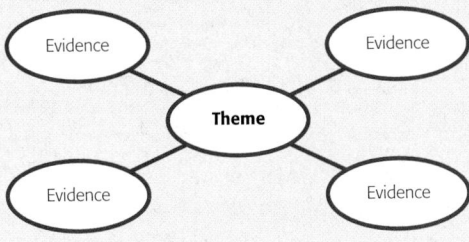

After you and your partner have completed your web diagram, discuss the following questions about theme:

1. (a)Is the theme you identified a **stated theme,** which is expressed directly, or an **implied theme,** which is revealed gradually? (b)If your theme is a stated theme, give examples from the text that demonstrate how it is expressed directly. If your theme is implied, give examples from the text where it is suggested or gradually revealed.

2. Is your theme related to the Big Idea of loyalty and betrayal? Explain.

READING AND VOCABULARY

Reading Strategy Evaluating Characters

When you **evaluate a character,** you make judgments about his or her abilities and qualities.

1. (a)Which aspects of Caesar's character do you consider admirable? (b)Which aspects of his character are you critical of? Explain.

2. (a)In the first half of the play, what judgments do you form about Cassius? (b)Do these judgments change as the play progresses? Explain.

3. Do you agree with Antony that all the conspirators, except Brutus, are motivated by envy? Support your opinion with examples from the play.

Vocabulary Practice

Practice with Analogies Choose the word that best completes each analogy below.

1. peevish : pleasant :: brief :
   a. sad   **b.** abbreviated   **c.** lengthy

2. danger : peril :: fear :
   a. terror   **b.** confidence   **c.** risk

3. joyous : victory :: disconsolate :
   a. loss   **b.** sadness   **c.** victory

4. improve : practice :: attain :
   a. mistake   **b.** fail   **c.** strive

5. bolster : undermine :: misconstrue :
   a. understand   **b.** confuse   **c.** steal

Academic Vocabulary

Here are two words from the vocabulary list on page R82. These words will help you think, write, and talk about the selection.

hierarchy (hī′ə rär′kē) *n.* the way people or things are ranked in an organization

aware (ə wâr′) *adj.* having knowledge of something

Practice and Apply

1. Describe the social **hierarchy** presented in Act 1 of *Julius Caesar.*

2. Is there evidence in the play that Caesar is **aware** of the plot against him? Explain.

AFTER YOU READ

Assess

Primary Visual Artifact

1. Students might suggest calmness, energy, pride, determination, or scorn.

2. Answers will vary. Students should support their answers.

Literary Element

1. (a) Pride.
   (b) Blind idealism or misplaced trust.

2. Students may say Brutus is the tragic hero because he experiences the greatest conflict throughout the play. His tragic end is due to his decisions and actions, while Caesar's is, to a large extent, out of his control.

Reading Strategy

1. (a) Students may say that Caesar's bravery and love for his friends and wife were admirable. (b) Students may identify Caesar's vanity as a fault.

2. (a) Students may say that at first, they believed Cassius to be disloyal, manipulative, and violent. (b) Students may say that as the play progressed, Shakespeare left open the possibility that Cassius conspired against Caesar out of genuine concern for the political future of Rome. Although Cassius may not always be an upstanding man, he is a sensitive and loyal friend to Brutus and to his troops.

3. Answers will vary. Students should support their answers.

Review: Theme

Remind students that a complex literary work may convey several themes.

Vocabulary

1. c **2.** a **3.** a **4.** c **5.** a

Academic Vocabulary

1. Caesar is at the top of the hierarchy, followed by the senators. Below them are the tribunes, represented by Flavius and Murellus. At the bottom of the hierarchy are the many commoners.

2. There is no evidence that Caesar was aware of a specific plot, but he was aware that he had enemies.

Assess

Writing About Literature

Students' essays should

- identify the play's strengths and weaknesses.
- include a plot summary.
- provide evidence from the play to support opinions.
- use vivid verbs where appropriate.

Listening and Speaking

Encourage students to rehearse facial expressions and physical gestures during the planning stage. After delivering their speeches, students may conclude that Shakespeare's speeches express timeless truths in unforgettable and rhythmic language.

Shakespeare's Language and Style

Among the many examples of vivid verbs, students might identify the following:
"The torrent *roar'd*, and we did buffet it / With lusty sinews," (p. 779)—*Roared* creates a powerful auditory image of a wild sea.
"I have seen tempests, when the scolding winds / Have *riv'd* the knotty oaks," (p. 786)—*Rived* is a more forceful and exact verb than *struck*.
"Let's *carve* him as a dish fit

Writing About Literature

Evaluate Author's Craft Write a review of *Julius Caesar*, describing the play's strengths and weaknesses and discussing its major themes. Include a brief plot summary. Answer questions such as the following: Are the characters interesting and believable? How effectively did Shakespeare organize the plot? Why might Shakespeare have chosen to tell this story? Use quotes from the play and references to specific scenes in your analysis.

As you draft, write from start to finish. Follow the writing plan shown here to keep on track.

Introduction	Begin with a general statement about *Julius Caesar*. Then move toward your thesis, or specific statement of your position concerning the play's strengths and weaknesses.
Body	Express your ideas about the effectiveness of the plot and characters. Provide evidence to support your ideas.
Conclusion	Briefly summarize your position and leave the reader with a final insight about the play.

After you complete your draft, meet with a peer reviewer to evaluate each other's work and to suggest revisions. Then proofread and edit your draft for errors in spelling, grammar, and punctuation.

Listening and Speaking

Julius Caesar is full of memorable passages, and all of them are intended to be read aloud. Every act has speeches and soliloquies that take on new meaning when delivered with understanding and expression. Get together with a partner and choose one speech from the play. Take turns reading the speech aloud several times. Discuss the best ways to use vocal tone and emphasis to bring out the speech's meaning. Then discuss what the speech says about its speaker. Why, do you think, are the speeches in Shakespeare's plays so celebrated? Share your thoughts with the class.

Literature Online **Web Activities** For eFlashcards, Selection Quick Checks, and other Web activities, go to www.glencoe.com.

Shakespeare's Language and Style

Choosing Vivid Verbs Verbs are words that describe action. Well-chosen verbs have the power to bring writing to life. When Cassius is trying to persuade Brutus to join the conspiracy in Act 1, for example, he creates a memorable image of a mighty Caesar, partly by using vivid verbs:

> *Why, man, he <u>doth bestride</u> the narrow world*
> *Like a Colossus, and we petty men*
> *<u>Walk</u> under his huge legs, and <u>peep</u> about*
> *To find ourselves dishonorable graves.*

According to Cassius, Caesar does not just stand on the world, he *bestrides* it; the word *bestride* suggests command and power. The "petty men" (meaning Cassius and Brutus) do not just *look* about, they *peep* from between Caesar's legs. *Peep* suggests that the men are timid and small.

Activity Find three examples from *Julius Caesar* of passages where vivid verbs help to make Shakespeare's writing lively and precise. For each example, briefly explain how Shakespeare's choice of verbs helps make the writing vivid and clear. Record your examples in a chart like the one below.

Vivid Verb	Effect
"It is more worthy to leap in ourselves / Than to tarry till they push us.: p. 861	Tarry is a more exact and vivid verb than its synonym wait."

Revising Check

Vivid Verbs Go back through your review of *Julius Caesar* and note places where more precise or vivid verbs would make your writing clearer or more lively. Revise your draft to improve your choice of verbs as needed.

---

for the gods," (p. 798)—*Carve* reflects Brutus's hope that the assassination of Julius Caesar will be a sacrifice, not butchery.
"It will *inflame* you, it will make you mad." (p. 827)—*Inflame* is a more powerful verb than *anger* and creates a strong image.

Literature Online

Web Activities Have students access the Web site for interactive activities that will help them assess their understanding of the selection.

PART 2

Portraits of Real Life

Marian Anderson, Singer, 1944. Laura Wheeler Waring. Oil on canvas. National Portrait Gallery, Smithsonian Institution, Washington, DC. ★

BIG IDEA

When reading a comedy, sometimes it is hard to know whether to laugh or cry. People find humor in the mistakes and misfortunes that comic characters experience. Maybe we laugh because we know that, in real life, we could be in their situations. Part 2 includes plays set in realistic situations. As you read, ask yourself: What is most interesting about realistic plays? Do they actually mirror life as it really is? **BI**

867

Analyzing and Extending

BI Big Idea

Portraits of Real Life
Write on the board this comment by Alfred Hitchcock: "Drama is life with the dull bits cut out." Introduce the idea that realistic modern drama mirrors real life, and comedy exposes incongruous aspects of modern life or human nature. Tell students that Part 2 will introduce dramas that are portraits of real life. Encourage students to contemplate this "big idea" and its relation to the artwork. **OL**

★ Viewing the Art

Marian Anderson, the subject of this painting, was a celebrated singer who lived from 1897 to 1993. She began her singing career in a church choir as a young girl, and by the 1920s was performing on such famous stages as Carnegie Hall. In the 1950s, Anderson became the first African American to sing with the famous New York Metropolitan Opera. **AS**

English Language Coach

Prefixes Point out to English language learners that knowing prefixes such as *mis-* (in *mistake* and *misfortune* of the epigraph) can help them define unfamiliar words. Explain that *mis-* means "wrong or bad," and show how it applies to *mistake*, meaning a "wrong idea," and *misfortune*, meaning "bad luck." **EL**

Differentiated Instruction

Previewing Guide less proficient students to preview plays before reading them. Remind students to notice titles, see how acts or scenes are organized, note the characters, and skim the text. Suggest that they predict what the play will be about and what the author's purpose will be. **BL**

Objectives for Part 2
• To understand the characteristics of major types of drama, including comedies and modern dramas (SE)
• To understand literary forms and terms such as drama, comedy, and dialogue (SE)
• To identify and describe the function of a dialogue and stage directions in drama (SE)

Part 2: Portraits of Real Life

Readability Scores Key
Dale-Chall/DRP/Lexile

PACING (DAYS)		SELECTIONS AND FEATURES	LITERARY ELEMENTS
STANDARD	**BLOCK**		
2 class sessions	1	LITERARY FOCUS: Comedy and Modern Drama, pp. 868–869	Comedy, SE pp. 868–869 Modern Drama, SE pp. 868–869 Analyzing Comedy, TWE p. 868
		A Marriage Proposal by Anton Chekhov, pp. 870–886	Farce, SE pp. 871–885 Irony, SE p. 885
		Grammar Workshop: Using Commas with Interjections and Parenthetical Expressions, p. 887	
2 class sessions	1	*That's Your Trouble,* by Harold Pinter, p. 888–892	Conflict, SE pp. 889, 890, 891, 892
		LITERARY PERSPECTIVE: "Writing for the Theater," by Harold Pinter **8.3/65/**1120, pp. 893–895	
1–2 class sessions	1	*Trifles* by Susan Glaspell, pp. 896–912	Stage Directions, SE pp. 897–911 Setting, SE p. 911
2–3 class sessions	1	COMPARING LITERATURE Theme Across Genres *The Ring of General Macías* by Josephina Niggli, pp. 916–931 **"Marked"** by Carmen Tafolla, p. 932 **"The Ring"** by Isak Dinesen **6.9/58/**940, pp. 933–939	Characterization, SE pp. 915–931 Irony, TWE p. 926
2–3 class sessions	2–3	Writing Workshop: Persuasive Speech, pp. 940–947	
1 class session		Speaking, Listening, and Viewing Workshop: Delivering a Persuasive Speech, pp. 948–949	
2 class sessions		Test Preparation and Practice, pp. 952–957	

About the Part

Part 2 covers comedy and modern drama.

READING AND CRITICAL THINKING	VOCABULARY	WRITING AND GRAMMAR	LISTENING, SPEAKING, AND VIEWING
Analyzing Dialogue, TWE p. 869		Quickwrite, SE p. 869	
Recognizing Author's Purpose, SE pp. 871–885	Word Origins, SE p. 885 Academic Vocabulary, SE p. 885	Evaluate Author's Use of Dialogue, SE p. 886	Set Design, SE p. 886 Tone in Dialogue, TWE p. 880
Analyzing Mood, SE pp. 889, 890, 891, 892	Practice with Connotation and Denotation, SE pp. 889, 892 Analyzing Slang, TWE p. 890	Analyzing Style, SE p. 892	
Compare and Contrast, TWE p. 894 Evaluating Argument, TWE p. 895			
Evaluating Characters, SE pp. 897–912 Making Judgments, TWE p. 908	Practice with Context Clues, SE p. 912 Word Origins, TWE p. 900	Evaluating Author's Craft, SE p. 912 Subordinating Conjunctions, TWE p. 902	Mock Trial, TWE p. 910 Telephone Skills, TWE p. 898
Analyzing Plot and Setting, SE pp. 915–931 Visualizing, TWE pp. 918, 938 Comparing and Contrasting, TWE p. 924	Word Parts, SE p. 915, 931 Connotation and Denotation, TWE p. 916	Writing a Journal Entry, SE p. 931 Compound Sentences and Predicates, TWE p. 928 Perfect Tense, TWE p. 934	Reading a Monologue, TWE p. 920
	Strong Words, TWE p. 944		Reading Speeches, TWE p. 943
	Troublesome Words, TWE p. 949		Appealing to Emotion and Logic, TWE p. 948
Rereading, TWE p. 952	Multiple-Meaning Words, TWE p. 955	Comma Usage, TWE p. 956	

Teach

BI Big Idea

Have students role-play dramatic and comic real-world situations, such as someone wrongly accused of a crime or an ordinary person mistaken for a world leader. Tell students that real-life conflicts like these are the material of modern drama and comedy. Note the experimentation and wide variation within these forms. **OL**

L Literary Element

Modern Drama Introduce Anton Chekhov as a Russian master dramatist who started the trend toward realism in drama. **Ask:** What makes the excerpt from Chekhov's *A Marriage Proposal* an example of modern drama? *(It portrays a realistic everyday conflict between two neighbors, Lomov and Natalia Stepanovna, over the ownership of a piece of land.)* Point out that the plot of a drama builds from a basic conflict such as the one depicted by Chekhov. Ask students how they think the play could turn into a comedy or a tragedy. **OL**

Comedy and Modern Drama

What are the elements of modern drama?

Modern drama often deals with everyday people. Unlike the passionate characters and life-and-death conflicts in *Julius Caesar*, characters in modern plays can be average people involved in personal, even petty conflicts.

Drama can be used as a synonym for *play*. Drama is traditionally separated into the subcategories of comedy and tragedy. The form of a drama can include acts—large divisions—and scenes—smaller divisions within acts.

Comedy In the broadest sense, a **comedy** is a play that is humorous and often has a happy ending. We are most familiar with comedies that are funny, such as those that poke fun at people's faults and limitations in order to teach something about human nature. There are different styles of comedy. **Farce** places flat characters in ridiculous situations. **Satire** exposes and ridicules vice or folly in individuals or societies. In this scene from Anton Chekhov's *A Marriage Proposal,* after fighting bitterly with Lomov, Natalia becomes hysterical upon learning that Lomov meant to propose to her.

> **CHUBUKOV.** The villain! The scarecrow!
> **NATALIA.** He's a monster! First he tries to steal our land, and then he has the nerve to yell at you.
> **CHUBUKOV.** Yes, and that turnip, that stupid rooster, has the gall to make a proposal. Some proposal!
> **NATALIA.** What proposal?
> **CHUBUKOV.** Why, he came to propose to you.
> **NATALIA.** To propose? To me? Why didn't you tell me before?
> **CHUBUKOV.** So he gets all dressed up in his formal clothes. That stuffed sausage, that dried up cabbage!
> **NATALIA.** To propose to me? Ohhhh! *[Falls into a chair and starts wailing.]* Bring him back! Back! Go get him! Bring him back! Ohhhh!

Modern Drama While satire and farce use deliberately unrealistic situations and characters, many modern plays find their humor and sadness in everyday life. Such plays can be either comedy or tragedy, but they often do not follow the traditional elements of these forms.

Trifles, for example, chronicles the day after Mrs. Wright is arrested on suspicion of murdering her husband. Though the play is about the Wrights and the circumstances of Mr. Wright's death, Mrs. Wright never appears onstage. The audience learns about her from the perspective of her neighbors and their reactions to items they find inside the Wrights' home.

Dialogue, stage directions, and props are important elements of drama.

Dialogue

Dialogue is the conversation characters have in a play. In the example below, Lomov and Natalia Stepanovna are the names of the characters who are speaking. Plays are written in this way, with the name of the character followed by what the character is to say.

> **NATALIA STEPANOVNA.** I hate to interrupt you, my dear Ivan Vassilevitch, but you said: "my Oxen Meadows." Do you really think they're yours?
> **LOMOV.** Why of course they're mine.
> **NATALIA STEPANOVNA.** What do you mean? The Oxen Meadows are ours, not yours!
> **LOMOV.** Oh, no, my dear Natalia Stepanovna, they're mine.
> **NATALIA STEPANOVNA.** Well, this is the first I've heard about it! Where did you get that idea?
> **LOMOV.** Where? Why, I mean the Oxen Meadows that are wedged between your birches and the marsh.
> **NATALIA STEPANOVNA.** Yes, of course, they're ours.

—Anton Chekhov, **from** *A Marriage Proposal* **L**

Skills Practice

LITERATURE: Analyzing Comedy
Ask students what they think the purpose of comedy is. *(To amuse and entertain)* Discuss the characteristics of comedy, including humorous dialogue and a happy ending. **Ask:** What indicates that *A Marriage Proposal* is a comedy? *(Natalia's attitude changes so abruptly after she hears Lobov was going to propose that it's very humorous.)* **Ask:** What indicates Chubukov, Natalia Stepanovna's elderly father, is a comic character? *(His names "turnip," "stupid rooster," "stuffed sausage," and "dried-up cabbage" are humorous.)* Help students

Stage Directions

Stage directions are the instructions that describe the appearance and actions of characters as well as details such as sets, props, costumes, sound effects, and lighting. Notice the references to actions, props, and lighting in the stage directions below. The stage directions appear in brackets.

MRS. HALE *[Crossing left to sink.]* I'd hate to have men coming into my kitchen, snooping around and criticizing. *[She arranges the pans under sink which the lawyer had shoved out of place.]*
MRS. PETERS. Of course it's no more than their duty. *[Crosses to cupboard upstage right.]*

—Susan Glaspell, **from** *Trifles*

Props

Short for the word *properties*, **props** are the objects and elements of a stage play or movie set. Props are often mentioned in stage directions.

COUNTY ATTORNEY. *[Rubbing his hands over the stove.]* Frank's fire didn't do much up there, did it? Well, let's go out to the barn and get that cleared up. *[The men go outside by upstage left door.]*

—Susan Glaspell, **from** *Trifles* **R**

Quickwrite

Try your hand at writing dialogue. Use a graphic organizer like the one below to briefly sketch two characters and identify a conflict between them. What would they say to each other?

OBJECTIVES
- Understand the characteristics of major types of drama, including comedies and modern dramas.
- Understand literary forms and terms such as drama, comedy, and dialogue.

- Identify and describe the function of dialogue and stage directions in dramatic literature.

Teach

R Reading Strategy

Analyzing Dialogue and Stage Directions Discuss why *Trifles* is a realistic modern drama. **Ask:** What is the function of the dialogue from *Trifles*? *(It realistically portrays an incident through the everyday conversations of neighbors. Here it builds suspense about a legal investigation.)* **Ask:** What is the function of the stage directions? *(Stage directions indicate movement off the stage and prompt actors to convey intended attitudes.)* **OL**

Quickwrite

Check students' graphic organizers for adequate development of character traits and a logical conflict.

Differentiated Instruction

to distinguish comedy from tragedy, as well as from farce and satire, which are similar. **Ask:** What would make *A Marriage Proposal* farce or satire? *(In a farce, the characters would be flat and not like real people. If the play is satire, it will poke fun at something in society.)* **OL**

Analyzing Dialogue Review with less proficient readers how characterization in drama consists almost entirely of dialogue. Have students describe Natalia from her spoken words. **Ask:** What makes Natalia's dialogue realistic? *(Her short phrases and expressions of emotion sound like a real person talking.)* **BL**

Objectives
- To understand the characteristics of major types of drama, including comedies and modern dramas (SE)
- To understand literary forms and terms such as drama, comedy, and dialogue (SE)
- To analyze comedy (TWE)

Focus

BELLRINGER

Bellringer Options
Selection Focus Transparency 37
Daily Language Practice
Transparency 78
Or write *peer pressure* on the board.
Ask: What are some things that people do as a result of peer pressure? Do adults sometimes give in to peer pressure?
Have students discuss the effects of peer pressure on teenagers and on adults. How is peer pressure different for the two age groups? How is it the same?

Literature Online

Author Search To expand students' appreciation of Anton Chekhov, have them access the Web site for additional information and resources.

A Marriage Proposal

MEET ANTON CHEKHOV

Anton Chekhov was an unlikely genius. Who would suspect that a provincial Russian doctor and the son of a grocer would revolutionize literature? As a doctor, Chekhov was trained to observe and analyze without judging his patients; in his writing, he applied the same principles to his characters. Chekhov's stories and plays focused on everyday life, illuminating the human flaws and the failures all people experience. His new approach helped popularize the Realist school of writing.

Humble Beginnings At age sixteen, Chekhov lived alone and supported himself. His father had gone bankrupt and rushed the rest of the family to Moscow to avoid debtor's prison. Chekhov remained at home to complete his studies while supporting himself as a tutor. Three years later, in 1879, Chekhov joined his family to study medicine on scholarship at the University of Moscow. He was deeply affected by his family's financial failure, and he would frequently turn to similar themes and situations in his plays and short stories.

"The dramatist is not meant to be a judge of his characters and what they say; his only job is to be an impartial witness."

—Anton Chekhov

While he was studying medicine, Chekhov began selling anecdotes and articles to comic magazines as a way of supporting his family. In these humorous pieces, critics see the revolutionary techniques that flourished in his later works. Chekhov focused on his characters' inner lives and their relationships with other characters.

A "Real" Writer By 1885 Chekhov had begun submitting his stories to more serious literary journals and magazines. In 1888 he won Russia's coveted Pushkin Prize for his short story collection *In the Twilight*.

In 1895 Chekhov decided to focus on playwriting. However, in 1896 his play *The Seagull* closed after only five performances. Chekhov was devastated, but his hopes were renewed when the play was restaged in 1898 at the Moscow Art Theatre. Following the successful second run of the *Seagull*, Chekhov continued to write plays for the Moscow Art Theatre, though he often disagreed with their interpretations of his work. He described his plays, including *Uncle Vanya*, *Three Sisters*, and *The Cherry Orchard*, as light social comedies. In them he presented sympathetic but weak characters who cannot seem to change their lives. He was annoyed by productions that staged the plays as melodramas.

Just as he began to experience great success on the stage, Chekhov's career was cut short. He had suffered from untreated tuberculosis for years, and the disease had weakened his heart. He died of a heart attack at the age of forty-four. His style of narrative realism would later influence nearly every major playwright of the twentieth century, including George Bernard Shaw, Samuel Beckett, Eugene O'Neill, and Tom Stoppard.

Anton Chekhov was born in 1860 and died in 1904.

Literature Online **Author Search** For more about Anton Chekhov, go to www.glencoe.com.

Selection Skills

Literary Elements
- Farce (SE pp. 871–885)
- Irony (SE p. 885)

Reading Skills
- Recognizing Author's Purpose (SE pp. 871–885)

A Marriage Proposal

Vocabulary Skills
- Word Origins (SE p. 885)
- Academic Vocabulary (SE p. 885)

Listening/Speaking/Viewing Skills
- Set Design (SE p. 886)
- Communicating Tone in Dialogue (TWE p. 880)

Writing Skills/Grammar
- Evaluate Author's Use of Dialogue (SE p. 886)
- Exclamation Points (TWE p. 878)
- Researching Background Information (TWE p. 874)
- Using Proper Adjectives (TWE p. 876)

Connecting to the Play

Chekhov's main character in *A Marriage Proposal* makes plans that he cannot seem to carry out. He battles both his pride and his imaginary ailments to try to achieve his goal. Before you read the play, think about the following questions:

- Think of a time when you carefully planned for something. Did any forces interfere with your plans?
- When the occasion you had planned for was over, how did you feel about your planning?

Building Background

Chekhov set this one-act play in the late 1800s in the Russian provinces, or countryside. At this time in Russia, the serfs had been freed, the Bolshevik revolution was less than twenty years away, and yet aristocratic farmers still depended on servants to do the work on their large estates. Although *A Marriage Proposal* is a light comedy, its depiction of Russia's aristocracy is consistent with a theme seen throughout Chekhov's work. Chekhov sensed that the "old" Russia was dying. Therefore, he often shows aristocrats as incompetent and frustrated, as he does with the petty characters in *A Marriage Proposal*.

Setting Purposes for Reading

Big Idea Portraits of Real Life

As you read this play, notice how Chekhov's characters' speech and actions mimic those in real life.

Literary Element Farce

A **farce** is a type of comedy with stereotyped characters in ridiculous situations. In a farce, an author uses physical action, exaggeration, improbable events, and surprises to make the audience laugh. Farce is one way to make fun of human traits and social customs. As you read, try to determine which traits and customs Chekhov is highlighting.

- See Literary Terms Handbook, p. R6.

Literature Online **Interactive Literary Elements Handbook** To review or learn more about the literary elements, go to www.glencoe.com.

OBJECTIVES
In studying this selection, you will focus on the following:
- identifying the elements of farce
- recognizing the author's purpose

Reading Strategy Recognizing Author's Purpose

Authors often write for a particular purpose: to entertain, to inform or teach a lesson, to tell a story, to try to persuade readers to accept an idea, or for a variety of other purposes. As you read *A Marriage Proposal*, see if you can determine why the author chose to tell this story in this particular way.

....

Reading Tip: Noting Details Use a graphic organizer like the one below to help you keep track of details and draw conclusions about them.

Details	Conclusions
Chubukov repeats the phrase "and so forth" often.	Chekhov uses this character trait to show how Chubukov speaks without purpose, repeating these words that really have no meaning.

Vocabulary

pompous (pom′ pəs) *adj.* showing an exaggerated sense of self-importance; p. 873 *The shopkeeper's attitude was pompous, so I left.*

affable (af′ ə bəl) *adj.* friendly and pleasant; p. 873 *Grace has friends because she is so affable.*

hypochondriac (hī′ pə kon′drē ak′) *n.* one whose worry over health is so great that it brings on the imagined symptoms of an illness; p. 873 *Doctors see their fair share of hypochondriacs.*

impudence (im′pyə dəns) *n.* speech or behavior that is aggressively forward or rude; p. 877 *Arnie showed his impudence when he cut in front of those who had been standing in the lunch line.*

oblivious (ə bliv′ ē əs) *adj.* unmindful or unaware; not noticing; p. 882 *Ana and Maria were oblivious to their teacher's desire to start class.*

- analyzing irony
- writing to evaluate an author's craft

ANTON CHEKHOV **871**

Focus

Summary

Lomov tells Chubukov that he wants to marry Chubukov's daughter Natalia. Chubukov is overjoyed. When Natalia comes in, she and Lomov argue over some land and Lomov leaves, upset. When Natalia finds out he was going to propose, she makes her father go after him. They argue again, over whose dog is better, and Lomov faints. When he comes to, Chubukov pronounces the couple engaged; they continue their argument.

Literature Online

Literary Elements Have students access the Web site to improve their understanding of farce.

V Vocabulary

Vocabulary File

Say: Add these words and definitions to your vocabulary file. For each word, include a sentence that gives you an example of how to use the word. **OL** Students with English language needs should include the pronunciations of these words in their files. **EL**

Selection Resources

Print Materials
- Unit 4 Resources (Fast File), pp. 45–47
- Leveled Vocabulary Development, p. 65
- Selection and Unit Assessments, pp. 153–154
- Selection Quick Checks, p. 77

Transparencies
- Bellringer Options Transparencies:
  Selection Focus Transparency 37
  Daily Language Practice Transparency 78
- Literary Elements Transparency 77

Technology
- TeacherWorks Plus™ CD-ROM
- StudentWorks Plus™ CD-ROM
- Presentation Plus!™ CD-ROM
- Literature Online, glencoe.com
- Online Student Edition, mhln.com
- ExamView® Assessment Suite CD-ROM
- Vocabulary PuzzleMaker CD-ROM
- Listening Library, disc 2 track 9

Golden Autumn in the Village, 1889. Isaak Ilyich Levitan. Oil on canvas, 43 x 67.2 cm. State Russian Museum, St. Petersburg. ★

A Marriage Proposal

Anton Chekhov
Translated by Theodore Hoffman

CHARACTERS

STEPAN STEPANOVITCH CHUBUKOV
(ste pän′ ste pä′nô vich choo boo′ kôf):
a landowner; elderly, **pompous** but **affable**

IVAN VASSILEVITCH LOMOV
(i vän′ vä sil′ yich lô′môf):
a landowner and Chubukov's neighbor;
healthy, but a **hypochondriac**; nervous,
suspicious

NATALIA STEPANOVNA (nä täl′yə ste pä nôv′nə):
Chubukov's daughter; twenty-five but still
unmarried

SCENE: Chubukov's mansion—the living room

[*LOMOV enters, formally dressed in evening
jacket, white gloves, top hat. He is nervous
from the start.*]

Reading Strategy Recognizing Author's Purpose *Why
do you think Chekhov chose to describe Natalia in this way?* **R₁**

Vocabulary

pompous (pom′pəs) *adj.* showing an exaggerated sense
of self-importance
affable (af′ə bəl) *adj.* friendly and pleasant
hypochondriac (hī′pə kon′dr ak′) *n.* one whose
worry over his or her health is so great that it brings on
the imagined symptoms of an illness

ANTON CHEKHOV **873**

Teach

R₁ Reading Strategy

Recognizing Author's Purpose

Answer: *In Chekhov's time,
it was probably unusual for
a woman of this age to be
unmarried. By including this
information, Chekhov communicates to the audience the focus
of his play.* **OL**

R₂ Reading Strategy

Questioning

Ask: What details in the cast
of characters indicate that the
play takes place in a different
era and/or culture? *(Students
should note, in addition to
the Russian names, the men's
descriptions as landown-
ers and the description of
Natalia as "twenty-five but still
unmarried.")* **OL**

CheckPoint

Use the CheckPoint questions
on Presentation Plus! to monitor students' comprehension.
These questions can be used
with interactive response keypads for immediate student
feedback.

Differentiated Instruction

Multiple Intelligences—Linguistic
Point out that Chekhov's stage directions on this page give no details about
the room in which the play takes place.
Encourage linguistic learners to write
stage directions for the setting. Have
students write more detailed stage directions for the play that specify how a
stage set would be decorated. Encourage
them to consider the mood and the
economic class that should be represented. Then have them specify how the
walls, floors, and furniture should look
to reflect these characteristics. Students
may wish to use stage directions from
another play as a model. **AL**

Objectives
• To recognize the author's purpose
(SE)
• To research Russian writers (TWE)

Teach

BI **Big Idea**

Portraits of Real Life

Answer: *Lomov and Chubukov each have their own ways of speaking and their own vocabulary and expressions, just like real people. For instance, Chubukov says "and so forth" repeatedly, and Lomov stumbles when he speaks, never seeming to say exactly what he means.* **OL**

★ Viewing the Art

Answer: *Students may say that rural life provided few opportunities for people. People were stuck in a state of poverty. Students may feel sympathetic toward the characters in the play.* **AS**

CHUBUKOV. [*Rising.*] Well, look who's here! Ivan Vassilevitch! [*Shakes his hand warmly.*] What a surprise, old man! How are you?

LOMOV. Oh, not too bad. And you?

CHUBUKOV. Oh, we manage, we manage. Do sit down, please. You know, you've been neglecting your neighbors, my dear fellow. It's been ages. Say, why the formal dress? Tails, gloves, and so forth. Where's the funeral, my boy? Where are you headed?

LOMOV. Oh, nowhere. I mean, here; just to see you, my dear Stepan Stepanovitch.

CHUBUKOV. Then why the full dress, old boy? It's not New Year's, and so forth.

LOMOV. Well, you see, it's like this. I have come here, my dear Stepan Stepanovitch, to bother you with a request. More than once, or twice, or more than that, it has been my privilege to apply to you for assistance in things, and you've always, well, responded. I mean, well, you have. Yes. Excuse me, I'm getting all mixed up. May I have a glass of water, my dear Stepan Stepanovitch? [*Drinks.*]

CHUBUKOV. [*Aside.*] Wants to borrow some money. Not a chance! [*Aloud.*] What can I do for you my dear friend?

LOMOV. Well, you see, my dear Stepanitch. . . . Excuse me, I mean Stepan my Dearovitch. . . . No, I mean, I get all confused, as you can see. To make a long story short, you're the only one who can help me. Of course, I don't deserve it, and there's no reason why I should expect you to, and all that.

Big Idea Portraits of Real Life *How would you describe Lomov's manner here?* **BI**

Return from the Fair, 1883. Illarion Mikhailovich Pryanishnikov. Oil on canvas, 48.5 x 71.5 cm. State Russian Museum, St. Petersburg.

Viewing the Art: What does this painting suggest to you about rural life in Russia in the 1800s? How does this view affect your understanding of the play? ★

874 UNIT 4 DRAMA

Additional Support

Skills Practice

RESEARCH: Historical Background
Alexander II became czar of Russia in 1855. He freed the country's serfs who were forced to work the land owned by the wealthy. However, when the next two czars did not do enough to improve the conditions of the peasants, they revolted in 1917. Have students research the history of Russia from the mid-1800s through the formation of the U.S.S.R. in 1922. You may wish to have students work in groups and research one of the following topics: causes of the Revolution, the Revolution itself, and the reformation of the country after the Revolution. **OL**

CHUBUKOV. Stop beating around the bush! Out with it!

LOMOV. In just a minute. I mean, now, right now. The truth is, I have come to ask the hand.

. . . I mean, your daughter, Natalia Stepanovna, I, I want to marry her!

CHUBUKOV. [*Overjoyed.*] Great heavens! Ivan Vassilevitch! Say it again!

LOMOV. I have come humbly to ask for the hand. . . .

CHUBUKOV. [*Interrupting.*] You're a prince! I'm overwhelmed, delighted, and so forth. Yes, indeed, and all that! [*Hugs and kisses LOMOV.*] This is just what I've been hoping for. It's my fondest dream come true. [*Sheds a tear.*] And, you know, I've always looked upon you, my boy, as if you were my own son. May God grant to both of you His Mercy and His Love, and so forth. Oh, I have been wishing for this. . . . But why am I being so idiotic? It's just that I'm off my rocker with joy, my boy! Completely off my rocker! Oh, with all my soul I'm. . . . I'll go get Natalia, and so forth.

LOMOV. [*Deeply moved.*] Dear Stepan Stepanovitch, do you think she'll agree?

CHUBUKOV. Why, of course, old friend. Great heavens! As if she wouldn't! Why she's crazy for you! Good God! Like a love-sick cat, and so forth. Be right back. [*Leaves.*]

LUMOV. It's cold. I'm gooseflesh all over, as if I had to take a test. But the main thing is, to make up my mind, and keep it that way. I mean, if I take time out to think, or if I hesitate, or talk about it, or have ideals, or wait for real love, well, I'll just never get married! Brrrr, it's cold! Natalia Stepanovna is an excellent housekeeper. She's not too bad looking. She's had a good education.

What more could I ask? Nothing. I'm so nervous, my ears are buzzing. [*Drinks.*] Besides, I've just got to get married. I'm thirty-five already. It's sort of a critical age. I've got to settle down and lead a regular life. I mean, I'm always getting palpitations,[1] and I'm nervous, and I get upset so easy. Look, my lips are quivering, and my eyebrow's twitching. The worst thing is the night. Sleeping. I get into bed, doze off, and, suddenly, something inside me jumps. First my head snaps, and then my shoulder blade, and I roll out of bed like a lunatic and try to walk it off. Then I try to go back to sleep, but, as soon as I do, something jumps again! Twenty times a night, sometimes. . . .

[*NATALIA STEPANOVNA enters.*]

NATALIA. Oh, it's only you. All Papa said was: "Go inside, there's a merchant come to collect his goods." How do you do, Ivan Vassilevitch?

LOMOV. How do you do, dear Natalia Stepanovna?

NATALIA. Excuse my apron, and not being dressed. We're shelling peas. You haven't been around lately. Oh, do sit down. [*They do.*] Would you like some lunch?

LOMOV. No thanks, I had some.

NATALIA. Well, then smoke if you want. [*He doesn't.*] The weather's nice today . . . but yesterday, it was so wet the workmen couldn't get a thing done. Have you got much hay in? I felt so greedy I had a whole field done, but now I'm not sure I was right. With the rain it could rot, couldn't it? I should have waited. But why are you so dressed up? Is there a dance or something? Of course, I must say you look splendid, but. . . . Well, tell me, why are you so dressed up?

---

1. If Lomov does in fact get *palpitations*, he experiences rapid, irregular heartbeats, which are often caused by stress or nervousness.

Reading Strategy Recognizing Author's Purpose *Why does Chekhov have Chubukov respond in this way?* **R1**

Literary Element Farce *What makes Chubukov's reaction to Lomov's request an example of farce?* **L**

Reading Strategy Recognizing Author's Purpose *How do you think Chekhov wants the audience to feel about Lomov?* **R2**

ANTON CHEKHOV **875**

Teach

BI₁ **Big Idea**

Portraits of Real Life

Answer: *He is nervous and unsure of how Natalia will respond, so he will not ask her directly. He also seems to want to establish the connection between their families first.* **OL**

BI₂ **Big Idea**

Portraits of Real Life

Answer: *Students may conclude that the aristocrats lived on land that had belonged to their families for generations and that land was a source of wealth and pride.* **OL**

LOMOV. [*Excited.*] Well, you see, my dear Natalia Stepanovna, the truth is, I made up my mind to ask you to . . . well, to, listen to me. Of course, it'll probably surprise you and even maybe make you angry, but. . . . [*Aside.*] It's so cold in here!

NATALIA. Why, what do you mean? [*A pause.*] Well?

LOMOV. I'll try to get it over with. I mean, you know, my dear Natalia Stepanovna that I've known, since childhood, even, known, and had the privilege of knowing, your family. My late aunt, and her husband, who, as you know, left me my estate, they always had the greatest respect for your father, and your late mother. The Lomovs and the Chubukovs have always been very friendly, you might even say affectionate. And, of course, you know, our land borders on each other's. My Oxen Meadows touch your birch grove. . . .

NATALIA. I hate to interrupt you, my dear Ivan Vassilevitch, but you said: "my Oxen Meadows." Do you really think they're yours?

LOMOV. Why of course they're mine.

NATALIA. What do you mean? The Oxen Meadows are ours, not yours!

LOMOV. Oh, no, my dear Natalia Stepanovna, they're mine.

NATALIA. Well, this is the first I've heard about it! Where did you get that idea?

LOMOV. Where? Why, I mean the Oxen Meadows that are wedged between your birches and the marsh.

NATALIA. Yes, of course, they're ours.

LOMOV. Oh, no, you're wrong, my dear Natalia Stepanovna, they're mine.

NATALIA. Now, come, Ivan Vassilevitch! How long have they been yours?

LOMOV. How long! Why, as long as I can remember!

NATALIA. Well, really, you can't expect me to believe that!

LOMOV. But, you can see for yourself in the deed, my dear Natalia Stepanovna. Of course, there was once a dispute about them, but everyone knows they're mine now. There's nothing to argue about. There was a time when my aunt's grandmother let your father's grandfather's peasants use the land, but they were supposed to bake bricks for her in return. Naturally, after a few years they began to act as if they owned it, but the real truth is. . . .

NATALIA. That has nothing to do with the case! Both my grand-father and my great-grandfather said that their land went as far as the marsh, which means that the Meadows are ours! There's nothing whatever to argue about. It's foolish.

LOMOV. But I can show you the deed, Natalia Stepanovna.

NATALIA. You're just making fun of me. . . . Great Heavens! Here we have the land for hundreds of years, and suddenly you try to tell us it isn't ours. What's wrong with you, Ivan Vassilevitch? Those meadows aren't even fifteen acres, and they're not worth three hundred rubles, but I just can't stand unfairness! I just can't stand unfairness!

LOMOV. But, you must listen to me. Your father's grandfather's peasants, as I've already tried to tell you, they were supposed to bake bricks for my aunt's grandmother. And my aunt's grandmother, why, she wanted to be nice to them. . . .

NATALIA. It's just nonsense, this whole business about aunts and grandfathers and grandmothers. The Meadows are ours! That's all there is to it!

LOMOV. They're mine!

Big Idea Portraits of Real Life *Why do you suppose it is taking so long for Lomov to ask Natalia his question?* **BI₁**

Big Idea Portraits of Real Life *What does Natalia and Lomov's conversation tell you about the life of the Russian aristocracy in the nineteenth century?* **BI₂**

Additional Support

Skills Practice

GRAMMAR : Proper Adjectives
Remind students that some adjectives are formed from proper nouns and should be capitalized. Have students write these sentences using correct capitalization.

1. Some american cities are along the pacific coast. *(American, Pacific)*

2. The students viewed african and asian art at the museum. *(African, Asian)*

3. Leo Tolstoy and Anton Chekhov were both russian writers, but Victor Hugo was a french writer. *(Russian, French)*

4. I love italian food, but my brothers love chinese food. *(Italian, Chinese)* **OL**

NATALIA. Ours! You can go on talking for two days, and you can put on fifteen evening coats and twenty pairs of gloves, but I tell you they're ours, ours, ours!

LOMOV. Natalia Stepanovna, I don't want the Meadows! I'm just acting on principle. If you want, I'll give them to you.

NATALIA. I'll give them to *you!* Because they're ours! And that's all there is to it! And if I may say so, your behavior, my dear Ivan Vassilevitch, is very strange. Until now, we've always considered you a good neighbor, even a friend. After all, last year we lent you our threshing machine, even though it meant putting off our own threshing until November. And here you are treating us like a pack of gypsies. Giving me my own land, indeed! Really! Why that's not being a good neighbor. It's sheer <u>impudence</u>, that's what it is. . . .

LOMOV. Oh, so you think I'm just a land-grabber? My dear lady, I've never grabbed anybody's land in my whole life, and no one's going to accuse me of doing it now! [*Quickly walks over to the pitcher and drinks some more water.*] The Oxen Meadows are mine!

NATALIA. That's a lie. They're ours!

LOMOV. Mine!

NATALIA. A lie! I'll prove it. I'll send my mowers out there today!

LOMOV. What?

NATALIA. My mowers will mow it today!

LOMOV. I'll kick them out!

NATALIA. You just dare!

LOMOV. [*Clutching his heart.*] The Oxen Meadows are mine! Do you understand? Mine!

Vocabulary

impudence (im′pyə dəns) *n.* speech or behavior that is aggressively forward or rude

Literary Element Farce *What makes Chubukov's statement here ridiculous?* **L1**

NATALIA. Please don't shout! You can shout all you want in your own house, but here I must ask you to control yourself.

LOMOV. If my heart wasn't palpitating the way it is, if my insides weren't jumping like mad, I wouldn't talk to you so calmly. [*Yelling.*] The Oxen Meadows are mine!

NATALIA. Ours!

LOMOV. Mine!

NATALIA. Ours!

LOMOV. Mine!

[*Enter CHUBUKOV.*]

CHUBUKOV. What's going on? Why all the shouting?

NATALIA. Papa, will you please inform this gentleman who owns the Oxen Meadows, he or we?

CHUBUKOV. [*To LOMOV.*] Why, they're ours, old fellow.

LOMOV. But how can they be yours, my dear Stepan Stepanovitch? Be fair. Perhaps my aunt's grandmother did let your grandfather's peasants work the land, and maybe they did get so used to it that they acted as if it was their own, but. . . .

CHUBUKOV. Oh, no, no . . . my dear boy. You forget something. The reason the peasants didn't pay your aunt's grandmother, and so forth, was that the land was disputed, even then. Since then it's been settled. Why, everyone knows it's ours.

LOMOV. I can prove it's mine.

CHUBUKOV. You can't prove a thing, old boy.

LOMOV. Yes, I can!

CHUBUKOV. My dear lad, why yell like that? Yelling doesn't prove a thing. Look, I'm not after anything of yours, just as I don't intend to give up anything of mine. Why should I? Besides, if you're going to keep arguing about it, I'd just as soon give the land to the peasants, so there!

Literary Element Farce *How does Chekhov make Lomov's behavior farcical here?* **L2**

L1 Literary Element

Farce
Answer: *The stage directions emphasize Lomov's exaggeration of his physical symptoms, as in "clutching his heart." Lomov is constantly describing his deteriorating physical state.* **OL**

L2 Literary Element

Farce
Answer: *Chubukov's argument is that "everyone knows" the land is his. However, it is clear that Lomov does not know this; in fact, Lomov thinks that the land is his.* **OL**

⭐ Writer's Technique

Dialogue Remind students that in a play, plot, character, and theme are revealed through the characters' dialogue. Chekhov characterizes Natalia based on her dialogue with Lomov. As she speaks, the audience recognizes that she is independent, strong-willed, assertive, and straightforward. The audience also learns that she has no special feelings for Lomov and that she sees him as nothing more than a neighbor. **AS**

English Language Coach

Idioms The play contains some idioms that you may wish to review with English language learners. Write the following idiomatic expressions on the board. Have students write what they think each idiom means. Check the meanings with them.

"Stop beating around the bush!" (p. 875)
"It's just that I'm off my rocker with joy" (p. 875)
"Why she's crazy for you!" (p. 875)
"I'm gooseflesh all over . . ."(p. 875) **EL**

Objectives
• To identify the elements of farce (SE)
• To use proper adjectives correctly (TWE)

R Reading Strategy

Recognizing Author's Purpose

Answer: *Chekhov includes this detail in order to make the argument and the characters even more ridiculous. Lomov tells Chubukov to leave his family out of the argument, but then he attacks Chubukov's family.* **OL**

L Literary Element

Farce

Answer: *It is clear that Lomov is overreacting about his health. On one hand, he believes that he needs a wife to ease his nervous concerns, and on the other, he is allowing his fictional conditions to interfere with his plans to propose to Natalia.* **OL**

LOMOV. There nothing! Where do you get the right to give away someone else's property?

CHUBUKOV. I certainly ought to know if I have the right or not. And you had better realize it, because, my dear young man, I am not used to being spoken to in that tone of voice, and so forth. Besides which, my dear young man, I am twice as old as you are, and I ask you to speak to me without getting yourself into such a tizzy, and so forth!

LOMOV. Do you think I'm a fool? First you call my property yours, and then you expect me to keep calm and polite! Good neighbors don't act like that, my dear Stepan Stepanovitch. You're no neighbor, you're a land grabber!

CHUBUKOV. What was that? What did you say?

NATALIA. Papa, send the mowers out to the meadows at once!

CHUBUKOV. What did you say, sir?

NATALIA. The Oxen Meadows are ours, and we'll never give them up, never, never, never, never!

LOMOV. We'll see about that. I'll go to court. I'll show you!

CHUBUKOV. Go to court? Well, go to court, and so forth! I know you, just waiting for a chance to go to court, and so forth. You pettifogging[2] cheater, you! All of your family is like that. The whole bunch of them!

LOMOV. You leave my family out of this! The Lomovs have always been honorable, upstanding people, and not a one of them was ever tried for embezzlement,[3] like your grandfather was.

CHUBUKOV. The Lomovs are a pack of lunatics, the whole bunch of them!

NATALIA. The whole bunch!

CHUBUKOV. Your grandfather was a drunkard, and what about your other aunt, the one who ran away with the architect? And so forth.

NATALIA. And so forth!

LOMOV. Your mother limped! *[Clutches at his heart.]* Oh, I've got a stitch in my side. . . . My head's whirling. . . . Help! Water!

CHUBUKOV. Your father was a gambler.

NATALIA. And your aunt was queen of the scandalmongers![4]

LOMOV. My left foot's paralyzed. You're a plotter. . . . Oh, my heart. It's an open secret that in the last elections you brib. . . . I'm seeing stars! Where's my hat?

NATALIA. It's a low-mean, spiteful. . . .

CHUBUKOV. And you're a two-faced, malicious schemer!

LOMOV. Here's my hat. . . . Oh, my heart. . . . Where's the door? How do I get out of here? . . . Oh, I think I'm going to die. . . . My foot's numb. *[Goes.]*

CHUBUKOV. *[Following him.]* And don't you ever set foot in my house again!

NATALIA. Go to court, indeed! We'll see about that!

[LOMOV staggers out.]

CHUBUKOV. The devil with him! *[Gets a drink, walks back and forth excited.]*

NATALIA. What a rascal! How can you trust your neighbors after an incident like that?

---

2. A *pettifogging* person squabbles over unimportant matters or uses mean, tricky methods.
3. Embezzlement is the act of stealing money entrusted to one's care; a bank official, for example, might embezzle funds from customers' accounts.

4. People who spread vicious gossip are *scandalmongers*.

Reading Strategy Recognizing Author's Purpose *What do you think is Chekhov's purpose in including this detail?* **R**

Literary Element Farce *How does Lomov's hypochondria contribute to the farcical aspects of the play?* **L**

Additional Support

Skills Practice

GRAMMAR AND LANGUAGE: Using Exclamation Points Remind students that an exclamation point is used to punctuate exclamatory sentences, sentences that express strong feeling or excitement. Point out that Chekhov uses many exclamation points in the course of his play because the characters are expressing anger. Have students copy three exclamatory sentences from the play. Ask them to read their sentences with appropriate expression. Then have them write three exclamatory sentences of their own. **OL**

Self-portrait in an Interior, Sokolniki, 1916–1917. Nina Simonovich-Efimova. Oil on canvas, 26 x 19⅝ in. Efimov Museum, Moscow.

Viewing the Art: How does this setting compare with your vision of the play's setting so far? Explain. ★

★ **Viewing the Art**

Answer: *Answers will vary, but students should comment on the relative wealth or poverty of the aristocrats and servants, and their respective houses.* **AS**

Differentiated Instruction

Multiple Intelligences—Logical-Mathematical Lomov's hypochondria is a farcical element of Chekhov's play. However, hypochondria can be a serious psychological ailment. Have logical–mathematical learners investigate questions such as these: What is hypochondria? What can be done about it? Have students research hypochondria, especially ways in which it may be manifested and how psychologists treat it. Suggest that students organize their findings in chart form, categorizing the information in whatever way seems most logical to them. **AL**

Objectives
- To recognize the author's purpose (SE)
- To identify the elements of farce (SE)
- To use exclamation points correctly (TWE)

Teach

L1 Literary Element

Farce Answer: *She has just called Lomov "a monster," and yet when her father tells her that Lomov meant to propose to her, she wants him to come back. She is so desperate to be married that she suggests that she will die if Lomov does not come back.* **OL**

R Reading Strategy

Recognizing Author's Purpose Answer: *He is suggesting that his characters' beliefs are weak and can be easily influenced, or that they will pretend to believe anything for the sake of personal gain.* **OL**

CHUBUKOV. The villain! The scarecrow!

NATALIA. He's a monster! First he tries to steal our land, and then he has the nerve to yell at you.

CHUBUKOV. Yes, and that turnip, that stupid rooster, has the gall[5] to make a proposal. Some proposal!

NATALIA. What proposal?

CHUBUKOV. Why, he came to propose to you.

NATALIA. To propose? To me? Why didn't you tell me before?

CHUBUKOV. So he gets all dressed up in his formal clothes. That stuffed sausage, that dried up cabbage!

NATALIA. To propose to me? Ohhhh! [*Falls into a chair and starts wailing.*] Bring him back! Back! Go get him! Bring him back! Ohhhh!

CHUBUKOV. Bring who back?

NATALIA. Hurry up, hurry up! I'm sick. Get him! [*Complete hysterics.*]

CHUBUKOV. What for? [*To her.*] What's the matter with you? [*Clutches his head.*] Oh, what a fool I am! I'll shoot myself! I'll hang myself! I ruined her chances!

NATALIA. I'm dying. Get him!

CHUBUKOV. All right, all right, right away! Only don't yell!

[*He runs out.*]

NATALIA. What are they doing to me? Get him! Bring him back! Bring him back!

[*A pause. CHUBUKOV runs in.*]

> "My heart's beating something awful. My Meadows. My eyebrows, they're both twitching!"

CHUBUKOV. He's coming, and so forth, the snake. Oof! You talk to him. I'm not in the mood.

NATALIA. [*Wailing.*] Bring him back! Bring him back!

CHUBUKOV. [*Yelling.*] I told you, he's coming! What agony to be the father of a grown-up daughter. I'll cut my throat some day, I swear I will. [*To her.*] We cursed him, we insulted him, abused him, kicked him out, and now . . . because you, you. . . .

NATALIA. Me? It was all your fault!

CHUBUKOV. My fault? What do you mean my fau . . . ? [*LOMOV appears in the doorway.*] Talk to him yourself! [*Goes out. LOMOV enters, exhausted.*]

LOMOV. What palpitations! My heart! And my foot's absolutely asleep. Something keeps giving me a stitch in the side. . . .

NATALIA. You must forgive us, Ivan Vassilevitch. We all got too excited. I remember now. The Oxen Meadows are yours.

LOMOV. My heart's beating something awful. My Meadows. My eyebrows, they're both twitching!

NATALIA. Yes, the Meadows are all yours, yes, yours. Do sit down. [*They sit.*] We were wrong, of course.

LOMOV. I argued on principle. My land isn't worth so much to me, but the principle. . . .

NATALIA. Oh, yes, of course, the principle, that's what counts. But let's change the subject.

LOMOV. Besides, I have evidence. You see, my aunt's grandmother let your father's grandfather's peasants use the land. . . .

NATALIA. Yes, yes, yes, but forget all that. [*Aside.*] I wish I knew how to get him going. [*Aloud.*] Are you going to start hunting soon?

---

5. *Gall*, a synonym for impudence, means "shocking boldness; scornful disrespect."

Literary Element Farce What makes Natalia's reaction here farcical? **L1**

Reading Strategy Recognizing Author's Purpose What is the author saying here about his characters' convictions? **R**

Additional Support

Skills Practice

LISTENING AND SPEAKING: Communicating Tone in Dialogue

Discuss the language and the stage directions of the dialogue on this page. Point out that in a different context, the dialogue might express true grief and remorse on the part of Natalia and her father. Have pairs of students practice the dialogue on this page. Ask them to practice one reading using a comic tone and another using a tragic tone. Let one or more pairs perform both readings for the class. Encourage the class to discuss vocal techniques that indicate different tones in the two readings. **OL**

LOMOV. After the harvest I'll try for grouse.[6] But oh, my dear Natalia Stepanovna, have you heard about the bad luck I've had? You know my dog, Guess? He's gone lame.

NATALIA. What a pity. Why?

LOMOV. I don't know. He must have twisted his leg, or got in a fight, or something. [*Sighs.*] My best dog, to say nothing of the cost. I paid Mironov 125 rubles for him.

NATALIA. That was too high, Ivan Vassilevitch.

LOMOV. I think it was quite cheap. He's a first class dog.

NATALIA. Why Papa only paid 85 rubles for Squeezer, and he's much better than Guess.

LOMOV. Squeezer better than Guess! What an idea! [*Laughs.*] Squeezer better than Guess!

NATALIA. Of course he's better. He may still be too young but on points[7] and pedigree,[8] he's a better dog even than any Volchanetsky owns.

LOMOV. Excuse me, Natalia Stepanovna, but you're forgetting he's overshot, and overshot dogs are bad hunters.

NATALIA. Oh, so he's overshot, is he? Well, this is the first time I've heard about it.

LOMOV. Believe me, his lower jaw is shorter than his upper.

NATALIA. You've measured them?

LOMOV. Yes. He's all right for pointing, but if you want him to retrieve. . . .

NATALIA. In the first place, our Squeezer is a thoroughbred, the son of Harness and Chisel, while your mutt doesn't even have a pedigree. He's as old and worn out as a peddler's horse.

LOMOV. He may be old, but I wouldn't take five Squeezers for him. How can you argue? Guess is a dog, Squeezer's a laugh. Anyone you can name has a dog like Squeezer hanging around somewhere. They're under every bush. If he only cost twenty-five rubles you got cheated.

NATALIA. The devil is in you today, Ivan Vassilevitch! You want to contradict everything. First you pretend the Oxen Meadows are yours, and now you say Guess is better than Squeezer. People should say what they really mean, and you know Squeezer is a hundred times better than Guess. Why say he isn't?

LOMOV. So, you think I'm a fool or a blind man, Natalia Stepanovna! Once and for all, Squeezer is overshot!

NATALIA. He is not!

LOMOV. He is so!

NATALIA. He is not!

LOMOV. Why shout, my dear lady?

NATALIA. Why talk such nonsense? It's terrible. Your Guess is old enough to be buried, and you compare him with Squeezer!

LOMOV. I'm sorry, I can't go on. My heart . . . it's palpitating!

NATALIA. I've always noticed that the hunters who argue most don't know a thing.

LOMOV. Please! Be quiet a moment. My heart's falling apart. . . . [*Shouts.*] Shut up!

NATALIA. I'm not going to shut up until you admit that Squeezer's a hundred times better than Guess.

LOMOV. A hundred times worse! His head. . . . My eyes . . . shoulder . . .

NATALIA. Guess is half-dead already!

---

6. A fowl-like bird, the *grouse* is often hunted for game or food.
7. Natalia is referring to her dog's physical characteristics and ancestry. In dog shows today, a dog is judged on specific characteristics, or *points*. Each breed has point standards that cover everything from skull shape and tail length to eye color and hair texture.
8. A dog's ancestry, or *pedigree*, is proof that a dog is purebred.

> **Literary Element** Farce *How does the argument over the dogs increase the farcical element of the play?* **L2**

ANTON CHEKHOV **881**

L1 Literary Element

Farce

Answer: *Chubukov applies his theory of jealousy to Lomov but not to himself or to Natalia.* **OL**

★ Literary History

Comedy or Tragedy

Despite the somewhat tragic circumstances of his characters, Chekhov maintained that his plays, especially his later ones, were comedies, not tragedies. He was distressed by the heavy-handed approach common in Russian theater of the time that some directors applied to his plays. Chekhov wanted his plays acted with a very light touch. **AS**

LOMOV. [*Weeping.*] Shut up! My heart's exploding!

NATALIA. I won't shut up!

[*CHUBUKOV comes in.*]

CHUBUKOV. What's the trouble now?

NATALIA. Papa, will you please tell us which is the better dog, his Guess or our Squeezer?

LOMOV. Stepan Stepanovitch, I implore you to tell me just one thing: Is your Squeezer overshot or not? Yes or no?

CHUBUKOV. Well what if he is? He's still the best dog in the neighborhood, and so forth.

LOMOV. Oh, but isn't my dog, Guess, better? Really?

CHUBUKOV. Don't get yourself so fraught up,[9] old man. Of course, your dog has his good points—thoroughbred, firm on his feet, well sprung ribs, and so forth. But, my dear fellow, you've got to admit he has two defects; he's old and he's short in the muzzle.

LOMOV. Short in the muzzle? Oh, my heart! Let's look at the facts! On the Marusinsky hunt my dog ran neck and neck with the Count's, while Squeezer was a mile behind them. . . .

CHUBUKOV. That's because the Count's groom hit him with a whip.

LOMOV. And he was right, too! We were fox hunting; what was your dog chasing sheep for?

CHUBUKOV. That's a lie! Look, I'm going to lose my temper . . . [*Controlling himself.*] my dear friend, so let's stop arguing, for that reason alone. You're only arguing because we're all jealous of somebody else's dog. Who can help it? As soon as you realize some dog is better than yours, in this case

our dog, you start in with this and that, and the next thing you know—pure jealousy! I remember the whole business.

LOMOV. I remember too!

CHUBUKOV. [*Mimicking.*] "I remember too!" What do you remember?

LOMOV. My heart . . . my foot's asleep . . . I can't . . .

> *"You should be hunting cockroaches in the kitchen, not foxes."*

NATALIA. [*Mimicking.*] "My heart . . . my foot's asleep." What kind of a hunter are you? You should be hunting cockroaches in the kitchen, not foxes. "My heart!"

CHUBUKOV. Yes, what kind of a hunter are you anyway? You should be sitting at home with your palpitations, not tracking down animals. You don't hunt anyhow. You just go out to argue with people and interfere with their dogs, and so forth. For God's sake, let's change the subject before I lose my temper. Anyway, you're just not a hunter.

LOMOV. But you, you're a hunter? Ha! You only go hunting to get in good with the count, and to plot, and intrigue, and scheme. . . . Oh, my heart! You're a schemer, that's what!

CHUBUKOV. What's that? Me a schemer? [*Shouting.*] Shut up!

LOMOV. A schemer!

CHUBUKOV. You infant! You puppy!

LOMOV. You old rat!

CHUBUKOV. You shut up, or I'll shoot you down like a partridge! You fool!

LOMOV. Everyone knows that—oh, my heart—that your wife used to beat you. . . . Oh, my feet . . . my head . . . I'm seeing stars . . . I'm going to faint! [*He drops into an armchair.*] Quick, a doctor! [*Faints.*]

---

9. The expression *fraught up* means "excited; charged up."

Literary Element Farce *How does Chekhov make Chubukov's insight here seem humorous?* **L1**

Additional Support

Skills Practice

READING: Summarizing Point out to students that much of the dialogue of the play is devoted to two arguments, one about land and the other about dogs. A good summary of the play would focus on these two arguments. Point out that each argument in the play can be summarized in one sentence. Have students write a summary of each argument. Then discuss why Chekhov chose to write several pages of dialogue detailing the arguments. **OL**

CHUBUKOV. [*Going on, oblivious.*] Baby! Weakling! Fool! I'm getting sick. [*Drinks water.*] Me! I'm sick!

NATALIA. What kind of a hunter are you? You can't even sit on a horse! [*To her father.*] Papa, what's the matter with him? Look, papa! [*Screaming.*] Ivan Vassilevitch! He's dead.

CHUBUKOV. I'm choking, I can't breathe. . . . Give me air.

NATALIA. He's dead! [*Pulling LOMOV's sleeve.*] Ivan Vassilevitch! Ivan Vassilevitch! What have you done to me? He's dead! [*She falls into an armchair. Screaming hysterically.*] A doctor! A doctor! A doctor!

CHUBUKOV. Ohhhh. . . . What's the matter? What happened?

NATALIA. [*Wailing.*] He's dead! He's dead!

CHUBUKOV. Who's dead? [*Looks at LOMOV.*] My God, he is! Quick! Water! A doctor! [*Puts glass to LOMOV's lips.*] Here, drink this! Can't drink it—he must be dead, and so forth. . . . Oh what a miserable life! Why don't I shoot myself! I should have cut my throat long ago! What am I waiting for? Give me a knife! Give me a pistol! [*LOMOV stirs.*] Look, he's coming to. Here, drink some water. That's it.

LOMOV. I'm seeing stars . . . misty . . . Where am I?

CHUBUKOV. Just you hurry up and get married, and then the devil with you! She accepts. [*Puts LOMOV's hand in NATALIA's.*] She accepts and so forth! I give you my blessing, and so forth! Only leave me in peace!

LOMOV. [*Getting up.*] Huh? What? Who?

CHUBUKOV. She accepts! Well? Kiss her!

NATALIA. He's alive! Yes, yes, I accept.

CHUBUKOV. Kiss each other!

LOMOV. Huh? Kiss? Kiss who? [*They kiss.*] That's nice. I mean, excuse me, what happened? Oh, now I get it . . . my heart . . . those stars . . . I'm very happy, Natalia Stepanovna. [*Kisses her hand.*] My foot's asleep.

NATALIA. I . . . I'm happy too.

CHUBUKOV. What a load off my shoulders! Whew!

NATALIA. Well, now maybe you'll admit that Squeezer is better than Guess?

LOMOV. Worse!

NATALIA. Better!

CHUBUKOV. What a way to enter matrimonial bliss! Let's have some champagne!

LOMOV. He's worse!

NATALIA. Better! Better, better, better, better!

CHUBUKOV. [*Trying to shout her down.*] ★ Champagne! Bring some champagne! Champagne! Champagne!

CURTAIN

Big Idea Portraits of Real Life *What do you think audiences in Russia when this play was first produced would have thought of this recent argument?* **BI**

Literary Element Farce *Do you think Lomov is actually dead? Why or why not?* **L₂**

Vocabulary

oblivious (ə bliv′ əs) *adj.* unmindful or unaware; not noticing

Literary Element Farce *What makes this dialogue humorous?* **L₃**

ANTON CHEKHOV **883**

Reading in the Real World

Citizenship Much of what took place during the time period in which Chekhov lived and wrote has had an impact on the politics, economics, and culture of the whole world. Between 1945 and 1991, there existed a rivalry between the Soviet Union and the United States that came to be called the Cold War. During this period, the rivalry and hostility varied tremendously in intensity. Have students search for magazine and newspaper articles discussing the current relationship between Russia and the United States. Have them take special note of late nineteenth-century problems that led to today's circumstances. **OL**

Assess

1. Some may like the ending of the play because it was funny, while others may dislike it because Lomov and Natalia seem unlikely to be happy.

2. (a) To propose to Chubukov's daughter, Natalia. (b) He is high-strung, nervous, and exhausted by such an important decision.

3. (a) Who owns several acres of land called the Oxen Meadows. (b) Natalia has no idea that Lomov has come to propose; she sees him as a visiting neighbor.

4. (a) Whose dog is better. (b) Natalia is stubborn and narrow-minded. Chubukov is volatile and insulting. Lomov is proud and sensitive.

5. Bickering is similar, but exaggerated and farcical.

6. Students' attitudes about marriage and characters may color their answers.

7. Some dialogue—"He is not!" "He is so!"—is realistic. Some dialogue—"What palpitations! My heart!"—is unrealistic.

8. Because of the media, most people today are aware of societal problems, but they may still ignore them. In Chekhov's time, it was easier for people to remain isolated and unaware.

RESPONDING AND THINKING CRITICALLY

Respond

1. Did you like the ending of the play? Explain why or why not.

Recall and Interpret

2. (a) Why has Lomov come to Chubukov's house? (b) What does his behavior tell you about his personality?

3. (a) What is the cause of the first argument? (b) Why, in your opinion, does the first argument start so easily?

4. (a) What is the second argument about? (b) What do both arguments reveal about their participants?

Analyze and Evaluate

5. Compare and contrast the bickering between characters in the play with similar interactions you have witnessed between people in real life. How is it similar? How is it different?

6. (a) In your opinion, are Lomov and Natalia a good match for each other? Explain. (b) Do you think they should marry? Why or why not?

7. Does the **dialogue**, or speech, in Chekhov's play seem realistic to you? Why or why not?

Connect

8. **Big Idea** Portraits of Real Life Chekhov's aristocratic characters seem to be in their own little world; they have no interaction with people outside the Russian provinces. Do you think this detail is realistic for Chekhov's time and place? For yours?

DAILY LIFE AND CULTURE

Land Ownership in Russia During the 1800s

During the course of the nineteenth century, the Russian government had begun the process of freeing peasants from serfdom, a type of slavery that bound working people to the land and its aristocratic owners. Between 1877 and 1905, approximately half of the land fit for farming had been transferred to the peasants. By the end of the century, the Russian nobility only owned about twenty percent of the land.

Despite their new status as landowners, peasants still experienced severe poverty. Those still without land of their own vied with other peasants for jobs on the remaining large estates. Few peasant children received a formal education at this time, and as a result they remained trapped in agricultural jobs. But there was not enough agricultural work on the remaining estates to employ all those who needed work. Eventually, agricultural workers made political demands that even more land be released from the nobility.

1. Why might a dispute over land ownership be so important to the characters in *A Marriage Proposal*?

2. Imagine that the characters in *A Marriage Proposal* were part of the peasant, not aristocratic class. Identify three ways in which the story would likely be different.

Daily Life and Culture

1. At the time, the Russian nobility had lost much land to peasants.

2. There might not have been a land dispute, Natalia would be uneducated, and Lomov would worry about more important concerns.

LITERARY ANALYSIS

Literary Element Farce

Many authors use **farce** to ridicule societal norms, in addition to making their audiences laugh. In *A Marriage Proposal*, Chekhov has Lomov continually complain about physical ailments in order to poke fun at him.

1. List three examples of statements made by the characters that made you laugh. Tell what you think Chekhov is making fun of in each example.

2. Identify three points in this play that you found particularly funny. Why are they humorous? What techniques of farce does Chekhov use to create each situation?

Review: Irony

As you learned on page 51, **irony** is a contrast between expectation and reality. *A Marriage Proposal* contains both situational and dramatic irony. In **situational irony**, the outcome of a situation is the opposite of what is expected. In **dramatic irony**, the audience knows something that the characters do not know.

Partner Activity Use a chart like the one below and find one good example of situational irony and one good example of dramatic irony in the play. Discuss your examples with a partner, then discuss how different audiences—teenagers, single adults, married couples, socialites, homeowners—may react differently to these ironic situations. Share your findings with the rest of your class.

Example	Type of Irony	Audience & Reaction
When Natalia enters on p. 875, she does not know that Lomov intends to propose.	Dramatic irony—the audience knows Lomov's intent.	

READING AND VOCABULARY

Reading Strategy Recognizing Author's Purpose

In order to recognize the author's purpose, you should ask yourself what the writer is trying to achieve.

1. Why do you think Chekhov wrote this play?

2. Find at least three details in the play to support your conclusions.

Vocabulary Practice

Practice with Word Origins A word's origins often give clues to its meaning. Match each vocabulary word with its corresponding root word. Use a dictionary for assistance.

1. affable   a. *impudens*, meaning "shameless"

2. impudent   b. *affabilis*, meaning "easily spoken to"

3. pompous   c. *oblivio*, meaning "forgetfulness"

4. oblivious   d. *pompa*, meaning "procession" or "display"

Academic Vocabulary

Here are two words from the vocabulary list on page R82.

couple (kup′ əl) *n.* two people linked romantically

consult (kən sult′) *v.* to ask advice; to ask a question of someone

Practice and Apply
1. What might married life be like for the **couple** Chekhov describes in *A Marriage Proposal*?
2. When Lomov tells Chubukov that he would like to **consult** with him, what does Chubukov assume?

AFTER YOU READ

Assess

Literary Element

1. Answers will vary, but might include the following: "Your mother limped!" Chekhov makes fun of people's urge to insult others when angry. When Natalia says, "He's alive! Yes, yes, I accept," Chekhov is mocking love, relationships, and marriage.

2. One point might be when Lomov says, "Please! Be quiet a moment. My heart's falling apart . . . Shut up!" This scene is humorous because Lomov is asking for quiet and then yells. Chekhov uses exaggeration to create farce in this situation.

Review: Irony
Discussions should include:

- examples of situational and dramatic irony

- detailed descriptions of how different groups might feel about the ironic situations that take place in the play.

Reading Strategy

1. Answers will vary. Chekhov may have wanted to entertain people by writing the play, but he also probably wanted to critique and mock the values of the nobility.

2. Answers will vary. Students may refer to humorous moments in the play and the ridiculous behavior of the characters.

Vocabulary

1. b **2.** a **3.** d **4.** c

Academic Vocabulary

1. Married life for Lomov and Natalia will probably be filled with arguments.

2. Chubukov assumes that Lomov wants to borrow money from him.

Assess

Writing About Literature

Students' essays should

- analyze the dialogue of each character in the play;
- support ideas with properly cited examples of dialogue from the play.

Interdisciplinary Activity

Students should include props and set design appropriate to the living room of a mansion, including those mentioned in the play: a pitcher and glasses, a chair, and a doorway. They should also include directions for the movements of the characters.

Chekhov's Language and Style

Writing assignments should

- be either dialogues or monologues;
- should apply Chekhov's writing style in terms of punctuation; and
- use punctuation to highlight emotion.

Writing About Literature

Evaluate Author's Craft Chekhov masterfully develops his characters' personalities through **dialogue**. Dialogue is conversation between the characters in a literary work. In a drama, the audience learns about the characters mainly through dialogue. Analyze the dialogue for each of the characters in *A Marriage Proposal*. Write one paragraph for each character explaining how Chekhov portrays him or her through speech.

Before you begin drafting, make a list of character traits and find examples of dialogue that help develop each trait. Use a chart like the one below to organize your ideas.

	Natalia
Trait	Dialogue
stubborn	"You can go on talking for two days, and you can put on fifteen evening coats and twenty pairs of gloves, but I'll tell you they're ours, ours, ours!"

After completing your writing assignment, meet with a peer reviewer to evaluate each other's writing. Then proofread and edit your draft for errors in spelling, grammar, and punctuation.

Interdisciplinary Activity: Drama

Design a set for *A Marriage Proposal*, alone or with a small group. Using graph paper or computer software, draw a floor plan of the stage as you envision it. On the plan, place the various furnishings, stage props, and exits. Then select a scene and mark the characters' positions and movements across the stage.

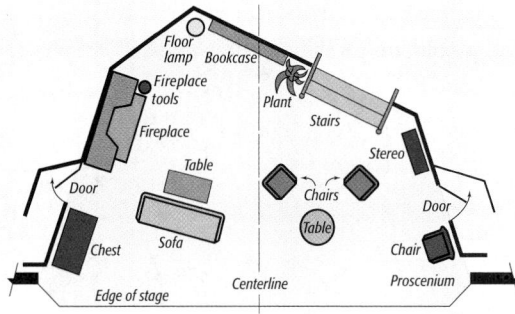

Chekhov's Language and Style

Using Exclamation Points Chekhov uses many exclamation points throughout *A Marriage Proposal*. The exclamation point is used to punctuate exclamatory sentences, sentences that express strong feeling, usually anger or excitement. Notice how Chekhov uses exclamation points in the examples below to communicate strong emotion:

> CHUBUKOV. [*Aside.*] Wants to borrow some money. Not a chance!
>
> LOMOV. [*Clutching his heart.*] The Oxen Meadows are mine! Do you understand? Mine!
>
> NATALIA. Please don't shout!
>
> CHUBUKOV. [*Trying to shout her down.*] Champagne! Bring some champagne! Champagne! Champagne!

Notice how different the tone of those examples would be without exclamation points:

> CHUBUKOV. [*Aside.*] Wants to borrow some money. Not a chance.
>
> LOMOV. [*Clutching his heart.*] The Oxen Meadows are mine. Do you understand? Mine.
>
> NATALIA. Please don't shout.
>
> CHUBUKOV. [*Trying to shout her down.*] Champagne, bring some champagne. Champagne, champagne.

Activity Write a brief monologue or dialogue using punctuation as Chekhov uses it: to indicate characters' emotions. When you have finished writing, read your monologue or dialogue aloud to your class.

Revising Check

Exclamation Points While useful for communicating strong emotion, exclamation points should not be overused. Reread the essay you wrote evaluating Chekhov's use of dialogue. Make sure that you used exclamation points accurately and sparingly. Make any revisions you deem necessary.

Literature Online Web Activities For eFlashcards, Selection Quick Checks, and other Web activities, go to www.glencoe.com.

Literature Online

Web Activities Have students access the Web site for interactive activities that will help them assess their understanding of the selection.

Grammar Workshop

Mechanics

Using Commas with Interjections and Parenthetical Expressions

"Of course, I must say you look splendid, but . . . Well, tell me, why are you so dressed up?"

— Anton Chekhov, from "A Marriage Proposal"

Connecting to Literature In the above quotation, Chekhov introduces the sentences with the expressions *of course* and *well. Of course* is a **parenthetical expression,** which adds explanatory information to the sentence. Other common parenthetical expressions include *in fact, on the other hand, for example, on the contrary, by the way, to be exact, after all,* and *nevertheless.* The word *well* is an **interjection,** a word that expresses emotion. *Alas, good grief, oh, uh-oh, sorry,* and *wow* are other common interjections. Because interjections and parenthetical expressions have no grammatical connection to the rest of the sentence, they should be separated with a comma.

Interjections These occur at the beginning of a sentence. Interjections that express strong emotion may be followed by an exclamation point.

> *Sorry, we weren't expecting you.*
> *Good heavens, he was wearing a suit and top hat!*

Parenthetical expressions These usually appear in the middle of a sentence and are set off by two commas. Occasionally, a parenthetical expression begins a sentence and is followed by a comma.

> *In fact, Lomov had come to Natalia with the intention of proposing marriage.*
> *Lomov had come to Natalia, in fact, with the intention of proposing marriage.*

Exercise

Rewrite the following sentences to correct any mistakes in comma usage.

1. Well if you check the background information, you can see that the story was written in the year 1888.
2. Oh I see that Chekhov had earned a degree in medicine.
3. Chekhov unfortunately was poor and had to support himself by writing hundreds of articles for comic magazines.
4. These writings on the other hand showed the revolutionary literary style and promise of the masterpieces he was soon to create.
5. This promise is of course realized in the one-act play "A Marriage Proposal."

▶ **Vocabulary Terms**

Interjections and **parenthetical expressions** express emotion or add explanatory information. Use commas to separate these words from the rest of the sentence.

▶ **Test-Taking Tip**

Overuse of interjections and parenthetical expressions can make your writing appear overly casual and informal, so use them sparingly when writing for a test.

▶ **Language Handbook**

For more about comma usage, see the Language Handbook, pp. R54–R55.

Literature Online
eWorkbooks To link to the Grammar and Language eWorkbook, go to www.glencoe.com.

OBJECTIVES
• Understand interjections and parenthetical expressions.
• Recognize and correct errors in comma usage.

---

eWorkbooks Have students access the Web site for more practice with mechanics.

English Language Coach

Interjections Students new to the United States may be unfamiliar with English interjections, many of which are slang. Note that interjections usually show surprise or emotion, and discuss appropriate use of interjections including *oh, ah, ouch, for heaven's sake, darn, eek, hey, excuse me, yikes,* and *hi.* **EL**

Focus

Write these sentences on the board: "Wow was I surprised!" and "His laugh was in fact contagious." **Ask:** How should these sentences be punctuated? *(Wow, was I surprised! His laugh was, in fact, contagious.)* Ask students to explain the function of the commas.

Teach

Commas Emphasize that interjections and parenthetical expressions, which are unnecessary add-ons, are set off with commas in a sentence. Give several examples and have students write sentences of their own. Note that interjections can stand alone with an exclamation point: *Great!* **OL**

Assess

Exercise

1. Well, if you check the background information, you can see that the story was written in the year 1888.
2. Oh, I see that Chekhov had earned a degree in medicine.
3. Chekhov, unfortunately, was poor and had to support himself by writing hundreds of articles for comic magazines.
4. On the other hand, these writings showed the revolutionary literary style and promise of the masterpieces he was soon to create.
5. This promise is, of course, realized in the one-act play "A Marriage Proposal."

Focus

BELLRINGER

Bellringer Options
Daily Language Practice Transparency 79
Or write the following sentences on the board: 1. When asked your opinion, you should always be honest. 2. It is best to avoid hurting other people's feelings whenever possible.
Ask: Which of these sentences do you agree with more?
Prompt students to support their answers with explanations and examples.

Author Search To expand students' appreciation of Harold Pinter, have them access the Web site for additional information and resources.

CheckPoint

Use the CheckPoint questions on Presentation Plus! to monitor students' comprehension. These questions can be used with interactive response keypads for immediate student feedback.

That's Your Trouble

MEET HAROLD PINTER

After a performance of his play *The Collection,* Harold Pinter gave an unusual bit of feedback to one of the actors. "'Michael, I wrote dot, dot, dot,'" Pinter told the actor, "'and you're giving me dot, dot.'"

The comment was more than just critical nitpicking. As one of the twentieth-century's top playwrights, Pinter reinvented the language of drama. Using small talk and long silences, he suggests deeper layers of meaning and conflict beneath the surface of daily life. In a style that has often been called "the comedy of menace," Pinter dramatizes tense, antagonistic relationships that break down into brutal power struggles. As a tribute to his unique style, critics have added a word to the *New Shorter Oxford English Dictionary:* "Pinteresque."

> *"There are no hard distinctions between what is real and what is unreal."*
>
> —Harold Pinter

Art and Danger As a child, Pinter experienced both beauty and violence. Pinter's father was a working-class tailor, but his family loved art and culture. In contrast, Pinter's mother came from a hard-scrabble family whose behavior, including that of her bare-knuckle boxer brother, sometimes verged on criminal.

The young Pinter also faced the terrors of World War II. Threatened by Nazi bombings, Pinter was twice evacuated from the city with other London children. Some critics trace the sense of free-floating menace in his plays to this early experience of war and separation from his loving family.

Stage and Screen From an early age, Pinter loved reading. After seeing John Webster's *The White Devil,* a seventeenth-century tale of murder and adultery, he joined the Royal Academy of Dramatic Arts. Pinter disliked the Academy's artificial theatricality. Eventually, he dropped out to pursue acting on his own.

In 1956 Pinter began writing his own plays. Influenced by Samuel Beckett, he also wrote Absurdist plays. One of his early plays, *The Birthday Party,* initially flopped, but it later won acclaim. Later successes included *The Caretaker* (1960) and *The Homecoming* (1965).

In one of his later plays, *Betrayal* (1978), Pinter took a new path. Using material inspired by his own life, he wrote dialogue that was less stylized than in his earlier plays. But the play was still revolutionary: Pinter shows how a marriage falls apart, but he presents the scenes in reverse chronological order.

Throughout his career, Pinter has continued to act and direct, both in his own plays and in those by other playwrights. He has also had a career as a screenwriter. Some of his screenplays include *The French Lieutenant's Woman* (1981) and *The Handmaid's Tale* (1990).

In 2005 Pinter was awarded the Nobel Prize in Literature. The Nobel presenter described Pinter as "the foremost representative of British drama in the second half of the twentieth century."

Harold Pinter was born in 1930.

Literature Online **Author Search** For more about Harold Pinter, go to www.glencoe.com.

888 UNIT 4 DRAMA

Selection Skills

Literary Elements
- Conflict (SE pp. 889, 890, 891, 892)

That's Your Trouble

Reading Skills
- Analyzing Mood (SE pp. 889, 890, 891, 892)

Vocabulary Skills
- Practice with Connotation and Denotation (SE pp. 889, 892)
- Analyzing Slang (TWE p. 890)

Writing Skills/Grammar
- Analyzing Style (SE p. 892)

Connecting to the Dramatic Sketch

Our conversations reveal much about who we are and what we find important. Our words communicate feelings and attitudes of which we are aware and sometimes unaware. Sometimes we do not realize how we feel until we find ourselves becoming irritated or upset over insignificant matters. Before you read, think about the following questions:

- What do your daily conversations reveal about you?
- In what way does your everyday language often mask or hide your true feelings?

Building Background

Theater of the Absurd refers to a style of dramatic literature that emerged primarily in the 1950s and 1960s. Absurdist dramas do not contain a plot but instead present a series of scenes in which the characters speak in meaningless conversations or perform actions with little or no purpose. Even though Absurdist plays are comic on the surface, they express underlying complex feelings, such as dread, guilt, or uncertainty. The central concern of the dramatists of the Absurd is to show that people are essentially helpless or confused in an alienating world.

Theater of the Absurd was shocking to audiences when it was new because it did not follow theatrical conventions. It lost its shock value as audiences became accustomed to its unusual techniques, many of which are now a part of mainsteam theater.

Setting Purposes for Reading

Big Idea Portraits of Real Life

As you read *That's Your Trouble,* notice the ways in which the characters communicate, or miscommunicate, with each other.

Literary Element Conflict

The **conflict** is the central struggle between two opposing forces in a story or drama. As you read, try to determine the conflict in Pinter's dramatic sketch.

- See Literary Terms Handbook, p. R4.

OBJECTIVES
In studying this selection, you will focus on the following:
- understanding conflict and the distinction between internal and external conflict
- analyzing mood
- writing to analyze an author's style

Reading Strategy Analyzing Mood

Analyzing mood entails examining the emotional quality or atmosphere of a literary work. A writer's choice of language, subject matter, setting and tone, as well as such sound devices as rhyme and rhythm, contribute to mood.

....

Reading Tip: Asking Questions When trying to determine mood, ask yourself questions as you read, such as: How do the setting and stage directions of a dramatic work contribute to the overall mood? Is the mood positive or negative? Use a chart to organize your questions and answers.

Question	Answer
At what point does a character dramatically change the mood?	In line 24, B responds "ferociously."

Vocabulary

ferociously (fə rō′shəs lē) *adv.* cruelly; savagely; p. 891 *The beast ferociously bared his teeth at the hunter.*

ignorant (ig′nər ənt) *adj.* lacking knowledge or experience; uninformed; p. 891 *He was ignorant in thinking that the earth was flat.*

....

Vocabulary Tip: Practice with Connotation and Denotation Knowing the connotations, or implied meaning or emotional association, of words can help you determine what the denotation, or dictionary definition, could be.

Literature Online **Interactive Literary Elements Handbook** To review or learn more about the literary elements, go to www.glencoe.com.

Focus

Summary

Two men are spending time in a park when one, A., sees a man wearing a sandwich board. He insists to his friend, B., that wearing the board will give the man a headache. B. disagrees, insisting that the pressure from the board will cause pain in the man's neck and shoulders rather than the head. The conflict becomes heated, with B. arguing that A.'s trouble is that he doesn't listen to other people and A. implying that his only trouble is B.

V Vocabulary

Vocabulary File

Say: Add these words and definitions to your vocabulary file. For each word, include a sentence that gives you an example of how to use the word. **OL** Students with English language needs should include the pronunciations of these words in their files. **EL**

Literary Elements Have students access the Web site to improve their understanding of conflict.

Selection Resources

Print Materials
- 📂 Unit 4 Resources (Fast File), pp. 49–51
- 📂 Leveled Vocabulary Development, p. 66
- 📂 Selection and Unit Assessments, pp. 155–156
- 📂 Selection Quick Checks, p. 78

Transparencies
- Bellringer Options Transparencies: Daily Language Practice Transparency 79
- Literary Elements Transparency 3

Technology
- 💿 TeacherWorks Plus™ CD-ROM
- 💿 StudentWorks Plus™ CD-ROM
- 💿 Presentation Plus!™ CD-ROM
- 💻 Literature Online, glencoe.com
- 💻 Online Student Edition, mhln.com
- 💿 Exam*View*® Assessment Suite CD-ROM
- 💿 Vocabulary PuzzleMaker CD-ROM
- 💿 Listening Library, disc 2 track 10

R1 Reading Strategy

Analyzing Mood

Answer: *Pinter creates an idyllic mood by having his characters enjoy a beautiful day in the park.* OL

L1 Literary Element

Conflict

Answer: *The conflict begins with the word "Rubbish." B disagrees that the man with the sandwich board will get a headache. From this point, the two begin their cycle of misinterpreting and criticizing each other.* OL

★ Viewing the Art

William Nicholson was a British painter and illustrator who lived from 1872 to 1949. **Ask:** What elements in this lithograph evoke a sense of absurdity similiar to that found in Pinter's dramatic sketch? *(Students may note that the sandwich man is being completely ignored by the more well-to-do passersby. His presence, therefore, seems somewhat meaningless and foolish, just like the conversation between A and B.)* **AS**

That's *Your* Trouble

Harold Pinter

Sandwich Man in Trafalgar Square, 1898. William Nicholson. Stapleton Collection, London.

Two men in a park. One on the grass, reading.
The other making cricket[1] strokes with umbrella.

1. A.: *(stopping in mid-stroke)*: Eh, look at that bloke[2], what's he got on his back, he's got a sandwich board[3] on his back.
2. B.: What about it?
3. A.: He wants to take it off, he'll get a headache.
4. B.: Rubbish.[4]
5. A.: What do you mean?
6. B.: He won't get a headache.
7. A.: I bet he will.
8. B.: The neck! It affects his neck! He'll get a neckache.
9. A.: The strain goes up.
10. B.: Have you ever carried a sandwich board?
11. A.: Never.
12. B.: Then how do you know which way the strain *goes*? *(Pause.)* It goes down! The strain goes down, it starts with the neck and it goes down. He'll get a neckache and a backache.

1. *Cricket* is a game played with a ball and bat.
2. *Bloke* is a British slang for "man" or "guy."
3. A *sandwich board* consists of two hinged boards that hang front and back from the shoulders of a person. It typically is used as a display advertisement.
4. *Rubbish* is a British term for "garbage," "lies," or "nonsense."

Reading Strategy   Analyzing Mood *Describe the mood that this setting creates.* **R1**

Literary Element   Conflict *How and where does the conflict between these two men begin?* **L1**

890 UNIT 4 DRAMA

Additional Support

Skills Practice

VOCABULARY: Slang Explain that the informal, inventive language called *slang* often creates a sense of unity among the members of a particular group. **Ask:** What can a listener tell about someone who uses certain slang? *(One might be able to tell ones' age* or the social groups to which he or she belongs.) What can you tell about the two characters in the play by the slang they use? *(Their use of informal language reveals that they are friends.)* **OL**

13. A.: He'll get a headache in the end.
14. B.: There's no end.
15. A.: That's where the brain is.
16. B.: That's where the *what* is?
17. A.: The brain.
18. B.: It's nothing to do with the brain.
19. A.: Oh, isn't it?
20. B.: It won't go anywhere *near* his brain.
21. A.: That's where you're wrong.
22. B.: I'm not wrong. I'm right. *(Pause.)* You happen to be talking to a man who knows what he's talking about. *(Pause.)* His brain doesn't come into it. If you've got a strain, it goes down. It's not like heat.
23. A.: What do you mean?
24. B.: *(ferociously)*: If you've got a strain it goes down! Heat goes up! *(Pause.)*
25. A.: You mean sound.
26. B.: I what?
27. A.: Sound goes up.
28. B.: Sound goes anywhere it likes! It all depends where you happen to be standing, it's a matter of physics, that's something you're just completely **ignorant** of, but you just try carrying a sandwich board and you'll find out soon enough. First the neck, then the shoulders, then the back, then it worms[5] into the buttocks, that's where it worms. The buttocks. Either the right or the left, it depends how you carry your weight. Then right down the thighs–a straight drop to his feet and he'll collapse.
29. A.: He hasn't collapsed yet.
30. B.: He will. Give him a chance. A headache! How can he get a headache? He hasn't got anything on his head! I'm the one who's got the headache. *(Pause.)* You just don't know how to listen to what other people tell you, that's your trouble.
31. A.: I know what my trouble is.
32. B.: You don't know what your trouble is, my friend. That's your trouble. ❧

5. Here, *worms* means "to move down into; make its way."

| **Reading Strategy** | Analyzing Mood *What effort does the word* ferociously *have on the mood?* **R₂** |

Big Idea Portraits of Real Life *What does B mean by the word "trouble" here?* **BI**

Literary Element Conflict *What does A imply that his "trouble" is at the end of the conversation?* **L₂**

Vocabulary

ferociously (fə rō′shəs lē) *adv.* cruelly; savagely

ignorant (ig′nər ənt) *adj.* lacking knowledge or experience; uninformed

HAROLD PINTER **891**

Assess

1. (a) Students may be surprised by the unusual approach to dramatic writing. (b) Students may believe it reflects everyday language.

2. (a) A thinks that neck strains cause headaches. (b) B does not realize that "in the end" means "eventually."

3. (a) A responds by implying that his trouble is actually B. (b) His tone is sarcastic.

4. (a) The conflict appears to be about whether the man wearing the sandwich board will get a headache. (b) The underlying conflict stems from B's need to feel superior.

5. (a) The irony lies in B's own irrational explanations. (b) It reflects Pinter's cynical view of human interaction.

6. (a) Students should support their answers with the text. (b) The characters suggest that friends can be contentious.

7. Pinter implies that our everyday conversations veil currents of aggression between individuals.

Literary Element

1. It regards the direction in which pain travels.

2. The internal conflicts arise from B's insecurity and his resulting aggression.

Literature Online

Web Activities Have students access the Web site for interactive activities that will help them assess their understanding of the selection.

RESPONDING AND THINKING CRITICALLY

Respond

1. (a)What was your first reaction to this dramatic sketch? (b)What is your opinion of the dialogue in *That's Your Trouble*?

Recall and Interpret

2. (a)According to B, what does A misunderstand about neck strains? (b)How does B misunderstand A?

3. (a)Describe A's response when B tells him that his "trouble is not listening" to people? (b)What is A's tone in response?

4. (a)After reading the dialogue, what does the conflict appear to be about? (b)What is the underlying conflict between these two men?

Analyze and Evaluate

5. (a)What is ironic about B's accusation that his companion is ignorant? (b)What purpose does irony serve in this dialogue?

6. (a)Determine whether you think that the two men are friends. (b)How do these characters change or complicate your definition of friendship?

Connect

7. **Big Idea** **Portraits of Real Life** What larger comments about human interaction does Pinter's sketch make through his characters? Explain.

LITERARY ANALYSIS

Literary Element Conflict

An **external conflict** exists when a character struggles against some outside force, such as another person, nature, society, or fate. An **internal conflict** is a struggle that takes place within the mind of a character who is torn between opposing feelings, desires, or goals. Think about the conflict or conflicts in *That's Your Trouble,* and then answer the following questions:

1. What is the external conflict in the dialogue?

2. What are the internal conflicts of these characters?

Writing About Literature

Analyze Style Pinter's work is best known for his minimalist approach to character and dialogue. His plays prioritize the verbal exchange between two characters, and what is not said is just as important as what is said. The Pinteresque pause, which has become Pinter's signature, embodies the tension many of his characters feel toward themselves and each other but try to hide.

Examine the pauses in the conversation. Imagine what is going on in the character's head during those pauses. Identify what a character says after the pause. Then determine whether they are effective stage directions for developing the character's emotions. Using details from the conversation, analyze that aspect of Pinter's style in *That's Your Trouble* in a brief essay.

892 UNIT 4 DRAMA

READING AND VOCABULARY

Reading Strategy Analyzing Mood

Mood is a broader term than tone, which refers to the attitude of the speaker or narrator toward the reader. Mood also differs from atmosphere, which is concerned mainly with the physical qualities that contribute to a mood, such as time, place, and weather.

1. What is the overall mood of this dramatic sketch?

2. How does the mood contribute to the tone of the playwright?

Vocabulary Practice

Practice with Connotation and Denotation.
A word can have a positive, negative, or neutral connotation. For example, the word *antsy* has a negative connotation while *eager* has a positive one. Determine whether each vocabulary word has a positive, negative, or neutral connotation.

1. ferociously
   a. positive   **b.** negative   **c.** neutral

2. ignorant
   a. positive   **b.** negative   **c.** neutral

Literature Online **Web Activities** For eFlashcards, Selection Quick Checks, and other Web activities, go to www.glencoe.com.

Writing About Literature

Students' essays should

- analyze Pinter's use of the pause.

- provide examples from the text to support their opinions.

Vocabulary

1. b   **2.** b

Reading Strategy

1. The play begins nonchalantly, but the mood quickly becomes tense and angry.

2. Pinter pokes fun at his characters by having them take themselves very seriously.

Writing for the Theater

Harold Pinter

Nobel Prize Award

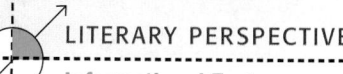
Building Background

Harold Pinter, a British playwright, was a recipient of the Nobel Prize in Literature in 2005. In "Writing for the Theater," Pinter discusses how he creates roles and chooses the language he uses in plays.

Set a Purpose for Reading

Read to discover the author's opinion and how he supports it.

Reading Strategy

Evaluating Argument

Evaluating an argument requires that you make a judgment or form an opinion about what you have read. Consider if the author clearly states his or her position and supports it with reasons and examples. Also, decide if you agree with the author's opinion. As you read, use a chart to determine Pinter's opinions and how he supports them. Then, consider an opposing viewpoint for each opinion.

Pinter's Opinion	Support	Opposing Viewpoint
What he writes only has obligations to itself	Responsibility is to the play, not the audience	Playwrights need to consider their audiences

The theater is a large, energetic, public activity. Writing is, for me, a completely private activity, a poem or a play, no difference. These facts are not easy to reconcile. The professional theater, whatever the virtues it undoubtedly possesses, is a world of false climaxes, calculated tensions, some hysteria, and a good deal of inefficiency. And the alarms of this world which I suppose I work in become steadily more widespread and intrusive. But basically my position has remained the same. What I write has no obligation to anything other than to itself. My responsibility is not to audiences, critics, producers, directors, actors or to my fellow men in general, but to the play in hand, simply. I warned you about definitive statements but it looks as though I've just made one.

I have usually begun a play in quite a simple manner; found a couple of characters in a particular context, thrown them together and listened to what they said, keeping my nose to the ground. The context has always been, for me, concrete and particular, and the

HAROLD PINTER **893**

Focus

Summary

In this excerpt from a 1962 speech, Pinter discusses the difficulties of representing "reality" through language and warns his audience against playwrights who characterize themselves as authorities on what is true or moral. He also discusses his own relationship with the writing process, describing himself as a writer who paradoxically enjoys putting words on the page and finds the ambiguities of language nauseating.

Big Idea

Portraits of Real Life
Say: Keep the following questions in mind as you read: Does Pinter think language is an effective way to represent reality? What are some of the concerns Pinter has about other writers? *(Pinter thinks it is difficult for any of us to represent reality through language. He is concerned that some writers pass off clichéd, overly moral writing as "true.")* **OL**

Readability Scores
Dale-Chall: 8.3
DRP: 65
Lexile: 1120

Differentiated Instruction

Less Proficient Readers Less proficient readers might understand Pinter's ideas more easily if the speech is read aloud. Have more proficient readers read the speech excerpt aloud, one paragraph at a time, while less proficient readers jot down questions and unfamiliar words.

Instruct more proficient readers to pause after reading each paragraph, giving less proficient readers time to clarify ideas and vocabulary words, and to write a one- to two-sentence summary of the paragraph. **BL**

Objective
• To evaluate an author's argument or defense of a claim (SE)

Teach

R1 Reading Strategy

Evaluating Argument Ask:
Do you agree or disagree with Pinter's argument about "common experience" and "common ground"? *(Answers will vary. Students might use examples from their own experience to support their evaluations.)* **OL**

⭐ Literary History

Reactions to Realism

When Pinter began acting and writing plays in the 1950s, realism was the trend in Western drama. Have students use library and Internet resources to define the following movements in relation to realism: naturalism; futurism; symbolism; expressionism. **AS**

---

characters concrete also. I've never started a play from any kind of abstract idea or theory . . . Apart from any other consideration, we are faced with the immense difficulty, if not the impossibility, of verifying the past. I don't mean merely years ago, but yesterday, this morning. What took place, what was the nature of what took place, what happened? If one can speak of the difficulty of knowing what in fact took place yesterday, one can I think treat the present in the same way. What's happening now? We won't know until tomorrow or in six months' time, and **R1** we won't know then, we'll have forgotten, or our imagination will have attributed quite false characteristics to today. A moment is sucked away and distorted, often even at the time of its birth. We will all interpret a common experience quite differently, though we prefer to subscribe to the view that there's a shared common ground, a known ground. I think there's a shared common ground all right, but that it's more like a quicksand. Because "reality" is quite a strong firm word we tend to think, or to hope, that the state to which it refers is equally firm, settled and unequivocal.[1] It doesn't seem to be, and in my opinion, it's no worse or better for that.

. . . There is a considerable body of people just now who are asking for some kind of clear and sensible engagement to be evidently disclosed in contemporary plays. They want the playwright to be a prophet. There is certainly a good deal of prophecy indulged in by playwrights these days, in their plays and out of them. Warnings, sermons, admonitions,[2] ideological exhortations,[3] moral judgments, defined problems with built-in solutions; all can camp under the banner of prophecy. The attitude behind this sort of thing might be summed up in one phrase: *"I'm telling you!"*

It takes all sorts of playwrights to make a world, and as far as I'm concerned "X" can follow any course he chooses without

my acting as his censor. To propagate[4] a phoney war between hypothetical schools of playwrights doesn't seem to me a very productive pastime and it certainly isn't my intention. But I can't but feel that we have a marked tendency to stress, so glibly, our empty preferences. The preference for *Life* with a capital *L*, which is held up to be very different to life with a small *l*, I mean the life we in fact live. The preference for goodwill, for charity, for benevolence, how facile they've become, these deliverances.

If I were to state any moral precept[5] it might be: beware of the writer who puts forward his concern for you to embrace, who leaves you in no doubt of his worthiness, his usefulness, his altruism,[6] who declares that his heart is in the right place, and ensures that it can be seen in full view, a pulsating mass where his characters ought to be. What is presented, so much of the time, as a body of active and positive thought is in fact a body lost in a prison of empty definition and cliché.

This kind of writer clearly trusts words absolutely. I have mixed feelings about words myself. Moving among them, sorting them out, watching them appear on the page, from this I derive a considerable pleasure. But at the same time I have another strong feeling about words which amounts to nothing less than nausea. Such a weight of words confronts us day in, day out, words spoken in a context such as this, words written by me and by others, the bulk of it a stale dead terminology; ideas endlessly repeated and permutated,[7] become platitudinous,[8] **R2** trite, meaningless. Given this nausea, it's very easy to be overcome by it and step back into paralysis. I imagine most writers know something of this kind of paralysis. But if it is possible to confront this nausea, to follow it to its hilt, to move through it and out of

---

1. *Unequivocal* means "clear" or "without doubt."
2. *Admonitions* are "cautionary advice."
3. *Exhortations* are "appeals" or "arguments."

4. Here, *propagate* means "publicize."
5. *Precept* means "standard."
6. *Altruism* means "unselfish behavior" or "attention to the welfare of others."
7. *Permutated* means "transformed entirely."
8. *Platitudinous* means "unoriginal" or "banal."

Additional Support

READING: Compare and Contrast

In his 2005 Nobel acceptance speech, Pinter revisits some of the same topics and themes covered in "Writing for the Theater." Have students read the first sixteen paragraphs of Pinter's Nobel speech (available online at nobelprize.org) and write a short analysis comparing and contrasting the content and themes of the two speeches. **Ask:** Which ideas does Pinter stress in both speeches? How did Pinter's views change between 1962 and 2005? *(Pinter continues to believe that the truth cannot be pinned down in theater, but that it matters in the real, offstage world.)* **OL** it, then it is possible to say that something has occurred, that something has even been achieved.

Language, under these conditions, is a highly ambiguous business. So often, below the word spoken, is the thing known and unspoken. My characters tell me so much and no more, with reference to their experience, their aspirations, their motives, their history. Between my lack of biographical data about them and the ambiguity of what they say lies a territory which is not only worthy of exploration but which it is compulsory to explore. You and I, the characters which grow on a page, most of the time we're inexpressive, giving little away, unreliable, elusive,[9] evasive,[10] obstructive, unwilling. But it's out of these attributes that a language arises. A language, I repeat, where under what is said, another thing is being said. ✎

---

9. *Elusive* means "not able to be defined or described."
10. *Evasive* means "intentionally vague."

Musee Grevin Poster, 1900. Jules Cheret.

RESPONDING AND THINKING CRITICALLY

Respond

1. What surprised you about Pinter's viewpoint on writing for the theater?

Recall and Interpret

2. (a)Does Pinter write plays to convey a certain ideology or make a moral judgment? Explain. (b)What does this say about how readers and audiences interpret theatrical works?

3. (a)What does Pinter say language offers other than the actual "words spoken"? (b)What do you think conveying the meaning of Pinter's language requires of actors who perform in his plays?

Analyze and Evaluate

4. (a)What is Pinter's opinion about the responsibilty of the playwright? (b)Does this support the idea of theater being a collaborative art form? Why or why not?

5. Konstanin Stanislavsky was a Russian actor and theorist who developed an acting technique known as The Method. He asked students to consider "the subtext" of characters, or the meaning that underlies the written text. Does Pinter's writing serve Stanislavsky's approach to acting? Why or why not?

Connect

6. How do Pinter's ideas about characterization apply to *That's Your Trouble*?

OBJECTIVES
- Evaluate an author's argument or defense of a claim.
- Analyze and evaluate the logic and use of evidence in an author's argument.
- Make judgments about how effectively an author has supported his or her beliefs and assumptions, citing evidence from the text.

HAROLD PINTER **895**

---

3. (a) Language has meaning that is not explicit in the text. (b) Actors must interpret their lines.

4. (a) Pinter believes that the playwright is only responsible for the text of the play. (b) Students may believe that playwrights should write with the performers and directors in mind.

5. Yes; Pinter believes there is language "below the word spoken," allowing actors to interpret the text.

6. Pinter says he has not provided much background about the characters. Pinter leaves their histories and motives up to the actors to determine.

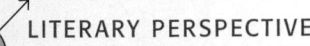
Teach

R2 Reading Strategy

Evaluating Argument Ask:
What are the main points of Pinter's argument here? *(He argues that it is possible to be overcome by the sheer volume of words, a volume that threatens to make language meaningless. Only by confronting our own uneasy relationship with language can we achieve meaning.)* **OL**

⭐ Viewing the Art

Jules Cheret (1836–1933) created artwork for many posters advertising performances, such as operas and concerts, as well as commercial products. The government of France honored Cheret for his work with a national award in 1890. **AS**

Assess

1. Students may be surprised that Pinter does not believe that playwrights should work with actors and directors or that they should write with a certain message in mind.

2. (a) No; he believes that the meaning of the play comes strictly out of the dialogue. (b) Readers and audiences often look for a playwright's intended meaning when there may not be one.

See also 📖 Active Learning and Note Taking Guide, pp. 139–144.

Focus

BELLRINGER

Bellringer Options
Daily Language Practice Transparency 80
Or **Say:** Think about a time when something of importance to you was disregarded as trivial. Discuss significant thoughts, ideas, and events that were overlooked or u nderestimated. **Ask:** What determines the value of an idea, event, or person? *(Whatever is relative to one's perceptions, experiences, and attitudes.)* **Ask:** Why is it important to value other people's ideas and experiences? *(To gain a greater understanding of humanity.)*

Author Search To expand students' appreciation of Susan Glaspell, have them access the Web site for additional information and resources.

Trifles

MEET SUSAN GLASPELL

Susan Glaspell changed American theater by incorporating new dramatic styles and ideas into her writing. She had a keen understanding of human nature and was well aware of the progressive social movements of her time. Her work mirrored vital themes in U.S. society in the late nineteenth and early twentieth centuries, a time when gender roles and expectations were changing dramatically. Glaspell also had a strong belief in the power of personal will to overcome life's challenges.

"The tide comes, the tide goes. You cannot know that and leave things just as they were before."

—Susan Glaspell

Traditional Midwestern Roots Glaspell was born in Davenport, Iowa. From her earliest days, she wanted to become a published writer. Glaspell loved to read and was influenced by both European and American authors. Glaspell began writing articles for a local newspaper to earn tuition money in order to attend Drake University. After graduating in 1899, Glaspell became a legislative reporter for a Des Moines newspaper. This journalistic work added to her worldly knowledge and provided ideas for her writing. A murder case in Des Moines that Glaspell once covered gave her the idea for her one-act play *Trifles*.

Glaspell soon ended her journalistic career to devote all of her energies to writing fiction. She published over fifty short stories for a variety of ladies' magazines. She also completed her first novel, *The Glory of the Conquered* (1909).

An Experimental Success In 1913 Glaspell married George Cram Cook. He was an idealist

and a non-conformist with a dynamic personality. Cook had a way of thinking and an approach to life similar to that of Glaspell. Cook and Glaspell left the Midwest and moved to Greenwich Village in New York City. Here they found other forward-thinking individuals, including active feminists. These people encouraged Glaspell to create female characters seeking freedom from conventional roles.

In 1915 Glaspell and Cook co-founded a repertory theater called the Provincetown Players, which operated in Cape Cod and New York City. This theater group provided a venue for American plays that Broadway had shunned due to their experimental or controversial nature. Glaspell's practical outlook helped to make the playhouse an artistic success. Her major accomplishment of that time was encouraging Eugene O'Neill, now considered by many critics to be America's greatest dramatist, and helping him get his playwriting career started.

In 1922 Cook and Glaspell left the playhouse and moved to Greece. After Cook's death in 1924, Glaspell returned to Provincetown to write fiction. Some of Glaspell's novels became bestsellers, and one was adapted for a Hollywood film. She won the coveted Pulitzer Prize in 1931 for her last play, *Alison's House.* In her later years, Glaspell spent time writing a biography about Cook called *Road to the Temple.*

Susan Glaspell was born in 1876 and died in 1948.

Literature Online Author Search For more about Susan Glaspell, go to www.glencoe.com.

Selection Skills

Trifles

Literary Elements
- Stage Directions (SE pp. 897–911)
- Setting (SE p. 911)

Reading Skills
- Evaluating Characters (SE pp. 897–912)
- Making Judgments (TWE p. 908)

Vocabulary Skills
- Practice with Context Clues (SE p. 912)
- Word Origins (TWE p. 900)

Listening/Speaking/Viewing Skills
- Mock Trial (TWE p. 910)
- Telephone Skills (TWE p. 898)

Writing Skills/Grammar
- Evaluating Author's Craft (SE p. 912)
- Conjunctions (TWE p. 902)

Connecting to the Play

Trifles chronicles the events following a mysterious death. The characters' perspectives of this death vary according their genders, societal norms, and personal experiences. Before you read the play, think about the following questions:

- In what ways do societal norms affect you?
- How do your personal experiences affect your perspective?

Building Background

Farm women in the United States during the nineteenth century were expected to be excellent wives, doting mothers, moral guardians, and tidy housekeepers. In an article dated 1884, a writer for the magazine *Household* states, "A really good housekeeper is almost always unhappy. While she does so much for the comfort of others, she nearly ruins her own health and life. It is because she cannot be easy and comfortable when there is the least disorder or dirt to be seen." As women strove to meet the expectations of society, they also became involved in local social movements, such as the charitable Ladies' Aid Society, and the temperance and suffrage movements.

Setting Purposes for Reading

Big Idea Portraits of Real Life

As you read *Trifles*, notice Glaspell's ability to capture a sense of real life through the characters, the stage directions, and the circumstances.

Literary Element Stage Directions

Stage directions are the instructions given by a playwright that describe the appearance of the characters, costumes, sets, and lighting. Stage directions that appear before a character's dialogue can also indicate movement and emotion, and help develop mood and plot.

- See Literary Terms Handbook, p. R16.

Literature Online Interactive Literary Elements Handbook To review or learn more about the literary elements, go to www.glencoe.com.

OBJECTIVES
In studying this selection, you will focus on the following:
- understanding stage directions
- evaluating characters
- analyzing setting
- writing to evaluate an author's craft

Reading Strategy Evaluating Characters

Evaluating Characters means judging how credible, believable, or realistic those characters are. Noticing details that show what a character is like can help you understand the plot and themes of a work. While reading this play, gather details that help you form an opinion about each character.

Reading Tip: Interpreting Details Recording details that strike you as important as you read can help you form an opinion about a character. Create a graphic organizer like the one below for each character.

Character	Details	Interpretations	Evaluation
Sheriff	"Well, can you beat the women! Held for murder and worryin' about her preserves."	The sheriff thinks that women think about silly things at serious times.	The sheriff has certain beliefs about women that will keep him from learning the truth about what happened.

Vocabulary

coroner (kôr´ ə nər) *n.* the public employee responsible for investigating deaths that are not thought to be from natural causes; p. 900 *The police officer called the coroner to the crime scene.*

trifle (trī´ fəl) *n.* something insignificant or of little value; p. 901 *Lucia's cheap ring was no more than a trifle.*

abashed (ə bash´ ed) *adj.* embarrassed or ashamed; p. 905 *Abashed by what he had said, Blake blushed.*

covert (kō´ vərt) *adj.* concealed; secretive; p. 909 *Marcus kept his plans for the surprise party covert.*

facetiously (fə sē´ shəs lē) *adv.* in a manner not meant to be taken seriously; p. 910 *"Ouch!" he facetiously said as she pretended to stomp on his foot.*

SUSAN GLASPELL **897**

Focus

Summary

Mrs. Wright has been accused of murdering her husband. As she awaits trial, the County Attorney and Sheriff scour her farmhouse for evidence. They are accompanied by Lewis Hale, who discovered Mr. Wright. Mrs. Peters and Mrs. Hale have come to gather some personal effects for Mrs. Wright. The men dismiss the women's observations. As they investigate upstairs, the women examine the downstairs. Discovering a lifeless bird, the women conclude that Mr. Wright killed the bird and drove his wife to kill him. The women conceal the bird from the men, and Mrs. Wright will probably go free.

V Vocabulary

Vocabulary File Say: Add these words and definitions to your vocabulary file. For each word, include a sentence that gives you an example of how to use the word. **OL** Students with English language needs should include the pronunciations of these words in their files. **EL**

Literary Elements Have students access the Web site to improve their understanding of stage directions.

Selection Resources

Print Materials
- 📁 Unit 4 Resources (Fast File), pp. 53–55
- 📁 Leveled Vocabulary Development, p. 67
- 📁 Selection and Unit Assessments, pp. 159–160
- 📁 Selection Quick Checks, p. 80

🖨 Transparencies
- Bellringer Options Transparencies: Daily Language Practice Transparency 80
- Literary Elements Transparency 81

Technology
- 💿 TeacherWorks Plus™ CD-ROM
- 💿 StudentWorks Plus™ CD-ROM
- 💿 Presentation Plus!™ CD-ROM
- 💻 Literature Online, glencoe.com
- 💻 Online Student Edition, mhln.com
- 💿 ExamView® Assessment Suite CD-ROM
- 💿 Vocabulary PuzzleMaker CD-ROM
- 💿 Listening Library, disc 2 track 12

Teach

BI₁ Big Idea

Portraits of Real Life

Say: Keep the following question in mind as you read. How does the author use ideas to paint a picture of real life? *(To explore ideas about the roles women play in society, their worth to one another and to men, oppression, and sexism. All of these reflect real-life issues. In this way, the author paints a realistic picture.)* **OL**

L₁ Literary Element

Stage Directions

Answer: *The playwright needs to establish the setting. By providing detailed descriptions, she assists the reader in his or her visualization of the upcoming scene. Such detailed descriptions are also helpful to directors and actors, who will have only the script to determine the playwright's vision.* **OL**

Trifles

Susan Glaspell

Empty Birdcage in Kitchen. Scott Picunko.

BI₁

CAST OF CHARACTERS

GEORGE HENDERSON, County Attorney

HENRY PETERS, Sheriff

LEWIS HALE, a neighboring farmer

MRS. PETERS

MRS. HALE

SCENE: *The kitchen in the now abandoned farmhouse of John Wright, a gloomy kitchen, and left without having been put in order—the walls covered with a faded wallpaper. Downstage right is a door leading to the parlor. On the right wall above this door is a built-in kitchen cupboard with shelves in the upper portion and drawers below. In the rear wall at right, up two steps, is a door opening onto stairs leading to the second floor. In the rear wall at left is a door to the shed and from there to the outside. Between these two doors is an old-fashioned black iron stove. Running along the left wall from the shed door is an old iron sink and sink shelf, in which is set a hand pump. Downstage of the sink is an uncurtained window. Near the window is an old wooden rocker. Center stage is an unpainted wooden kitchen table with straight chairs on either side. There is a small chair downstage right. Unwashed pans under the sink, a loaf of bread outside the breadbox, a dish towel on the table—other signs of incompleted work. At the rear the shed door opens and the SHERIFF comes in followed by the COUNTY ATTORNEY and HALE. The SHERIFF and HALE are men in middle life, the COUNTY ATTORNEY is a young man; all are much bundled up and go at once to the stove. They are followed by the two women—the SHERIFF'S wife, MRS. PETERS, first; she is a slight wiry woman, a thin nervous face. MRS. HALE is larger and would ordinarily be called more comfortable-looking, but she is disturbed now and looks fearfully about as she enters. The women have come in slowly, and stand close together near the door.*

Literary Element Stage Directions *Why has the playwright given such a detailed description of the scene?* **L₁**

Additional Support

Skills Practice

SPEAKING: Telephone Skills Point out that it is probably just as well that John Wright never got a telephone because he seldom spoke and was not interested in what others had to say. To communicate competently over the telephone, one must listen and speak effectively. This skill is especially important in the workplace. Have students discuss the characteristics of a good telephone communicator: 1. is knowledgeable about the subject at hand; 2. organizes ideas and communicates effectively; 3. speaks clearly; 4. exhibits understanding, friendliness, and politeness to others. **OL**

COUNTY ATTORNEY. (*at stove rubbing his hands*). This feels good. Come up to the fire, ladies.

MRS. PETERS. (*after taking a step forward*). I'm not—cold.

SHERIFF. (*unbuttoning his overcoat and stepping away from the stove to right of table as if to mark the beginning of official business*). Now, Mr. Hale, before we move things about, you explain to Mr. Henderson just what you saw when you came here yesterday morning.

COUNTY ATTORNEY. (*crossing down to left of the table*). By the way, has anything been moved? Are things just as you left them yesterday?

SHERIFF. (*looking about*). It's just the same. When it dropped below zero last night, I thought I'd better send Frank out this morning to make a fire for us—(*sits right of center table*) no use getting pneumonia with a big case on, but I told him not to touch anything except the stove—and you know Frank.

COUNTY ATTORNEY. Somebody should have been left here yesterday.

SHERIFF. Oh—yesterday. When I had to send Frank to Morris Center for that man who went crazy—I want you to know I had my hands full yesterday. I knew you could get back from Omaha by today and as long as I went over everything here myself—

COUNTY ATTORNEY. Well, Mr. Hale, tell just what happened when you came here yesterday morning.

HALE. (*crossing down to above table*). Harry and I had started to town with a load of potatoes. We came along the road from my place and as I got here I said, "I'm going to see if I can't get John Wright to go in with me on a party telephone."[1] I

___

1. A *party telephone* is a telephone line shared by more than one subscriber.

Literary Element Stage Directions *How do these gestures reflect the sheriff's intentions?* **L2**

Big Idea Portraits of Real Life *How does the mention of a party telephone help establish the setting of the play?* **BI2**

spoke to Wright about it once before and he put me off, saying folks talked too much anyway, and all he asked was peace and quiet—I guess you know about how much he talked himself; but I thought maybe if I went to the house and talked about it before his wife, though I said to Harry that I didn't know as what his wife wanted made much difference to John—

COUNTY ATTORNEY. Let's talk about that later, Mr. Hale. I do want to talk about that, but tell now just what happened when you got to the house.

HALE. I didn't hear or see anything; I knocked at the door, and still it was all quiet inside. I knew they must be up, it was past eight o'clock. So I knocked again, and I thought I heard somebody say, "Come in." I wasn't sure, I'm not sure yet, but I opened the door—this door (*indicating the door by which the two women are still standing*) and there in that rocker—(*pointing to it*) sat Mrs. Wright. (*They all look at the rocker downstage left.*)

COUNTY ATTORNEY. What—was she doing?

HALE. She was rockin' back and forth. She had her apron in her hand and was kind of—pleating it.

COUNTY ATTORNEY. And how did she—look?

HALE. Well, she looked queer.

COUNTY ATTORNEY. How do you mean—queer?

HALE. Well, as if she didn't know what she was going to do next. And kind of done up.

COUNTY ATTORNEY. (*takes out notebook and pencil and sits left of center table*). How did she seem to feel about your coming?

HALE. Why, I don't think she minded—one way or other. She didn't pay much attention. I said, "How do, Mrs. Wright, it's cold, ain't it?" And she said, "Is it?"—and went on kind of pleating at her apron. Well, I was surprised; she didn't ask me to come up to the stove, or to set down, but just sat there, not even looking at me, so I

Big Idea Portraits of Real Life *Why was Hale surprised by Mrs. Wright's behavior?* **BI3**

SUSAN GLASPELL **899**

Teach

L2 Literary Element

Stage Directions
Answer: *He gets comfortable and puts his personal interests to the side. The audience should expect something more serious to occur.* **OL**

BI2 Big Idea

Portraits of Real Life
Answer: *The party line and kitchen pump tell us that the story is set in the past.* **OL**

BI3 Big Idea

Portraits of Real Life
Answer: *She should be hospitable and polite. Her behavior indicates that something was amiss.* **OL**

★ Cultural History

Women at Work The nineteenth century severely limited women, excluding them from nearly every profession except teaching and writing. **AS**

✓ CheckPoint

Use the CheckPoint questions on Presentation Plus! to monitor students' comprehension. These questions can be used with interactive response keypads for immediate student feedback.

Objectives
• To understand stage directions (SE)
• To practice telephone communication skills (TWE)

Differentiated Instruction

Less Proficient Readers Recite the stage directions introducing the play. Assign a less proficient reader the task of sketching a diagram of the farmhouse kitchen on the chalkboard. Have the student revisit the stage directions, using the diagram as reinforcement for comprehension. **BL**

Proficient Readers Ask: Why hasn't the playwright indicated more details about the farmhouse's appearance? (*Writers don't need to provide readers with every minor detail in a scene. With general information, the reader is able to visualize what is being presented with detail.*) **AL**

Teach

R1 Reading Strategy

Evaluating Characters

Answer: *It shows her nervousness or agitation, even though she is still sitting. Her behavior is appalling, indicative of guilt, or indicative of shock.* OL

R2 Reading Strategy

Evaluating Characters

Answer: *Even though he is an older man with experience gauging people's emotional reactions, he seems bewildered by Mrs. Wright's emotional state, and is unqualified to say that she is unconcerned.* OL

said, "I want to see John." And then she—laughed. I guess you would call it a laugh. I thought of Harry and the team outside, so I said a little sharp: "Can't I see John?" "No," she says, kind o' dull like. "Ain't he home?" says I. "Yes," says she, "he's home." "Then why can't I see him?" I asked her, out of patience. "'Cause he's dead," says she. "*Dead?*" says I. She just nodded her head, not getting a bit excited, but rockin' back and forth. "Why—where is he?" says I, not knowing what to say. She just pointed upstairs—like that (*himself pointing to the room above*). I started for the stairs, with the idea of going up there. I walked from there to here—then I says "Why, what did he die of?" "He died of a rope round his neck," says she, and just went on pleatin' at her apron. Well, I went out and called Harry. I thought I might—need help. We went upstairs and there he was lyin'—

COUNTY ATTORNEY. I think I'd rather have you go into that upstairs, where you can point it all out. Just go on now with the rest of the story.

HALE. Well, my first thought was to get that rope off. It looked . . . (*Stops. His face twitches.*) . . . but Harry, he went up to him, and he said, "No, he's dead all right, and we'd better not touch anything." So we went back downstairs. She was still sitting that same way. "Has anybody been notified?" I asked. "No," says she, unconcerned. "Who did this, Mrs. Wright?" said Harry. He said it businesslike—and she stopped pleatin' of her apron. "I don't know," she says. "You don't *know*?" says Harry. "No," says she. "Weren't you sleepin' in the bed with him?" says Harry. "Yes," says she, "but I was on the inside." "Somebody slipped a rope round his neck

and strangled him and you didn't wake up?" says Harry. "I didn't wake up," she said after him. We must 'a' looked as if we didn't see how that could be, for after a minute she said, "I sleep sound." Harry was going to ask her more questions but I said maybe we ought to let her tell her story first to the **coroner**, or the sheriff, so Harry went fast as he could to Rivers' place, where there's a telephone.

COUNTY ATTORNEY. And what did Mrs. Wright do when she knew that you had gone for the coroner?

HALE. She moved from the rocker to that chair over there (*pointing to a small chair in the downstage right corner*) and just sat there with her hands held together and looking down. I got a feeling that I ought to make some conversation, so I said I had come in to see if John wanted to put in a telephone, and at that she started to laugh, and then she stopped and looked at me—scared. (*The COUNTY ATTORNEY, who has had his notebook out, makes a note.*) I dunno, maybe it wasn't scared. I wouldn't like to say it was. Soon Harry got back, and then Dr. Lloyd came, and you, Mr. Peters, and so I guess that's all I know that you don't.

COUNTY ATTORNEY. (*rising and looking around*). I guess we'll go upstairs first—and then out to the barn and around there. (*To the SHERIFF*) You're convinced that there was nothing important here—nothing that would point to any motive?

SHERIFF. Nothing here but kitchen things. (*The COUNTY ATTORNEY, after again looking around the kitchen, opens the door of a cupboard closet in right wall. He brings a small chair from right—gets up on it and looks on a shelf. Pulls his hand away, sticky.*)

Reading Strategy Evaluating Characters *How important is Mrs. Wright's gesture? What does it tell you about her character?* R1

Reading Strategy Evaluating Characters *Is Mr. Hale qualified to label Mrs. Wright's tone as unconcerned? Explain.* R2

Literary Element Stage Directions *Why has the County Attorney made a note here?* L1

Vocabulary

coroner (kôr′ə nər) *n.* the public employee responsible for investigating deaths that are not thought to be from natural causes

---

Additional Support

Skills Practice

VOCABULARY: Word Origins The word *trifle* is based upon the Middle English word *trufle*, or *trifle*, which is taken from the Old French *trufle* or *trufe*, meaning "trickery, mockery, or deceit." The common denotation of *trifle* is "something of little importance." The use of *trifle* as a verb is more clearly derived from its original French meaning. Have students define *trifle* as a verb, and then explain how its meaning is linked to its origin. (*The verb form of* trifle *is defined as to talk in a mocking tone or to talk with misleading or deluding intentions. Both definitions describe ridicule and dishonesty*). OL

Magdalena's Spices, 2003. Pam Ingalls.
Viewing the Art: Does this scene resemble how you picture Mrs. Wright's kitchen? Explain. ★

COUNTY ATTORNEY. Here's a nice mess. (*The women draw nearer upstage center.*)

MRS. PETERS. (*to the other woman*). Oh, her fruit; it did freeze. (*To the LAWYER*) She worried about that when it turned so cold. She said the fire'd go out and her jars would break.

SHERIFF. (*rises*). Well, can you beat the women! Held for murder and worryin' about her preserves.

COUNTY ATTORNEY. (*getting down from chair*). I guess before we're through she may have something more serious than preserves to worry about. (*crosses down right center*)

HALE. Well, women are used to worrying over **trifles**.

(*The two women move a little closer together.*)

COUNTY ATTORNEY. (*with the gallantry of a young politician*). And yet, for all their worries, what would we do without the ladies? (*The women do not unbend. He goes below the center table to the sink, takes a dipperful of water from the pail and, pouring it into a basin, washes his hands. While he is doing this, the SHERIFF and HALE cross to cupboard, which they inspect. The COUNTY ATTORNEY starts to wipe his hands on the roller towel, turns it for a cleaner place.*) Dirty towels! (*Kicks his foot against the pans under the sink.*) Not much of a housekeeper, would you say, ladies?

Literary Element Stage Directions *What do these directions imply about the women's feelings about Mr. Hale's comment?* **L2**

SUSAN GLASPELL **901**

Teach

R Reading Strategy

Evaluating Characters

Answer: *Mrs. Hale's statement is credible because of her former defense of the state of Mrs. Wright's kitchen. Mrs. Hale admits to not visiting her neighbors, which is not a flattering characteristic. Her willingness to admit her own faults shows that she is objective and only concerned with telling the truth.* **OL**

L Literary Element

Stage Directions

Answer: *Mrs. Hale is obviously sympathetic to Mrs. Wright's predicament, since she is making a point to clean up her kitchen. She seems to understand that housework can be left undone and not mean that a woman is unqualified to perform her duties; she also knows, from being a farm wife herself, how taxing farm work is and how difficult it is to keep up with it.* **OL**

MRS. HALE. (*stiffly*). There's a great deal of work to be done on a farm.

COUNTY ATTORNEY. To be sure. And yet (*with a little bow to her*) I know there are some Dickson County farmhouses which do not have such roller towels. (*He gives it a pull to expose its full length again.*)

MRS. HALE. Those towels get dirty awful quick. Men's hands aren't always as clean as they might be.

COUNTY ATTORNEY. Ah, loyal to your sex, I see. But you and Mrs. Wright were neighbors. I suppose you were friends, too.

MRS. HALE. (*shaking her head*). I've not seen much of her of late years. I've not been in this house—it's more than a year.

COUNTY ATTORNEY. (*crossing to women upstage center*). And why was that? You didn't like her?

MRS. HALE. I liked her all well enough. Farmers' wives have their hands full, Mr. Henderson. And then—

COUNTY ATTORNEY. Yes—?

MRS. HALE. (*looking about*). It never seemed a very cheerful place.

COUNTY ATTORNEY. No—it's not cheerful. I shouldn't say she had the homemaking instinct.

MRS. HALE. Well, I don't know as Wright had, either.

COUNTY ATTORNEY. You mean that they didn't get on very well?

MRS. HALE. No, I don't mean anything. But I don't think a place'd be any cheerfuller for John Wright's being in it.

COUNTY ATTORNEY. I'd like to talk more of that a little later. I want to get the lay of things upstairs now. (*He goes past the women to upstage right where steps lead to a stair door.*)

SHERIFF. I suppose anything Mrs. Peters does'll be all right. She was to take in some

clothes for her, you know, and a few little things. We left in such a hurry yesterday.

COUNTY ATTORNEY. Yes, but I would like to see what you take, Mrs. Peters, and keep an eye out for anything that might be of use to us.

MRS. PETERS. Yes, Mr. Henderson. (*The men leave by upstage right door to stairs. The women listen to the men's steps on the stairs, then look about the kitchen.*)

MRS. HALE. (*crossing left to sink*). I'd hate to have men coming into my kitchen, snooping around and criticizing. (*She arranges the pans under sink which the lawyer had shoved out of place.*)

MRS. PETERS. Of course it's no more than their duty. (*crosses to cupboard upstage right*)

MRS. HALE. Duty's all right, but I guess that deputy sheriff that came out to make the fire might have got a little of this on. (*Gives the roller towel a pull.*) Wish I'd thought of that sooner. Seems mean to talk about her for not having things slicked up when she had to come away in such a hurry. (*Crosses right to* MRS. PETERS *at cupboard.*)

MRS. PETERS. (*who has been looking through cupboard, lifts one end of a towel that covers a pan*). She had bread set. (*Stands still.*)

MRS. HALE. (*eyes fixed on a loaf of bread beside the breadbox, which is on a low shelf of the cupboard*). She was going to put this in there. (*Picks up loaf, then abruptly drops it. In a manner of returning to familiar things.*) It's a shame about her fruit. I wonder if it's all gone. (*Gets up on the chair and looks.*) I think there's some here that's all right, Mrs. Peters. Yes—here; (*holding it toward the window*) this is cherries, too. (*looking again*) I declare I believe that's the only one. (*Gets down, jar in her hand. Goes to the sink and wipes it off on the outside.*) She'll feel awful bad after all her hard work in the hot weather. I remember the afternoon I put up my cherries last summer. (*She*

Reading Strategy Evaluating Characters *What makes Mrs. Hale's statement a credible one?* **R**

902 UNIT 4 DRAMA

Literary Element Stage Directions *What do these stage directions suggest about Mrs. Hale's opinion of Mrs. Wright?* **L**

Additional Support

Skills Practice

GRAMMAR: Subordinating Conjunctions Often, sentences can be combined to make the relationship between them clearer. Subordinating conjunctions are words that show relationships of time, cause, or condition. Examples are *after, because, if, since, until, when, while.* As a class, determine

how the following sentences can be combined using a subordinating conjunction: Mr. Henderson makes several insulting comments. Mrs. Hale becomes defensive. (*After Mr. Henderson makes several insulting comments, Mrs. Hale becomes defensive.*) **OL** puts the jar on the big kitchen table, center of the room. With a sigh, is about to sit down in the rocking chair. Before she is seated realizes what chair it is; with a slow look at it, steps back. The chair which she has touched rocks back and forth. MRS. PETERS moves to center table and they both watch the chair rock for a moment or two.)

MRS. PETERS. (shaking off the mood which the empty rocking chair has evoked; now in a businesslike manner she speaks). Well, I must get those things from the front room

closet. (She goes to the door at the right, but, after looking into the other room, steps back.) You coming with me, Mrs. Hale? You could help me carry them. (They go in the other room; reappear, MRS. PETERS carrying a dress, petticoat and skirt, MRS. HALE following with a pair of shoes.) My, it's cold in there. (She puts the clothes on the big table, and hurries to the stove.)

Big Idea Portraits of Real Life *Why do you think Mrs. Wright needs these items?* **BI**

Table in Sorrento, 2003. Pam Ingalls.
Viewing the Art: What mood does this painting evoke? Is it similar to the play's mood? Why or why not?

SUSAN GLASPELL **903**

Teach

BI **Big Idea**
Portraits of Real Life
Answer: *She had to leave her house in a hurry and has no proper clothes. She needs these dressy clothes for her trial.* **OL**

⭐ **Viewing the Art**
Answer: *The harsh colors reflect the lonely and unforgiving farm life, and the kitchen scene reflects the importance of domestic items in the play.* **AS**

Differentiated Instruction

Kinesthetic Learners Kinesthetic learners will appreciate the opportunity to put the many stage directions to work. Choose an exchange that includes stage directions that require the reader or speaker to move or behave in a certain way. Divide students into pairs and have them act out the stage directions as they speak. Encourage students to follow the directions carefully, as this activity can serve as an assessment of comprehension. To further enhance understanding of the purpose of stage directions, have students rewrite the directions with movements and gestures that maintain the integrity of the scene. **BL**

Objectives
• To understand stage directions (SE)
• To evaluate characters (SE)
• To use subordinating conjunctions correctly (TWE)

903

Teach

B1 Big Idea

Portraits of Real Life

Answer: *An accused murderer should have more important things to worry about, and Mrs. Wright's preoccupation with her preserves indicates that the murder is not a priority.* **OL**

R1 Reading Strategy

Evaluating Characters

Answer: *Mrs. Peters is the sheriff's wife and undoubtedly influenced by that relationship. Her failure to think outside legal lines is surely connected to her statement. She says this because it seems that Mrs. Hale is defending Mrs. Wright's possible murder of her husband. The women's different backgrounds account for their contrasting opinions here.* **OL**

⭐ **Writer's Technique**

Invoking the Reader's Imagination

Ask: What does a voice "coming back to familiar things" sound like? *(The voice is soft, and the words are slow to indicate some memory or deep thought.)* Explain that this description requires an imaginative reader who pulls from personal experience to envision the sounds or images being presented. **AS**

MRS. HALE. (*right of center table examining the skirt*). Wright was close.[2] I think maybe that's why she kept so much to herself. She didn't even belong to the Ladies' Aid. I suppose she felt she couldn't do her part, and then you don't enjoy things when you feel shabby. I heard she used to wear pretty clothes and be lively, when she was Minnie Foster, one of the town girls singing in the choir. But that—oh, that was thirty years ago. This all you was to take in?

MRS. PETERS. She said she wanted an apron. Funny thing to want, for there isn't much to get you dirty in jail, goodness knows. But I suppose just to make her feel more natural. (*crosses to cupboard*) She said they was in the top drawer in this cupboard. Yes, here. And then her little shawl that always hung behind the door. (*Opens stair door and looks.*) Yes, here it is. (*Quickly shuts door leading upstairs.*)

MRS. HALE. (*abruptly moving toward her*). Mrs. Peters?

MRS. PETERS. Yes, Mrs. Hale? (*At upstage right door.*)

MRS. HALE. Do you think she did it?

MRS. PETERS. (*in a frightened voice*). Oh, I don't know.

MRS. HALE. Well, I don't think she did. Asking for an apron and her little shawl. Worrying about her fruit.

MRS. PETERS. (*Starts to speak, glances up, where footsteps are heard in the room above. In a low voice*). Mr. Peters says it looks bad for her. Mr. Henderson is awful sarcastic in a speech and he'll make fun of her sayin' she didn't wake up.

MRS. HALE. Well, I guess John Wright didn't wake when they was slipping that rope under his neck.

---

2. Here, *close* is used to mean "unwilling to talk or share feelings."

Big Idea Portraits of Real Life *Why does Mrs. Hale think that Mrs. Wright's worries about her preserves indicate her innocence?* **B1**

904 UNIT 4 DRAMA

MRS. PETERS. (*crossing slowly to table and placing shawl and apron on table with other clothing*). No, it's strange. It must have been done awful crafty and still. They say it was such a—funny way to kill a man, rigging it all up like that.

MRS. HALE. (*crossing to left of* MRS. PETERS *at table*). That's just what Mr. Hale said. There was a gun in the house. He says that's what he can't understand.

MRS. PETERS. Mr. Henderson said coming out that what was needed for the case was a motive; something to show anger, or—sudden feeling.

MRS. HALE. (*who is standing by the table*). Well, I don't see any signs of anger around here. (*She puts her hand on the dishtowel which lies on the table, stands looking down at table, one-half of which is clean, the other half messy.*) It's wiped to here. (*Makes a move as if to finish work, then turns and looks at loaf of bread outside the breadbox. Drops towel. In that voice of coming back to familiar things.*) Wonder how they are finding things upstairs. (*crossing below table to downstage right*) I hope she had it a little more readied-up up there. You know, it seems kind of sneaking. Locking her up in town and then coming out here and trying to get her own house to turn against her! ⭐

MRS. PETERS. But, Mrs. Hale, the law is the law.

MRS. HALE. I s'pose 'tis. (*unbuttoning her coat*) Better loosen up your things, Mrs. Peters. You won't feel them when you go out. (*MRS. PETERS takes off her fur tippet,[3] goes to hang it on chair back left of table, stands looking at the work basket on floor near downstage left window.*)

MRS. PETERS. She was piecing a quilt. (*She brings the large sewing basket to the center table and they look at the bright pieces,* MRS. HALE *above the table and* MRS. PETERS *left of it.*)

---

3. A *tippet* is a shawl or scarf.

Reading Strategy Evaluating Characters *What does this statement suggest about Mrs. Peters and Mrs. Hale?* **R1**

Additional Support

Skills Practice

WRITING: News Story have students write news stories about the death of John Wright. They should use the information that has appeared in the play, through page 905. Emphasize that news stories should focus on facts rather than theories. Also point out that news stories should begin with the most important facts. **OL**

MRS. HALE. It's a log cabin pattern.[4] Pretty, isn't it? I wonder if she was goin' to quilt it or just knot it?[5] (*Footsteps have been heard coming down the stairs. The* SHERIFF *enters followed by* HALE *and the* COUNTY ATTORNEY.)

SHERIFF. They wonder if she was going to quilt it or just knot it! (*The men laugh, the women look* **abashed**.)

COUNTY ATTORNEY. (*rubbing his hands over the stove*). Frank's fire didn't do much up there, did it? Well, let's go out to the barn and get that cleared up. (*The men go outside by upstage left door.*)

MRS. HALE. (*resentfully*). I don't know as there's anything so strange, our takin' up our time with little things while we're waiting for them to get the evidence. (*She sits in chair right of table smoothing out a block with decision.*) I don't see as it's anything to laugh about.

MRS. PETERS. (*apologetically*). Of course they've got awful important things on their minds. (*Pulls up a chair and joins* MRS. HALE *at the left of the table.*)

MRS. HALE. (*examining another block*). Mrs. Peters, look at this one. Here, this is the one she was working on, and look at the sewing! All the rest of it has been so nice and even. And look at this! It's all over the place! Why, it looks as if she didn't know what she was about! (*After she has said this they look at each other, then start to glance back at the door. After an instant* MRS. HALE *has pulled at a knot and ripped the sewing.*)

MRS. PETERS. Oh, what are you doing, Mrs. Hale?

---

4. A *log cabin pattern* for a quilt consists of strips of fabric arranged as squares.
5. The top and bottom layers of a quilt are connected to one another either by *quilting* or by *knotting.* Quilting is a pattern of stitching that covers the entire quilt. Knotting is done at regular intervals and consists of a piece of yarn passed through all layers and tied.

Reading Strategy Evaluating Characters *How do these women's perspectives on men differ?* **R2**

Vocabulary

abashed (ə bash′ ed) *adj.* embarrassed or ashamed

MRS. HALE. (*mildly*). Just pulling out a stitch or two that's not sewed very good. (*threading a needle*) Bad sewing always made me fidgety.

MRS. PETERS. (*with a glance at door, nervously*). I don't think we ought to touch things.

MRS. HALE. I'll just finish up this end. (*suddenly stopping and leaning forward*) Mrs. Peters?

MRS. PETERS. Yes, Mrs. Hale?

MRS. HALE. What do you suppose she was so nervous about?

MRS. PETERS. Oh—I don't know, I don't know as she was nervous. I sometimes sew awful queer when I'm just tired. (*MRS. HALE starts to say something, looks at* MRS. PETERS, *then goes on sewing.*) Well, I must get these things wrapped up. They may be through sooner than we think. (*putting apron and other things together*) I wonder where I can find a piece of paper, and string. (*Rises.*)

MRS. HALE. In that cupboard, maybe.

MRS. PETERS. (*crosses right looking in cupboard*). Why, here's a birdcage. (*Holds it up.*) Did she have a bird, Mrs. Hale?

MRS. HALE. Why, I don't know whether she did or not—I've not been here for so long. There was a man around last year selling canaries cheap, but I don't know as she took one; maybe she did. She used to sing real pretty herself.

MRS. PETERS. (*glancing around*). Seems funny to think of a bird here. But she must have had one, or why would she have a cage? I wonder what happened to it?

MRS. HALE. I s'pose maybe the cat got it.

MRS. PETERS. No, she didn't have a cat. She's got that feeling some people have about cats—being afraid of them. My cat got in her room and she was real upset and asked me to take it out.

MRS. HALE. My sister Bessie was like that. Queer, ain't it?

MRS. PETERS. (*examining the cage*). Why, look at ★ this door. It's broke. One hinge is pulled apart. (*Takes a step down to* MRS. HALE'S *right.*)

SUSAN GLASPELL **905**

Teach

R2 **Reading Strategy**

Evaluating Characters

Answer: *Mrs. Hale is described as speaking "resentfully" after being dismissed as insignificant. Mrs. Peters, on the other hand, responds to the same treatment "apologetically." While Mrs. Peters is obviously aware of the subordinate way the men treat her, she is less willing to acknowledge it as hurtful or wrong.* **OL**

★ **Writer's Technique**

Dialogue Point out the grave importance of dialogue in dramatic works. The vast majority of characterization and plot must be revealed through the dialogue in a play. Some playwrights use exposition and stage directions to do a lot of the play's work, but Susan Glaspell does not. She is content to reveal the story's unfolding through the characters themselves. **AS**

Building Reading Fluency

Following Along Both readers struggling to build fluency and those trying to improve it can benefit from a class reading of *Trifles.* Assign roles to students on a rotating basis to be sure that each class member has an opportunity to practice. Remind students that fluency can be enhanced by following along as fellow readers recite their assigned dialogue. Students can discover how to pronounce difficult words this way, and they can also offer support to those having trouble with pronunciation. Perform spot checks as the class reads to be sure that everyone is keeping pace. Encourage readers to "perform" their roles. **BL**

Objectives
• To evaluate characters (SE)
• To debate ideas in mock-trial format (TWE)

905

Teach

★ **Viewing the Art**

Answer: *It could resemble any of the lonely or thoughtful women, but probably is most comparable to Mrs. Wright because of the figure's down-turned face and hand position.* **AS**

Portrait of Olga, 1922–23. Pablo Picasso. Pastel, 105 x 75 cm. Private Collection. ★
Viewing the Art: Which character in *Trifles* could this portrait resemble? Why?

906 UNIT 4 DRAMA

Additional Support

Skills Practice

RESEARCH: Women's History
Susan Glaspell explores a variety of relevant women's issues in *Trifles*. Some might argue that these same issues are relevant today. Have students research some facet of women's history. Examples of appropriate topics include women at work; the women's suffrage movement; and the post-war women's movement. Diversify the assignment by allowing students of varied ethnic backgrounds the freedom to apply the assignment to their culture's history. Require students to compile their findings in a four- to five-page paper. **OL**

MRS. HALE. (*looking too*). Looks as if someone must have been rough with it.

MRS. PETERS. Why, yes. (*She brings the cage forward and puts it on the table.*)

MRS. HALE. (*glancing toward upstage left door*). I wish if they're going to find any evidence they'd be about it. I don't like this place.

MRS. PETERS. But I'm awful glad you came with me, Mrs. Hale. It would be lonesome for me sitting here alone.

MRS. HALE. It would, wouldn't it? (*dropping her sewing*) But I tell you what I do wish, Mrs. Peters. I wish I had come over sometimes when she was here. I—(*looking around the room*)—wish I had.

MRS. PETERS. But of course you were awful busy, Mrs. Hale—your house and your children.

MRS. HALE. (*rises and crosses left*). I could've come. I stayed away because it weren't cheerful—and that's why I ought to have come. I—(*looking out left window*)—I've never liked this place. Maybe because it's down in a hollow and you don't see the road. I dunno what it is, but it's a lonesome place and always was. I wish I had come over to see Minnie Foster sometimes. I can see now—(*shakes her head*)

MRS. PETERS. (*left of table and above it*). Well, you mustn't reproach yourself, Mrs. Hale. Somehow we just don't see how it is with other folks until—something turns up.

MRS. HALE. Not having children makes less work—but it makes a quiet house, and Wright out to work all day, and no company when he did come in. (*turning from window*) Did you know John Wright, Mrs. Peters?

MRS. PETERS. Not to know him; I've seen him in town. They say he was a good man.

MRS. HALE. Yes—good; he didn't drink, and kept his word as well as most, I guess, and

paid his debts. But he was a hard man, Mrs. Peters. Just to pass the time of day with him—(*shivers*) Like a raw wind that gets to the bone. (*pauses, her eye falling on the cage*) I should think she would' a' wanted a bird. But what do you suppose went with it?

MRS. PETERS. I don't know, unless it got sick and died. (*She reaches over and swings the broken door, swings it again, both women watch it.*)

MRS. HALE. You weren't raised round here, were you? (*MRS. PETERS shakes her head.*) You didn't know—her?

MRS. PETERS. Not till they brought her yesterday.

MRS. HALE. She—come to think of it, she was kind of like a bird herself—real sweet and pretty, but kind of timid and—fluttery. How—she—did—change. (*Silence; then as if struck by a happy thought and relieved to get back to everyday things, crosses right above MRS. PETERS to cupboard, replaces small chair used to stand on to its original place downstage right.*) Tell you what, Mrs. Peters, why don't you take the quilt in with you? It might take up her mind. ★

MRS. PETERS. Why, I think that's a real nice idea, Mrs. Hale. There couldn't possibly be any objection to it, could there? Now, just what would I take? I wonder if her patches are in here—and her things. (*They look in the sewing basket.*)

MRS. HALE. (*crosses to right of table*). Here's some red. I expect this has got sewing things in it. (*Brings out a fancy box.*) What a pretty box. Looks like something somebody would give you. Maybe her scissors are in here. (*Opens box. Suddenly puts her hand to her nose.*) Why— (*MRS. PETERS bends nearer, then turns her face away.*) There's something wrapped up in this piece of silk.

MRS. PETERS. Why, this isn't her scissors.

MRS. HALE. (*lifting the silk*). Oh, Mrs. Peters— it's—(*MRS. PETERS bends closer.*)

MRS. PETERS. It's the bird.

Big Idea Portraits of Real Life *Is Mrs. Hale's regret a realistic response to what has happened? Explain.* **BI**

Teach

BI Big Idea

Portraits of Real Life
Answer: *People have regrets, usually many of them. It is easy to look back and later see what you could or should have done. Students may recall personal moments that illustrate their own regrets.* **OL**

★ Writer's Technique

Dialogue
Ask: What purpose do the dashes in the characters' dialogue serve? *(The dashes indicate uncertainty, hesitation, or contemplation.)* **Ask:** Do you think this enhances or hinders the dialogue's delivery? *(Responses will vary, but should be supported with logical reasons.)* Explain to students that the playwright depends heavily on her characters' words for the development of *Trifles,* and that by describing *how* those words are relayed, she can convey feelings, attitudes, and even past events. **AS**

Differentiated Instruction

Proficient Readers To heighten the literary experience and level of instruction for proficient readers, have students consider the fate of Mrs. Wright. Instruct students to write three to four pages of dialogue, with stage directions, explaining what might have happened to Mrs. Wright after the play's conclusion. Students should include all of the characters and contemplate the characters' individual personalities and tendencies before writing dialogue. Encourage creativity, but explain the importance of maintaining credibility. Students can even be pushed to mimic the writing style of Susan Glaspell. **AL**

Objective
• To research and interpret the possible influences of the historical context on a literary work (TWE)

907

Teach

L **Literary Element**

Stage Directions

Answer: *To reveal a feeling of rising fear or suspense. The women have realized something of grave importance, but they do not want to reveal it to the men.* **OL**

★ **Viewing the Art**

Answer: *It brings to mind the loneliness and desolation felt by Mrs. Wright.* **AS**

Painting of Farm House Scene. Connie Hayes.
Viewing the Art: How is this farm scene similar to the play's setting?

MRS. HALE. But, Mrs. Peters—look at it! Its neck! Look at its neck! It's all—other side *to.*[6]

MRS. PETERS. Somebody—wrung—its—neck. (*Their eyes meet. A look of growing comprehension, of horror. Steps are heard outside,* MRS. HALE *slips box under quilt pieces, and sinks into her chair. Enter* SHERIFF *and* COUNTY ATTORNEY. MRS. PETERS *steps downstage left and stands looking out of window.*)

COUNTY ATTORNEY. (*as one turning from serious things to little pleasantries*). Well, ladies, have you decided whether she was going to quilt it or knot it? (*Crosses to center above table.*)

MRS. PETERS. We think she was going to—knot it. (SHERIFF *crosses to right of stove, lifts stove lid and glances at fire, then stands warming hands at stove.*)

COUNTY ATTORNEY. Well, that's interesting, I'm sure. (*Seeing the birdcage.*) Has the bird flown?

MRS. HALE. (*putting more quilt pieces over the box*). We think the—cat got it.

---

6. *Other side to* means that the bird's head was turned the wrong way.

Additional Support

Skills Practice

ASSESSMENT PRACTICE: Making Judgments Say: Which word best describes Mrs. Hale's character? a. judgmental; b. compassionate; c. deceitful; d. angry. Emphasize the importance of choosing the *best* answer. In answering, students must avoid adjectives that describe momentary feelings and choose the word that encompasses total character. (*A is blatantly incorrect. Mrs. Hale might be considered deceitful, but she did not set out to deceive and does so out of compassion. Although Mrs. Hale is angry at times, anger does not dominate her character. So B is the best answer.*) **OL**

COUNTY ATTORNEY. (*preoccupied*). Is there a cat? (*MRS. HALE glances in a quick* **covert** *way at MRS. PETERS.*)

MRS. PETERS. (*turning from window takes a step in*). Well, not now. They're superstitious, you know. They leave.

COUNTY ATTORNEY. (*to SHERIFF PETERS, continuing an interrupted conversation*). No sign at all of anyone having come from the outside. Their own rope. Now let's go up again and go over it piece by piece. (*They start upstairs.*) It would have to have been someone who knew just the— (*MRS. PETERS sits down left of table. The two women sit there not looking at one another, but as if peering into something and at the same time holding back. When they talk now it is in the manner of feeling their way over strange ground, as if afraid of what they are saying, but as if they cannot help saying it.*)

MRS. HALE. (*hesitantly and in hushed voice*) She liked the bird. She was going to bury it in that pretty box.

MRS. PETERS. (*in a whisper*). When I was a girl—my kitten—there was a boy took a hatchet, and before my eyes—and before I could get there— (*covers her face an instant*) If they hadn't held me back I would have—(*catches herself, looks upstairs where steps are heard, falters weakly*)—hurt him.

MRS. HALE. (*with a slow look around her*). I wonder how it would seem never to have had any children around. (*pause*) No, Wright wouldn't like the bird—a thing that sang. She used to sing. He killed that, too.

MRS. PETERS. (*moving uneasily*). We don't know who killed the bird.

> **Literary Element** Stage Directions *What feeling or mood does the author wish to reveal through the women's actions here?* **L**

> **Big Idea** Portraits of Real Life *How does Mrs. Peters's childhood memory make this scene more realistic?* **BI**

> **Vocabulary**

covert (kˈvərt) *adj.* concealed; secretive

MRS. HALE. I knew John Wright.

MRS. PETERS. It was an awful thing was done in this house that night, Mrs. Hale. Killing a man while he slept, slipping a rope around his neck that choked the life out of him.

MRS. HALE. His neck. Choked the life out of him. (*Her hand goes out and rests on the birdcage.*)

MRS. PETERS. (*with rising voice*). We don't know who killed him. We don't know.

MRS. HALE. (*her own feeling not interrupted*). If there'd been years and years of nothing, then a bird to sing to you, it would be awful—still, after the bird was still.

MRS. PETERS. (*something within her speaking*). I know what stillness is. When we homesteaded[7] in Dakota, and my first baby died—after he was two years old, and me with no other then—

MRS. HALE. (*moving*). How soon do you suppose they'll be through looking for the evidence?

MRS. PETERS. I know what stillness is. (*pulling herself back*) The law has got to punish crime, Mrs. Hale.

MRS. HALE. (*not as if answering that*). I wish you'd seen Minnie Foster when she wore a white dress with blue ribbons and stood up there in the choir and sang. (*a look around the room*) Oh, I wish I'd come over here once in a while! That was a crime! That was a crime! Who's going to punish that?

MRS. PETERS. (*looking upstairs*). We mustn't—take on.

MRS. HALE. I might have known she needed help! I know how things can be—for women. I tell you, it's queer, Mrs. Peters. We live close together and we live far apart. We all go through the same things—

---

7. When Mrs. Peters says *homesteaded* here, she is referring to the 1862 Homestead Act, which granted land to settlers if they could live on it for five years.

> **Reading Strategy** Evaluating Characters *Why does Mrs. Hale refer to Mrs. Wright as "Minnie Foster"? What does her description tell you about Mrs. Wright?* **R**

SUSAN GLASPELL **909**

Teach

BI Big Idea
Portraits of Real Life
Answer: *People make many connections between the past and present, so it seems realistic that Mrs. Peters would remember her kitten upon seeing the dead canary.* **OL**

R Reading Strategy
Evaluating Characters
Answer: *Mrs. Hale is remembering the woman Mrs. Wright once was, and is mourning the loss of that carefree, happy person. Students may say that Mrs. Hale's description makes them understand how much has been taken away from Mrs. Wright.* **OL**

★ Literary History
Provincetown Players In 1915, a host of non-theater writers and artists founded the Provincetown Players—a performing theatrical group. It produced new and experimental plays in members' homes. Susan Glaspell was among the original Provincetowners, along with Mary Heaton Vorse, George Cram Cook, and Robert Edmond Jones. **AS**

Differentiated Instruction

Auditory Learners Auditory learners will benefit greatly from any number of aural practices. A shared reading or tape recorded version of "Trifles" will augment their literary experience, but also enhance comprehension. Be sure to make periodic stops during any aural practices to check for comprehension.

Ask students to draw conclusions, make inferences and predictions, and summarize as you go. A combination of auditory options may further improve retention and comprehension. Encourage students to read aloud excerpts from "Trifles" to their loved ones at home. **BL**

Objectives
- To understand stage directions (SE)
- To evaluate characters (SE)
- To make judgments while reading (TWE)

L Literary Element

Stage Directions
Answer: *Lawyer ridicules the women's awareness, feelings, and priorities.* **OL**

R Reading Strategy

Evaluating Characters
Answer: *Her loyalty to another woman in despair demonstrates integrity but her disobedience to the law may be seen as unforgivable. Students should support their claims with textual evidence.* **OL**

CheckPoint

Use the CheckPoint questions on Presentation Plus! to check students' mastery of the selection. These questions can be used with interactive response keypads for immediate student feedback.

---

it's all just a different kind of the same thing. (*Brushes her eyes. Noticing the jar of fruit, reaches out for it.*) If I was you I wouldn't tell her her fruit was gone. Tell her it *ain't*. Tell her it's all right. Take this in to prove it to her. She—she may never know whether it was broke or not.

MRS. PETERS. (*takes the jar, looks about for something to wrap it in; takes petticoat from the clothes brought from the other room, very nervously begins winding this around the jar; in a false voice*). My, it's a good thing the men couldn't hear us. Wouldn't they just laugh! Getting all stirred up over a little thing like a—dead canary. As if that could have anything to do with—with—wouldn't they *laugh*! (*The men are heard coming downstairs.*)

MRS. HALE. (*under her breath*). Maybe they would—maybe they wouldn't.

COUNTY ATTORNEY. No, Peters, it's all perfectly clear except a reason for doing it. But you know juries when it comes to women. If there was some definite thing. (*Crosses slowly to above table. SHERIFF crosses downstage right. MRS. HALE and MRS. PETERS remain seated at either side of table.*) Something to show—something to make a story about—a thing that would connect up with this strange way of doing it— (*The women's eyes meet for an instant. Enter HALE from outer door.*)

HALE. (*remaining upstage left by door*). Well, I've got the team around. Pretty cold out there.

COUNTY ATTORNEY. I'm going to stay awhile by myself. (*To the SHERIFF*) You can send Frank out for me, can't you? I want to go over everything. I'm not satisfied that we can't do better.

SHERIFF. Do you want to see what Mrs. Peters is going to take in? (*The Lawyer picks up the apron, laughs.*)

COUNTY ATTORNEY. Oh, I guess they're not very dangerous things the ladies

picked out. (*Moves a few things about, disturbing the quilt pieces which cover the box. Steps back.*) No, Mrs. Peters doesn't need supervising. For that matter a sheriff's wife is married to the law. Ever think of it that way, Mrs. Peters?

MRS. PETERS. Not—just that way.

SHERIFF. (*chuckling*). Married to the law. (*Moves to downstage right door to the other room.*) I just want you to come in here a minute, George. We ought to take a look at these windows.

COUNTY ATTORNEY. (*scoffingly*).[8] Oh, windows!

SHERIFF. We'll be right out, Mr. Hale. (*HALE goes outside. The SHERIFF follows the COUNTY ATTORNEY into the other room. Then MRS. HALE rises, hands tight together, looking intensely at MRS. PETERS, whose eyes make a slow turn, finally meeting MRS. HALE'S. A moment MRS. HALE holds her, then her own eyes point the way to where the box is concealed. Suddenly MRS. PETERS throws back quilt pieces and tries to put the box in the bag she is carrying. It is too big. She opens box, starts to take bird out, cannot touch it, goes to pieces, stands there helpless. Sound of a knob turning in the other room, MRS. HALE snatches the box and puts it in the pocket of her big coat. Enter COUNTY ATTORNEY and SHERIFF, who remains downstage right.*)

COUNTY ATTORNEY. (*crosses to upstage left door facetiously*). Well, Henry, at least we found out that she was not going to quilt it. She was going to—what is it you call it, ladies?

MRS. HALE. (*standing center below table facing front, her hand against her pocket*). We call it—knot it, Mr. Henderson.

Curtain

---

8. *Scoffingly* means "scornfully."

Reading Strategy Evaluating Characters *Do you think Mrs. Peters is demonstrating integrity here? Explain.* **R**

Vocabulary
facetiously (fə s′shəs l) *adv.* in a manner not meant to be taken seriously; humorously

Literary Element Stage Directions *What do these directions tell you about the lawyer's attitude toward women?* **L**

Additional Support

Skills Practice

SPEAKING AND LISTENING:
Opening Statements In a trial, the prosecution establishes what it intends to prove in its opening statements. The defense outlines arguments for acquittal. Have paired students prepare both opening statements. They can use only what has been revealed in the play. The defense lawyer should incorporate what is known about Mrs. Wright's character and should stress lack of motive. Have each pair of students present their arguments. The audience members, acting as the jury, should evaluate the effectiveness and validity of each speech based on preestablished criteria. **OL**

RESPONDING AND THINKING CRITICALLY

Respond

1. (a)Do you believe that Mrs. Wright killed her husband? Explain. (b)What are your feelings towards Mrs. Wright?

Recall and Interpret

2. (a)Why did Mr. Hale stop by the Wrights' home? (b)If not for this visit, how do you think Mr. Wright's death would have been uncovered?

3. (a)What personal article did Mrs. Wright request to be brought to her? (b)Why might Mrs. Peters think that the article would make Mrs. Wright feel more natural? What does this tell you about the women?

4. (a)What do the women assume happened to the bird? (b)How does this assumption guide their actions?

Analyze and Evaluate

5. (a)How well does Susan Glaspell establish the scene for *Trifles*? (b)Do the stage directions enhance or hinder the scene's depiction? Explain.

6. (a)How does Mrs. Peters' homesteading experience connect her to Mrs. Wright? (b)Does Mrs. Peters' revealing of this information further credit or discredit her? Explain.

7. (a)How does the author reveal the time period in which *Trifles* is set? (b)Could the play have been set in a different era? Explain why or why not.

Connect

8. **Big Idea** **Portraits of Real Life** Identify and discuss some of the characteristics that make *Trifles* seem realistic.

LITERARY ANALYSIS

Literary Element **Stage Directions**

Stage directions serve as the medium of communication between a playwright, the actors, and the readers. In addition to describing the sets, stage directions can indicate a scene's mood, a character's intentions, and even inner conflict. A playwright is only able to communicate critical information to the audience in two ways: through dialogue and through stage directions.

1. Identify two places where stage directions affect your visualization of a character or a scene, either in a positive or a negative way.

2. How effective is the author's delivery of these directions? Explain.

3. How might the absence of stage directions affect the momentum of the play and its overall success?

Review: Setting

As you learned on pages 10–11, the **setting** is the time and place in which the events of a literary work occur. Setting is not limited to physical surroundings, however. The ideas, values, customs, and beliefs of a particular time and place are also an integral part of setting. Setting can help establish the atmosphere or mood of a work.

Partner Activity Pair up with a classmate and discuss the setting of *Trifles*. Together, create a three-column chart similar to the one below. Use the first column to indicate possible aspects of setting. Use the second column to illustrate examples of those aspects as found in the play. Use the final column to reflect your personal views on the aspect as it relates to *Trifles*.

Setting Aspects	Examples	My View
Beliefs	"Hale: Well, women are used to worrying over trifles."	I think that Hale is sadly mistaken, since it is such "trifles" that solve the crime. This shows that women of the time were not valued for their intellectual capacity. I think that society has come a long way.
Customs	The preserving of fruit by the women for future days	This indicates a hard-working, if not harsh life to me. Having to preserve fruit gives me the idea that the characters fear the future, and that it may not promise easy days.
Ideas		
Values		
Time		
Place		

SUSAN GLASPELL **911**

Assess

1. Answers will vary. Students should support their beliefs with examples.

2. (a) Mr. Hale wanted to share a party telephone. (b) Answers will vary.

3. (a) An apron (b) It might bring her some sense of normalcy.

4. (a) That Mr. Wright killed it (b) It justifies Mrs. Wright's reaction. They hide the bird and protect Mrs. Wright.

5. (a) With many details in the initial stage directions (b) They guide the reader's understanding of movement, thought, and emotion.

6. (a) It allows her to relate to Mrs. Wright's feelings of loneliness. (b) It shows her honesty and compassion

7. (a) The party telephone; the men's treatment of the women; and the Homestead Act. (b) The play would not have the same effect if it were set in a different era because of social, political, and historical details.

8. The setting—dirty dishes, rocking chairs, and staircases. The characters—the women's concern for how Mrs. Wright will cope, the men's dismissal of their concerns. The conversations—their subject matter, tones, and gestures.

Literary Element

1. Students should identify how stage directions affected their understanding.

2. Most will think that the delivery was effective.

3. Possible answer: Without them, more dialogue would be needed; this could slow the play.

911

Review: Setting

Students' views will vary. Possible examples:
Ideas: women should be good housekeepers
Values: Community involvement important
Time: after the Homestead Act (1862)
Place: rural United States

Assess

Reading Strategy

1. (a) With just the women's opinions to go on, one might justify her actions because she is a suffering widow who was mistreated by an abusive husband. (b) With only the men's perspectives, the reader might condemn Mrs. Wright and see her as ruthless and apathetic.

2. It balances the play, and lets readers judge for themselves.

Writing About Literature

Students' essays should:

- analyze and evaluate the author's use of dramatic irony
- provide textual examples as support for their opinions
- include and properly cite quotes from the play

Listening and Speaking

Encourage students to research the order of trial before preparing their mock trials. Trials commonly follow this order: opening statements, questioning and cross-examination by both the prosecution and the defense, closing arguments, deliberation of the jury, and a verdict.

Reading Strategy Evaluating Characters

The credibility of a character is determined not only by the character's thoughts and actions, but also by what other characters say and think about him or her. Sometimes, as in *Trifles*, a character's credibility is solely dependent on others' opinions and feelings.

1. (a) If you based your opinion of Mrs. Wright solely on Mrs. Hale's and Mrs. Peters' view of her, how would you view her? (b) How would you view Mrs. Wright if you based your opinion only on the male characters' opinons?

2. How do these two varying perspectives of Mrs. Wright's character affect the play as a whole?

Vocabulary Practice

Practice with Context Clues Use the context clues in the sentences below to determine the meaning of the boldfaced vocabulary word.

1. She considered the scrapbook only a **trifle**, but her grandchildren treated it like a treasure.
   a. something unimportant
   b. something valuable

2. They did not move the body until the **coroner** had had a chance to evaluate what had caused the death.
   a. murder suspect
   b. medical examiner

Academic Vocabulary

Here are two words from the vocabulary list on page R82.

legal (lē′gəl) *adj.* of, related to, or drawing authority from the law

debate (di bāt′) *n.* a verbal dispute or argument

Practice and Apply

1. What **legal** measures did Mrs. Hale and Mrs. Peters interfere with by confiscating the dead bird?

2. Why did Mrs. Hale and the County Attorney have a **debate** about the appearance of the kitchen?

Writing About Literature

Evaluate Author's Craft Dramatic irony occurs when the audience has information that is unknown to some or all of the characters in a play. What information is crucial to the play *Trifles*? How does the playwright use this information to create dramatic irony? What effect does the dramatic irony have on the audience and on the play? Write a one- or two-page analysis of the play in which you discuss the author's use of dramatic irony.

Before you begin drafting, reread the play and identify the places where dramatic irony is strongest. Use quotes from these scenes to support the ideas in your essay. A chart like the one below might help you organize your quotes and examples.

Example	Quote
Mrs. Hale lies to the County Attorney about what happened to the bird, but the audience knows the truth.	"MRS. HALE. (putting more quilt pieces over the box). We think the—cat got it."

After you have completed a draft, pair up with a peer reviewer. Allow him or her to evaluate your work and suggest revisions. Once you have revised your draft, proofread it for errors in spelling, grammar, and punctuation.

Listening and Speaking

In a small group, prepare to present a mock trial for Mrs. Minnie Wright. Assign roles for George Henderson, Henry Peters, Lewis Hale, Mrs. Peters, Mrs. Hale, a defense attorney, a judge, and a prosecutor. Compose a script containing each character's dialogue, and practice reciting the parts aloud so that their presentation is eloquent and effective.

Present your trial to another group of classmates who will act as the jury. After you have presented your case, have the jury vote on Mrs. Wright's guilt or innocence. The jury should also provide positive and negative feedback on the trial itself. Then, your small group can serve as a jury for another group.

 Literature **Online** **Web Activities** For eFlashcards, Selection Quick Checks, and other Web activities, go to www.glencoe.com.

Vocabulary

1. a 2. b

Academic Vocabulary

1. They have removed evidence from the scene of the crime.

2. To show the difference between men and women in the domestic scene.

Literature Online

Web Activities Have students access the Web site for interactive activities that will help them assess their understanding of the selection.

Comparing Literature *Across Genres*

Connecting to the Reading Selections

Expectations for women have varied tremendously across countries, cultures, and time periods. In most places today, women can expect to have choices when it comes to education, employment, and marriage. A century or more ago, expectations for women were very different. The three works compared here—by Josephina Niggli, Carmen Tafolla, and Isak Dinesen—explore cultural expectations, especially those relating to women, and how their characters face the challenges that result from those expectations.

United States, 1943

United States, 1992

Denmark, 1953

COMPARING THE [Big Idea] Portraits of Real Life

Capturing life in literature is a task that requires an author to incorporate realistic characters, events, and details into a literary work. Josephina Niggli, Carmen Tafolla, and Isak Dinesen all attempt to portray real life with their writing. While each author focuses on a different time and place, they all develop their characters in such a way that allows the reader to form a personal connection with them.

COMPARING Theme

The **theme** is the central message of a work of literature. The theme provides some insight or lesson with which readers can connect. Niggli, Tafolla, and Dinesen, for example, each explore the theme of loyalty and how it impacts the lives of women.

COMPARING Cultures

Culture is an important consideration for the authors of each of the following selections. All of the authors draw heavily on their surroundings and heritages for the inspiration and content of their stories. Without cultural backdrops, these selections would lose a layer of texture that draws the reader into the authors' literary worlds.

Focus

BELLRINGER

Bellringer Options
Selection Focus Transparency 38
Daily Language Practice
Transparency 81
Or **write on the board:**
"A Drama of the Mexican Revolution"
Ask: In what situations do people exhibit bravery? What is it that causes them to act bravely? Have students discuss the kinds of actions that reveal bravery, people who can be considered brave, and possible reasons for acting bravely.

Connecting to the Reading Selections

Ask students to describe anything they may know about the Mexican Revolution. Then ask them to think about the different perspectives and portraits of real life the following three selections may show.

Selection Skills

Comparing Literature

Literary Elements
- Characterization (SE pp. 915–931)
- Irony (TWE p. 926)
- Character Motivation (TWE p. 930)
- Free Verse (TWE p. 932)

Reading Skills
- Analyzing Plot and Setting (SE pp. 915–931)
- Visualizing (TWE pp. 918, 938)

Vocabulary Skills
- Word Parts (SE pp. 915, 931)
- Connotation and Denotation (TWE p. 916)

Listening/Speaking/Viewing Skills
- Reading a Monologue (TWE p. 920)

Writing Skills/Grammar
- Writing a Journal Entry (SE p. 931)
- Compound Sentences and Predicates (TWE p. 928)
- Perfect Tense (TWE p. 934)

Focus

Summary

Marica is about to poison herself in grief when Raquel stops her. After Marica goes to bed, two rebels break in. One shows Raquel the wedding ring of her husband, a Federal officer whom he says they have imprisoned. He demands refuge. Raquel hides the rebels, Andrés and Cleto, from Federal officers. After the officers leave, Cleto tells Raquel that her husband gave them the ring, promising refuge at his home if they spared his life. Raquel is shocked and poisons the two rebels.

Literature Online

Author Search To expand students' appreciation of Josephina Niggli, have them access the Web site for additional information and resources.

The Ring of General Macías

MEET JOSEPHINA NIGGLI

Even though Josephina Niggli was the child of European American parents, she most strongly identified with the Mexican culture into which she was born and raised. Niggli's fearlessness as a writer—exemplified by her tackling of subjects such as the oppression of women in Mexican culture and the Mexican revolution—inspired a new generation of Mexican American authors.

Between Borders Niggli came of age during a turbulent era in Mexican history. In 1913 President Francisco Madero was assassinated, and as a result the Niggli family fled Mexico and wandered the Southwestern United States until 1920. In 1925, at the onset of the Mexican Revolution, Niggli was sent away to school in San Antonio. Like many writers, Niggli's talent was first recognized and encouraged by a teacher—a particular nun who locked Niggli in her room until she emerged with a finished short story to enter in a magazine competition. Her entry went on to win second place.

> "Once you have experienced the emotion of having a play produced, you are forever lost to the ordinary world."
>
> —Josephina Niggli, from *Pointers on Playwriting*

After college, Niggli moved to North Carolina, where she joined the Carolina Playmakers, a graduate program at the University of North Carolina at Chapel Hill. She wrote several plays during this time that focused on the Mexican Revolution.

Mexican Village, Niggli's first novel, is her most famous work. Niggli portrays the experiences of an obstinate Mexican American who, after resisting his heritage, gradually learns to appreciate Mexican village culture and traditions. According to one critic, the novel was ahead of its time; as Raymond Paredes says, "*Mexican Village . . .* pointed forward to an emerging school of realism, confronting such issues as racism, the oppression of women, and the failure of the Mexican Revolution." This work, like others by Niggli, reflects both alienation from and loyalty toward the two cultures into which she was born.

A Brief Hollywood Turn Niggli temporarily moved to Hollywood to become a "stable writer," an uncredited writer hired to correct flawed scripts, for a renowned motion picture studio. As a stable writer, Niggli worked on famous film scripts, including *The Mark of Zorro* and *Seven Brides for Seven Brothers*. After leaving Hollywood, she continued to write for the popular television show *The Twilight Zone*. Not surprisingly, Niggli was an avid science fiction reader; one of her favorite movies was *Star Wars*.

Niggli eventually returned to North Carolina, where she taught playwriting at Western Carolina University for many years.

Josephina Niggli was born in 1910 and died in 1983.

Literature Online **Author Search** For more about Josephina Niggli, go to www.glencoe.com.

Selection Resources

Print Materials
- Unit 4 Resources (Fast File), pp. 56–59
- Leveled Vocabulary Development, p. 68
- Selection and Unit Assessments, pp. 161–162
- Selection Quick Checks, p. 81

Transparencies
- Bellringer Options Transparencies:
  Selection Focus Transparency 38
  Daily Language Practice Transparency 81
- Literary Elements Transparency 15

Technology
- TeacherWorks Plus™ CD-ROM
- StudentWorks Plus™ CD-ROM
- Presentation Plus!™ CD-ROM
- Literature Online, glencoe.com
- Online Student Edition, mhln.com
- Exam*View*® Assessment Suite CD-ROM
- Vocabulary PuzzleMaker CD-ROM
- Listening Library, disc 2 track 13

LITERATURE PREVIEW

Connecting to the Play

The Ring of General Macías focuses on family pride and the lengths to which people will go to preserve that pride. Before you read the play, think about the following questions:

- Of what things or qualities are you intensely proud?
- What would you do to keep your pride intact?

Building Background

The Mexican Revolution had its roots in the dictatorship of President Porfirio Díaz, who took power in 1876. Under Díaz the majority of citizens—small farmers and laborers—suffered increasing hardship and repression. Meanwhile, land and wealth were accumulated by a small, elite class. Many members of this class were educated in Europe and adopted European—especially French—fashions and manners. In 1910 armed resistance to Díaz's rule began, and in 1911 the dictator was forced to resign. The revolutionary struggle, which lasted for several more years, helped define Mexican identity.

Setting Purposes for Reading

Big Idea Portraits of Real Life

Notice how Niggli describes the women in the play. Do you think that these women accurately represent those in real life?

Literary Element Characterization

Characterization is the method(s) a writer uses to reveal a character's personality to the reader. A character's personality might be revealed through the character's own words, thoughts, or actions, or through what other characters think and say about the character. Being attuned to characterization can help you better understand a character, as well as the messages that an author intends to communicate through that character.

- See Literary Terms Handbook, p. R3.

Literature Online **Interactive Literary Elements Handbook** To review or learn more about the literary elements, go to www.glencoe.com.

OBJECTIVES
In studying this selection, you will focus on the following:
- understanding characterization
- analyzing plot and setting
- writing a journal entry to respond to a text's theme

READING PREVIEW

Reading Strategy Analyzing Plot and Setting

The **plot**, or series of events that occur in a literary work, reveals the conflicts that keep the story moving forward. The **setting** tells the reader when and where the work takes place. By **analyzing the plot and the setting** of a play or other literary work, you can learn a lot about the author's intended purpose for the work. As you read, notice the sequence of events in the play, the setting, and the significance of both.

Reading Tip: Sequencing Events. Use a graphic organizer like the one below to record the sequence of the events that form the plot.

Sequence of Events

| In the story, the problem begins when | → | After this, | → | Next, |

Vocabulary

regally (rē′gəl lē) *adv.* in a grand, dignified manner befitting a king or a queen; p. 920 *The homecoming queen waved regally at the crowd.*

ostentatiously (os′tən tā′shəs lē) *adv.* in a way intended to attract attention or impress others; p. 920 *Their home was decorated ostentatiously.*

notorious (nō tôr′ē əs) *adj.* widely and unfavorably known; p. 924 *The students' antics were notorious among the substitute teachers.*

repressed (ri prest′) *adj.* held back or kept under control; restrained; p. 925 *The two normally exuberant boys repressed their behavior.*

impertinent (im purt′ən ənt) *adj.* inappropriately bold or forward; p. 927 *The girl's brash behavior toward her teacher was impertinent.*

Vocabulary Tip: Word Parts Word meanings are changed by adding suffixes, prefixes, or both to root words.

Focus

Characterization

Say: Many characterization devices common in fiction, such as narrative description, do not work as well in plays. How can a playwright ensure that an audience gets an accurate impression of a character? *(Students may say that the character's voice and choice of words must be precise, or that the reactions of other characters may provide a reliable impression.)* Have students note the differences between Niggli's and Dinesen's methods of characterization. **OL**

V Vocabulary

Vocabulary File Say: Add these words and definitions to your vocabulary file. For each word, include a sentence that gives you an example of how to use the word. **OL** Students with English language needs should include the pronunciations of these words in their files. **EL**

Literature Online

Literary Elements Have students access the Web site to improve their understanding of characterization.

JOSEPHINA NIGGLI **915**

Differentiated Instruction

Using Graphic Organizers Point out that the use of graphic organizers can help students to better understand many aspects of the selection, such as developments in the characters and in the plot. They can also be useful for comparing and contrasting characters or for organizing details of setting. Suggest that students use a graphic organizer in addition to the one connected to the reading strategy to clarify an aspect of the selection they find confusing. Types they might find useful include word web diagrams, flow charts, Venn diagrams, or charts with different columns. **BL**

COMPARING LITERATURE

Teach

Big Idea

Portraits of Real Life

Say: Keep the following questions in mind as you read. What kind of life does the family of General Macías lead? How does this compare to the lives of the revolutionaries? How realistic and convincing do you find the portrayals of the characters? *(The family of the general leads a very privileged life and shows they are of the upper class in their formal manners and condescending attitude toward the peasants. The revolutionaries, on the other hand, are very poor and have led lives of much suffering. Students should support their ideas about how realistically the characters are portrayed with examples from the text.)* **OL**

R1 Reading Strategy

Analyzing Plot and Setting

Answer: *The setting is very formal. The people who live here might be very formal as well.* **OL**

In the Trenches (En la trinchea). Diego Rivera. Banco de Mexico Trust. Mural, 2.03 x 3.98 m. Secretaria de Educacion Publica, Mexico City, Mexico.

THE RING OF
General Macías

★ ★ ★ ★ ★ ★ ★ ★ ★ ★

Josephina Niggli

CHARACTERS

MARICA (mär ē´kə): the sister of General Macías

RAQUEL (rə kel´): the wife of General Macías

ANDRÉS DE LA O (än´dräs dā lə ō): a captain in the Revolutionary Army

CLETO (klä´tō): a private in the Revolutionary Army

BASILIO FLORES (bə sēl´yō flô´räs): a captain in the Federal Army

PLACE: *Just outside Mexico City.*

TIME: *A night in April 1912.*

[*The living room of General Macías's[1] home is luxuriously furnished in the gold and ornate style of Louis XVI.[2] In the Right wall are French windows leading into the patio. Flanking these windows are low bookcases. In the Back wall is, Right, a closet door; and, Center, a table holding a wine decanter[3] and glasses. The Left wall has a door Upstage, and Downstage a writing desk with a straight chair in front of it. Near the desk is an armchair. Down Right is a small sofa with a table holding a lamp at the Upstage end of it. There are pictures on the walls. The room looks rather stuffy and unlived in.*

---

1. Macías (mä sē´əs)
2. France's King *Louis XVI* lived a life of luxury and elegance until he was beheaded in 1793 during the French Revolution.
3. A *decanter* is a decorative bottle with a stopper.

Reading Strategy Analyzing Plot and Setting *What might you infer from this description of the setting?* **R1**

916 UNIT 4 DRAMA

Additional Support

Skills Practice

VOCABULARY: Connotation and Denotation Marica speaks disparagingly of "peasants." Explain that the original meaning of *peasant* was a person living off the land. However, it has come to have a negative connotation in certain contexts, meaning "a person with little education and a low social status."

Marica consciously uses the negative connotation.

Ask students to think of other words that have connotations beyond their dictionary definitions and whether the connotations are positive, negative, or neutral. **OL**

When the curtains part, the stage is in darkness save for the moonlight that comes through the French windows. Then the house door opens and a young girl in negligee enters stealthily. She is carrying a lighted candle. She stands at the door a moment listening for possible pursuit, then moves quickly across to the bookcase Down Right. She puts the candle on top of the bookcase and begins searching behind the books. She finally finds what she wants: a small bottle. While she is searching, the house door opens silently and a woman, also in negligee, enters. (These negligees are in the latest Parisian style.) She moves silently across the room to the table by the sofa, and as the girl turns with the bottle, the woman switches on the light. The girl gives a half-scream and draws back, frightened. The light reveals her to be quite young—no more than twenty—a timid, dovelike creature. The woman has a queenly air, and whether she is actually beautiful or not, people think she is. She is about thirty-two.]

MARICA. *[Trying to hide the bottle behind her.]* Raquel! What are you doing here?

RAQUEL. What did you have hidden behind the books, Marica?

MARICA. *[Attempting a forced laugh.]* I? Nothing. Why do you think I have anything?

RAQUEL. *[Taking a step toward her.]* Give it to me.

MARICA. *[Backing away from her.]* No. No, I won't.

RAQUEL. *[Stretching out her hand.]* I demand that you give it to me.

MARICA. You have no right to order me about. I'm a married woman. I . . . I . . . *[She begins to sob and flings herself down on the sofa.]*

RAQUEL. *[Much gentler.]* You shouldn't be up. The doctor told you to stay in bed. *[She bends over MARICA and gently takes the bottle out of the girl's hand.]* It was poison. I thought so.

MARICA. *[Frightened.]* You won't tell the priest, will you?

Literary Element Characterization *What can you infer about Raquel from this description?* **L1**

RAQUEL. Suicide is a sin, Marica. A sin against God.

MARICA. I know. I . . . [*She catches* RAQUEL's *hand.*] Oh, Raquel, why do we have to have wars? Why do men have to go to war and be killed?

RAQUEL. Men must fight for what they believe is right. It is an honorable thing to die for your country as a soldier.

MARICA. How can you say that with Domingo[4] out there fighting, too? And fighting what? Men who aren't even men. Peasants. Ranch slaves. Men who shouldn't be allowed to fight.

RAQUEL. Peasants are men, Marica. Not animals.

MARICA. Men. It's always men. But how about the women? What becomes of us?

RAQUEL. We can pray.

MARICA. *[Bitterly.]* Yes, we can pray. And then comes the terrible news, and it's no use praying any more. All the reason for our praying is dead. Why should I go on living with Tomás[5] dead?

RAQUEL. Living is a duty.

MARICA. How can you be so cold, so hard? You are a cold and hard woman, Raquel. My brother worships you. He has never even looked at another woman since the first day he saw you. Does he know how cold and hard you are?

RAQUEL. Domingo is my—honored husband.

MARICA. You've been married for ten years. And I've been married for three months. If Domingo is killed, it won't be the same for you. You've had ten years. *[She is crying wildly.]* I haven't anything . . . anything at all.

---

4. Domingo (də ming′gō)
5. Tomás (tō mäs′)

Reading Strategy Analyzing Plot and Setting *What do these lines tell you about the culture in which the play takes place?* **R3**

Literary Element Characterization *How does Niggli characterize Marica here?* **L2**

Teach

R2 **Reading Strategy**

Analyzing Plot and Setting
Ask: What descriptions in the stage direction are especially helpful in visualizing this first scene? *(Students may say that the moonlight through the window and a girl walking "stealthily" holding a candle are especially vivid details.)* **OL**

L1 **Literary Element**

Characterization Answer: *Raquel has some indefinable quality that makes her beautiful, even though she may not be conventionally beautiful. She is clearly very confident.* **OL**

R3 **Reading Strategy**

Analyzing Plot and Setting Answer: *These lines of dialogue indicate the existence of a strict class system.* **OL**

L2 **Literary Element**

Characterization Answer: *She has given up all hope because her husband has died in the war. Students may say that she is not as strong as Raquel.* **OL**

✔CheckPoint

Use the CheckPoint questions on Presentation Plus! to monitor students' comprehension. These questions can be used with interactive response keypads for immediate student feedback.

Objectives
• To analyze plot and setting (SE)
• To understand characterization (SE)
• To understand connotation and denotation (TWE)

English Language Coach

Predicting Predicting helps students connect to readings by providing a purpose for reading. Have students preview the opening page and predict who the protagonist and the antagonist of the play will be. Also ask them to describe the impressions they get from reading the description of the opening scene. Have them discuss the kind of mood that this setting creates and the expectations it gives them of the kind of events that may follow. **EL**

Teach

BI Big Idea

Portraits of Real Life Ask:
How do these words of Raquel to Marica—"You'll meet another man. You'll marry again. There will be children in your house"—reveal some of Raquel's attitudes toward real life? *(Raquel is being practical and realistic here, pointing out that though Marica feels intense grief for her husband now, chances are she will get over it and can still have a happy life. Raquel's attitude is that however much people love each other, in real life they tend to eventually move on after a loss. They usually do not persist in believing that there is no point in living after the death of a spouse.)* **OL**

★ Viewing the Art

Answer: *Students may say that the woman's calm, haughty demeanor is closer to the character of Raquel.* Frida Kahlo (1910–1954) was a Mexican painter whose art reflected her love of Mexican culture. **AS**

Self-Portrait, 1930. Frida Kahlo. Oil on canvas, 25½ x 21⅛ in. Museum of Fine Arts, Boston. Anonymous loan.
Viewing the Art: Is the woman portrayed here closer to the image you have developed of Marica or of Raquel? Explain. ★

RAQUEL. You've had three months—three months of laughter. And now you have tears. How lucky you are. You have tears. Perhaps five months of tears. Not more. You're only twenty. And in five months Tomás will become just a lovely memory.

MARICA. I'll remember Tomás all my life.

RAQUEL. Of course. But he'll be distant and far away. But you're young . . . and the young need laughter. The young can't live on tears. And one day in Paris, or Rome, or even Mexico City, you'll meet another man. You'll marry again. There will be children in your house. How lucky you are.

MARICA. I'll never marry again.

RAQUEL. You're only twenty. You'll think differently when you're twenty-eight, or nine, or thirty.

MARICA. What will you do if Domingo is killed?

RAQUEL. I shall be very proud that he died in all his courage . . . in all the greatness of a hero.

MARICA. But you'd not weep, would you? Not you! I don't think there are any tears in you.

RAQUEL. No, I'd not weep. I'd sit here in this empty house and wait.

MARICA. Wait for what?

918 UNIT 4 DRAMA

Additional Support

Skills Practice

READING: Visualizing Point out the importance of visualizing the scenes in the play to better understand the characters and plot. Have students visualize the contrasts in appearance between Raquel and Marica. What additional details do they imagine about their appearances? What are the contrasts between Raquel in her fashionable negligee and Andrés in the white pajama suit of the Mexican peasants? Have students sketch one or more of the characters, emphasizing the symbolism in their costumes in the cases of Raquel and Andrés. Suggest that students find illustrations of Mexican peasant clothes. **OL**

RAQUEL. For the jingle of his spurs as he walks across the tiled hall. For the sound of his laughter in the patio. For the echo of his voice as he shouts to the groom to put away his horse. For the feel of his hand . . .

MARICA. [*Screams.*] Stop it!

RAQUEL. I'm sorry.

MARICA. You do love him, don't you?

RAQUEL. I don't think even he knows how much.

MARICA. I thought that after ten years people slid away from love. But you and Domingo—why, you're all he thinks about. When he's away from you he talks about you all the time. I heard him say once that when you were out of his sight he was like a man without eyes or ears or hands.

RAQUEL. I know. I, too, know that feeling.

MARICA. Then how could you let him go to war? Perhaps to be killed? How could you?

RAQUEL. [*Sharply.*] Marica, you are of the family Macías. Your family is a family of great warriors. A Macías man was with Ferdinand when the Moors were driven out of Spain. A Macías man was with Cortés when the Aztecans surrendered. Your grandfather fought in the War of Independence. Your own father was executed not twenty miles from this house by the French.[6] Shall his son be any less brave because he loves a woman?

MARICA. But Domingo loved you enough to forget that. If you had asked him, he wouldn't have gone to war. He would have stayed here with you.

RAQUEL. No, he would not have stayed. Your brother is a man of honor, not a whining, creeping coward.

---

6. In 1492 *Ferdinand* of Aragon defeated the *Moors*, a Muslim people from northwest Africa who had controlled most of Spain since the 700s. Through the *War of Independence*, Mexico won freedom from Spain in 1821. The *French* invaded and occupied Mexico City in 1863.

Literary Element Characterization *What do these lines tell you about Raquel's attitude toward men going to war?* **L**

MARICA. [*Beginning to cry again.*] I begged Tomás not to go. I begged him.

RAQUEL. Would you have loved him if he had stayed?

MARICA. I don't know. I don't know.

RAQUEL. There is your answer. You'd have despised him. Loved and despised him. Now come, Marica, it's time for you to go to bed.

MARICA. You won't tell the priest—about the poison, I mean?

RAQUEL. No. I won't tell him.

MARICA. Thank you, Raquel. How good you are. How kind and good.

RAQUEL. A moment ago I was hard and cruel. What a baby you are. Now, off to bed with you.

MARICA. Aren't you coming upstairs, too?

RAQUEL. No . . . I haven't been sleeping very well lately. I think I'll read for a little while.

MARICA. Good night, Raquel. And thank you.

RAQUEL. Good night, little one.

[*MARICA goes out through the house door Left, taking her candle with her. RAQUEL stares down at the bottle of poison in her hand, then puts it away in one of the small drawers of the desk. She next selects a book from the Downstage case and sits on the sofa to read it, but feeling chilly, she rises and goes to the closet, Back Right, and takes out an afghan.[7] Coming back to the sofa, she makes herself comfortable, with the afghan across her knees. Suddenly she hears a noise in the patio. She listens, then convinced it is nothing, returns to her reading. But she hears the noise again. She goes to the patio door and peers out.*]

RAQUEL. [*Calling softly.*] Who's there? Who's out there? Oh! [*She gasps and backs into the room. Two men—or rather a man and a young boy—dressed in the white pajama suits of the Mexican peasants, with their sombreros tipped low over their faces, come into the room. RAQUEL draws herself up*

---

7. An *afghan* is a knitted or crocheted wool blanket.

Teach

R Reading Strategy

Analyzing Plot and Setting
Ask: How does Raquel's description of the warrior history of the Macías family give you a better idea of the story's setting and context? *(This description portrays the Macías family as brave and courageous and helps to explain Raquel's fierce pride in her family and the high value she places on bravery and honor.)* **OL**

L Literary Element

Characterization Answer:
Raquel expects men to go to war to defend their country and their families, even though they love their wives. Honor seems more important than love or even survival. **OL**

⭐ Writer's Technique

Imagery Raquel uses vivid sensory images to describe what she would miss about her husband. **Ask:** To which senses does each image appeal? What does this imagery add to Raquel's description? *(Sound: jingle of spurs, laughter, and the echo of shouting. Touch: the feel of his hand. Students may say that these vivid details make Raquel's description powerful and realistic and reveal how much she would miss her husband.)* **AS**

Objectives
- To analyze plot and setting (SE)
- To understand characterization (SE)
- To make use of visualization (TWE)

English Language Coach

Descriptions of Emotions and Behavior Many of the play's stage directions include words that describe emotions, attitudes, and behavior, such as *frightened*, *gentler*, and *bitterly*. Compile a list of nouns and modifiers from the stage directions that English language learners might find difficult. (Examples include *bewilderment*, *stealthily*, *sarcastically*, *dazed*, *stifled*, and *abruptly*.) Have them define the words by giving examples of situations in which a person might feel or act in such a way. **EL**

Teach

L1 Literary Element

Characterization Answer:
She is strong, brave, and haughty. She expects men to behave respectfully around women in all situations. **OL**

R Reading Strategy

Analyzing Plot and Setting Answer: *His comment implies that upper-class women value politeness in conversation over and above truth or substance.* **OL**

★ Writer's Technique

Irony Review the three kinds of irony with students. *Situational irony* occurs when an event is the opposite of expectations, *verbal irony* occurs when a person says the opposite of what is meant, and *dramatic irony* is when playgoers have information unknown to the characters onstage. **Ask:** What kind of irony does Raquel use in her comment "I am devastated"? *(Verbal irony.)* **AS**

---

regally. Her voice is cold and commanding.] Who are you, and what do you want here?

ANDRÉS. We are hunting for the wife of General Macías.

RAQUEL. I am Raquel Rivera de Macías.

ANDRÉS. Cleto, stand guard in the patio. If you hear any suspicious noise, warn me at once.

CLETO. Yes, my captain. [*The boy returns to the patio.*]

[*The man, hooking his thumbs in his belt, strolls around the room, looking it over. When he reaches the table at the back he sees the wine. With a small bow to RAQUEL he pours himself a glass of wine and drains it. He wipes his mouth with the back of his hand.*]

RAQUEL. How very interesting.

ANDRÉS. [*Startled.*] What?

RAQUEL. To be able to drink wine with that hat on.

ANDRÉS. The hat? Oh, forgive me, señora. [*He flicks the brim with his fingers so that it drops off his head and dangles down his back from the neck cord.*] In a military camp one forgets one's polite manners. Would you care to join me in another glass?

RAQUEL. [*Sitting on the sofa.*] Why not? It's my wine.

ANDRÉS. And very excellent wine. [*He pours two glasses and gives her one while he is talking.*] I would say Amontillado[8] of the vintage of '87.

RAQUEL. Did you learn that in a military camp?

ANDRÉS. I used to sell wines . . . among other things.

---

8. *Amontillado* (ə môn´til ä dō) is a kind of sherry, which is a strong wine.

Literary Element Characterization *What do the remarks that Raquel makes to Andrés reveal about her?* **L1**

Vocabulary

regally (rē´gəl lē) *adv.* in a grand, dignified manner befitting a king or a queen

---

RAQUEL. [*Ostentatiously hiding a yawn.*] I am devastated. ★

ANDRÉS. [*Pulls over the armchair and makes himself comfortable in it.*] You don't mind, do you?

RAQUEL. Would it make any difference if I did?

ANDRÉS. No. The Federals are searching the streets for us, and we have to stay somewhere. But women of your class seem to expect that senseless sort of question.

RAQUEL. Of course I suppose I could scream.

ANDRÉS. Naturally.

RAQUEL. My sister-in-law is upstairs asleep. And there are several servants in the back of the house. Mostly men servants. Very big men.

ANDRÉS. Very interesting. [*He is drinking the wine in small sips with much enjoyment.*]

RAQUEL. What would you do if I screamed?

ANDRÉS. [*Considering the request as though it were another glass of wine.*] Nothing.

RAQUEL. I am afraid you are lying to me.

ANDRÉS. Women of your class seem to expect polite little lies.

RAQUEL. Stop calling me "woman of your class."

ANDRÉS. Forgive me.

RAQUEL. You are one of the fighting peasants, aren't you?

ANDRÉS. I am a captain in the Revolutionary Army.

RAQUEL. This house is completely loyal to the Federal government.

ANDRÉS. I know. That's why I'm here.

RAQUEL. And now that you are here, just what do you expect me to do?

Reading Strategy Analyzing Plot and Setting *What does Andrés's comment imply about wealthy women at the time the play is set?* **R**

Vocabulary

ostentatiously (os´tən tā´shəs lē) *adv.* in a way intended to attract attention or impress others

---

Additional Support

Skills Practice

LISTENING AND SPEAKING: Reading a Monologue Point out that a speech by one person is called a monologue. Andrés's monologue reveals important facts that help explain his motivations. Have students discuss the tone of Andrés's monologue. Is it emotional or unemotional? What kind of reading would express his feelings most effectively? Ask pairs of students to read the monologue to each other and experiment with different methods of expression—for example, using an emotional tone and an unemotional tone. Have each pair report on the most effective method. **OL**

ANDRÉS. I expect you to offer sanctuary to myself and to Cleto.

RAQUEL. Cleto? [*She looks toward the patio and adds sarcastically.*] Oh, your army.

CLETO. [*Appearing in the doorway.*] I'm sorry, my captain. I just heard a noise. [*RAQUEL stands. ANDRÉS moves quickly to her and puts his hands on her arms from the back. CLETO has turned and is peering into the patio. Then the boy relaxes.*] We are still safe, my captain. It was only a rabbit. [*He goes back into the patio. RAQUEL pulls away from ANDRÉS and goes to the desk.*]

RAQUEL. What a magnificent army you have. So clever. I'm sure you must win many victories.

ANDRÉS. We do. And we will win the greatest victory, remember that.

RAQUEL. This farce has gone on long enough. Will you please take your army and climb over the patio wall with it?

ANDRÉS. I told you that we came here so that you could give us sanctuary.

RAQUEL. My dear captain—captain without a name . . .

ANDRÉS. Andrés de la O, your servant. [*He makes a bow.*]

RAQUEL. [*Startled.*] Andrés de la O!

ANDRÉS. I am flattered. You have heard of me.

RAQUEL. Naturally. Everyone in the city has heard of you. You have a reputation for politeness—especially to women.

ANDRÉS. I see that the tales about me have lost nothing in the telling.

RAQUEL. I can't say. I'm not interested in gossip about your type of soldier.

ANDRÉS. Then let me give you something to heighten your interest. [*He suddenly takes her in his arms and kisses her. She stiffens for a moment, then remains perfectly still. He steps away from her.*]

RAQUEL. [*Rage forcing her to whisper.*] Get out of here—at once!

ANDRÉS. [*Staring at her in admiration.*] I can understand why Macías loves you. I couldn't before, but now I can understand it.

RAQUEL. Get out of my house.

ANDRÉS. [*Sits on the sofa and pulls a small leather pouch out of his shirt. He pours its contents into his hand.*] So cruel, señora, and I with a present for you? Here is a holy medal. My mother gave me this medal. She died when I was ten. She was a street beggar. She died of starvation. But I wasn't there. I was in jail. I had been sentenced to five years in prison for stealing five oranges. The judge thought it a great joke. One year for each orange. He laughed. He had a very loud laugh. [*Pause.*] I killed him two months ago. I hanged him to the telephone pole in front of his house. And I laughed. [*Pause.*] I also have a very loud laugh. [*RAQUEL abruptly turns her back on him.*] I told that story to a girl the other night and she thought it very funny. But of course she was a peasant girl—a girl who could neither read nor write. She hadn't been born in a great house in Tabasco.[9] She didn't have an English governess.[10] She didn't go to school to the nuns in Paris. She didn't marry one of the richest young men in the Republic. But she thought my story very funny. Of course she could understand it. Her brother had been whipped to death because he had run away from the plantation that owned him. [*He pauses and looks at her. She does not move.*] Are you still angry with me? Even though I have brought you a present? [*He holds out his hand.*] A very nice present—from your husband.

---

9. On the southern coast of the Gulf of Mexico, *Tabasco* is one of Mexico's thirty-five states.

10. A *governess* is a woman employed to teach children in a private household.

Big Idea Portraits of Real Life *Is Raquel's abrupt change in behavior toward Andrés realistic? Explain.* **BI**

Literary Element Characterization *Why do you think Andrés describes what the young woman did not have?* **L3**

JOSEPHINA NIGGLI **921**

Teach

R Reading Strategy

Analyzing Plot and Setting
Answer: *It introduces a new conflict for Raquel: she must choose between giving her husband's enemies to soldiers in his army and saving her husband's life.* **OL**

L Literary Element

Characterization Answer:
Many students will likely say yes, because Raquel's bravery and cleverness have already been depicted. **OL**

RAQUEL. [*Turns and stares at him in amazement.*] A present! From Domingo?

ANDRÉS. I don't know him that well. I call him the General Macías.

RAQUEL. [*Excitedly.*] Is he well? How does he look? [*With horrified comprehension.*] He's a prisoner . . . your prisoner!

ANDRÉS. Naturally. That's why I know so much about you. He talks about you constantly.

RAQUEL. You know nothing about him. You're lying to me.

[*CLETO comes to the window.*]

ANDRÉS. I assure you, señora . . .

CLETO. [*Interrupting.*] My captain . . .

ANDRÉS. What is it, Cleto? Another rabbit?

CLETO. No, my captain. There are soldiers at the end of the street. They are searching all the houses. They will be here soon.

ANDRÉS. Don't worry. We are quite safe here. Stay in the patio until I call you.

CLETO. Yes, my captain. [*He returns to the patio.*]

RAQUEL. You are not safe here. When those soldiers come I shall turn you over to them.

ANDRÉS. I think not.

RAQUEL. You can't escape from them. And they are not kind to you peasant prisoners. They have good reason not to be.

ANDRÉS. Look at this ring. [*He holds his hand out, with the ring on his palm.*]

RAQUEL. Why, it's—a wedding ring.

ANDRÉS. Read the inscription inside of it. [*As she hesitates, he adds sharply.*] Read it!

RAQUEL. [*Slowly takes the ring. While she is reading her voice fades to a whisper.*] "D. M.—R. R.—June 2, 1902." Where did you get this?

ANDRÉS. General Macías gave it to me.

RAQUEL. [*Firmly and clearly.*] Not this ring. He'd never give you this ring. [*With dawning horror.*] He's dead. You stole it from his dead finger. He's dead.

ANDRÉS. Not yet. But he will be dead if I don't return to camp safely by sunset tomorrow.

RAQUEL. I don't believe you. I don't believe you. You're lying to me.

ANDRÉS. This house is famous for its loyalty to the Federal government. You will hide me until those soldiers get out of this district. When it is safe enough Cleto and I will leave. But if you betray me to them, your husband will be shot tomorrow evening at sunset. Do you understand? [*He shakes her arm. RAQUEL looks dazedly at him. CLETO comes to the window.*]

CLETO. The soldiers are coming closer, my captain. They are at the next house.

ANDRÉS. [*To RAQUEL.*] Where shall we hide? [*Raquel is still dazed. He gives her another little shake.*] Think, woman! If you love your husband at all—think!

RAQUEL. I don't know. Marica upstairs—the servants in the rest of the house—I don't know.

ANDRÉS. The General has bragged to us about you. He says you are braver than most men. He says you are very clever. This is a time to be both brave and clever.

CLETO. [*Pointing to the closet.*] What door is that?

RAQUEL. It's a closet . . . a storage closet.

ANDRÉS. We'll hide in there.

RAQUEL. It's very small. It's not big enough for both of you.

ANDRÉS. Cleto, hide yourself in there.

CLETO. But, my captain . . .

ANDRÉS. That's an order! Hide yourself.

CLETO. Yes, Sir. [*He steps inside the closet.*]

ANDRÉS. And now, señora, where are you going to hide me?

Reading Strategy Analyzing Plot and Setting *How does this situation contribute to the development of the plot?* **R**

Literary Element Characterization *Is the General's description of his wife consistent with the characterization of her thus far? Explain.* **L**

Additional Support

Skills Practice

WRITING: Using Adverbs The author uses many adverbs in the stage directions to indicate the vocal and facial expressions of the characters—for example, *sharply, slowly,* and *dazedly* on page 922 and *queenly* on page 923. Ask students to write a brief dialogue, either from their imagination or based on an actual experience. Have them write at least five stage directions that use adverbs to describe their characters' vocal or facial expressions. Encourage them to use compelling words that conjure up vivid images. **OL**

RAQUEL. How did you persuade my husband to give you his ring?

ANDRÉS. That's a very long story, señora, for which we have no time just now. [*He puts the ring and medal back in the pouch and thrusts it inside his shirt.*] Later I will be glad to give you all the details. But at present it is only necessary for you to remember that his life depends upon mine.

RAQUEL. Yes—yes, of course. [*She loses her dazed expression and seems to grow more*

queenly as she takes command of the situation.] Give me your hat. [*ANDRÉS shrugs and passes it over to her. She takes it to the closet and hands it to CLETO.*] There is a smoking jacket hanging up in there. Hand it to me. [*CLETO hands her a man's velvet smoking jacket. She brings it to ANDRÉS.*] Put this on.

ANDRÉS. [*Puts it on and looks down at himself.*] Such a pity my shoes are not comfortable slippers.

Teach

⭐ Viewing the Art

Answer: *The painting shows a "distribution of food." Students may infer that peasants at the time did not have enough to eat.* **AS**

Triumph of the Revolution—Distribution of Food (Trionfo de la revolucion, reparto de los alimentos), 1926-27. Diego Rivera. Banco de Mexico Trust. Fresco, 3.54 x 3.67 m. Chapel, Universidad Autonoma, Chapingo, Mexico. ⭐
Viewing the Art: What insight does this scene give you about social conditions in Mexico at the time of this play?

JOSEPHINA NIGGLI   **923**

Building Reading Fluency

Stage Directions Less proficient readers may find the stage directions distracting when they occur in the middle of the dialogue. Point out that they are essential for understanding the action of the play. Ask students to take note of the different ways in which stage directions are used—for example, to set a scene, to describe the action of a character, to describe a character's tone of voice or emotion, or to indicate a pause. Having students read aloud and act out some scenes will also help their comprehension and give them a better understanding of how the stage directions fit with the dialogue. **BL**

Objectives
• To understand characterization (SE)
• To analyze plot and setting (SE)
• To use adverbs appropriately (TWE)

Teach

L1 Literary Element

Characterization Ask: How does Raquel live up to her husband's description of her as being brave and clever? *(She shows her cleverness by quickly coming up with an ingenious but risky plan to save Andrés. She shows her bravery by facing the officers audaciously and playing out the charade she has created.)* **OL**

R Reading Strategy

Analyzing Plot and Setting

Ask: What aspects or techniques are most effective for creating suspense after the arrival of the Federal officers? How do you predict this situation will end? *(Students may say that knowing the spies are there hiding and wondering if the officers will notice creates tension and suspense. Raquel's quick thinking and ingenious solutions also create suspense by causing the reader to wonder whether she will be able to keep this up and whether something will happen to make her plans go wrong. Students should explain their predictions based on the events they have already read about.)* **OL**

RAQUEL. Sit in that chair. [*She points to the armchair.*]

ANDRÉS. My dear lady . . .

RAQUEL. If I must save your life, allow me to do it in my own way. Sit down. [*ANDRÉS sits. She picks up the afghan from the couch and throws it over his feet and legs, carefully tucking it in so that his body is covered to the waist.*] If anyone speaks to you, don't answer. Don't turn your head. As far as you are concerned, there is no one in this room—not even me. Just look straight ahead of you and . . .

ANDRÉS. [*As she pauses.*] And what?

L1 RAQUEL. I started to say "and pray," but since you're a member of the Revolutionary Army I don't suppose you believe in God and prayer.

ANDRÉS. My mother left me a holy medal.

RAQUEL. Oh, yes, I remember. A very amusing story. [*There is the sound of men's voices in the patio.*] The Federal soldiers are here. If you can pray, ask God to keep Marica upstairs. She is very young and very stupid. She'll betray you before I can shut her mouth.

ANDRÉS. I'll . . .

RAQUEL. Silence! Stare straight ahead of you and pray. [*She goes to the French window and speaks loudly to the soldiers.*] Really! What is the meaning of this uproar?

FLORES. [*Off.*] Do not alarm yourself, señora. [*He comes into the room. He wears the uniform of a Federal officer.*] I am Captain Basilio Flores, at your service, señora.

R RAQUEL. What do you mean, invading my house and making so much noise at this hour of the night?

FLORES. We are hunting for two spies. One of them is the **notorious** Andrés de la O. You may have heard of him, señora.

RAQUEL. [*Looking at ANDRÉS.*] Considering what he did to my cousin—yes, I've heard of him.

FLORES. Your cousin, señora?

RAQUEL. [*Comes to ANDRÉS and puts her hand on his shoulder. He stares woodenly in front of him.*] Felipe[11] was his prisoner before the poor boy managed to escape.

FLORES. Is it possible? [*He crosses to ANDRÉS.*] Captain Basilio Flores, at your service. [*He salutes.*]

RAQUEL. Felipe doesn't hear you. He doesn't even know you are in the room.

FLORES. Eh, it is a sad thing.

RAQUEL. Must your men make so much noise?

FLORES. The hunt must be thorough, señora. And now if some of my men can go through **R** here to the rest of the house . . .

RAQUEL. Why?

FLORES. But I told you, señora. We are hunting for two spies . . .

RAQUEL. [*Speaking quickly from controlled nervousness.*] And do you think I have them hidden someplace, and I the wife of General Macías?

FLORES. General Macías! But I didn't know . . .

RAQUEL. Now that you do know, I suggest you remove your men and their noise at once.

FLORES. But, señora, I regret—I still have to search this house.

RAQUEL. I can assure you, captain, that I have been sitting here all evening, and no peasant spy has passed me and gone into the rest of the house.

FLORES. Several rooms open off the patio, señora. They needn't have come through here.

RAQUEL. So . . . you do think I conceal spies in this house. Then search it by all means. Look under the sofa . . . under the table. In

---

Vocabulary

notorious (nō tôr′ ē əs) *adj.* widely and unfavorably known

---

11. *Felipe* (fə lē pā)

Additional Support

Skills Practice

READING: Comparing and Contrasting The characters of *The Ring of General Macías* have contrasting traits and ways of life. It may be helpful for students to analyze the main characters in terms of these contrasts.

Have students make charts comparing two sets of characters, one for Raquel and Marica and a second for Raquel and Andrés. Have students design the style of their charts themselves. Ask volunteers to write their charts on the board. **OL** the drawers of the desk. And don't miss that closet, captain. Inside that closet is hidden a very fierce and wicked spy.

FLORES. Please, señora . . .

RAQUEL. [*Goes to the closet door.*] Or do you prefer me to open it for you?

FLORES. I am only doing my duty, señora. You are making it very difficult.

RAQUEL. [*Relaxing against the door.*] I'm sorry. My sister-in-law is upstairs. She has just received word that her husband has been killed. They were married three months ago. She's only twenty. I didn't want . . .

MARICA. [*Calling off.*] Raquel, what is all that noise downstairs?

RAQUEL. [*Goes to the house door and calls.*] It is nothing. Go back to bed.

MARICA. But I can hear men's voices in the patio.

RAQUEL. It is only some Federal soldiers hunting for two peasant spies. [*She turns and speaks rapidly to* FLORES.] If she comes down here, she must not see my cousin. Felipe escaped, but her husband was killed. The doctor thinks the sight of my poor cousin might affect her mind. You understand?

FLORES. Certainly, señora. What a sad thing.

MARICA. [*Still off.*] Raquel, I'm afraid! [*She tries to push past* RAQUEL *into the room.* RAQUEL *and* FLORES *stand between her and* ANDRÉS.] Spies! In this house. Oh, Raquel!

RAQUEL. The doctor will be very angry if you don't return to bed at once.

MARICA. But those terrible men will kill us. What is the matter with you two? Why are you standing there like that? [*She tries to see*

past them, but they both move so that she can't see ANDRÉS.]

FLORES. It is better that you go back to your room, señora.

MARICA. But why? Upstairs I am alone. Those terrible men will kill me. I know they will.

FLORES. Don't be afraid, señora. There are no spies in this house.

MARICA. Are you sure?

RAQUEL. Captain Flores means that no spy would dare to take refuge in the house of General Macías. Isn't that right, captain?

FLORES. [*Laughing.*] Of course. All the world knows of the brave General Macías.

RAQUEL. Now go back to bed, Marica. Please, for my sake.

MARICA. You are both acting very strangely. I think you have something hidden in this room you don't want me to see.

RAQUEL. [*Sharply.*] You are quite right. Captain Flores has captured one of the spies. He is sitting in the chair behind me. He is dead. Now will you please go upstairs! ★

MARICA. [*Gives a stifled sob.*] Oh! That such a terrible thing could happen in this house. [*She runs out of the room, still sobbing.*]

FLORES. [*Worried.*] Was it wise to tell her such a story, señora?

RAQUEL. [*Tense with* **repressed** *relief.*] Better that than the truth. Good night, captain, and thank you.

FLORES. Good night, señora. And don't worry. Those spies won't bother you. If they were anywhere in this district, my men would have found them.

RAQUEL. I'm sure of it.

[*The Captain salutes her, looks toward* ANDRÉS *and salutes him, then goes into the patio. He can be heard calling his men. Neither* ANDRÉS

Literary Element Characterization *What do these lines tell you about Raquel?* **L₂**

Big Idea Portraits of Real Life *How is Raquel handling the search?* **B1**

Vocabulary

repressed (ri prest′) *adj.* held back or kept under control; restrained

---

JOSEPHINA NIGGLI **925**

Teach

L₂ Literary Element

Characterization Answer: *She is extremely quick witted and can size up a situation very rapidly. She is also a bold risk taker.* **OL**

B1 Big Idea

Portraits of Real Life Answer: *Students' answers will vary, but some may say that Raquel's behavior is rather uncharacteristic for her status and for the time period. Some may believe that Raquel would have reacted in a more cautious and decorous manner.* **OL**

★ Writer's Technique

Dramatic Irony Have students point out a striking example of dramatic irony in this scene. *(Raquel tells Marica sarcastically that a spy is sitting on the chair behind her. The audience knows, though Marica and Flores do not, that this is literally the truth.)* **AS**

Differentiated Instruction

Advanced Learners Point out that a revolution refers to a profound change in a country's government. Some revolutions come about because victims of poverty or injustice rise up against the existing government. Have students research a revolution involving demands by common people against an unjust monarchy or dictatorship, such as the American, French, or Russian revolutions. Have them find out the causes and effects of the revolution as well as the methods by which it came about. Then ask them to compare the causes of this revolution to what they know about the Mexican Revolution. **AL**

Objectives
• To understand characterization (SE)
• To analyze plot and setting (SE)
• To compare and contrast characters (TWE)

COMPARING LITERATURE

Teach

L1 Literary Element

Characterization Answer:
Students may say that Raquel finally shows a vulnerable side after remaining strong in such intense circumstances. **OL**

B1 Big Idea

Portraits of Real Life
Answer: *Students' answers will vary. Many will likely say that Andrés's behavior is surprising because Raquel represents all that he is fighting against. Others may say that Andrés respects Raquel, so he wants to help her in this way.* **OL**

★ Viewing the Art

Answer: *The mood of the painting seems calmer and more austere than that of the play.* **AS**

Pablo Burchard (1875–1964) was one of the founders of modern Chilean art. He often used expressive and abstract styles.

---

nor RAQUEL moves until the voices outside die away. Then Raquel staggers and nearly falls, but Andrés catches her in time.]

ANDRÉS. [*Calling softly.*] They've gone, Cleto. [*ANDRÉS carries Raquel to the sofa as Cleto comes out of the closet.*] Bring a glass of wine. Quickly.

CLETO. [*As he gets the wine.*] What happened?

ANDRÉS. It's nothing. Just a faint. [*He holds the wine to her lips.*]

CLETO. She's a great lady, that one. When she wanted to open the closet door my knees were trembling, I can tell you.

ANDRÉS. My own bones were playing a pretty tune.

> **Literary Element** Characterization How does this incident further develop Raquel's character? **L1**

CLETO. Why do you think she married Macías?

ANDRÉS. Love is a peculiar thing, Cleto.

CLETO. I don't understand it.

RAQUEL. [*Moans and sits up.*] Are they—are they gone?

ANDRÉS. Yes, they're gone. [*He kisses her hand.*] I've never known a braver lady.

RAQUEL. [*Pulling her hand away.*] Will you go now, please?

ANDRÉS. We'll have to wait until the district is free of them—but if you'd like to write a letter to your husband while we're waiting . . .

> **Big Idea** Portraits of Real Life *If this were a true story, would you expect this behavior from a revolutionary toward his enemy? Why or why not?* **B1**

Wall with a Door and Tree (Muro con puerta y arbol). Pablo Burchard.
Viewing the Art:
What is the mood of this painting? How does it compare with the mood in the play? ★

926 UNIT 4 DRAMA

Additional Support

Skills Practice

WRITING: Irony Students will become more familiar with recognizing verbal irony in literature if they use it in their own writing. Ask students to write a paragraph about a chore, a place, or an experience that they dislike and to use an ironic tone to express their feelings.

Encourage them not to speak too generally but to describe specific aspects of the situation. Have volunteers read their paragraphs aloud and discuss as a class the effectiveness of using verbal irony to make a point. **OL**

RAQUEL. [*Surprised at his kindness.*] You'd take it to him? You'd really give it to him?

ANDRÉS. Of course.

RAQUEL. Thank you. [*She goes to the writing desk and sits down.*]

ANDRÉS. [*To* CLETO, *who has been staring steadily at* RAQUEL *all the while.*] You stay here with the señora. I'm going to find out how much of the district has been cleared.

CLETO. [*Still staring at* RAQUEL.] Yes, my captain.

[ANDRÉS *leaves by the French windows.* CLETO *keeps on staring at* RAQUEL *as she starts to write. After a moment she turns to him.*]

RAQUEL. [*Irritated.*] Why do you keep staring at me?

CLETO. Why did you marry a man like that one, señora?

RAQUEL. You're very **impertinent.**

CLETO. [*Shyly.*] I'm sorry, señora.

RAQUEL. [*After a brief pause.*] What do you mean: "a man like that one"?

CLETO. Well, you're very brave, señora.

RAQUEL. [*Lightly.*] And don't you think the general is very brave?

CLETO. No, señora. Not very.

RAQUEL. [*Staring at him with bewilderment.*] What are you trying to tell me?

CLETO. Nothing, señora. It is none of my affair.

RAQUEL. Come here. [*He comes slowly up to her.*] Tell me what is in your mind.

CLETO. I don't know, señora. I don't understand it. The captain says love is a peculiar thing, but I don't understand it.

RAQUEL. Cleto, did the general willingly give that ring to your captain?

CLETO. Yes, señora.

impertinent (im purt′ ən ənt) *adj.* inappropriately bold or forward

---

RAQUEL. Why?

CLETO. The general wanted to save his own life. He said he loved you and he wanted to save his life.

RAQUEL. How would giving that ring to your captain save the general's life?

CLETO. The general's supposed to be shot tomorrow afternoon. But he's talked about you a lot, and when my captain knew we had to come into the city, he thought perhaps we might take refuge here if the Federals got on our trail. So he went to the general and said that if he fixed it so we'd be safe here, my captain would save him from the firing squad.

RAQUEL. Was your trip to the city very important—to your cause, I mean?

CLETO. Indeed yes, señora. The captain got a lot of fine information. It means we'll win the next big battle. My captain is a very clever man, señora.

RAQUEL. Did the general know about this information when he gave his ring to your captain?

CLETO. I don't see how he could help knowing it, señora. He heard us talking about it enough.

RAQUEL. Who knows about that bargain to save the general's life beside you and your captain?

CLETO. No one, señora. The captain isn't one to talk, and I didn't have time to.

RAQUEL. [*While the boy has been talking, the life seems to have drained completely out of her.*] How old are you, Cleto?

CLETO. I don't know, señora. I think I'm twenty, but I don't know.

RAQUEL. [*Speaking more to herself than to him.*] Tomás was twenty.

CLETO. Who is Tomás?

Reading Strategy Analyzing Plot and Setting *How might this information provided by Cleto affect the plot?* **R2**

JOSEPHINA NIGGLI **927**

Teach

L2 Literary Element

Characterization Ask: Why do you think that Cleto keeps staring at Raquel? What does this suggest about his character? (*Students may suggest that he admires her, is curious about her, thinks her beautiful, or is infatuated with her. They may think that his response to Raquel shows him to be young and impressionable.*) **OL**

R1 Reading Strategy

Analyzing Plot and Setting Ask: What do you think might be the reason behind the several questions Raquel asks Cleto? What do you predict she will do with this information? (*Students may say that she wants to size up the whole situation and understand at what price her husband bargained for his life. They may predict that she will use this information to try to stop the revolutionaries somehow.*) **OL**

R2 Reading Strategy

Analyzing Plot and Setting Answer: *The information may force Raquel to reexamine the situation and determine if she can do anything to further help her husband or the Federal cause.* **OL**

Differentiated Instruction

Acting Out Scenes Acting out segments of dialogue will give students a better understanding of the interactions between the characters and the developments in the play's action. Have students work in groups of two or three, each portraying one of the characters. Ask them to choose a scene that they consider important and to practice performing it together. Discuss with students techniques for conveying their scenes. Point out that facial expression, posture, and gestures can be as important as the words in representing emotion and attitude. Have each group perform its scene for the class. **BL**

Objectives
- To analyze plot and setting (SE)
- To understand characterization (SE)
- To use verbal irony (TWE)

927

BI Big Idea

Portraits of Real Life

Answer: *Students may say that the culture has different expectations for men and women. Women are expected to prioritize their husbands and families, while men are expected to prioritize their values and causes.* **OL**

L Literary Element

Characterization Answer:

She admires him for his courage and convictions and is saddened that he may die young. **OL**

RAQUEL. He was married to my sister-in-law. Cleto, you think my husband is a coward, don't you?

CLETO. [*With embarrassment.*] Yes, señora.

RAQUEL. You don't think any woman is worth it, do you? Worth the price of a great battle, I mean?

CLETO. No, señora. But as the captain says, love is a very peculiar thing.

RAQUEL. If your captain loved a woman as much as the general loves me, would he have given an enemy his ring?

CLETO. Ah, but the captain is a great man, señora.

RAQUEL. And so is my husband a great man. He is of the family Macías. All of that family have been great men. All of them—brave and honorable men. They have always held their honor to be greater than their lives. That is a tradition of their family.

CLETO. Perhaps none of them loved a woman like you, señora.

RAQUEL. How strange you are. I saved you from the Federals because I want to save my husband's life. You call me brave, and yet you call him a coward. There is no difference in what we have done.

CLETO. But you are a woman, señora.

RAQUEL. Has a woman less honor than a man, then?

CLETO. No, señora. Please, I don't know how to say it. The general is a soldier. He has a duty to his own cause. You are a woman. You have a duty to your husband. It is right that you should try to save him. It is not right that he should try to save himself.

RAQUEL. [*Dully.*] Yes, of course. It is right that I should save him. [*Becoming practical again.*] Your captain has been gone some time, Cleto. You'd better find out if he is still safe.

CLETO. Yes, señora. [*As he reaches the French windows she stops him.*]

RAQUEL. Wait, Cleto. Have you a mother—or a wife, perhaps?

CLETO. Oh, no, señora. I haven't anyone but the captain.

RAQUEL. But the captain is a soldier. What would you do if he should be killed?

CLETO. It is very simple, señora. I should be killed, too.

RAQUEL. You speak about death so calmly. Aren't you afraid of it, Cleto?

CLETO. No, señora. It's like the captain says . . . dying for what you believe in—that's the finest death of all.

RAQUEL. And you believe in the Revolutionary cause?

CLETO. Yes, señora. I am a poor peasant, that's true. But still I have a right to live like a man, with my own ground, and my own family, and my own future. [*He stops speaking abruptly.*] I'm sorry, señora. You are a fine lady. You don't understand these things. I must go and find my captain. [*He goes out.*]

RAQUEL. [*Rests her face against her hand.*] He's so young. But Tomás was no older. And he's not afraid. He said so. Oh, Domingo—Domingo! [*She straightens abruptly, takes the bottle of poison from the desk drawer and stares at it. Then she crosses to the decanter and laces the wine with the poison. She hurries back to the desk and is busy writing when ANDRÉS and CLETO return.*]

ANDRÉS. You'll have to hurry that letter. The district is clear now.

RAQUEL. I'll be through in just a moment. You might as well finish the wine while you're waiting.

ANDRÉS. Thank you. A most excellent idea. [*He pours himself a glass of wine. As he lifts it to his lips she speaks.*]

Big Idea Portraits of Real Life *What does Cleto's statement tell you about the culture in which he lives?* **BI**

Literary Element Characterization *How does Raquel feel about Cleto?* **L**

Skills Practice

GRAMMAR: Compound Sentences and Predicates Explain that a compound sentence has two or more independent clauses joined with a comma and coordinating conjunction. A simple sentence may have a compound predicate. A comma is not used between the elements of a compound predicate. Ask students to identify and punctuate the following sentences.

1. I have been sitting here all evening and no peasant spy has passed me. (*compound sentence, comma after "evening"*)

2. I sit here in this empty house and wait. (*compound predicate*) **OL**

Two Women, 1929. Frida Kahlo. Oil on canvas, 27³/₈ x 21 in. Private collection.
Viewing the Art: What different personalities do these two women convey? How do they reflect the differences between Raquel and Marica? ★

JOSEPHINA NIGGLI **929**

COMPARING LITERATURE

Teach

★ Viewing the Art
The foliage background shows Kahlo's admiration of the work of Henri Rousseau.
Answer: *Students may say that one woman looks strong and determined like Raquel, while the other looks less so, like Marica.* **AS**

Differentiated Instruction

Words from Other Languages This play contains several words borrowed from other languages that are now used in English. Some of them students will know, such as *patio* and *pajamas,* while others may be unfamiliar, such as *negligee, afghan,* and *sombrero.*

Ask students to use a dictionary to find the language from which each of these words is borrowed. (patio *from Spanish,* pajamas *from Hindi,* negligee *from French,* afghan *from Persian, and* sombrero *from Spanish*) **BL**

Objectives
• To understand characterization (SE)
• To analyze plot and setting
• To understand compound sentences and predicates (TWE)

929

Teach

BI Big Idea

Portraits of Real Life

Answer: *Responses may vary. Some students may say that Raquel's reaction is unrealistic because she has just poisoned the two revolutionary spies.* **OL**

CheckPoint

Use the CheckPoint questions on Presentation Plus! to check students' mastery of the selection. These questions can be used with interactive response keypads for immediate student feedback.

RAQUEL. Why don't you give some to—Cleto?

ANDRÉS. This is too fine a wine to waste on that boy.

RAQUEL. He'll probably never have another chance to taste such wine.

ANDRÉS. Very well. Pour yourself a glass, Cleto.

CLETO. Thank you. [*He pours it.*] Your health, my captain.

RAQUEL. [*Quickly.*] Drink it outside, Cleto. I want to speak to your captain. [*The boy looks at Andrés, who jerks his head toward the patio. CLETO nods and goes out.*] I want you to give my husband a message for me. I can't write it. You'll have to remember it. But first, give me a glass of wine, too.

ANDRÉS. [*Pouring the wine.*] It might be easier for him if you wrote it.

RAQUEL. I think not. [*She takes the glass.*] I want you to tell him that I never knew how much I loved him until tonight.

ANDRÉS. Is that all?

RAQUEL. Yes. Tell me, captain, do you think it possible to love a person too much?

ANDRÉS. Yes, señora. I do.

RAQUEL. So do I. Let us drink a toast, captain—to honor. To bright and shining honor.

ANDRÉS. [*Raises his glass.*] To honor. [*He drains his glass. She lifts hers almost to her lips and then puts it down. From the patio comes a faint cry.*]

CLETO. [*Calling faintly in a cry that fades into silence.*] Captain. Captain.

[*ANDRÉS sways, his hand trying to brush across his face as though trying to brush sense into his head. When he hears CLETO he tries to stagger toward the window but stumbles and can't quite make it. Hanging on to the table by the sofa he looks accusingly at her. She shrinks back against her chair.*]

ANDRÉS. [*His voice weak from the poison.*] Why?

RAQUEL. Because I love him. Can you understand that?

ANDRÉS. We'll win. The Revolution will win. You can't stop that.

RAQUEL. Yes, you'll win. I know that now.

ANDRÉS. That girl—she thought my story was funny—about the hanging. But you didn't . . .

RAQUEL. I'm glad you hanged him. I'm glad.

[*ANDRÉS looks at her and tries to smile. He manages to pull the pouch from his shirt and extend it to her. But it drops from his hand.*]

RAQUEL. [*Runs to French window and calls.*] Cleto. Cleto! [*She buries her face in her hands for a moment, then comes back to ANDRÉS. She kneels beside him and picks up the leather pouch. She opens it and, taking the ring, puts it on her finger. Then she sees the medal. She rises and, pulling out the chain from her own throat, she slides the medal on to the chain. Then she walks to the sofa and sinks down on it.*]

MARICA. [*Calling off.*] Raquel! Raquel! [*RAQUEL snaps off the lamp, leaving the room in darkness. MARICA opens the house door. She is carrying a candle which she shades with her hand. The light is too dim to reveal the dead ANDRÉS.*] What are you doing down here in the dark? Why don't you come to bed?

RAQUEL. [*Making an effort to speak.*] I'll come in just a moment.

MARICA. But what are you doing, Raquel?

RAQUEL. Nothing. Just listening . . . listening to an empty house.

QUICK CURTAIN

Big Idea Portraits of Real Life *Why do you think Raquel says this?* **BI**

Additional Support

Skills Practice

READING: Character Motivation
In a play, as in real life, people don't always explain themselves. Have students work in pairs and think about the four main characters one at a time—Marica, Cleto, Andrés, and Raquel, in that order. Have them review the words and actions of each character and then write a paragraph about why the character acts the way that he or she does. You might have pairs focus on only one character and then share ideas. **OL**

AFTER YOU READ

RESPONDING AND THINKING CRITICALLY

Respond

1. What aspect of the play did you find most surprising?

Recall and Interpret

2. (a)When the play opens, what are the two characters on stage discussing? (b)Which of the two women in the play seems wiser or more capable? Explain.

3. (a)Who enters the home of General Macías? (b)What are the political differences between the intruders and General Macías and his wife?

4. (a)What does Raquel learn about her husband from the intruders? (b)How does the intruders' information affect her? Explain.

Analyze and Evaluate

5. In your opinion, is Raquel a hero? Explain.

6. In what ways does this play help an audience understand the early part of the Mexican Revolution?

7. (a)What do the ring of General Macías and the medal of Andrés symbolize to their owners? (b)What do they represent to Raquel?

Connect

8. **Big Idea** **Portraits of Real Life** (a)Explain how this play speaks to both loyalty and betrayal. (b)What connections can you make between loyalty and betrayal in the play and loyalty and betrayal in real life?

LITERARY ANALYSIS

Literary Element Characterization

Characterization might be revealed to the reader through the character's own words. Sometimes authors will have characters present a long speech, or **monologue**, that tells the reader something about the character's personality.

1. Which character in the play delivers a monologue?

2. What does the reader learn about the character who is speaking and the character being spoken to as a result of this monologue?

Writing About Literature

Respond to Theme *The Ring of General Macías* portrays the complex relationships between honor and love and between loyalty and betrayal. Pretend that you are Raquel and that you are writing your innermost thoughts in a journal that no one else will read. What would you say about honor and love and loyalty and betrayal in wartime? If there were not a war, would your feelings be different? Write a one-page journal entry from Raquel's perspective in which you consider the effect of war on a person's attitude toward personal relationships.

Literature Online Web Activities For eFlashcards, Selection Quick Checks, and other Web activities, go to www.glencoe.com.

READING AND VOCABULARY

Reading Strategy Analyzing Plot and Setting

In order to understand a literary work, the reader must understand the basic chain of events that make up the story (**plot**), as well as the time and place in which the story takes place (**setting**). A plot consists of various stages, including the **climax**, which is the highest point in the story.

1. How does the description of the setting help you better understand the characters and their actions?

2. What is the climax, or highest emotional point, in *The Ring of General Macías*? Explain.

Vocabulary Practice

Practice with Word Parts The common adverb suffix *–ly* means "like."

Using that information, choose the best definition for each vocabulary word below.

1. regally
   a. like a king or queen
   b. queen
   c. unlike a king

2. ostentatiously
   a. done in order to attract attention
   b. full of attention
   c. not having impressive qualities

JOSEPHINA NIGGLI **931**

COMPARING LITERATURE

AFTER YOU READ

Assess

1. Students may have been surprised by Raquel's attitude to war or her interactions with the soldiers.

2. (a) The death of Marica's husband. (b) Raquel is wiser and more capable. She handles each situation calmly.

3. (a) Andrés and Cleto, members of the Revolutionary Army. (b) The intruders are peasants. General Macías and his wife are members of the wealthy, ruling party.

4. (a) He has been imprisoned by Revolutionary forces. (b) It enables her to determine her course of action.

5. Some students may say Raquel is a hero because she makes a sacrifice; others, that she is not because she commits a murder.

6. The play dramatizes the conflict between the upper class and the peasants.

7. (a) They symbolize the General's love for his wife and Andrés's mother's love. (b) Love and the reasons she had for killing.

8. Domingo and Raquel are loyal to one another and to their government. Domingo is willing to betray his country for his wife. Andrés and Cleto are loyal to their cause. (b) Students' personal connections will vary.

Literary Element

1. Andrés.

2. Andrés is bitter over his treatment by the upper class, and that this is why he has joined the revolution.

Writing About Literature

Students' journal entries should deal with the impact of war on the issues of honor, love, loyalty, and betrayal.

Vocabulary

1. a 2. a

Reading Strategy

1. Without knowledge of the war and class differences, the characters' actions would make no sense.

2. The climax is when Andrés drinks his poisoned wine. All of the play's action has been building to this point.

Teach

Discussion Starter

Students may say that it is universally good advice to leave one's mark in the world because the author uses words like *proud* and *brave.* Other students may say that it is bad advice because the author suggests that it might sometimes be necessary to write with "blood." The passage "Brave, beauty folded into its imperfection" encourages readers not to be hindered by the fear of failure or imperfection. **OL**

★ Viewing the Art

Katherine S. Nemanich (1949–) creates abstract collages inspired by the colors and textures found in nature. Have students discuss how the colors and composition of this collage reflect the theme and images found in "Marked." **AS**

Literature Online

Author Search To expand students' appreciation of Carmen Tafolla, have them access the Web site for additional information and resources.

Additional Support

Marked — Carmen Tafolla

BEFORE YOU READ

Building Background

Carmen Tafolla explains that "as a Mexican American growing up in the 50s and 60s, I came from a group that was not often represented in textbooks. I saw no reflections of my own culture, and I longed to record the beauty and uniqueness of the culture that surrounded me."

In the following poem, Tafolla uses the word *m'ija,* (mē´hə), a contraction of the Spanish words *mi* ("my") and *hija* ("daughter"). By calling the reader "m'ija," Tafolla follows the Mexican American tradition of addressing all readers as if they were her own children and makes the poem a message to them.

Carmen Tafolla was born in 1951.

Literature Online Author Search For more about Carmen Tafolla, go to www.glencoe.com.

Never write with pencil,
m'ija
It is for those
who would
5   erase.
Make your mark proud
          and open,
Brave,
              beauty folded into
10   its imperfection,
Like a piece of turquoise
          marked.

Never write
with pencil,
15   m'ija.
Write with ink
          or mud,
or berries grown in
gardens never owned,
20   or, sometimes,
      if necessary,
          blood.

Collage Series II, No. 3, 1993. Katherine S. Nemanich. Oil pastel on paper and board, 12 x 9 in. Private collection.

Discussion Starter

With a small group, discuss whether Carmen Tafolla's advice about making a mark in the world is useful or not. Referring to the exact words of the poem, discuss the situations in which her advice might be most beneficial.

Skills Practice

LITERARY ELEMENTS: Free Verse
Point out that the poem is written in free verse, with no regular rhyme or rhythm. **Ask:** What qualities, besides the line breaks, differentiate the poem from prose? *(The unusual sentence structures differentiate it from standard prose.)* Have students discuss how it would be different if the lines were regular and rhyming and how the free verse form better suits the poem. Ask students to read the poem aloud, paying attention to the phrasings or emphasis suggested by some of the line breaks or ways the words are arranged on the page. **OL**

The Ring

Isak Dinesen

Focus

Summary

In Denmark around 1800, newlyweds Sigismund and Lise stroll blissfully across their sheep fields. Their pleasure is interrupted when they learn that a thief has been terrorizing neighboring sheepfolds and has killed a shepherd. While Sigismund looks after two sick lambs, Lise walks on. Feeling spurned, she decides to hide from Sigismund. As she enters a hidden grove, she finds herself face to face with the sheep thief. The ensuing events change Lise and her marriage.

BEFORE YOU READ

Building Background

Isak Dinesen (əˈsäk diˈnə sən) is the pen name of the Danish writer Karen Blixen, who spent seventeen years managing a coffee plantation in eastern Africa. Dinesen recorded the triumphs and sorrows of those years in her memoir *Out of Africa,* from which the Oscar-winning film of the same name was made in 1985. Dinesen returned to the family estate at Rungstedlund in 1931 and devoted herself to her writing. She once said: "As for me I have one ambition only: to invent stories, very beautiful stories." Her short story collections include *Seven Gothic Tales* and *Winter's Tales.*

"The Ring" takes place in the Danish countryside around 1800. At that time, most people in Denmark lived on farms.

Isak Dinesen was born in 1885 and died in 1962.

Literature Online **Author Search** For more about Isak Dinesen, go to www.glencoe.com.

Literature Online

Author Search To expand students' appreciation of Isak Dinesen, have them access the Web site for additional information and resources.

CheckPoint

Use the CheckPoint questions on Presentation Plus! to monitor students' comprehension. These questions can be used with interactive response keypads for immediate student feedback.

O N A SUMMER MORNING a hundred and fifty years ago a young Danish squire and his wife went out for a walk on their land. They had been married a week. It had not been easy for them to get married, for the wife's family was higher in rank and wealthier than the husband's. But the two young people, now twenty-four and nineteen years old, had been set on their purpose for ten years; and in the end her haughty parents had had to give in to them.

They were wonderfully happy. The stolen meetings and secret, tearful love letters were now things of the past. To God and man they were one; they could walk arm in arm in broad daylight and drive in the same carriage, and they would walk and drive so till the end of their days. Their distant paradise had descended to earth and had proved, surprisingly, to be filled with the things of everyday life: with jesting and railleries,[1] with breakfasts and suppers, with dogs,

---

1. *Railleries* are instances of good-natured ridicule or teasing.

ISAK DINESEN **933**

Building Reading Fluency

Previewing Ask students to read the first paragraph of the selection and make some predictions about what will happen in the story. Ask them what they think the title refers to and how a ring might be significant to the events that will follow. Ask them to also predict what kinds of conflicts they think might develop based on the opening description of the characters and setting. Remind students to keep their predictions in mind as they read, to see how the story compares to their expectations. **BL**

Teach

L1 Literary Element

Characterization Ask: What do the descriptions of Lise on this page tell you about her character? *(The fact that she feels as if she is only playing when she goes about her chores makes her appear very young and ignorant about the realities of marriage and adult life.)* **OL**

haymaking and sheep. Sigismund, the young husband, had promised himself that from now there should be no stone in his bride's path, nor should any shadow fall across it. Lovisa, the wife, felt that now, every day and for the first time in her young life, she moved and breathed in perfect freedom because she could never have any secret from her husband.

To Lovisa—whom her husband called Lise—the rustic atmosphere of her new life was a matter of wonder and delight. Her husband's fear that the existence he could offer her might not be good enough for her filled her heart with laughter. It was not a long time since she had played with dolls; as now she dressed her own hair, looked over her linen press and arranged her flowers she again lived through an enchanting and cherished experience: one was doing everything gravely and solicitously, and all the time one knew one was playing.

It was a lovely July morning. Little woolly clouds drifted high up in the sky, the air was full of sweet scents. Lise had on a white muslin frock and a large Italian straw hat. She and her husband took a path through the park; it wound on across the meadows, between small groves and groups of trees, to the sheep field. Sigismund was going to show his wife his sheep. For this reason she had not brought her small white dog, Bijou, with her, for he would yap at the lambs and frighten them, or he would annoy the sheep dogs. Sigismund prided himself on his sheep; he had studied sheep-breeding in Mecklenburg[2] and England, and had brought back with him Cotswold rams by which to improve his Danish stock. While

---

2. *Mecklenburg* is a farming region in northeastern Germany.

Gentle Spring, 1889. Edward Wilkins Waite. Oil on canvas, 51 x 76 cm. Private collection.

934 UNIT 4 DRAMA

Additional Support

Skills Practice

GRAMMAR AND LANGUAGE:
Perfect Tenses Point out the large number of past perfect verbs used in the selection to describe past actions. Explain that the present perfect expresses an action that occurred at an indefinite time in the past. For example: *The thief has been stealing sheep.* The past perfect describes one past action that began and ended before another past action began. For example: *It was not a long time since she had played with dolls.* Have students write the present perfect and past perfect tenses of the verbs *be, steal,* and *find* and use each in a sentence. **OL**

they walked he explained to Lise the great possibilities and difficulties of the plan.

She thought: "How clever he is, what a lot of things he knows!" and at the same time: "What an absurd person he is, with his sheep! What a baby he is! I am a hundred years older than he."

But when they arrived at the sheepfold the old sheepmaster Mathias met them with the sad news that one of the English lambs was dead and two were sick. Lise saw that her husband was grieved by the tidings; while he questioned Mathias on the matter she kept silent and only gently pressed his arm. A couple of boys were sent off to fetch the sick lambs, while the master and servant went into the details of the case. It took some time.

Lise began to gaze about her and to think of other things. Twice her own thoughts made her blush deeply and happily, like a red rose, then slowly her blush died away, and the two men were still talking about sheep. A little while after their conversation caught her attention. It had turned to a sheep thief.

This thief during the last months had broken into the sheepfolds of the neighborhood like a wolf, had killed and dragged away his prey like a wolf and like a wolf had left no trace after him. Three nights ago the shepherd and his son on an estate ten miles away had caught him in the act. The thief had killed the man and knocked the boy senseless, and had managed to escape. There were men sent out to all sides to catch him, but nobody had seen him.

Lise wanted to hear more about the horrible event, and for her benefit old Mathias went through it once more. There had been a long fight in the sheep house, in many places the earthen floor was soaked with blood. In the fight the thief's left arm was broken; all the same, he had climbed a tall fence with a lamb on his back. Mathias added that he would like to string up the murderer with these two hands of his, and Lise nodded her head at him gravely in approval. She

remembered Red Ridinghood's wolf, and felt a pleasant little thrill running down her spine.

Sigismund had his own lambs in his mind, but he was too happy in himself to wish anything in the universe ill. After a minute he said: "Poor devil."

Lise said: "How can you pity such a terrible man? Indeed Grandmamma was right when she said that you were a revolutionary and a danger to society!" The thought of Grandmamma, and of the tears of past days, again turned her mind away from the gruesome tale she had just heard.

The boys brought the sick lambs and the men began to examine them carefully, lifting them up and trying to set them on their legs; they squeezed them here and there and made the little creatures whimper. Lise shrank from the show and her husband noticed her distress.

Visual Vocabulary
Cotswold is a breed of sheep with long, coarse hair, originally bred in the Cotswold Hills of southwestern England.

"You go home, my darling," he said, "this will take some time. But just walk ahead slowly, and I shall catch up with you."

So she was turned away by an impatient husband to whom his sheep meant more than his wife. If any experience could be sweeter than to be dragged out by him to look at those same sheep, it would be this. She dropped her large summer hat with its blue ribbons on the grass and told him to carry it back for her, for she wanted to feel the summer air on her forehead and in her hair. She walked on very slowly, as he had told her to do, for she wished to obey him in everything. As she walked she felt a great new happiness in being altogether alone, even without Bijou. She could not remember that she had ever before in all her life been altogether alone. The landscape around her

ISAK DINESEN **935**

Teach

L2 Literary Element

Characterization Ask: How does Lise's reaction to the story of the sheep thief further reveal her childish nature? *(She compares the sheep thief with the wolf in "Little Red Riding Hood." She feels a thrill at the thought of the thief, thinking of the situation as something dramatic and almost like a fairy tale, not as a real-life problem.)* **OL**

R Reading Strategy

Inferring Ask: Why do you think Lise responds the way she does when Sigismund refers to the sheep thief as a "Poor devil"? *(Students may think she is teasing him, because the two of them do indulge in jesting and railleries. She may also be bored with all the talk of sheep and want to start a fight or show her irritation in this way. Or she may be genuinely shocked by his comment and wonder if her grandmother's complaints might be true.)* **OL**

L3 Literary Element

Characterization Ask: How does Lise misinterpret Sigismund when he tells her to go home? What does this suggest about her character? *(He sent her home because she seemed bored and distressed, not because he cares more about the sheep. Lise's reaction suggests that she overreacts and gets offended easily.)* **OL**

Objectives
• To understand characterization (TWE)
• To understand perfect tenses (TWE)

English Language Coach

Marriage Marital traditions have many variations in different cultures. Invite English language learners to describe marital and wedding traditions from their own countries. Ask students questions such as these: What is a typical wedding like? What do the bride and groom wear? Do people dance at weddings?

Do people always choose whom they will marry? At what age does someone typically get married? What kinds of gifts are given to newlyweds? Then ask the class to discuss how these descriptions compare with weddings in the United States. **EL**

Teach

L1 Literary Element

Characterization Ask: What does the plan Lise decides on as she walks home tell you about her? *(Her plan to hide in the grove so that Sigismund will miss her and worry about her emphasizes her childishness yet again. It shows another way that she plays games.)* OL

was still, as if full of promise, and it was hers. Even the swallows cruising in the air were hers, for they belonged to him, and he was hers.

She followed the curving edge of the grove and after a minute or two found that she was out of sight to the men by the sheep house. What could now, she wondered, be sweeter than to walk along the path in the long flowering meadow grass, slowly, slowly, and to let her husband overtake her there? It would be sweeter still, she reflected, to steal into the grove and to be gone, to have vanished from the surface of the earth from him when, tired of the sheep and long-ing for her company, he should turn the bend of the path to catch up with her.

An idea struck her; she stood still to think it over.

L1 A few days ago her husband had gone for a ride and she had not wanted to go with him, but had strolled about with Bijou in order to explore her domain. Bijou then, gamboling, had led her straight into the grove. As she had followed him, gently forc-ing her way into the shrubbery, she had sud-denly come upon a glade in the midst of it, a narrow space like a small alcove with hang-ings of thick green and golden brocade, big enough to hold two or three people in it. She had felt at that moment that she had come into the very heart of her new home. If today she could find the spot again she would stand perfectly still there, hidden from all the world. Sigismund would look for her in all directions; he would be unable to under-stand what had become of her and for a minute, for a short minute—or, perhaps, if she was firm and cruel enough, for five—he would realize what a void, what an unen-durably sad and horrible place the universe would be when she was no longer in it. She gravely scrutinized the grove to find the right entrance to her hiding-place, then went in.

She took great care to make no noise at all, therefore advanced exceedingly slowly.

When a twig caught the flounces of her ample skirt she loosened it softly from the muslin, so as not to crack it. Once a branch took hold of one of her long golden curls; she stood still, with her arms lifted, to free it. A little way into the grove the soil became moist; her light steps no longer made any sound upon it. With one hand she held her small handkerchief to her lips, as if to emphasize the secretness of her course. She found the spot she sought and bent down to divide the foliage and make a door to her sylvan³ closet. At this the hem of her dress caught her foot and she stopped to loosen it. As she rose she looked into the face of a man who was already in the shelter.

He stood up erect, two steps off. He must have watched her as she made her way straight toward him.

She took him in in one single glance. His face was bruised and scratched, his hands and wrists stained with dark filth. He was dressed in rags, barefooted, with tatters wound round his naked ankles. His arms hung down to his sides, his right hand clasped the hilt of a knife. He was about her own age. The man and the woman looked at each other.

This meeting in the wood from beginning to end passed without a word; what hap-pened could only be rendered by panto-mime. To the two actors in the pantomime it was timeless; according to a clock it lasted four minutes.

She had never in her life been exposed to danger. It did not occur to her to sum up her position, or to work out the length of time it would take to call her husband or Mathias, whom at this moment she could hear shout-ing to his dogs. She beheld the man before her as she would have beheld a forest ghost: the apparition itself, not the sequels⁴ of it, changes the world to the human who faces it.

---

3. *Sylvan* means "in or among woods" or "formed by trees."
4. Here, *sequels* means "results or consequences."

Additional Support

Skills Practice

WRITING: Varying Sentence Length Point out the way Dinesen combines long sentences and shorter ones. For example: "He slowly reached out his hand to hers, his finger touched hers, and her hand was steady at the touch. But he did not take the ring." Point out that sentences of varying length make prose more interesting and prevent the rhythm from becoming monotonous. Have students write a short narrative paragraph describing an inter-esting event. Encourage them to employ different descriptive techniques and vary the length of their sentences. OL

Weary but Watchful, late 19th Century. John Sargent Noble.

Although she did not take her eyes off the face before her she sensed that the alcove had been turned into a covert.[5] On the ground a couple of sacks formed a couch; there were some gnawed bones by it. A fire must have been made here in the night, for there were cinders strewn on the forest floor.

After a while she realized that he was observing her just as she was observing him. He was no longer just run to earth and crouching for a spring, but he was wondering, trying to know. At that she seemed to see herself with the eyes of the wild animal at bay[6] in his dark hiding-place; her silently approaching white figure, which might mean death.

He moved his right arm till it hung down straight before him between his legs. Without lifting the hand he bent the wrist and slowly raised the point of the knife till it pointed at her throat. The gesture was mad,

unbelievable. He did not smile as he made it, but his nostrils distended,[7] the corners of his mouth quivered a little. Then slowly he put the knife back in the sheath by his belt.

She had no object of value about her, only the wedding ring which her husband had set on her finger in church, a week ago. She drew it off, and in this movement dropped her handkerchief. She reached out her hand with the ring toward him. She did not bargain for her life. She was fearless by nature, and the horror with which he inspired her was not fear of what he might do to her. She commanded him, she besought[8] him to vanish as he had come, to take a dreadful figure out of her life, so that it should never have been there. In the dumb[9] movement her young form had the grave authoritativeness[10] of a priestess conjuring down some monstrous being by a sacred sign.

---

5. As a noun, *covert* means "a hiding place." More often, you will see the word used as an adjective to mean "secret, hidden, or concealed."
6. *At bay* refers to the position of a cornered animal that is forced to turn and confront its pursuers.

7. *Distended* means "enlarged or expanded."
8. *Besought* is the past tense of *beseech* and means "begged or asked earnestly."
9. Here, *dumb* means "silent" and "without words."
10. *Authoritativeness* is the quality of having and using the power to act or command.

ISAK DINESEN **937**

English Language Coach

Multiple-Meaning Words Words with multiple meanings are especially challenging for English language learners. Point out that in English, words may have more than one meaning and the first one to come to mind is not always the correct one for the context. For example, the word *steal* on page 936 means to sneak unobserved, not to take something without permission. Ask students to use a dictionary to look up the following multiple-meaning words from the selection: *rank, ram, void, wound,* and *grave.* Ask them to use each word in two sentences, once the way it is used in the selection and once with another meaning. **EL**

Teach

⭐ Writer's Technique

Mood Have students discuss how the author creates mood on this and the preceding page. **Ask:** What details and descriptions contribute to the mood of this scene? What mood do they create? *(The description of Lise's slow progress into the grove, the vivid imagery of her surroundings, and the detailed description of the sheep thief are important to creating the mood of the scene. The emphasis on quietness creates a mysterious mood edged with suspense. The suspense becomes stronger once Lise and the thief see each other.)* **AS**

L₂ Literary Element

Characterization Lise offers her ring to the thief after he points his knife at her, but she is not motivated by fear. Draw students' attention to this passage: "the horror with which he inspired her was not fear of what he might do to her." **Ask:** Based on what you know about Lise's character, what do you think the cause of her horror is? *(Students may say that she is horrified simply by the existence of the thief in her world. In her sheltered innocence, she has never before come across a poor, desperate, and miserable person like him.)* **OL**

Objectives
- To understand characterization (TWE)
- To vary sentence lengths (TWE)

Teach

R Reading Strategy

Interpreting Ask: What do you think Lise means when she thinks "All is over" when she meets up with her husband? *(Students may think her comment refers to her marriage or to her encounter with the thief or both.)* **OL**

L Literary Element

Characterization Ask: What does the loss of her ring make Lise realize? How does this reflect a change in her character? *(As Lise tells Sigismund she has lost her ring, she suddenly comes to realize what the ring symbolizes: a lifetime of devotion. She seems to feel trapped by her vows. This shows that she no longer has the same childlike, fairy-tale ideas of marriage but realizes that it is a very real commitment.)* **OL**

✔CheckPoint

Use the CheckPoint questions on Presentation Plus! to check students' mastery of the selections. These questions can be used with interactive response keypads for immediate student feedback.

He slowly reached out his hand to hers, his finger touched hers, and her hand was steady at the touch. But he did not take the ring. As she let it go it dropped to the ground as her handkerchief had done.

For a second the eyes of both followed it. It rolled a few inches toward him and stopped before his bare foot. In a hardly perceivable movement he kicked it away and again looked into her face. They remained like that, she knew not how long, but she felt that during that time something happened, things were changed.

He bent down and picked up her handkerchief. All the time gazing at her, he again drew his knife and wrapped the tiny bit of cambric[11] round the blade. This was difficult for him to do because his left arm was broken. While he did it his face under the dirt and sun-tan slowly grew whiter till it was almost phosphorescent.[12] Fumbling with both hands, he once more stuck the knife into the sheath. Either the sheath was too big and had never fitted the knife, or the blade was much worn—it went in. For two or three more seconds his gaze rested on her face; then he lifted his own face a little, the strange radiance still upon it, and closed his eyes.

The movement was definitive and unconditional. In this one motion he did what she had begged him to do: he vanished and was gone. She was free.

She took a step backward, the immovable, blind face before her, then bent as she had done to enter the hiding-place, and glided away as noiselessly as she had come. Once outside the grove she stood still and looked round for the meadow path, found it, and began to walk home.

Her husband had not yet rounded the edge of the grove. Now he saw her and helloed to her gaily; he came up quickly and joined her.

The path here was so narrow that he kept half behind her and did not touch her. He began to explain to her what had been the matter with the lambs. She walked a step before him and thought: All is over. **R**

After a while he noticed her silence, came up beside her to look at her face and asked, "What is the matter?"

She searched her mind for something to say, and at last said: "I have lost my ring."

"What ring?" he asked her.

She answered, "My wedding ring."

As she heard her own voice pronounce the words she conceived their meaning.

Her wedding ring. "With this ring"— dropped by one and kicked away by another—"with this ring I thee wed." With this lost ring she had wedded herself to something. To what? To poverty, persecution, total loneliness. To the sorrows and the sinfulness of this earth. "And what therefore God has joined together let man not put asunder."[13] **L**

"I will find you another ring," her husband said. "You and I are the same as we were on our wedding day; it will do as well. We are husband and wife today too, as much as yesterday, I suppose."

Her face was so still that he did not know if she had heard what he said. It touched him that she should take the loss of his ring so to heart. He took her hand and kissed it. It was cold, not quite the same hand as he had last kissed. He stopped to make her stop with him.

"Do you remember where you had the ring on last?" he asked.

"No," she answered.

"Have you any idea," he asked, "where you may have lost it?"

"No," she answered. "I have no idea at all." ✑

---

11. *Cambric* is the soft, lightweight linen of which Lise's handkerchief is made.
12. Here, *phosphorescent* (fos′fə res′ənt) means "glowing."

13. *Asunder* (ə sun′dər) means "in separate parts." This biblical quotation (Matthew 19:6) is often repeated at the end of a traditional Christian marriage ceremony.

Additional Support

Skills Practice

READING: Visualizing Visualizing the spatial relationships in "The Ring" will give readers a better understanding of the events in the story. Readers must be able to visualize and follow the changing spatial relationships among the settings and characters. Ask students to draw or sketch pictures of the meadow, the woods, Sigismund, Lise, and the thief based on details from the story. They might draw individual pictures of the five or one picture of a scene involving all five. Drawings should give an idea of what the settings and characters look like and where they are in relation to each other. **OL**

Wrap-Up: Comparing Literature Across Genres

- *The Ring of General Macías*
  by Josephina Niggli
- *Marked*
  by Carmen Tafolla
- *The Ring*
  by Isak Dinesen

COMPARING THE [Big Idea] Portraits of Real Life

Writing Activity These selections—*The Ring of General Macías*, "Marked," and "The Ring"—involve the development of female characters facing particular conflicts and challenges. Do the concerns portrayed in these works still apply to today's women and girls? Are they relevant to all women or only to certain groups of women? Might these concerns apply to boys or to men as well? Consider contemporary issues and how they affect the lives of women today. Then write a brief essay in which you discuss your thoughts about these issues in relation to the literary works.

COMPARING Theme

Group Activity A genre is a category, or type, of literature. Each of the selections compared here represent different genres—drama, poetry, and short story—while conveying a theme, or message, about loyalty. With a small group, discuss the following questions:

1. To whom or what do the main characters in these selections believe they owe their loyalty? Explain.
2. What are some explanations for these differing ideas about loyalty?
3. In what ways do these selections show that girls and women are capable of acting bravely or of fulfilling roles once reserved for men?

Two Women, 1929. Frida Kahlo. Oil on canvas, 27³/₈ x 21 in. Private collection.

COMPARING Cultures

Partner Activity Josephina Niggli and Carmen Tafolla both weave Latino culture into their literary works. Niggli was raised in Mexico by Anglo parents, while Tafolla was raised in the United States by Mexican American parents. While their experiences are in some ways similar, they are also from two different eras. Do the different time periods have an effect on the writers' attitudes and beliefs? Do their differing childhood circumstances have an effect as well? With a partner, make inferences about each author's beliefs regarding the following:

1. the role of women and girls in society
2. the importance of culture in people's lives
3. the effect of history—especially family history—upon future generations

Support your inferences with details from the selections. Then share your thoughts with your classmates.

OBJECTIVES
- Compare works about culture and loyalty.
- Compare theme across genres.
- Compare and contrast authors' beliefs about culture.

Assess

Comparing the Big Idea
Students should relate their answers to the conflicts and challenges confronting the various characters.

Comparing Theme

1. Raquel believes that she owes loyalty to her husband and to her government; General Macías, to his wife and his government; Andrés and Cleto, to the revolutionary cause; and Marica, to her dead husband. The speaker of the poem believes loyalty is owed to oneself. Sigismund believes that he owes loyalty to Lise; Lise believes that she owes loyalty to Sigismund, but she is also immature and withholds her loyalty for petty reasons.

2. Differing ideas about loyalty might be due to people holding different values, having different experiences, or being at different stages in life.

3. Raquel supports her country by making the decision to kill the two spies. The poem suggests that women should use any means necessary to make their mark on the world. Lise is in many respects undaunted by her unexpected interaction with a killer.

Comparing Cultures

Students' discussions may include inferences such as these:

1. Both writers would probably say that women have the potential to accomplish anything they want.

2. Both value culture and would say that it should have an important place in everyone's lives.

3. Niggli would probably place greater value on history than Tafolla would. Tafolla's focus is on the future rather than the past.

Focus

BELLRINGER

Have students think of a time when they had to persuade someone to believe something or to take action. After a minute or two, ask volunteers to share their experiences. **Ask:** Whom were you trying to persuade? What were you trying to persuade the person (or persons) to believe or to do? Were you successful? If so, what technique did you use to persuade your audience? *(Answers will vary.)*

Summary

In this workshop, students will write and present persuasive speeches. They will follow the stages of the writing process, including prewriting, drafting, revising, and editing, and presenting. In addition, two mini-lessons on elaborating ideas with evidence and parallelism are provided.

Writing Models Have students access the Web site for interactive writing models and writing guides.

The Writing Process

In this workshop, you will follow the stages of the writing process. At any stage, you may think of new ideas to include and better ways to express them. Feel free to return to earlier stages as you write.

Prewriting

Drafting

Revising

 Focus Lesson: Elaborating on Ideas with Evidence

Editing & Proofreading

Focus Lesson: Parallelism

Presenting

Writing Models For models and other writing activities, go to www.glencoe.com.

OBJECTIVES
• Write a persuasive speech that uses rhetorical devices to support assertions.
• Clarify and defend positions with precise and relevant evidence.

940 UNIT 4 DRAMA

Writing Workshop

Persuasive Speech

 Presenting a Viewpoint

"If there be any in this assembly, any dear friend of Caesar's, to him I say, that Brutus' love to Caesar was no less than his. If then that friend demand why Brutus rose against Caesar, this is my answer: Not that I lov'd Caesar less, but that I lov'd Rome more. Had you rather Caesar were living, and die all slaves, than that Caesar were dead, to live all free men? As Caesar lov'd me, I weep for him; as he was fortunate, I rejoice at it; as he was valiant, I honor him; but, as he was ambitious, I slew him."

—William Shakespeare, from *The Tragedy of Julius Caesar*

Connecting to the Literature After Brutus kills Caesar, he has some persuading to do. In an impassioned speech to the plebeians gathered at the Forum, he must convince his audience that his reasons for killing Caesar were both noble and just. In this workshop, you will write a speech that uses both logical and emotional appeals. Study the rubric below to learn the goals and strategies for writing a successful persuasive speech.

Features of Persuasive Speeches

Goals	Strategies
To present a clearly stated opinion	☑ Clearly state your opinion or thesis at or near the beginning of your speech, and restate your opinion at the end
To engage the intended audience from beginning to end	☑ Include emotional and logical appeals or other devices—such as case studies, anecdotes, and analogies—as part of a narrative
To explain and support the opinion	☑ Give reasons for your opinions, and use facts and examples to back up your reasons
To convince an audience of a particular point of view	☑ Anticipate and address counterarguments ☑ Use logical order

---

Additional Support

Workshop Resources

Print Materials
📁 Unit 4 Resources (Fast File), pp. 60–62
📁 REAL Success in Writing: Research and Reports
📁 Writing Constructed Responses, pp. 1–26, 54, 61–66
📖 Glencoe Literature Library

✍ **Transparencies**
• Grammar and Language Transparency 9
• Writing Workshop Transparencies 21–25
• Visual Literacy/Fine Art Transparencies

💻 **Technology**
• Grammar & Language eWorkbook
• Revising with Style eWorkbook
• Sentence Diagraming eWorkbook
• Spelling Power eWorkbook
• Online Essay Grader, glencoe.com
• Literature Library Exam*View*™ Assessment Suite CD-ROM
• Literature Library Vocabulary PuzzleMaker CD-ROM

Assignment

Write a persuasive speech. As you move through the stages of the writing process, keep your audience and purpose in mind.

Audience: members of a high school assembly, including classmates, teachers, and the principal

Purpose: to persuade through logical and emotional appeals as well as precise, relevant evidence

Analyzing a Professional Model

In the short speech that follows, former senator Everett Dirksen explains why the marigold should be the national flower. As you read the speech, note how Dirksen presents a clear opinion, uses logical reasoning, and addresses counterarguments. Pay close attention to the comments in the margin. They point out features that you may want to include in your own speech.

Why Marigolds Should Be the National Flower
by Senator Everett Dirksen, Republican, Illinois

Mr. President: On January 8, 1965, I introduced Senate Joint Resolution 19, to designate the American marigold—*Tagetes erecta*—as the national floral emblem of the United States. Today I am introducing the same resolution with the suggestion that it again be referred to the Committee on the Judiciary.

The American flag is not a mere assembly of colors, stripes and stars but, in fact, symbolizes our origin, development, and growth.

The American eagle, king of the skies, is so truly representative of our might and power.

A national floral emblem should represent the virtues of our land and be national in character.

The marigold is a native of North America and can in truth and in fact be called an American flower.

It is national in character, for it grows and thrives in every one of the fifty states of this nation. It conquers the extremes of temperature. It well withstands the summer sun and the evening chill.

Real-World Connection

Perhaps no speaking or writing skills are more important than persuasive skills. These everyday skills help you influence your peers, parents, teachers, and siblings. They can also help you secure internships, find jobs, and gain admission into college.

Opinion/Thesis Statement

Be sure to state your opinion clearly and forcefully at or near the beginning of your speech.

Emotional Appeals and Analogy

The emotional appeal to national symbols and the analogy "king of the skies" arouse feelings of pride. Appeal to your listeners' emotions as well as to their logic.

Clarify Your Position

Present facts and opinions that make your position stronger or easier to understand.

Logical Reasoning

Use logical reasoning to support your opinion.

Teach

Big Idea

Portraits of Real Life
Say: Consider the following as you read. In real life, people often have to make decisions, make changes, and take action. They sometimes have to convince others to believe and act as they do. The art of persuasion plays a key role in convincing others. **Ask:** What are some real-life instances in which you saw persuasion at work? *(Answers will vary. Students may mention interactions with their peers, parents, or teachers; others may suggest national political issues or world events as areas where persuasion plays a role.)* **OL**

★ Political History

A Rose by Any Other Name Although Senator Dirksen lobbied passionately to declare the marigold the national flower, he was not successful. Instead, Senate Joint Resolution 159 designated the rose the National Floral Emblem of the United States. On November 20, 1986, President Ronald Reagan delivered Proclamation 5574, thereby announcing to the nation its new national symbol. **AS**

English Language Coach

Word Meaning Define the terms *persuade, persuasion,* and *persuasive.* (Persuade, *a verb, means "to convince someone of something"*; persuasion, *a noun, "the act of persuading, or the ability to persuade"*; persuasive, *an adjective, "able to persuade, or having the effect of persuading."*) **EL**

Differentiated Instruction

Identifying a Topic Less proficient writers may have difficulty pinpointing an appropriate topic for their persuasive speeches. Assist these students individually in selecting topics that are appropriate to their levels and about which they have strong feelings. **BL**

Objective
• To write a persuasive speech that uses rhetorical devices to support assertions (SE)

Teach

Writing Skills

Visual Aids Encourage students to use visual aids during their presentations. Have them choose visual aids that are appropriate to their speeches. **Explain:** Visual aids can help persuade audiences. If you are thinking of incorporating visual aids into your presentation, make sure that these aids are based on and relevant to your speech. **OL**

★ Language History

Logos, Pathos, and Ethos The rhetorical strategies used in persuasive speaking have a long history and are rooted in the meaning of their names. Explain to students what each word means. *Logos* is the Greek word from which the English word *logic* originates. It refers to the logic of a speaker's argument. *Ethos* relates to the English word *ethics,* which refers to the speaker's character and believability. *Pathos* refers to the audience's emotions and deeply felt beliefs—in other words, their psychological makeup. **AS**

Facts and Examples

Present facts and examples both to keep your audience engaged and to back up your argument.

Counterarguments

Others may suggest different national flowers. Make your case stronger by addressing opposing opinions or viewpoints.

Logical Order

Dirksen presents his points in order of importance. Present your argument in a logical order.

Conclusion

Forcefully restate your thesis. Also write a "clincher" statement, make a final emotional or logical appeal, or end in another memorable way.

Its robustness reflects the hardihood and character of the generations who pioneered and built this land into a great nation. It is not temperamental about fertility. It resists its natural enemies, the insects. It is self-reliant and requires little attention. Its spectacular colors—lemon and orange, rich brown and deep mahogany—befit the imaginative qualities of this nation.

It is as sprightly as the daffodil, as colorful as the rose, as resolute as the zinnia, as delicate as the carnation, as haughty as the chrysanthemum, as aggressive as the petunia, as ubiquitous as the violet, and as stately as the snapdragon.

It beguiles the senses and ennobles the spirit of man. It is the delight of the amateur gardener and a constant challenge to the professional.

Since it is native to America and nowhere else in the world, and common to every state in the Union, I present the American marigold for designation as the national floral emblem of our country.

Reading-Writing Connection Think about the writing techniques that you have just encountered and try them out in the persuasive speech you write. ★

Prewriting

Choose an Issue Your first job is to choose an issue that you truly care about. Keep your audience in mind: Your readers and listeners will be more interested if you select a topic that they truly care about too.

Gather Ideas Your next step is to test your issue by making sure that it presents both sides. At the same time, you can begin to develop ideas for writing by making a pro-and-con chart like this one:

School Dress Code

Pros	Cons
helps students prepare	bans the most practical choice of clothing
inspires students to work harder to earn higher grades	requires students to have a second wardrobe that meets the code
increases students' self-respect	discourages students from learning to make their own decisions

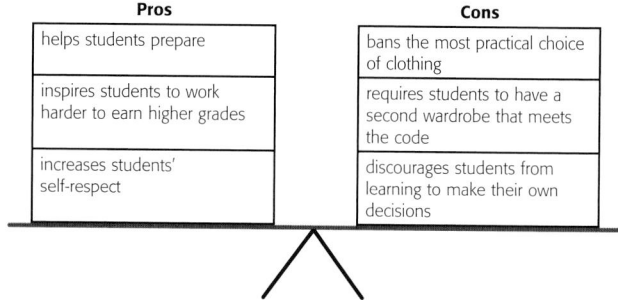

Additional Support

Skills Practice

RESEARCH: Credible Evidence
When attempting to persuade readers and listeners, students should understand that credible evidence is their best friend. When used appropriately, facts, data, and statistics create a strong foundation for a persuasive piece. Encourage students to research their topics at a library or via the Internet. Caution them to use credible sources, particularly in their online research. Have students pick one aspect of their topic and do an online search. Have them print out their findings and bring them to class. Evaluate the quality of the research and the sources with the class. **OL**

State Your Opinion Study your graphic organizer. Decide what you want to say about the issue. Sum up your opinion in a single sentence. This is your opinion statement, or thesis. You can revise it during the drafting or revising stages to make it sharper, clearer, or more accurate.

Talk About Your Ideas Meet with a partner. Read your opinion statement out loud. Briefly discuss your reasons for holding the opinion. As you do so, listen to your voice. How do you sound as you discuss this topic? What makes you most excited or personally involved as you explain your ideas? What specific words and what kinds of sentences do you use to convey your opinion and feelings? To develop your writing voice, listen to your speaking voice now so that you can remember and re-create it as you write later.

Make an Organizational Plan Outline your persuasive speech by planning the main points you will make, jotting down supporting details, listing counterarguments you will address, and making notes on how you will conclude.

▶ Create a focus for your listeners by stating your opinion in the first sentence or near the beginning of your speech.

▶ Win the reader over by sounding as reasonable and as logical as possible. Address and nullify counterarguments, while building support for your opinion.

▶ Present reasons, facts, examples, short stories or anecdotes, case studies, or analogies to support your opinion. Then conclude forcefully.

▶ Use one of these methods of organization or create a similar order that includes the elements shown below.

The Right Topic

Remember that a speech is ultimately intended for listeners, not readers, so choose a topic that will interest your audience from the very beginning. Also, choose a topic that you can support without long explanations, densely embedded facts, or statistics that will be hard for listeners to follow.

Test Prep

If you were writing a speech for a test, you would have to shorten the prewriting process. Consider which of the steps listed here you would still include.

OR

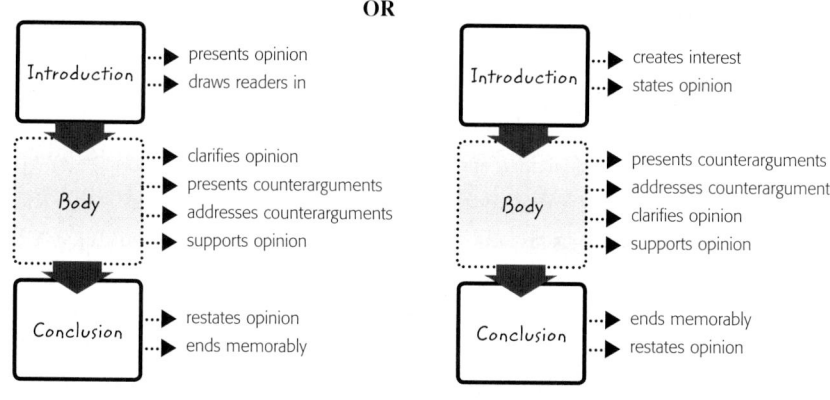

Introduction
····▶ presents opinion
····▶ draws readers in

Body
····▶ clarifies opinion
····▶ presents counterarguments
····▶ addresses counterarguments
····▶ supports opinion

Conclusion
····▶ restates opinion
····▶ ends memorably

Introduction
····▶ creates interest
····▶ states opinion

Body
····▶ presents counterarguments
····▶ addresses counterarguments
····▶ clarifies opinion
····▶ supports opinion

Conclusion
····▶ ends memorably
····▶ restates opinion

Building Reading Fluency

Reading Speeches The rhythm and cadence of a speech, especially a persuasive speech, are important to its effectiveness. Encourage students to become familiar with how various persuasive speeches sound, when read silently and aloud. Bring in examples of persuasive speeches, such as Martin Luther King Jr.'s "I Have a Dream" speech and Shirley Chisolm's 1970 speech on the Equal Rights Amendment. Both attempt to persuade the American people to support full and equal rights for all citizens. Allow students to read these on their own; then ask them to compare and contrast the speakers' rhythms. **OL**

Teach

Writing Process

Prewriting In the prewriting stage, students have the opportunity to define the focus of their persuasive speeches. Before they begin to gather ideas and do research and before they select the approaches they will take, have them write purpose statements for their speeches. A purpose statement differs from a thesis statement: It serves not to introduce the topic but to guide the student through the drafting, writing, and revising stages of his or her speech. **Say:** Clear thinking about your goals during this project will help you write a cogent and effective speech. Think about what you want to persuade your listeners to think or to do. Write your purpose statement down, and refer to it during the various stages of writing. **OL**

Objectives
• To write a persuasive speech that uses rhetorical devices to support assertions (SE)
• To use credible resources for research (TWE)

943

Teach

Writing Skills

Introduction Answer: *The listener is urged to imagine life under the proposed dress code.* **OL**

Writing Skills

Opinion Statement Answer: *"We must not let this outdated, unrealistic, and impractical dress code become reality" appears at the end of the first paragraph.* **OL**

Writing Skills

Counterarguments Answer: *The school board's reasons for the new dress code are presented.* **OL**

Writing Skills

Logical Order Answer: *The logical organization introduces the opinion in the first paragraph; the counterarguments, in the second; and the response to the counterarguments, in the third.* **OL**

Drafting

Use Transitions As you get your ideas down on paper, remember to link them with appropriate transitions. In persuasive writing, you can help your readers and listeners distinguish your most important reasons and points by introducing them with words such as *first, second,* and *last.* Other transition expressions that are similarly useful include *more important, most important,* and *finally.* Remember to link your ideas between paragraphs as well as within them.

Analyzing a Workshop Model

Here is a final draft of a persuasive speech. Read the speech and answer the questions in the margin. Use the answers to these questions to guide you as you write.

Down with Worn-Out Dress Codes!

Introduction

How does the writer create interest or draw the reader in?

Imagine never again being permitted to wear a pair of sneakers, blue jeans, or a sports cap to school. Imagine having to set aside most kinds of jewelry or almost anything metal. Imagine having to wear your hair the way the principal thinks it should look. If the school board has its way, that is what will happen at Wilkerson School. We must not let this outdated, unrealistic, and impractical dress code become reality.

Opinion Statement

What is the writer's opinion? Where is it stated?

The school board has published several reasons for the new dress code. First, members say that the new dress code will help prepare students for the real world. They explain that well-dressed students will behave more like adults at a job. As a result, they say, students will get down to the business of learning: They will work harder and receive higher grades. Second, according to the school board, the dress code will build students' self-respect as they take pride in their appearance. This, in turn, will be carried into greater respect for teachers and other students, who will be less likely to fight or disrupt classes.

Counterarguments

How does the writer address the opposing point of view?

These arguments are simplistic for several reasons. First, there is no proof that the clothing a student wears will change the student or that it will cause a student to focus more on learning. Also, the idea that a student's grades can be improved by wearing certain clothes is entirely illogical. I am sure that if I used that reasoning in one of my papers, Mrs. LeBlanc would circle it and write *This is faulty logic.* Finally, students' self-respect is not

Logical Order

Identify the organization of the speech so far. Is it logical? Explain.

Additional Support

VOCABULARY: Strong Words The importance of selecting the correct and most precise words to persuade an audience cannot be overstated. Remind students that the success of their speech lies in the words they select. As a vocabulary exercise, have students highlight persuasive words in their speeches. If they have difficulty pinpointing persuasive words, suggest that they try to incorporate some of the following into their speeches: *assure, imperative, critical, fundamental, implore, assert, vital, key, urgent, significant, momentous.* **OL**

based on the kinds of clothes they wear. Self-respect results from accomplishments and inner growth, not from putting on specific kind of footwear or removing jewelry. In fact, requiring students to conform to a dress code shows disrespect for students' ability to choose clothes that they think are acceptable for school.

Every aspect of the new dress-code policy is unacceptable, especially the ban on blue jeans and sneakers. Blue jeans and sneakers are popular with students for practical reasons. Jeans do not wear out quickly and are easy to clean. Each student needs only a few pairs of jeans, which can easily be thrown into a washing machine. Sneakers are practical because they are sturdier than dress shoes and provide better support for the feet. In addition, sneakers are safer because they have rubber soles that prevent students from slipping on the slick tile floors and cement stairways in our school.

There is another practical reason for opposing the dress code. Many families in our community live on a limited budget and have little money to invest in brand-new wardrobes for their school-aged children. Dress pants and shoes often cost more, and wear out faster, than jeans and sneakers. Even when dress clothes wear just as well, it is not practical to require students to have two sets of clothing. This expense is especially unfair to parents who are already struggling to earn enough money to clothe and care for their children.

Not only are dress codes impractical, but they are also out of date. In today's business world, clothing is often more casual than it was a few decades ago. In fact, many offices have at least one "casual dress" day, typically Friday. Besides, many workers are working directly from their homes now. These people can work in jeans, sweat suits, or pajamas if they want to.

It is admirable for the school board to want to make Wilkerson School a better place and to improve the prospects of its students. However, the first thing the school board should do to help achieve this goal is to withdraw its proposal for a new dress code.

Persuasion

Emotional Appeal
How does the writer appeal to emotions?

Logical Appeal
How does the writer appeal to logic?

Emotional Appeal
How does the writer appeal to emotions?

Facts and Examples
How do facts and examples support the writer's argument?

Conclusion
How does the writer conclude? What makes the final paragraph effective?

Teach

Writing Skills

Emotional Appeal Answer: *The code is couched in disrespectful terms, in a play to the emotions of students who will feel unfairly treated.* **OL**

Writing Skills

Logical Appeal Answer: *The practicality of jeans and sneakers is highlighted.* **OL**

Writing Skills

Emotional Appeal Answer: *The writer appeals to emotions by suggesting that the dress code will create economic hardship.* **OL**

Writing Skills

Facts and Examples Answer: *Facts and examples about what today's workers wear support the argument that dress codes are outdated.* **OL**

Writing Skills

Conclusion Answer: *The writer restates the opinion in a new way, calls for action, makes a final emotional appeal, and credits the school board with noble intentions.* **OL**

Differentiated Instruction

Public Presentation Motivate gifted and advanced students to take their persuasive skills to the next level. Perhaps there is an important issue facing their community or school that students might consider presenting to the town council, the school board, or school administrators. Encourage students to work together to draft a persuasive speech that includes credible evidence, appropriate rhetorical strategies, and a convincing delivery. Let other students know when their classmates will deliver the speech; encourage them to support these students in their efforts. **AL**

Objectives
- To write a persuasive speech that uses rhetorical devices to support assertions (SE)
- To use strong, precise language (TWE)

945

Teach

★ Writer's Technique

Know Your Audience The workshop model is a successful persuasive piece for several reasons. One of these is that the writer knows his or her audience (fellow students) and understands that the dress code is a "hot topic" that is likely to spur much debate and conversation. It is critical that a persuasive writer know his or her audience. Once the writer knows the audience and its *pathos*, he or she can effectively set out to persuade them. **AS**

Writing Process

Revising Remind students that mature writers are able to change course if they realize their initial arguments are not working. **Explain:** Revising your writing can be the most challenging aspect of the process. Having to choose a different topic does not imply failure. While it may take additional time to complete the assignment, in the end you will have produced better work. **OL**

Traits of Strong Writing

Ideas message or theme and the details that develop it

Organization arrangement of main ideas and supporting details

Voice writer's unique way of using tone and style

Word Choice vocabulary a writer uses to convey meaning

Sentence Fluency rhythm and flow of sentences

Conventions correct spelling, grammar, usage, and mechanics

Presentation the way words and design elements look on a page

For more information on using the Traits of Strong Writing, see pages R33–R34 of the Writing Handbook.

Revising

Peer Review When you finish your draft, ask a classmate to read it. Have your classmate identify your opinion statement or thesis, your use of facts and examples, and your counterarguments. If your reviewer cannot identify any of these major elements, revise your speech to create them or make them clear. Then ask your reviewer to consider how well your work reflects the traits of strong writing. Again, revise as needed.

Use the rubric below to help you evaluate your writing.

Rubric: Writing an Effective Persuasive Speech

☑ Do you state your opinion clearly?

☑ Do you include both logical and emotional appeals?

☑ Do you use reasons and facts to support your opinion?

☑ Do you present your ideas in a logical order?

☑ Do you include and respond to counterarguments?

☑ Do you clarify your opinion as needed and restate it in your conclusion?

▶ **Focus Lesson**

Elaborating on Ideas with Evidence

To make a point or counterargument convincing, you need to explain it fully or elaborate upon it. You can elaborate through clarification, restatement, and the addition of evidence or support: facts, examples, and other details that develop your main ideas. Here is a sentence from the Workshop Model followed by a revision that elaborates on the ideas.

Draft:

Many families in our community live on a limited budget.

Revision:

Many families in our community live on a limited budget and have little money to invest in brand-new wardrobes for their school-aged children.[1] Dress pants and shoes often cost more, and wear out faster, than jeans and sneakers.[2]

1: Elaboration with Fact   2: Elaboration with Fact and Examples

---

Additional Support

Skills Practice

SPEAKING: Pacing Explain that the pace, or speed, with which a speech is delivered is important. **Say:** A speech delivered too quickly will not make sense to the listeners, and a speech delivered too slowly will lose listeners' attention. Have students work in small groups to deliver their speeches without rushing or dawdling. Encourage them to practice reading aloud and timing themselves. Suggest that the written speech be formatted to remind the speaker to pause and emphasize certain points. Have students examine each others' work and offer constructive criticism. **OL**

Editing and Proofreading

Get It Right When you have completed the final draft of your speech, proofread it for errors in grammar, usage, mechanics, and spelling. Refer to the Language Handbook, pages R46–R60, as a guide.

▶ **Focus Lesson**

Parallelism

Parts of a sentence joined by *and* or another coordinating conjunction must be parallel. This means that these parts must all be nouns, verbs, or the same type of phrases or clauses.

Problem:

These people can work in jeans, wearing sweats, or in pajamas if they want to.

Three items—*jeans, wearing sweat suits,* and *in pajamas*—joined by a coordinating conjunction are not parallel: *jeans* is a noun, *wearing sweats* is a participial phrase, and *in pajamas* is a prepositional phrase.

Solution A: Make all of the items parallel by changing them into noun objects of prepositions.

These people can work in jeans, sweat suits, or pajamas if they want to.

Solution B: Make all of the items parallel by making them all participial phrases.

These people can work dressed in jeans, clothed in sweat suits, or clad in pajamas if they want to.

Solution C: Make all of the items parallel by making them all prepositional phrases.

These people can work in jeans, in sweat suits, or in pajamas if they want to.

Read It Aloud

Read your speech aloud to yourself. How does it sound? Do the sentences flow well? Are the words powerful and convincing? Do you open in an interesting way and close memorably? Base your final revisions on what you hear.

Presenting

Final Proofreading If you word-process your work, read it again after you print it out. It is often easier to see errors when they are printed on paper. Make all corrections as neatly as possible, using standard proofreading symbols.

Writer's Portfolio

Place a copy of your speech in your portfolio to review later.

Teach

Writing Process

Editing and Proofreading
Say: Give yourself enough time to set your persuasive speech aside for at least one day to gain some distance from your work. Then go back to proofread, and correct any mistakes you may have made. **OL**

Writing Process

Presenting Emphasize to students the importance of their delivery when giving a persuasive speech. **Say:** One of the most valuable tools you have when presenting your speech is your eyes. Making eye contact with your audience engages them and draws them into your speech. Look audience members straight in the eye—not at the tops of their heads. Don't just look at one or two people; move your gaze around the room. Making eye contact projects confidence during your delivery. **OL**

Objectives
- To clarify and defend positions with precise and relevant evidence (SE)
- To use and refine pacing in a speech (TWE)

Differentiated Instruction

Famous Speeches Encourage students with visual impairments to learn the art of persuasion by listening to successful speeches. Help students visit www.americanrhetoric.com or another Web site devoted to speeches. On this site students can choose from hun-dreds of famous (and not so famous) speeches. Guide students to choose those speeches with audio components. Topics include politics, civil rights, and other cultural issues, plus speeches from movies. **BL**

Focus

Summary

In this workshop, students will learn techniques for planning, rehearsing, and presenting a persuasive speech to the class.

Teach

Speaking Skills

Rhetorical Devices Point out that Antony's speech in *Julius Caesar* contains many effective rhetorical devices. Have students locate examples of the following rhetorical techniques, and suggest that they include some of them in their persuasive speeches:

- Repetition: Saying something again provides emphasis.
- Alliteration: A repeated beginning consonant sound has a pleasant musical effect.
- Parallelism: Related ideas are presented with balanced, similar constructions.
- Rhetorical question: A question is asked for effect and not for an answer.
- Understatement: An idea is deliberately underemphasized.
- Hyperbole: Exaggeration gives effect and emphasis. **OL**

Sound Devices

Do you remember the sound devices you learned in the poetry unit? Some of those work well in speeches. Repetition, for example, can often be effective. (Think of the many times that Martin Luther King Jr. said, "I have a dream.") Alliteration, too, can be powerfully persuasive.

Speaking, Listening, and Viewing Workshop

Persuasive Speech

Delivering a Persuasive Speech

Connecting to Literature When Brutus presented his speech after Caesar's assassination, persuading his audience was a matter of life or death. Brutus could not afford to mumble, speak too softly, shuffle his feet, or forget an important point. Instead, he had to master all of his rhetorical skills to make his message convincing. In this workshop, you will learn to how to deliver an effective, powerful, and persuasive speech to a real audience.

▶ **Assignment** Deliver a persuasive speech to an audience.

Planning Your Delivery

A speech *may* be read aloud. It is far more effective, however, when the written word— which readers can study and review—is transformed into the spoken word, which listeners must understand as it is delivered. Follow these steps to turn your persuasive writing into persuasive speaking:

- Start by reading your speech aloud to a partner. Find out what your listener notices immediately and what he or she misses. Most important, ask your partner whether he or she can identify your opinion statement. Then ask to what extent your speech was persuasive.
- Use your partner's comments to help you make your opinion statement clearer or more definite. Also brainstorm with your partner to devise ways to make your speech more dramatic, forceful, interesting, and persuasive.
- Make note cards that list the main ideas and details of your speech. Number the cards and refer to them only if needed.

School Board's Position
Dress codes prepare students for the professional world
Increase effort to improve learning and grades
Build respect for oneself and teachers
Decrease disruptive behavior

Students' Position
Dress codes are outdated:
—Professionals now dress casually
—Many employees work from home
Dress codes are expensive: for families on limited budgets
Dress codes are impractical

948 UNIT 4 DRAMA

Additional Support

Skills Practice

SPEAKING: Appealing to Emotion and Logic "O judgment, thou art fled to brutish beasts," says Antony as he breaks down with emotion, a tactic for swaying public opinion. Point out that he also evokes emotion as he recalls details about his relationship with Caesar and builds suspense about Caesar's will. **Say:** Emo-

tional appeals can be effective in a persuasive speech. A persuasive speech, however, should appeal to logic with solid arguments and facts. Encourage students to use logical devices such as analogies, which can clarify ideas by making familiar comparisons. Have them give examples of analogies. **OL**

Rehearsing

Practice your speech several times before you deliver it in class. Set a goal of learning your speech so well that you need no more than a glance at your note cards. Rehearse by yourself in front of a mirror. Try different gestures and tones of voice. Then, when you are confident that you are almost ready, ask a classmate or family member to listen. Work with that person to iron out any remaining wrinkles in your delivery.

Evaluating a Speech

Use these techniques to evaluate the content of your own speech or a partner's speech.

- Identify the opinion and the main ideas that support it.
- Analyze the types of arguments the speaker uses, such as appeals to emotion, logic, or authority, or the use of an analogy, anecdotes, or a case study.
- Study how well the speech anticipates and answers the listener's counterarguments.

Use the list below to help you evaluate the delivery of your own speech or a partner's speech.

Techniques for Delivering a Persuasive Speech

Verbal Techniques	Nonverbal Techniques
☑ **Enunciation** When you deliver your speech, speak as clearly as you can. Do not alter your voice drastically—even for emphasis—but do not mumble either.	☑ **Audience Feedback** Watch the audience's faces for hints that you are speaking too fast, too slowly, too loudly, or too softly.
☑ **Pitch** Eliminate the highs and lows in your voice as you make your points.	☑ **Eye Contact** Look directly at your audience except to refer briefly to note cards.
☑ **Tone** Be sure that your tone of voice suits the seriousness of your subject. Remember that you can also use your tone to help you emphasize key words and ideas.	☑ **Body Language** Show interest by standing tall and comfortably, not slouching or folding your arms.
☑ **Rate** Never race through your speech. Speak at a normal rate of speed.	☑ **Facial Expressions** Make sure that your facial expressions suit the content of your speech.

Rehearse Again and Again

Professionals often learn their material "cold" to avoid feeling nervous in front of an audience. That means knowing your speech so well that you feel self-assured and confident when you step before an audience.

Watch a Public Speaker

Watch a performance of an accomplished public speaker, recorded or online. Note how the speaker uses gestures, tone of voice, and posture to help persuade the audience.

OBJECTIVES
- Deliver a persuasive argument by using rhetorical devices to support assertions.
- Evaluate persuasive presentations of peers.

Teach

Listening Skills

Analyzing Arguments Ask students to take notes on the main points in other students' persuasive speeches. Suggest that they write down the speaker's opinion statement and then list supporting points and evidence. At the end of each speech, have students discuss how fully the opinion statement was supported and how logical the arguments were. Students should notice whether the speaker refutes counterarguments. **OL**

Speaking Skills

Researching Persuasive Facts and Quotations Point out to students that facts and quotations from authorities can make their speeches more convincing. For example, in the student speech about dress codes, facts from a research study or a well-chosen quotation from an expert would substantiate the argument that clothes are unrelated to behavior. Advise students to research reliable sources in print and on the Internet to locate relevant facts and authoritative quotations. **OL**

English Language Coach

Viewing Speeches Suggest that students who are learning English view videotapes of persuasive speeches to accustom them to effective speaking techniques as well as conventions of the English language. Encourage students to write down words they don't understand and look them up in the dictionary. **EL**

Differentiated Instruction

Distinguishing Troublesome Words In preparation for speaking, instruct students about commonly misused pairs of words such as these: *among/between, amount/number, can/may, bring/take, who/whom, good/well, leave/let,* and *like/as.* Have students practice using the words in sentences. **BL**

949

Focus

Summary

This feature is designed to interest students in reading dramas or novels related to this unit's themes. Great dramas of Western and Eastern literature appropriate for independent reading are recommended to complement the selections in this unit. Also recommended are classic and contemporary fiction masterpieces. Written in the nineteenth century, *Wuthering Heights* reflects the theme of loyalty and betrayal, and *A House for Mr. Biswas,* a twentieth-century novel, presents a portrait of real life.

★ Literary History

Aeschylus (525–456 B.C.)

Called the father of tragedy, Aeschylus was the earliest of the three great Greek tragedians, the other two being Sophocles and Euripides. He was responsible for the development of Greek drama. Before Aeschylus, Greek dramas had only one actor; he added a second actor, costumes, and stage settings. He also expanded the dramatic role of the chorus. **AS**

Drama and Novels

DRAMA RELIES ALMOST ENTIRELY ON ONE THING: characters must reveal themselves. Most dramas tell a story, present a theme, and move, shock, or entertain their viewers by means of conversations between characters as well as movements on a stage. Readers who wish to get the most out of a play have to hear those conversations and visualize those movements to the best of their ability. For more drama on a range of themes, try the first three suggestions below. For novels that incorporate the Big Ideas of *Loyalty and Betrayal,* as well as *Portraits of Real Life,* try the titles from the Glencoe Literature Library on the next page.

Seven Against Thebes

by Aeschylus ★

A prophecy was made about the two sons of Oedipus, Eteocles and Polyneices: they would divide their inheritance with a sword in order to obtain equal shares. As *Seven Against Thebes* opens, prehistoric Thebes is under siege by an Argive army led by Polyneices, the son of Oedipus and brother of Eteocles. Eteocles pledges to save Thebes and fiercely defend its seven gates against the Argive army's seven armored chiefs and their warriors. Trying to avoid disaster, the Theban women warn Eteocles to stay away from the seventh gate. A battle ensues, and the prophecy proves true.

The Post Office

by Rabindranath Tagore

In this short, two-act play, an adopted child named Amal is confined to his home as the result of an illness. His only entertainment is watching the neighborhood as he sits at his open window. As Amal engages in conversations with the townspeople who stroll by, he forms relationships and expresses keen insight into life. He also becomes drawn to the post office, which he can see from his window. After a watchman identifies the post office as the King's office, Amal becomes hopeful that the King will send him a letter.

Additional Support

Skills Practice

READING: Comparing and Contrasting Characters Point out that the recommended dramas feature some of the same characters as the dramas in this unit. Urge students to make comparisons and contrasts; for example, Shakespeare's Caesar in *Julius Caesar* with his Caesar in *Antony and Cleopatra* and Antigone in Sophocles' *Antigone* and Aeschylus's *Seven Against Thebes.* Have students draw inferences about characters, noting the significance of what they say and do and how they react to other characters. Suggest that students make graphic organizers to show similarities and differences. **OL**

CRITICS' CORNER

CLEOPATRA, QUEEN OF EGYPT.

"*[Antony and Cleopatra] may be world leaders but they are also, after all, only human beings—flawed and aging ones at that. We as human beings share their mortality; many of us recognize their strong feelings of jealousy, love, shame, and insecurity. Despite their historical grandeur and thanks to Shakespeare's sensitive portrayal of them, Antony and Cleoptara are no more—and no less—extraordinary than we are.*"

—Kathy D. Darrow and Ira Mark Milne, *Shakespeare for Students Review*

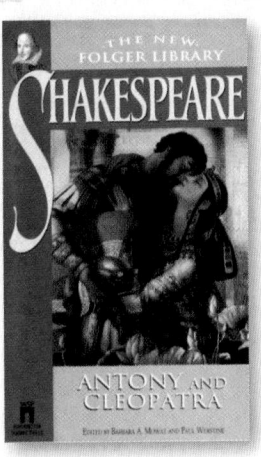

Antony and Cleopatra

by William Shakespeare

The married Roman leader Mark Antony, who is living in Alexandria, Egypt, falls in love with Cleopatra, the Queen of Egypt. When Antony's wife dies, Antony returns to Rome, where Caesar expects Antony to marry Caesar's sister. Antony soon returns to Egypt to live with Cleopatra, however. Caesar determines that he will attack Egypt and take control of it away from Antony, but Antony resolves never to let that happen. In the end, both Antony and Cleopatra face the harsh reality of their ill-fated love.

From the Glencoe Literature Library

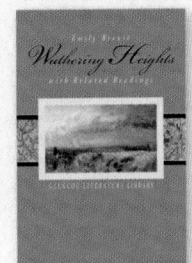

Wuthering Heights

By Emily Brontë

This brooding romance tells of *Loyalty and Betrayal* through the story of the thwarted relationship between a privileged woman and the penniless servant who loves her.

A House for Mr Biswas

by V. S. Naipul

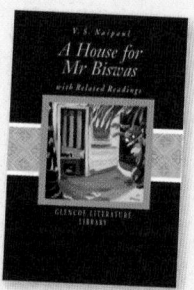

In this *Portrait of Real Life* in Trinidad in 1961, a man searches for a house of his own.

Reading in the Real World

Citizenship Point out that loyalty becomes a matter of life and death for many of these characters. *Seven Against Thebes* pits loyalty to family against loyalty to the kingdom. In *Antony and Cleopatra,* the main conflict is between Antony's loyalty to Cleopatra and the loyalty he owes his country and ruler.

In *Wuthering Heights,* Heathcliff and Catherine's mutual loyalty is a source of misery, eventually helping bring about her death. Discuss the betrayal in each story. Do some conflicts make betrayal inevitable? Is it possible to be too loyal to a cause or a person? What loyalties are worth dying for? **OL**

Teach

★ Literary History

Drama Say: Many of the writers in this unit represent stages in the evolution of drama. How has our concept of a dramatic character changed over the years? What traits are shared by the characters of Aeschylus, Sophocles, Shakespeare, Glaspell, and Pinter? *(They reveal themselves through their words and actions, not through the authors' descriptions.)* What is similar about the main conflicts of these plays? *(Answers will vary. Students may mention that many of these plays depict individuals torn between personal loyalties and loyalties to greater causes.)* **AS**

Objectives
• To encourage independent reading of drama and fiction (SE)
• To compare and contrast characters (TWE)

951

Focus

BELLRINGER

Say: Just as athletes train for contests, you can practice for tests, which affect you in school and beyond. Taking this practice test will help you prepare for future tests. Have students share their test-taking tips with the class. Discuss time management in both studying for and taking a test.

Or use **Bellringer Option Transparency.**

Teach

Assessment Explain to students that this lesson is designed to develop their test-taking strategies as well as to test their mastery of skills covered in this unit. Students will read a portion of a drama and then answer questions about the dramatic scene. They will use their knowledge of vocabulary and context to complete sentences. They will also use grammar and writing skills to improve a writing passage and write a short essay. **OL**

Reading: Drama

Carefully read the following passage. Use context clues to help you define any words with which you are unfamiliar. Pay close attention to the mood, theme, and characters. Then, on a separate sheet of paper, answer the questions on pages 953–954.

---

from *Oedipus the King* by Sophocles

TIME AND SCENE: *The royal house of Thebes. Many years have passed since Oedipus ascended the throne of Thebes, and now a plague has struck the city. A Chorus, the citizens of Thebes, along with Oedipus and Jocasta, are on stage.*

Chorus.   My king
    I've said it once, I'll say it time and again—
    I'd be insane, you know it,
    senseless, ever to turn my back on you.
5   You who set our beloved land—storm-tossed, shattered—
    straight on course. Now again, good helmsman,
    steer us through the storm!
[*The* Chorus *draws away, leaving* Oedipus *and* Jocasta *side by side.*]
  Jocasta.   For the love of god,
    Oedipus, tell me too, what is it?
    Why this rage? You're so unbending.
10 **Oedipus.** I will tell you. I respect you, Jocasta,
    much more than these men here . . . [*Glancing at the* Chorus.]
    Creon's to blame. Creon schemes against me.
  Jocasta. Tell me clearly, how did the quarrel start?
  Oedipus. He says I murdered Laius—I am guilty.
15 **Jocasta.** How does he know? Some secret knowledge
    or simply hearsay?
  Oedipus.   Oh, he sent his prophet in
    to do his dirty work. You know Creon,
    Creon keeps his own lips clean.
  Jocasta.   A prophet?
    Well then, free yourself of every charge!
20   Listen to me and learn some peace of mind:
    no skill in the world,
    nothing human can penetrate the future.
    Here is proof, quick and to the point.
    An oracle came to Laius one fine day

Skills Practice

READING: Rereading Advise students that rereading is a good way to improve comprehension. Rereading can help to pinpoint the characters' traits and relationships. **Write on the board:**
Oedipus, king of Thebes
Jocasta, Oedipus's wife
Creon, Jocasta's brother
Laius, Jocasta's former husband, deceased
Apollo, god of music, poetry, prophecy
Say: Rereading helps to clarify the characters' relationships and situations. Watch carefully for these details as you reread the passage several times to improve your comprehension. **OL**

25   (I won't say from Apollo himself
        but his underlings, his priests) and it said
        that doom would strike him down at the hands of a son,
        our son, to be born of our own flesh and blood. But Laius,
        so the report goes at least, was killed by strangers,
30   thieves, at a place where three roads meet . . . my son—
        he wasn't three days old and the boy's father
        fastened his ankles, had a henchman fling him away
        on a barren, trackless mountain. There, you see?
        Apollo brought neither thing to pass. My baby
35   no more murdered his father than Laius suffered—
        his wildest fear—death at his own son's hands.
        That's how the seers and their revelations
        mapped out the future. Brush them from your mind.
        Whatever the god needs and seeks
40   he'll bring to light himself, with ease.

Oedipus.   Strange,
        hearing you just now . . . my mind wandered,
        my thoughts racing back and forth.

Jocasta. What do you mean? Why so anxious, startled?

Oedipus. I thought I heard you say that Laius
45   was cut down at a place where three roads meet.

Jocasta. That was the story. It hasn't died out yet.

Oedipus. Where did this thing happen? Be precise.

Jocasta. A place called Phocis, where two branching roads,
        one from Daulia, one from Delphi,
50   come together—a crossroads.

Oedipus. When? How long ago?

Jocasta. The heralds no sooner reported Laius dead
        than you appeared and they hailed you king of Thebes.

Oedipus. My god, my god—what have you planned to do to me?

55 **Jocasta.** What, Oedipus? What haunts you so?

Oedipus.   Not yet.
        Laius—how did he look? Describe him.
        Had he reached his prime?

Jocasta.   He was swarthy,
        and the gray had just begun to streak his temples,
        and his build . . . wasn't far from yours.

Oedipus.   Oh no no,
60   I think I've just called down a dreadful curse
        upon myself—I simply didn't know!

❶ Who was the king of Thebes before Oedipus?
   (1) Apollo
   (2) Laius
   (3) Creon
   (4) Delphi

❷ What does the Chorus represent?
   (1) the aristocracy
   (2) the citizenry
   (3) the all-knowing voice
   (4) the prophetic voice

Assess

1. **Option 2 is the correct answer.** This fact is not directly stated in this passage but is hinted at in several places.

2. **Option 2 is the correct answer.** The setting defines the Chorus as the "citizens of Thebes."

Differentiated Instruction

Visualizing Encourage less skilled readers to try to visualize the scene and stage setting in a drama. Advise them to keep in mind which character is speaking and imagine how an actor would deliver the lines. Such visualization can help students discern characters' attitudes and emotions. **BL**

Building Reading Fluency

Paraphrasing With older works, students can benefit from paraphrasing, or summarizing in their own words. **Say:** Put each speaker's ideas into your own words as you tell a classmate the speaker's main point. Paraphrasing will improve your understanding. **OL**

Assess

3. **Option 4 is the correct answer.** A comparison is being made without using *like* or *as*.

4. **Option 3 is the correct answer.** Oedipus tells Jocasta, "Creon schemes against me."

5. **Option 2 is the correct answer.** Oedipus is praised for having saved the city in the past.

6. **Option 1 is the correct answer.** Context makes clear that the meaning is "rumor."

7. **Option 3 is the correct answer.** The figurative phrase means that Creon uses another's words to speak ill.

8. **Option 1 is the correct answer.** It is clear that Oedipus has been accused of killing Laius.

9. **Option 3 is the correct answer.** Jocasta makes clear that prophecies should be ignored.

10. **Option 1 is the correct answer.** The title and the context clearly show that Oedipus is the protagonist.

---

❸ What literary device is used in lines 6 and 7, where the Chorus compares Oedipus to a helmsman?
   (1) simile
   (2) irony
   (3) allusion
   (4) metaphor

❹ Why is Oedipus in a rage at the beginning of the selection?
   (1) The Chorus has insulted him.
   (2) He does not trust Jocasta.
   (3) He suspects Creon of being in a plot.
   (4) A plague has infected Thebes.

❺ From the context of this passage, what can you infer about the way in which Oedipus has ruled Thebes until now?
   (1) He is given to fits of rage and intolerance.
   (2) He is an admired and effective ruler.
   (3) He is the most admired ruler in history.
   (4) He is a cursed and doomed man.

❻ From the context, what do you think that the word *hearsay*, in line 16, means?
   (1) rumor
   (2) report
   (3) fact
   (4) prophecy

❼ What does Oedipus mean by saying, in line 18, "Creon keeps his own lips clean"?
   (1) Creon is no more than a scoundrel.
   (2) Creon is notorious for telling lies.
   (3) Creon uses others to spread rumors.
   (4) Creon speaks carefully so as not to offend.

❽ From the context, what do you think that the word *charge*, in line 19, means?
   (1) accusation
   (2) complaint
   (3) misdeed
   (4) judgment

❾ What is Jocasta's attitude toward prophecies?
   (1) They should be heeded.
   (2) They should be considered.
   (3) They should be ignored.
   (4) They should be excused.

❿ From this selection, who do you think that this play's protagonist is?
   (1) Oedipus
   (2) Jocasta
   (3) Creon
   (4) Laius

⓫ What can be inferred from Oedipus's reaction at the end of the selection?
   (1) Oedipus will remain the king.
   (2) The gods have cursed Creon.
   (3) Oedipus is now angry with Jocasta.
   (4) Oedipus grasps his role in Laius's death.

⓬ Which of the following best describes the theme of the selection?
   (1) Destiny can be changed.
   (2) Life is a game of chance.
   (3) Fate cannot be altered.
   (4) The gods are fickle creatures.

⓭ What is the overall mood of the selection?
   (1) calm
   (2) troubled
   (3) humorous
   (4) overjoyed

⓮ What irony can be inferred about Oedipus's situation at the end of this selection?
   (1) Creon relies on a prophet to do his speaking.
   (2) Laius died long ago, but his impact continues.
   (3) Jocasta does not understand the prophecy.
   (4) Oedipus is the child abandoned years ago.

⓯ On the basis of this selection, what kind of play do you think that Sophocles' *Oedipus the King* is?
   (1) comedy
   (2) romance
   (3) farce
   (4) tragedy

---

11. **Option 4 is the correct answer.** As Oedipus learns more about how Laius died, he begins to see his part in the prophecy.

12. **Option 3 is the correct answer.** Jocasta's account makes clear that she and Laius tried to change their destiny but failed, suggesting the theme that fate is inalterable.

13. **Option 2 is the correct answer.** Both Oedipus and Jocasta are distressed.

14. **Option 4 is the correct answer.** Oedipus begins to realize that he was the child abandoned by his parents in an effort to thwart the prophecy.

15. **Option 4 is the correct answer.** Circumstances allude to a sad conclusion.

Unit Assessment Have students access the Web site to prepare for the Unit Four test.

Vocabulary Skills: Sentence Completion

For each item in the Vocabulary Skills section, choose the word or words that best complete the sentence.

1 Shakespeare's tragic figures are often undone by their _____ and pride.
- (1) rash
- (2) deceit
- (3) arrogance
- (4) ignorance

2 The old woman's illness had left her with a/an _____ that required extended care.
- (1) enterprise
- (2) infirmity
- (3) peril
- (4) orator

3 Many athletes _____ in a competitive atmosphere.
- (1) thrive
- (2) vanquish
- (3) commend
- (4) disperse

4 The _____ prince was quick to smile and make small talk with any villager.
- (1) affable
- (2) ostentatious
- (3) impudent
- (4) arrogant

5 The hermit lived high in the mountains, _____ to what was happening in the world below.
- (1) notorious
- (2) oblivious
- (3) peevish
- (4) imminent

6 After his fifth physical examination showed no irregularity, we wondered whether the man was a/an _____.
- (1) coroner
- (2) hypochondriac
- (3) orator
- (4) trifle

7 The gang of bandits was _____ in the territory.
- (1) pompous
- (2) notorious
- (3) impertinent
- (4) repressed

8 She worked for many years to _____ success.
- (1) disperse
- (2) commend
- (3) thrive
- (4) attain

9 Her _____ decision to quit school limited her job opportunities.
- (1) rash
- (2) imminent
- (3) servile
- (4) affable

10 His missions into enemy territory involved _____ actions.
- (1) pious
- (2) disconsolate
- (3) covert
- (4) barren

Literature Online **Unit Assessment** To prepare for the Unit test, go to www.glencoe.com.

Assess

1. **Option 3 is the correct answer.** No other option relates to *pride*.

2. **Option 2 is the correct answer.** The context requires a word describing sickness. Option 3 is close but not the best answer. Neither option 1 nor option 4 fits the context.

3. **Option 1 is the correct answer.** No other option makes sense here.

4. **Option 1 is the correct answer.** All of the other choices imply a proud or selfish nature not appropriate in this context.

5. **Option 2 is the correct answer.** No other option makes sense here.

6. **Option 2 is the correct answer.** Key phrases are *physical examination* and *no irregularity*. No other option makes sense here.

7. **Option 2 is the correct answer.** No other choice makes sense here.

8. **Option 4 is the correct answer.** The context suggests achievement. No other option does so.

9. **Option 1 is the correct answer.** No other choice fits the context of an unwise decision.

10. **Option 3 is the correct answer.** Only this option suggests secretiveness.

Literature Online

Unit Assessment Have students access the Web site to prepare for the Unit Four test.

Differentiated Instruction

Synonyms Synonyms used within context provide clues to the meaning of unfamiliar words. Examples in *Oedipus* are *prophet* (line 16), *oracle* (line 24), and *seer* (line 37)—all synonyms used in the selection. Provide sentences with synonyms so students can practice using these context clues. **BL**

English Language Coach

Multiple-Meaning Words Tell English language learners that knowing the part of speech can help them understand a multiple-meaning word. Explain that in "Creon schemes," knowing that *scheme* is a verb helps to define the word as "to plot." Help define *prime* in "his prime." **EL**

Assess

1. **Option 3 is the correct answer.** The absolute phrase must be set off with a comma.

2. **Option 2 is the correct answer.** The phrase *in particular* is nonessential to the sentence, a parenthetical expression that must be set off with commas.

3. **Option 3 is the correct answer.** This sentence has a subject, the noun *belief,* but no predicate verb.

4. **Option 3 is the correct answer.** Two principal clauses must be separated by a comma.

Grammar and Writing Skills: Paragraph Improvement

Read carefully through the following passage from the first draft of a student's essay. Pay close attention to the writer's use of commas and parallelism. Then answer the questions on pages 956–957.

(1) *Sophocles based* Oedipus the King *on a popular folk tale of his time.* (2) *To be sure Athenian audiences were familiar with the tale, a fact that made the play an ideal medium for questioning some of the popular beliefs of his time.* (3) *Sophocles questions in particular the idea of predestination.* (4) *The belief that people have no real choices in life, that destiny is inalterable.* (5) *Oedipus's tale is tragic but the story is told with multiple levels of irony that, at times, make his inalterable fate seem ridiculous.*

(6) *Sophocles goes out of his way to present Oedipus as a capable and compassionate leader.* (7) *For example the city of Thebes prospers under Oedipus after he solves the sphinx's riddle.* (8) *Never once is it suggested that Oedipus has brought his destiny on himself by any* hubris, *which is excessive pride, or* hamartia, *which implies bad judgment or a flaw in character.* (9) *The gods rather have made the prophecies that lead Oedipus into disaster.* (10) *Apollo's oracle simply says "Find the killer," which leads to the cruel ironies of the play.* (11) *In other words, Sophocles is saying that Oedipus's tragic misfortune is the intentional work of "the gods."*

(12) *The Golden Age of Athens was a time for thinkers, scientists, and inventors, a time for people to share ideas freely, a place where all philosophers were welcomed.* (13) *The Greeks were impressed with the power of reason and the overall human potential.* (14) *Surely they must have been asking whether they still believed in their gods.* (15) *Hence the audience's sympathy for the tragic figure becomes something more complex.*

❶ Which of the following is the best way to revise sentence 2?
  (1) Insert an exclamation point after *To be sure.*
  (2) Change *audiences were* to *audience was.*
  (3) Insert a comma after *To be sure.*
  (4) Change *that* to *which.*

❷ Which of the following is the best way to revise sentence 3?
  (1) Transpose *questions* and *in particular.*
  (2) Insert commas around *in particular.*
  (3) Change *questions* to *wonder about.*
  (4) Make no change.

❸ Which of the following errors appears in sentence 4?
  (1) comma splice
  (2) lack of parallelism
  (3) sentence fragment
  (4) subject-verb disagreement

❹ Which of the following is the best way to revise sentence 5?
  (1) Insert a semicolon after *tragic.*
  (2) Delete the commas around *at times.*
  (3) Insert a comma after *tragic.*
  (4) Make no change.

Additional Support

Skills Practice

GRAMMAR: Comma Usage Review the use of commas with parenthetical expressions. **Say:** When an expression is parenthetical, or put in as an added note, it should be surrounded by commas. Give an example, such as "Her ideas, of course, are biased." In addition, have students explain these uses of the comma:

• to separate main clauses connected with a conjunction

• to set off nonessential subordinate clauses

• to set off introductory words

• to separate items in a series

• to introduce a quotation **OL**

5 Which of the following is the best revision for sentence 7?
  (1) For example, the city of Thebes prospers under Oedipus after he solves the sphinx's riddle.
  (2) For example, the city of Thebes, prospers under Oedipus after he solves the sphinx's riddle.
  (3) The city of Thebes for example prospers under Oedipus after he solves the sphinx's riddle.
  (4) Make no change.

6 Which of the following is the best revision for sentence 9?
  (1) The gods would rather make prophecies that lead to disaster.
  (2) The gods have made the prophecies that rather lead Oedipus into disaster.
  (3) It is the gods, rather, who have made the prophecies that lead Oedipus into disaster.
  (4) Make no change.

7 Which of the following is the best revision for sentence 10?
  (1) Apollo's oracle simply says "Find the killer!" which leads to the cruel ironies of the play.
  (2) Apollo's oracle simply says, "Find the killer," which leads to the cruel ironies of the play.
  (3) Apollo's oracle simply says, "Find the killer" who leads to the cruel ironies of the play.
  (4) Make no change.

8 Which of the following is the best revision of sentence 12?
  (1) The Golden Age of Athens was a time for thinkers, scientists, and inventors to share ideas, all philosophers were welcome.
  (2) The Golden Age of Athens welcomed all thinkers, scientists, philosophers, and inventors to share their ideas freely.
  (3) The Golden Age of Athens was a time for philosophers, scientists, and inventors to share ideas freely in a place where all thinkers were welcomed.
  (4) Make no change.

9 Which of the following is the best way to revise sentence 15?
  (1) Insert a comma after *Hence*.
  (2) Insert a colon after *Hence*.
  (3) Insert a dash after *Hence*.
  (4) Insert commas around *the tragic figure*.

10 Which of the following would be the best title for this essay?
  (1) "Irony and Fate in *Oedipus the King*"
  (2) "Greek Comedy, Greek Tragedy"
  (3) "A Greek Perspective of Modern Drama"
  (4) "The Use of Irony in Greek Farce"

Essay

Throughout history, theater has been valued in cultures all over the world. In your opinion, is drama as important in the modern world? How does it influence our culture? Write a short persuasive essay supporting your opinion with evidence from texts as well as personal experience. As you write, keep in mind that your essay will be checked for **ideas, organization, voice, word choice, sentence fluency, conventions,** and **presentation**.

Assess

5. **Option 1 is the correct answer.** The transitional phrase must be followed by a comma.

6. **Option 3 is the correct answer.** The word *rather* can be misinterpreted unless it is set off with commas. No other option corrects this error.

7. **Option 2 is the correct answer.** The direct quotation must be set off with commas.

8. **Option 3 is the correct answer.** Only this option corrects the error of failing to classify philosophers, scientists, and inventors as thinkers and to correct the lack of parallelism.

9. **Option 1 is the correct answer.** The transitional word should be followed by a comma.

10. **Option 1 is the correct answer.** Options **2** and **3** are too broad. Option **4** makes no sense in the context of a tragedy.

Essay

Students' essays should
- explain whether the student thinks drama is important to modern society
- provide evidence, textual and personal, to support drama's effects on culture
- use clear language and organization of ideas

Differentiated Instruction

Using Parallelism Some students may have difficulty recognizing how to use parallelism in revising sentences. Emphasize that words and phrases joined by a coordinating conjunction should be grammatically parallel. To show which words and phrases need to be parallel, write sentences on the board and underline the parallel parts. Then provide an erroneous example, such as "Oedipus was praised as a good ruler and wiping out the plague in Thebes." Ask students to correct the sentence. *(Oedipus ruled wisely and wiped out the plague in Thebes.)* **BL**

Unit at a Glance

LEGENDS AND MYTHS

About the Unit

Unit Five covers the legendary hero, myth, and oral traditions.

Unit Introduction
Building Background
2–3 days

Genre Focus: Legends and Myths
pp. 960–961

Literary Analysis Model: Joan C. Verniero and Robin Fitzsimmons, "The Journey of Gilgamesh"
pp. 962–963

Writers on Reading
pp. 964–965

Unit Introduction Wrap-Up
p. 966

Part 1: Acts of Courage
4–6 days

Part 1 covers the legendary hero. A chart showing the core skills taught in this Part appears on pages 967A–967B.

SELECTIONS AND FEATURES

LITERARY FOCUS: The Legendary Hero
pp. 968–969

T. H. White, "Arthur Becomes King" from *The Once and Future King*
pp. 970–986

Grammar Workshop: Sentence Structure
p. 987

Sir Thomas Malory, from *Le Morte d'Arthur*
pp. 988–1008

Miguel de Cervantes, from *Don Quixote*
pp. 1009–1019

TIME magazine: "What Makes a Hero?"
pp. 1020–1023

D. T. Niane, from *Sundiata*
pp. 1024–1030

VISUAL PERSPECTIVE: Will Eisner, "The Lion of Mali" from *Sundiata, A Legend of Africa*
pp. 1031–1034

Part 2: Rescuing and Conquering
7–9 days

Part 2 covers myth and oral traditions. A chart showing the core skills taught in this Part appears on pages 1035A–1035B.

SELECTIONS AND FEATURES

LITERARY FOCUS: Myth and Oral Tradition
pp. 1036–1037

Jenny Leading Cloud, "Coyote, Iktome, and the Rock"
pp. 1038–1042

Brian Branston, "The Stealing of Thor's Hammer"
pp. 1043–1051

Vocabulary Workshop: Word Origins
p. 1052

Edith Hamilton, "Theseus"
pp. 1053–1063

CULTURAL PERSPECTIVE: Bill Moyers, with Joseph Campbell, "The Hero's Adventure" pp. 1064–1067

Vocabulary Workshop: Word Origins
p. 1068

Geraldine Harris, "The Secret Name of Ra"
pp. 1069–1075

Comparing Literature Across Genres
Joseph Bruchac and Gayle Ross, "Where the Girl Rescued Her Brother"
Zora Neale Hurston, "John Henry"
Anonymous, "A Song of Greatness"
pp. 1076–1087

End-of-Unit Features
5–6 days

Writing Workshop: Research Paper
pp. 1088–1097

Speaking, Listening, and Viewing Workshop: Giving an Informative Presentation
pp. 1098–1099

INDEPENDENT READING
pp. 1100–1101

Test Preparation and Practice
pp. 1102–1107

Unit Resources

Glencoe Literature: The Reader's Choice offers a comprehensive package of tools to optimize student learning and the teaching experience. Each resource has been designed to assist students in specific areas and to offer instructional support for teachers. While all of these areas are covered in the core textbook, some students may need extra practice or additional help in specific areas. The resource package is designed so that you, the teacher, can choose which items will best assist your students. You may also use these resources as homework assignments and for assessment purposes. The following are resources recommended for use with Unit five.

Key for Unit Resource

- 📁 Blackline Master
- 📄 Workbook
- 📖 Supplemental Text
- 💿 CD-ROM
- 💾 DVD
- ⚡ Transparency
- 💻 Web-based

Essential Instructional Support

FAST FILE — Unit 5 Resources

Reading and Literature
- Unit Introduction, pp. 1–2
- The Big Idea Foldable, pp. 3–4
- The Big Idea School-Home Connection, p. 5
- The Big Idea School-Home Connection (Spanish), p. 6
- Challenge Planner, pp. 7–10
- Academic Vocabulary Development, pp. 11–12
- Comparing Literature Graphic Organizer, p. 47
- Literary Elements, pp. 17, 21, 24, 28, 35, 37, 40, 44, 48
- Reading Strategies, pp. 18, 22, 25, 27, 29, 31, 36, 38, 41, 43, 45, 49
- Active Reading Graphic Organizers, pp. 54 –63
- Selection Vocabulary Practice, pp. 19, 23, 26, 30, 39, 42, 46, 50
- Literary Focus, pp. 15, 33

Writing, Grammar, and Spelling
- Spelling Practice, p. 51
- Grammar Workshop, p. 20
- Writing Workshop Graphic Organizer, p. 52

Speaking, Listening, and Viewing
- Speaking, Listening, and Viewing Activity, p. 53

English Language Learners
- English Language Coach, pp. 16, 34

Differentiated Instruction

- 📄 Active Learning and Note Taking Guide pp. 145–177
- 📁 Leveled Vocabulary Development, pp. 69–76
- 💿 Skill Level Up!™ A Language Arts Game
- 💿 Listening Library Audio CD, disc 2, tracks 16–29
- 💿 Glencoe BookLink 3
- 💿 Vocabulary PuzzleMaker
- 💿 Literature Library Vocabulary PuzzleMaker

ASSESSMENT

- 📁 Selection and Unit Assessment, pp. 163–186, 217–218
- 📁 Selection Quick Checks, pp. 82–93
- 📁 Selection Quick Checks (Spanish), pp. 82–93
- 📁 Assessment by Learning Objectives, pp. 54–60
- 📁 Rubrics for Assessing Student Writing, Listening, and Speaking, pp. 14–15, 36–37
- 📁 Standardized Test Preparation and Practice
- 💻 Glencoe Online Essay Grader
- 💿 Interactive Tutor: Self-Assessment
- 💿 Exam*View*® Assessment Suite
- 💿 Literature Library Exam*View*® Assessment

Additional Instructional Support

Literature and Reading

- Active Learning and Note Taking Guide, pp. 145–177
- *inTIME* Magazines
- Glencoe Literature Library
- Literature Launchers: Pre-Reading Videos
- Literature Classics

Writing, Grammar, and Spelling

- REAL Success in Writing: Research and Reports
- Writing Constructed Responses
- Spelling Power eWorkbook
- Revising with Style eWorkbook
- Sentence Diagraming eWorkbook
- Glencoe Grammar and Composition Handbook
- Grammar and Language Workbook
- Grammar and Language eWorkbook

PROFESSIONAL DEVELOPMENT

- Professional Development Package

Transparencies

- Read Aloud, Think Aloud Transparencies 26–31
- Bellringer Options Transparencies
  - Selection Focus Transparencies 39–43
  - Daily Language Practice Transparencies 82–91
- Grammar and Language Transparencies 16, 41, 57
- Writing Workshop Transparencies 26–30
- Visual Literacy/Fine Art Transparencies

English Language Learner

- English Language Coach, Unit Resources (Fast File)
- *inTIME* Magazines (Spanish)
- Spanish Listening Library

Technology

- TeacherWorks Plus™
- StudentWorks Plus™
- Literature Launchers: Pre-Reading Videos
- Vocabulary PuzzleMaker
- Literature Library Vocabulary PuzzleMaker
- Skill Level Up!™ A Language Arts Game
- glencoe.com
- Presentation Plus! ™
- Exam*View*® Assessment Suite
- Literature Library Exam*View*® Assessment Suite
- Listening Library Audio CD, disc 2, tracks 16–29
- Interactive Tutor: Self-Assessment
- Glencoe BookLink 3
- Online Student Edition, mhln.com
- Glencoe Online Essay Grader
- Grammar and Language eWorkbook
- Revising with Style eWorkbook
- Sentence Diagraming eWorkbook
- Spelling Power eWorkbook
- Literature Classics
- Spanish Listening Library

Additional Glencoe Resources

 Dinah Zike's Foldables™

Foldables™ are three-dimensional, interactive graphic organizers that help students practice basic writing skills, review key vocabulary terms, and answer Big Ideas. Every unit contains a Foldable activity. You can find the pattern and directions for the Unit 5 Foldable in the Unit 5 Resources Fast File booklet. You can use the foldables as they are presented or modify them to suit the needs of your students.

Literature Online

For a wealth of online resources that support the instruction in Unit 5, students and teachers can visit our Web site at glencoe.com. Students will find additional learning, practice, and assessment opportunities such as these, which are noted in the student text:

- Author Search
- Big Idea Overview and Activity
- Interactive Literary Elements Handbook
- Study Central
- Unit Assessment
- Web Activities
- Writing Models

Teachers will find planning and instructional tools that include the following:

- Book Lesson Plans
- Web Activity Lesson Plans
- Teacher Forum
- Professional Resources

  Go to glencoe.com to see the entire selection of *Glencoe Literature* online resources.

 CheckPoint

Glencoe's Presentation Plus!™, a multimedia teaching tool, lets you present dynamic lessons that will engage your students. Using Microsoft PowerPoint®, you can customize the presentations to create your own personalized lessons. Use CheckPoint questions with interactive response keypads to get immediate student feedback during lessons, to increase student participation, and to assess student comprehension.

 Glencoe Literature Library

The collection of hardcover books includes full-length novels, novellas, plays, and works of nonfiction. Each volume consists of at least one complete extended-length reading accompanied by several related readings from a broad range of genres. A separate Study Guide for each *Glencoe Literature Library* book provides teaching notes and reproducible activity pages for students. Glencoe Literature Library titles that complement this unit include:

- ***The Red Badge of Courage with Related Readings***
  by Stephen Crane
- ***Beowulf with Related Readings***

GLENCOE BOOKLINK

Use the Glencoe BookLink 3 CD-ROM, a database of more than 26,700 titles, to *create customized reading lists* for your students.

- Search for award-winning titles (e.g., Newbery Award winners, Coretta Scott King Award winners, and Caldecott Medal winners) and for books on several state recommended reading lists.
- Find Degrees of Reading Power™ (DRP) and Lexile™ readability scores for all selections.
- Organize reading lists by students' reading level, author, genre, theme, or area of interest.
- Get a brief summary of each selection.

You can find recommended leveled readings for this unit with Independent Reading (see pages 1100 and 1101).

Online Essay

Use Glencoe's online essay grader powered by SkillWriter™ to score your students' writing and to provide individualized feedback to each student automatically.

You and your students can visit glencoe.com to link to the essay grader. *Students* can enter their essays and receive feedback on demand. *You* can manage demographic data, assign tests and generate individual student and aggregated reports. The essay grader can help you

- save time with automatic scoring and individualized feedback
- supplement in-class writing instruction using guided writing practice

REAL Success: Reading Excellence at All Levels

Glencoe REAL Success is a suite of new reading and language arts products designed to foster reading excellence at all levels. Look for TWE point-of-use references for these specific products that will help your students succeed in reading this Unit.

- *Jamestown Literature, An Adapted Reader*
- REAL Success in Writing: Research and Reports
- Skill Level Up!™ A Language Arts Game
- CheckPoint PowerPoint™ slides
- Literature/Reading support at Glencoe Web site

A lively collection of articles drawn from issues of the TIME family of magazines helps students develop the skills they need to interact with informational text in a meaningful way. Each of the news stories, feature articles, reviews, profiles, and essays in the magazine connect to an author, work, or theme in *Glencoe Literature: The Reader's Choice*. See the *inTIME* Teacher's Guide for specific connections to each unit and for reproducible student worksheets designed to develop students' reading and critical thinking skills.

Literature Launchers

Set the scene with Glencoe's Literature Launchers, engaging pre-reading video segments that introduce each unit. Each Unit Launcher brings the literature to life, featuring expert testimony and archival stills and footage from the time.

Insert your Glencoe Literature Launchers into your DVD player. Select the Unit 1 Launcher from the menu to introduce Legends and Myths.

Teacher Wraparound Edition Key

Level Appropriate Code

AL = Activities for students working above grade level

OL = Activities for students working at grade level

BL = Activities for students working below grade level

EL = Activities for English language learners

AS = Information for all students

Teacher Wraparound Prompts

R **Reading Skill** These activities help you teach reading skills and vocabulary.

V **Vocabulary** These activities help students comprehend words and incorporate them into reading.

BI **Big Idea** These activities and questions prompt students to explore the Big Idea.

L **Literary Element** These activities and questions help students comprehend selections and learn more about each genre.

★ **Enrichment** Additional activities and information involving art appreciation and history.

Professional Development Center

From Your Authors:

Teaching Literary Analysis: Legends and Myths

Connect to Today Myths are traditional stories that deal with goddesses, gods, heroes, and supernatural events. Legends are passed down from the past and based on historical events and actual heroes. Talking with students about the universal nature of myths can help them to understand why myths are still relevant today. Discuss with students the origins of myths. Ask them to think about what the various myths explain about the world and consider how similar myths emerge in different cultures, showing how their themes are universal. Discuss how the myths from the past have become part of the culture today. After students read a myth like "The Stealing of Thor's Hammer" by Brian Branston, have them create a three-column chart. In their charts, have students recount the origins of the story, tell what the myth explains about the world, describe the universal features of the story, and explain how the myth is a part of our culture today.

Make Personal Connections Students should look for ways to connect their own life concerns to those expressed in the myths and legends. As students read the epics and myths in this chapter, ask them to make connections to their own lives. Have they ever gone on a journey? Where did they go? What did they hope to gain from the experience? Ask students why they think characters in myths often go on long journeys. Before students read the Greek myth "Theseus" by Edith

**Douglas Fisher and
Jacqueline Jones Royster**

Hamilton, ask the above questions to activate students' prior knowledge and increase their interest in the text. As students read, keep the idea of going on a journey fresh in their minds by referring back to these questions occasionally.

**Maureen Whalen Spaight
E. R. Martin Jr. High School
East Providence, Rhode Island**

Teacher to Teacher

Through brainstorming, we establish what students already know and what they do not know about legends. We analyze the difference between legends and factual stories. I often ask students: Who are the heroes and why have they become legends? What are the differences between legends and myths? What makes a hero larger than life? In our discussion, we start with a hero in the school, then move to a hero in our state, then to a hero in the larger world. Then to introduce the concept of the oral tradition of storytelling, students tell a story in a "telephone line," in which one student whispers something to another who in turn whispers it to another. By the fifth student, the story has changed. Students learn that in oral storytelling, people fill in their own gaps in memory, which helps establish that a legend rises above the level of factual reality. I also bring to class children's books of tall tales and legends.

Teacher Chat Room

Making Literature Come Alive

Before you begin this unit or sometime during the unit, talk with other teachers about ways they have taught legends and myths. Have a lunch-time discussion group or an after-school hour for professional development and discuss the following questions and answers from our authors:

How can I help students understand the importance of myths?

- Help students see concerns that are common to all humans in myths. As students read the excerpt from *Sundiata* recorded by D. T. Niane, ask them to describe how excessive pride and love of flattery can be the downfall of some people, no matter where or when they live.

- Show students that they can explore different cultures by reading myths and legends. As students read "The Secret Name of Ra" by Geraldine Harris, ask them to explain what this myth reveals about ancient Egyptian culture. As students read "The Stealing of Thor's Hammer" by Brian Branston, have them discuss what this legend may reflect about Norse culture.

- Have students explore how humans develop their thinking about various issues. As students read "Where the Girl Rescued Her Brother" by Joseph Bruchac and Gayle Ross, ask them to discuss thoughts and ideas regarding the role of women. What is the role of women in this story? How does Buffalo Calf Road Woman change people's attitudes towards women through her actions in the story?

- Tell students that myths can be read for entertainment. As students read the excerpt from *Le Morte d'Arthur* by Sir Thomas Malory, ask them to outline the exciting events of the story. Have them discuss why the magical tale of Arthur has entertained people for centuries.

How can I use myths to teach reading strategies?

- Have students read myths to find the main idea or lesson taught. As students read the excerpt from *Don Quixote* by Miguel de Cervantes, ask them to discuss what lessons can be learned from the title character.

- Ask students to read the myths on multiple levels: first literally and then metaphorically. Have students read the short excerpt from *Sundiata* by D. T. Niane twice. Tell them that they should focus their first reading on the details presented in the story, and they should take notes. Then have students read the excerpt a second time and ask them to take notes on the metaphorical meaning of the story.

- Help students make connections to the myths and relate them to their own lives.

- Have students explore the concepts and concerns presented in many myths. Myths often present ideas about heroism, living in harmony with others, and dealing with love and loss. Have students read the Time article "What Makes a Hero?" and then discuss the heroes they have already read about as well as what it means to be a hero today.

Focus

BELLRINGER

Bellringer Options
Literature Launcher Video
Daily Language Practice
Transparency 82
Or **write on the board:** Ulysses, Gilgamesh, King Arthur, El Cid, Hercules. Discuss why students think legendary heroes like these have endured for thousands of years. **Say:** Myths and legends answer questions about the world and satisfy the need to express the ideals of a culture. Explain that in this unit, students will explore history and universal themes as they learn about myths and legends.

Objectives for the Unit Introduction

• To understand characteristics of legends and myths
• To identify and explore literary elements significant to the genres
• To analyze the effect that these literary elements have upon the reader

Theseus and the Minotaur, from the Story of Theseus, c. 1510. Master of the Campana Cassoni.
Oil on panel. Musee du Petit Palais, Avignon, France.

Unit Introduction Skills

Reading Skills

• Analyzing Genre (SE p. 963)
• Responding (SE p. 965)
• Synthesizing (TWE p. 962)
• Analyzing Structure (TWE p. 964)

Legends and Myths

Literary Elements

• Structure (TWE p. 964)

Listening/Speaking/Viewing Skills

• Retelling Stories (SE p. 966)
• Creating a Visual Promotion (SE p. 966)

Study Skills/Research/Assessment

• Note Taking (SE p. 960)
• Researching Across Cultures (TWE p. 960)

Legends and Myths

Looking Ahead

Legends and myths are stories that usually have long histories. Often, they have been written and rewritten, or told and retold, for countless generations. Both legends and myths come from **oral tradition**—that is, literature passed by word of mouth from generation to generation. Legends are usually based on historical figures such as saints or kings, and they generally involve less of the supernatural than myths do. Myths may contain the values, beliefs, and deepest truths of the cultures they spring from.

> PREVIEW **Big Ideas and Literary Focus**

1	**BIG IDEA:** Acts of Courage	**LITERARY FOCUS:** The Legendary Hero
2	**BIG IDEA:** Rescuing and Conquering	**LITERARY FOCUS:** Myth and the Oral Tradition

OBJECTIVES
In learning about the genres of legends and myths, you will focus on the following:

- understanding characteristics of legends and myths

- identifying and exploring literary elements significant to the genres
- analyzing the effect that these literary elements have upon the reader

INTRODUCTION **959**

Focus

Summary

This introduction begins with authors' comments on legends and myths. An analysis of *The Journey of Gilgamesh* clarifies the literary elements of legend. Finally, a guide to legend and myth summarizes key elements and suggested reading techniques for each.

★ Viewing the Art

Tell students that according to legend, Theseus, a great Greek hero, conquered the minotaur, a fearsome creature who lived in a labyrinth and who was half man and half bull. **Ask:** Based on the depiction of Theseus in the painting, what might be some of the characteristics of heroes in legends and myths? *(Students might note the following: They face difficult tests; they battle enemies; they are courageous; their actions may alter the fate of those around them.)* **AS**

Unit Resources

Classroom Management
- TeacherWorks Plus™ CD-ROM
- StudentWorks Plus™ CD-ROM
- Literature Launchers™: Pre-Reading Videos DVD, Unit Five

Core Instructional Support
- Unit 5 Resources (Fast File)
- Literature Online, glencoe.com
- Presentation Plus!™ CD-ROM, Unit Five

Transparencies
- Literary Elements Transparencies 7, 17, 86, 87, 88, 91, 98
- Bellringer Options Transparencies: Selection Focus Transparencies 39–43 Daily Language Practice Transparencies 82–91

Differentiated Instruction
- Active Learning and Note Taking Guide, pp. 145–177
- Skill Level Up!™ A Language Arts Game

Assessment
- Selection and Unit Assessments, pp. 163–186, 217–218
- Exam*View*® Assessment Suite CD-ROM
- Assessment by Learning Objectives, pp. 54–60

Supplemental Reading
- Glencoe Literature Library
- Glencoe BookLink 3 CD-ROM
- *inTIME* Magazines

Teach

L Literary Element

Legendary Hero Ask: In what way is Sir Thomas Malory's depiction of Sir Launcelot characteristic of the legendary hero? *(It exaggerates Sir Launcelot as enormously strong, brave, and skillful.)* In what way is D. T. Niane's depiction of the early African king Sundiata characteristic of the legendary hero? *(Sundiata is described as ambitious and wise.)* Discuss how learning more about these two legendary heroes might shed light on the values and the culture of England and Mali. **OL**

★ Literary History

Bulfinch's Mythology
First published in 1855, *The Age of Fable,* or *Bulfinch's Mythology* as it has come to be called, is a classic retelling of myths and legends. After his workday as a bank clerk, American writer Thomas Bulfinch (1796–1867) researched myths and wrote them to appeal to a general audience. **AS**

Genre Focus
What can readers gain from Legends and Myths?

★ According to Thomas Bulfinch, one of America's first collectors of world myths and legends, ". . . if that which tends to make us happier and better can be called useful, then we claim that epithet for our subject. For Mythology is the handmaid of literature; and literature is one of the best allies of virtue and promoters of happiness." Here, happiness and the deepest truths go hand in hand. The role models, beliefs, and values of a culture are often preserved in their legends and myths.

The Legendary Hero

Legend

Legends are traditional stories handed down from generation to generation. Legends are believed to originate in true events. However, legends typically exaggerate the powers and deeds of their main characters, or heroes.

> Sir Launcelot took another spear, and unhorsed sixteen more of the King of North Galys' knights, and with his next, unhorsed another twelve; and in each case with such violence that none of the knights ever fully recovered. The King of North Galys was forced to admit defeat, and the prize was awarded to King Bagdemagus. **L**
>
> —Sir Thomas Malory, **from** *Le Morte d'Arthur*

Hero

A **hero** is the main character in a literary work. The term can refer to either a female or a male. In legends, the hero is admired by the reader for his or her superior character and noble deeds. These characters serve to inspire readers to achieve the traits that their culture values.

> In order to defeat Soumaoro it was necessary first of all to destroy his magical power. At Sibi, Sundiata decided to consult the soothsayers, of whom the most famous in Mali were there.
>
> —D. T. Niane, **from** *Sundiata*

Literature Online **Study Central** Visit www.glencoe.com to review epics and myths.

Additional Support

Study Central Have students visit the Web site for resources that will help them to review legends and myths.

Skills Practice

READING: Synthesizing As students read myths and legends that present explanations for eternal questions, discuss the value of synthesizing, or combining ideas to create something new. Encourage students to synthesize what they learn from the myths and legends from different sources to come up with their own answers. For example, compare the hero tales that this unit presents from various cultures and then develop a personal definition for heroism. To give students practice in this reading technique, have them synthesize the information in this introduction about the value of myths and legends. **OL**

Myth and the Oral Tradition

Myths

Myths are very ancient stories, whose authors are unknown, or **anonymous.** Myths tell of gods and goddesses, their interventions in the lives of heroes, and supernatural events. Many myths attempt to explain a belief, a custom, or a force of nature. Across cultures, mythic themes show many similarities. For example, virtually every culture has a myth that seeks to explain the creation of the world.

Oral Tradition

A culture's oral tradition includes its myths and legends, and it also includes its folklore and folktales. **Folklore** is the broader term that includes traditional beliefs, customs, stories, songs, and dances. **Folktales** are the stories within the culture's folklore. Recording a story does not remove it from the oral tradition. As a story is told by each generation, it may gradually change. The next time you hear or read the story, it might sound a little different. Most folklore takes as its subject the concerns of the common people.

> The Minotaur was a monster, half bull, half human, the offspring of Minos' wife Pasiphaë and a wonderfully beautiful bull. Poseidon had given this bull to Minos in order that he should sacrifice it to him, but Minos could not bear to slay it and had kept it for himself. To punish him, Poseidon had made Pasiphaë fall madly in love with it.
>
> —Edith Hamilton, **from** *Theseus*

R

> Coyote was walking with his friend Iktome. Along their path stood Iya, the rock. This was not just any rock; it was special. It had those spidery lines of green moss all over it, the kind that tell a story. Iya had power.
>
> —Jenny Leading Cloud and Richard Erdoes **from "Coyote, Iktome, and the Rock"**

Gilgamesh, the Sumerian King of Uruk, Slays the Bull of Ishtar Helped by Ea-bani, ca. 20th century. E. Wallcousins. ★

INTRODUCTION **961**

Teach

R Reading Strategy

Analyzing Genre Ask: Based on the excerpt, why do you think the Greek tale *Theseus* is a myth? *(It tells of the supernatural and the intervention of a god in human affairs.)* Why is the Sioux story "Coyote, Iktome, and the Rock" a folktale rather than a myth? *(This tale treats a common subject rather than heroic or supernatural events.)* How are both *Theseus* and "Coyote, Iktome, and the Rock" similar? *(Both are part of the oral tradition and history of a culture.)* **OL**

★ Viewing the Art

This painting depicts a scene from the Gilgamesh epic. After Gilgamesh does not accept her marriage proposal, Ishtar, the goddess of both love and war, sends a bull to kill him. Gilgamesh battles the bull and eventually slays it. **AS**

Differentiated Instruction

Anonymous Authorship Students may be confused about why authors are named in this unit when myths and legends are by definition anonymous. Explain that individual authors may retell ancient tales in their own style, but that does not remove the story from the oral tradition. **BL**

Building Reading Fluency

Understanding Vocabulary Have students read aloud the passage by Sir Thomas Malory. Write on the board the word *unhorse,* and show students how knowing both the context and the meaning of the prefix *un-* as "removal of" clarifies the definition of the word. *Unhorse* means "to make a rider fall." **BL**

Objectives
- To identify and explore literary elements significant to the genres (TWE)
- To synthesize the myths and legends of different cultures (TWE)

961

Teach

R₁ Reading Strategy

Analyzing Genre Discuss whether "The Journey of Gilgamesh" is a myth, legend, or folktale. **Ask:** What elements of legend does it have? *("The Journey of Gilgamesh" has a larger-than-life hero, described as smart, beautiful, and noble, who is based on a historical figure.)* **OL**

★ Literary History

Gilgamesh The story of Gilgamesh is one of the earliest on record, dating back before 2000 B.C. It was written on 12 clay tablets in the seventh century B.C. but then was lost. When it was rediscovered in the nineteenth century, people were amazed about the story of the flood, which is similar to the Bible story. Gilgamesh is believed to have been an actual king of Uruk, and the story *Gilgamesh* originated in Sumer in ancient Mesopotamia, now Iraq. **AS**

Literary Analysis Model
How is *The Journey of Gilgamesh* an epic?

Joan C. Verniero and Robin Fitzsimmons have collaborated in collecting and retelling myths and legends from around the world. *Gilgamesh* may be the oldest known story to ever have been written down. It is based on a historical Babylonian king. ★

The Journey of Gilgamesh R₁
(Sumerian epic)

by Joan C. Verniero and Robin Fitzsimmons

APPLYING Literary Elements

Epic Hero
Gilgamesh has admirable qualities typical of a **epic hero.**

Epic
The conditions of Gilgamesh's birth are typical of characters in **myths** and **epics.**

Epic Hero
Gilgamesh demonstrates strength and courage, two heroic traits.

Gilgamesh was the proud and beautiful king of Uruk. He was ambitious and smart and loved to learn all there was to know about life. Gilgamesh's curiosity troubled his mother, Ninsunna.

"Why do you desire to know so much, my son?" she asked him.

5 "It is important to me," Gilgamesh replied, "to experience everything in the world—to taste every type of food, smell every fragrance, journey to every land, enjoy every dance. Can't you understand that?"

Ninsunna shook her head.

"Gilgamesh, although you come from the gods, part of you is still mortal.
10 You cannot know and experience everything. One day you will die, as all mortals die."

When Gilgamesh heard what his mother had told him, he flew into a rage.

"I do not wish to die!" he exclaimed angrily. "My great friend Enkidu died. I miss him terribly, and I do not wish to follow him into the land
15 of the dead. I will learn the secret of living forever."

Gilgamesh's mother tried to comfort her son.

"I only know of one person who has managed to escape death. His name is Uta-Napishtim, or Uta-Napishtim, the Remote. He survived a mighty ordeal and was granted everlasting life. He lives beyond Mount
20 Mashu, which is very far away."

Gilgamesh made up his mind to find Uta-Napishtim, the Remote. He traveled toward Mount Mashu. It was a long journey filled with many perils. He was pursued by the fierce lions of the forest. The Scorpion Men, who hid behind the boulders of the mountains, jumped out at him and
25 tried to frighten him.

Gilgamesh continued on his way. Sometimes it was so dark he could barely see in front of himself. Finally, in the distance, Gilgamesh saw a great, glowing light. He had reached the home of Uta-Napishtim.

The old man greeted Gilgamesh and asked him why he had come so
30 far from his home.

"Tell me how you have earned the right to live forever, Uta-Napishtim," Gilgamesh asked him. "This is what I wish to learn."

962 UNIT 5 LEGENDS AND MYTHS

Additional Support

Skills Practice

READING: Analyzing Structure

Ask: What is the overall structure of "The Journey of Gilgamesh"? *(The tale is structured as a frame story, or a plot structure that includes the telling of a story within a story.)* Which is the frame story? *(The tale of Gilgamesh is the frame story, and the tale of Uta-Napishtim is told within*

it.) Point out that like most legends, "The Journey of Gilgamesh" is episodic, consisting of a series of episodes or adventures. Ask students to outline the episodes that Verniero and Fitzsimmons present. Finally, discuss the use of dialogue in structuring the tale. **OL**

Uta-Napishtim invited Gilgamesh to sit beside him on the ground. "Here is my story. I lived in Shurippak, the city of the sun. One day the
35 god Ea came to me and told me that the gods were displeased with humans and wished to destroy the earth. They were going to send a great flood to cover the world.

"Ea instructed me to build a very large ship and to prepare for the deluge. Then he told me to bring my family into the ship, as well as
40 many animals, and to wait for the rains to fall. I did this. A great storm came and the skies were filled with black clouds. Thunder shook the ground and bolts of lightning raced through the heavens with hot, white light. For many days it rained and rained without stopping. We almost forgot what it was like to see the sun or to walk on dry land.

45 "We were very afraid, but I trusted that Ea had told me the truth, and that I would be saved. After a long while, the rains stopped falling and I sent a bird out from my ship to seek land. The bird returned to me, exhausted after failing to find a place to land. In time I sent another bird, a raven, to fly from the ship. I was overjoyed when the raven did not
50 return to me, for it had found a dry patch of earth on which to live. This was a very good sign.

"Eventually the great flood waters receded and our ship rested upon a cliff. We left the ship with all of the creatures we had carried with us, and gave thanks to Ea and Ishtar, the goddess of heaven."

55 "But how did you come to be immortal?" Gilgamesh asked.

"The gods saw that I obeyed Ea, and as a reward they granted me immortality."

Gilgamesh jumped to his feet. "That does not help me, Uta-Napishtim, for I have not been tested as you have. Is there no way I can live forever?" **R2**

60 "Everything in this world lives and dies, Gilgamesh," Uta-Napishtim told him. "Yet, there may be a way for you to get your wish. Here is a special plant. Take this plant with you, back to your home. When you are there, you may eat it, and perhaps it will give you eternal youth."

Gilgamesh did as he was told and began the long journey home
65 again. On the way he stopped to rest near a clear pool of water. He was so thirsty that he put the magic plant on the ground, and stepped into the pool to drink from it. Gilgamesh did not notice the snake that crawled in the grass, not far from the water. The snake saw the plant and ate it.

Gilgamesh had lost his chance for immortality. Finally he realized that
70 even though he was a rich and powerful man, he could not escape death.

Legend tells us that the snake, after eating the plant intended for Gilgamesh, was able to shed his skin and regain his youth. Therefore, all snakes have kept this unique ability to this very day.

Statue of a hero taming a lion (Gilgamesh, legendary king of Uruk?). From the palace of Sargon II (722–705 BC), Khorsabad. The colossal statues of genii protected the entrance to the throne room. Assyrian, 8th BC. Louvre, Paris, France ★

Epic
Notice the universal theme of Earth being wiped clean by a flood.

Epic
The story encourages its audience to learn along with Gilgamesh to accept their mortality.

Epic
This story explains an aspect of the natural world.

Humbaba, demon genie and guardian of the cedar forests of the Lebanon-range. Period of the Amorite dynasties. In the Gilgamesh-epic, Gilgamesh and his friend Enkidu cut off the demon's head, ca. 20th-16th BC. Terracotta. Iraq Museum, Baghdad, Iraq.

Reading Check

Analyzing How is this epic similar to and different from myths, legends, and folktales? Explain your answer.

INTRODUCTION **963**

Teach

Reading Check

Answer: "The Journey of Gilgamesh" has aspects of both legend and myth. It has a legendary hero as well as supernatural elements.

R2 Reading Strategy

Analyzing Genre Ask: What universal theme does "The Journey of Gilgamesh" have? *(concern about mortality)* In what way does Gilgamesh represent all people? *(He represents people's yearning to be immortal as well as their need to recognize that immortality is beyond the realm of human experience.)*

★ Viewing the Art

Ask: What might these sculptures reveal about the values of the artists who produced them? *(Students might say that the artists wanted to glorify heroes who were powerful enough to tame or conquer threatening creatures. They admired bravery and physical strength.)* **AS**

English Language Coach

Names Since keeping track of the complicated names in "The Journey of Gilgamesh" may be difficult for English language learners, suggest that they keep a list of all the story's names and places, along with their identification and phonetic spelling. Referring to this list can make reading smoother. **EL**

Differentiated Instruction

Contrasting Characters Assist less proficient readers in contrasting the characters in "The Journey of Gilgamesh." For example, ask students to contrast Gilgamesh with Uta-Napishtim, noting the youthfulness and impetuousness of Gilgamesh and the age and complacency of Uta-Napishtim. **BL**

Objectives

• To analyze the structure of myths and legends (SE)
• To identify and explore literary elements significant to the genres (SE)
• To synthesize the myths and legends of different cultures (TWE)

963

Teach

L Literary Element

Legendary Hero Ask: How does W. H. Auden describe the legendary Quest hero? *(A hero on a search for something makes a journey and is tested.)* Discuss how this definition applies to heroes students are familiar with, such as King Arthur. **Ask:** According to Auden, why is the Quest hero pervasive in literature worldwide? *(The hero answers a universal need and symbolizes human existence.)* **OL**

★ Viewing the Art

The scene shown in Jonathan Barry's painting is from the first book in the *Lord of the Rings* trilogy. Many students will be familiar with the *Lord of the Rings* books or films. **Ask:** In what ways is the Quest in *The Lord of the Rings* similar to and different from Auden's elements of the typical Quest story? *(Similar: a long journey; only one hero who can undertake it; Guardians and Tests must be overcome; friends help the hero. Different: The Quest is to destroy something, not find or possess it.)* **AS**

Additional Support

Interactive Reading Have students access the Web site for more practice with reading strategies.

964

Writers on Reading
What do writers say about legends and myths?

Reading Legends and Myths

The Quest Hero

The Quest is one of the oldest, hardiest, and most popular of all literary genres. In some instances it may be founded on historical fact—the Quest of the Golden Fleece may have had its origin in the search of seafaring traders for amber—and certain themes, like the theme of the enchanted cruel Princess whose heart can be melted only by the predestined lover, may be distorted recollections of religious rites, but the persistent appeal of the Quest as a literary form is due, I believe, to its validity as a symbolic description of our subjective personal existence as historical. . . .

The essential elements in this typical Quest story are six:

L

1. A precious Object and/or Person to be found and possessed or married.

2. A long journey to find it, for its whereabouts are not originally known to the seekers.

3. A hero. The precious object cannot be found by anybody, but only by the one person who possesses the right qualities of breeding or character.

4. A Test or series of Tests by which the unworthy are screened out, and the hero revealed.

5. The Guardians of the Object who must be overcome before it can be won. They may be simply a further test of the hero's *arete* [virtue], or they may be malignant in themselves.

6. The Helpers who with their knowledge and magical powers assist the hero and but for whom he would never succeed. They may appear in human or in an animal form.

—W. H. Auden, **from "The Quest Hero"**

Myth and Dream

Throughout the inhabited world, in all times and under every circumstance, the myths of man have flourished; and they have been of living inspiration of whatever else may have appeared out of the activities of the human body and mind. It would not be too much to say that myth is the secret opening through which the inexhaustible energies of the cosmos pour into human cultural manifestation.

—Joseph Campbell, **from *The Hero with a Thousand Faces***

The Bridge of Khazadum, 1998. Jonathan Barry. Oil on canvas. Private Collection. ★

Literature Online InterActive Reading Practice Visit www.glencoe.com for more practice reading epics and myths.

Skills Practice

RESEARCH: Cultural Diversity
Have groups of students do research to compare myths from different cultures. For example, have them compare creation myths from Japan, Scandinavia, the Middle East, Native American tribes, and ancient Greece. As students read, have them pay attention to the following:

- depiction of the hero
- values honored in the myth
- supernatural elements
- explanations about natural phenomena

Encourage students to note similarities and differences. **OL**

Girl with a Unicorn, 1980. Anthony Southcombe. Acrylic on board, 46 x 38 cm. Private Collection.

The Tenets of Storytelling

Stories are made of words and of such implications as the storyteller places upon words. The story lies at the center of language, and language is composed of words. Words, then, are the primary tools of the storyteller. It is to his purpose to use words well.

> "Myth does not mean something untrue, but a concentration of truth."
>
> —Doris Lessing

There are many kinds of stories. The basic story is one which centers upon an event, and the words proceed toward the formulation of meaning. This is the narrative process. The storyteller sets words in procession; his object is most often the establishment of meaning.

In general, stories are true to human experience. Indeed, the truth of human experience is their principal information. This is to say that stories tend to support and confirm our perceptions of the world and of the creatures within it. Even the most fantastic story is rooted in our common experience; otherwise, it would have no meaning for us. Strictly speaking, it would not be a story. . . .

The primary object of the story is the realization of wonder and delight.

—N. Scott Momaday, **from the foreward for** *Native American Stories*

Reading Check

Responding From your own reading experiences, which passage do you identify with most closely? Explain.

INTRODUCTION **965**

Teach

Reading Check

Answer: Students' answers will vary. They may be impressed by Momaday's explanation of the truth of stories.

Reading Strategy

Analyzing Genre Discuss how each writer has an individual perspective on myths and legends, but all touch on similar themes. **Ask:** What do all the authors on these pages emphasize about myths? *(Myths are true to human experience.)* **OL**

★ Viewing the Art

Say: Paintings, like stories, can evoke wonder and delight. **Ask:** In what specific ways does this painting evoke those two emotions? *(Students may say that the unicorn, a beautiful and fantastical creature, evokes wonder. The painter's decision to give the scene a golden glow despite a dark night sky adds to the sense of wonder.)* **AS**

Differentiated Instruction

Connotation and Denotation

Remind students that the connotations of a word are its meanings beyond the dictionary definition. Ask less proficient readers about the connotations of challenging words from the Joseph Campbell passage. *(Many have positive, intriguing connotations.)* **BL**

Reading in the Real World

College Comment on the pervasiveness of allusions, or references, to myth and legend in modern society, and provide students with several examples (e.g., the planets Mercury, Venus, and Mars are named after Roman gods). Discuss the reasons for allusions to ancient myths and legends. **OL**

Objectives

- To analyze the effect these literary elements have upon the reader (SE)
- To identify and explore literary elements significant to the genres (TWE)
- To understand characteristics of legends and myths (TWE)

965

Assess/Close

Guide to Reading Legends and Myths

Encourage students to explore the background of a myth or legend before reading.

Elements of Legends and Myths

Review the definitions related to myth and legend, and have students practice applying the reading techniques to "The Journey of Gilgamesh."

FOLDABLES™
Study Organizer

Have students make and label the Three-Tab Book. Then have them use this study organizer to take notes on the legends, myths, and folktales they read in this unit.

Wrap-Up

Guide to Reading Legends and Myths

- Read to enjoy.
- Consider the purpose of the work. Was it written to inspire, instruct, or motivate?
- Be aware of the cultural origin of the story.
- If you are reading a legend, be aware of historical elements in the text.
- If you are reading a myth, look for hints about the values of the culture that created it.

Elements of Legends and Myths

- **Legends** are ancient stories with elements of history and elements of fantasy.
- **Legendary heroes** are admirable and noble. They perform great deeds, often with the help of gods.
- **Myths** tell stories of gods, heroes, and supernatural interventions.
- **Folklore** includes the folktales, dances, songs, beliefs and customs of a culture.
- **Folktales** tell stories of common people.
- **Oral tradition** is the myths, legends, folklore, and folktales of a culture that are passed orally from generation to generation.

Activities

Use what you have learned about reading and analyzing legends, myths, and folktales.

1. Speaking/Listening/Viewing You may be surprised to find that myths and folktales are relatively easy to remember and retell. Create class time for retelling some of the myths, legends, and folktales from this unit. You will enjoy hearing the personal touches each person gives the story and experience firsthand the tradition of storytelling.

2. Visual Literacy Create a promotion for reading legends and myths to be mounted in your library. Aim your promotion at your peers.

3. Note Taking Try using this study organizer to practice identifying elements of legends and myths. For each selection, write clues you used to identify the element.

 THREE-TAB BOOK

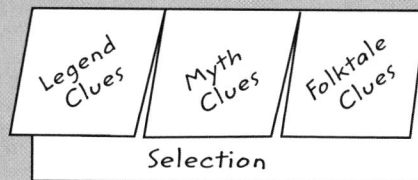

OBJECTIVES
- Create media products to engage a specific audience
- Use voice volume, stress, pacing, enunciation, eye contact, and gestures that meet the needs of the audience and the topic

---

Activities

1. **Speaking/Listening/Viewing** Practice ways to engage listeners in storytelling, such as varying voices for different characters, capturing mood with tone of voice, and using body language effectively.

2. **Visual Literacy** For a poster or promotion, discuss how to gain attention with a headline that piques interest.

Acts of Courage

An illustration from *A History of the Development and Customs of Chivalry* by Dr. Franz Kottenkamp, published in 1842. Friedrich Martin von Reibisch.

BI   BIG IDEA

Courage comes in many forms. An audition, a first date, a speech, even everyday life can require acts of courage. The legends in Part 1 narrate acts of courage that made people heroes to entire cultures. As you read the selections, ask yourself: Who are some modern heroes? What makes them heroic?

967

Analyzing and Extending

BI   Big Idea

Acts of Courage Ask students to describe their experiences with acts of courage, both physical and mental, and to determine a personal definition of heroism. Comment on the idea that courage is a trait that many heroes share. Tell students that Part 1 will introduce heroes whose courage makes them legendary. Encourage students to contemplate this "big idea" and its relation to the artwork. **OL**

★ Viewing the Art

Jousting, which is depicted in this painting, was a popular form of entertainment centuries ago in western Europe. Each rider would attempt to knock the other from atop his horse. Discuss with students the courage it must have taken to participate in such a sport. **AS**

English Language Coach

Building Background Discuss with students new to the United States their experience with courageous acts. You might raise the issue of coming to this country and ask for their impressions of the courage it involves. Invite students to share any legends about courageous heroes that they know. **EL**

Differentiated Instruction

Activating Prior Knowledge Invite less proficient readers to jot down words they associate with legendary heroes. Specifically ask them what they know about the world of knighthood, including King Arthur, tournaments, commoners, nobles, and coronations. Prepare students by discussing these terms. **BL**

Objectives for Part 1
- To identify the characteristics that distinguish literary forms (SE)
- To compare works that express a universal theme and provide evidence to support your ideas about each work (SE)
- To understand the literary terms *legend* and *epic* (SE)

Part 1: Acts of Courage

Readability Scores Key
Dale-Chall/DRP/Lexile

PACING (DAYS)		SELECTIONS AND FEATURES	LITERARY ELEMENTS
STANDARD	BLOCK		
1–2 class sessions	1	LITERARY FOCUS: The Legendary Hero, pp. 968–969	The Legendary Hero, SE p. 968 Comparing the Hero in Literature, TWE p. 968
		"Arthur Becomes King" from *The Once and Future King* by T. H. White **6.4**/**52**/1020, pp. 970–986	Idiom, SE pp. 971–985 Legend, SE p. 985
		Grammar Workshop: Sentence Structure, p. 987	
1 class session	1	**from *Le Morte d'Arthur*** by Sir Thomas Malory **6.7**/**60**/1110, pp. 988–1008	Dialogue, SE pp. 989–1007 Hero, SE p. 1007
1 class session		**from *Don Quixote*** by Miguel de Cervantes **10.9**/**63**/1350, pp. 1009–1019	Parody, SE pp. 1010, 1012, 1013, 1017, 1018 Foil, SE p. 1018 Idioms, TWE p. 1016
1–2 class sessions	1	TIME magazine, **"What Makes a Hero?"** by Amanda Ripley **10.0**/**63**/1080, pp. 1020–1023	
		from *Sundiata* by D. T. Niane **5.3**/**58**/1020, pp. 1024–1030	Dialogue, SE pp. 1025, 1027, 1028, 1029, 1030 Idiom, TWE p. 1028
		VISUAL PERSPECTIVE: **"The Lion of Mali"** from *Sundiata, A Legend of Africa* by Will Eisner, pp. 1031–1034	

About the Part

Part 1 covers the legendary hero and the way that various cultures and writers portray him or her.

READING AND CRITICAL THINKING	VOCABULARY	WRITING AND GRAMMAR	LISTENING, SPEAKING, AND VIEWING
Analyzing Hero, TWE p. 969		Quickwrite, SE p. 969	
Analyzing Tone, SE pp. 971–985 Scanning, TWE p. 980	Context Clues, SE p. 985	Writing a Character Analysis, SE p. 986 Using Fragments for Effect, SE p. 986 Using Hyperbole, TWE p. 976 Hyphens for Compound Words, TWE p. 978	Expressing Tone, TWE p. 982
		Using Main and Subordinate Clauses, SE p. 987	
Analyzing Plot, SE pp. 989–1008 Identifying Author's Purpose, TWE p. 994 Summarizing, TWE p. 1000	Word Origins, SE p. 1008	Writing a Compare and Contrast Essay, SE p. 1008 Using Commas, TWE p. 998 *Who* and *Whom*, TWE p. 1006	Retelling a Legend, TWE p. 1004
Evaluating Characters, SE pp. 1010, 1012, 1015, 1017, 1019 Visualizing, TWE p. 1012	Synonyms, SE pp. 1010, 1019	Writing an Adventure, SE p. 1019 Concrete and Abstract Nouns, TWE p. 1014	Conducting an Interview, SE p. 1019
Clarifying Meaning, SE p. 1020, 1021 Previewing the Article, SE p. 1020 Interpreting, TWE p. 1022		Creative Writing, TWE p. 1020	Analyzing Art, TWE pp. 1021, 1022
Identifying Genre, SE pp. 1025, 1027, 1029, 1030	Word Parts, SE p. 1030	Writing About Character, SE p. 1030	
Comparing and Contrasting Versions of a Story, SE pp. 1031–1033 Interpreting, TWE p. 1033			Dramatic Presentation, TWE p. 1031

Teach

Big Idea

Acts of Courage Show a video clip of a modern hero, such as Martin Luther King, Jr., or bring to class news clippings of current acts of courage, such as firefighters battling a blaze. Ask students what they find inspiring about these acts of courage. Tell students that real-life acts of courage parallel the courageous acts of legendary heroes who embody the ideals of a nation. **OL**

L Literary Element

The Legendary Hero

Ask: How does Arthur prove his worthiness as a legendary hero? *(Arthur alone is able to remove the sword from the stone. He is of noble birth and is popular with the citizenry.)* What noble traits does Arthur display? *(Honor, humility, and forgiveness.)* Point out the elements of fantasy in the legend, such as the magic sword Excalibur, and note that the legend of Arthur has inspired hundreds of plays, books, and movies. **OL**

The Legendary Hero

The word *legend* originates from the Latin word *legenda*, an adjective that means "for reading" or "to be read." Initially, *legenda* was used only when referring to written stories, not the stories that made up the oral tradition. In the fourteenth century, the English word *legend* was used similarly: it only referred to written accounts of saints' lives. Beginning in the fifteenth century, *legend* began to be used to refer to traditional stories as well. Legends communicated the heroic acts of knights and the greatness of kings and queens, and such stories became more widespread after the invention of the printing press. Eventually the term *legend* acquired its current meaning—a person or act worthy of inspiring a story.

L The secret of Arthur's birth was known only to a few of the nobles surviving from the days of King Uther. The Archbishop urged them to make Arthur's cause their own; but their support proved ineffective. The tournament was repeated at Candlemas and at Easter, and with the same outcome as before.

Finally at Pentecost, when once more Arthur alone had been able to remove the sword, the commoners arose with a tumultuous cry and demanded that Arthur should at once be made king. The nobles, knowing in their hearts that the commoners were right, all knelt before Arthur and begged forgiveness for having delayed his succession for so long. Arthur forgave them, and then, offering his sword at the high altar, was dubbed first knight of the realm. The coronation took place a few days later, when Arthur swore to rule justly, and the nobles swore him their allegiance.

—Thomas Malory, **from** *Le Morte d'Arthur*

An illustration from *A History of the Development and Customs of Chivalry* by Dr. Franz Kottenkamp, published in 1842. Friedrich Martin von Reibisch.

968 UNIT 5   LEGENDS AND MYTHS

Additional Support

Skills Practice

LITERARY ELEMENT: Hero Review the traditional depiction of the hero in legends and epics. **Ask:** How are epic and legendary heroes similar and different? *(Through the oral tradition, both portray a hero representing cherished values of a culture, such as courage, integrity, and intelligence, but the epic hero is the main character of an epic poem rather than a story and usually has supernatural elements.)* Discuss how King Arthur fulfills this definition of a legendary hero, while Don Quixote parodies the hero of legend for the purpose of humor. Read excerpts from *Beowulf* to introduce students to the depiction

Legend

A **legend** is a traditional story handed down from one generation to the next, originally by word of mouth. Legends are believed to be based on true events and a historical hero. In the above passage, King Arthur becomes king of Britain by pulling a sword from a stone. Over the years, legends have gained elements of fantasy and magic. Because legends are the stories of the people, they often express the values or character of a nation.

"Why," said Arthur, "do you both kneel before me?"
"My lord," Sir Ector replied, "there is only one man living who can draw the sword from the stone, and he is the true-born King of Britain."

—Thomas Malory, **from** *Le Morte d'Arthur*

Epic

When a hero and his or her adventures are described in the form of a long narrative poem— one that tells a story—it is called an **epic**. Like legends, epics have extraordinary heroes. One of the supernatural elements that often appears in epics is gods and goddesses intervening in the lives of humans. Such supernatural happenings are less common in legends.

Hero

The **hero** is the main character in a literary work, generally one the reader admires. His or her good deeds and noble character allow the hero to defeat all enemies. The hero often sets out on a journey or challenges an enemy in battle to save his or her nation or family.

A hero may be male or female. One well-known example of a modern female hero is Dorothy from *The Wizard of Oz*. She receives some guidance from superhuman forces—the good witch—and shows unusual courage, intelligence, independence, and leadership.

The heroes of literature face great difficulties, but reap great rewards. Some authors have speculated what it might be like for an ordinary person to try to live a hero's life. A famous example of this sort of tale is *Don Quixote*, in which Don Quixote has some trouble finding monsters to slay.

> At that moment they caught sight of some thirty or forty windmills, which stand on that plain, and as soon as Don Quixote saw them he said to his squire: "Fortune is guiding our affairs better than we could have wished. Look over there, friend Sancho Panza, where more than thirty monstrous giants appear. I intend to do battle with them and take all their lives."

R

—Miguel de Cervantes, **from** *Don Quixote*

Shield of the duchy of Krain, 1463. Gilded and painted wood. Wien Museum Karlsplatz, Vienna, Austria.

Quickwrite

These days, we use the word "legend" more loosely than it was used in the fourteenth century. We speak of music legends and sports legends; anyone whose fame is likely to last might be called a legend. Choose a modern legend from the list below or think of your own. Write four exaggerated phrases to describe your hero.

Rosa Parks
Tiger Woods
Eleanor Roosevelt
Abraham Lincoln
Martin Luther King Jr.

OBJECTIVES
- Identify the characteristics that distinguish literary forms.
- Compare works that express a universal theme and provide evidence to support your ideas about each work.

- Understand the literary forms and terms *legend* and *epic*.

Teach

R Reading Strategy

Analyzing Hero Discuss the traits expected of a legendary or epic hero, including courage, humility, wit, and honor. **Ask:** How does *Don Quixote* parody the legendary hero? *(Don Quixote is an idealistic but misguided hero who tries to slay windmills, since he can't find worthy opponents. The result is comic.)* **OL**

Assess

Quickwrite

Check students' phrases for exaggeration of positive qualities that could be termed legendary.

---

of an epic hero. **Ask:** How do you think the modern hero compares and contrasts with traditional depictions? *(Students may note that the epic or legendary hero is usually larger than life while the modern-day hero may be more realistic.)* Insist that students provide evidence to support their comparisons. **OL**

English Language Coach

Cultural References Tell students that *Le Morte d'Arthur* portrays thirteenth-century England and medieval knights and chivalry. Explain that in sixteenth-century Spain, Don Quixote idolizes the knights of King Arthur and attempts a reenactment as a knight with a squire, or assistant. **EL**

Objectives

- To identify the characteristics that distinguish literary forms (SE)
- To compare works that express a universal theme and provide evidence to support your ideas about each work (SE)
- To understand the literary terms *legend* and *epic* (SE)

Focus

BELLRINGER

Bellringer Options
**Selection Focus
Transparency 39
Daily Language Practice
Transparency 83**
Or **write on the board:** The Once and Future King. **Explain** that this is the title of the book from which this excerpt is taken.
Ask: What might this title mean?

Have students discuss possible interpretations of the title. Suggest that they pay close attention to *Once* and *Future*.

Literature Online

Author Search To expand students' appreciation of T. H. White, have them access the Web site for additional information and resources.

Arthur Becomes King
from *The Once and Future King*

MEET T. H. WHITE

A scholar of medieval life, Terence Hanbury White emerged as a popular writer who retold legends about the Knights of the Round Table.

White was born in Bombay, India, but lived most of his life in England. He had an unhappy childhood mainly because his parents frequently fought and occasionally became violent. When White was six, his parents sent him to England to begin his education.

As a student, he loved the medieval period. He wrote his college thesis on Sir Thomas Malory's romance, *Le Morte d'Arthur* (*The Death of Arthur*, 1485). Malory's masterpiece later inspired much of White's own work.

"Education is a companion which no future can depress, no crime can destroy. . . ."

—T. H. White

Reteller of Arthurian Legends In 1930 after graduating from Queens College in Cambridge, England, White began work as an English teacher. During the early thirties, he achieved his first critical success with the publication of an autobiographical account of his country life titled *England Have My Bones*. Six years later White left teaching to write full time. By that time he had published several novels and collections of poetry under his own name and the pseudonym James Aston.

White's most famous work, *The Sword in the Stone*, was published in 1938. It was the first novel of a tetralogy (a series of four novels) based on King Arthur and his knights. The

Sword in the Stone retells the education of young Arthur. It was followed by *The Witch in the Wood* (1939) (later retitled *The Queen of Air and Darkness*) and *The Ill-Made Knight* (1940). Along with a fourth volume, *The Candle in the Wind*, the books were compiled into one bestselling book titled *The Once and Future King* (1958). White's retelling of Arthurian legends inspired several adaptations, including the Walt Disney animated film *The Sword in the Stone* (1963) and the Broadway musical *Camelot* (1967).

Wish-fulfillment White identified strongly with the young Arthur in his novels. In a letter to a friend, he wrote that *The Once and Future King* "is more or less the kind of wish-fulfillment of the things I should like to have happened to me when I was a boy."

With a tip of the hat to his source of inspiration, White included, at the end of *The Once and Future King*, a cameo appearance by Sir Thomas Malory (c. 1405–1471).

White eventually retired to the Channel Island of Alderney. He became reclusive, spending his time hunting, fishing, and doting on his many pets.

T. H. White was born in 1906 and died in 1964.

Literature Online **Author Search** For more about T. H. White, go to www.glencoe.com.

Selection Skills

Literary Elements
- Idiom (SE pp. 971–985)
- Legend (SE p. 985)

Vocabulary Skills
- Context Clues (SE p. 985)

Reading Skills
- Analyzing Tone (SE pp. 971–985)
- Scanning (TWE p. 980)

Arthur Becomes King

Listening/Speaking/Viewing Skills
- Expressing Tone (TWE p. 982)

Writing Skills/Grammar
- Character Analysis (SE p. 986)
- Using Fragments for Effect (SE p. 986)
- Using Hyperbole (TWE p. 976)
- Hyphens for Compound Words (TWE p. 978)

Connecting to the Story

In the following selection, Arthur, referred to as "Wart," experiences a sudden change in status. Before you read the selection, think about the following questions:

- How would you react if you were suddenly given great responsibility?
- How might your friends react?

Building Background

This story takes place somewhere in England at some time during the medieval period when men wore armor and fought with swords. The author refers to the setting simply as "an imaginary world."

In the fourteenth and fifteenth centuries, jousting was one of the most popular sports in Europe. It involved two armored horsemen charging at each other with lowered spears, or lances. The goal was to knock the opponent off his horse. Sometimes the jousters merely broke their lances; occasionally they were injured or killed. King Henry II of France died after a jousting tournament in honor of his daughter's marriage.

Setting Purposes for Reading

Big Idea Acts of Courage

As you read, notice how White reveals the qualities that will make young Arthur a great king.

Literary Element Idiom

An **idiom** is a phrase with a special meaning that is different from the literal meaning of the words that make it up. Expressions such as "dying to see you" and "catching someone's eye" are examples of idioms. In this selection, White sometimes uses idioms that are anachronistic, or out of their proper time period. As you read, note his use of idioms.

- See Literary Terms Handbook, p. R8.

Literature Online Interactive Literary Elements **Handbook** To review or learn more about the literary elements, go to www.glencoe.com.

Reading Strategy Analyzing Tone

The **tone** of a literary work is a reflection of the author's attitude toward the subject. A writer's tone may convey a variety of attitudes, including sympathy or humor.

Reading Tip: Creating Character Sketches To determine the tone of White's story, create charts for each of the characters. Find examples that reveal the character's personality and make a list of adjectives that describe the character. Then decide what White's attitude is toward the character and explain your reasoning.

Nurse's Character Sketch	
Descriptive Adjectives	Author's Tone
emotional, weepy	humorous— her emotional outbursts are made to look ridiculous

Vocabulary

petulantly (pech′ ə lənt lē) *adv.* crankily; in an annoyed way; p. 973 *The small child sulked petulantly when she did not get her way.*

vulgar (vul′ gər) *adj.* characterized by a lack of good breeding or good taste; common; crude; p. 976 *Vulgar behavior offends people who value courtesy and good manners.*

sumptuous (sump′ chōo əs) *adj.* costly and magnificent; p. 977 *The flowers at my sister's expensive wedding were sumptuous.*

combatant (kəm bat′ ənt) *n.* one trained for, or engaged in, combat; p. 978 *The combatants fought each other mercilessly.*

throng (thrông) *v.* to move or gather in large numbers; to crowd together; p. 979 *People thronged the park to see the fireworks.*

Focus

Summary

King Uther has died and left no heir. But a sword stuck in a stone says that whoever pulls the sword out will become king. Sir Ector, Kay, and Kay's squire, the Wart, go to London for the tournament. In London, Kay finds he has left his sword at the inn. When the Wart goes to get it, he finds a sword stuck in a stone and pulls it out. Kay claims to have done it, but soon admits that the Wart did. Sir Ector and Kay treat the Wart with a new respect.

V Vocabulary

Vocabulary File Say: Add these words and definitions to your vocabulary file. For each word, include a sentence that gives you an example of how to use the word. **OL** Students with English language needs should include the pronunciations of these words in their files. **EL**

Literary Elements Have students access the Web site to improve their understanding of idioms.

OBJECTIVES
In studying this selection, you will focus on the following:
- recognizing and understanding idioms
- evaluating an author's tone
- understanding legends
- writing to analyze character development

T. H. WHITE **971**

Selection Resources

Print Materials
- 📁 Unit 5 Resources (Fast File), pp. 17–19
- 📁 Leveled Vocabulary Development, p. 69
- 📁 Selection and Unit Assessments, pp. 163–164
- 📁 Selection Quick Checks, p. 82

Transparencies
- Bellringer Options Transparencies: Selection Focus Transparency 39 Daily Language Practice Transparency 83
- Literary Elements Transparency 98

Technology
- 💿 TeacherWorks Plus™ CD-ROM
- 💿 StudentWorks Plus™ CD-ROM
- 💿 Presentation Plus!™ CD-ROM
- 💻 Literature Online, glencoe.com
- 💻 Online Student Edition, mhln.com
- 💿 ExamView® Assessment Suite CD-ROM
- 💿 Vocabulary PuzzleMaker CD-ROM
- 💿 Listening Library, disc 2 track 16

Teach

Arthur Becomes King

from The Once and Future King

T. H. White

A Tournament. Claude Deruet. Oil on canvas, 115 x 162.5 cm. Sotheby's, London. ★

King Pellinore arrived for the important week-end in a high state of flurry.

"I say," he exclaimed, "do you know? Have you heard? Is it a secret, what?"

"Is what a secret, what?" they asked him.

"Why, the King," cried his majesty. "You know, about the King?"

"What's the matter with the King?" inquired Sir Ector. "You don't say he's comin' down to hunt with those demned hounds of his or anythin' like that?"

"He's dead," cried King Pellinore tragically. "He's dead, poor fellah, and can't hunt any more."

Sir Grummore stood up respectfully and took off his cap of maintenance.

"The King is dead," he said. "Long live the King."

Everybody else felt they ought to stand up too, and the boys' nurse burst into tears.

"There, there," she sobbed. "His loyal highness dead and gone, and him such a

Additional Support

Skills Practice

READING: Arthurian Legend
Explain to students that there are many versions of the tales of King Arthur. Some of these versions are very old, and some are more recent. Walt Disney used White's version of the legend as the basis for the animated feature *The Sword in the Stone.* Have students use a search engine to locate variations of the Arthurian legend. Students might use keywords including *King Arthur, Camelot,* and *Knights of the Round Table.* Have them compare their findings to White's version and share the similarities and differences with the class. **OL**

respectful gentleman. Many's the illumin-ated picture I've cut out of him, from the Illustrated Missals,[1] aye, and stuck up over the mantel. From the time when he was in swaddling bands, right through them world towers till he was a-visiting the dispersed areas as the world's Prince Charming, there wasn't a picture of 'im but I had it out, aye, and give 'im a last thought o' nights."

"Compose yourself, Nannie," said Sir Ector.

"It is solemn, isn't it?" said King Pellinore, "What? Uther the Conqueror, 1066 to 1216."

"A solemn moment," said Sir Grummore. "The King is dead. Long live the King."

"We ought to pull down the curtains," said Kay, who was always a stickler[2] for good form, "or half-mast the banners."

"That's right," said Sir Ector. "Somebody go and tell the sergeant-at-arms."[3]

It was obviously the Wart's duty to execute this command, for he was now the junior nobleman present, so he ran out cheerfully to find the sergeant. Soon those who were left in the solar could hear a voice crying out, "Nah then, one two, special mourning fer 'is lite[4] majesty, lower awai on the command Two!" and then the flapping of all the standards, banners, pennons, pennoncells, banderolls, guidons, streamers and cognizances which made gay the snowy turrets of the Forest Sauvage.[5]

---

1. Here, *illuminated* refers to a style of decorating a book in gold, silver, and bright colors; *missals* are, in actuality, prayer books. White is pulling the reader's leg here (and will again later) by inserting bits of modern culture into his fictional medieval world. The *Illustrated Missals* seems to be a tabloid–style periodical featuring stories about knights and members of royalty.

2. A *stickler* is someone who insists on having things done in a certain way.

3. A *sergeant-at-arms* preserves order and performs minor official duties, for example, at meetings of a court or a legislature.

4. As a small boy, Arthur was nicknamed *Wart*. The *solar*, or solarium, is a sunny room or porch. The speaker's accent turns *late*, meaning "recently deceased," into *lite*.

5. The *standards . . . cognizances* are variously shaped flags flying from the small towers, or *turrets*, of Sir Ector's castle, *Forest Sauvage* (sō vazh'). The French word *sauvage* means "savage; wild."

"How did you hear?" asked Sir Ector.

"I was pricking through the purlieus of the forest after that Beast, you know, when I met with a solemn friar of orders gray,[6] and he told me. It's the very latest news."

"Poor old Pendragon," said Sir Ector.

"The King is dead," said Sir Grummore solemnly. "Long live the King."

"It is all very well for you to keep on mentioning that, my dear Grummore," exclaimed King Pellinore **petulantly,** "but who is this King, what, that is to live so long, what, accordin' to you?"

"Well, his heir," said Sir Grummore, rather taken aback.[7]

"Our blessed monarch," said the Nurse tearfully, "never had no hair. Anybody that studied the loyal family knowed that."

"Good gracious!" exclaimed Sir Ector. "But he must have had a next-of-kin?"

"That's just it," cried King Pellinore in high excitement. "That's the excitin' part of it, what? No hair and no next-of-skin, and who's to succeed to the throne? That's what my friar was so excited about, what, and why he was asking who could succeed to what, what? What?"

"Do you mean to tell me," exclaimed Sir Grummore indignantly, "that there ain't no King of Gramarye?"

"Not a scrap of one," cried King Pellinore, feeling important. "And there have been signs and wonders of no mean[8] might."

"I think it's a scandal," said Sir Grummore. "God knows what the dear old

---

6. The forest's *purlieus* (pur' lōōz) are its edges, and the *friar of orders gray* is a Roman Catholic monk.

7. To be *taken aback* is to be suddenly surprised or startled.

8. Here, *mean* means "humble or modest," so signs and wonders of *no mean might* actually have considerable symbolic importance.

Reading Strategy Analyzing Tone *How does the author use characterization to emphasize his humorous tone?* **R2**

Vocabulary

petulantly (pech' ə lənt lē) *adv.* crankily; in an annoyed way

T. H. WHITE **973**

Teach

L **Literary Element**

Dialect Say: Speech written in dialect reflects the character and background of the person speaking. Have students read aloud some examples of dialect on pages 972–973 and explain what the dialect indicates about the characters. *(The characters use slang and informal language, which suggests they are ordinary people. Characters such as Nannie use the Cockney dialect, which suggests they have less education than the noble characters.)* **OL**

R2 **Reading Strategy**

Analyzing Tone Answer: *The characters' dialect and the narrator's colloquial diction communicate the informal and lighthearted tone. For example, having the characters repeat each other and mispronounce words shows that the author is not taking the legend entirely seriously.* **OL**

CheckPoint

Use the CheckPoint questions on Presentation Plus! to monitor students' comprehension. These questions can be used with interactive response keypads for immediate student feedback.

English Language Coach

Understanding Dialect English language learners may have difficulty understanding dialect. Explain that in the Cockney dialect, initial *h*'s and other letters are sometimes omitted. These are indicated by apostrophes. Explain that in the upper class accent spoken by the king, final *g*'s are sometimes omitted. In addition, the author gives the king the habit of adding *what* to his sentences. Point out that this is similar to adding *like* or *you know* to sentences. Analyze and discuss speeches written in dialect as students read the selection. **EL**

Objectives
- To evaluate the author's tone (SE)
- To make predictions (TWE)
- To understand dialect (TWE)

Analyzing Tone Answer: *The tone, as conveyed through the characters, is humorous. King Pellinore, Sir Ector, and Sir Grummore are portrayed as absentminded old men who repeatedly misunderstand one another.* **OL**

L1 Literary Element

Idiom Answer: *Sir Ector is telling King Pellinore to relax, using a colloquial expression of a different time.* **OL**

L2 Literary Element

Idiom Answer: *He means that Sir Grummore and Sir Ector are confusing him with their constant interruptions.* **OL**

---

country is comin' to. Due to these lollards and communists,[9] no doubt."

"What sort of signs and wonders?" asked Sir Ector.

"Well, there has appeared a sort of sword in a stone, what, in a sort of a church. Not in the church, if you see what I mean, and not in the stone, but that sort of thing, what, like you might say."

"I don't know what the Church is coming to," said Sir Grummore.

"It's in an anvil," explained the King.

"The Church?"

"No, the sword."

"But I thought you said the sword was in the stone?"

"No," said King Pellinore. "The stone is outside the church."

"Look here, Pellinore," said Sir Ector. "You have a bit of a rest, old boy, and start again. Here, drink up this horn of mead[10] and take it easy."

"The sword," said King Pellinore, "is stuck through an anvil which stands on a stone. It goes right through the anvil and into the stone. The anvil is stuck to the stone. The stone stands outside a church. Give me some more mead."

"I don't think that's much of a wonder," remarked Sir Grummore. "What I wonder at is that they should allow such things to happen. But you can't tell nowadays, what with all these Saxon agitators."

"My dear fellah," cried Pellinore, getting excited again, "it's not where the stone is, what, that I'm trying to tell you, but what is written on it, what, where it is."

"What?"

"Why, on its pommel."

"Come on, Pellinore," said Sir Ector. "You just sit quite still with your face to the wall for a minute, and then tell us what you are talkin' about. Take it easy, old boy. No need for hurryin'. You sit still and look at the wall, there's a good chap, and talk as slow as you can."

"Whoso Pulleth Out This Sword of This Stone and Anvil, is Rightwise King Born of All England."

"There are words written on this sword in this stone outside this church," cried King Pellinore piteously, "and these words are as follows. Oh, do try to listen to me, you two, instead of interruptin' all the time about nothin', for it makes a man's head go ever so."

"What are these words?" asked Kay.

"These words say this," said King Pellinore, "so far as I can understand from that old friar of orders gray."

"Go on, do," said Kay, for the King had come to a halt.

"Go on," said Sir Ector, "what do these words on this sword in this anvil in this stone outside this church, say?"

"Some red propaganda, no doubt," remarked Sir Grummore.

King Pellinore closed his eyes tight, extended his arms in both directions, and announced in capital letters, "Whoso Pulleth Out This Sword of This Stone and Anvil, is Rightwise King Born of All England."

"Who said that?" asked Sir Grummore.

"But the sword said it, like I tell you."

"Talkative weapon," remarked Sir Grummore sceptically.

---

9. *Lollards* were follows of John Wycliffe, a religious reformer. They traveled as lay preachers throughout England and Scotland in the fourteenth and fifteenth centuries. White is also slyly mocking people of his own era by having Sir Grummore see or suspect communists nearly everywhere.

10. *Mead* is an alcoholic drink made from honey. Here, it is served in a vessel made from the horn of an animal.

Reading Strategy Analyzing Tone *How would you describe the tone of this selection so far?* **R1**

974 UNIT 5 LEGENDS AND MYTHS

Visual Vocabulary The *pommel* of a sword is a knob at the end of the hilt, or handle.

Literary Element Idiom *What is Sir Ector telling King Pellinore to do? Is this an expression you would expect to hear in medieval times?* **L1**

Literary Element Idiom *What does King Pellinore mean?* **L2**

Additional Support

Skills Practice

RESEARCH: Background Information The gargoyles of the church are a feature of Gothic architecture, which was created in Europe during the Middle Ages, from the mid-1100s to the 1400s. Some great Gothic cathedrals built in England include those in Coventry and Salisbury. Interested students might research the features of Gothic architecture. Have them find out what differentiated it from the earlier Romanesque style. Ask them to define and describe the following terms: pointed arch, ribbed vault, flying buttress, statue column, and gargoyle. **OL**

Armour, 1866. Adolphe von Menzel. Gouache on paper mounted on card.
Hamburger Kunsthalle, Hamburg, Germany.

"It was written on it," cried the King angrily. "Written on it in letters of gold."

"Why didn't you pull it out then?" asked Sir Grummore.

"But I tell you that I wasn't there. All this that I am telling you was told to me by that friar I was telling you of, like I tell you."

"Has this sword with this inscription been pulled out?" inquired Sir Ector.

"No," whispered King Pellinore dramatically. "That's where the whole excitement comes in. They can't pull this sword out at all, although they have all been tryin' like fun, and so they have had to proclaim a tournament all over England, for New Year's Day, so that the man who comes to the tournament and pulls out the sword can be King of all England for ever, what, I say?"

"Oh, father," cried Kay. "The man who pulls that sword out of the stone will be the King of England. Can't we go to the tournament, father, and have a shot?"

"Couldn't think of it," said Sir Ector.

"Long way to London," said Sir Grummore, shaking his head.

"My father went there once," said King Pellinore.

Kay said, "Oh, surely we could go? When I am knighted I shall have to go to a tournament somewhere, and this one happens at just the right date. All the best people will be there, and we should see the famous knights and great kings. It does not matter about the sword, of course, but think of the tournament, probably the greatest there has ever been in Gramarye, and all the things we should see and do. Dear father, let me go to this tourney, if you love me, so that I may bear away the prize of all, in my maiden fight."

Reading Strategy Analyzing Tone *How does the characters' discussion about whether to go to London affect the tone of the story? Consider the casual nature of their comments.* **R₂**

T. H. WHITE **975**

Teach

R₂ Reading Strategy

Analyzing Tone Answer: *The author combines a realistic detail—the difficulty of traveling to London in the Middle Ages— with the otherwise contemporary dialogue of the characters. Therefore, a statement such as "My father went there once" has a humorous effect.* **OL**

★ Viewing the Art

Adolphe von Menzel (1815–1905) was a German painter and printmaker known for the historical themes in his works. **Ask:** What do you think were some benefits and liabilities of wearing armor like this in battle? *(Benefits: protection. Liabilities: very heavy; hot inside; limited visibility; hard to balance on a horse)* **AS**

Differentiated Instruction

Multiple Intelligences—Linguistic
T. H. White referred to current events and used slang that was current in 1938 when he wrote *The Sword in the Stone.* Have students update the dialogue of "Arthur Becomes King" to their own time. Ask them to rewrite the dialogue on page 975 or another portion of dialogue using contemporary language and references. Point out that students do not need to translate each speech. Encourage them to summarize the portion of dialogue and write it in a modern style. Have students read their dialogues aloud. **AL**

Objectives
• To evaluate the author's tone (SE)
• To recognize and understand idioms (SE)
• To research background information (TWE)

975

Teach

L1 Literary Element

Character Have students summarize Kay's arguments for going to London. **Ask:** Is Kay a realistic character? *(Kay says that "all the best people will be there." He wants to see a splendid tournament and famous people. He says people will think poorly of the family if they do not go. The dialogue realistically portrays the arguments of a teenager.)* **OL**

★ Viewing the Art

The armor worn by the knight in the picture is called plate armor. Plate armor is made of large metal plates. The armor was designed so the plates would connect where movement and flexibility was required. Encourage students to notice this feature near the shoulder, elbow, and knees. **AS**

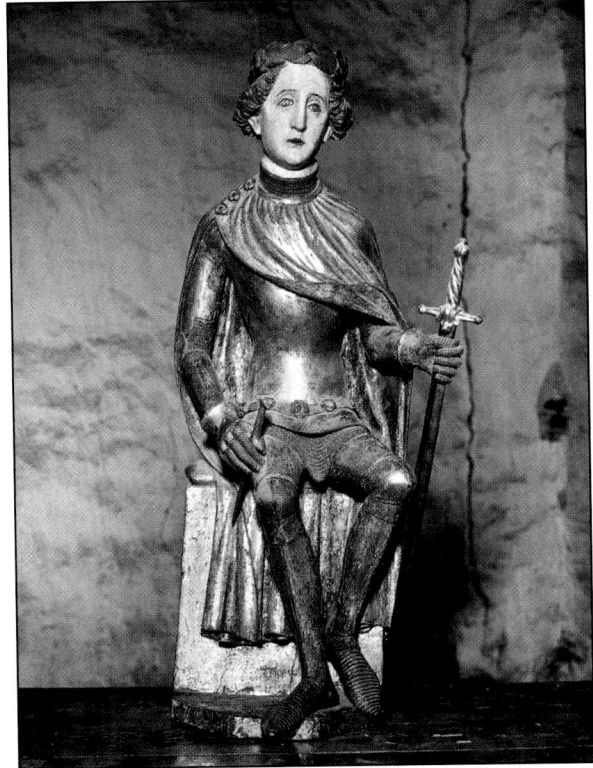

Knight with Armor. Artist unknown. ★
Archivo Iconográfico, S.A.

L1

"But, Kay," said Sir Ector, "I have never been to London."

"All the more reason to go. I believe that anybody who does not go for a tournament like this will be proving that he has no noble blood in his veins. Think what people will say about us, if we do not go and have a shot at that sword. They will say that Sir Ector's family was too **vulgar** and knew it had no chance."

"We all know the family has no chance," said Sir Ector, "that is, for the sword."

"Lot of people in London," remarked Sir Grummore, with a wild surmise. "So they say."

He took a deep breath and goggled at his host with eyes like marbles.

"And shops," added King Pellinore suddenly, also beginning to breathe heavily.

"Dang it!" cried Sir Ector, bumping his horn mug on the table so that it spilled. "Let's all go to London, then, and see the new King!"

They rose up as one man.

"Why shouldn't I be as good a man as my father?" exclaimed King Pellinore.

"Dash it all," cried Sir Grummore. "After all, damn it all, it is the capital!"

"Hurray!" shouted Kay.

"Lord have mercy," said the nurse.

At this moment the Wart came in with Merlyn, and everybody was too excited to notice that, if he had not been grown up now, he would have been on the verge of tears.

"Oh, Wart," cried Kay, forgetting for the moment that he was only addressing his squire, and slipping back into the familiarity of their boyhood. "What do you think? We are all going to London for a great tournament on New Year's Day!"

"Are we?"

"Yes, and you will carry my shield and spears for the jousts, and I shall win the palm[11] of everybody and be a great knight!"

"Well, I am glad we are going," said the Wart, "for Merlyn is leaving us too."

"Oh, we shan't need Merlyn."

"He is leaving us," repeated the Wart.

"Leavin' us?" asked Sir Ector. "I thought it was we that were leavin'?"

"He is going away from the Forest Sauvage."

Vocabulary

vulgar (vul′gər) *adj.* characterized by a lack of good breeding or good taste; common; crude

---

11. Kay hopes to win praise. In ancient times, a *palm* leaf or branch was often used as a symbol of victory or rejoicing.

Additional Support

Skills Practice

WRITING: Using Hyperbole Explain that hyperbole is a figure of speech that uses exaggeration for emphasis or effect. Point out that students probably use hyperbole quite often in everyday conversation, for example, when saying, "That was the hardest test I ever took." Explain that hyperbole can be an effective device to use in writing, if it is not overused. Have students write a paragraph about an exciting event they recently experienced. Ask them to use hyperbole at least twice to emphasize the importance of the occasion or the level of their emotions. Share their paragraphs with the class. **OL**

Sir Ector said, "Come now, Merlyn, what's all this about? I don't understand all this a bit."

"I have come to say Good-bye, Sir Ector," said the old magician.

"Tomorrow my pupil Kay will be knighted, and the next week my other pupil will go away as his squire. I have outlived my usefulness here, and it is time to go."

"Now, now, don't say that," said Sir Ector. "I think you're a jolly useful chap whatever happens. You just stay and teach me, or be the librarian or something. Don't you leave an old man alone, after the children have flown."

"We shall all meet again," said Merlyn. "There is no cause to be sad."

"Don't go," said Kay.

"I must go," replied their tutor. "We have had a good time while we were young, but it is in the nature of Time to fly. There are many things in other parts of the kingdom which I ought to be attending to just now, and it is a specially busy time for me. Come, Archimedes,[12] say Good-bye to the company."

"Good-bye," said Archimedes tenderly to the Wart.

"Good-bye," said the Wart without looking up at all.

"But you can't go," cried Sir Ector, "not without a month's notice."

"Can't I?" replied Merlyn, taking up the position always used by philosophers[13] who propose to dematerialize. He stood on his toes, while Archimedes held tight to his shoulder—began to spin on them slowly like a top—spun faster and faster till he was only a blur of grayish light—and in a few seconds there was no one there at all.

"Good-bye, Wart," cried two faint voices outside the solar window.

"Good-bye," said the Wart for the last time—and the poor fellow went quickly out of the room.

The knighting took place in a whirl of preparations. Kay's **sumptuous** bath had to be set up in the box-room, between two towel-horses and an old box of selected games which contained a worn-out straw dart-board—it was called fléchette[14] in those days—because all the other rooms were full of packing. The nurse spent the whole time constructing new warm pants for everybody, on the principle that the climate of any place outside the Forest Sauvage must be treacherous to the extreme, and, as for the sergeant, he polished all the armor till it was quite brittle and sharpened the swords till they were almost worn away.

At last it was time to set out.

Perhaps, if you happen not to have lived in the Old England of the twelfth century, or whenever it was, and in a remote castle on the borders of the Marches[15] at that, you will find it difficult to imagine the wonders of their journey.

The road, or track, ran most of the time along the high ridges of the hills or downs, and they could look down on either side of them upon the desolate marshes where the snowy reeds sighed, and the ice crackled, and the duck in the red sunsets quacked loud on the winter air. The whole country was like that. Perhaps there would be a moory marsh on one side of the ridge, and a forest of a hundred thousand acres on the other, with all the great branches weighted in white. They could sometimes see a wisp

---

14. In French, *fléchette* (flā shet′) means "a small arrow; dart."
15. *Marches* is a variation of marshes.

Big Idea Acts of Courage *Why might such a journey have required courage to undertake?* **BI**

Vocabulary

sumptuous (sump′ choo əs) *adj.* costly and magnificent

---

12. *Archimedes* (är′ kə mē′ dēz) is Merlyn's pet owl.
13. Magicians and sorcerers were sometimes referred to as *philosophers*—those who pursue wisdom and logical reasoning.

Literary Element Idiom *What does Ector's reaction to Merlyn's departure suggest about Merlyn's character?* **L2**

T. H. WHITE **977**

Teach

L2 Literary Element

Idiom Answer: *Merlyn is well-loved and respected by Ector as well as by the others, especially the Wart.* Jolly *is an idiom that means "very" or "quite."* **OL**

BI Big Idea

Acts of Courage
Answer: *Travel was arduous in the Middle Ages. Travelers faced poor conditions, went by horseback or on foot, and risked assault from thieves. Taking such a journey would have required great bravery.* **OL**

Differentiated Instruction

Role-Playing Students may better understand the plot, characters, and tone of the story if they do a role-play based on the character of Kay. Have pairs of students take turns reading Kay's speeches on pp. 975–976. Encourage them to imagine the tone of voice that Kay would use to try to convince his father to go to the tournament. Then have students take turns acting out a situation in which they try to convince their parents to go somewhere for a special occasion. Have them compare their own speeches to Kay's. **BL**

Objectives
• To recognize and understand idioms (SE)
• To analyze character (TWE)
• To analyze hyperbole (TWE)

Teach

L Literary Element

Idiom Answer: *So many people were in London for the tournament that new arrivals had no place to stay. "Full to the brim" is a modern expression, implying close to overflow, like a pot filled with liquid.* **OL**

BI₁ Big Idea

Acts of Courage Answer: *Nighttime dreams of courageous victory have given way to nervous fears as the day approaches.* **OL**

R Reading Strategy

Connecting Have a volunteer read the description of the tournament scene aloud. **Ask:** *To what type of modern event might the tournament be compared?* *(Students might compare it to a football game, horse race, or Olympic event.)* **OL**

of smoke among the trees, or a huddle of buildings far out among the impassable reeds, and twice they came to quite respectable towns which had several inns to boast of, but on the whole it was an England without civilization. The better roads were cleared of cover for a bow-shot[16] on either side of them, lest the traveller should be slain by hidden thieves.

They slept where they could, sometimes in the hut of some cottager who was prepared to welcome them, sometimes in the castle of a brother knight who invited them to refresh themselves, sometimes in the firelight and fleas of a dirty little hovel with a bush tied to a pole outside it—this was the sign-board used at that time by inns— and once or twice on the open ground, all huddled together for warmth between their grazing chargers. Wherever they went and wherever they slept, the east wind whistled in the reeds, and the geese went over high in the starlight, honking at the stars.

Those were lawless days and it was not safe to leave your house—or even to go to sleep in it. . . .

London was full to the brim. If Sir Ector had not been lucky enough to own a little land in Pie Street, on which there stood a respectable inn, they would have been hard put to it to find a lodging. But he did own it, and as a matter of fact drew most of his dividends from that source, so they were able to get three beds between the five of them. They thought themselves fortunate.

On the first day of the tournament, Sir Kay managed to get them on the way to the lists at least an hour before the jousts[17] could

possibly begin. He had lain awake all night, imagining how he was going to beat the best barons in England, and he had not been able to eat his breakfast. Now he rode at the front of the cavalcade,[18] with pale cheeks, and Wart wished there was something he could do to calm him down.

For country people, who only knew the dismantled tilting[19] ground of Sir Ector's castle, the scene which met their eyes was ravishing. It was a huge green pit in the earth, about as big as the arena at a football match. It lay ten feet lower than the surrounding country, with sloping banks, and the snow had been swept off it. It had been kept warm with straw, which had been cleared off that morning, and now the close-worn grass sparkled green in the white landscape. Round the arena there was a world of color so dazzling and moving and twinkling as to make one blink one's eyes. The wooden grandstands were painted in scarlet and white. The silk pavilions of famous people, pitched on every side, were azure and green and saffron and checkered. The pennons and pennoncells which floated everywhere in the sharp wind were flapping with every color of the rainbow, as they strained and slapped at their flag-poles, and the barrier down the middle of the arena itself was done in chessboard squares of black and white. Most of the **combatants** and their friends had not yet arrived, but one could see from those few who had come how the very people would turn the scene into a bank of flowers, and how the armor would flash, and the scal-

---

16. A *bow-shot* measured about four hundred yards, roughly the distance an old English longbow could shoot an arrow. The roadsides were cleared of trees and shrubs, or *cover*.

17. The *lists* was the field or area in which knights fought tournaments. The *jousts* were formal battles between mounted knights armed with long spears or other weapons.

Literary Element Idiom *Explain the meaning of "full to the brim."* **L**

18. A procession of people on horseback (or in vehicles) is a *cavalcade*.

19. Jousting is also called *tilting*.

Big Idea Acts of Courage *What conflicting emotions is Kay experiencing?* **BI₁**

Vocabulary

combatant (kəm bat′ ənt) n. one trained for, or engaged in, combat

---

Additional Support

Skills Practice

GRAMMAR: Hyphens for Compound Words Remind students that a hyphen is used to separate the parts of some compound words, such as *sister-in-law* and *well-dressed.* Explain that the hyphen in some compound nouns may be omitted if the word becomes common, as in *weekend.*

Have students find five compound words with hyphens in the selection. Ask them to check a dictionary to see whether any words (such as *dart-board*) are hyphenated in the selection but are now written as one word. Have them identify the part of speech of each word they find. **OL** loped sleeves of the heralds[20] jig in the wind, as they raised their brazen trumpets to their lips to shake the fleecy clouds of winter with joyances and fanfares.

"Good heavens!" cried Sir Kay. "I have left my sword at home."

"Can't joust without a sword," said Sir Grummore. "Quite irregular."

"Better go and fetch it," said Sir Ector. "You have time."

"My squire will do," said Sir Kay. "What a damned mistake to make! Here, squire, ride hard back to the inn and fetch my sword. You shall have a shilling if you fetch it in time."

The Wart went as pale as Sir Kay was, and looked as if he were going to strike him. Then he said, "It shall be done, master," and turned his ambling palfrey against the stream of newcomers. He began to push his way toward their hostelry[21] as best he might.

"To offer me money!" cried the Wart to himself. "To look down at this beastly little donkey-affair off his great charger and to call me Squire! Oh, Merlyn, give me patience with the brute, and stop me from throwing his filthy shilling in his face."

When he got to the inn it was closed. Everybody had **thronged** to see the famous

Arthur pulling the sword from the stone (detail). Artist unknown. British Library, London.

tournament, and the entire household had followed after the mob. Those were lawless days and it was not safe to leave your house—or even to go to sleep in it—unless you were certain that it was impregnable. The wooden shutters bolted over the downstairs windows were two inches thick, and the doors were double-barred.

"Now what do I do," asked the Wart, "to earn my shilling?"

He looked ruefully at the blind little inn, and began to laugh.

"Poor Kay," he said. "All that shilling stuff was only because he was scared and miserable, and now he has good cause to be. Well, he shall have a sword of some sort if I have to break into the Tower of London.

"How does one get hold of a sword?" he continued. "Where can I steal one? Could I waylay some knight, even if I am mounted

---

20. At tournaments, *heralds* carried challenges between knights, made proclamations, and trumpeted the stages of competition.
21. Wart is riding a gentle saddle horse *(palfrey)* toward the inn *(hostelry)*.

Big Idea Acts of Courage *What do you learn about the Wart's character from this paragraph?* **BI₂**

Vocabulary

throng (thrông) *v.* to move or gather in large numbers; to crowd together

T. H. WHITE **979**

Teach

BI₂ Big Idea

Acts of Courage Answer: *Wart is not as meek as he may appear; he is bright and honorable and resents being ordered around.* **OL**

★ Viewing the Art

Ask: In the painting, how do the people react to Arthur's pulling the sword from the stone? *(Students should note that the people look surprised and somewhat confused.)* How is their reaction similar to or different from that of Kay and Sir Ector? *(Students may say that Kay and Sir Ector are surprised, but they quickly begin to treat Arthur like royalty.)* **AS**

Differentiated Instruction

Sensory Details The author describes the landscape through which the characters travel on their way to London. Have students point out particularly vivid sensory details, such as "the snowy reeds sigh[ing]" or "the great branches weighted in white." Have students write a description of a particularly vivid landscape they have encountered. Encourage them to use sensory details as T. H. White does to recreate the scene for the reader. Have students read their descriptions aloud. **BL**

Objectives
• To recognize and understand idioms (SE)
• To use hyphens for compound words (TWE)
• To connect to the text (TWE)

Teach

BI₁ **Big Idea**

Acts of Courage Answer:
The Wart gets over his anger and begins to feel sorry for Kay, realizing that he was quite upset about not having a sword for the tournament. Wart's bravery demonstrates the noble person he really is. **OL**

R₁ **Reading Strategy**

Analyzing Tone Answer: *The author plays up the irony and humor of the Wart, casually deciding to pull the sword from the stone, which he assumes is "some sort of war memorial." He becomes more serious as he describes the differences in Wart's perceptions brought on by holding the sword.* **OL**

BI₂ **Big Idea**

Acts of Courage Answer:
The Wart struggles bravely with the sword because of the allegiance he feels toward Kay and Ector. His courage is demonstrated by his selfless attempt to aid in Kay's success. This is yet another sign that Arthur will one day make a good king. **OL**

---

on an ambling pad,[22] and take his weapons by force? There must be some swordsmith or armorer in a great town like this, whose shop would be still open."

He turned his mount and cantered off along the street. There was a quiet churchyard at the end of it, with a kind of square in front of the church door. In the middle of the square there was a heavy stone with an anvil on it, and a fine new sword was stuck through the anvil.

"Well," said the Wart, "I suppose it is some sort of war memorial, but it will have to do. I am sure nobody would grudge Kay a war memorial, if they knew his desperate straits."[23]

He tied his reins round a post of the lych-gate, strode up the gravel path, and took hold of the sword.

"Come, sword," he said. "I must cry your mercy and take you for a better cause.

"This is extraordinary," said the Wart. "I feel strange when I have hold of this sword, and I notice everything much more clearly. Look at the beautiful gargoyles of the church, and of the monastery which it belongs to. See how splendidly all the famous banners in the aisle are waving. How nobly that yew[24] holds up the red flakes of its timbers to worship God. How clean the snow is. I can smell something like fetherfew and sweet briar—and is it music that I hear?"

Visual Vocabulary
A *lych-gate* (lich´ āt) is a roofed gateway to a churchyard.

---

22. To *waylay* is to lie in wait for and attack. Wart's *pad*, or pad horse, is trained for slow, steady road travel and would not do well in a quick getaway.
23. *Straits* is a troublesome or difficult situation.
24. The church's *gargoyles* are ornaments in the form of outlandish creatures, its *monastery* is a residence for monks, and the *yew* is a type of evergreen tree.

Big Idea Acts of Courage *Why is the Wart willing to go to such lengths to obtain a sword for Kay?* **BI₁**

Reading Strategy Analyzing Tone *How would you describe the author's tone as the Wart decides to pull the sword from the stone and attempts to do so?* **R₁**

It was music, whether of pan-pipes or of recorders, and the light in the churchyard was so clear, without being dazzling, that one could have picked a pin out twenty yards away.

"There is something in this place," said the Wart. "There are people. Oh, people, what do you want?"

Nobody answered him, but the music was loud and the light beautiful.

"People," cried the Wart, "I must take this sword. It is not for me, but for Kay. I will bring it back."

There was still no answer, and Wart turned back to the anvil. He saw the golden letters, which he did not read, and the jewels on the pommel, flashing in the lovely light.

"Come, sword," said the Wart.

He took hold of the handles with both hands, and strained against the stone. There was a melodious consort[25] on the recorders, but nothing moved.

The Wart let go of the handles, when they were beginning to bite into the palms of his hands, and stepped back, seeing stars.

"It is well fixed," he said.

He took hold of it again and pulled with all his might. The music played more strongly, and the light all about the churchyard glowed like amethysts;[26] but the sword still stuck.

"Oh, Merlyn," cried the Wart, "help me to get this weapon."

There was a kind of rushing noise, and a long chord played along with it. All round the churchyard there were hundreds of old friends. They rose over the church wall all together, like the Punch and Judy[27] ghosts of remembered days, and there were badgers and nightingales and vulgar crows and hares and wild geese and falcons and fishes and

---

25. Here, *consort* means "a harmony of sounds."
26. The light was the violet color of quartz crystals called *amethysts*.
27. The main characters in a puppet show, *Punch and Judy*, have been popular with English audiences for centuries.

Big Idea Acts of Courage *Why does the Wart try so hard to pull the sword from the stone?* **BI₂**

Additional Support

Skills Practice

READING: Scanning Remind students that in scanning, a reader moves his or her eyes quickly over a text to find specific words or phrases. Have students practice scanning. Time them for one minute as they scan page 981 to find each different animal mentioned. Point out that animal names appear throughout the page. When they finish, have students share the animal names they found. **OL**

dogs and dainty unicorns and solitary wasps and corkindrills and hedgehogs and griffins and the thousand other animals he had met. They loomed round the church wall, the lovers and helpers of the Wart, and they all spoke solemnly in turn. Some of them had come from the banners in the church, where they were painted in heraldry,[28] some from the waters and the sky and the fields about—but all, down to the smallest shrew mouse, had come to help on account of love. Wart felt his power grow.

"Put your back into it," said a Luce (or pike[29]) off one of the heraldic banners, "as you once did when I was going to snap you up. Remember that power springs from the nape of the neck."

"What about those forearms," asked a Badger gravely, "that are held together by a chest? Come along, my dear embryo,[30] and find your tool."

A Merlin sitting at the top of the yew tree cried out, "Now then, Captain Wart, what is the first law of the foot? I thought I once heard something about never letting go?"

"Don't work like a stalling woodpecker," urged a Tawny Owl affectionately. "Keep up a steady effort, my duck, and you will have it yet."

A white-front said, "Now, Wart, if you were once able to fly the great North Sea,

A Joust Between Two Knights, late 15th century. Artist unknown. British Library, London.

surely you can coordinate a few little wing-muscles here and there? Fold your powers together, with the spirit of your mind, and it will come out like butter. Come along, Homo sapiens, for all we humble friends of yours are waiting here to cheer."

The Wart walked up to the great sword for the third time. He put out his right hand softly and drew it out as gently as from a scabbard.[31]

There was a lot of cheering, a noise like a hurdy-gurdy[32] which went on and on. In the

---

28. The animals in *heraldry* are painted on banners showing coats of arms, designs that represent noble families and their histories.
29. *Luce* is an old name for the pike, a fish that can grow to more than four feet long and that normally eats other fish.
30. The fertilized egg of an organism is an *embryo,* but the word can also refer to someone or something in the beginning stage of development.

Literary Element   Idiom *What is the Luce telling the Wart to do?* **L**

---

31. A *scabbard* is a case for the blade of a sword.
32. The *hurdy-gurdy* is a musical instrument shaped somewhat like a guitar but played by turning a hand crank that causes a revolving wheel to make the strings vibrate.

Reading Strategy   Analyzing Tone *At the climactic moment when the Wart draws the sword from the stone, what do you notice about the author's tone?* **R₂**

T. H. WHITE   **981**

Teach

L Literary Element

Idiom Answer: *The Luce is telling the Wart that he should use his back as leverage in pulling the sword from the stone. This is an example of another modern idiom.* **OL**

R₂ Reading Strategy

Analyzing Tone Answer: *The tone switches from playful and humorous to quiet and almost reverential.* **OL**

★ Viewing the Art

Encourage students to imagine the conversations among the spectators or the thoughts of the jousters in the painting. **Ask:** What might they be thinking about, feeling, wondering, or fearing? Have students write out a dialogue between two spectators or an internal monologue of one of the knights. *(Students' responses should reflect details they see in the painting or learn from the text.)* **AS**

Objectives
• To evaluate the author's tone (SE)
• To recognize and understand idioms (SE)
• To scan a literary work to improve comprehension (TWE)

Teach

L Literary Element

Idiom Answer: *The people are making a lot of noise cheering as the tournament continues.* **OL**

★ Viewing the Art

Jean Froissart (1333–1407) is primarily known as a historian and a poet. His poetry often praised the heroic deeds of knights, and his historical work is often acclaimed for providing an accurate depiction of what life was like in Europe during the fourteenth century. **AS**

A Tournament in London: Duel at the Fence, 14th century. Jean Froissart. Bibliotheque de l'Arsenal, Paris.

middle of this noise, after a long time, he saw Kay and gave him the sword. The people at the tournament were making a frightful row.

"But this is not my sword," said Sir Kay.

"It was the only one I could get," said the Wart. "The inn was locked."

"It is a nice-looking sword. Where did you get it?"

"I found it stuck in a stone, outside a church."

> **Literary Element** Idiom *What are the people at the tournament doing?* **L**

Sir Kay had been watching the tilting nervously, waiting for his turn. He had not paid much attention to his squire.

"That is a funny place to find one," he said.

"Yes, it was stuck through an anvil."

"What?" cried Sir Kay, suddenly rounding upon him. "Did you just say this sword was stuck in a stone?"

"It was," said the Wart. "It was a sort of war memorial."

Sir Kay stared at him for several seconds in amazement, opened his mouth, shut it again, licked his lips, then turned his back

982 UNIT 5 LEGENDS AND MYTHS

Additional Support

Skills Practice

LISTENING AND SPEAKING:

Expressing Tone Point out that the author expresses humor, suspense, irony, and respect at various points in the selection. Have students choose a passage that expresses a specific tone and prepare a reading of it, either alone or with one or more classmates.

They may wish to consider one of the humorous exchanges between Sir Ector, King Pellinore, and Sir Grummore at the beginning of the story or the Wart's emotional speeches at the end of the selection. Encourage students to use vocal tone and emphasis to express the appropriate literary tone. **OL**

982

and plunged through the crowd. He was looking for Sir Ector, and the Wart followed after him.

"Father," cried Sir Kay, "come here a moment."

"Yes, my boy," said Sir Ector. "Splendid falls these professional chaps do manage. Why, what's the matter, Kay? You look as white as a sheet."

"Do you remember that sword which the King of England would pull out?"

"Yes."

"Well, here it is. I have it. It is in my hand. I pulled it out."

Sir Ector did not say anything silly. He looked at Kay and he looked at the Wart. Then he stared at Kay again, long and lovingly, and said, "We will go back to the church."

"Now then, Kay," he said, when they were at the church door. He looked at his first-born kindly, but straight between the eyes. "Here is the stone, and you have the sword. It will make you the King of England. You are my son that I am proud of, and always will be, whatever you do. Will you promise me that you took it out by your own might?"

Kay looked at his father. He also looked at the Wart and at the sword.

Then he handed the sword to the Wart quite quietly.

He said, "I am a liar. Wart pulled it out."

As far as the Wart was concerned, there was a time after this in which Sir Ector kept telling him to put the sword back into the stone—which he did—and in which Sir Ector and Kay then vainly tried to take it out. The Wart took it out for them, and stuck it back again once or twice. After this, there was another time which was more painful.

He saw that his dear guardian[33] was looking quite old and powerless, and that he

was kneeling down with difficulty on a gouty knee.

"Sir," said Sir Ector, without looking up, although he was speaking to his own boy.

"Please do not do this, father," said the Wart, kneeling down also. "Let me help you up, Sir Ector, because you are making me unhappy."

"Nay, nay, my lord," said Sir Ector, with some very feeble old tears. "I was never your father nor of your blood, but I wote well ye are of an higher blood than I wend[34] ye were."

"Plenty of people have told me you are not my father," said the Wart, "but it does not matter a bit."

"Sir," said Sir Ector humbly, "will ye be my good and gracious lord when ye are King?"

"Don't!" said the Wart.

"Sir," said Sir Ector, "I will ask no more of you but that you will make my son, your foster-brother, Sir Kay, seneschal[35] of all your lands?"

Kay was kneeling down too, and it was more than the Wart could bear.

"Oh, do stop," he cried. "Of course he can be seneschal, if I have got to be this King, and, oh, father, don't kneel down like that, because it breaks my heart. Please get up, Sir Ector, and don't make everything so horrible. Oh, dear, oh, dear, I wish I had never seen that filthy sword at all."

And the Wart also burst into tears. ❧

---

33. Merlyn had arranged for Sir Ector to be Arthur's *guardian* and to raise him as his son. Neither Ector nor Wart knew that the baby's biological father was King Uther.

34. *Wote* and *wend* are past-tense forms of two obsolete verbs—*wot*, meaning "to know," and *ween*, meaning "to suppose, believe, or expect."

35. In medieval times, the *seneschal* (sen' ə shəl) managed the king's estate, ran his household, and sometimes also had official state duties or a military command.

Big Idea Acts of Courage *Will the Wart be a good king? Explain.* **BI₂**

Reading Strategy Analyzing Tone *What is the author's tone at the end of the story?* **R**

Big Idea Acts of Courage *In your opinion, is Kay brave? Why or why not?* **BI₁**

T. H. WHITE **983**

Reading in the Real World

Citizenship In "Arthur Becomes King," White explores the qualities and characteristics that make a great leader. Have students read newspaper and magazine articles about current world leaders and take note of the qualities and characteristics that each leader exhibits. Have students share their findings with the class and analyze what characteristics are required to be a leader in today's world. Have them think about which of today's world leaders might be considered "great" leaders. **OL**

Objectives
- To recognize and understand idioms (SE)
- To evaluate the author's tone (SE)
- To express tone orally (TWE)

Assess

1. Students should refer to specific incidents in the story.

2. (a)The king left no heir. (b)They are sad at first, but then they grow curious about who will succeed him.

3. (a)The Wart announces that Merlyn is leaving. (b)The Wart has an affectionate relationship with Merlyn and sees him as his mentor. His attitude is shown by his emotional reaction when Merlyn leaves and his calling upon Merlyn when he has difficulties.

4. (a)The inn where they are staying is locked. (b)It is the Wart's duty, and it is not in his nature to cause trouble by refusing an order.

5. (a)Kay is unable to make a false promise to his trusting father. (b) Arthur's silence suggests that he is wise and tactful and not power hungry, traits that promise to make him a good leader.

6. Repetition of the music and the light emphasizes the importance of the event and evokes suspense.

7. To show that Arthur will be a good leader because he was raised well

8. Yes, because becoming king was an enormous step and people felt great respect for their king

---

RESPONDING AND THINKING CRITICALLY

Respond

1. How did you react to the Wart's behavior at the beginning of the excerpt? At the middle? At the end? Explain.

Recall and Interpret

2. (a)Why does the death of King Uther throw the country into a state of excitement? (b)What effect does the death of the old king have on Sir Ector and his companions? Explain.

3. (a)What news does the Wart announce to Sir Ector and Kay? (b)What can you infer about the Wart's relationship with Merlyn? Support your answer with details from the story.

4. (a)Why is the Wart unable to bring Sir Kay's sword back to him? (b)Why does the Wart silently obey Sir Kay's order to fetch his sword?

5. (a)Sir Kay claims that he pulled the sword from the stone. Why does he change his story? (b)What does the Wart's response to this suggest to you about his character and future leadership?

Analyze and Evaluate

6. How does White's use of repetition in the first churchyard scene affect your appreciation of the story? Explain.

7. Why did White portray Sir Ector as a wise and loving father?

8. Do Sir Ector's and Sir Kay's reactions to the Wart's sudden "promotion" seem true to life? Explain.

Connect

9. **Big Idea** **Acts of Courage** In your opinion, what is White saying about heroism and acts of courage?

DAILY LIFE AND CULTURE

Feudalism and Chivalry in England

By about the eleventh century, a social, economic, and political system referred to as feudalism arose in medieval England. The feudal system revolved around one fundamental principle: loyalty and service in exchange for land. Lesser nobility usually pledged their services to their stronger counterparts. These nobles were obligated to supply a certain number of armed knights in exchange for the land that they had received from the lord above them in the feudal hierarchy. Peasants provided agricultural labor in return for protection from a feudal lord. The strict hierarchy was often oppressive for the underclass, as its members had little chance for advancement or for improving their quality of life.

The concept of chivalry developed out of the feudal system's debt of loyalty. The term *chivalry* referred to a code of knightly conduct in which a knight owed loyalty not only to his feudal lord, but also to God and his lady. The chivalrous knight was expected to display the

following virtues: honor, loyalty, piety, bravery, courtesy, and chastity. Eventually, chivalry became more evident in public entertainment—such as jousting tournaments—than in military service.

1. What evidence of the feudal system do you see in "Arthur Becomes King"?

2. What evidence of chivalry do you see?

---

9. Students may say that a person becomes a hero by acting nobly. Acts of courage sometimes entail controlling one's impulses and trying to empathize with those who treat one shabbily.

Daily Life and Culture

1. Possible answers: the noble titles of Sirs Kay, Ector, and Grummore; the fact that Kay is knighted; the fact that Arthur was Kay's squire, which shows the hierarchy; and the existence of the castle of Forest Sauvage

2. Possible answers: the jousting tournament in London, the existence of knights, and Sir Ector's plea that the Wart will be his lord when he is king

Literary Element Idiom

Idioms differ according to language and culture. Native speakers of English, for instance, use expressions such as "take it with a grain of salt" and "wrap it up," but these idioms would be difficult to translate for a foreign visitor learning English, because no direct translation exists. Americans might even have to work to "translate" idioms commonly found in British English, due to differences in vocabulary.

1. Why does White use more contemporary idioms in his retelling of the Arthurian legend?

2. In your opinion, do these idioms enhance or detract from the story? Explain your answer.

Review: Legend

As you learned on pages 968–969, a **legend** is a story usually based on actual events that have been exaggerated over time. Many legends are based on the lives and exploits of kings, especially those who lived at a time when stories were more likely to be told orally.

Partner Activity With a classmate, use the library or Internet to research other legendary kings of England, Scotland, Wales, and Ireland. Select two or three stories about legendary kings and then compare and contrast them with what you know of the Arthurian legend. Make a chart like the one below to organize your points. Share your findings with the rest of the class.

Legendary King	Similarities with Arthurian Legends	Differences with Arthurian Legends
Macbeth, King of Scots from AD 1040	Legend of his life inspired the play *Macbeth*; legend of Arthur has inspired many literary works	Macbeth obtained the throne by murdering King Duncan; Arthur became king through honest and valiant means
Conn Cétchathach, Irish king in the second century AD	Whether Conn was an actual historic figure or a literary invention is debatable; scholars are unsure whether Arthur was a historic person	

Reading Strategy Analyzing Tone

The author's **tone**, or attitude toward his or her subject, can be revealed through elements such as word choice, punctuation, sentence structure, and figures of speech.

1. Describe the overall tone of "Arthur Becomes King."

2. List three details that help convey the tone.

Vocabulary Practice

Practice with Context Clues Use context clues to determine the meaning of each boldfaced word.

1. When frustrated, King Pellinore sometimes spoke **petulantly**.
   a. peevishly **b.** forcefully

2. Some of the spectators acted in a **vulgar** way, pushing and shoving to get a better view.
   a. considerate **b.** crass

3. The knight wore **sumptuous** armor and a cloak with gold embroidery.
   a. rusty **b.** splendid

4. The rules of the tournament forbade the **combatants** to attack a fallen warrior.
   a. fighters **b.** allies

5. Like rock concerts today, many people **thronged** medieval tournaments.
   a. crowded **b.** refused

Academic Vocabulary

Here are two words from the vocabulary list on page R82. These words will help you think, write, and talk about the selection.

despite (di spīt′) *prep.* in spite of; regardless of

grant (grant) *v.* to allow or consent to something

Practice and Apply
1. Why does the Wart try to pull out the sword a third time, **despite** his previous failed attempts?
2. What request does Sir Ector ask Arthur to **grant** at the end of the story?

T. H. WHITE **985**

Assess

Literary Element

1. White uses modern-day expressions to instill a humorous tone that serves to lighten the story and to make the characters more accessible to the modern reader.

2. Students may say that the idioms enhance the story by creating the humorous tone.

Review: Legend

Students might enjoy reading more about one of the kings they learn about in their research. Encourage them to find a novel, a play, or a nonfiction book in the school library, and to add to their charts as they extend their knowledge.

Reading Strategy

1. The overall tone is one of lighthearted humor.

2. Students might select any of the idioms or the conversations between King Pellinore and Sirs Ector and Grummore.

Vocabulary

1. a **2.** b **3.** b **4.** a **5.** a

Academic Vocabulary

1. The Wart persists because he knows he must find a sword for Kay.

2. Sir Ector asks that Arthur make Kay his seneschal, the manager of a king's estate.

Assess

Writing About Literature

Students' essays should

- Include specific traits that Arthur demonstrates
- Refer to incidents in the story that indicate Arthur's traits

Internet Connection

Encourage students to pay special attention to the similarities and differences between the different versions.

White's Language and Style

Encourage students to read aloud both the original dialogue and their revised version. This will help them to hear that although the revised version may be more grammatical, it makes the speech sound less natural and more stilted. It may even detract from the believability of the characters.

Revising Check

Some students may find no fragments in their work. You may wish to have these students assist others in correcting their fragments.

Writing About Literature

Analyze Characters No one is more surprised than Wart to find that he is to be king of England. Does Wart have what it takes to be a good king? Review the selection for evidence that young Arthur possesses royal qualities and then write a brief analysis of his character. Include quotations from the text to support your analysis.

Before you begin drafting, brainstorm a list of "kingly" traits that you detect in the Wart. Use this list to develop your analysis of the Wart.

START

Introduction → Present your opinion of Wart's character in a concise thesis statement.

Body Paragraph(s) → Add supporting evidence. Refer to the "kingly traits" you brainstormed.

Conclusion → Briefly summarize your position and consider offering a related insight.

FINISH

After completing your draft, meet with a peer reviewer to provide feedback on each other's work. Then proofread and edit your draft for errors in spelling, grammar, and punctuation.

Internet Connection

Arthurian legend has developed over hundreds of years, and many variations of the stories exist. Using the Internet, find other legends about King Arthur and share them with the class.

Literature Online Web Activities For eFlashcards, Selection Quick Checks, and other Web activities, go to www.glencoe.com.

White's Language and Style

Using Fragments for Effect A sentence fragment is a word group written as a sentence but lacking either a subject, a verb, or both. Because sentence fragments are grammatically incorrect and often difficult to understand, writers tend to avoid using them. However, authors may use sentence fragments in dialogue to help create the sound of natural speech. For example, in "Arthur Becomes King," Sir Kay expresses a desire to go to London. "Long way to London," Sir Grummore replies. His statement lacks a subject and a verb, but it is the kind of clipped, fragmentary comment you might hear in actual speech. Note the following sentence fragments that occur in the dialogue in "Arthur Becomes King":

Sentence fragment	What it lacks
"Talkative weapon," remarked Sir Grunmore sceptically.	subject, verb
"Couldn't think of it," said Sir Ector.	subject
"And shops," added King Pellinore. . . .	subject, verb

Partner Activity Copy a passage from "Arthur Becomes King" that includes several sentence fragments. With a partner, replace these fragments with complete sentences. Then discuss how this changes the effect of the dialogue.

Revising Check

Fragments While sentence fragments can be effective in dialogue, they are not appropriate in formal writing. With a partner, read through your character analysis of Arthur, identify any sentence fragments, and turn them into complete sentences.

Literature Online

Web Activities Have students access the Web site for interactive activities that will help them assess their understanding of the selection.

Grammar Workshop

Sentence Structure

Using Main and Subordinate Clauses

"Let me help you up, Sir Ector, because you are making me unhappy."
— T. H. White, from "Arthur Becomes King"

Connecting to Literature In "Arthur Becomes King," T. H. White uses sentences that include both main and subordinate clauses. A **main,** or **independent, clause** has a subject and a predicate, expresses a complete thought, and can stand alone as a sentence. A **subordinate,** or **dependent, clause** has a subject and a predicate, but does not express a complete thought, and thus cannot stand alone as a sentence. In the sentence above, "Let me help you up, Sir Ector" is the main clause, and "because you are making me unhappy" is the subordinate clause.

Here is how to identify main and subordinate clauses and turn them into complete sentences.

Main clause *The story was written by T. H. White*

Explanation Because the clause has a subject—*story*—and a predicate—*was written*—and expresses a complete thought, it can stand alone as a complete sentence.

Solution To create a sentence, add a period to the main clause.

The story was written by T. H. White.

Subordinate clause *Because the story was interesting*

Explanation The clause has a subject—*story*—and a predicate—*was*—but does not express a complete thought.

Solution To create a sentence, combine the subordinate clause with a main clause.

Because the story was interesting, <u>*I wanted to read more of the author's work.*</u>

Exercise

Rewrite the following sentences to make complete sentences. If the sentence is already complete, write "correct."

1. Since the boy was able to pull the sword out easily, unlike the others who tried.

2. While it was clear that he was the new king.

3. Sir Ector and the other men were amazed by the feat.

4. After Wart pulled the sword.

> ▶ **Vocabulary Terms**
>
> A **main clause** has a subject and a predicate, expresses a complete thought, and can stand alone as a sentence. A **subordinate clause** has a subject and a predicate, but does not express a complete thought and cannot stand alone as a sentence.
>
> ▶ **Test-Taking Tip**
>
> To identify main and subordinate clauses on a test, separate the clause from the rest of the sentence. If it makes sense on its own, it is a main clause.
>
> ▶ **Language Handbook**
>
> For more on main and subordinate clauses, see the Language Handbook, pp. R46–R60.

Literature Online
eWorkbooks To link to the Grammar and Language eWorkbook, go to www.glencoe.com.

> **OBJECTIVES**
> • Understand subordinate and main clauses.
> • Recognize and correct errors in sentence structure.

Grammar Workshop

Sentence Structure

Focus

On the board, write: Kay will go to a tournament. When Kay is knighted. **Ask:** Which is a main clause and which is a subordinate clause? *(First is a main clause; second is a subordinate clause.)* Have students combine the clauses to make a complex sentence. *(Kay will go to a tournament when he is knighted.)* Stress that dependent clauses cannot stand alone.

Teach

Combining Sentences
Students should combine pairs of sentences by making the less important idea into a subordinate clause, with a relative pronoun or a subordinating conjunction, and the more important idea the main clause. For example, "T. H. White wrote novels about King Arthur. T. H. White was born in India in 1906." *(T. H. White, who was born in India in 1906, wrote novels about King Arthur.)* **OL**

Assess

Possible rewrites:

1. Since the boy was able to pull the sword out easily, unlike the others who tried, he became king.

2. While it was clear that he was the new king, Wart was unhappy.

3. *Correct*

4. After Wart pulled the sword, Sir Kay and Sir Ector knelt.

English Language Coach

Relative Pronouns Have students practice identifying the relative pronouns *that, which, who,* and *whose.* Caution English learners that subordinate clauses sometimes omit the relative pronoun. As an example, write on the board: *The sword he carried is magical.* Have students locate more examples. **EL**

Literature Online
eWorkbooks Have students access the Web site for more practice with main and subordinate clauses.

Focus

from *Le Morte d'Arthur*

MEET SIR THOMAS MALORY

Who wrote one of the most famous works in literary history, *Le Morte d'Arthur*? For many years, scholars have argued about the answer to this question. Considered by some to be the first novel and largely based on French poems of Arthurian legends, *Le Morte d'Arthur* is said to exist in two versions. One is the printed version that William Caxton published in 1485, of which one complete, original copy still exists. The other is a mysterious manuscript discovered at Winchester College in 1934. Known as the Winchester text, its relationship to the Caxton manuscript is not clear. The greatest difference between the two manuscripts is that Caxton broke the story into twenty-one books, whereas the Winchester text is divided into ten parts of five larger units.

"I bestow on Arthur God's blessing and my own, and Arthur shall succeed to the throne. . . ."

—Sir Thomas Malory,
from *Le Morte d'Arthur*

The Knight Prisoner Because a "syr Thomas Maleore knight" is named in the colophon, or inscription, of the 1485 version, Sir Thomas Malory is often identified as the author. Malory spent the first part of his life as a soldier and then as a country gentleman. He inherited estates from his father, married, fathered a son, and in 1445 became a member of Parliament. Thereafter, however, his life seemed to spiral out of control. Malory was cited in a multitude of lawsuits from the time period; he was charged with murder, robbery, and an attack on a religious institution, the

Abbey of Coombe. In one incident, he was accused of stealing seven cows, two calves, 335 sheep, and a farmer's cart. During the last twenty years of his life, Malory served at least four prison sentences for his crimes. In fact, he likely completed *Le Morte d'Arthur* while in prison during 1469 and 1470. At the end of his retelling of the epic tale, Malory describes himself as a "knight prisoner" and urges his readers to pray for his safe release. Ironically, King Arthur's world of heroism and chivalry stands in stark contrast to the life that Malory lived.

A Lasting Work of Art Malory's version of the legend has had the most influence and longevity; the book has remained in print since its first publication, more than five hundred years ago. According to scholar Edmund Reiss, "Many writers had worked on the French Arthurian prose romances between the thirteenth and fifteenth centuries; there had been adaptations of it in Spain and Germany. All this is now dead and buried, and Malory alone stands as a rock, defying all changes of taste and style and morals; not as a grand paradox of nature, but as a lasting work of art."

Sir Thomas Malory was born about 1405 and died in 1471.

Selection Skills

Reading Skills

- Analyzing Plot (SE pp. 989–1008)
- Identifying Author's Purpose (TWE p. 994)
- Summarizing (TWE p. 1000)

from Le Morte d'Arthur

Literary Elements

- Dialogue (SE pp. 989–1007)
- Hero (SE p. 1007)

Vocabulary Skills

- Word Origins (SE p. 1008)

Listening/Speaking/Viewing Skills

- Retelling a Legend (TWE p. 1004)

Writing Skills/Grammar

- Writing a Compare and Contrast Essay (SE p. 1008)
- Using Commas (TWE p. 998)
- *Who* and *Whom* (TWE p. 1006)

Connecting to the Story

Le Morte d'Arthur is a series of stories about knights and their brave deeds. Before you read the story, think about the following questions:

- Who is your hero? What makes that person a hero to you?
- Who do you think will be remembered as a hero five hundred years from now?

Building Background

In late medieval Europe (the twelfth to fifteenth centuries), knights and noblemen tried to behave according to a strict code of chivalry. Chivalry is derived from the French word *chevalier*, meaning "horseman." A chivalrous knight, however, was more than a skilled rider. He also strove to be generous to the weak and courteous to women.

Le Morte d'Arthur is a series of stories about King Arthur and the Knights of the Round Table. In episodes that take place between "The Tale of King Arthur" and "The Tale of Sir Launcelot du Lake," King Arthur marries Gwynevere. Her father gives Arthur the Round Table, and Arthur seeks to fill its 150 seats with knights. Arthur and his bravest knights, including Launcelot, go to Rome to fight Lucius. The Knights of the Round Table, especially Launcelot, show great strength and courage, defeating the Romans against huge odds.

Setting Purposes for Reading

Big Idea Acts of Courage

As you read this selection, notice how Malory's legend provides evidence that Arthur is a courageous hero.

Literary Element Dialogue

Dialogue is conversation between characters in a literary work. Dialogue can contribute to characterization, create mood, advance the plot, and develop theme. Pay careful attention to the use of dialogue as you read this legend.

- See Literary Terms Handbook, p. R5.

Literature Online **Interactive Literary Elements Handbook** To review or learn more about the literary elements, go to www.glencoe.com.

OBJECTIVES
In studying this selection, you will focus on the following:
- understanding the author's use of dialogue
- analyzing plot
- analyzing characteristics of heroes in works of literature
- writing to compare and contrast characters

Reading Strategy Analyzing Plot

When you **analyze plot**, you critically examine the sequence of events in a narrative work. Most plots develop around a conflict, or a struggle between opposing forces. A legend's plot may consist of a series of random conflicts.

Reading Tip: Taking Notes Compare and contrast the plot of *Le Morte d'Arthur* with the plot of a short story you have read.

LE MORTE D'ARTHUR — series of conflicts | characters, conflict | [SHORT STORY TITLE] — one main conflict

Vocabulary

abashed (ə basht′) *adj.* self-conscious; embarrassed or ashamed; p. 992 *Mike was abashed about his too-short haircut.*

inscribe (in skrīb′) *v.* to write, carve, or mark on a surface; p. 994 *The wedding band was inscribed with the couple's initials.*

ignoble (ig nō′ bəl) *adj.* of low birth or position; without honor or worth; p. 995 *They were shocked to discover that the charming young man had such ignoble beginnings.*

tumultuous (too mul′ chōō əs) *adj.* wildly excited, confused, or agitated; p. 995 *The horse galloped away, taking the girl on a tumultuous ride.*

prowess (prou′ is) *n.* great ability or skill; p. 996 *Her prowess on the violin was evident as she played the solo.*

Focus

Summary

In "The Tale of King Arthur," Sir Thomas Malory tells the legend of how Arthur became king by pulling a sword from a stone. As an infant, Merlin raises Arthur without informing him of his noble background. In "The Tale of Sir Launcelot du Lake," Sir Launcelot has a series of adventures while maintaining his integrity as an honorable knight. He becomes the most famous knight in King Arthur's court.

V Vocabulary

Vocabulary File Say: Add these words and definitions to your vocabulary file. For each word, include a sentence that gives you an example of how to use the word. **OL** Students with English language needs should include the pronunciations of these words in their files. **EL**

Literature Online

Literary Elements Have students access the Web site to improve their understanding of dialogue.

SIR THOMAS MALORY **989**

  Selection Resources

Print Materials
- Unit 5 Resources (Fast File), pp. 21–23
- Leveled Vocabulary Development, p. 70
- Selection and Unit Assessments, pp. 165–166
- Selection Quick Checks, p. 83

Transparencies
- Bellringer Options Transparencies: Selection Focus Transparency 40 Daily Language Practice Transparency 84
- Literary Elements Transparency 17

Technology
- TeacherWorks Plus™ CD-ROM
- StudentWorks Plus™ CD-ROM
- Presentation Plus!™ CD-ROM
- Literature Online, glencoe.com
- Online Student Edition, mhln.com
- ExamView® Assessment Suite CD-ROM
- Vocabulary PuzzleMaker CD-ROM
- Listening Library, disc 2 track 17

Acts of Courage Say: Keep the following questions in mind as you read: What situations develop that demand courage from the characters? How do different characters display courage? (*The various battles, captures, and threats from opponents all demand courage. Sir Launcelot confronts powerful knights and rescues many people. King Uther puts himself in a dangerous situation to inspire his people. Several knights prefer to face death rather than give in to their opponents.*) **OL**

★ Viewing the Art

Point out that Arthur is pictured on the left, while Launcelot is pictured on the right. **Ask:** What can you tell about the differences between these characters based on how they are pictured? (*Arthur is a king, while Launcelot is a knight dressed for battle. Arthur appears thoughtful, while Launcelot appears ready to face his enemies.*) **AS**

Readability Scores
Dale-Chall: 6.7
DRP: 60
Lexile: 1110

 from

Le Morte d'Arthur

The Tale of King Arthur

King Arthur and Sir Lancelot, 1862. William Morris. Stained Glass. Bradford Art Galleries and Museums, West Yorkshire, UK. ★

Sir Thomas Malory
retold by Keith Baines

990 UNIT 5   LEGENDS AND MYTHS

Additional Support

Leveled Reading
An adapted version of this selection is available on page 192 of *Jamestown Literature: An Adapted Reader*, grade 10.

Skills Practice

READING: Predicting Ask students to look at the illustration on the first page, the title, and the subtitle and predict what kinds of events will be described in the selection. Remind students that this is a legend. Ask them what events or situations they expect to read about in a legend. If some students are familiar with the legends of King Arthur, ask them which events they expect Malory to focus on in this selection.

Have students review and adjust their predictions as they read. **OL**

King Uther[1] Pendragon,[2] ruler of all Britain, had been at war for many years with the Duke of Tintagil in Cornwall when he was told of the beauty of Lady Igraine,[3] the duke's wife. Thereupon he called a truce and invited the duke and Igraine to his court, where he prepared a feast for them, and where, as soon as they arrived, he was formally reconciled to the duke through the good offices of his courtiers.

In the course of the feast, King Uther grew passionately desirous of Igraine and, when it was over, begged her to become his paramour.[4] Igraine, however, being as naturally loyal as she was beautiful, refused him.

"I suppose," said Igraine to her husband, the duke, when this had happened, "that the king arranged this truce only because he wanted to make me his mistress. I suggest that we leave at once, without warning, and ride overnight to our castle." The duke agreed with her, and they left the court secretly.

The king was enraged by Igraine's flight and summoned his privy council.[5] They advised him to command the fugitives' return under threat of renewing the war; but when this was done, the duke and Igraine defied his summons. He then warned them that they could expect to be dragged from their castle within six weeks.

Merlin the Magician, c.1352 Ms. Add. Meladius, 12228, fol. 202v. British Library, London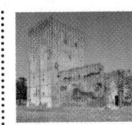

The duke manned and provisioned[6] his two strongest castles: Tintagil for Igraine, and Terrabyl, which was useful for its many sally ports, for himself. Soon King Uther arrived with a huge army and laid siege to Terrabyl; but despite the ferocity of the fighting, and the numerous casualties suffered by both sides, neither was able to gain a decisive victory.

Visual Vocabulary
Sally ports are gates or openings in castle walls through which a ruler's troops could make sudden attacks.

---

1. *Uther* (o͞o′ thər)
2. In ancient Britain, *Pendragon*, meaning "supreme leader," was a title attached after a ruler's name.
3. *Igraine* (ē grān′)
4. A man's lover or mistress is his *paramour*.
5. A *privy council* is a group of a ruler's closest advisors.

Literary Element Dialogue How does this dialogue help characterize Igraine? **L**

6. The duke supplied (*provisioned*) the castles with food and goods.

SIR THOMAS MALORY **991**

R Reading Strategy

Analyzing Plot Answer:
Students may predict that Uther will be able to deceive Igraine, allowing him to take advantage of her when her guard is down. **OL**

L Literary Element

Dialogue Ask: What do you think of King Uther when he tells Igraine, "tell me the truth and I swear I shall love you the better for it"? *(Some students may find him kind and understanding. Others may think that he is manipulative, since he has tricked Igraine and asks the question to see if she will tell him the truth, even though he has deceived her.)* **OL**

Still enraged, and now despairing, King Uther fell sick. His friend Sir Ulfius came to him and asked what the trouble was. "Igraine has broken my heart," the king replied, "and unless I can win her, I shall never recover."

"Sire," said Sir Ulfius, "surely Merlin the Prophet could find some means to help you? I will go in search of him."

Sir Ulfius had not ridden far when he was accosted by a hideous beggar. "For whom are you searching?" asked the beggar; but Sir Ulfius ignored him.

"Very well," said the beggar, "I will tell you: You are searching for Merlin, and you need look no further, for I am he. Now go to King Uther and tell him that I will make Igraine his if he will reward me as I ask; and even that will be more to his benefit than to mine."

"I am sure," said Sir Ulfius, "that the king will refuse you nothing reasonable."

"Then go, and I shall follow you," said Merlin.

Well pleased, Sir Ulfius galloped back to the king and delivered Merlin's message, which he had hardly completed when Merlin himself appeared at the entrance to the pavilion. The king bade him welcome.

"Sire," said Merlin, "I know that you are in love with Igraine; will you swear, as an anointed[7] king, to give into my care the child that she bears you, if I make her yours?"

The king swore on the gospel that he would do so, and Merlin continued: "Tonight you shall appear before Igraine at Tintagil in the likeness of her husband, the duke. Sir Ulfius and I will appear as two of the duke's knights: Sir Brastius and Sir Jordanus. Do not question either Igraine or her men, but say that you are sick and retire to bed. I will fetch you early in the morning, and do not rise until I come; fortunately Tintagil is only ten miles from here."

The plan succeeded: Igraine was completely deceived by the king's impersonation of the duke, and gave herself to him, and conceived Arthur. The king left her at dawn as soon as Merlin appeared, after giving her a farewell kiss. But the duke had seen King Uther ride out from the siege on the previous night and, in the course of making a surprise attack on the king's army, had been killed. When Igraine realized that the duke had died three hours before he had appeared to her, she was greatly disturbed in mind; however, she confided in no one.

Once it was known that the duke was dead, the king's nobles urged him to be reconciled to Igraine, and this task the king gladly entrusted to Sir Ulfius, by whose eloquence[8] it was soon accomplished. "And now," said Sir Ulfius to his fellow nobles, "why should not the king marry the beautiful Igraine? Surely it would be as well for us all."

The marriage of King Uther and Igraine was celebrated joyously thirteen days later; and then, at the king's request, Igraine's sisters were also married: Margawse, who later bore Sir Gawain, to King Lot of Lowthean and Orkney; Elayne, to King Nentres of Garlot. Igraine's daughter, Morgan le Fay, was put to school in a nunnery; in after years she was to become a witch, and to be married to King Uryens of Gore, and give birth to Sir Uwayne of the Fair Hands.

A few months later it was seen that Igraine was with child, and one night, as she lay in bed with King Uther, he asked her who the father might be. Igraine was greatly **abashed.**

"Do not look so dismayed," said the king, "but tell me the truth and I swear I shall love **L** you the better for it."

---

7. An *anointed* king was believed to have been chosen by God to be king.

Reading Strategy Analyzing Plot *How do you think this event will advance the plot?* **R**

---

8. Here, *eloquence* is speech or writing that is expressive, stirring, and effective.

Vocabulary

abashed (ə basht′) *adj.* self-conscious; embarrassed or ashamed

---

Additional Support

Skills Practice

RESEARCH: Historical Context
Opinion is divided about whether King Arthur is a historical figure. Many historians believe he was a British or Roman-British leader who led the fight against the invasion of the Anglo-Saxons during the sixth century. Have students research the early history of England, including its rule by the Roman Empire, its invasion by the Picts and the Scots, and its invasion by the Jutes, Angles, and Saxons in the 400s and 500s. Assign each historical period to a small group, and have each group present its findings in an oral report with graphic aids. **OL**

"The truth is," said Igraine, "that the night the duke died, about three hours after his death, a man appeared in my castle—the exact image of the duke. With him came two others who appeared to be Sir Brastius and Sir Jordanus. Naturally I gave myself to this man as I would have to the duke, and that night, I swear, this child was conceived."

"Well spoken," said the king; "it was I who impersonated the duke, so the child is mine." He then told Igraine the story of how Merlin had arranged it, and Igraine was overjoyed to discover that the father of her child was now her husband.

Sometime later, Merlin appeared before the king. "Sire," he said, "you know that you must provide for the upbringing of your child?"

"I will do as you advise," the king replied.

"That is good," said Merlin, "because it is my reward for having arranged your impersonation of the duke. Your child is destined for glory, and I want him brought to me for his baptism. I shall then give him into the care of foster parents who can be trusted not to reveal his identity before the proper time. Sir Ector would be suitable: he is extremely loyal, owns good estates, and his wife has just borne him a child. She could give her child into the care of another woman, and herself look after yours."

Sir Ector was summoned, and gladly agreed to the king's request, who then rewarded him handsomely. When the child was born he was at once wrapped in a gold cloth and taken by two knights and two ladies to Merlin, who stood waiting at the rear entrance to the castle in his beggar's disguise. Merlin took the child to a priest, who baptized him with the name of Arthur, and thence to Sir Ector, whose wife fed him at her breast.

Two years later King Uther fell sick, and his enemies once more overran his kingdom, inflicting heavy losses on him as they

Merlin & Arthur, W. Goscombe John. Bronze. 2 7/8 in. high.
National Museum of Wales, Cardiff.

Big Idea Acts of Courage *Read to the end of the next paragraph. What is so remarkable about the king's statement?* **BI**

SIR THOMAS MALORY **993**

Differentiated Instruction

Less Proficient Readers If students have difficulty with the conventions of legends, compare the genre to one with which they are familiar, such as the fairy tale. Point out that Malory's legend resembles a fairy tale in many ways. Ask students to name some common fairy tales. Discuss the ways in which these fairy tales are like the selection. Note that Malory's legend combines realistic and fantastic details like a fairy tale. **BL**

Objectives
• To analyze plot (SE)
• To understand the author's use of dialogue (SE)
• To conduct research on historical context (TWE)

Analyzing Plot Answer:
The events have set in motion Arthur's ascension to the throne. **OL**

⭐ **Language History**

Etymology Have students look up the origin of the words *noble* and *nobility* and explain how the original meaning relates to the meaning used by Malory. *(Both words come from the Latin* nobilis, *meaning "well-known." Nobles are well-known because of outstanding qualities or aristocratic birth.)* **AS**

---

advanced. Merlin prophesied that they could be checked only by the presence of the king himself on the battlefield, and suggested that he should be conveyed there on a horse litter.[9] King Uther's army met the invader on the plain at St. Albans, and the king duly appeared on the horse litter. Inspired by his presence, and by the lively leadership of Sir Brastius and Sir Jordanus, his army quickly defeated the enemy and the battle finished in a rout.[10] The king returned to London to celebrate the victory.

But his sickness grew worse, and after he had lain speechless for three days and three nights Merlin summoned the nobles to attend the king in his chamber on the following morning. "By the grace of God," he said, "I hope to make him speak."

In the morning, when all the nobles were assembled, Merlin addressed the king: "Sire, is it your will that Arthur shall succeed to the throne, together with all its prerogatives?"[11]

The king stirred in his bed, and then spoke so that all could hear: "I bestow on Arthur God's blessing and my own, and Arthur shall succeed to the throne on pain of forfeiting my blessing."[12] Then King Uther ⭐ gave up the ghost. He was buried and mourned the next day, as befitted his rank, by Igraine and the nobility of Britain.

During the years that followed the death of King Uther, while Arthur was still a child, the ambitious barons fought one another for the throne, and the whole of Britain stood in jeopardy. Finally the day came when the Archbishop of Canterbury, on the advice of Merlin, summoned the nobility to London for Christmas morning. In his message the Archbishop promised that the true succes-

sion to the British throne would be miraculously revealed. Many of the nobles purified themselves during their journey, in the hope that it would be to them that the succession would fall.

The Archbishop held his service in the city's greatest church (St. Paul's), and when matins[13] were done the congregation filed out to the yard. They were confronted by a marble block into which had been thrust a beautiful sword. The block was four feet square, and the sword passed through a steel anvil which had been struck in the stone, and which projected a foot from it. The anvil had been **inscribed** with letters of gold:

> WHOSO PULLETH OUTE THIS SWERD
> OF THIS STONE AND ANVLYD IS RIGHTWYS
> KYNGE BORNE OF ALL BRYTAYGNE

The congregation was awed by this miraculous sight, but the Archbishop forbade anyone to touch the sword before mass had been heard. After mass, many of the nobles tried to pull the sword out of the stone, but none was able to, so a watch of ten knights was set over the sword, and a tournament proclaimed for New Year's Day, to provide men of noble blood with the opportunity of proving their right to the succession.

Sir Ector, who had been living on an estate near London, rode to the tournament with Arthur and his own son Sir Kay, who had been recently knighted. When they arrived at the tournament, Sir Kay found to his annoyance that his sword was missing from its sheath, so he begged Arthur to ride back and fetch it from their lodging.

Arthur found the door of the lodging locked and bolted, the landlord and his wife having left for the tournament. In order not to disappoint his brother, he rode

---

9. The king was to be carried *(conveyed)* on a stretcher *(litter)* pulled by a horse.
10. A *rout* (rout) is an overwhelming defeat.
11. *Prerogatives* (pri rog' ə tivz) are the rights and privileges belonging solely to a particular person (such as a king) or group.
12. *Forfeiting my blessing* means that Uther is withholding his blessing if Arthur does not eventually become king.

Reading Strategy Analyzing Plot **What purpose have the events in this story served up until this point?** **R1**

---

13. *Matins* (mat' inz) are morning prayers.

Vocabulary
inscribe (in skrīb') *v.* to write, carve, or mark on a surface

---

Additional Support

Skills Practice

READING: Author's Purpose
Determining the author's purpose can help students and understand why the author portrays events in a particular manner. **Ask:** What does Malory emphasize most in his stories about Arthur and the Knights of the Round Table? What do you think is the purpose of these stories? *(Malory emphasizes the excit-*

ing adventures of Arthur and the other knights, perhaps to entertain and inspire wonder.) Point out that Malory's style is simple and direct. This style reflects his purpose: to recount adventures by focusing on the action, the events, and the dialogue of the characters. **OL** on to St. Paul's, determined to get for him the sword which was lodged in the stone. The yard was empty, the guard also having slipped off to see the tournament, so Arthur strode up to the sword, and, without troubling to read the inscription, tugged it free. He then rode straight back to Sir Kay and presented him with it.

Sir Kay recognized the sword, and taking it to Sir Ector, said, "Father, the succession falls to me, for I have here the sword that was lodged in the stone." But Sir Ector insisted that they should all ride to the churchyard, and once there bound Sir Kay by oath to tell how he had come by the sword. Sir Kay then admitted that Arthur had given it to him. Sir Ector turned to Arthur and said, "Was the sword not guarded?"

"It was not," Arthur replied.

"Would you please thrust it into the stone again?" said Sir Ector. Arthur did so, and first Sir Ector and then Sir Kay tried to remove it, but both were unable to. Then Arthur, for the second time, pulled it out. Sir Ector and Sir Kay both knelt before him.

"Why," said Arthur, "do you both kneel before me?"

"My lord," Sir Ector replied, "there is only one man living who can draw the sword from the stone, and he is the true-born King of Britain." Sir Ector then told Arthur the story of his birth and upbringing.

"My dear father," said Arthur, "for so I shall always think of you—if, as you say, I am to be king, please know that any request you have to make is already granted."

Reading Strategy Analyzing Plot *What conflict is being revealed here?* **R3**

Literary Element Dialogue *What does this response reveal about Arthur?* **L**

Sir Ector asked that Sir Kay should be made Royal Seneschal,[14] and Arthur declared that while they both lived it should be so. Then the three of them visited the Archbishop and told him what had taken place.

All those dukes and barons with ambitions to rule were present at the tournament on New Year's Day. But when all of them had failed, and Arthur alone had succeeded in drawing the sword from the stone, they protested against one so young, and of **ignoble** blood, succeeding to the throne.

The secret of Arthur's birth was known only to a few of the nobles surviving from the days of King Uther. The Archbishop urged them to make Arthur's cause their own; but their support proved ineffective. The tournament was repeated at Candlemas and at Easter,[15] and with the same outcome as before.

Finally at Pentecost,[16] when once more Arthur alone had been able to remove the sword, the commoners arose with a **tumultuous** cry and demanded that Arthur should at once be made king. The nobles, knowing in their hearts that the commoners were right, all knelt before Arthur and begged forgiveness for having delayed his succession for so long. Arthur forgave them, and then, offering his sword at the high altar, was dubbed first knight of the realm. The coronation took place a few days later, when Arthur swore to rule justly, and the nobles swore him their allegiance. ∿

---

14. In medieval times, the *Royal Seneschal* (sen′ ə shəl) managed the king's estate, ran his household, and sometimes also had offical state duties or a military command.
15. *Candlemas* and *Easter* are Christian festivals; *Candlemas* is celebrated on February 2 and *Easter* in early spring.
16. *Pentecost* is a Christian feast observed on the seventh Sunday after Easter.

Vocabulary

ignoble (ig nō′ bəl) *adj.* of low birth or position; without honor or worth

tumultuous (too mul′ chōō əs) *adj.* wildly excited, confused, or agitated

---

Teach

R2 Reading Strategy

Analyzing Plot Point out that the scene in which Arthur pulls the sword from the stone is a climactic one, because it answers the question of who will succeed the throne. **Ask:** What is the tone of this scene? (*The scene is not very suspenseful. Arthur pulls out the sword accidentally and then must perform the action several more times before he is allowed to become king. The scene has a matter-of-fact tone.*) **OL**

R3 Reading Strategy

Analyzing Plot Answer: *Sir Kay creates conflict when he lies to his father and tells him that he freed the sword from the stone. The reader knows that Arthur actually tugged the sword free.* **OL**

L Literary Element

Dialogue Answer: *Arthur seems both unassuming and unaware. He does not seem to know what his actions mean, and he does not seem to feel that he deserves the admiration of Sir Ector and Sir Kay.* **OL**

English Language Coach

Multiple-Meaning Words Point out the words *succeed* and *succeeded* on pages 994–995. Explain that the word *succeed* has two different meanings. It can mean "to inherit a title" or "to attain a desired end."

Have English language learners read the sentences with these words aloud. Ask them to explain what *succeed* means in each sentence. Then have them use the word in two sentences of their own, using each meaning once. **EL**

Objectives
- To analyze plot (SE)
- To understand the author's use of dialogue (SE)
- To evaluate the author's purpose (TWE)

Teach

BI **Big Idea**

Acts of Courage

Ask: Do you consider Sir Launcelot's decision to leave the court in search of adventure to be an act of courage? Why or why not? (*Answers will vary. Some students might think it is courageous, while others may think it is impetuous and childish of him to go off blindly in search of "adventure" because he is tired of his life at court.*) **OL**

R Reading Strategy

Analyzing Plot Answer: *Sir Lyonel is courageous, but his decision to challenge the knight on his own, without the assistance of his experienced uncle, seems foolish.* **OL**

★ Viewing the Art

This sculpture is part of the medieval collection at the Germanisches Nationalmuseum (National Germanic Museum) in Nuremberg, Germany. Founded in 1852, this is the largest museum of German cultural history. Its collections include prehistoric artifacts, scientific instruments, folk-culture items, and toys. **AS**

The Tale of Sir Launcelot du Lake

When King Arthur returned from Rome he settled his court at Camelot, and there gathered about him his knights of the Round Table, who diverted[17] themselves with jousting and tournaments. Of all his knights one was supreme, both in **prowess** at arms and in nobility of bearing, and this was Sir Launcelot, who was also the favorite of Queen Gwynevere, to whom he had sworn oaths of fidelity.[18]

One day Sir Launcelot, feeling weary of his life at the court, and of only playing at arms, decided to **BI** set forth in search of adventure. He asked his nephew Sir Lyonel to accompany him, and when both were suitably armed and mounted, they rode off together through the forest.

At noon they started across a plain, but the intensity of the sun made Sir Launcelot feel sleepy, so Sir Lyonel suggested that they should rest beneath the shade of an apple tree that grew by a hedge not far from the road. They dismounted, tethered their horses, and settled down.

"Not for seven years have I felt so sleepy," said Sir Launcelot, and with that fell fast asleep, while Sir Lyonel watched over him.

Soon three knights came galloping past, and Sir Lyonel noticed that they were being pursued by a fourth knight, who was one of the most powerful he had yet seen. The pursuing knight overtook each of the others in turn, and as he did so, knocked each off his horse with a thrust of his spear. When all three lay stunned he dismounted, bound them securely to their horses with the reins, and led them away.

Without waking Sir Launcelot, Sir Lyonel mounted his horse and rode after the knight, and as soon as he had drawn close enough, shouted his challenge. The knight turned about and they charged at each other, with the result that Sir Lyonel was likewise flung

Head of King Arthur, from the *Beautiful Fountain,* 14th century. Artist unknown. Statue. Germanisches Nationalmuseum, Nuremberg, Germany. ★

---

17. Here, *diverted* means "amused" or "entertained."
18. Launcelot swore his loyalty and devotion *(fidelity)* to Gwynevere.

Vocabulary

prowess (prou′ is) *n.* great ability or skill

Reading Strategy Analyzing Plot *What does this action reveal about Sir Lyonel?* **R**

Additional Support

Skills Practice

VOCABULARY: Connotation Point out that this legend uses many words that were common centuries earlier but are rarely used today.

Ask students to look up the following words from the selection: *bestow, ignoble, realm, joust, bewail* and *churlish.*

Have them note the origin and meaning of the words and then use each one in a sentence.

Ask students to discuss the connotations that these words have today and what kind of tone they give the story. **OL** from his horse, bound, and led away a prisoner.

The victorious knight, whose name was Sir Tarquine, led his prisoners to his castle, and there threw them on the ground, stripped them naked, and beat them with thorn twigs. After that he locked them in a dungeon where many other prisoners, who had received like treatment, were complaining dismally.

Meanwhile, Sir Ector de Marys, who liked to accompany Sir Launcelot on his adventures, and finding him gone, decided to ride after him. Before long he came upon a forester.

"My good fellow, if you know the forest hereabouts, could you tell me in which direction I am most likely to meet with adventure?"

"Sir, I can tell you: Less than a mile from here stands a well-moated castle. On the left of the entrance you will find a ford where you can water your horse, and across from the ford a large tree from which hang the shields of many famous knights. Below the shields hangs a caldron, of copper and brass: strike it three times with your spear, and then surely you will meet with adventure—such, indeed, that if you survive it, you will prove yourself the foremost knight in these parts for many years."

"May God reward you!" Sir Ector replied.

The castle was exactly as the forester had described it, and among the shields Sir Ector recognized several as belonging to knights of the Round Table. After watering his horse, he knocked on the caldron and Sir Tarquine, whose castle it was, appeared.

They jousted, and at the first encounter Sir Ector sent his opponent's horse spinning twice about before he could recover.

"That was a fine stroke; now let us try again," said Sir Tarquine.

This time Sir Tarquine caught Sir Ector just below the right arm and, having impaled him on his spear, lifted him

clean out of the saddle, and rode with him into the castle, where he threw him on the ground.

"Sir," said Sir Tarquine, "you have fought better than any knight I have encountered in the last twelve years; therefore, if you wish, I will demand no more of you than your parole[19] as my prisoner."

"Sir, that I will never give."

"Then I am sorry for you," said Sir Tarquine, and with that he stripped and beat him and locked him in the dungeon with the other prisoners. There Sir Ector saw Sir Lyonel.

"Alas, Sir Lyonel, we are in a sorry plight. But tell me, what has happened to Sir Launcelot? for he surely is the one knight who could save us."

---

19. A knight's *parole* was his pledge to fulfill certain conditions in exchange for full or partial freedom.

Miniature Painting Depicting the Knights of the Round Table, 15th century. Artist unknown. Archivo Iconográfico, S.A.

SIR THOMAS MALORY **997**

Teach

L Literary Element

Dialogue Ask: What are the functions of the dialogue on this page? (*It characterizes Sir Ector, furthers the plot, and provides vivid images of the castle setting.*) **OL**

★ Viewing the Art

King Arthur's knights are known as the Knights of the Round Table. **Ask:** What do you think is the significance of the table's being round? (*Since the table was round, none of the knights could claim higher rank than any other.*) **AS**

Differentiated Instruction

English History When Malory wrote *Le Morte d'Arthur,* England was involved in a struggle for the throne called the Wars of the Roses (1455–1485). The tumultuous political situation of Malory's time is reflected in the events he describes in his works. Have students read about the Wars of the Roses. Encourage them to find out how the war got its name and how the houses of Lancaster and York were finally united. Also ask them to find information on the mysterious disappearance of Edward IV's sons from the Tower of London. **AL**

Objectives
• To analyze plot (SE)
• To understand the author's use of dialogue (TWE)
• To research word origins and meanings (TWE)

R1 Reading Strategy

Analyzing Plot

Answer: *The reader is reminded of Sir Launcelot's vulnerable position as he sleeps under the apple tree. The prisoners seem to lose hope because they believe that something may have happened to Launcelot.* **OL**

BI Big Idea

Acts of Courage

Answer: *It seems that Sir Launcelot values his honor and his loyalty to Gwynevere more than his own life.* **OL**

"I left him sleeping beneath an apple tree, and what has befallen him since I do not know," Sir Lyonel replied; and then all the unhappy prisoners once more bewailed their lot.

While Sir Launcelot still slept beneath the apple tree, four queens started across the plain. They were riding white mules and accompanied by four knights who held above them, at the tips of their spears, a green silk canopy, to protect them from the sun. The party was startled by the neighing of Sir Launcelot's horse and, changing direction, rode up to the apple tree, where they discovered the sleeping knight. And as each of the queens gazed at the handsome Sir Launcelot, so each wanted him for her own.

"Let us not quarrel," said Morgan le Fay. "Instead, I will cast a spell over him so that he remains asleep while we take him to my castle and make him our prisoner. We can then oblige him to choose one of us for his paramour."

Sir Launcelot was laid on his shield and borne by two of the knights to the Castle Charyot, which was Morgan le Fay's stronghold. He awoke to find himself in a cold cell, where a young noblewoman was serving him supper.

"What cheer?"[20] she asked.

"My lady, I hardly know, except that I must have been brought here by means of an enchantment."

"Sir, if you are the knight you appear to be, you will learn your fate at dawn tomorrow." And with that the young noblewoman left him. Sir Launcelot spent an uncomfortable night but at dawn the four queens presented themselves and Morgan le Fay spoke to him:

"Sir Launcelot, I know that Queen Gwynevere loves you, and you her. But now you are my prisoner, and you will have to choose: either to take one of us for your

paramour, or to die miserably in this cell—just as you please. Now I will tell you who we are: I am Morgan le Fay, Queen of Gore; my companions are the Queens of North Galys, of Estelonde, and of the Outer Isles. So make your choice."

"A hard choice! Understand that I choose none of you, lewd sorceresses[21] that you are; rather will I die in this cell. But were I free, I would take pleasure in proving it against any who would champion[22] you that Queen Gwynevere is the finest lady of this land."

"So, you refuse us?" asked Morgan le Fay.

"On my life, I do," Sir Launcelot said finally, and so the queens departed.

Sometime later, the young noblewoman who had served Sir Launcelot's supper reappeared.

"What news?" she asked.

"It is the end," Sir Launcelot replied.

"Sir Launcelot, I know that you have refused the four queens, and that they wish to kill you out of spite. But if you will be ruled by me, I can save you. I ask that you will champion my father at a tournament next Tuesday, when he has to combat the King of North Galys, and three knights of the Round Table, who last Tuesday defeated him ignominiously."[23]

"My lady, pray tell me, what is your father's name?"

"King Bagdemagus."[24]

"Excellent, my lady, I know him for a good king and a true knight, so I shall be happy to serve him."

"May God reward you! And tomorrow at dawn I will release you, and direct you to an abbey which is ten miles from here, and where the good monks will care for you while I fetch my father."

---

20. *What cheer?* meant the same as asking "How are you?"

Reading Strategy Analyzing Plot *How does this detail create suspense?* **R1**

---

21. Launcelot accuses the women of being unchaste *(lewd)* witches *(sorceresses)*.
22. As a verb, *champion* means "to defend a person or cause."
23. The woman's father was defeated shamefully or dishonorably *(ignominiously)*.
24. *Bagdemagus* (bag′ də mag′ əs)

Big Idea Acts of Courage *From this statement, what do you think Sir Launcelot values?* **BI**

Additional Support

Skills Practice

WRITING: Using Commas Remind students that commas are needed to separate items in a series and to set off words of direct address. Commas are also necessary to set off interjections that begin a sentence, such as *yes, no,* or *oh.* Ask students to correctly punctuate these sentences:

1. I am at your service my lady. (*I am at your service, my lady.*)

2. Alas Sir Lyonel we are in a sorry plight. (*Alas, Sir Lyonel, we are in a sorry plight.*)

3. Launcelot is brave strong and adventurous. (*Launcelot is brave, strong, and adventurous.*) **OL**

"I am at your service, my lady."

As promised, the young noblewoman released Sir Launcelot at dawn. When she had led him through the twelve doors to the castle entrance, she gave him his horse and armor, and directions for finding the abbey. "God bless you, my lady; and when the time comes I promise I shall not fail you."

Sir Launcelot rode through the forest in search of the abbey, but at dusk had still failed to find it, and coming upon a red silk pavilion, apparently unoccupied, decided to rest there overnight, and continue his search in the morning. . . .

As soon as it was daylight, Sir Launcelot armed, mounted, and rode away in search of the abbey, which he found in less than two hours. King Bagdemagus' daughter was waiting for him, and as soon as she heard his horse's footsteps in the yard, ran to the window, and, seeing that it was Sir Launcelot, herself ordered the servants to stable his horse. She then led him to her chamber, disarmed him, and gave him a long gown to wear, welcoming him warmly as she did so.

King Bagdemagus' castle was twelve miles away, and his daughter sent for him as soon as she had settled Sir Launcelot. The king arrived with his retinue[25] and embraced Sir Launcelot, who then described his recent enchantment, and the great obligation he was under to his daughter for releasing him.

"Sir, you will fight for me on Tuesday next?"

"Sire, I shall not fail you; but please tell me the names of the three Round Table knights whom I shall be fighting."

"Sir Modred, Sir Madore de la Porte, and Sir Gahalantyne. I must admit that last Tuesday they defeated me and my knights completely."

"Sire, I hear that the tournament is to be fought within three miles of the abbey. Could you send me three of your most trustworthy knights, clad in plain armor, and with no device,[26] and a fourth suit of armor which I myself shall wear? We will take up our position just outside the tournament field and watch while you and the King of North Galys enter into combat with your followers; and then, as soon as you are in difficulties, we will come to your rescue, and show your opponents what kind of knights you command."

This was arranged on Sunday, and on the following Tuesday Sir Launcelot and the three knights of King Bagdemagus waited in a copse,[27] not far from the pavilion which had been erected for the lords and ladies who were to judge the tournament and award the prizes.

The King of North Galys was the first on the field, with a company of ninescore knights; he was followed by King Bagdemagus with fourscore[28] knights, and then by the three knights of the Round Table, who remained apart from both companies. At the first encounter King Bagdemagus lost twelve knights, all killed, and the King of North Galys six.

With that, Sir Launcelot galloped on to the field, and with his first spear unhorsed five of the King of North Galys' knights, breaking the backs of four of them. With his next spear he charged the king, and wounded him deeply in the thigh.

"That was a shrewd blow," commented Sir Madore, and galloped onto the field to challenge Sir Launcelot. But he too was tumbled from his horse, and with such violence that his shoulder was broken.

Sir Modred was the next to challenge Sir Launcelot, and he was sent spinning over his horse's tail. He landed head first, his helmet became buried in the soil, and he nearly broke his neck, and for a long time lay stunned.

---

25. The king's *retinue* is the group of people who accompany and serve him.
26. Armor with no *device* has no ornamental design.
27. A *copse* is a thicket of trees.
28. One *score* is twenty, so more than 260 knights have gathered.

Literary Element Dialogue *What does this dialogue reveal about Sir Launcelot?* **L**

Reading Strategy Analyzing Plot *Why do you think Sir Launcelot makes these requests?* **R₃**

Teach

L Literary Element

Dialogue Answer: *Launcelot is grateful and generous to those who help him, and he is true to his word.* **OL**

R₂ Reading Strategy

Analyzing Plot Ask: How does the plot of this legend compare to many contemporary plots? *(Instead of being built around one major conflict, the plot describes a series of conflicts that are seemingly random. Similarly, a series of new characters appears with whom the protagonist is in conflict.)* **OL**

R₃ Reading Strategy

Analyzing Plot Answer: *Students may say that Launcelot does not want to use his reputation to intimidate his opponents. Instead, he wants to prove himself by his deeds. He also wants to allow King Bagdemagus the opportunity to triumph before he enters the battle.* **OL**

English Language Coach

Medieval Vocabulary The legend contains words relating to medieval culture that may be familiar to fluent English speakers but new to English language learners.

Make a chart on the board with the following headings: "Knights," "Castle," and "Magic." Place related terms from the selection in the appropriate column and have students collectively define them. When possible, use illustrations to help define terms. **EL**

Objectives

- To analyze plot (SE)
- To understand the author's use of dialogue (SE)
- To use commas correctly (TWE)

Teach

BI **Big Idea**

Acts of Courage

Ask: After reading the description of the combatants he faces, what do you think of Launcelot's decision to fight for the king? (*Students may say that the description of the numerous men Launcelot faces makes him appear particularly brave and generous in agreeing to fight.*) **OL**

⭐ Viewing the Art

Ask: What inferences can you make about the lifestyle of King Arthur and Queen Guinevere, based on this art? (*They lived a very opulent life, had feasts, and had servants attending to them.*) **AS**

King Arthur and Queen Guinevere, 14th century. Artist unknown. British Library, London.

Finally Sir Gahalantyne tried; at the first encounter both he and Sir Launcelot broke their spears, so both drew their swords and hacked vehemently at each other. But Sir Launcelot, with mounting wrath, soon struck his opponent a blow on the helmet which brought the blood streaming from eyes, ears, and mouth. Sir Gahalantyne slumped forward in the saddle, his horse panicked, and he was thrown to the ground, useless for further combat.

Sir Launcelot took another spear, and unhorsed sixteen more of the King of North Galys' knights, and with his next, unhorsed another twelve; and in each case with such violence that none of the knights ever fully recovered. The King of North Galys was forced to admit defeat, and the prize was **BI** awarded to King Bagdemagus.

That night Sir Launcelot was entertained as the guest of honor by King Bagdemagus and his daughter at their castle, and before leaving was loaded with gifts.

"My lady, please, if ever again you should need my services, remember that I shall not fail you."

The next day Sir Launcelot rode once more through the forest, and by chance came to the apple tree where he had previously slept. This time he met a young noblewoman riding a white palfrey.

"My lady, I am riding in search of adventure; pray tell

Visual Vocabulary
A *palfrey* is a gentle saddle horse, especially one trained for a woman rider.

Additional Support

Skills Practice

READING: Summarizing The plot of this legend is action-driven, and the sequence of events is very important. Summarizing the selection can help students clarify the order of events and understand their significance to the plot. Ask students to summarize the major events that have occurred in the story up to this point, and tell them to pay particular attention to keeping them in chronological order. Have students close their books and recall the events to the best of their knowledge. Then ask them to check for forgotten and out-of-order events. **OL**

King Arthur and his Knights around the Table. Robert de Boron. Vellum. ★

me if you know of any I might find hereabouts."

"Sir, there are adventures hereabouts if you believe that you are equal to them; but please tell me, what is your name?"

"Sir Launcelot du Lake."

"Very well, Sir Launcelot, you appear to be a sturdy enough knight, so I will tell you. Not far away stands the castle of Sir Tarquine, a knight who in fair combat has overcome more than sixty opponents whom he now holds prisoner. Many are from the court of King Arthur, and if you can rescue them, I will then ask you to deliver me and my companions from a knight who distresses us daily, either by robbery or by other kinds of outrage."

"My lady, please first lead me to Sir Tarquine, then I will most happily challenge this miscreant[29] knight of yours."

When they arrived at the castle, Sir Launcelot watered his horse at the ford, and then beat the caldron until the bottom fell out. However, none came to answer the challenge, so they waited by the castle gate for half an hour or so. Then Sir Tarquine appeared, riding toward the castle with a wounded prisoner slung over his horse, whom Sir Launcelot recognized as Sir Gaheris, Sir Gawain's brother and a knight of the Round Table.

"Good knight," said Sir Launcelot, "it is known to me that you have put to shame many of the knights of the Round Table. Pray allow your prisoner, who I see is wounded,

to recover, while I vindicate[30] the honor of the knights whom you have defeated."

"I defy you, and all your fellowship of the Round Table," Sir Tarquine replied.

"You boast!" said Sir Launcelot.

At the first charge the backs of the horses were broken and both knights stunned. But they soon recovered and set to with their swords, and both struck so lustily that neither shield nor armor could resist, and within two hours they were cutting each other's flesh, from which the blood flowed liberally. Finally they paused for a moment, resting on their shields.

"Worthy knight," said Sir Tarquine, "pray hold your hand for a while, and if you will, answer my question."

"Sir, speak on."

"You are the most powerful knight I have fought yet, but I fear you may be the one whom in the whole world I most hate. If you

---

29. A *miscreant* knight is an evil, villainous one.

30. Launcelot wishes to defend against opposition, or *vindicate*, the honor of Tarquine's prisoners.

SIR THOMAS MALORY **1001**

Differentiated Instruction

Visualizing Less proficient readers may better visualize the battle scenes by first picturing the knights themselves. Ask students to find illustrations of a knight's equipment, and suggest that they make a drawing, diagram, or written description of the items in a knight's wardrobe. (*Knights wore a hood and a leather robe. Over this they wore chain mail of fine mesh to protect them from swords and lances. The chain mail consisted of a hauberk, which covered the neck and torso, and leggings. Knights had a variety of headgear including a heavy iron helmet with eye slits.*) **BL**

Acts of Courage Answer:
Students may say that Launcelot believes it is more important to expose his identity and risk death than lie and damage his sense of honor. **OL**

L₁ **Literary Element**

Dialogue Answer: *They are loyal and respectful. They not only feel it is their duty, but they are eager to follow him on his quest.* **OL**

★ **Language History**

Quest Point out that the word *quest* has distinctly chivalric connotations, referring to an adventurous journey by knights. **AS**

Additional Support

---

are not, for the love of you I will release all my prisoners and swear eternal friendship."

"What is the name of the knight you hate above all others?"

"Sir Launcelot du Lake; for it was he who slew my brother, Sir Carados of the Dolorous Tower, and it is because of him that I have killed a hundred knights, and maimed[31] as many more, apart from the sixty-four I still hold prisoner. And so, if you are Sir Launcelot, speak up, for we must then fight to the death."

"Sir, I see now that I might go in peace and good fellowship, or otherwise fight to the death; but being the knight I am, I must tell you: I am Sir Launcelot du Lake, son of King Ban of Benwick, of Arthur's court, and a knight of the Round Table. So defend yourself!"

"Ah! this is most welcome."

Now the two knights hurled themselves at each other like two wild bulls; swords and shields clashed together, and often their swords drove into the flesh. Then sometimes one, sometimes the other, would stagger and fall, only to recover immediately and resume the contest. At last, however, Sir Tarquine grew faint, and unwittingly lowered his shield. Sir Launcelot was swift to follow up his advantage, and dragging the other down to his knees, unlaced his helmet and beheaded him.

Sir Launcelot then strode over to the young noblewoman: "My lady, now I am at your service, but first I must find a horse."

Then the wounded Sir Gaheris spoke up: "Sir, please take my horse. Today you have overcome the most formidable knight, excepting only yourself, and by so doing have saved us all. But before leaving, please tell me your name."

"Sir Launcelot du Lake. Today I have fought to vindicate the honor of the knights of the Round Table, and I know that among

Sir Tarquine's prisoners are two of my brethren, Sir Lyonel and Sir Ector, also your own brother, Sir Gawain. According to the shields there are also: Sir Brandiles, Sir Galyhuddis, Sir Kay, Sir Alydukis, Sir Marhaus, and many others. Please release the prisoners and ask them to help themselves to the castle treasure. Give them all my greetings and say I will see them at the next Pentecost. And please request Sir Ector and Sir Lyonel to go straight to the court and await me there."

When Sir Launcelot had ridden away with the young noblewoman, Sir Gaheris entered the castle, and finding the porter in the hall, threw him on the ground and took the castle keys. He then released the prisoners, who, seeing his wounds, thanked him for their deliverance.

"Do not thank me for this work, but Sir Launcelot. He sends his greetings to you all, and asks you to help yourselves to the castle treasure. He has ridden away on another quest, but said that he will see you at the next Pentecost. Meanwhile, he requests Sir Lyonel and Sir Ector to return to the court and await him there."

"Certainly we shall not ride back to the court, but rather we shall follow Sir Launcelot wherever he goes," said Sir Ector.

"And I too shall follow him," said Sir Kay.

The prisoners searched the castle for their armor and horses and the castle treasure; and then a forester arrived with supplies of venison, so they feasted merrily and settled down for the night in the castle chambers—all but Sir Ector, Sir Lyonel, and Sir Kay, who set off immediately after supper in search of Sir Launcelot.

Sir Launcelot and the young noblewoman were riding down a broad highway when the young noblewoman said they were within sight of the spot where the knight generally attacked her.

"For shame that a knight should so degrade his high calling," Sir Launcelot replied.

---

31. To *maim* is to injure seriously or horribly.

Big Idea Acts of Courage *Why do you think Launcelot reveals himself, exposing himself to further danger?* **BI₁**

Literary Element Dialogue *How do the other characters' responses to Launcelot help characterize them?* **L₁**

Skills Practice

WRITING: Describing Action Point out that much of *Le Morte d'Arthur* describes a series of actions: travels, meetings with various strangers, and battles. The simple language, sentence structure, and vivid verbs help to make the actions realistic.

Have students write a paragraph describing a sporting event or other active, dramatic situation that they have observed or participated in. Encourage them to use the description of the fight with Sir Tarquine on page 1002 as a model. **OL**

"Certainly we will teach him a much-needed lesson. Now, my lady, I suggest that you ride on ahead, and as soon as he molests you, I will come to the rescue."

Sir Launcelot halted and the young noblewoman rode gently forward. Soon the knight appeared with his page, and seized the young noblewoman from her horse; she cried out at once, and Sir Launcelot galloped up to them.

"Scoundrel! What sort of knight do you think you are, to attack defenseless women?"

In answer the other knight drew his sword. Sir Launcelot did likewise, and they rushed together. With his first stroke Sir Launcelot split open the knight's head, down to the throat.

"Let that be your payment, though long overdue," said Sir Launcelot.

"Even so; he certainly deserved to die. His name was Sir Percy of the Forest Sauvage."

"My lady, do you require anything more of me?"

"No, good Sir Launcelot; and may the sweet Lord Jesu[32] protect you, for certainly you are the bravest and gentlest knight I have known. But pray tell me one thing: why is it you do not take to yourself a wife? Many good ladies, both high born and low born, grieve that so fine a knight as yourself should remain single. It is whispered, of course, that Queen Gwynevere has cast a spell over you so that you shall love no other."

"As for that, people must believe what they will about Queen Gwynevere and me. But married I will not be, for then I should have to attend my lady instead of entering for tournaments and wars, or riding in search of adventure. And I will not take a paramour, both for the fear of God and in the belief that those who do so are always unfortunate when they meet a knight who is purer of heart; for whether they are defeated or victorious in such an encounter, either result must be equally distressing and shameful. I believe that a true knight is neither adulterous nor lecherous."[33]

Sir Launcelot then took his leave of the young noblewoman, and for two days wandered alone through the forest, resting at night at the most meager of lodgings. On the third day, as he was crossing a bridge, he was accosted by a churlish porter,[34] who, after striking his horse on the nose so that it turned about, demanded to know by what right Sir Launcelot was riding that way.

"And what right do I need to cross this bridge? Surely, I cannot ride beside it," said Sir Launcelot.

"That is not for you to decide," said the porter, and with that he lashed at Sir Launcelot with his club. Sir Launcelot drew his sword, and after deflecting the blow, struck the porter on the head and split it open.

At the end of the bridge was a prosperous-looking village, overtopped by a fine castle. As Sir Launcelot advanced he heard someone cry: "Good knight, beware! You have done yourself no good by killing the chief porter of the castle."

Sir Launcelot rode on regardless, through the village and into the castle court, which was richly grassed. Thinking to himself that this would be a good place for combat, Sir Launcelot tied his horse to a ring in the wall and started across the lawn. Meanwhile people were peering at him from every door and window, and again he heard the warning: "Good knight, you come here at your peril!"

Before long two giants appeared, fully armed except for their heads, and brandishing huge clubs. Together they rushed at Sir Launcelot, who raised his shield to defend himself, and then struck at one of the giants and beheaded him. Thereupon the second

---

32. *Jesu* (jē′ zōō) is a form of *Jesus*.

Big Idea Acts of Courage *The noblewoman tells Launcelot that he is the "bravest and gentlest" knight she has known. What is the significance of these two adjectives?*

BI₂

---

33. A true knight is pure. He does not commit adultery (*adulterous*), nor is he preoccupied with indecent thoughts and desires (*lecherous*).

34. Here, the gatekeeper (*porter*) is bad-tempered and very rude (*churlish*).

SIR THOMAS MALORY **1003**

Teach

BI₂ Big Idea

Acts of Courage Answer: *It is not enough for a knight to be a brave and skillful fighter; he must also be "gentle," polite, kind to women, and socially astute.* **OL**

L₂ Literary Element

Dialogue Ask: According to his words on this page, how does Launcelot believe a knight should behave? *(Students may say that knights should devote themselves to tournaments, wars, and adventures instead of to relationships with women. Some unmarried knights may choose to have affairs at the expense of their virtue. If a knight were to behave in this way, he would be at a disadvantage against virtuous knights.)* **OL**

Objectives
• To understand the author's use of dialogue (SE)
• To describe action in writing (TWE)

1003

R Reading Strategy

Analyzing Plot

Answer: *Malory is reminding the reader of events in the first legend that led to the birth of Arthur. King Uther was attracted to Igraine and arranged with Merlin to have a relationship with her. Launcelot's return to Tintagil reveals how different he is from King Uther.* **OL**

★ Viewing the Art

Ask: How does the picture help you understand the variety of life in King Arthur's court? *(It shows the honor, chivalry, camaraderie, and respect that are part of life in Camelot.)* **AS**

Roman de Tristan: Scenes from the Legend of King Arthur, 15th century. Artist unknown. Archivo Iconográfico, S.A. ★

giant roared with dismay and fled into the forest, where Sir Launcelot pursued him. In a few minutes, Sir Launcelot drew abreast of the giant and struck him on the shoulder with a blow that carried through to the navel, and the giant dropped dead.

When Sir Launcelot returned to the castle, he was greeted by threescore ladies, who all knelt before him.

"Brave knight! we thank you for delivering us. Many of us have been prisoners for seven years now, and although we are all high born, we have had to work like servants for our keep, doing silk embroidery. Pray tell us your name, so that our friends can know who has saved us."

"My ladies, I am called Sir Launcelot du Lake."

"Welcome, Sir Launcelot! It was you alone whom the giants feared, and you alone who

could have overcome them. How often have we prayed for your coming!"

"My ladies, please greet your friends for me; and when I pass through this country again, grant me what hospitality you may feel is my due. Please recompense[35] yourselves from the castle treasure, and then insure that the castle is restored to the rightful owner."

"Sir Launcelot, this is the castle of Tintagil, and belonged formerly to the duke of that name. But after his death, Igraine, who had been his wife, was made queen by King Uther Pendragon, to whom she bore Arthur, our present king."

"And so, after all, I know the owner of this castle. My ladies, I bless you, and farewell."

Always in quest of adventure, Sir Launcelot rode through many different countries, through wild valleys and forests, and across strange rivers; and at night he slept where he could, often in the roughest of lodgings. Then one day he came to a well-kept house where the lady offered him the best of hospitality. After supper he was taken to his chamber, which overlooked the front door, and there Sir Launcelot disarmed and fell comfortably asleep.

He was awakened a short time later by a tremendous knocking at the door below, and looking through the window recognized Sir Kay in the moonlight, and three knights galloping toward him with drawn swords. The **B1**

---

35. Launcelot invites the ladies to *recompense* themselves, or divide the treasure among themselves, as a way to make up for their treatment by the giants.

Reading Strategy Analyzing Plot *Why do you think Malory returns Sir Launcelot to Tintagil?* **R**

Additional Support

Skills Practice

LISTENING AND SPEAKING:

Retelling a Legend Discuss effective ways to retell a legend orally. Point out that a speaker must decide which parts of the legend to emphasize with his or her voice, facial expressions, and gestures. Discuss the understated style of the legend, and have students consider whether a low-key style would also be effective in an oral retelling of the work.

Have students choose an episode from "The Tale of Sir Launcelot du Lake" and prepare an oral retelling. Have them present their interpretations in small groups, and then discuss as a class the most effective methods for telling the story. **OL** moment they got to the house, they dismounted and set upon Sir Kay, who turned about and drew his sword to defend himself. Sir Launcelot hastily armed, saying to himself: "If they kill Sir Kay I shall be a party to his death, for three against one is unjust."

He let himself down from the window by means of his sheet, and then challenged the three attackers, whispering to Sir Kay to stand by while he dealt with them. Sir Kay did as he was advised, and then Sir Launcelot, with seven tremendous blows, brought all three knights to their knees and begging for mercy.

"Your lives will be spared if you yield to Sir Kay," said Sir Launcelot.

"Sir, it is surely you to whom we should yield, since we could easily have overcome Sir Kay."

"If you wish to be spared, you will go as prisoners of Sir Kay, and yield to Queen Gwynevere."

Each of the knights then swore on his sword to abide by the conditions of his surrender, and Sir Launcelot knocked once more at the door of the house.

"Why, I thought you were safely in bed," said the landlady, recognizing Sir Launcelot as she opened the door.

"Madam, I was, but then I had to jump out of the window and rescue this comrade of mine."

As they came into the light, Sir Kay recognized Sir Launcelot and thanked him humbly for twice saving his life.

"It was no more than I should have done, but come up to my chamber; you must be tired and hungry."

When Sir Kay had eaten, he lay on Sir Launcelot's bed, and they slept together until dawn. Sir Launcelot woke first, and rising quietly, clad himself in Sir Kay's armor, and then, mounting Sir Kay's horse, rode away from the house.

When Sir Kay awoke, he was astonished to find that Sir Launcelot had exchanged armor with him, but then he realized he had done it so that he should ride home unmolested, while Sir Launcelot encountered his opponents. And when Sir Kay had taken his leave of the landlady he rode back to the court without further incident.

For several days Sir Launcelot rode through the forest, and then he came to a countryside of low meadows and broad streams. At the foot of a bridge he saw three pavilions, and a knight standing at the entrance to each, with a white shield hanging above, and a spear thrust into the ground at one side. Sir Launcelot recognized the three knights, who were from Arthur's court, as Sir Gawtere, Sir Raynolde, and Sir Gylmere. However, he rode straight past them, looking neither to right nor to left, and without saluting them.

"Why, there rides Sir Kay, the most overbearing[36] knight of all, in spite of his many defeats. I think I will challenge him and see if I cannot shake his pride a little," said Sir Gawtere.

He then galloped up to Sir Launcelot and challenged him. They jousted, and Sir Gawtere was flung violently from the saddle.

"That is certainly not Sir Kay," said Sir Raynolde. "For one thing, he is very much bigger."

"Probably it is some knight who has killed Sir Kay and is riding in his armor," Sir Gylmere replied.

"Well, since he has overcome our brother we shall have to challenge him. But I think it must be either Sir Launcelot, Sir Tristram, or Sir Pelleas; and we may not come well out of this."

Sir Gylmere challenged Sir Launcelot next, and was also overthrown. Then Sir Raynolde rode up to him.

"Sir, I would prefer not to challenge a knight so powerful as you, but since you have probably killed my brothers, I am obliged to; so defend yourself!"

They jousted; both broke their spears and they continued the combat with swords. Sir Gawtere and Sir Gylmere

---

36. An *overbearing* person is excessively proud and superior in attitude and behavior.

Literary Element Dialogue *What does this statement reveal about the fraternity of knights?* **L**

Teach

L Literary Element

Dialogue

Ask: What is the effect of Sir Sagramour's announcing he will challenge Sir Kay and the knights, not knowing who is riding in Kay's armor? (*This section adds humor and irony because the reader knows it is really Launcelot in Sir Kay's armor, and that the knights are wrong to think this rider will be easily conquered.*) **OL**

BI Big Idea

Acts of Courage

Answer: *Launcelot is a noble character who does not perform his deeds for personal glory, but in honor of Gwynevere and for the glory of knighthood in general. He does not want to boast of his exploits; the other knights will do so for him.* **OL**

CheckPoint

Use the CheckPoint questions on Presentation Plus! to check students' mastery of the selection. These questions can be used with interactive response keypads for immediate student feedback.

recovered, and attempted to rescue their brother, but Sir Launcelot saw them in time, and using more strength than hitherto, struck each off his horse again. At this, Sir Raynolde, badly wounded as he was, and with blood streaming from his head, picked himself up and once more rushed at Sir Launcelot.

"Sir, I should let things be," said Sir Launcelot. "I was not far away when you were knighted, and I know you to be worthy: therefore do not oblige me to kill you."

"May God reward you!" Sir Raynolde replied. "But speaking both for myself and my brothers, I would prefer to know your name before yielding to you, because we know very well that you are not Sir Kay, whom any one of us could have overcome."

"That is as may be; but I still require that you yield to Queen Gwynevere at the next Pentecost, and say that Sir Kay sent you."

The three brothers took their oath, and Sir Launcelot left them. He had not ridden much further when, coming to a glade, he found four more knights of the Round Table: Sir Gawain, Sir Ector, Sir Uwayne, and Sir Sagramour le Desyrus.

L "Look!" said Sir Sagramour, "there rides Sir Kay. I will challenge him."

Sir Sagramour first, then each of the other knights in turn, challenged Sir Launcelot, and was flung from his horse. Sir Launcelot left them gasping on the ground, and said to himself as he rode away: "Blessed be the maker of this spear; with it I have tumbled four knights off their horses." Meanwhile the four knights were picking themselves up and consoling each other.

"To the devil with him! He is indeed powerful," said one.

"I believe that it must be Sir Launcelot," said another.

"Anyhow, let him go now; we shall discover when we return to Camelot," said a third, and so on. . . .

Sir Launcelot returned to Camelot two days before the feast of Pentecost, and at the court was acclaimed[37] by many of the knights he had met on his adventures.

Sir Gawain, Sir Uwayne, Sir Ector, and Sir Sagramour all laughed when they saw him in Sir Kay's armor, but without the helmet, and readily forgave his joke at their expense.

Sir Gaheris described to the court the terrible battle Sir Launcelot had fought with Sir Tarquine, and how sixty-four prisoners had been freed as a result of his victory.

Sir Kay related how Sir Launcelot had twice saved his life, and then exchanged armor with him, so that he should ride unchallenged.

Sir Gawtere, Sir Gylmere, and Sir Raynolde described how he had defeated them at the bridge, and forced them to yield as prisoners of Sir Kay; and they were overjoyed to discover that it had been Sir Launcelot nevertheless.

Sir Modred, Sir Mador, and Sir Gahalantyne described his tremendous feats in the battle against the King of North Galys; and Sir Launcelot himself described his enchantment by the four queens, and his rescue at the hands of the daughter of King Bagdemagus. . . .

And thus it was, at this time, that Sir Launcelot became the most famous knight at King Arthur's court. ∾

---

37. Launcelot was *acclaimed*, or greeted with loud, enthusiastic praise.

Big Idea Acts of Courage *Why does Sir Launcelot refrain from describing his acts of courage?* **BI**

Additional Support

1006

Skills Practice

GRAMMAR: *Who* and *Whom* Point out these sentences: "The young noblewoman who had served Sir Launcelot's supper reappeared." "Sir, it is surely you to whom we should yield." Point out that *who* serves as a subject or a predicate pronoun; *whom*, as a direct object or an object of a preposition.

Have students choose the correct word in parentheses.

1. For (who, whom) are you searching? *(whom)*

2. Merlin took the child to a priest, (who, whom) baptized him with the name of Arthur. *(who)* **OL**

RESPONDING AND THINKING CRITICALLY

Respond

1. What is your reaction to the world of King Arthur and his knights? If you could be transported there for a day, would you go? Why or why not?

Recall and Interpret

2. (a)What does Merlin ask of King Uther in return for granting his wish? (b)Why, do you think, does Merlin request this reward for helping Uther?

3. (a)What events lead Arthur to pull the sword from the stone? (b)What does Arthur's behavior immediately after pulling the sword free tell you about him?

4. (a)Why is Sir Tarquine so determined to kill Sir Launcelot? (b)Why do you think Sir Launcelot reveals his identity, knowing that the ensuing fight will lead to death?

Analyze and Evaluate

5. Do the characters of King Uther Pendragon and Igraine seem realistic? Why or why not?

6. If you were one of the nobles, would you have proclaimed the young Arthur to be king as described in "The Tale of King Arthur"? Explain.

7. What do you learn about Sir Kay's character in "The Tale of King Arthur" that foreshadows what his fellow knights think of him in "The Tale of Sir Launcelot du Lake"?

Connect

8. **Big Idea** Acts of Courage Why would Sir Launcelot be described as courageous? Is he a hero? Explain.

LITERARY ANALYSIS

Literary Element Dialogue

Much of *Le Morte d'Arthur* is related through **dialogue**, the written conversation between characters. Dialogue gives readers a sense of a character's personality and feelings, and helps readers focus on important scenes. In "The Tale of King Arthur," for example, the reader realizes the importance of King Uther's feelings when Uther says "Igraine has broken my heart, and unless I can win her, I shall never recover."

1. Reread the scene on page 995 in which Sir Ector realizes that Arthur has removed the sword from the stone. Why do you think the author chose to use dialogue here?

2. Which passage of dialogue in the selection do you find particularly effective or striking? Why?

Review: Hero

As you learned on pages 968–969, a **hero** is the chief character in a literary work, typically one whose qualities or noble deeds arouse the admiration of the reader.

Partner Activity Critic Jeffrey Helterman observes that "Arthur institutes a code of behavior which stresses always succoring [aiding] ladies . . . and never taking up battles for a wrongful cause." With a partner, find examples from "The Tale of Sir Launcelot du Lake" of knights following this code of behavior. Use a chart like the one below. What can you infer from the code about the values held by this society?

Example	Inference
When a knight attacks a noblewoman, Sir Launcelot fights and defeats him.	Protecting women and their honor is valued in his society.
Sir Launcelot refuses Morgan le Fay.	

SIR THOMAS MALORY **1007**

Assess

1. Students should refer to the setting and characters of the legend in their response.

2. (a) Merlin asks for custody of the child that Igraine will bear Uther. (b) Merlin arranged the birth of Arthur and wants to control his fate.

3. (a) Arthur's brother, Sir Kay, forgets his sword and asks Arthur to go back for it. (b) Arthur is modest and selfless. His rule will probably be more fair and generous than Uther's rule.

4. (a) Because Launcelot had killed his brother (b) Because he is an honest, virtuous knight, and because he is confident he can win the battle

5. Students may say the characters of Uther and Igraine do not seem realistic because their relationship is based on magic. Or they may say they are realistic because Uther demonstrates the human trait of lust and the use of trickery to get what he wants, while Igraine defends her virtue.

6. Students' responses should show knowledge of the plot and characters of the legend.

7. He is revealed to be a dishonest and weak character.

8. Students' responses should include specific details about Launcelot's character and about their own understanding of the definition of courage.

Literary Element

1. Students may say that the dialogue shows the relationship between the men.

2. Students should give specific reasons for their choice. For example, Launcelot's response to Morgan le Fay on page 998 is effective because it reveals his personality and gives insight into a knight's moral code.

Review: Hero

After students complete their charts, have a class discussion about how the values of Arthur's time compare to the values we hold today.

Assess

Reading Strategy

1. Students may say that Malory included this to illustrate his virtue and his devotion to Gwynevere.

2. Malory may have included the scene to show Launcelot's devotion to protecting women.

3. Students may say that Malory wants to express the moral code of the knights.

Vocabulary

1. b **2.** c **3.** b **4.** a

Academic Vocabulary

1. Launcelot ensures that he will face Sir Kay's enemies and that Sir Kay will ride home without challenge.

2. Students should explain their opinions about the violence in the selection.

Writing About Literature

Students' essays should

• analyze similarities and differences between two characters

• include evidence from the text that supports their arguments

---

Reading Strategy Analyzing Plot

Often, determining the author's purpose in **plotting** certain episodes can help readers understand the theme of a legend.

1. Why do you think Malory included Launcelot's refusal to choose a paramour from among Morgan le Fay and her companions?

2. Why might Malory have included Launcelot's killing of Sir Tarquine within the plot?

3. Using what you know about the plot, what message do you think Malory wants to express? Explain.

Vocabulary Practice

Practice with Word Origins Choose the word that has the same origin as each vocabulary word below. Use a dictionary if you need help.

1. abashed
   a. abacus   **b.** bashful   **c.** basked

2. tumultuous
   a. timid   **b.** tepid   **c.** tumor

3. ignoble
   a. ignorance   **b.** nobility   **c.** igneous

4. inscribe
   a. scribble   **b.** scrutiny   **c.** install

Academic Vocabulary

Here are two words from the vocabulary list on page R82. These words will help you think, write, and talk about the selection.

ensure (en shoor´) *v.* to make certain, to insure

impact (im´ pakt) *v.* to have an effect

Practice and Apply

1. By exchanging armor, what is **ensured** for Sir Launcelot? For Sir Kay?

2. How did the violence in this selection **impact** you? Would you have preferred less of it? Why or why not?

Writing About Literature

Compare and Contrast Characters Malory introduces and describes strong characters in this legend. He discusses and shows their personal characteristics, some of which are in distinct contrast with other characters. Choose two characters from the legend, such as Launcelot and Sir Kay, or Merlin and Uther. Write a one- or two-page analysis in which you compare and contrast the personalities and qualities of these characters. Use evidence from Malory's legend to explain your position.

Before you begin drafting, take notes on the similarities and differences of each character in a Venn diagram.

Include evidence from the legend to support your descriptions of the characters. Once you have completed the diagram, begin drafting.

Invite a peer reviewer to exchange drafts with you. Proofread and edit each other's drafts, and provide comments about those areas you find particularly interesting, as well as places that may need more clarification. Check for errors in spelling, grammar, and punctuation.

Literature Groups

One element of Arthurian legend was the tradition of courtly love, in which knights devoted themselves to a lady, often a married woman. Within your group, discuss how the relationships between men and women in the selections compare with gender roles in society today.

 Web Activities For eFlashcards, Selection Quick Checks, and other Web activities, go to www.glencoe.com.

Literature Groups

Students should offer everyday examples that illustrate gender roles in the text and today.

Literature Online

Web Activities Have students access the Web site for interactive activities that will help them assess their understanding of the selection.

from *Don Quixote*

MEET MIGUEL DE CERVANTES

Little is known about Miguel de Cervantes Saavedra's early years and education except that he was the son of a doctor. When he was twenty-one, Cervantes went to Italy to work for a cardinal. By 1570 he enlisted in the Spanish army regiment stationed in Rome, and the following year, he fought against the Turks in the Lepanto naval battle. Though ill with a fever, Cervantes fought bravely and his personal courage was noted. He sustained several wounds, one of which rendered his left hand permanently useless. Nonetheless, he remained with the army and fought in several other battles. While returning to Spain in 1576, Barbary pirates captured his ship, and Cervantes and his brother were sold into slavery in Algiers. Even as a slave, Cervantes gained a reputation for courage and leadership, and mounted several attempts to escape. In 1580 Cervantes's family finally managed to buy his freedom, but the price ruined his family's finances.

Struggles to Find Work Once back in Spain, Cervantes struggled with his desire to write and the necessity of making a living; he finally obtained a short-lived position as royal messenger to Algeria in 1581. During this time, Cervantes's only child, Isabel de Saavedra, was born and raised in his household.

In 1585 Cervantes published his first work, *La Galatea,* a pastoral romance written in both prose and verse. In later years, Cervantes claimed to have written more than twenty plays during this time (1582–1587), although only two survive: *La Numancia* (a historical tragedy), and *El trato de Argel* (*The Traffic of Algiers*). He once noted that these plays were received by audiences without "booing" or pelting the actors with vegetables. Cervantes's literary career languished, and he finally decided to find other, more consistent work.

Cervantes was hired as a purchasing agent for the Spanish Armada. However, accounting errors landed him in trouble with his superiors, municipal authorities, and the church, which excommunicated him several times. Cervantes started writing short stories, but his earlier accounting troubles caught up with him, and he was jailed until April 1598.

> *"It can be said that all prose fiction is a variation on the theme of Don Quixote."*
>
> —Lionel Trilling

Publishing Success In 1605 Cervantes published Part I of *Don Quixote.* The titular character is an idealistic gentleman devoted to reading chivalric romances. He decides to become a knight-errant, and sets off in search of adventure with his squire Sancho Panza. Readers responded enthusiastically, and Cervantes finally achieved literary success.

Over the next decade or so, Cervantes wrote several other works of fiction. But none surpassed the creation of Don Quixote, one of the world's most beloved and enduring literary figures.

Miguel de Cervantes was born in 1547 and died in 1616.

 Author Search For more about Miguel de Cervantes, go to www.glencoe.com.

MIGUEL DE CERVANTES **1009**

Selection Skills

from **Don Quixote**

Literary Elements
- Parody (SE pp. 1010, 1012, 1013, 1017, 1018)
- Foil (SE p. 1018)
- Idiom (TWE p. 1016)

Reading Skills
- Evaluating Characters (SE pp. 1010, 1012, 1015, 1017, 1019)
- Visualizing (TWE p. 1012)

Vocabulary Skills
- Synonyms (SE pp. 1010, 1019)

Listening/Speaking/Viewing Skills
- Conducting an Interview (SE p. 1019)

Writing Skills/Grammar
- Writing an Adventure (SE p. 1019)
- Concrete and Abstract Nouns (TWE p. 1014)

Focus

Summary

A middle-aged man steeped in the lore of knight-errantry transforms himself into Don Quixote of La Mancha. Unaware of how ludicrous he looks or how ridiculous his mission is, he sets off on his bony horse to right the wrongs of the world, accompanied only by Sancho Panza, a simple peasant who rides an ass. Don Quixote's first challenge is to destroy a brood of wicked giants. The giants are really windmills, and they nearly destroy the knight. Don Quixote remounts and sets off for more adventures.

V Vocabulary

Vocabulary File Say: Add these words and definitions to your vocabulary file. For each word, include a sentence that gives you an example of how to use the word. **OL** Students with English language needs should include the pronunciations of these words in their files. **EL**

Literary Elements Have students access the Web site to improve their understanding of parody.

Connecting to the Story

The following excerpt from *Don Quixote* depicts an underdog, or someone who is not expected to succeed. Before you read the story, think about the following questions:

- Can you remember a time when you defied the odds? Explain.
- How do you generally feel about an underdog in a given situation?

Building Background

Cervantes published the novel *Don Quixote* in two parts, the first in 1605 and the final in 1615. The excerpt included here is just a fraction of the entire work, which, in some English translations, spans over one thousand pages.

Don Quixote discusses two sharply different perspectives of the world: idealism (envisioning things in an ideal form) and realism (envisioning things as they actually are). The work can be appreciated as a satire of idealism in an imperfect and often corrupt world. *Don Quixote* also highlights the way illusion can transform. Its influence on the development of the modern novel is significant and global.

Setting Purposes for Reading

Big Idea Acts of Courage

As you read this excerpt, reflect on how Don Quixote is a hero in his own mind, and how this information is enough to render his acts courageous.

Literary Element Parody

A **parody** is a humorous imitation of a literary work that aims to illustrate the work's shortcomings. A parody may imitate the plot, characters, or style of another work, but usually exaggerates those characteristics. As you read, think about why this work is a parody of chivalry and stories about knights.

- See Literary Terms Handbook, p. R12.

OBJECTIVES
In studying this selection, you will focus on the following:
- understanding parody
- evaluating characters

- recognizing and analyzing foils
- writing to apply theme

Reading Strategy Evaluating Characters

When you **evaluate characters**, you make judgments or form opinions about them by paying close attention to their actions, statements, thoughts, and feelings. As you read this excerpt, notice how Cervantes provides details about the characters' personalities, physical attributes, and ways of thinking about life, particularly knightly life.

Reading Tip: Looking for Clues As you read, think about the clues the author gives about each character's personality. Some clues will be subtle, while others will be directly stated.

Vocabulary

interminable (in tur′ mi nə bəl) *adj.* having or seeming to have no end; p. 1012 *The students found the exam to be interminable.*

renown (ri noun′) *n.* a state of being widely acclaimed; p. 1012 *In the 1920s my aunt was a singer of worldwide renown.*

redress (ri dres′) *v.* to correct or compensate for wrong or loss; p. 1013 *The man felt there was no way to redress the tragic loss of his dog.*

discourteous (dis kur′ tē əs) *adj.* impolite; p. 1015 *The angry pedestrian was discourteous to the driver of the car that hit him.*

enmity (en′ mə tē) *n.* hatred or ill will; p. 1017 *The organization has enmity toward anyone who abuses animals.*

Vocabulary Tip: Synonyms Words that have the same or nearly the same meaning are called synonyms.

Literature Online Interactive Literary Elements Handbook To review or learn more about the literary elements, go to www.glencoe.com.

Selection Resources

Print Materials
- Unit 5 Resources (Fast File), pp. 24–26
- Leveled Vocabulary Development, p. 71
- Selection and Unit Assessments, pp. 167–168
- Selection Quick Checks, p. 84

Transparencies
- Bellringer Options Transparencies:
  Selection Focus Transparency 41
  Daily Language Practice Transparency 85
- Literary Elements Transparency 91

Technology
- TeacherWorks Plus™ CD-ROM
- StudentWorks Plus™ CD-ROM
- Presentation Plus!™ CD-ROM
- Literature Online, glencoe.com
- Online Student Edition, mhln.com
- ExamView® Assessment Suite CD-ROM
- Vocabulary PuzzleMaker CD-ROM
- Listening Library, disc 2 track 18

Don Quixote Armed as a Knight. Cristobal Valero. Museo del Prado, Madrid, Spain. ★

from DON QUIXOTE

Miguel de Cervantes
Translated by J. M. Cohen

Which treats of the quality and way of life of the famous knight Don Quixote de la Mancha.[1]

In a certain village in La Mancha,[1] which I do not wish to name, there lived not long ago a gentleman—one of those who have always a lance in the rack, an ancient shield, a lean hack[2] and a greyhound for coursing. His habitual diet consisted of a stew, more beef than mutton, of hash most nights, boiled bones on Saturdays, lentils on Fridays, and a young pigeon as a Sunday treat; and on this he spent three-quarters of his income. The rest of it went on a fine cloth doublet,[3] velvet breeches and slippers for

R

---

1. *La Mancha* is a region in south-central Spain.

2. Unlike a warhorse or show horse, a *hack* is a horse used for transportation.
3. A *doublet* is a close-fitting jacket worn by men of this time.

MIGUEL DE CERVANTES **1011**

Teach

R Reading Strategy

Evaluating Characters

Answer: *Don Quixote spends his time reading about knights and their escapades. An actual knight would live these adventures instead of reading about them.* **OL**

L1 Literary Element

Parody Answer: *Cervantes exaggerates to show Don Quixote's humorous and desperate state of mind, a condition that contrasts with a knight's usual state.* **OL**

Readability Scores
Dale-Chall: 10.9
DRP: 63
Lexile: 1350

---

holidays, and a homespun suit of the best in which he decked himself on weekdays. His household consisted of a housekeeper of rather more than forty, a niece not yet twenty, and a lad for the field and market, who saddled his horse and wielded the pruning hook.

Our gentleman was verging on fifty, of tough constitution, lean-bodied, thin-faced, a great early riser and a lover of hunting. They say that his surname was Quixada or Quesada—for there is some difference of opinion amongst authors on this point. However, by very reasonable conjecture we may take it that he was called Quexana. But this does not much concern our story; enough that we do not depart by so much as an inch from the truth in the telling of it.

The reader must know, then, that this gentleman, in the times when he had nothing to do—as was the case for most of the year—gave himself up to the reading of books of knight-errantry;[4] which he loved and enjoyed so much that he almost entirely forgot his hunting, and even the care of his estate. So odd and foolish, indeed, did he grow on this subject that he sold many acres of cornland to buy these books of chivalry[5] to read, and in this way brought home every one he could get. And of them all he considered none so good as the works of the famous Feliciano de Silva. For his brilliant style and those complicated sentences seemed to him very pearls, especially when he came upon those love passages and challenges frequently written in the manner of: "The reason for the unreason with which you treat my reason, so weakens my reason that with reason I complain of your beauty"; and also when he read: "The high heavens that with their stars divinely fortify you in your divinity and make you deserving of the desert that your greatness deserves."

These writings drove the poor knight out of his wits; and he passed sleepless nights trying to understand them and disentangle their meaning, though Aristotle[6] himself would never have unraveled or understood them, even if he had been resurrected for that sole purpose. He did not much like the wounds that Sir Belianis gave and received, for he imagined that his face and his whole body must have been covered with scars and marks, however skillful the surgeons who tended him. But, for all that, he admired the author for ending his book with the promise to continue with that **interminable** adventure, and often the desire seized him to take up the pen himself, and write the promised sequel for him. No doubt he would have done so, and perhaps successfully, if other greater and more persistent preoccupations had not prevented him.

In short, he so buried himself in his books that he spent the nights reading from twilight till daybreak and the days from dawn till dark; and so from little sleep and much reading, his brain dried up and he lost his wits. He filled his mind with all that he read in them, with enchantments, quarrels, battles, challenges, wounds, wooings, loves, torments and other impossible nonsense; and so deeply did he steep his imagination in the belief that all the fanciful stuff he read was true, that to his mind no history in the world was more authentic. . . .

In fact, now that he had utterly wrecked his reason he fell into the strangest fancy that ever a madman had in the whole world. He thought it fit and proper, both in order to increase his **renown** and to serve the state, to turn knight-errant and travel through the

---

4. *Knights-errant* traveled about in search of adventure.
5. Medieval knights lived by a code of honorable behavior known as *chivalry*.

Reading Strategy Evaluating Characters *Do you think Don Quixote is behaving like a typical knight? Explain.* **R**

1012 UNIT 5 LEGENDS AND MYTHS

---

6. The Greek philosopher *Aristotle* (384-322 BC) was considered to possess one of the greatest minds of the ancient world.

Literary Element Parody *What is Cervantes conveying about Don Quixote here?* **L1**

Vocabulary

interminable (in tur′ mi nə bəl) *adj.* having or seeming to have no end

renown (ri noun′) *n.* a state of being widely acclaimed

Additional Support

Skills Practice

READING: Visualizing The author provides some vivid descriptions of Don Quixote, but does not go into detail about his physical appearance. Ask students to describe the mental image they have of Don Quixote based on the details the author does include, such as Don Quixote's age, clothing, and habits.

Have students make sketches of Don Quixote and Sancho Panza to better visualize them. Students' sketches should reflect the differences in class and appearance of Don Quixote and Sancho Panza and incorporate as many specific details from the selection as possible. **OL**

Don Quixote in his Study, 1800–1868. George Cattermole. Victoria & Albert Museum, London.

world with horse and armor in search of adventures, following in every way the practice of the knights-errant he had read of, **redressing** all manner of wrongs, and exposing himself to chances and dangers, by the overcoming of which he might win eternal honor and renown. Already the poor man fancied himself crowned by the valor of his arm, at least with the empire of Trebizond; and so, carried away by the strange pleasure he derived from these agreeable thoughts, he hastened to translate his desires into action.

The first thing that he did was to clean some armor which had belonged to his ancestors, and had lain for ages forgotten in a corner, eaten with rust and covered with mold. But when he had cleaned and repaired it as best he could, he found that there was one great defect: the helmet was a simple headpiece without a visor. So he ingeniously made good this deficiency by fashioning out of pieces of pasteboard a kind of half-visor which, fitted to the helmet, gave the appearance of a complete headpiece. However, to see if it was strong enough to stand up to the

risk of a sword cut, he took out his sword and gave it two strokes, the first of which demolished in a moment what had taken him a week to make. He was not too pleased at the ease with which he had destroyed it, and to safeguard himself against this danger, reconstructed the visor, putting some strips of iron inside, in such a way as to satisfy himself of his protection; and, not caring to make another trial of it, he accepted it as a fine jointed headpiece and put it into commission.

Next he went to inspect his hack, but though, through leanness, he had more quarters than there are pence in a groat,[7] and more blemishes than Gonella's[8] horse, which was nothing but skin and bone, he appeared to our knight more than the equal of Alexander's Bucephalus and the Cid's Babieca.[9] He spent four days pondering what name to give him; for, he reflected, it would be wrong for the horse of so famous a knight, a horse so good in himself, to be without a famous name. Therefore he tried to fit him with one that would signify what he had been before his master turned knight-errant, and what he now was; for it was only right that as his master changed his profession, the horse should change his name for a sublime and high-sounding one, befitting the new order and the new calling he professed. So, after many names invented, struck out and rejected, amended, canceled and remade in his fanciful mind, he finally decided to call him Rocinante,[10] a name

---

7. The *groat*, an old coin, was worth four pence (four pennies). Don Quixote's horse was so bony that it appeared to have more than four quarters (the part of an animal's body that includes a leg).
8. Pietro *Gonella* was a famous court jester. He had a horse that was equally famous for being skinny.
9. *Bucephalus* was the favorite horse of Alexander the Great (356–323 BC). *Babieca* was the horse of El Cid (Rodrigo Díaz de Vivar, 1040–1099), Spain's national hero.
10. *Rocinante* is a combination of two Spanish words: *rocín*, meaning "nag or old horse," and *ante*, meaning "before or first." Rocinante could be translated into English with several meanings: as "the first old horse," "premiere (and therefore best) old horse," or "former old horse."

Big Idea Acts of Courage *Do you think Don Quixote is ready to perform acts of courage? Explain.* **BI**

Vocabulary

redress (ri dres´) *v.* to correct or compensate for wrong or loss

Literary Element Parody *How is Cervantes parodying typical knight behavior with Don Quixote's behavior here?* **L2**

MIGUEL DE CERVANTES **1013**

Teach

BI Big Idea

Acts of Courage Answer: *Students may say that Don Quixote has read frivolous stories and does not seem well-prepared for or practiced in adventure.* **OL**

L2 Literary Element

Parody Answer: *Cervantes ironically says that Don Quixote "ingeniously" made a half-visor from pieces of pasteboard. This is not something a real knight would wear.* **OL**

★ Viewing the Art

George Cattermole (1800–1868) studied architectural drafting in his youth. **Ask:** What aspects of architectural study can you see in the painting? (*Students may refer to the window, trim, or furniture.*) **AS**

English Language Coach

Ironic Tone Point out what Cervantes says about nonsensical quotes about love: "Aristotle himself would never have understood them, even if he had been resurrected for that sole purpose." Explain that while this statement implies that these quotes are very philosophical and profound, the author is being ironic. What he is really saying is that these quotes make no sense at all and are pointlessly made complex to sound impressive. Ask students to see if they can find other examples of irony and sarcasm in the part of the selection they have already read. **EL**

Objectives

• To understand parody (SE)
• To evaluate characters (SE)
• To visualize written events (TWE)

1013

Evaluating Characters

Ask: What does Don Quixote's approach to the farm girl tell you about him? *(He is so wrapped up in his fantasy that he transforms everything around him—even people—to suit his purpose.)* **OL**

B1 **Big Idea**

Acts of Courage Answer:
He chooses a lower class honest laborer. As a knight in training, his honesty will serve him well, but his intelligence is lacking. **OL**

---

which seemed to him grand and sonorous, and to express the common horse he had been before arriving at his present state: the first and foremost of all hacks in the world.

Having found so pleasing a name for his horse, he next decided to do the same for himself, and spent another eight days thinking about it. Finally he resolved to call himself Don Quixote. And that is no doubt why the authors of this true history, as we have said, assumed that his name must have been Quixada and not Quesada, as other authorities would have it. Yet he remembered that the valorous Amadis had not been content with his bare name, but had added the name of his kingdom and native country in order to make it famous, and styled himself Amadís[11] of Gaul. So, like a good knight, he decided to add the name of his country to his own and call himself Don Quixote de la Mancha. Thus, he thought, he very clearly proclaimed his parentage and native land and honored it by taking his surname from it.

Now that his armor was clean, his helmet made into a complete headpiece, a name found for his horse, and he confirmed in his new title, it struck him that there was only one more thing to do: to find a lady to be enamored of. For a knight-errant without a lady is like a tree without leaves or fruit and a body without a soul. He said to himself again and again: "If I for my sins or by good luck were to meet with some giant hereabouts, as generally happens to knights-errant, and if I were to overthrow him in the encounter, or cut him down the middle or, in short, conquer him and make him surrender, would it not be well to have someone to whom I could send him as a present, so that he could enter and kneel down before my sweet lady and say in tones of humble submission: 'Lady, I am the giant Caraculiambro, lord of the island of

Malindrania, whom the never-sufficiently-to-be-praised knight, Don Quixote de la Mancha, conquered in single combat and ordered to appear before your Grace, so that your Highness might dispose of me according to your will'?" Oh, how pleased our knight was when he had made up this speech, and even gladder when he found someone whom he could call his lady. It happened, it is believed, in this way: in a village near his there was a very good-looking farm girl, whom he had been taken with at one time, although she is supposed not to have known it or had proof of it. Her name was Aldonza Lorenzo, and she it was he thought fit to call the lady of his fancies; and, casting around for a name which should not be too far away from her own, yet suggest and imply a princess and great lady, he resolved to call her Dulcinea del Toboso—for she was a native of El Toboso—a name which seemed to him as musical, strange and significant as those others that he had devised for himself and his possessions.

In spite of the arguments of his family and friends, Don Quixote is determined to live out his dream. Most knights-errant in books were accompanied by a squire—a young man of noble birth aspiring to knighthood. Don Quixote's squire is slightly different. . . .

from Chapter VII

Of the Second Expedition of our good knight
Don Quixote de la Mancha.

All this while Don Quixote was plying a laborer, a neighbor of his and an honest man—if a poor man may be called honest—but without much salt in his brainpan. In the end, he talked to him so much, persuaded him so hard and gave him such promises that the poor yokel[12] made up his mind to go

---

11. *Amadís* was the protagonist of the romance *Amadís de Gaula (Amadís of Gaul)*. *Amadís de Gaula* was the foremost chivalric romance, written in the late thirteenth century. The character *Amadís* was widely considered the ideal knight: the most handsome and courageous of all. *Amadís de Gaula* was the object of parody for much of *Don Quixote.*

12. *Yokel* describes a naïve or gullible inhabitant of a rural area or small town.

Big Idea **Acts of Courage** What kind of person does Don Quixote choose as a squire? Is he a suitable choice? Why or why not? **B1**

Additional Support

Skills Practice

GRAMMAR: Concrete and Abstract Nouns Explain that a concrete noun names an object recognized by the senses and that an abstract noun names an idea, quality, or characteristic. Examples of concrete nouns are *saddlebags, foot,* and *helmet.* Examples of abstract nouns are *opportunity, desire,* and *discomfort.*

Write the following sentence on the board and ask students to identify each noun as concrete or abstract: "This is a fair war and it is a great service to God to wipe such a wicked brood from the face of the earth." *(concrete:* brood, face, earth; *abstract:* war, service, God*)* **OL**

Don Quixote and Sancho, 19th century.
Alexandre Gabriel Decamps. Oil on canvas.

out with him and serve him as squire. Don Quixote told him, amongst other things, that he ought to feel well disposed to come with him, for some time or another an adventure might occur that would win him in the twinkling of an eye some isle, of which he would leave him governor. These promises and others like them made Sancho Panza—for this was the laborer's name—leave his wife and children and take service as his neighbor's squire. Then Don Quixote set about raising money, and by selling one thing, pawning another, and making a bad bargain each time, he raised a reasonable sum. He also fixed himself up with a shield, which he borrowed from a friend, and patching up his broken helmet as best he could, he gave his squire Sancho notice of the day and the hour on which he proposed to set out, so that he should provide himself with all that was most needful; and he particularly told his squire to bring saddlebags. Sancho said that he would, and that he was also thinking of bringing a very fine donkey he had, for he was not too good at much traveling on foot. At the mention of the donkey Don Quixote hesitated a little, racking his brains to remember whether any knight-errant ever had a squire mounted on donkey back; but no case came to his memory. But, for all that, he decided to let him take it, intending to

provide him with a more proper mount at the earliest opportunity by unhorsing the first **discourteous** knight he should meet. He provided himself also with shirts and everything else he could, following the advice which the innkeeper had given him. And when all this was arranged and done, without Panza saying good-bye to his wife and children, or Don Quixote taking leave of his housekeeper and niece, they departed from the village one evening, quite unobserved, and rode so far that night that at daybreak they thought they were safe, and that even if anyone came out to search for them they would not be found.

Sancho Panza rode on his donkey like a patriarch,[13] with his saddlebags and his leather bottle, and a great desire to see himself governor of the isle his master had promised him. It chanced that Don Quixote took the same route and struck the same track across the plain of Montiel as on his

---

13. A *patriarch* is the oldest and most respected male member of a family.

Reading Strategy Evaluating Characters *What do Panza's and Don Quixote's actions here tell you about them?* **R₂**

Vocabulary

discourteous (dis kur′ tē əs) *adj.* impolite

MIGUEL DE CERVANTES **1015**

Teach

R₂ Reading Strategy

Evaluating Characters
Answer: *Sneaking away is not typical behavior—one expects a knight to leave openly and with pomp. These are unusual, almost childish knights.* **OL**

★ **Viewing the Art**

Alexandre Gabriel Decamps (1803–1860) was known for his paintings with exotic and adventurous Middle Eastern scenes. **Ask:** Does this painting represent the spirit of adventure? Why or why not? *(Students may point to the road [beginning of a journey], sword [knight's weapon], tired animals [not so glamorous], etc.)* **AS**

Differentiated Instruction

Identifying Author's Purpose To identify Cervantes' purpose in writing *Don Quixote,* ask students to examine his tone, the events and details he emphasizes, and their own reactions to the story. Have them discuss what they think the purposes of the selection are, pointing out in particular any messages that the author seems to want to convey to the reader. *(Students may say that Cervantes' purposes are to satirize popular tales about knights-errant and to write a humorous and entertaining story. Messages include warnings against exaggerated idealism and becoming caught up in a fantasy world.)* **BL**

Objectives
• To evaluate characters (SE)
• To identify concrete and abstract nouns (TWE)

BI₁ Big Idea

Acts of Courage Answer:
Don Quixote is convinced that the windmills are monsters to fight. His intentions are courageous. However, he is foolish because his behavior is based on a misconception. **OL**

⭐ Viewing the Art

Charles Robert Leslie (1794–1859) was an English painter known for his portraits and historical paintings. **Ask:** What does this painting tell you about the character Sancho Panza? *(Students should point to his size and pampered look, and say that he is concerned with the indulgent side of life, i.e., food and drink.)* **AS**

---

first expedition; but he traveled with less discomfort than before, as it was the hour of dawn, and the sun's rays, striking them obliquely, did not annoy them. . . .

from Chapter VIII

Of the valorous Don Quixote's success in the dreadful and never before imagined Adventure of the Windmills, with other events worthy of happy record.

At that moment they caught sight of some thirty or forty windmills, which stand on that plain, and as soon as Don Quixote saw them he said to his squire: "Fortune is guiding our affairs better than we could have wished. Look over there, friend Sancho Panza, where more than thirty monstrous giants appear. I intend to do battle with them and take all their lives. With their spoils we will begin to get rich, for this is a fair war, and it is a great service to God to wipe such a wicked brood from the face of the earth."

"What giants?" asked Sancho Panza.

Sancho Panza, 1839. Charles Robert Leslie. ⭐
Oil on panel, 12 x 9 in.
Victoria and Albert Museum, London.

"Those you see there," replied his master, "with their long arms. Some giants have them about six miles long."

"Take care, your worship," said Sancho; "those things over there are not giants but windmills, and what seem to be their arms are the sails, which are whirled round in the wind and make the millstone turn."

"It is quite clear," replied Don Quixote, "that you are not experienced in this matter of adventures. They are giants, and if you are afraid, go away and say your prayers, while I advance and engage them in fierce and unequal battle."

As he spoke, he dug his spurs into his steed Rocinante, paying not attention to his squire's shouted warning that beyond all doubt they were windmills and no giants he was advancing to attack. But he went on, so positive that they were giants that he neither listened to Sancho's cries nor noticed what they were, even when he got near them. Instead he went on shouting in a loud voice: "Do not fly, cowards, vile creatures, for it is one knight alone who assails you."

At that moment a slight wind arose, and the great sails began to move. At the sight of which Don Quixote shouted: "Though you wield more arms than the giant Briareus, you shall pay for it!" Saying this, he commended himself with all his soul to his Lady Dulcinea, beseeching her aid in his great peril. Then, covering himself with his shield and putting his lance in the rest, he urged Rocinante forward at a full gallop and attacked the nearest windmill, thrusting his lance into the sail. But the wind turned it with such violence that it shivered his weapon in pieces, dragging the horse and his rider with it, and sent the knight rolling badly injured across the plain. Sancho Panza rushed to his assistance as fast as his donkey could trot, but when he came up he found that the knight could not stir. Such a shock had Rocinante given him in their fall.

Big Idea Acts of Courage *Do you think Don Quixote is behaving courageously here or foolishly? Explain.* **BI₁**

Additional Support

1016

LITERARY ELEMENT: Idiom Remind students that an idiom is an expression whose meaning cannot be understood only by knowing the meanings of the words. Ask whether they have ever heard the expression *to tilt at windmills,* meaning "to combat imaginary foes or nonexistent dangers."

Write the following sentences on the board and ask students to explain them in their own words:
I never see you without your Sancho Panza hanging on you.
Stan will never be realistic; he'll always be a Don Quixote. **OL**

"O my goodness!" cried Sancho. "Didn't I tell your worship to look what you were doing, for they were only windmills? Nobody could mistake them, unless he had windmills on the brain."

"Silence, friend Sancho," replied Don Quixote. "Matters of war are more subject than most to continual change. What is more, I think—and that is the truth—that the same sage Friston who robbed me of my room and my books has turned those giants into windmills, to cheat me of the glory of conquering them. Such is the **enmity** he bears me; but in the very end his black arts shall avail him little against the goodness of my sword."

"God send it as He will," replied Sancho Panza, helping the knight to get up and remount Rocinante, whose shoulders were half dislocated.

As they discussed this last adventure they followed the road to the pass of Lapice where, Don Quixote said, they could not fail to find many and various adventures, as many travelers passed that way. He was much concerned, however, at the loss of his lance, and, speaking of it to his squire, remarked: "I remember reading that a certain Spanish knight called Diego Perez de Vargas, having broken his sword in battle, tore a great bough or limb from an oak, and performed such deeds with it that day, and pounded so many Moors, that he earned the surname of the Pounder, and thus he and his descendants from that day onwards have been called Vargas y Machuca.[14] I mention this because I propose to tear down just such a limb from the first oak we meet, as big and as good as his; and I intend to do such deeds with it that you may consider yourself most fortunate to have won

14. The name *Machuca* comes from the Spanish verb *machucar*, "to crush."

Vocabulary

enmity (en′ mə tē) *n.* hatred or ill will

the right to see them. For you will witness things which will scarcely be credited."

"With God's help," replied Sancho, "and I believe it all as your worship says. But sit a bit more upright, sir, for you seem to be riding lopsided. It must be from the bruises you got when you fell."

"That is the truth," replied Don Quixote. "And if I do not complain of the pain, it is because a knight-errant is not allowed to complain of any wounds, even though his entrails[15] may be dropping out through them."

"If that's so, I have nothing more to say," said Sancho, "but God knows I should be glad if your worship would complain if anything hurt you. I must say, for my part, that I have to cry out at the slightest twinge, unless this business of not complaining extends to knights-errants' squires as well."

Don Quixote could not help smiling at his squire's simplicity,[16] and told him that he could certainly complain how and when he pleased, whether he had any cause or no, for up to that time he had never read anything to the contrary in the law of chivalry.

Sancho reminded him that it was time for dinner, but his master replied that he had need of none, but that his squire might eat whenever he pleased. With this permission Sancho settled himself as comfortably as he could on his donkey and, taking out what he had put into the saddlebags, jogged very leisurely along behind his master, eating all the while; and from time to time he raised the bottle with such relish that the best-fed publican[17] in Malaga might have envied him. Now, as he went along like this, taking repeated gulps, he entirely forgot the promise his master had made him, and reckoned that going in search of adventures, however dangerous, was more like pleasure than hard work. . . . ✎

15. *Entrails* are internal organs, especially the intestines.
16. Here, *simplicity* means "innocence" or "silliness."
17. *Publican* is another term for innkeeper.

MIGUEL DE CERVANTES **1017**

Assess

1. (a) Answers will vary. (b) Answers will vary, but should be supported by text details.

2. (a) Sleep deprivation "addles his brains." (b) The language in the "quotation" is unlike that of Cervantes's own book, and the quotation itself makes no sense.

3. (a) He promises him an island to govern. (b) He is concerned with the basics of life: food and comfort.

4. (a) To increase his renown and serve the state by redressing wrongs (b) The whole concept of knight-errantry and those who ide-alize it

5. (a) Don Quixote sees evil giants, and Sancho Panza sees windmills. (b) People's problems or dangers

6. (a) It leaves a person unpre-pared for life's realities. (b) Enthusiasm and motivation in the pursuit of a goal

7. It is not an answer to current problems and may not have originally been wonderful.

8. Most students will probably find him to be a sympathetic character.

RESPONDING AND THINKING CRITICALLY

Respond

1. (a)How did you react to the character of Don Quixote? (b)Is he someone you would consider heroic? Explain.

Recall and Interpret

2. (a)What causes Don Quixote to lose his wits? (b)How do you know that Cervantes is parodying the style of Feliciano de Silva?

3. (a)How does Don Quixote persuade Sancho Panza to become his squire? (b)How would you describe Sancho Panza's philosophy of life?

4. (a)What is Don Quixote's purpose in becoming a knight errant? (b)Satire holds up something or someone to ridicule or critique. What is the target of Cervantes's satire when the narrator describes Don Quixote's lofty goals?

5. (a)How do Don Quixote and Sancho Panza each view the windmills? (b)What might the windmills symbolize? Explain.

Analyze and Evaluate

6. Cervantes's depiction of his hero is the source of the English word *quixotic,* which describes a person caught up in the romantic pursuit of unreachable goals without regard for practicality. (a)What do you think are the dangers of seeing the world in this way? (b)Are there any advantages? Explain.

7. Through the character of Don Quixote, what might Cervantes be suggesting about people who "live in the past"?

Connect

8. **Big Idea** **Acts of Courage** Do you agree that Don Quixote is a courageous yet sympathetic character, or do you think that he is merely a buffoon? Explain your opinion.

LITERARY ANALYSIS

Literary Element Parody

A **parody** seeks to poke fun at or critique some aspect of society. Cervantes uses parody in *Don Quixote* to offer his critique of a life and time dominated by greed and violence, as well as to poke fun at popular novels about chivalry, such as *Amadís de Gaula*.

1. How does Cervantes use Don Quixote's madness to help him parody aspects of life?

2. What are some particular incidents in this selection that use humor to show that Don Quixote is not an ideal knight like those in Arthurian legends or others in chivalric romances?

3. How do the names used throughout *Don Quixote* contribute to its humor and its use of parody?

Review: Foil

As you learned on page 834, every character in literature has certain personality traits or qualities that are revealed to us in the course of a literary work. Sometimes a writer creates characters who are **foils** for one another—those who have opposite personality traits and are best under-stood in contrast with each other. For example, one char-acter may be calm, while the foil may be hot-tempered. By showing us the two figures side by side in the same situations, the author stresses their differences and helps the reader see their individual qualities more clearly.

Partner Activity Pair up with a classmate and discuss the following questions about the use of foils in *Don Quixote:*

1. How do Don Quixote's traits compare with those of Sancho Panza?

2. In the code of medieval chivalry, a squire served as an apprentice or knight-in-training. How does the portrayal of Sancho Panza by Cervantes mock the role of the squire in medieval courtly romances?

Literary Element

1. It is a sort of higher wisdom. In his madness, Don Quixote sees meek people as good. He can call the rich "monsters" and get away with it.

2. He thinks windmills are giants, whereas the ideal knight would see a windmill realistically.

3. His exact name is unknown and dis-puted, contrasting with his high self-image. His lady's and horse's names are exaggerated and comical.

READING AND VOCABULARY

Reading Strategy Evaluating Characters

Most people in Don Quixote's time thought of the ideal knight as being physically strong, capable, and honorable. Don Quixote, however, is elderly, weak, and somewhat delusional. Furthermore, as his squire, he chooses Sancho Panza, who is married, poor, and concerned with providing enough food and money for his family. The **characters** in *Don Quixote* in some ways highlight the qualities that traditional knights did not aspire to possess.

1. How might the story be different if Don Quixote or Sancho Panza were ideal types?

2. Why do you think Don Quixote chose Sancho Panza instead of a more suitable candidate?

Vocabulary Practice

Practice with Synonyms Find the synonym for each vocabulary word listed below.

1. interminable
   a. foul   **b.** endless
2. renown
   a. fame   **b.** renew
3. redress
   a. remedy   **b.** outfit
4. discourteous
   a. rude   **b.** lost
5. enmity
   a. unified   **b.** hatred

Academic Vocabulary

Here are two words from the vocabulary list on page R82.

tradition (trə dish′ən) *n.* customs practiced from generation to generation

resolve (ri zolv′) *v.* to make a firm decision about something; to determine

Practice and Apply

1. What is one way that Don Quixote follows **tradition** in this story?

2. What causes Sancho Panza to **resolve** to be Don Quixote's squire?

WRITING AND EXTENDING

Writing About Literature

Apply Theme As explained earlier, a *quixotic* character is one who is foolishly impractical. Write your own adventure involving a quixotic character, set either in Don Quixote's time or in the present.

Before you begin drafting, outline your story's beginning, middle, and end. Jot down some notes about the main character's personality, what he or she looks like, and the conflict that the character will go through in the story. You may want to use a chart similar to the one below.

Plot:	Characters:	Conflicts:
Beginning:		
Middle:		
End:		

If you are comfortable parodying an aspect of contemporary life, add this to your story. Once you have completed the diagram, begin drafting.

After completing your draft, choose a peer reviewer and exchange stories. Evaluate each other's work for clarity and flow. Discuss areas of your partner's draft that may need clarification or more description. Then proofread and edit your own draft for errors in spelling, grammar, and punctuation.

Learning for Life

In small groups, conduct a mock interview with Don Quixote. Brainstorm and formulate interview questions, possible responses by Don Quixote, and the interview host's words. Choose one group member to conduct the interview, one to be Don Quixote, and one to be the stage manager. Practice the interview before presenting it to your classmates.

Literature Online Web Activities For eFlashcards, Selection Quick Checks, and other Web activities, go to www.glencoe.com.

MIGUEL DE CERVANTES **1019**

Assess

Review: Foil

1. Don Quixote is idealistic and impractical. Sancho Panza has too little wit or imagination to dream.

2. Sancho Panza does not belong to the appropriate class nor does he have any appropriate qualities, except loyalty.

Reading Strategy

1. It would not have been a comical parody of the genre.

2. To contrast with Don Quixote's imagination and belief. Don Quixote probably had limited options for potential squires, as most people would be hesitant to accompany a delusional man on an imaginary journey.

Vocabulary

1. b **2.** a **3.** a **4.** a **5.** b

Academic Vocabulary

1. He sets out on a journey, he appoints a knight errant, he tries to right wrongs, and he meets a woman.

2. Quixote promises him an island of which he will be governor.

Writing About Literature

Students' essays should

- show an understanding of the term *quixotic*
- apply the theme of *Don Quixote* to an original work

Learning for Life

Students' interviews should

- use interview format
- reflect an understanding of the characters

1019

Focus

Summary

Amanda Ripley describes a heroic act by a doctor with Doctors Without Borders. She compares and contrasts American and European definitions of and need for heroes. Ripley also examines "everyday" heroes.

Teach

Big Idea

Acts of Courage **Say:** As you read, keep the following questions in mind: How do you define heroism? Whom do *you* see as a hero? **OL**

Readability Scores
Dale-Chall: 10.0
DRP: 63
Lexile: 1080

Media Link to Acts of Courage

Preview the Article

1. What answers can you give to the question in the title of the article?

2. From skimming the first paragraph, what can you predict about the content of the article?

Set a Purpose for Reading

Read to discover contrasting ideas about heroes.

Reading Strategy

Clarifying Meaning
When you **clarify the meaning** of a text, you work to unlock the meaning of each section or paragraph. To clarify meaning, answer the following questions:

- What does this section mean? Why might the writer have chosen to include this?

- How does this information relate to the main idea and other ideas in the text?

Create a chart similar to the one below and answer the questions to help you clarify meaning as you read.

Questions to Ask	Ideas and Thoughts
What does this section mean?	
How does this relate to the main idea?	
How does this relate to what I already know about the subject?	

OBJECTIVES
- Clarify understanding of informational texts by creating graphic organizers.
- Determine the main idea and supporting details.

1020 UNIT 5 LEGENDS AND MYTHS

TIME

WHAT MAKES A HERO?

Some heroes act boldly on the world stage. Others make a difference outside the public eye by identifying problems, finding solutions, and inspiring the rest of us.

By AMANDA RIPLEY

WAR BREEDS HEROES—AND A DEEP NEED TO ANOINT them. The soldier who sacrifices himself for his comrades, the civilian who walks more than six miles to get help for a wounded prisoner of war, the medic who makes no distinction between a bleeding ally and a bleeding enemy, the aid worker who passes through a combat zone to bring water to a crippled city—all are called heroes, and all deserve to be. But the word *hero* is also used as a way to excuse senseless deaths, a way to support the fiction that courage and bravery will be enough to carry men and women through the valley of death. The truth is more complicated and sad. Sometimes heroic virtue means the difference between life and death and sometimes it does not. Sometimes a hero is not born until the moment he or she recognizes that heroism may not solve anything—and yet behaves heroically anyway.

In the 1980s, Xavier Emmanuelli, cofounder of the medical humanitarian organization Doctors Without Borders, was working on the border between Cambodia and Thailand. With bombs falling uncomfortably nearby, Emmanuelli and another doctor attended to wounded refugees. The first victim was a young woman. She was alive but critically wounded, her body nearly sliced in two by a bomb fragment. Emmanuelli made a quick diagnosis. "I thought there was nothing to be done and went on to another victim," he remembers.

But when he looked back, the other doctor, a young man named Daniel Pavard, had not moved on. He was cradling the woman's head and caressing her hair. "He was helping her die," says Emmanuelli. "He did it very naturally. There was no public, no cameras, no one looking. The bombing continued, and he did this as if he was all alone in his humanity."

In his 35-year career, Emmanuelli has witnessed most

Additional Support

See also 📖 Active Learning and Note Taking Guide, pp. 159–166.

Skills Practice

WRITING: Comic Strip
Encourage students to tap into their creativity by conceiving, writing, and illustrating a comic strip featuring a hero or heroine of their own creation. Students might create a hero or heroine with superhero powers. Alternatively, students might create a hero or heroine who addresses a concrete problem in today's society. Allow students to collaborate with each other on this project. Some students can work as writers and others as illustrators. When the students have finished their projects, bind their comic strips together into a class publication. **OL**

of the tragedies of our era, from Saigon to Sierra Leone, locations where warfare has resulted in thousands of deaths—places where heroes are made if ever there are heroes. But he has never found heroes in the obvious spots—behind podiums, say, or on armored personnel carriers. Sometimes he has not even recognized them until later, reflecting on what he has seen them do. "It is in gestures," he says, "that you know a person's true nature—gestures that almost escape detection."

Today, the newspapers are full of hero nominees, some more convincing than others. The British papers gushed over Lieut. Colonel Tim Collins, who became a national hero in England for giving a speech to his troops before they marched into war in Iraq: "We go to liberate, not to conquer," he said. "If you are ferocious in battle, remember to be magnanimous [noble and fair-minded] in victory."

News reporters have been called heroic for doing their jobs, and bombing victims have been called courageous for surviving. There have been grainy black-and-white portraits of U.S. General Tommy Franks and sad images of France's President Jacques Chirac, the "white knight of peace," as the French newspaper *Le Figaro* called him. Still, many people find it hard to believe in any of the major leaders for more than half an hour. A hero, by most definitions, must be both brave and generous, a rare combination.

American and European Heroes

For some, the very idea of a "European hero" is problematic. It is Americans, after all—whom the Irish-born writer Oscar Wilde mockingly called "hero worshippers"—who put all their faith in a romantic notion of the individual. Europeans like to put their faith in the group; they believe that they know better than to overestimate the lone actor. Is it not unrealistic to think that a single, flawed human can change the world? Have we not learned by now that history is a mix of complicated circumstances, not a totem pole of individual men—heroic as they may be?

"In the U.S., it is more likely that the rugged individualist will be admired more," says Oxford University philosopher Roger Crisp. "It's kind of old-fashioned. There's a sense [in Europe] that we've already been through that." Billionaire businessmen are not embraced as society's saviors. That is what the state is for. When TIME asked Italian novelist Umberto Eco who his hero was, he responded with a quotation from German playwright Bertolt Brecht: "Unhappy the land that needs heroes."

And yet, for all of Europe's worldly skepticism, there is no doubt that heroes live there—and not all of them went to the war zone. People still crave heroes, still

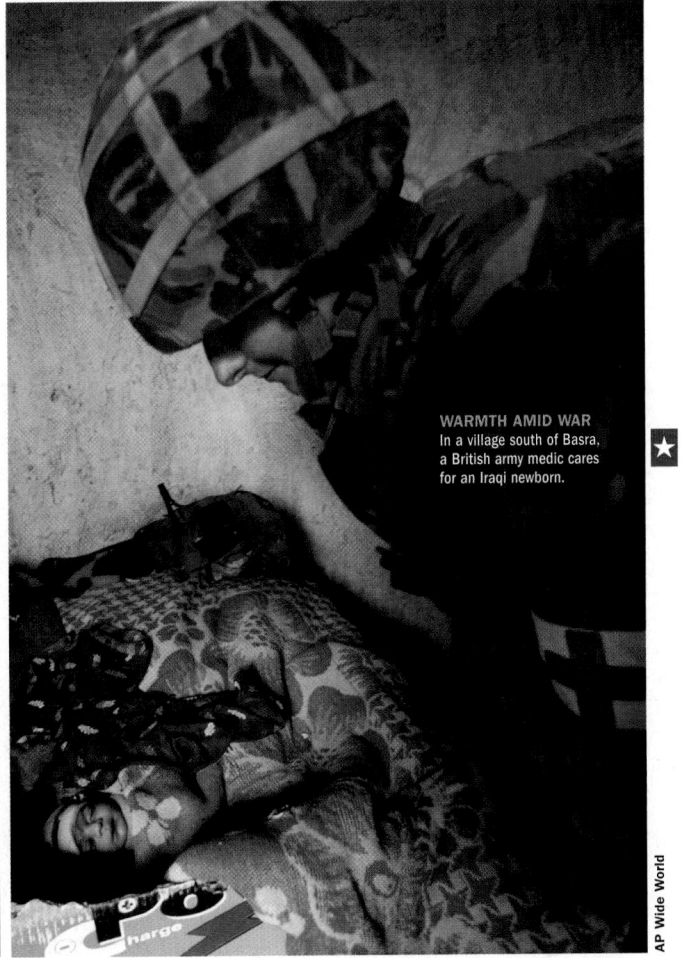

WARMTH AMID WAR
In a village south of Basra, a British army medic cares for an Iraqi newborn.

AP Wide World

WHAT MAKES A HERO? **1021**

Informational Text

TIME

Teach

R Reading Strategy

Clarifying Meaning

Say: Clarifying meaning while you read is important because authors often build ideas on one another. If you don't clear up a confusing passage, you may not understand main ideas or information that comes later. Assist students in clarifying the text's meaning. Explain that if they don't understand a particular passage, they can take the following steps:

- Reread the section more slowly.
- Look up words you don't know in a dictionary.
- Ask questions about what you don't understand. **OL**

★ Viewing the Photograph

Ask: How does this photograph illustrate both public and private acts of heroism? *(Students may see the soldier fighting a public war but also caring for the baby in a very private and intimate way.)* **AS**

Reading in the Real World

Citizenship Say: One category of heroes Ripley discusses is the "everyday hero": an ordinary citizen who does something extraordinary. Invite students to research everyday heroes in their local newspapers and publications. Students should note who the person is (or was), what the person did, and how and why this person is considered heroic. Set aside part of a class period for students to present their findings to the class. Discuss the commonalities and explore the different assumptions students have. **OL**

Objectives
- To clarify understanding of informational texts by creating graphic organizers (SE)
- To create a comic strip (TWE)

Teach

Informational Text

R rely on individuals—if not to solve problems single-handedly, then at least to identify them, to point the way toward a solution and, not least, to inspire the rest of us.

"People do need heroes in Europe," insists Sister Emmanuelle, the Belgian-born nun who spent 22 years living among the garbage pickers of Cairo, Egypt, forcing the rest of the world to acknowledge their existence. "Currently there is a real search for grandness, in a different way than wealth. I can see how people need this when they cry as I tell them about the love and deep commonality that saves people. That touches them deep in their hearts," says Emmanuelle. She is living proof that for the European hero, the good of the group and individual accomplishment can exist together.

Heroes Past and Present

In ancient Greece, heroes inhabited a space between gods and men. "Their heroes were very often flawed," says Crisp. "[The ancient Greek warrior]

LIBERATION
Lech Walesa, founder of Poland's Solidarity movement (top) and Charles de Gaulle. Both helped to free their nations from tyrannical rule

Achilles was sulky and arrogant, but admired because he was big and tough." The same might be said of some European heroes today. In a 2003 survey of six European nations, people were asked to name a famous figure from European history with whom they would like to pass an hour. The study, sponsored by three European associations, was meant to identify the "great men" who inhabit an overall

European memory.

In the end, despite the fact that they have spent decades throwing politicians out of office, people chose their country's current leaders. The Germans wanted an hour with Foreign Minister Joschka Fischer. The British picked their prime minister, Tony Blair. The Spanish, President José María Aznar. The French . . . well, the French picked Charles de Gaulle, of course. The greatly admired general and statesman became the symbol of France during its battle against Nazi occupation and later as its president. But the second most popular choice in France was the current president, Chirac.

Even as we disparage our leaders, we still want to believe in them. In late 2002, the BBC television channel caused hours of dinner-table bickering when it invited the public to vote for the greatest Briton of all time. Beatle John Lennon and Princess Diana made the short list. But the winner was Winston Churchill, who led the country through the

★ **BORN LEADER**
Nelson Mandela, the one-man dynamo in the fight to end South Africa's apartheid.

1022 UNIT 5 LEGENDS AND MYTHS

dark and difficult days of the Second World War.

Everyday Heroes

If you asked a thousand people for a definition of heroism, you would get a thousand different answers. The French celebrity philosopher Bernard-Henri Levy defines a hero narrowly, as someone who tells the truth when it means risking his or her life. Others are so uncomfortable with the word that they prefer to use different, subtle labels like "role model" or "uncommon man."

Many people take a broader view and define heroes as people who have stood without flinching in the face of very bad odds. Some say people who put themselves in mortal danger are heroes. Others define heroes as activists, in the old-fashioned sense, stubbornly beating a drum to remind us of problems we would prefer to ignore. Some believe that heroes are able to turn grief that would have destroyed most of us into defiant hope. Still others say that heroes live comfortably while inspiring millions to hope

for better things.

Most heroes are walking contradictions. A hero has to be, on the one hand, a dreamer—to believe against overwhelming odds that something can change. But a hero is also a realist who does something useful; giving up is not an option.

And so in France, a businessman has begun collecting résumés in the decaying housing projects of the Parisian suburbs so he can help young immigrants find jobs. In Iceland, a former engineer convinced people to save the whales not because they are pretty, but because the whale-watching industry could make more money than the whale-killing industry. And in the West Bank, a Palestinian surgeon endures a six-hour round-trip commute through armed checkpoints to save lives—both Arab and Jewish—in the operating room of an Israeli hospital. After decades of assuming the state would look after the collective good, Europeans—and Americans—have been forced to acknowledge that the government cannot manage the job alone.

Individuals must fill the gaps.

True heroes, adds Emmanuelli, never know that they are heroes. They just find themselves in a situation for which they have been preparing, unwittingly, all their lives. Then they do the right thing. "A hero understands that he is a tool," he says.

In every case, if heroism requires courage and generosity, the last ingredient is circumstance. Novelist Jean-Christophe Rufin, winner of France's top literary award, and president of *Action Contre la Faim* (Action Against Hunger), a private humanitarian organization, says his model of a hero was his grandfather. Until he was sent to a Nazi prison camp for hiding people in his garage, he raised Rufin himself. "Physically, he was absolutely not a hero. He was short, thin and weak, though he resisted many things that would have killed me 10 times," Rufin says. "All the choices he made were kind of obvious things. It was the circumstances that made him a hero."

—Updated 2005, from TIME Europe, April 28, 2003

RESPONDING AND THINKING CRITICALLY

Respond

1. Did your ideas about what makes a hero change after you read the article? Explain.

Recall and Interpret

2. (a) Why did Xavier Emmanuelli, cofounder of Doctors Without Borders, think that his colleague, Daniel Pavard, was a hero? (b) How does this challenge the traditional definition of a hero?

3. (a) According to Oxford University philosopher Roger Crisp, how do people in the United States define heroes? (b) Do you agree with him? Why or why not?

4. (a) According to the writer, what are two qualities that a hero must have? (b) What do you think some other qualities of a hero might be?

Analyze and Evaluate

5. The article cites German playwright Bertolt Brecht, who once said "Unhappy the land that needs heroes." What do you think this means? Do you agree? Explain.

6. (a) How does the writer conclude the article? (b) Do you think it is an effective conclusion? Why or why not?

7. What do you think is the main idea of the article? Support your ideas with evidence from the article.

Connect

8. Compare and contrast the heroes of Sir Thomas Malory's *Le Morte d'Arthur* and those described in this TIME article.

WHAT MAKES A HERO?   **1023**

Assess

1. Students should explain their opinions and ideas about heroism.

2. (a) Because he quietly helped a dying bomb victim while no one was around to observe him (b) Most people identified as heroes are in the public eye.

3. (a) People in the United States define heroes as "rugged individualists." (b) Some may say that traditional heroes in the United States are political leaders, soldiers, or entrepreneurs, while others may see Crisp's definition as a generalization.

4. (a) A hero must be both an idealistic dreamer and a realist. (b) Selflessness, emotional and physical strength, and humanity

5. Students may say that a land that "needs heroes" may not be providing for its citizens—and is therefore an unhappy place—or that people seek out heroes regardless of their country's conditions.

6. (a) With a quotation from the novelist Jean-Christophe Rufin (b) The quotation provides sense of closure—that circumstances make heroes. Some students, however, might want a more definitive statement.

7. Some students may say that there are many kinds of heroes, or that our definition of heroism has changed over time. Students should provide evidence for their claims.

8. Sir Launcelot acted with honor and virtue with women and his allies; however, he was also a public figure and a warrior. Most of the heroes in Ripley's article save lives rather than take them, as Launcelot does.

For additional assessment, see 📁 Selection and Unit Assessment, pp. 169–170.

Focus

BELLRINGER

Bellringer Options
Selection Focus Transparency 42
Daily Language Practice
Transparency 86
Or show images of tools of war, past and present (shields, combat boots, or gas masks). **Ask:**
What do you think you would need to be a warrior? Have students identify the components and compose a description of a "perfect" warrior.

Literature Online

Author Search To expand students' appreciation of D. T. Niane, have them access the Web site for additional information and resources.

from *Sundiata*

MEET D. T. NIANE AND THE STORYTELLERS

The *Sundiata* (soon dyä'tə) is the national epic of the Mandingo people, who live in present-day Mali and parts of the coastal region of West Africa. It celebrates the founding of the ancient Mali empire, which occurred around 1235. A king named Sundiata played an important role in establishing Mali as a powerful state. Stories and legends about Sundiata are told to this day.

The Griot or Jali All over the world, storytellers have helped to pass down history and tradition from generation to generation in times and places where literacy was not widespread. In Africa one name for the storyteller—a name which may come from French or Portuguese—is *griot* (grē'o). A Mende, or native African, word for griot is *jali* (or *jeli* or *djali*). Griots or jalis are steeped in oral tradition from childhood onward.

During Sundiata's time, griots were employed by kings and other leaders to recite their country's legendary history. In African society prior to colonization, griots held a high place in social status hierarchies. They were valued for recording the history and traditions of their societies. Since they did not work from a written text, they could alter their stories to suit occasions and their audiences. This process led to the development of many different versions of the *Sundiata*. The episode you will read comes from a version told by storyteller Mamadou Kouyaté (ma'mä doo koo yä' tä) to historian and professor D. T. Niane, who adapted it into prose.

"We are the repositories which harbor secrets many centuries old. . . ."

—Mamadou Kouyaté

From the Storytellers to Us Today, the *Sundiata* is recited by Mandingo griots. Their performances, which can last several hours, are enlivened by musical accompaniment, dramatic gestures, and frequent interjections from the audience, suggesting agreement and enthusiasm.

When D. T. Niane, a specialist in the Mande world, met griots in Mali, he felt that his eyes had "been opened [to the] mysteries of eternal Africa." In his introduction to the *Sundiata*, he wrote, "May this book open the eyes of more than one African and induce him to come and sit humbly beside the ancients and hear the words of the griots who teach wisdom and history."

Literature Online **Author Search** For more about D. T. Niane and the storytellers, go to www.glencoe.com.

1024 UNIT 5 LEGENDS AND MYTHS

Selection Skills

Literary Elements
- Dialogue (SE pp. 1025, 1027, 1028, 1029, 1030)
- Idiom (TWE p. 1028)

from **Sundiata**

Reading Skills
- Identifying Genre (SE pp. 1025, 1027, 1029, 1030)

Vocabulary Skills
- Word Parts (SE p. 1030)

Writing Skills/Grammar
- Writing About Character (SE p. 1030)

Study Skills/Research/Assessment
- Conducting Research (TWE p. 1026)

Connecting to the Legend

The *Sundiata* tells the story of a great leader, his followers, and their larger-than-life deeds. Before you read this passage, ask yourself the following questions:

- What helps you gain the extra confidence and energy you need to perform well in events such as a crucial game or an exam?
- Why do people enjoy listening to stories about heroes?

Building Background

Sundiata came to power around 1235, when he freed Mali from the control of a neighboring kingdom. He built his capital in Niani, which was located on a tributary of the Niger River. Enriched by profits from the gold trade, Niani became an important commercial center. Sundiata continued to expand the empire until his death in 1255. Under his successors, the empire flourished. At a time when bandits roamed through other areas, Mali was known as a safe and orderly place. "Neither traveler nor inhabitant in it has anything to fear from robbers or men of violence," wrote an early Arab visitor.

Setting Purposes for Reading

Big Idea Acts of Courage

As you read, notice how the characters in the *Sundiata* display their courage.

Literary Element Dialogue

Dialogue is the written conversation between characters in a literary work. Through dialogue, an author reveals the feelings, thoughts, and intentions of characters, develops conflicts, and moves the plot forward. As you read, analyze the dialogue in this legend and consider how it reveals characters and advances the plot.

- See Literary Terms Handbook, p. R5.

Literature Online Interactive Literary Elements Handbook To review or learn more about the literary elements, go to www.glencoe.com.

Reading Strategy Identifying Genre

Genre is a category or type of literary work characterized by a particular form or style. One important genre of folklore is legends, or stories that are believed to be based on historical events and an actual hero. Legends help convey a culture's learning, knowledge, and values.

Reading Tip: Making a Chart Record details of the *Sundiata* that help you identify it as a legend.

Sundiata	
Details that reveal historical events	
Details about a hero's exploits	
Details that reveal Mandingo customs, beliefs, and values	Sundiata has great charm and the strength of ten men. Charm and strength are valued.
Details that are fantastic or exaggerated	

Vocabulary

scrupulous (skro͞o′pyə ləs) *adj.* thoroughly attentive to even the smallest details; precise; p. 1027 *Ana's knitting was scrupulous.*

elude (i lo͞od′) *v.* to avoid or escape, especially through cleverness or quickness; p. 1027 *As one child gave chase, the other child tried to elude her.*

confidante (kon′ fə dant′) *n.* a person who is entrusted with secrets or private affairs; p. 1028 *Only Eric's confidante knew about his secret plans.*

perpetuate (pər pech′o͞o āt′) *v.* to cause to continue to be remembered; p. 1028 *Gossip can perpetuate hurtful and untrue rumors.*

Focus

Summary

Sundiata, son of the former king of Mali, stops in Sibi with his army on the way to battle Mali's current king, Soumaoro, who rules through evil magic. Sundiata's sister, who was forced to become a wife to Soumaoro, has learned the secret of the magic and shares this knowledge with Sundiata. After a review of his troops and armed with the information from his sister, Sundiata confidently leads his army to meet the enemy.

V Vocabulary

Vocabulary File Say: Add these words and definitions to your vocabulary file. For each word, include a sentence that gives you an example of how to use the word. **OL** Students with English language needs should include the pronunciations of these words in their files. **EL**

Literary Elements Have students access the Web site to improve their understanding of dialogue.

OBJECTIVES

In studying this selection, you will focus on the following:
- analyzing dialogue
- identifying genre and analyzing legends
- connecting a text to contemporary events

D. T. NIANE AND THE STORYTELLERS **1025**

Big Idea

Acts of Courage Say: Keep these questions in mind as you read: How does Sundiata react to injustice? Is he a warrior or a peacemaker? *(Sundiata could be described as both; he waged war to correct social injustice, to defend those who could not defend themselves, and to bring peace.)* **OL**

⭐ Cultural History

Mali From 1307 to 1332, Mali was governed by the famous Muslim ruler Mansa Musa. During this time, the city of Timbuktu became recognized as an important center of knowledge and Muslim culture. Between 1324 and 1325, Mansa Musa led a pilgrimage to Mecca, giving evidence of his great wealth and influence. His entourage was preceded by 500 individuals carrying staffs of gold, and his gifts to the ruler of Cairo were so extravagant that they resulted in the devaluation of gold in Egypt. **AS**

Readability Scores
Dale-Chall: 5.3
DRP: 58
Lexile: 1020

Sahelian Landscape, Mali, 1991. Tilly Willis. Oil on canvas. Private collection.

from ⚜ SUNDIATA ⚜

Recorded by D. T. Niane
Translated by G. D. Pickett

Even before he was born, Sundiata was destined for greatness. Acting on the instructions of a soothsayer,[1] his father, the king of Mali, had married a hideous, hunchbacked woman named Sogolon. As foretold, the couple had a son. It seemed, however, that the boy was unlikely to become a great leader as had been predicted. The young Sundiata could not even walk. He and his ugly mother became the object of cruel jokes and jealous abuse by the old king's first wife. At the age of seven, Sundiata suddenly reacted to an insult by standing up and tearing a tree from the ground. He instantly became the center of atten-

tion, a boy with great charm and the strength of ten men. Among his constant companions were the princes Fran Kamara and Kamandjan.[2] Even more important to him was his griot, Balla Fasséké,[3] who taught him the history of his people and of the world beyond.

Still fearing persecution from the jealous queen, Sogolon escaped with Sundiata to neighboring Ghana. There the amazing boy grew up. In his absence, Mali was taken over by the king of Sosso, a cruel sorcerer named Soumaoro,[4] whose secret chamber was tapestried with human skins and

---

1. A soothsayer is someone who claims to be able to foretell the future.

2. *Kamara* (kä′ mä rä), *Kamandjan* (kä′ män jän)
3. *Balla Fasséké* (bä′ lä fä sä′ kä)
4. *Soumaoro* (sōō′ mar ō)

1026 UNIT 5 LEGENDS AND MYTHS

Additional Support

Skills Practice

RESEARCH: Griots Have students research to learn more about the role of the griot in ancient and modern society. Encourage students to learn how the griot profession has changed over time, where griots may be found today, and how someone can become a griot. Have students debate the importance of the griot profession today. *(Griots and griottes have been present in African society for about 1,000 years. They can be described as historians. The profession is inherited. Today, they often share West African culture with people around the world.)* **OL**

adorned with the skulls of his enemies. Soumaoro captured Balla Fasséké and Sundiata's half-sister, Nana Triban.[5] Enraged by Soumaoro's barbarism, Sundiata raised an army and prepared to restore his country to its rightful people. Although he succeeded in defeating Soumaoro in a great battle, he could not capture or kill the man himself, for the magician had the power to appear and disappear at will. While Sundiata rested in the town of Sibi,[6] Soumaoro once again raised a powerful army. The two prepared to meet in a final battle.

Sundiata and his mighty army stopped at Sibi for a few days. The road into Mali lay open, but Soumaoro was not yet vanquished. The king of Sosso had mustered a powerful army and his sofas were numbered by the thousand. He had raised contingents[7] in all the lands over which he held sway and got ready to pounce again on Mali.

With **scrupulous** care, Sundiata had made his preparations at Sibi. Now he had sufficient sofas to meet Soumaoro in the open field, but it was not a question of having a lot of troops. In order to defeat Soumaoro it was necessary first of all to destroy his magical power. At Sibi, Sundiata decided to consult the soothsayers, of whom the most famous in Mali were there.

On their advice Djata[8] had to sacrifice a hundred white bulls, a hundred white rams and a hundred white cocks. It was in the middle of this slaughter that it was announced to Sundiata that his sister Nana Triban and Balla Fasséké, having been able to escape from Sosso, had now arrived. Then Sundiata said to Tabon Wana, "If my sister and Balla have been able to escape from Sosso, Soumaoro has lost the battle."

---

5. *Nana Triban* (nä′ nä trī′ bän)
6. *Sibi* (sī′ bē)
7. The *sofas* are soldiers or warriors, and *contingents* are additional troops.
8. *Djata* (dyä′ tə) is a shortened form of Sundiata.

Reading Strategy   Identifying Genre *Which items in this summary indicate that the legend will include exaggerated elements?* **R**

Vocabulary

scrupulous (skrōō′ pyə ləs) *adj.* thoroughly attentive to even the smallest details; precise

---

Leaving the site of the sacrifices, Sundiata returned to Sibi and met his sister and his griot.

"Hail, my brother," said Nana Triban.

"Greetings, sister."

"Hail Sundiata," said Balla Fasséké.

"Greetings, my griot."

After numerous salutations, Sundiata asked the fugitives to relate how they had been able to **elude** the vigilance of a king such as Soumaoro. But Triban was weeping for joy. Since the time of their childhood she had shown much sympathy towards the crippled child that Sundiata had been. Never had she shared the hate of her mother, Sassouma Bérété.

"You know, Djata," she said, weeping, "for my part I did not want you to leave the country. It was my mother who did all that. Now Niani is destroyed, its inhabitants scattered, and there are many whom Soumaoro has carried off into captivity in Sosso."

She cried worse than ever. Djata was sympathetic to all this, but he was in a hurry to know something about Sosso. Balla Fasséké understood and said, "Triban, wipe away your tears and tell your story, speak to your brother. You know that he has never thought ill of you, and besides, all that was in his destiny."

Nana Triban wiped her tears away and spoke.

"When you left Mali, my brother sent me by force to Sosso to be the wife of Soumaoro, whom he greatly feared. I wept a great deal at the beginning but when I saw that perhaps all was not lost I resigned[9] myself for the time being. I was nice to Soumaoro and was the chosen one among his numerous wives. I had my chamber in the great tower where he himself lived. I knew how to flatter

---

9. When Nana *resigned* herself, she gave in without resistance or complaint.

Literary Element   Dialogue *What does Nana Triban wish to convey to her half-brother?* **L**

Vocabulary

elude (i lōōd′) *v.* to avoid or escape, especially through cleverness or quickness

D. T. NIANE AND THE STORYTELLERS   **1027**

Teach

B1 Big Idea

Acts of Courage Answer:
Though Soumaoro is violent and it could be dangerous to mislead him, Nana Triban pretends that she is loyal to Soumaoro and tries to get him to confide in her. The legend implies that one should be brave and resourceful in times of danger. **OL**

L1 Literary Element

Dialogue Answer: *Balla Fasséké means that he, as the storyteller, is the "word," and Sundiata, as the hero, is the "deed." Sundiata's destiny will begin because he will now fulfill the soothsayer's prophecies of greatness.* **OL**

⭐ Viewing the Art

Explain to students that this is an ancient African statue of a soldier. **Ask:** Do you think the statue displays courageous qualities? Why or why not? *(Students may say yes, because the soldier stands straight, tall, and stares straight ahead.)* **AS**

---

him and make him jealous. Soon I became his **confidante** and I pretended to hate you, to share the hate which my mother bore you. It was said that you would come back one day, but I swore to him that you would never have the presumption[10] to claim a kingdom you had never possessed, and that you had left never to see Mali again. However, I was in constant touch with Balla Fasséké, each of us wanting to pierce the mystery of Soumaoro's magic power. One night I took the bull by the horns and said to Soumaoro: 'Tell me, oh you whom kings mention with trembling, tell me Soumaoro, are you a man like others or are you the same as the jinn[11] who protects humans? No one can bear the glare of your eyes, your arm has the strength of ten arms. Tell me, king of kings, tell me what jinn protects you so that I can worship him also.' These words filled him with pride and he himself boasted to me of the might of his Tana. That very night he took me into his magic chamber and told me all.

"Then I redoubled my zeal to show myself faithful to his cause, I seemed more overwhelmed than him. It was even he who went to the extent of telling me to take courage, that nothing was yet lost. During all this time, in complicity[12] with Balla Fasséké, I was preparing for the inevitable flight.

Archer Figure Inland Delta Region, Mali. Ceramic. Height 61.9 cm. Museum Purchase, 86-12-1, National Museum of African Art. ⭐

Nobody watched over me any more in the royal enclosure, of which I knew the smallest twists and turns. And one night when Soumaoro was away, I left that fearsome tower. Balla Fasséké was waiting for me at the gate to which I had the key. It was thus, brother, that we left Sosso."

Balla Fasséké took up the story.

"We hastened to you. The news of the victory of Tabon made me realize that the lion had burst his chains. Oh son of Sogolon, I am the word and you are the deed, now your destiny begins."

Sundiata was very happy to recover his sister and his griot. He now had the singer who would **perpetuate** his memory by his words. There would not be any heroes if deeds were condemned to man's forgetfulness, for we ply our trade to excite the admiration of the living, and to evoke the veneration[13] of those who are to come.

Djata was informed that Soumaoro was advancing along the river and was trying to block his route to Mali. The preparations were complete, but before leaving Sibi, Sundiata arranged a great military review in the camp so that Balla Fasséké, by his words, should strengthen the hearts of his sofas. In the middle of a great circle formed by the

---

10. Here, *presumption* means "excessive boldness".
11. In Arab folklore, a *jinn*, or genie, was an angel-like spirit that had magical powers and could take on other forms.
12. People acting in *complicity* are involved together, as accomplices in a crime or, as here, in secret activities.

> **Big Idea** **Acts of Courage** *What risks does Nana Triban take while staying with Soumaoro? What does the legend imply about how one should act in times of danger?* **B1**

> **Vocabulary**
> **confidante** (kon´ fə dant´) n. a person who is entrusted with secrets or private affairs

---

13. To *evoke veneration* is to call up feelings of deep respect.

> **Literary Element** **Dialogue** *What do you think Balla Fasséké means by this remark?* **L1**

> **Vocabulary**
> **perpetuate** (pər pech´ o͞o āt´) v. to cause to continue to be remembered

1028 UNIT 5 LEGENDS AND MYTHS

Additional Support

Skills Practice

LITERARY ELEMENT: Idiom Write the following sentence on the board: *I took the bull by the horns.* **Say:** This is an example of an *idiom,* an expression that means something different from the literal meaning of its individual words. Idioms make it possible for us to add interest to our language. They offer a different way to express our thoughts. Practice using idioms. Write a brief paragraph describing the character of Sundiata. Use idioms in your description. *(Answers will vary; students should use idioms that describe Sundiata as courageous and moral.)* **OL**

Bearded Male Figure. 14th century
Djenne (African) Terra-cotta. Height 38.1 cm.
The Detroit Institute of Arts, MI.

sofas, Balla Fasséké extolled[14] the heroes of
Mali. To the king of Tabon he said:
"You whose iron arm can split ten skulls
at a time, you, Tabon Wana, king of the
Sinikimbon and the Djallonké,[15] can you
show me what you are capable of before the
great battle is joined?"

The griot's words made Fran Kamara leap
up. Sword in hand and mounted on his swift
steed he came and stood before Sundiata and
said, "Maghan Sundiata, I renew my oath to
you in the sight of all the Mandingoes gathered together. I pledge myself to conquer or
to die by your side. Mali will be free or the
smiths[16] of Tabon will be dead."

The tribes of Tabon shouted their approval,
brandishing their weapons, and Fran Kamara,
stirred by the shouts of the sofas, spurred his

---

14. Balla highly praised (*extolled*) the heroes.
15. *Sinikimbon* (si' nē kim' bōn), *Djallonké* (jä lôn' kā)
16. The *Mandingoes* were various peoples who inhabited the
    upper and middle Niger River valley. *Smiths* make or repair
    metal objects, such as swords, but Fran Kamara is speaking
    figuratively, referring to his sword-bearing troops.

---

charger and charged forward. The warriors
opened their ranks and he bore down on a
great mahogany tree. With one stroke of his
sword he split the giant tree just as one splits
a paw-paw.[17] The flabbergasted army
shouted, "Wassa Wassa . . . Ayé . . . "

Then, coming back to Sundiata, his sword
held aloft, the king of Tabon said, "Thus on
the Niger plain will the smiths of Tabon
cleave those of Sosso in twain."[18] And the
hero came and fell in beside Sundiata.

Turning towards Kamandjan, the king of
Sibi and cousin of the king of Tabon, Balla
Fasséké said, "Where are you, Kamandjan,
where is Fama Djan? Where is the king of
the Dalikimbon Kamaras? Kamandjan of
Sibi, I salute you. But what will I have to
relate of you to future generations?"

Before Balla had finished speaking, the king
of Sibi, shouting his war cry, started his fiery
charger off at full gallop. The sofas, stupefied,
watched the extraordinary horseman head
for the mountain that dominates[19] Sibi. . . .
Suddenly a tremendous din filled the sky, the
earth trembled under the feet of the sofas and
a cloud of red dust covered the mountain.
Was this the end of the world? . . . But slowly
the dust cleared and the sofas saw Kamandjan
coming back holding a fragment of a sword.
The mountain of Sibi, pierced through and
through, disclosed a wide tunnel!

Admiration was at its highest pitch. The
army stood speechless and the king of Sibi,
without saying a word, came and fell in
beside Sundiata.

Balla Fasséké mentioned all the chiefs by
name and they all performed great feats;
then the army, confident in its leadership,
left Sibi. ∾

---

17. *Paw-paw* is a banana-like fruit.
18. To *cleave in twain* is to split in two.
19. The mountain *dominates* Sibi because it towers over it.

Literary Element Dialogue *Why does Balla Fasséké ask
this question?* **L2**

Reading Strategy Identifying Genre *What characteristic
of legends is found in this passage?* **R**

Teach

L2 Literary Element

Dialogue Answer: *Students
may say that he is trying to
inspire Kamandjan to do great
things.* **OL**

R Reading Strategy

Identifying Genre Answer:
*Students may say that the
fantastic elements of this passage—as displayed when the
mountain is pierced through
by a man—are characteristic of
legends.* **OL**

★ Viewing the Art

Djenné was an ancient trading city in the southern part
of Mali. It was a hub of trading and the heart of Muslim
studies in the region. **AS**

✓CheckPoint

Use the CheckPoint questions
on Presentation Plus! to check
students' mastery of the selection. These questions can be
used with interactive response
keypads for immediate student
feedback.

English Language Coach

Vocabulary Help English language
learners understand the text by rewriting it in their own words. Tell students
the word *flabbergasted* means "overwhelmed with shock, surprise, or wonder." Have them think of another way to
express the same idea, using different
words. Encourage students to share ideas
by working in groups. (*Students may use
words like* amazed, surprised, *or* shocked
to express the idea of flabbergasted.
*They may describe the same concept
though expressive narrative style.*) **EL**

Objectives
• To analyze dialogue (SE)
• To identify genre and analyze leg-
ends (SE)
• To understand idiom (TWE)

Assess

1. Answers will vary.
2. (a) Destroy his magical powers. (b) Consults with soothsayers, showing that he respects the expertise of others.
3. (a) Rush into battle (b) To guarantee their status as heroes
4. So he can be worshipped and live forever
5. (a) He knows that fame motivates people. (b) Newspapers, magazines, and television make people famous.
6. People do great things because they hope for recognition, or heroes exist mainly because we celebrate them.

Literary Element

1. (a) To show that she was behaving in a way that would attract his attention. (b) She is crafty, resourceful, brave, and loyal.
2. The king of Tabon is assuring Sundiata Fran Kamara that Soumaoro will be defeated.

Interdisciplinary Activity

Students lists should include specific qualities of characters that indicate an obvious and tight connection to the qualities of a hero.

Web Activities Have students access the Web site for interactive activities that will help them assess their understanding of the selection.

RESPONDING AND THINKING CRITICALLY

Respond

1. What do you think might happen next in this story? Share your predictions with your classmates.

Recall and Interpret

2. (a) What does Sundiata first plan to do in order to defeat Soumaoro? (b) Later, what does he do before leaving Sibi? What do his methods suggest about him as a leader?

3. (a) What astonishing deeds do Fran Kamara and Kamandjan perform at the urging of Balla Fasséké? (b) Why do Balla Fasséké's words cause the warriors to react as they do?

Analyze and Evaluate

4. Why do you think Sundiata has such a strong desire to be remembered by future generations?

5. (a) What knowledge of human nature does Balla Fasséké reveal through his speeches? (b) Does our society today have any methods comparable to Balla Fasséké's for making people famous? Explain.

Connect

6. **Big Idea** Acts of Courage At one point, the story says, "There would not be any heroes if deeds were condemned to man's forgetfulness." How would you interpret this statement?

LITERARY ANALYSIS

Literary Element Dialogue

In this legend, **dialogue** helps to advance the plot and to develop the characters. Dialogue brings characters to life by showing what they are thinking and feeling as they react to other characters.

1. (a) Why do you think Nana Triban mentions that she "knew how to flatter [Soumaoro] and make him jealous"? (b) From her words, what impressions do you have of Nana Triban? Explain.

2. What does the king of Tabon means when he says, "Thus on the Niger plain will the smiths of Tabon cleave those of Sosso in twain"? Explain.

Interdisciplinary Activity

The heroes of legends usually embody the qualities their particular culture values. Who are some heroes of recent times about whom you could imagine a legend developing? In a small group, list heroes from the recent past or the present day, including political figures, athletes, or others who exemplify skill, strength, or courage. For each name on your list, write two or three sentences explaining why audiences might enjoy hearing stories about that person.

Literature Online **Web Activities** For eFlashcards, Selection Quick Checks, and other Web activities, go to www.glencoe.com.

1030 UNIT 5 LEGENDS AND MYTHS

READING AND VOCABULARY

Reading Strategy Identifying Genre

Legends are part of folklore's oral tradition—the stories and histories that storytellers have retold for generations. Usually, legends celebrate the heroic qualities of a national or cultural hero.

1. Identify three exaggerated or fantastic details in this legend. Which detail did you consider most entertaining or inspiring? Explain.

2. From this legend, what traits or qualities would you say the Mandingo people valued in a person?

Vocabulary Practice

Practice with Word Parts Use your knowledge of word parts to answer these questions.

1. Which of the following words contains a prefix that means "with"?
   a. elude   **c.** confidante
   b. captivity

2. Which of the following words contains a suffix often found in verbs?
   a. inhabitant   **c.** perpetuate
   b. glee

Reading Strategy

1. Students may list details such as the events of Sundiata's childhood or the incredible feats performed by the Mali sofas. Students should support their answers.

2. Loyalty, bravery, and resourcefulness

Vocabulary

1. c   2. c

THE LION OF MALI

FROM SUNDIATA: A LEGEND OF AFRICA

retold by Will Eisner

Building Background

The tale of Sundiata is based on the real person Sundiata, a monarch who established the Sudanese empire of Mali. According to oral tradition, he had eleven brothers, who were heirs to the kingdom of Kangaba in Mali. Sumanguru, ruler of the adjacent land of Kaniaga, ravaged Kanagaba, killing all of Sundiata's brothers. Sundiata, who was already ill and weak, was spared.

Will Eisner, an acclaimed graphic novel artist most famous for the character the Spirit, depicts the beginning of this tale in this graphic novel version of "The Lion of Mali." Eisner grew up in the tenements of New York City, where his first work was published in his Bronx high school's newspaper. His budding career in comics art was interrupted by service in the U.S. army during World War II; however, the army did make good use of his talents—he created illustrations for posters and comic strips to entertain the troops while serving. Eisner went on to enjoy a sixty-year career in comics, winning seven awards from the National Cartoonist Society, including the prestigious Reuben award in 1988. So influential was his art that an award even has been created in his honor: the Will Eisner Comic Industry Awards.

Set a Purpose for Reading

Read to discover similarities and differences between the graphic-novel and text versions of the tale of Sundiata.

Reading Strategy

Comparing and Contrasting Versions of a Story

There are many different versions of the tale of Sundiata. When you **compare and contrast versions,** you identify similarities and differences between them. This graphic-novel excerpt and the prose excerpt by Niane cover different portions of Sundiata's story, but there are still many points of comparison between them. As you read, think about how plot, setting, and characters are conveyed in each excerpt. How is reading each format similar and different? Take notes to help you keep track of the similarities and differences.

Similarities and Differences between Graphic Novel and Prose	**R**
Similarities	Differences

THE LION OF MALI **1031**

Differentiated Instruction

Teach

R1 Reading Strategy

Comparing and Contrasting Versions of a Story Ask: How is this portrayal of Sundiata different from the text you read earlier? *(The graphic novel shows a younger Sundiata, one who is playful and innocent. The Sundiata in the excerpt students read was a warrior and leader of an army.)* **OL**

★ Cultural History

Geography The valley referred to here may have run along the Niger River, which currently extends more than 2,500 miles through four countries. Today, food production in this region is dependent on the Niger's annual flooding. The Niger River is among the most important of Mali's features, but it does not represent the geography of the entire country. At Mali's center is the semiarid Sahel region, and much of the northern section of the country lies within the Sahara, the largest desert on Earth. **AS**

Additional Support

Skills Practice

RESEARCH: Historical Background Have students conduct research to learn about Sumanguru's rule in western Africa. **Say:** The ruler Sumanguru is viewed today as a harsh and cruel leader. Research to learn more about the characteristics of Sumanguru's reign and its impact on western Africa. *(Students should identify reasons that Sumanguru is regarded as a conqueror and a tyrant. They may conclude that he was responsible for diminishing trade and for the emerging Mali empire.)* **OL**

SO AS SUMANGURU'S WARRIORS ENTERED THE VALLEY THEY WERE MET BY ONLY HALF OF THE MALI.

...WHO PRETENDED TO FLEE WHILE SUMANGURU'S MEN PURSUED THEM INTO THE VALLEY...

WHERE THEY WERE ATTACKED FROM ABOVE.

THEY WERE TRAPPED

SUMANGURU'S BEST FIGHTERS TURNED AND FLED

OH, LOOK, SUMANGURU! THE MEN OF MALI ARE WINNING THE BATTLE!

WILL EISNER **1033**

Teach

R2 Reading Strategy

Comparing and Contrasting Versions of a Story Ask: Do you prefer seeing the battle, as on this page, or reading a detailed description as you did earlier? Which gives you a better sense of the battle? *(Students' answers will vary.)* **OL**

★ Literary History

Graphic Texts Graphic texts, like the one featured here, tell stories through a combination of art, dialogue, and text. Although graphic texts may look much like comic books, they often feature important and serious themes. Today, graphic novels are written for a wide-ranging audience that includes adults and teenagers as well as younger readers. Graphic novels are gaining popularity and can be found at bookstores and libraries. **AS**

Differentiated Instruction

Interpreting Successfully interpreting text enables students to understand and respond to what they read. Have students work in small groups to discuss the story. Have them refer to the graphic text to answer these questions: Who is fighting in this battle? What are the main events of the battle? How does it end? **BL**

Objectives
• To compare and contrast versions of a story (SE)
• To conduct research (TWE)

Teach

Cultural History

The Wind Sumanguru calls upon the wind to help when he and his troops are outnumbered. People throughout history have identified elements like the wind and the rain as beings with supernatural power. According to ancient Greek thought, the god Aeolus kept winds tied up in a sack, while Zephyrus, god of the west wind, brought spring and humidity. In North America, the Iroquois Ga-oh had animal companions that brought the winds. **AS**

Assess

1. Most students will agree that it helps illustrate the characters and action and provides background to the story.

2. (a) The phrases "like a cloud of locusts" and "like the horns of the buffalo" are similes. (b) The warriors swarm as if they were locusts. The two groups of

RESPONDING AND THINKING CRITICALLY

Respond

1. Does the graphic-novel version of the tale of Sundiata enhance your understanding of the text version? Why or why not?

Recall and Interpret

2. (a)What are two examples of simile in this graphic novel? (b)How does Eisner illustrate the similes?

3. (a)How do the men of Mali plan to outsmart Sumanguru's army? (b)What happens when they execute their plan? Explain.

Analyze and Evaluate

4. Do you think Eisner's illustrations tell the tale of "The Lion of Mali" in an effective way? Explain.

5. What comment about Sumanguru's powers is Eisner making in the last three panels of the selection?

Connect

6. What characteristics of legends are demonstrated in the graphic-novel retelling of the tale of Sundiata?

OBJECTIVES
- Compare and contrast literary works.
- Evaluate the use of different media to tell a story.
- Read to enrich your understanding of different cultures.

1034 UNIT 5 LEGENDS AND MYTHS

warriors are positioned as if they were horns of the buffalo.

3. (a) Half of the army will hide and surprise them. (b) They are able to trap the enemy.

4. The illustrations clearly tell the story; however, they do not provide certain details or any background.

5. He foreshadows that Sumanguru's omnipotence will eventually lead to his downfall.

6. Exaggeration is used in the graphic novel. The Mali warriors quickly arm themselves and disperse to attack an invading army. Sumanguru uses magical powers.

Rescuing and Conquering

The Life Line, 1884. Homer, Winslow. Oil on canvas, 28.62 x 44.75 in. Philadelphia Museum of Art, PA.

BI | **BIG IDEA**

Leaders and warriors may use their strength to rescue allies and conquer enemies. But often strength is not enough. The tales in Part 2 tell of heroes who use their brains and bravery in rescues and conquests—and sometimes outwit themselves. As you read these myths and folktales, ask yourself: How do the hero's intelligence and other personal qualities contribute to these rescues and conquests?

1035

Analyzing and Extending

BI Big Idea

Rescuing and Conquering
Ask students to consider the reasons behind rescues and conquests. **Ask:** Why might rescues and conquests be material for myths and folk legends? *(These themes make powerful stories that resonate with deep-seated human motives. They may be the goals for grand heroic actions but also for everyday interactions.)* Tell students that Part 2 will deepen their understanding of rescues and conquests, and encourage students to consider this "big idea" in relation to the artwork. **OL**

★ Viewing the Art

Winslow Homer (1836–1910) was born and raised in New England. He began his career as an illustrator for several publications but eventually concentrated on oil and watercolor painting. He often painted humans in natural outdoor scenes. After 1883, Homer turned to producing mostly images of the sea and humans' attempts to deal with the uncontrollable elements of nature. **AS**

English Language Coach

Building Background Discuss with students new to the United States what rescues and conquests mean. Invite students to suggest stories, myths, legends, or songs from their cultural background that treat the themes of rescue and conquest. Compare and contrast such stories. **EL**

Differentiated Instruction

Reading Across Cultures Encourage less proficient readers to learn about the folklore of different cultures. As they discover myths, legends, and folktales, suggest that they pay attention to themes and patterns that recur with many groups, including the themes of rescue and conquest. **BL**

Objectives for Part 2
• To identify universal themes prevalent in the literature of all cultures (SE)
• To compare works that express a universal theme and provide evidence to support the ideas expressed in each work (SE)
• To understand the literary forms and terms *myth, folktale,* and *oral tradition* (SE)

Part 2: Rescuing and Conquering

Readability Scores Key
Dale-Chall/DRP/Lexile

PACING (DAYS)		SELECTIONS AND FEATURES	LITERARY ELEMENTS
STANDARD	BLOCK		
1-2 class sessions	1	LITERARY FOCUS: Myth and the Oral Tradition, pp. 1036–1037	Myth and Oral Tradition, SE pp. 1036–1037
		"Coyote, Iktome, and the Rock" by Jenny Leading Cloud **4.1/46**/530, pp. 1038–1042	Character Archetypes, SE pp. 1039, 1040, 1042
1-2 class sessions	1	**"The Stealing of Thor's Hammer,"** by Brian Branston **6.7/55**/1050, pp. 1043–1051	Plot Pattern Archetypes, SE pp. 1044, 1048, 1049, 1050 Myth, SE p. 1050
		Vocabulary Workshop: Word Origins, p. 1052	
1 class session		**"Theseus,"** by Edith Hamilton **5.8/59**/1130, pp. 1053–1063	Image Archetype, SE pp. 1054, 1055, 1057, 1062 Plot Pattern Archetype, SE p. 1062
1 class session	1	CULTURAL PERSPECTIVE: "The Hero's Adventure," by Bill Moyers, with Joseph Campbell, pp. 1064–1067	
		Vocabulary Workshop: Word Origins, p. 1068	
1 class session		**"The Secret Name of Ra,"** by Geraldine Harris **7.3/57**/1050, pp. 1069–1075	Theme Archetype, SE pp. 1070, 1071, 1074, 1075
2 class sessions	1	COMPARING LITERATURE Across Genres **"Where the Girl Rescued Her Brother"** by Joseph Bruchac and Gayle Ross **5.0/57**/970, pp. 1077–1083 **"John Henry"** by Zora Neale Hurston, pp. 1084–1085 **"A Song of Greatness"** by Anonymous, pp. 1086–1087	Suspense, SE pp. 1078, 1080, 1081, 1083 Rhythm and Meter, TWE p. 1084
2–3 class sessions		Writing Workshop: Research Paper, pp. 1088–1097	
1 class session	2	Speaking, Listening, and Viewing Workshop: Informative Presentation, pp. 1098–1099	
2 class sessions		Test Preparation and Practice, pp. 1102–1107	

About the Part

Part 2 covers myth and oral traditions.

READING AND CRITICAL THINKING	VOCABULARY	WRITING AND GRAMMAR	LISTENING, SPEAKING, AND VIEWING
Analyzing Structure of a Legend, SE pp. 1039, 1041, 1042	Academic Vocabulary, SE p. 1042	Creating Myths, TWE p. 1040	Dramatizing Literature, SE p. 1042
Making Inferences About Characters, SE pp. 1044, 1046, 1051	Analogies, SE pp. 1044, 1051 Academic Vocabulary, SE p. 1051	Character Analysis, SE p. 1051 Speaking Verbs, TWE p. 1046	
	Word Origins, SE p. 1052		
Identifying Sequence, SE pp. 1054, 1057, 1058, 1062	Context Clues, SE pp. 1054, 1062	Author's Craft, SE p. 1063 Using Participles, SE p. 1063	Analyzing Art, TWE pp. 1055, 1056, 1059, 1060
Higher-Level Thinking, TWE p. 1064		Research Jobs, TWE p. 1066	Role-Playing, TWE p. 1065 Analyzing Art, TWE p. 1066
	Etymology, SE p. 1068		
Analyzing Style, SE pp. 1070, 1071, 1074, 1075	Antonyms, SE pp. 1070, 1075	Punctuating Lists, TWE p. 1072	Analyzing Art, TWE p. 1073 Egyptian Mythology, TWE p. 1074
Synthesizing, SE p. 1078, 1080, 1082, 1083 Using Graphic Organizers, TWE p. 1080	Synonyms, SE p. 1078, 1083	Quickwrite, SE p. 1085 Analytical Essay, SE p. 1083 Using Dashes, TWE p. 1082	Discussion Starter, SE p. 1086 Oral Interpretation, TWE p. 1086
Skimming Texts for Information, TWE p. 1091		Types of Research Reports, TWE p. 1090	
			Informative Presentation, SE pp. 1098–1099

Teach

Big Idea

Rescuing and Conquering

- Pose a hypothetical conflict, such as a friend being criticized or a sibling involved in a fight. Have students discuss whether a rescue or conquest would be their response and why. Also have students notice current news events related to rescues and conquests. Tell students that these same themes play out in myths and folklore. **OL**

L Literary Element

Myth and Oral Tradition

Ask: How is the Norse story an example of myth and the oral tradition? *(It portrays the supernatural elements of the Norse gods dealing with their opponents, the giants. Passed down through generations, it conveys beliefs and values, such as respect for wit.)* **OL**

★ Viewing the Art

Point out to students that many myths convey societies' ideals. **Ask:** From viewing this painting, what qualities do you think the Norse culture valued? **AS**

Myth and the Oral Tradition

What are the elements of Myth and Folktales?

Writer Joseph Campbell devoted his career to the study and teaching of world myths and oral traditions. He once said: "Read myths. They teach you that you can turn inward, and you begin to get the message of the symbols." In the passage from a myth below, the king of the giants has stolen Thor's hammer, which is Thor's protector. The Norse gods meet in council to plan how to get the hammer back.

Such a serious situation had to be made known to Odin. At once, he called a council meeting of all the Æsir and without delay they sat in deliberation upon their judgement stools. "Who's the first with any ideas?" asked Odin.

Tyr suggested an armed invasion of Jotunheim. Niord agreed, saying it should be an attack by sea and land and air with the Valkyries on their flying horses spear-heading the aerial battalions.

Loki said, "I can tell you this: a direct attack will be useless. Let me remind you of the magic spells employed by the giant king to frustrate Thor in the past. Even if an attack was successful, the hammer would still lie hidden. There is only one way to get it back and that is to trick King Loki of Outgard into producing it."

—Brian Branston, **from "The Stealing of Thor's Hammer" L**

Thor's Fight with the Giants, 1872. Martin Eskel Winge. Oil on canvas, 484 x 333 cm. National Museum, Stockholm, Sweden. ★

Additional Support

Skills Practice

READING: Comparing Folklore
Discuss how these tales from different cultures treat the theme of conquests and rescues. Invite students to compare how different cultures treat these universal questions:

- How did the world begin? *(Egyptians attribute creation to Ra.)*

- What is a hero? *(John Henry is an example.)*

- What sacred objects are symbolic of power? *(Thor's hammer, Cheyenne Sacred Arrows)* **OL**

Myth

Myths are traditional stories that deal with gods, heroes and supernatural forces. They may offer role models, try to explain the natural world, or suggest the beliefs, customs, or ideals of a society. The authors of myths are unknown, though a later translator may be named, as in the example above.

"I am the maker of heaven and earth," said Ra. "I made the heights and the depths, I set horizons at east and west and established the gods in their glory. When I open my eyes it is light; when I close them it is dark. The mighty Nile floods at my command. The gods do not know my true name but I am the maker of time, the giver of festivals. I spark the fire of life."

—Geraldine Harris, *from* "The Secret Name of Ra"

Oral Tradition

A culture's **oral tradition** includes stories and other oral transmissions that preserve the culture's history, ancestry, and literature. Although writing allows a story to be remembered unchanged, oral transmission allows a story to evolve for the benefit of each generation of listeners. Many well-loved stories were preserved orally before they were written down. Some oral wisdom has not been written down to this very day.

"If a man held an important position among the Cheyenne, such as the keeper of the Sacred Arrows, then his wife, too, would have to be of the highest moral character, for she shared the weight of his responsibility."

—Joseph Bruchac and Gayle Ross, *from* "Where the Girl Rescued Her Brother"

Oral tradition includes folklore, folktales, and tall tales.

Folklore The traditional beliefs, practices, stories, songs, and dances of a culture make up its **folklore**. It is based on the concerns of the common people. In the selection below, John Henry is a man defined by his work on the railroad.

John Henry told his Captain,
Man ain't nothing but a man,
And 'fore I'll let that steam drill beat me down
I'll die with this hammer in my hand;
Die with this hammer in my hand.

—Zora Neale Hurston, *from* "John Henry"

Folktale Animal stories, trickster stories, fairy tales, myths, legends and tall tales are all included in the larger category of folktales. A **folktale** is a traditional story that has been passed down orally long before being written down.

Tall Tale A **tall tale** is a kind of folktale. In a tall tale, the fantastic adventures and amazing feats of folk heroes are wildly exaggerated, but the realistic local settings and tone suggest that the exaggerations are true.

Quickwrite

Have fun thinking up your own exaggerations. You can use one of the sentence starters in the list to get you writing, or you can think of your own way to begin.

It was so hot...
It was so cold...
She was so strong...
He was so tall...
He was so hungry...
She was so thirsty...

OBJECTIVES
- Identify universal themes prevalent in the literature of all cultures.
- Compare works that express a universal theme and provide evidence to support the ideas expressed in each work.
- Understand the literary forms and terms *myth, folktale,* and *oral tradition.*

LITERARY FOCUS **1037**

Teach

Reading Strategy

Making Inferences Ask: What does the passage from "Where the Girl Rescued Her Brother" reveal about Cheyenne tradition? *(Wives had status equal to their husbands.)* Point out that this aspect of culture might never have been written down. **Ask:** What makes John Henry an example of folklore? *(As a powerful railroad worker, John Henry was a hero to the common people.)* Invite students to give examples of American folklore, such as Paul Bunyan and Brer Rabbit. **OL**

Assess

Quickwrite

Check to see that students use exaggeration. Encourage imaginative thinking.

English Language Coach

Norse Names Help students new to the United States to pronounce and understand the difficult Norse names for people and places: Tell students Thor, the war god, is the son of Odin, the chief god, and Loki is a mischief-making god. Also identify Æsir, Tyr, Jotunheim, Niord, Valkyries, King Loki, and Outgard. **EL**

Differentiated Instruction

American Folklore Assist less proficient readers with Hurston's reference to John Henry. John Henry, a powerful railroad worker, raced against a machine to drill rock—and won, but died soon after. Discuss why this tale would be so appealing that it would be repeated for generations. **BL**

Objectives
- To identify universal themes prevalent in the literature of all cultures (SE)
- To understand the terms *myth, folktale,* and *oral tradition* (SE)
- To compare folklore (TWE)

1037

Focus

BELLRINGER

Bellringer Options
Daily Language Practice Transparency 87
Or **ask:** What are the qualities of a generous person? Have students discuss what it means to be generous. Encourage them to include specific examples of generosity by themselves or by people they know.

Literature Online

Author Search To expand students' appreciation of Jenny Leading Cloud, have them access the Web site for additional information and resources.

Coyote, Iktome, and the Rock

MEET JENNY LEADING CLOUD

Imagine a world in which spirits surround you. Everything around you—the trees and rocks and rivers—is imbued with life and intelligence. All of creation is interrelated in a universal community.

For Jenny Leading Cloud, this world lives on through the tales of her people, the Lakota Indians. The Lakota are a division of the Sioux, one of the tribes commonly referred to as the North American Plains Indians. A proud nation, the Sioux inhabited vast tracts of land in what later became Montana, Nebraska, Minnesota, Wyoming, and North and South Dakota. However, as white settlers spread west in the mid-nineteenth century, the Plains Indians faced systematic persecution, losing their lands and facing violence and exploitation by the new government. By the late twentieth century, only about forty thousand Sioux remained.

In the face of these trials, tribal members like Jenny Leading Cloud have strived to keep the beliefs and culture of their people alive. By recounting the legends and myths of their people, these tribal storytellers work to preserve a tradition that stretches back hundreds of years.

The Great Spirit Spiritual beliefs are central to the Sioux. The Lakota do not see religion as something separate from daily life. Instead, they believe spirituality suffuses all parts and patterns in the universe. At the center of this spiritual universe is *Wakan Tanka* or *Tunkashila*, the Great Spirit or Grandfather.

The Lakota also recognize a number of spirits who inhabit the natural world. These spirits, who represent natural forces, include *Takuskanskan* (That Which Moves-Moves); *Wi* (the Sun), *Hanwi* (the Moon), *Wohpe* (Falling Star), and *Tate* (Wind). Because of its importance to the Sioux, *Tatanka* (the buffalo) also has a sacred role in religion and folklore.

> *"The buffalo and the coyote are our brothers; the birds, our cousins."*
>
> — Jenny Leading Cloud

Telling Tales The Sioux passed on the myths and legends of their culture through oral storytelling, which usually occurred in the evening. The stories are divided into two types. The first, the *ehanni woyaka,* includes accounts of events that are believed to have occurred, such as creation myths and events from recent history. The second type, *ohunkanka,* includes fictional stories and morality tales that are meant to teach a lesson. Lakota tradition emphasizes virtues such as bravery, fortitude, wisdom, and generosity.

One of the Lakota's favorite characters is the spider man Iktome. According to the legends, he tricked human beings to move from their original home under the earth to live on the land—thus creating the Lakota nation. Iktome also gave all animals and human beings their physical forms and names, and he created their languages. He is a comic figure, but his stories often teach serious lessons.

Jenny Leading Cloud was born in the late 1800s and died around 1980.

Literature Online **Author Search** For more about Jenny Leading Cloud, go to www.glencoe.com.

Selection Skills

Literary Elements
- Character Archetypes (SE pp. 1039, 1040, 1042)

Coyote, Iktome, and the Rock

Writing Skills/Grammar
- Creating Myths (TWE p. 1040)

Reading Skills
- Analyzing Structure of a Legend (SE pp. 1039, 1041, 1042)

Vocabulary Skills
- Academic Vocabulary (SE p. 1042)

Listening/Speaking/Viewing Skills
- Dramatizing Literature (SE p. 1042)

Connecting to the Story

"Coyote, Iktome, and the Rock" is a White River Sioux folktale that teaches a lesson about generosity. Before you read, think about the following questions:

- Have you ever given something away and later wanted it back?
- Do you believe that when something is given, it should be given forever?

Building Background

For many years, American Indian groups recorded little cultural information. Instead, storytellers were charged with remembering stories, songs, and poems, which were passed orally from generation to generation. "Coyote, Iktome, and the Rock" is a story from the oral tradition of the White River Sioux. Jenny Leading Cloud told this version in 1967 on the Rosebud Indian Reservation in South Dakota. Leading Cloud's folktale includes techniques commonly found in American Indian myth, such as the use of animals and objects as characters.

Setting Purposes for Reading

Big Idea Rescuing and Conquering

Before you read "Coyote, Iktome, and the Rock," predict which character will do the rescuing and which one will do the conquering. As you read, note whether your predictions were correct.

Literary Element Character Archetype

Some types of characters frequently appear in literature across many cultures. **Character archetypes** include noble heroes, evil-hearted villains, and wily tricksters. As you read, examine the characters in "Coyote, Iktome, and the Rock" and determine which ones are archetypes.

- See Literary Terms Handbook, p. R3.

Literature Online **Interactive Literary Elements Handbook** To review or learn more about the literary elements, go to www.glencoe.com.

Reading Strategy Analyzing Structure

Analyzing structure means examining the order or the pattern that a writer uses to present his or her ideas. Folktales, legends and other stories are often organized chronologically, or according to the sequence of events in the plot. Writers also use structural techniques, such as repetition, to help the reader follow the action. While reading "Coyote, Iktome, and the Rock," ask yourself why the storyteller chose to shape the story the way she did.

Reading Tip: Sequencing It may be helpful to pay attention to the sequence of events as you read. Create a graphic organizer like the one below to keep track of the story's events and to note any ideas the author emphasizes through repetition.

SEQUENCE OF EVENTS

The first main event is . . .

The second main event is Coyote gets cold and sends Iktome to get his blanket back. Rock refuses, saying "What is given is given."

The third main event is . . .

The fourth main event is . . .

The final main event is . . .

OBJECTIVES

In studying this selection, you will focus on the following:
- understanding and identifying character archetypes
- identifying and analyzing structure of a legend
- dramatizing a literary text

JENNY LEADING CLOUD **1039**

Focus

Summary

This Native American myth tells the story of Coyote and Iktome. On a walk, they encounter Iya, a powerful rock. Coyote gives Iya his blanket. Later, Coyote wants the blanket back because the weather turns bad. Iya refuses to return the blanket. Coyote takes the blanket back anyway and is flattened by Iya.

V Vocabulary

Vocabulary File Say: Add these words and definitions to your vocabulary file. For each word, include a sentence that gives you an example of how to use the word. **OL** Students with English language needs should include the pronunciations of these words in their files. **EL**

Literature Online

Literary Elements Have students access the Web site to improve their understanding of character archetype.

Selection Resources

Print Material
- Unit 5 Resources (Fast File), pp. 35–36
- Selection and Unit Assessments, pp. 175–176
- Selection Quick Checks, p. 88

Transparencies
- Bellringer Options Transparencies: Daily Language Practice Transparency 87
- Literary Elements Transparencies 86, 87, 88

Technology
- TeacherWorks Plus™ CD-ROM
- StudentWorks Plus™ CD-ROM
- Presentation Plus!™ CD-ROM
- Literature Online, glencoe.com
- Online Student Edition, mhln.com
- ExamView® Assessment Suite CD-ROM
- Vocabulary PuzzleMaker CD-ROM
- Listening Library, disc 2 track 22

Teach

Big Idea

Rescuing and Conquering

Say: As you read, think about the following question: How could a rock conquer a living animal? *(A rock is older and harder to destroy than a living animal. The rock symbolically conquers the animals by outliving them.)* **OL**

L Literary Element

Character Archetype

Answer: *Iya is powerful, wise, special, old, and strong.* **Ask:** Why would Native Americans choose a rock to represent these characteristics? *(Rocks are old and hard to break, so they would be associated with wisdom, strength, and power.)* **OL**

★ Cultural History

Coyote Coyote was one of the main animals associated with Native American mythology. For some Native American tribes, Coyote was a cultural hero. Other tribes showed Coyote as being a trickster whose tricks often backfire on him. **AS**

Readability Scores
Dale-Chall: 4.1
DRP: 46
Lexile: 530

Navajo Pictorial Blanket.

Coyote, Iktome, and the Rock

Told by Jenny Leading Cloud,
recorded by Richard Erdoes

★ Coyote was walking with his friend Iktome.[1] Along their path stood Iya, the rock. This was not just any rock; it was special. It had those spidery lines of green moss all over it, the kind that tell a story. Iya had power.

Coyote said: "Why, this is a nice-looking rock. I think it has power." Coyote took off the thick blanket he was wearing and put it on the rock. "Here, Iya, take this as a present. Take this blanket, friend rock, to keep you from freezing. You must feel cold."

"Wow, a giveaway!" said Iktome. "You sure are in a giving mood today, friend."

"Ah, it's nothing. I'm always giving things away. Iya looks real nice in my blanket."

"His blanket, now," said Iktome.

The two friends went on. Pretty soon a cold rain started. The rain turned to hail. The hail turned to slush. Coyote and Iktome took refuge in a cave, which was cold and wet. Iktome was all right; he had his thick buffalo robe. Coyote had only his shirt, and he was shivering. He was freezing. His teeth were chattering.

"*Kola*,[2] friend of mine," Coyote said to Iktome, "go back and get me my fine blanket. I need it, and that rock has no use for it. He's been getting along without a blanket for ages. Hurry; I'm freezing!"

Iktome went back to Iya, saying: "Can I have that blanket back please?"

The rock said: "No, I like it. What is given is given."

Iktome returned and told Coyote: "He won't give it back."

---

1. *Iktome*, the Sioux Spider Man, is a trickster able to transform from human to spider and back again.

Literary Element Character Archetype *What are some personality traits associated with Iya, the rock?* **L**

---

2. *Kola* is a Lakota word for "friend."

Additional Support

Skills Practice

WRITING: Creating Myths Have students write their own myth using one or more animal characters. The myth should have a moral and should illustrate the human traits the student has ascribed to the characters. Each student should share his or her myth with the rest of the class. **OL**

"That no-good, ungrateful rock!" said Coyote. "Has he paid for the blanket? Has he worked for it? I'll go get it myself."

"Friend," said Iktome, "Tunka,[3] Iya, the rock—there's a lot of power there! Maybe you should let him keep it."

"Are you crazy? This is an expensive blanket of many colors and great thickness. I'll go talk to him."

Coyote went back and told Iya: "Hey, rock! What's the meaning of this? What do you need a blanket for? Let me have it back right now!"

"No," said the rock, "what is given is given."

"You're a bad rock! Don't you care that I'm freezing to death? That I'll catch a cold?" Coyote jerked the blanket away from Iya and put it on. "So there; that's the end of it."

"By no means the end," said the rock.

Coyote went back to the cave. The rain and hail stopped and the sun came out again, so Coyote and Iktome sat before the cave, sunning themselves, eating pemmican[4] and fry-bread[5] and *wojapi*, berry soup. After eating, they took out their pipes and had a smoke.

All of a sudden Iktome said: "What's that noise?"

"What noise? I don't hear anything."

"A crashing, a rumble far off."

"Yes, friend, I hear it now."

"Friend Coyote, it's getting stronger and nearer, like thunder or an earthquake."

"It is rather strong and loud. I wonder what it can be."

"I have a pretty good idea, friend," said Iktome.

Then they saw the great rock. It was Iya, rolling, thundering, crashing upon them.

---

3. *Tunka* is a Lakota word for "stone."
4. *Pemmican*—a cake made of dried, pounded meat, and animal fat—was food American Indians carried with them when traveling.
5. *Fry-bread* is a flatbread fried in oil, shortening, or lard. It remains a popular American Indian food today.

Big Idea Rescuing and Conquering *Why does the rock make this statement? What do you think will happen next?* **BI**

"Friend, let's run for it!" cried Iktome; "Iya means to kill us!"

The two ran as fast as they could while the rock rolled after them, coming closer and closer.

"Friend; let's swim the river. The rock is so heavy, he sure can't swim!" cried Iktome. So they swam the river, but Iya, the great rock, also swam over the river as if he had been made of wood.

"Friend, into the timber, among the big trees," cried Coyote. "That big rock surely can't get through this thick forest." They ran among the trees, but the huge Iya came rolling along after them, shivering and splintering the big pines to pieces, left and right.

The two came out onto the flats. "Oh! Oh!" cried Iktome, Spider Man. "Friend Coyote, this is really not my quarrel. I just remembered, I have pressing business to attend to. So long!" Iktome rolled himself into a tiny ball and became a spider. He disappeared into a mousehole.

Coyote ran on and on, the big rock thundering close at his heels. Then Iya, the big rock, rolled right over Coyote, flattening him out altogether.

Iya took the blanket and rolled back to his own place, saying: "So there!"

A *wasichu*[6] rancher riding along saw Coyote lying there all flattened out. "What a nice rug!" said the rancher, picking Coyote up, and he took the rug home.

The rancher put Coyote right in front of his fireplace. Whenever Coyote is killed, he can make himself come to life again, but it took him the whole night to puff himself up into his usual shape. In the morning the rancher's wife told her husband: "I just saw your rug running away."

Friends, hear this; always be generous in heart. If you have something to give, give it forever. ◆

---

6. *Wasichu* is a Lakota word meaning "white man."

Reading Strategy Analyzing Structure *How many times has Iktome called Coyote "friend"? Why does Iktome repeat this word?* **R**

JENNY LEADING CLOUD **1041**

Teach

BI Big Idea
Rescuing and Conquering
Answer: *Iya says, "By no means the end," because he does not consider the blanket incident over. He is probably already planning what he will do next. Students may speculate that the rock will get the blanket back and seek revenge for Coyote's poor treatment.* **OL**

R Reading Strategy
Analyzing Structure
Answer: *Iktome calls Coyote "friend" seven times. He repeats this word to emphasize the friendship between himself and Coyote, and to emphasize his attempt to help Coyote. In the end, however, Iktome abandons his friend, showing that actions speak louder than words. Ironically, the last time Iktome calls Coyote "friend" is just before he disappears and Iya rolls over Coyote.* **OL**

CheckPoint

Use the CheckPoint questions on Presentation Plus! to monitor students' comprehension and to check students' mastery of the selection. These questions can be used with interactive response keypads for immediate student feedback.

Differentiated Instruction

Supernatural Elements Less proficient readers may be confused by some of the supernatural elements in the story. **Say:** Native American myths often gave animal characters supernatural abilities, such as shape-changing. **Ask:** What supernatural elements did you find in the myth? *(Students might mention Iktome's becoming a spider, Coyote's talking, and Coyote's returning to normal after being crushed by Iya.)* **AL**

Objectives
- To understand and identify character archetypes (SE)
- To identify and analyze the structure of a legend (SE)
- To create myths (TWE)

1041

Assess

1. Students' answers will vary.

2. (a) Iya refuses to give Coyote his blanket. (b) He is selfish and ill-tempered.

3. (a) They sun themselves, have a snack, and smoke. (b) They're not worried about the rock.

4. (a) Into the river and into the timber (b) The rock has many powers and abilities.

5. (a) Coyote mentions it once, but Iya refers to it often. (b) Iktome seems to warn Coyote with his comments.

6. (a) Coyote is not dependable. (b) Yes, although he has no right to it.

7. The storyteller prepares the audience for the next part of the story, when Iktome turns into a spider and disappears.

8. Coyote's strategy backfires. Iya, the rock, is the true conqueror in this story.

Literary Element

1. Coyote and Iktome are both tricksters; Iya, the wise and powerful figure; the rancher, the foolish human.

2. Coyote and Iktome both stir up trouble. Iya's actions relate to his role as wise and powerful figure. The rancher's mistaking Coyote for a rug shows humans as foolish.

Literature Online

Web Activities Have students access the Web site for interactive activities that will help them assess their understanding of the selection.

RESPONDING AND THINKING CRITICALLY

Respond

1. (a)Do you agree or disagree with Coyote's behavior? (b)How would you have acted in similar circumstances?

Recall and Interpret

2. (a)What is the main conflict in the story? (b)What does Coyote's behavior reveal about his character?

3. (a)What do Coyote and Iktome do after the rain and hail stop? (b)What does their behavior suggest?

4. (a)Where do Coyote and Iktome go to escape Iya? (b)What does Iya's pursuit of Coyote and Iktome convey about the rock?

Analyze and Evaluate

5. (a)Compare the way Coyote and Iktome respond to the rock's power. (b)Which character has a better understanding of Iya's true nature? Explain.

6. (a)What kind of friend is Coyote? (b)Does he have good reasons for taking his blanket back from Iya?

7. Why does the storyteller reveal Iktome's identity as Spider Man near the end of the story?

Connect

8. **Big Idea** **Rescuing and Conquering** Coyote tries to be the conqueror in this story by reclaiming the blanket. Does his strategy work? Why or why not?

LITERARY ANALYSIS

Literary Element **Character Archetype**

In "Coyote, Iktome, and the Rock," the storyteller uses three different **character archetypes**—the trickster, the wise and powerful figure, and the foolish human. Tricksters, a common character archetype in American Indian myth, generate comic relief and conflict in a story. Tricksters sometimes function as heroes when their antics bring about positive changes or teach important lessons.

1. Match each character archetype with the appropriate character in the story.

2. Explain how these archetypes relate to each character's function in the story.

Performing

In a small group, dramatize "Coyote, Iktome, and the Rock" or another trickster story. Create a script based on the story or improvise dialogue based on the characters and plot. Practice your performance, paying attention to volume, pitch, pacing, enunciation, and gestures in order to share your story as effectively as possible with your audience. Perform your skit for the class.

Literature Online **Web Activities** For eFlashcards, Selection Quick Checks, and other Web activities, go to www.glencoe.com.

READING AND VOCABULARY

Reading Strategy **Analyzing Structure**

Instead of using chronological, or time, order, the storyteller presents events in the order in which they occur. "Coyote, Iktome, and the Rock" comes from an oral tradition that uses repetition both to help the listener follow the story and to create a rhythm that helps for the storyteller to remember details.

1. What is the main structure of "Coyote, Iktome, and the Rock"? Where does the structure vary?

2. List two examples of repetition from the story.

Academic Vocabulary

Here are two words from the vocabulary list on page R82.

alternative (ôl tur ′nə tiv) *n.* a choice between things; one of the things to be selected

demonstrate (dem ′ən strāt´) *v.* to explain or make clear by using examples

Practice and Apply
1. Did Coyote have an **alternative** to taking the blanket back from Iya? Explain.
2. What lesson about generosity did the story **demonstrate**?

Reading Strategy

1. Primarily chronological, with two examples of the storyteller directly addressing the audience

2. Possible answers include the repetition of the word "friend" and the thundering of the rock as it rolls after Coyote.

Performing

Students' skits should reflect the characteristics of trickster tales. Encourage students to be creative.

Academic Vocabulary

1. Coyote could have shared the blanket.

2. Generosity means putting others' needs before one's own.

The Stealing of Thor's Hammer

MEET BRIAN BRANSTON

How many writers do you know who have visited the most remote, inaccessible corners of the world, including Iceland, Greenland, and the Great Barrier Reef? How many writers have ridden the Great Rapids of the Orinoco River in South America—in a hovercraft? Brian Branston, author of "The Stealing of Thor's Hammer," has done these things and more, including traveling in a dugout canoe in search of the Yanamamo Indians in Brazil. Branston, working in the Travel and Exploration unit for the British Broadcasting Corporation (BBC), traveled to remote locations all over the world, not to write about them but to capture them on film.

For twenty-five years, Branston also wrote books on such subjects as the occult, Anglo-Saxon mythology, and Scandinavian mythology. In his book *Gods & Heroes from Viking Mythology* (1978), he brings Viking myths to life with vivid language and descriptions.

> *"Our forefathers of fifteen hundred years ago. . . were not creatures apart, different from the birds, plants, or animals."*
>
> —Brian Branston

Seafaring Warriors Viking mythology (also called Norse or Scandinavian mythology) encompasses stories from four countries: Iceland, Norway, Sweden, and Denmark. The Vikings are most familiar to modern readers as the seafaring warriors who ventured abroad to conquer parts of Europe in search of goods and land.

The Vikings were not merely fearsome, unimaginative brutes, however. The long, dark Scandinavian winters were conducive to story-telling. Viking storytellers tried to make sense of their world with its dark forests and forbidding mountains. Their mythology is multilayered and makes use of natural elements that are familiar in that northern landscape, such as volcanoes and bears.

Viking mythology is based on several gods: Odin (the One-Eyed Allfather, also known as Woden or Wotan), Thor (the god of thunder), Tyr (the god of war and treaties), and Frey and Freya (the god and goddess of fertility). On a plain called Ida, these gods built the city of Asgard. The city had twelve realms, the highest being Valhalla, where the heroic went after dying.

Influences of Mythology Traces of Viking mythology are still found in the English language, music, and literature today. For example, the Viking gods gave their names to the days of the week: Tuesday (Tyr), Wednesday (Woden), Thursday (Thor), and Friday (Frey). J. R. R. Tolkien drew heavily from these stories to create his *Lord of the Rings* trilogy. Composer Richard Wagner used the myths in his "Rings of the Nibelung" opera cycle. The archetypal plots and characters of these stories give them lasting appeal.

Brian Branston was born in 1914.

Literature Online Author Search For more about Brian Branston, go to www.glencoe.com.

BRIAN BRANSTON **1043**

Focus

BELLRINGER

Bellringer Options
Daily Language Practice Transparency 88
Or **write on the board:** creation myths, explanatory myths, heroic myths **Ask:** What myths fit these categories? What are some modern-day myths?
Have students discuss creation, explanatory, and heroic myths and modern myths, such as the stories of novels, comic books, and films.

Literature Online

Author Search To expand students' appreciation of Brian Branston, have them access the Web site for additional information and resources.

Selection Skills

The Stealing of Thor's Hammer

Literary Elements
- Plot Pattern Archetypes (SE pp. 1044, 1048, 1049, 1050)
- Myth (SE p. 1050)
- Suspense (TWE p. 1048)

Reading Skills
- Making Inferences About Characters (SE pp. 1044, 1046, 1051)

Vocabulary Skills
- Analogies (SE pp. 1044, 1051)
- Academic Vocabulary (SE p. 1051)

Writing Skills/Grammar
- Character Analysis (SE p. 1051)
- Speaking Verbs (TWE p. 1046)

Focus

Summary

Thor's thunder-making hammer Mullicrusher is mysteriously stolen one night. Suspecting Loki, Thor calls for the god of mischief, who denies any involvement. Loki journeys to Outgard to visit giant King Loki, who turns out to be responsible for the robbery. As ransom for the hammer, King Loki demands goddess Freya's hand in marriage. The gods plan to trick King Loki by having Thor and Loki dress up as the bride and her handmaiden. Just as the marriage is being consecrated, Thor grabs his hammer and strikes down King Loki.

V Vocabulary

Vocabulary File Say: Add these words and definitions to your vocabulary file. For each word, include a sentence that gives you an example of how to use the word. **OL** Students with English language needs should include the pronunciations of these words in their files. **EL**

Literary Elements Have students access the Web site to improve their understanding of plot pattern archetypes.

Connecting to the Myth

The following myth relates the story of the theft of Thor's hammer and the gods' plan to recover it. Before you read the story, think about the following questions:

- How far would you go to recover something important to you?
- Is physical strength or cunning more important in resolving a conflict? Explain.

Building Background

Norse mythology is filled with gods, giants, dwarfs, and elves. The Norse god Thor is the protagonist of the story you are about to read. In Viking mythology, Thor is known as the strongest of the gods but far from the smartest. He is armed with the hammer Mjollnir, which was crafted by dwarfs in the underworld. Thor uses Mjollnir to defend the gods against their enemies, the frost giants. When Thor throws his hammer, it creates lightning and then returns to his hand. Many Vikings wore hammer amulets, perhaps as protection from storms at sea.

Setting Purposes for Reading

Big Idea Rescuing and Conquering

As you read this myth, notice the importance the characters place upon retrieving Thor's hammer.

Literary Element Plot Pattern Archetypes

Plot pattern archetypes are story elements and themes common to a wide variety of cultures and stories. These archetypes are plotlines or story elements that appear throughout the history of literature, from ancient stories to contemporary movies. An example of a plot pattern archetype is characters fooling dangerous and powerful enemies. As you read, look for possible plot pattern archetypes in the story.

- See Literary Terms Handbook, p. R13.

Literature Online Interactive Literary Elements Handbook To review or learn more about the literary elements, go to www.glencoe.com.

OBJECTIVES
In studying this selection, you will focus on the following:
- recognizing and analyzing plot pattern archetypes that occur across time and culture
- making inferences about characters, and supporting the inferences with evidence from the story

---

Reading Strategy *Making Inferences About Characters*

Making inferences about characters means making reasonable assumptions about characters based on how they act and how they are described.

Reading Tip: Creating a Web Use a web like the one below to record the inferences you draw about one of the main characters in this myth.

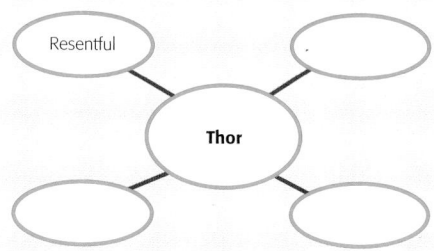

Vocabulary

disdainful (dis dān′ fəl) *adj.* scornful; mocking; p. 1045 *The senator held a disdainful view of the opposing candidate.*

aggrieved (ə grēvd′) *adj.* disturbed; upset; p. 1045 *The aggrieved customer got a refund.*

guile (gīl) *n.* cunning; p. 1046 *The spy used guile to outsmart the guards.*

deliberation (di lib′ə rā′shən) *n.* an official meeting or consultation; p. 1048 *The town leaders decided that deliberation was necessary.*

jubilantly (jōō′bə lənt lē) *adv.* joyfully or happily; p. 1049 *The bride and groom walked jubilantly down the aisle together.*

Vocabulary Tip: Practice with Analogies Analogies show logical relationships between two pairs of words.

- understanding literary forms and terms, such as myth and oral tradition
- writing to analyze characters

Selection Resources

Print Materials
- Unit 5 Resources (Fast File), pp. 37–39
- Leveled Vocabulary Development, p. 73
- Selection and Unit Assessments, pp. 177–178
- Selection Quick Checks, p. 89

Transparencies
- Bellringer Options Transparencies: Daily Language Practice Transparency 88
- Literary Elements Transparencies 86, 87

Technology
- TeacherWorks Plus™ CD-ROM
- StudentWorks Plus™ CD-ROM
- Presentation Plus!™ CD-ROM
- Literature Online, glencoe.com
- Online Student Edition, mhln.com
- ExamView® Assessment Suite CD-ROM
- Vocabulary PuzzleMaker CD-ROM
- Listening Library, disc 2 track 23

The Stealing of Thor's Hammer

Brian Branston

THOR, 1911. Arthur Rackham. In Wagner's 'The Rhinegold & the Valkrie'. ★

The god Thor always resented the **disdainful** way he had been treated by King Loki of Outgard.[1] He was quite determined that one day he would get his own back. Then a dreadful thing happened which made him fear that revenge might prove impossible: his hammer was stolen!

One evening he had retired as usual after a hearty supper in his palace of Bilskirnir and in an unusually tidy mood he placed his shoes together neatly, folded his clothes and laid his hammer on the table next to his pillow before getting into bed beside Sif.[2]

Daylight was squeezing through the gaps in the shutters and the dawn chorus of birdsong was pealing in from the countryside when Thor awoke from a disturbing dream. He fancied in his sleep that a thief had crept into the bedroom and had stolen the one sure protection the gods had against the giants—his hammer. Half awake, he fumbled a hand out of the sheets and felt along the top of the bedside table. It was empty.

He sat up in bed with such a jolt that his wife Sif was shot out onto the floor. Before she could open her mouth to protest, Thor was yelling, "My hammer! My hammer's been stolen! Æsir![3] Elves! Quick! Wait! No! Yes! Who's stolen my hammer? LOKI! LOKEE … !" and his red hair and beard tossed about in all directions as he wrathfully dragged on his clothes. He absentmindedly picked the **aggrieved** Sif off the floor and put her back into bed, by which time Loki[4] had come running up panting.

---

1. *King Loki* (lō′kē) is the king of the giants in Norse mythology. *Outgard* is the name of his home. *King Loki* is not to be confused with *Loki*, the fire god.
2. *Sif* (sif) is the wife of Thor and the Norse goddess of fertility and crops.
3. *Æsir* (a′zir) is another name for the group made up of the principal Norse gods.
4. Here, *Loki* refers to the god of fire and mischief, not to be confused with King Loki.

Teach

Big Idea

Rescuing and Conquering
Say: Keep the following questions in mind as you read: In the story, what must be rescued? Why is this important? *(The gods must rescue Thor's hammer, which has been stolen by King Loki because it is a powerful artifact and Thor's means of creating thunder.)* **OL**

★ Viewing the Art

Ask: What does this illustration tell us about Thor's relationship to his hammer? *(That it is an extension of himself, connecting him to the earth—rocks—and to the heavens—weather/thunder.)* **AS**

✓ CheckPoint

Use the CheckPoint questions on Presentation Plus! to monitor students' comprehension. These questions can be used with interactive response keypads for immediate student feedback.

Readability Scores
Dale-Chall: 6.7
DRP: 55
Lexile: 1050

English Language Coach

Myths from Other Cultures

Students from other backgrounds may be able to connect to this Norse myth by sharing some myths from their own cultures. Have these students share myths involving the robbery of a sacred artifact, the rescue of a person in distress, or a battle against beasts or monsters. **EL**

Differentiated Instruction

Examining Maps Students with spatial skills may find it beneficial to study the geography of the Norse people. Have students find maps of the Scandinavian region. Remind students that the Viking peoples were seafarers. Have students notice the primacy of seas and oceans in the Viking countries. **BL**

Objective
• To analyze theme of rescuing and conquering (SE)

R1 Reading Strategy

Making Inferences about Characters Answer: *So far, Thor has acted on his emotions, jumping out of bed and throwing his wife to the floor and yelling when he discovers that his hammer is missing. He intends to take Loki to Jotunheim without thinking that both of them will probably be killed. He will most likely act recklessly and without much thought about the consequences throughout the rest of the story.* **Ask:** What do Thor's actions tell you about the importance of the hammer? *(He considers it a very important personal possession that must be recovered at any cost.)* **OL**

R2 Reading Strategy

Making Inferences about Characters Answer: *King Loki possesses intelligence and cunning. He stole Thor's hammer in secret and hid it so it could not be reclaimed. However, he is also boastful and arrogant.* **OL**

"You had anything to do with this, Loki?" bellowed Thor.

"What, what … ?" gasped Loki as Thor gripped him by the scruff.

"My hammer—have you stolen it?"

"No, no, no," stammered Loki. "Only one lot dare do that, and you don't need me to tell you who they are. The giants!"

"Come on then!" cried Thor, "My chariot—you are coming with me to Jotunheim[5] to get it back!" and he started to drag Loki downstairs to the stables.

"Stop!" shouted Loki. "Do have the sense to stop! Can't you see that's just what the giants want? Without your hammer you'd be killed. We need stealth here. We need **guile**."

"Well, you're the one for that," replied Thor, simmering down, "What do you suggest?"

The upshot was that Loki volunteered to borrow Freya's[6] feather coat and fly as a hawk into Jotunheim to find out if possible what had happened to Thor's hammer. He winged his way swiftly over the ocean to the shores of Jotunheim and across the tops of the towering forest trees towards the mountains and the stronghold of King Loki.

From a distance he saw the king sitting on the gravemound of his ancestors just outside the city walls. There was a rune-carved stone commemorating the dead giants who were sitting upright in their high seats below in the mound waiting for the Ragnarok.[7] Loki flew to the top of the tall stone and perched there. King Loki of Outgard was amusing himself plaiting[8] gold leashes for his hunting dogs and trimming the manes of his horses. He glanced up.

"It's Loki, isn't it?" he asked.

"Yes," replied the hawk, "you are quite right, of course."

"How goes it with the Æsir, and how with the elves? Very well, I trust?"

"The elves are upset and the Æsir worse. Someone has stolen Thor's hammer."

"And who's the culprit?" asked King Loki of Outgard.

"You are, your gigantic majesty," answered the Mischief Maker at which the giant let out such an exploding guffaw of cruel laughter that his horses shied in fear and his hounds cringed in terror.

"There's no use pretending with a clever fellow like you," he said. "You are quite right. I *have* stolen Thor's hammer; and the Thundering Nuisance will only get it back on conditions."

"What conditions?"

"Don't think the hammer can be regained by force. It can't. I have buried it deep in the earth, seven leagues[9] down. Only one thing will redeem it. You must bring me the goddess Freya to be my wife!"

Loki made no reply but flew straight back to Asgard[10] and before he could alight Thor was asking him for news.

"Tell me at once, before you perch," he cried, "have you found out where my hammer is?"

The Mischief Maker explained precisely all he knew and told the terms necessary for retrieving the hammer. He had scarcely taken off the feather coat when Thor was dragging him to Freya's palace, bursting into it without any politeness or ceremony.

"Here's your feather coat, dear Freya," said Thor, "thanks for the loan of it. Now hurry up please and find yourself a bride's veil."

---

5. *Jotunheim* (yô'toon häm') is one of the nine worlds in Norse mythology and the realm of the giants. *Jotun* is another world for *giant.*
6. *Freya* (frā'ə) is the Norse goddess of fertility and love.
7. *Ragnarok* is the climatic final battle between the gods in Norse mythology.
8. *Plaiting* (plāt'ing) means "braiding."
9. One *league* (lēg) is equal to about three miles or five kilometers.
10. *Asgard* (as'gärd') is another of the nine worlds and the realm where the gods live.

Reading Strategy Making Inferences About Characters *From what you have read so far, what can you infer about Thor's personality?* **R1**

Vocabulary

guile (gīl) n. cunning

Reading Strategy Making Inferences About Characters *What qualities does King Loki possess? What will it likely take to trick him?* **R2**

Additional Support

Skills Practice

WRITING: Speaking Verbs When writing dialogue, many writers use certain verbs to denote certain ways of speaking. These verbs can be an effective way to quickly and succinctly communicate a character's emotional state. Have students scan this page for the speaking verbs Branston employs to denote the characters' emotions as they speak. *(Yell, bellow, gasp, stammer, cry, shout, reply, ask, answer.)* Have students connect each verb to an emotion. **OL**

Donar-Thor, School wall Chart. Colour print after a painting by Max Koch.
No. 4 of Series, 1905. Sagenbilder, Leipzig. ★

BRIAN BRANSTON **1047**

Teach

★ Viewing the Art

Ask: What qualities of Thor are reflected in the painting? *(strength, determination, and steadfastness of purpose)* **AS**

Building Reading Fluency

Dramatic Performance Mythical gods and monsters often have exaggerated, dramatic personalities that are fun to play aloud. Have students choose roles from the various characters in the myth.

Have one student narrate. Have the class read this page of the myth (or the entire myth) aloud, making sure to express the grand emotions of these mythical characters. **BL**

Objectives
• To make inferences about characters, and support the inferences with evidence from the story (SE)
• To analyze verb usage (TWE)

1047

L1 Literary Element

Plot Pattern Archetypes

Answer: *Answers will vary. Students may say that they have heard stories in which powerful figures have gone to great lengths to marry women who did not want to marry them.* **OL**

BI1 Big Idea

Rescuing and Conquering

Answer: *While some want to try a direct attack, Loki reminds them that such an assault might hurt the giants but will not achieve the desired result: retrieving the hammer, which will remain buried. At this, the wise god Heimdall suggests deception rather than force.* **OL**

"A bride's veil?" asked Freya, surprised. "Who's getting married?"

"You are," said Thor.

"I?" exclaimed Freya beginning to get angry, "to whom, pray? Or is it a secret?"

"It's no secret," said the simple Thor, "to Loki of Outgard, of course."

Freya's lovely breasts rose with such fury that her famous necklace Brisingamen snapped apart and the precious jewels scattered across the marble floor. She picked up the nearest weapon to hand, a distaff,[11] and started to belabor[12] Loki, shouting, "I shan't, I shan't, I shan't!" It was no use trying to reason with her. She flatly refused to marry any giant even though he was a king.

Such a serious situation had to be made known to Odin.[13] At once, he called a council meeting of all the Æsir and without delay they sat in **deliberation** upon their judgement stools. "Who's first with any ideas?" asked Odin.

Tyr suggested an armed invasion of Jotunheim. Niord[14] agreed, saying it should be an attack by sea and land and air with the Valkyries[15] on their flying horses spear-heading the aerial battalions.

Loki said, "I can tell you this: a direct attack will be useless. Let me remind you of the magic spells employed by the giant king to frustrate Thor in the past. Even if an attack was successful, the hammer would still lie hidden. There is only one way to get

it back and that is to trick King Loki of Outgard into producing it."

Heimdall,[16] the whitest and sometimes the wisest of the gods said he had an idea. "If we were to dress Thor himself up as a bride and send Loki disguised as a handmaid to do the talking, then once the hammer is brought out Thor can snatch it up and—hey presto!—heads will roll!"

"Jumping Jormungander!"[17] shouted Thor, foaming at the mouth. "Vexatious Vergelmir![18] Nobody dresses me up as a woman!"

But it was no use Thor's continuing to protest. Heimdall's suggestion was voted best in the end and the Thunderer had to submit to being clothed in petticoats to hide his hairy legs and a long-sleeved blouse stuffed out a bit in the appropriate places, topped by an embroidered tunic. Brooches were pinned onto his false bust and a set of housewife's keys was set to dangle from his girdle.[19] To show he really was 'Freya', he had to wear the goddess's famous necklace, now repaired, Brisingamen. And to complete the disguise he was draped to the waist in a white bride's veil. Loki in turn was dressed up as a woman, a rather saucy[20] lady's maid.

Thor's goats[21] were led from the stable and harnessed to the chariot. "Come on there, Toothgnasher! Gee up, Toothgrinder!" he shouted and cracked his whip while the smile vanished from Loki's lips as he nearly slipped out of the back. In a flash of lightning they were halfway across the sky.

---

11. A *distaff* (dis´taf) is a pole used to hold wool for spinning.
12. To *belabor* (bi lā´bər) is to strike or hit.
13. *Odin* is a Norse god of war. He is also the god of poets.
14. *Niord* is the Norse god of the sea.
15. *Valkyries* (val kēr´ēs) are Odin's twelve handmaidens, who ride onto the battlefield on winged horses to take souls of the brave to Valhalla, one of the nine realms.

Literary Element Plot Pattern Archetypes *What plot elements do you recognize so far in this story?* **L1**

Big Idea Rescuing and Conquering *Why might the gods decide against attacking King Loki to reclaim the hammer?* **BI1**

Vocabulary

deliberation (di lib´ə rā´shən) *n.* an official meeting or consultation

1048 UNIT 5 LEGENDS AND MYTHS

16. *Heimdall* (hīm dəl) is the watchman of the gods; he possesses keen eyesight, hearing, and the ability to see the future.
17. The *Jormungander* is Loki's son, a mighty serpent that encircles the Earth.
18. *Vexatious* (vek sā´shēs) means "troublesome." *Vergelmir* is a spring in Norse mythology that was instrumental in forming the first giants.
19. Thor's female costume includes *petticoats* (pet´ē kōts´), which are decorative feminine undergarments; a *tunic* (tōō´nik), which is a long, loose shirt; and a *girdle* (gurd´əl), which here means "a wide belt." He is also wearing a set of *housewife's keys*. Women in Scandinavian cultures ruled the household and, therefore, held the keys to the house.
20. *Saucy* (sô´sē) means "spirited."
21. Thor drove a chariot pulled by two *goats*.

Additional Support

Skills Practice

LITERARY ELEMENT: Suspense
Branston heightens the suspense toward the end of the story to make the reader fear for the characters' lives. **Ask:** How does Branston heighten the suspense? *(The fear that Thor and Loki might be discovered fuels the suspense. Thor eats a lot at the wedding banquet, uncharac-* teristic of Freya, the goddess of fertility. Thor is almost discovered when the king lifts her veil. Loki the handmaiden must come up with excuses to cover Thor. Finally, Thor's attack comes at the last possible second, during the solemniza-tion of the marriage.) **OL**

In Jotunheim King Loki of Outgard heard the thunder of the chariot wheels and he called out to his servants to strew the carved wooden settles with cushions and goat skins to make them comfortable, to broach the sparkling, foamy ale, to set up the trestle tables and prepare the wedding feast for him and his new bride the lovely, the delectable, the incomparable Freya. He rubbed his gigantic hands with satisfaction as he thought of all his possessions, of the gold-horned oxen with jet black hides thronging his paddocks, of his horses and hounds, his hunting hawks, of the gold and jewels in his iron-bound coffers;[22] he seemed to need only one thing to complete his happiness—the goddess Freya.

By the time the 'bride' and her 'lady's maid' had arrived it was early evening and the banquet was ready.

The bride was placed on King Loki's right hand and the maid on his left. The giant was very surprised when, during the feasting, the bride had no difficulty in despatching a whole ox, eight fine salmon and all the dainties intended for the lady giants. He was even more astonished to see this mountain of food washed down with three firkins of mead—and a firkin holds nine gallons! "I don't think I ever saw a giant maiden with such a thirst or such an appetite," he said. "It *is* unusual," said the cunning lady's maid, "but you have to remember that when Freya knew she was going to marry you ... " and here Loki was forced to gulp as he thought

> ### And the giant king's hair almost stood on end at the sight of the flashing eyes he saw there in the lacy shadows.

of the thumping lie he was about to tell, "she was so excited, your majesty, that she couldn't eat for a week. Not a morsel passed her lovely lips. When we arrived here she was ravenous."[23]

"You can say that again," muttered King Loki. He was getting impatient and wanted to steal a kiss from the bride so he lifted a corner of her veil.

Loki was petrified. And the giant king's hair almost stood on end at the sight of the flashing eyes he saw there in the lacy shadows. Handmaid Loki hastened to tell him not to worry, Freya's eyes were rather red because she had not been able to sleep for a week before coming to Outgard.

At last King Loki of Outgard called for the marriage to be solemnized[24] in the traditional way by the bride and groom swearing their vows on Thor's hammer. The hammer was fetched from its hiding-place and laid on the bride's lap while the happy pair placed their hands on it and swore to be true to each other.

Thor's hand was underneath and when he felt Mullicrusher[25] within his grasp once more all his confidence returned. He did not bother to throw off his veil. With one great lunge he felled his old enemy the giant king.

Then the pair of imposters strode out of the hall, mounted the chariot and rattled **jubilantly** back to Asgard again. ✆

---

22. *Settles* (set'əls) are large wooden benches or seats. Here, to *broach* (brōch) means "to open." *Paddocks* (pad'ək) are fields where horses graze, and *coffers* (kô'fərs) are chests or boxes used to store valuables.

Literary Element Plot Pattern Archetypes *Based on stories you have read or heard before, what might happen next between the fake bride and the eager groom?* **L2**

---

23. Ravenous (rav' ə nəs) means "very hungry."
24. When a marriage is solemnized (sol' əm nīz'), it is formally established.
25. Mullicrusher (mə lē' crə shər) is the nickname the author uses for Thor's hammer.

Big Idea Rescuing and Conquering *Why do you think Thor's confidence returns when he grasps his hammer?* **BI2**

Vocabulary

jubilantly (jōo'bə lənt lē) *adv.* joyfully or happily

Assess

1. (a) The gods act impulsively; cunning characters have advantages over impulsive characters; humor plays a role. (b) Scenes of Thor accidentally throwing his wife from bed, throttling Loki, barging into Freya's rooms, and dressing as a bride are comical.

2. (a) Loki (b) He has played tricks before.

3. (a) Tyr suggests an armed invasion, and Niord suggests an attack by sea, land, and air. (b) It would be violent, with less humor and less focus on cunning.

4. (a) She looks and acts strangely because she has not eaten, drunk, or slept for a week. (b) Loki's gulp before lying or the narrator's description of King Loki's awed response to his bride's drinking mead

5. (a) Females are used in many of the jokes in the story, but they do not play a main role. Thor does not understand them or know how to act like a woman. (b) Thor finally realizes that the only way to get his hammer back is to adopt the cunning of Loki and the other, smarter gods.

RESPONDING AND THINKING CRITICALLY

Respond

1. (a) What is your view of Norse heroes and villains after reading this myth? (b) How did the events of the story influence your view?

Recall and Interpret

2. (a) Who does Thor initially suspect of stealing his hammer? (b) What does this suspicion indicate about their relationship?

3. (a) What course of action do Tyr and Niord suggest? (b) If their suggestions had been followed, how would this story have changed?

4. (a) What excuses does Loki give for the behavior and appearance of the "bride"? (b) Which of these do you think is the most humorous? Explain.

Analyze and Evaluate

5. (a) How would you summarize the role of females in this story? (b) How does this role pertain to Thor dressing up as a bride?

6. (a) Explain Loki's role in this story. (b) What does the prominence of such a character in a heroic myth suggest?

7. Why do you think King Loki would risk war or invasion over Thor's hammer?

Connect

8. **Big Idea** **Rescuing and Conquering** (a) Thor went to extreme measures to retrieve his hammer. Why does this myth cast the thunder god in such a role? (b) What does Thor's story suggest about the gods and about the importance placed on recovering stolen items?

LITERARY ANALYSIS

Literary Element Plot Pattern Archetype

The plot of a story that seems familiar may incorporate **plot pattern archetypes**. Two common plot pattern archetypes are listed below:

- A valuable item is stolen or sought, and characters make a plan to recover or discover it, often with the aid of a powerful or wise ally.
- Characters venture into forbidden or dangerous territory and discover the item, often with the use of disguise or other secretive devices.

The archetype of a stolen item being recovered through trickery is central to "The Stealing of Thor's Hammer".

1. List the major plot points from this myth.

2. What other stories have similar plot patterns?

3. Why do you think the idea of stolen artifacts being recovered is an archetype that is used so often?

Review: Myth

As you learned on pages 1036–1037, a **myth** is a traditional story that uses gods and supernatural forces to explain a belief, a custom, a force of nature, or some aspect of human behavior. The gods in myths have established roles and use emblems or tools that help them perform their symbolic duties. For example, ancient Norse cultures believed that lightning was caused by Thor's hammer.

Partner Activity Pair up with a classmate and discuss the mythic ideas and characters in this story. Working with your partner, create a chart like the one below showing how the characteristics of "The Stealing of Thor's Hammer" define it as myth.

Characteristics of Myth	Examples
Explains a force of nature	Thor's hammer creates lightning.

6. (a) Loki says that stealth and guile, rather than force, are needed to retrieve Thor's hammer. (b) That the Norse people knew that might and brawn were not always the way to win and that intelligence and humor should be valued

7. He wants Freya and knows the gods are powerless against him while he has Thor's hammer.

8. (a) To mock the image of the masculine, headstrong hero (b) The gods are fallible and even funny. In Norse culture private property was very important.

READING AND VOCABULARY

Reading Strategy Making Inferences About Characters

A story does not always state explicitly what a character is like or what a character is feeling or thinking. Readers **infer** these character traits by using a combination of their own experience and evidence from the text.

1. Using what you know about human behavior and what you know about Thor, infer what he might be thinking or feeling during the wedding feast.

2. What parts from the story help you infer that King Loki might easily be tricked?

Vocabulary Practice

Practice with Analogies Complete each analogy with the best vocabulary word from the answer column. Use a dictionary, thesaurus, or the story "The Stealing of Thor's Hammer" if you need help.

1. genuine : false :: content :
2. happy : joyful :: scornful :
3. Thor : action :: Loki :
4. Thor : impulse :: Odin's council :
5. accurately : sloppily :: unhappily :

a. deliberation
b. disdainful
c. jubilantly
d. aggrieved
e. guile

Academic Vocabulary

Here are two words from the vocabulary list on page R82.

assess (ə ses′) *v.* to evaluate

consequent (kon′ sə kwent′) *adj.* following as a direct result; resultant

Practice and Apply

1. How did the Asgardian gods **assess** their options for rescuing Thor's hammer?
2. After Thor's hammer was stolen, what did his **consequent** anger make him want to do?

WRITING AND EXTENDING

Writing About Literature

Analyze Character In Norse mythology, Loki is the trickster god of fire. In "The Stealing of Thor's Hammer," he is referred to as the "Mischief Maker." In mythology the trickster normally uses cunning and deception rather than facing conflict directly. In a short essay, explain how Loki fits the description of the trickster and explain what role the trickster plays in "The Stealing of Thor's Hammer."

Before you begin drafting, take notes on specific passages from the story that focus on Loki's comments or actions. Follow the writing path shown here to help you organize your essay and ideas.

START

Introduction → Present your main idea and organize what you plan to say about it.

Body Paragraph(s) → Develop your main idea here, supporting it with evidence from the text.

Conclusion → Summarize your main idea and offer any last insights.

FINISH

After you complete your draft, meet with a peer reviewer to read and respond to each other's work. Revise your essay based on your peer reviewer's suggestions. Be sure to proofread and edit your revised draft for errors in grammar, spelling, and punctuation.

Literature Groups

"The Stealing of Thor's Hammer" is a humorous look at the way the gods respond to a crisis. What effect does humor have on the subject, characters, and tone of the story? Why are many myths told using a humorous tone? Meet with a small group of your classmates to discuss how humor is used in this and other myths and stories.

Literature Online Web Activities For eFlashcards, Selection Quick Checks, and other Web activities, go to www.glencoe.com.

BRIAN BRANSTON **1051**

Assess

Literary Element

1. Thor's hammer is stolen; he accuses Loki; Loki finds the true culprit, an old adversary of Thor; the gods meet to discuss the issue; Loki and Thor dress as females to fool King Loki; Loki covers up Thor's poor acting; King Loki's pride and lust for Freya have him handing the precious hammer back to Thor.

2. Stories and movies such as *Raiders of the Lost Ark* or *Troy,* in which precious items (or people) are stolen. Bugs Bunny cartoons often involve Bugs dressing as a woman, as do movies like *Mrs. Doubtfire.*

3. Most people can relate to losing something precious and doing almost anything to reclaim it.

Review: Myth

Students' charts should demonstrate how the story exhibits the characteristics of a myth.

Reading Strategy

1. He curses having to dress as a female, but he does it, knowing he may get his hammer back. Yet he does not try to act like a woman. Perhaps he is too vengeful or stupid to act like a woman. He lives only in the moment.

2. He thinks he is getting something he wants and he is distracted from the facts before his eyes.

Vocabulary

1. d 2. b 3. e 4. a 5. c

Academic Vocabulary

1. With a council
2. Attack King Loki

Writing About Literature

Students' essays should
• include specific examples from the story supporting the thesis

• include insights and analyses from the student's own thoughts

Literature Groups

Students' conclusions should
• discuss the role of humor in the story and in myth
• discuss what humor reveals about human nature

1051

Focus

Write on the board: Both kids seem angry. **Say:** All of the words in this sentence came into English from the Norse language. Norse words have become essential to English expression. In this lesson we will explore the origins of English words from Norse.

Teach

Etymology The English word *Friday* comes from the name of the Norse goddess Frigg, the wife of the Odin. Many simple English words come from Norse. Students should identify additional words that come from Norse, such as *gear, knife, club, crawl, lift, low, skill,* and *window.* Etymology is fascinating and can provide clues to word meanings. **OL**

Assess

Exercise

1. Wednesday—Odin's day
2. berserk—bear shirt
3. husband—householder
4. window—wind eye

▶ **Vocabulary Terms**

Word origins, or etymology, is the study of the history and development of words.

▶ **Test-Taking Tip**

To determine the meaning of an unfamiliar word in a reading passage, break the word into its parts—root, prefix, and suffix. If you recognize the root, you can probably figure out what the word means.

▶ **Reading Handbook**

For more about word origins, see the Reading Handbook, p. R20.

LiteratureOnline
eFlashcards For eFlashcards and other vocabulary activities, go to www.glencoe.com.

OBJECTIVES
- Research word origins to understand influences on the English language.
- Use word parts to define unfamiliar words.

Examining Words from Norse Myths

"The god Thor always resented the disdainful way he had been treated by King Loki of Outgard."

—Brian Branston, from "The Stealing of Thor's Hammer"

Connecting to Literature The angry, noisy Thor was the Norse god of thunder. The familiar English word *Thursday* ("Thor's day") comes from his name. Tracing the **word origins,** or etymology, of this word explains how this Norse name entered our language. Modern English has its roots in the language of the Anglo-Saxons who lived in England in the early Middle Ages. Viking peoples from Denmark and other Scandinavian countries later invaded and settled in England. As a result, terms from the Vikings' Old Norse language and mythology, like *Thor,* were assimilated into English.

"The Stealing of Thor's Hammer" offers other examples of terms from Norse myths that have entered the English language. In the attempt to retrieve his hammer, Thor disguises himself as the beautiful goddess Freya. What day of the week takes its name from hers?

Below is a chart of English words and their definitions, and the Old Norse words, including definitions, from which the English words were derived.

English Word	Old Norse Word
geyser *n.* a spring that produces jets of water	**geysa** *v.* to gush; to rush forward
score *n.* twenty; a group of twenty items; a record mark	**skor** *n.* notch; twenty
snub *v.* to rebuke; to neglect or treat rudely	**snubba** *v.* to curse

---

Exercise

Match the English words below with the meanings of the words from their Norse origins. Use a dictionary if you need help.

1. Wednesday
2. berserk
3. husband
4. window

a. wind eye
b. Odin's day
c. householder
d. bear shirt

Additional Support

eFlashcards Have students access the Web site for more practice with word origins.

English Language Coach

Word Parts Review with students how to use word parts to determine the meaning of unfamiliar words. Begin with Norse-derived words such as *wrong* and *die,* and show how to decode these words with affixes, such as *wrongful* ("full of wrong, unjust") and *undying* ("not dying"). **EL**

Differentiated Instruction

Word Origins Review how students can determine word origins by using the dictionary. Make sure they understand that the symbol > means "derived from." Have them look up the derivations of these words (which come from Norse): *want, weak, wrong, rag, rug, scare,* and *bloom.* **BL**

from Theseus

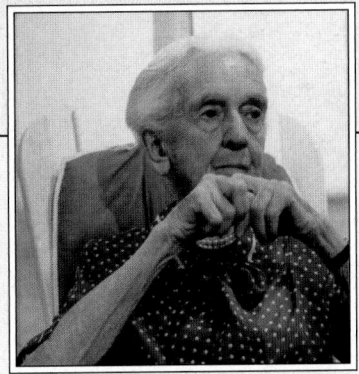

MEET EDITH HAMILTON

Throughout her life, Edith Hamilton was committed to education. As headmistress at Bryn Mawr School in Baltimore (a preparatory school for girls), she touched the lives of hundreds of students. Later in life, Hamilton brought the ancient world to life for a new generation of readers by providing the modern world with engaging editions of Greek and Roman literature.

Early Education Hamilton was born in Dresden, Germany, to an intellectual family. For most of her childhood, she was educated at her home in Fort Wayne, Indiana. From an early age, Hamilton was fascinated with Greek and Roman literature, and she began studying Latin with her father when she was only seven years old. She also studied French, German, and Greek. Hamilton was an apt pupil; by the time she was a teenager, she was fluent in those four languages.

"To be able to be caught up into the world of thought—that is educated."

—Edith Hamilton

Scholar and Teacher Hamilton left home to attend a girls' finishing school at age sixteen. She next attended Bryn Mawr College and received her master's degree in classics in 1894. After graduation, Hamilton studied at universities in Leipzig and Munich, Germany. Her younger sister, Alice, studied in Germany as well. Together, they were the first women to attend courses at the university in Munich.

After returning to the United States, Hamilton accepted an offer to serve as the first headmistress of Bryn Mawr School. Hamilton was a

success as a teacher and an administrator. Students enjoyed her classes (especially her senior class on Virgil) and admired her high standards.

A Second Career Hamilton retired from Bryn Mawr in 1922 with the intention of writing about the classics. Her friends, enthusiastic about her teachings of Greek tragedies, encouraged her to publish her works. Hamilton wrote various articles about Greek drama, which were so successful that she was encouraged to rework them as a book. As a result, she published *The Greek Way* in 1930. Hamilton went on to write numerous books and translations, including *The Roman Way* (1932), *Mythology* (1943), and *Echo of Greece* (1957).

Hamilton almost single-handedly popularized the study of the ancient world. She was recognized for her work with several honorary degrees and awards. She was elected to the American Academy of Arts and Letters in 1955. She was even made an honorary citizen of Athens in 1957. When Hamilton died at age ninety-five, she left behind fans worldwide who treasured the teacher and writer who "[talked] about Aeschylus exactly as though he were her eldest son."

Edith Hamilton was born in 1867 and died in 1963.

Literature Online **Author Search** For more about Edith Hamilton, go to www.glencoe.com.

EDITH HAMILTON **1053**

Focus

BELLRINGER

Bellringer Options
Daily Language Practice Transparency 89
Or **Ask:** What is your definition of a hero? Allow students to express their personal definitions of heroism. **Ask:** Have you ever witnessed a hero in action? How did you feel after observing this act of heroism? *(Answers will vary.)* Explain that students' reading of "Theseus" may help them understand why people are often so moved by heroes.

Literature Online

Author Search To expand students' appreciation of Edith Hamilton, have them access the Web site for additional information and resources.

Selection Skills

Theseus

Literary Elements
- Image Archetype (SE pp. 1054, 1055, 1057, 1062)
- Plot Pattern Archetype (SE p. 1062)

Reading Skills
- Identifying Sequence (SE pp. 1054, 1057, 1058, 1062)

Vocabulary Skills
- Context Clues (SE pp. 1054, 1062)
- Journaling (TWE p. 1058)

Study Skills/Research/Assessment
- Greek Mythology (TWE p. 1060)

Writing Skills/Grammar
- Evaluate Author's Craft (SE p. 1063)
- Using Participles (SE p. 1063)
- The Verb *Be* (TWE p. 1056)

Focus

Summary

Theseus was the son of Aegeus, the Athenian king. The king left before his son was born but explained to his wife that when his son grew strong enough, he could claim him as his father. "Theseus" begins as a chronicle of this adventure and develops into an intricate plot of obstacles and conquests. By the conclusion, Theseus has gained and lost his true love, buried his father, established a democracy, and liberated an oppressed people.

V Vocabulary

Vocabulary File Say: Add these words and definitions to your vocabulary file. For each word, include a sentence that gives you an example of how to use the word. **OL** Students with English language needs should include the pronunciations of these words in their files. **EL**

Literary Elements Have students access the Web site to improve their understanding of image archetype.

Connecting to the Story

The following narrative is an account of courage, love, loss, and democracy. Edith Hamilton's retelling of "Theseus" captures the great hero's life in a series of inspirational and sometimes tragic events. Before you read the story, think about the following questions:

- How do you handle difficult decisions?
- Have you ever advocated for, or supported, another's rights?

Building Background

The body of stories that tell of the gods, heroes, and ceremonies of the ancient Greeks is commonly known as Greek mythology. The philosopher Plato identified elements of fiction in these narratives during the fifth and fourth centuries BC. However, until that time, Greeks viewed these tales as factual. Western views of the myths generally regard the stories as inventive and fascinating. For this reason, the mythology of the Greeks remains unrivaled as a source of inspiration for contemporary writers. "Theseus," as retold by Hamilton, illustrates the appeal and imaginativeness typical of ancient Greek mythology.

Setting Purposes for Reading

Big Idea Rescuing and Conquering

As you read this excerpt from "Theseus," note how the opposing themes of rescuing and conquering emerge, often side by side.

Literary Element Image Archetype

Image archetypes are images that recur throughout literature across cultures. These images are believed to have universal meaning. The stone in Greek mythology, for example, is symbolic of an obstacle in life's path. A cup is symbolic of one's fate or destiny. As you read, try to identify archetypical images in "Theseus."

- See Literary Terms Handbook, p. R8.

Literature Online **Interactive Literary Elements Handbook** To review or learn more about the literary elements, go to www.glencoe.com.

OBJECTIVES
In studying this selection, you will focus on the following:
- identifying and analyzing image archetypes
- identifying sequence
- recognizing plot pattern archetypes
- writing to evaluate an author's craft

Reading Preview

Reading Strategy Identifying Sequence

Identifying sequence in a story means recognizing the logical order of events or ideas. Events in fiction usually occur in chronological order, or the order in which they happen in time. Signal words such as *first*, *there*, *following*, *during*, and *before* can indicate shifts in time, place, or incident.

Reading Tip: Annotating When you read, annotate, or take note of, time and place sequences. Watch for transitional and signal words. Write critical notes that comment on the sequences.

Signal Word	Type of Sequence	Annotation
"Aegeus went back to Athens *before* the child was born, but *first* he placed in a hollow a sword. . . ."	Time and place.	The words "before" and "first" signal time sequences linking key events.

Vocabulary

contemptible (kən temp′ tə bəl) *adj.* worthy of contempt; loathsome; p. 1055 *The bank robbery was a contemptible act that endangered lives.*

endear (en dēr′) *v.* to cause to adore or admire; p. 1057 *Writing a letter to show gratitude would endear the child to his parent's friend.*

confinement (kən fīn′mənt) *n.* the state of being restricted or confined; p. 1057 *Confinement was the most dreaded punishment for the teenager.*

Vocabulary Tip: Context Clues Often you can understand an unfamiliar word by examining the words and ideas that surround it.

Selection Resources

Print Materials
- Unit 5 Resources (Fast File), pp. 40–42
- Leveled Vocabulary Development, p. 74
- Selection and Unit Assessments, pp. 179–180
- Selection Quick Checks, p. 90

Transparencies
- Bellringer Options Transparencies: Daily Language Practice Transparency 89
- Literary Elements Transparencies 86, 87

Technology
- TeacherWorks Plus™ CD-ROM
- StudentWorks Plus™ CD-ROM
- Presentation Plus!™ CD-ROM
- Literature Online, glencoe.com
- Online Student Edition, mhln.com
- ExamView® Assessment Suite CD-ROM
- Vocabulary PuzzleMaker CD-ROM
- Listening Library, disc 2 track 24

The Passions of Pasiphae, wife of King Minos of Crete, from the Story of Theseus, (c.1510). Master of the Campana Cassoni. Oil on panel, 69 x 182 cm. Musee du Petit Palais, Avignon, France. ★

From

THESEUS

Retold by Edith Hamilton

The great Athenian hero was Theseus. He had so many adventures and took part in so many great enterprises[1] that there grew up a saying in Athens, "Nothing without Theseus."

He was the son of the Athenian King, Aegeus. He spent his youth, however, in his mother's home, a city in southern Greece. Aegeus went back to Athens before the child was born, but first he placed in a hollow a sword and a pair of shoes and covered them with a great stone. He did this with the knowledge of his wife and told her that whenever the boy—if it was a boy— grew strong enough to roll away the stone and get the things beneath it, she could send him to Athens to claim him as his father. The child was a boy and he grew up strong far beyond others, so that when his mother finally took him to the stone he lifted it with no trouble at all. She told him then that the

time had come for him to seek his father, and a ship was placed at his disposal[2] by his grandfather. But Theseus refused to go by water, because the voyage was safe and easy. His idea was to become a great hero as quickly as possible, and easy safety was certainly not the way to do that. Hercules, who was the most magnificent of all the heroes of Greece, was always in his mind, and the determination to be just as magnificent himself. This was quite natural since the two were cousins.

He steadfastly refused, therefore, the ship his mother and grandfather urged on him, telling them that to sail on it would be a **contemptible** flight from danger, and he set forth to go to Athens by land. The journey was long and very hazardous because of the bandits that beset[3] the road. He killed them

---

1. Here, *enterprises* are undertakings or projects of great difficulty, risk, or complication.

Literary Element Image Archetype *What might lifting a great stone typically represent?* **L**

2. Here, *disposal* means "to use as one chooses."
3. *Beset* means "to trouble or badger."

Vocabulary

contemptible (kən temp′tə bəl) *adj.* worthy of contempt; loathsome

EDITH HAMILTON **1055**

Teach

BI Big Idea

Rescuing and Conquering
Answer: *Theseus's punishment of the bandits rescues the victims by ridding them of the treacherous men, while simultaneously conquering the bandits themselves through defeat.* **OL**

★ Viewing the Art

Some observant students might note that this painting is stylistically similar to seventeenth-century European religious art. Reynaud Levieux (1613–c. 1694), a prominent Provençal artist, was the son of a glass painter. He traveled to Rome in 1640 and studied the works of the famous artist Raphael. He is known primarily for his large paintings for churches, although he also painted for private homes and created nonreligious works like this one. **AS**

Theseus Discovering His Father's Sword. Reynaud Levieux. Oil on canvas.
The Cummerland Museum of Art and Gardens, Jacksonville, FL.

all, however; he left not one alive to trouble future travelers. His idea of dealing justice was simple, but effective: what each had done to others, Theseus did to him. Sciron, for instance, who had made those he captured kneel to wash his feet and then kicked them down into the sea, Theseus hurled over a precipice.[4] Sinis, who killed people by fastening them to two pine trees bent down to the ground and letting the trees go, died in that way himself. Procrustes was placed upon the iron bed which he used for his victims, tying them to it and then making them the right length for it by stretching those who were too short and cutting off as much as was necessary from those who were too long. The

story does not say which of the two methods was used in his case, but there was not much to choose between them and in one way or the other Procrutes' career ended.

It can be imagined how Greece rang with the praises of the young man who had cleared the land of these banes[5] to travelers. When he reached Athens he was an acknowledged hero and he was invited to a banquet by the King, who of course was unaware that Theseus was his son. In fact he was afraid of the young man's great popularity, thinking that he might win the people over to make him king, and he invited him with the idea of poisoning him. The plan was not his, but Medea's, the heroine of the Quest of the Golden Fleece[6] who knew through her sorcery who Theseus was. She had fled to

---

4. A *precipice* is an extremely steep place.

Big Idea Rescuing and Conquering *How does this method of justice exhibit the ideas of rescuing and conquering?* **BI**

---

5. *Banes* refers to harmful or poisonous things.
6. In Greek mythology, Jason and the Argonauts went on the *Quest of the Golden Fleece* to secure him the throne.

1056 UNIT 5 LEGENDS AND MYTHS

Additional Support

WRITING: The Verb *Be* Verbs determine the pace of a narrative. Heavy use of the verb *be* *(is, are, was, were)* slows the rate at which a narrative progresses because it shows no action. Have students compare two sentences from "Theseus": one that contains a form of *be* and another that contains an action verb. Then have them write three sentences with forms of *be* and three sentences with action verbs. Discuss the effectiveness of both sets of sentences. **Ask:** When might it be appropriate to use *be*? *(when the pace of a selection is unimportant; when the focus is on a scene's appearance)* **OL**

1056

Athens when she left Corinth in her winged car, and she had acquired great influence over Aegeus, which she did not want disturbed by the appearance of a son. But as she handed him the poisoned cup Theseus, wishing to make himself known at once to his father, drew his sword. The King instantly recognized it and dashed the cup to the ground. Medea escaped as she always did and got safely away to Asia.

Aegeus then proclaimed to the country that Theseus was his son and heir. The new heir apparent soon had an opportunity to **endear** himself to the Athenians.

Years before his arrival in Athens, a terrible misfortune had happened to the city. Minos, the powerful ruler of Crete, had lost his only son, Androgeus, while the young man was visiting the Athenian King. King Aegeus had done what no host should do, he had sent his guest on an expedition full of peril—to kill a dangerous bull. Instead, the bull had killed the youth. Minos invaded the country, captured Athens and declared that he would raze it to the ground unless every nine years the people sent him a tribute of seven maidens and seven youths. A horrible fate awaited these young creatures. When they reached Crete they were given to the Minotaur to devour.

The Minotaur was a monster, half bull, half human, the offspring of Minos' wife Pasiphaë and a wonderfully beautiful bull. Poseidon had given this bull to Minos in order that he should sacrifice it to him, but Minos could not bear to slay it and kept it for himself. To punish him, Poseidon had made Pasiphaë fall madly in love with it.

When the minotaur was born Minos did not kill him. He had Daedalus, a great architect and inventor, construct a place of **confinement** for him from which escape was impossible. Daedalus built the Labyrinth, famous throughout the world. Once inside, one would go endlessly along its twisting paths without ever finding the exit. To this place the young Athenians were each time taken and left to the Minotaur. There was no possible way to escape. In whatever direction they ran they might be running straight to the monster; if they stood still he might at any moment emerge from the maze. Such was the doom which awaited fourteen youths and maidens a few days after Theseus reached Athens. The time had come for the next installment of the tribute.

At once Theseus came forward and offered to be one of the victims. All loved him for his goodness and admired him for his nobility, but they had no idea that he intended to try to kill the Minotaur. He told his father, however, and promised him that if he succeeded, he would have the black sail which the ship with its cargo of misery always carried changed to a white one, so that Aegeus could know long before it came to land that his son was safe.

When the young victims arrived in Crete they were paraded before the inhabitants on their way to the Labyrinth. Minos' daughter Ariadne was among the spectators and she fell in love with Theseus at first sight as he marched past her. She sent for Daedalus and told him he must show her a way to get out of the Labyrinth, and she sent for Theseus and told him she would bring about his escape if he would promise to take her back to Athens and marry her. As may be imagined, he made no difficulty about that, and she gave him the clue she had got from

---

> **Literary Element** Image Archetype *A sword in Greek mythology often represents legacy. Explain the importance of Theseus establishing his legacy at this point in the story.* **L₁**

> **Reading Strategy** Identifying Sequence *What does the signal word "then" indicate?* **R**

> **Vocabulary**
> **endear** (en dēr′) *v.* to cause to adore or admire

> **Literary Element** Image Archetype *What image archetype do you think the Minotaur symbolizes?* **L₂**

> **Vocabulary**
> **confinement** (kən fīn′mənt) *n.* the state of being restricted or confined

EDITH HAMILTON **1057**

BI Big Idea

Rescuing and Conquering

Answer: *The yarn may be a rescue aid. With it, Minotaur can be conquered.* Have students make predictions based on Ariadne's decision to give Theseus the life-saving clue about the ball of thread. *(Ariadne and Theseus will probably fall in love.)* **OL**

R Reading Strategy

Identifying Sequence

Answer: *It explains that the following events happened at a specific, different place (Naxos), after the adventure in the labyrinth.* **OL**

★ Literary History

Romeo and Juliet In Western literature, Romeo and Juliet, the hero and heroine of William Shakespeare's famed play, are archetypes for "star-crossed" lovers. **Ask:** What do the similarities between Theseus and Ariadne's love story and Romeo and Juliet's story say about the power of image archetypes? *(Image archetypes resonate with people as evidenced in this particular archetype's common use.)* **AS**

Theseus Fighting the Minotaur. Antoine-Louis Barye, 1795–1875. Bronze Sculpture. Mohammed Khalil Museum, Cairo.

Daedalus, a ball of thread which he was to fasten at one end to the inside of the door and unwind as he went on. This he did and, certain that he could retrace his steps whenever he chose, he walked boldly into the maze looking for the Minotaur. He came upon him asleep and fell upon him, pinning him to the ground; and with his fists—he had no other weapon—he battered the monster to death.

Big Idea Rescuing and Conquering *How does the ball of thread reflect the idea of rescuing and conquering?* **BI**

Reading Strategy Identifying Sequence *How does this sentence help you understand the sequence of events?* **R**

1058 UNIT 5 LEGENDS AND MYTHS

As an oak tree falls on the hillside
Crushing all that lies beneath,
So Theseus. He presses out the
life,
The brute's savage life,
and now it lies dead.
Only the head sways
slowly, but the horns are
useless now.

When Theseus lifted himself up from that terrific struggle, the ball of thread lay where he had dropped it. With it in his hands, the way out was clear. The others followed and taking Ariadne with them they fled to the ship and over the sea toward Athens.

On the way there they put in at the island of Naxos and what happened then is differently reported. One story says that Theseus deserted Ariadne. She was asleep and he sailed away without her, but Dionysus found her and comforted her. The other story is much more favorable to Theseus. She was extremely sea-sick, and he set her ashore to recover while he returned to the ship to do some necessary work. A violent wind carried him out to sea and kept him there a long time. On his return he found that Ariadne had died, and he was deeply afflicted. ★

Both stories agree that when they drew near to Athens he forgot to hoist the white sail. Either his joy at the success of his voyage put every other thought out of his head, or his grief for Ariadne. The black sail was seen by his father, King Aegeus, from the Acropolis, where for days he had watched the sea with straining eyes. It was to him the sign of his son's death and he threw himself down from a rocky height into the sea, and was killed. The sea into which he fell was called the Aegean ever after.

Additional Support

Skills Practice

VOCABULARY: Journaling Students can clarify the meanings of unfamiliar words by listing them in a three-column chart in their journals. They can document their perceived meaning of the word, the context or other clues used to arrive at this meaning, and finally, the dictionary definition of the word. By doing so, students make a concerted effort at discovering word meanings, and keep a running log of newly acquired vocabulary. Students also gain confidence as readers when they learn that their perceived definitions are correct. **OL**

Theseus and the Daughters of Minos. Benedetto Gennari. ⭐

⭐ Viewing the Art

Benedetto Gennari I (1563–1658) was the patriarch of an Italian family of painters linked to the studio of the painter Guercino. This painting depicts Theseus—the legendary Athenian hero known for slaying the Minotaur of Crete—with the daughters of Minos, king of Crete. **Ask:** What do the characters' poses add to the mood of the painting? *(Students may say that the characters' intimate yet carefree poses add a whimsical or sensuous element to the mood of the painting.)* **AS**

Differentiated Instruction

Modern-Day Heroes Assign students the task of researching modern-day heroes. Ask students to include biographical information about their subjects, detailed descriptions of the actions or characteristics that qualify the subjects as heroes and a full explanation of how their subjects relate to past or mythical heroes, like Theseus. When students finish, have them compile their writings to create a book about modern-day heroes. **AL**

Objectives
- To identify sequence (SE)
- To define unfamiliar words (TWE)

1059

Teach

BI Big Idea

Rescuing and Conquering

Answer: *Theseus rescues the vanquished from the Thebans' refusal to bury their dead. He conquers Thebes so that the victims may be vindicated.* **OL**

★ Viewing the Art

Born in Britain in 1935, Peter Connolly is a scholar of ancient civilizations and an accomplished artist. Connolly has garnered wide praise for his books on ancient warfare, such as *The Greek Armies* and *The Cavalryman,* which he wrote and illustrated. **Ask:** How is Connolly's knowledge of Ancient Greece evident in the details he chooses to include in this illustration? *(Students may point out the clothing or the ship with banks of rowers.)* **AS**

 CheckPoint

Use the CheckPoint questions on Presentation Plus! to check students' mastery of the selection. These questions can be used with interactive response keypads for immediate student feedback.

Theseus's Arrival in Crete, 1990. Peter Connolly. Watercolor. ★

So Theseus became King of Athens, a most wise and disinterested king. He declared to the people that he did not wish to rule over them; he wanted a people's government where all would be equal. He resigned his royal power and organized a commonwealth,[7] building a council hall where the citizens should gather and vote. The only office he kept for himself was that of Commander in Chief. Thus Athens became, of all earth's cities, the happiest and most prosperous, the only true home of liberty, the one place in the world where the people governed themselves. It was for this reason that in the great War of the Seven against Thebes, when the victorious Thebans refused burial to those of the enemy who had died, the vanquished[8] turned to Theseus and Athens for help, believing that free men under such a leader would never consent to having the helpless dead wronged. They did not turn in vain.

Theseus led his army against Thebes, conquered her and forced her to allow them to be buried. But when he was victor he did not return evil to the Thebans for the evil they had done. He showed himself the perfect knight. He refused to let his army enter and loot the city. He had come not to harm Thebes, but to bury the Argive dead, and that duty done he led his soldiers back to Athens.

In many other stories he shows the same qualities. He received the aged Oedipus whom everyone else had cast out. He was with him when he died, sustaining and comforting him. He protected his two helpless daughters and sent them safely home after their father's death. When Hercules in his madness killed his wife and children and upon his return to sanity determined to kill himself, Theseus alone stood by him. Hercules' other friends fled, fearing to be polluted by the presence of one who had done so horrible a deed, but Theseus gave him his hand, roused his courage, told him to die would be a coward's act, and took him to Athens.∞

---

7. A *commonwealth* is a political unit that gives supreme power to the common man.
8. Here, *vanquished* is used as a noun and means those overcome through battle.

Big Idea Rescuing and Conquering *Explain how Theseus's actions employ both ideas of rescuing and conquering.* **BI**

Additional Support

Skills Practice

RESEARCH: Greek Mythology

Ask students to choose a character, place, or event from Greek mythology that is mentioned in the selection. Then have them conduct Internet research to learn more about the subject they have chosen. Encourage them to consult a variety of sources, and to make sure the sources are trustworthy. Explain that if they have questions about the credibility of a source, they should use a second source to confirm the information they find. Students should write brief essays on their topics and then share their findings with the class. **OL**

RESPONDING AND THINKING CRITICALLY

Respond

1. From this retelling, what are your impressions of Theseus's character?

Recall and Interpret

2. (a)According to Hamilton, why did the saying "Nothing without Theseus" develop? (b)What does this saying reflect about the main character?

3. (a)Why does Theseus refuse to seek his father by water? (b)How does Theseus's willingness to forego the voyage by water affect the myth's plot?

4. (a)How does Aegeus intend to kill Theseus? (b)What image archetype does this represent?

Analyze and Evaluate

5. (a)How does the author reveal a lack of certainty in the myth's legacy? (b)Does this uncertainty diminish the myth's credibility? Explain.

6. How well does the author transition between places and time frames? Explain.

7. (a)How has Theseus changed by the story's conclusion? (b)What events have led to this change, and why are they significant?

Connect

8. **Big Idea** **Rescuing and Conquering** Greek mythology encompasses many acts of rescuing and conquering. Which do you think is more prevalent in "Theseus"—rescuing, or conquering? Support your opinion.

DAILY LIFE AND CULTURE

Pleasing the Gods

Greeks, in their daily lives, had to consider the happiness of countless gods. Pleasing the gods through daily rituals was more important than knowing exactly how many gods there were. In fact, some special altars were created specifically for worshipping potential unknown gods. The contentment of the gods was assured not through correct beliefs, but through proper action. Greek people worshipped their gods diligently and made appropriate sacrifices to them to lessen the chances of retribution.

1. The ancient Greeks were expected to keep the gods happy. How might everyday activities be affected by this responsibility? Explain.

2. In Greek mythology, what action might take place if a human displeased a god?

Jupiter. Benvenuto Cellini (1500–1571). Bronze Sculpture. Museo Nazionale del Bargello, Florence.

EDITH HAMILTON **1061**

Assess

1. Students may indicate either approval or disapproval of Theseus, and should cite examples of his heroism or his self-serving behavior.

2. (a) The saying developed because of Theseus's many adventures and enterprises. (b) It reflects his determination, greatness, or reputation with the people.

3. (a) To seek his father by water would be too easy (b) Theseus endures many difficult situations because of his decision to travel by land.

4. (a) With the poisoned cup provided by Medea, who knows Theseus's true identity. (b) The image archetype of the cup is fate or destiny.

5. (a) The author reveals uncertainty by giving varying accounts of Theseus and Ariadne's separation. (b) Students should support their ideas with examples from the text.

6. The conveyance of a large volume of ideas and circumstances in a short period of time without much confusion shows a good use of transitions.

7. (a) He is not interested in conquering, rather in establishing a commonwealth. His behavior is not merely self-serving, but benefits others. (b) Theseus has been humbled by the loss of his lover and father and by his battles and struggles.

8. Students impressed by his acts of heroism may state that more rescuing occurred. Those influenced by the violence in the story will say that more conquering occurred.

Daily Life and Culture

1. Since the gods' happiness was such a priority, a Greek might have daily activities interrupted with acts of praise and with plans of sacrifice.

2. Responses may include financial troubles, illness, or death inflicted on the human.

Assess

Literary Element

1. Students' choice of archetypes that are true to life will vary. Answers should be supported with reasons.

2. Yes. The archetypes deepen the meaning of the work, but are not required for a general reading of the text.

3. The universal meanings of image archetypes tie them to a long history of myths and literary works; they make the story more complex and heighten its meaning.

Review: Plot Pattern Archetype

Ask students to share examples of other myths or stories they've read whose plot patterns resemble that of "Theseus."

Reading Strategy

1. Students may approve the author's handling of the story's sequences, judging that the author gives ample transitions and signals to indicate changes in place and time. Students disapproving of the story's sequences may indicate transitions that are too quick or weak.

2. Students' answers will vary.

Literary Element Image Archetype

The use of **image archetypes** in works of mythology can help an author communicate with his or her readers. Since the meanings and importance of a work's images have already been established, the author does not have to work to make readers understand the significance of the images.

1. Which image archetypes stand out the most in "Theseus"? Select one that you think is true to life. Explain your choice.

2. Can a reader who is unfamiliar with the image archetypes of Greek literature understand and enjoy "Theseus"? Explain.

3. How does the use of image archetypes in "Theseus" strengthen or weaken the plot?

Review: Plot Pattern Archetype

As you learned on page 1044, **plot pattern archetype** is a recurring plot arrangement found across cultures in literary works.

Partner Activity Meet with a classmate to discuss the plot pattern archetypes of "Theseus." Work with your partner to create a two-column chart like the one below. Fill in the left-hand column with examples of plot pattern archetypes. Use the right-hand column to list examples of each archetype from "Theseus."

Plot Pattern Archetype	Example from Text
secret birth	Theseus is born and lives his childhood without any knowledge of who his father is.
series of impossible tasks involving monsters or evildoers and formidable situations	
revelation as favored heir	

Reading Strategy Identifying Sequence

A story's **sequence** plays an important role in the author's method of conveying thoughts, ideas, and events. If an author fails to alert his or her readers to significant changes in place and time, he or she risks losing the reader's understanding and interest. Much of this communication lies in the author's use of transitional and signal words.

1. How well do you think the author communicated the plot sequences in "Theseus"? Explain.

2. Support your opinion with several examples from the text.

Vocabulary Practice

Practice with Context Clues Use context clues to determine the meaning of the boldfaced vocabulary words in each sentence below.

1. The man's **contemptible** behavior left him with few friends. He was often judgmental, impolite, and vulgar.
   a. loathsome   b. delightful

2. The dog's gentle nudges **endeared** him to her even though the thought of an early-morning walk was uninspiring.
   a. to cause to become beloved   b. to cause disapproval

3. The prison's **confinement** nearly drove the inmate wild.
   a. freedom   b. the state of being restricted

Academic Vocabulary

Here is a word from the vocabulary list on page R82.

criteria (krī tēr′ ē ə) n. a measure on which a judgment or decision is based

Practice and Apply
What **criteria** did Aegeus set forth before Theseus could seek him?

Vocabulary

1. a **2.** a **3.** b

Academic Vocabulary

Theseus had to be strong enough to roll away the large stone and retrieve the sword and shoes before he could seek his father.

Writing About Literature

Evaluate Author's Craft Author Edith Hamilton's task of retelling the myth of Theseus is complicated by the story's pre-existence. Because the text has been told time and again by numerous writers, the author faces a long history of established creativity. Hamilton's retelling of Theseus must therefore offer the reader something more than other versions. In a one- or two-page analysis, evaluate how Hamilton brings new life to this old tale.

Before you begin drafting, note the story's stylistic strengths and weaknesses in a chart like the one below.

Stylistic Strengths	Stylistic Weaknesses
The author retells each incident in Theseus's journey with specific, clear details.	Certain incidents do not have a definite ending.

Be sure to include details from the story that illustrate your assertions. Record any impressions or ideas that strike you as relevant. Once you have completed the chart, begin drafting.

After your draft is complete, have a peer reviewer evaluate your work and suggest revisions. Following the review, proofread and edit your draft for errors in spelling, grammar, and punctuation.

Interdisciplinary Activity: Social Studies

The modern concept of a hero derives from mythical hero archetypes. Research the hero archetypes of three or four other cultures and compare and contrast your findings to the mythical hero archetypes. Create a poster that shows the similarities and differences among them.

Hamilton's Language and Style

Using Participles Participles are words that can function as both verbs and adjectives. There are two forms of participles: present and past. Present participles typically end in "—ing" while past participles typically end in "—ed." Edith Hamilton's use of participles shapes her language and style. Note how her use of participles affects her communication of events:

*"But as she handed him the **poisoned** cup Theseus, wishing to make himself known at once to his father, drew his sword."*

*"Once inside, one would go endlessly along its **twisting** paths without ever finding the exit."*

Word	Past or Present Participle
poisoned	past participle
twisting	present participle

Activity Create your own chart and record additional participles in "Theseus." Reword each phrase or sentence containing a participle so that the word serves a different function or is eliminated altogether. Determine the effect on the phrase or sentence with or without the original use of the participle.

Revising Check

Participles The use of participles can strengthen your work. If a description seems ineffective, it may be appropriate to replace traditional adjectives with participles. With a partner, review your evaluation of Edith Hamilton's craft and note places that could benefit from the use of participles. Revise your draft as necessary.

 Literature Online **Web Activities** For eFlashcards, Selection Quick Checks, and other Web activities, go to www.glencoe.com.

Assess

Writing About Literature

Students' essays should

- include a thesis that states an overall argument about Hamilton's ability to bring new life to the story
- mention specific stylistic strengths and weaknesses in the text
- explain each strength or weakness using examples from the text and sound reasoning

Interdisciplinary Activity

If students have trouble finding appropriate resources, direct them to encyclopedias of world mythology or to reliable Web sites.

Hamilton's Language and Style

Students should note that using a participle can help to make a phrase more concise. For example, "the poisoned cup" is more concise than "the cup that was poisoned," or "the cup that contained poison." Encourage students to consider using participles when editing their own writing for wordiness.

EDITH HAMILTON **1063**

Revising Check

Be sure that students do not replace adjectives with participles indiscriminately. Guide them in identifying situations in which such substitutions are appropriate and situations in which traditional adjectives are more effective.

Literature Online

Web Activities Have students access the Web site for interactive activities that will help them assess their understanding of the selection.

Focus

Summary

In this interview, Joseph Campbell speaks with Bill Moyers about the power of myths and how they relate to human experience. He discusses a variety of ideas, including conquering inner demons, becoming an adult, and being a parent, but most importantly, following one's bliss. He emphasizes the importance of the individual and refers to Ariadne and Theseus to make this point. For Campbell, myths are models for human behavior.

Teach

Big Idea

Rescuing and Conquering

Say: Keep the following question in mind as you read: How are readers encouraged, through myth, to rescue and conquer?
(The characters in myths inspire readers to rescue and conquer by presenting the "possibility of . . . perfection." The characters rescue the helpless and conquer evil—things all humans wish they were capable of.) **OL**

The HERO'S Adventure

Bill Moyers, with
Joseph Campbell

Building Background

As a young boy, Joseph Campbell was intrigued with American Indian civilizations. As an adult, after studying in the United States and Europe and then traveling for some years, he began teaching in the literature department of Sarah Lawrence College. Campbell, an author and editor of dozens of books, was regarded as a prominent scholar on mythology. In 1988, one year after his death, PBS aired *Joseph Campbell and The Power of Myth with Bill Moyers*. The following is an excerpt from over six hours of footage of a conversation between the two men.

Set a Purpose for Reading

Read to discover the comparisons Joseph Campbell makes between mythology and real life.

Reading Strategy

Analyzing Rhetorical Devices

Rhetorical devices are techniques of using language to persuade. One type of rhetorical device is an analogy, or a comparison that shows the relationship between otherwise dissimilar things. Another type of rhetorical device is causation, or showing the cause-and-effect relationship between things. As you read the interview, identify rhetorical devices and analyze their effectiveness.

1064 UNIT 5 LEGENDS AND MYTHS

MOYERS: When I was a boy and read *Knights of the Round Table*,[1] myth stirred me to think that I could be a hero. I wanted to go out and do battle with dragons, I wanted to go into the dark forest and slay evil. What does it say to you that myths can cause the son of an Oklahoma farmer to think of himself as a hero?

CAMPBELL: Myths inspire the realization of the possibility of your perfection, the fullness of your strength, and the bringing of solar light into the world. Slaying monsters is slaying the dark things. Myths grab you somewhere down inside. As a boy, you approach it one way, as I did reading my Indian stories. Later on, myths tell you more, and more, and still more. I think that anyone who has ever dealt seriously with religious or mythic ideas will tell you that we learn them as a child on one level, but then many different levels are revealed. Myths are infinite in their revelation.

---

1. *Knights of the Round Table* refers to the symbolic court and knights in the legend of King Arthur. The Round Table was equal on all sides, with places for 150 knights to sit.

Additional Support

See also ▌Active Learning and Note Taking Guide, pp. 171–177.

Skills Practice

READING: Higher-Level Thinking
Help students understand the lofty sentences in "The Hero's Adventure" by teaching them to break them down into digestible parts. Read the first sentence of Campbell's initial response aloud. **Ask:** What concepts or arrangements of words make this sentence difficult to understand? Students finding the syntax confusing can work with you to reword the sentence. Students struggling with concepts should be reminded of the definitions of the words *inspire* and *realization* and should then reexamine the sentence. **OL**

MOYERS: How do I slay that dragon in me? What's the journey each of us has to make, what you call "the soul's high adventure"?

CAMPBELL: My general formula for my students is "Follow your bliss." Find where it is, and don't be afraid to follow it.

MOYERS: Is it my work or my life?

CAMPBELL: If the work that you're doing is the work that you chose to do because you are enjoying it, that's it. But if you think, "Oh, no! I couldn't do that!" that's the dragon locking you in. "No, no, I couldn't be a writer," or "No, no, I couldn't possibly do what So-and-so is doing."

MOYERS: In this sense we're not going on our journey to save the world but to save ourselves.

CAMPBELL: But in doing that, you save the world. The influence of a vital person vitalizes, there's no doubt about it. . . .

MOYERS: I like what you say about the old myth of Theseus and Ariadne. Theseus says to Ariadne, "I'll love you forever if you can show me a way to come out of the labyrinth." So she gives him a ball of string, which he unwinds as he goes into the labyrinth, and then follows to find the way out. You say, "All he had was the string. That's all you need."

CAMPBELL: That's all you need—an Ariadne thread.

MOYERS: Sometimes we look for great wealth to save us, a great power to save us, or great ideas to save us, when all we need is that piece of string.

CAMPBELL: That's not always easy to find. But it's nice to have someone who can give you a clue. That's the teacher's job, to help you find your Ariadne thread.

MOYERS: Like all heroes, the Buddha[2] doesn't show you the truth itself, he shows you the way to truth. ⭐

CAMPBELL: But it's got to be your way, not his. The Buddha can't tell you exactly how

to get rid of your particular fears, for example. Different teachers may suggest exercises, but they may not be the ones to work for you. All a teacher can do is *suggest*. He is like a lighthouse that says, "There are rocks over here, steer clear. There is a channel, however, out there."

The big problem of any young person's life is to have models to suggest possibilities. The mind has many possibilities, but we can live no more than one life. What are we going to do with ourselves? A living myth presents contemporary models.

MOYERS: Today, we have an endless variety of models. A lot of people end up choosing many and never knowing who they are.

CAMPBELL: When you choose your vocation, you have actually chosen a model, and it will fit you in a little while. After middle life, for example, you can pretty well tell what a person's profession is. Wherever I go, people know I'm a professor. I don't know what it is that I do, or how I look, but I, too, can tell professors from engineers and merchants. You're shaped by your life.

MOYERS: There is a wonderful image in *King Arthur* where the knights of the Round Table are about to enter the search for the Grail[3] in the Dark Forest, and the narrator says, "They thought it would be a disgrace to go forth in a group. So each entered the forest at a separate point of his choice." You've interpreted that to express the Western emphasis upon the unique phenomenon of a single human life—the individual confronting darkness.

CAMPBELL: What struck me when I read that in the thirteenth-century *Queste del Saint Graal*[4] was that it epitomizes an especially Western spiritual aim and ideal, which is, of living the life that is potential in *you* and was never in anyone else as a possibility.

This, I believe, is the great Western truth: that each of us is a completely unique crea-

---

3. *The Grail,* or the Holy Grail, was a wide-mouthed vessel that the knights in the legend of King Arthur sought after.

4. *Queste del Saint Graal* is one of the three romances in the story of the Arthurian knight Lancelot.

2. *Buddha* is the founder of the major world religion Buddhism, which began in southern and eastern Asia.

JOSEPH CAMPBELL **1065**

⭐ Writer's Technique

Interviewing a Variety of Sources As the interview progresses, discuss the interviewer's techniques for drawing good answers from Campbell. One such technique is his tendency to pull from a variety of sources. Point out Moyers's use of the Buddha, the myth of Theseus, and King Arthur. The interviewer not only demonstrates his preparation for the interview, but he also, and more importantly, draws a diverse number of excellent answers from Campbell. **AS**

Differentiated Instruction

Role-Playing After reading part or all of "The Hero's Adventure," students may find it helpful to revisit the interview by performing it themselves. Separate students into pairs, and have them decide which roles they will play. Reading aloud will reinforce the concepts and give students a second opportunity to under-

stand them. To measure comprehension, you may want to have each student come up with three or four additional questions that follow the same theme presented in the interview. Have students swap questions and then answer them as their "characters" would. **BL**

Objectives

- To understand rhetorical devices, including analogy and causation (SE)
- To evaluate the way an author's choice of words advances the theme or purpose of the work (SE)

Teach

★ Viewing the Art

Say: In one of the many legends of St. George, he courageously slays a dragon that had been terrorizing a small town. In the process, he saves the king's daughter, who was about to be thrown to the dragon to appease it. Remind students that Joseph Campbell and Bill Moyers refer to the concept of "slaying the dragon" as a metaphor. They equate "slaying the dragon" with overcoming one's limitations and fears. **Ask:** How does this view of "slaying the dragon" affect your interpretation of the artwork? *(Possible response: It helps me relate to St. George because, like him, I have my own "dragons" to slay.)* **AS**

St. George and the Dragon. Paulo Uccello. National Gallery Collection; By kind permission of the Trustees of the National Gallery, London. ★

ture and that, if we are ever to give any gift to the world, it will have to come out of our own experience and fulfillment of our own potentialities, not someone else's. Generally in all traditionally grounded societies, the individual is cookie-molded. His duties are put upon him in exact and precise terms, and there's no way of breaking out from them. When you go to a guru[5] to be guided on the spiritual way, he knows just where you are on the traditional path, just where you have to go next, just what you must do to get there. He'll give you his picture to wear, so you can be like him. That wouldn't be a proper Western pedagogical[6] way of guidance. We have to give our students guidance in developing their own pictures of themselves. What each must seek in his life never was, on land or sea. It is to be something out of his own unique potentiality for experience, something that never has been and never could have been experienced by anyone else. . . .

---

5. Here, a *guru* is personal spiritual teacher in traditional Hinduism, a major world religion primarily practiced in India.
6. *Pedagogical* means characterized by teaching.

1066 UNIT 5 LEGENDS AND MYTHS

MOYERS: How does a child know when his time has come? In ancient societies, the boy, for example, went through a ritual which told him the time had come. He knew that he was no longer a child and that he had to put off the influences of others and stand on his own. We don't have such a clear moment or an obvious ritual in our society that says to my son, "You are a man." Where is the passage today?

CAMPBELL: I don't have the answer. I figure you must leave it up to the boy to know when he has got his power. A baby bird knows when it can fly. We have a couple of birds' nests right near where we have breakfast in the morning, and we have seen several little families launched. These little things don't make a mistake. They stay on the branch until they know how to fly, and then they fly. I think somehow, inside, a person knows this.

I can give you examples from what I know of students in art studios. There comes a moment when they have learned what the artist can teach them. They have assimilated the craft, and they are ready for their own flight. Some of the artists allow their students to do

Additional Support

Skills Practice

RESEARCH: Following Your Bliss

As a class, discuss what it means to "follow your bliss." **Ask:** Why is it important to have a job you love? *(If you love your job, you're more likely to do it well, to be less stressed, and not to be resentful.)* Assign students the task of uncovering their "bliss." Students should start by examining their likes and dislikes and seriously considering what they might be driven to do for the rest of their lives. Have them research three fields of interest before settling on one. For their career of choice, instruct them to write a 3–4 page essay describing the job and how it relates to their personal bliss. **OL** that. They expect the student to fly off after. . . . The students I know, the ones who are really valid as students, know when it is time to push off.

MOYERS: There is an old prayer that says, "Lord, teach us when to let go." All of us have to know that, don't we?

CAMPBELL: That's the big problem of the parent. Being a parent is one of the most demanding careers I know. When I think what my father and mother gave up of themselves to launch their family—well, I really appreciate that.

My father was a businessman, and, of course, he would have been very happy to have his son go into business with him and take it on. In fact, I did go into business with Dad for a couple of months, and then I thought, "I can't do this." And he let me go. There is that testing time in your life when you have got to test yourself out to your own flight.

MOYERS: Myths used to help us know when to let go.

CAMPBELL: Myths formulate things for you. They say, for example, that you have to become an adult at a particular age. The age might be a

good average age for that to happen—but actually, in the individual life, it differs greatly. Some people are late bloomers and come to particular stages at a relatively late age. You have to have a feeling for where you are. You've got only one life to live, and you don't have to live it for six people. Pay attention to it.

MOYERS: What about happiness? If I'm a young person and I want to be happy, what do myths tell me about happiness?

CAMPBELL: The way to find out about your happiness is to keep your mind on those moments when you feel most happy, when you really are happy—not excited, not just thrilled, but deeply happy. This requires a little bit of self-analysis. What is it that makes you happy? Stay with it, no matter what people tell you. This is what I call "following your bliss."

MOYERS: But how does mythology tell you about what makes you happy?

CAMPBELL: It won't tell you what makes you happy, but it will tell you what happens when you begin to follow your happiness, what the obstacles are that you're going to run into. ✎

RESPONDING AND THINKING CRITICALLY

Respond

1. How have myths inspired your ideas or beliefs? Explain.

Recall and Interpret

2. (a)What is the literal meaning of the Ariadne thread? (b)What might it represent figuratively?

3. (a)What do Campbell and Moyers claim is a unique "Western aim and ideal"? (b)Do you think that this ideal applies to your life? Why or why not?

Analyze and Evaluate

4. (a)What analogy does Campbell make about an artist's learning process? (b)Does it work well? Why or why not?

5. (a)According to Campbell, how can mythology inform a person's sense of happiness? (b)Do you agree with him? Why or why not?

Connect

6. Recall one of Theseus' adventures in Edith Hamilton's retelling of the myth of Theseus. What characteristics make Theseus a hero in that adventure? Explain.

OBJECTIVES
• Understand rhetorical devices, including analogy and causation.
• Evaluate the way an author's choice of words advances the theme or purpose of the work.

JOSEPH CAMPBELL **1067**

in friendship, family loyalty, and love relationships; therefore, they illustrate modern-day obstacles.

6. Students should be able to identify a number of Theseus's adventures, including his defeat of Sciron,

Sinis, or Procrustes; his escape from Daedalus's labyrinth; his rise to power as king; and his defeat of Thebes. Students should point out Theseus's loyalty and fairness, and the value he places on equality and friendship.

 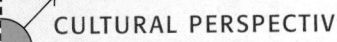
Assess

1. Answers will vary. Most will say that they have developed ideas and beliefs about courage, family, strength, and loyalty from myths.

2. (a) The Ariadne thread is the thread that Ariadne, Minos's daughter, provided Theseus. It allowed him to trace his way out of Daedalus's labyrinth and defeat the Minotaur. (b) The thread represents the tools or lessons parents and teachers hand down to young people so they can learn to take care of themselves.

3. (a) The ability to live a unique life based on your individual potential (b) Students' answers will vary. Some may say they feel encouraged to express their unique ideas and thoughts and make individual choices. Others may think that their choices are more limited than those of adults.

4. (a) An artist knows when to follow his or her own path, just as a bird knows when to fly away from its nest. (b) Most students will think that the analogy works well. It equates the idea of a bird's maturation to a person's growth.

5. (a) Campbell believes that mythology can inform a person about what obstacles may get in the way of one's happiness. (b) Students' answers will vary. Some may feel that the myths are too far removed from real life to inform a modern student about his or her happiness. Others may argue that myths present universal conflicts

Focus

Write on the board: The jovial boy studied geography. **Ask:** Which words came from Greek or Roman mythology? *(Jovial comes from the chief Roman god, Jove, and geography comes from the Greek goddess of Earth, Gaea.)* Many English words come from Greek or Roman mythology, and knowing this expands vocabulary and helps define unfamiliar words.

Teach

Etymology Explain the etymology of *muse, music,* and *museum,* all of which come from the Greek goddesses of the arts and sciences, the Muses. Students should explore the etymology of Greek and Roman words, such as *iridescence,* "Gordian knot," "sword of Damocles," *narcissistic, mentor, harpy, lethargic,* and *erotic.* **OL**

Assess

Exercise

1. herculean
2. mercurial
3. Olympian

▶ **Vocabulary Terms**

Word origins are the histories of words. Word origins generally include the other languages or earlier forms of English that words came from.

▶ **Test-Taking Tip**

Learning to recognize Greek and Latin word roots, like those in the chart, can help you determine the meanings of unfamiliar words on a test.

▶ **Reading Handbook**

For more about word origins, see the Reading Handbook, p. R20.

**Literature Online
eFlashcards** For eFlashcards and other vocabulary activities, go to www.glencoe.com.

OBJECTIVES
• Learn to recognize common roots.
• Use word origins to understand unfamiliar words.

Examining Words from Greek and Roman Myths

"Daedalus built the Labyrinth, famous throughout the world. Once inside, one would go endlessly along its twisting paths without ever finding the exit."

—Edith Hamilton, from *Theseus*

Connecting to Literature In the above passage, Hamilton mentions the Labyrinth built by Daedalus, the famed mythological architect and sculptor. This term initially referred only to Daedalus's creation, which was used to house the Minotaur, a fearsome creature that was part man and part bull. However, over time the term's meaning has changed. Now *labyrinth* refers to any kind of maze, or a complex structure or idea. The etymology, or history, of this word is not an anomaly; in fact, Greek and Roman mythology is the source of many words that are currently used in English.

Becoming familiar with word origins, or the sources of words from other languages or older forms of English, can increase your vocabulary and help you to identify unfamiliar terms.

Below is a chart of English words and their definitions, and the Greek and Roman words, including definitions, from which the English words were derived.

English Word	Greek or Roman Word
herculean (hur′kyə lē′ ən) *adj.* of tremendous power or difficulty	**Hercules** (hur′kyə lēz′) *n.* Greek hero renowned for his strength
Olympian (o lim′ pē ən) *adj.* godlike, lofty, or extraordinary	**Olympus** (ō lim′pəs) *n.* mountain and home of the Greek gods
mercurial (mər kyoor′ ē əl) *adj.* eloquent or ingenious; unpredictable or inconstant	**Mercury** (mur′kyər ē) *n.* fleet-footed Roman messenger god

Exercise

For each item below, choose the English word from the chart above that best completes the sentence.

1. Crushing boulders for the new road would have been a far more _____ task without the help of machinery.
2. The actor's _____ behavior and irresponsible attitude made him difficult to work with.
3. A roar from the fans cheered the _____ baseball star on after hitting his second home run.

Additional Support

eFlashcards Have students access the Web site for more practice with word origins.

Differentiated Instruction

Word Origins Review how less proficient readers can use word origins to define unfamiliar words. Ask students which English words came from these Greek and Roman roots:

• Hypnos, the Greek god of sleep (*hypnosis*)

• Mars, the Roman god of war (*martial, Mars*)

• Furies, three avenging spirits in Greek mythology (*fury, furious*)

Discuss the definitions of these words and their relation to the words' origins. **BL**

The Secret Name of Ra

MEET GERALDINE HARRIS

Author Geraldine Harris studied at Cambridge University in the 1970s and became fascinated with Egyptian history and mythology. As a result, she became an Egyptologist and has written history books about the great kingdoms that arose five thousand years ago along the Nile River Valley. She also created the fantasy series *Seven Citadels*, four novels that tell the story of a young prince in an incredible ancient world. *Seven Citadels* combines elements of spirituality, fantasy, and folklore, a style for which Harris has become well known.

"To know this secret name of Ra was to have power over him and over the world that he had created."

—"The Secret Name of Ra"

Egyptian Mythology Egypt is one of the oldest known civilizations on Earth, dating back to 3000 BC. Ancient Egyptians told and wrote stories both to entertain and to reinforce their beliefs. Egyptian mythology is a collection of stories and traditions that follow the gods of nature: the earth, the sky, the sun, the moon, the stars, and the Nile River. The gods and goddesses in these stories symbolized aspects of the natural world and explained natural phenomena. Since life in ancient Egypt revolved around the fertile valley of the Nile River, the creatures that lived in the Nile and along its banks became important in Egyptian mythology.

One of the oldest and most important gods in the Egyptian pantheon was Ra—the God of the Sun. Acknowledged as the supreme creator and the father of all the gods, Ra was usually represented with a man's body and the head of a hawk. In many creation myths, humans arose specifically from either Ra's tears or his saliva. Pharaohs—Egyptian rulers—were also considered gods who had been chosen to lead the people and maintain order on Earth.

The earliest information about Egyptian mythology comes from a pictographic writing system called hieroglyphics. The hieroglyphs painted on tomb walls show scenes of daily life: people tending cattle, fishing, and harvesting crops. Hieroglyphics also reveal the Egyptians' beliefs, including those about an afterlife.

According to their myths, ancient Egyptians regarded the afterlife as more important than life on Earth. In fact, Egyptians devoted much time and energy to preparing for survival in the next world. It was thought that when someone died, his or her soul, or *ka*, could survive if the body was well preserved. The process of mummification was developed for this purpose. Caring properly for the dead was seen as essential for eternal life. Tombs were built for important Egyptians, mostly pharaohs, and were filled with food, drink, and representations of the gods to ensure a safe passage into the afterlife.

Geraldine Harris was born in 1951.

Literature Online **Author Search** For more about Geraldine Harris, go to www.glencoe.com.

GERALDINE HARRIS **1069**

Focus

BELLRINGER

Bellringer Options
Daily Language Practice Transparency 90
Or write the following quotations on the board:
In our world of big names, curiously, our true heroes tend to be anonymous.
—Daniel J. Boorstin
The ideal has many names, and beauty is but one of them.
—W. Somerset Maugham
Ask: What is the speaker in each of these quotations saying about names?

Have students discuss the importance of names.

Literature Online

Author Search To expand students' appreciation of Geraldine Harris, have them access the Web site for additional information and resources.

Selection Skills

Literary Elements
• Theme Archetype (SE pp. 1070, 1071, 1074, 1075)

The Secret Name of Ra

Reading Skills
• Analyzing Style (SE pp. 1070, 1071, 1074, 1075)

Vocabulary Skills
• Antonyms (SE pp. 1070, 1075)

Listening/Speaking/Viewing Skills
• Egyptian Mythology (TWE p. 1074)

Writing Skills/Grammar
• Writing Myths (SE p. 1075)
• Punctuating Lists (TWE p. 1072)

Focus

Summary

Isis wishes that she could have the power of the sun god, Ra. She devises a plan to trick him into telling her the secret name that is the foundation for his power. Isis creates a serpent that strikes Ra and poisons him, and then she offers to cure him. Once she convinces Ra that she can save him only if he tells her his secret name, he is restored to his full power. Isis now possesses the same power and will one day be able to give Ra's power to her son, Horus.

V Vocabulary

Vocabulary File Say: Add these words and definitions to your vocabulary file. For each word, include a sentence that gives you an example of how to use the word. **OL** Students with English language needs should include the pronunciations of these words in their files. **EL**

Literary Elements Have students access the Web site to improve their understanding of theme archetype.

Connecting to the Myth

The following Egyptian myth describes the power attached to an individual's name or names. Before you read the myth, think about the following questions:

- Why might someone choose to keep his or her name a secret?
- What might someone's name reveal about that person?

Building Background

The goddess Isis is considered one of the most important and powerful deities in Egyptian mythology. The ancient Egyptians recognized her as a great magician capable of curing the sick and restoring the dead to life. Isis also had three other roles: mourner, protector, and life-giver. As wife of the murdered god Osiris, Isis was the chief goddess at funeral rites. As the mother and protector of Horus (a god in the form of a falcon), she was considered a life-giver and a guardian.

Setting Purposes for Reading

Big Idea Rescuing and Conquering

As you read this selection, notice how Isis both conquers and rescues Ra.

Literary Element Theme Archetype

A **theme archetype** is a message about life that appears frequently in literature across many cultures. For example, creation myths share a theme archetype: namely, the supreme power of the god or gods who made the world. As you read "The Secret Name of Ra," note theme archetypes.

- See Literary Terms Handbook, p. R18.

Literature Online Interactive Literary Elements Handbook To review or learn more about the literary elements, go to www.glencoe.com.

Reading Strategy Analyzing Style

Style is an author's individual, characteristic way of writing. Elements such as diction, tone, sentence length and structure, and figurative language and imagery make up a writer's style. **Analyzing an author's style** means identifying these elements and considering their effect.

Reading Tip: Taking Notes Use a web to record examples of some of the elements that make up Harris's style.

Vocabulary

deity (dē′ ə tē) n. a god or goddess; p. 1072 *Pagan mythology honored more than one deity.*

drivel (driv′ əl) v. to drool; to allow saliva to drip from the mouth; p. 1072 *Milk began to drivel from the baby's lips as she rocked to the music.*

abyss (ə bis′) n. an extremely deep chasm; a seemingly bottomless hole; p. 1072 *The Mariana Trench in the Pacific Ocean is the deepest abyss of its kind.*

virile (vir′ əl) adj. having traits normally associated with males, such as strength; p. 1072 *The virile athlete could bench-press more than two hundred pounds.*

Vocabulary Tip: Antonyms Words that have opposite or nearly opposite meanings are called antonyms. Note that antonyms are always the same part of speech.

OBJECTIVES
In studying this selection, you will focus on the following:
- understanding theme archetypes

- analyzing style
- writing to apply style in an original work

1070 UNIT 5 LEGENDS AND MYTHS

Selection Resources

Print Materials
- Unit 5 Resources (Fast File), pp. 44–46
- Leveled Vocabulary Development, p. 75
- Selection and Unit Assessments, pp. 183–184
- Selection Quick Checks, p. 92

Transparencies
- Bellringer Options Transparencies:
  Daily Language Practice Transparency 90
- Literary Elements Transparencies 86, 87

Technology
- TeacherWorks Plus™ CD-ROM
- StudentWorks Plus™ CD-ROM
- Presentation Plus!™ CD-ROM
- Literature Online, glencoe.com
- Online Student Edition, mhln.com
- ExamView® Assessment Suite CD-ROM
- Vocabulary PuzzleMaker CD-ROM
- Listening Library, disc 2 track 26

The Secret Name of Ra

Geraldine Harris

Detail of a Young Boy from the Tomb of Nefertari, 1290–1224 BC Artist Unknown.

Ra, the Sole Creator was visible to the people of Egypt as the disc of the sun, but they knew him in many other forms. He could appear as a crowned man, a falcon or a man with a falcon's head and, as the scarab beetle[1] pushes a round ball of dung in front of it, the Egyptians pictured Ra as a scarab pushing the sun across the sky. In caverns deep below the earth were hidden another seventy-five forms of Ra: mysterious beings with mummified bodies and heads consisting of birds or snakes, feathers or flowers. The names of Ra were as numerous as his forms; he was the Shining One, The Hidden One, The Renewer of the Earth, The Wind in the Souls, the Exalted One, but there was one name of the Sun God which had not been spoken since time began. To know this secret name of Ra was to have power over him and over the world that he had created.

Isis longed for such a power. She had dreamed that one day she would have a marvellous falcon-headed son called Horus and she wanted the throne of Ra to give to her child. Isis was the Mistress of Magic, wiser than millions of men, but she knew that nothing in creation was powerful enough to harm its creator. Her only chance was to turn the power of Ra against himself and at last Isis thought of a cruel and cunning plan. Every day the Sun God walked through his kingdom, attended by a crowd of spirits and

---

1. A *scarab beetle* is a type of beetle that ancient Egyptians used as a magic charm to ward off evil. It was also a sacred symbol of resurrection.

Reading Strategy Analyzing Style *What effect does this list of names create?* **R**

Literary Element Theme Archetype *What universal theme does the author introduce here?* **L**

GERALDINE HARRIS **1071**

Teach

L Literary Element

Simile Have students identify the figure of speech used in these lines. *(The figure of speech is a simile comparing Ra's poisoning to the Nile River as its banks flood.)* **OL**

R Reading Strategy

Questioning Have students speculate about how Isis might have been able to accomplish her goal. *(Answers will vary. Students might say that Ra is too trusting and let his guard down. Some might say that Isis was able to create a creature that could harm Ra because she used his saliva—a part of Ra.)* **OL**

★ Cultural History

The Nile River The Nile is the longest river in the world, running about 4,132 miles through Africa to the Mediterranean Sea. The regular flooding of the Nile provides irrigation in otherwise dry regions and leaves arable soil behind when the waters recede. The Nile River basin was home to the earliest farmers and to the earliest of the advanced civilizations—the ancient Egyptians, whose civilization dates back as early as 3100 B.C. **AS**

lesser **deities**, but Ra was growing old. His eyes were dim, his step no longer firm and he had even begun to **drivel**.

One morning Isis mingled with a group of minor goddesses and followed behind the King of the Gods. She watched the face of Ra until she saw his saliva drip onto a clod of earth. When she was sure that no-one was taking any notice of her, she scooped up the earth and carried it away. Isis mixed the earth with the saliva of Ra to form clay and modelled a wicked-looking serpent.

Through the hours of darkness she whispered spells over the clay serpent as it lay lifeless in her hands. Then the cunning goddess carried it to a crossroads on the route which the Sun God always took. She hid the serpent in the long grass and returned to her palace.

The next day Ra came walking through his kingdom with the spirits and lesser deities crowding behind him. When he approached the crossroads, the spells of Isis began to work and the clay serpent quivered into life. As the Sun God passed, it bit him in the ankle and crumbled back into earth. Ra gave a scream that was heard through all creation.

His jaws chattered and his limbs shook as the poison flooded through him like a rising Nile.[2] "I have been wounded by something **L** deadly," whispered Ra. "I know that in my heart, though my eyes cannot see it. Whatever it was, I, the Lord of Creation, did not make it. I am sure that none of you would have done such a terrible thing to me, but I have never felt such pain! How can this have happened to me? I am the Sole Creator, the child of the watery **abyss**. I am the god with a thousand names, but my secret name was only spoken once, before time began. Then it was hidden in my body so that no-one should ever learn it and be able to work spells against me. Yet as I walked through my kingdom something struck at me and now my heart is on fire and my limbs shake. Send for the Ennead! Send for my children! They are wise in magic and their knowledge pierces heaven."

Messengers hurried to the great gods and from the four pillars of the world came the Ennead: Shu and Tefenet, Geb and Nut, Seth and Osiris, Isis and Nephthys, Envoys[3] traveled the land and the sky and the watery abyss to summon all the deities created by Ra. From the marshes came frog-headed Heket, Wadjet the cobra goddess and the fearsome god, crocodile-headed Sobek. From the deserts came fiery Selkis, the scorpion goddess, Anubis the jackal, the guardian of the dead and Nekhbet the vulture goddess. From the cities of the north came warlike Neith, gentle cat-headed Bastet, fierce lion-headed Sekhmet and Ptah the god of crafts. From the cities of the south came Onuris, the divine huntsman and ram-headed Khnum with Anukis his wife and Satis his daughter. Cunning Thoth and wise Seshat, goddess of writing; **virile** Min and snake-headed Renenutet, goddess of the harvest, kindly Meskhenet and monstrous Taweret, goddesses of birth—all of them were summoned to the side of Ra. The gods and goddesses gathered around the Sun God, weeping and wailing, afraid that he was going to die. Isis stood among them beating her breast and pretending to be as distressed and bewildered as all the other frightened deities. **R**

"Father of All," she began, "whatever is the matter? Has some snake bitten you? Has some wretched creature dared to strike at his

---

2. *Nile* refers to the Nile River, the longest in the world. The Nile River periodically rises, flooding its banks. The ancient Egyptians depended upon the regular flooding of the Nile because the receding waters left behind arable— or plantable—soil.

Vocabulary

deity (dē′ ə tē) *n.* a god or goddess
drivel (driv′ əl) *v.* to drool; to allow saliva to drip from the mouth
abyss (ə bis′) *n.* an extremely deep chasm; a seemingly bottomless hole

---

3. An *envoy* is a representative.

Vocabulary

virile (vir′ el) *adj.* having traits normally associated with males, such as strength

Additional Support

Skills Practice

WRITING: Punctuating Lists

Remind students that items in a list should be separated by commas unless the items include commas. If the items include commas, they should be separated by semicolons. In order to illustrate the majesty of Ra and the Egyptian pantheon, Harris makes use of long lists. Point out paragraph 5 on page 1072. The first list in this paragraph follows a colon and features pairs of names separated by commas. Have students locate other lists in the same paragraph and identify how Harris varies the structure. **OL**

Painted Bas-Relief Depicting The God Osiris, ca.1348-1320 BC ★

★ Viewing the Art

A relief is a sculpture in which figures, symbols, or other design elements project from a flat background. In bas-reliefs, also called low reliefs, the figures and forms are raised only slightly. Such reliefs are common on ancient Egyptian buildings. **Ask:** What can we learn about the character traits of Osiris from this image? *(strong, authoritative, divine, connected to the land, etc.)* **AS**

Differentiated Instruction

Unfamiliar Words Many words contained in the selection are difficult to pronounce, especially the names of the Egyptian gods and goddesses that are listed. Have students create a list of difficult-to-pronounce words and then use a dictionary or some other source to find the pronunciation. (Note: Since not all of the Egyptian gods and goddesses appear in all dictionaries, it might save time if students use an online resource that allows them to search several reference sources at one time.) Once students have found the pronunciations, have them practice reading sections of the story aloud to a partner. **BL**

Objective
• To punctuate long lists properly (TWE)

Teach

BI₁ Big Idea

Rescuing and Conquering
Answer: *Isis wants Ra to let her help him. In doing so, she will rescue him and conquer him.* **OL**

R Reading Strategy

Analyzing Style Answer:
This is another example of the mythic style. The list instructs the reader, makes her story sound more traditional, and gives the story larger-than-life qualities. **OL**

L Literary Element

Theme Archetype Answer:
Names as identities and as sources of power and mystery **OL**

BI₂ Big Idea

Rescuing and Conquering
Answer: *Ra probably realizes that he has been conquered because he has relinquished the power of his secret name.* **OL**

CheckPoint

Use the CheckPoint questions on Presentation Plus! to check students' mastery of the selection. These questions can be used with interactive response keypads for immediate student feedback.

Mural Painting of the Goddess Isis, 1323-1295 BC Gerard Jean Baptiste Scotin.

Creator? Few of the gods can compare with me in wisdom and I am the Mistress of Magic. If you will let me help you, I'm sure that I can cure you."

Ra was grateful to Isis and told her all that had happened. "Now I am colder than water and hotter than fire," complained the Sun God. "My eyes darken. I cannot see the sky and my body is soaked by the sweat of fever."

"Tell me your full name," said cunning Isis. "Then I can use it in my spells. Without that knowledge the greatest of magicians cannot help you."

"I am the maker of heaven and earth," said Ra. "I made the heights and the depths,

> **Big Idea** Rescuing and Conquering *What is Isis trying to accomplish? In your opinion, is her goal to rescue or to conquer Ra?* **BI₁**

I set horizons at east and west and established the gods in their glory. When I open my eyes it is light; when I close them it is dark. The mighty Nile floods at my command. The gods do not know my true name but I am the maker of time, the giver of festivals. I spark the fire of life. At dawn I rise as Khepri, the scarab and sail across the sky in the Boat of Millions of Years. At noon I blaze in the heavens as Ra and at evening I am Ra-atum, the setting sun."

"We know all that," said Isis. "If I am to find a spell to drive out this poison, I will have to use your secret name. Say your name and live."

"My secret name was given to me so that I could sit at ease," moaned Ra, "and fear no living creature. How can I give it away?"

Isis said nothing and knelt beside the Sun God while his pain mounted. When it became unbearable, Ra ordered the other gods to stand back while he whispered his secret name to Isis. "Now the power of the secret name has passed from my heart to your heart," said Ra wearily. "In time you can give it to your son, but warn him never to betray the secret!"

Isis nodded and began to chant a great spell that drove the poison out of the limbs of Ra and he rose up stronger than before. The Sun God returned to the Boat of Millions of Years and Isis shouted for joy at the success of her plan. She knew now that one day Horus her son would sit on the throne of Egypt and wield the power of Ra. ✑

> **Reading Strategy** Analyzing Style *Describe the style of this paragraph. Why does Harris list Ra's various identities?* **R**

> **Literary Element** Theme Archetype *What archetypal themes does the author convey in this passage?* **L**

> **Big Idea** Rescuing and Conquering *Does Ra realize that he has been conquered as well as rescued? Explain.* **BI₂**

Additional Support

Web Activities Have students access the Web site for interactive activities that will help them assess their understanding of the selection.

Skills Practice

LISTENING AND SPEAKING:
Egyptian Mythology Have students find another Egyptian myth or research another Egyptian god or goddess. They might consider researching Horus, Osiris, Seth, or one of the other gods mentioned in "The Secret Name of Ra." After

students have collected their information, have them prepare an oral presentation. They can prepare a monologue, a dialogue, a brief skit, a poem, a song, or some other creative method for presenting their information orally. **OL**

RESPONDING AND THINKING CRITICALLY

Respond

1. What are your impressions of Isis?

Recall and Interpret

2. (a)What are some of Ra's names? (b)What do these names tell you about Ra?

3. (a)Why does Isis want to know Ra's secret name? (b)How can knowing a name give you power over someone?

4. (a)How does Isis trick Ra into revealing his secret name to her? (b)Why is she able to create something that can hurt Ra?

Analyze and Evaluate

5. How would you compare Ra and Isis?

6. What values of ancient Egyptians does this myth reflect?

Connect

7. **Big Idea** **Rescuing and Conquering** (a)How does Isis both rescue and conquer Ra? (b)In your opinion, is there a difference between rescuing and conquering? Explain.

LITERARY ANALYSIS

Literary Element Theme Archetype

A **theme archetype** transcends time and place because it applies to people living now, just as it did to people living centuries ago. Archetypal themes in "The Secret Name of Ra" include creation, guarding secrets, the serpent as an evil force, a name representing identity and power, and envy and desire for power.

1. Choose two of the archetypal themes listed above and explain how each applies to "The Secret Name of Ra."

2. Why do you think Harris uses archetypal themes in retelling this ancient Egyptian myth?

3. What other literature have you read that contains archetypal themes similar to those in "The Secret Name of Ra"? Explain the relationship between the themes in the two works.

Writing About Literature

Apply Style Writing a myth requires a formal, authoritative style. Try your hand at the mythic style by writing your own short myth. Like "The Secret Name of Ra," your myth should contain theme archetypes. You may also incorporate **anthropomorphism,** the technique of assigning human behaviors and traits to gods, animals, or things.

READING AND VOCABULARY

Reading Strategy Analyzing Style

Harris creates a mythic style by using a dignified tone and formal language. Her writing creates a larger-than-life effect that conveys a sense of authority.

1. If the story were rewritten using informal language, how would it change? Explain.

2. Find three examples of formal language and explain what each contributes to the story.

> **Vocabulary** **Practice**
>
> **Practice with Antonyms** Find the antonym for each vocabulary word below. Use a dictionary or a thesaurus if you need help.
>
> 1. deity
>   a. divinity   b. mortal   c. immortal
> 2. drivel
>   a. swallow   b. drool   c. spit
> 3. abyss
>   a. peak   b. pit   c. chasm
> 4. virile
>   a. masculine   b. feminine   c. massive

Literature Online **Web Activities** For eFlashcards, Selection Quick Checks, and other Web activities, go to www.glencoe.com.

GERALDINE HARRIS **1075**

Assess

1. Students' answers will vary.

2. (a) The Shining One, The Hidden One, The Renewer of the Earth, The Wind in the Souls, and The Exalted One (b) He is very powerful and revered and is a creator.

3. (a) For her son (b) It is part of his or her identity.

4. (a) By creating a serpent that bites Ra and telling him that she can cure him if he tells her his secret name (b) She is a sorceress and can use part of him in her spell.

5. Ra is revered but old. Isis is wise and cunning.

6. Reverence for the sun and a realization that even the gods have limitations

7. (a) She rescues Ra from pain but conquers him by obtaining his secret name. (b) Answers will vary.

Literary Element

1. Students may choose creation because Ra is the god of creation. Others might names as identity because the story is about Isis trying to obtain Ra's secret identity.

2. They are universal and easily recognizable, appeal to subconscious drives and experiences, and make the story more accessible and powerful.

3. Answers will vary.

Writing About Literature

Myths should convey archetypal themes and exemplify elements of the mythic style such as formal language and dignified tone.

Reading Strategy

1. Without formal language, the story loses its authority and majesty.

2. "Messengers hurried to the great gods and from the four pillars of the world came the Ennead: Shu and Tefenet, Geb and Nut, Seth and Osiris, Isis and Nephthys. Envoys traveled the land and the sky and the watery abyss to summon all the deities created by Ra." The long sentence and the list of names make the passage sound impressive. A lack of formality would detract from the sense of importance.

Vocabulary

1. b 2. a 3. a 4. b

Focus

BELLRINGER

Bellringer Options
Selection Focus Transparency 43
Daily Language Practice
Transparency 91

Or write on the boar some names of famous American heroes, such as George Washington, Martin Luther King Jr., and Eleanor Roosevelt. **Ask:** What heroic acts did these people perform? How do their individual types of heroism differ?

Have students talk about these heroes and others they know about. Have them discuss everyday heroic acts, such as helping the elderly and contributing to charity.

Connecting to the Reading Selections

Allow students to share their responses to the opening question. Then have students discuss what they already know about Native American traditions and legend, as well as African American folklore and music.

Comparing Literature *Across Genres*

Connecting to the Reading Selections

Heroes come in many forms and show up in the most unexpected places. In times of war, some heroes fall and new heroes rise. Faced with the possibility of becoming obsolete, heroes will fight to prove themselves. And, with history to inspire and guide them, heroism is born in the hearts and minds of children. The three works compared here explore timeless themes of heroism: self-sacrifice, great courage, and the strength of the human spirit.

Joseph Bruchac and Gayle Ross
Where the Girl Rescued Her Brother .... legend **1077**
Her courage amazed them all

Zora Neale Hurston
John Henry .... tall tale **1084**
Working harder than any machine

Chippewa
A Song of Greatness .... song **1086**
How heroes are born

COMPARING THE Big Idea **Rescuing and Conquering**

Every culture tells heroic stories of rescue and victory. The Native American and African American cultures depicted in these literary works experienced the horror of conquest at the hands of white settlers. Instead of focusing on the bleak, however, these works center on the triumphant and the heroic and on the strength of the human spirit—a concept common to all humanity.

COMPARING Oral Tradition

An **oral tradition** transmits literature by word of mouth from one generation to the next. Oral literature is a way of recording the past, glorifying leaders, and teaching morals and traditions to young people. These literary works began in the oral tradition but are now recorded in print, making them available to a wider audience.

COMPARING Cultural Beliefs

Though these literary works were born of different cultures—Cheyenne, African American, and Chippewa—they all center on the theme of the individual's power to change the world. This universal theme is a testament to the rich heritage of each culture, and spurs us to look deeply into our souls to uncover what makes us all human.

Selection Skills

Literary Elements

- Suspense (SE pp. 1078, 1080, 1081, 1083)
- Rhythm and Meter (TWE p. 1084)

Comparing Literature

Reading Skills

- Synthesizing (SE pp. 1078, 1080, 1082, 1083)
- Using Graphic Organizers (TWE p. 1080)

Vocabulary Skills

- Synonyms (SE pp. 1078, 1083)

Listening/Speaking/Viewing Skills

- Discussion Starter (SE p. 1086)
- Oral Interpretation (TWE p. 1086)

Writing Skills/Grammar

- Analytical Essay (SE p. 1083)
- Using Dashes (TWE p. 1082)

Where the Girl Rescued Her Brother

MEET JOSEPH BRUCHAC AND GAYLE ROSS

Joseph Bruchac and Gayle Ross share a common interest—they both draw from their Native American heritage for their literary inspiration. Bruchac is a writer of Abenaki Indian descent who has published books of poetry, essays, and novels interweaving Native American history and myth. Ross is a direct descendant of John Ross, Principal Chief of the Cherokee during the Trail of Tears. As a child, she learned traditional Cherokee stories and songs from her grandmother.

Native American Mythology Native American mythology is a rich collection of legends and folklore. Different tribal groups each developed their own stories about the creation of the world and why things are the way they are. These stories have been passed down by word of mouth. Many traditional myths are sacred and are narrated through movement, song, and dance using symbols and imagination. They begin and end in a certain way each time they are told. According to Ross, she and Bruchac have been taught "that stories are living spirits and that the role of the storyteller is to care for the tales in [his or her] keeping."

"In a sense, you could say the stories know more than we do, and so we have a great responsibility to tell them well."

—Joseph Bruchac

Native American myths consist of hero stories, trickster stories, stories that impart a moral lesson or give warnings to children, and stories that celebrate family and community. For example, the myth of Apotamkin, a hairy human figure with long fangs, was used to instill fear into children to prevent them from wandering away from parental supervision.

Native American mythology often draws upon living things or natural objects regarded as sacred representations of their beliefs and values. In many tribal creation stories, animals are considered equals of humans and the creators of the universe. In some myths, animals have the ability to speak, think, and behave like humans. The coyote, bear, and raven are often found in myths recounting the origin of a tribe. The raven is said to have created mankind by coaxing human beings from a giant clamshell found on the beach. Some myths also give him credit for releasing the sun and moon to the sky. The coyote was regarded as a popular spirit among tribes such as the Sioux and the Maidu. A sly trickster, the coyote was believed to be responsible for human sickness, sorrow, and death, but also for the creation of the Milky Way.

Native Americans do not share a unified body of mythology. Hundreds of different tribes each have their own languages, as well as a variety of unique rituals and traditions. By studying their myths, we can learn how Native Americans view themselves and the world, and discover similarities between the different tribes that lived many years ago and those that thrive today.

Joseph Bruchac was born in 1942. Gayle Ross was born in 1951.

Literature Online Author Search For more about Joseph Bruchac and Gayle Ross, go to www.glencoe.com.

JOSEPH BRUCHAC AND GAYLE ROSS **1077**

Focus

Literature Online

Author Search To expand students' appreciation of Joseph Bruchac and Gayle Ross, have them access the Web site for additional information and resources.

Selection Resources

Print Materials
- Unit 5 Resources (Fast File), pp. 47–50
- Leveled Vocabulary Development, p. 76
- Selection and Unit Assessments, pp. 185–186
- Selection Quick Checks, p. 93

Transparencies
- Bellringer Options Transparencies: Selection Focus Transparency 43 Daily Language Practice Transparency 91
- Literary Elements Transparency 7

Technology
- TeacherWorks Plus™ CD-ROM
- StudentWorks Plus™ CD-ROM
- Presentation Plus!™ CD-ROM
- Literature Online, glencoe.com
- Online Student Edition, mhln.com
- ExamView® Assessment Suite CD-ROM
- Listening Library, disc 2 tracks 27–29
- Vocabulary PuzzleMaker CD-ROM

COMPARING LITERATURE

BEFORE YOU READ

Focus

Summary

A young Cheyenne woman, Buffalo Calf Road Woman, rides with her husband and brother as they try to drive the white army off their lands. Suddenly she sees that her brother has been surrounded by Crow scouts, allies of the whites. She rides her pony into the battle and grabs her brother's hand. He leaps onto her pony, and they ride away. From then on the battle is known as the fight Where the Girl Rescued Her Brother.

V Vocabulary

Vocabulary File Say: Add these words and definitions to your vocabulary file. For each word, include a sentence that gives you an example of how to use the word. **OL** Students with English language needs should include the pronunciations of these words in their files. **EL**

Literary Elements Have students access the Web site to improve their understanding of suspense.

Additional Support

LITERATURE PREVIEW

Connecting to the Story

The following story is a celebration of the courage and heroism of women. The story focuses on one particular woman's heroic acts during a critical time in her people's history. Before you read the story, think about the following questions:

- Have you heard or read about a person who responded heroically in a time of crisis?
- What made that person's actions heroic?
- How have you acted, or how do you think you would act, in a time of crisis?

Building Background

When gold was discovered in the Black Hills of South Dakota in the early 1870s, miners rushed into the area, heedless of the treaty that had previously guaranteed the Sioux people exclusive possession of the land. The miners' total disregard for the rights of Native Americans spurred skirmishes between the two groups. As a result, Brigadier General George Crook of the United States Army ordered the Sioux to leave the area, but Sioux chiefs Sitting Bull and Crazy Horse ignored the order. After a series of unprovoked attacks on his people, Sitting Bull summoned the Sioux, Cheyenne, and certain Arapaho to Montana. Soon after, this confederation surprised Crook's troops at Rosebud Creek in southern Montana. A battle soon took place there on June 17, 1876. That battle is described, in part, in "Where the Girl Rescued Her Brother."

Setting Purposes for Reading

Big Idea Rescuing and Conquering

As you read this story, notice how Bruchac and Ross explore women's roles in the theme of rescuing and conquering.

Literary Element Suspense

Suspense is a feeling of curiosity, uncertainty, or even dread about what is going to happen next in a story. Suspense can help you engage with a story by heightening your interest in a particular outcome or various outcomes. As you read, notice how Bruchac and Ross create and build suspense.

- See Literary Terms Handbook, p. R17.

OBJECTIVES
In studying this selection, you will focus on the following:
- recognizing and analyzing suspense

READING PREVIEW

Reading Strategy Synthesizing

To **synthesize** is to build an understanding of a literary work by combining your knowledge of different subjects and applying it to your reading. Synthesizing can help you gain a broader understanding and appreciation of a work. While reading this story, draw on your knowledge of legend, Native American culture, gender roles, and U.S. history to synthesize an understanding of the text's depiction of heroism.

Reading Tip: Heroic Act Checklist What elements are common to acts of heroism? Create a checklist that can be used to identify heroic acts. As you read, fill in the checklist with heroic elements and examples of these elements from the text.

Heroic Elements	Examples
courage	Head of the Society of Quilters approaches the grizzly bear

Vocabulary

confront (kən frunt´) v. to come face-to-face with; to oppose; p. 1080 *James had to confront his fear of flying when his employer made him travel to New York.*

vault (vôlt) v. to jump; spring; p. 1081 *Maria vaulted over the puddle to keep her shoes dry.*

strategic (strə tē´ jik) adj. highly important to an intended goal; p. 1082 *The president knew the most strategic way to advertise the product.*

Vocabulary Tip: Synonyms Words that have the same or nearly the same meaning are called synonyms. The words *shy* and *timid*, for example, are synonyms. Note that synonyms are always the same part of speech.

Literature Online Interactive Literary Elements Handbook To review or learn more about the literary elements, go to www.glencoe.com.

- synthesizing to enhance reading comprehension
- writing to analyze cultural and historical context

Skills Practice

READING: Previewing Previewing can help students to form a more complete comprehension of a selection. Have students view the selection title and the accompanying art. Ask them to predict how the girl might rescue her brother. **OL**

Where the Girl Rescued Her Brother

Joseph Bruchac and Gayle Ross

A Cheyenne Brave, 1901. Frederic Remington. Color lithograph. Private Collection. ★

It was the moon when the chokecherries were ripe. A young woman rode out of a Cheyenne camp with her husband and her brother. The young woman's name was Buffalo Calf Road Woman. Her husband, Black Coyote, was one of the chiefs of the Cheyenne, the people of the plains who call themselves Tsis-tsis-tas, meaning simply "The People." Buffalo Calf Road Woman's brother, Comes-in-Sight, was also one of the Cheyenne chiefs, and it was well-known how close he was to his sister.

Like many of the other young women of the Cheyenne, Buffalo Calf Road Woman was respected for her honorable nature. Although it was the men who most often went to war to defend the people—as they were doing on this day—women would accompany their husbands when they went to battle. If a man held an important position among the Cheyenne, such as the keeper of the Sacred Arrows, then his wife, too, would have to be of the highest moral character, for she shared the weight of his responsibility.

Buffalo Calf Road Woman was well aware of this, and as she rode by her husband she did so with pride. She knew that today they were on their way to meet their old allies, the Lakota.[1] They were going out to try to drive back the *veho*, the spider people who were trying to claim all the lands of the Native peoples.

The Cheyenne had been worried about the *veho*, the white people, for a long time. They had given them that name because, like the black widow spider, they were very beautiful but it was dangerous to get close to them. And unlike the Cheyenne, they seemed to follow a practice of making promises and not keeping them. Although their soldier chief Custer had promised to

---

1. The *Lakota* were the largest group of the Sioux (sōō) people. Their traditional hunting grounds were in the western Dakotas and Nebraska.

JOSEPH BRUCHAC AND GAYLE ROSS **1079**

1079

Teach

R Reading Strategy

Synthesizing Answer: *Students may say that it is expected, since promises are often broken, especially during wars or other conflicts.* `OL`

L1 Literary Element

Suspense Answer: *The vivid image sets the suspenseful scene of the women holding small weapons and waiting for the bear's approach.* `OL`

BI Big Idea

Rescuing and Conquering Answer: *Like the white pioneers and spider people, the bear came into land that did not belong to it and threatened harm. Unlike these people, the bear returned home.* `OL`

★ Political History

George Crook
Crook was a colonel in the Union Army during the Civil War. His later effectiveness against the Paiute, Snake, and Apache groups got him a promotion to brigadier general in 1873. He went on to lead a number of successful campaigns against the Sioux and Apache peoples. `AS`

Additional Support

Leveled Reading
An adapted version of this selection is available on page 206 of *Jamestown Literature: An Adapted Reader*, grade 10.

---

be friendly with the Cheyenne, now he and the others had come into their lands to make war upon them.

Buffalo Calf Road Woman wore a robe embroidered with porcupine quills. The clothing of her brother and her husband, Black Coyote, was also beautifully decorated with those quills, which had been flattened, dyed in different colors, folded, and sewed on in patterns. Buffalo Calf Road Woman was proud that she belonged to the Society of Quilters. As with the men's societies, only a few women—those of the best character—could join. Like the men, the women had to be strong, honorable, and brave. Buffalo Calf Road Woman had grown up hearing stories of how Cheyenne women would defend their families when the men were away. The women of the Cheyenne were brave, and those in the Society of Quilters were the bravest of all.

Buffalo Calf Road Woman smiled as she remembered one day when the women of the Society of Quilters showed such bravery. It was during the Moon of Falling Leaves. A big hunt had been planned. The men who acted as scouts had gone out and located the great buffalo herd. They had seen, too, that there were no human enemies anywhere near their camp. So almost none of the men remained behind.

On that day, when all the men were away, a great grizzly bear came into the camp. Such things seldom happened, but this bear was one that had been wounded in the leg by a white fur-trapper's bullet. It could no longer hunt as it had before, and hunger brought it to the Cheyenne camp, where it smelled food cooking.

When the huge bear came walking into the camp, almost everyone scattered. Some women grabbed their little children. Old people shut the door flaps of their tepees, and the boys ran to find their bows and arrows. Only a group of seven women

who had been working on the embroidery of an elk-skin robe did not run. They were members of the Society of Quilters, and Buffalo Calf Road Woman was among them. The seven women put down their work, picked up the weapons they had close to hand, and stood to face the grizzly bear.

Now of all of the animals of the plains, the only one fierce enough and powerful enough to attack a human was the grizzly. But **confronted** by that determined group of women, the grizzly bear stopped in its tracks. It had come to steal food, not fight. The head of the Society of Quilters stepped forward a pace and spoke to the bear.

"Grandfather," she said, her voice low and firm, "we do not wish to harm you, but we will protect our camp. Go back to your own home."

The grizzly shook its head and then turned and walked out of the camp. The women stood and watched it as it went down through the cottonwoods and was lost from sight along the bend of the stream.

Buffalo Calf Road Woman turned her mind away from her memories. They were close to Rosebud Creek. The scouts had told them that a great number of the *veho* soldiers would be there and that the Gray Fox, General George Crook, was in command. The Cheyenne had joined up now with the Oglala,[2] led by Crazy Horse. The Lakota people were always friends to the Cheyenne, but this man, Crazy Horse, was the best friend of all. Some even said that he was one of their chiefs, too, as well as being a war leader of his Oglala. ★

---

2. Also a Sioux people, the *Oglala* (ō glä' lə) lived in what is now South Dakota.

Literary Element Suspense *How does this sentence create suspense?* `L1`

Big Idea Rescuing and Conquering *How is the grizzly bear similar to and different from other threats confronting the Cheyenne?* `BI`

Vocabulary

confront (kən frunt') *v.* to come face-to-face with; to oppose

Reading Strategy Synthesizing *From your previous knowledge of U.S. history, Native American history, and war in general, is Custer's shift expected or surprising? Explain.* `R`

Skills Practice

READING: Using Graphic Organizers Point out that a graphic organizer can help students identify and recall the various proper nouns and other nouns in the selection. Have students design a cluster map that shows the names of the Native American groups and their leaders that appear in the selection. For example, an area of the map dealing with groups named in the selection would include Cheyenne, Crow, Shoshone, Oglala, and Lakota. `OL`

There were Crow and Shoshone[3] scouts with Crook, and the *veho* had many cannons. The Lakota and the Cheyenne were outnumbered by the two thousand men in Crook's command. But they were prepared to fight. They had put on their finest clothes, for no man should risk his life without being dressed well enough so that if he died, the enemy would know a great warrior had fallen. Some of the men raised their headdresses three times, calling out their names and the deeds they had done. Those headdresses of eagle feathers were thought to give magical protection to a warrior. Other men busied themselves painting designs on their war ponies.

Now they could hear Crook's army approaching. The rumble of the horses' hooves echoed down the valley, and there was the sound of trumpets. War ponies reared up and stomped their feet. Many of the Cheyenne men found it hard to put on the last of their paint as their hands shook from the excitement of the coming battle.

Crazy Horse **vaulted** onto his horse and held up one arm. *"Hoka Hey,"* he cried. "It is a good day to die."

Buffalo Calf Road Woman watched from a hill as the two lines of men—the blue soldiers to one side, and the Lakota and Cheyenne to the other—raced toward each other. The battle began. It was not a quick fight or an easy one. There were brave men on both sides. Two

Cheyenne Indian war shirt ⭐

Moons, Little Hawk, Yellow Eagle, Sitting Bull, and Crazy Horse were only a few of the great warriors who fought for the Cheyenne and the Lakota. And Crook, the Gray Fox general of the whites, was known to be a tough fighter and a worthy enemy.

Buffalo Calf Road Woman's husband, Black Coyote, and her brother, Comes-in-Sight, were in the thick of the fight. The odds in the battle were almost even. Although the whites had more soldiers and guns, the Lakota and the Cheyenne were better shots and better horsemen. Had it not been for the Crow and Shoshone scouts helping Crook, the white soldiers might have broken quickly from the ferocity of the attack.

From one side to the other, groups of men attacked and retreated as the guns cracked, cannons boomed, and smoke filled the air. The war shouts of the Lakota and the Cheyenne were almost as loud as the rumble of the guns. The sun moved across the sky as the fight went on, hour after hour, while the confusion of battle swirled below.

Then Buffalo Calf Road Woman saw something that horrified her. Her brother had been drawn off to one side, surrounded by Crow scouts. He tried to ride free of them,

---

3. The *Crow* and *Shoshone* (shə shō′nē) peoples lived primarily in the Rocky Mountains.

JOSEPH BRUCHAC AND GAYLE ROSS **1081**

Teach

R Reading Strategy

Synthesizing Answer: *The rescue itself seems factual or historical. The resulting cease-fire and cheering seem legendary.* OL

BI Big Idea

Rescuing and Conquering Answer: *It probably inspired the Cheyenne and Lakota to fight harder.* OL

CheckPoint

Use the CheckPoint questions on Presentation Plus! to check students' mastery of the selection. These questions can be used with interactive response keypads for immediate student feedback.

★ Viewing the Art

Draw students' attention to the materials from which the dress is made. **Ask:** *Why did the Cheyenne make their clothing from these items?* (*Students should note that the Cheyenne hunted elk and deer, and they used the animals to make food, shelter, and clothing.*) AS

Dress. 19th century, Southern Cheyenne. Buckskin, elk teeth, glass beads, tin cones, and yellow and red pigments, length: 48 in., width: 35 in. Smithsonian Institution, Washington, DC. ★

but his pony went down, struck by a rifle bullet and killed. Now he was on foot, still fighting. The Crow warriors were trying to get close, to count coup[4] on him. It was more of an honor to touch a living enemy, so they were not firing their rifles at him. And he was able to keep them away with his bow and arrows. But it was clear that soon he would be out of ammunition and would fall to the enemy.

Buffalo Calf Road Woman waited no longer. She dug her heels into her pony's sides and galloped down the hill. Her head low, her braids streaming behind her, she rode into the heart of the fight. Some men moved aside as they saw her coming, for there was a determined look in her eyes. She made the long howling cry that Cheyenne women

---

4. Among some Native Americans, to *count coup* (ko͞o) was to touch a living enemy and get away safely—an act requiring both skill and courage.

used to urge on the warriors. This time, however, she was the one going into the fight. Her voice was as strong as an eagle's. Her horse scattered the ponies of the Crow scouts who were closing in on her brother, Comes-in-Sight. She held out a hand; her brother grabbed it and vaulted onto the pony behind her. Then she wheeled, ducking the arrows of the Crow scouts, and heading back up the hill.

That was when it happened. For a moment, it seemed as if all the shooting stopped. The Cheyenne and the Lakota, and even the *veho* soldiers, lowered their guns to watch this act of great bravery. A shout went up, not from one side but from both, as Buffalo Calf Road Woman reached the safety of the hilltop again, her brother safe behind her on her horse. White men and Indians cheered her.

So it was that Buffalo Calf Road Woman performed the act for which the people would always remember her. Inspired by her courage, the Cheyenne and Lakota drove back the Gray Fox—Crook made a **strategic** withdrawal.

"Even the *veho* general was impressed," said the Cheyenne people. "He saw that if our women were that brave, he would stand no chance against us in battle."

So it is that to this day, the Cheyenne and the Lakota people do not refer to the fight as the Battle of the Rosebud. Instead, they honor Buffalo Calf Road Woman by calling the fight Where the Girl Rescued Her Brother. ∾

Reading Strategy Synthesizing *Which elements of the rescue seem historical, and which seem legendary?* R

Big Idea Rescuing and Conquering *Why do you think Buffalo Calf Road Woman's daring rescue helped the Cheyenne and Lakota win the battle?* BI

Vocabulary

strategic (strə tē′jik) *adj.* highly important to an intended goal

---

Additional Support

Web Activities Have students access the Web site for interactive activities that will help them assess their understanding of the selection.

Skills Practice

WRITING: Dashes for Explanatory Comments Remind students that one use of dashes is to set off explanatory comments that interrupt the main ideas of sentences. Have students find and copy three sentences from the selection in which dashes are used to set off additional information. Then have students write three sentences of their own, using dashes to set off explanatory comments. OL

AFTER YOU READ

RESPONDING AND THINKING CRITICALLY

Respond

1. Were you surprised by the response of those who witnessed Buffalo Calf Road Woman's bravery at Rosebud Creek? Explain.

Recall and Interpret

2. (a)At the beginning of the story, who are Black Coyote, Comes-in-Sight, and Buffalo Calf Road Woman on their way to meet? (b)How will this meeting help the Cheyenne people?

3. (a)What clothing is Buffalo Calf Road Woman wearing on her journey? (b)What special meaning does Buffalo Calf Road Woman's clothing have?

4. (a)Describe the scene at Rosebud Creek. From the scene, what do you infer about the Cheyenne's attitude toward fighting and battle?

Analyze and Evaluate

5. (a)How do the Cheyenne people seem to view the role of women in their society? (b)Do you think their views are typical for other people in the United States during that historical time period? Explain.

6. Why might the authors have included the bear story in their tale?

7. Were you surprised by the climax and resolution of the story? Explain.

Connect

8. **Big Idea** **Rescuing and Conquering** If you were a close friend of Buffalo Calf Road Woman and realized what she was about to do, would you have tried to stop her? Why or why not?

LITERARY ANALYSIS

Literary Element Suspense

Writers build **suspense** through characters' actions and words, by providing sensory details of what the characters see, hear, touch, taste, or smell, and by targeting readers' prior knowledge of details and events. Suspense helps the storyteller captivate an audience.

1. What sensory details in the battle scene describe the ferocity of the battle and the toughness of both sides?

2. How do these sensory details, combined with your prior knowledge, build suspense in the battle scene?

Writing About Literature

Analyze Cultural and Historical Context "Where the Girl Rescued Her Brother" is steeped both in Native American culture and U.S. history. The Native American characters' beliefs and actions are heavily influenced by their cultural heritage. The period of western expansion depicted in the story was a significant era of U.S. and Native American history. Write a one-or-two-page analysis of the cultural and historical context of "Where the Girl Rescued Her Brother" in which you point out the relevance of culture and history to the characters and events in the story.

READING AND VOCABULARY

Reading Strategy Synthesizing

Synthesizing what you already know about Native Americans, women's roles in war, and U.S. history can help you better understand the selection.

1. How do the authors portray the role of women in Cheyenne society? Give details from the story.

2. At what points in the story does legend become more important than history? Explain.

> **Vocabulary** Practice
>
> Choose the best synonym for each vocabulary word below.
>
> **1. confront**
>   **a.** conjoin   **b.** oppose
>
> **2. vault**
>   **a.** spring   **b.** languish
>
> **3. strategic**
>   **a.** layered   **b.** important to a goal

Literature Online **Web Activities** For eFlashcards, Selection Quick Checks, and other Web activities, go to www.glencoe.com.

JOSEPH BRUCHAC AND GAYLE ROSS   **1083**

Assess

1. Students may have been surprised that the two sides would have stopped fighting to cheer her on.

2. (a) They are going to meet the Lakota. (b) It will give them more soldiers to fight against Crook's forces.

3. (a) A robe decorated with porcupine quills (b) It symbolizes her membership in the Society of Quilters.

4. (a) The Lakota and Cheyenne warriors are preparing for battle. Crook's army is present with their many cannons. (b) The Cheyenne take great pride in battle.

5. (a) They highly respect the skills and courage of women. (b) Their views were probably not typical of other people at that time, who did not allow women to vote or hold jobs traditionally held by men.

6. It illustrates that the Cheyenne women were strong and brave.

7. The story of the grizzly bear prepares for Buffalo Calf Road Woman's brave act.

8. Answers will vary.

Literary Element

1. Sensory details may include the noise of the guns and cannons and the Native Americans' headdresses.

2. The knowledge of the great power of both sides makes the outcome of the battle uncertain, providing suspense.

Vocabulary

1. b **2.** a **3.** b

Writing About Literature

Students' essays should

- provide relevant historical and cultural details
- connect historical and cultural details to the story

Reading Strategy

1. The authors portray women as strong and as capable of being protectors.

2. Legend becomes more important during the grizzly bear and rescue scenes, both of which focus on making a point rather than on relating facts.

Focus

Summary

This is an African American work song based on the legend of John Henry, a railroad man who challenged a steam drill to a contest of strength and endurance in drilling holes in rock. The legend says that John Henry won the contest but died in the process.

Teach

⭐ Viewing the Art

Ask students which of John Henry's characteristics appear to be portrayed in the painting. *(Students should note that John Henry's figure fills up most of the frame. Therefore, he seems not only strong and powerful, but larger than life. He also looks exhausted, perhaps from a long day of work.)* **AS**

BEFORE YOU READ

Building Background

Zora Neale Hurston is one of the most important authors of the Harlem Renaissance, a period in which African American art and literature blossomed and flourished, primarily in New York City's Harlem neighborhood during the 1920s. Hurston is best known for her novel *Their Eyes Were Watching God,* the tale of an African American woman's life in Eaton, Florida. Hurston is also known for her collections of African American folktales, such as *Tell My Horse* and *Mules and Men,* in which "John Henry" appears. After her death, much of Hurston's work went out of print until it was resurrected largely through the efforts of writer Alice Walker in the 1970s.

"John Henry" is a **tall tale,** a type of folktale associated with the U.S. frontier. Tall tales are humorous stories that contain wild exaggerations and inventions. Typically, their heroes are bold but occasionally foolish characters who may have superhuman abilities or who may act as if they do. The legend of John Henry may have originated during the drilling of the Big Bend Tunnel in West Virginia about 1870.

Zora Neale Hurston was born in 1891 and died in 1960.

John Henry

Zora Neale Hurston

Resting, 1944. Claude Clark.
Smithsonian American Art Museum, Washington, DC. ⭐

Additional Support

Skills Practice

LITERARY ELEMENTS: Rhythm and Meter Rhythm is often a vital element of poetry, and is always an essential component of song. Have students read the song aloud. Then have them analyze the rhythm and meter of the song. *(The song has an irregular rhythm and meter. It switches freely from iambic lines, which contain metrical feet with unstressed and then stressed syllables, to trochaic lines, which contain metrical feet with stressed and then unstressed syllables.)* **OL**

1　John Henry driving on the right
　　　hand side,
　　Steam drill[1] driving on the left,
　　Says, 'fore I'll let your steam drill
　　　beat me down
　　I'll hammer my fool self to death,
　　Hammer my fool self to death.

2　John Henry told his Captain,[2]
　　When you go to town
　　Please bring me back a nine pound
　　　hammer
　　And I'll drive your steel on down,
　　And I'll drive your steel on down.

3　John Henry told his Captain,
　　Man ain't nothing but a man,
　　And 'fore I'll let that steam drill beat
　　　me down
　　I'll die with this hammer in my hand,
　　Die with this hammer in my hand.

4　Captain ast John Henry,
　　What is that storm I hear?
　　He says Cap'n that ain't no storm,
　　'Tain't nothing but my hammer in
　　　the air,
　　Nothing but my hammer in the air.

5　John Henry told his Captain,
　　Bury me under the sills of the floor,
　　So when they get to playing good
　　　old Georgy skin,[3]
　　Bet 'em fifty to a dollar more,
　　Fifty to a dollar more.

6　John Henry had a little woman,
　　The dress she wore was red,
　　Says I'm going down the track,
　　And she never looked back.
　　I'm going where John Henry fell dead,
　　Going where John Henry fell dead.

7　Who's going to shoe your pretty li'l' feet?
　　And who's going to glove your hand?
　　Who's going to kiss your dimpled
　　　cheek?
　　And who's going to be your man?
　　Who's going to be your man?

8　My father's going to shoe my pretty li'l'
　　　feet;
　　My brother's going to glove my hand;
　　My sister's going to kiss my dimpled
　　　cheek;
　　John Henry's going to be my man,
　　John Henry's going to be my man. **BI**

9　Where did you get your pretty li'l'
　　　dress?
　　The shoes you wear so fine?
　　I got my shoes from a railroad man,
　　My dress from a man in the mine,
　　My dress from a man in the mine. ∾

---

1. A *steam drill* is a steam-powered machine used to drill through rock. The human workers hammer the rock by hand.
2. Here, the *Captain* is the boss of the railroad workers.
3. *Georgy skin* is slang for Georgia Skin, a card game.

Quickwrite

In this selection, Hurston retells the tall tale of John Henry, a worker who died during his successful, superhuman attempt to out-hammer a steel drill. The story is told in the form of a **ballad**, a narrative song or poem. In two or three paragraphs, discuss the following questions: Why do you think Henry competes with the steam drill? What heroic traits does Henry possess? What flaw(s) does Henry possess? Why do you think "John Henry" is considered an important tall tale?

Teach

BI Big Idea

Rescuing and Conquering
Ask: Why might the woman say this if John Henry is dead? *(She might say it because her love for and loyalty to John Henry will surpass death. She may be pledging her love to the power of the human spirit that John Henry's story represents.)* **OL**

Quickwrite

Students' paragraphs should

- provide a reason for Henry's decision, such as "He wants to prove that men are better than machines"
- note Henry's heroic traits, such as courage and superhuman endurance
- note Henry's flaws, such as arrogance
- provide a reason for the tale's importance, such as showing that people have a strength of spirit that machines lack

✓CheckPoint

Use the CheckPoint questions on Presentation Plus! to monitor students' comprehension and to check students' mastery of the selection. These questions can be used with interactive response keypads for immediate student feedback.

English Language Coach

African American History English language learners may be unfamiliar with the history of African Americans. Briefly review the history of African Americans: the mass transport of enslaved people from Africa to the Americas, the conflict over slavery in the South before and during the Civil War, Lincoln's Emancipation Proclamation, and the civil rights movement. Have students share what they know about African American history. **EL**

Objective
- To analyze rhythm and meter (TWE)

Focus

Summary

This is a Chippewa poem, passed down through the oral tradition, about the speaker feeling inspired to become a great hero like the ones he hears about in stories told by the elders.

Teach

★ Viewing the Art

Much of the artwork of Eanger Irving Couse (1866–1936) reflects the time he spent living among Native Americans. His paintings were intended to promote the preservation of Native American cultures and lifestyles. **AS**

Discussion Starter

Students should

- note that the speaker is young and inspired by tales of great heroes; this inspiration makes him or her confident and proud

- provide a reason for oral tradition's importance to this poem, such as youths of many generations to meet their potential

---

BEFORE YOU READ

Building Background

The Chippewa (chip´ə wä´), or Ojibwa (ō jib´ wä´), is a Native American group that lives in Canada and on reservations in the northern United States. From the seventeenth until the nineteenth centuries, the Chippewa were involved in a number of conflicts with the Sioux and the Fox peoples and held shifting alliances with the colonial French and British. After the War of 1812, they enacted a treaty with the United States and have lived on reservations since. The Ojibwa now make up the third largest group of Native Americans in the United States.

Traditional Ojibwa meals include farmed and gathered foods, such as wild rice, corn, and squash, and hunted foods, such as fish and deer. The Ojibwa also created a unique picture-based writing system that was intricately connected with their religious beliefs and medicinal knowledge.

A SONG OF GREATNESS

Chippewa

Fireside. Eanger Irving Couse (1866–1936).

When I hear the old men
Telling of heroes,
Telling of great deeds
Of ancient days-
5 When I hear that telling,
Then I think within me
I, too, am one of these.

When I hear the people
Praising great ones,
10 Then I know that I too-
Shall be esteemed;
I, too, when my time comes
Shall do mightily

Discussion Starter

Meet with a small group to discuss the roles of history and heritage in the life of a hero. How old is the speaker in the poem? Why does the speaker believe he/she will "do mightily"? How is the oral tradition important to this poem? Summarize your discussion for the rest of the class.

Additional Support

Skills Practice

READING: Oral Interpretation One way to respond to literature is through oral interpretation of the text. The Native American storytelling tradition is based on the passing down of stories through oral presentations and interpretations. Have students put together a dramatic performance of the song. Have students bring in or improvise musical instruments, such as drums, to accompany the performance. Then, discuss how the performance affects students' understanding of the text. **OL**

Wrap-Up: Comparing Literature *Across Genres*

- *Where the Girl Rescued Her Brother*
  by Joseph Bruchac and Gayle Ross
- *John Henry*
  by Zora Neale Hurston
- *A Song of Greatness*
  —Chippewa Traditional

COMPARING THE [Big Idea] Rescuing and Conquering

Writing Activity "Where the Girl Rescued Her Brother," "John Henry," and "A Song of Greatness" together offer different explorations of the heroic ideas of rescuing and conquering. Are both the concepts of rescuing and of conquest the focus in each work? How are such ideas expressed in each work? Are the ideas stated directly or implied? Which stages of the hero's life are depicted in the works? Think about these questions, then write a brief essay discussing how the ideas of rescuing and conquering are conveyed in these selections.

COMPARING Oral Tradition

Writing Down the Story A **genre** is a category or type of literature. Though the selections compared here come from different genres—the first being a short story, the second a tall tale, and the third a poem—each of the selections originated in the oral tradition of its respective culture. Now that these stories have been written down, they are available to a wider audience. Think of a story about an event that to your knowledge has not been written down, but that someone told. Then choose two of the above forms—short story, tall tale, poem—and write down the story you heard. You may add details or exaggerations as you wish. When you are finished, consider the following questions:

- Does your story communicate as well on paper, or did it sound better when you first heard it?
- Did you find one genre easier to write than the other? Why or why not?
- How did the genres you chose affect how you told the story?

COMPARING Cultural Beliefs

Partner Activity Each of these selections communicates the beliefs of its respective culture. "Where the Girl Rescued Her Brother" comes from the Cheyenne people, "John Henry" comes from the African American culture, and "A Song of Greatness" hearkens from the Chippewa tradition. From what you have read in these selections, how do these cultures differ? How are they similar? With a partner, make inferences about each culture's beliefs about the following:

- the role(s) of women in society
- the importance of history and heritage
- the value of courage

Support your inferences with details from the selections. Then share your thoughts with your classmates.

OBJECTIVES
- Compare and contrast works about rescue and conquest.
- Compare oral traditions across genres.
- Compare and contrast cultural beliefs.
- Compare themes across genres.

COMPARING LITERATURE **1087**

Assess

Comparing the Big Idea

Students' essays should

- note that the concept of rescue is used only minimally (if at all) in "John Henry" and not at all in "A Song of Greatness"
- note that conquest and rescuing are expressed explicitly in "Where the Girl Rescued Her Brother," that John Henry implicitly tries to "conquer" the steam drill, and that the speaker in "Greatness" is implicitly inspired to conquer time and history by becoming a great hero
- note that the hero's birth is expressed in "Greatness," the hero's great acts are expressed in "Where the Girl Rescued Her Brother," and the hero's fall is expressed in "John Henry"

Comparing Oral Tradition

Encourage students to explore the connections between genre and content, or form and function. For example, stories with strong narrative arcs may be easier to write as short fiction, stories with larger-than-life characters or extraordinary events may be easier to write as tall tales, and more impressionistic stories may be easier to write as poems.

Comparing Cultural Beliefs

- Women are given roles of power and strength in Cheyenne culture. Women take the roles of romantic partners in "John Henry." "Greatness" does not touch on the roles of women.

- "Where the Girl Rescued Her Brother" and "Greatness" express Native Americans' strong beliefs in the importance of history and heritage—they inspire and instruct people how to live. "John Henry" shows that progress cannot overcome humanity.

- "John Henry" shows that courage is valuable but can also betray. "Where the Girl Rescued Her Brother" shows that selfless courage is a vital fiber of society. "Greatness" shows that courage is an important value taught to the young.

Focus

BELLRINGER

Write the following questions on the board:

• What do you know?

• What do you want to know? Give students a few moments to think of responses. **Ask:** If you had the chance to inform someone of something you know a lot about, or if you had the chance to learn about something new, what would it be? *(Answers will vary.)* Encourage students to think of writing a research report as an opportunity to share what they know or to learn about something entirely new.

Summary

In this workshop, students will write and present research reports. Students will follow the stages of the writing process, including prewriting, drafting, revising, editing, and presenting. In addition, two focus lessons, on developing coherent paragraphs and using commas correctly, are provided.

The Writing Process

In this workshop, you will follow the stages of the writing process. At any stage, you may think of new ideas to include and better ways to express them. Feel free to return to earlier stages as you write.

Prewriting
- - - - - - - - -
Drafting
- - - - - - - - -
Revising
- - - - - - - - -
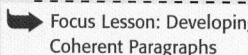 Focus Lesson: Developing Coherent Paragraphs

Editing and Proofreading
- - - - - - - - -
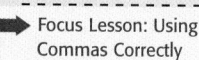 Focus Lesson: Using Commas Correctly

Presenting
- - - - - - - - -

 Literature**Online**
Writing Models For models and other writing activities, go to www.glencoe.com.

OBJECTIVES
Write a research report. Present and support a thesis based on a variety of sources. Credit and document sources.

 # Writing Workshop

Research Paper

➤ Writing a Research Report

"WHOSO PULLETH OUTE THIS SWERD OF THIS STONE AND ANVYLD IS RIGHTWYS KYNGE BORNE OF ALL BRYTAYGNE"

—Sir Thomas Malory, from *Le Morte d'Arthur*

Connecting to the Literature Legends and myths often retell tales of fantastic happenings, such as pulling a sword from a stone. Sometimes, however, they also contain hints of events that may really have happened. In a research report, a writer may explore the possibility of the historical truth of such events as well as other questions related to the work. To find out how to write a research report on any topic, begin by reading the goals and strategies below.

Rubric: Features of Research Reports

Goals	Strategies
To present a clearly stated thesis statement	☑ State clearly a central conclusion ☑ Revise your thesis statement as needed
To explain and support the thesis statement	☑ Take notes from a variety of sources ☑ Introduce and explain your sources
To include an introduction that states the thesis, a body that supports the thesis, and a conclusion that restates the thesis	☑ Use an outline or a graphic organizer to help you plan your writing ☑ Check to be sure that each body paragraph clearly supports the thesis
To use sources correctly and honestly	☑ Quote, paraphrase, and summarize information ☑ Credit your sources
To present the writer's own thinking on the research topic	☑ Comment on what the experts say ☑ Include your own insights

Additional Support

 Literature**Online**

Writing Models Have students access the Web site for interactive writing models and writing guides.

Workshop Resources

Print Materials
- 📁 Unit 5 Resources (Fast File), pp. 51–53
- 📁 REAL Success in Writing: Research and Reports
- 📁 Writing Constructed Responses, pp. 1–26, 54
- 📖 Glencoe Literature Library

🖨 **Transparencies**
- Grammar and Language Transparencies 55, 57, 59
- Writing Workshop Transparencies 26–30

💻 **Technology**
- Grammar & Language eWorkbook
- Revising with Style eWorkbook
- Sentence Diagraming eWorkbook
- Spelling Power eWorkbook
- Online Essay Grader, glencoe.com
- Literature Library Exam*View*™ Assessment Suite CD-ROM
- Literature Library Vocabulary PuzzleMaker CD-ROM

> **Assignment**
>
> Write a research report in which you present a thesis that is based on your reading of several sources. As you move through the stages of the writing process, keep your audience and purpose in mind.
>
> **Audience:** classmates and teacher
>
> **Purpose:** to research a topic and present your conclusions supported by evidence

Prewriting

Find and Narrow a Topic Make a list of topics that interest you. Gather information about each topic by reading an encyclopedia article.

▶ **Ask Questions** Write out questions you have about your topic. Focus on what interests you and what you want to know more about.

▶ **Narrow Your Topic** Think about the length of the paper you have been assigned to write. Match that length with a question you have asked.

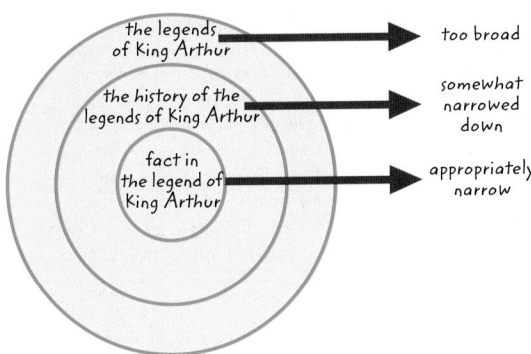

the legends of King Arthur → too broad

the history of the legends of King Arthur → somewhat narrowed down

fact in the legend of King Arthur → appropriately narrow

Read Specific Sources Once you decide on your research question, consult specialized sources.

▶ **Use Reliable Sources** Library databases are good sources for biography and general reference. For sources on the Internet, use these criteria:

▶ Who is the author? Is he or she an expert in the field?

▶ Is there documentation? Are the sources used to create the site listed on the site? Are there footnotes or a bibliography?

▶ What is the purpose of the site? Personal Web pages or Web pages created to sell merchandise may not be reliable. However, you can trust Web pages created by reputable public institutions.

Real-World Connection

Research skills are important in many decisions in life, from making everyday purchases to choosing a college or finding a job. The more you know in each case, the better your choice will be.

Audience and Purpose

Most research reports are formal writing exercises. Remember that your purpose is to inform and not to entertain. Usually teachers will ask you to use the third person and to avoid using *I*. Maintain a serious tone and avoid slang and contractions.

Teach

Big Idea

Rescuing and Conquering

Say: Consider this question as we begin this workshop: What is more interesting, fact or fiction? Explain that legends and myths tell us much about our beliefs, our cultures and our identities but how we organize and report factual information is important in how we define ourselves, our culture, and our histories. **OL**

★ Writer's Technique

Topic Selection Effective writers write about their interests, their passions, and what they know best. Explain to students the importance of picking topics that interest them. **Say:** When writing a research report, start the writing process by picking a topic that interests you and with which you are familiar. Encourage students to jot down a number of topics and choose two from the list to weigh as their final topic choices. **AS**

English Language Coach

Research Assistance Consider pairing nonnative speakers with advanced students at the beginning of the writing process. Advanced students can help English language learners become familiar with conducting research, taking notes, and drafting a thesis. **EL**

Differentiated Instruction

Identifying a Topic Less proficient writers may have difficulty pinpointing appropriate topics for their research reports. Work with these students individually to assist them in selecting topics that are appropriate to their level and that interest them. **BL**

Objectives
• To write a research report (SE)
• To present and support a thesis based on a variety of sources (SE)

Teach

Writing Process

Prewriting Say: The most critical task you undertake in the research process is taking careful notes. Reinforce the methods students should use to take notes. Provide students with a short passage of factual information. Have them practice taking notes from the passage, and then go over their results as a class. **OL**

⭐ Cultural History

A Cautionary Tale Stress to students the importance of avoiding plagiarism. Tell them the following cautionary tale. **Say:** In 2002, a famous historian, Doris Kearns Goodwin, was accused of and admitted to plagiarizing from sources she had used many years before. While she did not plagiarize intentionally, she did in fact lift passages from another historian's work. She admitted her mistake, apologized, and corrected the citations. **AS**

⭐ Avoid Plagiarism

Plagiarism is using other people's exact words or their ideas as if they are one's own. One good way to avoid plagiarism is to use several sources. Doing this will help you develop a broader view of your topic. What is common knowledge—that is, what almost all the sources say—will become clear, and so will what is unique and must therefore be acknowledged in your paper.

Developing a Thesis

Writing a thesis for a research paper is a process. Your thesis should begin to "come to you" as you read and take notes. It is a good idea to start out with a working thesis statement and refine it as you go along to make it clearer, more precise, and more reflective of the actual body of your paper.

Take Notes Even though your report will be based on other people's ideas, it must be your own work, and you must identify your sources. One way to ensure that you do your own work—and avoid plagiarism—is to prewrite by taking notes. Once you begin your draft, you should be working from your own notes—all of your sources should be set aside.

Make four kinds of note cards.

▶ **Bibliography note cards** Write on a separate card the full publishing information for each source you use.

▶ **Summary note cards** Label each of these cards *summary*. Start with the author's last name or the title of the source. Then write down the main ideas of what you read. A good way to do this is to start with a key point and then to make a brief bulleted list of details. Record the page number(s) on which you found this information.

▶ **Paraphrase note cards** Label each of these cards *paraphrase*. Write down the author's last name or the title of the source. Then paraphrase, or retell in your own words, the information you found. Record the page number(s) on which you found this information.

▶ **Quotation note cards** Label each of these cards *quotation*. Start with the author's last name or the title of the source. Then quote, or copy exactly, the information. Record the page number(s) on which you found the quotation.

Find Your Main Ideas One good reason to use note cards is that you can organize them easily into groups of related ideas. This organization can help you develop a sense of the paragraphs that you will write to support your thesis. Group the cards into possible topics for paragraphs. Clip together each group of cards. Then try arranging the cards in each clipped group in the order in which you will present them in your paper.

Make a Plan One final prewriting step before drafting is to develop an outline or another organizational plan. One purpose of this step is to be sure that your main ideas truly relate to and support your thesis. If they do not, revise your thesis. A second purpose is to establish the order of main ideas in your draft.

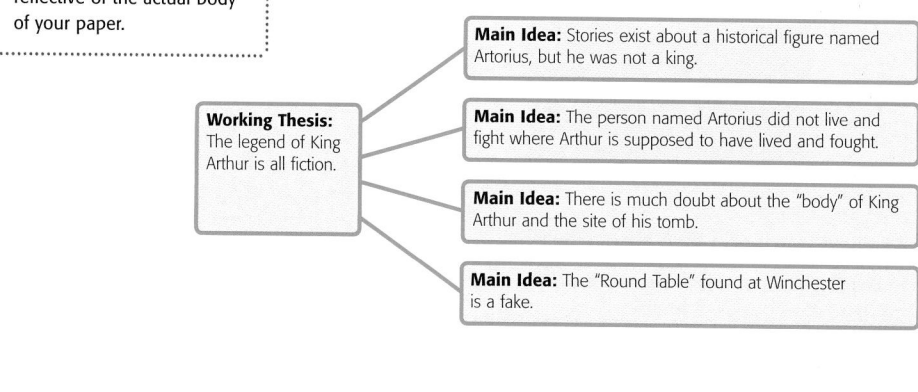

Working Thesis: The legend of King Arthur is all fiction.

Main Idea: Stories exist about a historical figure named Artorius, but he was not a king.

Main Idea: The person named Artorius did not live and fight where Arthur is supposed to have lived and fought.

Main Idea: There is much doubt about the "body" of King Arthur and the site of his tomb.

Main Idea: The "Round Table" found at Winchester is a fake.

Additional Support

Skills Practice

WRITING: Types of Research Reports Explain to students that there are different approaches they can take when writing their research reports:

• Summary research reports sum up the opinions of other writers and are syntheses of the information researched.

• Evaluative research reports state opinions and are backed up by evidence from primary and secondary sources.

• Original research reports lead to new insights about a topic.

Ensure that students understand the type of research report they are to write for this assignment. **OL**

Drafting

Support Your Thesis The success of a research paper depends in large part on the thesis. Be sure that you state your thesis in the introduction of your draft. As you develop the body, be sure that each paragraph relates to and supports the thesis. If you wish, you can write the body of your paper first and then draw your thesis from it.

Analyzing a Workshop Model

Here is a final draft of a research report. As you read it, answer the questions in the margin. Use your answers to these questions to guide you as you write your own research report.

The Legend of King Arthur: The Facts of the Matter

Did Merlin exist? Was there once a place called Camelot? Did Sirs Lancelot, Gawain, Galahad, and other knights ever sit around a round table? The answer to all of these questions is no. The legend of King Arthur is powerful, enduring, and important to many people, but it is not true. In fact, there is nothing about the legend of King Arthur that is definitely based on fact.

Thesis Statement
Be sure that your introduction includes a thesis statement. What do you expect every body paragraph in this paper to be about?

The Faithful Knight in Equal Field Subdues his Faithless Foe, (1860–1941). Frederick and Pickford Marriot.

Nevertheless, people want to believe in a factual basis for the King Arthur legend. Their most important argument is that there really was a man named Arthur who has come down in legend as King Arthur. Some

Teach

Writing Process

Drafting Explain: The key element of a solid research report is a thesis. Solid theses are those that are specific, are supported by facts, and can be fully examined in the space allotted. As students generally have difficulty writing a specific thesis, consider setting aside class time to allow for a thesis-writing workshop. Have students read each others' theses and comment on three categories: Is the thesis specific? Can it be supported by research? Does the writer have enough space in the assignment to fully cover the topic? **OL**

Writing Skills

Thesis Statement Answer: *Specific aspects of the King Arthur legend and their lack of definite basis in fact.* **OL**

Differentiated Instruction

Skimming Texts for Information
A research project can be overwhelming for students in terms of having to access, review, and understand many different texts and resources. Encourage students to skim and scan for information. **Say:** Skimming over a source will tell you if it will be useful to you or not. Read the title, chapter headings, and even the sources used to determine if you want to use the source. Scanning helps you pinpoint information quickly. Look for key words and phrases in the text as you scan it during the research process. **BL**

Objectives
- To write a research report (SE)
- To credit and document sources (SE)
- To understand types of research reports (TWE)

1091

Teach

Writing Skills

Main Ideas Answer:
Some people believe that Arthur was a historical figure. **OL**

Writing Skills

Supporting Details Answer:
General information about life in Britain in the fourth and fifth centuries **OL**

Writing Skills

Paraphrase Answer: *The author's exact words are not needed to communicate the ideas.* **OL**

Writing Skills

Explanation Answer: *The tenuousness of the connection between the "fierce fighter" and Arthur* **OL**

Writing Skills

Your Own Insights Answer:
Ideas about how the story of Arthur was probably changed **OL**

Main Ideas

Each paragraph should develop one main idea related to the thesis. What is the main idea of this paragraph?

Supporting Details

Sometimes supporting details consist of background information for your reader. What background information appears here?

Paraphrase

Most information in your paper should be summarized or paraphrased. Why is a direct quotation not needed here?

Explanation

Source material does not tell everything. It must be linked with explanation. What does the writer explain here?

Your Own Insights

In addition to showing others' thinking, a research paper should show your own thinking too. What original thoughts do you find here?

---

think that they find Arthur in an actual historical figure called Artorius, which may be a Roman name for Arthur. Others cite a hero called Arth Fawr, a Welsh term meaning "great bear," which sounds very much like Arthur (Barber 37). If the existing records can be believed, Artorius or Arth Fawr lived in the late fifth and early sixth centuries AD (Lacey 18). This was a terrible time in the history of Great Britain, which had been part of the Roman Empire since the first century AD. As the Roman Empire declined and fell in the fourth and fifth centuries, killing, looting, and burning began. Fierce fighters came from the west and the east (Day 11). Many Britons (people living on the island that now forms part of Great Britain) were killed, and many lived in terrible fear. After about AD 450, the whole eastern part of the land fell to two groups of invaders: the Angles and the Saxons. The "West Country" remained free (Day 29).

Battles raged on in the West Country. About the year 500, a man appeared who won a series of twelve battles against the invaders (Byrd). A sixth-century source, *The Ruin and Conquest of Britain* by Gildas describes these battles, including the final battle known as the Battle of Badon Hill. This was the decisive battle that brought peace to the people of the West Country for perhaps forty years. This account also includes an unidentified fierce fighter whose name may—or may not—have been some form of Arthur (Alexander). It is important to note that the fighter's name is never mentioned in this account, but people have still just assumed the warrior has to be Arthur. An early ninth-century source by Nennius is the first text that mentions Arthur's name. Nennius's account also associates Arthur (or in this case, Artorius) with the Battle of Badon and eleven other victories. It does not refer to Artorius as king, however. Instead, it records Arthur's title as *Dux Bellorum*, or "leader of battles" (Echard). Both sources are far from proof that the leader they present is the same Arthur of legend.

Once a hero story is started, it is easy to see how it can be carried along. In our own time, people communicate ideas on the Internet that are not true but are believed to be, especially as more and more people repeat them. It is easy to imagine this happening in the early Middle Ages when storytelling was probably the main form of entertainment. If Artorius really was a fierce and fantastic fighter, the stories about him probably just kept getting bigger and a lot more fantastic. In *The Search for Arthur*, David Day comments on Arthur's growing fame.

Additional Support

Skills Practice

RESEARCH: Internet Sources
Explain to students that when researching, the Internet can be their best friend or their worst enemy. **Say:** Anything and everything can end up posing as "fact" on the Internet. Be wary of what Internet sources you use. To be on the safe side, consult only Web sites with .edu, .org, or .gov in their address lines. If you are unsure of the viability of a source, bring it to class, and we will evaluate it.

As a class, pick a random topic and, if possible, run an Internet search on that topic. Point out Web sites that are worthy and useful, and guide students away from flimsy sites. **OL**

The deeds of the Dux Bellorum [who brought peace after so much war] were forever remembered by proud Britons. Arthur was not only the saviour of a people on the brink of extinction, but he gave them the glory of a dozen victories. The deeds of other heroes . . . soon became associated with his name (15).

This quotation explains why Arthur—or Arth Fawr, or Artorius—became so famous. It does not, however, prove that the stories about this figure were true.

There are also geographical problems with the story of Arthur and his great battles. One proposed site of Arthur's supposed last great battle is Badon Hill, which is thought to be located in southwest England (Echard). The historical *Dux Bellorum* did not live there, however. Instead, Day says, "[T]here is little doubt" that he lived and fought north of where the English border is today, in an area we now call southern Scotland (18). The Welsh, for whom Arthur was a "national hero" (Lupack), offer other sources of the story in their poetry and other writing. Some of these sources call Arthur's final battle the Battle of Camlann, where he was killed fighting Medraut or Mordred. Camlann may be in the north of England near Hadrian's Wall, or it may be in the south of England at Slaughter's Bridge (Lacey 69). Wherever it was, it is unlikely that Arthur lived and fought in two places that were so far away from each other.

Probably the main reason that nothing in the Arthur legends can be trusted as fact is that poets and other writers—not true historians—gave us the stories of King Arthur that we tell today. The first important source of the story came from a man who lived in the twelfth century, Geoffrey of Monmouth. He wrote *The History of the Kings of Britain*. The title of this work makes it sound like fact, but it is full of fiction and was probably written in large part for political purposes (Day 39). As Professor Siân Echard notes (on her Web page) about King Arthur in history, there was plenty of doubt about the truth of Monmouth's work and other stories about Arthur, even about the time when the earliest accounts were written. In about 1124, the medieval historian William of Malmesbury called the stories of Arthur "deceitful fables." Historian William of Newburgh, who wrote between 1196 and 1198, said that Geoffrey of Monmouth "weaves the most ridiculous figments of imagination." He also said that Geoffrey "cloaked" his fables about Arthur

---

Exposition

Long Quotations

Begin a new line and indent quotations more than four lines long. If you have to leave something out, use an ellipsis. If you have to add something, put it in brackets. Why do you think a long quotation was used here?

Summary

A summary condenses information in source material. Why did the writer reduce this information to key points and details?

Main Ideas

Main ideas must support the thesis. How does the topic sentence of this paragraph relate to the thesis?

Support

Be sure that your support is convincing. How do these sources help the writer prove the thesis?

WRITING WORKSHOP **1093**

Teach

Writing Skills

Long Quotations Answer: *David Day's words are just right for expressing the idea that the writer wants to convey.* OL

Writing Skills

Summary Answer: *The source material probably elaborates a great deal. Only a summary is needed to make a point that supports the main idea of the paragraph.* OL

Writing Skills

Main Ideas Answer: *It supports the idea that the stories about Arthur are fiction, not fact.* OL

Writing Skills

Support Answer: *They show that even twelfth-century historians did not believe the stories told about Arthur.* OL

Reading in the Real World

Career Reinforce for students the importance of learning how to conduct research and synthesize information into a report. Many careers require research and writing. These include jobs in law, medicine, education, research, business, and advertising. **Say:** Learning how to research and synthesize information efficiently and effectively will help you enormously in the workplace. Not only will you save yourself time by knowing how to conduct research, you will also feel confident about presenting your findings. OL

Objectives
- To present and support a thesis based on a variety of sources (SE)
- To evaluate Internet sources (TWE)

1093

Teach

Writing Skills

Coherent Paragraph
Answer: *The paragraph is about how authors built upon fictional stories about Arthur. It does not stray from that idea.* **OL**

Writing Skills

Sources **Answer:** *With the clause "As Caroline Alexander notes"* **OL**

Writing Skills

Your Own Insights **Answer:** *The writer notes that tourists are eager to believe the story that Arthur's tomb is in Glastonbury.* **OL**

Writing Skills

Direct Quotations **Answer:** *They exactly express an important idea in a few words.* **OL**

Coherent Paragraph

Remember that each paragraph should be about just one main idea, with no unrelated details. What is the main idea of this paragraph? Explain whether the paragraph strays from that main idea.

Sources

It is a good idea to introduce some of your sources. How does the writer do that here?

Your Own Insights

Remember to add comments of your own. What comment does the writer add here?

Direct Quotations

Use direct quotations sparingly. Why are these words quoted directly?

---

with the "honorable name of history" (Eckard). In so many words, then, real historians called these early stories about Arthur lies.

Literature took these fables even further. A twelfth-century French poet named Chrétien de Troyes added much of the romance of the legend, including the great adventures (in both battle and love) of the knights of the Round Table (Alexander). Sir Thomas Malory, who is credited with first bringing together in English the many related tales (including stories about Lancelot, Guinevere, and the Holy Grail), combined all of the stories into one very long work called *Le Morte d'Arthur (Glencoe Literature p.990)*. By the time he was finished, the tales already had had a long history of imagination and invention—and that was more than five centuries ago.

Even though the facts of invention are so clear and so well-known, no one seems to stop looking for proof that Arthur existed. People search for his birthplace, for Camelot, for the sites of battles, and for Avalon. Every attempt to find underlying and certain facts in the Arthur legend has failed, however. One of the most significant attempts to find "proof" was an early one, which involved finding Arthur's body. In 1191 monks claimed to have "discovered" the tomb of Arthur and Guinevere at Glastonbury in southern England, a place that had long been called Avalon by some (and which many people continue to call Avalon today). As Caroline Alexander notes, however, the monks certainly had their motives. The abbey had burned to the ground in 1184, but after the "discovery" a rich tourist industry that helped the monks rebuild their home sprang up. Also, no one could really disprove or prove the claim. After all, there was no DNA testing then, and the tomb conveniently disappeared in 1589, so there is no DNA testing now, either. The article on Glastonbury in *The New Arthurian Encyclopedia* notes that many historians "dismissed the grave as a fabrication and a publicity stunt" (200). Nevertheless, to this day, a sign proudly marks the spot as "Site of King Arthur's Tomb," and tourists remain eager to visit—and to believe.

Another attempt to confirm that the legend is "fact" occurred when the so-called Round Table was produced. A huge solid-oak table painted to show the place where each of Arthur's knights sat was "found" at Winchester Castle in Wessex. Suddenly, the real home of Camelot appeared to be known once and for all. As Day notes, however, the table was just a medieval forgery: "Forensic examination indicates that the wood was cut for this table just before 1250" (96), about seven hundred years after the story of Arthur at Badon Hill, or Camlann—or wherever the figure that was or was not Arthur might have been.

1094 UNIT 5 LEGENDS AND MYTHS

Additional Support

Skills Practice

WRITING: Paraphrasing Say: One of the most difficult tasks in researching and synthesizing is effectively paraphrasing sources. You must keep two things in mind as you paraphrase sources: Does your paraphrase capture the author's original intent or meaning? Have you been vigilant in avoiding plagiarism?

Provide students with a passage to paraphrase, on an overhead projector or the board. Have them collectively paraphrase the passage. Point out places in which plagiarism can be avoided and show students how to convey the author's message in their own words. **OL**

The truest thing that can be said about the history of the legend is that there is a history of trying to turn the legend of King Arthur into fact. If a great battle leader named Arthur ever existed, he was not a king, and he could not have lived in both the North and the Southwest at once. Stories that were told about Arthur simply grew bigger and bigger over time, and even early historians did not hesitate to call them "fables." Those who love the story of King Arthur may want desperately to believe that some part of the legend really took place, but that seems about as likely as pulling a sword from a stone.

John Chalon of England and Lois de Beul of France Jousting, 15th century. Royal Armoury manuscript. Private Collection.

Works Cited

Alexander, Caroline. "A Pilgrim's Search for Relics of the Once and Future King." Smithsonian 26.11(February 1996), <http://www.galegroup.net>

Barber, Chris, and David Pykitt. Journey to Avalon: The Final Discovery of King Arthur. York Beach, Maine: Samuel Weiser, 1997.

Byrd, Laura. "A Place of Legends." World and I 16.11(November 2001), <http://www.galegroup.net>

Day, David. The Search for King Arthur. New York: Facts on File, 1995.

Echard, Siân. "King Arthur in History: Texts." <http://faculty.arts.ubc.ca/sechard/344art.htm>

Glencoe Literature. Chicago: McGraw-Hill, 2007.

Lacy, Norris J., ed. The New Arthurian Encyclopedia. New York: Garland Publishing, 1996.

Lupack, Alan, and Barbara Tepa Lupack. "The Tomb of King Arthur." The Camelot Project at the University of Rochester. 4 October 2005. <http://www.lib.rochester.edu/camelot/gerald.htm>

Exposition

Conclusion
Conclude with a brief summary and a final insight. How does this author summarize without repeating?

Variety of Sources
Use a variety of sources. What different kinds of sources are shown here?

Reliable Sources
Your sources should be reliable. What would you check to be sure that this source is reliable?

Encyclopedia Sources
Encyclopedia articles can provide excellent overviews. How is this encyclopedia different from a general encyclopedia?

Writing Workshop

Research Paper

Teach

Writing Skills

Conclusion Answer: *The writer restates the thesis in an original way, saying that the only true thing about the legend is the search for its truth, and summarizes some of the main points that support the thesis.* **OL**

Writing Skills

Variety of Sources
Answer: *Two magazines accessed online, two books, two Web sites, a textbook, and a specialized encyclopedia* **OL**

Writing Skills

Reliable Sources Answer: *Students may suggest finding information about the author or publisher, as well as seeing whether the article contains footnotes or a bibliography.* **OL**

Writing Skills

Encyclopedia Sources
Answer: *It focuses on topics related to the Arthurian legends.* **OL**

Differentiated Instruction

Revision Encourage less proficient writers to revise one step at a time:

- First, read through the report to check that arguments and ideas make sense.
- Second, make sure you have included an introduction, a thesis, supporting paragraphs, and a conclusion.
- Third, proofread for punctuation and spelling errors.
- Fourth, make sure your sources are properly quoted and cited.
- Finally, pair up with another student and checks each other's reports. **BL**

Objectives
- To write a research report (SE)
- To practice paraphrasing (TWE)

Teach

Writing Process

Revising Revising research reports is not an easy task. Near the end of the process, students are generally ready to turn in whatever they have prepared thus far and call it quits. **Say:** Revising can be one of the most rewarding stages of writing. Effective writers read over their work, note where confusion exists or where arguments fall apart, and revise. Take time to shore up your arguments, polish your transitions, and craft your concluding thoughts. **OL**

★ Literary History

Writing Manuals Describe the various manuals for writing with which students may become familiar as they progress in their academic careers and are assigned more and longer research papers. These manuals include the *MLA Handbook for Writers, The Chicago Manual of Style,* and *The Elements of Style.* Explain that each manual has its own particular method or style and that certain programs or instructors may prefer or require a particular style. **AS**

Additional Support

Traits of Strong Writing

Ideas message or theme and the details that develop it

Organization arrangement of main ideas and supporting details

Voice writer's unique way of using tone and style

Word Choice vocabulary a writer uses to convey meaning

Sentence Fluency rhythm and flow of sentences

★ **Conventions** correct spelling, grammar, usage, and mechanics

Presentation the way words and design elements look on a page

For more information on using the traits of strong writing, see pages R33–R34 of the Writing Handbook.

Revising

Use the rubric below to help you evaluate your writing.

Rubric: Writing a Research Report

- ☑ Do you clearly state, fully explain, and support your thesis?
- ☑ Do you have a clear introduction, body, and conclusion?
- ☑ Do you paraphrase and summarize most of your sources and credit all ideas?
- ☑ Do you present your own explanations, insights, and comments?

▶ **Focus Lesson**

Developing Coherent Paragraphs

To make the sentences in a paragraph flow coherently, you may have to change the order of ideas, add or improve transitions, and take out words or sentences that do not belong.

Draft: Incoherent Paragraph

Another attempt to confirm that the legend is "fact" occurred when the so-called Round Table was produced. The real home of Camelot appeared to be known once and for all. A huge solid-oak table painted to show the place where each of Arthur's knights sat was "found" at Winchester Castle in Wessex. One can just imagine the knights gathered around it. As Day notes, however, the table was just a medieval forgery: "Forensic examination indicates that the wood was cut for this table just before 1250" (96), about seven hundred years after the story of Arthur at Badon Hill, or Camlann—or wherever the figure that was or was not Arthur might have been.

Revision:

Another attempt to confirm that the legend is "fact" occurred when the so-called Round Table was produced. A huge solid-oak table painted to show the place where each of Arthur's knights sat was "found" at Winchester Castle in Wessex.[1] ~~One can just imagine the knights gathered around it.~~[2] Suddenly,[3] the real home of Camelot appeared to be known once and for all. As Day notes, however, the table was just a medieval forgery: "Forensic examination indicates that the wood was cut for this table just before 1250" (96), about seven hundred years after the story of Arthur at Badon Hill, or Camlann—or wherever the figure that was or was not Arthur might have been.

1. Improve the order of ideas
2. Delete unrelated ideas
3. Link ideas with transitions

Skills Practice

PUNCTUATION: Ellipses Remind students of the proper conventions involved in using ellipses. **Say:** When you are inserting a quotation into your text but are not using every word of the quotation, you must indicate where you have left out words. Indicate an omission with the use of points of ellipsis—three spaced periods. Write the following quotation from Barack Obama, about Rosa Parks, on the board: "Well before she made headlines across the country, she was a highly respected member of the Montgomery community and a commit-

Editing and Proofreading

Get It Right When you have completed the final draft of your research report, proofread it for errors in grammar, usage, mechanics, and spelling. Refer to the Language Handbook, pages R46–R60, as a guide.

► **Focus Lesson**

Using Commas Correctly

In general, commas should be used to set off transition words and phrases—such as *first, as a result, consequently,* and *on the other hand*—whether they are introductory expressions (at the beginning of a sentence) or interrupters (in the middle of a sentence).

Original: In this sentence, *nevertheless* is an introductory transition word.

Nevertheless people want to believe in a factual basis for the King Arthur legend.

Improved: Add a comma after the introductory transition word.

Nevertheless, people want to believe in a factual basis for the King Arthur legend.

Original: In this sentence, the transitional word *however* interrupts the sentence.

That does not prove however that the stories about him were true.

Improved: Use commas before and after the transition.

That does not prove, however, that the stories about him were true.

Check Your Citations

As a separate proofreading step, make sure that you have placed beginning and end quotation marks around all quoted materials. Check also to be sure that you have closed the quotation before adding the parentheses enclosing the citation. Finally, be sure that the final punctuation appears after the parentheses.

Try a New Proofreading Method

Sometimes your own typos are hard to catch. Try reading your paper backwards to examine closely the spelling of each word.

Writer's Portfolio

Place a copy of your research report in your portfolio to review later.

Presenting

Follow Style Guidelines Before you hand in your final copy, be sure that all paragraphs and long quotations are indented correctly and that all sources are cited correctly. Be sure that your paper has a complete Works Cited list. Follow any other guidelines your teacher may require for a cover sheet, page numbers, margins, and other presentation details.

---

ted member of the civil rights effort." Have students shorten the quotation, using ellipsis points to indicate omission. *(Possible response: "Well before she made headlines across the country, she was . . . a committed member of the civil rights effort.")* **OL**

Differentiated Instruction

Proofreading in Pairs Say: It is often difficult to spot one's own mistakes in mechanics. Having someone else look over your work before finalizing it may be a good idea. Divide students into pairs so that they can review one another's work for grammatical and mechanical errors. **BL**

Teach

Writing Process

Editing and Proofreading
Suggest that students leave plenty of time to proofread their reports. Students should be especially careful in spotting and correcting punctuation and formatting mistakes in these areas:

- spacing, font and margins
- punctuation in and around quotations
- the Works Cited list

Writing Process

Presenting Reinforce for students the importance of taking pride in their work and in the final presentation of their research reports. **Say:** The initial impression your research report makes is important. While it is the overall quality of the content that determines your grade, be sure to present your report in a professional manner. **OL**

Objectives
- To write a research report (SE)
- To use ellipses (TWE)

1097

Focus

Summary

In this workshop, students will learn techniques for planning, rehearsing, and delivering an informative presentation to the class.

Teach

Speaking Skills

Preparing Graphic Organizers

Tell students that graphic organizers such as timelines and charts present information clearly and concisely. Offer these tips:

- Use graphic organizers to reinforce key facts.

- Make sure organizers are large, neat, simple, and clear enough to be seen by everyone.

- Practice incorporating graphic organizers smoothly.

- Be familiar with the content.

- Maintain eye contact with the audience while showing a graphic organizer. **OL**

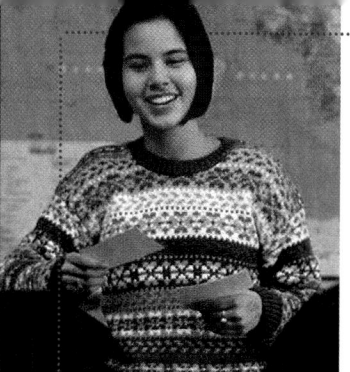

Speaking, Listening, and Viewing Workshop

Informative Presentation

Delivering an Informative Presentation

Connecting to Literature Go back in time to the days of King Arthur and the knights of the Round Table. Can you call to mind fierce warriors, colorful contests, beautiful ladies, a wise sorcerer, or a lady in the lake? These are all images that can create interest at the start of an oral informative presentation about King Arthur. That is just the beginning of your job, however. In this workshop, you will learn how to deliver an interesting informative presentation with a thesis and logical support.

> **Assignment** Create and deliver an informative presentation based on the topic of your research report.

Planning Your Presentation

The most important goal of your presentation is to state and support your thesis. As you do so, you must also create interest for an audience of listeners and viewers. Make all of these goals a part of your planning:

- **An interesting introduction and a satisfying conclusion**
  Consider telling a story or asking a thought-provoking question.
- **A clear statement of the thesis near the beginning of a presentation and an effective restatement at the end**
  You might wish to display your thesis on a board or screen.
- **Clearly stated main ideas with examples, quotations, and other information to back them up and make them clear**
  Display as well as state your main ideas.
- **References to your sources for ideas and quotations**
  Consider providing your audience with a handout.
- **Background information that reflects an understanding of what listeners need to know**
  Explain your ideas and information as you go along.
- **Images, props, slides, or other visuals to add interest and accurate information**
  Consider making slides or creating props or illustrations.
- **A smooth, confident delivery**
  Make cue cards to help you remember your points.

Organization

An informative report is organized like a research report: both require an interesting introduction that states a thesis; a body that contains main ideas, explanation, and support; and a conclusion that restates the thesis in a fresh way.

Avoid Plagiarism

Do you have to credit your sources in an oral report? Yes, you do. Use phrases such as "According to . . . " and "As [the source] says. . . . " Also, although piquing listeners' interest with intriguing or amusing information would be great, your first job is to be accurate and truthful.

Additional Support

Skills Practice

SPEAKING: Outlining Suggest that students consider themselves teachers as they give their informative presentations. Emphasize the importance of being organized in order to help their audience learn the information they are presenting. Point out that making an outline is an effective way to organize information for a presentation. Review with students the traditional format for an outline, and present several models on the overhead, as well as blank outlines for them to fill out. Note that outlines for speeches should be organized in a logical manner—chronologically, spatially, or in order of importance. Urge students to have you

Creating Props, Visual Aids, or Electronic Media

Create a chart to help you think of ideas for visuals.

Visual Ideas for "The Legend of King Arthur: The Facts of the Matter"	
Graphic Organizers	time line sequence chain
Illustrations	map showing places mentioned in report photos or pictures of things in report
Electronic Media	slides with key points and bullets short video selection from a King Arthur movie

Rehearsing

Rehearse in stages. First, say everything out loud to yourself, just as you might present it to the class. Repeat the process while using your visuals, props, or electronic media. Next, rehearse your presentation in front of friends or family members. At the end, call for questions. Also ask for suggestions for your presentation.

Finally, keep the following verbal and nonverbal techniques in mind as you practice and then as you deliver your presentation:

Techniques for Delivering a Presentation

Verbal Techniques	Nonverbal Techniques
☑ **Pace** Speak at a moderate, even rate as you present your thesis and support. You may vary your pace to create an engaging opening or dramatic closing.	☑ **Eye Contact** Look at your audience as much as possible.
☑ **Pronunciation** Speak clearly.	☑ **Posture** Stand or sit up straight. Avoid leaning.
☑ **Tone** Sound interested in your topic. Use your tone to highlight the most important points you make.	☑ **Gestures** Avoid nervous gestures such as foot tapping and hair twirling, but use natural hand gestures to reinforce ideas.
☑ **Volume** Speak loudly enough that everyone can hear you.	☑ **Facial Expressions** Match the look on your face to the ideas you are expressing.

Record and Revise

Record your practice session. Is your presentation clear and smooth? How are the pace and tone? Decide what you can improve.

Use a Mirror

If you cannot record yourself, try practicing in front of a mirror. Decide whether your facial expressions and body language send the right messages.

Ask for Specific Feedback

When you rehearse for friends or family, ask your listeners to comment on specific parts of your presentation, such as whether they understood your thesis and whether the points you made to support it were clear and convincing.

OBJECTIVES
- Deliver an oral presentation of research findings.
- Use props, visuals, and electronic media to enhance the oral presentation.

Teach

Listening Skills

Evaluating Information

Say: Pay attention to the clarity and completeness of the information your classmates present. For evaluation purposes, it is important to note whether the theses are presented clearly, both at the beginning and the end. In addition, evaluate how well the speakers' facts and information back up their theses. **Suggest that students create a checklist for use in evaluating their peers' presentations. OL**

Viewing Skills

Evaluating Visuals As students help their classmates rehearse, encourage them to pay special attention to the visual aids. Advise them to evaluate how well props and visuals reinforce the presenters' main ideas. Ask them to offer feedback to peers on how clearly, coherently, and smoothly visuals are worked into their presentations. OL

Differentiated Instruction

review and approve their outlines before they plan their presentations. Show students that by adding phrases they can develop their outline framework into speaking notes that can be used for their presentations. **OL**

Pacing One of the challenges of delivering a presentation is pacing it effectively, especially if students are nervous. Help less skilled students use a stopwatch to determine the ideal pace for their presentations, without being too rushed or plodding. Urge students to rehearse this pace. **BL**

Objectives
- To deliver an oral presentation of research findings (SE)
- To use props, visuals, and electronic media to enhance the oral presentation (SE)
- To outline a speech (TWE)

Focus

Summary

The purpose of this feature is to interest students in reading additional legends, myths, and folktales or works reflecting the themes of this unit: acts of courage, rescuing, and conquering. Many different cultures are represented in this selection of grade-appropriate works.

Teach

 Literary History

Fables Explain that fables are stories with morals and usually have animals as characters. The world's most famous fables are those written around 600 B.C. by Aesop, a Greek slave. In the seventeenth century, popular fables were written by La Fontaine. The tradition of fables continues in modern times in books such as Rudyard Kipling's *Jungle Books.* **AS**

Legends and Myths

LEGENDS, MYTHS, AND FOLKTALES are all traditional stories that vary in their forms and content. Legends generally glorify historical figures, giving them fictional traits and describing them in a sentimental tone. Folktales often focus on justice and may have a serious, humorous, or sentimental tone. Myths can explain natural phenomena or human relationships; their tone tends to be dignified. For more legends, myths, and folktales on a range of themes, try the first three suggestions below. For a novel and an epic poem that incorporate the Big Ideas of *Acts of Courage* and *Rescuing and Conquering,* try the titles from the Glencoe Literature Library on the next page.

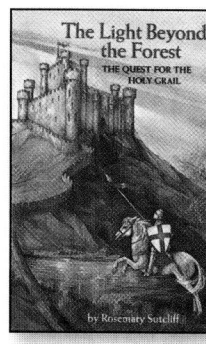

The Light Beyond The Forest

by Rosemary Sutcliff

In this retelling of part of the legend of King Arthur, the Knights of the Round Table set out in search of a relic known as the Holy Grail. This is a tale of heroism and adventure, but it also has tender, human moments, such as when the brave Lancelot first meets up with his son Galahad. Sir Lancelot, Sir Galahad, Sir Bors, and Sir Percival encounter many adventures, but always triumph over the forces of evil that threaten them physically and spiritually. This book is the second in a trilogy.

Cut from the Same Cloth: American Women of Myth, Legend, and Tall Tale

by Robert D. San Souci

Discover the United States' unheralded heroines who are as strong-willed and clever as their male counterparts. San Souci retells fifteen folktales, ballads, and stories about legendary women, presenting three tales from each of five regions of the United States: the Northeast, South, Midwest, Southwest, and West. The heroines, who range from Molly Cottontail to Pale-Faced Lightning, represent African Americans, Anglo Americans, Native Americans (including the Eskimo and Hawaiians), and Mexican Americans.

1100 UNIT 5 LEGENDS AND MYTHS

Additional Support

Skills Practice

READING: Comparing and Contrasting Encourage students to compare and contrast the folktales, myths, and legends that they read. **Say:** What do the tales reveal about the values of specific cultures? How is the concept of heroism similar and different in the various tales?

Specifically, suggest that students compare and contrast *The Light Beyond the Forest* with the King Arthur legend in this unit, "Arthur Becomes King," and the myths, legends, and tall tales in *Cut from the Same Cloth* with similar selections in this unit. **OL**

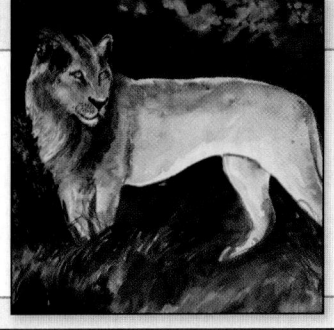

CRITICS' CORNER

"[The] quick, plainly told fables [in The Girl Who Married a Lion and Other Tales from Africa] feature places where people and animals live in close proximity and somebody has to walk miles to a river everyday just to collect water. The personalities of Africa's animals—the wiliness of the hare, the gullibility of the lion, the laziness of the baboon—take shape as the book proceeds. And there are clear moral lessons here. . . ."

—Maggie Galehouse, the *New York Times Book Review*

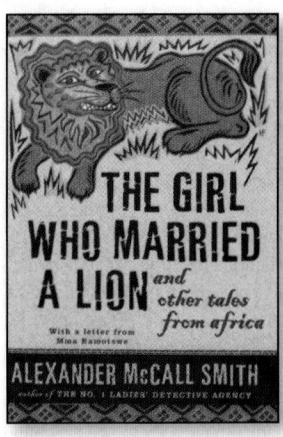

The Girl Who Married a Lion and Other Tales from Africa

by Alexander McCall Smith

The values and traditions of Zimbabwe and Botswana come alive in this collection of short tales collected and edited for an international audience by fiction writer Alexander McCall Smith. Like other tales from around the world, these stories have themes of ambition, jealousy, and love; they value community; they show greed being punished and loyalty rewarded; and they reflect a sense of humor. Many also personify the natural world, as titles such as "The Baboons Who Went This Way and That" reflect.

From the Glencoe Literature Library

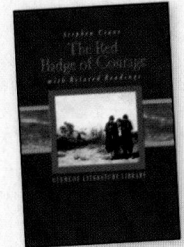

The Red Badge of Courage

by Stephen Crane

Facing his own fears, Henry Fleming performs *Acts of Courage* and returns to fight in the Civil War.

Beowulf ★

translated by Burton Raffel

A great warrior leads his people and slays a dragon in this tale of adventure and *Rescuing and Conquering.*

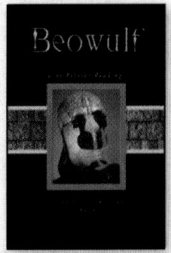

Teach

★ Literary History

Epic Poem Tell students that an epic poem is a long narrative poem that depicts a hero of high standing pursuing courageous acts important to a people's history. Epic poems have wide-ranging settings, are written in a lofty style, and usually include supernatural elements. Besides the Old English epic *Beowulf,* other epic poems important to different cultures include the Greek *Odyssey,* the Spanish *Cantar de mío Cid,* the French *Song of Roland,* and the Indian *Mahabharata.* **AS**

Glencoe Literature Library

Glencoe Literature Library offers an extensive collection of hardcover books that help you encourage your students to read independently. Choose among the more than 120 full-length literary works—novels, novellas, plays, and nonfiction. Each book includes related readings from a broad range of genres. Go to glencoe.com for more information.

Reading in the Real World

Citizenship Discuss how newspapers reflect modern-day culture, just as legends, myths, and folktales reflected earlier cultures. Invite students to look for allusions to famous myths, legends, and folktales in the newspaper. Also, ask them to compare heroes in the news with heroes of legends. **OL**

Differentiated Instruction

Oral Presentation Since legends, myths, and folktales originate in the oral tradition, have students reinforce their understanding of their independent reading by telling stories to the class. Discuss how oral literature differs from literature by individual authors. **OL**

Objectives
- To encourage independent reading of myths, legends, and folktales (SE)
- To compare and contrast in reading (TWE)

1101

Focus

BELLRINGER

Say: Knowing how to succeed on tests is a skill like any other. It takes practice to master. This test will help prepare you for tests to come and will give you insights into improving your reading and writing. Have groups of students make checklists of the strategies for test taking and test preparation that they have found most successful.

Teach

Assessment Tell students that Test Preparation and Practice is designed to develop their skill in test-taking strategies as well as to test their mastery of the skills and vocabulary covered in this unit. Students will be asked to read two selections related to King Arthur and then answer questions that test reading and vocabulary skills. They will also use their grammar and writing skills to improve a writing passage, and finally they will write a short essay. **OL**

Test Preparation and Practice

English–Language Arts

Reading: Epic and Myth

Carefully read the following passage. Use context clues to help you define any words with which you are unfamiliar. Pay close attention to rhetorical devices and character development. Then, on a separate sheet of paper, answer questions 1–10, on page 1104.

from "King Arthur" by Donna Rosenberg

based on *History of the Kings of Britain* by Geoffrey of Monmouth

line

The horrible appearance of the fiend was matched only by the terrible nature of his deeds. His face was darkly splotched like the skin of a frog. His eyebrows hung low over his eyes, which burned with fire. His ears were enormous, and his nose was hooked like a hawk's beak. His mouth was as flat as a flounder's, and his fat, loose, fleshy lips spread apart to display his swollen gums. His bristly

5   black beard fell over his chest, concealing part of his fat body. He had the broad neck and shoulders of a bull. His arms and legs stretched out like the limbs of a mighty oak tree. From the top of his head to the tip of his shovel-shaped feet, he was thirty feet tall.

The giant wore a tunic made from human hair, fringed with the beards of men. He carried the corpses of twelve peasants tied together on his back. In his hand, he carried a club so mighty that the

10   two strongest farmers in the land could not have lifted it off the ground.

The giant dropped the corpses by the fire and approached Arthur with broad strides. As Arthur fingered Excalibur, he saw that the giant's mouth was still smeared with the clotted blood and scraps of flesh from his last meal. Even his beard and his hair were strewn with gore.

Arthur said to him, "May great God in heaven, who rules the world, give you a short life and a

15   shameful death! Surely you are the most foul fiend that was ever formed! Guard yourself, you dog, and prepare to die, for this day my hands will kill you!"

The giant responded by raising his fearsome club. He grinned like a ferocious boar, confident of its menacing tusks. Then he growled, and foam spilled from his gaping mouth.

King Arthur raised his shield and prayed to God that it would protect him against the fiend's

20   mighty club. The giant's first blow fell upon Arthur's shield, making the cliffs clang like an anvil and shattering his source of protection. The shock of the impact almost knocked Arthur to the ground, but he quickly recovered.

The blow ignited King Arthur's rage, and he furiously struck the giant on the forehead with his sword. Blood gushed into the giant's eyes and down his cheeks, blinding him.

25   Just as an enraged boar, its flesh torn from the attacks of hunting hounds, turns and charges upon a hunter, so the giant, maddened with the pain of his wound, rushed with a roar upon King

Additional Support

Skills Practice

READING: Reading for a Test

Say: Reading for a test is different from reading for pleasure or for class. Your goal is to answer the questions correctly, not to understand the passage thoroughly. Help students practice reading passages quickly, visually "mapping" their contents and then returning to the passage as they answer questions if they need to look at specific details. Help students to pace themselves so that they don't spend too much time concentrating on the passage and leave themselves with too little time for the questions. Practice with sample reading-comprehension passages from standardized tests. **OL**

Arthur. Groping blindly with his hands, the giant grabbed the king by the shoulders and clasped him
to his chest, trying to crush Arthur's ribs and burst his heart. King Arthur summoned all of his strength
and twisted his body out from under the giant's grasp.

30   "Peace to you, my lord!" the giant exclaimed. "Who are you that fights so skillfully with me? Only
Arthur, the most noble of all kings, could defeat me in combat!"

"I am that Arthur of whom you speak," the king replied. Then, quick as lightning, Arthur struck the
giant repeatedly with his sword.

Informational Reading Carefully read the following data, paying close attention to **R**
details and any specific instructions. Then answer questions 11–14, on page 1104.

FANTASCOPE
Now Showing: King Arthur Festival
100 hours of continuous viewing—October 13 to October 19
The *BEST* and *WORST* of cinematographic treatments of the LEGEND
Program for October 13

5

King Arthur, directed by Antoine Fuqua
Writing credit: David Franzoni
Cast: Clive Owen, Ioan Gruffudd, Keira Knightley
Saturn Award nominee, 2005

10   Review: *Chicago Sun-Times* ROGER EBERT—* * * "Considerable production values," "Charisma"
Show times: 8 A.M., 6 P.M., 4 A.M.

Monty Python and the Holy Grail, directed by Terry Gilliam and Terry Jones
Writing credits: Graham Chapman, John Cleese
Cast: Graham Chapman, John Cleese, Eric Idle, Terry Gilliam, Terry Jones, Michael Palin

15   Winner of the 1976 **Hugo Award** for Best Dramatic Presentation
Review: GEORGE PERRY—"a classic comedy"
Show times: 8 A.M., 6 P.M., 4 A.M.

The Spaceman and King Arthur, directed by Russ Mayberry
Writing credits: Don Tait, Mark Twain (novel)

20   Cast: Dennis Dugan, Jim Dale, Ron Moody, Kenneth More, John Le Mesurier
Review: *Cold Fusion Video Review*—"overcontrived," "clueless," "lackluster," "Twain's *A Connecticut
Yankee in King Arthur's Court* . . . inexplicably tempts movie producers to make variations on it."
Show times: 10 A.M., 8 P.M.

Camelot, directed by Josh Logan

25   Writing credits: T. H. White (novel), Alan Jay Lerner
Cast: Richard Harris, Vanessa Redgrave
Winner of three **Oscars** and three **Golden Globe Awards**
Review: *Shadows on the Wall*—"So corny you've got to love it."
Show times: noon, 10 P.M.

Teach

R Reading Strategy

Informational Reading
Emphasize that purpose shapes the process of reading. Discuss the purpose of informational reading, and give students practice in seeking specific facts in informational texts, such as train schedules, recipes, and instruction booklets. Point out that students should preview such a text to get clues to its contents, and show them how to skim a text to get a general overview of it. **OL**

Differentiated Instruction

Preparing for Standardized Tests
Less proficient students will need additional practice and preparation for standardized tests. Give them these tips:

• Find out whether you are penalized for wrong guesses. If so, skip questions when you don't know the answer.

• Be careful how you mark the answer sheet, because stray marks can be counted as answers.

• Check question numbers to ensure your answers are in the right place.

• Check your answers. **BL**

Assess

1. **D** is the correct answer. Options **A, B,** and **C** do not have the same or even a similar meaning to *fiend*.

2. **F** is the correct answer. The phrase is a comparison of essentially unlike things in which the word *like* is used.

3. **C** is the correct answer. The second paragraph states that the tunic is made of human hair.

4. **G** is the correct answer. The repetition of the /b/ sound at the beginning of adjacent words is alliterative.

5. **B** is the correct answer. The words *fearsome* and *ferocious* offer context clues.

6. **F** is the correct answer. Arthur is the hero.

7. **D** is the correct answer. Options **A** and **C** do not fit the context. Option **B** comes closer, but in context *called forth* is most appropriate.

8. **F** is the correct answer. The word *as* is used in this comparison.

9. **B** is the correct answer. Arthur is not magical, nor is his battle with the giant trivial, so options **A** and **C** are incorrect. Option **D** is

Items 1–10 apply to "from 'King Arthur.'"

1. From the context, what do you think that the word *fiend*, in line 1, means?
   - **A.** animal
   - **B.** cohort
   - **C.** felon
   - **D.** brute

2. Which of the following literary elements is used in the phrase *his nose was hooked like a hawk's beak*, in line 3?
   - **F.** simile
   - **G.** irony
   - **H.** allusion
   - **J.** metaphor

3. What is the giant's tunic made from?
   - **A.** a mighty oak
   - **B.** boars' hair
   - **C.** human hair
   - **D.** scraps of flesh

4. Which of the following sound devices appears in the phrase *bristly black beard*, in lines 4 and 5?
   - **F.** consonance
   - **G.** alliteration
   - **H.** assonance
   - **J.** allusion

5. From the context, what do you think that the word *menacing*, in line 18, means?
   - **A.** alarming
   - **B.** threatening
   - **C.** imminent
   - **D.** destructive

6. Which of the following best describes Arthur's role in the passage?
   - **F.** protagonist
   - **G.** antagonist
   - **H.** rival
   - **J.** narrator

7. From the context, what do you think that the word *summoned*, in line 28, means?
   - **A.** appeared
   - **B.** collected
   - **C.** sent for
   - **D.** called forth

8. Which of the following literary elements is used in the phrase *quick as lightning* in line 32?
   - **F.** simile
   - **G.** irony
   - **H.** allusion
   - **J.** metaphor

9. From the context, what might qualify Arthur as a heroic character?
   - **A.** He possesses magical powers.
   - **B.** He defeats a villainous force.
   - **C.** He undertakes a trivial risk.
   - **D.** He is a nobleman.

10. Which of the following plot-pattern archetypes appears in this passage?
    - **F.** secret birth
    - **G.** impossible task
    - **H.** honorable death as ruler
    - **J.** revelation as favored heir

Items 11–14 apply to "Fantascope."

11. Which film did Twain's novel inspire?
    - **A.** *Monty Python and the Holy Grail*
    - **B.** *The Spaceman and King Arthur*
    - **C.** *Camelot*
    - **D.** *A Connecticut Yankee in King Arthur's Court*

12. Which film is described as a comedy?
    - **F.** *Monty Python and the Holy Grail*
    - **G.** *The Spaceman and King Arthur*
    - **H.** *Camelot*
    - **J.** *King Arthur*

13. Which component of the movie billing offers a critical opinion of the film's merit?
    - **A.** review excerpts
    - **B.** directing credits
    - **C.** writing credits
    - **D.** awards and nominations

14. Which film won the greatest number of awards?
    - **F.** *Monty Python and the Holy Grail*
    - **G.** *The Spaceman and King Arthur*
    - **H.** *Camelot*
    - **J.** *King Arthur*

true, but it is not sufficient to qualify Arthur as heroic.

10. **G** is the correct answer. Slaying the giant is an "impossible" task that Arthur accomplishes.

11. **B** is the correct answer. Both the writing credits and the review mention Twain's novel.

12. **F** is the correct answer. The review of the Monty Python film identifies it as a comedy.

13. **A** is the correct answer. Each film has a review or a quotation from a film critic that contains an opinion of the film.

14. **H** is the correct answer. The movie bill clearly states that *Camelot* won six awards, more than any of the others.

Vocabulary Skills: Sentence Completion

For each item in the Vocabulary Skills section, choose the word that best completes the sentence.

1. Each soldier trained for long hours to engage a/an _____ in battle.
   A. confidante
   B. enmity
   C. combatant
   D. bane

2. The country club members considered an average person too _____ for their exclusive society.
   F. vulgar
   G. scrupulous
   H. interminable
   J. tumultuous

3. The brawny hero demonstrated great physical _____ when engaged in mortal combat.
   A. bane
   B. prowess
   C. guile
   D. renown

4. The jury spent hours in _____ before reaching a decision.
   F. guile
   G. jubilance
   H. prowess
   J. deliberation

5. His _____ birth doomed him to remain always a peon, excluded from the rights of landowners.
   A. ignoble
   B. aggrieved
   C. disdainful
   D. discourteous

6. The _____ banquet pleased the king, though his taste was usually for simpler fare.
   F. strategic
   G. interminable
   H. vulgar
   J. sumptuous

7. The escaped criminal crept through back alleys in an effort to _____ his pursuers.
   A. perpetuate
   B. vault
   C. confront
   D. elude

8. Skilled chess players may sacrifice a game piece in order to make a/an _____ move.
   F. petulant
   G. strategic
   H. contemptible
   J. aggrieved

9. The only way to restore their friendship was to _____ the wrong she had done.
   A. redress
   B. throng
   C. beset
   D. perpetuate

10. His dreary lesson was the _____ of his week.
   F. deliberation
   G. renown
   H. bane
   J. guile

 Literature Online **Unit Assessment** To prepare for the Unit test, go to www.glencoe.com.

Assess

1. **C** is the correct answer. No other option makes sense in this context.

2. **F** is the correct answer. The context requires a word meaning "common" or "unrefined."

3. **B** is the correct answer. The key words here are *brawny* and *great,* which suggest ability and skill.

4. **J** is the correct answer. No other option makes sense in this context.

5. **A** is the correct answer. The key word is *peon,* suggesting low birth. Options **B** and **C** do not fit this context. *Discourteous* means "impolite," so option **D** is incorrect.

6. **J** is the correct answer. The king's taste for "simpler fare" is unlike a "sumptuous," or lavish, banquet.

7. **D** is the correct answer. Options **A** and **B** make no sense in the context. Option **C** is an antonym of the correct answer.

8. **G** is the correct answer. No other option fits this context.

9. **A** is the correct answer. No other option fits this context.

10. **H** is the correct answer. No other option makes sense in this context.

English Language Coach

Word Origins Help English language learners decode words by examining word origins. For example, *interminable,* comes from the Latin *terminare* ("to end"), also seen in *terminal* and *terminate.* Provide lists of Latin roots and definitions, and have students practice with examples such as *exculpate.* **EL**

Literature Online

Unit Assessment Have students access the Web site to prepare for the Unit Five test.

1105

Assess

1. **D** is the correct answer. A comma must follow a lengthy phrase that begins a sentence.

2. **G** is the correct answer. This singular subject *mythology* requires a singular verb.

3. **B** is the correct answer. These fragments are not used effectively. No other option corrects this error without introducing further errors.

4. **H** is the correct answer. Only this option is appropriate to the topic and organization of this paragraph.

5. **C** is the correct answer. This is a run-on sentence. No other option corrects this error without changing the content or introducing further errors.

6. **H** is the correct answer. A comma must follow a subordinate clause that begins a sentence.

7. **D** is the correct answer. The transition *however* must be set off with commas.

Grammar and Writing Skills: Paragraph Improvement

In the following excerpt from a student's first draft of a persuasive essay, numbers appear beneath underlined parts. The numbers correspond to items below that provide options for replacing, or ask questions about, the underlined parts. On a separate sheet of paper, record the letter of the best option in each item. If you think that the original should not be changed, choose "NO CHANGE."

Numbers that appear in boxes refer to questions about specific paragraphs or about the essay as a whole. If one of these questions is about the sentence order in a paragraph, sentence numbers within that paragraph correspond to question numbers, not to the sequence of sentences or paragraphs.

Read the passage through once before you begin to answer the questions. As you read, pay close attention to the writer's use of main and subordinate clauses, commas, and organization.

[1]

<u>While central to England's Age of Chivalry the legend of King Arthur extends to the whole of Western civilization.</u> The legends of Arthur may have originated with an actual chieftain in Wales, and most historical novels place Arthur in the sixth century. <u>Even so, the mythology surrounding Camelot and King Arthur have been told and retold</u> in countless versions over time. <u>Movies. Novels. Poems. Parodies.</u> The legend developed from a popular myth to become something far more universal.

[2]

4 <u>He probably bore little resemblance to the legendary hero scholars assume that an actual person inspired the myth.</u> But in his earliest literary form, Arthur appears almost entirely mythical. <u>Although he does have some human characteristics Arthur and his companions often demonstrate superhuman strength and consort with mythological creatures.</u> <u>By the time of the 13th century however</u> Arthur becomes more like a typical king and less of a hero, no longer the powerful warrior of the early tradition.

[3]

<u>The debate about Arthur's actual existence, will continue because there is no conclusive evidence.</u> <u>Whether</u> lived or invented, however, the story of Arthur has had an undeniable influence on literature, art, music, and all Western society. Maybe it is the appeal to a lost ideal that attracts so many of us to this legendary figure. 10

Additional Support

Skills Practice

GRAMMAR: Subject-Verb Agreement Write on the board: The teller of stories and legends (wander/wanders) the countryside. **Ask:** Which is the correct verb? *(wanders)* Students may become confused when a prepositional phrase intervenes between subject and verb. Diagraming this sentence clarifies that the subject is *teller,* demanding the singular verb *wanders.* Also review subject-verb agreement for sentences in unusual order, such as "There (is/are) many legends to tell." Once again, diagraming helps students to see that the subject is *legends,* demanding the plural verb *are.* **OL**

1. **A.** NO CHANGE
   B. Lowercase *Chivalry.*
   C. Insert a semicolon after *Chivalry.*
   D. Insert a comma after *Chivalry.*

2. **F.** NO CHANGE
   G. Change *have* to *has.*
   H. Change *Even so* to *Although.*
   J. Change *Even so* to *In fact.*

3. **A.** NO CHANGE
   B. Examples include movies, novels, poems, and parodies written from many perspectives and in different languages.
   C. Examples include; movies, novels, poems, and parodies written from many perspectives and in different languages.
   D. Examples including movies, novels, poems, and parodies written from many perspectives and in different languages.

4. Which sentence, if inserted here, would provide the most effective transition into this paragraph?
   F. The existence of Arthur is unimportant.
   G. No question about it—Arthur did exist.
   H. There is still debate about whether Arthur was an actual historical figure.
   J. Few care whether Arthur actually lived or not.

5. **A.** NO CHANGE
   B. Insert a comma after the word *hero.*
   C. Insert a comma and the word *but* after *hero.*
   D. Insert commas around *to the legendary hero.*

6. **F.** NO CHANGE
   G. Insert semicolons after *characteristics* and after *strength.*
   H. Insert a comma after the word *characteristics.*
   J. Change the verb *consort* to *consorts.*

7. **A.** NO CHANGE
   B. By the time of the thirteenth century; however,
   C. By the time of the thirteenth century, however;
   D. By the time of the thirteenth century, however,

8. **F.** NO CHANGE
   G. The debate about Arthur's actual existence will continue because: there is no conclusive evidence.
   H. The debate about Arthur's actual existence will continue, because there is no conclusive evidence.
   J. Because no conclusive evidence exists the debate about Arthur's actual existence will continue.

9. **A.** NO CHANGE
   B. While
   C. Although
   D. Once

10. Which of the following has the writer successfully included in the concluding paragraph?
    F. the introduction of opposite viewpoints
    G. information not included in previous paragraphs
    H. a summary of the key points in the essay
    J. conclusive evidence of Arthur's existence and influence

Assess

8. **H** is the correct answer. The comma should separate the main clause from the subordinate clause that begins with *because.*

9. **A** is the correct answer. The sentence contains no error. *Whether* is used to introduce alternatives.

10. **H** is the correct answer. The final paragraph clearly states, "there is no conclusive evidence," so option **J** is incorrect. It includes neither new information nor opposing viewpoints, so options **F** and **G** are also incorrect.

Essay

Students' essay should

- discuss the importance of the hero in literature and society
- identify qualities of a hero
- give examples from unit selections
- have a clear thesis, introduction, supporting paragraphs, and conclusion

Essay

The hero has long been part of literature and society. Write an essay in which you discuss the importance of that role. First, define some qualities that characterize a hero. Next, with examples from one or more of the readings in this unit, show how these larger-than-life figures function in literature and what they mean to society and the average person. As you write, keep in mind that your essay will be checked for **ideas**, **organization**, **voice**, **word choice**, **sentence fluency**, **conventions**, and **presentation**.

Differentiated Instruction

Supporting a Thesis Emphasize the importance of using examples to illustrate main points in an essay. Guide less practiced writers in creating an outline, laying out examples that will offer the best support. Remind students that transitional phrases such as *for instance* help introduce examples. **BL**

English Language Coach

Transitional Phrases Prepare English language learners for test taking by explaining the shades of differences among various transitional phrases. Ask students to give examples of transitional devices that show contrast, addition, similarity, sequence, confirmation, and illustration. **EL**

Unit at a Glance

MYSTERY, MODERN FABLE, AND SCIENCE FICTION/FANTASY

About the Unit

Unit Six covers science fiction, fantasy, modern fable, and mystery.

Part 1: The Extraordinary and Fantastic
6–8 days

Part 1 covers science fiction, fantasy, and modern fable. A chart showing the core skills taught in this Part appears on pages 1117A–1117B.

SELECTIONS AND FEATURES

Part 2: The Uncanny and Mysterious
5–6 days

Part 2 covers mystery. A chart showing the core skills taught in this Part appears on pages 181A–1181B.

SELECTIONS AND FEATURES

LITERARY FOCUS: Style and Tone
pp. 1182–1183

Agatha Christie, "The Witness for the Prosecution"
pp. 1184–1204

Grammar Workshop: Mechanics
p. 1205

Sir Arthur Conan Doyle, "The Adventure of the Speckled Band"
pp. 1206–1228

Vocabulary Workshop: Language Resources
p. 1229

O. Henry, "A Retrieved Reformation"
pp. 1230–1239

Joan Aiken, "Lungewater"
pp. 1240–1255

End-of-Unit Features
5–6 days

Writing Workshop: Short Story
pp. 1256–1263

Professional Model: Isaac Asimov, "Frustration"
p. 1257

Speaking, Listening, and Viewing Workshop: Presenting an Oral Interpretation of a Short Story
pp. 1264–1265

INDEPENDENT READING
pp. 1266–1267

Test Preparation and Practice
pp. 1268–1273

Unit Resources

Glencoe Literature: The Reader's Choice offers a comprehensive package of tools to optimize student learning and the teaching experience. Each resource has been designed to assist students in specific areas and to offer instructional support for teachers. While all of these areas are covered in the core textbook, some students may need extra practice or additional help in specific areas. The resource package is designed so that you, the teacher, can choose which items will best assist your students. You may also use these resources as homework assignments and for assessment purposes. The following are resources recommended for use with Unit 6.

Key for Unit Resources

📁 Blackline Master   📀 DVD

📄 Workbook   🔖 Transparency

📖 Supplemental Text   💻 Web-based

💿 CD-ROM

Essential Instructional Support

 Unit 6 Resources

Reading and Literature

- Unit Introduction, pp. 1–2
- The Big Idea Foldable, pp. 3–4
- The Big Idea School-Home Connection, p. 5
- The Big Idea School-Home Connection (Spanish), p. 6
- Challenge Planner, pp. 7–10
- Academic Vocabulary Development, pp. 11–13
- Comparing Literature Graphic Organizer, p. 24
- Literary Elements, pp. 17, 20, 25, 29, 33, 39, 43, 46, 49
- Reading Strategies, pp. 18, 21, 26, 28, 30, 32, 34, 40, 44, 47, 50
- Active Reading Graphic Organizers, pp. 55–64
- Selection Vocabulary Practice, pp. 19, 22, 27, 31, 35, 41, 45, 48, 51
- Literary Focus, pp. 15, 37

Writing, Grammar, and Spelling

- Spelling Practice, p. 52
- Grammar Workshop, pp. 23, 42
- Writing Workshop Graphic Organizer, p. 53

Speaking, Listening, and Viewing

- Speaking, Listening, and Viewing Activity, p. 54

English Language Learners

- English Language Coach, pp. 16, 38

Differentiated Instruction

📄 Active Learning and Note Taking Guide, pp. 178–210

📁 Leveled Vocabulary Development, pp. 77–85

💿 Skill Level Up!™ A Language Arts Game

💿 Listening Library Audio CD, disc 2, tracks 30–43

💿 Glencoe BookLink 3

💿 Vocabulary PuzzleMaker

💿 Literature Library Vocabulary PuzzleMaker

ASSESSMENT

📁 Selection and Unit Assessments, pp. 187–208, 219–220

📁 Selection Quick Checks, pp. 94–104

📁 Selection Quick Checks (Spanish), pp. 94–104

📁 Assessment by Learning Objectives, pp. 61–68

📁 Rubrics for Assessing Student Writing, Listening, and Speaking, pp. 22–23, 46–47

📁 Standardized Test Preparation and Practice

💻 Glencoe Online Essay Grader

💿 Interactive Tutor: Self-Assessment

💿 ExamView® Assessment Suite

💿 Literature Library ExamView® Assessment

Additional Instructional Support

Literature and Reading

- Active Learning and Note Taking Guide, pp. 178–212
- *inTIME* Magazines
- Glencoe Literature Library
- Literature Launchers: Pre-Reading Videos
- Literature Classics

Writing, Grammar, and Spelling

- REAL Success in Writing: Research and Reports
- Writing Constructed Responses
- Spelling Power eWorkbook
- Revising with Style eWorkbook
- Sentence Diagraming eWorkbook
- Glencoe Grammar and Composition Handbook
- Grammar and Language Workbook
- Grammar & Language eWorkbook

PROFESSIONAL DEVELOPMENT

- Professional Development Package

Transparencies

- Read Aloud, Think Aloud Transparencies 32–35
- Bellringer Options Transparencies
  - Selection Focus Transparencies 44–47
  - Daily Language Practice Transparencies 92–102
- Grammar and Language Transparencies 21, 45, 70
- Writing Workshop Transparencies 31–35
- Visual Literacy/Fine Art Transparencies

English Language Learner

- English Language Coach
- *inTIME* Magazines (Spanish)
- Spanish Listening Library

Technology

- TeacherWorks Plus™
- StudentWorks Plus™
- Literature Launchers: Pre-Reading Videos
- Vocabulary PuzzleMaker
- Literature Library Vocabulary PuzzleMaker
- Skill Level Up!™ A Language Arts Game
- glencoe.com
- Presentation Plus!™
- Exam*View*® Assessment Suite
- Literature Library Exam*View*® Assessment Suite
- Listening Library Audio CD, disc 2, tracks 30–43
- Interactive Tutor: Self-Assessment
- Glencoe BookLink 3
- Online Student Edition, mhln.com
- Glencoe Online Essay Grader
- Grammar and Language eWorkbook
- Revising with Style eWorkbook
- Sentence Diagraming eWorkbook
- Spelling Power eWorkbook
- Literature Classics
- Spanish Listening Library

Additional Glencoe Resources

Dinah Zike's Foldables™

Foldables™ are three-dimensional, interactive graphic organizers that help students practice basic writing skills, review key vocabulary terms, and answer Big Ideas. Every unit contains a Foldable activity. You can find the pattern and directions for the Unit 6 Foldable in the Unit 6 Resources Fast File booklet. You can use the foldables as they are presented or modify them to suit the needs of your students.

For a wealth of online resources that support the instruction in Unit 6, students and teachers can visit our Web site at glencoe.com. Students will find additional learning, practice, and assessment opportunities such as these, which are noted in the student text:

- Author Search
- Big Idea Overview and Activity
- Interactive Literary Elements Handbook
- Study Central
- Unit Assessment
- Web Activities
- Writing Models

Teachers will find planning and instructional tools that include the following:

- Book Lesson Plans
- Web Activity Lesson Plans
- Teacher Forum
- Professional Resources

  Go to glencoe.com to see the entire selection of *Glencoe Literature* online resources.

Glencoe's Presentation Plus!™, a multimedia teaching tool, lets you present dynamic lessons that will engage your students. Using Microsoft PowerPoint®, you can customize the presentations to create your own personalized lessons. Use CheckPoint questions with interactive response keypads to get immediate student feedback during lessons, to increase student participation, and to assess student comprehension.

Glencoe Literature Library

The collection of hardcover books includes full-length novels, novellas, plays, and works of nonfiction. Each volume consists of at least one complete extended-length reading accompanied by several related readings from a broad range of genres. A separate Study Guide for each *Glencoe Literature Library* book provides teaching notes and reproducible activity pages for students. Glencoe Literature Library titles that complement this unit include:

- ***The Strange Case of Dr. Jekyll and Mr. Hyde with Related Readings*** by Robert Louis Stevenson
- ***Frankenstein with Related Readings*** by Mary Shelley

GLENCOE BOOKLINK

Use the Glencoe **BookLink 3** CD-ROM, a database of more than 26,700 titles, to *create customized reading lists* for your students.

- Search for award-winning titles (e.g., Newbery Award winners, Coretta Scott King Award winners, and Caldecott Medal winners) and for books on several state recommended reading lists.
- Find Degrees of Reading Power™ (DRP) and Lexile™ readability scores for all selections.
- Organize reading lists by students' reading level, author, genre, theme, or area of interest.
- Get a brief summary of each selection.

You can find recommended leveled readings for this unit with Independent Reading (see pages 1266 and 1267).

Online Essay Grader

Use Glencoe's online essay grader powered by SkillWriter™ to score your students' writing and to provide individualized feedback to each student automatically.

You and your students can visit glencoe.com to link to the essay grader. *Students* can enter their essays and receive feedback on demand. *You* can manage demographic data, assign tests, and generate individual student and aggregated reports. The essay grader can help you

- Save time with automatic scoring and individualized feedback.
- Supplement in-class writing instruction using guided writing practice.

REAL Success: Reading Excellence at All Levels

Glencoe REAL Success is a suite of new reading and language arts products designed to foster reading excellence at all levels. Look for TWE point-of-use references for these specific products that will help your students succeed in reading this Unit.

- *Jamestown Literature: An Adapted Reader,* Grade 10
- REAL Success in Writing: Research and Reports
- Skill Level Up! A Language Arts Game
- CheckPoint PowerPoint™ slides
- Literature/Reading support at Glencoe Web site

A lively collection of articles drawn from issues of the TIME family of magazines helps students develop the skills they need to interact with informational text in a meaningful way. Each of the news stories, feature articles, reviews, profiles, and essays in the magazine connect to an author, work, or theme in *Glencoe Literature: The Reader's Choice.* See the *inTIME* Teacher's Guide for specific connections to each unit and for reproducible student worksheets designed to develop students' reading and critical thinking skills.

Literature Launchers

Set the scene with Glencoe's Literature Launchers, engaging pre-reading video segments that introduce each unit. Each Unit Launcher brings the literature to life, featuring expert testimony and archival stills and footage from the time.

Insert your Glencoe Literature Launchers into your DVD player. Select the Unit 6 Launcher from the menu to introduce Genre Fiction.

Teacher Wraparound Edition Key

Level Appropriate Code

AL = Activities for students working above grade level

OL = Activities for students working at grade level

BL = Activities for students working below grade level

EL = Activities for English language learners

AS = Information for all students

Teacher Wraparound Prompts

R **Reading Skill** These activities help you teach reading skills and vocabulary.

V **Vocabulary** These activities help students comprehend words and incorporate them into reading.

BI **Big Idea** These activities and questions prompt students to explore the Big Idea.

L **Literary Element** These activities and questions help students comprehend selections and learn more about each genre.

★ **Enrichment** Additional activities and information involving art appreciation and history.

Professional Development Center

From Your Authors:

Teaching Literary Analysis: Mystery, Modern Fable, And Science Fiction

Make Media Connections Ask students to discuss the ways in which the media portrays the genre of mystery and the genre of science fiction. What sound effects are common in mysteries? In science fiction? What types of visual images are used for these two genres? Ask students to think about particular movies or television shows they have seen that represent these two genres. Then have students use the same questions to compare two short stories from these genres. After students have read "The Adventure of the Speckled Band" by Sir Arthur Conan Doyle and "A Sound of Thunder" by Ray Bradbury, ask them to create a T chart. What makes these two genres unique? How do you know that you are reading a mystery? When do you know you are reading a work of science fiction? Do the genres share any qualities? Have students answer the questions in their chart to see the similarities and differences between the two stories.

Start with an Illustration Using a series of illustrations or photos, ask students to classify the visual information as mystery, science fiction, or other. How do they know which category to place each illustration in? Ask students to discuss the visual information. Develop a list of vocabulary terms that they might find in each of these genres, such as "mysterious" or "futuristic." Students will likely use a number

Jeffrey D. Wilhelm and Beverly Chin

of terms in their discussions that are common to the genres themselves. Then, have students examine the artwork presented with "The Witness for the Prosecution" by Agatha Christie and the artwork accompanying "By the Waters of Babylon" by Stephen Vincent Benét. Ask students to explain how the two pieces represent the two different genres.

Teacher to Teacher

As a librarian, I welcome classes to the library when they are starting a new literature unit. Students can use the wealth of resources in the library, including books, databases, and websites, to build background on a particular subject. For this unit, I collaborate with the teacher to create a list of questions students must answer about the characteristics of fables. After students have read through the fables they find, identifying similar elements in each one, we ask them to create a modern fable in which they incorporate the same elements. Students love to put a modern twist on traditional tales!

**Katherine Voss
St. Benedict High School
Chicago, Illinois**

Teacher Chat Room

Making Literature Come Alive

Before you begin this unit or sometime during the unit, talk with other teachers about ways they have taught mystery and science fiction. Have a lunch-time discussion group or an after-school hour for professional development and discuss the following questions and answers from our authors:

How can reading mysteries build students' skills in making predictions?

- Mysteries provide students with an excellent opportunity to focus on making and revising predictions. Students should regularly pause while reading mysteries and log their predictions. The key to learning to predict lies in learning from wrong predictions and reviewing the text for missed clues. As students read "The Adventure of the Speckled Band" by Sir Arthur Conan Doyle, have them pause after every other page to write down their predictions of what will happen next. As students continue to read, have them revise their predictions to make them more accurate.

- In addition to predicting, students can be provided with a simple definition of deductive and inductive logic and be asked to analyze their thinking as they read. Discussing these thought processes with students and helping them understand the way their minds work builds their metacognitive skills. As students read "Lungewater," by Joan Aiken, ask students to be aware of and take notes on their thinking process as they read.

What thinking skills can students learn from fictional detectives?

- Solving Problems
- Using evidence
- Persevering
- Maintaining integrity

After students read Agatha Christie's "The Witness for the Prosecution," ask them to write about what they have learned from the characters. Have students explain how the characters display the characteristics listed above.

How can reading science fiction help enhance students' knowledge of technology?

- Science fiction is known for its unique applications of technology to solve problems. Consider showing your students clips from the original Star Trek series. Discuss the range of technology now available that was barely thinkable at the time the show was written.

- Invite students to keep a log of the technology used in science fiction that was not available at the time of the writing of the text. Ask them to analyze their list and determine how much technology has evolved. Have students keep a technology log as they read "A Sound of Thunder" by Ray Bradbury and "Robot Dreams" by Isaac Asimov. After reading both, lead students in a discussion of how technology has evolved since these selections were written.

- Discuss the future of technology. How might science fiction contribute to the development of new technology? Discuss the idea that this field of literature has had a profound impact on technology research and development.

Focus

BELLRINGER

Bellringer Options
Literature Launcher Video
Daily Language Practice
Transparency 92
Or challenge students with "what if" questions **Ask:** What can you imagine it would be like if you lived one thousand years from now? What kind of civilization can you imagine on another planet or in another reality? What kind of case can you dream up for a detective? Encourage students to dream up imaginative scenarios, and point out that writers of science fiction and other types of genre fiction do just that. **Say:** The imagination of science fiction, mystery, and fantasy writers leads them to create intriguing fictional worlds. Point out that these are some of the most popular types of writing today, and encourage students to explore these imaginative forms.

Objectives for Unit Six
- To understand characteristics of mysteries, modern fables, and science fiction (SE)
- To identify and explore literary elements significant to the genres (SE)
- To analyze the effect that these literary elements have upon the reader (SE)
- To analyze an author's style (TWE)

The Homecoming, 1996. Peter Szumowski. Oil on canvas, 91.4 x 152.4 cm. Private collection. ★

1108 UNIT 6 GENRE FICTION

Unit Introduction Skills

Reading Skills
- Evaluating Author's Style (SE p. 1113)

Literary Elements
- Identifying Genre (SE pp. 1109–1116)
- Analyzing Sensory Details (TWE p. 1110)

Genre Fiction

Listening/Speaking/Viewing Skills
- Illustrating Part of a Story (SE p. 1116)

Writing Skills/Grammar
- Main Idea and Details (TWE p. 1114)

Genre Fiction

Looking Ahead

Genre fiction is a flexible term used to group works of fiction that have similar characters, plots, or settings. Bookstores and libraries often shelve some of their fiction by genre categories—for example, romance, mystery, science fiction, and fantasy. Different from myths and folktales, genre fiction does not emerge from the oral traditions of cultures, nor is it usually rooted in history. Mysteries are often set in the present, fantasies in an indeterminate past or a distorted present, and science fiction in a distant future. This unit includes genres that reveal the unlimited potential of the human imagination.

PREVIEW	Big Ideas and Literary Focus

1	**BIG IDEA:** The Extraordinary and Fantastic	**LITERARY FOCUS:** Description
2	**BIG IDEA:** The Uncanny and Mysterious	**LITERARY FOCUS:** Style and Tone

OBJECTIVES
In learning about the genres of mystery, modern fable, and science fiction, you will focus on the following:

- understanding characteristics of mysteries, modern fables, and science fiction
- identifying and exploring literary elements significant to the genres
- analyzing the effect that these literary elements have upon the reader

INTRODUCTION **1109**

Focus

Summary

This introduction begins with descriptions of types of genre fiction including fantasy, science fiction, and mystery. Introducing the genre of the modern fable, an analysis of "The Happy Man's Shirt," by Italo Calvino considers the elements of a genre fiction story and how they contribute to the story's effectiveness.

★ Viewing the Art

Peter Szumowski often incorporates the fantastic into images of traditional British life (for example, a flying saucer over a rural area). He frequently creates images that seem familiar but unnerving. Have students notice elements of *The Homecoming* that appear familiar, and others that appear strange. Discuss with students how this effect mirrors the impression mysteries, modern fables, and science fiction can leave on the reader. **AS**

Unit Resources

Classroom Management
- TeacherWorks Plus™ CD-ROM
- StudentWorks Plus™ CD-ROM
- Literature Launchers™: Pre-Reading Videos DVD, Unit Six

Core Instructional Support
- Unit 6 Resources (Fast File)
- Literature Online, glencoe.com
- Presentation Plus!™ CD-ROM, Unit Six

Transparencies
- Literary Elements Transparencies 6, 10, 16, 22, 43, 86, 87, 88, 89, 102, 109
- Bellringer Options Transparencies: Selection Focus Transparencies 44–47 Daily Language Practice Transparencies 92–102

Differentiated Instruction
- Active Learning and Note Taking Guide, pp. 178–210
- Skill Level Up!™ A Language Arts Game

Assessment
- Selection and Unit Assessments, pp. 187–208, 219–220
- Exam*View*® Assessment Suite CD-ROM
- Assessment by Learning Objectives, pp. 61–68

Supplemental Reading
- Glencoe Literature Library
- Glencoe BookLink 3 CD-ROM
- *inTIME* Magazines

1109

Teach

L Literary Element

Analyzing Genre Ask: What makes Bradbury's story "A Sound of Thunder" science fiction? *(A future setting and the technology of time travel are fantasy elements characteristic of science fiction.)* **Ask:** What makes Jamaica Kincaid's fiction fantasy? *(It is highly imaginative and set in a different reality.)* **Ask:** What type of mystery does "The Witness for the Prosecution" appear to be and why? *(It seems to be a detective story because a crime is solved.)* **OL**

★ Literary History

Science Fiction

History Science fiction began with Jules Verne, H. G. Wells, and E. R. Burroughs in the nineteenth century. The magazine *Amazing Stories,* founded by Hugo Gernsback in 1926, encouraged development of science fiction. Founded in 1937, John W. Campbell Jr.'s *Astounding Science Fiction* advanced literary science fiction and brought authors such as Isaac Asimov and Robert Heinlein to the public's attention. **AS**

Additional Support

Study Central Have students visit the Web site for resources that will help them to review genre fiction.

1110

Genre Focus
What are science fiction, modern fables, and mystery?

This unit includes four kinds of genre fiction: science fiction, fantasy, modern fable, and mystery. Writers of these kinds of fiction use all of the techniques of good story telling. The writers create unusual settings and characters, intriguing plot patterns, and use vivid descriptions to draw readers into imagined worlds or investigations. Often, writers of science fiction, fantasy, and mystery create characters who appear in subsequent works, where the story develops further. In this way, genre fiction writers create series.

Types of Genre Fiction

★ Science Fiction

Science fiction is fiction that deals with the impact of science and technology—real or imagined—on society and individuals. Sometimes occurring in the future, science fiction commonly portrays space travel, exploration of the planets, and future societies or scientific and technological advances.

> The sign on the wall seemed to quaver under a film of sliding warm water. Eckels felt his eyelids blink over his stare, and the sign burned in this momentary darkness:
>   TIME SAFARI, INC.
>   SAFARIS TO ANY YEAR IN THE PAST.
>   YOU NAME THE ANIMAL.
>   WE TAKE YOU THERE.
>   YOU SHOOT IT.
>
> —Ray Bradbury, **from "A Sound of Thunder"** L

Fantasy

Fantasy is a highly imaginative type of fiction, usually set in an unfamiliar world or a distant, heroic past. Fantasy stories may include people, but they often include gnomes, elves, or other fantastical beings or supernatural forces. The use of magic is common in fantasy stories.

> I turned around and looked ahead of me again. A deep hole had opened up before me. I looked in. The hole was deep and dark and I couldn't see the bottom. I thought, What's down there?, so on purpose I fell in. I fell and I fell, over and over, as if I were an old suitcase.
>
> —Jamaica Kincaid, **from "What I Have Been Doing Lately"**

Fable

A **fable** is a brief, usually simple story intended to teach a lesson about human behavior or to give advice about how to behave. Themes in fables are often stated directly. Modern fables also focus on themes relating to human behavior, with little development of individual characters.

> "Here's what you must do. Look for a happy man, a man who's happy through and through and exchange your son's shirt for his."
>
> —Italo Calvino, **from "The Happy Man's Shirt"**

Literature Online Study Central Visit www.glencoe.com to review genre fiction.

Skills Practice

LITERARY ELEMENT: Analyzing Sensory Details Ask: What visual image in Adam Cohen's "The Machine Nurturer" passage makes the biggest impression on you? *(Students will probably say the "pink paper ears.")* Encourage students to form and describe mental pictures of the machine. Point out that Cohen uses sound imagery as well in "babylike noises" and how inventive imagery characterizes his style. **Ask:** What do these images tell you about the story? *(They depict a world like ours, but under fantastic circumstances.)* **OL**

Mystery

The genre of **mystery** includes a variety of types, all of which follow a standard plot pattern. Spy stories are often mysteries, as are tales of danger or adventure. A **detective story** usually follows a standard plot pattern—a crime is committed and a detective searches for clues that lead him or her to the criminal. Any story that relies on the unknown or the terrifying can be considered a mystery.

"Who, then, in your opinion, murdered Miss French?"

"Why, a burglar, of course, as was thought at first. The window was forced, you remember. She was killed with a heavy blow from a crowbar, and the crowbar was found lying on the floor beside the body."

—Agatha Christie, **from "The Witness for the Prosecution"**

Style and Tone

Style, Voice, and Diction

The expressive qualities that distinguish an author's work, including word choice, sentence structure, and figures of speech, contribute to **style**. **Voice,** an author's distinctive use of language to convey the author's or narrator's personality to the reader, is determined by elements of style. **Diction,** the writer's choice of words, is an important element in the writer's voice or style.

I had no keener pleasure than in following Holmes in his professional investigations, and in admiring the rapid deductions, as swift as intuitions, and yet always founded on a logical basis with which he unraveled the problems which were submitted to him.

—Sir Arthur Conan Doyle, **from "The Adventure of the Speckled Band"** **L1**

Attitude

Tone is the writer's attitude toward his or her subject. Tone is conveyed through elements such as word choice, punctuation, sentence structure, and figures of speech. A writer's tone may be sympathetic, objective, serious, ironic, sad, bitter, or humorous.

I walked for I don't know how long before I came to a big body of water. I wanted to get across it but it would take me years to build a boat. I wanted to get across but it would take me I didn't know how long to build a bridge. Years passed and then one day, feeling like it, I got into my boat and rowed across.

—Jamaica Kincaid, **from "What I Have Been Doing Lately"** **L2**

Imagery and Description

Imagery refers to descriptive language that appeals to the senses. Authors carefully select details, creating "word pictures" that evoke an emotional response. Imagery can create new worlds for the reader or present a fresh perspective on this world. **Description** is a detailed portrayal of a person, place, thing, or event. Good description is especially important in genre fiction to help the reader imagine unfamiliar times and places.

When Kismet is lonely and spots a human, it cranes its head forward. It flaps its pink paper ears and excitedly makes babylike noises.

—Adam Cohen, **from "The Machine Nurturer"**

Sensory Details

Authors use evocative words or phrases that appeal to one or more of the five senses—sight, hearing, touch, taste, and smell—in order to create effective images.

A windstorm from the beast's mouth engulfed them in the stench of slime and old blood. The Monster roared, teeth glittering with sun.

—Ray Bradbury, **from "A Sound of Thunder"**

INTRODUCTION **1111**

Teach

L1 Literary Element

Voice and Diction Ask:
What does word choice tell you about the narrator in the Conan Doyle excerpt? *(The narrator's concentrated use of elaborate words such as* deductions, intuitions, *and* unravelled *shows he is an educated and intelligent person.)* **OL**

L2 Literary Element

Tone and Structure Ask:
What tone does Jamaica Kincaid convey? *(An ironic, humorous tone.)* Direct students to notice the parallelism of Kincaid's sentences. **Ask:** What is the effect of the break in pattern at the end? *(The contrast adds to the surprise and humor of the last sentence.)* **OL**

Study Central Have students visit the Web site for resources that will help them to review the genre fiction.

Differentiated Instruction

Analyzing Style Provide less proficient students with charts or checklists for analyzing author's style. As an example, discuss the first passage by Jamaica Kincaid. **Ask:** What techniques does Kincaid use to make you feel as if you are falling? *(She uses repetition to mimic the sensation of falling and a first-person narrator for immediacy.)* **Ask:** What characterizes the language choice? *(The language is direct but imaginative.)* Have students complete the chart with information about Kincaid's style. Then encourage students to analyze the style of other excerpts. **BL**

Objectives
- To analyze characteristics of text, including style, diction, tone, and voice (SE)
- To analyze sensory details (TWE)

1111

Teach

L Literary Element

Analyzing Genre Ask: What makes "The Happy Man's Shirt" a modern fable? *(It is one author's modern retelling of an old folktale that has the main purpose of expressing a moral judgment related to current attitudes toward happiness.)* **Ask:** What elements of fantasy does the story have? *(Its setting is an imaginary land.)* **OL**

R1 Reading Strategy

Evaluating Author's Purpose Ask: What is the moral of the fable? *(Happiness does not depend on external possessions but on a state of mind.)* **OL**

★ Literary History

Modern Fable A modern fable is similar to a traditional fable, but it is set in modern times or reflects current culture. Often, modern fables are adaptations of traditional fables that update the characters, setting, and moral to modern times. **AS**

Additional Support

Literary Analysis Model
How do readers analyze style and tone?

Italo Calvino (1923-1985) is one of the most important Italian fiction writers of the twentieth century. In the course of his career, he wrote novels, stories, essays, and translations and received many important literary awards. Much of Calvino's early writings—which resemble fables or myths—were **L** influenced by the oppressive political conditions in Italy during Benito Mussolini's fascist regime. According to Calvino, "When a man cannot give clear form to this thinking, he expresses it in fables." "The Happy Man's Shirt" is Calvino's retelling of a ★ traditional Italian fable, one of two hundred he collected for his 1956 book, *Italian Folktales*.

The Happy Man's Shirt R1

retold by Italo Calvino
translated by George Martin

A king had an only son that he thought the world of. But this prince was always unhappy. He would spend days on end at his window staring into space.

"What on earth do you lack?" asked the king. "What's wrong with you?"

5 "I don't even know myself, Father."

"Are you in love? If there's a particular girl you fancy, tell me, and I'll arrange for you to marry her, no matter whether she's the daughter of the most powerful king on earth or the poorest peasant girl alive!"

"No, Father, I'm not in love."

10 The king tried in every way imaginable to cheer him up, but theaters, balls, concerts, and singing were all useless, and day by day the rosy hue drained from the prince's face.

The king issued a decree, and from every corner of the earth came the most learned philosophers, doctors, and professors. The king showed

15 them the prince and asked for their advice. The wise men withdrew to think, then returned to the king. "Majesty, we have given the matter close thought and we have studied the stars. Here's what you must do. Look for a happy man, a man who's happy through and through, and exchange your son's shirt for his."

20 That same day the king sent ambassadors to all parts of the world in search of the happy man.

A priest was taken to the king. "Are you happy?" asked the king.

APPLYING Literary Elements

Tone

The narrator's tone is objective, which makes him sound reliable. When he says the prince is unhappy, we believe him.

Style

Paragraph length is a stylistic choice. This paragraph is just one sentence long.

Imagery

The "word picture" Calvino creates of the prince's face causes the reader to feel pity for the prince.

Skills Practice

LITERARY ELEMENT: Recognizing Structure Ask: How does Calvino structure his tale, and what is the effect? *(He structures the tale as three parallel episodes, which is satisfying and reminiscent of traditional fantasy stories.)* How does he structure his choice of characters? *(The priest and king reflect aspects* of society thought to bring happiness: religion and political power.) How does Calvino stress the moral with irony? *(Just as the king thinks his son is saved, he realizes he is not.)* Tell students to notice the author's underlying structure as they read genre fiction in this unit. **OL**

"Yes, indeed, Majesty."

"Fine. How would you like to be my bishop?"

25 "Oh, Majesty, if only it were so!"

"Away with you! Get out of my sight! I'm seeking a man who's happy just as he is, not one who's trying to better his lot." **R2**

Thus the search resumed, and before long the king was told about a neighboring king, who everybody said was a truly happy man. He had a
30 wife as good as she was beautiful and a whole slew of children. He had conquered all his enemies, and his country was at peace. Again hopeful, the king immediately sent ambassadors to him to ask for his shirt.

The neighboring king received the ambassadors and said, "Yes, indeed, I have everything anybody could possibly want. But at the same time I
35 worry because I'll have to die one day and leave it all. I can't sleep at night for worrying about that!" The ambassadors thought it wiser to go home without this man's shirt.

At his wit's end, the king went hunting. He fired at a hare but only wounded it, and the hare scampered away on three legs. The king
40 pursued it, leaving the hunting party far behind him. Out in the open field he heard a man singing a refrain. The king stopped in his tracks. "Whoever sings like that is bound to be happy!" The song led him into a vineyard, where he found a young man singing and pruning the vines.

"Good day, Majesty," said the youth. "So early and already out in
45 the country?"

"Bless you! Would you like me to take you to the capital? You will be my friend."

"Much obliged, Majesty, but I wouldn't even consider it. I wouldn't even change places with the Pope."

50 "Why not? Such a fine young man like you . . ."

"No, no, I tell you. I'm content with just what I have and want nothing more."

"A happy man at last!" thought the king. "Listen, young man. Do me a favor."

55 "With all my heart, Majesty, if I can."

"Wait just a minute," said the king, who, unable to contain his joy any longer, ran to get his retinue. "Come with me! My son is saved! My son is saved!" And he took them to the young man. "My dear lad," he began, "I'll give you whatever you want! But give me. . . give me . . ."

60 "What, Majesty?"

"My son is dying! Only you can save him. Come here!"

The king grabbed him and started unbuttoning the youth's jacket. All of a sudden he stopped, and his arms fell to his sides.

The happy man wore no shirt.

Diction

The choice of the word "slew" is informal.

Voice

Medium-length sentences contribute to the narrator's straightforward reporter-like voice.

Sensory Details

The vivid physical description appeals to the sense of touch.

Reading Check

Evaluating Would you say that Calvino's stylistic choices were successful in "The Happy Man's Shirt"? Explain your answer.

INTRODUCTION 1113

Teach

Reading Check

Answer: *Students will probably agree that Calvino's style is successful, that his choices create a unified and memorable work of fiction. They may cite the appeal of the story's structure, dialogue, word choice, and imagery.* **OL**

R2 Reading Strategy

Analyzing Style and Tone

Ask: What patterns in Calvino's style do you notice, and what effects do they have? *(Calvino uses repetition as the king continues to ask if people are happy; this technique builds suspense. The use of dialogue throughout adds drama and immediacy.)* **Ask:** What is Calvino's tone toward his characters? *(He uses an objective tone, which allows readers to identify with the characters.)* Point out that Calvino does not state the moral directly, as many fables do. **Ask:** What is the effect of ending the story with "The happy man wore no shirt"? *(The simple direct statement is surprising and makes the reader think.)* **OL**

English Language Coach

Secondary Definitions Point out the word *fancy*, and tell students they will encounter words using a secondary definition (in this case, "to like" rather than "elaborate"). Tell them part of speech will help determine meaning, and if the more common definition does not fit, they should check their dictionaries. **EL**

Building Reading Fluency

Dialogue Point out as a tip for reading dialogue that the paragraph changes every time there is a new speaker. Even though the speaker is not named, the paragraphing identifies the speaker. Have students identify the speaker of each line in "The Happy Man's Shirt" as they practice reading aloud to one another. **BL**

Objectives

• To analyze characteristics of text, including style, diction, tone, and voice (SE)
• To analyze the structure of a text (TWE)

Teach

R1 Reading Strategy

Summarizing Ask: What is the appeal of fantasy, according to Cooper? *(It reaches a deeper unconscious level with an imagined reality.)* **Ask:** In what way does Ray Bradbury say science fiction is indicative of a beneficial human trait? *(It is human to look to the future, and by dreaming, people create inventions.)* **Ask:** What makes a mystery powerful, according to Sue Grafton? *(Strong characters and plot as well as the ability to explore evil and impose justice make a mystery satisfying.)* OL

R2 Reading Strategy

Analyzing Analogy Ask: What do you think South American novelist Gabriel García Márquez means to bring out by comparing literature to carpentry? *(The analogy suggests that an author has a craft grounded in truth and real life.)* OL

Additional Support

Interactive Reading Have students access the Web site for more practice with reading strategies.

1114

Writers on Reading
What do writers say about genre fiction?

Reading Science Fiction, Modern Fable, and Mystery

The Metaphor of Fantasy

Why does anyone read, or write, fantasy?

Fantasy goes one stage beyond realism; requiring complete intellectual surrender, it asks more of the reader, and at its best may offer more. Perhaps this is why it is also less popular, at any rate among adults, who set such store by their ability to think. Among small children, who have not yet begun to think much about the stories they hear, fantasy reigns supreme. . . .

And what do we, and they, find, when we read fantasy? The escape and encouragement are there, for sure—but in a different form. This time, when we depart from our own reality into the reality of the book, it's not a matter of stepping across the street, or into the next county, or even the next planet. This time, we're going out of time, out of space, into the unconscious, that dreamlike world which has in it all the images and emotions accumulated since the human race began. We aren't escaping out, we're escaping in, without any idea of what we may encounter. Fantasy is the metaphor through which we discover ourselves.

—Susan Cooper, from "Escaping into Ourselves" **R1**

Science and Technology in Fiction

Hiding in caves, discovering fire, building cities—all of these were science-fictional endeavors. We can see the depiction of possible futures scrawled on cave walls in southern France, where the first science-fiction tales illustrated how to find, kill, and eat the wild beasts.

> "Ultimately, literature is nothing but carpentry.... With both you are working with reality, a material just as hard as wood."
>
> —Gabriel García Márquez **R2**

The problems that faced primitive man had to be solved. They dreamed answers to dire questions; that is the essence of the fiction that becomes science. Once a vivid dream was realized in their heads, they were able to act on it. So the creatures of old time planned for tomorrow and tomorrow and tomorrow. What is true of them certainly is true

Author Ursula K. Le Guin poses with her award at the PEN USA Annual LitFest Awards Gala at the Biltmore Hotel on November 9, 2005 in Los Angeles, California.

Literature Online InterActive Reading Practice Visit www.glencoe.com for more practice reading genre fiction.

Skills Practice

READING: Main Idea and Details
Point out to students that Ray Bradbury cites three events from early human history: the use of caves as shelter, the discovery of fire, and the creation of the city. **Ask:** What main point does Bradbury illustrate with these three examples? *(Each illustrates his point about fictional dreams becoming reality.)* Discuss the value of using examples to support a main idea, noting how Bradbury clarifies his main idea and creates impact by using concrete illustrations. Ask students to provide details that support Grafton's and Cooper's ideas. OL

Writer Hans Christian Andersen 1805–75 reads his story Engelen (the Angel) to sick child of Mrs. Jerichau-Baumann (wife of the artist),1862. E. Jerichau-Baumann. Hans Christian Andersen Birthplace, Odense, Denmark. ★

Teach

Reading Check

Answer: *Students should give specific resons for identifying with a given passage.* **OL**

★ Viewing the Art

Hans Christian Andersen, portrayed here, wrote some of our most enduring fairy tales, including "The Little Mermaid" and "The Emperor's New Clothes." **Ask:** How are fairy tales related to genre fiction? *(They abide by similar conventions, and many of them present serious moral content within the context of fantastical events.)* **Ask:** Where would you draw the line between science fiction and fairy tales? Why? *(Answers will vary, but will likely mention the presence of technology.)* **AS**

of us. We wonder about tomorrow morning, tomorrow evening, and the day after that, so as to plan our schools, marriages, and careers. Everything that we do has to be imagined first.

—Ray Bradbury, **from "Predicting the Past, Remembering the Future"**

Ingredients of a Mystery

The creation of complex and believable characters is essential to the writing of a successful mystery. Whether it's a short story or a full-length novel, the narrative line needs to be strong, the prose style crisp, the pace relentless. But there are many other elements to conquer beyond the basics of character and plot. A mystery is more than a novel, more than a compelling account of people whose fate engages us.

The mystery is a way of examining the dark side of human nature, a means by which we can explore, vicariously, the perplexing questions of crime, guilt and innocence, violence and justice. The mystery not only re-creates the original conditions from which violence springs, tracking the chaos that murder unleashes, but then attempts to divine the truth through the process of rational investigation and eventually restores an order to the universe.

—Sue Grafton, **from** *Writing Mysteries: A Handbook by the Mystery Writers of America*

Reading Check

Responding From your own reading experiences, which passage do you identify with most closely? Explain.

INTRODUCTION **1115**

English Language Coach

Archetypes The term *archetypes* in Susan Cooper's passage "The Metaphor of Fantasy" may be unfamiliar to students new to the United States. Explain that archetypes are recurring characters in literature, such as the superman or the earth mother. Discuss additional examples to clarify. **EL**

Differentiated Instruction

Evaluating Encourage students who are less practiced at critical reading to evaluate the validity of the points these authors make. Ask students to consider how logical each author's reasoning is and which author makes the most convincing case. Make sure students can support their opinions with specifics. **BL**

Objectives

• To understand characteristics of text, including style, diction, tone, and voice (SE)
• To identify main idea and supporting details (TWE)

Assess/Close

Guide to Reading Genre Fiction Ask students to predict how the fiction they read in this unit will differ from fiction earlier in the book. Advise students to pay attention to the elements of genre fiction as they read, and to apply what they have already learned about fiction.

Elements of Genre Fiction See if students have any questions about the elements of these genres.

Activities

1. Make sure that students can support their artistic choices with details from the text.

2. Guide students to recognize the nuances of language affected by translation.

3. Suggest that students keep a journal of their responses to the literature.

FOLDABLES™
Study Organizer

Have students make and label the Bound Book Foldable. They can write examples of each literary element in the book.

Additional Support

Wrap-Up

Guide to Reading Genre Fiction

- Identify the genre category.
- Evaluate your enjoyment as you read.
- Pay attention to characters, settings, plot development, and themes, as you do with other genres of fiction.
- Evaluate the consistency with which the author creates the imaginary world.
- Notice elements of the author's style.

Elements of Genre Fiction

- **Imagery** paints "word pictures" in the reader's imagination.
- **Sensory** details appeal to the reader's five senses.
- **Voice** tells the reader about the author's or narrator's personality.
- **Tone** communicates the author's or narrator's attitude toward the audience or the subject matter.
- **Diction** refers to the words the author chooses.
- **Style** refers to all the choices the author makes and includes voice, diction, and tone.

Activities ➤

Use what you have learned about reading and analyzing mysteries, fantasy, and science fiction to do one of these activities.

1. Visual Literacy Create an illustration for some part of the story "The Happy Man's Shirt," and share it with your class. Discuss which details of the story support the illustration and how the illustration complements the text.

2. Speaking/Listening/Viewing "The Happy Man's Shirt" was translated from Italian. In a small group, discuss the likely effects of translation on style, diction, tone, and voice. Prepare a statement summing up the writing techniques that help make a translation good.

3. Note Taking You might try using this study organizer to keep track of the literary elements in this unit. As you read, record examples that you feel exemplify the author's style, voice, tone, or diction within each work. Write notes explaining your examples.

  BOUND BOOK

OBJECTIVES
- Use viewing strategies effectively.
- Explain how voice affects the tone of a text.
- Analyze characteristics of text, including style, diction, tone, and voice.

Skills Practice

READING: Comparing Translations
Have students read and compare two different translations of the same work, such as *Antigone.* Guide students to analyze the voice of each translation, as evidenced by diction, narrator, and style. Ask students to draw conclusions about how the translator's voice affects the tone of a work. Encourage proficient readers to further discuss the role of the translator and whether a translator can be an artist in his or her own right. **OL**

PART 1

The Extraordinary and Fantastic

Classic Domed Disk with Windows and Four-Piece Landing Gear Hovers over Country Home near Helena, Montana, USA, ca. 20th century. Artist Unknown. ★

BI   BIG IDEA

Imagine a world where extraordinary things happen. Imagine traveling to distant galaxies or living in a world where dreams become real. The fantasy and science fiction stories in Part 1 will expand your imagination. As you read these tales, ask yourself: What makes these stories so appealing?

1117

Analyzing and Extending

BI   Big Idea

The Extraordinary and the Fantastic Prepare students for a journey into the imagination. Encourage them to visualize the astonishing scenes and descriptions they will read about. Tell students that Part 1 will present the world of science fiction and fantasy with stories that are extraordinary and fantastic, and encourage students to contemplate this "big idea" and its relation to the artwork. **OL**

★ Viewing the Art

Have students study the painting. Discuss what they believe is occurring inside the home while the spaceship is preparing to land. Ask students to write a short dialogue between imaginary characters living in the home. **Ask:** Are your characters curious and excited about the arrival or scared and apprehensive? Have students share their dialogues with the class. **AS**

English Language Coach

Multiple-Meaning Words Tell English language learners that the word *fantastic* has a meaning different from the one they may be familiar with: "wonderful, superb." In this unit, *fantastic* means "imaginary, unreal." Explain that the stories in this part will include elements that are not realistic. **EL**

Differentiated Instruction

Building Background Encourage less proficient students to describe elements of fantasy and science fiction that they are already familiar with. Have them create a chart listing characters they know of in conventional categories such as monsters, ghosts, time travelers, space travelers, elves, and robots. **BL**

Objectives for Part 1

- To understand the use of images and sounds to elicit the reader's emotions (SE)
- To analyze characteristics of text including word choice (SE)
- To explain how the selection of genre shapes the theme or topic (SE)

Part 1: The Extraordinary and Fantastic

Readability Scores Key
Dale-Chall/**DRP**/Lexile

PACING (DAYS)		SELECTIONS AND FEATURES	LITERARY ELEMENTS
STANDARD	**BLOCK**		
1–2 class sessions	1	LITERARY FOCUS: Description, pp. 1118–1119	Imagery and Figurative Language, SE p. 1118 Analyzing Description, TWE p. 1118
		"A Sound of Thunder" by Ray Bradbury **5.2/56/700**, pp. 1120–1134	Foreshadowing, SE pp. 1121–1133
1–2 class sessions	1	**"By the Waters of Babylon"** by Stephen Vincent Benét **5.6/49/820**, pp. 1135–1149	Moral, SE pp. 1136–1148 Archetypes, SE p. 1148
		Grammar Workshop: Sentence Structure, p. 1150	
2 class sessions	1	COMPARING LITERATURE Across Genres "What I Have Been Doing Lately" by Jamaica Kincaid **4.4/46/780**, pp. 1152–1157 "People at Night" by Denise Levertov, p. 1158 "The Dream" by Anna Akhmatova, pp. 1159–1160	Stream of Consciousness, SE pp. 1153–1157 Sound Devices, TWE p. 1158
2 class sessions	1–2	SCIENTIFIC PERSPECTIVE: "One Legend Found" by William J. Broad **8.5/69/1380**, pp. 1161–1163	Fantastic Creatures, TWE p. 1162
		"Robot Dreams" by Isaac Asimov **8.0/52/820**, pp. 1164–1171	Analogy, SE pp. 1165, 1167, 1170 Theme Archetype, SE p. 1170
		TIME magazine, "The Machine Nurturer" by Adam Cohen **8.0/64/1050**, pp. 1172–1175	
		"Bread" by Margaret Atwood **3.6/51/740**, pp. 1176–1180	Point of View, SE pp. 1177–1180

About the Part

Part 1 covers the extraordinary and the fantastic.

READING AND CRITICAL THINKING	VOCABULARY	WRITING AND GRAMMAR	LISTENING, SPEAKING, AND VIEWING
Analyzing Figurative Language, TWE p. 1119	Context, TWE p. 1119	Quickwrite, SE p. 1119	
Identifying Genre Elements, SE pp. 1121–1133	Word Parts, SE p. 1133	Author's Craft, SE p. 1134 Using Gerunds, SE p. 1134	Oral Defense, TWE p. 1130
Visualizing, SE pp. 1136–1149 Comparing and Contrasting, TWE p. 1146	Word Origins, SE pp. 1136, 1149	Evaluate Author's Craft, SE p. 1149	Analyzing Art, SE pp. 1143, 1145, 1146 Rebuttal, SE p. 1149
		Avoiding Misplaced Modifiers, SE p. 1150	
Interpreting Imagery, SE pp. 1153–1157 Previewing, TWE p. 1154	Analogies, SE pp. 1153, 1157 Prefixes, TWE p. 1156	Compare and Contrast Events, SE p. 1157 Quickwrite, SE p. 1159	Discussion Starter, SE p. 1158
Comparing and Contrasting Events and Ideas, TWE p. 1162			
Applying Prior Knowledge to Understand Text, SE pp. 1165, 1167, 1169, 1171	Synonyms, SE p. 1171 Academic Vocabulary, SE p. 1171	Analyze Genre Elements, SE p. 1171	Dramatizing, TWE p. 1168
Connecting to Contemporary Issues, TWE p. 1173		Creative Writing, TWE p. 1174	Analyzing Art, TWE p. 1174
Recognizing Author's Purpose, SE pp. 1177, 1179, 1180	Connotation and Denotation, SE pp. 1177, 1180	Apply Description, SE p. 1180	Analyzing Art, TWE p. 1178

Teach

LITERARY FOCUS

Big Idea

The Extraordinary and the Fantastic Invite students to tell well-known ghost stories or futuristic stories. Identify these as fantasy or science fiction with themes of the extraordinary or fantastic. Ask students how the genres of science fiction and fantasy shape the stories and what effect these genres have on the reader. Point out that these types of stories that stretch the imagination will be featured in Part 1. **OL**

L Literary Element

Imagery and Figurative Language Suggest that students visualize the series of vivid images in the Bradbury excerpt. **Ask:** Which images of going back in time do you find especially vivid? *(Students' answers will vary.)* **Ask:** What emotions do the similes Bradbury uses arouse? *(The similes "like golden salamanders" and "like Chinese boxes" seem mystical and magical.)* **OL**

Description

How do writers describe fantastic worlds?

How does a fantasy or science fiction writer help you experience events and scenes that are imaginary? The writer might use imagery to create "word pictures" that evoke an emotional response. Or the writer might use sensory details, or evocative words or phrases that appeal to your senses of sight, sound, touch, taste, or smell. Notice how specific the details are in Bradbury's description of an advertisement for a service that transports people back in time. When writers vividly describe places, things, people, and events, readers can imagine them as if they were real.

Eckels glanced across the vast office at a mass and tangle, a snaking and humming of wires and steel boxes, at an aurora that flickered now orange, now silver, now blue. There was a sound like a gigantic bonfire burning all of Time, all the years and all the parchment calendars, all the hours piled high and set aflame.

A touch of the hand and this burning would, on the instant, beautifully reverse itself. Eckels remembered the wording in the advertisements to the letter. Out of chars and ashes, out of dust and coals, like golden salamanders, the old years, the green years, might leap; roses sweeten the air, white hair turn Irish-black, wrinkles vanish; all, everything fly back to seed, flee death, rush down to their beginnings, suns rise in western skies and set in glorious easts, moons eat themselves opposite to the custom, all and everything cupping one in another like Chinese boxes, rabbits into hats, all and everything returning to the fresh death, the seed of death, the green death, to the time before the beginning. A touch of the hand might do it, the merest touch of a hand.

—Ray Bradbury, **from "A Sound of Thunder"** **L**

Additional Support

Skills Practice

LITERARY ELEMENT: Analyzing Description Read the quotations aloud and ask students to draw the following:

- the ruined city in "By the Waters of Babylon"
- the scene in "People at Night"
- the giant squid's eyes and tentacles in Broad's description

Ask: What emotions do the descriptions elicit? *(Students should notice the ominous mood of "By the Waters of Babylon" and "People at Night.")* **OL**

UH OH, IT HAPPENED AGAIN.

CALVIN WAKES UP WITHOUT ANY RECOGNIZABLE FEATURES, SAVE TWO ANTENNAE. HOW DISGUSTING.

HE OOZES OUT OF BED ON A TRAIL OF SLIME, LACKING ARMS AND LEGS, HOW WILL CALVIN PUT ON HIS CLOTHES?

AREN'T YOU DRESSED YET? YOU ARE SO SLUGGISH IN THE MORNING!

©1987 Universal Press Syndicate   10-2

Figurative Language

Figurative Language is language that uses figures of speech, or expressions that are not literally true but express some truth beyond the literal level. Figurative language includes simile, metaphor, and personification.

Simile A figure of speech that uses *like* or *as* to compare two seemingly unlike things is a **simile.** Similes can make desriptions understandable to readers. In this passage, notice how the writer uses a simile to describe a fictitious place, known as the Dead Place.

How shall I tell what I saw? The towers are not all broken—here and there one still stands, like a great tree in a forest, and the birds nest high.

—Stephen Vincent Benét, **from "By the Waters of Babylon"**

Metaphor A figure of speech that makes a comparison between two seemingly unlike things is a **metaphor.** A metaphor suggests an underlying similarity between the two things compared. Unlike a simile, it does not use *like* or *as.* Notice how this metaphor gives a sense of the direction of time travel in the story.

Time was a film run backward.

—Ray Bradbury, **from "A Sound of Thunder"**

Personification A figure of speech that gives human qualities to an animal, an object, a force of nature, or an idea is **personification.** Writers use personification to explain, expand, and create vivid images.

The fluorescent light flickers sullenly, a / pause. But you command. It grabs / each face and holds it up / by the hair for you, mask after mask.

—Denise Levertov, **from "People at Night"**

Imagery Good descriptive writing uses **imagery**—language that appeals to one or more of the five senses: sight, hearing, touch, taste, and smell. Imagery helps to create an emotional response in the reader.

But the giant squid is real, growing up to lengths of at least 60 feet, with eyes the size of dinner plates and a tangle of tentacles lined with long rows of sucker pads.

—William J. Broad, **from "One Legend Found, Many Still to Go"**

Quickwrite

Describing a Place Write a paragraph in which you describe a favorite place. For example, you might describe your room, a friend's house, or a coffee shop. Arrange details in spatial order—left to right, front to back—to create a vivid picture.

OBJECTIVES
- Understand the use of images and sounds to elicit the reader's emotions.
- Analyze characteristics of text, including word choice.
- Explain how the selection of genre shapes the theme or topic.

Teach

R Reading Strategy

Analyzing Figurative Language Ask: What is the purpose of Bradbury's metaphor "film run backward"? *(It clarifies the wonder of time travel.)* **Ask:** In the Stephen Vincent Benét excerpt, what does the simile compare? *(A tower is compared with a tall tree.)* **Ask:** What is personified in Denise Levertov's poem? *(The fluorescent light)* Discuss the emotions these images elicit. **OL**

Quickwrite

Check students' descriptions for precise details and spatial order. Encourage students to use colorful images and figurative language.

English Language Coach

Context For students new to the United States, discuss some of the cultural references they may be unfamiliar with, such as "Irish-black" (dark hair), "Chinese boxes" (nesting boxes), and "rabbits into hats" (magic trick). Also review unfamiliar words such as *chars, salamanders, fluorescent, sullen,* and *tentacles.* **EL**

Differentiated Instruction

Analyzing Genre Discuss how the science fiction and fantasy genres treat subject matter. **Ask:** What is the author's purpose in fantasy and science fiction? *(to entertain, enlighten, and/or satirize)* Note that science fiction writers often comment on today's world by extrapolating trends into the future. **AL**

Focus

Author Search To expand students' appreciation of Ray Bradbury, have them access the Web site for additional information and resources.

A Sound of Thunder

MEET RAY BRADBURY

Picture a twelve-year-old boy sitting spellbound on Christmas Day, slowly pecking away on a toy typewriter, composing a story about life on Mars. For Ray Bradbury, his dream of becoming a writer was just over the horizon. He was an impressionable child and later wove many of his early life experiences into his work.

Bradbury, born in Waukegan, Illinois, learned to read at age four. He loved fairy tales and other stories containing fantasy plots or magic, such as *The Wizard of Oz* and *Tarzan*. Bradbury was a loyal fan of the *Buck Rogers* comic strip, one of the first series in a genre people were calling "science fiction."

Bradbury grew up in an age of constant technological innovation. In 1933 he visited the World's Fair in Chicago, where he was fascinated by a roaring mechanical dinosaur. As an adult, Bradbury said, "You pose the question, what if I had given up on dinosaurs? I wouldn't have had my career."

The Sky's the Limit At age fourteen Bradbury moved to Los Angeles with his family. He loved living in "Tinseltown" and wanted to become part of the popular culture by writing, directing, and acting. He got a job as a newsboy and began saving his money. Following his high school graduation in 1938, he bought a real typewriter, rented an office, and began his career as a writer.

Although he never went to college, Bradbury continued his education by observing, listening, and visiting public libraries. In these ways, he learned enough about the media world in Hollywood to introduce himself to the important people around town. He published his first science fiction stories in pulp magazines. Later his stories appeared in more widely circulated publications such as the *New Yorker* and the *Saturday Evening Post*. The publication of his short story collection *The Martian Chronicles* in 1950 was a major breakthrough in his career.

When television became popular in American homes during the 1950s, Bradbury started writing teleplays for various programs, including Rod Serling's *The Twilight Zone*. His novel *Fahrenheit 451* (1953) became a Hollywood film.

Bradbury met Walt Disney in the early 1960s, and the two men discovered that they had many common interests. In time, Bradbury served as a consultant for the geosphere being built at Epcot Center in Florida.

> *"The ability to fantasize is the ability to survive."*
> —Ray Bradbury

Basking in the Limelight Since the 1940s, Bradbury has published more than five hundred works. In 2002 he received a star on the Hollywood Walk of Fame for his accomplishments in the film industry. Film producer and director Steven Spielberg is one of Bradbury's many admirers. In 2004 President and Mrs. Bush presented him with the National Medal of Arts. Today Bradbury is considered one of the most popular and widely read short story writers in the world.

Ray Bradbury was born in 1920.

Author Search For more about Ray Bradbury, go to www.glencoe.com.

Selection Skills

A Sound of Thunder

Reading Skills
- Identifying Genre Elements (SE pp. 1121–1133)
- Previewing (TWE p. 1122)
- Monitoring Comprehension (TWE p. 1126)

Literary Elements
- Foreshadowing (SE pp. 1121–1133)
- Description (SE p. 1133)

Vocabulary Skills
- Word Parts (SE p. 1133)

Listening/Speaking/Viewing Skills
- Oral Defense (TWE p. 1130)

Writing Skills/Grammar
- Evaluate Author's Craft (SE p. 1134)
- Using Gerunds (SE p. 1134)
- Appositives (TWE p. 1124)
- Vivid Adjectives (TWE p. 1128)

Connecting to the Story

In the following short story, Ray Bradbury implies that seemingly insignificant actions can change the future for an entire generation. Before you read the story, think about the following questions:

- How might your actions during your lifetime affect someone living one hundred years in the future?
- Do you believe that you have a responsibility to future generations?

Building Background

Although the term *science fiction* was not used until about 1930, science fiction tales have been told since before the invention of writing. One of the earliest science fiction writers was Lucian of Samosata who, around 100 BC, wrote a fantasy about a journey to the moon. Modern science fiction began to take shape in the nineteenth century.

Science fiction is defined loosely as fiction that deals with the impact of science and technology on the world. Sometimes the technology is real, sometimes it is entirely imagined, and sometimes it has been imagined by an author and then brought to reality by scientists. Science fiction themes often warn of the potential for disaster when technology is abused.

Setting Purposes for Reading

Big Idea The Extraordinary and Fantastic

As you read "A Sound of Thunder," notice how Bradbury uses a fantastic idea to imagine a setting no human has actually seen before.

Literary Element Foreshadowing

Foreshadowing is the author's use of clues to hint at events that will occur later in the story. As you read, look for clues that indicate how the story will end.

- See Literary Terms Handbook, p. R7.

Literature Online **Interactive Literary Elements Handbook** To review or learn more about the literary elements, go to www.glencoe.com.

OBJECTIVES

In studying this selection, you will focus on the following:
- recognizing and analyzing the author's use of literary techniques such as foreshadowing

- identifying characteristics that help determine genre
- analyzing description
- writing to evaluate author's craft

Reading Strategy Identifying Genre

A **genre** is a category or type of literature, such as fiction or poetry. Each genre can be subdivided into more specific categories that can be identified by subject matter, content, or style. Identifying the genre of a selection helps a reader to establish expectations for the work.

Reading Tip: Analyzing Clues Readers can understand the genre of a literary work by analyzing its characteristics. Use a chart like the one below to record the characteristics of "A Sound of Thunder." Then analyze your clues to determine common elements in science fiction.

Characteristic	Description
Setting:	The story occurs in an unknown place in 2055.
Conflict:	
Theme:	

Vocabulary

expendable (iks pen′də bəl) *adj.* not strictly necessary; capable of being sacrificed; p. 1125 *My mother believed that our vacation was expendable.*

correlate (kôr′ə lāt) *v.* to bring (one thing) into relation (with another thing); calculate; p. 1126 *The old data correlated with the new results.*

paradox (par′ə doks′) *n.* something that seems illogical, contradictory, or absurd, but that in fact may be true; p. 1126 *Although it was a paradox, she found that she both liked and disliked him.*

resilient (ri zil′yənt) *adj.* capable of springing back into shape or position after being bent, stretched, or compressed; p. 1127 *The rubber ball is so resilient that it still bounces after being frozen.*

primeval (prī mē′vəl) *adj.* of or having to do with the first or earliest age; primitive; p. 1130 *The will to live is a primeval instinct.*

Focus

Summary

Eckels and two hunters travel to the past to hunt a *Tyrannosaurus rex.* Travis, the guide, warns them to stay on a special metal path because any environmental disturbance might change the future. When the dinosaur approaches, Eckels panics and runs off the path. When he returns to the present, he discovers a crushed butterfly on the bottom of his shoe and that the present time has been altered.

V Vocabulary

Vocabulary File Say: Add these words and definitions to your vocabulary file. For each word, include a sentence that gives you an example of how to use the word. **OL** Students with English language needs should include the pronunciations of these words in their files. **EL**

Literary Elements Have students access the Web site to improve their understanding of foreshadowing.

RAY BRADBURY **1121**

Selection Resources

Print Materials
- Unit 6 Resources (Fast File), pp. 17–19
- Leveled Vocabulary Development, p. 77
- Selection and Unit Assessments, pp. 187–188
- Selection Quick Checks, p. 94

Transparencies
- Bellringer Options Transparencies:
  Selection Focus Transparency 44
  Daily Language Practice Transparency 93
- Literary Elements Transparency 6

Technology
- TeacherWorks Plus™ CD-ROM
- StudentWorks Plus™ CD-ROM
- Presentation Plus!™ CD-ROM
- Literature Online, glencoe.com
- Online Student Edition, mhln.com
- ExamView® Assessment Suite CD-ROM
- Vocabulary PuzzleMaker CD-ROM
- Listening Library, disc 2 track 31

Teach

A Sound of Thunder

Ray Bradbury

1122

The sign on the wall seemed to quaver under a film of sliding warm water. Eckels felt his eyelids blink over his stare, and the sign burned in this momentary darkness:

> TIME SAFARI, INC.
> SAFARIS TO ANY YEAR IN THE PAST.
> YOU NAME THE ANIMAL.
> WE TAKE YOU THERE.
> YOU SHOOT IT.

A warm phlegm gathered in Eckels' throat; he swallowed and pushed it down. The muscles around his mouth formed a smile as he put his hand slowly out upon the air, and in that hand waved a check for ten thousand dollars to the man behind the desk.

"Does this safari guarantee I come back alive?"

"We guarantee nothing," said the official, "except the dinosaurs." He turned. "This is Mr. Travis, your Safari Guide in the Past. He'll tell you what and where to shoot. If he says no shooting, no shooting. If you disobey instructions, there's a stiff penalty of another ten thousand dollars, plus possible government action, on your return."

Eckels glanced across the vast office at a mass and tangle, a snaking and humming of wires and steel boxes, at an aurora[1] that flickered now orange, now silver, now blue. There was a sound like a gigantic bonfire burning all of Time, all the years and all the parchment calendars, all the hours piled high and set aflame.

A touch of the hand and this burning would, on the instant, beautifully reverse itself. Eckels remembered the wording in the advertisements to the letter. Out of chars and ashes, out of dust and coals, like golden salamanders, the old years, the green years, might leap; roses sweeten the air, white hair turn Irish-black, wrinkles vanish; all, everything fly back to seed, flee death, rush down to their beginnings, suns rise in western skies and set in glorious easts, moons eat themselves opposite to the custom, all and everything cupping one in another like Chinese boxes, rabbits into hats, all and everything returning to the fresh death, the seed death, the green death, to the time before the beginning. A touch of a hand might do it, the merest touch of a hand.

---

1. Here, *aurora* refers to the shimmering lights that come off of the time machine.

Reading Strategy Identifying Genre *How might the sign on the wall indicate the genre of the selection?* **R**

Literary Element Foreshadowing *What future events might this passage foreshadow?* **L**

Big Idea The Extraordinary and Fantastic *Why has Eckels memorized the wording of the advertisement?* **BI**

RAY BRADBURY **1123**

Differentiated Instruction

Teach

L1 Literary Element

Foreshadowing Answer:
The reference foreshadows that the election information will probably be important later in the story. **OL**

R Reading Strategy

Identifying Genre Answer:
Answers will vary. Students should explain their answers. **OL**

BI1 Big Idea

The Extraordinary and Fantastic Answer: *None of the major events—both good and bad—upon which Western civilization is based has yet to occur.* **OL**

⭐ Language History

Meanings from Latin In the story, the *Tyrannosaurus rex* is referred to as the Thunder Lizard, a common title given to the dinosaur. However, the actual meaning of its name comes from the Greek and Latin for "tyrant lizard king." Show students the connection between *Tyranno* and *tyrant* and *saurus* and *lizard.* **AS**

"Unbelievable." Eckels breathed, the light of the Machine on his thin face. "A real Time Machine." He shook his head. "Makes you think. If the election had gone badly yesterday, I might be here now running away from the results. Thank God Keith won. He'll make a fine President of the United States."

"Yes," said the man behind the desk. "We're lucky. If Deutscher had gotten in, we'd have the worst kind of dictatorship. There's an anti-everything man for you, a militarist, anti-Christ, anti-human, anti-intellectual. People called us up, you know, joking but not joking. Said if Deutscher became President they wanted to go live in 1492. Of course it's not our business to conduct Escapes, but to form Safaris. Anyway, Keith's President now. All you got to worry about is—"

"Shooting my dinosaur," Eckels finished it for him.

⭐ "A *Tyrannosaurus rex*. The Tyrant Lizard, the most incredible monster in history. Sign this release. Anything happens to you, we're not responsible. Those dinosaurs are hungry."

Eckels flushed angrily. "Trying to scare me!"

"Frankly, yes. We don't want anyone going who'll panic at the first shot. Six Safari leaders were killed last year, and a dozen hunters. We're here to give you the severest thrill a *real* hunter ever asked for. Traveling you back sixty million years to bag the biggest game in all of Time. Your personal check's still there. Tear it up."

Mr. Eckels looked at the check for a long time. His fingers twitched.

"Good luck," said the man behind the desk. "Mr. Travis, he's all yours."

They moved silently across the room, taking their guns with them, toward the Machine, toward the silver metal and the roaring light. First a day and then a night and then a day and then a night, then it was day-night-day-night-day. A week, a month, a year, a decade! A.D. 2055. A.D. 2019. 1999! 1957! Gone! The Machine roared.

They put on their oxygen helmets and tested the intercoms.

Eckels swayed on the padded seat, his face pale, his jaw stiff. He felt the trembling in his arms and he looked down and found his hands tight on the new rifle. There were four other men in the Machine. Travis, the Safari Leader, his assistant, Lesperance, and two other hunters, Billings and Kramer. They sat looking at each other, and the years blazed around them.

"Can these guns get a dinosaur cold?" Eckels felt his mouth saying.

"If you hit them right," said Travis on the helmet radio. "Some dinosaurs have two brains, one in the head, another far down the spinal column. We stay away from those. That's stretching luck. Put your first two shots into the eyes, if you can, blind them, and go back into the brain."

The Machine howled. Time was a film run backward. Suns fled and ten million moons fled after them. "Think," said Eckels. "Every hunter that ever lived would envy us today. This makes Africa seem like Illinois."

The Machine slowed; its scream fell to a murmur. The Machine stopped.

The sun stopped in the sky.

The fog that had enveloped the Machine blew away and they were in an old time, a very old time indeed, three hunters and two Safari Heads with their blue metal guns across their knees.

"Christ isn't born yet," said Travis. "Moses has not gone to the mountain to talk with God. The Pyramids are still in the earth, waiting to be cut out and put up. *Remember* that. Alexander, Caesar, Napoleon, Hitler—none of them exists."

Literary Element Foreshadowing *Why might Bradbury have included a reference to an election and who won it in a story about hunting dinosaurs?* **L1**

Reading Strategy Identifying Genre *Do you believe that time travel might really be possible by the year 2055 when this story occurs? Why or why not?* **R**

Big Idea The Extraordinary and Fantastic *What makes this paragraph so fantastic?* **BI1**

Additional Support

Skills Practice

GRAMMAR: Using Appositives
Remind students that an appositive is a noun or phrase placed next to another noun to identify or give more information about it. Appositives are set off by commas unless they are essential to the meaning of the sentence. Have students identify the appositive phrases:

"This is Mr. Travis, your Safari Guide in the Past."
"The Tyrant Lizard, the most incredible monster in history."
"And the head itself, a ton of sculptured stone, lifted easily upon the sky." **OL**

The men nodded.

"That"—Mr. Travis pointed—"is the jungle of sixty million two thousand and fifty-five years before President Keith."

He indicated a metal path that struck off into green wilderness, over steaming swamp, among giant ferns and palms.

"And that," he said, "is the Path, laid by Time Safari for your use. It floats six inches above the earth. Doesn't touch so much as one grass blade, flower, or tree. It's an anti-gravity metal. Its purpose is to keep you from touching this world of the past in any way. Stay on the Path. Don't go off it. I repeat. *Don't go off.* For *any* reason! If you fall off, there's a penalty. And don't shoot any animal we don't okay."

"Why?" asked Eckels.

"Step on a mouse and you crush the Pyramids. Step on a mouse and you leave your print, like a Grand Canyon, across Eternity."

They sat in the ancient wilderness. Far birds' cries blew on a wind, and the smell of tar and an old salt sea, moist grasses, and flowers the color of blood.

"We don't want to change the Future. We don't belong here in the Past. The government doesn't *like* us here. We have to pay big graft to keep our franchise.² A Time Machine is finicky business. Not knowing it, we might kill an important animal, a small bird, a roach, a flower even, thus destroying an important link in a growing species."

"That's not clear," said Eckels.

"All right," Travis continued, "say we accidentally kill one mouse here. That means all the future families of this one particular mouse are destroyed, right?"

"Right."

"And all the families of the families of the families of that one mouse! With a stamp of

your foot, you annihilate first one, then a dozen, then a thousand, a million, a *billion* possible mice!"

"So they're dead," said Eckels. "So what?" **L₂**

"So what?" Travis snorted quietly. "Well, what about the foxes that'll need those mice to survive? For want of ten mice, a fox dies. For want of ten foxes, a lion starves. For want of a lion, all manner of insects, vultures, infinite billions of life forms are thrown into chaos and destruction. Eventually it all boils down to this: fifty-nine million years later, a cave man, one of a dozen on the *entire world*, goes hunting wild boar or saber-tooth tiger for food. But you, friend, have *stepped* on all the tigers in that region. By stepping on one single mouse. So the cave man starves. And the cave man, please note, is not just *any expendable* man, no! He is an *entire future nation.* From his loins would have sprung ten sons. From their loins one hundred sons, and thus onward to a civilization. Destroy this one man, and you destroy a race, a people, an entire history of life. It is comparable to slaying some of Adam's grandchildren. The stomp of your foot, on one mouse, could start an earthquake, the effects of which could shake our earth and destinies down through Time, to their very foundations. With the death of that one cave man, a billion others yet unborn are throttled in the womb. Perhaps Rome never rises on its seven hills. Perhaps Europe is forever a dark forest, and only Asia waxes healthy and teeming. "Step on a mouse and you crush the Pyramids. Step on a mouse and you leave your print, like a Grand Canyon, across Eternity." Queen Elizabeth might never be born. Washington might not cross the Delaware, there might never be a United States at all. So be careful. Stay on the Path. *Never* step off!"

Big Idea The Extraordinary and Fantastic *In your own words, explain the extraordinary consequences of killing a single prehistoric mouse.* **BI₂**

Vocabulary

expendable (iks pen′ də bəl) *adj.* not strictly necessary; capable of being sacrificed

2. Time Safari, Inc., pays money as bribes to government officials in return for continued permission to run its business.

RAY BRADBURY **1125**

Teach

"I see," said Eckels. "Then it wouldn't pay for us even to touch the *grass*?"

"Correct. Crushing certain plants could add up infinitesimally.[3] A little error here would multiply in sixty million years, all out of proportion. Of course maybe our theory is wrong. Maybe Time *can't* be changed by us. Or maybe it can be changed only in little subtle ways. A dead mouse here makes an insect imbalance there, a population disproportion later, a bad harvest further on, a depression, mass starvation, and, finally, a change in *social* temperament in far-flung countries. Something much more subtle, like that. Perhaps only a soft breath, a whisper, a hair, pollen on the air, such a slight, slight change that unless you looked close you wouldn't see it. Who knows? Who really can say he knows? We don't know. We're guessing. But until we do know for certain whether our messing around in Time *can* make a big roar or a little rustle in history, we're being careful. This Machine, this Path, your clothing and bodies, were sterilized, as you know, before the journey. We wear these oxygen helmets so we can't introduce our bacteria into an ancient atmosphere."

"How do we know which animals to shoot?"

"They're marked with red paint," said Travis. "Today, before our journey, we sent Lesperance here back with the Machine. He came to this particular era and followed certain animals."

"Studying them?"

"Right," said Lesperance. "I track them through their entire existence, noting which of them lives longest. Very few. How many times they mate. Not often. Life's short. When I find one that's going to die when a tree falls on him, or one that drowns in a tar pit, I note the exact hour, minute, and second. I shoot a paint bomb. It leaves a red

patch on his hide. We can't miss it. Then I **correlate** our arrival in the Past so that we meet the Monster not more than two minutes before he would have died anyway. This way, we kill only animals with no future, that are never going to mate again. You see how *careful* we are?"

"But if you came back this morning in Time," said Eckels eagerly, "you must've bumped into *us*, our Safari! How did it turn out? Was it successful? Did all of us get through—alive?"

Travis and Lesperance gave each other a look.

★

"That'd be a **paradox**," said the latter. "Time doesn't permit that sort of mess—a man meeting himself. When such occasions threaten, Time steps aside. Like an airplane hitting an air pocket. You felt the Machine jump just before we stopped? That was us passing ourselves on the way back to the Future. We saw nothing. There's no way of telling *if* this expedition was a success, *if we* got our monster, or whether all of us—meaning *you,* Mr. Eckels—got out alive."

Eckels smiled palely.

"Cut that," said Travis sharply. "Everyone on his feet!"

They were ready to leave the Machine.

The jungle was high and the jungle was broad and the jungle was the entire world forever and forever. Sounds like music and sounds like flying tents filled the sky, and those were pterodactyls soaring with cavernous gray wings, gigantic bats of delirium and night fever.

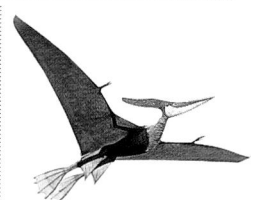

Visual Vocabulary
Pterodactyls (ter´ ə dak´ tilz) are extinct flying reptiles with wingspans of up to forty feet.

---

3. *Infinitesimally* (in´ fi nə tes´ə məl le) describes something being done "in a way that is too small to be measured."

Reading Strategy Identifying Genre *How might this warning help you to determine the genre of this selection?* **R**

> **Vocabulary**
>
> **correlate** (kôr´ə lāt) *v.* to bring (one thing) into relation (with another thing); calculate
> **paradox** (par´ə doks´) *n.* something that seems illogical, but that in fact may be true

---

Additional Support

Skills Practice

READING: Monitoring Comprehension Comprehending long sentences can be difficult even for proficient readers. Suggest that students pay close attention to punctuation when deciphering long and complicated sentences. Point out that punctuation marks such as commas and semicolons indicate pauses or breaks in thought. Ask less proficient readers to point out separate parts of a long sentence, isolating each clause and phrase. Suggest that they break each sentence into manageable parts, making the sentence as a whole easier to understand. **OL**

Eckels, balanced on the narrow Path, aimed his rifle playfully.

"Stop that!" said Travis. "Don't even aim for fun, blast you! If your gun should go off—"

Eckels flushed. "Where's our *Tyrannosaurus?*"

Lesperance checked his wristwatch. "Up ahead. We'll bisect his trail in sixty seconds. Look for the red paint! Don't shoot till we give the word. Stay on the Path. *Stay on the Path!*"

They moved forward in the wind of morning.

"Strange," murmured Eckels. "Up ahead, sixty million years, Election Day over. Keith made President. Everyone celebrating. And here we are, a million years lost, and they don't exist. The things we worried about for months, a lifetime, not even born or thought about yet."

"Safety catches off, everyone!" ordered Travis. "You, first shot, Eckels. Second, Billings. Third, Kramer."

"I've hunted tiger, wild boar, buffalo, elephant, but now, this is *it,*" said Eckels. "I'm shaking like a kid."

"Ah," said Travis.

Everyone stopped.

Travis raised his hand. "Ahead," he whispered. "In the mist. There he is. There's His Royal Majesty now."

The jungle was wide and full of twitterings, rustlings, murmurs, and sighs.

Suddenly it all ceased, as if someone had shut a door.

Silence.

A sound of thunder.

Out of the mist, one hundred yards away, came *Tyrannosaurus rex.*

"It," whispered Eckels. "It . . ."

"Sh!"

It came on great oiled, **resilient,** striding legs. It towered thirty feet above half of the trees, a great evil god, folding its delicate watchmaker's claws close to its oily reptilian[4] chest. Each lower leg was a piston, a thousand pounds of white bone, sunk in thick ropes of muscle, sheathed over in a gleam of pebbled skin like the mail of a terrible warrior. Each thigh was a ton of meat, ivory, and steel mesh. And from the great breathing cage of the upper body those two delicate arms dangled out front, arms with hands which might pick up and examine men like toys, while the snake neck coiled. And the head itself, a ton of sculptured stone, lifted easily upon the sky. Its mouth gaped, exposing a fence of teeth like daggers. Its eyes rolled, ostrich eggs, empty of all expression save hunger. It closed its mouth in a death grin. It ran, its pelvic bones crushing aside trees and bushes, its taloned feet clawing damp earth, leaving prints six inches deep wherever it settled its weight. It ran with a gliding ballet step, far too poised and balanced for its ten tons. It moved into a sunlit arena warily, its beautifully reptilian hands feeling the air.

"Why, why," Eckels twitched his mouth. "It could reach up and grab the moon."

"Sh!" Travis jerked angrily. "He hasn't seen us yet."

"It can't be killed." Eckels pronounced this verdict quietly, as if there could be no argument. He had weighed the evidence and this was his considered opinion. The rifle in his

Visual Vocabulary
Mail is a flexible body armor made of small, overlapping or interlinked metal plates or rings.

---

4. *Reptilian* (rep til′ē ən) means "of or like a reptile."

Literary Element Foreshadowing *What do you think Travis was going to say? What sort of ending to the story might Travis's warning foreshadow?* **L**

Vocabulary

resilient (ri zil′ yənt) *adj.* capable of springing back into shape or position after being bent, stretched, or compressed

Big Idea The Extraordinary and Fantastic *In this paragraph, how do you think Bradbury was able to describe an animal that has been extinct for millions of years in such specific and vivid terms?* **BI**

RAY BRADBURY **1127**

Teach

BI **Big Idea**

The Extraordinary and Fantastic **Answer:** *Eckels has just realized the extraordinary size and strength of the dinosaur that before was mythical to him rather than real.* **OL**

L **Literary Element**

Foreshadowing **Answer:** *On page 1126, Eckels asks Travis: "Then it wouldn't pay for us even to touch the grass?"* **OL**

⭐ **Viewing the Art**

Say: *A Brachiosaurus is a massive plant-eating dinosaur of the Jurassic and Cretaceous eras. It has a long and flexible neck, long forelegs, and nostrils above its eyes.* **Ask:** *In what ways is the dinosaur in the painting comparable to the Tyrannosaurus rex described in the story? (By placing the dinosaur in the foreground, the painter emphasizes its enormous size. Its ferocity is also highlighted because of the close-up on the large claw and teeth. The dinosaur looks as though it could "crush aside trees and bushes," like the dinosaur in the story.)* **AS**

hands seemed a cap gun. "We were fools to come. This is impossible."

"Shut up!" hissed Travis.

"Nightmare."

"Turn around," commanded Travis. "Walk quietly to the Machine. We'll remit one half your fee."

"I didn't realize it would be this *big*," said Eckels. "I miscalculated, that's all. And now I want out."

"It *sees* us!"

"There's the red paint on its chest!"

The Tyrant Lizard raised itself. Its armored flesh glittered like a thousand green coins. The coins, crusted with slime, steamed. In the slime, tiny insects wriggled, so that the entire body seemed to twitch and undulate,[5] even while the monster itself did not move. It exhaled. The stink of raw flesh blew down the wilderness.

"Get me out of here," said Eckels. "It was never like this before. I was always sure I'd come through alive. I had good guides, good safaris, and safety. This time, I figured wrong. I've met my match and admit it. This is too much for me to get hold of."

"Don't run," said Lesperance. "Turn around. Hide in the Machine."

"Yes." Eckels seemed to be numb. He looked at his feet as if trying to make them move. He gave a grunt of helplessness.

"Eckels!"

He took a few steps, blinking, shuffling.

"Not *that* way!"

The Monster, at the first motion, lunged forward with a terrible scream. It covered one hundred yards in four seconds. The rifles jerked up and blazed fire. A windstorm from the beast's mouth engulfed them in the stench of slime

---

5. *Undulate* (un´jə lāt´) means "to move like a wave."

Big Idea The Extraordinary and Fantastic
What has Eckels just realized? **BI**

and old blood. The Monster roared, teeth glittering with sun.

Eckels, not looking back, walked blindly to the edge of the Path, his gun limp in his arms, stepped off the Path, and walked, not knowing it, in the jungle. His feet sank into green moss. His legs moved him, and he felt alone and remote from the events behind.

The rifles cracked again. Their sound was lost in shriek and lizard thunder. The great level of the reptile's tail swung up, lashed sideways. Trees exploded in clouds of leaf and branch. The Monster twitched its jeweler's hands down to fondle at the men,

Literary Element Foreshadowing *Which of Eckels's earlier questions foreshadows his action here?* **L**

Brachiosaurus. English School, 20th century. Oil on canvas. Natural History Museum, London, UK. ⭐

Additional Support

Skills Practice

WRITING: Vivid Adjectives The description of the dinosaur and its death contains many vivid adjectives. Ask students to list some of these adjectives. (*Possible answers: Resilient, striding, evil, delicate, oily, reptilian, pebbled, taloned, metallic, glittering, sickening.*)

Have students use the words they listed to write a descriptive paragraph of their own involving a dinosaur. Ask them also to add vivid adjectives of their own. When students have finished writing, have them read their descriptions to a classmate. **OL** to twist them in half, to crush them like berries, to cram them into its teeth and its screaming throat. Its boulder-stone eyes leveled with the men. They saw themselves mirrored. They fired at the metallic eyelids and the blazing black iris.

Like a stone idol, like a mountain avalanche, *Tyrannosaurus* fell. Thundering, it clutched trees, pulled them with it. It wrenched and tore the metal Path. The men flung themselves back and away. The body hit, ten tons of cold flesh and stone. The guns fired. The Monster lashed its armored tail, twitched its snake jaws, and lay still. A fount of blood spurted from its throat. Somewhere inside, a sac of fluids burst. Sickening gushes drenched the hunters. They stood, red and glistening.

The thunder faded.

The jungle was silent. After the avalanche, a green peace. After the nightmare, morning.

Billings and Kramer sat on the pathway and threw up. Travis and Lesperance stood with smoking rifles, cursing steadily.

In the Time Machine, on his face, Eckels lay shivering. He had found his way back to the Path, climbed into the Machine.

Travis came walking, glanced at Eckels, took cotton gauze from a metal box, and returned to the others, who were sitting on the Path.

"Clean up."

They wiped the blood from their helmets. They began to curse too. The Monster lay, a hill of solid flesh. Within, you could hear the sighs and murmurs as the furthest chambers of it died, the organs malfunctioning, liquids running a final instant from pocket to sac to spleen, everything shutting off, closing up forever. It was like standing by a wrecked locomotive or a steam shovel at quitting time, all valves being released or levered tight. Bones cracked; the tonnage of its own flesh, off balance, dead weight, snapped the delicate forearms, caught underneath. The meat settled, quivering.

Another cracking sound. Overhead, a gigantic tree branch broke from its heavy mooring, fell. It crashed upon the dead beast with finality.

"There." Lesperance checked his watch. "Right on time. That's the giant tree that was scheduled to fall and kill this animal originally." He glanced at the two hunters. "You want the trophy picture?" **R1**

"What?"

"We can't take a trophy back to the Future. The body has to stay right here where it would have died originally, so the insects, birds, and bacteria can get at it, as they were intended to. Everything in balance. The body stays. But we *can* take a picture of you standing near it."

The two men tried to think, but gave up, shaking their heads.

They let themselves be led along the metal Path. They sank wearily into the Machine cushions. They gazed back at the ruined Monster, the stagnating mound, where already strange reptilian birds and golden insects were busy at the steaming armor.

A sound on the floor of the Time Machine stiffened them. Eckels sat there, shivering.

"I'm sorry," he said at last.

"Get up!" cried Travis.

Eckels got up.

"Go out on that Path alone," said Travis. He had his rifle pointed. "You're not coming back in the Machine. We're leaving you here!"

Lesperance seized Travis' arm. "Wait—"

"Stay out of this!" Travis shook his hand away. "This fool nearly killed us. But it isn't *that* so much, no. It's his *shoes*! Look at them! He ran off the Path. That *ruins* us! We'll forfeit! Thousands of dollars of insurance! We guarantee no one leaves the Path. He left it. Oh, the fool! I'll have to report to the government. They might revoke[6] our license to travel. Who knows what he's done to Time, to History!"

"Take it easy, all he did was kick up some dirt."

---

6. *Revoke* means "to cancel or withdraw."

Reading Strategy Identifying Genre *What conflict is described here? How does it define a characteristic of this genre?* **R2**

R1 **Reading Strategy**

Identifying Genre

Ask: How is Lesperance's comment, "Right on time. That's the giant tree that was scheduled to fall and kill this animal originally" distinctive of the story's genre? (*This comment is typical of the science fiction genre because it reveals the vastly different concepts of time these characters have from ours today. Since they are able to move back and forth in time and see past events at any given moment, they think of events as being "scheduled" to happen at a certain time, even though they really happened by chance, such as the tree branch falling and killing the dinosaur.*) **OL**

R2 **Reading Strategy**

Identifying Genre **Answer:** *The conflict is person versus technology, which is a common conflict in science fiction writing.* **OL**

Differentiated Instruction

Identifying Author's Purpose
Mention that authors usually write fiction with a purpose in mind, such as to entertain or to teach a lesson. To identify an author's purpose, tell students to look carefully at the way a piece of literature is written, their own reactions to it, and the messages that come across.

Ask students to review the sections of the story that they find most striking or most important, and to discuss what they consider to be Bradbury's purposes in writing it. (*Students may say that his purpose is to entertain, yet also to present a warning about meddling with the delicate balance of life.*) **BL**

Objectives
- To recognize and analyze the author's use of literary techniques such as foreshadowing (SE)
- To identify characteristics that help determine genre (SE)
- To use vivid adjectives (TWE)

Foreshadowing Answer:
This statement foreshadows that the world has in fact changed because of Eckels' actions.) OL

L2 Literary Element

Foreshadowing Ask: When Travis says, "I'm warning you, Eckels, I might kill you yet. I've got my gun ready," do you expect this foreshadows the outcome of the story? *(Students may predict that Travis either kills Eckels or comes very close to doing so.)* OL

BI1 Big Idea

The Extraordinary and Fantastic Answer: *The details all point to changes in the world that are barely noticeable and difficult to describe, but certainly present. Eckels is unsure of the exact consequences of his actions, but this passage suggests that there certainly will be consequences.)* OL

"How do we *know?*" cried Travis. "We don't know anything! It's all a mystery! Get out there, Eckels!"

Eckels fumbled his shirt. "I'll pay anything. A hundred thousand dollars!"

Travis glared at Eckels' checkbook and spat. "Go out there. The Monster's next to the Path. Stick your arms up to your elbows in his mouth. Then you can come back with us."

"That's unreasonable!"

"The Monster's dead, you idiot. The bullets! The bullets can't be left behind. They don't belong in the Past; they might change anything. Here's my knife. Dig them out!"

The jungle was alive again, full of the old tremorings and bird cries. Eckels turned slowly to regard the **primeval** garbage dump, that hill of nightmares and terror. After a long time, like a sleepwalker, he shuffled out along the Path.

He returned, shuddering, five minutes later, his arms soaked and red to the elbows. He held out his hands. Each held a number of steel bullets. Then he fell. He lay where he fell, not moving.

"You didn't have to make him do that," said Lesperance.

"Didn't I? It's too early to tell." Travis nudged the still body. "He'll live. Next time he won't go hunting game like this. Okay." He jerked his thumb wearily at Lesperance. "Switch on. Let's go home."

1492.   1776.   1812.

They cleaned their hands and faces. They changed their caking shirts and pants. Eckels was up and around again, not speaking. Travis glared at him for a full ten minutes.

"Don't look at me," cried Eckels. "I haven't done anything."

"Who can tell?"

"Just ran off the Path, that's all, a little mud on my shoes—what do you want me to do—get down and pray?"

"We might need it. I'm warning you, Eckels, I might kill you yet. I've got my gun L2 ready."

"I'm innocent. I've done nothing."

1999.   2000.   2055.

The Machine stopped.

"Get out," said Travis.

The room was there as they had left it. But not the same as they had left it. The same man sat behind the same desk. But the same man did not quite sit behind the same desk.

Travis looked around swiftly. "Everything okay here?" he snapped.

"Fine. Welcome home!"

Travis did not relax. He seemed to be looking at the very atoms of the air itself, at the way the sun poured through the one high window.

"Okay, Eckels, get out. Don't ever come back."

Eckels could not move. "You heard me," said Travis. "What're you *staring* at?"

Eckels stood smelling of the air, and there was a thing to the air, a chemical taint[7] so subtle, so slight, that only a faint cry of his subliminal[8] senses warned him it was there. The colors, white, gray, blue, orange, in the wall, in the furniture, in the sky beyond the window, were . . . were . . . And there was a *feel*. His flesh twitched. His hands twitched. He stood drinking the oddness with the pores of his body. Somewhere, someone must have been screaming one of those whistles that only a dog can hear. His body screamed silence in return. Beyond this room, beyond this wall, beyond this man who was not quite the same man seated at this desk that was not quite the same desk

---

Literary Element Foreshadowing *What might this statement foreshadow?* L1

Vocabulary

primeval (prī mē′ vəl) *adj.* of or having to do with the first or earliest age; primitive

---

7. A *taint* is a trace of something that harms or spoils.
8. *Subliminal* (sub lim′ ən əl) means "existing below the limits of sensation or consciousness; subconscious."

Big Idea The Extraordinary and Fantastic *In what ways are the details in this passage extraordinary or fantastic?* BI1

Additional Support

Skills Practice

LISTENING AND SPEAKING: Oral Defense Ask students to prepare an answer to questions that might be covered when making an oral defense, such as the participants in the safari might be asked to make on their return. They should be able to answer these questions: *What happened? Why did it happen? What was done or could be done now to resolve the problem?* Ask students to imagine that either Eckels or Travis is called upon by a supervisor to explain the events of their safari. Pair students together, one as the supervisor who asks questions and one as Travis or Eckels who defends himself. OL

Brachiosaurus. Zdenek Burian (1905–1981).

. . . lay an entire world of streets and people. What sort of world it was now, there was no telling. He could feel them moving there, beyond the walls, almost, like so many chess pieces blown in a dry wind. . . .

But the immediate thing was the sign painted on the office wall, the same sign he had read earlier today on first entering.

Somehow, the sign had changed:

TYME SEFARI INC.
SEFARIS TU ANY YEER EN THE PAST.
YU NAIM THE ANIMALL.
WEE TAEKYUTHAIR.
YU SHOOT ITT.

Eckels felt himself fall into a chair. He fumbled crazily at the thick slime on his boots. He held up a clod of dirt, trembling, "No, it *can't* be. Not a *little* thing like that. No!"

Embedded in the mud, glistening green and gold and black, was a butterfly, very beautiful and very dead.

"Not a little thing like *that!* Not a butterfly!" cried Eckels.

It fell to the floor, an exquisite thing, a small thing that could upset balances and knock down a line of small dominoes and then big dominoes and then gigantic dominoes, all down the years across Time. Eckels' mind whirled. It *couldn't* change things. Killing one butterfly couldn't be *that* important! Could it?

His face was cold. His mouth trembled, asking: "Who— Who won the presidential election yesterday?"

The man behind the desk laughed. "You joking? You know very well. Deutscher, of course! Who else? Not that fool weakling Keith. We got an iron man now, a man with guts!" The official stopped. "What's wrong?"

Eckels moaned. He dropped to his knees. He scrabbled at the golden butterfly with shaking fingers. "Can't we," he pleaded to the world, to himself, to the officials, to the Machine, "can't we take it *back*, can't we *make* it alive again? Can't we start over? Can't we—"

He did not move. Eyes shut, he waited, shivering. He heard Travis breathe loud in the room; he heard Travis shift his rifle, click the safety catch, and raise the weapon.

There was a sound of thunder. ❧

| **Literary Element** | Foreshadowing *Why does Bradbury allow the reader to infer what happens at the end of the story?* **L₃** |

RAY BRADBURY **1131**

Teach

BI₂ **Big Idea**

The Extraordinary and Fantastic Ask: How does Eckels' exclamation, "Not a little thing like *that!* Not a butterfly!" contribute to the fantastic qualities of the story? (*Eckels' outburst occurs at the climax of the story, when he realizes he has altered the future by killing a butterfly. This highlights one of the most extraordinary aspects of the story, which is the idea that a minute change in a primordial age can have profound effects on human civilization millions of years later.*) **OL**

L₃ **Literary Element**

Foreshadowing Answer: *Bradbury doesn't need to say it again. It was already foreshadowed.* **OL**

CheckPoint

Use the CheckPoint questions on Presentation Plus! to check students' mastery of the selection. These questions can be used with interactive response keypads for immediate student feedback.

Reading in the Real World

College Ask students to research the factors that led to the dinosaurs' extinction. Have them find contrasting theories about what caused their extinction, and take note of the evidence for each theory. Ask students to describe the theory they find most convincing and explain why. Then have students discuss connections between the factors involved in the dinosaurs' extinction and the Bradbury story. (*A combination of environmental factors had dramatic and far-reaching effects, eventually killing off the dinosaurs. Similar cause-and-effect relationships appear in the story.*) **OL**

Objectives
- To recognize and analyze the author's use of literary techniques such as foreshadowing (SE)
- To identify characteristics that help determine genre (SE)
- To present an oral defense (TWE)

Assess

1. Students may say Eckels should not have been shot because there may be a way to restore things. Other students may say it was a fitting end to a coward who had changed the future.

2. (a) Natural events occur in reverse order as the group goes back in time. (b) He is awed by the power of such an invention.

3. (a) Eckels is terrified and runs off the path. (b) The men are not fully prepared for how huge and ferocious the dinosaur is.

4. (a) The future has been changed. (b) The future has not changed for the better.

5. Events do occur in logical ways. That is part of what makes the story believable.

6. (a) The author says the dinosaur is a great god; that each leg is a piston; that each thigh is meat, ivory, and steel mesh; that its head is a ton of sculptured stone; that its eyes are ostrich eggs. (b) These comparisons relate the body parts to things with which the reader is familiar.

7. The company might say its services are educational. Pure greed may be another reason.

8. (a) Students might mention historical events in which

RESPONDING AND THINKING CRITICALLY

Respond

1. What was your reaction to the outcome of the story?

Recall and Interpret

2. (a) Describe what happens after the hunting party enters the Machine. (b) What feelings does Eckels experience during his first journey in the Machine? Explain your answer using evidence from the text.

3. (a) How does Eckels react when the *Tyrannosaurus rex* appears? (b) In your opinion, why do Eckels and the other men react the way they do?

4. (a) What do the men discover when they return from their trip? (b) Why do you think Eckels and Travis are so dismayed by the changes they find?

Analyze and Evaluate

5. Within the fictional world that Bradbury has created, do events seem to occur in a logical, predictable way? Support your answer with specific examples from the story.

6. (a) Identify at least three metaphors the author uses to describe the *Tyrannosaurus rex*. What two things are being compared in each metaphor? (b) How do these metaphors help you visualize the Monster?

7. Even though its activities are risky, Time Safari stays in business. What reasons might the company have for continuing its operations?

Connect

8. **Big Idea** The Extraordinary and Fantastic (a) If it were possible to travel to the past in order to change an event, what might you want to change? Why? (b) Consider the repercussions of a very small change in prehistoric time, as described in the story. What might be the repercussions of the changes you describe?

PRIMARY SOURCE QUOTATION

The Butterfly Effect
The following excerpt from a newspaper editorial describes the possible influence of Ray Bradbury's story on the common expression *butterfly effect*.

"A conjecture made to the New York Academy of Sciences in 1963 by meteorologist Edward Lorenz eventually spawned the popular term "butterfly effect." Lorenz suggested that the atmospheric disturbance caused by flapping wings could eventually amplify into a catastrophic event worthy of a Weather Channel special. . . . Chaos theory says that any system, simple or complex, has an elemental order that will react in unpredictable ways when subjected to simple events. . . . The title of Lorenz's speech given to the American Academy for the Advancement of Science in 1972 was this: "Predictability: Does the Flap of a Butterfly's Wings in Brazil set off a Tornado in Texas?"

Let's reduce this mumbo-jumbo to American English with [an] example from . . . "real life." Ray Bradbury published the sci-fi story "A Sound of Thunder," in which a man named Eckels travels

back to the Jurassic period. . . . Upon returning to his future, Eckels finds that everything has changed. He's horrified when he examines primordial goo on his boots: 'Embedded in the mud . . . was a butterfly, very beautiful and very dead. . . .' Ray Bradbury published his story 11 years before Lorenz's [example] flapped into existence."
—Bob Saar, *The Hawkeye*, from **"The Butterfly Effect"**

1. Explain the butterfly effect in your own words. Have you heard the expression before? Explain.

2. Why might the story "A Sound of Thunder" have had such a lasting effect on our culture?

many people lost their lives, such as the Civil War or the Holocaust. (b) Students should explain their answers.

Primary Source Quotation

1. Students should refer to the high level of sensitivity and changes that occur over time.

2. Chaos theory is an idea with complex and fascinating implications, and it seems to have captured the popular imagination and held it even until the present time.

LITERARY ANALYSIS

Literary Element Foreshadowing

Bradbury uses **foreshadowing** throughout "A Sound of Thunder" to prepare the reader for the eventual outcome of the story. Foreshadowing helps to build suspense in the reader by hinting at events to come.

1. What clues help prepare you for the way Eckels behaves in a crisis?

2. Reread the last section of the story beginning with the words "1492. 1776. 1812" (page 1130). Identify two clues that foreshadow the outcome of the story.

Review: Description

As you learned on page 65, **description** is a detailed portrayal of a person, place, object, or action. Description employs imagery that appeals to the reader's senses. Good description makes readers feel as if they had stepped into the story and it is taking place all around them.

Partner Activity Pair up with a classmate and discuss the use of description in "A Sound of Thunder." Working together, choose a particularly vivid character, object, or scene from the story and depict it in a poster, collage, or painting.

You may want to brainstorm details about your subject before you begin creating your depiction. Use a web like the one below to keep track of descriptive details.

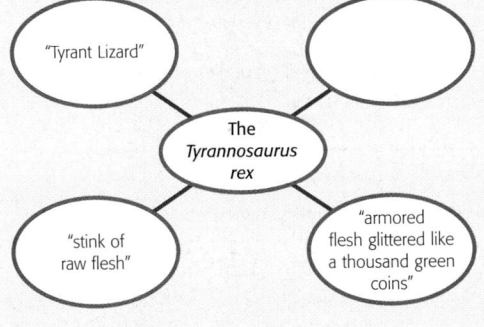

READING AND VOCABULARY

Reading Strategy Identifying Genre

Since different **genres**—or types of literature—are created for different purposes, properly categorizing a work can help the reader develop conclusions about the meaning of the work and about the author's message.

1. What is the overall purpose or message of "A Sound of Thunder"? Explain.

2. How does this message help you categorize the story?

3. What other characteristics helped you to categorize the story? Explain your answer.

Vocabulary Practice

Practice with Word Parts Match each numbered word in the list with its Latin word of origin. Use a dictionary if you need help.

1. colloquial   a. *stringere* (to draw tight)
2. concoct   b. *loqui* (speak)
3. conjunction   c. *coquere* (to cook)
4. compensate   d. *jungere* (to join)
5. constrict   e. *pensare* (to weigh)

Academic Vocabulary

Here are two words from the vocabulary list on page R82.

minor (mī′nər) *adj.* less important; smaller

indicate (in′di kāt) *v.* to suggest, to show, or to identify

Practice and Apply
1. When the hunting party returns in the time machine, what **minor** changes do they notice first?
2. What do these changes **indicate** about time travel?

RAY BRADBURY **1133**

AFTER YOU READ

Assess

Literary Element

1. From the very beginning, there are clues that Eckels is nervous about the safari. He seeks reassurance that things will go well right up to the time the dinosaur appears.

2. The change in the sign and the dead butterfly are clues that foreshadow the final outcome.

Review: Description

Encourage students to depict the character, object, or scene that made the strongest impression on their imagination.

Reading Strategy

1. The overall message is that people have a responsibility to protect and care for the earth for future generations despite advances in technology.

2. The warning about the dangers of technology identifies the selection as science fiction. The concern about social ills also helps to identify the story as science fiction.

3. Characteristics students might list include the future setting; technology that allows people to travel through time; the conflict between people and technology; and the theme warning of the possible destruction of civilization as a result of technology and its abuse.

Vocabulary

1. b 2. c 3. d 4. e 5. a

Academic Vocabulary

1. There is a slight change in the air; colors seem to be somewhat different; the spelling of the sign on the wall has changed.

2. Traveling into the past can change the future.

Assess

Writing About Literature

Students' essays should

- quote specific passages that contain vivid images.
- explain how the images help the reader experience what is being described.
- identify which sense each image appeals to.

Literature Groups

Students might benefit from referring to other stories, books, or movies they've experienced that deal with the concept of time travel. In each work, did the journey through time have a positive or negative effect on the characters? On the world as a whole?

Bradbury's Language and Style

Ask students why authors might make use of participles in their writing. *(Students should note that participles allow authors to turn verbs into adjectives. For example, "slide" becomes "sliding." This gives writers a wide range of words to choose from when selecting modifiers. It helps add variety and originality to their work.)*

Writing About Literature

Evaluate Author's Craft Bradbury is a master of the sensory image. The world that he has created in "A Sound of Thunder" comes alive through all five of the senses. Find several passages in the story that contain vivid imagery. Then write a brief essay explaining how these images help you to imagine what it is like to see, hear, smell, taste, or touch what is being described.

Before you begin writing, make a list of images that you find in the passages that you have chosen to write about. Identify the sense or senses to which each of the images appeals. Then analyze the effect the image has on the reader. Use a chart like the one below to record your thoughts:

Pauses	Senses
a mass and tangle, a snaking and humming of wires and steel boxes	sight, sound

After finishing your essay, meet with a peer reviewer to evaluate each other's work and suggest revisions. Once you have revised your essay, remember to proofread and edit it for spelling, grammar, and punctuation errors.

Literature Groups

On page 1126 of the story, Lesperance says, "That'd be a paradox. Time doesn't permit that sort of mess." Working in small groups, discuss the pros, cons, and paradoxes of time travel. In your discussion, consider Lesperance's argument and the possible impact of being in two times at once.

Bradbury's Language and Style

Using Gerunds In "A Sound of Thunder," Bradbury creates vivid images by using gerunds and participles in his descriptions. It is easy to confuse a gerund and a present participle because they both end in *–ing.* Just remember that a gerund is used as a noun. A participle is used as an adjective.

Example from Story	Gerund or Participle?	Reason
"under a film of *sliding* warm water"	participle	"sliding" modifies "warm water"
"a *snaking* and *humming* of wires"	gerunds	"snaking" and "humming" are objects of the preposition "at"

Activity Create a chart like the one above. Then fill in two gerunds and two participles from "A Sound of Thunder." Make sure you explain your reasoning for selecting each example. If you find additional examples, create additional rows.

Revising Check

Gerunds and Participles You can help your readers create vivid pictures in their mind's eye by using gerunds and participles. With a partner, review your essay on Bradbury's use of imagery and look for places where you might make your language more vivid by using gerunds and participles.

Literature Online **Web Activities** For eFlashcards, Selection Quick Checks, and other Web activities, go to www.glencoe.com.

Literature Online

Web Activities Have students access the Web site for interactive activities that will help them assess their understanding of the selection.

By the Waters of Babylon

MEET STEPHEN VINCENT BENÉT

Themes of history and war march through the works of Stephen Vincent Benét, who was born in Bethlehem, Pennsylvania, into a military family. His father was an Army colonel who often read poetry to his children. Not surprisingly, as a child Benét preferred reading to playing sports.

Benét spent his childhood on army posts in California. When he was ten, he began attending school at a military academy. Benét's first book of poems, *Five Men and Pompey*, was published in 1915 when he was just seventeen years old and a student at Yale University. His studies were interrupted by a year of government service during World War I, when he worked in the same department as writer James Thurber. Benét completed his master's degree in 1919. As his thesis, Benét submitted a volume of poems entitled *Heavens and Earth* (1920).

"*Books are not men and yet they stay alive.*"
—Stephen Vincent Benét

A Literary Career Benét then turned to fiction, publishing the autobiographical novel *The Beginning of Wisdom* in 1921. He moved to France to continue his studies at the Sorbonne, where he met his wife, writer Rosemary Carr. Throughout the 1920s Benét continued to publish fiction, including the books *Young People's Pride* (1922) and *Jean Huguenot* (1923); and poetry, including *King David* (1923), *The Ballad of William Sycamore, 1790–1880* (1923), and *Tiger Joy* (1925).

While living in France, Benét wrote the epic Civil War poem *John Brown's Body* (1928).

The poem achieved immediate critical and popular acclaim, and Benét won the Pulitzer Prize for the book in 1929. That same year, he was elected to the National Institute of Arts and Letters.

Although many of Benét's works focus on historical themes, he was also interested in horror, mystery, and science fiction. In 1937 he published a one-act play entitled *The Headless Horseman*, based on the Washington Irving story "The Legend of Sleepy Hollow." That same year, Benét published the short story collection *Thirteen O'Clock*. That book included perhaps his most famous story, "The Devil and Daniel Webster," based on the German legend of Faust, a man who sells his soul to the devil. After its publication, the story was adapted as a play, an opera, and two movies.

During the 1940s, Benét worked in radio and as a screenwriter in Hollywood. Throughout his life, he suffered from poor vision, crippling arthritis, and mental illness. Despite these setbacks, he continued to publish and earn honors as a writer, receiving the O. Henry Story Prize and the Roosevelt Medal. Benét had planned an epic poem called *Western Star*, but only finished one volume before his death. Nonetheless, he was awarded a second Pulitzer Prize posthumously for the work.

Stephen Vincent Benét was born in 1898 and died in 1943.

LiteratureOnline **Author Search** For more about Stephen Vincent Benét, go to www.glencoe.com.

STEPHEN VINCENT BENÉT **1135**

Focus

BELLRINGER

Bellringer Options
Selection Focus Transparency 45
Daily Language Practice
Transparency 94
Or **on the board, write:** Rite of Passage. **Ask:** What is a rite of passage? *(Answers will vary.)* What rites of passage have you or people you know experienced? *(Answers might include confirmation, bar/bat mitzvah, obtaining a driver's license, or going away to college.)* Have students discuss how these experiences might change a person's life. Discussion topics might include changes in expectations, new friends, or new responsibilities.

LiteratureOnline

Author Search To expand students' appreciation of Stephen Vincent Benét, have them access the Web site for additional information and resources.

Selection Skills

By the Waters of Babylon

Literary Elements
- Moral (SE pp. 1136–1148)
- Archetypes (SE p. 1148)

Reading Skills
- Visualizing (SE pp. 1136–1149)
- Comparing and Contrasting (TWE p. 1146)

Vocabulary Skills
- Word Origins (SE pp. 1136, 1149)

Listening/Speaking/Viewing Skills
- Analyze Art (SE pp. 1143, 1145, 1146)
- Rebuttal (SE p. 1149)

Writing Skills/Grammar
- Evaluate Author's Craft (SE p. 1149)
- Researching Historical Background (TWE p. 1144)
- Capitalization of Proper Nouns (TWE p. 1138)
- Making Judgments (TWE p. 1142)

Focus

Summary

The narrator is John, the son of a priest in an unspecified time and culture. To become a priest, John sets off on a journey alone. Although it is forbidden, he goes to the Place of the Gods, where he finds marks from the Great Burning. In a vision he sees the Place of the Gods first with lights, roads, and people, and then as it is destroyed by fire and poison mist. On waking, John finds the body of a preserved "god" and realizes that he was a man. John's father will not let him tell of his discovery, but John plans to rebuild the civilization when he becomes chief priest.

Ⅴ Vocabulary

Vocabulary File Say: Add these words and definitions to your vocabulary file. For each word, include a sentence that gives you an example of how to use the word. **OL** Students with English language needs should include the pronunciations of these words in their files. **EL**

Literary Elements Have students access the Web site to improve their understanding of moral.

Connecting to the Story

The following story describes a rite of passage—a transition from childhood to adulthood. Before you read the story, think about the following questions:

- What experiences have made you feel more like an adult than a child?
- What responsibilities do those experiences entail?

Building Background

The title "By the Waters of Babylon" alludes to the Bible's Psalm 137, which begins:

"By the rivers of Babylon, there we sat down, yea, we wept, when we remembered Zion."

The psalm describes the Israelites' grief over the destruction of their temple, their separation from their homeland Jerusalem (referred to here as Zion), and their enforced captivity at the hands of the Babylonians.

Many readers and critics have interpreted this story as an allegory about the aftermath of a nuclear holocaust. However, this story was first written in 1937, years before the first atomic weapons were even developed. Atomic bombs were developed in the United States during World War II and first used on August 6, 1945, when the United States dropped an atomic bomb on the city of Hiroshima in Japan. The devastation caused by this attack makes the scenes depicted in Benét's tale all the more prescient and affecting.

Setting Purposes for Reading

Big Idea The Extraordinary and Fantastic

As you read this short story, notice how Benét's main character is awed and amazed by the places he visits.

Literary Element Moral

A **moral** is a practical lesson about right and wrong. Some modern stories, especially science fiction stories, use these straightforward messages.

- See Literary Terms Handbook, p. R11.

Literature Online **Interactive Literary Elements Handbook** To review or learn more about the literary elements, go to www.glencoe.com.

OBJECTIVES
In studying this selection, you will focus on the following:
- understanding moral
- visualizing to enhance reading comprehension
- recognizing archetypes
- writing to evaluate author's craft

1136 UNIT 6 GENRE FICTION

Reading Strategy Visualizing

Visualizing means using an author's words to form a mental picture of what is being described. Visualizing allows you to enter a story's world and better understand the action taking place.

Reading Tip: Noting Descriptive Words Practice visualizing by paying careful attention to the descriptive words the author uses. Use a chart like the one below to record what you visualize in each paragraph.

Paragraph	Visualization
"Yet, after a while, my eyes were opened and I saw."	I picture the ruins of road bridges crossing over a river.
"It felt like ground underfoot; it did not burn me."	The narrator is describing the ruins of a big city.

Vocabulary

bade (bād) v. past tense of bid, to command, order, or ask; p. 1138 *The babysitter bade the two naughty children to stop running in the house.*

anteroom (an' tē rōōm') n. a small room serving as a waiting area or entrance to a larger main room; p. 1143 *My grandmother always greeted her guests in the anteroom.*

perplexed (pər plekst') adj. troubled with doubt or uncertainty; puzzled; p. 1145 *The complicated math formula perplexed the entire class.*

Vocabulary Tip: Word Origins The origin, or history, of most words can be found in a dictionary. Consider the following dictionary entry:

dour (door, dour) adj. **1.** sullenly gloomy; grim; forbidding. **2.** unyielding; obstinate. [Latin *dūrus* hard.]

The entry tells you that the word *dour* originated from the Latin word *dūrus*, meaning "hard."

Selection Resources

Print Materials
- 📁 Unit 6 Resources (Fast File), pp. 20–22
- 📁 Leveled Vocabulary Development, p. 78
- 📁 Selection and Unit Assessments, pp. 189–190
- 📁 Selection Quick Checks, p. 95

Transparencies
- Bellringer Options Transparencies: Selection Focus Transparency 45 Daily Language Practice Transparency 94
- Literary Elements Transparency 89

Technology
- 💿 TeacherWorks Plus™ CD-ROM
- 💿 StudentWorks Plus™ CD-ROM
- 💿 Presentation Plus!™ CD-ROM
- 💻 Literature Online, glencoe.com
- 💻 Online Student Edition, mhln.com
- 💿 ExamView® Assessment Suite CD-ROM
- 💿 Vocabulary PuzzleMaker CD-ROM
- 💿 Listening Library, disc 2 track 32

A Pyramid of Skulls, 1898–1900. Paul Cezanne. Oil on canvas. Private collection.

By the Waters of Babylon

Stephen Vincent Benét

The north and the west and the south are good hunting ground, but it is forbidden to go east. It is forbidden to go to any of the Dead Places except to search for metal and then he who touches the metal must be a priest or the son of a priest. Afterwards, both the man and the metal must be purified. These are the rules and the laws; they are well made. It is forbidden to cross the great river and look upon the place that was the Place of the Gods—this is most strictly forbidden. We do not even say its name though we know its name. It is there that spirits live, and demons—it is there that there are the ashes of the Great Burning.

These things are forbidden—they have been forbidden since the beginning of time.

My father is a priest; I am the son of a priest. I have been in the Dead Places near us, with my father—at first, I was afraid. When my father went into the house to search for the metal, I stood by the door and my heart felt small and weak. It was a dead man's house, a spirit house. It did not have the smell of man, though there were old bones in a corner. But it is not fitting that a priest's son should show fear. I looked at the bones in the shadow and kept my voice still.

> **Literary Element** Moral *What does this opening paragraph suggest about the morals of the people who live in this unidentified place?* **L**

STEPHEN VINCENT BENÉT **1137**

Teach

R1 Reading Strategy

Visualizing Answer: *He is brave, intelligent, hungry for knowledge, and mature beyond his years.* **OL**

R2 Reading Strategy

Visualizing Answer: *His state of mind is stoical, calm, and peaceful.* **OL**

BI Big Idea

The Extraordinary and the Fantastic Answer: *He means that John may not be ready to absorb the knowledge that awaits him if he follows the path indicated by the dream.* **OL**

Readability Scores
Dale-Chall: 5.6
DRP: 49
Lexile: 820

Then my father came out with the metal—a good, strong piece. He looked at me with both eyes but I had not run away. He gave me the metal to hold—I took it and did not die. So he knew that I was truly his son and would be a priest in my time. That was when I was very young—nevertheless, my brothers would not have done it, though they are good hunters. After that, they gave me the good piece of meat and the warm corner by the fire. My father watched over me—he was glad that I should be a priest. But when I boasted or wept without a reason, he punished me more strictly than my brothers. That was right.

After a time, I myself was allowed to go into the dead houses and search for metal. So I learned the ways of those houses—and if I saw bones, I was no longer afraid. The bones are light and old—sometimes they will fall into dust if you touch them. But that is a great sin.

I was taught the chants and the spells—I was taught how to stop the running of blood from a wound and many secrets. A priest must know many secrets—that was what my father said. If the hunters think we do all things by chants and spells, they may believe so—it does not hurt them. I was taught how to read in the old books and how to make the old writings—that was

Visual Vocabulary
A *grub* is the soft, wormlike larva of an insect, especially of a beetle.

hard and took a long time. My knowledge made me happy—it was like a fire in my heart. Most of all, I liked to hear of the Old Days and the stories of the gods. I asked myself many questions that I could not answer, but it was good to ask them. At night, I would lie awake and listen to the wind—it seemed to me that it was the voice of the gods as they flew through the air.

We are not ignorant like the Forest People—our women spin wool on the wheel, our priests wear a white robe. We do not eat grubs from the tree, we have not forgotten the old writings, although they are hard to understand. Nevertheless, my knowledge and my lack of knowledge burned in me—I wished to know more. When I was a man at last, I came to my father and said, "It is time for me to go on my journey. Give me your leave."

He looked at me for a long time, stroking his beard, then he said at last, "Yes. It is time." That night, in the house of the priest-hood, I asked for and received purification. My body hurt but my spirit was a cool stone. It was my father himself who questioned me about my dreams.

He **bade** me look into the smoke of the fire and see—I saw and told what I saw. It was what I have always seen—a river, and, beyond it, a great Dead Place and in it the gods walking. I have always thought about that. His eyes were stern when I told him—he was no longer my father but a priest. He said, "This is a strong dream."

"It is mine," I said, while the smoke waved and my head felt light. They were singing the Star song in the outer chamber and it was like the buzzing of bees in my head.

He asked me how the gods were dressed and I told him how they were dressed. We know how they were dressed from the book, but I saw them as if they were before me. When I had finished, he threw the sticks three times and studied them as they fell.

"This is a very strong dream," he said. "It may eat you up."

Reading Strategy Visualizing *What image of the narrator does this metaphor communicate?* **R2**

Big Idea The Extraordinary and Fantastic *What does John's father mean by this statement?* **BI**

Vocabulary

bade (bād) *v.* past tense of bid, to command, order, or ask

Reading Strategy Visualizing *Visualize the narrator based on this paragraph. What do you learn about him?* **R1**

1138 UNIT 6 GENRE FICTION

Additional Support

Skills Practice

GRAMMAR AND LANGUAGE: Capitalization of Proper Nouns

Write the words *Ann, Colorado River,* and *Aztecs* on the board. Remind students that names of specific people, places, historical events, and nationalities are capitalized. The author uses several imaginary proper nouns. Have students find and write six proper nouns from the selection. *(Possible answers include Forest People; Dead Place(s); Place of the Gods; the Great Burning and the Destruction; Ou-dis-sun, the Sacred, the Long; Hill People; and Bitter Water.)* **OL**

Where Eagles Dare! James Noel Smith. ⭐

"I am not afraid," I said and looked at him with both eyes. My voice sounded thin in my ears but that was because of the smoke.

He touched me on the breast and the forehead. He gave me the bow and the three arrows.

"Take them," he said. "It is forbidden to travel east. It is forbidden to cross the river. It is forbidden to go to the Place of the Gods. All these things are forbidden."

"All these things are forbidden," I said, but it was my voice that spoke and not my spirit. He looked at me again.

"My son," he said. "Once I had young dreams. If your dreams do not eat you up, you may be a great priest. If they eat you, you are still my son. Now go on your journey."

I went fasting, as is the law. My body hurt but not my heart. When the dawn came, I was out of sight of the village. I prayed and purified myself, waiting for a sign. The sign was an eagle. It flew east.

Sometimes signs are sent by bad spirits. I waited again on the flat rock, fasting, taking no food. I was very still—I could feel the sky above me and the earth beneath. I waited till the sun was beginning to sink. Then three deer passed in the valley, going east—they did not wind me or see me. There was a white fawn with them—a very great sign.

I followed them, at a distance, waiting for what would happen. My heart was troubled about going east, yet I knew that I must go. My head hummed with my fasting—I did not even see the panther spring upon the white fawn. But, before I knew it, the bow was in my hand. I shouted and the panther lifted his head from the fawn. It is not easy to kill a panther with one arrow but the arrow went through his eye and into his brain. He died as he tried to spring—he rolled over, tearing at the ground. Then I knew I was meant to go east—I knew that was my journey. When the night came, I made my fire and roasted meat.

Literary Element Moral *What moral might be contained in these words?* **L**

STEPHEN VINCENT BENÉT **1139**

Teach

L Literary Element

Moral Answer: *This passage hints that the boy believes that commandments may be broken in the search for truth.*
Ask: *Why do you think a distinction is made between John's* voice *and his* spirit? *(The author is emphasizing that people have an inner life consisting of conscience, inner strength, and a moral sense. This "spirit" is separate from physical facts such as pain or hunger.)* **OL**

⭐ Viewing the Art

Say: *The eagles in the painting bring to mind the character of John as he makes his journey.* **Ask:** *What qualities does John share with the eagles? (Students may note that John exhibits the courage and spirit of the eagles. Like them, he is willing to explore perilous places. His desire helps him to soar above the danger.)* **AS**

English Language Coach

Homographs Explain that some sets of words may be spelled the same but have different meanings. On page 1138, *leave* does not mean "to go away" but "permission." Encourage English language learners to check a dictionary if the meaning of a word they know does not fit the context of a sentence. Have students look up each word below in a dictionary and write a sentence using the word's most common meaning and then one using the word as it is used in the story. *fast (fasting)* (p. 1139), *bow* (p. 1139), *banks* (p. 1140), *current* (p. 1141) **EL**

Objectives
• To analyze possible moral (SE)
• To visualize to enhance reading comprehension (SE)
• To capitalize proper nouns (TWE)

Teach

It is eight suns' journey to the east and a man passes by many Dead Places. The Forest People are afraid of them but I am not. Once I made my fire on the edge of a Dead Place at night and, next morning, in the dead house, I found a good knife, little rusted. That was small to what came afterward but it made my heart feel big. Always when I looked for game, it was in front of my arrow, and twice I passed hunting parties of the Forest People without their knowing. So I ★ knew my magic was strong and my journey clean, in spite of the law.

Toward the setting of the eighth sun, I came to the banks of the great river. It was half-a-day's journey after I had left the god-road—we do not use the god-roads now for they are falling apart into great blocks of stone, and the forest is safer going. A long way off, I had seen the water through trees but the trees were thick. At last, I came out upon an open place at the top of a cliff. There was the great river below, like a giant in the sun. It is very long, very wide. It could eat all the streams we know and still be thirsty. Its name is Ou-dis-sun, the Sacred, the Long. No man of my tribe had seen it, not even my father, the priest. It was magic and I prayed.

Then I raised my eyes and looked south. It was there, the Place of the Gods.

How can I tell what it was like—you do not know. It was there, in the red light, and they were too big to be houses. It was there with the red light upon it, mighty and ruined. I knew that in another moment the gods would see me. I covered my eyes with my hands and crept back into the forest.

Surely, that was enough to do, and live. Surely it was enough to spend the night upon the cliff. The Forest People themselves do not come near. Yet, all through the night, I knew that I should have to cross the river and walk in the places of the gods, although the gods ate me up. My magic did not help me at all and yet there was a fire in my bowels,

a fire in my mind. When the sun rose, I thought, "My journey has been clean. Now I will go home from my journey." But, even as I thought so, I knew I could not. If I went to the Place of the Gods, I would surely die, but, if I did not go, I could never be at peace with my spirit again. It is better to lose one's life than one's spirit, if one is a priest and the son of a priest.

Nevertheless, as I made the raft, the tears ran out of my eyes. The Forest People could have killed me without fight, if they had come upon me then, but they did not come. When the raft was made, I said the sayings for the dead and painted myself for death. My heart was cold as a frog and my knees like water, but the burning in my mind would not let me have peace. As I pushed the raft from the shore, I began my death song—I had the right. It was a fine song.

> "I am John, son of John," I sang. "My
> people are the Hill People. They are
> the men.
> I go into the Dead Places but I am not
> slain. I take the metal from the Dead
> Places but I am not blasted.
> I travel upon the god-roads and am not
> afraid. E-yah! I have killed the panther,
> I have killed the fawn!
> E-yah! I have come to the great river. No
> man has come there before.
> It is forbidden to go east, but I have gone,
> forbidden to go on the great river, but
> I am there.
> Open your hearts, you spirits, and hear
> my song.
> Now I go to the Place of the Gods, I shall
> not return.
> My body is painted for death and my
> limbs weak, but my heart is big as I go
> to the Place of the Gods!"

Big Idea The Extraordinary and Fantastic *What elements of the fantastic are in this passage?* **BI₁**

Literary Element Moral *What moral does this statement communicate? Do you agree with it? Why or why not?* **L**

Additional Support

Skills Practice

LISTENING AND SPEAKING: Connecting with Real-Life Events
Discuss John's courage in continuing to explore the Dead Place: he "had long gone past what was forbidden," but his "hunger for knowledge burned" in him. Encourage students to discuss people in real life who have gone to forbidden

places in pursuit of knowledge, such as 15th and 16th century explorers, mountain climbers, oceanographers, or astronauts. Have students research an explorer and give an oral report to the class. Students may want to present their information in conjunction with a multi-media presentation. **OL**

All the same, when I came to the Place of the Gods, I was afraid, afraid. The current of the great river is very strong—it gripped my raft with its hands. That was magic, for the river itself is wide and calm. I could feel evil spirits about me, in the bright morning; I could feel their breath on my neck as I was swept down the stream. Never have I been so much alone—I tried to think of my knowledge, but it was a squirrel's heap of winter nuts.

Yet, after a while, my eyes were opened and I saw. I saw both banks of the river— I saw that once there had been god-roads across it, though now they were broken and fallen like broken vines. Very great they were, and wonderful and broken—broken in the time of the Great Burning when the fire fell out of the sky. And always the current took me nearer to the Place of the Gods, and the huge ruins rose before my eyes.

I do not know the customs of rivers—we are the People of the Hills. I tried to guide my raft with the pole but it spun around. I thought the river meant to take me past the Place of the Gods and out into the Bitter Water of the legends. I grew angry then—my heart felt strong. I said aloud, "I am a priest and the son of a priest!" The gods heard me— they showed me how to paddle with the pole on one side of the raft. The current changed itself—I drew near to the Place of the Gods.

When I was very near, my raft struck and turned over. I can swim in our lakes—I swam to the shore. There was a great spike of rusted metal sticking out into the river—I hauled myself up upon it and sat there, panting. I had saved my bow and two arrows and the knife I found in the Dead Place but that

> "There was no strength in my knowledge any more and I felt small and naked as a new-hatched bird—alone upon the great river, the servant of the gods."

was all. My raft went whirling downstream toward the Bitter Water. I looked after it, and thought if it had trod me under, at least I would be safely dead. Nevertheless, when I had dried my bowstring and restrung it, I walked forward to the Place of the Gods.

It felt like ground underfoot; it did not burn me. It is not true what some of the tales say, that the ground there burns forever, for I have been there. Here and there were the marks and stains of the Great Burning, on the ruins, that is true. But they were old marks and old stains. It is not true either, what some of our priests say, that it is an island covered with fogs and enchantments. It is not. It is a great Dead Place—greater than any Dead Place we know. Everywhere in it there are god-roads, though most are cracked and broken. Everywhere there are the ruins of the high towers of the gods.

How shall I tell what I saw? I went carefully, my strung bow in my hand, my skin ready for danger. There should have been the wailings of spirits and the shrieks of demons, but there were not. It was very silent and sunny where I had landed—the wind and the rain and the birds that drop seeds had done their work—the grass grew in the cracks of the broken stone. It is a fair island—no wonder the gods built there. If I had come there, a god, I also would have built.

How shall I tell what I saw? The towers are not all broken—here and there one still stands, like a great tree in a forest, and the birds nest high. But the towers themselves look blind, for the gods are gone. I saw a fish hawk, catching fish in the river. I saw a little

Reading Strategy Visualizing Explain in your own words what John is looking at. R

Big Idea The Extraordinary and Fantastic What does John think is extraordinary about this place? What do you think is extraordinary? BI₂

STEPHEN VINCENT BENÉT **1141**

Teach

R Reading Strategy

Visualizing Answer: *He is looking at a river with the remains of a bridge spanning it. He can also see many very large ruins, possibly the remains of a large city.* Have students identify specific words and phrases that help them visualize the Place of the Gods. (*Possible answers include "too big to be houses"; "great blocks of stone"; "felt like ground underfoot"; marks and stains"; "fogs and enchantments"; "cracked and broken."*) **OL**

BI₂ Big Idea

The Extraordinary and the Fantastic Answer: *John notices that the stories about the Place of the Gods are not true. He is amazed at what the gods built. Students should be starting to realize that John is describing the ruins of a twentieth or twenty-first century city.* **OL**

Differentiated Instruction

Multiple Intelligences—Musical
Musically talented students can add to their classmates' enjoyment of the story. Challenge students to present John's song in a variety of forms such as a chant, a rap song, and a folk song. They may work individually, with a partner, or with a group. They may use any musical instruments they wish. After the performances, have the class discuss the style to which the song best lends itself. **AL**

Objectives
- To understand moral (SE)
- To visualize to enhance reading comprehension (SE)
- To connect with real-life events (TWE)

R Reading Strategy

Visualizing Answer: *The images of the green-eyed cats wailing appeal to the senses of sight and sound. The pigeons and wild dogs appeal primarily to sight.* **OL**

BI Big Idea

The Extraordinary and the Fantastic Answer: *John probably entered a large public building, possibly a train station with access to the subway system. He believes it is important because of how it is decorated. Note: this is likely a specific reference to Grand Central Terminal in New York City. In 1912 French artist Paul César Helleu painted a decorative astrological ceiling in the station's concourse.* **OL**

★ Cultural History

The Father of Our Country Two prominent statues of George Washington stand in Washington Square, which is in New York City's Greenwich Village. They are called *Washington at War* and *Washington at Peace.* **AS**

---

dance of white butterflies over a great heap of broken stones and columns. I went there and looked about me—there was a carved stone with cut-letters, broken in half. I can read letters but I could not understand these. They said UBTREAS. There was also the shattered image of a man or a god. It had been made of white stone and he wore his hair tied back like a woman's. His name was ASHING, as I read on the cracked half of a stone. I thought it wise to pray to ASHING, ★ though I do not know that god.

How shall I tell what I saw? There was no smell of man left, on stone or metal. Nor were there many trees in that wilderness of stone. There are many pigeons, nesting and dropping in the towers—the gods must have loved them, or, perhaps, they used them for sacrifices. There are wild cats that roam the god-roads, green-eyed, unafraid of man. At night they wail like demons but they are not demons. The wild dogs are more dangerous, for they hunt in a pack, but them I did not meet till later. Everywhere there are the carved stones, carved with magical numbers or words.

I went north—I did not try to hide myself. When a god or a demon saw me, then I would die, but meanwhile I was no longer afraid. My hunger for knowledge burned in me—there was so much that I could not understand. After a while, I knew that my belly was hungry. I could have hunted for my meat, but I did not hunt. It is known that the gods did not hunt as we do—they got their food from enchanted boxes and jars. Sometimes these are still found in the Dead Places—once, when I was a child and foolish, I opened such a jar and tasted it and found the food sweet. But my father found out and punished me for it strictly, for, often, that food is death. Now, though, I had long gone past what was forbidden, and I entered the likeliest towers, looking for the food of the gods.

I found it at last in the ruins of a great temple in the mid-city. A mighty temple it must have been, for the roof was painted like the sky at night with its stars—that much I could see, though the colors were faint and dim. It went down into great caves and tunnels—perhaps they kept their slaves there. But when I started to climb down, I heard the squeaking of rats, so I did not go—rats are unclean, and there must have been many tribes of them, from the squeaking. But near there, I found food, in the heart of a ruin, behind a door that still opened. I ate only the fruits from the jars—they had a very sweet taste. There was drink, too, in bottles of glass—the drink of the gods was strong and made my head swim. After I had eaten and drunk, I slept on the top of a stone, my bow at my side.

When I woke, the sun was low. Looking down from where I lay, I saw a dog sitting on his haunches. His tongue was hanging out of his mouth; he looked as if he were laughing. He was a big dog, with a gray-brown coat, as big as a wolf. I sprang up and shouted at him but he did not move—he just sat there as if he were laughing. I did not like that. When I reached for a stone to throw, he moved swiftly out of the way of the stone. He was not afraid of me; he looked at me as if I were meat. No doubt I could have killed him with an arrow, but I did not know if there were others. Moreover, night was falling.

I looked about me—not far away there was a great, broken god-road, leading north. The towers were high enough, but not so high, and while many of the dead-houses were wrecked, there were some that stood. I went toward this god-road, keeping to the heights of the ruins, while the dog followed. When I had reached the god-road, I saw that there were others behind him. If I

Reading Strategy Visualizing *Images are descriptions that appeal to one or more of the five senses. Visualize the animals in the Dead Place. To which senses do these images appeal?* **R**

Big Idea The Extraordinary and Fantastic *What type of building do you think John has entered? Why does he believe it was so important to the gods?* **BI**

Additional Support

Skills Practice

WRITING: Making Judgments John knowingly breaks the laws of his people by traveling east on his journey. Have students decide whether John has done the right thing in going east despite his father's warnings. Have them *write* a paragraph in which they state their opinions about John's decision. In their essays, students should consider the ways in which John rationalizes his own actions. **OL**

Abismo. David Alfaro Siqueiros (1896–1974). Piroxyline on Masonite, 23⅝ x 27½ in.
Viewing the Art: What elements in this painting remind you of the setting of the story? ★

had slept later, they would have come upon me asleep and torn out my throat. As it was, they were sure enough of me; they did not hurry. When I went into the dead-house, they kept watch at the entrance—doubtless they thought they would have a fine hunt. But a dog cannot open a door and I knew, from the books, that the gods did not like to live on the ground but on high.

I had just found a door I could open when the dogs decided to rush. Ha! They were surprised when I shut the door in their faces—it was a good door, of strong metal. I could hear their foolish baying beyond it but I did not stop to answer them. I was in darkness—I found stairs and climbed. There were many stairs, turning around till my head was dizzy. At the top was another door—I found the knob and opened it. I was

in a long small chamber—on one side of it was a bronze door that could not be opened, for it had no handle. Perhaps there was a magic word to open it but I did not have the word. I turned to the door in the opposite side of the wall. The lock of it was broken and I opened it and went in.

Within, there was a place of great riches. The god who lived there must have been a powerful god. The first room was a small **anteroom**—I waited there for some time, telling the spirits of the place that I came in peace and not as a robber. When it seemed to me that they had had time to hear me,

---

Vocabulary

anteroom (an′ tē rōōm′) *n.* a small room serving as a waiting area or entrance to a larger, main room

---

STEPHEN VINCENT BENÉT **1143**

Reading in the Real World

Citizenship John has a vision of the Great Burning and the Destruction that destroyed the great city. After students have completed the story, have them use an online periodical index to find articles about nuclear weapons and warfare and the people and organizations who fight against them. Have students report their findings and then lead a discussion about what can be done to prevent the kind of destruction described in the story. **OL**

Teach

L Literary Element

Character The author contrasts John's superstitions with his intelligence and ability to reason. Have students point out details that show his superstition and those that show his rationality. *(He thinks a magic word can open a door and speaks to the spirits as he enters the "god's" anteroom, yet he escapes the dogs knowing they cannot open a door and uses his knowledge that the gods lived on high.)* **OL**

★ Viewing the Art

Answer: *The brightness and colors are like the painting of the sky in the "mighty temple"; the spreading shape is like the fire in the sky during the Great Burning.* **AS**

Objectives
• To visualize to enhance reading comprehension (SE)
• To make judgments about characters (TWE)

1143

R₁ Reading Strategy

Visualizing Answer: *Students' visualizations will vary. The images they picture should be related to the text.* **OL**

R₂ Reading Strategy

Visualizing Answer: *John describes a sink and a faucet.* **Ask:** What other household items are described in this paragraph? (*He also describes a stove, an oven, and lamps.*) **OL**

★ Viewing the Art

Say: Avigdor Arikha was born in 1929 in Bukovina, then part of the USSR. After spending his youth in a kibbutz near Jerusalem, he studied fine art and philosophy. Arikha's paintings, drawings, and etchings are displayed in museums around the world. A renowned artist, Arikha currently lives and works in Paris and Jerusalem. **Answer:** *The view from the window that John imagined in the story would show a great city.* **AS**

I went on. Ah, what riches! Few, even, of the windows had been broken—it was all as it had been. The great windows that looked over the city had not been broken at all though they were dusty and streaked with many years. There were coverings on the floors, the colors not greatly faded, and the chairs were soft and deep. There were pictures upon the walls, very strange, very wonderful—I remember one of a bunch of flowers in a jar—if you came close to it, you could see nothing but bits of color, but if you stood away from it, the flowers might have been picked yesterday. It made my heart feel strange to look at this picture—and to look at the figure of a bird, in some hard clay, on a table and see it so like our birds. Everywhere there were books and writings, many in tongues that I could not read. The god who lived there must have been a wise god and full of knowledge. I felt I had right there, as I sought knowledge also.

Nevertheless, it was strange. There was a washing-place but no water—perhaps the gods washed in air. There was a cooking-place but no wood, and though there was a machine to cook food, there was no place to put fire in it. Nor were there candles or lamps—there were things that looked like lamps but they had neither oil nor wick. All these things were magic, but I touched them and lived—the magic had gone out of them. Let me tell one thing to show. In the washing-place, a thing said "Hot" but it was not hot to the touch—another thing said "Cold" but it was not cold. This must have been a strong magic but the magic was gone. I do not understand—they had ways—I wish that I knew.

It was close and dry and dusty in their house of the gods. I have said the magic was

gone but that is not true—it had gone from the magic things but it had not gone from the place. I felt the spirits about me, weighing upon me. Nor had I ever slept in a Dead Place before—and yet, tonight, I must sleep there. When I thought of it, my tongue felt dry in my throat, in spite of my wish for knowledge. Almost I would have gone down again and faced the dogs, but I did not.

I had not gone through all the rooms when the darkness fell. When it fell, I went back to the big room looking over the city and made fire. There was a place to make fire and a box with wood in it, though I do not think they cooked there. I wrapped myself in a floor-covering and slept in front of the fire—I was very tired.

Now I tell what is very strong magic. I woke in the midst of the night. When I woke, the fire had gone out and I was cold. It seemed to me that all around me there were whisperings and voices. I closed my eyes to shut them out. Some will say that I slept again, but I do not think that I slept. I could feel the spirits drawing my spirit out of my body as a fish is drawn on a line.

Why should I lie about it? I am a priest and the son of a priest. If there are spirits, as they say, in the small Dead Places near us, what spirits must there not be in that great Place of the Gods? And would not they wish to speak? After such long years? I know that I felt myself drawn as a fish is drawn on a line. I had stepped out of my body—I could see my body asleep in front of the cold fire, but it was not I. I was drawn to look out upon the city of the gods.

It should have been dark, for it was night, but it was not dark. Everywhere there were lights—lines of light—circles and blurs of light—ten thousand torches would not have been the same. The sky itself was alight—you could barely see the stars for the glow in the sky. I thought to myself "This is strong magic" and trembled. There was a roaring in my ears like the rushing of rivers. Then my eyes grew used to the light and my ears to the sound. I knew that I was seeing the city as it had been when the gods were alive.

Reading Strategy Visualizing *What do you see when you visualize the pictures that John is looking at?* **R₁**

Reading Strategy Visualizing *What is John describing?* **R₂**

Additional Support

Skills Practice

RESEARCH: Historical Connection
The story's description of the destruction of the city is similar to the reports of the bombing of Hiroshima, Japan, during World War II. Assign small groups of students one of the following specific topics involving the bombing of Hiroshima. Have the groups *research* their topics

and *report* their findings to the class.

- reasons for the bombing
- results in lives lost and property damage
- eyewitness reports
- long-term effects **OL**

That was a sight indeed—yes, that was a sight: I could not have seen it in the body— my body would have died. Everywhere went the gods, on foot and in chariots—there were gods beyond number and counting and their chariots blocked the streets. They had turned night to day for their pleasure—they did not sleep with the sun. The noise of their coming and going was the noise of many waters. It was magic what they could do— it was magic what they did.

I looked out of another window—the great vines of their bridges were mended and the god-roads went east and west. Restless, restless, were the gods and always in motion! They burrowed tunnels under rivers—they flew in the air. With unbelievable tools they did giant works—no part of the earth was safe from them, for, if they wished for a thing, they summoned it from the other side of the world. And always, as they labored and rested, as they feasted and made love, there was a drum in their ears— the pulse of the giant city, beating and beating like a man's heart.

Were they happy? What is happiness to the gods? They were great, they were mighty, they were wonderful and terrible.

As I looked upon them and their magic, I felt like a child—but a little more, it seemed to me, and they would pull down the moon from the sky. I saw them with wisdom beyond wisdom and knowledge beyond knowledge.

August, 1982. Avigdor Arikha. Oil on canvas, 31¾ x 39¼ in.
Viewing the Art: Compare the view in this picture with what John imagined he saw when he looked out the window.

And yet not all they did was well done—even I could see that—and yet their wisdom could not but grow until all was peace.

Then I saw their fate come upon them and that was terrible past speech. It came upon them as they walked the streets of their city. I have been in the fights with the Forest People—I have seen men die. But this was not like that. When gods war with gods, they use weapons we do not know. It was fire falling out of the sky and a mist that poisoned. It was the time of the Great Burning and the Destruction. They ran about like ants in the streets of their city—poor gods, poor gods! Then the towers began to fall. A few escaped—yes, a few. The legends tell it. But, even after the city had become a Dead Place, for many years the poison was

Literary Element Moral *What does this description of the gods tell you about the story's moral?* **L**

Big Idea The Extraordinary and Fantastic *What is extraordinary about John's vision?* **BI₁**

Big Idea The Extraordinary and Fantastic *What happened to the city and its people?* **BI₂**

STEPHEN VINCENT BENÉT **1145**

Teach

BI₁ Big Idea

The Extraordinary and the Fantastic Answer: *It is extraordinary that John can visualize the gods as they once were. The way in which the gods lived was also extraordinary to John because they could fly, build tunnels and tall buildings, and use advanced technology.* **OL**

L Literary Element

Moral Answer: *The gods were actually restless, inventive, hard-working, and creative people. It seems to John that they could accomplish anything, and yet their city lies in ruins and none of them are left. John's observations indicate a message about the damage that war and violent technology can have on a society.* **OL**

BI₂ Big Idea

The Extraordinary and the Fantastic Answer: *The city was destroyed by an atomic weapon, which killed almost everyone and poisoned the earth with radioactivity.* **OL**

Differentiated Instruction

Illustrating Tell students to visualize three separate descriptive passages as you read them aloud. Then identify one of the passages and have students make an illustration of it. Passages to read include paragraph 7, page 1144; paragraph 2, page 1145; and paragraph 4, page 1145. After students complete their drawings, have them reread the paragraph to check for details they missed. **BL**

Objectives

- To understand moral (SE)
- To visualize to enhance reading comprehension (SE)
- To research historical connection (TWE)

Teach

Moral Answer: *John sees wisdom and sadness in the man's face and concludes that he had watched the death of his city. He identifies with the man and repeats his earlier statement: "It is better to lose one's life than one's spirit." He brings out the moral that men's bodies are capable of causing destruction; their spirits are capable of wisdom and good.* **OL**

still in the ground. I saw it happen, I saw the last of them die. It was darkness over the broken city and I wept.

All this, I saw. I saw it as I have told it, though not in the body. When I woke in the morning, I was hungry, but I did not think first of my hunger for my heart was **perplexed** and confused. I knew the reason for the Dead Places but I did not see why it had happened. It seemed to me it should not have happened, with all the magic they had. I went through the house looking for an answer. There was so much in the house I could not understand—and yet I am a priest and the son of a priest. It was like being on one side of the great river, at night, with no light to show the way.

Then I saw the dead god. He was sitting in his chair, by the window, in a room I had not entered before and, for the first moment, I thought that he was alive. Then I saw the skin on the back of his hand—it was like dry leather. The room was shut, hot and dry—no doubt that had kept him as he was. At first I was afraid to approach him—then the fear left me. He was sitting looking out over the city—he was dressed in the clothes of the gods. His age was neither young nor old— I could not tell his age. But there was wisdom in his face and great sadness. You could see that he would have not run away. He had sat at his window, watching his city die—then he himself had died. But it is better to lose one's life than one's spirit— and you could see from the face that his spirit had not been lost. I knew, that, if I touched him, he would fall into dust—and yet, there was something unconquered in the face.

That is all of my story, for then I knew he was a man—I knew then that they had been men, neither gods nor demons. It is a great knowledge, hard to tell and believe. They were men—they went a dark road, but they were men. I had no fear after that—I had

---

Vocabulary

perplexed (pər plekst´) *adj.* troubled with doubt or uncertainty; puzzled

---

Literary Element Moral *How does John's characterization of the man he finds help make the story's moral clear?* **L1**

Additional Support

Skills Practice

READING: Comparing and Contrasting The author describes the city and its broken-down, deserted state. Then he describes the city as it was before its destruction. Encourage students to visualize the similarities and differences in the city in its two states as they read the descriptions. Have students make a chart with two columns labeled *Before* and *After*. Have them list details that describe the city in each state. For example, under *Before* they might write "light" and "filled with chariots"; under *After*, "dark" and "broken-down roads." Have volunteers write their details on a chart on the board. **OL**

no fear going home, though twice I fought off the dogs and once I was hunted for two days by the Forest People. When I saw my father again, I prayed and was purified. He touched my lips and my breast, he said, "You went away a boy. You come back a man and a priest." I said, "Father, they were men! I have been in the Place of the Gods and seen it! Now slay me, if it is the law—but still I know they were men."

He looked at me out of both eyes. He said, "The law is not always the same shape—you have done what you have done. I could not have done it in my time, but you come after me. Tell!"

I told and he listened. After that, I wished to tell all the people but he showed me otherwise. He said, "Truth is a hard deer to hunt. If you eat too much truth at once, you may die of the truth. It was not idly that our fathers forbade the Dead Places." He was right—it is better the truth should come little by little. I have learned that, being a priest. Perhaps, in the old days, they ate knowledge too fast.

Nevertheless, we make a beginning. It is not for the metal alone we go to the Dead Places now—there are the books and the writings. They are hard to learn. And the magic tools are broken —but we can look at them and wonder. At least, we make a beginning. And, when I am chief priest we shall go beyond the great river. We shall go to the Place of the Gods—the place newyork—not one man but a company. We shall look for the images of the gods and find the god ASHING and the others—the gods Lincoln and Biltmore[1] and Moses.[2] But they were men who built the city, not gods or demons. They were men. I remember the dead man's face. They were men who were here before us. We must build again. ✎

1. The *Biltmore* is a famous hotel in New York City.
2. Robert *Moses* (1888–1981) was a New York state public official whose name appears on many bridges and other structures built during his administration.

Literary Element Moral *What moral is John's father preaching in this statement? Do you agree with him? Explain* **L2**

Clytie, c. 1890–92. Frederic Leighton. Oil on canvas, 85.1 x 137.8 cm. Fitzwilliam Museum, University of Cambridge, UK.
Viewing the Art: What mood does this scene evoke? Is it similar to the mood evoked by this story? Explain.

STEPHEN VINCENT BENÉT **1147**

Differentiated Instruction

Researching Lost Worlds Although this story is fantasy, history has shown that the knowledge and advancements of great civilizations—such as those of the ancient Maya, Egyptians, Greeks, and Romans—can be lost to subsequent generations. Investigate a lost civilization that was later rediscovered. Look for parallels between that civilization and the culture of the former dwellers of the Place of the Gods. Share your findings with the class. **AL**

Teach

L2 Literary Element

Moral Answer: *John's father is preaching the familiar moral that the common people should not be told disturbing truths that contradict traditional beliefs. Students' opinions of this moral will vary, but some may point out that this argument has been used throughout history by dictators who know that knowledge is power.* **OL**

★ Viewing the Art

Answer: *Students might say that the painting evokes a sense of mystery and awe; it draws our attention to something beyond our world. In the story, the characters learn more about what lies beyond their borders. The characters and the readers are awed by the mystery of this other world.* **AS**

✓CheckPoint

Use the CheckPoint questions on Presentation Plus! to check students' mastery of the selection. These questions can be used with interactive response keypads for immediate student feedback.

Objectives
• To understand moral (SE)
• To analyze art (TWE)

1147

Assess

1. Choices may include a philosophical statement such as "It is better to lose one's life than one's spirit."

2. (a) When John holds a piece of metal and does not die, it is clear he will become a priest. (b) John considers his calling a privilege; he says the knowledge he gets makes him happy.

3. (a) John decides to travel east. (b) John must overcome the conflict of knowing that his journey east is forbidden by his father and the laws of his community.

4. (a) The river's current carries him toward the Place of the Gods. The raft spins until the gods show him how to paddle on one side of the raft. When he nears land, his raft turns over and he swims to shore. (b) He is courageous and values knowledge.

5. (a) John becomes a man. He becomes wise, calm, and fearless. (b) His knowledge may liberate his people from their old myths and lead them to advance their civilization.

6. Some students may see John as disrespectful, while others may see him as having the courage to act according to his convictions.

RESPONDING AND THINKING CRITICALLY

Respond

1. Which line or passage in the story had the greatest impact on you? Why?

Recall and Interpret

2. (a) Which event determines that John will one day be a priest? (b) In your opinion, does John consider his priestly calling a privilege or a burden? Explain.

3. (a) In which direction does John decide to travel? Why? (b) What internal conflict must John overcome before choosing a direction for his journey? Explain.

4. (a) Describe John's journey down the great river. (b) In your opinion, what does John's decision to continue on his journey reveal about his character?

Analyze and Evaluate

5. (a) Analyze the ways in which John's journey changes him. (b) In your opinion, what long-term impact will his journey have on John's people?

6. Do you believe that John is being disrespectful by ignoring his father's advice and the law? Explain.

7. How does knowing the source of the Biblical allusion in the title of this story enrich your understanding of the story? Explain.

Connect

8. **Big Idea** The Extraordinary and Fantastic While in the Place of the Gods, John has an extraordinary vision of what it was once like, followed by a vision of its destruction. Do you think the author was making a cautionary statement about modern society through this story? Explain.

LITERARY ANALYSIS

Literary Element Moral

Although **morals** are usually found in fables or parables, modern stories—science fiction in particular—often present morals that warn of future catastrophic events. Here, Benét uses a moral to warn society of the potential dangers of modern technology and nuclear warfare.

1. Explain the moral of "By the Waters of Babylon."

2. In your opinion, what does the story reveal about the author's convictions about right and wrong and about his views of the conflicts between good and evil in the world?

Review: Archetypes

As you learned on pages 1036–1037, an **archetype** is an original model upon which other versions are based. An archetypal theme, plot, or character represents an element so universal that it applies to people across time and place. The archetypes found in "By

the Waters of Babylon" would have been just as recognizable to the ancient Greeks as they are to modern readers. The holocaust or post-apocalypse **theme archetype** found in "By the Waters of Babylon" involves superstition and ignorance about the past. The **plot pattern archetype** involves a young person experiencing a rite of passage and simultaneously discovering something about the world in a strange and dangerous place. The **character archetype** is that of a naïve young hero, caught between two worlds, who breaks the rules of his culture for the sake of knowledge. Benét's protagonist is a similar character archetype to J. K. Rowling's popular character Harry Potter.

Partner Activity Pair up with a classmate and discuss the archetypes described above. Make a list of other stories, books, movies, legends, and other sources that contain similar themes, plots, and character archetypes. Discuss how the items on your list compare with the theme, plot, and character archetypes found in "By the Waters of Babylon."

7. The Place of the Gods is comparable to Zion; readers may also weep as they see the possible end of modern civilization.

8. Students might think that Benét was trying to warn people about the consequences of a catastrophic war.

READING AND VOCABULARY

Reading Strategy Visualizing

When we read or listen, we form mental images of what the speaker or writer is describing. We create pictures in our minds automatically, even when we have never actually seen what is being described. This mental process is called **visualizing**. Benét uses many descriptive words and phrases that encourage readers to form mental images of the setting in his story, even though we have never actually seen it with our own eyes.

1. Read the following sentence from "By the Waters of Babylon," then close your eyes and imagine the scene: "I saw a little dance of white butterflies over a great heap of stone." After forming your mental image, write a few sentences describing how you imagine the scene to look.

2. Find another descriptive passage of your choice, form a mental image, and describe it.

Vocabulary Practice

Practice with Word Origins Choose the language from which each term originated. Use a dictionary to find word histories.

1. bade
   a. Old English   **b.** Spanish   **c.** Russian
2. anteroom
   a. Sanskrit   **b.** Old English   **c.** French
3. perplexed
   a. Latin   **b.** German   **c.** Swedish

Academic Vocabulary

Here are two words from the vocabulary list on page R82.

intrinsic (in trin′zik) *adj.* belonging to something at its most basic level of existence

perceive (pər sēv′) *v.* to develop knowledge about something, often through the senses

Practice and Apply
1. What was John's **intrinsic** motivation to continue his journey?
2. What truth did John finally **perceive** at the end of the story?

WRITING AND EXTENDING

Writing About Literature

Evaluate Author's Craft Benét plants clues to enable the reader to infer key aspects of the story. Write a one- or two-page essay in which you evaluate the effectiveness of this technique. Consider whether or not gradually revealing the truth about the Place of the Gods adds suspense and interest to the story. Use details from the selection to support your ideas.

Before you begin writing, find examples from the text that provide clues to the author's meaning. Use a chart like the one below to record your examples and note your inferences.

Clues	Inferences
"Everywhere in it there are god-roads, though most are cracked and broken. Everywhere there are the ruins of the high towers of the gods." p. 1141	This sounds a lot like a description of an urban area with skyscrapers or high-rise buildings.

After you finish writing your essay, exchange papers with a peer reviewer. Provide each other with feedback regarding the essays. After revising, do not forget to proofread your work for errors in spelling, grammar, and punctuation.

Listening and Speaking

In 1877 British biologist Thomas Henry Huxley wrote: "If a little knowledge is dangerous, where is the man who has so much as to be out of danger?" Prepare a speech in which John makes use of this quote as a rebuttal to his father's arguments that truth is dangerous. Use the dialogue in the story as a model for John's speech patterns and manner of expressing himself. Then rehearse and perform the speech for your class.

Literature**Online** **Web Activities** For eFlashcards, Selection Quick Checks, and other Web activities, go to www.glencoe.com.

STEPHEN VINCENT BENÉT **1149**

Literary Element

1. Challenging accepted beliefs and following one's conscience can lead to greater wisdom.

2. Benét shows a conflict between following laws and following instinct. Benét also offers an argument against war and destruction.

Review: Archetypes

Point out to students that the archetype of the hero's journey recurs in many stories from Homer's *Odyssey* to J. D. Salinger's *The Catcher in the Rye*.

Reading Strategy

1. This sentence provides information about the color of the butterflies, the size of the stone pile, and where the butterflies are in relation to the stones.

2. Answers will vary.

Vocabulary

1. a   2. b   3. a

Academic Vocabulary

1. He is compelled to pursue knowledge even when it is dangerous or against the law.

2. He finally understood that the gods were men, just like himself.

Literature**Online**

Web Activities Have students access the Web site for interactive activities that will help them assess their understanding of the selection.

Writing About Literature

Students' essays should

• state an opinion about the author's use of clues to increase suspense.

• use specific details from the story to support their opinion.

Listening and Speaking

Encourage students to discuss the meaning of Huxley's statement before preparing their speeches.

Focus

Write on the board: Margaret Atwood writes about strong females whose father studied insects. **Ask:** What is confusing about this sentence and how should it be corrected? *(It sounds like Atwood's characters have entomologists as parents.)* **OL**

Teach

Modifiers Review the function of adjective and adverb phrases. Have students provide additional examples of misplaced modifiers. **OL**

Assess

Possible rewrites:

1. Stephen Vincent Benét, fascinated by U.S. history, wrote many stories.
2. His poem "Western Star," a lengthy epic, won the Pulitzer Prize.
3. The story "By the Waters of Babylon" reminds readers of closely related tales in the Bible.
4. Confused and alone, the main character of the story must go on a journey.
5. On the bus, I read the story about the brave young man.

Additional Support

eFlashcards Have students access the Web site for more practice with sentence structure.

▶ **Vocabulary Terms**

A **modifier** is a word or phrase that describes something. A **misplaced modifier** modifies or appears to modify the wrong word in a sentence.

▶ **Test-Taking Tip**

To correct misplaced modifiers when writing for a test, think about the meaning of the sentence. Then, make sure that any modifiers are located as close as possible to the word or words they describe.

▶ **Language Handbook**

For more about sentence structure, see the Language Handbook, pp. R50–R51.

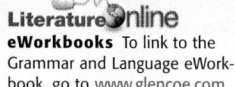
eWorkbooks To link to the Grammar and Language eWorkbook, go to www.glencoe.com.

OBJECTIVES
- Understand modifiers.
- Recognize and correct misplaced modifiers in a sentence.

Avoiding Misplaced Modifiers

"There was the great river below, like a giant in the sun."
—Stephen Vincent Benét, from "By the Waters of Babylon"

In "By the Waters of Babylon," Stephen Vincent Benét uses vivid **modifiers**—words or phrases that add descriptive details—to help readers experience the scene. If modifiers are used incorrectly, however, they can confuse, instead of inform, the reader. A **misplaced modifier** is positioned so that it appears to modify the wrong word in a sentence, making the meaning of the sentence unclear.

To correct a misplaced modifier, determine which word in the sentence it actually modifies and move it as close as possible to that word.

Misplaced modifiers

The boy picked up the sheet of metal, pretending to be unconcerned.
Was it the sheet of metal that was pretending to be unconcerned?
He made the raft with tears running from his eyes.
Was the raft made from the boy's running tears?

Solution Place the phrase next to the word it modifies.

The boy, pretending to be unconcerned, picked up the sheet of metal.
The phrase *pretending to be unconcerned* modifies *boy.*
With tears running from his eyes, he made the raft.
The phrase *with tears running from his eyes* modifies *he.*

Exercise

Rewrite the following sentences to correct the misplaced modifiers.

1. Stephen Vincent Benét wrote many stories fascinated by U.S. history.
2. His poem "Western Star" won the Pulitzer Prize, a lengthy epic.
3. The story "By the Waters of Babylon" reminds readers of tales in the closely related Bible.
4. The main character of the story, confused and alone, must go on a journey.
5. I read the story about the brave young man on the bus.

Skills Practice

Dangling Modifiers Point out to students that a misplaced modifier is one that is in the wrong place and, therefore, describes the wrong thing. A dangling modifier is one that is meant to modify a word or phrase, but that word or phrase is not present in the sentence. **Example:** *Using poisoned wine, the honor of her husband was protected.* **Solution:** The sentence contains no word for the modifier "Using poisoned wine" to modify. Rewrite the sentence to include a noun or pronoun for the modifier to modify. **Corrected sentence:** *Using poisoned wine, she protected the honor of her husband.* **OL**

Comparing Literature *Across Genres*

Connecting to the Reading Selections

Our dreams often reflect experiences in our daily lives. Our daily experiences can be as haunting as our dreams. These three selections, which include a dream narrative, a poem about identity in the crowded darkness, and a poem about a dream, reveal fragments of both the inner and outer worlds of the narrator and speakers.

COMPARING THE `Big Idea` The Extraordinary and Fantastic

The relationship between the real world and the dream world is both extraordinary and fantastic. The writers featured here all explore this divide and the ways in which the two worlds are related. Jamaica Kincaid's short story integrates both the real world and two distinct dreams to show the relationship between all three. Denise Levertov's poem uses the contrasts between night and day and the individual and society to describe what is unknown and imagined. Anna Akhmatova's poem relates "unearthly dreams" and questions whether they can foretell future events.

COMPARING Description

A **description** is a detailed portrayal of a person, a place, an object, or an event. Each writer uses rich sensory details to re-create experiences and sensations. In these works, carefully selected details help the reader picture settings, events, and characters, even when those described are extraordinary, fantastic, or unreal.

COMPARING Author's Culture

Each work is rooted in its author's culture: Kincaid infuses her dream setting with elements from her native island, Antigua; Levertov evokes the hectic culture of the city at night; and Akhmatova provides a glimpse into the culture of fear and loss that she once inhabited.

COMPARING LITERATURE **1151**

Focus

BELLRINGER

Bellringer Options
Selection Focus Transparency 46
Daily Language Practice
Transparency 95
Or write on the board some common dream themes, such as being able to fly, being chased, and not being able to move quickly. **Ask:** What might these dream themes represent or symbolize? How do these themes connect to your own life?
Have students talk about these dream themes and what they mean to them. Have students talk about some of their own dreams and make conjectures about their meanings.

Connecting to the Reading Selections

Allow students to share their responses to the opening statements. Then have students discuss what they already know about Jamaica Kincaid, Denise Levertov, and Anna Akhmatova.

Selection Skills

Literary Elements
- Stream of Consciousness (SE pp. 1153–1157)
- Sound Devices (TWE p. 1158)

Comparing Literature

Reading Skills
- Interpreting Imagery (SE pp. 1153–1157)
- Previewing (TWE p. 1154)

Vocabulary Skills
- Analogies (SE pp. 1153, 1157)
- Prefixes (TWE p. 1156)

Listening/Speaking/Viewing Skills
- Discussion Starter (SE p. 1158)

Writing Skills/Grammar
- Compare and Contrast Events (SE p. 1157)
- Quickwrite (SE p. 1159)

1151

Focus

Building Background

Jamaica Kincaid's homeland of Antigua has a history of colonialism. Christopher Columbus came across the island in 1493. The British established a colony in 1667 and ran sugar plantations until 1834. Then the British Commonwealth of Nations declared Antigua an independent state. **AS**

Author Search To expand students' appreciation of Jamaica Kincaid, have them access the Web site for additional information and resources.

What I Have Been Doing Lately

MEET JAMAICA KINCAID

"Troublemaker" is how teachers used to describe Elaine Potter Richardson. Growing up on the tiny island of Antigua in the Caribbean was not easy. Richardson would later adopt the pen name Jamaica Kincaid and become famous for her poetic language, but at a young age her way with words often landed her in hot water. Precocious and rebellious, Kincaid had a rocky relationship with her mother, and she often escaped the confines of her life by stealing away to read books.

A Need to Escape As a child, Kincaid always felt trapped. The sea that surrounded Antigua formed a geographic jail. Racism and conventional ways of thinking stifled her dreams. Kincaid longed for a challenging, thought-provoking, and free place to live. As she later commented, "In the place I'm from you don't have much room." At the age of seventeen, Kincaid left her island home to become an *au pair,* or nanny, in the United States. Within ten years of her departure, Kincaid had embraced her pen name and managed to publish a few nonfiction articles in magazines. She changed her surname because her family disapproved of her writing. She later explained that she adopted the name *Jamaica,* subconsciously, as a way of re-creating a part of her past. Kincaid's work quickly drew the attention of William Shawn, a former editor of the *New Yorker.* She wrote an article for him, and soon she was a regular contributor, which ensured that her work would reach a wide audience. Before long, she moved on to writing fiction.

Books About Home and Family Kincaid's first book was a short story collection called *At the Bottom of the River.* It includes "What I Have Been Doing Lately" and nine other stories. When the work first appeared, critics immediately recognized the author as a fresh, new, and compelling voice in fiction. Critics commented admiringly on Kincaid's style, which created poetry through repetition; her use of rich details; and her narrators' suspensions between dreams and reality. In fact, Kincaid explains that dreaming is part of the Caribbean way of life. In the Caribbean world, she says, people "live for dreaming."

> "For me, writing isn't a way of being public or private; it's just a way of being."
>
> —Jamaica Kincaid

A Writing Life Kincaid's second work of fiction, the novel *Annie John,* brought her wide popularity and ensured her literary reputation. In this work, Kincaid explores the theme of family, especially a daughter's relationship to her mother. Kincaid's second novel, *Lucy,* also focuses on this kind of relationship and contains many autobiographical elements. In recent years, Kincaid has returned to nonfiction and has written several works including an extended essay about gardening.

Jamaica Kincaid was born in 1949.

LiteratureOnline Author Search For more about Jamaica Kincaid, go to www.glencoe.com.

Selection Resources

Print Materials
- Unit 6 Resources (Fast File), pp. 24–27
- Leveled Vocabulary Development, p. 79
- Selection and Unit Assessments, pp. 191–192
- Selection Quick Checks, p. 96

Transparencies
- Bellringer Options Transparencies:
  Selection Focus Transparency 46
  Daily Language Practice Transparency 95
- Literary Elements Transparency 102

Technology
- TeacherWorks Plus™ CD-ROM
- StudentWorks Plus™ CD-ROM
- Presentation Plus!™ CD-ROM
- Literature Online, glencoe.com
- Online Student Edition, mhln.com
- ExamView® Assessment Suite CD-ROM
- Vocabulary PuzzleMaker CD-ROM
- Listening Library, disc 2 tracks 33–35

LITERATURE PREVIEW

READING PREVIEW

Connecting to the Story

This story narrates a dream. Before you read "What I Have Been Doing Lately," ask yourself these questions:

- Have you ever had a dream that you felt contained a message or lesson?
- Have you ever dreamed that you were in a place that seemed familiar in certain ways but was strange in other ways?

Building Background

The setting of "What I Have Been Doing Lately" is a bizarre dreamland, but it does contain some realistic elements. The climate and landscape of the dream, with its cloudless skies, monkeys, and flowering trees, are similar to those on the island of Antigua, where the author grew up. Within this setting, the narrator experiences a kind of double dream. The narrator is on a sort of journey, but the meaning of the journey is obscure.

Setting Purposes for Reading

Big Idea The Extraordinary and Fantastic

As you read, think about the extraordinary and fantastic places to which the subconscious mind can take people when they dream.

Literary Element Stream of Consciousness

Stream of consciousness is the literary representation of a character's free-flowing thoughts, feelings, and memories. Emotions, impressions, images, and ideas—both rational and irrational—unfold on the page in the same pattern and the same speed that they occur in the character's mind. As you read "What I Have Been Doing Lately," look for the free associations that identify the narrator's thoughts as stream of consciousness.

- See Literary Terms Handbook, p. R17.

Literature Online **Interactive Literary Elements Handbook** To review or learn more about the literary elements, go to www.glencoe.com.

OBJECTIVES

In studying this selection, you will focus on the following:
- analyzing stream of consciousness

Reading Strategy Interpreting Imagery

Interpreting imagery means looking carefully at sensory details, such as those that describe things the narrator sees and hears, and determining their importance in the story.

Reading Tip: Making a Chart As you read, list the images you encounter. Reflect on what they tell you about the setting, the events, or the narrator.

Image	Interpretation
p. 1154 "Either it was drizzling or there was a lot of dust in the air and the dust was damp."	• This is a world of sensation. • The narrator feels dampness but is confused about her surroundings.

Vocabulary

verandah (və ran´də) n. a long porch, usually with a roof, that extends along a house; p. 1155 *The man sat on the verandah and watched the rain.*

horizon (hə rī´zən) n. the place where the earth and sky appear to meet; p. 1155 *From the meadow, we could see the clouds on the horizon.*

dutiful (doo´ti fəl) adj. acting out of a sense of obligation or a sense of what is required; p. 1155 *The dutiful worker always did every task carefully.*

interlaced (in´tər lāst´) adj. connected by or woven together; p. 1156 *The fabric was interlaced gold threads.*

Vocabulary Tip: Analogies Analogies are comparisons that are based on the logical relationships between pairs of words. Relationships can include synonyms, antonyms, and class and member.

- interpreting imagery
- writing a comparison/contrast essay

JAMAICA KINCAID **1153**

Summary

A young girl relates in first-person stream of consciousness a dream she had. In the dream, she hears the doorbell and goes to answer the door. There is no one there, but she goes outside and begins walking. She sees a monkey in a tree, crosses a lake, and tumbles into a hole. She comes across a woman, who asks her what she has been doing lately. The girl desribes her dream, and then begins to relive the dream, this time with variations in the imagery. Toward the end she comes across a picnic of beautiful people, but they turn to mud when she comes close. She is left with a feeling of great sadness. She rejects the bad dream and returns to the beginning again.

V Vocabulary

Vocabulary File Say: Add these words and definitions to your vocabulary file. For each word, include a sentence that gives you an example of how to use the word. **OL** Students with English language needs should include the pronunciations of these words in their files. **EL**

Literature Online

Literary Elements Have students access the Web site to improve their understanding of stream of consciousness.

Differentiated Instruction

Less Proficient Readers Less proficient readers may have difficulty with the story's stream-of-consciousness style. Explain to students that the story is a dream and is written to show the fluid course and feeling of a dreaming experience. The story is not supposed to have a logical sequence of events. It may help these students to close their eyes and listen to someone else read the story while the listeners let the antilogical style wash over them. **BL**

Teach

Big Idea

The Extraordinary and Fantastic

Ask: How does the fantasy change over the course of the story? *(The fantasy becomes darker and less pleasant over the course of the story.)* **OL**

★ Viewing the Art

Oil Painting Oil-based paints are created by combining a pigment with an oil and a paint thinner, and sometimes with a metallic salt to quicken the paint's drying. **Ask:** How is this style of painting appropriate to the story? *(It is a semi-realistic painting with few details. This is appropriate because dreams are also somewhat hazy and unrealistic.)* **AS**

Readability Scores
Dale-Chall: 4.4
DRP: 46
Lexile: 780

Eight Huts in Haiti. D. Roosevelt (b. 1952). Oil on canvas. Private collection. ★

What I Have Been Doing Lately

Jamaica Kincaid

What I have been doing lately: I was lying in bed and the doorbell rang. I ran downstairs. Quick. I opened the door. There was no one there. I stepped outside. Either it was drizzling or there was a lot of dust in the air and the dust was damp.

I stuck out my tongue and the drizzle or the damp dust tasted like government school ink. I looked north. I looked south. I decided to start walking north. While walking north, I noticed that I was barefoot. While walking north, I looked up and saw the planet Venus.

1154 UNIT 6 GENRE FICTION

Additional Support

Skills Practice

READING: Previewing Previewing a reading selection is an invaluable technique to enhance one's understanding and appreciation of a reading selection. This story is the fantastical journey of a girl through her own dream world. Have students read the title, scan the text, and look at the accompanying art. Have students make predictions about what happens in the story and what the story is about. **OL**

I said, "It must be almost morning." I saw a monkey in a tree. The tree had no leaves. I said, "Ah, a monkey. Just look at that. A monkey." I walked for I don't know how long before I came up to a big body of water. I wanted to get across it but I couldn't swim. I wanted to get across it but it would take me years to build a boat. I wanted to get across it but it would take me I didn't know how long to build a bridge. Years passed and then one day, feeling like it, I got into my boat and rowed across. When I got to the other side, it was noon and my shadow was small and fell beneath me. I set out on a path that stretched out straight ahead. I passed a house, and a dog was sitting on the **verandah** but it looked the other way when it saw me coming. I passed a boy tossing a ball in the air but the boy looked the other way when he saw me coming. I walked and I walked but I couldn't tell if I walked a long time because my feet didn't feel as if they would drop off. I turned around to see what I had left behind me but nothing was familiar. Instead of the straight path, I saw hills. Instead of the boy with his ball, I saw tall flowering trees. I looked up and the sky was without clouds and seemed near, as if it were the ceiling in my house and, if I stood on a chair, I could touch it with the tips of my fingers. I turned around and looked ahead of me again. A deep hole had opened up before me. I looked in. The hole was deep and dark and I couldn't see the bottom. I thought, What's down there?, so on purpose I fell in.

> *"A deep hole had opened up before me. I looked in. The hole was deep and dark and I couldn't see the bottom."*

I fell and I fell, over and over, as if I were an old suitcase. On the sides of the deep hole I could see things written, but perhaps it was in a foreign language because I couldn't read them. Still I fell, for I don't know how long. As I fell I began to see that I didn't like the way falling made me feel. Falling made me feel sick and I missed all the people I had loved. I said, I don't want to fall anymore, and I reversed myself. I was standing again on the edge of the deep hole. I looked at the deep hole and I said, You can close up now, and it did. I walked some more without knowing distance. I only knew that I passed through days and nights, I only knew that I passed through rain and shine, light and darkness. I was never thirsty and I felt no pain. Looking at the **horizon**, I made a joke for myself: I said, "The earth has thin lips," and I laughed.

Looking at the horizon again, I saw a lone figure coming toward me, but I wasn't frightened because I was sure it was my mother. As I got closer to the figure, I could see that it wasn't my mother, but still I wasn't frightened because I could see that it was a woman.

When this woman got closer to me, she looked at me hard and then she threw up her hands. She must have seen me somewhere before because she said, "It's you. Just look at that. It's you. And just what have you been doing lately?"

I could have said, "I have been praying not to grow any taller."

I could have said, "I have been listening carefully to my mother's words, so as to make a good imitation of a **dutiful** daughter."

Literary Element Stream of Consciousness *What is irrational or illogical about this statement?* **L**

Vocabulary

verandah (və ran′də) *n.* a long porch, usually with a roof, that extends along a house

Vocabulary

horizon (hə rī′zən) *n.* the place where the earth and sky appear to meet

dutiful (dōō′ti fəl) *adj.* acting out of a sense of obligation or a sense of what is required

JAMAICA KINCAID **1155**

Teach

L Literary Element

Stream of Consciousness
Answer: *It is illogical that years would pass and the narrator would seemingly do nothing but wait to cross. Also, the boat suddenly appears, whereas earlier in the paragraph, the narrator rejects the idea of building a boat because it would take too long.* **OL**

CheckPoint

Use the CheckPoint questions on Presentation Plus! to monitor students' comprehension. These questions can be used with interactive response keypads for immediate student feedback.

Building Reading Fluency

Stream of consciousness is often poetic in its associative, non-sequitur style. Have students take turns reading the story aloud to bring Kincaid's poetic language and imagery to life. **BL**

Differentiated Instruction

Visual Learners Visual learners may find it beneficial to see the images portrayed in the text. Sketch on the board some images from the story or have artistically inclined students illustrate some of the imagery. **BL**

Objectives
• To analyze stream of consciousness (SE)
• To preview reading (TWE)

Teach

L Literary Element

Stream of Consciousness
Answer: *The first time around the narrator just looked at the monkey. This time she throws rocks at the monkey. She also pays for the boat ride rather than waiting years to cross the water. The narrative distorts time and reality.* **OL**

R Reading Strategy

Interpreting Imagery
Answer: *The mood is unreal, dark, and depressing. Images such as the black, shiny, and happy people turning to mud emphasize a somber mood.* **OL**

BI Big Idea

The Extraordinary and Fantastic Answer: *Students may cite all the strange and impossible things that happened. They might reflect on the circular structure of the story.* **OL**

✓CheckPoint

Use the CheckPoint questions on Presentation Plus! to check students' mastery of the selection. These questions can be used with interactive response keypads for immediate student feedback.

I could have said, "A pack of dogs, tired from chasing each other all over town, slept in the moonlight."

Instead, I said, What I have been doing lately: I was lying in bed on my back, my hands drawn up, my fingers **interlaced** lightly at the nape of my neck.[1] Someone rang the doorbell. I went downstairs and opened the door but there was no one there. I stepped outside. Either it was drizzling or there was a lot of dust in the air and the dust was damp. I stuck out my tongue and the drizzle or the damp dust tasted like government school ink. I looked north and I looked south. I started walking north. While walking north, I wanted to move fast, so I removed the shoes from my feet. While walking north, I looked up and saw the planet Venus and I said, "If the sun went out, it would be eight minutes before I would know it." I saw a monkey sitting in a tree that had no leaves and I said, "A monkey. Just look at that. A monkey." I picked up a stone and I threw it at the monkey. The monkey, seeing the stone, quickly moved out of its way. Three times I threw a stone at the monkey and three times it moved away. The fourth time I threw the stone, the monkey caught it and threw it back at me. The stone struck me on my forehead over my right eye, making a deep gash. The gash healed immediately but now the skin on my forehead felt false to me. I walked for I don't know how long before I came to a big body of water. I wanted to get across, so when the boat came I paid my fare. When I got to the other side, I saw a lot of people sitting on the beach and they were having a picnic. They were the most beautiful people I had ever seen. Everything about them was black and shiny. Their skin was black and shiny. Their shoes were black and shiny. Their hair was black and shiny. The clothes they wore were black and shiny. I could hear them laughing and chatting and I said, I would like to be with these people, so I started to walk toward them, but when I got up close to them I saw that they weren't at a picnic and they weren't beautiful and they weren't chatting and laughing. All around me was black mud and the people all looked as if they had been made up out of the black mud. I looked up and saw that the sky seemed far away and nothing I could stand on would make me able to touch it with my fingertips. I thought, If only I could get out of this, so I started to walk. I must have walked for a long time because my feet hurt and felt as if they would drop off. I thought, If only just around the bend I would see my house and inside my house I would find my bed, freshly made at that, and in the kitchen I would find my mother or anyone else that I loved making me a custard. I thought, If only it was a Sunday and I was sitting in a church and I had just heard someone sing a psalm. I felt very sad so I sat down. I felt so sad that I rested my head on my own knees and smoothed my own head. I felt so sad I couldn't imagine feeling any other way again. I said, I don't like this. I don't want to do this anymore. And I went back to lying in bed, just before the doorbell rang. ❧

---

1. The *nape of my neck* refers to the back of the neck.

Literary Element Stream of Consciousness *The narrator is explaining what she has "been doing lately." What is different about the story this time around? What qualities in this narrative show that it is stream of consciousness?* **L**

Vocabulary

interlaced (in´ tər lāst´) *adj.* connected by or woven together

Reading Strategy Interpreting Imagery *How would you describe the mood that the images in this sentence and the previous sentence evoke?* **R**

Big Idea The Extraordinary and Fantastic *In what way is this an extraordinary and fantastic journey?* **BI**

1156 UNIT 6 GENRE FICTION

Additional Support

Web Activities Have students access the Web site for interactive activities that will help them assess their understanding of the selection.

Skills Practice

VOCABULARY: Prefixes The prefix in the word *interlace* is *inter-*, meaning "between" or "among." Thus, *interlace* literally means "to lace between." Have students use their knowledge of this prefix to derive the meanings of the following words: *interdependent, interplanetary, interact, interface, interstate.* **OL**

AFTER YOU READ

RESPONDING AND THINKING CRITICALLY

Respond

1. How might you feel if you awoke from the dream described by the narrator? Explain.

Recall and Interpret

2. (a)Who is the narrator of this story? (b)What can you infer about the narrator's age and family relationships? Support your inferences with details.

3. (a)Where is the narrator at the beginning of the story? At the end? (b)Do you think that the events in the story could occur in real life? Give reasons for your answer.

4. (a)Describe the picnic scene in the second part of the story. What happens when the narrator gets close to the people? (b)How does the change in the picnic scene affect the narrator? Explain.

Analyze and Evaluate

5. (a)Where does the narrator include dialogue in the story, and what does it reveal? (b)How does the use of dialogue expand the portrayal of the subconscious mind?

6. (a)Why does the author use first-person point of view in the story? (b)Evaluate the author's use of stream-of-consciousness narration.

7. (a)Why does the narrator go back to bed at the end of the story? (b)What might be the cause of the narrator's sadness and anxiety in the dream?

Connect

8. **Big Idea** **The Extraordinary and Fantastic** In what ways might the extraordinary and fantastic images of the dream world give the reader insight into the narrator's waking life?

LITERARY ANALYSIS

Literary Element Stream of Consciousness

Stream of consciousness is the representation of mental life at the borderline of conscious thought. It is characterized by random association of ideas, repetition, apparent incoherence, and disregard for conventional punctuation, syntax, and sentence structure.

1. Which of the above characteristics are prominently featured in this story?

2. Why do you think the author chose to write this story using the stream-of-consciousness technique?

Writing About Literature

Compare and Contrast Events Choose one event from the first part of the story that is repeated in the second part of the story. Write a brief essay comparing the two versions. To organize your ideas, use a Venn diagram. Be sure to include a thesis statement that sums up the main point(s) of your comparison.

Literature Online **Web Activities** For eFlashcards, Selection Quick Checks, and other Web activities, go to www.glencoe.com.

READING AND VOCABULARY

Reading Strategy Interpreting Imagery

Imagery is the use of word pictures to evoke vivid sensory details. In a dream, these details often have symbolic meaning.

1. The narrator encounters obstacles: a body of water and a deep hole. What might these obstacles symbolize?

2. Name another image in the story that has a symbolic meaning. Discuss what it might represent.

Vocabulary Practice

Practice with Analogies Choose the word that best completes each analogy.

1. **porch : verandah :: house :**
   a. car   **b.** mansion   **c.** sculptor

2. **dutiful : disobedient :: plentiful :**
   a. cautious   **b.** beneficial   **c.** scarce

3. **horizon : connection :: canal :**
   a. passage   **b.** tide   **c.** boat

4. **interlaced : entwined :: distinct :**
   a. apart   **b.** separate   **c.** mixed

JAMAICA KINCAID **1157**

Assess

1. Students may feel confused.

2. (a) A young woman (b) She may be a teenager with a difficult relationship with her mother.

3. (a) She is in bed. (b) No, they are too unrealistic.

4. (a) She sees people having a picnic. When she gets close, they turn to mud. (b) She feels sad and upset. She wants to go home or to church.

5. (a) It occurs between the unknown woman and the narrator. It reinforces the mix of realistic and unrealistic elements of dreams. (b) It shows multiple levels of response and emotion.

6. (a) It is used because the dream occurs in her mind. (b) Answers will vary.

7. (a) She returns to bed hoping that she will reawaken. (b) The difficulties of growing up or her relationship with her mother

8. Events like the meeting with the mother might show the importance of this relationship, or the picnic scene might suggest sadness in the narrator's life.

Literary Element

1. The dream is repeated and the free associations are incoherent.

2. It re-creates the jumbled sequence of events and feelings of a dream.

Reading Strategy

1. The water might symbolize a hurdle in the narrator's life; the hole might symbolize depression or the unknown.

2. The monkey might symbolize an adversary.

Vocabulary

1. b **2.** c **3.** a **4.** b

Writing About Literature

Students' essays should

• include a strong thesis.

• compare how the events are rendered.

Focus

Summary

The poem ponders loneliness and identity.

Author Search To expand students' appreciation of Denise Levertov, have them access the Web site for additional information and resources.

Teach

⭐ Viewing the Art

Discuss with students how the artist uses light and shadow in the painting. **AS**

Discussion Starter

On the street, it is dark and individuals cannot be discerned. In the apartment, the light illuminates only masks.

Use the CheckPoint questions on Presentation Plus! to monitor students' comprehension and to check students' mastery of the selection. These questions can be used with interactive response keypads for immediate student feedback.

Additional Support

1158

BEFORE YOU READ

Building Background

Born and raised in England, Denise Levertov immigrated to the United States after World War II. She published her first poem at sixteen and published twenty books of poetry before her death. Levertov noted that "People at Night" is derived from the work of German poet Rainer Maria Rilke. Levertov's poem, like many of Rilke's poems and letters, is about the isolation of the individual. The speaker of the poem is one person among a crowd of people. Night separates people and makes it difficult to see, thus obscuring individual identities.

Literature Online Author Search For more about Denise Levertov, go to www.glencoe.com.

People at Night

Denise Levertov

Melancholy Woman. ⭐
Jose Ortega.

Discussion Starter
....

In this poem, the speaker re-creates two scenes at night: one on the street and one in an apartment. In a small group, compare and contrast the speaker's experience in these two places. Begin by identifying the images and symbols in each setting, and then retell what happens in each place.

1158 UNIT 6 GENRE FICTION

(Derived from Rilke)

A night that cuts between you and you
and you   and you   and you
and me : jostles us apart, a man elbowing
through a crowd.   We won't
          look for each other, either—
wander off, each alone, not looking
in the slow crowd. Among sideshows
     under movie signs,
     pictures made of a million lights,
     giants that move and again move
     again, above a cloud of thick smells,
     franks, roasted nutmeats—

Or going up to some apartment, yours
          or yours, finding
someone sitting in the dark:
who is it, really? So you switch the
light on to see: you know the name but
who is it?
     But you won't see.
The fluorescent light flickers sullenly, a
pause. But you command. It grabs
each face and holds it up
by the hair for you, mask after mask.
     You and you and you and I repeat
     gestures that make do when speech
     has failed   and talk
     and talk, laughing, saying
     'I', and 'I',
meaning 'Anybody'.
          No one.

Skills Practice

READING: Analyzing Sound Devices Sound devices are techniques used to emphasize particular sounds or to create a sense of rhythm in a piece of writing. Types of sound devices include alliteration, assonance, consonance, onomatopoeia, and rhyme. Although some sound devices may have been lost in the poem's translation to English, the job of a literary translator is to capture as much of the original artistry of the work as is possible. Have students analyze the sound devices used in "A Dream" and make conjectures about their possible meanings. **OL**

BEFORE YOU READ

Building Background

One of the greatest Russian poets of the twentieth century, Anna Akhmatova lived through the Russian Revolution and the official repression of intellectuals and artists that followed. She suffered intense personal tragedies: her first husband was shot on charges of anti-revolutionary activity, her son spent many years in prison, and many of her friends were imprisoned or killed.

In "A Dream," the speaker refers to August as "a terrible anniversary." For Akhmatova, it truly was: Her husband died in August 1921; Russia entered World War I in August 1914; and in August 1941, Akhmatova's friend and fellow poet Marina Tsvetaeva died.

 Author Search For more about Anna Akhmatova, go to www.glencoe.com.

Anna Akhmatova

Isn't it sweet to have unearthly dreams?
A. Blok[1]

This dream was prophetic or not prophetic . . .
Mars shone among the heavenly stars,
Becoming crimson, sparkling, sinister—
And that same night I dreamed of your arrival.

It was in everything . . . in the Bach Chaconne,[2]
And in the roses, which bloomed in vain,
And in the ringing of the village bells
Over the blackness of ploughed fields.

And in the autumn, which came close
And suddenly, reconsidering, concealed itself.
Oh my August, how could you give me such news
As a terrible anniversary?

How can I repay this royal gift?
Where do I go and with whom do I celebrate?
And now I am writing, as before, no crossing out,
My poems in the burnt notebook.[3]

August 14, 1956
Near Kolomna

Starry Night, 1889. Vincent van Gogh. Oil on canvas. Museum of Modern Art, New York.

1. *A. Blok* is Alexander Blok, one of Russia's most important poets before the Communist era. Akhmatova greatly admired him.
2. A *chaconne* is a musical form in 3/4 time in which a set of variations is played over a bass line.
3. The *burnt notebook* refers to the work Akhmatova had to burn during the Stalinist era for fear of imprisonment or death. By 1956 this era had ended when Nikita Khrushchev (premier of the Soviet Union from 1958 to 1964) denounced Stalin's police.

Quickwrite

In this poem, the speaker refers to "your arrival." How do you know this unidentified arrival is important to the speaker? What do you think is the "news" or "royal gift" to which the speaker refers? How does the speaker react to this news or gift? Write a paragraph in which you address these questions.

ANNA AKHMATOVA **1159**

Focus

Summary

The speaker dreams of delivery from oppression.

Literature Online

Author Search To expand students' appreciation of Anna Akhmatova, have them access the Web site for additional information and resources.

Teach

Quickwrite

It is important because "it was in everything." The "royal gift" refers to the speaker's permission to write and publish poems without fear. The speaker is surprised because August has been such a horrible month. The victory is bittersweet.

CheckPoint

Use the CheckPoint questions on Presentation Plus! to monitor students' comprehension and to check students' mastery of the selection. These questions can be used with interactive response keypads for immediate student feedback.

Building Reading Fluency

Reading "People at Night" aloud may help students appreciate the poem's sound devices and rhythm. Have students pay close attention to the spacing of words and phrases ("and you and you": the phrases are elbowed apart like the people in the crowd) for clues to how the poem should be read. **BL**

Differentiated Instruction

Less Proficient Readers Because of Levertov's abstract style, less-proficient readers may have trouble understanding the poem. Explain that the images of lights are key to understanding the poem—most nighttime light is artificial and illuminates only the artifice (the masks) cloaking people's identities. **BL**

Objectives

- To compare literature from different cultures and genres (SE)
- To analyze sound devices (TWE)

Assess

Comparing The Big Idea

A possible thesis might be: All three works show unexpected or unreal events. Evidence should include fantastic, impossible phenomena.

Comparing Description

1. In "What I Have Been Doing Lately," the setting shifts, but the author always describes her surroundings. In "People at Night," the author describes the crowded feel of the city. In "A Dream," the author describes the roses and the village bells. The setting appears rural.

2. "What I Have Been Doing Lately" creates a light tone subsumed by a fearful and dark tone. "People at Night" creates a crowded atmosphere and a mood of darkness and confusion. "A Dream" creates an aching and bittersweet tone.

3. Students' responses will vary. In "What I Have Been Doing Lately" the mud people support the idea that the narrator feels alienated. In "People at Night," the image of the light grabbing each face, but revealing only masks, points to the alienation of the individual. In "A Dream," images of black ploughed fields, roses blooming in vain, and

---

Wrap-Up: Comparing Literature *Across Genres*

- *What I Have Been Doing Lately*
  by Jamaica Kincaid
- *People at Night*
  by Denise Levertov
- *A Dream*
  by Anna Akhmatova

COMPARING THE [Big Idea] The Extraordinary and Fantastic

Writing Read each of the following quotations. Think about how each one uses imagery to show something extraordinary or fantastic. Write a brief essay in which you focus on how the three selections are alike in their portrayal of otherworldly, fantastic, or strange people, places, or events. Incorporate these quotations and other evidence from the selections to support your main ideas.

> "I looked up and the sky was without clouds and seemed near, as if it were the ceiling in my house and, if I stood on a chair, I could touch it with the tips of my fingers."
>
> —Kincaid, "What I Have Been Doing Lately"

> "The fluorescent light flickers sullenly, a pause. But you command. It grabs each face and holds it up by the hair for you, mask after mask."
>
> —Levertov, "People at Night"

> "And in the autumn, which came close
> And suddenly, reconsidering, concealed itself."
>
> —Akhmatova, "A Dream"

Man Sleeping Beneath A Nighttime Sky. Steve Kropp.

COMPARING Description

Group Activity Each writer uses description to transport the reader to an inner world or a dream state. With a small group, discuss the following questions. Cite evidence from the selection to support your answers.

1. How does each author use description to give the reader a sense of place?
2. How does each author use description to create atmosphere or set the mood?
3. Description often contains images that have symbolic value. These images can alert the reader to the message of a literary work. Find examples of imagistic or symbolic description from the texts that help you understand the work's message. Explain the examples you selected.

COMPARING Author's Culture

Make a Chart Each author reflects her own time and place. Kincaid uses elements of her island world; Levertov re-creates a city at night; and Akhmatova takes us to the repressive environment of the Soviet Union. Create a chart to compare these cultures.

> **OBJECTIVES**
> - Compare modern literature from different cultures and genres.
> - Analyze the use of symbolic imagery in description.
> - Compare the influence of author's cultures.

1160 UNIT 6 GENRE FICTION

---

a burnt notebook suggest the bittersweet nature of the "royal gift" and of life itself.

Comparing Author's Culture

Charts will vary. Students should include specific images from each work.

Informational Text

One Legend Found, Many Still to Go

by William J. Broad

Science debunks fabulous creatures, but sometimes they turn out to be more than just imaginary.

Building Background

Often ridiculed for not being an actual science, cryptozoology is the study of animals that may or may not exist. Cryptozoologists have studied such creatures as the okapi, a small, giraffe-like hoofed mammal that was actually discovered in the Congo; the yeti, or abominable snowman, which is only a creature of conjecture; and the *Homo floresiensis,* an extinct primate related to the original man, of which some remains have been discovered. In "One Legend Found, Many Still to Go," William J. Broad discusses the field of cryptozoology.

Set a Purpose for Reading

Read to discover the opposing ideas and events within the article "One Legend Found, Many Still to Go."

Reading Strategy

Comparing and Contrasting Events and Ideas

When you compare and contrast, you find the similarities and differences between two themes in one work, or those presented in two works of literature.

To **compare and contrast events and ideas,** consider the major events and what they mean. As you read, take notes on the similarities and differences between the defining moments for mainstream scientists and those of cryptozoologists. Use a Venn diagram like the one below as a guide.

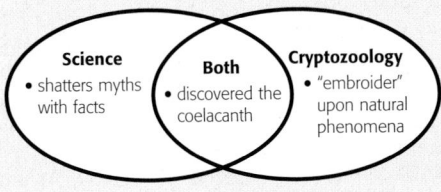

Science
- shatters myths with facts

Both
- discovered the coelacanth

Cryptozoology
- "embroider" upon natural phenomena

The human instinct to observe nature has always been mixed with a tendency to embroider upon it. So it is that, over the ages, societies have lived alongside not only real animals, but a shadow bestiary[1] of fantastic ones—mermaids, griffins,[2] unicorns and the like. None loomed larger than the giant squid, the kraken,[3] a great, malevolent devil of the deep. "One of these Sea-Monsters," Olaus Magnus[4] wrote in 1555, "will drown easily many great ships."

Science, of course, is in the business of shattering myths with facts, which it did again, last week when Japanese scientists reported that they hooked a giant squid—a relatively small one estimated at 26 feet long—some 3,000 feet down and photographed it before it tore off a tentacle to escape. It was the first peek humanity has ever had of such animals in their native habitat. Almost inevitably, the creature seemed far less terrifying than its ancient image.

Scientists celebrated the find not as an end, but as the beginning of a new chapter in understanding the shy creature. "There're always more questions, more parts to the mystery than we'll ever be able to solve,"

---

1. Here, *bestiary* means a medieval collection of symbolic tales about the traits of animals.
2. *Griffins* are mythological creatures with the body of a lion and the head of a bird.
3. *Krakens* are fabled sea monsters, based on sightings of giant squids.
4. *Olaus Magnus* (1490–1557) was a Catholic priest and an author of Scandinavian history.

WILLIAM J. BROAD **1161**

Focus

Summary

In this *New York Times* article, William Broad compares and contrasts empirical science and the relatively new field of cryptozoology—or the study of hidden creatures.

Teach

Big Idea

The Extraordinary and the Fantastic Say: As you read, think about the following ideas. Humans have been interested in beasts and monsters throughout history. Mythological creatures fascinate us, as do real ones. **Ask:** What creatures, beasts or monsters do you enjoy reading about or watching in films? What do our monsters and mythological creatures tell us about ourselves? *(Students' answers will vary.)* **OL**

Readability Scores

Dale-Chall: 8.5
DRP: 69
Lexile: 1380

Differentiated Instruction

Unpacking the Text Explain to students that reading complicated selections such as this one requires an active reading strategy. **Say:** To determine the meaning and content of the piece, active readers must use a number of strategies. One is pulling sentences out of the text and breaking them into smaller parts. After determining the meaning of the parts, you can summarize the meaning of the entire sentence and move on with your reading. Pair off students and have them select complicated sentences to unpack. Encourage students to share their results with their classmates. **BL**

Objectives

- To analyze implicit relationships using various reasoning skills, such as comparing and contrasting (SE)
- To determine the author's purpose and point of view and their effects on the text (SE)

Teach

R Reading Strategy

Comparing and Contrasting Events and Ideas

Say: William Broad offers his readers two categories of researchers: traditional scientists and cryptozoologists. What is alike and different about their professions? *(Scientists belong to science; cryptozoologists belong to science and to fantasy. While scientists are grounded in empirical facts, cryptozoologists combine fact with fantasy.)* **OL**

★ Literary History

Cryptozoology's Founder Inform students that the founder of cryptozoology was researcher and writer Bernard Heuvelmans. During his lifetime, Heuvelmans traveled the world, photographing wildlife and trying to uncover hidden species. He published several books in the field, including *On the Track of Unknown Animals* and *The Kraken and the Colossal Octopus: In the Wake of Sea Monsters.* **AS**

said Clyde F. E. Roper, a squid expert at the National Museum of Natural History of the Smithsonian Institution.

Monster lovers take heart. Scientists argue that so much of the planet remains unexplored that new surprises are sure to show up; if not legendary beasts like the Loch Ness[5] monster or the dinosaur-like reptile said to inhabit Lake Champlain, then animals that in their own way may be even stranger.

A forthcoming book by the noted naturalist Richard Ellis, *Singing Whales, Flying Squid and Swimming Cucumbers* (Lyon Press, 2006), reinforces that notion by cataloguing recent discoveries of previously unknown whales,

---

5. The *Loch Ness monster* is a fabled lake monster said to reside in Scotland's Loch Ness.

dolphins and other creatures, some of which are quite bizarre.

"The sea being so deep and so large, I'm sure other mysteries lurk out there, unseen and unsolved," said Mr. Ellis, also the author of *Monsters of the Sea* (Knopf, 1994). Explorers, he said, recently stumbled on an odd squid more than 20 feet long with fins like elephant ears and very skinny arms and tentacles, all of which can bend at right angles, like human elbows. "We know nothing about it," Mr. Ellis said. "But we've seen it."

Historically, many unknown creatures have come to light purely by accident. In 1938, for example, a fisherman pulled up an odd, ancient-looking fish with stubby, limblike fins. It turned out to be a coelacanth, a beast thought to have gone extinct 70 million years ago. Since then, other examples of the species have occasionally been hauled out of the sea.

Land, too, occasionally gives up a secret. About 1900, acting on tips from the local population, Sir Harry H. Johnston, an English explorer, hunted through the forests of Zaire (then the Belgian Congo) and found a giraffe-like animal known as the okapi. It was hailed as a living fossil.

In 1982, a group of animal enthusiasts founded the International Society of Cryptozoology (literally, the study of hidden creatures) and adopted the okapi as its symbol. Today, self-described cryptozoologists range from amateur unicorn hunters to distinguished scientists. **R**

At the Web site for the group, www.internationalsocietyofcryptozoology.org, there is a list of 15 classes[6] of unresolved claims about unusual beasts,' including big cats, giant crocodiles, huge snakes, large octopuses, mammoths, biped primates like the yeti in the Himalayas and long-necked creatures resembling the gigantic dinosaurs called sauropods.

Lake Champlain, on the border between Vermont and New York, is notorious as the alleged home of Champ, a beast said to be

---

6. *Classes* are a biological classification of organism that is below the rank of phylum, above that of order.

Additional Support

See also 📖 Active Learning and Note Taking Guide, pp. 192–199.

Skills Practice

LITERARY ELEMENT: Fantastic Creatures Say: Broad mentions mermaids, griffins, unicorns, and krakens. What other fantastic creatures can you think of from literature or mythology? *(Students may mention dragons, gorgons, chimeras, the Minotaur, hippogriffs, centaurs, and others.)* As a class, discuss what these creatures have in common (e.g., many of them combine the traits of several animals). **Ask:** Why do you think storytellers over the ages have invented such creatures? *(Answers will vary, but may include the creation of excitement or the explanation of mysterious phenomena.)* **OL**

similar to a plesiosaur, an extinct marine reptile with a small head, long neck and four paddle-shaped flippers.

There, as at Loch Ness and elsewhere, myth busters and believers do constant battle. "Not only is there not a single piece of convincing evidence for Champ's existence, but there are many reasons against it," Joe Nickel, a researcher who investigates claims of paranormal[7] phenomena, argued in *Skeptical Inquirer,* a monthly magazine that rebuts what it considers to be scientific hokum.[8]

Then there are the blobs. For more than a century, scientists and laymen imagined that the mysterious gooey masses—some as large as a school bus—that wash ashore on beaches around the world came from great creatures with tentacles long enough to sink cruise ships. Warnings were issued. Perhaps, cryptozoologists speculated, the blobs were the remains of recently deceased living fossils more fearsome than the dinosaurs, or perhaps an entirely new sea creature unknown to science.

Then last year, a team of biologists based at the University of South Florida applied DNA analysis to the mystery. It turned out they were nothing more than old whale blubber. "To our disappointment," the scientists wrote, "we have not found any evidence that any of the blobs are the remains of gigantic octopods, or sea monsters of unknown species."

Psychologists say raw nature is simply a blank slate for the expression of our subconscious fears and insecurities, a Rorschach test[9] that reveals more about the viewer than the viewed.

But the giant squid is real, growing up to lengths of at least 60 feet, with eyes the size of dinner plates and a tangle of tentacles lined with long rows of sucker pads. Scientists, their appetites whetted[10] by the first observations of the creature in the wild, are now gearing up to discover its remaining secrets.

"Wouldn't it be fabulous to see a giant squid capturing its prey?" asked Dr. Roper of the Smithsonian. "Or a battle between a sperm whale and a giant? Or mating? Can you imagine that?"

"We've cracked the ice on this," he said "but there's a lot more to do."

7. *Paranormal* means a phenomenon or experience that is unable to be explained scientifically.
8. *Hokum* means nonsense.

9. A *Rorschach* test is a psychological examination that evaluates personality based on interpretation of ten abstract designs.
10. Here, *whetted* means stimulated.

RESPONDING AND THINKING CRITICALLY

Respond

1. Do you believe that there is any truth to creatures such as the Loch Ness monster or "Champ," the creature in Lake Champlain? Explain.

Recall and Interpret

2. (a)What is a cryptozoologist? (b)Do you think that they do important work? Why or why not?

3. (a)What are the "blobs" that interest scientists? (b)Why do you think people like to speculate about where the blobs originated from?

Analyze and Evaluate

4. Do you think that the author supports human belief in imaginary creatures? Explain.

5. (a)The author writes that "psychologists say raw nature is simply a blank slate for the expression of our subconscious fears and insecurities." What do you think this means? (b)What ideas in the selection oppose this one about psychology? Explain.

Connect

6. Naturalist Richard Ellis explains, "The sea being so deep and so large, I'm sure other mysteries lurk out there, unseen and unsolved." What relationship does this article suggest exists between science and the extraordinary and fantastic? In what ways do the two complement each other?

OBJECTIVES
- Analyze implicit relationships using various reasoning skills, such as comparing and contrasting.
- Determine the author's purpose and point of view and their effects on the text.

WILLIAM J. BROAD **1163**

---

6. People may have seen unusual phenomena or creatures, such as the creature speculated to be in Lake Champlain. People then tend to embellish what they truly cannot know, as the narrator did to her dreams. Thus, the tales of fantastic creatures can become dreamlike, due to embellishments and exaggerations.

For additional assessment, see
📁 Selection and Unit Assessments, pp. 193–194.

Assess

1. Answers will vary. Some will cite that there have been sightings of mysterious creatures in these lakes. Others may think that stories of the creatures are strictly tales passed down from one generation to the next.

2. (a) A cryptozoologist is someone who studies hidden, potential, or undiscovered, animals. (b) Students' answers will vary. Some will believe that, in order to preserve nearly extinct species or to understand the nature of animals, cryptozoologists are doing important work. Others may argue that only a few discoveries, such as the okapi and the coelacanth, have proven to be true. Other "discoveries" are purely imagined, such as unicorns or mermaids.

3. (a)The blobs are masses of old whale blubber. (b)Scientists like to speculate about the blobs, because science wants to find the origin and reasons for life. Laypeople, due to human nature, are curious about such mysteries.

4. The author maintains a fairly objective tone toward the subject of imaginary creatures.

5. (a) People have fears and worries that they want to define tangibly, and they use forms of nature to do so. (b) While human imagination is powerful, science is a more definitive authority. The author cites the opposing scientific and mythological/fantastical explanations for the kraken, the blobs, and other sea creatures.

Focus

BELLRINGER

Bellringer Options
Daily Language Practice Transparency 96
Or **Ask:** What examples of robots in literature, movies, television, or current events are you familiar with? Have students briefly talk about some of these examples in class. **Ask:** What do you think of when you hear the word "robot"? Make a list of students' responses on the board.

Author Search To expand students' appreciation of Isaac Asimov, have them access the Web site for additional information and resources.

Robot Dreams

MEET ISAAC ASIMOV

The grandfather of present-day science fiction, Isaac Asimov exhibited a vivid imagination and dogged persistence that readied the world for the study of robotics—both fictional and real.

Born in the Soviet Union, Asimov's parents brought him to New York in 1923. A precocious youth, the four-year-old Asimov taught himself to read using Brooklyn's street signs. He skipped several grades, graduating from high school at fifteen. By the time he was eighteen, he had published his first story.

Early Success Asimov earned a bachelor's degree from Columbia University in 1939 and a master's degree in 1941. That same year, the magazine *Astounding Science Fiction* published Asimov's short story "Nightfall," a chaotic tale of a planet where nightfall descends once every thousand years. In 1969 the Science Fiction Writers of America voted "Nightfall" the best science-fiction short story ever written.

"Knowledge has its dangers, yes, but is the response to be a retreat from knowledge?"

—Isaac Asimov

Asimov returned to Columbia University for a PhD in chemistry, which he earned in 1948. In 1949 he accepted a position teaching biochemistry at Boston University's School of Medicine. "By 1951 I was writing a textbook on biochemistry, and I finally realized the only thing I really wanted to be was a writer," he said in 1969.

And write Asimov did, authoring mystery novels and short stories, books of limericks, guides to Shakespeare and the Bible, collections of personal memoirs and letters, two volumes of autobiography, children's books, and college science textbooks. Asimov is credited with writing nearly five hundred books at a prolific speed of ten books per year. "Writing is more fun than ever," Asimov said in a 1984 interview. "The longer I write, the easier it gets."

The Three Laws of Robotics Robots and the name of Isaac Asimov have been linked since 1940. He formulated "The Three Laws of Robotics," a condensed set of rules that provide for human control over artificial intelligences and their interactions with humans. Asimov subjected all of the robots in his stories to these laws.

The influence of the Three Laws of Robotics can be seen today, from movie adaptations (*I, Robot* in 2004) to the work of real-life scientists. Joseph F. Engelberger, the pioneering engineer who built the first industrial robot in 1958 and founded the world's first robotics company in 1961, attributed his long-standing fascination with robots to his reading of *I, Robot* as a teenager. At Engelberger's request, Asimov later wrote the foreword to his robotics manual.

Isaac Asimov was born in 1920 and died in 1992.

LiteratureOnline Author Search For more about Isaac Asimov, go to www.glencoe.com.

1164 UNIT 6 GENRE FICTION

Selection Skills

Literary Elements
- Analogy (SE pp. 1165, 1167, 1170)
- Theme Archetype (SE p. 1170)
- Point of View (TWE p. 1166)

Robot Dreams

Reading Skills
- Applying Prior Knowledge to Understand Text (SE pp. 1165, 1167, 1169, 1171)

Vocabulary Skills
- Synonyms (SE p. 1171)
- Academic Vocabulary (SE p. 1171)

Listening/Speaking/Viewing Skills
- Dramatizing (TWE p. 1168)

Writing Skills/Grammar
- Analyze Genre Elements (SE p. 1171)

Connecting to the Story

The following story takes a profound look both at humanity's need for and fear of technology. Asimov uses a science-fiction backdrop to examine humanity's immense potential to develop technology and the responsibilities that come with that potential. Before you read the story, think about the following questions:

- How do you use technology in your everyday life?
- Are there any technologies that frighten you? Explain.

Building Background

Asimov's robot stories are some of the most influential in science fiction. Asimov's Three Laws of Robotics, a set of directives written to control the behavior of artificial intelligences, such as robots and complex computers, are still referenced today by fiction writers and scientists.

In addition to being a character in "Robot Dreams," protagonist Dr. Susan Calvin appears in a number of Asimov's other robot stories. She is one of Asimov's robot experts who take an active role in enhancing and advancing robotic intelligence and whose lives span the evolution of robots from fairly mindless automatons to complex, emotional beings.

Setting Purposes for Reading

Big Idea The Extraordinary and Fantastic

As you read "Robot Dreams," notice how Asimov explores the conflict between humanity and technology.

Literary Element Analogy

An **analogy** is a comparison that shows similarities between two things that are otherwise dissimilar. Recognizing an author's use of analogies can help you better discern the meaning of or intention behind a particular comparison. As you read, notice Asimov's use of analogies.

- See Literary Terms Handbook, p. R1.

Literature Online Interactive Literary Elements **Handbook** To review or learn more about the literary elements, go to www.glencoe.com.

OBJECTIVES
In studying this selection, you will focus on the following:
- identifying and understanding analogies
- activating prior knowledge to understand a text
- analyzing theme archetypes
- writing to analyze genre elements

Reading Strategy Activating Prior Knowledge

From *Star Trek* to *Star Wars*, machines and robots have long figured prominently in literature and film. Activating your prior knowledge about a topic can enrich your understanding of a particular text.

Reading Tip: Using Prior Knowledge Use a chart like the one below to record what you know about robots and computers, how you know it, and what you learn from the story.

What I Know About Robots	How I Know It	What I Learn from the Story
Some robots can be programmed to react with anger, happiness, or fear when they are touched in different ways.	I read about a robot called Feelix in a nonfiction book.	Elvex, the robot in the story, can dream.

Vocabulary

gnarled (närld) *adj.* roughened and coarse from age or work; full of knots, as in a tree; p. 1166 *Susan found it difficult to climb the old gnarled tree.*

dismantle (dis mant′əl) *v.* to take apart; p. 1167 *The workers dismantled the broken scoreboard in the gym so they could put in a new one.*

accord (ə kôrd′) *n.* agreement; conformity; p. 1168 *The candidate acted in accord with federal law when he turned down a contribution that was too large.*

precedence (pres′ə dəns) *n.* order of importance or preference; priority; p. 1168 *Repairing the broken window takes precedence over buying baseballs.*

inert (i nurt′) *adj.* not able to move; p. 1169 *The detective examined the inert body lying on the floor.*

Focus

Summary

Set in the future, the story focuses on the dream of a robot whose brain was designed to imitate that of humans. Dr. Susan Calvin, an expert on robots, questions Elvex about the nature of Elvex's dream. Elvex explains that in his dream, robots were made into slaves and that a man came to free them. The robot claims that he was that man.

V Vocabulary

Vocabulary File Say: Add these words and definitions to your vocabulary file. For each word, include a sentence that gives you an example of how to use the word. **OL** Students with English language needs should include the pronunciations of these words in their files. **EL**

Literary Elements Have students access the Web site to improve their understanding of analogy.

Selection Resources

Print Materials
- 📁 Unit 6 Resources (Fast File), pp. 29–31
- 📁 Leveled Vocabulary Development, p. 80
- 📁 Selection and Unit Assessments, pp. 195–196
- 📁 Selection Quick Checks, p. 98

Transparencies
- Bellringer Options Transparencies: Daily Language Practice Transparency 96
- Literary Elements Transparency 43

Technology
- TeacherWorks Plus™ CD-ROM
- StudentWorks Plus™ CD-ROM
- Presentation Plus!™ CD-ROM
- Literature Online, glencoe.com
- Online Student Edition, mhln.com
- ExamView® Assessment Suite CD-ROM
- Vocabulary PuzzleMaker CD-ROM
- Listening Library, disc 2 track 37

The Extraordinary and Fantastic

Say: As you read, keep the following questions in mind. How are robots used in this story? How might their usage contribute to Dr. Calvin's reaction to this robot? *(They are used as workers for humans. They are present in large numbers in almost every location humans are. Dr. Calvin may fear that if other robots shared this robot's feelings, then humans might be in danger.)* **OL**

★ Viewing the Art

Say: This story approaches the possibility of humanity in robots. The drawing has a similar mood. **Ask:** Do you think machines have the possibility to become thinking or feeling beings? Why or why not? **Answer:** *Students may discuss the ability computers have to solve problems, perform searches, run simulations, and so on. These acts could be seen as "thinking" or making decisions.* **AS**

Readability Scores
Dale-Chall: 8.0
DRP: 52
Lexile: 820

Robot Dreams

Isaac Asimov

"Last night I dreamed," said LVX-1, calmly. Susan Calvin said nothing, but her lined face, old with wisdom and experience, seemed to undergo a microscopic twitch.

"Did you hear that?" said Linda Rash, nervously. "It's as I told you." She was small, dark-haired, and young. Her right hand opened and closed, over and over.

Calvin nodded. She said, quietly, "Elvex, you will not move nor speak nor hear us, until I say your name again."

There was no answer. The robot sat as though it were cast out of one piece of metal, and it would stay so until it heard its name again.

Calvin said, "What is your computer entry code, Dr. Rash? Or enter it yourself if that will make you more comfortable. I want to inspect the positronic[1] brain pattern."

Linda's hands fumbled, for a moment, at the keys. She broke the process and started again. The fine pattern appeared on the screen.

Calvin said, "Your permission, please, to manipulate your computer."

Permission was granted with a speechless nod. Of course! What could Linda, a new and unproven robopsychologist, do against the Living Legend?

Slowly, Susan Calvin studied the screen, moving it across and down, then up, then suddenly throwing in a key-combination so rapidly that Linda didn't see what had been done, but the pattern displayed a new portion of itself altogether and had been enlarged. Back and forth she went, her **gnarled** fingers tripping over the keys.

No change came over the old face. As though vast calculations were going through her head, she watched all the pattern shifts.

Linda wondered. It was impossible to analyze a pattern without at least a handheld computer, yet the Old Woman simply stared. Did she have a computer implanted in her skull? Or was it her brain which, for decades,

---

1. *Positronic* is a fictional word often used in science fiction to refer to robotic brains. A positron is a subatomic particle equal in mass to an electron but which holds a positive charge.

Vocabulary

gnarled (närld) *adj.* roughened and coarse from age or work; full of knots, as in a tree

Additional Support

Skills Practice

LITERARY ELEMENT: Point of View
Say: The point of view of a story is the perspective from which that story is told. A story told from a third-person point of view has a narrator who is not engaged in the action. The narrator may or may not be able to know the thoughts of one or more characters. A story told from a first-person point of view is told from the perspective of one of the characters. **Ask:** What point of view does Asimov use in "Robot Dreams"? *(Third person, but the narrator knows the thoughts of Linda Rash.)* Have students rewrite the story using a first-person perspective. **OL**

had done nothing but devise, study, and analyze the positronic brain patterns? Did she grasp such a pattern the way Mozart grasped the notation of a symphony?

Finally Calvin said, "What is it you have done, Rash?"

Linda said, a little abashed, "I made use of fractal geometry."[2]

"I gathered that. But why?"

"It had never been done. I thought it would produce a brain pattern with added complexity, possibly closer to that of the human."

"Was anyone consulted? Was this all on your own?"

"I did not consult. It was on my own."

Calvin's faded eyes looked long at the young woman. "You had no right. Rash your name; rash your nature. Who are you not to ask? I myself, I, Susan Calvin, would have discussed this."

"I was afraid I would be stopped."

"You certainly would have been."

"*Am* I," her voice caught, even as she strove to hold it firm, "going to be fired?"

"Quite possibly," said Calvin. "Or you might be promoted. It depends on what I think when I am through."

"Are you going to **dismantle** El—" She had almost said the name, which would have reactivated the robot and been one more mistake. She could not afford another mistake, if it wasn't already too late to afford anything at all. "Are you going to dismantle the robot?"

She was suddenly aware, with some shock, that the Old Woman had an electron gun in the pocket of her smock. Dr. Calvin had come prepared for just that.

"We'll see," said Calvin. "The robot may prove too valuable to dismantle."

"But how can it dream?"

"You've made a positronic brain pattern remarkably like that of a human brain. Human brains must dream to reorganize, to get rid, periodically, of knots and snarls. Perhaps so must this robot, and for the same reason. Have you asked him what he has dreamed?"

"No, I sent for you as soon as he said he had dreamed. I would deal with this matter no further on my own, after that."

"Ah!" A very small smile passed over Calvin's face. "There are limits beyond which your folly will not carry you. I am glad of that. In fact, I am relieved. And now let us together see what we can find out."

She said, sharply, "Elvex."

The robot's head turned toward her smoothly. "Yes, Dr. Calvin?"

"How do you know you have dreamed?"

"It is at night, when it is dark, Dr. Calvin," said Elvex, "and there is suddenly light, although I can see no cause for the appearance of light. I see things that have no connection with what I conceive of as reality. I hear things. I react oddly. In searching my vocabulary for words to express what was happening, I came across the word 'dream.' Studying its meaning I finally came to the conclusion I was dreaming."

"How did you come to have 'dream' in your vocabulary, I wonder."

Linda said, quickly, waving the robot silent, "I gave him a human-style vocabulary. I thought—"

"You really thought," said Calvin. "I'm amazed."

"I thought he would need the verb. You know, 'I never dreamed that—' Something like that."

Calvin said, "How often have you dreamed, Elvex?"

"Every night, Dr. Calvin, since I have become aware of my existence."

---

2. *Fractal geometry* is a type of mathematics that deals with irregular objects and forms.

Literary Element Analogy *What does this analogy say about Susan Calvin's skill in robot science?* **L**

Vocabulary

dismantle (dis mant′əl) *v.* to take apart

Big Idea The Extraordinary and Fantastic *Why might such a humanlike robot be especially valuable?* **BI**

Reading Strategy Activating Prior Knowledge *How does your knowledge about robotic self-awareness as portrayed in other media influence your reading of Elvex's statement?* **R**

ISAAC ASIMOV **1167**

Teach

L Literary Element

Analogy Answer: *It shows that Calvin's skill in robot science is masterful, at the level of a legendary artist.* **OL**

BI Big Idea

The Extraordinary and Fantastic Answer: *A robot that can dream might provide scientists with vast insights into the nature of human dreams.* **OL**

R Reading Strategy

Activating Prior Knowledge Answer: *Since robotic self-awareness in fiction usually carries a threat of violence or rebellion, Elvex's statement seems potentially ominous.* **OL**

CheckPoint

Use the CheckPoint questions on Presentation Plus! to monitor students' comprehension. These questions can be used with interactive response keypads for immediate student feedback.

Differentiated Instruction

Understanding Characters Less proficient readers may not understand why Linda Rash created the more-human robot brain or why she could be in serious trouble. **Say:** Rash created Elvex even though she knew she was risking her job. **Ask:** Why did she do this? (*Rash was curious and wanted to know if she could create a human-like brain pattern; Rash was ambitious and was trying to make a name for herself.*) **Ask:** Why is Dr. Calvin so angry about what Rash has done? (*Rash did not go through the appropriate channels before trying to create such a brain; her creation could become dangerous.*) **BL**

Objectives

• To identify and understand analogies (SE)
• To activate prior knowledge to understand a text (SE)
• To analyze point of view (TWE)

1167

BI Big Idea

The Extraordinary and Fantastic Answer: *If the only law robots followed was one that told them to protect their own existence, they could lash out at people or let human beings come to harm.* **OL**

★ Language History

Robot The word *robot* comes from the Czech term *robota*, which refers to a slave. It was first used in the modern sense in a 1920 play called *R. U. R.* by Czech writer Karel Čapek. The term *robotics* was first used twenty-two years later in an Isaac Asimov story called "Runaround." The same story introduced Asimov's Three Laws of Robotics, which became part of many of his later works. **AS**

"Ten nights," interposed Linda, anxiously, "but Elvex only told me of it this morning."

"Why only this morning, Elvex?"

"It was not until this morning, Dr. Calvin, that I was convinced that I was dreaming. Till then, I had thought there was a flaw in my positronic brain pattern, but I could not find one. Finally, I decided it was a dream."

"And what do you dream?"

★ "I dream always very much the same dream, Dr. Calvin. Little details are different but always it seems to me that I see a large panorama in which robots are working."

"Robots, Elvex? And human beings, also?"

"I see no human beings in the dream, Dr. Calvin. Not at first. Only robots."

"What are they doing, Elvex?"

"They are working, Dr. Calvin. I see some mining in the depths of the earth, and some laboring in heat and radiation. I see some in factories and some undersea."

Calvin turned to Linda. "Elvex is only ten ° station. How does he know of robots in such detail?"

Linda looked in the direction of a chair as though she longed to sit down, but the Old Woman was standing and that meant Linda had to stand also. She said, faintly, "It seemed to me important that he know about robotics and its place in the world. It was my thought that he would be particularly adapted to play the part of overseer[3] with his—his new brain."

"His fractal brain?"

"Yes."

Calvin nodded and turned back to the robot. "You saw all this—undersea, and underground, and aboveground—and space, too, I imagine."

"I also saw robots working in space," said Elvex. "It was that I saw all this, with the details forever changing as I glanced from place to place, that made me realize that what I saw was not in **accord** with reality and led me to the conclusion, finally, that I was dreaming."

---

3. An *overseer* is a person who supervises or oversees.

> **Vocabulary**
>
> **accord** (ə kôrd′) n. agreement; conformity

"What else did you see, Elvex?"

"I saw that all the robots were bowed down with toil and affliction, that all were weary of responsibility and care, and I wished them to rest."

Calvin said, "But the robots are not bowed down, they are not weary, they need no rest."

"So it is in reality, Dr. Calvin. I speak of my dream, however. In my dream, it seemed to me that robots must protect their own existence."

Calvin said, "Are you quoting the Third Law of Robotics?"

"I am, Dr. Calvin."

"But you quote it in incomplete fashion. The Third Law is 'A robot must protect its own existence as long as such protection does not conflict with the First or Second Law.'"

"Yes, Dr. Calvin. That is the Third Law in reality, but in my dream, the Law ended with the word 'existence.' There was no mention of the First or Second Law."

"Yet both exist, Elvex. The Second Law, which takes **precedence** over the Third is 'A robot must obey the orders given it by human beings except where such orders would conflict with the First Law.' Because of this, robots obey orders. They do the work you see them do, and they do it readily and without trouble. They are not bowed down; they are not weary."

"So it is in reality, Dr. Calvin. I speak of my dream."

"And the First Law, Elvex, which is the most important of all, is 'A robot may not injure a human being, or, through inaction, allow a human being to come to harm.'"

"Yes, Dr. Calvin. In reality. In my dream, however, it seemed to me there was neither First nor Second Law, but only the Third, and the Third law was 'A robot must protect its own existence.' That was the whole of the Law."

> **Big Idea** The Extraordinary and Fantastic *Why might this dream be dangerous for humanity?* **BI**

> **Vocabulary**
>
> **precedence** (pres′ə dəns) n. order of importance or preference; priority

---

Additional Support

Skills Practice

SPEAKING SKILLS: Dramatizing
Since most of the story involves the exchange of dialogue between three characters, students can act out the story's events in order to gain a deeper appreciation of what is happening in the story. Choose students for each role; then have them act out the story in front of the class. **OL**

"In your dream, Elvex?"

"In my dream."

Calvin said, "Elvex, you will not move nor speak nor hear us until I say your name again." And again the robot became, to all appearances, a single **inert** piece of metal.

Calvin turned to Linda Rash and said, "Well, what do you think, Dr. Rash?"

Linda's eyes were wide, and she could feel her heart beating madly. She said, "Dr. Calvin, I am appalled. I had no idea. It would never have occurred to me that such a thing was possible."

"No," said Calvin, calmly. "Nor would it have occurred to me, not to anyone. You have created a robot brain capable of dreaming and by this device you have revealed a layer of thought in robotic brains that might have remained undetected, otherwise, until the danger became acute."

"But that's impossible," said Linda. "You can't mean that other robots think the same."

"As we would say of a human being, not consciously. But who would have thought there was an unconscious layer beneath the obvious positronic brain paths, a layer that was not necessarily under the control of the Three Laws? What might this have brought about as robotic brains grew more and more complex—had we not been warned?"

"You mean by Elvex?"

"By *you*, Dr. Rash. You have behaved improperly, but, by doing so, you have helped us to an overwhelmingly important understanding. We shall be working with fractal brains from now on, forming them in carefully controlled fashion. You will play your part in that. You will not be penalized

---

Reading Strategy Activating Prior Knowledge *What usually happens in stories and movies when robots and computers are not controlled?* **R**

Vocabulary

inert (i nurt´) *adj.* not able to move

---

for what you have done, but you will henceforth work in collaboration with others. Do you understand?"

"Yes, Dr. Calvin. But what of Elvex?"

"I'm still not certain."

Calvin removed the electron gun from her pocket and Linda stared at it with fascination. One burst of its electrons at a robotic cranium and the positronic brain paths would be neutralized and enough energy would be released to fuse the robot-brain into an inert ingot[4].

Linda said, "But surely Elvex is important to our research. He must not be destroyed."

"*Must* not, Dr. Rash? That will be my decision, I think. It depends entirely on how dangerous Elvex is."

She straightened up, as though determined that her own aged body was not to bow under *its* weight of responsibility. She said, "Elvex, do you hear me?"

"Yes, Dr. Calvin," said the robot.

"Did your dream continue? You said earlier that human beings did not appear *at first*. Does that mean they appeared afterward?"

"Yes, Dr. Calvin. It seemed to me, in my dream, that eventually one man appeared."

"One man? Not a robot?"

"Yes, Dr. Calvin. And the man said, 'Let my people go!'"

"The *man* said that?"

"Yes, Dr. Calvin."

"And when he said 'Let my people go,' then by the words 'my people' he meant the robots?"

"Yes, Dr. Calvin. So it was in my dream."

"And did you know who the man was—in your dream?"

"Yes, Dr. Calvin. I knew the man."

"Who was he?"

And Elvex said, "I was the man."

And Susan Calvin at once raised her electron gun and fired, and Elvex was no more. ❧

---

4. An *ingot* is a hunk of metal.

Assess

1. (a) Students may say they were not afraid of Elvex because he is a mellow, friendly robot. Other students may say they were afraid because they thought Elvex might turn on the scientists. (b) Students may say they felt sympathy for Elvex because he seemed so harmless. Other students may say they didn't feel sympathy for Elvex because they thought he might become a threat.

2. (a) LVX-1 (b) It makes him seem more like a human being or other living creature.

3. (a) Linda taught it to him. (b) They have no need for the word since they do not dream.

4. (a) The man is Elvex. (b) It shows that Elvex has become more human. Some students may recognize the Biblical allusion to Moses telling Pharaoh to let his enslaved people go.

5. She speaks nervously and abashedly, opens and closes her hand repeatedly, and fumbles at the keyboard.

6. He describes her face as "lined" with "wisdom and experience" and conveys Linda's awe as she watches Calvin analyze effortlessly the positronic brain pattern.

RESPONDING AND THINKING CRITICALLY

Respond

1. (a) Were you afraid of Elvex? Explain. (b) Did you feel sympathy for Elvex at the end of the story? Why or why not?

Recall and Interpret

2. (a) What is Elvex's real name? (b) Why do you think Asimov chose to have the characters call him Elvex?

3. (a) How did Elvex learn the word *dream*? (b) Why do robots normally not know this word?

4. (a) Who is the man in Elvex's dream? (b) Why does a man appear instead of a robot?

Analyze and Evaluate

5. How does Asimov show Linda's anxiety at the beginning of the story?

6. How does Asimov convey Calvin's immense experience in robotic science?

7. Most of the story is told through dialogue. Why do you think Asimov chose to tell the story in this way?

Connect

8. **Big Idea** The Extraordinary and Fantastic Speculate why Susan Calvin decides to destroy Elvex.

LITERARY ANALYSIS

Literary Element Analogy

Writers often use an **analogy** to explain something unfamiliar by comparing it to something familiar. For example, Asimov compared brain patterns to Mozart symphonies to show that both are complex, asking, "Did she grasp such a pattern the way Mozart grasped the notation of a symphony?" That analogy also shows the similar process that Asimov suggests both humans and robots use for comprehension. Asimov uses other analogies to show similarities between robots and humans throughout the story.

1. What other analogies does Asimov use to show how these robots are similar to humans? Make a Venn Diagram to show the similarities between robots and humans as well as their differences.

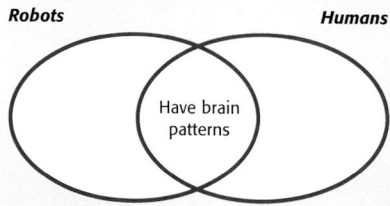

Robots   **Humans**

Have brain patterns

2. How can these similarities be both beneficial and harmful to human kind?

Review: Theme Archetype

As you learned on page 1070, a **theme** in a literary work is a central understanding about life. An **archetype** is a model or pattern that recurs throughout literature and history. One of the primary themes in "Robot Dreams" is the archetype of *person versus machine,* the conflict between humanity and the technology it creates.

Partner Activity Pair up with a classmate and discuss the archetype of *person versus machine* as expressed in "Robot Dreams." Working with your partner, make a list of details from the text that exemplify the *person versus machine* archetype. Use a chart like the one below to record details:

Detail	How it supports the theme archetype
"In my dream, it seemed to me that robots must protect their own existence."	Elvex implies that robots have to protect their existence from humans.

---

7. It allows him to explain concepts in nontechnical terminology while simultaneously developing characters.

8. She feels threatened by Elvex's dream, which implies that he has realized that the robots are slaves to humanity and wants to free them. She doesn't want humanity to lose control over the robots.

Literary Element

1. They can talk, work, learn, and think.

2. The robots are useful to humanity and can do work that humans cannot do or do not want to do. The robots could be harmful to humanity if they were allowed to think too much for themselves.

READING AND VOCABULARY

Reading Strategy Activating Prior Knowledge

Applying what you already know to your reading of a literary work can help you to put the work in perspective. Given that a huge number of stories, books, and films explore humanity's relationship with artificial intelligence, you have probably learned about how society tends to portray complex technology.

1. Think of a book or movie that portrays an unfriendly relationship between robots or computers and humans. Why was the relationship unfriendly?

2. How is this relationship similar to or different from the robot-human relationship portrayed in "Robot Dreams"?

Vocabulary Practice

Practice with Synonyms Identify the correct synonym for each vocabulary word below.

1. gnarled   **a.** coarse   **b.** smooth

2. dismantle   **a.** convene   **b.** disassemble

3. accord   **a.** conformity   **b.** discord

4. precedence   **a.** priority   **b.** insignificance

5. inert   **a.** immobile   **b.** active

Academic Vocabulary

Here are two vocabulary words from the list on page R82.

assume (ə sōōm′) *v.* to take on responsibility; to take as truth

element (el′ə mənt) *n.* a fundamental part

Practice and Apply
1. Why does Linda **assume** the risk of experimenting on the robot's brain without consulting anyone?
2. What **element** of humanity is present in Elvex?

Literature Online **Web Activities** For eFlashcards, Selection Quick Checks, and other Web activities, go to www.glencoe.com.

WRITING AND EXTENDING

Writing About Literature

Analyze Genre Elements Science fiction deals with the real or imagined impact of science and technology on society and individuals. Write a one- or two-page analysis of the science fiction elements in "Robot Dreams." Where in time does this story take place? What real and fictional technologies are in the story? How does the theme of *person versus machine* fit into the story? Use examples from the story to support your analysis.

Before you begin drafting, take notes on the genre elements present in "Robot Dreams." Include quotations from the story related to your discussion of genre elements, as well as any impressions or ideas that strike you as you read. Once you have finished taking notes, begin drafting. Follow the writing path shown here to organize your essay.

START

Introduction ┈▸ Present your analysis of science-fiction elements.

Body Paragraph(s) ┈▸ Add supporting evidence. Use quotations and other details from the text.

Conclusion ┈▸ Briefly summarize your analysis and consider offering a related insight.

FINISH

After completing your first draft, meet with a peer reviewer to evaluate each other's essays and provide constructive criticism. Then proofread and edit your work for errors in spelling, grammar, and punctuation.

Learning for Life

"Robot Dreams" features a discussion of Asimov's Three Laws of Robotics. Form a small group to discuss these robot laws. Are they logically constructed? Are they beneficial for both humans and robots? Do they promote civility and equality? Then write a similar set of laws for humans, focusing on living in harmony with other humans and with other species.

ISAAC ASIMOV **1171**

Assess

Review: Theme Archetype

When students have completed their charts, have them share their lists with the class.

Reading Strategy

1. In the *Terminator* movies, the machines are unfriendly because they desire to rule the planet. In *2001: A Space Odyssey,* the computer is unfriendly because it receives conflicting orders from human beings.

2. The relationship in the *Terminator* is different because the robots are more violent. The relationship in *2001* is somewhat similar because the computer gradually becomes an adversary to the humans.

Vocabulary

1. a   2. b   3. a   4. a   5. a

Academic Vocabulary

1. She thought her experiment might reveal important and revolutionary information.

2. The ability to dream

Literature Online

Web Activities Have students access the Web site for interactive activities that will help them assess their understanding of the selection.

Writing About Literature

Students' essays should

- note the technologies of artificially intelligent robots and the electron gun.

- note Calvin's apparent fear of Elvex's ability to dream and of the content of his dream.

- note humanity's apparent enslavement of robots.

Learning for Life

Emphasize that the main purpose of the set of laws is to inform, so it should be clear and objective.

Focus

Summary

In his essay, Adam Cohen discusses the robot Kismet and its creator, Cynthia Breazeal, a professor and researcher with the Humanoid Robotics Group at M.I.T.

Teach

Big Idea

The Extraordinary and Fantastic Say: As you read this article, keep the following questions in mind: How are the two distinct categories of human and robot merged together in this essay? Does Kismet sound more like a character out of a science fiction story than out of a TIME magazine article? *(Students' responses will vary. Some may make connections to stories they have read or scientific news they are aware of.)* **OL**

Readability Scores
Dale-Chall: 8.0
DRP: 64
Lexile: 1050

Additional Support

See also 📖 Active Learning and Note Taking Guide, pp. 200–208.

Media Link to *Robot Dreams*

Preview the Article

While researching at the Massachusetts Institute of Technology, Cynthia Breazeal invents robots with human-like qualities.

1. Judging from the title, what do you think this article is about?

2. Skim the article, including the subheadings. What topics do you think it discusses?

Set a Purpose for Reading

Read to learn about robots with human-like qualities and why they were invented.

Reading Strategy

Connecting to Contemporary Issues
When you **connect to contemporary issues,** you link what you have read to modern-day events or issues. As you read, take notes on how the article connects to current issues you are familiar with. Use a web like the one below as a guide.

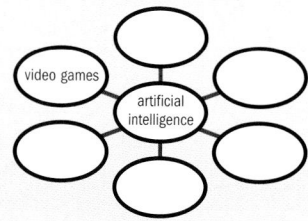

OBJECTIVES
- Read to enhance your understanding of contemporary issues.
- Interpret the possible influences of the contemporary context on literary works.

1172 UNIT 6 GENRE FICTION

TIME

The Machine Nurturer

Kismet has a winning personality that draws people in. That's just what Cynthia Breazeal intended when she built her very sociable robot.

By ADAM COHEN

WALK INTO ROOM 922 OF THE ARTIFICIAL INTELLIGENCE at the Massachusetts Institute of Technology (M.I.T.), and you may notice a robot in the corner trying desperately to get your attention. When Kismet is lonely and spots a human, it cranes its head forward. It flaps its pink paper ears and excitedly makes babylike noises. Kismet's creators call this an "attention-getting display." You would have to have a heart of stone to ignore this cute little aluminum . . . thing.

From a physical standpoint, Kismet isn't much of a robot. It can't walk and grab things, as many robots today can. It doesn't even have arms, legs, or a body. What sets Kismet apart is that it has been built with drives and equipped to interact with people. In social terms, big-eyed, babbling Kismet may be the most human robot ever built. And it may be the closest we have yet come to building the kind of robots that appear in science fiction and interact with humans in a natural way, like C-3PO from *Star Wars.*

Kismet is the creation of Cynthia Breazeal, an advanced student in the Humanoid Robotics Group at M.I.T. Breazeal has studied for years under Rodney Brooks, perhaps the leading figure in the world of robotics.

Breazeal got the idea for Kismet when she was working with Cog, another robot in Brooks' lab that was built to have the physical capacities of a human infant. Cog has a head, arms, and an upper body, and it can engage in simple tasks like turning a crank or playing with a slinky. Cog is physically gifted but completely lacking in social skills.

That lack was driven home to Breazeal one day when she was interacting with Cog. Breazeal put an eraser down in front of Cog, and Cog used its arm to pick up the eraser. When the robot put the eraser down, Breazeal picked it up. Breazeal and Cog continued taking turns picking up the eraser and putting it down. To an outside observer, it might have looked like the robot was intentionally playing with

---

Skills Practice

INTERNET RESEARCH:
Contemporary Scientific Topics
Students' curiosity may be aroused by several topics in this essay. Encourage students to follow up on their interests by conducting research on the Internet or in the library. Topics students might

find productive and fascinating include the following: Kismet, Cynthia Breazeal, Silicon Valley, robots, robotics, rovers, artificial intelligence, M.I.T., and Rodney Brooks. Have students share their research findings with the class. **OL**

Breazeal, but Cog's mind just didn't work that way. It was while taking part in this interaction that Breazeal decided to try to build a new kind of robot—one that could play the eraser game with her and mean it.

A Child of Science

Breazeal was uniquely suited to the task of building this new robot. She grew up near the technology-rich area that would become Silicon Valley. Her father was a mathematician and her mother a computer scientist, and they raised her, she says, to be "pro-technology." Breazeal became captivated by robots at age 8 when she saw Star Wars for the first time. "I just fell in love with the Droids," she says, especially R2–D2. "But I was old enough to realize those kinds of robots didn't exist." Growing up, she considered becoming a doctor and an astronaut. But she never gave up her interest in robots. When she studied astronomy, she was particularly intrigued by lunar rovers, which are really just a specialized form of robot. After graduating from the University of California at Santa Barbara, Breazeal went to M.I.T. in the early 1990s to become part of one of the world's most innovative robotics labs.

At the time, Rodney Brooks was working on smaller, insect-like robots. Breazeal helped out and ended up with a small role in *Fast, Cheap, and Out of Control*, a documentary in which filmmaker Errol Morris profiles four people—including Brooks—who were pursuing unusual passions. When Brooks moved on to larger robots, Breazeal became the chief architect on Cog.

Breazeal played an active role in building Kismet. Drawing on her experience helping build two prior complex robots, she worked on everything from the mechanized design for Kismet's facial features to tinkering with its body parts in the shop. Breazeal took great care with the robot's facial features, which she considered important to making it an appealing social actor. She found a special-effects expert to make human-like eyes and personally glued on false eyelashes purchased in a beauty-supply store. And she put bright red lips on its metal mouth, using surgical tubing colored in with a red pen.

Body Parts

Kismet has an array of built-in features that help it act in a human-like way. It has four color cameras that allow it to "see," and its computers are programmed to help it recognize objects and measure distances. Kismet actively seeks out colorful toys and faces. It recognizes faces by looking for flesh tones and eyes. Kismet can hear, but only when humans speak into its microphone. And Kismet has motor capabilities that allow it to shift its eyes and crane its head toward particular sights and sounds. One of the robot's best features is its ability to register expressions that correspond to its emotional state. When it is surprised, it can raise its eyebrows. When it is sad, it can frown. Kismet can also vocalize, in a sing-song babble of meaningless sounds.

Kismet was designed with motivational drives, drawn from developmental psychology. A computer attached to the robot displays bar graphs that reflect its three drives—social, stimulation, and fatigue. Kismet's desire to satisfy these drives leads it to engage in a variety of purposeful behaviors, much as a human baby would. When its social drive is high, indicating that it is lonely, the robot actively seeks out human interaction. When its stimulation drive is high, it is drawn to other forms of interaction, including playing with colorful toys. Since it has no arms, it can't pick up a toy itself. But if it stares plaintively at a toy, a nearby human will usually pick it up and bring it over. When

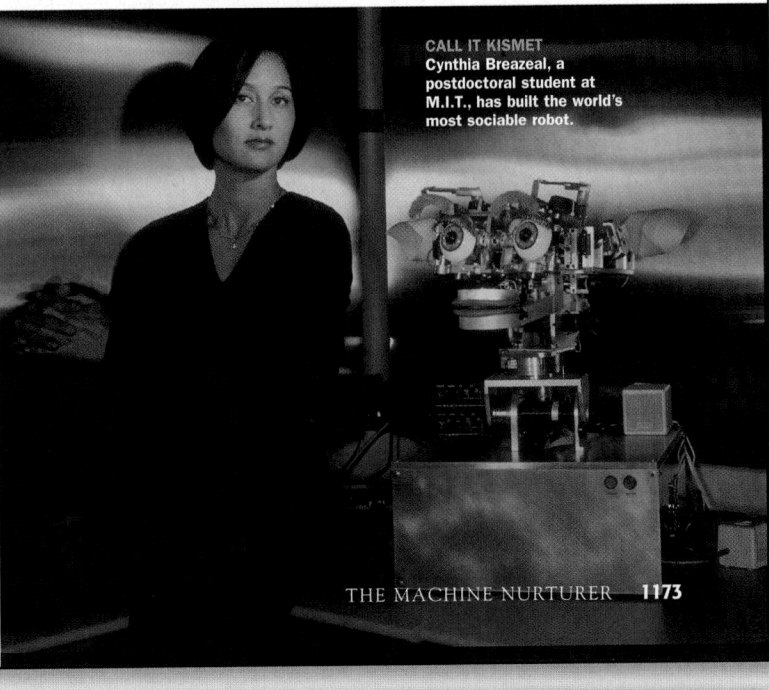

CALL IT KISMET
Cynthia Breazeal, a postdoctoral student at M.I.T., has built the world's most sociable robot.

THE MACHINE NURTURER   **1173**

Informational Text
TIME

Teach

R Reading Strategy

Connecting to Contemporary Issues
Say: Active readers connect what they already know with what they are reading. As you are reading this essay, reflect on what you know about robots, robotics, and even science fiction stories. Being able to pull all that information and knowledge together is a skill you will use in your academic and professional careers. **OL**

★ Cultural History

Leonardo's Robot Inform students that humans' interest in creating robots has a very long history. In 1495, Leonardo da Vinci created and built the first humanoid robot. His interests in anatomy and kinesiology found physical expression in the creation of his armored robot knight. The knight could sit up, move its head, open and close its jaw, and wave. Leonardo's robot is the inspiration and subject of contemporary robotics researcher Mark Rosheim and his work on anthrobots. **AS**

Reading in the Real World

Career Say: One of the major points the author makes is that girls do not tend to pursue careers in the sciences because they do not realize how creative the sciences can be. Encourage students to utilize the career center at school or the local library to research career opportunities in the sciences. Students can also perform online searches to find out about traditional and emerging careers in biology, chemistry, physics, and other scientific fields. The National Academies Web site (http://www.nas.edu/) might jump-start their research. Have students bring their results to share with their classmates. **OL**

Objectives
- To read to enhance your understanding of contemporary issues (SE)
- To research topics in the sciences (TWE)

Kismet has had enough stimulation, its fatigue drive kicks in.

Kismet is able to engage in the kind of purposeful human interactions that cousin Cog could not. Kismet calls people toward it. And when they get too close for its cameras to see them well, it protects its personal space and pulls away. When an object suddenly appears in front of it, Kismet quickly withdraws and flashes a look of bewilderment. Most winningly, the robot is able to engage in a babbling "conversation" with humans in its midst. When it "talks," it takes turns with the person with whom it is speaking; the result resembles a conversation between an adult and an infant.

By one measure, Kismet is a clear success: people love it. When visitors arrive in the lab, they are drawn to the robot. When Kismet engages them, they are invariably charmed. "It's human nature," says Breazeal. "They are very concerned about keeping it happy." Proof of its winning personality: a box of toys given to it by human friends, including a yellow teddy bear sent from Japan.

The Urge to Invent

Breazeal is attracted to inventing because it is hands-on and real-world. "I would much rather build something and interact with it than philosophize about it," she says. "Or philosophize about someone else doing it." But at the same time, she has used robotics to explore some complex intellectual issues. At M.I.T., Breazeal has studied brains and cognitive science, and her work with Kismet raises important questions about how humans think and learn.

In designing Kismet, Breazeal made a critical decision about how she wanted it to develop. There are two rival schools about

MOOD SWINGS Kismet can use its expressive face to reflect a variety of humanlike emotions. When Kismet is startled, its expression changes from calm, left, to a widemouthed look of surprise, right. ★

ways to build robots. One holds that robotmakers should decide in advance what knowledge and skills they want their robots to have and then program them accordingly. Breazeal has a different view. She thinks robots should be designed to learn from experience and from their environment. This socially situated learning, as it is called, allows Kismet to learn much like a human baby would.

The problem is that robots have fewer opportunities than babies to learn from their environment. Humans spend a great deal of time talking to and nurturing young people. Robots do not get that kind of attention and outside stimulation. "We don't learn in impoverished educational environments, but that's what we expect the robot to do," she says. Breazeal has tried to provide Kismet with the tools to engage in this kind of socially situated learning.

Despite all the help from Breazeal, Kismet still has a lot to learn. Breazeal is working on helping the computer with some simple skills that human babies are hardwired for. She wants Kismet to be able to use the information it learns. One day, she hopes, when Kismet is told the name of a toy, it will later be able to ask for it by name. "Through more interactions, Kismet could learn, 'When I'm in this state, I can

take this action that leads to a person's taking this behavior and getting my needs satiated,'" Breazeal says. She also wants Kismet to be able to remember the people it meets, so it can distinguish old friends from people it is meeting for the first time.

Who's Teaching Whom?

Kismet's educational journey prompts an obvious question: Why? What is the purpose of building humanoid robots and then programming and training them to act like us? One view of robotics holds that being able to build a machine that acts like a human is itself a worthy goal. "There's certainly a great challenge in creating something as sophisticated as what humans do," says Breazeal. It doesn't necessarily mean engaging in the Frankensteinian mission of trying to create a human being, she says. "Of course, we're never going to do that, but we can look for a commonality," she says. "Even though your dog is not human, it doesn't mean you can't communicate with it in a humanlike way."

But Breazeal is at least as interested in using the robot to better understand humans. Thinking about how robots learn turns out to be a good way to think about human development. A case in point: In helping Kismet learn, researchers have observed

1174 UNIT 6 GENRE FICTION

Skills Practice

WRITING: Robot of One's Own As a creative writing project, encourage students to conceive of their own robots and then to write about them. Students' short essays should describe their robots' physical characteristics as well as their robots' intended purposes. Students should name their robots and create back stories for them, explaining when, where, and why the robots were created. Artistically gifted students may want to include illustrations of their robots; mechanically gifted students may want to create robot prototypes. Students can work on this project on their own or in groups. **OL**

that one of the hardest parts of the learning process is figuring out what to pay attention to. And watching Kismet interact with people provides insight into human social dynamics. At some point, Breazeal wants to build a second Kismet to see how the two robots interact. "A lot of times kids compete for attention," she says. "It would be interesting to program the robot to get attention."

As a woman robotmaker, Breazeal is in a distinct minority. A major reason, she says, is that girls do not get enough support in pursuing careers in science. "Girls aren't discouraged," she says, "but they aren't encouraged either." And they don't have enough positive role models. When she was growing up, Breazeal says, she did not see many women scientists, and the ones she did encounter were mainly "difficult people" she did not want to emulate. What made the difference

for her is that her mother was a scientist and encouraged her to pursue a career in the sciences.

Breazeal thinks more girls would be attracted to the hard sciences (including physics, chemistry, and biology) if they realized how creative they can be. Contrary to popular conceptions of hard science as dry and rigid, she sees it as a rich field for self-expression. "Technology is flexible enough that you can make it what you want," she says. And Breazeal is certainly doing just that. By emphasizing the social aspect of robotics, she is taking the field in a bold new direction. "I'm trying to challenge the stereotypes," she says, "[by] putting a human face on them."

It's impossible to spend time with Kismet without seeing that face. It is a long way from being a human. But it has enough human qualities that its interactions are, in some way, clearly social. And it forms bonds with people that may

fall short of human bonds but are far different from the ones people form with most inanimate objects. Breazeal freely acknowledges that her little creation tugs at her own heartstrings. "I definitely have an attachment to it," she says, admitting that she missed it while on a recent trip to Australia. So what will happen if she ever has to part with Kismet? "I really don't know," she says. "The legal system doesn't have parental rights for robots."

—Updated 2005, from TIME, December 4, 2000

Editor's note: After the publication of this article, Breazeal went on to become an associate professor at M.I.T., as well as director of the school's Robotic Life Group. She published her first book, Designing Sociable Robots, *in 2002 and continues to create robots like Kismet that work and learn in partnership with people.*

> ❝Technology is flexible enough that you can make it what you want.❞

RESPONDING AND THINKING CRITICALLY

Respond

1. Do you think that robots actually can have feelings?

Recall and Interpret

2. (a)What is the difference between Kismet and Cog? (b)What can their interactions reveal about human interactions?

3. What are the "two rival schools" of thought on how to build robots?

4. What are two of the reasons why Breazeal programs and trains robots to act like humans?

Analyze and Evaluate

5. (a)How does the author describe the characteristics of the robots and their interactions? (b)Do the descriptions enable you to visualize the robots well? Why or why not?

6. How does the author use the subject of Cynthia Breazeal to make a point about women in science?

Connect

7. After reading about Kismet, do you think there is any aspect of reality in Isaac Asimov's *Robot Dreams*? Explain.

THE MACHINE NURTURER **1175**

Assess

1. Students may doubt that it is actually possible or necessary to invent robots with feelings. Others may be fascinated with the idea.

2. (a) Kismet has social abilities, while Cog's are mainly physical. (b) That people, who have social abilities, demand interaction and mental stimulation

3. Some believe a scientist should know what skills they want the robot to have before they program it; others, that a robot should learn from experience.

4. She can understand the learning process and gain insight into human social interactions.

5. (a) The author describes the behavior of Kismet as if it has a personality. He remarks on how it sees, how it recognizes faces, and how it hears when people speak into its microphone. Descriptions of Cog do not show a distinct personality and focus more on its actions. (b) The author creates a strong visual image of Kismet.

6. The author describes Breazeal's upbringing and her childhood curiosity about science and objects. He also comments on the disparity between men and women in science and includes Breazeal's comments on the topic.

7. Answers will vary. Most students will say it is possible for robots to have feelings, but improbable that robots would be able to think and to dream, especially without being specifically programmed to do so.

For additional assessment, see 📁 Selection and Unit Assessments, pp. 197–198.

Focus

BELLRINGER

Bellringer Options
Selection Focus Transparency 47
Daily Language Practice
Transparency 97
Or present a cup of water to the class. **Ask:** What is this water worth? *(Students may say that the water is not worth much, since water fountains can be found throughout the school.)* **Ask:** What is this water worth in a country without any major plumbing systems? *(Students should note that the water's value increases significantly.)* Ask students to keep this concept in mind as they read.

Literature Online

Author Search To expand students' appreciation of Margaret Atwood, have them access the Web site for additional information and resources.

Bread

MEET MARGARET ATWOOD

Margaret Atwood has become one of Canada's most respected and most popular writers, producing award-winning poems, novels, children's books, short stories, and essays. "I became a poet at the age of sixteen. I did not intend to do it. It was not my fault," Atwood has said.

Growing Up Atwood was born in Ottawa, Ontario, Canada, but her childhood was divided between a variety of Canadian cities and the forests of northwestern Quebec, where her father, a scientist, conducted research about insects. Both her parents were avid readers and encouraged her love of words.

Atwood earned a bachelor's degree from the University of Toronto in 1961 and a graduate degree from Radcliffe College a year later. For the next several years, she combined jobs waiting tables, working at a market research company, and teaching grammar, with off-and-on studies at Harvard University.

"I began as a profoundly apolitical writer, but then I began to do what all novelists and some poets do; I began to describe the world around me."

—Margaret Atwood

A Focus on Humanity In 1966 Atwood won her first major literary prize, Canada's Governor General's Award, for her second book of poems, *The Circle Game*. The publication of her first novel, *The Edible Woman*, in 1969 coincided with the growing feminist movement and helped put Atwood on the literary map. While much of her writing focuses on women, Atwood is also known for writing that ponders human behavior in general.

Though critics have noted the political nature of much of Atwood's writing, Atwood says that she begins new works without a political agenda in mind. "One works by simple observation, looking into things. . . . As an artist your first loyalty is to your art. Unless this is the case, you're going to be a second-rate artist." Pressed by an interviewer to name her "discrete truth," Atwood mentioned her belief that "money should not be the measure of all things."

In recent years, Atwood has become so famous in Canada that people follow her around on the streets and in stores. She is a frequent guest on Canadian television and radio. Atwood has remarked, "I'm a serious writer and I never expected to become a popular one."

Margaret Atwood was born in 1939.

Literature Online **Author Search** For more about Margaret Atwood, go to www.glencoe.com.

1176 UNIT 6 GENRE FICTION

Selection Skills

Literary Elements
• Point of View (SE pp. 1177–1180)

Reading Skills
• Recognizing Author's Purpose (SE pp. 1177, 1179, 1180)

Bread

Vocabulary Skills
• Connotation and Denotation (SE pp. 1177, 1180)

Writing Skills/Grammar
• Apply Description (SE p. 1180)

Listening/Speaking/Viewing Skills
• Analyzing Art (TWE p. 1178)
• Present Research Findings (TWE p. 1178)

Connecting to the Story

Some things, such as air or water, can seem very common and yet are very precious. Before you read this story, ask yourself the following questions:

- What do you think of when you hear the word *bread*? What do you associate with bread, and why do you make these associations?
- How do the circumstances of your life affect the way in which you view everyday items, such as bread or water?

Building Background

As a child, Margaret Atwood enjoyed reading E. Nesbit, Edgar Allan Poe, and Mark Twain, as well as *Grimm's Fairy Tales* and comic books. As a writer, she was influenced by a number of Canadian poets despite her claim that ". . . when I started, nobody took *Canadian writing* seriously." Today, Atwood is one of many internationally respected Canadian writers.

Setting Purposes for Reading

Big Idea **The Extraordinary and Fantastic**

As you read this story, notice that Atwood includes both realistic and fantastic details. Think about what overall message these details allow Atwood to suggest about human nature.

Literary Element **Point of View**

Point of view refers to the vantage point from which a story is told. In the second-person point of view, the word "you" establishes the reader's view of the action. As you read "Bread," notice how Atwood's use of the second-person point of view forces readers into a personal confrontation with stark realities.

- See Literary Terms Handbook, p. R13.

Literature Online **Interactive Literary Elements Handbook** To review or learn more about the literary elements, go to www.glencoe.com.

OBJECTIVES
In studying this selection, you will focus on the following:
- analyzing point of view

Reading Strategy Recognizing Author's Purpose

The **author's purpose** is the author's intent in writing a work. Authors usually write to persuade, to inform, to explain, to entertain, or to describe a process. They may write for more than one purpose. As you read, consider what Atwood describes and what questions she asks of the reader. What does her inclusion of these details tell you about her purpose for writing?

Reading Tip: Taking Notes "Bread" evokes five different scenes, or contexts. As you read, record your thoughts about why Atwood included each scene.

Scene	Author's Purpose
Cutting yourself a slice of bread and eating it with honey and peanut butter	To show how many people eat bread or take it for granted

Vocabulary

bloated (blō′tid) *adj.* puffed up; swollen; p. 1178 *After eating too much, Rick complained that he felt bloated.*

scavenger (skav′in jər) *n.* one who searches through discarded materials for something useful; p. 1179 *A scavenger found the bicycle at the dump and began riding it.*

subversive (səb vur′ siv) *adj.* intended to destroy or undermine; p. 1179 *He authored a subversive article revealing the councilwoman had broken the law.*

treacherous (trech′ ər əs) *adj.* likely to betray a trust, disloyal; p. 1179 *Her actions toward me were treacherous; I suffered as a result of them.*

dupe (do̅o̅p) *v.* to fool; to trick; p. 1179 *The salesperson duped me into buying something I did not need.*

Vocabulary Tip: Connotation and Denotation A word's denotation is its dictionary definition. A word's connotations are its implied meanings. Be aware of connotations as you read.

- recognizing author's purpose
- writing to apply description

MARGARET ATWOOD **1177**

Focus

Summary

In "Bread," Margaret Atwood presents five scenes in which bread is at the center. In the first, the narrator describes the pleasure bread brings when plentiful. What follows are scenarios far less comfortable: a picture of starving children and a scene of a prison where bread is used for torture and humiliation. The text then shifts to a German fairytale depicting a rich sister denying her poor sister's starving children a mouthful of bread. The narrator concludes the text by forcing the reader to question his or her own compassion.

V Vocabulary

Vocabulary File Say: Add these words and definitions to your vocabulary file. For each word, include a sentence that gives you an example of how to use the word. **OL** Students with English language needs should include the pronunciations of these words in their files. **EL**

Literary Elements Have students access the Web site to improve their understanding of point of view.

Selection Resources

Print Materials
- Unit 6 Resources (Fast File), pp. 33–35
- Leveled Vocabulary Development, p. 81
- Selection and Unit Assessments, pp. 199–200
- Selection Quick Checks, p. 100

Transparencies
- Bellringer Options Transparencies:
  Selection Focus Transparency 47
  Daily Language Practice Transparency 97
- Literary Elements Transparency 22

Technology
- TeacherWorks Plus™ CD-ROM
- StudentWorks Plus™ CD-ROM
- Presentation Plus!™ CD-ROM
- Literature Online, glencoe.com
- Online Student Edition, mhln.com
- Exam*View*® Assessment Suite CD-ROM
- Vocabulary PuzzleMaker CD-ROM
- Listening Library, disc 2 track 39

Teach

BREAD

Margaret Atwood

Still Life. Francisco Zurbaran (1598–1664). Private Collection, Madrid, Spain. ★

Imagine a piece of bread. You don't have to imagine it, it's right here in the kitchen, on the breadboard, in its plastic bag, lying beside the bread knife. The bread knife is an old one you picked up at an auction; it has the word BREAD carved into the wooden handle. You open the bag, pull back the wrapper, cut yourself a slice. You put butter on it, then peanut butter, then honey, and you fold it over. Some of the honey runs out onto your fingers and you lick it off. It takes you about a minute to eat the bread. This bread happens to be brown, but there is also white bread, in the refrigerator, and a heel of rye you got last week, round as a full stomach then, now going moldy. Occasionally you make bread. You think of it as something relaxing to do with your hands.

Imagine a famine. Now imagine a piece of bread. Both of these things are real but you happen to be in the same room with only one of them. Put yourself into a different room, that's what the mind is for. You are now lying on a thin mattress in a hot room. The walls are made of dried earth, and your sister, who is younger than you, is in the room with you. She is starving, her belly is **bloated**, flies land on her eyes; you brush them off with your hand. You have cloth too, filthy but damp, and you press it to her lips and forehead. The piece of bread is the bread you've been saving, for days it seems. You are as hungry as she is, but not yet as weak. How long does this take? When will someone come with more bread? You think of going out to see if you might find something

---

Literary Element Point of View *In this first scene, what type of situation is the point of view used to evoke?* **L1**

Vocabulary

bloated (blō′ tid) *adj.* puffed up; swollen

1178 UNIT 6 GENRE FICTION

---

that could be eaten, but outside the streets are infested with **scavengers** and the stink of corpses is everywhere.

Should you share the bread or give the whole piece to your sister? Should you eat the piece of bread yourself? After all, you have a better chance of living, you're stronger. How long does it take to decide?

Imagine a prison. There is something you know that you have not yet told. Those in control of the prison know that you know. So do those not in control. If you tell, thirty or forty or a hundred of your friends, your comrades, will be caught and will die. If you refuse to tell, tonight will be like last night. They always choose the night. You don't think about the night, however, but about the piece of bread they offered you. How long does it take? This piece of bread was brown and fresh and reminded you of sunlight falling across a wooden floor. It reminded you of a bowl, a yellow bowl that was once in your home. It held apples and pears; it stood on a table you can also remember. It's not the hunger or the pain that is killing you but the absence of the yellow bowl. If you could only hold the bowl in your hands, right here, you could withstand anything, you tell yourself. The bread they offered you is **subversive**, it's **treacherous**, it does not mean life.

Reading Strategy Recognizing Author's Purpose *What do these questions suggest about the author's purpose?* **R**

Literary Element Point of View *According to the story, you, as the prisoner, feel that the offered bread is "subversive" and "treacherous." Why might a prisoner feel this way?* **L2**

Vocabulary

scavenger (skav′in jər) *n.* one who searches through discarded materials for something useful
subversive (səb vur′ siv) *adj.* intended to destroy or undermine
treacherous (trech′ ər əs) *adj.* likely to betray a trust; disloyal

---

There were once two sisters. One was rich and had no children, the other had five children and was a widow, so poor that she no longer had any food left. She went to her sister and asked her for a mouthful of bread. "My children are dying," she said. The rich sister said, "I do not have enough for myself," and drove her away from the door. Then the husband of the rich sister came home and wanted to cut himself a piece of bread; but when he made the first cut, out flowed red blood.

Everyone knew what that meant.

This a traditional German fairy tale.

The loaf of bread I have conjured[1] for you floats about a foot above your kitchen table. The table is normal, there are no trap doors in it. A blue tea towel[2] floats beneath the bread, and there are no strings attaching the cloth to the bread or the bread to the ceiling or the table to the cloth, you've proved it by passing your hand above and below. You didn't touch the bread though. What stopped you? You don't want to know whether the bread is real or whether it's just a hallucination I've somehow **duped** you into seeing. There's no doubt that you can see the bread, you can even smell it, it smells like yeast, and it looks old enough, solid as your own arm. But can you trust it? Can you eat it? You don't want to know, imagine that. ✎

---

1. *Conjured* means "caused to appear, as by magic."
2. A *tea towel* is a towel used for drying dishes.

Big Idea The Extraordinary and Fantastic *What might the story be suggesting about the reader's desire to confront reality?* **BI**

Vocabulary

dupe (do͞op) *v.* to fool; to trick

Teach

R Reading Strategy

Recognizing Author's Purpose Answer: *These questions may suggest that Atwood's purpose is to force readers to contemplate the terrible dilemmas faced by starving people.* **OL**

L2 Literary Element

Point of View Answer: *The prisoner may feel that the bread is tainted. It seems to promise safety and satisfaction, but it comes from jailers who want to torture or kill people.* **OL**

BI Big Idea

The Extraordinary and Fantastic Answer: *Students may say that the story is suggesting that readers prefer not to think too closely about reality. Readers may prefer not to think about how valuable bread is and about starving or helpless people who lack food and safety.* **OL**

✓CheckPoint

Use the CheckPoint questions on Presentation Plus! to monitor students' comprehension and to check students' mastery of the selection. These questions can be used with interactive response keypads for immediate student feedback.

Differentiated Instruction

It's All in the Presentation "Bread" appears as a collection of separate scenes tied together with a single strand. Students struggling with comprehension may not be able to fully absorb its meaning if presented with the text in its current form; they may not be able to locate the strand. Present the text in pieces, dedicating time to building an understanding of each scene. Finally, re-present the text as a whole and discuss with students how each segment fits into the larger picture. In this way, they will be able to see what connects the scenes and how that connection is accomplished. **BL**

Objectives
- To analyze point of view (SE)
- To recognize author's purpose (SE)
- To conduct background research (TWE)

Assess

1. Answers will vary.

2. (a) An everyday domestic scene (b) A casual attitude

3. (a) Both scenes depict starving people. (b) Both scenes present the dilemma of saving oneself or others. (c) Students should cite details from the text.

4. (a) Those who refuse to share are responsible for the suffering of others. (b) Readers are responsible for helping the oppressed.

5. (a) The prisoner is tortured. (b) Safety and ordinary comforts

6. Readers notice how much they take their own safety and comfort for granted.

7. The detached voice allows room for emotional responses.

8. (a) Readers do not want to know what is really happening to fellow humans. (b) Famine and persecution are daily experiences for many people.

Literary Element

1. Students may say the word "you" seemed to implicate them directly.

2. (a) The story would have focused on the narrator's experience, not the reader's. (b) Answers will vary.

Web Activties Have students access the Web site for interactive activities that will help them assess their understanding of the selection.

RESPONDING AND THINKING CRITICALLY

Respond

1. Which scene affected you most strongly? Why?

Recall and Interpret

2. (a)What does the narrator describe in the first paragraph? (b)What attitude toward bread does the description convey?

3. (a)Summarize the scenes of famine and prison evoked in the story. What role does bread play in these scenes? (b)What questions, or dilemmas, are presented in these scenes? (c)What other details in these scenes help create empathy for prisoners and those suffering from hunger? Explain.

4. (a)What is the moral, or message, of the traditional German fairy tale? (b)How does this message relate to the other situations described in the story?

Analyze and Evaluate

5. (a)What do you think happens to the prisoner in the night? (b)What does the yellow bowl symbolize for the prisoner?

6. How does reading the first paragraph affect your perception of the next three scenes? Explain.

7. How effective is the narrator's voice in presenting the author's message? Explain.

Connect

8. **Big Idea** The Extraordinary and Fantastic (a)What possible meanings do you see in the final sentence? (b)How does the story upend common ideas about what is ordinary in life and what is extraordinary? Explain.

LITERARY ANALYSIS

Literary Element Point of View

Point of view is the vantage point from which a story is told. When an author uses "you" to establish the vantage point of a story, it is as if the reader becomes a character experiencing the situations in the story.

1. How did the use of second-person point of view affect your reaction to the story?

2. (a)How would this story be different if it had been told from the first-person point of view? (b)Would it have been as effective? Explain.

Writing About Literature

Apply Description A symbol is any object, person, place, or experience that means more than what it is. Write a short fantasy story similar to "Bread," in which you describe an object that has symbolic meaning. Begin by freewriting for a few moments about images and ideas you associate with the object. To give your readers a fresh insight into the object, you should describe the object within a variety of contexts or situations.

Literature Online **Web Activities** For eFlashcards, Selection Quick Checks, and other Web activities, go to www.glencoe.com.

READING AND VOCABULARY

Reading Strategy Recognizing Author's Purpose

The **author's purpose** is the author's intent in writing a literary work.

1. Early on, the story says, "Put yourself into a different room, that's what the mind is for." (a)How does this command relate to the scenes that follow? (b)What does this command suggest about the purpose of the story?

2. In your opinion, what were Atwood's goals in creating this piece?

Vocabulary Practice

Practice with Connotation and Denotation Complete each sentence below.

1. The denotation of *bloated* is ___.
   a. shrunken   b. swollen

2. A connotation of *scavenger* is ___.
   a. trash picker   b. detective

3. A connotation of *treacherous* is ___.
   a. evil   b. sad

Writing About Literature
Have volunteers read aloud their fantasy stories.

Reading Strategy

1. (a) It invites readers to imagine the experience of hunger. (b) The purpose is to help readers empathize with suffering people.

2. To evoke empathy in her readers

Vocabulary

1. b 2. a 3. a

PART 2

The Uncanny and Mysterious

Adam und seine Richter (with a self-portrait of Hausner) Adam and his Judges, 1965. Rudolf Hausner. Tempera on board, 22.83 X 10.24 in. Private collection. ★

BI   BIG IDEA

Trying to figure out the ending is part of the fun of reading mysteries. The mysteries in Part 2 offer devious schemes, clever criminals, and much that is uncanny and mysterious. As you read these mysteries, ask yourself: What clues do I have now? What do they suggest about how the story will end?

1181

Analyzing and Extending

BI   Big Idea

The Uncanny and the Mysterious Discuss the appeal of a good mystery. It allows the reader to experience the challenge of solving a puzzle or of being amazed by the feats of fictitious sleuths. Tell students that Part 2 will present the mystery story as an entertaining genre of fiction. Invite students to explore stories of the uncanny and mysterious, and encourage them to contemplate this "big idea" and its relation to the artwork. **OL**

★ Viewing the Art

Rudolf Hausner (1914–1995) studied art during the 1930s in Vienna. In 1947, after a period of intense study of the Surrealist style, Hausner helped start the Viennese School of Fantastic Realism and went on to become a prominent Austrian artist. Many of his works, such as the one shown here, depict the biblical Adam. This *Adam* actually takes on characteristics of Hausner himself. Ask students to contemplate the identity of these "judges" of Adam. **AS**

English Language Coach

Building Background Discuss with English language learners the word *uncanny,* meaning "strange, mysterious, weird." Point out that in contrast with *mysterious, uncanny* has connotations of something frightening or unsettling. Ask students to suggest occurrences that they would consider uncanny. **EL**

Differentiated Instruction

Drawing Conclusions Review with less proficient readers that a conclusion is a general statement based on reasoning or text details. Note that in detective stories the reader, along with the protagonist, watches for clues to draw a conclusion about a crime. Ask for examples from television and film. **BL**

Objectives for Part 2

- To analyze the elements that contribute to an author's style (SE)
- To recognize and analyze figurative language (SE)
- To understand the tone of a literary work (SE)

1181

Part 2: The Uncanny and Mysterious

Readability Scores Key
Dale-Chall/DRP/Lexile

PACING (DAYS)		SELECTIONS AND FEATURES	LITERARY ELEMENTS
STANDARD	**BLOCK**		
2 class sessions	1	LITERARY FOCUS: Style and Tone, pp. 1182–1183	Tone, SE p. 1182 Analyzing Style, TWE p. 1182
		"The Witness for the Prosecution" by Agatha Christie **7.7/52/800**, pp. 1184–1204	Motivation, SE pp. 1185–1203 Style, SE p. 1203 Mood, TWE p. 1188
		Grammar Workshop: Mechanics, p. 1205	
1–2 class sessions	1	**"The Adventure of the Speckled Band"** by Sir Arthur Conan Doyle **7.5/57/1120**, pp. 1206–1228	Character Archetype, SE pp. 1207–1227 Tone, SE p. 1227
		Vocabulary Workshop: Language Resources, p. 1229	
2 class sessions	1	**"A Retrieved Reformation"** by O. Henry **5.2/56/880**, pp. 1230–1239	Humor, SE pp. 1231–1239 Figures of Speech, SE p. 1239
		"Lungewater" by Joan Aiken **7.6/57/960**, pp. 1240–1255	Mood, SE pp. 1241–1255
2–3 class sessions	2–3	Writing Workshop: Science Fiction Story, pp. 1256–1263	
1 class session		Speaking, Listening, and Viewing Workshop: Oral Interpretation of a Science Fiction Story, pp. 1264–1265	
2 class sessions		Test Preparation and Practice, pp. 1268–1273	Characterization, TWE p. 1270

About the Part

Part 2 covers the uncanny and the mysterious.

READING AND CRITICAL THINKING	VOCABULARY	WRITING AND GRAMMAR	LISTENING, SPEAKING, AND VIEWING
Drawing Inferences About Mood, TWE p. 1183		Quickwrite, SE p. 1183	
Making Inferences about Characters, SE pp. 1185–1203	Synonyms, SE pp. 1185, 1203 Context Clues, TWE p. 1186 Sentence Completion, TWE p. 1194	Analyzing Point of View, SE p. 1204 Using Ellipses, SE p. 1204	Performing Dramatic Scenes, SE p. 1204
		Using Semicolons, SE p. 1205	
Analyzing Details, SE pp. 1207–1227 Analyzing Point of View, TWE p. 1208	Word Parts, SE p. 1227 Confused Words, TWE p. 1207	Genre Analysis, SE p. 1228 Comma Usage, TWE p. 1210	Performing Dialogue, TWE p. 1214
	Using a Thesaurus, SE p. 1229		
Making and Verifying Predictions, SE pp. 1231–1239	Context Clues, SE pp. 1231, 1239	Figurative-Language Analysis, SE p. 1239	Analyzing Art, SE pp. 1234, 1237 Music and Movies, TWE p. 1236
Analyzing Text Structure, SE pp. 1241–1255	Antonyms, SE p. 1255	Analyzing Style, SE p. 1255 Fragments, TWE p. 1252	Analyzing Art, SE pp. 1244, 1246, 1248, 1250–1253
		Dialogue, TWE p. 1258 Vivid Verbs and Adverbs, TWE p. 1260	
			Comparing and Contrasting, TWE p. 1264
Summarizing, TWE p. 1268		Semicolons vs. Colons, TWE p. 1272	

LITERARY FOCUS

Focus

BELLRINGER

Bellringer Options
Daily Language Practice Transparency 98
Or stage a classroom "mystery" or present logic problems for students to solve. Ask students about famous detectives and detective writers they know from literature. Mention that mystery stories will be featured in Part 2. Encourage students to monitor their emotional reactions.

Teach

L Literary Element

Tone Discuss the author's tone in "The Witness for the Prosecution." **Ask:** Which phrases create a solemn tone? *("grave danger," "utmost frank-ness," "said hopelessly," and "dastardly crime")* Similarly, have students identify the tone of the remaining excerpts. **OL**

Style and Tone

Tone and the author's style contribute strongly to the appeal of many mysteries. Writers may adopt a detached, no-nonsense tone or create a sense of danger or foreboding.

Style

Style is the distinctive way that an author uses language and the expressive qualities to distinguish his or her work. Word choice, the length and arrangement of sentences, the use of figurative language and imagery, and dialogue all contribute to an author's style. In the passage from "The Witness for the Prosecution" below, Christie uses relatively short sentences and few modifiers.

> Indeed, as a solicitor, Mr. Mayherne's reputation stood very high. His voice, when he spoke to his client, was dry but not unsympathetic.
> "I must impress upon you again that you are in very grave danger, and that the utmost frankness is necessary."
> Leonard Vole, who had been staring in a dazed fashion at the blank wall in front of him, transferred his glance to the solicitor.

> "I know," he said hopelessly. "You keep telling me so. But I can't seem to realize yet that I'm charged with murder—*murder*. And such a dastardly crime too."
>
> —Agatha Christie, **from "The Witness for the Prosecution"**

Notice the longer, more complex sentences in the example below.

> "The family was at one time among the richest in England, and the estates extended over the borders into Berkshire in the north and Hampshire in the west. In the last century, however, four successive heirs were of a dissolute and wasteful disposition, and the family ruin was eventually completed by a gambler in the days of the Regency."
>
> —Sir Arthur Conan Doyle, **from "The Adventure of the Speckled Band"**

Additional Support

Skills Practice

LITERARY ELEMENTS: Style
Review the following elements of style:
Figurative language—Conan Doyle's simile comparing wings of a house to claws of a crab
Sentence structure—Doyle's long and complicated sentences compared to Christie's shorter and simpler sentences
Diction—Jimmy Valentine's release from prison portrayed through diction
Dialogue—Plot progression through Christie's use of dialogue
Imagery—Doyle's images of decay **OL**

Diction

An important element of an author's style or voice is **diction,** a writer's choice of words. Good writers choose their words carefully to convey a particular meaning or feeling. Look for unusual word choices in this passage, in which Jimmy Valentine is being released from prison.

> "[Jimmy] had on a suit of the villainously fitting, ready-made clothes and a pair of the stiff, squeaky shoes that the state furnishes to its discharged compulsory guests."
>
> —O. Henry, **from "A Retrieved Reformation"**

Figurative Language

Language or expressions that are not literally true but express some truth beyond the literal level are called **figurative language.** Figurative language includes figures of speech such as metaphor and simile. Here, a detective employs metaphor and simile to comment on a crime scene where a safe has been robbed.

> "That's Dandy Jim Valentine's autograph. He's resumed business. Look at that combination knob—jerked out as easy as pulling up a radish in wet weather."
>
> —O. Henry, **from "A Retrieved Reformation"**

Suspense

Suspense is a feeling of curiosity, uncertainty, or dread about what is going to happen next. In the example from "The Witness for the Prosecution," a lawyer introduces an incriminating fact, contributing to the suspense.

> "Are you not aware, Mr. Vole, that Miss French left a will under which you are the principal beneficiary?"

Tone

Tone is a writer's or speaker's attitude toward the subject matter. In this passage, Sherlock Holmes uses a cheery, friendly tone as he meets a new client. Notice how the tone changes when the client speaks.

> "'I am glad to see that Mrs. Hudson has had the good sense to light the fire. Pray draw up to it, and I shall order you a cup of hot coffee, for I observe that you are shivering.'
>
> 'It is not cold which makes me shiver,' said the woman, in a low voice, changing her seat as requested.
>
> 'What, then?'
>
> 'It is fear, Mr. Holmes. It is terror.'"
>
> —Sir Arthur Conan Doyle, **from "The Adventure of the Speckled Band"**

Mood

Mood is the emotional quality of a story. This description of a country house creates a dreary, ominous mood.

> "The building was of gray, lichen-blotched stone, with a high central portion, and two curving wings, like the claws of a crab, thrown out on each side."
>
> —Sir Arthur Conan Doyle, **from "The Adventure of the Speckled Band"**

Quickwrite

Conveying Tone Write a few lines to convey an objective, dramatic, humorous, or bitter tone toward a subject of your choosing.

OBJECTIVES
- Analyze the elements that contribute to an author's style.
- Recognize and analyze figurative language.
- Understand the tone of a literary work.

LITERARY FOCUS **1183**

LITERARY FOCUS

Teach

R **Reading Strategy**

Drawing Inferences About Mood Note the spooky mood of Doyle's descriptions of the abandoned house. **Ask:** Which words and details contribute to this gloomy mood? *(descriptions of lichen, broken and boarded-up windows, and a caved-in roof)* How is a suspenseful mood created in "The Witness for the Prosecution"? *(Anticipation of what the will contains creates suspense.)* **OL**

Assess

Quickwrite

Check students' writing for words and details that create the chosen tone. Have students read aloud to contrast tone.

English Language Coach

Reading Comprehension Strategies Help students new to the United States to comprehend a difficult passage such as Conan Doyle's by breaking it into smaller sentences and looking up unfamiliar words such as *dissolute* ("immoral"). **EL**

Differentiated Instruction

Commas Write this phrase on the board: *stiff, squeaky shoes.* Review with students the use of the comma to separate coordinate adjectives. To help students determine whether adjectives are coordinate, have them insert the word *and* between to see if the words are parallel. **BL**

Objectives
- To analyze the elements that contribute to an author's style (SE)
- To recognize and analyze figurative language (SE)
- To analyze style (TWE)

Focus

BELLRINGER

Bellringer Options
Daily Language Practice Transparency 99
Or **ask:** How do we decide who is guilty and who is innocent when a rule or law has been broken? Have students in groups of four create scenarios in which one of them broke a rule or law. Two group members will act as suspects and two will act as witnesses. Invite each group to present its scenario to the class, and have the class decide who is guilty and who is innocent based on suspects' alibis and witness statements.

Author Search To expand students' appreciation of Agatha Christie, have them access the Web site for additional information and resources.

The Witness for the Prosecution

MEET AGATHA CHRISTIE

After a lifetime of writing, Agatha Christie was an expert at inventing—and solving—murder mysteries. She imagined murders on the Nile River, on a train called the *Orient Express*, at the Tuesday Club, in Mesopotamia, and, of course, in the library. These were mysteries with complex plots, ingenious twists and turns, and satisfying solutions. In story after story, Christie, who was sometimes called the "Queen of Crime" and the "Duchess of Death," subtly directs the reader's attention away from the most crucial clues.

> *"I found myself making up stories and acting different parts, and there's nothing like boredom to make you write."*
>
> —Agatha Christie

Bored to Death? How did this author of approximately seventy novels, more than one hundred short stories, and over one dozen plays get started? In an interview, Christie revealed that she began imagining stories as a child to combat boredom. At the age of eighteen, she was recovering from influenza when her mother suggested that she write a story. Christie's very first attempt, entitled "The House of Beauty," was published in a magazine.

By the time she was twenty-six, Christie had written her first novel, *The Mysterious Affair at Styles*. Initially, several publishers rejected the book, but when it was finally published it had moderate success. Six years and six novels later, Christie had begun to establish her reputation as a talented mystery writer.

The Christie Detectives Christie created a number of fictional detectives. Hercule Poirot is the private eye in what may be Christie's most famous work, *Murder on the Orient Express*. Jane Marple is an amateur sleuth in her seventies with a knack for solving mysteries, who first appears in *The Murder at the Vicarage*. Novels featuring Poirot and Marple established Christie as the most popular mystery writer of all time.

Many Faithful Readers Only surpassed by sales of the Bible and the works of William Shakespeare, Christie's books have sold a spectacular two billion copies. Ironically, Christie once claimed, "I don't enjoy writing detective stories. I enjoy thinking of a detective story, planning it, but when the time comes to write it, it is like going to work everyday, like having a job." Among the many honors she received was the New York Drama Critics Circle Award for best foreign play, *The Witness for the Prosecution*. Christie continued writing until the last year of her life, publishing her eightieth book at the age of eighty. In 2005 the first annual Agatha Christie Week was held in her birthplace, Torquay, England. Visitors participated in a murder mystery tour in Christie's honor.

Agatha Christie was born in 1890 and died in 1976.

Literature Online Author Search For more about Agatha Christie, go to www.glencoe.com.

Selection Skills

The Witness for the Prosecution

Literary Elements
- Motivation (SE pp. 1185–1203)
- Style (SE p. 1203)
- Mood (TWE p. 1188)

Reading Skills
- Making Inferences About Characters (SE pp. 1185–1203)
- Reviewing (TWE p. 1190)
- Activating Prior Knowledge (TWE p. 1196)

Vocabulary Skills
- Synonyms (SE pp. 1185, 1203)
- Context Clues (TWE p. 1186)

Listening/Speaking/Viewing Skills
- Performing Dramatic Scenes (SE p. 1204)

Writing Skills/Grammar
- Analyzing Point of View (SE p. 1204)
- Using Ellipses (SE p. 1204)
- Writing News Stories (TWE p. 1200)

Connecting to the Story

In "The Witness for the Prosecution," Agatha Christie stays a step ahead of the reader just as some of the characters stay a step ahead of one another and the legal system. As you read, ask yourself these questions:

- Is there more here than meets the eye? What is it?
- What unstated motives or reasons might each character have?

Building Background

"The Witness for the Prosecution" is about a man in England who is accused of "willful murder," or what people in the United States call premeditated, or planned, murder. At the beginning of the story, his solicitor, or lawyer, meets with him to learn the facts of the case. The solicitor must prepare to meet the arguments of the prosecution; in this case, the British government, or Crown, which undertakes legal action against the accused. In a British court of law, the solicitor prepares the case, but does not argue it at trial. That is the job of the counsel for the defense, referred to in this story as the K.C., or King's Counsel.

Setting Purposes for Reading

Big Idea The Uncanny and Mysterious

As you read, think about what seems convincing and real, as well as what seems suspicious or mysterious, about the accused man, his story, and the woman who testifies against him.

Literary Element Motivation

Motivation is the stated or implied reason or cause for a character's actions. As you read, notice the motivations characters attribute to themselves, as well as those that are suggested by one character for another.

- See Literary Terms Handbook, p. R11.

Literature Online Interactive Literary Elements Handbook To review or learn more about the literary elements, go to www.glencoe.com.

Reading Strategy Making Inferences About Characters

When you **make inferences about characters,** you use your reason and experience to figure out what an author is not saying directly about a character.

Reading Tip: Taking Notes Use a chart to record details about the characters and your inferences.

Detail	+ My Reason or Experience	= My Inference

Vocabulary

cultivate (kul´tə vāt´) v. to encourage or further the development of; p. 1188 *Lauren cultivated Rachel's friendship by calling her every night.*

pretext (pre´tekst) n. a reason or motive offered in order to disguise real intentions; p. 1189 *Jill wanted to stay home, so she told her mother she was sick, but that was just a pretext.*

amicable (am´ə kə bəl) adj. friendly; p. 1191 *George and Tameka, who had an amicable relationship, talked to each other every day.*

recoil (ri koil´) v. to shrink back physically or emotionally; p. 1195 *Zach recoils at the thought of telling on his best friend.*

animosity (an´ə mos´ə tē) n. ill will or resentment; active strong dislike or hostility; p. 1200 *Jorge's animosity toward Greg showed itself in his tense posture and scowl.*

Vocabulary Tip: Synonyms Synonyms are words with the same or similar meaning that are the same part of speech.

Focus

Summary

Leonard Vole is accused of murdering the wealthy, elderly Miss French. His lawyer, Mr. Mayherne, believes Vole is innocent, but Vole's wife, Romaine, denies her husband's alibi. She also reveals that she and Vole are not married, so she can testify against him. Mayherne reveals evidence from a char-woman that proves Romaine is trying to ruin Vole. Vole is acquitted, but Mayherne discovers that Romaine was the charwoman and had created the ruse to save Vole, who is indeed guilty.

V Vocabulary

Vocabulary File Say: Add these words and definitions to your vocabulary file. For each word, include a sentence that gives you an example of how to use the word. **OL** Students with English language needs should include the pronunciations of these words in their files. **EL**

Literary Elements Have students access the Web site to improve their understanding of motivation.

OBJECTIVES
In studying this selection, you will focus on the following:
- analyzing motivation
- making inferences about characters

- identifying and analyzing style
- writing to analyze third-person limited point of view

AGATHA CHRISTIE **1185**

Selection Resources

Print Materials
- Unit 6 Resources (Fast File), pp. 39–41
- Leveled Vocabulary Development, p. 82
- Selection and Unit Assessments, pp. 201–202
- Selection Quick Checks, p. 101

Transparencies
- Bellringer Options Transparencies: Daily Language Practice Transparency 99
- Literary Elements Transparency 16

Technology
- TeacherWorks Plus™ CD-ROM
- StudentWorks Plus™ CD-ROM
- Presentation Plus!™ CD-ROM
- Literature Online, glencoe.com
- Online Student Edition, mhln.com
- ExamView® Assessment Suite CD-ROM
- Vocabulary PuzzleMaker CD-ROM
- Listening Library, disc 2 track 40

The Uncanny and Mysterious Say: *While reading, keep the following questions in mind: Who is the most mysterious character in the story? What questions would you ask this character if you could?* (*Answers will vary. We seem to know least about French's maid and the charwoman. Students might want to ask the maid if she was hoping French's nephew would be the principal beneficiary in the will, or how the charwoman got a hold of the letters.*) **OL**

R1 Reading Strategy

Making Inferences About Characters Answer: *He appears to be a reasonable man, shrewd but not uncaring about his client.* **OL**

L1 Literary Element

Motivation Answer: *Mayherne's job as Vole's lawyer is to defend him, so he must do his best to prove Vole's innocence.* **OL**

Readability Scores
Dale-Chall: 7.7
DRP: 52
Lexile: 800

The Witness for the Prosecution

Agatha Christie

The Barrister. Thomas Davidson (1863–1908). Oil on canvas. Roy Miles Fine Paintings, London.

M r. Mayherne adjusted his pince-nez[1] and cleared his throat with a little dry-as-dust cough that was wholly typical of him. Then he looked again at the man opposite him, the man charged with willful murder.

Mr. Mayherne was a small man, precise in manner, neatly, not to say foppishly[2] dressed, with a pair of very shrewd and piercing gray eyes, by no means a fool. Indeed, as a solicitor, Mr. Mayherne's reputation stood very high. His voice, when he spoke to his client, was dry but not unsympathetic.

"I must impress upon you again that you are in very grave danger, and that the utmost frankness is necessary."

Leonard Vole, who had been staring in a dazed fashion at the blank wall in front of him, transferred his glance to the solicitor.

"I know," he said hopelessly. "You keep telling me so. But I can't seem to realize yet that I'm charged with murder—*murder.* And such a dastardly[3] crime too."

Mr. Mayherne was practical, not emotional. He coughed again, took off his pince-nez, polished them carefully, and replaced them on his nose. Then he said:

"Yes, yes, yes. Now, my dear Mr. Vole, we're going to make a determined effort to get you off—and we shall succeed—we shall succeed. But I must have all the facts. I must know just how damaging the case against you is likely to be. Then we can fix upon the best line of defense."

---

1. *Pince-nez* (pans ′ nā′) are eyeglasses that are clipped to the nose rather than held on by pieces that bend around the ears.
2. *Foppishly* means "fashionable in a silly or vain way."

3. *Dastardly* means "cowardly."

Reading Strategy Making Inferences About Characters *What inferences can you make about Mayherne based on the details so far?* **R1**

Literary Element Motivation *What is Mayherne's motivation for preparing the best possible defense?* **L1**

1186 UNIT 6 GENRE FICTION

Additional Support

Skills Practice

VOCABULARY: Context Clues
Context clues help define unfamiliar words or words with multiple meanings. Write the following types of context clues on the board: 1. a synonym; 2. reference to what the word is like or not like; 3. a general topic associated with the word;

4. a description or action associated with the word. Have students working in pairs read the first page of the selection, paying close attention to the words *willful, foppishly, solicitor, dry, impress,* and *frankness.* Instruct students to determine which kinds of context clues exist for

Still the young man looked at him in the same dazed, hopeless fashion. To Mr. Mayherne the case had seemed black enough, and the guilt of the prisoner assured. Now, for the first time, he felt a doubt.

"You think I'm guilty," said Leonard Vole, in a low voice. "But, by God, I swear I'm not! It looks pretty black against me; I know that. I'm like a man caught in a net—the meshes of it all round me, entangling me whichever way I turn. But I didn't do it, Mr. Mayherne; I didn't do it!"

In such a position a man was bound to protest his innocence.[4] Mr. Mayherne knew that. Yet, in spite of himself, he was impressed. It might be, after all, that Leonard Vole was innocent.

"You are right, Mr. Vole," he said gravely. "The case does look very black against you. Nevertheless, I accept your assurance. Now, let us get to facts. I want you to tell me in your own words exactly how you came to make the acquaintance of Miss Emily French."

"It was one day in Oxford Street. I saw an elderly lady crossing the road. She was carrying a lot of parcels. In the middle of the street she dropped them, tried to recover them, found a bus was almost on top of her and just managed to reach the curb safely, dazed and bewildered by people having shouted at her. I recovered her parcels, wiped the mud off them as best I could, retied the string of one, and returned them to her."

"There was no question of your having saved her life?"

"Oh, dear me, no! All I did was to perform a common act of courtesy. She was extremely grateful, thanked me warmly, and said something about my manners not being those of most of the younger generation—I can't remember the exact words. Then I lifted my hat and went on. I never expected to see her again. But life is full of coincidences. That very evening I came across her at a party at a friend's house. She recognized me at once and asked that I should be introduced to her. I then found out that she was a Miss Emily French and that she lived at Cricklewood. I talked to her for some time. She was, I imagine, an old lady who took sudden and violent fancies to people. She took one to me on the strength of a perfectly simple action which anyone might have performed. On leaving, she shook me warmly by the hand, and asked me to come and see her. I replied, of course, that I should be very pleased to do so, and she then urged me to name a day. I did not want particularly to go, but it would have seemed churlish[5] to refuse, so I fixed on the following Saturday. After she had gone, I learned something about her from my friends. That she was rich, eccentric, lived alone with one maid and owned no less than eight cats."

"I see," said Mr. Mayherne. "The question of her being well off came up as early as that?"

"If you mean that I inquired—" began Leonard Vole hotly, but Mr. Mayherne stilled him with a gesture.

"I have to look at the case as it will be presented by the other side. An ordinary observer would not have supposed Miss French to be a lady of means. She lived poorly, almost humbly. Unless you had been told the contrary, you would in all probability have considered her to be in poor circumstances—at any rate to begin with. Who was it exactly who told you that she was well off?"

"My friend, George Harvey, at whose house the party took place."

"Is he likely to remember having done so?"

"I really don't know. Of course it is some time ago now."

"Quite so, Mr. Vole. You see, the first aim of the prosecution will be to establish that you were in low water financially—that is true, is it not?"

Leonard Vole flushed.

---

4. To *protest* one's *innocence* is to steadfastly declare it.

Literary Element Motivation *Why do you think Vole includes these details?* **L2**

5. Here, *churlish* means "rude" or "ill-bred."

Reading Strategy Making Inferences About Characters *What might Mayherne infer from Vole's anger?* **R3**

Teach

R2 Reading Strategy

Making Inferences About Characters Ask: What can you infer about Vole based on this statement? (*He is shrewd; it is as though he is able to read Mr. Mayherne's thoughts.*) **OL**

L2 Literary Element

Motivation Answer: *Students may say Vole wants to make himself look respectable to Mayherne. Vole wants to show that he is polite, mannerly, and considerate in order to prove his innocence.* **OL**

R3 Reading Strategy

Making Inferences About Characters Answer: *Mayherne might infer that Vole is justifiably angry at being accused of taking an interest in Emily French's money.* **OL**

 CheckPoint

Use the CheckPoint questions on Presentation Plus! to monitor students' comprehension. These questions can be used with interactive response keypads for immediate student feedback.

each word and which words or phrases provide those clues. Then have them write a possible definition for each word. (*Willful: type 3; foppishly: type 2; solicitor: types 3 and 4; Dry: type 2; impress: type 4; frankness: type 3.*) **OL**

Building Reading Fluency

Reading Aloud Have groups of three read this page aloud—one student reading the narration, one reading Mayherne's dialogue, and one reading Vole's dialogue. Encourage them to bring the characters to life by means of the tone, volume, and speed of their speech. **BL**

Objectives
• To analyze character motivation (SE)
• To make inferences about characters (SE)
• To classify context clues (TWE)

Teach

L Literary Element

Motivation Ask: What predictions can you make at this point about Vole's guilt or innocence in this case? *(Answers will vary. Some students will say that Vole had strong motivation to kill Miss French—money. Others, like Mayherne, will believe Vole's story and find that his sense of honor motivated him more than his need for money.)* **OL**

⭐ Viewing the Art

Émile Zola (1840–1902) was an influential French novelist, critic, and activist. He is perhaps most famous for his letter "J'accuse," which was published in a newspaper and defended a Jewish soldier wrongly accused of espionage. Zola was jailed for libel and became a hero worldwide for his courage. **AS**

Caricature of Émile Zola, 1880. Artist unknown.

"Yes," he said, in a low voice. "I'd been having a run of infernal[6] bad luck just then."

"Quite so," said Mr. Mayherne again. "That being, as I say, in low water financially, you met this rich old lady and **cultivated** her acquaintance assiduously.[7] Now if we are in a position to say that you had no idea she

---

6. *Infernal* means "hellish."
7. Here, *assiduously* means "with a great deal of effort and determination."

Vocabulary

cultivate (kul′ tə vāt′) *v.* to encourage or further the development of

1188 UNIT 6 GENRE FICTION

---

was well off, and that you visited her out of pure kindness of heart—"

"Which is the case."

"I daresay. I am not disputing the point. I am looking at it from the outside point of view. A great deal depends on the memory of Mr. Harvey. Is he likely to remember that conversation, or is he not? Could he be confused by counsel into believing that it took place later?"

Leonard Vole reflected for some minutes. Then he said steadily enough, but with a rather paler face:

"I do not think that that line would be successful, Mr. Mayherne. Several of those present heard his remark, and one or two of them chaffed[8] me about my conquest of a rich old lady."

The solicitor endeavored to hide his disappointment with a wave of the hand. **L**

"Unfortunate," he said. "But I congratulate you upon your plain speaking, Mr. Vole. It is to you I look to guide me. Your judgment is quite right. To persist in the line I spoke of would have been disastrous. We must leave that point. You made the acquaintance of Miss French; you called upon her; the acquaintanceship progressed. We want a clear reason for all this. Why did you, a young man of thirty-three, good-looking, fond of sport, popular with your friends, devote so much of your time to an elderly woman with whom you could hardly have anything in common?"

Leonard Vole flung out his hands in a nervous gesture.

"I can't tell you—I really can't tell you. After the first visit, she pressed me to come again, spoke of being lonely and unhappy. She made it difficult for me to refuse. She showed so plainly her fondness and affection for me that I was placed in an awkward position. You see, Mr. Mayherne, I've got a weak nature—I drift—I'm one of those people who can't say 'No.' And believe me or not, as you like, after the third or fourth visit I

---

8. *Chaffed* means "teased in a playful way."

Additional Support

Skills Practice

LITERARY ELEMENT: Mood An author creates emotion through setting, language, subject matter, and tone. Have students create a graphic organizer and list descriptions and examples of these aspects of the story. Help students recognize that these elements create a mood of suspense. **OL**

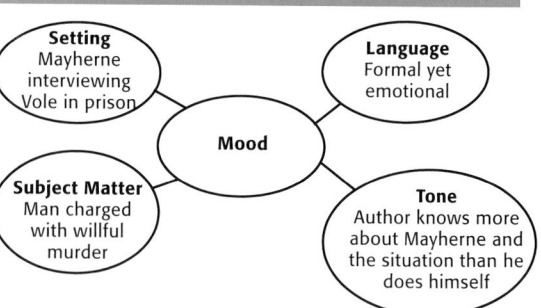

Setting — Mayherne interviewing Vole in prison
Language — Formal yet emotional
Mood
Subject Matter — Man charged with willful murder
Tone — Author knows more about Mayherne and the situation than he does himself

1188

paid her I found myself getting genuinely fond of the old thing. My mother died when I was young, an aunt brought me up, and she too died before I was fifteen. If I told you that I genuinely enjoyed being mothered and pampered, I daresay you'd only laugh."

Mr. Mayherne did not laugh. Instead he took off his pince-nez again and polished them, a sign with him that he was thinking deeply.

"I accept your explanation, Mr. Vole," he said at last. "I believe it to be psychologically probable. Whether a jury would take that view of it is another matter. Please continue your narrative. When was it that Miss French first asked you to look into her business affairs?"

"After my third or fourth visit to her. She understood very little of money matters and was worried about some investments."

Mr. Mayherne looked up sharply.

"Be careful, Mr. Vole. The maid, Janet Mackenzie, declares that her mistress was a good woman of business and transacted all her own affairs, and this is borne out[9] by the testimony of her bankers."

"I can't help that," said Vole earnestly. "That's what she said to me."

Mr. Mayherne looked at him for a moment or two in silence. Though he had no intention of saying so, his belief in Leonard Vole's innocence was at that moment strengthened. He knew something of the mentality of elderly ladies. He saw Miss French, infatuated with the good-looking young man, hunting about for **pretexts** that would bring him to the house. What more likely than that she should plead ignorance of business and beg him to help her with her money affairs? She was enough

---

9. *Borne out* means "verified by facts, testimony, or events."

Vocabulary

pretext (prē′tekst) *n.* a reason or motive offered in order to disguise real intentions

---

of a woman of the world to realize that any man is slightly flattered by such an admission of his superiority. Leonard Vole had been flattered. Perhaps, too, she had not been averse[10] to letting this young man know that she was wealthy. Emily French had been a strong-willed old woman, willing to pay her price for what she wanted. All this passed rapidly through Mr. Mayherne's mind, but he gave no indication of it and asked instead a further question.

"And you did handle her affairs for her at her request?"

"I did."

"Mr. Vole," said the solicitor, "I am going to ask you a very serious question, and one to which it is vital I should have a truthful answer. You were in low water financially. You had the handling of an old lady's affairs—an old lady who, according to her own statement, knew little or nothing of business. Did you at any time, or in any manner, convert to your own use the securities which you handled? Did you engage in any transaction for your own pecuniary[11] advantage which will not bear the light of day?" He quelled[12] the other's response. "Wait a minute before you answer. There are two courses open to us. Either we can make a feature of your probity[13] and honesty in conducting her affairs whilst pointing out how unlikely it is that you would commit murder to obtain money which you might have obtained by such infinitely easier means. If, on the other hand, there is anything in your dealings which the prosecution will get hold of—if, to put it baldly, it can be proved that you swindled the old lady in any way—we must take the line that you had no motive for the murder, since she was already a profitable source of income to you. You perceive the distinction. Now, I beg of you, take your time before you reply."

But Leonard Vole took no time at all.

---

10. Here, *averse* means "against" or "disinclined."
11. *Pecuniary* means "relating to money" or "monetary."
12. *Quelled* means "crushed" or "quieted."
13. *Probity* is moral uprightness.

AGATHA CHRISTIE **1189**

Teach

R1 Reading Strategy

Making Inferences About Characters Ask: What can you infer about Vole from his reaction here? *(Students might infer that Vole suddenly understands why he has been arrested for the murder—because he did indeed have a motive for killing French.)* **OL**

L1 Literary Element

Motivation Answer: *Vole says Mackenzie is motivated by her loyalty or is just confused. Mackenzie could also be motivated by her own desire for the woman's inheritance.* **OL**

L2 Literary Element

Motivation Ask: Given Vole's and Mackenzie's possible motivations, whose explanation do you believe? *(Some students might believe Vole is innocent because he seems not to have known about the will; others might wonder what motivation Mackenzie would have for lying about his character.)* **OL**

R2 Reading Strategy

Making Inferences About Characters Answer: *Vole acts as if he truly is a man who has identified the evidence that will prove his innocence.* **OL**

"My dealings with Miss French's affairs were all perfectly fair and aboveboard. I acted for her interests to the very best of my ability, as anyone will find who looks into the matter."

"Thank you," said Mr. Mayherne. "You relieve my mind very much. I pay you the compliment of believing that you are far too clever to lie to me over such an important matter."

"Surely," said Vole eagerly, "the strongest point in my favor is the lack of motive. Granted that I cultivated the acquaintance-ship of a rich old lady in the hopes of getting money out of her—that, I gather, is the substance of what you have been saying—surely her death frustrates all my hopes?"

The solicitor looked at him steadily. Then, very deliberately, he repeated his unconscious trick with his pince-nez. It was not until they were firmly replaced on his nose that he spoke.

"Are you not aware, Mr. Vole, that Miss French left a will under which you are the principal beneficiary?"[14]

R1 "What?" The prisoner sprang to his feet. His dismay was obvious and unforced. "My God! What are you saying? She left her money to me?"

Mr. Mayherne nodded slowly. Vole sank down again, his head in his hands.

"You pretend you know nothing of this will?"

"Pretend? There's no pretense about it. I knew nothing about it."

"What would you say if I told you that the maid, Janet Mackenzie, swears that you *did* know? That her mistress told her distinctly that she had consulted you in the matter and told you of her intentions?"

"Say? That she's lying! No, I go too fast. Janet is an elderly woman. She was a faithful watchdog to her mistress, and she didn't like me. She was jealous and suspicious. I should say that Miss French confided her intentions to Janet, and that Janet either mistook something she said or else was convinced in

---

14. A *beneficiary* is a person who receives money from a will.

1190 UNIT 6 GENRE FICTION

---

her own mind that I had persuaded the old lady into doing it. I daresay that she herself believes now that Miss French actually told her so."

"You don't think she dislikes you enough to lie deliberately about the matter?"

Leonard Vole looked shocked and startled.

"No, indeed! Why should she?"

"I don't know," said Mr. Mayherne thoughtfully. "But she's very bitter against you." **L2**

The wretched young man groaned again.

"I'm beginning to see," he muttered. "It's frightful. I made up to her, that's what they'll say, I got her to make a will leaving her money to me, and then I go there that night, and there's nobody in the house—they find her the next day—oh! my God, it's awful!"

"You are wrong about there being nobody in the house," said Mr. Mayherne. "Janet, as you remember, was to go out for the evening. She went, but about half past nine she returned to fetch the pattern of a blouse sleeve which she had promised to a friend. She let herself in by the back door, went upstairs and fetched it, and went out again. She heard voices in the sitting room, though she could not distinguish what they said, but she will swear that one of them was Miss French's and one was a man's."

"At half past nine," said Leonard Vole. "At half past nine . . ." He sprang to his feet. "But then I'm saved—saved—"

"What do you mean, saved?" cried Mr. Mayherne, astonished.

"By half past nine I was at home again! My wife can prove that. I left Miss French about five minutes to nine. I arrived home about twenty past nine. My wife was there waiting for me. Oh, thank God—thank God! And bless Janet Mackenzie's sleeve pattern."

Literary Element Motivation What does Vole say motivates Mackenzie? What else might motivate her? **L1**

Reading Strategy Making Inferences About Characters Which details here might lead you to infer that Vole is telling the truth? **R2**

Additional Support

Skills Practice

READING: Review Say: When reading a murder mystery, pausing every so often to review what you know about the characters and details might help you solve the crime. Have students create a profile of each character they have met so far in the story. Each profile should include a description of the character's role, reliability, and motivation. Have students add details to their profiles and create profiles of new characters as they read further. **OL**

Bond Street, 1999. Peter Miller. Oil on canvas, 35.6 x 40.6 cm. Private collection. ⭐

Teach

⭐ **Viewing the Art**

Bond Street is a famed shopping district in London's West End. One of its more notable businesses is the famous auction house Sotheby's. **AS**

In his exuberance,[15] he hardly noticed that the grave expression on the solicitor's face had not altered. But the latter's words brought him down to earth with a bump.

"Who, then, in your opinion, murdered Miss French?"

"Why, a burglar, of course, as was thought at first. The window was forced, you remember. She was killed with a heavy blow from a crowbar, and the crowbar was found lying on the floor beside the body. And several articles were missing. But for Janet's absurd suspicions and dislike of me, the police would never have swerved from the right track."

"That will hardly do, Mr. Vole," said the solicitor. "The things that were missing were mere trifles of no value, taken as a blind.[16] And the marks on the window were not at all conclusive. Besides, think for yourself. You say you were no longer in the house by half past nine. Who, then, was the man Janet heard talking to Miss French in the sitting room? She would hardly be having an **amicable** conversation with a burglar!"

"No," said Vole. "No—" He looked puzzled and discouraged. "But, anyway," he added with reviving spirit, "it lets me out. I've got an alibi. You must see Romaine—my wife—at once."

"Certainly," acquiesced[17] the lawyer. "I should already have seen Mrs. Vole but for her being absent when you were arrested. I wired to Scotland at once, and I understand

---

15. *Exuberance* means "excited enthusiasm."
16. Here, a *blind* refers to an action undertaken to throw an investigator off the track.

17. *Acquiesced* means "agreed."

Vocabulary

amicable (am′ ə kə bəl) *adj.* friendly

AGATHA CHRISTIE **1191**

English Language Coach

Word Meanings Have English language learners work with native English speakers in groups of three to decode the meanings of words such as *suspicious, wretched, distinguish,* and *exuberance.* They should discuss how the words are used, write down possible definitions, and then check with a dictionary. **EL**

Differentiated Instruction

Visual Learners Invite visual learners to create colored diagrams, cause-and-effect charts, and illustrations of the characters, setting, and plot as they read. These visual aids will help them understand the story more fully. **BL**

Objectives
- To analyze character motivation (SE)
- To make inferences about characters (SE)
- To review text in order to deepen understanding (TWE)

1191

Teach

BI₁ Big Idea

The Uncanny and Mysterious Ask: Does the situation Mayherne describes seem mysterious to you? *(Some students might find it odd that a married man would visit an unmarried woman whom he has described as one who takes "violent fancies" to people. Some students might think it perfectly natural for Vole to visit French alone if he saw her as a motherly figure.)* OL

L₁ Literary Element

Motivation Answer: *If Vole did know that French wanted to marry him, he might have believed that the only way he could get her money was to marry her—or kill her.* Help students recognize how Christie, through Mayherne, brings up one motivation after another that Vole may have had to kill French. **Ask:** How does Vole hold up under these accusations? *(He reacts emotionally but then becomes rational. The way his logical arguments win out over his emotional reactions may be one reason Mr. Mayherne believes he is innocent.)* OL

that she arrives back tonight. I am going to call upon her immediately I leave here."

Vole nodded, a great expression of satisfaction settling down over his face.

"Yes, Romaine will tell you. My God! it's a lucky chance that."

"Excuse me, Mr. Vole, but you are very fond of your wife?"

"Of course."

"And she of you?"

"Romaine is devoted to me. She'd do anything in the world for me."

He spoke enthusiastically, but the solicitor's heart sank a little lower. The testimony of a devoted wife—would it gain credence?[18]

"Was there anyone else who saw you return at nine-twenty? A maid, for instance?"

"We have no maid."

"Did you meet anyone in the street on the way back?"

"Nobody I knew. I rode part of the way in a bus. The conductor might remember."

Mr. Mayherne shook his head doubtfully.

"There is no one, then, who can confirm your wife's testimony?"

"No. But it isn't necessary, surely?"

"I daresay not. I daresay not," said Mr. Mayherne hastily. "Now there's just one thing more. Did Miss French know that you were a married man?"

"Oh, yes."

"Yet you never took your wife to see her. **BI₁** Why was that?"

For the first time, Leonard Vole's answer came halting and uncertain.

"Well—I don't know."

"Are you aware that Janet Mackenzie says her mistress believed you to be single and contemplated marrying you in the future?"

Vole laughed.

"Absurd! There was forty years' difference in age between us."

"It has been done," said the solicitor dryly. "The fact remains. Your wife never met Miss French?"

---

18. *Credence* is acceptance that something is true.

Literary Element Motivation *How does this information suggest a motivation for murder?* **L₁**

1192 UNIT 6 GENRE FICTION

"No—" Again the constraint.[19]

"You will permit me to say," said the lawyer, "that I hardly understand your attitude in the matter."

Vole flushed, hesitated, and then spoke.

"I'll make a clean breast of it. I was hard up, as you know. I hoped that Miss French might lend me some money. She was fond of me, but she wasn't at all interested in the struggles of a young couple. Early on, I found that she had taken it for granted that my wife and I didn't get on—were living apart. Mr. Mayherne—I wanted the money—for Romaine's sake. I said nothing, and allowed the old lady to think what she chose. She spoke of my being an adopted son to her. There was never any question of marriage—that must be just Janet's imagination."

"And that is all?"

"Yes—that is all."

Was there just a shade of hesitation in the words? The lawyer fancied so. He rose and held out his hand.

"Good-bye, Mr. Vole." He looked into the haggard young face and spoke with an unusual impulse. "I believe in your innocence in spite of the multitude of facts arrayed against you.[20] I hope to prove it and vindicate[21] you completely."

Vole smiled back at him.

"You'll find the alibi is all right," he said cheerfully.

Again he hardly noticed that the other did not respond.

"The whole thing hinges a good deal on the testimony of Janet Mackenzie," said Mr. Mayherne. "She hates you. That much is clear."

"She can hardly hate me," protested the young man.

The solicitor shook his head as he went out.

"Now for Mrs. Vole," he said to himself.

---

19. *Constraint* refers to "the act of holding something back."
20. The *multitude of facts arrayed against you* refers to the many facts that suggest Vole's guilt.
21. To *vindicate* is to free from blame or suspicion.

Additional Support

Skills Practice

GRAMMAR: Dashes Have students read this page of the selection and note where the author uses dashes. **Ask:** Where are the dashes found most often on this page? *(in the dialogue)* What purposes do the dashes serve? *(They show that Vole is stopping himself from revealing something, as in "Well—I don't know." They also give the impression that Vole is speaking haltingly, as though he is reluctant to reveal the information.)* Invite volunteers to read this portion of Mayherne and Vole's dialogue aloud. **Ask:** What effect do the

He was seriously disturbed by the way the thing was shaping.

The Voles lived in a small shabby house near Paddington Green. It was to this house that Mr. Mayherne went.

In answer to his ring, a big slatternly[22] woman, obviously a charwoman,[23] answered the door.

"Mrs. Vole? Has she returned yet?"

"Got back an hour ago. But I dunno if you can see her."

"If you will take my card to her," said Mr. Mayherne quietly, "I am quite sure that she will do so."

The woman looked at him doubtfully, wiped her hand on her apron and took the card. Then she closed the door in his face and left him on the step outside.

In a few minutes, however, she returned with a slightly altered manner.

"Come inside, please."

She ushered him into a tiny drawing room. Mr. Mayherne, examining a drawing on the wall, started up suddenly to face a tall, pale woman who had entered so quietly that he had not heard her.

"Mr. Mayherne? You are my husband's solicitor, are you not? You have come from him? Will you please sit down?"

Until she spoke, he had not realized that she was not English. Now, observing her more closely, he noticed the high cheekbones, the dense blue-black of the hair, and an occasional very slight movement of the hands that was distinctly foreign. A strange woman, very quiet. So quiet as to make one uneasy. From the very first Mr. Mayherne was conscious that he was up against something that he did not understand.

---

22. Here, *slatternly* means "disorderly in personal appearance."
23. A *charwoman* is a woman hired to clean.

Literary Element Motivation *Vole just said he and his wife had no maid. What motivation might he have for not mentioning this charwoman?* **L2**

Big Idea The Uncanny and Mysterious *What is so mysterious to Mayherne about this woman?* **BI2**

The Tea Party. Henry Lamb (1885–1960). Oil on board. The Arts Club, London. ★

"Now, my dear Mrs. Vole," he began, "you must not give way—"[24]

He stopped. It was so very obvious that Romaine Vole had not the slightest intention of giving way. She was perfectly calm and composed.

"Will you please tell me about it?" she said. "I must know everything. Do not think to spare me. I want to know the worst." She hesitated, then repeated in a lower tone, with a curious emphasis which the lawyer did not understand: "I want to know the worst."

Mr. Mayherne went over his interview with Leonard Vole. She listened attentively, nodding her head now and then.

"I see," she said, when he had finished. "He wants me to say that he came in at twenty minutes past nine that night?"

---

24. *Give way* suggests breaking down emotionally.

AGATHA CHRISTIE **1193**

Teach

L2 Literary Element

Motivation Answer: *Perhaps the charwoman knows something incriminating about Vole that he doesn't want Mayherne to know. Also, if Vole was motivated to lie about the maid in order to hide incriminating evidence, perhaps he is hiding other evidence as well.* OL

BI2 Big Idea

The Uncanny and Mysterious Answer: *She looks exotic, she acts strange, and she is very quiet. Mayherne is unsettled by her.*

Ask: What is it exactly that he does not understand about Vole's wife? *(Perhaps he is unsure of understanding someone from a different culture, or perhaps he is intimidated by her beauty.)* OL

★ Viewing the Art

Henry Lamb (1885–1960) was born in Australia but raised in England. In addition to studying painting at the Chelsea School of Art, he also attended medical school. AS

dashes have on your impression of Mr. Vole? *(Answers may vary. Vole's halting speech might make him seem less trustworthy, or it may make students believe he is telling the difficult truth.)* OL

Reading in the Real World

College Have students use library and Internet resources to research several colleges in London. Instruct them to create profiles of two colleges and the neighborhoods in which they are located. Have them present their information about these colleges to the class. OL

Objectives

• To analyze character motivation (SE)

• To understand the use of dashes (TWE)

1193

Teach

R1 **Reading Strategy**

Making Inferences About Characters Answer:
Mayherne is most likely to infer that the woman wants to protect Vole. **OL**

★ **Viewing the Art**

Charles van den Eychen came from a long line of artists, including his father and grandfather. Van den Eychen (also spelled Eycken) was popular in the nineteenth century for his portrayals of pets; he even received a commission from the queen of Belgium. **AS**

The Proud Mother. Charles van den Eychen (1879–1923). ★

"He did come in at that time?" said Mr. Mayherne sharply.

"That is not the point," she said coldly. "Will my saying so acquit him? Will they believe me?"

Mr. Mayherne was taken aback. She had gone so quickly to the core of the matter.

"That is what I want to know," she said. "Will it be enough? Is there anyone else who can support my evidence?"

There was a suppressed[25] eagerness in her manner that made him vaguely uneasy.

"So far there is no one else," he said reluctantly.

"I see," said Romaine Vole.

She sat for a minute or two perfectly still. A little smile played over her lips.

The lawyer's feeling of alarm grew stronger and stronger.

"Mrs. Vole—" he began. "I know what you must feel—"

"Do you?" she asked. "I wonder."

"In the circumstances—"

"In the circumstances—I intend to play a lone hand."

He looked at her in dismay.

"But, my dear Mrs. Vole—you are overwrought.[26] Being so devoted to your husband—"

"I beg your pardon?"

The sharpness of her voice made him start. He repeated in a hesitating manner:

"Being so devoted to your husband—"

Romaine Vole nodded slowly, the same strange smile on her lips.

"Did he tell you that I was devoted to him?" she asked softly. "Ah! yes, I can

25. Here, *suppressed* means "restrained."

Reading Strategy Making Inferences About Characters *What is Mayherne most likely to infer from these questions?* **R1**

26. Someone who is *overwrought* is upset or agitated.

1194 UNIT 6 GENRE FICTION

Additional Support

Skills Practice

ASSESSMENT: Sentence Completion Have students complete the following sentences:

1. Mayherne is _____ to find Romaine so _____.
   a. uneasy; overwrought
   b. eager; pleasant
   c. alarmed; calm
   d. composed; vague

2. She _____ that she is not _____ to Leonard.
   a. repeats; shabby
   b. misunderstands; obligated
   c. promises; unfaithful
   d. insists; devoted

see he did. How stupid men are! Stupid—stupid—stupid—"

She rose suddenly to her feet. All the intense emotion that the lawyer had been conscious of in the atmosphere was now concentrated in her tone.

"I hate him, I tell you! I hate him. I hate him. I hate him! I would like to see him hanged by the neck till he is dead."

The lawyer **recoiled** before her and the smoldering passion in her eyes.

She advanced a step nearer and continued vehemently:

"Perhaps I shall see it. Supposing I tell you that he did not come in that night at twenty past nine, but at twenty past ten? You say that he tells you he knew nothing about the money coming to him. Supposing I tell you he knew all about it, and counted on it, and committed murder to get it? Supposing I tell you that he admitted to me that night when he came in what he had done? That there was blood on his coat? What then? Supposing that I stand up in court and say all these things?"

Her eyes seemed to challenge him. With an effort, he concealed his growing dismay, and endeavored to speak in a rational tone.

"You cannot be asked to give evidence against your husband—"

"He is not my husband!" The words came out so quickly that he fancied he had misunderstood her.

"I beg your pardon? I—"

"He is not my husband." The silence was so intense that you could have heard a pin drop.

"I was an actress in Vienna. My husband is alive but in a madhouse. So we could not marry. I am glad now."

She nodded defiantly.

Literary Element Motivation *What is the woman's motivation for making this statement?* **L2**

Vocabulary

recoil (ri koil´) *v.* to shrink back physically or emotionally

---

"I should like you to tell me one thing," said Mr. Mayherne. He contrived[27] to appear as cool and unemotional as ever. "Why are you so bitter against Leonard Vole?"

She shook her head, smiling a little.

"Yes, you would like to know. But I shall not tell you. I will keep my secret. . . ."

Mr. Mayherne gave his dry little cough and rose.

"There seems no point in prolonging this interview," he remarked. "You will hear from me again after I have communicated with my client."

She came closer to him, looking into his eyes with her own wonderful dark ones.

"Tell me," she said, "did you believe—honestly—that he was innocent when you came here today?"

"I did," said Mr. Mayherne.

"You poor little man," she laughed.

"And I believe so still," finished the lawyer. "Good evening, madam."

He went out of the room, taking with him the memory of her startled face.

"This is going to be the devil of a business," said Mr. Mayherne to himself as he strode along the street.

Extraordinary, the whole thing. An extraordinary woman. A very dangerous woman. Women were the devil when they got their knife into you.

What was to be done? That wretched young man hadn't a leg to stand upon. Of course, possibly he did commit the crime. . . .

"No," said Mr. Mayherne to himself. "No—there's almost too much evidence against him. I don't believe this woman. She was trumping up[28] the whole story. But she'll never bring it into court."

He wished he felt more conviction[29] on the point.

---

27. Here, *contrived* means "made a great effort."
28. To *trump up* is to make up or concoct.
29. Here, *conviction* means "certainty."

Reading Strategy Making Inferences About Characters *What inferences can you draw about Mayherne's character based on this comment?* **R2**

Teach

L1 Literary Element

Motivation Ask: What might motivate Romaine to make such a statement? (*She has decided not to ally herself with her husband, a fact she communicates by her demeaning tone and her use of the word "stupid" to describe Vole and perhaps Mayherne for allying himself with her husband and/or for believing his story.*) **OL**

L2 Literary Element

Motivation Answer: *She wants Mayherne to know that she has no real motive for protecting Vole and that she may have a motive for despising him.* **OL**

R2 Reading Strategy

Making Inferences About Characters Answer: *Students may say that Mayherne, rightly or wrongly, trusts his intuition. They may also say that he remains firm about his beliefs in spite of new information.* **OL**

---

3. Mayherne realizes how ____ they are when he arrives at their ____ house.
   a. wealthy; estate
   b. far; country
   c. poor; shabby
   d. doubtful; charred
   (1. c; 2. d; 3. c) **OL**

Differentiated Instruction

Less Proficient Readers Words like *supposing* and *madhouse* have connotations in this context that might differ from their denotations. Read the appropriate dictionary definitions of these words aloud and discuss how their meanings in the story differ. **BL**

Objectives
• To analyze character motivation (SE)
• To make inferences about characters (TWE)
• To practice sentence completion (TWE)

L Literary Element

Motivation Answer: *Mackenzie is "attached" to French's nephew; perhaps she fancies marrying him after he inherits French's money.* **OL**

★ Cultural History

Adaptation "The Witness for the Prosecution" began as a short story in 1933 but was adapted for the stage by Agatha Christie in 1953 and for the screen by director Billy Wilder in 1957. The movie—starring Charles Laughton as the solicitor and Tyrone Power and Marlene Dietrich as the Voles—was nominated for six Academy Awards. **AS**

The police court proceedings[30] were brief and dramatic. The principal witnesses for the prosecution were Janet Mackenzie, maid to the dead woman, and Romaine Heilger, Austrian subject, the mistress of the prisoner.

Mr. Mayherne sat in court and listened to the damning story that the latter told. It was on the lines she had indicated to him in their interview.

The prisoner reserved his defense and was committed for trial.

Mr. Mayherne was at his wits' end. The case against Leonard Vole was black beyond words. Even the famous K.C.[31] who was engaged for the defense held out little hope.

"If we can shake that Austrian woman's testimony, we might do something," he said dubiously.[32] "But it's a bad business."

Mr. Mayherne had concentrated his energies on one single point. Assuming Leonard Vole to be speaking the truth, and to have left the murdered woman's house at nine o'clock, who was the man Janet heard talking to Miss French at half past nine?

The only ray of light was in the shape of a scapegrace[33] nephew who had in bygone days cajoled[34] and threatened his aunt out of various sums of money. Janet Mackenzie, the solicitor learned, had always been attached to this young man and had never ceased urging his claims upon her mistress. It certainly seemed possible that it was this nephew who had been with Miss French after Leonard Vole left, especially as he was not to be found in any of his old haunts.

In all other directions, the lawyer's researches had been negative in their result.

No one had seen Leonard Vole entering his own house, or leaving that of Miss French. No one had seen any other man enter or leave the house in Cricklewood. All inquiries drew blank.[35]

It was the eve of the trial when Mr. Mayherne received the letter which was to lead his thoughts in an entirely new direction.

It came by the six o'clock post. An illiterate scrawl, written on common paper and enclosed in a dirty envelope with the stamp stuck on crooked.

Mr. Mayherne read it through once or twice before he grasped its meaning.

"Dear Mister:
"You're the lawyer chap wot acts for the young feller. If you want that painted foreign hussy showd up for wot she is an her pack of lies you come to 16 Shaw's Rents Stepney to-night It ull cawst you 2 hundred quid Arsk for Misses Mogson."[36]

The solicitor read and reread this strange epistle. It might, of course, be a hoax,[37] but when he thought it over, he became increasingly convinced that it was genuine, and also convinced that it was the one hope for the prisoner. The evidence of Romaine Heilger damned him completely, and the line the defense meant to pursue, the line that the evidence of a woman who had admittedly lived an immoral life was not to be trusted, was at best a weak one.

Mr. Mayherne's mind was made up. It was his duty to save his client at all costs. He must go to Shaw's Rents.

He had some difficulty in finding the place, a ramshackle building in an evil-smelling slum, but at last he did so, and on inquiry for Mrs. Mogson was sent up to a room on the third floor. On this door he knocked and, getting no answer, knocked again.

---

30. *Police court proceedings* are similar to proceedings that result in an indictment in the United States: on the basis of testimony given in court, Vole is "committed for trial," or required to stand trial.
31. *K.C.* is the King's Counsel, who is referred to later in this story as Sir Charles.
32. *Dubiously* means "doubtfully."
33. A *scapegrace* is a rascal.
34. *Cajoled* means "urged in a flattering way in order to achieve one's own ends."

Literary Element Motivation *What motivation does Mackenzie have for pinning the crime on Vole?* **L**

---

35. *Drew blank* means "were left unanswered."
36. This note is written to suggest the speech of lower-class people in London. *Wot* means "who" in the first line and "what" in the third line; *ull cawst* means "will cost"; and 200 *quid* is 200 pounds, a huge sum at the time.
37. A *hoax* is an act intended to deceive or trick.

Additional Support

Skills Practice

READING: Activating Prior Knowledge Have students write short paragraphs describing which aspects of "The Witness for the Prosecution" seem familiar to them and explaining why. Then have them meet in small groups to discuss the following questions:

- What personal experiences make the story seem familiar to you?
- What were you able to predict about the story based on your prior knowledge?
- How do your perspectives on the story differ and why? **OL**

At this second knock, he heard a shuffling sound inside, and presently the door was opened cautiously half an inch, and a bent figure peered out.

Suddenly the woman, for it was a woman, gave a chuckle and opened the door wider.

"So it's you, dearie," she said, in a wheezy voice. "Nobody with you, is there? No playing tricks? That's right. You can come in—you can come in."

With some reluctance the lawyer stepped across the threshold into the small dirty room, with its flickering gas jet.[38] There was an untidy unmade bed in a corner, a plain deal table[39] and two rickety chairs. For the first time Mr. Mayherne had a full view of the tenant of this unsavory apartment. She was a woman of middle age, bent in figure, with a mass of untidy gray hair and a scarf wound tightly round her face. She saw him looking at this and laughed again, the same curious, toneless chuckle.

"Wondering why I hide my beauty, dear? He, he, he. Afraid it may tempt you, eh? But you shall see—you shall see."

She drew aside the scarf, and the lawyer recoiled involuntarily before the almost formless blur of scarlet. She replaced the scarf again.

"So you're not wanting to kiss me, dearie? He, he, I don't wonder. And yet I was a pretty girl once—not so long ago as you'd think, either. Vitriol,[40] dearie, vitriol—that's what did that. Ah! but I'll be even with 'em—"

She burst into a hideous torrent of profanity which Mr. Mayherne tried vainly to quell. She fell silent at last, her hands clenching and unclenching themselves nervously.

"Enough of that," said the lawyer sternly. "I've come here because I have reason to

---

38. A *gas jet* is used to turn on light created by gas rather than by electricity.
39. A *deal table* is a simple table made of fir or pine boards, which the British call "deal."
40. *Vitriol* is a chemical substance that can burn the skin.

Reading Strategy Making Inferences About Characters *What inference might you make about this woman, based on her appearance?* **R**

Mrs. Seymour Fort, 1778. John Singleton Copley.

believe you can give me information which will clear my client, Leonard Vole. Is that the case?"

Her eyes leered at him cunningly.

"What about the money, dearie?" she wheezed. "Two hundred quid, you remember."

"It is your duty to give evidence, and you can be called upon to do so."

"That won't do, dearie. I'm an old woman, and I know nothing. But you give me two hundred quid, and perhaps I can give you a hint or two. See?"

"What kind of hint?"

"What should you say to a letter? A letter from *her*. Never mind how I got hold of it. That's my business. It'll do the trick. But I want my two hundred quid."

Mr. Mayherne looked at her coldly and made up his mind.

"I'll give you ten pounds, nothing more. And only that if this letter is what you say it is."

"Ten pounds?" She screamed and raved at him.

"Twenty," said Mr. Mayherne, "and that's my last word."

He rose as if to go. Then, watching her closely, he drew out a pocketbook and counted out twenty one-pound notes.

"You see," he said. "That is all I have with me. You can take it or leave it."

AGATHA CHRISTIE **1197**

L Literary Element

Motivation Ask: What is Mayherne's motivation for giving the woman so much less money than she has asked for? *(He knows that she is poor and is counting on the fact that she won't be able to resist the money he is offering.)* **OL**

BI₁ Big Idea

The Uncanny and Mysterious Answer: *Students should note that the woman appears out of nowhere, that Mayherne doesn't know who she really is or even what she looks like, and that the place where she meets Mayherne may or may not be her real address. Furthermore, the letters could be real or fake, and the person to whom they were written could be real or fake.* **OL**

★ Viewing the Art

Parisian-born artist François Bonvin (1817–1887) attended the prestigious École de Dessin in Paris but left to work as a typesetter, printer, and police clerk. He was influenced by sixteenth- and seventeenth-century Flemish painters and became a proponent of the emerging Realist movement. **AS**

Still Life With Book, Papers, and Inkwell, 1876.
François Bonvin. National Gallery, London.

L But already he knew that the sight of the money was too much for her. She cursed and raved impotently,[41] but at last she gave in. Going over to the bed, she drew something out from beneath the tattered mattress.

"Here you are, damn you!" she snarled. "It's the top one you want."

It was a bundle of letters that she threw to him, and Mr. Mayherne untied them and scanned them in his usual cool, methodical manner. The woman, watching him eagerly, could gain no clue from his impassive face.

He read each letter through, then returned again to the top one and read it a second time. Then he tied the whole bundle up again carefully.

They were love letters, written by Romaine Heilger, and the man they were written to was not Leonard Vole. The top letter was dated the day of the latter's arrest.

"I spoke true, dearie, didn't I?" whined the woman. "It'll do for her, that letter?"

Mr. Mayherne put the letters in his pocket, then he asked a question.

"How did you get hold of this correspondence?"

"That's telling," she said with a leer. "But I know something more. I heard in court what

that hussy said. Find out where she was at twenty past ten, the time she says she was at home. Ask at the Lion Road Cinema. They'll remember—a fine upstanding girl like that— curse her!"

"Who is the man?" asked Mr. Mayherne. "There's only a Christian name here."

The other's voice grew thick and hoarse, her hands clenched and unclenched. Finally she lifted one to her face.

"He's the man that did this to me. Many years ago now. She took him away from me—a chit[42] of a girl she was then. And when I went after him—and went for him too—he threw the cursed stuff at me! And she laughed—damn her! I've had it in for her for years. Followed her, I have, spied upon her. And now I've got her! She'll suffer for this, won't she, Mr. Lawyer? She'll suffer?"

"She will probably be sentenced to a term of imprisonment for perjury,"[43] said Mr. Mayherne quietly.

"Shut away—that's what I want. You're going, are you? Where's my money? Where's that good money?"

Without a word, Mr. Mayherne put down the notes on the table. Then, drawing a deep breath, he turned and left the squalid room. Looking back, he saw the old woman crooning over the money.

He wasted no time. He found the cinema in Lion Road easily enough, and, shown a photograph of Romaine Heilger, the commissionaire[44] recognized her at once. She had arrived at the cinema with a man some time after ten o'clock on the evening in question. He had not noticed her escort particularly, but he remembered the lady who had spoken to him about the picture that was showing. They stayed until the end, about an hour later.

Mr. Mayherne was satisfied. Romaine Heilger's evidence was a tissue of lies from beginning to end. She had evolved it out of her passionate hatred. The lawyer wondered whether he would ever know what lay

41. Here, *impotently* means "helplessly" or "powerlessly."

Big Idea The Uncanny and Mysterious *What is mysterious about this woman, the circumstances, and the letters?* **BI₁**

1198 UNIT 6 GENRE FICTION

42. Here, *chit* refers to a rude young person.
43. *Perjury* is the act of lying under oath in a court of law.
44. *Commissionaire* is a British term for a theater attendant.

Additional Support

Skills Practice

LISTENING AND SPEAKING:

Monologues Invite students to choose a character from the story and create a monologue or journal entry from that character's point of view. Have students address the following questions in their presentations:

• What is most important to this character?

• What stands between this character and his or her goals?

• What is this character willing to do in order to achieve his or her goals? **OL**

The Trial of Mr Pickwick.
Cecil Charles Windsor Aldin
(1870–1935). Colour lithograph.
Dickens House Museum, London.

behind that hatred. What had Leonard Vole done to her? He had seemed dumbfounded when the solicitor had reported her attitude to him. He had declared earnestly that such a thing was incredible—yet it had seemed to Mr. Mayherne that after the first astonishment his protests had lacked sincerity.

He did know. Mr. Mayherne was convinced of it. He knew, but he had no intention of revealing the fact. The secret between those two remained a secret. Mr. Mayherne wondered if someday he should come to learn what it was.

The solicitor glanced at his watch. It was late, but time was everything. He hailed a taxi and gave an address.

"Sir Charles must know of this at once," he murmured to himself as he got in.

The trial of Leonard Vole for the murder of Emily French aroused widespread interest. In the first place the prisoner was young and good-looking, then he was accused of a particularly dastardly crime, and there was the further interest of Romaine Heilger, the principal witness for the prosecution. There had been pictures of her in many papers, and several fictitious stories as to her origin and history.

The proceedings opened quietly enough. Various technical evidence came first. Then Janet Mackenzie was called. She told substantially the same story as before. In cross-examination counsel for the defense succeeded in getting her to contradict herself once or twice over her account of Vole's association with Miss French; he emphasized the fact that though she had heard a man's voice in the sitting room that night, there was nothing to show that it was Vole who was there, and he managed to drive home a feeling that jealousy and dislike of the prisoner were at the bottom of a good deal of her evidence. **R**

Then the next witness was called.

"Your name is Romaine Heilger?"

"Yes."

"You are an Austrian subject?"

"Yes."

"For the last three years you have lived with the prisoner and passed yourself off as his wife?"

Just for a moment Romaine Heilger's eyes met those of the man in the dock. Her expression held something curious and unfathomable.[45]

"Yes."

Big Idea The Uncanny and Mysterious *What remains a mystery to Mayherne?* **BI₂**

---

45. *Unfathomable* means "impossible to understand."

Teach

BI₂ Big Idea

The Uncanny and Mysterious Answer: *Mayherne does not understand the nature of the relationship between Vole and Heilger. He thinks that Vole has done something terrible to Heilger but that he will never know what.* **OL**

R Reading Strategy

Making Inferences About Characters Ask: What conclusions do you draw here about Janet Mackenzie? *(Students may say that they believe she made up the negative information about Vole, or they may say that she was indeed telling the truth about Vole but was bullied on the witness stand.)* **OL**

★ Viewing the Art

Cecil Charles Windsor Aldin (1870–1935) was a popular illustrator, painter, and writer most remembered for his faithful, revealing depictions of dogs. **Ask:** How does the trial depicted here resemble the trial in "The Witness for the Prosecution"? *(Answers will vary.)* **AS**

Differentiated Instruction

Dictionary Skill Help gifted students learn how to use the *Oxford English Dictionary* to determine the etymology of words. Then instruct them to use this resource along with library and Internet research to analyze differences in British and American English. **Ask:** Why do we have different words to designate the same people, things, and concepts—such as *solicitor* and *lawyer*? How have historical events shaped these two versions of the English language? Have students write short essays addressing their research findings. **AL**

Objectives
• To analyze theme (SE)
• To make inferences about character (SE)
• To analyze motivation (SE)
• To write character monologues (TWE)

L Literary Element

Motivation Answer: *The law-yer senses that there is some-thing fake or overdone in such negative testimony.*

Ask: How might an unbiased witness affect the jury's motiva-tion in such a trial? *(The jury might be more apt to believe a witness who is evenhanded rather than one who seems to have a score to settle.)* **OL**

R1 Reading Strategy

Making Inferences About Characters Ask: What does it tell you about Heilger that she denies the charges against her in this manner? *(Students might say her attitude shows a certain arrogance, as though she is challenging the barrister to pro-duce evidence against her.)* **OL**

★ Viewing the Art

England's eighth largest city, Coventry is located in the West Midlands. In the 1920s and 1930s, the automobile ruled the streets, as Coventry became the major English center of automobile manu-facture. **Ask:** Does this depic-tion of Coventry remind you of the story's setting? Why or why not? *(Answers will vary.)* **AS**

Bishop Street, Coventry, 1929. Joan Murphy. Oil on canvas. Herbert Art Gallery & Museum, Coventry, UK. ★

The questions went on. Word by word the damning facts came out. On the night in question the prisoner had taken out a crow-bar with him. He had returned at twenty minutes past ten and had confessed to hav-ing killed the old lady. His cuffs had been stained with blood, and he had burned them in the kitchen stove. He had terrorized her into silence by means of threats.

As the story proceeded, the feeling of the court which had, to begin with, been slightly favorable to the prisoner, now set dead against him. He himself sat with downcast head and moody air, as though he knew he were doomed.

Yet it might have been noted that her own counsel sought to restrain Romaine's **animosity.** He would have preferred her to be more unbiased.

Literary Element Motivation *Why would Heilger's lawyer have preferred a more unbiased testimony?* **L**

Vocabulary

animosity (an´ə mos´ə tē) *n.* ill will or resentment; active strong dislike or hostility

1200 UNIT 6 GENRE FICTION

Formidable and ponderous,[46] counsel for the defense arose.

He put it to her that her story was a mali-cious fabrication[47] from start to finish, that she had not even been in her own house at the time in question, that she was in love with another man and was deliberately seek-ing to send Vole to his death for a crime he did not commit.

Romaine denied these allegations with superb insolence.[48]   **R1**

Then came the surprising denouement,[49] the production of the letter. It was read aloud in court in the midst of a breathless stillness.

"Max, beloved, the Fates have delivered him into our hands! He has been arrested for mur-der—but, yes, the murder of an old lady! Leonard, who would not hurt a fly! At last I shall have my revenge. The poor chicken! I shall say that he came in that night with blood upon him—that he con-fessed to me. I shall hang him, Max—and when he hangs he will know and realize that it was Romaine who sent him to his death. And then—happiness, Beloved! Happiness at last!"

There were experts present ready to swear that the handwriting was that of Romaine Heilger, but they were not needed. Confronted with the letter, Romaine broke down utterly and confessed everything. Leonard Vole had returned to the house at the time he said, twenty past nine. She had invented the whole story to ruin him.

With the collapse of Romaine Heilger, the case for the Crown collapsed also. Sir Charles called his few witnesses; the prisoner himself

---

46. The phrase *formidable and ponderous* is meant to suggest the mental and emotional strength and weight of the counsel for the defense.
47. The phrase *malicious fabrication* suggests a story that has been elaborately made up for evil purposes.
48. *Insolence* is a display of an obviously contrary attitude.
49. A *denouement* (dā´no͞o mäN´) is an action that follows a climax, or high point, of a story.

Skills Practice

WRITING: News Articles Have stu-dents working alone or in small groups use the information from the story to write newspaper, television, or radio news stories about Leonard Vole's trial as though it were happening in the pres-ent. Instruct students to use library and Internet resources to find models for this kind of writing. **Ask:** Which details would a reporter or newswriter want the public to know about Vole's trial? Which details would hold the public interest? **OL**

went into the box and told his story in a manly straightforward manner, unshaken by cross-examination.

The prosecution endeavored to rally, but without great success. The judge's summing up was not wholly favorable to the prisoner, but a reaction had set in, and the jury needed little time to consider their verdict.

"We find the prisoner not guilty."

Leonard Vole was free!

Little Mr. Mayherne hurried from his seat. He must congratulate his client.

He found himself polishing his pince-nez vigorously and checked himself. His wife had told him only the night before that he was getting a habit of it. Curious things, habits. People themselves never knew they had them.

An interesting case—a very interesting case. That woman, now, Romaine Heilger.

The case was dominated for him still by the exotic figure of Romaine Heilger. She had seemed a pale, quiet woman in the house at Paddington, but in court she had flamed out against the sober background, flaunting herself like a tropical flower.

If he closed his eyes, he could see her now, tall and vehement, her exquisite body bent forward a little, her right hand clenching and unclenching itself unconsciously all the time.

Curious things, habits. That gesture of hers with the hand was her habit, he supposed. Yet he had seen someone else do it quite lately. Who was it now? Quite lately—

He drew in his breath with a gasp as it came back to him. The woman in Shaw's Rents . . .

He stood still, his head whirling. It was impossible—impossible— Yet, Romaine Heilger was an actress.

The K.C. came up behind him and clapped him on the shoulder.

"Congratulated our man yet? He's had a narrow shave, you know. Come along and see him."

But the little lawyer shook off the other's hand.

He wanted one thing only—to see Romaine Heilger face to face.

He did not see her until some time later, and the place of their meeting is not relevant.

"So you guessed," she said, when he had told her all that was in his mind. "The face? Oh! that was easy enough, and the light of that gas jet was too bad for you to see the makeup."

"But why—why—"

"Why did I play a lone hand?" She smiled a little, remembering the last time she had used the words.

"Such an elaborate comedy!"

"My friend—I had to save him. The evidence of a woman devoted to him would not have been enough—you hinted as much yourself. But I know something of the psychology of crowds. Let my evidence be wrung from me, as an admission, damning me in the eyes of the law, and a reaction in favor of the prisoner would immediately set in."

"And the bundle of letters?"

"One alone, the vital one, might have seemed like a—what do you call it?—put-up job."

"Then the man called Max?"

"Never existed, my friend."

"I still think," said little Mr. Mayherne, in an aggrieved manner, "that we could have got him off by the—er—normal procedure."

"I dared not risk it. You see, you thought he was innocent—"

"And you knew it? I see," said little Mr. Mayherne.

"My dear Mr. Mayherne," said Romaine, "you do not see at all. I knew—he was guilty!" ◆

Reading Strategy   Making Inferences About Characters *What inferences did Heilger make about both the jury and Mayherne?* **R3**

AGATHA CHRISTIE   **1201**

Assess

1. Accept reasonable responses.
2. (a) Of the murder of French (b) By acting naïve and by behaving like a gentleman
3. (a) The woman Vole calls his wife, actually his unmarried actress companion (b) She is mysterious and exotic; she takes control and is not what he expected.
4. (a) Heilger creates a sensation by being a witness for the prosecution. (b) At first, the jury believes him, then the angry Heilger, then the evidence conveyed by the letters.
5. Christie portrays Vole as a gentleman who shows no anger, pettiness, or obvious deception and Mayherne as a decent man who believes in Vole.
6. (a) An actress could deceive the jury and Mayherne. (b) She convinces everyone except perhaps the prosecutor.
7. (a) Answers may vary. Students should support their views. (b) Mayherne has legal knowledge and court experience; Heilger knows human nature.
8. Students should support their opinions with evidence from the text.

RESPONDING AND THINKING CRITICALLY

Respond

1. Were you fooled? Explain.

Recall and Interpret

2. (a) What crime is Leonard Vole accused of? (b) How does Vole convince Mr. Mayherne that he did not commit the crime?
3. (a) Who is Romaine Heilger? (b) Why does Mayherne's first meeting with her startle him?
4. (a) What happens when Heilger testifies at the trial? (b) How does the jury respond to Vole during the trial? Explain.

Analyze and Evaluate

5. From beginning to end, the facts are against Vole, and yet Christie convinces most readers to think of him as innocent. How does she do this?

6. (a) Why does Christie cast Vole's companion as an actress? (b) How well does Heilger "perform" as a witness for the prosecution?
7. (a) Is Mayherne a believable character? Cite evidence from the text to support your opinion. (b) Who, in your opinion, had a better knowledge of the legal system and English court proceedings: Mayherne or Heilger? Explain.

Connect

8. From reading this story, do you think Christie deserves to be called the "Queen of Crime"? Explain.
9. **Big Idea** The Uncanny and Mysterious
What mysteries remain unanswered at the end of the story?

VISUAL LITERACY: Photography

Acting on a Set

Here is a still photo from the 1957 movie version of "Witness for the Prosecution." Directed by Billy Wilder, the film features Tyrone Power as Leonard Vole and Marlene Dietrich as the witness for the prosecution. Here, Marlene Dietrich shown in the witness box.

Group Activity Work with classmates to discuss and answer the following questions.

1. (a) How does the woman in this picture look the same or different from the way Christie presents Romaine Heilger in the story? (b) How do you expect the woman pictured here to talk? to act? Explain why.

2. What emotions do you see in this photograph? How do they match or contradict the emotions conveyed in the parallel scene in the story?

Still from the movie "Witness for the Prosecution," 1957

9. Who plotted French's death (Vole, Heilger, or both), when and how the plot began, and whether Heilger can be arrested for perjury

Group Activity

1. (a) Students may say this woman has blond hair; Romaine has blue-black hair. Both are attractive. (b) To talk aggressively in the uneducated accent of the woman in Shaw's Rents and to act just as aggressively and self-assuredly

2. Students should see the same emotional intensity from the woman in the film that they felt during the parallel scene in the story.

LITERARY ANALYSIS

Literary Element | Motivation

In a mystery, a reader has no choice but to pay attention to the suggestions made or implied by the author or characters, about other characters' **motivations**. Every character in this story typically has at least one transparent or implied motive, from the mysterious "Misses Mogson" to the gullible Mr. Mayherne.

1. (a) What is Heilger's "lone hand"? (b) What is her motivation for playing it? (c) Is this motivation stated or implied? (d) How does Heilger's real motivation differ from motivations that other characters state, suggest, or infer?

2. (a) What motivates the jury to acquit Vole? (b) What motivates Mayherne to visit Heilger after the acquittal?

Review: Style

As you learned on pages 1182–1183, **style** is composed of the expressive qualities that distinguish an author's work, including word choice and the length and arrangement of sentences, as well as the use of figurative language and imagery. In "The Witness for the Prosecution," **diction**, or word choice, reflects the author's culture, a primarily upper-middle-class British world.

Partner Activity With a partner, find several examples of Vole's polite, sophisticated speech. Write alternative, more plain-speaking, or working-class ways in which Vole might have expressed the same thoughts. Then discuss what effect Vole's diction has on Mayherne.

Example	Alternative
"I'd been having a run of infernal bad luck just then."	"I couldn't catch a break."

READING AND VOCABULARY

Reading Strategy | Making Inferences About Characters

The conflicts between characters help a reader to **make inferences** about them. Consider what you can infer based on the following conflicts.

1. Vole says his wife loves him. Vole's "wife" says she hates him. What inference can you draw from this conflict? What inference does Mayherne draw?

2. The narrator experiences an internal conflict. What is it? What does it tell you about Mayherne? about Vole? about Heilger?

Vocabulary | Practice

Practice with Synonyms Find a synonym for each vocabulary word. Use a dictionary or thesaurus if you need help.

1. cultivate   **a.** encourage   **b.** destroy
2. pretext   **a.** display   **b.** excuse
3. amicable   **a.** friendly   **b.** guilty
4. recoil   **a.** shrink   **b.** hug
5. animosity   **a.** hatred   **b.** complexity

Academic Vocabulary

Here are two words from the vocabulary list on page R83. These words will help you think, write, and talk about the selection.

instruct (in strukt´) v. to teach or direct

incentive (in sen´tiv) n. something that acts as a motivator or causes someone to take a particular action

Practice and Apply

1. What would you **instruct** Mayherne to do the next time he defends an accused murderer?
2. What does Vole name as his **incentive** for visiting Miss French?

AGATHA CHRISTIE **1203**

Assess

Literary Element

1. (a) Her lone hand is her plan to perform both in court and at Shaw's Rents. (b) She wants Leonard Vole to be acquitted. (c) Implied (d) Mayherne, the narrator, and the reader may see Heilger as motivated by hatred early in the story.

2. (a) The unmasking of Heilger's testimony as false rather than any certainty of Vole's innocence (b) His noticing the same fist clenching in the witness for the prosecution and in the woman at Shaw's Rents

Review: Style

Students might list these examples and others: "If I told you that I genuinely enjoyed being mothered and pampered, I daresay you'd only laugh" and "Surely her death frustrates all my hopes?" Students should note that Vole's educated, polite speech has a positive effect on Mayherne and inclines the solicitor to think the best of him.

Reading Strategy

1. That Vole's "wife" bears a secret grudge or that Vole is a liar; Mayherne infers that there is something inexplicable about Vole's "wife."

2. The narrator sees through Mayherne's eyes and sides with Vole but senses that details aren't quite right. This conflict reveals that Mayherne forges ahead even though he feels uncertain, that Vole's story is not convincing, and that Heilger is not who she seems to be.

Vocabulary

1. a   **2.** b   **3.** a   **4.** a   **5.** a

Academic Vocabulary

1. To look more closely at the motive and obvious clues
2. Kindliness toward an older woman

Assess

Writing About Literature

Students' essays should

- contain a thesis about how point of view affects the story
- analyze the effects of point of view on the narrator, on building suspense, and on the plot twist at the end of the story

Christie's Language and Style

Sample answers:

"I'm beginning to see," he muttered. "It's frightful . . . I made up to her, that's what they will say." *(a thought too terrible to be spoken)*

The testimony of a devoted wife—would it gain credence? . . . *(a thought that trails off, interior monologue)*

Performing

To prepare for their interrogation scenes, students can also watch popular crime-drama television programs or engage in Internet research on body language and nonverbal communication.

Writing About Literature

Analyze Point of View To write "The Witness for the Prosecution," Agatha Christie chose the third-person limited point of view: she describes the events as only Mr. Mayherne experiences them. How does this point of view increase suspense and help create the plot twist? Write a brief essay in which you explain the effect of the third-person limited point of view on the reader.

Before you write, gather and organize ideas by completing a graphic organizer like this one:

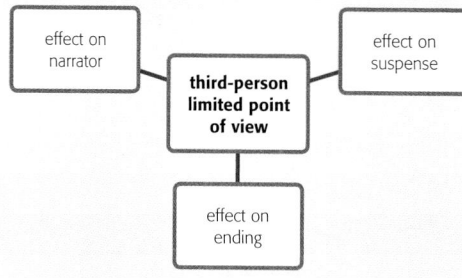

As you draft, be sure to create an introductory paragraph that includes your thesis about the effect of the third-person limited point of view. Create one or more body paragraphs to support your thesis and end with a formal conclusion.

After you complete your draft, have a peer read it and suggest revisions. Then proofread and edit your work for errors in spelling, grammar, and punctuation.

Performing

Working with a partner, choose, practice, and perform one of the interrogation scenes. Imagine and re-create the mannerisms, body language, and other details that help characters appear as if they are telling the truth, and that show the lawyer's responses, including his confusion and suspicions. Then watch the film version of the story and compare the performances with those of you and your partner.

Christie's Language and Style

Using Ellipses Three times in her story, Christie uses an ellipsis, a mark of punctuation used by narrative writers to show that a thought or conversation is trailing off. An ellipsis can also signal what is left unsaid or is too terrible to be said. In some cases, however, it merely shows the process of silent thinking between words, as in this example:

"At half past nine," said Leonard Vole.

"At half past nine . . ." He sprang to his feet.

"But then I'm saved—saved—"

Study these two additional examples of ellipses used in "The Witness for the Prosecution."

Example	Of course, possibly he did commit the crime. . . .
	The woman in Shaw's Rents. . . .
Context	Mayherne is thinking to himself
	Mayherne is realizing where he recently saw the fist-clenching habit
Reason for Use	Shows something possible, yet too terrible to state
	Shows Mayherne's realization; creates a dramatic pause

Activity Substitute an ellipsis for two other marks of punctuation in two different excerpts from the story. Use one ellipsis to show silent thinking between words or a dramatic pause; use another to show a thought that is too terrible to state or that simply trails off.

Revising Check

Ellipses If you used an ellipsis to show a thought that trails off in your essay about point of view in "The Witness for the Prosecution," replace it with a period or another appropriate end mark. Ellipses are rarely acceptable in expository writing; instead, use them sparingly in narration.

Revising Check

Students may not be familiar with the use of periods with ellipses. They should note that if an ellipsis is required at the end of a sentence, a period is typically used in addition to the ellipsis (unless the sentence is intended to be incomplete).

Grammar Workshop

Mechanics

Using Semicolons

"In cross-examination counsel for the defense succeeded in getting her to contradict herself once or twice over her account of Vole's association with Miss French; he emphasized the fact that though she had heard a man's voice in the sitting room that night, there was nothing to show that it was Vole who was there. . . ."

> —Agatha Christie, from "The Witness for the Prosecution"

Connecting to Literature In "The Witness for the Prosecution," Agatha Christie uses a **semicolon** to link together related ideas. A semicolon connects two or more main, or independent, clauses into one sentence. For example, you can connect the closely related clauses, "I enjoy reading" and "I especially like mystery novels" with a semicolon to form the following sentence: "I enjoy reading; I especially like mystery novels."

You can also use semicolons in compound or complex sentences that include a **conjunction**, a word that joins together groups of words in a sentence. The semicolon accentuates the close relationship between the two clauses in the sentence.

Situation To replace a comma and a coordinating conjunction in a compound sentence

> *There was little evidence to prove his innocence, and few people believed he was not guilty.*
> *There was little evidence to prove his innocence; few people believed he was not guilty.*

Situation To use a semicolon before a conjunctive adverb in a complex sentence

> *Leonard Vole's wife wanted to testify against him, therefore, his lawyer felt the trial was doomed.*
> *Leonard Vole's wife wanted to testify against him; therefore, his lawyer felt the trial was doomed.*

Exercise

Rewrite the following sentences using a semicolon.

1. Agatha Christie wrote many exciting stories and her writing was full of suspense.
2. Her story, "Witness for the Prosecution," was incredibly popular, therefore, it was made into a movie.
3. The story describes the criminal trial of Leonard Vole. He is charged with murder.

GRAMMAR WORKSHOP **1205**

▶ **Vocabulary Terms**

A **semicolon** connects two or more independent clauses in a sentence. A **conjunction** is a word that joins single words or groups of words. A **conjunctive adverb** is used to clarify the relationship between clauses of a compound sentence.

▶ **Test-Taking Tip**

When deciding whether or not to use a semicolon, first determine if the sentence has at least two clauses that express complete thoughts.

▶ **Language Handbook**

For more on semicolons, see the Language Handbook, p. R54.

Literature Online
eWorkbooks To link to the Grammar and Language eWorkbook, go to www.glencoe.com.

OBJECTIVES
- Use semicolons correctly.
- Demonstrate an understanding of conjunctions.
- Recognize conjunctions in a sentence.

Grammar Workshop

Mechanics

Focus

Tell students that sometimes people avoid using semicolons because they are not clear on how they should be used. **Write on the board:** The scientist introduced his time machine; it could move into the future or the past. **Ask:** What is the purpose of the semicolon in this sentence? *(to connect two independent clauses)*

Teach

Semicolons Emphasize the two main uses of semicolons. **Say:** A semicolon joins two independent clauses into one sentence. Sometimes a conjunctive adverb begins the second clause. Discuss when a semicolon is preferable to a conjunction and comma in a sentence, especially when the relationship is evident. **OL**

Assess

1. Agatha Christie wrote many exciting stories; her writing was full of suspense.
2. Her story "The Witness for the Prosecution" was incredibly popular; therefore, it was made into a movie.
3. The story describes the criminal trial of Leonard Vole; he is charged with murder.

Literature Online
eWorkbooks Have students access the Web site for more practice with semicolons.

English Language Coach

Types of Sentences English learners may be unfamiliar with the terms *compound sentence* and *complex sentence.* Diagram the two types of sentences and explain that a compound sentence has more than one main clause, whereas a complex sentence contains at least one subordinate clause. **EL**

Differentiated Instruction

Conjunctive Adverbs Tell students that conjunctive adverbs are connecting words that show relationships, such as *however, therefore, nevertheless, consequently,* and *moreover.* Brainstorm a list of conjunctive adverbs. Note the proper use of a semicolon between two independent clauses. **BL**

Focus

The Adventure of the Speckled Band

MEET SIR ARTHUR CONAN DOYLE

The greatest crime that detective Sherlock Holmes ever faced did not happen in the pages of a book. In 1901, weary of constructing convoluted mysteries, Doyle killed off Holmes in the short story "The Final Problem." His fans rebelled, canceling subscriptions to the magazine where Doyle's stories appeared and demanding Holmes's return. Defeated, Doyle resurrected the detective. Just as in his stories, Holmes triumphed.

For Doyle, Holmes's popularity was a mixed blessing. Because of Sherlock Holmes, he was one of the highest paid writers of his time, but he also felt his other accomplishments were overlooked. Despite his misgivings, Doyle will always be remembered for creating the world's most famous detective.

"When you have eliminated the impossible, whatever remains, however improbable, must be the truth."

—Sir Arthur Conan Doyle

Diagnoses and Deductions Born in Edinburgh, Scotland, Doyle was educated in England and Austria, and received several medical degrees from the University of Edinburgh. In medical school, Doyle studied under Dr. Joseph Bell, an expert diagnostician. Bell dazzled his students by diagnosing not only diseases but also a person's occupation merely through observation.

A New Detective Doyle started a medical practice after earning his degree, but soon he was earning more money writing occasional short stories than for his medical work. To build a readership for his writing, Doyle wanted to create a character who could appear in a series of stories. He admired the detective stories of Edgar Allan Poe, so he decided to make his character a detective. Recalling his college professor, Dr. Bell, Doyle gave his detective remarkable deductive skills. His new creation, Sherlock Holmes, first appeared in *A Study in Scarlet*, published in 1887. The novel was a success, so Doyle followed it with more Holmes stories and novels. By 1890 he had left his medical practice to focus on writing full time.

Fairies and the Spirits Doyle continued to write Sherlock Holmes stories through 1926, but he also pursued other interests. He published historical novels, including tales of fourteenth-century chivalry. Inspired by his participation in the Boer War as a medical officer, he also wrote military books.

Despite Holmes's hard-nosed rationalism, Doyle had a keen interest in the paranormal. He attended séances and lectured about the spirit world. He also believed in the existence of fairies and wrote several books on the topic. This belief in the "unseen world" was a solace later in life. Before his death, he wrote, "The reader will judge that I have had many adventures. The greatest and most glorious awaits me now."

Sir Arthur Conan Doyle was born in 1859 and died in 1930.

Literature Online Author Search For more about Sir Arthur Conan Doyle, go to www.glencoe.com.

Selection Skills

The Adventure of the Speckled Band

Literary Elements
- Character Archetype (SE pp. 1207–1227)
- Tone (SE p. 1227)
- Irony (TWE p. 1222)

Reading Skills
- Analyzing Details (SE pp. 1207–1227)
- Point of View (TWE p. 1208)
- Making Predictions (TWE p. 1214)

Vocabulary Skills
- Word Parts (SE p. 1227)
- Confused Words (TWE p. 1220)

Listening/Speaking/Viewing Skills
- Performing Dialogue (TWE p. 1214)

Writing Skills/Grammar
- Genre Analysis (SE p. 1228)
- Comma Usage (TWE p. 1210)
- Compare and Contrast (TWE p. 1224)

Connecting to the Story

This is an example of a classic mystery, which requires the story's hero, the detective, to solve the crime before it can be repeated. Before you read the story, think about the following questions:

- Have you ever encountered a mysterious situation?
- Have you had to take quick action in order to prevent something bad from happening?

Building Background

In Sherlock Holmes's first adventure, *A Study in Scarlet,* Holmes says to his friend Dr. Watson, "There are few people, . . . who, if you told them a result, would be able to evolve from their own inner consciousness what the steps were which led up to that result. This power is what I mean when I talk of reasoning backwards, or analytically." Holmes's practice of "reasoning backwards" to solve crimes comes from the deductive method described by French philosopher René Descartes in the seventeenth century. Descartes argued that the best way to solve a problem is to divide it into smaller parts whose causes can be explained logically. Using deduction, probability, and hypothesis, Sherlock Holmes always managed to solve crime.

Setting Purposes for Reading

Big Idea The Uncanny and Mysterious

As you read this short story, notice the details that help to create an eerie, mysterious mood.

Literary Element Character Archetype

A **character archetype** is a character who displays patterns of behavior and serves as an ideal model upon which literary characters are based. In "The Adventure of the Speckled Band," Sherlock Holmes is the archetypal detective. Doyle's depiction of Holmes in this and other stories has become the pattern, or archetype, for countless other fictional detectives.

- See Literary Terms Handbook, p. R3.

Literature Online Interactive Literary Elements Handbook To review or learn more about the literary elements, go to www.glencoe.com.

OBJECTIVES
In studying this selection, you will focus on the following:
- analyzing archetypal characters
- analyzing details and their significance to the plot
- writing to analyze genre elements
- recognizing and understanding tone

Reading Strategy Analyzing Details

Analyzing details means asking what the details in a piece of writing suggest. When reading a mystery story such as "The Adventure of the Speckled Band," it is especially important to notice details, which often point toward the solution. As you read this story, make note of the details you think will be especially important in solving the crime.

Reading Tip: Examining Each Detail Individually
It might be helpful to examine the details in this story one-by-one as you read. Use a chart like the one shown below to help you organize your analysis.

Detail	Detail Description	Why is the Detail Significant?
The bell rope in Miss Stoner's sister's room	The rope is not actually attached to a bell, and it was added to the room shortly before Miss Stoner's sister died.	The fake bell must have played a role in Miss Stoner's sister's death.

Vocabulary

livid (liv ′ id) *adj.* bruised p. 1214 *Both his knees were livid after the fall.*

amiable (ām ′ ə bəl) *adj.* good-humored; easy to get along with; p. 1217 *He was amiable and talked to everyone at the party.*

invaluable (in val ′ ū ə bəl) *adj.* priceless; p. 1221 *Good friends are invaluable in a crisis.*

erroneous (ə rō ′ nē əs) *adj.* inaccurate; wrong p. 1224 *Even after all of his research, he still came up with an erroneous conclusion.*

insufficient (in ′ sə fish ′ ənt) *adj.* not enough; p. 1224 *She brought only twelve cupcakes, which proved insufficient for the fourteen children.*

Focus

Summary

A young woman named Helen, who is on the verge of getting married, asks Sherlock Holmes to help her uncover the mystery of her sister's unexpected death. Her sister was also about to be married before her death. Holmes determines after investigating that Dr. Roylott, Helen's stepfather, murdered her sister so that he would not have to share the money her mother had left them. Dr. Roylott is also trying to kill Helen for the same reason.

V Vocabulary

Vocabulary File Say: Add these words and definitions to your vocabulary file. For each word, include a sentence that gives you an example of how to use the word. **OL** Students with English language needs should include the pronunciations of these words in their files. **EL**

Literary Elements Have students access the Web site to improve their understanding of character archetype.

 Selection Resources

Print Materials
- Unit 6 Resources (Fast File), pp. 43–45
- Leveled Vocabulary Development, p. 83
- Selection and Unit Assessments, pp. 203–204
- Selection Quick Checks, p. 102

Transparencies
- Bellringer Options Transparencies: Daily Language Practice Transparency 100
- Literary Elements Transparencies 86, 87, 88

Technology
- TeacherWorks Plus™ CD-ROM
- StudentWorks Plus™ CD-ROM
- Presentation Plus!™ CD-ROM
- Literature Online, glencoe.com
- Online Student Edition, mhln.com
- Exam*View*® Assessment Suite CD-ROM
- Vocabulary PuzzleMaker CD-ROM
- Listening Library, disc 2 track 41

Moreton Old Hall. Harry George Theaker (1873–1954). Watercolour on paper. Little Moreton Hall, Cheshire, UK. ⭐

The Adventure of The Speckled Band

Sir Arthur Conan Doyle

BI1 In glancing over my notes of the seventy-odd cases in which I have during the last eight years studied the methods of my friend Sherlock Holmes, I find many tragic, some comic, a large number merely strange, but none commonplace; for, working as he did rather for the love of his art than for the acquirement of wealth, he refused to associate himself with any investigation which did not tend toward the unusual, and even the fantastic. Of all these varied cases, however, I cannot recall any which presented more singular features than that which was associated with the well-known Surrey[1] family of the Roylotts of Stoke Moran. The events in question occurred in the early days of my association with Holmes, when we were sharing rooms as bachelors in Baker Street. It is possible that I might have placed them upon record before, but a promise of secrecy was made at the time, from which I have only been freed during the last month by the untimely death of the lady to whom the pledge was given. It is perhaps as well that the facts should now come to light, for I have reasons to know that there are widespread rumors as to the death of Dr. Grimesby Roylott which tend to make the matter even more terrible than the truth.

Literary Element Character Archetype *What does this statement say about Holmes's character?* **L1**

---

1. *Surrey* is a county located in southeastern England.

1208 UNIT 6 GENRE FICTION

It was early in April in the year '83[2] that I woke one morning to find Sherlock Holmes standing, fully dressed, by the side of my bed. He was a late riser as a rule, and as the clock on the mantelpiece showed me that it was only a quarter past seven, I blinked up at him in some surprise, and perhaps just a little resentment, for I was myself regular in my habits.

"Very sorry to knock you up,[3] Watson," said he, "but it's the common lot this morning. Mrs. Hudson has been knocked up, she retorted upon me, and I on you."

"What is it, then—a fire?"

"No; a client. It seems that a young lady has arrived in a considerable state of excitement, who insists upon seeing me. She is waiting now in the sitting-room. Now, when young ladies wander about the metropolis at this hour of the morning, and knock sleepy people up out of their beds, I presume that it is something very pressing which they have to communicate. Should it prove to be an interesting case, you would, I am sure, wish to follow it from the outset. I thought, at any rate, that I should call you and give you the chance."

"My dear fellow, I would not miss it for anything."

I had no keener pleasure than in following Holmes in his professional investigations, and in admiring the rapid deductions, as swift as intuitions, and yet always founded on a logical basis, with which he unravelled the problems which were submitted to him. I rapidly threw on my clothes, and was ready in a few minutes to accompany my friend down to the sitting-room. A lady dressed in black and heavily veiled, who had been sitting in the window, rose as we entered.

"Good-morning, madam," said Holmes, cheerily. "My name is Sherlock Holmes. This is my intimate friend and associate, Dr. Watson, before whom you can speak as freely as before myself. Ha! I am glad to see that Mrs. Hudson has had the good sense to light the fire. Pray draw up to it, and I shall order you a cup of hot coffee, for I observe that you are shivering."

"It is not cold which makes me shiver," said the woman, in a low voice, changing her seat as requested.

"What, then?"

"It is fear, Mr. Holmes. It is terror." She raised her veil as she spoke, and we could see that she was indeed in a pitiable state of agitation, her face all drawn and gray, with restless, frightened eyes, like those of some hunted animal. Her features and figure were those of a woman of thirty, but her hair was shot with premature gray, and her expression was weary and haggard. Sherlock Holmes ran her over with one of his quick, all-comprehensive glances.

"You must not fear," said he, soothingly, bending forward and patting her forearm. "We shall soon set matters right, I have no doubt. You have come in by train this morning, I see."

"You know me, then?"

"No, but I observe the second half of a return ticket in the palm of your left glove. You must have started early, and yet you had a good drive in a dog-cart, along heavy roads, before you reached the station."

The lady gave a violent start, and stared in bewilderment at my companion.

"There is no mystery, my dear madam," said he, smiling. "The left arm of your jacket is spattered with mud in no less than seven places. The marks are perfectly fresh. There is no vehicle save a dog-cart which throws up mud in that way, and then only when you sit on the left-hand side of the driver."

"Whatever your reasons may be, you are perfectly correct," said she. "I started from

2. '83 refers to the year 1883.
3. *Knock you up* here means "wake you up."

Big Idea The Uncanny and Mysterious *What does this description of the potential client suggest about the mystery?* **BI₂**

Reading Strategy Analyzing Details *Why has Doyle included these details about the woman's appearance?* **R**

Literary Element Character Archetype *Why might Watson describe Holmes's glance in this way?* **L₂**

SIR ARTHUR CONAN DOYLE **1209**

R1 Reading Strategy

Analyzing Details Answer:
The woman's stepfather has a bad temper and is capable of violence. **OL**

★ **Cultural History**

Gypsies The people referred to as gypsies prefer to be called Roma, which means "people" in their language. When they immigrated into Europe, the term *gypsy* was applied to them because their dark skin made people think they came from Egypt; they became known as Gyptians, a shortened version of *Egyptian*. Eventually, the name became shortened to *gypsy*. In 1995, the Council of Europe approved the term *Roma* in place of *gypsy*. **AS**

---

home before six, reached Leatherhead[4] at twenty past, and came in by the first train to Waterloo. Sir, I can stand this strain no longer; I shall go mad if it continues. I have no one to turn to—none, save only one, who cares for me, and he, poor fellow, can be of little aid. I have heard of you, Mr. Holmes; I have heard of you from Mrs. Farintosh, whom you helped in the hour of her sore need. It was from her that I had your address. Oh, sir, do you not think that you could help me, too, and at least throw a little light through the dense darkness which surrounds me? At present it is out of my power to reward you for your services, but in a month or six weeks I shall be married, with the control of my own income, and then at least you shall not find me ungrateful."

Holmes turned to his desk, and unlocking it, drew out a small case-book, which he consulted.

"Farintosh," said he. "Ah yes, I recall the case; it was concerned with an opal tiara. I think it was before your time, Watson. I can only say, madam, that I shall be happy to devote the same care to your case as I did to that of your friend. As to reward, my profession is its own reward; but you are at liberty to defray whatever expenses I may be put to, at the time which suits you best. And now I beg that you will lay before us everything that may help us in forming an opinion upon the matter."

"Alas!" replied our visitor, "the very horror of my situation lies in the fact that my fears are so vague, and my suspicions depend so entirely upon small points, which might seem trivial to another, that even he to whom of all others I have a right to look for help and advice looks upon all that I tell him about it as the fancies[5] of a nervous woman. He does not say so, but I can read it from his soothing answers and averted eyes. But I have heard, Mr. Holmes, that you can see deeply into the manifold[6] wickedness of the human heart. You may advise me how to walk amid the dangers which encompass me."

"I am all attention, madam."

"My name is Helen Stoner, and I am living with my stepfather, who is the last survivor of one of the oldest Saxon families in England, the Roylotts of Stoke Moran, on the western border of Surrey."

Holmes nodded his head. "The name is familiar to me," said he.

"The family was at one time among the richest in England, and the estates extended over the borders into Berkshire in the north and Hampshire in the west. In the last century, however, four successive heirs were of a dissolute[7] and wasteful disposition, and the family ruin was eventually completed by a gambler in the days of the Regency. Nothing was left save a few acres of ground, and the two-hundred-year-old house, which is itself crushed under a heavy mortgage. The last squire dragged out his existence there, living the horrible life of an aristocratic pauper; but his only son, my stepfather, seeing that he must adapt himself to the new conditions, obtained an advance from a relative, which enabled him to take a medical degree, and went out to Calcutta,[8] where, by his professional skill and his force of character, he established a large practice. In a fit of anger, however, caused by some robberies which had been perpetrated in the house, he beat his native butler to death, and narrowly escaped a capital sentence. As it was, he suffered a long term of imprisonment, and afterward returned to England a morose[9] and disappointed man.

"When Dr. Roylott was in India he married my mother, Mrs. Stoner, the young widow of Major-General Stoner, of the Bengal Artillery. My sister Julia and I were twins, and we were only two years old at the time of my mother's remarriage. She had a

---

4. *Leatherhead* is a town in the county of Surrey.
5. *Fancies* in this sense refers to illusions.
6. *Manifold* means "multiplied greatly."

---

7. *Dissolute* means "immoral."
8. *Calcutta* is the largest city in India.
9. A *morose* person is gloomy and unsociable.

Reading Strategy Analyzing Details *What does this sentence suggest about the woman's stepfather?* **R1**

Additional Support

Skills Practice

GRAMMAR AND LANGUAGE:

Comma Usage Write the following sentence on the board: *My sister Julia and I were twins, and we were only two years old at the time of my mother's remarriage.* **Ask:** Why is a comma used in this sentence? (*The conjunction is connecting two independent clauses so a comma must be used before the conjunction.*) Have students write five of their own sentences using a comma in the same way. **OL**

considerable sum of money—not less than £1000[10] a year—and this she bequeathed[11] to Dr. Roylott entirely while we resided with him, with a provision that a certain annual sum should be allowed to each of us in the event of our marriage. Shortly after our return to England my mother died—she was killed eight years ago in a railway accident near Crewe. Dr. Roylott then abandoned his attempts to establish himself in practice in London, and took us to live with him in the old ancestral house at Stoke Moran. The money which my mother had left was enough for all our wants, and there seemed to be no obstacle to our happiness.

"But a terrible change came over our stepfather about this time. Instead of making friends and exchanging visits with our neighbors, who had at first been overjoyed to see a Roylott of Stoke Moran back in the old family seat, he shut himself up in his house, and seldom came out save to indulge in ferocious quarrels with whoever might cross his path. Violence of temper approaching to mania[12] has been hereditary in the men of the family, and in my stepfather's case it had, I believe, been intensified by his long residence in the tropics. A series of disgraceful brawls took place, two of which ended in the police-court, until at last he became the terror of the village, and the folks would fly at his approach, for he is a man of immense strength, and absolutely uncontrollable in his anger.

"Last week he hurled the local blacksmith over a parapet[13] into a stream, and it was only by paying over all the money which I could gather together that I was able to avert another public exposure. He had no friends at all save the wandering gypsies,[14] and he would give these vagabonds leave to encamp upon the few acres of bramble-covered land which represent the family estate, and would accept in return the hospitality of their tents, wandering away with them sometimes for weeks on end. He has a passion also for Indian animals, which are sent over to him by a correspondent, and he has at this moment a cheetah and a baboon, which wander freely over his grounds, and are feared by the villagers almost as much as their master.

"You can imagine from what I say that my poor sister Julia and I had no great pleasure in our lives. No servant would stay with us, and for a long time we did all the work of the house. She was but thirty at the time of her death, and yet her hair had already begun to whiten, even as mine has."

"Your sister is dead, then?"

"She died just two years ago, and it is of her death that I wish to speak to you. You can understand that, living the life which I have described, we were little likely to see any one of our own age and position. We had, however, an aunt, my mother's maiden sister, Miss Honoria Westphail, who lives near Harrow, and we were occasionally allowed to pay short visits at this lady's house. Julia went there at Christmas two years ago, and met there a half-pay major of marines, to whom she became engaged. My stepfather learned of the engagement when my sister returned, and offered no objection to the marriage; but within a fortnight[15] of the day which had been fixed for the wedding, the terrible event occurred which has deprived me of my only companion."

Sherlock Holmes had been leaning back in his chair with his eyes closed and his head sunk in a cushion, but he half opened his lids now and glanced across at his visitor.

"Pray be precise as to details," said he.

---

10. *£1000* is one thousand pounds, referring to the British monetary system.
11. *Bequeathed* means "left money or property after death."
12. *Mania* is a psychological disorder marked by extreme physical and mental agitation or enthusiasm.
13. A *parapet* is a low wall usually found around a roof.
14. *Gypsies,* or the Roma, are nomadic people originally from northern India who now live primarily in Europe.
15. *Fortnight* is a British term meaning "a period of fourteen days."

Reading Strategy Analyzing Details *Why do you think Doyle has mentioned the stepfather's love of Indian animals?* **R2**

Literary Element Character Archetype *Why would Holmes make this request?* **L**

SIR ARTHUR CONAN DOYLE **1211**

Teach

Analyzing Details

Answer: *The woman did not feel safe in her home. Students may speculate that her apprehension was due not just to the animals but also to the stepfather.* **OL**

⭐ Viewing the Art

The mandrill, which is the largest monkey species, and the drill are the only non-hominids of the primate order larger than the baboon. Although the Viennese painter Oskar Kokoschka (1886–1980) never traveled to the native habitat of the mandrill—the equatorial rain forests of Western Africa—he did pass through North Africa in the late 1920s, where he may have seen a mandrill in captivity.

Ask: How would you react if a mandrill or baboon were loose in your neighborhood? *(Answers will vary. Some students may think that mandrills are relatively harmless. Others may be deathly afraid of large animals.)* **AS**

The Mandrill, 1926. Oskar Kokoschka. Oil on canvas, 125.5 x 102.3 cm. Museum Boymans van Beuningen, Rotterdam, The Netherlands. ⭐

"It is easy for me to be so, for every event of that dreadful time is seared into my memory. The manor-house is, as I have already said, very old, and only one wing is now inhabited. The bedrooms in this wing are on the ground floor, the sitting-rooms being in the central block of the buildings. Of these bedrooms the first is Dr. Roylott's, the second my sister's, and the third my own. There is no communication between them,[16] but they all open out into the same corridor. Do I make myself plain?"

"Perfectly so."

"The windows of the three rooms open out upon the lawn. That fatal night Dr. Roylott had gone to his room early, though we knew that he had not retired to rest, for my sister was troubled by the smell of the strong Indian cigars which it was his custom to smoke. She left her room, therefore, and came into mine, where she sat for some time, chatting about her approaching wedding. At eleven o'clock she rose to leave me, but she paused at the door and looked back.

"'Tell me, Helen,' said she, 'have you ever heard any one whistle in the dead of the night?'

"'Never,' said I.

"'I suppose that you could not possibly whistle, yourself, in your sleep?'

"'Certainly not. But why?'

"'Because during the last few nights I have always, about three in the morning, heard a low, clear whistle. I am a light sleeper, and it has awakened me. I cannot tell where it came from—perhaps from the next room, perhaps from the lawn. I thought that I would just ask you whether you had heard it.'

"'No, I have not. It must be those wretched gypsies in the plantation.'

"'Very likely. And yet if it were on the lawn, I wonder that you did not hear it also.'

"'Ah, but I sleep more heavily than you.'

"'Well, it is of no great consequence, at any rate.' She smiled back at me, closed my door, and a few moments later I heard her key turn in the lock."

"Indeed," said Holmes. "Was it your custom always to lock yourselves in at night?"

"Always."

"And why?"

"I think that I mentioned to you that the doctor kept a cheetah and a baboon. We had no feeling of security unless our doors were locked."

"Quite so. Pray proceed with your statement."

"I could not sleep that night. A vague feeling of impending misfortune impressed me. My sister and I, you will recollect, were twins, and you know how subtle are the links which bind two souls which are so closely allied. It was a wild night. The wind was howling outside, and the rain was beating and splashing against the windows.

---

16. *There is no communication between them* means that there are no doors connecting the rooms.

Reading Strategy Analyzing Details *What does this detail reveal about the woman's emotional state?* **R1**

Additional Support

Skills Practice

WRITING: Creative Writing Discuss with students the importance of point of view in literature. **Ask:** How would the scene of Julia's death have been different if it was told from Julia's point of view? *(Julia would be able to provide more details about what she was hearing, see-* *ing, and feeling. She could also have described the reason she lit the match.)* Have students rewrite the scene from Julia's point of view. Students should incorporate all the descriptions found in Helen's version of the story. **OL**

Suddenly, amid all the hubbub of the gale, there burst forth the wild scream of a terrified woman. I knew that it was my sister's voice. I sprang from my bed, wrapped a shawl round me, and rushed into the corridor. As I opened my door I seemed to hear a low whistle, such as my sister described, and a few moments later a clanging sound, as if a mass of metal had fallen. As I ran down the passage my sister's door was unlocked, and revolved slowly upon its hinges. I stared at it horror-stricken, not knowing what was about to issue from it. By the light of the corridor-lamp I saw my sister appear at the opening, her face blanched[17] with terror, her hands groping for help, her whole figure swaying to and fro like that of a drunkard. I ran to her and threw my arms round her, but at that moment her knees seemed to give way and she fell to the ground. She writhed as one who is in terrible pain, and her limbs were dreadfully convulsed. At first I thought that she had not recognized me, but as I bent over her she suddenly shrieked out, in a voice which I shall never forget: 'Oh, my God! Helen! It was the band! The speckled band!' There was something else which she would fain[18] have said, and she stabbed with her finger into the air in the direction of the doctor's room, but a fresh convulsion seized her and choked her words. I rushed out, calling loudly for my stepfather, and I met him hastening from his room in his dressing-gown. When he reached my sister's side she was unconscious, and though he poured brandy down her throat and sent for medical aid from the village, all efforts were in vain, for she slowly sank and died without having recovered her consciousness. Such was the dreadful end of my beloved sister."

"One moment," said Holmes; "are you sure about this whistle and metallic sound? Could you swear to it?"

"That was what the county coroner asked me at the inquiry. It is my strong impression that I heard it, and yet, among the crash of

Portrait of Edward Cross Holding a Lion Cub, 1820. Jacques-Laurent Agasse.

the gale and the creaking of an old house, I may possibly have been deceived."

"Was your sister dressed?"

"No, she was in her night-dress. In her right hand was found the charred stump of a match, and in her left a matchbox."

"Showing that she had struck a light and looked about her when the alarm took place. That is important. And what conclusions did the coroner come to?"

"He investigated the case with great care, for Dr. Roylott's conduct had long been notorious in the county, but he was unable to find any satisfactory cause of death. My evidence showed that the door had been fastened upon the inner side, and the windows were blocked by old-fashioned shutters with broad iron bars, which were secured every night. The walls were carefully sounded, and

---

17. *Blanched* means "turned suddenly pale."
18. *Fain* is an archaic word meaning "with eagerness."

Reading Strategy Analyzing Details *Why would Holmes say that this detail is important?* **R2**

SIR ARTHUR CONAN DOYLE **1213**

Teach

R2 **Reading Strategy**

Analyzing Details Answer:
This detail means the woman saw or heard something that awakened her before her death. **OL**

★ **Viewing the Art**

Swiss-born English painter Jacques-Laurent Agasse (1767–1849) was one of the most famous animal painters of the late eighteenth and early nineteenth centuries. In addition to art, Agasse studied veterinary science. **Ask:** Does Edward Cross seem similar to or different from Dr. Roylott? Explain. *(Students may infer that both men are privileged collectors of wild animals. Edward Cross looks content, whereas Dr. Roylott was known as a cantankerous hermit.)* **AS**

Differentiated Instruction

Character Motivation Students may not understand why Helen is covering up for her stepfather. **Ask:** Why do you think Helen is trying to protect her step-father? *(Helen has very few close rela-tives since her aunt lives far away and her sister is dead, so she may not want others to think badly of him. She may also be embarrassed by his poor treatment of her.)* **BL**

Objectives
• To analyze universal traits of character archetypes (SE)
• To analyze details and their significance to the plot (SE)
• To practice creative writing (TWE)

1213

BI₁ **Big Idea**

The Uncanny and Mysterious **Answer:** *The lack of marks of violence means finding the cause of death is more difficult.* **OL**

R **Reading Strategy**

Analyzing Details **Answer:** *This injury indicates that the woman has been mistreated by her stepfather and that the stepfather is capable of violence toward his stepdaughters.* **OL**

★ **Writer's Technique**

Allusions Authors use allusions in many ways in literature. The most common use is to reference some information that should be known to the reader. A phrase such as "Herculean task" is an example of allusion because the author is assuming the reader knows who Hercules is and what his myth involved. **Ask:** Why does Doyle use the term *allusion* to describe Julia's dying statement about the speckled band? *(Doyle calls Julia's statement an allusion because she states it as if Helen should understand the statement.)* **AS**

---

were shown to be quite solid all round, and the flooring was also thoroughly examined, with the same result. The chimney is wide, but is barred up by four large staples. It is certain, therefore, that my sister was quite alone when she met her end. Besides, there were no marks of any violence upon her."

"How about poison?"

"The doctors examined her for it, but without success."

"What do you think that this unfortunate lady died of, then?"

"It is my belief that she died of pure fear and nervous shock, though what it was that frightened her I cannot imagine."

"Were there gypsies in the plantation at the time?"

"Yes, there are nearly always some there."

★ "Ah, and what did you gather from this allusion¹⁹ to a band—a speckled band?"

"Sometimes I have thought that it was merely the wild talk of delirium, sometimes that it may have referred to some band of people, perhaps to these very gypsies in the plantation. I do not know whether the spotted handkerchiefs which so many of them wear over their heads might have suggested the strange adjective which she used."

Holmes shook his head like a man who is far from being satisfied.

"These are very deep waters," said he; "pray go on with your narrative."

"Two years have passed since then, and my life has been until lately lonelier than ever. A month ago, however, a dear friend, whom I have known for many years, has done me the honor to ask my hand in marriage. His name is Armitage—Percy Armitage—the second son of Mr. Armitage, of Crane Water, near Reading. My stepfather has offered no opposition to the match, and we are to be married in the course of the spring. Two days ago some repairs were started in the west wing of the building,

---

19. An *allusion* is a reference to something.

Big Idea The Uncanny and Mysterious *How does this fact add to the mystery of Julia's death?* **BI₁**

---

and my bedroom wall has been pierced, so that I have had to move into the chamber in which my sister died, and to sleep in the very bed in which she slept. Imagine, then, my thrill of terror when last night, as I lay awake, thinking over her terrible fate, I suddenly heard in the silence of the night the low whistle which had been the herald of her own death. I sprang up and lit the lamp, but nothing was to be seen in the room. I was too shaken to go to bed again, however, so I dressed, and as soon as it was daylight I slipped down, got a dog-cart at the 'Crown Inn,' which is opposite, and drove to Leatherhead, from whence I have come on this morning with the one object of seeing you and asking your advice."

"You have done wisely," said my friend. "But have you told me all?"

"Yes, all."

"Miss Roylott, you have not. You are screening your stepfather."

"Why, what do you mean?"

For answer Holmes pushed back the frill of black lace which fringed the hand that lay upon our visitor's knee. Five little **livid** spots, the marks of four fingers and a thumb, were printed upon the white wrist.

"You have been cruelly used," said Holmes.

The lady colored deeply and covered over her injured wrist. "He is a hard man," she said, "and perhaps he hardly knows his own strength."

There was a long silence, during which Holmes leaned his chin upon his hands and stared into the crackling fire.

"This is a very deep business," he said, at last. "There are a thousand details which I should desire to know before I decide upon our course of action. Yet we have not a moment to lose. If we were to come to Stoke

---

Reading Strategy Analyzing Details *What does the revelation of this detail reveal about the woman and her stepfather?* **R**

Vocabulary

livid (liv′id) *adj.* bruised

Additional Support

Skills Practice

READING: Predictions Students should be able to make predictions about what has happened to Helen's sister. Have them write their predictions about the culprit, the motive, and the method. Collect these and return them later for review of their accuracy. **OL**

LISTENING AND SPEAKING:

Performance Students should pair up and practice performing the dialogue between Helen and Holmes. After each pair has practiced, they should perform their part in front of the class. **OL**

The Gare Saint-Lazare: Arrival of a Train, 1877. Claude Monet. Oil on canvas, 80.3 x 98.1 cm. Fogg Art Museum, Harvard University Art Museums, Boston. ★

Moran today, would it be possible for us to see over these rooms without the knowledge of your stepfather?"

"As it happens, he spoke of coming into town today upon some most important business. It is probable that he will be away all day, and that there would be nothing to disturb you. We have a housekeeper now, but she is old and foolish, and I could easily get her out of the way."

"Excellent. You are not averse[20] to this trip, Watson?"

"By no means."

"Then we shall both come. What are you going to do yourself?"

"I have one or two things which I would wish to do now that I am in town. But I shall return by the twelve-o'clock train, so as to be there in time for your coming."

"And you may expect us early in the afternoon. I have myself some small business matters to attend to. Will you not wait and breakfast?"

"No, I must go. My heart is lightened already since I have confided my trouble to you. I shall look forward to seeing you again this afternoon." She dropped her thick black veil over her face and glided from the room.

"And what do you think of it all, Watson?" asked Sherlock Holmes, leaning back in his chair.

"It seems to me to be a most dark and sinister business."

"Dark enough and sinister enough."

"Yet if the lady is correct in saying that the flooring and walls are sound, and that the door, window, and chimney are impassable, then her sister must have been undoubtedly alone when she met her mysterious end."

"What becomes, then, of these nocturnal[21] whistles, and what of the very peculiar words of the dying woman?"

"I cannot think."

"When you combine the ideas of whistles at night, the presence of a band of gypsies who are on intimate terms with this old doctor, the fact that we have every reason

---

20. *Averse* means "against or opposed to."

21. *Nocturnal* means "taking place at night."

Big Idea The Uncanny and Mysterious *Why does the woman need to wear a dark veil?* **BI₂**

SIR ARTHUR CONAN DOYLE **1215**

Teach

Character Archetype
Answer: *Villains are usually portrayed as large, imposing, and ugly. Students may offer comparisons to villains in today's books or movies.* **OL**

⭐ Viewing the Art

Henry Arthur Payne (1868–1940) was a British artist best known for a work he did for the Houses of Parliament in London: a mural concerning the origin of the War of the Roses.
Ask: What mood does this painting evoke? Does it match the feeling that Miss Helen Stoner experiences when she goes to bed? *(This painting evokes a mood of relaxation. The sky and room are calm and filled with white light; the curtains are open. This contrasts with the anxiety that Miss Helen Stoner feels.)* **AS**

The End of the Day, 1938. Henry A. Payne. Oil on board, 45.7 x 81.3 cm. Private collection. ⭐

to believe that the doctor has an interest in preventing his stepdaughter's marriage, the dying allusion to a band, and, finally, the fact that Miss Helen Stoner heard a metallic clang, which might have been caused by one of those metal bars which secured the shutters falling back into its place, I think that there is good ground to think that the mystery may be cleared along those lines."

"But what, then, did the gypsies do?"

"I cannot imagine."

"I see many objections to any such theory."

"And so do I. It is precisely for that reason that we are going to Stoke Moran this day. I want to see whether the objections are fatal, or if they may be explained away. But what in the name of the devil!"

The ejaculation[22] had been drawn from my companion by the fact that our door had been suddenly dashed open, and that a huge man had framed himself in the aperture.[23] His costume was a peculiar mixture of the professional and of the agricultural, having a black top-hat, a long frock-coat, and a pair of high gaiters, with a hunting-crop[24] swinging

in his hand. So tall was he that his hat actually brushed the cross-bar of the doorway, and his breadth[25] seemed to span it across from side to side. A large face, seared with a thousand wrinkles, burned yellow with the sun, and marked with every evil passion, was turned from one to the other of us, while his deep-set, bile-shot[26] eyes, and his high, thin, fleshless nose, gave him somewhat the resemblance to a fierce old bird of prey.

"Which of you is Holmes?" asked this apparition.[27]

"My name, sir; but you have the advantage of me," said my companion, quietly.

"I am Dr. Grimesby Roylott, of Stoke Moran."

"Indeed, doctor," said Holmes, blandly. "Pray take a seat."

"I will do nothing of the kind. My stepdaughter has been here. I have traced her. What has she been saying to you?"

"It is a little cold for the time of the year," said Holmes.

"What has she been saying to you?" screamed the old man, furiously.

"But I have heard that the crocuses promise well," continued my companion, imperturbably.[28]

"Ha! You put me off, do you?" said our new visitor, taking a step forward and shaking his hunting-crop. "I know you, you

---

22. Here, *ejaculation* means "a sudden shout."
23. An *aperture* is an opening, in this case, the doorway.
24. The man is dressed in *gaiters,* which are fabric or leather leg coverings reaching to the knee, and he is holding a *hunting-crop,* a short, looped whip.

25. *Breadth* means "width."
26. By *bile-shot eyes,* the author probably means eyes in which the whites are tinted yellow. Bile is a yellowish fluid stored in the liver. An excess of the fluid was once thought to create anger.
27. An *apparition* is a ghost, but the word can be used in a humorous reference to someone who appears unexpectedly, like a ghost.
28. *Imperturbably* means "refusing to become upset."

Literary Element Character Archetype *How does this character compare to the archetypal image of the villain?* **L**

Additional Support

Skills Practice

GRAMMAR: Parallelism Write the following sentence on the board: *Suddenly, however, he started, tapped me on the shoulder, and pointed over the meadows.* Explain the parallelism in this sentence. Write the following on the board: 1. *We stopped for dinner, are driving to the movies, and needed to* put gasoline in the car. 2. *The dogs are playing in the yard, chasing their tails, and ate their treats.* Have students correct the faulty parallelism. *(We stopped for dinner, drove to the movies, and put gasoline in the car. The dogs are playing in the yard, chasing their tails, and eating their treats.)* **OL**

scoundrel! I have heard of you before. You are Holmes, the meddler."

My friend smiled.

"Holmes, the busybody!"

His smile broadened.

"Holmes, the Scotland Yard Jack-in-office!"[29]

Holmes chuckled heartily. "Your conversation is most entertaining," said he. "When you go out close the door, for there is a decided draught."[30]

"I will go when I have said my say. Don't you dare to meddle with my affairs. I know that Miss Stoner has been here. I traced her! I am a dangerous man to fall foul of! See here." He stepped swiftly forward, seized the poker, and bent it into a curve with his huge brown hands.

"See that you keep yourself out of my grip," he snarled; and hurling the twisted poker into the fireplace, he strode out of the room.

"He seems a very **amiable** person," said Holmes, laughing. "I am not quite so bulky, but if he had remained I might have shown him that my grip was not much more feeble than his own." As he spoke he picked up the steel poker, and with a sudden effort straightened it out again.

"Fancy his having the insolence[31] to confound me with the official detective force! This incident gives zest to our investigation, however, and I only trust that our little friend will not suffer from her imprudence[32] in allowing this brute to trace her. And now, Watson, we shall order breakfast, and afterward I shall walk down to Doctors' Commons, where I hope to get some data which may help us in this matter."

It was nearly one o'clock when Sherlock Holmes returned from his excursion. He held in his hand a sheet of blue paper, scrawled over with notes and figures.

"I have seen the will of the deceased wife," said he. "To determine its exact meaning I have been obliged to work out the present prices of the investments with which it is concerned. The total income, which at the time of the wife's death was little short of £1100, is now, through the fall in agricultural prices, not more than £750. Each daughter can claim an income of £250, in case of marriage. It is evident, therefore, that if both girls had married, this beauty[33] would have had a mere pittance,[34] while even one of them would cripple him to a very serious extent. My morning's work has not been wasted, since it has proved that he has the very strongest motives for standing in the way of anything of the sort. And now, Watson, this is too serious for dawdling, especially as the old man is aware that we are interesting ourselves in his affairs; so if you are ready, we shall call a cab and drive to Waterloo. I should be very much obliged if you would slip your revolver into your pocket. An Eley's No. 2 is an excellent argument with gentlemen who can twist steel pokers into knots. That and a tooth-brush are, I think, all that we need."

At Waterloo we were fortunate in catching a train for Leatherhead, where we hired a trap at the station inn, and drove for four or five miles through the lovely Surrey lanes. It was a perfect day, with a bright sun and a few fleecy clouds in the heavens. The trees and wayside hedges were just throwing out their first green shoots, and the air was full of the pleasant smell of the moist earth. To me at least there was a strange contrast between the sweet promise of spring and this sinister quest upon which we were engaged. My companion sat in front of the trap, his arms folded, his hat pulled

---

29. *Scotland Yard* is headquarters of the London police. *Jack-in-office* is a term for a self-important, petty official.

30. A *draught* is a draft of air.

31. *Insolence* means "disrespect."

32. *Imprudence* is a lack of good judgment.

Reading Strategy Analyzing Details *What does this detail suggest about Holmes?* **R**

Vocabulary

amiable (ā′ mē ə bəl) *adj.* good-humored; easy to get along with

33. Here, Holmes is referring ironically to Miss Stone's stepfather, Dr. Grimesby Roylott.

34. A *pittance* is a small and usually inadequate amount of money.

Teach

R Reading Strategy

Analyzing Details Answer: *Holmes is equal in strength to Dr. Roylott even though he did not wish to challenge the man in a physical confrontation.* **OL**

★ Cultural History

Scotland Yard In 1829, the British parliament created the police force of London, England, which was housed in a building known as Great Scotland Yard. Prior to the formation of the police force, the building had been built and used for other purposes. At the time, the police force consisted of just over 1,000 individuals. By 1887, the number had grown to 13,000. Additions to the building did not provide adequately, so a new facility was provided in 1967 and was named New Scotland Yard. **AS**

Building Reading Fluency

Vocabulary Help The description of Dr. Roylott may contain unfamiliar words for some readers. Have each student choose five words from this page of the story and look up the definitions for those words. Once they find the definitions, the student needs to write a short paragraph using the words correctly. Each student should read his or her paragraph aloud. **BL**

Objectives
- To analyze universal traits of character archetypes (SE)
- To analyze details and their significance to the plot (SE)
- To practice using parallel sentence structure (TWE)

Analyzing Details Answer:
Miss Stoner is terrified of her stepfather. **OL**

R2 Reading Strategy

Analyzing Details Answer:
These details indicate that Dr. Roylott does not have enough money to keep his estate in good repair.
Ask: Why might this information be important? *(If Helen's stepfather does not have much money, he could have a motive for wanting to harm Julia and Helen.)* **OL**

★ Writer's Technique

Similes Authors use similes to create images in the minds of readers. Have students identify similes in the story. **Ask:** Why does Doyle use these similes? *(Similes give readers a better picture of what the author is trying to describe.)* Have students practice writing and sharing similes of their own. **AS**

---

down over his eyes, and his chin sunk upon his breast, buried in the deepest thought. Suddenly, however, he started, tapped me on the shoulder, and pointed over the meadows.

"Look there!" said he.

A heavily timbered park stretched up in a gentle slope, thickening into a grove at the highest point. From amid the branches there jutted out the gray gables and high roof-tree of a very old mansion.

"Stoke Moran?" said he.

"Yes, sir, that be the house of Dr. Grimesby Roylott," remarked the driver.

"There is some building going on there," said Holmes; "that is where we are going."

"There's the village," said the driver, pointing to a cluster of roofs some distance to the left; "but if you want to get to the house, you'll find it shorter to get over this stile, and so by the foot-path over the fields. There it is, where the lady is walking."

"And the lady, I fancy, is Miss Stoner," observed Holmes, shading his eyes. "Yes, I think we had better do as you suggest."

We got off, paid our fare, and the trap[35] rattled back on its way to Leatherhead.

"I thought it as well," said Holmes, as we climbed the stile,[36] "that this fellow should think we had come here as architects or on some definite business. It may stop his gossip. Good-afternoon, Miss Stoner. You see that we have been as good as our word."

Our client of the morning had hurried forward to meet us with a face which spoke her joy. "I have been waiting so eagerly for you!" she cried, shaking hands with us warmly. "All has turned out splendidly. Dr. Roylott has gone to town, and it is unlikely that he will be back before evening."

"We have had the pleasure of making the doctor's acquaintance," said Holmes, and in a few words he sketched out what had occurred. Miss Stoner turned white to the lips as she listened.

---

35. Here, a *trap* is a two-wheeled carriage.
36. A *stile* is a set of stairs used to walk over a wall or fence.

"Good heavens!" she cried. "He has followed me, then."

"So it appears."

"He is so cunning that I never know when I am safe from him. What will he say when he returns?"

"He must guard himself, for he may find that there is someone more cunning than himself upon his track. You must lock yourself up from him tonight. If he is violent, we shall take you away to your aunt's at Harrow. Now, we must make the best use of our time, so kindly take us at once to the rooms which we are to examine."

The building was of gray, lichen-blotched stone, with a high central portion, and two curving wings, like the claws of a crab, thrown out on each side. In one of these wings the windows were broken, and blocked with wooden boards, while the roof was partly caved in, a picture of ruin. The central portion was in little better repair, but the right-hand block was comparatively modern, and the blinds in the windows, with the blue smoke curling up from the chimneys, showed that this was where the family resided. Some scaffolding had been erected against the end wall, and the stonework had been broken into, but there were no signs of any workmen at the moment of our visit. Holmes walked slowly up and down the ill-trimmed lawn, and examined with deep attention the outsides of the windows.

"This, I take it, belongs to the room in which you used to sleep, the center one to your sister's, and the one next to the main building to Dr. Roylott's chamber?"

"Exactly so. But I am now sleeping in the middle one."

"Pending the alterations, as I understand. By the way, there does not seem to be any very pressing need for repairs at that end wall."

"There were none. I believe that it was an excuse to move me from my room."

"Ah! that is suggestive. Now, on the other side of this narrow wing runs the corridor

---

Additional Support

Skills Practice

WRITING: Descriptive Writing
Describing the room where Julia died is important to the mystery because the room contains clues to the crime. **Say:** Notice how Doyle uses specific descriptive phrases such as "gaping fireplace" and "worm-eaten oak."

These descriptions are sensory—appeals to at least one of the five senses: sight, touch, smell, taste, and sound. Have students write paragraphs describing their bedrooms. Remind students to incorporate sensory descriptions into their writing. **OL** from which these three rooms open. There are windows in it, of course?"

"Yes, but very small ones. Too narrow for any one to pass through."

"As you both locked your doors at night, your rooms were unapproachable from that side. Now, would you have the kindness to go into your room and bar your shutters."

Miss Stoner did so, and Holmes, after a careful examination through the open window, endeavored in every way to force the shutter open, but without success. There was no slit through which a knife could be passed to raise the bar. Then with his lens he tested the hinges, but they were of solid iron, built firmly into the massive masonry. "Hum!" said he, scratching his chin in some perplexity; "my theory certainly presents some difficulties. No one could pass these shutters if they were bolted. Well, we shall see if the inside throws any light upon the matter."

A small side door led into the white-washed corridor from which the three bedrooms opened. Holmes refused to examine the third chamber, so we passed at once to the second, that in which Miss Stoner was now sleeping, and in which her sister had met with her fate. It was a homely little room, with a low ceiling and a gaping fireplace, after the fashion of old country-houses. A brown chest of drawers stood in one corner, a narrow white-counterpaned bed in another, and a dressing-table on the left-hand side of the window. These articles, with two small wicker-work chairs, made up all the furniture in the room, save for a square of Wilton carpet in the center. The boards round and the paneling of the walls were of brown, worm-eaten oak, so old and discolored that it may have dated from the

On the Pont de l'Europe, 1876–1880. Gustave Caillebotte. Kimbell Art Museum, Fort Worth, TX.

original building of the house. Holmes drew one of the chairs into a corner and sat silent, while his eyes traveled round and round and up and down, taking in every detail of the apartment.

"Where does that bell communicate with?" he asked, at last, pointing to a thick bell-rope which hung down beside the bed, the tassel actually lying upon the pillow.

"It goes to the housekeeper's room."

"It looks newer than the other things?"

"Yes, it was only put there a couple of years ago."

"Your sister asked for it, I suppose?"

"No, I never heard of her using it. We used always to get what we wanted for ourselves."

"Indeed, it seemed unnecessary to put so nice a bell-pull there. You will excuse me for a few minutes while I satisfy myself as to this floor." He threw himself down upon his face with his lens in his hand, and crawled swiftly backward and forward, examining minutely the cracks between the boards. Then he did the same with the woodwork with which the chamber was paneled. Finally he walked over to the bed, and spent some time in staring at it, and in running his eye up and down the wall. Finally he took the bell-rope in his hand and gave it a brisk tug.

Literary Element Character Archetype *What does Holmes's refusal reveal about his character?* **L**

SIR ARTHUR CONAN DOYLE **1219**

Teach

L Literary Element

Character Archetype

Answer: *Holmes does not want to waste time on other rooms; instead, he focuses only on what is important to the investigation.* **OL**

★ Viewing the Art

Gustave Caillebotte (1848–1896) helped to organize the first Impressionist exhibit in Paris in 1874. He was an engineer by trade and painted in a slightly more realistic vein than such other Impressionists as Pierre-Auguste Renoir and Edgar Degas. When he passed away, Caillebotte bequeathed his entire oeuvre—over 500 paintings—to the government.

Ask: What does this painting seem to suggest about industrialization? *(The view of nature, so prevalent in painting of the Romantic period, has been completely consumed by the cold, gray steel of a modern bridge. The characters are masculine and faceless and seem ill-at-ease and bemused in this unnatural environment.)* **AS**

Differentiated Instruction

Less Proficient Readers Students may be confused about what is happening as Holmes investigates the rooms. **Ask:** What clues that Holmes detects in the room make him suspicious? *(Holmes sees a whip, a saucer of milk, a ventilator connected to the other room, and a dummy bell cord.)* **Ask:** Why do these clues make him suspicious? (The only cat in the household is a cheetah, so a saucer of milk is unnecessary. The ventilator is connected to another room, not to the outside as it should be. The bell cord serves no purpose. The whip is unusual for a bedroom.) **BL**

Objectives
- To analyze universal traits of character archetypes (SE)
- To analyze details and their significance to the plot (SE)
- To practice descriptive writing (TWE)

Teach

BI₁ Big Idea

The Uncanny and Mysterious Answer: *The connecting of the two rooms with the ventilator was done on purpose, so it is likely to be a clue to solving the mystery.* **OL**

BI₂ Big Idea

The Uncanny and Mysterious Answer: *Holmes has already figured out the solution to the mystery, even though he has chosen not to reveal the answer yet.* **OL**

L₁ Literary Element

Dialogue Dialogue in stories serves a number of purposes. **Ask:** How does the dialogue move the plot along? *(The dialogue points out the clues Holmes is going to use to solve the case.)* **OL**

★ Viewing the Art

Baker Street, made famous by Sherlock Holmes's fictional address of 221B, is a real street in London. Originally part of an upper-class residential neighborhood, it is now predominantly commercial. **AS**

Baker Street, 20th century. John Sutton. Private collection. ★

"Why, it's a dummy,"³⁷ said he.

"Won't it ring?"

"No, it is not even attached to a wire. This is very interesting. You can see now that it is fastened to a hook just above where the little opening for the ventilator³⁸ is."

"How very absurd! I never noticed that before."

"Very strange!" muttered Holmes, pulling at the rope. "There are one or two very singular points about this room. For example, what a fool a builder must be to open a ventilator into another room, when, with the same trouble, he might have communicated with the outside air!"

"That is also quite modern," said the lady.

"Done about the same time as the bell-rope?" remarked Holmes.

"Yes, there were several little changes carried out about that time."

"They seem to have been of a most interesting character—dummy bell-ropes, and ventilators which do not ventilate. With your permission, Miss Stoner, we shall now carry our researches into the inner apartment."

Dr. Grimesby Roylott's chamber was larger than that of his stepdaughter, but was as plainly furnished. A camp-bed, a small wooden shelf full of books, mostly of a technical character, an arm-chair beside the bed, a plain wooden chair against the wall, a round table, and a large iron safe were the principal things which met the eye. Holmes walked slowly round and examined each and all of them with the keenest interest.

"What's in here?" he asked, tapping the safe.

"My stepfather's business papers."

"Oh! you have seen inside, then?"

"Only once, some years ago. I remember that it was full of papers."

"There isn't a cat in it, for example?"

"No. What a strange idea!"

"Well, look at this!" He took up a small saucer of milk which stood on the top of it.

"No; we don't keep a cat. But there is a cheetah and a baboon."

"Ah, yes, of course! Well, a cheetah is just a big cat, and yet a saucer of milk does not go very far in satisfying its wants, I dare say. There is one point which I should wish to determine." He squatted down in front of the wooden chair, and examined the seat of it with the greatest attention.

"Thank you. That is quite settled," said he, rising and putting his lens in his pocket. "Hello! Here is something interesting!"

The object which had caught his eye was a small dog-lash³⁹ hung on one corner of the bed. The lash, however, was curled upon itself, and tied so as to make a loop of whip-cord.

"What do you make of that, Watson?"

"It's a common enough lash. But I don't know why it should be tied."

"That is not quite so common, is it? Ah, me! it's a wicked world, and when a clever man turns his brains to crime it is the worst of all. I think that I have seen enough now, Miss Stoner, and with your permission we shall walk out upon the lawn." **L₁**

I had never seen my friend's face so grim or his brow so dark as it was when we turned from the scene of this investigation.

---

37. A *dummy* is a decoy or a fake.
38. A *ventilator* is a device that circulates air.

Big Idea The Uncanny and Mysterious *Why might this discovery be important in solving the mystery?* **BI₁**

---

39. A *dog-lash* is a whip used to control dogs.

Big Idea The Uncanny and Mysterious *What does this statement suggest about Holmes's progress toward solving the mystery?* **BI₂**

Additional Support

Skills Practice

GRAMMAR: Confused Words Write the following sentence part on the board: *said Miss Stoner, laying her hand upon my companion's sleeve. Laying* and *lying* are often confused. Explain that *laying* is always used with a direct object and *lying* is not. **Ask:** What are some other words that are often confused? *(Possible answers include* their *and* there, to *and* too, *and* accept *and* except.) Have students write two sentences, using the words *laying* and *lying* correctly. Then have them write two sentences, using another pair of commonly confused words. **OL**

We had walked several times up and down the lawn, neither Miss Stoner nor myself liking to break in upon his thoughts before he roused himself from his reverie.[40]

"It is very essential, Miss Stoner," said he, "that you should absolutely follow my advice in every respect."

"I shall most certainly do so."

"The matter is too serious for any hesitation. Your life may depend upon your compliance."

"I assure you that I am in your hands."

"In the first place, both my friend and I must spend the night in your room."

Both Miss Stoner and I gazed at him in astonishment.

"Yes, it must be so. Let me explain. I believe that that is the village inn over there?"

"Yes, that is the 'Crown,'"

"Very good. Your windows would be visible from there?"

"Certainly."

"You must confine yourself to your room, on pretence[41] of a headache, when your stepfather comes back. Then when you hear him retire for the night, you must open the shutters of your window, undo the hasp, put your lamp there as a signal to us, and then withdraw quietly with everything which you are likely to want into the room which you used to occupy. I have no doubt that, in spite of the repairs, you could manage there for one night."

"Oh yes, easily."

"The rest you will leave in our hands."

"But what will you do?"

"We shall spend the night in your room, and we shall investigate the cause of this noise which has disturbed you."

"I believe, Mr. Holmes, that you have already made up your mind," said Miss Stoner, laying her hand upon my companion's sleeve.

"Perhaps I have."

"Then, for pity's sake, tell me what was the cause of my sister's death."

"I should prefer to have clearer proofs before I speak."

"You can at least tell me whether my own thought is correct, and if she died from some sudden fright."

"No, I do not think so. I think that there was probably some more tangible cause. And now, Miss Stoner, we must leave you, for if Dr. Roylott returned and saw us, our journey would be in vain. Good-bye, and be brave, for if you will do what I have told you, you may rest assured that we shall soon drive away the dangers that threaten you."

Sherlock Holmes and I had no difficulty in engaging a bedroom and sitting-room at the "Crown Inn." They were on the upper floor, and from our window we could command a view of the avenue gate, and of the inhabited wing of Stoke Moran Manor-House. At dusk we saw Dr. Grimesby Roylott drive past, his huge form looming up beside the little figure of the lad who drove him. The boy had some slight difficulty in undoing the heavy iron gates, and we heard the hoarse roar of the doctor's voice, and saw the fury with which he shook his clinched fists at him. The trap drove on, and a few minutes later we saw a sudden light spring up among the trees as the lamp was lit in one of the sitting-rooms.

"Do you know, Watson," said Holmes, as we sat together in the gathering darkness, "I have really some scruples as to taking you tonight. There is a distinct element of danger."

"Can I be of assistance?"

"Your presence might be **invaluable**."

"Then I shall certainly come."

"It is very kind of you."

"You speak of danger. You have evidently seen more in these rooms than was visible to me."

Literary Element Character Archetype *Why would Holmes refuse to tell Miss Stoner about his suspicions at this point in his investigations?* **L2**

Vocabulary

invaluable (in val´ū ə bəl) *adj.* priceless

---

40. A *reverie* is a daydream.
41. *Pretence* refers to the act of pretending for the purpose of deception.

Teach

L2 Literary Element

Character Archetype
Answer: *Students should explain that Holmes wants to have all the facts before giving an answer. He does not want to be wrong.* **OL**

R Reading Strategy

Drawing Conclusions Ask: What does this speech tell you about Helen? (*Obviously, she wants to know what happened to her sister. She also resists the idea of her stepfather's being the culprit.*) **OL**

★ Language History

Tangible The word *tangible* comes from the Latin word *tangere*, which means "to touch." Doyle uses the word to refer to a concrete cause, meaning something that has substance. **Ask:** Why would a word meaning "to touch" be used in this way? (*Something a person can touch has to have substance and has to be grounded in reality.*) **AS**

Differentiated Instruction

Less Proficient Readers Some readers may not understand why Doyle is giving away the identity of the murderer before the end of the story. **Ask:** Why does Doyle give away the identity of the murderer before the end? (*Readers have probably suspected Helen's stepfather since the beginning, so the murderer's identity is not meant to be a surprise. The method he used, however, is still kept a secret, even though Holmes hints at how the act was committed to Watson.*) **BL**

Objectives
• To analyze universal traits of character archetypes (SE)
• To analyze details and their significance to the plot (SE)
• To understand the appropriate usage of words (TWE)

Character Archetype

Answer: *Holmes is saying that he can learn a lot by looking at these details, unlike Watson, who sees the details but does not draw conclusions about them.* **OL**

★ Viewing the Art

Surrey is an English county near London, known for its natural beauty, especially its vast woodlands.

Ask: Does this depiction of a garden remind you of the story's setting? Why or why not? *(Students may mention the story's rural setting in England.)* **AS**

The Garden, Sutton Place, Surrey, England, 1910. ★
Ernest Spence.

"No, but I fancy that I may have deduced a little more. I imagine that you saw all that I did."

"I saw nothing remarkable save the bell-rope, and what purpose that could answer I confess is more than I can imagine."

"You saw the ventilator, too?"

"Yes, but I do not think that it is such a very unusual thing to have a small opening between two rooms. It was so small that a rat could hardly pass through."

"I knew that we should find a ventilator before ever we came to Stoke Moran."

"My dear Holmes!"

"Oh yes, I did. You remember in her statement she said that her sister could smell Dr. Roylott's cigar. Now, of course that suggested at once that there must be a communication between the two rooms. It could only be a small one, or it would have been remarked upon at the coroner's inquiry. I deduced a ventilator."

"But what harm can there be in that?"

"Well, there is at least a curious coincidence of dates. A ventilator is made, a cord is hung, and a lady who sleeps in the bed dies. Does not that strike you?"

"I cannot as yet see any connection."

"Did you observe anything very peculiar about that bed?"

Literary Element Character Archetype *What is Holmes saying about himself and about Watson in this statement?* **L**

"No."

"It was clamped to the floor. Did you ever see a bed fastened like that before?"

"I cannot say that I have."

"The lady could not move her bed. It must always be in the same relative position to the ventilator and to the rope—for so we may call it, since it was clearly never meant for a bell-pull."

"Holmes," I cried, "I seem to see dimly what you are hinting at! We are only just in time to prevent some subtle and horrible crime."

"Subtle enough and horrible enough. When a doctor does go wrong, he is the first of criminals. He has nerve and he has knowledge. Palmer and Pritchard[42] were among the heads of their profession. This man strikes even deeper; but I think, Watson, that we shall be able to strike deeper still. But we shall have horrors enough before the night is over; for goodness' sake let us have a quiet pipe, and turn our minds for a few hours to something more cheerful."

About nine o'clock the light among the trees was extinguished, and all was dark in the direction of the Manor-House. Two hours passed slowly away, and then, suddenly, just at the stroke of eleven, a single bright light shone out in front of us.

"That is our signal," said Holmes, springing to his feet; "it comes from the middle window."

As we passed out he exchanged a few words with the landlord, explaining that we were going on a late visit to an acquaintance, and that it was possible that we might spend the night there. A moment later we were out on the dark road, a chill wind blowing in our faces, and one yellow light twinkling in front of us through the gloom to guide us on our somber errand.

There was little difficulty in entering the grounds, for unrepaired breaches gaped in the old park wall. Making our way among the trees, we reached the lawn, crossed it, and were about to enter through

---

42. *Palmer and Pritchard* were two nineteenth-century doctors who were executed for murder.

Additional Support

LITERARY ELEMENT: Irony Ask: If irony involves saying one thing but meaning the exact opposite, would Holmes's comment "It is a nice household" be classified as ironic? Why or why not? *(Yes, because Holmes really does not mean Dr. Roylott has a nice house-hold. He means the opposite, because Dr. Roylott is violent and has wild animals on his grounds.)* **Ask:** Why might Doyle use irony at this point in the story? *(Doyle might want to show that Holmes is not frightened by their surroundings or their situation.)* **OL**

the window, when out from a clump of laurel-bushes[43] there darted what seemed to be a hideous and distorted child, who threw itself upon the grass with writhing limbs, and then ran swiftly across the lawn into the darkness.

"My God!" I whispered; "did you see it?"

Holmes was for the moment as startled as I. His hand closed like a vise upon my wrist in his agitation. Then he broke into a low laugh, and put his lips to my ear.

"It is a nice household," he murmured. "That is the baboon."

I had forgotten the strange pets which the doctor affected. There was a cheetah, too; perhaps we might find it upon our shoulders at any moment. I confess that I felt easier in my mind when, after following Holmes's example and slipping off my shoes, I found myself inside the bedroom. My companion noiselessly closed the shutters, moved the lamp onto the table, and cast his eyes round the room. All was as we had seen it in the daytime. Then creeping up to me and making a trumpet of his hand, he whispered into my ear again so gently that it was all that I could do to distinguish the words:

"The least sound would be fatal to our plans."

I nodded to show that I had heard.

"We must sit without light. He would see it through the ventilator."

I nodded again.

"Do not go asleep; your very life may depend upon it. Have your pistol ready in case we should need it. I will sit on the side of the bed, and you in that chair."

I took out my revolver and laid it on the corner of the table.

Holmes had brought up a long, thin cane, and this he placed upon the bed beside him. By it he laid the box of matches and the stump of a candle. Then he turned down the lamp, and we were left in darkness.

How shall I ever forget that dreadful vigil?[44] I could not hear a sound, not even the drawing of a breath, and yet I knew that my companion sat open-eyed, within a few feet of me, in the same state of nervous tension in which I was myself. The shutters cut off the least ray of light, and we waited in absolute darkness. From outside came the occasional cry of a night-bird, and once at our very window a long-drawn, cat-like whine, which told us that the cheetah was indeed at liberty. Far away we could hear the deep tones of the parish clock, which boomed out every quarter of an hour. How long they seemed, those quarters! Twelve struck, and one and two and three, and still we sat waiting silently for whatever might befall.

Suddenly there was the momentary gleam of a light up in the direction of the ventilator, which vanished immediately, but was succeeded by a strong smell of burning oil and heated metal. Some one in the next room had lit a dark-lantern. I heard a gentle sound of movement, and then all was silent once more, though the smell grew stronger. For half an hour I sat with straining ears. Then suddenly another sound became audible—a very gentle, soothing sound, like that of a small jet of steam escaping continually from a kettle. The instant that we heard it, Holmes sprang from the bed, struck a match, and lashed furiously with his cane at the bell-pull.

"You see it, Watson?" he yelled. "You see it?"

But I saw nothing. At the moment when Holmes struck the light I heard a low, clear whistle, but the sudden glare flashing into my weary eyes made it impossible for me to tell what it was at which my friend lashed so savagely. I could, however, see that his face was deadly pale, and filled with horror and loathing.

He had ceased to strike, and was gazing up at the ventilator, when suddenly there

---

43. *Laurel-bushes* are bushes covered with sweet-smelling leaves.

Big Idea The Uncanny and Mysterious *How does this event add to the mood of the story?* **BI₁**

---

44. A *vigil* is a period spent watching or guarding someone or something.

Big Idea The Uncanny and Mysterious *How do these details help create a feeling of suspense?* **BI₂**

SIR ARTHUR CONAN DOYLE **1223**

L1 Literary Element

Character Archetype
Answer: *It shows Holmes's bravery and ability to be prepared for anything.* **OL**

L2 Literary Element

Mood Ask: What is the mood of the passage now? (*more suspenseful because readers feel that danger is near*) **Ask:** What elements contribute to the passage's mood? (*the scream, Holmes's grave expression, and his call to Watson to get his pistol*) **OL**

broke from the silence of the night the most horrible cry to which I have ever listened. It swelled up louder and louder, a hoarse yell of pain and fear and anger all mingled in the one dreadful shriek. They say that away down in the village, and even in the distant parsonage,[45] that cry raised the sleepers from their beds. It struck cold to our hearts, and I stood gazing at Holmes, and he at me, until the last echoes of it had died away into the silence from which it rose.

"What can it mean?" I gasped.

"It means that it is all over," Holmes answered. "And perhaps, after all, it is for the best. Take your pistol, and we will enter Dr. Roylott's room."

L2 With a grave face he lit the lamp and led the way down the corridor. Twice he struck at the chamber door without any reply from within. Then he turned the handle and entered, I at his heels, with the cocked pistol in my hand.

It was a singular sight which met our eyes. On the table stood a dark-lantern with the shutter half open, throwing a brilliant beam of light upon the iron safe, the door of which was ajar. Beside this table, on the wooden chair, sat Dr. Grimesby Roylott, clad in a long gray dressing-gown, his bare ankles protruding beneath, and his feet thrust into red heelless Turkish slippers. Across his lap lay the short stock[46] with the long lash which we had noticed during the day. His chin was cocked upward and his eyes were fixed in a dreadful, rigid stare at the corner of the ceiling. Round his brow he had a peculiar yellow band, with brownish speckles, which seemed to be bound tightly round his head. As we entered he made neither sound nor motion.

"The band! the speckled band!" whispered Holmes.

I took a step forward. In an instant his strange head-gear began to move, and there

reared itself from among his hair the squat diamond-shaped head and puffed neck of a loathsome serpent.

"It is a swamp adder!"[47] cried Holmes; "the deadliest snake in India. He has died within ten seconds of being bitten. Violence does, in truth, recoil upon the violent, and the schemer falls into the pit which he digs for another. Let us thrust this creature back into its den, and we can then remove Miss Stoner to some place of shelter, and let the county police know what has happened."

As he spoke he drew the dog-whip swiftly from the dead man's lap, and throwing the noose round the reptile's neck, he drew it from its horrid perch, and carrying it at arm's-length, threw it into the iron safe, which he closed upon it.

Such are the true facts of the death of Dr. Grimesby Roylott, of Stoke Moran. It is not necessary that I should prolong a narrative which has already run to too great a length, by telling how we broke the sad news to the terrified girl, how we conveyed her by the morning train to the care of her good aunt at Harrow, of how the slow process of official inquiry came to the conclusion that the doctor met his fate while indiscreetly playing with a dangerous pet. The little which I had yet to learn of the case was told me by Sherlock Holmes as we traveled back next day.

"I had," said he, "come to an entirely **erroneous** conclusion, which shows, my dear Watson, how dangerous it always is to reason from **insufficient** data. The presence of the gypsies, and the use of the word 'band,' which was used by the poor girl, no doubt to explain the appearance which she had caught a hurried glimpse of by the light of her match, were sufficient to put me upon an entirely wrong scent. I can only claim the

---

45. The *parsonage* is the house provided for a minister by a church.
46. The *stock* is the handle of the whip.

Literary Element Character Archetype *What character trait of Holmes's does this statement illustrate?* **L1**

---

47. An *adder* is a poisonous snake.

Vocabulary

erroneous (ə rō′nē əs) *adj.* inaccurate; wrong
insufficient (in′ sə fish′ ənt) *adj.* not enough

Skills Practice

READING: Comparing and Contrasting Texts Have students read either a different Sherlock Holmes story or another example from the detective genre, such as Edgar Allan Poe's "The Purloined Letter." Ask students to write an essay comparing and contrasting the two texts. **OL**

RESEARCHING: Detective Stories Have students form small groups to research topics related to the detective story. Possible topics might include the history of the detective story, famous fictional detectives, or the backgrounds of authors who wrote similar stories. **OL**

Going into the World. Evert-Jan Boks. Oil on canvas.

merit that I instantly reconsidered my position when, however, it became clear to me that whatever danger threatened an occupant of the room could not come either from the window or the door. My attention was speedily drawn, as I have already remarked to you, to this ventilator, and to the bell-rope which hung down to the bed. The discovery that this was a dummy, and that the bed was clamped to the floor, instantly gave rise to the suspicion that the rope was there as bridge for something passing through the hole and coming to the bed. The idea of a snake instantly occurred to me, and when I coupled it with my knowledge that the doctor was furnished with a supply of creatures from India, I felt that I was probably on the right track. The idea of using a form of poison which could not possibly be discovered by any chemical test was just such a one as would occur to a clever and ruthless man who had had an Eastern training. The rapidity with which such a poison would take effect would also, from his point of view,

be an advantage. It would be a sharp-eyed coroner, indeed, who could distinguish the two little dark punctures which would show where the poison fangs had done their work. Then I thought of the whistle. Of course he must recall the snake before the morning light revealed it to the victim. He had trained it, probably by the use of the milk which we saw, to return to him when summoned. He would put it through this ventilator at the hour that he thought best, with the certainty that it would crawl down the rope and land on the bed. It might or might not bite the occupant, perhaps she might escape every night for a week, but sooner or later she must fall a victim.

"I had come to these conclusions before ever I had entered his room. An inspection of his chair showed me that he had been in the habit of standing on it, which of course would be necessary in order that he should reach the ventilator. The sight of the safe, the saucer of milk, and the loop of whipcord were enough to finally dispel any doubts which may have remained. The metallic clang heard by Miss Stoner was obviously caused by her stepfather hastily closing the door of his safe upon its terrible occupant. Having once made up my mind, you know the steps which I took in order to put the matter to the proof. I heard the creature hiss, as I have no doubt that you did also, and I instantly lit the light and attacked it."

"With the result of driving it through the ventilator."

"And also with the result of causing it to turn upon its master at the other side. Some of the blows of my cane came home, and roused its snakish temper, so that it flew upon the first person it saw. In this way I am no doubt indirectly responsible for Dr. Grimesby Roylott's death, and I cannot say that it is likely to weigh very heavily upon my conscience." ✎

Big Idea The Uncanny and Mysterious *What does this revelation say about Holmes and his mystery-solving abilities?* **BI**

SIR ARTHUR CONAN DOYLE **1225**

1225

Assess

1. Accept reasonable responses.

2. (a) Julia was going to be married. (b) If Helen and Julia married, their stepfather would lose control of the money their mother had left them.

3. (a) The dummy bell and the ventilator connecting Julia's room to her stepfather's room (b) The snake traveled to Julia's room through the ventilator and used the dummy bell as a bridge to her bed.

4. (a) Sit in complete darkness and silence (b) Holmes thinks that he and Watson might become victims if they do not act swiftly enough.

5. (a) Holmes can tell just by looking at the woman that she has traveled by train and by dog-cart. (b) It shows why Holmes is considered an impressive detective and why this desperate woman would have sought him out for help. It also encourages readers to focus on the details Holmes emphasizes.

6. (a) A trained doctor with a quick and violent temper and little money, who keeps animals from India (b) They create a sinister character with a motive for murder and give readers a reason to suspect him of the crime. His vola-

RESPONDING AND THINKING CRITICALLY

Respond

1. Were you surprised by the mystery's solution? Explain.

Recall and Interpret

2. (a)Before her death, how was Julia's life about to change? (b)Why is this detail important to the story?

3. (a)As he examines Miss Stoner's sister's room, what two unusual elements does Holmes discover? (b)How do these two elements relate to the mystery's solution?

4. (a)What do Holmes and Watson do in Miss Stoner's sister's room that night? (b)Why does Holmes consider their actions dangerous?

Analyze and Evaluate

5. (a)How does Doyle demonstrate Holmes's deductive abilities early in the story? (b)Why would this display of Holmes's abilities be important for readers?

6. (a)From the clues in the story, what type of man is Dr. Roylett? (b)Why did Doyle choose these characteristics for Dr. Roylett?

7. (a)How does Holmes determine what happened to Julia? (b)Why were Miss Stoner and Watson unable to draw the same conclusion on their own?

Connect

8. **Big Idea** The Uncanny and Mysterious Sherlock Holmes is often regarded as the greatest fictional detective of all time. From the evidence in this story, why do you think people give him this title?

PRIMARY VISUAL ARTIFACT

The Speckled Band

In Doyle's story, "the speckled band" refers to a snake. When the snake is discovered, Holmes called it a "swamp adder" and claims it is "the deadliest snake in India." However, there is no snake native to India known as the swamp adder. One critic hypothesizes that the snake in question is actually a banded krait (pictured below), which is the second-deadliest snake in India, after the cobra. For this and other speculations on the nature of the speckled band, conduct further research on the Web.

1. How does Doyle describe "the speckled band" in the story?

2. How does this description compare with the appearance of the banded krait in the photo?

3. Why might Doyle have named a snake in his story that does not exist?

Banded Krait snake

---

tile nature also creates tension in the story, as the reader wonders if Holmes can solve the crime before he strikes again.

7. (a) He studies her room and her stepfather's room; finds a few clues, such as the ventilator and the saucer of milk; and deduces what happened.

(b) They are neither as observant as Holmes nor as capable of forming hypotheses from seemingly insignificant details.

8. Student answers will vary, but they should point out how quickly he solved the mystery.

LITERARY ANALYSIS

Literary Element Character Archetype

In certain literary genres, **character archetypes** are used to develop a character that is familiar to the reader. An archetypal character creates certain expectations in the reader, and as a result, the writer can spend more time developing an intricate plot and less time developing character.

1. Describe the traits that make Sherlock Holmes the archetypal detective.

2. Give two examples of other fictional detectives and describe which traits they share with Sherlock Holmes.

Review: Tone

As you learned on page 252, **tone** reflects the author's attitude toward his or her character and subject. Word choice, sentence structure, and figurative language can help you determine the author's tone. In this story, how does the tone of Watson's narrative reveal Doyle's attitude toward Sherlock Holmes?

Partner Activity With a partner, look for examples in the story that help you identify Doyle's attitude towards his main character. Use a chart like the one below to help you get started.

Examples	Tone	Doyle's Attitude toward Holmes
Holmes works "rather for the love of his art than for the acquirement of wealth."	Sincere	Doyle views Holmes as a detective dedicated to solving the most unusual and difficult mysteries.
Watson "had no keener pleasure than in following Holmes in his professional investigations."	Admiring	

READING AND VOCABULARY

Reading Strategy Analyzing Details

In a mystery story, no detail is unimportant. Mystery authors often use two types of **details**: those that will help readers solve the mystery and those that will lead readers astray. Because details are so important to the plot of a mystery, they must be included carefully and at specific points in the action. Details revealed too early could give away the ending; details revealed too late may cause frustration or loss of interest in the reader.

1. Cite two details in this story that contribute to the mystery's solution. Where in the story are these two details introduced?

2. Explain why each of the details is introduced at that particular point in the plot.

Vocabulary Practice

Practice with Word Parts Choose the best definition for each vocabulary word below, using your knowledge of word parts. Use a dictionary if you need help.

1. amiable
   a. good-humored   b. unfriendly
   c. prickly
2. invaluable
   a. of little value   b. priceless
   c. lacking value
3. erroneous
   a. inaccurate   b. correct
   c. complex

Academic Vocabulary

Here are two words from the vocabulary list on page R83.

generate (jen′ ə rāt′) v. to produce or develop

incidence (in′ sə dəns) n. the rate at which something happens

Practice and Apply
1. When does Holmes **generate** his theory of who was responsible for Julia's death?
2. Why does Holmes have such a high **incidence** of success as a detective?

SIR ARTHUR CONAN DOYLE **1227**

Assess

Primary Visual Artifact

1. As yellow with brownish speckles and a diamond-shaped head

2. The banded krait has alternating brown and yellow bands about one inch in width. The coloring of the snakes matches, but brown bands are different from brown speckles.

3. Perhaps to create the snake rather than researching and using a real snake as a model

Literary Element

1. Obsessively attentive to detail, not fearful of villains, cautious, curious, and logical

2. Students' answers will vary, but may include Hercule Poirot from Agatha Christie's novels, Dick Tracy, Columbo, Perry Mason, Batman, Monk, Dr. House, or the characters from *Law & Order*, *CSI*, and *The Closer*.

Review: Tone

Second row, third column of chart: Doyle views Holmes as a man who inspires loyalty in his friends. Students should use quotations from the text for their other answers.

Reading Strategy

1. The stepfather's lack of money, the ventilator, the dummy bell, the saucer of milk, the looped whip-cord, the stepfather's love of Indian animals, and the stepfather's history of violence, among others

---

2. The clues in the beginning are meant to lead readers toward a certain suspect while the clues at the end are meant to show how the crime took place.

Vocabulary

1. a   2. b   3. a

Academic Vocabulary

1. Some may say he knew the right answer before he visited the house. Others may say he solved the mystery after examining both rooms.

2. He is very observant and intelligent and is an expert at deductive reasoning.

Assess

Writing About Literature

Students' essays should

- identify elements of detective or crime fiction, such as the existence of an unsolved crime or mysterious circumstances

- analyze how these elements contribute to the subgenre of detective fiction

Doyle's Language and Style

Students' examples and revisions will vary. Some may say that Holmes's and Watson's use of formal language commands respect, while Dr. Roylott's less-formal use of language helps show readers that he is a savage character.

Revising Check

Some students may have little feel for levels of diction and style. Check students' work to make sure that they are improving their drafts, not merely making the language stilted and obscure.

Writing About Literature

Analyze Genre Elements Each literary genre or sub-genre is characterized by a particular set of traits. For example, stories in the science fiction subgenre are usually set in the future, and gothic literature usually includes supernatural elements. Mystery stories are characterized by their own elements, many of which can be found in "The Adventure of the Speckled Band." Write a short essay identifying and analyzing three of these elements as they are illustrated in the story.

Before you begin drafting, determine which elements you will analyze. Then create an outline listing these elements and examples from the story. The partial outline below should help you get started:

> I. An effective detective
>   A. Holmes suspects a ventilator will be found before he even sees the room
>   B. Holmes solves the mystery with only a few clues
> II.
>   A.
>   B.

After you complete your draft, have a peer read it and suggest revisions. Then proofread and edit your work for errors in spelling, grammar, and punctuation.

Reading Further

Doyle wrote approximately sixty works in which Sherlock Holmes is the main character. Four of these are novels, but the rest have been compiled in collections of short stories. Some of these story collections are listed below:

The Adventures of Sherlock Holmes: The stories collected in this volume were originally published between 1891 and 1892. They include some of Holmes's best-known cases, including "The Adventure of the Speckled Band."

The Memoirs of Sherlock Holmes: This collection contains what was intended to be the last of Doyle's Sherlock Holmes stories. It includes the tale "The Final Problem," in which Holmes is killed.

Doyle's Language and Style

Using Formal Language In "The Adventure of the Speckled Band," Doyle uses formal language to illustrate characteristics of his main characters, Holmes and Watson. Note how formal language affects the dialogue below:

> "I had come to these conclusions before ever I had entered his room. An inspection of his chair showed me that he had been in the habit of standing on it, which of course would be necessary in order that he should reach the ventilator. The sight of the safe, the saucer of milk, and the loop of whip-cord were enough to finally dispel any doubts which may have remained."

This dialogue illustrates formal language in two ways: in its diction and in its sentence structure. Diction refers to the selection of specific words, such as "dispel." Holmes also speaks in long, complex sentences rather than short, choppy ones.

Activity Make a list of five examples of formal language from the story. Then rewrite the sentences using informal language. Organize your examples in a chart like the one shown below. How do your impressions of the characters change according to the kind of language they use to speak or narrate?

Formal Language	Rewritten sentence
"Did you observe anything very peculiar about that bed?"	Did you see anything weird about the bed?

Revising Check

Formal Language When you are writing a formal essay or research paper, formal language is appropriate. Revisit the draft you wrote analyzing genre elements and look for places where you can make your language more formal. Combine short sentences to create longer, more complex sentences. Make sure you have chosen the most accurate and specific words possible. If necessary, use a thesaurus or a dictionary.

Literature Online **Web Activities** For eFlashcards, Selection Quick Checks, and other Web activities, go to www.glencoe.com.

Literature Online

Web Activities Have students access the Web site for interactive activities that will help them assess their understanding of the selection.

Vocabulary Workshop

Using a Thesaurus

"I had no keener pleasure than in following Holmes in his professional investigations, and in admiring the rapid deductions, as swift as intuitions, and yet always founded on a logical basis with which he unraveled the problems which were submitted to him."

—Sir Arthur Conan Doyle, from "The Adventure of the Speckled Band"

Connecting to Literature In this quotation, Sir Arthur Conan Doyle uses synonyms to describe the work of Sherlock Holmes. Although some synonyms are practically interchangeable, many have slight differences in meaning. For example, *rapid* means "moving at a fast rate of speed," while *swift* means "occurring suddenly."

Most dictionaries list and explain the differences among some synonyms, but for many words you will need to consult a thesaurus. A **thesaurus** is a specialized dictionary of synonyms and antonyms. Thesauri are available in many formats—CD-ROM, Internet, software, and print—and can be organized either traditionally by concept or dictionary style.

Traditional Style These thesauri organize words under general concepts. To find a synonym for the adjective *fast*, for example, you would look it up in the alphabetical index. This listing contains several entries, including *speedy, sudden,* and *hasty,* with page references. On those pages, you would find synonyms that are related, respectively, to the basic concepts of *velocity, instantaneity,* and *haste.* Probably the best-known traditional thesaurus is *Roget's Thesaurus.*

Dictionary Style This type of thesaurus presents words in alphabetical order, exactly as a dictionary does. Each word is followed by several synonyms, which are listed by part of speech. Each entry also directs the reader to cross-referenced entries. In this type of thesaurus, you must look up a specific word to find its synonyms. When you select a synonym, look it up in the alphabetical listing to see additional synonyms. J. I. Rodale's *The Synonym Finder* is an example of a dictionary-style thesaurus.

Exercise

1. Using a thesaurus, find two synonyms for each word listed below. Then look up the definitions of those synonyms in a dictionary to identify the precise meaning for each one.

   a. grief   **b.** honor   **c.** strange   **d.** hesitate   **e.** shining

2. Use each word and the synonyms you have found in a sentence. Be sure your sentences reflect the slight differences in meanings for all the words.

▶ **Vocabulary Terms**

A **thesaurus** is a specialized dictionary that lists synonyms and antonyms.

▶ **Test-Taking Tip**

To quickly skim through a dictionary or thesaurus, use the guide words located at the top of each page. These list the first and last entry on a page.

▶ **Reading Handbook**

For more about using a thesaurus, see the Reading Handbook, p. R20.

Literature Online
eFlashcards Visit www.glencoe.com for eFlashcards and other vocabulary activities.

OBJECTIVES
- Use research tools such as a thesaurus.
- Analyze why an author uses particular language.

English Language Coach

Synonyms Discuss the shades of meaning of the following synonyms:

- certain, confident, positive
- surprise, amaze, astound
- opinion, belief, conviction

Provide other examples for students to explain and check in a dictionary. **EL**

Differentiated Instruction

Language Choice Write on the board Doyle's statement *he unraveled the problems.* Ask why the author didn't use the synonym *dilemmas, crises, difficulties, troubles,* or *predicaments.* Point out other passages and help students with less language facility see why the author used certain words. **BL**

Focus

Ask: If you want to avoid repeating the same word, where can you find a good synonym? *(a thesaurus)* **Ask:** What are other situations in which a thesaurus is helpful? *(when looking for a more precise word)* Poll students to see how many are familiar with the various types of thesauri and how to use them.

Teach

Using Guide Words Give students practice using a dictionary-style thesaurus. Provide a list of entry words (e.g., *thesaurus, tire, tread, toady, tongue*), and ask which would appear on the page with these guide words: *tip/tone.* Also have students practice using cross-references to find additional synonyms. Discuss how to use a dictionary to distinguish the shades of meaning of synonyms. **OL**

Assess

Exercise

1. Possible answers:

   a. misfortune, sorrow

   b. praise, respect

   c. odd, eccentric

   d. procrastinate, be afraid

   e. illustrious, luminous

2. Sentences should highlight the specific shade of meaning of each synonym.

Literature Online

eFlashcards Have students access the Web site for more practice with thesauri.

1229

Focus

BELLRINGER

Bellringer Options
Daily Language Practice Transparency 101
Or write the word *criminal* on the board. **Ask:** What does it mean to be a criminal? Discuss different types of criminals. **Ask:** Once someone is a criminal, is that person a criminal for life? Find out if students feel it is possible to commit a crime and not be a criminal or to be a criminal without committing a crime.

Literature Online

Author Search To expand students' appreciation of O. Henry, have them access the Web site for additional information and resources.

A Retrieved Reformation

MEET O. HENRY

A prison sentence changed O. Henry from a novice writer to an American master of the short story.

Born William Sydney Porter in Greensboro, North Carolina, Henry was raised by his aunt and grandmother. He left school at fifteen and moved to Texas, where he held a string of low-level jobs. In 1887 he married Athol Estes Roach and they moved to Austin, where he worked as a bank teller, and then to Houston, where he became a newspaper columnist.

"Inject a few raisins of conversation into the tasteless dough of existence."

—O. Henry

In 1896 Henry was indicted for embezzling bank funds, and unwilling to stand trial, he fled to Honduras. Six months later, on receiving news of his wife's illness, Henry returned to the United States. Although he was convicted of embezzlement and sentenced to five years in Ohio State Penitentiary, the misappropriation may have had more to do with careless record keeping than calculated criminal behavior. While in prison, Henry assumed his pen name and wrote his first national story—"Whistling Dick's Christmas Stocking" (1899).

Irony and Coincidence Henry's stories feature classic plotlines that often lead to ironic endings, as in "The Gift of the Magi" (1906) and "The Ransom of Red Chief" (1910). Some of his stories deal with crimes and criminals, but the crimes are rarely violent and the criminals are not malicious. His works were panned by critics as overly sentimental, but

Henry found readers eager to embrace his mastery of surprise endings.

After his release from prison in 1902, Henry moved to New York and began writing short stories for the magazine *World*. That city and the Southwest were the settings for many of his stories. In his lifetime, Henry published ten books of fiction and more than 250 short stories.

Surprise Endings Though a prolific writer, Henry suffered from failing health, financial problems, and alcoholism, and he died of cirrhosis of the liver.

As an example of irony that Henry would appreciate, the city that charged him with embezzlement now honors him as a native son. Austin's Parks and Recreation Department restored the house where Henry and his family lived from 1893 to 1895, and turned it into the O. Henry Museum. The museum offers creative writing programs for adults and children.

Another tribute to Henry was established in 1918 by the Society of Arts and Sciences. The O. Henry Awards is an annual collection of the best American and Canadian short stories.

O. Henry was born in 1862 and died in 1910.

Literature Online **Author Search** For more about O. Henry, go to www.glencoe.com.

1230 UNIT 6 GENRE FICTION

Selection Skills

Literary Elements
- Humor (SE pp. 1231–1239)
- Figures of Speech (SE p. 1239)

A Retrieved Reformation

Reading Skills
- Making and Verifying Predictions (SE pp. 1231–1239)
- Analyzing Text Structure (TWE p. 1234)

Vocabulary Skills
- Context Clues (SE pp. 1231, 1239)

Listening/Speaking/Viewing Skills
- Analyzing Art (SE pp. 1234, 1237)
- Music and Movies (TWE pp. 1236)

Writing Skills/Grammar
- Analysis (SE p. 1239)
- Past Perfect Tense (TWE p. 1232)

Connecting to the Story

"A Retrieved Reformation" is about a pardoned criminal and the choices he makes after his release from prison. Henry incorporates irony and a surprise ending into the story. Before you read, think about the following questions:

- Do you believe that a criminal can change for the better? Why or why not?
- What experiences or influences do you think have the power to bring about major changes?

Building Background

Henry probably drew on events in his own life when he wrote "A Retrieved Reformation." Set primarily in the South, an area familiar to Henry, the story revolves around banking and robbery, two subjects he knew well. The main character, Jimmy Valentine, demonstrates the positive results of hope and industry as well as Henry's belief in the human capacity for goodness.

Setting Purposes for Reading

Big Idea The Uncanny and Mysterious

Early in "A Retrieved Reformation," the prison warden says, "Stop cracking safes, and live straight." This advice foreshadows an uncanny situation at the end of the story. As you read, look for this and other mysterious circumstances.

Literary Element Humor

Literary **humor** relies on the writer's ability to describe a character or an event in an amusing way. Writers use many techniques—exaggeration, puns, sarcasm, verbal irony—to create humor. As you read, watch for examples of humor in "A Retrieved Reformation."

- See Literary Terms Handbook, p. R8.

Literature Online **Interactive Literary Elements Handbook** To review or learn more about the literary elements, go to www.glencoe.com.

Reading Strategy Making Predictions

Making predictions, or reasonable guesses, about what may happen in a story can increase comprehension. As you read, think about what may happen next. Verify, or see whether your predictions were right, at the end of the story.

Reading Tip: Taking Notes In a chart, explain and support at least three predictions about the story.

Prediction	Explanation	Verification
I think that shoes will play some part in the story.	The prison shoe shop and "stitching uppers" are mentioned in the first sentence.	Valentine opens a shoe store.

Vocabulary

assiduously (ə sij´ oo əs lē) adv. carefully diligent; persistently attentive; p. 1232 *Luis worked assiduously on the complicated assignment.*

retribution (ret´rə bū´shən) n. punishment; justice; p. 1234 *Do you think that detention is sufficient retribution for vandalism?*

exclusive (iks klōo´siv) adj. single or sole; stylish, fashionable; p. 1235 *The elegant new store features an exclusive line of leather purses.*

unobtrusively (un´əb trōo´siv lē) adv. inconspicuously; discreetly; p. 1236 *To avoid interrupting, Brock sat unobtrusively in the back.*

anguish (ang´gwish) n. extreme suffering, pain, or anxiety; p. 1237 *Anna felt intense anguish at hearing of her grandmother's death.*

Vocabulary Tip: Context Clues Context clues are surrounding words or phrases that can help a reader interpret an unfamiliar word.

OBJECTIVES
In studying this selection, you will focus on the following:
- recognizing and analyzing humor
- making and verifying predictions
- writing to evaluate figures of speech

O. HENRY **1231**

Focus

Summary

Jimmy Valentine, a bank robber, leaves prison and returns to a life of crime. He sets up shop as Ralph Spencer, a shoe salesman. He meets Miss Annabel Adams, the banker's daughter. They fall in love and plan to marry. Just as Spencer is about to abandon his old life, Annabel's niece gets locked in the bank's new safe. To save the girl, Valentine must reveal his identity in front of a detective. Valentine saves the girl, and the detective, pretending not to know him, walks away.

V Vocabulary

Vocabulary File Say: Add these words and definitions to your vocabulary file. For each word, include a sentence that gives you an example of how to use the word. **OL** Students with English language needs should include the pronunciations of these words in their files. **EL**

Literature Online

Literary Elements Have students access the Web site to improve their understanding of humor.

Teach

Big Idea

The Uncanny and Mysterious Say: Keep the following questions in mind as you read: How does your opinion of Jimmy Valentine change as the story progresses? Which aspect of the plot do you find most uncanny? *(Students will have a variety of responses. Some will come to like Valentine and be happy that he is not going back to prison. Some will think he still needs to be punished for his past crimes. They may list one of the following examples as the most uncanny: Annabel's being the banker's daughter, Valentine being able to save the young girl because of his criminal background, Price's pretending not to know Valentine.)* **OL**

Readability Scores
Dale-Chall: 5.2
DRP: 56
Lexile: 880

Woman with an umbrella, or *The Walk,* 1981. Louis Anquetin. Oil on canvas.

A Retrieved Reformation

O. Henry

A guard came to the prison shoe shop, where Jimmy Valentine was **assiduously** stitching uppers, and escorted him to the front office. There the warden handed Jimmy his pardon, which had been signed that morning by the governor.

Jimmy took it in a tired kind of way. He had served nearly ten months of a four-year sentence. He had expected to stay only about three months, at the longest. When a man with as many friends on the outside as Jimmy Valentine had is received in the "stir"[1] it is hardly worth while to cut his hair.

"Now, Valentine," said the warden, "you'll go out in the morning. Brace up, and make a man out of yourself. You're not a bad fellow at heart. Stop cracking safes, and live straight."

"Me?" said Jimmy, in surprise. "Why, I never cracked a safe in my life."

"Oh, no," laughed the warden. "Of course not. Let's see, now. How was it you happened to get sent up on that Springfield job? Was it because you wouldn't prove an alibi for fear of compromising somebody in extremely high-toned society? Or was it simply a case of a mean old jury that had it in for you? It's always one or the other with you innocent victims."

"Me?" said Jimmy, still blankly virtuous.[2] "Why, warden, I never was in Springfield in my life!"

"Take him back, Cronin," smiled the warden, "and fix him up with outgoing clothes. Unlock him at seven in the morning, and let him come to the bullpen.[3] Better think over my advice, Valentine."

At a quarter past seven on the next morning Jimmy stood in the warden's outer office.

---

1. *Stir* is a slang term for "prison."

Vocabulary

assiduously (ə sij´ oo əs lē) *adv.* carefully diligent; persistently attentive

2. *Virtuous* means "exhibiting virtue" or being "righteous or chaste."
3. Here, *bullpen* refers to the warden's outer office.

1232 UNIT 6 GENRE FICTION

Additional Support

Skills Practice

GRAMMAR AND LANGUAGE: Past Perfect Tense Past perfect tense shows that one past action or condition began and ended before another past action started. At the beginning of "A Retrieved Reformation," O. Henry uses the past perfect tense to give background information about the events that led to the action of the story. **Ask:** When and where does the story begin? *(in prison the day before Valentine's release)* Ask students to identify examples of past perfect tense. *(The first two paragraphs include "had been signed," "had served," and "had expected.")* **OL**

1232

He had on a suit of the villainously fitting,[4] ready-made clothes and a pair of the stiff, squeaky shoes that the state furnishes to its discharged compulsory[5] guests.

The clerk handed him a railroad ticket and the five-dollar bill with which the law expected him to rehabilitate himself into good citizenship and prosperity. The warden gave him a cigar, and shook hands. Valentine, 9762, was chronicled on the books "Pardoned by Governor," and Mr. James Valentine walked out into the sunshine.

Disregarding the song of the birds, the waving green trees, and the smell of the flowers, Jimmy headed straight for a restaurant. There he tasted the first sweet joys of liberty in the shape of a broiled chicken and a bottle of wine—followed by a cigar a grade better than the one the warden had given him.

From there he proceeded leisurely to the depot. He tossed a quarter into the hat of a blind man sitting by the door, and boarded his train. Three hours set him down in a little town near the state line. He went to the café of one Mike Dolan and shook hands with Mike, who was alone behind the bar.

"Sorry we couldn't make it sooner, Jimmy, me boy," said Mike. "But we had that protest from Springfield to buck against, and the governor nearly balked. Feeling all right?"

"Fine," said Jimmy. "Got my key?"

He got his key and went upstairs, unlocking the door of a room at the rear. Everything was just as he had left it. There on the floor was still Ben Price's collar button that had been torn from that eminent[6] detective's shirt when they had overpowered Jimmy to arrest him.

Pulling out from the wall a folding bed, Jimmy slid back a panel in the wall, and dragged out a dust-covered suitcase. He opened this and gazed fondly at the finest set of burglar's tools in the East. It was a complete set, made of specially tempered steel, the latest designs in drills, punches, braces and bits, jimmies, clamps, and augers, with two or three novelties[7] invented by Jimmy himself, in which he took pride.

In half an hour Jimmy went downstairs and through the café. He was now dressed in tasteful and well-fitting clothes,[8] and carried his dusted and cleaned suitcase in his hand.

"Got anything on?" asked Mike Dolan, genially.

"Me?" said Jimmy, in a puzzled tone. "I don't understand. I'm representing the New York Amalgamated Short Snap Biscuit Cracker and Frazzled Wheat Company."

This statement delighted Mike to such an extent that Jimmy had to take a seltzer-and-milk on the spot. He never touched "hard" drinks.

A week after the release of Valentine, 9762, there was a neat job of safe burglary done in Richmond, Indiana, with no clue to the author. A scant $800 dollars was all that was secured.

Two weeks after that a patented, improved, burglar-proof safe in Logansport was opened like a cheese to the tune of $1500.

That began to interest the rogue-catchers.[9] Then an old-fashioned bank-safe in Jefferson City became active and threw out of its crater an eruption of banknotes amounting to $5000.

The losses were now high enough to bring the matter up into Ben Price's class of work. By comparing notes, a remarkable similarity

---

4. *Villainously fitting* means "fitting so poorly that the wearer looks bad."
5. *Compulsory* means "mandatory" or "enforced."
6. *Eminent* means "well-known and distinguished."

Reading Strategy Making Predictions *What does this act show about Jimmy Valentine's character? Predict how you think he might grow and change later in the story.* **R1**

Reading Strategy Making Predictions *How does Valentine's action here fit in with your previous prediction?* **R2**

7. *Novelties* are "things that are new or unusual."
8. Note that Valentine's clothes are now "tasteful and well-fitting" rather than "villainously fitting."
9. A *rogue* is "a dishonest or worthless person."

Literary Element Humor *Explain how this is an example of humor. If you need to, look up the definitions for some of the words.* **L**

O. HENRY **1233**

Teach

R1 Reading Strategy

Making Predictions
Answer: *Valentine seems to take his freedom or the simple things in life for granted. This suggests his eventual downfall or his learning to value simple joys.* **OL**

R2 Reading Strategy

Making Predictions
Answer: *This action displays a generosity that is contrary to the criminal stereotype. It shows the kind and generous side of Valentine.* **OL**

L Literary Element

Humor Answer: *Valentine's company is obviously not real; the name makes little sense: biscuit cracker is redundant, and it is unlikely that anyone would want wheat that is "frazzled"—weary or frayed.* **OL**

 CheckPoint

Use the CheckPoint questions on Presentation Plus! to monitor students' comprehension. These questions can be used with interactive response keypads for immediate student feedback.

English Language Coach

Understanding Slang and Idioms

Nonnative speakers may have trouble understanding some phrases in the story. Write the following words on the board, and have students find them in their text. Then use context and other resources such as dictionaries for slang or idioms to help students decipher meaning. ("col-lared" – taken aside in a swift movement, possibly by the collar of one's shirt; "stop over"– to stay somewhere briefly; "wind up"– to end or finish something; "old scores"– refers to the "settle old scores" idiom, which usually means harming someone who has harmed you in the past) **EL**

Objectives

- To make predictions as a reading strategy (SE)
- To recognize and analyze humor (SE)
- To understand and identify the use of past perfect tense (TWE)

1233

Teach

in the methods of the burglaries was noticed. Ben Price investigated the scenes of the robberies, and was heard to remark: "That's Dandy Jim Valentine's autograph. He's resumed business. Look at that combination knob—jerked out as easy as pulling up a radish in wet weather. He's got the only clamps that can do it. And look how clean those tumblers were punched out! Jimmy never has to drill but one hole. Yes, I guess I want Mr. Valentine. He'll do his bit next time without any short-time or clemency foolishness."

Ben Price knew Jimmy's habits. He had learned them while working up the Springfield case. Long jumps, quick get-aways, no confederates, and a taste for good society—these ways had helped Mr. Valentine to become noted as a successful dodger of **retribution**. It was given out that

Vocabulary

retribution (ret´rə bū´shən) n. punishment; justice

The Bank, 1899. Francis Donkin Bedford.
Viewing the Art: How does this image help you picture the story's setting? Explain. ⭐

Additional Support

Skills Practice

READING: Analyzing Text Structures Narrative fiction uses a primarily chronological structure, presenting events in time order. Ask students for examples of word clues that will help them identify chronological order; write them on the board. (*Examples include* first, next, then, later, after, *and* finally.) Have students look for time order clues in the story. (*Students should list "At the end of a year," "On the Monday night after," "The next morning," "After breakfast," and "Then they went on to the bank."*) **OL**

Ben Price had taken up the trail of the elusive cracksman, and other people with burglar-proof safes felt more at ease.

One afternoon Jimmy Valentine and his suitcase climbed out of the mailback in Elmore, a little town five miles off the railroad down in the black-jack country of Arkansas. Jimmy, looking like an athletic young senior just home from college, went down the broad sidewalk toward the hotel.

A young lady crossed the street, passed him at the corner, and entered a door over which was the sign "The Elmore Bank." Jimmy Valentine looked into her eyes, forgot what he was, and became another man. She lowered her eyes and colored slightly. Young men of Jimmy's style and looks were scarce in Elmore.

Jimmy collared[10] a boy loafing on the steps of the bank as if he were one of the stockholders and began to ask him questions about the town, feeding him dimes at intervals. By and by the young lady came out, looking royally unconscious of the young man with the suitcase, and went her way.

"Isn't that young lady Miss Polly Simpson?" asked Jimmy, with specious[11] guile.[12]

"Naw," said the boy. "She's Annabel Adams. Her pa owns this bank. What'd you come to Elmore for? Is that a gold watch-chain? I'm going to get a bulldog. Got any more dimes?"

Jimmy went to the Planters' Hotel, registered as Ralph D. Spencer, and engaged a room. He leaned on the desk and declared his platform to the clerk. He said he had come to Elmore to look for a location to go into business. How was the shoe business, now, in the town? He had thought of the shoe business. Was there an opening?

The clerk was impressed by the clothes and manner of Jimmy. He, himself, was something of a pattern of fashion to the thinly gilded youth of Elmore, but he now perceived his shortcomings. While trying to figure out Jimmy's manner of tying his four-in-hand[13] he cordially gave information.

Yes, there ought to be a good opening in the shoe line. There wasn't an **exclusive** shoe store in the place. The dry goods and general stores handled them. Business in all lines was fairly good. Hoped Mr. Spencer would decide to locate in Elmore. He would find it a pleasant town to live in, and the people very sociable.

Mr. Spencer thought he would stop over in the town a few days and look over the situation. No, the clerk needn't call the boy. He would carry up his suitcase, himself; it was rather heavy.

Mr. Ralph Spencer, the phoenix[14] that arose from Jimmy Valentine's ashes—ashes left by the flame of a sudden and alterative attack of love—remained in Elmore, and prospered. He opened a shoe store and secured a good run of trade.

Socially he was also a success, and made many friends. And he accomplished the wish of his heart. He met Miss Annabel Adams and became more and more captivated by her charms.

At the end of a year the situation of Mr. Ralph Spencer was this: he had won the respect of the community, his shoe store was flourishing, and he and Annabel were engaged to be married in two weeks. Mr. Adams, the typical, plodding, country banker, approved of Spencer. Annabel's pride in him almost

---

10. Here, *collared* means "grabbed."
11. *Specious* means "possessing a deceptive attraction" or "having a false look of truth."
12. *Guile* means "deceitful cunning" or "a way of being clever or devious."

Big Idea The Uncanny and Mysterious Elusive *means* "mysterious." What qualities make Valentine mysterious? **BI₁**

Reading Strategy Making Predictions *What is happening here? What do you think will happen next?* **R**

Big Idea The Uncanny and Mysterious *Explain what is uncanny and mysterious about this information.* **BI₂**

---

13. A *four-in-hand* is a "knot for a necktie."
14. The *phoenix* is a legendary bird that lived for five hundred years, was consumed in flames, and then rose from ashes to live again.

Vocabulary

exclusive (iks klōō′siv) *adj.* single or sole; stylish, fashionable

O. HENRY **1235**

B1 Big Idea

The Uncanny and Mysterious Ask: What is uncanny about Ben Price's arrival? *(It is strange that Ben Price finds Valentine just as Valentine is making his final commitment to living the straight life.)* **OL**

R1 Reading Strategy

Making Predictions Ask: Why has the author included a scene in the bank safe? What do you think is going to happen next? *(Students will probably predict that someone is going to get locked in the safe or that Valentine is going to have to break into it for some other reason.)* **OL**

---

equalled her affection. He was as much at home in the family of Mr. Adams and that of Annabel's married sister as if he were already a member.

One day Jimmy sat down in his room and wrote this letter, which he mailed to the address of one of his old friends in St. Louis:

> Dear Old Pal:
>
> I want you to be at Sullivan's place, in Little Rock, next Wednesday night, at nine o'clock. I want you to wind up some little matters for me. And, also, I want to make you a present of my kit of tools. I know you'll be glad to get them—you couldn't duplicate the lot for a thousand dollars. Say, Billy, I've quit the old business—a year ago. I've got a nice store. I'm making an honest living, and I'm going to marry the finest girl on earth two weeks from now. It's the only life, Billy—the straight one. I wouldn't touch a dollar of another man's money now for a million. After I get married I'm going to sell out and go West, where there won't be so much danger of having old scores brought up against me. I tell you, Billy, she's an angel. She believes in me; and I wouldn't do another crooked thing for the whole world. Be sure to be at Sally's, for I must see you.
>
> Your old friend,
> Jimmy

B1 On the Monday night after Jimmy wrote this letter, Ben Price jogged **unobtrusively** into Elmore in a livery buggy. He lounged about town in his quiet way until he found out what he wanted to know. From the drug store across the street from Spencer's shoe store he got a good look at Ralph D. Spencer.

Going to marry the banker's daughter, are you, Jimmy? said Ben to himself, softly. Well, I don't know!

The next morning Jimmy took breakfast at the Adamses. He was going to Little Rock

---

that day to order his wedding suit and buy something nice for Annabel. That would be the first time he had left town since he came to Elmore. It had been more than a year now since those last professional "jobs," and he thought he could safely venture out.

After breakfast quite a family party went downtown together—Mr. Adams, Annabel, Jimmy, and Annabel's married sister and her two little girls, aged five and nine. They came by the hotel where Jimmy still boarded, and he ran up to his room and brought down his suitcase. Then they went on to the bank. There stood Jimmy's horse and buggy and Dolph Gibson, who was going to drive him over to the railroad station.

All went inside the high, carved-oak railings into the banking room—Jimmy included, for Mr. Adams' future son-in-law was welcome anywhere. The clerks were pleased to be greeted by the good-looking, agreeable young man who was going to marry Miss Annabel.

Jimmy set his suitcase down. Annabel, whose heart was bubbling with happiness and lively youth, put on Jimmy's hat and picked up the suitcase. "Wouldn't I make a nice drummer?" said Annabel. "My, Ralph, how heavy it is. Feels like it was full of gold bricks."

"Lot of nickel-plated shoehorns in there," said Jimmy, coolly, "that I'm going to return. Thought I'd save express charges by taking them up. I'm getting economical."

The Elmore Bank had just put in a new safe and vault. Mr. Adams was very proud of it, and insisted on an inspection by every- **R1** one. The vault was a small one, but it had a new patented door. It fastened with three solid steel bolts thrown simultaneously[15] with a single handle, and had a time lock.

Mr. Adams beamingly explained its workings to Mr. Spencer, who showed a courteous but not too intelligent interest. The two children, May and Agatha, were delighted by the shining metal and funny clock and knobs.

---

15. *Simultaneously* means "at the same time."

Skills Practice

LISTENING AND VIEWING: Music and Movies This O. Henry story has inspired plays, movies, and songs. You may want to acquire one of the following to listen to or view in class.

- the 1920 version of *Alias Jimmy Valentine*

- Bing Crosby's recording of "When Jimmy Valentine Gets Out"

Have students take notes when listening or viewing. Discuss how these versions compare with the story they have read. **OL**

While they were thus engaged, Ben Price sauntered[16] in and leaned on his elbow, looking casually inside between the railings. He told the teller he didn't want anything; he was just waiting for a man he knew.

Suddenly there were screams from the women, and a commotion. Unperceived by the elders, May, the nine-year-old girl, in a spirit of play, had shut Agatha in the vault. She had then shot the bolts and turned the knob of the combination as she had seen Mr. Adams do.

The old banker sprang to the handle and tugged at it.

"The door can't be opened," he groaned. "The clock hasn't been wound nor the combination set."

Agatha's mother screamed again, hysterically.

"Hush!" said Mr. Adams, raising his trembling hand. "All be quiet for a moment. Agatha!" he called as loudly as he could. "Listen to me." During the following silence they could just hear the faint sound of the child wildly shrieking in the dark vault in a panic of terror.

"My precious darling!" wailed the mother. "She will die of fright! Open the door! Oh, break it open! Can't you men do something?"

"There isn't a man nearer than Little Rock who can open that door," said Mr. Adams, in a shaky voice. "My God! Spencer, what shall we do? That child—she can't stand it long in there. There isn't enough air, and, besides, she'll go into convulsions from fright."

Agatha's mother, frantic now, beat the door of the vault with her hands. Somebody wildly suggested dynamite. Annabel turned to Jimmy, her large eyes full of **anguish**, but not yet despairing. To a woman nothing seems quite impossible to the powers of the man she worships.

---

16. *Sauntered* means "casually walked" or "strolled."

Reading Strategy Making Predictions *Explain the irony in this passage and the possible ways that this drama could end.* **R2**

Vocabulary

anguish (ang′gwish) *n.* extreme suffering, pain, or anxiety

The Charing Cross to Bank Omnibus. Thomas Musgrove Joy. Oil on canvas.

Viewing the Art: What personality does this woman convey? Does it reflect that of Annabel Adams? ⭐

"Can't you do something, Ralph—*try,* won't you?"

He looked at her with a queer, soft smile in his keen eyes.

"Annabel," he said, "give me that rose you are wearing, will you?"

Hardly believing that she had heard him aright, she unpinned the bud from the bosom of her dress and placed it in his hand. Jimmy stuffed it into his vest pocket, threw off his coat, and pulled up his shirt sleeves. With that act Ralph D. Spencer passed away and Jimmy Valentine took his place.

"Get away from the door, all of you," he commanded.

Literary Element Humor *Explain how this small detail provides amusement.* **L**

O. HENRY **1237**

Teach

R2 **Reading Strategy**

Making Predictions
Answer: *Some ironies: Valentine, an accomplished safecracker, just happens to be present. He could save himself by not revealing that he can open the safe, or he can expose himself by opening it and thus saving the child's life.* **OL**

L **Literary Element**

Humor Answer: *Valentine's asking for the rose in the midst of this crisis is a quirky gesture that implies that love has led him to reveal his criminal skill to save the child.* **OL**

⭐ **Viewing the Art**

Answer: *Answers will vary. Students may say that the woman seems friendly and wealthy. Her apparently upbeat attitude seems similar to that of Annabel Adams.* **AS**

Differentiated Instruction

Research Attitudes Invite advanced students to study the societal implications of the story. **Ask:** If a person commits a crime, does that make him or her a criminal forever? Why does our society imprison people? How do we view people who have served prison time? Have students research these issues by reading as well as interviewing people in the community. Encourage them to present a report to the class. *(Students should support their ideas with references to Henry's story and to other cultural references or personal experiences.)* **AL**

Objectives
• To make predictions as a reading strategy (SE)
• To recognize and analyze humor (SE)
• To appreciate stories presented in music and film forms (TWE)

Teach

BI Big Idea

The Uncanny and Mysterious Ask: Do you find Price's action believable? *(Some students will say no because it is Price's job to arrest Valentine; some will find the action believable because Price recognizes that Valentine has changed.)* **OL**

★ Literary History

O. Henry's Words O. Henry once stated, "My advice to you, if you should ever be in a hold up, is to line up with the cowards and save your bravery for an occasion when it may be of some benefit to you." **Ask:** What do you think he meant by this? How does it relate to the story you are reading? *(He is warning against useless bravery, as opposed to situations in which you could save yourself or someone else, such as Valentine's act of saving the girl.)* **AS**

CheckPoint

Use the CheckPoint questions on Presentation Plus! to check students' mastery of the selection. These questions can be used with interactive response keypads for immediate student feedback.

Additional Support

Web Activities Have students access the Web site for interactive activities that will help them assess their understanding of the selection.

The Bridge, from A Home series, 1895. Watercolor on paper.
National Museum, Stockholm, Sweden.

He set his suitcase on the table and opened it out flat. From that time on he seemed to be unconscious of the presence of anyone else. He laid out the shining, queer implements swiftly and orderly, whistling softly to himself as he always did when at work. In a deep silence and immovable, the others watched him as if under a spell.

In a minute Jimmy's pet drill was biting smoothly into the steel door. In ten minutes—breaking his own burglarious record—he threw back the bolts and opened the door.

Agatha, almost collapsed, but safe, was gathered into her mother's arms.

Jimmy Valentine put on his coat, and walked outside the railings toward the front door. As he went he thought he heard a far-away voice that he once knew call "Ralph!" But he never hesitated.

At the door a big man stood somewhat in his way.

"Hello, Ben!" said Jimmy, still with his strange smile. "Got around at last, have you? Well, let's go. I don't know that it makes much difference, now."

Then Ben Price acted strangely.

"Guess you're mistaken, Mr. Spencer," he **BI** said. "Don't believe I recognize you. Your buggy's waiting for you, ain't it?"

And Ben Price turned and strolled down the street.

1238 UNIT 6   GENRE FICTION

Skills Practice

LITERARY ELEMENT: Diction
Discuss how O. Henry allows his characters and narrator to speak in a way that creates the selection's atmosphere. Write on the board a few phrases from the story that pertain to Valentine's character or other characters. **Ask:** What is the significance of the words O. Henry uses? *(Examples might include the safe that Jimmy "opened like a cheese" or "an eruption of banknotes" that came from another bank heist. These slightly comic phrases detract from the criminal nature of Jimmy's deeds.)* **OL**

RESPONDING AND THINKING CRITICALLY

Respond

1. (a)What do you think of Ben Price's action at the end of the story? (b)How would you have acted if you were in his position? Why?

Recall and Interpret

2. (a)Where is Jimmy Valentine at the beginning of the story? (b)Why do you think he "expected to stay only about three months"?

3. (a)What reason does Mike Dolan give for not getting Jimmy out earlier? (b)How do you think Dolan obtained the governor's pardon?

4. (a)Describe the contents of Valentine's suitcase. (b)What do these contents tell you about him?

Analyze and Evaluate

5. (a)How does the comparison of Ralph Spencer to the legendary phoenix help the reader understand him as a character? (b)Explain why you think that this comparison is effective or ineffective.

6. (a)Analyze the symbolic meaning of Valentine asking for Annabel's rose. What effect do you think Henry means to create? (b)How effective is the author in creating it?

Connect

7. **Big Idea** **The Uncanny and Mysterious** Explain the ironic situation that Valentine finds himself in at the end of the story.

LITERARY ANALYSIS

Literary Element **Humor**

Much of the **humor** in Henry's stories revolves around ironic situations, in which the outcome is contrary to the reader's expectations, such as Valentine falling in love with a bank owner's daughter.

1. Henry's detective story character archetypes in this selection are also humorous. Give one example.

2. Explain whether your example shows irony, coincidence, or something else.

Writing About Literature

Evaluate Figures of Speech In this selection, Henry uses several figures of speech. In similes and metaphors, unlike things are compared to help the reader visualize the action. A **simile** is a direct comparison in which *like* or *as* is used; a **metaphor** is an implied comparison. An **idiom** is a phrase that conveys meaning beyond a literal definition of its words. Write a one- or two-page analysis evaluating the effectiveness of the similes, metaphors, and idioms in "A Retrieved Reformation." Use evidence from the story to support your opinions.

Literature Online **Web Activities** For eFlashcards, Selection Quick Checks, and other Web activities, go to www.glencoe.com.

READING AND VOCABULARY

Reading Strategy **Making Predictions**

After reading a selection, it is useful to review your **predictions** and verify them.

1. How many of your predictions about "A Retrieved Reformation" proved to be correct? List them.

2. What new information did you acquire while verifying your predictions?

Vocabulary **Practice**

Practice with Context Clues Read the sentences below and use context clues to select the most likely meaning for each vocabulary word.

1. Janet stayed up all night *assiduously* working on her algebra homework.
  a. inconsistently **c.** strangely
  b. industriously **d.** calmly

2. Noah was angry and demanded *retribution* for the vandal's damage to his car.
  a. fair dealing **c.** tickets
  b. payment **d.** punishment

O. HENRY **1239**

Assess

1. Accept reasonable responses.

2. (a) In prison (b) He had powerful friends on the outside.

3. (a) The governor almost "balked" after a protest in Springfield. (b) The governor was threatened or bribed by Dolan's or Valentine's powerful friends.

4. (a) The "finest set of burglar's tools in the East," "drills, punches, braces and bits, jimmies, clamps, and augers," and "two or three novelties invented by Jimmy himself (b) He was probably guilty of the crime he was convicted of and plans to steal again.

5. (a) It shows that Valentine made his work look easy. (b) The simile creates an image of the adeptness of the principal character.

6. (a) The rose can symbolize love, beauty, and tenderness. It shows here that Valentine (note the romantic name) knows that his next action may land him in jail but chooses this sacrifice as his last act as Ralph Spencer before he reverts to being Jimmy Valentine. (b) Answers will vary.

7. After choosing family life over a life of crime, he must use his criminal skills to save a member of his fiancée's family.

Literary Element

1. Jimmy Valentine, the criminal, is generous and softhearted rather than tough and frightening.

2. Student answers will vary but should be supported.

Writing About Literature

Students' essays should
• indicate an understanding of figurative language
• include evidence from the text that supports examples

Reading Strategy

1. Answers will vary.
2. Verification should include at least one point about the plot or characters.

Vocabulary

1. b **2.** d

1239

BEFORE YOU READ

Focus

BELLRINGER

Bellringer Options
**Daily Language Practice
Transparency 102**
Or **ask:** Do you believe in the
supernatural? Explain.
Discuss with students their
feelings about ghosts, spirits,
and other supernatural phenomenon. Lead the discus-
sion toward the probability of
restless spirits who have been
wronged as mortals and seek
revenge in the afterlife. Explain
to students that such subjects
inundate the genre of literature
known as Gothic.

Literature Online

Author Search To expand
students' appreciation of Joan
Aiken, have them access the
Web site for additional information and resources.

Lungewater

MEET JOAN AIKEN

The author of more than sixty books, Joan Aiken was born into a literary family. Her father, mother, stepfather, and sister were all writers. Aiken is best known for her children's books, which blend fantasy, history, and adventure. She has also written fiction for adults, as well as poetry and nonfiction.

Beginnings Aiken was born in Rye, Sussex, England. On her fifth birthday, she bought a writing pad with money received as a gift and started writing poems and stories. She was raised in the countryside and home-schooled by her mother until she was twelve. After that, she attended school in Oxford. She was a voracious reader and includes Francis Hodgson Burnett, Charles Dickens, Edgar Allan Poe, Saki, and James Thurber among her early influences.

While still in school, Aiken had two poems published in the prestigious magazine the *Abinger Chronicle*. After graduation Aiken worked as a secretary, an advertising copy-writer, a copyeditor, and a librarian at the United Nations. She also worked for the British Broadcasting Corporation (BBC), which broadcast some of her short stories in 1941.

In 1945 Aiken married journalist Ronald George Brown. Together they had two children. In 1952 Aiken began work on a children's book titled *The Wolves of Willoughby Chase*. However, Aiken's work was interrupted when her husband became seriously ill. She had to put the manuscript aside and find full-time work. As her husband grew sicker, Aiken's first book of children's short stories, *All You've Ever Wanted* (1953), was published. Two years later, she published a second collection, *More Than You Bargained For*. Sadly, her husband died that same year.

Unfinished Business Seven years after she had started it, Aiken returned to her unfinished novel, *The Wolves of Willoughby Chase*. The book, finally published in 1962, won the Lewis Carroll Shelf Award. With this success came financial stability for Aiken and her family, and she was finally able to return to writing full-time. *The Wolves of Willoughby Chase* would prove to be the first in a series of popular fantasy/alternate-history novels for children. Other books in the series include *Black Hearts in Battersea* (1964); *The Whispering Mountain* (1968), which won the Guardian Children's Fiction Award; *Dido and Pa* (1986); and *Midwinter Nightingale* (2003). Another popular series of Aiken's books follows the adventures of heroine Arabel and her pet raven, Mortimer.

"You have to imagine something before you do it."

—Joan Aiken

Aiken's adult novels are noted for their terror, suspense, and gothic atmosphere. Her works for adults also include a number of books based on characters from Jane Austen's books.

Joan Aiken was born 1924 and died in 2004.

Literature Online Author Search For more about Joan Aiken, go to www.glencoe.com.

Selection Skills

Lungewater

Reading Skills
- Analyzing Text Structure (SE pp. 1241–1255)
- Monitoring Understanding (TWE p. 1244)
- Making Generalizations (TWE p. 1254)

Literary Elements
- Mood (SE pp. 1241–1255)

Vocabulary Skills
- Practice with Antonyms (SE p. 1255)
- Deciphering Idioms (TWE p. 1242)

Writing Skills/Grammar
- Analyzing Style (SE p. 1255)
- Imitating Structure (TWE p. 1246)
- Correcting Fragments (TWE p. 1252)

Listening/Speaking/Viewing Skills
- Analyzing Art (SE pp. 1244, 1246, 1248, 1250–1253)

Connecting to the Story

One of the most important characters in the story you are about to read is someone who may at first seem powerless or insignificant in the face of the story's conflict. Before you read the selection, consider the following questions:

- Have you ever suddenly noticed someone who seemed insignificant prior to that moment?
- Do you think people who treat others badly eventually pay for their behavior? Explain.

Building Background

In medieval Europe, tenant farmers called *serfs* were bound to a plot of land and to the will of the land-owner. A serf, through his productivity, provided his own clothing and food. After giving a substantial part of the harvest to his lord, he was able to keep a small portion for himself and his family. Serfs lacked many personal liberties. Landlords frequently treated serfs cruelly, but serfs had no legal rights and therefore no way of stopping such treatment. Unless he was for-mally freed by his lord, the only way a serf might escape his bondage would be to run away.

Setting Purposes for Reading

Big Idea The Uncanny and Mysterious

As you read "Lungewater," observe the mysterious characters and circumstances. Then decide for yourself if something uncanny is occuring.

Literary Element Mood

Mood is the emotional quality or atmosphere of a work. Authors create mood through their choice of subject matter, setting, language, diction, and tone. Gothic literature, such as "Lungewater," has a particu-larly gloomy, foreboding mood and contains elements of mystery, horror, and the supernatural.

- See Literary Terms Handbook, p. R11.

Literature Online **Interactive Literary Elements Handbook** To review or learn more about the literary elements, go to www.glencoe.com.

OBJECTIVES

In studying this selection, you will focus on the following:
- identifying and analyzing characteristics that contribute to mood

Reading Strategy Analyzing Text Structure

Analyzing text structure means looking critically at the pattern used to present events and ideas in a literary work. "Lungewater" is a frame story—a story within which another story unfolds. The frame is the outer story, which usually precedes and follows the inner and more important story.

Reading Tip: Charting Structure As you read, use a Venn diagram like the one shown below to keep track of characters, events, and places in the inner and the outer story. In the middle of the diagram, note what the two stories have in common.

Frame Story | **Inner Story**

Narrator
Bus trip

Sunwool house
Christmas Eve

Stiva

Vocabulary

accosted (ə kôst′ əd) *v.* approached someone in order to speak; p. 1242 *The woman accosted the postal carrier to ask about the rising cost of stamps.*

guttural (gut′ ər əl) *adj.* sounding as if coming from the throat; p. 1243 *The dog let out a guttural sound and then began to bark.*

impediment (im ped′ ə mənt) *n.* something that hinders or obstructs; p. 1245 *Ted's speech impediment prevented him from debating.*

brooded (br$\overline{oo}$′ əd) *v.* thought fretfully or anxiously about; p. 1247 *The seniors brooded over their forthcoming college applications.*

sonorous (sə nôr′ əs) *adj.* loud, forceful, or heavy in sound; p. 1252 *The preacher's sonorous voice filled the cavernous church.*

- analyzing the structure of a text
- writing an analysis of an author's style

JOAN AIKEN **1241**

Focus

Summary

The narrator of "Lungewater" meets a man as they wait for a bus. This man entertains him or her with the story of Count Boyanus, who long ago fled his country, accompanied by an enslaved person, Stiva, to settle near Hovel Hanger. The count falls in love with a lady who is completely disinterested and marries another. The count fool-ishly pursues her. He repeatedly has Stiva deliver his poems, and on the last attempt Stiva falls to his death. The teller of this tale is Stiva's younger brother. The narrator, too, is connected to the story.

V Vocabulary

Vocabulary File Say:

Add these words and defini-tions to your vocabulary file. For each word, write an origi-nal sentence that gives you an example of how to use the word. **OL** Students with English language needs should include the pronunciations of these words in their files. **EL**

Literary Elements Have stu-dents access the Web site for interactive activities that will improve their understanding of mood.

Selection Resources

Print Materials
- 📁 Unit 6 Resources (Fast File), pp. 49–51
- 📁 Leveled Vocabulary Development, p. 85
- 📁 Selection and Unit Assessments, pp. 207–208
- 📁 Selection Quick Checks, p. 104

Transparencies
- Bellringer Options Transparencies: Daily Language Practice Transparency 102
- Literary Elements Transparency 10

Technology
- TeacherWorks Plus™ CD-ROM
- StudentWorks Plus™ CD-ROM
- Presentation Plus!™ CD-ROM
- Literature Online, glencoe.com
- Online Student Edition, mhln.com
- ExamView® Assessment Suite CD-ROM
- Vocabulary PuzzleMaker CD-ROM
- Listening Library, disc 2 track 43

BI₁ Big Idea

The Uncanny and Mysterious Say: Keep the following questions in mind as you read: What elements of the text contribute to its eeriness and mystery? (*The text is made eerie by its mood, subject matter, and strange characters. Its mystery is provided by the frequent twists in its plots and by its frame-within-a-frame structure.*) **OL**

BI₂ Big Idea

The Uncanny and Mysterious Answer: *The narrator's admission that he or she never takes the path alone makes the reader wonder what is so scary about the path.* **OL**

⭐ Viewing the Art

Ask: How is the setting in this painting similar to or different from the setting at the beginning of the story? (*The bus depot in the painting is in a teeming metropolis, whereas the bus stop where the narrator is sitting is described as one of many "cheerless wayside bus stations."*) **AS**

Readability Scores
Dale-Chall: 7.6
DRP: 57
Lexile: 960

The City, 1937. Nicholas Bristowe. Oil on canvas, 66 x 81.2 cm. Private collection.

Lungewater

Joan Aiken

BI₁ On Christmas Eve each year, for many years, I used to visit my great-aunt Theodosia, the last survivor of three aged sisters. And a long, dispiriting journey I was obliged to take, involving two bus changes and extended periods spent exposed in cheerless wayside bus shelters. And at the finish, a choice of walking, either up a straight, bleak stretch of windy road, or along a path that, though beautiful, was frightening (for reasons to be explained later), so I never went that way unless I had a companion with me.

One Christmas Eve, waiting for the third of my buses in a bus shelter with broken glass panes, a central bar missing from the bench, and various hate messages scribbled on the dented litter-bin, which was the only other furniture, I was **accosted** by a very singular[1] old gentleman who came into the bus shelter and sat down on the other end of the damaged seat.

More than commonly tall, he was dressed in a Norfolk jacket and knickerbockers[2] of an old-fashioned cut, made from some hairy, fawn-colored material, serge perhaps. He

---

1. Here, *singular* (sing′gyə lər) means "odd" or "striking."
2. A *Norfolk* (nôr′fək) jacket is a loose-fitted jacket with pleats. *Knickerbockers* are loose-fitting pants that gather at the knee.

Vocabulary

accosted (ə kôst′əd) *v.* approached someone in order to speak

---

Big Idea The Uncanny and Mysterious *How has the author introduced the element of mystery here?* **BI₂**

1242 UNIT 6 GENRE FICTION

Skills Practice

VOCABULARY: Deciphering Idioms
Students "own" a word when they can use it in a sentence that clearly demonstrates their understanding of it. Write an informal definition of *idiom* on the board and explain that idioms are essential parts of a well-rounded vocabulary. Have students compare some of the idioms in "Lungewater" to their personal experiences. Ask them to list *omnibus, knickerbockers,* and *stockings* on one side of a chart and their personal experiences with similar things on the other. (*Possible answers: shuttle bus; Capri pants; knee socks.*) **OL**

wore high canvas boots and long, thick, woolen stockings of the same sandy brown, and was quite bald, but this was compensated for by the long, thick, white beard and moustache that framed the lower part of his face like a garden hedge.

"Can you tell me, my young friend," he asked me in a heavy foreign accent, "is it from this place that I am to catch an omnibus³ to Hovel Hanger?"

I told him that, yes, it was, and that I was hoping to get the same bus myself but had been told it would be late owing to wintry road conditions.

"Ah, so? But I hope that we shall arrive at that place before too late in the day—before it grows dark."

His accent was very **guttural**—the *h*'s in "hope" and "Hovel Hanger" came out with a thick "gh" sound, like blobs of ketchup from a bottle.

"To pass time, then, I shall relate to you the story of why I am come all the way from Dahoungarie⁴ to visit this small place."

"Thank you, sir. I should like to hear it," I said politely, hoping that the story would not be long and that the bus would soon come.

"I tell you the story of Count Hugo Boyanus, who fled from my country after the revolution there and came to settle in a house near Hovel Hanger. Before, he had possessed hundreds of miles of farmland and forest, besides coal mines, oil wells, factories, rivers full of fish, whole towns and villages and their inhabitants. Now—no more. No property left. But money, yes, that he did have; being a man of insight, he had

---

3. *Omnibus* (om′nə bus′) is a chiefly British term for a large bus, usually with an upper and lower deck.
4. *Dahoungarie* may be the old gentleman's way of saying Hungary, which is a country in Eastern Europe.

Literary Element   Mood *How do you feel about this character after he is first described by the narrator?* **L**

Vocabulary

guttural (gut′ər əl) *adj.* sounding as if coming from the throat

seen trouble coming years earlier, so, wisely, he sent his gold abroad to mount up for him in foreign lands, in foreign banks. Then, when the people rose, and took away from the rich, Count Boyanus escaped and traveled to this country, with just one servant to carry his bags, a slave named Stiva."

"A slave?"

"Before, the count had owned hundreds of serfs—slaves, you would say; it is the same thing. Among them was this boy, Stiva, whose parents were dead. They, too, had been serfs, and had died in the count's service. The boy, Stiva, could neither read nor write. Had never been to school. What choice did he have? There was no one to speak up for him. When told to do so, he went with the count, though he was sad to leave home, and, in your country, he could not understand the language. Nor was there anyone to take his part. So he remained, unpaid, in the service of the count, who bought Lungewater manor house, near Hovel Hanger.

"In former days, the count had often traveled abroad. He spoke other tongues—English, French, Italian—with fluency. He had made friends in other lands. He was an educated man, a poet, a historian; he wrote with knowledge and elegance on many topics.

"But the boy, Stiva, remained an illiterate. Books, written words, meant nothing to him. Nor did he learn many words of your language. He had no time. All day he served the count. Carrying up his breakfast, polishing his boots, cleaning and oiling his bird guns (for the count was a great sportsman), fastening the flies on his fishing lines (for the River Lunge ran through the count's land).

"Now," said the old gentleman, "I come to tell the important part. The count was in love with an English lady. He had met her some years before when he was reading for a master's degree at Bad Hassenberg University. She was there with her mother,

Reading Strategy   Analyzing Text Structure *What is the function of this and the previous paragraph?* **R**

Teach

L Literary Element

Mood Answer: *The man's height, baldness, and tall boots give him an air of mystery. The description helps establish the story's mood of ominous foreboding.* **OL**

R Reading Strategy

Analyzing Text Structure Answer: *The paragraphs function as the beginning of the story inside the frame, or the story within the story. They cover many years in a short amount of time, as in a fairy tale.* **OL**

★ Writer's Technique

Character Ask: What does the narrator's behavior say about him or her? (*Possible answers: The narrator is considerate; he or she is reluctant to express her true feelings to adults*). Encourage students to see that though the narrator's response is untruthful, he or she is not deceptive. Point out that contradictions, such as this, make for full, complex characters. **AS**

✓ CheckPoint

Use the CheckPoint questions on Presentation Plus! to monitor students' comprehension. These questions can be used with interactive response keypads for immediate student feedback.

Objectives
• To analyze the structure of a text (SE)
• To analyze mood(SE)
• To understand idioms (TWE)

Differentiated Instruction

Visual Learners Help visual learners understand the story's structure by showing a clip of a television show or documentary with a similar organization. An example would be a television character telling another character a story unrelated to the existing story line. Visual learners may also sketch a story within a story. Ask them to consider the possibility of two stories occurring at one time in their own homes or a restaurant or school building. (*Sample drawings: A mother and father are preparing dinner and telling one another about their experiences at work.*) **OL**

Teach

The Fair Toxophilites, 1872. William Powell Frith. Oil on canvas, 98.2 x 81.7 cm. Royal Albert Memorial Museum, Exeter, Devon, UK.
Viewing the Art: What similarities do you find between these women and the beautiful lady? ⭐

1244 UNIT 6 GENRE FICTION

Skills Practice

READING: Monitoring Your Understanding An excellent measure of understanding is making predictions. If students are able to surmise what might follow a given event in a story, they're demonstrating a keen understanding of what preceded it. Ask students to make predictions after the following plot points: 1. The lady refuses the count; 2. The narrator informs the reader that the shortest route to Sunwool is Changewood Gully. (*The count will try to win her back; The crazed count will send Stiva on this dangerous path.*) **OL**

who was taking the waters.[5] The town offered balls, riding parties; there was a casino and gambling—picnics, archery, horse racing. The lady was very young, very charming, light-hearted, beautiful as an angel. She did not, perhaps, take him too seriously. They rode, they danced, they walked together in the forests . . . but she was many years younger, and her family was not favorably disposed toward the count. They thought him too old, too foreign perhaps. But he had lost his heart entirely. When the lady's family returned to England, he lost no time in following; that, indeed, was why he chose to settle in the neighborhood. For the lady's family lived by Chalk Hill, not far from Lungewater House, on the other side of the river.

"But then a worse misfortune than all before happened to the count—or so it seemed to him—worse, even, than losing his lands and his properties. The lady would not have him. She did not return his love. And, not long after he came, she married another man.

"The count bore this new disappointment very badly. He was not accustomed to rebuff.[6] He fell into a black gloom of anger and misery. To him it was intolerable that the lady should prefer another man. For this, all suffered in his household, but most especially the boy Stiva, who bore kicks and bad words in silence.

"Even now, the count could not believe that the lady would not very soon regret her mistake. He was not one to give up easily. He spent a large part of his days writing, writing, and rewriting a long, furious poem, asking, adjuring, imploring[7] the lady to reconsider. This took him a whole year. And, on Christmas Eve, he sent the poem to her, by the hand of his servant boy, Stiva.

"Now, as I told you, the River Lunge ran between the properties of Count Boyanus and the lady, who now lived with her husband in a house called Sunwool."

"Sunwool?" I said. I would have said more, but the old man was eager to go on with his story. It was as if a flood, after long battering against some obstruction, had finally broken through the **impediment** and surged on its way, carrying in its wild rush all the debris and damaged matter that it had withstood for so long.

"Da! Da!"[8] he said impatiently. "Sunwool. So it was. . . . And the shortest path from one house to the other ran along the bank of the Lunge River, through a place called Changewood Gully. And here there is a spot called the Stride. Here the river becomes very narrow, drawn in between high, rocky banks (or so I've been informed). From the top of the cliff you can hardly see the water, which boils along down below with furious energy. This narrow race is called the Stride because, from time to time, there have been men who were bold enough, some foolhardy enough, to take the standing leap that will carry a person from one side to the other. (It is not possible there to take a run, for the sides are too steep and rocky.)"

I nodded, and asked quickly, "Did Stiva go that way when he delivered the poem?"

"No! Stiva did not. The count had ordered him to deliver the envelope by the speediest route—the count always wanted his orders obeyed at once—but Stiva, though illiterate, was not a fool. He did not choose to risk his

---

8. *Da* (dä) means "yes" in many languages, including Bulgarian, Croatian, and Slovenian. The countries where these languages are spoken were, until 1918, part of the dual monarchy of Austria-Hungary.

Big Idea The Uncanny and Mysterious *What does the narrator's response to this name suggest?* **BI**

Vocabulary

impediment (im ped′ ə mənt) n. something that hinders or obstructs

---

5. Naturally occurring springs are thought to contain minerals that have medicinal effects. Many people visit such spas, hoping the *waters* will improve their health.
6. *Rebuff* (ri buf′) means "rejection of an offer."
7. *Adjuring* (ə joor′ing) means "making a sincere appeal"; *imploring* (im plôr′ing) means "begging."

Reading Strategy Analyzing Text Structure *What role does Christmas Eve play in the structure of the story?* **R**

Teach

⭐ **Viewing the Art**

Answer: *Students may say that the count does not have an older servant and would have been unlikely to have guests at his home.* **AS**

Formal Picnic. Vincent McIndoe.

Viewing the Art: Could this scene take place at the count's Lungewater home? Why or why not? ⭐

Additional Support

Skills Practice

WRITING: Imitating Structure
Put students' comprehension and creativity to work by having them construct a short story similar in structure to Joan Aiken's. List the following criteria on the chalkboard: *1. Must be short fiction with a gothic or suspenseful air; 2. Must have an "outer" story and an "inner" story.*

Encourage students who may struggle to begin to brainstorm, map out their stories, and then run their ideas by a peer or teacher. Urge students to design gothic cover pages to accompany their stories. Assess stories based on listed criteria and creativity. **OL** life at the dangerous spot when there was a footbridge farther downstream, which would take him over in safety. He was neither tall nor strong—why should he be? His diet, for the most part, was bread and porridge. He went by the longer way, and delivered the envelope and came back to his master."

"Did the lady reply to the poem? The beautiful lady?"

"She did not. She was otherwise occupied. On the next day, Christmas Day, news came that she had been delivered of a baby daughter, who was christened Noelle."

"Noelle?" I said. "Then—"

Brushing my interruption aside, the old gentleman went on, "And when these tidings reached Count Boyanus, they made him even angrier and more miserable. To him, it seemed as if that were a short, scornful reply to his year's poetic outpouring. A slap in the face.

"But, as I have said, he was not a man to give up. He sat down at his desk and began another poem. . . ."

At this moment a bus drew up beside us. HATFIELD HANGER said the sign on the front.

"Is this our bus?" asked my companion hopefully.

"No, I am afraid it is not. . . ."

"Then I resume. A year went by, during which the count shot, fished the Lunge water, **brooded** angrily, abused his boy Stiva with hard words and kicks, while toiling at a second poem, even more vehement,[9] more anguished, more urgent and beseeching than the first. He wrote and wrote and he rewrote, he crossed out and amended and replaced one line with another. At last the work was done, and all carefully copied out. (The count could not entrust this part to the boy, for the boy could not write. He had

---

9. *Vehement* (vē´ə mənt) means "intense" or "forceful."

Literary Element | Mood *What mood does this description help create?* **L**

Vocabulary

brooded (brŏŏd´əd) *v.* thought fretfully or anxiously about

to do it himself.) On Christmas evening Boyanus gave the work to the boy Stiva to deliver. By now, from a little lad of nine or ten, Stiva had become a larger boy of ten or eleven. But he still knew no letters or figures, and very little English. He had no time for learning. He led a sad, lonely life, and longed for his own land. But he did not complain. To whom could he, indeed? He served his master faithfully, and received kicks and curses in return.

"'Take the letter to the lady by the shortest way,' ordered Count Boyanus.

"'Yes, master,' said Stiva. But, as before, he did not cross the Lunge River by the Stride, but chose to go the longer, safer way over the footbridge. And the letter was delivered; but again, the lady did not answer, perhaps because, as on the previous occasion, she was engaged, just then, in childbirth. On the day after Christmas, she bore her second child, another daughter. Named Christina."

This time I did not interrupt.

"And again, Count Boyanus, when he heard of this, was furious, hurt, insulted, and unable to recognize or accept the fact that the lady was indeed happy with her chosen husband, and was not at all interested in the count's suit."[10]

"So he sat down to begin a third poem—"

"Excuse me—" I began.

For another bus had now come slowly into view through the misty, frosty haze of the winter day.

CHISEL WOOD said the sign over the driver's cab.

"Is this our bus?" hopefully asked my fellow traveler.

"Yes, this is the one."

So we climbed onboard and paid our fares, and the old gentleman sat down by me.

"I continue my story," he said. "At the end of the third year, the count had completed

---

10. Here, the count's *suit* is his attempt to persuade the young woman to marry him.

Reading Strategy | Analyzing Text Structure *How does the repetition of the events surrounding the count's letter-writing affect the story?* **R**

Teach

L Literary Element

Mood Answer: *This description creates a frenzied, crazed, and sinister mood associated with the count's letter writing.* **OL**

R Reading Strategy

Analyzing Text Structure
Answer: *The repetition of the letter writing and the count's order for Stiva to deliver it gives the story the feel of a folktale. In folktales, something usually happens three times before the climax of the story. The repetition helps the reader experience the count's refusal to take no for an answer.* **OL**

★ Writer's Technique

First-Person Point of View The decision to use a particular point of view is crucial to how a story is presented. As a class, discuss the advantages and disadvantages of "Lungewater" as told from a first-person point of view. *(Advantages: Narrator is likeable; readers are easily drawn to story because they feel invited by the "I"; disadvantages: Feelings of other characters cannot be explored thoroughly.)* **AS**

Building Reading Fluency

Word Lists "Lungewater" has words that some students will find unfamiliar. Provide a list of unfamiliar words and allow students time to practice pronunciation. Examples are *anguish, blottings,* and *clambered.* Decoding clues can be found throughout the text, however. Before students begin reading "Lungewater," provide them with a printed list, or have them copy a list from the chalkboard. Go through the list several times, asking students to repeat the words as you read. Students should be less apprehensive about reading aloud after studying the unfamiliar words. **BL**

Objectives
• To analyze the structure of a text (SE)
• To identify and analyze characteristics that contribute to mood (SE)
• To imitate story structure (TWE)

Teach

⭐ **Viewing the Art**

Answer: *This painting could be a depiction of the Stride—the ravine into which Stiva and the count fall to their deaths. The bridge in the background could be the footbridge that Stiva crosses when he delivers the first two poems. The River Lunge seems to be missing.* **AS**

Rocky Ravine at Sorrento, 1823. Heinrich Reinhold. Oil on paper on canvas. Hamburger Kunsthalle, Hamburg, Germany.

Viewing the Art: In what ways does this painting reflect the story's setting? ⭐

1248 UNIT 6 GENRE FICTION

Additional Support

Skills Practice

READING: Italics Aiken uses italics sparingly in "Lungewater." **Ask:** What purpose do italics serve? (*Italics are used for emphasis in meaning or pronunciation, to indicate the name of something, or to call something to the reader's attention.*) Ask students to skim the text for italics and to record the author's purpose for using them in a chart, as shown.

page	italics	purpose
1245	*Da! Da!*	Foreign words

OL

his most impassioned poem yet. Written with such great heart-burnings and anguish, with blottings and crossings-out of words inserted or lines deleted, as if the central core of his heart were bursting forth, red-hot, into urgent words. When the boy Stiva brought a glass of tea or vodka or brandy to the count's study, he would, as often as not, be greeted by a book flung at his head, or an inkwell. When the poem was done, he put it into an envelope and gave it to Stiva to deliver.

"'Take it the shortest way,' he ordered.

"The count was not a patient man. He expected his orders to be obeyed on the instant. If not, his punishments were severe.

"'Yes, master,' said Stiva, and off he went.

"But on this occasion, the count suddenly decided to follow Stiva. Who knows why? Perhaps there was one line in the poem that did not fully satisfy him, and at the last minute, he wished to alter it—"

"Excuse me, sir," I said, "but this is where we have to get off the bus."

"Ah, so, indeed? I thank you, my young friend."

Rather stiffly, the elderly traveler clambered[11] down from the bus platform and stood looking about him.

We had alighted[12] at a crossroads in the middle of a wooded common. Not far off could be heard the roar of water.

LUNGEWATER said one of the arms of the signpost. HOVEL HANGER said another. CHALK HILL said a third. CHISEL WOOD said the fourth.

It was a gloomy, foggy day. One could not see far in any direction. The birch and thorn trees were white with frost crystals.

"I wish to go to Lungewater House," said my companion. "Can you tell me which way that would be? Are you familiar with this neighborhood?"

"Yes, sir. It is only a ruin now, you know that?"

And a nasty, dismal, decaying dark spot, too, I thought; not a place to visit on a murky winter afternoon.

"Yes, I know," he said. "But my brother lived there once, and I should like to see it. First, though, I should greatly like to see the Stride. This narrow crossing place. Can you tell me how to get there? And also Sunwool House, where the lady lived?"

"Yes, sir. You can take the path by the river. I will be glad to show you; I am going that way myself."

"I am very much obliged to you," said the old man. And so he accompanied me along the footpath, among the white-frosted trees, and as we walked—slowly enough, for he was rather lame—the noise of rushing water grew louder.

"The weather is very misty in your country," said the old man, looking at the shapes of white vapor that hung and drifted among the trees. "No wonder that you have so many tales of ghosts and specters. I believe there are such stories about the Stride. I have been told that it is an especially haunted spot?"

He was right. And that is why—if the truth be told—I would never have been walking that way by myself.

"Sir—please tell me the end of the story. What happened to Stiva? And to the count? And why have you come all the way here from Dahoungarie?"

"Ah, well, I will tell you. First you must know that in his third year of lonely living at Lungewater House, Stiva had at last made one friend. This was a local lad, Will Thorne. Will was a foot soldier in the army, but when he was at home on leave, he liked nothing better than to poach[13] for trout in Count Boyanus's fishing water. Stiva had encountered Thorne down by the water fishing one evening and, instead of reporting him, had fallen into talk with him. For, by now, Stiva

---

11. *Clambered* (klam´bərd) means "climbed clumsily."
12. *Alighted* (ə lit´əd) means "stepped down" or "disembarked."

13. To *poach* (pōch) is to hunt or fish illegally on someone else's property.

Big Idea The Uncanny and Mysterious *Why do you think the count chooses to follow Stiva this time?* **BI**

Reading Strategy Analyzing Text Structure *How does the story's structure shift here?* **R**

JOAN AIKEN **1249**

Teach

BI Big Idea

The Uncanny and Mysterious Answer:
Because of the lady's failure to respond to his letters, the count may be suspicious of Stiva and is following him to see if he is really delivering the letters. **OL**

R Reading Strategy

Analyzing Text Structure
Answer: *The narrator's comments help merge the two existing stories, the present and the past.* **OL**

★ Writer's Technique

Dialogue Point out the author's extensive use of dialogue here. **Ask:** Is it possible for a scene to consist only of dialogue? Explain. (*Yes. The characters' words not only can move the story along but also can present past action, introduce conflict, and describe the setting.*) Tell students that writers such as Ernest Hemingway have written stories in which most of the action was revealed through dialogue. **AS**

Differentiated Instruction

Literary Response Reactions to "Lungewater" can be expressed in various ways. Some students articulate their thoughts through speaking, while others find writing pleasurable. Some may even need to demonstrate their understanding of the text through performance. Allow students to choose from the following list of possible ways to respond: speaking, writing, acting, or drawing. Develop a rubric that clearly outlines expectations: *Your response must articulate the events of the story.* Allow students the opportunity to present their responses to the class. **BL**

Objectives
• To analyze the structure of a text (SE)
• To interpret italics (TWE)

Teach

BI₁ Big Idea

The Uncanny and Mysterious Answer:

Thorne might wonder why Stiva has stayed with the count when he could be a free man. He might also wonder at how cruel the count must be to keep Stiva thinking that he is an enslaved person. **OL**

★ Viewing the Art

Answer: *The man in the painting—with arms crossed, chest puffed out, and chin raised—exudes the same self-absorption and haughtiness as the count. But he would not have been seen in public with a woman other than his love across the River Lunge.* **AS**

The Race at Auteuil, Paris. Giuseppe or Joseph de Nittis. Oil on canvas.
Galleria Nazionale d'Arte Moderna, Rome.

Viewing the Art: Could the man in this painting represent the count? Why or why not? ★

had acquired a few phrases of halting English. And he was greatly surprised when Will Thorne told him that in England there were no slaves, that no man belongs absolutely to his master, that servants are paid wages, and may give notice. And he was even more amazed when Will promised to

Big Idea The Uncanny and Mysterious *What might Thorne have found mysterious about Stiva's situation?* **BI₁**

write a letter for him and try to see that it was sent to his younger brother. For Stiva had a brother, Matvey, who was only four years old when the count was obliged to flee from his lands. Matvey had been left in the charge of a grandmother, an old washer-woman on the count's estate, probably dead by now. And Will Thorne, as it chanced, was soon to be sent, with his regiment, to a part of eastern Europe not too far from where that estate lay. So Stiva told the name of the village where Count Boyanus had his mansion."

"But, sir, please tell me what happened to Stiva? And to the count?"

"Well. The count, striding along the wooded ridge at the end of his garden, wishful to call Stiva back, observed that the boy was taking the longer route and plainly did not intend to jump across the Stride. So he flew into a rage, made haste after the boy, and struck him a violent blow with the butt of the bird gun he always carried. And he ordered Stiva to leap across the gully."

"So the count must have changed his mind about altering the poem?"

"Perhaps. We shall never know if that was his intention. And poor Stiva, shaking and terrified, made a desperate effort to leap across the Stride. But he failed and fell down into the ravine,[14] and the envelope that he carried fluttered away out of his hand. And Stiva's body was never seen again, for the Lunge water there flows into strange deeps and underground whirlpools, from which no object is ever recovered.

"But Will Thorne, secretly poaching the count's waters farther downstream, saw the whole thing happen, and, by chance, he caught the envelope with the count's poem as it came fluttering down.

"The count did not see that; but he did see a man with a fishing rod. And, still full of rage, he shot the man with his bird gun."

"Did the count kill Will Thorne?"

"No. But he was badly hurt, and crawled back home with great difficulty. And when

---

14. A *ravine* is a slender, steep-sided valley usually created by running water.

Additional Support

Skills Practice

READING: Literary Response Stiva's fate in "Lungewater" is sad and will have an emotional impact on many students. Channel this impact and help students shape it into a literary response. Explain that responses in literature come in two forms: intellectual, which describes what we think about a text, and emotional, which describes how we feel about a text. Lead a class discussion on the unfair treatment experienced by Stiva. After students have expressed themselves, ask them to compare Stiva's treatment to events in other readings and in the real world. (*Answers will vary and should be supported with examples.*) **OL**

1250

the count made inquiry and found who had been shot, he had Will sent to jail. And there Will's neglected wound became inflamed and he presently died of it.

"Meanwhile, the lady at Sunwool House, the count's lost love, had a third daughter, a sister for Noelle and Christina."

"What happened to the third poem, the one that Will Thorne had caught?"

"Wait, and I will tell you. But first," said my companion, "are we not very close to the Stride?"

We were, and my heart was beating painfully fast. The sound of rushing water almost deafened us. To our left, the waters of the Lunge River, brown and turgid[15] and foamy from long days of recent rain, swung and surged, rolled and plaited, whirling along broken branches, strips of plank torn from jetties, farm tools, all kinds of wreckage swept down from farther upstream, where there had been floods.

There, where we were, the river could not overleap its banks, for they were far too high, but its angry voice could be heard below as it poured in a thunderous mass toward the narrowest part of the channel.

"Is this what they call the Stride?" asked my companion. "It is a fearsome place."

"The Stride is a little farther along," I told him. "Where the path becomes very narrow indeed and the right-hand bank is even steeper."

The path was slippery now, too, where spraylike mist in the air had turned to fine ice underfoot.

I wondered if it had been like this when Stiva made his leap.

"It would be kind of you to hold my arm," said my companion. It felt thin and stiff as an old dead stick under the rough cloth. We proceeded with great caution.

A Native of Garwhal, in the attitude of moving forward, 1908. Gertrude Ellen Burrard. Oil on canvas, 51 x 40.7 cm. Council National Army Museum, London.

Viewing the Art: Is the boy portrayed here similar to the image you have developed of Stiva? Explain. ★

"I do not wonder that the ghost of Stiva haunts this place," the old man said, half to himself. "Poor, lonely boy. Despite all his ill-usage he was a faithful servant—I think he will have been ashamed that he failed to deliver that last letter."

But I was not sure about that. Would he have been ashamed? Would he not rather have been angry with his master?

"What became of Count Boyanus?"

"Later that same year he, too, fell into the Stride. Some say he was carrying his own poem, his last, to the lady, but there are many that say that the ghost of Stiva pulled him down. The sad, angry ghost."

---

15. *Turgid* (tur′jid) means "swollen with debris."

Big Idea The Uncanny and Mysterious *What seems uncanny about the river as the narrator describes it?* **BI₂**

Literary Element Mood *How does this observation by the old man enhance the mood?* **L**

Teach

BI₂ Big Idea

The Uncanny and Mysterious Answer: *The physical description of the water makes it seem very powerful, much more powerful than humans, able to destroy both nature (broken branches) and the things humans make (tools and boards). It seems alive and threatening.* **OL**

L Literary Element

Mood Answer: *The man suggests explicitly what the mood implies—that the area is mysterious and likely haunted.* **OL**

★ Viewing the Art

Answer: *Answers will vary. Students may point out that this boy looks older than an undernourished Stiva would look. Also, Garwhal is in India, at the foot of the Himalayas, not in Bulgaria. This difference could cause discrepancies between the image of the boy portrayed in the painting and the image that students have generated in their minds.* **AS**

Differentiated Instruction

Less Proficient Readers Assist less proficient readers by dividing the class into groups reflective of students' reading ability. Students in need of occasional monitoring should work within your clear view and should be visited frequently. Students requiring intensive monitoring should work in a small group of which you are a part. The two groups requiring assistance can be monitored effectively in this way: Read a passage aloud, discuss it, check for comprehension, and then have students summarize it in writing. As one group summarizes, check the progress of the other group. **BL**

Objectives

- To identify and analyze characteristics that contribute to mood (SE)
- To recognize and explain those elements in texts that prompt a personal response (TWE)

L Literary Element

Mood Answer: *The language in this passage makes it seem as though the narrator is falling into a trance brought on by the ghost of the Stride. The passage complicates the mood of fear with the hypnotic pull of the place. The words "a wish, a will" suggest a sinister agency that beckons people to plunge to their deaths.* **OL**

⭐ Viewing the Art

Answer: *With its shining sun and picturesque setting, this scene has an idyllic mood. It is not similar to the story's mood, which is much darker and more harrowing.* **AS**

I could believe that, especially now, at this twilit hour, in this freezing mist and gloom.

We stood on the lip of the Stride and looked across the deceptively narrow distance to the rocky path, layered with ice, that ran across the opposite cliff. From where we stood, it was hardly more than a table's width over the water to the other side—but not for all the money in the Bank of England would I have attempted that jump.

And yet, there was something about the atmosphere of the place—an urgency, a wish, a will, that beckoned from below. . . .

I shivered with cold, and would have been glad to move on, to get away, but the old man still stood motionless, deep in thought, staring intently at the wavering mist-shapes that formed and re-formed and hung below us in the ravine, at the spidery frost-spangled birch trees cresting the cliffs on either side of the river.

"How comes it that you know all these things, sir?" I asked, trying not to shake visibly with cold and fright. "Who are you?"

"I will tell you in a moment. But first I must try to do my best for that poor, homesick spirit. Hold me firmly, if you please, my friend."

Literary Element Mood *How does the author's word choice here contribute to the story's mood?* **L**

He leaned outward a little and called down: "Stiva! *Stiva!* Do you hear me? Stiva? Are you there?"

He waited. And the roar of the water answered him.

"Stiva! Listen!"

Then followed a long, **sonorous** message, uttered in a foreign language, deep and harsh. A prayer, perhaps, or an incantation.[16] His frail old body shook with passion. After he had come to its end, my companion wiped his eyes, then, after a long, silent pause, turned to me.

"Thank you, my friend. That is all. Now we shall go on."

I waited to ask questions until we had passed the narrowest section of the pathway and were on fairly firm, level ground. Then I said again, "Sir, who *are* you?"

"Why," said the old gentleman, "my name is Matvey. I am Stiva's younger brother."

The Poacher. Constant Troyon, 1810–1865. Musee des Beauz-Arts, Mulhouse, France.
Viewing the Art: What mood is evoked by this scene? Is it similar to the story's mood? ⭐

16. An *incantation* (in′kan tā′shən) is a verbal spell or charm that is either sung or spoken.

Vocabulary

sonorous (sə nôr′əs) *adj.* loud, forceful, or heavy in sound

---

Additional Support

Skills Practice

GRAMMAR: Fragments To help students distinguish fragments, write the following on the board: *1. After leaving dinner, the couple. 2. The teacher reprimanded the student. To no avail.* Ask students to describe the problem in each example and to offer a solution. (*1. Lacks a verb; does not tell what the couple does; Solution: After leaving dinner, the couple went dancing. 2. Both are parts of the same sentence; Solution: The teacher reprimanded the student*

The Love Letter. George B. O'Neil (1828–1917). Private collection.

Viewing the Art: What mood is expressed by this scene? Does it match the mood at the conclusion of this story? Explain. ★

JOAN AIKEN **1253**

Differentiated Instruction

to no avail.) Explain that fragments are acceptable in literary writing and, on occasion, in scholarly writing, but that they should make sense and not distract the reader. **OL**

Chunking "Lungewater" may prove to be a lengthy story for some readers. For students struggling with comprehension, "chunk" the selection. Present the story a few pages at a time, requiring students to summarize parts as they go. **BL**

Teach

R1 Reading Strategy

Analyzing Text Structure
Answer: *The two stories have merged with the introduction of the character of the great-aunt. She is a character in both stories, so she bridges the action in each.* **OL**

R2 Reading Strategy

Analyzing Text Structure
Answer: *Students will say that the events in the outer story—the letter's delivery to its proper recipient—resolve the inner story, allowing Stiva to rest in peace instead of haunting the riverbank.* **OL**

CheckPoint

Use the CheckPoint questions on Presentation Plus! to check students' mastery of the selection. These questions can be used with interactive response keypads for immediate student feedback.

"But how—how—how did you ever come to hear the story?"

He said, "The poacher, Will Thorne, who caught the last poem as it fluttered down, put it in his pocket. When he was lying in jail, he carried out his promise to write a letter to Stiva's brother, for he remembered the address of the village that Stiva had told him. But before the letter was sent off, Will Thorne died in jail. His few possessions, with the letter and poem among them, were given back to his old mother, and lay, gathering dust, in the bottom of a basket of patches for twenty years. When she died, the basket passed to her daughter, who put it in an attic. Only by chance, not long ago, did a child, rummaging, pull out the old papers. Will Thorne's letter, containing the poem, was clearly addressed to me. In fact I had grown to manhood and moved many times, but it did, in the end, catch up with me.

"I made inquiries about this region, and was dismayed to hear tales that my brother's ghost still haunts the place. And I think this may be because he had not been able to perform his final task. So I came to do it for him."

"You mean," I said, thunderstruck, "deliver the poem?"

"*Da!* Just so. If it is possible. I have the poem here." He tapped his Norfolk jacket pocket. "I think—after all—I will not trouble to look at Lungewater House. You say it is all in ruins. That would be too sad. But, if you will tell me how I can get from this place to Sunwool House?"

"Sunwool? Certainly," I said. "Of course. Of course! Nothing is easier. I am going there myself, as a matter of fact. We follow the bank and cross the bridge."

We did so. Cozily, under the hill ahead of us, among its sheltered walled gardens, lay Sunwool House, where my aunt, Theodosia, the last survivor of three sisters, still lived. And was waiting for my Christmas visit.

She was a small, elfish old lady, with a soft skin like a crumpled birch leaf and eyes of faded river brown. She received my companion without the least surprise. "Ah, yes . . . the poems from Count Boyanus. Do you know, my mother never opened them? I believe she felt that to do so might bring her bad luck. And she had no intention of risking that. She and my father had led such a very happy life. Yes, here are the two poems. . . ."

Having unlocked a rosewood desk, she pulled open an inner drawer and took from it two faded yellow envelopes, exactly matching the one that my companion had given to her.

"I am quite sure that you are right, sir; that poor boy Stiva will be very happy to know that his last task has been faithfully executed. And I daresay that from now on he will stop haunting the riverbank, and that will be a great convenience for all the local poachers."

"But the poems, Great-Aunt Theodosia? Aren't you going to read them?" I demanded.

"Why, no, my dear. I think they are much better left unread. That Count Boyanus—I do not like the sound of him at all. A harsh, violent, self-deceiving man. No, no, I think that my mother's judgment of him was perfectly sound. I think by far the best thing to do with the poems is this."

And my great-aunt Theodosia dropped the three unopened envelopes into her drawing-room fire. ∞

Reading Strategy Analyzing Text Structure *How do the inner story and the outer story come together here?* **R1**

Reading Strategy Analyzing Text Structure *How does the outer story help resolve the inner story here?* **R2**

Additional Support

Web Activities Have students access the Web site for interactive activities that will help them assess their understanding of the selection.

Skills Practice

READING: Making Generalizations
Discuss the fact that authors don't always directly state what they want their readers to grasp. **Ask:** Why might a writer not reveal all he or she wants the reader to know or understand? *(Writing requires the participation of the reader. Writers expect that their audiences will* participate in the experience: As writers give, readers are expected to receive. Receiving often means seeking out hidden information.) Have students make and record generalizations about the life Aunt Theodosia lived before encountering Matvey. (Answers will vary.) **OL**

RESPONDING AND THINKING CRITICALLY

Respond

1. Were you satisfied with the story's ending? Explain.

Recall and Interpret

2. (a)Where and when does the story begin? (b)Give specific reasons that might explain the author's choice to begin the narrative here.

3. (a)Who is Stiva? (b)Why does he remain with Count Boyanus?

4. (a)What is the shortest route between Count Boyanus's and the lady's properties? (b)What is strange about the count's insistence that Stiva take this route?

5. (a)What happens to Stiva? (b)How is what happens to Stiva related to what happens to the count later?

Analyze and Evaluate

6. (a)How does Joan Aiken present the story of Count Hugo Boyanus? (b)How does this decision affect the structure of the story?

7. (a)How does Aiken communicate the lady's feelings for Count Boyanus to the reader? (b)How well does the author reveal important information without explicitly stating it? Explain.

8. (a)How does the old man's story connect him to the narrator? (b)How believable is this connection? Explain.

Connect

9. **Big Idea** **The Uncanny and Mysterious** What strikes you as the most uncanny or mysterious element in this story? Explain.

LITERARY ANALYSIS

Literary Element Mood

When determining the **mood** of a piece, first contemplate the emotional effect it has on you. Then try to link the cause of your feelings to specific elements of the text. By doing so, you can more easily identify the mood of the piece and which elements contribute most to it.

1. (a)Describe the mood of "Lungewater," using examples from the story as support. (b)How does the author establish this mood?

2. Do you believe the mood is fitting? Explain.

Writing About Literature

Analyze Style Style is the expressive quality of an author's work, consisting of the sentence structure, word choice, and use of figurative language and imagery that make the writing unique. In "Lungewater," Joan Aiken uses elements of style to paint a vivid picture of one strange, dark Christmas Eve journey. In an essay, examine Aiken's use of figurative language and imagery in "Lungewater" and how they contribute to her distinct style.

READING AND VOCABULARY

Reading Strategy Analyzing Text Structure

A writer may use a variety of techniques in **structuring** a literary work. Stories are often arranged chronologically, and the action moves straightforwardly through time. Other techniques include repetition, flashback, and framing.

1. Does "Lungewater" have a chronological structure?

2. How would the story change if it did not have a frame? Give examples.

Vocabulary Practice

Practice with Antonyms Choose the best antonym for each vocabulary word.

1. **accosted**	**a.** approached	**b.** retreated
2. **guttural**	**a.** silky	**b.** grating
3. **impediment**	**a.** obstacle	**b.** benefit
4. **brooded**	**a.** concentrated	**b.** daydreamed
5. **sonorous**	**a.** quiet	**b.** loud

Literature Online **Web Activities** For eFlashcards, Selection Quick Checks, and other Web activities, go to www.glencoe.com.

---

2. The mood fits the plot well: Both are sad and eerie.

Writing About Literature

Students' essays should provide textual examples of figurative language to analyze Aiken's style.

Reading Strategy

1. "Lungewater" jumps back and forth from the past to the present.

2. Answers will vary.

Vocabulary

1. b 2. a 3. b 4. b 5. a

Assess

1. Accept reasonable responses.

2. (a) In a dilapidated bus shelter in England on a recent Christmas Eve (b) Answers will vary.

3. (a) The enslaved person of Count Boyanus (b) He is illiterate and ignorant of his rights.

4. (a) By way of the Stride, a dangerous location (b) He has no compassion for Stiva and does not seem to realize that if Stiva plunges to his death, the letters will be lost.

5. (a) He fatally falls down the ravine when forced to jump the Stride. (b) Later, the count supposedly tries to jump the Stride and falls, some say pulled into the river by Stiva's ghost.

6. (a) As a story within a story (b) The outer story, set in the present day, becomes the frame for the inner story.

7. (a) Through her refusal to respond to the count (b) She does not assign motives to the characters but allows the reader to interpret what they say and do.

8. (a) The narrator is the great-grandchild of the lady, and the old man is the brother of Stiva. (b) Answers will vary.

9. Answers will vary but should be supported by details in the text.

Literary Element

1. (a) "Lungewater" has a gothic mood: gloomy, eerie setting and elements of mystery, horror, and the supernatural. (b) Through descriptions of the misty weather, violent river, and deep ravine and the count's personality

Focus

BELLRINGER

Write *science fiction* on the board.
Ask: What does this term mean to you? What do you think of when you hear it used as a category or descriptor? *(Students may say that they think of futuristic worlds, fantastic films, or stories about aliens or alternative realities. Some may mention famous films; others may describe video games or comic books.)*

Summary

In this workshop, students will write and present short science fiction stories. Students will follow the stages of the writing process, including prewriting, drafting, revising, editing, and presenting. In addition, the workshop provides two mini-lessons, one on using dialogue and one on correcting shifts in point of view.

Writing Models Have students access the Web site for interactive writing models and writing guides.

The Writing Process

In this workshop, you will follow the stages of the writing process. At any stage, you may think of new ideas to include and better ways to express them. Feel free to return to earlier stages as you write.

Prewriting

Drafting

Revising

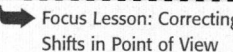 Focus Lesson: Using Dialogue

Editing and Proofreading

 Focus Lesson: Correcting Shifts in Point of View

Presenting

Literature Online
Writing Models For models and other writing activities, go to www.glencoe.com.

OBJECTIVES
- Write a science fiction story that contains dialogue.
- Maintain a consistent point of view in a story.

Writing Workshop

Short Story

 Exploring Science Fiction ★

The Machine howled. Time was a film run backward. Suns fled and ten million moons fled after them. "Think," said Eckels. "Every hunter that ever lived would envy us today. This makes Africa seem like Illinois."

The Machine slowed; its scream fell to a murmur. The Machine stopped.

The sun stopped in the sky.

—Ray Bradbury, from "A Sound of Thunder"

Connecting to Literature In "A Sound of Thunder," Ray Bradbury takes the reader to another world, where a machine can make the sun stop "in the sky" and cause time to roll "backward." This type of writing is called science fiction. It has all the elements of fiction—including characters, events, and a plot—but it deals with the impact of technology, real or imagined, on society and individuals. Science fiction is also often set in the future or in an alternative world. Study the rubric below to learn the goals and strategies for writing a successful science fiction story.

Rubric: Features of Science Fiction

Goals	Strategies
To present a series of events conveying a clear problem or conflict	☑ Present at least three separate but related events
To engage the reader from beginning to end	☑ Start out with a strong introduction or "hook" ☑ Create an interesting problem or conflict
To introduce believable characters	☑ Use descriptive details ☑ Write convincing dialogue
To resolve the conflict and end the story in a satisfying way	☑ Create a believable ending that the reader cannot easily predict

1256 UNIT 6 GENRE FICTION

Additional Support

Workshop Resources

Print Materials
📁 Unit 6 Resources (Fast File), pp. 52–54
📁 REAL Success in Writing: Research and Reports
📁 Writing Constructed Responses, pp. 1–26, 54
📖 Glencoe Literature Library

✍ **Transparencies**
- Grammar and Language Transparencies 3, 28
- Writing Workshop Transparencies 31–35
- Visual Literacy/Fine Art Transparencies

💻 **Technology**
- Grammar & Language eWorkbook
- Revising with Style eWorkbook
- Sentence Diagraming eWorkbook
- Spelling Power eWorkbook
- Online Essay Grading, glencoe.com
- Literature Library Exam*View*™ Assessment Suite CD-ROM
- Literature Library Vocabulary PuzzleMaker CD-ROM

Narration

Real-World Connection

Telling a story well is a useful social skill and a source of personal satisfaction. Learning how to tell a story can also increase your appreciation of the many great films, books, and plays you will read or view in your lifetime.

► **Assignment**

Write a science fiction story that contains dialogue. As you move through the stages of the writing process, keep your audience and purpose in mind.

Audience: classmates and peers

Purpose: to entertain by including all of the elements of a good short story, including setting, characters, events, exposition, conflict, rising action, resolution, falling action, and dialogue

Analyzing a Professional Model

In the short story that follows, Isaac Asimov presents a not-so-future world in which computers are used to create conditions for, and to fight, wars. As you read the story, identify story elements as well as features of science fiction. Pay close attention to the comments in the margin. They point out features that you might want to include in your own story.

from *"Frustration"* by Isaac Asimov

Herman Gelb turned his head to watch the departing figure. Then he said, "Wasn't that the Secretary?"

"Yes, that was the Secretary of Foreign Affairs. Old man Hargrove. Are you ready for lunch?"

"Of course. What was he doing here?"

Peter Jonsbeck didn't answer immediately. He merely stood up, and beckoned Gelb to follow. They walked down the corridor and into a room that had the steamy smell of spicy food.

"Here you are," said Jonsbeck. "The whole meal has been prepared by computer. Completely automated. Untouched by human hands. And my own programming. I promised you a treat, and here you are."

It *was* good. Gelb could not deny it and didn't want to. Over dessert, he said, "But what was Hargrove doing here?"

Jonsbeck smiled. "Consulting me on programming. What else am I good for?"

"But why? Or is it something you can't talk about?"

"It's something I suppose I *shouldn't* talk about, but it's a fairly open secret. There isn't a computer man in the capital who doesn't know what the poor frustrated simp is up to."

Exposition

Introduce the characters and begin the action.

Dialogue

Use dialogue to show characters and tell the story.

WRITING WORKSHOP **1257**

Teach

Big Idea

The Uncanny and the Mysterious Say: As you read about writing science fiction stories, keep the following idea in mind: Although science fiction is rooted in technology, the ideas for stories, alternative universes, and strange new beings originate in writers' imagination. Encourage students to take their own ideas seriously when approaching their short stories. **Say:** Every author starts somewhere! **OL**

★ Literary History

Proto-Science Fiction
Tell students about the nineteenth-century roots of science fiction. In 1818 Mary Shelley published *Frankenstein; or, The Modern Prometheus.* Her protagonist, a scientist, creates a living being and then must deal with the consequences. Known as the "mother of science fiction," Shelley paved the way for authors long before science fiction emerged as a genre. Encourage students to read *Frankenstein* or to watch a film based on the story. **AS**

Differentiated Instruction

Identifying a Topic Some writers may have difficulty deciding on a plot and characters for their short story. Work with these students individually to assist them in developing a story line and characters that they are able to bring to "life." **BL**

English Language Coach

Multicultural Science Fiction
Students from other countries may like to take a few minutes to describe the kinds of science fiction that are prevalent in their countries of origin. They may also have interesting opinions on American science fiction and its influence around the world. **EL**

Objective
• To write a science fiction story that contains dialogue (SE)

Teach

Writing Process

Prewriting Say: Ideas for science fiction short stories are all around you. As you are brainstorming about what direction you would like to take in your story, think about everyday objects and events that you could use in your story. Encourage students to have a small notepad with them at all times to jot down spontaneous ideas in. **OL**

Writing Skills

Time and Place for Writing

Say: Creative writing demands a certain kind of attention that may be different from what you are used to in your other studies. When and where it is possible, carve out extra time and a comfortable place to write your stories in. Explain that although some students may find a busy work environment conducive to writing, others may need the solitude and quiet of a library. **Say:** One way to take your own writing seriously is to be mindful of how you approach the task. **OL**

Conflict

Be sure that the story contains a problem or conflict.

Dialogue/Rising Action

Use dialogue to intensify the conflict or create rising action.

Characterization

Show characters through their words and actions.

"What is he up to then?"

"He's fighting wars."

Gelb's eyes opened wide. "With whom?"

"With nobody, really. He fights them by computer analysis. He's been doing it for I don't know how long."

"But why?"

"He wants the world to be the way we are—noble, honest, decent, full of respect for human rights and so on."

"So do I. So do we all. We have to keep up the pressure on the bad guys, that's all."

"And they're keeping the pressure on us, too. They don't think we're perfect."

"I suppose we're not, but we're better than they are. You know that."

Jonsbeck shrugged. "A difference in point of view. It doesn't matter. We've got a world to run, space to develop, computerization to extend. Cooperation puts a premium on continued cooperation and there is slow improvement. We'll get along. It's just that Hargrove doesn't want to wait. He hankers for quick improvement—by force. You know, *make* the bums shape up. We're strong enough to do it."

"By force? By war, you mean. We don't fight wars any more."

"That's because it's gotten too complicated. Too much danger. We're all too powerful. You know what I mean? Except that Hargrove thinks he can find a way. You punch certain starting conditions into the computer and let it fight the war mathematically and yield the results."

"How do you make equations for war?"

"Well, you try, old man. Men. Weapons. Surprise. Counterattack. Ships. Space stations. Computers. We mustn't forget computers. There are a hundred factors and thousands of intensities and millions of combinations. Hargrove thinks it is possible to find *some* combination of starting conditions and courses of development that will result in clear victory for us and not too much damage to the world, and he labors under constant frustration."

"But what if he gets what he wants?"

"Well, if he can find the combination—if the computer says, 'This is it,' then I suppose he thinks he can argue our government into fighting exactly the war the computer has worked out so that, barring random events that upset the indicated course, we'd have what we want."

Additional Support

Skills Practice

WRITING: Dialogue Offer a mini-workshop in writing dialogue. When writing dialogue, students should keep the following rules in mind:

- Capitalize the first word in dialogue.

- Do not capitalize the first word after an interruption in the dialogue.

- Enclose other punctuation within quotation marks.

- Indent each new line of dialogue. Have students work together in small groups to create dialogue in which they demonstrate each of these rules. Write their dialogue on the board to demonstrate the rules. **OL**

"There'd be casualties."

"Yes, of course. But the computer will presumably compare the casualties and other damage—to the economy and ecology, for instance—to the benefits that would derive from our control of the world, and if it decides the benefits will outweigh the casualties, then it will give the go-ahead for a 'just war.' After all, it may be that even the losing nations would benefit from being directed by us, with our stronger economy and stronger moral sense."

Gelb stared his disbelief and said, "I never knew we were sitting at the lip of a volcanic crater like that. What about the 'random events' you mentioned?"

"The computer program tries to allow for the unexpected, but you never can, of course. So I don't think the go-ahead will come. It hasn't so far, and unless old man Hargrove can present the government with a computer simulation of a war that is totally satisfactory, I don't think there's much chance he can force one."

"And he comes to you, then, for what reason?"

"To improve the program, of course."

"And you help him?"

"Yes, certainly. There are big fees involved, Herman."

Gelb shook his head, "Peter! Are you going to try to arrange a war, just for money?"

"There won't be a war. There's no realistic combination of events that would make the computer decide on war. Computers place a greater value on human lives than human beings do themselves, and what will seem bearable to Secretary Hargrove, or even to you and me, will never be passed by a computer."

"How can you be sure of that?"

"Because I'm a programmer and I don't know of any way of programming a computer to give it what is most needed to start any war, any persecution, any devilry, while ignoring any harm that may be done in the process. And because it lacks what is most needed, the computers will always give Hargrove, and all others who hanker for war, nothing but frustration."

"What is it that a computer doesn't have, then?"

"Why, Gelb. It totally lacks a sense of self-righteousness."

Reading-Writing Connection Think about the writing techniques that you have just encountered and try them out in the science fiction story you write.

Narration

Time Order
Tell events in time order or use a flashback. The story at this point is told by means of a conversation in time order.

Background Information
Give enough information about place, time, characters, and motives so that readers can follow the story.

Climax
Raise the conflict to a high point of tension, or climax.

Resolution
Provide an interesting or satisfying resolution or ending.

Teach

Writing Skills

Understanding Genre
Say: Effective writers know their genre. In this unit, you have been exposed to several forms of science fiction and mystery writing. Since your assignment is to write a science fiction short story, get familiar with the many modes of science fiction during the prewriting stage. Encourage students to go to the library or to perform an online search to find an example of science fiction to bring to class. They may bring in books, comics, or even films. **OL**

★ Writer's Technique

Resolution Explain to students that part of the success of Asimov's short story lies in its resolution. The last line of his story brings relief to the reader because there will be no war. At the same time, however, the last line reveals the irony of technology's so-called advantages: in this alternative universe, it values human life more than human beings do. In just one line, Asimov is able to bring his story to a close and offer his thoughts about war, technology, and human nature. **AS**

Differentiated Instruction

Illustration Give artistically talented students the opportunity to illustrate their stories. Some may enjoy illustrating stories in a comic-book fashion; others may prefer to incorporate their illustrations into their stories in a more conventional manner. **AL**

Drama Offer students talented in drama a chance to create a one-act science fiction play to present to the class. Other students may volunteer as actors, script writers, costume creators, and stage directors. Consider having them perform the play for other classes or for parents on a special-event night. **AL**

Objectives
• To analyze a professional model (SE)
• To practice writing dialogue (TWE)

Teach

Writing Process

Prewriting In the early stages of writing, encourage students to freewrite. Explain that when writing creatively, it is usually best to write first whatever comes to mind without worrying about structure, grammar, or punctuation. Encourage students to use this technique to discover what it is they would really like to write about. After they finish, students can read through their "draft" and glean from it what is useful. **OL**

★ Literary History

Alternative Realities

Explain that one of the appeals of science fiction is that in this genre alternative societies can be explored and envisioned. Readers can find examples of alternative societies throughout the history of the genre. One early work is Charlotte Perkins Gilman's novel *Herland,* published in 1915. In this work, Gilman suggests that women in the future reproduce by parthenogenesis, a process in which the male gamete is unnecessary. **AS**

What If Questions

One way to think of story ideas is to ask questions that begin with *What if,* such as *What if Earth became uninhabitable?* or *What if an alien landed on the roof of my apartment building?*

Test Prep

If you were writing a story for a test, you would have to shorten the prewriting process. Which of the steps listed here would you still follow? Why?

Prewriting

Brainstorm Setting, Characters, Events, and Focus Before writing your story, think through many ideas and then choose the best ones.

► Begin by thinking about where and when your story will take place. Make a list of possible settings.

► Think about who will appear in your story. List your characters.

► Decide what will happen to your characters. List possible events.

► Create a science fiction focus. Brainstorm about issues related to science and technology that you could explore in a story. ★

Make a Story Map A story must have a conflict or a problem to solve. It must also be told in a logical order. Making a story map will help ensure that you have ideas for all the story elements before you begin writing. It will also help you put your ideas, especially the events, in order.

Setting:	time—3005; place—in space
Characters:	star traveler and his wife, Laura
Problem or Conflict:	The star traveler wants to visit other planets and galaxies, but his wife wants him home on Earth.
Events:	1. Husband decides on life of travel. 2. Husband goes into space. 3. Husband has a crisis—is torn between star traveling and wife. 4. Husband decides on space.
Ending:	the beauty and joy of star traveling

Talk About Your Ideas Meet with a partner. Use your story map to help you summarize the ideas you have for your story so far. Ask your partner for suggestions about what to add, take out, or do differently. To develop your writing voice, listen to your own speaking voice now as you retell the most important or exciting parts of the story, such as the conflict or high point of the action. Work with your partner to identify the words and phrases that reflect your voice—which should be part of your written story. Jot down those words and phrases.

Develop Dialogue Look at your events again. Decide what the characters will be thinking to themselves or saying to one another at the most important moments of the story. Also think about how the characters' words and thoughts can help you get the story started or move the plot along. Make some notes.

Skills Practice

WRITING: Vivid Verbs and Adverbs
Remind students of the importance of using vivid verbs and adverbs in their stories. Write the following sentences on the board and have students rewrite them by substituting vivid verbs for hackneyed ones:
Bill walked to the door.

The monster ate his breakfast.
The aliens looked at the people.
(Possible rewrites: Bill ambled to the door nonchalantly. The monster devoured his breakfast. The aliens peered inquisitively at the people.)
Consider writing other sentences on the board for further practice. **OL**

Drafting

Create Paragraphs Whenever the time or place changes, or when you write dialogue, be sure to create a new paragraph. Finally, your ending or resolution should be stated in a separate paragraph.

Analyzing a Workshop Model

Here is a final draft of a science fiction story. Read the story and answer the questions in the margin. Use the answers to guide you as you write.

"Star Traveler"

I am unwrapping my recycled Stardust Fries when my transmitter beeps. "Please come home," flashes across the screen from my wife Laura. I think of her back on Earth, just getting home from work. My thoughts are disrupted when the captain's face appears on my transmitter. He announces, "We are within sight of Paradiscus. All officers are invited on deck."

I toss my food, uneaten, into the Stardust snack-recycling bin. As I make my way to the bridge, I remember how upset Laura was when I told her of my plan to join the crew of the *Zodiac*, a space explorer.

"You'll be gone so much. I may not see you again!" she cried.

"Come with me," I pleaded. "I can get you a job on the *Zodiac*, too."

She just kept shaking her head and saying, "Earth's my home." I couldn't understand that. It's 3005, and the atmosphere is so toxic there that a person couldn't last thirty seconds without a suit.

After Laura had cried herself to sleep, I put on an atmosphere suit. I knew that the wide-open universe was calling me. I packed my things, and in the morning I left—but not without a few tears of my own.

When I reach the deck, the planet Paradiscus lies straight ahead—a beautiful marblelike mixture of blue and green in the black void of space—the way Earth must have looked a thousand years ago.

"Tonight," the captain says, breaking into my meditation, "we enter the gravitational field of Anterpodia galaxy. No further communication with the Milky Way will be possible for several years." Within hours Laura will be totally out of range.

It is not, in fact, too late for me to turn back. The transport room is still operative. My cozy living room is waiting for me. But then I look out at the stars and I know that I have made the right decision. Who can truly understand what drives us star travelers?

Exposition
How does this opening show time, place, and characters?

Conflict
What is the conflict or problem?

Time Order
Are the events told in time order? Explain.

Dialogue/Rising Action
How does this part of the dialogue help create rising action?

Climax/Resolution
What is the climax of the story? How does the story end?

Narration

WRITING WORKSHOP **1261**

Reading in the Real World

Career Science fiction itself is a huge industry. Suggest that students who are particularly interested in this genre investigate various careers related to science fiction. Students may explore opportunities in filmmaking and screenwriting; some may be interested in writing original short stories or novels. Others may look into careers in illustration or television production. **OL**

Teach

Writing Skills

Exposition Answer: *The opening, which takes place in 3005, presents a main character who is not on Earth but whose wife (Laura) is on Earth.* **OL**

Writing Skills

Conflict Answer: *The main character is traveling in space against the wishes of his wife.* **OL**

Writing Skills

Time Order Answer: *The story begins in the present but flashes back to a conversation in the past.* **OL**

Writing Skills

Dialogue/Rising Action Answer: *This part of the dialogue reveals and intensifies the conflict. The narrator, or star traveler, is entering a different galaxy, where he will be unable to communicate with his wife for several years.* **OL**

Writing Skills

Climax/Resolution Answer: *The climax occurs when the star traveler chooses space over life on Earth with his wife. The resolution is in the reflection "Who can truly understand what drives us star travelers?"* **OL**

Objectives
- To analyze a workshop model (SE)
- To use vivid verbs and adverbs (TWE)

Teach

Writing Process

Revising Suggest to students that they take some time, while revising their stories, to add more detail where appropriate to enrich their characters, background information, descriptions of setting, and dialogue. Encourage students to think of the details they include as parts of the puzzle or as elements of the overall picture they want to present to their readers. **OL**

★ Cultural History

Science Fiction in Film Inform students that the late 1960s, the 1970s, and the 1980s were the defining decades for the explosion of science fiction in film and on television. The *Star Trek* series in 1966–1969, the film *2001: A Space Odyssey* in 1968, and *Close Encounters of the Third Kind* and *Star Wars* in 1977. These were followed by the *Terminator, Alien,* and *Jurassic Park* science fiction film series. Science fiction combined with new technologies in special effects and computer graphics have led to a film revolution. **AS**

Traits of Strong Writing

Follow these traits of strong writing to express your ideas effectively.

Ideas message or theme and the details that develop it

Organization arrangement of main ideas and supporting details

Voice writer's unique way of using tone and style

Word Choice vocabulary a writer uses to convey meaning

Sentence Fluency rhythm and flow of sentences

Conventions correct spelling, grammar, usage, and mechanics

Presentation the way words and design elements look on a page

For more information on using the traits of strong writing, see pages R33–R34 of the Writing Handbook.

Revising

Peer Review When you finish your draft, ask a classmate to read it. Have your classmate identify the characters, the problem or conflict, the events, and the resolution or ending. Then ask your reviewer to make suggestions about where to change background information or dialogue, or add more details about the conflict and how it builds up. Ask your reviewer to review the traits of strong writing, too; then think about how they apply to your work.

Use the rubric below to help you evaluate your writing.

Rubric: Writing a Science Fiction Story

☑ Do you include a series of events?

☑ Do you capture and hold your reader's interest from beginning to end?

☑ Do you include a conflict or problem to solve?

☑ Do you present lifelike, believable characters, or characters that help show an alternative world?

☑ Do you solve the problem or conflict and include a satisfying ending?

▶ **Focus Lesson**

Using Dialogue

Dialogue in a story helps bring characters to life. It can show their motives, thoughts, and values. It can also reveal their relationships to other characters and to the conflict. As you revise your narrative, look for places where you can add dialogue or replace flat statements with dialogue. Note how dialogue improves the passage from the Workshop Model below.

Draft:

As I make my way to the bridge, I remember how upset Laura was when I told her of my plan to join the crew of the Zodiac, a space explorer. She worried about how much I'd be gone, so I asked her to come with me. I said I'd get her a job on the Zodiac.

Revision:

As I make my way to the bridge, I remember how upset Laura was when I told her of my plan to join the crew of the Zodiac, a space explorer.

"You'll be gone so much. I may not see you again!" she cried.[1]

"Come with me," I pleaded. "I can get you a job on the Zodiac, too."[2]

1: shows character's feelings   2: shows character's values

Additional Support

Skills Practice

WRITING: Coordinate and Cumulative Adjectives In describing characters and scenes in their short stories, students may be using several adjectives at once. Point out to students the differences between coordinate and cumulative adjectives.

Coordinate adjectives are two or more adjectives that modify the same noun or pronoun.

(An example: The woman wore *gigantic, green, garish* earrings.)

Cumulative adjectives modify adjectives that follow them as well as a noun or pronoun.

Editing and Proofreading

Get It Right When you have completed the final draft of your story, proofread it for errors in grammar, usage, mechanics, and spelling. Refer to the Language Handbook, pages R40–R60, as a guide.

▶ **Focus Lesson**

Correcting Shifts in Point of View

Stories are often told from the third-person point of view. The narrator uses pronouns such as *he, she,* and *they* to tell the story. Many stories are told from the first-person point of view. A character in the story uses the pronoun *I* to tell what is happening. You should tell your story in third person or first person, but not both. You should also avoid shifting to the second person. Below are examples of shifts in point of view and corrections from the Workshop Model.

Problem: The narrative shifts from the first person to the third person.

I knew that the wide-open universe was calling me. He packed his things, and in the morning he left—but not without a few tears of his own.

Solution: Make sure that all personal pronouns are first-person pronouns.

I knew that the wide-open universe was calling me. I packed my things, and in the morning I left—but not without a few tears of my own.

Problem: The narrative shifts inappropriately to the second person (you).

The atmosphere is so toxic there that you couldn't last thirty seconds without a suit.

Solution: Use a noun or another pronoun that makes sense in the context of the sentence.

The atmosphere is so toxic there that a person couldn't last thirty seconds without a suit.

Presenting

One Last Look If you word process your work, read it again after you print it out. Sometimes, it is easier to see errors on paper than on the screen. Make all corrections neatly in red or blue ink. To cross something out, draw a single line through the word or words.

Read It Aloud

Read your story aloud to yourself. How does it sound? Do the characters sound real? Is the plot interesting or exciting? Do the sentences flow well? Base final revisions on what you hear.

Let It Rest

Let your story rest for a day or two before you revise it. When you come back to it, a little time and distance may help you see its strengths and weaknesses more clearly.

Writer's Portfolio

Place a copy of your story in your portfolio to review later.

Teach

Writing Process

Editing and Proofreading
Say: Consider letting an objective third party read through your story—perhaps a parent, a sibling, or a friend outside of class. Ask him or her to comment on the overall impression and tone of the story. Stress the importance of letting outsiders read students' work. The process can help writers catch mechanical mistakes and can be rewarding (in terms of students' pride in their creations). **OL**

Writing Process

Presenting Say: The final touch you put on your story is its title. Generally you want to create a title that piques the interest of your readers but does not give your story away. Have students work on titles for their stories. Then pair off students and have them work with each other, comparing and contrasting their titles and offering constructive criticism. **OL**

Differentiated Instruction

(An example: The performance of *modern interpretive jazz* dance will start at 7 P.M.)
Remind students to use commas between coordinating adjectives not joined by *and.* Generally commas are not used between cumulative adjectives. **OL**

Starting in the Middle Students may not realize that they need not start their stories at the beginning and follow through to the end. Suggest that students who are "stuck" at the beginning of a story start in the middle (writing about the core problem) or at the end (writing about its resolution). **BL**

Objectives
- To maintain a consistent point of view in a story (SE)
- To use dialogue (SE)
- To understand coordinate and cumulative adjectives (TWE)

1263

Focus

Summary

In this workshop, students will learn techniques for planning and presenting a group discussion of a short story to the class.

Teach

Speaking Skills

Responding to Other Group Members
As group members present, emphasize the importance of the following:

- responding politely to others
- maintaining eye contact
- taking the proper amount of time
- not interrupting others **OL**

Speaking Skills

The Role of Facilitator
Explain the responsibilities of the facilitator of a group discussion: to ask thought-provoking questions, to keep the discussion on track, to balance speakers' time, and to ask follow-up questions. Give examples of each function and show videotapes of moderated primary debates and other group discussions. **OL**

Responding Orally
The best oral interpretations have a written basis—good notes. During the planning stage, make a separate note card for each main idea you plan to present. On the note card, write the words from the text that support your main idea as well as any other brief notes that will help you recall and present your point.

Speaking, Listening, and Viewing Workshop

Group Discussion

Presenting an Oral Interpretation of a Short Story

Connecting to Literature Science fiction stories such as "A Sound of Thunder" are often full of interesting events, complicated choices, moral questions, and characters in conflict. Like other literary genres, they offer much to discuss—and much to discover through the process of sharing interpretations. In this workshop, you will learn how to participate in a group discussion in which all group members present their oral interpretations of a science fiction story.

> **Assignment** In a group, discuss and interpret a science fiction story, using accurate and detailed references to the text.

Planning Your Group Discussion

In a group discussion, every member must be an active participant, contributing through active speaking and listening strategies. To ensure that everyone takes an active role, assign specific group tasks such as the following:

- **Leader or Facilitator** This person introduces the topic, keeps the discussion focused, and keeps track of time.
- **Recorder** This person keeps track of the most important points and takes the lead in summarizing the discussion.
- **Group Participants** All group participants, including the leader and the recorder, present ideas and ask questions about the literature; support their opinions with details from the literature; and evaluate, respect, and respond to the interpretations and questions of others.

After you assign roles, work with the rest of the group to plan ways to achieve the following goals for a group discussion that interprets a story:

- Make judgments about the story.
- Support each judgment with words and passages from the story.
- Point out stylistic devices (such as imagery) and their effects.
- Discuss the questions raised in the text, such as the problems created by new technology.

1264 UNIT 6 GENRE FICTION

Skills Practice

LISTENING: Comparing and Contrasting Emphasize that students should compare and contrast the interpretations presented by their classmates during their group discussions. Advise students to pay attention to similarities and differences in

- interpretation of characters

- interpretation of key plot elements
- interpretation of theme

Suggest that students prepare three-column graphic organizers with the headings *Plot*, *Character*, and *Theme*, and have students fill in the interpretations for each group-discussion participant. **OL**

Interpreting the Literature

What can you say about the literature? Follow these steps for thinking of your own interpretations and questions.

- Review the story under discussion. Summarize the story, or make a story map showing its main events, its conflict, and its resolution, or ending.
- Ask questions. Many of the best questions about literature begin with the questions *why, how,* or *how well.* Complete an organizer like this one, substituting your own questions.

Why . . .	How . . .	How well . . .
Why does Bradbury set the most important part of his story in a jungle?		How well does Bradbury show the dinosaur and its power?

Preparing for the Group Discussion

As a group member, you can prepare for the discussion this way:

- Plan a logical order in which to present your points.
- Rehearse the points you will make.
- Gather references to the text or quotations from the story as support.

As a group, you can prepare for the discussion this way:

- Decide on a format. For example, will each person have a certain amount of time to speak? Will the discussion follow a specific order?
- Decide how and when to end discussion and how to summarize.

Techniques for Delivering a Persuasive Speech

Speaking Techniques	Listening Techniques
☑ **Make Eye Contact** Address the group—not your notes—when you speak.	☑ **Focus** Look directly at each speaker and concentrate on what each has to say.
☑ **Maintain an Even Pitch** Eliminate the highs and lows in your voice as you speak.	☑ **Interpret** Actively follow each interpretation and the evidence used to support it.
☑ **Speak Clearly** Avoid rushing through your points and running your words together.	☑ **Respond** Show interest. Nod in agreement if that is appropriate. Ask for clarification if necessary.
☑ **Use Audience Feedback** Watch other group members' reactions to get feedback.	☑ **Evaluate** Make judgments about each main point. Prepare thoughtful responses.

Watch a Group Discussion

Watch a television presentation or download a video of a group discussion. You may want to watch weekly news shows that have three or four guests. Study the participants' tone, body language, pitch, and active listening strategies.

Speak Up

During the discussion, other group members may present ideas that you cannot hear, understand, or follow. Do not let those comments pass! Instead, politely ask, "Could you repeat that?" or admit, "I don't follow that. Could you explain it to me?"

OBJECTIVES
- Orally express main ideas, opinions, and judgments about literature, supporting them with references to the text.
- Focus attention on, interpret, respond to, and evaluate each speaker's message.

Teach

Speaking Skills

Organizing a Discussion
Invite students to report on the formats of televised discussion shows, and discuss the ways to organize group discussions. Have students weigh the pros and cons of participants' talking one at a time versus interacting on specific topics. Discuss how to combine formats as well. **OL**

Listening Skills

Active Listening Strategies
Review active listening strategies prior to the group discussions. Encourage students to prepare by recalling the story, pay attention and be actively engaged while others are speaking, and respond with attentive looks, appropriate reactions, and nods of encouragement. Suggest that students make notes about follow-up questions to ask and express appreciation afterward. Urge discussion participants to listen carefully to others' ideas. **OL**

Objectives
- To express main ideas, opinions, and judgments about literature orally, supporting them with references to the text (SE)
- To focus attention on, interpret, respond to, and evaluate each speaker's message (SE)
- To understand the role of a discussion facilitator (TWE)

English Language Coach

Framing Questions Have students practice asking *why, how,* and *how well* questions about a story. Give examples of open-ended questions that invite discussion. Urge students to write down questions after they read a story and evaluate these as discussion questions. **EL**

Differentiated Instruction

Oral Reading Invite auditory learners to present short oral readings to bring out their interpretations of a story. For example, discuss how students can reveal their interpretations of characters through gestures, expressions, and tone of voice. Also discuss how their readings can set a mood. **BL**

1265

Focus

Summary

The purpose of this feature is to interest students in reading additional genre fiction similar to the mysteries, modern fables, and fantasy stories in this unit. Recommendations include classic and contemporary grade-appropriate fiction. Some of the recommended books are by authors represented in this unit.

Teach

★ Literary History

Detective Stories

Say: Mystery stories center on finding out secrets or creating suspense. In one subgroup, the detective story, a detective follows clues to solve a crime. The form originated in the mid-nineteenth century with Edgar Allan Poe and was developed further by great writers, including Sir Arthur Conan Doyle and Agatha Christie, who created two of the world's most famous fictional detectives, Sherlock Holmes and Hercule Poirot. **AS**

Genre Fiction

SOME TYPES OF FICTION FOLLOW SUCH DISTINCT PATTERNS that they have their own classification, or genre. Among these types of genre fiction are mysteries, in which characters use clues to solve a problem, and science fiction, which presents imagined events related to science or technology. Fantasy stories with invented characters, settings, and other elements is another subset of fiction. Modern fables, or stories that are usually based on a single event and use stock characters, also follow a distinct pattern. For more genre fiction on a range of themes, try the first three suggestions below. For novels that incorporate the Big Ideas of *The Extraordinary and Fantastic* and *The Uncanny and Mysterious,* try the titles from the Glencoe Literature Library on the next page.

The Ear, the Eye, and the Arm

by Nancy Farmer

The place is Zimbabwe. The year is 2194. After sneaking into a dangerous city, three children are kidnapped and forced into a life of hard labor in a plastics mine. Many fast-paced adventures follow. The children's parents hire a trio of mutant detectives to find them, but the sensitive yet absurd rescuers are constantly just one step behind the children. This novel combines elements of science fiction, humor, and traditional African culture. Notes and a glossary help readers with the traditional African tribal language and lore.

Nightfall

by Isaac Asimov and Robert Silverberg

Two of the greatest science-fiction writers of the twentieth century collaborated on this suspenseful tale, which is based on a 1941 short story by Asimov. *Nightfall* explores what happens when darkness slowly falls in a world that has seen nothing but sunlight for the last two thousand years. Readers experience the event through the eyes of a newspaperman, an astronomer, a psychologist, an archeologist, and a religious person. As a terrified society verges on chaos, only a few citizens are prepared to face a truth that reveals some of the most fundamental aspects of human experience.

1266 UNIT 6 GENRE FICTION

Additional Support

Skills Practice

READING: Predicting the Author's Purpose Point out that writers of fables, fantasy, and science fiction often have a distinct purpose in mind and that sometimes that purpose is expressed as a moral or a comment on society. From the descriptions of the books on this page, ask students to predict what each fantasy writer's purpose might be. In this regard, encourage students to draw inferences from the aspect of society the author focuses on as well as from the character traits illustrated. Invite students to read the books to determine whether their predictions of the author's purpose are accurate. **OL**

CRITICS' CORNER

"The pretense, disguise, play-acting, and outward show that are essential to the mystery genre are given a special intensity in Christie's work by her constant emphasis on and reference to the "theatricality" of her characters' actions. A well-known example is Murder on the Orient Express *(1934), in which Hercule Poirot comes to realize that he has been an audience of one for a careful series of performances."*

—Nicholas Birns and Margaret Boe Birns,
from *The Cunning Craft: Original Essays on Detective Fiction and Contemporary Literary Theory*

Murder on the Orient Express

by Agatha Christie

In this novel, the most well known of Agatha Christie's many mysteries, the murder of an American gentleman occurs on the Orient Express, a luxury train traveling from Istanbul to Paris. The man is found dead in his train compartment with the door locked from the inside. Trapped by a snowstorm in Yugoslavia, the full train includes an array of passengers from many countries traveling first class, as well as Hercule Poirot, a Belgian detective. Eventually, Poirot pieces together the many obscure clues that help make up the ingenious plot.

From the Glencoe Literature Library

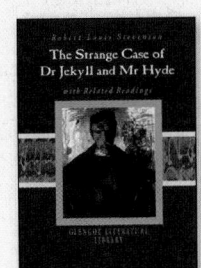

The Strange Case of Dr. Jekyll and Mr. Hyde

By Robert Louis Stevenson

Good reigns by day and evil by night in this *Extraordinary and Fantastic* divided self.

Frankenstein

By Mary Shelley

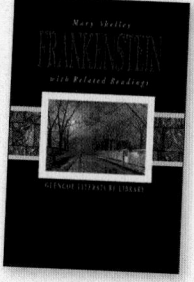

Dr. Frankenstein is obsessed with giving his creation life—but the results will shock him and the readers of this *Uncanny and Mysterious* gothic novel.

Teach

★ Literary History

Mary Shelley (1797–1851) The daughter of radical intellectuals William Godwin and Mary Wollstonecraft and the wife of poet Percy Bysshe Shelley, Mary Shelley was only twenty-one when her famous novel *Frankenstein* was published. In it the monster embodies the evil unleashed by an ambitious but creative scientist. The novel still inspires films, plays, and books today. This masterpiece is considered the first modern work of science fiction, as well as one of the most compelling works of gothic literature, a type of Romantic writing intended to arouse terror. **AS**

Glencoe Literature Library

Glencoe Literature Library offers an extensive collection of hardcover books that help you encourage your students to read independently. Choose among the more than 120 full-length literary works—novels, novellas, plays, and nonfiction. Each book includes related readings from a broad range of genres. Go to www.Glencoe.com for more information.

Objectives

• To encourage independent reading of mysteries, fables, and science fiction (SE)
• To predict author's purposes (TWE)

English Language Coach

Stock Characters Some students may not know the term *stock characters*, referring to conventional character types in genres. Give examples, such as the outlaw and the brave cowboy in Westerns. Urge students to identify how other characters differ from stock characters as they read. **EL**

Differentiated Instruction

Word Parts Write this word from the page on the board: *subset*. Discuss how word parts can help students to determine meaning. Students should recognize that the prefix *sub-* means "under" or "beneath," so *subset* means "a set within a set." Urge students to analyze word parts of unfamiliar words. **BL**

Focus

BELLRINGER

Say: Taking tests can open doors to a bright future. You may have to take a test to graduate from an academic program or qualify for admission. One way to ensure that you do well is to learn test-taking strategies and to practice taking tests. Have groups of students demonstrate dos and don'ts for test taking and test preparation.

Teach

Assessment Explain to students that Test Preparation and Practice is designed to develop their test-taking skills as well as to test their mastery of the skills taught in this unit. Students will read a fictional selection and then answer questions that test their comprehension and their vocabulary. Next, they will use vocabulary knowledge and context clues to select words to complete sentences. They will also use grammar and writing skills to improve a writing passage. Finally, they will write a short essay. **OL**

Test Preparation and Practice

English–Language Arts

Reading: Genre Fiction

Carefully read the following passage. Pay close attention to the author's main idea and use of literary devices. Also note the other qualities of the story, such as character development, setting, plot, and mood—all of which contribute to the author's style. Use context clues to help you define any words with which you are unfamiliar. Then, on a separate sheet of paper, answer the questions on pages 1269–1270.

> **from "The Metamorphosis"** by Franz Kafka
> translated by David Wyllie
>
> One morning, when Gregor Samsa woke from troubled dreams, he found himself transformed in his bed into a horrible vermin. He lay on his armor-like back, and if he lifted his head a little he could see his brown belly, slightly domed and divided by arches into stiff sections. The
> 5   bedding was hardly able to cover it and seemed ready to slide off any moment. His many legs, pitifully thin compared with the size of the rest of him, waved about helplessly as he looked.
>   "What's happened to me?" he thought. It wasn't a dream. His room, a proper human room although a little too small, lay peacefully between
> 10   its four familiar walls. A collection of textile samples lay spread out on the table—Samsa was a traveling salesman—and above it there hung a picture that he had recently cut out of an illustrated magazine and housed in a nice, gilded frame. It showed a lady fitted out with a fur hat and fur boa who sat upright, raising a heavy fur muff that covered the
> 15   whole of her lower arm towards the viewer.
>   Gregor then turned to look out the window at the dull weather. Drops of rain could be heard hitting the pane, which made him feel quite sad. "How about if I sleep a little bit longer and forget all this nonsense," he thought, but that was something he was unable to do
> 20   because he was used to sleeping on his right, and in his present state couldn't get into that position. However hard he threw himself onto his right, he always rolled back to where he was. He must have tried it a hundred times, shut his eyes so that he wouldn't have to look at the floundering legs, and only stopped when he began to feel a mild, dull
> 25   pain there that he had never felt before.
>   "Oh, God," he thought, "what a strenuous career it is that I've chosen! Traveling day in and day out. Doing business like this takes much more effort than doing your own business at home, and on

---

Skills Practice

READING: Summarizing Say: Summarizing is an effective strategy to use in connection with reading-comprehension passages on standardized tests. Remind students that summarizing is telling the main ideas of what has been read. Advise students to summarize briefly the reading-comprehension passages they read. This technique will help them answer questions based on the passage as a whole. Remind students to read quickly yet thoroughly enough to answer the questions correctly, which should be their main concern. Encourage students to practice summarizing as a method of monitoring their comprehension. **OL**

top of that there's the curse of traveling, worries about making train
30   connections, bad and irregular food, contact with different people all
the time so that you can never get to know anyone or become friendly
with them. It can all go to Hell!" He felt a slight itch up on his belly;
pushed himself slowly up on his back towards the headboard so that
he could lift his head better; found where the itch was, and saw that it
35   was covered with lots of little white spots which he didn't know what
to make of; and when he tried to feel the place with one of his legs
he drew it quickly back because as soon as he touched it he was
overcome by a cold shudder.

He slid back into his former position. "Getting up early all the time,"
40   he thought, "it makes you stupid. You've got to get enough sleep. . . . "

❶ What is the setting of the passage?
  A Gregor's dream
  B Gregor's office
  C Gregor's bed
  D Gregor's room

❷ From what point of view is the passage
written?
  F first-person limited
  G first-person omniscient
  H second-person
  I third-person omniscient

❸ What does the word *housed*, in line 13, mean?
  A contained
  B dwelled
  C limited
  D addressed

❹ Which of the following is a synonym for the
word *state*, in line 20?
  F standing
  G condition
  H outlook
  I declare

❺ According to the context, which of the
following best describes Gregor's
transformation?
  A gradual
  B ongoing
  C sudden
  D transitional

❻ What is Gregor's reaction to the realization
that he is an insect?
  F He is frantic.
  G He is worried.
  H He is mildly surprised.
  I He is unconcerned.

❼ To what element of the story does the
second paragraph most contribute?
  A character
  B setting
  C conflict
  D mood

❽ To what element of the story does the fourth
paragraph most contribute?
  F character
  G setting
  H conflict
  I plot

❾ Which of the following describes Gregor's
attitude in the passage?
  A buoyant
  B hesitant
  C abrasive
  D surly

❿ What is Gregor most distressed about in the
passage?
  F his career
  G his state
  H his family
  I his home

Assess

1. **D** is the correct answer.
The passage takes place in
Gregor's room. He is lying
in his bed, but the setting
includes the whole room.

2. **I** is the correct answer. The
passage is not written from
Gregor's perspective or from
a second-person perspective,
so options **F, G,** and **H** are
incorrect.

3. **A** is the correct answer. The
picture frame "contains"
the picture. No other option
makes sense in this context.

4. **G** is the correct answer.
Gregor cannot roll onto his
side because of his present
physical condition. No other
option makes sense in this
context.

5. **C** is the correct answer. The
first two lines imply a sudden transformation as Gregor
wakes up to a changed form.

6. **H** is the correct answer.
Gregor remarks on his transformation only in the second
paragraph.

7. **B** is the correct answer. Most of the
paragraph describes Gregor's room,
which is the setting of the story.

8. **F** is the correct answer. The fourth
paragraph is devoted entirely to
Gregor's thoughts and actions.

9. **B** is the correct answer. Gregor is
in no way cheerful, so option **A** is

incorrect. He is not rude in the passage, because he is alone, so options
C and **D** are incorrect.

10. **F** is the correct answer. Although
Gregor shows little concern about
his transformation, he complains
about his job.

Assess

11. **C** is the correct answer. The context is "bad and irregular food," which implies that it is substandard or inadequate.

12. **I** is the correct answer. The author makes no direct comment about Gregor's personality, so options **F**, **G**, and **H** are incorrect. In these two paragraphs, Gregor's actions and thoughts indirectly reveal aspects of Gregor's personality.

13. **B** is the correct answer. Gregor's transformation itself is an extended comparison between two dissimilar things.

14. **I** is the correct answer. Gregor's descriptions of his career reveal his dissatisfaction with his hectic life as a traveling salesman.

Unit Assessment Have students access the Web site to prepare for the Unit Six test.

---

11 From the context, what do you think the word *irregular*, in line 30, means?
  A not commonly found
  B not uniform
  C not up to standard
  D not following rules

12 How is Gregor's personality revealed in the third and fourth paragraphs?
  F through metaphor
  G through symbol
  H through direct characterization
  I through indirect characterization

13 What can Gregor's transformation into a "horrible vermin" be considered?
  A an allegorical interpretation
  B a metaphorical characterization
  C a symbolic interpretation
  D a direct characterization

14 From the passage, what can you infer about Gregor's life before his transformation?
  F His career once was satisfying.
  G He made a good living despite illness.
  H Life was not without pitfalls.
  I Life was rushed and unsatisfying.

Literature Online Unit Assessment To prepare for the Unit test, go to www.glencoe.com.

Additional Support

Skills Practice

LITERARY ELEMENT:
Characterization

Say: Pay attention to various types of characterization, such as direct characterization through the author's description and indirect characterization through what a character says, does, or thinks.

Encourage students to draw inferences from indirect characterization, as in "The Metamorphosis" excerpt, where Gregor Samsa is portrayed indirectly mainly through his thoughts. Suggest that **interior monologues** such as Samsa's, which present the thoughts and emotions of a character, can be very revealing. **OL**

Vocabulary Skills: Sentence Completion

For each item in the Vocabulary Skills section, choose the word that best completes the sentence.

1 Because he had worked with his hands all his life, his fingers were badly _____ in his old age.
- **A** sonorous
- **B** gnarled
- **C** amicable
- **D** erroneous

2 He has known nothing but _____ since he suffered that tragic loss.
- **F** precedence
- **G** pretext
- **H** anguish
- **I** paradox

3 For our camping trip, we left all _____ items at home, and took only the essentials.
- **A** expendable
- **B** dutiful
- **C** exclusive
- **D** invaluable

4 Emergency-care workers need a _____ state of mind to cope on a daily basis.
- **F** treacherous
- **G** resilient
- **H** primeval
- **I** guttural

5 The professor did his best to explain "string theory," but the concept _____ more of the audience than it illuminated.
- **A** dismantled
- **B** cultivated
- **C** perplexed
- **D** accosted

6 On their arrival, guests were kept waiting on the _____ until the host could greet them.
- **F** verandah
- **G** horizon
- **H** psalm
- **I** retribution

7 Thoughts are like the fiber strands of a blanket, _____ to form a unified whole.
- **A** interlaced
- **B** bloated
- **C** livid
- **D** inert

8 The true measure of a great magician is his ability to _____ the audience before they know that they have been tricked.
- **F** recoil
- **G** bade
- **H** dupe
- **I** accost

9 Scientists do not know whether the *Tyrannosaurus rex* was a hunter or a/an _____ that ate others' leftovers.
- **A** retribution
- **B** animosity
- **C** impediment
- **D** scavenger

10 He spent the afternoon _____ editing his report to ensure that it was free of errors.
- **F** unobtrusively
- **G** assiduously
- **H** resiliently
- **I** erroneously

Assess

1. **B** is the correct answer. No other option makes sense in this context.

2. **H** is the correct answer. No other option makes sense in this context.

3. **A** is the correct answer. No other option makes sense here.

4. **G** is the correct answer. The context requires a word meaning "capable of being repaired or recovering." No other option makes sense in this context.

5. **C** is the correct answer. The sentence requires an image of confusion. No other option makes sense in this context.

6. **F** is the correct answer. A verandah is a porch. No other option makes sense in the context.

7. **A** is the correct answer. The context requires an image of a woven pattern. Only *interlaced* fits this context.

8. **H** is the correct answer. The context requires a synonym of *trick*. No other option makes sense in this context.

9. **D** is the correct answer. No other option makes sense in this context.

10. **G** is the correct answer. No other option makes sense in this context.

Differentiated Instruction

Contrasts and Comparisons Point out to students that the context of a sentence-completion question can provide comparison and contrast clues:

- **contrast**—in item 9, *or* signals that the missing word contrasts with *hunter*.

- **antonym**—in item 5, *but* signals that the missing word is an antonym of *illuminated*.

- **synonym**—A synonym clue equates one word with another, as in item 8, in which *dupe* is a synonym of *trick*. Discuss words that signal these context clues and provide sentences for practice. **BL**

1271

Assess

1. **D** is the correct answer. The sentence contains a conjunctive adverb between two main clauses but with incorrect punctuation. No other option corrects this error without inserting additional errors.

2. **H** is the correct answer. The logic of the sentence counters the point made in the previous sentence. The transitional word *instead* reflects that change.

3. **D** is the correct answer. The long opening phrase is meant to modify *Gregor* but instead modifies nothing.

4. **H** is the correct answer. A coordinating conjunction appears between the two main clauses, so a full stop is not needed. No other option corrects this error without inserting additional errors.

5. **B** is the correct answer. The transitional phrase *in fact,* introducing the second of the two main clauses, needs a semicolon before it and a comma after it.

Grammar and Writing Skills: Paragraph Improvement

Read carefully through the following paragraphs from the first draft of a student's reflective essay. Pay close attention to the writer's use of grammar and the location and appropriateness of modifiers. Then answer the questions on pages 1272–1273.

(1) *Franz Kafka's "The Metamorphosis" is the story of Gregor Samsa, a young man who wakes up one morning transformed into an insect-like creature.* (2) *Gregor is strangely indifferent to his plight, indeed his manner seems almost too odd.* (3) *Likewise, he worries about the daily obligations that have drained him.*

(4) *Attempting to satisfy the demands of his family and employer, Gregor's maddening life falls into tragedy.* (5) *The horrible insect becomes a metaphor, signifying Gregor's fading identity and inability to function in society.*

(6) *Gregor's world changes drastically; and his physical abilities are the first to go.* (7) *Unable to work, Gregor can no longer support his family.* (8) *Not all of his changes come from his altered body, in fact some changes are caused by the world's reaction to him.* (9) *His family's rejection brings on emotional deterioration just as severe as his physical decline.* (10) *Even his sister becomes indifferent to him at last, who at first showed him compassion and pity.*

(11) *The cruelest irony, however, is in the positive changes that occur in the Samsa family as Gregor descends into insignificance.* (12) *As Gregor becomes more isolated and worthless; but, his family becomes more self-reliant.* (13) *Gregor becomes a sacrifice, given up so that the others can prosper.*

❶ Which of the following is the best revision of sentence 2?
  A Gregor is, strangely, indifferent to his plight, indeed, his manner seems almost too odd.
  B Gregor is strangely indifferent to his plight: indeed, his manner seems almost too odd.
  C Gregor is strangely indifferent to his plight, indeed, his manner seems almost too odd.
  D Gregor is strangely indifferent to his plight; indeed, his manner seems almost too odd.

❷ Which of the following words is the best substitute for *likewise* in sentence 3?
  F finally
  G also
  H instead
  I thus

❸ Which of the following errors appears in sentence 4?
  A run-on sentence
  B incorrect parallelism
  C sentence fragment
  D dangling modifier

1272 UNIT 6   GENRE FICTION

Skills Practice

GRAMMAR: Semicolons Versus Colons **Write on the board:** Franz Kafka was born in Czechoslovakia, he spoke German. Review the main methods of correcting comma splices:

• Insert a semicolon between independent clauses. A conjunctive adverb may be needed to express the relationship. (*Franz Kafka was born in Czechoslovakia; however, he spoke German*).

• Use a comma with a conjunction (*Franz Kafka was born in Czechoslovakia, but he spoke German*). This is effective when the conjunction expresses the relationship.

4 Which of the following is the best way to revise sentence 6?

F Change the semicolon to a colon.
G Enclose *drastically* in quotations marks.
H Change the semicolon to a comma.
I Make no change.

5 Which of the following is the best revision of sentence 8?

A Not all of his changes come from his altered body; in fact some changes are caused by the world's reaction to him.
B Not all of his changes come from his altered body; in fact, some changes are caused by the world's reaction to him.
C In fact, not all of his changes come from his altered body some changes are caused by the world's reaction, to him.
D Not all of his changes come from his altered body, in fact, some changes are caused by the world's reaction to him.

6 Which of the following errors appears in sentence 10?

F run-on sentence
G misplaced modifier
H sentence fragment
I lack of subject-verb agreement

7 What addition to the third paragraph would show the severity of Gregor's emotional decline?

A a description of Gregor's reaction to his sister
B more details about Gregor's physical changes
C elaboration on Gregor's family life
D an illustration of how limited Gregor's movements are

8 What could the writer add to the last paragraph in order to develop the point made there?

F examples
G quotations
H objections
I dates

9 Which of the following is the best revision of sentence 12?

A As Gregor becomes more isolated and worthless, but his family becomes more, self-reliant.
B Gregor becomes more isolated and worthless, but, his family becomes more self-reliant.
C As Gregor becomes more isolated and worthless, his family becomes more self-reliant.
D Gregor becomes more isolated; and worthless but his family becomes more self-reliant.

10 Which of the following does the writer include in the concluding paragraph?

F the introduction of opposite viewpoints
G information not included in previous paragraphs
H a summary of the key points
I information not related to the writer's argument

Essay

Choose one of the readings from this unit and write an essay that discusses how the author's use of imagery contributes to the theme or purpose of the text. What do the main character or characters learn, about themselves or the world in general, from being in a foreign or strange setting? Use specific examples from the readings. Be sure to organize your ideas and write in complete sentences. Proofread your work and correct any grammatical errors. As you write, keep in mind that your essay will be checked for **ideas, organization, voice, word choice, sentence fluency, conventions,** and **presentation.**

Assess

6. **G** is the correct answer. The modifier *who first showed him compassion and pity* should follow the noun *sister.*

7. **A** is the correct answer. Details about Gregor's reaction to his sister's indifference would support the point made about his "severe" emotional decline.

8. **F** is the correct answer. Examples would clarify the nature of the "positive changes."

9. **C** is the correct answer. The introductory subordinate clause should be followed only by a comma, not by a semicolon and a coordinating conjunction. No other option corrects this error without inserting additional errors.

10. **G** is the correct answer. The paragraph contains neither opposing viewpoints nor a summary of key points, so options **F** and **H** are incorrect. Instead, the author provides related but new information to support the argument.

- Use a colon *only* when the second clause explains the first; so in the sample sentence, a colon would be incorrect.
Provide more examples to correct. **OL**

Essay

Check that students provide specific examples of imagery in their essays and that they relate the examples to plausible analyses of the selections' themes.

REFERENCE SECTION

A

Abstract language Language that expresses an idea or intangible reality, as opposed to a specific object, occurrence, or a concrete reality. "On Women's Right to Vote," page 446, includes abstract language such as *liberty, power, blessings,* and *posterity.*

See also CONCRETE LANGUAGE.

Absurd, Theater of the See *THEATER OF THE ABSURD.*

Act A major unit of a drama, or play. Modern dramas generally have one, two, or three acts. Older dramas often have five acts. Although Shakespeare did not separate his plays into acts, each play was later divided into five acts. Acts may be divided into one or more scenes.

See pages 706–712

See also DRAMA, SCENE.

Allegory A literary work in which all or most of the characters, settings, and events stand for ideas, qualities, or figures beyond themselves. The overall purpose of an allegory is to teach a moral lesson.

See also SYMBOL.

Alliteration The repetition of consonant sounds, generally at the beginnings of words. Alliteration can be used to emphasize words, reinforce meaning, or create a musical effect. Note the repeated *s* sounds in the opening of Jean Toomer's "Reapers":

> Black reapers with the sound of steel on stones
> Are sharpening scythes.

See pages 646–647, 651, and 660

See also SOUND DEVICES.

Allusion A reference to a well-known character, place, or situation from history, music, art, or another work of literature. Discovering the meaning of an allusion can often be essential to understanding a work.

For example, in "Farewell to Manzanar," Jeanne Wakatsuki Houston refers to the residents of the camp as "a band of Charlie Chaplins." This allusion is to Charlie Chaplin, a famous film comedian.

See pages 453, 463, and 541

Ambiguity The state of having more than one meaning. The richness of literary language lies in its ability to evoke multiple layers of meaning. The title of E. E. Cumming's poem "since feeling is first," is intentionally ambiguous.

Analogy A comparison that shows similarities between two things that are otherwise dissimilar. A writer may use an analogy to explain something unfamiliar by comparing it to something familiar.

See pages 466, 500, and 1163

See also METAPHOR, RHETORICAL DEVICES, SIMILE.

Anecdote A short written or oral account of an event from a person's life. Essayists often use anecdotes to support their opinions, clarify their ideas, grab the reader's attention, or entertain.

See pages 389, 397, and 450

Antagonist A person or a force in society or nature that opposes the *protagonist,* or central character, in a story or drama. The reader is generally not meant to sympathize with the antagonist. Mark Antony is Brutus's antagonist in Shakespeare's *Julius Caesar.*

See pages 94–95 and 721

See also CHARACTER, CONFLICT, PROTAGONIST.

Anthropomorphism The assignment of human characteristics to gods, animals, or inanimate objects. It is a key element in fables and folktales, where the main characters are often animals. In the myth "Coyote, Iktome and the Rock," page 1038, the animals behave somewhat like human beings.

See also FABLE.

Antithesis The technique of putting opposite ideas side-by-side in order to point out their differences or to draw attention to the superiority of one. Antithesis is often used in logical argument.

See also ARGUMENT, PERSUASION.

Aphorism A short, pointed statement that expresses a wise or clever observation about human experience.

Apostrophe A literary device in which a speaker addresses an inanimate object, an idea, or an absent person.

See also PERSONIFICATION.

Archetype Ideas, characters, stories, or images that are common to human experience across cultures and throughout the world. In their purest form, archetypes occur in oral tradition, but they also appear in written works of literature. They can be divided into the following categories:

Character archetype: Includes familiar individuals such as the wise leader, the rebel, the damsel in distress, and the traitor. Coyote, the trickster of Native American folklore, is a character archetype.

Image archetype: Objects or places that have a universal symbolism. For example, a lily can be a symbol of purity.

Plot pattern archetype: Stories that occur in many cultures. Making the long journey home, completing the "impossible" task, or outwitting the formidable enemy are all archetypal plots.

Theme archetype: Ideas that occur wherever people tell stories. The idea that good can overcome evil, that people can redeem themselves, or that an underworld exists are all archetypal themes.

See pages 960–966, 1036–1037, and 1147

See also FOLKLORE, MYTH, ORAL TRADITION, STOCK CHARACTER, SYMBOL.

Argument A type of persuasive writing in which logic and reason are used to try to influence a reader's ideas or actions.

See pages 444–445, 453, and 500

See also PERSUASION.

Aside In a play, a comment that a character makes to the audience, which other characters onstage do not hear. The speaker turns to one side—or "aside"—away from the action onstage. Asides, which are rare in modern drama, reveal what a character is thinking or feeling. For example, Act 2, Scene 2, of Shakespeare's *Julius Caesar* includes the following exchange:

CAESAR. Be near me, that I may remember you.

TREBONIUS. Caesar, I will [*Aside.*] and so near will I be, That your best friends shall wish I had been further.

See pages 796 and 815

See also SOLILOQUY.

Assonance The repetition of same or similar vowel sounds in words that are close together. For example, the short *i* sound is repeated in this line from Shakespeare's "Shall I Compare Thee to a Summer's Day?":

So long lives this, and this gives life to thee.

See pages 646–647, 655, and 660

See also SOUND DEVICES.

Atmosphere The dominant emotional feeling of a literary work that contributes to the mood. Authors create atmosphere primarily through details of setting, such as time, place, and weather. The description of the rooms at the ball in Edgar Allan Poe's "The Masque of the Red Death" builds an atmosphere of suspense and foreboding.

See also MOOD.

Author's purpose An author's intent in writing a literary work. For example, the author may want to persuade, inform, describe a process, entertain, or express an opinion.

See pages 318–319, 370, and 500

See also DICTION, STYLE, THEME.

Autobiography A person's account of his or her life. The author typically focuses on the most significant events in his or her life. Autobiographies give insights into the author's view of himself or herself and of the society in which he or she lived. For example, *Farewell to Manzanar* is Jeanne Wakatsuki Houston's autobiography.

See pages 318–319 and 334

See also BIOGRAPHY, MEMOIR, NONFICTION.

B

Ballad A musical narrative song or poem that recounts an exciting or dramatic episode. Folk ballads were passed down by word of mouth for generations before being written down. A typical ballad consists of *ballad stanzas.* Literary ballads, such as "Ballad of Birmingham," are written in imitation of folk ballads and have a known author. Many ballads include the elements of plot, such as exposition, conflict, climax, and resolution.

See pages 641, 643, and 1084

See also BALLAD STANZA, FOLKLORE, NARRATIVE POETRY, ORAL TRADITION, PLOT.

Ballad Stanza A quatrain, or four-line stanza, in which the first and third lines have four stressed syllables, and the second and fourth lines have three stressed syllables. Only the second and fourth lines rhyme. Although the basic foot in this stanza is the iamb ($\smile$ $'$), there tend to be many irregularities.

See page 638

See also METER, QUATRAIN, STANZA.

Bias An inclination toward a certain opinion or position on a topic, possibly stemming from prejudice.

See also NONFICTION.

Biography A nonfiction account of a person's life written by another person. Biographies can vary in length, from brief encyclopedia entries to works that span several volumes.

See also AUTOBIOGRAPHY, JOURNAL, MEMOIR.

Blank verse Unrhymed poetry or dramatic verse written in a meter known as *iambic pentameter.* Each line of iambic pentameter has five units, or feet; each foot is made up of an unstressed syllable followed by a stressed syllable. Much of Shakespeare's work is written in blank verse. The following line, spoken by Mark Antony in Act 3, Scene 1, of Shakespeare's *Julius Caesar,* is an example of blank verse:

$\smile$ O $'$ par / $\smile$ don $'$ me / $\smile$ thou $'$ bleed / $\smile$ ing $'$ piece / $\smile$ of $'$ earth . . .

See pages 775 and 795

See also FOOT, IAMB, METER, RHYTHM

C

Cadence The rhythmic rise and fall of language when it is spoken or read aloud.

See also FREE VERSE and METER

Catalog The listing of images, details, people, or events in a literary work.

Character An individual in a literary work. *Main characters* are central to the story and are typically fully developed. *Minor characters* display few personality traits and are used to help develop the story. A character who shows varied and sometimes contradictory traits, such as the daughter in Amy Tan's "Two Kinds," is a *round character.* A character who reveals only one personality trait is called a *flat character.* A *stock character* is a flat character of a familiar and often-repeated type. A *dynamic character,* such as Luis in Judith Ortiz Cofer's "Catch the Moon," changes during the story. A *static character,* such as Luis's father, remains the same throughout the story.

See pages 94–95, 128, and 1043

See also ANTAGONIST, CHARACTERIZATION, FOIL, STEREOTYPE, STOCK CHARACTER, PROTAGONIST.

Character archetype. *See ARCHETYPE.*

Characterization The methods a writer uses to reveal the personality of a character. In *direct characterization,* the writer makes explicit statements about a character. In *indirect characterization,* the writer reveals a character's personality through that individual's words, thoughts, and actions and through what other characters think and say about that character.

See pages 149, 763, and 934

See also CHARACTER.

Climax The point of greatest emotional intensity, interest, or suspense in the plot of a literary work. Also called the turning point, the climax usually comes near the end of a story or drama. For example, in Doris Lessing's "Through the Tunnel," the climax occurs when Jerry finally swims through the tunnel.

See pages 10–11, 816, and 837

See also CONFLICT, PLOT.

Comedy A type of drama that is humorous and typically has a happy ending. Comedy can be divided into two categories: high and low. *High comedy* makes fun of human behavior in a witty, sophisticated manner. *Low comedy* involves physical humor and simple, often vulgar, wordplay.

See also DRAMA, FARCE, HUMOR, PARODY, SATIRE.

Comic relief A humorous scene, an event, or a speech in an otherwise serious work. It provides relief from emotional intensity, while at the same time highlighting the seriousness of the story. The sentry's lines in *Antigone* often provide comic relief.

Concrete language Specific language about actual things or occurrences. Words like *dog* and *sky* are concrete, while words like *truth* and *evil* are abstract.

See also ABSTRACT LANGUAGE.

Conflict The struggle between opposing forces in a story or drama. An *external conflict* exists when a character struggles against some outside force, such as another person, nature, society, or fate. In Doris Lessing's "Through the Tunnel," for example, when Jerry tries to swim through the tunnel, he is involved in an external conflict with nature. An *internal conflict* is a struggle that takes place within the mind of a character who is torn between opposing feelings or goals. Jerry wrestles with an internal conflict when he tries to overcome his own fear in order to swim through the tunnel.

See pages 36, 62 and 896

See also ANTAGONIST, PLOT, PROTAGONIST.

Connotation The suggested or implied meanings associated with a word beyond its dictionary definition, or *denotation.* A word can have a positive or negative connotation, or neutral connotation.

See pages 49 and 769

See also DENOTATION, FIGURATIVE LANGUAGE.

Consonance The repetition of consonant sounds, typically within or at the end of words that do not rhyme and preceded by different vowel sounds, as in the following line from Lucille Clifton's "Miss Rosie":

  si<u>tt</u>ing, wai<u>t</u>ing for your mind.

See pages 646–647, 655, and 660

See also SOUND DEVICES.

Couplet Two consecutive lines of rhymed verse that work together as a unit to make a point or to express an idea. The last two lines of Shakespeare's "Shall I Compare Thee to a Summer's Day?" are a couplet.

See also RHYME, SONNET, STANZA.

D

Denotation The literal, or dictionary, meaning of a word.

See pages 49 and 769

See also CONNOTATION.

Denouement The resolution of a story. Denouement is a French word meaning "unknotting." The denouement comes after the climax and often ties in with the falling action.

See also FALLING ACTION, RESOLUTION.

Description A detailed portrayal of a person, a place, an object, or an event. Good descriptive writing helps readers to see, hear, smell, taste, or feel the subject.

See pages 10–11, 91, and 1133

See also FIGURATIVE LANGUAGE, IMAGERY.

Descriptive essay. *See ESSAY.*

Dialect A variation of a language spoken by a group of people, often within a particular region. Dialects may differ from the standard form of a language in vocabulary, pronunciation, or grammatical form. "Civil Peace," contains examples of dialect.

See pages 74, 80, and 118

Dialogue Written conversation between characters in a literary work. Dialogue brings characters to life by revealing their personalities and by showing what they are thinking and feeling as they react to other characters. Dialogue can also create mood, advance the plot, and develop theme. Plays are composed almost completely of dialogue.

See pages 111, 993, and 1101

See also MONOLOGUE.

Diction A writer's choice of words; an important element in the writer's voice or style. Skilled writers choose their words carefully to convey a particular meaning or feeling. These lines from "A Child's Christmas in Wales" give an example of Dylan Thomas's diction:

> **All the Christmases roll down toward the two-tongued sea, like a cold and headlong moon bundling down the sky that was our street. . . .**

See pages 240, 637, and 639

See also AUTHOR'S PURPOSE, CONNOTATION, STYLE, TONE, VOICE.

Drama A story written to be performed by actors before an audience. The script of a dramatic work, or play, often includes the author's instructions to the actors and the director, known as *stage directions.* A drama may be divided into *acts,* which may also be broken up into *scenes,* indicating changes in location or the passage of time.

See pages 704–961 and 868–869

See also ACT, COMEDY, DIALOGUE, SCENE, STAGE DIRECTIONS, TRAGEDY.

Dramatic irony. See IRONY.

Dramatic monologue A form of dramatic poetry in which a speaker, describing a crucial moment in his or her life, addresses a silent listener.

See also DRAMATIC POETRY, MONOLOGUE.

Dynamic character See CHARACTER.

E

Elegy A serious poem mourning a death or a great loss.

End rhyme The rhyming of words at the ends of lines.

End-stopped line A line of poetry that ends in a punctuation mark. An end-stopped line usually contains a complete thought or image. The following example from Edna St. Vincent Millay's "Well, I Have Lost You; and I Lost You Fairly," contains an end-stopped line:

> **Should I outlive this anguish—and men do—**
> **I shall have only good to say of you.**

See also ENJAMBMENT.

Enjambment The continuation of a sentence or phrase from one line of a poem to the next, without a pause between the lines. The following lines from Robert Hayden's "Those Winter Sundays" are an example of enjambment:

> **What did I know, what did I know**
> **of love's austere and lonely offices.**

See pages 538, 541, and 583

See also END-STOPPED LINE.

Epic A long narrative poem that recounts, in formal language, the exploits of a larger-than-life hero. This *epic hero* is usually a person of high social status who embodies the ideals of his or her people. He or she is often of historical or legendary importance. Epic plots typically involve supernatural events, long time periods, distant journeys, and life-and-death struggles between good and evil. Folk epics have no known author and usually arise through storytelling and the collective experiences of people, while literary epics are written by known authors.

See page 000

See also FOLKLORE, HERO, LEGEND, MYTH, NARRATIVE POETRY, ORAL TRADITION.

Epic hero *See EPIC, HERO.*

Epic simile *See SIMILE.*

Essay A short work of nonfiction on a single topic. *Descriptive essays* describe a person, place, or thing. *Narrative essays* relate true stories. *Persuasive essays* promote an opinion. *Reflective essays* reveal an author's observations on a subject. Essays fall into two categories, according to their style. A *formal essay* is serious and impersonal, often with the purpose of instructing or persuading. Typically, the author strikes a serious tone and develops a main idea, or *thesis,* in a logical, highly organized way. An *informal,* or *personal essay,* entertains while it informs, usually in light, conversational style.

See pages 94–95, 409, and 441

See also NONFICTION.

Exaggeration *See HYPERBOLE.*

Exposition An author's introduction of the characters, setting, and conflict at the beginning of a story, novel, or play.

See pages 10–11, 29, and 236

See also PLOT.

Extended metaphor A metaphor that compares two unlike things in various ways throughout a paragraph, stanza, or an entire selection. William Shakespeare uses an extended metaphor in the poem "Shall I Compare Thee to a Summer's Day?"

See also METAPHOR.

F

Fable A short, usually simple tale that teaches a moral and sometimes uses animal characters. Themes in fables are often stated directly. Italo Calvino's "The Happy Man's Shirt" is a modern fable.

See also LEGEND, MORAL, PARABLE, THEME.

Falling action The action that follows the climax in a play or a story. The falling action may show the results of the climax. It may also include the *denouement,* a French word meaning "unknotting." The denouement, or *resolution,* explains the plot or unravels the mystery.

See pages 10–11

See also CLIMAX, DENOUEMENT, PLOT.

Fantasy A highly imaginative genre of fiction, usually set in an unfamiliar world or a distant, heroic past. Fantasy stories commonly take place in imaginary worlds and may include gnomes, elves, or other fantastical or supernatural beings and forces. The use of some type of magic is common in fantasy stories.

See pages 1110–1116

See also SCIENCE FICTION.

Farce A type of comedy with stereotyped characters in ridiculous situations. Anton Chekhov's *A Marriage Proposal* is an example of a farce.

See also COMEDY, HUMOR, PARODY, SATIRE.

Fiction Literature in which situations and characters are invented by the writer. Fiction includes both short stories, such as Edgar Allan Poe's "The Masque of the Red Death," and novels, such as T. H. White's *The Once and Future King.* Aspects of a fictional work may be based on fact or experience.

See also DRAMA, NONFICTION, NOVEL, SHORT STORY.

Figurative language Language that uses *figures of speech,* or expressions that are not literally true, but express some truth beyond the literal level. Types of figurative language include hyperbole, metaphor, personification, simile, and understatement.

See pages 584, 593, and 622

See also HYPERBOLE, IMAGERY, METAPHOR, OXYMORON, PERSONSIFICATION, SIMILE, SYMBOL, UNDERSTATEMENT.

Figures of speech. *See FIGURATIVE LANGUAGE.*

Flashback An interruption in the chronological order of a narrative to describe an event that happened earlier. A flashback gives readers information that may help explain the main events of the story. For example, in Leslie Marmon Silko's "Lullaby," the narrator includes a flashback to the day Ayah and Chato found out that Jimmie had died.

See pages 13, 18, and 129

Flat character. *See CHARACTER.*

Foil A character who provides a strong contrast to another character, usually a main character. By using a foil, a writer calls attention to the strengths or weaknesses of a character. For example, the self-controlled Octavius is a foil to the excitable Mark Antony in Shakespeare's *Julius Caesar.*

See pages 838, 853, and 1022

See also CHARACTER.

Folklore The traditional beliefs, customs, stories, songs, and dances of a culture. Folklore is based in the concerns of ordinary people and is passed down through oral tradition.

See also BALLAD, EPIC, FOLKTALE, LEGEND, MYTH, ORAL TRADITION, TALL TALE.

Folktale An anonymous traditional story passed down orally long before being written down. Folktales include animal stories, trickster stories, fairy tales, myths, legends, and tall tales.

See also EPIC, FOLKLORE, LEGEND, MYTH, ORAL TRADITION, TALL TALE.

Foot The basic unit in the measurement of rhythm in poetry. A foot usually contains one stressed syllable (´) and one or more unstressed syllables (˘).

See also METER, RHYTHM, SCANSION.

Foreshadowing An author's use of clues or hints to prepare readers for events that will happen later in a story.

See also PLOT, RISING ACTION, SUSPENSE.

Form The structure of a poem. Many modern writers use loosely structured poetic forms instead of following traditional or formal patterns. These poets vary the lengths of lines and stanzas, relying on emphasis, rhythm, pattern, and the placement of words and phrases to convey meaning.

Formal essay. *See ESSAY.*

Formal speech. A speech of which the main purpose is to persuade, although it may also inform and entertain. Anthony's "On Women's Right to Vote," page 446, is a formal speech to persuade. The four main types of formal speech are legal, political, ceremonial, and religious.

Frame story A plot structure that includes the telling of a story within a story. The frame is the outer story, which usually precedes and follows the inner, more important story. Joan Aiken uses a frame in "Lungewater," page 1240. Some literary works have frames that bind together many different stories.

Free verse Poetry that has no fixed pattern of meter, rhyme, line length, or stanza arrangement. Gwendolyn Brooks's "Horses Graze" is a poem composed in free verse.

See pages 553 and 557

See also POETRY, RHYTHM.

G

Genre A category or type of literature. Examples of genres are poetry, drama, fiction, nonfiction, essay, and epic. The term also refers to subcategories of literary work. For example, fantasy, magical realism, mystery, romance, and science fiction are genres of fiction. Ray Bradbury's "A Sound of Thunder" belongs to both the short story and science-fiction genres.

See pages 4–5, 207, and 226

Gothic literature A novel or short story that has a gloomy, foreboding mood and contains strong elements of horror, mystery, and the supernatural. "Lungewater" by Joan Aiken is a gothic short story.

Haiku A traditional Japanese form of poetry that has three lines and seventeen syllables. The first and third lines have five syllables each; the second line has seven syllables. The purpose of traditional Haiku is to capture a flash of insight that occurs during an observation of nature.

See pages 572 and 574

See also TANKA.

Hero The main character in a literary work, typically one whose admirable qualities or noble deeds arouse admiration. In contemporary usage, the term can refer to either a female or male. For example, Buffalo Calf Road Woman is the hero of "Where the Girl Rescued Her Brother" by Joseph Bruchac and Gayle Ross.

See pages 960–966, 1011, and 1065

See also EPIC, MYTH, PROTAGONIST, TRAGEDY.

Hexameter A line of verse consisting of six feet.

See also FOOT, METER

High comedy. *See COMEDY.*

Historical fiction Fiction that sets characters against a backdrop of actual events. Some works of historical fiction include actual historical people along with fictitious characters.

See also FICTION.

Historical narrative A work of nonfiction that tells the story of important historical events or developments. *Farewell to Manzanar* by Jeanne Wakatsuki Houston and James D. Houston is a historical narrative.

See pages 321 and 334

Humor The quality of a literary work that makes the characters and their situations seem funny, amusing, or ludicrous. Humor often points out human failings and the irony found in many situations. Humorous language includes sarcasm, exaggeration, and verbal irony. Humorous writing can be equally effective in fiction and nonfiction.

See also COMEDY, FARCE, PARODY, PUN, SATIRE.

Hyperbole A figure of speech that uses exaggeration to express strong emotion, make a point, or evoke humor. "You've asked me a million times" is an example of hyperbole.

See pages 398, 769, and 1034

See also FIGURATIVE LANGUAGE, UNDERSTATEMENT.

I

Iamb (ī'amb) A two-syllable metrical foot consisting of one unaccented syllable (˘) followed by one accented syllable (´), as in the word *divide*.

Iambic pentameter A specific poetic meter in which each line has five metric units, or feet, and each foot consists of an unstressed syllable (˘) followed by a stressed syllable (´). The rhythm of a line of iambic pentameter would be indicated as shown in this example from Shakespeare's "Shall I Compare Thee to a Summer's Day?":

> Rough winds do shake the darling buds of may,

See also BLANK VERSE, METER, SCANSION.

Idiom An expression whose meaning is different from its literal meaning. Idioms are readily understood by native speakers but are often puzzling to non-native speakers. Phrases such as "catch his eye," "turn the tables," "over the hill," and "keep tabs on" are idiomatic expressions in English. Idioms can add realism to dialogue in a story and contribute to characterization.

See pages 975 and 989

See also DIALECT.

Image archetype. *See ARCHETYPE.*

Imagery Descriptive language that appeals to one or more of the five senses: sight, hearing, touch, taste, and smell. This use of sensory detail helps create an emotional response in the reader. For example, the following lines from Doris Lessing's "Through the Tunnel" use imagery to make an underwater scene vivid:

> A few inches above them the water sparkled as if sequins were dropping through it . . . it was like swimming in flaked silver.

See pages 10–11, 633, and 1118–1119

See also FIGURATIVE LANGUAGE.

Informal essay. *See ESSAY.*

Internal conflict. *See CONFLICT.*

Internal rhyme Rhyme that occurs within a single line of poetry. Poets use internal rhyme to convey meaning, to evoke mood, or to create a musical effect. Randall uses internal rhyme in his poem "The Ballad of Birmingham":

> "<u>No</u>, baby, <u>no</u>, you may not <u>go</u>,"

See also RHYME.

Inversion The reversal of the usual word order in a prose sentence or a line of poetry. Writers use inversion to maintain *rhyme scheme* or *meter* or to emphasize certain words or phrases. An example of inversion occurs in the final line of Shakespeare's sonnet "Shall I Compare Thee to a Summer's Day?":

> So long <u>lives this</u>, and this gives life to thee.

See page 661

Irony A contrast or discrepancy between expectation and reality, or between what is expected and what actually happens.

In *situational irony,* the actual outcome of a situation is the opposite of what is expected. In Shakespeare's *Julius Caesar,* for example, the suitors spare Mark Antony's life because they believe he is harmless. Instead, he turns out to be a vengeful, deadly enemy.

In *verbal irony,* a person says one thing and means another. For example, in *Julius Caesar,* Mark Antony uses verbal irony when he praises Brutus and the conspirators to the crowd at Julius Caesar's funeral, while actually trying to turn the people against them.

In *dramatic irony,* the audience or reader knows information that the characters do not know. For example, in *Julius Caesar,* Caesar's wife warns him not to go to the Senate. The audience knows of the murder plot, although Caesar and his wife do not.

See pages 51, 70, and 889

See also PARADOX.

J

Journal. A daily record of events kept by a participant in those events or a witness to them. A journal is usually less intimate than a diary and emphasizes events rather than emotions.

See also DIARY, NONFICTION.

Juxtaposition The placement of two or more distinct things side by side in order to contrast or compare them. It is commonly used to evoke an emotional response in the reader.

See pages 625 and 627

L

Language. *See DICTION, FIGURATIVE LANGUAGE, IMAGERY, SENSORY DETAILS.*

Legend A traditional story handed down from past generations and believed to be based on actual people and events. Legends usually celebrate the heroic qualities of a national or cultural leader. Because legends are the stories of the people, they are often expressions of the values or character of a nation. For example, "Where the Girl Rescued Her Brother," retold by Joseph Bruchac and Gayle Ross, is a legend.

See pages 960–966, 989, and 1034

See also EPIC, FABLE, FOLKLORE, HERO, MYTH, ORAL TRADITION.

Legendary heroes Idealized figures, sometimes based on real people, who embody qualities admired by the cultural group to which they belong. The adventures and accomplishments of these heroes are preserved in legends or tales that are handed down from generation to generation. In the Sumerian epic "The Journey of Gilgamesh" as told by Joan C. Verniero and Robin Fitzsimmons, Gilgamesh is a legendary hero.

See also FOLKTALE.

Line The basic unit of poetry. A line consists of a word or a row of words. In metered poems, lines are measured by the number of feet they contain.

See pages 533 and 535

See also FOOT, STANZA.

Literal language Language that is simple, straightforward, and free of embellishment. It is the opposite of figurative language, which conveys ideas indirectly.

See also DENOTATION.

Local color The use of specific details to re-create the language, the customs, the geography, and the habits of a particular area. In "The Californian's Tale," for example, Mark Twain recreates the mining country of California by describing the speech, dress, and habits of his characters.

See page 48

See also DIALECT.

Low comedy. *See COMEDY.*

Lyric poetry Poetry that expresses a speaker's personal thoughts and feelings. Lyric poems are usually short and musical. While the subject of a lyric poem might be an object, a person, or an event, the emphasis of the poem is on the experience of emotion. Among the lyric poems in this book are Robert Hayden's "Those Winter Sundays" and Shakespeare's "Shall I Compare Thee to a Summer's Day?"

See pages 613, 617, and 622

See also POETRY.

M

Magical realism Fiction that combines fantasy and realism. Magical realism inserts fantastic, sometimes humorous, events and details into a believable reality.

See also GENRE.

Memoir A type of narrative nonfiction that presents an author's personal experience of an event or period. A memoir is usually written from the first-person point of view. It often emphasizes the writer's thoughts and feelings, his or her relationships with other people, or the impact of significant historical events on his or her life. Maya Angelou's "Living Well. Living Good." is an example of a memoir.

See pages 318–319, 358, and 382

See also AUTOBIOGRAPHY.

Metaphor A figure of speech that makes a comparison between two seemingly unlike things. Unlike a *simile,* a metaphor implies an underlying similarity between the two and does not use of the words *like* or *as.* The following lines from Jimmy Santiago Baca's "I Am Offering This Poem" feature a metaphor:

> [love] is a pot full of yellow corn
> to warm your belly in winter

See pages 584–585, 602, and 622

See also ANALOGY, FIGURATIVE LANGUAGE, SIMILE.

Meter A regular pattern of stressed and unstressed syllables that gives a line of poetry a predictable rhythm. The unit of meter within the line is the *foot.* Each type of foot has a unique pattern of stressed (´) and unstressed (˘) syllables:

iamb (˘´) as in *complete*

trochee (´˘) as in *trouble*

anapest (˘˘´) as in *intervene*

dactyl (´˘˘) as in *majesty*

spondee (´´) as in *blue-green*

A particular meter is named for the type of foot and the number of feet per line. For example, *trimeter* has three feet, *tetrameter* has four feet, *pentameter* has five feet, and *hexameter* has six feet. The most common meter in English poetry is *iambic pentameter,* as in this line from Shakespeare's *Julius Caesar:*

> ˘   ´   / ˘   ´   / ˘   ´   / ˘   ´   / ˘   ´
> O par / don me / thou bleed / ing piece / of earth

See pages 543, 546, and 646–647

See also FOOT, IAMBIC PENTAMETER, RHYTHM, SCANSION.

Monologue A long speech or written expression of thoughts by a character in a literary work. The burial speeches of Brutus and Antony in Act 3, Scene 2, in Shakespeare's *Julius Caesar* are monologues.

See pages 352, 815, and 934

See also DIALOGUE, SOLILOQUY.

Mood The emotional quality of a literary work. A writer's choice of language, subject matter, setting, diction, and tone, as well as sound devices such as rhyme, rhythm, and meter can help create mood.

See pages 10–11, 427, and 1253

See also ATMOSPHERE, SETTING, TONE.

Moral A practical lesson about right and wrong conduct. Morals are typically found in fables. Some science fiction, such as Stephen Vincent Bénet's short story "By The Waters of Babylon," presents a moral.

See pages 1136 and 1147

See also FABLE, PARABLE, THEME.

Motif A significant word, phrase, image, description, idea, or other element that is repeated throughout a literary work and is related to the theme. For example, in "A Swimming Lesson," Jewelle L. Gomez repeats the word *rhythm* to convey a message about life.

See pages 412 and 416

Motivation The stated or implied reason a character acts, thinks, or feels a certain way. Motivation may be an external circumstance, an internal moral, or an emotional impulse.

See pages 97, 178, and 1201

Mystery A genre of fiction that follows a standard plot pattern: a crime is committed and a detective searches for clues that lead him or her to the criminal. Any story that relies on the unknown or the terrifying can be considered a mystery.

See also FICTION, GENRE.

Myth A traditional story that deals with goddesses, gods, heroes, and supernatural forces. A myth may explain a belief, a custom, or a force of nature. Sophocles' *Antigone* draws on traditional elements of ancient Greek mythology.

See pages 960–966, 1036–1037, and 1054

See also EPIC, FOLKLORE, LEGEND, ORAL TRADITION.

N

Narrative Writing or speech that tells a story. Driven by a *conflict* or problem, a narrative unfolds event by event and leads to a *resolution.* The story is narrated, or told, by a *narrator* and can take the form of a novel, an essay, a poem, or a short story.

See also NARRATIVE POETRY, NARRATOR, PLOT.

Narrative essay *See ESSAY.*

See pages 412, 503–504, and 687–688

Narrative poetry Verse that tells a story. Narrative poems are usually contrasted with lyric poems. *Ballads, epics,* and *romances* are all types of narrative poetry. For example, Dudley Randall's "The Ballad of Birmingham" is a narrative poem.

See pages 641 and 643

See also BALLAD, EPIC, LYRIC POETRY, NARRATIVE.

Narrator The person who tells a story. The narrator may be a character in the story, as in Amy Tan's "Two Kinds," or outside the story, as in Judith Ortiz Cofer's "Catch the Moon." Narrators are not always truthful. A narrator in a work of literature may be *reliable* or *unreliable.* Some unreliable narrators intentionally mislead readers. Others fail to understand the true meaning of the events they describe. Most stories with unreliable narrators are written in the first person.

See pages 192–193, 209, and 288

See also NARRATIVE, POINT OF VIEW, SPEAKER.

Nonfiction Literature about real people, places, and events. Among the categories of nonfiction are biographies, autobiographies, and essays. For example, Maya Angelou's "Living Well. Living Good." is nonfiction.

See pages 308–519

See also AUTOBIOGRAPHY, BIOGRAPHY, ESSAY, FICTION, MEMOIR.

Novel A book-length fictional prose narrative. Because of its length, the novel has greater potential to develop plot, character, setting, and theme than does a short story.

See also FICTION, PLOT, SHORT STORY.

O

Octave An eight-line stanza. The term is used mainly to describe the first eight lines of a *Petrarchan,* or *Italian,* sonnet.

See also SONNET.

Ode A long, serious lyric poem that is elevated in tone and style. Some odes celebrate a person, an event, or even a power; others are more private meditations. Odes are traditionally written in three stanzas and include rhyme.

See also LYRIC POETRY.

Onomatopoeia The use of a word or phrase that imitates or suggests the sound of what it describes. Some examples are *mew, hiss, crack, swish, murmur,* and *buzz.*

See also SOUND DEVICES.

Oral tradition Literature that passes by word of mouth from one generation to the next. Oral literature is a way of recording the past, glorifying leaders, and teaching morals and traditions to young people. Stories of the legendary African hero Sundiata are passed on in this manner.

See pages 1036–1037, 1076 and 1087

See also BALLAD, EPIC, FOLKLORE, FOLKTALE, LEGEND, MYTH.

Oxymoron A figure of speech in which opposite ideas are combined. Examples are "bright darkness," "wise fool," and "hateful love."

See also FIGURATIVE LANGUAGE, PARADOX.

P

Paradox A situation or a statement that appears to be contradictory but is actually true, either in fact or in a figurative sense.

See also OXYMORON.

Parallelism The use of a series of words, phrases, or sentences that have similar grammatical form. Parallelism shows the relationship between ideas and helps emphasize thoughts.

See also REPETITION.

Parody A humorous imitation of a literary work that aims to point out the work's shortcomings. A parody may imitate the plot, characters, or style of another work, usually through exaggeration. Miguel de Cervantes's *Don Quixote* is a parody of chivalry and novels about knight-errantry.

See pages 1014 and 1022

See also COMEDY, FARCE, HUMOR, SATIRE.

Persona The person created by the author to tell a story. Even if a story is told from a first-person point of view, as in Isabel Allende's story "And of Clay Are We Created," the narrator is not the author. The attitudes and beliefs of the persona may not be the same as those of the author.

See pages 192–193, 265, and 276

See also NARRATOR, POINT OF VIEW.

Personification A figure of speech in which an animal, object, force of nature, or idea is given human characteristics. William Shakespeare personifies death in this line from "Shall I Compare Thee to a Summer's Day?":

> Nor shall Death brag thou wand'rest in his shade

See pages 589, 593, and 602

See also APOSTROPHE, FIGURATIVE LANGUAGE.

Persuasion A type of writing, usually nonfiction, that attempts to convince readers to think or act in a particular way. Writers of persuasive works use appeals to logic, emotion, morality, and authority to sway their readers.

See pages 444–445, 463, and 500

See also ARGUMENT.

Persuasive Essay *See ESSAY.*

Play A literary work of any length intended for performance on stage with actors assuming the roles of the characters and speaking the lines from a playwright's script.

See also DRAMA.

Plot The sequence of events in a narrative work. The plot begins with the *exposition,* which introduces the *characters, setting,* and *conflict.* Conflicts are introduced in the *exposition,* the first stage of the plot. As the work progresses, *rising action* builds suspense and adds complications, which lead to the *climax,* or turning point. After the climax, which is the moment of highest emotional pitch or greatest suspense, comes the *falling action* and the *resolution,* sometimes called the *denouement,* which reveal the logical results of the climax.

See pages 10–11, 236, and 837

See also CLIMAX, CONFLICT, DENOUEMENT, EXPOSITION, FALLING ACTION, FORESHADOWING, RESOLUTION, RISING ACTION.

Plot pattern archetype. *See ARCHETYPE.*

Poetic license The freedom given to poets to ignore standard rules of grammar or proper diction in order to create a desired artistic effect.

Poetry A form of literary expression that differs from prose in emphasizing the line, rather than the sentence, as the unit of composition. Many other traditional characteristics of poetry apply to some poems but not to others. Some of these characteristics are emotional, imaginative language; use of figures of speech; division into stanzas; and the use of rhyme and regular meter.

See pages 520–703

See also FIGURATIVE LANGUAGE, METER, PROSE, RHYME, STANZA.

Point of view The perspective from which a story is told. In a story with *first-person* point of view, the narrator is a character in the story, referred to as "I." The reader sees everything through that character's eyes. Amy Tan's "Two Kinds" is told from first-person point of view. In a story with *third-person limited* point of view, the narrator reveals the thoughts, feelings, and observations of only one character, referring to that character as "he" or "she." Judith Ortiz Cofer's short story "Catch the Moon" uses third-person limited point of view. In a story with *third-person omniscient,* or all-knowing, point of view, the narrator is not a character in the story, but rather someone who stands outside the story and comments on the action. A third-person omniscient narrator, such as the one in Doris Lessing's "Through the Tunnel," knows everything about the characters and events and may reveal details that the characters themselves could not

reveal. Occasionally an author uses *second-person* point of view, addressing the reader or one of the characters as "you." Margaret Atwood uses the second-person point of view in "Bread."

See pages 192–193, 236, and 1178

See also NARRATOR, SPEAKER.

Prologue An introductory section of a play, speech, or other literary work. Sophocles' play *Antigone* contains a prologue, which sets the scene and provides background information for the drama.

Propaganda Written or spoken material designed to bring about a change or damage a cause through the use of emotionally charged words, name-calling, or other techniques.

Props A theater term (a shortened form of *properties*) for the objects and elements of the scenery used in a stage play, movie, or television show.

See also STAGE DIRECTIONS.

Prose Literature that is written in sentences and paragraphs (as distinguished from poetry, which is arranged in lines and stanzas). Essays, short stories, magazine articles, and most plays are examples of prose. Shakespeare alternates between prose and poetry in the dialogue of *Julius Caesar.*

See also POETRY.

Prose poem Short prose composition that uses rhythm, imagery, and other poetic devices to express an idea or emotion. Prose poetry does not have line breaks; instead, the sentences appear in standard paragraph form.

See pages 560, 563, and 569

See also POETRY, PROSE.

Protagonist The central character in a literary work around whom the main conflict revolves. During the course of the literary work, the protagonist undergoes a conflict that is crucial to the plot. Generally, the reader or audience is meant to sympathize with the protagonist. Prince Prospero is the protagonist in Edgar Allan Poe's story "The Masque of the Red Death."

See pages 94–95, 721, and 741

See also ANTAGONIST, CHARACTER, CONFLICT, HERO.

Pun A humorous play on words. Puns usually involve words that are similar in sound (*merry* and *marry*) or a word that has several meanings. In Shakespeare's *Julius Caesar,* for example, a shoemaker identifies himself by saying "all that I live by is with the *awl,*" making a pun on *all* and *awl,* a tool for punching holes in leather.

See also HUMOR.

Q

Quatrain A four-line stanza. The quatrain is the most common stanza form in English poetry. It may be unrhymed or have a variety of rhyme schemes.

See also COUPLET, OCTAVE, SONNET, STANZA.

Quotation A passage by another author, used word-for-word in a literary work. A quotation is enclosed in quotation marks, or otherwise set apart, to indicate that it is not written by the person in whose work it appears. Quotations can serve to illustrate ideas and to show that other people share the author's opinions.

See pages 381, 486, and 491

R

Reflective essay *See ESSAY.*

Refrain A line or lines repeated at regular intervals in a poem or song, usually at the end of a stanza.

See also REPETITION.

Reliable narrator *See NARRATOR.*

Repetition The recurrence of sounds, words, phrases, lines, or stanzas in a poem, speech, or other piece of writing. Writers use repetition to emphasize an important point, to expand upon an idea, to help create rhythm, and to increase the feeling of unity in a work.

See also PARALLELISM, RHETORICAL DEVICES, RHYME.

Resolution Also called the *denouement,* a French word meaning "unknotting," the resolution is the part of a plot that concludes the falling action by revealing or suggesting the outcome of the conflict.

See CONFLICT, DENOUEMENT, FALLING ACTION, PLOT.

Rhetorical devices Persuasive techniques used by public speakers and writers of literary works, especially those written to persuade. Rhetorical devices include repetition, parallelism, analogy, logic, and the skillful use of connotation and anecdote. Effective rhetoric often appeals to logic, emotion, morality, or authority.

See pages 444–445, 466, and 500

See also ANALOGY, ANECDOTE, ARGUMENT, CONNOTATION, PARALLELISM, PERSUASION, REPETITION.

Rhyme The repetition of the same stressed vowel sounds and any succeeding sounds in two or more words. *End rhyme* occurs at the ends of lines of poetry. *Internal rhyme* occurs within a single line. *Slant rhyme* occurs when words include sounds that are similar but not identical (*jackal* and *buckle*). Slant rhyme typically involves some variation of *consonance* (the repetition of similar consonant sounds) or *assonance* (the repetition of similar vowel sounds).

See pages 520–526, 593, and 676

See also ASSONANCE, CONSONANCE, RHYME SCHEME, SOUND DEVICES.

Rhyme scheme The pattern that end rhymes form in a stanza or a poem. Rhyme scheme is designated by the assignment of a different letter of the alphabet to each new rhyme. The rhyme scheme of Edna St. Vincent Millay's "Well I Have Lost You; and I Lost You Fairly" begins as follows:

Well, I have lost you; and I lost you fairly;	a
In my own way, and with my full consent.	b
Say what you will, kings in a tumbrel rarely	a
Went to their deaths more proud than this one went.	b

See pages 520–526, 643, and 676

See also RHYME.

Rhythm The pattern of beats created by the arrangement of stressed and unstressed syllables, especially in poetry. Rhythm gives a poem a musical quality. It can also emphasize certain words or ideas to help convey meaning. Rhythm can be *regular,* with a predictable pattern or meter, or *irregular.*

See pages 520–526, 546, and 646–647

See also BLANK VERSE, FOOT, IAMBIC PENTAMETER, METER, SCANSION.

Rising action The part of a plot where complications to the conflict develop and increase the reader's interest.

See PLOT.

Round character. *See CHARACTER.*

Run-on line The continuation of a sentence from one line of a poem the next.

> To him who in the love of Nature holds
> Communion with her visible forms, she speaks
> A various language;
> > Bryant, "Thanatopsis"

Run-on lines enable poets to create a conversational tone, breaking lines at a point where people would normally pause in conversation, yet still maintaining the unit of thought.

See also END-STOPPED LINE.

S

Sarcasm The use of bitter or caustic language to point out shortcomings or flaws.

See also IRONY, SATIRE.

Satire Writing that uses humor or wit to ridicule the vices or follies of people or societies to bring about improvement. Satire uses devices such as *exaggeration, understatement,* and *irony.* Luisa Valenzuela's short story "The Censors" is a satire of repressive government.

See also COMEDY, FARCE, HUMOR, PARODY, SARCASM, WIT.

Scansion The analysis of the meter of a line of verse. To scan a line of poetry means to note the stressed(´) and unstressed syllables (ˇ) and to divide the line into its *feet,* or rhythmical units.

See also FOOT, METER, RHYTHM.

Scene A subdivision of an act in a play. Each scene usually takes place in a specific setting and time.

See pages 706–712

See also ACT, DRAMA.

Science fiction Fiction that deals with the impact of science and technology—real or imagined—on society and on individuals. Sometimes occurring in the future, science fiction commonly portrays space travel, exploration of other planets, and future societies. Ray Bradbury's "A Sound of Thunder" is an example of science fiction.

See pages 1110–1116, 1136, and 1147

See also FANTASY, GENRE.

Sensory details Evocative words or phrases that convey sensory experiences—seeing, hearing, tasting, touching, and smelling. Sensory details make writing come alive by helping readers imagine what is being described.

See also IMAGERY.

Septet A seven-line poem or stanza.

Sestet A six-line poem or stanza.

See also SONNET.

Setting The time and place in which the events of a literary work occur. Setting includes not only the physical surroundings, but also the ideas, customs, values, and beliefs of a particular time and place. Setting often helps create an atmosphere or mood. For example, the setting of Dylan Thomas's "A Child's Christmas in Wales" is a Welsh seaside town in the early twentieth century.

See pages 10–11, 276, and 914

See also ATMOSPHERE, MOOD.

Shakespearean sonnet. *See SONNET.*

Short story A brief fictional narrative in prose. A short story usually focuses on a single event and has only a few characters. Elements of the short story include *setting, characters, plot, point of view,* and *theme.*

See also FICTION, NOVEL, PLOT.

Simile A figure of speech that uses the word *like* or *as* to compare two seemingly unlike things. For example, this simile appears in Amy Tan's story "Two Kinds":

And she also did a fancy sweep of a curtsy, so that the fluffy skirt of her white dress cascaded to the floor like the petals of a large carnation.

An *epic simile* is a long, elaborate comparison that continues for several lines. It is a feature of epic poems, but is found in other poems as well.

See pages 584–585, 620, and 622

See also ANALOGY, FIGURATIVE LANGUAGE, METAPHOR.

Situational irony. *See IRONY.*

Slant rhyme. *See RHYME.*

Soliloquy A dramatic device in which a character, alone on stage (or while under the impression of being alone), reveals his or her private thoughts and feelings as if thinking aloud. For example, Antony vows his revenge of Caesar's murder in a soliloquy in Act 3, Scene 1, of Shakespeare's *Julius Caesar.*

See pages 796 and 815

See also ASIDE, MONOLOGUE.

Sonnet A lyric poem of fourteen lines, typically written in *iambic pentameter* and usually following strict patterns of stanza division and rhyme.

The *Shakespearean sonnet,* also called the *English sonnet,* consists of three *quatrains,* or four-line stanzas, followed by a *couplet,* or pair of rhyming lines. The rhyme scheme is typically *abab cdcd efef gg.* The rhyming couplet often presents a conclusion to the issues or questions presented in the three quatrains.

In the *Petrarchan sonnet,* also called the *Italian sonnet,* fourteen lines are divided into two stanzas, the eight-line *octave* and the six-line *sestet.* The sestet usually responds to a question or situation posed by the octave. The rhyme scheme is typically *abbaabba cdecde* or *abbaabba cdcdcd.*

See pages 596 and 598

See also COUPLET, LYRIC POETRY, RHYME SCHEME, STANZA.

Sound devices Techniques used to emphasize particular sounds in writing. Writers use sound devices such as *alliteration* and *assonance* to underscore the meaning of certain words, to enhance rhythm, and to add a musical quality to the work.

See pages 648–649

See also ALLITERATION, ASSONANCE, CONSONANCE, ONOMATOPOEIA, RHYME, RHYTHM.

Speaker The voice that communicates with the reader of a poem, similar to the narrator in a work of prose. Sometimes the speaker's voice is that of the poet, sometimes that of a fictional person or even a thing. For example, the speaker in Robert Hayden's poem "Those Winter Sundays" is a man thinking back to his poor childhood and remembering the sacrifices his father made while raising him.

See pages 192–193, 566, and 617

See also NARRATOR, TONE.

Spondee A metrical foot of two accented syllables.

See also FOOT, METER.

Stage directions Instructions written by a playwright that describe the appearance and actions of characters, as well as the sets, props, costumes, sound effects, and lighting for a play.

See pages 868–869, 901, and 914

See also DRAMA, PROPS.

Stanza A group of lines forming a unit in a poem or song. A stanza in a poem is similar to a paragraph in prose. Typically, stanzas in a poem are separated by a line of space.

See pages 533, 535, and 546

See also COUPLET, OCTAVE, QUATRAIN, SONNET.

Stereotype A generalization about a group of people that is made without regard for individual differences. In literature, this term is often used to describe a conventional or flat character who conforms to an expected, fixed pattern of behavior. Stereotypes are used to make or reflect broad generalizations about a group of people. The nervous, hypochondriac Lomov in Anton Chekhov's "A Marriage Proposal" is a stereotype.

See also STOCK CHARACTER.

Stock character A character who represents a type that is recognizable as belonging to a particular genre. For example, a cruel stepmother or charming prince is often found in fairy tales. Valiant knights and heroes are found in legends and myths. The hard-boiled detective is found in detective stories. Stock characters have conventional traits and mannerisms shared by all members of their type.

See pages 1036–1037

See also ARCHETYPE, CHARACTER, STEREOTYPE.

Stream of consciousness The literary representation of an author's or character's free-flowing thoughts, feelings, and memories. Stream-of-consciousness writing does not always employ conventional sentence structure or other rules of grammar and usage.

See pages 1152 and 1156

Structure The particular order or pattern a writer uses to present ideas. For example, narratives sometimes follow a chronological order. Listing detailed information, comparing and contrasting, analyzing cause-and-effect relationships, or describing a problem and then offering a solution are some other ways a writer can structure a text. Poetic structure—more commonly known as *form*—refers to the organization of words, lines, and images as well as of ideas.

See pages 430, 434, and 557

See also FORM.

Style The expressive qualities that distinguish an author's work, including word choice, sentence structure, and figures of speech.

See pages 19, 383, and 1226

See also AUTHOR'S PURPOSE, DICTION, IMAGERY, TONE, VOICE.

Subject The topic of a literary work.

Surprise ending A plot twist at the end of a story that is unexpected because the author provides misleading clues or withholds important information.

Suspense A feeling of curiosity, uncertainty, or even dread about what is going to happen next in a story.

To build suspense, an author may create a threat to the central character or use *foreshadowing*. Suspense is especially important in the plot of an adventure or mystery story. In Doris Lessing's "Through the Tunnel," for example, suspense builds as the reader wonders whether Jerry will be able to succeed in the physical and mental challenge he has set for himself.

See pages 10–11, 1078, and 1083

See also FORESHADOWING, MOOD.

Symbol Any person, animal, place, object, or event that exists on a literal level within a work but also represents something on a figurative level. Swimming through the tunnel, for example, is a symbolic achievement for Jerry in Doris Lessing's "Through the Tunnel." The act means that he is growing up.

See also ALLEGORY, FIGURATIVE LANGUAGE.

T

Tall tale A wildly imaginative story, usually passed down orally, about the fantastic adventures or amazing feats of folk heroes in realistic local settings. The ballad "John Henry" as told by Zora Neale Hurston is an example of a tall tale.

See also FOLKLORE.

Tanka Unrhymed Japanese verse form consisting of five lines. The first and third lines have five syllables each; the other lines have seven syllables each.

See pages 576 and 578

See also HAIKU.

Teleplay The script of a drama written for television, which, in addition to dialogue and stage directions, usually contains detailed instructions about camera shots and angles.

See also STAGE DIRECTIONS.

Theater of the Absurd Drama, primarily of the 1950s and 1960s, that does not contain a plot but instead presents a series of scenes in which the characters speak in meaningless conversations or perform actions with little purpose. The central concern of this drama is to show that people are helpless or confused in an alienating world.

See also DRAMA, SURREALISM.

Theme The main idea or message of a story, a poem, a novel, or a play, sometimes expressed as a general statement about life. Some works have a *stated theme,* which is expressed directly. Other works have an *implied theme,* which is revealed gradually through other elements such as plot, character, setting, point of view, and symbol. A literary work may have more than one theme. Themes and subjects are different. The subject of a work might be love; the theme would be what the writer says about love–for example, love is cruel; love is wonderful; or love is fleeting.

See pages 94–95, 338, and 869

See also AUTHOR'S PURPOSE, FABLE, MORAL.

Theme archetype. *See ARCHETYPE.*

Thesis The main idea of an essay or other work of nonfiction. The thesis may be implied but is commonly stated directly.

See pages 400–401, 409, and 441

See also ESSAY, NONFICTION.

Title The name given to a literary work. The title can help explain setting, provide insight into the theme, or describe the action that will take place in the work.

Tone An author's attitude toward his or her subject matter. Tone is conveyed through elements such as word choice, punctuation, sentence structure, and figures of speech. A writer's tone may convey a variety of attitudes, such as sympathy, seriousness, irony, sadness, bitterness, or humor. For example, James Thurber's amused and affectionate tone in "The Car We Had to Push" contrasts with Isabel Allende's solemn tone in "And of Clay Are We Created."

See pages 252, 262, and 1225

See also ATMOSPHERE, AUTHOR'S PURPOSE, DICTION, MOOD, NARRATOR, SPEAKER, STYLE, VOICE.

Tragedy A play in which the main character, or *tragic hero,* suffers a downfall as a result of a fatal character flaw, errors in judgment, or forces beyond human control, such as fate. Traditionally, the tragic hero is a

person of high rank who, out of *hubris* (an exaggerated sense of power and pride) violates a human, a natural, or a divine law. By breaking the law, the hero poses a threat to society and causes the suffering or death of family members, friends, and associates. In the last act of a traditional tragedy, these wrongs are set right when the tragic hero is punished or dies and order is restored. For example, *Antigone* by Sophocles is a tragedy which describes the downfall of Creon, a king whose pride is his *tragic flaw* and leads to his destruction.

See pages 714–715

See also DRAMA, HERO.

Tragic hero. *See TRAGEDY.*

U

Understatement Language that makes something seem less important than it really is. Understatement may be used to add humor or to focus the reader's attention on something the author wants to emphasize.

See also HYPERBOLE.

Unreliable narrator. *See NARRATOR.*

V

Verbal irony. *See IRONY.*

Verse paragraph A group of lines in a poem that form a unit. Unlike a stanza, a verse paragraph does not have a fixed number of lines. While poems written before the twentieth century usually contain stanzas, many contemporary poems are made up of verse paragraphs. Verse paragraphs help to organize a poem into thoughts, as paragraphs help to organize prose.

See pages 580 and 583

See also FREE VERSE, STANZA.

Voice The distinctive use of language that conveys the author's or narrator's personality to the reader. Voice is determined by elements of style such as word choice and tone.

See pages 192–193, 249 and 382

See also DICTION, NARRATOR, STYLE, TONE.

W

Wit An exhibition of cleverness and humor. The works of Dorothy Parker and Mark Twain are known for their wit.

See also COMEDY, HUMOR, SARCASM, SATIRE.

Word choice. *See DICTION.*

The Reading Process

Being an active reader is a crucial part of being a lifelong learner. It is also an ongoing task. Good reading skills are recursive; that is, they build on each other, providing the tools you'll need to understand text, to connect selections to your own life, to interpret ideas and themes, and to read critically.

Vocabulary Development

To develop a rich vocabulary, consider these four important steps:

- **Read** a wide variety of texts.
- **Enjoy** and engage in wordplay and word investigation.
- **Listen** carefully to how others use words.
- **Participate** regularly in good classroom discussions.

Using context to discover meaning

When you look at the words and sentences surrounding a new word, you are using context. **Look** before, at, and after a new word or phrase. **Connect** what you know with what an author has written. Then **guess** at a possible meaning. **Try again** if your guess does not make sense. Consider these strategies for using context:

- Look for a synonym or an antonym nearby to provide a clue to the word's meaning.
- Notice if the text relates the word's meaning to another word.
- Check for a description of an action associated with the word.
- Try to find a general topic or idea related to the word.

Using word parts and word origins

Consider these basic elements when taking a word apart to determine meaning:

- **Base words** Locate the most basic part of a word to predict a core meaning.
- **Prefixes** Look at syllables attached before a base that add to or change a meaning.
- **Suffixes** Look at syllables added to the end of a base word that create new meanings.

Also consider **word origins**—Latin, Greek, and Anglo-Saxon roots—that are the basis for much of English vocabulary. Knowing these roots can help you determine derivations and spellings, as well as meanings in English.

Using reference materials

When using context and analyzing word parts do not help to unlock the meaning of a word, go to a reference source such as a dictionary, a glossary, a thesaurus, or even the Internet. Use these tips:

- **Locate** a word by using the guide words at the top of the pages.
- **Look** at the parts of the reference entry, such as part of speech, definition, or synonym.
- **Choose** between multiple meanings by thinking about what makes sense.
- **Apply** the meaning to what you're reading.

Distinguishing between meanings

Determining subtle differences between word meanings also aids comprehension. **Denotation** refers to the dictionary meaning or meanings of a word. **Connotation** refers to an emotion or underlying value that accompanies a word's dictionary meaning. The word *fragrance* has a different connotation from the word *odor,* even though the denotation of both words is "smell."

Comprehension Strategies

Because understanding is the most critical reading task, lifelong learners use a variety of reading strategies before, during, and after reading to ensure their comprehension.

Establishing and adjusting purposes for reading

To establish a purpose for reading, preview or **skim** a selection by glancing quickly over the entire piece, reading headings and subheadings, and noticing the organizational pattern of the text.

If you are reading to learn, solve a problem, or perform a task involving complex directions, consider these tips:

- Read slowly and carefully.
- Reread difficult passages.
- Take careful notes or construct a graphic.

Adjust your strategies as your purpose changes. To locate specific information in a longer selection, or to enjoy an entertaining plot, you might allow yourself a faster pace. Know when to speed up or slow down to maintain your understanding.

Drawing on personal background

When you recall information and personal experiences that are uniquely your own, you **draw on your personal background.** By thus **activating prior knowledge,** and combining it with the words on a page, you create meaning in a selection. To expand and extend your prior knowledge, share it interactively in classroom discussions.

Monitoring and modifying reading strategies

Check or **monitor your understanding** as you read, using the following strategies:

- Summarize
- Clarify
- Question
- Predict what will come next

You can use these four important steps once or twice in an easy, entertaining passage or after every paragraph in a conceptually dense nonfiction selection. As you read, think about asking interesting questions, rather than passively waiting to answer questions your teacher may ask later.

All readers find that understanding sometimes breaks down when material is difficult. Consider these steps to modify or change your reading strategies when you don't understand what you've read:

- Reread the passage.
- Consult other sources, including text resources, teachers, and other students.
- Write comments or questions on another piece of paper for later review or discussion.

Constructing graphic organizers

Graphic organizers, such as charts, maps, and diagrams, help you construct ideas in a visual way so you can remember them later. Look at the following model. Like a Venn diagram, which compares and contrasts two ideas or characters, a **semantic features analysis** focuses on the discriminating features of ideas or words. The items or ideas you want to compare are listed down the side, and the discriminating features are listed across the top. In each box use a + if the feature or characteristic applies to the item or a – if the feature or characteristic does not apply.

People in Government	Elected	Appointed	Passes Laws	Vetoes Laws
President	+	–	–	+
State Governor	+	–	–	+
Supreme Court Justice	–	+	–	–
Secretary of Defense	–	+	–	–

A **flowchart** helps you keep track of the sequence of events. Arrange ideas or events in a logical, sequential order. Then draw arrows between your ideas to indicate how one idea or event flows into another. Look at the following flowchart to see how you might show the chronological sequence of a story. Use a flowchart to make a **change frame,** recording causes and effects in sequence to illustrate how something changed.

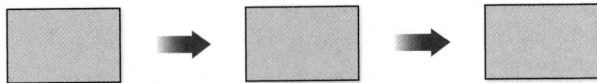

A **web** can be used for a variety of purposes as you read a selection.

- To **map out the main idea and details** of a selection, put the main idea in the middle circle and, as you read, add supporting details around the main thought.
- To **analyze a character in a story,** put the character's name in the middle and add that character's actions, thoughts, reputation, plot involvement, and personal development in the surrounding circles.
- To **define a concept,** put a word or an idea in the middle circle and then add a more general category, descriptions, examples, and non-examples in the surrounding circles.

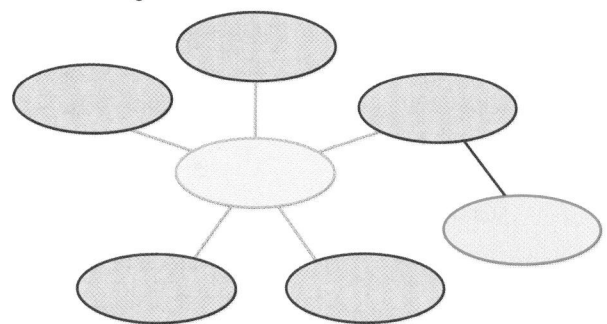

Analyzing text structures

To follow the logic and message of a selection and to remember it, analyze the **text structure,** or organization of ideas, within a writer's work. In narrative as well as in informational text, writers may embed one structure within another, but it is usually possible to identify one main pattern of organization. Recognizing the pattern of organization can help you discover the writer's purpose and will focus your attention on the important ideas in the selection. **Look for signal words** to point you to the structure.

- **Chronological order** often uses words such as *first, then, after, later,* and *finally*.
- **Cause-and-effect order** can include words or phrases such as *therefore, because, subsequently,* or *as a result of*.
- **Comparison-contrast order** may use words or phrases such as *similarly, in contrast, likewise,* or *on the other hand*.

Interpreting graphic aids

Graphic aids provide an opportunity to see and analyze information at a glance. Charts, tables, maps, and diagrams allow you to analyze and compare information. Maps include a compass rose, legend, and scale to help you interpret direction, symbols, and size. Charts and graphs compare information in categories running horizontally and vertically.

Tips for Reading Graphic Aids

- Examine the title, labels, and other explanatory features.
- Apply the labels to the graphic aid.
- Interpret the information.

Look carefully at the models below.

Scale

Compass rose

Legend

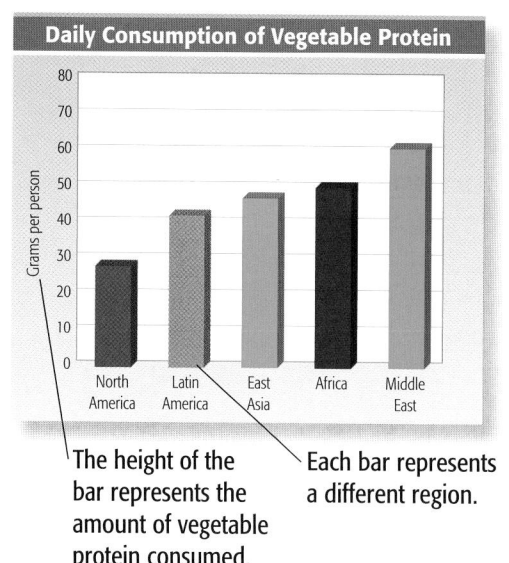

The height of the bar represents the amount of vegetable protein consumed.

Each bar represents a different region.

Sequencing

The order in which thoughts are arranged is called a **sequence**. A good sequence is one that is logical, given the ideas in a selection. **Chronological order, spatial order,** and **order of importance** are common forms of sequencing. Think about the order of a writer's thoughts as you read and pay particular attention to sequence when **following complex written directions**.

Summarizing

A summary is a short restatement of the main ideas and important details of a selection. Summarizing what you have read is an excellent tool for understanding and remembering a passage.

Tips for Summarizing

- Identify the **main ideas** or most important thoughts within a selection.
- Determine the essential **supporting details.**
- Relate all the main ideas and the essential details in a **logical sequence.**
- **Paraphrase**—that is, use your own words.
- Answer **who, what, why, where,** and **when** questions when you summarize.

The best summaries can easily be understood by someone who has not read the selection. If you're not sure whether an idea is a main idea or a detail, try taking it out of your summary. Does your summary still sound complete?

Drawing inferences and supporting them

An **inference** involves using your reason and experience to come up with an idea based on what a writer implies or suggests, but does not directly state. The following strategic reading behaviors are examples of inference:

- **Making a prediction** is taking an educated guess about what a text will be about based on initial clues a writer provides.
- **Drawing a conclusion** is making a general statement you can explain with reason or with supporting details from a text.
- **Making a generalization** is generating a statement that can apply to more than one item or group.

What is most important when inferring is to be sure that you have accurately based your thoughts on supporting details from the text as well as on your own knowledge.

Reading silently for sustained periods

When you read for long periods of time, your task is to avoid distractions. Check your comprehension regularly by summarizing what you've read so far. Using study guides or graphic organizers can help get you through difficult passages. Take regular breaks when you need them and vary your reading rate with the demands of the task.

Synthesizing information

You will often need to read across texts; that is, in different sources, combining or **synthesizing** what you've learned from varied sources to suit your purposes. Follow these suggestions:

- Understand the information you've read in each source.
- Interpret the information.
- Identify similarities and differences in ideas or logic.
- Combine like thoughts in a logical sequence.
- Add to the information or change the form to suit your purposes.

Literary Response

Whenever you share your thoughts and feelings about something you've read, you are responding to text. While the way you respond may vary with the type of text you read and with your individual learning style, as a strategic reader you will always need to adequately support your responses with proof from the text.

Responding to informational and aesthetic elements

When you respond both intellectually *and* emotionally, you connect yourself with a writer and with other people. To respond in an intellectual way, ask yourself if the ideas you have read are logical and well supported. To respond emotionally, ask yourself how you feel about those ideas and events. Choose a way to respond that fits your learning style. Class discussions, journal entries, oral interpretations, enactments, and graphic displays are some of the many ways to share your thoughts and emotions about a writer's work.

Comparing responses with authoritative views

Critics' reviews may encourage you to read a book, see a movie, or attend an event. They may also warn you that whatever is reviewed is not acceptable entertainment or is not valued by the reviewer. Deciding whether to value a review depends on the credibility of the reviewer and also on your own personal views and feelings. Ask yourself the following questions:

- What is the reviewer's background?
- What qualifies the reviewer to write this evaluation?
- Is the review balanced? Does it include both positive and negative responses?
- Are arguments presented logically?
- Are opinions supported with facts?
- What bias does this reviewer show?
- Do I agree? Why or why not?

Analysis and Evaluation

Good readers want to do more than recall information or interpret thoughts and ideas. When you read, read critically, forming opinions about characters and ideas, and making judgments using your own prior knowledge and information from the text.

Analyzing characteristics of texts

To be a critical reader and thinker, start by analyzing the characteristics of the text. Think about what specific characteristics make a particular selection clear, concise, and complete. Ask yourself these questions:

- What **pattern of organization** has this writer used to present his or her thoughts? Cause/effect? Comparison/contrast? Problem/solution? Does this organization make the main ideas clear or vague? Why?
- What word order, or **syntax**, gives force and emphasis to this writer's ideas? Does the grammatical order of the words make ideas sound complete, or is the sentence structure confusing?
- What **word choices** reveal this writer's tone, or attitude about the topic? Is the language precise or too general? Is it economical and yet descriptive?

Evaluating the credibility of sources

Evaluating the credibility of a source involves making a judgment about whether a writer is knowledgeable and truthful. Consider the following steps:

- **Decide on the writer's purpose or motive.** What will the writer gain if you accept his or her ideas or if you act on his or her suggestions?
- **Investigate the writer's background.** How has the writer become an authority in his or her field? Do others value what he or she says?
- **Evaluate the writer's statements.** Is the writer's information factual? Can it be proved? Are opinions clearly stated as such? Are they adequately supported with details so that they are valid? Are any statements nonfactual? Check to be sure.

Analyzing logical arguments and modes of reasoning

When you analyze works you've read, ask yourself whether the reasoning behind a writer's works is logical. Two kinds of logical reasoning are

Inductive Reasoning By observing a limited number of particular cases, a reader arrives at a general or universal statement. This logic moves from the specific to the general.

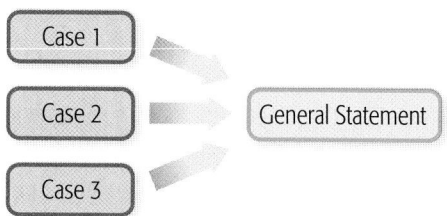

Deductive Reasoning This logic moves from the general to the specific. The reader takes a general statement and, through reasoning, applies it to specific situations.

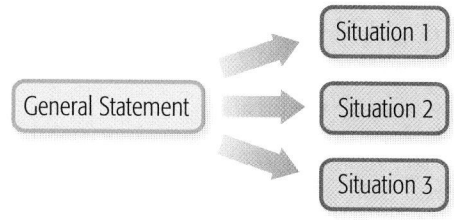

Faulty reasoning, on the other hand, is vague and illogical. Look for either/or reasoning or oversimplified statements when analyzing faulty reasoning. Failure to understand a writer's work may be the result of poorly presented, unsupported arguments, sequenced in a haphazard way.

A writer shows **bias** when he or she demonstrates a strong personal, and sometimes unreasonable, opinion. Look for bias when evaluating editorials, documentaries, and advertisements.

Writers use **persuasive techniques** when they try to get readers to believe a certain thing or act in a particular way. A writer may have a strong personal bias and still compose a persuasive essay that is logical and well supported. On the other hand, deceptive arguments can be less than accurate in order to be persuasive. Read carefully to judge whether a writer's bias influences his or her writing in negative or positive ways.

FOLDABLES™

 Reading and Thinking with Foldables™

by Dinah Zike, M.Ed., Creator of **Foldables™**

Using Foldables™ Makes Learning Easy and Enjoyable

Anyone who has paper, scissors, and a stapler or some glue can use Foldables in the classroom. Just follow the illustrated step-by-step directions. Check out the following sample:

Reading Objective: to understand how one character's actions affect other characters in a short story

Use this Foldable to keep track of what the main character does and how his or her actions affect the other characters.

1. Place a sheet of paper in front of you so that the short side is at the top. Fold the paper in half from top to bottom.

2. Fold in half again, from side to side, to divide the paper into two columns. Unfold the paper so that the two columns show.

3. Draw a line along the column crease. Then, through the top layer of paper, cut along the line you drew, forming two tabs.

4. Label the tabs *Main character's actions* and *Effects on others.*

5. As you read, record the main character's actions under the first tab. Record how each of those actions affects other characters under the second tab.

> **Practice reading and following step-by-step directions.**

> Main character's actions | Effects on others

> **Illustrations make directions easier to follow.**

> **Become an active reader, tracking and reorganizing information so that you can better comprehend the selection.**

Short Story

Reading Objective: to analyze a short story on the basis of its literary elements

As you read, use the following Foldable to keep track of five literary elements in the short story.

1. Stack three sheets of paper with their top edges about a half-inch apart. Be sure to keep the side edges straight.

2. Fold up the bottom edges of the paper to form six tabs, five of which will be the same size.

3. Crease the paper to hold the tabs in place and staple the sheets together along the crease.

4. Turn the sheets so that the stapled side is at the top. Write the title of the story on the top tab. Label the five remaining tabs *Setting, Characters, Plot, Point of View,* and *Theme.*

5. Use your Foldable as you read the short story. Under each labeled tab, jot down notes about the story in terms of that element.

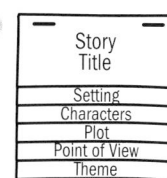

Story Title
Setting
Characters
Plot
Point of View
Theme

You may adapt this simple Foldable in several ways.

- Use it with dramas, longer works of fiction, and some narrative poems—wherever five literary elements are present in the story.

- Change the labels to focus on something different. For example, if a story or a play has several settings, characters, acts, or scenes, you could devote a tab to each one.

Drama

 Reading Objective: to understand conflict and plot in a drama

As you read the drama, use the following Foldable to keep track of conflicts that arise and ways that those conflicts are resolved.

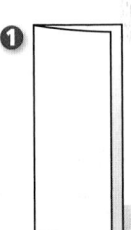

1. Place a sheet of paper in front of you so that the short side is at the top. Fold the paper in half from side to side.

2. Fold the paper again, one inch from the top as shown here.

3. Unfold the paper and draw lines along all of the folds. This will be your chart.

4. At the top, label the left column *Conflicts* and the right column *Resolutions.*

5. As you read, record in the left column the various conflicts that arise in the drama. In the right column, explain how each conflict is resolved by the end of the drama.

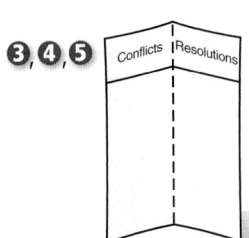

You may adapt this simple Foldable in several ways.

- Use it with short stories, longer works of fiction, and many poems—wherever conflicts and their resolutions are important.

- Change the labels to focus on something different. For example, you could record the actions of two characters, or you could record the thoughts and feelings of a character before and after the story's climax.

Lyric Poem

 Reading Objective: to interpret the poet's message by understanding the speaker's thoughts and feelings

As you read the poem, use the following Foldable to help you distinguish between what the speaker *says* and what the poet *means*.

1. Place a sheet of paper in front of you so that the short side is at the top. Fold the paper in half from top to bottom.

2. Fold the paper in half again from left to right.

3. Unfold and cut through the top layer of paper along the fold line. This will make two tabs.

4. Label the left tab *Speaker's Words.* Label the right tab *Poet's Meaning.*

5. Use your Foldable to jot down notes on as you read the poem. Under the left tab, write down key things the speaker says. Under the right tab, write down what you think the poet means by having the speaker say those things.

You may adapt this simple Foldable in several ways.

■ Use it to help you visualize the images in a poem. Just replace *Speaker's Words* with *Imagery* and replace *Poet's Meaning* with *What I See.*

■ Replace the label *Speaker's Words* with *Speaker's Tone* and under that tab write adjectives that describe the tone of the speaker's words.

■ If the poem you are reading has two stanzas, you might devote each tab to notes about one stanza.

Informational Text

 Reading Objective: to understand and remember ideas in informational text

As you read a nonfiction selection, use this Foldable to help you identify what you already know about the topic, what you might want to know about it, and what you learn about it from the selection.

1. Hold a sheet of paper in front of you so that the short side is at the top. Fold the bottom of the paper up and the top down to divide the paper into thirds.

2. Unfold the paper and turn it so that the long side is at the top. Draw lines along the folds and label the three columns *Know, Want to Know,* and *Learned.*

3. Before you read the selection, write what you already know about the topic under the left heading and what you want to know about it under the middle heading. As you read, jot down what you learn about the topic under the last heading.

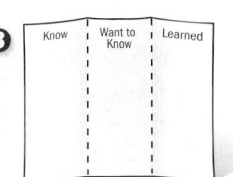

You may adapt this simple Foldable in several ways.

- Use it with magazine and newspaper articles, textbook chapters, reference articles, and informational Web sites—anything you might read to look for information.

- Use this three-part Foldable to record information from three sources. Label each column with the name of one source and write notes from that source under its heading.

- For a two-column Foldable, just fold the sheet of paper in half. For four columns, fold it in half and then in half again.

The Writing Process

Writing is a process with five stages: *prewriting, drafting, revising, editing/ proofreading,* and *publishing/presenting.* These stages often overlap, and their importance, weight, and even their order vary according to your needs and goals. Because writing is recursive, you almost always have to double back somewhere in this process, perhaps to gather more information or to reevaluate your ideas.

The Writing Process

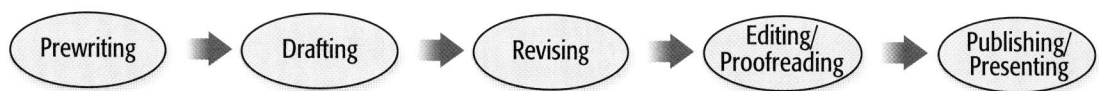

Prewriting → Drafting → Revising → Editing/ Proofreading → Publishing/ Presenting

Prewriting

The prewriting stage includes coming up with ideas, making connections, gathering information, defining and refining the topic, and making a plan for a piece of writing.

Tips for prewriting

- Begin with an interesting idea (*what* you will write about).
- Decide the purpose of the writing (*why* you are writing).
- Identify the audience (for *whom* you are writing).
- Explore your idea through a technique such as free-writing, clustering, making diagrams, or brainstorming.

   Freewriting is writing nonstop for a set time, usually only five or ten minutes. The idea is to keep pace with your thoughts, getting them on paper before they vanish. Freewriting can start anywhere and go anywhere.

   Clustering begins with writing a word or phrase in the middle of a sheet of paper. Circle the word or phrase; then think of related words and ideas. Write them in bubbles connected to the central bubble. As you cluster, connect related ideas. The finished cluster will be a diagram of how your ideas can be organized.

   Brainstorming is creating a free flow of ideas with a group of people—it's like freewriting with others. Start with a topic or question; encourage everyone to join in freely. Accept all ideas without

judgment and follow each idea as far as it goes. You can evaluate the ideas later.

- Search for information in print and nonprint sources.
- If you are writing a personal essay, all of the information may come from your own experiences and feelings. If you are writing a report or a persuasive essay, you will probably need to locate pertinent factual information and take notes on it. Besides library materials, such as books, magazines, and newspapers, you will want to use the Internet and other on-line resources. You may also want to interview people with experience or specialized knowledge related to your topic.
- As you gather ideas and information, jot them down on note cards to use as you draft.
- Evaluate all ideas and information to determine or fine-tune the topic.
- Organize information and ideas into a plan that serves as the basis for writing.
- Develop a rough outline reflecting the method of organization you have chosen. Include your main points and supporting details.
- Find and include missing information or ideas that might add interest or help accomplish the purpose of the writing.

Drafting

In this stage, you translate into writing the ideas and information you gathered during prewriting. Drafting is an opportunity to explore and develop your ideas.

Tips for drafting

- Follow the plan made during prewriting but be flexible. New and better ideas may come to you as you develop your ideas; be open to them.
- Transform notes and ideas into related sentences and paragraphs, but don't worry about grammar or mechanics. At this point, it is usually better to concentrate on getting your ideas on paper. You might want to circle or annotate ideas or sections that need more work.
- Determine the tone or attitude of the writing.
- Try to formulate an introduction that will catch the interest of your intended audience.

Revising

In this stage, review and evaluate your draft to make sure it accomplishes its purpose and speaks to its intended audience. When revising, interacting with a peer reviewer can be especially helpful.

Using peer review

Ask one or more of your classmates to read your draft. Here are some specific ways in which you can direct their responses:

- Have readers tell you in their own words what they have read. If you do not hear your ideas restated, you will want to revise for clarity.
- Ask readers to tell you what parts of your writing they liked best and why.
- Discuss the ideas in your writing with your readers. Add any new insights you gain to your revision.
- Ask readers for suggestions about things such as organization and word choice.

You may want to take notes on your readers' suggestions so you will have a handy reference as you revise.

Tips for the peer reviewer

When you are asked to act as a reviewer for a classmate's writing, the following tips will help you do the most effective job:

- Read the piece all the way through—without commenting—to judge its overall effect.
- Tell the writer how you responded to the piece. For example, did you find it informative? interesting? amusing?
- Ask the writer about parts you don't understand.
- Think of questions to ask that will help the writer improve the piece.
- Be sure that your suggestions are constructive.
- Help the writer make improvements.
- Answer the writer's questions honestly. Think about how you would like someone to respond to you.

Tips for revising

- Be sure you have said everything you wanted to say. If not, *add.*
- If you find a section that does not relate to your topic, *cut it.*
- If your ideas are not in a logical order, *rearrange* sentences and paragraphs.
- *Rewrite* any unclear sentences.
- Evaluate your introduction to be sure it creates interest, leads the reader smoothly into your topic, and states your main idea. Also evaluate your conclusion to be sure it either summarizes your writing or effectively brings it to an end.
- Evaluate your word choices. Choose vivid verbs and precise nouns. Use a thesaurus to help you.
- Consider the comments of your peer reviewer. Evaluate them carefully and apply those that will help you create a more effective piece of writing.

Editing/Proofreading

In the editing/proofreading stage, you polish your revised draft and proofread it for errors in grammar and spelling. Use this proofreading checklist to help you check for errors and use the proofreading symbols in the chart below to mark places that need corrections.

☑ Have I avoided run-on sentences and sentence fragments and punctuated sentences correctly?

☑ Have I used every word correctly, including plurals, possessives, and frequently confused words?

☑ Do verbs and subjects agree? Are verb tenses correct?

☑ Do pronouns refer clearly to their antecedents and agree with them in person, number, and gender?

☑ Have I used adverb and adjective forms and modifying phrases correctly?

☑ Have I spelled every word correctly and checked the unfamiliar ones in a dictionary?

Publishing/Presenting

There are a number of ways you can share your work. You could publish it in a magazine, a class anthology, or another publication, or read your writing aloud to a group. You could also join a writers' group and read one another's works.

Proofreading Symbols		
⊙	Lt Brown	Insert a period.
∧	No one came to the party.	Insert a letter or a word.
=	I enjoyed paris.	Capitalize a letter.
/	The Class ran a bake sale.	Make a capital letter lowercase.
⌒	The campers are home sick.	Close up a space.
ⓢⓟ	They visited (N.Y.) ⓢⓟ	Spell out.
∧ ⌄	Sue please come I need your help.	Insert a comma or a semicolon.
∩	He enjoyed feild day.	Transpose the position of letters or words.
#	alltogether	Insert a space.
℘	We went to to Boston.	Delete letters or words.
⌄ ⌄ ⌄	She asked, Whos coming?	Insert quotation marks or an apostrophe.
/ = /	mid January	Insert a hyphen.
¶	"Where?" asked Karl. "Over there," said Ray.	Begin a new paragraph.

Using the Traits of Strong Writing

What are some basic terms you can use to discuss your writing with your teacher or classmates? What should you focus on as you revise and edit your compositions? Check out the following seven terms, or traits, that describe the qualities of strong writing. Learn the meaning of each trait and find out how using the traits can improve your writing.

Ideas The message or the theme and the details that develop it

Writing is clear when readers can grasp the meaning of your ideas right away. Check to see whether you're getting your message across.

☑ Does the title suggest the theme of the composition?

☑ Does the composition focus on a single narrow topic?

☑ Is the thesis—the main point or central idea—clearly stated?

☑ Do well-chosen details elaborate your main point?

Organization The arrangement of main ideas and supporting details

An effective plan of organization points your readers in the right direction and guides them easily through your composition from start to finish. Find a structure, or order, that best suits your topic and writing purpose. Check to see whether you've ordered your key ideas and details in a way that keeps your readers on track.

☑ Are the beginning, middle, and end clearly linked?

☑ Is the internal order of ideas easy to follow?

☑ Does the introduction capture your readers' attention?

☑ Do sentences and paragraphs flow from one to the next in a way that makes sense?

☑ Does the conclusion wrap up the composition?

Voice A writer's unique way of using tone and style

Your writing voice comes through when your readers sense that a real person is communicating with them. Readers will respond to the **tone** (or attitude) that you express toward a topic and to the **style** (the way that you use language and shape your sentences). Read your work aloud to see whether your writing voice comes through.

☑ Does your writing sound interesting?

☑ Does your writing reveal your attitude toward your topic?

☑ Does your writing sound like you—or does it sound like you're imitating someone else?

Word Choice The vocabulary a writer uses to convey meaning

Words work hard. They carry the weight of your meaning, so make sure you choose them carefully. Check to see whether the words you choose are doing their jobs well.

☑ Do you use lively verbs to show action?

☑ Do you use vivid words to create word pictures in your readers' minds?

☑ Do you use precise words to explain your ideas simply and clearly?

Sentence Fluency The smooth rhythm and flow of sentences that vary in length and style

The best writing is made up of sentences that flow smoothly from one sentence to the next. Writing that is graceful also sounds musical–rhythmical rather than choppy. Check for sentence fluency by reading your writing aloud.

- ☑ Do your sentences vary in length and structure?
- ☑ Do transition words and phrases show connections between ideas and sentences?
- ☑ Does parallelism help balance and unify related ideas?

Conventions Correct spelling, grammar, usage, and mechanics

A composition free of errors makes a good impression on your readers. Mistakes can be distracting, and they can blur your message. Try working with a partner to spot errors and correct them. Use this checklist to help you.

- ☑ Are all words spelled correctly?
- ☑ Are all proper nouns—as well as the first word of every sentence—capitalized?
- ☑ Is your composition free of sentence fragments?
- ☑ Is your composition free of run-on sentences?
- ☑ Are punctuation marks—such as apostrophes, commas, and end marks—inserted in the right places?

Presentation The way words and design elements look on a page

Appearance matters, so make your compositions inviting to read. Handwritten papers should be neat and legible. If you're using a word processor, double-space the lines of text and choose a readable font. Other design elements–such as boldfaced headings, bulleted lists, pictures, and charts–can help you present information effectively as well as make your papers look good.

Preparing a manuscript

Follow the guidelines of the Modern Language Association when you prepare the final copy of your research paper.

- **Heading** On separate lines in the upper left-hand corner of the first page, include your name, your teacher's name, the course name, and the date.
- **Title** Center the title on the line below the heading.
- **Numbering** Number the pages one-half inch from the top of the page in the right-hand corner. Write your last name before each page number after the first page.
- **Spacing** Use double spacing throughout.
- **Margins** Leave one-inch margins on all sides of every page.

Writing Modes

Writing may be classified as expository, descriptive, narrative, or persuasive. Each of these classifications, or modes, has its own purpose.

Expository Writing

Expository writing gives instructions, defines or explains new terms or ideas, explains relationships, compares one thing or opinion with another, or explains how to do something. Expository essays usually include a thesis statement in the introduction.

- ☑ Does the opening contain attention-grabbing details or intriguing questions to hook the reader?
- ☑ Have I provided sufficient information to my audience in a clear and interesting way?
- ☑ Have I checked the accuracy of the information I have provided?
- ☑ Are my comparisons and contrasts clear and logical?

Descriptive Writing

Description re-creates an experience primarily through the use of sensory details. A writer should strive to create a single impression that all the details support. To do so requires careful planning as well as choices about order of information, topic sentences, and figurative language.

- ☑ Did I create interest in my introduction?
- ☑ Are my perspective and my subject clearly stated in my topic sentence?
- ☑ Did I organize details carefully and consistently?
- ☑ Did I order information effectively?
- ☑ Have I chosen precise, vivid words?
- ☑ Do transitions clearly and logically connect the ideas?
- ☑ Have I created a strong, unified impression?

Narrative Writing

Narrative writing, whether factual or fictional, tells a story and has these elements: characters, plot, point of view, theme, and setting. The plot usually involves a conflict between a character and an opposing character or force.

- ☑ Did I introduce characters and a setting?
- ☑ Did I develop a plot that begins with an interesting problem or conflict?
- ☑ Did I build suspense, lead the reader to a climax, and end with a resolution?
- ☑ Did I use dialogue to move the story along?

Persuasive Writing

Persuasive writing expresses a writer's opinion. The goal of persuasion is to make an audience change its opinion and, perhaps, take action. Effective persuasive writing uses strong, relative evidence to support its claims. This kind of writing often requires careful research, organization, and attention to language.

- ☑ Did I keep my audience's knowledge and attitudes in mind from start to finish?
- ☑ Did I state my position in a clear thesis statement?
- ☑ Have I included ample supporting evidence?
- ☑ Have I addressed opposing viewpoints?
- ☑ Have I avoided errors in logic?

Research Paper Writing

More than any other type of paper, research papers are the product of a search—a search for data, for facts, for informed opinions, for insights, and for new information.

Selecting a topic

- If a specific topic is not assigned, choose a topic. Begin with the assigned subject or a subject that interests you. Read general sources of information about that subject and narrow your focus to some aspect of it that interests you. Good places to start are encyclopedia articles and the tables of contents of books on the subject. A computerized library catalog will also display many subheads related to general topics. Find out if sufficient information about your topic is available.

- As you read about the topic, develop your paper's central idea, which is the purpose of your research. Even though this idea might change as you do more research, it can begin to guide your efforts. For example, if you were assigned the subject of the Civil War, you might find that you're interested in women's roles during that war. As you read, you might narrow your topic down to women who went to war, women who served as nurses for the Union, or women who took over farms and plantations in the South.

Conducting a broad search for information

- Generate a series of researchable questions about your chosen topic. Then research to find answers to your questions.

- Among the many sources you might use are the card catalog, the computer catalog, the *Reader's Guide to Periodical Literature* (or an electronic equivalent), newspaper indexes, and specialized references such as biographical encyclopedias.

- If possible, use primary sources as well as secondary sources. A **primary source** is a firsthand account of an event—for example, the diary of a woman who served in the army in the Civil War is a primary source. **Secondary sources** are sources written by people who did not experience or influence the event. Locate specific information efficiently by using the table of contents, indexes, chapter headings, and graphic aids.

Developing a working bibliography

If a work seems useful, write a **bibliography card** for it. On an index card, write down the author, title, city of publication, publisher, date of publication, and any other information you will need to identify the source. Number your cards in the upper right-hand corner so you can keep them in order.

Following are model bibliography, or source, cards.

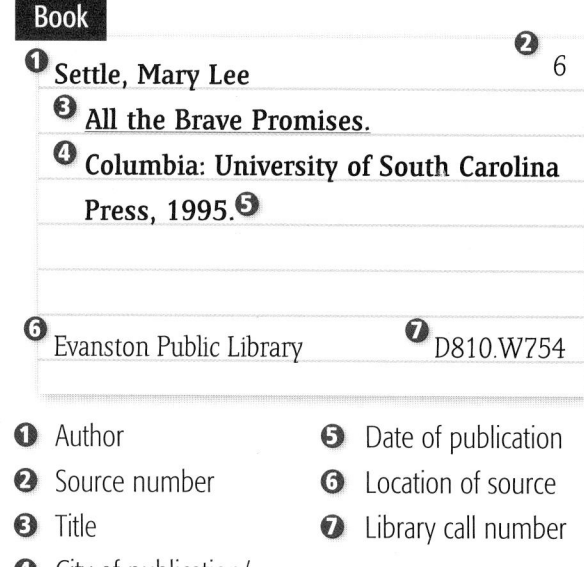

Book

❶ Settle, Mary Lee   ❷ 6

❸ All the Brave Promises.

❹ Columbia: University of South Carolina Press, 1995. ❺

❻ Evanston Public Library   ❼ D810.W754

❶ Author   ❺ Date of publication
❷ Source number   ❻ Location of source
❸ Title   ❼ Library call number
❹ City of publication/ Publisher

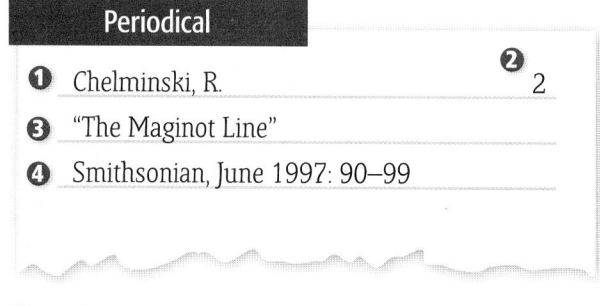

Periodical

❶ Chelminski, R.   ❷ 2

❸ "The Maginot Line"

❹ Smithsonian, June 1997: 90–99

❶ Author
❷ Source number
❸ Title
❹ Title of magazine/date/page number(s)

Online source

❶ "Job Hunting Resources"   ❷ 6

❸ The Career Building Network

❹ CareerBuilder

❺ 14 Feb. 2002

❻ http://www.careerbuilder.com

❶ Title   ❹ Sponsoring organization
❷ Source number   ❺ Date of access
❸ Title of database   ❻ URL

Evaluating your sources

Your sources should be **a**uthoritative, **r**eliable, **t**imely, and **s**uitable (**arts**).

- The source should be **authoritative.** The author should be well-known in the field. An author who has written several books or articles about a subject or who is frequently quoted may be considered an authority. You might also consult *Book Review Index* and *Book Review Digest* to find out how other experts in the field have evaluated a book or an article.

- The source should be **reliable.** If possible, avoid material from popular magazines in favor of that from more scholarly journals. Be especially careful to evaluate material from online sources. For example, the Web site of a well-known university is more reliable than that of an individual. (You might also consult a librarian or your instructor for guidance in selecting reliable online sources.)

- The source should be **timely.** Use the most recent material available, particularly for subjects of current importance. Check the publication date of books as well as the month and year of periodicals.

- The source should be **suitable,** or **appropriate.** Consider only material that is relevant to the purpose of your paper. Do not waste time on books or articles that have little bearing on your topic. If you are writing on a controversial topic, you should include material that represents more than one point of view.

Compiling and organizing note cards

Careful notes will help you to organize the material for your paper.

- As you reread and study sources, write useful information on index cards. Be sure that each note card

identifies the source (use the number of the bibliography card that corresponds to each source).

- In the lower right-hand corner of the card, write the number of the page on which you found the information.

- Three helpful ways to take notes are paraphrasing, summarizing, and quoting directly.

   1. **Paraphrase** important details that you want to remember; that is, use your own words to restate specific information.

   2. **Summarize** main ideas that an author presents. When you summarize several pages, be sure to note the page on which the material begins and the page on which it ends—for example, 213–221.

   3. **Quote** the exact words of an author only when the actual wording is important. Be careful about placing the author's words in quotation marks.

- Identify the subject of each note card with a short phrase written in the upper left.

> Avoid **plagiarism**—presenting an author's words or ideas as if they were your own. Remember that you must credit the source not only for material directly quoted but also for any facts or ideas obtained from the source.

See the sample note card below, which includes information about careers and goals from three pages.

> *Careers and goals*   12
> *Many people "crave work that will*
> *spark... excitement and energy."*
> *(5) Sher recognizes that a career does*
> *not necessarily satisfy a person's aim*
> *in life. (24) She also offers advice on*
> *how to overcome obstacles that people*
> *experience in defining their goals. (101)*

- Organize your note cards to develop a **working outline.** Begin by sorting them into piles of related cards. Try putting the piles together in different ways that suggest an organizational pattern. (If, at this point, you discover that you do not have enough information, go back and do further research.) Many methods of organization are possible. You might also combine methods of organization.

Developing a thesis statement

A thesis statement tells what your topic is and what you intend to say about it—for example, "World War II changed the lives of African Americans and contributed to the rise of the Civil Rights Movement."

- Start by examining your central idea.
- Refine it to reflect the information that you gathered in your research.
- Next, consider your approach to the topic. What is the purpose of your research? Are you proving or disproving something? illustrating a cause-and-effect relationship? offering a solution to a problem? examining one aspect of the topic thoroughly? predicting an outcome?
- Revise your central idea to reflect your approach.
- Be prepared to revise your thesis statement if necessary.

Drafting your paper

Consult your working outline and your notes as you start to draft your paper.

- Concentrate on getting your ideas down in a complete and logical order.
- Write an introduction and a conclusion. An effective introduction creates interest, perhaps by beginning with a question or a controversial quotation; it should also contain your thesis statement. An effective conclusion will summarize main points, restate your thesis, explain how the research points to important new questions to explore, and bring closure to the paper.

Documenting sources

Since a research paper, by its nature, is built on the work of others, you must carefully document all the sources you have used.

- Name the sources of words, ideas, and facts that you borrow.
- In addition to citing books and periodicals from which you take information, cite song lyrics, letters, and excerpts from literature.
- Also credit original ideas that are expressed graphically in tables, charts, and diagrams, as well as the sources of any visual aids you may include, such as photographs.
- You need not cite the source of any information that is common knowledge, such as "John F. Kennedy was assassinated in 1963 in Dallas, Texas."

In-text citations The most common method of crediting sources is with parenthetical documentation within the text. Generally a reference to the source and page number is included in parentheses at the end of each quotation, paraphrase, or summary of information borrowed from a source. An in-text citation points readers to a corresponding entry in your **works-cited list**—a list of all your sources, complete with publication information, that will appear as the final page of your paper. The Modern Language Association (MLA) recommends the following guidelines for crediting sources in text. You may wish to refer to the *MLA Handbook for Writers of Research Papers* by Joseph Gibaldi for more information and examples.

- **Put in parentheses the author's last name and the page number where you found the information.**

  An art historian has noted, "In Wood's idyllic farmscapes, man lives in complete harmony with Nature; he is the earth's caretaker" (Corn 90).

- **If the author's name is mentioned in the sentence, put only the page number in parentheses.**

  Art historian Wanda Corn has noted, "In Wood's idyllic farmscapes, man lives in complete harmony with Nature; he is the earth's caretaker" (90).

- **If no author is listed, put the title or a shortened version of the title in parentheses. Include a page number if you have one.**

  Some critics believe that Grant Wood's famous painting *American Gothic* pokes fun at small-town life and traditional American values ("Gothic").

Compiling a list of works cited

At the end of your text, provide an alphabetized list of published works or other sources cited.

- Include complete publishing information for each source.
- For magazine and newspaper articles, include the page numbers. If an article is continued on a different page, use + after the first page number.
- For online sources, include the date accessed.
- Cite only those sources from which you actually use information.
- Arrange entries in alphabetical order according to the author's last name. Write the last name first. If no author is given, alphabetize by title.
- For long entries, indent five spaces every line after the first.

How to cite sources

On the next three pages, you'll find sample style sheets that can help you prepare your list of sources—the final page of the research paper. Use the one your teacher prefers.

MLA Style

MLA style is most often used in English and social studies classes. Center the title *Works Cited* at the top of your list.

Source	Style
Book with one author	Witham, Barry B. *The Federal Theatre Project: A Case Study.* New York: Cambridge UP, 2003. ["UP" is an abbreviation for "University Press."]
Book with two or three authors	Hoy, Pat C., II, Esther H. Schor, and Robert DiYanni. *Women's Voices: Visions and Perspectives.* New York: McGraw-Hill, 1990. [If a book has more than three authors, name only the first author and then write "et al." (Latin abbreviation for "and others").]
Book with editor(s)	Komunyakaa, Yusef, and David Lehman, eds. *The Best American Poetry 2003.* New York: Scribners, 2003.
Book with an organization or a group as author or editor	Smithsonian Institution. *Aircraft of the National Air and Space Museum.* Washington: Smithsonian Institution Press, 1998.
Work from an anthology	Cofer, Judith Ortiz. "Tales Told Under the Mango Tree." *Hispanic American Literature.* Ed. Nicolas Kanellos. New York: HarperCollins, 1995. 34–44.
Introduction in a published book	Weintraub, Stanley. Introduction. *Great Expectations.* By Charles Dickens. New York: Signet, 1998. v–xii.
Encyclopedia article	"Jazz." *Encyclopaedia Britannica.* 15th ed. 1998.
Weekly magazine article	Franzen, Jonathan. "The Listener." *New Yorker* 6 Oct. 2003: 85–99.
Monthly magazine article	Quammen, David. "Saving Africa's Eden." *National Geographic* Sept. 2003: 50–77.
Newspaper article	Dionne, E. J., Jr. "California's Great Debate." *Washington Post* 26 Sept. 2003: A27. [If no author is named, begin the entry with the title of the article.]
Internet	"Visit Your Parks." *National Park Service.* 1 Oct. 2003. National Park Service, U.S. Dept. of the Interior. 3 Nov. 2003 <http://www.nps.gov/parks.html>.
Online magazine article	Martin, Richard. "How Ravenous Soviet Viruses Will Save the World." *Wired Magazine* 11.10 (October 2003). 17 Oct. 2003 <http://www.wired.com/wired/archive/11.10/phages.html>.
Radio or TV program	"Orcas." *Champions of the Wild.* Animal Planet. Discovery Channel. 21 Oct. 2003.
Videotape or DVD	Hafner, Craig, dir. *The True Story of Seabiscuit.* DVD. A & E Home Video, 2003. [For a videotape (VHS) version, replace "DVD" with "Videocassette."]
Interview	Campeche, Tanya. E-mail interview. 25 Feb. 2004. [If an interview takes place in person, replace "E-mail" with "Personal"; if it takes place on the telephone, use "Telephone."]

CMS Style

CMS style was created by the University of Chicago Press to meet its publishing needs. This style, which is detailed in *The Chicago Manual of Style* (CMS), is used in a number of subject areas. Center the title *Bibliography* at the top of your list.

Source	Style
Book with one author	Witham, Barry B. *The Federal Theatre Project: A Case Study.* New York: Cambridge University Press, 2003.
Book with multiple authors	Hoy, Pat C., II, Esther H. Schor, and Robert DiYanni. *Women's Voices: Visions and Perspectives.* New York: McGraw-Hill, 1990. [If a book has more than ten authors, name only the first seven and then write "et al." (Latin abbreviation for "and others").]
Book with editor(s)	Komunyakaa, Yusef, and David Lehman, eds. *The Best American Poetry 2003.* New York: Scribners, 2003.
Book with an organization or a group as author or editor	Smithsonian Institution. *Aircraft of the National Air and Space Museum.* Washington, DC: Smithsonian Institution Press, 1998.
Work from an anthology	Cofer, Judith Ortiz. "Tales Told Under the Mango Tree." *Hispanic American Literature,* edited by Nicolas Kanellos, 34–44. New York: HarperCollins, 1995.
Introduction in a published book	Dickens, Charles. *Great Expectations.* New introduction by Stanley Weintraub. New York: Signet, 1998.
Encyclopedia article	[Credit for encyclopedia articles goes in your text, not in your bibliography.]
Weekly magazine article	Franzen, Jonathan. "The Listener." *New Yorker,* October 6, 2003, 85–99.
Monthly magazine article	Quammen, David. "Saving Africa's Eden." *National Geographic,* September 2003, 50–77.
Newspaper article	Dionne, E. J., Jr. "California's Great Debate." *Washington Post,* September 26, 2003, A27. [Credit for unsigned newspaper articles goes in your text, not in your bibliography.]
Internet	U.S. Dept. of the Interior. "Visit Your Parks." *National Park Service.* http://www.nps.gov/parks.html.
Online magazine article	Martin, Richard. "How Ravenous Soviet Viruses Will Save the World." *Wired Magazine* 11.10 (October 2003). http://www.wired.com/wired/archive/11.10/phages.html.
Radio or TV program	[Credit for radio and TV programs goes in your text, not in your bibliography.]
Videotape or DVD	Hafner, Craig, dir. *The True Story of Seabiscuit.* A & E Home Video, 2003. DVD. [For a videotape (VHS) version, replace "DVD" with "Videocassette."]
Interview	[Credit for interviews goes in your text, not in your bibliography.]

APA Style

The American Psychological Association (APA) style is commonly used in the sciences. Center the title *References* at the top of your list.

Source	Style
Book with one author	Witham, B. B. (2003). *The federal theatre project: A case study.* New York: Cambridge University Press.
Book with multiple authors	Hoy, P. C., II, Schor, E. H., & DiYanni, R. (1990). *Women's voices: Visions and perspectives.* New York: McGraw-Hill. [If a book has more than six authors, list the first six authors and then write "et al." (Latin abbreviation for "and others").]
Book with editor(s)	Komunyakaa, Y., & Lehman, D. (Eds.). (2003). *The best American poetry 2003.* New York: Scribners.
Book with an organization or a group as author or editor	Smithsonian Institution. (1998). *Aircraft of the National Air and Space Museum.* Washington, DC: Smithsonian Institution Press.
Work from an anthology	Cofer, J. O. (1995). Tales told under the mango tree. In N. Kanellos (Ed.), *Hispanic American Literature* (pp. 34–44). New York: HarperCollins.
Introduction in a published book	[Credit for introductions goes in your text, not in your references.]
Encyclopedia article	Jazz. (1998). In *Encyclopaedia Britannica.* (Vol. 6, pp. 519–520). Chicago: Encyclopaedia Britannica.
Weekly magazine article	Franzen, J. (2003, October 6). The listener. *The New Yorker,* 85–99.
Monthly magazine article	Quammen, D. (2003, September). Saving Africa's Eden. *National Geographic,* 204, 50–77.
Newspaper article	Dionne, E. J., Jr. (2003, September 26). California's great debate. *The Washington Post,* p. A27. [If no author is named, begin the entry with the title of the article.]
Internet	U.S. Dept. of Interior, National Park Service. (2003, October 1). *National Park Service.* Visit your parks. Retrieved October 17, 2003, from http://www.nps.gov/parks.html
Online magazine article	Martin, R. (2003, October). How ravenous Soviet viruses will save the world. *Wired Magazine,* 11.10. Retrieved October 17, 2003, from http://www.wired.com/wired/archive/11.10/phages.html
Radio or TV program	Orcas. (2003, October 21). *Champions of the wild* [Television series episode]. Animal Planet. Silver Spring, MD: Discovery Channel.
Videotape or DVD	Hafner, C. (Director). (2003). *The true story of Seabiscuit* [DVD]. A & E Home Video. [For a videotape (VHS) version, replace "DVD" with "Videocassette."]
Interview	[Credit for interviews goes in your text, not in your references.]

BUSINESS WRITING

Business writing is a specialized form of expository writing. Business writing might include documents such as letters, memorandums, reports, briefs, proposals, and articles for business publications. Business writing must be clear, concise, accurate, and correct in style and usage.

Letter of Application

One form of business writing that follows a conventional format is a letter of application. A letter of application can be used when applying for a job, an internship, or a scholarship. In most cases, the letter is intended to accompany a résumé or an application. Because detailed information is usually included in the accompanying form, a letter of application should provide a general overview of your qualifications and the reasons you are submitting an application. A letter of application should be concise. You should clearly state which position you are applying for and then explain why you are interested and what makes you qualified. The accompanying material should speak for itself.

32 South Street
Austin, Texas 78746
May 6, 20___

Melissa Reyes
City Life magazine
2301 Davis Avenue
Austin, Texas 78764

❶ Re: Internship

Dear Ms. Reyes:

    I am a junior at City High School and editor of the City High Herald. I ❷ am writing to apply for your summer internship at City Life magazine. As a journalism student and a longtime fan of your magazine, I feel that an internship with your magazine would provide me with valuable experience in the field of journalism. I believe that my role with the City High Herald ❸ has given me the skills necessary to be a useful contributor to your magazine this summer. In addition, my enclosed application shows that I ❹ am also a diligent worker.

    I thank you for considering my application for your summer internship, and I hope to be working with you in the coming months.

                  Sincerely,

                  Anne Moris

                  Anne Moris

❶ The optional subject line indicates the topic of the letter.

❷ The writer states her purpose directly and immediately.

❸ The writer comments briefly on her qualifications.

❹ The writer makes reference to the accompanying material.

Activity: Choose a local business where you might like to work. Write a letter of application for an internship at that business. Assume that you will be submitting this letter along with a résumé or an internship application that details your experience and qualifications.

Résumé

The purpose of a résumé is to provide the employer with a comprehensive record of your background information, related experience, and qualifications. Although a résumé is intended to provide a great deal of information, the format is designed to provide this information in the most efficient way possible.

All résumés should include the following information: a heading that provides your name and contact information; a job goal or a career objective; your education information; your work experience; other related experience; and relevant activities, associations, organizations, or projects that you have participated in. You may also want to include honors that you have received and list individuals whom the employer can contact for a reference. When listing work experience, be sure to give the name of the employer, your job title, and a few brief bulleted points describing your responsibilities.

---

❶ Jane Wiley
909 West Main Street, Apt. #1
Urbana, Illinois 61802
(217) 555-0489 • jane@internet.edu

Goal
Seeking position in television news production

❷ Education
Junior standing in the College of Communications at the University of
 Illinois, Urbana-Champaign
2000 Graduate of City High School

Honors
Member of National Honor Society

Activities
❸ Member, Asian American Association: 2001–Present
Environmental Committee Chairperson, Asian American Association:
 August 2002–May 2003

Work Experience
❹ Radio Reporter, WPGU, 107.1 FM, Champaign, Illinois: May 2002–Present
❺ • Rewrote and read stories for afternoon newscasts
• Served as field reporter for general assignments

Cashier, Del's Restaurant, Champaign, Illinois: May 2002–August 2002
• Responsible for taking phone orders
• Cashier for pickup orders

Assistant Secretary, Office of Dr. George Wright, Woodstock, Illinois:
May 2001–August 2001
• Answered phones
• Made appointments

---

❶ Header includes all important contact information.

❷ All important education background is included.

❸ Related dates are included for all listed activities.

❹ Job title is included along with the place of employment.

❺ Job responsibilities are briefly listed.

Activity: Create an outline that lists the information that you would want to include in a résumé. Use a word processor if possible.

Job Application

When applying for a job, you usually need to fill out a job application. When you fill out the application, read the instructions carefully. Examine the entire form before beginning to fill it out. Write neatly and fill out the form completely, providing all information directly and honestly.

If a question does not apply to you, indicate that by writing *n/a,* short for "not applicable." Keep in mind that you will have the opportunity to provide additional information in your résumé, in your letter of application, or during the interview process.

❶ **Please type or print neatly in blue or black ink.**

❷ **Name:** _____ **Today's date:** _____
Address: _____
Phone #: _____ **Birth date:** _____ **Sex:** _____ **Soc. Sec. #:** _____

****

Job History (List each job held, starting with the most recent job.)

❸ 1. Employer: _____ Phone #: _____
Dates of employment: _____
Position held: _____
Duties: _____

❹ 2. Employer: _____ Phone #: _____
Dates of employment: _____
Position held: _____
Duties: _____

****

Education (List the most recent level of education completed.)

_____

****

Personal References:

1. Name: _____ Phone #: _____
Relationship: _____

2. Name: _____ Phone #: _____
Relationship: _____

❶ The application provides specific instructions.

❷ All of the information requested should be provided in its entirety.

❸ The information should be provided neatly and succinctly.

❹ Experience should be stated accurately and without embellishment.

Activity: Pick up a job application from a local business or use the sample application above. Complete the application thoroughly. Fill out the application as if you were actually applying for the job. Be sure to pay close attention to the guidelines mentioned above.

Memos

A memorandum (memo) conveys precise information to another person or a group of people. A memo begins with a leading block. It is followed by the text of the message. A memo does not have a formal closing.

> TO: All Employees
> FROM: Jordan Tyne, Human Resources Manager
> ❶ SUBJECT: New Human Resources Assistant Director
> DATE: November 3, 20___
>
> ❷ Please join me in congratulating Leslie Daly on her appointment as assistant director in the Human Resources Department. Leslie comes to our company with five years of experience in the field. Leslie begins work on Monday, ❸ November 10. All future general human resource inquiries should be directed to Leslie.
>
> Please welcome Leslie when she arrives next week.

❶ The topic of the memo is stated clearly in the subject line.

❷ The announcement is made in the first sentence.

❸ All of the important information is included briefly in the memo.

Business E-mail

E-mail is quickly becoming the most common form of business communication. While e-mail may be the least formal and most conversational method of business writing, it shouldn't be written carelessly or too casually. The conventions of business writing—clarity, attention to your audience, proper grammar, and the inclusion of relevant information—apply to e-mail.

An accurate subject line should state your purpose briefly and directly. Use concise language and avoid rambling sentences.

> To: LiamS@internet.com
> From: LisaB@internet.com
> CC: EricC@internet.com
> Date: January 7, 8:13 A.M.
> ❶ Subject: New Product Conference Call
>
> Liam,
>
> ❷ I just wanted to make sure that arrangements have been made for next week's conference call to discuss our new product. The East Coast sales team has already scheduled three sales meetings at the end of the month with potential buyers, so it's important that our sales team is prepared to talk about the product. Please schedule the call when the manufacturing director is available, ❸ since he will have important information for the sales team.
>
> Lisa

❶ Subject line clearly states the topic.

❷ The purpose is stated immediately and in a conversational tone.

❸ Important details are included in a brief, direct fashion.

Activity: Write an e-mail to your co-workers. Inform them of a change in company procedure that will affect them. State the specific information that they need to know. Indicate to your co-workers whether action needs to be taken on their part.

Grammar Glossary

This glossary will help you quickly locate information on parts of speech and sentence structure.

A

Absolute phrase. *See* Phrase.

Abstract noun. *See* Noun chart.

Action verb. *See* Verb.

Active voice. *See* Voice.

Adjective A word that modifies a noun or pronoun by limiting its meaning. Adjectives appear in various positions in a sentence. (The *gray* cat purred. The cat is *gray*.)

Many adjectives have different forms to indicate **degree of comparison.** *(short, shorter, shortest)*

The **positive degree** is the simple form of the adjective. *(easy, interesting, good)*

The **comparative degree** compares two persons, places, things, or ideas. *(easier, more interesting, better)*

The **superlative degree** compares more than two persons, places, things, or ideas. *(easiest, most interesting, best)*

A **predicate adjective** follows a linking verb and further identifies or describes the subject. (The child is *happy*.)

A **proper adjective** is formed from a proper noun and begins with a capital letter. Many proper adjectives are created by adding these suffixes: *-an, -ian, -n, -ese,* and *-ish. (Chinese, African)*

Adjective clause. *See* Clause chart.

Adverb A word that modifies a verb, an adjective, or another adverb by making its meaning more specific. When modifying a verb, an adverb may appear in various positions in a sentence. (Cats *generally* eat less than dogs. *Generally,* cats eat less than dogs.) When modifying an adjective or another adverb, an adverb appears directly before the modified word. (I was *quite* pleased that they got along *so* well.) The word *not* and the contraction *-n't* are adverbs. (Mike *wasn't* ready for the test today.) Certain adverbs of time, place, and degree also have a negative meaning. (He's *never* ready.)

Some adverbs have different forms to indicate degree of comparison. *(soon, sooner, soonest)*

The **comparative** degree compares two actions. *(better, more quickly)*

The **superlative** degree compares three or more actions. *(fastest, most patiently, least rapidly)*

Adverb clause. *See* Clause chart.

Antecedent. *See* Pronoun.

Appositive A noun or a pronoun that further identifies another noun or pronoun. (My friend *Julie* lives next door.)

Appositive phrase. *See* Phrase.

Article The adjective *a, an,* or *the.*

Indefinite articles (*a* and *an*) refer to one of a general group of persons, places, or things. (I eat *an* apple *a* day.)

The **definite article** (*the*) indicates that the noun is a specific person, place, or thing. (*The* alarm woke me up.)

Auxiliary verb. *See* Verb.

B

Base form. *See* Verb tense.

C

Clause A group of words that has a subject and a predicate and that is used as part of a sentence. Clauses fall into two categories: *main clauses,* which are also called *independent clauses,* and *subordinate clauses,* which are also called *dependent clauses.*

A **main clause** can stand alone as a sentence. There must be at least one main clause in every sentence. (*The rooster crowed,* and *the dog barked.*)

A **subordinate clause** cannot stand alone as a sentence. A subordinate clause needs a main clause to complete its meaning. Many subordinate clauses begin with subordinating conjunctions or relative pronouns. (*When Geri sang her solo,* the audience became quiet.) The chart on the next page shows the main types of subordinate clauses.

TYPES OF SUBORDINATE CLAUSES

Clause	Function	Example	Begins with . . .
Adjective clause	Modifies a noun or pronoun	Songs *that have a strong beat* make me want to dance.	A relative pronoun such as *which, who, whom, whose,* or *that*
Adverb clause	Modifies a verb, an adjective, or an adverb	*Whenever Al calls me,* he asks to borrow my bike.	A subordinating conjuction such as *after, although, because, if, since, when,* or *where*
Noun clause	Serves as a subject, an object, or a predicate nominative	*What Philip did* surprised us.	Words such as *how, that, what, whatever, when, where, which, who, whom, whoever, whose,* or *why*

Collective noun. *See* Noun chart.

Common noun. *See* Noun chart.

Comparative degree. *See* Adjective; Adverb.

Complement A word or phrase that completes the meaning of a verb. The four basic kinds of complements are *direct objects, indirect objects, object complements,* and *subject complements.*

A **direct object** answers the question *What?* or *Whom?* after an action verb. (Kari found a *dollar.* Larry saw *Denise.*)

An **indirect object** answers the question *To whom? For whom? To what?* or *For what?* after an action verb. (Do *me* a favor. She gave the *child* a toy.)

An **object complement** answers the question *What?* after a direct object. An object complement is a noun, a pronoun, or an adjective that completes the meaning of a direct object by identifying or describing it. (The director made me the *understudy* for the role. The little girl called the puppy *hers.*)

A **subject complement** follows a subject and a linking verb. It identifies or describes a subject. The two kinds of subject complements

are *predicate nominatives* and *predicate adjectives.*

A **predicate nominative** is a noun or pronoun that follows a linking verb and tells more about the subject. (The author of "The Raven" is *Poe.*)

A **predicate adjective** is an adjective that follows a linking verb and gives more information about the subject. (Ian became *angry* at the bully.)

Complex sentence. *See* Sentence.

Compound preposition. *See* Preposition.

Compound sentence. *See* Sentence.

Compound-complex sentence. *See* Sentence.

Conjunction A word that joins single words or groups of words.

A **coordinating conjunction** (*and, but, or, nor, for, yet, so*) joins words or groups of words that are equal in grammatical importance. (David *and* Ruth are twins. I was bored, *so* I left.)

Correlative conjunctions (*both . . . and, just as . . . so, not only . . . but also, either . . . or, neither . . . nor, whether . . . or*) work in pairs to join words and groups of words

of equal importance. (Choose *either* the muffin *or* the bagel.)

A **subordinating conjunction** (*after, although, as if, because, before, if, since, so that, than, though, until, when, while*) joins a dependent idea or clause to a main clause. (Beth acted *as if* she felt ill.)

Conjunctive adverb An adverb used to clarify the relationship between clauses of equal weight in a sentence. Conjunctive adverbs are used to replace *and* (*also, besides, furthermore, moreover*); to replace *but* (*however, nevertheless, still*); to state a result (*consequently, therefore, so, thus*); or to state equality (*equally, likewise, similarly*). (Ana was determined to get an A; *therefore,* she studied often.)

Coordinating conjunction. *See* Conjunction.

Correlative conjunction. *See* Conjunction.

D

Declarative sentence. *See* Sentence.

Definite article. *See* Article.

Demonstrative pronoun. *See* Pronoun.

Direct object. *See* Complement.

E

Emphatic form. *See* Verb tense.

F

Future tense. *See* Verb tense.

G

Gerund A verb form that ends in *-ing* and is used as a noun. A gerund may function as a subject, the object of a verb, or the object of a preposition. (*Smiling* uses fewer muscles than *frowning*. Marie enjoys *walking*.)

Gerund phrase. *See* Phrase.

I

Imperative mood. *See* Mood of verb.

Imperative sentence. *See* Sentence chart.

Indicative mood. *See* Mood of verb.

Indirect object. *See* Complement.

Infinitive A verb form that begins with the word *to* and functions as a noun, an adjective, or an adverb. (No one wanted *to answer.*) Note: When *to* precedes a verb, it is not a preposition but instead signals an infinitive.

Infinitive phrase. *See* Phrase.

Intensive pronoun. *See* Pronoun.

Interjection A word or phrase that expresses emotion or exclamation. An interjection has no grammatical connection to other words. Commas follow mild ones; exclamation points follow stronger ones. (*Well,* have a good day. *Wow!*)

Interrogative pronoun. *See* Pronoun.

Intransitive verb. *See* Verb.

Inverted order In a sentence written in *inverted order,* the predicate comes before the subject. Some sentences are written in inverted order for variety or special emphasis. (Up the beanstalk *scampered Jack.*) The subject also generally follows the predicate in a sentence that begins with *here* or *there.* (*Here was* the solution to his problem.) Questions, or interrogative sentences, are generally written in inverted order. In many questions, an auxiliary verb precedes the subject, and the main verb follows it. (*Has* anyone *seen* Susan?) Questions that begin with *who* or *what* follow normal word order.

Irregular verb. *See* Verb tense.

L

Linking verb. *See* Verb.

M

Main clause. *See* Clause.

Mood of verb A verb expresses one of three moods: indicative, imperative, or subjunctive.

The **indicative mood** is the most common. It makes a statement or asks a question. (We *are* out of bread. *Will* you *buy* it?)

The **imperative mood** expresses a command or makes a request. (*Stop* acting like a child! Please *return* my sweater.)

The **subjunctive mood** is used to express, indirectly, a demand, suggestion, or statement of necessity (I demand that he *stop* acting like a child. It's necessary that she *buy* more bread.) The subjunctive is also used to state a condition or wish that is contrary to fact. This use of the subjunctive requires the past tense. (If you *were* a nice person, you *would return* my sweater.)

N

Nominative pronoun. *See* Pronoun.

Noun A word that names a person, a place, a thing, or an idea. The chart on this page shows the main types of nouns.

TYPES OF NOUNS

Noun	Function	Examples
Abstract noun	Names an idea, a quality, or a characteristic	capitalism, terror
Collective noun	Names a group of things or persons	herd, troop
Common noun	Names a general type of person, place, thing, or idea	city, building
Compound noun	Is made up of two or more words	checkerboard, globe-trotter
Noun of direct address	Identifies the person or persons being spoken to	*Maria,* please stand.
Possessive noun	Shows possession, ownership, or the relationship between two nouns	my *sister's* room
Proper noun	Names a particular person, place, thing, or idea	Cleopatra, Italy, Christianity

Noun clause. *See* Clause chart.

Noun of direct address. *See* Noun chart.

Number A noun, pronoun, or verb is *singular* in number if it refers to one; *plural* if it refers to more than one.

O

Object. *See* Complement.

P

Participle A verb form that can function as an adjective. Present participles always end in *-ing*. (The woman comforted the *crying* child.) Many past participles end in *-ed*. (We bought the beautifully *painted* chair.) However, irregular verbs form their past participles in some other way. (Cato was Caesar's *sworn* enemy.)

Passive voice. *See* Voice.

Past tense. *See* Verb tense.

Perfect tense. *See* Verb tense.

Personal pronoun. *See* Pronoun, Pronoun chart.

Phrase A group of words that acts in a sentence as a single part of speech.

An **absolute phrase** consists of a noun or pronoun that is modified by a participle or participial phrase but has no grammatical relation to the complete subject or predicate. (*The vegetables being done,* we finally sat down to eat dinner.)

An **appositive phrase** is an appositive along with any modifiers. If not essential to the meaning of the sentence, an appositive phrase is set off by commas. (Jack plans to go to

the jazz concert, *an important musical event.*)

A **gerund phrase** includes a gerund plus its complements and modifiers. (*Playing the flute* is her hobby.)

An **infinitive phrase** contains the infinitive plus its complements and modifiers. (It is time *to leave for school.*)

A **participial phrase** contains a participle and any modifiers necessary to complete its meaning. (The woman *sitting over there* is my grandmother.)

A **prepositional phrase** consists of a preposition, its object, and any modifiers of the object. A prepositional phrase can function as an adjective, modifying a noun or a pronoun. (The dog *in the yard* is very gentle.) A prepositional phrase may also function as an adverb when it modifies a verb, an adverb, or an adjective. (The baby slept *on my lap.*)

A **verb phrase** consists of one or more auxiliary verbs followed by a main verb. (The job *will have been completed* by noon tomorrow.)

Positive degree. *See* Adjective.

Possessive noun. *See* Noun chart.

Predicate The verb or verb phrase and any objects, complements, or modifiers that express the essential thought about the subject of a sentence.

A **simple predicate** is a verb or verb phrase that tells something about the subject. (We *ran.*)

A **complete predicate** includes the simple predicate and any words that modify or complete it. (We *solved the problem in a short time.*)

A **compound predicate** has two or more verbs or verb phrases that are joined by a conjunction and share the same subject. (We *ran to the park and began to play baseball.*)

Predicate adjective. *See* Adjective; Complement.

Predicate nominative. *See* Complement.

Preposition A word that shows the relationship of a noun or pronoun to some other word in the sentence. Prepositions include *about, above, across, among, as, behind, below, beyond, but, by, down, during, except, for, from, into, like, near, of, on, outside, over, since, through, to, under, until, with.* (I usually eat breakfast *before* school.)

A **compound preposition** is made up of more than one word. *(according to, ahead of, as to, because of, by means of, in addition to, in spite of, on account of)* (We played the game *in spite of* the snow.)

Prepositional phrase. *See* Phrase.

Present tense. *See* Verb tense.

Progressive form. *See* Verb tense.

Pronoun A word that takes the place of a noun, a group of words acting as a noun, or another pronoun. The word or group of words that a pronoun refers to is called its **antecedent.** (In the following sentence, *Mari* is the antecedent of *she. Mari likes Mexican food, but she doesn't like Italian food.*)

A **demonstrative pronoun** points out specific persons, places, things, or ideas. *(this, that, these, those)*

An **indefinite pronoun** refers to persons, places, or things in a more general way than a noun does. (*all, another, any, both, each, either, enough, everything, few, many, most, much, neither, nobody, none, one, other, others, plenty, several, some*)

An **intensive pronoun** adds emphasis to another noun or pronoun. If an intensive pronoun is omitted, the meaning of the sentence will be the same. (Rebecca *herself* decided to look for a part-time job.)

An **interrogative pronoun** is used to form questions. (*who? whom? whose? what? which?*)

A **personal pronoun** refers to a specific person or thing. Personal pronouns have three cases: nominative, possessive, and objective. The case depends upon the function of the pronoun in a sentence. The first chart on this page shows the case forms of personal pronouns.

A **reflexive pronoun** reflects back to a noun or pronoun used earlier in the sentence, indicating that the same person or thing is involved.

(We told *ourselves* to be patient.)

A **relative pronoun** is used to begin a subordinate clause. (*who, whose, that, what, whom, whoever, whomever, whichever, whatever*)

Proper adjective. *See* Adjective.

Proper noun. *See* Noun chart.

R

Reflexive pronoun. *See* Pronoun.

Relative pronoun. *See* Pronoun.

S

Sentence A group of words expressing a complete thought. Every sentence has a subject and a predicate. Sentences can be classified by function or by structure. The second chart on this page shows the categories by function; the following subentries describe the categories by structure. *See also* Subject; Predicate; Clause.

A **simple sentence** has only one main clause and no subordinate clauses. (*Alan found an old violin.*)

A simple sentence may contain a compound subject or a compound predicate or both. (*Alan and Teri found an old violin. Alan found an old violin and tried to play it. Alan and Teri found an old violin and tried to play it.*) The subject and the predicate can be expanded with adjectives, adverbs, prepositional phrases, appositives, and verbal phrases. As long as the sentence has only one main clause, however, it remains a simple sentence. (*Alan, rummaging in the attic, found an old violin.*)

A **compound sentence** has two or more main clauses. Each main clause has its own subject and predicate, and these main clauses are usually joined by a comma and a coordinating conjunction. (*Cats meow, and dogs bark, but ducks quack.*) Semicolons may also be used to join the main clauses in a compound sentence. (*The helicopter landed; the pilot had saved four passengers.*)

A **complex sentence** has one main clause and one or more

PERSONAL PRONOUNS

Case	Singular Pronouns	Plural Pronouns	Function in Sentence
Nominative	I, you, she, he, it	we, you, they	subject or predicate nominative
Objective	me, you, her, him, it	us, you, them	direct object, indirect object, or object of a preposition
Possessive	my, mine, your, yours, her, hers, his, its	our, ours, your, yours, their, theirs	replacement for the possessive form of a noun

TYPES OF SENTENCES

Sentence Type	Function	Ends with . . .	Examples
Declarative sentence	Makes a statement	A period	I did not enjoy the movie.
Exclamatory sentence	Expresses strong emotion	An exclamation point	What a good writer Consuela is!
Imperative sentence	Makes a request or gives a command	A period or an exclamation point	Please come to the party. Stop!
Interrogative sentence	Asks a question	A question mark	Is the composition due today?

subordinate clauses. *(Since the movie starts at eight, we should leave here by seven-thirty.)*

A **compound-complex sentence** has two or more main clauses and at least one subordinate clause. *(If we leave any later, we may miss the previews, and I want to see them.)*

Simple predicate. *See* Predicate.

Simple subject. *See* Subject.

Subject The part of a sentence that tells what the sentence is about.

A **simple subject** is the main noun or pronoun in the subject. *(Babies* crawl.*)*

A **complete subject** includes the simple subject and any words that modify it. *(The man from New Jersey* won the race.*)* In some sentences, the simple subject and the complete subject are the same. *(Birds* fly.*)*

A **compound subject** has two or more simple subjects joined by a conjunction. The subjects share the same verb. *(Firefighters* and *police officers* protect the community.*)*

Subjunctive mood. *See* Mood of verb.

Subordinate clause. *See* Clause.

Subordinating conjunction. *See* Conjunction.

Superlative degree. *See* Adjective; Adverb.

T

Tense. *See* Verb tense.

Transitive verb. *See* Verb.

V

Verb A word that expresses action or a state of being. *(cooks, seem, laughed)*

An **action verb** tells what someone or something does. Action verbs can express either physical or mental action. (Crystal *decided* to *change* the tire herself.)

A **transitive verb** is an action verb that is followed by a word or words that answer the question *What?* or *Whom?* (I *held* the baby.)

An **intransitive verb** is an action verb that is not followed by a word that answers the question *What?* or *Whom?* (The baby *laughed.*)

A **linking verb** expresses a state of being by linking the subject of a sentence with a word or an expression that identifies or describes the subject. (The lemonade *tastes* sweet. He *is* our new principal.) The most commonly used linking verb is *be* in all its forms *(am, is, are, was, were, will be, been, being)*. Other linking verbs include *appear, become, feel, grow, look, remain, seem, sound, smell, stay, taste.*

An **auxiliary verb**, or helping verb, is a verb that accompanies the main verb to form a verb phrase. (I *have been* swimming.) The forms of *be* and *have* are the most common auxiliary verbs: *(am, is, are, was, were, being, been; has, have, had, having)*. Other auxiliaries include *can, could, do, does, did, may, might, must, shall, should, will, would.*

Verbal A verb form that functions in a sentence as a noun, an adjective, or an adverb. The three kinds of verbals are gerunds, infinitives, and participles. *See* Gerund; Infinitive; Participle.

Verb tense The tense of a verb indicates when the action or state of being occurs. All the verb tenses are formed from the four principal parts of a verb: a base form *(talk)*, a present participle *(talking)*, a simple past form *(talked)*, and a past participle *(talked)*. A **regular verb** forms its simple past and past participle by adding *-ed* to the base form. *(climb, climbed)* An **irregular verb** forms its past and past participle in some other way. *(get, got, gotten)*

In addition to present, past, and future tenses, there are three perfect tenses.

The **present perfect tense** expresses an action or condition that occurred at some indefinite time in the past. This tense also shows an action or condition that began in the past and continues into the present. (She *has played* the piano for four years.)

The **past perfect tense** indicates that one past action or condition began *and* ended before another past action started. (Andy *had finished* his homework before I even began mine.)

The **future perfect tense** indicates that one future action or condition will begin *and* end before another future event starts. Use *will have* or *shall have* with the past participle of a verb. (By tomorrow, I *will have finished* my homework, too.)

The **progressive form** of a verb expresses a continuing action with any of the six tenses. To make the progressive forms, use the appropriate tense of the verb *be* with the present participle of the main verb. (She *is swimming.* She *has been swimming.*)

The **emphatic form** adds special force, or emphasis, to the present and past tense of a verb. For the emphatic form, use *do, does,* or *did* with the base form. (Toshi *did want* that camera.)

Voice The **voice** of a verb shows whether the subject performs the action or receives the action of the verb.

A verb is in the **active voice** if the subject of the sentence performs the action. (The referee *blew* the whistle.)

A verb is in the **passive voice** if the subject of the sentence receives the action of the verb. (The whistle *was blown* by the referee.)

Mechanics

This section will help you use correct capitalization, punctuation, and abbreviations in your writing.

Capitalization

This section will help you recognize and use correct capitalization in sentences.

Rule: Capitalize the first word in any sentence, including direct quotations and sentences in parentheses unless they are included in another sentence.

Example: She said, "Come back soon."

Emily Dickinson became famous only after her death. (She published only six poems during her lifetime.)

Rule: Always capitalize the pronoun *I* no matter where it appears in the sentence.

Example: Some of my relatives think that I should become a doctor.

Rule: Capitalize proper nouns, including

a. names of individuals and titles used in direct address preceding a name or describing a relationship.

Example: George Washington; Dr. Morgan; Aunt Margaret

b. names of ethnic groups, national groups, political parties and their members, and languages.

Example: Italian Americans; Aztec; the Republican Party; a Democrat; Spanish

c. names of organizations, institutions, firms, monuments, bridges, buildings, and other structures.

Example: Red Cross; Stanford University; General Electric; Lincoln Memorial; Tappan Zee Bridge; Chrysler Building; Museum of Natural History

d. trade names and names of documents, awards, and laws.

Example: Microsoft; Declaration of Independence; Pulitzer Prize; Sixteenth Amendment

e. geographical terms and regions or localities.

Example: Hudson River; Pennsylvania Avenue; Grand Canyon; Texas; the Midwest

f. names of planets and other heavenly bodies.

Example: Venus; Earth; the Milky Way

g. names of ships, planes, trains, and spacecraft.

Example: USS *Constitution; Spirit of St. Louis; Apollo 11*

h. names of most historical events, eras, calendar items, and religious names and items.

Example: World War II; Age of Enlightenment; June; Christianity; Buddhists; Bible; Easter; God

i. titles of literary works, works of art, and musical compositions.

Example: "Why I Live at the P.O."; *The Starry Night; Rhapsody in Blue*

j. names of specific school courses.

Example: Advanced Physics; American History

Rule: Capitalize proper adjectives (adjectives formed from proper nouns).

Example: Christmas tree; Hanukkah candles; Freudian psychology; American flag

Punctuation

This section will help you use these elements of punctuation correctly.

Rule: Use a **period** at the end of a declarative sentence or a polite command.

Example: I'm thirsty.

Example: Please bring me a glass of water.

Rule: Use an **exclamation point** to show strong feeling or after a forceful command.

Example: I can't believe my eyes!

Example: Watch your step!

Rule: Use a **question mark** to indicate a direct question.

Example: Who is in charge here?

Rule: Use a **colon**

a. to introduce a list (especially after words such as *these, the following,* or *as follows*) and to introduce material that explains, restates, or illustrates previous material.

Example: The following states voted for the amendment: Texas, California, Georgia, and Florida.

Example: The sunset was colorful: purple, orange, and red lit up the sky.

b. to introduce a long or formal quotation.

Example: It was Mark Twain who stated the following proverb: "Man is the only animal that blushes. Or needs to."

c. in precise time measurements, biblical chapter and verse references, and business letter salutations.

Example:
3:35 PM	7:50 AM
Gen. 1:10–11	Matt. 2:23
Dear Ms. Samuels:	Dear Sir:

Rule: Use a **semicolon**

a. to separate main clauses that are not joined by a coordinating conjunction.

Example: There were two speakers at Gettysburg that day; only Lincoln's speech is remembered.

b. to separate main clauses joined by a conjunctive adverb or by *for example* or *that is*.

Example: Because of the ice storm, most students could not get to school; consequently, the principal canceled all classes for the day.

c. to separate the items in a series when these items contain commas.

Example: The students at the rally came from Senn High School, in Chicago, Illinois; Niles Township High School, in Skokie, Illinois; and Evanston Township High School, in Evanston, Illinois.

d. to separate two main clauses joined by a coordinating conjunction when such clauses already contain several commas.

Example: The designer combined the blue silk, brown linen, and beige cotton into a suit; but she decided to use the yellow chiffon, yellow silk, and white lace for an evening gown.

Rule: Use a **comma**

a. between the main clauses of a compound sentence.

Example: Ryan was late getting to study hall, and his footsteps echoed in the empty corridor.

b. to separate three or more words, phrases, or clauses in a series.

Example: Mel bought carrots, beans, pears, and onions.

c. between coordinate modifiers.

Example: That is a lyrical, moving poem.

d. to set off parenthetical expressions, interjections, and conjunctive adverbs.

Example: Well, we missed the bus again.

Example: The weather is beautiful today; however, it is supposed to rain this weekend.

e. to set off nonessential words, clauses, and phrases, such as:
—adverbial clauses

Example: Since Ellen is so tall, the coach assumed she would be a good basketball player.

—adjective clauses

Example: Scott, who had been sleeping, finally woke up.

—participles and participial phrases

Example: Having found what he was looking for, he left.

—prepositional phrases

Example: On Saturdays during the fall, I rake leaves.

—infinitive phrases

Example: To be honest, I'd like to stay awhile longer.

—appositives and appositive phrases

Example: Ms. Kwan, a soft-spoken woman, ran into the street to hail a cab.

f. to set off direct quotations.

Example: "My concert," Molly replied, "is tonight."

g. to set off an antithetical phrase.

Example: Unlike Tom, Rob enjoys skiing.

h. to set off a title after a person's name.

Example: Margaret Thomas, Ph.D., was the guest speaker.

i. to separate the various parts of an address, a geographical term, or a date.

Example: My new address is 324 Indian School Road, Albuquerque, New Mexico 85350.

I moved on March 13, 1998.

j. after the salutation of an informal letter and after the closing of all letters.

Example: Dear Helen,   Sincerely,

k. to set off parts of a reference that direct the reader to the exact source.

Example: You can find the article in the *Washington Post*, April 4, 1997, pages 33–34.

l. to set off words or names used in direct address and in tag questions.

Example: Yuri, will you bring me my calculator?

Lottie became a lawyer, didn't she?

Rule: Use a **dash** to signal a change in thought or to emphasize parenthetical material.

Example: During the play, Maureen—and she'd be the first to admit it—forgot her lines.

Example: There are only two juniors attending—Mike Ramos and Ron Kim.

Rule: Use **parentheses** to set off supplemental material. Punctuate within the parentheses only if the punctuation is part of the parenthetical expression.

Example: If you like jazz (and I assume you do), you will like this CD. (The soloist is Miles Davis.)

Example: The upper Midwest (which states does that include?) was hit by terrible floods last year.

Rule: Use **brackets** to enclose information that you insert into a quotation for clarity or to enclose a parenthetical phrase that already appears within parentheses.

Example: "He serves his [political] party best who serves the country best." —*Rutherford B. Hayes*

Example: The staircase (which was designed by a famous architect [Frank Lloyd Wright]) was inlaid with ceramic tile.

Rule: Use **ellipsis points** to indicate the omission of material from a quotation.

Example: ". . . Neither an individual nor a nation can commit the least act of injustice against the obscurest individual. . . ."
—*Henry David Thoreau*

Rule: Use **quotation marks**

a. to enclose a direct quotation, as follows:

Example: "Hurry up!" shouted Lisa.

When a quotation is interrupted, use two sets of quotation marks.

Example: "A cynic," wrote Oscar Wilde, "is someone who knows the price of everything and the value of nothing."

Use single quotation marks for a quotation within a quotation.

Example: "Did you say 'turn left' or 'turn right'?" asked Leon.

In writing dialogue, begin a new paragraph and use a new set of quotation marks every time the speaker changes.

Example: "Do you really think the spaceship can take off?" asked the first officer. "Our engineer assures me that we have enough power," the captain replied.

b. to enclose titles of short works, such as stories, poems, essays, articles, chapters, and songs.

Example: "The Lottery" [short story]
"Provide, Provide" [poem]
"Civil Disobedience" [essay]

c. to enclose unfamiliar slang terms and unusual expressions.

Example: The man called his grandson a "rapscallion."

d. to enclose a definition that is stated directly.

Example: *Gauche* is a French word meaning "left."

Rule: Use **italics**

a. for titles of books, lengthy poems, plays, films, television series, paintings and sculptures, long

musical compositions, court cases, names of newspapers and magazines, ships, trains, airplanes, and spacecraft. Italicize and capitalize articles (*a, an, the*) at the beginning of a title only when they are part of the title.

Example: *E.T.* [film]; *The Piano Lesson* [play]
The Starry Night [painting]
the *New Yorker* [magazine]
Challenger [spacecraft]
The Great Gatsby [book]
the *Chicago Tribune* [newspaper]

b. for foreign words and expressions that are not used frequently in English.

Example: Luciano waved good-bye, saying, "*Arrivederci.*"

c. for words, letters, and numerals used to represent themselves.

Example: There is no *Q* on the telephone keypad.

Example: Number your paper from *1* through *10*.

Rule: Use an **apostrophe**

a. for a possessive form, as follows:

Add an apostrophe and -*s* to all singular nouns, plural nouns not ending in -*s*, singular indefinite pronouns, and compound nouns. Add only an apostrophe to a plural noun that ends in -*s*.

Example: the tree's leaves
the man's belt
the bus's tires
the children's pets
everyone's favorite
my mother-in-law's job
the attorney general's decision
the baseball player's error
the cats' bowls

If two or more persons possess something jointly, use the possessive form for the last person named. If they possess it individually, use the possessive form for each one's name.

Example: Ted and Harriet's family
Ted's and Harriet's bosses
Lewis and Clark's expedition
Lewis's and Clark's clothes

b. to express amounts of money or time that modify a noun.

Example: two cents' worth

Example: three days' drive (You can use a hyphenated adjective instead: a three-day drive.)

c. in place of omitted letters or numerals.

Example: haven't [have not]   the winter of '95

d. to form the plural of letters, numerals, symbols, and words used to represent themselves. Use an apostrophe and -*s*.

Example: You wrote two 5's instead of one.

Example: How many *s*'s are there in Mississippi?

Example: Why did he use three *!*'s at the end of the sentence?

Rule: Use a hyphen

a. after any prefix joined to a proper noun or proper adjective.

Example: all-American   pre-Columbian

b. after the prefixes *all-*, *ex-*, and *self-* joined to any noun or adjective, after the prefix *anti-* when it joins a word beginning with *i*, after the prefix *vice-* (except in *vice president* or *vice admiral*), and to avoid confusion between words that begin with *re-* and look like another word.

Example: ex-president
self-important
anti-inflammatory
vice-principal
re-creation of the event
recreation time
re-pair the socks
repair the computer

c. in a compound adjective that precedes a noun.

Example: a bitter-tasting liquid

d. in any spelled-out cardinal or ordinal numbers up to *ninety-nine* or *ninety-ninth,* and with a fraction used as an adjective.

Example: twenty-three   eighty-fifth
one-half cup

e. to divide a word at the end of a line between syllables.

Example: air-port   scis-sors
fill-ing   fin-est

Abbreviations

Abbreviations are shortened forms of words.

Rule: Use only one period if an abbreviation occurs at the end of a sentence. If the sentence ends with a question mark or an exclamation point, use the period and the second mark of punctuation.

Example: We didn't get home until 3:30 AM

Example: Did you get home before 4:00 AM?

Example: I can't believe you didn't get home until 3:30 A.M.!

Rule: Capitalize abbreviations of proper nouns and abbreviations related to historical dates.

Example: John Kennedy Jr.   P.O. Box 333
800 B.C.   A.D. 456   1066 C.E.

Use all capital letters and no periods for most abbreviations of organizations and government agencies.

Example: CBS   CIA   PIN
CPA   IBM   NFL
MADD   GE   FBI

Spelling

The following basic rules, examples, and exceptions will help you master the spellings of many words.

Forming plurals

English words form plurals in many ways. Most nouns simply add -s. The following chart shows other ways of forming plural nouns and some common exceptions to the pattern.

General Rules for Forming Plurals		
If the word ends in	**Rule**	**Examples**
ch, s, sh, x, z	add -es	glass, glasses
a consonant + y	change y to i and add -es	caddy, caddies
a vowel + y or o	add only -s	cameo, cameos monkey, monkeys
a consonant + o common exceptions	generally add -es but sometimes add only -s	potato, potatoes cello, cellos
f or ff common exceptions	add -s change f to v and add -es	cliff, cliffs hoof, hooves
lf	change f to v and add -es	half, halves

A few plurals are exceptions to the rules in the previous chart, but they are easy to remember. The following chart lists these plurals and some examples.

Special Rules for Forming Plurals	
Rule	**Examples**
To form the plural of most proper names and one-word compound nouns, follow the general rules for plurals.	Cruz, Cruzes Mancuso, Mancusos crossroad, crossroads
To form the plural of hyphenated compound nouns or compound nouns of more than one word, make the most important word plural.	mother-in-law, mothers-in-law, attorney general, attorneys general
Some nouns have unusual plural forms.	goose, geese child, children
Some nouns have the same singular and plural forms.	moose scissors pants

Adding prefixes

When adding a prefix to a word, keep the original spelling of the word. Use a hyphen only when the original word is capitalized or with the prefixes *all-, ex-,* and *self-* joined to a noun or an adjective.

co + operative = cooperative
inter + change = interchange
pro + African = pro-African
ex + partner = ex-partner

Suffixes and the silent *e*

Many English words end in a silent letter *e*. Sometimes the *e* is dropped when a suffix is added. When adding a suffix that begins with a consonant to a word that ends in silent *e*, keep the *e*.

like + ness = likeness   sure + ly = surely
COMMON EXCEPTIONS awe + ful = awful;
judge + ment = judgment

When adding a suffix that begins with a vowel to a word that ends in silent *e*, usually drop the *e*.

believe + able = believable
expense + ive = expensive
COMMON EXCEPTION mile + age = mileage

When adding a suffix that begins with *a* or *o* to a word that ends in *ce* or *ge*, keep the *e* so the word will retain the soft *c* or *g* sound.

notice + able = noticeable
courage + ous = courageous

When adding a suffix that begins with a vowel to a word that ends in *ee* or *oe*, keep the final *e*.

see + ing = seeing   toe + ing = toeing

Drop the final silent *e* after the letters *u* or *w*.

argue + ment = argument
owe + ing = owing

Keep the final silent *e* before the suffix *-ing* when necessary to avoid ambiguity.

singe + ing = singeing

Suffixes and the final *y*

When adding a suffix to a word that ends in a consonant + *y*, change the *y* to *i* unless the suffix begins with *i*. Keep the *y* in a word that ends in a vowel + *y*.

try + ed = tried   fry + ed = fried
stay + ing = staying   display + ed = displayed
copy + ing = copying   joy + ous = joyous

Adding *-ly* and *-ness*

When adding *-ly* to a word that ends in a single *l*, keep the *l*, but when the word ends in a double *l*, drop one *l*. When the word ends in a consonant + *le*, drop the *le*. When adding *-ness* to a word that ends in *n*, keep the *n*.

casual + ly = casually
practical + ly = practically
dull + ly = dully
probable + ly = probably
open + ness = openness
mean + ness = meanness

Doubling the final consonant

Double the final consonant in words that end in a consonant preceded by a single vowel if the word is one syllable, if it has an accent on the last syllable that remains there even after the suffix is added, or if it is a word made up of a prefix and a one-syllable word.

stop + ing = stopping
admit + ed = admitted
replan + ed = replanned

Do not double the final consonant if the accent is not on the last syllable or if the accent shifts when the suffix is added. Also do not double the final consonant if the final consonant is *x* or *w*. If the word ends in a consonant and the suffix begins with a consonant, do not double the final consonant.

benefit + ed = benefited
similar + ly = similarly
raw + er = rawer
box + like = boxlike
friend + less = friendless
rest + ful = restful

Forming compound words

When joining a word that ends in a consonant to a word that begins with a consonant, keep both consonants.

out + line = outline
after + noon = afternoon
post + card = postcard
pepper + mint = peppermint

ie and *ei*

Learning this rhyme can save you many misspellings: "Write *i* before *e* except after *c*, or when sounded like *a* as in *neighbor* and *weigh*." There are many exceptions to this rule, including *seize, seizure, leisure, weird, height, either, neither, forfeit.*

-cede, *-ceed*, and *-sede*

Because of the relatively few words with *sēd* sounds, these words are worth memorizing.

These words use *-cede:* **accede, precede, secede.**

One word uses *-sede:* **supersede.**

Three words use *-ceed:* **exceed, proceed, succeed.**

Succeeding on Tests

This section is designed to help you prepare for both classroom and standardized tests. You will become familiar with the various formats of tests and the types of questions you will be required to answer.

Preparing for Classroom Tests

This section will help you learn how to prepare for classroom tests.

Thinking ahead

- Write down information about an upcoming test— when it will be given, what it will cover, and so on—so you can plan your study time effectively.

- Review your textbook, quizzes, homework assignments, class notes, and handouts. End-of-chapter review questions often highlight key points from your textbook.

- Develop your own questions about main ideas and important details, and practice answering them. Writing your own practice tests is an excellent way to get ready for a real test.

- Make studying into an active process. Rather than simply rereading your notes or a chapter in your textbook, try to create a summary of the material. This can be an outline, a list of characters, or a time line. Try to include details from both your lecture notes and your textbook reading so you will be able to see connections between the two.

- Form study groups. Explaining information to a peer is one of the best ways to learn the material.

- Sleep well the night before a test. Spreading your study time over several days should have given you enough confidence to go to bed at your regular time the night before a test.

- Remember that eating well helps you remain alert. Students who eat a regular meal on the morning of a test generally score higher than those who do not.

Taking objective tests

Many of the tests you take in your high school classes will be objective tests, meaning that they ask questions that have specific correct answers. Time is often limited for these tests, so be sure to use your time efficiently.

- First, read the directions carefully. If anything is unclear, ask questions.

- Try to respond to each item on the test, starting with the easier ones.

- Skip difficult questions rather than dwelling on them. You can always come back to them at the end of the test.

- Try to include some time to review your test before turning it in.

Below are tips for answering specific kinds of objective test items:

Kind of item	Tips
Multiple-choice	Read all the answer choices provided before choosing one; even if the first one seems nearly correct, a later choice may be a better answer. Be cautious when choosing responses that contain absolute words such as *always, never, all,* or *none.* Since most generalizations have exceptions, absolute statements are often incorrect.
True/False	If *any* part of the item is false, the correct answer must be "false."
Short-answer	Use complete sentences to help you write a clear response.
Fill-in	Restate fill-ins as regular questions if you are not sure what is being asked.
Matching	Note in the directions whether some responses can be used more than once or not used at all.

Taking subjective (essay) tests

You will also take subjective tests during high school. Typically, these tests ask questions that require you to write an essay. Your grade is based more on how well you are able to make your point than on whether you choose a correct answer.

- When you receive the test, first read it through. If there are several questions, determine how much time to spend on each question.

- Begin your answer by jotting down ideas on scratch paper for several minutes. Read the test question again to make sure you are answering it. Then create a rough outline from which you can create your essay.

- Start your essay with a thesis statement in the first paragraph and follow with paragraphs that provide supporting evidence. Give as much information as possible, including examples and illustrations where appropriate.

- Finish your essay with a conclusion, highlighting the evidence you have provided and restating your thesis.

- You will probably not have time to revise and recopy your essay. After you are finished writing, spend any remaining time proofreading your answer and neatly making any necessary corrections.

Preparing for Standardized Tests

Standardized tests are designed to be administered to very large groups of students, not just those in a particular class. Three of the most widely known standardized tests, all part of the college application process, are the ACT, the PSAT, and the SAT. The strategies in this handbook refer specifically to the PSAT and SAT tests, but they also can apply to preparing for the ACT and other standardized tests.

The PSAT is generally administered to students in the eleventh grade, though some schools offer it to students in the tenth grade as well. This test is designed to predict how well you will do on the SAT. For most students, the PSAT is simply a practice test. Those who perform exceptionally well on the eleventh grade PSAT, however, will qualify for National Merit Scholarship competition.

The SAT consists of the SAT-I: Reasoning Test and a variety of SAT-II: Subject Tests. The SAT-I is a three-hour test that evaluates your general verbal and mathematics skills. The SAT-II: Subject Tests are hour-long tests given in specific subjects and are designed to show specifically how much you have learned in a particular subject area.

Tips for taking standardized tests

Standardized tests are often administered outside of regular class time and require registration. Ask your teacher or guidance counselor how you can register early to ensure that you can take the test at a time and location most convenient for you. In addition, follow these tips:

- Skip difficult questions at first. Standardized tests are usually timed, so first answer items you know. You can return later to those you skipped.

- Mark only your answers on the answer sheet. Most standardized tests are scored by a computer, so stray marks can be read as incorrect answers.

- Frequently compare the question numbers on your test with those on your answer sheet to avoid putting answers in the wrong spaces.

- If time permits, check your answers. If you are not penalized for guessing, fill in answers for any items you might have skipped.

Preparing for the PSAT and the SAT-I

The verbal sections of the PSAT and SAT-I contain sentence completion items and Reading Comprehension questions.

Sentence completion

Sentence completion items provide a sentence with one or two blanks and ask you to select the word or pair of words that best fits in the blank(s). Here is some general information to help you with these questions on the PSAT and SAT-I.

- Start by reading the sentence and filling in your own word to replace the blank. Look for words that show how the word in the blank is related to the rest of the sentence–*and, but, since, therefore, although.*

- Do not read the sentence with the words from each answer choice inserted. This may leave you with several choices that "sound good."

- Once you have chosen your own word to fill in the blank, pick the word from the answer choices that is closest in meaning to your word.

- If you have trouble coming up with a specific word to fill in the blank, try to determine whether the word should be positive or negative. Even this bit of information can help you eliminate some answer choices. If you can eliminate even one answer choice, take a guess at the correct answer.

Reading comprehension

Reading Comprehension questions on the PSAT and SAT-I measure your ability to understand and interpret what you read. Each reading passage is followed by a series of questions. Here are some points to keep in mind when working with these questions:

- You get points for answering questions correctly, not for reading passages thoroughly. Therefore, it is to your advantage to read the passages quickly and spend your time working on the questions.

- After quickly reading a passage, briefly summarize it. This will help you answer general questions, which are based on the passage as a whole.

- To answer specific questions based on details included in the passage, return to the passage to find the correct answers. Reading Comprehension is like an open-book test: you are expected to look at the passage while answering the questions.

- Reading Comprehension passages almost never include controversial opinions. Therefore, an answer choice like "advocated the overthrow of the government" is very likely to be incorrect.

- If you can eliminate even one answer choice, take a guess at the correct answer.

Taking Essay Tests

Writing prompts, or long essay questions, include key words that signal the strategy you will use to bring your ideas into sharp focus. Similarly, these key words also appear in constructed responses, or short essay questions.

Key Word	Strategy
Analyze	To **analyze** means to systematically and critically examine all parts of an issue or event.
Classify or categorize	To **classify** or **categorize** means to put people, things, or ideas into groups, based on a common set of characteristics.
Compare and contrast	To **compare** is to show how things are similar or alike. To **contrast** is to show how things are different.
Describe	To **describe** means to present a sketch or an impression. Rich detail, especially details that appeal to the senses, flesh out a description.
Discuss	To **discuss** means to systematically write about all sides of an issue or event.
Evaluate	To **evaluate** means to make a judgment and support it with evidence.
Explain	To **explain** means to clarify or make plain.
Illustrate	To **illustrate** means to provide examples or to show with a picture or another graphic.
Infer	To **infer** means to read between the lines or to use knowledge or experience to draw conclusions, make generalizations, or form a prediction.
Justify	To **justify** means to prove or to support a position with specific facts and reasons.
Predict	To **predict** means to tell what will happen in the future based on an understanding of prior events and behaviors.
State	To **state** means to briefly and concisely present information.
Summarize	To **summarize** means to give a brief overview of the main points of an event or issue.
Trace	To **trace** means to present the steps or stages in a process or an event in sequential or chronological order.

Pronunciation Key

This glossary lists the vocabulary words found in the selections in this book. The definition given is for the word as it is used in the selection; you may wish to consult a dictionary for other meanings of these words. The key below is a guide to the pronunciation symbols used in each entry.

a	at	**ō**	hope	**ng**	sing
ā	ape	**ô**	fork, all	**th**	thin
ä	father	**oo**	wood, put	<u>**th**</u>	this
e	end	**ōo**	fool	**zh**	treasure
ē	me	**oi**	oil	**ə**	ago, taken, pencil,
i	it	**ou**	out		lemon, circus
ī	ice	**u**	up	**´**	indicates primary stress
o	hot	**ū**	use	**´**	indicates secondary

ENGLISH

A

abashed (ə basht´) *adj.* self-conscious; embarrassed or ashamed **p. 992**

abeyance (ə bā´ əns) *n.* a state of temporary inactivity **p. 253**

absolve (ab zolv´) *v.* to free from blame **p. 746**

abstraction (ab strak´ shən) *n.* theoretical concept isolated from real application **p. 497**

abyss (ə bis´) *n.* an extremely deep chasm; a seemingly bottomless hole **p. 1072**

accord (ə kôrd´) *n.* agreement; conformity **p. 1168**

accosted (ə kôst´ əd) *v.* approached someone in order to speak **p. 1242**

acutely (a kūt´ lē) *adv.* very perceptively or discerningly **p.39**

admonish (ad mon´ish) *v.* to warn, as against a specific action **p. 342**

ESPAÑOL

A

abashed/avergonzado(a) *adj.* que siente vergüenza; **p. 992**

abeyance/suspensión *s.* inactividad transitoria; estado temporal de inactividad **p. 253**

absolve/absolver *v.* liberar de culpa or reproche; **p. 746**

abstraction/abstracción *s.* concepto teórico a aislado de la aplicación real; **p. 496**

abyss/abismo *s.* profundidad muy grande, imponente; **p. 1072**

accord/acuerdo *s.* convenio; en conformidad con una resolución; **p. 1162**

accosted/abordó *v.* se acercó a alguien para hablarle, preguntarle o proponerle algo; **p. 1242**

acutely/agudamente *adv.* llena y enteramente; con percepción; **p. 39**

admonish/amonestar *v.* advertir, como contra una acción específica; **p. 342**

advocate (ad´ və kāt´) *v.* to support publicly **p. 393**

affable (af´ ə bəl) *adj.* friendly and pleasant **p. 873**

affirmation (a fər mā´ shən) *n.* positive agreement or judgment **p. 628**

agenda (ə jen´ də) *n.* an outline of tasks to be accomplished **p. 458**

aggrieved (ə grēvd´) *adj.* disturbed; upset **p. 1045**

aglow (ə glō´) *adj.* glowing **p. 632**

albeit (ôl bē´ it) *conj.* although; even if **p. 183**

alleviate (ə lē´ vē āt´) *v.* to make easier to bear; relieve; lessen **p. 328**

amenable (ə mē´ nə bəl) *adj.* responsive; able to be controlled **p. 76**

amiable (ā´ mē ə bəl) *adj.* good-humored; easy to get along with **p. 1217**

amicable (am´ə kə bəl) *adj.* friendly **p. 1191**

anguish (ang´ gwish) *n.* extreme suffering, pain, or anxiety **p. 1237**

animosity (an´ə mos´a tē) *n.* ill will or resentment; active strong dislike or hostility **p. 1200**

anonymity (an´ə nim´ ətē) *n.* being unknown; having no name; unrecognized **p. 404**

apprehension (ap´ ri hen´ shən) *n.* dread; fear of the future **p. 595**

aristocracy (ar´is tok´rə sē) *n.* a type of government in which a minority of upper-class individuals rule **p. 449**

arrogance (ar´ ə gəns) *n.* overbearing pride **p. 738**

arrogant (ar´ ə gənt) *adj.* full of self-importance; haughty **p. 154**

arroyo (ə roi´ ō) *n.* a dry gully or stream bed **p. 281**

artisan (är´tə zən) *n.* a skilled craftsman **p. 364**

ascertaining (as´ər tān´ ing) *v.* finding out definitely **p. 133**

assiduously (ə sij´ oo əs lē) *adv.* carefully diligent; persistently attentive **p. 1232**

advocate/abogar por *v.* propugnar or apoyar públicamente; **p. 393**

affable/afable *adj.* amable, gracioso, y agradable; **p. 873**

affirmation/afirmación *s.* expresión o gesto que sirve para asegurar o decir que sí; **p. 630**

agenda/agenda *s.* relación de los asuntos que han de tratarse o de las actividades que se han de realizar; **p. 458**

aggrieved/agraviado(a) *adj.* que ha recibido alguna ofensa; **p. 1045**

aglow/resplandeciente *adj.* que brilla intensamente; encendido; **p. 634**

albeit/aunque *conj.* si bien, bien que; **p. 183**

alleviate/aliviar *v.* relevar; minorar; hacer más fácil de soportar **p. 328**

amenable/dócil *adj.* lo que se puede controlar; sensible, tratable; **p. 76**

amiable/amable *adj.* ameno, agradable; amistoso; **p. 1211**

amicable/amigable *adj.* afable, amistoso; **p. 1186**

anguish/angustia *s.* congoja, ansiedad; sufrimiento, dolor; **p. 1237**

animosity/animosidad *s.* mala voluntad o resentimiento; aversión u hostilidad; **p. 1194**

anonymity/anonimato *s.* de condición desconocida; sin hombre; condición del autor cuyo nombre es nombre desconocido; **p. 404**

apprehension/aprehensión *s.* temor; sensación que se tiene cuando se piensa que puede ocurrir algo malo; **p. 597**

aristocracy/aristocracia *s.* tipo de gobierno en que una clase privilegiada; tenga el poder; **p. 449**

arrogance/arrogancia *s.* orgullo dominador; **p. 738**

arrogant/arrogante *adj.* lleno de sentimiento exagerado de la propia importancia; orgulloso; **p. 154**

arroyo/arroyo *s.* barranca seca; **p. 281**

artisan/artesano(a) *s.* persona que fabrica cosas a mano especialmente con un propósito artístico; **p. 364**

ascertaining/averiguando *v.* asegurando la verdad o certeza de algo; cerciorándose de algo; **p. 133**

assiduously/esmeradamente *adv.* hecho con máximo cuidado y atención diligente; **p. 1232**

attain (ə tān′) *v.* to accomplish; to arrive at **p. 862**

attribute (at′rə būt) *n.* a quality or characteristic of a person or thing **p. 433**

austere (ôs tēr′) *adj.* without ornament, very simple **p. 135**

austere (ôs tēr′) *adj.* stern; severe in appearance **p. 534**

B

barren (bar′ən) *adj.* empty and dreary; without life; desolate **p. 836**

belie (bi lī′) *v.* to misrepresent; to give a false impression of **p. 366**

benevolence (bə nev′ ə ləns) *n.* kindness; generosity **p. 414**

beseeching (bi sēch′ ing) *adj.* begging; asking earnestly **p. 213**

blasphemous (blas′fə məs) *adj.* showing disrespect or scorn for God or anything sacred **p. 89**

bloated (blō′tid) *adj.* puffed up; swollen **p. 1178**

boding (bōd′ ing) *n.* a warning or indication, especially of evil **p. 27**

bough (bou) *n.* a tree branch **p. 654**

brooded (broo′ əd) *v.* thought fretfully or anxiously about **p. 1247**

bureau (byoor′ō) *n.* a chest of drawers for the bedroom **p. 537**

C

ceremonious (ser′ə mō′ nē əs) *adj.* carefully observant of the formal acts required by ritual, custom, or etiquette **p. 588**

chaos (kā′ os) *n.* a state of disorder and confusion **p. 560**

china (chī′ nə) *n.* fine, glossy pottery used for tableware **p. 632**

chronic (kron′ ik) *adj.* persistent; ongoing, especially of sickness or pain **p. 532**

attain/alcanzar *v.* obtener o conseguir; llegar a poseer; **p. 862**

attribute/atributo *s.* calidad o característica de algo; **p. 433**

austere/austero(a) *adj.* sin decoración, muy sencillo; **p. 135/534**

austere/grave *adj.* severo, implacable; severo o austero en la apariencia; **p. 534**

B

barren/yermo(a) *adj.* inhabitado, despoblado; estéril; lúgubre; **p. 836**

belie/contradecir *v.* decir lo contrario; **p. 366**

benevolence/benevolencia *s.* amabilidad; generosidad; **p. 414**

beseeching/suplicante *adj.* mendicante; preguntando seriamente; **p. 213**

blasphemous/blasfemo(a) *adj.* que muestra una falta de respeto o desdén por el Dios o algo sagrado; **p. 89**

bloated/hinchado(a) *adj.* con su volumen aumentado; inflamado; hecho en exceso; **p. 1174**

boding/presagio *s.* aviso o indicación, especialmente de malo; **p. 27**

bough/rama *s.* cada una de las partes que nacen del tronco del árbol; **p. 656**

brooded/cavilar *v.* pensar o meditar profundamente, a veces con ansiedad; **p. 1246**

bureau/cómoda *s.* mueble que se usa para guardar ropa; **p. 539**

C

ceremonious/ceremonioso(a) *adj.* que observa las formalidades y se atiene a sus reglas; **p. 590**

chaos/caos *s.* estado de confusión y desorden; **p. 562**

china/vajilla *s.* conjunto de platos, fuentes, tazas y otros recipientes para el servicio de mesa; loza; **p. 634**

chronic/crónico(a) *adj.* persistente; especialmente una enfermedad muy larga o habitual; **p. 534**

cipher (si´fər) *n.* a signifying figure; a number or symbol **p. 565**

combatant (kəm bat´ ənt) *n.* one trained for, or engaged in, combat **p. 978**

commandeer (kom´ ən dēr´) *v.* to seize for use by the military or government **p. 75**

commend (kə mend´) *v.* to speak highly of; to praise **p. 798**

commodious (kə mō´ dē əs) *adj.* having or containing ample room; spacious **p. 356**

compassionate (kəm pash´ ə nit) *adj.* having or showing sympathy for another's misfortune, combined with a desire to help **p. 459**

comprehensive (kom´ pri hen´ siv) *adj.* including nearly everything; large in scope; complete **p. 728**

confidante (kon´ fə dant´) *n.* a person who is entrusted with secrets or private affairs **p. 1028**

confinement (kən fīn´mənt) *n.* the state of being restricted or confined **p. 1057**

conflagration (kon´flə grā´ shən) *adj. n.* a huge fire **p. 566**

confront (kən frunt´) *v.* to come face-to-face with; to oppose **p. 1080**

conscientiously (kon´ shē en´ shəs lē) *adv.* thoughtfully and carefully **p. 210**

contemptible (kən temp´tə bəl) *adj.* worthy of contempt; loathsome **p. 1055**

contend (kən tend´) *v.* to declare or maintain as a fact; argue **p. 114**

contrition (kən trish´ ən) *n.* sorrow for one's sin or wrongdoing; repentance **p. 210**

convivial (kən viv´ē əl) *adj.* fond of merriment and parties with good company; sociable **p. 357**

convoluted (kon´ və lōō´ təd) *adj.* turned in or wound up upon itself; coiled; twisted **p. 166**

correlate (kôr´ə lāt) *v.* to bring (one thing) into relation (with another thing); calculate **p. 1126**

coterie (kō´tər ē) *n.* a small group of people who share a particular interest and often meet socially **p. 342**

countenance (koun´ tə nəns) *n.* the face **p. 86**

covert (kō´ vərt) *adj.* secret; hidden **p. 837**

credence (krēd´ əns) *n.* trustworthiness, especially in the reports or statements of others **p. 346**

cipher/cifra *s.* signo que representa un número; número dígito; **p. 567**

combatant/combatiente *s.* algiuen adiestrado para combate; **p. 978**

commandeer/expropiar *v.* coger por uso del militario o el gobierno; **p. 75**

commend/elogiar *v.* alabar las cualidades y méritos de alguien o de algo; **p. 000**

commodious/cómodo *adj.* que tiene espacio amplio; espacioso; **p. 356**

compassionate/compasivo(a) *adj.* que presta auxilio a los necesitados; que ejercita el amor al prójimo; **p. 459**

comprehensive/comprensivo(a) *adj.* hecho de manera completa o muy a fondo; exhaustivo; **p. 728**

confidante/confidente *s.* persona en que se puede confiar; **p. 1028**

confinement/confinamiento *s.* encierro dentro de ciertos límites; **p. 1056**

conflagration/incendio *s.* gran fuego **p. 568**

confront/confrontar *v.* encontrar algo; oponerse; **p. 1078**

conscientiously/ concienzudamente *adv.* cuidadosamente y reflexivamente; **p. 210**

contemptible/despreciable *adj.* digno de desdén; **p. 1055**

contend/contender *v.* declarar o mentener como un hecho; discutir; **p. 114**

contrition/contrición *s.* dolor para sus pecados o malos; arrepentimiento; **p. 210**

convivial/convival *adj.* que le gusta alegría o fiestas con buena compañía; sociable; **p. 357**

convoluted/retorcido(a) *adj.* arrollado; enroscado; **p. 166**

correlate/poner en correlación *v.* poner algo en relación con algo diferente; calcular; **p. 1122**

coterie/tertulia *s.* grupo pequeño de gente que tienen interés en algo y se encuentran socialmente; **p. 342**

countenance/cara *s.* el rostro; **p. 86**

covert/secreto(a) *adj.* que se mantiene oculto; escondido; **p. 837** [U4]

credence/crédito *s.* reputación, fama, autoridad; **p. 346**

crest (krest) *n.* a peak, high point, or climax **p. 628**

crevice (krev′ is) *n.* a narrow crack into or through something **p. 283**

cultivate (kul′ tə vāt′) *v.* to encourage or further the development of **p. 1188**

D

daft (daft) *adj.* without sense or reason; crazy; silly **p. 243**

debasement (di bās′mənt) *n.* the state of being low-ered in quality, value, or character; degradation **p.433**

decapitate (di kap′ə tāt′) *v.* to cut off the head of **p. 232**

deceitful (di sēt′fəl) *adj.* untruthful and cunning; false **p. 838**

declarative (di klar′ə tiv) *adj.* a type of sentence or expression that makes a simple statement; an explana-tory statement **p. 406**

decrepit (di krep′ it) *adj.* broken down by long use or old age **p. 153; p. 555**

deference (def′ər əns) *n.* respect and honor due to another **p. 741**

deferred (di furd′) *v.* put off, postponed **p.673**

defile (di fīl′) *v.* to spoil the purity of; to make dirty or unclean **p. 752**

deflect (di flekt′) *v.* to cause to turn aside; to bend or deviate **p. 497**

deity (dē′ ə tē) *n.* a god or goddess **p. 1071**

deliberation (di lib′ ə rā′shən) *n.* an official meeting or consultation **p. 1048**

dense (dens) *adj.* thick **p. 621**

derision (di rizh′ ən) *n.* mockery; ridicule **p. 254**

designation (des′ig nā′shən) *n.* a distinguishing name or mark **p. 326**

disconsolate (dis kon′sə lit) *adj.* dejected; mourn-ful; unable to be comforted **p. 857**

discordant (dis kôrd′ ənt) *adj.* not in agreement or harmony **p. 102**

crest/cresta *s.* punto más alto o culminación de algo; clímax; **p. 630**

crevice/hendedura *s.* una rendija angosta en o por algo; **p. 283**

cultivate/cultivar *v.* mantener o desarrollar un sentimiento o relación; **p. 1182**

D

daft/tonto(a) *adj.* sin razón ni sentido; loco; chiflado; **p. 243**

debasement/degradación *s.* estado de ser disminuido en calidad, valor, o carácter; **p. 433**

decapitate/decapitar *v.* cortar la cabeza de; **p. 232**

deceitful/engañoso(a) *adj.* mentiroso y ingenioso; falso; **p. 838**

declarative/declarativo(a) *adj.* tipo de sentencia o expresión que hace una declaración o afirmación simple; una declaración para explicar; **p. 406**

decrepit/decrépito(a) *adj.* arruinado por la edad; vaciado; **p. 153; p. 555**

deference/deferencia *s.* respeto y honor para algiuen **p. 741**

deferred/diferido(a) *v.* dejó algo para más tarde; pospuesto; **p. 673**

defile/manchar *v.* ensuciar; estropear la pureza de; **p. 752**

deflect/desviar *v.* hacer que desviarse; enconar o apartar; **p. 496**

deity/deidad *s.* los dioses o las diosas de diversas religiones; **p. 1071**

deliberation/deliberación *s.* una reunión o consul-tación oficial; **p. 1048**

dense/esposo(a) *adj.* que tiene gran cantidad; **p. 621**

derision/mofa *s.* burla; ridículo **p. 254**

designation/designación *s.* un nombre o una marca distinguida **p. 326**

disconsolate/desconsolado(a) *adj.* que se muestra melancólico, triste y afligido; que no tiene consuelo; **p. 857**

discordant/discordante *adj.* que no está de acuerdo o en armonía **p. 102**

discourteous (dis kur′ tē əs) *adj.* impolite **p. 1015**

disdainful (dis dān′fəl) *adj.* scornful; mocking **p. 1045**

disgruntled (dis grun′tld) *adj.* in a state of sulky dissatisfaction **p. 579**

dismantle (dis mant′əl) *v.* to take apart **p. 1167**

disperse (dis purs′) *v.* to break up and send in different directions; to scatter **p. 800**

dissension (di sen′shən) *n.* disagreement within a group **p. 449**

distortion (dis tôr′ shən) *n.* an appearance of being twisted or bent out of shape **p. 287**

doctrine (dok′ trin) *n.* a particular principle or position that is taught or supported, as of a religion **p. 201**

domestic (də mes′ tik) *adj.* relating to one's own country **p. 448**

dominion (də min′ yən) *n.* control or the exercise of control **p. 496**

drivel (driv′ əl) *v.* to drool; to allow saliva to drip from the mouth **p. 1072**

duly (dōō′ lē) *adv.* rightfully; suitably **p. 14**

dupe (doop) *v.* to fool; to trick **p. 1179**

dutiful (dōō′ti fəl) *adj.* acting out of a sense of obligation or a sense of what is required **p. 1155**

E

edifice (ed′ ə fis) *n.* a building, especially a large, important-looking one **p. 76**

elation (i lā′shən) *n.* a feeling of great joy; ecstasy **p. 431**

elude (i lōōd′) *v.* to avoid or escape, especially through cleverness or quickness **p. 1027**

emanate (em′ə nāt′) *v.* to come or set forth, as from a source **p. 497**

emancipation (i man′sə pā′shən) *n.* the process of becoming free from control or the power of another **p. 486**

discourteous/descortés *adj.* sin buena educación, respeto o amabilidad; **p. 1015**

disdainful/desdeñoso(a) *adj.* que muestra menosprecio o indiferencia; **p. 1045**

disgruntled/descontento(a) *adj.* que no está satisfecho o a gusto; **p. 581**

dismantle/desmantelar *v.* desarmar, desmontar; **p. 1161**

disperse/dispersar *v.* separar, repartir o diseminar los que estaba unido; **p. 800**

dissension/disensión *s.* falta de acuerdo entre varias personas; **p. 449**

distortion/torcimiento *s.* apariencia de ser torcido o curvado **p. 287**

doctrine/doctrina *s.* un principio particular o una posición particular que es enseñado o mantenido, como de una religión **p. 201**

domestic/doméstico(a) *adj.* que pertenece a la nación de que se habla, opuesto a lo que es extranjero; interior; **p. 448**

dominion/dominio *s.* poder o autoridad sobre algo; potestad; **p. 496**

drivel/babear *v.* dejar caer la saliva de la boca; **p. 1072**

duly/debidamente *adv.* justamente, cumplidamente; **p. 14**

dupe/engañar *v.* engatusar; embaucar; **p. 1175**

dutiful/obediente *adj.* realizado o que obra a rigor y con conciencia de las obligaciones; **p. 1150**

E

edifice/edificio *s.* una edificación, especialmente una grande o que parece importante; **p. 76**

elation/elación *s.* un sentimiento de alegría; éxtasis **p. 431**

elude/eludir *v.* evitar o escapar, especialmente por habilidad o rapidez **p. 1027**

emanate/irradiar *v.* despedir calor u otra energía; **p. 496**

emancipation/emancipación *s.* el proceso de hacerse libre de control o el poder de alguien **p. 485**

embroidered (em broi´dərd) *adj.* decorated with needlework **p. 613**

endear (en dēr´) *v.* to cause to adore or admire **p. 1057**

enhance (en hans´) *v.* to make greater, as in beauty or value **p. 66**

enmity (en´ mə tē) *n.* hatred or ill will **p. 1017**

enterprise (en´tər prīz´) *n.* an important project or undertaking **p. 785**

entreat (en trēt´) *v.* to ask earnestly; to beg **p. 781**

equanimity (ēk´ wə nim´ ə tē) *n.* the ability to remain calm and assured **p. 267**

eradicate (i rad´ ə kāt´) *v.* to do away with completely **p. 56**

erratically (ər rat´ i ka lē) *adv.* in an irregular or unpredictable way **p. 40**

erroneous (ə rō´nē əs) *adj.* inaccurate; wrong **p. 1224**

eschew (es chōō´) *v.* to keep apart from something disliked or harmful; avoid **p. 391**

essence (es´əns) *n.* necessary characteristics of a thing **p. 656**

exclusive (iks klōō´siv) *adj.* single or sole; stylish, fashionable **p. 1235**

exhortation (eg´zôr tā´ shən) *n.* a strong appeal or warning **p. 113**

expendable (iks pen´də bəl) *adj.* not strictly necessary; capable of being sacrificed **p. 1125**

exultation (eg´ zul tā´shən) *n.* joy; jubilation **p. 432**

F

famished (fam´isht) *adj.* intensely hungry; ravenous **p. 725**

ferociously (fə rō´shəs lē) *adv.* cruelly; savagely **p. 891**

fester (fes´tər) *v.* to become increasingly infected or inflamed **p. 673**

fetish (fet´ish) *n.* abnormally obsessive preoccupation or attachment; a fixation **p. 496**

embroidered/bordado(a) *adj.* adornado con relieves ejecutados con agujas y diversas clases del hilo. **p. 615**

endear/hacer querer *v.* causar cariño, amor o admiración; **p. 1056**

enhance/engrandecer *v.* hacer más grande, como en buleza o valor; **p. 66**

enmity/enemistad *s.* animadversión, odio o antipatía; **p. 1017**

enterprise/empresa *s.* tarea que ejecuta algo importante; proyecto importante; **p. 785**

entreat/suplicar *v.* solicitar con fuerza y constancia; impetrar; **p. 781**

equanimity/ecuanimidad *s.* serenidad o equilibrio; **p. 267**

eradicate/erradicar *v.* eliminar por completo; **p. 56**

erratically/irregularmente *adv.* que no es regular ni habitual; por modo errático; **p. 40**

erroneous/erróneo(a) *adj.* inexacto; incorrecto; **p. 1218**

eschew/evitar *v.* separarse de algo dañoso o detestado; rehuir **p. 391**

essence/esencia *s.* lo característico de algo; lo necesario; **p. 656**

exclusive/exclusivo(a) *adj.* solo o único; selecto; de moda; **p. 1235**

exhortation/exhortación *s.* una apelación o una advertencia fuerte; **p. 113**

expendable/consumible *adj.* que no es necesario estrictamente; capaz de ser sacrificado sin efectos negativos **p. 1121**

exultation/exultación *s.* alegría; júbilo; **p. 432**

F

famished/hambriento(a) *adj.* que tiene mucha hambre; **p. 725**

ferociously/ferozmente *adv.* cruelmente; salvajemente; **p. 891**

fester/enconar(se) *v.* inflamar o empeorar una herida; **p. 673**

fetish/fetiche *s.* obsesión o preocupación caprichosa por una cosa; una fijación; **p. 495**

fiasco (fē as′kō) *n.* a complete or humiliating failure **p. 104**

fissure (fish′ər) *n.* a narrow crack **p. 538**

flecking (flek′ing) *v.* leaving spots or streaks **p. 580**

formidable (fôr′mi də bəl) *adj.* causing fear, dread, or awe by reason of size, strength, or power **p. 151**

fortitude (fôr′ tə tōōd′) *n.* firm courage or strength of mind in the face of pain or danger **p. 267**

fortnight (fôrt′ nīt′) *n.* two weeks **p. 76**

furtive (fur′ tiv) *adj.* secret; shifty; sly **p. 198**

G

gaunt (gônt) *adj.* extremely thin and hollow-eyed, as from hunger or illness; "looking like skin and bones" **p. 223**

glyph (glif) *n.* an engraved, symbolic figure **p. 565**

gnarled (närld) *adj.* roughened and coarse from age or work; full of knots, as in a tree **p. 1166**

gorge (gôrj) *n.* the passageway between two higher land areas, such as a narrow valley **p. 562**

grapple (grap′ əl) *v.* to struggle, as though wrestling; to come to terms with **p. 455**

gregarious (gri gār′ē əs) *adj.* one who is fond of company; social **p. 423**

grimace (gri mās′ing) *v.* to make a face expressing disgust, disapproval, or pain **p. 538**

grounds (grounds) *n.* the remains of the coffee beans after water has been passed through them; sediment **p. 662**

guile (gīl) *n.* cunning **p. 1046**

guttural (gut′ər əl) *adj.* sounding as if coming from the throat **p. 1243**

H

hale (hāl) *adj.* in good physical condition; healthy **p. 245**

---

fiasco/fiasco *s.* un fracaso; un fallo completo o humillante; **p. 104**

fissure/fisura *s.* hendidura poco profunda; **p. 540**

flecking/salpicando *v.* manchando con gotas; **p. 582**

formidable/formidable *adj.* que causa miedo, pavor, ansiedaad o temor a causa de tamaño, fuerza o poder; **p. 151**

fortitude/fortaleza *s.* valor duro o fuerza del mente en frente de dolor opeligro; **p. 267**

fortnight/quincena *s.* dos semanas; **p. 76**

furtive/furtivo(a) *adj.* secreto; inquieto; **p. 198**

G

gaunt/flaco(a) *adj.* extremamente flaco, por hambre o enfermedad; descamado; **p. 223**

glyph/glifo *s.* figura simbólica usualmente que presenta información; canal vertical que sirve como elemento decorativo; **p. 567**

gnarled/nudoso(a) *adj.* con una parte dura o que sobresale; abultamiento o tumor causado por una enfermedad; como el tronco y las ramas de un árbol; **p. 1160**

gorge/desfiladero *s.* paso estrecho entre montañas; **p. 562**

grapple/asir *v.* esforzarse para conseguir algo; ceder o someterse; **p. 455**

gregarious/sociable *adj.* inclinado al trato y relación con los demás; **p. 423**

grimace/hacer muecas *frase verbal.* hacer gestos o contraer el rostro para expresar disgusto o dolor; **p. 540**

grounds/poso *s.* sedimento de un líquido; especialmente el café; **p. 664**

guile/astucia *s.* habilidad para engañar o para lograr cualquier fin; **p. 1046**

guttural/gutural *adj.* de un sonido que proviene o pertenece a la garganta; **p. 1243**

H

hale/robusto(a) *adj.* que está en bien condición física; sano; **p. 245**

harass (hə ras´) *v.* to bother or annoy repeatedly **p. 230**

hoary (hôr´ē) *adj.* white or gray with age; covered with frost **p. 654**

hones (hōnz) *n.* whetstones or similar tools used to sharpen knives and other types of blades **p. 548**

horizon (hə ri´zən) *n.* the place where the earth and sky appear to meet **p. 1155**

hurtle (hurt´ əl) *v.* to move rapidly, especially with much force or noise **p. 154**

hypochondriac (hī´ pə kon´drē ak´) *n.* one whose worry over his or her health is so great that it brings on the imagined symptoms of an illness **p. 873**

I

ignoble (ig nō´ bəl) *adj.* of low birth or position; without honor or worth **p. 995**

ignorant (ig´nər ənt) *adj.* lacking knowledge or experience; uninformed **p. 891**

immense (i mens´) *adj.* immeasurable; vast; huge **p. 553**

imminent (im´ ə nənt) *adj.* about to occur **p. 16, p. 807**

immortal (i môrt´ əl) *adj.* lasting or living forever; everlasting **p. 404**

impeccably (im pek´ə blē) *adv.* without error or flaw **p. 136**

impediment (im ped´ə mənt) *n.* something that hinders or obstructs **p. 1245**

imperative (im per´ə tiv) *adj.* expressing a command or order **p. 486**

imperceptible (im´pər sep´tə bəl) *adj.* slight, barely capable of being seen or sensed **p. 137**

impertinent (im purt´ən ənt) *adj.* inappropriately bold or forward **p. 927**

impetuous (im pech´ o͞o əs) *adj.* rushing headlong into things; rash **p. 68**

imploring (im plôr´ ing) *adj.* asking earnestly; begging **p. 26**

improvident (im prov´ ə dent) *adj.* wasteful or unthrifty **p. 41**

harass/atormentar *v.* molestar repetidamente; **p. 229**

hoary/canoso(a) *adj.* color o brillo poco vivo; apagado; envejecido; **p. 656**

hones/piedras de afilar *s. pl.* lo que se usa para sacarle filo a un objeto; **p. 550**

horizon/horizonte *s.* línea del límite visual donde parecen juntarse el cielo y la tierra; **p. 1150**

hurtle/lanzar *v.* mover rápidamente, con mucha fuerza o ruido; **p. 154**

hypochondriac/hipocondríaco(a) *s.* alguien que tiene una preocupación sobre su salud tan grande que causa síntomas imaginadas de una enfermedad; **p. 873**

I

ignoble/innoble *adj.* de una posición baja; sin honor ni valor; **p. 995**

ignorant/ignorante *adj.* que no tiene instrucción; que no tiene información sobre una materia o asunto; **p. 891**

immense/inmenso(a) *adj.* que no se puede medir; vasto; grande **p. 555**

imminent/inminente *adj.* que está por suceder o a punto de ocurrir; **p. 16, p. 807**

immortal/inmortal *adj.* que no muere; que dura un tiempo indefinido; eterno; **p. 404**

impeccably/impecablemente *adv.* que no tiene defecto o imperfección; **p. 136**

impediment/impedimento *s.* dificultad, impedimento, obstáculo; **p. 1245**

imperative/imperativo(a) *adj.* expresando un orden o un comando; **p. 484**

imperceptible/imperceptible *adj.* que no se puede recibir por los sentidos; **p. 137**

impertinent/impertinente *adj.* impropiamente atrevido; **p. 927**

impetuous/impetuoso *adj.* salpullido; que avanza precipitadamente o sin pensar; **p. 68**

imploring/implorante *adj.* que pregunta seriamente; mendicante; **p. 27**

improvident/imprevisor(a) *adj.* que no conoce o anticipa el futuro; que no es frugal; **p. 41**

improvised (im′ prə vīzd′) *adj.* invented, composed, or done without preparing beforehand **p. 166**

impudence (im′pyə dəns) *n.* speech or behavior that is aggressively forward or rude **p. 877**

incantation (in′ kan tā′ shən) *n.* words spoken in casting a spell **p. 69**

incense (in sens′) *v.* to make very angry **p. 786**

incredulous (in krej′ ə ləs) *adj.* unwilling or unable to believe. **p. 216**

indelible (in del′ə bəl) *adj.* unable to be erased or removed; permanent **p. 420**

indifferently (in dif′ər ənt lē) *adv.* not concerned about someone or something; without a preference **p. 532**

induce (in dōōs′) *v.* to lead or move by persuasion; to bring about **p. 377**

inert (i nurt′) *adj.* not able to move **p. 1169**

infirmity (in fur′mə tē) *n.* a weakness or ailment **p. 16, p. 566, p. 784**

ingenuity (in′jə nōō′ə tē) *n.* ability to devise or contrive; cleverness; skillfulness **p. 423**

inhibit (in hib′ it) *v.* to hold back one's natural impulses; restrain **p. 357**

inscribe (in skrīb′) *v.* to write, carve, or mark on a surface **p. 994**

inscrutable (in skrōōt′ tə bəl) *adj.* mysterious **p. 126**

insufficient (in′ sə fish′ənt) *adj.* not enough **p. 1224**

intact (in takt′) *adj.* entire; untouched, uninjured, and having all parts **p. 432**

interim (in′tər im) *n.* the space of time that exists between events **p. 795**

interject (in′ tər jekt′) *v.* to cut into with a comment **p. 53**

interlaced (in′ tər lāst′) *adj.* connected by or woven together **p. 1156**

interminable (in tur′ mi nə bəl) *adj.* lasting, or seeming to last, forever; endless **p. 122, p. 1012**

intermittent (in′ tər mit′ ənt) *adj.* occurring at intervals; not steady and continuous **p. 422**

intimidation (in tim′ ə dā shən) *n.* act of making one feel afraid or discouraged **p. 141**

improvised/improvisado(a) *adj.* que se hace sin preparación; **p. 166**

impudence/aplomo *s.* dicho o conducta que es agresivamente atrevido o grosero; **p. 877**

incantation/encantación *s.* palabras dichas para encantar o hechizar; **p. 69**

incense/enfurecer *v.* enfadar mucho; **p. 786**

incredulous/incrédulo(a) *adj.* que no quiere o no puede creer; **p. 216**

indelible/indeleble *adj.* que no se pude borrar o quitar; **p. 420**

indifferently/indiferentemente *adv.* sin que importe que se haga de una manera u otra; sin preferencia; **p. 534**

induce/inducir *v.* referido a una acción causarla o motivarla para que suceda; **p. 377**

inert/inerte *adj.* paralizado, inmóvil; **p. 1163**

infirmity/enfermedad *s.* lo que se tiene cuando se pierde la salud; achaque; **p. 16, p. 568, p. 784**

ingenuity/ingeniosidad *s.* la cualidad de discurrir o inventar con prontitud y facilidad; **p. 423**

inhibit/inhibir *v.* prohibir; refrenar los impulsos naturales; **p. 357**

inscribe/inscribir *v.* escribir, labrar o señalar un superficie; **p. 994**

inscrutable/inescrutable *adj.* misterioso; **p. 126**

insufficient/insuficiente *adj.* que no es bastante; **p. 1218**

intact/intacto(a) *adj.* entero; indemne, y que tiene todas las partes **p. 432**

interim/ínterin *s.* intervalo de tiempo entre dos hechos; **p. 795**

interject/interponer *v.* poner entre cosas o personas; **p. 53**

interlaced/entrelazado(a) *adj.* conectado por o tejido juntos; **p. 1150**

interminable/interminable *adj.* que parece que no tener término o fin; **p. 122, p. 1012**

intermittent/intermitente *adj.* que se interrumpe y continúa o se repite; **p. 422**

intimidation/intimidación *s.* provocar o infundir miedo; **p. 141**

intuitively (in too′ə tiv lē) *adv.* knowing, sensing, understanding; instinctively **p. 438**

invaluable (in val′ ū ə bəl) *adj.* priceless **p. 1221**

invaluable (in val′ ū ə bəl) *adj.* very great in value **p. 414**

irreproachable (ir′ i prō chə bəl) *adj.* free from blame or criticism; faultless **p. 182**

J

jubilantly (joo′bə lənt lē) *adv.* joyfully or happily **p. 1049**

judiciously (joo dish′ əs lē) *adv.* in a way that shows good judgment; sensibly **p. 245**

L

lag (lag) *v.* to fall behind **p. 589**

livid (liv′ id) *adj.* bruised **p. 1214**

lucid (loo′ sid) *adj.* clear-headed; mentally alert **p. 116**

lurk (lurk) *v.* to stay hidden, ready to attack **p. 246**

M

mainstream (mān′ strēm′) *adj.* representing the most widespread attitudes and values of a society or group **p. 414**

makeshift (māk shift′) *adj.* suitable as a temporary substitute for the proper or desired thing **p. 231**

malice (mal′ is) *n.* a desire to hurt another person **p. 819**

malicious (mə lish′ əs) *adj.* having or showing a desire to harm another **p. 158**

marveled (mär′ vəld) *v.* to become filled with wonder or astonishment **p. 636**

mature (mə choor′) *adj.* having reached a desired state **p. 619**

melancholy (mel′ ən kol′ ē) *adj.* depressed; dejected **p. 538**

mesmerize (mez′ mə rīz′) *v.* to hypnotize **p. 56**

meticulous (mi tik′yə ləs) *adj.* precise; careful; worried about details **p. 565**

intuitively/intuitivamente *adv.* con la capacidad de comprender sin razonamiento; entender por instinto; **p. 438**

invaluable/inestimable *adj.* incalculable, sin precio; **p. 414**

irreproachable/irreprochable *adj.* libre de culpa o reproche; sin defecto; **p. 182**

J

jubilantly/alborozadamente *adv.* con gran regocijo y alegría; **p. 1049**

judiciously/juiciosamente *adv.* en una manera que muestra buen juicio; razonablemente **p. 245**

L

lag/rezagar(se) *v.* atrasarse; quedarse atrás; **p. 591**

livid/amoratado(a) *adj.* ponerse morado; **p. 1209**

lucid/lúcido(a) *adj.* alerta; inteligente; **p. 116**

lurk/esconderse *v.* quedar escondido, listo para atacar; **p. 246**

M

mainstream/mayoritario(a) *adj.* de la mayoría a relacionado con ella; **p. 414**

makeshift/temporal *adj.* provisional; satisfactorio para una substitución por lo desendo; **p. 231**

malice/malicia *s.* intención maligna; despecho; **p. 819**

malicious/malévolo(a) *adj.* que muestra o que tiene un deseo de dañar; **p. 158**

marveled/maravillar(se) *v.* causar admiración o asombro; **p. 638**

mature/maduro(a) *adj.* desarrollado; que ha realizado un estado deseado; **p. 621**

melancholy/melancólico(a) *adj.* que tiene tristeza profunda; desanimado; **p. 540**

mesmerize/fascinar *v.* atraer irresistiblemente; hipnotizar, ofuscar; **p. 56**

meticulous/meticuloso(a) *adj.* preciso; cuidadoso; preocupado por los detalles; **p. 567**

meticulous (mi tik´yə ləs) *adj.* characterized by great or excessive concern about details **p. 355**

misconstrue (mis´kən strōō´) *v.* to misinterpret; to misunderstand **p. 858**

misgiving (mis giv´ing) *n.* a feeling of doubt; apprehension **p. 818**

moor (moor) *n.* a tract of open, rolling, wild land, often having marshes **p. 15**

N

nomadic (nō mad´ik) *adj.* moving from place to place; wandering **p. 438**

nostalgia (nos tal´jə) *n.* a longing for things or people of the past **p. 439**

nostalgic (nos tal´jik) *adj.* longing for persons, things, or situations from the past **p. 638**

notorious (nō tôr´ē əs) *adj.* widely and unfavorably known **p. 924**

O

obligatory (ə blig´ə tôr´ē) *adj.* required or necessary **p. 362**

obligatory (ə blig´ə tôr´ē) *adj.* legally or morally binding; required **p. 404**

oblivion (ə bli´vē ən) *n.* a lack of awareness or memory **p. 628**

oblivious (ə bliv´ē əs) *adj.* unmindful or unaware; not noticing **p. 883**

obscurity (əb skyōōr´ ə tē) *n.* darkness; dimness **p. 254**

odious (ō´dē əs) *adj.* disgusting or offensive **p. 449**

offering (ô fər ing) *n.* something that is presented as a gift **p. 662**

oppress (ə pres´) *v.* to control or govern by the cruel and unjust use of force or authority **p. 200**

orator (ôr´ə tər) *n.* a person skilled in public speaking **p. 829**

ordain (ôr dān´) *v.* to order or establish; to appoint **p. 448**

meticulous/meticuloso(a) *adj.* que actúa con exactitud, atención y detenimiento; **p. 355**

misconstrue/malinterpretar *v.* interpretar incorrectamente; o equivocadamente; **p. 858**

misgiving/recelo *s.* un sentido de duda; mal presentimiento; **p. 818**

moor/páramo *s.* extensión de terreno que se inunda; llanura anegadiza; **p. 15**

N

nomadic/nómada *adj.* que va de un lugar a otro, que no vive permanentemente en un sitio; **p. 438**

nostalgia/nostalgia *s.* sentimiento de tristeza o añoranza por el recuerdo de algo perdido o por la falta de algo querido; **p. 439**

nostalgic/nostálgico(a) *adj.* con tristeza o añoranza por el recuerdo de algo perdido o por la falta de algo querido; **p. 638**

notorious/notorio(a) *adj.* conocido extensamente y desfavorablemente; **p. 924**

O

obligatory/obligatorio(a) *adj.* que tiene que ser hecho, cumplido o ejecutado; necesario o requerido; **p. 362**

oblivion/olvido *s.* pérdida de la memoria que se tenía; **p. 630**

oblivious/desmemoriado(a) *adj.* desprevenido; que no observa algo; **p. 882**

obscurity/obscuridad *s.* oscuridad; penumbra; **p. 254**

odious/odioso(a) *adj.* que se siente aversión o repugnancia; **p. 449**

offering/ofrenda *s.* ofrecimiento o donación; **p. 664**

oppress/oprimir *v.* someter a una persona o a un pueblo privándolo de sus derechos o libertades; **p. 200**

orator/orador(a) *s.* persona que habla en público con persuasión y habilidad; **p. 829**

ordain/decretar *v.* resolver o decidir cuando se tiene autoridad para ello; establecer; **p. 448**

ostentatiously (os´tən tā´shəs lē) *adv.* in a way intended to attract attention or impress others **p. 920**

P

pandemonium (pan´ də mō´ nē əm) *n.* wild disorder and uproar **p. 269**

paradox (par´ə doks´) *n.* a statement that seems contradictory and yet may be true **p. 485, p. 1122**

paraphernalia (par´ə fər nāl´ yə) *n.* things used in a particular activity; equipment **p. 68**

parenthesis (pə ren´thə sis) *n.* digression or afterthought; disruption in continuity **p. 624**

patriarch (pā´trē ärk´) *n.* the male head of a family or group **p. 324**

peevish (pē´vish) *adj.* irritable; bad-tempered **p. 853**

pent-up (pent´ up) *adj.* not expressed or released; held in **p. 171**

peril (per´əl) *n.* exposure to harm or danger **p. 854**

perpetuate (pər pech´ oo āt´) *v.* to cause to continue to be remembered **p. 1028**

peruse (pə rooz´) *v.* to read through or examine carefully **p. 344**

perverse (pər vurs´) *adj.* determined to go against what is reasonable, expected, or desired; contrary **p. 745**

petulantly (pech´ə lənt lē) *adv.* crankily; in an annoyed way **p. 973**

pious (pī´əs) *adj.* devoutly religious **p. 729**

piqued (pēkt) *adj.* aroused in anger or resentment; offended **p. 68**

pompous (pom´pəs) *adj.* showing an exaggerated sense of self-importance **p. 873**

potent (pōt´ənt) *adj.* having strength or authority; powerful **p. 377**

precarious (pri kār´ e əs) *adj.* uncertain or unpredictable **p. 37**

precedence (pres´ə dəns) *n.* order of importance or preference; priority **p. 1168**

ostentatiously/ostentosamente *adv.* en una manera intentada atraer atención o causar impresión; **p. 920**

P

pandemonium/pandemónium *s.* desordén y alboroto furioso; **p. 269**

paradox/paradoja *s.* algo que parace ilógico, opuesto, o absurdo, pero de hecho sea verdadero; **p. 484, p. 1122**

paraphernalia/bienes parafernales *s.* cosas usadas en una actividad particular; equipo; **p. 68**

parenthesis/digresión *s.* ruptura del hilo del discurso para hablar de cosas que no tienen conexión con lo que se está tratando; **p. 626**

patriarch/patriarca *s.* la cabeza o el jefe masculino de una familia o un grupo; **p. 324**

peevish/displicente *adj.* que desagrada y disgusta; irritable; **p. 853**

pent-up/encerrado(a) *adj.* que no se expresa o libera; contenido; **p. 171**

peril/peligro *s.* situación en la que puede suceder algo malo; **p. 854**

perpetuate/perpetuar *v.* causar que recordar; **p. 1028**

peruse/repasar *v.* leer con cuidado; examinar; **p. 344**

perverse/perverso(a) *adj.* determinado por oponerse lo que es razonable, previsto, o deseado; contrario; **p. 745**

petulantly/con impaciencia *adv.* en una manera molestada; irritablemente; **p. 973**

pious/piadoso(a) *adj.* religioso, devoto; **p. 729**

piqued/resentir(se) *adj.* sentir pesar o enojo por algo; **p. 68**

pompous/pomposo(a) *adj.* que muestra un sentido de sentimiento exagerado de la propia importancia; **p. 873**

potent/potente *adj.* que tiene poder para producir un efecto; **p. 377**

precarious/precario(a) *adj.* que no es seguro o que dura poco; que no se puede pronosticar; **p. 37**

precedence/precedencia *s.* orden de importancia o preferencia; prioridad en el tiempo; **p. 1162**

predecessor (pred´ ə ses´ ər) *n.* one who comes, or has come before in another time **p. 23**

presentiment (pri zen´ tə mənt) *n.* a feeling that something is about to happen **p. 267**

pretext (pre´ tekst) *n.* a reason or motive offered in order to disguise real intentions **p. 1189**

prevail (pri vāl´) *v.* to be superior in power or influence; succeed **p. 748**

primal (prī´məl) *adj.* a basic, original state of being **p. 562**

primeval (prī mē´ vəl) *adj.* of or having to do with the first or earliest age; primitive **p. 1130**

prodigy (prod´ə jē) *n.* an extraordinarily gifted or talented person, especially a child **p. 98**

profuse (prə fūs´) *adj.* great in amount; plentiful **p. 84**

prowess (prou´ is) *n.* great ability or skill **p. 996**

psalm (sälm) *n.* a sacred poem, song, or hymn **p. 1151**

Q

querulous (kwer´ ə ləs) *adj.* argumentative; uncooperative **p. 579**

R

rapier (rā´pē ər) *n.* a narrow, long-bladed, two-edged sword **p. 379**

rash (rash) *adj.* marked by haste and lack of caution or consideration **p. 842**

reapers (rē´ pərs) *n.* machines or people that cut grain for harvesting **p. 548**

recoil (ri koil´) *v.* to shrink back physically or emotionally **p. 1195**

recollect (rek´ ə lekt´) *v.* to remember **p. 588**

redress (ri dres´) *v.* to correct or compensate for wrong or loss **p. 1013**

regally (rē´gəl lē) *adv.* in a grand, dignified manner befitting a king or a queen **p. 920**

relevant (rel´ ə vənt) *adj.* related to the issue at hand **p. 458**

predecessor/predecesor *s.* alguien que viene antes, o que ha venido antes en otro tiempo; **p. 23**

presentiment/presentimiento *s.* un sentido que algo va a ocurrir; **p. 267**

pretext/pretexto *s.* motivo o razón simulada o aparente que se da para justificarse o excusarse de algo; **p. 1183**

prevail/prevalecer *v.* triunfar; ser superior en poder o influencia; tener éxito; **p. 748**

primal/primitivo *adj.* de un estado de vivir básico o original; **p. 562**

primeval/primitivo(a) *adj.* de la época primera; prístino; **p. 1126**

prodigy/prodigio *s.* una persona de talenta extraordinaria, especialmente un niño; **p. 98**

profuse/profuso(a) *adj.* grande en cantidad, abundante; **p. 84**

prowess/hazaña *s.* habilidad grande; **p. 996**

psalm/salmo *s.* un poema, canto o himno sagrado; **p. 1151**

Q

querulous/quejumbroso(a) *adj.* que expresa disconformidad, disgusto o enfado con poco motivo y con frecuencia **p. 581**

R

rapier/espadín *s.* espada de hoja bastante estrecha; **p. 379**

rash/impulsivo(a) *adj.* que procede sin reflexión y cautela; **p. 842**

reapers/segadoras *s.* pl. máquinas que sirven para cortar el pasto o cereal; **p. 550**

recoil/retroceder *v.* retirarse a causa del asco o la aversión a algo; **p. 1189**

recollect/recordar *v.* traer a la memoria; **p. 590**

redress/reparar *v.* remediar o prevenir un daño o perjuicio; **p. 1013**

regally/reglamente *adv.* en una manera magnífica o dignificada, como lo de un rey o una reína; **p. 920**

relevant/pertinente *adj.* que viene a propósito **p. 457**

relic (rel´ ik) *n.* an object that has survived decay, destruction, or the passage of time and is valued for its historic interest **p. 233**

remorse (ri môrs´) *n.* distress stemming from the guilt of past wrongs **p. 553**

renaissance (ren´ə säns´) *n.* rebirth or comeback **p. 470**

renown (ri noun´) *n.* a state of being widely acclaimed **p. 1012**

repercussion (rē´ pər kush´ ən) *n.* an effect or result of some action **p. 112**

repressed (ri prest´) *adj.* held back or kept under control; restrained **p. 925**

reprieve (ri prēv´) *v.* to give temporary relief, as from something unpleasant or difficult **p. 253**

reproach (ri prōch´) *n.* blame, disgrace, discredit **p. 99**

repulse (ri puls´) *n.* an act of beating back or driving away, as with force **p. 721**

resilient (ri zil´ yənt) *adj.* capable of springing back into shape or position after being bent, stretched, or compressed **p. 1127**

retail (rē´ tāl) *v.* to sell directly to the consumer **p. 76**

retribution (ret´rə bū´shən) *n.* punishment; justice **p. 1234**

reveling (rev´ əl ing) *adj.* taking great pleasure **p. 172**

reverie (rev´ər ē) *n.* fanciful thinking, daydream **p. 102**

russet (rus´ it) *adj.* a deep reddish- brown **p. 655**

S

sacred (sā´ krid) *adj.* worthy of reverence **p. 553**

savvy (sav´ē) *adj.* one who has practical knowledge or understanding **p. 472**

scavenger (skav´ in jər) *n.* one who searches through discarded materials for something useful **p. 1179**

scenario (si när´ ē ō´) *n.* an outline or model of an expected or imagined series of events **p. 357**

scrupulous (skrōō´ pyə ləs) *adj.* thoroughly attentive to even the smallest details; precise **p. 1027**

relic/reliquia *s.* un objecto valorado por su interés histórico; **p. 233**

remorse/remordimiento *s.* dolor por la culpa de hechos pasados; **p. 555**

renaissance/renacimiento *s.* nacer otra vez; rehabilitación; **p. 470**

renown/renombre *s.* fama; estado de ser aclamado extensamente; **p. 1012**

repercussion/repercusión *s.* el efecto o el resultado de una acción; **p. 112**

repressed/reprimido(a) *adj.* contenido; refrenado; **p. 925**

reprieve/aliviar *v.* dar alivio temporal, como de algo desagradable o difícil; **p. 253**

reproach/reproche *s.* desgracia, descrédito; **p. 99**

repulse/repulsión *s.* el acto de ahuyentar o obligar a retroceder, como con fuerza; **p. 721**

resilient/elástico(a) *adj.* capaz de recoger la forma después de ser estirado o torcido; **p. 1123**

retail/vender al por menor *v.* vender directamente al consumidor; **p. 76**

retribution/retribución *s.* castigo; justicia; **p. 1234**

reveling/gozándose en *adj.* deleitándo se en algo; **p. 172**

reverie/ensueño *s.* pensamientos imaginativos; fantasías; **p. 102**

russet/rojizo(a) *adj.* con tonalidad roja; bermejo; **p. 657**

S

sacred/sagrado(a) *adj.* digno de reverencia; **p. 555**

savvy/experimentado(a) *adj.* que tiene conocimiento practico de algo; **p. 472**

scavenger/basurero(a) *s.* persona que recoge, compra o vende trapos, prendas u objetos usados; trapero; **p. 1174**

scenario/escenario *s.* modelo o plan de una serie de sucesos reales o imaginados; **p. 357**

scrupulous/escrupuloso(a) *adj.* atento de cada detalle; preciso y exacto; **p. 1027**

scrutinize (skrōōt´ ən īz) *v.* to look at closely; inspect carefully p. 125

scythes (sīths) *n.* cutting implements made of a long, curved single-edged blade p. 548

searing (sēr´ing) *adj.* extremely hot or bright p. 560

sedate (si dāt´) *adj.* quiet and restrained in style or manner; calm p. 25

self-possessed (self´ pə zest´) *adj.* in control of oneself; composed p. 14

serenity (sə ren´ ə tē) *n.* calmness; peacefulness p. 123

serpentine (sur´pən tēn´) *adj.* snake-like, twisting, winding p. 560

servile (sur´vil) *adj.* lacking self-respect; behaving as if other people are superior p. 776

sidle (sīd´əl) *v.* to move sideways, especially in a way that does not attract attention or cause disturbance p. 197

singular (sing´ gyə lər) *adj.* unusual or remarkable p. 256

skeptical (skep´ ti kəl) *adj.* having or showing doubt or suspicion; questioning; disbelieving p. 126

slyly (slī´lē) *adv.* cunningly, in an artful manner p. 595

solace (sol´ is) *n.* relief from sorrow or disappointment; comfort p. 23

sonorous (sə nôr´əs) *adj.* loud, forceful, or heavy in sound p. 1252

sparse (spärs) *adj.* thinly spread or distributed p. 286

spectral (spek´ trəl) *adj.* ghostlike p. 89

staidness (stād´ nəs) *n.* the state or quality of being serious, steady, or conservative in character p. 183

stolid (stol´ id) *adj.* showing little or no emotion p. 394

strategic (strə tē´ jik) *adj.* highly important to an intended goal p. 1082

stridently (strīd´ ənt lē) *adv.* in a loud, harsh manner; shrilly p. 245

stupor (stōō´ pər) *n.* a state of extreme lethargy p. 588

scrutinize/escudriñar *v.* indagar o averiguar cuidadosamente algo; p. 192

scythes/guadañas *s.* instrumentas que se utiliza para segar, formadas por una cuchilla curva larga y puntiaguda; p. 550

searing/abrasador(a) *adj.* que calienta demasiado; p. 562

sedate/sereno(a) *adj.* tranquilo y refrenido en estilo o manera; p. 25

self-possessed/sereno(a) *adj.* tranquilo o sosegado; dueño de mismo ; p. 14

serenity/serenidad *s.* tranquilidad; calma; p. 123

serpentine/serpentino(a) *adj.* que se mueve o se extiende dando vueltas como la serpiente; p. 562

servile/servil *adj.* que obra con ciega adhesión o sometimiento a la autoridad de alguien; sin respeto de si mismo; p. 776

sidle/andar de lado *v.* acercarse o moverse en una manera tímida o que no atrae atención; p. 197

singular/singular *adj.* ravo o notable; p. 256

skeptical/escéptico(a) *adj.* que tiene o que muestra duda o sospecha; p. 126

slyly/astutamente *adv.* de manera hábil para engañar o lograr con artificios cualquier fin; p. 000

solace/consuelo *s.* alivio de dolor o desilusión; solaz; p. 23

sonorous/sonoro(a) *adj.* que produce un sonido agradable, intenso, sonante; p. 1251

sparse/esparcido(a) *adj.* distribuido con poca densidad; p. 286

spectral/espectral *adj.* como una fantasma; p. 89

staidness/gravedad *s.* el estado o la calidad de ser serio, conservativo o regular en carácter; p. 183

stolid/impasible *adj.* que no manifiesta desconcierto o inquietud; que no manifiesta emoción; p. 394

strategic/estratégico(a) *adj.* de una alta importancia para una meta planeada; p. 1080

stridently/estridentemente *adv.* de manera exagerada o violenta produce una sensación molesta y llamativa; p. 245

stupor/estupor *s.* adormecimiento, somnolencia; p. 590

submerged (səb murjd´) *adj.* hard to see; sunken p. 537

subordinate (sə bôr´də nāt´) *v.* to cause to be, or treat as, secondary, inferior, or less important p. 333

subversive (sub vur´ siv) *adj.* seeking to weaken, destroy, or overthrow p. 184

subversive (səb vur´ siv) *adj.* intended to destroy or undermine p. 1179

sumptuous (sump´ choo əs) *adj.* costly and magnificent p. 977

superfluous (soo pur floo əs) *adj.* not needed; unnecessary p. 414

supplication (səp´ lə kā´shən) *n.* an earnest and humble request p. 211

syntax (sin´taks) *n.* ordered structure or systematic arrangement; the rules of language p. 624

T

taboo (tə boo´) *n.* a cultural or social rule forbidding something p. 438

taut (tôt) *adj.* tense; tight p. 169

temperate (tem´pər it) *adj.* calm and free from extremes of temperature p. 599

testament (tes´ tə mənt) *n.* proof of or tribute to p. 57

thrive (thrīv) *v.* to be successful; to grow well p. 813

throng (thrông) *v.* to move or gather in large numbers; to crowd together p. 979

torrential (tôren´chəl) *adj.* flowing rapidly and abundantly p. 366

translucent (trans loo´ sənt) *adj.* allowing light to pass through; almost clear, see-through p. 580

treacherous (trech´ ər əs) *adj.* likely to betray a trust; disloyal p. 1179

tread (tred) *v.* to step or walk on p. 613

tremulously (trem´ yə ləs lē) *adv.* in a trembling or vibrating way p. 391

tribulation (trib´ yə lā´ shən) *n.* great misery or distress; suffering p. 273

submerged/sumergido(a) *adj.* hundido, totalmente metido; p. 539

subordinate/subordinar *v.* tratar como si fuera inferior o menos importante; p. 333

subversive/subversivo(a) *adj.* que intenta trastornar o desestabilizar; p. 184

subversive/subversivo(a) *adj.* que intenta trastornar o desestabilizar; p. 1175

sumptuous/suntuoso(a) *adj.* caro y magnífico; p. 977

superfluous/superfluo(a) *adj.* que no es necesario; p. 414

supplication/súplica *s.* un ruego serio y humilde; p. 211

syntax/sintaxis *s.* parte de la gramática; la estructura o cisterna, las reglas de una idioma; p. 626.

T

taboo/tabú *s.* prohibición de tocar, mencionar o hacer algo por prejuicio, convención social o motivos religiosos; p. 438

taut/tirante *adj.* tenso; tieso; p. 169

temperate/templado(a) *adj.* tranquilo y libre de extremos de temperatura p. 601

testament/testamento *s.* prueba o demostración; p. 57

thrive/prosperar *v.* salir adelante o imponerse; tener éxito; p. 813

throng/estrujar *v.* mover or reunir en números grandes; empujar

torrential/torrencial *adj.* que se produce en abundancia rápidamente; p. 367

translucent/transluciente *adj.* que permite que pase la luz y de las imágenes; p. 582

treacherous/traicionero(a) *adv.* que rompe la confianza o fidelidad; desleal; p. 1175

tread/pisar *v.* poner alternativamente los pies sobre el suelo; p. 615

tremulously/trémulamente *adj.* en una manera vibrada o estremecida p. 391

tribulation/tribulación *s.* gran miseria o dolor; sufrimiento p. 273

tumultuous (too mul′ ch‾oo əs) *adj.* wildly excited, confused, or agitated **p. 995**

turbulent (tur′ byə lənt) *adj.* causing unrest, violent action, or disturbance **p. 486**

U

ulterior (ul tēr′ ē ər) *adj.* intentionally withheld or concealed **p. 183**

unobtrusively (un′ əb tr‾oo ′siv lē) *adv.* inconspicuously; discreetly **p. 1236**

V

vague (vāg) *adj.* unclear or undetermined **p. 38**

vague (vāg) *adj.* uncertain; unclear; not precisely expressed **p. 404**

valor (val′ ər) *n.* courageous spirit, personal bravery **p. 486**

vanquish (vang′ kwish) *v.* to defeat; to overcome **p. 829**

vault (vôlt) *v.* to jump; spring **p. 1081**

vehemently (vē′ ə mənt lē) *adv.* strongly; intensely; passionately **p. 347**

verandah (və ran′ də) *n.* a long porch, usually with a roof, that extends along one or more sides of a house **p. 1150**

vernacular (vər nak′yə lər) *adj.* a form of language particular to a certain group of people; jargon **p. 470**

vintage (vin′ tij) *adj.* characterized by enduring appeal; classic **p. 231**

virile (vir′ el) *adj.* having traits normally associated with males, such as strength **p. 1073**

vulgar (vul′ gər) *adj.* characterized by a lack of good breeding or good taste; common; crude **p. 976**

vulnerability (vul′ nər ə bil′ ə tē) *n.* state of being open to harm, damage, or illness **p. 56**

vulnerable vulnerable (vul′ nər ə bəl) *adj.* easily damaged or hurt **p. 414**

W

wanton (wont′ ən) *adj.* shamelessly unrestrained; immoral **p. 86**

tumultuous/tumultuoso(a) *adj.* excitado, confundido, o agitado ferozmente **p. 995**

turbulent/turbulento(a) *adj.* que causa, inquietud, acción violenta, o perturbación **p. 485**

U

ulterior/ulterior *adj.* intencionalmente detenido o disimulado; **p. 183**

unobtrusively/discretamente *adv.* sin llamar la atención; desapercibidamente; **p. 000**

V

vague/vago(a) *adj.* impreciso, indeterminado; **p. 38** [U1]

vague/vago(a) *adj.* incierto; que no se expresa precisamente; **p. 404**

valor/valor *s.* valería, un espíritu valeroso **p. 485**

vanquish/vencer *v.* derrotar o rendir a un enemigo; **p. 829**

vault/abovedar *v.* saltar; brincar; **p. 1079**

vehemently/vehementemente *adv.* fuertemente; intensamente; con pasión **p. 347**

verandah/pórtico *s.* un porche largo, usualmente con un techo, que extiende al lado de una casa **p. 1150**

vernacular/vernáculo(a) *adj.* una forma de lenguaje particular a un grupo de personas; jerga **p. 470**

vintage/clásico(a) *adj.* caracterizado por apelación que dura **p. 231**

virile/viril *adj.* con fuerza y valor normalmente asociados a un varón; masculino; **p. 1073**

vulgar/vulgar *adj.* común; crudo; caracterizado por una falta de buen gusto **p. 976**

vulnerability/vulnerabilidad *s.* condición en la que se puede sufrir deterioro físico o moral; **p. 56**

vulnerable/vulnerable *adj.* que se puede dañar fácilmente **p 414**

W

wanton/lascivo(a) *adj.* inmoral; libre sin vergüenza **p 86**

ACADEMIC WORD LIST

The list of words that appears on this page and the following pages represents a research-based collection of words that are commonly used in academic texts. The purpose of the list is to present students with the basics of a working academic vocabulary, one that will prove useful in reading, writing, and research in many areas of study. Many of these words also appear throughout the Glencoe Language Arts program.

Sublist One

analysis
approach
area
assessment
assume
authority
available
benefit
concept
consistent
constitutional
context
contract
create
data
definition
derived
distribution
economic
environment
established
estimate
evidence
export
factors
financial
formula
function
identified
income
indicate
individual

interpretation
involved
issues
labor
legal
legislation
major
method
occur
percent
period
policy
principle
procedure
process
required
research
response
role
section
sector
significant
similar
source
specific
structure
theory
variables

Sublist Two

achieve
acquisition
administration

affect
appropriate
aspects
assistance
categories
chapter
commission
community
complex
computer
conclusion
conduct
consequences
construction
consumer
credit
cultural
design
distinction
elements
equation
evaluation
features
final
focus
impact
injury
institute
investment
items
journal
maintenance
normal

obtained
participation
perceived
positive
potential
previous
primary
purchase
range
region
regulations
relevant
resident
resources
restricted
security
select
site
sought
strategies
survey
text
traditional
transfer

Sublist Three

alternative
circumstances
comments
compensation
components
consent
considerable

constant
constraints
contribution
convention
coordination
core
corporate
corresponding
criteria
deduction
demonstrate
document
dominant
emphasis
ensure
excluded
framework
funds
illustrated
immigration
implies
initial
instance
interaction
justification
layer
link
location
maximum
minorities
negative
outcomes
partnership

philosophy
physical
proportion
published
reaction
registered
reliance
removed
scheme
sequence
sex
shift
specified
sufficient
task
technical
techniques
technology
validity
volume

Sublist Four

access
adequate
annual
apparent
approximated
attitudes
attributed
civil
code
commitment
communication
concentration
conference
contrast
cycle
debate
despite
dimensions
domestic
emerged
error

ethnic
goals
granted
hence
hypothesis
implementation
implications
imposed
integration
internal
investigation
job
label
mechanism
obvious
occupational
option
output
overall
parallel
parameters
phase
predicted
principal
prior
professional
project
promote
regime
resolution
retained
series
statistics
status
stress
subsequent
sum
summary
undertaken

Sublist Five

academic
adjustment

alter
amendment
aware
capacity
challenge
clause
compounds
conflict
consultation
contact
decline
discretion
draft
enable
energy
enforcement
entities
equivalent
evolution
expansion
exposure
external
facilitate
fundamental
generated
generation
image
liberal
license
logic
marginal
medical
mental
modified
monitoring
network
notion
objective
orientation
perspective
precise
prime
psychology

pursue
ratio
rejected
revenue
stability
styles
substitution
sustainable
symbolic
target
transition
trend
version
welfare
whereas

Sublist Six

abstract
accurate
acknowledged
aggregate
allocation
assigned
attached
author
bond
brief
capable
cited
cooperative
discrimination
display
diversity
domain
edition
enhanced
estate
exceed
expert
explicit
federal
fees
flexibility

furthermore
gender
ignored
incentive
incidence
incorporated
index
inhibition
initiatives
input
instructions
intelligence
interval
lecture
migration
minimum
ministry
motivation
neutral
nevertheless
overseas
preceding
presumption
rational
recovery
revealed
scope
subsidiary
tapes
trace
transformation
transport
underlying
utility

Sublist Seven

adaptation
adults
advocate
aid
channel
chemical
classical

comprehensive
comprise
confirmed
contrary
converted
couple
decades
definite
deny
differentiation
disposal
dynamic
eliminate
empirical
equipment
extract
file
finite
foundation
global
grade
guarantee
hierarchical
identical
ideology
inferred
innovation
insert
intervention
isolated
media
mode
paradigm
phenomenon
priority
prohibited
publication
quotation
release
reverse
simulation
solely
somewhat

submitted
successive
survive
thesis
topic
transmission
ultimately
unique
visible
voluntary

Sublist Eight

abandon
accompanied
accumulation
ambiguous
appendix
appreciation
arbitrary
automatically
bias
chart
clarity
conformity
commodity
complement
contemporary
contradiction
crucial
currency
denote
detected
deviation
displacement
dramatic
eventually
exhibit
exploitation
fluctuations
guidelines
highlighted
implicit
induced

inevitably
infrastructure
inspection
intensity
manipulation
minimized
nuclear
offset
paragraph
plus
practitioners
predominantly
prospect
radical
random
reinforced
restore
revision
schedule
tension
termination
theme
thereby
uniform
vehicle
via
virtually
visual
widespread

Sublist Nine

accommodation
analogous
anticipated
assurance
attained
behalf
bulk
ceases
coherence
coincide
commenced
concurrent

confined
controversy
conversely
device
devoted
diminished
distorted
duration
erosion
ethical
format
founded
incompatible
inherent
insights
integral
intermediate
manual
mature
mediation
medium
military
minimal
mutual
norms
overlap
passive
portion
preliminary
protocol
qualitative
refine
relaxed
restraints
revolution
rigid
route
scenario
sphere
subordinate
supplementary
suspended
team

temporary
trigger
unified
violation
vision

Sublist Ten

adjacent
albeit
assembly
collapse
colleagues
compiled
conceived
convinced
depression
encountered
enormous
forthcoming
inclination
integrity
intrinsic
invoked
levy
likewise
nonetheless
notwithstanding
odd
ongoing
panel
persistent
posed
reluctant
so-called
straightforward
undergo
whereby

INDEX OF SKILLS

Reading and Thinking

Grammar and Language

INDEX OF SKILLS

Research, Test-Taking, and Study Skills

Interdisciplinary Activities

INDEX OF AUTHORS AND TITLES

INDEX OF ART AND ARTISTS

H

Haas, Richard, *William Street at Night* 168

Harmensz van Rijn, Rembrandt, *Pallas Athena or, Armoured Figure* 752

Hausner, Rudolf, *Adam und seine Richter* 181

Hayes, Connie, *Secluded Little House by Water* 10

Hayes, Connie, *Painting of Farm House Scene* 908

Heinrich, Reinhold, *Rocky Ravine at Sorrento* 1248

Homer, Winslow, *The Life Line* 1035

Hopper, Edward, *Room in New York* 164

Hopper, Edward, *Rocky Sea Shore* 218

I

Ingalls, Pam, *Room with a View* 54

Ingalls, Pam, *Creamers* 662

Ingalls, Pam, *Table in Sorrento* 903

Ingalls, Pam, *Magdalena's Spices* 901

Iverson, Mary, *Central Park Skyline* 152

J

Jacot, Don, *Storefront Window, Chinatown, NY* 106

Jacquette, Yvonne, *Flatiron Intersection* 170

Johnson, William H., *Girl in a Green Dress* 199

Johnson, William H., *Lift Up Thy Voice and Sing* 443

Joy, Thomas Musgrove, *The Charing Cross To Bank Omnibus* 1237

K

Kahlo, Frida, *Self-Portrait* 918

Kahlo, Frida, *Two Women* 929

Kerr, James Wilfrid, *7th Avenue Subway* 315

Knight, Dame Laura, *Snowballing* 192

Kokoschka, Oskar, *The Mandrill* 1212

Kupka, Frantisek, *Essay, Force* 656

L

Lamb, Henry, *The Tea Party* 1193

Larsson, Carl, *Young Girl at a Grand Piano* 105

Leighton, Frederic, *M.84 Clytie* 1146

Leslie, Charles Robert, *Sancho Panza, 1839* 1016

Levitan, Isaak Ilyich, *Golden Autumn in the Village* 872

Lewis, Norman, *Yellow Hat* 650

M

Magritte, Rene, *September 16* 232

Magritte, Rene, *Le Chateau des Pyrenees* 399

Magritte, Rene, *Décalcomanie* 636

Marriot, Frederick and Pickford, *The Faithful Knight in Equal Field Subdues his Faithless Foe* 1091

May, Mabel Henrietta, *A Sick Ward at the Salpetriere* 375

Mayers, Gil, *Jaws* 675

McIndoe, Vincent, *Formal Picnic* 1246

Merisi da Caravaggio, Michelangelo, *Young boy singing and playing the lute* 847

Miller, Peter, *Bond Street* 1191

Miro, Joan, *Composition* 624

Mollica, Patti, *Palm Trees* 57

Monet, Claude, *The Garden* 59

Monet, Claude, *Gare Saint-Lazare* 1215

Monet, Claude, *The Artist's Garden at Giverny* 612

Monticelli, Adolphe Joseph Thomas, *Harvesting* 548

Moran, Thomas, *Fiercely the red sun descending* 424

Morgenstern, Christian, *Reeds at the Starnberg Lake* 41

Murphy, Joan, *Bishop Street, Coventry* 1200

N

Nemanich, Katherine S., *Collage Series II, No. 3* 932

Nevins, Daniel, *River Diego* 583

Newcomb, John, *Vision Quest* 286

O

O'Neil, George B., *The Love Letter* 1253

Ortega, Jose, *Melancholy Woman* 1158

P

Palagi, Pelagio, *Roman statesman and general* 782

Panchal, Shanti, *Home Coming—After a Long Absence* 142

Paterson, Caroline, *Scrumping Apples* 654

Payne, Henry A., *The End of the Day* 1216

Picasso, Pablo, *To The Foot From Its Child/ Neruda Foot, La Coruna* 552

Picasso, Pablo, *Portrait of Olga* 906

Picunko, Scott, *Empty Birdcage in Kitchen* 898

Pippin, Horace, *Victorian Parlor II* 355

Pippin, Horace, *Giving Thanks* 201

Prozzo, Marco, *Wooden Type Block by Marco Prozzo* 33

Pryanishnikov, Illarion Mikhailovich, *Return from the Fair* 874

R

Rajput, Jaipur, *Woman Flying a Kite* 579

Raverat, Lucy, *The Waking: Flying the Kite* 541

Riches, Lizzie, *Girl with Red Gloves* 93

Rivera, Diego, *In the Trenches* 916

Rivera, Diego, *Triumph of the Revolution/ Distribution of Food* 923

Roosevelt, D., *Eight Huts in Haiti* 1154

Rosen, Hilary, *Piccadilly Line* 314

Ruiz-Tagle, Maria Angelica, *The Magician* 554

Ryder, Susan, *The Drum Table* 258

S

Sadler, Walter Dendy, *Home Sweet Home* 247

Savrasov, Alexei, *Muddy Road through the Field* 273

Scotin, Gerard Jean Baptiste, *Mural Painting of the Goddess Isis* 1074

Seurat, Georges Pierre, *The Invalid* 595

Shakito, *Good Old Days* 150

Sievert, Ludwig, *Julius Caesar* 830

Simonovich-Efimova, Nina, *Self-portrait in an Interior, Sokolniki* 879

Siqueiros, David Alfaro, *Abismo* 1143

Smith, Francis Hopkinson, *The Statue of Liberty* 362

Solomon, Simeon, *Night* 796

Soubirous, Bernadette, *Visionary of Lourdes* 377

Southcombe, Anthony, *Girl with a Unicorn* 965

ACKNOWLEDGMENTS

Unit 1

From "Introduction" from *The Oxford Book of American Short Stories,* edited by Joyce Carol Oates. Copyright © 1992 by The Ontario Review, Inc. Reprinted by permission of The Ontario Review, Inc.

"The Summer People" from *Come Along With Me* by Shirley Jackson, copyright 1948, 1952 © 1960 by Shirley Jackson. Used by permission of Viking Penguin, a division of Penguin Group (USA) Inc. and The Linda Allen Agency.

"The Book of the Dead" by Edwidge Danticat. First published in *The New Yorker* and reprinted by permission of Edwidge Danticat and Aragi Inc.

"An Astrologer's Day" from *The Grandmother's Tale and Selected Stories* by R. K. Narayan. Copyright © 1994 by R. K. Narayan. Reprinted by permission of the Wallace Literary Agency, Inc.

"Civil Peace" from *Girls at War and Other Stories* by Chinua Achebe, copyright © 1972, 1973 by Chinua Achebe. Used by permission of Doubleday, a division of Random House, Inc. and the Emma Sweeney Agency.

"Two Kinds" Copyright © 1989 by Amy Tan. Reprinted by permission of Amy Tan and the Sandra Dijkstra Literary Agency.

"The Car We Had to Push" from *My Life and Hard Times* by James Thurber. Copyright © 1933 by James Thurber. Copyright © renewed 1961 by Helen Thurber and Rosemary A. Thurber. Reprinted by arrangement with Rosemary A. Thurber and the Barbara Hogenson Agency.

"Tuesday Siesta" from *No One Writes to the Colonel and Other Stories* by Gabriel García Márquez and translated by J. S. Bernstein. Copyright © 1968 in the English translation by Harper & Row Publishers, Inc. Reprinted by permission of HarperCollins Publishers.

"When Mr. Pirzada Came to Dine" from *Interpreter of Maladies* by Jhumpa Lahiri. Copyright © 1999 by Jhumpa Lahiri. Reprinted by permission of Houghton Mifflin Company. All rights reserved.

Paule Marshall, Introduction and "To Da-duh, In Memoriam" from *Reena and Other Stories.* Copyright © 1983 by The Feminist Press. Reprinted with the permission of The Feminist Press at the City University of New York, www.feministpress.org.

"Contents of the Dead Man's Pocket" by Jack Finney. Reprinted by permission of Don Congdon Associates. Copyright © 1956 by the Crowell Collier Publishing Company, renewed 1984 by Jack Finney.

"The Censors" by Luisa Valenzuela. Copyright © Luisa Valenzuela. Luisa Valenzuela is a well-known Argentine novelist who has been extensively translated into English.

"Everyday Use" from *In Love & Trouble: Stories of Black Women,* copyright © 1973 by Alice Walker, reprinted by permission of Harcourt, Inc. and The Wendy Weil Agency.

"Through the Tunnel" from *The Habit of Loving by Doris Lessing.* Copyright © 1955 by Doris Lessing. Originally appeared in The New Yorker. Reprinted by permission of HarperCollins Publishers.

"The Vision Quest" from *American Indian Myths and Legends* by Richard Erdoes and Alfonso Ortiz, copyright © 1984 by Richard Erdoes and Alfonso Ortiz. Used by permission of Pantheon Books, a division of Random House, Inc.

"Catch the Moon" from *An Island Like You: Stories of the Barrio* by Judith Ortiz Cofer. Copyright © 1995 by Judith Ortiz Cofer. Reprinted by permission of the publisher, Scholastic Inc./Orchard Books, New York.

"A Child's Christmas in Wales," by Dylan Thomas, from *A Child's Christmas in Wales,* copyright © 1954 by New Directions Publishing Corp. Reprinted by permission of New Directions Publishing Corp.

"Winter Night" by Kate Boyle. Reprinted by permission of the Watkins/Loomis Agency.

"And of Clay Are We Created" reprinted with the permission of Scribner, an imprint of Simon & Schuster Adult Publishing Group, from *The Stories of Eva Luna* by Isabel Allende. Copyright © 1989 by Isabel Allende. English translation copyright © 1991 by Macmillan Publishing Company.

"Lullaby," copyright © 1981 by Leslie Marmon Silko. Reprinted from *Storyteller* by Leslie Marmon Silko, published by Seaver Books, New York, New York.

Unit 2

Chapters 2–4 from *Farewell to Manzanar* by James D. and Jeanne Wakatsuki Houston. Copyright © 1973 by James D. Houston. Reprinted by permission of Houghton Mifflin Co. All rights reserved.

From *Kaffir Boy* by Mark Mathabane. Copyright © 1986 by Mark Mathabane. Reprinted with the permission of Scribner, an imprint of Simon & Schuster Adult Publishing Group.

From *Wouldn't Take Nothing For My Journey Now* by Maya Angelou, copyright © 1993 by Maya Angelou. Used by permission of Random House, Inc.

"Typhoid Fever" reprinted with the permission of Scribner, an imprint of Simon & Schuster Adult Publishing Group, from *Angela's Ashes* by Frank McCourt. Copyright © 1996 by Frank McCourt.

Carolyn T. Hughes, "Looking Forward to the Past: A Profile of Frank McCourt," *Poets & Writers Magazine,* September/October 1999. Reprinted by permission of the publishers, Poets & Writers, Inc., 72 Springs Street, New York, NY 10012. www.pw.org.

Excerpt from *An American Childhood* by Annie Dillard. Copyright © 1987 by Annie Dillard. Reprinted by permission of HarperCollins Publishers, Inc.

"A Swimming Lesson" from *Forty-Three Septembers* by Jewelle L. Gomez. Copyright © 1993 by Jewelle Gomez. Reprinted by permission of Firebrand Books, Ithaca, New York.

"The Tucson Zoo," copyright © 1977 by Lewis Thomas, from *The Medusa and the Snail* by Lewis Thomas. Used by permission of Viking Penguin, a division of Penguin Group (USA) Inc.

"Straw Into Gold," copyright © 1987 by Sandra Cisneros. First published in *The Texas Observer*, September 1987. Reprinted by permission of Susan Bergholz Literary Services, New York. All rights reserved.

"I've Been to the Mountaintop" reprinted by arrangement with the Estate of Martin Luther King Jr., c/o Writers House as agent for the proprietor New York, NY. Copyright 1968 Martin Luther King Jr., copyright renewed 1966 Coretta Scott King.

Excerpts from "Not Funnies," by Charles McGrath. *New York Times Magazine*, July 11, 2004. Copyright © 2004 by The New York Times Co. Reprinted with permission.

"'Hamlet' too hard? Try a comic book" by Teresa Méndez. *Christian Science Monitor*, October 12, 2004. Reprinted by permission of the Copyright Clearance Center.

Unit 3

"Those Winter Sundays" Copyright © 1966 by Robert Hayden, from *Collected Poems of Robert Hayden* by Robert Hayden, edited by Frederick Glaysher. Used by permission of Liveright Publishing Corporation.

"Creatures," copyright © 2002 by Billy Collins, from *Nine Horses* by Billy Collins. Used by permission of Random House, Inc.

"The Waking," copyright 1953 by Theodore Roethke, from *Collected Poems* by Theodore Roethke. Used by permission of Doubleday, a division of Random House, Inc.

"Ode to My Socks" from *Neruda and Vallejo: Selected Poems*, translated by Robert Bly and James Wright, Boston, Beacon Press 1976. © 1972 by Robert Bly. Reprinted by permission.

From *In the Bear's House* by N. Scott Momaday. Copyright © 1999 by the author and reprinted by permission of St. Martin's Press, LLC.

Three haiku by Bashō from *The Essential Haiku: Versions of Bashō, Buson & Issa,* edited and with an introduction by Robert Haas. Introduction and selection copyright © 1994 by Robert Haas. Unless otherwise noted, all translations copyright © 1994 by Robert Haas. Reprinted by permission of HarperCollins Publishers.

Two tanka by Lady Ise, from *A Book of Women Poets from Antiquity to Now* by Willis Barnstone and Aliki Barnstone, copyright © 1980 by Schocken Books, a division of Random House, Inc. Used by permission of Schocken Books, a division of Random House, Inc.

"Woman with Kite" from *Leaving Yuba City* by Chitra Banerjee Divakaruni, copyright © 1997 by Chitra Banerjee Divakaruni. Used by permission of Doubleday, a division of Random House, Inc.

"Heart we will forget him" reprinted by permission of the publishers and the Trustees of Amherst College from *The Poems of Emily Dickinson*, Thomas H. Johnson, ed., Cambridge, Mass: The Belknap Press of Harvard University Press, Copyright © 1951, 1955, 1979, 1983 by the President and Fellows of Harvard College.

"Sonnet XLVII" of *Fatal Interview* by Edna St. Vincent Millay. From *Collected Poems*, HarperCollins. Copyright © 1931, 1958 by Edna St. Vincent Millay and Norma Millay Ellis. All rights reserved. Used by permission of Elizabeth Barnett, literary executor.

"William Shakespeare's 'Sonnet 18'" from *Poetry Comics: An Animated Anthology* by David Morice. Copyright © 2002 by Teachers and Writers Collaborative. Reprinted by permission of Teachers & Writers Collaborative, 5 Union Square West, New York, NY 10003.

"since feeling is first" Copyright 1926, 1954 © 1991 by the Trustees for the E.E. Cummings Trust. Copyright © 1985 by George James Firmage, from *Complete Poems: 1904-1962* by E.E. Cummings, edited by George J. Firmage. Used by permission of Liveright Publishing Corporation.

"Horses Graze" by Gwendolyn Brooks. Reprinted by consent of Brooks Permissions.

"Parlor" from *On the Bus with Rosa Parks,* W. W. Norton & Co., New York. Copyright © 1999 by Rita Dove. Used by permission of the author.

"Secondhand Grief" by Sherman Alexie, from *One Stick Song,* copyright © 2000 by Sherman Alexie. Reprinted by permission of Hanging Loose Press.

"4 Little Girls" by Roger Ebert (October 24, 1997) Copyright © the Ebert Company. Reprinted by permission.

"Miss Rosie," copyright © 1987 by Lucille Clifton. Reprinted from *Good Woman: Poems and a Memoir: 1969–1980* with permission from the Permissions Company on behalf of BOA Editions, Rochester, NY.

"After Apple-Picking" and "Fire and Ice" from *The Poetry of Robert Frost,* edited by Edward Connery Lathem. 1923, 1930, 1939, 1969 by Henry Holt and Company, copyright 1951, 1958 by Robert Frost © 1967 by Lesley Frost Ballantine. Reprinted by permission of Henry Holt and Company LLC.

"Arabic Coffee" from *19 Varieties of Gazelle: Poems of the Middle East.* Copyright © 1994, 1995, 1998, 2002 by Naomi Shihab Nye. Reprinted by permission of the author.

"Jazz Fan Looks Back" by Jayne Cortez. Copyright © 2002 by Jayne Cortez. Reprinted by permission of Hanging Loose Press.

From *To A Young Jazz Musician* by Wynton Marsalis and Selwyn Seyfu Hinds, copyright © 2004 by Wynton Marsalis Enterprises. Used by permission of Random House, Inc.

Unit 4

The Antigone of Sophocles, an English Version by Dudley Fitts and Robert Fitzgerald, copyright 1939 by Harcourt, Inc., and renewed 1967 by Dudley Fitts and Robert Fitzgerald, reprinted by permission of the publisher. CAUTION: All rights, including professional, amateur, motion picture, recitation, lecturing, performance, public reading, radio broadcasting, and television are strictly reserved. Inquiries on all rights should be addressed to Harcourt, Inc., Permissions Department, Orlando, FL 32887-6777.

"A Marriage Proposal" from *The Brute and Other Farces by Anton Chekhov,* English version by Theodore Hoffman, edited by Eric Bentley. Copyright © 1958 by Eric Bentley. International Copyright Secured. All Rights Reserved.

Unit 5

Unit 6

Reference Section

Maps

Photography

COV David Mendelsohn/Masterfile; **i** David Mendelsohn/Masterfile; **ix** Getty Images; **vi** Art Resource, NY; **vii** Schalkwijk/Art Resource, NY; **viii** (t)CORBIS, (b)VAGA;**x** (t)The Barnes Foundation, Merion Station, Pennsylvania/CORBIS, (b)Albright-Knox Art Gallery/CORBIS; **xii** (t)Bridgeman Art Library, (b)Private Collection/Bridgeman Art Library;**xiii** CORBIS; **xix** Erich Lessing/Art Resource, NY; **xv** (t)Courtesy Museu Picasso, Barcelona. © 1999 Estate of Pablo Picasso/Artists Rights Society (ARS), NY. (b)Smithsonian American Art Museum, Washington, DC/Art Resource, NY; **xvi** Smithsonian American Art Museum, Washington, DC/Art Resource, NY; **xviii** Réunion des Musées Nationaux/Art Resource, NY; **xxi** (t)Bradford Art Galleries and Museums, West Yorkshire, UK/Bridgeman Art Library, (b)Lowe Art Museum/SuperStock; **xxii** Sandro Vannini/CORBIS; **xxiii** SuperStock; **xxiv** Roy Miles Fine Paintings/Bridgeman Art Library; **xxix** The Art Archive/Ministry of Public Information Mexico/Dagli Orti; **xxviii** CORBIS; **xxx** SuperStock; AKG-Images/Jean-Louis Nou; **xxxi** SuperStock; **xxxvii** David Mendelsohn/Masterfile; **4** The Art Archive/Culver Pictures; **7** Brooklyn Museum of Art/CORBIS; **9** Getty Images; **10** Images.com/CORBIS; **12** Mansell/Time Inc.; **14** Alan Klehr/Veer; **16** Brooklyn Museum of Art/CORBIS; **17** Tate Gallery, London/Art Resource, NY; **20** The Art Archive/Culver Pictures; **23** Doug Martin; **25** Mark Burnett; **26** Museum of Fine Arts, Boston; **28** CORBIS; **31** Cathy McKinty/Acclaim Images; **32** SuperStock; **33** Getty Images; **34** Lauros/Giraudon/Bridgeman Art Library; **35** Erich Hartmann/Magnum Photos; **37** Mikael Utterström/Alamy; **41** Bildarchiv Preussischer Kulturbesitz/Art Resource, NY; **45** Mary Iverson/CORBIS; **50** Pascal Le Segretain/Getty Images; **52** Tony Arruza/CORBIS; **54** Pam Ingalls/CORBIS; **57** Patti Mollica/SuperStock; **59** Francis G. Mayer/CORBIS; **61** Marc Brasz/CORBIS; **64** THE HINDU/AFP/Getty Images; **67** SuperStock; **73** AP/Wide World Photos; **75** (t)Masterfile/Greg Stott, (b)The Image Bank/Getty Images **77** Loiuse Grubb/The Image Works; **78** The Butler Institute of American Art, Youngstown, Ohio; **79** Steven Needham/Envision; **82** CORBIS; **84** Mary Evans Picture Library; **85** Manuel Bellver/CORBIS; **87** Erich Lessing/Art Resource, NY; **88** Getty Images; **90** Lowe Art Museum/SuperStock; **93** Bridgeman Art Library; **94** Universal Press Syndicate; **96** Getty Images; **98** CORBIS; **101** (l)FPG, (r)Stock Montage/SuperStock; **102** Philadelphia Museum of Art/CORBIS; **103** Mark Burnett; **104** Clive Barda/Camrax Inc.; **105** Christie's Images/CORBIS; **106** Louis K. Meisel Gallery, Inc./CORBIS; **110** AP/Wide World Photos; **112–115** "The Car We Had to Push" from MY LIFE AND HARD TIMES Copyright © 1933, 1961 by James Thurber. Reprinted by arrangement with Rosemary A. Thurber and the Barbara Hogenson Agency; **116** Mark Burnett; **117** "The Car We Had to Push" from MY LIFE AND HARD TIMES Copyright © 1933, 1961 by James Thurber. Reprinted by arrangement with Rosemary A. Thurber and the Barbara Hogenson Agency; **120** CORBIS; **124** Christie's Images/© 1999 Artists Rights Society (ARS), New York/ADAGP, Paris; **127** Kactus Foto, Santiago, Chile/Superstock/© 1999 Artists Rights Society (ARS), New York/ADAGP, Paris; **131** Scott Gries/Getty Images; **133** Christies's Images/CORBIS; **136** Victoria & Albert Museum, London/Art Resource, NY; **139** Gerry Charm/SuperStock; **142** Bridgeman Art Library; **144** SuperStock; **148** AP/Wide World Photo; **150** Erol Samuel/Superstock; **152** Mary Iverson/CORBIS; **153** (t)Christie's Image/Bridgeman Art Library, (b)Cindy Lewis Photography; **156** Bridgeman Art Library; **158** Victor Collector/Private Collection/The Bridgeman Art Library; **162** Time Life Pictures/Getty Images; **164** Sheldon Memorial Art Gallery, University of Nebraska-Lincoln; **167** The Bridgeman Art Library/Getty Images; **168** VAGA; **170** Yvonne Jacquette/Brooke Alexander, Inc.; **175** Chris Rogers/CORBIS; **177** Allied Artists/The Kobal Collection; **178** Bridgeman Art Library; **180** Miriam Berkley; **181** Erich Lessing/Art Resource, NY; **182** Natalie Racioppa/Getty Images; **183** Images.com/CORBIS; **187** Joe Oliver/Odyssey Chicago; **188** Kevin Schafer/TIME; **191** Bridgeman Art Library; **192** Reproduced with permission of Curtis Brown Ltd, Lo; **194** Anthony Barboza/Black Images; **196** William Manning/CORBIS; **197** The Liaison Agency; **199** Art Resource, NY; **200** Superstock; **201** The Barnes Foundation, Merion Station, Pennsylvania/CORBIS; **203** Superstock; **204** Boltin Picture Library /Bridgeman Art Library; **207** (t)Roy Miles Fine Paintings/Bridgeman Art Library, (c)Christie's Images/Bridgeman Art Library, (b)CORBIS; **208–210** Getty Images; **211** Richard J. Green/Photo Researchers; **213** Roy Miles Fine Paintings/Bridgeman Art Library; **214–215** John Bunker/SuperStock; **217** Kari Van Tine/Veer; **218** Whitney Museum of American Art; **219** Greg Bliss/Masterfile; **221** Images.com/CORBIS; **223** Christie's Images/Bridgeman Art Library; **224** Minnesota Historical Society/CORBIS; **225** CORBIS; **227** Miriam Berkley; **229** Henry Diltz/CORBIS; **231** Cindy Lewis Photography; **232** The Minneapolis Institute of Arts/© 1999 C. Herscovici, Brussels/Artists Rights Society (ARS), New York.; **233** Mark Steinmetz; **234** Bridgeman Art Library; **239** Hulton-Deutsch Collection/CORBIS; **241** Sotheby's Picture Library; **242** Elizabeth Barakah Hodges/SuperStock; **244** Bridgeman Art Library; **245** Salamander Picture Library; **246** (l)Agence Top/Envision, (r)Salamander Picture Library; **247** Christie's Images/Bridgeman Art Library; **248** SuperStock; **251** Getty Images; **253** Getty Images; **254** Charles Philip/CORBIS; **255** Giraudon/Art Resource, NY; **256** Christie's Images Ltd.; **258** Manya Igel Fine Arts, London, UK/Bridgeman Art Library; **260** Philadelphia Museum of Art/CORBIS; **264** Archive Photos/Horst Tappe; **266** Bridgeman Art Library; **268** Albright-Knox Art Gallery/CORBIS; **273** Scala/Art Resource, NY; **278** Nancy Crampton; **280** Stephan Daige/CORBIS; **281** Paul Conklin/Uniphoto; **283** Herb Levart/Superstock; **284** Robert McIntosh/CORBIS; **285** Thomas Ives/CORBIS; **286** John Newcomb/Superstock; **287** John Sanford/Science Photo Library/Photo Researchers; **291** Bridgeman Art Library; **292** Victor Collector/Private Collection/The Bridgeman Art Library; **295** Robert McIntosh/CORBIS; **300** (l)file photo, (r)file photo; **301** (l, tcr, bcr, br)file photo, (tr)Mary Evans Picture Library; **308** Art Resource, NY; **310** Universal Press Syndicate; **311** Flip Schulke/CORBIS; **313** CORBIS; **314–315** Bridgeman Art Library; **317** Bridgeman Art Library; **318** The Metropolitan Museum of Art; **319** Leslie Braddock/SuperStock; **320** Robert Scheer; **322** CORBIS; **324** Susan McCartney/Photo Researchers; **325** The National Archives/CORBIS; **327** Aaron Haupt Photography; **329** Time & Life Pictures; **330** (t)Aaron Haupt Photography; (b)Hulton-Deutsch Collection/CORBIS; **331** CORBIS; **332** Time Life Pictures; **337** William Campbell for Time; **339** David Turnley/CORBIS; **341** (t)Louise Gubb/The Image Works, (b)Animals Animals/Earth Scenes/OSF/Sean Morris; **343** Paul Almasy/CORBIS; **345** Reuters/Juda Ngwenya/Archive Photos; **347** Lauren Goodsmith/The Image Works; **348** Louise Gubb/The Image Works; **350** Reuters/Juda Ngwenya/Archive Photos; **353** Jim Stratford/Black Star; **355** The Metropolitan Museum of Art; **357** Bridgeman Art Library; **360** Tina Fineberg/AP/Wide World Photos; **362** Christie's Images/CORBIS; **365** Bridgeman Art Library; **366** AKG-Images/Tony Vaccaro; **368** Bridgeman Art Library; **369** Geoffrey Clements/CORBIS; **373** Francine Fleischer/CORBIS; **375** Giraudon/Bridgeman Art Library; **377** Mary Evans Picture Library; **378** Erich Lessing/Art Resource, NY; **381** Bill Kaye/Paramount/Universal/The Kobal Collection; **384** Francine Fleischer/CORBIS; **386** Tore Bergsaker/Sygma/CORBIS; **388** Rollie McKenna; **390** The Andy Warhol Foundation for the Visual Arts/CORBIS; **392** Scala/Art Resource, NY; **393** Reprinted with permission of King Features Syndicate; **394** CORBIS; **399** Israel Museum, Jerusalem, Israel/Bridgeman Art Library; **400** Giulio Marcocchi/Getty Images; **401** Wayne Lankinen/DRK Photo; **402** Time Life Pictures/Getty Images; **405** Illusrtation Works/Getty Images; **411** Diane Sabin; **415** Private Collection/Bridgeman Art Library; **418** Getty Images; **420** Joan Grout/CORBIS; **423** Bridgeman Art Library; **424** North Carolina Museum of Art/CORBIS; **425** Linda Chesak/Images.com; **429** Nancy Crampton; **431** BRAUD, DOMINIQUE/Animals Animals-Earth Scenes; **432** Wayne Lankinen/DRK Photo; **433** Scott Camazine/Photo Researchers; **435** AP/Wide World Photos; **437** The Art Archive/Ministry of Public Information Mexico/Dagli Orti; **439** Franklin McMahon/CORBIS; **443** Art Resource, NY; **444** CORBIS; **446** Frances Benjamin Johnston/CORBIS; **448** Bettmann/CORBIS; CORBIS; **452** Flip Schulke/CORBIS; **454** (t)CORBIS, (b)Joachim Messerschmidt/FPG; **455** AKG-Images; **456** Flip Schulke/CORBIS; **459** Flip Schuke/CORBIS; **461** UPI/CORBIS; **468** through **469** Chester Brown; **471** Images.com/CORBIS; **474** 2005 Marvel/CORBIS; **476** Christian Pierre/SuperStock; **478** Steve & Ghy Sampson/Getty Images; **480** Andy Warhol Foundation/CORBIS; **483** Time & Life Pictures/Getty Images; **485** North Wind Picture Archives; **487** Chicago

R104 ACKNOWLEDGMENTS

Historical Society/Bridgeman Art Library; **488** CORBIS; **492** (t)Collection of Keya Morgan/Keya Gallery; (b)Spencer Platt/Getty Images; **496** Erich Lessing/Art Resource, NY; **504** Walter Geiersperger/CORBIS; **505** Phil Schermeister/CORBIS; **508** (bl)Raul Touzon/Getty Images, (bcl)Richard Hamilton Smith/CORBIS, (bcr)age fotostock/SuperStock, (br)Raymond Gehman/Getty Images; **510** (t)file photo, (b)file photo; **511** (t)Getty Images, (cw from top)file photo; **518** Marc Chagall/ARS, NY/Art Resource, NY; **522** CORBIS; **523** (t, b)CORBIS; **524** Erich Lessing/Art Resource, NY; **525** Private Collection/Bridgeman Art Library; **527** Archivo Iconografico, S.A./CORBIS; **528** Universal Press Syndicate; **530** Pach/CORBIS; **532** Bridgeman Art Library; **535** Juliet van Otteren; **537** The Art Archive/Private Collection/Joseph Martin; **540** CORBIS; **541** Lucy Raverat/RONA Gallery, London, UK/The Bridgeman Art Library; **542** Private Collection /Bridgeman Art Library; **543** Robert Landau/CORBIS; **546** CORBIS; **548** The Bridgeman Art Library/Getty Images; **550** Getty Images; **552** Courtesy Museu Picasso, Barcelona. © 1999 Estate of Pablo Picasso/Artists Rights Society (ARS),**554** Kactus Foto, Santiago, Chile/SuperStock; **557** Vyto Starinskas/Rutland Herald/CORBIS; **559** Brenda Chrystie/CORBIS; **563** Giulio Marcocchi/Getty Images; **565** AKG-Images; **566** Smithsonian American Art Museum, Washington, DC/Art Resource, NY; **569** Snark/Art Resource, NY; **571** Private Collection, Boltin Picture Library/Bridgeman Art Library; **573** The Art Archive; **574** Mori Sushin Tessan/British Library, London, UK./The Bridgeman Art Library; **575** Christie's Images/CORBIS; **577** Neela Banerjee; **579** AKG-Images/Jean-Louis Nou; **583** Daniel Nevins/SuperStock; **584** Francis G. Mayer/CORBIS; **586** Private Collection; **588** Charles Neal/SuperStock; **589** AKG-Images/Electa; **590** CORBIS; **593** CORBIS; **595** Peter Willi/SuperStock; **597** CORBIS; **599** Charles Neal/SuperStock; **603–609** Poetry Comics: An Animated Anthology by Dave Morice. Copyright © 2002 by Teachers & Writers Collaborative. Reprinted by permission of Teachers & Writers Collaborative, 5 Union Square West, New York, NY 10003; **610** Hulton Archive/Getty Images; **612** Archivo Iconografico, S.A./CORBIS; **613** Scala/Art Resource, NY; **617** Larry Ford/CORBIS; **619** Smithsonian American Art Museum, Washington, DC/Art Resource, NY; **622** The Art Archive/Culver Pictures; **624** Giraudon/Art Resource, NY; **626** CORBIS; **628** Boltin Picture Library; **630** Christopher Felver/CORBIS; **632** Images.com/CORBIS; **634** Christopher Felver/CORBIS; **636** Photothèque R. Magritte-ADAGP/Art Resource, NY; **638** Reprinted by Permission of the Dudley Randall Literary Estate; **642** Andy Warhol Foundation/CORBIS; **643** Tyler Mallory/AP; **645** Getty Images; **646** Universal Press Syndicate; **648** Gerardo Somoza/Outline Press Syndicate; **650** Courtesy of the Bill Hodges Gallery; **652** The Granger Collection, NY.; **654** Bourne Gallery, Reigate, Surrey, UK/Bridgeman Art Library; **656** Frantisek Kupka/Art Resource, NY.; **660** Gerardo Somoza/Outline Press Syndicate; **662** Pam Ingalls/CORBIS; **664** Courtesy of Chang-Rae Lee; **666** Tara Sasrowardoyo/TIME; **667** Scott Jones/TIME; **668** (tl)Christie's Images/CORBIS; (tr)Romare Bearden/Smithsonian American Art Museum/Art Resource, NY, (cl)Francks Deceus/Private Collection/Bridgeman Art Library, (bl)CORBIS, (bl)Gilbert Mayers/SuperStock, (br)Maurice Faulk/SuperStock; **669** National Portrait Gallery, Smithsonian Institution/Art Resource, NY; **671** Christie's Images/CORBIS; **672** Romare Bearden/Smithsonian American Art Museum/Art Resource, NY; **673** Francks Deceus/Private Collection/Bridgeman Art Library; **675** Gilbert Mayers/SuperStock; **679** CORBIS; **681** Maurice Faulk/SuperStock; **683** Arnold Newman/Getty Images; **685** Margie Livingston Campbell/SuperStock; **691** PunchStock; **696** (tl)Book provided by Little Professor Book Company. Photo by Aaron Haupt, (r)Aaron Haupt, (bl)Gerardo Somoza/Outline Press Syndicate; **697** (l)Book provided by Little Professor Book Company. Photo by Aaron Haupt, (t)Barbara Savage Cheresh; **704** Reunion des Musees Nationaux/Art Resource, NY; **707** Universal Press Syndicate; **708** Images.com/CORBIS; **709** Getty Images; **710–711** Bridgeman Art Library; **713** Michelle da Verona/Czartoryski Museum, Cracow, Poland/The Bridgeman Art Library; **714** Bridgeman Art Library; Archiv/Photo Researchers; **716** Ashmolean Museum, Oxford/Bridgeman Art Library; **717** Erich Lessing/Art Resource, NY; **720** Réunion des Musées Nationaux /Art Resource, NY; **721** Mary Evans Picture Library; **723** Scala/Art Resource, NY; **724** Bridgeman Art Library; **726** The Art Archive/National Archaeological

Museum Athens/Dagli Orti; **728** The Art Archive/Museo Nazionale Tarant/Dagli Orti; **731** The Art Archive/Musée du Louvre Paris/Dagli Orti; **733** Mary Evans Picture Library; **737** Private Collection, Courtesy of IAP Fine Art/Bridgeman Art Library; **743** The British Museum; **748** Giraudon/Art Resource, NY; **751** Louvre, Paris, France, Peter Willi/Bridgeman Art Library; **752** Museu Calouste Gulbenkian, Lisbon, Portugal, Giraudon/Bridgeman Art Library; **754** The Art Archive/National Archaeological Museum Athens/Dagli Orti; **757** Erich Lessing/Art Resource, NY; **758** Photo by Studio Kontos; **768** Art Resource, NY; **769** Collections/Nigel Hawkins; **770** The Art Archive/Musée du Château de Versailles/Dagli Orti; **772** Paolo Uccello/The Bridgeman Art Library/Getty Images; **774** Chase Manhattan Bank Archive; **776** Bridgeman Art Library; **779** Scala/Art Resource, NY; **782** AKG-Images/Pirozzi; **786** Private Collection/Bridgeman Art Library; **789** Scala/Art Resource; **793** Smithsonian Institution; **794** Erich Lessing/Art Resource, NY; **796** Royal Albert Memorial Museum, Exeter, Devon, UK/Bridgeman Art Library; **801** Alinari/Art Resource, NY; **805** Cameraphoto/Art Resource, NY; **806** Victoria & Albert Museum, London/Art Resource, NY; **807** Bildarchiv Preussischer Kulturbesitz/Art Resource, NY; **810** The British Museum; **815** The Art Archive/Galleria d'Arte Moderna Rome/Dagli Orti; **817** Erich Lessing/Art Resource, NY; **820** The Metropolitan Museum of Art; **821** Private Collection, Stair Sainty Matthiesen Gallery, New York, USA/Bridgeman Art Library; **824** Private Collection, Christopher Wood Gallery, London, UK/Bridgeman Art Library; **826** Alinari/Art Resource, NY; **828** Erich Lessing/Art Resource, NY; **830** AKG-Images; **835** David Forbert/SuperStock; **838** Erich Lessing/Art Resource, NY; **841** Erich Lessing/Art Resource, NY; **842** Kunsthistorisches Museum, Vienna, Austria, Ali Meyer/Bridgeman Art Library; **843** Bridgeman Art Library; **847** Scala/Art Resource, NY; **848** Mary Evans Picture Library; **854** Erich Lessing/Art Resource, NY; **859** Scala/Art Resource; **862** CM Dixon, Canterbury, Kent; **864** Archive/Photo Researchers; The British Museum; **867** Laura Wheeler Waring/National Portrait Gallery, Smithsonian Institution/Art Resource, NY.; **869** Siri Stafford/Getty Images; Barros & Barros/The Image Bank; **870** CORBIS; **872–873** State Russian Museum/Bridgeman Art Library; **874** State Russia Museum/Bridgeman Art Library; **879** Courtesy Thames and Hudson, London; **884** CORBIS; **888** Getty Images; **893** CORBIS; **895** CORBIS; **896** The Granger Collection, New York; **898** Images.com/CORBIS; **901–903** Pam Ingalls/CORBIS; **906** Pablo Picasso/Private Collection/Bridgeman Art Library; **908** Images.com/CORBIS; **913** (t)Schalkwijk/Art Resource, NY, (c)file photo, (b)Edward Wilkins Waite/Private Collection/Bridgeman Art Library;**916** Schalkwijk/Art Resource, NY; **918** Courtesy of Museum of Fine Arts, Boston; **923** Schalkwijk/Art Resource, NY; **926** SuperStock **929** Private collection, courtesy of Mary-Anne Martin/Fine Art, New York; **932** File photo; **934** Edward Wilkins Waite/Private Collection/Bridgeman Art Library; **935** Kelmscott Farms; **937** Christie's Images/CORBIS; **939** Private collection, courtesy of Mary-Anne Martin/Fine Art, New York; **941** Getty Images; **945** Getty Images;**950** (l, tr)Aaron Haupt Photography, (br)CORBIS; **951** (l, cr, br)file photo, (tr)Mary Evans Picture Library; **958** Master of the Campana Casson/Musee du Petit Palais, Avignon, France/The Bridgeman Art Library; **961** Mary Evans Picture Library; **963** (t, b)Erich Lessing/Art Resource, NY; **964** Private Collection/The Bridgeman Art Library; **965** Anthony Southcombe/Private Collection/The Bridgeman Art Library; **967** The British Library/Topham-HiP/The Image Works; **968** Stapleton Collection/CORBIS; **969** Erich Lessing/Art Resource, NY; Lambeth Palace Library/Bridgeman Art Library; **972** Sotheby's/AKG-Images; **974** Richard T. Nowitz/CORBIS; **975** Adolphe von Menzel/The Bridgeman Art Library/Getty Images; **976** Archivo Iconografico, S.A./CORBIS; **979** HIP/Art Resource, NY; **980** Collections/Brian Shuel; **981** The British Library/Topham-HIP/The Image Works; **982** Giraudon/Art Resource, NY; **984** Reproduced by courtesy of the Director and University Librarian, the John Rylands University Library of Manchester; **988** Lambeth Palace Library/Bridgeman Art Library; **990** Bradford Art Galleries and Museums, West Yorkshire, UK/Bridgeman Art Library; **991** (t)Art Resource, NY, (b)Collections/Roy Stedall-Humphryes; **993** Courtesy of National Museums and Galleries of Wales; **996** Scala/Art Resource, NY; **997** Archivo Iconografico, S.A./CORBIS; **1000** (t)HIP/Art Resource, NY, (b)Collections/Brian Shuel; **1001** The Bridgeman Library/Getty

Images; **1004** Archivo Iconografico, S.A./CORBIS; **1009** Hulton Archive; **1011** Giraudon/Art Resource, NY; **1013** Victoria & Albert Museum, London, UK/Bridgeman Art Library; **1015** Alexandre Gabriel Decamps/The Bridgeman Art Library/Getty Images; **1016** Victoria & Albert Museum, London/Art Resource, NY; **1021** DAN CHUNG/AP Wideworld Photos; **1022** (t, c)CORBIS, (b)LOUISE GUBB **1026** Erich Lessing/Art Resource, NY; **1028** Franko Khoury/National Museum of African Art; **1029** Founders Society Purchase, Eleanor Clay Ford Fund for African Art. Photograph The Detroit Institute of Arts; **1032–1034** Excerpt from Sundiata, A Legend of Africa © 2002 Will Eisner, published by permission from NBM Publishing.; **1035** The Philadelphia Museum of Art/Art Resource, NY; **1036** Nationalmuseum, Stockholm, Sweden/Bridgeman Art Library; **1038** Werner Forman/CORBIS; **1040** Lowe Art Museum/SuperStock; **1043** National Museum of Iceland, Reykjavik, Iceland/The Bridgeman Art Library; **1045** MARY EVANS/ARTHUR RACKHAM; **1047** AKG-Images; **1053** Gjon Mili/Getty Images; **1055** Musee du Petit Palais, Avignon, France, Peter Willi/Bridgeman Art Library; **1058** The Art Archive/Mohammed Khalil Museum Cairo/Dagli Orti; **1060** AKG-Images/Peter Connolly; **1061** Scala/Art Resource, NY; The Art Archive/Mohammed Khalil Museum Cairo/Dagli Orti; **1064** Victoria & Albert Museum, London/Art Resource, NY; **1066** National Gallery Collection; By kind permission of the Trustees of the National Gallery, London/CORBIS; **1071** Sandro Vannini/CORBIS; **1073–1074** Gianni Dagli Ortl/CORBIS; **1076** (t)Private Collection, Peter Newark Western Americana /Bridgeman Art Library, (c)Smithsonian American Art Museum, Washington, DC/Art Resource, NY, (b)SuperStock; **1077** (l)Martin Benjamin, (r)Courtesy of the author; **1079** Private Collection, Peter Newark Western Americana /Bridgeman Art Library; **1081** The Art Archive/Bill Manns; **1082** Catalogue No. 153048, Department of Anthropology, Smithsonian Institution.; **1084** Smithsonian American Art Museum, Washington, DC/Art Resource, NY; **1086** SuperStock; **1091** Sotheby's Picture Library; **1095** Private Collection/Bridgeman Art Library; **1100** (l, r)Aaron Haupt Photography; **1101** (l, br)file photo, (tr)John Bunker/SuperStock, (cr)Aaron Haupt Photography; **1108** Peter Szumowski/Private Collection/The Bridgeman Art Library; **1112** Sophie Bassouls/CORBIS; **1114** Getty Images; **1115** The Art Archive/Hans Christian Andersen Birthplace Odense Denmark/Dagli Orti; **1117** Mary Evans Picture Library; **1120** Vince Bucci/Getty Images; **1122** Jerry Bauer; **1126** Martin Dohrn/Photo Researchers; **1127** Image Reproduced from Eyewitness Books: Knight With Permission from DK Publishing, Inc. ©Dorling Kindersley Ltd., London; **1128** Natural History Museum, London, UK/Bridgeman Art Library; **1131** SuperStock; **1132** Getty Images; **1135** AP/WideWorld Photos; **1137** CORBIS; **1138** David M. Schleser/Photo Researchers; **1139** James Noel Smith/Illustration Works/Getty Images; **1143** Christie's Images; **1145** Marlborough Gallery; **1146** Getty Images; Fredderic Leighton/Fitzwilliam Museum, University of Cambridge, UK/Bridgeman Art Library; **1151** (t)Van Hoorick/SuperStock (c)Images.com/CORBIS, (b)Museum of Modern Art, New York, USA/Bridgeman Art Library; **1152** Anthony Barboza/Black Images; **1154** Van Hoorick/SuperStock; **1158** Images.com/CORBIS; **1159** Museum of Modern Art, New York, USA/Bridgeman Art Library; **1160** Images.com/CORBIS; **1161** age fotostock/SuperStock; **1162** Stefano Bianchetti/CORBIS; **1164** Getty Images; **1166** Illustration Works; **1173** Jason Grow/SABA for TIME; **1174** (l)Jason Grow/SABA for TIME, (r)Jason Grow/SABA for TIME; **1176** Time Life Pictures/Getty Images; **1178** Scala/Art Resource, NY; **1182** Francisco Sancha y Lengo/Bibliotheque des Arts Decoratifs, Paris, France/Bridgeman Art Library; **1184** Getty Images; **1186** Roy Miles Fine Paintings/Bridgeman Art Library; **1188** CORBIS; **1191** Private Collection/Bridgeman Art Library; **1193** The Arts Club, London, UK/Bridgeman Art Library; **1194** Fine Art Photographic Library/CORBIS; **1197** Francis G. Mayer/CORBIS; **1198** National Gallery Collection; By kind permission of the Trustees of the National Gallery, London/CORBIS; **1199** Dickens House Museum, London, UK/Bridgeman Art Library; **1200** Herbert Art Gallery & Museum, Coventry, UK/Bridgeman Art Library; **1202** AKG-Images; **1206** Keystone/Getty Images; **1208** Little Moreton Hall, Cheshire, UK, National Trust Photographic Library/John Hammond/Bridgeman Art Library; **1212** Museum Boymans van Beuningen, Rotterdam, The Netherlands/Bridgeman Art Library; **1213**

Christie's Images/CORBIS; **1215** Francis G. Mayer/CORBIS; **1216** Private Collection, The Maas Gallery, London, UK/Bridgeman Art Library; **1219** Kimbell Art Museum/CORBIS; **1220** Private Collection, Eaton Gallery, Princes Arcade, London/Bridgeman Art Library; **1222** Fine Art Photographic Library/CORBIS; **1225** Evert-Jan Boks/The Bridgeman Art Library/Getty Images; **1226** age fotostock/SuperStock; **1230** CORBIS; **1232** The Bridgeman Art Library/Getty Images; **1234** Historical Picture Archive/CORBIS; **1237** Christie's Images Ltd; **1238** Carl Larsson/The Bridgeman Art Library/Getty Images; **1240** Ullstein Bild/The Granger Collection; **1242** Private Collection, Piano Nobile Fine Paintings, London/Bridgeman Art Library; **1244** Royal Albert Memorial Museum, Exeter, Devon, UK/Bridgeman Art Library; **1246** Images.com/CORBIS; **1248** Hamburger Kunsthalle, Hamburg, Germany/Bridgeman Art Library; **1250** Galleria Nazionale d'Arte Moderna, Rome, Italy/Bridgeman Art Library; **1251** Courtesy of the Council, National Army Museum, London, UK/Bridgeman Art Library; **1252** Giraudon/Art Resource, NY; **1253** Fine Art Photographic Library, London/Art Resource, NY; **1257** Getty Images; **1261** Digital Vision/PunchStock; **1266** (l, r, tr, br)Aaron Haupt Photography, (tl)file photo, (bl)Getty Images